# Countries of the World

## and Their Leaders
## Yearbook 2002

ISSN 0196-2809

# Countries of the World

## and Their Leaders
## Yearbook 2002

A Compilation of U.S. Department of State Reports on Contemporary Political and Economic Conditions, Government Personnel and Policies, Political Parties, Religions, History, Education, Press, Radio and TV, Climate, and Other Characteristics of Selected Countries of the World; Together with Travel Alerts, Passport and Visa Information, World Health Information for Travelers, and Customs and Duty Tips for Returning Residents

## Volume 1

Chiefs of State and Cabinet Members of Foreign Governments
Status of the World's Nations
U.S. Embassies, Consulates, and Foreign Service Posts
Background Notes: Afghanistan – St. Lucia

**GALE GROUP**
—★—
**THOMSON LEARNING**

*Detroit • New York • San Diego • San Francisco*
*Boston • New Haven, Conn. • Waterville, Maine*
*London • Munich*

*Countries of the World* was produced by
**Eastword Publications Development, Inc., Cleveland, Ohio**

Jennifer L. Jackson, *Editor*


**Gale Group Staff**

Rita M. Runchock, *Managing Editor*
Mary Rose Bonk, *Project Editor*

Dorothy Maki, *Manufacturing Manager*
Nekita McKee, *Buyer*

Mike Logusz, *Graphic Artist*
Kenn Zorn, *Product Design Manager*

**ISBN 0-7876-3489-1 (Set)**
**ISBN 0-7876-3490-5 (Volume 1)**
**ISBN 0-7876-3491-3 (Volume 2)**

**Printed in the United States of America**

10  9  8  7  6  5  4  3  2  1

# CONTENTS

## VOLUME 2

Background Notes (continued): St. Vincent & the Grenadines—Zimbabwe; Foreign Travel, including Health and Travel Warnings; and International Treaty Organizations

### Background Notes on Countries of the World (Vol. 2)

## Foreign Travel (Vol. 2)

## Travel Warnings and Consular Information Sheets from U.S. State Department (Vol.2)

## International Treaty Organizations (Vol.2)

# Introduction

Events in all parts of the world—Europe, Asia, the Americas, and Africa—demonstrate the dynamic changes that can quickly change the world's political and economic structures. This 2002 edition continues the tradition of *Countries of the World* in meeting the need for current information by monitoring and presenting pertinent U.S. Government publications to update the annual volume. The U.S. Department of the State and Central Intelligence Agency publications present the most current basic information available on the countries of the world, their leaders, and U.S. Embassies worldwide.

For this 2002 edition, over eighty-four "Background Notes" have been updated since the publication of last year's edition of *Countries of the World*. In addition, "Editor's Updates" have been included for thirty-five "Background Notes" that the State Department has not recently updated. The "updates" contain information on recent events reported in the following sources: the *New York Times*, *The Economist*, and the *Far Eastern Economic Review*.

Although the "Background Notes" section fills a significant portion of *Countries of the World,* the other sections of this year's edition have not been forgotten. The "Chiefs of State and Cabinet Members of Foreign Governments" and the "Status of the World's Nations" sections have both been updated. In the "Foreign Travel" section, the "International Travelers' Health Information," "Visa Requirements of Foreign Governments," "Patterns of Global Terrorism," and several of the government advice articles have also been updated.

Government data is current as of June 2001. Because events and conditions in the world can change dramatically and quickly, readers are encouraged to consult the website of the U.S. State Department at http://www.state.gov for the latest information releases.

# Chiefs of State
## and
## Cabinet Members of
## Foreign Governments

May 2001

## PREFACE

This directory of *Chiefs of State and Cabinet Members of Foreign Governments* is updated monthly. It is intended to be used primarily as a reference aid and includes as many governments of the world as is considered practicable, some of them not officially recognized by the United States. Regimes with which the United States has no diplomatic exchanges are indicated by the initials "NDE".

Governments are listed in alphabetical order according to the most commonly used version of each country's name. The spelling of the personal names in this directory follows transliteration systems generally agreed upon by Government agencies, except in the case in which officials have stated a preference for alternate spellings of their names.

NOTE: Although the head of the central bank is listed for each country, in most cases he or she is not a Cabinet member. Ambassadors to the United States and Permanent Representatives to the UN, New York, have also been included.

## KEY TO ABBREVIATIONS

| | | | |
|---|---|---|---|
| Adm. | Admiral | Fd. Mar. | Field Marshal |
| Admin. | Administrative Administration | Fed. | Federal |
| | | Gen. | General |
| Asst. | Assistant | Govt. | Government |
| Brig. | Brigadier | Intl. | International |
| Capt. | Captain | Lt. | Lieutenant |
| Cdr. | Commander | Maj. | Major |
| Cdte. | Comandante | Mar. | Marshal |
| Chmn. | Chairman | Mbr. | Member |
| Col. | Colonel | Min. | Minister, Ministry |
| Comdr. | Commodore | NDE | No Diplomatic Exchange |
| Ctte. | Committee | Org. | Organization |
| Del. | Delegate | Pres. | President |
| Dep. | Deputy | Prof. | Professor |
| Dept. | Department | RAdm. | Rear Admiral |
| Dir. | Director | Ret. | Retired |
| Div. | Division | Sec. | Secretary |
| Dr. | Doctor | VAdm. | Vice Admiral |
| Eng. | Engineer | VMar. | Vice Marshal |

# AFGHANISTAN

(Last updated: 8/30/2000)

*On 27 September 1996, the ruling members of the Afghan Government were displaced by members of the Islamic Taliban movement. Afghanistan has no functioning government at this time, and the country remains divided among fighting factions.*

# ALBANIA, REPUBLIC OF

(Last updated: 4/20/2001)

| | |
|---|---|
| President | **Meidani,** Rexhep |
| Prime Minister | **Meta,** Ilir |
| Dep. Prime Min. | **Ceco,** Makbule |
| Min. of Agriculture | **Xhuveli,** Lufter |
| Min. of Construction | **Demeti,** Arben |
| Min. of Culture, Youth, & Sports | **Uruci,** Esmeralda |
| Min. of Defense | **Lleshi,** Ismail |
| Min. of Economic Cooperation & Trade | **Meksi,** Ermelinda |
| Min. of Education | **Ruka,** Et'hem |
| Min. of Finance | **Angjeli,** Anastas |
| Min. of Foreign Affairs | **Milo,** Paskal |
| Min. of Health | **Solis,** Leonard |
| Min. of Information | **Ulqini,** Musa |
| Min. of Justice | **Imami,** Arben |
| Min. of Labor | **Ceco,** Makbule |
| Min. of Local Govt. | **Fino,** Bashkim |
| Min. of Public Order | **Gjoni,** Ilir |
| Min. of Public Sector Economy & Privatization | |
| Min. of Public Works | **Poci,** Spartak |
| Min. of State at the Prime Minister's Office | **Legisi,** Ndre |
| Min. of Transport | |
| State Sec. for European Integration | **Lakrori,** Maqo |
| Chmn., of the National Intelligence Service | **Klosi,** Fatos |
| Governor, Albanian State Bank | **Cani,** Shkelqim |
| Ambassador to the US | **Bushati,** Petrit |
| Permanent Representative to the UN, New York | **Nesho,** Agim |

# ALGERIA, DEMOCRATIC AND POPULAR REPUBLIC OF

(Last updated: 9/21/2000)

| | |
|---|---|
| President | **Bouteflika,** Abdelaziz |
| Prime Minister | **Benflis,** Ali |
| Min. of Agriculture | **Berkat,** Said |
| Min. of Commerce | **Medelsi,** Mourad |
| Min. of Culture & Communications | **Teboune,** Abdelmadjid |
| Min. of Energy & Mines | **Khalil,** Chekib |
| Min. of Finance | **Benachenou,** Abdellatif |
| Min. of Fishing & Marine Resources | **Ghoul,** Omar |
| Min. of Foreign Affairs | **Belkhadem,** Abdelaziz |
| Min. of Health & Population | **Abdelmoumene,** Mohamed |
| Min. of Higher Education & Scientific Research | **Fakhri,** Amar |
| Min. of Housing | **Bounekraf,** Abdelkader |
| Min. of Industry & Restructuring | **Menasra,** Abdelmadjid |
| Min. of Interior & Local Authorities | **Zerhouni,** Yazid |
| Min. of Justice | **Ouyahia,** Ahmed |
| Min. of Labor & Social Protection | **Bougerra,** Soultani |
| Min. of National Education | **Benbouzid,** Boubker |
| Min. of Participation & Coordination of Reforms | **Tammar,** Hamid |
| Min. of Posts & Telecommunications | **Meghlaoui,** Mohamed |
| Min. of Public Works, Territorial Management, Environment & Urban Planning | **Rahmani,** Cherif |
| Min. of Religious Affairs & Endowments | **Ghlamallah,** Bouabdellah |
| Min. of Small & Medium-sized Enterprises | **Boukrouh,** Noureddine |
| Min. of State | **Ouyahia,** Ahmed |

## ALGERIA, DEMOCRATIC AND POPULAR REPUBLIC OF (cont.)

Min. of Tourism & Handicrafts ............................................ **Derbani,** Lakhdar
Min. of Transportation .................................................. **Lounaoussi,** Hamid
Min. of Vocational Training .............................................. **Younes,** Karim
Min. of War Veterans .................................................. **Abbes,** Mohamed Cherif
Min. of Water Resources ................................................ **Saadi,** Salim
Min. of Youth & Sports ................................................. **Sellal,** Abdelmalik
Min. in Charge of National Solidarity ..................................... **Abbes,** Djamel Ouled
Min. in Charge of Relations with Parliament ............................... **Derbal,** Abdelouhab
Min. to the Prime Minister in Charge of Greater Algiers ................... **Rahmani,** Cherif
Min. Del. for Budget .................................................. **Brahiti,** Ali
Min. Del. to the Min. of Foreign Affairs in Charge of the National
Community Abroad & Regional Cooperation .......................... **Ziari,** Abdelaziz
Sec. Gen. of the Government ............................................ **Noui,** Ahmed
Governor, Central Bank ................................................ **Keramane,** Abdelouahab
Ambassador to the US .................................................. **Jazairy,** Driss
Permanent Representative to the UN, New York ........................... **Bali,** Abdellah

## ANDORRA, PRINCIPALITY OF

(Last updated: 7/27/2000)

Head of Government ................................................... **Forne,** Marc Molne
Head of State (Co-Prince) .............................................. **Alanis,** Joan Marti, *Bishop*
Head of State (Co-Prince) .............................................. **Chirac,** Jacques
Min. of Agriculture & the Environment ................................... **Adellach,** Olga Coma
Min. of Culture & Tourism .............................................. **Pujal,** Enric Areny
Min. of the Economy ................................................... **Casadevall,** Enric Medrano
Min. of Education, Youth, & Sports ...................................... **Cervos,** Pere Cardona
Min. of Finance & Interior .............................................. **Sangra,** Estanislau Cardona
Min. of Foreign Affairs ................................................. **Pintat,** Albert Santor Iaria
Min. of Health & Welfare ............................................... **Goicoechea,** Josep Maria Utrillo
Min. of Territorial Planning ............................................ **Naudi,** Candid Mora
Ambassador to the US .................................................. **Minoves-Triquell,** Juli
Permanent Representative to the UN, New York ........................... **Minoves-Triquell,** Juli

## ANGOLA, REPUBLIC OF

(Last updated: 2/27/2001)

President ............................................................. **dos Santos,** Jose Eduardo
Min. of Agriculture & Rural Development ................................. **Lutucuta,** Gilberto
Min. of Assistance & Social Reintegration ................................ **Malungo,** Albino
Min. of Commerce ..................................................... **Hossi,** Victorino Domingos
Min. of Education & Culture ............................................ **Neto,** Antonio Burity da Silva
Min. of Energy & Water ................................................ **da Silva,** Luis Filipe
Min. of External Relations .............................................. **de Miranda,** Joao Bernardo
Min. of Family & Women's Affairs ....................................... **da Silva,** Candida Celeste
Min. of Finance ...................................................... **Bessa,** Julio
Min. of Fisheries & Environment ........................................ **Jardim,** Maria de Fatima Monteiro
Min. of Geology & Mines ............................................... **Africano,** Manuel Antonio
Min. of Health ....................................................... **Hamukuya,** Albertina Julia
Min. of Hotels & Tourism .............................................. **Valentim,** Jorge Alicerces
Min. of Industry ..................................................... **David,** Joaquim Duarte da Costa
Min. of Interior ...................................................... **dos Santos "Nando",** Fernando da Piedade Dias
Min. of Justice ...................................................... **Tjipilica,** Paulo
Min. of National Defense ............................................... **Paihama,** Kundi
Min. of Petroleum .................................................... **de Vasconcelos,** Jose Maria Botelho
Min. of Planning ..................................................... **Lourenco,** Ana Dias
Min. of Posts & Telecommunications ..................................... **Ribeiro,** Licinio Tavares
Min. of Public Administration, Employment, & Social Welfare .............. **Neto,** Antonio Domingos Pitra Costa
Min. of Public Works & Urban Affairs ................................... **da Silva,** Antonio Henriques
Min. of Science & Technology ........................................... **Nganda Gina,** Joao Baptista
Min. of Social Communication .......................................... **Neto,** Pedro Hendrick Vaal
Min. of Territorial Admin. ............................................. **Muteka,** Fernando Faustino

## ANGOLA, REPUBLIC OF (cont.)

| | |
|---|---|
| Min. of Transport | **Brandao,** Andre Luis |
| Min. of War Veterans | **van Dunem,** Pedro Jose |
| Min. of Youth & Sports | **Barrica,** Jose Marcos |
| Min. in the Office of the Presidency, Civil Affairs | **Leitao,** Jose da Costa e Silva |
| Min. in the Office of the Presidency, General Secretariat | **Peixoto,** Jose Mateus de Adelino |
| Min. in the Office of the Presidency, Military Affairs | **Dias "Kopelipa",** Manuel Helder |
| Governor, Central Bank | **Jaime,** Aguinaldo |
| Ambassador to the US | **Diakidi,** Josefina Perpetua Pitra |
| Permanent Representative to the UN, New York | **Patricio,** Jose Goncalves Martins |

## ANTIGUA AND BARBUDA

(Last updated: 2/2/2001)

| | |
|---|---|
| Governor General | **Carlisle,** James B. |
| Prime Minister | **Bird,** Lester |
| Min. of Agriculture, Lands, & Fisheries | **Bird,** Vere, Jr. |
| Min. of Caricom & OECS Affairs | **Bird,** Lester |
| Min. of Defense | **Bird,** Lester |
| Min. of Education, Culture, & Technology | **Williams,** Rodney |
| Min. of External Affairs | **Bird,** Lester |
| Min. of Finance | **Bird,** Lester |
| Min. of Health & Social Improvement | **St. Luce,** John |
| Min. of Home Affairs, Urban Development, Renewal, & Social Development | **Percival,** Bernard |
| Min. of Information & Public Broadcasting | **Yearwood,** Guy |
| Min. of Justice & Legal Affairs | **Cort,** Errol |
| Min. of Labor, Public Safety, & Cooperatives | **Benjamin,** Steadroy |
| Min. of Legislature, Privatization, Printing, & Electoral Affairs | **Bird,** Lester |
| Min. of Planning, Implementation, & Public Service | **Browne,** Gaston |
| Min. of Public Utilities, Aviation, International & Local Transport, & Housing | **Yearwood,** Robin |
| Min. of Public Works, Sewage, Energy, Urban Development, & Renewal | **Bird,** Lester |
| Min. of Social Improvement, Urban Development, Renewal, & Community Development | **St. Luce,** John |
| Min. of State in the Ministries of Information, Broadcasting, & Public Works | **Walker,** Bernard |
| Min. of State in the Office of the Prime Minister | **Michael,** Asot |
| Min. of Telecommunications & Gaming | **Bird,** Lester |
| Min. of Tourism & Environment | **Joseph,** Molwyn |
| Min. of Trade, Industry, & Business Development | **Humphreys,** Hilroy |
| Min. of Youth Empowerment, Sports, Community Development, & Carnival | **Yearwood,** Guy |
| Attorney General | **Cort,** Errol |
| Ambassador to the US | **Hurst,** Lionel |
| Permanent Representative to the UN, New York | **Lewis,** Patrick |

## ARGENTINA (ARGENTINE REPUBLIC)

(Last updated: 3/27/2001)

| | |
|---|---|
| President | **De La Rua,** Fernando |
| Vice President | |
| Min. Coordinator | **Colombo,** Chrystian |
| Min. of Defense | **Jaunarena,** Jose Horacio |
| Min. of Economy | **Cavallo,** Domingo |
| Min. of Education | **Delich,** Andres Guillermo |
| Min. of Environment & Social Action | |
| Min. of Foreign Relations, International Trade, & Worship | **Rodriguez Giavarini,** Adalberto |
| Min. of Infrastructure & Housing | **Bastos,** Carlos Manuel |
| Min. of Interior | **Mestre,** Ramon Bautista |
| Min. of Justice & Human Rights | **De La Rua,** Jorge |
| Min. of Labor, Employment, & Human Resources Formation | **Bullrich,** Patricia |
| Min. of Public Health | **Lombardo,** Hector |
| Sec. Gen. of the Pres. | **Gallo,** Nicolas |
| Pres., Central Bank | **Pou,** Pedro |
| Ambassador to the United States | **Gonzalez,** Guillermo |
| Permanent Representative to the UN, New York | **Listre,** Arnoldo M |

## ARMENIA

(Last updated: 2/15/2001)

President . . . . . . . . . . . . . . . . . . . . . . . . . . . . . . . . . . . . . . . . . . . . . . . . . . . . . **Kocharian,** Robert
Prime Minister . . . . . . . . . . . . . . . . . . . . . . . . . . . . . . . . . . . . . . . . . . . . . . **Markaryan,** Andranik
Min. of Agriculture . . . . . . . . . . . . . . . . . . . . . . . . . . . . . . . . . . . . . . . . . . **Gevorgian,** Zaven
Min. of Culture, Youth, & Sports . . . . . . . . . . . . . . . . . . . . . . . . . . . . . . . **Sharoyan,** Roland
Min. of Defense . . . . . . . . . . . . . . . . . . . . . . . . . . . . . . . . . . . . . . . . . . . . . . **Sarkisyan,** Serzhik
Min. of Education & Science . . . . . . . . . . . . . . . . . . . . . . . . . . . . . . . . . . . **Ghazarian,** Edward
Min. of Energy . . . . . . . . . . . . . . . . . . . . . . . . . . . . . . . . . . . . . . . . . . . . . . . **Galustian,** Karen
Min. of Environment . . . . . . . . . . . . . . . . . . . . . . . . . . . . . . . . . . . . . . . . . . **Muradian,** Murad
Min. of Finance . . . . . . . . . . . . . . . . . . . . . . . . . . . . . . . . . . . . . . . . . . . . . . **Khachatryan,** Vartan
Min. of Foreign Affairs . . . . . . . . . . . . . . . . . . . . . . . . . . . . . . . . . . . . . . . . **Oskanyan,** Vartan
Min. of Health . . . . . . . . . . . . . . . . . . . . . . . . . . . . . . . . . . . . . . . . . . . . . . . **Mkrtchian,** Ararat
Min. of Industrial Infrastructure . . . . . . . . . . . . . . . . . . . . . . . . . . . . . . . **Zadoyan,** David
Min. of Industry & Trade . . . . . . . . . . . . . . . . . . . . . . . . . . . . . . . . . . . . . . **Jshmartian,** Karen
Min. of Interior . . . . . . . . . . . . . . . . . . . . . . . . . . . . . . . . . . . . . . . . . . . . . . **Harutyunian,** Haik
Min. of Justice . . . . . . . . . . . . . . . . . . . . . . . . . . . . . . . . . . . . . . . . . . . . . . **Harutyunian,** David
Min. of Management of State Property . . . . . . . . . . . . . . . . . . . . . . . . . . . **Vardanian,** David
Min. of National Security . . . . . . . . . . . . . . . . . . . . . . . . . . . . . . . . . . . . . . **Petrossian,** Karlos
Min. of Revenue . . . . . . . . . . . . . . . . . . . . . . . . . . . . . . . . . . . . . . . . . . . . . **Manukyan,** Andranik
Min. of Social Welfare . . . . . . . . . . . . . . . . . . . . . . . . . . . . . . . . . . . . . . . . **Martirosian,** Razmik
Min. of Territorial Administration . . . . . . . . . . . . . . . . . . . . . . . . . . . . . . **Abramyan,** Ovik
Min. of Transport & Communication . . . . . . . . . . . . . . . . . . . . . . . . . . . . **Zakharyan,** Yervand
Min. of Urban Planning . . . . . . . . . . . . . . . . . . . . . . . . . . . . . . . . . . . . . . . **Lokyan,** David
Chmn., National Bank . . . . . . . . . . . . . . . . . . . . . . . . . . . . . . . . . . . . . . . . **Sarkisyan,** Tigran
Ambassador to the US . . . . . . . . . . . . . . . . . . . . . . . . . . . . . . . . . . . . . . . . **Kirakosian,** Arman
Permanent Representative to the UN, New York . . . . . . . . . . . . . . . . . . . **Abelian,** Movses

## ARUBA

(Last updated: 3/27/2001)

Governor . . . . . . . . . . . . . . . . . . . . . . . . . . . . . . . . . . . . . . . . . . . . . . . . . . . . **Koolman,** Olindo
Prime Minister . . . . . . . . . . . . . . . . . . . . . . . . . . . . . . . . . . . . . . . . . . . . . . **Eman,** Henny
Dep. Prime Min. . . . . . . . . . . . . . . . . . . . . . . . . . . . . . . . . . . . . . . . . . . . . . **Croes,** Glenbert
Min. of Economic Affairs, Tourism, & Social Affairs . . . . . . . . . . . . . . . . **Beke,** Lilia
Min. of Education & Labor . . . . . . . . . . . . . . . . . . . . . . . . . . . . . . . . . . . . . **Wever-Lacle,** Mary
Min. of Finance . . . . . . . . . . . . . . . . . . . . . . . . . . . . . . . . . . . . . . . . . . . . . . **Croes,** Robertico
Min. of General Affairs . . . . . . . . . . . . . . . . . . . . . . . . . . . . . . . . . . . . . . . **Eman,** Henney
Min. of Health . . . . . . . . . . . . . . . . . . . . . . . . . . . . . . . . . . . . . . . . . . . . . . . **Posner,** Israel
Min. of Justice & Public Works . . . . . . . . . . . . . . . . . . . . . . . . . . . . . . . . . **Croes,** Eddy
Min. of Transport & Communications . . . . . . . . . . . . . . . . . . . . . . . . . . . . **Croes,** Glenbert
Attorney General . . . . . . . . . . . . . . . . . . . . . . . . . . . . . . . . . . . . . . . . . . . . . **Rosingh,** Ruud
Pres., Central Bank . . . . . . . . . . . . . . . . . . . . . . . . . . . . . . . . . . . . . . . . . . . **Caram,** A.R.

## AUSTRALIA, COMMONWEALTH OF

(Last updated: 2/5/2001)

Governor General . . . . . . . . . . . . . . . . . . . . . . . . . . . . . . . . . . . . . . . . . . . . **Deane,** William
Prime Minister . . . . . . . . . . . . . . . . . . . . . . . . . . . . . . . . . . . . . . . . . . . . . . **Howard,** John
Dep. Prime Min. . . . . . . . . . . . . . . . . . . . . . . . . . . . . . . . . . . . . . . . . . . . . . **Anderson,** John
Min. for Aged Care . . . . . . . . . . . . . . . . . . . . . . . . . . . . . . . . . . . . . . . . . . . **Bishop,** Bronwyn
Min. for Agriculture, Fisheries, & Forestry . . . . . . . . . . . . . . . . . . . . . . . . **Truss,** Warren
Min. for the Arts & the Centenary of Federation . . . . . . . . . . . . . . . . . . . **McGauran,** Peter
Min. for Communications, Information Technology, & the Arts . . . . . . . . . . . . . **Alston,** Richard
Min. for Community Services . . . . . . . . . . . . . . . . . . . . . . . . . . . . . . . . . . . **Anthony,** Larry
Min. for Defense . . . . . . . . . . . . . . . . . . . . . . . . . . . . . . . . . . . . . . . . . . . . . **Reith,** Peter
Min. for Education, Training, & Youth Affairs . . . . . . . . . . . . . . . . . . . . . . **Kemp,** David
Min. for Employment, Workplace Relations, & Small Business . . . . . . . . . . . . . **Abbott,** Anthony (Tony)
Min. for the Environment & Heritage . . . . . . . . . . . . . . . . . . . . . . . . . . . . **Hill,** Robert
Min. for Family & Community Services . . . . . . . . . . . . . . . . . . . . . . . . . . . **Vanstone,** Amanda
Min. for Finance & Administration . . . . . . . . . . . . . . . . . . . . . . . . . . . . . . **Fahey,** John
Min. for Financial Services & Regulation . . . . . . . . . . . . . . . . . . . . . . . . . . **Hockey,** Joe

## AUSTRALIA, COMMONWEALTH OF (cont.)

| | |
|---|---|
| Min. for Foreign Affairs | **Downer,** Alexander |
| Min. for Forestry & Conservation | **Tuckey,** Wilson |
| Min. for Health & Aged Care | **Woolridge,** Michael, *M.D.* |
| Min. for Immigration & Multicultural Affairs | **Ruddock,** Phillip |
| Min. for Industry, Science, & Resources | **Minchin,** Nick |
| Min. for Justice & Customs | **Ellison,** Christopher (Chris) |
| Min. for Reconciliation & Aboriginal & Torre Strait Islanders Affairs | **Ruddock,** Philip |
| Min. for Regional Services, Territories, & Local Government | **McDonald,** Ian |
| Min. for Small Business | **Macfarlane,** Ian |
| Min. for Sports & Tourism | **Kelly,** Jackie |
| Min. for Trade | **Vaile,** Mark |
| Min. for Transport & Regional Services | **Anderson,** John |
| Min. for Veterans' Affairs | **Scott,** Bruce |
| Min. Assisting the Min. for Defense | **Scott,** Bruce |
| Min. Assisting the Prime Minister | **Tuckey,** Wilson |
| Min. Assisting the Prime Minister for Public Service | **Worth,** Trish |
| Min. Assisting the Prime Minister for the Status of Women | **Anthony,** Larry |
| Treasurer | **Costello,** Peter |
| Asst. Treasurer | **Kemp,** Rod |
| Special Min. of State | **Ellison,** Chris |
| Attorney General | **Williams,** Daryl |
| Chmn., Reserve Bank | **Macfarlane,** Ian J. |
| Ambassador to the US | **Thawley,** Michael |
| Permanent Representative to the UN, New York | **Wensley,** Penelope |

## AUSTRIA, REPUBLIC OF

(Last updated: 12/21/2000)

| | |
|---|---|
| President | **Klestil,** Thomas |
| Chancellor | **Schuessel,** Wolfgang |
| Vice Chancellor | **Riess-Passer,** Susanne |
| Min. for Agriculture & Environment | **Molterer,** Wilhelm |
| Min. for Defense | **Scheibner,** Herbert |
| Min. for Economic Affairs | **Bartenstein,** Martin |
| Min. for Education & Culture | **Gehrer,** Elizabeth |
| Min. for Finance | **Grasser,** Karl-Heinz |
| Min. for Foreign Affairs | **Ferrero-Waldner,** Benita-Maria |
| Min. of Infrastructure, Future, & Innovation | **Forstinger,** Monika |
| Min. for the Interior | **Strasser,** Ernst |
| Min. for Justice | **Boehmdorfer,** Dieter |
| Min. of Social, Family, Youth, & Women's Affairs | **Haupt,** Herbert |
| State Sec., in the Chancellery | **Morak,** Franz |
| State Sec., in the Finance Ministry | **Finz,** Alfred |
| State Sec., for Health Affairs in the Social Affairs Ministry | **Waneck,** Reinhard |
| State Sec., Tourism in the Economic Ministry | **Rossmann,** Mares |
| Pres., Austrian National Bank | **Liebscher,** Klaus |
| Ambassador to the US | **Moser,** Peter |
| Permanent Representative to the UN, New York | **Pfanzelter,** Gerhard |

## AZERBAIJAN (AZERBAIJANI REPUBLIC)

(Last updated: 3/15/2001)

| | |
|---|---|
| President | **Aliyev,** Heydar |
| Chmn., National Assembly (Milli Majlis) | **Aleskerov,** Murtuz |
| Prime Minister | **Rasizade,** Artur |
| First Dep. Prime Min. | **Abbasov,** Abbas |
| Dep. Prime Min. | **Efendiyev,** Elchin |
| Dep. Prime Min. | **Eyyubov,** Yagub |
| Dep. Prime Min. | **Hasanov,** Ali |
| Dep. Prime Min. | **Sharifov,** Abid |
| Min. of Agriculture & Food | **Aliyev,** Irshad |

## AZERBAIJAN (AZERBAIJANI REPUBLIC) (cont.)

| | |
|---|---|
| Min. of Communications | **Akhmadov,** Nadir |
| Min. of Culture | **Bulbuloglu,** Polad |
| Min. of Defense | **Abiyev,** Safar, *Lt. Gen.* |
| Min. of Economics | **Nasrullayev,** Namiq |
| Min. of Education | **Mardanov,** Misir |
| Min. of Finance | **Alekperov,** Avaz |
| Min. of Foreign Affairs | **Quliyev,** Vilayat |
| Min. of Health | **Insanov,** Ali |
| Min. of Internal Affairs | **Usubov,** Ramil |
| Min. of Justice | **Mamedov,** Fikret |
| Min. of Labor & Social Security | **Nagiyev,** Ali |
| Min. of National Security | **Abbasov,** Namiq |
| Min. of Press & Information | **Tabrizili,** Siruz |
| Min. of State Property | **Aliyev,** Farhad |
| Min. of Taxation | **Mamedov,** Fazil |
| Min. of Trade | **Bagirov,** Huseyngulu |
| Min. of Youth & Sports | **Harayev,** Abulfaz |
| Pres., State Oil Company | **Aliyev,** Natiq |
| Chmn., National Bank | **Rustamov,** Elman |
| Ambassador to the US | **Pashayev,** Hafiz |
| Permanent Representative to the UN, New York | **Quliyev,** Eldar |

## THE BAHAMAS

(Last updated: 3/27/2001)

| | |
|---|---|
| Governor General | **Turnquest,** Orville |
| Prime Minister | **Ingraham,** Hubert A. |
| Dep. Prime Min. | **Watson,** Frank |
| Min. of Agriculture & Fisheries | **Knowles,** James |
| Min. of Economic Development | **Laing,** Zhivargo |
| Min. of Education, Youth, & Sports | **Foulkes,** Dion |
| Min. of Finance & Planning | **Allen,** William |
| Min. of Foreign Affairs | **Bostwick,** Janet |
| Min. of Health & the Environment | **Knowles,** Ronald |
| Min. of Housing & Social Development | **Allen,** Algernon |
| Min. of Justice | **Bethel,** Carl |
| Min. of Labor & Immigration | **Deveaux,** Earl |
| Min. of Local Govt. | **Thompson,** David C. |
| Min. of National Security | **Watson,** Frank |
| Min. of Public Service & Cultural Affairs | **Moxey-Ingraham,** Teresa |
| Min. of Public Works | **Russell,** Kenneth |
| Min. of Tourism | **Turnquest,** Tommy |
| Min. of Transport, Aviation, & Local Government | **Smith,** Cornelius A. |
| Attorney General | **Bethel,** Carl |
| Governor, Central Bank | **Francis,** Julian W. |
| Ambassador to the US | **Sears,** Joshua |
| Permanent Representative to the UN, New York | **Rolle,** Anthony |

## BAHRAIN, STATE OF

(Last updated: 4/20/2001)

| | |
|---|---|
| Amir | **Khalifa, HAMAD,** bin Isa Al |
| Prime Minister | **Khalifa, KHALIFA,** bin Salman Al |
| Min. of Amiri Court Affairs | **Khalifa, ALI bin ISA,** bin Salman Al |
| Min. of Cabinet Affairs | **Mutawa,** Muhammad bin Ibrahim al- |
| Min. of Commerce & Industry | **Salih,** Ali Salih Abdallah al- |
| Min. of Defense | **Khalifa, KHALIFA bin AHMAD,** Al, *Maj.Gen.* |
| Min. of Education | **Ghatam,** Muhammad Jasim al-, *Dr.* |
| Min. of Electricity & Water | **Khalifa, DAIJ,** bin Khalifa Al |
| Min. of Finance & National Economy | **Saif,** Abdallah Hasan al- |
| Min. of Foreign Affairs | **Khalifa, MUHAMMAD,** bin Mubarak Al |

## BAHRAIN, STATE OF (cont.)

| | |
|---|---|
| Min. of Health | **Musawi,** Faysal Radhi al- |
| Min. of Housing & Agriculture | **Khalifa, KHALID,** bin Abdallah Al |
| Min. of Information | **Hamir,** Nabil Yaqub al- |
| Min. of Interior | **Khalifa, MUHAMMAD bin KHALIFA,** bin Hamad Al |
| Min. of Justice & Islamic Affairs | **Khalifa, ABDALLAH bin KHALID,** Al |
| Min. of Labor & Social Affairs | **Shuala,** Abd al-Nabi al- |
| Min. of Municipalities & Environment | **Khalifa, KHALID,** bin Abdallah Al |
| Min. of Oil | **Khalifa, ISA bin ALI,** bin Hamad Al |
| Min. of Public Works | **Jawdar,** Fahmi Ali al- |
| Min. of State | **Kamal-al-Din,** Muhammad Hasan |
| Min. of State for Foreign Affairs | **ABD AL-GHAFFAR Abdallah,** Muhammad, *Dr.* |
| Min. of State for Municipalities & Environment Affairs | **Urayid,** Jawad Salim al- |
| Min. of State for Shura Council Affairs | **Fadhil,** Abd al-Aziz Muhammad al- |
| Min. of Transportation & Communication | **Khalifa, ALI bin KHALIFA,** bin Salman Al |
| Chmn., Bahrain Monetary Agency | **Khalifa, KHALIFA,** bin Salman Al |
| Governor, Bahrain Monetary Agency | **Khalifa, AHMAD,** bin Muhammad bin Hamad bin Abdallah Al |
| Ambassador to the US | |
| Permanent Representative to the UN, New York | **Bu Alai,** Jasim bin Muhammad |

## BANGLADESH, PEOPLE'S REPUBLIC OF

(Last updated: 1/17/2001)

| | |
|---|---|
| President | **Ahmed,** Shahabuddin |
| Prime Minister | **Hasina,** Sheikh |
| Min. of Agriculture | **Chowdhury,** Begum Matia |
| Min. of Cabinet Affairs | **Hasina,** Sheikh |
| Min. of Chittagong Hill Tracts Affairs | **Chakma,** Kalpa Ranjan |
| Min. of Civil Aviation & Tourism | **Hossain,** Mosharraf |
| Min. of Commerce | **Jalil,** Abdul |
| Min. of Communications | **Monju,** Anwar Hossain |
| Min. of Defense | **Hasina,** Sheikh |
| Min. of Education, Primary & Mass Education | **Sadique,** A. S. H. K. |
| Min. of Energy & Mineral Resources | **Hasina,** Sheikh |
| Min. of Environment & Forests | **Chowdhury,** Syeda Sajeda |
| Min. of Establishment | **Hasina,** Sheikh |
| Min. of Finance | **Kibria,** S. A. M. S. |
| Min. of Fisheries & Livestock | **Rob,** A. S. M. Abdur |
| Min. of Food | **Amu,** Amir Hossain |
| Min. of Foreign Affairs | **Azad,** Abdus Samad |
| Min. of Health & Family Welfare | **Selim,** Sheikh Fazlul Karim |
| Min. of Home Affairs | **Nasim,** Mohammad |
| Min. of Housing & Public Works | **Hossain,** Mosharraf |
| Min. of Industries | **Ahmed,** Tofael |
| Min. of Labor & Employment | **Mannan,** M. A. |
| Min. of Law, Justice, & Parliamentary Affairs | **Khasru,** Abdul Matin |
| Min. of Local Govt. | **Rahman,** Zillur |
| Min. of Post & Telecommunications | **Nasim,** Mohammad |
| Min. of Science & Technology | **Khan,** Noor Uddin, *Lt. Gen. (Ret.)* |
| Min. of Special Affairs | **Hasina,** Sheikh |
| Min. of Textiles | **Hasina,** Sheikh |
| Min. of Water Resources | **Razzaq,** Abdur |
| Min. Without Portfolio | **Yusuf,** Salahuddin |
| Min. of State for Civil Aviation | **Islam,** Syed Ashraful |
| Min. of State for Communications | **Chowdhury,** Anisul Haq |
| Min. of State for Environment & Forests | **Rahman,** H. N. Ashiqur |
| Min. of State for Fisheries & Livestock | **Quddus,** Abdul |
| Min. of State for Foreign Affairs | **Chowdhury,** Abul Hasan |
| Min. of State for Health & Family Welfare | **Amanullah,** M., *Dr.* |
| Min. of State for Housing & Public Works | **Alauddin,** Mohammad |
| Min. of State for Textiles | **Zahangir,** A. K. M. |
| Min. of State for Youth & Sports | **Quader,** Obaidul |

## BANGLADESH, PEOPLE'S REPUBLIC OF (cont.)

| | |
|---|---|
| Min. of State with Independent Charge for Children Affairs & Social Welfare | **Hossain,** Mozammel |
| Min. of State with Independent Charge for Cultural Affairs | **Quader,** Obaidul |
| Min. of State with Independent Charge for Disaster Management & Relief | **Talukder,** Abdul Khaleque |
| Min. of State with Independent Charge for Energy & Mineral Resources | **Islam,** Rafiqul |
| Min. of State with Independent Charge for Information | **Sayeed,** Abu |
| Min. of State with Independent Charge for Jute | **Huq,** Faezul |
| Min. of State with Independent Charge for Land | **Mosharraf,** Alhaj Rashed |
| Min. of State with Independent Charge for Planning | **Alamgir,** Mohiuddin Khan |
| Min. of State with Independent Charge Post & Telecommunications | **Rouf,** Abdur, |
| Min. of State with Independent Charge for Primary & Mass Education | **Roy,** Satish Chandra |
| Min. of State with Independent Charge for Religious Affairs | **Islam,** Moulana Mohammad Nurul |
| Min. of State with Independent Charge for Rural Development & Cooperatives | **Ali,** Rahmat |
| Min. of State with Independent Charge for Shipping | **Maya,** Mofazzal Hossain Chowdhury |
| Min. of State with Independent Charge for Social Welfare | **Hosain,** Mozammel, *Dr.* |
| Min. of State with Independent Charge for Women, Children, & Social Welfare | **Talukdar,** Zinatun Nesa |
| Chief Justice | **Rahman,** Latifur |
| Governor, Central Bank | **Farashuddin,** Mohammed |
| Speaker of Parliament | **Chowdhury,** Humayun Rashid |
| Ambassador to the US | **Shehabuddin,** Khwaja Mohammad |
| Permanent Representative to the UN, New York | **Chowdhury,** Anwarul Karim |

## BARBADOS

(Last updated: 4/11/2001)

| | |
|---|---|
| Governor General | **Husbands,** Clifford, *Sir* |
| Prime Minister | **Arthur,** Owen |
| Dep. Prime Min. | **Miller,** Billie |
| Min. of Agriculture & Rural Development | **Wood,** Anthony |
| Min. of Commerce, Consumer Affairs, & Business Development | **Toppin,** Ronald |
| Min. of Defense & Security | **Arthur,** Owen |
| Min. of Economic Affairs | **Arthur,** Owen |
| Min. of Education, Youth Affairs, & Culture | **Mottley,** Mia |
| Min. of Environment, Energy, & Natural Resources | **Eastmond,** Rawle |
| Min. of Finance | **Arthur,** Owen |
| Min. of Foreign Affairs | **Miller,** Billie |
| Min. of Foreign Trade | **Miller,** Billie |
| Min. of Health | **Goddard,** Phillip |
| Min. of Home Affairs | **Simmons,** David |
| Min. of Housing & Lands | **Clarke,** Gline |
| Min. of Industry & International Business | **Farley,** Reginald |
| Min. of Information | **Arthur,** Owen |
| Min. of Labor, Sports, & Public Sector Reform | **Greenidge,** Rudolph |
| Min. of Public Works & Transportation | **Marshall,** Rommel |
| Min. of Social Transformation | **Lashley,** Hamilton |
| Min. of State | **Toppin,** Ronald |
| Min. of Tourism & International Transport | **Lynch,** Noel Anderson |
| Attorney General | **Simmons,** David |
| Governor, Central Bank | **Williams,** Marion |
| Ambassador to the US | **King,** Michael |
| Permanent Representative to the UN, New York | **Clarke,** June Yvonne |

## BELARUS, REPUBLIC OF

(Last updated: 2/6/2001)

| | |
|---|---|
| President | **Lukashenko,** Aleksandr |
| Prime Minister | **Yermoshin,** Vladimir |
| First Dep. Prime Min. | **Kobyakov,** Andrey |
| Dep. Prime Min. | |
| Dep. Prime Min. | **Demchuk,** Mikhail |
| Dep. Prime Min. | **Khvostov,** Mikhail |
| Dep. Prime Min. | **Kokorev,** Valeriy |
| Dep. Prime Min. | **Kozik,** Leonid |

## BELARUS, REPUBLIC OF (cont.)

| | |
|---|---|
| Dep. Prime Min. | **Novitskiy**, Gennadiy |
| Dep. Prime Min. | **Popkov**, Aleksandr |
| Min. of Agriculture & Food | **Rusy**, Mikhail |
| Min. of Architecture & Construction | **Kurachkin**, Henadz |
| Min. of Communications | **Goncharenko**, Vladimir |
| Min. of Culture | **Hulyaka**, Leonid |
| Min. of Defense | **Chumakov**, Aleksandr, *Col. Gen.* |
| Min. of Economy | **Shimov**, Vladimir |
| Min. of Education | **Strazhev**, Vasiliy |
| Min. of Emergency Situations | **Astapov**, Valery |
| Min. of Enterprise & Investment | **Sazonov**, Aleksandr |
| Min. of Finance | **Korbut**, Nikolay |
| Min. of Foreign Affairs | **Khvostov**, Mikhail |
| Min. of Forestry | **Zorin**, Valentin |
| Min. of Fuel & Energy | |
| Min. of Health | **Zelenkevich**, Igor |
| Min. of Housing & Municipal Services | **Milkota**, Alexsandr |
| Min. of Industry | **Kharlap**, Anatoliy |
| Min. of Interior | **Naumov**, Vladimir |
| Min. of Justice | **Vorontsov**, Gennadiy |
| Min. of Labor | **Lyakh**, Ivan |
| Min. of Natural Resources & Environmental Protection | **Rusyy**, Mikhail |
| Min. of Social Security | **Dargel**, Olga |
| Min. of Sports & Tourism | **Vorsin**, Yavhen |
| Min. of State Property & Privitization | **Novak**, Vasiliy |
| Min. of Statistics & Analysis | **Zinowski**, Vladzimir |
| Min. of Trade | **Kozlov**, Petr |
| Min. of Transport | **Lukashev**, Aleksandr |
| Chmn., State Committee for Control | **Kobyakov**, Aleksandr |
| Chmn., State Committee for Security (KGB) | **Yerin**, Leonid |
| Chmn., National Bank | **Prokopovich**, Petr |
| Prosecutor General | **Sheyman**, Viktor |
| State Sec., Security Council | **Latpov**, Ural |
| Ambassador to the US | **Tsepkalo**, Valeriy |
| Permanent Representative to the UN, New York | **Ling**, Sergey |

## BELGIUM, KINGDOM OF

(Last updated: 3/27/2001)

| | |
|---|---|
| King | **Albert II** |
| Prime Minister | **Verhofstadt**, Guy |
| Vice Prime Min. | **Durant**, Isabelle |
| Vice Prime Min. | **Lanotte**, Johan Vande |
| Vice Prime Min. | **Michel**, Louis |
| Vice Prime Min. | **Onkelinx**, Laurette |
| Min. of Agriculture | **Gabriels**, Jaak |
| Min. of Budget | **Lanotte**, Johan Vande |
| Min. of Consumer Affairs, Health, & Environment | **Aelvoet**, Magda |
| Min. of Defense | **Flahaut**, Andre |
| Min. of Economic Affairs & Research | **Picque**, Charles |
| Min. of Employment | **Onkelinx**, Laurette |
| Min. of Finance | **Reynders**, Didier |
| Min. of Foreign Affairs | **Michel**, Louis |
| Min. of the Interior | **Duquesne**, Antoine |
| Min. of Justice | **Verwilghen**, Marc |
| Min. of Public Administration | **van den Bossche**, Luc |
| Min. of Social Affairs & Pensions | **Vandenbroucke**, Frank |
| Min. of Telecommunications & State-owned Companies | **Daems**, Rik |
| Min. of Transportation | **Durant**, Isabelle |
| Sec. of State for Development Aid | **Boutmans**, Eddy |
| Sec. of State for Foreign Affairs & Trade | **Neyts**, Annemie |
| Sec. of State for Transport & Sustainable Development | **Deleuze**, Olivier |
| Governor, National Bank | **Quaden**, Guy |
| Ambassador to the US | **Reyn**, Alexis |
| Permanent Representative to the UN, New York | **Adam**, Andre |

## BELIZE

(Last updated: 4/11/2001)

| | |
|---|---|
| Governor General | **Young,** Colville, *Sir* |
| Prime Minister | **Musa,** Said Wilbert |
| Dep. Prime Min. | **Briceno,** John |
| Senior Min. | **Price,** George |
| Min. of Agriculture, Fisheries, & Cooperatives | **Silva,** Daniel |
| Min. of Budget Management, Investment, & Trade | **Fonseca,** Ralph |
| Min. of Education & Sports | **Hyde,** Cordel |
| Min. of Environment & Industry | **Briceno,** John |
| Min. of Finance | **Musa,** Said |
| Min. of Foreign Affairs | **Musa,** Said |
| Min. of Health, Public Services, Labor, & Civil Society | **Castillo,** Valdemar |
| Min. of Housing, Urban Renewal, & Home Affairs | **Bradley,** Richard "Dickie" |
| Min. of Human Development & Women | **Oolores,** Garcia Balderamose |
| Min. of Information | **Smith,** Godfrey |
| Min. of National Coordination & Mobilization | **Campos,** Ruben |
| Min. of National Security & Economic Development | **Espat,** Jorge |
| Min. of Natural Resources | **Briceno,** John |
| Min. of Public Utilities, Energy, Communications, Immigration, & Nationality | **Samuels,** Maxwell |
| Min. of Rural Development & Culture | **Mes,** Marcial |
| Min. of State in the Ministry of Economic Development | **Baeza,** Servulo |
| Min. of State in the Ministry of Industry | **Arceo,** Patricia |
| Min. of Sugar Industry, Local Government, & Latin American Affairs | **Marin,** Florencio |
| Min. of Tourism & Youth | **Espat,** Mark |
| Min. of Works, Transportation, Citrus & Banana Industries | **Canton,** Henry |
| Attorney General | **Smith,** Godfrey |
| Governor, Central Bank | **Arnold,** Keith |
| Ambassador to the US | **Shoman,** Lisa M. |
| Permanent Representative to the UN, New York | **Stuart,** Leslie W. |

## BENIN, REPUBLIC OF

(Last updated: 11/17/2000)

| | |
|---|---|
| President | **Kerekou,** Mathieu |
| Min. of Civil Service, Labor, & Administrative Reform | **Batoko,** Ousmane |
| Min. of Culture & Communications | **Zossou,** Gaston |
| Min. of Education & Scientific Research | **Alahassa,** Damien Zinsou |
| Min. of Energy, Mining, & Water Resources | **Dansou,** Felix Essou |
| Min. of Environment, Housing, & Urban Affairs | **Gnacadja,** Luc |
| Min. of Finance & Economy | **Tchane,** Abdoulaye Bio |
| Min. of Foreign Affairs & Cooperation | **Idji,** Antoine Kolawole |
| Min. of Health | **D'Almeida-Massougbodji,** Marina |
| Min. of Industry & Small to Medium-Sized Businesses | **Igue,** Pierre John |
| Min. of Interior, Security, & Territorial Administration | **Tawema,** Daniel |
| Min. of Justice, Legislative Affairs, & Human Rights | **Gnonlonfoun,** Joseph H. |
| Min. of National Defense | **Osho,** Pierre |
| Min. of Public Works & Transportation | **Attin,** Joseph Sourou |
| Min. for Relations with Institutions | **Akindes,** Sylvain Adekpedjou |
| Min. of Rural Development | **Nata,** Theophile |
| Min. of State for Coordination of Govt. Actions, Economic Development, & Job Creation | **Amoussou,** Bruno |
| Min. of Social Welfare & Women's Affairs | **Baba-Moussa,** Ramatou |
| Min. of Trade, Artisanry, & Tourism | **Adjovi,** Severin |
| Min. of Youth, Sports, & Recreation | **Houde,** Valentin Aditi |
| Ambassador to the US | **Tonoukouin,** Lucien |
| Permanent Representative to the UN, New York | **Adechi,** Joel |

## BERMUDA (BRITISH COLONY)

(Last updated: 9/21/2000)

| | |
|---|---|
| Governor | **Masefield,** Thorold |
| Premier | **Smith,** Jennifer |
| Dep. Premier | |
| Min. of Community & Cultural Affairs | **Lister,** Terry |
| Min. of Development, Opportunity, & Government Services | **Lister,** Terry |
| Min. of Education & Human Affairs | **Smith,** Jennifer |
| Min. of Environment, Planning, & Natural Resources | **Hodgson,** Arthur |
| Min. of Finance | **Cox,** Eugene |
| Min. of Health, Family Services, Housing, & Women's Issues | **Bascome,** Nelson |
| Min. of Labor, Home Affairs & Public Safety | **Cox,** Paula |
| Min. of Legislative Affairs | **Brown Evans,** Lois |
| Min. of Sports, Youth Development, Parks, & Recreation | **Lister,** Dennis |
| Min. of Telecommunications | **Webb,** Maurine |
| Min. of Tourism & Marine Services | **Allen,** David |
| Min. of Transport & Aviation Services | **Brown,** Ewart, *Dr.* |
| Min. of Works, Engineering, Parks, & Housing | **Scott,** Alex |
| Attorney General | **Evans,** Lois Browne |
| Cabinet Sec. | |
| Chmn., Bermuda Monetary Authority | |

## BHUTAN, KINGDOM OF—NDE

(Last updated: 11/17/2000)

| | |
|---|---|
| King | **Wangchuck,** Jigme Singye |
| Min. of Agriculture | **Dorji,** Kinzang |
| Min. of Education & Health | **Dorji,** Sanjay Nedup |
| Min. of Finance | **Zimba,** Hishey |
| Min. of Foreign Affairs | **Thinley,** Jigme |
| Min. of Home Affairs | **Gyamtso,** Thinley |
| Min. of Law | **Tobgye,** Sonam |
| Min. of Trade & Industry | **Wangchuk,** Khandu |
| Chmn., Royal Advisory Council | **Tsangbi,** Kungang |
| Chmn., Third Committee (Social, Humanitarian, Cultural) | **Tsering,** Ugyen |
| Permanent Representative to the UN, New York | **Pradhan,** Om |

## BOLIVIA, REPUBLIC OF

(Last updated: 3/27/2001)

| | |
|---|---|
| President | **Banzer,** Suarez, Hugo |
| Vice President | **Quiroga,** Ramirez, Jorge Fernando |
| Min. of Agriculture | **Carvajal,** Donoso, Hugo Arturo |
| Min. of Economic Development | **Saavedra,** Bruno, Carlos |
| Min. of Education, Culture, & Sports | **Hoz de Vila,** Tito |
| Min. of Finance | **Lupo,** Flores, Jose Luis |
| Min. of Foreign Affairs & Worship | **Murillo de la Rocha,** Javier |
| Min. of Foreign Trade & Investment | **Mansila,** Pena, Claudio |
| Min. of Govt. | **Fortun,** Suarez, Guillermo |
| Min. of Health | **Cuentas,** Guillermo |
| Min. of Housing & Basic Services | **Poma Rojas,** Ruben Enrique |
| Min. of Information | **Kempf,** Suarez, Manfredo |
| Min. of Justice & Human Rights | **Vasquez,** Villamor, Luis Angel |
| Min. of Labor & Microbusiness | **Pacheco,** Franco, Jorge |
| Min. of National Defense | **Vargas,** Lorenzetti, Oscar |
| Min. of the Presidency | **Perez Monasterios,** Marcelo |
| Min. of Sustainable Development & Planning | **Maclean,** Abaroa, Ronald |
| Pres., Central Bank | **Morales,** Juan Antonio |
| Prosecutor Gen. | **Crespo,** Solis, Oscar, *Dr.* |
| Ambassador to the US | **Fernandez,** Marlene |
| Permanent Representative to the UN, New York | **Jordan,** Pando, Roberto |

# BOSNIA AND HERZEGOVINA

(Last updated: 4/3/2001)

*(Bosnia's central government is headed by a tri-partite presidency with one representative of each of the three major ethnic constituencies.)*

### National Government

| | |
|---|---|
| Presidency Chairman (Serb) | **Radisic,** Zivko |
| Presidency Member (Muslim) | **Belkic,** Beriz |
| Presidency Member (Croat) | **Krizanovic,** Jozo |
| Prime Minister | **Matic,** Bozidar |
| Min. of Civil Works & Communications | **Mihajlovic,** Svetozar |
| Min. of European Integration | **Mikerevic,** Dragan |
| Min. of Foreign Affairs | **Lagumdzija,** Zlatko |
| Min. of Foreign Trade & Economic Relations | **Hadziahmetovic,** Azra |
| Min. of Human Rights & Refugees | **Zubak,** Kresimir |
| Min. of Treasury of the Institutions of Bosnia-Herzegovina | **Matic,** Bozidar |
| Chmn., House of Representatives | **Avdic,** Sead |
| Chmn., House of Peoples | **Tosic,** Momir |
| Dep. Min. of Civil Works & Communications | **Halilagic,** Jusuf |
| Dep. Min. of Civil Works & Communications | **Lovric,** Milan |
| Dep. Min. of European Integration | **Kadic,** Rasim |
| Dep. Min. of European Integration | **Marijanovic,** Zora |
| Dep. Min. of Foreign Affairs | **Misic,** Ivica |
| Dep. Min. of Foreign Affairs | **Blagojevic,** Milovan |
| Dep. Min. of Foreign Trade & Economic Relations | **Prlic,** Jadranko |
| Dep. Min. of Foreign Trade & Economic Relations | **Kragulj,** Nikola |
| Dep. Min. of Human Rights & Refugees | **Haracic-Sabic,** Kadrija |
| Dep. Min. of Human Rights & Refugees | **Vladicic,** Vladislav |
| Dep. Min. of Treasury of the Institutions of Bosnia-Herzegovina | **Inamovic,** Muharem |
| Dep. Min. of Treasury of the Institutions of Bosnia-Herzegovina | **Kovic,** Gordana |
| Dep. Chmn., House of Representatives | **Ljubic,** Mariofil |
| Dep. Chmn., House of Representatives | **Mirjanic,** Zeljko |
| Dep. Chmn., House of Peoples | **Campara,** Avdo |
| Dep. Chmn., House of Peoples | **Majic,** Petar |
| Governor, Central Bank | **Nicholl,** Peter |
| Ambassador to the US | **Davidovic,** Igor |
| Permanent Representative to the UN, New York | **Zivalj,** Husein |

### Federation Government (Muslim and Croat)

| | |
|---|---|
| President | **Filipovic,** Karlo |
| Vice President | **Halilovic,** Safet |
| Prime Minister | **Behmen,** Alija |
| Dep. Prime Min. | **Grabovac,** Nikola |
| Min. of Agriculture, Water Industry, & Forestry | **Hadzihajdarevic,** Behija |
| Min. of Defense | **Anic,** Nijo |
| Min. of Education, Science, Culture, & Sports | **Demirovic,** Mujo |
| Min. of Energy, Mining, & Industry | **Becirovic,** Hasan |
| Min. of Finance | **Grabovac,** Nikola |
| Min. of Health | **Misanovic,** Zeljko |
| Min. of Interior | **Besic,** Muhamed |
| Min. of Justice | **Mijan,** Zvonko |
| Min. for Labour, Social Affairs, Displaced People & Refugees | **Halilovic,** Sefer |
| Min. of Refugees, Displaced Persons & Social Welfare | **Garib,** Sulejman |
| Min. of Trade | **Jurkovic,** Andrija |
| Min. of Transportation & Communications | **Mehmedic,** Besim |
| Min. of Urban Planning & Environmental Protection | **Mehmedovic,** Ramiz |
| Min. of Veterans Affairs | **Hadzovic,** Suada |
| Dep. Min. of Agriculture, Water Industry, & Forestry | **Ivic,** Kazimir |
| Dep. Min. of Defense | **Buljbasic,** Ferid |
| Dep. Min. of Education, Science, Culture, & Sports | **Lovrenovic,** Dubravko |
| Dep. Min. of Energy, Mining, & Industry | **Bosnjak,** Vinko |
| Dep. Min. of Finance | **Hafizovic,** Sefik |
| Dep. Min. of Health | **Ajanovic,** Ekrem |
| Dep. Min. of Interior | **Limov,** Tomislav |
| Dep. Min. of Justice | **Dzihanovic,** Sahbaz |

## BOSNIA AND HERZEGOVINA (cont.)

Dep. Min. of Labour, Social Affairs, Displaced People & Refugees .......... **Tuka,** Mijat
Dep. Min. of Refugees, Displaced Persons, & Social Welfare ................ **Cordas,** Davor
Dep. Min. of Trade ................................................ **Baksic,** Alija-Remzo
Dep. Min. of Transport & Communications ........................... **Brdar,** Stipo
Dep. Min. of Urban Planning & Environmental Protection ................. **Britvar,** Boris
Dep. Min. of Veterans Affairs ....................................... **Jonjic,** Dobrica
Min. Without Portfolio .............................................. **Ivankovic,** Mladen
Min. Without Portfolio .............................................. **Grahovac,** Gavrilo
Republika Srpska ...................................................
President .......................................................... **Sarovic,** Mirko
Vice President ...................................................... **Cavic,** Dragan
Prime Minister ..................................................... **Ivanic,** Mladen
Dep. Prime Min. .................................................... **Kunic,** Petar
Min. of Agriculture, Forestry, & Water Management ..................... **Latinovic,** Rajko
Min. of Defense .................................................... **Bilic,** Slobodan
Min. of Education .................................................. **Savanovic,** Gojko
Min. of Finance .................................................... **Vracar,** Milenko
Min. of Foreign Trade .............................................. **Turalic,** Fuad
Min. of Health ..................................................... **Balaban,** Milorad
Min. of Industry ................................................... **Bukejlovic,** Pero
Min. of Internal Affairs ............................................ **Bundalo,** :Perica
Min. of Justice .................................................... **Maric,** Biljana
Min. of Local Administration ........................................ **Kunic,** Petar
Min. of Mining & Energy ............................................ **Lemez,** Bosko
Min. of Refugees ................................................... **Micic,** Mico
Min. of Religion ................................................... **Antelj,** Dusan
Min. of Science .................................................... **Novakovic,** Mitar
Min. of Sports ..................................................... **Tesanovic,** Zoran
Min. of Trade & Tourism ............................................ **Tadic,** Zeljko
Min. of Transport & Communications .................................. **Dokic,** Branko
Min. of Urban Planning ............................................. **Djuric,** Nedjo
Min. of War Veterans ............................................... **Solaja,** Dragan
Speaker of the Serb Assembly ....................................... **Kalinic,** Dragan

## BOTSWANA, REPUBLIC OF

(Last updated: 3/15/2001)

President ........................................................... **Mogae,** Festus Gontebanye
Vice President ...................................................... **Khama,** Seretse Ian
Min. of Agriculture ................................................ **Swarts,** Johnny
Min. of Commerce & Industry ........................................ **Seretse,** Tebelelo
Min. of Education .................................................. **Kedikilwe,** Pontashego
Min. of Finance & Development Planning ............................... **Goalathe,** Baledzi
Min. of Foreign Affairs ............................................. **Merahfe,** Mompati, *Lt. Gen. (Ret)*
Min. of Health ..................................................... **Phumaphi,** Joy
Min. of Labor & Home Affairs ....................................... **Kwelagobe,** Daniel
Min. of Lands & Housing ............................................ **Nkate,** Jacob
Min. of Local Government ........................................... **Nasha,** Margaret
Min. of Mineral, Energy, & Water Affairs .............................. **Mokgothu,** Boometswe
Min. of Presidential Affairs & Public Administration ..................... **Mogami,** Thebe
Min. of Works, Transport, & Commmunications ......................... **Magang,** David
Asst. Min. of Agriculture ........................................... **Seloma,** Pelokgale
Asst. Min. of Finance & Development Planning ......................... **Sebetele,** Boyce
Asst. Min. of Local Government ...................................... **Kokorwe,** Gladys
Asst. Min. of President Affairs & Public Administration. ...................
Attorney General ................................................... **Skelemani,** Phandu T. C.
Governor, Central Bank ............................................. **Mohohlo,** Lena
Ambassador to the US .............................................. **Seepapitso IV,** Kgosi, *Chief*
Permanent Representative to the UN, New York ........................ **Legwaila,** Joseph

## BRAZIL, FEDERATIVE REPUBLIC OF

(Last updated: 3/13/2001)

President . . . . . . . . . . . . . . . . . . . . . . . . . . . . . . . . . . . . . . . . . . . . . . . . **Cardoso,** Fernando Henrique
Vice President . . . . . . . . . . . . . . . . . . . . . . . . . . . . . . . . . . . . . . . . . . . **Maciel,** Marco
Min. of Agricultural Reform . . . . . . . . . . . . . . . . . . . . . . . . . . . . . . . **Jungmann,** Raul
Min. of Agriculture . . . . . . . . . . . . . . . . . . . . . . . . . . . . . . . . . . . . . . . **Pratini de Moraes,** Marcus Vinicius
Min. of Budget & Management . . . . . . . . . . . . . . . . . . . . . . . . . . . . **Tavares,** Martus
Min. of Communications . . . . . . . . . . . . . . . . . . . . . . . . . . . . . . . . . . **Pimenta da Veiga,** Joao
Min. of Culture . . . . . . . . . . . . . . . . . . . . . . . . . . . . . . . . . . . . . . . . . . **Weffort,** Francisco Correa
Min. of Defense . . . . . . . . . . . . . . . . . . . . . . . . . . . . . . . . . . . . . . . . . **Quintao,** Geraldo Magela da Cruz
Min. of Development, Industry, & Commerce . . . . . . . . . . . . . . . . **Tapias,** Alcides
Min. of Education . . . . . . . . . . . . . . . . . . . . . . . . . . . . . . . . . . . . . . . **Renato de Souza,** Paulo
Min. of Environment . . . . . . . . . . . . . . . . . . . . . . . . . . . . . . . . . . . . . **Sarney Filho,** Jose
Min. of Finance . . . . . . . . . . . . . . . . . . . . . . . . . . . . . . . . . . . . . . . . . **Malan,** Pedro
Min. of Foreign Affairs . . . . . . . . . . . . . . . . . . . . . . . . . . . . . . . . . . . **Lafer,** Celso
Min. of Health . . . . . . . . . . . . . . . . . . . . . . . . . . . . . . . . . . . . . . . . . . **Serra,** Jose
Min. of Justice . . . . . . . . . . . . . . . . . . . . . . . . . . . . . . . . . . . . . . . . . . **Gregori,** Jose
Min. of Labor & Employment . . . . . . . . . . . . . . . . . . . . . . . . . . . . . **Dornelles,** Francisco
Min. of Mines & Energy . . . . . . . . . . . . . . . . . . . . . . . . . . . . . . . . . . **Jorge,** Jose
Min. of National Integration . . . . . . . . . . . . . . . . . . . . . . . . . . . . . . **Bezerra,** Fernando
Min. of Science & Technology . . . . . . . . . . . . . . . . . . . . . . . . . . . . . **Sardenberg,** Ronaldo
Min. of Social Security . . . . . . . . . . . . . . . . . . . . . . . . . . . . . . . . . . . **Brant,** Roberto
Min. of Sports & Tourism . . . . . . . . . . . . . . . . . . . . . . . . . . . . . . . . **Melles,** Rafael
Min. of Transport . . . . . . . . . . . . . . . . . . . . . . . . . . . . . . . . . . . . . . . **Padilha,** Eliseu
Pres., Central Bank . . . . . . . . . . . . . . . . . . . . . . . . . . . . . . . . . . . . . . **Fraga Neto,** Arminio
Ambassador to the US . . . . . . . . . . . . . . . . . . . . . . . . . . . . . . . . . . . **Barbosa,** Rubens Antonio
Permanent Representative to the UN, New York . . . . . . . . . . . . . . **Fonseca Jr.,** Gelson

## BRUNEI (NEGARA BRUNEI DARUSSALAM)

(Last updated: 11/17/2000)

Sultan . . . . . . . . . . . . . . . . . . . . . . . . . . . . . . . . . . . . . . . . . . . . . . . . . **HASSANAL Bolkiah,** *Sir*
Prime Minister . . . . . . . . . . . . . . . . . . . . . . . . . . . . . . . . . . . . . . . . . . **HASSANAL Bolkiah,** *Sir*
Min. of Communications . . . . . . . . . . . . . . . . . . . . . . . . . . . . . . . . . **ZAKARIA bin Sulaiman**
Min. of Culture, Youth, & Sports . . . . . . . . . . . . . . . . . . . . . . . . . . **HUSSAIN bin Mohamed Yusof**
Min. of Defense . . . . . . . . . . . . . . . . . . . . . . . . . . . . . . . . . . . . . . . . . **HASSANAL Bolkiah,** *Sir*
Min. of Development . . . . . . . . . . . . . . . . . . . . . . . . . . . . . . . . . . . . . **ISMAIL bin Damit**
Min. of Education . . . . . . . . . . . . . . . . . . . . . . . . . . . . . . . . . . . . . . . **Abdul AZIZ bin Umar**
Min. of Finance . . . . . . . . . . . . . . . . . . . . . . . . . . . . . . . . . . . . . . . . . **HASSANAL Bolkiah,** *Sir*
Min. of Foreign Affairs . . . . . . . . . . . . . . . . . . . . . . . . . . . . . . . . . . . **MOHAMED Bolkiah**
Min. of Health (Acting) . . . . . . . . . . . . . . . . . . . . . . . . . . . . . . . . . . . **Abdul AZIZ bin Umar**
Min. of Home Affairs . . . . . . . . . . . . . . . . . . . . . . . . . . . . . . . . . . . . **ISA bin Ibrahim**
Min. of Industry & Primary Resources . . . . . . . . . . . . . . . . . . . . . . **ABDUL RAHMAN bin Mohamed Taib**
Min. of Religious Affairs . . . . . . . . . . . . . . . . . . . . . . . . . . . . . . . . . . **Mohamed ZAIN bin Serudin**
Ambassador to the US . . . . . . . . . . . . . . . . . . . . . . . . . . . . . . . . . . . **PUTEH ibni Mohammad Alam**
Permanent Representative to the UN, New York . . . . . . . . . . . . . .

## BULGARIA, REPUBLIC OF

(Last updated: 3/2/2001)

President . . . . . . . . . . . . . . . . . . . . . . . . . . . . . . . . . . . . . . . . . . . . . . . **Stoyanov,** Petar
Vice President . . . . . . . . . . . . . . . . . . . . . . . . . . . . . . . . . . . . . . . . . . . **Kavaldzhiev,** Todor
Prime Minister . . . . . . . . . . . . . . . . . . . . . . . . . . . . . . . . . . . . . . . . . . **Kostov,** Ivan
Dep. Prime Min. . . . . . . . . . . . . . . . . . . . . . . . . . . . . . . . . . . . . . . . . . **Zhotev,** Petur
Min. of Agriculture & Forests . . . . . . . . . . . . . . . . . . . . . . . . . . . . . **Vurbanov,** Ventsislav
Min. of Culture . . . . . . . . . . . . . . . . . . . . . . . . . . . . . . . . . . . . . . . . . . **Moskova,** Ema
Min. of Defense . . . . . . . . . . . . . . . . . . . . . . . . . . . . . . . . . . . . . . . . . **Noev,** Boyko
Min. of Economy . . . . . . . . . . . . . . . . . . . . . . . . . . . . . . . . . . . . . . . . **Zhotev,** Petur
Min. of Education & Sciences . . . . . . . . . . . . . . . . . . . . . . . . . . . . . **Dimitrov,** Dimitur

## BULGARIA, REPUBLIC OF (cont.)

Min. of Environment & Water .......................................... **Maneva,** Evdokiya
Min. of Finance ...................................................... **Radev,** Muravey
Min. of Foreign Affairs ............................................... **Mikhaylova,** Nadezhda
Min. of Health ....................................................... **Semerdzhiev,** Ilko
Min. of Interior ...................................................... **Yordanov,** Emanuil
Min. of Justice ...................................................... **Simeonov,** Teodosiy
Min. of Labor & Social Policy .......................................... **Neykov,** Ivan
Min. of State Administration ........................................... **Kostov,** Ivan
Min. of Territorial Development & Urbanization .......................... **Chachev,** Evgeniy
Min. of Transportation & Communications ................................ **Slavinski,** Antoniy
Min. Without Portfolio ................................................ **Pramatarski,** Aleksandur
Chmn., Bulgarian National Bank ........................................ **Gavriyski,** Svetoslav
Ambassador to the US ................................................ **Dimitrov,** Filip
Permanent Representative to the UN, New York ........................... **Sotirov,** Vladimir

## BURKINO FASO

(Last Updated: 2/14/2001)

Head of State......................................................... **Compaore,** Blaise, *Capt.*
Prime Minister ....................................................... **Yonli,** Paramango Ernest
Min. of Agriculture ................................................... **Diallo,** Salif
Min. of Animal Resources ............................................. **Bonou,** Alphonse
Min. of Arts & Culture ................................................ **Ouedrago,** Mahamoudou
Min. of Basic Education & Mass Literacy ................................. **Kietga,** Fidele
Min. of Civil Service & Institutional Development ......................... **Somda,** Jean Emile
Min. of Commerce & Finance .......................................... **Yonli,** Paramango Ernest
Min. of Communications ............................................... **Hien,** Theodore Kilmite
Min. of Defense ...................................................... **Lougue,** Kouame
Min. of Employment, Labor, & Social Security ............................ **Tou,** Alain Lodovic
Min. of Environment & Water Resources ................................. **Hien,** Fidele
Min. of Foreign Affairs ................................................ **Ouedraogo,** Youssouf
Min. of Health ....................................................... **Tapsoba,** Pierre Joseph Emmanuel
Min. of Higher Education & Scientific Research ........................... **Dabire,** Christophe
Min. of Information ................................................... **Hien,** Theodore Kilimite
Min. of Infrastructure, Housing, & Urban Planning ........................ **Lingani,** Hippolyte
Min. of Justice & Human Rights Promotion ............................... **Badini,** Boureima
Min. of Parliamentary Relations ........................................ **Topan,** Sanne Mohamed
Min. of Post & Telecommunications ..................................... **Thombiano,** Justin Tieba
Min. of Regional Integration ........................................... **Kabore,** Nayabtigungu Congo
Min. of Secondary & Higher Education & Scientific Research ............... **Sawadogo,** Laya
Min. of Security ...................................................... **Bassole,** Djibril Yipene
Min. of Social & Family Affairs.......................................... **Ouedraogo,** Gilbert
Min. of State Without Portfolio ......................................... **Ouedraogo,** Ram
Min. of Territorial Administration & Decentralization ...................... **Nabare,** Bernard
Min. of Trade, Industry, & Crafts ....................................... **Yoda,** Bedouma Alain
Min. of Transport & Tourism ........................................... **Yameogo,** Salvador
Min. of Women's Affairs ............................................... **Guigma,** Gisele
Min. of Youth & Sports ............................................... **Kabore,** Rene Emile
Governor, Central Bank ............................................... **Ouedraogo,** Boukary
Ambassador to the US ................................................ **Zidouemba,** Bruno
Permanent Representative to the UN, New York ........................... **Kafando,** Michel

## BURMA, UNION OF (MYANMAR)

(Last updated: 3/15/2001)

*(Burma is governed by a military junta—the State Law and Order Council (SLORC)—that has been in place since a military coup on 18 September 1988. On 15 November 1997 the SLORC changed its name to the State Peace and Development Council (SPDC) and made cabinet changes removing most of the former SLORC members. Burmese name elements are not separated.)*

Prime Minister ....................................................... **THAN SHWE,** *Sr. Gen.*
Chmn., State Peace and Development Council (SPDC) ..................... **THAN SHWE,** *Sr. Gen.*

## BURMA, UNION OF (MYANMAR) (cont.)

| | |
|---|---|
| Vice Chmn., State Peace and Development Council (SPDC) | MAUNG AYE, *Gen.* |
| Secretary 1, State Peace and Development Council (SPDC) | KHIN NYUNT, *Lt. Gen.* |
| Secretary 2, State Peace and Development Council (SPDC) | |
| Secretary 3, State Peace and Development Council (SPDC) | WIN MYINT, *Lt. Gen.* |
| Dep. Prime Min. | TIN HLA, *Lt. Gen.* |
| Dep. Prime Min. | TIN TUN, *Lt. Gen.* |
| Min. of Agriculture & Irrigation | NYUNT TIN, *Maj. Gen.* |
| Min. of Commerce | PYEI SONE, *Brig. Gen.* |
| Min. of Communications, Post, & Telegraph | WIN TIN, *Brig. Gen.* |
| Min. of Construction | SAW TUN, *Maj. Gen.* |
| Min. of Cooperatives | AUNG SAN, *Col.* |
| Min. of Culture | WIN SEIN, *Col. (Ret.)* |
| Min. of Defense | THAN SHWE, *Sr. Gen.* |
| Min. of Education | THAN AUNG |
| Min. of Electric Power | TIN HTUT, *Maj. Gen.* |
| Min. of Energy | LUN THI, *Brig. Gen.* |
| Min. of Finance & Revenue | KHIN MAUNG THEIN, *Lt. Col. (Ret.)* |
| Min. of Foreign Affairs | WIN AUNG |
| Min. of Forestry | AUNG PHONE, *Col. (Ret.)* |
| Min. of Health | KET SEIN, *Maj. Gen.* |
| Min. of Home Affairs | TIN HLAING, *Lt. Gen.* |
| Min. of Hotels & Tourism | SAW LWIN, *Lt. Gen.* |
| Min. of Immigration & Population | SAW TUN |
| Min. of Industry No. 1 | AUNG THAUNG, *Col.* |
| Min. of Industry No. 2 | SAW LWIN, *Maj. Gen.* |
| Min. of Information | KYI AUNG, *Maj. Gen.* |
| Min. of Labor | TIN AYE, *VAdm.* |
| Min. of Livestock Breeding & Fisheries | MAUNG MAUNG THEIN, *Brig. Gen.* |
| Min. of Military Affairs | TIN HLA, *Lt. Gen.* |
| Min. of Mines | OHN MYINT, *Brig. Gen.* |
| Min. of National Planning & Economic Development | SOE THA |
| Min. of Progress of Border Areas, National Races, & Development Affairs | THEIN NYUNT, *Col.* |
| Min. of Rail Transport | PAN AUNG, *Lt. Col. (Ret.)* |
| Min. of Religious Affairs | U AUNG KHIN, *Col. (Ret.)* |
| Min. of Science & Technology | U THAUNG, *Lt. Col. (Ret.)* |
| Min. of Social Welfare, Relief, & Resettlement | SEIN HTWA, *Maj. Gen.* |
| Min. of Sports | THURA AYE MYINT, *Brig. Gen.* |
| Min. of Transport | HLA MYINT SWE, *Maj. Gen.* |
| Min. Without Portfolio | MAUNG MAUNG KHIN, *VAdm.* |
| Min. in the Office of the Chairman of SPDC | ABEL, David Oliver, *Brig. Gen.* |
| Min. in the Office of the Chairman of SPDC | MIN THEIN, *Lt. Gen.* |
| Min. in the Office of the Prime Min. | |
| Min. in the Office of the Prime Min. | THAN SHWE |
| Min. in the Office of the Prime Min. | TIN NGWE, *Lt. Gen.* |
| Dep. Min. of Agriculture & Irrigation | KHIN MAUNG, *Brig. Gen.* |
| Dep. Min. of Agriculture & Irrigation | OHN MYINT |
| Dep. Min. of Commerce | KYAW SAN, *Col.* |
| Dep. Min. of Commerce | KYAW SHWE, *Col.* |
| Dep. Min. of Commerce | MYO TINT, *Brig. Gen.* |
| Dep. Min. of Construction | MYINT THEIN, *Brig. Gen.* |
| Dep. Min. of Construction | TINT SWE |
| Dep. Min. of Culture | SOE NYUNT, *Lt. Col. (Ret.)* |
| Dep. Min. of Defense | KHIN MAUNG WIN, *Brig. Gen.* |
| Dep. Min. of Education | SOE WIN MAUNG, *Brig. Gen.* |
| Dep. Min. of Education | THAN NYUNT |
| Dep. Min. of Education | U MYO NYUNT |
| Dep. Min. of Electric Power | MAUNG MAUNG, *Brig. Gen.* |
| Dep. Min. of Electric Power | U MYO MYINT |
| Dep. Min. of Energy | THEIN AUNG, *Brig. Gen.* |
| Dep. Min. of Energy | TIN TUN |
| Dep. Min. of Finance & Revenue | THAN TUN, *Brig. Gen.* |
| Dep. Min. of Foreign Affairs | KHIN MAUNG WIN |
| Dep. Min. of Foreign Affairs | NYUNT SWE, *Col. (Ret.)* |
| Dep. Min. of Information | SOE MYINT, *Brig. Gen.* |
| Dep. Min. of Information | THAIK TUN, *Brig. Gen.* |
| Dep. Min. of Health | MYA OO, *M.D.* |

## BURMA, UNION OF (MYANMAR) (cont.)

| | |
|---|---|
| Dep. Min. of Home Affairs | THURA MYINT MAUNG, *Brig. Gen.* |
| Dep. Min. of Hotels & Tourism | AYE MYINT KYU, *Brig. Gen.* |
| Dep. Min. of Immigration & Population | MAUNG AUNG |
| Dep. Min. of Industry No. 1 | KYAW WIN, *Brig. Gen.* |
| Dep. Min. of Industry No. 1 | THEIN TUN, *Brig. Gen.* |
| Dep. Min. of Industry No. 2 | AUNG THEIN LINN, *Brig.Gen.* |
| Dep. Min. of Industry No. 2 | KHIN MAUNG KYA, *Lt.Col.* |
| Dep. Min. of Information | AUNG THEIN, *Brig. Gen.* |
| Dep. Min. of Information | THEIN SEIN |
| Dep. Min. of Labor | WIN SEIN, *Brig. Gen.* |
| Dep. Min. of Livestock Breeding & Fisheries | AUNG THIEN |
| Dep. Min. of Mines | HLAING WIN, *Col. (Ret.)* |
| Dep. Min. of Mines | MYINT THEIN |
| Dep. Min. of National Planning & Economic Development | |
| Dep. Min. of Progress of Border Areas, National Races, & Development Affairs | KYAW TIN |
| Dep. Min. of Progress of Border Areas, National Races, & Development Affairs | THAN TUN, *Brig. Gen.* |
| Dep. Min. of Rail Transport | THURA U THAUNG LWIN |
| Dep. Min. of Religious Affairs | |
| Dep. Min. of Science & Technology | THURA AUNG KO, *Brig. Gen.* |
| Dep. Min. of Social Welfare, Relief, & Resettlement | MAUNG KYI, *Brig. Gen.* |
| Dep. Min. of Transport | KYAW MYINT, *Brig. Gen.* |
| Dep. Min. of Transport | PE THAN |
| Dep. Min. in the Office of the Chairman of SPDC | SET MAUNG |
| Governor, Central Bank of Burma | KYI AYE |
| Ambassador to the US | TIN WINN |
| Permanent Representative to the UN, New York | WIN MRA |

## BURUNDI, REPUBLIC OF

(Last updated: 11/17/2000)

| | |
|---|---|
| President | **Buyoya,** Pierre |
| First Vice President | **Bamvuginyumvira,** Frederic |
| Second Vice President | **Sinamenye,** Mathias |
| Min. of Agriculture & Livestock | **Ntihabose,** Salvator |
| Min. of Civil Service, Labor, & Vocational Training | **Tungamwese,** Emmanuel |
| Min. of Commerce, Industry, & Tourism | **Ntanyotora,** Joseph |
| Min. of Communal Development & Handicrafts | **Nshimirimana,** Denis |
| Min. of Defense | **Ndayirukiye,** Cyrille |
| Min. of Development & Reconstruction | **Nimbona,** Leon |
| Min. of Education | **Mpawenayo,** Prosper |
| Min. of Energy & Mines | **Barandereka,** Bernard |
| Min. of External Relations & Cooperation | **Ntahomvukiye,** Severin |
| Min. of Finance | **Nihangaza,** Charles |
| Min. of Health | **Ntahobari,** Stanislas |
| Min. of Human Rights, Institutional Reform, & Relations with the National Assembly | **Nindorera,** Eugene |
| Min. of Information & Government Spokesman | **Rukingama,** Luc, *Dr.* |
| Min. of Internal Affairs & Security | **Twagiramungu,** Ascension, *Col.* |
| Min. of Justice | **Sinunguruza,** Terence |
| Min. of Land & Environment | **Nsengiyumva,** Jean-Pacifique |
| Min. of Peace Process | **Niyonsaba,** Ambroise |
| Min. of Public Works & Housing | **Ntirampeba,** Gaspard |
| Min. of Reintegration of Refugees, Displaced Persons, & Repatriates | **Nkurunziza,** Pascal |
| Min. of Transport, Post, & Telecommunications | **Mbon'gaba,** Cyprien |
| Min. of Women, Welfare, & Social Affairs | **Ndorimana,** Romaine |
| Min. of Youth, Sports, & Culture | **Nyamwiza,** Gerard |
| Governor, Central Bank | |
| Permanent Representative to the UN, New York | **Nteturuye,** Marc |

# CAMBODIA, KINGDOM OF

(Last updated: 4/10/2001)

*The government coalition includes - the Cambodian People's Party (CPP) and the National United Front for an Independent, Neutral, Peaceful and Cooperative Cambodia (FUNCINPEC)(F).*

| | |
|---|---|
| King | **Norodom SIHANOUK** |
| Pres., National Assembly | **Norodom RANARIDDH,** *Prince (F)* |
| Prime Minister | **HUN SEN,** *(CPP)* |
| Dep. Prime Min. | **SAR KHENG,** *(CPP)* |
| Dep. Prime Min. | **TOL LAH,** *(F)* |
| Min. of State | **CHHIM SIEKLENG,** *(F)* |
| Min. of State | **HONG SUN HUOT,** *M.D. (F)* |
| Min. of State | **HOR NAMHONG,** *(CPP)* |
| Min. of State | **KEAT CHHON,** *(CPP)* |
| Min. of State | **LU LAY SRENG,** *(F)* |
| Min. of State | **SOK AN,** *(CPP)* |
| Min. of State | **TIE BANH,** *Gen. (CPP)* |
| Min. of State | **YU HOKKRI,** *(F)* |
| Min. in the Council of Ministers | **SOK AN,** *(CPP)* |
| Min. of Agriculture, Forestry, & Fishing | |
| Min. of Commerce | **CHAM PRASIT,** *(CPP)* |
| Min. of Culture & Fine Arts | **Norodom BOPHA DEVI,** *Princess (F)* |
| Min. of Economy & Finance | **KEAT CHHON,** *(CPP)* |
| Min. of Education, Youth, & Sports | **TOL LAH,** *(F)* |
| Min. of Environment | **MOK MARET,** *(CPP)* |
| Min. of Foreign Affairs & International Cooperation | **HOR NAMHONG,** *(CPP)* |
| Min. of Health | **HONG SUN HUOT,** *M.D. (F)* |
| Min. of Industry, Mines, & Energy | **SUY SEM,** *(CPP)* |
| Min. of Information & Press | **LU LAY SRENG,** *(F)* |
| Co-Min. of Interior | **SAR KHENG,** *(CPP)* |
| Co-Min. of Interior | **YU HOKKRI,** *(F)* |
| Min. of Justice | **UK VITHUN,** *(F)* |
| Co-Min. of National Defense | **SISOWATH SIRIRATH,** *Prince (F)* |
| Co-Min. of National Defense | **TIE BANH,** *Gen. (CPP)* |
| Min. of Planning | **CHHAY THAN,** *(CPP)* |
| Min. of Posts & Telecommunications | **SO KHUN,** *(CPP)* |
| Min. of Public Works & Transportation | **KHY TAINGLIM,** *(F)* |
| Min. of Relations with Parliament & Inspection | **KHUN HANG,** *(F)* |
| Min. of Religious Affairs | **CHEA SAVOEUN,** *(F)* |
| Min. of Rural Development | **CHHIM SIEKLENG,** *(F)* |
| Min. of Social Affairs, Labor, Vocational Training, & Youth Rehabilitation | **IT SAM-HENG,** *(CPP)* |
| Min. of Tourism | **VENG SEREYVUTH,** *(F)* |
| Min. of Urbanization & Construction | **IM CHHUNLIM,** *(CPP)* |
| Min. of Water Resources & Meteorology | **LIM KEAN-HAO,** *(CPP)* |
| Min. of Women's Affairs & War Veterans | **MU SOCHUA,** *(F)* |
| State Sec. in the Council of Ministers | **CHEA SAOPHOAN,** *(F)* |
| State Sec. in the Council of Ministers | **SUM MANITH,** *(CPP)* |
| State Sec. of Agriculture, Forestry, & Fishing | **CHAN TONG IV,** *(CPP)* |
| State Sec. of Agriculture, Forestry, & Fishing | **MAY SAM OEUN,** *(F)* |
| State Sec. of Commerce | **KHEK VANDY,** *(F)* |
| State Sec. of Commerce | **PEN SIMAN,** *(CPP)* |
| State Sec. of Culture & Fine Arts | **PEN YET,** *(CPP)* |
| State Sec. of Culture & Fine Arts | **SISOWATH PANARA SIRIVUT,** *Prince (F)* |
| State Sec. of Economy & Finance | **KONG VIBOL,** *(F)* |
| State Sec. of Economy & Finance | **UK RABUN,** *(CPP)* |
| State Sec. of Education, Youth, & Sports | **IM SOTHI,** *(CPP)* |
| State Sec. of Education, Youth, & Sports | **POK THAN,** *(F)* |
| State Sec. of Environment | **KHAN SAPHAN,** *(CPP)* |
| State Sec. of Environment | **SO GARI,** *(F)* |
| State Sec. of Foreign Affairs & International Cooperation | **SOENG CHAMRAEUN,** *(F)* |
| State Sec. of Foreign Affairs & International Cooperation | **UCH KIM AN,** *(CPP)* |
| State Sec. of Health | **MAM BUN HENG,** *M.D. (CPP)* |
| State Sec. of Health | **UNG PHIRUN,** *(F)* |
| State Sec. of Industry, Mines, & Energy | **ITH PRANG,** *(CPP)* |
| State Sec. of Industry, Mines, & Energy | **NHEP BUNCHIN,** *(F)* |

## CAMBODIA, KINGDOM OF (cont.)

| | |
|---|---|
| State Sec. of Information & Press | KHIEU KANHARITH, *(CPP)* |
| State Sec. of Information & Press | UM DARAVUT, *(F)* |
| State Sec. of Interior | EM SAM AN, *(CPP)* |
| State Sec. of Interior | KIENG VANG, *(F)* |
| State Sec. of Interior | PHAN SINA, *(F)* |
| State Sec. of Interior | PRUM SOKHA, *(CPP)* |
| State Sec. of Justice | LI VUOCHLENG, *(CPP)* |
| State Sec. of Justice | SUY NU, *(F)* |
| State Sec. of National Defense | CHAY SANGYUN, *(CPP)* |
| State Sec. of National Defense | PAO BUNSROE, *(F)* |
| State Sec. of Planning | LAY PROHOAH, *(F)* |
| State Sec. of Planning | U AOHAT, *(CPP)* |
| State Sec. of Post & Telecommunications | LAM PU-AN, *(F)* |
| State Sec. of Post & Telecommunications | PHAN PHIN, *(CPP)* |
| State Sec. of Public Works & Transportation | AHMAD YAHYA, *(F)* |
| State Sec. of Public Works & Transportation | TRAM IV-TOEK, *(CPP)* |
| State Sec. of Relations with Parliament & Inspection | KHOV MENG HEANG, *(F)* |
| State Sec. of Relations with Parliament & Inspection | HONG CHHEM, *(CPP)* |
| State Sec. of Religious Affairs | CHUON IEM, *(CPP)* |
| State Sec. of Religious Affairs | |
| State Sec. of Rural Development | LY THUCH, *(F)* |
| State Sec. of Rural Development | YIM CHHAILI, *(CPP)* |
| State Sec. of Social Affairs, Labor, Vocational Training, & Youth Rehabilitation | NIM THOT, *(CPP)* |
| State Sec. of Social Affairs, Labor, Vocational Training, & Youth Rehabilitation | PRAK CHANTHA, *(F)* |
| State Sec. of Tourism | NUT NINDOEUN, *(F)* |
| State Sec. of Tourism | THONG KHON, *(CPP)* |
| State Sec. of Urbanization & Construction | NU SANGKHAN, *(F)* |
| State Sec. of Urbanization & Construction | TI YAV, *(CPP)* |
| State Sec. of Water Resources & Meteorology | NGO PIN, *(F)* |
| State Sec. of Water Resources & Meteorology | YU KEAHEANG, *(CPP)* |
| State Sec. of Women's Affairs & War Veterans | UNG KUNTHAVI, *(F)* |
| State Sec. of Women's Affairs & War Veterans | YU AY, *(CPP)* |
| Governor, State Bank | CHEA CHANTO, *(CPP)* |
| Ambassador to the US | ROLAND ENG, *(F)* |
| Permanent Representative to the UN, New York | OUCH BORITH, *(CPP)* |

## CAMEROON, REPUBLIC OF

(Last updated: 11/17/2000)

| | |
|---|---|
| President | **Biya,** Paul |
| Prime Minister | **Musonge,** Peter Mafany |
| Min. of Agriculture | **Perevet,** Zacharie |
| Min. of Communication | **Ndongo,** Jacques Fame |
| Min. of Culture | **Oyono,** Ferdinand Leopold |
| Min. of Economy & Finance | **Mfoumou,** Edouard Akame |
| Min. of Employment, Labor, & Social Insurance | **Ondoua,** Pius Scurity |
| Min. of Environment & Forests | **Ondoua,** Sylvestre Naah |
| Min. of External Relations | **Kontchou Kouomegni,** Augustin |
| Min. of Higher Education | **Mebara,** Antangana Jean-Marie |
| Min. of Industrial & Commercial Development | **Bouba,** Maigari Bello |
| Min. of Justice & Keeper of the Seals | **Mbappe,** Robert Mbella |
| Min. of Livestock, Fisheries, & Animal Industries | **Hamadjoda,** Adjoudi |
| Min. of Mines, Water Resources, & Energy | **Mbele,** Yves, *Dr.* |
| Min. of National Education | **Owona,** Joseph |
| Min. of Posts & Telecommunication | |
| Min. of Public Health | **Monekosso,** Gotlieb |
| Min. of Public Investments & Territorial Development | **Edima,** Ferdinand Koungou |
| Min. of Public Service & Administrative Reform | **Dairou,** Sali |
| Min. of Public Works | **Etah,** Jerome |
| Min. of Scientific & Technical Research | **Nlend,** Henri Hogbe |
| Min. of Social Affairs | **Fouda,** Madeleine |
| Min. of Special Duties | **Abety,** Pierre |
| Min. of Special Duties | **Hamadou,** Baba |
| Min. of Special Duties | **Ngole,** Elvis Ngole |

21

## CAMEROON, REPUBLIC OF (cont.)

Min. of Special Duties .............................................. **Okouda,** Martin Aristide
Min. of Superior State Control ........................................ **Owona,** Joseph
Min. of Territorial Administration ..................................... **Ename,** Samson Ename
Min. of Tourism ................................................... **Mbafou,** Claude Joseph
Min. of Town Planning & Housing .................................... **Hele,** Pierre
Min. of Towns .................................................... **Zanga,** Antoine
Min. of Transport ................................................. **Abanda,** Joseph Tsanga
Min. of Women's Affairs .............................................
Min. of Youth & Sports .............................................
Min. Del. at the Presidency in Charge of Defense ........................ **Ali,** Amadou
Min. Del. at the Presidency for Higher State Control ..................... **Gwanmesia,** Lucy
Min. Del. at the Presidency for Relations with Assemblies ................. **Owona,** Gregoire
Min. Del. at External Relations for the Commonwealth .................... **Ngute,** Joseph Ndion
Min. Del. at External Relations for Relations with the Islamic World ......... **Gargoum,** Adoum
Min. Del. at Economic Affairs for Budget ............................. **Melingui,** Roger
Min. Del. at Economic Affairs for the Stabilization Plan ................... **Gankou,** Jean-Marie
Sec. of State for Agriculture ........................................ **Abdoulaye,** Aboubacar
Sec. of State for External Relations .................................. **Kouomegni,** Augustin Kontchou
Sec. of State for Industrial & Commercial Development ................... **Mbio,** Edmond Moampea
Sec. of State for Lands ............................................. **Yembe,** Jones Shey
Sec. of State for National Education .................................. **Teghen,** Joseph Yunga
Sec. of State for National Gendarmerie ................................ **Meka,** Remi Ze
Sec. of State for Posts & Telecommunications .......................... **Oumarou,** Denis
Sec. of State for Prison Administration ................................ **Gassagaye,** Antar
Sec. of State for Public Health ...................................... **Hayatou,** Alim
Sec. of State for Public Investments & Territorial Development ............. **Messi,** Tsala
Sec. of State for Public Works ....................................... **Bonde,** Emmanuel
Sec. of State for Transport .......................................... **Djalloh,** Nana Aboubakar, *Dr.*
Governor, Central Bank ............................................. **Mba,** Casimir Oye
Ambassador to the US .............................................. **Mendouga,** Jerome
Permanent Representative to the UN, New York ......................... **Belinga Eboutou,** Martin

## CANADA

(Last updated: 2/14/2001)

Governor General .................................................. **Clarkson,** Adrienne
Prime Minister .................................................... **Chretien,** Jean
Dep. Prime Min. ................................................... **Gray,** Herb
Min. of Agriculture ................................................ **Van Clief,** Lyle
Min. of Canadian Heritage .......................................... **Copps,** Sheila
Min. of Citizenship & Immigration .................................... **Caplan,** Elinor
Min. of Defense ................................................... **Eggleton,** Arthur
Min. of Environment ............................................... **Anderson,** David
Min. of Finance ................................................... **Martin,** Paul
Min. of Fisheries & Oceans ......................................... **Dhaliwal,** Herb
Min. of Foreign Affairs ............................................. **Manley,** John
Min. of Health .................................................... **Rock,** Allan
Min. of Human Resources Development ................................ **Jane,** Stewart
Min. of Indian Affairs & Northern Development ......................... **Nault,** Robert
Min. of Industry .................................................. **Tobin,** Brian
Min. of Intergovernmental Affairs ..................................... **Dion,** Stephane
Min. of International Cooperation & the Francophonie .................... **Minna,** Maria
Min. of International Trade .......................................... **Pettigrew,** Pierre
Min. of Justice ................................................... **McLellan,** Anne
Min. of Labor .................................................... **Bradshaw,** Claudette
Min. of National Revenue ........................................... **Cauchon,** Martin
Min. of Natural Resources & Wheat Board ............................. **Goodale,** Ralph
Min. of Public Works & Government Services ........................... **Gagliano,** Alfonso
Min. of State for the Atlantic Canada Opportunities Agency ................ **Boudreau,** Bernard
Min. of Transport ................................................. **Collenette,** David
Min. of Veterans Affairs ............................................ **Duhamel,** Ronald
Sec. of State for Asia-Pacific ........................................ **Chan,** Raymond
Sec. of State for the Federal Office of Regional Development-Quebec ......... **Cauchon,** Martin
Sec. of State for International Financial Institutions ...................... **Peterson,** James

## CANADA (cont.)

Sec. of State for Latin America and Africa ............................... **Kilgour,** David
Sec. of State for Multiculturalism and the Status of Women ............... **Fry,** Hedy
Sec. of State for Parks ........................................... **Mitchell,** Andrew
Sec. of State for Science, Research, & Development ..................... **Duhamel,** Ronald
Sec. of State for Training, & Youth ................................. **Blondin-Andrew,** Ethel
Sec. of State for Western Economic Diversification & La Francophonie ........
Pres., Treasury Board & Infrastucture ............................... **Robillard,** Lucienne
Attorney General .................................................. **McLellan,** Anne
Solicitor General ................................................. **MacAulay,** Lawrence
Govt. Leader in the House ......................................... **Boudria,** Don
Govt. Leader in the Senate ........................................ **Graham,** Alasdair
Governor, Bank of Canada .......................................... **Thiessen,** Gordon
Ambassador to the US .............................................. **Kergin,** Michael
Permanent Representative to the UN, New York ....................... **Heinbecker,** Paul

## CAPE VERDE, REPUBLIC OF

(Last updated: 3/13/2001)

President ......................................................... **Pires,** Pedro
Prime Minister .................................................... **Neves,** Jose Maria Pereira
Min. of Agriculture & Fisheries ................................... **Couto de Matos,** Mario Anselmo
Min. of Defense ................................................... **Neves,** Jose Maria Pereira
Min. of Education, Culture & Sports ............................... **Borges,** Victor
Min. of Finance & Economic Planning ............................... **Burgo,** Carlos Augusto Duarte
Min. of Foreign Affairs, Co-operation & Communities ............... **Sousa,** Manuel Inocencio
Min. of Health, Employment, & Solidarity .......................... **Dantas Dos Reis,** Dario Laval Rezende
Min. of Infrastructure & Transport ................................ **Lopes,** Jorge Lima Delgado
Min. of Justice & Local Administration ............................ **Fones,** Cristina *Mrs.*
Min. of Tourism, Industry, & Trade ................................ **Duarte,** Jose Armando
Sec. of State for Foreign Affairs ................................. **Veiga,** Fatima Lima *Mrs.*
Sec. of State for Parliamentary Affairs & Defense ................. **Mauricio,** Armindo Cipriano
Sec. of State for State Reforms, Public Administration, & Local Government ... **Neves,** Edeltrudes Pires
Sec. of State for Youth Affairs ................................... **Mascarenhas,** Maria de Jesus Veiga Miranda

## CENTRAL AFRICAN REPUBLIC

(Last updated: 4/11/2001)

President ......................................................... **Patasse,** Ange-Felix
Prime Minister .................................................... **Ziguele,** Martin
Min. of Agriculture ............................................... **Dede,** Daniel Emery
Min. of Civil Service & Employment ................................ **Gonbala,** Laurent
Min. of Commerce, Industry, & Tourism ............................. **Koyassambia,** Jean-Baptiste
Min. of Communication, Postal, & Telecommunications ............... **Wakanga,** Albert Francis
Min. of Culture & Relations with Parliament ....................... **Doko,** Michel
Min. of Defense ................................................... **Demafouth,** Jean Jacques
Min. of Economy, Planning, & International Coop. ................... **Gomba,** Alexis
Min. of Education & Scientific Research ............................ **Anguimate,** Eloi
Min. of Environment, Water Resources, & Forestry .................. **Gounebana,** Constance
Min. of Finance & Budget .......................................... **Dabanga,** Theodore
Min. of Foreign Affairs & Francophonie ............................ **Mezode,** Agba Otikpo
Min. of Higher Education & Research ............................... **Mbaikoa,** Thimoleon
Min. of Housing, Town Planning, & Public Building ................. **Sama,** Armand
Min. of Interior & Territorial Administration ..................... **Biko,** Theodore
Min. of Justice ................................................... **Metefara,** Marcel
Min. of Mining & Energy ........................................... **Nalke-Dorogo,** Andre
Min. of Posts & Telecommunications ................................ **Vickos,** Jean Bruno
Min. of Presidential Affairs ...................................... **Gbezera-Bria,** Michel
Min. of Public Health ............................................. **Kalite,** Joseph
Min. of Public Works .............................................. **Mazette,** Jacquesson
Min. of Social Affairs & Family ................................... **Francoise,** Ibrahim
Min. of Territory Administration & Public Security ................ **Sokambi,** Aristide
Min. of Tourism, Arts, & Culture .................................. **Gounebana,** Constance Nathalie

## CENTRAL AFRICAN REPUBLIC (cont.)

| | |
|---|---|
| Min. of Trade, Industry, & Private Sector Promotion | **Mbaitadjim,** Jacob |
| Min. of Transportation & Civil Aviation | **Pendemou,** Desire |
| Min. of Youth & Sports | **Ndarata,** Jean-Dominque |
| Min. Del. for Disarmament | **Doyene,** Michel |
| Min. Del. for Finance | **Dokoula,** Lazarre |
| Min Del. for Foreign Affairs | **Boucher,** Victor |
| Min. Del. for Planning & International Cooperation | **Eregani,** Clement |
| Min. Del. for Public Security | **Zana,** Robert |
| Min. with Special Responsibility for Relations with the Arab World | **Mamadou,** Bello |
| Min. of State for Finance | **Sorongope,** Eric |
| Min. of State for Posts & Telecommunications | **Koyambonou,** Gabriel Jean Edouard |
| Sec. of State for Administration | **Dahomondo,** Gilbert Moussa Labbe |
| Sec. of State for National Solidarity | **Mbissa,** Albertine |
| Dir., Central Bank | **Koyamba,** Alphonse |
| Ambassador to the US | **Koba,** Henri |
| Permanent Representative to the UN, New York | **Fernandez,** Antonio Diende |

## CHAD, REPUBLIC OF

(Last updated: 3/15/2001)

| | |
|---|---|
| President | **Deby,** Idriss, *Lt. Gen.* |
| Prime Minister | **Yamassoum,** Nagoum |
| Min. of Agriculture | **Kebzabo,** Saleh |
| Min. of Civil Service & Employment | **Golom,** Routang Yoma |
| Min. of Commerce, Industry, & Crafts | **Tahini,** Kalzuede |
| Min. of Communications | **Abdelkerim,** Nadjo |
| Min. of Culture, Youth, & Sports | **Djouassab,** Abba Koi *Dr.* |
| Min. of Development & Economic Promotion | **Hassan,** Mahamat Ali |
| Min. of Environment & Water | **Kadjallami,** Oumar Boukar |
| Min. of Finance | **Louani,** Mahamat |
| Min. of Foreign Affairs & Cooperation | **Annadif,** Mahamat Saleh |
| Min. of Higher Education | **Nissala,** Laoukissam |
| Min. of Interior, Security, & Decentralization | **Moussa,** Abderaman |
| Min. of Justice & Keeper of the Seals | **Ahlhabo,** Mahamat Ahamat |
| Min. of Livestock | **Assour,** Weiding Assi |
| Min. of Mines, Energy, & Petroleum | **Moussa,** Moukhtar |
| Min. of National Defense & Reinsertion | **Nouri,** Mahamat |
| Min. of National Education | **Hamid,** Abderahim Breme |
| Min. of Post & Telecommunications | **Garba,** Salibou |
| Min. of Public Health | **Kimto,** Faime |
| Min. of Public Works & Transportation | **Daoussa,** Bichara Cherif |
| Min. of Social Affairs & Family | **Atahir,** Mariam |
| Min. of State | **Kebzabo,** Saleh |
| Min. of Tourism Development | **Choukou,** Mahamat Ahmat |
| Min., Sec. Gen. of the Govt. | **Houdeingar,** David |
| Asst. Sec. Gen. of the Govt. | **Maki,** Mahamat Saleh |
| Min. Delegate to the Prime Minister for Decentralization | **Lapia,** Djimtedaye |
| Sec. of State for Civil Service, Labor & Job Promotion | **Boukar,** Oumar |
| Sec. of State for Finance | **Pahimi,** Albert |
| Sec. of State for the Interior | **Djeme,** Ganda Djaha |
| Sec. of State for National Education | **Abdoulaye,** Ahmat |
| Sec. of State for Public Health | **Maryoud,** Attamar |
| Sec. of State for Public Works | **Ndikibeulngar,** Bassounda |
| Ambassador to the US | **Soubiane,** Ahmat Hassaballah |
| Permanent Representative to the UN, New York | **Guelnodji,** Koumtog Laoteg |

## CHILE, REPUBLIC OF

(Last updated: 3/19/2001)

| | |
|---|---|
| President | **Lagos,** Ricardo |
| Min. of Agriculture | **Campos Quiroga,** Jaime |
| Min. of Defense | **Fernandez,** Mario |
| Min. of Economy, Mining, & Energy | **De Gregorio,** Jose |
| Min. of Education | **Aylwin Oyarzun,** Mariana |
| Min. of Finance | **Eyzaguirre Guzman,** Nicolas |
| Min. of Foreign Relations | **Alvear Valenzuela,** Maria Soledad |
| Min. of Health | **Bachelet,** Michelle |
| Min. of Housing, Urbanism, & Public Lands | **Ravinet,** Jaime |
| Min. of Interior | **Insulza,** Jose Miguel |
| Min. of Justice | **Gomez Urrutia,** Jose Antonio |
| Min. of Labor & Social Security | **Solari Saavedra,** Ricardo |
| Min. of National Women's Service | **Delpiano,** Adriana |
| Min. of Planning & Cooperation | **Krauss,** Alejandra |
| Min. of Public Works, Transportation, & Telecommunications | **Cruz,** Carlos |
| Min. Sec. Gen. of Govt. | **Huepe Garcia,** Claudio |
| Min. Sec. Gen. of the Presidency | **Garcia Hurtado,** Alvaro |
| Pres., Central Bank | **Massad,** Carlos |
| Ambassador to the US | **Bianchi,** Andres |
| Permanent Representative to the UN, New York | **Valdes,** Juan |

## CHINA, PEOPLE'S REPUBLIC OF

(Last updated: 3/28/2001)

| | |
|---|---|
| President | **Jiang,** Zemin |
| Vice President | **Hu,** Jintao |
| Premier, State Council | **Zhu,** Rongji |
| Vice Premier, State Council | **Li,** Lanqing |
| Vice Premier, State Council | **Qian,** Qichen |
| Vice Premier, State Council | **Wen,** Jiabao |
| Vice Premier, State Council | **Wu,** Bangguo |
| State Councilor, State Council | **Chi,** Haotian |
| State Councilor, State Council | **Ismail,** Amat |
| State Councilor, State Council | **Luo,** Gan |
| State Councilor, State Council | **Wang,** Zhongyu |
| State Councilor, State Council | **Wu,** Yi |
| Sec. Gen., State Council | **Wang,** Zhongyu |
| Chmn., Central Military Commission | **Jiang,** Zemin |
| Min. in Charge of National Defense Science, Technology, & Industry Commission | **Liu,** Jibin |
| Min. in Charge of State Development Planning Commission | **Zeng,** Peiyan |
| Min. in Charge of State Economic & Trade Commission | **Sheng,** Huaren |
| Min. in Charge of State Family Planning Commission | **Zhang,** Weiqing |
| Min. in Charge of State Nationalities Affairs Commission | **Li,** Dezhu |
| Min. of Agriculture | **Chen,** Yaobang |
| Min. of Civil Affairs | **Doje,** Cering |
| Min. of Communications | **Huang,** Zhendong |
| Min. of Construction | **Yu,** Zhengsheng |
| Min. of Culture | **Sun,** Jiazheng |
| Min. of Education | **Chen,** Zhili |
| Min. of Finance | **Xiang,** Huaicheng |
| Min. of Foreign Affairs | **Tang,** Jiaxuan |
| Min. of Foreign Trade & Economic Cooperation | **Shi,** Guangsheng |
| Min. of Information Industry | **Wu,** Jichuan |
| Min. of Justice | **Zhang,** Fusen |
| Min. of Labor & Social Security | **Zhang,** Zuoji |
| Min. of Land & Natural Resources | **Zhou,** Yongkang |
| Min. of National Defense | **Chi,** Haotian |
| Min. of Personnel | **Zhang,** Xuezhong |
| Min. of Public Health | **Zhang,** Wenkang |
| Min. of Public Security | **Jia,** Chunwang |
| Min. of Railways | **Fu,** Zhihuan |

## CHINA, PEOPLE'S REPUBLIC OF (cont.)

Min. of Science & Technology ................................................ **Zhu,** Lilan
Min. of State Security ....................................................... **Xu,** Yongyue
Min. of Supervision ......................................................... **He,** Yong
Min. of Water Resources .................................................... **Wang,** Shucheng
Pres., People's Bank of China .............................................. **Dai,** Xianglong
Ambassador to the US ...................................................... **Yang,** Jiechi
Permanent Representative to the UN, New York ........................... **Qin,** Huasun
Hong Kong ................................................................
(Special Administrative Region of the People's Republic of China) ...........
Chief Executive ............................................................ **Tung,** Chee-hwa
Chief Secretary for Administration ......................................... **Chan,** Anson
Sec. for Civil Service ....................................................... **Wong,** Joseph W. P.
Sec. for Commerce & Trade ................................................ **Chau,** Tak-hay
Sec. for Constitutional Affairs .............................................. **Suen,** Michael M. Y.
Sec. for Economic Services ................................................. **Lee,** Sandra
Sec. for Education and Manpower ........................................... **Law,** Fanny
Sec. for Environment & Food ............................................... **Yam,** Lily
Sec. for Finance ........................................................... **Tsang,** Donald
Sec. for Financial Services ................................................. **Ip,** Stephen
Sec. for Health & Welfare .................................................. **Yeoh,** E. K., *Dr.*
Sec. for Home Affairs ...................................................... **Lam,** W. K.
Sec. for Housing .......................................................... **Wong,** Dominic S. W.
Sec. for Information Technology & Broadcasting ............................ **Yau,** Carrie
Sec. for Justice ............................................................ **Leung,** Elsie
Sec. for Planing & Lands ................................................... **Siu,** Gordon
Sec. for Security .......................................................... **Ip,** Regina
Sec. for Transport ......................................................... **Ng,** Nicholas
Sec. for Treasury .......................................................... **Yue,** Denise
Sec. for Works ............................................................ **Lee,** Shing-see
Chief Executive, Hong Kong Monetary Authority .......................... **Yam,** Joseph
Convenor, Executive Council ............................................... **Leung,** Chun-ying
Chief Justice .............................................................. **Li,** Andrew
Pres., Legislative Council .................................................. **Fan,** Rita
Commissioner, Independent Commission Against Corruption ............... **Lai,** Alan
Dir., Audit Commission .................................................... **Chan,** Dominic Yin-tat
Macau ...................................................................
(Special Administrative Region of the People's Republic of China) ...........
Chief Executive ............................................................ **Ho,** Hau-wah (Edmund)
Sec for Administration & Justice ............................................ **Chan,** Florinda Da Rosa Silva
Sec for Economics & Finance ............................................... **Tam,** Francis Pak-un
Sec for Security ........................................................... **Cheong,** Kuoc Va
Sec for Social Affairs & Culture ............................................ **Chui,** Fernando Sai-on
Sec for Transportation & Public Works ..................................... **Ao,** Man Long
Procurator Gen. ........................................................... **Ho Chio,** Meng
Pres., Court of Final Appeal ............................................... **Sam,** Hou Fai
Pres., Legislative Council .................................................. **Chou,** Susana
Commissioner, Audit ...................................................... **Choi,** Fatima Mei-lei
Commissioner, Independent Commission Against Curruption ............... **Cheong,** U

## COLOMBIA, REPUBLIC OF

(Last updated: 4/3/2001)

President .................................................................. **Pastrana,** Andres
Vice President ............................................................. **Bell,** Lemus, Gustavo
Min. of Agriculture & Livestock ............................................ **Villalba,** Rodrigo
Min. of Communication .................................................... **Rosario,** Sintes, Maria del
Min. of Culture ............................................................ **Morales,** Lopez, Aracely
Min. of Economic Development ............................................. **Ramirez,** Ocampo, Augusto
Min. of Energy & Mines .................................................... **Valencia,** Cossio, Ramiro
Min. of Environment ....................................................... **Mayr,** Maldonaldo, Juan
Min. of Finance ........................................................... **Santos,** Calderon, Juan Manuel
Min. of Foreign Relations .................................................. **Fernandez,** de Soto, Guillermo
Min. of Foreign Trade ..................................................... **Ramirez,** Marta Lucia
Min. of Health ............................................................ **Ordonez,** Sara

## COLOMBIA, REPUBLIC OF (cont.)

Min. of Interior .......... **Estrada,** Villa, Armando
Min. of Justice .......... **Gonzalez,** Romulo
Min. of Labor & Social Security ..........
Min. of Mines & Energy .......... **Caballero,** Argaez, Carlos
Min. of National Defense .......... **Ramirez,** Acuna, Luis Fernando
Min. of National Education .......... **Lloreda,** Mera, Francisco Jose
Min. of Planning .......... **Herrera,** Vergara, Hernando
Min. of Public Health ..........
Min. of Sustainable Development ..........
Min. of Transportation .......... **Canal,** Gustavo
Dir., National Planning .......... **Echeverri,** Juan Carlos
Pres., Central Bank .......... **Urrutia,** Montoya, Miguel
Prosecutor General .......... **Gomez,** Mendez, Alfonso
Ambassador to the US .......... **Moreno,** Mejia, Luis Alberto
Permanent Representative to the UN, New York .......... **Valdivieso,** Sarmiento, Alfonso

## COMOROS, FEDERAL ISLAMIC REPUBLIC OF

(Last updated: 3/16/2001)

*On April 30 1999 the Comoros transitional government—which had been in place since the death of President Taki in October 1998—was toppled by a coup led by the Army Chief of Staff, Col. Assoumani Azzali. This is the 18th coup or coup attempt in the Comoros.*

Head of State .......... **Azzali,** Assoumani
Prime Minister .......... **Madi,** Hamada
Min. of Culture, Youth, & Sports .......... **Madi,** Ahamada
Min. of Defense .......... **M'Radabi,** Fakhri Mahmoud
Min. of Economy, Commerce, Artisanry, & Investments .......... **Bacar,** Harithi
Min. of Equipment, Energy, & Urban Affairs .......... **Abdallah,** Charif
Min. of Finance, Budget, & Planning .......... **Aboudou,** Assoumany
Min. of Foreign Affairs & Cooperation .......... **el-Amine,** Souefou Mohamed
Min. of Interior & Decentralization .......... **Djalim,** Ahmed ali
Min. of Justice & Islamic Affairs .......... **Iliasse,** Yahaya Mohamed
Min. of National Education, Professional Formation, & Human Rights .......... **Soilihi,** Said Abdallah Cheikh
Min. of Production & Environment .......... **Ali,** Said Ali Boina
Min. of Public Employees & Labor .......... **Mmadi,** Djaffar
Min. of Public Health, Population, & Women's Affairs .......... **Abbas,** Attoumane Jaffar
Min. of Public Service, Employment, & Work .......... **Hamdia,** Milissane
Min. of Transport, Tourism, Posts, & Telecommunications .......... **Athoumani,** Mohamed Ali
Min. Delegate of the Prime Minister in Charge of Communication & National Reconciliation .......... **Soimadou,** Mohamed Abdou
Dir. Gen., Central Bank .......... **Halifa,** Mohamed
Ambassador-Designate to the US .......... **Djabir,** Ahmed
Permanent Representative-designate to the UN, New York .......... **Djabir,** Ahmed

## CONGO, DEMOCRATIC REPUBLIC OF

(Last updated: 4/20/2001)

President .......... **Kabila,** Joseph
Min. of Agriculture, Fisheries, & Livestock .......... **Futa,** Andre Phillipe
Min. of Civil Service .......... **Lwanghy,** Celestin
Min. of Communications & Press .......... **Karubi,** Kikaya Bin
Min. of Culture & Arts .......... **Wafwana,** Marthe Ngalula
Min. of Defense .......... **Kabila,** Joseph
Min. of Economy, Finance, & Budget .......... **Mbuyamu,** Matungulu
Min. of Education .......... **Rwakaikara Kamara,** Augustin
Min. of Energy .......... **Buse Falay,** Georges
Min. of Enterprises .......... **Bolongo,** Norbert Likulia
Min. of Finance & Budget .......... **Kalondaya,** Jean Amisi
Min. of Fisheries, & Livestock .......... **Mawampanga,** Mwana Nanga
Min. of Foreign Affairs & International Cooperation .......... **Okitundu,** Leonard She ..........

## CONGO, DEMOCRATIC REPUBLIC OF (cont.)

| | |
|---|---|
| Min. of Health | **Mamba,** Mashako |
| Min. of Housing, Environment, & Tourism Development | **Sakanya,** Henri Mova |
| Min. of Human Rights | **Luaba,** Ntumba |
| Min. of Industry & Commerce | **Mateyibo,** Helene |
| Min. of Interior | **Manyanga,** Mira Ndjokou |
| Min. of Information & Tourism | **Ilongo,** Sakombi |
| Min. of Justice | **Masudi,** Ngele |
| Min. of Labor & Social Security | **Mufwankol,** Marie Ange Lukiana |
| Min. of Land Registration, Environment, & Tourism | **Banamuhere,** Salomon |
| Min. of Mining & Petroleum | **Bavangu,** Simon Tumawako |
| Min. of National Education | **Kiota,** Kutumisa |
| Min. of National Security & Public Order | **Kongolo,** Mwenze |
| Min. of Petroleum Resources | **Chubaka,** Anatole Bishikwabo |
| Min. of Planning & Reconstruction | **Numbi,** Denis Kalume |
| Min. of Post, Telephone, & Telecommunications | **Mawoko,** Phillipe Kuwutama |
| Min. of the Presidency | **Mwanke,** Augustin Katumba |
| Min. of Public Administration | **Mukulungu,** Benjamin |
| Min. of Public Works | **Mbaki,** Nkondi |
| Min. of Regional Cooperation | **Mutombo Mudiay,** Odelive Meta |
| Min. of Social Affairs | **Ebamba,** Jeanne |
| Min. of Transport & Communication | **Minada,** Dakarudino Wakale |
| Min. of Youth & Sports | **Nzulama,** Thimothee Moleka |
| Min. of State for Education | **Yerodia Ndombasi,** Abdoulaye |
| Min. of State for Internal Affairs | **Kakudji,** Gaetan |
| Min. of State (without portfolio) | **Mpoyo,** Pierre-Victor |
| Del. Min. of Defense | **Awan,** Irung Ilunga |
| Head, National Intelligence Agency | **Kazadi,** Didier |
| Governor, Central Bank | **Masangu,** Jean-Claude |
| Ambassador to the US | |
| Permanent Representative to the UN, New York | |

## CONGO, REPUBLIC OF THE

(Last updated: 3/15/2001)

| | |
|---|---|
| President | **Sassou-Nguesso,** Denis |
| Min. of the Presidency in Charge of National Defense | **Lekoundzou Ossetoumba,** Justin Itihi |
| Min. of the Presidency in Charge of the Presidential Cabinet & State Control | **Bitsindou,** Gerard |
| Min. of Agriculture & Livestock | **Nkoua Gongara,** Celestin |
| Min. of Commerce and Small & Medium-Sized Enterprises | **Boussoukou Boumba,** Pierre Damien |
| Min. of Communication & Relations with Parliament | **Ibovi,** Francois |
| Min. of Culture & Tourism | **Mambou Gnali,** Aimee |
| Min. of Economy, Finance, & Budget | **Dzon,** Mathias |
| Min. of Education & Scientific Research | **Nzila,** Pierre |
| Min. of Energy & Water Resources | **Tassoua,** Jean-Marie |
| Min. of Foreign Affairs & Cooperation | **Adada,** Rodolphe |
| Min. of Forestry & Fisheries | **Djombo,** Henri |
| Min. of Health & National Solidarity | **Opimbat,** Leon Alfred |
| Min. of Industrial Development & Private Sector Promotion | **Obama,** Alphonse |
| Min. of Industry, Mines, & Environment | **Mampouya,** Michel |
| Min. of Interior | **Oba,** Pierre |
| Min. of Justice & Keeper of the Seals | **Mbemba,** Jean Martin |
| Min. of Labor & Social Security | **Ndouane,** Lambert |
| Min. of Petroleum Affairs | **Taty Loutard,** Jean-Baptiste |
| Min. of Posts & Telecommunications | **Dello,** Jean |
| Min. of Public Service, Administrative Reform, & Women's Affairs | **Dambenze,** Jeanne |
| Min. of Public Works | **Tsiba,** Florent |
| Min. of Reconstruction & Urban Development | **Mberi,** Martin |
| Min. of Regional Development | **Moussa,** Pierre |
| Min. of Technical Education, Professional Training, Youth, Civic Education, & Sports | **Okombi Salissan,** Andre |
| Min. of Transport, Civil Aviation, & Merchant Marine | **Mvouba,** Isidore |
| Dir., Central Bank | **Poungui,** Ange Edouard |
| Permanent Representative to the UN, New York | **Ikouebe,** Basile |

## COOK ISLANDS

(Last updated: 2/15/2001)

*(Self-governing in free association with New Zealand)*

| | |
|---|---|
| Prime Minister | **Maoate,** Terepai, *Dr.* |
| Dep. Prime Min. | **George,** Norman |
| Min. of Agriculture | **Woonton,** Robert |
| Min. of Broadcasting | **George,** Norman |
| Min. of Civil Aviation | **Munokoa,** Ngamau |
| Min. of Communication | **George,** Norman |
| Min. of Conservation | |
| Min. of Corrective Services | |
| Min. of Crown Law | **George,** Norman |
| Min. of Cultural Development | **Marurai,** Jim |
| Min. of Customs | **George,** Norman |
| Min. of Economic Development & Planning | |
| Min. of Education | **Marurai,** Jim |
| Min. of the Electoral Office | |
| Min. of Energy | **Munokoa,** Ngamau |
| Min. of Finance | **Maoate,** Terepai, *Dr.* |
| Min. of Foreign Affairs | **Woonton,** Robert |
| Min. of General Licensing Authority | |
| Min. of Health | **George,** Norman |
| Min. of Housing | |
| Min. of Immigration | **Woonton,** Robert |
| Min. of Information Services | |
| Min. of Inland Revenue | |
| Min. of Internal Affairs | **Munokoa,** Ngamau |
| Min. of Justice | **Vavia,** Tangata |
| Min. of Legislative Services | **George,** Norman |
| Min. of Marine Resources | **Woonton,** Robert |
| Min. of Outer Islands Development | **Vavia,** Tangata |
| Min. of Parliamentary Services | **Woonton,** Robert |
| Min. of Police | **George,** Norman |
| Min. of State Owned Enterprises | |
| Min. of Telecommunications | **George,** Norman |
| Min. of Tourism & Transportation | **Woonton,** Robert |
| Min. of Trade, Labor, & Shipping | |
| Min. of Water Supply | **Munokoa,** Ngamau |
| Min. of Women, Youth & Sports | **Munokoa,** Ngamau |
| Min. of Works, Energy, & Physical Planning | **Munokoa,** Ngamau |
| Min. Responsible for Affairs of the Aronga Mana | |
| Min. Responsible for the Prime Minister's Department | |
| Min. Responsible for the Public Service Commission | **Marurai,** Jim |
| Min. Responsible for Waterfront Commission | |
| Attorney General | **George,** Norman |

## COSTA RICA, REPUBLIC OF

(Last updated: 1/24/2001)

| | |
|---|---|
| President | **Rodriguez,** Miguel Angel |
| First Vice Pres. | **Fischel,** Volio, Astrid |
| Second Vice Pres. | **Odio,** Benito, Elizabeth |
| Min. of Agriculture & Livestock | **Dent-Zeledon,** Alberto |
| Min. of Culture, Youth, & Sports | **Fischel,** Voilo, Astrid |
| Min. of Economy | **Barrantes,** Gilberto |
| Min. of Education | **Vargas,** Guillermo |
| Min. of Environment & Energy | **Odio,** Benito, Elizabeth |
| Min. of Finance | **Baruch,** Goldberg, Leonel |
| Min. of Foreign Relations & Religion | **Rojas,** Lopez, Roberto |
| Min. of Foreign Trade | **Duenas,** Thomas |
| Min. of Health | **Pardo,** Evans, Rogelio |
| Min. of Housing | **Monroe,** Donald |

## COSTA RICA, REPUBLIC OF (cont.)

Min. of Justice ............................................................... **Nagel,** Berger, Monica
Min. of Labor & Social Security ...................................... **Morales,** Mora, Victor
Min. of the Presidency ................................................... **Chaverri,** Danilo
Min. of Public Education ................................................ **Gutierrez,** Carranza, Claudio
Min. of Public Security, Government, & Police ............... **Ramos,** Martinez, Rogelio
Min. of Public Works & Transportation ......................... **Fernandez,** Mario
Min. of Science & Technology ....................................... **De Taramond,** Guy
Min. of Women's Situation ............................................ **Ingianna,** Yolanda
Pres., Central Bank ...................................................... **Lizano,** Fait, Eduardo
Ambassador to the US .................................................. **Daremblum,** Rosenstein, Jaime
Permanent Representative to the UN, New York ............. **Niehaus,** Quesada, Bernd

## CÔTE D'IVOIRE, REPUBLIC OF

(Last updated: 2/15/2001)

President .................................................................... **Gbagbo,** Laurent
Prime Minister ............................................................ **N'Guessan,** Affi
Min. of Agriculture & Animal Resources ....................... **Douati,** Alphonse
Min. of Commerce & Industry ....................................... **Bohoun,** Bouabre
Min. of Communication & Culture .................................. **Kone,** Dramane
Min. of Construction & Environment .............................. **Assia,** Abou
Min. of Defense & Civil Protection ................................ **Kouassi,** Moise Lida
Min. of Economic Infrastructure .................................... **Achi,** Patrick
Min. of Economy & Finance .......................................... **Koulibaly,** Mamadou
Min. of Environment .................................................... **Boka,** Cahterine Ohouchi
Min. of Family & Promotion .......................................... **Lagou,** Adjoua Henriette
Min. of Foreign Affairs ................................................. **Sangare,** Abou Drahamane
Min. of Higher Education & Scientific Research .............. **Bailly,** Sery
Min. of Interior & Decentralization ............................... **Dudou,** Emile Boga
Min. of Justice ............................................................ **Oulai,** Siene
Min. of Labor & Civil Service ....................................... **Oulaye,** Hubert
Min. of Mines & Energy ............................................... **Monnet,** Leon Emanuel
Min. of National Education ........................................... **N'guessan,** Michel Amani
Min. of Planing & Development ..................................... **N'Guessan,** Affi
Min. of Public Health & Social Protection ...................... **N'Dori,** Raymond Aboudoh
Min. of Social Affairs & National Solidarity ................... **Yapi,** Clotilde Ohouochi
Min. of Sports ............................................................ **Bro-Grebe,** Genevieve
Min. of Tourism & Handicrafts ...................................... **Likikouet,** Odette Bako
Min. of Transport ........................................................ **Kabran,** Appiah Aime
Min. of Youth ............................................................. **Dano,** Djedje Sebastien
Ambassador to the US .................................................. **Bamba,** Youssouf
Permanent Representative to the UN, New York ............. **Bouah-Kamon,** Claude Stanislas

## CROATIA, REPUBLIC OF

(Last updated: 3/16/2001)

President .................................................................... **Mesic,** Stjepan
Prime Minister ............................................................ **Racan,** Ivica
Dep. Prime Min. .......................................................... **Antunovic,** Zeljka
Dep. Prime Min. .......................................................... **Granic,** Goran
Dep. Prime Min. .......................................................... **Linic,** Slavko
Min. of Agriculture & Forestry ..................................... **Pankretic,** Bozidar
Min. of Culture ........................................................... **Vujic,** Antun
Min. of Defense .......................................................... **Rados,** Jozo
Min. of Economy & Privatization. .................................. **Fizulic,** Goranko
Min. of Education & Sport ............................................ **Strugar,** Vladimir
Min. of European Integration ....................................... **Jakovcic,** Ivan
Min. of Finance .......................................................... **Crkvenac,** Mato
Min. of Foreign Affairs ................................................. **Picula,** Tonino
Min. of Health ............................................................ **Stavljevic-Rukavina,** Maja
Min. of Homeland War Defenders .................................. **Pandic,** Ivica
Min. of Immigration, Development, & Reconstruction ...... **Cacic,** Radimir

## CROATIA, REPUBLIC OF (cont.)

| | |
|---|---|
| Min. of Internal Affairs | **Lucin,** Sime |
| Min. of Justice | **Ivanisevic,** Stjepan |
| Min. of Labor & Social Welfare | **Vidovic,** Davorko |
| Min. of Science & Technology | **Kraljevic,** Hrvoje |
| Min. of Small & Medium Businesses | **Pecek,** Zeljko |
| Min. of Tourism | **Zupan Ruskovic,** Pave |
| Min. of Transportation and Telecommunications | **Tusek,** Alojz |
| Min. of Urban Development, Construction, & Housing | **Kovacevic,** Bozo |
| Governor, National Bank of Croatia | **Rohatinski,** Zeljko |
| Ambassador-Designate to the US | **Grdesic,** Ivan |
| Permanent Representative to the UN, New York | **Simonovic,** Ivan |

## CUBA, REPUBLIC OF—NDE

(Last updated: 3/26/2001)

| | |
|---|---|
| President of the Council of State | **Castro,** Ruz, Fidel |
| First Vice Pres. of the Council of State | **Castro,** Ruz, Raul, *Gen.* |
| Vice Pres. of the Council of State | **Almeida,** Bosque, Juan |
| Vice Pres. of the Council of State | **Colome,** Ibarra, Abelardo, *Corps. Gen.* |
| Vice Pres. of the Council of State | **Lage,** Davila, Carlos |
| Vice Pres. of the Council of State | **Lazo,** Hernandez, Esteban |
| Vice Pres. of the Council of State | **Machado,** Ventura, Jose Ramon |
| Min. Sec. of the Council of State | **Miyar,** Barruecos, Jose M. |
| Pres. of the Council of Ministers | **Castro,** Ruz, Fidel |
| First Vice Pres. of the Council of Ministers | **Castro,** Ruz, Raul, *Gen.* |
| Vice Pres. of the Council of Ministers | **Cienfuegos,** Gorriaran, Osmani |
| Vice Pres. of the Council of Ministers | **Diaz,** Suarez, Adolfo |
| Vice Pres. of the Council of Ministers | **Fernandez,** Alvarez, Jose Ramon |
| Vice Pres. of the Council of Ministers | **Miret,** Prieto, Pedro |
| Vice Pres. of the Council of Ministers | **Rodriguez Garcia,** Jose Luis |
| Sec. of the Council of Ministers | **Lage,** Davila, Carlos |
| Min. of Agriculture | **Jordan Morales,** Alfredo |
| Min. of Basic Industries | **Portal,** Leon, Marcos |
| Min. of Construction | **Junco del Pino,** Juan Mario |
| Min. of Culture | **Prieto Jimenez,** Abel |
| Min. of Domestic Trade | **Castillo,** Cuesta, Barbara |
| Min. of Economy & Planning | **Rodriguez,** Garcia, Jose Luis |
| Min. of Education | **Gomez,** Gutierrez, Luis I. |
| Min. of Finance & Prices | **Millares,** Rodriguez, Manuel |
| Min. of the Fishing Industry | **Lopez Valdes,** Alfredo |
| Min. of the Food Industry | **Roca,** Iglesias, Alejandro |
| Min. of Foreign Investment & Economic Cooperation | **Lomas,** Morales, Marta |
| Min. of Foreign Relations | **Perez,** Roque, Felipe |
| Min. of Foreign Trade | **de la Nuez Ramirez,** Raul |
| Min. of Higher Education | **Vecino,** Alegret, Fernando |
| Min. of Information Science & Communication | **Gonzalez,** Planas, Ignacio |
| Min. of Interior | **Colome,** Ibarra, Abelardo, *Corps. Gen.* |
| Min. of Justice | **Diaz,** Sotolongo, Roberto |
| Min. of Labor & Social Security | **Morales,** Cartaya, Alfredo |
| Min. of Light Industry | **Perez,** Othon, Jesus |
| Min. of Public Health | **Dotres,** Martinez, Carlos |
| Min. of the Revolutionary Armed Forces | **Castro,** Ruz, Raul, *Gen.* |
| Min. of Science, Technology, & Environment | **Simeon,** Negrin, Rosa Elena |
| Min. of the Sugar Industry | **Rosales del Toro,** Ulises, *Div. Gen.* |
| Min. of Tourism | **Ferradaz,** Ibrahim |
| Min. of Transportation | **Perez,** Morales, Alvaro |
| Min. Without Portfolio | **Cabrisas Ruiz,** Ricardo |
| Min. Without Portfolio | **Lopez,** Rodriguez, Wilfredo |
| Pres., Central Bank of Cuba | **Soberon Valdes,** Francisco |
| Attorney General | **Escalona,** Reguera, Juan |
| Permanent Representative to the UN, New York | **Rodriguez Parrilla,** Bruno |

## CYPRUS, REPUBLIC OF

(Last updated: 11/17/2000)

President . . . . . . . . . . . . . . . . . . . . . . . . . . . . . . . . . . . . . . . . . . **Clerides,** Glafcos
Dep. Min. to the Pres. . . . . . . . . . . . . . . . . . . . . . . . . . . . . . . . **Kouros,** Pandelis
Min. of Agriculture, Natural Resources, & Environment . . . . . . . . . . . . . . . . . . . . **Themistokleous,** Konstandinos
Min. of Commerce, Industry, & Tourism . . . . . . . . . . . . . . . . . . . . **Rolandis,** Nicos
Min. of Communications, Public Works, & Transport . . . . . . . . . . . . . . . . . . . . **Neophytou,** Averof
Min. of Defense . . . . . . . . . . . . . . . . . . . . . . . . . . . . . . . . . . . . . **Hasikos,** Socrates
Min. of Education & Culture . . . . . . . . . . . . . . . . . . . . . . . . . . . . **Ioannides,** Ouranios
Min. of Finance . . . . . . . . . . . . . . . . . . . . . . . . . . . . . . . . . . . . . **Clerides,** Takis
Min. of Foreign Affairs . . . . . . . . . . . . . . . . . . . . . . . . . . . . . . . **Kasoulides,** Ioannis
Min. of Health . . . . . . . . . . . . . . . . . . . . . . . . . . . . . . . . . . . . . . **Savvides,** Frixos
Min. of Interior . . . . . . . . . . . . . . . . . . . . . . . . . . . . . . . . . . . . . **Christodoulou,** Christodoulos
Min. of Justice & Public Order . . . . . . . . . . . . . . . . . . . . . . . . . . **Koshis,** Nicos
Min. of Labor . . . . . . . . . . . . . . . . . . . . . . . . . . . . . . . . . . . . . . . **Mousiouttas,** Andreas
Governor, Central Bank . . . . . . . . . . . . . . . . . . . . . . . . . . . . . . . **Afxentiou,** Afxentios
Ambassador to the US . . . . . . . . . . . . . . . . . . . . . . . . . . . . . . . . **Kozakou-Marcoullis,** Erato
Permanent Representative to the UN, New York . . . . . . . . . . . . . . . . . . . . . . . **Zackheos,** Sotos

## CZECH REPUBLIC

(Last updated: 4/19/2001)

President . . . . . . . . . . . . . . . . . . . . . . . . . . . . . . . . . . . . . . . . . . . **Havel,** Vaclav
Prime Minister . . . . . . . . . . . . . . . . . . . . . . . . . . . . . . . . . . . . . . **Zeman,** Milos
Dep. Prime Min. . . . . . . . . . . . . . . . . . . . . . . . . . . . . . . . . . . . . . **Kavan,** Jan
Dep. Prime Min. . . . . . . . . . . . . . . . . . . . . . . . . . . . . . . . . . . . . .
Dep. Prime Min. . . . . . . . . . . . . . . . . . . . . . . . . . . . . . . . . . . . . . **Rychetsky,** Pavel
Dep. Prime Min. . . . . . . . . . . . . . . . . . . . . . . . . . . . . . . . . . . . . . **Spidla,** Vladimir
Min. of Agriculture . . . . . . . . . . . . . . . . . . . . . . . . . . . . . . . . . . **Fencl,** Jan
Min. of Culture . . . . . . . . . . . . . . . . . . . . . . . . . . . . . . . . . . . . . **Dostal,** Pavel
Min. of Defense . . . . . . . . . . . . . . . . . . . . . . . . . . . . . . . . . . . . . **Vetchy,** Vladimir
Min. of Education . . . . . . . . . . . . . . . . . . . . . . . . . . . . . . . . . . . **Zeman,** Eduard
Min. of Environment . . . . . . . . . . . . . . . . . . . . . . . . . . . . . . . . . **Kuzvart,** Milos
Min. of Finance . . . . . . . . . . . . . . . . . . . . . . . . . . . . . . . . . . . . . **Rusnok,** Jiri
Min. of Foreign Affairs . . . . . . . . . . . . . . . . . . . . . . . . . . . . . . . **Kavan,** Jan
Min. of Health . . . . . . . . . . . . . . . . . . . . . . . . . . . . . . . . . . . . . . **Fiser,** Bohumil
Min. of Industry & Trade . . . . . . . . . . . . . . . . . . . . . . . . . . . . . . **Gregr,** Miroslav
Min. of Interior . . . . . . . . . . . . . . . . . . . . . . . . . . . . . . . . . . . . . **Gross,** Stanislav
Min. of Justice . . . . . . . . . . . . . . . . . . . . . . . . . . . . . . . . . . . . . **Bures,** Jaroslav
Min. of Labor & Social Affairs . . . . . . . . . . . . . . . . . . . . . . . . . . **Spidla,** Vladimir
Min. of Local Development . . . . . . . . . . . . . . . . . . . . . . . . . . . . **Lachnit,** Petr
Min. of Transport & Communication . . . . . . . . . . . . . . . . . . . . . . **Schling,** Jaromir
Min. Without Portfolio . . . . . . . . . . . . . . . . . . . . . . . . . . . . . . . . **Brezina,** Karel
Governor, Czech National Bank . . . . . . . . . . . . . . . . . . . . . . . . . **Tuma,** Zdenek
Ambassador to the US . . . . . . . . . . . . . . . . . . . . . . . . . . . . . . . . **Vondra,** Aleksandr
Permanent Representative to the UN, New York . . . . . . . . . . . . . . . . . . . . . . . **Galuska,** Vladimir

## DENMARK, KINGDOM OF

(Last updated: 3/15/2001)

Head of State . . . . . . . . . . . . . . . . . . . . . . . . . . . . . . . . . . . . . . . **Queen Margrethe II**
Prime Minister . . . . . . . . . . . . . . . . . . . . . . . . . . . . . . . . . . . . . . **Rasmussen,** Poul Nyrup
Dep. Prime Min. . . . . . . . . . . . . . . . . . . . . . . . . . . . . . . . . . . . . . **Jelved,** Marianne
Min. of Culture . . . . . . . . . . . . . . . . . . . . . . . . . . . . . . . . . . . . . **Gerner Nielsen,** Elsebeth
Min. of Defense . . . . . . . . . . . . . . . . . . . . . . . . . . . . . . . . . . . . . **Troejborg,** Jan
Min. of Developmental Aid . . . . . . . . . . . . . . . . . . . . . . . . . . . . . **Bundegaard,** Anita Bay
Min. of Ecclesiastical Affairs . . . . . . . . . . . . . . . . . . . . . . . . . . . **Lebech,** Johannes
Min. of Economic Affairs & Nordic Cooperation . . . . . . . . . . . . . . . . . . . . . . . **Jelved,** Marianne
Min. of Education . . . . . . . . . . . . . . . . . . . . . . . . . . . . . . . . . . . . **Margrethe,** Vestager
Min. of Environment & Energy . . . . . . . . . . . . . . . . . . . . . . . . . . **Auken,** Svend
Min. of Finance . . . . . . . . . . . . . . . . . . . . . . . . . . . . . . . . . . . . . **Gjellerup,** Pia
Min. of Food, Agriculture, & Fisheries . . . . . . . . . . . . . . . . . . . . . **Bjerregaard,** Ritt

## DENMARK, KINGDOM OF (cont.)

| | |
|---|---|
| Min. of Foreign Affairs | **Lykketoft,** Mogens |
| Min. of Gender Equality | **Bundsgaard,** Lotte |
| Min. of Health | **Rolighed,** Arne |
| Min. of Housing & Urban Affairs | **Bundsgaard,** Lotte |
| Min. of Interior | **Jespersen,** Karen |
| Min. of Justice | **Jensen,** Frank |
| Min. of Labor | **Hygum,** Ove |
| Min. of Research & Information Technology | **Weiss,** Birthe |
| Min. of Social Affairs | **Kristensen,** Henrik Dam |
| Min. of Taxation | **Sorensen,** Frode |
| Min. of Trade & Industry | **Stavad,** Ole |
| Min. of Transportation & Communication | **Buksti,** Jacob |
| Governor, Central Bank | **Andersen,** Bodil Nyboe |
| Ambassador to the US | **Federspiel,** Ulrik |
| Permanent Representative to the UN, New York | **Bojer,** Jorgen Rud Hansen |

## DJIBOUTI, REPUBLIC OF

(Last updated: 3/15/2001)

| | |
|---|---|
| President | **Guelleh,** Ismail Omar |
| Prime Minister | **Dilleita,** Mohamed Dilleita |
| Min. of Agriculture, Livestock, & Fishing | **Daoud,** Ali Mohamed |
| Min. of Commerce, Industry, & Crafts | **Wais,** Elmi Obsieh |
| Min. of Communication, Culture, Post Office, & Telecoms | |
| Min. of Defense | **Ahmed,** Ougoureh Kifleh |
| Min. of Economy, Finance, & Privatization | **Bouh,** Yacin Elmi |
| Min. of Education | **Absieh,** Abdi Ibrahim |
| Min. of Employment & National Solidarity | **Abdillahi,** Mohamed Barkat |
| Min. of Energy & Natural Resources | **Mohamed,** Mohamed Ali |
| Min. of Equipment & Transportation | **Djama,** Osman Idriss |
| Min. of Foreign Affairs, International Cooperation, & Parliamentary Relations | **Farah,** Ali Abdi |
| Min. of Health | **Mohamed,** Dini Farah |
| Min. of Interior | **Miguil,** Abdallah Aboillahi |
| Min. of Justice, Muslim & Penal Affairs, & Human Rights | **Djibril,** Ibrahim Idriss |
| Min. of Presidential Affairs & Investment Promotion | **Moussa,** Osman Ahmed |
| Min. of Urban Planning, Housing, Environment, National, & Regional Development | **Oudine,** Souleiman Omar |
| Min. of Youth, Sports, Leisure, & Tourism | **Bililis,** Dini Abdallah |
| Min. Del. to the Prime Min. for Decentralization | **Waberi,** Ahmed Guirreh |
| Min. Del. to the Prime Min. for Mosque Properties & Muslim Affairs | **Dirir,** Cheik Mogueh |
| Min. Del. to the Prime Min. for the Promotion of Women, Family Well-Being, & Social Affairs | **Youssouf,** Hawa Ahmed |
| Governor, Central Bank | **Djama,** Mahamoud Haid |
| Ambassador to the US | **Roble,** Olhaye Oudine |
| Permanent Representative to the UN, New York | **Roble,** Olhaye Oudine |

## DOMINICA, COMMONWEALTH OF

(Last updated: 4/12/2001)

| | |
|---|---|
| President | **Sorhaindo,** Crispin Anselm |
| Prime Minister | **Charles,** Pierre |
| Dep. Prime Min. | |
| Min. of Agriculture & Environment | **Pascal,** Lloyd |
| Min. of Communications & Works | **Charles,** Pierre |
| Min. of Community Development | **Walter,** Matthew |
| Min. of Education | **Sabroache,** Herbert |
| Min. of Finance & Economic Planning | **George,** Ambrose |
| Min. of Foreign Affairs | **Charles,** Pierre |
| Min. of Health & Social Security | **Toussaint,** John |
| Min. of Housing & Physical Planning | **Henderson,** Vince |
| Min. of Immigration & Labor | **Austrie,** Reginald |
| Min. of National Security | **Charles,** Pierre |

## DOMINICA, COMMONWEALTH OF (cont.)

| | |
|---|---|
| Min. of Planning & Environment | **Martin,** Atherton |
| Min. of Tourism | **Savarin,** Charles |
| Min. of Trade, Industry, & Manufacturing | **Riviere,** Osborne |
| Attorney General | **Bruney,** David |
| Permanent Representative to the UN, New York | **Richards,** Simon Paul |

## DOMINICAN REPUBLIC

(Last updated: 9/15/2000)

| | |
|---|---|
| President | **Mejia,** Dominguez, Rafael Hipolito |
| Vice Pres. | **Ortiz Bosch,** Milagros |
| Sec. of State for Agriculture | **Jaquez,** Eligio |
| Sec. of State for the Armed Forces | **Soto,** Jimenez, Jose Miguel |
| Sec. of State for Culture | **Raful,** Tony |
| Sec. of State for Education, Fine Arts, & Public Worship | **Ortiz Bosch,** Milagros |
| Sec. of State for Environment | **Moya,** Pons, Frank |
| Sec. of State for Finance | **Alvarez,** Bogaert, Fernando |
| Sec. of State for Foreign Relations | **Tolentino,** Dipp, Hugo |
| Sec. of State for Industry & Commerce | **Lockward,** Angel |
| Sec. of State for Interior & Police | **Subervi,** Bonilla, Rafael |
| Sec. of State for the Presidency | **Grullon,** Sergio |
| Sec. of State for Public Health | **Rodriguez,** Soldevilla, Jose |
| Sec. of State for Public Works & Communications | **Vargas,** Miguel |
| Sec. of State for Sports, Physical Education, & Recreation | **Cedeno,** Cesar |
| Sec. of State for Tourism | **Alfredo,** Bordas, Ramon |
| Sec. of State for Women | **Henriquez,** Yadira |
| Sec. of Work | **Ray,** Guevara, Milton |
| Sec. of Youth | **Pena,** Guaba, Antonio |
| Attorney General | **Bello,** Rosa, Virgilio |
| Governor, Central Bank | **Guerrero,** Prats, Frank |
| Ambassador to the US | **Saladin,** Selin, Roberto |
| Permanent Representative to the UN, New York | **Aguiar,** Cristina |

## ECUADOR, REPUBLIC OF

(Last updated: 4/19/2001)

| | |
|---|---|
| President | **Noboa,** Bejarano, Gustavo |
| Vice Pres. | **Pinto,** Rubianes, Pedro |
| Min. of Agriculture | |
| Min. of Education | **Hanasse,** Salem, Roberto |
| Min. of Energy & Mines | **Teran,** Ribadeneira, Pablo |
| Min. of Environment & Tourism | **Vazquez,** Rocio |
| Min. of Finance & Credit | **Gallardo,** Jorge |
| Min. of Foreign Relations | **Moeller,** Heinz |
| Min. of Foreign Trade | **Pallares,** Galo Plaza |
| Min. of Government & Police | **Manrique,** Juan |
| Min. of Health | **Bustamante,** Fernando |
| Min. of Labor | **Insua,** Chang, Alberto |
| Min. of National Defense | **Unda,** Hugo |
| Min. of the Presidency | **Perez,** Monasterios, Marcelo |
| Min. of Public Works | **Machiavello,** Jose |
| Min. of Social Welfare | **Patino,** Arcoa, Raul |
| Min. of Urban Development & Housing | **Murgueytio,** Nelson |
| Pres., Central Bank | **Ycaza,** Jose Luis |
| Ambassador to the US | **A-Baki,** Ivonne |
| Permanent Representative to the UN, New York | **Aleman,** Mario |

## EGYPT, ARAB REPUBLIC OF

(Last updated: 11/17/2000)

| | |
|---|---|
| President | **Mubarak**, Mohammed Hosni |
| Prime Minister | **Ebeid**, Atef Mohamed |
| Dep. Prime Min. | **Wally**, Youssef Amin |
| Min. of Agriculture & Land Reclamation | **Wally**, Youssef Amin |
| Min. of Awqaf (Religious Affairs) | **Zaqzouq**, Mahmoud Hamdy |
| Min. of Communications & Information Technology | **Nazif**, Ahmed Mahmoud Mohamed |
| Min. of Construction, Housing, & New Urban Communities | **Soliman**, Mohamed Ibrahim |
| Min. of Culture | **Hosni**, Farouq |
| Min. of Defense & Military Production | **Tantawi**, Mohamed Hussein, *Fd. Mar.* |
| Min. of Economy & Foreign Trade | **Boutros-Ghali**, Youssef |
| Min. of Education | **Baha al-Din**, Hussein Kamel |
| Min. of Electricity & Energy | **Saiedi**, Ali Fahmy El- |
| Min. of Finance | **Hassanein**, Muhammad Medhat |
| Min. of Foreign Affairs | **Moussa**, Amre Mahmoud |
| Min. of Health & Population | **Sallam**, Ismail Awadallah, *Dr* |
| Min. of Higher Education | **Shehab**, Moufed Mahmoud |
| Min. of Industry & Technology Development | **Rifa'i**, Mustafa Mohamed El- |
| Min. of Information | **Sherif**, Mohamed Safwat El- |
| Min. of Insurance & Social Affairs | **Guindi**, Amina El- |
| Min. of Interior | **Adli**, Habib El- |
| Min. of Justice | **Seif al-Nasr**, Farouq |
| Min. of Manpower & Immigration | **Amawy**, Ahmed El- |
| Min. of Petroleum | **Fahmy**, Sameh |
| Min. of Planning | **Dersh**, Ahmed Mahrus El- |
| Min. of Public Business Sector | **Khattab**, Mokhtar |
| Min. of Supply & Internal Trade | **Khedr**, Hassan Ali |
| Min. of Tourism | **Beltagui**, Mamdouh El- |
| Min. of Transport | **Demeri**, Ibrahim El- |
| Min. of Water Resources & Irrigation | **Abu Zeid**, Mahmoud Abd al-Halim |
| Min. of Youth | **Dessouki**, Ali al-Din Hillal |
| Min. of State for Administrative Development | **Abu Amer**, Mohamed Zaki |
| Min. of State for Environment Affairs | **Ebeid**, Nadia Riad Makram |
| Min. of State for International Co-operation | **Dersh**, Ahmed Mahrus El- |
| Min. of State for Local Development | **Abdel Qader**, Mustafa |
| Min. of State for Military Production | **Mesh'al**, Sayrd |
| Min. of State for People's Assembly & Consultative Council Affairs | **Shazly**, Kamal El- |
| Min. of State for Scientific Research | **Shehab**, Moufed Mahmoud |
| Governor, Central Bank | **Hassan**, Ismail |
| Ambassador to the US | **Fahmy**, Nabil |
| Permanent Representative to the UN, New York | **Aboul Gheit**, Ahmed Ali |

## EL SALVADOR, REPUBLIC OF

(Last updated: 11/17/2000)

| | |
|---|---|
| President | **Flores Perez**, Francisco |
| Vice Pres. | **Quintanilla**, Carlos |
| Chief of the Cabinet | **Daboub**, Juan Jose |
| Min. of Agriculture & Livestock | **Urrutia**, Loucel, Salvador |
| Min. of Defense | **Varela**, Juan Antonio Martinez, *Maj. Gen.* |
| Min. of Economy | **Lacayo**, Miguel |
| Min. of Education | **Jacir de Lovo**, Ana Evelyn |
| Min. of Environment & Natural Resources | **Majano**, Guerrero, Ana Maria |
| Min. of Finance | **Trigueros**, Jose Luis |
| Min. of Foreign Relations | **De Avila**, Maria Eugenia Brizuela |
| Min. of Health | **Lopez Beltran**, Jose |
| Min. of Interior | **Acosta Oertel**, Mario Ernesto |
| Min. of Labor & Social Welfare | **Nieto**, Menendez, Jorge Isidoro |
| Min. of Public Security & Justice | **Galindo**, Francisco Bertrand |
| Min. of Public Works | **Quiros**, Jose Angel |
| Sec. Presidency Information | **Imendia**, Francisco |
| Attorney General | **Artiga**, Belisario |
| Pres., Central Reserve Bank | **Barraza**, Rafael |

## EL SALVADOR, REPUBLIC OF (cont.)

Ambassador to the US . . . . . . . . . . . . . . . . . . . . . . . . . . . . . . . . . . . . . . . . **Leon,** Rodriguez, Rene Antonio
Permanent Representative to the UN, New York . . . . . . . . . . . . . . . . . . . . . . . **Andino Salazar,** Jose Roberto


## EQUATORIAL GUINEA

(Last updated: 3/20/2001)

President . . . . . . . . . . . . . . . . . . . . . . . . . . . . . . . . . . . . . . . . . . . . . . . . . . . . **Obiang Nguema Mbasogo,** Teodoro, *Brig. Gen.*
*(Ret.)*
Prime Minister . . . . . . . . . . . . . . . . . . . . . . . . . . . . . . . . . . . . . . . . . . . . . . **Rivas,** Candido Muatetema
First Dep. Prime Min. . . . . . . . . . . . . . . . . . . . . . . . . . . . . . . . . . . . . . . . . . **Oyono Ndong,** Miguel
Dep. Prime Min. . . . . . . . . . . . . . . . . . . . . . . . . . . . . . . . . . . . . . . . . . . . . . **Ndong,** Demetrio Elo
Sec. Gen. of the Govt. . . . . . . . . . . . . . . . . . . . . . . . . . . . . . . . . . . . . . . . . **Eyegue Obama Asue,** Francisco Pascual
Min. of State for Agriculture, Fisheries, & Animal Husbandry . . . . . . . . . . . . . . **Camo,** Gregorio Boho
Min. of State in Charge of Economy & Commerce . . . . . . . . . . . . . . . . . . . . . . **Nguema Onguene,** Marcelino, *M.D.*
Min. of State in Charge of Planning & International Cooperation . . . . . . . . . . . . **Ndong Mba,** Anatolio
Min. of State for Economy & Commerce . . . . . . . . . . . . . . . . . . . . . . . . . . . . **Nguema Onguene,** Marcelina *M.D.*
Min. of State for Education & Science . . . . . . . . . . . . . . . . . . . . . . . . . . . . . . **Ngu,** Antonio Fernando Nve
Min. of State for Forestry, Fishing, & Environment . . . . . . . . . . . . . . . . . . . . . **Obiang,** Teodoro Nguema
Min. of State for Health & Social Welfare . . . . . . . . . . . . . . . . . . . . . . . . . . . **Onguene,** Marcelino Nguema
Min. of State for Information, Tourism, and Culture . . . . . . . . . . . . . . . . . . . . **Esono,** Lucas Nguema
Min. of State for Labor & Social Security . . . . . . . . . . . . . . . . . . . . . . . . . . . . **Nfube,** M. Ricardo Mangue Obama
Min. of State for the Interior & Local Corporations . . . . . . . . . . . . . . . . . . . . **Ndong,** Demetrio Elo
Min. of State for Missions . . . . . . . . . . . . . . . . . . . . . . . . . . . . . . . . . . . . . . **Evuna Owono Asangono,** Alejandro
Min. of State at the Presidency in Charge of Relations with
Assemblies & Legal Matters . . . . . . . . . . . . . . . . . . . . . . . . . . . . . . . . . . . . **Boriko,** Miguel Abia Biteo
Min. of State at the Presidency in Charge of Special Duties . . . . . . . . . . . . . . . **Evuna Owono Asangono,** Alejandro
Min. of State for Transport & Communication . . . . . . . . . . . . . . . . . . . . . . . . **Ntutumu,** Marcelino Oyono
Min. of Agriculture, Fisheries, & Animal Husbandry . . . . . . . . . . . . . . . . . . . . **Nsue,** Constantine Eko
Min. of Civil Service & Administrative Reforms . . . . . . . . . . . . . . . . . . . . . . . **Tang,** Ignacio Milam
Min. of Culture, Tourism, & Francophone Affairs . . . . . . . . . . . . . . . . . . . . . . **Nse Nfumu,** Augustin
Min. of Economic Affairs & Finance . . . . . . . . . . . . . . . . . . . . . . . . . . . . . . . **Edjo,** Baltasar Engonga
Min. of Education, Science, & Francophone Affairs . . . . . . . . . . . . . . . . . . . . . **Nfumu,** Santiago Ngua
Min. of Employment & Social Security . . . . . . . . . . . . . . . . . . . . . . . . . . . . . **Congue,** Constantino
Min. of Foreign Affairs, International Cooperation, & Francophone Affairs . . . . . **Efuman,** Santiago Nsobeya
Min. of Forestry & Environment . . . . . . . . . . . . . . . . . . . . . . . . . . . . . . . . . . **Obiang,** Teodoro Nguema
Min. of Health & Social Welfare . . . . . . . . . . . . . . . . . . . . . . . . . . . . . . . . . . **Ntutumu,** Juan Antonio
Min. of Industry, Commerce, & Small Enterprises . . . . . . . . . . . . . . . . . . . . . **Nsue,** Constantino Ekong
Min. of Information, Tourism, & Culture . . . . . . . . . . . . . . . . . . . . . . . . . . . . **Esono,** Lucas Nguema
Min. of Interior & Local Corporations . . . . . . . . . . . . . . . . . . . . . . . . . . . . . . **Onguene,** Clemente Engonga Nguema
Min. of Justice & Religion . . . . . . . . . . . . . . . . . . . . . . . . . . . . . . . . . . . . . . **Nsue,** Ruben Maye
Min. of Labor & Social Promotion . . . . . . . . . . . . . . . . . . . . . . . . . . . . . . . . **Cayetano Toherida,** Ernesto Maria
Min. of Mines & Energy . . . . . . . . . . . . . . . . . . . . . . . . . . . . . . . . . . . . . . . . **Ela,** Cristobal Menana
Min. of Planning & Economic Development . . . . . . . . . . . . . . . . . . . . . . . . . . **Mbo,** Fortunato Ofa
Min. of Public Works, Housing, & Urban Affairs . . . . . . . . . . . . . . . . . . . . . . . **Ndong,** Florentino Nkogo
Min. of Social Affairs & Women's Development . . . . . . . . . . . . . . . . . . . . . . . **Asangono,** Teresa Efua
Min. of Territorial Admin. & Local Govt. . . . . . . . . . . . . . . . . . . . . . . . . . . . . **Ndong Ela Mangue,** Julio
Min. of Youth & Sports . . . . . . . . . . . . . . . . . . . . . . . . . . . . . . . . . . . . . . . . **Ntutumu,** Juan Antonio Bibang`
Min. Del. to Agriculture, Livestock, & Rural Development . . . . . . . . . . . . . . . . **Obama,** Carlos Eyi
Min. Del. for Civil Service & Administrative Reform . . . . . . . . . . . . . . . . . . . . **Borilo,** Caridad Besari
Min. Del. for Communications & Transports . . . . . . . . . . . . . . . . . . . . . . . . . **Ngomo,** M. Jeremias Ondo
Min. Del. of Economic Affairs & Finance . . . . . . . . . . . . . . . . . . . . . . . . . . . **Abia,** Miguel
Min. Del. of Foreign Affairs, International Cooperation, & Francophone Affairs . **Ebang,** Jos Ela
Min. Del. for Justice & Religion . . . . . . . . . . . . . . . . . . . . . . . . . . . . . . . . . . **Ebule,** Filomena Evangelina Oyo
Min. Del. for Labor & Social Security . . . . . . . . . . . . . . . . . . . . . . . . . . . . . . **Awong,** Secundino Oyono
Min. Del. of National Defense . . . . . . . . . . . . . . . . . . . . . . . . . . . . . . . . . . . **Nsomo,** Melanio Ebendeng *Brig. Gen.*
Min. Del. for National Security . . . . . . . . . . . . . . . . . . . . . . . . . . . . . . . . . . . **Mba,** Manuel Nguema *Col.*
Min. Del. for Public Works, Housing, & Urgan Affairs . . . . . . . . . . . . . . . . . . . **Acuse,** Carmelo Modu
Min. Del. to the Presidency in Charge of Youth & Sports . . . . . . . . . . . . . . . . . **Eyegue Obama Asue,** Francisco Pascual
Vice Min. of Culture, Tourism, & Crafts Promotion . . . . . . . . . . . . . . . . . . . . . **Mibuy,** Anacleto Olo
Vice Min. of Economy & Finance . . . . . . . . . . . . . . . . . . . . . . . . . . . . . . . . . **Edu,** Marcelino Oyono
Vice Min. of Education & Science . . . . . . . . . . . . . . . . . . . . . . . . . . . . . . . . . **Nguema,** Filiberto Ntutumu
Vice Min. of Forestry, Fishing, & Environment . . . . . . . . . . . . . . . . . . . . . . . . **Ivina,** Joaquin Mecheba
Vice Min. of Health & Social Welfare . . . . . . . . . . . . . . . . . . . . . . . . . . . . . . **Fernandex,** Tomas Mecheba
Vice Min. of Industry, Commerce, & Small Enterprises . . . . . . . . . . . . . . . . . . **Ava,** Basilio

## EQUATORIAL GUINEA (cont.)

Vice Min. of Justice & Religious Affairs .................................................. **Ngomo Mbengono,** Francisco Javier
Vice Min. of Planning & Economic Development ............................... **Nchama,** Antonio Javier Nguema
Vice Min. of Press, Radio, & Television ................................................ **Mokuy,** Alfonso Nsue
Vice Min. of Public Works, Housing, & Urban Affairs .................... **Matta,** Ceferino Eburi
Vice Min. of Tourism & Culture ............................................................ **Torrez,** Hilario Sisa
Sec. of State for Energy .......................................................................... **Ondo,** Miguel Ekua
Sec. of State for International Cooperation & Francophone Affairs ........... **Ekua,** Lino Sima
Sec. of State for Mines ........................................................................... **Lima,** Gabriel Mbega Obiang
Sec. of State for National Defense ........................................................ **Ngua,** Francisco Edu *Col.*
Sec. of State for National Security ........................................................ **Mba Nguema,** Antonio
Sec. of State for Press, Radio, & Television ........................................ **Ngua Nfumu,** Santiago
Sec. of State for Treasury & Budget ..................................................... **Edjo,** Melchor Esono
Ambassador to the US ............................................................................ **Ondo Bile,** Pastor Micha
Permanent Representative to the UN, New York ................................. **Nsue,** Teodoro Biyogo

## ERITREA, STATE OF

(Last updated: 1/5/2001)

President ................................................................................................... **Isaias,** Afworki
Vice President ......................................................................................... **Mahmud,** Ahmed Sherifo
Min. of Agriculture ................................................................................ **Arefaine,** Berhe
Min. of Construction .............................................................................. **Abraha,** Asfaha
Min. of Defense ...................................................................................... **Sebhat,** Ephrem
Min. of Education ................................................................................... **Osman,** Saleh
Min. of Energy & Mines ........................................................................ **Tesfai,** Ghebreselassie
Min. of Finance ...................................................................................... **Gebreselassie,** Yoseph
Min. of Fisheries .................................................................................... **Petros,** Solomon
Min. of Foreign Affairs .......................................................................... **Ali,** Said Abdella
Min. of Health ........................................................................................ **Saleh,** Meki
Min. of Information & Culture ............................................................... **Beraki,** Gebre Selasie
Min. of Justice ........................................................................................ **Fozia,** Hashim
Min. of Labor & Human Welfare .......................................................... **Askalu,** Menkerios
Min. of Land, Water, & Environment .................................................... **Tesfai,** Ghirmazion
Min. of Local Government ..................................................................... **Mahmoud,** Ahmed Sherifo
Min. of Tourism ..................................................................................... **Ahmed,** Haj Ali
Min. of Trade & Industry ....................................................................... **Ali,** Said Abdella
Min. of Transport & Communications ................................................... **Saleh,** Idris Kekia
Governor, Bank of Eritrea ...................................................................... **Beyene,** Tekie
Ambassador to the US ............................................................................ **Asmerom,** Girma
Permanent Representative to the UN, New York ................................. **Baduri,** Ahmed Tahir

## ESTONIA, REPUBLIC OF

(Last updated: 11/17/2000)

President ................................................................................................... **Meri,** Lennart
Prime Minister ........................................................................................ **Laar,** Mart
Min. of Agriculture ................................................................................ **Padar,** Ivari
Min. of Culture ....................................................................................... **Kivi,** Signe
Min. of Defense ...................................................................................... **Luik,** Juri
Min. of Economics ................................................................................. **Parnoja,** Mihkel
Min. of Education ................................................................................... **Lukas,** Tonis
Min. of Environment .............................................................................. **Kranich,** Heiki
Min. of Finance ...................................................................................... **Kallas,** Siim
Min. of Foreign Affairs........................................................................... **Ilves,** Toomas Hendrick
Min. of Interior ...................................................................................... **Loodus,** Tarmo
Min. of Justice ........................................................................................ **Rask,** Mart
Min. of Population .................................................................................. **Saks,** Katrin
Min. for Regional Affairs ....................................................................... **Asmer,** Toivo
Min. of Social Affairs ............................................................................ **Nestor,** Eiki
Min. of Transport & Communications ................................................... **Jurgenson,** Toivo
Pres., Estonian Central Bank ................................................................. **Kraft,** Vahur
Ambassador to the US ............................................................................ **Juergenson,** Sven
Permanent Representative to the UN, New York ................................. **Pajula,** Merle

## ETHIOPIA (FEDERAL DEMOCRATIC REPUBLIC OF ETHIOPIA)

(Last updated: 3/15/2001)

President . . . . . . . . . . . . . . . . . . . . . . . . . . . . . . . . . . . . . . . . . . . . . . . . **Negasso,** Gidada
Prime Minister . . . . . . . . . . . . . . . . . . . . . . . . . . . . . . . . . . . . . . . . . . **Meles,** Zenawi
Dep. Prime Min. . . . . . . . . . . . . . . . . . . . . . . . . . . . . . . . . . . . . . . . . . **Kassu,** Ilala
Dep. Prime Min. . . . . . . . . . . . . . . . . . . . . . . . . . . . . . . . . . . . . . . . . . **Legese,** Adisu
Min. of Agriculture . . . . . . . . . . . . . . . . . . . . . . . . . . . . . . . . . . . . . . **Mengistu,** Hulukai
Min. of Culture & Information . . . . . . . . . . . . . . . . . . . . . . . . . . . **Wolde,** Michael Chamo
Min. of Defense . . . . . . . . . . . . . . . . . . . . . . . . . . . . . . . . . . . . . . . . . **Legese,** Adisu
Min. of Economic Planning & Cooperation . . . . . . . . . . . . . . . . **Ghirma,** Biru
Min. of Education . . . . . . . . . . . . . . . . . . . . . . . . . . . . . . . . . . . . . . . **Genet,** Zewde
Min. of Finance . . . . . . . . . . . . . . . . . . . . . . . . . . . . . . . . . . . . . . . . . **Sufian,** Ahmed
Min. of Foreign Affairs . . . . . . . . . . . . . . . . . . . . . . . . . . . . . . . . . . **Seyoum,** Mesfin
Min. of Health . . . . . . . . . . . . . . . . . . . . . . . . . . . . . . . . . . . . . . . . . **Adem,** Ibrahim
Min. of Justice . . . . . . . . . . . . . . . . . . . . . . . . . . . . . . . . . . . . . . . . . **Wolde,** Werede
Min. of Labor & Social Affairs . . . . . . . . . . . . . . . . . . . . . . . . . . . **Hassan,** Abdella
Min. of Mines & Energy . . . . . . . . . . . . . . . . . . . . . . . . . . . . . . . . . **Izzedin,** Ali
Min. of State Farms, Coffee & Tea Development . . . . . . . . . . . . **Hassan,** Abdella
Min. of Trade & Industry . . . . . . . . . . . . . . . . . . . . . . . . . . . . . . . . **Kassahun,** Ayele
Min. of Transport & Communications . . . . . . . . . . . . . . . . . . . . . **Muhammad,** Diriri
Min. of Water Resources . . . . . . . . . . . . . . . . . . . . . . . . . . . . . . . . **Shiferaw,** Jarso
Min. of Works & Urban Development . . . . . . . . . . . . . . . . . . . . . **Haile,** Assegide
Governor, National Bank . . . . . . . . . . . . . . . . . . . . . . . . . . . . . . . . **Teklewold,** Atnafu
Ambassador to the US . . . . . . . . . . . . . . . . . . . . . . . . . . . . . . . . . . **Berhane,** Gebre-Christos
Permanent Representative to the UN, New York . . . . . . . . . . . . **Fisseha,** Yimer

## FIJI ISLANDS, REPUBLIC OF THE

(Last updated: 11/17/2000)

*Following an attempted coup and declaration of marshal law by the military, Fiji will now have an interim government to serve until new elections are held and a new constitution is instituted.*

President . . . . . . . . . . . . . . . . . . . . . . . . . . . . . . . . . . . . . . . . . . . . . . . **Iloilo,** Josefa
Vice President . . . . . . . . . . . . . . . . . . . . . . . . . . . . . . . . . . . . . . . . . **Seniloli,** Jope
Prime Minister . . . . . . . . . . . . . . . . . . . . . . . . . . . . . . . . . . . . . . . . . **Qarase,** Laisenia
Dep. Prime Min. . . . . . . . . . . . . . . . . . . . . . . . . . . . . . . . . . . . . . . . **Nailatikau,** Epeli
Min. for Agriculture, Fisheries, Forests, & Alta . . . . . . . . . . . . . **Tora,** Apisai
Min. for Commerce, Business Development, & Investment . . . . **Vuetilovoni,** Tomasi
Min. for Education . . . . . . . . . . . . . . . . . . . . . . . . . . . . . . . . . . . . . **Delailomaloma,** Nelson
Min. for Fijian Affairs . . . . . . . . . . . . . . . . . . . . . . . . . . . . . . . . . . **Nailatikau,** Epeli
Min. for Finance & National Planning . . . . . . . . . . . . . . . . . . . . . **Kubuabola,** Jone
Min. for Foreign Affairs, External Trade, & Sugar . . . . . . . . . . . **Tavola,** Kaliopate
Min. for Health . . . . . . . . . . . . . . . . . . . . . . . . . . . . . . . . . . . . . . . . **Nacuva,** Pita
Min. for Home Affairs & Immigration . . . . . . . . . . . . . . . . . . . . . **Ratakele,** Talemo
Min. for Information & Communication . . . . . . . . . . . . . . . . . . . . **Kubuabola,** Inoke
Min. for Justice . . . . . . . . . . . . . . . . . . . . . . . . . . . . . . . . . . . . . . . . **Qetaki,** Alipate
Min. for Labor & Industrial Relations . . . . . . . . . . . . . . . . . . . . . **Momeodonu,** Tevita
Min. for Lands & Mineral Resources . . . . . . . . . . . . . . . . . . . . . . **Bulanauca,** Mitieli
Min. for Local Govt, Housing, & Environment . . . . . . . . . . . . . . **Cokanauto,** Tuqakitau
Min. for National Reconciliation . . . . . . . . . . . . . . . . . . . . . . . . . . **Qarase,** Laisenia
Min. for Public Enterprises & Public Sector Reform . . . . . . . . . . **Hatch,** Hector
Min. for Regional Development & Multi-Ethnic Affairs . . . . . . . **Tuisese,** Ilaitia
Min. for Tourism & Transport . . . . . . . . . . . . . . . . . . . . . . . . . . . . **Koroitamana,** Jone
Min. for Women, Culture, & Social Welfare . . . . . . . . . . . . . . . . **Kepa,** Ro Teimumu
Min. for Works & Energy . . . . . . . . . . . . . . . . . . . . . . . . . . . . . . . . **Cokanasiga,** Joketani
Min. for Youth, Employment, & Sports . . . . . . . . . . . . . . . . . . . . **Dakuidreketi,** Keni
Attorney General . . . . . . . . . . . . . . . . . . . . . . . . . . . . . . . . . . . . . . . **Qetaki,** Alipate
Governor, Reserve Bank . . . . . . . . . . . . . . . . . . . . . . . . . . . . . . . . . **Narube,** Savenaca
Ambassador to the US . . . . . . . . . . . . . . . . . . . . . . . . . . . . . . . . . . **Masirewa,** Napolioni, *Ratu*
Permanent Representative to the UN, New York . . . . . . . . . . . . **Naidu,** Amraiya

## FINLAND, REPUBLIC OF

(Last updated: 11/17/2000)

President . . . . . . . . . . . . . . . . . . . . . . . . . . . . . . . . . . . . . . . . . . . . . . . . . . . . . . . **Halonen,** Tarja
Prime Minister . . . . . . . . . . . . . . . . . . . . . . . . . . . . . . . . . . . . . . . . . . . . . . . . . **Lipponen,** Paavo
Min. of Agriculture & Forestry . . . . . . . . . . . . . . . . . . . . . . . . . . . . . . . **Hemila,** Kalevi
Min. of Basic Services . . . . . . . . . . . . . . . . . . . . . . . . . . . . . . . . . . . . . . . . **Soininvaara,** Osmo
Min. of Culture . . . . . . . . . . . . . . . . . . . . . . . . . . . . . . . . . . . . . . . . . . . . . . . **Linden,** Suvi
Min. of Defense . . . . . . . . . . . . . . . . . . . . . . . . . . . . . . . . . . . . . . . . . . . . . . **Enestam,** Jan Erik
Min. of Education . . . . . . . . . . . . . . . . . . . . . . . . . . . . . . . . . . . . . . . . . . . . **Rask,** Maija
Min. of Environment . . . . . . . . . . . . . . . . . . . . . . . . . . . . . . . . . . . . . . . . . **Hassi,** Satu
Min. of Finance . . . . . . . . . . . . . . . . . . . . . . . . . . . . . . . . . . . . . . . . . . . . . . **Niinisto,** Sauli
Min. of Foreign Affairs . . . . . . . . . . . . . . . . . . . . . . . . . . . . . . . . . . . . . . **Tuomioja,** Erkki
Min. of Foreign Trade . . . . . . . . . . . . . . . . . . . . . . . . . . . . . . . . . . . . . . . **Sasi,** Kimmo
Min. of Interior . . . . . . . . . . . . . . . . . . . . . . . . . . . . . . . . . . . . . . . . . . . . . . **Itala,** Ville
Min. of Justice . . . . . . . . . . . . . . . . . . . . . . . . . . . . . . . . . . . . . . . . . . . . . . . **Koskinen,** Johannes
Min. of Labor . . . . . . . . . . . . . . . . . . . . . . . . . . . . . . . . . . . . . . . . . . . . . . . **Filatov,** Tarja
Min. of Local & Regional Affairs . . . . . . . . . . . . . . . . . . . . . . . . . . . . **Korhonen,** Martti
Min. of Social Affairs & Health . . . . . . . . . . . . . . . . . . . . . . . . . . . . . **Perho,** Maija
Min. of Trade & Industry . . . . . . . . . . . . . . . . . . . . . . . . . . . . . . . . . . . . **Monkare,** Sinikka
Min. of Transport & Communications . . . . . . . . . . . . . . . . . . . . . . . . **Heinonen,** Olli-Pekka
Governor, Bank of Finland . . . . . . . . . . . . . . . . . . . . . . . . . . . . . . . . . . **Vanhala,** Matti
Ambassador to the US . . . . . . . . . . . . . . . . . . . . . . . . . . . . . . . . . . . . . . . **Laajava,** Jaakko
Permanent Representative to the UN, New York . . . . . . . . . . . . . . . **Rasi,** Satu Marjatta

## FRANCE (FRENCH REPUBLIC)

(Last updated: 4/6/2001)

President . . . . . . . . . . . . . . . . . . . . . . . . . . . . . . . . . . . . . . . . . . . . . . . . . . . . . **Chirac,** Jacques
Prime Minister . . . . . . . . . . . . . . . . . . . . . . . . . . . . . . . . . . . . . . . . . . . . . . . **Jospin,** Lionel
Min. of Agriculture & Fisheries . . . . . . . . . . . . . . . . . . . . . . . . . . . . . . **Glavany,** Jean
Min. of Civil Service & State Reform . . . . . . . . . . . . . . . . . . . . . . . . . **Sapin,** Michel
Min. of Culture & Communication . . . . . . . . . . . . . . . . . . . . . . . . . . . **Tasca,** Catherine
Min. of Defense . . . . . . . . . . . . . . . . . . . . . . . . . . . . . . . . . . . . . . . . . . . . . . **Richard,** Alain
Min. of Economy, Finance, & Industry . . . . . . . . . . . . . . . . . . . . . . . **Fabius,** Laurent
Min. of Employment & Solidarity . . . . . . . . . . . . . . . . . . . . . . . . . . . . **Guigou,** Elisabeth
Min. of Foreign Affairs . . . . . . . . . . . . . . . . . . . . . . . . . . . . . . . . . . . . . . **Vedrine,** Hubert
Min. of Infrastructure, Transport, & Housing . . . . . . . . . . . . . . . . . . **Gayssot,** Jean-Claude
Min. of the Interior . . . . . . . . . . . . . . . . . . . . . . . . . . . . . . . . . . . . . . . . . . **Vaillant,** Daniel
Min. of Justice . . . . . . . . . . . . . . . . . . . . . . . . . . . . . . . . . . . . . . . . . . . . . . . **Lebranchu,** Marylise
Min. of National Education . . . . . . . . . . . . . . . . . . . . . . . . . . . . . . . . . . **Lang,** Jack
Min. of Regional Development & Environment . . . . . . . . . . . . . . . . . **Voynet,** Dominique
Min. of Relations with Parliament . . . . . . . . . . . . . . . . . . . . . . . . . . . . **Queyranne,** Jean-Jack
Min. of Research . . . . . . . . . . . . . . . . . . . . . . . . . . . . . . . . . . . . . . . . . . . . **Schwartzenberg,** Roger-Gerard
Min. of Youth & Sports . . . . . . . . . . . . . . . . . . . . . . . . . . . . . . . . . . . . . . **Buffet,** Marie-George
Min. Del. for European Affairs . . . . . . . . . . . . . . . . . . . . . . . . . . . . . . . **Moscovici,** Pierre
Min. Del. for Family & Children . . . . . . . . . . . . . . . . . . . . . . . . . . . . . . **Royal,** Segolene
Min. Del. for Health . . . . . . . . . . . . . . . . . . . . . . . . . . . . . . . . . . . . . . . . . **Kouchner,** Bernard
Min. Del. for Towns . . . . . . . . . . . . . . . . . . . . . . . . . . . . . . . . . . . . . . . . . **Bartolone,** Claude
Sec. of State for Budget . . . . . . . . . . . . . . . . . . . . . . . . . . . . . . . . . . . . . . **Parly,** Florence
Sec. of State for Cooperation & Francophonie . . . . . . . . . . . . . . . . . **Josselin,** Charles
Sec. of State for Defense . . . . . . . . . . . . . . . . . . . . . . . . . . . . . . . . . . . . . **Masseret,** Jean-Pierre
Sec. of State for Economic Solidarity . . . . . . . . . . . . . . . . . . . . . . . . . **Hascoet,** Guy
Sec. of State for Elderly & the Handicapped . . . . . . . . . . . . . . . . . . . **Guinchard-Kunstler,** Paulette
Sec. of State for Foreign Trade . . . . . . . . . . . . . . . . . . . . . . . . . . . . . . . **Huwart,** Francois
Sec. of State for Housing . . . . . . . . . . . . . . . . . . . . . . . . . . . . . . . . . . . . . **Lienemann,** Marie-Noelle
Sec. of State for Industry . . . . . . . . . . . . . . . . . . . . . . . . . . . . . . . . . . . . **Pierret,** Christian
Sec. of State for Overseas Territories . . . . . . . . . . . . . . . . . . . . . . . . . **Paul,** Christian
Sec. of State for Patrimony & Cultural Decentralization . . . . . . . . . **Duffour,** Michel
Sec. of State for Professional Teaching . . . . . . . . . . . . . . . . . . . . . . . . **Melenchon,** Jean-Luc
Sec. of State for Small & Medium Business, Commerce,
Craft, & Consumer Affairs . . . . . . . . . . . . . . . . . . . . . . . . . . . . . . . . . . . **Patriat,** Francois
Sec. of State for the Elderly & the Handicapped . . . . . . . . . . . . . . . . **Gillot,** Dominique
Sec. of State for Tourism . . . . . . . . . . . . . . . . . . . . . . . . . . . . . . . . . . . . . **Demessine,** Michelle
Sec. of State for Women's Rights & Professional Training . . . . . . . . **Pery,** Nicole

## FRANCE (FRENCH REPUBLIC) (cont.)

Governor, Bank of France . . . . . . . . . . . . . . . . . . . . . . . . . . . . . . . . . . . . . . . . . . . . . . . **Trichet,** Jean-Claude
Ambassador to the US . . . . . . . . . . . . . . . . . . . . . . . . . . . . . . . . . . . . . . . . . . . . . . . . . . **Bujon de l'Estang,** Francois
Permanent Representative to the UN, New York . . . . . . . . . . . . . . . . . . . . . . . . . **Levitte,** Jean-David

## GABON (GABONESE REPUBLIC)

(Last updated: 2/23/2001)

President . . . . . . . . . . . . . . . . . . . . . . . . . . . . . . . . . . . . . . . . . . . . . . . . . . . . . . . . . . . . . . **Bongo,** El Hadj Omar
Vice President . . . . . . . . . . . . . . . . . . . . . . . . . . . . . . . . . . . . . . . . . . . . . . . . . . . . . . . . . **Di Ndinge,** Didjob Divungi
Prime Minister . . . . . . . . . . . . . . . . . . . . . . . . . . . . . . . . . . . . . . . . . . . . . . . . . . . . . . . . **Ntoutoume-Emane,** Jean-Francois
Min. of Agriculture, Livestock, & Rural Economy . . . . . . . . . . . . . . . . . . . . . . . . **Owono Essono,** Fabian
Min. of Civil Services & Administrative Reforms . . . . . . . . . . . . . . . . . . . . . . . . . **Nziengui,** Patrice
Min. of Commerce, Tourism, & Industial Development . . . . . . . . . . . . . . . . . . . . **Mabika-Mouyama,** Alfred
Min. of Defense . . . . . . . . . . . . . . . . . . . . . . . . . . . . . . . . . . . . . . . . . . . . . . . . . . . . . . . **Bongo,** Ali-Ben
Min. of Equipment, Construction, & the City . . . . . . . . . . . . . . . . . . . . . . . . . . . . **Boundono Simangoye,** Egide
Min. of Family & Women's Affairs . . . . . . . . . . . . . . . . . . . . . . . . . . . . . . . . . . . . . . **Ngoma,** Angelique
Min. of Finance, Economy, Budget, & Privatization . . . . . . . . . . . . . . . . . . . . . . **Doumba,** Emile
Min. of Health & Population . . . . . . . . . . . . . . . . . . . . . . . . . . . . . . . . . . . . . . . . . . . **Boukoudi,** Faustin
Min. of Higher Education & Scientific Research . . . . . . . . . . . . . . . . . . . . . . . . . . **Berre,** Andre Diaudonne
Min. of Justice . . . . . . . . . . . . . . . . . . . . . . . . . . . . . . . . . . . . . . . . . . . . . . . . . . . . . . . . **Missongo,** Pascal Desire
Min. of National Education . . . . . . . . . . . . . . . . . . . . . . . . . . . . . . . . . . . . . . . . . . . . **Mba Obame,** Andre
Min. of Small Enterprises . . . . . . . . . . . . . . . . . . . . . . . . . . . . . . . . . . . . . . . . . . . . . **Biyoghe-Mba,** Paul
Min. of Social Affairs & National Solidarity . . . . . . . . . . . . . . . . . . . . . . . . . . . . . **Ondo Metogho,** Emmanuel
Min. of Transport & Merchant Marine . . . . . . . . . . . . . . . . . . . . . . . . . . . . . . . . . . **Ngari,** Idriss
Min. of Water & Forests . . . . . . . . . . . . . . . . . . . . . . . . . . . . . . . . . . . . . . . . . . . . . . . **Onouviet,** Richard
Min. of Youth, Culture, Arts, & Sports . . . . . . . . . . . . . . . . . . . . . . . . . . . . . . . . . . **Ona Ondo,** Daniel
Min. of State for Communication . . . . . . . . . . . . . . . . . . . . . . . . . . . . . . . . . . . . . . . **Pendy-Bouyiki,** Jean-Remy
Min. of State for Equipment & Construction . . . . . . . . . . . . . . . . . . . . . . . . . . . . . **Myboto,** Zacharie
Min. of State for Foreign Affairs, Cooperation, & Francophonie Affairs . . . . . . . **Ping,** Jean
Min. of State for Housing, Zoning, & Urban Affairs . . . . . . . . . . . . . . . . . . . . . . . **Adiahenot,** Jacques
Min. of State for Interior, Public Security, & Decentralization . . . . . . . . . . . . . . . **Miyakou,** Antoine Mboumbou
Min. of State for Labor & Human Resources . . . . . . . . . . . . . . . . . . . . . . . . . . . . . **Missambo,** Paulette
Min. of State for Mines & Energy . . . . . . . . . . . . . . . . . . . . . . . . . . . . . . . . . . . . . . . **Toungui,** Paul
Min. of State for Planning . . . . . . . . . . . . . . . . . . . . . . . . . . . . . . . . . . . . . . . . . . . . . **Oye Mba,** Casimir
Min. Del. of Agriculture, Livestock, & Rural Economy . . . . . . . . . . . . . . . . . . . . . **Ndaki,** Barnabe
Min. Del. of Commerce, Tourism, & Industrial Development . . . . . . . . . . . . . . . . **Ekie,** Ursala
Min. Del. of Equipment & Construction . . . . . . . . . . . . . . . . . . . . . . . . . . . . . . . . . **Ngoma Madoungou,** S.
Min. Del. of Finance, Economy, Budget, & Privatization . . . . . . . . . . . . . . . . . . . **Assele Ebinda,** Yolande
Min. Del. of Foreign Affairs, Cooperation, & Francophonie Affairs . . . . . . . . . . **Mabala,** Martin
Min. Del. of Interior, Public Security, & Decentralization . . . . . . . . . . . . . . . . . . **Mangwang Me Nguema,** Jean Pierre
Min. Del. of Justice . . . . . . . . . . . . . . . . . . . . . . . . . . . . . . . . . . . . . . . . . . . . . . . . . . . **Ebome,** Pierre-Claver
Min. Del. of National Education, Youth, & Sports . . . . . . . . . . . . . . . . . . . . . . . . .
Min. Del. of Planning . . . . . . . . . . . . . . . . . . . . . . . . . . . . . . . . . . . . . . . . . . . . . . . . . **Siby,** Felix
Min. Del. to the Prime Minister for Interior, Decentralization, & Security . . . . . . **Akolghe Mba,** Emmanuel
Min. Del. of Transport, Tourism, & National Parks . . . . . . . . . . . . . . . . . . . . . . . . **Magouindi,** Joachim
Dir., Central Bank . . . . . . . . . . . . . . . . . . . . . . . . . . . . . . . . . . . . . . . . . . . . . . . . . . . . **Leyimangoye,** Jean-Paul
Ambassador to the US . . . . . . . . . . . . . . . . . . . . . . . . . . . . . . . . . . . . . . . . . . . . . . . . . **Boundoukou-Latha,** Paul
Permanent Representative to the UN, New York . . . . . . . . . . . . . . . . . . . . . . . . . **Dangue-Rewaka,** Denis

## GAMBIA, REPUBLIC OF THE

(Last updated: 4/19/2001)

Head of State . . . . . . . . . . . . . . . . . . . . . . . . . . . . . . . . . . . . . . . . . . . . . . . . . . . . . . . . . **Jammeh,** Yahya
Vice President . . . . . . . . . . . . . . . . . . . . . . . . . . . . . . . . . . . . . . . . . . . . . . . . . . . . . . . . . **Saidy,** Isatou Njie, *Mrs.*
Sec. of State in the Office of the President . . . . . . . . . . . . . . . . . . . . . . . . . . . . . . . **Singhatey,** Edward
Sec. of State for Agriculture . . . . . . . . . . . . . . . . . . . . . . . . . . . . . . . . . . . . . . . . . . . . **Dumbuya,** Fa Sainey
Sec. of State for Education . . . . . . . . . . . . . . . . . . . . . . . . . . . . . . . . . . . . . . . . . . . . . **Jow,** Satang
Sec. of State for External Affairs . . . . . . . . . . . . . . . . . . . . . . . . . . . . . . . . . . . . . . . . **Jobe,** Momodou Lamin Sedat, *Dr.*
Sec. of State for Finance & Economic Affairs . . . . . . . . . . . . . . . . . . . . . . . . . . . . . **Jatta,** Famara
Sec. of State for Health & Social Affairs . . . . . . . . . . . . . . . . . . . . . . . . . . . . . . . . . **Gassama,** Yankuba
Sec. of State for Information & Tourism . . . . . . . . . . . . . . . . . . . . . . . . . . . . . . . . . **Wafa-Ogoo,** Susan
Sec. of State for Interior . . . . . . . . . . . . . . . . . . . . . . . . . . . . . . . . . . . . . . . . . . . . . . . **Bajo,** Lamin

## GAMBIA, REPUBLIC OF THE (cont.)

| | |
|---|---|
| Sec. of State for Justice | **Seck,** Pap Cheyassin |
| Sec. of State for Lands & Local Govt. | **Bajo,** Lamine |
| Sec. of State for Public Works & Communications | **Jallow,** Momodou Sarjo |
| Sec. of State for Trade, Industry, & Employment | **Sillah,** Musa Hassan |
| Sec. of State for Youth, Sports, & Culture | **Touray,** Yankuba |
| Attorney General | **Seck,** Pap Cheyassin |
| Chief of Defense Staff | **Jatta,** Bubacar |
| Ambassador to the US | |
| Permanent Representative to the UN, New York | **Jagne,** Baboucarr-Blaise |

## GEORGIA

(Last updated: 4/10/2001)

| | |
|---|---|
| President | **Shevardnadze,** Eduard |
| Speaker, Parliament | **Zhvania,** Zurab |
| Min. of Agriculture | **Kirvalidze,** Davit |
| Min. of Construction | **Chkhenkeli,** Merab |
| Min. of Culture | **Gogiberidze,** Sesili |
| Min. of Defense | **Tevzadze,** David |
| Min. of Economy & Industry | **Chkhartishvili,** Vano |
| Min. of Education | **Kartozia,** Merab |
| Min. of Energy | **Mirtskhulava,** David |
| Min. of Environment | **Chkhobadze,** Nino |
| Min. of Finance | **Noghaideli,** Zurab |
| Min. of Foreign Affairs | **Menagharishvili,** Irakli |
| Min. of Health & Social Security | **Jorbenadze,** Avtandil |
| Min. of Interior | **Targamadze,** Kakha |
| Min. of Justice | **Saakashvili,** Mikheil |
| Min. of Privatization | |
| Min. of Refugee | **Vashakidze,** Valeri |
| Min. of Revenues | **Machavariani,** Michael |
| Min. of Security | **Kutateladze,** Vakhtang |
| Min. of State | **Arsenishvili,** Giorgi |
| Min. of State Property | **Dzneladze,** Levan |
| Min. of Transport & Communication | **Adeishvili,** Merab |
| Min. Without Portfolio | **Kakabadze,** Malkhaz |
| Sec., National Security Council | **Sajaia,** Nugzar |
| Chmn., National Bank | **Managadze,** Irakli |
| Ambassador to the US | **Japaridze,** Tedo |
| Permanent Representative to the UN, New York | **Chkheidze,** Petr |

## GERMANY (FEDERAL REPUBLIC OF GERMANY)

(Last updated: 2/15/2001)

| | |
|---|---|
| President | **Rau,** Johannes |
| Chancellor | **Schroeder,** Gerhard |
| Vice Chancellor | **Fischer,** Joschka |
| Min. of Agriculture | **Kuenast,** Renate |
| Min. of Defense | **Scharping,** Rudolf |
| Min. for Economic Cooperation | **Wieczorek-Zeul,** Heidemarie |
| Min. of Economics | **Mueller,** Werner |
| Min. for Education & Research | **Bulmahn,** Edelgard |
| Min. for Environment | **Trittin,** Juergen |
| Min. for Family | **Bergmann,** Christine |
| Min. of Finance | **Eichel,** Hans |
| Min. of Foreign Affairs | **Fischer,** Joschka |
| Min. for Health | **Schmidt,** Ullaa |
| Min. of the Interior | **Schily,** Otto |
| Min. of Justice | **Daeubler-Gmelin,** Herta |
| Min. for Labor & Social Affairs | **Riester,** Walter |
| Min. for Transport & Construction | **Bodewig,** Kurt |
| Pres., German Federal Bank | **Welteke,** Ernst |

## GERMANY (FEDERAL REPUBLIC OF GERMANY) (cont.)

Ambassador to the US . . . . . . . . . . . . . . . . . . . . . . . . . . . . . . . . . . . . . . . . **Chrobog**, Juergen
Permanent Representative to the UN, New York . . . . . . . . . . . . . . . . . . . . . . . **Kastrup**, Dieter

## GHANA, REPUBLIC OF

(Last updated: 4/19/2001)

President . . . . . . . . . . . . . . . . . . . . . . . . . . . . . . . . . . . . . . . . . . . . . . . . . . . **Kufuor**, John Agyekum
Vice President . . . . . . . . . . . . . . . . . . . . . . . . . . . . . . . . . . . . . . . . . . . . . . . **Mahama**, Aliu, *Alhaji*
Min. of Agriculture . . . . . . . . . . . . . . . . . . . . . . . . . . . . . . . . . . . . . . . . . . . **Quarshigah**, Courage, *Major (Ret.)*
Min. of Communication . . . . . . . . . . . . . . . . . . . . . . . . . . . . . . . . . . . . . . . . **Agyapong**, Owusu
Min. of Defense . . . . . . . . . . . . . . . . . . . . . . . . . . . . . . . . . . . . . . . . . . . . . . **Kufuor**, Kwame Addo, *Dr.*
Min. of Economic Planning & Regional Cooperation . . . . . . . . . . . . . . . . . . . **Nduom**, Kwesi, *Dr.*
Min. of Education . . . . . . . . . . . . . . . . . . . . . . . . . . . . . . . . . . . . . . . . . . . . . **Ameyaw-Akumfi**, Christopher
Min. of Energy . . . . . . . . . . . . . . . . . . . . . . . . . . . . . . . . . . . . . . . . . . . . . . . **Kan-Dapaah**, Albert
Min. of Environment, Science, & Technology . . . . . . . . . . . . . . . . . . . . . . . . **Fobih**, Dominic
Min. of Finance . . . . . . . . . . . . . . . . . . . . . . . . . . . . . . . . . . . . . . . . . . . . . . **Osafu-Marfo**, Yaw
Min. of Foreign Affairs . . . . . . . . . . . . . . . . . . . . . . . . . . . . . . . . . . . . . . . . **Owusu-Agyeman**, Hackman
Min. of Health . . . . . . . . . . . . . . . . . . . . . . . . . . . . . . . . . . . . . . . . . . . . . . . **Anane**, Richard, *Dr.*
Min. of Interior . . . . . . . . . . . . . . . . . . . . . . . . . . . . . . . . . . . . . . . . . . . . . . **Yakubu**, Malik Alhassan, *Alhaji*
Min. of Justice . . . . . . . . . . . . . . . . . . . . . . . . . . . . . . . . . . . . . . . . . . . . . . . **Addo**, Nana Akufo
Min. of Lands, Forestry, & Mines . . . . . . . . . . . . . . . . . . . . . . . . . . . . . . . . **Afriyie**, Kweku, *Dr.*
Min. of Local Govt. & Rural Development . . . . . . . . . . . . . . . . . . . . . . . . . . **Baah-Wiredu**, Kwadwo
Min. of Manpower Development & Employment . . . . . . . . . . . . . . . . . . . . . . **Bannerman**, Cecilia
Min. of Parliamentary Affairs . . . . . . . . . . . . . . . . . . . . . . . . . . . . . . . . . . . **Mensah**, J. H.
Min. of Presidential Affairs . . . . . . . . . . . . . . . . . . . . . . . . . . . . . . . . . . . . . **Obetsebi-Lamptey**, Jake
Min. of Roads & Transportatoin . . . . . . . . . . . . . . . . . . . . . . . . . . . . . . . . . **Adjei-Dako**, K.
Min. of Tourism . . . . . . . . . . . . . . . . . . . . . . . . . . . . . . . . . . . . . . . . . . . . . **Yakubu**, Hawa
Min. of Trade & Industry . . . . . . . . . . . . . . . . . . . . . . . . . . . . . . . . . . . . . . **Apraku**, Kofi Konadu, *Dr.*
Min. of Women's Affairs . . . . . . . . . . . . . . . . . . . . . . . . . . . . . . . . . . . . . . . **Asmah**, Gladys
Min. of Works & Housing . . . . . . . . . . . . . . . . . . . . . . . . . . . . . . . . . . . . . . **Bartels**, Kwamena
Min. of Youth & Sports . . . . . . . . . . . . . . . . . . . . . . . . . . . . . . . . . . . . . . . . **Issah**, Ali Yussif, *Mallam*
Min. of State for Agriculture . . . . . . . . . . . . . . . . . . . . . . . . . . . . . . . . . . . . **Ashitey**, Ishmael
Min. of State for Education . . . . . . . . . . . . . . . . . . . . . . . . . . . . . . . . . . . . . **Churcher**, Christine
Min. of State in Charge of Media Relations . . . . . . . . . . . . . . . . . . . . . . . . . **Ohene**, Elizabeth
Min. of State in Charge of Private Sector Development . . . . . . . . . . . . . . . . . **Nyannor**, Charles
Attorney General . . . . . . . . . . . . . . . . . . . . . . . . . . . . . . . . . . . . . . . . . . . . . **Addo**, Nana Akufu
Governor, Central Bank . . . . . . . . . . . . . . . . . . . . . . . . . . . . . . . . . . . . . . . . **Agama**, G. K.
Ambassador to the US . . . . . . . . . . . . . . . . . . . . . . . . . . . . . . . . . . . . . . . . . **Koomson**, Kobena
Permanent Representative to the UN, New York . . . . . . . . . . . . . . . . . . . . . . **Effah-Apenteng**, Nana

## GREECE (HELLENIC REPUBLIC)

(Last updated: 1/18/2001)

President . . . . . . . . . . . . . . . . . . . . . . . . . . . . . . . . . . . . . . . . . . . . . . . . . . . **Stephanopoulos**, Konstandinos "Kostis"
Prime Minister . . . . . . . . . . . . . . . . . . . . . . . . . . . . . . . . . . . . . . . . . . . . . . **Simitis**, Konstandinos
Min. of the Aegean . . . . . . . . . . . . . . . . . . . . . . . . . . . . . . . . . . . . . . . . . . . **Sifounakis**, Nikolaos
Min. of Agriculture . . . . . . . . . . . . . . . . . . . . . . . . . . . . . . . . . . . . . . . . . . . **Anomeritis**, Yeoryios
Min. of Culture . . . . . . . . . . . . . . . . . . . . . . . . . . . . . . . . . . . . . . . . . . . . . . **Venizelos**, Evangelos
Min. of Development . . . . . . . . . . . . . . . . . . . . . . . . . . . . . . . . . . . . . . . . . . **Khristodhoulakis**, Nikos
Min. of Environment, Town Planning, & Public Works . . . . . . . . . . . . . . . . . **Laliotis**, Konstandinos
Min. of Finance . . . . . . . . . . . . . . . . . . . . . . . . . . . . . . . . . . . . . . . . . . . . . . **Papandoniou**, Ioannis
Min. of Foreign Affairs . . . . . . . . . . . . . . . . . . . . . . . . . . . . . . . . . . . . . . . . **Papandreou**, Yeoryios
Min. of Foreign Affairs (Alternate) . . . . . . . . . . . . . . . . . . . . . . . . . . . . . . . **Papazoi**, Elisavet
Min. of Health & Welfare . . . . . . . . . . . . . . . . . . . . . . . . . . . . . . . . . . . . . . **Papadhopoulos**, Alexandros
Min. of Interior, Public Administration, & Decentralization . . . . . . . . . . . . . . **Papandreou**, Vasiliki "Vasso"
Min. of Justice . . . . . . . . . . . . . . . . . . . . . . . . . . . . . . . . . . . . . . . . . . . . . . . **Stathopoulos**, Mikhail
Min. of Labor & Social Insurance . . . . . . . . . . . . . . . . . . . . . . . . . . . . . . . . **Yiannitsis**, Anastasios
Min. of Macedonia & Thrace . . . . . . . . . . . . . . . . . . . . . . . . . . . . . . . . . . . . **Paskhalidhis**, Yeoryios
Min. of Merchant Marine . . . . . . . . . . . . . . . . . . . . . . . . . . . . . . . . . . . . . . **Papoutsis**, Khristos
Min. of National Defense . . . . . . . . . . . . . . . . . . . . . . . . . . . . . . . . . . . . . . . **Tsokhatzopoulos**, Apostolos-Athanasios "Akis"
Min. of National Economy . . . . . . . . . . . . . . . . . . . . . . . . . . . . . . . . . . . . . **Papandoniou**, Ioannis

## GREECE (HELLENIC REPUBLIC) (cont.)

| | |
|---|---|
| Min. of National Education & Religions | **Efthimiou,** Petros |
| Min. of Press & Mass Media | **Reppas,** Dhimitrios |
| Min. to the Prime Minister | **Papaioannou,** Miltiadhis |
| Min. of Public Order | **Khrisokhoidhis,** Mikhail |
| Min. of Transport & Communications | **Varelis,** Khristos |
| Governor, Bank of Greece | **Papademos,** Loukas |
| Ambassador to the US | **Philon,** Alexandros |
| Permanent Representative to the UN, New York | **Gounaris,** Ilias |

## GRENADA

(Last updated: 4/6/2001)

| | |
|---|---|
| Governor General | **Williams,** Daniel |
| Prime Minister | **Mitchell,** Keith |
| Min. of Agriculture, Lands, Forestry, & Fisheries | **Charles,** Claris |
| Min. of Carriacou & Petit Martinique Affairs | **Nimrod,** Elvin |
| Min. of Communications | **Bowen,** Gregory |
| Min. of Works, Public Utilities, & Transport | **Bowen,** Gregory |
| Min. of Education | **John,** Augustine |
| Min. of Finance, Trade, & Planning | **Boatswain,** Anthony |
| Min. of Foreign Affairs | **Nimrod,** Elvin |
| Min. of Health & Environment | **Modeste-Curwen,** Clarice |
| Min. of Housing, Social Services, Culture, & Cooperatives | **McQueen,** Brian |
| Min. of Implementation | **Whiteman,** Joslyn |
| Min. of Information | **Mitchell,** Keith |
| Min. of International Trade | **Nimrod,** Elvin |
| Min. of Labor | **Nimrod,** Elvin |
| Min. of Labor & Local Affairs | **Joseph,** Lawrence |
| Min. of Legal Affairs | **Anthony,** Raymond |
| Min. of Local Government (Carriacou & Petite Martinique) | **Nimrod,** Elvin |
| Min. of National Security, Mobilisation & Information | **Mitchell,** Keith |
| Min. of Tourism, Civil Aviation, Women's Affairs, & Social Security | **Hood,** Brenda |
| Min. of Youth, Sports, Culture, & Community Development | **Mitchell,** Adrian |
| Attorney General | **Anthony,** Raymond |
| Permanent Representative to the UN, New York | **Stanislaus,** Lamuel |

## GUATEMALA, REPUBLIC OF

(Last updated: 4/19/2001)

| | |
|---|---|
| President | **Portillo,** Cabrera, Alfonso Antonio |
| Vice President | **Reyes,** Lopez, Juan Francisco |
| Min. of Agriculture | **Sandoval,** Villeda, Leopoldo |
| Min. of Communications | **Rabbe,** Luis |
| Min. of Culture | **Lux De Coti,** Otilia |
| Min. of Defense | **Arevalo,** Eduardo Lacs, *Gen.* |
| Min. of Economy | **Ventura,** Marco Antonio |
| Min. of Education | **Torres,** Mario |
| Min. of Energy & Mines | **Archila,** Raul |
| Min. of Environment & Natural Resources | **Arango,** Leonel Soto |
| Min. of Foreign Relations | **Orellana,** Gabriel |
| Min. of Government | **Barrientos,** Byron |
| Min. of Labor | **Alfaro,** Juan Francisco |
| Min. of Public Finance | **Maza,** Castellanos, Manuel Hiram |
| Min. of Public Health | **Bolanos,** Mario |
| Prosecutor General | **Gonzalez,** Rodas, Adolfo |
| Solicitor General | **Garcia,** Regas, Carlos |
| Pres., Bank of Guatemala | **Sosa,** Lopez, Lizardo |
| Ambassador to the US | **Rivera,** Ariel |
| Permanent Representative to the UN, New York | **Rosenthal,** Gert |

## GUINEA, REPUBLIC OF

(Last updated: 3/15/2001)

President .............................................................. **Conte,** Lansana, *Gen.*
Prime Minister ........................................................ **Sidime,** Lamine
Min. of Agriculture & Animal Husbandry ............................. **Sarr,** Jean-Paul
Min. of Commerce, Industry, Small & Medium-Scale Enterprise .......... **Balde,** Adama
Min. of Communication ................................................ **Conde,** Mamadi
Min. of Defense ......................................................
Min. of Economy & Finance ............................................ **Camara,** Sheik Amadou
Min. of Employment & Public Administration ........................... **Kamara,** Lamine
Min. of Fishing & Aquaculture ........................................ **Sidibe,** Mansa Musa
Min. of Foreign Affairs .............................................. **Camara,** Mahawa Bangoura
Min. of Higher Education & Scientific Research ....................... **Camara,** Eugene
Min. of Justice & Keeper of the Seals ................................ **Togba,** Maurice Zogbelemou
Min. of Mining, Geology, & Environment ............................... **Souma,** Ibrahima
Min. of Pre-University & Civic Education .............................. **Doualamou,** Germain
Min. of Public Health ................................................ **Diallo,** Mamadou Saliou, *Dr.*
Min. of Public Works & Transport ..................................... **Diallo,** Cellou Dalein
Min. of Social Affairs, Promotion of Women, & Children ............... **Aribot,** Mariama
Min. of Technical Teaching & Professional Training ................... **Sylla,** Almamy Fode
Min. of Territorial Administration & Decentralization ................ **Solano,** Moussa
Min. of Tourism, Hotels, & Handicrafts ............................... **Diakite,** Sylla Koumba
Min. of Urban Planning & Housing ..................................... **Foromo,** Blaise
Min. of Water Power & Energy ......................................... **Niankoye,** Fassou
Min. of Youth, Sports, & Culture ..................................... **Sangare,** Abdel Kadr
Sec. Gen. of the Government ........................................... **Sanoko,** Ousmane
Sec. Gen. of the Presidency .......................................... **Bangoura,** Fode
Governor, Central Bank ............................................... **Bah,** Ibrahim Cherif
Ambassador to the US ................................................. **Thiam,** Mohamed
Permanent Representative to the UN, New York ......................... **Fall,** Francois

## GUINEA-BISSAU, REPUBLIC OF

(Last updated: 4/2/2001)

President ............................................................. **Koumba,** Yalla
Prime Minister ....................................................... **Imbali,** Faustino
Min. of Agriculture, Forestry & Livestock ............................ **Nhasse,** Alamara
Min. of Defense ...................................................... **Soares,** Lucio
Min. of Economy & Finance ............................................ **Duarte de Barros,** Rui
Min. of Education, Science, & Technology ............................. **Martins,** Geraldo
Min. of Fisheries & Sea .............................................. **Balde,** Oscar
Min. of Foreign Affairs & International Cooperation ................... **Gomes,** Antonieta Rosa
Min. of Interior ..................................................... **Sanha,** Antonio Artur
Min. of Justice ...................................................... **Cabi,** Dionisio
Min. of Natural Resources & Energy ................................... **Balde,** Julio
Min. of Parliamentary Affairs ........................................ **Balde,** Joaquim
Min. of Presidential Affairs ......................................... **da Costa,** Pedro
Min. of Public Administration & Labor ................................ **Pereira,** Carlos Pinto
Min. of Public Health ................................................ **Dias,** Francisco
Min. of Public Service & Employment .................................. **Balde,** Joaquim
Min. of Social Equipment ............................................. **Barai,** Carlitos
Min. of Social Infrastructure ........................................ **Barrai,** Carlitos
Min. of Social Solidarity, Employment, & Fight Against Poverty ........ **Tipote,** Mascarenhas
Min. of Trade, Industry, Tourism, and Handicrafts .................... **Embalo,** Antonio Serifo
Chmn. of the Min. Council & News Media ............................... **Balde,** Joaquim
Sec. of State for Commerce, Industry, & Artifacts .................... **Embalo,** Antenio Serifo
Sec. of State for Employment & Poverty Alleviation ................... **Tipote,** Filomena Mascarenhas
Sec. of State for Fisheries .......................................... **Paquena,** Augusto
Sec. of State for International Cooperation ........................... **Mane,** Malam
Sec. of State for Planning & Regional Development .................... **Bia,** Purna
Sec. of State for Social Solidarity & the Reintegration of War Veterans ........ **Cabral,** Marcelino Lopes
Sec. of State for Tourism ............................................ **Conduto de Pina,** Francisco
Sec. of State for Trade & Handicraft ................................. **Djallo,** Abubacar Rachid
Sec. of State for Transport & Communications ......................... **Seidi,** Andala

## GUINEA-BISSAU, REPUBLIC OF (cont.)

| | |
|---|---|
| Sec. of State for Treasury, Budget, & Fiscal Affairs | **Quade,** Usna |
| Sec. of State for Veterans | **Cabral,** Marcelino Lopes |
| Sec. of State for Youth, Culture, & Sports | **Namone,** Brum Sitna |
| Ambassador to the US | **Lopes da Rosa,** Mario |

## GUYANA, REPUBLIC OF

(Last updated: 4/20/2001)

| | |
|---|---|
| President | **Jagdeo,** Bharrat |
| Prime Minister | **Hinds,** Samuel |
| First Vice President | |
| Second Vice President | **Persaud,** Reepu Daman |
| Min. Office of the President (Public Service) | **Fung-On,** George |
| Min. of Agriculture | **Chandarpal,** Navin |
| Min. of Amerindian Affairs | **Rodrigues,** Carolyn |
| Min. of Economic Planning | |
| Min. of Education | **Jeffrey,** Henry *Dr.* |
| Min. of Finance | **Kowlessar,** Saisnarine |
| Min. of Fisheries, Crops, & Livestock | **Sawh,** Satyadeow |
| Min. of Foreign Affairs | **Rohee,** Clement |
| Min. of Foreign Trade | **Rohee,** Clement |
| Min. of Health & Labor | **Ramsammy,** Leslie *Dr.* |
| Min. of Home Affairs | **Gajraj,** Ronald |
| Min. of Housing & Water | **Baksh,** Shaik |
| Min. of Human Services, Social Security & Labour | **Bisnauth,** Dale *Dr.* |
| Min. of Information | |
| Min. of Legal Affairs | **Ramson,** Charles Rishiram |
| Min. of Local Government | **Nokta,** Harripersaud |
| Min. of Marine Resources | **Sawah,** Satyadeow |
| Min. of Parliamentary Affairs | **Persaud,** Reepu Daman |
| Min. of Public Service Management | **Westford,** Jennifer *Dr.* |
| Min. of Public Works | **Hinds,** Samuel |
| Min. of Trade, Industry, & Tourism | |
| Min. of Transport, Communication, & Hydraulics | **Xavier,** Anthony |
| Min. of Youth & Sports | **Texeira,** Gail |
| Min. Within Local Government | **Collymore,** Clinton |
| Head of Presidential Secretariat | **Luncheon,** Roger |
| Attorney General | |
| Governor, Bank of Guyana | **Meredith,** Archibald |
| Ambassador to the US | **Ishmael,** Odeen |
| Permanent Representative to the UN, New York | **Insanally,** Rudolph |

## HAITI, REPUBLIC OF

(Last updated: 3/13/2001)

| | |
|---|---|
| President | **Aristide,** Jean-Bertrand |
| Prime Minister | **Cherestal,** Jean-Marie Antoine Polynice |
| Min. of Agriculture, Natural Resources, & Rural Development | **Hilaire,** Sebastien |
| Min. of Commerce & Industry | **Theard,** Stanley |
| Min. of Culture | **Paul,** Guy |
| Min. of Economy & Finance | **Joseph,** Fred |
| Min. of Education, Youth, & Sports | **Bien-Aime,** Paul Antoine |
| Min. of Environment | **Cadet,** Yves |
| Min. of Finance | **Flaubert,** Gustave |
| Min. of Foreign Affairs | **Antonio,** Joseph Philippe |
| Min. of Haitians Living Abroad | **Voltaire,** Leslie |
| Min. of Interior | **Menard,** Henri-Claude |
| Min. of Justice & Public Security | **Lissade,** Gary |
| Min. of Labor & Social Affairs | **Flambert,** Mathilde |
| Min. of National Education, Youth, & Sports | **Merisier,** Georges |
| Min. of Planning & External Cooperation | **Bazin,** Marc |
| Min. of Public Health & Population | **Voltaire,** Henri-Claude |

## HAITI, REPUBLIC OF (cont.)

| | |
|---|---|
| Min. of Public Service | **Pierre**, Webster |
| Min. of Public Works, Transportation & Communications | **Laraque**, Ernst |
| Min. of Social Affairs | **Saint-Preux**, Eudes |
| Min. of Women's Affairs | **Lubin**, Ginette |
| Sec. of State for Labor | **Joseph**, Ronald |
| Sec. of State for Population | **Andre**, Jean |
| Sec. of State for Public Security | |
| Sec. of State for Tourism | **Deverson**, Martine |
| Sec. of State for Youth, Sports, & Civic Service | **Lescouflair**, Evans |
| Sec. of State for Finance | **Privert**, Jocelerme |
| Governor, Central Bank | **Jean**, Fritz |
| Ambassador to the US | |
| Permanent Representative to the UN, New York | **Lelong**, Pierre |

## HOLY SEE (STATE OF THE VATICAN CITY)

(Last updated: 11/17/2000)

| | |
|---|---|
| Head, Roman Catholic Church | **Pope John Paul II** |
| Secretary of State | **Sodano**, Angelo Cardinal |
| Secretary for Relations with States | **Tauran**, Jean-Louis |
| Papal Nuncio to the US | **Montalvo**, Gabriel |

## HONDURAS

(Last updated: 2/2/2001)

| | |
|---|---|
| President | **Flores**, Facusse, Carlos Roberto |
| First Vice Pres. | **Handal**, William |
| Second Vice Pres. | **Caballero**, de Arevalo, Gladys |
| Third Vice Pres. | **Cerrato**, Hernandez, Hector Vidal |
| Min. of Agriculture & Livestock | **Alvarado**, Downing, Guillermo |
| Min. of Culture, Arts, & Sports | **Padgett**, Herman Allan |
| Min. of Defense | **Flores**, Valeriano, Enrique |
| Min. of Education | **Calix**, Figueroa, Ramon |
| Min. of Finance | **Nunez**, Gabriela |
| Min. of Foreign Relations | **Flores Bermudez**, Roberto |
| Min. of Government & Justice | **Rubi**, Vera Sofia |
| Min. of Industry & Commerce | **Kafati**, Oscar |
| Min. of Labor | **Miranda**, de Galo, Rosa America |
| Min. of Natural Resources & Environment | **Gomez**, de Caballero, (Silvia) Xiomara |
| Min. of Presidency | **Alfaro**, Zelaya, Gustavo Adolfo |
| Min. of Public Health | **Castellanos**, Plutarco |
| Min. of Public Works, Transportation, & Housing | **Lozano**, Reyes, Tomas |
| Min. of Security | **Fonseca Zuniga**, Gautama |
| Min. of Tourism | **Abarca**, de Perdomo, Ana del Socorro |
| Min. Without Portfolio | **Leiva**, Roberto |
| Min. Without Portfolio | **Reina**, Jorge Arturo |
| Min. Without Portfolio | **Valladares**, Nahun |
| Dir. of the Social Investment Fund | **Starkman**, Moises |
| Pres., Central Bank | **Asfura**, Violeta |
| Ambassador to the US | **Noe Pino**, Hugo |
| Permanent Representative to the UN, New York | **Orellana**, Edmundo |

## HUNGARY, REPUBLIC OF

(Last updated: 3/27/2001)

| | |
|---|---|
| President | **Madl**, Ferenc |
| Prime Minister | **Orban**, Viktor |
| Min. of Agriculture & Regional Development | **Vonza**, Andras |
| Min. of Culture | **Rockenbauer**, Zoltan |
| Min. of Defense | **Szabo**, Janos |

## HUNGARY, REPUBLIC OF (cont.)

| | |
|---|---|
| Min. of Economics | **Matolcsy,** Gyorgy |
| Min. of Education | **Pokorni,** Zoltan |
| Min. of Environmental Protection | **Turi-Kovacs,** Bela |
| Min. of Finance | **Varga,** Mihaly |
| Min. of Foreign Affairs | **Martonyi,** Janos |
| Min. of Health | **Mikola,** Istvan |
| Min. of Interior | **Pinter,** Sandor |
| Min. of Justice | **David,** Ibolya |
| Min. for National Cultural Heritage | **Hamori,** Jozsef |
| Min. of Social & Family Affairs | **Harrach,** Peter |
| Min. of Transport & Water Management | **Fonagy,** Janos |
| Min. of Youth & Sports | **Deutsch,** Tamas |
| Min. Without Portfolio in Charge of Civilian National Security Services | **Demeter,** Ervin |
| Min. Without Portfolio in Charge of Prime Minister's Office | **Stumpf,** Istvan |
| Min. Without Portfolio for PHARE Program | **Boros,** Imre |
| Pres., Hungarian National Bank | **Jarai,** Zsigmond |
| Ambassador to the US | **Jeszenszky,** Geza |
| Permanent Representative to the UN, New York | **Erdos,** Andre |

## ICELAND, REPUBLIC OF

(Last updated: 2/20/2001)

| | |
|---|---|
| President | **Grimsson,** Olafur |
| Prime Minister | **Oddsson,** David |
| Min. of Agriculture | **Agustsson,** Gudni |
| Min. of Education & Culture | **Bjarnasson,** Bjorn |
| Min. of Environment | **Fridleifsdottir,** Siv |
| Min. of Finance | **Haarde,** Geir |
| Min. of Fisheries | **Mathiesen,** Arni |
| Min. of Foreign Affairs | **Asgrimsson,** Halldor |
| Min. of Health & Social Security | **Palmadottir,** Ingiborg |
| Min. of Industry & Trade | **Sverrisdottir,** Valgerdur |
| Min. of Justice & Church Affairs | **Petursdottir,** Solveig |
| Min. of Social Affairs | **Petursson,** Paul |
| Min. of Transport | **Bodvarsson,** Sturla |
| Dir., Central Bank of Iceland | **Ingolfsson,** Finnur |
| Ambassador to the US | **Hannibalsson,** Jon Baldvin |
| Permanent Representative to the UN, New York | **Ingolfsson,** Thorsteinn |

## INDIA, REPUBLIC OF

(Last updated: 3/15/2001)

| | |
|---|---|
| President | **Narayanan,** Kocheril Raman |
| Vice President | **Kant,** Krishnan |
| Prime Minister | **Vajpayee,** Atal Bihari |
| Principal Sec. | **Mishra,** Brajesh |
| Min. of Agriculture | **Kumar,** Nitish |
| Min. of Chemicals & Fertilizers | **Dhindsa,** Sukhdev Singh |
| Min. of Civil Aviation | **Yadav,** Sharad |
| Min. of Commerce & Industry | **Maran,** Murasoli |
| Min. of Communications | **Paswan,** Ram Vilas |
| Min. of Consumer Affairs & Public Distribution | **Kumar,** Shanta |
| Min. of Defense | **Fernandes,** George |
| Min. of Environment & Forests | **Baalu,** T. R. |
| Min. of External Affairs | **Singh,** Jaswant |
| Min. of Finance | **Sinha,** Yashwant |
| Min. of Health & Family Welfare | **Thakur,** C.P. |
| Min. of Heavy Industries & Public Enterprises | **Joshi,** Manohar Gajanan |
| Min. of Home Affairs | **Advani,** Lal Krishna |
| Min. of Human Resource Development, Science & Technology, With Additional Charge of Ocean Development | **Joshi,** Murli Manohar, *Dr.* |
| Min. of Information & Broadcasting | **Swaraj,** Sushma |

## INDIA, REPUBLIC OF (cont.)

| | |
|---|---|
| Min. of Labor | **Jatiya,** Satyanarayan |
| Min. of Law | **Jaitely,** Arun |
| Min. of Mines | **Patwa,** Sunder Lal |
| Min. of Parliamentary Affairs, Information & Technology | **Mahajan,** Pramod |
| Min. of Petroleum & Natural Gas | **Naik,** Ram |
| Min. of Power With Additional Charge of Mines &Minerals | **Prabhu,** Suresh |
| Min. of Railways | **Banerjee,** Mamata |
| Min. of Rural Development | **Naidu,** Venkaiah |
| Min. of Textiles | **Rana,** Kanshi Ram |
| Min. of Tourism & Culture | **Kumar,** Ananth |
| Min. of Tribal Affairs | **Oram,** Jual |
| Min. of Urban Development & Poverty Alleviation | **Jagmohan,** |
| Min. of Water Resources | **Sethi,** Arjun Charan |
| Min. of Youth Affairs & Sports | **Bharati,** Uma |
| Min. of State for Agriculture | **Naik,** Shripad Yasso |
| Min. of State for Agriculture | **Pradhan,** Debendra, *Dr.* |
| Min. of State for Chemicals & Fertilizers | **Mukherjee,** Satyabrata |
| Min. of State for Civil Aviation | **Gupta,** Chaman Lal |
| Min. of State for Coal With Independent Charge | **Hussain,** Syed Shahnawaz |
| Min. of State for Commerce & Industry | **Abdullah,** Omar |
| Min. of State for Commerce & Industry | **Raman,** *Dr.* |
| Min. of State for Communications | **Sikdar,** Tapan |
| Min. of State for Consumer Affairs & Public Distribution | **Chauhan,** Sriram |
| Min. of State for Consumer Affairs & Public Distribution | **Prasad,** V. Sreenivasa |
| Min. of State for External Affairs | **Panja,** Ajit Kumar |
| Min. of State for External Affairs | **Uppalapati,** Venkata Krishnam Raju |
| Min. of State for Food Processing | **Singh,** T. Chaoba |
| Min. of State for Finance | **Patil,** Balasaheb Vikhe |
| Min. of State for Finance | **Ramachandran,** Ginjee N. |
| Min. of State for Health & Family Welfare | **Raja,** A. |
| Min. of State for Heavy Industries & Public Enterprises | **Kathiria,** Vallabhbhai |
| Min. of State for Home | **Rao,** Chennamaneni Vidyasagar |
| Min. of State for Home | **Swami,** I. D. |
| Min. of State for Human Resource Development | **Mahajan,** Sumitra |
| Min. of State for Information & Broadcasting | **Bais,** Ramesh |
| Min. of State for Labor & Employment | **Muni,** Lall |
| Min. of State for Mines | **Patil,** Jaisingrao Gaikwadh |
| Min. of State for Nonconventional Energy Sources With Independent Charge | **Kannappan,** M. |
| Min. of State for Parliamentary Affairs & Railways | **Rajagopal,** Olenchery |
| Min. of State for Petroleum | **Ponnuswamy,** E. |
| Min. of State for Petroleum & Natural Gas, With Additional Charge of Parliamentary Affairs | **Gangwar,** Santosh Kumar |
| Min. of State for Planning Statistics & Programme Implementation | **Shourie,** Arun |
| Min. of State for Power | **Mehta,** Jayawanti |
| Min. of State for Railways | **Singh,** Digvijay |
| Min. of State for Road Transport & Highways With Independent Charge | **Khandhuri,** Bhuwan Chandra, *Maj. Gen. (Ret.)* |
| Min. of State for Rural Development | **Maharia,** Subhash |
| Min. of State for Rural Development | **Verma,** Rita |
| Min. of State for Science & Technology | **Rawat,** Bachi Singh |
| Min. of State for Shipping | **Yadav,** Hukemdeo Narayan |
| Min. of State for Small Scale, Agro/Rural Industries With Independent Charge | **Vasundhara,** Raje |
| Min. of State for Social Justice & Empowerment with Independent Charge | **Gandhi,** Maneka |
| Min. of State for Steel With Independent Charge | **Tripath,** B.K. |
| Min. of State for Textiles | **Dhananjaya,** Kumar, Venur |
| Min. of State for Tribal Affairs | **Kuleste,** Faggan Singh |
| Min. of State for Urban Development & Poverty Alleviation | **Dattatreya,** Bandaru |
| Min. of State for Water Resources | **Chakravarty,** Bijoya |
| Min. of State for Youth Affairs & Sports | **Radhakrishnan,** Pon |
| Governor, Reserve Bank | **Jalan,** Bimal Nayan |
| Ambassador to the US | **Chandra,** Naresh |
| Permanent Representative to the UN, New York | **Sharma,** Kamalesh |

## INDONESIA, REPUBLIC OF

(Last updated: 3/20/2001)

| | |
|---|---|
| President | **Abdurrahman WAHID** |
| Vice President | **MEGAWATI Sukarnoputri** |
| Coordinating Min. for Political, Social, & Security Affairs | **Susilo Bambang YUDHOYONO,** *Lt. Gen. (Ret.)* |
| Coordinating Min. for Economy, Finance, & Industry | **Razil RAMLI** |
| Min. of Agriculture | **Bunngaran SARAGIH** |
| Min. of Culture & Tourism | **I Gede ARDIKA** |
| Min. of Defense | **Mohammad MAHFUD Mahmodin** |
| Min. of Education | **YAHYA Muhaimin** |
| Min. of Energy & Mineral Resources | **PURNOMO Yusgiantoro** |
| Min. of Finance | **PRIJADI Praptosuhardjo** |
| Min. of Foreign Affairs | **Alwi Abdurrahman SHIHAB** |
| Min. of Health | **Ahmad SUJUDI,** *M.D.* |
| Min. of Home Affairs | **SURJADI Soedirdja,** *Lt. Gen. (Ret.)* |
| Min. of Housing & Regional Infastructure | **Erna WITOELAR** |
| Min. of Industry & Trade | **Luhut B. PANJAITAN,** *Lt. Gen. (Ret.)* |
| Min. of Justice & Human Rights | **Baharuddin LOPA** |
| Min. of Manpower & Transmigration | **Al Hilal HAMDI** |
| Min. of Maritime Exploration | **SARWONO Kusumaatmadja** |
| Min. of Religious Affairs | **Mohammad TOLCHAH Hasan** |
| Min. of Tranportation & Communications | **Agum GUMELAR,** *Lt. Gen. (Ret.)* |
| Non-Departmental Min. for Cooperatives, Small & Medium Enterprises | **ZARKASIH Nur** |
| Non-Departmental Min. for the Empowerment of Women's Affairs | **Khofifah Indar PARAWANSA** |
| Non-Departmental Min. for Environment | **Alexander Sonny KERAF** |
| Non-Departmental Min. for Reform of the State Apparatus | **Ryaas RASYID** |
| Non-Departmental Min. for Research & Technology | **A. S. HIKAM** |
| Junior Min. for Acceleration of Development in Eastern Indonesia | **Manuel KAISIEPO** |
| Junior Min. for Forestry | **MARZUKI Usman** |
| Junior Min. for Restructuring the National Economy | **CACUK Sudariyanto** |
| State Secretary | **Djohan EFFENDI** |
| Attorney General | **MARZUKI Darusman** |
| Cdr., Armed Forces | **WIDODO A. S.,** *Adm.* |
| Governor, Bank Indonesia | **Anwar NASUTION** |
| Ambassador to the US | **DORODJATUN Kuntjoro-Jakti** |
| Permanent Representative to the UN, New York | **Makarim WIBISONO,** |

## IRAN, ISLAMIC REPUBLIC OF

(Last updated: 4/10/2001)

| | |
|---|---|
| Supreme Leader | **KHAMENEI,** Ali Hoseini-, *Ayatollah* |
| President | **KHATAMI-Ardakani,** (Ali) Mohammad, *Hojjat ol-Eslam* |
| Speaker of the Islamic Consultative Assembly (Majles) | **Mahdavi-KARUBI,** Mehdi, *Hojjat ol-Eslam* |
| First Vice Pres. | **Habibi,** Hasan Ebrahim, *Dr.* |
| Vice Pres. for Atomic Energy | **Aqazadeh-Khoi,** Qolam Reza |
| Vice Pres. for Development & Social Affairs | |
| Vice Pres. for Environmental Protection | **Ebtekar,** Masumeh, *Dr., Mrs.* |
| Vice Pres. for Executive Affairs | **Hashemi-Rafsanjani,** Mohammad |
| Vice Pres. for Legal & Parliamentary Affairs | **Saduqi,** Mohammad Ali, *Hojjat ol-Eslam* |
| Vice Pres. for Physical Training | **Hashemi-Taba,** Mostafa |
| Vice Pres. for Planning & Management | **Aref-Yazdi,** Mohammad Reza, *Dr.* |
| Min. of Agriculture Jihad | **Hojati,** Mahmud |
| Min. of Commerce | **Shariat-Madari,** Mohammad |
| Min. of Cooperatives | **Haji-Qaem,** Morteza |
| Min. of Defense & Armed Forces Logistics | **Shamkhani,** Ali, *VAdm.* |
| Min. of Economic Affairs & Finance | **Namazi,** Hosein, *Dr.* |
| Min. of Education & Training | **Mozafar,** Hosein |
| Min. of Energy | **Bitaraf,** Habibollah |
| Min. of Foreign Affairs | **Kharazi,** (Ali Naqi) Kamal, *Dr.* |
| Min. of Health, Treatment, & Medical Education | **Farhadi,** Mohammad, *Dr.* |
| Min. of Housing & Urban Development | **Abdol-Alizadeh,** Ali, *Dr.* |
| Min. of Industries & Mines | **Jahangiri,** Eshaq |

## IRAN, ISLAMIC REPUBLIC OF (cont.)

| | |
|---|---|
| Min. of Intelligence & Security | **Yunesi,** (Mohammad) Ali, *Hojjat ol-Eslam* |
| Min. of Interior | **Musavi-Lari,** Abdol Vahed, *Hojjat ol-Eslam* |
| Min. of Islamic Culture & Guidance | **Masjed-Jamei,** Ahmad |
| Min. of Justice | **Shoshtari,** Mohammad Esmail, *Hojjat ol-Eslam* |
| Min. of Labor & Social Affairs | **Kamali,** Hosein |
| Min. of Petroleum | **Namdar-Zanganeh,** Bijan |
| Min. of Post, Telegraph & Telephone | **Motamedi,** Ahmad, *Dr.* |
| Min. of Roads & Transport | **Dadman,** Rahman, *Dr.* |
| Min. of Science, Research & Technology | **Moin-Najafabadi,** Mostafa, *Dr.* |
| Governor, Central Bank | **Nurbakhsh,** Mohsen, *Dr.* |
| Head of Interest Section in the US | **Jahansuzan,** Fariborz |
| Permanent Representative to the UN, New York | **Nejad-Hoseinian,** Mohammad Hadi |

## IRAQ, REPUBLIC OF

(Last updated: 4/20/2001)

| | |
|---|---|
| President | **Husayn,** SADDAM |
| Vice President | **Maruf,** Taha Muhyi al-Din |
| Vice President | **Ramadan,** Taha Yasin |
| Prime Minister | **Husayn,** SADDAM |
| Dep. Prime Min. | **Aziz,** Tariq Mikhail |
| Dep. Prime Min. | **Azzawi,** Hikmat Mizban Ibrahim al- |
| Dep. Prime Min. | **Zubaydi,** Muhammad Hamza al- |
| Dep. Prime Min. | **Aziz,** Tariq |
| Min. of Agriculture | **Salih,** Abd al-Ilah Hamid Mahmud al- |
| Min. of Awqaf & Religious Affairs | **Salih,** Abd al-Munim Ahmad |
| Min. of Culture & Information | **Sahhaf,** Muhammad Said Qasim |
| Min. of Defense | **Jabburi Tai,** Sultan Hashim Ahmad al-, *Lt. Gen.* |
| Min. of Education | **Shaqrah,** Fahd Salim |
| Min. of Finance | **Azzawi,** Hikmat Mizban Ibrahim al- |
| Min. of Foreign Affairs (Acting) | **Aziz,** Tariq Mikhail |
| Min. of Health | **Mubarak,** Umid Midhat |
| Min. of Higher Education & Scientific Research | **Abd al-Ghafur,** Humam Abd al-Khaliq, *Dr.* |
| Min. of Housing & Reconstruction | **Sarsam,** Maan Abdallah al- |
| Min. of Industry & Minerals | **Ani,** Adnan Abd al-Majid Jasim al- |
| Min. of Interior | **Abd al-Razzaq,** Muhammad Zimam |
| Min. of Irrigation | **Ahmad,** Mahmud Dhiyab al- |
| Min. of Justice | **Shawi,** Mundhir Ibrahim al- |
| Min. of Labor & Social Affairs | **Jabburi,** Sadi Tumah |
| Min. of Oil | **Ubaydi,** Amir Rashid Muhammad al- |
| Min. of Planning | |
| Min. of Trade | **Salih,** Muhammad Mahdi al- |
| Min. of Transport & Communications | **Khalil,** Ahmad Murtada Ahmad, *Dr.* |
| Min. of State | **Atrush,** Abd al-Wahhab Umar Mirza al- |
| Min. of State | **Zibari,** Arshad Muhammad Ahmad Muhammad al- |
| Min. of State for Foreign Affairs | **Ahmad,** Naji Sabri |
| Min. of State for Military Affairs | **Shanshal,** Abd al-Jabbar Khalil, *Staff Gen.* |
| Adviser to the Pres. | **Azzawi,** Hatim Hamdan al- |
| Adviser to the Pres. | **Habubi,** Safa Hadi Jawad, *Dr.* |
| Adviser to the Pres. | **Qasir,** Nizar Jumah Ali al- |
| Adviser to the Pres. | **Tikriti,** Barzan Ibrahim Hasan al- |
| Adviser to the Pres. | **Tikriti,** Watban Ibrahim al-Hasan al- |
| Adviser to the Pres. for Military Affairs | **Jabburi,** Sadi Tuma Abbas al- |
| Governor, Central Bank | **Huwaysh,** Isam Rashid al- |
| Head of Interests Section in the US | **Duri,** Akram Jasim al- |
| Permanent Representative to the UN, New York | **Duri,** Muhammad Abdallah Ahmad Shati |

# IRELAND

(Last updated: 2/9/2000)

| | |
|---|---|
| President | **McAleese,** Mary |
| Prime Minister | **Ahern,** Bertie |
| Dep. Prime Min. | **Harney,** Mary |
| Min. for Agriculture, Food, & Forestry | **Walsh,** Joe |
| Min. for Arts, Culture, & the Gaeltacht | **de Valera,** Sile |
| Min. for Defense | **Smith,** Michael |
| Min. for Education, Science, & Technology | **Woods,** Michael |
| Min. for Enterprise & Employment | **Harney,** Mary |
| Min. for Environment & Rural Development | **Dempsey,** Noel |
| Min. for Finance | **McCreevy,** Charlie |
| Min. for Foreign Affairs | **Cowen,** Brian |
| Min. for Health & Children | **Martin,** Michael |
| Min. for Justice, Equality & Law Reform | **O'Donoghue,** John |
| Min. for Marine & Natural Resources | **Fahey,** Frank |
| Min. for Social, Community, & Family Affairs | **Ahern,** Dermot |
| Min. for Tourism & Trade | **McDaid,** Jim, *Dr.* |
| Min. for Transport, Energy, & Communications | **O'Rourke,** Mary |
| Attorney General | **McDowell,** Michael |
| Governor, Central Bank of Ireland | **O'Connell,** Maurice |
| Ambassador to the US | **O'hUiginn,** Sean |
| Permanent Representative to the UN, New York | **Ryan,** Richard |

# ISRAEL, STATE OF

(Last updated: 3/27/2001)

| | |
|---|---|
| President | **Katzav,** Moshe |
| Prime Minister | **Sharon,** Ariel |
| Dep. Prime Min. | **Shalom,** Silvan |
| Dep. Prime Min. | **Yishai,** Eli |
| Min. of Agriculture | **Simhon,** Shalom |
| Min. of Communications | **Rivlin,** Reuven |
| Min. of Construction & Housing | **Sharansky,** Natan |
| Min. of Defense | **Ben Eliezer,** Binyamin |
| Min. of Education | **Livnat,** Limor |
| Min. of Environment | **Hanegbi,** Tzahi |
| Min. of Finance | **Shalom,** Silvan |
| Min. of Foreign Affairs | **Peres,** Shimon |
| Min. of Health | **Dahan,** Nissim |
| Min. of Immigrant Absorption | **Sharon,** Ariel |
| Min. of Industry & Trade | **Itzik,** Dalia |
| Min. of Infrastructure | **Lieberman,** Avigdor |
| Min. of Interior | **Yishai,** Eli |
| Min. of Internal Security | **Landau,** Uzi |
| Min. of Justice | **Sheetrit,** Meir |
| Min. of Labor & Social Affairs | **Benizri,** Shlomo |
| Min. of Regional Affairs | **Ohana,** Asher |
| Min. of Regional Cooperation | **Livni,** Tzipi |
| Min. of Jerusalem Affairs | **Suissa,** Eli yahu |
| Min. of Science, Culture, & Sport | **Vilnai,** Matan |
| Min. for Social & Jewish Diaspora Affairs | |
| Min. of Tourism | **Rehavam,** Ze'evi |
| Min. of Transportation | **Sneh,** Ephraim |
| Min. Without Portfolio | **Avital,** Shmuel |
| Min. Without Portfolio | **Cohen,** Ra'anan |
| Min. Without Portfolio | |
| Min. Without Portfolio | **Naveh,** Danny |
| Min. Without Portfolio | **Tarif,** Salah |
| Dep. Min. of Defense | **Rabin-Pelossof,** Dalia |
| Governor, Bank of Israel | **Klein,** David |
| Ambassador to the US | **Ivry,** David |
| Permanent Representative to the UN, New York | **Lancry,** Yehuda |

## ITALY (ITALIAN REPUBLIC)

(Last updated: 4/19/2001)

| | |
|---|---|
| President | **Ciampi,** Carlo Azeglio |
| Prime Minister | **Amato,** Giuliano |
| Under Sec. for the Cabinet | **Micheli,** Enrico |
| Min. of Agriculture | **Pecoraro Scanio,** Alfonso |
| Min. of Communications | **Cardinale,** Salvatore |
| Min. of Civil Service | **Bassanini,** Franco |
| Min. of Culture | **Melandri,** Giovanna |
| Min. of Defense | **Mattarella,** Sergio |
| Min. of Education | **De Mauro,** Tullio |
| Min. of Environment | **Bordon,** Willer |
| Min. of Equal Opportunity | **Bellillo,** Katia |
| Min. of European Affairs | **Mattioli,** Gianni |
| Min. of Finance | **Del Turco,** Ottaviano |
| Min. of Foreign Affairs | **Dini,** Lamberto |
| Min. of Health | **Veronesi,** Umberto |
| Min. of Industry, Commerce, & Foreign Trade | **Letta,** Enrico |
| Min. of Institutional Reform | **Maccanico,** Antonio |
| Min. of Interior | **Bianco,** Enzo |
| Min. of Justice | **Fassino,** Piero Franco |
| Min. of Labor & Social Security | **Salvi,** Cesare |
| Min. of Public Administration | **Bassanini,** Franco |
| Min. of Public Works | **Nesi,** Nerio |
| Min. of Regional Affairs | **Loiero,** Agazio |
| Min. of Relations with Parliament | **Toia,** Patrizia |
| Min. of Social Affairs | **Turco,** Livia |
| Min. of Transport | **Bersani,** Pierluigi |
| Min. of Treasury & Budget | **Visco,** Vincenzo |
| Min. of University & Science | **Zecchino,** Ortensio |
| Pres. of the Chamber of Deputies | **Violante,** Luciano |
| Pres. of the Senate | **Mancino,** Nicola |
| Governor, Bank of Italy | **Fazio,** Antonio |
| Ambassador to the US | **Salleo,** Ferdinando |
| Permanent Representative to the UN, New York | **Vento,** Sergio |

## JAMAICA

(Last updated: 11/22/2000)

| | |
|---|---|
| Governor General | **Cooke,** Howard, *Sir* |
| Prime Minister | **Patterson,** Percival James (P.J.) |
| Dep. Prime Min. | **Mullings,** Seymour |
| Min. of Agriculture | **Clarke,** Roger |
| Min. of Defense | **Patterson,** Percival James (P.J.) |
| Min. of Education & Culture | **Whiteman,** Burchell |
| Min. of Finance & Planning | **Davies,** Omar *Dr.* |
| Min. of Foreign Affairs | **Robertson,** Paul, *Dr.* |
| Min. of Foreign Trade | **Hylton,** Anthony |
| Min. of Health | **Junor,** John |
| Min. of Industry, Commerce & Technology | **Paulwell,** Phillip |
| Min. of Information | **Henry-Wilson,** Maxine |
| Min. of Labor & Social Security | **Buchanan,** Donald |
| Min. of Land & the Environment | **Mullings,** Seymour |
| Min. of Local Government, Youth, & Community Development | **Bertram,** Arnold |
| Min. of Mining & Energy | **Pickersgill,** Robert |
| Min. of National Security & Justice | **Knight,** K. D. |
| Min. of Tourism & Sports | **Simpson-Miller,** Portia |
| Min. of Transport & Works | **Phillips,** Peter, *Dr.* |
| Min. of Water & Housing | **Blythe,** Karl, *Dr.* |
| Attorney General | **Nicholson,** A. J. |
| Governor, Central Bank | **Latibeaudiere,** Derick |
| Ambassador to the US | **Bernal,** Richard |
| Permanent Representative to the UN, New York | **Durrant,** Mignonette Patricia |

## JAPAN

(Last updated: 3/7/2001)

Emperor .......................................................... **Akihito**
Prime Minister .................................................. **Mori,** Yoshiro
Chief Cabinet Sec. ............................................. **Fukuda,** Yasuo
Min. of Agriculture, Forestry, & Fisheries ............................ **Yatsu,** Yoshio
Min. of Economy, Trade, & Industry ................................. **Hiranuma,** Takeo
Min. of Education, Culture, Sport, Science & Technology ................. **Machimura,** Nobutaka
Min. of Environment .............................................. **Kawaguchi,** Yoriko
Min. of Finance ................................................. **Miyazawa,** Kiichi
Min. of Foreign Affairs .......................................... **Kono,** Yohei
Min. of Health, Labor, & Welfare ................................. **Sakaguchi,** Chikara
Min. of Justice ................................................. **Koumura,** Masahiko
Min. of Land, Infrastructure, & Transport ........................ **Ogi,** Chikage
Min. of Public Management, Home Affairs, Posts & Telecommunications ..... **Katayama,** Toranosuke
Dir. Gen., Defense Agency ........................................ **Toshitsugu,** Saito
State Min., Administrative Reform, Okinawa & Northern Territories ......... **Hashimoto,** Ryutaro
State Min., Economic & Fiscal Policy, Information Technology ............. **Aso,** Taro
State Min., Financial Services Agency ............................ **Yanagisawa,** Hakuo
State Min., Science & Technology Policy ........................... **Sasagawa,** Takashi
Chmn., National Pulbic Safety Commission ......................... **Ibuki,** Bunmei
Governor, Central Bank ........................................... **Hayami,** Masaru
Ambassador to the US ............................................ **Yanai,** Shunji
Permanent Representative to the UN, New York ..................... **Sato,** Yukio

## JORDAN, HASHEMITE KINGDOM OF

(Last updated: 4/2/2001)

King ............................................................ **Abdallah II**
Crown Prince .................................................... **Hamzah**
Prime Minister .................................................. **Ragheb,** Ali Abu al-
First Dep. Prime Min. ........................................... **Hmoud,** Marwan al-
Dep. Prime Min. ................................................. **Halaiqa,** Mohammad
Dep. Prime Min. ................................................. **Irsheidat,** Salah
Dep. Prime Min. ................................................. **Khleifat,** Awad
Dep. Prime Min. ................................................. **Nabulsi,** Faris
Min. of Administrative Development & Social Development ...............
Min. of Agriculture ............................................. **Zannouneh,** Zuhair
Min. of Awqaf & Islamic Affairs .................................
Min. of Culture ................................................. **Kayed,** Mahmoud
Min. of Defense ................................................. **Ragheb,** Ali Abu al-
Min. of Economic Affairs ........................................ **Halaiqa,** Mohammad
Min. of Education ............................................... **Touqan,** Khalid
Min. of Energy & Mineral Resources .............................. **Sabri,** Wael
Min. of Finance ................................................. **Marto,** Michel
Min. of Foreign Affairs ......................................... **Khatib,** Abdul Ilah al-
Min. of Health .................................................. **Suheimat,** Tareq
Min. of Information ............................................. **Rifal,** Taleb al-
Min. of Interior ................................................ **Khleifat** Awad
Min. of Justice ................................................. **Nabulsi,** Faris
Min. of Labor ................................................... **Fayez,** Eid al-
Min. of Municipal, Rural & Environmental Affairs ................. **Akour,** Abdul Rahim
Min. of Planning ................................................ **Hadid,** Jawad
Min. of Post & Telecommunications ............................... **Zobi,** Fawaz Hatem
Min. of Prime Ministry Affairs .................................. **Irsheidat,** Saleh
Min. of Public Works & Housing .................................. **Gheida,** Hosni Abu
Min. of Religious Affairs ....................................... **Abbadi,** Abdul Salam
Min. of Social Development ...................................... **Ghoul,** Tamam
Min. of State ................................................... **Shreideh,** Adel
Min. of State for Administrative Development ..................... **Thneibat,** Mohammad
Min. of State for Legal Affairs ................................. **Masadeh,** Daifallah Salem
Min. of State for Parliamentary Affairs ......................... **Dalabih,** Yousef
Min. of Trade & Industry ........................................ **Azar,** Wasif
Min. of Transport ............................................... **Kalaldeh,** Mohammed Farhan

## JORDAN, HASHEMITE KINGDOM OF (cont.)

| | |
|---|---|
| Min. of Tourism & Antiquities | **Biltaji,** Akel |
| Min. of Water | **Halawani,** Hatim |
| Min. of Youth & Sports | **Shuqom,** Said |
| Chief of the Royal Court | **Tarawneh,** Fayez |
| Gov., Central Bank | **Touqan,** Umayid |
| Ambassador to the US | **Muasher,** Marwan |
| Permanent Representative to the UN, New York | **Abu Nimah,** Hasan |

## KAZAKHSTAN, REPUBLIC OF

(Last updated: 1/10/2001)

| | |
|---|---|
| President | **Nazarbayev,** Nursultan |
| Chmn., Senate (upper house) | **Abdukarimov,** Oralbai |
| Chmn., Majlis (lower house) | **Tuyakbayev,** Zharmakan |
| Prime Minister | **Tokayev,** Kasymzhomart |
| First Dep. Prime Min. | **Akhmetov,** Daniyal |
| Dep. Prime Min. | **Shkolnik,** Vladimir |
| Dep. Prime Min. | **Tasmagambetov,** Imangali |
| Dep. Prime Min. | **Zhandosov,** Uraz |
| Min. of Agriculture | **Mynbayev,** Sauat |
| Min. of Culture & Information | **Sarsenbayev,** Altynbek |
| Min. of Defense | **Tokpakbayev,** Sat, *Lt. Gen.* |
| Min. of Economy & Trade | **Kulekeyev,** Zhaksibek |
| Min. of Education & Science | **Bekturganov,** Nuraly |
| Min. of Energy & Natural Resources | **Shkolnik,** Vladimir |
| Min. of Finance | **Yesenbayev,** Mazhit |
| Min. of Foreign Affairs | **Idrisov,** Yerlan |
| Min. of Internal Affairs | **Iskakov,** Bulat |
| Min. of Justice | **Rogov,** Igor |
| Min. of Labor & Social Security | **Baymenov,** Alikhan |
| Min. of Natural Resources & Environmental Protection | **Shukputov,** Andar |
| Min. of Revenues | **Kakimzhanov,** Zianulla |
| Min. of Transport & Communications | **Masimov,** Kasim |
| Min. Without Portfolio | **Samakova,** Aytkul |
| Chmn., Central Bank | **Marchenko,** Grigoriy |
| Chmn., Kazakhoil National Oil & Gas Company | **Balgimbayev,** Nurlan |
| Chmn., National Security Committee (KNB) | **Musayev,** Alnur |
| Chmn., Presidential Agency for Strategic Planning | **Kelimbetov,** Kairat |
| Sec., Security Council | **Tazhin,** Marat |
| Ambassador to the US-Designate | **Saudabayev,** Kanat |
| Permanent Representative to the UN, New York | **Sarbyssynova,** Madina |

## KENYA, REPUBLIC OF

(Last updated: 4/6/2001)

| | |
|---|---|
| President | **Moi,** Daniel T. Arap |
| Vice President | **Saitoti,** George |
| Min. for Agriculture | **Obure,** Chris Mogere |
| Min. for Education | **Musyoka,** Stephen Kalonzo |
| Min. for Energy | **Masakhalia,** Yekoyada F. O. |
| Min. for Energy | |
| Min. for Environment | **Nyenze,** Francis |
| Min. for Finance | **Okemo,** Chrysanthus |
| Min. for Foreign Affairs & International Cooperation | **Godana,** Bonaya A. |
| Min. for Home Affairs, Heritage, & Sports | **Ngala,** Noah Katana |
| Min. for Information, Transport & Communications | **Mudavadi,** Musalia |
| Min. for Labor | **Ngutu,** Joseph K. |
| Min. for Lands & Settlement | **Nyagah,** Joseph |
| Min. for Local Government | **Kamotho,** Joseph J. |
| Min. for Medical Services | |
| Min. for Planning | **Ndambuki,** Gideon M. |
| Min. for Public Health | **Ongeri,** Sam, *Prof.* |

## KENYA, REPUBLIC OF (cont.)

| | |
|---|---|
| Min. for Roads & Public Works | **Kiptoon,** Andrew |
| Min. for Rural Development | **Mohammed,** Hussein Maalim |
| Min. for Science & Technology | **Kosgey,** Henry |
| Min. for Tourism, Trade & Industry | **Biwott,** Nicholas K. |
| Min. for Vocational Training | **Kones,** Kipkalia |
| Min. for Water | **Ng'eny,** Kipng'eno Arap |
| Min. of State in the Office of the Pres. | **Madoka,** Marsden H. |
| Min. of State in the Office of the Pres. | **Ntimama,** William ole |
| Min. of State in the Office of the Pres. | **Sunkuli,** Julius L. O. |
| Min. of State in the Office of the Pres. | **Taib,** Shariff Nassir |
| Attorney General | **Wako,** Amos |
| Governor, Central Bank | **Nyagah,** Nahashon |
| Ambassador to the US | **Nzibo,** Yusuf Abdulraham *Dr.* |
| Permanent Representative to the UN, New York | **Kuindwa,** Fares |

## KIRIBATI, REPUBLIC OF

(Last updated: 11/17/2000)

| | |
|---|---|
| President | **Tito,** Teburoro |
| Vice President | **Tentoa,** Tewareka |
| Min. of Commerce, Industry, & Employment | **Awerika,** Tanieru |
| Min. of Education, Science, & Technology | **Tokataake,** Willie |
| Min. of Environment & Natural Resource Development | **Tong,** Anote |
| Min. of Finance & Economic Planning | **Tinga,** Beniamina |
| Min. of Foreign Affairs & International Trade | **Tito,** Teburoro |
| Min. of Health, Family Planning, & Social Welfare | **Teeke,** Kataotika |
| Min. of Home Affairs | **Tentoa,** Tewareka |
| Min. of Line & Phoenix Islands Development | **Tatabea,** Teiraoi |
| Min. of Rural Development | **Tentoa,** Tewareka |
| Min. of Transport, Communications, & Tourism | **Kaiea,** Manraoi |
| Min. of Works & Energy | **Schutz,** Emile |

## KOREA, NORTH (DEMOCRATIC PEOPLE'S REPUBLIC OF KOREA)—NDE

(Last updated: 4/3/2001)

| | |
|---|---|
| General Secretary, Korean Workers' Party (KWP) | **Kim,** Chong-il, *Mar.* |
| Supreme Cdr. of Korean People's Army (KPA) | **Kim,** Chong-il, *Mar.* |
| Chmn., National Defense Commission (NDC) | **Kim,** Chong-il, *Mar.* |
| First Vice Chmn. of NDC | **Cho,** Myong-nok, *VMar.* |
| Vice Chmn. of NDC | **Kim,** Il-ch'ol, *VMar.* |
| Vice Chmn. of NDC | **Yi,** Yong-mu, *VMar.* |
| Member, NDC | **Chon,** Pyong-ho |
| Member, NDC | **Kim,** Ch'ol-man |
| Member, NDC | **Kim,** Yong-ch'un, *VMar.* |
| Member, NDC | **Paek,** Hak-nim, *VMar.* |
| Member, NDC | **Yi,** Ul-sol |
| Member, NDC | **Yon,** Hyong-muk |
| Pres., Supreme People's Assembly (SPA) Presidium | **Kim,** Yong-nam |
| Vice Pres., SPA | **Kim,** Yong-t'ae |
| Vice Pres., SPA | **Yang,** Hyong-sop |
| Honorary Vice Pres., SPA | **Kim,** Yong-chu |
| Honorary Vice Pres., SPA | **Pak,** Song-ch'ol |
| Premier | **Hong,** Song-nam |
| Vice Premier | **Cho,** Ch'ang-tok |
| Vice Premier | **Kwak,** Pom-ki |
| Min. of Agriculture | **Kim,** Ch'ang-sik |
| Min. of Chemical Industry | **Pak,** Pong-chu |
| Min. of City Management | **Ch'oe,** Chong-kon |
| Min. of Commerce | **Yi,** Yong-son |
| Min. of Construction & Building-Materials Industries | **Cho,** Yun-hui |
| Min. of Culture | **Kang,** Nung-su |
| Min. of Education | **Pyon,** Yong-rip |

## KOREA, NORTH (DEMOCRATIC PEOPLE'S REPUBLIC OF KOREA)—NDE (cont.)

| | |
|---|---|
| Min. of Electronic Industry | **O,** Su-yong |
| Min. of Extractive Industries | **Son,** Chong-ho |
| Min. of Finance | **Mun,** Il-Pong |
| Min. of Fisheries | **Yi,** Song-un |
| Min. of Foreign Affairs | **Paek,** Nam-sun |
| Min. of Foreign Trade | **Yi,** Kwang-kun |
| Min. of Forestry | **Yi,** Sang-mu |
| Min. of Labor | **Yi,** Won-il |
| Min. of Land & Environment Protection | **Chang,** Il-son |
| Min. of Land & Marine Transport | **Kim,** Yong-il |
| Min. of Light Industry | **Yi,** Yon-su |
| Min. of Metal & Machine-Building Industries | **Chong,** Sung-hun |
| Min. of People's Armed Forces | **Kim,** Il-ch'ol, *VMar.* |
| Min. of Post & Telecommunications | **Yi,** Kum-pom |
| Min. of Power & Coal Industries | **Sin,** T'ae-nok |
| Min. of Procurement & Food Administration | **Paek,** Ch'ang-yong |
| Min. of Public Health | **Kim,** Su-hak |
| Min. of Public Security | **Paek,** Hak-nim, *VMar.* |
| Min. of Railways | **Kim,** Yong-sam |
| Min. of State Construction Control | **Pae,** Tal-chun |
| Min. of State Inspection | **Kim,** Ui-sun |
| Chmn., State Planning Ctte. | **Pak,** Nam-ki |
| Chmn., Physical Culture & Sports Guidance Ctte. | **Pak,** Myong-ch'ol |
| Pres., National Academy of Sciences | **Yi,** Kwang-ho |
| Pres., Central Bank | **Kim,** Wan-su |
| Dir., Central Statistics Bureau | **Kim,** Ch'ang-su |
| Chief Sec. | **Chong,** Mun-san |
| Permanent Representative to the UN, New York | **Yi,** Hyong-ch'ol |

## KOREA, SOUTH (REPUBLIC OF KOREA)

(Last updated: 3/29/2001)

| | |
|---|---|
| President | **Kim,** Dae-jung |
| Prime Minister | **Lee,** Han-Dong |
| Dep. Prime Minister | **Jin,** Nyum |
| Dep. Prime Minister | **Han,** Wan-Sang |
| Min. of Agriculture & Forestry | **Han,** Kap-soo |
| Min. of Budget & Planning | **Chon,** Yun-col |
| Min. of Commerce, Industry, & Energy | **Chang,** Che-Shik |
| Min. of Construction & Transportaiton | **Oh,** Jang-Seop |
| Min. of Culture & Tourism | **Kim,** Han-Gill |
| Min. of Defense | **Kim,** Dong-Shin |
| Min. of Education | **Han,** Wan-Sang |
| Min. of Environment | **Kim,** Myong-Ja |
| Min. of Finance & Economy | **Jin,** Nyum |
| Min. of Foreign Affairs & Trade | **Han,** Seung-Soo |
| Min. of Gender Equality | **Han,** Myung-Sook |
| Min. of Govt. Administration | **Lee,** Keun-Sik |
| Min. of Govt. Policy Coordination | **Na,** Seung-Po |
| Min. of Health & Welfare | **Kim,** Won-Gil |
| Min. of Information & Communication | **Yang,** Seung-Taik |
| Min. of Justice | **Kim,** Jung-kil |
| Min. of Labor Affairs | **Kim,** Ho-Jin |
| Min. of Maritime Affairs & Fisheries | **Chung,** Woo-Taik |
| Min. of National Defense | **Cho,** Song-tae |
| Min. of Planning & Budget | **Jeon,** Yun-Chrul |
| Min. of Policy Coordination | **Choi,** Chae-uk |
| Min. of Science & Technology | **Kim,** Young-Hwan |
| Min. of State for Trade | **Hwang,** Tu-yun |
| Min. of Unification | **Lim,** Dong-Won |
| Dir., National Intelligence Service | **Shin,** Kuhn |
| Dir., Office of Legislation | **Song,** Chong-ui |
| Dir., Office of Patriots & Veterans Affairs | **Pak,** Sang-pom |
| Chmn., Central Personnel Committee | **Kim,** Kwang-wong |

## KOREA, SOUTH (REPUBLIC OF KOREA) (cont.)

| | |
|---|---|
| Chmn., Emergency Planning Committee | **Kim,** Chin-son |
| Chmn., Fair Trade Commission | **Chon,** Yun-chol |
| Chmn., Financial Supervisory Commission | **Yi,** Kun-yong |
| Chmn., Special Commission on Women's Affairs | **Yun,** Ho-chung, *Ms.* |
| Sec. Gen., Board of Audit & Inspection | **An,** Pon-il |
| Governor, Central Bank | **Chon,** Chol-hwan |
| Dir., Central Personnel Committee | **Kim,** Kwang-wong |
| Ambassador to the US | **Yang,** Song-chol |
| Permanent Representative to the UN, New York | **Son,** Chun-yong |

## KUWAIT, STATE OF

(Last updated: 2/16/2001)

| | |
|---|---|
| Amir | **Sabah, JABIR,** al-Ahmad al-Jabir Al |
| Prime Minister | **Sabah, SAAD,** al-Abdallah al-Salim Al |
| First Dep. Prime Min. | **Sabah, SABAH,** al-Ahmad al-Jabir Al |
| Dep. Prime Min. | **Sabah, JABIR MUBARAK,** al-Hamad Al |
| Dep. Prime Min. | **Sabah, MUHAMMAD KHALID,** al-Hamad Al |
| Dep. Prime Min. | **Sharar,** MUHAMMAD Dayfallah al- |
| Min. of Communications | **Sabah, AHMAD ABDALLAH,** Al-Ahmad Al |
| Min. of Defense | **Sabah, JABIR MUBARAK,** al-Hamad Al |
| Min. of Education & Higher Education | **Harun,** Musaid Rashid Ahmad Al |
| Min. of Electricity & Water | **Ayyar,** Talal al- |
| Min. of Finance | **Ibrahim,** Yusif Hamad al- *Dr.* |
| Min. of Foreign Affairs | **Sabah, SABAH,** al-Ahmad al-Jabir Al |
| Min. of Information | **Sabah,** AHMAD FAHD al-Ahmad Al |
| Min. of Interior | **Sabah, MUHAMMAD KHALID,** al-Hamad Al |
| Min. of Justice | **Baqir,** Ahmad Yaqub |
| Min. of Oil | **Subih,** Adil Khalid al-, *Dr.* |
| Min. of Planning | **Ibrahim,** Yusif Hamad al-, *Dr.* |
| Min. of Public Health | **Jarallah,** Muhammad Ahmad, *Dr.* |
| Min. of Public Works | **Azimi,** Fahd Dhaisan Mai al- |
| Min. of Religious Endowment & Islamic Affairs | **Baqir,** Ahmad Yaqub |
| Min. of Social Affairs & Labor | **Ayyar,** Talal al- |
| Min. of Trade & Industry | **Khurshid,** Salih Abd al-Rida |
| Min. of State for Administrative Development Affairs | **Ibrahim,** Yusif Hamad al-, *Dr.* |
| Min. of State for Amiri Diwan Affairs | **Sabah, NASIR,** Muhammad Ahmad Al |
| Min. of State for Cabinet Affairs | **Sharar,** Muhammad Dayfallah al- |
| Min. of State for Foreign Affairs | **Sabah, MUHAMMAD SABAH,** al-Salim Al, *Dr.* |
| Min. of State for Housing Affairs | **Azimi,** Fahd Dhaisan Mai al- |
| Min. of State for National Assembly Affairs | **Sharar,** Muhammad Dayfallah al- |
| Speaker, Parliament | **Khurafi,** Jasim al- |
| Governor, Central Bank | **Sabah, SALIM,** Abd al-Aziz Saud Al |
| Ambassador to the US | |
| Permanent Representative to the UN, New York | **Abul Hasan,** Muhammad Abdallah Abbas |

## KYRGYZSTAN (KYRGYZ REPUBLIC)

(Last updated: 3/27/2001)

| | |
|---|---|
| President | **Akayev,** Askar |
| Supreme Council (Zhogorku Kenesh) | |
| Chmn., Assembly of People's Representatives | **Borubayev,** Altay |
| Chmn., Legislative Assembly | **Erkebayev,** Abdygany |
| Prime Minister | **Bakiyev,** Kurmanbek |
| First Dep. Prime Min. | **Tanayev,** Nikolai |
| Dep. Prime Min. | **Sulaimankulov,** Arzymat |
| Chief of Staff | **Ukulov,** Kurmanbek |
| Min. of Agriculture & Water & Processing Industries | **Kostyuk,** Alexander |
| Min. of Defense | **Topoyev,** Esen, *Col. Gen.* |

## KYRGYZSTAN (KYRGYZ REPUBLIC) (cont.)

| | |
|---|---|
| Min. of Ecology & Emergency Situations | **Eshmambetov,** Ratbek |
| Min. of Education, Science, & Culture | **Sharshekeyeva,** Kamila |
| Min. of Finance | **Akmataliyev,** Temirbek |
| Min. of Foreign Affairs | **Imanaliyev,** Muratbek |
| Min. of Foreign Trade & Industry | **Sulaimankulov,** Arzymat |
| Min. of Health | **Meymanaliyev,** Tilekbek |
| Min. of Internal Affairs | **Aitbayev,** Tashtemir |
| Min. of Justice | **Abdyrahmanov,** Jakyp |
| Min. of Labor & Social Welfare | **Aknazarova,** Roza |
| Min. of Transportation & Communications | **Jumaliyev,** Kubanychbek |
| Sec., National Security Council | **Januzakov,** Bolot |
| Chmn., National Security Service | **Januzakov,** Bolot |
| Chmn., State Commission for Procurement & Material Reserves | **Kereksizov,** Tashkul |
| Chmn., State Commission for Management of State Property & Attraction of Direct Investments | **Jiyenbekov,** Sadriddin |
| Dir., Agency for Registration of Real Estate Rights | **Omuraliyev,** Tolobek |
| Dir., Agency for Science & Copyright | **Omorov,** Roman |
| Dir., State Communication Agency | **Titov,** Andrei |
| Chmn., National Bank | **Sarbanov,** Ulan |
| Ambassador to the US | **Abdrisayev,** Bakyt |
| Permanent Representative to the UN, New York | **Ibraimova,** Elmira |

## LAOS (LAO PEOPLE'S DEMOCRATIC REPUBLIC)

(Last updated: 4/2/2001)

*Laotion officials are addressed by the first element in their names.*

| | |
|---|---|
| President | **Khamtai Siphandon,** *Gen.* |
| Vice President | **Choummali Saignason,** *Lt. Gen.* |
| Prime Minister | **Boungnang Volachit** |
| Dep. Prime Min. | **Thongloun Sisolit** |
| Dep. Prime Min. | **Somsavat Lengsavat** |
| Min. of Agriculture & Forestry | **Sian Saphangthong** |
| Min. of Commerce | **Phoumi Thipphavon** |
| Min. of Communications, Transport, Posts, & Construction | **Bouathong Vonglokham** |
| Min. of Education | **Phimmason Leuangkhamma** |
| Min. of Finance | **Soukan Mahalat** |
| Min. of Foreign Affairs | **Somsavat Lengsavat** |
| Min. of Industry & Handicrafts | **Soulivong Daravong** |
| Min. of Information & Culture | **Phandouangchit Vongsa** |
| Min. of Interior | **Asang Laoli,** *Maj. Gen.* |
| Min. of Justice | **Khamouan Boupha** |
| Min. of Labor & Social Welfare | **Somphan Phengkhammi** |
| Min. of National Defense | **Douangchai Phichit,** *Maj. Gen.* |
| Min. of Public Health | **Ponmek Dalaloi,** *M.D.* |
| Min., Perm. Secy., Office of the President | **Soubanh Srithirath** |
| Min., Attached to the Office of the Prime Min. | **Bountiam Phitsamai** |
| Min., Attached to the Office of the Prime Min. | **Somphong Mongkhonvilai** |
| Min., Attached to the Office of the Prime Min. | **Saisengliteng Bliachu** |
| Min., Attached to the Office of the Prime Min. | **Somphavan Inthavong** |
| Min., Attached to the Office of the Prime Min. | **Souli Nanthavong** |
| Chmn. State Planning Committee | **Thongloun Sisoulit** |
| Governor, National Bank | |
| Ambassador to the US | **Vang Rattanavong** |
| Permanent Representative to the UN, New York | **Alounkeo Kittikhoun,** |

## LATVIA, REPUBLIC OF

(Last updated: 11/17/2000)

| | |
|---|---|
| President | **Vike-Freiberga,** Vaira |
| Prime Minister | **Berzins,** Andris |
| Min. of Agriculture | **Slakteris,** Atis |

## LATVIA, REPUBLIC OF (cont.)

| | |
|---|---|
| Min. of Culture | **Petersone,** Karina |
| Min. of Defense | **Kristovskis,** Girts Valdis |
| Min. of Economics | **Kalvitis,** Aigars |
| Min. of Education & Science | **Greiskalns,** Karlis |
| Min. of Environmental Protection & Regional Development | **Makarovs,** Vladimirs |
| Min. of European Integration | **Krasts,** Guntars |
| Min. of Finance | **Berzins,** Gundars |
| Min. of Foreign Affairs | **Berzins,** Indulis |
| Min. of Internal Affairs | **Seglins,** Mareks |
| Min. of Justice | **Labucka,** Ingrida |
| Min. of State for State Revenue | **Poca,** Alja |
| Min. of Transport | **Gorbunovs,** Anatolijs |
| Min. of Welfare | **Pozarnovs,** Andrejs |
| Special Min. for Cooperation with International Financial Institutions | **Zile,** Roberts |
| Special Min. for Regional and Local Govt. | **Bunkss,** Janis |
| Special Min. for State Reform | **Krumins,** Janis |
| Pres., Central Bank of Latvia | **Repse,** Einars |
| Ambassador to the US | **Ronis,** Aivis |
| Permanent Representative to the UN, New York | **Priedkalns,** Janis |

## LEBANON (LEBANESE REPUBLIC)

(Last updated: 2/20/2001)

| | |
|---|---|
| President | **Lahud,** Emile |
| Prime Minister | **Hariri,** Rafiq |
| Dep. Prime Min. | **Fares,** Issam |
| Min. of Agriculture | **Abdallah,** Ali |
| Min. of Culture | **Salameh,** Ghassan |
| Min. of Displaced | **Hamadeh,** Marwan |
| Min. of Economy & Trade | **Flayhan,** Basil |
| Min. of Education & Higher Education | **Murad,** Abed Al-Rahim |
| Min. of Energy & Water | **Baydun,** Mohammad Abed Al-Hamid |
| Min. of Environment | **Moussa,** Michel |
| Min. of Finance | **Siniora,** Fuad |
| Min. of Foreign Affairs & Emigres | **Hammud,** Mahmud |
| Min. of Health | **Franjiyah,** .Sulayman |
| Min. of Industry | **Frem,** George |
| Min. of Information | **Aridi,** Ghazi |
| Min. of Interior & Municipalities | **Murr,** Elias |
| Min. of Justice | **Al-Jisr,** Samir |
| Min. of Labor | **Qanso,** Ali |
| Min. of National Defense | **Hrawi,** Khalil |
| Min. of Public Works & Transport | **Mikati,** Najib |
| Min. of Social Affairs | **Diab,** Asad |
| Min. of State | **Arslan,** Talal |
| Min. of State | **Baydun,** Nazih |
| Min. of State | **Helu,** Pierre |
| Min. of State | **Merhej,** Bishara |
| Min. of State | **Pharaon,** Michel |
| Min. of State | **Tabbarah,** Bahej |
| Min. of State for Administrative Reform Affairs | **Saad,** Fuad |
| Min. of Telecommunications | **Cordahi,** Jean Louis |
| Min. of Tourism | **Karam,** Karam |
| Min. of Youth & Sports | **Hovnanian,** Sebouh |
| Governor, Central Bank | **Salimi,** Riyad |
| Ambassador to the US | **Abboud,** Farid |
| Permanent Representative to the UN, New York | **Tadmoury,** Selim |

# LESOTHO, KINGDOM OF

(Last updated: 11/17/2000)

King ............................................................... **Letsie III**
Prime Minister .................................................... **Mosisili**, Pakalitha
Dep. Prime Min. .................................................. **Maope**, Kelebone Albert
Min. to the Prime Min. ........................................... **Motanyane**, Sephiri Enoch
Min. of Agriculture, Cooperatives, & Land Reclamation ........... **Bulane**, Vova
Min. of Communications Information, Broadcasting,
Posts, & Telecommunications ..................................... **Mphafi**, Qnyane
Min. of Defense ................................................... **Mosisili**, Pakalitha
Min. of Education ................................................. **Lehohla**, Lesao Archibald
Min. of Employment & Labor ....................................... **Molopo**, Nots'i Victor
Min. of Environment, Gender, & Youth Affairs ..................... **Lepono**, Mathabiso
Min. of Finance & Development Planning ........................... **Maope**, Kelebone Albert
Min. of Foreign Affairs .......................................... **Thabane**, Motsoahae Thomas
Min. of Health & Social Welfare .................................. **Mabote**, Tefo
Min. of Industry, Trade, & Marketing ............................. **Malie**, Mpho Meli
Min. of Justice, Human Rights, Law, & Constitutional Affairs ..... **Mokhehle**, Shakane
Min. of Local Government & Home Affairs .......................... **Mabitle**, Mopshatla
Min. of Natural Resources ........................................ **Moleleki**, Monyane
Min. of Public Works & Transport ................................. **Moerane**, Mofelehetsi
Min. of Tourism, Sports, & Culture ............................... **Motaung**, Mlalele
Governor, Central Bank ........................................... **Maruping**, Anthony
Ambassador to the US ............................................. **Moleko**, Lebohang Kenneth
Permanent Representative to the UN, New York ..................... **Mangoaela**, Percy Metsing

# LIBERIA, REPUBLIC OF

(Last updated: 2/8/2001)

President ......................................................... **Taylor**, Charles
Vice President .................................................... **Blah**, Moses Zeh
Min. of Agriculture .............................................. **Massaquoi**, Roland
Min. of Commerce & Industry ...................................... **Peabody**, Cora
Min. of Defense ................................................... **Chea**, Daniel
Min. of Education ................................................. **Kandakai**, Evelyne
Min. of Finance .................................................. **Barnes**, Nathaniel
Min. of Foreign Affairs .......................................... **Captan**, Monie
Min. of Health & Social Welfare .................................. **Coleman**, Peter
Min. of Information, Culture, & Tourism .......................... **Mulbah**, Joe W.
Min. of Internal Affairs ......................................... **Poe**, Maxwell
Min. of Justice .................................................. **Varmah**, Eddington
Min. of Labor .................................................... **Neufville**, Christian
Min. of Land, Mines, & Energy .................................... **Dunbar**, Jenkins
Min. of National Security ........................................ **Kammah**, Philip
Min. of Planning & Economic Affairs .............................. **Ward**, Amelia
Min. of Posts & Telecommunications ............................... **Bright**, John
Min. of Public Works ............................................. **Taylor**, Emmett
Min. of Rural Development ......................................... **Bowen**, Hezekiah
Min. of Transport ................................................ **Carbah**, Francis
Min. of Youth & Sports ........................................... **Massaquoi**, Francois
Min. of State for Planning & Economic Affairs .................... **McClain**, Wisseh
Min. of State for Presidential Affairs ........................... **Taylor**, Jonathan
Min. of State Without Portfolio .................................. **Zayzay**, Augustine
Governor, National Bank .......................................... **Bright**, Charles
Ambassador to the US ............................................. **Bull**, William
Permanent Representative to the UN, New York ..................... **Kawah**, Lamine

# LIBYA (SOCIALIST PEOPLE'S LIBYAN ARAB JAMAHIRIYA)

(Last updated: 4/3/2001)

*(Col. Muammar al-Qadhafi has no official title but he runs Libya and is de facto chief of state. The Secretary of the General People's Congress is chief of state in theory but is not treated as such. The Secretary of the General People's Committee plays the role of prime minister.)*

## LIBYA (SOCIALIST PEOPLE'S LIBYAN ARAB JAMAHIRIYA) (cont.)

| | |
|---|---|
| Leader | **Qadhafi,** Muammar Abu Minyar al-, *Col.* |
| Sec. Gen., People's Congress | **Zanati,** Muhammad al- |
| Asst. Sec. Gen., People's Congress | **Ibrahim,** Ahmad Mohamed |
| Sec. Gen., People's Committee | **Al-Shamikh,** Mubarak Abdullah |
| Sec. of the Gen. People's Committee for Economy & Trade | **Juwayd,** Abd Al-SSalam Ahmed |
| Sec. of the Gen. People's Committee for African Unity | **Al-Turayki,** Ali Abd Al-Salam |
| Sec. of the Gen. People's Committee for Finance | **Al-Burayni,** Al-'Ujayli Abd Al-Salam |
| Sec. of the Gen. People's Committee for Foreign Liaison & International Cooperation | **Shalgam,** Abd Al-Rahman |
| Sec. of Gen. People's Committee for Justice & Public Security | **Al-Abbar,** Abd al-Rahman |
| Governor, Central Bank | **Al-Hamid,** Ahmed Munaysi Abd |
| Permanent Representative to the UN, New York | **Dorda,** Abuzed |

## LIECHTENSTEIN, PRINCIPALITY OF

(Last updated: 11/17/2000)

| | |
|---|---|
| Head of State | **Hans,** Adam II |
| Head of Government (Prime Minister) | **Frick,** Mario |
| Deputy Head of Government | **Ritter,** Michael |
| Govt. Councillor for Construction | **Frick,** Mario |
| Govt. Councillor for Culture & Sport | **Willi,** Andrea |
| Govt. Councillor for Economy | **Ritter,** Michael |
| Govt. Councillor for Education | **Marxer,** Norbert |
| Govt. Councillor for Environment, Agriculture, & Forestry | **Marxer,** Norbert |
| Govt. Councillor for Family Affairs & Equal Rights | **Willi,** Andrea |
| Govt. Councillor for Finance | **Frick,** Mario |
| Govt. Councillor for Foreign Relations | **Willi,** Andrea |
| Govt. Councillor for Health & Social Services | **Ritter,** Michael |
| Govt. Councillor for Interior | **Ritter,** Michael |
| Govt. Councillor for Justice | **Frommelt,** Heinz |
| Govt. Councillor for Transportation | **Marxer,** Norbert |
| Chmn., Liechtenstein State Bank | **Kindle,** Herbert |
| Permanent Representative to the UN, New York | **Fritsche,** Claudia |

## LITHUANIA, REPUBLIC OF

(Last updated: 2/9/2001)

| | |
|---|---|
| President | **Adamkus,** Valdas |
| Prime Minister | **Paksas,** Rolandas |
| Min. of Administration Reforms & Municipal Affairs | **Rudalevicius,** Jonas |
| Min. of Agriculture & Forestry | **Kristinatis,** Kestutis |
| Min. of Culture | **Kevisas,** Gintautas |
| Min. of Defense | **Linkevicius,** Linas |
| Min. of Economy | |
| Min. of Education & Science | **Monkevicius,** Algirdas |
| Min. of Environmental Protection | |
| Min. of Finance | **Lionginas,** Jonas |
| Min. of Foreign Affairs | **Valionis,** Antanas |
| Min. of Health | **Janusonis,** Vincas |
| Min. of Internal Affairs | **Markevicius,** Vytautas |
| Min. of Justice | **Bartkus,** Gintautas |
| Min. of Social Security & Labor | **Blinkeviciute,** Vilija |
| Min. of Transportation & Communication | **Barakauskas,** Dailis |
| Chmn., Bank of Lithuania | **Sarkinas,** Reinoldijus |
| Ambassador to the US | **Sakalauskas,** Stasys |
| Permanent Representative to the UN, New York | **Jusys,** Oskaras |

## LUXEMBOURG, GRAND DUCHY OF

(Last updated: 3/16/2001)

| | |
|---|---|
| Grand Duke | **Henri** |
| Prime Minister | **Juncker**, Jean-Claude |
| Vice Prime Min. | **Polfer**, Lydie |
| Min. of Agriculture, Viticulture, & Rural Development | **Boden**, Fernand |
| Min. of Civil Service & Administrative Reform | **Polfer**, Lydie |
| Min. of Communications | **Biltgen**, Francois |
| Min. of Cooperation Humanitarian Action, & Defense | **Goerens**, Charles |
| Min. of Cults | **Biltgen**, Francois |
| Min. of Culture, Higher Education, & Research | **Hennicot-Schoepges**, Erna |
| Min. of Economy | **Grethen**, Henri |
| Min. of Education & Vocational Training | **Hennicot-Schoepges**, Erna |
| Min. of Employment | **Biltgen**, Francois |
| Min. of Environment | **Goerens**, Charles |
| Min. of Family, Social Solidarity, & Youth | **Jacobs**, Marie-Josee |
| Min. of Finance | **Juncker**, Jean-Claude |
| Min. of Foreign Affairs & External Commerce | **Polfer**, Lydie |
| Min. of Health | **Wagner**, Carlo |
| Min. of Interior | **Wolter**, Michel |
| Min. of Justice | **Frieden**, Luc |
| Min. of Middle Class, Housing, & Tourism | **Boden**, Fernand |
| Min. of National Education, Professional Training, & Sports | **Brasseur**, Anne |
| Min. of Promotion of Women | **Jacobs**, Marie-Josee |
| Min. of Public Works | **Hennicot-Schoepges**, Erna |
| Min. of Relations with Parliament | **Biltgen**, Francois |
| Min. of Social Security | **Wagner**, Carlo |
| Min. of State | **Juncker**, Jean-Claude |
| Min. of Transportation | **Grethen**, Henri |
| Min. of Treasury and the Budget | **Frieden**, Luc |
| Sec. of State for the Environment | **Berger**, Eugene |
| Sec. of State for Public Function & Administrative Reform | **Schaack**, Joseph |
| Chief of Defense Staff | **Lenz**, Guy, *Col.* |
| Chmn., Luxembourg Central Bank | **Mersch**, Yves |
| Ambassador to the US | **Conzemius**, Arlette |
| Permanent Representative to the UN, New York | **Wurth**, Hubert |

## MACEDONIA, THE FORMER YUGOSLAV REPUBLIC OF

(Last updated: 2/23/2001)

| | |
|---|---|
| President | **Trajkovski**, Boris |
| Prime Minister | **Georgievski**, Ljubco |
| Dep. Prime Min. | **Ibrahimi**, Bedredin |
| Dep. Prime Min. | **Krstevski**, Zoran |
| Min. of Agriculture, Forestry, & Water Management | **Gjorcev**, Marjan |
| Min. of Culture | **Samoilova-Cvetanova**, Ganka |
| Min. of Defense | **Paunovski**, Ljuben |
| Min. of Economy | **Fetai**, Besnik |
| Min. of Education & Science | **Novkovski**, Nenad |
| Min. of Environment & Urban Planning | **Dodovski**, Marjan |
| Min. of Finance | **Gruevski**, Nikola |
| Min. of Foreign Affairs | **Kerim**, Srgjan |
| Min. of Health | **Danailovski**, Dragan |
| Min. of Internal Affairs | |
| Min. of Justice | **Nasufi**, Xhevdet |
| Min. of Labor & Social Welfare | **Ibrahimi**, Bedredin |
| Min. of Local Self Government | **Saiti**, Xhemail |
| Min. of Transportation & Communication | **Balkovski**, Ljubco |
| Min. Without Portfolio | **Fejzulahu**, Ernad |
| Min. Without Portfolio | **Krstevski**, Zoran |
| Speaker, Assembly | **Andov**, Stojan |
| Governor, Macedonian Central Bank | **Trenevski**, Martin |
| Ambassador to the US | **Acevska**, Ljubica |
| Permanent Representative to the UN, New York | **Calovski**, Naste |

## MADAGASCAR

(Last updated: 1/19/2001)

| | |
|---|---|
| President | **Ratsiraka,** Didier, *Adm. (Ret.)* |
| Prime Minister | **Andrianarivo,** Tantely |
| Vice Prime Min. in Charge of Budget & Development of Autonomous Provinces | **Rajaonarivelo,** Pierrot Jocelyn |
| Min. of Agriculture | **Raveloarijaona,** Marcel Theophile |
| Min. of Armed Forces | **Ranjeva,** Marcel, *lt. Gen.* |
| Min. of Civil Service, Labor, & Social Laws | **Razafinakanga,** Alice |
| Min. of Commerce & Consumer Affairs | **Randrianambinina,** Alphonse |
| Min. of Economy & Finance | **Andrianarivo,** Tantely |
| Min. of Energy & Mines | **Rasoza,** Charles |
| Min. of Environment | **Alphonse** |
| Min. of Fisheries & Maritime Resources | **Abdallah,** Houssen |
| Min. of Foreign Affairs | **Ratsifandrihamanana,** Lila |
| Min. of Health | **Rahantalalao,** Henriette |
| Min. of Higher Education | **Sydson,** Joseph |
| Min. of Industry & Crafts | **Ratovomalala,** Mamy |
| Min. of Information, Culture, & Communication | **Betsimifira,** Fredo |
| Min. of Interior | **Rasolondraibe,** Jean-Jacques, *Brig. Gen.* |
| Min. of Justice | **Imbiky,** Anaclet |
| Min. of Livestock | **Rakotondrasoa** |
| Min. of Population, Women's Issues, & Childhood | **Jaotody,** Noeline |
| Min. of Posts & Telecommunications | **Andriamanjato,** Ny Hasina |
| Min. of Primary & Secondary Education | **Jacquit,** Simon |
| Min. of Private Sector Economy & Privatization | **Constant,** Horace |
| Min. of Public Works | **Tsaranazy,** Jean Emile, *Col.* |
| Min. of Scientific Research | **Rakotonirainy,** Georges Solay |
| Min. of Technical & Professional Education | **Levelo,** Boniface |
| Min. of Territorial Management & Cities | **Ramamantsoa,** Herivelona |
| Min. of Tourism | **Razafimanjato,** Blandin |
| Min. of Transport & Meteorology | **Rasolonay,** Charles |
| Min. of Waters & Forrests | **Rajohnson,** Rija |
| Min. of Youth & Sports | **Ndrianasolo** |
| Sec. of State in the Ministry of Interior for Public Security | **Azaly,** Ben Marofo |
| Sec. of State in the Ministry of the Armed Forces for the Gendarmerie | **Bory,** Jean Paul, *Lt. Gen.* |
| Governor, Central Bank | **Ravelojaona,** Gaston |
| Ambassador to the US | **Andrianarivelo-Razafy,** Zina |
| Permanent Representative to the UN, New York | **Bakoniarivo,** Jean De La Croix |

## MALAWI, REPUBLIC OF

(Last updated: 3/20/2001)

| | |
|---|---|
| President | **Muluzi,** Bakili, *Dr.* |
| Vice President | **Malewezi,** Justin |
| Min. of Agriculture & Irrigation | **Mangulama,** Leonard |
| Min. of Commerce & Industry | **Kaleso,** Peter |
| Min. of Defense | **Munyenyembe,** Rodwell |
| Min. of Education | **Mtafu,** George, *Dr.* |
| Min. of Finance & Economic Planning | **Chikaonda,** Mathews |
| Min. of Foreign Affairs & International Cooperation | **Patel,** Lilian |
| Min. of Gender, Youth & Community Services | **Banda,** Mary |
| Min. of Health & Population | **Banda,** Aleke |
| Min. of Home Affairs & Internal Security | **Maloza,** Mangeza |
| Min. of Information | **Stambuli,** Clement |
| Min. of Justice | **Fachi,** Peter |
| Min. of Labor | **Mwawa,** Yusuf |
| Min. of Lands, Housing, Physical Planning, & Surveys | **Maloya,** Thengo |
| Min. of Natural Resources & Environmental Affairs | **Thomson,** Harry |
| Min. for Privatization | **Malewezi,** Justin |
| Min. of Sports & Culture | **Dossi,** Moses |
| Min. of Tourism | **Lipenga,** Ken *Dr.* |
| Min. of Transport & Public Works | **Phumisa,** Kaliyoma |
| Min. of Water Development | **Mlanga,** Lee |
| Min. Without Portfolio | **Mussa,** Uladi |

## MALAWI, REPUBLIC OF (cont.)

| | |
|---|---|
| Min. of State in the President's Office for District & Local Government Administration | Mbewe, Patrick |
| Min. of State in the President's Office for People with Disablilites | Claver, George |
| Min. of State in the President's Office for Poverty Alleviation | Sumani, Alice |
| Min. of State in the President's Office for Presidential Affairs | Lemani, Dumbo |
| Min. of State in the President's Office for Statutory Corporations | Khamisa, Bob |
| Dep. Min. of Agriculture | Mtewa, Mekki *Dr.* |
| Dep. Min. of Commerce | Bwanalt, Phillip |
| Dep. Min. of Education, Science & Technology | Kaphuka, Samuel |
| Dep. Min. of Finance & Economic Planning | Sonke, Jan Jaap |
| Dep. Min. of Foreign Affairs & International Cooperation | Katsonga, Davis |
| Dep. Min. of Health | Kaliati, Patricia |
| Dep. Min. of Lands | Nasho, Martha |
| Dep. Min. of Natural Resources & Environment | Shati, Ludoviko |
| Dep. Min. of Sports & Culture | |
| Dep. Min. of Transport & Public Works | Omar, Iqbar |
| Dep. Min. in the President's Office for Public Events, Relief & Rehabilitation | Mkandawire, Chenda |
| Attorney General | Fachi, Peter |
| Governor, Reserve Bank | |
| Ambassador to the US | Kandiero, Paul Tony Steven |
| Permanent Representative to the UN, New York | Juwayeyi, Yusuf McDadlly |

## MALAYSIA

(Last updated: 3/28/2001)

| | |
|---|---|
| Paramount Ruler | TUANKU JA'AFAR, ibni Al-Marhum Tuanku Abdul Rahman |
| Dep. Paramount Ruler | Sultan TUNKU SALAHUDDIN Abdul Aziz Shah ibni Al-Marhum Sultan Hisammuddin Alam Shah |
| Prime Minister | MAHATHIR bin Mohamad |
| Dep. Prime Min. | ABDULLAH bin Ahmad Badawi |
| Min. of Agriculture | Mohamed EFFENDI Norwawi |
| Min. of Culture, Arts, & Tourism | Abdul KADIR bin Sheik Fadzir |
| Min. of Defense | Mohamed NAJIB bin Abdul Razak |
| Min. of Domestic Trade & Consumer Affairs | MUHYIDDIN bin Mohamed Yassin |
| Min. of Education | MUSA Mohamad |
| Min. of Energy, Communications, & Multimedia | Leo MOGGIE Anak Irok |
| Min. of Entrepreneur Development | Mohamed NAZRI bin Abdul Aziz |
| Min. of Finance | DAIM Zainuddin |
| Min. of Foreign Affairs | Syed HAMID bin Syed Jaafar Albar |
| Min. of Health | CHUA Jui Meng |
| Min. of Home Affairs | ABDULLAH bin Ahmad Badawi |
| Min. of Housing & Local Government | ONG Kah Ting |
| Min. of Human Resources | FONG Chan Ong |
| Min. of Information | KHALIL Yaakob |
| Min. of Intl. Trade & Industry | RAFIDAH binti Abdul Aziz |
| Min. of Land & Cooperative Development | KASITAH bin Gaddam |
| Min. of National Unity & Social Development | Siti ZAHARAH binti Sulaiman |
| Min. of Primary Industries | LIM Keng Yaik |
| Min. of Rural Development | AZMI bin Khalid |
| Min. of Science, Technology, & Environment | LAW Hieng Ding |
| Min. of Special Functions in the Dept. of the Prime Min. | DAIM Zainuddin |
| Min. of Transport | LING Liong Sik |
| Min. of Women's Affairs | SHAHRIZAT binte Abdul Jalil |
| Min. of Works | S. Samy VELLU |
| Min. of Youth & Sports | HISHAMMUDDIN bin Hussein |
| Min. in the Dept. of the Prime Min. | Bernard Biluk DOMPOK |
| Min. in the Dept. of the Prime Min. | Abdul HAMID bin Zainal Abidin |
| Min. in the Dept. of the Prime Min. | PANDIKAR AMIN Mulia |
| Min. in the Dept. of the Prime Min. | RAIS YATIM |
| Dep. Min. of Agriculture | Mohamed SHARIFF omar |
| Dep. Min. of Culture, Arts, & Tourism | NG Yen Yen |
| Dep. Min. of Defense | Mohamed SHAFIE Apdal |

## MALAYSIA (cont.)

| | |
|---|---|
| Dep. Min. of Domestic Trade & Consumer Affairs | **S. SUBRAMANIAM** |
| Dep. Min. of Education | **ABDUL AZIZ Samsuddin** |
| Dep. Min. of Education | **CHOON Kim** |
| Dep. Min. of Energy, Communications, & Multimedia | **TAN Chai Ho** |
| Dep. Min. of Finance | **SHAFIE Mohamed Salleh** |
| Dep. Min. of Finance | **CHAN Kong Choy** |
| Dep. Min. of Foreign Affairs | **Leo Francis Michael TOYAD** |
| Dep. Min. of Health | **SULEIMAN Mohamed** |
| Dep. Min. of Home Affairs | **CHOR Chee Heung** |
| Dep. Min. of Home Affairs | **ZAINAL Abidin Zin** |
| Dep. Min. of Housing & Local Government | **M. KAYVAES** |
| Dep. Min. of Human Resources | **ABDUL LATIFF Ahmad** |
| Dep. Min. of Information | **Mohamed KHALID Mohamed Yunus** |
| Dep. Min. of Intl. Trade & Industry | **KERK Choo Ting** |
| Dep. Min. of Land & Cooperative Development | **TAN Kee Kwong** |
| Dep. Min. of National Unity & Social Development | **Tiki Anak Lafe** |
| Dep. Min. of Rural Development | **G. Palanivel** |
| Dep. Min. of Science, Technology, & Environment | **ZAINAL Dahalan** |
| Dep. Min. of Transport | **RAMLI Ngah Talib** |
| Dep. Min. of Works | **Mohamed KHALED Nordin** |
| Dep. Min. of Youth & Sports | **ONG Tee Keat** |
| Dep. Min. in the Dept. of the Prime Min. | **ADNAN bin Mansor** |
| Dep. Min. in the Dept. of the Prime Min. | **AZLAN Abu Bakar** |
| Governor, Central Bank | **ZETI Akhtar Aziz** |
| Ambassador to the US | **GHAZZALI bin Sheikh Abdul Khalid** |
| Permanent Representative to the UN, New York | **HASMY bin Agam,** |

## MALDIVES, REPUBLIC OF

(Last updated: 11/17/2000)

| | |
|---|---|
| President | **Gayoom,** Maumoon Abdul |
| Speaker of People's Majlis | **Hameed,** Abdulla |
| Min. of Atolls Administration | **Hameed,** Abdulla |
| Min. of Construction & Public Works | **Zahir,** Umar |
| Min. of Defense & National Security | **Gayoom,** Maumoon Abdul |
| Min. of Education | **Latheef,** Mohamed |
| Min. of Finance & Treasury | **Gayoom,** Maumoon Abdul |
| Min. of Fisheries, Agriculture, & Marine Resources | **Hussain,** Abdul Rasheed |
| Min. of Foreign Affairs | **Jameel,** Fathulla |
| Min. of Health | **Abdulla,** Ahmed |
| Min. of Home Affairs, Housing, & Environment | **Shafeeu,** Ismail |
| Min. of Human Resources, Employment, & Labor | **Kamaluddeen,** Abdulla |
| Min. of Information, Arts, & Culture | **Manik,** Ibrahim |
| Min. of Justice | **Zahir,** Ahmed |
| Min. of Planning & National Development | **Zaki,** Ibrahim Hussain |
| Min. of the President's Office | **Jameel,** Abdulla |
| Min. of Science & Technology | |
| Min. of Tourism | **Sobir,** Hassan |
| Min. of Trade & Industries | **Yameen,** Abdulla |
| Min. of Transport & Civil Aviation | **Ibrahim,** Ilyas |
| Min. of Women's Affairs & Social Security | **Yoosuf,** Raashida |
| Min. of Youth & Sports | **Hussain,** Mohamed Zahir |
| Min. of State & Auditor-General | **Fathy,** Ismail |
| Min. of State for Defense & National Security | **Sattar,** Anbaree Abdul |
| Min. of State for Finance & Treasury | **Hilmy,** Arif |
| Min. of State for Pres. Affairs | **Hussain,** Mohamed |
| Iman, of the Islamic Center | **Shathir,** Ahmed |
| Special Advisor, Supreme Council of Islamic Affairs | **Fathy,** Moosa |
| Attorney General | **Munavvar,** Mohammed |
| Governor, Central Bank | **Gayoom,** Maumoon Abdul |
| Permanent Representative to the UN, New York | **Shihab,** Hussain |

## MALI, REPUBLIC OF

(Last updated: 11/17/2000)

President .............................................................. **Konare,** Alpha Oumar
Prime Minister ........................................................ **Sidibe,** Mande
Min. of Armed Forces & Veterans .................................... **Maiga,** Soumeylou Boubeye
Min. of Communications .............................................. **Tamboura,** Ascofare Ouleymatou
Min. of Culture ...................................................... **Coulibaly,** Pascal Baba
Min. of Economy & Finance ........................................... **Kone,** Bacari
Min. of Education .................................................... **Dicko,** Moustapha
Min. of Employment .................................................. **Sissoko,** Makan Moussa
Min. of Environment ................................................. **Cisse,** Soumailia
Min. of Foreign Affairs & Malians Abroad ............................. **Sidibe,** Modibo
Min. of Health ...................................................... **Nafo,** Traore Fatoumata
Min. of Industry, Commerce, & Transport ............................. **Traore,** Toure Alimata
Min. of Justice & Keeper of the Seals ................................ **Poudiougou,** Abdoulaye Ogotembely
Min. of Labor & Professional Training ................................ **Sissoko,** Mankan Moussa
Min. of Mines, Energy, & Water Resources ............................ **Coulibaly,** Aboubacary
Min. for the Promotion of Women, Child & Family Affairs ............... **Thierro,** Diarra Hafsatou
Min. of Rural Development ........................................... **Diallo,** Ahmed el Madani
Min. of Security & Civil Protection .................................. **Doumbia,** Tiecoura, *Gen.*
Min. of Social Development .......................................... **M'Daiye,** Diukite Fatoumata
Min. of State Building & Housing Affairs ............................. **Sissoko,** Bouare Fily
Min. of Territorial Administration & Local Communitites ............... **Sy,** Ousmane
Min. of Tourism ..................................................... **Halatine,** Zakyatou Oualett
Min. of Youth & Sports .............................................. **Kone,** Adama
Ambassador to the US ................................................ **Diarrah,** Cheick Oumar
Permanent Representative to the UN, New York ......................... **Ouane,** Moctar

## MALTA, REPUBLIC OF

(Last updated: 11/17/2000)

President .............................................................. **De Marco,** Guido
Prime Minister ........................................................ **Fenech Adami,** Eddie
Dep. Prime Min. ...................................................... **Borg,** Joseph, *Dr.*
Min. for Agriculture & Fisheries ..................................... **Zammit,** Ninu
Min. for the Economic Services ....................................... **Bonnici,** Josef
Min. for Education ................................................... **Galea,** Louis
Min. for Environment ................................................ **Zammit Dimech,** Francis
Min. for Finance ..................................................... **Dalli,** John
Min. for Foreign Affairs ............................................. **Borg,** Joseph, *Dr.*
Min. for Health ...................................................... **Deguara,** Louis
Min. for Home Affairs ................................................ **Borg,** Tonio
Min. for Social Policy ............................................... **Gonzi,** Lawrence
Min. for Tourism ..................................................... **Refalo,** Michael
Min. for Transport & Communications ................................. **Galea,** Censu
Governor, Central Bank ............................................... **Ellul,** Emanuel
Ambassador to the US ................................................ **Saliba,** George
Permanent Representative to the UN, New York ......................... **Balzan,** Walter

## MARSHALL ISLANDS, REPUBLIC OF THE

(Last updated: 11/17/2000)

President .............................................................. **Note,** Kessai
Min. of Assistance to the President .................................. **Zackios,** Gerald
Min. of Education .................................................... **Kendall,** Wilfred
Min. of Finance ...................................................... **Konelios,** Michael
Min. of Foreign Affairs & Trade ...................................... **Jacklick,** Alvin
Min. of Health & Environment ........................................ **Lometo,** Tadashi
Min. of Internal Affairs & Welfare ................................... **Lorak,** Nidel
Min. of Public Works ................................................ **Morris,** Rien
Min. of Resources, Development, & Works ............................. **Silk,** John
Min. of Transportation & Communications ............................. **Wase,** Brenson

## MARSHALL ISLANDS, REPUBLIC OF THE (cont.)

Ambassador to the US .................................................. **de Brum,** Banny
Permanent Representative to the UN, New York ......................... **Relang,** Jackeo A.

## MAURITANIA, ISLAMIC REPUBLIC OF

(Last updated: 3/16/2001)

President ............................................................. **Taya,** Maaouya Ould Sid Ahmed
Prime Minister ....................................................... **El Avia,** Ould Mohamed
Min. of Civil Service, Labor, Youth & Sports .......................... **Sidi,** Baba Ould
Min. of Commerce, Handicrafts, & Tourism ............................. **Hamet,** Diop Abdoul
Min. of Communications & Relations with Parliament ................... **Saleh,** Rachid Ould
Min. of Culture & Islamic Orientation ................................ **Isselmou,** Moustaph Ould
Min. of Defense ...................................................... **Elewa,** Kaba Ould
Min. of Economic & Development Affairs ............................... **Nani,** Mohamed Ould
Min. of Education .................................................... **Abdallahi,** Deddoud Ould
Min. of Equipment & Transportation ................................... **Gueladio,** Kamara Ali
Min. of Finance ...................................................... **Ali,** Mahfoudh Ould Mohamed
Min. of Fisheries & Maritime Economy ................................. **Zamel,** Mohamed el Moctar Ould
Min. of Foreign Affairs .............................................. **Abdi,** Dah Ould
Min. of Hydraulics & Energy .......................................... **Moustafa,** Kane
Min. of Interior, Post, & Telecommunications ......................... **Jelil,** Dahould Abdel
Min. of Justice ...................................................... **Lemrabott,** Sidi Mahmoud Ould Cheikh Ahmed
Min. of Mines & Industry ............................................. **Rajel,** Ishagh Ould
Min. of National Defense ............................................. **Elewa,** Kaba Ould
Min. of Public Health ................................................ **Houmeid,** Bodiel Ould
Min. of Rural Development & Environment .............................. **Hamady,** Ahmedy Ould
Min. of Women's Rights & Family Welfare .............................. **Hedeid,** Mintata Mint
Sec. of State Delegate to the Prime Minister in Charge of
Developing the Use of Informatics .................................... **Saleck,** Fatimetou Mint Mohamed
Ambassador to the US ................................................. **Ben Jidou,** Ahmed Ben Khalifa
Permanent Representative to the UN, New York ......................... **Deddach,** Mahfoudh Ould

## MAURITIUS

(Last updated: 10/26/2000)

President ............................................................. **Uteem,** Cassam, *Sir*
Vice President ....................................................... **Chettiar,** Angidi
Prime Minister ....................................................... **Jugnauth,** Anerood
Dep. Prime Min. ...................................................... **Berenger,** Paul
Min. of Agriculture .................................................. **Jugnauth,** Pravin
Min. of Arts & Culture ............................................... **Ramdass,** Motee
Min. of Civil Service Affairs & Administrative Reforms ............... **Jeewah,** Ahmad
Min. of Commerce, Industry, & International Trade .................... **Cuttaree,** Jayen
Min. of Cooperatives ................................................. **Koonjoo,** Prem
Min. of Defense & Home Affairs ....................................... **Jugnauth,** Anerood
Min. of Education .................................................... **Obeegadoo,** Steve
Min. of Environment .................................................. **Bhagwan,** Rajesh
Min. of Finance ...................................................... **Berenger,** Paul
Min. of Fisheries .................................................... **Michel,** Sylvio
Min. of Foreign Affairs .............................................. **Gayan,** Ali
Min. of Health ....................................................... **Jugnauth,** Ashok
Min. of Housing & Land ............................................... **Choonee,** Mukeshwar
Min. of Justice & Human Rights ....................................... **Shing,** Emmanuel Leung
Min. of Labor & Industrial Relations ................................. **Soodhun,** Showkatally
Min. of Public Infrastructure & Internal Transport ................... **Baichoo,** Anil
Min. of Public Utilities ............................................. **Ganoo,** Alan
Min. of Regional Administration, Rodrigues, Urban & Rural Development ..... **Lesjongard,** Joe
Min. of Social Security & Institutional Reform ....................... **Lauthan,** Samioulah
Min. of Telecommuications & Technology Information ................... **Jeeha,** Pradeep
Min. of Tourism ...................................................... **Bodha,** Nando
Min. of Training, Skills Development & Productivity .................. **Fowdar,** Sangeet
Min. of Women Rights & Family Welfare ................................ **Navarre-Marie,** Arianne

## MAURITIUS (cont.)

Min. of Youth & Sports .............................................. **Yerrigadoo**, Ravi
Attorney General .................................................... **Shing**, Emmanuel Leung
Governor, Central Bank .............................................. **Maraye**, M. Dan
Ambassador to the US ............................................... **Jesseramsing**, Chitmansing
Permanent Representative to the UN, New York ...................... **Wan Chat Kwong**, Taye Wah Michel

## MEXICO (UNITED MEXICAN STATES)

(Last updated: 4/11/2001)

President ........................................................... **Fox**, Quesada, Vicente
Sec. of Agrarian Reform ............................................ **Herrera**, Tello, Maria Teresa
Sec. of Agriculture ................................................ **Usabiaga**, Arroyo, Javier
Sec. of Communications & Transport ................................. **Cerisola y Weber**, Pedro
Sec. of Comptroller General ........................................ **Barrio**, Terrazas, Francisco
Sec. of Economy .................................................... **Derbez**, Bautista, Luis Ernesto
Sec. of Energy ..................................................... **Martens**, Rebolledo, Ernesto
Sec. of Environment & Natural Resources ............................ **Lichtinger**, Victor
Sec. of Finance & Public Credit .................................... **Gil**, Diaz, Francisco
Sec. of Foreign Relations .......................................... **Castaneda**, Gutman, Jorge
Sec. of Government ................................................. **Creel**, Miranda, Santiago
Sec. of Health ..................................................... **Frenk**, Mora, Julio
Sec. of Labor & Social Welfare ..................................... **Abascal**, Carranza, Carlos
Sec. of National Defense ........................................... **Vega**, Garcia, Gerardo Clemente Ricardo, *Gen.*
Sec. of Navy ....................................................... **Peyrot**, Gonzalez, Marco Antonio, *Vice Adm.*
Sec. of Public Education ........................................... **Tamez**, Guerra, Reyes
Sec. of Public Security & Justice Services ......................... **Gertz**, Manero, Alejandro
Sec. of Social Development .......................................... **Vazquez**, Mota, Josefina
Sec. of Tourism .................................................... **Navarro**, Leticia
Attorney General ................................................... **Macedo**, de la Concha, Rafael
Chief, Dept. of the Fed. District .................................. **Lopez**, Obrador, Andres Manuel
Attorney General, Fed. District .................................... **Batiz**, Vazquez, Bernardo
Governor, Bank of Mexico ........................................... **Ortiz**, Martinez, Guillermo
Ambassador to the US ............................................... **Bremer Martino**, Juan Jose
Permanent Representative to the UN, New York ...................... **Tello**, Macias, Manuel

## MICRONESIA, FEDERATED STATES OF

(Last updated: 1/19/2001)

President ........................................................... **Falcam**, Leo A.
Vice President ..................................................... **Killion**, Redley
Sec. of Economic Affairs ........................................... **Anefal**, Sebastian
Sec. of Foreign Affairs ............................................ **Ilon**, Epel
Sec. of Finance & Administration ................................... **Ehsa**, John
Sec. of Health, Education, & Social Services ....................... **Pretrick**, Eliuel
Sec. of Justice .................................................... **Musrasrik**, Emilio
Sec. of Transportation, Communications, & Infrastructure ........... **Weilbacher**, Lukner
Dep. Sec. of Economic Affairs ...................................... **McKenzie**, Patrick
Dep. Sec. of Foreign Affairs ....................................... **Iehsi**, Ieske
Dep. Sec. of Health, Education, & Social Services .................. **Cantero**, Catalino
Speaker of the Congress ............................................ **Fritz**, Jack
Ambassador to the US ............................................... **Marehalau**, Jesse
Permanent Representative to the UN, New York ...................... **Nakayama**, Masao

## MOLDOVA, REPUBLIC OF

(Last updated: 12/11/2000)

President ........................................................... **Lucinschi**, Petru
Chairman of Parliament ............................................. **Diacov**, Dumitru
Prime Minister ..................................................... **Braghis**, Dumitru
First Dep. Prime Min. .............................................. **Cucu**, Andrei

## MOLDOVA, REPUBLIC OF (cont.)

| | |
|---|---|
| Dep. Prime Min. | **Cosarciuc,** Valeriu |
| Dep. Prime Min. | **Gutu,** Lidia |
| Min. of Agriculture | **Russu,** Ion |
| Min. of Cabinet | **Petrache,** Mihai |
| Min. of Culture | **Ciobanu,** Gennadie |
| Min. of Defense | **Gamurari,** Boris |
| Min. of Economy & Reform | **Cucu,** Andrei |
| Min. of Education | **Gutu,** Ion |
| Min. of Environment | **Raileanu,** Ion |
| Min. of Finance | **Manoli,** Mihai |
| Min. of Foreign Affairs | **Cernomaz,** Nicolae |
| Min. of Health | **Parasca,** Vasile |
| Min. of Industry & Energy | **Lesanu,** Ion |
| Min. of Internal Affairs | **Turcan,** Vladimir |
| Min. of Justice | **Sterbet,** Valeria |
| Min. of Labor | **Revenco,** Valerian |
| Min. of State | **Filat,** Vladimir |
| Min. of Territory Development, Construction, & Communal Services | **Severovan,** Mihai |
| Min. of Transportation & Communications | **Smochin,** Afanasie |
| Dir., Intelligence & Security Service (ISS) | **Pasat,** Valeriu |
| Prosecutor General | **Iuga,** Mircea |
| Pres., National Bank | **Talmaci,** Leonid |
| Secretary of National Security | **Plamadeala,** Mihai |
| Ambassador to the US | **Ciobanu,** Ceslav |
| Permanent Representative to the UN, New York | **Botnaru,** Ion |

## MONACO, PRINCIPALITY OF

(Last updated: 11/17/2000)

| | |
|---|---|
| Chief of State | **Rainier III,** *Prince* |
| Min. of State | **Leclercq,** Patrick |
| Govt. Councilor for Finance & Economics | **Biancheri,** Franck |
| Govt. Councilor for the Interior | **Deslandes,** Philippe |
| Govt. Councilor for Public Works & Social Affairs | **Badia,** Jose |
| Pres., National Council | **Campora,** Jean-Louis |
| Permanent Representative to the UN | **Boisson,** Jacques |

## MONGOLIA

(Last updated: 7/17/2000)

| | |
|---|---|
| President | **Bagabandi,** Natsagiyn |
| Prime Minister | **Amarjargal,** Rinchinnyamin |
| Chief of the General Police | **Muren,** Dashdorjiyn |
| Min. of Agriculture and Industry | **Sodnomtseren,** Choinzongiin |
| Min. of Defense | **Tuvdendorj,** Sharavdorjiin |
| Min. of Education | **Battur,** A. |
| Min. of Environment | **Mendsaikhan,** |
| Min. of External Relations | **Tuya,** Nyam-Osorin |
| Min. of Finance | **Ochirsukh,** Yansanjavin |
| Min. of Health and Welfare | **Sonin,** Sodov, Dr. |
| Min. of Infrastructure Development | **Batkhuu,** Gavaagiin |
| Min. of Justice | **Ganbold,** Dash |
| Chief of the General Staff | **Dashzeveg,** Tserenbaljdyn |
| Secretary, National Security Council | **Bold,** Ravdangiyn |
| Pres., Central Bank of Mongolia | **Unenbat,** J. |
| Ambassador to the US | **Choinhor,** Jalbuugiyn |
| Permanent Representative to the UN, New York | **Enkhsaikhan,** Jargalsaihany |

## MOROCCO, KINGDOM OF

(Last updated: 4/5/2001)

King ............................................................. **Mohamed VI**
Prime Minister ................................................... **Youssoufi,** Abderrahmane
Min. of Agriculture & Rural Development ........................... **Alaoui,** Ismail
Min. of Awqaf & Islamic Affairs .................................. **Alaoui,** Abdelkebir M'Daghri
Min. in Charge of Relations with Parliament ...................... **Bouzouba,** Mohamed
Min. in Charge of Territorial Management, Urbanism, Housing, & Environment . **El Yazghi,** Mohamed
Min. of Cultural & Communications ................................ **Achari,** Mohamed
Min. of Economy, Finance, & Tourism .............................. **Oulalou,** Fathallah
Min. of Economic Forecasts & Planning ............................ **Aouad,** Abdelhamid
Min. of Employment, Vocational Training, Social Development, & Solidarity ... **Fassi,** Abbas
Min. of Equipment ................................................ **Tighouane,** Bouamar
Min. for Foreign Affairs & Cooperation ........................... **Benaissa,** Mohamed
Min. of Health ................................................... **Khiari,** Thami
Min. of Higher Education ......................................... **Zerouali,** Najib
Min. of Human Rights ............................................. **Oujar,** Mohamed
Min. of Industry, Trade, Energy & Mines .......................... **Mansouri,** Mustapha
Min. of Interior ................................................. **Midaqui,** Ahmed
Min. of Justice .................................................. **Azziman,** Omar
Min. of Marine Fisheries ......................................... **Chbaatou,** Said
Min. of National Education ....................................... **Saaf,** Abdallah
Min. of Social Economy, Small & Medium Enterprises &
Handicraft in Charge of the General Affairs of the Govt. ......... **Alami,** Ahmed Halimi
Min. of Transport & Merchant Marine .............................. **Zhined,** Abdeslam
Min. of Youth & Sports ........................................... **Moussaoui,** Ahmed
Sec. Gen. of the Government ...................................... **Rabi,** Abdessadek
Min. Delegate to the Minister of Agriculture & Rural
Development in Charge of Rural Development ........................ **Naouni,** Hassan
Min. Delegate to the Minister of Employment, Vocational Training, Social
Development, & Solidarity in Charge of Women Situation, Family, Child
Care, & Handicapped's Integration ................................ **Chakrouni,** Nazha
Min. Delegate to the Prime Minister in Charge of the Administration
of National Defense .............................................. **Sbai,** Abderrahmane
Sec. of State for Foreign Affairs & Cooperation .................. **Fehri,** Taieb Fassi
Sec. of State for Interior ....................................... **El Hemma,** Fouad
Sec. of State to the Minister of Territorial Management, Urbanism, Housing, &
Environment in Charge of Housing ................................. **M'Barki,** Mohamed
Sec. of State to the Minister of Higher Education in Charge of
Scientific Research .............................................. **Fehri,** Omar Fassi
Sec. of State to the Prime Minister in Charge of Post, Telecommunication
Technologies & Information ....................................... **Hajji,** Nasr
Sec. of State to the Minister of Social Economy, Small & Medium
Enterprises & Handicraft ......................................... **Benatik,** Abdelkrim
Gov., Central Bank ............................................... **Sakkat,** Mohamed
Ambassador to the US ............................................. **Maaroufi,** Abdullah
Permanent Representative to the UN, New York ..................... **Bennouna,** Ahmed

## MOZAMBIQUE, REPUBLIC OF

(Last updated: 3/15/2001)

President ........................................................ **Chissano,** Joaquim Alberto
Prime Minister ................................................... **Mocumbi,** Pascoal Manuel
Min. of Agriculture & Rural Development ........................... **Muteia,** Helder
Min. of Culture .................................................. **Mkaima,** Miguel
Min. of Defense .................................................. **Dai,** Tobias
Min. of Education ................................................ **Nguenha,** Alcido
Min. of Environmental Coordination ............................... **Kachamila,** John
Min. of Fisheries ................................................ **Muthemba,** Cadmiel
Min. of Foreign Affairs & Cooperation ............................ **Simao,** Leonardo
Min. of Health ................................................... **Songane,** Franciso
Min. of Higher Education, Science & Technology ................... **Brito,** Lidia
Min. of Industry & Commerce ...................................... **Morgado,** Carlos
Min. of Interior ................................................. **Manhenje,** Almerino

## MOZAMBIQUE, REPUBLIC OF (cont.)

Min. of Justice .............................................. **Abudo,** Jose Ibraimo
Min. of Labor ............................................... **Sevene,** Mario
Min. of Mineral Resources & Energy ......................... **Langa,** Castigo
Min. of Planning & Finance ................................. **Diogo,** Luisa
Min. of Public Works & Housing ............................. **White,** Robert
Min. of State Administration ............................... **Chichava,** Jose
Min. of Tourism ............................................ **Sumbana,** Fernando
Min. of Transport & Communications ......................... **Salomao,** Tomas
Min. of Women's & Social Affairs ........................... **Matable,** Virginia
Min. of Veteran's Affairs .................................. **Thai,** Antonio Hama
Min. of Youth & Sport ...................................... **Libombo,** Joel
Min. in the Presidency for Defense & Security Affairs ...... **Manhenje,** Almerino
Min. in the Presidency for Parliamentary & Diplomatic Affairs .............. **Madeira,** Francisco
Attorney General ........................................... **Namburete,** Antonio
Governor, Central Bank ..................................... **Maleiane,** Adriano Afonso
Ambassador to the US ....................................... **Namashulua,** Marcos Geraldo
Permanent Representative to the UN, New York ............... **dos Santos,** Carlos

## NAMIBIA, REPUBLIC OF

(Last updated: 11/17/2000)

President .................................................. **Nujoma,** Sam
Prime Minister ............................................. **Geingob,** Hage
Dep. Prime Min. ............................................ **Witbooi,** Hendrik
Min. of Agriculture, Water, & Rural Development ............ **Angula,** Helmut
Min. of Basic Education, Sport, & Culture .................. **Mutorwa,** John
Min. of Defense ............................................ **Nghimtina,** Erkki
Min. of Environment & Tourism .............................. **Malima,** Philemon
Min. of Finance ............................................ **Mbumba,** Nangolo
Min. of Fisheries & Marine Resources ....................... **Iyambo,** Abraham
Min. of Foreign Affairs, Information, & Broadcasting ....... **Gurirab,** Theo-Ben
Min. of Health & Social Services ........................... **Amathila,** Libertine, *Dr.*
Min. of Higher Education, Training, & Employment Creation .. **Angula,** Nahas
Min. of Home Affairs ....................................... **Ekandjo,** Jerry
Min. of Justice ............................................ **Tjiriange,** Ngarikutuke
Min. of Labor .............................................. **Toivo ya Toivo,** Andimba
Min. of Lands, Resettlement, & Rehabilitation ............. **Ithana,** Pendukeni
Min. of Mines & Energy ..................................... **Nyamu,** Jesaya
Min. of Prisons & Correctional Services .................... **Hausiko,** Marco
Min. of Regional, Local Govt., & Housing .................. **Iyambo,** Nicky
Min. of Trade & Industry ................................... **Hamutenya,** Hidipo
Min. Without Portfolio .....................................
Min. of Women Affairs & Child Welfare ..................... **Ndaitwah,** Netumbo
Min. of Works, Transport, & Communications ................ **Amweelo,** Moses
Dir Gen., National Planning Commission .................... **Kuugongelwa,** Saara
Attorney General ........................................... **Tjiriange,** Ngarikutuke
Special Advisor on Economics .............................. **Hanekom,** Gert
Special Advisor on Political Matters ...................... **Hishoono,** Kanana
Special Advisor on Security ............................... **Tsheehama,** Peter
Governor, Central Bank .................................... **Jafar,** Ahmad, *Dr.*
Ambassador to the US ...................................... **Iipumbu,** Leonard
Permanent Representative to the UN, New York .............. **Andjaba,** Martin

## NAURU, REPUBLIC OF

(Last updated: 11/17/2000)

President .................................................. **Dowiyogo,** Bernard
Min. of Business Development & Consumer Affairs ........... **Clodumar,** Kinza
Min. of Civil Aviation & Transportation .................. **Clodumar,** Kinza
Min. of Education & Vocational Training ................... **Namaduk,** Remy
Min. of Finance & Economic Reforms ....................... **Dowiyogo,** Bernard
Min. of Foreign Affairs .................................. **Dowiyogo,** Bernard

## NAURU, REPUBLIC OF (cont.)

Min. of Home Affairs & Culture .......................................... **Audoa**, Anthony
Min. of Human Resources, Development, & Employment .................. **Dowiyogo**, Bernard
Min. of Industry & Economic Development ............................ **Clodumar**, Kinza
Min. of Justice ...................................................... **Gadoengin**, Vassal
Min. of Public Service ................................................ **Dowiyogo**, Bernard
Min. of Sports ...................................................... **Gioura**, Derog
Min. of Telecommunications .......................................... **Dowiyogo**, Bernard
Min. of Tourism ...................................................... **Clodumar**, Kinza
Min. of Works, Planning, & Housing Development ...................... **Gioura**, Derog
Min. Assisting the President ......................................... **Gioura**, Derog
Permanent Representative to the UN, New York ........................ **Clodumar**, Vinci Niel

## NEPAL, KINGDOM OF

(Last updated: 11/17/2000)

King ................................................................ **Birendra**, Bir Bikram Shah Dev
Prime Minister ...................................................... **Koirala**, Girija Prasad
Dep. Prime Min. ..................................................... **Poudel**, Ram Chandra
Min. of Agriculture and Cooperatives ................................ **Bastola**, Chakra Prasad
Min. of Culture, Tourism, & Civil Aviation .......................... **Chataut**, Tarini Dutta
Min. of Defense ..................................................... **Koirala**, Girija Prasad
Min. of Education and Sports ........................................ **Chataut**, Tarini Dutta
Min. of Finance ..................................................... **Acharya**, Mahesh
Min. of Foreign Affairs ............................................. **Bastola**, Chakra Prasad
Min. of Forest & Soil Conservation .................................. **Thakur**, Mahantha
Min. of General Administration ...................................... **Koirala**, Girija Prasad
Min. of Health ...................................................... **Yadav**, Ram Baran
Min. of Home Affairs ................................................ **Joshi**, Govinda Raj
Min. of Industries, Commerce, & Supplies ............................ **Tamrakar**, Ram Krishna
Min. of Information & Communications ................................ **Gupta**, Jaya Prakash
Min. of Labor & Transport Management ................................ **Koirala**, Gigija Prasad
Min. of Land Reform & Management .................................... **Ojha**, Siddha Raj
Min. of Law, Justice, & Parliamentary Affairs ....................... **Thakur**, Mahanta
Min. of Local Development ........................................... **Poudel**, Ram Chandra
Min. of Physical Planning & Works ................................... **Khadka**, Khum Bahadur
Min. of Population & Environment .................................... **Shrestha**, Omkar Prasad
Min. of Science and Technology ...................................... **Chaudhari**, Surendra Prasad
Min. of Water Resources ............................................. **Khadka**, Khum Bahadur
Min. of Women, Children, & Social Welfare ........................... **Koirala**, Girija Prasad
Governor, Central Bank .............................................. **Shrestha**, Satyendra Ryara
Ambassador to the US ................................................ **Thapa**, Bekh Bahadur
Permanent Representative to the UN, New York ........................ **Shah**, Narendra M.

## NETHERLANDS, KINGDOM OF THE

(Last updated: 11/21/2000)

Queen ............................................................... **Beatrix**
Prime Minister ...................................................... **Kok**, Wim
Vice Prime Min. ..................................................... **Borst**, Els
Vice Prime Min. ..................................................... **Jorritsma**, Annemarie
Min. of Agriculture, Nature Management, & Fisheries ................. **Brinkhorst**, Laurens-Jan
Min. of Defense ..................................................... **de Grave**, Frank
Min. of Development Cooperation ..................................... **Herfkens**, Eveline
Min. of Economic Affairs ............................................ **Jorritsma**, Annemarie
Min. of Education, Culture, & Science ............................... **Hermans**, Loek
Min. of Finance ..................................................... **Zalm**, Gerrit
Min. of Foreign Affairs ............................................. **Van Aartsen**, Jozias
Min. of Home Affairs ................................................ **de Vries**, Klaas
Min. of Housing, Physical Planning, & Environment ................... **Pronk**, Jan
Min. of Justice ..................................................... **Korthals**, Benk
Min. of Social Affairs & Employment ................................. **Vermeend**, Willem
Min. of Transport, Public Works & Water Management .................. **Netelenbos**, Tineke

## NETHERLANDS, KINGDOM OF THE (cont.)

| | |
|---|---|
| Min. of Urban & Minority Policies | **van Boxtel,** Roger |
| Min. of Welfare, Health, & Sports | **Borst,** Els |
| State Sec. for Agriculture | **Faber,** Geke |
| State Sec. for Culture | **van der Ploeg,** Rick |
| State Sec. for Defense | **van Hoof,** Henk |
| State Sec. for Economic Affairs & Foreign Trade | **Ybema,** Gerrit |
| State Sec. for Education | **Adelmund,** Karin |
| State Sec. for Financial Affairs | **Bos,** Wouter |
| State Sec. for Foreign Affairs (European Affairs) | **Benschop,** Dick |
| State Sec. for Health, Welfare, & Sports | **Vliegenhart,** Margo |
| State Sec. for Housing | **Remkes,** Johan |
| State Sec. for Justice | **Cohen,** Job |
| State Sec. for Kingdom Affairs | **de Vries,** Gijs |
| State Sec. for Social Affairs (Equal Opportunity) | **Verstand,** Annelies |
| State Sec. for Social Affairs (Social Security) | **Hoogervorst,** Hans |
| State Sec. for Transportation & Public Works | **deVries,** Monique |
| Chief of the Defense Staff | **Kroon,** Luuk, *VAdm.* |
| President, The Netherlands Central Bank | **Wellink,** Nout |
| Ambassador to the US | **Vos,** Joris |
| Permanent Representative to the UN, New York | **van Walsum,** Peter |

## NETHERLANDS ANTILLES

(Last updated: 3/27/2001)

*(Self-governing part of Netherlands realm)*

| | |
|---|---|
| Governor | **Saleh,** Jaime |
| Prime Minister | **Pourier,** Miguel |
| Dep. Prime Min. | **Camelia-Romer,** Susanne |
| Min. of Education, Culture, Youth & Sports | **Lamp,** Stanley |
| Min. of Finance | **Voges,** Russell |
| Min. of National Recovery Plan & Economic Affairs | **Camelia-Romer,** Susanne |
| Min. of Public Health, Environment, & Humanitarian Affairs | **Abraham,** Jopie |
| Min. of Justice | **Martha,** Rutsel |
| Min. of Interior Affairs, Labor, & Social Affairs | **Rafael,** Magda |
| Min. of Transportation & Telecommunication | **Bulo,** Ensley |
| Attorney General | **Goedgedrag,** Fritz |
| Dir., Bank of the Nertherlands Antilles | **Tromp,** Emsley |

## NEW ZEALAND

(Last updated: 4/16/2001)

| | |
|---|---|
| Governor General | **Cartwright,** Silvia, *Dame* |
| Prime Minister | **Clark,** Helen |
| Dep. Prime Min. | **Anderton,** James (Jim) |
| Min. of Accident Insurance | **Dalziel,** Lianne |
| Min. of Agriculture | **Sutton,** James (Jim) |
| Min. of the America's Cup | **Mallard,** Trevor |
| Min. of Arts, Culture, & Heritage | **Clark,** Helen |
| Min. of Biosecurity | **Sutton,** James (Jim) |
| Min. of Broadcasting | **Hobbs,** Marian |
| Min. of Civil Defense | **Hawkins,** George |
| Min. of Commerce | **Swain,** Paul |
| Min. of Communications | **Swain,** Paul |
| Min. of Conservation | **Lee,** Sandra |
| Min. of Corrections | **Robson,** Matt |
| Min. of Courts | **Robson,** Matt |
| Min. of Crown Research Institutes | **Hodgson,** Peter (Pete) |
| Min. of Defense | **Burton,** Richard (Mark) |
| Min. of Disarmament & Arms Control | **Robson,** Matt |
| Min. of Economic Development | **Anderton,** James (Jim) |
| Min. of Education | **Mallard,** Trevor |

## NEW ZEALAND (cont.)

Min. of Energy ............................................................. **Hodgson,** Peter (Pete)
Min. of the Environment ............................................... **Hobbs,** Marian
Min. of Finance .......................................................... **Cullen,** Michael
Min. of Fisheries ........................................................ **Hodgson,** Peter (Pete)
Min. of Foreign Affairs & Trade ...................................... **Goff,** Philip (Phil)
Min. of Forestry ......................................................... **Hodgson,** Peter (Pete)
Min. of Health ........................................................... **King,** Annette
Min. of Housing .......................................................... **Gosche,** Mark
Min. of Information Technology ....................................... **Swain,** Paul
Min. of Immigration .................................................... **Dalziel,** Lianne
Min. of Industry & Regional Development ........................... **Anderton,** James (Jim)
Min. of Internal Affairs ............................................... **Hawkins,** George
Min. of Justice .......................................................... **Goff,** Philip (Phil)
Min. of Labor ............................................................ **Wilson,** Margaret
Min. of Land Information ............................................... **Robson,** Matt
Min. of Local Government ............................................. **Lee,** Sandra
Min. of Maori Affairs .................................................. **Horomia,** Parekura
Min. of Pacific Island Affairs ......................................... **Gosche,** Mark
Min. of Police ........................................................... **Hawkins,** George
Min. of Racing ........................................................... **King,** Annette
Min. of Research, Science, & Technology ............................ **Hodgson,** Peter (Pete)
Min. of Revenue ......................................................... **Cullen,** Michael
Min. of Senior Citizens ................................................ **Dalziel,** Lianne
Min. of Social Services & Employment ............................... **Maharey,** Steven (Steve)
Min. of Sports, Fitness, & Leisure .................................... **Mallard,** Trevor
Min. of State Owned Enterprises ...................................... **Burton,** Richard (Mark)
Min. of State Services .................................................. **Mallard,** Trevor
Min. of Statistics ....................................................... **Harre,** Laila
Min. of Tourism ......................................................... **Burton,** Richard (Mark)
Min. of Trade Negotiations ............................................ **Sutton,** James (Jim)
Min. of Transport ....................................................... **Gosche,** Mark
Min of Veterans Affairs ................................................ **Burton,** Richard (Mark)
Min. of Women's Affairs ............................................... **Harre,** Laila
Min. of Youth Affairs .................................................. **Harre,** Laila
Min. in Charge of the Treaty of Waitangi Negotiations ............ **Wilson,** Margaret
Min. Responsible for Adult & Community Education ................ **Mallard,** Trevor
Min. Responsible for Civil Aviation .................................. **Gosche,** Mark
Min. Responsible for Disability Issues ............................... **Dalziel,** Lianne
Min. Responsible for Ethnic Affairs .................................. **Hawkins,** George
Min. Responsible for the National Library & the National Archives ........... **Hobbs,** Marian
Min. Responsible for Rural Affairs ................................... **Sutton,** James (Jim)
Min. Responsible for Small Business .................................. **Hodgson,** Peter (Pete)
Min. Responsible for Timberlands West Coast Ltd. .................. **Hodgson,** Peter (Pete)
Associate Min. of Biosecurity ......................................... **Hobbs,** Marian
Associate Min. of Commerce .......................................... **Harre,** Laila
Associate Min. of Community & Voluntary Sector ................... **Maharey,** Steven (Steve)
Associate Min. of Economic Development ............................ **Hodgson,** Peter (Pete)
Associate Min. of Education ........................................... **Hobbs,** Marian
Associate Min. of Education ........................................... **Maharey,** Steven (Steve)
Associate Min. of Energy .............................................. **Swain,** Paul
Associate Min. of Finance ............................................. **Swain,** Paul
Associate Min. of Fisheries ........................................... **Horomia,** Parekura
Associate Min. of Foreign Affairs & Trade ........................... **Robson,** Matt
Associate Min. of Industry & Regional Development ................ **Hodgson,** Peter (Pete)
Associate Min. of Justice .............................................. **Swain,** Paul
Associate Min. of Justice .............................................. **Wilson,** Margaret
Associate Min. of Labor ............................................... **Hare,** Laila
Associate Min. of Land Information ................................... **Swain,** Paul
Associate Min. of Maori Affairs ...................................... **Lee,** Sandra
Associate Min. of Revenue ............................................. **Swain,** Paul
Associate Min. of State Services ...................................... **Wilson,** Margaret
Associate Min. of Tourism ............................................ **Horomia,** Parekura
Associate Min. of Transportation ..................................... **Tizard,** Judith
Associate Min. of Arts, Culture & Heritage .......................... **Tizard,** Judith
Associate Min. of Corrections ......................................... **Turia,** Tariana
Associate Min. of Education ........................................... **Horomia,** Parekura

## NEW ZEALAND (cont.)

| | |
|---|---|
| Associate Min. of Health | **Dyson,** Ruth |
| Associate Min. of Housing | **Turia,** Tariana |
| Associate Min. of Maori Affairs | **Turia,** Tariana |
| Associate Min. of Social Services & Employment | **Horomia,** Parekura |
| Associate Min. of Social Services & Employment | **Turia,** Tariana |
| Associate Min. to the Prime Min. on Auckland Issues | **Tizard,** Judith |
| Parliamentary Under Sec. to the Min. of Econ. Development & of Industry & Regional Development | **Samuels,** Dover |
| Parliamentary Under Sec. to the Min. of Econ. Development, of Industry & Regional Development, of Revenue, & of Racing | **Wright,** John |
| Treasurer | **Cullen,** Michael |
| Attorney General | **Wilson,** Margaret |
| Governor, Reserve Bank | **Brash,** Donald |
| Ambassador to the US | **Bolger,** James (Jim) |
| Permanent Representative to the UN, New York | **MacKay,** Donald J. (Don) |

## NICARAGUA, REPUBLIC OF

(Last updated: 3/26/2001)

| | |
|---|---|
| President | **Aleman,** Lacayo, Arnoldo |
| Vice President | **Navarro,** Leopoldo |
| Min. of Agriculture & Forestry | **Augusto,** Navarro, Jose |
| Min. of Defense | **Guerra,** Jose Adan |
| Min. of Development, Industry, & Commerce | **Sacasa,** Noel |
| Min. of Education, Culture, & Sports | **Robleto,** Fernando |
| Min. of Environment & Natural Resources | **Stadhagen,** Roberto |
| Min. of Family | **Lopez,** Prado, Rosa Argentina |
| Min. of Finance | **Duque,** Estrada, Esteban |
| Min. of Foreign Affairs | **Aguirre,** Sacasa, Francisco |
| Min. of Government | **Marenco,** Jose |
| Min. of Health | **Arguello,** Mariangeles |
| Min. of Industry, Development, & Trade | **Caldera,** Norman |
| Min. of Labor | **Montenegro,** Mario |
| Min. of Transportation & Infrastructure | **Bohorquez Ocampo,** Edgard |
| Attorney General | **Centeno,** Julio |
| Pres., Central Bank | **Ramirez,** Noel |
| Ambassador to the US | **Ortega,** Urbina, Alfonso |
| Permanent Representative to the UN, New York | **Sevilla,** Somoza, Eduardo |

## NIGER, REPUBLIC OF

(Last updated: 11/17/2000)

| | |
|---|---|
| President | **Tandja,** Mamadou |
| Prime Minister | **Amadou,** Hama |
| Min. of Animal Resources | **Maoude,** Koroney |
| Min. of Commerce & Energy | **Oumarou,** Seyne |
| Min. of Communications | **Salifou,** Amadou Elhadj |
| Min. of Defense | **Gaoh,** Sabiou Dady |
| Min. of Education | **Ibrahim,** Ari |
| Min. of Environment | **Assoumane,** Issoufou |
| Min. of Finance | **Gamatie,** Ali Badjo |
| Min. of Foreign Affairs | **Sabo,** Nassirou |
| Min. of Health | **Adamou,** Assoumane |
| Min. of Higher Education, Reserach, & Technology | **Edmond,** Amadou Laousal dit |
| Min. of Interior | **Manzo,** Mahamane |
| Min. of Justice | **Sirfi,** Ali |
| Min. of Mines | **Baare,** Yahaya |
| Min. of Plan | **Maliki,** Barhouni |
| Min. of Privatization | **Oumarou,** Alma |
| Min. of Public Works | **Mireille,** Ausseil |
| Min. of Rural Development | **Boukary,** Wassalke |
| Min. of Small Business Development | **Bonto,** Souley Hassane dit |

## NIGER, REPUBLIC OF (cont.)

| | |
|---|---|
| Min. of Social Development | **Foumakoye,** Aichatou |
| Min. of Transportation | **Labo,** Abdou |
| Min. of Tourism | **Boula,** Rhissa Ag |
| Min. of Water Resources | **Daouel,** Akoli |
| Min. of Youth, Sports, & Culture | **Lamine,** Issa |

## NIGERIA, FEDERAL REPUBLIC OF

(Last updated: 2/15/2001)

| | |
|---|---|
| President | **Obasanjo,** Olusegun |
| Vice President | **Abubakar,** Atiku |
| Min. of Agriculture | **Bello,** Adamu |
| Min. of Aviation | **Chikwe,** Kema, *Mrs.* |
| Min. of Commerce | **Bello,** Mustapha |
| Min. of Communications | **Arzika,** Mohammed |
| Min. of Culture & Tourism | **Jack,** Boma Bromilo *Miss* |
| Min. of Defense | **Danjuma,** Theophilus Yakubu, *Gen.* |
| Min. of Education | **Borishade,** Babalola |
| Min. of Environment | **Said,** Mohammed Kabir |
| Min. of Federal Capital Territory | **Abba-Gana,** Mohammed |
| Min. of Finance | **Ciroma,** Malam Adamu |
| Min. of Foreign Affairs | **Lamido,** Sule |
| Min. of Health | **Nwosu,** Alphonsus |
| Min. of Industries | **Jamodu,** Kolawole |
| Min. of Information | **Gana,** Jerry |
| Min. of Internal Affairs | **Afolabi,** Sunday M., *Chief* |
| Min. of Justice | **Ige,** Bola |
| Min. of Labor & Productivity | **Gwadabe,** Musa |
| Min. of Police Affairs | **Akiga,** Steven |
| Min. of Power & Steel | **Agagu,** Olusegun |
| Min. of Presidency (Civil Service) | **Usman,** Bello Alhaji |
| Min. of Presidency (Economic Matters) | **Ogbuleafor,** Vincent |
| Min. of Presidency (Inter-Gov't.) | **Kida,** Ibrahim Umar |
| Min. of Presidency (Special Project) | **Edu,** Yomi |
| Min. of Regional Integration & Cooperation | **Ogunkelu,** Bimbola |
| Min. of Science & Technology | **Isong,** Tuner |
| Min. of Solid Minerals | **Agabi,** Kanu Godwin |
| Min. of Sports & Social Development | **Aku,** Ishaya Mark |
| Min. of Transport | **Madueke,** Ojo |
| Min. of Water Resources | **Kaliel,** Mohammed Bello, *Col.* |
| Min. of Women & Youth | **Ismail,** Aishat |
| Min. of Works & Housing | **Anenih,** Tony, *Chief* |
| Min. of State for Agriculture | **Agbobu,** Chris |
| Min. of State for Communications | **Haruna-Elewi,** Ade |
| Min. of State for the Air Force | **Chuke,** Dan |
| Min. of State for the Army | **Batagarawa,** Lawal |
| Min. of State for the Navy | **Adelaja,** Dupe |
| Min. of State for Education | **Usman,** Bello |
| Min. of State for Environment | **Okopido,** Bello |
| Min. of State for the Federal Capital Territory | **Ewugu,** Solomon |
| Min. of State for Finance | **Martins-Kuye,** Jubril |
| Min. of State for Foreign Affairs | **Onyia,** Dubem |
| Min. of State for Health | **Ndalolo,** Amina |
| Min. of State for Industries | **Nwuruku,** Lawrence |
| Min. of State for Internal Affairs | **Shata,** Mohammed |
| Min. of State for Justice | **Abdulahi,** Musa Elayo |
| Min. of State for Power & Steel | **Goje,** Danjuma |
| Min. of State for Science & Technology | **Tallen,** Pauline |
| Min. of State for Transport | **Yuguda,** Isa |
| Min. of State for Water Resources | **Ngelale,** Precious |
| Min. of State for Works & Housing | **Ali,** Garba Madaki |

## NORWAY, KINGDOM OF

(Last updated: 11/17/2000)

| | |
|---|---|
| King | **Harald V** |
| Prime Minister | **Stoltenberg,** Jens |
| Min. of Agriculture | **Hanssen,** Bjarne Hakon |
| Min. of Children & Family Affairs | **Orheim,** Karita Bekkemellem |
| Min. of Cultural Affairs | **Horn,** Ellen |
| Min. of Defense | **Godal,** Bjorn Tore |
| Min. of Education, Research, & Church Affairs | **Giske,** Trond |
| Min. of the Environment | **Bjerke,** Siri |
| Min. of Finance | **Schjott-Pedersen,** Karl Eirik |
| Min. of Fisheries | **Gregussen,** Otto |
| Min. of Foreign Aid | **Sydnes,** Ann Kristin |
| Min. of Foreign Affairs | **Jagland,** Thorbjorn |
| Min. of Health | **Tonne,** Tore |
| Min. of Justice & Police | **Harlem,** Hanne |
| Min. of Labor & Govt. Admin. | **Kosmo,** Jorgen |
| Min. of Local Govt. & Regional Development | **Brustad,** Sylvia |
| Min. of Oil & Energy | **Akselsen,** Olav |
| Min. of Social Affairs | **Ingebrigtsen,** Guri |
| Min. of Trade & Industry | **Knudsen,** Grete |
| Min. of Transport & Communications | **Gustavsen,** Terje Moe |
| Governor, Bank of Norway | **Gjedrem,** Svein |
| Ambassador to the US | **Vraalsen,** Tom |
| Permanent Representative to the UN, New York | **Ole Peter,** Kolby |

## OMAN, SULTANATE OF

(Last updated: 11/17/2000)

| | |
|---|---|
| Sultan | **Said, QABOOS,** bin Said Al |
| Special Representative for His Majesty the Sultan | **Said, THUWAYNI,** bin Shihab Al |
| Prime Minister | **Said, QABOOS,** bin Said Al |
| Dep. Prime Min. for Cabinet Affairs | **Said, FAHD,** bin Mahmud Al |
| Min. of the Royal Office | **Mamari,** Ali bin Majid al-, *Gen.* |
| Min. of Agriculture & Fisheries | **Rawahi,** Ahmad bin Khalfan bin Muhammad al-, *Dr.* |
| Min. of Awqaf & Religious Affairs | **Salimi,** Abdallah bin Muhammad bin Abdallah al- |
| Min. of Civil Service | **Azizi,** Abd al-Aziz bin Matar al- |
| Min. of Commerce, Industry, & Minerals | **Sultan,** Maqbul bin Ali bin |
| Min. of Communications | **Shamas,** Suhail bin Mustahail |
| Min. of Defense | **Said, QABOOS,** bin Said Al |
| Min. of Defense Affairs | **Busaidi, BADR,** bin Saud bin Harib Al |
| Min. of Diwan of Royal Court | **Busaidi, SAYF,** bin Hamad bin |
| Min. of Education | **Busaidi, SAUD,** bin Ibrahim bin Saud Al |
| Min. of Electricity & Water | **Qutaybi,** Muhammad bin Ali al- |
| Min. of Finance | **Said, QABOOS,** bin Said Al |
| Min. of Foreign Affairs | **Said, QABOOS,** bin Said Al |
| Min. of Health | **Musa,** Ali bin Muhammad bin, *Dr.* |
| Min. of Higher Education | **Manthiri,** Yahya bin Mahfudh al- |
| Min. of Information | **Ruwas,** Abd al-Aziz bin Muhammad al- |
| Min. of Interior | **Busaidi, ALI,** bin Hamud bin Ali Al |
| Min. of Justice | **Hinai,** Muhammad bin Abdallah bin Zahir al- |
| Min. of Legal Affairs | **Alawi,** Muhammad bin Ali bin Nasir al- |
| Min. of National Economy | **Makki,** Ahmad bin Abd al-Nabi al- |
| Min. of National Heritage & Culture | **Said, FAYSAL,** bin Ali Al |
| Min. of Oil & Gas | **Rumhi,** Muhammad bin Hamad bin Sayf al- |
| Min. of Regional Municipalities & Environment | **Alawi,** Khamis bin Mubarak bin Isa al-, *Dr.* |
| Min. Responsible for Foreign Affairs | **Alawi,** bin Abdallah, Yusuf bin |
| Min. of Social Affairs, Labor & Vocational Training | **Husni,** Amir bin Shuwayn al- |
| Min. of State | **Busaidi, MUSALAM,** bin Ali Al |
| Min. of State | **Busaidi, MUTASIM,** bin Hamud bin Nasir Al |
| Min. of Transportation & Housing | **Mamari,** Malik bin Sulayman al- |
| Min. of Water Resources | **Aufi,** Hamid Said al-, *Lt. Gen.* |

## OMAN, SULTANATE OF (cont.)

| | |
|---|---|
| Special Adv. to His Majesty | **Ghazali,** Salim bin Abdallah al- |
| Special Adv. to His Majesty for Economic Planning Affairs | **Zubayr,** Muhammad bin |
| Special Adv. to His Majesty for Environmental Affairs | **Said, SHABIB,** bin Taymur Al |
| Special Adv. to His Majesty for External Liaison | **Zawawi,** Umar bin Abd al-Munim al- |
| Pres. Majlis al-Dawlah (Council of State) (Upper House) | **Harthi,** Hamud bin Abdallah al- |
| Pres. Majlis al-Shura (Advisory Council) (Lower House) | **Qatabi,** Abdallah Ali al- |
| Chmn., Central Bank | **Said, QABOOS,** bin Said Al |
| Executive Pres., Central Bank | **Zadjali,** Hamud bin Sangur Hashim |
| Ambassador to the US | **Dhahab,** Abdallah bin Muhammad bin Aqil al- |
| Permanent Representative to the UN, New York | **Hinai,** Fuad bin Mubarak al- |

## PAKISTAN, ISLAMIC REPUBLIC OF

(Last updated: 1/19/2001)

*On 12 May 2000 Pakistan's Supreme Court unanimously validated the October 1999 coup and granted Musharraf executive and legislative authority for three years from the coup date. Musharraf acts as Pakistan's Minister of Defense and Minister of Information, but he has not officially taken up the posts.*

| | |
|---|---|
| President | **Tarar,** Mohammad Rafiq |
| Chief Executive | **Musharraf,** Pervez, *Lt. Gen.* |
| Min. for Commerce, Industries, & Production | **Daud,** Abdul Razzaq |
| Min. of Communications & Railways | **Ashraf,** Javed, *Lt. Gen. (Ret.)* |
| Min. of Defense | |
| Min. for Education | **Jalal,** Zubeda |
| Min. for Environment, Labor, & Rural Development | **Khan,** Omar Asghar |
| Min. of Finance | **Aziz,** Shaukat |
| Min. for Food, Agriculture, & Livestock | **Junejo,** Khair Muhammad |
| Min. of Foreign Affairs | **Sattar,** Abdus |
| Min. for Health | **Kansi,** Abdul Malik |
| Min. of Information | |
| Min. of Interior & Narcotics | **Haider,** Moinuddin, *Lt. Gen. (Ret.)* |
| Min. for Kashmir, Northern Areas, Housing, & Works | **Khan,** Abbas Sarfaz |
| Min. of Law, Human Rights & Parliamentary Affairs | **Jameel,** Shahida |
| Min. of Parliamentary Affairs | |
| Min. for Petroleum & Natural Resources | **Aminuddin,** Usman |
| Min. of Privatization | **Saleem,** Altaf |
| Min. of Religious Affairs | **Ghazi,** Mahmood |
| Min. of Science & Technology | **Rehman,** Attaur |
| Min. of Sports, Culture, Tourism, Youth & Minorities | **Tresslor,** S. K. *Col. (Ret.)* |
| Min. of Water & Power | |
| Min. of Women's Development, Social Welfare, Special Education, & Population | **Inayatullah,** Attiya |
| Attorney General | **Munshi,** Aziz A. |
| Governor, State Bank | **Hussain,** Ishrat |
| Ambassador to the US | **Lodhi,** Maleeha |
| Permanent Representative to the UN, New York | **Ahmad,** Shamshad |

## PALAU, REPUBLIC OF

(Last updated: 2/2/2001)

*The new cabinet will be named following the inaguration of the new President and Vice President.*

| | |
|---|---|
| President (Elect) | **Remengesau,** Tommy, *Jr.* |
| Vice President (Elect) | **Pierantozzi,** Sandra |
| Ambassador to the US | **Kyota,** Hersey |

## PANAMA, REPUBLIC OF

(Last updated: 3/30/2001)

| | |
|---|---|
| President | **Moscoso,** Mireya Elisa |
| First Vice President | **Vallarino,** Arturo Ulises |

## PANAMA, REPUBLIC OF (cont.)

| | |
|---|---|
| Second Vice President | **Bazan**, Jimenez, Dominador "Kaiser" |
| Min. of Agrarian Development | **Adan**, Gordon, Pedro |
| Min. of Agriculture | **ADAN**, Gordon, Pedro |
| Min. for Canal Affairs | **Martinelli**, Berrocal, Ricardo |
| Min. of Commerce & Industry | **Jacome**, Diaz, Joaquin |
| Min. of Economy & Finance | **Delgado**, Duran, Norberto |
| Min. of Education | **Mata**, Doris Rosas de |
| Min. of Foreign Relations | **Aleman**, Jose Miguel |
| Min. of Government & Justice | **Spadafora**, Winston |
| Min. of Health | **Gracia Garcia**, Fernando |
| Min. of Housing | **Cardenas**, Miguel |
| Min. of Labor & Labor Development | **Vallarino III**, Joaquin Jose |
| Min. of Presidency | **Young**, Valdez, Ivonne |
| Min. of Public Works | **Juliao**, Gelonch, Victor Nelson |
| Min. of Women, Youth, Family, & Childhood | **Rolla**, Alba Esther Tejada de |
| Attorney General | **Sossa**, Jose Antonio |
| Manager, National Bank of Panama | **Urriola**, Eduardo |
| Ambassador to the US | **Ford**, Guillermo |
| Permanent Representative to the UN, New York | **Morales**, Quijano, Ramon |

## PAPUA NEW GUINEA, INDEPENDENT STATE OF

(Last updated: 3/8/2001)

| | |
|---|---|
| Governor General | **Atopare**, Silas, *Sir* |
| Prime Minister | **Morauta**, Mekere, *Sir* |
| Dep. Prime Min. | **Ogio**, Michael |
| Min. for Agriculture & Livestock | **Taranupi**, Muki |
| Min. Assisting the Prime Minister | |
| Min. for Bougainville Affairs | **Philemon**, Bart |
| Min. for Communications & High Technology | **Kaputin**, John |
| Min. for Corporatization & Privatization | **Auali**, Vincent |
| Min. for Correctional Services | **Smith**, Henry |
| Min. for Culture & Tourism | **Napo**, Samson |
| Min. for Defense | **Genia**, Kilroy |
| Min. for Education | **Waiko**, John |
| Min. for Environment & Conservation | **Agiwa**, Herowa |
| Min. for Finance | **Kumbakor**, Andrew |
| Min. for Fisheries | **Ganarafo**, Ron |
| Min. for Foreign Affairs | **Philemon**, Bart |
| Min. for Forestry | **Ogio**, Michael |
| Min. for Health | **Mond**, Ludger |
| Min. for Home Affairs | **Ebenosi**, William |
| Min. for Housing | **Lus**, Pita, *Sir* |
| Min. for Justice | **Ruing**, Puri |
| Min. for Labor & Employment | **Benjamin**, Charlie |
| Min. for Lands & Fiscal Planning | **Pundari**, John |
| Min. for Mining | **Laimo**, Michael |
| Min. for Petroleum & Energy | **Haiveta**, Chris |
| Min. for Planning & Implementation | **Avei**, Moi |
| Min. for Police | **Jimson**, Sauk |
| Min. for Privitization & Corporatization | **Auali**, Vincent |
| Min. for Provincial & Local Government | **Lasaro**, Iairo |
| Min. for Public Service | **Embel**, Philemon |
| Min. for Rural Development | **Kumbakor**, Andrew |
| Min. for Trade & Industry | **Tekwie**, John |
| Min. for Transport, Works, & Civil Aviation | **Pogo**, Alfred |
| Min. for Treasury | |
| Attorney General | **Gene**, Michael |
| Governor, Central Bank | **Kamit**, Wilson |
| Ambassador to the US | **Bogan**, Nagora |
| Permanent Representative to the UN, New York | **Donigi**, Peter |

## PARAGUAY, REPUBLIC OF

(Last updated: 3/27/2001)

| | |
|---|---|
| President | **Gonzalez Macchi,** Luis |
| Vice President | **Franco,** Julio Cesar |
| Min. of Agriculture & Livestock | **Zuniga,** Enrique |
| Min. of Education & Worship | **Duarte Frutos,** Nicanor |
| Min. of Finance & Economy | **Oviedo,** Francisco |
| Min. of Foreign Relations | **Moreno Ruffinelli,** Jose |
| Min. of Industry & Commerce | **Acevedo,** Euclides |
| Min. of Interior | **Fanego Arellano,** Julio Cesar |
| Min. of Justice & Labor | **Ferreira,** Silvio |
| Min. of National Defense (Acting) | **Fanego Arellano,** Julio Cesar |
| Min. of Public Health & Social Welfare | **Chiola,** Martin |
| Min. of Public Works & Communications | **Bower,** Walter |
| Min. of Secretary General for the Presidency | **Bestard,** Jaime |
| Dir., Secretariat of National Intelligence | **Gomez de la Fuente,** Mario *Lt. Gen. (Ret.)* |
| Sec., for Women's Affairs | **Munoz,** Cristina |
| Pres., Central Bank | **Ashwell,** Washington |
| Ambassador to the US | **Rachid,** Leila |
| Permanent Representative to the UN, New York | **Lara Castro,** Jorge |

## PERU, REPUBLIC OF

(Last updated: 2/2/2001)

| | |
|---|---|
| President | **Paniagua Corazao,** Valentin |
| Prime Minister | **Perez de Cuellar,** Javier |
| Min. of Agriculture | **Amat Y Leon Chavez,** Carlos |
| Min. of Defense | **Ledesma Rebaza,** Walter |
| Min. of Economy & Finance | **Silva Ruete,** Javier |
| Min. of Education | **Rubio Correa,** Marcial |
| Min. of Energy & Mines | **Herrera, Descalzi,** Carlos |
| Min. of Fisheries | **Meier Cornejo,** Ludwig |
| Min. of Foreign Affairs | **Perez de Cuellar,** Javier |
| Min. of Health | **Pretell Zarate,** Eduardo |
| Min. of Industry, Tourism, Integration, & International Trade Negotiations | **Inchaustegui Vargas,** Juan |
| Min. of Interior | **Vidal Herrera,** Ketin |
| Min. of Justice | **Garcia Sayan,** Diego |
| Min. of Labor | **Zavala Costa,** Jaime |
| Min. of Presidency | **Navarro Castaneda,** Emilio |
| Min. for Promotion of Women & Human Development | **Villaran de la Puente,** Susana |
| Min. of Transport, Communications, Housing, & Construction | **Ortega Navarrete,** Luis |
| President, Central Bank | **Suarez,** German |
| Ambassador to the US | **Alzamora Traverso,** Carlos |
| Permanent Representative to the UN, New York | **Valdez Carrillo,** Jorge |

## PHILIPPINES, REPUBLIC OF THE

(Last updated: 4/2/2001)

| | |
|---|---|
| President | **Macapagal-Arroyo,** Gloria |
| Vice President | **Guingona,** Teofisto |
| Executive Secretary | **De Villa,** Renato, *Gen. (Ret.)* |
| Sec. of Agrarian Reform | **Braganza,** Hernani |
| Sec. of Agriculture | **Montemayor,** Leonardo |
| Sec. of the Budget & Management | **Boncodin,** Emilia |
| Sec. of Education, Culture, & Sports | **Roco,** Raul |
| Sec. of Energy | **Camacho,** Jose |
| Sec. of Environment & Natural Resources | **Alvarez,** Heherson |
| Sec. of Finance | **Romulo,** Alberto |
| Sec. of Foreign Affairs | **Guingona,** Teofisto |
| Sec. of Health | **Dayrit,** Manuel, *M.D.* |
| Sec. of Interior & Local Govt. | **Lina,** Jose |
| Sec. of Justice | **Perez,** Hernando |

## PHILIPPINES, REPUBLIC OF THE (cont.)

Sec. of Labor & Employment ............................................. **Santo Thomas**, Patricia
Sec. of National Defense ............................................. **Reyes**, Angelo, *Gen. (Ret.)*
Sec. of Public Works & Highways ...................................... **Datumanong**, Simeon
Sec. of Science & Technology .......................................... **Alabastro**, Estrella
Sec. of Social Welfare & Development .................................. **Soliman**, Corazon
Sec. of Socio-Economic Planning ...................................... **Canlas**, Dante
Sec. of Tourism ....................................................... **Gordon**, Richard
Sec. of Trade & Industry .............................................. **Roxas**, Manuel
Sec. of Transportation & Communications ............................... **Alvarez**, Panteleon
Governor, Central Bank ................................................ **Buenaventura**, Rafael
Ambassador to the US (Acting) ......................................... **Abadilla**, Ariel
Permanent Representative to the UN, New York .......................... **Mabilangan**, Felipe H.

## POLAND, REPUBLIC OF

(Last updated: 2/28/2001)

President ............................................................. **Kwasniewski**, Aleksander
Prime Minister ....................................................... **Buzek**, Jerzy
Dep. Prime Min. ...................................................... **Komolowski**, Longin
Dep. Prime Min. ...................................................... **Steinhoff**, Janusz
Min. of Agriculture .................................................. **Balazs**, Artur
Min. of Communications ............................................... **Srebro**, Maciej
Min. of Culture & Art ................................................ **Zakrzewski**, Andrzej
Min. of Economy ...................................................... **Steinhoff**, Janusz
Min. of Education .................................................... **Wittbrodt**, Edmund
Min. of Environmental Protection ..................................... **Tokarczuk**, Antoni
Min. of Finance ...................................................... **Bauc**, Jaroslaw
Min. of Foreign Affairs .............................................. **Bartoszewski**, Wladyslaw
Min. of Health ....................................................... **Opala**, Grzegorz
Min. of Internal Affairs & Administration ............................ **Biernacki**, Marek
Min. of Justice ...................................................... **Kaczynski**, Lech
Min. of Labor & Social Policy ........................................ **Komolowski**, Longin
Min. of National Defense ............................................. **Komorowski**, Bronislaw
Min. for Regional Development & Housing ............................... **Kropiwinicki**, Jerzy
Min. of Transport & Maritime Economy ................................. **Widzyk**, Jerzy
Min. of Treasury ..................................................... **Kamela-Sowinska**, Aldona
Min. Without Portfolio (Center for Strategic Studies) ................ **Kropiwnicki**, Jerzy
Min. Without Portfolio (Coordinator of Special Services) ............. **Palubicki**, Janusz
Min. Without Portfolio (Family Affairs) ..............................
Chmn., Scientific Research Committee ................................. **Wiszniewski**, Andrzej
Pres., Polish National Bank .......................................... **Balcerowicz**, Leszek
Ambassador to the US ................................................. **Grudzinski**, Przemyslaw
Permanent Representative to the UN, New York .......................... **Stanczyk**, Janusz

## PORTUGAL (PORTUGUESE REPUBLIC)

(Last updated: 3/8/2001)

President ............................................................. **Sampaio**, Jorge
Prime Minister ....................................................... **Guterres**, Antonio
Min. of Agriculture, Rural Development, & Fisheries .................. **Capoulas Santos**, Luis Manuel
Min. of Culture ...................................................... **Sasportes**, Jose
Min. of Defense ...................................................... **Caldas**, Julio Castro
Min. of Economy ...................................................... **De Sousa**, Mario Cristina
Min. of Education .................................................... **Silva**, Augusto Santos
Min. of the Environment , Territorial Planning, & Urban Development ... **Socrates**, Jose
Min. of Finance ...................................................... **Pina Moura**, Joaquim
Min. of Foreign Affairs .............................................. **Gama**, Jaime
Min. of Health ....................................................... **Arcanjo**, Maria Manuela
Min. of Infrastructure & Public Works ................................ **Ferro Rodrigues**, Eduardo
Min. of Internal Administration ...................................... **Teixeira**, Nuno Severiano
Min. of Justice ...................................................... **Costa**, Antonio
Min. of Labor & Solidarity ........................................... **Pedroso**, Paulo

## PORTUGAL (PORTUGUESE REPUBLIC) (cont.)

| | |
|---|---|
| Min. of Planning | **Ferreira,** Maria Elisa |
| Min. of the Presidency | **Martins,** Guilherme D'Oliveira |
| Min. of Science & Technology | **Mariano Gago,** Jose |
| Min. of Social Security & Labor Ferro Rodrigues Eduardo | |
| Min. of State | **Gama,** Jamie |
| Min. of State | **Coelho,** Jorge |
| Min. of Public Administration Reforms Martins Alberto | |
| Min. of Youth & Sports | **Lello,** Jose |
| Governor, Bank of Portugal | **Constancio,** Vitor |
| Ambassador to the US | **Rocha Paris,** Joao |
| Permanent Representative to the UN, New York | **Monteiro,** Antonio Victor Martins |

## QATAR, STATE OF

(Last updated: 1/4/2001)

| | |
|---|---|
| Amir | **Thani, HAMAD,** bin Khalifa Al |
| Prime Minister | **Thani, ABDALLAH,** bin Khalifa Al |
| Dep. Prime Min. | **Thani, MUHAMMAD,** bin Khalifa Al |
| Min. of Communications & Transport | **Thani, AHMAD bin NASIR,** Al |
| Min. of Defense | **Thani, HAMAD,** bin Khalifa Al |
| Min. of Education & Higher Education | **Kafud,** Muhammad Abd al-Rahim al- |
| Min. of Endowments & Islamic Affairs | **Marri,** Ahmad Abdallah al- |
| Min. of Energy, Industry, Water & Electricity | **Attiyah,** Abdallah bin Hamad al- |
| Min. of Finance, Economy, & Trade | **Kamal,** Yusif Husayn al- |
| Min. of Foreign Affairs | **Thani, HAMAD bin JASIM bin JABIR,** Al |
| Min. of Housing & Civil Service Affairs | **Thani, FALAH,** bin Jasim bin Jabir Al |
| Min. of Interior | **Thani, ABDALLAH,** bin Khalid Al |
| Min. of Justice | **Ghanim,** Hasan bin Abdallah al- |
| Min. of Municipal Affairs & Agriculture | **Khatir,** Ali bin Muhammad al- |
| Min. of Public Health | **Hajar,** Hajar bin Ahmad al-, *Dr.* |
| Min. of State | **Thani, AHMAD bin SAYF,** Al |
| Min. of State | **Thani, HAMAD bin ABDALLAH,** bin Muhammad Al |
| Min. of State | **Thani, HAMAD bin SUHAYM,** Al |
| Min. of State | **Thani, HASAN,** bin Abdallah bin Muhammad Al |
| Min. of State | **Thani, MUHAMMAD,** bin Khalid Al |
| Min. of State for Cabinet Affairs | **Kawari,** Ali bin Said al- |
| Min. of State for Foreign Affairs | **Mahmud,** Ahmad Abdallah al- |
| Min. of State for Interior Affairs | **Thani, HAMAD bin NASIR bin JASIM,** AL |
| Pres., Sharia Court | **Mahmud,** Abd al-Rahman Abdallah Zayid al- |
| Governor, Central Bank | **Attiyah,** Abdallah bin Khalid al- |
| Ambassador to the US | **Dafa,** Badr Umar al- |
| Permanent Representative to the UN, New York | **Nasir,** Nasir Abd al-Aziz al- |

## ROMANIA

(Last updated: 2/2/2001)

| | |
|---|---|
| President | **Iliescu,** Ion |
| Prime Minister | **Nastase,** Adrian |
| Dep. Prime Min. | |
| Dep. Prime Min. | |
| Dep. Prime Min. | |
| Dep. Prime Min. | |
| Min. of Agriculture & Food | **Sarbu,** Illie |
| Min. of Communication & Information Technology | **Nica,** Dan |
| Min. of Culture | **Theodorescu,** Razvan |
| Min. of Defense | **Pascu,** Ioan Mircea |
| Min. Del. for National Minorities | **Eckstein-Kovacs,** Peter |
| Min. of Education | **Andronescu,** Ecaterina |
| Min. of European Integration | **Puwak,** Hildergard Carola |
| Min. of Finance | **Tanasescu,** Mihai Nicolae |

## ROMANIA (cont.)

Min. of Foreign Affairs .......................................................... **Geoana**, Mircea Dan
Min. of Health .......................................................... **Bartos**, Daniela
Min. of Industry & Resources .......................................................... **Popescu**, Dan Ioan
Min. of Interior .......................................................... **Rus**, Ioan
Min. of Justice .......................................................... **Stanoiu**, Rodica Mihaela
Min. of Labor & Social Protection .......................................................... **Sarbu**, Marian
Min. of Public Administration .......................................................... **Cozmanca**, Octav
Min. of Public Works, Transport & Housing .......................................................... **Mitrea**, Miron Tudor
Min. of Tourism .......................................................... **Agathon**, Dan Matei
Min. of Waters & Environmental Protection .......................................................... **Ilie**, Aurel Constantin
Min. of Youth & Sports .......................................................... **Gingaras**, Giorgiu
Chmn., Romanian National Bank .......................................................... **Isarescu**, Mugur
Ambassador to the US ..........................................................
Permanent Representative to the UN, New York .......................................................... **Gorita**, Ion

## RUSSIA (RUSSIAN FEDERATION)

(Last updated: 3/29/2001)

President .......................................................... **Putin**, Vladimir Vladimirovich
Premier .......................................................... **Kasyanov**, Mikhail Mikhaylovich
Dep. Premier .......................................................... **Gordeyev**, Aleksey Vasilyevich
Dep. Premier .......................................................... **Khristenko**, Viktor Borisovich
Dep. Premier .......................................................... **Klebanov**, Ilya Iosifovich
Dep. Premier .......................................................... **Kudrin**, Aleksey Leonidovich
Dep. Premier .......................................................... **Matviyenko**, Valentina Ivanovna
Min. of Agriculture .......................................................... **Gordeyev**, Aleksey Vasilyevich
Min. of Anti-Monopoly Policy & Enterprise Support .......................................................... **Yuzhanov**, Ilya Arturovich
Min. of Atomic Energy .......................................................... **Rumyantsev**, Aleksandr Yuryevich
Min. of Civil Defense, Emergencies, & Natural Disasters .......................................................... **Shoygu**, Sergey Kuzhugetovich
Min. of Culture .......................................................... **Shvydkoy**, Mikhail Yefimovich
Min. of Defense .......................................................... **Ivanov**, Sergey Borisovich
Min. of Economic Development & Trade .......................................................... **Gref**, German Oskarovich
Min. of Education .......................................................... **Filippov**, Vladimir Mikhaylovich
Min. of Energy ..........................................................
Min. of Federation Affairs & Nationalities and Migration Policy .......................................................... **Blokhin**, Aleksandr Viktorovich
Min. of Finance .......................................................... **Kudrin**, Aleksey Leonidovich
Min. of Foreign Affairs .......................................................... **Ivanov**, Igor Sergeyevich
Min. of Health .......................................................... **Shevchenko**, Yuriy Leonidovich
Min. of Industry, Science, & Technology .......................................................... **Dondukov**, Aleksandr Nikolayevich
Min. of Internal Affairs (MVD) .......................................................... **Gryzlov**, Boris Vyacheslavovich
Min. of Justice .......................................................... **Chayka**, Yuriy Yakovlevich
Min. of Labor & Social Development .......................................................... **Pochinok**, Aleksandr Petrovich
Min. of Natural Resources .......................................................... **Yatskevich**, Boris Aleksandrovich
Min. of Press, Television & Radio Broadcasting, & Mass Communications ..... **Lesin**, Mikhail Yuryevich
Min. of Property Relations .......................................................... **Gazizullin**, Farit Rafikovich
Min. of Railways .......................................................... **Aksenenko**, Nikolay Yemelyanovich
Min. of Socioeconomic Development in Chechnya .......................................................... **Yelagin**, Vladimir Vasilyevich
Min. of Taxes & Levies .......................................................... **Bukayev**, Gennadiy Ivanovich
Min. of Telecommunications & Information .......................................................... **Reyman**, Leonid Dododzhonovich
Min. of Transportation .......................................................... **Frank**, Sergey Ottovich
CINC, Federal Border Service .......................................................... **Totskiy**, Konstantin Vasilyevich
Dir., Foreign Intelligence Service (SVR) .......................................................... **Lebedev**, Sergey Nikolayevich
Head, Federal Security Service (FSB) .......................................................... **Patrushev**, Nikolay Platonovich
Head, Government Apparatus .......................................................... **Shuvalov**, Igor Ivanovich
Sec., Security Council .......................................................... **Rushaylo**, Vladimir Borisovich
Chmn., Central Bank of Russia .......................................................... **Gerashchenko**, Viktor Vladimirovich
Procurator General .......................................................... **Ustinov**, Vladimir Vasilyevich
Ambassador to the US .......................................................... **Ushakov**, Yuriy Viktorovich
Permanent Representative to the UN, New York .......................................................... **Lavrov**, Sergey Viktorovich

## RWANDA (RWANDESE REPUBLIC)

(Last updated: 3/21/2001)

President . . . . . . . . . . . . . . . . . . . . . . . . . . . . . . . . . . . . . . . . . . . . . . . . . . . **Kagame,** Paul
Vice President . . . . . . . . . . . . . . . . . . . . . . . . . . . . . . . . . . . . . . . . . . . . . . .
Prime Minister . . . . . . . . . . . . . . . . . . . . . . . . . . . . . . . . . . . . . . . . . . . . . **Makuza,** Bernard
Min. of Agriculture . . . . . . . . . . . . . . . . . . . . . . . . . . . . . . . . . . . . . . . . . **Kabayija,** Ephrem
Min. of Commerce, Industry, & Tourism . . . . . . . . . . . . . . . . . . . . . . . . **Lyambabaje,** Alexandre
Min. of Defense & National Security . . . . . . . . . . . . . . . . . . . . . . . . . . . **Habyarimana,** Emmanuel, *Col.*
Min. of Education . . . . . . . . . . . . . . . . . . . . . . . . . . . . . . . . . . . . . . . . . . **Mudidi,** Emmanuel
Min. of Energy, Water, & Natural Resources . . . . . . . . . . . . . . . . . . . . **Bahude,** Marcel
Min. of Finance & Planning . . . . . . . . . . . . . . . . . . . . . . . . . . . . . . . . . **Kaberuka,** Donat
Min. of Foreign Affairs & Regional Cooperation . . . . . . . . . . . . . . . . . **Bumaya,** Andre
Min. of Gender & Womens Development . . . . . . . . . . . . . . . . . . . . . . . . **Muganza,** Angeline
Min. of Health . . . . . . . . . . . . . . . . . . . . . . . . . . . . . . . . . . . . . . . . . . . . **Rwabuhihi,** Ezechias
Min. of Information . . . . . . . . . . . . . . . . . . . . . . . . . . . . . . . . . . . . . . . . **Iyamuremye,** Augustin
Min. of Interior & Security . . . . . . . . . . . . . . . . . . . . . . . . . . . . . . . . . . **Ntiruhungwa,** Jean de Dieu
Min. of Justice . . . . . . . . . . . . . . . . . . . . . . . . . . . . . . . . . . . . . . . . . . . **Mucyo,** Jean de Dieu
Min. of Land Resettlement & Environment . . . . . . . . . . . . . . . . . . . . . . **Nkusi,** Laurent
Min. of Local Government . . . . . . . . . . . . . . . . . . . . . . . . . . . . . . . . . . . **Nyandwi,** Desire
Min. of Public Service & Labor . . . . . . . . . . . . . . . . . . . . . . . . . . . . . . . **Kayitesi,** Sylvie Zainab
Min. of Public Works, Transport, & Telecommunications . . . . . . . . . . . **Silas,** Kalinganire
Min. of Social Affairs . . . . . . . . . . . . . . . . . . . . . . . . . . . . . . . . . . . . . .
Min. of State for Agriculture . . . . . . . . . . . . . . . . . . . . . . . . . . . . . . . . **Makuba,** Aaron
Min. of Youth, Culture, & Sports . . . . . . . . . . . . . . . . . . . . . . . . . . . . . **Ngarambe,** Francois
Min. to the President's Office . . . . . . . . . . . . . . . . . . . . . . . . . . . . . . . . **Mutaboba,** Joseph
Governor, Central Bank . . . . . . . . . . . . . . . . . . . . . . . . . . . . . . . . . . . . . **Mutemberezi,** Francois
Ambassador to the US . . . . . . . . . . . . . . . . . . . . . . . . . . . . . . . . . . . . . . **Sezibera,** Richard
Permanent Representative to the UN, New York . . . . . . . . . . . . . . . . . . **Mutaboba,** Joseph W.

## SAINT KITTS AND NEVIS, FEDERATION OF

(Last updated: 11/17/2000)

Governor General . . . . . . . . . . . . . . . . . . . . . . . . . . . . . . . . . . . . . . . . . **Sebastian,** Cuthbert Montraville
Prime Minister . . . . . . . . . . . . . . . . . . . . . . . . . . . . . . . . . . . . . . . . . . . . **Douglas,** Denzil, *Dr.*
Dep. Prime Min. . . . . . . . . . . . . . . . . . . . . . . . . . . . . . . . . . . . . . . . . . . **Condor,** Sam
Min. of Agriculture, Fisheries, Co-operatives, Lands, & Housing . . . . . . **Liburd,** Cedric Roy
Min. of Communications, Works, & Public Utilities . . . . . . . . . . . . . . . **Herbert,** Rupert Emanuel
Min. of Community & Social Development . . . . . . . . . . . . . . . . . . . . . . . **Condor,** Sam
Min. of Education, Labor, & Social Security . . . . . . . . . . . . . . . . . . . . . **Harris,** Timothy
Min of Finance, Development, & Planning . . . . . . . . . . . . . . . . . . . . . . . **Douglas,** Denzil, *Dr.*
Min. of Foreign & Caricom Affairs . . . . . . . . . . . . . . . . . . . . . . . . . . . . **Condor,** Sam
Min. of Health & Environment . . . . . . . . . . . . . . . . . . . . . . . . . . . . . . . . **Martin,** Earl Asim, *Dr.*
Min. of International Trade . . . . . . . . . . . . . . . . . . . . . . . . . . . . . . . . . . **Condor,** Sam
Min. of National Security . . . . . . . . . . . . . . . . . . . . . . . . . . . . . . . . . . . **Douglas,** Denzil, *Dr.*
Min. of Tourism, Information, Telecomm., Commerce, & Consumer Affairs . . . . **Astaphan,** G. A. Dwyer
Min. of Youth, Sports, & Culture . . . . . . . . . . . . . . . . . . . . . . . . . . . . . **Henry-Martin,** Jacinth Lorna
Ambassador to the US . . . . . . . . . . . . . . . . . . . . . . . . . . . . . . . . . . . . . . **Liburd,** Osbert
Permanent Representative to the UN, New York . . . . . . . . . . . . . . . . . .

## SAINT LUCIA

(Last updated: 4/12/2001)

Governor General . . . . . . . . . . . . . . . . . . . . . . . . . . . . . . . . . . . . . . . . . **Louisy,** Perlette, *Dr.*
Prime Minister . . . . . . . . . . . . . . . . . . . . . . . . . . . . . . . . . . . . . . . . . . . . **Anthony,** Kenny
Dep. Prime Min. . . . . . . . . . . . . . . . . . . . . . . . . . . . . . . . . . . . . . . . . . . **Michel,** Mario
Min. of Agriculture & Fisheries . . . . . . . . . . . . . . . . . . . . . . . . . . . . . . **Elias,** Cassius
Min. of Commerce, International Financial Services, & Consumer Affairs . . . . . . **Pierre,** Philip
Min. of Communications, Works, Transport, & Public Utilities . . . . . . . . . . . . . **George,** Calixte
Min. of Community Development, Culture, Local Government, & Cooperatives . **Greaves,** Damian
Min. of Development, Planning, Environment, & Housing . . . . . . . . . . . . . . . **Francois,** Walter
Min. of Education, Human Resource Development, Youth & Sports . . . . . . . . . . **Michel,** Mario
Min. of Finance, Economic Affairs, & Information . . . . . . . . . . . . . . . . . . . . **Anthony,** Kenny

## SAINT LUCIA (cont.)

Min. of Foreign Affairs & International Trade ........................... **Hunte,** Julian Robert
Min. of Health, Human Services, Family Affairs, & Women ................. **Flood,** Sarah
Min. of Legal Affairs, Home Affairs, & Labor ........................... **John,** Velon
Min. of Public Service ................................................ **Compton,** Petros
Min. of Tourism & Civil Aviation ...................................... **Rambally,** Menissa
Attorney General ..................................................... **Compton,** Petros
Ambassador to the US ................................................. **Johnny,** Sonia
Permanent Representative to the UN, New York ..........................

## SAINT VINCENT AND THE GRENADINES

(Last updated: 4/6/2001)

Governor General .................................................... **Jack,** David
Prime Minister ...................................................... **Gonsalves,** Ralph
Dep. Prime Minister ................................................. **Straker,** Louis
Min. of Agriculture, Lands, & Fisheries ............................. **Walters,** Selmon
Min. of Commerce & Trade ............................................ **Straker,** Louis
Min. of Education, Youth Affairs, & Sports .......................... **Browne,** Mike
Min. of Finance ..................................................... **Gonsalves,** Ralph
Min. of Foreign Affairs ............................................. **Straker,** Louis
Min. of Grenadine Affairs & Legal Affairs ........................... **Gonsalves,** Ralph
Min. of Health & the Environment .................................... **Slater,** Douglas
Min. of Information ................................................. **Gonsalves,** Ralph
Min. of Labor ....................................................... **Gonsalves,** Ralph
Min. of National Security ........................................... **Beache,** Vincent
Min. of Planning & Economic Development ............................. **Gonsalves,** Ralph
Min. of Social Development, Family, Gender Affairs, & Ecclesiastical Affairs .. **Miguel,** Girlyn
Min. of Telecommunications, Science, Technology, & Industry ............. **Thompson,** Jerrol
Min. of Tourism & Culture ........................................... **Baptiste,** Rene
Min. of Transport, Works, & Housing ................................. **Francis,** Julian
Attorney General .................................................... **Joseph,** Carl
Ambassador to the US ................................................ **Layne,** Kingsley C. A.
Permanent Representative to the UN, New York ..........................

## SAMOA, INDEPENDENT STATE OF

(Last updated: 11/17/2000)

Head of State ....................................................... **Malietoa,** Tanumafili II
Prime Minister ...................................................... **Tuila'epa,** Sailele Malielegaoi
Min. of Agriculture, Forestry, Fisheries, & Meteorological Services .......... **Molio'o,** Teofilo
Min. of Commerce, Trade, & Industry ................................. **Tuila'epa,** Sailele Malielegaoi
Min. of Education ................................................... **Fiame,** Naomi Mata'afa
Min. of Finance ..................................................... **Tuila'epa,** Sailele Malielegaoi
Min. of Foreign Affairs ............................................. **Tuila'epa,** Sailele Malielegaoi
Min. of Health ...................................................... **Misa,** Telefoni Retzlaff
Min. of Immigration ................................................. **Tofilau,** Eti Alesana
Min. of Internal Affairs ............................................ **Tofilau,** Eti Alesana
Min. of Justice ..................................................... **Solia,** Papu Vaai
Min. of Labor ....................................................... **Polataivao,** Fosi
Min. of Lands, Survey, & Environment ................................ **Tuala,** Sale Tagaloa Kerslake
Min. of Police & Prisons ............................................ **Tofilau,** Eti Alesana
Min. of Public Service .............................................. **Tofilau,** Eti Alesana
Min. of Public Works ................................................ **Luagalau,** Levaula Kamu
Min. of Transportation & Civil Aviation ............................. **Hans,** Joachim Keil
Min. of Treasury, Inland Revenue, & Customs ......................... **Tuila'epa,** Sailele Malielegaoi
Min. of Women's Affairs ............................................. **Leniu,** Tofaeono Avamagalo
Min. Without Portfolio .............................................. **Tofilau,** Eti Alesana
Attorney General .................................................... **Heather,** Brenda
Governor, Central Bank .............................................. **Scanlan,** Papali'i Tommy
Ambassador to the US ................................................ **Slade,** Tuiloma Neroni
Permanent Representative to the UN, New York ........................ **Slade,** Tuiloma Neroni

## SAN MARINO, REPUBLIC OF

(Last updated: 11/17/2000)

Captain Regent (Joint Chiefs of State) .................................... **Francini,** Loris
Captain Regent (Joint Chiefs of State) .................................... **Cecchetti,** Alberto
Sec. of State for Finance, Welfare & Information ......................... **Galassi,** Clelio
Sec. of State for Foreign & Political Affairs ............................. **Gatti,** Gabriele
Sec. of State for Internal Affairs ........................................ **Volpinari,** Antonio Lazzaro
Permanent Representative to the UN, New York ......................... **Filippi Balestra,** Gian Nicola

## SAO TOME AND PRINCIPE, DEMOCRATIC REPUBLIC OF

(Last updated: 3/19/2001)

President ................................................................ **Trovoada,** Miguel
Prime Minister .......................................................... **Posser da Costa,** Guilherme
Dep Sec of State to the Prime Min. ...................................... **Lima,** Emilio Guadalupe Fernandes
Min. of Agriculture & Fisheries ......................................... **Santos,** Hermenilgido De Assuncao Sousa
Min. of Commerce, Industry, & Tourism ................................. **Rita,** Cosme Afonso Da Trindade
Min. of Defense ......................................................... **Bexigas,** Joao Quaresma Viegas, *Col.*
Min. of Economics ...................................................... **Batista de Sousa,** Maria Das Neves Ceita
Min. of Education, Culture, & Youth .................................... **Da Costa,** Sacramento
Min. of Equipment & Environment ...................................... **Carvalho,** Arlindo Afonso
Min. of Foreign Affairs & Cooperation ................................. **Branco,** Joaquim Rafael
Min. of Health & Sports ................................................ **De Lima,** Antonio Soares Marques
Min. of Infrastructure & Natural Resources ............................ **Dos Prazeres,** Luis Alberto Carneiro
Min. of Internal & Territorial Administration .......................... **Lima,** Manuel Da Cruz Margal
Min. of Justice, Parliamentary Affairs, Labor, & Public Administration ....... **Paulino,** Alberto
Min. of Planning & Finance ............................................ **David,** Adelino Castelo
Sec. of State for Youth, Sport, & Professional Training .................. **Bastos,** Luis
Governor, Bank of Sao Tome & Principe .................................
Ambassador to the US ..................................................
Permanent Representative to the UN, New York ......................... **Augusto,** Domingos Ferreira

## SAUDI ARABIA, KINGDOM OF

(Last updated: 1/19/2001)

King .................................................................... **Saud, FAHD,** bin Abd al-Aziz Al
Prime Minister .......................................................... **Saud, FAHD,** bin Abd al-Aziz Al
First Dep. Prime Min. ................................................... **Saud, ABDALLAH,** bin Abd al-Aziz Al
Second Dep. Prime Min. ................................................ **Saud, SULTAN,** bin Abd al-Aziz Al
Min. of Agriculture & Water ............................................ **Muammar,** Abdallah bin Abd al-Aziz al-
Min. of Civil Service ................................................... **Fayiz,** Muhammad bin Ali
Min. of Commerce ..................................................... **Faqih,** Usama Jafar
Min. of Communications ................................................ **Salum,** Nasir bin Muhammad al-, *Dr.*
Min. of Defense & Aviation ............................................. **Saud, SULTAN,** bin Abd al-Aziz Al
Min. of Education ...................................................... **Rashid,** Muhammad Ahmad al-
Min. of Finance & National Economy ................................... **Asaf,** Ibrahim Abd al-Aziz al-
Min. of Foreign Affairs ................................................. **Saud, SAUD al-FAYSAL,** bin Abd al-Aziz Al
Min. of Health ......................................................... **Shubukshi,** Usama bin Abd al-Majid, *Dr.*
Min. of Higher Education ............................................... **Angari,** Khalid bin Muhammad al-
Min. of Industry & Electricity .......................................... **Yamani,** Hashim bin Abdallah bin Hashim
Min. of Information .................................................... **Farsi,** Fuad Abd al-Salam
Min. of Interior ........................................................ **Saud, NAYIF,** bin Abd al-Aziz Al
Min. of Islamic Guidance ............................................... **Shaykh,** Salih bin Abd al-Aziz bin Muhammad
  bin Ibrahim
Min. of Justice ......................................................... **Shaykh,** Abdallah Muhammad Ibrahim Al al-
Min. of Labor & Social Affairs ......................................... **Namla,** Ali bin Ibrahim
Min. of Municipal & Rural Affairs ...................................... **Jarallah,** Muhammad bin Ibrahim al-
Min. of Petroleum & Mineral Resources ................................ **Naimi,** Ali Ibrahim
Min. of Pilgrimage Affairs & Religious Trusts .......................... **Madani,** Iyyad bin Amin
Min. of Planning ....................................................... **Ghusaybi,** Khalid bin Muhammad
Min. of Post, Telephone, & Telegraph .................................. **Ghusaybi,** Khalid bin Muhammad
Min. of Public Works & Housing ....................................... **Saud, MITIB,** bin Abd al-Aziz Al

## SAUDI ARABIA, KINGDOM OF (cont.)

| | |
|---|---|
| Min. of State | **Alaqi,** Madani bin Abd al-Qadir al- |
| Min. of State | **Assaf,** Ibrahim bin Muhammad al-, *Dr.* |
| Min. of State | **Ayban,** Musaid bin Muhammad al- |
| Min. of State | **Jihani,** Ali bin Talal al-, *Dr.* |
| Min. of State | **Khuwaytir,** Abd al-Aziz bin Abdallah al- |
| Min. of State | **Mani,** Abd al-Aziz bin Ibrahim al- |
| Min. of State | **Nafisa,** Mutalib bin Abdallah al- |
| Min. of State | **Saud, ABD AL-AZIZ,** bin Fahd bin Abd al-Aziz Al |
| Min. of State | **Shaykh,** Muhammad bin Abd al-Aziz al- |
| Pres. of the Higher Council of Ulema | **Shaykh,** Abd al-Aziz Abdallah al- |
| Governor, Saudi Arabian Monetary Agency | **Sayyari,** Hamad al- |
| Ambassador to the US | **Saud, BANDAR,** bin Sultan bin Abd al-Aziz Al |
| Permanent Representative to the UN, New York | **Shubukshi,** Fawzi bin Abd al-Majid al- |

## SENEGAL, REPUBLIC OF

(Last updated: 3/14/2001)

| | |
|---|---|
| President | **Wade,** Abdoulaye |
| Prime Minister | **Boye,** Madior |
| Min. of African Integration | **Sow,** Amadou |
| Min. of Agriculture & Stockbreeding | **Diouf,** Pape |
| Min. of Armed Forces | **Sambo,** Youba |
| Min. in Charge of Relations with Assemblies | **Dja,** Haoua |
| Min. of Civil Service, Labor, & Employment | **Dem,** Yero |
| Min. of Culture & Communication | **Mbow,** Penda |
| Min. Del. for Budget | **Diop,** Abdoulaye |
| Min. Del. for Literacy, Technical, & Vocational Training | **Diop,** Becaye |
| Min. of Energy & Water Resources | **Bathily,** Abdoulaye |
| Min. of Environment | **Ba,** Lamine |
| Min. of Equipment & Transportation | **Seck,** Mamadou |
| Min. of Finance & Economic Affairs | **Diop,** Moctar |
| Min. of Fisheries | **Sarr,** Oumar |
| Min. of Foreign Affairs & Senegalese Abroad | **Gadio,** Cheikh Tidiane |
| Min. of Health | **Fall,** Abdoul |
| Min. of Higher Education | **Diagne,** Mousee |
| Min. of Interior | **Niang,** Mamadou, *Maj. Gen.* |
| Min. of Justice & Keeper of the Seals | **Madior Boye,** Mame |
| Min. of Mines, Handicrafts, & Industry Landing | **Savane,** Landing |
| Min. of National Education, Technical, & Vocational Training | **Ndiaye,** Kansoumbaly |
| Min. of National Soldarity & Family Affairs | **Tall,** Aminata |
| Min. of Planning | **Thima,** Samba Dioulde |
| Min. of Sports & Leisure | **Ndong,** Joseph |
| Min. of Tourism | **Toure,** Ndiawar |
| Min. of Town Planning & Housing | **Fall,** Pape Sadibou |
| Min. of Trade | **Thiam,** Horatius |
| Min. of Youth | **Diagne,** Momodou Fada |
| Ambassador to the US | **Seck,** Mamadou Mansour |
| Permanent Representative to the UN, New York | **Ka,** Ibra Deguene |

## SEYCHELLES, REPUBLIC OF

(Last updated: 11/17/2000)

| | |
|---|---|
| President | **Rene,** France Albert |
| Vice President | **Michel,** James |
| Min. of Administration | **Alexander,** Noellie |
| Min. of Agriculture & Marine Resources | **Dolor,** Ernesta |
| Min. of Culture & Information | **Jumeau,** Ronny |
| Min. of Education | **Faure,** Danny |
| Min. of Foreign Affairs, Planning, & Environment | **Bonnelame,** Jeremie |
| Min. of Health | **Dugasse,** Jacqueline |
| Min. of Housing and Land Use | **Belmont,** Joseph |

## SEYCHELLES, REPUBLIC OF (cont.)

Min. of Industries & International Business ............................. **Pillay,** Patrick
Min. of Internal Affairs, Defense, & Legal Affairs ........................ **Rene,** France Albert
Min. of Local Government & Sports ..................................... **Frichot,** Sylvette
Min. of Social Affairs & Manpower Development ....................... **Herminie,** William
Min. of Tourism & Civil Aviation ....................................... **De Comarmond,** Simone
Governor, Central Bank ................................................ **Weber,** Norman
Ambassador to the US .................................................. **Morel,** Claude
Permanent Representative to the UN, New York ......................... **Morel,** Claude

## SIERRA LEONE, REPUBLIC OF

(Last updated: 3/13/2001)

President ............................................................. **Kabbah,** Ahmad Tejan
Vice President ....................................................... **Demby,** Albert Joe
Min. of Agriculture, Forestry, & Marine Resources ....................... **Adams,** Okere
Min. of Defense ...................................................... **Kabbah,** Ahmad Tejan
Min. of Development & Economic Planning ............................ **Sesay,** Kadi, *Dr.*
Min. of Education, Youth, & Sports .................................... **Wurie,** Alpha T., *Dr.*
Min. of Finance ...................................................... **Kuyembeh,** Peter
Min. of Foreign Affairs & International Cooperation ..................... **Dumbuya,** Ahmed Ramadan
Min. of Health & Sanitation .......................................... **Tejan-Jalloh,** Ibrahim I., *Dr.*
Min. of Information & Broadcasting ................................... **Spencer,** Julius, *Dr.*
Min. of Justice ...................................................... **Berewa,** Solomon E.
Min. of Labor & Industrial Relations .................................. **Timbo,** Alpha
Min. of Lands, Housing, Country Planning & the Environment .............. **Sessay,** Alfred Bobson
Min. of Mineral Resources ............................................ **Deen,** Mohamed Alhaji
Min. of Political & Parliamentary Affairs .............................. **Koroma,** Abu Aya
Min. of Rural Development & Local Government ......................... **Danda,** J. B.
Min. of Safety & Security ............................................ **Margai,** Charles
Min. of Social Welfare, Gender, & Children's Affairs ..................... **Gbujama,** Shirley Yema
Min. of Tourism & Culture ............................................ **Jomo-Jalloh,** A. B. S.
Min. of Trade & Industry ............................................. **Kamara,** Osman
Min. of Transport & Communications .................................. **Pujey,** Momoh
Min. of Works & Maintenance ......................................... **Jah,** S. U. M., *Dr.*
Min. of State for Eastern Region ...................................... **Fillie-Faboe,** S. R.
Min. of State for Northern Region ..................................... **Sesay,** Ibrahim
Min. of State for Presidential Affairs .................................. **Koroma,** Momodu
Min. of State for Public Affairs ....................................... **Ngombu,** Dominic
Min. of State for Southern Region ..................................... **Sesay,** Foday
Attorney General ..................................................... **Berewa,** Solomon E.
Ambassador to the US ................................................ **Leigh,** John Ernest
Permanent Representative to the UN, New York ......................... **Kamara,** Ibrahim M.

## SINGAPORE, REPUBLIC OF

(Last updated: 2/20/2001)

President ............................................................. **Nathan,** Sellapan Rama (S. R.)
Prime Minister ....................................................... **Goh,** Chok Tong
Dep. Prime Min. ...................................................... **Lee,** Hsien Loong, *Brig. Gen. (Res.)*
Dep. Prime Min. ...................................................... **Tan,** Keng Yam Tony
Senior Minister ...................................................... **Lee,** Kuan Yew
Min. of Communications & Information Technology ....................... **Yeo,** Cheow Tong
Min. of Community Development & Muslim Affairs ....................... **Abdullah,** Tarmugi
Min. of Defense ...................................................... **Tan,** Keng Yam Tony
Min. of Education .................................................... **Teo,** Chee Hean, *RAdm. (Res.)*
Min. of the Environment (Acting) ...................................... **Lim,** Swee Say
Min. of Finance ...................................................... **Hu,** Tsu Tau Richard
Min. of Foreign Affairs ............................................... **Jayakumar,** Shunmugam
Min. of Health ....................................................... **Lim,** Hng Kiang, *Lt. Col. (Res.)*
Min. of Home Affairs ................................................. **Wong,** Kan Seng
Min. of Information & the Arts ........................................ **Lee,** Yock Suan
Min. of Law .......................................................... **Jayakumar,** Shunmugam

## SINGAPORE, REPUBLIC OF (cont.)

Min. of Manpower .................................................... **Lee,** Boon Yang
Min. of Law .......................................................... **Jayakumar,** Shunmugam
Min. of National Development ....................................... **Mah,** Bow Tan
Min. of Trade & Industry ............................................ **Yeo,** Yong Boon George, *Brig. Gen. (Res.)*
Min. Without Portfolio ............................................... **Lim,** Boon Heng
Chmn., The Monetary Authority of Singapore ......................... **Lee,** Hsien Loong, *Brig. Gen. (Res.)*
Ambassador to the US ................................................ **Chan,** Heng Chee
Permanent Representative to the UN, New York ........................ **Mahbubani,** Kishore

## SLOVAKIA (SLOVAK REPUBLIC)

(Last updated: 1/10/2001)

President ............................................................ **Schuster,** Rudolf
Prime Minister ...................................................... **Dzurinda,** Mikulas
Dep. Prime Min. ..................................................... **Csaky,** Pal
Dep. Prime Min. ..................................................... **Fogas,** Lubomir
Dep. Prime Min. ..................................................... **Hamzik,** Pavol
Dep. Prime Min. ..................................................... **Miklos,** Ivan
Min. of Agriculture ................................................. **Koncos,** Pavel
Min. of Construction & Regional Development ......................... **Harna,** Istvan
Min. of Culture ..................................................... **Knazko,** Milan
Min. of Defense ..................................................... **Stank,** Jozef
Min. of Economy ..................................................... **Harach,** Lubomir
Min. of Education ................................................... **Ftacnik,** Milan
Min. of Environment ................................................. **Miklos,** Laszlo
Min. of Finance ..................................................... **Schmognerova,** Brigita
Min. of Foreign Affairs ............................................. **Kukan,** Eduard
Min. of Health ...................................................... **Kovac,** Roman
Min. of Interior .................................................... **Pittner,** Ladislav
Min. of Justice ..................................................... **Carnogursky,** Jan
Min. of Labor ....................................................... **Magvasi,** Peter
Min. of Privatization ............................................... **Machova,** Maria
Min. of Transportation, Post, & Telecommunications ................. **Macejko,** Jozef
Governor, Central Bank of Slovakia .................................. **Jusko,** Marian
Chief of General Staff .............................................. **Cerovsky,** Milan
Ambassador to NATO .................................................. **Burian,** Peter
Ambassador to the US ................................................ **Butora,** Martin
Permanent Representative to the UN, New York ........................ **Tomka,** Peter

## SLOVENIA, REPUBLIC OF

(Last updated: 4/3/2001)

President ............................................................ **Kucan,** Milan
Prime Minister ...................................................... **Drnovsek,** Janez
Min. of Agriculture, Forestry, & Nutrition ......................... **But,** Franc
Min. of Culture ..................................................... **Rihter,** Andreja
Min. of Defense ..................................................... **Grizold,** Anton
Min. of Economic Affairs ............................................ **Petrin,** Tea
Min. of Education & Sports .......................................... **Cok,** Lucija
Min. of Environment & Town Planning ................................. **Kopac,** Janez
Min. of Finance ..................................................... **Rop,** Anton
Min. of Foreign Affairs ............................................. **Rupel,** Dimitrij
Min. of Health ...................................................... **Keber,** Dusan
Min. of Interinal Affairs ........................................... **Bohinc,** Rado
Min. of Justice ..................................................... **Bizjak,** Ivan
Min. of Labor, Family & Social Affairs .............................. **Dimovski,** Vlado
Min. of Transport & Communication ................................... **Presecnik,** Jakob
Min. Without Portfolio for European Affairs ......................... **Bavcar,** Igor
Governor, National Bank ............................................. **Gaspari,** Mitja
Ambassador to the US ................................................ **Kracun,** Davorin
Permanent Representative to the UN, New York ........................ **Petric,** Ernest

## SOLOMON ISLANDS

(Last updated: 8/15/2000)

| | |
|---|---|
| Governor General | **Lapli,** John *Sir* |
| Prime Minister | **Sogavare,** Mannaseh Damukana |
| Asst. Prime Minister | **Waena,** Nathaniel |
| Dep. Prime Min. | **Kemakeza,** Allan |
| Min. of Agriculture & Primary Industries | **Kwan,** Moon P. |
| Min. of Commerce, Employment, Trade, &Indigenous Business | **Holosivi,** David |
| Min. of Culture, Tourism, & Aviation | **Koli,** Johnson |
| Min. of Education | |
| Min. of Finance | **Rini,** Snyder |
| Min. of Fisheries & Marine Resources | **Luialamo,** George |
| Min. of Foreign Affairs | **Philip,** Danny |
| Min. of Forestry, Environment, & Conservation | **Chan,** Tommy Koh |
| Min. of Health & Medical Services | **Paul,** Allan |
| Min. of Home & Ecclesiastical Affairs | |
| Min. of Lands & Housing | |
| Min. of Mines & Energy | |
| Min. of National Planning & Human Resource Development | **Maena,** Michael |
| Min. of Police, Justice, & Legal Affairs | **Haomae,** William |
| Min. of Provincial Govt. & Rural Development | **Waena,** Nathaniel |
| Min. of Transport, Works, & Communications | **Tahua,** Joses |
| Min. of Women, Youth, & Sports | **Laore,** Albert |
| Governor, Central Bank | **Houenipwela,** Richard |
| Ambassador to the US | **Horoi,** Rex |
| Permanent Representative to the UN, New York | **Horoi,** Rex |

## SOMOLIA, REPUBLIC OF

(Last updated: 11/29/2000)

*Abdikassim Salad Hassan was elected President of an interim government at the Djibouti-sponsored Arta Peace Conference on 27 August 2000 by a broad representation of Somali clans that compromised the Transitional Assembly.*

| | |
|---|---|
| President | **Abdikassim,** Salad Hassan |
| Prime Minister | **Ali,** Khalifa Galaydh |
| Min. of Agriculture | **Yousuf,** Moalin Amin |
| Min. of Commerce | **Mohamed,** Warsame Ali |
| Min. of Defense | **Abdullahi,** Baqor Musa |
| Min. of Education | **Mohamed,** Maydhane Burale |
| Min. of Finance | **Sayid,** Sheikh Dahir |
| Min. of Fishing | **Mohamed,** Nur Bakar |
| Min. of Foreign Affairs | **Ismael,** Mahmoud Hourreh |
| Min. of Health & Rural Development | |
| Min. of Higher Education | **Mohamed,** Ali Ahmed |
| Min. of Industry | **Hassan,** Mohamud Hassan |
| Min. of Information | **Zakaria,** Mohamud Haji Abdi |
| Min. of Interior | **Dahir,** Sheikh Mohamed |
| Min. of Inter-Regions Cooperation | **Hassan,** Farah Hugale |
| Min. of Justice | **Mohamed,** Omar Fara |
| Min. of Livestock Development | **Abdulwahab,** Moalin Mohamud |
| Min. of Planning | **Hussein,** Elabe Fahiye |
| Min. of Ports & Marine Transport | **Abdiwali,** Jama Warsame |
| Min. of Posts & Communications | **Abdulkadir,** Moalin |
| Min. of Public works | **Said,** Warsame |
| Min. of Reconstruction & Rehabilitation | **Abdullahi,** Ga'al Abdi |
| Min. of Science & Technology | **Abdulkadir,** Mohamed Abdulle |
| Min. of Sports & Employment | **Abdulasis,** Mukhtar Qaridi |
| Min. of Transport | **Abdi,** Gouled Mohamed |
| Min. of Water & Mineral Resources | **Hassan,** Abshir Farah |

## SOUTH AFRICA, REPUBLIC OF

(Last updated: 4/19/2001)

| | |
|---|---|
| State President | **Mbeki,** Thabo Mvuyelwa |
| Executive Deputy President | **Zuma,** Jacob |
| Min. of Agriculture & Land Affairs | **Msane-Didiza,** Thoko |
| Min. of Arts, Culture, Science, & Technology | **Ngubane,** Baldwin "Ben" |
| Min. of Correctional Services | **Skosana,** Ben |
| Min. of Defense | **Lekota,** Mosiuoa |
| Min. of Education | **Asmal,** Kader |
| Min. of Environment Affairs & Tourism | **Moosa,** Mohamed Valli |
| Min. of Finance | **Manuel,** Trevor |
| Min. of Foreign Affairs | **Dlamini-Zuma,** Nkosazana Clarice |
| Min. of Health | **Tshabalala-Msimang,** Manto |
| Min. of Home Affairs | **Buthelezi,** Mangosuthu |
| Min. of Housing | **Mthembi-Mahanyele,** Sankie |
| Min. of Intelligence | **Nhlanhla,** Joe |
| Min. of Justice & Constitutional Development | **Maduna,** Penuell |
| Min. of Labor | **Mdladlana,** Membathisi Shepherd |
| Min. of Mineral & Energy Affairs | **Mlambo-Ngcuka,** Phumzile |
| Min. of Posts, Telecommunications, & Broadcasting | **Matsepe-Cassaburri,** Ivy |
| Min. of Provincial & Local Government | **Mufamadi,** Sydney |
| Min. of Public Enterprises | **Radebe,** Jeff |
| Min. of Public Service & Administration | **Fraser-Moleketi,** Geraldine |
| Min. of Public Works | **Sigcau,** Stella |
| Min. of Safety & Security | **Tshwete,** Steve |
| Min. of Sport & Recreation | **Balfour,** Ngconde |
| Min. of Trade & Industry | **Erwin,** Alec |
| Min. of Water Affairs & Forestry | **Kasrils,** Ronnie |
| Min. of Welfare & Population Development | **Skweyiya,** Zola |
| Min. in the Office of the President | **Pahad,** Essop |
| Governor, Reserve Bank | **Mboweni,** Tito |
| Ambassador to the US | **Sisulu,** Sheila |
| Permanent Representative to the UN, New York | **Kumalo,** Dumisani Shadrack |

## SPAIN, KINGDOM OF

(Last updated: 2/27/2001)

| | |
|---|---|
| Chief of State | **Juan Carlos I,** *King* |
| President of the Government | **Aznar,** Jose Maria |
| First Vice President | **Lucas,** Juan Jose |
| Second Vice President | **Rato,** Figaredo, Rodrigo |
| Min. of Agriculture, Fisheries, & Food | **Canete,** Miguel Arias |
| Min. of Defense | **Trillo,** Federico |
| Min. of Development | **Alvarez-Cascos,** Francisco |
| Min. of Economy | **Rato,** Figaredo, Rodrigo |
| Min. of Education, Culture, & Sport | **Castillo,** Pilar Del |
| Min. of Environment | **Matas,** Jaume |
| Min. of Finance | **Montoro,** Cristobal |
| Min. of Foreign Affairs | **Pique,** Josep |
| Min. of Health | **Villalobos,** Celia |
| Min. of Interior | **Rajoy,** Mariano Brey |
| Min. of Justice | **Acebes,** Angel |
| Min. of Labor & Social Issues | **Aparicio,** Juan Carlos |
| Min. of the Presidency | **Rajoy,** Mariano |
| Min. of Public Administration | **Posada,** Jesus |
| Min. of Science & Technology | **Birules,** Anna |
| Min. Without Portfolio (Spokesman) | **Cabanillas,** Pio |
| Governor, Bank of Spain | **Caruana,** Jaime |
| Ambassador to the US | **Ruperez,** Francisco Javier |
| Permanent Representative to the UN, New York | **Arias,** Inocencio Felix Llamas |

# SRI LANKA, DEMOCRATIC SOCIALIST REPUBLIC OF

(Last updated: 11/17/2000)

| | |
|---|---|
| President | **Kumaratunga**, Chandrika Bandaranaike |
| Prime Minister | **Wickramanayake**, Ratnasiri |
| Min. of Agriculture & Lands | **Jayaratna**, D. M. |
| Min. of Buddha Sasana | **Jayakody**, Lakshman |
| Min. of Cooperative Development | **Wickremasinghe**, D. P. |
| Min. of Cultural & Religious Affairs | **Jayakody**, Lakshman |
| Min. of Defense | **Kumaratunga**, Chandrika Bandaranaike |
| Min. of Education & Higher Education | **Pathirana**, Richard |
| Min. of Finance & Planning | **Kumaratunga**, Chandrika Bandaranaike |
| Min. of Fisheries & Aquatic Resources Development | **Rajapakse**, Mahinda |
| Min. of Foreign Affairs | **Kadirgamar**, Lakshman |
| Min. of Forestry & Environment | **Wijesekera**, Mahinda |
| Min. of Health & Indigenuous Medicine | **de Silva**, Nimal Siripala |
| Min. of Housing & Urban Development | **Gunawardena**, Indika |
| Min. of Industrial Development | **Gooneratne**, Clement V. |
| Min. of Internal Trade, International Commerce, & Food | **Wickramaratne**, Kingsley |
| Min. of Irrigation & Power | **Ratwatte**, Anuruddha, *Gen.* |
| Min. of Justice, Constitutional Affairs, Ethnic Affairs, & National Integration | **Peiris**, Gamini L., *Prof.* |
| Min. of Labor | **Seneviratne**, John |
| Min. of Livestock Development & Estate Infrastructure | |
| Min. of Mahaweli Development | **Sirsena**, Maithripala |
| Min. of Plan Implementation & Parliamentary Affairs | **Fernandopulle**, Jeyaraj |
| Min. of Port Development , Rehabilitation, & Reconstruction | **Ashraff**, Mohamed H. M. |
| Min. of Posts, Telecommunications, & Media | **Samaraweera**, Mangala |
| Min. of Provincial Councils & Local Government | **Moulana**, S. Alavi |
| Min. of Public Administration, Home Affairs, & Plantation Industries | |
| Min. of Samurdhi, Youth Affairs, & Sports | **Dissanayaka**, D. M. S. B. |
| Min. of Science & Technology | **Weerakoon**, Batty |
| Min. of Social Services | **Jayasena**, Sumedha |
| Min. of Tourism & Civil Aviation | **Senanayake**, Dharmasiri |
| Min. of Transport & Highways | **Fowzie**, A. H. M. |
| Min. of Vocational Training & Rural Industries | **Dodangoda**, Amarasiri |
| Min. of Women's Affairs | **Ratnayake**, Hema |
| Dep. Min. for Agriculture & Land | **Rajapaksa**, Chamal |
| Dep. Min. for Buddha Sasana | **Premaratna**, Ediriweera |
| Dep. Min. for Cooperative Development | **Balasuriya**, Jagath |
| Dep. Min. for Cultural & Religious Affairs | **Alahapperuma**, Dalas |
| Dep. Min. for Defense | **Ratwatte**, Anuruddha, *Gen.* |
| Dep. Min. for Education & Higher Education | **Cooray**, Reginald |
| Dep. Min. for Finance | **Peiris**, Gamini L., *Prof.* |
| Dep. Min. for Fisheries & Aquatic Resources Development | **Fernando**, Milroy |
| Dep. Min. for Foreign Affairs | **Kiriella**, Lakshman |
| Dep. Min. for Forestry & Environment | **Premachandra**, Munidasa |
| Dep. Min. for Health & Indigenous Medicine | **Karalliyadda**, Tissa |
| Dep. Min. for Home Affairs | **Gopallawa**, Monty |
| Dep. Min. for Housing & Urban Development | **Herath**, Mahiepala |
| Dep. Min. for Industrial Development | **Jayasinghe**, Athula Nimalsiri |
| Dep. Min. for Internal & International Commerce, & Food | **Gunawardena**, Lionel |
| Dep. Min. for Irrigation | **Basnayake**, Bandula |
| Dep. Min. for Justice, Constitutional Affairs, & National Integration | **Perera**, Dilan |
| Dep. Min. for Labor | **Perera**, Dilan |
| Dep. Min. for Livestock Development & Estate Infrastructure | **Kariyawasam**, Noel Padmasiri |
| Dep. Min. for Mahaweli Development | **Jayatissa**, A. R. |
| Dep. Min. for Plan Implementation & Parliamentary Affairs | **Premaratne**, Shantha |
| Dep. Min. for Planning | **Weerawanni**, Samaraweera |
| Dep. Min. for Port Development, Rehabilitation, & Reconstruction | **Ranatunga**, Reggie |
| Dep. Min. for Posts, Telecommunications, & Media | **Hisbullah**, M. L. A. M. |
| Dep. Min. for Power | **Perera**, Felix |
| Dep. Min. for Public Administration, Plantation Industries, & Home Affairs | **Gopallawa**, Monty |
| Dep. Min. for Public Utilities & Estate Housing | **Chandrasekeran**, P. |
| Dep. Min. for Samurdhi, Youth Affairs, & Sports | **Gamage**, Piyasena |
| Dep. Min. for Science & Technology | **Peiris**, J. Yooses |
| Dep. Min. for Social Services | **Abu**, Bakkar |

## SRI LANKA, DEMOCRATIC SOCIALIST REPUBLIC OF (cont.)

Dep. Min. for Tourism & Civil Aviation .................................. **Semasinghe,** H. B.
Dep. Min. for Transport & Highways ..................................... **Weerasinghe,** H. M.
Dep. Min. for Vocational Training & Rural Industries ..................... **Gajadeera,** Chandrasiri
Dep. Min. for Women's Affairs ......................................... **Rajapakse,** Nirupama
Dep. Min. for Youth Affairs & Sports ................................... **Kumaranatunga,** Jeewan
Governor, Central Bank ................................................ **Jayawardena,** A. S.
Ambassador to the US ................................................. **Rasaputram,** Warnasena
Permanent Representative to the UN, New York ......................... **De Saram,** John Henricus

## SUDAN, REPUBLIC OF THE

(Last updated: 4/6/2001)

President ............................................................. **Bashir,** Umar Hasan Ahmad al-, *Lt. Gen.*
First Vice President .................................................... **Taha,** Ali Osman Mohamed
Second Vice President ................................................. **Machar Kacoul,** Moses
Chmn., Bureau of Federal Rule ........................................ **Muhammad,** Ali al-Haj
Min. of Agriculture & Forests ......................................... **Al-Khalifa,** Magzoub *Dr.*
Min. of Animal Resources ............................................. **Guy,** Riak *Dr.*
Min. of Cabinet Affairs ............................................... **Malwal,** Martin
Min. of Civil Aviation ................................................ **Malwal,** Joseph
Min. of Communications & Roads ...................................... **Eila,** Mohamed Tahir
Min. of Defense ...................................................... **Salih,** Bekri Hassan *Maj. Gen.*
Min. of Education .................................................... **Fartak,** Ali Tamim
Min. of Energy ...................................................... **al-Jaz,** Awad, *Dr.*
Min. of Environment & Construction .................................. **Tahir,** Al-Tigani Adam *Maj. Gen.*
Min. of External Relations ............................................ **Ismail,** Mustafa Osman *Dr.*
Min. of External Trade ............................................... **Kasha,** Abd Al-Hameed Musa
Min. of Federal Relations ............................................. **Suleiman,** Ibrahim *Gen.*
Min. of Federal Rule ................................................. **Nafie,** Nafie Ali *Dr.*
Min. of Finance & National Economy .................................. **Hamadi,** Abd Al-Rahim *Dr.*
Min. of Foreign Affairs ............................................... **Ismail,** Mustafa Osman
Min. of Guidance & Endowment ...................................... **Al-Basheir,** Isam Ahmed *Dr.*
Min. of Health ...................................................... **Ballal,** Ahmed *Dr.*
Min. of Higher Education ............................................. **Magzoub,** Mubarak *Dr.*
Min. of Industry .................................................... **al-Mutaafi,** Abdal Halim
Min. of Industry & Investment ....................................... **Al-Diggeir,** Galal *Dr.*
Min. of Information & Culture ........................................ **Salahn Addin,** Ghazi
Min. of Interior .................................................... **Hussein,** Abdelrahim Mohamed, *Brig.*
Min. of International Cooperation .................................... **Al-Hindi,** Siddiq
Min. of International Cooperation & Investment ......................
Min. of Irrigation ................................................... **Mohamed,** Kamal Ali
Min. of Justice ..................................................... **Yassin,** Ali Mohamed Osman
Min. of Labor ...................................................... **Magaya,** Alison Manani *Maj. Gen.*
Min. of Manpower .................................................. **Manani,** Alison
Min. for Presidential Affairs ......................................... **Salih,** Salah Ahmed Mohamed *Maj. Gen.*
Min. of Relations at the National Assembly ............................ **Sabdarat,** Abd Al-Basit
Min. of Roads & Bridges ............................................. **Eila,** Mohamed Tahir
Min. of Science & Technology ........................................ **Taha,** Al-Zubeir Basheir
Min. of Social Planning .............................................. **Mohamed,** Samia Ahmed
Min. of Sports & Youth .............................................. **Riziq,** Hassan Osman
Min. of Survey ...................................................... **Malwal,** Joseph
Min. of Tourism & Culture ........................................... **Al-Magid,** Abd Al-Basit Abd
Min. of Transportation .............................................. **Akhol,** Lam *Dr.*
State Minister of Agriculture ......................................... **Hussein,** Abd Al-Jabbar
State Minister of Cabinet Affairs ..................................... **Al-Latief,** Kamal Abd
State Minister of Civil Aviation ...................................... **Al-Bahi,** Mohamed Hassan
State Minister of Culture & Tourism .................................. **Al-Mugtaba,** Siddiq
State Minister of Defense ............................................ **Addin,** Ibrahim Shams *Col.*
State Minister of Education .......................................... **Zeid,** Mohamed Abu
State Minister of External Relations .................................. **Al-Fadil,** Al-Tigani
State Minister of External Relations .................................. **Deng,** Chol
State Minister of Federal Rule ....................................... **Al-Fadul,** Mohamed Ahmed
State Minister of Federal Rule ....................................... **Al-Safi,** Sulieman Salman
State Minister of Federal Rule ....................................... **Teny,** Makwac

## SUDAN, REPUBLIC OF THE (cont.)

State Minister of Finance . . . . . . . . . . . . . . . . . . . . . . . . . . . . . . . **Al-Hassan,** Al-Zubeir Ahmed
State Minister of Health . . . . . . . . . . . . . . . . . . . . . . . . . . . . . . . . . **Ahmed,** Abdalla Sid *Dr.*
State Minister of Industry . . . . . . . . . . . . . . . . . . . . . . . . . . . . . . . **Osman,** Ali Ahmed
State Minister of Information . . . . . . . . . . . . . . . . . . . . . . . . . . . . **Mustafa,** Al-Tayeb
State Minister of Internal Affairs . . . . . . . . . . . . . . . . . . . . . . . . . **Al-Aas,** Ahmed Mohamed
State Minister of International Cooperation . . . . . . . . . . . . . . . . . **Balouh, Adam,** *Dr.*
State Minister of Irrigation . . . . . . . . . . . . . . . . . . . . . . . . . . . . . . **Abdalla,** Osman
State Minister of Justice . . . . . . . . . . . . . . . . . . . . . . . . . . . . . . . . . **Karti,** Ali Ahmed
State Minister of Science & Technology . . . . . . . . . . . . . . . . . . . . **Hassan,** Jamal Mohamed
State Minister of Transport . . . . . . . . . . . . . . . . . . . . . . . . . . . . . . **Al-Sheikh,** Hassan Musa
State Minister of Youth & Sports . . . . . . . . . . . . . . . . . . . . . . . . . **Zein,** Abd Al-Gadir Mohamed
Asst. to the Pres. . . . . . . . . . . . . . . . . . . . . . . . . . . . . . . . . . . . . . . . **Omer,** Ibrahim Ahmed
Political Adviser to the Pres. . . . . . . . . . . . . . . . . . . . . . . . . . . . . . **Sabdarat,** Abdalbasit
Religious Adviser to the Pres. . . . . . . . . . . . . . . . . . . . . . . . . . . . . **Alimam,** Ahmed Ali
Presidential Councilor for Peace Affairs . . . . . . . . . . . . . . . . . . . **Nafi,** Nafi Ali, *Dr.*
Sec. of the Higher Council for Peace . . . . . . . . . . . . . . . . . . . . . . **Khalifa,** Mohamed al-Amin
Attorney General . . . . . . . . . . . . . . . . . . . . . . . . . . . . . . . . . . . . . . **Yassin,** Ali Mohamed Osman
Governor, Central Bank of Sudan . . . . . . . . . . . . . . . . . . . . . . . . . **Sabir,** Muhammad al-Hasan
Ambassador to the US . . . . . . . . . . . . . . . . . . . . . . . . . . . . . . . . . .
Permanent Representative to the UN, New York . . . . . . . . . . . . **Erwa,** el-Fatik Mohamed Ahmed

## SURINAME, REPUBLIC OF

(Last updated: 11/17/2000)

President . . . . . . . . . . . . . . . . . . . . . . . . . . . . . . . . . . . . . . . . . . . . . **Venetiaan,** Runaldo Ronald
Vice President . . . . . . . . . . . . . . . . . . . . . . . . . . . . . . . . . . . . . . . . **Ajodhia,** Jules Rattankoemar
Min. of Agriculture & Fishing . . . . . . . . . . . . . . . . . . . . . . . . . . . **Panday,** Geetapersad Gangaram
Min. of Defense . . . . . . . . . . . . . . . . . . . . . . . . . . . . . . . . . . . . . . . **Assen,** Ronald
Min. of Education & Human Development . . . . . . . . . . . . . . . . . . **Sandriman,** Walter
Min. of Finance . . . . . . . . . . . . . . . . . . . . . . . . . . . . . . . . . . . . . . . **Hildenberg,** Humphrey
Min. of Foreign Affairs . . . . . . . . . . . . . . . . . . . . . . . . . . . . . . . . . **Levens,** Marie
Min. of Health . . . . . . . . . . . . . . . . . . . . . . . . . . . . . . . . . . . . . . . . **Khudabux,** Mohamed Rakieb
Min. of Home Affairs . . . . . . . . . . . . . . . . . . . . . . . . . . . . . . . . . . **Joella-Sewnundun,** Urmila
Min. of Justice & Police . . . . . . . . . . . . . . . . . . . . . . . . . . . . . . . . **Gilds,** Siegfried
Min. of Labor . . . . . . . . . . . . . . . . . . . . . . . . . . . . . . . . . . . . . . . . . **Marica,** Clifford
Min. of Natural Resources . . . . . . . . . . . . . . . . . . . . . . . . . . . . . . **Demon,** Franco Rudy
Min. of Planning & Development Cooperation . . . . . . . . . . . . . . **Raghoebarsingh,** Keremchand
Min. of Public Works . . . . . . . . . . . . . . . . . . . . . . . . . . . . . . . . . . **Balesar,** Dewanand
Min. of Regional Development . . . . . . . . . . . . . . . . . . . . . . . . . . . **Russel,** Romeo van
Min. of Social Affairs . . . . . . . . . . . . . . . . . . . . . . . . . . . . . . . . . . **Somohardjo,** Paul
Min. of Trade & Industry . . . . . . . . . . . . . . . . . . . . . . . . . . . . . . . **Tjon Tjin Joe,** Jack
Min. of Transportation, Communication, & Tourism . . . . . . . . . **Castelen,** Guno
Pres., Central Bank . . . . . . . . . . . . . . . . . . . . . . . . . . . . . . . . . . . . **Telting,** Andre
Ambassador to the US . . . . . . . . . . . . . . . . . . . . . . . . . . . . . . . . . .
Permanent Representative to the UN . . . . . . . . . . . . . . . . . . . . . . **Mungra,** Subhas

## SWAZILAND, KINGDOM OF

(Last updated: 3/20/2001)

King . . . . . . . . . . . . . . . . . . . . . . . . . . . . . . . . . . . . . . . . . . . . . . . . **Mswati III**
Prime Minister . . . . . . . . . . . . . . . . . . . . . . . . . . . . . . . . . . . . . . . **Dlamini,** Barnabas Sibusiso, *Dr.*
Dep. Prime Min. . . . . . . . . . . . . . . . . . . . . . . . . . . . . . . . . . . . . . . **Khoza,** Arthur R. V.
Min. for Agriculture & Cooperatives . . . . . . . . . . . . . . . . . . . . . **Fanourakis,** Roy
Min. for Economic Planning & Development . . . . . . . . . . . . . . . **Prince,** Guduza
Min. for Education . . . . . . . . . . . . . . . . . . . . . . . . . . . . . . . . . . . . **Carmichael,** John
Min. for Enterprise & Employment . . . . . . . . . . . . . . . . . . . . . . . **Dlamini,** Lufto E.
Min. for Finance . . . . . . . . . . . . . . . . . . . . . . . . . . . . . . . . . . . . . . **Sithole,** Majozi
Min. for Foreign Affairs & Trade . . . . . . . . . . . . . . . . . . . . . . . . . **Ntshangase,** Abednego
Min. for Health & Social Welfare . . . . . . . . . . . . . . . . . . . . . . . . . **Dlamini,** Phetsile, *Dr.*
Min. for Home Affairs . . . . . . . . . . . . . . . . . . . . . . . . . . . . . . . . . **Sobandla,** *Prince*
Min. for Housing & Urban Development . . . . . . . . . . . . . . . . . . . **Shabangu,** Albert
Min. for Justice & Constitutional Affairs . . . . . . . . . . . . . . . . . . . **Simelane,** Maweni, *Chief*

## SWAZILAND, KINGDOM OF (cont.)

| | |
|---|---|
| Min. for Natural Resources & Energy | **Guduza,** *Prince* |
| Min. for Public Service & Information | **Mdluli,** Magwagwa |
| Min. for Public Works & Transport | **Mlangeni,** Titus |
| Min. for Tourism, Environment, & Communication | **Lukhele,** Stella |
| Governor, Central Bank | **Dlamini,** Martin |
| Ambassador to the US | **Kanya,** Mary Madzandza |
| Permanent Representative to the UN, New York | **Mamba,** Clifford Sibusiso |

## SWEDEN, KINGDOM OF

(Last updated: 1/19/2001)

| | |
|---|---|
| King | **Carl XVI Gustav** |
| Prime Minister | **Persson,** Goran |
| Dep. Prime Min. | **Hjelm-Wallen,** Lena |
| Min. of Agriculture & Lapp Affairs | **Winberg,** Margareta |
| Min. of Culture | **Ulvskog,** Marita |
| Min. of Defense | **Von Sydow,** Bjorn |
| Min. of Education | **Ostros,** Thomas |
| Min. of Environment | **Larsson,** Kjell |
| Min. of Finance | **Ringholm,** Bo |
| Min. of Foreign Affairs | **Lindh,** Anna |
| Min. of Justice | **Bodstrom,** Thomas |
| Min. of Social Affairs | **Engqvist,** Lars |
| Min. of Trade and Industry | **Rosengren,** Bjorn |
| Dep. Min. of Culture | **Messing,** Ulrika |
| Dep. Min. of Education | **Warnersson,** Ingegerd |
| Dep. Min. of Finance | **Lovden,** Lars-Erik |
| Dep. Min. of Foreign Affairs (Aid and Migration) | **Schori,** Pierre |
| Dep. Min. of Foreign Affairs (Trade and Baltic Issues) | **Pagrotsky,** Leif |
| Dep. Min. of Justice | **Liejon,** Britta |
| Dep. Min. of Social Affairs | **Klingvall,** Maj-Inger |
| Dep. Min. of Trade and Industry | **Sahlin,** Mona |
| Gov. of Swedish Central Bank | **Backstrom,** Urban |
| Ambassador to the US | **Eliasson,** Jan |
| Permanent Representative to the UN, New York | **Schori,** Pierre |

## SWITZERLAND (SWISS CONFEDERATION)

(Last updated: 1/5/2001)

| | |
|---|---|
| President | **Leuenberger,** Moritz |
| Vice President | **Villiger,** Kasper |
| Chief, Federal Dept. of Defense, Civil Protection, & Sports | **Schmid,** Samuel |
| Chief, Federal Dept. of Economic Affairs | **Couchepin,** Pascal |
| Chief, Federal Dept. of Finance | **Villiger,** Kasper |
| Chief, Federal Dept. of Foreign Affairs | **Deiss,** Joseph |
| Chief, Federal Dept. of Home Affairs | **Dreifuss,** Ruth |
| Chief, Federal Dept. of Justice & Police | **Metzler-Arnold,** Ruth |
| Chief, Federal Dept. of Transportation, Communications & Energy | **Leuenberger,** Moritz |
| Federal Chancellor | **Huber-Hotz,** Annemarie |
| Pres., Swiss National Bank | **Hans,** Meyer |
| Ambassador to the US | **Defago,** Alfred |

## SYRIA (SYRIAN ARAB REPUBLIC)

(Last updated: 11/17/2000)

| | |
|---|---|
| President | **al-Asad,** Bashar |
| Vice President | **Khaddam,** Abd al-Halim ibn Said |
| Vice President | **Mashariqa,** Muhammad Zuhayr |
| Prime Minister | **Miru,** Muhammad Mustafa |
| Dep. Prime Min. | **Talas,** Mustafa, *First Lt. Gen.* |

## SYRIA (SYRIAN ARAB REPUBLIC) (cont.)

Dep. Prime Min. for Economic Affairs ................................. **Rad,** Khalid
Dep. Prime Min. for Services Affairs................................. **Najiutri,** Muhammad
Min. of Agriculture & Agrarian Reform ........................... **Mustafa,** Asad
Min. of Awqaf ................................................. **Ziyadah,** Muhammad bin- abd-al-Rauf
Min. of Communications .......................................
Min. of Construction ........................................... **Mushantat,** Nuhad
Min. of Culture ............................................... **Qannut,** Maha *Dr.*
Min. of Defense ............................................... **Talas,** Mustafa, *First Lt. Gen.*
Min. of Economy & Foreign Trade ............................... **Imadi,** Muhammad al- *Dr.*
Min. of Education ............................................. **Sayyid,** Mahmud al- *Dr.*
Min. of Electricity ............................................ **Dahar,** Munib bin Asad Saim al-
Min. of Finance .............................................. **Mahayni,** Khalid al-
Min. of Foreign Affairs ........................................ **Shara,** Farouk al-
Min. of Health ............................................... **Shatti,** Muhammad Iyad al-, *M.D.*
Min. of Higher Education ...................................... **Rishah,** Hassan *Dr.*
Min. of Housing & Utilities .................................... **Safadi,** Hussam al-
Min. of Industry ............................................. **Hamu,** Ahmad
Min. of Information ........................................... **Umran,** Adnan
Min. of Interior ............................................. **Harba,** Muhammad *Dr.*
Min. of Irrigation ............................................ **Atrash,** Taha al-
Min. of Justice .............................................. **Khatib,** Nabil al-
Min. of Local Government ..................................... **Yasin,** Salam al-
Min. of Oil & Mineral Resources ............................... **Jamal,** Muhammad Maher bin-Husni
Min. for Presidential Affairs ................................... **Duwayhi,** Haytham
Min. of Religious Trusts ......................................
Min. of Social Affairs & Labor ................................. **Qudsi,** Bariah al- *Dr.*
Min. of Supply & Internal Trade ................................ **Barid,** Usamah Ma al- *Dr.*
Min. of Telecommunications .................................... **Martini,** Radwan
Min. of Tourism .............................................. **Miqdad,** Qasim
Min. of Transportation ........................................ **Ubayd,** Makram
Min. of State ................................................ **Hamidah,** Makhul abu
Min. of State ................................................ **Nuri,** Hassan al-
Min. of State ................................................ **Shuraytih,** Ihsan *Dr.*
Min. of State for Cabinet Affairs ............................... **Sayfu,** Muhammad Mufdi
Min. of State for Environmental Affairs ......................... **Adili,** Faruq al- *Dr.*
Min. of State for Foreign Affairs ............................... **Qaddur,** Nasir
Min. of State for Planning Affairs .............................. **Zaim,** Isam al- *Dr.*
Governor, Central Bank ....................................... **Mutawalli,** Hisham
Ambassador to the US ........................................ **Mualem,** Walid
Permanent Representative to the UN, New York ................... **Wahba,** Mikhail

## TAIWAN—NDE

(Last updated: 2/9/2001)

President ................................................... **Chen,** Shui-bian
Vice President .............................................. **Lu,** Annette
Pres., Executive Yuan (Premier) ............................... **Chang,** Chun-hsiung
Vice Pres., Executive Yuan (Vice Premier) ...................... **Lai,** In-jaw
Sec. Gen., Executive Yuan .................................... **Chiou,** I-jen
Pres., Control Yuan ......................................... **Chien,** Fredrick
Pres., Examination Yuan ..................................... **Hsu,** Shui-teh
Pres., Judicial Yuan ......................................... **Weng,** Yueh-sheng
Pres., Legislative Yuan ...................................... **Wang,** Jin-ping
Min. of Economic Affairs ..................................... **Lin,** Hsin-yi
Min. of Education ........................................... **Tseng,** Chih-lang
Min. of Finance ............................................ **Yen,** Ching-chang
Min. of Foreign Affairs ...................................... **Tien,** Hung-mao
Min. of Interior ............................................ **Chang,** Po-ya
Min. of Justice ............................................. **Chen,** Ting-nan
Min. of National Defense ..................................... **Wu,** Shih-wen
Min. of Transportation & Communications ....................... **Yeh,** Chu-lan
Min. Without Portfolio ....................................... **Chang,** Yu-hui
Min. Without Portfolio ....................................... **Chen,** Ching-huang
Min. Without Portfolio ....................................... **Hu,** Chien-biao

## TAIWAN—NDE (cont.)

| | |
|---|---|
| Min. Without Portfolio | **Huang,** Jung-tsun |
| Min. Without Portfolio | **Lin,** Neng-pai |
| Min. Without Portfolio | **Tsay,** Ching-yen |
| Chmn., Aborgines Commission | **Youharni,** Yisicacafute |
| Chmn., Agricultural Council | **Chen,** Hsi-huang |
| Chmn., Atomic Energy Council | **Hsia,** Teh-yu |
| Chmn., Central Election Commission | **Huang,** Hsih-cheng |
| Chmn., Consumer Protection | **Lai,** In-jaw |
| Chmn., Cultural Affairs | **Chen,** Yu-hsiu |
| Chmn., Economic Planning & Development Council | **Chen,** Po-chih |
| Chmn., Fair Trade Commission | **Chao,** Yang-ching |
| Chmn., Labor Affairs Council | **Chen,** Chu |
| Chmn., Mainland Affairs Council | **Tsai,** Ying-wen |
| Chmn., Mongolian & Tibetan Affairs Commission | **Hsu,** Cheng-kuang |
| Chmn., National Palace Museum | **Tu,** Cheng-sheng |
| Chmn., National Science Council | **Weng,** Cheng-yi |
| Chmn., National Youth Commission | **Lin,** Feng-mei |
| Chmn., Overseas Chinese Affairs Commission | **Chang,** Fu-mei |
| Chmn., Physical Education & Sports Commission | **Hsu,** Hsin-yi |
| Chmn., Public Construction Commission | **Lin,** Neng-pai |
| Chmn., Research Development & Evaluation Commission | **Lin,** Chia-cheng |
| Chmn., Veterans Affairs Commission | **Yang,** Te-chih |
| Chmn., Vocational Assistance for Retired Veterans Affairs | **Tang,** Teh-chih |
| Sec. Gen. of National Security Council | **Chiu,** I-jen |
| Dir. Gen., Budget, Accounting & Statistics | **Lin,** Chuan |
| Dir. Gen., Central Personnel Administration | **Chu,** Wu-hsien |
| Dir. Gen., Department of Health | **Lee,** Ming-liang |
| Dir. Gen., Environmental Protection Administration | **Lin,** Chun-yi |
| Dir. Gen., Government Information Office | **Chung,** Ching |
| Dir. Gen., National Police Administration | **Wang,** Chin-wang |
| Representative to the US | **Chen,** Chien-jen |
| Governor, Central Bank of China | **Perng,** Fai-nan |

## TAJIKISTAN, REPUBLIC OF

(Last updated: 3/1/2001)

| | |
|---|---|
| President | **Rahmonov,** Emomali |
| Chmn., National Assembly (upper house) | **Ubaydulloyev,** Makhmadsaid |
| Chmn., Assembly of Representatives (lower house) | **Khayrulloyev,** Sadullo |
| Prime Minister | **Oqilov,** Oqil |
| First Dep. Prime Min. | **Turajonzoda,** Hajji Akbar |
| Dep. Prime Min. | |
| Dep. Prime Min. | **Koimdodov,** Kozidavlat |
| Dep. Prime Min. | **Sharopova,** Nigina |
| Dep. Prime Min. | **Vazirov,** Zokir |
| Dep. Prime Min. | **Zuhurov,** Saidamir, *Maj. Gen.* |
| Min. of Agriculture | **Rahmatov,** Tursun |
| Min. of Culture | **Rahimov,** Abdurahim |
| Min. of Defense | **Khayrulloyev,** Sherali, *Col. Gen.* |
| Min. of Economy & Trade | **Soliyev,** Hakim |
| Min. of Education | **Rajabov,** Safarali |
| Min. of Emergency Situations | **Ziyoyev,** Mirzo |
| Min. of Energy | **Yorov,** Abdullo |
| Min. of Environmental Protection | **Shokirov,** Usmonqul |
| Min. of Finance | **Najmuddinov,** Safarali |
| Min. of Foreign Affairs | **Nazarov,** Talbak |
| Min. of Grain Products | **Uroqov,** Bekmurod |
| Min. of Health | **Ahmadov,** Alamkhon |
| Min. of Internal Affairs | **Sharipov,** Khomiddin |
| Min. of Justice | **Hamidov,** Halifabobo |
| Min. of Labor, Employment, & Social Welfare | **Musoyeva,** Rafiqa |
| Min. of Land Improvement & Water Economy | **Nazirov,** Abduqohir |
| Min. of Security | **Abdurahimov,** Khayriddin |
| Min. of Transport | **Salimov,** Abdujalol |

## TAJIKISTAN, REPUBLIC OF (cont.)

Chmn., State Committee for Administration of Affairs of State .............. **Davlatov,** Matlubkhon
Chmn., State Committee on Construction & Architecture ................... **Eshmirzoyev,** Ismat
Chmn., State Committee on Industry & Mining .......................... **Aliyev,** Ayub
Chmn., State Committee on Land Resources & Reclamation ................ **Gulmahmadov,** Davlatsho
Chmn., State Committee for Oil & Gas ................................. **Muhabbatov,** Salamsho
Chmn., State Committee on Precious Metals ........................... **Davlatov,** Muhammadjon
Chmn., State Committee for Radio & Television ........................ **Rajabov,** Ubaydullo
Sec., Security Council ............................................... **Azimov,** Amirkul
Chmn., National Bank ............................................... **Alimardonov,** Murodali
Ambassador to the US ............................................... **Alimov,** Rashid
Permanent Representative to the UN, New York ........................ **Alimov,** Rashid

## TANZANIA, UNITED REPUBLIC OF

(Last updated: 2/23/2001)

President ........................................................... **Mkapa,** Benjamin William
Vice President ...................................................... **Juma,** Omar Ali
Prime Minister ...................................................... **Sumaye,** Frederick
Pres. of Zanzibar ................................................... **Karume,** Amani Abeid
Min. of Agriculture & Food .......................................... **Kennja,** Charles
Min. of Communications & Transport ................................. **Mwandosya,** Mark
Min. of Community Development, Women's Affairs, & Children ............ **Migiro,** Asha Rose
Min. of Cooperatives & Marketing .................................... **Kahama,** George
Min. of Defense ..................................................... **Sarungi,** Philemon
Min. of Education ................................................... **Mungai,** James
Min. of Energy & Mineral Resources .................................. **Maokola-Majogo,** Edgar
Min. of Finance ..................................................... **Mramba,** Basil
Min. of Foreign Affairs & International Cooperation ..................... **Kikwete,** Jakay Mrisho
Min. of Health ...................................................... **Abdalla,** Anna
Min. of Home Affairs ................................................ **Khatib,** Mohammed Seif
Min. of Industries & Trade .......................................... **Simba,** Iddi
Min. of Justice & Constitutional Affairs ............................... **Mwapachu,** Harish Bakari
Min. of Labor, Youth Development, & Sports .......................... **Kapuya,** Juma
Min. of Lands & Human Settelement .................................. **Cheyo,** Gideon
Min. of Regional Administration & Local Government ................... **Nigwilizi,** Hassan, *Brig. Gen.*
Min. of Science, Technology, & Higher Education ....................... **Pius,** Ng'wandu
Min. of Tourism, Natural Resources, & Environment .................... **Meghji,** Zakhia
Min. of Water & Livestock Development ............................... **Lowassa,** Edward
Min. of Works ...................................................... **Magufuli,** John
Min. of State, President's Office ..................................... **Masilingi,** Wilson
Min. of State for Planning, President's Office .......................... **Malocho,** Nassoro
Min. of State, Prime Minister's Office ................................ **Mohammed,** Ali Ameir
Min. of State, Prime Minister's Office ................................ **Mkangaa,** Juma
Min. of State, Vice President's Office ................................. **Lowassa,** Edward
Governor, Central Bank .............................................. **Ballali,** Daudi
Ambassador to the US ............................................... **Nyang'anyi,** Mustafa Salim
Permanent Representative to the UN, New York ........................ **Mwakawago,** Daudi Ngelautwa

## THAILAND, KINGDOM OF

(Last updated: 2/23/2001)

King ............................................................... **PHUMIPHON Adunyadet**
Prime Minister ..................................................... **THAKSIN Chinnawat**
Dep. Prime Min. .................................................... **CHAWALIT Yongchaiyut,** *Gen. (Ret.)*
Dep. Prime Min. .................................................... **DET Bunlong**
Dep. Prime Min. .................................................... **PHITHAK Intharawithayanan**
Dep. Prime Min. .................................................... **PONGPHON Adireksan**
Dep. Prime Min. .................................................... **SUWIT Khunkitti**
Min. Attached to Office of Prime Min. ................................ **CHATURON Chaisaeng**
Min. Attached to Office of Prime Min. ................................ **CHUCHIP Hansawat**
Min. Attached to Office of Prime Min. ................................ **KRASAE Chanawong**
Min. Attached to Office of Prime Min. ................................ **SOMSAK Thepsuthin**

## THAILAND, KINGDOM OF (cont.)

| | |
|---|---|
| Min. Attached to Office of Prime Min. | THAMMARAK Isarangkun na Ayutthaya, *Gen. (Ret.)* |
| Min. of Agriculture & Cooperatives | CHUCHIP Hansawat |
| Min. of Commerce | ADISAI Photharamik |
| Min. of Communications & Transportation | WANMUHAMATNO Matha |
| Min. of Defense | CHAWALIT Yongchaiyut, *Gen. (Ret.)* |
| Min. of Education | KASEM Watthanachai |
| Min. of Finance | SOMKHIT Chatusiphithak |
| Min. of Foreign Affairs | SURAKIAT Sathianthai |
| Min. of Industry | SURIYA Chungrungruangkit |
| Min. of Interior | PURACHAI Piamsombun, *Capt. (Ret.)* |
| Min. of Justice | PHONGTHEP Thepkanchana |
| Min. of Labor & Social Welfare | DET Bunlong |
| Min. of Public Health | SUDARAT Keyuraphan |
| Min. of Science, Technology, & Environment | SONTHAYA Khunplum |
| Min. of State University Bureau | SUTHAM Saengprathum |
| Dep. Min. of Agriculture & Cooperatives | PRAPHAT Panyachatrak |
| Dep. Min. of Agriculture & Cooperatives | NATHI Khlipthong |
| Dep. Min. of Commerce | SUWAN Walaisathian |
| Dep. Min. of Communications & Transportation | PRACHA Malinon |
| Dep. Min. of Communications & Transportation | PHONGSAKON Laohawichian |
| Dep. Min. of Defense | YUTTHASAK Sasiprapha, *Gen. (Ret.)* |
| Dep. Min. of Education | CHALONG Khrutkhunthot |
| Dep. Min. of Finance | WARATHEP Rattanakon |
| Dep. Min. of Finance | SUCHAT Chaowisit, *Capt. (Ret.)* |
| Dep. Min. of Industry | PHICHET Sathirachawan |
| Dep. Min. of Interior | SORA-AT Klinprathum |
| Dep. Min. of Interior | SOMBAT Uthaisang |
| Dep. Min. of Labor & Social Welfare | LADAWAN Wongsiwong |
| Dep. Min. of Public Health | SURAPHONG Supwongli |
| Governor, Central Bank | CHATUMONGKHON Sonakun |
| Ambassador to the US | TEJ Bunnag |
| Permanent Representative to the UN, New York | ATSADA Chaiyanam, |

## TOGO (TOGOLESE REPUBLIC)

(Last updated: 11/17/2000)

| | |
|---|---|
| President | **Eyadema,** Gnassingbe, *Gen.* |
| Prime Minister | **Kodjo,** Agbeyome |
| Min. of Agriculture, Animal Breeding, & Fisheries | **Bamenante,** Komikpine |
| Min. of Communication & Civic Education | **Bawa,** Semedo |
| Min. of Democracy & Rule of Law Promotion | **Olympio,** Harry Octavian |
| Min. of Economy & Finance | **Lalle,** Takpandja |
| Min. of Environment & Forest Resources | **Adade,** Koffi |
| Min. of Foreign Affairs & Cooperation | **Panou,** Kaffi |
| Min. of Health | **Agba,** Kondi Charles |
| Min. of Industry & the Dev. of the Free Trade Zone | **Osseyi,** Rudolph Kossivi |
| Min. of Interior & Security | **Wala,** Sizing Akawilou |
| Min. of Justice & Human Rights and Keeper of the Seals | **Memene,** Seyi, *Gen.* |
| Min. of Labor & Civil Service | **Tozoun,** Kokou Biossey |
| Min. of Mines, Energy, Posts & Telecommunications | **Andjo,** Tchamdja |
| Min. of National Defense | **Tidjani,** Assani, *Gen.* |
| Min. of National Education & Research | **Sama,** Koffi |
| Min. of Planning & Territorial Dev. | **Pre,** Simfe Tchaeou |
| Min. of Relations with the National Assembly | **Amoudokpo,** Komi Dotse |
| Min. of Tech. Education, Prof. Training & Cottage Industry | **Kodjo,** Maurille |
| Min. of Tourism & Leisure | **Assimadiou,** Kossi |
| Min. of Town Planning, & Housing | **Agboli,** Hope |
| Min. of Transport & Water Resources | **Dramani,** Dama |
| Min. of Women's Affairs & Social Welfare | **Aissah,** Irene Ashira |
| Min. of Youth, Sports & Culture | **Klassou,** Komi |
| Min. Del. at the Prime Minister's Office in charge of Relations with Parliament and the European Union | **Devo,** Hodeminou |
| Sec. of State at the Prime Min.'s Office in charge of the Private Sector | **Aguigah,** Angela |

## TOGO (TOGOLESE REPUBLIC) (cont.)

Sec. of State at the Prime Ministry in Charge of Planning & Territorial Dev. .... **Ati,** Atcha Tcha-Gouni
Sec. of State at the Ministry of Finance in Charge of Finance & Budget ....... **Guenou,** Assiba Amoussou
Dir., Central Bank ................................................. **Aho,** Yao Messan
Ambassador to the US ............................................. **Bodjona,** Akoussoulelou
Permanent Representative to the UN, New York ...................... **Kpotstra,** Roland Yao

## TONGA, KINGDOM OF

(Last updated: 2/5/2001)

King ......................................................... **Tupou,** IV, Taufa'ahau
Prime Minister ............................................... **Ulukalala,** Lavaka ata, *Prince*
Dep. Prime Min. .............................................. **Topou,** Tevita
Min. of Agriculture .......................................... **Ulukalala,** Lavaka ata, *Prince*
Min. of Civil Aviation ....................................... **Ulukalala,** Lavaka ata, *Prince*
Min. of Defense .............................................. **Ulukalala,** Lavaka ata, *Prince*
Min. of Education ............................................ **Fakafanua,** Tutoatasi
Min. of Finance .............................................. **Utoikamanu,** Siosiua
Min. of Fisheries ............................................ **Ulukalala,** Lavaka ata, *Prince*
Min. of Foreign Affairs ...................................... **Ulukalala,** Lavaka ata, *Prince*
Min. of Forestry ............................................. **Ulukalala,** Lavaka ata, *Prince*
Min. of Health ............................................... **Tangi,** Vailami, *Dr.*
Min. of Justice .............................................. **Tupou,** Tevita
Min. of Labor, Commerce, Industries, & Tourism ............... **Paunga,** Hulioo Tukikolongahau, *Dr.*
Min. of Lands, Survey, & Natural Resources ................... **Fielakepa**
Min. of Marine Affairs ....................................... **Ulukalala,** Lavaka ata, *Prince*
Min. of Police & Prisons ..................................... **Edwards,** Clive William
Min. of Public Works & Disaster Relief Actitivies ............ **Cocker,** Cecil James
Min. of Telecommunication .................................... **Ulukalala,** Lavaka ata, *Prince*
Attorney General ............................................. **Tupou,** Tevita
Governor (Acting), National Reserve Bank ..................... **Utoikamanu,** Siosiua
Ambassador to the US ......................................... **Fineanganofo,** Akosita
Permanent Representative to the UN, New York ................. **Tupou,** Sonatane Tua Taumoepeau

## TRINIDAD AND TOBAGO, REPUBLIC OF

(Last updated: 2/26/2001)

President .................................................... **Robinson,** Arthur Napoleon Raymond
Prime Minister .............................................. **Panday,** Basdeo
Min. of Agriculture, Lands, & Marine Resources ..............
Min. of Communications & Information Technology .............. **Maraj,** Ralph
Min. of Community Development ................................ **Rafeeq,** Hamza, *Dr.*
Min. of Education ........................................... **Persad-Bissessar,** Kamal
Min. of Energy .............................................. **Gillette,** Lindsay
Min. of Enterprise Development .............................. **Assam,** Mervyn
Min. of Environment ......................................... **Nanan,** Adesh
Min. of Finance ............................................. **Yetming,** Gerald
Min. of Food Production & Marine Affairs .................... **Sudama,** Trevor
Min. of Foreign Affairs ..................................... **Assam,** Mervyn
Min. of Health .............................................. **Khan, Rafeeq,** Hamza
Min. of Housing & Settlement ................................ **Baksh,** Sadiq
Min. of Human Development, Youth, & Culture ................. **Singh,** Ganga
Min. of Infrastructure Development .......................... **John,** Carlos
Min. of Labor & Cooperatives ................................ **Partap,** Harry
Min. of Legal Affairs ....................................... **Maharaj,** Ramesh
Min. of Local Government .................................... **Singh,** Dhanraj
Min. of National Security ................................... **Panday,** Basdeo
Min. of Planning & Development .............................. **Humphrey,** John
Min. of Public Administration ............................... **Wade,** Mark
Min. of Public Utilities ....................................
Min. of Social & Community Development ...................... **Ramsaran,** Manohar
Min. of Sports, Youth Affairs, Culture, & Human Resources ... **Ramsarran,** Manohar
Min. of Tobago Affairs ...................................... **Job,** Morgan

## TRINIDAD AND TOBAGO, REPUBLIC OF (cont.)

Min. of Tourism ....................................................... **Assam,** Mervyn
Min. of Transportation ............................................... **John,** Jearlean
Attorney General ...................................................... **Maharaj,** Ramesh
Governor, Central Bank .............................................. **Dookeran,** Winston
Ambassador to the US ............................................... **Arneaud,** Michael
Permanent Representative to the UN, New York ......................... **McKenzie,** George Winston

## TUNISIA, REPUBLIC OF

(Last updated: 3/27/2001)

President ............................................................. **Ben Ali,** Zine El Abidine
Prime Minister ....................................................... **Ghannouchi,** Mohamed
Min. of Agriculture .................................................. **Rabah,** Sadok
Min. of Communications .............................................. **Friaa,** Ahmed
Min. of Culture ...................................................... **Hermassi,** Abdelbaki
Min. of Economic Development ....................................... **Saddam,** Abdellatif
Min. of Education .................................................... **Rouissi,** Moncer
Min. of Environment & Land Development .............................. **Nabli,** Mohamed
Min. of Equipment & Housing ......................................... **Belaid,** Slaheddine
Min. of Finance ...................................................... **Baccar,** Taoufik
Min. of Foreign Affairs .............................................. **Ben Yahia,** Habib
Min. of Higher Education ............................................. **Chaabane,** Sadok
Min. of Human Rights, Communications, & Relations with the Chamber
of Deputies .......................................................... **Maqoui,** Slaheddine
Min. of Industry ..................................................... **Ben Abdallah,** Moncef
Min. of Interior ..................................................... **Kaabi,** Abdallah
Min. of International Coop. & Foreign Investments .................... **Merdassi,** Fethi
Min. of Justice ...................................................... **Tekkari,** Bechir
Min. of National Defense ............................................. **Jazi,** Dali
Min. of the Presidential Office ...................................... **Ouederni,** Ahmen Eyadh
Min. of Public Health ................................................ **Zbidi,** Abdelkarim
Min. of Religious Affairs ............................................ **Jeribi,** Jelloul
Min. of Social Affairs ............................................... **M'henni,** Hedi
Min. of State ........................................................ **Ben Dhia,** Abdelaziz
Min. for State Property & Property Affairs ........................... **Grira,** Ridha
Min. of Tourism, Entertainment, & Handicrafts ....................... **Zenaidi,** Mondher
Min. of Trade ........................................................ **Sioud,** Taher
Min. of Transport .................................................... **Chouk,** Hassine
Min. of Vocational Training & Employment ............................ **Kefi,** Faiza
Min. of Women's & Fmaily Affairs ..................................... **Zarrouk,** Naziha
Min. of Youth, Childhood, & Sport .................................... **Zouari,** Abderrahim
Min. Delegate to the Prime Minister in Charge of Human
Rights, Communication & Relations With the House of Deputies ............ **Hindaoui,** Afif
Sec. Gen., of the Government ......................................... **Kecyhiche,** Mohamed Rachid
Governor, Central Bank .............................................. **Daous,** Mohamed
Ambassador to the US ............................................... **Atallah,** Hatem
Permanent Representative to the UN, New York ......................... **Mustapha,** Said Ben

## TURKEY, REPUBLIC OF

(Last updated: 3/5/2001)

President ............................................................. **Sezer,** Ahmed Necdet
Prime Minister ....................................................... **Ecevit,** Bulent
Dep. Prime Min. ...................................................... **Bahceli,** Devlet
Dep. Prime Min. ...................................................... **Ozkan,** Husamettin
Dep. Prime Min. ...................................................... **Yilmaz,** Mesut
Min. of State ........................................................ **Bahceli,** Devlet
Min. of State ........................................................ **Bal,** Faruk
Min. of State ........................................................ **Cay,** Abdulhaluk
Min. of State ........................................................ **Dervis,** Kemal
Min. of State ........................................................ **Gaydali,** Edip Safter
Min. of State ........................................................ **Gemici,** Hasan

## TURKEY, REPUBLIC OF (cont.)

| | |
|---|---|
| Min. of State | **Gurel,** Sukru Sina |
| Min. of State | **Kececiler,** Mehmet |
| Min. of State | **Mirzaoglu,** Ramazan |
| Min. of State | **Onal,** Recep |
| Min. of State | **Ozkan,** Husamettin |
| Min. of State | **Toskay,** Tunca |
| Min. of State | **Tumen,** Aydin |
| Min. of State | **Unlu,** Fikret |
| Min. of State | **Usenmez,** Suayip |
| Min. of State | **Yilmaz,** Mustafa |
| Min. of State | **Yalova,** Yuksel |
| Min. of State | **Yucelen,** Rustu Kazim |
| Min. of Agriculture & Village Affairs | **Gokalp,** Husnu Yusuf |
| Min. of Culture | **Talay,** Istemihan |
| Min. of Energy & National Resources | **Ersumer,** Cumhur |
| Min. of Environment | **Aytekin,** Fevzi |
| Min. of Finance | **Oral,** Sumer |
| Min. of Foreign Affairs | **Cem,** Ismail |
| Min. of Forestry | **Cagan,** Nami |
| Min. of Health | **Durmus,** Osman |
| Min. of Industry & Trade | **Tanrikulu,** Ahmet Kenan |
| Min. of Interior | **Tantan,** Saadettin |
| Min. of Justice | **Turk,** Hikmet Sami |
| Min. of Labor & Social Security | **Okuyan,** Yasar |
| Min. of National Defense | **Cakmakoglu,** Sabahattin |
| Min. of National Education | **Bostancioglu,** Metin |
| Min. of Public Works & Housing | **Aydin,** Koray |
| Min. of Tourism | **Mumcu,** Erkan |
| Min. of Transportation | **Oksuz,** Enis |
| Governor, Central Bank | **Serdengecti,** Sureyya |
| Ambassador to the US | **Ilkin,** Baki |
| Permanent Representative to the UN, New York | **Pamir,** Umit |

## TURKMENISTAN

(Last updated: 4/4/2001)

*According to the Turkmen constitution, the President serves as de facto head of the cabinet.*

| | |
|---|---|
| President | **Niyazov,** Saparmurat |
| Chmn., Supreme Council (Mejlis) | **Muradov,** Sakhat |
| Dep. Chmn., Cabinet of Ministers (Agriculture, Business Development, & Light Industry) | **Saparov,** Rejep |
| Dep. Chmn., Cabinet of Ministers (Banking & Currency Affairs) | **Gandymov,** Seitbay |
| Dep. Chmn., Cabinet of Ministers (Communications & Transport) | **Kerkawov,** Rovshen |
| Dep. Chmn., Cabinet of Ministers (Construction) | **Hudayguliyev,** Mukhammetnazar |
| Dep. Chmn., Cabinet of Ministers (Culture & Mass Media) | **Aydogdiyev,** Orazgeldy |
| Dep. Chmn., Cabinet of Ministers (Defense) | **Sarjayev,** Batyr |
| Dep. Chmn., Cabinet of Ministers (Economics & Finance) | **Begmyradov,** Orazmut |
| Dep. Chmn., Cabinet of Ministers (Energy) | **Gurbanmuradov,** Yolly |
| Dep. Chmn., Cabinet of Ministers (Healthcare) | **Berdimukhamedov,** Gurbanguly |
| Dep. Chmn., Cabinet of Ministers (Textiles & Foreign Trade) | **Geoklenova,** Jemal |
| Min. of Agriculture | **Saparov,** Rejep |
| Min. of Culture | **Aydogdiyev,** Orazgeldy |
| Min. of Defense | **Sarjayev,** Batyr |
| Min. of Economics & Finance | **Begmyradov,** Orazmut |
| Min. of Education | **Ashirov,** Annagurban |
| Min. of Energy & Industry | **Atayev,** Amangeldy |
| Min. of Environmental Protection | **Rajapov,** Matkarim |
| Min. of Foreign Affairs | **Berdiyev,** Batyr |
| Min. of Health & Medical Industry | **Berdimukhamedov,** Gurbanguly |
| Min. of Industry & Construction Materials | **Hudayguliyev,** Mukhammetnazar |
| Min. of Internal Affairs | **Berdiyev,** Poran, *Maj. Gen.* |
| Min. of Justice | **Kasimov,** Gurban |
| Min. of Oil & Gas Industry & Mineral Resources | **Nazarov,** Gurban |

## TURKMENISTAN (cont.)

Min. of Trade & Resources .............................................. **Aidogdyev,** Dortguly
Min. of Transportation & Communication ............................... **Halykov,** Hudayguly
Min. of Water Resources ............................................... **Tekebayev,** Altybay
Chmn., Central Bank ................................................... **Gandymov,** Seitbay
Chmn., National Committee for Security (KNB) ......................... **Nazarov,** Muhamet, *Lt. Gen.*
Ambassador to the US .................................................. **Orazov,** Mered
Permanent Representative to the UN, New York ......................... **Atayeva,** Aksoltan

## TUVALU

(Last updated: 2/2/2001)

Governor General ...................................................... **Puapua,** Tomasi, *Sir, M.D.*
Prime Minister (Acting) ............................................... **Tuilimu,** Lagitupu (of Nanumea)
Dep. Prime Min. .......................................................
Min. for Education, Sports, & Culture ................................. **Esekia,** Teagai
Min. for Finance & Economic Planning .................................. **Tuilimu,** Lagitupu (of Nanumea)
Min. for Foreign Affairs .............................................. **Ionatana,** Ionatana
Min. for Health, Women's, & Community Affairs ........................ **Esekia,** Teagai
Min. for Internal Affairs & Rural & Urban Development ................. **Luka,** Faimalaga (of Nukufetau)
Min. for Natural Resources & Environment ............................. **Luka,** Faimalaga (of Nukufetau)
Min. for Tourism, Trade, & Commerce .................................. **Tuilimu,** Lagitupu (of Nanumea)
Min. for Works, Energy, & Communications ............................. **Teo,** Samuelu (of Niutao)
Attorney General ...................................................... **Teo,** Teleti
Speaker of the House ..................................................

## UGANDA, REPUBLIC OF

(Last updated: 12/21/2000)

President ............................................................. **Museveni,** Yoweri Kaguta
Vice President ........................................................ **Kazibwe,** Wandira Specioza, *Dr.*
Prime Minister ........................................................ **Nsibambi,** Apollo
First Dep. Prime Min. ................................................. **Kategaya,** Eriya
Second Dep. Prime Min. ............................................... **Ali,** Moses, *Brig. Gen.*
Third Dep. Prime Min. ................................................. **Butime,** Tom, *Maj.*
Min. of Agriculture, Animal Industry, & Fisheries .................... **Mugerwa,** Kisamba
Min. in Charge of the Presidency ..................................... **Rugunda,** Ruhakana
Min. of Defense ....................................................... **Museveni,** Yoweri Kaguta
Min. of Disaster Preparedness & Refugees ............................. **Butiime,** Tom, *Maj.*
Min. of Economic Monitoring .......................................... **Ruhemba,** Kweronda
Min. of Education & Sports ............................................ **Kdihu,** Makubuya
Min. of Energy & Mineral Development ................................. **Bbumba,** Syda
Min. of Ethics & Integrity ............................................ **Matembe,** Miriam
Min. of Finance, Planning, & Economic Development .................... **Ssendawula,** Gerald
Min. of Foreign Affairs ............................................... **Kategaya,** Eriya
Min. of Gender, Labor & Social Development ........................... **Mukwaya,** Janati B.
Min. of Health ....................................................... **Kiyonga,** Crispus W. C. B., *Dr.*
Min. of Information ................................................... **Basoga,** Nsadhu
Min. of Internal Affairs .............................................. **Ali,** Moses, *Brig. Gen.*
Min. of Justice & Constitutional Affairs .............................. **Mayanja-Nkangi,** Joshua S.
Min. of Local Govt. ................................................... **Bidandi,** Sali
Min. in the Office of the Vice President .............................. **Okwir,** Betty
Min. of Parliamentary Affairs ......................................... **Kadaga,** Rebecca
Min. of Public Service & Labor ........................................ **Musheja,** Amanya
Min. of Public Works, Housing, & Communications ..................... **Nasasira,** John
Min. of Security ...................................................... **Muruli,** Wilson Mukasa
Min. of Tourism, Trade, & Industry ................................... **Rugumayo,** Edward
Min. of Water, Lands, & Environment .................................. **Kajura,** Muganwa Henry
Min. of State for Agriculture ......................................... **Sebunya,** Kibirige, *Dr.*
Min. of State for Animal Industry ..................................... **Byaruhanga,** Fabius
Min. of State for Communication ...................................... **Kafabusa,** Werike
Min. of State for Defense ............................................. **Kavuma,** Stephen
Min. of State for Disaster Preparedness & Refugees ................... **Kuka,** Jane Frances

## UGANDA, REPUBLIC OF (cont.)

Min. of State for Energy & Mineral Development .......................... **Kiryapayo,** Thomas
Min. of State for Environment ............................................. **Muyingo,** Kezimbira
Min. of State for Fisheries ................................................ **Mukisa,** Fred
Min. of State for Gender & Cultural Affairs .............................. **Nyanzi,** Vincent
Min. of State for General Health ......................................... **Omeda,** Max
Min. of State for Higher Education & Sports .............................. **Aketch,** Betty
Min. of State for Housing ................................................ **Babu,** Francis, *Capt.*
Min. of State for Industry & Technology .................................. **Rwendeire,** Abel, *Dr.*
Min. of State for Labor & Industrial Relations ........................... **Mateke,** Philemon
Min. of State for Lands .................................................. **Isoke,** Baguma
Min. of State for Local Government ....................................... **Byaruhanga,** Philip, *Dr.*
Min. of State for Northern Uganda ....................................... **Omwony,** Ojok
Min. of State for Planning & Investment ..................................
Min. of State for Primary Health Care .................................... **Wabudeya,** Beatrice
Min. of State for Privatization .......................................... **Tumubweine,** Manzi
Min. of State for Public Service ......................................... **Mavenjina,** C.
Min. of State for Regional Cooperation ................................... **Mbabazi,** Amama
Min. of State for Security ............................................... **Mukasa,** Muruli
Min. of State for Tourism, Wildlife, & Antiquities ....................... **Akaki,** Jovina Ayuma
Min. of State for Transport .............................................. **Awuzu,** Andruale
Min. of State for Water .................................................. **Othieno,** Akiika
Min. of State for Youth & Child Affairs .................................. **Nayiga,** Florence
Min. of State in Charge of Karamoja ..................................... **Lokeris,** Peter Aparite
Min. of State in Charge of Luwero ....................................... **Nankabirwa,** Ruth
Min. of State in Charge of Northern Uganda & Reconstruction ..............
Attorney General ........................................................ **Katureebe,** Balthazar Bart Magunda
Governor, Bank of Uganda ................................................ **Mutebile,** Emmanuel Tumusiime
Ambassador to the US .................................................... **Ssempala,** Edith Grace
Permanent Representative to the UN, New York ............................ **Kiwanuka,** Matia Semakula Mulumba

## UKRAINE

(Last updated: 3/27/2001)

President ................................................................ **Kuchma,** Leonid
Chmn., Rada (parliament) ................................................ **Plyushch,** Ivan
Prime Minister .......................................................... **Yushchenko,** Viktor
First Dep. Prime Min. ................................................... **Yekhanurov,** Yuriy
Dep. Prime Min. for Agroindustrial Complex ..............................
Dep. Prime Min. for Industrial Policy ................................... **Dubyna,** Oleh
Dep. Prime Min. for Humanitarian Affairs ................................ **Zhulinskiy,** Mykola
Min. of Agriculture ..................................................... **Kyrylenko,** Ivan
Min. of Culture & Arts .................................................. **Stupka,** Bohdan
Min. of Defense ......................................................... **Kuzmuk,** Oleksandr, *Gen.*
Min. of Ecology & Natural Resources ..................................... **Zayets,** Ivan
Min. of Economy ......................................................... **Rohovyy,** Vasyl
Min. of Education & Science ............................................. **Kremen,** Vasyl
Min. of Emergency Situations ............................................ **Durdynets,** Vasyl
Min. of Finance ......................................................... **Mityukov,** Ihor
Min. of Foreign Affairs ................................................. **Zlenko,** Anatoliy
Min. of Fuel & Energy ................................................... **Stashevskyy,** Stanislav
Min. of Health .......................................................... **Moskalenko,** Vitaliy
Min. of Internal Affairs ................................................ **Smirnov,** Yuriy
Min. of Justice ......................................................... **Stanik,** Syuzanna
Min. of Labor & Social Policy ........................................... **Sakhan,** Ivan
Min. of Transportation .................................................. **Kostyuchenko,** Leonid
Sec. of the Government .................................................. **Lysytsky,** Viktor
Sec., National Security & Defense Council ............................... **Marchuk,** Yevhen
Chief, Presidential Administration ...................................... **Lytvyn,** Volodymyr
Chmn., National Bank .................................................... **Stelmakh,** Volodymyr
Chmn., Security Service ................................................. **Radchenko,** Oleksandr
Chmn., State Property Fund .............................................. **Bondar,** Oleksandr
Procurator General ...................................................... **Potybenko,** Mykhaylo
Ambassador to the US .................................................... **Hryshchenko,** Konstantin
Permanent Representative to the UN, New York ............................

## UNITED ARAB EMIRATES

(Last updated: 8/11/2000)

President .................................................... **Nuhayyan, ZAYID,** bin Sultan Al
Vice President ............................................... **Maktum, MAKTUM,** bin Rashid al-
Prime Minister .............................................. **Maktum, MAKTUM,** bin Rashid al-
Dep. Prime Min. ............................................ **Nuhayyan, SULTAN,** bin Zayid Al
Min. of Agriculture & Fisheries ............................ **Raqabani,** Said Muhammad al-
Min. of Communications .................................... **Tayir,** Ahmad bin Humayd al-
Min. of Defense ............................................. **Maktum, MUHAMMAD,** bin Rashid al-
Min. of Economy & Commerce .............................. **Qasimi, FAHIM,** bin Sultan al-
Min. of Education & Youth .................................. **Sharhan,** Ali Abd al-Aziz al-, *Dr.*
Min. of Electricity & Water ................................. **Uways,** Humayd bin Nasir al-
Min. of Finance & Industry ................................. **Maktum, HAMDAN,** bin Rashid al-
Min. of Foreign Affairs ..................................... **Nuaymi, RASHID,** bin Abdallah al-
Min. of Health ............................................. **Madfa,** Hamad bin Abd al-Rahman al-
Min. of Higher Education & Scientific Research ............ **Nuhayyan, NUHAYYAN,** bin Mubarak Al
Min. of Information & Culture .............................. **Nuhayyan, ABDALLAH,** bin Zayid Al
Min. of Interior ........................................... **Badi,** Muhammad Said al-, *Lt. Gen.*
Min. of Justice & Islamic Affairs & Awqaf ................. **Dhahiri,** Muhammad Nakhira al-
Min. of Labor & Social Affairs ............................. **Tayir,** Matar bin Humayd al-
Min. of Petroleum & Mineral Resources .................... **Nasiri,** Ubayd Saif al-
Min. of Planning ........................................... **Mualla,** Humayd bin Ahmad al-
Min. of Public Works & Housing ........................... **Raqad,** Raqad bin Salim al-
Min. of State for Cabinet Affairs .......................... **Ghayth,** Said Khalfan al-
Min. of State for Financial & Industrial Affairs ........... **Kharbash,** Muhammad Khalfan bin, *Dr.*
Min. of State for Foreign Affairs .......................... **Nuhayyan, HAMDAN,** bin Zayid Al
Min. of State for Supreme Council Affairs ................. **Nuaymi, MAJID,** bin Said al-
Governor, Central Bank .................................... **Suwaydi,** Sultan bin Nasir al-
Ambassador to the US ..................................... **Dhahiri,** Asri Said Ahmad al-
Permanent Representative to the UN, New York ........... **Samhan,** Muhammad Jasim

## UNITED KINGDOM OF GREAT BRITAIN AND NORTHERN IRELAND

(Last updated: 2/2/2001)

Queen ...................................................... **Elizabeth II**
Prime Minister & First Lord of the Treasury ............... **Blair,** Tony
Dep Prime Min. ............................................ **Prescott,** John
Chancellor of the Exchequer ............................... **Brown,** Gordon
Sec. of State for Defense .................................. **Hoon,** Geoffrey
Sec. of State for Education & Employment ................. **Blunkett,** David
Sec. of State for the Environment, Transport & The Regions ... **Prescott,** John
Sec. of State for Foreign & Commonwealth Affairs ......... **Cook,** Robin
Sec. of State for Health ................................... **Milburn,** Alan
Sec. of State for the Home Department ..................... **Straw,** Jack
Sec. of State for National Heritage ........................ **Smith,** Chris
Sec. of State for Northern Ireland ......................... **Reid,** John, *Dr.*
Sec. of State for Scotland ................................. **Reid,** John
Sec. of State for Social Security .......................... **Darling,** Alistair
Sec. of State for Trade & Industry & President of The Board of Trade ........ **Byers,** Stephen
Sec. of State for Wales .................................... **Murphy,** Paul
Min. of Agriculture, Fisheries, & Food .................... **Brown,** Nick
Min. for the Cabinet Office ................................ **Mowlam,** Marjorie, *Dr.*
Min. of Overseas Development Assistance ................... **Short,** Clare
Chief Secretary to the Treasury ........................... **Smith,** Andrew
Lord Chancellor ........................................... **Irvine,** *Lord*
Chancellor of the Duchy of Lancaster ...................... **Mowlam,** Marjorie, *Dr.*
Lord Privy Seal, Leader of the House of Lords, and Minister for Women ....... **Jay,** *Baroness*
Lord Pres. of the Council & Leader of the House of Commons .............. **Beckett,** Margaret
Chief Whip ................................................ **Taylor,** Ann
Governor, Bank of England ................................ **George,** Edward
Ambassador to the US ..................................... **Meyer,** Christopher
Permanent Representative to the UN, New York ........... **Greenstock,** Jeremy

## URUGUAY, ORIENTAL REPUBLIC OF

(Last updated: 4/9/2001)

| | |
|---|---|
| President | **Batlle,** Jorge |
| Vice President | **Hierro,** Luis |
| Min. of Agriculture & Fishing | **Gonzalez,** Gonzalo |
| Min. of Economy & Finance | **Bension,** Alberto |
| Min. of Education & Culture | **Mercader,** Antonio |
| Min. of Foreign Affairs | **Opertti,** Didier |
| Min. of Health | **Ameglio,** Horacio Fernandez |
| Min. of Housing & Environment | **Cat,** Carlos |
| Min. of Industry, Energy, & Mines | **Abreu,** Sergio |
| Min. of Interior | **Stirling,** Guillermo |
| Min. of Labor & Social Welfare | **Alonso,** Alvaro |
| Min. of National Defense | **Brezzo Pardes,** Luis |
| Min. of Public Health | **Fernandez,** Horacio |
| Min. of Sports & Youth | **Trobo,** Jaime |
| Min. of Tourism | **Varela,** Alfonso |
| Min. of Transportation & Public Works | **Caceres,** Lucio |
| President, Central Bank | **Rodriguez,** Batlle, Cesar |
| Ambassador to the US | **Fernandez,** Faingold, Hugo |
| Permanent Representative to the UN, New York | **Paolillo,** Felipe H. |

## UZBEKISTAN, REPUBLIC OF

(Last updated: 2/27/2001)

| | |
|---|---|
| President | **Karimov,** Islom |
| Chmn., Supreme Assembly (Oliy Majlis) | **Halilov,** Erkin |
| Prime Minister | **Sultonov,** Otkir |
| First Dep. Prime Min. | **Azimov,** Rustam |
| Dep. Prime Min. | **Ghulomova,** Dilbar |
| Dep. Prime Min. | **Isayev,** Anatoliy |
| Dep. Prime Min. | **Ismailov,** Uktam |
| Dep. Prime Min. | **Karamatov,** Hamidulla |
| Dep. Prime Min. | **Kholtoyev,** Torup |
| Dep. Prime Min. | **Mukhiddinov,** Azimjan |
| Dep. Prime Min. | **Otayev,** Valeriy |
| Dep. Prime Min. | **Usmonov,** Mirabror |
| Dep. Prime Min. | **Yunosov,** Rustam |
| Min. of Agriculture & Water Resources | **Kholtoyev,** Torup |
| Min. of Communications | **Abdullaev,** Fahtullah |
| Min. of Culture | **Jurayev,** Hairulla |
| Min. of Defense | **Ghulomov,** Kodir |
| Min. of Education | **Jorayev,** Risboy |
| Min. of Emergency Situations | **Kasymov,** Bahodir, *Maj. Gen.* |
| Min. of Energy & Fuel | **Atayev,** Valery |
| Min. of Finance | **Normuradov,** Mamarizo |
| Min. of Foreign Affairs | **Kamilov,** Abdulaziz |
| Min. of Foreign Economic Relations | **Ghaniyev,** Elyor |
| Min. of Health | **Nazirov,** Feruz |
| Min. of Higher & Secondary Specialized Education | **Ghulomov,** Saidakhror |
| Min. of Internal Affairs | **Almatov,** Zokirjon |
| Min. of Justice | **Polvon-Zoda,** Abdusamad |
| Min. of Labor & Social Security | **Abidov,** Okiljon |
| Min. of Macroeconomics & Statistics | **Azimov,** Rustam |
| Sec., National Security Council | **Rakhmonkulov,** Mirakbar |
| Chmn., State Bank | **Mullajanov,** Fayzulla |
| Chmn., State Committee for Customs | **Oripov,** Said-Azim |
| Chmn., State Taxation Committee | **Khojayev,** Botir |
| Chmn., National Bank for Foreign Economic Activity | **Mirkhojaev,** Zanutdin |
| Chmn., National Security Service (SNB) | **Inoyatov,** Rustam, *Col. Gen.* |
| Ambassador to the US | **Safayev,** Sadiq |
| Permanent Representative to the UN, New York | **Vohidov,** Alisher |

## VANUATU, REPUBLIC OF

(Last updated: 4/20/2001)

President . . . . . . . . . . . . . . . . . . . . . . . . . . . . . . . . . . . . . . . . . . . . . . . . . . . . . . . **Bani,** John, Father
Prime Minister . . . . . . . . . . . . . . . . . . . . . . . . . . . . . . . . . . . . . . . . . . . . . . . . **Natapei,** Edward
Dep. Prime Min. . . . . . . . . . . . . . . . . . . . . . . . . . . . . . . . . . . . . . . . . . . . . . . . **Vohor,** Serge
Min. of Agriculture, Forestry, & Fisheries . . . . . . . . . . . . . . . . . . . . . . . . . . . .
Min. of the Comprehensive Reform Program . . . . . . . . . . . . . . . . . . . . . . . . .
Min. of Education . . . . . . . . . . . . . . . . . . . . . . . . . . . . . . . . . . . . . . . . . . . . . .
Min. of Finance . . . . . . . . . . . . . . . . . . . . . . . . . . . . . . . . . . . . . . . . . **Bomal Carlo,** Joe
Min. of Foreign Affairs . . . . . . . . . . . . . . . . . . . . . . . . . . . . . . . . . . . . . . . . . . .
Min. of Health . . . . . . . . . . . . . . . . . . . . . . . . . . . . . . . . . . . . . . . . . . . . . . . . .
Min. of Infrastructure & Public Utilities . . . . . . . . . . . . . . . . . . . . . . . . . . . . .
Min. of Internal Affairs . . . . . . . . . . . . . . . . . . . . . . . . . . . . . . . . . . . . . . . . . .
Min. of Lands & Mineral Resources . . . . . . . . . . . . . . . . . . . . . . . . **Molisa,** Sela
Min. of Ni-Vanuatu Business Development . . . . . . . . . . . . . . . . . . . . . . . . . .
Min. of Trade Development . . . . . . . . . . . . . . . . . . . . . . . . . . . . . . . . . **Vohor,** Serge
Min. of Youth & Sports . . . . . . . . . . . . . . . . . . . . . . . . . . . . . . . . . . . . . . . . . .
Permanent Representative to the UN, New York (Acting) . . . . . . . . . . . . . . . . . **Carlot,** Alfred

## VENEZUELA, REPUBLIC OF

(Last updated: 2/20/2001)

President . . . . . . . . . . . . . . . . . . . . . . . . . . . . . . . . . . . . . . . . . . . . . . **Chavez,** Frias, Hugo
Vice President . . . . . . . . . . . . . . . . . . . . . . . . . . . . . . . . . . . . . . . . . . . . **Bastidas,** Adina
Min. of Defense . . . . . . . . . . . . . . . . . . . . . . . . . . . . . . . . . . . . . . . . **Rangel,** Jose Vicente
Min. of Education, Culture, & Sports . . . . . . . . . . . . . . . . . . . . . . . . . . **Navarro,** Hector
Min. of Energy & Mines . . . . . . . . . . . . . . . . . . . . . . . . . . . . . . **Silva,** Calderon, Alvaro
Min. of Environment & Natural Resources . . . . . . . . . . . . . . . . . . . **Osario,** Ana Elisa
Min. of Finance . . . . . . . . . . . . . . . . . . . . . . . . . . . . . . . . . . . . . . . . . . . **Rojas,** Jose
Min. of Foreign Affairs . . . . . . . . . . . . . . . . . . . . . . . . . . . . . . . **Davila,** Luis Alfonso
Min. of Health & Social Development . . . . . . . . . . . . . . . . . . . . **Rodriguez,** Ochoa, Gilberto
Min. of Infrastructure . . . . . . . . . . . . . . . . . . . . . . . . . . . . **Hurtado,** Ismael Eliezer, *Maj. Gen.*
Min. of Interior & Justice . . . . . . . . . . . . . . . . . . . . . . . . . . . . . . . . **Miguilena,** Luis
Min. of Labor . . . . . . . . . . . . . . . . . . . . . . . . . . . . . . . . . **Portocarrero,** Blancanieves
Min. of Planning & Development . . . . . . . . . . . . . . . . . . . . . . . . . **Giordani,** Jorge
Min. of Production & Commerce . . . . . . . . . . . . . . . . . . . . . . . . . . **Romero,** Luisa
Min. of Science & Technology . . . . . . . . . . . . . . . . . . . . . . . . . . . . **Genatios,** Carlos
Sec., Office of the Presidency . . . . . . . . . . . . . . . . . . . . . . . . . . . . . . . **Jaua,** Elias
Prosecutor General . . . . . . . . . . . . . . . . . . . . . . . . . . . . . . . . . . . . **Rodriguez,** Isaias
Pres., Central Bank . . . . . . . . . . . . . . . . . . . . . . . . . . . . . . . . . . **Castellanos,** Diego
Ambassador to the US . . . . . . . . . . . . . . . . . . . . . . . . . . . . . . **Toro,** Hardy, Alfredo
Permanent Representative to the UN, New York . . . . . . . . . . . . . . . . . **Arcaya,** Ignacio

## VIETNAM, SOCIALIST REPUBLIC OF

(Last updated: 2/6/2001)

*Vietnamese officials are addressed by the last element in their names.*

Chairman, National Assembly . . . . . . . . . . . . . . . . . . . . . . . . . . . . . . . **Nong Duc Manh**
President . . . . . . . . . . . . . . . . . . . . . . . . . . . . . . . . . . . . . . . . . . . . . . **Tran Duc Luong**
Vice President . . . . . . . . . . . . . . . . . . . . . . . . . . . . . . . . . . . . . . . . **Nguyen Thi Binh**
Prime Minister . . . . . . . . . . . . . . . . . . . . . . . . . . . . . . . . . . . . . . . . **Phan Van Khai**
First Dep. Prime Min. . . . . . . . . . . . . . . . . . . . . . . . . . . . . . . . . . . **Nguyen Tan Dung**
Dep. Prime Min. . . . . . . . . . . . . . . . . . . . . . . . . . . . . . . . . . . . . . **Nguyen Cong Tan**
Dep. Prime Min. . . . . . . . . . . . . . . . . . . . . . . . . . . . . . . . . . . . . . **Nguyen Manh Cam**
Dep. Prime Min. . . . . . . . . . . . . . . . . . . . . . . . . . . . . . . . . . . . . . . **Pham Gia Khiem**
Min. of Agriculture & Rural Development . . . . . . . . . . . . . . . . . . . . . . . **Le Huy Ngo**
Min. of Construction . . . . . . . . . . . . . . . . . . . . . . . . . . . . . . . . . . **Nguyen Manh Kiem**
Min. of Culture & Information . . . . . . . . . . . . . . . . . . . . . . . . . . . **Nguyen Khoa Diem**
Min. of Education & Training . . . . . . . . . . . . . . . . . . . . . . . . . . . . **Nguyen Minh Hien**
Min. of Finance . . . . . . . . . . . . . . . . . . . . . . . . . . . . . . . . . . . . . **Nguyen Sinh Hung**
Min. of Foreign Affairs . . . . . . . . . . . . . . . . . . . . . . . . . . . . . . . . . **Nguyen Dy Nien**

## VIETNAM, SOCIALIST REPUBLIC OF (cont.)

| | |
|---|---|
| Min. of Industry | **Dang Vu Chu** |
| Min. of Justice | **Nguyen Dinh Loc** |
| Min. of Labor, War Invalids, & Social Welfare | **Nguyen Thi Hang** |
| Min. of Marine Products | **Ta Quang Ngoc** |
| Min. of National Defense | **Pham Van Tra**, *Sr. Lt. Gen.* |
| Min. of Planning & Investment | **Tran Xuan Gia** |
| Min. of Public Health | **Do Nguyen Phuong**, *M.D.* |
| Min. of Public Security | **Le Minh Huong**, *Maj. Gen.* |
| Min. of Science, Technology, & Environment | **Chu Tuan Nha** |
| Min. of Trade | **Vu Khoan** |
| Min. of Transportation & Communications | **Le Ngoc Hoan** |
| Chmn., State Child Protection & Childcare Comm. | **Tran Thi Thanh Thanh** |
| Chmn., State Ethnic Minorities & Mountain Regions Ctte. | **Hoang Duc Nghi** |
| Chmn., State Inspection Ctte. | **Ta Huu Thanh** |
| Chmn., State Population & Family Planning Ctte. | **Tran Thi Trung Chien** |
| Chmn., State Youth, Sports, & Physical Training Affairs Ctte. | **Ha Quang Du** |
| Chmn., Govt. Office | **Doan Manh Giao** |
| Chmn., Govt. Personnel & Organization Ctte. | **Do Quang Trung** |
| Governor, State Bank | **Le Duc Thuy** |
| Chief, General Staff, People's Army of Vietnam | **Le Van Dung** |
| Ambassador to the US | **Le Van Bang** |
| Permanent Representative to the UN, New York | **Ngyen Thanh Chau,** |

## YEMEN, REPUBLIC OF

(Last updated: 4/20/2001)

| | |
|---|---|
| President | **Salih,** Ali Abdallah, *Fd. Mar.* |
| Vice President | **Hadi,** Abd al-Rab Mansur al-, *Maj. Gen.* |
| Prime Minister | **Ba Jamal,** Abd al-Qadir |
| Dep. Prime Min. | **Salami,** Alawi Salah al- |
| Min. of Agriculture & Irrigation | **Jabali,** Ahmad Salim al- |
| Min. of Awqaf & Religious Guidance | **Ajam,** Qasim al- |
| Min. of Civil Service & Social Security | **Rawih,** Abd al-Wahhab, *Dr.* |
| Min. of Communications | **Muallimi,** Abd al-Malik al- |
| Min. of Construction, Housing, & Urban Planning | **Dafai,** Abdallah Husayn al- |
| Min. of Culture | **Rawhani,** Abd al-Wahhab al- |
| Min. of Defense | **Alaywa,** Abdallah Ali, *Brig. Gen.* |
| Min. of Education | **Abu Ghanim,** Fadl, *Dr.* |
| Min. of Electricity & Water | **Abyad,** Yahya al- |
| Min. of Expatriate Affairs | **Qubati,** Abduh Ali |
| Min. of Finance | **Salami,** Alawi Salah al- |
| Min. of Fisheries | **Ahmadi,** Ali Hasan al-, *Dr.* |
| Min. of Foreign Affairs | **Qurbi,** Abu Bakr al-, *Dr.* |
| Min. of Higher Education & Scientific Research | **Shuaybi,** Yahya al-, *Dr.* |
| Min. of Industry & Trade | **Uthman,** Abd al-Rahman Muhammad Ali al- |
| Min. of Information | **Awadi,** Husayn Dayfallah al- |
| Min. of Interior | **Alimi,** Rashid Muhammad al-, *Dr.* |
| Min. of Justice | **Akabat,** Ahmad, *Qadi* |
| Min. of Labor & Vocational Training | **Tayib,** Muhammad Muhammad al- |
| Min. of Legal Affairs | **Ghanim,** Abdallah Ahmad al- |
| Min. of Local Administration | **Abu Ras,** Sadiq Amin Husayn |
| Min. of Oil & Mineral Resources | **Ba Rabba,** Rashid, *Dr.* |
| Min. of Planning & Development | **Sufan,** Ahmad Muhammad Abdallah al- |
| Min. of Public Health & Population | **Munibari,** Abd al-Nasir al-, *Dr.* |
| Min. of Public Works & Urban Development | **Dafi,** Abdallah Husayn al- |
| Min. of Social & Labor Affairs | **Arhabi,** Abd al-Karim al- |
| Min. of Social Security & Social Affairs | **Batani,** Muhammad Abdallah al- |
| Min. of State & Secretary General Presidency | **Bashiri,** Abdallah, *Maj. Gen.* |
| Min. of Supply & Trade | **Kumaim,** Abd al-Aziz al- |
| Min. of Technical Education & Vocational Training | **Batani,** Muhammad Abdallah al- |
| Min. of Tourism & Environment | **Iryani,** Abd al-Malik al- |
| Min. of Transportation & Maritime Affairs | **Yafai,** Said, *Capt.* |
| Min. of Youth & Sports | **Akwa,** Abd al-Rahman al- |
| Min. of State | **Ali,** Faysal Mahmud |

## YEMEN, REPUBLIC OF (cont.)

| | |
|---|---|
| Min. of State for Cabinet Affairs | **Saidi,** Mutahir al-, *Dr.* |
| Min. of State for Human Rights | **Farah,** Wahiba, *Dr.* |
| Min. of State for Parliamentary & Shura Council Affairs | **Attas,** Alawi Hasan al- |
| Chief of Staff, Armed Forces | **Ulaywah,** Ali Abdallah, *Maj. Gen.* |
| Speaker, Parliament | **Ahmar,** Abdallah Husayn al- |
| Governor, Central Bank | **Samawi,** Ahmad Abdul-Rahman al- |
| Ambassador to the US | **Hajri,** Abd al-Wahhab Abdallah al- |
| Permanent Representative to the UN, New York | **Ashtal,** Abdallah Salih al- |

## YUGOSLAVIA, FEDERAL REPUBLIC OF—NDE

(Last updated: 3/5/2001)

| | |
|---|---|
| President | **Kostunica,** Vojislav |
| Prime Minister | **Zizic,** Zoran |
| Dep. Prime Min. | **Labus,** Miroljub |
| Min. of Agriculture | **Vitosevic,** Sasa |
| Min. of Defense | **Krapovic,** Slobodan |
| Min. for Economy | **Vuksanovic,** Danilo |
| Min. of Finance | **Pesic,** Dragisa |
| Min. of Foreign Affairs | **Svilanovic,** Goran |
| Min. of Health | **Kovac,** Miodrag |
| Min. of Internal Affairs | **Zivkovic,** Zoran |
| Min. of Justice | **Grubac,** Momcilo |
| Min. of Minorities | **Ljajic,** Rasim |
| Min. of Religion | **Sijakovic,** Bogoljub |
| Min. of Sport | **Andric,** Vojislav |
| Min. of Telecommunication | **Tadic,** Boris |
| Min. of Transportation | **Sami,** Zoran |
| Min. Without Portfolio | **Radojevic,** Velimir |
| Federal Sec. for Information | **Matic,** Goran |
| Governor, National Bank of Yugoslavia | **Dinkic,** Mladjan |
| Head of the Mission to the UN, New York | **Jovanovic,** Vladislav |
| Montenegro, Republic of | |
| President | **Djukanovic,** Milo |
| Prime Minister | **Vujanovic,** Filip |
| Dep. Prime Min. | **Burzan,** Dragisa |
| Dep. Prime Min. | **Krivokapic,** Ranko |
| Dep. Prime Min. | **Krgovic,** Ljubisa |
| Dep. Prime Min. | **Telacevic,** Asim |
| Min. of Agriculture & Forestry | **Simovic,** Milutin |
| Min. of Culture | **Luburic,** Radojica |
| Min. of Environment | **Gomilanovic,** Miodrag |
| Min. of Education & Science | **Kujovic,** Dragan |
| Min. of Finance | **Ivanisevic,** Miroslav |
| Min. of Foreign Affairs | **Lukovac,** Branko |
| Min. of Health | **Micevic,** Zarko |
| Min. of Industry, Power Industry, & Mining | **Djukanovic,** Vojin |
| Min. of Internal Affairs | **Maras,** Vukasin |
| Min. of Justice | **Radulovic,** Branislav |
| Min. of Labor & Social Security | **Stijepovic.,** Slavoljub |
| Min. of Minority Issues | **Juncaj,** Ljujidj |
| Min. of Religion | **Vujanovic,** Filip |
| Min. of Sport | **Stijepovic,** Slavoljub |
| Min. of Tourism | **Mitrovic,** Vlado |
| Min. of Trade | **Bralic,** Ramo |
| Min. of Transport & Maritime Affairs | **Kalamperovic,** Jusuf |
| Min. of Urban Planning | **Gregovic,** Rade |
| Chmn., Montenegrin Central Bank | **Goranovic,** Predrag |
| Republican Sec. of Information | **Jaredic,** Bozidar |
| Serbia, Republic of | |
| President | **Milutinovic,** Milan |
| Prime Minister | **Djindjic,** Zoran |
| Dep. Prime Min. | **Covic,** Nebojsa |
| Dep. Prime Min. | **Kasza,** Jozsef |

## YUGOSLAVIA, FEDERAL REPUBLIC OF—NDE (cont.)

| | |
|---|---|
| Dep. Prime Min. | **Korac,** Zarko |
| Dep. Prime Min. | **Mihajlovic,** Dusan |
| Dep. Prime Min. | **Obradovic,** Vuk |
| Dep. Prime Min. | **Perisic,** Momcilo |
| Dep. Prime Min. | **Pravdic,** Aleksandar |
| Min. of Agriculture | **Veselinov,** Dragan |
| Min. of Culture | **Branislav,** Lecic |
| Min. of Economy & Privatization | **Vlahovic,** Aleksandar |
| Min. of Education & Sports | **Knezevic,** Gazo |
| Min. of Finance | **Djelic,** Bozidar |
| Min. of Foreign Economic Relations | **Pitic,** Goran |
| Min. of Health | **Joksimovic,** Obren |
| Min. of Housing | **Sumarac,** Dragoslav |
| Min. of Interior (interim) | **Mihajlovic,** Dusan |
| Min. of Justice & Local Administration | **Batic,** Vladan |
| Min. of Labor | **Milovanovic,** Dragan |
| Min. of Mining | **Novakovic,** Goran |
| Min. of Religion | **Milovanovic,** Vojislav |
| Min. of Science | **Domazet,** Dragan |
| Min. of Social Welfare | **Matkovic,** Gordana |
| Min. of Trade & Tourism | **Milosavljevic,** Slobodan |
| Min. of Transport & Telecommunications | **Vukosavljevic,** Marija |

## ZAMBIA, REPUBLIC OF

(Last updated: 4/19/2001)

| | |
|---|---|
| President | **Chiluba,** Frederick |
| Vice President | **Tembo,** Christon |
| Min. of Agriculture, Fisheries, & Food Security | **Desai,** Suresh |
| Min. of Commerce, Trade, & Industry | **Mpamba,** David |
| Min. of Community Development & Social Welfare | **Lapunga,** Dawson |
| Min. of Defense | **Sampa,** Chitalu |
| Min. of Education | **Miyanda,** Godfrey, *Brig. Gen.* |
| Min. of Energy & Water Development | **Saviye,** David |
| Min. of Environment & Natural Resources | **Miyanda,** Samuel |
| Min. of Finance | **Kalumba,** Katele, *Dr.* |
| Min. of Foreign Affairs | **Walubita,** Sipakeli |
| Min. of Health | **Kavindele,** Enock |
| Min. of Home Affairs | **Machungwa,** Peter, *Dr.* |
| Min. of Information & Broadcasting | **Zimba,** Newstead |
| Min. of Labor & Social Services | **Nawakwi,** Edith |
| Min. of Lands | **Chambeshi,** Abel |
| Min. of Legal Affairs | **Malambo,** Vincent |
| Min. of Local Government & Housing | **Namuyamba,** Bates |
| Min. of Mines & Mineral Development | **Syamujaye,** Syamukayumbu |
| Min. of Science, Technology &Vocational Training | **Kayope,** Valentine |
| Min. of Sport, Youth & Child Development | **Chambesi,** Abel |
| Min. of State for Presidential Affairs | **Silwamba,** Eric |
| Min. of Tourism | **Harrington,** William |
| Min. of Transport & Communications | **Luo,** Nkandu |
| Min. of Works & Supply | **Mandandi,** Godden |
| Min. Without Portfolio | **Sata,** Michael |
| Permanent Sec., Office of the President | **Zimba,** Gibson |
| Attorney General | **Chilupe,** George |
| Solicitor General | **Siame,** Fred |
| Governor, Central Bank | **Mwanza,** Jacob |
| Ambassador to the US | **Kamana,** Dunstan Weston |
| Permanent Representative to the UN, New York | **Musambachime,** Mwelwa |

## ZIMBABWE, REPUBLIC OF

(Last updated: 11/17/2000)

President .............................................................. **Mugabe,** Robert
Vice President .......................................................... **Muzenda,** Simon Vengai
Vice President .......................................................... **Msika,** Joseph
Min. of Defense ....................................................... **Mahachi,** Moven
Min. of Education, Sports, & Culture ............................. **Mumbengegwi,** Simbarashe
Min. of Environment & Tourism ................................... **Nhema,** Francis
Min. of Finance & Economic Development ...................... **Makoni,** Simba
Min. of Foreign Affairs ............................................. **Mudenge,** Stanislaus
Min. of Health & Child Welfare .................................. **Stamps,** Timothy
Min. of Higher Education & Technology ......................... **Murerwa,** Herbert
Min. of Home Affairs ............................................... **Nkomo,** John
Min. of Industry & International Trade ........................... **Moyo,** Nkosana
Min. of Justice, Legal, & Parliamentary Affairs ................ **Chinamasa,** Patrick
Min. of Lands, Agriculture, & Rural Development ............. **Made,** Joseph
Min. of Local Govt., Public Works, & National Housing ...... **Chombo,** Ignatius
Min. of Mines & Energy ............................................ **Sekeramayi,** Sydney
Min. of Public Service, Labor, & Social Welfare .............. **Moyo,** July
Min. of Rural Resources & Water Development ................. **Mujuru,** Joyce
Min. of Transport & Energy ....................................... **Mombeshora,** Swithen
Min. of Youth Development, Gender, & Employment Creation ... **Gezi,** Border
Min. of State for Information & Publicity ........................ **Moyo,** Jonathan
Min. of State for National Security ............................... **Goche,** Nicholas
Governor, Central Bank ............................................. **Tsumba,** Leonard
Ambassador to the US ............................................... **Mubako,** Simbi Veke
Permanent Representative to the UN, New York ................. **Jokonya,** Tichaona Joseph Benjamin

# Status of the
# World's Nations

# Status of the World's Nations

Listing of Nations, Dependencies, and Areas of Special Sovereignty

---

**Editor's note: This information was created by** *Geographic Notes*, **issued by the Bureau of Intelligence, U.S. State Department circa April 15, 1992 and was updated January 19, 2001.**

---

## OVERVIEW

In this survey, the term "nation" refers to a people politically organized into a sovereign state with a definite, internationally recognized territory. The number of such nations has almost tripled since the end of World War II. On the eve of the war there were 70 nations; by January 1995, there were 190.

In 1990 and 1991 several important change took place in the status of the world's nations. Two nations, Yemen and Germany, were formed in 1990, each by unification of two formerly separate nations. In the case of Germany, the former German Democratic Republic was subsumed by the Federal Republic of Germany. The Republic of Yemen was formed by union of the former Yemen Arab Republic and the People's Democratic Republic of Yemen. Also in 1990, Namibia finally realized its Independence; the UN had terminated its status as a South African mandate in 1966.

The year 1990 also began a period of turmoil in the former Soviet Union. The independence of the three Baltic States—Estonia, Latvia, and Lithuania—was recognized by the central Soviet government in August 1991. The United States established diplomatic relations with the democratically elected governments of the Baltic States in September 1991. In December 1991 the 12 former Soviet republics became separate sovereign nations. Eleven of the 12 have formed a Commonwealth of Independent States (Georgia has not joined). The role and powers of the CIS are in the process of being defined.

The magnitude of these changes, though noteworthy, is not unprecedented in recent history. The unsettled international situations following each of the World Wars fostered the creation of new nations without an equal dissolution of existing ones. As a result of World War I, three nations in Europe ceased to exist—Austria, Hungary, Montenegro, and Serbia—but they were replaced by four new nations: Austria, Hungary, Czechoslovakia, and Yugoslavia. Poland reappeared on the map of Europe after an interval of almost a century and a quarter during which it had been partitioned among Austria-Hungary, Germany, and Russia.

In the early part of World War II, Estonia, Latvia, and Lithuania were forcibly incorporated into the USSR. Other nations disappeared temporarily from the world community during the period that led up to World War II. These include Ethiopia in 1936, Austria in 1938, and Czechoslovakia in 1939. In the aftermath of World War II, however, two new nations emerged through the partition of Germany, and Israel was created within the United Kingdom's Palestine League of Nations Mandate.

## Proliferation of Nations

The dramatic increase in the number of nations since World War II has occurred primarily through the breakup of larger territorial entities, particularly in Africa, along the southern periphery of Asia, in the Caribbean, and in the Pacific Ocean. The dissolution of the Soviet Union follows this proliferation pattern.

Several periods since 1945 were marked particularly by the emergence of new nations from colonial powers. In 1960 alone, 14 new nations appeared from French-controlled parts of Africa. Of the 69 nations formed worldwide between 1961 and 1992, 42 had been wholly or partly under British sovereignty at some time in their history, including seven of the 11 new Pacific island nations. Between September 1974 and November 1975, all five of Portugal's overseas provinces in Africa became nations.

Several exceptional situations since World War II have caused irregularities in the sovereignty structure. Syria in 1958 joined Egypt to form the United Arab Republic, a union that endured three years. In 1962 the West Indies Federation, just a few months before its scheduled independence, was dissolved in favor of sovereignty for Jamaica and Trinidad and Tobago.

In another instance in which nations unsuccessfully attempted to merge, Kenya, Uganda, Tanganyika, and Zanzibar considered the creation of an East African federation with a single national government. These plans failed to materialize, but in April 1964 Tanganyika and Zanzibar merged to become one nation, Tanzania.

## Geographical Attributes

The largest nation by size of territory is Russia, followed, in order by Canada, China, the United States, Brazil, and Australia, all with more than 5 million square kilometers of total area. The largest nation by population is China, followed, in order by India, the United States, and Indonesia, all with more than 190 million people. The Holy See (Vatican City) is the world's smallest nation, in both land area and population.

Of the 190 nations, 44 are insular, including parts of islands; 40 are landlocked; and the remaining 106 face one or more oceans or their embayments. As nations delimit their 200-nautical-mile exclusive economic zones (EEZs) under the provisions of the 1982 United Nations Convention on the Law of the Sea, including negotiating maritime boundaries with neighboring nations, some may face the possibility of being "zonelocked."

## Dependent Areas

Government control over land areas varies widely, from full sovereignty to none. The term "dependent areas" encompasses a broad category of political entities that fall in some way within the jurisdiction of a nation. In this survey, dependent areas are "overseas" territories associated with a nation; they do not include offshore islands that belong to or make up civil divisions of a nation. Australia, Denmark, France, Netherlands, New Zealand, Norway, Portugal, Spain, the United Kingdom, and the United States maintain dependent areas. The level of political dependence ranges from self-governing in domestic affairs

to administered directly from the national capital. The latter case often includes minor scattered islands with little or no permanent population.

Except for a sector of Antarctica, there are no significant land areas that are not either under the control of a nation or claimed by one. Antarctic claims have been made by seven of the 26 consultative nations to the 1959 Antarctic Treaty,* although the legal status of those claims remains in suspension under the provisions of the treaty. The unclaimed sector of Antarctica is between 90 and 150 degrees west longitude.

The United States has asserted no claim of sovereignty in Antarctica, although it reserves the right to make one; it recognizes none of the claims within the Antarctic Treaty area (south of 60 degrees south latitude) made by other nations.

*Argentina, Australia, Chile, France, New Zealand, Norway, and the United Kingdom are the seven signatories of the 1959 Antarctic Treaty which have claims in Antarctica. The 19 remaining consultative nations are Belgium, Brazil, China, Ecuador, Finland, Germany, India, Italy, Japan, Netherlands, Peru, Poland, South Africa, South Korea, Spain, Sweden, USSR, United States, and Uruguay.

# NATIONS, DEPENDENCIES, AREAS OF SPECIAL SOVEREIGNTY

The following information is provided as reference material only. The data do not necessarily correspond to official statistics published by the various states. Status of the World's Nations should not be considered legally definitive.

## Diplomatic Relations

The United States has established diplomatic relations with 180 of the listed nations. These are designated by an asterisk (*).

## Name of Nation

The short-form name of the nation (printed in bold type) is commonly used; the long form is used for official documents and formal occasions. In a few instances no short form exists; the long form must serve for all usages. Conversely, a long form may not exist or may seldom be used.

## Sovereignty

The sovereignty of dependencies and areas of special sovereignty is identified; where required, a note clarifies an entity's political status.

## Capitals

For each state the conventionally accepted capital city name, recommended for use on maps, is listed. In the several instances where states have more than one capital, information on each is given. Some dependencies have no capital city and may be administered from another dependency of the same nation. In the case of small multi-island insular states or dependencies, the island on which the capital is located is given, unless it has the same name.

## UN Membership

UN membership is indicated by a (+).

# Independent States[1] in the World as of January 2001

| Nation | | Code[2] | Capital |
|---|---|---|---|
| **Short-form name** | Long-form name | | |
| 001. Afghanistan *+ | **Islamic State of Afghanistan** | AF | *Kabul* |
| 002. Albania *+ | **Republic of Albania** | AL | *Tirana* |
| 003. Algeria *+ | **Democratic and Popular Republic of Algeria** | AG | *Algiers* |
| 004. Andorra *+ | **Principality of Andorra** | AN | *Andorra la Vella* |
| 005. Angola *+ | **Republic of Angola** | AO | *Luanda* |
| | | | |
| 006. Antigua and Barbuda *+ | (no long-form name) | AC | *Saint John's* |
| 007. Argentina *+ | **Argentine Republic** | AR | *Buenos Aires* |
| 008. Armenia *+ | **Republic of Armenia** | AM | *Yerevan* |
| 009. Australia *+ | **Commonwealth of Australia** | AS | *Canberra* |
| 010. Austria *+ | **Republic of Austria** | AU | *Vienna* |
| | | | |
| 011. Azerbaijan *+ | **Republic of Azerbaijan** | AJ | *Baku* |
| 012. Bahamas, The *+ | **Commonwealth of The Bahamas** | BF | *Nassau* |
| 013. Bahrain *+ | **State of Bahrain** | BA | *Manama* |
| 014. Bangladesh *+ | **People's Republic of Bangladesh** | BG | *Dhaka* |
| 015. Barbados *+ | (no long-form name) | BB | *Bridgetown* |
| | | | |
| 016. Belarus *+ | **Republic of Belarus** | BO | *Minsk* |
| 017. Belgium *+ | **Kingdom of Belgium** | BE | *Brussels* |
| 018. Belize *+ | (no long-form name) | BH | *Belmopan* |
| 019. Benin *+ | **Republic of Benin** | BN | *Porto-Novo* |
| 020. Bhutan + | **Kingdom of Bhutan** | BT | *Thimphu* |
| | | | |
| 021. Bolivia *+ | **Republic of Bolivia** | BL | *La Paz (administrative)* <br> *Sucre (legislative/judiciary)* |
| 022. Bosnia and Herzegovina *+ | (no long-form name) | BK | *Sarajevo* |
| 023. Botswana *+ | **Republic of Botswana** | BC | *Gaborone* |
| 024. Brazil *+ | **Federative Republic of Brazil** | BR | *Brasília* |
| 025. Brunei *+ | **Negara Brunei Darussalam** | BX | *Bandar Seri Begawan* |
| | | | |
| 026. Bulgaria *+ | **Republic of Bulgaria** | BU | *Sofia* |
| 027. Burkina Faso *+ | **Burkina Faso** | UV | *Ouagadougou* |
| 028. Burma *+ | **Union of Burma** | BM | *Rangoon* |
| 029. Burundi *+ | **Republic of Burundi** | BY | *Bujumbura* |
| 030. Cambodia *+ | **Kingdom of Cambodia** | CB | *Phnom Penh* |
| | | | |
| 031. Cameroon *+ | **Republic of Cameroon** | CM | *Yaoundé* |
| 032. Canada *+ | (no long-form name) | CA | *Ottawa* |
| 033. Cape Verde *+ | **Republic of Cape Verde** | CV | *Praia* |
| 034. Central African Republic *+ | **Central African Republic** | CT | *Bangui* |
| 035. Chad *+ | **Republic of Chad** | CD | *N'Djamena* |
| | | | |
| 036. Chile *+ | **Republic of Chile** | CI | *Santiago* |
| 037. China *+ [3] | **People's Republic of China** | CH | *Beijing* |
| 038. Colombia *+ | **Republic of Colombia** | CO | *Bogotá* |
| 039. Comoros *+ | **Federal Islamic Republic of the Comoros** | CN | *Moroni* |
| 040. Congo (Brazzaville) *+[4] | **Republic of the Congo** | CF | *Brazzaville* |
| | | | |
| 041. Congo (Kinshasa) *+[4] | **Democratic Republic of the Congo** | CG | *Kinshasa* |
| 042. Costa Rica *+ | **Republic of Costa Rica** | CS | *San José* |
| 043. Côte d'Ivoire *+ | **Republic of Côte d'Ivoire** | IV | *Yamoussoukro* |
| 044. Croatia *+ | **Republic of Croatia** | HR | *Zagreb* |
| 045. Cuba + | **Republic of Cuba** | CU | *Havana* |

* Diplomatic relations with the United States  + Member of United Nations

Status of the World's Nations

# Nations, Dependencies, and Areas of Special Sovereignty

| Nation | | Code[2] | Capital |
|---|---|---|---|
| Short-form name | Long-form name | | |
| 046. Cyprus *+ | Republic of Cyprus | CY | Nicosia |
| 047. Czech Republic *+ | Czech Republic | EZ | Prague |
| 048. Denmark *+ | Kingdom of Denmark | DA | Copenhagen |
| 049. Djibouti *+ | Republic of Djibouti | DJ | Djibouti |
| 050. Dominica *+ | Commonwealth of Dominica | DO | Roseau |
| 051. Dominican Republic *+ | Dominican Republic | DR | Santo Domingo |
| 052. Ecuador *+ | Republic of Ecuador | EC | Quito |
| 053. Egypt *+ | Arab Republic of Egypt | EG | Cairo |
| 054. El Salvador *+ | Republic of El Salvador | ES | San Salvador |
| 055. Equatorial Guinea *+ | Republic of Equatorial Guinea | EK | Malabo |
| 056. Eritrea *+ | State of Eritrea | ER | Asmara |
| 057. Estonia *+ | Republic of Estonia | EN | Tallinn |
| 058. Ethiopia *+ | Federal Democratic Republic of Ethiopia | ET | Addis Ababa |
| 059. Fiji *+ | Republic of the Fiji Islands | FJ | Suva |
| 060. Finland *+ | Republic of Finland | FI | Helsinki |
| 061. France *+ | French Republic | FR | Paris |
| 062. Gabon *+ | Gabonese Republic | GB | Libreville |
| 063. Gambia, The *+ | Republic of The Gambia | GA | Banjul |
| 064. Georgia *+ | Republic of Georgia | GG | T'bilisi |
| 065. Germany *+ | Federal Republic of Germany | GM | Berlin |
| 066. Ghana *+ | Republic of Ghana | GH | Accra |
| 067. Greece *+ | Hellenic Republic | GR | Athens |
| 068. Grenada *+ | (no long-form name) | GJ | Saint George's |
| 069. Guatemala *+ | Republic of Guatemala | GT | Guatemala |
| 070. Guinea *+ | Republic of Guinea | GV | Conakry |
| 071. Guinea-Bissau *+ | Republic of Guinea-Bissau | PU | Bissau |
| 072. Guyana *+ | Co-operative Republic of Guyana | GY | Georgetown |
| 073. Haiti *+ | Republic of Haiti | HA | Port-au-Prince |
| 074. Holy See * | Holy See | VT | Vatican City |
| 075. Honduras *+ | Republic of Honduras | HO | Tegucigalpa |
| 076. Hungary *+ | Republic of Hungary | HU | Budapest |
| 077. Iceland *+ | Republic of Iceland | IC | Reykjavík |
| 078. India *+ | Republic of India | IN | New Delhi |
| 079. Indonesia *+ | Republic of Indonesia | ID | Jakarta |
| 080. Iran + | Islamic Republic of Iran | IR | Tehran |
| 081. Iraq + | Republic of Iraq | IZ | Baghdad |
| 082. Ireland *+ | (no long-form name) | EI | Dublin |
| 083. Israel *+ | State of Israel | IS | (see note 5) |
| 084. Italy *+ | Italian Republic | IT | Rome |
| 085. Jamaica *+ | (no long-form name) | JM | Kingston |
| 086. Japan *+ | (no long-form name) | JA | Tokyo |
| 087. Jordan *+ | Hashemite Kingdom of Jordan | JO | Amman |
| 088. Kazakhstan *+ | Republic of Kazakhstan | KZ | Astana |
| 089. Kenya *+ | Republic of Kenya | KE | Nairobi |
| 090. Kiribati *+ | Republic of Kiribati | KR | Tarawa |
| 091. Korea, North + | Democratic People's Republic of Korea | KN | P'yongyang |
| 092. Korea, South *+ | Republic of Korea | KS | Seoul |
| 093. Kuwait *+ | State of Kuwait | KU | Kuwait |

* Diplomatic relations with the United States  + Member of United Nations

| Nation | | Code[2] | Capital |
|---|---|---|---|
| Short-form name | Long-form name | | |
| 094. Kyrgyzstan *+ | Kyrgyz Republic | KG | *Bishkek* |
| 095. Laos *+ | Lao People's Democratic Republic | LA | *Vientiane* |
| 096. Latvia *+ | Republic of Latvia | LG | *Riga* |
| 097. Lebanon *+ | Lebanese Republic | LE | *Beirut* |
| 098. Lesotho *+ | Kingdom of Lesotho | LT | *Maseru* |
| 099. Liberia *+ | Republic of Liberia | LI | *Monrovia* |
| 100. Libya *+ | Great Socialist People's Libyan Arab Jamahiriya | LY | *Tripoli* |
| 101. Liechtenstein *+ | Principality of Liechtenstein | LS | *Vaduz* |
| 102. Lithuania *+ | Republic of Lithuania | LH | *Vilnius* |
| 103. Luxembourg *+ | Grand Duchy of Luxembourg | LU | *Luxembourg* |
| 104. Macedonia, The Former Yugoslav Republic of *+ | The Former Yugoslav Republic of Macedonia | MK | *Skopje* |
| 105. Madagascar *+ | Republic of Madagascar | MA | *Antananarivo* |
| 106. Malawi *+ | Republic of Malawi | MI | *Lilongwe* |
| 107. Malaysia *+ | (no long-form name) | MY | *Kuala Lumpur* |
| 108. Maldives *+ | Republic of Maldives | MV | *Male* |
| 109. Mali *+ | Republic of Mali | ML | *Bamako* |
| 110. Malta *+ | Republic of Malta | MT | *Valletta* |
| 111. Marshall Islands *+ | Republic of the Marshall Islands | RM | *Majuro* |
| 112. Mauritania *+ | Islamic Republic of Mauritania | MR | *Nouakchott* |
| 113. Mauritius *+ | Republic of Mauritius | MP | *Port Louis* |
| 114. Mexico *+ | United Mexican States | MX | *Mexico* |
| 115. Micronesia, Federated States of *+ | Federated States of Micronesia | FM | *Palikir* |
| 116. Moldova *+ | Republic of Moldova | MD | *Chisinau* |
| 117. Monaco *+ | Principality of Monaco | MN | *Monaco* |
| 118. Mongolia *+ | (no long-form name) | MG | *Ulaanbaatar* |
| 119. Morocco *+ | Kingdom of Morocco | MO | *Rabat* |
| 120. Mozambique *+ | Republic of Mozambique | MZ | *Maputo* |
| 121. Namibia *+ | Republic of Namibia | WA | *Windhoek* |
| 122. Nauru *+ | Republic of Nauru | NR | *Yaren District (no capital city)* |
| 123. Nepal *+ | Kingdom of Nepal | NP | *Kathmandu* |
| 124. Netherlands *+ | Kingdom of the Netherlands | NL | *Amsterdam, The Hague* |
| 125. New Zealand *+ | (no long-form name) | NZ | *Wellington* |
| 126. Nicaragua *+ | Republic of Nicaragua | NU | *Managua* |
| 127. Niger *+ | Republic of Niger | NG | *Niamey* |
| 128. Nigeria *+ | Federal Republic of Nigeria | NI | *Abuja* |
| 129. Norway *+ | Kingdom of Norway | NO | *Oslo* |
| 130. Oman *+ | Sultanate of Oman | MU | *Muscat* |
| 131. Pakistan *+ | Islamic Republic of Pakistan | PK | *Islamabad* |
| 132. Palau *+ | Republic of Palau | PS | *Koror* |
| 133. Panama *+ | Republic of Panama | PM | *Panama* |
| 134. Papua New Guinea *+ | Independent State of Papua New Guinea | PP | *Port Moresby* |
| 135. Paraguay *+ | Republic of Paraguay | PA | *Asunción* |
| 136. Peru *+ | Republic of Peru | PE | *Lima* |
| 137. Philippines *+ | Republic of the Philippines | RP | *Manila* |
| 138. Poland *+ | Republic of Poland | PL | *Warsaw* |

* Diplomatic relations with the United States  + Member of United Nations

Status of the World's Nations

| Nation | | Code[2] | Capital |
|---|---|---|---|
| Short-form name | Long-form name | | |
| 139. Portugal *+ | **Portuguese Republic** | PO | Lisbon |
| 140. Qatar *+ | **State of Qatar** | QA | Doha |
| 141. Romania *+ | (no long-form name) | RO | Bucharest |
| 142. Russia *+ | **Russian Federation** | RS | Moscow |
| 143. Rwanda *+ | **Rwandese Republic** | RW | Kigali |
| 144. Saint Kitts and Nevis *+ | **Federation of Saint Kitts and Nevis** | SC | Basseterre |
| 145. Saint Lucia *+ | (no long-form name) | ST | Castries |
| 146. Saint Vincent and the Grenadines *+ | (no long-form name) | VC | Kingstown |
| 147. Samoa *+ | **Independent State of Samoa** | WS | Apia |
| 148. San Marino *+ | **Republic of San Marino** | SM | San Marino |
| 149. Sao Tome and Principe *+ | **Democratic Republic of Sao Tome and Principe** | TP | São Tomé |
| 150. Saudi Arabia *+ | **Kingdom of Saudi Arabia** | SA | Riyadh |
| 151. Senegal *+ | **Republic of Senegal** | SG | Dakar |
| 152. Seychelles *+ | **Republic of Seychelles** | SE | Victoria |
| 153. Sierra Leone *+ | **Republic of Sierra Leone** | SL | Freetown |
| 154. Singapore *+ | **Republic of Singapore** | SN | Singapore |
| 155. Slovakia *+ | **Slovak Republic** | LO | Bratislava |
| 156. Slovenia *+ | **Republic of Slovenia** | SI | Ljubljana |
| 157. Solomon Islands *+ | (no long-form name) | BP | Honiara |
| 158. Somalia *+ | (no long-form name) | SO | Mogadishu |
| 159. South Africa *+ | **Republic of South Africa** | SF | Pretoria (administrative) Cape Town (legislative) Bloemfontein (judiciary) |
| 160. Spain *+ | **Kingdom of Spain** | SP | Madrid |
| 161. Sri Lanka *+ | **Democratic Socialist Republic of Sri Lanka** | CE | Colombo Sri Jayewardenepura |
| 162. Sudan *+ | **Republic of the Sudan** | SU | Khartoum |
| 163. Suriname *+ | **Republic of Suriname** | NS | Paramaribo |
| 164. Swaziland *+ | **Kingdom of Swaziland** | WZ | Mbabane (administrative) Lobamba (legislative) |
| 165. Sweden *+ | **Kingdom of Sweden** | SW | Stockholm |
| 166. Switzerland * | **Swiss Confederation** | SZ | Bern |
| 167. Syria *+ | **Syrian Arab Republic** | SY | Damascus |
| 168. Tajikistan *+ | **Republic of Tajikistan** | TI | Dushanbe |
| 169. Tanzania *+ | **United Republic of Tanzania** | TZ | Dar es Salaam Dodoma (legislative) |
| 170. Thailand *+ | **Kingdom of Thailand** | TH | Bangkok |
| 171. Togo *+ | **Togolese Republic** | TO | Lomé |
| 172. Tonga *+ | **Kingdom of Tonga** | TN | Nuku'alofa |
| 173. Trinidad and Tobago *+ | **Republic of Trinidad and Tobago** | TD | Port-of-Spain |
| 174. Tunisia *+ | **Republic of Tunisia** | TS | Tunis |
| 175. Turkey *+ | **Republic of Turkey** | TU | Ankara |
| 176. Turkmenistan *+ | (no long-form name) | TX | Ashgabat |
| 177. Tuvalu * | (no long-form name) | TV | Funafuti |
| 178. Uganda *+ | **Republic of Uganda** | UG | Kampala |
| 179. Ukraine *+ | (no long-form name) | UP | Kiev |
| 180. United Arab Emirates *+ | **United Arab Emirates** | TC | Abu Dhabi |

* Diplomatic relations with the United States  + Member of United Nations

## Nation

| Short-form name | Long-form name | Code[2] | Capital |
|---|---|---|---|
| 181. United Kingdom *+ | United Kingdom of Great Britain and Northern Ireland | UK | London |
| 182. United States + | United States of America | US | Washington, DC |
| 183. Uruguay *+ | Oriental Republic of Uruguay | UY | Montevideo |
| 184. Uzbekistan *+ | Republic of Uzbekistan | UZ | Tashkent |
| 185. Vanuatu *+ | Republic of Vanuatu | NH | Port-Vila |
| 186. Venezuela *+ | Republic of Venezuela | VE | Caracas |
| 187. Vietnam *+ | Socialist Republic of Vietnam | VM | Hanoi |
| 188. Yemen *+ | Republic of Yemen | YM | Sanaa |
| 189. Yugoslavia | Federal Republic of Yugoslavia | YI | Belgrade |
| 190. Zambia *+ | Republic of Zambia | ZA | Lusaka |
| 191. Zimbabwe *+ | Republic of Zimbabwe | ZI | Harare |

## Other

| Short-form name | Long-form name | Code[2] | Capital |
|---|---|---|---|
| Taiwan[6] | (no long-form name) | TW | T'ai-pei |

* Diplomatic relations with the United States  + Member of United Nations

# Notes

Note 1: In this listing, the term "independent state" refers to a people politically organized into a sovereign state with a definite territory recognized as independent by the US.

Note 2: Federal Information Processing Standard (FIPS) 10-4 codes.

Note 3: With the establishment of diplomatic relations with China on January 1, 1979, the US Government recognized the People's Republic of China as the sole legal government of China and acknowledged the Chinese position that there is only one China and that Taiwan is part of China.

Note 4: "Congo" is the official short-form name for both the Republic of the Congo and the Democratic Republic of the Congo. To distinguish one from the other, the U.S. Department of State adds the capital in parentheses. This practice is unofficial and provisional.

Note 5: In 1950 the Israel Parliament proclaimed Jerusalem as the capital. The US, like most other countries that have embassies in Israel, maintains its Embassy in Tel Aviv.

Note 6: Claimed by both the Government of the People's Republic of China and the authorities on Taiwan (see note 3)

Source: Office of The Geographer and Global Issues, Bureau of Intelligence and Research, U.S. Department of State, Washington, D.C.

Status of the World's Nations

## Dependencies and Areas of Special Sovereignty as of November 2000

| | Short-form name | Long-form name | Sovereignty | Code[1] | Capital |
|---|---|---|---|---|---|
| 01. | American Samoa | **Territory of American Samoa** | United States | AQ | *Pago Pago* |
| 02. | Anguilla | (no long-form name) | United Kingdom | AV | *The Valley* |
| 03. | Antarctica | (no long-form name) | None (see note 2) | AY | *None* |
| 04. | Aruba | (no long-form name) | Netherlands | AA | *Oranjestad* |
| 05. | Ashmore and Cartier Islands | **Territory of Ashmore and Cartier Islands** | Australia | AT | *Administered from Canberra* |
| 06. | Baker Island | (no long-form name) | United States | FQ | *Administered from Washington, D.C.* |
| 07. | Bermuda | (no long-form name) | United Kingdom | BD | *Hamilton* |
| 08. | Bouvet Island | (no long-form name) | Norway | BV | *Admin. from Oslo* |
| 09. | British Indian Ocean Territory[3] | **British Indian Ocean Territory** | United Kingdom | IO | *None* |
| 10. | Cayman Islands | (no long-form name) | United Kingdom | CJ | *George Town* |
| 11. | Christmas Island | **Territory of Christmas Island** | Australia | KT | *The Settlement (Flying Fish Cove)* |
| 12. | Clipperton Island | (no long-form name) | France | IP | *Administered from French Polynesia* |
| 13. | Cocos (Keeling) Islands | **Territory of Cocos (Keeling) Islands** | Australia | CK | *West Island* |
| 14. | Cook Islands | (no long-form name) | New Zealand | CW | *Avarua* |
| 15. | Coral Sea Islands | **Coral Sea Islands Territory** | Australia | CR | *Administered from Canberra* |
| 16. | East Timor | **(no long-form name)** | Temporarily administered by the United Nations | TT | *Dili* |
| 17. | Falkland Islands (Islas Malvinas) | **Colony of the Falkland Islands** | United Kingdom[4] | FK | *Stanley* |
| 18. | Faroe Islands | (no long-form name) | Denmark | FO | *Tórshavn* |
| 19. | French Guiana[5] | **Department of Guiana** | France | FG | *Cayenne* |
| 20. | French Polynesia | **Territory of French Polynesia** | France | FP | *Papeete* |
| 21. | French Southern & Antarctic Lands[6] | **Territory of the French Southern and Antarctic Lands** | France | FS | *Administered from Paris* |
| 22. | Gibraltar | (no long-form name) | United Kingdom | GI | *Gibraltar* |
| 23. | Greenland | (no long-form name) | Denmark | GL | *Nuuk (Godthåb)* |
| 24. | Guadeloupe[5] | **Department of Guadeloupe** | France | GP | *Basse-Terre* |
| 25. | Guam | **Territory of Guam** | United States | GQ | *Hagatna* |
| 26. | Guernsey[7] | **Bailiwick of Guernsey** | British Crown Dependency | GK | *Saint Peter Port* |
| 27. | Heard Island & McDonald Islands | **Territory of Heard Island and McDonald Islands** | Australia | HM | *Administered from Canberra* |
| 28. | Hong Kong | **Hong Kong Special Administrative Region** | China[7] | HK | *Victoria* |
| 29. | Howland Island | (no long-form name) | United States | HQ | *Administered from Washington, D.C.* |
| 30. | Jan Mayen | (no long-form name) | Norway | JN | *Administered from Oslo[8]* |
| 31. | Jarvis Island | (no long-form name) | United States | DQ | *Administered from Washington, D.C.* |
| 32. | Jersey | **Bailiwick of Jersey** | British Crown Dependency | JE | *Saint Helier* |
| 33. | Johnston Atoll | (no long-form name) | United States | JQ | *Administered from Washington, D.C.* |
| 34. | Kingman Reef | (no long-form name) | United States | KQ | *Administered from Washington, D.C.* |

| Short-form name | Long-form name | Sovereignty | Code[1] | Capital |
|---|---|---|---|---|
| 35. Macau | **Macau Special Administrative Region** | China[9] | MC | *Macau* |
| 36. Man, Isle of | (no long-form name) | British Crown Dependency | IM | *Douglas* |
| 37. Martinique[2] | **Department of Martinique** | France | MB | *Fort-de-France* |
| 38. Mayotte | **Territorial Collectivity of Mayotte** | France | MF | *Mamoudzou* |
| 39. Midway Islands | (no long-form name) | United States | MQ | *Administered from Washington, D.C.* |
| 40. Montserrat | (no long-form name) | United Kingdom | MH | *Plymouth* |
| 41. Navassa Island | (no long-form name) | United States | BQ | *Administered from Washington, D.C.* |
| 42. Netherlands Antilles[10] | (no long-form name) | Netherlands | NT | *Willemstad* |
| 43. New Caledonia | **Territory of New Caledonia and Dependencies** | France | NC | *Nouméa* |
| 44. Niue | (no long-form name) | New Zealand | NE | *Alofi* |
| 45. Norfolk Island | **Territory of Norfolk Island** | Australia | NF | *Kingston* |
| 46. Northern Mariana Islands | **Commonwealth of the Northern Mariana Islands** | United States | CQ | *Saipan* |
| 47. Palmyra Atoll | (no long-form name) | United States | LQ | *Administered from Washington, D.C.* |
| 48. Paracel Islands | (no long-form name) | undetermined[11] | PF | *None* |
| 49. Pitcairn Islands | **Pitcairn, Henderson, Ducie, and Oeno Islands** | United Kingdom | PC | *Adamstown* |
| 50. Puerto Rico | **Commonwealth of Puerto Rico** | United States | RQ | *San Juan* |
| 51. Reunion[5] | **Department of Reunion** | France | RE | *Saint-Denis* |
| 52. Saint Helena[13] | (no long-form name) | United Kingdom | SH | *Jamestown* |
| 53. Saint Pierre & Miquelon | **Territorial Collectivity of Saint Pierre and Miquelon** | France | SB | *Saint-Pierre* |
| 54. South Georgia & the South Sandwich Islands | **South Georgia and the South Sandwich Islands** | United Kingdom[4] | SX | *None* |
| 55. Spratly Islands | (no long-form name) | undetermined[14] | PG | *None* |
| 56. Svalbard | (no long-form name) | Norway | SV | *Longyearbyen* |
| 57. Tokelau | (no long-form name) | New Zealand | TL | *None* |
| 58. Turks & Caicos Islands | (no long-form name) | United Kingdom | TK | *Grand Turk* |
| 59. Virgin Islands, U.S. | **United States Virgin Islands** | United States | VQ | *Charlotte Amalie* |
| 60. Virgin Islands, British | (no long-form name) | United Kingdom | VI | *Road Town* |
| 61. Wake Island | (no long-form name) | United States | WQ | *Administered from Washington, D.C.* |
| 62. Wallis and Futuna | **Territory of the Wallis and Futuna Islands** | France | WF | *Matâ'utu* |
| 63. Western Sahara | (no long-form name) | undetermined | WI | *None* |

# Notes

Note 1: Federal Information Processing Standard (FIPS) 10-4 codes.

Note 2: Antarctica consists of the territory south of 60 degrees south latitude. This area includes claims by Argentina, Australia, Chile, France, New Zealand, Norway, and the United Kingdom, the legal status of which remains in suspense under the terms of the Antarctic Treaty of 1959. The United States recognizes no claims to Antarctica.

Note 3: Chagos Archipelago (including Diego Garcia).

Note 4: Dependent territory of the United Kingdom (also claimed by Argentina).

Note 5: French Guiana, Guadeloupe, Martinique and

Reunion are departments (first-order administrative units) of France, and are therefore not dependencies or areas of special sovereignty. They are included in this list only for the convenience of the user. The Department of Guadeloupe includes the nearby islands of Marie-Galante, La Desirade, and Iles des Saintes, as well as Saint Barthelemy and the northern three-fifths of Saint Martin (the rest of which belongs to Netherlands Antilles). The islands of Bassas da India, Europa Island, Glorioso Islands, Juan de Nova Island, and Tromelin Island are administered from Reunion; all these islands are claimed by Madagascar, and Tromelin Island is claimed by Mauritius.

Note 6: "French Southern and Antarctic Lands" includes Île Amsterdam, Île Saint-Paul, Îles Crozet, and Îles Kerguelen in the southern Indian Ocean, along with the French-claimed sector of Antarctica, "Terre Adélie." The United States does not recognize the French claim to "Terre Adélie" (see note 2).

Note 7: The Bailiwick of Guernsey includes the islands of Alderney, Guernsey, Herm, Sark, and nearby smaller islands.

Note 8: Under a Sino-British declaration of September 1984, Hong Kong reverted to Chinese control on July 1, 1997. It is now a semi-autonomous entity that exists pursuant to international agreement and maintains its own government apart from the People's Republic of China.

Note 9: Administered from Oslo, Norway, through a governor resident in Longyearbyen, Svalbard.

Note 10: Under the Sino-Portuguese Joint Declaration on the Question of Macau signed in 1987, Macau reverted to Chinese control on December 20, 1999. It is now a semi-autonomous entity that exists pursuant to international agreement and maintains its own government apart from the People's Republic of China.

Note 11: Netherlands Antilles comprises two groupings of islands: Curaçao and Bonaire are located off the coast of Venezuela; Saba, Sint Eustatius, and Sint Maarten (the Dutch two-fifths of the island of Saint Martin) lie 800 km to the north.

Note 12: South China Sea islands occupied by China but claimed by Vietnam.

Note 13: The territory of Saint Helena includes the Island group of Tristan da Cunha; Saint Helena also administers Ascension Island.

Note 14: South China Sea islands claimed in entirety by China and Vietnam and in part by the Philippines and Malaysia; each of these states occupies some part of the islands.

Source: Office of the Geographer and Global Issues, Bureau of Intelligence and Research, U.S. Department of State, Washington, D.C.

# Alphabetical Checklist of 124 New Nations Since 1943

Algeria .................................................................. July 5, 1962
Angola ...................................................................Nov. 11, 1976
Antigua and Barbuda .......................................Nov. 1, 1981
Armenia .............................................................Sept. 23, 1991
Azerbaijan .........................................................Aug. 30, 1991
Bahamas, The .................................................... July 10, 1973
Bahrain ..............................................................Aug. 14, 1971
Bangladesh ............................................................ Apr. 4, 1972
Barbados ............................................................Nov. 30, 1966
Belarus ..............................................................Aug. 25, 1991
Belize ................................................................Sept. 21, 1981
Benin ...................................................................Aug. 1, 1960
Bosnia and Herzegovina ...................................April 1, 1992
Botswana ...........................................................Sept. 30, 1966
Brunei .................................................................. Jan. 1, 1984
Burkina ...............................................................Aug. 5, 1960
Burma ................................................................. Jan. 4, 1948
Burundi ................................................................ July 1, 1962
Cambodia ........................................................... Nov. 8, 1949
Cameroon ............................................................ Jan. 1, 1960
Cape Verde .......................................................... July 5, 1975
Central African Republic ...................................Aug. 13, 1960
Chad ...................................................................Aug. 11, 1960
Comoros ............................................................. Dec. 31, 1976
Congo, Dem. Rep. of (Zaire) .............................June 30, 1960
Congo, Rep. of ..................................................Aug. 15, 1960
Côte d'Ivoire (Ivory Coast) ..............................Aug. 7, 1960
Croatia ...............................................................June 25, 1991
Cyprus ...............................................................Aug. 16, 1960
Czech Republic ................................................... Jan. 1, 1993
Djibouti ..............................................................June 27, 1977
Dominica ............................................................. Nov. 3, 1978
Equatorial Guinea ............................................Oct. 12, 1968
Eritrea ...............................................................April 27, 1993
Estonia ................................................................ Sept. 6, 1991
Fiji ......................................................................Oct. 10, 1970
Gabon .................................................................Aug. 17, 1960
Gambia, The ........................................................ Feb. 18, 1965
Georgia ..............................................................April 9, 1991
Ghana .................................................................. Mar. 6, 1957
Grenada ............................................................... Feb. 7, 1974
Guinea ................................................................Oct. 2, 1958
Guinea-Bissau ...................................................Sept. 10, 1974
Guyana ...............................................................May 26, 1966
Iceland ...............................................................June 17, 1944
India ...................................................................Aug. 15, 1947
Indonesia ...........................................................Dec. 28, 1949
Israel ....................................................................May 15, 1948
Jamaica ...............................................................Aug. 6, 1962
Jordan .................................................................. Mar. 22, 1946
Kazakhstan ......................................................... Dec. 6, 1991
Kenya ................................................................. Dec. 12, 1963
Kiribati ................................................................ July 12, 1979
Korea, North .....................................................Sept. 9, 1948
Korea, South ......................................................Aug. 15, 1948
Kuwait ................................................................June 19, 1961
Kyrgyzstan ........................................................Aug. 31, 1991
Laos ..................................................................... July 19, 1949
Latvia .................................................................. Sept. 6, 1991
Lebanon .............................................................Nov. 22, 1943
Lesotho ................................................................Oct. 4, 1966
Libya ..................................................................Dec. 24, 1951
Lithuania ............................................................. Sept. 6, 1991
Macedonia ..........................................................Nov. 20, 1991
Madagascar ........................................................June 27, 1960
Malawi ................................................................. July 6, 1964

Malaysia ............................................................Aug. 31, 1957
Maldives ............................................................July 26, 1966
Mali ...................................................................Sept. 22, 1960
Malta ..................................................................Sept. 21, 1964
Marshall Islands ............................................... Oct. 21, 1986
Mauritania ........................................................ Nov. 28, 1960
Mauritius ...........................................................Mar. 12, 1968
Micronesia, Federated States of ...................... Nov. 3, 1986
Moldova .............................................................Aug. 27, 1991
Morocco .............................................................Mar. 2, 1956
Mozambique ......................................................June 25, 1975
Namibia ............................................................. March 21, 1990
Nauru .................................................................Jan. 31, 1968
Niger .................................................................. Aug. 3, 1960
Nigeria ............................................................... Oct. 1, 1960
Pakistan .............................................................Aug. 14, 1947
Palau ..................................................................Jan. 1, 1981
Papua New Guinea ............................................Sept. 16, 1976
Philippines......................................................... July 4, 1946
Qatar..................................................................Sept. 3, 1971
Russia ................................................................ Aug. 24, 1991
Rwanda ...............................................................July 1, 1962
Saint Kitts and Nevis .......................................Sept. 19, 1983
Saint Lucia ........................................................ Feb. 22, 1979
Saint Vincent and the Grenadines.................... Oct. 27, 1979
São Tomé and Príncipe .....................................July 12, 1975
Senegal .............................................................. Aug. 20, 1960
Serbia and Montenegro* ..................................April 11, 1992
Seychelles ..........................................................June 28, 1976
Sierra Leone ......................................................Apr. 27, 1961
Singapore .......................................................... Aug. 9, 1965
Slovakia .............................................................Jan. 1, 1993
Slovenia .............................................................June 25, 1991
Solomon Islands ............................................... July 7, 1978
Somalia ..............................................................July 1, 1960
Sri Lanka ........................................................... Feb. 4, 1948
Sudan .................................................................Jan. 1, 1956
Suriname ........................................................... Nov. 25, 1975
Swaziland ...........................................................Sept. 6, 1968
Syria...................................................................Jan. 1, 1944
Tajikistan ...........................................................Sept. 9, 1991
Tanzania ............................................................. Dec. 9, 1961
Togo....................................................................Apr. 27, 1960
Tonga ..................................................................June 4, 1970
Trinidad and Tobago ........................................Aug. 31, 1962
Tunisia ...............................................................Mar. 20, 1956
Turkmenistan.................................................... Oct. 27, 1991
Tuvalu................................................................ Oct. 1, 1978
Uganda .............................................................. Oct. 9, 1962
Ukraine..............................................................Dec. 1, 1991
Uzbekistan.........................................................Aug. 31, 1991
United Arab Emirates ...................................... Dec. 2, 1971
Vanuatu..............................................................July 30, 1980
Vietnam ............................................................. Mar. 8, 1949
Western Samoa ................................................. Jan. 1, 1962
Yemen.................................................................May 22, 1990
Zambia ...............................................................Oct. 24, 1964
Zimbabwe ..........................................................Apr. 18, 1980

*Serbia and Montenegro have asserted the formation of a joint independent state and wish to be recognized as a continuation of the former Republic of Yugoslavia. The US view is that the Socialist Federal Republic of Yugoslavia has dissolved and no successor state represents its continuation. As a result, this entity (new Yugoslavia) has not been formally recognized as a state by the U.S.

## Chronological Checklist of 124 New Nations Since 1943

| | | |
|---|---|---|
| 1943 | Nov. 22 | Lebanon |
| 1944 | Jan. 1 | Syria |
| | June 17 | Iceland |
| 1946 | Mar. 22 | Jordan |
| | July 4 | Philippines |
| 1947 | Aug. 14 | Pakistan |
| | Aug. 15 | India |
| 1948 | Jan. 4 | Burma |
| | Feb. 4 | Sri Lanka |
| | May 15 | Israel |
| | Aug. 15 | Korea, South |
| | Sept. 9 | Korea, North |
| 1949 | Mar. 8 | Vietnam |
| | July 19 | Laos |
| | Nov. 8 | Cambodia |
| | Dec. 28 | Indonesia |
| 1951 | Dec. 24 | Libya |
| 1956 | Jan. 1 | Sudan |
| | Mar. 2 | Morocco |
| | Mar. 20 | Tunisia |
| 1957 | Mar. 6 | Ghana |
| | Aug. 31 | Malaysia |
| 1958 | Oct. 2 | Guinea |
| 1960 | Jan. 1 | Cameroon |
| | Apr. 27 | Togo |
| | June 27 | Madagascar |
| | June 30 | Congo, Dem. Rep. of (Zaire) |
| | July 1 | Somalia |
| | Aug. 1 | Benin |
| | Aug. 3 | Niger |
| | Aug. 5 | Burkina |
| | Aug. 7 | Côte d'Ivoire |
| | Aug. 11 | Chad |
| | Aug. 13 | Central African Republic |
| | Aug. 15 | Congo, Rep of |
| | Aug. 16 | Cyprus |
| | Aug. 17 | Gabon |
| | Aug. 20 | Senegal |
| | Sept. 22 | Mali |
| | Oct. 1 | Nigeria |
| | Nov. 28 | Mauritania |
| 1961 | Apr. 27 | Sierra Leone |
| | June 19 | Kuwait |
| | Dec. 9 | Tanzania |
| 1962 | Jan. 1 | Western Samoa |
| | July 1 | Burundi |
| | July 1 | Rwanda |
| | July 5 | Algeria |
| | Aug. 6 | Jamaica |
| | Aug. 31 | Trinidad and Tobago |
| | Oct. 9 | Uganda |
| 1963 | Dec. 12 | Kenya |
| 1964 | July 6 | Malawi |
| | Sept. 21 | Malta |
| | Oct. 24 | Zambia |
| 1965 | Feb. 18 | Gambia, The |
| | July 26 | Maldives |
| | Aug. 9 | Singapore |
| 1966 | May 26 | Guyana |
| | Sept. 30 | Botswana |
| | Oct. 4 | Lesotho |
| | Nov. 30 | Barbados |
| 1968 | Jan. 31 | Nauru |
| | Mar. 12 | Mauritius |
| | Sept. 6 | Swaziland |
| | Oct. 12 | Equatorial Guinea |
| 1970 | June 4 | Tonga |
| | Oct. 10 | Fiji |
| 1971 | Aug. 14 | Bahrain |
| | Sept. 3 | Qatar |
| | Dec. 2 | United Arab Emirates |
| 1972 | Apr. 4 | Bangladesh |
| 1973 | July 10 | Bahamas, The |
| 1974 | Feb. 7 | Grenada |
| | Sept. 10 | Guinea-Bissau |
| 1975 | June 25 | Mozambique |
| | July 6 | Cape Verde |
| | July 12 | São Tomé and Príncipe |
| | Sept. 16 | Papua New Guinea |
| | Nov. 11 | Angola |
| | Nov. 26 | Surname |
| | Dec. 31 | Comoros |
| 1976 | June 28 | Seychelles |
| 1977 | June 27 | Djibouti |
| 1978 | July 7 | Solomon Islands |
| | Oct. 1 | Tuvalu |
| | Nov. 3 | Dominica |
| 1979 | Feb. 22 | Saint Lucia |
| | July 12 | Kiribati |
| | Oct. 27 | Saint Vincent and the Grenadines |
| 1980 | Apr. 18 | Zimbabwe |
| | July 30 | Vanuatu |
| 1981 | Jan. 1 | Palau |
| | Sept. 21 | Belize |
| | Nov. 1 | Antigua and Barbuda |
| 1983 | Sept. 19 | Saint Kitts and Nevis |
| 1984 | Jan. 1 | Brunei |
| 1986 | Oct. 21 | Marshall Islands |
| | Nov. 3 | Micronesia, Federated States of |
| 1990 | Mar. 21 | Namibia |
| | May 22 | Yemen |
| 1991 | April 9 | Georgia |
| | June 25 | Croatia |
| | June 25 | Slovenia |
| | Aug. 24 | Russia |
| | Aug. 25 | Belarus |
| | Aug. 27 | Moldova |
| | Aug. 30 | Azerbaijan |
| | Aug. 31 | Uzbekistan |
| | Aug. 31 | Kyrgyzstan |
| | Sept. 6 | Latvia |
| | Sept. 6 | Lithuania |
| | Sept. 6 | Estonia |
| | Sept. 9 | Tajikistan |
| | Sept. 23 | Armenia |
| | Oct. 27 | Turkmenistan |
| | Nov. 20 | Macedonia |
| | Dec. 1 | Ukraine |
| | Dec. 6 | Kazakhstan |
| 1992 | April 1 | Bosnia and Herzegovina |
| | April 11 | Serbia and Montenegro* |
| 1993 | Jan. 1 | Czech Republic |
| | Jan. 1 | Slovakia |
| | April 27 | Eritrea |

*Serbia and Montenegro have asserted the formation of a joint independent state and wish to be recognized as a continuation of the former Republic of Yugoslavia. The US view is that the Socialist Federal Republic of Yugoslavia has dissolved and no successor state represents its continuation. As a result, this entity (new Yugoslavia) has not been formally recognized as a state by the U.S.

# U.S. Embassies, Consulates, and Foreign Service Posts

# How and Where to Seek the State Department's Assistance When Doing Business Abroad

## DOING BUSINESS OVERSEAS— YOUR FIRST POINT OF CONTACT

If you are planning a trip overseas or need information about doing business overseas, your first point of contact should be the nearest U.S. Department of Commerce District Office. (See page 127.)

There are 47 District Offices and 21 Branch Offices in cities throughout the United States and Puerto Rico staffed by trade specialists from the United States and Foreign Commercial Service (US&FCS). These District Offices provide information on foreign markets, agent/distributor location services, trade leads, and counseling on business opportunities.

All District Offices have access to the National Trade Data Bank, a one-stop computerized source for current export promotion and country-specific trade data collected by 17 U.S. Government agencies. U.S. Export Assistance Centers, which combine the export promotion and trade finance services of the Department of Commerce, the Export-Import Bank, the Small Business Administration, and the Agency for International Development, now are open in Miami, Chicago, Long Beach, and Baltimore.

It is strongly recommended that business representatives inform the District Office of their plans to travel overseas. The District Office will notify Commercial Sections in overseas posts of the upcoming visit to ensure that they are adequately prepared to help.

The *Key Officers Guide* (page 132) lists key officers at Foreign Service posts with whom American business representatives would most likely have contact. All embassies, missions, consulates general, and consulates are listed.

At the head of each U.S. diplomatic mission are the Chief of Mission (with the title of **Ambassador**, **Minister**, or **Charge d'Affaires**) and the Deputy Chief of Mission. These officers are responsible for all components of the U.S. Mission within a country, including consular posts.

A **Chief of Mission Secretary** is responsible for the scheduling of appointments for that official. In addition to other duties, this secretary may also assist business persons by directing inquiries to the appropriate Mission office.

**Commercial Officers** advise U.S. business on local trade and tariff laws, government procurement procedures, and business practices; identify potential importers, agents, distributors, and joint venture partners; provide information on local government tenders; and assist with resolution of trade and investment disputes. At smaller posts, commercial interests are represented by Economic/Commercial Officers from the Department of State.

**Commercial Officers for Tourism** promote the U.S. travel and tourism industry.

**Economic Officers** advise U.S. business on the local investment climate and economic trends; negotiate trade and investment agreements to open markets and level the playing field; and analyze and report on macroeconomic trends and trade policies and their potential impact on U.S. interests.

**Resource Officers** counsel U.S. business on issues related to natural resources, including minerals, oil and gas and energy; and analyze and report on local natural resource trends and trade policies and their potential impact on U.S. interests.

**Agricultural Officers** promote the export of U.S. agricultural products and report on agricultural production and market developments in their area.

**Animal and Plant Health Inspection Service Officers** are responsible for animal and plant health issues as they impact U.S. trade and in protecting U.S. agriculture from foreign pests and diseases. They expedite U.S. exports in the area of technical sanitary and phytosanitary (S&P) regulations.

**Environment, Science and Technology (EST) Officers** analyze and report on EST developments and their potential impact on U.S. policies and programs.

**Financial Attaches** analyze and report on major financial developments.

**Consular Officers** extend to U.S. citizens and their property abroad the protection of the U.S. Government. They maintain lists of local attorneys, act as liaison with police and other officials, and have the authority to notarize documents. The Department recommends that business representatives residing overseas register with the consular officer; in troubled areas, even travelers are advised to register.

**Immigration and Naturalization Service Officers** are responsible for enforcing the laws regulating the admission of foreign-born persons (i.e., aliens) to the United States and for administering various immigration benefits, including the naturalization of resident aliens.

**Regional Security Officers** are responsible for providing physical, procedural, and personnel security services to U.S. diplomatic facilities and personnel; they also provide local in-country security briefings and threat assessments to business executives.

**AID Mission Directors** are responsible for AID programs, including dollar and local currency loans, grants, and technical assistance.

**Political Officers** advise U.S. business executives on the local political climate and analyze and report on political developments and their potential impact on U.S. interests.

**Labor Officers** follow the activities of labor organizations to supply such information as wages, nonwage costs, social security regulations, labor attitudes toward American investments, etc. Advise U.S. business on local labor laws and practices and analyze and report on activities of local labor organizations, labor laws and practices, and their potential impact on U.S. interests.

**Administrative Officers** are responsible for normal business operations of the post, including purchasing for the post and its commissary.

**Security Assistance Officers** are responsible for Defense Cooperation in Armaments and foreign military sales to include functioning as primary in-country point of contact for U.S. Defense Industry.

**Information Systems Managers** are responsible for the post's unclassified information systems, database management, programming, and operational needs. They provide liaison with appropriate commercial contacts in the information field to enhance the post's systems integrity.

**Communications Programs Officers** are responsible for the telecommunications, telephone, radio, diplomatic pouches, and records management programs within the diplomatic mission. They maintain close contact with the host government's information/communications authorities on operational matters.

**Public Affairs Officers** are the press and cultural affairs specialists and maintain close contact with the local press.

**Legal Attaches** serve as representatives to the U.S. Department of Justice on criminal matters.

## U.S. Department of State and Commerce Country Desk Officers

Both the Departments of State and Commerce have country desk officers based in Washington, D.C. who have comprehensive, up-to-date information on particular countries and can advise U.S. companies of the political and economic climate.

International Economic Policy (IEP) country desk officers in the Department of Commerce collect information on individual country regulations, tariffs, business practices, economic and political developments, trade data, and market size and growth, keeping a current pulse on the potential markets for U.S. products, services, and investments.

IEP has several regional business information centers that focus on new opportunities for trade and investment in various parts of the world: the former Soviet Union, Eastern Europe, Japan, Latin America and the Caribbean, and the European Community.

For a specific country desk officer or regional business center, call (202) 482–3022.

Country desk officers at the Department of State maintain regular contact with overseas diplomatic missions and can provide country-specific economic and political analysis for U.S. companies.

For a specific State Department country desk officer, call (202) 647–4000.

The Department of State, Bureau of Diplomatic Security, can also provide current data on the security situation to interested persons planning trips abroad. American business representatives desiring this information should contact the Overseas Security Advisory Council at (202) 663–0533.

## Department of State Coordinator for Business Affairs

The Coordinator for Business Affairs coordinates the Department's advocacy for U.S. companies overseas competing in international bids; problem-solving assistance to U.S. companies; dialogue with the U.S. private sector to ensure that business concerns are appropriately factored into foreign policy; and programs and practices to improve the Department's support for business. You should consider the Coordinator for Business Affairs your principal point of contact for business concerns within the Department of State. Tel. (202) 647–1942; FAX (202) 647–5713.

## Trade Information Center

For general information about U.S. Government export promotion programs, you should contact the Trade Information Center. It provides information on Federal programs and activities that support U.S. exports, information on overseas markets and industry trends, and a computerized calendar of U.S Government-sponsored domestic and overseas trade events. The center's nationwide toll-free number is: 1–800–USA–TRADE (1–800–872–8723).

A special line is available for those who are deaf or hearing-impaired: TDD 1–800–833–8723.

# EXAMPLES OF ACCEPTED FORMS FOR ADDRESSING MAIL

It is most important that correspondence to a Foreign Service post be addressed to a section or position rather than to an officer by name. This will eliminate delays resulting from the forwarding of official mail to officers who have transferred. Normally, correspondence concerning commercial matters should be addressed simply "Commercial Section" followed by the name and correct mailing address of the post. (See below for examples of correct mailing addresses.)

## Posts with APO/FPO Numbers:

*APO/FPO Address\**

> Name
> Organization
> PSC or Unit number, Box number
> APO AE 09080 **or** APO AA 34038 **or**
> APO AP 96337

*International Address\*\**

> Name of Person/Section
> American Embassy
> P.O. Box 26431\*\*\*
> Manama, Bahrain

## Posts without APO/FPO Numbers:

*Diplomatic Pouch Address\**
> Name of Person/Section
> Name of Post
> Department of State
> Washington, D.C. 20521–four digit add-on
> (*see* 9-digit ZIP Code explanation and listing)

*International Address\*\**
> Name of Person/Section
> American Embassy
> Jubilaeumstrasse 93\*\*\*
> 3005 Bern, Switzerland

\*    Use domestic postage.

\*\*    Use international postage.

\*\*\*    Use street address only when P.O. box is not supplied.

---

**NOTE: Do not combine any of the above forms (e.g., international plus APO/FPO addresses). This will only result in confusion and possible delays in delivery. Mail sent to the Department for delivery through its pouch system for posts with APO/FPO addresses cannot be accepted and will be returned to the sender.**

# STATE ZIP CODES

In conjunction with the U.S. Postal Service's system of 9-digit ZIP Codes, the Department of State has assigned a unique 4-digit number to each Foreign Service post. All mail sent through the Department's pouch system (for posts without APO/FPO addresses) should add the 4-digit number to the current ZIP Code 20521. For example, the ZIP Code for Abidjan would be 20521–2010;  for Abu Dhabi, 20521–6010. Refer to the following list for each Foreign Service post's unique  number.

| Post | Code | Post | Code |
|------|------|------|------|
| Abidjan | 2010 | Buenos Aires | 3130 |
| Abu Dhabi | 6010 | Bujumbura | 2100 |
| Accra | 2020 | Bukavu | 2240 |
| Adana | 5020 | Cairo | 7700 |
| Addis Ababa | 2030 | Calcutta | 6250 |
| Algiers | 6030 | Calgary | 5490 |
| Almaty | 7030 | Canberra | 7800 |
| Amman | 6050 | Cape Town | 2480 |
| Amsterdam | 5780 | Caracas | 3140 |
| Ankara | 7000 | Casablanca | 6280 |
| Antananarivo | 2040 | Chengdu | 4080 |
| Ashgabat | 7070 | Chiang Mai | 4040 |
| Asmara | 7170 | Chisinau | 7080 |
| Asuncion | 3020 | Ciudad Juarez | 3270 |
| Athens | 7100 | Cluj-Napoca | 1315 |
| Auckland | 4370 | Colombo | 6100 |
| Baghdad | 6060 | Conakry | 2110 |
| Baku | 7050 | Copenhagen | 5280 |
| Bamako | 2050 | Cotonou | 2120 |
| Bandar Seri Begawan | 4020 | Curacao | 3160 |
| Bangkok | 7200 | Dakar | 2130 |
| Bangui | 2060 | Damascus | 6110 |
| Banjul | 2070 | Dar Es Salaam | 2140 |
| Barcelona | 5400 | Dhahran | 6310 |
| Beijing | 7300 | Dhaka | 6120 |
| Beirut | 6070 | Djibouti | 2150 |
| Belfast | 5360 | Doha | 6130 |
| Belgrade | 5070 | Dubai | 6020 |
| Belize | 3050 | Dublin | 5290 |
| Berlin | 5090 | Durban | 2490 |
| Bern | 5110 | Dushanbe | 7090 |
| Bishkek | 7040 | Dusseldorf | 5160 |
| Bissau | 2080 | Edinburgh | 5370 |
| Bogota | 3030 | Florence | 5670 |
| Bombay | 6240 | Frankfurt | 7900 |
| Bonn | 7400 | Freetown | 2160 |
| Brasilia | 7500 | Fukuoka | 4310 |
| Bratislava | 5840 | Gaborone | 2170 |
| Brazzaville | 2090 | Geneva (M) | 5120 |
| Bridgetown | 3120 | Georgetown | 3170 |
| Brussels (USNATO - M) | 5230 | Grenada | 3180 |
| Brussels (E) | 7600 | Guadalajara | 3280 |
| Bucharest | 5260 | Guangzhou | 4090 |
| Budapest | 5270 | Guatemala City | 3190 |
|  |  | Guayaquil | 3430 |
|  |  | (The) Hague | 5770 |

| | | | |
|---|---|---|---|
| Hamburg | 5180 | Monterrey | 3330 |
| Hamilton | 5300 | Montevideo | 3360 |
| Hanoi | 4550 | Montreal | 5510 |
| Harare | 2180 | Moscow | 5430 |
| Havana | 3200 | Munich | 5190 |
| Helsinki | 5310 | Muscat | 6220 |
| Hermosillo | 3290 | Naha | 4320 |
| Ho Chi Minh City | 7160 | Nairobi | 8900 |
| Hong Kong | 8000 | Naples | 5700 |
| Islamabad | 8100 | Nassau | 3370 |
| Istanbul | 5030 | N'Djamena | 2410 |
| Jakarta | 8200 | New Delhi | 9000 |
| Jeddah | 6320 | Niamey | 2420 |
| Jerusalem | 6350 | Nice | 5610 |
| Johannesburg | 2500 | Nicosia | 5450 |
| Kampala | 2190 | Nouakchott | 2430 |
| Karachi | 6150 | Nuevo Laredo | 3340 |
| Kathmandu | 6190 | Oporto | 5330 |
| Khabarovsk | 5870 | Osaka-Kobe | 4330 |
| Khartoum | 2200 | Oslo | 5460 |
| Kiev | 5850 | Ottawa | 5480 |
| Kigali | 2210 | Ouagadougou | 2440 |
| Kingston | 3210 | Panama City | 9100 |
| Kinshasa | 2220 | Paramaribo | 3390 |
| Kolonia | 4120 | Paris | 9200 |
| Krakow | 5140 | Perth | 4160 |
| Kuala Lumpur | 4210 | Peshawar | 6170 |
| Kuwait | 6200 | Phnom Penh | 4540 |
| Lagos | 8300 | Ponta Delgada | 5340 |
| La Paz | 3220 | Port-au-Prince | 3400 |
| Lahore | 6160 | Port Louis | 2450 |
| Leipzig | 5860 | Port Moresby | 4240 |
| Libreville | 2270 | Port-of-Spain | 3410 |
| Lilongwe | 2280 | Poznan | 5050 |
| Lima | 3230 | Prague | 5630 |
| Lisbon | 5320 | Praia | 2460 |
| Ljubljana | 7140 | Pretoria | 9300 |
| Lome | 2300 | Pusan | 4270 |
| London | 8400 | Quebec | 5520 |
| Luanda | 2550 | Quito | 3420 |
| Lusaka | 2310 | Rabat | 9400 |
| Luxembourg | 5380 | Rangoon | 4250 |
| Madras | 6260 | Recife | 3080 |
| Madrid | 8500 | Reykjavik | 5640 |
| Majuro | 4380 | Riga | 4520 |
| Malabo | 2320 | Rio de Janeiro | 3090 |
| Managua | 3240 | Riyadh | 6300 |
| Manama | 6210 | Rome | 9500 |
| Manila | 8600 | St. George's | 3180 |
| Maputo | 2330 | St. Petersburg | 5440 |
| Marseille | 5600 | San Jose | 3440 |
| Maseru | 2340 | San Salvador | 3450 |
| Matamoros | 3300 | Sanaa | 6330 |
| Mbabane | 2350 | Santiago | 3460 |
| Melbourne | 4140 | Santo Domingo | 3470 |
| Merida | 3320 | Sao Paulo | 3110 |
| Mexico City | 8700 | Sapporo | 4340 |
| Milan | 5690 | Sarajevo | 7130 |
| Minsk | 7010 | Seoul | 9600 |

| | | | |
|---|---|---|---|
| Shanghai | 4100 | Tokyo | 9800 |
| Shenyang | 4110 | Toronto | 5530 |
| Singapore | 4280 | Trieste | 5720 |
| Skopje | 7120 | Tunis | 6360 |
| Sofia | 5740 | Ulaanbaatar | 4410 |
| Stockholm | 5750 | Valletta | 5800 |
| Strasbourg | 5620 | Vancouver | 5540 |
| Surabaya | 4200 | Vatican City | 5660 |
| Suva | 4290 | Vienna | 9900 |
| Sydney | 4150 | Vientiane | 4350 |
| Taipei, AIT | 4170 | Vilnius | 4510 |
| Tallinn | 4530 | Vladivostok | 5880 |
| Tashkent | 7110 | Warsaw | 5010 |
| Tbilisi | 7060 | Wellington | 4360 |
| Tegucigalpa | 3480 | Windhoek | 2540 |
| Tel Aviv | 9700 | Yaounde | 2520 |
| Thessaloniki | 5060 | Yekaterinburg | 5890 |
| Tijuana | 3350 | Yerevan | 7020 |
| Tirana | 9510 | Zagreb | 5080 |

# TELEPHONING A FOREIGN SERVICE POST

Below is the procedure for telephoning a Foreign Service Post. American Embassy Canberra is used as an example.

**Calling from a U.S. Government Agency:**

Dial 9 + international access code + country code + city code + local number

Eg. 9 + 011 + [61] + (6) + 2705000

**Others:**

Dial international access code + country code + city code + local number

Eg. 011 + [61] + (6) + 2705000

**NOTE: Some international calls will require operator assistance because the country is not an international dial country. The telephone listing of these countries will not be proceded by a country code and city code (always shown in brackets and parentheses).**

Calls to certain points outside the continental U.S. can be dialed in the same manner as long distance. Simply dial the area code or country code and the local number. For these locations, no city code will appear with the telephone number.

# IVG USAGE DIAL PREFIX CODES

The International Voice Gateway (IVG) switch is located in Beltsville, Maryland and provided interconnectivity from 99 overseas locations to all Department of State and government agencies located in the Washington, D.C. metropolitan area. Through the use of calling cards, it also enables users to access the FTS networks, GETS, WITS, as well as commercial numbers for international direct dialing at substantially reduced rates.

| Post | Access Code | Post | Access Code |
|------|------------|------|------------|
| Abu Dhabi | 845 | Lilongwe | 835 |
| AIT Taipei | 844 | Lima | 549 |
| Algiers | 928 | London | 492 |
| Almaty | 927 | Madrid | 559 |
| Ankara | 295 | Manila | 678 |
| Ashgaba | 962 | Mexico | 578 |
| Asuncion | 642 | Milan | 481 |
| Athens | 869 | Minsk | 577 |
| Baku | 841 | Moscow | 435 |
| Bangkok | 675 | Ndjamena | 924 |
| Berlin | 292 | New Delhi | 840 |
| Bern | 873 | OSIA Moscow | 995 |
| Bogota | 879 | Ottawa | 834 |
| Bonn | 496 | Panama City | 833 |
| Brandy | 490 | Paris | 498 |
| Brasilia | 921 | Port au Prince | 271 |
| Bratislava | 560 | Pretoria | 685 |
| Brussels | 694 | Quito | 644 |
| Buenos Aires | 878 | Riga | 868 |
| Cairo | 870 | Rome | 674 |
| Canberra | 679 | San Salvador | 830 |
| Caracas | 643 | Santiago | 843 |
| Chisinau | 548 | Sarajevo | 837 |
| Croughton | 573 | Seoul | 725 |
| DTSPO | 671 | Singapore | 726 |
| Dublin | 693 | Stockholm | 993 |
| Dushanbe | 752 | Tallinn | 969 |
| Frankfurt | 568 | Tbilisi | 997 |
| Ft. Lauderdale | 798 | Tegucigalpa | 539 |
| Gaborone | 846 | Tel Aviv | 751 |
| Geneva | 493 | Tirana | 970 |
| Guatemala | 799 | Tokyo | 688 |
| Hong Kong | 727 | USNATO | 641 |
| Jakarta | 386 | Valletta | 753 |
| Kampala | 838 | Vienna | 872 |
| Kiev | 788 | Vilnius | 973 |
| Kigali | 988 | Wellington | 847 |
| Kingston | 929 | Yekaterinburg | 757 |
| Lagos | 261 | Yerevan | 996 |
| La Paz | 547 | Zagreb | 444 |

# DEPARTMENT OF COMMERCE DISTRICT OFFICES

(*)-Denotes Trade Specialist at a Branch Office.
(**)-Denotes a U.S. Export Assistance Center.
(***)-Office with managerial and administrative oversight responsibilities (offers no direct business counseling).

### ALABAMA
Birmingham—George Norton (Dir.)
Medical Forum Building, 7th Fl.
950 – 22d Street North, ZIP: 35203
Tel.: (205) 731–1331, FAX: (205) 731–0076

### ALASKA
Anchorage—Charles Becker (Dir.)
World Trade Center, 421 W. First St.,
ZIP: 99501
Tel.: (907) 271–6237, FAX: (907) 271–6242

### ARIZONA
Phoenix—Frank Woods (Dir.)
Tower One, Suite 970
2901 N. Central Avenue, ZIP: 85012
Tel.: (602) 640–2513, FAX: (602) 640–2518

### ARKANSAS
Little Rock—Lon J. Hardin (Dir.)
TCBY Tower Building, Suite 700
425 West Capitol Avenue, ZIP: 72201
Tel.: (501) 324–5794, FAX: (501) 324–7380

### CALIFORNIA
Los Angeles—Sherwin Chen (Mgr.)
11000 Wilshire Blvd., Rm 9200, ZIP: 90024
Tel.: (310) 235–7104, FAX: (310) 235–7220

Newport Beach—Paul Tambakis (Dir.)
3300 Irvine Avenue, Suite 305, ZIP: 92660
Tel.: (714) 660–1688, FAX: (714) 660–8039

Oxnard—Gerald Vaughn (Mgr.)
300 Esplanade Drive, Suite 2090, ZIP: 93030
Tel.: (805) 981–8150, FAX: (805) 981–1855

(**)Long Beach—Joe Sachs (Dir.)
US&FCS Director— Mary Delmege, Acting
One World Trade Center., Suite 1670,
ZIP: 90831
Tel.: (310) 980–4551, FAX: (310) 980–4561

(***)Ontario—Fred Latuperissa (Mgr.)
Inland Empire
2940 Inland Empire Blvd, Ste. 121, ZIP: 91764
Tel.: (909) 466–4134, FAX: (909) 466–4140

San Diego—Mary Delmege (Dir.)
6363 Greenwich Dr., Suite 230, ZIP: 92122
Tel.: (619) 557–5395, FAX: (619) 557–6176

(**)San Jose—James S. Kennedy (Dir.)
101 Park Center Plaza, Suite 1001, ZIP: 95113
Tel.: (408) 271–7300, FAX: (408) 271–7307

(*)Monterey—Joe Katz (Mgr.)
c/o Center for Trade & Commercial
Diplomacy
411 Pacific St., Suite 200, ZIP: 93940
Tel.: (408) 641–9850, FAX: (408) 641–9849

(*)Novato—Elizabeth Krauth (Mgr.)
330 Ignacio Blvd, Suite 102, ZIP: 94949
Tel.: (415) 883–1966, FAX: (415) 883–2711

(*)Oakland—Raj Shea (Mgr.)
530 Water Street, Suite 740, ZIP: 94607
Tel.: (510) 273–7350, FAX: (510) 251–7352

Sacramento—Brooks Ohlson (Mgr.)
917 – 7th Street, 2nd Floor, ZIP: 95814
Tel.: (916) 498–5155, FAX: (916) 498–5923

San Francisco—Matt Andersen (Mgr.)
250 Montgomery St., 14th Fl., ZIP: 94104
Tel.: (415) 705–2300, FAX: (415) 705–2297

(*)Santa Clara—James Rigassio (Mgr.)
5201 Great Amer. Pkwy., #456, ZIP: 95054
Tel.: (408) 970–4610, FAX: (408) 970–4618

**COLORADO**
**Denver—(Vacant)
1625 Broadway, Suite 680, ZIP: 80202
Tel.: (303) 844–6622, FAX: (303) 844–5651

**CONNECTICUT**
Middletown—Carl Jacobsen (Dir.)
213 Court Street, Suite 903, ZIP: 06457–3346
Tel.: (860) 638–6950, FAX: (860) 638–6970

**DELAWARE**
Served by the Philadelphia EAC.

**FLORIDA**
(**)Miami—Karl Koslowski (Dir.)
P.O. Box 590570, ZIP: 33159
5600 Northwest 36th St., Ste. 617, ZIP: 33166
Tel.: (305) 526–7425, FAX: (305) 526–7434

(*)Clearwater—George Martinez (Mgr.)
1130 Cleveland Street, ZIP: 34615
Tel.: (813) 461–0011, FAX: (813) 449–2889

(*)Orlando—Philip A. Ouzts (Mgr.)
Eola Park Centre, Suite 1270
200 E. Robinson Street, ZIP: 32801
Tel.: (407) 648–6235, FAX: (407) 648–6756

(*)Tallahassee
Michael Higgins (Mgr.)

The Capitol, Suite 2001, ZIP: 32399–0001
Tel.: (904) 488–6469, FAX: (904) 921–5395

**GEORGIA**
**Atlanta—Tapan Banerjee (Dir.)
285 Peachtree Center Avenue, NE
Marquis Two Tower, Suite 200,
ZIP: 30303–1229
Tel.: (404) 657–1900, FAX: (404) 657–1970

Savannah—Barbara Prieto (Mgr.)
6001 Chatham Center Dr., Suite 100,
ZIP: 31405
Tel.: (912) 652–4204, FAX: (912) 652–4241

**HAWAII**
Honolulu—George B. Dolan (Mgr.)
P.O. Box 50026
300 Ala Moana Blvd., Room 4106, ZIP: 96850
Tel.: (808) 541–1782, FAX: (808) 541–3435

**IDAHO**
(*)Boise—Steve Thompson (Mgr.)
700 West State Street, 2d Fl., ZIP: 83720
Tel.: (208) 334–3857, FAX: (208) 334–2783

**ILLINOIS**
(**)Chicago—(Vacant)
Xerox Center
55 West Monroe Street, Suite 2440, ZIP: 60603
Tel.: (312) 353–8040, FAX: (312) 353–8098

(*)Highland Park—Robin F. Mugford (Mgr.)
610 Central Avenue, Suite 150, ZIP: 60035
Tel: (847) 681–8010, FAX: (847) 681–8012

(*)Wheaton—Roy Dube (Mgr.)
c/o Illinois Institute of Technology
201 East Loop Road, ZIP: 60187
Tel.: (312) 353–4332, FAX: (312) 353–4336

(*)Rockford—James Mied (Mgr.)
P.O. Box 1747
515 North Court Street, ZIP: 61110
Tel.: (815) 987–8123, FAX: (815) 963–7943

**INDIANA**
Indianapolis—Dan Swart (Mgr.)
Penwood One, Suite 106
11405 N. Pennsylvania Street
Carmel, IN 46032
Tel.: (317) 582–2300, FAX: (317) 582–2301

**IOWA**
Des Moines—(Vacant)
Federal Building, Room 817
210 Walnut Street, ZIP: 50309
Tel.: (515) 284–4222, FAX: (515) 284–4021

## KANSAS
(*)Wichita—George D. Lavid (Mgr.)
151 N. Volutsia, ZIP: 67214
Tel.: (316) 269–6160, FAX: (316) 683–7326

## KENTUCKY
Louisville—John Autin (Dir.)
601 W. Broadway, Room 634B, ZIP: 40202
Tel.: (502) 582–5066, FAX: (502) 582–6573

(***)Somerset—Sara Melton (Mgr.)
246 Poplar Avenue, P.O. Box 50, ZIP: 42501
Tel. (606) 678–2029, FAX: (606) 678–2267

## LOUISIANA
New Orleans—David Spann (Dir.)
1 Canal Place
365 Canal Street, Suite 2150, ZIP: 70130
Tel.: (504) 589–6546, FAX: (504) 589–2337

Shreveport—Norbert O. Gannon (Mgr.)
5210 Hollywood Avenue, Annex, ZIP: 71109
Tel.: (318) 676–3064, FAX: (318) 676–3063

## MAINE
(*)Portland—Jeffrey Porter (Mgr.)
511 Congress Street, ZIP: 04101
Tel.: (207) 541–7400, FAX: (207) 541–7420

## MARYLAND
(**)Baltimore—Michael Keaveny (Dir.)
World Trade Center, Suite 2432
401 E. Pratt Street, ZIP: 21202
Tel.: (410) 962–4539, FAX: (410) 962–4529

## MASSACHUSETTS
Boston—Frank J. O'Connor (Dir.)
World Trade Center, Suite 307
164 Northern Avenue, ZIP: 02210
Tel.: (617) 424–5990, FAX: (617) 424–5992

(*)Marlborough—William Davis (Mgr.)
100 Granger Boulevard, Unit 102, ZIP: 01752
Tel.: (508) 624–6000, FAX: (508) 624–7145

## MICHIGAN
Detroit—Neil Hesse (Dir.)
211 W. Fort Street, Suite 2220 ZIP: 48226
Tel.: (313) 226–3650, FAX: (313) 226–3657

(***)Pontiac—Richard Corson (Mgr.)
Oakland Pointe Office Building
250 Elizabeth Lake Road, ZIP: 48341
Tel.: (810) 975–9600, FAX: (810) 975–9606

(***)Ann Arbor—Paul Litton (Mgr.)
425 S. Main Street, Suite 103, ZIP: 48104
Tel.: (313) 741–2430, FAX: 741–2432

(*)Grand Rapids—Thomas Maguire (Mgr.)
301 W. Fulton St., Suite 718–S, ZIP: 49504
Tel.: (616) 458–3564, FAX: (616) 458–3872

## MINNESOTA
Minneapolis—Ronald E. Kramer (Dir.)
Federal Building, Room 108
110 South 4th Street, ZIP: 55401
Tel.: (612) 348–1638, FAX: (612) 348–1650

## MISSISSIPPI
Jackson—(Vacant)
201 W. Capitol Street, Suite 310, ZIP: 39201
Tel.: (601) 965–4388, FAX: (601) 965–5386

## MISSOURI
(**)St. Louis—Randall J. LaBounty (Dir.)
8182 Maryland Avenue, Suite 303, ZIP: 63105
Tel.: (314) 425–3302, FAX: (314) 425–3381

Kansas City—Rick Villalobos (Dir.)
601 East 12th Street, Room 635, ZIP: 64106
Tel.: (816) 426–3141, FAX: (816) 426–3140

## MONTANA
Served by the Boise Export Assistance Center.

## NEBRASKA
(*)Omaha—Allen Patch (Mgr.)
11135 "O" Street, ZIP: 68137
Tel.: (402) 221–3664, FAX: (402) 221–3668

## NEVADA
Reno—Jere Dabbs (Mgr.)
1755 East Plumb Lane, Suite 152, ZIP: 89502
Tel.: (702) 784–5203, FAX: (702) 784–5343

## NEW HAMPSHIRE
(*)Portsmouth—Susan Berry (Mgr.)
17 New Hampshire Avenue, ZIP: 03801–2838
Tel.: (603) 334–6074, FAX: (603) 334–6110

## NEW JERSEY
Trenton—Rod Stuart (Dir.)
3131 Princeton Pike, Bldg. #6,
Suite 100, ZIP: 08648
Tel.: (609) 989–2100, FAX: (609) 989–2395

(*)Newark—Tom Rosengren (Mgr.)
One Gateway Center, 9th Floor, ZIP: 07102
Tel.: (201) 645–4682. FAX: (201) 645–4783

## NEW MEXICO
(*)Santa Fe—Sandra Necessary (Mgr.)
c/o New Mexico Dept. of Economic
Development
P.O. Box 20003, ZIP: 87504–5003
Tel.: (505) 827–0350, FAX: (505) 827–0263

## NEW YORK
Buffalo—George Buchanan (Dir.)
Federal Building, Room 1304
111 West Huron Street, ZIP: 14202
Tel.: (716) 551–4191, FAX: (716) 551–5290

(***)Long Island—George Soteros (Mgr.)
1550 Franklin Avenue, Room 207
Mineola, ZIP: 11501
Tel.: (516) 571–3921, FAX: (516) 571–4161

(*)Rochester—James C. Mariano (Mgr.)
111 East Avenue, Suite 220, ZIP: 14604
Tel.: (716) 263–6480, FAX: (716) 325–6505

(*)Harlem—K.L. Fredericks (Mgr.)
163 West 125th Street, Suite 904, ZIP 10027
New York, New York ZIP: 10027
Tel.: (212) 860–6200, FAX (212) 860–6203

(**) New York—Joel W. Barkan (Acting Dir.)
6 World Trade Center, Rm. 635, ZIP: 10048
Tel.: (212) 264–0634, FAX: (212) 264–1356

(***)Westchester—William Spitler (Dir.)
707 West Chester Avenue, White Plains,
ZIP: 10604
Tel.: (914) 682–6218, FAX: (914) 682–6698

## NORTH CAROLINA
Greensboro—Samuel P. Troy (Dir.)
400 West Market Street, Suite 400, ZIP: 27401
Tel.: (910) 333–5345, FAX: (910) 333–5158

(*)Charlotte—Roger Fortner (Dir.)
521 E. Morehead Street, Suite 435, ZIP: 28202
Tel.: (704) 333–4886, FAX: (704) 332–2681

## NORTH DAKOTA
Served by the Minneapolis EAC.

## OHIO
Cincinnati—Michael Miller (Dir.)
36 East 7th Street, Suite 2650, ZIP: 45202
Tel.: (513) 684–2944, FAX: (513) 684–3227

(***)Columbus—Michael Miller (Dir.)
37 North High Street, 4th Fl, ZIP: 43215
Tel.: (614) 365–9510, FAX: (614) 365–9598

Cleveland—John McCartney (Dir.)
Bank One Center
600 Superior Avenue, East, Suite 700,
ZIP: 44114
Tel.: (216) 522–4750, FAX: (216) 522–2235

(***)Toledo—Robert Abrams (Mgr.)
300 Madison Avenue, ZIP: 43604
Tel.: (419) 241–0683, FAX: (419) 241–0684

## OKLAHOMA
Oklahoma City—Ronald L. Wilson (Dir.)
301 Northwest 63rd Street, Suite 330,
ZIP: 73116
Tel.: (405) 231–5302, FAX: (405) 231–4211

(*) Tulsa—Thomas Strauss (Mgr.)
440 South Houston Street, Room 505,
ZIP: 74127
Tel.: (918) 581–7650, FAX: (918) 581–2844

## OREGON
Portland—Denny Barnes (Dir.)
One World Trade Center, Suite 242
121 SW Salmon Street, ZIP: 97204
Tel.: (503) 326–3001, FAX: (503) 326–6351

(*)Eugene—Pamela Ward (Mgr.)
1445 Willamette St., Suite 13, ZIP: 97401–4003
Tel.: (541) 465–6575, FAX (541) 465–6704

## PENNSYLVANIA
(**)Philadelphia—Maria Galindo (Dir.)
615 Chestnut Street, Suite 1501, ZIP: 19106
Tel.: (215) 597–6101, FAX (215) 597–6123

Pittsburgh—Ted Arnn (Mgr.)
2002 Federal Building
1000 Liberty Avenue, ZIP: 15222
Tel.: (412) 395–5050, FAX: (412) 395–4875

## PUERTO RICO
San Juan (Hato Rey)—J. Enrique Vilella (Dir.)
525 F.D. Roosevelt Ave, Suite 905, ZIP: 00918
Tel.: (787) 766–5555, FAX: (787) 766–5692

## RHODE ISLAND
(*) Providence—Raimond Meerbach (Mgr.)
One West Exchange Street, ZIP: 02903
Tel.: (401) 528–5104, FAX: (401) 528–5067

## SOUTH CAROLINA
Columbia—Ann Watts (Dir.)
Strom Thurmond Federal Bldg., Suite 172
1835 Assembly Street, ZIP: 29201
Tel.: (803) 765–5345, FAX: (803) 253–3614

(*)Charleston—David Kuhlmeier
P.O. Box 975, ZIP: 29402
81 Mary Street, ZIP: 29403
Tel: (803) 727–4051, FAX: (803) 727–4052

(***)Greenville—Denis Csizmadia (Mgr.)
Upstate Export Assistance Center
Park Central Office Park, Building 1, Ste. 109
555 North Pleasantburg Dr., ZIP: 29607
Tel.: (864) 271–1976, FAX: (864) 271–4171

## SOUTH DAKOTA
(*)Sioux Falls—Harvey Timberlake (Mgr.)
Augustana College, 2001 S. Summit Avenue,

Room SS–29A, ZIP: 57197
Tel: (605) 330–4264, FAX: (605) 330–4266

**TENNESSEE**
Nashville—Jim Charlet (Dir.)
Parkway Towers, Suite 114
404 James Robertson Parkway, ZIP: 37219
Tel.: (615) 736–5161, FAX: (615) 736–2454

(*)Memphis
Ree Russell (Mgr.)
22 North Front Street, Suite 200, ZIP: 38103
Tel.: (901) 544–4137, FAX: (901) 544–3646

(*)Knoxville
Thomas McGinty (Mgr.)
301 East Church Avenue, ZIP: 37915
Tel.: (423) 545–4637, FAX: (615) 545–4435

**TEXAS**
(**)Dallas—Bill Schrage (Dir.)
2050 N. Stemmons Fwy., Suite 170,
ZIP: 75258
P.O. Box 420069, ZIP: 75342–0069
Tel.: (214) 767–0542, FAX: (214) 767–8240

(*)Austin—Karen Parker (Mgr.)
P.O. Box 12728, Suite 300R
1700 Congress, 2d Fl., ZIP: 78701
Tel.: (512) 482–5939, FAX: (512) 482–5940

(*)Fort Worth—Vavie Sellschopp (Mgr.)
100 E. 15th Street, ZIP: 76102
Tel.: (817) 871–6001, FAX: (817) 871–6031

Houston—James D. Cook (Dir.)
#1 Allen Center, Suite 1160
500 Dallas, ZIP: 77002
Tel.: (713) 229–2578, FAX: (713) 229–2203

(*)San Antonio—Mitchel Auerbach (Mgr.)
1222 N. Main, Suite 450, ZIP: 78212
Tel.: (210) 228–9878, FAX (210) 228–9874

**UTAH**
Salt Lake City—Stephen P. Smoot (Dir.)
324 S. State Street, Suite 105, ZIP: 84111
Tel.: (801) 524–5116, FAX: (801) 524–5886

**VERMONT**
(*) Montpelier—James Cox (Mgr.)
109 State Street, 4th Fl., ZIP: 05609
Tel.: (802) 828–4508, FAX: (802) 828–3258

**VIRGINIA**
Richmond—(Vacant)

700 Centre
704 East Franklin Street, Suite 550, ZIP: 23219
Tel.: (804) 771–2246, FAX: (804) 771–2390

**WASHINGTON**
(***)Seattle—Lisa Kjaer–Schade (Dir.)
Westin Building, 2001 6th Avenue,
Suite 650, ZIP: 98121
Tel.: (206) 553–5615, FAX: (206) 553–7253

(*)Spokane—James K. Hellwig (Mgr.)
1020 West Riverside, ZIP: 99201
Tel.: (509) 353–2625, FAX: (509) 353–2449

**WEST VIRGINIA**
Charleston—W. Davis Coale, Jr. (Dir.)
405 Capitol Street, Suite 807, ZIP: 25301
Tel.: (304) 347–5123, FAX: (304) 347–5408

(***)Wheeling—Martha Butwin (Mgr.)
1310 Market St., 2d Fl., ZIP: 26003
Tel.: (304) 233–7472, FAX: (304) 233–7492

**WISCONSIN**
Milwaukee—Paul D. Churchill (Dir.)
517 E. Wisconsin Avenue, Room 596,
ZIP: 53202
Tel.: (414) 297–3473, FAX: (414) 297–3470

**WYOMING**
Served by the Denver Export Assistance Center.

# Regional Offices

(*)Eastern Region
Thomas Cox (Regional Dir.)
World Trade Center, Suite 2450
401 East Pratt Street, Baltimore, MD,
ZIP: 21202
Tel.: (410) 962–2805, FAX: (410) 962–2799

(*)Mid–Eastern Region
Gordon Thomas (Regional Dir.)
36 East 7th Street, Suite 2025
Cincinnati, OH, ZIP: 45202
Tel.: (513) 684–2947, FAX: (513) 684–3200

(*)Mid–Western Region Sandy Gerley (Regional Dir.)
8182 Maryland Avenue, Suite 1011,
St. Louis, MO, ZIP: 63105
Tel.: (314) 425–3300, FAX: (314) 425–3375

(*)Western Region Keith Bovetti (Regional Dir.)
250 Montgomery St., 14th Fl.,
San Francisco, CA, ZIP: 94104
Tel.: (415) 705–2310, FAX: (415) 705–2299

# U.S. Embassies
# Office Addresses and Key Officers List
## Country-by-country listing

**Editor's note:** Address and telephone number of each embassy, consulate or foreign service post are listed on the following pages for the benefit of the U.S. resident traveling overseas. Names and assignments are shown for each post to aid in making the most direct inquiry. It should be noted, however, that in sending mail to an embassy, consulate or post from the United States, the U.S. Department of State advises use of the address forms shown on page 125; they are more dependable and usually faster routing than using the addresses shown on the following pages. The Department also advises that inquiries be addressed not by name but by title. This will avoid undesirable forwarding of inquiries and response delays in instances where personnel shifts have occurred. Titles have been abbreviated in these listings. A key to those abbreviations is provided below.

# ABBREVIATIONS AND SYMBOLS

| | |
|---|---|
| ACM | Assistant Chief of Mission |
| ADM | Administrative Section |
| ADV | Adviser |
| AGR | Agricultural Section (USDA/FAS) |
| AID | Agency for International Development |
| ALT | Alternate |
| AMB | Ambassador |
| AMB SEC | Ambassador's Secretary |
| APHIS | Animal and Plant Health Inspection Service Officer |
| APO | Army Post Office |
| ARSO | Assistant Regional Security Officer |
| ATO | Agricultural Trade Office (USDA/FAS) |
| BCAO | Branch Cultural Affairs Officer (USIS) |
| Bg | Brigadier General |
| BIB | Board for International Broadcasting |
| BO | Branch Office (of Embassy) |
| BOB/EUR | Board of Broadcasting, European Office |
| BPAO | Branch Public Affairs Officer (USIS) |
| B.P. | Boite Postale |
| BUD | Budget |
| C | Consulate |
| CA | Consular Agency/Agent |
| CAO | Cultural Affairs Officer (USIS) |
| Capt | Captain (USN) |
| CDC | Centers for Disease Control |
| Cdr | Commander |
| CEO | Cultural Exchange Officer (USIS) |
| CG | Consul General, Consulate General |
| CG SEC | Consul General's Secretary |
| CHG | Charge d'Affaires |
| CINCAFSOUTH | Commander-in-Chief Allied Forces Southern Europe |
| CINCEUR | Commander-in-Chief U.S. European Command |
| CINCUSAFE | Commander-in-Chief U.S. Air Forces Europe |
| CINCUSAREUR | Commander-in-Chief U.S. Army Europe |
| Col | Colonel |
| CM | Chief of Mission |
| COM | Commercial Section (FCS) |
| CON | Consul, Consular Section |
| COUNS | Counselor |
| C.P. | Caixa Postal |
| CUS | Customs Service (Treasury) |
| DAC | Development Assistance Committee |
| DCM | Deputy Chief of Mission |
| DEA | Drug Enforcement Agency |
| DEP | Deputy |
| DEP DIR | Deputy Director |
| DIR | Director |
| DOE | Department of Energy |
| DPAO | Deputy Public Affairs Officer (USIS) |
| DPO | Deputy Principal Officer |
| DSA | Defense Supply Adviser |
| E | Embassy |
| ECO | Economic Section |
| ECO/COM | Economic/Commercial Section |
| EDO | Export Development Officer |
| ERDA | Energy Research and Development Administration |
| EST | Environment, Science, and Technology |
| EX-IM | Export-Import |
| FAA | Federal Aviation Administration |
| FAA/CASLO | Federal Aviation Administration Civil Aviation Security Liaison Officer |
| FAA/FSIDO | Federal Aviation Administration Flight Standards International District Office |
| FIC/JSC | Finance Committee and Joint Support Committee |
| FIN | Financial Attache (Treasury) |

| | |
|---|---|
| FODAG | Food and Agriculture Organizations |
| FPO | Fleet Post Office |
| IAEA | International Atomic Energy Agency |
| IAGS | Inter-American Geodetic Survey |
| IBB | International Broadcasting Bureau |
| ICAO | International Civil Aviation Organization |
| IMO | Information Management Officer |
| IO | Information Officer (USIS) |
| IPO | Information Program Officer |
| IRM | Information Resources Management |
| IRS | Internal Revenue Service |
| ISM | Information Systems Manager |
| JUS/CIV | Department of Justice, Civil Division |
| JUSMAG | Joint US Military Advisory Group |
| LAB | Labor Officer |
| LO | Liaison Officer |
| Ltc | Lieutenant Colonel |
| LEGATT | Legal Attache |
| M | Mission |
| Mg | Major General |
| MAAG | Military Assistance Advisory Group |
| MILGP | Military Group |
| MSG | Marine Security Guard |
| MSC | Military Staff Committee |
| MIN | Minister |
| MLO | Military Liaison Office |
| MNL | Minerals Officer |
| NARC | Narcotics |
| NATO | North Atlantic Treaty Organization |
| NAS | Narcotics Affairs Section |
| NCIS | Naval Criminal, U.S. |
| OAS | Organization of American States |
| ODA | Office of the Defense Attache |
| ODC | Office of Defense Cooperation |
| OIC | Officer in Charge |
| OMC | Office of Military Cooperation |
| PAO | Public Affairs Officer (USIS) |
| PC | Peace Corps |
| PO | Principal Officer |
| PO SEC | Principal Officer's Secretary |
| POL | Political Section |
| POL/LAB | Political and Labor Section |
| POLAD | Political Adviser |
| POL/ECO | Political/Economic Section |
| Radm | Rear Admiral |
| RCON | Regional Consular Affairs Officer |
| REDSO | Regional Economic Development Services Office |
| REF | Refugee Coordinator |
| REP | Representative |
| RES | Resources |
| RHUDO | Regional Housing and Urban Development Office |
| RMO | Regional Medical Officer |
| ROCAP | Regional Officer for Central American Programs |
| RPSO | Regional Procurement and Support Office |
| RSO | Regional Security Officer |
| SAO | Security Assistance Office |

| | |
|---|---|
| SCI | Scientific Attache |
| SCO | Senior Commercial Office |
| SEC DEL | Secretary of Delgation |
| SHAPE | Supreme Headquarters Allied Powers Europe |
| SLG | State and Local Government |
| SR | Senior |
| STC | Security Trade Control |
| UNEP | United Nations Environment Program |
| UNESCO | United Nations Educational, Scientific, & Cultural Organizations |
| UNIDO | United Nations Industrial Development Organization |
| USA | United States Army |
| USAF | United States Air Force |
| USDA/APHIS | Animal and Plant Health Inspection Serv. |
| USEU | US Mission to the European Union |
| USGS | US Geological Survey |
| USINT | United States Interests Section |
| USIS | United States Information Service |
| USLO | United States Liaison Office |
| USMC | United States Marine Corps |
| USMTM | US Military Training Mission |
| USN | United States Navy |
| USNATO | US Mission to the North Atlantic Treaty Organization |
| USOAS | US Mission to the Organization of American States |
| USOECD | US Mission to the Organization for Economic Cooperation and Development |
| USTTA | US Travel and Tourism Agent |
| USUN | US Mission to the United Nations |
| VC | Vice Consul |
| VOA | Voice of America |

# KEY OFFICERS OF FOREIGN SERVICE POSTS

## ALBANIA

**Tirana (E),** Tirana Rruga Elbasanit 103—AmEmbassy Tirana, Department of State, Washington, D.C. 20521-9510, Tel [355] (42) 47285 thru 89, Fax 232222

| | |
|---|---|
| AMB: | Joseph Limprecht |
| AMB OMS: | Judith A. Franco |
| DCM: | Robert A. Sorenson |
| POL: | Thomas K. Yasdgerdi |
| ECO/COM: | Charles W. Levesque |
| CON: | Laurence K. Jones |
| ADM: | William D. Downer |
| GSO: | Wanda M. Washington |
| RSO: | Matthew J. Dooley |
| IPO: | Dwaine Jefferson |
| DAO: | Cdr. Michael R. Thompson |
| ODC: | Maj. Sean M. Callahan |
| PAO: | Deborah A. Jones |

| | |
|---|---|
| AID: | Howard J. Sumka |
| AGR: | Holly Higgins (resident in Sofia) |
| FAA: | Steven B. Wallace (resident in Rome) |
| DEA: | James Soiles (resident in Athens) |

Last Modified: Wednesday, November 08, 2000

# ALGERIA

**Algiers (E),** 4 Chemin Cheikh Bachir El-Ibrahimi—B.P. Box 408 (Alger-Gare) 16000, Tel [213] (2) 69-12-55, 69-32-22, 69-11-86, 69-14-25, Fax 69-39-79; GSO Fax 69-17-82; COM Tel 69-23-17, Fax 69-18-63; PAO Fax 69-14-88. Internet address: us-embassy.eldjazair.net.dz

| | |
|---|---|
| AMB: | Janet A. Sanderson |
| AMB OMS: | Kristyna Rabassa |
| DCM: | Lucien S. Vandenbroucke |
| POL/ECO: | David Scott |
| PAO: | Therese M. Clavet |
| ECO/COM: | Marc Tejtel |
| CON: | Andrew Mitchell |
| ADM: | Alberta G. J. Mayberry |
| RSO: | Robert Q. Blackburn |
| DAO: | Col. Theodore Kissel |
| FAS: | Merrit Chesley(resident in Rabat) |
| FAA: | Kurt H. Edwards(resident in Paris) |
| IRS: | Marlene M. Sartipi, Acting (resident in Paris) |
| DEA: | Eugene Habib (resident in Paris) |
| FCS: | Kathleen Kriger (resident in Casablanca) |
| IMO: | Dominick Logalbo |
| LEGATT: | Enrique H. Ghimenti (resident in Paris) |
| O: | Georges McCormick (resident in Cairo) |

Last Modified: Friday, March 09, 2001

# ANGOLA

**Luanda (E),** Rua Houari Boumedienne No. 32, Miramar, Luanda, Angola;—International Mail: Caixa Postal 6484, Luanda, Angola, or Pouch: Department of State. 2550 Luanda Place, Washington, D.C. 20521-2550; INMARSAT: Int'l operator 873-151-7430, Tel [244] (2) 447-028/445-481, Fax 446-924; DAO Fax 447-217; Admin/Consular Annex: Casa Inglesa, Rua Major Kanhangula No. 132/135, Angola, or use above pouch address; ADMIN Tel 392-498; CON Tel 396-927, Fax 390-515

| | |
|---|---|
| AMB: | Joseph G. Sullivan |
| AMB OMS: | Nancy Rasari |
| DCM: | Todd R. Greentree |
| POL/ECO: | Joao Ecsodi |
| POL/MIL: | John Pardue |
| ADM: | Rosalyn Anderson |
| ECO/COM: | Jill A. Derderian |
| CON: | Christina Huth |
| IPO: | Donald Snead |
| RSO: | Donald Schenck |
| PAO: | Jan Hartman |
| DAO: | Major Gregory Furbish, USA |
| AID: | Keith Simmons |
| FAA: | Edward Jones (resident in Dakar) |
| IRS: | James P. Beene (resident in London) |
| AGR: | Richard Helm (resident in Pretoria) |

Last Modified: Friday, November 17, 2000

# ARGENTINA

**Buenos Aires (E),** International Mail: 4300 Colombia, 1425 Buenos Aires—APO Address: Unit 4334, APO AA 34034, Tel [54] (1) 777-4533 and 777-4534, Fax 777-0197; COM Fax 777-0673, Telex 18156 AMEMBAR

| | |
|---|---|
| AMB: | James D. Walsh |
| AMB OMS: | Nancy L. Graham |
| POL: | Michael Matera |
| ECO: | Stephen Thompson |
| COM: | James Wilson |
| ADM: | Norman D. Milford |
| GSO: | Donald Hunt |
| RSO: | Walter Huscilowitc |
| CON: | Robert Raymer |
| PAO: | Guy Burton |
| IRM: | Ronnie Fontenot |
| EST: | Marshall Carter-Tripp |
| DAO: | Col. Robert Adams |
| MILGP: | Col. Clark Lynn |
| AGR: | Philip Shull |
| APHIS: | Thomas Schissel |
| LAB: | Thomas J. Morgan |
| FAA: | Santiago Garcia (resident in Miami) |
| FAA/CASLO: | Hector Vela |
| IRS: | Frederick Dulas (resident in Mexico City) |
| DEA: | Thomas R. Polimine |
| DCM: | Milton Drucker |

Last Modified: Thursday, December 28, 2000

# ARMENIA

**Yerevan (E),** 18 Gen Bagramian (local address)—American Embassy Yerevan, Dept. of State, Washington, D.C. 20521-7020 (pouch address), Tel 3741-151-551, Fax 3742-151-550, Telex 243137 AMEMY. Internet address: embgso@arminco.com

| | |
|---|---|
| AMB: | Michael Craig Lemmon |
| AMB OMS: | Jana Amon |
| DCM: | Patricia Moller |
| POL/ECO: | Mark Tauber |
| POL/NARC: | Brad Johnson |
| ADM: | Robert Bryson |
| ECON/COM: | Jeffrey Horwitz |
| CON: | Lily Kosier |
| IRM: | Rudolph Szabados |
| AID: | [Vacant] |
| PAO: | John Balian |
| RSO: | Marian Cotter |
| FAA: | Dennis B. Cooper (resident in Brussels) |
| AGR: | Geoff Wiggin (resident in Moscow) |
| IRS: | Margaret J. Lullo (resident in Berlin) |
| PC: | William Benjamin |
| DAO: | Eric J. Von Tersch |
| TREAS: | David Gentry |
| DEA: | Lex Henderson (resident in Ankara) |
| RMO: | Bruce T. Miller, MD. (resident in Frankfurt) |
| IPO: | Clifford Brzozowski |
| USDA: | Craig Infanger |

Last Modified: Wednesday, November 08, 2000

## AUSTRALIA

**Canberra (E)**, Moonah Pl., Canberra, A.C.T. 2600—APO AP 96549, Tel [61] (2) 6214-5600, afterhours Tel 6214-5900, Fax 6214-5970. Internet address: usaembassy@bigpond.com Internet website: usis-australia.gov

| | |
|---|---|
| AMB: | Edward W. Gnehm, Jr. |
| AMB OMS: | Debra Nelson |
| DCM: | Michael P. Owens |
| POL: | Stephen Engelken |
| ECO: | Michael Delaney |
| CON: | Steven P. Coffman (resident in Sydney) |
| COM: | Robert Connan (resident in Sydney) |
| ADM: | Jo Ellen Powell |
| GSO: | E. [Charles] Ash |
| RSO: | Kim Starke |
| PAO: | Don Q. Washington |
| IRM: | Janice Fedak |
| PER: | [Vacant] |
| DAO: | Col. Rick Lester |
| AGR: | Randy Zeitner |
| APHIS: | Eric Hoffman |
| CUS: | Robert F. Tine. (resident in Singapore) |
| FAA: | Donald Slechta (resident in Sydney) |
| LAB: | [Vacant] |
| LEGATT: | Lou Caprino |
| DEA: | Gene Sugimoto |

**Melbourne [CG]**, 553 St. Kilda Road, P.O. Box 6722, Melbourne, Vic 3004—Unit 11011, APO AP 96551-0002, Tel [61] (8) 9202-1224, afterhours Tel 9389-3601; Fax 9510-4646; CON Fax 9525-0769; COM Fax 9510-4660;Internet address: melbourne@state.gov

| | |
|---|---|
| CG: | David Lyon |
| POL/ECO: | Abigail Aronson |
| COM: | Mitchell G. Larson |
| CON: | George Brazier |
| ADM: | Louise Veenstra |
| DCMC: | Cdr. Barbara Bell, USN |
| IRM: | Linda Howard |

**Sydney [CG]**, 59th Fl., MLC Centre, 19-29 Martin Place, Sydney N.S.W. 2000—PSC 280, Unit 11026, APO AP 96554-0002, Tel [61] (2) 9373-9200, afterhours Tel 4422-2201; ADMIN Fax 9373-9125; COM Fax 9221-0573; CON Fax 9373-9184. Internet website: http://usembassy-australia.state.gov/sydney

| | |
|---|---|
| CG: | Richard Greene |
| CG SEC: | Paolina Milasi |
| POL/ECO: | Virginia Murray |
| COM: | Robert Connan |
| CON: | Steven P. Coffman |
| ADM: | Alaina Teplitz |
| PAO: | David Gilmour |
| IRM: | Barton Hoskins |
| IRS: | Billy J. Brown (resident in Singapore) |
| FAA/CASLO: | Donald Slechta |

**Perth [CG]**, 13th Fl., 16 St. George's Terr., Perth, WA 6000—APO AP 96530, Tel [61] (8) 9202-1224, afterhours Tel 9476-0081, Fax 9231-9444. Internet address: usgperth@starwon.com.au

| | |
|---|---|
| CG: | Sallybeth Bumbrey |
| CON: | Roger Skavdahl |
| USN: | Cdr. Bruce A. Vandenbos |

Last Modified: Thursday, April 05, 2001

## AUSTRIA

**Vienna (E)**, Boltzmanngasse 16, A-1091, Vienna, Tel [43] (1) 313-39, Fax [43] (1) 310-0682; CON: Garten-bauprome-nade 2, 4th Floor, A-1010 Vienna, Tel [43] (1) 313-39, Fax 513-4351; COM Fax [43] (1) 310-6917 or 31339-2911; EXEC Fax [43] (1) 317-7826; ADM Fax [43] (1) 31339-2510; ECON/POL Fax [43] (1) 313-2916; Web site address www.usembassy-vienna.at; E-mail address usis@usia.co.at.

| | |
|---|---|
| AMB: | Kathryn W. Hall |
| AMB OMS: | Patricia J. Able |
| DCM: | Robert S. Deutsch |
| ECO/POL: | Lee Brudvig |
| CON: | James Pettit |
| COM: | Joseph Kaesshaefer |
| ADM: | Timothy E. Roddy |
| RSO: | Todd M. Keil |
| PAO: | Andrew J. Schilling |
| IMO: | Terry Branstner |
| DAO: | Col. Bruce E. Boevers, USA |
| AGR: | Robert C. Curtis |
| APHIS: | Dr. Christopher Groocock |
| INS: | William Griffen |
| PA/RPO: | Renate Coleshill |
| LEGAT: | Steven Grantham |
| CUS: | Robin Avers |
| DEA: | Thomas Slovenkay |
| FAA: | Amy Becke |
| FBIS: | Michael Petty |
| ISO: | Dustin Lumley |
| IPO: | Mark S. Buske |

**US Mission to International Organizations in Vienna (UNVIE)**, Obersteinergasse 11/1, A-1190 Vienna, EXEC Tel [43] (1) 31339-74-3501, direct – 369-2095, Fax 31339-74-3504; IAEA Tel [43] (1) 31339-74-3322, Fax 369-8392; POL/ECO Tel 31339-74-3521, Fax 31339-74-3531; CTBT Tel 31339-74-3223, Fax 31339-74-3531. Web site address: www.usun-vienna.usia.co.at

| | |
|---|---|
| US REP: | John B. Ritch III |
| AMB OMS: | Karen S. Schoppl |
| DCM: | Laura E. Kennedy |
| POL/ECO: | Kathleen W. Barmon |
| CTBT: | Charles R. Oleszycki |
| IAEA: | Mark Fitzpatrick |
| SCI: | Lisa Hilliard |
| NRC: | Charles Z. Serpan |
| ISPO: | Joseph M. Carelli |
| ADM: | David W. Ball |
| IRM: | Randal F. Jennison |
| SCI [TC]: | Ira N. Goldman |

**U.S. Delegation to the Organization for Security and Cooperation in Europe (OSCE)**, Obersteinergasse 11/1, A-1190 Vienna, Tel [43] (1) 31339, Fax 368-6385

| | |
|---|---|
| AMB: | David T. Johnson |
| AMB OMS: | Donna Scott |
| DCM: | Josiah Rosenblatt |
| POL: | Andrew Steinfeld |

| PAA: | Charles Walsh |
|---|---|
| WASS: | Paul Van Son |
| ASG: | Richard Pabst |
| JCS: | Col. Terrence Tallent |
| ACDA: | Gregory G. Govan |
| OSD: | Col. John Albert |
| COM: | Janice Helwig |
| ADM: | David W. Ball |
| IRM: | Randal F. Jennison |

**Salzburg (CA),** Alter Markt 1, 5202; Tel. [43] (662) 84-87-76, Fax [43] (662) 84-97-77; afterhours Tel [43] (1) 31339-75-32

| CA: | Jeanie DeGraff Mayer |
|---|---|

Last Modified: Thursday, March 29, 2001

# AZERBAIJAN

**Baku (E),** Azadliq Prospekt 83, Baku 370007, Azerbaijan—AmEmbassy Baku, Dept. of State, Washington, D.C. 20521-7050 (pouch address), Tel [9] (9412) 98-03-35, 36, 37, Fax 90-66-71; Tie Line 841-0289; EXEC Fax 98-91-79; CON Fax 98-37-55; COM Fax 98-61-17; PAO Tel & Fax 98-93-12. Internet address: http://www.usia.gov/posts/baku.html

| AMB: | Ross L. Wilson |
|---|---|
| AMB OMS: | Louise Nash |
| DCM: | Elizabeth W. Shelton |
| POL: | Sherry A. Holiday |
| ECO: | Debra Juncker |
| REO: | Laura A. Griesmer |
| ADM: | Joseph T. Zuccarini |
| IRM: | Rick Fasciglione |
| RSO: | Joseph Hooten |
| CON: | Inger Tangborn |
| DAO: | Maj. Mitchell Biondich, USMC |
| COM: | Michael Lally |
| PAO: | James Seward |
| AGR: | Susan R. Schayes resident in Ankara) |
| FAA: | Dennis B. Cooper (resident in Brussels) |
| IRS: | Margaret J. Lullo (resident in Berlin) |
| DEA: | Lex Henderson (resident in Ankara) |
| RMO: | Bruce T. Miller, MD. |

Last Modified: Wednesday, January 31, 2001

# BAHAMAS, THE

**Nassau (E),** Queen St. (local/express mail address) P.O. Box N-8197; Amembassy Nassau, P.O. Box 599009, Miami, Fl. 33159-9009 (stateside address);—Nassau, Dept. of State, Wash., D.C. 20521-3370 (pouch address), Tel (242) 322-1181, afterhours Tel 328-2206, EXEC Fax (242) 356-0222; ECO/COM Fax 328-3495; ADM Fax 328-7838; NAS Fax 356-0918; PAO Fax 326-5579; Visas Fax 356-7174

| AMB: | [Vacant] |
|---|---|
| AMB OMS: | [Vacant] |
| CHG: | Daniel A. Clune |
| POL/ECO: | Elizabeth L. Martinez |
| ECO/COM: | Thomas W. Ohlson |
| CON: | Edward J. Ramotowski |
| ADM: | Andrew W. Oltyan |
| RSO: | Marc A. Garcia |

| PAO: | Elizabeth L. Martinez (Acting) |
|---|---|
| APHIS: | Gary Timmons |
| ATO: | Willis Collie  (resident in Miami) |
| IRM: | Diane B. Peterson |
| NAS: | Glen Smith |
| NLO: | Lt. Cmdr. William Ridings |
| CGLO: | Lt. Cmdr. Lance Rocks |
| CUS/INC: | George F. St. Clair |
| DEA: | Thomas M. Hill |
| FAA: | Ruben Quinones (resident in Miami) |
| INS: | James S. Carbonneau |
| IRS: | Frederick Dulas (resident in Mexico City) |
| LAB: | John J. Muth (resident in Washington, D.C.) |

Last Modified: Thursday, April 05, 2001

# BAHRAIN

**Manama (E),** Building No. 979, Road 3119, Block 331, Zinj District—AmEmbassy Manama, PSC 451, FPO AE 09834-5100; International Mail: American Embassy, Box 26431, Manama, Bahrain, Tel [973] 273-300, afterhours Tel 275-126, Fax 272-594; ADM Fax 275-418; ECON/COM Fax 256-717; PAO Tel 276-180, Fax 270-547; OMC Tel 276-962, Fax 276-046. Web site address: http://www.usembassy.com.bh

| AMB: | Johnny Young |
|---|---|
| AMB OMS: | Gloria Kilgore |
| DCM: | Joseph A. Mussomeli |
| POL: | Alfred F. Fonteneau |
| POL/MIL: | Douglas E. Miller |
| ECO: | Tracy Hailey |
| CON: | Karen B. Zareski |
| ADM: | Martin P. Hohe |
| RSO: | Kevin W. Bauer |
| PAO: | Donna J. Winton |
| IRM: | [Vacant] |
| OMC: | Col. Thomas A. Gilkey, USAF |
| ANNEX: | Thomas E. Davies |
| FAA: | Lynn Osmus (resident in Brussels) |
| FAA/CASLO: | Ronald N. Reynolds (resident in Rome) |
| LEGATT: | Bassem Youssef (resident in Riyadh) |
| ATO: | Ron Verdonk (resident in Dubai) |
| IRS: | Larry LeGrand (resident in Rome) |
| ENV: | George Sibley (resident in Amman) |
| DEA: | Robert Clark (resident in Islamabad) |
| IMO: | [Vacant] |

Last Modified: Wednesday, March 21, 2001

# BANGLADESH

**Dhaka (E),** Diplomatic Enclave, Madani Ave., Baridhara, Dhaka 1212 or—G.P.O. Box 323, Dhaka 1000, Tel [880] (2) 882-4700-22, Fax 882-3744; USAID Fax 882-3648; PAO address: House No. 110, Road No. 27, Banani, Dhaka 1213, Tel [880] (2) 881-3440-44, Fax 988-1677; PC address: House No. 57, Ishakhan Ave., Sector-6, Uttara Model Town, Tel [880] (2) 891-8435, 891-1017, Fax 891-7654, PC Internet Address: mbedford@bd.peacecorps.gov; Embassy Internet Address: dhaka@exchange.gov.

| AMB: | Mary Ann Peters |
|---|---|
| AMB OMS: | Karen Landherr |
| DCM: | Christopher W. Webster |
| POL: | Dan W. Mozena |

| | |
|---|---|
| ECO: | Cleveland Charles |
| CON: | Steven Harper |
| ADM: | Robert W. Pons |
| RSO: | Daniel C. Becker |
| PAO: | John S. Kincannon |
| IMO: | Robert L. Olson |
| AID: | Gordon West |
| DAO: | Ltc. Robert Wilkinson |
| PC: | Michael Bedford |
| AGR: | Weyland Beeghly (resident in New Delhi) |
| LAB: | Faye Von Wrangel |
| FAA: | David L. Knudson (resident in Singapore) |
| LOC: | Lygia M. Ballantyne (resident in New Delhi) |

Last Modified: Thursday, November 09, 2000

# BARBADOS

**Bridgetown (E),** Canadian Imperial Bank of Commerce Bldg., Broad Street—P.O. Box 302 or FPO AA 34055, Tel (246) 436-4950, Fax 429-5246, Telex 2259 USEMB BG1 WB, Marine Sec. Guard, Tel 436-8995; CON Fax 431-0179; AID Fax 429-4438; PAO Fax 429-5316; MLO Fax 427-1668; LEGATT Fax 437-7772

| | |
|---|---|
| AMB: | [Vacant] |
| AMB OMS: | Barbara Treharne |
| CHG: | Roland W. Bullen |
| POL/ECO: | D. Brent Hardt |
| ECO: | Mary Doetsch |
| COM: | Larry Farris (res. in Dominican Republic) |
| CON: | Theorphilus J. Rose |
| ADM: | Paul S. Carpenter |
| RSO: | William K. Pennebaker |
| PAO: | Emila Puma |
| IRM: | Ronnie J. Fontenot |
| AID: | Paul Bisek |
| DAO: | Ltc. John L. Churchill |
| MLO: | Ltc. Ronald Jenkins, USN |
| REA: | Lawrence J. Gumbiner (resident in Costa Rica) |
| AGR: | Rod McSherry (resident in Caracas) |
| LAB: | Terrence Daru |
| LEGATT: | Donovan J. Leighton |
| IRS: | Frederick Dulas (resident in Mexico City) |
| FAA: | Ruben Quinones (resident in Miami) |
| DEA: | James Agee, Jr. |

Last Modified: Thursday, November 09, 2000

# BELARUS

**Minsk (E),** 46 Starovilenskaya Str., 220002 Minsk &#8721; PSC 78, Box B Minsk, APO 09723, Tel [375] (17) 210-12-83 and 234-77-61, afterhours Tel 226-1601, Fax 234-78-53, CON Fax 217-7160; Fax 577-4650; PAO Tel [375] (17) 217-04-81, Fax 217-88-28

| | |
|---|---|
| AMB: | Michael G. Kozak |
| AMB OMS: | Linda L. Jackson |
| DCM: | Joseph Kunstadter |
| ECO/COM: | Christopher T. Robinson |
| CON: | Joan M. Christini |
| ADM: | Thomas Burke |
| GSO: | Jeff Reneau |
| IRM: | Paul J. Wright |
| RSO: | Bradford McDougle |

| | |
|---|---|
| PAO: | Michael Reinert |
| AGR: | Geoff Wiggin (resident in Moscow) |
| AID: | Christine Sheckler |
| FAA: | Dennis B. Cooper (resident in Brussels) |
| IRS: | Margaret J. Lullo (resident in Berlin) |
| DAO: | Ltc. Jeffrey S. Haschak |
| RMO: | Dr. Ronald A. Larsen (resident in Moscow) |
| DEA: | Thomas C. Slovenkay (resident in Vienna) |
| IPO: | Lester Brayshaw |

Last Modified: Friday, March 16, 2001

# BELGIUM

**Brussels (E),** 27 Boulevard du Regent, B-1000 Brussels—PSC 82, Box 002, APO AE 09710, Tel [32] (2) 508-2111; Fax [32] (2) 511-2725; EXEC Fax 508-2160; POL/ECON Fax 513-5333; COM Fax 512-6653; direct-in-dial: Amb [32] (2) 508-2444; AMB OMS 508-2444; DCM 508-2446; POL 508-2475; ECO 508-2448; COM 508-2425; CON 508-2382; ADM 508-2350; RSO 508-2370; PAO 508-2412; IMO 508-2200; DAO 508-2505; ODC 508-2664; FAS 508-2437; FAA 508-2703.

| | |
|---|---|
| AMB: | Paul L. Cejas |
| AMB OMS: | Michelle V. Edwards |
| DCM: | P. Michael McKinley |
| POL: | Robyn Hinson-Jones |
| ECO: | Eric D. Benjaminson |
| COM: | George W. Knowles |
| CON: | Joseph M. Pomper |
| ADM: | Penelope W. Snider, Acting |
| RSO: | Daniel J. Pocus |
| PAO: | Joseph E. MacManus |
| DAO: | Col. William Zekas |
| ODC: | Col. George A. Reed |
| FAA: | Lynn Osmus |
| IRS: | Frederick Pablo (resident in Paris) |
| LEGATT: | Sandra L. Fowler |
| DEA: | Stephen Luzinski |
| USSS: | Patrick C. Miller (resident in Paris) |
| IMO: | Durwood L. Franke |
| FAS: | Philip A. Letarte (resident in The Hague) |

**US Mission to the North Atlantic Treaty Organization (USNATO),** Autoroute de Zaventem, B-1110 Brussels—PSC 81 APO AE 09724, Tel [32] (2) 724-3111, Fax 724-3403; PA Fax 726-9368; direct in dial: Amb Tel 724-3230; AMB OMS Tel 724-3230; DCM Tel 724-3232; DEF ADV Tel 724-3218; POL/ECO Tel 724-3226; PA Tel 724-3237; ADMIN Tel 724-3240; IMO Tel 724-3244

| | |
|---|---|
| US PERM REP: | Alexander R. Vershbow |
| PERM REP SEC: | Regina D. Olton |
| DEP PERM/ | |
| REP/DCM: | Victoria J. Nuland |
| DEF ADV: | Robert B. Hall |
| POL ADV: | Andrew L. Goodman |
| PUB AFF ADV: | Elizabeth B. Pryor |
| ADM ADV: | Henry M. Reed II |
| IMO: | Danny D. Lockwood |

**US Mission to the European Union (USEU),** 13 rue Zinner, 1000 Brussels—APO AE 09724, Tel [32] (2) 508-2222, Fax 502-8117; COM Fax 513-1228; direct in dial: AMB [32] (2) 508-2750; AMB OMS 508-2750; DCM 508-

2752; POL 508-2772; ECO 508-2780; PAO 508-2774; FAS 508-2760; CUS 508-2770; TRADE 508-2780; LAB 508-2773; COM 508-2745; TREAS 508-2668; NAS 508-2667; AID 508-2626; SCI TECH AFF 508-2781; APHIS 508-2762; ADM 508-2647

| | |
|---|---|
| AMB: | Richard L. Morningstar |
| AMB OMS: | Valerie J. Towns |
| DCM: | John A. Cloud |
| POL: | Robert W. Becker |
| ECO: | Anne E. Derse |
| PAO: | Laurence D. Wohlers |
| AGR: | Mary E. Revelt |
| CUS: | Robert E. Mall |
| TRADE: | Nancy J. Adams |
| LAB: | David G. Wagner |
| COM: | Kenneth Moorefield |
| TREAS: | Gregory J. Berger |
| NAS: | Jimmie E. Wagner |
| EST: | Colin S. Helmer |
| APHIS: | Alejandro B. Thiermann |
| JUST: | Mark Richards |
| AID: | Kurt Fuller |
| ADM: | Jennifer L. Barnes |

**European Logistical Support Office** (ELSO - Antwerp), Noorderlaan 147, BUS 12A, B-2030 Antwerp—APO AE 09710, Tel [32] (3) 540-2010, Fax [32] (3) 540-2040.

| | |
|---|---|
| DIR: | Steven G. Hartman |
| DEP DIR: | [Vacant] |

**SHAPE Belgium,** B-7010—APO AE 09705, Tel [32] (65) 445-000

| | |
|---|---|
| POLAD: | Michael L. Durkee |
| DEP POLAD: | Col. Charles M. Kuzell, USA |

Last Modified: Wednesday, February 07, 2001

# BELIZE

**Belize City (E),** Gabourel Lane—P.O. Box 286, Unit 7401, APO AA 34025, Tel [501] (2) 77161 thru 63, Fax 30802; ADM Fax 35321; DAO Fax 32795; DEA Fax 33856; PC Fax 30345; IBB Tel [501] (7) 22091/22063, Fax 22147; MLO Tel 25-2009/2019, Fax 25-2553. Internet address: embbelize@belizwpoa.us-state.gov. Web site address: http://www.usemb-belize.gov

| | |
|---|---|
| AMB: | Carolyn Curiel |
| AMB OMS: | Nancy M. Rasari |
| DCM: | Robert Fretz |
| ECO/POL: | George Aldridge |
| CON: | David Chang |
| IRM: | Thomas Zuraw |
| ADM: | Joel Danies |
| IBB: | Carl G. Britt, Jr. |
| MLO: | Ltc. Rogelio Diaz, USA |
| FAA: | Ruben Quinones (resident in Miami) |
| DEA: | Ruth Higgs |

Last Modified: Thursday, November 09, 2000

# BENIN

**Cotonou (E),** rue Caporal Bernard Anani, B.P. 2012, Tel [229] 30-06-50, 30-05-13, 30-17-92, Fax 30-14-39 and 30-

19-74, workweek: Monday through Friday. Internet address: amemb.coo@intnet.bj

| | |
|---|---|
| AMB: | [Vacant] |
| AMB OMS: | Bermadine B. Phillips |
| CHG: | Liam J. Humphreys |
| CON/POL/COM: | Elizabeth Brandon |
| ADM: | Matthew B. Dever |
| RSO: | Scott Campbell |
| RPO: | Ola Criss (resident Accra) |
| GSO: | David Lamontagne |
| IPO: | Eley M. Johnson |
| PC: | Geremie Sawadogo |
| PAO: | Andree Johnson |
| RFMO: | Jose Irizarry |
| FMS: | Matthew Jennings (resident in Accra) |
| AID: | Harry Lightfoot |
| DAO: | Col. Daniel Pike (resident in Abidjan) |
| DEA: | Edgar L. Moses (resident in Lagos) |
| FAA: | Edward Jones (resident in Dakar) |
| FCS: | Todd Hansen (resident in Abidjan) |
| IRS: | Frederick Pablo (resident in Paris) |

Last Modified: Tuesday, December 19, 2000

# BERMUDA

**Hamilton (CG),** Crown Hill, 16 Middle Road, Devonshire—P.O. Box HM325, Hamilton HMBX, Bermuda, or AmConGen Hamilton, Department of State, Wash., D.C. 20520-5300, Tel [441] 295-1342, Fax 295-1592 or 296-9233

| | |
|---|---|
| CG: | Lawrence D. Owen |
| POL/ADM: | Douglas Dobson |
| CON: | Sylvia Hammond |
| INS: | Warren Burr |
| CUS: | Vincent Priore |
| ATO: | Willis Collie (resident in Miami) |
| APHIS: | Thomas J. Andre, Jr. |
| FAA: | Ruben Quinones (resident in Miami) |
| RSO: | John A. Hurley III resident in Ottawa) |
| IRS: | Frederick Dulas resident in Mexico City) |
| NASA: | William Way |
| DEA: | Michael S. Vigil res. in Caribbean Field Div.) |

# BOLIVIA

**La Paz (E),** Ave. Arce No. 2780—P.O. Box 425, La Paz, Bolivia, APO AA 34032, Tel [591] (2) 430251, Fax 433900; USAID Tel 786544, Fax 786654; Direct lines: AMB [591] (2) 432524; DCM 431340; POST 1 432540; DEA 431481; CON 433758, Fax 433854; PAO Tel 432621; USAID DIR Tel 786179, USAID EXEC OFF Tel 786399

| | |
|---|---|
| AMB: | Donna J. Hrinak |
| AMB OMS: | Sonia D. Ramirez |
| DCM: | George C. Lannon |
| ECO/POL: | Hugh Neighbour |
| CON: | Thomas H. Lloyd |
| ADM: | Frederick B. Cook |
| RSO: | [Vacant] |
| LAB: | Kenneth R. Audroue |
| AID: | Liliana Ayalde |
| AGR: | Larry Fuell (resident in Lima) |
| COM: | [Vacant] |
| PAO: | Donald E. Terpstra |
| IRM: | Gregory Tyson |

| | |
|---|---|
| DAO: | Col. Dennis Fowler, USAF |
| MILGP: | Col. Dennis E. Keller, USA |
| NIMA: | John Tomasovich (resident in Asuncion) |
| ICITAP: | [Vacant] |
| PC: | Meredith Smith |
| FAA: | Santiago Garcia (resident in Miami) |
| FAA/CASLO: | Hector Vella(resident in Buenos Aires) |
| NAS: | J. Richard Baca |
| IRS: | Frederick Dulas (resident in Mexico City) |
| DEA: | Anthony Placido |

**Cochabamba [CA],** Avenida Oquendo No. 654, Torres Sofer 6to Piso, Of. 601, Tel. [591] (42) 56714; DEA address: Cruce Taquiqa, Zona Linde, Tel [591] (42) 88896, 98; AID address: Edificio Los Tiempos, Clase Quatanilla, Tel. [591] (42) 33992, 50155; NAS address: Calle Jacaranda No. 0237, Tel. [591] (42) 72972/73/74; PC address: Calle Thomas Frias No. 1250, Tel. [591] (42) 40425

| | |
|---|---|
| CA: | William Scarborough |
| DEA: | John Emerson |
| AID: | Richard Fisher |
| NAS: | Francisco Alvarez |
| PC: | Remigio Ancalle |

**Santa Cruz [CA],** 313 Calle Guemes No. 6, Zona Equipetrol, Tel. [591] (03) 330725, 363842, Fax 32554; DEA address: PC address: Calle Campero No. 91, Tel. [591] (03) 451887; NAS address: Ber. Anillo No. 1008, Tel. [591] (03) 420935/423367

| | |
|---|---|
| CA: | Mary F. Telchi |
| DEA: | James R. White |
| PC: | Trevor Murray |
| NAS: | Pedro T. Hernandez |

**Trinidad,** DEA address- AmEmbassy La Paz, Unit 3913, (Trinidad), APO AA 34032, Tel. [591] (04) 625432; NA address: Av. Panamericana Kilometro No. 1.5, Tel [591] (04) 621974, 621880

| | |
|---|---|
| DEA: | Pedro Janier |
| NAS: | Rural R. Gusler |

**Sucre,** Av. Kilometro 7, Edificio No. 218, Office 226 Tel. [591] (06) 444411

| | |
|---|---|
| PC: | Eduardo Avila |

**Tarija,** Calle Bolivar Esq. Colon, Tel. [591] (06) 812205

| | |
|---|---|
| PC: | David Chambi |

**Chimore,** AmEmbassy La Paz, Unit 3913, (Chimore), APO AA 34032, Tel. [591] (04) 114305; NAS address: Cal Jacaranda No. 0237, [591] (04) 114366, 4303, 4320

| | |
|---|---|
| DEA: | John Emerson |
| NAS: | Francisco Alvarez |

Last Modified: Thursday, November 09, 2000

# BOSNIA-HERZEGOVINA

**Sarajevo (E),** Alipasina 43, 71000 Sarajevo, Tel [387] (71) 445-700, Fax [387] (71) 659-722

| | |
|---|---|
| AMB: | Thomas J. Miller |
| AMB OMS: | Lynn Bitters |

| | |
|---|---|
| DCM: | Sylvia J. Bazala |
| POL/ECO: | Robert B. Ehrnman |
| COM: | Patrick Hughes (resident in Zagreb) |
| CON: | Ann B. Sides |
| ADM: | Douglas B. Leonnig |
| RSO: | Michael G. Considine |
| PAO: | Janet E. Garvey |
| DAO: | Ltc. Raymond Hodgkins, USA |
| REF AFF: | John Wysham |
| INL: | Eric Gaudiosi |
| IRM: | James G. Williamson |
| FAA: | Steven B. Wallace (resident in Rome) |
| AGR: | Allan Mustard (resident in Vienna) |
| DEA: | Thomas C. Slovenkay (resident in Vienna) |
| IRS: | Larry J. LeGrand (resident in Rome) |

**Banja Luka [BO],** Jovana Ducicav 5, Banja Luka, Tel [387] (58) 211-500, Fax 218-291

| | |
|---|---|
| POL: | Dean Pittman |

**Mostar [BO],** Mostarkog Bataljona BB, Mostar, Tel [387] (88) 580-580, Fax 580-581

| | |
|---|---|
| POL: | Martha Patterson |

Last Modified: Thursday, November 09, 2000

# BOTSWANA

**Gaborone (E),** P.O. Box 90, Tel [267] 353-982, afterhours Tel 357-111 or 374-498, Fax 356-947; AID Tel 324-449, Fax 324-404; CDC Tel 301-696; VOA Tel 810-932. E-mail address: usembgab@mega.bw or usambgav@it.bw

| | |
|---|---|
| AMB: | John E. Lange |
| AMB OMS: | Kam Ting Wong |
| DCM: | Scott H. Delisi |
| POL/ECO: | Michael Morrow |
| CON/COM: | Katherine Flachsbart |
| ADM: | Melinda Tabler-Stone |
| RSO: | James Combs |
| PAO: | Damaris Kirchhofer |
| EST: | Mario E. Merida |
| IPO: | Bruce MacEwen |
| IBB: | Jack Fisher |
| IRM: | Bruce MacEwen |
| AID: | Edward Spriggs |
| AGR: | Richard Helm (resident in Pretoria) |
| FAA: | Edward Jones (resident in Dakar) |
| FCS: | Roger Ervin (resident in Johannesburg) |
| LAB: | Frederick J. Kaplan (resident in Johannesburg) |
| ODC: | Maj. Ronald L. Kinser, USA |
| DAO: | Maj. Scott Hathaway, USA |
| VOA: | Jack Fisher |
| CDC: | Tom Kenyon |
| IRS: | James P. Beene (resident in London) |
| DEA: | Larry W. Frye (resident in Pretoria) |

Last Modified: Wednesday, November 29, 2000

# BRAZIL

**Brasilia (E),** Avenida das Nacoes, Quadra 801, Lote 3, Brasilia, D.F. Cep 70403-900 Brazil—American Embassy Brasilia, Unit 3500, APO AA 34030, Tel [55] (61) 321-7272, Fax 225-9136 (Stateside address); ADM Fax 225-5857; COM Fax 225-3981; PAO Fax 321-2833, 322-0554;

AID Fax 323-6875; FCS Fax 225-3981; NAS Fax 226-0171; SCI Fax 321-3615; POL Fax 223-0497; ECO Fax 224-9477. Internet address: http://www.embaixada-americana.org.br/

| | |
|---|---|
| AMB: | Anthony S. Harrington |
| AMB OMS: | [Vacant] |
| DCM: | Cristobal Orozco |
| POL: | William R.Barr |
| ECO: | Brian R. Stickney |
| SCI: | Marc Nicholson |
| COM: | Richard Lenahan |
| NIST: | Ileana Martinez |
| CON: | Gregory Frost |
| ADM: | Jeffrey D. Levine |
| GSO: | John Manuel |
| RSO: | Christopher J. Paul |
| PAO: | Gail Gulliksen |
| IRM: | Alan Roecks |
| AID: | Janice Weber |
| FAA: | Santiago Garcia (resident in Miami) |
| DEA: | Patrick Healy |
| DAO: | Col. Charles Rowcliffe, USA |
| MLO: | Col. Donald Belche, USAF |
| AGR: | Herbert ""Finn"" Rudd |
| BUREC: | Peter Hradilek |

**Rio de Janeiro [CG]**, Avenida Presidente Wilson, 147 Castelo, Rio de Janeiro-RJ 20030-020—Unit 3501, APO AA 34030, Tel [55] (21) 292-7117, Fax 220-0439; PAO Fax 262-1820, PAO Telex 22831, Fax 262-5131

| | |
|---|---|
| CG: | Cristobal R. Orozco |
| ECO/POL: | Robert Taylor |
| COM: | Judith Henderson |
| CON: | Ronald Sinclair |
| ADM: | Christopher A. Lambert |
| RSO: | Foon C. Chung |
| IRM: | Simon Guerrero |
| PAO: | Michael Hahn |
| DAO: | Cdr. Craig J. Baranowski |
| MLO: | Lcdr. Michael Rabang |
| AGR: | Herbert ""Finn"" Rudd (resident in Brasilia) |
| VOA: | William Rodgers |
| LOC: | Pamela Howard-Reguindin |

**Sao Paulo [CG]**, Rua Padre Joao Manoel, 933 Sao Paulo 01411-001—P.O. Box 2489, Unit 3502, APO AA 34030, Tel [55] (11) 881-6511, Fax 852-5154; PAO Fax 852-1395; Press Fax 852-4438, Internet address: www.amcham.com.br/consulate

| | |
|---|---|
| CG: | Carmen Martinez |
| ECO: | Kenneth B. Davis |
| POL: | Maria Sanchez |
| CON: | Rudolph Boone |
| COM: | Richard Lenahan |
| ADM: | Jesse I. Coronado |
| RSO: | Jackson Booth |
| PAO: | David Kurakane |
| ATO: | Mark Lower |
| IRM: | Christopher D. Dye |
| LAB: | Mark A. Mittlehauser |
| IRS: | Frederick Dulas (resident in Mexico City) |
| DEA: | Jeffrey J. Fitzpatrick |

**Recife [C]**, Rua Goncalves Maia, 163, Boa Vista, Recife—APO AA 34030, Tel [55] (81) 421-2441, Emergency Tel 421-5641, Fax 231-1906

| | |
|---|---|
| PO: | Francisco J. Fernandez |
| CON: | Duncan H. Walker |

Commercial Office [Trade Center], Rua Estados Unidos, 1812, 01427-002, Sao Paulo, S.P. Tel [55] (11) 853-2811, Fax 853-2744

| | |
|---|---|
| COM: | Richard Lenehan |

Commercial and Agricultural offices are also located at Belo Horizonte (PAO and COM Branch), Rua Fernades Tourinho 147-14th Fl., 302112-000, Belo Horizonte MG, Tel. [55] (31) 281-7271, Fax 281-6551

| | |
|---|---|
| COM: | Sean Kelly |

**Belem [CA]**, Rua Oswaldo Cruz 165 66, 017-090 Belem, Para, Brazil, Tel 55-91-223-0800/0413, Fax 091-223-0413, Telex 91-1092

| | |
|---|---|
| CA: | Christine Serrao |

**Fortaleza [CA]**, Instituto Brasil-Estados Unidos, Rua Nogueria Acioly, 891, Aldeota, Fortaleza, Brazil; Tel/Fax [55] (85) 252-1539

| | |
|---|---|
| CA: | Patricia C. Cavin |

**Manaus [CA]**, Rua Recife 1010, 67, 057, Amazonas, Brazil, Tel [55] (92) 234-4546, Fax (92) 234-4546

| | |
|---|---|
| CA: | James R. Fish |

**Porto Alegre [CA]**, Rua Riachuelo, 1257, 90010-271, Centro, Porto Alegre, RS

| | |
|---|---|
| CA: | Debra T. Godoy |

**Salvador da Bahia [CA]**, Av. Antonio Carlos Magalhaes S/N-Ed. Cidadella Center 1, Sala 410, 40, 275-440 Salvador, Bahia, Brazil, Tel [55] 071-358-9166, Telex 712780, Fax 071-351-0717

| | |
|---|---|
| CA: | Heather M. Marques |

Last Modified: Thursday, November 09, 2000

# BRUNEI

**Bandar Seri Begawan (E)**, Third Floor - Teck Guan Plaza, Jalan Sultan, Bandar Seri Begawan, Brunei Darussalam—PSC 470 (BSB), FPO AP 96507, Emb Tel [673] (2) 220-384, 229-670, Fax [673] (2) 225-293; Amb direct line 240-763; DCM direct line 241-645; COM Fax 226-523; STU III Fax 240-761. E-mail: amembbsb@brunet.bn. Embassy website: http://members.xoom.com/amembrunei

| | |
|---|---|
| AMB: | Sylvia G. Stanfield |
| AMB OMS: | Elizabeth J. Ryley |
| DCM: | Georgia T. Wright |
| ADM/CON: | [Vacant] |
| IRM/GSO: | Donald J. Connolly |
| RSO: | Robert Valenti (resident in Kuala Lumpur) |
| ODC: | Col. Robert C. McAdams, USA (resident in Singapore) |
| RMO: | Dr. Michael E. Nesemann (resident in Singapore) |
| PER: | Melvin Spence (resident in Kuala Lumpur) |
| ATO: | Dale Good (resident in Singapore) |

| | |
|---|---|
| FAA: | David L. Knudson (resident in Singapore) |
| DAO: | Capt. Terry S. Douglas, USN (resident in Singapore) |
| CUS: | Donald K. Shruhan, Jr. (resident in Singapore) |
| IRS: | Billy J. Brown (resident in Singapore) |
| PAO: | Charles Barclay (resident in Kuala Lumpur) |
| SAO: | Col. Robert McAdams, USAF (resident in Singapore) |
| RSO: | Robert Valenti (resident in Kuala Lumpur) |
| DEA: | Larry M. Hahn (resident in Singapore) |

Last Modified: Thursday, November 09, 2000

# BULGARIA

**Sofia (E),** 1 Saborna St.—AMEmbassy Sofia, Dept. of State, 5740 Sofia Place, Washington, D.C. 20521-5740, Tel [359] (2) 937-5100, Fax 981-8977; CON Fax 963-2859; ADM/GSO/HR Fax 963-0086; FMO Fax 963-2759; CLO Fax 971-2022; HU Fax 971-3561; PAO Fax 980-3646; COM Fax 980-6850; AGR Fax 981-6568; AID Fax 964-0102; PC Tel 980-0217, Fax 981-7525; ODC Fax 980-9114, DOJ Fax 953-3386. Website: www.usembassy.bg; Consular Section: niv@usconsulate.bg - for NIV information, nivappt@usconsulate.bg - for NIV appointments, iv-dv@usconsulate.bg - for immigrant visa-diversity visa lottery information, acs@usconsulate.bg - for info for American citizens

| | |
|---|---|
| AMB: | Richard M. Miles |
| AMB OMS: | Hortencia Gencalp |
| DCM: | Roderick Moore |
| DCM OMS: | Marilyn Wigle Connors |
| POL/ECO: | John Winant |
| ADM: | William Loskot |
| COM: | Richard Kanter |
| CON: | Laurence Tobey |
| RSO: | Keith LaRochelle |
| GSO: | Gregory MacDonald |
| IPO: | John Moore |
| PAO: | Michael Seidenstricker |
| ODC: | Maj. Perry Teague, USA |
| AID: | Debra Farland |
| DAO: | Col. Barry Shade, USAF |
| AGR: | Holly Higgins |
| PC: | Steven Taylor |
| FMO: | Michael Roche |
| DOJ: | Karen Kramer>BR> FAA: [Vacant] (resident in Rome) |
| DEA: | James Soiles (resident in Athens) |
| IRS: | Frederick Pablo (resident in Rome) |

Last Modified: Wednesday, April 04, 2001

# BURKINA FASO

**Ouagadougou (E),** 602 Avenue Raoul Follerau, 01 B.P. 35, Tel (226) 30-67-23, afterhours Tel 31-26-60 and 31-27-07, Fax (226) 30-38-90. Internet address: amemb-ouaga@ouagadougb.us-state.gov

| | |
|---|---|
| AMB: | Jimmy Kolker |
| AMB OMS: | Karen Waltz-Davis |
| DCM: | Daniel Santos, Jr. |
| POL/ECO/COM: | Christopher Palmer |
| ADM: | Terrence Wong |

| | |
|---|---|
| RSO: | [Vacant] |
| PAO: | Richard Johannsen |
| IRM: | (Vacant) |
| DAO: | Col. Daniel W. Pike, USA (resident in Abidjan) |
| FAA: | Edward Jones resident in Dakar) |
| RETO: | Robert Lindsey resident in Dakar) |

Last Modified: Friday, January 19, 2001

# BURMA

**Rangoon (E),** 581 Merchant St. (GPO 521). Box B, APO AP 96546, Tel [95] (1) 282055, 282182, Fax [95] (1) 280409, direct-in-dial: EXEC Tel [95] (1) 283668; DAO Tel 277507; GSO Tel 543354, 542608, Fax 543353; Health Unit Tel 511072, Fax 511069; PAO Tel 221585, 223106, 223140, Fax 221262. Internet address: rangoon-info@state.gov

| | |
|---|---|
| CHG: | Priscilla A. Clapp |
| CHG SEC: | Patricia J. Youmans |
| DCM: | Karl E. Wycoff |
| POL/ECO: | Paul B. Daley |
| PAO: | Ronald J. Post |
| ECO/COM: | Anthony C. Woods |
| CON: | Kristin M. Hagerstrom |
| ADM: | Stanley E. Gibson |
| FMO: | Laurence Rigg |
| GSO: | David T. Rockey |
| RSO: | Patrick McCreary |
| IPO: | Daniel L. Reagan |
| AGR: | Maurice W. House (resident in Bangkok) |
| DAO: | Col. Jack C. Dibrell, USA |
| DEA: | John M. Whalen |

Last Modified: Tuesday, September 05, 2000

# BURUNDI

**Bujumbura (E),** B.P. 1720, Avenue Des Etas-Unis, Tel [257] 22-34-54, afterhours Tel 21-48-53, Fax 22-29-26; AID/OFDA Tel 22-59-51, Fax 22-29-86. E-mail: (user last name plus initials) @bujumburab.us-state.gov

| | |
|---|---|
| AMB: | Mary C. Yates |
| AMB OMS: | Nancy Alain |
| DCM: | Roger J. Moran |
| ECO/CON: | David G. Mosby |
| POL/CON: | Karl Olsen |
| ADM: | Thomas Doherty |
| RSO: | Patrick McGhee |
| PAO: | Judith M. Kaula |
| GSO: | Richard Yoneoka |
| IPO: | Rose Safir |
| FAA: | Ronald L. Montgomery (resident in Dakar) |
| AID/OFDA: | Miriam Lutz |
| AID/REDSO: | David Aasen |
| DAO/OPSCO: | Ralph Lankford |
| RETO: | Melvia Hasman (resident in Dakar) |
| IRS: | Frederick Pablo (resident in Paris) |
| DEA: | Robert Shannon (resident in Cairo) |

Last Modified: Tuesday, November 07, 2000

# CAMBODIA

**Phnom Penh (E),** 27 EO Street 240—Box P, APO AP 96546, Tel [855] 23-216-436/438, Fax 23-216-811; ADM Fax 23-216437

| | |
|---|---|
| AMB: | Kent M. Wiedemann |
| AMB OMS: | Elka H. Hortoland |
| DCM: | Alexander A. Arvizu |
| DCM OMS: | Sharon F. Walton |
| POL: | Theodore Allegra |
| ECO/COM: | Bruce L. Levine |
| CON: | [Vacant] |
| ADM: | Henry M. Kaminski |
| GSO: | Stephen A. Druzak |
| IPO: | Monte R. Marchant |
| AID: | Lisa Chiles |
| PAO: | [Vacant] |
| RSO: | Phil A. Whitney |
| FAA: | David L. Knudson (resident in Singapore) |
| APHIS: | Dale Maki (resident in Beijing) |
| DAO: | Col. Michael A. Norton |
| CINCPACREP: | Maj.Ralph A. Skeba |
| NAMRU: | Dr. James G. Olson |
| IRS: | Billy J. Brown (resident in Singapore) |
| DEA: | William Simpson, Jr. (resident in Bangkok) |

Last Modified: Wednesday, October 18, 2000

# CAMEROON

**Yaounde (E),** rue Nachtigal, B.P. 817—Pouch address: American Embassy, Dept. of State, Washington, D.C. 20521-2520; Tel (237) 23-40-14, or (237) 22-25-89, Fax 23-07-53; ADM Tel 23-13-87; IRM Tel [237] 23-43-72; DAO Tel 22-03-17. Internet address: http//usembassy@state.gov/Yaounde.

| | |
|---|---|
| AMB: | John M. Yates |
| AMB OMS: | Diane Manago |
| DCM: | Frances T. Jones |
| DCM OMS: | Barbara Jensen |
| PAO: | J. Thomas Dougherty |
| POL/ECO: | Robert S. Ford |
| CON: | Marinda Harpole |
| ADM: | Lawrence G. Richter |
| RSO: | Alfred P. Vincent |
| GSO: | Kathleen Roberts |
| BFO: | Kevin T. Crews |
| FMS: | V. Ray Meininger |
| DAO: | Scott Rutherford |
| PC: | James Dobson |
| IMO: | Jean Chapoteau |

**Douala [BO],** Tel (237) 42-53-31 and 42-03-03, Fax 42-77-90

| | |
|---|---|
| DIR: | William Philo |

Last Modified: Wednesday, February 07, 2001

# CANADA

**Ottawa, Ontario (E),** 490 Sussex Drive, Ottawa, Ontario, Canada KIN 1G8,— P.O. Box 5000, Ogdensburg, NY 13669-0430, Tel (613) 238-5335; Fax 688-3097 COM Fax 688-3088

| | |
|---|---|
| AMB: | Gordon D. Giffin |
| AMB OMS: | Joanne P. Holliday |
| DCM: | Stephen R. Kelly |
| POL: | Patrick Del Vecchio |
| ECO: | Robert Smolik |
| COM: | Dolores F. Harrod |
| CON: | Michael D. Bellows |
| ADM: | Warren P. Nixon |
| RSO: | John Hurley |
| PAO: | Mary Ellen Gilroy |
| IMO: | David R. Miller |
| EST: | Susan M. Lysyshyn |
| DAO: | Col. Lowell Boyd |
| FAS: | Norval Francis |
| DEA: | Anthony Pratapas |
| CUS: | [Vacant] |
| LAB: | Karen E. Krueger |
| FAA: | Leann Moore (resident in Washington, D.C.) |
| IRS/CID: | Peggy E. Mullins |
| LEGATT: | Stewart Sturm |
| ATF: | David Kreighbaum |
| INS: | [Vacant] |
| USSS: | [Vacant] |
| APHIS: | Mark Knez |

**Calgary, Alberta [CG],** Suite 1050, 615 Macleod Trail, S.E., Calgary, Alberta, Canada T2G 4T8, Tel (403) 266-8962, Fax 264-6630; COM Fax 264-6630

| | |
|---|---|
| CG: | Roy E. Chavera |
| CON: | Richard Appleton |
| COM: | Michael Speck |
| VC: | Kirby Nelson |

**Halifax, Nova Scotia (CG),** Suite 910, Cogswell Tower, Scotia Sq., Halifax, NS, Canada B3J 3K1, Tel (902) 429-2480, Fax 423-6861; COM Tel (902) 429-2482, Fax 429-7690

| | |
|---|---|
| CG: | Elo-Kai Ojamaa |
| CON: | Mark Seibel |

**Montreal, Quebec (CG),** P.O. Box 65, Postal Station Desjardins, H5B 1G1—P.O. Box 847, Champlain, NY 12919-0847, Tel (514) 398-9695, EXEC Fax 398-9430; ADM Fax 398-0711; COM Fax 398-0711

| | |
|---|---|
| CG: | Mary C. Pendleton |
| CG SEC: | Loretta Hight |
| COM: | Donald Businger |
| CON: | Douglas V. Ellice |
| ADM: | Lynn Donovan |
| PAO: | Janet Wilgus |
| IRM: | Warren L. Gilsdorf |
| USSS: | Thomas Greenaway |

**U.S. Mission to the International Civil Aviation Organization (ICAO),** Suite 14.10, 999 University St., Montreal, Quebec, Canada H3C-5J9, Tel (514) 954-8304, Fax 954-8021

| | |
|---|---|
| US REP: | Amb. Edward W. Simpson |
| OMS: | Maryann Hughes |
| DEP US REP: | Wm. Frank Price |
| ALT US REP: | David M. Shapiro |

**Quebec, Quebec (CG),** 2 Place Terrasse Dufferin, C.P. 939, G1R 4T9—P.O. Box 1547, Champlain, NY 12919-1547, Tel (418) 692-2095, Fax 692-4640

| | |
|---|---|
| CG: | Lois Aroian |
| CON: | Hazel R. Boone |

**Toronto, Ontario (CG),** 360 University Ave., M5G 2S4—P.O. Box 135, Lewiston, NY 14092-0135, Tel (416) 595-1700, Fax 595-0051

| | |
|---|---|
| CG: | Franklin P. Huddle, Jr. |
| CG OMS: | Karen Heide |
| POL/ECON: | Mitchell E. Optican |
| COM: | Patrick O. Santillo |
| CON: | John D. Morris |
| ADM: | Ralph S. Kwong |
| RSO: | Vance R. Witmer |
| CUS: | Diane Gie-George |
| IRM: | John N. Wickersham |
| PAO: | Phillip P. Hoffman |
| INS: | John T. Smarsh |

**Vancouver, British Columbia (CG),** 1095 West Pender St., V6E 2M6—P.O. Box 5002, Point Roberts, WA 98281-5002, Tel (604) 685-4311, Fax 685-5285; CON GEN Tel 685-4311, ext. 269, Fax 685-7304; ADMIN Tel 685-4311, ext. 250; CON/ACS Tel 685-4311; CON/NIV Tel 685-4311; CON Fax 685-7175; COM Fax 687-6095

| | |
|---|---|
| CG: | Hugo Llorens |
| CG ASST: | Holly Wazelle |
| ECO/ADM: | Chris Lambert |
| COM: | John W. Avard |
| CON: | Michael B. Chang |
| PAO: | Meg Gilroy (resident in Ottawa) |
| USSS: | Robert Bond |

Last Modified: Thursday, December 14, 2000

# CAPE VERDE

**Praia (E),** Rua Abilio Macedo 81, C.P. 201, Tel [238] 61-56-16, Fax 61-13-55

| | |
|---|---|
| AMB: | Michael D. Metelits |
| AMB OMS: | Audrey J. Ley |
| DCM/ADM: | Elizabeth B. McGaffey |
| CON: | Leilani L. Straw |
| RSO: | George G. Fredericks (resident in Dakar) |
| AID: | [Vacant] |
| DAO: | Ltc. Todd Coker, USMC (resident in Dakar) |
| LAB: | Jay T. Smith] (resident in Washington, D.C.) |
| IMO: | David Odette (resident at RIMC Frankfurt) |
| M: | Susan Hullinger (resident in Dakar) |
| FAA: | Edward Jones (resident in Dakar) |
| IRS: | Frederick D. Pablo (resident in Paris) |
| RCON: | Ann Gordon (resident in Dakar) |

Last Modified: Thursday, November 09, 2000

# CENTRAL AFRICAN REPUBLIC

**Bangui (E),** Avenue David Dacko, B.P. 924, Tel [236] 61-02-00, 61-02-10, 65-25-78, Fax 61-44-94, duty phone (236) 50-12-08

| | |
|---|---|
| AMB: | Robert C. Perry |
| AMB OMS: | Cynthia Newman |
| DCM: | Judith D. Francis |
| ADM: | Mark J. Biedlingmaier |
| RSO: | Timothy Laas (resident in N'Djamena) |

| | |
|---|---|
| DAO: | Ltc. Terence M. Tidler, USA (resident in N'Djamena) |
| FAA: | Ronald L. Montgomery (resident in Dakar) |
| IRM: | Santiago Urieta |
| RBFO: | Linda K. Green |
| RMO: | Dr. William Green |
| RPO: | C. Allison Barkley (resident in Yaounde) |
| IRS: | Frederick D. Pablo (resident in Paris) |
| DEA: | Robert Shannon (resident in Cairo) |

Last Modified: Thursday, November 09, 2000

# CHAD

**N'Djamena (E),** Ave. Felix Eboue, B.P. 413, Tel [235] (51) 70-09, 51-90-52, 51-92-33, Telex 5203 KD, Fax 51-56-54, or 56-54; Direct system dialing via system 85/IVG in Dept: AMB 924-1702, DCM 924-1712; POL/ECO 924-1732; POL/MIL 924-2852; RSO 924-1352; IPC 924-1672, Fax 924-3292.

| | |
|---|---|
| AMB: | Christopher E. Goldthwait |
| AMB OMS: | Niceta D. Lowry |
| DCM: | Paul E. Rowe |
| POL: | R. Wayne Boyls |
| POL/MIL: | Francis P. Peck |
| ADM: | Richard C. Paschall III |
| IPO: | Joseph W. Cole |
| RSO: | Timothy E. Laas |
| PAO: | Dr. Katharine P. Moseley |
| DAO: | MAJ. Christopher E. Brown |
| FAA: | Edward Jones (resident in Dakar) |
| RELO: | Robert Lindsey (resident in Dakar) |

Last Modified: Wednesday, January 03, 2001

# CHILE

**Santiago (E),** Av. Andres Bello 2800, APO AA 34033, Tel [56] (2) 232-2600, Fax 330-3710; COM Fax 330-3172; AID Fax 638-0931; AGR Fax 56-2-330-3203; FBO Fax 233-4108; CON 56-2-330-3710; GSO Fax 330-3020

| | |
|---|---|
| AMB: | John O'Leary |
| AMB OMS: | Rosalie B. Kahn |
| DCM: | James J. Carragher |
| ECO/POL: | Brian J. Blood |
| COM: | John A. Harris |
| CON: | Carl F. Troy |
| ADM: | David F. Davison |
| RSO: | John J. Root |
| PAO: | Kathleen A. Brion |
| IRM: | Patrick Meagher |
| DAO: | Capt. Larry Pacentrilli, USN |
| MILGP: | Col. Alexander Trujillo |
| IRS: | Frederick Dulas (resident in Mexico City) |
| AGR: | Lewis J. Stockard |
| APHIS: | Eric R. Hoffman |
| LAB: | Thomas D. Mittnacht |
| DEA: | Victor Olivieri |
| LEGATT: | Kevin Currier |
| FAA: | Santiago Garcia (resident in Miami) |
| DEA: | Victor L. Olivieri |

Last Modified: Thursday, January 25, 2001

# CHINA (See also Taiwan)

**Beijing (E),** Xiu Shui Bei Jie 3, 100600—PSC 461, Box 50, FPO AP 96521-0002, Tel [86] (10) 6532-3831, Telex AMEMB CN 22701; EXEC/ECO Fax 6532-6422; POL/ES&T/RSO Fax 6532-6423; ESO/MSG Fax 6532-6421; GSO Travel Fax 6532-2483; Health Unit Fax 6532-6424; AGR Fax 6532-2962; CUS Fax 6500-3032; INS Fax 6561-4507; PAO Fax 6532-2039; CON Fax 6532-3178; COM Tel 6532-6924 thru 27, Fax 6532-3297; ADM/Personnel Fax 6532-5141; APHIS address: 12-21 China World Trade Ctr., No. 1 Jianguomenwai Ave., Beijing, FAX [86] (10) 6505-4574; American Center for Education Exchange (ACEE) address: Jing Guang Center, Tel 6510-5242, Fax 6501-5247; Federal Aviation Administration (FAA) address: No. 15 Guang Hua Li, Jian Guo Men Wai, Chao Yang District, Tel 6504-2571, Fax 6504-5154

| | |
|---|---|
| AMB: | Joseph W. Prueher |
| AMB OMS: | Lynette Tanibe |
| DCM: | Michael W. Marine. |
| POL: | James Moriarty |
| ECO: | Lauren Moriarty |
| COM: | Lee Boam |
| CON: | David Hopper |
| ADM: | Raymond Boneski |
| GSO: | Dan Christenson |
| RSO: | James McWhirter |
| PAO: | Lloyd Neighbors |
| IRM: | [Vacant] |
| ES&T: | Kurt Tong |
| DAO: | Bg. Gratton Sealock |
| LAB: | [Vacant] |
| AGR: | Larry Senger |
| APHIS: | Dale Maki |
| CUS: | David Benner |
| FAA: | Elizabeth Keck |
| INS: | Jeannette Chu |
| IRS: | Stanley Beesley (resident in Tokyo) |
| DEA: | Luis A. Burgos |

**Guangzhou [CG],** No. 1 Shamian Street South, Guangzhou 510133, Pouch address: U.S. Dept. of State, Wash, D.C.20521-4090—PSC 461, Box 100, FPO AP 96521-0002, Tel [86] (20) 8188-8911, Duty Officer Tel.139-0229-3169,CONS Fax 8186-2341; 7553, Fax 8666-0703; EXEC/ADM Fax: 8186-4001; PAO Tel 8335-4269, Fax 8335-4764; American School of Guangzhou: Tel 8758-0001, Fax 8758-0002

| | |
|---|---|
| CG: | Edward McKeon |
| ECO/POL: | Paul Hacker |
| COM: | Ned Quistorff |
| CON: | Allen Kong |
| ADM: | Dan Romano |
| RSO: | Martin Chu |
| GSO: | DeAngela Burns |
| PAO: | Mark Canning |
| IRM: | William Dunkel |
| INS: | Jeanette Chu |

**Shanghai [CG],** 1469 Huai Hai Zhong Lu, Shanghai 200031 China; FPO address: AmConGen Shanghai—PSC 461, Box 200 FPO AP 96521, Tel [86] (21) 6433-3936, Fax 6433-4122

| | |
|---|---|
| CG: | Henry Levine |

| | |
|---|---|
| POL/ECON: | Robert Griffiths |
| ADM: | Robert Frazier |
| CON: | Anne Hall |
| COM: | Catherine Houghton |
| PAO: | Anthony Hutchinson |
| RSO: | Pittman Orr |
| ATO: | Laverne Brabant |

**Shenyang [CG],** 52, 14th Wei Road, Heping District, 110003—PSC 461, Box 45, FPO AP 96521-0002, Tel [86] (21) 6433-6880, Duty Officer Tel 137-401-9790, Fax 2322-2374; PAO Fax 2322-1505; FCS Fax 2322-2206

| | |
|---|---|
| CG: | Augus Simmons |
| COM: | Erin Sullivan |
| CON: | RIchard Walsh |
| POL/ECON: | John Hoover |
| ADM: | Won Y. Lee |
| PAO: | Salome Hernandez |
| IRM: | Roger Bjorkdahl |
| RSO: | Paul Vallee |

**Chengdu [CG],** 4 Lingshiguan Road, Chengdu 610041, Sichuan—PSC 461, Box 85, FPO AP 96521-0002, Tel [86] (28) 558-3992, 558-9642, Duty Officer Tel 1370-800-1422; Peace Corps Tel 541-2234/2340/2436, Fax 541-7152, Peace Corps Duty Officer 139-8005-9990; Consulate Fax 558-3520; PAO Fax 558-3792; COM Fax 558-9221.

| | |
|---|---|
| CG: | David L. Bleyle |
| CG SEC: | Cheryl C. Cruise |
| ECO/POL: | John Fogarty |
| POL/ECO: | Marc D. Koehler |
| CON/POL: | Douglas G. Kelly |
| ADM: | Sean B. Stein |
| IRM: | Christopher House |
| FMS: | Modesto Gutierrez |
| COM: | Thomas Sims |
| PAO: | Cynthia Caples |
| GSO: | Josephine J. Dumm |

Last Modified: Thursday, March 08, 2001

# COLOMBIA

**Bogota (E),** Calle 22D-BIS, No. 47-51, Apartado Aereo 3831,—APO AA 34038, Tel [57] (1) 315-0811, Fax 315-2197; CON Tel. 315-1566; FCS Fax [571] (315) 2171/2190; GSO Fax [571] (315) 2207

| | |
|---|---|
| AMB: | Curtis W. Kamman |
| AMB OMS: | Sheila M. Jones |
| DCM: | Barbara C. Moore |
| POL/ECO: | Leslie A. Bassett |
| COM: | Karla King |
| CON: | Kenneth F. Sackett |
| ADM: | Robert E. Davis |
| RSO: | Seymour C. Dewitt |
| PAO: | James H. Williams |
| IRM: | Michael J. Kovich |
| AID: | [Vacant)] |
| DAO: | Col. Leocadio Muniz, USA |
| USMILGP: | Col. James C. Hiett, USA |
| AGR: | David G. Salmon |
| APHIS: | John L. Shaw |
| FAA: | Victor Tamariz (resident in Miami) |
| NAS: | Luis G. Moreno |
| IRS: | Luis O. Rivera |

CUS:     Stephen J. Hayward
ATF:     David O. Navarrete
IRM:     Michael F. Ingram
DEA:     Leo Arreguin, Jr.
LEGATT:     Joseph L. Rodriguez
USSS:     Anthony M. Chapa

**Barranquilla (CA),** Calle 77, No. 68-15; Tel. (95) 353-0970 or 0974; Fax (95) 353-5216

CA:     David S. Parrish

Last Modified: Thursday, November 09, 2000

## COMOROS (See Mauritius)

Last Modified: Monday, January 08, 2001

## CONGO, DEMOCRATIC REPUBLIC OF THE (formerly Zaire)

**Kinshasa (E),** 310 Avenue des Aviateurs—Unit 31550, APO AE 09828, Tel [243] (12) 21804, 21807, cellular line: [243] (88) 43608; CON (88) 46859; COM Fax (88) 03276; PROC Fax (88) 43805; USAID Fax (88) 03274; PAO Fax (88) 46592

AMB:     William L. Swing
AMB OMS:     Mary J. Jazynka
DCM:     R. Barrie Walkley
POL:     Susan W. Zelle
ECO/COM:     Katherine Simonds
CON:     Daphne M. Titus
ADM:     Dean B. Wooden
RSO:     Donald W. Weinberg
S/GSO:     Danny E. Corsbie
PAO:     Judith D. Trunzo
IRM:     Janette M. Corsbie
DAO:     Ltc. Sue A. Sandusky, USA
AID:     John A. Grayzel
FAA:     Ronald L. Montgomery (resident in Dakar)

Last Modified: Thursday, November 09, 2000

## CONGO, REPUBLIC OF THE

**Brazzaville (E),** The Brazzaville Embassy Office is co-located with Embassy Kinshasa at 310 Avenue Des Aviateurs, Kinshasa, DRC, Tel [243] (88) 43608, Fax (88) 41036. Address/phone of temporary office in Brazzaville: 70 rue Bayardelle, Tel [242] 81-14-72; additional information: [243] (88) 40520 or (88) 40252

AMB:     David H. Kaeuper
DCM:     James C. Swan
CON:     William S. Rowland
ECO:     Ava Rogers
DAO:     [Vacant]
ADM:     John F. Moos
RSO:     Laviris Stubblefield
PAO:     Thomas J. Dougherty
IRM:     Thomas Rebarick
FAA:     Ronald L. Montgomery (resident in Dakar)
IRS:     Frederick D. Pablo (resident in Paris)

## COSTA RICA

**San Jose (E),** Pavas, San Jose—APO AA 34020, Tel (506) 220-3939, afterhours Tel 220-3127, Fax 220-2305; COM Fax 231-4783

AMB:     Thomas J. Dodd
AMB OMS:     Laura A. Bailey
DCM:     Linda Jewell
POL/ECO:     Perry E. Ball
COM:     Frank Foster
CON:     Janet M. Weber
ADM:     Clarke W. Allard
RSO:     William J. Griffin
PAO:     Gary McElhiney
IRM:     Cynthia M. Ruby
DEA:     Vance W. Stacy
FAA:     Ruben Quinones (resident in Miami)
ODR:     Mark Wilkins
AGR:     Charles Bertsch
APHIS Region V:     Harold C. Hofmann
APHIS Region VI:     Mark Knez
ENVIR HUB:     Lawrence Gumbiner
IRS:     Frederick Dulas (resident in Mexico City)

Last Modified: Thursday, November 09, 2000

## COTE D'IVOIRE (in English, Ivory Coast)

**Abidjan (E),** 5 rue Jesse Owens, 01 B.P. 1712, Tel [225] 20-21-09-79 or 20-21-46-72, Fax 20-22-32-59

AMB:     George Mu
AMB OMS:     Cheryl Dukelow
DCM:     Jackson McDonald
POL/ECO:     Robert P. Jackson
COM:     Johnny Brown
CON:     Nan Stewart
ADM:     James D. McGee
RSO:     Gregory Levin
PAO:     Patricia M. Hawkins
ESC:     William G. Springmeier
IRM:     William Walls
DAO:     Col. Daniel Pike
AGR:     Bruce J. Zanin
CDC:     Dr. Terence Chorba
FAA:     Edward Jones (resident in Dakar)
FBIS:     David Lastova
PC:     Martin Mueller
AID:     James Hradsky (resident in Bamako)
VOA:     Luis Ramirez
RMO:     Dr. Charles Rosenfarb
RMOP:     Dr. Michael Gershon
DEA:     Edgar L. Moses (resident in Lagos)
IRS:     Frederick D. Pablo (resident in Paris)
ISO:     Miller I. Vinson

**African Development Bank/Fund,** Ave. Joseph Anoma, 01—B.P. 1387 Abidjan 01, Tel [225] 20-40-15, Fax 33-14-34; COM Tel 21-46-16, Fax 22-24-37

EXEC DIR:     Alice Dear
ALT DIR:     Jeannie Scott
COM:     Angela Chatman-Williams

Last Modified: Friday, March 02, 2001

# CROATIA

**Zagreb (E),** Andrije Hebranga 2, 1000 Zagreb, Croatia, Tel [385] (1) 661-2200, afterhours Tel 661-2400, Fax 455-8585; EXEC Fax 455-0394; ADM Fax 455-0892; GSO Fax 481-7711. Website address: www.usembassy.hr

| | |
|---|---|
| AMB: | Lawrence G. Rossin |
| AMB OMS: | Kathy Chelsen |
| DCM: | Charles L. English |
| CON: | Russel Brown |
| POL/ECO: | William Mozdzierz |
| RSO: | Jack Picardy |
| COM: | Patrick C. Hughes |
| ADM: | Mary Teirlynck |
| PAO: | Allen Docal |
| IRM: | Charles C. Reitz |
| AID: | Pamela Baldwin |
| DAO: | Col. John Adams, USA |
| AGR: | Allan Mustard (resident in Vienna) |
| FAA: | Steven B. Wallace (resident in Rome) |
| IRS: | Larry J. LeGrand (resident in Rome) |
| REF: | Kevin Carew |
| SAO: | Maj. Kris Wheaton, USA |
| DLA/SPLIT: | Cpt. Dean Wilt, USA |

Last Modified: Friday, April 06, 2001

# CUBA

**Havana (USINT),** Swiss Embassy, Calzada between L and M Sts., Vedado, Havana, USINT Tel [53] (7) 33-3551/9, 33-3543/5, Fax 33-3700; Refugee inquiries telephone numbers 33-3546/7, afterhours Marine Post 1 33-3026; PAO direct line 33-3967, Fax 33-3869; T+T Fax 33-3975, FBO direct line: 33-4096/97, Fax 33-3975; ADM Fax 66-2095, INS switchboard 33-4511/33-3586, Fax 33-4512

| | |
|---|---|
| PO: | Vikki Huddleston |
| DPO: | John Boardman |
| POL/ECO: | Jeffrey Delaurentis |
| CON: | Patricia Murphy |
| ADM: | Joseph Hilliard |
| RSO: | Michael French |
| PAO: | Janet Edmunson |
| IRM: | Paula Marx |
| FAA: | Ruben Quinones (resident in Miami) |
| FBO: | James C. McQueen |
| INS (OIC) | |

# CYPRUS

**Nicosia (E),** Metochiou and Ploutarchou Streets, Engomi, Nicosia, Cyprus—P.O. Box 24536, PSC 815 FPO AE 09836, Tel [357] (2) 776400, afterhours Tel 776934, Fax 780944; CON Fax 781146; PAO Tel 677143, Fax 668003; Internet address: amembsys@spidernet.com.cy

| | |
|---|---|
| AMB: | Donald K. Bandler |
| AMB OMS: | Nelia G. Adanza |
| DCM: | Daniel R. Russel |
| POL: | Donald R. Shemanski |
| ECO/COM: | Woodward C. Price |
| CON: | David R. Dreher |
| ADM: | Thomas M. Young |
| RSO: | Thomas F. Grey, Jr. |
| PAO: | Walter Douglas |
| IRM: | Matthew E. McClammy |

| | |
|---|---|
| DAO: | Col. Philip C. Rusciolelli, USA |
| FAA: | Steven B. Wallace (resident in Rome) |
| IRS: | Larry J. LeGrand (resident in Rome) |
| DEA: | Perry Felecos |
| USSS: | Robert E. Blatner |

Last Modified: Thursday, November 09, 2000

# CZECH REPUBLIC

**Prague (E),** Trziste 15, 11801 Prague 1, Tel [420] (2) 5753-0663, Fax 5753-0920; Emerg after hrs 5753-2716; GSO Fax 5753-0584; DAO Fax 5753-2718; ODC Fax 5753-1175; CON Fax 5753-4028; POL/ECO Fax 5753-2717; COM Fax 5753-1165 or 5753-1168; AGR Fax 5753-1173; Pub. Diplomacy and IRC: Hybernska 7A 11716 Prague 1, PAO Tel Fax 2422-0983

| | |
|---|---|
| AMB: | [Vacant] |
| AMB OMS: | [Vacant] |
| CHG: | Steven J. Coffey |
| POL/ECO: | John J. Boris |
| COM: | Richard Steffens |
| CON: | Elizabeth Barnett |
| ADM: | [Vacant] |
| RSO: | Dennis W. Bochantin |
| PAO: | Evelyn Early |
| IMO: | David L. Patterson |
| DAO: | Col. Marc J. Neifert, USAF |
| AGR: | Robert H. Curtis (resident in Vienna) |
| EST: | Keith A. Eddins |
| FAA: | [Vacant] |
| IBB: | Tadeausz Lipien |
| IRS: | [Vacant] |
| LEGATT: | Eliska Tretera |

Last Modified: Thursday, April 05, 2001

# DENMARK

**Copenhagen (E),** Dag Hammarskjolds Alle 24, 2100 Copenhagen—PSC 73, APO AE 09716, Tel [45] 3555-3144, afterhours Tel 3555-9270, Fax 3543-0223; POL/ECO/EST Fax 3542-8075; ADM Fax 3526-9611; CON Fax 3538-9616; PAO Fax 3542-7273; AGR Fax 3543-0278; USAF Fax 3526-5108; COM Fax 3542-0175; DAO Fax 3542-2516. Embassy home page: www.usembassy.dk

| | |
|---|---|
| AMB: | Richard N. Swett |
| AMB ASST: | Robert D. Quinn |
| DCM: | Lawrence E. Butler |
| POL/ECO: | Francis T. Scanlan |
| EST: | Paul D. Stephenson |
| COM: | Rizwan Khaliq |
| CON: | Dennis W. Merz |
| ADM: | Sarah F. Drew |
| RSO: | Claude J. Nebel |
| PAO: | H. Lela Margiou |
| IRM: | Joyce E. Snider |
| DAO: | Capt. Michael G. Watson, USN |
| ODC: | Col. Edwin E. Noble, USAF |
| DEA: | Arthur L. Kersey |
| INS: | John G. Hughes |
| GSO: | Peter A. Siegwald |
| FAA/CASLO: | Walter W. Parks III |
| AGR: | Philip A. Letarte (resident in The Hague) |
| IRS: | James P. Beene (resident in London) |
| LAB: | Elaine Papazian-Etienne |

FBI:                   Robert Patton
RMO:                   Bruce T. Miller, MD. (resident of Frankfurt)

# DJIBOUTI

**Djibouti (E),** Plateau du Serpent, Blvd. Marechal Joffre, B.P. 185, Tel [253] 35-39-95, Fax 35-39-40, afterhours 35-13-43

| | |
|---|---|
| AMB: | Lange Schermerhorn |
| OMS: | Donna Linchangco |
| DCM/ECO/COM: | Edward P. Malcik |
| ADM: | Christopher K. Derrick |
| POL/CON: | Lauren L. May |
| IPO: | Carl E. Stefan |
| IMS: | Ruth Ann Kleinfelt |
| USLO: | Maj. Joseph J. Bovy, USA |
| RSO: | Michael J. Stutzman |
| DAO: | Ltc. Kevin Kenny, USA  (resident in Addis Ababa) |
| DEA: | Robert Shannon (resident in Cairo) |
| FAA: | Ronald L. Montgomery (resident in Dakar) |
| IRS: | Frederick D. Pablo  (resident in Paris) |
| LAB: | Ralph Anske (resident in Nairobi) |

Last Modified: Friday, December 01, 2000

# DOMINICAN REPUBLIC

**Santo Domingo (E),** corner of Calle Cesar Nicolas Penson and Calle Leopoldo Navarro—Unit 5500, APO AA 34041-5500, Tel [809] 221-2171, afterhours Tel 221-8100 or 562-3560, Fax 686-7437; Fax 685-6959; AID Tel 221-1100, Fax 221-0444; INS Tel 731-4390, Fax 731-4350; PC Tel 685-4102, Fax 686-3241. Fax 686-4326; ADM 731-4255, Fax 731-4280; FCS 227-2121, Fax 540-1267; PAO 731-4614, Fax 541-1828; DEA 731-4381, Fax 685-7507; DAO 731-4220, Fax 687-5222; MAAG 682-1953, Fax 682-3991; APHIS 227-0111, Fax 732-9454; AGR 227-0112, Fax 732-9454; ECO/POL 731-4335; website: www.usia. gov/posts/santodomingo. E-mail: Last name first, initial, middle initial@state.gov

| | |
|---|---|
| AMB: | [Vacant] |
| AMB OMS: | [Vacant] |
| CHG: | Janice L. Jacobs |
| DCM OMS: | Irene Buentello |
| ECON/POL: | Krishna R. Urs |
| COM: | Carol M. Kim |
| CON: | Joan V. Smith |
| PAO: | Merrie D. Blocker |
| ADM: | Harry A. Blanchette |
| RSO: | Paul T. Peterson |
| IRM: | Jamie Esquivel |
| AID: | Elena Brineman |
| DEA: | Ruben S. Prieto |
| INS: | Bartolome Rodriguez |
| DAO: | Lt Col John T. Hennessey, USMC |
| MAAG: | Cdr. Larry McCabe, USN |
| TAT: | Anthony Patton |
| APHIS: | Carolyn Cohen |
| AGR: | Kevin Smith |
| PC: | Anita Friedman |
| IRS: | Frederick Dulas (resident in Mexico City) |
| FAA: | Ruben Quinones (resident in Miami) |
| NAS: | Gaye G. Maris (resident in Miami) |
| LEGATT: | Armando Rodriguez |

**Puerto Plata [CA],** Calle Beller 51, 2nd Fl., Office No. 6; Tel. [809] 586-4204, Sousa Office Tel 571-3880

CA:                    William G. Kirkman

Last Modified: Thursday, April 05, 2001

# ECUADOR

**Quito (E),** Avenida 12 de Octubre y Avenida Patria—APO AA 34039, Tel [593] (2) 562-890, afterhours Tel 561-749, voice mail 561-624, Fax 502-052; COM Fax 504-550; direct-in-dialing: 644-6-0000 or office ext. E-mail: last name/middle initial/@state.gov

| | |
|---|---|
| AMB: | Gwen C. Clare |
| AMB OMS: | Linda Hartsock |
| DCM: | Larry Palmer |
| POL: | W. Stuart Symmington IV |
| ECO: | Thomas Kelly |
| COM: | Robert Jones |
| CON: | Suzanne Payne |
| ADM: | Christopher Stillman |
| RSO: | Barry M. Moore |
| PAO: | James Moore |
| IRM: | Michael Cesena |
| NAS: | Joel Cassman |
| AID: | Hilda Arellano |
| DAO: | Col. Martin Reyes, USA |
| MILGP: | Col. Joseph Contarino, USA |
| DEA: | William Hudson |
| PC: | Marcy Kelley |
| INS: | Charles Aycock |
| AGR: | Lawrence D. Fuell (resident in Lima) |
| FAA: | Victor Tamariz (resident in Miami) |

**Guayaquil (CG),** 9 de Octubre y Garcia Moreno—APO AA 34039, Tel [593] (4) 323-570, afterhours Tel 321-152, Fax 325-286; COM Fax 324-558

| | |
|---|---|
| CG: | Michael Glover |
| CG SEC: | Deanna Cotter |
| CON: | Steve Hardesty |
| ADM: | Gayle Hamilton |
| IRM: | Barbara Darnielle |
| COM: | Rodrigo Morales |
| DEA: | Victor Cortez |
| INS: | Robert Hlavac |

Last Modified: Monday, January 22, 2001

# EGYPT

**Cairo (E),** (North Gate) 8, Kamal el-Din Salah St., Garden City—Unit 64900, APO AE 09839-4900, Tel [20] (2) 795-7371, Telex 93773 AMEMB UN, 23227 AMEMB UN, Fax 797-3200; ADM Fax 797-2875; COM/CON Fax 795-8368; AID Fax 797-2233; PAO Fax 797-3591; DAO Fax 797-3049; AGR Fax 356-3989; LOC Fax 356-0233; OMC Fax 797-2273; ECO/POL Fax 797-2181, 797-3491; RSO Fax 797-2828; LEGATT Fax 797-2932; Workweek: Sunday through Thursday

| | |
|---|---|
| AMB: | Daniel C. Kurtzer |
| AMB OMS: | Jacalyn M. Stein |
| DCM: | Reno L. Harnish III |
| ECO/POL: | Richard Lebaron |
| COM: | Bobette Orr |
| CON: | Roger Pierce |

| | |
|---|---|
| ADM: | Stephen T. Smith |
| RSO: | John H. Frese |
| GSO: | James Alderman |
| PAO: | Marcelle Wahba |
| IRM: | Roger Cohen |
| AID: | Richard Brown |
| DAO: | Col. Mark Victorson, USA |
| FAA: | Steven B. Wallace (resident in Rome) |
| IRS: | Larry LeGrand (resident in Rome) |
| LAB: | Paul Fruell |
| PER: | Florence Crisp |
| DEA: | Robert Shannon |
| OMC: | Mg. John Vines, USA |
| AGR: | Thomas Pomeroy |
| LEGATT: | John Morton |
| LOC: | Laila Mulgaokar |

Last Modified: Monday, February 05, 2001

# EL SALVADOR

**San Salvador (E),** Final Blvd. Santa Elena, Antiguo Cuscatlan, Unit 3116, APO AA 34023, Tel (503) 278 – 4444, Fax 278 – 6011; USAID Tel (503) 298 – 1666, Fax (503) 298 – 0885; ECO/COM Fax (503) 298 – 2336; GSO Fax (503) 278 – 3347; ADMIN Tel (503) 228 – 2860, Fax (503) 289 – 4591; PC Tel (503) 263 – 8517/8604/03; Fax (503) 263-8420. Internet address: www.usinfo.org.sv/ www.sansalvador.state.gov

| | |
|---|---|
| AMB: | Anne W. Patterson |
| AMB OMS: | Carol L. Scannel |
| DCM: | Mark M. Boulware |
| POL: | Kevin M. Johnson |
| ECO/COM: | Bruce Williamson |
| CON: | William M. Bartlett |
| ADM: | Jorge Cintron |
| RSO: | Kevin M. Barry |
| PAO: | Marjorie Coffin |
| IRM: | Richard J. Herkert |
| GSO: | Rosina Schacknies |
| FMO: | Thomas A. Lyman |
| PER: | Marianne Kompa |
| DAO: | Col. Richard Nazario, USA |
| AID/DIR: | Kenneth C. Ellis |
| MILGP: | Col. John L. Goetchius, Jr. |
| AGR: | Suzanne Heinen (resident in Guatemala City) |
| APHIS/DIR: | [Vacant] |
| PC: | Michael L. Wise |
| DEA: | Vincent J. Sparacino, Acting |
| DOJ: | Robert Loosle |
| FAA: | Ruben Quinones (resident in Miami) |
| RIG: | Timothy E. Cox |
| LAB: | Edmund K. Sutow |
| IRS: | Frederick Dulas (resident in Mexico City) |
| ICITAP: | Louis Cobarruviaz |
| LEGATT: | Fernando M. Rivero (resident in Miami) |
| INS: | Victor W. Johnston |

Last Modified: Thursday, November 09, 2000

# ERITREA

**Asmara (E),** Franklin D. Roosevelt St.—P.O. Box 211, Asmara, Eritrea, Tel [291] (1) 120004, Fax 127584; USAID Tel 121895, Fax 123093; Peace Corps Tel 126354, Fax 122870; DAO/SAO Tel 126381, DOD/SAO Fax 126339

| | |
|---|---|
| AMB: | William D. Clarke |
| AMB OMS: | Sharron McGlathery |
| DCM: | Howard T. Perlow |
| CON: | James J. Hunter |
| ADM: | Johanna E. Schoeppl |
| POL: | David E. Manuel |
| POL/MIL: | [Vacant] |
| COM: | Howard T. Perlow |
| IRM: | Paul Rogers |
| AID: | [Vacant] |
| PAO: | [Vacant] |
| PC: | Tim Donnay |
| SAO: | Lt. Kenneth B. Agosta, USA |
| GSO: | Elizabeth A. Bowers |
| DAO: | Ltc. David Crawford, USA |
| RSO: | Michael J. Stutzman (resident in Addis Ababa) |
| FAA: | Ronald L. Montgomery (resident in Dakar) |
| IRS: | James P. Beene (resident in London) |
| DEA: | Robert Shannon (resident in Cairo) |

Last Modified: Thursday, November 09, 2000

# ESTONIA

**Tallinn (E),** Kentmanni 20, Tallinn 15099, Tel [372] 668-8100, Duty Officer Cell Phone Tel [372] (5) 092-129, Fax [372] 668-8134 or 668-8117; Direct-dialing: EXEC Tel 668-8103; ADM Tel 668-8105, Fax 668-8266; CON Tel 668-8111; IPO Tel 668-8277; PAO Tel 668-8124 or 668-8125; PA Fax 668-8253; Fax 631-2026; DAO Tel 668-8200, Fax 668-8257

| | |
|---|---|
| AMB: | Melissa F. Wells |
| DCM: | Dolores M. Brown |
| AMB OMS: | Rita Solis |
| POL: | Robert W. Filby |
| ECO/COM: | Nancy J. Nelson |
| CON: | Ellen B. Thorburn |
| ADM: | Michael S. Tulley |
| PAO: | Richard C. Lundberg |
| IPO: | Timothy W. Tickner |
| COM: | Thomas M. Kelsey (resident in Stockholm) |
| GSO: | William Slaven |
| RSO: | Gary Sheppard |
| RAO: | Daniel N. Hoffman |
| ODC: | Ltc John Suprin, USA |
| DAO: | Lcdr Patrick McCabe, USN |
| LEGATT: | William Moschella III |
| AGR: | Robert C. Tetro (resident in Stockholm) |
| EST: | David W. Mulenex (resident in Copen-hagen) |
| FAA: | Dennis Cooper (resident in Brussels) |
| IRS: | Margaret J. Lullo (resident in Berlin) |
| DEA: | Arthur L. Kersey (resident in Copenhagen) |

Last Modified: Thursday, April 05, 2001

# ETHIOPIA

**Addis Ababa (E),** Entoto St.—P.O. Box 1014, Tel [251] (1) 550-666, Fax 551-328, Telex 21282; PAO Tel 550-007, Fax 551-748; USAID Tel 510-088, Fax 510-043; ADM/GSO Fax 550-774; POL/ECO Fax 550-174. Internet address: usembassy@telecom.net.et

| | |
|---|---|
| AMB: | Tibor P. Nagy |
| AMB OMS: | Patricia M. McCarthy |

| | |
|---|---|
| DCM: | William P. Lukasavich |
| POL/ECON: | Atim E. Ogunba |
| ECO/COM: | Stuart A. Zimmer |
| CON: | Michael E. Thurston |
| ADM: | William N. Campbell |
| RSO: | Lee R. Marple |
| IMO: | Douglas G. McGifford |
| RPO: | Steven C. Lemelin |
| REO: | Larry E. Andre, Jr. |
| REF: | John Egan McAteer |
| AID: | Douglas Sheldon |
| ORA: | Michael R. Pastirik |
| PAO: | Alice C. Lemaistre |
| DATT: | LTC Kevin B. Kenny |
| LAB: | Ralph D. Anske (resident in Nairobi) |
| AGR: | Fred R. Kessel (resident in Nairobi) |
| FAA: | Ronald L. Montgomery (resident in Dakar) |
| IRS: | James P. Beene (resident in London) |
| DEA: | Robert Shannon (resident in Cairo) |

Last Modified: Thursday, November 09, 2000

# FIJI

**Suva (E),** 31 Loftus St.—P.O. Box 218, Tel [679] 314-466, Fax 300-081; EXEC OFF Fax 303-872; CON Fax 302 – 267; ADM Fax 305 – 106; DAO Fax 312 – 603; PAO Fax 308-685. Internet address: usembsuva@is.com.fj

| | |
|---|---|
| AMB: | M. Osman Siddique |
| AMB OMS: | Phyllis Williams |
| DCM: | Ronald K. McMullen |
| POL/ECO: | John Hennessey-Niland |
| ECO/COM: | Christopher Hodges |
| CON: | Howard Betts |
| ADM: | Michael Bakalar |
| RSO: | Brent Barker |
| GSO/IRM: | Ryan C. Rhea |
| DAO: | Ltc. Cletis R. Davis, USMC |
| FAA: | Donald A. Slechta (resident in Sydney) |
| IRS: | Karen Sena (resident in Singapore) |
| DEA: | Gene Sugimoto (resident in Canberra) |

Last Modified: Thursday, February 15, 2001

# FINLAND

**Helsinki (E),** Itainen Puistotie 14A, FIN-00140 Helsinki—APO AE 09723, Tel [358] (9) 171-931, EXEC Fax 174-681; ADM Fax 171-546; POL/ECO Fax 621-4778; COM Fax 635-332; PAO Fax 656-846

| | |
|---|---|
| AMB: | Eric S. Edelman |
| AMB OMS: | Karen Starr |
| DCM: | Carol Van Voorst |
| POL: | Stephen A. Cristina |
| ECO: | Ingrid M. Kollist |
| COM: | Thomas M. Kelsey (resident in Stockholm) |
| CON: | Constance Anderson |
| ADM: | Suneta L. Halliburton |
| RSO: | David J. Benson |
| PAO: | Stacy White |
| IRM: | Aila Long |
| DAO: | James R. Luntzel, USAF |
| AGR: | Robert C. Tetro (resident in Stockholm) |
| FAA: | Joseph Teixera (resident in London) |
| LAB: | Frank Collins III |
| IRS: | James P. Beene (resident in London) |

| | |
|---|---|
| DEA: | Arthur L. Kersey (resident in Copenhagen) |

Last Modified: Thursday, November 09, 2000

# FRANCE

**Paris (E),** 2 Avenue Gabriel, 75382 Paris Cedex 08—PSC 116, APO AE 09777, Tel [33] (1) 4312-2222, AMEMB Fax 4266-9783; AMB/AMB OMS/SA 4312-2700; DCM 4312-2800; POL 4312-2783; ECO 4312-2654; FCS 4312-2357, Fax 4312-2172 CON Fax 4312-4691; ADM 4312-2009; DSS 4312-2119; FSC 4312-7054; PA 4312-4898; IMO 4312-2141; EST 4312-2563; DAO 4312-2669; ODC 4312-4695; AGR 4312-2277; LAB 4312-2393; CUS 4312-7400; FAA 4312-2225; FAA/CASLO 4312-2629; FIN 4312-2446; IRS 4312-4560; website: http://www.amb-usa.fr

| | |
|---|---|
| AMB: | [Vacant] |
| CHG: | Douglas L. McElhaney |
| AMB OMS: | [Vacant] |
| DCM: | Alejandro D. Wolff |
| POL: | Sharon A. Wiener |
| ECO: | Joel S. Spiro |
| FCS: | Kenneth P. Moorefield |
| CON: | Larry Colbert |
| ADM: | Howard C. Wiener |
| DSS: | Timothy W. Burchfield |
| FSC: | Robert J. McAnneny |
| PA: | C. Miller Crouch |
| IMO: | Frontis Wiggins, Acting |
| EST: | Raymond E. Clore |
| DAO: | RADM Larry Poe, USN |
| ODC: | Col. Thomas A. Lyons, Jr., USAF |
| AGR: | Frank Piason |
| LAB: | William W. Jordan III |
| CUST: | Michael P. Looney, Acting |
| DEA: | Eugene Habib |
| FAA: | Kurt H. Edwards |
| FAA/CASLO: | Jess Presas |
| IRS: | Marlene M. Sartipi, Acting |
| USSS: | Patrick C. Miller |
| LEGATT: | Enrique H. Ghimenti |

**US Mission to the Organization for Economic Cooperation and Development (USOECD),** 19 rue de Franqueville, 75016 Paris—PSC 116 (USOECD), APO AE 09777, Tel [33] (1) 4524-7477, Fax 4524-7480. Website: http://www.amb usa.fr/usoecd/usoecdto.htm

| | |
|---|---|
| AMB: | Amy L. Bondurant |
| AMB OMS: | [Vacant] |
| DCM: | Richard Behrend |
| ECO/FIN: | John L. Weeks |
| ECO/SOC: | Robert S. Luke |
| FCS: | Margaret A. Keshishian |
| LAB: | Alonzo SIbert |
| TRADE DIV: | Mary A. Gorjance |
| ADM: | Ronna S. Pazdral |
| DOE: | Elisabeth G. Lisann |
| AID: | Kelly C. Kammener |
| INVES ADV: | Brian D. McFeeters |
| ENERGY ADV: | [Vacant] |
| SEC/DEL/PAO: | Evan T. Hough |
| EPA: | Breck Milroy |
| FIN: | Robert R. Winship |
| PAO: | Rio C. Howard |

**US Observer Mission to the United Nations Educational, Scientific, and Cultural Organization (UNESCO),** 2 Avenue Gabriel, 75382, Paris CEDEX 08—APO AE 09777, Tel [33] (1) 4312-2016, Fax 4312-2218

OBSERVER:      Shirley M. Hart

**Bordeaux [C],** 10, Place de la Bourse, 33025 Bordeauz Cedex, Tel [33] (5) 5648-6380, Fax 5651-6197

CON:      Nancy J. Cooper

**Lille[C],** Tel [33] (3) 2078-2960, Fax 2055-6432

CON:      Katharine Koch

**Lyon[C],** 16 Rue de la Republique, 69002 Lyon, Tel [33] (4) 7838-3688 or 7838-3303, or c/o Lyon Commerce International 69289 Lyon Cedex 02—PSC 116, APO AE 09777. Tel 7838-3688; PA 7837-8569; FCS 7838-0592; Fax 7241-7181. E-mail:lyons@calva.net.

CON:      Cameron S. Thompson

**Marseille [CG],** 12 Boulevard Paul Peytral, 13286 Marseille Cedex 6, Paris Embassy (MAR)—PSC 116 (MAR), APO AE 09777, Tel [33] (4) 91-54-92-00, Telex 430597, Fax 91-55-09-47. E-mail: amcongen-mars@calva.net

| | |
|---|---|
| CG: | Samuel V. Brock |
| DPO: | Martha Melzow |
| NCIS: | Dwight E. Clayton |
| NCIS: | Janice Grandmarie |

**Martinique [CA],** No. 23 Lot La Norville, 5KM500, Route de Balata, Fort de France, Martinique, Tel 596-71-9690, Fax 596-71-9689

CA:      Henry Ritchie

**Montferrier** [EBCL]-European Biological Control Laboratory, USDA ARS EBCL, Campus International de Baillarguet, 34980 Montferrier-sur-Lez, Tel [33] (4) 9962-3000; Fax 9962-3049

LAB DIR:      Paul C. Quimby

**Nice[CA],** 31 rue du Marechal Joffre, 06000 Nice, Tel [33] (4) 9388-8955, or 9302-3098, Fax 9387-0738

CA:      Lucien LeLievre

**Rennes [C],** 30 Quai Duguay-Trouin, 35000 Rennes, Tel [33] (2) 2344-0960; Fax 9935-0092

CON:      Maureen E. Cormack

**Strasbourg [CG],** 15 Ave. D'Alsace, 67082 Strasbourg CEDEX—PSC 116, APO AE 09777, Tel [33] (3) 88-35-31-04, Fax 24-06-95; E-mail:congenusa@mail.sdv.fr. website:http://www.ambusa.fr/consul/strasbourg.htm

CG:      Gayleatha B. Brown

**Toulon [Sixth Fleet Liason Office],** Olus-Prefecture Maritime, 83800 Toulon, Tel: [33] (4) 9402-0853; Fax 9402-1915

USN:      Kevin L. Little

**Toulouse [C],** 25 Allee Jean-Jaures (2nd floor), 3100 Toulouse, Tel [33] (5) 3441-3619; Fax 3441-1619

CON:      Laurie A. Farris

Last Modified: Wednesday, February 21, 2001

# GABON

**Libreville (E),** Blvd. de la Mer—B.P. 4000; Tel [241] 74-34-92, 76-20-03/04, 72-12-39/41, Fax: (241) 74-55-07; Direct Lines: EXEC 74-34-93, PC 73-33-33; EXEC Fax: 77-37-39, CON Fax: 76-88-49, GSO Fax: 73-98-74, PC Fax: 73-84-70. Internet Address: usembassy.state.gov.

| | |
|---|---|
| AMB: | James V. Ledesma |
| AMB OMS: | Genie Wray |
| DCM: | Thomas F. Daughton |
| ADM: | Nathan M. Bluhm |
| ECO/COM: | John J. Hillmeyer |
| CON/POL: | Mary Margaret Knudson |
| GSO: | Keith L. Heffern |
| RSO: | Alfred Vincent (resident in Yaounde) |
| IPO: | James W. Miles |
| PC: | Janice Wessel |
| IBB/SAO: | Gaines Johnson |
| DAO: | Ltc. Scott Rutherford (resident in Yaounde) |
| FAA: | Edward Jones (resident in Dakar) |
| IRS: | Frederick D. Pablo (resident in Paris) |

Last Modified: Tuesday, January 02, 2001

# GAMBIA, THE

**Banjul (E),** Fajara, Kairaba Ave., P.M.B. 19, Banjul, Tel (220) 392-856, 392-858, 391-970, 391-971, Fax 392-475

| | |
|---|---|
| AMB: | George W. B. Haley |
| AMB OMS: | Jeanne M. Leonard |
| DCM/ADM: | Brian L. Browne |
| POL/ECO/CON: | Rhett D. Taylor |
| RCON: | Ann Gordon (resident in Dakar) |
| GSO: | Don D. Curtis |
| RSO: | James C. Moss |
| IPO: | Don D. IJames |
| DAO: | Ltc. Todd Coker (resident in Dakar) |
| LAB: | Jay T. Smith (resident in Washington, D.C.) |
| FAA: | Edward Jones (resident in Dakar) |
| IRS: | Frederick D. Pablo  (resident in Paris) |
| IMO: | Susan Hullinger (resident in Dakar) |

Last Modified: Thursday, November 09, 2000

# GEORGIA

**Tbilisi (E),** 25 Atoneli, 995-32-982-393 or 989-967; Tie-line Fax 997-4200, Fax 995-32-933-759; GSO Fax 001-012; ADM Fax 938-951; AID Tel 778-541 or 778-542, Fax 001-013

| | |
|---|---|
| AMB: | Kenneth S. Yalowitz |
| AMB OMS: | Mary Metzger |
| DCM: | Philip N. Remler |
| POL/ECO: | Sandra Clark |
| COM: | John D. Breidenstine (resident in Ankara) |
| ADM: | David F. Schafer |
| PAO: | Victoria Sloan |
| CON: | Steven Fagin |
| RSO: | Gerald D'Antonio |
| AGR: | Geoff Wiggin (resident in Moscow) |

| | |
|---|---|
| IRM: | Richard Fasciglioni |
| DAO: | Ltc. David Penn, USMC |
| AID: | Michael Farbman |
| FAA: | Dennis Cooper (resident in Brussels) |
| DEA: | Lex Henderson (resident in Ankara) |
| CUS: | George Levitsky |
| JUS: | Peter Sprung |
| MLT: | Col. Charles Bradley, Jr. |
| RMO: | Bruce T. Miller, MD. (resident in Frankfurt) |

Last Modified: Thursday, November 09, 2000

# GERMANY, FEDERAL REPUBLIC OF

**Berlin (E),** Neustaedtische Kirchstrasse 4-5, 10017 Berlin—PSC 120, Box 1000, APO AE 09265, Tel [49] (30) 238-5174, Fax 238-6290; COM Fax 238-6296. CON/ADM address: Clayallee 170, 14195 Berlin—PSC 120, Box 3000, APO AE 09265, CON Tel [40] (30) 832-9233, Fax 831-4926; ADM Tel 8305-1500, Fax 8305-1555

| | |
|---|---|
| AMB: | John C. Kornblum |
| AMB OMS: | Dona Fay Richard |
| DCM: | Michael C. Polt |
| POL: | David Wolfson |
| ECO: | Joseph A. Saloom |
| COM: | Kay R. Kuhlmam |
| CON: | Brian W. Flora |
| ADM: | Lynwood M. Dent |
| RSO: | Edward Gaffney |
| PAO: | David L. Arnett |
| IMO: | Joseph Devlin |
| FAA: | Anthony Fazio (resident in Paris) |
| CUS: | John C. Kelly |
| GAO: | Richard Rorvig |
| DAO & ARMA: | Col. Frederick Hammerson |
| ODC: | Col. Robert Stratton, USAF |
| AGR: | Peter Kurz |
| LAB: | Curtis A. Stone |
| FIN: | T. Ashby McCown (resident in Frankfurt) |
| IRS: | Margaret J. Lullo |
| LEGATT: | Klaus Wolfenberger |
| DEA: | Frederic J. Geiger |
| RMO: | Bruce T. Miller, MD. (resident in Frankfurt) |

**Dusseldorf [CG],** Kennedydamm 17, 40476 Dusseldorf, Unit 22115, APO AE 09103, Tel [49] (211) 470-610, afterhours [49] (172) 970-2456, Fax [49] (211) 431-448; COM Tel 470-6136, Fax 431-431

| | |
|---|---|
| CG: | Daniel E. Harris |
| POL/ECO: | Jules D. Silberberg |
| CON/ADM: | Linda E. Daetwyler |
| COM: | Edward C. Fantasia |
| RSO: | Edward Gaffney (resident in Berlin) |
| IRS: | Margaret J. Lullo (resident in Berlin) |

**Frankfurt Am Main (CG),** Siesmayerstrasse 21, 60323 Frankfurt—PSC 115, APO AE 09213-0115, Tel [49] (69) 7535-0, Fax 748-938; COM Tel 956-2040, Fax 561-114; ADM/RSC 7535-3441, Fax 7535-3450

| | |
|---|---|
| CG: | Edward B. O'Donnell |
| CG SEC: | Suzanne Chapman |

| | |
|---|---|
| POL: | Kenneth B. Davis |
| POL/ECO: | Micheal Detar |
| COM: | Peter B. Alois |
| CON: | Kathleen M. Cayer |
| ADM: | Mike Rafferty |
| RSC: | Sidney V. Reeves |
| RPSO: | Walter R. Cate |
| RSO: | George G. Lambert |
| PAO: | David R. Farrar |
| IRM: | Thomas Schuh |
| INS: | William D. McNamee |
| FAA/CASIFO: | Dave Orochena |
| FAA/CASLO: | Christopher Glasow |
| FAA/FSIFO: | John Barbagalo |
| CUS: | Craig Stevens |
| RIMC: | James Van Derhoff |
| LEGATT: | Robert L. Fricke |
| ESC: | Kenneth Stanley |
| IRS: | William Gilligan |
| FIN: | James G. Wallar |
| DEA: | James A. Shroba |
| GSA: | Thomas D. Meiron |
| FRDCD: | Patrick Connelly |
| RMO: | Bruce T. Miller, MD. |

**Hamburg [CG],** Alsterufer 27/28, 20354 Hamburg, Tel [49] (40) 41171-100, afterhours Tel (49) (173) 208 3038; Fax [49] (40) 41171-222; ADM Fax 417-665; CONS Fax 443-004; COM Fax 410-6598; PAO Tel 413279-0, Fax 413279-33; ATO Tel 414607-0, Fax 414607-20; E-mail: hamburginfo@state.gov

| | |
|---|---|
| CG: | Christopher F. Lynch |
| RSO: | Edward Gaffney (resident in Berlin) |
| POL/ECO: | John R. Rodgers |
| COM: | James Finlay |
| ADM/CON: | Martha L. Loverde |
| PAO: | William H. Cook |
| ATO: | Jeffrey W. Jones |
| IRS: | Margaret J. Lullo (resident in Berlin) |

**Leipzig [CG],** Wilhelm-Seyfferth-Strasse 4, 04107 Leipzig—PSC 120, Box 1000, APO AE 09265, Tel [49] (341) 213-840, Fax 213-8417; COM Tel 213-8440, Fax 213-8441; PAO Tel 213-8420, Fax 213-8432; ADM Fax 213-8461

| | |
|---|---|
| CG: | Timothy M. Savage |
| CG SEC: | Petra Beier |
| POL/ECO: | Phillip X. Linderman |
| COM: | Kay Kullmann (resident in Berlin) |
| ADM/CON: | Sabine Klaube |
| PAO: | John A. Quintus |
| RSO: | Edward F. Gaffney (resident in Berlin) |
| IRS: | Margaret J. Lullo (resident in Berlin) |

**Munich [CG],** Koeniginstrasse 5, 80539 Muenchen—Unit 24520, APO AE 09053-4520, Tel [49] (89) 2888-0, afterhours Tel [49] (171) 815-4805; ADM Fax [49] (89) 283-047; EXEC Tel 2888-608, Fax 280-2317; CON Tel 2888-722 thru 729, Fax 280-9998; COM Tel 2888-735, Fax 285-261; PAO Tel 2888-620, Fax 2899-8021

| | |
|---|---|
| CG: | Robert W. Boehme |
| CG OMS: | Carol A. Bryan |

| | |
|---|---|
| POL/ECON: | Theodore Tanoue |
| COM: | John McCaslin |
| CON: | Linda R. Hoover |
| ADM: | Jeffrey R. Cellars |
| IRM: | Robert P. McCumber |
| RSO: | Martin F. Kraus |
| PAO: | Robert L. Hugins |
| IBB: | [Vacant] |

Last Modified: Thursday, February 08, 2001

# GHANA

**Accra (E),** Ring Road East—P.O. Box 194, Tel [233] (21) 775-348, Annex Tel 776-601, Fax 776-008; COM Tel 235-096, Fax 765-712 Internet address: [addressee]@dos.us-state.gov. E-mail address: [addressee]@admin accra-emba. Homepage address: http:www.usembassy.org.gh

| | |
|---|---|
| AMB: | Kathryn D. Robinson |
| AMB OMS: | Monika D. Jennings |
| DCM: | Gail D. Mathieu |
| POL: | Stephanie Sullivan |
| ECO/COM: | Michael S. Owen |
| CON: | Michael R. Schimmel |
| ADM: | Isiah L. Parnell |
| GSO: | Raymond D. Maxwell |
| RSO: | Vincent D. Graham |
| DAO: | Lt. Col. Dean F. Bland |
| SAO: | Sam Acquah |
| PAO: | Brooks Robinson |
| IRM: | Duane Bredeck |
| USAID: | Frank Young |
| PC: | Leonard B. Floyd |
| AGR: | David Rosenbloom (resident in Lagos) |
| DEA: | Edgar L. Moses (resident in Lagos) |
| FAA: | Edward Jones (resident in Dakar) |
| IRS: | Frederick D. Pablo (resident in Paris) |
| INS: | Hailu Kebede |

Last Modified: Tuesday, December 19, 2000

# GREECE

**Athens (E),** 91 Vasilissis Sophias Blvd., 10160 Athens—PSC 108, APO AE 09842-0108, Tel [30] (1) 721-2951, AmEmb Fax 645-6282; COM Fax 721-8660; PAO Fax 729-4311; AMEMB SEC 720-2478; DCM/DCM SEC 720-2379; POL 720-2381; ECON 720-2312; COM ) 720-2302; CON 720-2403; ADM 720-2279; RSO 720-2286; PAO 720-2361; IRM 720-2347; IPU 720-2340; DAO 720-2753; ODC 720-2602; AGR 720-2798; DEA 720-2785; INS 720-2781; LEGATT 720-2457; FAA 720-2089. Internet address: usembassy@usisathens.gr

| | |
|---|---|
| AMB: | R. Nicholas Burns |
| AMB OMS: | Ellen Morrissey |
| DCM: | J. Michael Cleverley |
| POL: | J. Brady Kiesling |
| ECO: | John P. Felt |
| COM: | Walter Hage |
| CON: | Betsy Anderson |
| ADM: | Jacquelyn O. Briggs |
| RSO: | William G. Gaskill |
| PAO: | Arlene R. Jacquette |
| IRM: | Richard Kwiatkowski |
| DEA: | James Soiles |
| INS: | Evangelia Klapakis |

| | |
|---|---|
| LEGATT: | Robert F. Clifford |
| DAO: | Capt. Ted Venable, USA |
| ODC: | Col. Robert M. Corrie |
| AGR: | Elizabeth Berry (resident in Rome) |
| FAA: | [Vacant] |
| IRS: | [Vacant] |

**Thessaloniki [CG],** 43 Tsimiski St., 7th floor, Commercial Center "Plateia," GR-546 23 Thessaloniki—PSC 108, Box 37, APO AE 09842-0108, Tel [30] (31) 242905 or 720-400, Fax 242927. E-mail address: cons@compulink.gr Website: http://www.compulink.gr/us-consulate

| | |
|---|---|
| CG: | John M. Koenig |
| POL/ADM: | Marilynn Gurian |
| PCO: | Jeremy Keller |

Last Modified: Thursday, November 09, 2000

# GRENADA

**St. George's (E),** P.O. Box 54, St. George's, Grenada, W.I., Tel [473] 444-1173/6, Fax 444-4820. E-mail address: usemb-gd@caribsurf.com

| | |
|---|---|
| AMB: | [Vacant](resident in Bridgetown) |
| DCM: | Lloyd W. Moss |
| CON: | Theorphilus J. Rose (resident in Bridgetown) |
| RSO: | William Pennebaker (resident in Bridgetown) |
| PAO: | Emilia Puma (resident in Bridgetown) |
| ADM: | Paul Carpenter (resident in Bridgetown) |
| DAO: | Ltc. John Churchill (resident in Bridgetown) |
| MLO: | Ltc. Ronald Jenkins, USN (resident in Bridgetown) |
| LAB: | Terrence Daru (resident in Bridgetown) |
| LEGATT: | Donovan Leighton (resident in Bridgetown) |
| FAA: | Ruben Quinones (resident in Miami) |
| IRS: | Frederick Dulas (resident in Mexico City) |
| DEA: | James Agee, Jr. (resident in Bridgetown) |

# GUATEMALA

**Guatemala City (E),** Avenida Reforma 7-01 Zone 10—APO AA 34024, Tel (502) 331-1541, Fax 334-8477; POL/ECON Fax 334-8474; INS Fax 339-2472; PER Fax 331-6660; CON Fax 331-0564; COM Fax 331-7373; PC Tel 334-8263, Fax 334-4121; AID Tel 332-0202, Fax 331-1511

| | |
|---|---|
| AMB: | Prudence Bushnell |
| AMB OMS: | Linda Howard |
| DCM: | Stephen G. McFarland |
| POL: | David Van Valkenburg |
| ECO: | Brendan Hanniffy |
| COM: | Daniel J. Thompson |
| CON: | Peter Kaestner |
| ADM: | Brian W. Wilson |
| RSO: | Charlene Lamb |
| PAO: | Mary Deane Conners |
| IRM: | Thomas P. Phalen |
| AID: | George Carner |
| DAO: | Col. Mario Jimenez, USA |
| MILGP: | Col. Jorge Matos, USA |
| AGR: | Frank Coolidge |
| APHIS: | Gordon Tween |
| NAS: | Perry Holloway |

| | |
|---|---|
| NIMA: | Glen Ramsey |
| PC: | Charles Reilly |
| ICITAP: | Joseph Gannon |
| FAA: | Ruben Quinones (resident in Miami) |
| DEA: | Pedro Velazco |
| INS: | Arturo Gutierrez |
| LAB: | William Owen |
| IRS: | Frederick Dulas (resident in Mexico City) |
| LEGATT: | Fernando M. Rivero (resident in Miami) |
| CUS: | Ed Mederos (resident in Miami) |
| ENVIR/HUB: | Lawrence Gumbiner (resident in San Jose) |

Last Modified: Wednesday, March 14, 2001

# GUINEA

**Conakry (E),** rue KA 038, B.P. 603, Tel [224] 41-15-20, 41-15-21, or 41-15-23, Fax 41-15-22; AMB cellular Tel [224] 21-86-26; USAID Tel 41-25-02, Fax 41-19-85; PAO Tel 46-14-24 or 41-36-78, Fax 41-29-21; Peace Corps Tel 46-31-57 or 40-22-98, Fax 46-34-84. E-mail addresses: amemconakry.adm@eti-bull.net; amemconakry.cons@eti-bull.net. Embassy web page:www.eti-bull.net/usembassy

| | |
|---|---|
| AMB: | Joyce E. Leader |
| AMB OMS: | [Vacant] |
| DCM: | Louis J. Nigro, Jr. |
| POL/ECO: | Lori Shoemaker |
| ECO/COM: | Jay Tetrault |
| ADM: | Larry E. Andre, Jr. |
| CON: | Elizabeth Gracon |
| RCON: | Ann Gordon (resident in Dakar) |
| RSO: | Richard L. Fuller |
| GSO: | Kay Crawford |
| PAO: | Amelia Broderick |
| IRM: | David Adams |
| DAO: | Ltc. William Watson III, USMC (resident in Dakar) |
| AID: | Harry Birnholz |
| FAA: | Edward L. Jones (resident in Dakar) |
| LAB: | [Vacant] (resident in Washington, D.C.) |
| PC: | Kathleen Tilford |
| RELO: | Robert Lindsey (resident in Dakar) |
| RETO: | Timothy H. Robinson (resident in Dakar) |
| IRS: | Frederick D. Pablo (resident in Paris) |
| DEA: | Edgar L. Moses (resident in Lagos) |

Last Modified: Wednesday, January 03, 2001

# GUINEA-BISSAU

**Bissau (E),** 1 Rua Ulysses S. Grant, Bairro de Penha, Bissau,—C.P. 297, 1067 Bissau Codex, Guinea-Bissau, Tel [245] 25-2273/76, Fax 25-2282; tie line (8) 760-0000; USAID Tel [245] 20-1817/19, Fax 20-1808; PC Tel 20-2312, Fax 20-2314

(Operations temporarily suspended).

# GUYANA

**Georgetown (E),** 100 Young and Duke Streets, Kingston, Georgetown, Guyana—P.O. Box 10507; Tel [592] (2) 54900-9, and 57961-3, Fax 58497 and 57968; USAID Fax 57316, Peace Corps Fax 53202; direct-in-dial: DCM [592] (2) 62326; RSO 73918; IPU 66491; ADM 73949; P/E 64309; MLO 57863; USAID 57315, 57318-9; Peace Corps 55072-3. Internet www.usembguyana.com

| | |
|---|---|
| AMB: | James F. Mack |
| AMB OMS: | Louise Nash |
| DCM: | Sheila J. Peters |
| POL: | Henry L. Bischarat |
| ECO/COM: | Thomas P. Carroll |
| CON: | Vincent A. Principe |
| ADM: | Patrick Hotze |
| RSO: | Wendy A. Bashnan |
| MLO: | Maj. David V. Nabor |
| IRM: | Dominick Logalbo |
| AID: | Carol R. Becker |
| DAO: | Col. Gregory Landers, USAF (resident in Caracas) |
| AGR: | Rod McSherry (resident in Caracas) |
| LEGATT: | Hector Rodriguez (resident in Caracas) |
| LAB: | Terrence Daru (resident in Bridgetown) |
| IRS: | Frederick Dulas (resident in Mexico City) |
| PC: | Gary Thompson |
| DEA: | Paul A. Herring (resident in Caracas) |

Last Modified: Thursday, November 09, 2000

# HAITI

**Port-au-Prince (E),** 5 Harry Truman Blvd.—P.O. Box 1761, Tel [509]222-0354, 222-0368, 222-0200, 222-0612, Fax 509 223-1641; Consular Annex: 104, rue Oswald Durand, Tel (509) 223-7011, Fax 223-9665; USAID: 17, Harry Truman Blvd. Port-au-Prince, Haiti, Tel 222-5500, Fax (509) 223-9503

| | |
|---|---|
| AMB: | Dean Curran |
| CHG: | Kenneth A. Duncan |
| POL: | [Vacant] |
| ECON: | Martha Kelley |
| CON: | Roger Daley |
| ADM: | Edmund Atkins |
| PAO: | Daniel Whitman |
| RSO: | John Burton Young |
| GSO: | Nicholas Quackenbush |
| IMO: | Bruce Warren |
| AID: | Louis Lucke |
| COM: | Janice Bruce |
| DAO: | Mark Gillette |
| MLO: | Cdr. Michael Brennan |
| CGLO: | Lt. Cdr. Mark Cawthorne |
| AGR: | Kevin Smith (resident in Santo Domingo) |
| APHIS: | Kelan Evans |
| DEA: | Sam Gaye, Acting |
| FAA: | Ruben Quinones (resident in Miami) |
| DCMCI: | Maj. Chailendreia Dickens |
| IRS: | Frederick Dulas (resident in Mexico City) |
| INS: | Charles Jean |
| PC: | Mary Hogan |

Last Modified: Tuesday, December 19, 2000

# HOLY SEE, THE

**Vatican City (E),** Villa Domiziana, Via Delle Terme Deciane 26, 00153 Rome, Italy—PSC 59, Box 66, APO AE 09624, Tel (3906) 4674-3428, Fax (3906) 575-8346 or 5730-0682. E-mail: usemb.holysee@agora.it; website: www.usis.it/usembvat

| | |
|---|---|
| AMB: | Corinne C. Boggs |
| AMB SA: | Jennifer D. Dudley |
| AMB OMS: | Hedy V. Kane |

| | |
|---|---|
| DCM: | Joseph Merante |
| POL: | Mark J. Powell |
| ADM: | Howell Howard |
| RSO: | George J. Goldstein (resident in Rome) |
| FAA: | Steven B. Wallace (resident in Rome) |
| DEA: | Vincent J. Di Stefano (resident in Rome) |

Last Modified: Thursday, November 09, 2000

# HONDURAS

**Tegucigalpa (E),** Avenida La Paz, Apartado Postal No. 3453—APO AA 34022, Tel [504] 238-5114 or 236-9320, afterhours Tel. 236-9325; EXEC OFF Tel [504] 237-0696, Fax [504] 236-9037; COM Fax [504] 238-2888; Public Diplomacy Fax 236-9309; USAID Fax 236-7776; CON Fax 237-1792.Website:www.usia.gov/abttusia/posts/hoi/wwwhmain.html

| | |
|---|---|
| AMB: | Frank Almaguer |
| AMB OMS: | Mary Navarro |
| DCM: | Paul A. Trivelli |
| POL: | Edward J. Michal |
| ECO: | David C. Wolfe |
| CON: | Catherine M. Barry |
| FCS: | Daniel J. Thompson (resident in Guatemala City) |
| JAO: | Samuel G. Durrett |
| RSO: | John B. McKennan |
| PAO: | Gregory M. Adams |
| IRM: | Leon G. Galanos |
| AID: | Joesph Lombardo |
| DAO: | Col. David Kuhns, USAF |
| MILGP: | Ltc. Miquel Morales |
| DEA: | Thomas Berger |
| AGR: | Suzanne Heinen(resident in Guatemala City) |
| INS: | Joseph Banda, Jr. |
| FAA: | Ruben Quinones (resident in Miami) |
| PC: | Stephen Miller |
| IRS: | Frederick Dulas (resident in Mexico City) |
| GSO: | Alan Smiley |
| FBO : | Michael Stinger |
| FMO: | Marie Bohlmann |
| ICITAP: | Sharon Banda |
| COE: | Maj. Jeffrey Duarte |

Last Modified: Thursday, November 09, 2000

# HONG KONG

**Hong Kong (CG),** 26 Garden Rd.—PSC 461, Box 1, FPO AP 96521-0006, Tel [852] 2523-9011(after hours/emergency: 2841-2230); CON Fax 2147-5790; ADM Fax 2524-0860; FAS Address: 18th Fl., St. John's Bldg., 33 Garden Rd., Tel 2841-2350, Fax 2845-0943; COM Address: 17th Fl., St. John's Bldg., 33 Garden Rd., Tel 2521-1467, Fax 2845-9800. IVG No. 727-0000 (after hours 727-2230). Web site address: www.usconsulate.org.hk

| | |
|---|---|
| CG: | Michael Klosson |
| DPO: | John Medeiros |
| ECO/POL: | Lisa J. Kubiske |
| COM: | Barry Friedman] |
| CON: | Alice C. Moore |
| ADM: | Jay N. Anania |
| GSO: | Geoffrey H. Moore |
| RSO: | Patrick J. Moore |

| | |
|---|---|
| PAO: | Robert B. Laing |
| OLA: | John W. Reddinger |
| FAS: | Howard Wetzel |
| APHIS: | Dale Maki (resident in Beijing) |
| INS: | Dow J. Clark |
| CUS: | Thomas J. Howe |
| DEA: | Thomas Ma |
| FAA: | Elizabeth Keck (resident in Beijing) |
| IRS: | Stanley Beesley (resident in Tokyo) |
| FBI: | William Liu |
| FIN: | Lois E. Quinn |
| USSS: | James P. Crowe |
| IMO: | Kirk W. Ingvoldstad |

Last Modified: Monday, October 02, 2000

# HUNGARY

**Budapest (E),** 1054 Szabadsag Ter 12—American Embassy Budapest, Department of State, Washington, D.C. 20521-5270, Tel [36] (1) 475-4400, Fax 475-4764; CON Fax 475-4188; USAID Tel 302-6400, Fax 302-0693 or 302-0720; PA Tel 475-4606, Fax 475-4708; USCS Tel 475-4282, Fax 475-4676. Internet address: usembudap-est@pronet.hu

| | |
|---|---|
| AMB: | Peter F. Tufo |
| AMB OMS: | S. Virginia Parker |
| DCM: | Thomas B. Robertson |
| ADM: | Jeffry R. Olesen |
| COM: | Scott E. Bozek |
| CON: | Susan E. Alexander |
| POL: | Kyle R. Scott |
| ECO: | Jean A. Bonilla |
| RSO: | David R. Haag |
| EST: | Nina M. Fite |
| IRM: | Jerry W. Lester |
| ODC: | Col. Michael Hart, USAF |
| DAO: | Col. James P. Mault, USA |
| PAO: | James D. Nealon |
| AID/RIG: | Donna M. Dinkler |
| AID/RSC: | Patricia Lerner |
| AGR: | Robert H. Curtis(resident in Vienna) |
| FAA: | Amy Becke(resident in Vienna) |
| IRS: | Margaret J. Lullo(resident in Berlin) |
| INS: | William Gilligan(resident in Vienna) |
| DEA: | Thomas Slovenkay(resident in Vienna) |
| LEGATT: | Miles Burden |
| CUS: | Robin Avers (resident in Vienna) |

Last Modified: Thursday, February 15, 2001

# ICELAND

**Reykjavik (E),** Laufasvegur 21—PSC 1003, Box 40, FPO AE 09728-0340, Tel (354) 562-9100, AMB OMS direct dial 562-9125, Fax 562-9118; PAO Tel 562-1020 and 562-1022, Fax 552-9529; ECO/COM Fax 354-562-9139; CON Fax 354-562-9110; ADM Fax 354-562-9123

| | |
|---|---|
| AMB: | Barbara J. Griffiths |
| AMB OMS: | Diana F. McGee |
| DCM: | Robert Sorenson |
| POL/CON: | William E. Moeller III |
| ECO/COM: | Edward P. Brown |
| ADM: | Mary T. Gudjonsson |
| RSO: | Claude J. Nebel (resident in Copenhagen) |
| PAO: | [Vacant] |

IRM:    Philip L. Bunch
FAA:    Joseph Teixera (resident in London)
IRS:    James P. Beene (resident in London)
DEA:    Arthur L. Kersey (resident in Copenhagen)

Last Modified: Thursday, November 09, 2000

# INDIA

**New Delhi (E),** Shanti Path, Chanakyapuri 110021, Tel [91] (11) 419-8000,611-3033, Fax 419-0017; COM Fax 331-5172; USAID Tel 419-8000, USAID Fax 419-8454; 419-8612

| | |
|---|---|
| AMB: | Richard F. Celeste |
| AMB OMS: | Betty C. Taylor |
| DCM: | Albert A. Thibault |
| POL: | Robert K. Boggs |
| ECO: | Robert G. Rapson |
| ORA: | John E. Ferguson |
| COM: | Samuel Kidder |
| CON: | John R. Nay |
| ADM: | Steven J. White |
| RSO: | Daniel R. McCarthy |
| LEGATT: | Ralph P. Horton |
| PAO: | James J. Callahan |
| DEA: | Robert B. Barnes |
| IMO: | Frederick R. Sadler |
| AID: | Walter E. North |
| ODA: | Col. Mark S. Pernell, U.S. ARMY |
| AGR: | Weyland Beeghly |
| INS: | Kathy A. Redman |
| DSA: | Maj. Richard B. White, U.S. ARMY |
| FAA: | David L. Knudson (resident in Singapore) |
| FAA/CASLO: | Steve Tochterman |

**Mumbai [CG],** Lincoln House, 78 Bhulabhai Desai Rd. 400026, Tel [91] (22) 363-3611, CONGEN Fax 363-0350; PUBLIC AFFAIRS Tel 262-4590, Fax 262-4595; COM Tel 265-2511, COM Fax 262-3850

| | |
|---|---|
| CG: | David P. Good |
| CG OMS: | Wendy A. Maalouf |
| POL/ECO: | Scott B. Ticknor |
| COM: | Richard Rotham |
| CON: | Frederick Polasky |
| ADM: | Bernard J. Woerz |
| PA: | Elizabeth A. Corwin |
| IPC: | [Vacant] |

**Calcutta [CG],** 5/1 Ho Chi Minh Sarani, Calcutta 700071, Tel [91] (33) 282-3611 thru 15, 282-5757, CONGEN Fax 282-2335. CONGEN internet address: consulat@cal.vsnl.net.in; COM Fax 282-1074. COM internet address: Office.Calcutta@mail.doc.gov; PAO Tel 245-1211, Fax 245-1616. PAO internet address: usis@usis-cal.ernet.in

| | |
|---|---|
| CG: | Christopher Sandrolini |
| CON: | Katherine M. Perez |
| ADM: | Michelle Esperdy |
| PA: | [Vacant] |

**Chennai [CG],** 220 Anna Salai 600006, Tel [91] (44) 827-3040/827-7542/827-7835, Fax 825-02440; CON Fax 826-2538; COM Tel 811-2024, Fax 811-2036; PA Fax 826-3407; FCS Bangalore: W-202, II floor, West Wing "Sunrise Chambers," 22 Ulsoor Road, Bangalore 560042, Tel [91] (80) 558-1452, Fax 558-3630

| | |
|---|---|
| CG: | Bernard Alter |
| CG OMS: | Cheryl L. Vanallen |
| ADM: | Lyngrid S. Rawlings |
| POL/ECO: | R. Bruce Neuling |
| COM: | Donald G. Nay |
| CON: | Clyde L. Jones |
| PA: | Mark Larsen |
| IPO: | Frank W. Landymore |

Last Modified: Tuesday, December 12, 2000

# INDONESIA

**Jakarta (E),** Medan Merdeka Selatan 5—Unit 8129, Box 1, APO AP 96520, Tel [62] (21) 3435-9000, Fax 386-2259; PAO Fax 381-0243; COM Fax 385-1632; USAID Fax 380-6694; AGR Fax 3435-9920; OMADP Fax 384-3339

| | |
|---|---|
| AMB: | Robert S. Gelbard |
| AMB OMS: | Janice Smith |
| DCM: | Stephen Mull |
| POL: | Pamela Slutz |
| ECO: | Judith R. Fergin |
| COM: | Alice A. Davenport |
| CON: | Stephen A. Edson |
| ADM: | Robert Weisberg |
| RSO: | Jacob Wohlman |
| PAO: | Greta Morris |
| IRM: | Doyle Lee |
| AID: | Desaix Meyers |
| AGR: | Kent Sisson |
| LAB: | Gregory G. Fergin |
| EST: | Robin McCllellan |
| GSO: | Margaret Uyehara |
| DAO: | COL Joseph Daves, USA |
| OMADP: | LTC Derek Wheeler, USA |
| FAA: | David L. Knudson (resident in Singapore) |
| CUS: | [Vacant] (resident in Singapore) |
| IRS: | Billy J. Brown (resident in Singapore) |
| DEA: | Larry M. Hahn (resident in Singapore) |

**Surabaya [CG],** Jalan Raya Dr., Sutomo 33, Surabaya 60264; Am Con Gen—Box 1, Unit 8131, APO AP 96520-0002, Tel [62] (31) 567-6880 or 568-2287, Fax 567-4492; COM Fax 567-7748. E-mail address: amconsby@rad.net.id

| | |
|---|---|
| CG: | Robert Pollard |
| POL/ECO: | Jaoquin Monseratte |
| COM: | Alice A. Davenport (resident in Jakarta) |
| ADM/CON: | G. Craig Combs |

**Bali [CA],** Jl. Hayam Wuruk 188, Denpasar 80235, Tel. [62] (361) 233-605, Fax 222-426. E-mail address: tabuh@denpasar.wasantara.net.id

| | |
|---|---|
| CA: | Andrew Toth |

Last Modified: Monday, December 04, 2000

# IRELAND

**Dublin (E),** 42 Elgin Rd., Ballsbridge, Tel [353] (1) 668-8777, afterhours Tel 668-9612, Fax 668-9946; EXEC Tel 668-2302, EXEC Fax 660-3217; POL/ECO Tel 668-2328, Fax 667-0056; ADM Tel 668-2221, Fax 668-7734; COM

Tel 668-2350, Fax 667-4754; DAO Tel 668-2200, Fax 668-8698. Internet address: aedublin@indigo.ie

| AMB: | Michael J. Sullivan |
|---|---|
| AMB OMS: | Colleen Kozubek |
| DCM: | Earle St. A. Scarlett |
| ECO: | Edwin R. Nolan |
| POL: | Richard M. Mills |
| COM: | William M. Crawford |
| CON: | Leigh G. Carter |
| ADM: | Mark X. Perry |
| RSO: | James J. Murphy |
| PAO: | Barbara S. Scarlett |
| IRM: | James E. Barclay |
| DAO: | Col. Gerald D. Saltness |
| AGR: | Thomas A. Hamby (resident in London) |
| INS: | Arnold K. Ellis |
| CUS: | John Martinez, Jr. (resident in London) |
| FAA: | Joseph Teixera (resident in London) |
| IRS: | James P. Beene (resident in London) |
| DEA: | Michael J. McManamon (resident in London) |

Last Modified: Thursday, November 09, 2000

# ISRAEL

*The Consulate General in Jerusalem is an independent U.S. Mission, established in 1928, whose members are not accredited to a foreign government.

**Tel Aviv (E),** 71 Hayarkon St., Tel Aviv—PSC 98, Unit 7228, APO AE 09830, Tel [972] (3) 519-7575, afterhours Tel 519-7551, Fax 517-3227; ADM/GSO Fax 510-2444; CON Fax 516-0744; PAO Fax 510-3830; RSO Fax 510-1233 FCS Fax 510-7215; AGR Fax 510-2565. PAO internet: usisisrl@usis.rog.il

| AMB: | Martin S. Indyk |
|---|---|
| AMB OMS: | Barbara E. Simpson |
| DCM: | Richard A. Roth |
| POL: | John F. Scott |
| ECO: | Deborah R. Schwartz |
| PAO: | William D. Cavness |
| COM: | Ann M. Bacher |
| CON: | Marsha D. von Duerckheim |
| ADM: | Lawrence Mandel |
| RSO: | Gregory B. Starr |
| IRM: | Sandra M. Muench |
| DAO: | Col. William Clark, USAF |
| LAB: | Theodore A. Mann |
| SCI: | William H. Crane |
| AGR: | Thomas Pomeroy (resident in Cairo) |
| AID: | Larry Garber |
| DCMC: | Ltc. George A. Sears |
| FAA: | Steven B. Wallace (resident in Rome) |
| DEA: | Perry Felecos (resident in Nicosia) |
| IRS: | Larry J. LeGrand (resident in Rome) |
| LEGATT: | Scott G. Jessee |
| BRX-IFO: | Samuel Aaron (resident in Brussels) |

**Jerusalem (CG),** 18 Agron Rd., Jerusalem 94190—Unit 7228, P.O. Box 0039, APO AE 09830, Tel [972] (2) 6227230, afterhours Tel 6227250, EXEC Fax 6249462; ADM Fax 6240071; USAID Fax 6259484. Consular and PAO sections: 27 Nablus Rd., Jerusalem 97200—Unit 7228, P.O. Box 0039, APO AE 09830; CON Tel 6227230,

afterhours Tel 6227250, Fax 6272233; PAO Tel 6282456, Fax 6282454

| CG: | John E. Herbst |
|---|---|
| DPO: | Gerald M. Feierstein |
| POL: | Jason L.Davis |
| ECO/COM: | Timothy E. Wilder |
| CON: | Suzanne I. Lawrence |
| ADM: | Jennifer V. Bonner |
| RSO: | Dale E. McElhattan |
| PAO: | Jane C. Gaffney |
| IRM: | Stephen P. Provencal |
| COM: | [Vacant] (resident in Tel Aviv) |
| AID: | Larry Garber (resident in Tel Aviv) |
| IRS: | Larry J. LeGrand (resident in Rome) |
| LEGATT: | Scott G. Jessee (resident in Tel Aviv) |

**Haifa [CA],** 12 Jerusalem Street, 33132, Haifa, Tel. 972-04-670615

| CA: | Jonathan D. Friedland |
|---|---|

Last Modified: Thursday, November 09, 2000

# ITALY

**Rome (E),** Via Veneto 119/A, 00187 Rome—PSC 59 Box 100, APO AE 09624, Tel [39] (06) 46741, Telex 622322 Ambrma, Fax 488-2672; PAO Via Boncompagni 2,00187 Rome, PAO Fax 4674-2655. Internet address: www.usembassy.it. Tel 4674-2321, Fax 4674-2113

| AMB: | Thomas M. Foglietta |
|---|---|
| AMB OMS: | Elizabeth A. Roberts-Strang |
| DCM: | William P. Pope |
| POL: | Eric R. Terzuolo |
| POL/MIL: | Gary D. Robbins |
| ECO: | Margaret M. Dean |
| COM: | Eric R. Weaver |
| CON: | Charles F. Keil |
| ADM C: | Catherine M. Smith |
| ADM O: | Grace C. Stettenbauer |
| RSO: | Richard Gaiani |
| PAO: | Robert J. Callahan |
| IRM: | Harry W. Lumley |
| EST: | David W. Mulenex |
| DAO: | Capt. Thaddeus J. Moyseowicz, USN |
| AGR: | Elizabeth Berry |
| ODC: | Col. Mark J. Devlin |
| LAB: | James J. Ehrman |
| CUS: | [Vacant] |
| FAA: | [Vacant] |
| FAA/CASIFO: | Daniel Prevo |
| FBO: | Eric N. Rumpf |
| IRS: | Frederick Pablo |
| INS: | Gregory B. Smith |
| USSS: | Raphael A. Gonzales |
| DEA: | [Vacant] |
| RMO: | Bruce T. Miller, MD. (resident if Frankfurt) |

**US Mission to the United Nations Agencies for Food and Agriculture (FODAG),** Via Sardegna 49, 00187 Rome—PSC 59, Box 31, APO AE 09624, Tel [39] (0) (6) 4674-3500, Fax 4788-7043

| AMB: | George S. McGovern |
|---|---|
| AMB OMS: | Judy M. Edelhoff |

| DCM: | Carolee Heileman |
| POL/ECO: | Lucy Tamlyn |
| AID: | Timothy Lavelle |
| AGR: | David P. Lambert |

**Milan [CG],** Via Principe Amedeo, 2/10, 20121 Milan; APO address PSC 59, Box 60 (M), APO AE 09624, Tel [39] (02) 290-351, Fax 2900-1165; CG Tel 290-35300, Fax 290-35410; COM Tel 659-2260, Fax 659-6561, COM E-mail: milan.office.box@mail.doc.gov; DPO/POL/ECO Tel 290-35304, Fax 290-35410; POL/MIL Tel 290-35387, Fax 2900-1165; ECO Tel 290-35306, Fax 2900-1165; CON Tel 290-351, Fax 290-35273, E-mail: uscitizensmilan@state.gov and usvisamilan@state.gov; CON Visa Tel info 290-35280; ADM Tel 290-35287, Fax 2900-1165; GSO Tel 290-35329, Fax 290-35390; RSO Tel 290-35287, Fax 2900-1165; PAO Tel 290-35503, Fax 290-35525; DAO Tel 290-35340, Fax 2900-1165, E-mail: daomilan@state.gov; DEA Tel 655-5766, Fax 2900-0739, E-mail: am.con.gen.milan5@agora.stm.it; USSS Tel 290-35447, Fax 2900-1673, E-mail: usssmilan@state.gov

| CG: | Ruth van Heuven |
| DPO/POL/ECO: | Mary Jo Willis |
| POL/MIL: | Robert Lady |
| COM: | Maria Andrews |
| ECO: | David Reimer |
| CON: | Brian Oberle |
| ADM: | Eric Nelson |
| GSO: | David Elmo |
| RSO: | Melissa McPeak |
| PAO: | Eugene Santoro |
| IRM: | J. Michael Suddath |
| DEA: | Paul Campo |
| USSS: | Thomas Impastato |
| RMO: | Bruce T. Muller  (resident in Frankfurt) |

**Naples [CG],** Piazza Della Repubblica 80122 Naples—PSC 810 Box 18, FPO AE 09619-0002, Tel [39] (081) 583-8111, or 583-8245, Fax 761-1869 or 68-0982

| CG: | Marianne M. Myles |
| POL/ECO: | Michael A. Feldman |
| CON: | Fabio M. Saturni |
| COM: | Albina Parente |
| ADM: | Lee R. Brown |
| RSO: | George J. Goldstein (resident in Rome) |
| PAO: | Leslie W. McBee |
| POLAD: | Arnold J. Croddy (resident in NATO, Naples) |

**Florence [CG],** Lungarno Amerigo Vespucci, 38, 50123 Firenze—PSC 59 Box F, APO AE 09624, Tel [39] (055) 239 8276/7/8/9, 217-605, Fax 284-088; COM Tel 211-676, Fax 283-780

| CG: | Hilarion A. Martinez |
| DPO/CON/ADM: | Alma J. Engel |
| COM: | Barbara Lapini |
| RSO: | Richard Gaiani |

**U.S. Commercial Office** (Genoa), Via Dante 2/43 (Palazzo Borsa), 16121 Genoa, Tel (39) (010) 543-877, Fax 576-1678

| CA: | Anna Maria Saiano |
| COM: | Susanna Lezzi |

**Palermo [CA],** Via Vaccarini 1, 90143 Palermo, Tel [39] (091) 305-857, Fax 625-6026, afterhours/emergencies Tel (081) 583-8111 (Naples duty officer)

| CA: | Barbara Cucinella |

**Trieste [CA],** Via Roma 15, 34132 Trieste, Off. Tel. [39] (040) 660-177, Home (040) 302-354, Fax (040) 631-240

| CA: | Paolo Bearz |

Last Modified: Thursday, February 22, 2001

# IVORY COAST (See Cote D'Ivoire)

# JAMAICA

**Kingston (E),** Jamaica Mutual Life Center, 2 Oxford Rd., 3rd Fl., Tel (876) 929-4850 thru 9, Fax 935-6001. Direct-in-dial numbers: NAS (876) 935-6080; PC 929-0495; DAO 935-6021; MLO 935-6074; DEA 929-4956; COM 926-8115; AGR 920-2827; INS 935-6095; PAO Tel (876) 935-6053, Fax (876) 929-3637. PAO internet address: opa-kgn@pd.state.gov

| AMB: | (Vacant) |
| AMB OMS: | Beverly Harrison |
| CHG: | Richard H. Smyth |
| CON: | Don Wells |
| COM: | Carol M. Kim  (resident in Santo Domingo) |
| ADM: | Moosa A. Valli |
| ECO/POL: | Michael Koplovsky |
| RSO: | Robert Reed |
| PAO: | J. Michael Korff |
| IRM: | Ron Coles |
| AID: | Mosina Jordan |
| DAO: | Cdr. Craig D. Powell, USN |
| MLO: | LTC Cyril M. Ferenchak, USA |
| AGR: | Kevin N. Smith (resident in Santo Domingo) |
| APHIS: | Art Flores |
| NAS: | Edmund R. Leather |
| PC: | Suchet Loois |
| IRS: | Frederick Dulas (resident in Mexico City) |
| INS: | Gil Valencia, Acting |
| FAA: | Ruben Quinones (resident in Miami) |
| LAB: | John J. Muth (resident in Washington, D.C.) |
| DEA: | John H. Reape, Jr. |

**Montego Bay (CA),** P.O. Box 212 St. James Place, 2nd floor, Glouchester Avenue; Tel. (876) 952-0160/5050

| CA: | Robert T. Garth |

Last Modified: Thursday, April 05, 2001

# JAPAN

Tokyo (E), 10-5, Akasaka 1-chome, Minato-ku, Tokyo 107-8420—Unit 45004, Box 258, APO AP 96337-5004, general Tel [81] (3) 3224-5000, Fax 3505-1862; American Center Tel 3436-0901, Fax 3436-0900. Tokyo home page is http://www.usia.gov/posts/japan.html. ECO internet E-mail address: ustkyecn@ppp.bekkoame.or.jp

| AMB: | Thomas S. Foley |
| AMB OMS: | Freddie A. Barron |

| | |
|---|---|
| DCM: | Christopher J. Lafleur |
| POL: | James J. Foster |
| ECO: | C. Lawrence Greenwood, Jr. |
| COM: | Samuel H. Kidder |
| CON: | John R. Dinger |
| ADM: | Cornelius M. Keur |
| RSO: | Darwin D. Cadogan |
| PAO: | Louise K. Crane |
| IRM: | Thomas A. Bell |
| EST: | James H. Hall |
| DAO: | Capt. Jeffrey W. Crews, USN |
| MDO: | Col. David W. Yauch, USAF |
| AGR: | W. John Child |
| APHIS: | Ralph H. Iwamoto, Jr. |
| ATO: | David C. Miller |
| LAB: | William B. Clatanoff, Jr. |
| IRS: | Stanley Beesley |
| CUS: | James P. McElwain |
| DOE: | [Vacant] |
| FAA: | Bob Jensen |
| FIN: | Robert S. Dohner |
| LEGATT: | James E. Moynihan |
| AID: | [Vacant] |
| DEA: | Peter Shigeta |

**US Trade Center**, World Import Mart, 7th Fl., 1-3 Higashi Ikebukuro 3-chome, Toshima-ku, Tokyo 107-8630, Tel [81] (3) 3987-2441, Fax 3987-2447. COM home page is http://www.csjapan.doc.gov/

| | |
|---|---|
| DIR: | E. Keith Kirkham |

**Agricultural Trade Office**, Tameike Tokyo Bldg., 7th Fl., 1-14, Akasaka 1-chome Minato-ku, Tokyo 107-0052, Tel [81] (3) 3505-6050, Fax 3582-6429

| | |
|---|---|
| EXEC DIR: | Terrence Barber |
| DIR: | David C. Miller |

**Naha, Okinawa (CG)**, No. 2564 Nishihara, Urasoe, Okinawa 901-2101— PSC 556, Box 840, FPO AP 96386-0840, Tel [81] (98) 876-4211, Fax 876-4243. Internet E-mail address: cgnaha2@sunnynet.or.jp

| | |
|---|---|
| CG: | Robert S. Luke |
| POL/MIL: | Lawrence J. Mire |
| ADM: | George T. Novinger |
| CON: | Alan R. Holst |
| PAO: | Karen D. Kelley |

**Osaka-Kobe [CG]**, 11-5, Nishitenma 2-chome, Kita-Ku, Osaka 530-8543—Unit 45004, Box 239, APO AP 96337-5004, Tel [81] (6) 6315-5900, Fax (6) 6315-5915; ADM Fax (6) 6315-5915; CON Fax (6) 6315-5930; COM Fax (6) 6315-5963; ATO Fax (6) 6315-5906; PAO (6) 6315-5965, Fax (6) 6361-5987. Osaka home page- http://www.senri-i.or.jp/amcons. E-mail for CON: acsok@gol.com and aok@state.gov; E-mail for ADM: oad@state.gov.

| | |
|---|---|
| CG: | Robert P. Ludan |
| CON: | Clarence A. Hudsonl |
| POL/ECO: | Douglas J. Meurs |
| COM: | Kenneth B. Reidbord |
| ADM: | Stewart T. Devine |
| PAO: | Max Kwak |
| ATO: | Daniel A. Martinez |
| IRM: | Wayne D. Payton |

**Sapporo [CG]**, Kita 1-Jo Nishi 28-chome, Chuo-ku, Sapporo 064-0821—Unit 45004, Box 276, APO AP 96337-5004, Tel [81] (11) 641-1115/7, Fax 643-1283; COM Fax 643-0911. Sapporo home page address: http://plaza12.mbn.or.jp/amcongensapporo/ E-mail addresses: meservewm@state.gov and gaylema@state.gov

| | |
|---|---|
| CG: | Michael Meserve |
| CON/COM: | Michael Gayle |

**Fukuoka [C]**, 5-26 Ohori 2-chome, Chuo-ku, Fukuoka 810-0052—Unit 45004, Box 242, APO AP 96337-5004, Tel [81] (92) 751-9331/4, Fax 713-9222; COM Fax 725-3772; PAO 761-6661, Fax 721-0109. Fukuoka home page: http://www.usia.gov/posts/fukuoka.html

| | |
|---|---|
| PO: | Kevin K. Maher |
| ECO/COM: | Scott A. Smith |
| ADM/CON: | Gary S. Wakahiro |
| PAO: | Bruce P. Kleiner |

**Nagoya [C]**, Nishiki SIS Building, 6th Fl., 10 – 33 Nishiki 3-chome, Naka-ku, Nagoya 460-0003—Unit 45004, Box 280, APO AP 96337-5004, Tel [81] (52) 203-4011, Fax 201-4612; COM Tel 203-4277; PAO 581-8631, Fax 581-3190. Nagoya home pages: http://www.japan-net.ne.jp/>amcon-ngo/cshome.html and usia.gov/posts/nagoya/ E-mail address: amconngo@japan-net.ne.jp

| | |
|---|---|
| PO: | Andrew J. Quinn |
| COM: | Gary E. Konop |
| PAO: | Jeffrey M. Jamison |

Last Modified: Thursday, November 09, 2000

# JORDAN

**Amman (E)**, P.O. Box 354, Amman 11118 Jordan—APO AE 09892-0200, Tel [962](6)592-0101, direct line to Post 1 [962](6)592-2500; USAID Office Tel 592-0101; EXEC/POL Fax 592-0159; ADMIN Fax 592-0163; CON Fax 592-4102; ECO Fax 592-7653; COM Fax 592-0146; AID Fax 592-0143; PAO Fax 592-0121; MAP Fax 592-0160. Internet address: http://www.usembassy-Amman.org.jo

| | |
|---|---|
| AMB: | William J. Burns |
| AMB OMS: | Mary Dubose |
| DCM: | Janet A. Sanderson |
| POL: | Roberta Newell |
| ECO/COM: | James V. Soriano |
| CON: | Steven S. Maloney |
| ADM: | Kathleen T. Austin |
| RSO: | David Bettis |
| PAO: | Alberto Fernandez |
| IRM: | David R. Chinn |
| AID: | Lewis W. Lucke |
| DAO: | Col. Wallace Dees |
| AGR: | Thomas Pomeroy (resident in Cairo) |
| IRS: | Larry J. LeGrand (resident in Rome) |
| FAA: | Steven B. Wallace (resident in Rome) |
| DEA: | Perry Felecos (resident in Nicosia) |

Last Modified: Thursday, November 09, 2000

# KAZAKHSTAN

**Almaty (E)**, 99/97A Furmanova St., Almaty, Republic of Kazakstan 480091, Tel [7] (3272) 63-39-21, 63-13-75, or

50-76-23, afterhours Tel 50-76-27, Fax 63-38-83; ADM Fax 63-29-42; PAO Fax 63-30-45; PC Fax 62-40-30; FCS Fax 63-88-11; AID Fax 69-64-90; DAO Fax 50-76-20; tie line [8] 927-0000

| | |
|---|---|
| AMB: | Richard H. Jones |
| AMB OMS: | Mary Lee |
| DCM: | Daniel Russell |
| POL/ECO: | Ann Breiter |
| ADM: | John Kuschner |
| CON: | Sara Craig |
| COM: | Julie Snyder |
| IRM: | Bradley Gabler |
| PAO: | Vivian Walker |
| AID: | Glenn Anders |
| PC: | Wylie Williams |
| RSO: | Thomas Huey |
| DAO: | Col. Nilgun O. Nesbett |
| FAA: | Dennis B. Cooper (resident in Brussels) |
| AGR: | James R. Dever (resident in Islamabad) |
| IRS: | Margaret J. Lullo (resident in Berlin) |
| RMO: | Dr. Christine Kwik |
| DEA: | Robert Clark (resident in Islamabad) |

Last Modified: Thursday, March 01, 2001

## KENYA

**Nairobi (E),** Mombasa Road, P.O. Box 30137, Unit 64100, APO AE 09831-4100, Tel [254] (2) 537-800, Fax 537-810; IRM STU-III 537-851, COM Fax [254] (2) 537-846

| | |
|---|---|
| AMB: | Johnnie Carson |
| AMB OMS: | Anna Marie Bustamante |
| DCM: | Michael W. Marine |
| POL: | Walter N.S. Pflaumer |
| ECO: | Harold Foster |
| COM: | August Maffrey |
| CON: | Kay Anske |
| ADM: | Mark Jackson |
| RSO: | Paul T. Peterson |
| PAO: | Thomas Hart |
| IRM: | Kay Gotoh |
| LEGATT: | Bill Corbett |
| PC: | Winne D. Emoungu |
| LOC: | Ruth A. Thomas |
| AID: | Jonathan Conly |
| AID/REDSO: | Donald MacKeenzie |
| AGR: | Fred Kessel |
| APHIS: | James P. Cavanaugh |
| FAA: | Ronald L. Montgomery (resident in Dakar) |
| LAB: | Ralph D. Anske |
| UNEP: | Scott Danaher |
| CDC: | Bernard Nahlen, MD |
| INS: | Joseph Martin |
| KULSO: | Col. Ronald Roughead |
| MRU: | Col. Ronald Rosenberg |
| DAO: | Ltc. Thomas F. Westfall |
| MLO: | Col. David Swartzlander, USA |
| IRS: | Jame P. Beene (resident in London) |
| DEA: | Robert Shannon (resident in Cairo) |

Last Modified: Thursday, November 09, 2000

## KOREA

**Seoul (E),** 82 Sejong-Ro, Chongro-ku—Unit 15550, APO AP 96205-0001, Tel [82] (2) 397-4114, Fax 738-8845; USATO address: Room 303, Leema Bldg, 146-1, Susong-dong, Chongro-ku, Tel 397-4188, Fax 720-7921

| | |
|---|---|
| AMB: | Stephen W. Bosworth |
| AMB OMS: | Teressa D. Roller |
| DCM: | Richard A. Christenson |
| POL: | William D. Strub |
| ECO: | Frederic W. Maerkle |
| CONS: | Richard C. Hermann |
| COM: | John Peters |
| ADM: | Alphonse Lopez |
| RSO: | James T. Cronin |
| PAO: | Jeremy F. Curtin |
| IRM: | Danny D. Lockwood |
| CUS: | William Allen |
| POL/LAB: | Marc Knapper |
| DAO: | Col. Thomas R. Riley, USA |
| MAAG: | Col. Claude Crabtree |
| AGR: | William L. Brant |
| APHIS: | Robert Tanaka |
| ATO: | Daryl Brehm |
| DEA: | Michael L. Chapman |
| INS: | Lolita K. Parocua |
| FAA: | Elizabeth Keck (resident in Beijing) |
| IRS: | Stanley Beesley (resident in Tokyo) |

**US Export Development Office/U.S. Commercial Center, c/o US Embassy,** Tel [82] (2) 397-4356, Fax 739-1628 DIR:Camille Sailer

Last Modified: Thursday, November 09, 2000

## KUWAIT

**Kuwait (E),** P.O. Box 77 Safat, 13001 Safat, Kuwait—Unit 69000, APO AE 09880-9000, Tel [965] 539-5307/5308, afterhours [965] 538-2097/2098, Fax [965] 538-0282; GSO Fax 539-0938; COM Fax 538-0281; PAO Fax 538-0294; OMC-K Fax 539-0974; CON Fax 538-0449; DIALO Fax 538-0443; workweek: Saturday through Wednesday. Embassy web page: http//www.usembassy.gov.kw. Embassy internet address:usisirc@qualitynet.net. PAO internet address: usiskwt@kuwait.net or usisirc@kuwait.net. COM internet address: tcs@kuwait.net

| | |
|---|---|
| AMB: | James A. Larocco |
| AMB OMS: | Patricia K. Keegan |
| DCM: | William T. Monroe |
| POL: | Ethan A. Goldrich |
| POL/MIL: | Norman T. Roule |
| ECO: | Michael E. McNaull |
| COM: | Robert J. Bucalo |
| CON: | Donald E. Ahern |
| ADM: | Brian H. McIntosh |
| ATO: | Ronald Verdonk (resident in Dubai) |
| FAA: | Lynn Osmus (resident in Brussels) |
| CUS: | Joda C. Taylor |
| RSO: | Michael T. Manegan |
| ATO: | Ronald Verdonk (resident in Cairo) |
| IRM: | Thomas Smith |
| PAO: | Susan L. Ziadeh |
| OMC-K: | Walter Wojdakowski, USA |
| IBB/VOA: | Walter D. Patterson |

| | |
|---|---|
| DEA: | Robert Clark (resident in Islamabad) |

Last Modified: Wednesday, March 28, 2001

## KYRGYZSTAN

**Bishkek (E),** 171 Prospect Mira, Bishkek 720016, The Kyrgyz Republic, Tel [996] (312) 551-241, [996] (517) 777-217, Fax [996] (312) 551-264; CON Fax [996] (517) 777-202; USAID Fax [996] (517) 777-203; IVG line: 964; night/emergency numbers [996] (312) 551-262 (post one-marines)

| | |
|---|---|
| AMB: | John M. O'Keefe |
| AMB OMS: | Glenda Wright |
| DCM: | Sheila S. Gwaltney |
| POL/ECO: | Peter T. Eckstrom |
| CON: | Gregory N. Gardner |
| ADM: | Daniel M. Hirsch |
| GSO: | Gary L. Anderson |
| PAO: | Edward J. Kulakowski |
| DAO: | Ltc. Maria C. Constantine |
| IPO: | Raymond H. Harger |
| RSO: | Edward C. Phillips |
| PC: | Joseph S. Curtin |
| AID: | Tracy G. Atwood |
| RMO: | Dr. Christine Kwik (resident in Almaty) |

Last Modified: Tuesday, November 07, 2000

## LAOS

**Vientiane (E),** rue Bartholonie, P.O. 114—Box V, APO AP 96546, Tel [856] (21) 212581/582/585, afterhours Tel 212581, Fax 212584

| | |
|---|---|
| AMB: | [Vacant] |
| AMB OMS: | Louise C. Ramirez |
| CHG: | Karen B. Stewart |
| POL: | Gregory L. Lawless |
| ECO/COM: | Patricia A. Mahoney |
| CON: | Joseph de Maria |
| ADM: | Brian R. Moran |
| GSO: | Michael E. Bakalar |
| NAS: | Peter M. Haymond |
| PAO: | M. Elizabeth McKay |
| RSO: | John P. Gaddis (resident in Bangkok) |
| FAA: | David L. Knudson (resident in Singapore) |
| APHIS: | Dale Maki (resident in Beijing) |
| IRM: | Gary L. Cook |
| DEA: | Michael Dugan |
| IRS: | Billy J. Brown (resident in Singapore) |

Last Modified: Thursday, November 09, 2000

## LATVIA

**Riga (E),** Raina Boulevard 7, LV-1510, Riga, Latvia—PSC 78, Box Riga, APO AE 09723, Tel [371]703-6200, afterhours Tel [371] 730-6200, Fax 782-0047. PAO Tel 721-6478, Fax 782-0077, MLT Tel 732-6299, Fax 783-0222; Med Unit Fax 782-0049; CON recording [371] 782-0045

| | |
|---|---|
| AMB: | James H. Holmes |
| AMB OMS: | Teresa Chupp |
| DCM: | Tracey Jacobson |
| DCM OMS: | Sharon O'Neal |
| POL/ECO: | Bruce D. Rogers |

| | |
|---|---|
| ECO/COM: | Anne L. Chick |
| COM: | Karen S. Pilmanis |
| COM: | Thomas M. Kelsey (resident in Stockholm) |
| CON: | Karen E. Martin |
| ADM: | John C. Lamson |
| GSO: | Jonathan Schools |
| ORA: | William Pennington |
| ORA: | Stephen McFarland |
| IRM: | Paul J. Wright |
| PAO: | Gregory B. Elftmann |
| DOJ: | Mark J. McKeon |
| PC: | Coralie J. Turbitt |
| RSO: | Leroy M. Bowers |
| AGR: | Lana Bennett (resident in Stockholm) |
| FAA: | Dennis Cooper (resident in Brussels) |
| DAO: | Ltc. Jeffrey M. Seng, USMC |
| ODC: | Maj. Charles Cox |
| EST: | David W. Mulenex (resident in Copenhagen) |
| MLT: | Col. Gery W. Kosel |
| IRS: | Margaret J. Lullo (resident in Berlin) |
| DEA: | Arthur L. Kersey (resident in Copenhagen) |

Last Modified: Thursday, April 05, 2001

## LEBANON

**Beirut (E),** Antelias—P.O. Box 70-840, or PSC 815, Box 2, FPO AE 09836-0002, Tel [961] (4) 543-600, 542-600, 544-130/131/133, Fax 544-136; ADM Fax 544-604

| | |
|---|---|
| AMB: | David M. Satterfield |
| AMB OMS: | Antonette Schroeder |
| DCM: | David M. Hale |
| POL: | Karen H. Sasahara |
| ECO/COM: | Elizabeth Fritschle |
| CON: | Patricia J. Raikes |
| ADM: | Roger C. Nottingham |
| RSO: | Walter B. Deering |
| PAO: | Anne H. O'Leary |
| IRM: | Michael Reed |
| AID: | James E. Stephenson |
| DAO: | Ltc. Patrick Michelson, USA |
| OMC: | Maj. Ivar S. Tait |
| AGR: | Thomas Pomeroy (resident in Cairo) |
| LEGATT: | Thomas Knowles (resident in Athens) |
| FAA: | Steven B. Wallace (resident in Rome) |
| IRS: | Margaret J. Lullo (resident in Berlin) |
| DEA: | Perry Felecos (resident in Nicosia) |

Last Modified: Wednesday, January 03, 2001

## LESOTHO

**Maseru (E),** P.O. Box 333, Maseru 100 Lesotho, Tel [266] 312-666, Fax 310-116; E-mail address: amles@lesoff.co.za

| | |
|---|---|
| AMB: | Katherine H. Peterson |
| AMB OMS: | Linda DeSola |
| DCM: | Daniel P. Bellegarde |
| ADM: | J.A. Diffily |
| PC: | Carol Chappell |
| RSO: | James Combs (resident in Gaborone) |
| FAA: | Edward Jones (resident in Dakar) |
| DAO: | COL. Richard Dennis Rider (resident in Pretoria) |
| AGR: | Richard Helm (resident in Pretoria) |

| | |
|---|---|
| LAB: | Frederick J. Kaplan (resident in Johannesburg) |
| IRS: | James P. Beene (resident in London) |
| DEA: | Larry W. Frye (resident in Pretoria) |

Last Modified: Thursday, November 30, 2000

# LIBERIA

**Monrovia (E),** 111 United Nations Dr., P.O. Box 10-0098, Mamba Point, Tel [231] 226-370-380, Front Office 220-150; Fax 226-148, Front Office 226-154; GSO 226-149; USAID 226-152. No APO/FPO is available.

| | |
|---|---|
| AMB: | Bismarck Myrick |
| AMB OMS: | Judith Glen |
| DCM: | Walter Greenfield |
| POL/ECO: | Hartford T. Jennings |
| COM: | Johnny Brown (resident in Abidjan) |
| CON: | Anthony Beaver |
| ADM: | Michael L. Bajek |
| RSO: | Frank C. Benevento |
| PAO: | Sarah C. Morrison |
| AID: | Rudolph Thomas |
| IRM: | Aurelius J. Manupella |
| DAO: | Maj. Frank Lactignola |
| FAA: | Ronald L. Montgomery (resident in Dakar) |
| AGR: | Bruce J. Zanin (resident in Abidjan) |
| CDC (WHO): | Dennis King |
| DOJ: | William Wagner |
| RMO: | Dr. Georges F. McCormick (resident in Abidjan) |
| LAB: | [Vacant] (resident in Washington, D.C.) |
| IRS: | Frederick D. Pablo (resident in Paris) |
| DEA: | Edgar L. Moses (resident in Lagos) |

Last Modified: Thursday, November 09, 2000

# LITHUANIA

**Vilnius (E),** Akmenu 6, 2600 Vilnius, Lithuania—PSC 78, Box V, APO AE 09723, Tel [370] (2) 223-031 (24 hours), [370] (8) 733-309 (24-hour cellular), Fax [370] [2] 312-819; USAID [370] (2) 221-666, Fax 222-954; PAO Tel 220-481, Fax 220-445

| | |
|---|---|
| AMB: | Keith C. Smith |
| AMB OMS: | Vianna Fieser |
| DCM: | Anthony Spakauskas |
| POL/ECO: | Marilyn Ereshefsky |
| CON: | Linda Eichblatt |
| REGA: | Jennifer Ewbank |
| COM: | Thomas M. Kelsey (resident in Stockholm) |
| ADM: | Susan Page |
| IRM: | James Fieser |
| GSO: | Andrew Graves |
| AID: | Christine Sheckler |
| PAO: | Michael Boyle |
| RSO: | Kenneth Luzzi |
| AGR: | James Higgiston (resident in Warsaw) |
| DAO: | Maj. Albert M. Zaccor, USA |
| SAO: | Maj. Maella Lohman |
| FAA: | Dennis Cooper (resident in Brussels) |
| IRS: | Margaret J. Lullo (resident in Berlin) |
| FBI: | Bill Moschella (resident in Tallinn) |
| DEA: | Arthur L. Kersey (resident in Copenhagen) |

Last Modified: Thursday, November 09, 2000

# LUXEMBOURG

**Luxembourg (E),** 22 Blvd. Emmanuel-Servais, 2535 Luxembourg—official mail: name/office, American Embassy Luxembourg, Unit 1410, APO AE 09126-1410; personal mail: name, American Embassy Luxembourg, PSC 9, Box 9500, APO AE 09123, Tel [352] 460123, Fax 46 14 01 (Consular/ADM); 22 64 57 (Exec. Office)

| | |
|---|---|
| AMB: | [Vacant] |
| CHG: | Gerald J. Loftus |
| OMS: | Sharon S. Wells |
| POL/MIL: | Joan B. Vandaveer |
| POL/ECO: | Patricia Kim-Scott |
| ADM: | Michaelene F. Kaczmarek |
| CON: | Ronald A. Johnson |
| RSO: | C. Kevin Scott |
| IPO: | David Hazzard |
| AGR: | Philip A. Letarte (resident in The Hague) |
| COM: | George Knowles (resident in Brussels) |
| DEA: | Stephen Luzinski (resident in Brussels) |
| DAO: | Col. William Zekas (resident in Brussels) |
| ODC: | Col. George A. Reed (resident in Brussels) |
| FAA: | Paul H. Feldman, Acting (resident in Brussels) |
| DOJ: | Mark Richard (resident in Brussels) |
| FBI: | Sandra Fowler (resident in Brussels) |
| IRS: | Margaret J. Lullo (resident in Berlin) |
| CUS: | Michael Looney (resident in Paris) |

Last Modified: Wednesday, February 14, 2001

# MACEDONIA, Former Yugoslav Republic of

**Skopje (E),** Bul. Ilinden bb, 91000 Skopje—Pouch address: Embassy Skopje, Department of State, Washington, D.C. 20521-7120, Tel [389] (91) 116-180, Fax 117-103; USAID: Veljko Vlahovich, 26/5, 91000 Skopje, Tel 117-211, 117-032, Fax 118-105; PAO Tel 116-623, 117-129; Fax 118-431; USDAO Tel 118-690

| | |
|---|---|
| AMB: | E. Michael Einik |
| AMB/DCM OMS: | Marjie J. Douglas |
| DCM: | Laura J. Kirkconnell |
| POL: | Charles A. Stonecipher |
| ECO/COM: | Anton K. Smith |
| CON: | Patrick W. Walsh |
| ADM: | Sandra R. Smith |
| GSO: | Cheryl N. Johnson |
| RSO: | Michael K. Brown |
| IRM: | Arthur J. Hermanson |
| DAO: | Col. Robert Lynch |
| PAO: | Yolanda Richardson |
| FAA: | Steven B. Wallace (resident in Rome) |
| AGR: | Holly Higgins (resident in Sofia) |
| AID: | Stephen Haynes |
| PRM: | Frances R. Culpepper |
| IRS: | Larry J. LeGrand (resident in Rome) |
| DEA: | James Soiles (resident in Athens) |

Last Modified: Wednesday, December 13, 2000

# MADAGASCAR

**Antananarivo (E),** 14 & 16, rue Rainitovo Antsahavola Antananarivo 101, Republic of Madagascar, Tel [261] (20)

22 21257 or (20) 22 20956, Cellular [261] 030 23 80900, Fax (20) 22 34539

| | |
|---|---|
| AMB: | Shirley E. Barnes |
| AMB OMS: | Kay Woodhouse-Maury |
| DCM: | June Carter Perry |
| DCM OMS: | Linda L. Wood |
| POL: | James A. Knight |
| ECO/CON/COM: | Stuart A. Zimmer |
| ADM: | Donald B. Andrus |
| RSO: | Yann E. Stephan |
| GSO: | Katherine A. Radcliffe |
| FMO: | Natalie B. Cropper |
| PAO: | Joan McKniff |
| IRM: | Raymond Shankweiler |
| AID: | Karen M. Poe |
| LAB: | Ralph D. Anske (resident in Nairobi) |
| LEGATT: | Robert H. Wright (resident in Pretoria) |
| FAA: | Ronald L. Montgomery (resident in Dakar) |
| PCD: | John A. Reddy |
| IRS: | Frederick Pablo (resident in Paris) |
| DEA: | Larry W. Frye (resident in Pretoria) |

Last Modified: Wednesday, December 13, 2000

# MALAWI

**Lilongwe (E),** P.O. Box 30016, Lilongwe 3, Malawi, Tel [265] 773-166, 773-342, 773-367; Fax [265] 770-471; EXEC Fax [265] 772-316; ADMIN Fax 773-169; USAID [265] 772-455; Fax [265] 773-181; PC [265] 757-157; Fax [265] 751-008.

| | |
|---|---|
| AMB: | Roger A. Meece |
| AMB OMS: | Doris M. McCourt |
| DCM: | Marcia Bernicat |
| ECO/COM: | Charles Randolph |
| CON/POL: | Mitchell B. Benedict |
| ADM: | Frank W. Skinner |
| RSO: | Ronald J. Elkins |
| IMO: | Lloyd Cammel |
| RMO: | Lawrence Hill (resident in Pretoria) |
| PAO: | Vicki Adair |
| AID: | Kiertisak Toh |
| PC: | Terry Murphree |
| DATT: | Col. James Smaugh (resident in Harare) |
| AGR: | Fred Kessel (resident in Nairobi) |
| LAB: | Ralph D. Anske (resident in Nairobi) |

Last Modified: Wednesday, February 21, 2001

# MALAYSIA

**Kuala Lumpur (E),** 376 Jalan Tun Razak, 50400 Kuala Lumpur—P.O. Box 10035, 50700 Kuala Lumpur, APO AP 96535-8152, Tel [60] (3) 2168-5000; ADM Tel 2168-4800, Fax 2168-4961; GSO Fax 2168-4948 or 2168-4951. Internet address: http://www.aring.my/usiskl

| | |
|---|---|
| AMB: | B. Lynn Pascoe |
| AMB OMS: | Ginny Phillips |
| DCM: | Robert C. Reis, Jr. |
| POL: | James F. Entwistle |
| ECO: | Christopher J. Marut |
| COM: | Michael J. Hand |
| CON: | Sylvia Johnson |
| ADM: | An T. Le |
| GSO: | Chris J. Laycock |
| RSO: | Robert F. Valente |

| | |
|---|---|
| PAO: | Charles Barclay |
| IRM: | Donald P. Clayton |
| SAO: | Col. Mark Swarigen |
| DAO: | Col. Donald R. Moran |
| DEA: | James Tse |
| AGR: | Abdullah Saleh |
| FAA: | David L. Knudson (resident in Singapore) |
| CUS: | Donald K. Shruhan, Jr. (resident in Singapore) |
| IRS: | Billy J. Brown (resident in Singapore) |
| LEGATT: | Ralph P. Horton (resident in Bangkok) |

Last Modified: Thursday, November 09, 2000

# MALI

**Bamako (E),** rue Rochester NY and rue Mohamed V, B.P. 34, Tel [223] 22-54-70, afterhours Tel 22-38-33, Telex 2448 AMEMB MJ, Fax 223712. Internet address: ipc@usa.org.ml

| | |
|---|---|
| AMB: | Michael E. Ranneberger |
| AMB OMS: | Carolyn J. Kite |
| DCM: | John O'Leary |
| POL/ECO: | George M. Frederick |
| CON: | Susan K. Archer |
| ADM: | Catherine I. Ebert-Gray |
| RSO: | [Vacant] |
| PAO: | Robin L. Yeager |
| RMO: | Dr. Patrick Sterling |
| IPO: | Marv A. Allie |
| AID: | Paul C. Tuebner |
| DAO: | Ltc Todd Coker (resident in Dakar) |
| LAB: | James Maxstadt (resident in Washington, D.C.) |
| FAA: | Edward Jones (resident in Dakar) |
| CDC: | Dr. Enias Baganizi |
| PC: | Gene Neill |
| RCON: | Ann Gordon (resident in Dakar) |
| RELO: | Robert Lindsey (resident in Dakar) |

Last Modified: Wednesday, January 03, 2001

# MALTA

**Valletta (E),** 3rd Fl., Development House, St. Anne St., Floriana, Malta—P.O. Box 535, Valletta, Tel [356] 235-960, Fax (EXO) [356] 223-322, COM/CON/ADM [356] 243-229; PAO [356] 246-917, Fax 22-33-22. Internet address: usembassy@kemmunet.net.mt

| | |
|---|---|
| AMB: | Kathryn L. H. Proffitt |
| AMB OMS: | Melanie G. Gisler |
| DCM: | Deborah A. Bolton |
| SA: | Teresa J. Ensor |
| ECO/COM/CON: | James M. Perez |
| POL: | [Vacant] |
| ADM: | Randall C. Budden |
| RSO: | George J. Goldstein (resident in Rome) |
| PAO: | Keith E. Peterson |
| IRM: | Stephen J. Weaver |
| DAO: | Capt. Vincent P. Mocini, USN (resident in Rome) |
| AGR: | Elizabeth Berry (resident in Rome) |
| FAA: | Steven B. Wallace (resident in Rome) |
| IRS: | Larry J. LeGrand (resident in Rome) |
| DEA: | Vincent J. Di Stefano (resident in Rome) |

Last Modified: Thursday, November 09, 2000

## MARSHALL ISLANDS

**Majuro (E),** Oceanside Mejen Weto, Long Island, Majuro, Republic of the Marshall Islands, Tel (692) 247-4011, Fax 247-4012; COM FAX 247-7533—Pouch: Majuro, 20521-4380, via U.S. Mail, P.O. Box 1379, Majuro, MH 96960-1379. No APO/FPO is available; workweek M – F: 8 am-12 noon and 1-5 pm

| | |
|---|---|
| AMB: | Joan M. Plaisted |
| AMB OMS: | Ann J. Key |
| DCM: | Michael A. Spangler |
| ADM: | Carolyn Pittman |
| MILOFF: | Dr. Thomas Keene |
| RSO: | Ronald M. Mazer (resident in Manila) |
| FAA: | Barry Brayer (resident in Los Angeles) |
| CUS: | Donald K. Shruhan, Jr. (resident in Singapore) |
| IRS: | Stanley Beesley (resident in Tokyo) |
| DEA: | Jeffrey L. Wendling (resident in Manila) |

Last Modified: Thursday, November 09, 2000

## MAURITANIA

**Nouakchott (E),** rue Abdallaye, Nouakchott, B.P. 222, Tel (222) 25-26-60, 25-26-63, 25-11-41 or 25-11-45, Fax 25-15-92; STU III classified Fax 25-36-04; workweek: Sunday through Thursday. Internet address: aemnouak@opt.mr

| | |
|---|---|
| AMB: | Timberlake Foster |
| AMB OMS: | Jana A. Amon |
| DCM: | Carol A. Colloton |
| ECO/CON: | Katherine M. Metres |
| RCON: | Ann Gordon (resident in Dakar) |
| ADM: | Sonya K. Rix |
| RSO: | George G. Frederick (resident in Dakar) |
| RMO: | Dr. Jesse Monestersky (resident in Dakar) |
| IRM: | Walter H. Yates III |
| DAO: | Ltc Todd Coker, USMC (resident in Dakar) |
| R/PER: | Judith E. Picardi (residnet in Bamako) |
| RFMO: | Mary J. Snyder (resident in Dakar) |
| FAA: | Edward L. Jones (resident in Dakar) |
| LAB: | [Vacant] (resident in Washington, D.C.) |
| IRS: | Frederick D. Pablo (resident in Paris) |
| DEA: | Edgar L. Moses (resident in Lagos) |

Last Modified: Wednesday, January 03, 2001

## MAURITIUS*

**Port Louis (E),** Rogers House (4th Fl.), John Kennedy St., Tel [230] 208-2347, 208 – 2354, 208 – 9763 thru 9767, Fax 208-9534; Int'l. mail: P.O. Box 544, Port Louis, Mauritius; U.S. mail: Am. Emb., Port Louis, Dept. of State, Wash., D.C. 20521 – 2450. Internet address: usembass@intnet.mu*Note: Port Louis is now responsible for Comoros and assumed responsibility for Seychelles on October 1, 1996.

| | |
|---|---|
| AMB: | Mark W. Erwin |
| AMB OMS: | [Vacant] |
| DCM: | Alexander H. Marguiles |
| POL/ECO/CON: | Heather C.Variava |
| ADM: | Charles Slater |
| RSO: | Wayne Algire (resident in Antananarivo) |
| PAO: | Daniel P. Claffey |
| IRM: | Elizabeth Slater |
| FAA: | Ronald L. Montgomery (resident in Dakar) |

| | |
|---|---|
| LAB: | Ralph D. Anske (resident in Nairobi) |
| IRS: | Frederick Pablo (resident in Paris) |

Last Modified: Thursday, November 09, 2000

## MEXICO

**Mexico City (E),** Paseo de la Reforma 305, 06500 Mexico, D.F.—P.O. Box 3087, Laredo, TX 78044-3087, Tel [52] (5) 209-9100, Fax (52) (5) 208-3373 and 511-9980

| | |
|---|---|
| AMB: | Jeffrey Davidow |
| AMB OMS: | Celestina Renteria |
| DCM: | James M. Derham |
| POL: | J. Christian Kennedy |
| ECO: | William R. Brew |
| COM: | Dale Slaght |
| CON: | Thomas P. Furey |
| CG: | Victor A. Abeyta |
| ADM: | James B. Lane |
| RSO: | Kenneth E. Sykes |
| EST: | S. Ahmed Meer |
| IRM: | Wayne G. Adams |
| RAMC: | Frederic C. Hassani |
| PAO: | John S. Dickson |
| NAS: | Gaye Maris |
| DAO: | Col. Richard Downie |
| MLO: | Col. Francisco Pedrozo |
| FBU: | Bernardino G. Gonzalez |
| SCI: | Lawrence M. Kerr |
| AID: | Paul White |
| EPA: | Lawrence Sperling |
| AGR: | Frank Lee |
| APHIS [Reg. 6]: | Scott D. Saxe |
| APHIS [Reg. 5]: | Elba Quintero |
| FAA: | Ruben Quinones (resident in Miami) |
| LAB: | John Ritchie |
| INS: | Hipolito Acosta |
| CUS: | Pete Gonzalez, Acting |
| ATF: | Keith Heinzerling |
| LEGATT: | Edmundo L. Guevara |
| DEA: | Michael G. Garland |
| IRS: | Frederick Dulas |
| FIN: | Steve Backes |

**USDA/AGR Trade Office (ATO),** Jaime Balmer no. 8-201, Colonia Polanco, 11560 Mexico, D.F. Mail: P.O. Box 3087, Laredo, TX 78044-3087, Tel [52] (5) 280-5291, 280-5277, Fax 281-6093

| | |
|---|---|
| ATO: | Chad R. Russell |

**US Export Development Office,** Liverpool 31, 06600 Mexico, D.F., Tel [52] (5) 591-0155, Fax 566-1115

| | |
|---|---|
| DIR/COM: | Jon Kuehner |

**Ciudad Juarez [CG],** Chihuahua, Avenue Lopez Mateos 924 Norte, 32300 Ciudad Juarez, Chihuahua—P.O. Box 10545, El Paso, TX 79995-0545, Tel [52] (16) 113000, Fax 169056

| | |
|---|---|
| CG: | Edward H. Vazquez |
| DPO: | Philip Egger |
| RSO: | Robert D. Barton |
| ADM: | Jacqueline Holland |
| INS: | Robert Ballow |
| DEA: | Javier Jacquez |

**Guadalajara [CG],** JAL, Progreso 175, 44100 Guadalajara, Jalisco, Mexico—Box 3088, Laredo, TX 78044-3088, Tel [52] (3) 825-2998, 825-2700, Fax 826-6549. E-mail Address: consuladousa@megared.net.mx

| | |
|---|---|
| CG: | Edward H. Wilkinson |
| COM: | Virginia Krivis |
| CON: | Derwood K. Staeben |
| ADM: | Joanne Edwards |
| PAO: | Judith L. Bryan |
| GSO: | Craig A. Anderson |
| APHIS: | Ivette Perez-Marcano |
| LEGATT: | Andrew Diaz |
| DEA: | Pedro Pena |

**Monterrey [CG],** N. L. Ave., Constitucion 411 Poniente 64000 Monterrey, N.L., Box 3098, Laredo, TX 78044-3098, Tel [52] (8) 345-2120, 342-0177; ADM Fax 343-7283

| | |
|---|---|
| CG: | Robert A. Nolan |
| CG SEC: | Ana Silva |
| POL/ECO: | Otto H. Van Maerssen |
| COM: | Janice Corbett |
| CON: | Daniel D. Darrach |
| ADM: | Naomi Lyew |
| RSO: | Gregory Houston |
| PAO: | Rebecca Winchester |
| INS: | Arthur Nieto |
| CUS: | Ventura Cerda |
| DEA: | Jose A. Baeza |
| LEGATT: | Ed Preciado |

**Tijuana [CG],** B.C.N., Tapachula 96, 22420 Tijuana, Baja California Norte—P.O. Box 439039, San Diego, CA 92143-9039, Tel [52] (66) 81-7400, Answering Serv. Tel., (619) 692-2154, Fax (52) (66) 81-8016, 81-7113

| | |
|---|---|
| CG: | Richard Gonzalez |
| CON: | Phillip Egger |
| COM: | Renato Davia |
| ADM: | Susan L. Pazina |
| PAO: | H. Clinton Wright |
| INS: | Scott Hatfield |
| NIV: | Sandra Raynes |
| DEA: | Alexander G. Toth |
| CUS: | Sonny Manzano |
| RSO: | Joel Henderson |
| ACS: | :Lisa A. Gamble-Barker |

**Hermosillo [C],** Sonora, Monterrey 141 Pre. 83260 Hermosillo, Sonora Mail: Box 3598, Laredo, TX 78044-3598, Tel [52] (62) 17-2375, Fax 17- 2578. E-mail address: amconsul@rtn.uson.mx

| | |
|---|---|
| PO: | Ronald Kramer |
| CON: | William E. Fitzgerald |
| ADM: | Stephen Weed |
| IRM: | Rudy R. Garcia |
| CUS: | Terry Kirkpatrick |
| APHIS: | Dale Rush |
| DEA: | Harvey Goehring |
| RSO: | Robert Barton (resident of Ciudad Juarez) |

**Matamoros [C],** Tamps., Ave. Primera 2002, 87330 Matamoros, Tamaulipas—Box 633, Brownsville, TX 78522-0633, Tel [52] (88) 12-44-02, Fax 12-21-71

| | |
|---|---|
| PO: | David L. Stone |

| | |
|---|---|
| CON: | Kelly S. Cecil |
| ADM: | Vera Pauli-Widenhouse |

**Merida [C],** Yuc., Paseo Montejo 453, 97000 Merida, Yucatan—Box 3087, Laredo, TX 78044 – 3087, Tel [52] (99) 25 – 5011, Fax 25 – 6219

| | |
|---|---|
| PO: | David R. Ramos |
| CON: | Joseph Gallazzi |
| NIV: | Anthony J. Kleiber |
| ADM: | Kurt J. Hoyer |
| DEA: | Jaime Camacho |

**Nuevo Laredo [C],** Tamps., Calle Allende 3330, Col. Jardin, 88260 Nuevo Laredo, Tamps.—Drawer 3089, Laredo, TX 78044-3089, Tel [52] (87) 14-0512, Fax 14-7984, ext. 128; AGR Tel 191-603, Fax 191-605. Internet address: Watkinsra@state.gov

| | |
|---|---|
| PO: | Thomas Hart Armbruster |
| ADM: | Juan Aguero |
| CON: | Lana Chumley |
| AGR: | Richard T. Drennan |

**Nogales, Sonora (C)** Calle San Jose s/n, 84065, Nogales, Sonora &#8721; P.O. Box 1729, Nogales, AZ 85628 (U.S. mailing address); Apartado Postal No. 267, C.P. 8400, Nogales, Sonora, Mexicio (Mexican mailing address), Tel [52] (631) 34820, Fax [52] (631) 34797 or 34652

| | |
|---|---|
| PO: | Jane Gray |
| CON: | Sean Murphy |
| ADM: | David J. Savastuk |

**Acapulco [CA],** Hotel Acapulco Continental, Costera M. Aleman 121-Local 14, Acapulco, Gro. 39580, Tel. [52] (74) 81-16-99, Fax (74) 84-03-00. Internet address: consular@grol.telmex.net.mx

| | |
|---|---|
| CA: | Alexander Richards |

**Cabo San Lucas (CA),** Blvd. Marina y Pedregal No. 1 Local No. 3, Zona Centro Cabo San Lucas, B.C.S., Tel and Fax (114)-3-35-66

| | |
|---|---|
| CA: | Michael J. Houston |

**Cancun [CA],** Plaza Caracol Dos, Segundo Nivel No. 320-323, Blvd. Kukulkan, J., 8.5 Zona Hotelera, Cancun, Q.R. 77500, Tel [52] 98-83-2450, Fax 83-1373

| | |
|---|---|
| CA: | Lynette Belt |

**Cozumel [CA],** Av. Juarez 33 Local 8, Centro Commercial ""Villa Mar""; Plaza Principal 2do. Nivel, Cozumel, QR 77600, Mexico. Tel (52) (987) 245-74, Fax (52) (987) 223-39. Internet address: anne@cozumel.net

| | |
|---|---|
| CA: | Anne R. Harris |

**Ixtapa [CA],** Local 9 Plaza Ambiente, Ixtapa, Zihuatanejo, Gro. 40880, Mexico. Tel (52) (755) 3-1108, Fax (52) (755) 4-62-76, Cell 52-755-7-1106. Internet address: lizwilliams@diplomats.com

| | |
|---|---|
| CA: | Elizabeth Williams |

**Mazatlan [CA],** Hotel Playa Mazatlan, Rodolfo T. Loaiza No. 202 Zona Dorada, 82100, Mazatlan, Sin, Tel [52] 69 16-58-89/13-44-44, ext. 285. Internet address: mazagent@red2000.com.mx

CA:                        Gerianne N. Gallardo

**Oaxaca [CA],** Macedonio Alcala No. 201, Desp. 206 68000 Oaxaca, Tel and Fax [951] 4-30-54. Internet address: conagent@oax.1.telmex.net.mx

CA:                        Mark A. Leyes

**Puerto Vallarta[CA],** Plaza Zaragoza 166, Piso 2-18, Edif. Vallarta Plaza, Puerto Vallarta, Jalisco, 48300, Tel [52] (322)-2-00-69, Fax (322)-2-00-74

CA:                        Kelly A. Trainor

**San Luis Potosi [CA],** Edificio Las Terrazas, Av. Venustiano Carranza 2076, Int.41; 40 Piso, Colonia Polanco, San Luis Potosi 78220, Mexico. Tel (52) (48) 11-78-02, Fax (52) (48) 11-78-03. Internet address: fercar@infosel.net.mx

CA:                        Carolyn Lazaro

**San Miguel de Allende (CA),** Dr. Hernandez Macias 72, San Miguel de Allende, Gto., Tel (415) 2-23-57, Fax 2-15-88. E-mail address: coromar@unisono.net.mx

CA:                        Col. Philip J. Maher

Last Modified: Thursday, March 29, 2001

# MICRONESIA

**Kolonia (E),** P.O. Box 1286, Pohnpei, Federated States of Micronesia 96941, Tel [691] 320-2187, Fax 320-2186

| | |
|---|---|
| AMB: | Diane E. Watson |
| OM/VC/COMM: | Sally J. Mitchell |
| DCM/POL/ECO: | Mary Ann Wright |
| ADM: | Jewellene E. Wilson (resident in Majuro) |
| RSO: | Gordon Sjue (resident in Manila) |
| FAA: | Barry Brayer (resident in Hawthorne, CA) |
| CUS: | Donald K. Shruhan, Jr. (resident in Singapore) |
| IRS: | Stanley Beesley (resident in Tokyo) |
| DEA: | Jeffrey L. Wendling |

# MOLDOVA

**Chisinau (E),** Strada Alexei Mateevici, No. 103, 2009, Tel [373] (2) 233-772, afterhours Tel 237-345, Fax 233-044. Tie lines: ADM 8-548-0123; POL/ECO 8-548-0103; PAO 8-548-0101; USAID 8-548-0163; DAO 8-548-0104; AMB 8-548-0174. Internet address: chisinau@amemb.mld-net.com. E-mail address: angel.ac@owh.moldnet.md. State Dept. E-mail address: clo33123@state.gov

| | |
|---|---|
| AMB: | Rudolf V. Perina |
| AMB OMS: | Christine Rosenquist |
| DCM: | William G. Perett |
| ADM: | Warren Hadley |
| POL/ECO: | John K. Madden |
| GSO: | Judson Scott |
| CON: | Michael J. Sears |
| IRM: | Ricardo Cabrera |
| PAO: | Lisa Heilbronn |

| | |
|---|---|
| AID: | Thomas Lofgren |
| DAO: | Lt. Col. William C. Vogt |
| RSO: | Richard A. Colquhoun |
| RMO: | Ron Larsen (resident in Moscow) |
| FAA: | Dennis B. Cooper (resident in Brussels) |
| DEA: | Thomas C. Slovenkay (resident in Vienna) |

Last Modified: Thursday, November 09, 2000

# MONGOLIA

**Ulaanbaatar (E),** Micro Region 11, Big Ring Road, C.P.O. 1021, Ulaanbaatar 13, Mongolia (international address)—PSC 461, Box 300, FPO AP 96521-0002 (U.S. address), Tel [976] (11) 329095, Fax 320776; USAID Fax 310440; PAO Fax 312380; PC Fax 311520. Internet E-mail address: receptionist@usembassy.mn. Website address:

www.us-mongolia.com

| | |
|---|---|
| AMB: | John Dinger |
| OMS: | Carole Akgun |
| DCM: | Mark Willis |
| POL: | Lynn Roche |
| CON: | Timothy P. Roche |
| ECO: | Laura Byergo |
| FMS: | Dale Kerksiek |
| GSO: | Kristi Hogan |
| IRM: | Anthony Weller |
| AID: | Edward Birgells |
| APHIS: | Dale Maki (resident in Beijing) |
| PC: | Ken Heldenfels |
| PAO: | Theresa Markiw |
| RSO: | James McWhirter (resident in Beijing) |
| DAO: | (Vacant) |
| FAA: | Elizabeth Keck (resident in Beijing) |
| IRS: | Stanley Beesley (resident in Tokyo) |
| DEA: | Thomas Ma (resident in Hong Kong) |

Last Modified: Wednesday, March 28, 2001

# MOROCCO

**Rabat (E),** 2 Ave. de Marrakech—PSC 74, Box 3, APO AE 09718, Tel [212] (3) 776-2265, Fax 776-5661, afterhours Tel 776-9639; PAO Tel 775-8181, Fax 775-0863; USAID 763,2001, Fax 763-2012. Internet address: http://www.usembassy-morocco.org.ma

| | |
|---|---|
| AMB: | Edward M. Gabriel |
| AMB OMS: | Lisa Williams |
| DCM: | Maureen E. Quinn |
| POL: | Robert M. Holley |
| ECO: | Richard G. Johnson |
| LAB: | Paul R. Malik (resident in Casablanca) |
| CON: | Evan G. Reade (resident in Casablanca) |
| ADM: | Christopher R. Riche |
| RSO: | Nanette A. Krieger |
| PAO: | Jack McCreary |
| COM: | Kathleen Kriger (resident in Casablanca) |
| IRM: | Lloyd Stevenson |
| AGR: | Quintin Gray |
| AID: | James Bednar |
| ODA: | Col. Richard H. Estes, USAF |
| ODC: | Col. Bradley Anderson, USA |
| IRS: | Frederick D. Pablo (resident in Paris) |
| FAA: | Anthony Fazio  (resident in Paris) |
| DEA: | Eugene Habib (resident in Paris) |

**Casablanca (CG),** 8 Blvd. Moulay Youssef—PSC 74, Box 24, APO AE 09718 (CAS), Tel [212] (2) 226-4550, Fax 220-8096; COM Fax 222-0259; PAO Tel 222-1460, Fax 229-9136; duty officer cellular Tel [212] (06) 113-40-65

| | |
|---|---|
| CG: | Nabeel A. Khoury |
| LAB/ECO: | Paul R. Malik |
| CON: | Evan G. Reade |
| ADM: | Lawrence F. Connell |
| IRM: | Naseem A. Ioane |
| PAO: | William B. Armbruster |

Last Modified: Monday, March 05, 2001

## MOZAMBIQUE

**Maputo (E),** Avenida Kenneth Kaunda 193—P.O. Box 783, Tel [258] (1) 49-27-97,Fax 49-01-14; Internet Address: ww.usembassy-maputo.gov.mz; USAID Tel 49-07-26, Fax 49-20-98.

| | |
|---|---|
| AMB: | Sharon Wilkinson |
| AMB OMS: | Carol R. Johnson |
| OCM: | Robert Loftis |
| ECO/POL: | Eric P. Whitaker |
| CON: | John Hickey |
| ADM: | Jonita Whitaker |
| RSO: | Paul W. Kennedy |
| IPO: | Stephen Widenhouse |
| RFMO: | Francis Conte (resident in Harare) |
| RMO: | Lawrence Hill (resident Pretoria) |
| RPO: | Cecelia K. Elkhatis (resident in Gaborone) |
| PC: | John Grabowski |
| AID: | Cynthia Rozell |
| DAO: | Bernard R. Sparrow |

Last Modified: Wednesday, November 08, 2000

## NAMIBIA

**Windhoek (E),** Ausplan Building, 14 Lossen St., Private Bag 12029 Ausspannplatz, Windhoek, Namibia, Tel [264] (61) 221-601, Fax 229-792. Website: www.usemb.org.na

| | |
|---|---|
| AMB: | Jeffrey A. Bader |
| AMB OMS: | Michele L. Willoughby |
| DCM: | Thurmond H. Borden |
| POL: | Joseph P. Cassidy |
| ECO/COM: | John E. Warner |
| CON: | Harmony E. Caton |
| ADM: | Michael A. Raynor |
| RSO: | Donald A. Schenck |
| GSO: | Judith W. Semilota |
| PAO: | Ruby M. Apsler |
| IRM: | Fredrick E. Ogg |
| B&F/PER: | R. Douglas Brown |
| AID: | Carole S. Scherrer-Palma |
| FACILITIES: | Jerry D. Pifer |
| FAA: | Ronald L. Montgomery (resident in Dakar) |
| ODA: | Lili D. Dawidowicz |
| AGR: | Richard Helm (resident in Pretoria) |
| LAB: | Frederick J. Kaplan (resident in Johannesburg) |
| IRS: | James P. Beene (resident in London) |
| DEA: | Larry W. Frye (resident in Pretoria) |

Last Modified: Thursday, November 09, 2000

## NEPAL

**Kathmandu (E),** Pani Pokhari, P.O. Box 295, Tel [977] (1) 411179, (Chancery); 270144 (USAID); and 415845 (Public Diplomacy); Fax: [977] (1) 419963 (Chancery); 272357 (USAID); and 415847 (Public Diplomacy).

| | |
|---|---|
| AMB: | Ralph Frank |
| AMB OMS: | Suzonne M. Woytovech |
| DCM: | Larry M. Dinger |
| POL/ECO: | John Dyson |
| POL/MIL: | Peter S. Sherman |
| ENV: | Deborah J. Seligsohn |
| CON: | Paul Cantrell |
| ADM: | Michael S. Hoza |
| RSO: | Kevin E. Wetmore |
| IPO: | Randal E. Meyers |
| PAO: | Robert C. Kerr |
| AID: | Joanne T. Hale |
| DAO: | Ltc. John M. Wilkinson, USA (resident in Dhaka) |
| SAO: | Maj. Richard B. White, USA (resident in New Delhi) |
| IRS: | Billy J. Brown (resident in Singapore) |
| FAA: | David L. Knudson (resident in Singapore) |

Last Modified: Thursday, November 09, 2000

## NETHERLANDS

**The Hague (E),** Lange Voorhout 102, 2514 EJ, The Hague—PSC 71, Box 1000, APO AE 09715, Tel [31] (70) 310-9209, Fax 361-4688; COM Fax 363-2985; POL/ECO Fax 31-70-310-9348; ADM Fax [31] (70) 3109-232

| | |
|---|---|
| AMB: | Cynthia P. Schneider |
| AMB OMS: | Janet Leane |
| DCM: | Reed Fendrick |
| POL: | Mary Daly |
| ECO: | Mark Tokola |
| COM: | Terry Sorgi, Acting |
| ADM: | Robert Wood |
| RSO: | Rebecca Dockery |
| PAO: | Angier Peavy |
| IRM: | Mari Jain Womack |
| APHIS: | Ken Nagata |
| DAO: | Capt. Derek Offer, USN |
| ODC: | Col. Paul Van Gorden |
| AGR: | Philip Letarte |
| FAA: | Joseph Teixera (resident in London) |
| IRS: | Margaret J. Lullo (resident in Berlin) |
| LAB: | Philip Kosnett |
| DEA: | David Borah |
| CWDEL: | Col. William Miller, USAF (Ret'd) |
| USIR: | Allen Weiner |
| LEGATT: | Sandra Fowler (resident in Brussels) |

**Amsterdam [CG],** Museumplein 19, 1071 DJ Amsterdam—PSC 71, Box 1000, APO AE 09715, Tel [31] (20) 5755 309, CG Fax 5755 310; COM Fax 5755 350

| | |
|---|---|
| CG: | Arnold Campbell |
| CON: | Cynthia Wood |
| COM: | Terry Sorgi |

Last Modified: Thursday, March 15, 2001

# NETHERLANDS ANTILLES

**Curacao (CG),** J.B. Gorsiraweg #1—P.O. Box 158, Willemstad, Curacao, Tel [599] (9) 461-3066, Fax 461-6489, Duty Tel 560-6870; DEA Tel 461-6985/560-2575/560-2573, Fax 461-3192. Internet address: info@amcongencuracao.an

| | |
|---|---|
| CG: | Barbara J. Stephenson |
| CG SEC: | Willem Remie |
| DEA: | Patrick P. Stenkamp |
| ADMIN ASST: | Dirk Dijkhuizen |
| VC: | Patricia Aguilera |
| CON ASST: | Saskia Rozier |
| RSO: | John Davis (resident in Caracas) |
| PAO: | [Vacant] |
| AGR: | Rod McSherry (resident in Caracas) |
| ATO: | Willis Collie (resident in Miami) |
| LEGATT: | Hector Rodriguez (resident in Caracas) |
| FAA: | Ruben Quinones (resident in Miami) |
| IRS: | Frederick Dulas (resident in Mexico City) |
| GSO: | Patricia Aguilera |

**Aruba [INS],** Queen Beatrix Airport, Oranjestad, Aruba, Tel. [297] (8) 31316, Fax 31665

| | |
|---|---|
| Port DIR: | Manny Garcia |

Last Modified: Thursday, March 01, 2001

# NEW ZEALAND

**Wellington (E),** 29 Fitzherbert Terr., Thorndon, Wellington—P.O. Box 1190, Wellington, PSC 467 Box 1, APO AP 96531-1001, Tel [64] (4) 472-2068, Fax 471-2380; ADM Fax 472-3478; EXEC Fax 472-3537. PAO internet address: http://usembassy.state.gov/wellington. POL internet address: amembpol@ihug.co.nz. GSO internet address: amembass@ihug.co.nz

| | |
|---|---|
| AMB: | Carol Moseley Braun |
| AMB OMS: | Pamela Loring |
| DCM: | Philip Wall |
| POL/ECO: | James A. Pierce |
| ADM: | Timothy W. Harley |
| COM: | Edward Cannon (resident in Auckland) |
| CON: | Eric N. Richardson |
| RSO: | Robert W. Starnes |
| PAO: | John T. Ohta |
| IRM: | Jorge Viscal |
| DAO: | Capt. Hartwell T. Trotter, Jr., USN |
| AGR: | David Young |
| DEA: | Gene Sugimoto (resident in Canberra) |
| FAA: | Bob Jensen (resident in Tokyo) |
| LEGATT: | Lou Caprino (resident in Canberra) |
| CUS: | [Vacant] (resident in Singapore) |
| IRS: | Billy J. Brown (resident in Singapore) |
| GSO: | Joseph Blais |

**Auckland [CG],** 3rd Fl., Citibank Center, 23 Custom St., East, (Corner of Commerce St.,) , Auckland; Private Bag 92022, Auckland 1—PSC 467, Box 1, APO AP 96531-1001, Tel [64] (9) 303-2724, Fax 366-0870; Internet address: amcongen@ihug.co.nz COM Tel [64] (9) 303-2038, Fax 302-3156; Internet address:auckland.office.box@mail.doc.gov

| | |
|---|---|
| CG: | Douglas M. Berry |
| COM: | Edward Cannon |

| | |
|---|---|
| POL: | Andrew Young |

Last Modified: Wednesday, March 14, 2001

# NICARAGUA

**Managua (E),** Km. 41/2 Carretera Sur.—APO AA 34021, Tel [505] (2) 66-2298, 666010, 666012-13, 666015-18, 666026-27, 666032-33; AMB Fax 669074; ADM Fax 663865; GSO Fax 666046; CON Fax 669943, ECO/COM Fax 669056; PAO Fax 663861; AGR Fax 667006; AID Fax 783828; DAO Fax 668022. Webpage: www.amemb.org.ni

| | |
|---|---|
| AMB: | Oliver. P. Garza |
| AMB OMS: | Patricia A. Brania |
| DCM: | Deborah A. McCarthy |
| POL: | Casey H. Christensen |
| ECO/COM: | Anthony J. Interlandi |
| ADM: | Robert D. Goldberg |
| CON: | Celio F. Sandate |
| RSO: | Frederick A. Byron |
| IRM: | Craig W. Specht |
| PAO: | Edward Loo |
| AID: | Marilyn Zak |
| DAO: | Ltc. Gerry G. Turnbow |
| PC: | Howard T. Lyon |
| DEA: | Joseph Petrauskas |
| AGR: | Charles R. Bertsch (resident in San Jose) |
| APHIS: | Dr. Alan Terrell |
| FAA: | Ruben Quinones (resident in Miami) |
| IRS: | Frederick Dulas (resident in Mexico City) |

Last Modified: Thursday, November 09, 2000

# NIGER

**Niamey (E),** rue Des Ambassades, B.P. 11201, Tel [227] 72-26-61 thru 4, afterhours Tel 72-31-41, Fax 73-31-67, Telex EMB NIA 5444 NI; INMARSAT line 011-874-154-1474; E-mail address: usemb@intnet.ne

| | |
|---|---|
| AMB: | Barbo A. Owens-Kirkpatrick |
| AMB OMS: | Judy R. Snyder |
| DCM: | Douglas Rohn |
| ECO/CON: | Matthew McKeever |
| ADM: | Carol L. Stricker |
| RSO: | Albert E. De Jong |
| PAO: | Louis P. Lantner |
| IPO: | Todd D. Roe |
| FAO: | Capt. Jason J. Turner |
| PC: | James Bullington |
| DAO: | Major Christopher Brown (resident in N'Djamena) |
| FSC: | Johnny Brown (resident in Abidjan) |
| RELO: | Robert Lindsey (resident in Dakar) |

Last Modified: Wednesday, January 03, 2001

# NIGERIA

**Abuja U.S. Embassy Office (E),** 9 Mambilla St., Off Aso Drive, Maitama District—P.O. Box 5760, Garki, Abuja, Tel [234] (9) 523-0960, 523-0916, 523-5857, Fax 523-0353.

| | |
|---|---|
| AMB: | Howard Jeter |
| AMB OMS: | Diane McBride |
| DCM: | Nancy M. Serpa |
| POL: | Kathleen Fitzgibbon |
| ECO: | Lawrence Cohen |
| COM: | Miguel P. de Zela |

| | |
|---|---|
| CON: | Ronald Robinson |
| ADM: | Alex Kirkpatrick |
| IRM: | Richard Carpenter |
| RSO: | Gary Gibson |
| RMO: | Dr. William Green |
| PAO: | Donald Bishop |
| AID: | Thomas Hobgood |
| DAO: | [Vacant] |
| FAA: | Ronald L. Montgomery (resident in Dakar) |
| FBI: | Weldon M. Burt |
| SAO: | [Vacant] |
| AGR: | David Rosenbloom |
| DEA: | Andre Kellum |
| LAB: | Nicholas J. Levintow |
| IRS: | Federick D. Pablo (resident in Paris) |

**Lagos (CG),** 2 Walter Carrington Crescent, Victoria Island, Lagos, Tel [234] (1) 261-0050, Fax 261-9856; CON Tel 261-1215; COM Tel 261-0241, Fax 261-1863; ADM Tel 261-1303; AID Tel 261-4621

| | |
|---|---|
| CG: | Charles N. Patterson, Jr. |
| CG OMS: | Roxie O. Gilmore |
| ADM: | Barbara J. Martin |
| CON: | Rafael P. Foley |
| POL/ECO: | John Bauman |
| PAO: | Timothy F. Smith |

Last Modified: Friday, February 16, 2001

# NORWAY

**Oslo (E),** Drammensveien 18, 0244 Oslo—PSC 69, Box 1000, APO AE 09707, Tel [47] (22) 44-85-50, Fax [47] (22) 44-33-63; ADM Tel [47] (21) 30-88-05, Fax [47] (22) 43-07-77; COM Tel [47] (21) 30-88-66, Fax [47] (22) 55-88-03; POL/ECO Tel [47] (21) 30-88-90, Fax [47] (22) 55-43-13; PAO Tel [47] (21) 30-85-94, Fax [47] (22) 44-04-36; DAO Tel [47] (21) 30-87-81, Tel [47] (21) 30-88-20, Unclassified fax [47] (22) 55-28-77, Unclassified fax [47] (22) 44-37-34; ODC Tel [47] (21) 30-86-60, Fax [47] (22) 44-98-92. Internet address: www.usa.no

| | |
|---|---|
| AMB: | Robin Chandler Duke |
| AMB OMS: | Sharon Sweeting |
| DCM: | Jon Gundersen |
| POL/ECO: | Pamela J. Pearson |
| COM: | James Koloditch |
| CON: | Glenn W. Carey |
| ADM: | Leo J. Hession, Jr. |
| RSO: | Bruce T. Mills |
| PAO: | Neil Klopfenstein |
| IRM: | Kenneth P. Knudsen |
| DAO: | Capt. John Evanoff II, USN |
| DEA: | Arthur L. Kersey (resident in Copenhagen) |
| ODC: | Col. Gregory J. Berlan, USAF |
| AGR: | Lana Bennett (resident in Stockholm) |
| LAB: | Raymond S. Dalland |
| FAA: | Joseph Teixeira (resident in London) |
| FAA/CASLO: | Walter Parks III (resident in Copenhagen) |
| IRS: | James P. Beene (resident in London) |
| FBI: | Robert Patton (resident in London) |
| FBU/SSA: | Barbara Wilson (resident in Frankfurt) |

Last Modified: Thursday, November 09, 2000

# OMAN

**Muscat (E),** P.O. Box 202, Code No. 115, Medinat Qaboos, Tel. [968] 698-989, afterhours Tel [968] 699-049; DAO Fax 699-779; ECA Fax 699-669; POL/ECO/COM Fax 604-316; OMC Fax 604-327; PAO Fax 699-771; Health Unit Fax 699-088. Workweek: Saturday through Wednesday, 8 am to 4:30 pm. Embassy internet address: aemctgnr@omantel.net.om. POL/ECO/COM internet address: aemcteco@gto.net.om. CON internet address: aemctcons@gto.net.om. PAO internet address: aemctlib@gto.net.om. Website address: http://www.usia.gov/posts/muscat/

| | |
|---|---|
| AMB: | John B. Craig |
| AMB OMS: | Maria Beck |
| DCM: | Gary A. Grappo |
| POL/ECO: | Bill Stewart |
| POL/MIL: | Mark Westfall |
| ECO/COM: | Uzra S. Zeya |
| CON: | Wendy Crook |
| ADM: | Lois A. Price |
| RSO: | Mike Hall |
| IRM: | David P. Jesser |
| PAO: | Richard M. Wilbur |
| DAO: | Col John Wahlquist |
| OMC: | Col Rodger Oetjen |
| ECA: | Ltc. Eric J. Brooks |
| FMO: | Jeff Hill |
| ATO: | Ronald P. Verdonk (resident in Dubai) |
| FAA: | Lynn Osmus (resident in Brussels) |
| LEGATT: | Bassem Youssef (resident in Riyadh) |
| ALAT: | Mark C. Sofia (resident in Riyadh) |
| DEA: | Robert Clark (resident in Islamabad) |

Last Modified: Tuesday, February 06, 2001

# PAKISTAN

**Islamabad (E),** Diplomatic Enclave, Ramna 5—P.O. Box 1048, Unit 62200, APO AE 09812-2200, Tel [92] (51) 2080-0000, Fax 2276427. Workweek: Monday thru Friday; internet address: isl@state.gov.

| | |
|---|---|
| AMB: | William B. Milam |
| AMB OMS: | Judy J. Copenhaver |
| DCM: | Michelle J. Sison |
| POL: | John R. Schmidt |
| ECO: | James S. Elliott |
| ADM: | W. Douglas Frank |
| CON: | David T. Donahue |
| RSO: | Martin T. Donnelly |
| IRM: | Kevin N. Bradshaw |
| AGR: | James R. Dever |
| PAO: | Lee J. Irwin |
| LOC: | James C. Armstrong |
| LEGATT: | Christopher Reimann |
| COM: | Amer M. Kayani |
| NAS: | Jon F. Danilowicz |
| REF: | Thomas J. Hushek |
| DEA: | Robert Clark |
| DAO: | Col. Herbert Stoddard, USAF |
| ODRP: | Col. Tod J. Wilson |
| IRS: | Billy J. Brown (resident in Singapore) |
| FAA: | David L. Knudson (resident in Singapore) |

**Karachi (CG),** 8 Abdullah Haroon Rd.—Unit 62400, APO AE 09814-2400, Tel [92] (21) 568-5170 thru 79, Fax 568-

0496; GSO Fax 568-3089. Workweek: Monday through Friday. Internet address: unconkh@cyber.net.pk

| | |
|---|---|
| CG: | John E. Bennett |
| CG SEC: | Jill McNeilly |
| POL: | Bruce R. Nelson |
| ECO: | Michael J. Mates |
| CON: | Tricia Cypher |
| ADM: | Edward D. Booth |
| RSO: | Randall D. Bennett |
| PAO: | Joseph J. Brennig |
| IRM: | Shannon G. Lankford |
| DEA: | Robert Clark (resident in Islamabad) |

**Lahore [C],** 50 Shahrah-e-Bin Badees Empress Rd., near Simla Hills—Unit 62216, APO AE 09812 -- 2216, Tel [92] (42) 6365530 thru 6365540, Fax 636-5177. Workweek: Monday through Friday. Internet address: amconsul@brain.net.pk

| | |
|---|---|
| PO: | Sheldon J. Rapoport |
| POL/CON: | Angela A. Bryan |
| PAO: | Bonnie S. Gutman |
| DEA: | Robert Clark (resident in Islamabad) |
| RSO: | Randy G. Crawford |

**Peshawar [C],** 11 Hospital Road, Peshawar Cantt—NWFP Unit 62217, APO AE 09812-2217, Tel [92] (91) 279801-803, 285496-497, Fax 276712. Workweek: Monday through Friday. Internet address: http://www.brain.net.pk/consul E-mail address: consul@brain.net.pk

| | |
|---|---|
| PO: | David J. Katz |
| PO SEC: | Cherisa K. Harwell |
| DPO/ADM: | Lawrence L. Hess |
| CON: | Roger T. Kenna |
| POL: | J. Peter McIllwain |
| RSO: | [Vacant] |
| IRM: | Lawrence J. Long |
| DEA: | Steven G. Dunn |
| NAS: | Robert M. Traister |

Last Modified: Tuesday, November 14, 2000

# PALAU

**Koror (E),** P.O. Box 6028, Republic of Palau 96940, Tel (680) 488-2920/2990, Fax 488-2911. E-mail address: usembassykoror@palaunet.com

| | |
|---|---|
| CHG: | Allen E. Nugent |
| DEA: | Joseph W. Hoban (resident in Guam) |
| FAA: | Barry Brayer (resident in Hawthorne, CA) |
| RSO: | Ronald M. Mazer (resident in Manilla) |

# PANAMA

**Panama City (E),** Apartado 6959, Panama 5, Rep. de Panama—Unit 0945, APO AA 34002, Tel [507] 207-7000, Fax 227-1964; GSO Fax 225-2720; PER Fax 227-6850

| | |
|---|---|
| AMB: | Simon Ferro |
| AMB OMS: | Yolanda Norvell |
| DCM: | Frederick A. Becker |
| POL/ECO: | W. Lewis Amselem |
| CON/GEN: | Robert J. Blohm |
| ADM: | Trevor A. Snellgrove |
| IRM: | Terrence K. Williamson |

| | |
|---|---|
| RSO: | Edward A. Lennon |
| PC: | Janice Jorgensen |
| APHIS: | Dr. John H. Wyss |
| ARS: | [Vacant] |
| FAS: | Charles R. Bertsch (resident in San Jose) |
| DEA: | Jay Bergman |
| ABMC: | Dannie Cooper |
| COM: | Richard F. Benson |
| PAO: | Joao M. Ecsodi |
| ICITAP: | [Vacant] |
| AID: | Lawrence J. Klassen |
| CUS: | Robert J. Benavente |
| IRS: | Frederick Dulas (resident in Mexico City) |
| FAA: | Victor Tamariz (resident in Miami) |
| DAO: | Col. David Bruening, USA |
| NAS: | Laura L. Livingston |
| ICITAP: | [Vacant] |
| LEGATT: | Gilbert C. Torrez |
| USCG: | Cdr. James Parker |
| INS: | John A. Mata |

**Cristobal, Colon (CA),** Panama Agencias Bldg., Terminal and Pedro Prestan Sts., Cristobal, Colon Province; No residential or office mail delivery in Colon. Send all mail to: c/o American Embassy, Panama, Box E, APO Miami 34002; Tel; (507) 41-2440/2478; Fax (507) 41-6039

| | |
|---|---|
| CA: | Frank X. Zeimetz |

Last Modified: Thursday, November 09, 2000

# PAPUA NEW GUINEA

**Port Moresby (E),** Douglas St.—P.O. Box 1492—Tel [675] 321-1455, Fax 321-3423; ADM Fax 320-0637

| | |
|---|---|
| AMB: | Arma Jane Karaer |
| AMB OMS: | Mary F. Roberts |
| DCM: | Alan B. Latimer |
| POL: | John Cushing |
| ECO/COM: | James C. Garry |
| CON: | Aaron Hellman |
| ADM: | Ken Miller |
| GSO: | Beryle Randall |
| ATO: | Dale Good (resident in Singapore) |
| RSO: | Marilyn Wanner |
| DAO: | Col. Charles Scaperotto, USAF (resident in Canberra) |
| FAA: | Bob Jensen (resident in Tokyo) |
| DEA: | Gene Sugimoto (resident in Canberra) |

Last Modified: Thursday, November 09, 2000

# PARAGUAY

**Asuncion (E),** 1776 Mariscal Lopez Ave., Casilla Postal 402—Unit 4711, APO AA 34036-0001, Tel [595] (21) 213-715, Fax 213-728

| | |
|---|---|
| AMB: | [Vacant] |
| AMB OMS: | Ann Granatino |
| CHG: | Stephen G. McFarland |
| POL: | David Lindwall |
| ECO/COM: | Richard Boly |
| CON: | Julie L. Grant |
| ADM: | Frank Ledahawsky |
| FMO: | James H. Basso |
| RSO: | William Vancio |
| IRM: | Michael W. Meyers |

| | |
|---|---|
| AID: | Wayne Tate |
| DAO: | Ltc. William G. Graves, USA |
| DEA: | Lewis R. Adams, Jr. |
| FBIS: | Nancy Johnson |
| NIMA: | John Tomasovichi |
| ODC: | Col. Ahmed E. Labault, USA |
| PAO: | James C. Dickmeyer |
| PC: | John McCloskey |
| AGR: | Philip Shull (resident in Buenos Aires) |
| FAA: | Santiago Garcia (resident in Miami) |
| IRS: | Frederick Dulas (resident in Mexico City) |

Last Modified: Thursday, November 09, 2000

# PERU

**Lima (E)**, Avenida Encalada, Cuadra 17, Monterrico, Lima—P.O. Box 1995, Lima 1, or American Embassy (Lima), APO AA 34031-5000, Tel [51] (1) 434-3000, Fax 434-3037, afterhours Tel 434-3032 (RNX: 549-0000 or 549 + four-digit ext.); RSO Fax 437-2012; AGR Fax 434-3043; APHIS Fax 434-3043; COM Fax 434-3041; PAO Fax 434-1299; DAO Fax 434-0117; DEA Fax 434-3054; MAAG Fax 434-1199; NAMRID Tel 561-2733, Fax 561-3042; NIMA Tel 475-1945, Fax 476-3618; USAID address: Av. Arequipa 351, Lima 1, Tel 433-3200, Fax 433-7034. Internet address: last name and initials of recipient@limawpoa.us-state.gov

| | |
|---|---|
| AMB: | John Hamilton |
| AMB OMS: | Maria D. Guillory |
| DCM: | Heather M. Hodges |
| CON: | Annette L. Veler |
| ADM: | James G. Williard |
| PAO: | Douglas M. Barnes |
| RSO: | Gordon A. Sjue |
| POL: | Arnold A.Chacon |
| ORA: | Robert E. Gorelick |
| ECO: | Krishna Urs |
| COM: | Andrew Wylegala |
| IRM: | Richard L. Gunn |
| AID: | Thomas Geiger |
| INS: | Michael E. Wojticki |
| DAO: | Col. Michael McCarthy, USAF |
| DEA: | Randy K. Sales |
| MAAG: | Col. Gilberto Perez |
| NAMRID: | Cdr. Trueman W. Sharp, USN |
| NAS: | Candis L. Cunningham |
| NIMA: | Eduardo Elinan |
| AGR: | Lawrence D. Fuell |
| APHIS: | Donald R. Wimmer |
| LAB: | Timothy Pounds |
| IRS: | Frederick Dulas (resident in Mexico City) |
| LEGATT: | Kevin Currier (resident in Santiago) |
| FAA: | Victor Tamariz (resident in Miami) |

**Cuzco (CA)**, Avenida Tullumayo 125, Tel. [51] (84) 24-5102, 23-9451, 22-4112, Fax 23-3541

| | |
|---|---|
| CA: | Olga Villagarcia |

Last Modified: Thursday, November 09, 2000

# PHILIPPINES

**Manila (E)**, 1201 Roxas Blvd., FPO AP 96515, Tel [63] (2) 523-1001, Telex 722-27366 AME PH, Fax [63] (2) 522-4361; COM Off 395 Senator Gil J. Puyat Ave., Makati City, Tel [63] (2) 890-9717, 890-9362, Fax [63] (2) 895-3028

| | |
|---|---|
| AMB: | Thomas C. Hubbard |
| AMB OMS: | [Vacant] |
| DCM: | Michael E. Malinowski |
| POL: | Aloysius M. O'Neill |
| ECO: | Terry A. Breese |
| CON: | John Caulfield |
| COM: | George Ruffner |
| ADM: | Raymond J. Pepper |
| GSO: | Elizabeth Hinson, Acting |
| RSO: | Ronald M. Mazer |
| PAO: | Greta N. Morris |
| IRM: | William K. Curry |
| AID: | Patricia K. Buckles |
| FAA: | David L. Knudson (resident in Singapore) |
| FAA/CASLO: | Richard W. Hyman |
| DAO: | Col. Robert Worthington, USAF |
| DEA: | Jeffrey L. Wendling |
| JUSMAG: | Col. Danwill A. Lee, USA |
| AGR: | Charles Alexander |
| LAB: | Richard W. Nelson |
| INS: | Harold E. Woodward |
| IRS: | Billy J. Brown (resident in Singapore) |

**Asian Development Bank (Manila)**, #6 ADB Avenue, 0401 Mandaluyong City, Metro Manila—P.O. Box 789, 0980 Manila, Tel [632] 632-6050, 632-4444; Telex 63587 ADB PN; 42205 ADB PM, and 29066 ADB PH; Fax 632-4003, 632-2084; COM ADB Off, 395 Senator Gil Puyat Ave., Makati, Metro Manila, Tel [632] 890-9364, 895-3020, Fax 890-9713

| | |
|---|---|
| US EXEC DIR: | Linda Tsao Yang |
| US ALT EXEC DIR: | N. Cinnamon Dornsife |
| COM/ADB: | Dennis Barnes |

**Cebu [CA]**, 3rd Fl., PCI Bank Bldg., Gorordo Avenue, Lahug, Cebu City 6000; FPO AP 96515; Tel. [63] (32) 311-261/2, 310-671; Fax 310-174

| | |
|---|---|
| CON AGT: | John Frank Domingo |

Last Modified: Thursday, November 09, 2000

# POLAND

**Warsaw (E)**, Aleje Ujazdowskie 29/31 00-054 Warsaw Pl—AmEmb Warsaw, Dept. of State, Washington, D.C., 20521-5010 (pouch address), Tel [48] (22) 628-3041, afterhours Tel 625-0055, 625-0133, 629-0638, or 629-3651, IVG Operator 628-0000; EXEC Fax [48] (22) 625-6731, IVG x2510; PC Tel 843-5011, Fax 843-4200; POL Fax 625-7710, IVG x2272; ECO Fax 625-7494, IVG x2528; CON Fax 627-4734, IVG x2542; ADM Fax 628-7431, IVG x2507; ISC Fax 625-6382; HR Fax 625-2400, IVG x2545; BUD/FISC Fax 625-3536, IVG x2539; GSO Fax 628-9326, IVG x2540; MED Fax 625-7518, IVG x2080; PAS Fax 621-6907; RSO Fax 627-2316; mailroom Fax 628-8298, IVG x2340; Telex 817771 Emusa Pl.

| | |
|---|---|
| AMB: | Christopher R. Hill |
| AMB OMS: | Linda Price |
| DCM: | Michael C. Mozur |
| POL: | Gerald C. Anderson |

| | |
|---|---|
| ECO: | Richard Huff |
| COM: | David Fulton |
| CON: | Patricia A. Butenis |
| ADM: | Andrea J. Nelson |
| HR: | Steven R. Slatin |
| GSO: | Marcia E. Cole |
| RSO: | Larry D. Salmon |
| IMO: | Robert Burkhart |
| ISO: | Janet A. Cote |
| PAO: | Cesar D. Beltran |
| DAO: | COL. Roy J. Panzarella |
| AGR: | James Higgiston |
| LAB: | Marc E. Norman |
| DEA: | Frederic J. Geiger (resident in Berlin) |
| FAA: | Dennis Cooper (resident in Brussels) |
| FAA/CASLO: | George D. Pfromm (resident in Brussels) |
| FAA/FSIDO: | Chris Glasgow (resident in Frankfurt) |
| IRS: | Margaret J. Lullo (resident in Berlin) |

**US Commercial Service** (Warsaw), Aleje Jerozolimskie 56C, Ikea Building, 2nd Fl., 00-803 Warsaw—Am Emb Warsaw, Dept. of State, 5010 Warsaw Pl., Wash., D.C., 20521-5010 (pouch address), Tel [48] (22) 625-4374, Fax 621-6327

| | |
|---|---|
| DIR: | David Fulton |

**Krakow [CG]**, Ulica Stolarska 9, 31043 Krakow—Am Con Gen Krakow, Dept. of State, 5040 Krakow Pl., Wash., D.C., 20521-5140 (pouch address), Tel [48] (12) 429-6655, Fax 421-8292

| | |
|---|---|
| CG: | Siria R. Lopez |
| POL/ECO: | Douglas J. Apostol |
| CON: | Timothy C. Sandusky |
| ADM: | Jefferson K. Dubel |
| BPAO: | Leslie High |

**Poznan [CA]**, Paderwskiego 7, 61-770, Poznan, Tel [48] (61) 851-8966, Fax 851-8516

| | |
|---|---|
| CA: | Urszula Dziuba |

Last Modified: Tuesday, December 19, 2000

# PORTUGAL

**Lisbon (E)**, Avenida das Forcas Armadas, 1600 Lisbon—PSC 83, APO AE 09726, Tel [351] (21) 727-3300, Fax [351] (21) 726-9109; FCS Fax [351] (21) 726-8914; PAO Fax [351] (21) 726-8814; FAS Fax [351] (21) 726-9721

| | |
|---|---|
| AMB: | Gerald S. McGowan |
| AMB OMS: | Carolyn P. Smith |
| DCM: | Kathleen Stephens |
| POL/ECO: | Dennis B. Hankins |
| COM: | Robert M. Shipley |
| ORA: | Robert Papp |
| CON: | Luis Espada-Platet |
| ADM: | Gary G. Bagley |
| RSO: | Thomas E. Stocking |
| PAO: | Jeffrey Murray |
| AGR: | Robert Wicks (resident in Madrid) |
| FAS: | Lloyd Fleck |
| DEA: | Yvette Torres (resident in Madrid) |
| SCI: | Marshall H. Carter-Tripp (resident in Madrid) |
| FAA: | Anthony Fazio (resident in Paris) |
| IRM: | Michael M. Chiaventone |
| DAO: | Col. Earl L. Hanson, USAF |

| | |
|---|---|
| IRS: | Frederick D. Pablo (resident in Paris) |
| ODC: | Capt. Roy A. Merrill, USAF |

**Ponta Delgada (C)**, Sao Miguel, Azores, Avenida Infante D Henrique—PSC 76, Box 3000, APO AE 09720-0002, Tel [351] 296-282216, Fax [351] 296-287216

| | |
|---|---|
| PO: | Bernice A. Powell |
| VC: | Marc H. Williams |

**American Business Center** (Oporto), Av. da Boavista, 3523, Sala 501, 4000 Porto—APO AE 09726, Tel [351] (2) 618-6607, Fax [351] (2) 618-6625

| | |
|---|---|
| DIR: | Robert Shipley (resident in Lisbon) |

**Funchal (CA)**, Edificio Infante, Bloco B, 4 Andar, Apt. B, Rua Tenente Coronel Sarmento, 9000 Funchal, Tel [351] (91) 743-429; Fax [351] (91) 743-808

| | |
|---|---|
| CA: | Antonio D. Borges |

Last Modified: Tuesday, March 27, 2001

# QATAR

**Doha (E)**, 22 February Road, Doha, Qatar (P.O. Box 2399), Tel [974] 884-101; EXEC ASST Tel [974] 884-367, Fax 884-150; DCM Tel 884-068; CON Tel 884-020; POL/MIL Tel 884-161; POL Tel 884-137; ADM Tel 884-164, Fax 884-298; RSO Tel 884-067; PAO Tel 884-105; E/COMM Tel 884-220; IRM Tel 884-223. Workweek: Saturday thru Wednesday

| | |
|---|---|
| AMB: | Elizabeth D. McKune |
| EXEC ASST: | Jean Atkinson |
| DCM: | Matthew Tueller |
| CON: | Kevin Kabumoto |
| POL/MIL: | James Vail |
| POL: | Steven Butler |
| ADM: | Bonnie Bissonette |
| RSO: | Jeffrey C. Breed |
| ECO/COM: | David Hinkle |
| PAO: | Aleta Wenger |
| IRM: | Juan Bacerra |
| ATO: | Ronald Verdonk (resident in Dubai) |
| IRS: | Margaret J. Lullo (resident in Berlin) |
| FAA: | Lynn Osmus (resident in Brussels) |
| USLO: | Ltc. Brian Kerins, USAF |
| DAO: | Cmd. George Zimmerman, USN |
| RMO: | Dr. Scott Kennedy (resident in Riyadh) |
| DEA: | Robert Clark (resident in Islamabad) |

# ROMANIA

**Bucharest (E)**, Strada Tudor Arghezi 7-9—Pouch: American Embassy Bucharest, Department of State, Washington, D.C. 20521-5260, Tel [40] (1) 210-4042, emergency afterhours 210-0149, Fax 210-0395, EXEC Fax 212-3604, CON Tel 210-4042, Fax 211-3360; AID Tel [40] (1) 336-8851, Fax 312-0508; AGR Tel 210-4042, Fax 210-0395; GSO Tel 211-5658, Fax 210-5567; Peace Corps Tel 312-1289, Fax 312-3004; Public Diplomacy Information Resources B&F/PER ext. 262; CON ext. 270 CLO ext. 256; GSO ext. 777; IRM ext. 229; MED ext. 211; PD ext. 888; POL/ECO ext. 205; RSO ext. 249; AID ext. 444; DAO ext.

240; FSC ext. 350; RLA ext. 254. Internet address: http://www.usembassy.ro

| | |
|---|---|
| AMB: | James C. Rosapepe |
| AMB OMS: | Rose Stafiej |
| DCM: | Susan Johnson |
| POL/ECO: | Carolyn Johnson |
| COM: | Jeremy Keller |
| CON: | Stephen Pattison |
| ADM: | Ronna S. Pazdral |
| RSO: | Nace Crawford |
| IRM: | Harry Moore |
| AID: | Denny Robertson |
| DAO: | Col. Robert Veale, USAF |
| PAO: | Stephan Strain |
| PC: | Ken Ayars |
| RLA: | Charles Lewis |
| AGR: | Holly Higgins (resident in Sofia) |
| FAA: | Steven B. Wallace (resident in Rome) |
| IRS: | Margaret J. Lullo (resident in Berlin) |

**Cluj-Napoca** (BO), International address US Branch Office, Universitatii 7-9, Etage 1, Cluj-Napoca, Romania 3400, Tel [40] (64) 19-38-15, Fax 19-38-68

| | |
|---|---|
| PO: | [Vacant] |

Last Modified: Thursday, November 09, 2000

# RUSSIA

**Moscow (E),** Bolshoy Devyatinckiy Pereulok No. 8, 121099 Moscow, Russian Federation—PSC-77, APO AE 09721, Tel [7] (095) 728-5000, Fax 728-5090, emergency after hours Tel 728-5025, USAID Tel 728-5262, Fax 960-2141/2, PAO Tel 728-5067, PAO Cultural 728-5242, PAO Press 728-5131, PAO Fax 728-5203, RIMC Tel 728-5656, Fax 728-5003, CONS Tel 728-5217, Fax 728-5358.

| | |
|---|---|
| AMB: | James F. Collins |
| AMB EXEC ASST: | Cynthia Doell |
| DCM: | John M. Ordway |
| POL: | George Krol |
| ECO: | A. Daniel Weygandt |
| COM: | Stephan Wasylko |
| CON: | Laura Clerici |
| ADM: | Richard Kramer |
| RSO: | John Rendeiro |
| PAO: | Alexander Almasov |
| IMO: | Lawrence Krause |
| EST: | Deborah Linde |
| AID: | Carol Peasley |
| DAO: | Brig. Gen. Frank Klotz |
| PC: | Timothy Douglas |
| AGR: | Geoffrey Wiggin |
| ATO: | Robert Walker |
| FAA: | Dennis B. Cooper (resident in Brussels) |
| IRS: | Margaret J. Lullo (resident in Bonn) |
| INS: | Donald Monica |
| VOA: | Pete Heinlein |
| NASA: | Dennis McSweeney, Acting |
| DOE: | Cynthia Lersten |
| LES: | Karen Aguilar |
| RIMC: | Randy Kreft |
| TREAS: | Brian Cox |
| LAB: | Karen Enstrom |
| DOJ: | Michael Pyszczymuka |
| CUST: | Michael Woodworth |

**U.S. Foreign Commercial Service** (Moscow), 23/38 Bolshaya Molthanovka, 121069 Moscow, Russian Federation, Tel [7] (095) 737-5030, Fax 737-5033, e-mail moscow.office.box@mail.doc.gov

| | |
|---|---|
| DIR: | [Vacant] |

**St. Petersburg [CG],** Furshtadtskaya Ulitsa 15, 191028, St. Petersburg, Russia—PSC 78, Box L, APO AE 09723, Tel [7] (812) 275-1701, afterhours Tel 274-8692, Fax 110-7022; GSO Fax 275-3295; ADM Fax 275-4735. E-mail address: usa.consulate@cltele.com

| | |
|---|---|
| CG: | Paul Smith |
| DPO: | Michael Klecheski |
| CG SEC: | Caryn Solomon |
| POL/ECO: | Kathleen Morenski |
| COM: | Michael Richardson |
| CON: | Robin Morritz |
| ADM: | Douglas Ellrich |
| GSO: | Vangala S. Ram |
| RSO: | David Hall |
| BPAO: | Thomas M. Leary |
| IM-IPO: | Harry Chamberlain |

**U.S. Foreign Commercial Service**, American Consulate General, 25 Nevskiy Prospect, St. Petersburg, 191186 Russia, Tel [7] (812) 326-2560, Fax 326-2561PAO- The American Center, Millionnaya Ulitsa 5/1, 191186 St. Petersburg, Tel [7] (812) 311-8905 or 325-8050, Fax 325-8052

**Vladivostok [CG],** Ulitsa Pushkinskaya 32, Vladivostok, Russia, 690001—Pouch address: AmConGen Vladivostok, Dept. of State, Washington, D.C. 20521-5880, Tel [7] (4232) 30 – 00 – 70 (Note: if calling from the U.S., and the U.K., dial 7-501-4232), 30 – 00 – 72, Fax (7) (4232) 26-02-48 (if faxing from the U.S. or U.K.: (7-501) (4232) 26-02-48); CON Fax 30 – 00 – 91 (if faxing from the U.S. or U.K.: (7-501) (4232) 30 – 00 – 91); COM Tel 30 – 00 – 93, Fax 30-00-92; PAO Tel 26 – 70 – 17, Fax 30 – 00 – 95 (if faxing from the U.S. or U.K., (7-501) (4232) 30 – 00 – 95); FCS Tel. 30 – 00 – 93, Fax 30 – 00 – 92, Peace Corps Tel 22-11-31, Fax 49-69-23

| | |
|---|---|
| CG: | Lysbeth J. Rickerman |
| POL/ECO: | [Vacant] |
| ADM: | James Doty |
| CON: | Elizabeth K. Thompson |
| RSO: | Karen R. Schaeffer |
| BPAO: | [Vacant] |
| PC: | Valerie Ann Ibaan |

**Yekaterinburg [CG],** Ulitsa Gogolya 15A—P.O. Box 400, 620151 Yekaterinburg, AmConGen Yekaterinburg, Dept. of State, Wash., D.C., 20521-5890, Tel [7] (3432) 564-619, 564-691, 629-888; COM 564-736; CON 564-744; PAO 564-760; Fax [7] (3432) 564-515. E-mail: uscgyekat(at sign)gin.ru; website: www.uscgyekat.ur.ru

| | |
|---|---|
| CG: | James Bigus |
| POL/ECO/COM: | Scott Hamilton |
| ADM: | James Leaf |
| CON: | Andrew L. Flashberg |
| BPAO: | Kimberly G. Hargan |

Last Modified: Thursday, December 28, 2000

# RWANDA

**Kigali (E),** Blvd. de la Revolution, B.P. 28, Int'l (250) 75601/2/3, (250) 72126, (250) 77147, Fax 419-710-9346; IRM direct INMARSAT 873-150-7503, Fax (250) 72128, 7:30 am-5:30 pm, afterhours, contact will be AMB res, 83219; DCM res. 75314; POL 75632; ECON 77228; IRM 73501; USAID Tel 74719, (250) 73251/52/53; USAID Fax 73950, DIR res. 75981; PAO-same number as Embassy. Internet address: amembkigali@hotmail.com

| | |
|---|---|
| AMB: | George M. Staples |
| AMB OMS: | Diana Kniazuk |
| DCM: | Donald W. Koran |
| POL: | Ronald N. Capps |
| ECO/COM/CON: | Beth A. Payne |
| ADM: | Salvatore Piazza |
| RSO: | William I. Mellott |
| PAO: | Ergibe A. Boyd |
| IRM: | James A. Harrison |
| GSO: | Charles G. Chandler |
| AID: | Richard H. Goldman |
| DAO: | Maj. Richard W. Skow, USA |
| FAA: | Ronald L. Montgomery (resident in Dakar) |
| RETO: | Melvia Hansen (resident in Dakar) |
| IRS: | Frederick Pablo (resident in Paris) |
| DEA: | Robert Shannon (resident in Cairo) |

Last Modified: Thursday, April 05, 2001

# SAMOA

**Apia (E)**—P.O. Box 3430, Apia, Tel [685] 21-631, afterhours Tel 23-617, Fax 22-030. Mobile Tel [685] 7-1776. Internet address: usembassy@samoa.net

| | |
|---|---|
| AMB: | Carol Moseley-Braun (resident in Wellington) |
| CHG: | William Warren |
| RSO: | Kim Starke (resident in Canberra) |
| DAO: | Capt. J. Jeffrey Langer, USN (resident in Wellington) |

# SAUDI ARABIA

**Riyadh (E),** Collector Road M, Riyadh Diplomatic Quarter or American Embassy, Unit 61307, APO AE 09803-1307, international mail: P.O. Box 94309, Riyadh 11693, Tel 966 (1) 488-3800, Fax 488-7360; PAO address: P.O. Box 94310, Riyadh 11693, Fax 488-3989; COM Fax 488-3237; POL/ECO Fax 488-3278; RSO Fax 488-7867; FMC Fax 482-2765; GSO Fax 488-7939; ATO Tel 488-4364, ext. 1560, Fax 482-4364; ISC Fax 488-7867; ADM/HR Fax 488-7765; workweek: Saturday – Wednesday

| | |
|---|---|
| AMB: | Wyche Fowler, Jr. |
| AMB OMS: | Deborah Burns |
| DCM: | Charles Brayshaw |
| POL: | Marc J. Sievers |
| POL/MIL: | Frederick W. Axelgard |
| ECON: | Alice A. Dress |
| COM: | Charles Kestenbaum |
| CON: | Tom Furey |
| ADM: | Lawrence Blackburn |
| RSO: | William Lamb |
| PAO: | Rick Roberts |
| IRM: | Leo Bourne |
| FAA: | Lynn Osmus (resident in Brussels) |
| DAO: | Col. Bernard J. Dunn |
| ATO: | Quintin Gray |
| USMTM: | Maj. Gen. Silas R. Johnson, Jr. |
| FIN: | Leticia Macapinlac |
| OPMSANG: | BG Buford C. Blount |
| IRS: | Larry J. LeGrand (resident in Rome) |
| DEA: | Robert O. Shannon (resident in Cairo) |
| LEGATT: | Wilfred Rattigan |

**Dhahran [CG],** Between ARAMCO HdQtrs and King Abdulaziz Airbase—P.O. Box 38955, Dhahran (Doha) 31942 or Unit 66803, APO AE 09858-6803, Tel [966] (3) 330-3200; ADM Fax 330-2123; COM Fax 330-2190; CON Fax 330-6816; EXEC Fax 330-0464; GSO Fax 330-3296; workweek Saturday through Wednesday

| | |
|---|---|
| CG: | Marc Desjardins |
| OMS: | Phyllis DeSmet-Howard |
| RAO: | Donald Hepburn |
| ECON: | Andrew Boyd |
| COM: | Nasir Abbasi |
| CON: | Ann O'Barr-Breedlove |
| ADM: | Jewellene Wilson |
| IRM: | Eric Schaffner |
| RSO: | Richard C. Ober |

**Jeddah [CG],** Palestine Rd., Ruwais—P.O. Box 149, Jeddah 21411, or Unit 62112, APO AE 09811, Tel [966] (2) 667-0080, Fax 669-2991; ADM Fax 669-3074; CON Fax 669-3078; COM Tel 606-2479, Fax 606-2567; ATO Tel 661-2408, Fax 667-6196; PAO Tel 660-0080, Fax 660-6367; workweek: Saturday through Wednesday

| | |
|---|---|
| CG: | Richard Baltimore |
| CG SEC: | Catheline Garrity |
| POL/ECON: | Michael Snowden |
| COM: | David Rundell |
| CON: | Art Mills |
| RSO: | Laurie Darlow |
| ADM: | William S. Holden |
| PAO: | Geraldine Keener |
| IRM: | Kirol Barbour |
| ATO: | Quintin Gray (resident in Riyadh) |
| FAA/CAAG: | John Waltz |
| USGS: | Ronald Worl |
| USMTM: | Maj. Peter Ahl |

U.S. Representative to the Saudi Arabian U.S. Joint Commission on Economic Cooperation (USREP/-JECOR), P.O. Box 5927, Riyadh, Tel [966] (1) 248-3471, ext. 263, Fax 248-3471, ext. 857

| | |
|---|---|
| DIR: | George A. Matter |

Last Modified: Thursday, November 09, 2000

# SENEGAL

**Dakar (E),** B.P. 49, Avenue Jean XXIII, Tel [221] 823-4296 or 823-7384, Fax 822-2991; PAO Tel 823-1185 or 823-8124; AID Tel 823-5880, 823-1602, 823-6680, Fax 823-2965, Telex 21793 AMEMB SG, Fax 822-2991; E-mail user last name and initials, i.e. doejt@state.gov

| | |
|---|---|
| AMB: | Harriet L. Elam-Thomas |
| AMB OMS: | Ruth Walker |
| DCM: | Terence McCulley |
| POL: | Deborah Malac |
| ECO: | Tim Forsyth |

| | |
|---|---|
| RCON: | Ann Gordon |
| ADM: | Mark Stevens |
| RSO: | George G. Frederick |
| PAO: | Chris Datta |
| IRM: | Susan Hullinger |
| ODC: | Maj. Robert Gaddis |
| RMO: | Dr. Nancy Manahan |
| AID: | Donald Clark |
| DEA: | Edgar L. Moses (resident in Lagos) |
| RIG: | Henry Barrett |
| DAO: | Ltc Todd Coker, USMC |
| AGR: | Bruce Zanin (resident in Abidjan) |
| IPO: | Isis M. Ortiz |
| FAA: | Edward Jones |
| LAB: | Anthony C. Newton (resident in Washington, D.C.) |
| RELO: | Robert Lindsey |
| IRS: | Frederick D. Pablo (resident in Paris) |

Last Modified: Wednesday, January 03, 2001

# SEYCHELLES (See Mauritius)

# SIERRA LEONE

**Freetown (E),** corner of Walpole and Siaka Stevens Sts., Tel [232] (22) 226-481 through 226-485, AMB Tel 226-155, DCM Tel 227-192, Fax 225-471

| | |
|---|---|
| AMB: | Joseph H. Melrose, Jr. |
| EXEC SEC: | [Vacant] |
| DCM: | Cheryl A. Martin |
| POL/ECO/GSO: | Maria Brewer |
| CON: | Marlee K. Anderson |
| RCON: | Reginald J. McHugh (resident in Accra) |
| ADM: | Robert B. Houston |
| RSO: | Richard Ingram |
| PAO: | Patricia L. Sharpe |
| IRM: | Mark A Brewer |
| LAB: | [Vacant] (resident in Washington, D.C.) |
| DAO: | Ltc. William Watson III, USN (resident in Dakar) |
| IRS: | James P. Beene (resident in London) |
| FAA: | Ronald L. Montgomery (resident in Dakar) |
| DEA: | Edgar L. Moses (resident in Lagos) |

Last Modified: Wednesday, April 18, 2001

# SINGAPORE

**Singapore (E),** 27 Napier Rd., Singapore 258508—PSC Box 470, FPO AP 96534-0001, Tel [65] 476-9100, Fax 476-9340. Internet home page address: http://www.usembassyingapore.org.sg.

| | |
|---|---|
| AMB: | Steven J. Green |
| AMB OMS: | Virginia Ann Crawford |
| DCM: | Herbert W. Schulz |
| ECO/POL: | Douglas G. Spelman |
| ADM: | James A. Forbes |
| PAO: | Thomas D. Gradisher |
| IMO: | Jeffrey R. Hill |
| GSO: | Peter W. Drew |
| CON: | Kevin L. Richardson |
| RMO: | Dr. Michael E. Nesemann |
| RPSO: | Paula B. Compton |
| RSO: | Wayne E. May |
| ATO: | Bonnie Borris (resident in Kuala Lumpur) |

| | |
|---|---|
| COM: | Jonathan M. Bensky |
| CUS: | Robert F. Tine |
| LEGATT: | Pedro Rubio, Jr. |
| DAO: | Capt. Carlton E. Soderholm |
| ODC: | Col. Robert C. McAdams |
| DEA: | Michael J. Ferguson |
| FAA: | [Vacant] |
| FAA/CASIFO: | Wilson E. Fisher |
| FAA/CASLO: | Steven J. Tochterman |
| FAA/IFO: | David E. Hegy |
| INS: | Mario R. Ortiz |
| IRS: | Billy J. Brown |
| USCG: | Lamberto D. Sazon |

**FAA,** Changi Airport Terminal 2, South Finger, 4th Fl.,—Unit No. 048-006/009, Singapore, FAA Tel [65] 543-1466, Fax 543-1952; IFO Tel 545-5822, Fax 545-9772; CASIFO/CASLO Tel 545-8077, Fax 545-2318

**AGR/ATO,** 541 Orchard Road,—Unit No. 15-03. Liat Towers, Singapore 238881, Tel [65] 737-1233, Fax 732-8307:

**LEGATT c/o American Embassy,** PSC 470, FPO AP 96507. Tel [65] 750-2404, Fax 750-2075USCG USCG Midet Singapore, PSA Sembawang Wharves.

Last Modified: Thursday, November 09, 2000

# SLOVAK REPUBLIC

**Bratislava (E),** Hviezdoslavovo Namestie 4, 81102 Bratislava (int'l address), Tel [421] (7) 5443-3338, ADM Fax 5441-5148; CONS Tel 5443-3338, GSO Fax 5922-3044, CONS Fax 5441-8861, POL Tel 5922-3343, POL/ECO Fax 5443-0096. Internet address: www.usis.sk

| | |
|---|---|
| AMB: | Carl Spielvogel |
| AMB OMS: | Yvonne DeRuiz |
| DCM: | Douglas C. Hengel |
| POL: | Michael Martin |
| ECO: | Mark Bocchetti |
| ADM: | Sarah Solberg |
| CON: | Sara E. Potter |
| PAO: | Gregory John Orr |
| GSO: | Mona Kuntz |
| IRM: | Joyce Clark |
| DAO: | Ltc. Peter Brigham, USA |
| PC: | Philip Stantial |
| COM: | Joseph Kaesshaefer (resident in Vienna) |
| RSO: | Rob Myers |
| FAA: | Steven B. Wallace (resident in Rome) |
| DEA: | Alfred A. Alexander (resident in Moscow) |
| AGR: | Allan Mustard (resident in Vienna) |
| CUS: | Peter Liston (resident in Vienna) |
| LEGATT: | Eliska Tretera (resident in Prague) |
| INS: | William Griffin (resident in Vienna) |
| IRS: | Margaret J. Lullo (resident in Berlin) |

Last Modified: Thursday, March 22, 2001

# SLOVENIA

**Ljubljana (E),** Presernova 31, 1000 Ljubljana or —7140 Ljublijana Place Dept. of State, Washington, D.C. 20521-7140, Tel [01] 200-5000, Fax 200-5555; PAO address: Fax 426-4284. Email address: Email@usembassy.si

| | |
|---|---|
| AMB: | Nancy H. Ely-Raphel |
| AMB OMS: | Hulya Kilgore |
| DCM/SEP: | Trevor J. Evans |
| ADM: | John M. Lipinski |
| POL: | Edmond E. Seay III |
| ECO: | Douglas E. Sonnek |
| CON: | Patricia L. Endresen |
| PAO: | William J. Millman |
| IRM: | Arthur T. Day |
| COM: | Patrick C. Hughes (resident in Zagreb) |
| RSO: | Todd R. Ziccarelli |
| DAO: | Ltc. Keith R. Laverty, USA |
| AGR: | Robert Curtis (resident in Vienna) |
| DEA: | Kevin Scully (resident in Vienna) |
| FAA: | Dennis Cooper (resident in Brussels) |
| IRS: | Fred D. Pablo (resident in Paris) |
| GSO: | Leslie C. Schaar |
| ODC: | Maj. Kelly A. Ziccarello |

Last Modified: Thursday, January 04, 2001

# SOUTH AFRICA

**Pretoria (E),** 877 Pretorius St., Arcadia 0083—P.O. Box 9536, Pretoria 0001, Tel [27] (12) 342-1048, Fax 342-2244; PAO Tel 342-3006, Fax 342-2090; AID Tel 323-8869, Fax 323-6443

| | |
|---|---|
| AMB: | Delano E. Lewis, Sr. |
| AMB OMS: | Marilynne Bonner |
| DCM: | John M. Blaney |
| DCM OMS: | Kim Carlin |
| POL: | Marguerita Ragsdale |
| ECO: | Robert F. Godec |
| COM: | Johnnie Brown |
| CON: | Sharyl Brower |
| ADM: | Steven R. Buckler |
| RSO: | William L. Adams |
| MNL: | James F. Freund |
| IRM: | Raymond C. Langston |
| PAO: | Thomas N. Hull |
| CUS: | Forrest Ward, Acting |
| EST: | W. Brent Christensen |
| AID: | Stacey Rhodes |
| FAA: | Edward Jones (resident in Dakar) |
| DAO: | Col. Richard D. Rider, USAF |
| LEGATT: | Robert H. Wright |
| AGR: | Richard Helm |
| IRS: | James P. Beene (resident in London) |
| DEA: | Larry W. Frye |
| RMO: | Dr. Lawrence N. Hill |
| USSS: | Paul M. Price |

**Cape Town [CG],** Broadway Industries Center, Heerengracht, Foreshore, Cape Town 8001, P.O. Box 6773, Roggebaai 8012, Tel [27] (21) 421-4280 thru 90, ADM/GSO Fax 418-1989; CG/POL/RSO Fax 421-1230; CON Fax 425-3014; COM/FCS Fax 421-4269; PUBLIC AFFAIRS SECTION Fax 425-2536.

| | |
|---|---|
| CG: | Stephen J. Nolan |
| DPO: | Mary B. Leonard |
| COM/FCS: | Robert Farris |
| CON: | Tina D. Stixrude |
| IPO: | Martin H. Myers |
| ADM: | Alan D. Troxel |
| RSO: | Thomas Colin |
| PAO: | Louis Mazel |

**Durban [CG],** 2901 Durban Bay House, 333 Smith St., Durban 4001, Tel [27] (31) 304-4737, Fax 301-8206; COM Tel 304-4737, Fax 301-0577

| | |
|---|---|
| CG: | Craig L. Kuehl |
| ADM/CON: | Joshua D. Glazeroff |
| COM: | Henry S. Richmond |
| PAO: | Amelia Broderick |

**Johannesburg (CG)** B>1 River Street—corner of Riviera, Killarney—P.O. Box 1762, Houghton, 2041, Tel [27] (11) 644-8000, Fax 646-6913; COM Tel 778-4800, Fax 442-3770; PAO Tel 838-2231, Fax 838-3920; SCO Tel 778-4800, Fax 442-3770. E-mail address: amcongen.jhb@pixie.co.za

| | |
|---|---|
| CG: | Sue F. Patrick |
| CG SEC: | Terri L. Tedford |
| COM: | Johnnie Brown |
| CON: | Mary Sue Conaway |
| ADM: | Amy Pitts |
| IRM: | Jeffrey Koch |
| INS: | Phyllis Coven |
| PAO: | Matthew McGrath |
| LAB: | Frederick J. Kaplan |
| SCO: | William Center |
| RSO: | Tedd Archabal |

Last Modified: Wednesday, April 04, 2001

# SPAIN

**Madrid (E),** Serrano 75, 28006 Madrid—PSC 61, APO AE 09642, Tel [34] (1) 91587-2200, Fax 91587-2303. Inward dial (DID) numbers: AMB [34] 91587-2201; DCM 91587-2205; POL 91587-2387; ECO 91587-2286; ADM 91587-2208; IRM 91587-2308; DAO 91587-2278; PAO 91587-2502; DEA 91587-2280; FAA 91587-2300; ODC 91549-1339; CON 91587-2236; B&F 91587-2211; PER 91587-2226; RSO 91587-2230; IRM duty phone 91587-2355; EMB duty phone 619-276-782; Duty Officer Cell 609-373-385. Internet address: http://www.embusa.es

| | |
|---|---|
| AMB: | Edward L. Romero |
| AMB OMS: | Maria DeLourdes Fernandez |
| DCM: | Heather M. Hodges |
| POL: | Michael Butler |
| COM: | Michael Liikala |
| ECO: | Stephen V. Noble |
| CON: | Philip French |
| ADM: | Cathy T. Chikes |
| RSO: | Stanley J. Joseph |
| IRM: | Nicodemo Romeo |
| PAO: | Pamela Corey-Archer |
| AGR: | Robert Wicks |
| LAB: | Colin M. Cleary |
| EST/SCI: | Laura A. Lochman |
| DAO: | Capt. John B. Gregor, USN |
| DEA: | Yvette Torres |
| ODC: | Col. Jere S. Medaris, US Army |
| FAA: | Kurt Edwards  (resident in Paris) |
| FAA/CASLO: | Mike Galvan |
| FAA/CAAG: | Miriam Santana |
| LEGATT: | Eduardo Sanchez |
| IRS: | Frederick Pablo (resident in Paris) |
| NASA: | Ingrid Desilvestre |
| DCMC: | Maj. Stephen C. Smith |
| INS: | Kent Johansson |

**Barcelona [CG],** Paseo Reina Elisenda de Moncada 23, 08034 Barcelona—PSC 61, Box 0005, APO AE 09642, Tel [34] (93) 280-2227, Fax (93) 205-5206; ADM Fax (93) 205-7764; PAO Fax (93) 205-5857; COM Fax (93) 205-7705

| | |
|---|---|
| CG: | Douglas R. Smith |
| COM: | Louis Santamaria |
| CON/ADM: | Marc J. Meznar |
| PAO: | Deborah Glassman |
| IBB: | Rodney A. Nelson |

**La Coruna [CA],** Canton Grande, 6-8E, 15003; Tel. [34] 981213-233; Fax [34] 981228 808

| | |
|---|---|
| CA: | Marcelino Fuentes- Ramos |

**Las Palmas [CA],** Los Martinez De Escobar, 3 Oficina 7-35007, Tel 34-928-271 259, Fax 34-928-22-58-63

| | |
|---|---|
| CA: | Ana Maria Quintana-Figueroa |

**Fuengirola (Malaga) (CA),** Avenida Juan Gomez "Juanito", 8, Edificio Lucia 1C Fuengirola, 29640 Malaga, Tel. 34-952-47-48-91, Fax 34-952-46-51-89

| | |
|---|---|
| CA: | Roberta G. Aaron |

**Palma de Mallorca (CA),** Avenida Jaime II, No. 26, Entresuelo H-1 07012; Tel. 34-971-725051, Fax 34-971-71-87-55

| | |
|---|---|
| CA: | Bartolome Bestard |

**Seville [CA],** Paseo de las Delicias, 7 Seville, 41012, Tel. 34-95-42 31885, Fax 34-95-42 32040

| | |
|---|---|
| CA: | Jerry Lee Johnson |

**Valencia [CA],** Dr. Romagosa, 1, 2, J, 46002 Valencia; Tel. 34-96-351-6973, Fax 34-96-352-9565

| | |
|---|---|
| CA: | Mary A. Garrity |

Last Modified: Thursday, November 09, 2000

# SRI LANKA

**Colombo (E),** 210 Galle Road, Colombo 3 - P.O. Box 106 Tel [94] (1) 448007; Main Fax 437345; CONSULAR Fax 436943; ADMIN Fax 471091; USAID 44 Galle Rd, Colombo 3, Tel 472855; Fax 472850; PUBLIC AFFAIRS 44 Galle Rd, Colombo 3, Tel 421270; Fax 449070; IBB (Formerly VOA) Tel 032-55931/32; Fax 032-55822.

| | |
|---|---|
| AMB: | Shaun E. Donnelly |
| DCM: | Lewis Amselem |
| POL: | Andrew C. Mann |
| ECO: | Thomas A. Cadogan |
| COM/LAB: | Ian M. Sheridan |
| CON: | William M. Howe |
| ADM: | Long N. Lee |
| RSO: | Stephen V. Wright |
| PAO: | Stephen W. Holgate |
| DAO: | Ltc. Frank L. Rindone |
| AID: | [Vacant] |
| IBB: | Gary Wise |
| IMO: | Russell F. Himmelsbach |
| FAA: | David L. Knudson (resident in Singapore) |
| FAS: | Weyland Beeghly (resident in New Delhi) |

| | |
|---|---|
| IRS: | Billy J. Brown (resident in Singapore) |

Last Modified: Thursday, November 09, 2000

# SUDAN

**Khartoum (E),** Sharia Ali Abdul Latif—P.O. Box 699, APO AE 09829, Tel [249] (11) 774611 or 77-47 – 00, Fax [249] (11) 774137, Telex 22619 AMEM SD, Fax (873) (151) 6770

| | |
|---|---|
| AMB: | [Vacant] |
| AMB OMS: | Linda Clark |
| CHG: | Donald Teitelbaum |
| ADM: | Bruce Knotts |
| CON: | Roger Pierce (resident in Cairo) |
| PAO: | [Vacant] |
| LAB: | Ralph D. Anske (resident in Nairobi) |
| FAA: | Ronald L. Montgomery (resident in Dakar) |
| DEA: | Robert Shannon (resident in Cairo) |

Last Modified: Thursday, November 09, 2000

# SURINAME

**Paramaribo (E),** Dr. Sophie Redmondstraat 129—P.O. Box 1821, AmEmbassy Paramaribo, Dept. of State, Washington, D.C., 20521 – 3390, Tel [597] 472900, 477881, 476459; AMB 478300; DCM 476507; IRM 476793; GSO Fax 479829; AMB Fax 420800; ADM Fax 410972. Internet address: embuscen@sr.net

| | |
|---|---|
| AMB: | Dennis K. Hays |
| AMB OMS: | Carol Virginia Oakley |
| DCM: | Arnold H. Campbell |
| POL/ECO: | Martha L. Campbell |
| CON: | Eric A. Fichte |
| ADM: | Russell W. Jones |
| ECO/COM: | Robin D. Diallo |
| GSO: | Matthew G. Johnson |
| RSO: | Howard A. Hicks (resident in Georgetown) |
| PAO: | David A. Bustamante (resident in Port-of-Spain) |
| DAO: | Maj. Frank P. Wagdalt, USA |
| PC: | Edward Stice |
| IRM: | Alfred F. Begin |
| AGR: | Shawn R. McSherry (resident in Caracas) |
| FAA: | Victor Tamariz (resident in Miami) |
| LAB: | Terrence Daru (resident in Bridgetown) |
| LEGATT: | Hector Rodriguez (resident in Caracas) |
| DEA: | Patrick P. Stenkamp (resident in Curacao) |
| IRS: | Frederick Dulas (resident in Mexico City) |

Last Modified: Thursday, November 09, 2000

# SWAZILAND

**Mbabane (E),** 7th Fl., Central Bank Bldg., Warner Street—P.O. Box 199, Mbabane, Swaziland, Tel [268] 404-6441/5, Fax [268] 404-5959 E-mail address: usemb-swd@realnet.co.sz

| | |
|---|---|
| AMB: | Gregory Johnson |
| AMB OMS: | Marva L. Long |
| DCM: | Katherine J. Millard |
| POL/ECO/CON: | Thomas Jung |
| IRM: | Marv Adams |
| PAO: | Bruce A. Lohof |
| GSO: | Ellen Langston |

| | |
|---|---|
| RSO: | Paul Kennedy (resident in Maputo) |
| FAA: | Ronald L. Montgomery (resident in Dakar) |
| AGR: | Richard Helm (resident in Pretoria) |
| DAO: | Col. Richard D. Rider, USAF (resident in Pretoria) |
| LAB: | Frederick J. Kaplan (resident in Johannesburg) |
| IRS: | James P. Beene (resident in London) |
| DEA: | Larry W. Frye (resident in Pretoria) |

Last Modified: Wednesday, February 28, 2001

# SWEDEN

**Stockholm (E),** Dag Hammarskjölds Väg 31, S-115 89 Stockholm, Sweden—pouch address: AmEmb Stockholm, Dept. of State, Wash, D.C. 20521-5750, Tel [46] (8) 783-5300, Fax (46) (8) 661-1964; AMB OMS Tel 783-5314; afterhours Tel 783-5310; CON Fax 660-5879; COM: Fax 660-9181; AGR: Fax 662-8495; PAO Fax 665-3303; DAO Fax 662-8046

| | |
|---|---|
| AMB: | Lyndon L. Olson, Jr. |
| AMB OMS: | Carolyn Gough |
| DCM: | Gillian M. Milovanovic |
| POL: | Jack M. Zetkulic |
| ECO: | Bruce E. Carter |
| COM: | Thomas M. Kelsey |
| CON: | Linda M. Brown |
| ADM: | Martha L. Campbell |
| GSO: | Mark R. Brandt |
| RSO: | Kurt E. Olsson |
| PAO: | Viktor Sidabras |
| IRM: | Russell LeClair |
| DAO: | Capt. Michael D. Andersen, Acting |
| FAA: | Joseph Teixera (resident in London) |
| AGR: | Lana Bennett |
| IRS: | James P. Beene (resident in London) |
| DEA: | Arthur L. Kersey (resident in Copenhagen) |

Last Modified: Friday, February 16, 2001

# SWITZERLAND

**Bern (E),** Jubilaumsstrasse 93, 3005 Bern, Tel [41] (31) 357-7011, Fax 357-7344; Telex (845) 912603, AMB Tel 357-7259; DCM Tel 357-7258; POL/ECO Tel 357-7424; ADM Tel 357-7295; PAO Tel 357-7238, Fax 357-7379; IRM Tel 357 – 7201; RSO Tel 357-7296; DEA Tel 357-7367, Fax 357-7253; DAO Tel 357-7244, Fax 357-7381; AGR Tel 357-7279, Fax 357-7363; LEGATT Tel 357-7340, Fax 357-7268; CON Fax 357-7398; FCS Fax 357-7336; COM Fax 357-7336. Embassy website: www.usembassy.ch

| | |
|---|---|
| AMB: | J. Richard Fredericks |
| EXEC OMS: | Sonja Seitamo |
| DCM: | George Glass |
| POL/ECO: | Dennis J. Ortblad |
| COM: | Michael Keaveny |
| CON: | Cassius C. Johnson |
| ADM: | Jeffrey A. VanDreal |
| AGR: | Kenneth Roberts (resident in Geneva/USTR) |
| RSO: | John Davis |
| PAO: | Mary Ellen Koenig |
| IRM: | Ricardo E. Diez De Medina |
| DAO: | Col. Stefan Aubrey, USA |

| | |
|---|---|
| DEA: | David Michael |
| LEGATT: | Herbert Cohrs |
| IRS: | Frederick D. Pablo (resident in Paris) |
| FAA: | Anthony Fazio (resident in Paris) |
| RMO: | Bruce T. Miller, MD. (resident in Frankfurt) |

**US Mission to the European Office of the UN and Other International Organizations** (Geneva), Mission Permanente Des Etats-Unis, Route de Pregny 11, 1292 Chambesy-Geneva, Switzerland, Tel [41] (22) 749-4111, Fax 749-4880, Amb. Tel 749-4300, Fax 749-4892; DCM Tel 749-4302; PSA (POL) Tel 749-4621; IAEA (ECON) Tel 749-4629, Fax 749-4883; RMA Tel 749-4617, Fax 4671; LEGATT: 749-4460; ADM Tel 749-4391, Fax 749-4491; PAO Tel 749-4360, Fax 749-4314; RSO Tel 749-4397; LAB Tel 749-4624; IRM Tel 749-4306

| | |
|---|---|
| CM: | George E. Moose |
| EXEC ASST: | [Vacant] |
| DCM: | James B. Foley |
| IEA [ECO]: | Michael Meigs |
| PSA [POL]: | John Long |
| RMA: | Linda Thomas-Greenfield |
| LEGATT: | Michael Peay |
| EST: | Lynette Poulton |
| ADM: | Warrington E. Brown |
| PAO: | John D. Hamill |
| RSO: | Jeremy S. Zeikel |
| LAB: | Robert S. Hagen |
| IRM: | M. Audrey Anderson |
| IMO: | Peter Jensen |

**US Trade Representative (USTR),** Botanic Bldg., 1-3 Avenue de la Paix, 1202 Geneva, Switzerland, Tel [41] (22) 749-4111, Fax 749-5308

| | |
|---|---|
| CM: | Rita Derrick Hayes |
| DCM: | Andrew L. Stoler |
| COM: | David Nicholson |
| AGR: | Kenneth Roberts |

**US Delegation to the Conference on Disarmament (CD),** U.S. Mission Bldg., Route de Pregny 11, 1292 Chambesy-Geneva, Tel [41] (22) 749-4407, Fax 749-4833

| | |
|---|---|
| US REP: | Robert T. Grey, Jr. |
| REP SEC: | Maria J. King |
| DEP REP: | Katherine C. Crittenberger |
| EXEC SEC: | John H. King |
| DOE REP: | [Vacant] |
| JCS REP: | [Vacant] |
| OSD REP: | [Vacant] |
| STATE REP: | [Vacant] |

**Geneva [CA],** 11 route de Pregny, 1292 Chambesy/Geneva, Tel [41] (22) 798-1605, Fax 798-1630

| | |
|---|---|
| CA: | Mary P. Genoud |
| RMO: | Bruce T. Miller, MD. (resident in Frankfurt) |

**Zurich (CA),** Dufourstrasse 101, 8008 Zurich, Tel [41] (01) 422-2566, Fax 383-9814

| | |
|---|---|
| CA: | Ellen Bruckmann |

Last Modified: Thursday, April 05, 2001

# SYRIA

**Damascus (E),** Abou Roumaneh, Al-Mansur St., No. 2—P.O. Box 29, Damascus, Syria, Tel [963] (11) 333-1342, Fax 224-7938; 24 hours: 333-3232; PAO Tel 333-1878, 333-8413, Fax 332-1456; CON Fax 331-9678

| | |
|---|---|
| AMB: | Ryan C. Crocker |
| AMB OMS: | Betty L. McNaughton |
| DCM: | David D. Pearce |
| DCM OMS: | Suan Hamric |
| POL: | Lisa Carle |
| ECO/COM: | Daniel H. Rubinstein |
| CON: | Roberto Powers |
| ADM: | Paul G. Churchill |
| RSO: | George Tietjen |
| PAO: | Stephen A. Seche |
| IRM: | Norman R. McKone |
| DAO: | LTCOL Timothy Grimmett |
| AGR: | Thomas Pomeroy (resident in Cairo) |
| FAA: | Steven B. Wallace (resident in Rome) |
| IRS: | Margaret J. Lullo (resident in Berlin) |
| DEA: | Perry Felecos (resident in Nicosia) |
| IMO: | Robert King |

Last Modified: Wednesday, December 13, 2000

# TAIWAN

Unofficial commercial and other relations with the people of Taiwan are conducted through an unofficial instrumentality, the American Institute in Taiwan, which has offices in Taipei and Kaohsiung. AIT Taipei operates an American Trade Center, located at the Taipei World Trade Center. The addresses of these offices are:

# TAJIKISTAN

**Dushanbe (E),** Dushanbe in Almaty, Kazakhstan: 531 Seyfullin St., Tel 7(3272)58-79-61, Fax 7(3272)58079-68, IVG (through Embassy Almaty) 8-927-0000. Dushanbe in Dushanbe, Tajikistan: 10 Pavlova St., Tel: 992(372)21-03-48, Fax 992(372)21-03-62. Internet address: amemb@usis.td.silk.org

| | |
|---|---|
| AMB: | Robert P.J. Finn (resident in Almaty) |
| AMB OMS: | [Vacant] |
| DCM: | James A. Boughner |
| POL/ECO/CON: | Gregory M. Marchese (resident in Almaty) |
| ADM: | [Vacant] |
| RSO: | James R. Callaway |
| DAO: | Maj. David Brigham USA |

Last Modified: Thursday, March 01, 2001

# TANZANIA

**Dar Es Salaam (E),** 140 Msese Road, Kinondoni District—P.O. Box 9123, Tel [255] (22) 2666010/1/2/3/4/5, Telex 41250 USA TZ; Fax 2666701. Internet address: usembassy-dar2@cats-net.com

| | |
|---|---|
| AMB: | [Vacant] |
| AMB OMS: | Victoria Q. Spiers |
| CHG: | Wanda L. Nesbitt |
| POL/ECO: | Michael G. Heath |
| COM: | Colin Green |
| CON: | Charles S. Smith |
| ADM: | Paul A. Folmsbee |

| | |
|---|---|
| RSO: | Jeffery W. Culver |
| IPO: | John E. Combs |
| PAO: | Dudley O. Sims |
| RAO: | Christopher Bane |
| CDC: | Cheryl Scott |
| AGR: | Fred Kessel (resident in Nairobi) |
| LAB: | Ralph D. Anske (resident in Nairobi) |
| DOD: | Major James P. Sweeney |
| AID: | Lucretia Taylor |
| FAA: | Edward Jones (resident in Dakar) |
| PC: | Joel Wallach |
| RRC: | Randy Berry (resident in Kampala) |

Last Modified: Wednesday, April 04, 2001

# THAILAND

**Bangkok (E),** 120 Wireless Rd.—APO AP 96546, Tel [66] (2) 205-4000, Fax 205-4131; COM 3rd Fl., Diethelm Towers Bldg., Tower A, 93/1 Wireless Rd., 10330, Tel 255-4365 thru 7, Fax 255-2915

| | |
|---|---|
| AMB: | Richard E. Hecklinger |
| AMB OMS: | Jennifer V. Texeira |
| DCM: | Marie T. Huhtala |
| POL: | Eric C. Sandberg |
| ECO: | Robert W. Fitts |
| COM: | Karen L. Ware |
| CON: | Alice C. Moore |
| ADM: | Kathleen V. Hodai |
| GSO: | Gerald L. Hanisch |
| RSO: | John P. Gaddis |
| PAO: | Virginia L. Farris |
| IRM: | David M. Yeutter |
| NAS: | Donald E. Stader |
| FSC: | Howard A. Renman |
| REF: | Jeffrey Rock |
| LAB: | William Weinstein |
| DAO: | Col. E. Lauderdale, USAF |
| EST: | James C. Martin |
| JUSMAG: | Col. Lance Booth |
| JTF/FA: | Ltc. Jeffrey E. Smith |
| CDC/HIV: | Timothy D. Mastro |
| CUS: | Scott A. Davis |
| INS: | Jean Christiansen |
| DEA: | William Simpson, Jr. |
| LEGATT: | Ralph P. Horton |
| AGR: | Maurice House |
| FAA: | David L. Knudson (resident in Singapore) |
| FAA/CASLO: | George B. Brennan |
| IRS: | Billy J. Brown (resident in Singapore) |

**Chiang Mai (CG),** 387 Vidhayanond Rd., Chaing Mai 50300—U.S. Embassy, Box C, APO AP 96546, Tel [66] (53) 252-629, Fax 252-633

| | |
|---|---|
| PO: | Thomas Murphy |
| ADM: | Karen L. Emmerson |
| POL/CON: | Miguel A. Ordonez |

Last Modified: Thursday, November 09, 2000

# TOGO

**Lome (E),** rue Pelletier Caventou and rue Vauban, B.P. 852, Tel [228] 21-29-91/4; AMB/DCM/ECO 21-53-91; ADM/B&F/GSO 21-79-52; CON 22-70-89; PAO 21-77-94;

Internet Addresses: PAO: lomepas@pd.state.gov; Chancery: ustogo1@cafe.tg;

| | |
|---|---|
| AMB: | Karl W. Hofmann |
| AMB OMS: | Diane G. Mooney |
| DCM: | William Fitzgerald |
| ECO/COM: | Jennifer Rasamimanana |
| POL/CON: | Matthew Rosenstock |
| ADM: | Kay Crawford |
| RSO: | Jerald Barnes |
| PDO: | Jeffrey Robertson |
| IPO: | Joellis Smith |
| FAA: | Edward Jones (resident in Dakar) |
| PCD: | Miguel Reabold |
| DAO: | Col. Daniel W. Pike, USA (resident in Abidjan) |
| FMS: | Matt Jennings (resident in Accra) |
| IRS: | Frederick D. Pablo (resident in Paris) |
| GSO: | Hughes Ogier |

Last Modified: Wednesday, December 20, 2000

# TRINIDAD AND TOBAGO

**Port-of-Spain (E),** 15 Queen's Park West—P.O. Box 752, Tel (868) 622-6372/6, 6176, Fax 628-5462; EXEC OFF Fax 628-8134; ECO/COM Fax 622-2444

| | |
|---|---|
| AMB: | Edward E. Shumaker III |
| AMB OMS: | Shirley Habib |
| DCM: | David C. Stewart |
| POL: | Imre Lipping |
| ECO/COM: | Albert Nahas |
| CON: | Richard Sherman |
| ADM: | Cherie Jackson |
| IPO: | Robert L. Browning |
| RSO: | Alan Sheely |
| GSO: | John McIntyre |
| PAO: | Gonzalo Gallegos |
| COM: | Carol Kim (resident in Santo Domingo) |
| AGR: | Rod McSherry (resident in Caracas) |
| DAO: | Ltc. John L. Churchill, USA (resident in Bridgetown) |
| DEA: | Gary Davis |
| LAB: | Terrence Daru Zabriskie (resident in Bridgetown) |
| IRS: | Richard Lee |
| FAA: | Ruben Quinones (resident in Miami) |

Last Modified: Wednesday, November 08, 2000

# TUNISIA

**Tunis (E),** 144 Ave. de la Liberte, 1002 Tunis-Belvedere, Tel [216] (1) 782-566, Fax 789-719; USATO Fax 785-345; CON Fax 788-923; FSI Tel 741-672 or 746-991, Fax 741-062; GSO Tel 707-166 or 715-785, Fax 715-735; PAO Tel 799-895, 789-800, 798-833, Fax 789-313; DAO Fax 794-677; ODC Fax 788-609; AGR Fax 785-345

| | |
|---|---|
| AMB: | [Vacant] |
| AMB OMS: | [Vacant] |
| CHG: | Joseph D. Stafford |
| POL/ECO: | Susan W. Zelle |
| COM: | Edward V. O'Brien |
| CON: | Thomas E. Cairns |
| ADM: | Judith A. Chammas |
| RSO: | Christian J. Schurman |

| | |
|---|---|
| PAO: | David A. Queen |
| IMO: | Raymond W. Horning |
| ISO: | David M. Mueller |
| FSI: | Adnan A. Siddiqi |
| AGR: | Merritt Chesley (resident in Rabat) |
| ODC: | Col. Michael Blatti |
| DAO: | Col. Roger S. Bass II, USA |
| IRS: | Frederick D. Pablo (resident in Paris) |
| FAA: | Kurt H. Edwards (resident in Paris) |
| ABMC: | Fred M. Rhodes |
| LAB: | Mary T. Curtin |

Last Modified: Tuesday, December 19, 2000

# TURKEY

**Ankara (E),** 110 Ataturk Blvd.—PSC 93, Box 5000, APO AE 09823, Tel [90] (312) 468-6110, Fax 467-0019; ADM/ECO Fax 468-6138; GSO Fax 467-0057; PER Fax 467-8847; POL Fax 468-4775; CON Fax 468-6131; PAO Tel 468-6102 thru 6106; PAO EXEX OFF Fax 467-3624 and 468-6145; AGR Fax 467-0056; COM Fax 467-1366. Internet address: http://www.usis-ankara.orgt.tr.

| | |
|---|---|
| AMB: | Mark R. Parris |
| AMB OMS: | Mary C. Jorgenson |
| DCM: | James F. Jeffrey |
| POL: | Gene B. Christy |
| POL/MIL: | Stuart V. Brown |
| ECO: | Madelyn Spirnak |
| COM: | John D. Breidenstine |
| CON: | Jacqueline Ratner |
| RAO: | Terry Percival |
| ADM: | Arthur F. Salvaterra |
| GSO: | Kimberlee Fordyce-App |
| RSO: | Rosa E. Trainham |
| IRM: | Harold E. Spake |
| PAO: | Helena K. Finn |
| AGR: | Susan Schayes |
| LAB: | Dorothy A. Delahanty |
| DAO: | Col. James M. Carlin, USAF |
| EX/IM: | Julie Panaro |
| ODC: | Mg. R. J. Mike Boots |
| FAA: | Steven B. Wallace (resident in Rome) |
| TDA: | Deborah Forhan |
| IRS: | Larry LeGrand (resident in Rome) |
| DEA: | Lex Henderson |
| OPIC: | Peter Ballinger |

**Istanbul [CG],** 104-108 Mesrutiyet Caddesi, Tepebasi, 80050 Istanbul, Turkey—PSC 97, Box 0002, APO AE 09827-0002, Tel [90] (212) 251-3602, Fax 251-3218; ADM Fax 251-3632; CON Fax 252-7851; DEA Fax 251-5213; FAS Fax 243-5262; FCS/COM Fax 252-2417; GSO Fax 251-2554; PAO Fax 252-7986. Web site address: http://www.usisist.org.tr

| | |
|---|---|
| CG: | Frank C. Urbanic |
| CG SEC: | Karen L. Nickel |
| POL: | Gregory D. Fukutomi |
| ECO: | Juan A. Alsace |
| COM: | James M. Fluker |
| CON: | Gary L. Sheaffer |
| ADM: | Mary L. Schertz |
| RSO: | John C. Taylor |
| PAO: | Mary Ann Whitten |

| | |
|---|---|
| IRM: | Donald L. Greer |
| DEA: | Russell Benson |

**Adana [C],** Ataturk Caddesi—PSC 94, APO AE 09824, Tel [90] (322) 459-1551, Fax 457-6591. Website address: http://www.usconadana.org.tr

| | |
|---|---|
| PO: | Stuart E. Jones |
| POL/ECO: | Charles O. Blaha |
| ADM/CON: | Mark M. Cameron |

**Izmir [CA],** PSC 88, Box 5000, APO AE 09821, Tel [90] (232) 441-0072 and 441-2203; Fax 441-2373; COM: c/o Izmir Chamber of Commerce, Ataturk Caddesi 126, Kat 5, 35210 Pasaport, Izmir, PSC 88 Box 5000, APO AE 09821, Tel 441-2446, Fax 489-0267

| | |
|---|---|
| CA: | Jale Kaptaner |
| COM: | Berrin Erturk |

Last Modified: Thursday, December 28, 2000

# TURKMENISTAN

**Ashgabat (E),** 9 Puskin Street, Tel [9] (9312) 35-00-45, 35-0 0-42, 51-13-06, tie line 962-0000, Fax 51-13-05, tie line 962-2159

| | |
|---|---|
| AMB: | Stephen R. Mann |
| OMS: | Robert Durham |
| DCM: | Eric Schultz |
| POL/ECO: | Eileen Kropf |
| ADM: | Sarah Penhune |
| IRM: | Ronald M. Grider. |
| CON: | Alexander Kasanof |
| AGR: | Susan Schayes (resident in Ankara) |
| RSO: | Paul R. Pettit |
| GSO: | Doug Dykhouse |
| DAO: | Maj. Kurt H. Meppen |
| FAA: | Dennis B. Cooper (resident in Brussels) |
| IRS: | Margaret J. Lullo (resident in Berlin) |
| DEA: | Lex Henderson (resident in Ankara) |

Last Modified: Thursday, March 01, 2001

# UGANDA

**Kampala (E),** Parliament Ave.—P.O. Box 7007, Tel [256] (41) 259792/3/5, Fax 259794; ADM Tel 234142, Fax 341863; PAO Tel 233231, Fax 250314; AID Tel 235879, Fax 233417

| | |
|---|---|
| AMB: | Martin G. Brennan |
| AMB OMS: | [Vacant] |
| DCM: | Donald Teitelbaum |
| POL: | Randy Berry |
| COM: | Donald L. Brown |
| CON: | Helen Johnston |
| ADM: | Herbert L. Treger |
| AGR: | Fred Kessel (resident in Nairobi) |
| GSO: | Gloria J. Junge |
| RSO: | Raymond Bassi |
| PAO: | Virgil D. Bodeen |
| IRM: | Vella Wells |
| AID: | Dawn Liberi |
| FAA: | Ronald L. Montgomery (resident in Dakar) |
| LAB: | Ralph D. Anske (resident in Nairobi) |
| IRS: | James P. Beene (resident in London) |

| | |
|---|---|
| DAO: | Maj. Mark R. Ellington |
| DEA: | Robert Shannon (resident in Cairo) |

Last Modified: Monday, November 20, 2000

# UKRAINE

**Kiev (E),** 10 Yuria Kotsubynskoho, 2..54053 Kiev 53, Tel [380] (44) 490-4000, afterhours Tel 216-3805, Fax 244-7350; PAO Tel 213-2532, Fax 213-3386; USAID Tel 462-5678, Fax 462-5834; COM Tel 417-2669, Fax 417-1419; PC Tel 220-1183; AGR Tel 417-1268

| | |
|---|---|
| AMB: | Carlos E. Pascual |
| AMB OMS: | Mary Ann Lucey |
| DCM: | David M. Hess |
| DCM OMS: | Ruth Underwood |
| POL: | Kathleen A. Kavalec |
| ECO: | Kenneth Fairfax |
| COM: | David W. Hunter |
| CON: | Lauren H. Marcott |
| ADM: | Bohdan Dmytrewycz |
| RSO: | Vida M. Gecas |
| IRM: | Dennis L. Severns |
| PAO: | Mark Taplin |
| AGR: | James Higgiston (resident in Warsaw) |
| FAA: | Dennis Cooper (resident in Brussels) |
| DAO: | Col. Robert W. Hughes, USAF |
| PC: | Karl Beck |
| AID: | Christopher Crowley |
| ODC: | Major John Kershaw |
| RLA: | Walter R. Sulsynsky |
| ATRA: | Maj. Gregory Wright |
| DEA: | Alfred A. Alexander (resident in Moscow) |
| LEGATT: | Mark Jimerson |
| IRS: | Margaret J. Lullo (resident in Berlin) |

Last Modified: Tuesday, November 28, 2000

# UNITED ARAB EMIRATES

**Abu Dhabi (E),*** Al-Sudan St.—P.O. Box 4009, Pouch: AmEmbassy Abu Dhabi, Dept. of State, Washington, D.C. 20521-6010, Tel [971] (2) 443-6691 or 443-6692, afterhours Tel 443-4457, Fax 443-4771; ADM Fax 443-5441; CON Fax 443-5786; PAO Fax 443-4802; USLO Fax 443-4604; COM: Blue Tower Bldg., 8th Fl., Sheikh Khalifa Bin Zayed St., Tel 273-666, Fax (2) 271-377, workweek: Saturday – Wednesday. Internet address: usembabu@emirates.net.ae*Note: Neither post has access to APO/FPO.
AMB:Theodore H. Kattouf

| | |
|---|---|
| AMB OMS: | Donna L. Millet |
| DCM: | Deborah Jones |
| POL: | Stephanie Williams |
| ECO: | Thomas Williams |
| COM: | Nancy Charles-Parker |
| CON: | Charles Glatz |
| ADM: | Ernest J. Parkin |
| RSO: | John F. Rooney |
| PAO: | Katherine Van DeVate |
| ATO: | Ronald Verdonk |
| IRM: | Mark J. Davis |
| DAO: | Col. Michael E. Vrosh |
| USLO: | Col. Bruce Deane |
| IRS: | Larry LeGrand (resident in Rome) |

FAA:    Lynn Osmus (resident in Brussels)
LEGATT:    Bassem Youssef (resident in Riyadh)
DEA:    Robert Clark (resident in Islamabad)

**Dubai (CG),*** Dubai World Trade Center, 21st Fl.—P.O. Box 9343, Pouch AMCONGEN Dubai, Dept. of State, Washington, D.C., 20521-6020, Tel [971] (4) 3313-115, Fax 3314-043; COM Tel 3313-584, Fax 3313-121; PAO Tel 3314-882, Fax 3314-254; ATO Tel 3313-612/3314-063, Fax 3314-998; NRCC Tel 3311-888, Fax 3315-764, workweek: Saturday – Wednesday. Internet E-mail address: max@emirates.net.ae

| | |
|---|---|
| CG: | Thomas C. Krajeski |
| ADM: | Daniel F. Romano |
| RSO: | Mike S. Zupan |
| COM: | John Lancia |
| CON: | Mary E. Earl |
| ATO: | Ronald P. Verdonk |
| POL/MIL: | Joseph Forcier |
| NCIS: | Randy Hughes |
| NRCC: | Lcdr. Joseph Russell |

Last Modified: Wednesday, January 31, 2001

# UNITED KINGDOM

**London, England (E),** 24/31 Grosvenor Sq., W1A 1AE—PSC 801, Box 40; FPO AE 09498-4040, Tel [44] (020) 7499-9000; ECO Fax [44] (20) 7409-1637; COM/FCS Fax [44] (20) 7408-8020; CONS Fax [44] (20) 7495-5012; ADM Fax [44] (20) 7629-9124. Website: www.usembassy.org.uk

| | |
|---|---|
| AMB: | [Vacant] |
| AMB OMS: | [Vacant] |
| CHG: | Glyn T. Davies |
| POL: | Morton R. Dworken |
| ECO: | Peter H. Chase |
| COM: | David Katz |
| COM rep to the EBRD: | Gene Harris |
| CON: | Wayne G. Griffith |
| ADM: | Lee R. Lohman |
| RSO: | Tony R. Bell |
| PAO: | Pamela H. Smith |
| IMO: | Jane S. Norris |
| SCI: | Alyce J. Tidball |
| INS: | Edward H. Skerrett |
| DAO: | Capt. Stewart R. Barnett III |
| ODC: | Col. Joseph Niemeyer |
| AGR: | Thomas A. Hamby |
| LAB: | George S. Dragnich |
| JUS/CIV: | James A. Gresser |
| CUS: | John Martinez, Jr. |
| DEA: | Michael J. McManamon |
| FAA: | Joseph Teixeira |
| FAA/CASLO: | Elizabeth Mullikin |
| FAA/IFO: | Tony Kijek |
| FIN: | Louellen Stedman |
| SAO: | Barbara McNamara |
| USSS: | Glen S. Colvin |
| IRS: | J. Paul Beene |
| FBI: | A. Lance Emory |

**Belfast, Northern Ireland (CG),** Queen's House, 14 Queen St., BT1 6EQ—PSC 801, Box 40, FPO AE 09498-4040, Tel [44] (2890) 328-239, Fax [44] (2890) 248-482

| | |
|---|---|
| CG: | Jane Benton Fort |

| | |
|---|---|
| CON: | Nicholas Manring |
| POL/ECO: | Eric Green |

**Edinburgh, Scotland (CG)** B>3 Regent Ter. EH7 5BW—PSC 801, Box 40, FPO AE 09498-4040, Tel [44] (131) 556-8315, Fax [44] (131) 557-6023. Website: www.usembassy.org.uk/scotland/

| | |
|---|---|
| CG: | Liane R. Dorsey |

**European Bank for Reconstruction and Development**, 24/31 Grosvenor Square, London W1A 1AE

Tel [44] (20) 7588-4028

| | |
|---|---|
| EXEC DIR: | [Vacant] |
| ALT DIR: | [Vacant] |
| COM: | Gene Harris |

**Cayman Islands [CA],** Office of Adventure Travel, Seven Mile Beach, Georgetown, Grand Cayman, Tel 345-945-1511, Fax 345-945-1811

| | |
|---|---|
| CA: | Gail Duquesnay |

Last Modified: Thursday, March 22, 2001

# UNITED STATES

**US Mission to the United Nations (USUN),** 799 United Nations Plaza, New York, NY 10017-3505, Tel (212) 415-4000, afterhours Tel 415-4444, Fax 415-4443

| | |
|---|---|
| US REP: | Amb. Richard C. Holbrooke |
| US REP SEC: | Patsy Agee |
| DEP US REP: | James B. Cunningham |
| DEP US REP SEC: | Eunhee Jeong |
| US REP FOR SPEC POL AFF: | Amb. Nancy Soderberg |
| US REP TO ECOSOC: | Amb. Betty King |
| US REP FOR UN MANAGEMENT AND REFORM: | Donald S. Hays |
| DIR/WASHINGTON OFF: | Bob Orr |
| CHIEF OF STAFF: | Rosemarie Pauli |
| DIR OF COMM: | Mary E. Glynn |
| POL: | Mark Minton |
| INT LEGAL: | Robert B. Rosenstock |
| HOST COUNTRY: | Robert C. Moller |
| UN REFORM MGT: | Susun Shearhouse |
| ADM: | Harry Young |
| MSC: | Col. James Bagley |
| RSO: | James Bacigalupo |
| IRM: | [Vacant] |

**US Mission to the Organization of American States (USOAS),** Department of State, Washington, D.C. 20520, Tel (202) 647-9376, Fax 647-0911

| | |
|---|---|
| US REP: | Amb. Luis J. Lauredo |
| DEP US REP: | Ronald D. Godard |
| POL/ECO: | Charlotte Roe |
| TECH COOP: | Margarita Riva-Geoghegan |
| RESOURCES: | Joan E. Segerson |

Last Modified: Monday, November 20, 2000

# URUGUAY

**Montevideo (E),** Lauro Muller 1776—APO AA 34035, Tel [598] (2) 203-60-61 or 418-77-77, Fax 598-2-4188611. Internet address: www.embeeuu.gub.uy.

| | |
|---|---|
| AMB: | Christopher C. Ashby |
| AMB OMS: | [Vacant] |
| DCM: | Marianne M. Myles |
| PLEC: | Paul T. Belmont |
| ECO: | Stephen K. Keat |
| RSO: | Dean L. DeVilla |
| ADM: | Michael K. St. Clair |
| CON: | Denise A. Boland |
| PAO: | Jean E. Manes |
| IPO: | John C. Adams |
| ODC: | Col Randall L. James, USAF |
| AGR: | Phil Shull (resident in Buenos Aires) |
| DAO: | LTC Albert F. Leftwich, USA |
| CUS: | Lawrence L. Mulkearns |
| FAA/CASLO: | Hector Vela (resident in Buenos Aires) |

Last Modified: Thursday, November 09, 2000

# UZBEKISTAN

**Tashkent (E),** 82 Chilanzarskaya, Tel [998] 71 120-5450, Fax 120-6335, tie-line Tel 793-0000, tie-line Fax 793-0131; PAO Fax [998] (71) 120-6224; USAID Fax 120-6309; COM Fax 120-6692; duty officer cellular Tel [998] (71) 180-4060

| | |
|---|---|
| AMB: | John E. Herbst |
| AMB OMS: | Mary Cross |
| DCM: | Molly O'Neal |
| POL/ECO: | Larry Memmott |
| ADM: | Elizabeth L. Cobb |
| FCS: | Tyrena Holley |
| PAO: | Mark Asquino |
| AID: | Jim Goggin |
| PC: | Lawrence Leahy |
| RSO: | Randy Steen |
| IRM: | Jimmie Rabourn |
| AGR: | James R. Dever (resident in Islamabad) |
| GSO: | Jack Anderson |
| CON: | Phillip Slattery |
| FAA: | Dennis B. Cooper (resident in Brussels) |
| DEA: | Robert Clark (resident in Islamabad) |

Last Modified: Thursday, April 05, 2001

# VENEZUELA

**Caracas (E),** Calle F con Calle Suapure, Colinas de Valle Arriba—P.O. Box 62291, Caracas 1080-A or APO AA 34037, Tel [58] (2) 975-6411/975-7811 or 975-9821 (after-hours); IVG 643 plus ext. or 643-0000 (operator); MILGP [58] (2) 682-7749/2877, Emb Fax 975-6710; ADM Fax 975-9429; AGR Fax 975-7615; CON Fax 753-4534; CON ACS FAX 975-8991; COM and FCS Fax 975-9643; CUS Fax 975-6556; DAO Fax 975-6542; DEA Fax 975-8519; ECO Fax 975-9778; FAS Fax 975-7615; FMC Fax 975-7903; GSO Fax 975-8406; LEGATT Fax 975-9629; MILGP Fax 682-5844; NAS Fax 975-9685; PAO Fax PER Fax 975-6292. Website address: www.usia.gov/posts/caracas

| | |
|---|---|
| AMB: | John F. Maisto |
| AMB OMS: | Ann Kirlian |
| DCM: | Nancy Mason |
| POL: | Thomas H. Ochiltree |
| ECO: | Gary Maybarduk |
| COM: | Louis Santamaria |
| CON: | Marilyn F. Jackson |
| ADM: | Robert Weisberg |
| RSO: | Henry N. Jenkins |

| | |
|---|---|
| PAO: | Phillip Parkerson |
| IRM: | John H. Varner, Jr. |
| GSO: | Thomas F. Burke |
| CUS: | Percival A. Jordan |
| DEA: | Paul A. Herring |
| DAO: | Col. Gregory H. Landers, USAF |
| MILGP: | Col. William C. Hunter, USA |
| PER: | Eleanor Akahloun |
| AGR: | Rod McSherry |
| LAB: | Bruce W. Friedman |
| FAA: | Victor Tamariz (resident in Miami) |
| FMO: | Robert A. Wert |
| IRS: | Frederick Dulas (resident in Mexico City) |
| NAS: | Michael Corbin |
| LEGATT: | Hector Rodriguez |

**Maracaibo [CA],** CEVAZ — Centro Venezolano-Americano del Zulia, Calle 63 Numero 3E60, Apartado 419, Maracaibo, Estado Zulia, Venezuela, Tel 58-61-982-164 or 58-61-925-953, Fax 58-61-921-098

| | |
|---|---|
| CA: | George Quintero |

Last Modified: Thursday, November 09, 2000

# VIETNAM

**Hanoi (E),** 7 Lang Ha Road, Ba Dinh District, Hanoi, Vietnam (Int'l mail), U.S. Embassy-Hanoi, PSC 461, Box 400, FPO AP 96521-0002 (U.S. mail), U.S. Embassy-Hanoi, Dept. of State, Washington, D.C. 20521-4500 (pouch address), Tel [84] (4) 772-1500, EXEC Fax 772-2615; ADM Fax 772-1510; CON Fax 831-3017; USDAO Fax 831-3239; AGR Fax 843-8932; POL/ECO Fax 772-2614; PAO Tel 822-5439, Fax 822-5435; USCS Tel 824-2422, Fax 824-2421; DEA Fax 772-4932; GSO Fax 772-3351/2613.

| | |
|---|---|
| AMB: | Douglas B. "Pete" Peterson |
| AMB OMS: | Lavay L. Miler |
| DCM: | Dennis G. Harter |
| ADM: | Raymond J. Pepper |
| POL: | James L. Bruno |
| ECO: | Robert W. Dry |
| CON: | Amy Monk |
| S&T: | Gary R. Sigmon |
| COM: | Michael R. Frisby |
| AGR: | Leon H. Schmick |
| APHIS: | Dale Maki (resident in Beijing) |
| HHS: | Michael J. Linnan |
| PAO: | David B. Monk |
| GSO: | [Vacant] |
| IMO: | Kenneth J. Hoeft |
| DAO: | Ltc. Frank L. Miller, Jr., USA |
| RSO: | Douglas P. Quiram |
| FAA: | David L. Knudson (resident in Singapore) |
| LAB: | Linda S. Specht |
| DEA: | David F. Lytal |
| USAID: | Jean M. Gilson |

**Ho Chi Minh City (CG),** 4 Le Duan, District 1—PSC 461, P.O. Box 500, FPO AP 96521-0002, Tel [84] (8) 822-9433, Fax 822-9434; COM, INS, PAS and FAS Address: 65 Le LOI, District 1, Ho Chi Minh City: COM Tel 825-0490, Fax 825-0491; INS Tel 821-6237, Fax 821-6241; PAS Tel 821-6400, Fax 821-6405; FAS Tel 825-0528, Fax 825-0503.

| CG: | Charles A. Ray |
|---|---|
| DPO: | Eric G. John |
| POL: | James M. Waller |
| ECO: | Jeffery A. Beller |
| CON: | Jane J. Tannenbaum |
| ADM: | Michael C. Mullins |
| RSO: | John R. Myers |
| IPO: | James H. Porter |
| COM: | Gregory Loose |
| GSO: | Sau Ching Yip |
| PAS: | Scott D. Weinhold |
| INS: | Larry F. Crider |
| RRS: | David Greene |

Last Modified: Thursday, February 15, 2001

# YEMEN

**Sanaa (E),** Dhahr Himyar Zone, Sheraton Hotel District—P.O. Box 22347, Sanaa, Republic of Yemen, Tel [967] (1)303-155/6/7/8/9, 303-160/1/2, 303-183, 303-256, 303-164, 303-242, 303-165, Fax 303-182; CON Fax 303-175; PAO Tel 303-180/1, Fax 303-163; post one/afterhours: 303-261; RMO Fax303-184; workweek: Saturday – Wednesday, 8:00 a.m. to 4:30 p.m. Internet address: usembassyol@y.net.ye

| AMB: | Barbara K. Bodine |
|---|---|
| AMB OMS: | Virginia S. Burns |
| DCM: | Bradford Hanson |
| POL: | Steven C. Walker |
| POL/MIL: | Jonathan D. Rice |
| ECO/COM: | Donna Visocan |
| CON: | Patricia W. Johnson |
| ADM: | Sandra M. Wenner-Yeaman |
| RSO: | Victor DeWindt |
| PAO: | A. Chris Eccel |
| RMO: | Jesse H. Monestersky |
| DAO: | Ltc. Robert Newman |
| IRM: | Steven J. Derrick |
| AID: | Richard Brown (resident in Cairo) |
| ATO: | Quintin Gray (resident in Riyadh) |
| FAA: | Lynn Osmus (resident in Brussels) |
| IRS: | Magaret J. Lullo (resident in Berlin) |
| DEA: | Robert Clark (resident in Islamabad) |

Last Modified: Monday, January 22, 2001

# YUGOSLAVIA

**Belgrade (E),** American Embassy Belgrade—U.S. Department of State, Washington, D.C. 20521-5070, Tel [381] (11) 645-655, afterhours Tel 646-481, tie line (8) 754-0000, Fax [381] (11) 645-221; Exec Fax 645-332; POL/ECO Fax 646-054; PAO Fax 646-924; CON Fax 644-053; GSO Fax 645-221. Internet address: amembassybelgrade@dos.us-state.gov

(Operations temporarily suspended).

**Pristina (USOP),** 30 Nazim Hikmet 38000 Pristina, Kosovo Province—Pouch address: 9520 Pristina Place, Washington, DC 20521-9520, Tel [381](38)549-516, Satellite Tel 873-761-912-435, Satellite Fax 873-761-912-436, Duty Officer 377-044-153-594 USAID: Dragodan – Nazim Hikmet, 38000 Pristina, Kosovo Province Tel [381](38)590 174, Fax [381] (38) 590438, Satellite Tel 873-761-393-321

| CM: | Christopher W. Dell |
|---|---|
| CM OMS: | Marcia W. Vajay |
| DPO: | Nicholas A. Sherwood |
| POL: | Karen T. Levine |
| ECO/COM: | Theresa Grencik |
| ADM: | Dwight R. Rhoades |
| GSO: | Gyorgy Vajay |
| RSO: | Steven J. Chalupsky |
| FMO: | Raymond H. Murphy, II |
| IPO: | Richard McInturff |
| DAO: | Col. John Pemberton |
| AID DIR: | Craig Buck |
| INL: | Henry Wilkins |
| JUS/OPDAT: | James Cowles |
| REF: | Bruce Boardsley |

Last Modified: Thursday, April 05, 2001

# ZAIRE (See Congo, Democratic Republic of the)

# ZAMBIA

**Lusaka (E),** corner of Independence and United Nations Aves.—P.O. Box 31617, Tel [260] (1) 250-955 or 252-230, front office Tel 254-301, afterhours Tel 252-234, Telex AMEMB ZA 41970, Fax 252-225; AID Tel 254-303 thru 6, ext. 212, Fax 254-532; PAO Tel 227-993 thru 4, ext. 211, Fax 226-523

| AMB: | David B. Dunn |
|---|---|
| AMB OMS: | Barbara J. Rangel |
| DCM: | Robert E. Whitehead |
| POL: | Lisa J. Peterson |
| ECO/COM: | Troy D. Fitrell |
| CON: | Simone Baer |
| ADM: | Clyde L. Jardine |
| RSO: | John L. Walker |
| PAO: | George P. Newman |
| IRM: | Alberta Ortiz |
| DAO: | Ltc. James Cobb, USA (resident in Harare) |
| FAA: | Ronald L. Montgomery (resident in Dakar) |
| AGR: | Fred Kessel (resident in Nairobi) |
| LAB: | Ralph D. Anske (resident in Nairobi) |
| AID: | Walter E. North |
| IRS: | James P. Beene (resident in London) |
| DEA: | Larry W. Frye (resident in Pretoria) |

Last Modified: Thursday, November 09, 2000

# ZIMBABWE

**Harare (E),** 172 Herbert Chitepo Ave.—P.O. Box 3340, Tel [263] (4) 250-593/4/5, Fax 796-488; Executive Office direct line 704679, Fax 796487; Embassy Fax 797488; IVG Prefix 778; IPU direct tel line 708941; DAO Fax 705752; PAS Tel 758800/1, Fax 758802; USAID Tel 252593/4, Fax 252478, 25259; PC Tel 752273/4/5. Internet address: paslan@zimweb.co.zw

| AMB: | Thomas McDonald |
|---|---|
| AMB OMS: | Nelda Villines |
| DCM: | Earl Irving |
| POL: | Matthew Harrington |
| ECO/COM: | Mark Prokop |
| CON: | Theresa Hebron |

# U.S. Embassies, Consulates, and Foreign Service Posts

ADM:            Mark Woerner
RSO:            George Word
PAO:            Bruce Wharton
IMO:            Dennis Thatcher
ECO/LAB:        Scott Remington
AID:            Rose Maire Depp

AGR:            Richard Helm (resident in Pretoria)
DAO:            LTCOL James Smaugh
FAA:            Edward Jones (resident in Dakar)
IRS:            J. Paul Beene (resident in London)

Last Modified: Tuesday, December 19, 2000

# Background Notes
## on
## Countries of the World

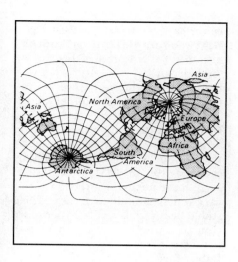

# THE WORLD

1999

Editor's Note: This entry on The World is an abstract of current, key facts to provide a global context for the various national entries in this Yearbook. This information was provided by the U.S. Central Intelligence Agency; Background Notes on individual countries are from the U.S. Department of State.

## GEOGRAPHY

**Map references:** World, Time Zones
**Area:** *total:* 510.072 million sq km; *land:* 148.94 million sq km; *water:* 361.132 million sq km; *note:* 70.8% of the world's surface is water, 29.2% is land

**Area—comparative:** land area about 15 times the size of the US

**Land boundaries:** the land boundaries in the world total 251,480.24 km (not counting shared boundaries twice)

**Coastline:** 356,000 km

**Maritime claims:** *contiguous zone:* 24 nm claimed by most, but can vary; *continental shelf:* 200-m depth claimed by most or to depth of exploitation; others claim 200 nm or to the edge of the continental margin; *exclusive fishing zone:* 200 nm claimed by most, but can vary; *exclusive economic zone:* 200 nm claimed by most, but can vary; *territorial sea:* 12 nm claimed by most, but can vary; *note:* boundary situations with neighboring states prevent many countries from extending their fishing or economic zones to a full 200 nm; 43 nations and other areas that are landlocked include Afghanistan, Andorra, Armenia, Austria, Azerbaijan, Belarus, Bhutan, Bolivia, Botswana, Burkina Faso, Burundi, Central African Republic, Chad, Czech Republic, Ethiopia, Holy See (Vatican City), Hungary, Kazakh- stan, Kyrgyzstan, Laos, Lesotho, Liechtenstein, Luxembourg, Malawi, Mali, Moldova, Mongolia, Nepal, Niger, Paraguay, Rwanda, San Marino, Slovakia, Swaziland, Switzerland, Tajikistan, The Former Yugoslav Republic of Macedonia, Turkmenistan, Uganda, Uzbekistan, West Bank, Zambia, Zimbabwe

**Climate:** two large areas of polar climates separated by two rather narrow temperate zones from a wide equatorial band of tropical to subtropical climates

**Terrain:** the greatest ocean depth is the Mariana Trench at 10,924 m in the Pacific Ocean

**Elevation extremes:** *lowest point:* Dead Sea -408 m; *highest point:* Mount Everest 8,848 m

**Natural resources:** the rapid using up of nonrenewable mineral resources, the depletion of forest areas and wetlands, the extinction of animal and plant species, and the deterioration in air and water quality (especially in Eastern Europe, the former USSR, and China) pose serious long-term problems that governments and peoples are only beginning to address

**Land use:** *arable land:* 10%; *permanent crops:* 1%; *permanent pastures:* 26%; *forests and woodland:* 32%; *other:* 31% (1993 est.)

**Irrigated land:** 2,481,250 sq km (1993 est.)

**Natural hazards:** large areas subject to severe weather (tropical cyclones), natural disasters (earthquakes, landslides, tsunamis, volcanic eruptions)

**Environment—current issues:** large areas subject to overpopulation, industrial disasters, pollution (air, water, acid rain, toxic substances), loss of vegetation (overgrazing, deforestation, desertification), loss of wildlife, soil degradation, soil depletion, erosion

**Environment—international agreements:** selected international environmental agreements are included under the Environment—international agreements entry for each country and in the Selected International Environmental Agreements appendix.

## PEOPLE

**Population:** 5,995,544,836 (July 1999 est.)

**Age structure:** *0-14 years:* 30% (male 934,816,288; female 884,097,095); *15-64 years:* 63% (male 1,905,701,066; female 1,861,265,079); *65 years and over:* 7% (male 179,094,601; female 230,570,707) (1999 est.)

**Population growth rate:** 1.3% (1999 est.)

**Birth rate:** 22 births/1,000 population (1999 est.)

**Death rate:** 9 deaths/1,000 population (1999 est.)

**Sex ratio:** *at birth:* 1.06 male(s)/female; *under 15 years:* 1.06 male(s)/female; *15-64:* 1.02 male(s)/female; *65 years and over:* 0.78 male(s)/female; *total population:* 1.02 male(s)/female (1999 est.)

**Infant mortality rate:** 56 deaths/1,000 live births (1999 est.)

**Life expectancy at birth:** *total population:* 63 years; *male:* 61 years; *female:* 65 years (1999 est.)

**Total fertility rate:** 2.8 children born/woman (1999 est.)

# GOVERNMENT

**Data code:** none; there is no FIPS 10-4 country code for the World, so the Factbook uses the "W" data code from DIAM 65-18 "Geopolitical Data Elements and Related Features," Data Standard No. 3, March 1984, published by the Defense Intelligence Agency; see the Cross-Reference List of Country Data Codes appendix

**Administrative divisions:** 266 nations, dependent areas, other, and miscellaneous entries

**Legal system:** all members of the UN (excluding Yugoslavia) plus Nauru and Switzerland are parties to the statute that established the International Court of Justice (ICJ) or World Court

# ECONOMY

**Economy—overview:** Growth in global output (gross world product, GWP) dropped to 2% in 1998 from 4% in 1997 because of continued recession in Japan, severe financial difficulties in other East Asian countries, and widespread dislocations in the Russian economy. The US economy continued its remarkable sustained prosperity, growing at 3.9% in 1998, and accounted for 22% of GWP. Western Europe's economies grew at roughly 2.5%, not enough to cut deeply into the region's high unemployment; these economies produced 21% of GWP. China, the second largest economy in the world, continued its rapid growth and accounted for 11% of GWP. Japan posted a decline of 2.6% in 1998 and its share in GWP

dropped to 7.4%. As usual, the 15 successor nations of the USSR and the other old Warsaw Pact nations experienced widely different rates of growth. Russia's national product dropped by 5% whereas the nations of central and eastern Europe grew by 3.4% on average. The developing nations varied widely in their growth results, with many countries facing population increases that eat up gains in output. Externally, the nation-state, as a bedrock economic-political institution, is steadily losing control over international flows of people, goods, funds, and technology. Internally, the central government finds its control over resources slipping as separatist regional movements—typically based on ethnicity—gain momentum, e.g., in the successor states of the former Soviet Union, in the former Yugoslavia, in India, and in Canada. In Western Europe, governments face the difficult political problem of channeling resources away from welfare programs in order to increase investment and strengthen incentives to seek employment. The addition of more than 80 million people each year to an already overcrowded globe is exacerbating the problems of pollution, desertification, underemployment, epidemics, and famine. Because of their own internal problems, the industrialized countries have inadequate resources to deal effectively with the poorer areas of the world, which, at least from the economic point of view, are becoming further marginalized. In 1998, serious financial difficulties in several high-growth East Asia countries cast a shadow over short-term global economic prospects. The introduction of the euro as the common currency of much of Western Europe in January 1999 poses serious economic risks because of varying levels of income and cultural and political differences among the participating nations. (For specific economic developments in each country of the world in 1998, see the individual country entries.)

**GDP:** GWP (gross world product)—purchasing power parity—$39 trillion (1998 est.)

**GDP—real growth rate:** 2% (1998 est.)

**GDP—per capita:** purchasing

power parity—$6,600 (1998 est.)

**GDP—composition by sector:** *agriculture:* NA%; *industry:* NA%; *services:* NA%

**Household income or consumption by percentage share:** *lowest 10%:* NA%; *highest 10%:* NA%

**Inflation rate (consumer prices):** all countries 25%; developed countries 2% to 4% typically; developing countries 10% to 60% typically (1998 est.); *note:* national inflation rates vary widely in individual cases, from stable prices in Japan to hyperinflation in a number of Third World countries

**Labor force:** NA

**Labor force—by occupation:** NA

**Unemployment rate:** 30% combined unemployment and underemployment in many non-industrialized countries; developed countries typically 5%-12% unemployment (1998 est.)

**Industries:** dominated by the onrush of technology, especially in computers, robotics, telecommunications, and medicines and medical equipment; most of these advances take place in OECD nations; only a small portion of non-OECD countries have succeeded in rapidly adjusting to these technological forces; the accelerated development of new industrial (and agricultural) technology is complicating already grim environmental problems

**Industrial production growth rate:** 5% (1997 est.)

**Electricity—production:** 12.3427 trillion kWh (1994)

**Electricity—production by source:** *fossil fuel:* NA%; *hydro:* NA%; *nuclear:* NA%; *other:* NA%

**Electricity—consumption:** 12.3427 trillion kWh (1994)

**Exports:** $5 trillion (f.o.b., 1998 est.)

**Exports—commodities:** the whole range of industrial and agricultural goods and services

**Exports—partners:** in value, about 75% of exports from the developed countries

**Imports:** $5 trillion (f.o.b., 1998 est.)

**Imports—commodities:** the whole range of industrial and agricultural goods and services

**Imports—partners:** in value, about 75% of imports by the developed countries

**Debt—external:** $2 trillion for less

developed countries (1998 est.)
**Economic aid—recipient:** traditional worldwide foreign aid $50 billion (1995 est.)

# TRANSPORTATION

**Railways:** *total:* 1,201,337 km includes about 190,000 to 195,000 km of electrified routes of which 147,760 km are in Europe, 24,509 km in the Far East, 11,050 km in Africa, 4,223 km in South America, and 4,160 km in North America; note—fastest speed in daily service is 300 km/hr attained by France's Societe Nationale des Chemins-de-Fer Francais (SNCF) Le Train a Grande Vitesse (TGV)—Atlantique line;

*broad gauge:* 251,153 km; *standard gauge:* 710,754 km; *narrow gauge:* 239,430 km

**Highways:** *total:* NA km; *paved:* NA km; *unpaved:* NA km

**Ports and harbors:** Chiba, Houston, Kawasaki, Kobe, Marseille, Mina' al Ahmadi (Kuwait), New Orleans, New York, Rotterdam, Yokohama

**Merchant marine:** *total:* 28,310 ships (1,000 GRT or over) totaling 495,299,489 GRT/764,129,056 DWT; *ships by type:* barge carrier 23, bulk 5,745, cargo 8,766, chemical tanker 1,326, combination bulk 319, combination ore/oil 227, container 2,615, liquefied gas tanker 802, livestock carrier 60, multifunction large-load carrier 90, oil tanker 4,521, passenger 392, passenger-cargo 126, railcar

carrier 19, refrigerated cargo 1,067, roll-on/roll-off cargo 1,117, short-sea passenger 484, specialized tanker 118, vehicle carrier 493 (1998 est.)

# MILITARY

**Military branches:** ground, maritime, and air forces at all levels of technology

**Military expenditures—dollar figure:** aggregate real expenditure on arms worldwide in 1998 remained at approximately the 1997 level, about three-quarters of a trillion dollars (1998 est.)

**Military expenditures—percent of GDP:** roughly 2% of gross world product (1998 est.)

# AFGHANISTAN

July 1994

Official Name:
**Islamic State of Afghanistan**

## PROFILE

### Geography

**Area:** 648,000 sq. km. (252,000 sq. mi.); slightly smaller than Texas.
**Cities (1993 est.):** Capital—Kabul (est. 800,000). Other cities—Kandahar (226,000); Herat (177,000); Mazar-e-Sharif (131,000); Jalalabad (58,000); Konduz (57,000).
**Terrain:** Landlocked; mostly mountains and desert.
**Climate:** Dry, with cold winters and hot summers.

### People

**Nationality:** Noun and adjective—Afghan(s).
**Population:** 17.7 million (1993 estimate, including about 1.4 million refugees in Pakistan and 2 million refugees in Iran).
**Annual growth rate:** 2.5% (1993 est.).
**Ethnic groups:** Pashtun, Tajik, Uzbek, Hazara, Aimaq, Turkmen, Baluch, Nuristani.
**Religions:** Sunni Muslim 84%, Shi'a Muslim 15%.
**Languages:** Pashto, Dari (Afghan Persian).
**Education:** Years compulsory—6. Literacy—about 29%.
**Health:** Infant mortality rate (1993)—169 /1,000. Life expectancy (1992 est.)—45 yrs. (male); 43 yrs. (female).
**Work force:** Mostly in rural agriculture; number cannot be estimated due to conflict.

### Government

**Type:** Afghanistan identifies itself as an "Islamic state."
**Independence:** August 19, 1919.
**Organization:** Interim government is a presidential system with a prime minister and cabinet.
**Political parties:** The 10 major Afghan political factions are largely based on the former resistance organizations. About half are Islamist in orientation; the other are more traditional or secular. President Burhanuddin Rabbani's Jamiat-i-Islami (Islamic Society) and Prime Minister Gulbuddin Hekmatyar's Hezb-i-Islami (Islamic Party) have been bitter rivals for political influence in Afghanistan.
**Flag:** Adopted in 1992, the flag has three horizontal bands—green, white, and black—with the great seal of Afghanistan superimposed on the bands.

### Economy

**GDP:** $3 billion (1991 est.).
**Natural resources:** Natural gas, oil, coal, copper, talc, barites, sulfur, lead, zinc, iron, salt, precious and semiprecious stones.
**Agriculture (at least 65% of GDP):** Wheat, corn, barley, rice, cotton, fruit, nuts, karakul pelts, wool, mutton.
**Industry (estimated 20% of GDP):** Small-scale production for domestic use of textiles, soap, furniture, shoes, fertilizer, and cement; handwoven carpets for export.
**Trade (1992 est.):** Exports—$1 billion: carpets, rugs, fruit and nuts, natural gas, cotton, oil-cake, karakul. Major markets—Central Asian Republics, EEC, India, Pakistan. Imports—$1.7 billion: petroleum products, sugar, manufactured goods, edible oils, tea. Major suppliers—Central Asian Republics, Japan, Singapore, France, India, Pakistan.
**1994 market exchange rate:** 2,400 Afghanis=U.S. $1.

## PEOPLE

Afghanistan's ethnically and linguistically mixed population reflects its location astride historic trade and invasion routes leading from Central Asia into South and Southwest Asia. Pashtuns are the dominant ethnic group, accounting for about 38% of the population. Tajik (25%), Hazara (19%), Aimaq (6%), Uzbek (6%), Turkmen (2%), and other small groups are also represented. Dari (Afghan Persian) and Pashto are official languages. Dari is spoken by more than one-third of the population as a first language and serves as a lingua franca for most Afghans. Tajik, Uzbek, and Turkmen are spoken widely in the north. More than 70 other languages and numerous dialects are also spoken by smaller groups throughout the country.

Afghanistan is an Islamic country. An estimated 84% of the population is Sunni; the remainder is predominantly Shi'a, including Isma'ilis, Hazaras, and the Qizilbash. Despite attempts during the years of communist rule to secularize Afghan society, Islamic practices still pervade all aspects of life. Likewise, Islamic religious tradition and codes provide the principal means of controlling personal conduct and settling legal disputes. Excluding urban populations in the principal cities, most Afghans are divided into clans and tribal groups, which follow centuries-old customs and religious practices.

# HISTORY

Afghanistan, often called the crossroads of Central Asia, has had a turbulent history. In 328 BC, Alexander the Great entered the territory of present-day Afghanistan, then part of the Persian Empire, to capture Bactria (present-day Balkh). Invasions by the Scythians, White Huns, and Turks followed in succeeding centuries. In AD 642, Arabs invaded the entire region and introduced Islam.

Arab rule quickly gave way to the Persians, who controlled the area until conquered by the Turkic Ghaznavids in 998. Mahmud of Ghazni (998–1030) consolidated the conquests of his predecessors and turned Ghazni into a great cultural center as well as a base for frequent forays into India. Following Mahmud's shortlived dynasty, various princes attempted to rule sections of the country until the Mongol invasion of 1219. The Mongol invasion, led by Genghis Khan, resulted in the destruction of many cities, including Herat, Ghazni, and Balkh, and the despoliation of fertile agricultural areas.

Following Genghis Khan's death in 1227, a succession of petty chieftains and princes struggled for supremacy until late in the 14th century, when one of his descendants, Tamerlane, incorporated Afghanistan into his own vast Asian empire. Babur, a descendant of Tamerlane and the founder of India's Moghul dynasty at the beginning of the 16th century, made Kabul the capital of an Afghan principality.

In 1747, Ahmad Shah Durrani, the founder of what is known today as Afghanistan, established his rule. A Pashtun, Durrani was elected king by a tribal council after the assassination of the Persian ruler Nadir Shah at Khabushan in the same year. Throughout his reign, Durrani consolidated chieftainships, petty principalities, and fragmented provinces into one country. His rule extended from Mashhad in the west to Kashmir and Delhi in the east, and from the Amu Darya (Oxus) River in the north to the Arabian Sea in the south. All of Afghanistan's rulers until the 1978 Marxist coup were from Durrani's Pashtun tribal confederation, and all were members of that tribe's Mohammadzai clan after 1818.

## European Influence

Collision between the expanding British and Russian Empires significantly influenced Afghanistan during the 19th century. British concern over Russian advances in Central Asia and growing influence in Persia culminated in two Anglo-Afghan wars. The first (1839–42) resulted not only in the destruction of a British army, but is remembered today as an example of the ferocity of Afghan resistance to foreign rule. The second Anglo-Afghan war (1878–80) was sparked by Amir Shir Ali's refusal to accept a British mission in Kabul. This conflict brought Amir Abdur Rahman to the Afghan throne. During his reign (1880–1901), the British and Russians officially established the boundaries of what would become modern Afghanistan. The British retained effective control over Kabul's foreign affairs.

Afghanistan remained neutral during World War I, despite German encouragement of anti-British feelings and Afghan rebellion along the borders of British India. The Afghan king's policy of neutrality was not universally popular within the country, however.

Habibullah, Abdur Rahman's son and successor, was assassinated by members of an anti-British movement in 1919. His third son, Amanullah, regained control of Afghanistan's foreign policy after launching the Third Anglo-Afghan war with an attack on India in the same year. During the ensuing conflict, the war-weary British relinquished their control over Afghan foreign affairs by signing the Treaty of Rawalpindi in August 1919. In commemoration of this event, Afghans celebrate August 19 as their Independence Day.

## Reform and Reaction

King Amanullah (1919–29) moved to end his country's traditional isolation in the years following the Third Anglo-Afghan war. He established diplomatic relations with most major countries and, following a 1927 tour of Europe and Turkey—which had seen modernization and secularization under Attaturk—introduced several reforms intended to modernize the country. Some of these, such as the abolition of the traditional Muslim veil for women and the opening of a number of coeducational schools, quickly alienated many tribal and religious leaders. The weakness of the army under Amanullah further jeopardized his position. He was forced to abdicate in January 1929 after Kabul fell to forces led by Bacha-i-Saqao, a Tajik brigand. Prince Nadir Khan, a cousin of Amanullah's, in turn defeated Bacha-i-Saqao in October of the same year. With considerable Pashtun tribal support, Khan was declared King Nadir Shah. Four years later, however, he was assassinated in a revenge killing by a Kabul student.

Mohammad Zahir Shah, Nadir Khan's 19-year-old son, succeeded to the throne and reigned from 1933 to 1973. In 1964, King Zahir Shah promulgated a liberal constitution providing for a two-chamber legislature to which the king appointed one-third of the deputies. The people elected another third, and the remainder were selected indirectly by provincial assemblies. Although Zahir's "experiment in democracy" produced few lasting reforms, it permitted the growth of unofficial extremist parties of both left and right. This included the communist People's Democratic Party of Afghanistan (PDPA), which had close ideological ties to the Soviet

Union. In 1967, the PDPA split into two major rival factions: the Khalq (Masses) faction headed by Nur Muhammad Taraki and supported by the military, and the Parcham (Banner) faction led by Babrak Karmal. The split reflected deep ethnic, class, and ideological divisions within Afghan society.

Zahir's cousin, Sardar Mohammad Daoud, served as his Prime Minister from 1953 to 1963. During his tenure as Prime Minister, Daoud solicited military and economic assistance from both Washington and Moscow and introduced controversial social policies. Daoud's alleged support for

the creation of a Pashtun state in the Pakistan-Afghan border area heightened tensions with Pakistan and eventually resulted in Daoud's dismissal in March 1963.

Daoud's Republic (1973–78) and the April 1978 Coup Amid charges of corruption and malfeasance against the royal family and poor economic conditions caused by the severe 1971–72 drought, former Prime Minister Daoud seized power in a military coup on July 17, 1973. Daoud abolished the monarchy, abrogated the 1964 constitution, and declared Afghanistan a republic with himself as its first President and Prime Minister. His attempts to carry out badly needed economic and social reforms met with little success, and the new constitution promulgated in February 1977 failed to quell chronic political instability.

Seeking to exploit more effectively mounting popular disaffection, the PDPA reunified with Moscow's support. On April 27–28, 1978, the PDPA initiated a bloody coup which resulted in the overthrow and death of Daoud and most of his family. Nur Muhammad Taraki, Secretary General of the PDPA, became President of the Revolutionary Council and Prime Minister of the newly established Democratic Republic of Afghanistan.

Opposition to the Marxist government emerged almost immediately. During its first 18 months of rule, the PDPA brutally imposed a Marxist-style "reform" program which ran counter to deeply rooted Islamic traditions.

Decrees advocating the abolition of usury, changes in marriage customs, and land reform were particularly misunderstood and upsetting to highly conservative villagers. In addition, thousands of members of the traditional elite, the religious establishment, and the intelligentsia were imprisoned, tortured, or murdered. Conflicts within the PDPA also surfaced early and resulted in exiles, purges, imprisonments, and executions.

By the summer of 1978, a major revolt in the Nuristan region of eastern Afghanistan spread into a country-wide insurgency. In September 1979, Hafizullah Amin, who had earlier been the Prime Minister and minister of defense, seized power from Taraki after a palace shootout. Over the next two months, instability plagued Amin's regime as he moved against perceived enemies in the PDPA. By December, party morale was crumbling, and the insurgency was growing.

## The Soviet Invasion

The Soviet Union moved quickly to take advantage of the April 1978 coup. In December 1978, Moscow signed a new bilateral treaty of friendship and cooperation with Afghanistan, and the Soviet military assistance program increased significantly. The regime's survival increasingly was dependent upon Soviet military equipment and advisers as the insurgency spread and the Afghan army began to collapse.

By October 1979, however, relations between Afghanistan and the Soviet Union were tense as Hafizullah Amin refused to take Soviet advice on how to stabilize and consolidate his government. Faced with a deteriorating security situation on December 24, 1979, large numbers of Soviet airborne forces, joining thousands of Soviet troops already on the ground, began to land in Kabul under the pretext of a field exercise. On December 26, these invasion forces killed Hafizullah Amin and installed Babrak Karmal, exiled leader of the Parcham faction, as Prime Minister. Massive Soviet ground forces invaded from the north on December 27.

Following the invasion, the Karmal regime, although backed by an expeditionary force of about 120,000 Soviet troops, was unable to establish authority outside Kabul. As much as 80% of the countryside, including parts of Herat and Kandahar, eluded effective government control. An overwhelming majority of Afghans opposed the communist regime, either actively or passively. Afghan freedom fighters (mujahidin) made it almost impossible for the regime to maintain a system of local government outside major urban centers. Poorly armed at first, in 1984 the mujahidin began receiving substantial assistance in the form of weapons and training from the U.S. and other outside powers.

In May 1985, the seven principal Peshawar-based guerrilla organizations formed an alliance to coordinate their political and military operations against the Soviet occupation. Late in 1985, the mujahidin were active in

and around Kabul, launching rocket attacks and assassinating high government officials. The failure of the Soviet Union to win over a significant number of Afghan collaborators or to rebuild a viable Afghan army forced it to bear an increasing responsibility for fighting the resistance and for civilian administration.

Soviet and popular displeasure with the Karmal regime led to its demise in May 1986. Karmal was replaced by Muhammad Najibullah, former chief of the Afghan secret police (KHAD). Najibullah had established a reputation for brutal efficiency during his tenure as KHAD chief.

As Prime Minister, though, Najibullah was ineffective and highly dependent on Soviet support. Undercut by deepseated divisions within the PDPA, regime efforts to broaden its base of support proved futile.

## The Geneva Accords and Aftermath

By the mid-1980s, the tenacious Afghan resistance movement—aided by the United States, Saudi Arabia, Pakistan, and others—was exacting a high price from the Soviets, both militarily within Afghanistan and by souring the U.S.S.R.'s relations with much of the Western and Islamic world. Although informal negotiations for a Soviet withdrawal from Afghanistan had been underway since 1982, it was not until 1988 that the Governments of Pakistan and Afghanistan, with the United States and Soviet Union serving as guarantors, signed an agreement settling the major differences between them. The agreement, known as the Geneva accords, included five major documents, which, among other things, called for U.S. and Soviet non-interference in the internal affairs of Pakistan and Afghanistan, the right of refugees to return to Afghanistan without fear of persecution or harassment, and, most importantly, a timetable that ensured full Soviet withdrawal from Afghanistan by February 15, 1989. About 14,500 Soviet and an estimated one million Afghan lives were lost between 1979 and the Soviet withdrawal in 1989.

Significantly, the mujahidin were neither party to the negotiations nor to the 1988 agreement and, consequently, refused to accept the terms of the accords. As a result, civil war did not end with the Soviet withdrawal, completed as scheduled in February 1989. Instead, it escalated. Najibullah's regime, though failing to win popular support, territory, or international recognition, was able to remain in power until 1992.

# GOVERNMENT AND POLITICAL CONDITIONS

The Soviet-supported Najibullah regime did not collapse until the defection of General Abdul Rashid Dostam and his Uzbek militia in March 1992. However, as the victorious mujahidin entered Kabul to assume control over the city and the central government, a new round of internecine fighting began between the various militias, which had coexisted only uneasily during the Soviet occupation. With the demise of their common enemy, the militias' ethnic, clan, religious, and personality differences surfaced, and the civil war continued.

Seeking to resolve these differences, the leaders of the Peshawar-based mujahidin groups agreed in mid-April to establish a 51-member interim Islamic Jihad Council to assume power in Kabul. Moderate leader Professor Sibghatullah Mojaddedi was to chair the council for three months, after which a 10-member leadership council composed of mujahidin leaders and presided over by the head of the Jamiat-i-Islami, Professor Burhanuddin Rabbani, was to be set up for a period of four months. During this six-month period, a Loya Jirga, or grand council of Afghan elders and notables, would convene and designate an interim administration which would hold power up to a year, pending elections.

But in May 1992, Rabbani prematurely formed the leadership council, undermining Mojaddedi's fragile authority. In June, Mojaddedi surrendered power to the Leadership Council, which then elected Rabbani as President. Nonetheless, heavy fighting broke out in August 1992 in Kabul between forces loyal to President Rabbani and rival factions, particularly those who supported Gulbuddin Hekmatyar's Hezb-i-Islami. After Rabbani convened a highly controversial council to extend his tenure in December 1992, fighting in the capital flared up in January and February 1993. The Islamabad accord, signed in March 1993, which appointed Hekmatyar as Prime Minister, failed to have a lasting effect. A follow-up agreement, the Jalalabad accord, called for the militias to be disarmed but was never fully implemented. Through 1993, Hekmatyar's Hezb-i-Islami forces, allied with the Shi'a Hezb-i-Wahdat militia, clashed intermittently with Rabbani and Masood's Jamiat forces. Cooperating with Jamiat were militants of Sayyaf's Ittehad-i-Islami and, periodically, troops loyal to ethnic Uzbek strongman Abdul Rashid Dostam. On January 1, 1994, Dostam switched sides, precipitating large-scale fighting in Kabul and in northern provinces, which caused thousands of civilian casualties in Kabul and elsewhere and created a new wave of displaced persons and refugees.

The central government exercises only limited control over the countryside, where local leaders and militia commanders, some with only nominal allegiance to any of the national figures battling for power in Kabul, hold sway. A date for elections in Afghanistan has yet to be established.

## Principal Government Officials

For up-to-date information on Principal Government Officials, see the Chiefs of State and Cabinet Members of Foreign Governments section starting on page 1.

Afghanistan maintains an embassy in the United States at 2341 Wyoming Avenue, NW, Washington, DC 20008 (tel. 202-234-3770/71/72).

# ECONOMY

Historically, there has been a dearth of information and reliable statistics about Afghanistan's economy. This was exacerbated by the Soviet invasion and ensuing civil war, which destroyed much of the underdeveloped country's infrastructure and disrupted normal patterns of economic activity.

## Agriculture

The Afghan economy continues to be overwhelmingly agricultural, despite the fact that only 15% of its total land area is arable and less than 6% currently is cultivated. Agricultural production is constrained by an almost total dependence on erratic winter snows and spring rains for water; irrigation is primitive. Relatively little use is made of machines, chemical fertilizer, or pesticides.

Grain production is Afghanistan's traditional agricultural mainstay. Overall agricultural production declined an average of 3.5% per year between 1978 and 1990. This can be attributed to sustained fighting, instability in rural areas, prolonged drought, and deteriorated infrastructure. Soviet efforts to disrupt production in resistance-dominated areas also contributed to this decline. Furthermore, Soviet efforts to centralize the economy through state ownership and control and consolidation of farmland into large collective farms contributed to lower production.

The war against the Soviet Union and the ensuing civil war also led to migration to the cities and refugee flight to Pakistan and Iran, further disrupting normal agricultural production. Recent studies indicate that agricultural production and livestock numbers are less than one-half of what they were in 1978. It is estimated that Afghanistan's food production levels are about 15% lower than what is necessary to feed the population. Shortages are exacerbated by the country's already limited transportation network, which has deteriorated due to damage and neglect resulting from war and the absence of an effective central government.

Opium is increasingly becoming a source of cash for many Afghans, especially since the breakdown in central authority after the Soviet withdrawal. Opium is easy to cultivate and transport and offers a quick source of income for returning refugees and other impoverished Afghans. Afghanistan is the second-largest producer of raw opium in the world, after Burma. In 1993, despite efforts by the U.S. and others to encourage alternative crops, poppy and opium production increased 8% and 7%, respectively, from a year earlier. Much of Afghanistan's opium production is shipped to laboratories in Pakistan and refined into heroin which is either consumed by a growing South Asian addict population or exported, primarily to Europe and North America.

## Trade and Industry

Trade accounts for a small portion of the Afghan economy, and there are no reliable statistics relating to trade flows. Since the Soviet withdrawal and the collapse of the Soviet Union, other limited trade relationships appear to be emerging with Iran, Pakistan, and the West. Afghanistan trades little with the United States; its 1992 trade is estimated at $6 million. Afghanistan does not enjoy U.S. most-favored-nation (MFN) trading status, which was revoked in 1986.

Afghanistan is endowed with a wealth of natural resources, including extensive deposits of coal, salt, chromium, iron ore, gold, fluorite, talc, copper, and lapis lazuli. Unfortunately, the country's remote and rugged terrain, and inadequate transportation network, usually have made mining these resources unprofitable.

The most important resource has been natural gas, first tapped in 1967. At their peak during the 1980s, natural gas sales accounted for $300

million a year in export revenues (56% of the total). Ninety percent of these exports went to the Soviet Union to pay for imports and debts. However, during the withdrawal of Soviet troops in 1989, Afghanistan's natural gas fields were capped to prevent sabotage by the mujahidin. Restoration of gas production has been hampered by internal strife and the disruption of traditional trading relationships following the collapse of the Soviet Union.

## Transportation

Landlocked Afghanistan has no railways, but the Amu Darya (Oxus) River, which forms part of Afghanistan's border with Turkmenistan, Uzbekistan, and Tajikistan, has barge traffic. During their occupation of the country, the Soviets completed a bridge across the Amu Darya and built a motor vehicle and railroad bridge between Termez and Jeyretan.

Most roadbuilding occurred in the 1960s, funded by the U.S. and the Soviet Union. The Soviets built a road and tunnel through the Salang Pass in 1964, connecting northern and southern Afghanistan. A highway connecting the principal cities of Herat, Kandahar, Ghazni, and Kabul forms the primary road system.

The highway system requires significant reconstruction, and regional roads are in a state of disrepair. The poor state of the Afghan transportation and communication networks has further fragmented and hobbled the struggling economy.

## Economic Development and Recovery

Afghanistan embarked on a modest economic development program in the 1930s. The government founded banks, introduced paper money, established a university, expanded primary, secondary, and technical schools, and sent students abroad for education. In 1956, the Afghan Government promulgated the first in a long series of ambitious development plans. By the late 1970s, these had achieved only mixed results due to flaws in the planning process as well

as inadequate funding and a shortage of the skilled managers and technicians needed for implementation.

These constraints on development have been exacerbated by the flight of refugees and the disruption and instability stemming from the Soviet occupation and ensuing civil war. Today, economic recovery and long-term development will depend on establishing an effective and stable political system.

The UN and the international donor community continue to provide considerable humanitarian relief. Since its inception in 1988, the umbrella UN Office for the Coordination of Humanitarian Assistance to Afghanistan (UNOCHA) has channeled $512 million in multilateral cash assistance to Afghan refugees and vulnerable persons inside Afghanistan. The U.S. and Japan are the leading contributors to this relief effort. One of its key tasks is to eliminate from priority areas (such as villages, arable fields, and roads) some of the estimated 10 million landmines which continue to litter the Afghan landscape. Afghanistan is the most heavily mined country in the world; mine-related injuries number up to 100 per month. Without successful mine clearance, refugee repatriation, political stability, and economic reconstruction will be severely constrained.

The UN, through the UN Development Program (UNDP), is expected to play a major role in post-war recovery and reconstruction of Afghanistan. In November 1993, the UNDP Action Plan for the Immediate Rehabilitation of Afghanistan identified more than $600 million in quick-impact development projects which could be implemented within two years where security conditions permit.

# FOREIGN RELATIONS

Before the Soviet invasion, Afghanistan pursued a policy of neutrality and nonalignment in its foreign relations. In international forums, Afghanistan generally followed the voting patterns of Asian and African non-aligned countries. Following the Marxist coup of April 1978, the Taraki Government developed significantly closer ties with the Soviet Union and its communist satellites.

After the December 1979 invasion, Afghanistan's foreign policy mirrored that of the Soviet Union. Afghan foreign policy-makers attempted, with little success, to increase their regime's low standing in the non-communist world. With the signing of the Geneva accords, Najibullah unsuccessfully sought to end Afghanistan's isolation within the Islamic world and in the Non-Aligned Movement.

Most Western countries, including the United States, maintained small diplomatic missions in Kabul during the Soviet occupation. Many subsequently closed their missions due to instability and heavy fighting in Kabul. Although a few states have reestablished a diplomatic presence in Kabul, most embassies, including that of the United States, remain closed.

## Pakistan

Two areas—Pashtunistan and Baluchistan—have long complicated Afghanistan's relations with Pakistan. Controversies involving these areas date back to the establishment of the Durand Line in 1893 dividing Pashtun and Baluch tribes living in Afghanistan from those living in what later became Pakistan. Afghanistan vigorously protested the inclusion of Pashtun and Baluch areas within Pakistan without providing the inhabitants with an opportunity for self-determination. Since 1947, this problem has led to incidents along the border, with extensive disruption of normal trade patterns. The most serious crisis lasted from September 1961 to June 1963, when diplomatic, trade, transit, and consular relations between the countries were suspended.

The 1978 Marxist coup further strained relations between the two countries. Pakistan took the lead diplomatically in the United Nations, the Non-Aligned Movement, and the

Organization of the Islamic Conference in opposing the Soviet occupation. During the war against the Soviet occupation, Pakistan served as the primary logistical conduit for the Afghan resistance. Pakistan, aided by UN agencies, private groups, and many friendly countries, continues to provide refuge to about 1.4 million Afghans.

Much of Afghanistan remains dependent on Pakistani links for trade and travel to the outside world, and Pakistan views Afghanistan as eventually becoming its primary route for trade with Central Asia.

## Iran

Afghanistan's relations with Iran have fluctuated over the years, with periodic disputes over the water rights of the Helmand River as the main issue of contention.

Following the Soviet invasion, which Iran opposed, relations deteriorated.

The Iranian consulate in Herat closed, as did the Afghan consulate in Mashhad. The Iranians complained of periodic border violations following the Soviet invasion. In 1985, they urged feuding Afghan Shi'a resistance groups to unite to oppose the Soviets. Iran supported the cause of the Afghan resistance and provided limited financial and military assistance to rebel leaders who pledged loyalty to the Iranian vision of Islamic revolution. Iran provides refuge to about 2 million Afghans.

## Russia

In the 19th century, Afghanistan served as a strategic buffer state between czarist Russia and the British Empire in the sub-continent. Afghanistan's relations with Moscow became more cordial after the Bolshevik Revolution in 1917. The Soviet Union was the first country to establish diplomatic relations with Afghanistan after the Third Anglo-Afghan war and signed an Afghan-

Soviet non-aggression pact in 1921, which also provided for Afghan transit rights through the Soviet Union. Early Soviet assistance included financial aid, aircraft and attendant technical personnel, and telegraph operators.

The Soviets began a major economic assistance program in Afghanistan in the 1950s. Between 1954 and 1978, Afghanistan received more than $1 billion in Soviet aid, including substantial military assistance. In 1973, the two countries announced a $200-million assistance agreement on gas and oil development, trade, transport, irrigation, and factory construction. Following the 1979 invasion, the Soviets augmented their large aid commitments to shore up the Afghan economy and rebuild the Afghan military. They provided the Karmal regime an unprecedented $800 million. The Soviet Union supported the Najibullah regime even after the withdrawal of Soviet troops in February 1989. Today, unresolved questions concerning Soviet MIA/POWs in Afghanistan remain an issue between Russia and Afghanistan.

Tajik rebels based in Afghanistan in July 1993 attacked a Russian border outpost in Tajikistan, killing 25 Russians and prompting Russian retaliatory strikes which caused extensive damage in northern Afghanistan. Reports of Afghan support for the Tajik rebels have led to cool relations between the two countries.

## Tajikistan

Afghanistan's relations with newly independent Tajikistan have been complicated by ongoing political upheaval and civil war in Tajikistan which spurred some 100,000 Tajiks to seek refuge in Afghanistan in late 1992 and early 1993. Tajik rebels seeking to overthrow the regime of Russian-backed former communist Imamali Rahmanov began operating from Afghan bases and recruiting Tajik refugees into their ranks. These rebels, reportedly aided by Afghans and a number of foreign Islamic extremists, conduct cross-border raids against Russian and Tajik security posts and seek to infiltrate fight-

ers and materiel from Afghanistan into Tajikistan.

# U.S.-AFGHAN RELATIONS

The first extensive American contact with Afghanistan was made by Josiah Harlan, an adviser in Afghan politics in the 1830s. After the establishment of diplomatic relations in 1934, the U.S. policy of helping developing nations raise their standard of living was an important factor in maintaining and improving U.S.-Afghan ties. From 1950 to 1979, U.S. foreign assistance provided Afghanistan with more than $500 million in loans, grants, and surplus agricultural commodities to develop transportation facilities, increase agricultural production, expand the educational system, stimulate industry, and improve government administration.

In the 1950s, the U.S. declined Afghanistan's request for defense cooperation but extended an economic assistance program focused on the development of Afghanistan's physical infrastructure—roads, dams, and power plants. Later, U.S. aid shifted from infrastructure projects to technical assistance programs to help develop the skills needed to build a modern economy. The Peace Corps was active in Afghanistan between 1962 and 1979.

After the April 1978 coup, relations deteriorated. In February 1979, U.S. Ambassador Adolph Dubs was murdered after Afghan security forces burst in on his kidnapers. The U.S. then reduced bilateral assistance and terminated a small military training program. All remaining assistance agreements were ended after the Soviet invasion.

Following the Soviet invasion, the United States supported diplomatic efforts to achieve a Soviet withdrawal. In addition, generous U.S. contributions to the refugee program in Pakistan played a major part in efforts to assist Afghans in need. U.S. efforts also included helping Afghans

living inside Afghanistan. This cross-border humanitarian assistance program increased Afghan self-sufficiency and helped Afghans resist Soviet attempts to drive civilians out of the rebel-dominated countryside. During the period of Soviet occupation of Afghanistan, the U.S. provided about $3 billion in military and economic assistance to Afghans and the resistance movement.

The U.S. Embassy in Kabul was closed in January 1989 for security reasons. The U.S. has supported the peaceful emergence of a broad-based government representative of all Afghans and has been active in encouraging a UN role in the national reconciliation process in Afghanistan. The U.S. provides financial aid for mine-clearing activities and other humanitarian assistance to Afghans through international organizations.

In addition to the efforts of the UN and other donors, the U.S. has provided $328 million in direct bilateral assistance to Afghanistan since 1985 through its crossborder program based in Islamabad, Pakistan. However, assistance levels have fallen dramatically in recent years due to overall budgetary constraints in the U.S. and the difficulties inherent in administering a crossborder aid program.

## Principal U.S. Officials

**For up-to-date information on Principal U.S. Officials, see the U.S. Embassies, Consulates, and Foreign Service section starting on page 139.**

# UN EFFORTS

During the Soviet occupation, the United Nations was highly critical of the U.S.S.R.'s interference in the internal affairs of Afghanistan and was instrumental in obtaining a negotiated Soviet withdrawal under the terms of the Geneva accords.

In the aftermath of the accords and subsequent Soviet withdrawal, the

*A report on important events that have taken place since the last State Department revision of this* Background Note.

Despite attempts to end the civil war which began in 1978 with Soviet support for the former Communist government, fighting continued to plague Afghanistan into the spring of 1997. By that time, 1.5 million Afghans had died and the Taliban, a militant Islamic faction, had consolidated its control over 90 percent of the nation.

Early in 1996, the warring factions that drove Soviet troops out of the country in 1989 agreed to establish a multiparty council to serve for six months and attempt to set the pattern for a future government. Fighting continued, however, and rebel leader Gulbuddin Hekmatyar was driven from his headquarters by the new militia just a few days after the announcement of the multiparty council.

Soon afterward, a UN diplomat arrived on a mission to bring the warring groups into a coalition government. The UN peace plan was delayed while a group close to former King Zakir Shah tried to settle differences between the government and the Taliban army. The Taliban, a Sunni Muslim movement which rose from the villages of the southwest, was accorded little influence under the original coalition plan despite the strength of its army, which had grown into the country's most powerful military force.

The government launched a major assault against rival Islamic factions in early March of 1996. The action was seen as an attempt by President Burhandoin Rabbani to gain control of the entire capital before the UN-sponsored cease-fire could go into effect.

President Rabbani's government and rival faction Hezb-i-Islami, led by former Prime Minister Hekmatyar, signed a peace agreement in May of 1996. Under the agreement, Mr. Hekmatyar was to have been returned to his former position in the government. He served as Prime Minister until January 1994 in a government comprised of Islamic factions that seized control after the Soviet-backed government was ousted in 1992. But war broke out between government troops and Hekmatyar's supporters, destroying the capital, Kabul, and killing an estimated 45,000 civilians.

The Taliban have successfully battled the government and imposed strict Islamic rule on most of Afghanistan. Women have been forced to resign from their jobs and girls are not allowed to attend government schools. Punishment of criminals is conducted in public and includes amputation for thieves and stoning adulterers to death.

In early 1998, the Taliban militia controlled about two-thirds of Afghanistan. Opposition forces under Ahmad Shah Masoud controlled the northeast of the country. Taliban forces mounted another offensive against their opponents in August-September 1998 and nearly sparked a war with neighboring Iran after a series of Shiite villages were pillaged and Iranian diplomats killed. Iran, which supplies Masoud's forces, countered by massing troops along its border with Afghanistan. Although the crisis subsided, tensions between the Taliban and Iran remained high.

A persistent problem for the Taliban has been their lack of diplomatic recognition. Only Pakistan, Saudi Arabia, and the United Arab Emirates recognize the Taliban as the legitimate government of Afghanistan; most of the world, as well as international organizations such as the UN continue to recognize the ousted government of Hekmatyar as the legitimate government of the country. Despite their lack of recognition, in October 1997, the Taliban announced a $2 billion possible pipeline plan to transport natural gas from Turkmenistan to Pakistan through Afghanistan.

While lacking a functioning central government, Afghanistan fell victim to deforestation, poor water management, and overgrazing. Bob McKerrow, the leader of the Kabul delegation of the International Federation of Red Cross and Red Crescent Societies, predicted a major ecological disaster affecting the entire Hindu Kush mountain range. Triggered by melting snow and heavy rains, floods have occurred in at least seven provinces, covering more than a quarter of Afghanistan and killing over 100 people. By June 2001 severe international sanctions, poor harvest, devastation of livestock, and the country's worst drought in thirty years had put five million Afghans at risk of starvation. An estimated 800,000 people fled their homes as a result of the drought and continued civil war.

Despite attempts to broker a peace settlement, fighting between the Taliban and opposition factions continued through late spring of 2001. In March 1999, the warring factions agreed to enter a coalition government, but by July these UN-sponsored peace talks broke down and the Taliban renewed its offensive against opposition forces. In May 2001, the Taliban controlled 95 percent of the country. The warfare led to more displacement among the civilian population and led to UN condemnation of the Taliban. Growing disputes between the Taliban and the UN have threatened any future humanitarian assistance. The Taliban also found itself on the receiving end of U.S. sanctions and a global trade embargo for its continued harboring of Saudi terrorist Osama bin Laden. The Taliban continued to draw global criticism for their harsh version of Islam and crackdown on "un-Islamic" Afghans. In March 2001 they ordered all statues of Buddha be destroyed and in May they required Hindus to wear yellow tags to distinguish them from Muslims.

United Nations has assisted in the repatriation of refugees and has provided humanitarian aid such as health care, educational programs, and food and has supported mine-clearing operations. The UNDP and associated agencies have undertaken a limited number of development projects. However, the UN reduced its role in Afghanistan in 1992 in the wake of fierce factional strife in and around Kabul.

# ALBANIA

March 1999

Official Name:
**Republic of Albania**

# PROFILE

## Geography

**Area:** 28,750 square km, slightly larger than Maryland.
**Cities:** Capital—Tirana (est. pop 312,220). Other cities—Durres (100,405), Elbasan (87,711), Shkoder (82,097), Vlore (71,089).
**Terrain:** Mostly mountains and hills; small plains along coast.
**Climate:** Mild temperate; cool, cloudy, wet winters; hot, clear, dry summers; interior colder.

## People

**Nationality:** Albanian(s).
**Population (1995 est.):** 3,413,904.
**Population growth rate (1995 est.):** 1.16%.
**Ethnic groups:** Albanian 95%; Greek 3-4%; other 1-2%.
**Religions:** Muslim 70%; Orthodox 20%; Catholic 10%.
**Languages:** Albanian (Tosk is the official dialect), Greek.
**Education:** Years compulsory—9. Attendance—96.6% in urban areas, 41.1% in rural areas. Literacy—72%.
**Health:** Infant mortality rate—30/ 1000. Life expectancy—males 70 yrs., females 76 yrs.
**Workforce (1.5 million):** Agriculture 60%; industry and commerce 40%.

## Government

**Type:** Parliamentary democracy.
**Constitution:** The People's Assembly approved an interim basic law on April 29, 1991; a draft constitution was rejected by popular referendum in the fall of 1994. A revised draft was subsequently approved in a referendum on November 22, 1998.
**Independence:** November 28, 1912 (from the Ottoman Empire).
**Branches:** Executive—President (head of state); Prime Minister (head of government), Council of Ministers (cabinet). Legislative—unicameral People's Assembly (parliament). Judicial—Constitutional Court, Court of Cassation, appeals courts, and district courts.
**Subdivisions:** 36 Rreths (districts).
**Political parties:** Socialist Party (PS); Democratic Party (PD); Republican Party (PR); Unity for Human Rights Party (PBDNJ, Greek minority party); Social Democratic Party (PSD); Democratic Alliance Party (PAD); Legality Party (LLP, monarchist), Balli Kombetar (BK, National Front); National Unity Party (PUK); National Unity Party (PNU); Social Democratic Union Party (PBSD); Christian Democratic Party (PCD); Democratic Party of the Right (PDD); Agrarian Party (PA); and up to 20 other parties registered.
**Suffrage:** Universal and compulsory at age 18.

## Economy

**GDP (1998 est.):** $2.88 billion.
**GDP growth rate (1998 est.):** 10%.
**GNP per capita (1998 est.):** $830.
**Natural resources:** Oil, gas, coal, chromium, copper, iron, nickel.
**Agriculture (55% of GDP):** Wheat, corn, potatoes, sugar beets, cotton, and tobacco.
**Industry (16% of GDP):** Textiles, timber, construction materials, fuels, semi-processed minerals.
**Trade (1998 est.):** Exports—$343 million. Major markets—(The EU accounts for two-thirds of market); Italy, Greece, Macedonia. Imports— $1.09 billion. Major suppliers—Italy, Greece, Macedonia, Germany.

# PEOPLE AND HISTORY

The name Albania is derived from an ancient Illyrian tribe, the Albanoi, forbears of the modern Albanians. The Albanian name for their country is Shqiperia.

Prior to the 20th century, Albania was subject to foreign domination except for a brief period (1443-1478) of revolt from Ottoman rule. Albania declared its independence during the first Balkan War in 1912 and remained independent after the World War I largely through the intercession of U.S. President Woodrow Wilson at the Paris peace conference.

In 1939, Italy under Mussolini annexed Albania. Following Italy's 1943 surrender to Allied Powers during World War II, German troops occupied the country. Partisan bands, including the communist-led National Liberation Front (NLF), gained control in November 1944 following the German withdrawal. Since Yugoslav communists were instrumental in creating the Albanian communist Party of Labor in November 1941, the NLF regime, led by Enver Hoxha, became a virtual satellite of Yugoslavia until the Tito-Stalin split in 1948. Subsequently, Albania's hard-line brand of communism led to growing difficulties with the Soviet Union under Krushchev, coming to a head in 1961 when the Soviet leaders openly denounced Albania at a party congress. The two states broke diplomatic relations later that year. However, Albania continued nominal membership in the Warsaw Pact until the 1968 invasion of Czechoslovakia.

In 1945, an informal U.S. mission was sent to Albania to study the possibility of establishing relations with the NLF regime. However, the regime refused to recognize the validity of prewar treaties and increasingly harassed the U.S. mission until it was withdrawn in November 1946. The U.S. maintained no contact with the Albanian Government between 1946 and 1990.

During the 1960s, China emerged as Albania's staunch ally and primary source of economic and military assistance. However, the close relationship faltered during the 1970s when China decided to introduce some market reforms and seek a rapprochement with the U.S. After years of rocky relations, the open split came in 1978 when the Chinese Government ended its aid program and terminated all trade. Hoxha, still communist dictator, opted to pursue an isolationist course. The result was financial ruin for Albania.

By 1990, changes elsewhere in the communist bloc began to influence thinking in Albania. The government

## Travel Notes

**Travel Advice:** For up-to-date information from the U.S. State Department on possible inconvenient or hazardous situations, see the **Travel Warnings and Consular Information Sheets from the U.S. Government** section starting on page 1723. For the latest information on health requirements and conditions, see the **International Travelers' Health Information** section starting on page 1351. For further information dealing with non-urgent matter, see the **Tips for Travelers to...** section starting on page 1546.

began to seek closer ties with the West in order to improve the economic conditions in the country. The People's Assembly approved an interim basic law in April 1991. Short-lived governments introduced initial democratic reforms throughout 1991. In 1992, the victorious Democratic Party government under President Sali Berisha began a more deliberate program of market economic and democratic reform. Progress stalled in 1995, however, resulting in declining public confidence in government institutions and an economic crisis spurred on by the proliferation and collapse of several pyramid financial schemes. The implosion of authority in early 1997 alarmed the world and prompted intense international mediation and pressure. Early elections held in June 1997 led to the victory of a Socialist-led coalition of parties, which remains in power today.

# GOVERNMENT AND POLITICAL CONDITIONS

Albania's 1976 socialist constitution was declared invalid in April 1991, and an interim basic law was adopted. The country remains without a permanent constitution; a draft constitution was rejected in a November 1994 referendum.

## Principal Government Officials

**For up-to-date information on Principal Government Officials, see the Chiefs of State and Cabinet Members of Foreign Governments section starting on page 1.**

## President and Cabinet

The Head of State in Albania is the President of the Republic. The President is elected to a 5-year term by the People's Assembly by secret ballot, requiring a two-thirds majority of the votes of all deputies. The next election is expected in 2002.

The President has the power to guarantee observation of the Constitution and all laws, act as Commander-in-Chief of the armed forces; exercise the duties of the People's Assembly when the Assembly is not in session, and appoint the Chairman of the Council of Ministers (Prime Minister).

Executive power rests with the Council of Ministers (cabinet). The Chairman of the Council (Prime Minister) is appointed by the President, ministers are nominated by the President on the basis of the Prime Minister's recommendation. The People's Assembly must give final approval of the composition of the Council. The Council is responsible for carrying out both foreign and domestic policies. It directs and controls the activities of the ministries and other state organs.

The Council consists of 17 ministers and nine state secretaries. The Socialist Party occupies the bulk of the cabinet positions, though the Democratic Alliance, the Social Democratic Party, and the Agrarian Party each head one ministry.

## Legislature

The Kuvendi Popullor, or People's Assembly, is the law-making body of the Albanian Government. There are 155 deputies in the Assembly, of which 115 are directly elected by an absolute majority of the voters and 40 are chosen by their parties on the basis of proportional representation. The President of the Assembly (or Speaker) has two deputies and chairs the Assembly. There are 15 permanent commissions, or committees. Parliamentary elections are held at least every 4 years.

The parliament that emerged from elections in June 1997 was led by the Socialist Party, which took 101 of the 155 seats. The Democratic Party won 27 seats. The Social Democrats won eight seats (including the Speaker's), and the Unity for Human Rights party won four. Among the remaining seats, the Democratic Alliance, Republican, and Legality and Unity of the Right parties won two each; Balli Kombetar, the Agrarian, Christian Democrat, and National Unity Party won one each.

The Assembly has the power to decide the direction of domestic and foreign policy; approve or amend the Constitution; declare war on another state; ratify or annul international treaties; elect the President of the Republic, the Supreme Court, the Attorney General and his or her deputies; and control the activity of state radio and television, state news agency and other official information media.

## Judicial System

The court system consists of a Constitutional Court, the Court of Cassation, appeals courts, and district courts. The Constitutional Court is comprised of nine members appointed by the People's Assembly for maximum 9-year terms. The Constitutional Court interprets the Constitution, determines the constitutionality of laws, and resolves disagreements between local and federal authorities. The remaining courts are each divided into three jurisdictions: criminal, civil, and military. The Court of Cassation is the highest court of appeal and consists of 11 members appointed by the People's Assembly and serving 7-year terms. The President of the Republic chairs the High Council of Justice (HCJ) charged with appointing and dismissing other judges. The HCJ was expanded in late 1997 to comprise 13 members from among the various branches of government.

A college of three judges renders Albanian court verdicts; there is no jury trial, though the college is sometimes referred to in the Albanian press as the "jury."

## Administrative Divisions

Albania is divided into 12 prefectures. Prefects are appointed by the Council of Ministers. Each prefecture comprises several districts (Rreths), of which there are 36. Each district

**Editor's Update**                                          **June 2001**

*A report on important events that have taken place since the last State Department revision of this* Background Note.

The war in the neighboring Serbian province of Kosovo dominated Albanian affairs throughout the early part of 1999. Efforts to negotiate a settlement to the conflict between Serb security forces and Kosovar Albanians in March 1999 failed. When the talks collapsed, the Serbs continued their attacks and NATO responded with air strikes against Serbian communications, industrial, and military sites throughout Serbia (including Kosovo) and Montenegro. By mid-May 1999, it was estimated that roughly 700,000 Albanians fled Kosovo altogether while another 600,000 were displaced within Kosovo. Albania received over 450,000 refugees. Others fled to the Former Yugoslav Republic of Macedonia (FYROM), Montenegro, or NATO countries, including the United States.

The NATO air campaign continued into early June and calls mounted in hawkish Western circles for the introduction of ground forces to stop the ethnic cleansing. The Serbian forces withdrew from Kosovo in early June, and Kosovar Albanian refugees began returning to their homes, thus easing the strain on Albania.

Ironically, the refugee influx proved positive to the Albanian economy. Under the reformist leadership of Prime Minister Ilir Meta, Albania registered an economic growth of 8 percent. and is expected to continue the trend in the 2001 fiscal year.

In February 2001, an ethnic Albanian revolt broke out in Macedonia, with the goal of creating a Greater Albania. President Rexhep Meidani called for an end to the fighting in order to aid the Balkan pursuit of European integration. A truce was made in June 2001 but its stability has yet to be determined.

has its own local administration and governor. District governors are elected by the District Council, whose members are selected from party lists made public to voters before local elections, on the basis of proportional representation. City mayors are directly elected by voters, while city councils are chosen by proportional representation.

Albania maintains an embassy in the United States at 2100 S Street NW, Washington, DC 20008 (telephone: 202-223-4942; fax: 202-628-7342).

# ECONOMY

The collapse of communism in Albania came later and was more chaotic than in other eastern European countries and was marked by a mass exodus of refugees to Italy and Greece in 1991 and 1992. Attempts at reform began in earnest in early 1992 after real GDP fell by more than 50% from its peak in 1989.

The democratically elected government that assumed office in April 1992 launched an ambitious economic reform program to halt economic deterioration and put the country on the path toward a market economy. Key elements included price and exchange system liberalization, fiscal consolidation, monetary restraint, and a firm income policy. These were complemented by a com-

prehensive package of structural reforms including privatization, enterprise, and financial sector reform, and creation of the legal framework for a market economy and private sector activity. Most prices were liberalized and are now at or near international levels. Most agriculture, state housing, and small industry were privatized. Progress continued in the privatization of transport, services, and small and medium-sized enterprises. In 1995, the government began privatizing large state enterprises.

Results of Albania's efforts were initially encouraging. Led by the agricultural sector, real GDP grew by an estimated 11% in 1993, 8% in 1994, and more than 8% in 1995, with most of this growth in the private sector. Annual inflation dropped from 250% in 1991 to single-digit numbers. The Albanian currency, the lek, stabilized. Albania became less dependent on food aid. The speed and vigor of private entrepreneurial response to Albania's opening and liberalizing was better than expected. Beginning in 1995, however, progress stalled, with negligible GDP growth in 1996 and a 9% contraction in 1997. Inflation approached 20% in 1996 and 50% in 1997. The lek initially lost up to half of its value during the 1997 crisis, before rebounding to its January 1998 level of 143 to the dollar.

Albania is currently undergoing an intensive macroeconomic restructuring regime with the IMF and World Bank. The need for reform is profound, encompassing all sectors of the economy. However, reforms are constrained by limited administrative capacity and low-income levels, which make the population particularly vulnerable to unemployment, price fluctuation, and other variables that negatively affect income. Albania is still dependent on foreign aid and remittances from expatriates abroad. Large scale investment from outside is still hampered by poor infrastructure, lack of a fully functional banking system, untested or incompletely developed investment, tax, and contract laws, and an enduring mentality that discourages bureaucratic initiative.

# FOREIGN RELATIONS

Albanian foreign policy has concentrated on maintaining good relations with its Balkan neighbors, gaining access to European-Atlantic security institutions, and securing close ties with the United States. The crisis of 1997 spurred an intensive period of international involvement in Albania, led by the Organization for Security and Cooperation in Europe (OSCE). Italy hosted a series of international conferences and led a multinational force of about 7,000 troops to help stabilize the country and facilitate OSCE election monitoring. The United States has worked closely with European partners and various multilateral fora to ensure that international efforts are coordinated.

The Government of Albania is very concerned with developments in the ethnic Albanian province of Kosovo in neighboring Serbia, particularly in the post-Dayton agreement period. While maintaining a responsible and non-provocative position, the Albanian Government has made it clear that the status and treatment of the Albanian population in Kosovo is a principal national concern. Bilateral relations with Greece have improved dramatically since 1994. In 1996, the two countries signed a Treaty of Peace and Friendship and discussed the issues of the status of Albanian refugees in Greece and education in the mother tongue for the ethnic Greek minority in southern Albania. Tirana's relations with Macedonia remain friendly, despite occasional incidents involving ethnic Albanians there. Tirana has repeatedly encouraged the Albanian minority's continued participation in the government of F.Y.R.O.M.

## Foreign Aid

Through FY 1998, the U.S. committed approximately $300 million to Albania's economic and political transformation and to address humanitarian needs. This figure comprises about 10% of all bilateral and multilateral assistance offered since 1991. Italy ranks first in bilateral assistance and

## Travel Notes

**Travel Advice:** For up-to-date information from the U.S. State Department on possible inconvenient or hazardous situations, see the **Travel Warnings and Consular Information Sheets from the U.S. Government** section starting on page 1723. For the latest information on health requirements and conditions, see the **International Travelers' Health Information** section starting on page 1385. For further information dealing with non-urgent matter, see the **Tips for Travelers to...** section starting on page 1588.

Germany third. The EU has given about $800 million since 1991 and pledged $175 million in 1996-1999.

In FY 1999, the U.S. will provide $30 million through the Support for East European Democracy (SEED) Act, up from $27 million the previous year. The U.S. also will provide an agricultural commodities grant of $10 million. The $30 million Albanian-American Enterprise Fund (AAEF), launched in 1994, is actively making debt and equity investments in local businesses. AAEF is designed to harness private sector efforts to assist in the economic transformation. U.S. assistance priorities include promotion of agricultural development and a market economy, advancement of democratic institutions (including police training), and improvements in

quality of life. The SEED funding request for Albania for FY 2000 is $25 million.

# U.S.- ALBANIAN RELATIONS

The U.S. and Albania had no diplomatic relations between 1946 and 1991. Following the Albanian Government's lifting in March 1991 of restrictions on religious and political activity and on travel, the U.S. reestablished diplomatic relations with Albania. The U.S. Embassy in Tirana reopened October 1, 1991. Since 1991, the U.S. has maintained close relations with a series of Albanian Governments. The U.S. Government has provided more than $250 million in technical and humanitarian assistance to support Albania's political and economic development.

## Principal U.S. Embassy Officials

For up-to-date information on Principal U.S. Officials, see the U.S. Embassies, Consulates, and Foreign Service section starting on page 139.

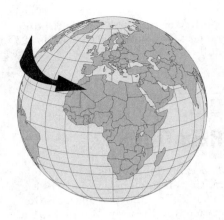

# ALGERIA
November 1988

Official Name:
## Democratic and Popular Republic of Algeria

# PROFILE

## Geography

**Area:** 2.4 million sq. km. (918,497 sq. mi.); almost one-third the size of the continental US.
**Cities:** Capital—Algiers metropolitan area (pop. 2.8 million, 1987 est. ). Other cities (1987)—Oran (590,818), Constantine (438,717), Annaba (310,106).
**Terrain:** Three zones roughly parallel to the Mediterranean Sea and divided by mountain ranges, a relatively fertile coastal plain, Tellian Atlas Mountains, high plateau region, Saharan Atlas Mountains, and desert. About 3% cultivated land; 16% pasture; and 80% desert, wasteland, and mountains.
**Climate:** Mild winters and hot summers in coastal plain; less rain and cold winters in high plateau. February-May, sandstorms and considerable daily temperature variation in the desert.

## People

**Nationality:** Noun and adjective—Algerian(s).
**Population (1987):** 23 million.
**Annual growth rate (1986 est.):** 3.1%.
**Ethnic groups:** Arab and Berber.
**Religion:** 99% Sunni Islam.
**Languages:** Arabic (official), Berber dialects, French.

**Education (1986):** Years compulsory—to age 16. Attendance—94% primary, 47% secondary. Literacy (1983)—52%; 65%—males, 40%—females.
**Health:** Infant mortality rate (1986)—82.4/1,000. Life expectancy (1986)—60 yrs.
**Work force (1986):** 4.7 million. Agriculture—22%. Industry and commerce—32%. Services and government—33%.

## Government

**Type:** Republic.
**Independence:** July 5, 1962.
**Constitution:** November 19, 1976.
**Branches:** Executive—president. Legislative—National Popular Assembly. Judicial—Supreme Court and Higher Judicial Council.
**Subdivisions:** 48 *wilayaat* (provinces).
**Political party:** National Liberation Front (FLN).
**Suffrage:** Universal adult (age 18).
**Central government budget (1987):** $21.3 billion.
**Defense (1980 est.):** 2.4% of GDP
**Flag:** Staff side green, other half white; red star in a red crescent, centered.

## Economy

**Nominal GDP (1986):** $59 billion.
**Real growth rate (1986):** 2%.
**Per capita income (est.):** $2,645.
**Avg. inflation rate (1986):** 10%.
**Natural resources:** Crude oil, natural gas, iron ore, phosphates, uranium, lead, zinc, mercury.
**Agriculture (8% of GDP):** Products—wheat, barley, oats, olives, dates, citrus fruits, sheep, cattle. Arable land-6.7 million hectares (about 13% of total land).
**Industry (73% of 1986 GDP):** Types—crude oil, natural gas, petrochemicals, refined petroleum products, iron and steel, home appliances, transportation equipment, food processing.
**Trade (1986):** Exports—$8.1 billion: crude oil, condensates and refined products, liquefied natural gas, mercury, phosphates, wine. Major markets—US, France, FRG, Spain. Imports—$7.9 billion: wheat, corn, soybeans, meat, milk, eggs, machinery and vehicles, aircraft, capital goods. Major suppliers—France, Belgium, Italy, Netherlands, FRG, Canada, US. External debt (1987 est.)—$17 billion. Debt service (1986 est.)—$4.9 billion, or 60% of exports.
**Official exchange rate:** 4.89 dinars=US$1 (September 1987). The controlled Algerian dinar is permitted to fluctuate very narrowly against the US dollar.
**Fiscal year:** Calendar year.

## Membership in International Organizations

UN and some of its specialized and related agencies, Organization of African Unity (OAU), Arab League,

Nonaligned Movement, Organization of Petroleum Exporting Countries (OPEC), Organization of Arab Petroleum Exporting Countries (OAPEC), INTELSAT, Organization of the Islamic Conference (OIC).

# GEOGRAPHY

Algeria, the second largest state in Africa, has a Mediterranean coastline of about 998 kilometers (620 mi.). The Tellian and Saharan Atlas mountain ranges cross the country from east to west, dividing it into three zones. Between the northern zone, Tellian Atlas, and the Mediterranean is a narrow fertile coastal plain—the Tell (Arabic for hill)—with a moderate climate year round and rainfall adequate for agriculture. A high plateau region, averaging 914 meters (3,000 ft.) above sea level, with limited rainfall and great rocky plains and desert, lies between the two mountain ranges. It is generally barren except for scattered clumps of trees and intermittent bush and pasture land. The third and largest zone, south of the Saharan-Atlas range, is mostly desert. About 80% of the country is desert, steppes, wasteland, and mountains.

Algeria's weather is irregular from year to year, but in the north, the summers are usually hot with little rainfall. Winter rains begin in the north in October. Frost and snow are rare, except on the highest slopes of the Tellian Atlas mountains. Dust and sandstorms occur most frequently between February and May.

# PEOPLE

Ninety-one percent of the Algerian population lives along the Mediterranean coast on 12% of the land. Forty-five percent of the population are urban, and urbanization continues despite efforts to discourage migration to the cities. About 1.5 million nomads and semisettled bedouin still live in the Saharan area. According to 1986 data, 45% of the population is under age 15.

Nearly all Algerians are Muslim, of Arab, Berber, or mixed Arab-Berber stock. A mostly foreign Roman Catholic community of about 45,000 exists, as do very small Protestant and Jewish communities. Many foreign technicians and teachers, including about 45,000 French and about 2,000 Americans, reside in Algeria. The total foreign (non-Arab) population is estimated at 75,000.

Algeria's educational system has grown remarkably since 1962; in the last 12 years, attendance has doubled to more than 5 million students. Education is free and compulsory to age 16. Despite government allocation of substantial educational resources (15.8% of the 1985 state budget), population pressures and a serious shortage of teachers have severely strained the system. In 1985, foreign teachers accounted for 71% of all secondary-level instructors. Algeria has begun to emphasize establishment of technical institutes for training in the skills necessary to operate the country's burgeoning industrial sector. Each year, Algeria sends some 7,000 university-level students overseas, particularly to Western Europe and the United States but also to Eastern Europe and the Soviet Union.

Algeria's free national medical program emphasizes preventive care. Newly qualified medical personnel are required by law to serve in state medical facilities for several years.

Housing is one of Algeria's most pressing problems because of the high rate of population increase and the influx of people from rural to urban areas. The 1985–89 development plan calls for the construction of 250,000 housing units per year. In 1986, 115,000 units were built.

# HISTORY

Since the 5th century B.C., the indigenous tribes of northern Africa (identified by the Romans as "Berbers") have been pushed back from the coast by successive waves of Phoenician, Roman, Vandal, Byzantine, Arab, Turkish, and, finally, French invaders. The greatest cultural impact came from the Arab invasions of the 8th and 11th centuries A.D., which brought Islam and the Arabic language. The effects of the most recent (French) occupation—French language and European-inspired socialism—are still pervasive.

North African boundaries have shifted during various stages of the conquests. The borders of modern Algeria were created by the French, whose colonization began in 1830. To benefit French colonists, most of whom were farmers and businessmen, northern Algeria was eventually organized into overseas departments of France, with representatives in the French National Assembly. France controlled the entire country, but the traditional Muslim population in the rural areas remained separated from the modern economic infrastructure of the European community.

Indigenous Algerians began their revolt on November 1, 1954, to gain rights denied them under French rule. The revolution, launched by a small group of nationalists who called themselves the National Liberation Front (FLN), was a guerrilla war in which both sides used terrorist tactics. Eventually, protracted negotiations led to a cease-fire signed by France and the FLN on March 18, 1962, at Evian, France. The Evian accords also provided for continuing economic, financial, technical, and cultural relations along with interim administrative arrangements until a referendum on self-determination could be held.

The referendum was held in Algeria on July 1, 1962, and France declared Algeria independent on July 3. On September 8, 1963, a constitution was adopted by referendum, and later that month, Ahmed Ben Bella was formally elected president. On June 19, 1965, President Ben Bella was replaced in a bloodless coup by a Council of the Revolution headed by Minister of Defense Col. Houari Boumediene.

The National Assembly was dissolved and the constitution suspended after

Algeria

the overthrow of the Ben Bella government; 11 years of rule by decree followed. A new constitution was approved by popular referendum on November 19, 1976, and Houari Boumediene was elected president of the republic on December 10, 1976. He died 2 years later.

Following nomination by an FLN Party Congress, Col. Chadli Bendjedid was elected president on Febru-ary 7, 1979; he was elected to a second 5-year term in January 1984.

# GOVERNMENT

Algeria has a centralized government. Under the 1976 constitution, the government administers the country, taking its guidance on fundamental policy issues from periodic congresses of the FLN party and from the party's Central Committee between congresses. From 1965 until the election of the National Popular Assembly in 1977 and creation of the FLN Political Bureau in 1979, all executive and legislative power was concentrated in the Council of the Revolution and the Council of Ministers (both headed by President Boumediene).

A process of building new political institutions began in 1967 when the

212

communal (township) assemblies were created. *Wilaya* (provincial) assemblies were added in 1969. Movement toward forming national political institutions started on dune 19, 1975, when President Boumediene announced that a new constitution would be drafted. A National Charter stating the goals and principles of the Algerian revolution was put forward and approved by plebiscite in June 1976. The new constitution, providing for a presidential system of government and a National Popular Assembly, was promulgated in November. In elections under the new constitution, President Boumediene, the sole candidate (FLN), was elected to a 6-year term on December 10, 1976. Elections for the National Popular Assembly took place in February 1977.

After President Boumediene's death, the country returned to a more collegial leadership representing a diversity of opinion. With strong military backing, the first FLN Party Congress since 1964 named Col. Chadli Bendjedid Secretary General of the FLN in January 1979 and the only presidential candidate. Constitutional amendments recommended by the FLN party congress and adopted by the National Popular Assembly in July 1979 reduced the presidential term from 6 to 5 years, required the designation of a prime minister and established procedures in the event the chief of state is incapacitated. The FLN also was restructured-the Council of the Revolution was replaced with a 17-member political bureau of senior political personalities, and a 160-member central committee was created to make policy between party congresses.

Chadli Bendjedid was elected president on February 7, 1979, and named his first cabinet 1 month later. He affirmed continuity with the prior administration and with the Algerian revolution but also announced a review of national priorities. President Bendjedid consolidated his political position at the extraordinary FLN congress of June 15-19, 1980, which confirmed his mandate of "full power" and authorized him to make major personnel and policy changes.

President Bendjedid was reelected to a second 5-year term in January 1984.

Prior to local elections in December 1984, provincial authority was increased, and 17 new provinces *(wilayaat)* were created. Algeria's 48 *wilayaat* are further subdivided into districts and communes. Each *wilaya* is administered by a *wali* (governor), appointed by decree and responsible to the minister of interior.

Civil, criminal, public, commercial, and family legislation that remained from the French colonial system was reviewed by the National Commission of Legislation. In July 1985, all French laws were proclaimed invalid. Commercial and family law have been revised extensively, and new codes were prepared in the areas of customs, labor, water usage, forests, and grazing lands. The code dealing with family and personal status is based on Muslim law but is administered by the civil courts. The new system retained the Supreme Court, established in 1963, with responsibility for regulating jurisprudence.

## Principal Government Officials

For up-to-date information on Principal Government Officials, see the Chiefs of State and Cabinet Members of Foreign Governments section starting on page 1.

Algeria maintains an embassy in the United States at 2118 Kalorama Road NVV., Washington, D.C. 20008 (tel. 202-32300). The visa section is located at 2137 Wyoming Avenue NW., 20008 (same phone number as the Embassy).

# POLITICAL CONDITIONS

Since 1965, Algeria has enjoyed relative political stability, including a peaceful and constitutional transition to President Bendjedid's leadership.

The FLN seeks to mobilize popular participation in politics through its own countrywide structures and those of its mass organizations for peasants, youth, veterans, and women. In keeping with the National Charter and the constitution, the Algerian Government espouses revolutionary socialism and applies this philosophy to its domestic and foreign policies. Its principal domestic objectives are to achieve economic development through industrialization and increased agricultural productivity and to raise the standard of living under a socialist system.

President Bendjedid seeks to revitalize FLN party and government structures as well as the economy. The government's 1987 economic slogan, "autonomy for enterprises," reflects its current effort to grant greater financial and managerial autonomy to state-owned enterprises, which account for 80% of the country's GDP.

Population growth and associated problems—unemployment and underemployment, inability of social services to keep pace with rapid urban migration, inadequate industrial management and productivity, insufficient agricultural production, and inefficient distribution of consumer goods—are being addressed by the government.

# ECONOMY

The planning, development, and administration of the Algerian economy traditionally has been almost totally under State control, though the government has in recent years sought to reduce the level of such control. Government agencies and numerous state enterprises have controlled foreign trade and operated almost all major industries, much of the distribution and retail systems, all public utilities, and the entire banking and credit system. Under President Bendjedid, the government has launched an effort to foster greater autonomy in agricultural and

**Customs:** US citizens need a visa to enter Algeria. Travelers should clearly stipulate the intended date of entry and planned duration of stay on their visa applications.

Visitors are permitted to bring in any amount of foreign exchange, provided it is declared at customs. A special currency form is provided at the frontier; complete and retain it after authentication by airport customs authorities. Foreign currency can be exchanged at all banks, seaports, and airports and in some hotels and vacation villages. Unused foreign currency is reexportable, provided it was properly declared upon entry and amounts were duly recorded by the exchange authorities on the currency form.

**Climate and clothing:** The coastal areas have a mild climate, hot in summer and cool and rainy for several months in winter. Winter clothing is worn almost continuously from November until April, particularly at night, and rainwear is advisable. Rooms are not always warmly heated in winter.

**Health:** No vaccinations are required for entry. Typhoid, tetanus, polio, and cholera inoculations are recommended. Tapwater is not potable; bottled water is available.

**Transportation:** The domestic airline serves Oran, Constantine, Annaba, and many of the Saharan cities, including Tamanrasset. There is railway passenger service between the major northern cities and bus service to many of the smaller cities and towns. Good paved roads, one of which links Morocco and Tunisia, cover the northern region and connect some oases. The Trans-Saharan Highway is surfaced from Ghardaia to Tamanrasset. Rental cars are available but expensive.

**Telecommunications:** There are international airmail, telegraph, telex, and telephone services to the US and Europe. Long-distance calls may be made from any post office, but it is not possible to reverse charges or to use a credit card. Algeria is five time zones ahead of eastern standard time.

**Tourist attractions:** Obtain information on Saharan travel from the Algerian Tourist office (ONAT), 25-27 rue Khelifa Boukhalfa, Algiers; Algerian consulates; and the Amicale des Sahariens (Paris: 33, rue Paul Valery, 16e, tel. KLE 20-24; Algiers: 14, Avenue du 1er Novembre, tel. 62-22-02).

Algiers has a chronic shortage of hotel rooms, so make reservations in advance.

**National holidays:** New Year's Day, January 1; Labor Day, May 1; Independence Day, July 5 (National Day); Anniversary of the Outbreak of the Revolution, November 1. Islamic holidays, which follow the lunar cycle (and advance roughly 10 days annually): Id al-Fitr (end of Ramadan), May 28-29 (1987); Id al-Adha (Feast of Sacrifice), August 5-6 (1987); Islamic New Year (First of Muharram), August 25 (1987); Achoura (10th of Muharram), September 4 (1987); Mawlid an-Nabi (Prophet's Birthday), November 4 (1987)

**Travel Advice:** For up-to-date information from the U.S. State Department on possible inconvenient or hazardous situations, see the **Travel Warnings and Consular Information Sheets from the U.S. Government** section starting on page 1723. For the latest information on health requirements and conditions, see the **International Travelers' Health Information** section starting on page 1385. For further information dealing with nonurgent matter, see the **Tips for Travelers to...** section starting on page 1588.

other economic sectors as a means to improve production and economic performance.

In the decade following independence, Algeria nationalized all major foreign business interests as well as many private Algerian companies and about one-third of the arable farm land. (Some land was redistributed to private owners in early 1985 and much larger redistribution occurred in 1987-88.) Nationalization ranged from the assumption of a controlling interest to complete take-overs. The Algerian Government has settled most of the claims for compensation of nationalized properties by foreign firms and in 1982 began settling individual claims.

Government efforts to attract foreign capital recently have led to changes in laws affecting foreign investment, including a 1986 revised joint venture law that relaxed past restrictive provisions and a new law on hydrocarbon exploration. Normally, only those foreign private investments involving the formation of joint ventures between foreign firms and appropriate Algerian state enterprises are allowed, with the latter retaining a controlling interest. Some U.S. firms have joint venture agreements with Algerian state enterprises, all in petroleum or mining activities; joint ventures in other areas are being discussed with U.S. firms.

The hydrocarbon sector is of major importance to the Algerian economy, representing more than 97% of the country's hard currency earnings in 1987. The Algerian economy weathered the recession of the early 1980s better than many other hydrocarbon producers because of the diversification of its hydrocarbon export mix and the development of a relatively large industrial sector. However the significant decline in hydrocarbon earnings since 1986 because of the downturn in oil prices has forced the government to reduce expenditures and adopt other austerity measures.

Real gross domestic product (GDP) grew only 2.2% in 1986 to 59 billion, less than one-half its 1985 level. Hydrocarbons, primarily crude oil, gas, condensates, and refined products, accounted for 29%, construction for 14%, and agriculture for 8%.

With crude oil production of about 635,000 barrels per day (1987), Algeria accounts for less than 4% of total production by the Organization of Petroleum Exporting Countries. However its known natural gas reserves are the fourth largest in the world, after the U.S.S.R., Iran, and the United States. The government has adopted a development strategy that links the country's future to production and export of gas, both by pipeline and in liquid form (liquefied. natural gas-LNG), and gas derivatives such as condensate and liquid petroleum gas (LPG-mainly butane and propane). Algeria has pioneered the development of LNG technology and, with Italy, has constructed the first trans-Mediterranean gas pipeline. Algeria's move into the condensate, LPG, and refined products markets has cushioned the country fluctuations in the global hydrocarbon market. However the economy has felt keenly the effects of the recent downturn in oil prices, and the government has had to reduce imports and government expenditures.

The Algerian Government has defended high oil and gas prices on the grounds that past prices for petroleum and other raw materials, and especially nonrenewable hydrocarbon resources, brought inadequate returns to producer countries that need this income to advance their economies. Algeria's policy of high gas prices has dampened sales; recently, the government has begun to accommodate market forces in its pricing policies.

The current 5-year economic development plan (1985-90) continues to be financed by hydrocarbon income, but there have been major changes in expenditures. Emphasis has been shifted away from heavy industrial development and toward the agricultural sector with the ultimate goal of agricultural self-sufficiency. Although new heavy industry has been given reduced priority, industrial development still receives major allocations under the plan.

Algeria has 80,000 kilometers (48,000 mi.) of national and provincial roads, 75% of which are hard surfaced 4,000 kilometers (2,400 mi.) of railway, 8 international airports-Algiers, Annaba, Constantine, Tebessa, Ghardaia, Tamanrasset, Oran, and Tlemcen—and 57 other airfields and landing strips. The railroad system is being modernized and expanded. Air Algerie, the state-owned airline, is expanding its fleet of jet aircraft and is improving its ground facilities. Although U.S. airlines do not serve Algeria, 18 foreign airlines, including most of the major West European airlines, operate regularly to Algiers, and other cities. Nearly 7,000 merchant ships carried 15 million tons of cargo to Algeria in 1981 and 18.5 million tons in 1982. Seventy percent of the cargo passed through the main ports of Algiers, Annaba, and Oran.

Photo credit: Gordon Barbery.

**Ancient Roman ruins. For several centuries, the northern region of Algeria, known then as Numidia, was a center of Roman culture.**

The state-owned shipping line, CNAN, is being expanded rapidly. It operates special tank ships to carry LNG, conventional oil tankers, and several types of dry cargo ships. Algeria continues to improve its communications and was among the first countries in the world to adopt earth satellite telecommunications for domestic and international use.

Although 30% of Algeria's population depend directly on agriculture for a living, less than 10% of the GDP is generated by this sector. The "socialist sector" of Algerian agriculture controls one-third of the best land in the country, mostly properties abandoned by the French, who left Algeria at the time of independence. This land was until 1987 organized into worker-managed state farms (*domaines autogres*). As a first step in the new development plan, some land (mostly in the less arable southern provinces) was redistributed to private owners, and further incentives are being given to private farmers who account for about 50% of farm output; more resources are being allocated to agriculture in an effort to improve and expand production. In 1987-88, large state farms have been dismantled and parceled out on long-

Background Notes

term leases to cooperatives of four or five leaseholders for each farm.

Algeria produces large quantities of wheat and barley, wine, olives and olive oil, citrus fruits, and dates. Nevertheless, it must import at least one-third of its food to feed its growing population.

Algerian trade is primarily with Western Europe, Japan, and the United States. Algeria accords most-favored-nation status to all countries and has special trade arrangements with its immediate neighbors and the European Community.

In 1986, Algeria exported an estimated $8.1 billion in goods, almost totally hydrocarbons. It imported $7.9 billion in goods in 1986. Since the oil price fall in 1982, U.S. exports to Algeria have declined from high of $1 billion to $530 million in 1986. France has been a principal trading partner since 1981.

Despite the decline in U.S. sales, new measures to make Algerian commercial laws more flexible, an aggressive development plan, the investment rate, and high foreign exchange earnings continue to offer excellent prospects for U.S. business. Subsidized exports to Algeria by foreign governments create obstacles for American companies, but these are not insurmountable.

Algeria receives economic development assistance, including grants, technical assistance, and concessionary loans, from West and East European countries, China, Canada, Saudi Arabia, the UN Development Program, and specialized agencies of the United Nations, including the World Bank. France, the U.S.S.R., and East European countries maintain several thousand technical specialists in educational, military, industrial, and health-related activities in Algeria, although the government seeks to reduce its dependence on foreign specialists. The United States provided direct economic assistance (PL-480 grain) to Algeria in 1966-67 and, since then, has contributed foodstuffs for the World Food Program's school feeding program in

Algeria. In 1980-81, the United States contributed $4 million in disaster relief to earthquake victims. Algeria cooperated with the United States on the transit of U.S. aid to Sahelian and Saharan African nations and, in addition, made major efforts to assist drought-afflicted economic immigrants in southern Algeria.

Algeria provides assistance of unknown dollar value to many African states, much of it as scholarships for students to study at Algerian universities. In 1985, the Government of Algeria organized and contributed $ 10 million to an Organization of African Unity relief fund for victims of the African drought in addition to an unspecified amount of monetary aid on a bilateral basis. It also provides shelter and food in Algeria for more than 40,000 non-Algerian drought victims. The Algerian Government, in conjunction with the Office of the UN High Commissioner for Refugees, provides food and shelter to an estimated 165,000 (Algerian Government estimates) refugees from the Western Sahara conflict who live in camps near the town of Tindouf in southwestern Algeria.

# DEFENSE

Algeria's armed forces, known collectively as the Popular National Army, total about 135,000 members, with some 100,000 reservists, and are under the control of the president, who is also minister of national defense. Defense expenditures accounted for approximately $1.2 billion or 9.2% of Algeria's 1988 budget.

Algeria is a leading military power in the region and has its forces oriented toward its western (Morocco) and eastern (Libya) borders. Its primary military supplier has been the Soviet Union, which has sold various types of sophisticated equipment under military trade agreements. Algeria has attempted, in recent years, to diversify its sources of military materiel. Military forces are supplemented by a 15,000-member gendarmerie or rural police force under the control of the president and a 30,000-member

*Surete Nationale* role or metropolitan police force under the Ministry of the Interior.

# FOREIGN RELATIONS

Algeria defines its foreign policy as one of independence and nonalignment. It is often a leading proponent of the Third World viewpoint in international affairs and has taken an active role in the Nonaligned Movement. Algeria advocates securing a greater share of the world's wealth for developing countries by obtaining higher prices for the raw materials they produce. In 1988, Algeria assumed a 2-year seat as a non-permanent member of the UN Security Council.

As a result of its own revolutionary experience, Algeria supports what it considers to be legitimate "national liberation movements," including the Palestine Liberation Organization and southern African nationalist groups. Since 1976, Algeria has supported the Polisario, a group claiming to represent the population of Western (formerly Spanish) Sahara. Although cautious about escalation of the conflict, the government has provided the Polisario materiel, financial and political support, and sanctuary in southwestern Algeria around Tindouf for its fighters and refugees of the conflict. Diplomatic relations were broken with Morocco and Mauritania after they partitioned and occupied the former Spanish colony under the terms of a November 1975 agreement with Spain. Mauritania withdrew from the Western Sahara conflict in August 1979 and reestablished relations with Algeria. Algeria and Morocco reestablished diplomatic relations in May 1988. Diplomatic efforts to resolve the dispute under the auspices of the UN Secretary General and the OAU have been underway. Algeria also has maintained active relations with Libya, and has no major problems with its eastern neighbor, Tunisia, nor with its southern neighbors, Mali and Niger.

Algerian relations with France traditionally have been colored by problems of Algerian residents in France, French transfer payments to Algerians, and unsettled claims dating from Algerian independence.

Algeria is interested in developing political and commercial relations with African countries to the south and looks to sub-Saharan Africa as well as to the Maghreb as eventual markets for its industrial products. The government has paved a trans-Saharan highway from Algiers to Tamanrasset. Paving of forks to Niger and Mali should further facilitate expanded trade between North and West Africa.

# U.S.-ALGERIAN RELATIONS

U.S.-Algerian relations have progressed steadily since the 1979 accession of President Bendjedid and his 1985 visit to the United States. During the June 1967 Arab-Israeli war Algeria had severed diplomatic relations with the United States. Relations improved gradually after 1969, however partly as a result of growing mutual interest in trade, development of energy resources, and Algeria's interest in acquiring American technology. In 1973-74, the U.S. Secretary of State visited Algeria several times for talks with former President Boumediene and other Algerian officials, and the Algerian president made an unofficial visit to Washington, D.C. in April 1974. Full diplomatic relations were resumed on November 12, 1974, and the new U.S. Ambassador presented his credentials in January 1975. Algeria sent an ambassador to Washington in June 1977. Relations have improved markedly since then.

The major political differences that marked U.S.-Algerian relations in the early years of Algerian independence have been ameliorated. Following the rupture of U.S.-Iranian relations in April 1980, Algeria became the protecting power for Iranian interests in the United States. Algeria served as the intermediary for the release of U.S. hostages held in Tehran. Relations have improved in recent years and can now be characterized as good. President Bendjedid visited Washington in April 1985—the first state visit by an Algerian head of state—demonstrating the extent of improved U.S.-Algerian relations. During the visit, an agreement establishing a Joint Economic Commission was signed, and a cultural agreement was initialed and subsequently signed in 1987. A Consular Convention was initialed in December 1986.

For many years, Algeria's export earnings derived mainly from sales of crude oil, more than one-half of which went to the United States. Since 1979, however Algeria has reduced its exports of crude oil and increased exports of condensate, natural gas, and refined products. U.S. imports of Algerian crude and refined hydrocarbons, which totaled some $5.2 billion in 1981, dropped to about $1.9 billion in 1986. The U.S. trade deficit with Algeria is about $1.5 billion.

Improving political relations between the United States and Algeria have seen a corresponding increase in cooperation in the economic area. The first U.S.-Algerian Joint Economic Commission met in Algiers in 1986, and the second may meet in Washington in 1989. Algeria is a major participant in the U.S. Department of Agriculture's Export Enhancement Program and its credit guarantee programs for agricultural commodities, such as wheat. The U.S. Feed Grains Council, which opened an office in Algiers in late 1985, is spearheading the development of a modern demonstration and dairy and poultry farm. U.S. firms are engaged in irrigation projects in the country. The Export-Import Bank is engaged in a new credit guarantee program with Algeria, and discussions are underway for a framework agreement with the Overseas Private Investment Corporation.

The United States has no Agency for International Development or Peace Corps programs in Algeria. More than 1,000 Algerian students are enrolled in U.S. universities in any given year. A number of professionally distinguished Algerians have visited the United States under the auspices of U.S. Information Agency cultural exchange programs, which have included a limited number of grants to U.S. citizens to teach and conduct research at Algerian universities. Teams of Algerian agricultural and irrigation experts also have visited the United States, under the auspices of the U.S. Department of Agriculture.

The United States has a small ($100,000 per year) International Military Education and Training (IMET) program for training Algerian military personnel. The Department of Agriculture has proposed a $172,000 program to train Algerian agronomists. In 1980–81, the United States provided $4 million in disaster relief to victims of a major earthquake at El Asnam (now "Chleff"). For 1983-86, the UN Development Plan had programmed expenditures of $36 million. In 1987–88, the United States assisted Algeria in its efforts to control locust infestation.

## Principal U.S. Officials

For up-to-date information on Principal U.S. Officials, see the U.S. Embassies, Consulates, and Foreign Service section starting on page 139.

The U.S. Embassy is located at 4 Chemin Cheich Bachir Brahimi, Algiers; mailing address B.P. Box 549 (Alger-Gare), (tel.213 (2)601425;telex 66047).

The consulate in Oran is located at 14 Square de Bamako (tel.390972; telex 22310 AMCONRN).

*A report on important events that have taken place since the last State Department revision of this* Background Note.

Fighting between the government that seized power in 1992 and Muslim fundamentalists continued throughout the first half of 1997, even as new Parliamentary elections were held in June.

On Christmas Eve 1994, four armed suspected Muslim fundamentalists seized an Air France jet with 283 people aboard in Algiers. After killing three hostages and releasing 61 others, the gunmen ordered the plane flown to Marseilles, France. It was on the runway there that French commandos stormed the jet, killed the hijackers, and freed the remaining hostages. French authorities said they ordered the assault after learning the hijackers planned to blow up the plane over Paris. Soon afterward, four Roman Catholic priests were killed in Algeria in what radicals called a reprisal for the deaths of the four hijackers.

In April 1997, government authorities reported that Islamic radicals attacked a village near Algiers, hacking to death 93 people, bringing the total dead in a wave of massacres to about 300.

Otherwise, the Algerian civil war continued to take a toll of 600–1,000 dead per month. Since 1992, the Algerian government estimates that there have been 27,000 terrorist-related deaths, while human rights monitors put the estimate at close to 100,000.

The fundamentalists said their goal was to turn Algeria into a pure Islamic state. As part of pursuing that end, they said they were killing intellectuals, writers, artists, and journalists who opposed their goal. The five years of violence had claimed 59 journalists.

There were occasional movements toward a peaceful settlement. In March 1995, the leading figure among the Islamic rebels called on the government for a negotiated peace. That appeal came from Madani Merzak, head of the Islamic Salvation Army, the armed faction of the Islamic Salvation Front. Chances for peace dimmed in early May 1995, when the alliance of two Islamic militant groups split.

Algerian President Liamine Zeroual announced in December 1995 the appointment of Ahmen Ouyahia as Prime Minister. Ouyahia, 43, became the youngest Prime Minister in the country's modern history. A career diplomat, Ouyahia brokered a peace agreement in 1993 between the Government and guerrillas.

On June 5, 1997, the parliamentary elections President Zeroual announced more than one year earlier were held. The ruling military-backed parties were returned to power amid a low voter turnout and charges of fraud. The opposition Islamic Salvation Front and all other parties based on religion were banned from the election. Mr. Zeroual's National Democratic Rally, a party formed two months before the election, captured 155 of the assembly's 380 seats. The National Liberation Front, also supporting Mr. Zeroual, won 64 seats, giving the president control of 57 percent of Parliament and reuniting in power the coalition discredited as corrupt during a move toward democracy in the late 1980s.

Two moderate opposition parties participated in the election, the largest of which, the Movement for a Peaceful Society, alleged widespread voting irregularities. The 200 international observers on hand to monitor the elections also questioned the vote, claiming the government blocked their efforts to investigate charges of ballot stuffing. However, the Organization for African Unity, which also monitored the vote, said the election was legitimate.

A low 65 percent voter turnout was viewed as a response to the Islamic Front's call for an election boycott, and to a 1996 constitutional referendum regarded as flawed. The government claimed victory as 79 percent of eligible voters approved a Constitution giving Mr. Zeroual the power to invalidate Parliamentary legislation. The military-backed Government's cancellation of legislative elections in January 1992 triggered the Islamic revolt.

In September 1997, there were three nighttime massacres made upon civilians in Algiers, killing hundreds of people. No one claimed responsibility, but the government blamed Islamic rebels. The Algerian government, however, has refused to let international agencies investigate the mass killings, which has increased the suspicion that the government itself may somehow be involved with the slayings. The nighttime raids sometimes occur two or three times a week in Algeria. In March 1998, Algeria made an appeal to the UN Human Rights Commission for help with its domestic terrorism problem. The government, however, stated that it would not allow the UN to send human rights experts into the country.

Unrest continued into 1999. The governing coalition set new presidential elections for April, but one day before the voters went to the polls six of the seven candidates withdrew claiming that the government had rigged the results. The sole candidate to remain in the race was Abdelaziz Bouteflika, Algeria's foreign minister in the 1960s and 1970s, and the candidate who held the backing of the military-backed government coalition. With no opposition, Mr. Bouteflika won an overwhelming majority.

Once in power, Mr. Bouteflika made the return of stability his top priority. In an effort at reconciliation, he pardoned thousands of prisoners implicated in political terrorism. Despite his peace initiative, Islamic militants continue violent attacks and riots. In late 2000 during the Muslim holy month of Ramadan, upwards of 250 people, including women and children, were slaughtered. Over 500 had been murdered in the first two months of 2001. As of June 2001, random attacks on civilians continued to occur with regularity.

On June 14, 2001, nearly 500 people were injured during a "march for democracy" in Algiers. Nearly half a million protestors hit the streets and headed for the Algerian presidential compound. They objected to the military-controlled government's abuse of power and demanded more freedom and justice for the people. Mr. Bouteflika has also tried to end Algeria's international isolation. After a three-year absence, Amnesty International was allowed to visit. Ties between Algeria and France improved when France reopened its consulates and cultural centers in July 1999.

# ANDORRA

March 2000

Official Name:
**Principality of Andorra**

# PROFILE

## Geography

**Area:** 467 sq. km. (180 sq. mi.); about half the size of New York City.
**Cities:** Capital—Andorra la Vella.
**Terrain:** Mountainous.
**Climate:** Temperate, cool, dry.

## People

**Nationality:** Noun and adjective—Andorran(s).
**Population:** 65,000.
**Annual growth rate:** 1.5%
**Ethnic Groups:** Catalan, Spanish, French, Portuguese.
**Religion:** Roman Catholic.
**Languages:** Catalan (official), Spanish, French.
**Education:** Years compulsory—to age 16; Attendance—100%; literacy—100%.
**Health:** Infant mortality rate—8/1,000; life expectancy—76 yrs. male, 81 yrs. female.

## Government

**Type:** Parliamentary democracy that retains as its heads of state a co-principality.
**Constitution:** Ratified in March 1993.
**Independence:** 1278.
**Branches:** Head of State—Two co-princes (President of France, Bishop of Seu d'Urgell in Spain). Executive—head of government (Cap de Govern) and eight ministers. Legislative—General Council (founded 1419) consisting of 28 members. Judicial—Civil cases heard in first instance by four judges (batlles) and in appeals by the one-judge Court of Appeals. The highest body is the five-member Superior Council of Justice. Criminal cases are heard by the Tribunal of Courts in Andorra la Vella.
**Subdivisions:** Seven parishes (parroquies)—Andorra la Vella, Canillo, Encamp, La Massana, Ordino, Sant Julia de Loria, and Escaldes make up the districts represented in the General Council.
**Political parties/groups:** Liberal Union (UL), National Andorran Coalition (CAN), Social Democrat Party (PSD), various minor groups.
**Suffrage:** Universal at 18.

## Economy

**GDP:** $1.2 billion.
**Natural resources:** Hydroelectric power, mineral water, timber, iron ore, lead.
**Agriculture:** Products—tobacco, sheep.
**Industry:** Types—tourism, (mainstay of the economy), tobacco products, furniture.
**Trade:** Major activities are commerce and banking; no official figures are available. Duty-free status.

**Official currencies:** Spanish peseta and French franc.

# PEOPLE

Andorrans live in seven urbanized valleys that form Andorra's political districts. Andorrans are a minority in their own country; Spanish, French, and Portuguese residents make the up 67.7% of the population. The national language is Catalan, a romance language related to the Provençal groups. It is spoken by more than 6 million people in the region comprising French and Spanish Catalonia. French and Spanish also are spoken. Education law requires school attendance for children up to age 16. A system of French, Spanish and Andorran lay schools provide education up to the secondary level. Schools are built and maintained by Andorran authorities, but teachers are paid for the most part by France or Spain. About 50% of Andorran children attend the French primary schools, and the rest attend Spanish or Andorran schools. In July 1997, the Andorran Government passed a law on universities and shortly afterward, the University of Andorra was established. Neither the geographically complex country nor the number of students makes it possible for the University of Andorra to develop a full academic program, and it serves principally as a center for virtual studies, connected to Spanish and French universities. The only two graduate schools in Andorra are the Nursing School and the School of Computer Science.

# HISTORY

Andorra is the last independent survivor of the March states, a number of buffer states created by Charlemagne to keep the Muslim Moors from advancing into Christian France. Tradition holds that Charlemagne granted a charter to the Andorran people in return for their fighting the Moors. In the 800s, Charlemagne's grandson, Charles the Bald, named the Count of Urgel as overlord of Andorra. A descendant of the count later gave the lands to the diocese of Urgel, headed by Bishop of Urgel. In the 11th century, fearing military action by neighboring lords, the bishop placed himself under the protection of the Lord of Caboet, a Spanish nobleman. Later, the Count of Foix, a French noble, became heir to Lord Caboet through marriage, and a dispute arose between the French Count and the Spanish bishop over Andorra. In 1278, the conflict was resolved by the signing of a pareage, which provided that Andorra's sovereignty be shared between the Count of Foix and the Bishop of Seu d'Urgell of Spain. The pareage, a feudal institution recognizing the principle of equality of rights shared by two rulers, gave the small state its territory and political form.

Over the years, the title was passed between French and Spanish rule until, under the French throne of Henry IV, an edict in 1607 established the head of the French state and the Bishop of Urgel as co-princes of Andorra. Given its relative isolation, Andorra has existed outside the mainstream of European history, with few ties to countries other than France and Spain. In recent times, however, its thriving tourist industry along with developments in transportation and communications have removed the country from its isola-

## Travel Notes

**Travel Advice:** For up-to-date information from the U.S. State Department on possible inconvenient or hazardous situations, see the **Travel Warnings and Consular Information Sheets from the U.S. Government** section starting on page 1723. For the latest information on health requirements and conditions, see the **International Travelers' Health Information** section starting on page 1385. For further information dealing with non-urgent matter, see the **Tips for Travelers to...** section starting on page 1588.

# GOVERNMENT

Until very recently, Andorra's political system had no clear division of powers into executive, legislative, and judicial branches. A constitution was ratified and approved .in 1993. The constitution establishes Andorra as a sovereign parliamentary democracy that retains as its heads of state a co-principality. The fundamental impetus for this political transformation was a recommendation by the Council of Europe in 1990 that, if Andorra wished to attain full integration in the European Union (EU), it should adopt a modern constitution which guarantees the rights of those living and working there. A Tripartite Commission—made up of representatives of the co-princes, the General Council, and the Executive Council—was formed in 1990 and finalized the draft constitution in April 1991.

Under the new 1993 constitution, the co-princes continue as heads of state, but the head of government retains executive power. The two co-princes serve coequally with limited powers that do not include veto over government acts.

They are represented in Andorra by a delegate. As co-princes of Andorra, the President of France and the Bishop of Seu d'Urgell maintain supreme authority in approval of all international treaties with France and Spain, as well as all those which

deal with internal security, defense, Andorran territory, diplomatic representation, and judicial or penal cooperation. Although the institution of the co-princes is viewed by some as an anachronism, the majority sees them as both a link with Andorra's traditions and a way to balance the power of Andorra's two much larger neighbors.

Andorra's main legislative body is the 28-member General Council (Parliament). The sindic (president), the subsindic and the members of the Council are elected in the general elections to be held every 4 years. The Council meets throughout the year on certain dates set by tradition or as required.

At least one representative from each parish must be present for the General Council to meet. Historically, within the General Council, four deputies apiece from each of the seven individual parishes have provided representation. This system allowed the smaller parishes, who have as few as 350 voters, the same number of representatives as larger parishes which have up to 2,600 voters. To correct this imbalance, a provision in the new constitution introduces a modification of the structure and format for electing the members of the Council; under this new format, half of the representatives are to be chosen by the traditional system, while the other half are selected from nationwide lists. A sindic and a subsindic are chosen by the General Council to implement its decisions. They serve 3-year terms and may be reappointed once. They receive an annual salary. Sindics have virtually no discretionary powers, and all policy decisions must be approved by the Council as a whole. In 1981, the Executive Council, consisting of the head of government and seven ministers, was established. Every 4 years, after the general elections, the General Council elects the head of government, who, in turn, chooses the other members of the Executive Council.

The judicial system is independent. Courts apply the customary laws of Andorra, supplemented with Roman law and customary Catalan law. Civil cases are first heard by the batlles court—a group of four judges, two chosen by each co-prince. Appeals are heard in the Court of Appeals. The highest body is the five-member Superior Council of Justice.

Andorra has no defense forces and only a small internal police force. All able-bodied men who own firearms must serve, without remuneration, in the small army, which is unique in that all of its men are treated as officers. The army has not fought for more than 700 years, and its main responsibility is to present the Andorran flag at official ceremonies.

# POLITICAL CONDITIONS

Andorra's young democracy is in the process of redefining its political party system. Three out of the five parties that dominated the political scene in past years have dissolved. The Liberal Union or UL, (current head of government Forne's party) is trying to reshape itself and change its name to that of the Andorran Liberal Party (PLA), thus offering a political umbrella to small parties and groups that have not yet found their place. Another party by the name of the Social Democratic Party has been formed and is designed to attract parties previously aligned with socialist ideals. Given the number of parties and Andorra's relative size, no one party controls the General Council; therefore, legislative majorities arise through coalitions. Since the 1993 constitutional ratification, three coalition governments have formed. The current government unites the UL, the CNA (National Andorran Coalition), and another relatively small party with Marc Forne Molne, a Liberal Unionist, as Cap de Govern, or head of government.

The government has continued to address many long-awaited reforms. In addition to legalizing political parties and trade unions for the first time, freedom of religion and assembly also have been legally guaranteed.

teed. Most significant has been a redefinition of the qualifications for Andorran citizenship, a major issue in a country where only 13,000 of 65,000 are legal citizens. In 1995, a law to broaden citizenship was passed but citizenship remains hard to acquire, with only Andorran nationals being able to transmit citizenship automatically to their children. Lawful residents in Andorra may obtain citizenship after 25 years of residency. Children of residents may opt for Andorran citizenship after age 18 if they resided virtually all of their lives in Andorra. Mere birth on Andorran soil does not confer citizenship. Dual nationality is not permitted. Noncitizens are allowed to own only a 33% share of a company. Only after they have resided in the country for 20 years, will they be entitled to own a 100% of a company. A

proposed law to reduce the necessary years from 20 to 10 is being debated in Parliament.

By creating a modern legal framework for the country, the 1993 constitution has allowed Andorra to begin a shift from an economy based largely on duty-free shopping to one based on international banking and finance. Despite promising new changes, it is likely that Andorra will, at least for the short term, continue to confront a number of difficult issues arising from the large influx of foreign residents and the need to develop modern social and political institutions. In addition to questions of Andorran nationality and immigration policy, other priority issues will include allowing freedom of association, dealing with housing scarcities and speculation in real state, developing the tourist industry and renegotiating the relationship with the European Union.

## Principal Government Officials

For up-to-date information on Principal Government Officials, see the Chiefs of State and Cabinet Members of Foreign Governments section starting on page 1.

# ECONOMY

Andorra's GDP for 1998 was $1.2 billion, with tourism as its principal component. Attractive for shoppers from France and Spain as a free port, the country also has developed active summer and winter tourist resorts. With some 270 hotels and 400 restaurants, as well as many shops, the tourist trade employs a growing portion of the domestic labor force.

There is a fairly active trade in consumer goods, including imported manufactured items, which, because they are duty-free, are less expensive in Andorra than in neighboring countries. As a result, smuggling is commonplace. Andorra's duty free status also has had a significant effect on the controversy concerning its relationship with the European Union. Its negotiations on duty-free status and relationship with the union began in 1987, soon after Spain joined. An agreement that went into effect in July 1991 sets duty-free quotas and places limits on certain items—mainly milk products, tobacco, and alcoholic beverages. Andorra is permitted to maintain

price differences from other EU countries, and visitors enjoy limited duty-free allowances.

The results of Andorra's elections thus far indicate that many support the government's reform initiatives and believe Andorra must, to some degree, integrate into the European Union in order to continue to enjoy its prosperity. Although less than 2% of the land is arable, agriculture was the mainstay of the Andorran economy until the upsurge in tourism. Sheep raising has been the principal agricultural activity, but tobacco growing is lucrative. Most of Andorra's food is imported.

In addition to handicrafts, manufacturing includes cigars, cigarettes, and furniture for domestic and export markets. A hydroelectric plant at Les Escaldes, with a capacity of 26.5 megawatts, provides 40% of Andorra's electricity; Spain provides the rest.

# FOREIGN RELATIONS

Since the establishment of sovereignty with the ratification of the constitution in 1993, Andorra has moved to become an active member of the international community. In July 1993, Andorra established its first diplomatic mission in the world to the United Nations. In early 1995, the United States and Andorra established formal diplomatic relations. Andorra also has expanded relations with other nations.

Andorra is a full member of the United Nations (UN), United Nations Educational, Scientific and Cultural Organization (UNESCO), United Nations Conference for Commerce

and Development (UNCCD), International Center of Studies for Preservation and Restoration of Cultural Heritage (ICCROM), Telecommunications International Union (UIT), International Red Cross, Universal Copyright Convention, European Council, EUTELSAT, World Tourism Organization, Organization for Security and Cooperation in Europe (OSCE), Customs Cooperation Council (CCC), and Interpol. Since 1991 Andorra has had a special agreement with the European Union.

# U.S.-ANDORRAN RELATIONS

As noted, the United States established diplomatic relations with Andorra in early 1995. The two countries are on excellent terms. The U.S. Ambassador to Spain also is accredited as Ambassador to Andorra. United States Consulate General officials based in Barcelona visit Andorra regularly.

## Principal U.S. Official

For up-to-date information on Principal U.S. Officials, see the U.S. Embassies, Consulates, and Foreign Service section starting on page 139.

Edward L. Romero is the U.S. Ambassador in Madrid to Andorra. The U.S. Embassy is at Serrano, 75—08006 Madrid and the Consulate General is at Passeig Reina Elisenda, 23-25, 08034 Barcelona, Spain (tel. 932 802 227).

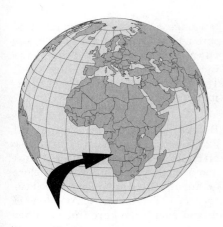

# ANGOLA

June 1987

Official Name:
**People's Republic of Angola**

# PROFILE

## Geography

**Area:** 1,246,700 sq. km. (481,351 sq. mi.); about twice the size of Texas.
**Cities:** Capital—Luanda (pop. 1 million). Other cities—Huambo (500,000).
**Terrain:** Varied.
**Climate:** Tropical to subtropical.

## People

**Nationality:** Noun and adjective—Angolan.
**Population (1986 est.):** 8.5 million.
**Annual growth rate (1986 est.):** 2.7%.
**Ethnic groups:** Ovimbundu 37%, Kimbundu 25%, Bakongo 15%, Lunda-Chokwe 8%, Nganguel 6%, Haneca and Humbe 3%, Ovambo 2%, mestico and European 2%, other 2%.
**Religions:** Roman Catholic, Protestant, traditional.
**Languages:** Portuguese (official), African (dialects).
**Education:** Attendance—75%. Literacy—30%.
**Health:** Infant mortality rate—148/1000. Life expectancy—42 yrs.
**Work force:** Agriculture—75%

## Government

**Type:** Marxist people's republic, one party rule.
**Independence:** November 11, 1975.
**Branches:** Executive—president, three ministers of state, Council of Ministers. Legislative—People's Assembly. Judicial—military and civilian courts.
**Administrative subdivisions:** 18 provinces
**Political party:** Popular Movement for the Liberation of Angola-Labor Party (MPLA-PT).
**Suffrage:** Universal adult (candidates limited to those approved by MPLA-PT).
**Flag:** Two horizontal bars, red over black; centered, a yellow five-pointed star half encircled by a machine gear crossed by a machete.

## Economy*

**GDP (1986):** $45 billion.
**Real growth rate (1985 est.):** 0%.
**Natural resources:** Petroleum diamonds, iron, phosphate, copper, feldspar gold bauxite, uranium.
**Agriculture (42% of GNP):** Products—cassava, maize, plantains, sweet potatoes, milk, millet, citrus, beans, potatoes, sugar, beef, palm oil, sisal, coffee.
**Industry (28% of GNP):** Types—petroleum, mining, food processing, beer, tires, textiles.
**Trade (1986):** Exports—$1.4 billion: petroleum, gas, coffee, diamonds. Partners—US, Bahamas, Netherlands, Spain, Belgium, Brazil, Algeria. Imports—$1. 1 billion: foodstuffs, textiles, machinery, raw materials, consumer goods, tools, medical supplies, chemicals. Major suppliers—US, France, Brazil, Spain, Portugal, Italy, FRG, Japan.
**Official exchange rate:** Approx. 35 kwanzas=US$1.
**Economic aid received:** Primarily from Western private and public sectors; mostly military but some economic aid from Eastern bloc.

## Membership in International Organizations

UN, Organization of African Unity (OAU), African Development Bank (ADB), Nonaligned Movement, Southern Africa Development Coordination Conference.

# GEOGRAPHY

Angola, on the west coast of southern Africa, has an area of 1,246,699 square kilometers (451,351 sq. mi.)-about twice the size of Texas. Angola proper lies south of the Congo River and is hounded by Zaire on the north and northeast, Zambia on the east,

---

\* Data for the period since independence have been extremely limited due to the continuing civil war.

Namibia on the south, and the Atlantic Ocean on the west. The enclave of Cabinda lies on the seacoast northwest of Angola proper and is bordered by the Congo, the Atlantic Ocean, and the strip of Zairian territory that separates Cabinda from Angola proper.

The flat land that lies in a narrow strip along Angola's coast rises abruptly toward the interior, a vast plateau and upland region ranging from 900-2,100 meters (3,000 ft.-7,000 ft.) in elevation and forming one of Africa's great watershed areas.

Because of its size, variations in terrain, and exposure to ocean currents of varying temperatures, Angola's climate is diverse. The southern regions and the coastal plain up to Luanda are semiarid, particularly in the Namib Desert in the southwest. The north has two seasons, especially on the plateau; from May to October, it is dry and cool with occasional freezing temperatures; during the November to April rainy season, it is extremely hot and humid.

# PEOPLE

Angola's average population density is 6.9 persons per square kilometer, but more than 70% of the people are concentrated in the west, central highlands, and north. Density on the eastern and southeastern savanna is less than 1 person per square kilometer.

Angolans are almost entirely Bantu of various ethnic groupings. Three-fourths of Angola's approximately 5.5 million people are accounted for by the three most important ethnic groupings.

- The Ovimbundu, in central and southeastern Angola, are the largest group, consisting of about 37% of the population. They are farmers and traders, who have traditionally been the underpinning of agriculture in the central highlands.

- The Bakongo, concentrated in the northwest but also living in areas adjacent to the Congo and Zaire as well as Cabinda, constitute about 15%. This ethnic group at one time formed a loose federation—the Kingdom of the Kongo—with which European contact was made in the 15th century when Portuguese caravels landed at the mouth of the Congo River.

- The Kimbundu, about 25%, are concentrated in the area around Luanda and out toward the east. Having had prolonged, intensive contact with Portuguese colonial rulers, the Kimbundu have the highest proportion of people assimilated into the European culture.

- The Lunda and Chokwe live in northeastern Angola, with branches in Zaire, and make up about 8% of the population. These ethnic groups once comprised a great kingdom in the Angolan interior and were barely touched by Portuguese influence. Those who remain are relatively isolated from national politics.

Other ethnic groups include the Nganguela in the southeast and the Ovambo and Herero in the southwest. The Ovambo and Herero are migratory cattle herders, with branches in Namibia, who regularly migrate across the Angola-Namibia border.

The Portuguese brought the Catholic religion with them, and toward the end of the 19th century, Protestant missionaries arrived from the United States, Canada, and the United Kingdom. Catholic and Protestant missionaries have played a significant role in educating black Angolans. At the time of independence, leaders of Angola's three major liberation movements had been educated at Protestant missions. Many Angolans, however, continue to adhere to traditional beliefs.

The diverse ethnic backgrounds of the population suggest the wide range of languages spoken. No one African language extends beyond its ethnic area. Portuguese is the official language, and the only language used throughout the country. Literacy, less than 10% at independence, has increased significantly since then. The Angolan Government gives priority to promoting education.

Before the 1975 civil war, about 325,000 whites, primarily Portuguese citizens, lived in Angola. All but about 30,000 fled to Portugal before or during the war; only a few have returned. The mesticos, Angolans of mixed racial background, number only about 1% of the population but are influential politically, culturally, and economically beyond their numbers. They are the most highly skilled and educated group.

# HISTORY

Angola was settled by the Portuguese in the 15th century and remained a Portuguese colony until it received independence in 1975. The first European to reach Angola was the Portuguese explorer Diogo Cao, who landed at the mouth of the Congo River in 1483. The land was then ruled by an African monarch, the King of the Kongo, whose capital became the present day M'banza-Congo (Sao Salvador). In 1490, the Portuguese sent a small fleet of ships carrying priests, skilled workers, and tools to the Kongolese King who received the mission warmly, accepted Christianity, and agreed to send his son, later King Afonso, to Lisbon.

Soon, however, the slave trade led to the deterioration of Portugal's relations with King Afonso and his successors, and internal revolts hastened the decline of the Kongo Kingdom. Meanwhile, the Portuguese expanded their contacts southward along the coast, founding Luanda in 1576.

In 1641, a Dutch fleet seized the rich slave ports of Luanda and Benguela, and the Portuguese retreated to the interior. They held out stubbornly until 1648, when a powerful expedition from Brazil restored the coast to Portuguese control.

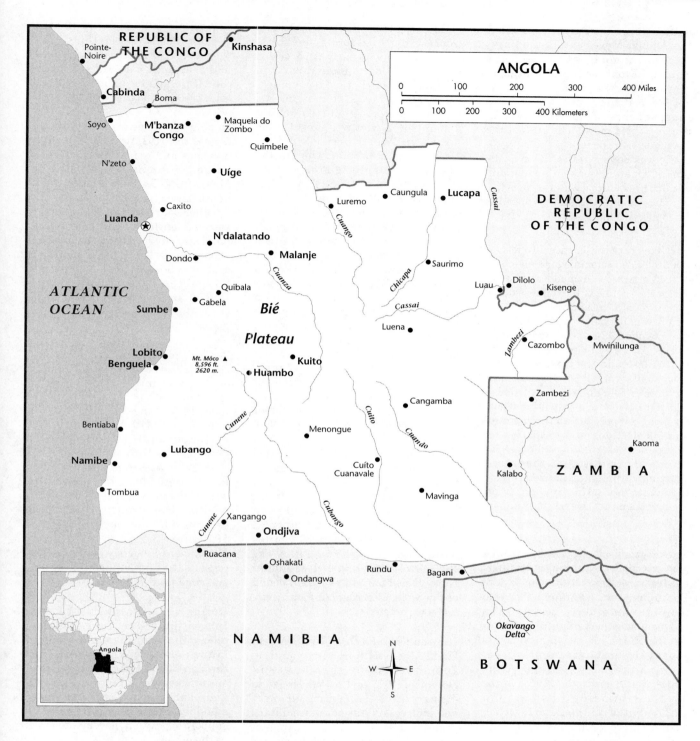

The slave trade continued until the mid-19th century, with Angola serving as a major source of supply for Brazilian plantations. Some 3 million Angolans are estimated to have been transported to the New World during the three centuries of the slave trade.

Angola's boundaries were formally established by the Berlin West Africa Congress in 1884-85, in which France, Germany, and Portugal won recognition of the borders of their colonies with the Congo. The frontier, including Northern Rhodesia (now Zambia), was established in 1905. Tribal wars and uprisings were common, continuing into the early part of the 20th century, when separate uprisings were put down by the Por-

tuguese in northern, central, and southern Angola. Following World War II, Portuguese interest in colonizing Angola increased considerably. Black and mestico discontent over Portuguese unwillingness to concede eventual independence led to the outbreak of two separate wars for independence in 1961. While initially hard pressed, Portuguese forces gradually reduced the guerrilla efforts of the Popular Movement for the Liberation of Angola (MPLA) and the National Front for the Liberation of Angola (FNLA) to relatively low levels. The National Union for the Total Independence of Angola (UNITA), began a third movement against the Portuguese in the late 1960s but generally was no more effective than the others. Open dissension among and within these groups was a serious factor in reducing the effectiveness of Angolan nationalists.

Partly as a result of discontent over the prolonged colonial wars, elements of the Portuguese Armed Forces overthrew the regime of Portuguese dictator Marcelo Caetano in April 1974, and it was decided to grant immediate independence to the African colonies. In January 1975, the Portuguese and the three liberation movements worked out a complicated agreement—the Alvor Accord—which provided for a transitional government composed of all three groups and for elections in preparation for independence in November 1975. After a shaky existence, the transitional government collapsed during the summer of 1975. By then, fighting had begun in several cities among MPLA, FNLA, and UNITA forces.

The history of the Alvor Accord period is unclear and subject to different interpretations. However, lack of Portuguese will and/or ability to maintain an orderly transition to independence made fighting inevitable. The three liberation movements sought to consolidate control over their natural areas of support-the FNLA in the north, the MPLA in the area surrounding Luanda, and UNITA in the south-and to establish a secure presence in Luanda, the capital. As these areas overlapped, clashes were frequent. Because each group had a long list of external supporters-the MPLA from the Soviets, Cubans, Nigeria, Sweden, and Denmark, and FNLA, UNITA from the United States, the People's Republic of China, France, Great Britain, Romania, North Korea, Zaire, and South Africa-internationalization of the conflict was not improbable.

In late 1974, the FNLA, with help from Zaire, moved forces into northern Angola and, in early 1975, seized the town of Caxito (35 mi. north of Luanda). In March, the MPLA, a self-proclaimed Marxist movement, began receiving considerable amounts of Soviet weapons. Cuban military advisers arrived in June 1975. By midsummer, the United States was supplying arms to both the FNLA and UNITA. The FNLA, led by Holden Roberto, and UNITA, led by Jonas Savimbi, had indicated a pro-Western orientation. In August, South African forces occupied Angolan territory along the Namibian border, ostensibly to protect a hydroelectric project. By October 1975, some 5,000 South African troops were fighting alongside UNITA and FNLA troops in a march toward Luanda that covered 500 miles in 3 weeks. Additional Cuban advisers arrived in early October and, at the MPLA's request, Cuban combat troops began landing in Angola soon after. By February 1976, the number of Cubans had grown to about 15,000.

In October 1975, the FNLA, once again supported by Zaire, began a final attempt to capture Luanda before independence day. The MPLA, using the edge it had acquired in modern Soviet-supplied weaponry, stopped the FNLA drive 12 miles north of the capital. The MPLA was therefore in control of Luanda on November 11 when Portugal ceded power without recognizing an Angolan government.

U.S. assistance to the FNLA and UNITA ceased following congressional votes—by the Senate in December 1975 and by the House in January 1976—prohibiting all direct and indirect military or paramilitary assistance to any group in Angola. South African forces withdrew and, by March, Cuban and Soviet support for the MPLA proved decisive. The MPLA established control over most of Angola. The FNLA reverted to guerrilla warfare in northern Angola, and Holden Roberto permanently left the country. UNITA retreated to the southeastern corner of Angola and carried out low-level guerrilla operations in the central highlands and

eastern areas. In February 1976, the Organization of African Unity (which before the South African intervention had been split between support for the MPLA and for national reconciliation) recognized the MPLA.

During the 11 years since independence, the FNLA has been rent by divisions and reorganizations and is no longer a military threat to the MPLA. UNITA, which appealed to South Africa for continued assistance as other sources of external support were discontinued, has on the other hand steadily increased the level and expanded the scope of its operations and now poses a major challenge. Savimbi has remained leader of UNITA and has remained in Angola throughout the post-independence period.

Angola's history since 1975 has been characterized by intensification of the civil war, its involvement in regional conflicts, and turmoil within the ruling MPLA. Long-standing divisions within the MPLA resulted in an uprising against the government led by Interior Minister Nito Alves in May 1977. Although several MPLA leaders were killed, the government, with Cuban assistance, succeeded in quelling the revolt. President Dos Santos, who became president in 1979 after the death of Agostinho Neto, spent his early years in office consolidating power under these difficult conditions.

During 1977–78, the Front for the Liberation of the Congo (FLNC), operating from bases in Angola, launched two invasions of Zaire through Shaba Province. These invasions were defeated, and in 1978 Zaire and Angola reached an understanding that neither country would support opposition movements aimed at the other.

Since independence, Angola has been deeply involved in efforts to obtain independence for Namibia. The South West African People's Organization (SWAPO) conducts operations into Namibia from Angolan territory, and negotiations to implement UN Security Council Resolution 435 of 1978, providing for Namibian independence, have directly or indirectly focused on the issue of Cuban combat forces in Angola. Angola also provides assistance to the African National Congress.

# GOVERNMENT

Angola is a one-party state ruled by the MPLA. Political power is concentrated in the party's 12-member Political Bureau (10 full members and 2 alternates) and 90-member Central Committee. The Central Committee meets several times annually, with day-to-day oversight carried out by the party secretariat and Political Bureau. The secretariat is organized with areas of responsibility parallel to those of the government ministries. The Council of Ministers, comprised of the various government ministers, meets regularly to implement policy decisions made by the party. In addition, three "super-ministries" were created in 1986—the Ministers of State for Production and Economic Coordination, Inspection and State Control, and Social and Economic Affairs—which coordinate the work of various government ministries and report directly to the president. President Dos Santos is head of government and head of the party. Below this level, however, the MPLA generally has maintained a policy of not allowing a single individual to hold both government and party posts. Some ministers are also members of the Central Committee and Political Bureau. The People's Assembly meets biannually, largely to implement policy decisions made by the party.

Government and party administration at the provincial and local levels parallels that at the national level. For example, there are provincial people's assemblies and party committees and respective party and government posts. Regional Military Councils are now the supreme authority at the provincial level.

The constitution establishes the broad outlines of the government structure and delineates the rights and duties of citizens. Although the

constitution provides for free elections, all parties other than the MPLA are banned, and opposing views, either in the media or in public demonstrations, are not allowed. Membership in the MPLA is tightly restricted.

The constitution provides for an independent judiciary and for the right of the accused to a fair public trial, but, in practice, the judiciary follows party guidelines. Areas of jurisdiction within the judiciary are unclear. Military and civilian courts exist, and the Regional Military Councils have authority to try crimes against the state. There have been reports of prolonged detention without trial, unfair trials, and arbitrary executions.

The country is divided into 17 provinces, along with Cabinda.

## Principal Government Officials

**For up-to-date information on Principal Government Officials, see the Chiefs of State and Cabinet Members of Foreign Governments section starting on page 1.**

# POLITICAL CONDITIONS

Since 1976, Angola has been politically unstable because of political maneuvering within the ruling MPLA, civil war with UNITA, and repeated incursions by South African forces operating from Namibia.

During the past 5 years, UNITA has expanded its operations from bases in southeastern Angola to virtually all areas of the country. With the exception of a lower level of fighting in Namibe and Luanda, sustained, intensified fighting between MPLA forces and UNITA guerrilla forces is taking place in most of the provinces. UNITA has publicly emphasized its intention to expand the fighting to all areas of Angola, including Cabinda,

and has warned foreigners against traveling in contested areas. Estimates of the area that UNITA controls vary, but it appears to hold most of Moxico and Cuando Cubango provinces, about one-quarter of the country. UNITA's base of support has been among the Ovimbundu, Chokwe, and Nganguela, but dissatisfaction with the MPLA is not confined to those groups. UNITA has made a sustained effort to be self-sufficient but continues to rely on South African and other sources of external support.

Savimbi has emphasized that UNITA's goal is national reconciliation in Angola and that UNITA is prepared to enter into talks with the MPLA toward this objective. He has also stated that he supports a settlement in southern Africa involving implementation of the UN plan for Namibia and the withdrawal of foreign forces from Angola.

UNITA's military operations have disrupted the economy and have made effective MPLA administration throughout much of the countryside and small towns difficult, but the MPLA maintains control over all provincial capitals. UNITA administers areas it controls but has never established a separate government structure; in fact, Savimbi has emphasized his support for national unity and has condemned separatism.

The FNLA, sometimes referred to as the Military Committee for the Resistance in Angola (COMIRA), no longer poses a military threat to the government. The Front for the Liberation of Cabinda (FLEC), in conjunction with UNITA, carries out low-level activity in Cabinda.

Factionalism within the MPLA has also contributed to political instability. Since independence, there have been frequent personnel shifts within the party, in part reflecting maneuvering between various party factions.

Factional divisions are based on personality, ethnic and racial lines, and ideological differences. Although since 1977 open conflict generally has not characterized the leadership, decision making remains largely immobilized by political infighting. President Dos Santos so far has been unable to unite the various factions around common approaches to Angola's most pressing problems.

The MPLA's Second Party Congress, held in December 1985, purged or demoted many prominent ideologues and mesticos from top positions. Dos Santos replaced them with his closest supporters. However, leadership changes in the government that were expected after the Party Congress, including the appointment of a prime minister, did not materialize. Instead, Dos Santos created three superministries in the economic sphere. Reportedly, these three ministries, with overlapping responsibilities, have been a further focus of infighting. (Dos Santos did not create a similar superministry for defense and security; these ministers report directly to him.) Dos Santos recently has stressed, in public, the need to combat corruption and has been openly critical of past performance by government and party officials.

The intensification and expansion of the war has led to increasing charges and countercharges by the MPLA and UNITA of alleged human rights violations, including arbitrary executions, intimidation of civilian populations, and detention of political prisoners. In November 1982, President Dos Santos was given special emergency powers to deal with economic and security problems. During 1983 he established Regional Military Councils throughout Angola with special powers to confiscate goods and personnel without compensation and to try crimes against the state. People's vigilante brigades also have been established. In the absence of a negotiated settlement to the war, security is expected to continue to deteriorate, with concomitant effects on the political situation within the country.

# ECONOMY

The Angolan economy deteriorated severely as a result of the abrupt transition to independence in 1975 and the fighting during the pre- and post independence periods. The departure at independence of most of the 350,000 Portuguese, who had run the economy, caused severe disruption. Intensification of the civil war during the past 5 years has caused further serious deterioration of the economy and the quality of life. UNITA has targeted economic sites, attacking industrial centers, power facilities, petroleum installations, transportation infrastructure, mining areas, and agricultural projects.

Angola is potentially one of the richest countries in sub-Saharan Africa with extensive petroleum potential, rich agricultural land, and valuable mineral resources. Before independence, Angola exported oil, coffee, diamonds, iron ore, sisal, fish, and cement and earned about $100 million annually from Zairian and Zambian traffic on the Benguela Rail road. UNITA operations, however, have kept the Benguela Railroad effectively closed for the past several years.

Petroleum, the only bright spot in an otherwise progressively deteriorating economic picture, has kept the economy afloat. Petroleum production is expanding, and Angola has sufficient proven reserves to increase production significantly over the next 10 years, if the producing areas do not become enmeshed in the growing civil war. Petroleum production at the end of 1986 was about 250,000 barrels per day.

Most of Angola's petroleum still comes from fields off the Cabinda coast. Angola has divided its entire coastal area into exploration blocks and is attempting to encourage exploration by foreign companies in these areas. Results are encouraging; a number of West European and U.S. oil companies are active in Angola: Chevron, Texaco, Conoco, the French company Elf Aquitaine, the Brazilian company Braspetro, the Italian-owned AGIP, and the Japanese company Mitsubishi being the most extensively involved. Most of the companies participate in production-sharing arrangements with the Angolan Government through the Angolan

**Travel Notes**

**Travel Advice:** For up-to-date information from the U.S. State Department on possible inconvenient or hazardous situations, see the **Travel Warnings and Consular Information Sheets from the U.S. Government** section starting on page 1723. For the latest information on health requirements and conditions, see the **International Travelers' Health Information** section starting on page 1385. For further information dealing with non-urgent matter, see the **Tips for Travelers to...** section starting on page 1588.

state oil company, Sonangol. Angola has opened a marketing office in London and generally has been flexible on pricing in order to facilitate sales. U.S. imports of Angolan petroleum amounted to over $700 million in 1986, or somewhat more than half of total Angolan production. Angola also sells petroleum to Brazil, Western Europe, and some African countries. An increasing amount of petroleum production has been committed to covering financing arrangements for other areas of the economy and petroleum production expansion costs.

Angola still exports diamonds and coffee but at declining levels. By 1980, diamond production had reached a post-independence peak of 1.5 million carats (compared with 2.4 million carats the year before independence), but has declined since to about 370,000 carats in 1986. Most of these are gem diamonds, and the country has therefore suffered as a result of a decline in gem prices. Diamond exports have accounted for 8%-10% of Angola's export earnings, but because of extensive smuggling and intensified UNITA guerrilla operations in the northeastern diamond production area, production has decreased.

Coffee production has dropped from 3.4 million bags annually during the pre-independence period to about 310,000 bags in 1985. Angola is a member of the International Coffee Organization.

During the pre-independence period, Angola was also a major African food exporter but is now forced to import most of its food. Intensive UNITA activities in the central highlands Angola's breadbasket-have severely disrupted agricultural production, reducing it largely to subsistence levels. The fighting between UNITA and MPLA forces, coupled with the effects of drought in previous years, have displaced as many as 500,000 persons in the central highlands area, many of whom are suffering from severe malnutrition and starvation. The United States under the Food for Peace program has, since 1977, contributed foodgrains to UNICEF (United Nations Children's Fund) to feed displaced persons in central Angola. The International Committee of the Red Cross has had an extensive food distribution program in central Angola which, however, has at times been disrupted for prolonged periods by fighting between MPLA and UNITA. Some Western countries and the European Economic Community have also provided food assistance.

Angola produced about 20,000 metric tons of sugar in 1982-83, but production has declined somewhat to about 18,000 tons in 1985. It also has extensive fisheries resources and has given priority to developing this sector. A fishing agreement with the Soviet Union resulted in heavy Soviet exploitation and has limited the usefulness of this resource.

The effect of steadily rising defense costs to meet the increasing threat posed by UNITA and the declining prices for petroleum, as well as the overall deterioration of the economy, has been a steady rise in Angola's long- and short-term debt to Western and Eastern bloc creditors. Total foreign debt at the end of 1986 was estimated at about $2.5 billion. Angola has made expansion of petroleum production its highest economic priority, which has helped to keep the debt problem within manageable limits. Whether the expansion of petroleum production can offset deterioration of the rest of the economy and meet steadily rising defense costs is the key economic question

facing Angola. Some estimates suggest that as much as 50% of the country's export earnings are allocated to defense costs. In addition to military hardware, Angola reportedly pays for Cuban forces stationed there. The economic squeeze has forced Angola to approach both Western and Eastern bloc creditors to seek debt rescheduling. During 1986, Angola occasionally fell behind in payments to Western creditors but eventually managed to make payments. Payments to Soviet and bloc creditors have apparently been in arrears.

During recent years, the Angolan Government has emphasized to the population the need for austerity and increased productivity. In order to pay creditors and finance petroleum expansion, it has been forced to cut back on the import of basic necessities as well as raw materials. Food shortages exist throughout the country. The government has greatly expanded the money supply, causing inflation to skyrocket, while shortages and inflation have resulted in a thriving black market, including illegal currency exchange.

Angola is the third largest trading partner of the United States in sub-Saharan Africa because of petroleum exports. U.S. imports from Angola in 1985 were $1.09 billion; exports were $137 million. In part, due to a drop in oil prices, trade figures declined in 1986. U.S. imports from Angola in 1986 were $729 million, exports fell to $86.5 million. The United States exports industrial goods and services, primarily oil-field equipment, mining equipment, and chemicals-aircraft, and food to Angola; the primary U.S. import from Angola is petroleum. U.S. investment in Angola is centered on the petroleum sector. The Export-Import Bank (EXIM) had not been active in taking on new Angola-related business even before-the congressional ban of 1986. EXIM's exposure is about $200 million. No legal prohibition exists on U.S. business activity with Angola except for normal export licensing restrictions.

Most of Angola's trade is with the West; in fact, most West European countries trade with Angola and pro-

vide limited economic assistance. Portugal is particularly active and has a number of technicians there. France, Italy, Brazil, and Spain have also been active. A number of Arab countries, the EEC, and the UN Development Program have provided assistance for the fisheries sector. Although Marxist in orientation, the Angolan Government has adopted a pragmatic economic approach and has encouraged Western investment. Angola joined the Lome Convention in April 1985. It is a member of the African Development Fund and Bank but not of any other multilateral development banks. Angola's economic dealings with the Eastern bloc, particularly the Soviet Union, center on the purchase of military equipment and payment for troops and advisers. In 1982, Angola and the Soviet Union signed an economic cooperation agreement for $2 billion over a 10-year period, but this has resulted in little concrete Soviet economic assistance.

Angola has nationalized most of its economy but has allowed some private sector activity to continue, particularly in agriculture. Strikes are prohibited by law, and the Union of Angolan Workers is controlled by the state.

Angola's GDP was approximately $4.5 billion in 1985. Adjusted for inflation, however, it remains substantially below pre-independence levels. Despite continued expansion of the oil sector, overall growth is essentially static. Angolan exports fell from $2.1 billion in 1985 to $1.4 billion in 1986. Imports fell from $1.4 billion in 1985 to $1.1 billion in 1986.

# FOREIGN RELATIONS

Since independence, Angola has depended upon the Soviet Union and Cuba for security assistance and has adopted a pro-Soviet foreign policy. Angola maintains various agreements with the Soviet Union, the centerpiece being a 20-year treaty of friendship and cooperation signed in October 1976.

In 1986, Luanda and Moscow exchanged several high-level delegations, and President Dos Santos visited the Soviet Union twice. The Angolans received pledges of support for defense against South Africa and alleged Western support for UNITA. Since 1983, the Soviets have supplied extensive amounts of -sophisticated military hardware to Angola. Estimates indicate that in addition to military personnel, there are about 1,200 Soviet civilian advisers 1,500 other Eastern bloc advisers, and 5,000-9,000 Cuban civilian advisers in Angola. Angola regularly exchanges official visits with Cuba and the Eastern bloc. President Dos Santos visited Cuba in March 1984 and signed a joint Angola-Cuba communique that stated conditions for the removal of Cuban forces from the country.

Although the Angolan Government maintains close links with the Soviet Union and the Eastern bloc, it has sought better relations with the West and with moderate African states. This apparently has been done in an effort to bolster Angola's economy, to gain increased political support in its confrontation with South Africa, and to undercut outside support for UNITA. Angola maintains diplomatic relations with most West European states.

Angola has consistently called for the immediate implementation of UN Security Council Resolution 435, which provides for internationally acceptable independence for Namibia, the territory on Angola's southern border illegally controlled by South Africa. Since 1978, when Resolution 435 was passed, Angola has been involved in the intermittent negotiations concerning Namibia. At the same time, the MPLA allows SWAPO to maintain bases in southern Angola and to carry out military operations against South African forces in Namibia. South Africa has regularly retaliated by launching operations into southern Angola directed against SWAPO and Angolan forces stationed along the border. Following Operation Protea in August 1981, South Africa occupied a salient in Cunene Province in southern Angola.

With the Lusaka Accord of February 1984, the South African Government began the process of disengagement from Angola. This process was completed by early 1985. However, Angola has consistently rejected South Africa's condition that in order for South Africa to agree to implement Resolution 435, Angola must agree to a parallel withdrawal of Cuban combat forces. For its part, South Africa has continued to use Namibia as a base for cross-border raids into Angola in pursuit of SWAPO and in support of UNITA.

During the past 5 years, Angola has gained better relations with moderate African states. During 1982, it established diplomatic relations with Senegal and Cote d'Ivoire. Angola has sought to work with Zaire and Zambia in order to resolve security problems. As a result of Zairian support for UNITA at the time of independence and the unsuccessful invasions of Shaba in 1977-78 by the Angola-based anti-Mobutu Front for the Liberation of the Congo, Angola's relationship with Zaire has been uneasy. Angola continues to be concerned by alleged UNITA activities from Zaire. Angola, Zambia, and Zaire held a series of high-level meetings in 1986 to discuss regional security and transportation problems. Zambian relations with Angola are considered good. Angola works closely with the other frontline states (states bordering South Africa and Namibia) and is responsible for energy coordination within the Southern Africa Development Coordination Council. It also maintains close ties with the other Portuguese-speaking African states of Mozambique, Cape Verde, Guinea Bissau, and Sao Tome and Principe.

The Angolan Government officially espouses a policy of nonalignment, and article 14 of the Angolan constitution states that Angola shall respect the principles of the UN Charter and the Charter of the Organization of African Unity. Article 16 of the constitution states that Angola shall not join any international military organization or allow the installation of foreign military bases on its territory. Consistent with the official policy of nonalignment, Angola plays an active role within the Nonaligned Movement. Angola regularly supports the Soviet line at the United Nations.

# DEFENSE

The Angolan Armed Forces number about 80,000, and service by all males 18 years and older is mandatory. The People's Militia number about 10,000, but these forces are lightly armed and are used only for defensive duties within their localities. The Soviets continue to supply the Angolan Armed Forces with equipment, which includes sophisticated surface-to-air missiles, tanks, and aircraft. Soviet military aid since 1976 has totaled more than $4 billion. Some 35,000 Cuban military personnel, including combat forces and military trainers and advisers, are in Angola as well as 1,500 Soviet and Eastern bloc military advisers.

# U.S.-ANGOLA RELATIONS

The United States does not maintain diplomatic relations with Angola, but since 1978 the two countries have had frequent contacts to discuss regional and bilateral matters.

The United States intensified its dialogue with the Angolan Government in 1981, when Assistant Secretary of State for African Affairs Chester A. Crocker visited Luanda in conjunction with the Reagan administration's initiative aimed at bringing about a settlement of the long-standing Namibia problem. In launching its initiative on southern Africa, the United States made clear its assessment that achieving internationally recognized independence for Namibia was intimately connected with the problem of bringing about a withdrawal of Cuban combat forces. That assessment was based on South African emphasis of the security threat to Namibia and the southern Africa

## Editor's Update

*A report on important events that have taken place since the last State Department revision of this* Background Note.

The Angolan government and the opposition movement UNITA (Union for the Total Independence of Angola) reached agreement in January 1996 on a timetable to disarm fighters on both sides of a civil war halted in 1994. UNITA suspended the demobilization of its fighters under a 13-month old peace accord in late-1995 after Government troops commenced a fresh offensive against them in northern Angola. But the government of President Jose Eduardo dos Santos and the UNITA rebels renewed the peace agreement in January 1996, and by August had demobilized some 100,000 troops.

Angola has been plagued by war since 1961, when nationalists launched an uprising against their Portuguese colonizers. Independence was achieved in 1975 but war soon broke out between the victors. The current treaty, known as the Lusaka Protocol, is the third peace effort between the opposing groups. But it is the first to guarantee a share of power to UNITA and the first to be supported by 6,500 armed United Nations peacekeepers.

During most of the fighting, the United States and South Africa backed UNITA. The Soviet Union and Cuban troops backed the Government of Jose Eduardo dos Santos. President Jose dos Santos said in a recent visit to the United States that his faith in Marxism-Leninism was misplaced.

In February 1996, the United Nations Security Council approved a three-month extension of a $1 million-per-day strategy that sought to verify implementation of the 1994 peace accord signed by the government and Jonas Savimbi, the UNITA rebel leader. A dozen small-scale military battles were reported in February 1996, but by August the government had pledged $73 million to disarm fighters, rebuild the country, and support the peace process.

Renewed fighting broke out in June 1997, however, as government troops attacked rebel-controlled territory near the border with the Democratic Republic of the Congo (the former Zaire). Government spokesmen said troops were trying to close the border to armed troops escaping the Zairian civil war. UNITA rebels had supported Zairian president Mobutu Sese Seko, who was driven from power in May. However, UN officials said the fighting took place away from the border in the diamond-mining region of the north, raising the possibility that the government was moving to eliminate the rebel organization. In October 1997, the UN imposed new sanctions which further weakened UNITA. The government made Savimbi a stakeholder in the mines, in exchange for UNITA giving up control over the main diamond-mining areas. By mid-January 1998, UNITA had withdrawn from these areas.

UNITA was supposed to officially disarm and join Angolan politics at the end of February 1998. The deadline passed but there was no disarmament or reconciliation. Full-scale warfare between Mr. dos Santos's government and Mr. Savimbi's UNITA resumed by December 1998.

Since then, the situation has become increasingly precarious. On February 26, 1999 the UN withdrew its observer mission. Late that same month, the government began conscripting young males. UNITA forces control much of the countryside, particularly in central Angola, while the government retains the cities. Mr. Savimbi, whose forces control the major roadways, refuses to allow humanitarian aid to pass through his territory. Moreover, UNITA still has rebel bases across the border in Zambia and Congo where they back the efforts of Congolese rebels to overthrow Laurent Kabila (who is supported by Mr. dos Santos). A fresh government offensive against UNITA rebels began in the fall of 1999 and resulted in the capture of Bailundo. In December, the war spread to Namibia after that country allowed Mr. do Santos's forces to mount attacks against UNITA from Namibian territory.

In May 2001, Mr. dos Santos made a renewed effort to seek peace and democracy within Angola. At that time the kidnapping and killing of civilians by UNITA had sharply increased. As of June, both the government and UNITA claimed to accept the Lusaka Protocol, but no serious efforts had been made to end the war.

According to a report by the Human Rights Watch Arms Project in Washington, both sides in the Angolan conflict are guilty of serious abuses, including assaults on relief personnel, the continuing laying of landmines, weapons imports and the forced recruitment of juvenile soldiers.

region posed by the Cuban presence, and on South Africa's refusal to implement the UN plan for Namibia without a reciprocal Angolan commitment to Cuban troop withdrawal in tandem with implementation of the UN plan. U.S. discussions with Angola have taken place within the context of the U.S. role as intermediary with the parties in an effort to resolve the Namibia issue. Since 1976, the United States has consistently expressed its concern about the Cuban presence, which it regards as destabilizing to the region.

The negotiations between Angola and South Africa have been long and diffi-

cult. Confidence between the parties has been and remains low. It took 2 years to engage Luanda and Pretoria in a substantive negotiation, and another year until 1984—to begin to erode the mutual mistrust and to construct a negotiating framework acceptable to both sides. But with the Lusaka Accord of February 1984, the South Africans began the process of disengagement from Angola. In November 1984, the Angolans said they were ready to commit themselves to withdraw 20,000 Cuban troops within 3 years of the beginning of implementation of Security Council Resolution 435. While this proposal was in itself not sufficient to

conclude an agreement-South Africa responded to the Angolan "Plataforma" with a proposal for complete Cuban troop withdrawal in 12 weeks-it was an important step forward in that Luanda had accepted the principle that the independence of Namibia could take place only within the context of withdrawal of Cuban troops from Angola.

At present, the negotiations are effectively at a standstill. Luanda suspended its substantive participation in the talks in June 1985—purportedly in reaction to repeal of the Clark Amendment forbidding U.S. aid to UNITA as well as to South African cross-border raids, including a failed attack on Angolan oil facilities in Cabinda. Under Secretary for Political Affairs Michael Armacost met with Angolan President Dos Santos in September 1985 and with Foreign Minister Van Dunem Mbinda in 1986, and there have been other diplomatic contacts at lower levels. The negotiations were tentatively resumed in April 1987 in a meeting between Assistant Secretary Crocker and Angolan interior Minister Rodrigues "kito" in Brazzaville, Congo.

The United States has made clear to the Angolan Government that it is ready to help achieve a settlement of the Namibia problem that will protect the security interests of Angola as well as the other parties involved. The United States also has made clear that normalization of U.S.-Angolan relations can be considered only within the context of a comprehensive settlement involving implementation of the UN Plan for Namibia and the withdrawal of Cuban combat forces from Angola.

The United States has stated publicly that it believes UNITA to be a legitimate nationalist movement that cannot be excluded from a role in the political life of Angola. There must be a genuine process of national reconciliation if there is to be real peace in Angola. The United States supports UNITA's struggle against Soviet-Cuban imperialism and, in this regard, is providing it with appropriate and effective assistance. During a private visit to the United States in January 1986, UNITA leader Savimbi met with President Reagan and other high U.S. officials. But U.S. policy is based on the belief that military solutions are not viable and does not seek to impose a solution to the internal Angolan conflict. The United States regards the Angolan conflict as an Angolan problem that should be resolved without outside interference.

U.S. policy attempts to help realize both Namibian independence and peace in Angola by addressing Angola's and South Africa's security concerns vis-a-vis each other. The withdrawal of foreign forces that has been the objective of the U.S. brokered negotiations—the withdrawal of Cubans from Angola and South Africans from Namibia—would leave it to the Angolans to work out a solution to their internal problems. Savimbi has publicly stated that he supports U.S. efforts to achieve a negotiated regional settlement.

Since 1977, the United States has provided indirect humanitarian food aid to Angola through UNICEF. There are no general prohibitions against U.S. private sector involvement in Angola. However, the U.S. Government does not approve American exports to Angola with a military end-use. In 1986, the U.S. Congress passed legislation prohibiting new EXIM financing, except agricultural exports, in Angola.

The U.S. Government has asked American companies operating in Angola to consider U.S. national interests as well as their own in making business decisions. These companies are also alerted to the risks involved in doing business in the midst of a civil war. Direct bilateral assistance to Angola is prohibited by U.S. law.

## Principal U.S. Officials

**For up-to-date information on Principal U.S. Officials, see the U.S. Embassies, Consulates, and Foreign Service section starting on page 139.**

# ANTIGUA AND BARBUDA

April 2000

Official Name:
**Antigua and Barbuda**

## PROFILE

### Geography

**Area:** Antigua—281 sq. km. (108 sq. mi.); Barbuda—161 sq. km. (62 sq. mi.).
**Cities:** Capital—St. John's (pop. 30,000).
**Terrain:** Generally low-lying, with highest elevation 405 m. (1,330 ft.).
**Climate:** Tropical maritime.

### People

**Nationality:** Noun and adjective—Antiguan(s), Barbudan(s).
**Population (1998):** 69,006.
**Annual population growth rate (1998):** 1.5%.
**Ethnic groups:** Almost entirely of African origin; some of British, Portuguese, and Levantine Arab origin.
**Religions:** Principally Anglican, with evangelical Protestant and Roman Catholic minorities.
**Language:** English.
**Education:** Years compulsory—9. Literacy—about 90%.
**Health:** Life expectancy—71 yrs. male; 75 yrs. female. Infant mortality rate—18/1,000.
**Work force (32,000):** Commerce and services, agriculture, other industry.
**Unemployment (1996):** 7.0%

### Government

**Type:** Constitutional monarchy with Westminster-style Parliament.
**Constitution:** 1981.
**Independence:** November 1, 1981.
**Branches:** Executive—governor general (representing Queen Elizabeth II, head of state), prime minister (head of government), and cabinet. Legislative—a 17-member Senate appointed by the governor general (mainly on the advice of the prime minister and the leader of the opposition) and a 17-member popularly elected House of Representatives. Judicial—magistrate's courts, Eastern Caribbean Supreme Court (High Court and Court of Appeals, privy council in London).
**Administrative subdivisions:** Six parishes and two dependencies (Barbuda and Redonda).
**Political parties:** Antigua Labor Party (ALP, incumbent), United Progressive Party (UPP), Barbuda People's Movement (BPM).
**Suffrage:** Universal at 18.

### Economy

**GDP (1999, current U.S. dollars):** $175.7 million.
**GDP growth rate (1998):** 3.9%.
**Per capita GDP (1999):** $2,745.
**Natural resources:** Negligible.
**Agriculture (1998, 4.0% of GDP):** Products—cotton, livestock, vegetables, pineapples.
**Services:** Tourism, banking, and other financial services.
**Trade (1998):** Exports—$41 million—OECS (26%), United States (.03%), Trinidad and Tobago (2%), Barbados (15%). Imports—$373.6 million—United States (27%), U.K. (16%), OECS (3%).

## HISTORY

Antigua was first inhabited by the Siboney ("stone people") whose settlements date at least to 2400 BC. The Siboney were succeeded by the Arawaks who originated in Venezuela and gradually migrated up the chain of islands now called the Lesser Antilles. The warlike Carib people drove the Arawaks from neighboring islands but apparently did not settle on either Antigua or Barbuda.

Christopher Columbus landed on the islands in 1493 naming the larger one "Santa Maria de la Antigua." The English colonized the islands in 1632. Sir Christopher Codrington established the first large sugar estate in Antigua in 1674, and leased Barbuda to raise provisions for his plantations. Barbuda's only town is named after him. Codrington and others brought slaves from Africa's west coast to work the plantations.

Antiguan slaves were emancipated in 1834 but remained economically

**Galley Bay, one of Antigua's 365 beaches.**

Photo credit: Corel Corporation.

dependent on the plantation owners. Economic opportunities for the new freedmen were limited by a lack of surplus farming land, no access to credit, and an economy built on agriculture rather than manufacturing. Poor labor conditions persisted until 1939 when a member of a royal commission urged the formation of a trade union movement.

The Antigua Trades and Labor Union, formed shortly afterward, became the political vehicle for Vere Cornwall Bird who became the union's president in 1943. The Antigua Labor Party (ALP), formed by Bird and other trade unionists, first ran candidates in the 1946 elections and became the majority party in 1951 beginning a long history of electoral victories.

Voted out of office in the 1971 general elections that swept the progressive labor movement into power, Bird and the ALP returned to office in 1976; the party won renewed mandates in the general elections in 1984 and 1989. In the 1989 elections, the ruling ALP won all but two of the 17 seats.

During elections in March 1994, power passed from Vere Bird to his son, Lester Bird, but remained within the ALP which won 11 of the 17 parliamentary seats. In the last elections

in March 1999, the ALP gained another seat resulting in a distribution of 12 seats to the ALP, four seats to the opposition United Progressive Party (UPP) led by Baldwin Spencer, and one seat to the Barbuda People's Movement (BPM).

# GOVERNMENT AND POLITICAL CONDITIONS

As head of state, Queen Elizabeth II is represented in Antigua and Barbuda by a governor general who acts on the advice of the prime minister and the cabinet. Antigua and Barbuda has a bicameral legislature: a 17-member Senate appointed by the governor general—mainly on the advice of the prime minister and the leader of the opposition—and a 17-member popularly elected House of Representatives. The prime minister is the leader of the majority party in the House and conducts affairs of state with the cabinet. The prime minister and the cabinet are responsible to the Parliament. Elections must be held at least every five years but may be called by the prime minister at any time.

Antigua and Barbuda has a multiparty political system with a long history of hard fought elections, two of which have resulted in peaceful changes of government. The opposition, however, claims to be disadvantaged by the ruling party's longstanding monopoly on patronage and its control of the electronic media.

Constitutional safeguards include freedom of speech, press, worship, movement, and association. Antigua and Barbuda is a member of the eastern Caribbean court system. Jurisprudence is based on English common law.

## Principal Government Officials

**For up-to-date information on Principal Government Officials, see the Chiefs of State and Cabinet Members of Foreign Governments section starting on page 1.**

Antigua and Barbuda maintain an embassy in the United States at 3216 New Mexico Ave. NW, Washington, DC 20016 (tel. 202-362-5122).

# ECONOMY

Tourism is the key industry and the principal earner of foreign exchange in Antigua and Barbuda. However, a series of violent hurricanes since 1995 resulted in serious damage to tourist infrastructure and periods of sharp reductions in visitor numbers. Overall economic growth for 1998 was 3.9%.

Inflation has been moderate, averaging 3%-4% annually, since 1993. Antigua and Barbuda is a beneficiary of the U.S. Caribbean Basin Initiative. Its 1995 exports to the U.S. were valued at $3 million and its U.S. imports totaled $97 million. It also belongs to the predominantly English-speaking Caribbean Community and Common Market (CARICOM).

# FOREIGN RELATIONS

Antigua and Barbuda maintains diplomatic relations with the United States, Canada, the United Kingdom, and the People's Republic of China, as well as with many Latin American countries and neighboring Eastern Caribbean states. It is a member of the United Nations, the Commonwealth of Nations, the Organization of American States, the Organization of Eastern Caribbean States, and the Eastern Caribbean's Regional Security System (RSS).

As a member of CARICOM, Antigua and Barbuda supported efforts by the United States to implement UN Security Council Resolution 940, designed to facilitate the departure of Haiti's de facto authorities from power. The country agreed to contribute personnel to the multinational force which restored the democratically elected government of Haiti in October 1994.

In May 1997, Prime Minister Bird joined 14 other Caribbean leaders and President Clinton for the first-ever U.S.-regional summit in Bridgetown, Barbados. The summit strengthened the basis for regional cooperation on justice and counternarcotics issues, finance and development, and trade.

# U.S.-ANTIGUA AND BARBUDA RELATIONS

## Principal U.S. Embassy Officials

**For up-to-date information on Principal U.S. Officials, see the U.S. Embassies, Consulates, and Foreign Service section starting on page 139.**

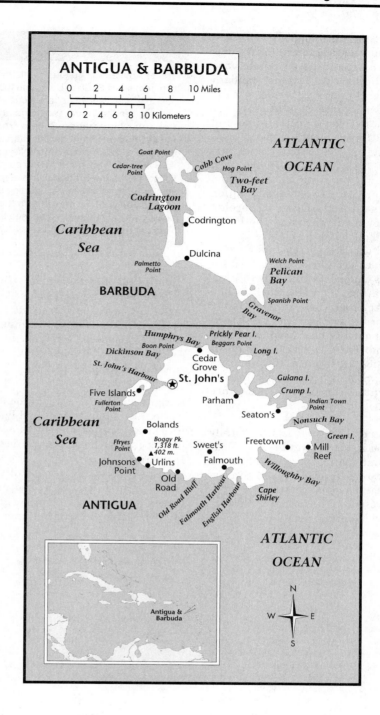

The United States maintains no official presence in Antigua.

The ambassador and embassy officers are resident in Barbados and travel to Antigua frequently. However, a U.S. consular agent resident in Antigua assists U.S. citizens in Antigua and Barbuda.

The U.S. embassy in Barbados is located in the Canadian Imperial Bank of Commerce Building, Broad Street, Bridgetown (tel: 246-436-4950; fax: 246-429-5246).

*Consular Agent*
Juliet Ryder
Hospital Hill, English Harbor
Antigua
Tel: (268) 463-6531

The United States has maintained friendly relations with Antigua and Barbuda since its independence. The

United States has supported the Government of Antigua and Barbuda's effort to expand its economic base and to improve its citizens' standard of living. However, concerns over the lack of adequate regulation of the financial services sector prompted the U.S. Government to issue a financial advisory for Antigua and Barbuda in 1999. The U.S. also has been active in supporting post-hurricane disaster assistance and rehabilitation through USAID's Office of Foreign Disaster Assistance and the Peace Corps. Following the closure in July 1996 of the USAID regional mission for the eastern Caribbean, U.S. assistance is channeled primarily through multilateral agencies such as the Inter-American Development Bank, the World Bank, and the Caribbean Development Bank. In addition, Antigua and Barbuda receives counter-narcotics assistance and benefits from U.S. military exercise-related and humanitarian civic assistance construction projects.

Antigua and Barbuda is strategically situated in the Leeward Islands near maritime transport lanes of major importance to the United States. Antigua has long hosted a U.S. military presence. The former U.S. Navy support facility, turned over to the

## Travel Notes

**Travel Advice:** For up-to-date information from the U.S. State Department on possible inconvenient or hazardous situations, see the **Travel Warnings and Consular Information Sheets from the U.S. Government** section starting on page 1723. For the latest information on health requirements and conditions, see the **International Travelers' Health Information** section starting on page 1385. For further information dealing with non-urgent matter, see the **Tips for Travelers to...** section starting on page 1588.

Government of Antigua and Barbuda in 1995, is now being developed as a regional Coast Guard training facility. The U.S. Air Force continues to maintain a space-tracking facility on Antigua. The U.S. embassy in Antigua closed on June 30, 1994.

Antigua and Barbuda's location close to the U.S. Virgin Islands and Puerto Rico makes it an attractive transshipment point for narcotics traffickers. International concerns have also been raised by the vulnerability of the off-shore financial sector to money laundering. To address these problems, the U.S. and Antigua and

Barbuda have signed a series of counter-narcotic and counter-crime treaties and agreements, including a maritime law enforcement agreement (1995), subsequently amended to include overflight and order-to-land provisions (1996); a bilateral extradition treaty (1996); and a mutual legal assistance treaty (1996).

In 1997, Antigua and Barbuda had more than 57,000 U.S. visitors. It is estimated that 4,500 Americans reside in the country.

## Other Contact Information

**U.S. Department of Commerce**
International Trade Administration
Trade Information Center
14th and Constitution Avenue, NW
Washington, DC 20230
Tel: 1-800-USA-Trade

**Caribbean/Latin American Action**
1818 N Street, NW
Suite 310
Washington, DC 20036
Tel: 202-466-7464
Fax: 202-822-0075

# ARGENTINA

October 2000

Official Name:
**The Argentine Republic**

# PROFILE

## Geography

**Area:** 2.8 million sq. km. (1.1 million sq. mi.); about the size of the U.S. east of the Mississippi River; second-largest country in South America.
**Cities:** Capital—Buenos Aires (city 3 million; metropolitan area 13 million). Other major cities—Cordoba (1.2 million); Rosario (950,000); Mar del Plata (900,000); Mendoza (400,000).
**Terrain:** Andes mountains and foothills in the west. Aconcagua (7,021 m; 23,034 ft) is highest peak in the Western Hemisphere; remainder of country is lowland; central region characterized by vast grassy plains (pampas).
**Climate:** Varied—predominantly temperate with extremes ranging from subtropical in the north to arid/subantarctic in far south.

## People

**Nationality:** Noun and adjective—Argentine(s).
**Population:** (2000 est.) 37.0 million.
**Annual population growth rate:** (1999 est.) 1.3%.
**Ethnic Groups:** European 85%, mostly of Spanish and Italian descent. Mestizo, Amerindian or other nonwhite groups 15%.

**Religion:** Roman Catholic 92%, Protestant 2%, Jewish 2%, other 4%.
**Language:** Spanish.
**Education:** Years compulsory—9. Adult literacy (1995)—96.2%.
**Health:** Infant mortality rate—18.41/1000. Life expectancy (1995 est.)—74.76 yrs.
**Work force:** Industry and commerce—36%; agriculture—19%; transport and communications—6%.

## Government

**Type:** republic.
**Independence:** July 9, 1816.
**Constitution:** 1853, revised 1994.
**Branches:** Executive—president, vice president, cabinet. Legislative—bicameral congress (72-member Senate, 257-member Chamber of Deputies). Judicial—Supreme Court, federal and provincial trial courts.
**Administrative subdivisions:** 23 provinces and one autonomous federal capital district.
**Political parties:** Justicialist (Peronist), Radical Civic Union (UCR), FREPASO, numerous smaller national and provincial parties. In 1997, UCR and FREPASO formed a coalition called the Alliance for Work, Justice, and Education.
**Suffrage:** Universal adult.

## Economy

**Year:** (1999).
**GDP:** $283 billion.

**Annual real growth rate:** -3.1%.
**Per capita GDP:** $7,700.
**Natural resources:** Fertile plains (pampas). Minerals: lead, zinc, tin, copper, iron, manganese, oil, uranium.
**Agriculture:** (5% of GDP, about 40% of exports by value) Products—grains, oilseeds and by-products, livestock products.
**Industry:** (28% of GDP) Types—food processing, oil refining, machinery and equipment, textiles, chemicals and petrochemicals.
**Trade:** Exports ($23.3 billion)—grains, meats, oilseeds, manufactured products. Major markets—Brazil 25%; EU 20%; U.S. 11%; Chile 7%. Imports ($25.5 billion)—machinery, vehicles and transport products, chemicals. Major suppliers—EU 28%; Brazil 22%; U.S. 20%.

# U.S.-ARGENTINE RELATIONS

The United States and Argentina currently enjoy a close bilateral relationship, which was highlighted by President Clinton's visit to Argentina in October 1997 and President De la Rua's visit to Washington in June 2000. The efforts of the Menem (1989-99) and De la Rua (1999-) administrations to open Argentina's economy and realign its foreign policy have contributed to the improvement in these relations, and the interests and policies of the two countries coincide on many issues. Argentina and the United States often vote together in the United Nations and other multilateral fora. Argentina has participated in many multilateral forces deployments mandated by the United Nations Security Council, including recent missions to Haiti and the former Yugoslavia. Reflecting the growing partnership that marks ties between the two countries, the U.S. Secretary of State and Argentine Foreign Minister chaired 1997 and 1999 meetings of the Special Consultative Process to address important issues in the bilateral relationship. Argentina was designated a major non-NATO ally in 1998.

## U.S. Embassy Functions

The U.S. Mission in Buenos Aires carries out the traditional diplomatic function of representing the U.S. Government and people in discussions with the Argentine Government, and more generally, in relations with the people of Argentina. The excellent political relationship between the United States and Argentina is increasingly reflected in the U.S. Embassy's efforts to facilitate cooperation in nontraditional areas such as counter-terrorism, anti-narcotics, and scientific cooperation on space, peaceful uses of nuclear energy, and the environment. The embassy also provides a wide range of services to U.S. citizens and businesses in Argentina. Officers from the U.S. Foreign Service, Foreign Commercial Service, and Foreign Agricultural Service work closely with the thousands of U.S. companies which do business in Argentina, providing information on Argentine trade and industry regulations and assisting U.S. companies starting or maintaining business ventures in Argentina.

Attaches accredited to Argentina from the Department of Justice (including the Drug Enforcement Administration and the Federal Bureau of Investigation), U.S. Customs, the Federal Aviation Administration, and other federal agencies work closely with Argentine counter-

parts on international crime and other issues of concern. An active, sophisticated, and expanding media environment, together with growing positive interest in American culture and society, make Argentina an uncommonly receptive environment for the information and cultural exchange work of the U.S. Embassy as well. The number of Argentines studying in U.S. universities is rapidly growing, and the Fulbright fellowship program has more than tripled the annual number of U.S. and Argentine academic grantees since 1994.

The embassy's consular section monitors the welfare and whereabouts of more than 20,000 U.S. citizen residents of Argentina and more than 300,000 U.S. tourists each year. Consular personnel also provide American citizens passport, voting, notarial, Social Security, and other services. Although the U. S. since 1996 has permitted Argentine tourists to visit without visas, the consular section does issue nonimmigrant visas to persons who travel for other purposes, such as students and those who seek to work in the U.S., as well as immigrant visas to those who seek U.S. permanent residence.

## Principal U.S. Embassy Officials

For up-to-date information on Principal U.S. Officials, see the U.S. Embassies, Consulates, and Foreign Service section starting on page 139.

## Contact Information

The U.S. Embassy and Consulate General in Argentina are located at 4300 Colombia Avenue in the Palermo district of Buenos Aires.
Mission offices can be reached at tel (54)(11) 4777-4533/34; fax (54)(11) 4777-0197.
Mailing addresses : U.S. Embassy Buenos Aires, APO AA 34034; or 4300 Colombia, 1425 Buenos Aires, Argentina. Embassy home page:

usembassy@state.gov/baires_embassy.

# ECONOMY

Argentina has resumed modest economic growth in 2000, after suffering a significant recession which began in the last quarter of 1998. President Fernando de la Rua, who took office in December 1999 following the 10-year administration of former President Carlos Menem, has appointed a respected economic team which is continuing and building on past economic policies. During the 1990s, Argentina implemented a successful economic restructuring based on macroeconomic stabilization, trade liberalization, privatization, and public administrative reform, which placed the country on a relatively sound economic footing after decades of decline and chronic bouts of high inflation. However, Argentina still needs to complete some difficult structural reforms to ensure a steady growth path.

The 1991 convertibility law established a quasicurrency board, which has been a pillar of price stability. The government privatized most state-controlled companies, opened the economy to foreign trade and investment, improved tax collection, and created private pension and workers compensation systems. As a result of these policies, Argentina experienced a boom in economic growth in the early 1990s, followed by a period of somewhat more erratic growth in the second half of the decade when the country was hit by a series of external economic shocks. While the economy recovered fairly quickly from the effects of the "Tequila" crisis of 1995, Argentina is finding it harder to return to strong growth after the recession that followed successive shocks from East Asia, Russia, and Brazil.

Structural reforms, coupled with monetary stability, fostered major new investment in services and industry in the 1990s, particularly in the telecommunications, food-processing, banking, energy, and mining sectors. As a result, Argentina's exports more than doubled, from about $12 billion in 1992 to around $25 billion in 1999. Imports also grew rapidly during the same period, from $15 billion to over $25 billion. However, Argentina's international trade still remains a relatively small part of its economy. This is in part a heritage of decades of import-substitution policies, but it also reflects the country's relatively diversified economy.

One of Argentina's challenges is to generate growth with more equitable distribution of income and reduced unemployment. The country has seen double-digit unemployment since the mid-1990s (peaking at 18.4% midyear 1995); the May 2000 unemployment rate was 15.4%. Over the long term, significant declines in unemployment will come slowly; labor productivity will rise as major private investments are implemented, and future growth will be strongest in capital-intensive sectors. There is broad support for the key elements of Argentina's economic model. However, a growing awareness exists that important structural reforms are still needed, primarily in the labor market, tax administration, and delivery of public services. Inefficiencies in these areas need to be addressed to ensure stable growth. Public sector corruption, commonly acknowledged as being widespread, is another subject of public debate. The Argentine justice system can be politically influenced, is often inefficient, and provides slow due process.

## Banking
The past few years have seen a significant consolidation and strengthening of Argentina's banking system, in large part through foreign investments. In addition to high reserve and capital-adequacy requirements, the Central Bank of Argentina maintains a repurchase agreement with a consortium of international banks to provide a $6 billion safety net in the event of a liquidity squeeze. Mergers and acquisitions, which decreased the number of Argentine banks from nearly 300 in 1990 to fewer than 100 at the end of 1999, are expected to continue and lead to improvements in

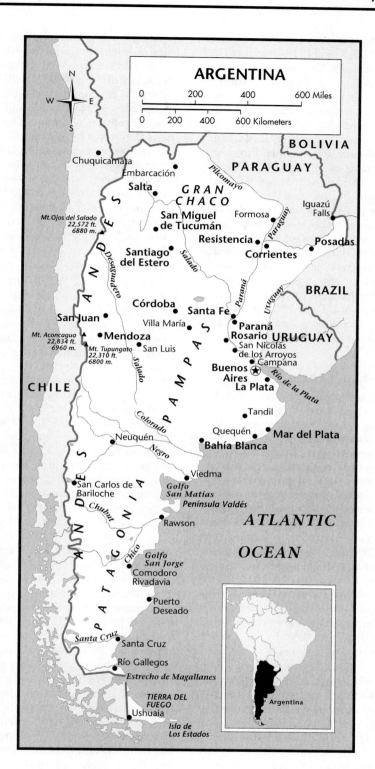

management and efficiency. The foreign currency reserves of the Central Bank stood at nearly $25 billion in December 1999, or over 9 months of imports. However, by law, these reserves are used to back the monetary liabilities of the Central Bank and are not available for conducting monetary policy.

Despite the recession, bank deposits continued to grow during 1999, although at a much slower rate than in previous years. Total deposits in the banking system stood at nearly $80 billion in December 1999—twice that of June 1995, when deposits hit a low of $37 billion. Foreign-controlled banks now hold over 40% of total deposits, and six of the top 10 commercial banks are in the hands of U.S. and European financial institutions. Still, the level of bank utilization in Argentina remains relatively low, and bank intermediation represents only about 30% of GDP—a much lower ratio than that in Chile, Mexico, or Brazil, for example. Financing and lending costs, high by industrialized country standards, were further increased by the late-1990s turmoil in emerging markets. Annual interest rates which banks charge large preferred businesses were around 10% in 2000. For consumer overdrafts or higher-risk firms (typically small businesses), annual rates approach 25%. Given Argentina's extremely low rates of inflation, those interest rates, which reflect lenders' risk calculations, are very high in real terms.

## Foreign Trade

Strong growth in Argentina's foreign trade since 1990 has been key to meeting its external payments. Foreign trade now equals about 17% of GDP—up from 11% in 1990—and plays an increasingly important role in Argentina's economic development. Still, exports represent only 8% of Argentine GDP, almost unchanged since 1990. The U.S. recorded trade surpluses with Argentina every year from 1993-99, as Argentina's firms increased capital goods purchases during that period. This trend reflected the Argentine Government's policy of encouraging modernization and improved competitiveness in Argentine industry through lower tariffs on capital goods.

Argentina's trade deficit dropped from $5 billion in 1998 to $2.2 billion in 1999, primarily because the recession lowered demand for imports. The overall value of 1999 Argentine exports fell 12%, due mainly to low international commodity prices, while imports dropped 19% from 1998. Argentine exports began to increase significantly in the last months of 1999 and continued their upward trend in early 2000. Exports should continue to rise throughout 2000 as rebounding economies in Brazil and Asia increase demand and prices for Argentine commodities

move upward; rising oil prices have been particularly significant. The U.S. trade surplus with Argentina was $2.4 billion in 1999, down from 1998 as U.S exports to the country declined from $5.9 to $5.0 billion. Fresh Argentine beef was exported to the U.S. market in 1997 for the first time in over 60 years, and in 1999 its export quota of 20,000 tons was filled. However, beef exports to the U.S. were suspended in August 2000 when some Argentine cattle (near Paraguay) were discovered to have antibodies for hoof and mouth disease.

Mercosur, the customs union that includes Argentina, Brazil, Paraguay, and Uruguay, entered into force January 1, 1995. Chile and Bolivia joined the pact subsequently as associate members. Close cooperation between Brazil and Argentina—historic competitors—is the key to Mercosur's integration process, which includes political and military elements in addition to a customs union. Brazil accounts for more than 70% of Mercosur GDP and Argentina about 27%. Mercosur has been one of the largest and most successful integrated markets in the developing world, with substantial foreign investment going to its members. Intra-Mercosur trade also rose dramatically from $4 billion in 1991 to over $23 billion in 1998. More than 90% of intra-Mercosur trade is duty-free, while the group's common external tariff (CET) applies to more than 85% of imported goods. Remaining goods will be phased into the CET by 2006. Argentina adheres to most treaties and international agreements on intellectual property. It is a member of the World Intellectual Property Organization and signed the Uruguay Round agreements in December 1993, including measures related to intellectual property. However, extension of adequate patent protection to pharmaceuticals has been a highly contentious bilateral issue. In May 1997, the U.S. suspended 50% of Argentina's GSP benefits because of its unsatisfactory pharmaceutical patent law. In May 1999, The U.S. Government initiated consultations under WTO procedures to address these inadequacies and expanded the consultations in May 2000.

## Investment

U.S. direct investment in Argentina is concentrated in telecommunications, petroleum and gas, electric energy, financial services, chemicals, food processing, and vehicle manufacturing. The stock of U.S. direct investment in Argentina approached $16 billion at the end of 1999, according to embassy estimates. Canadian, European, and Chilean firms—other important sources of capital—also have invested significant amounts. Spanish companies in particular have entered the Argentine market aggressively, with major investments in the petroleum and gas, telecommunications, banking, and retail sectors. Several bilateral agreements play an important role in promoting U.S. private investment. Argentina has an Overseas Private Investment Corporation (OPIC) agreement and an active program with the U.S. Export-Import Bank. Under the 1994 U.S.-Argentina Bilateral Investment Treaty, U.S. investors enjoy national treatment in all sectors except shipbuilding, fishing, nuclear-power generation, and uranium production. The treaty allows for international arbitration of investment disputes.

# GOVERNMENT AND POLITICAL CONDITIONS

After years of post-World War II instability, Argentina is today a fully functioning democracy. Former President Carlos Menem's administration (1989-99) reordered Argentina's foreign and domestic policies. His reelection in May 1995—in the face of hardships caused by economic restructuring and exacerbated by the Mexico peso crisis—provided a mandate for Menem's free-market economic strategy and pro-U.S. foreign policy. Menem's second term ended in December 1999; the constitution does not provide for a sitting president to succeed himself more than once. Argentina's current President, Fernando de la Rua, has continued the economic and foreign policy strategies begun by Menem.

The constitution of 1853, as revised in 1994, mandates a separation of powers into executive, legislative, and judicial branches at the national and provincial level. Each province also has its own constitution, roughly mirroring the structure of the national constitution. The president and vice president were traditionally elected indirectly by an electoral college to a single 6-year term and not allowed to seek immediate reelection. Constitutional reforms adopted in August 1994 reduced the presidential term to 4 years, abolished the electoral college in favor of direct voting, and limited the president and vice president to two consecutive terms; they are allowed to stand for a third term or more after an interval of at least one term. The president appoints cabinet ministers and the constitution grants him considerable power, including a line-item veto.

Provinces traditionally sent two senators, elected by provincial legislatures, to the upper house of Congress. Voters in the federal capital of Buenos Aires elected an electoral college which chose the city's senators. The constitution now mandates a transition (beginning in 2001) to direct election for all senators, and the addition of a third senator representing the largest minority party from each province and the capital. The revised constitution reduces senatorial terms from 9 to 6 years. One-third of the Senate will stand for reelection every 2 years.

Members of the Chamber of Deputies are directly elected to 4-year terms. Voters elect half the members of the lower house every 2 years through a system of proportional representation. Other important 1994 constitutional changes included the creation of a senior coordinating minister to serve under the president and autonomy for the city of Buenos Aires, which now elects its own mayor. The constitution establishes the judiciary as an independent government entity. The president appoints members of the Supreme Court with the consent of the Senate. Other federal judges are appointed by the president on the recommendation of a magistrates' council. The Supreme Court has the power, first asserted in 1854, to declare legislative acts unconstitutional.

## Political Parties

The two largest political parties are the Justicialist (PJ) or Peronist Party, which evolved out of Juan Peron's efforts in the 1940s to expand the role of labor in the political process, and the Union Civica Radical (UCR), or Radical Civic Union, founded in 1890. Traditionally, the UCR has had more urban middle-class support and the PJ more labor support, but both parties are now broadly based.

A grouping of mostly left-leaning parties and former Peronists—the Front for a Country in Solidarity (FREPASO)—emerged in the 1990s as a serious political contender, especially in the federal capital. In August 1997, the UCR and FREPASO formed a coalition called the Alliance for Work, Justice and Education (the Alliance). Smaller parties occupy various positions on the political spectrum and some are active only in certain provinces. Historically, organized labor (largely tied to the Peronist Party) and the armed forces also have played significant roles in national life. However, labor's political power has been significantly weakened by free market reforms, and the armed forces are firmly under civilian control. Repudiated by the public after a period of military rule (1976-83) marked by human rights violations, economic decline, and military defeat in the 1982 Falkland/Malvinas Islands conflict, the Argentine military today is a downsized, volunteer force focused largely on international peacekeeping.

## Government Policy

The De la Rua administration has continued wideranging economic reforms begun by Menem designed to open the Argentine economy and enhance its international competitiveness. Privatization, deregulation, fewer import barriers, and a fixed exchange rate have been corner- stones of this effort. All of these changes have dramatically reduced the role of the Argentine state in regulating the domestic market. The reform agenda, however, remains incomplete, and improvements in the judicial system and provincial administration are still needed, among other areas.

## National Security

The president and a civilian minister of defense control the Argentine armed forces. The paramilitary forces under the control of the Interior Ministry are the Gendarmeria (border police) and the Prefectura Naval (coast guard). The Argentine armed forces maintain close defense cooperation and military-supply relationships with the United States. Other countries also have military relationships with the Argentine forces, principally Israel, Germany, France, Spain, and Italy.

Lack of budgetary resources is the most serious problem facing the Argentine military today. Current economic conditions and the government's commitment to reduce public sector spending have slowed modernization and restructuring efforts. Under Presidents Menem and De la Rua, Argentina's traditionally difficult relations with its neighbors have improved dramatically, and Argentine officials publicly deny seeing a potential threat from any neighboring country. Mercosur has exercised a useful role in supporting democracy in the region, intervening, for example, to discourage the Paraguayan military during an attempted coup in early 2000.

# PEOPLE

Argentines are a fusion of diverse national and ethnic groups, with descendants of Italian and Spanish immigrants predominant. Waves of immigrants from many European countries arrived in the late 19th and early 20th centuries. Syrian, Lebanese, and other Middle Eastern immigrants number about 500,000, mainly in urban areas. Argentina has the largest Jewish population in Latin America, about 250,000 strong. In recent years, there has been a substantial influx of immigrants from neighboring Latin American countries. The indigenous population, estimated at 700,000, is concentrated in the provinces of the north, northwest, and south. The Argentine population has one of Latin America's lowest growth rates. Eighty percent of the population resides in cities or towns of more than 2,000, and over one-third lives in the greater Buenos Aires area. With 13 million inhabitants, this sprawling metropolis serves as the focus for national life. Argentines enjoy comparatively high standards of living; half the population considers itself middle class.

# HISTORY

Europeans arrived in the region with the 1502 voyage of Amerigo Vespucci. Spanish navigator Juan Diaz de Solias visited what is now Argentina in 1516. Spain established a permanent colony on the site of Buenos Aires in 1580, although initial settlement was primarily overland from Peru. The Spanish further integrated Argentina into their empire by establishing the Vice Royalty of Rio de la Plata in 1776, and Buenos Aires became a flourishing port.

Buenos Aires formally declared independence from Spain on July 9, 1816. Argentines revere Gen. Jose de San Martin, who campaigned in Argentina, Chile, and Peru as the hero of their national independence. Following the defeat of the Spanish, centralist and federalist groups waged a lengthy conflict between themselves to determine the future of the nation. National unity was established, and the constitution promulgated in 1853. Two forces combined to create the modern Argentine nation in the late 19th century: the introduction of modern agricultural techniques and integration of Argentina into the world economy. Foreign investment and immigration from Europe aided this economic revolution. Investment, primarily British, came in such fields as railroads and ports. The migrants

## Travel Notes

**Travel Advice:** For up-to-date information from the U.S. State Department on possible inconvenient or hazardous situations, see the **Travel Warnings and Consular Information Sheets from the U.S. Government** section starting on page 1723. For the latest information on health requirements and conditions, see the **International Travelers' Health Information** section starting on page 1385. For further information dealing with non-urgent matter, see the **Tips for Travelers to...** section starting on page 1588.

who worked to develop Argentina's resources—especially the western pampas—came from throughout Europe, just as in the United States.

Conservative forces dominated Argentine politics until 1916, when their traditional rivals, the Radicals, won control of the government . The Radicals, with their emphasis on fair elections and democratic institutions, opened their doors to Argentina's expanding middle class as well as to elites previously excluded from power . The Argentine military forced aged Radical President Hipolito Yrigoyen from power in 1930 and ushered in another decade of Conservative rule. Using fraud and force when necessary, the governments of the 1930s attempted to contain the currents of economic and political change that eventually led to the ascendance of Juan Domingo Peron (b. 1897). New social and political forces were seeking political power, including a modern military and labor movements that emerged from the growing urban working class.

The military ousted Argentina's constitutional government in 1943. Peron, then an army colonel, was one of the coup's leaders, and he soon became the government's dominant figure as Minister of Labor. Elections carried him to the presidency in 1946. He aggressively pursued policies aimed at giving an economic and political voice to the working class and greatly expanded the number of unionized workers. In 1947, Peron announced the first 5-year plan based

on the growth of nationalized industries. He helped establish the powerful General Confederation of Labor (CGT). Peron's dynamic wife, Eva Duarte de Peron, known as Evita (1919-52), helped her husband develop strength with labor and women's groups; women obtained the right to vote in 1947. Peron won reelection in 1952, but the military deposed him in 1955. He went into exile, eventually settling in Spain. In the 1950-60s, military and civilian administrations traded power, trying, with limited success, to deal with diminished economic growth and continued social and labor demands. When military governments failed to revive the economy and suppress escalating terrorism in the late 1960s and early 1970s, the way was open for Peron's return.

On March 11, 1973, Argentina held general elections for the first time in 10 years. Peron was prevented from running, but voters elected his stand-in, Dr. Hector Campora, as President. Peron's followers also commanded strong majorities in both houses of Congress. Campora resigned in July 1973, paving the way for new elections. Peron won a decisive victory and returned as President in October 1973 with his third wife, Maria Estela Isabel Martinez de Peron, as Vice President. During this period, extremists on the left and right carried out terrorist acts with a frequency that threatened public order. The government resorted to a number of emergency decrees, including the implementation of special executive authority to deal with violence. This allowed the government to imprison persons indefinitely without charge.

Peron died on July 1, 1974. His wife succeeded him in office, but her administration was undermined by economic problems, Peronist intraparty struggles, and growing terrorism. A military coup removed her from office on March 24, 1976, and the armed forces formally exercised power through a junta composed of the three service commanders until December 10, 1983. The armed forces applied harsh measures against terrorists and many suspected of being their sympathizers. They restored basic order, but the costs of what became known as the "Dirty War" were high in terms of lives lost and basic human rights violated. Conservative counts list over 10,000 persons as "disappeared" during the 1976-83 period.

Serious economic problems, mounting charges of corruption, public revulsion in the face of human rights abuses and, finally, the country's 1982 defeat by the U.K. in an unsuccessful attempt to seize the Falklands/Malvinas Islands all combined to discredit the Argentine military regime. Under strong public pressure, the junta lifted bans on political parties and gradually restored basic political liberties. On October 30, 1983, Argentines went to the polls to choose a president; vice president; and national, provincial, and local officials in elections found by international observers to be fair and honest. The country returned to constitutional rule after Raul Alfonsin, candidate of the Radial Civic Union, received 52% of the popular vote for president. He began a 6-year term of office on December 10, 1983.

In 1985 and 1987, large turnouts for mid-term elections demonstrated continued public support for a strong and vigorous democratic system. The UCR-led government took steps to resolve some of the nation's most pressing problems, including accounting for those who disappeared during military rule, establishing civilian control of the armed forces, and consolidating democratic institutions. However, constant friction with the military, failure to resolve endemic economic problems, and an inability to maintain public confidence undermined the effectiveness of the Alfonsin government, which left office 6 months early after Peronist candidate Carlos Saul Menem won the 1989 presidential elections.

As President, Menem launched a major overhaul of Argentine domestic policy. Large-scale structural reforms dramatically reversed the role of the state in Argentine economic life. A decisive leader pressing a controversial agenda, Menem was not reluc-

tant to use the presidency's extensive powers to issue decrees when the Congress was unable to reach consensus on his proposed reforms. Those powers were curtailed somewhat when the constitution was reformed in 1994 as a result of the so-called Olivos Pact with the opposition Radical Party. That arrangement opened the way for Menem to seek and win reelection with 50% of the vote in the three-way 1995 presidential race.

The 1995 election saw the emergence of the moderate-left FREPASO political alliance. This alternative to the two traditional political parties in Argentina is particularly strong in Buenos Aires but as yet lacks the national infrastructure of the Peronists and Radicals. In an important development in Argentina's political life, all three major parties in the 1999 race espoused free market economic policies. In October 1999, the UCR-FREPASO Alliance's presidential candidate, Fernando de la Rua, defeated Peronist candidate Eduardo Duhalde. Taking office in December 1999, De la Rua has not only continued the previous administration's free market economic policies but has followed an IMF-sponsored program of government spending cuts, revenue increases, and provincial revenue-sharing reforms to get the federal deficit under control. De la Rua also has pursued labor law reform and business-promotion measures aimed at stimulating the economy and increasing employment. Despite these measures, Argentine economic growth remained nearly flat in 2000.

# FOREIGN RELATIONS

In recent years, Argentina has had a strong partnership with the United States. Argentina was the only Latin American country to participate in the Gulf war and all phases of the Haiti operation. It has contributed to UN peacekeeping operations worldwide, with Argentine soldiers and police serving in Guatemala, Ecuador-Peru, Western Sahara, Angola, Cyprus, Kosovo, Bosnia, and East Timor. In recognition of its contribu-

tions to international security and peacekeeping, the U.S. Government designated Argentina as a major non-NATO ally in January 1998. Argentina has been an enthusiastic supporter of the Summit of the Americas process, and currently chairs the Free Trade of the Americas initiative leading to the Buenos Aires Ministerial in April 2001. At the UN, Argentina is a close U.S. collaborator, supporting the U.S. campaign to improve human rights in Cuba and the fight against international terrorism and narcotics trafficking. In November 1998, Argentina hosted the United Nations conference on climate change, and in October 1999 in Berlin, became one of the first nations worldwide to adopt a voluntary greenhouse-gas emissions target.

Eager for closer ties to industrialized nations, Argentina left the Non-Aligned Movement in the early 1990s and has pursued a relationship with the OECD. It has become a leading advocate of nonproliferation efforts worldwide. A strong proponent of enhanced regional stability in South America, Argentina has revitalized its relationship with Brazil; settled lingering border disputes with Chile; discouraged military takeovers in Ecuador and Paraguay; served with the U.S., Brazil, and Chile as one of the four guarantors of the Ecuador-Peru peace process; and restored diplomatic relations with the United Kingdom. In 1998, President Menem made a state visit to the U.K., and Prince Charles reciprocated with a visit to Argentina. In 1999, the two countries agreed to normalize travel to the Falklands/Malvinas from the mainland and resumed direct flights.

## Principal Government Officials

**For up-to-date information on Principal Government Officials, see the Chiefs of State and Cabinet Members of Foreign Governments section starting on page 1.**

Argentina maintains an embassy in the United States at 1600 New Hampshire Ave. NW, Washington DC 20009; tel (202) 238-6400; fax (202) 332-3171. It has consular offices in the following locations:

**Atlanta:**

245 Peachtree Center Ave., Suite 2101 Atlanta, GA 30303 Tel: (404) 880-0805; Fax (404) 880-0806

**Chicago:**

205 North Michigan Ave., Suite 4209 Chicago, IL 60601 Tel (312) 819-2620; Fax (312) 819-2612

**Houston:**

3050 Post Oak Blvd., Suite 1625 Houston, TX 77056 Tel (713) 871-8935; Fax (713) 871-0639

**Los Angeles**:

5055 Wilshire Blvd., Suite 210 Los Angeles, CA 90036 Tel (213) 954-9155; Fax (713) 871-9076

**Miami:**

800 Brickell Ave., PH1 Miami, FL 33131 Tel (305) 373-7794; Fax (305) 371-7108

**New York:**

12 West 56th St. New York, NY 10019 Tel (212) 603-0400; Fax (212) 541-7746

**Washington, DC:**

1811 Q St. NW Washington, DC 20009 Tel: (202) 238-6460; Fax (202) 332-3171

# Other Contact Information

American Chamber of Commerce in Argentina Viamonte 1133, 8th floor Buenos Aires, Argentina; Tel (54)(11) 4371-4500; Fax (54)(11) 4371-8400 Home page: http://www.amchamarg.com

U.S. Department of Commerce Office of Latin America and the Caribbean International Trade Administration 14th and Constitution Avenue, NW Washington, DC 20230 Tel (202) 482-2436; (800) USA-TRADE; Fax (202) 482-4726; Internet: http://www.ita.doc.gov Automated fax service for trade-related information: (202) 482-4464

# ARMENIA

March 1996

Official Name:
## Republic of Armenia

# PROFILE

## Geography

**Area:** 29,800 sq. km. (11,500 sq. mi.); slightly larger than Maryland.
**Cities:** Capital—Yerevan.
**Terrain:** High plateau with mountains, little forest land.
**Climate:** Highland continental, hot summers, cold winters.

## People

**Nationality:** Noun—Armenian(s). Adjective—Armenian.
**Population:** 3.7 million; 700,000 people are estimated to have left Armenia during the last five years.
**Ethnic groups:** Armenian 96%; Kurd 2%; Russian, Greek, and other 2%.
**Religion:** Armenian Apostolic Church (more than 90% nominally affiliated).
**Languages:** Armenian (96%), Russian, other.
**Education:** Literacy—99%.
**Health:** Infant mortality rate—20/1,000. Life expectancy—72 years.
**Work force (1.6 million):** Industry and construction—30%. Agriculture and forestry—35%. Other—35%.

## Government

**Type:** Republic.
**Constitution:** Approved in 1995 ref-erendum.
**Independence:** 1918 (First Armenian Republic); 1991 (from Soviet Union).
**Branches:** Executive—president (head of state) with wider powers relative to other branches, prime minister (head of cabinet), Council of Ministers (cabinet). Legislative—unicameral National Assembly (parliament). Judicial—Constitutional Court.
**Administrative subdivisions:** 10 marzer (provinces) in addition to the city of Yerevan, which has the status of a province.
**Political parties:** Armenian National Movement (ruling party), Shamiram Women's Party, National Democratic Union, National Self-Determination Union, Liberal Democratic Party, Christian Democratic Party, Republican Party, Communist Party of Armenia, Armenian Ramkavar Azatakan Party, Armenian Revolutionary · Federation-Dashnaktsutyun (temporarily banned under a December 28, 1994, presidential decree), plus 34 marginal parties.
**Suffrage:** Universal at 18.

## Economy (1995)

**GDP:** $1.4 billion.
**GDP growth rate:** 5%.
**Per capita GDP:** $450.
**Natural resources:** Copper, zinc, gold, and lead; hydroelectric power; small amounts of gas and petroleum.
**Agriculture:** Products—fruits and vegetables, wines, some livestock.
**Industry:** Types—chemicals, electronic products, machinery, processed food, synthetic rubber, and textiles.
**Trade:** Exports—$264 million (of which 39% to countries outside the former Soviet Union): precious stones and jewelry 34%, machinery and equipment 22%, minerals and metals 24%, plastics and chemicals 7%. Imports—$669 million (of which 50% from countries outside the former Soviet Union), including $152 million of humanitarian assistance: minerals and metals 35%, food and foodstuffs 34%, machinery and equipment 10%, chemicals 9%, precious stones and jewelry 9%. Major trade partners—Russia 24%, Turkmenistan 20%, Iran 13%, Georgia 7%, EU countries 15%.
**Exchange rate:** 402 dram=U.S.$1.

# U.S.-ARMENIAN RELATIONS

The dissolution of the Soviet Union in December 1991 brought an end to the Cold War and created the opportunity to build bilateral relations with the New Independent States (NIS) as they began a political and economic transformation. The U.S. recognized the independence of Armenia on December 25, 1991, and opened an embassy in Yerevan in February 1992.

The United States has made a concerted effort to help Armenia and the other NIS during their difficult transition from totalitarianism and a command economy to democracy and open markets. The cornerstone of this continuing partnership has been the Freedom for Russia and Emerging Eurasian Democracies and Open Markets (FREEDOM) Support Act, enacted in October 1992, under which the U.S. to date has provided nearly $500 million in humanitarian and technical assistance for Armenia.

In addition, the U.S. has played a leading role in the Minsk Group, which was created in 1992 by the Conference of Security and Cooperation in Europe—now the Organization for Security and Cooperation in Europe (OSCE)—to encourage a peaceful, negotiated resolution to the conflict between Azerbaijan and Armenia over the Nagorno-Karabakh region. That conflict has cost several thousand lives, created nearly one million refugees and displaced persons, and caused economic hardships for Armenia.

## U.S.-Armenian Economic Relations

In April 1992, the U.S. and Armenia concluded a trade agreement which provides reciprocal most-favored-nation status to the products of each country and guarantees intellectual property protection.

An Overseas Private Investment Corporation agreement with Armenia, which encourages U.S. private investment by providing direct loans and loan guarantees and by assisting with project/investor matching, entered into force in April 1992. A bilateral investment treaty was signed on September 23, 1992, and was ratified by the Armenian parliament in September 1995. Armenia has also expressed interest in negotiating a tax treaty and is receiving U.S. technical assistance in revising its tax structure.

## U.S. Support to Build a Market Economy

The U.S. continues to work closely with international financial institutions like the International Monetary Fund (IMF) and the World Bank to help Armenia in its transition to a free-market economy.

Armenia has embarked upon an ambitious reform program, which should eventually allow a move away from humanitarian aid toward more development assistance. U.S. economic assistance programs have three objectives: to help create a legal, regulatory, and policy framework for competition and economic growth in energy, agriculture, housing, and other sectors; to promote fiscal reform; and to develop a competitive and efficient private financial sector. The Peace Corps is also very active in Armenia, with a focus on small business development and English language education.

The U.S. Department of Agriculture's (USDA) Extension Program provides advisory services and support to private farmers in all Armenian provinces, facilitates the formation of farmer associations and marketing initiatives, and has laid the groundwork for several agribusiness associations. USDA's Cochran Fellowship Program provides training to Armenian agriculturists. USDA and USAID have also launched an effort to revive production and export of Armenian vegetables and fruits. Under the Farmer-to-Farmer Program, Volunteers for Overseas Cooperative Assistance provides production and marketing assistance to Armenia's farmers, including the first farmer-owned winery, which is now producing and selling wine under its own label.

USAID's Energy-Sector Reform Project funded technical assistance and training (implemented by a resident energy advisor), feasibility and technical studies, and the purchase of critically needed equipment and commodities to support the Armenian energy sector's transition to a market economy.

The International City/County Manager Association (ICMA), also funded by USAID, facilitates the drafting and enactment of laws that promote the development of a private housing market, including a mortgage law, a condominium law, and a draft real estate law. Largely because of ICMA's efforts, more than half of all public housing in Yerevan has been privatized.

The Eurasia Foundation, working with a local bank in Yerevan, has established the first line of credit for small to medium-sized enterprises in Armenia. Lending began in late 1995, backed by a $2 million grant from USAID.

## U.S. Humanitarian Assistance

The United States provided $138 million in assistance to Armenia in FY 1995, the highest per capita amount in the NIS. Humanitarian aid accounted for 85% of this total, reflecting the economic effects caused by Turkish and Azerbaijani embargoes related to the Nagorno-Karabakh conflict, destruction in northern Armenia left from the devastating 1988 earthquake, and the virtual paralysis of most of the country's factories. In 1995, this aid included 138,000 tons of wheat, 25,000 metric tons of kerosene, and 81,000 tons of mazout (low-grade fuel oil), which was especially crucial during the cold winter months when electricity was available for only two to four hours a day in the cities and is virtually unavailable elsewhere. The U.S. Kerosene Program, administered by USAID, targets 210,000 of the most poverty-stricken families throughout Armenia, as well as 1,100 schools. The U.S., in collaboration with U.S.-based private voluntary organizations, also organized nine flights and shipped 202 containers by surface to Armenia to supply food, medicine, and clothing valued at $28 million.

## U.S. Support to Achieve Democracy

Technical assistance and training programs have been provided in municipal administration, intergovernmental relations, public affairs, foreign policy, diplomatic training, rule of law, and development of a constitution. Specific programs are targeted at promoting free and fair elections, strengthening political parties, and promoting the establishment of an independent judiciary and independent media.

Educational exchange programs play an important role in supporting democratic and free-market reforms. Assistance in the translation and publication of printed information also has been provided.

The U.S. Information Agency (USIA) sponsored in 1995 a range of exchange programs in the U.S. for Armenian lawyers, judges, political party members, and journalists to study the American judicial and political system and participate in programs on privatization, the media, and civil society. USIA continues to support Hai-FM, an independent, privately owned radio station that ran voter education programming before the July 1995 elections. In addition, USIA also funded a project by the National Democratic Institute (NDI) to print several thousand brochures showing people how to participate in the elections.

USAID helped fund international and domestic groups to monitor the parliamentary elections held July 1995. USAID has also funded programs run by NDI to monitor the July elections and strengthen an array of democratic and civic organizations.

## Principal U.S. Embassy Officials

**For up-to-date information on Principal U.S. Officials, see the U.S. Embassies, Consulates, and Foreign Service section starting on page 139.**

The U.S. embassy in Yerevan, Armenia is at 18 Marshal Bagramyan; tel: 3742-151-144 or 3742-524-661; fax: 3742-151-138.

# HISTORICAL HIGHLIGHTS

After the destruction of the Seleucid Empire, the first Armenian state was founded in 190 BC. At its zenith, from 95 to 55 BC, Armenia extended its rule over the area of what is now eastern Turkey. For a time, Armenia was the strongest state in the Roman East. It became part of the Roman Empire and adopted a Western political, philosophical, and religious orientation.

In 301 AD, Armenia became the first nation to adopt Christianity as a state religion, establishing in the 6th century a church that still exists independently of both the Catholic and the Eastern Orthodox churches.

During its later political eclipses, Armenia depended on the church to preserve and protect its unique identity.

Between the 4th and 19th centuries, Armenia was conquered and ruled by, among others, Persians, Byzantines, Arabs, Mongols, and Turks.

For a brief period from 1918 to 1920, it was an independent republic.

In late 1920, the communists came to power, and in 1922, Armenia became part of the Trans-Caucasian Soviet Socialist Republic. In 1936, it became the Armenian Soviet Socialist Republic. Armenia declared its independence from the Soviet Union on September 23, 1991.

# ECONOMY

Armenia is the second most densely populated of the former Soviet republics. It is a landlocked country between the Black and the Caspian Seas, bordered on the north and east by Georgia and Azerbaijan and on the south and west by Iran and Turkey. Armenia's economy has been based largely on industry—chemicals, electronic products, machinery, processed food, synthetic rubber, and textiles—and highly dependent on outside resources. Agriculture accounted for only 20% of net material product and 10% of employment before the breakup of the Soviet Union in 1991. Armenian mines produce copper, zinc, gold, and lead.

About 95% of energy is imported; the main domestic energy source is hydroelectric. Small amounts of gas and petroleum could be developed.

Like other New Independent States, Armenia's economy suffers from the legacy of a centrally planned economy and the breakdown of former Soviet trading patterns. In addition, the effects of the 1988 earthquake, which killed more than 25,000 people and made 500,000 homeless, are still being felt. Finally, the ongoing conflict with Azerbaijan over Nagorno-Karabakh has led to a blockade which has devastated the economy because of Armenia's dependence on outside supplies of energy and most raw materials. Land routes through Azerbaijan and Turkey are closed; routes through Georgia and Iran are inadequate or unreliable. In 1992-93, GDP fell nearly 60% from its 1989 level.

Nevertheless, the Government of Armenia, helped by the cease-fire that has been in effect in Nagorno-Karabakh since 1994, has been able to carry out wide-ranging economic reforms which paid off in dramati-

## Travel Notes

**Travel Advice:** For up-to-date information from the U.S. State Department on possible inconvenient or hazardous situations, see the **Travel Warnings and Consular Information Sheets from the U.S. Government** section starting on page 1723. For the latest information on health requirements and conditions, see the **International Travelers' Health Information** section starting on page 1385. For further information dealing with non-urgent matter, see the **Tips for Travelers to...** section starting on page 1588.

cally lower inflation. Armenia also registered strong economic growth in 1995, building on the turnaround that began the previous year.

In December 1994, the IMF approved the first tranche of a systemic transformation facility to support Armenia's macroeconomic reform program. As part of the program, the government pledged to strengthen its macroeconomic management (including increasing revenue collection), move toward full price liberalization, eliminate most exchange and trade restrictions, and accelerate the privatization process.

Privatization in agriculture has gone furthest. About 87% of farm land has been distributed, and the sale of land has been permitted since February 1994. Privatization in other areas of the economy is moving more slowly. Distribution of privatization vouchers began in October 1994; the government accelerated the pace of small-scale privatization and began to convert larger enterprises to joint stock companies as a first step toward full privatization. More than half of the housing stock has been privatized. Most prices have now been completely liberalized.

A liberal foreign investment law was approved in June 1994. A national currency, the dram, was introduced in late November 1993 and was very stable in 1995.

## Environmental Issues

Armenia is trying to address its environmental problems. It has established a Ministry of Environment and has introduced a pollution fee system by which taxes are levied on air and water emissions and solid waste disposal, with the resulting revenues used for environmental protection activities. Armenia is interested in cooperating with other members of the Commonwealth of Independent States (a group of 12 former Soviet republics) and with members of the international community on environmental issues.

# GOVERNMENT AND POLITICAL CONDITIONS

Armenians voted overwhelmingly for independence in a September 1991 referendum, followed by a presidential election in October 1991 that gave 83% of the vote to Levon Ter-Petrossian. Ter-Petrossian had been elected head of government in 1990, when the Armenian National Movement defeated the Communist Party. The next presidential elections are slated for the fall of 1996.

The government is dominated by the anti-communist, nationalist Armenian National Movement, which is the largest party in the parliament. Opposition parties exist but have limited support. In November 1990, the Armenian Communist Party declared itself independent. In 1991, after the August coup in Moscow, a large group of party members split from the Armenian Communist Party and formed a separate Democratic Party.

The Government of Armenia's stated aim is to build a Western-style parliamentary democracy as the basis of its form of government.

However, international observers questioned the inherent fairness of the parliamentary elections and constitutional referendum conducted in July 1995, citing polling deficiencies, lack of cooperation by the electoral commission, and the failure to register opposition parties and candidates. Observers noted, though, that several opposition parties and candidates were able to mount credible campaigns and proper polling procedures were generally followed. The new constitution greatly expands the powers of the executive branch and gives it much more influence over the judiciary and municipal officials.

The observance of human rights in Armenia is uneven and was marked by serious shortcomings in 1995. Police brutality goes largely unreported, while observers note that defendants are often beaten to extract confessions and are denied visits from relatives and lawyers.

Public demonstrations usually take place without government interference, though one rally in June 1995 by opposition parties was broken up by paramilitary troops. Freedom of religion is not protected under existing law. Non-apostolic churches have been subjected to harassment, sometimes violently. Non-apostolic churches must register with the government, and proselytizing is forbidden by law. Most of Armenia's ethnic Azeri population was deported in 1988-89 and remain refugees, largely in Azerbaijan. Armenia's record on discrimination toward the few remaining national minorities is generally good. The government does not restrict internal or international travel. Although freedom of the press and speech are guaranteed, the government maintains its monopoly over television and radio broadcasting.

## Principal Government Officials

For up-to-date information on Principal Government Officials, see the Chiefs of State and Cabinet Members of Foreign Governments section starting on page 1.

Armenia's embassy in the U.S. is at 2225 R Street, NW, Washington, DC, 20008; tel: 202-319-1976 or 202-319-2983; fax: 202-319-2984.

# DEFENSE AND MILITARY ISSUES

Armenia established a Ministry of Defense in 1992. Border guards subject to the ministry patrol Armenia's borders with Georgia and Azerbaijan, while Russian troops continue to monitor its borders with Iran and Turkey.

The Conventional Armed Forces in Europe (CFE) Treaty was ratified by the Armenian parliament in July 1992. The treaty establishes comprehensive limits on key categories of military equipment, such as tanks, artillery, armored combat vehicles, combat aircraft, and combat helicopters, and provides for the destruction of weaponry in excess of those limits. Armenian officials have consistently expressed determination to comply with its provisions. Armenia has provided data on armaments as required under the CFE Treaty. There are indications that Armenia is trying to establish mechanisms to ensure fulfillment of its arms control obligations. Armenia is not a significant exporter of conventional weapons, but it has provided substantial support, including materiel, to separatists in the Nagorno-Karabakh region of Azerbaijan.

In March 1993, Armenia signed the multilateral Chemical Weapons Convention, which calls for the eventual elimination of chemical weapons. Armenia acceded to the Nuclear Non-Proliferation Treaty as a non-nuclear weapons state in July 1993. The U.S. and other Western governments have discussed efforts to establish effective nuclear export control systems with Armenia.

# FOREIGN RELATIONS

Armenia is a member of the Commonwealth of Independent States, the United Nations, the Organization for Security and Cooperation in Europe, NATO's Partnership for Peace, the North Atlantic Cooperation Council, the International Monetary Fund, and the International Bank for Reconstruction and Development.

## Nagorno-Karabakh

In 1988, the territory of Nagorno-Karabakh, a predominantly ethnic Armenian enclave within Azerbaijan, voted to secede and join Armenia. This eventually developed into a full-scale armed conflict.

Armenian support for the separatists led to an economic embargo by Azerbaijan, which has crippled Armenia's foreign trade and restricted its imports of food and fuel, three-quarters of which transited Azerbaijan under Soviet rule.

Peace talks in early 1993 were disrupted by the seizure of Azerbaijan's Kelbajar district by Nagorno-Karabakh Armenian forces and the forced evacuation of thousands of ethnic Azeris. Turkey in protest then followed with an embargo of its own against Armenia. President Ter-Petrossian has thus far resisted domestic pressure to recognize the self-proclaimed independence of the "Nagorno-Karabakh Republic." Some 750,000 ethnic Azeris who fled during the Karabakhi offensives still live as internally displaced persons in Azerbaijan, while roughly 400,000 ethnic Armenians who fled Azerbaijan since 1988 remain refugees.

Negotiations to peacefully resolve the conflict have been ongoing since 1992 under the aegis of the Minsk Group of the OSCE. The Minsk Group is currently co-chaired by Finland and Russia and comprises Armenia, Azerbaijan, Turkey, the U.S., several Western European nations, and representatives of the Armenian and Azeri communities of Nagorno-Karabakh. The talks have focused on the status of Nagorno-Karabakh, the return of refugees, the lifting of blockades, the withdrawal from occupied territories, and the status of the Lachin corridor, which connects Nagorno-Karabakh to Armenia.

Karabakhi Armenians, supported by the Republic of Armenia, now hold about one-fifth of Azerbaijan and have refused to withdraw from occupied territories until an agreement on the status of Nagorno-Karabakh is reached. Armenia and Azerbaijan continue to observe the cease-fire which has been in effect since May 1994, and in late 1995 both also agreed to OSCE field representatives based in Tbilisi, Georgia to help facilitate the peace process. The United States has supported OSCE efforts to work toward deploying a multinational peacekeeping operation for the region as part of a broader political settlement.

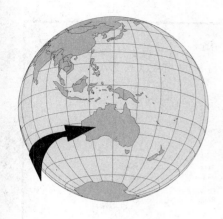

# AUSTRALIA

October 2000

Official Name:
**Commonwealth of Australia**

# PROFILE

## Geography

**Area:** 7.7 million sq. km. (3 million sq. mi.); about the size of the 48 continental United States.
**Cities:** (1998) Capital—Canberra (pop. 310,100). Other cities—Sydney (4.0 million), Melbourne (3.5 million), Brisbane (1.5 million), Perth (1.3 million).
**Terrain:** Varied, but generally low-lying.
**Climate:** Relatively dry, ranging from temperate in the south to tropical in the north.

## People

**Nationality:** Noun and adjective—Australian(s).
**Population:** (2000): 19.1 million.
**Annual growth rate:** 1.3%.
**Ethnic groups:** European 92%, Asian 7%, Aboriginal 1%.
**Religions:** Anglican 22%, Roman Catholic 27%, other Christian 22%, other non-Christian 3%, no religion 17%.
**Languages:** English.
**Education:** Years compulsory—to age 15 in all states except Tasmania, where it is 16. Literacy—99%.
**Health:** Infant mortality rate—6/1,000. Life expectancy—males 75 yrs., females 81 yrs.

**Work force:** 9.2 million: agriculture—5%; mining, manufacturing, and utilities—22%; services—69%; public administration and defense—4%.

## Government

**Type:** Democratic, federal-state system recognizing British monarch as sovereign.
**Constitution:** July 9, 1900.
**Independence:** (federation) January 1, 1901.
**Branches:** Head of state is the governor general, who is appointed by the Queen of Australia (the British Monarch). Legislative—bicameral Parliament (76-member Senate, 148-member House of Representatives). The House of Representatives selects as head of government the Prime Minister, who then appoints his cabinet. Judicial—independent judiciary.
**Administrative subdivisions:** Six states and two territories.
**Political parties:** Liberal, National, Australian Labor, Australian Democrats. Liberal and National parties form the governing coalition.
**Suffrage:** Universal and compulsory over 18.
**Central government budget:** (FY 1998-99) $85 billion.
**Defense:** (est.1998-99) 1.9% of GDP or 8.7% of government budget.
**Flag:** On a blue field, U.K. Union Jack in the top left corner, a large white star directly beneath symboliz-

ing federation, and five smaller white stars on the right half representing the Southern Cross constellation.

## Economy

**GDP:** (1999) $390 billion.
**Inflation rate:** (1999) 1.8% p.a.
**Trade:** Exports ($58 billion, 1999)—coal, gold, wool, meat, iron ore, wheat, alumina, aluminum, machinery and transport equipment. Major markets—Japan, U.S. ($5.5 billion), New Zealand, South Korea. Imports ($65 billion, 1999)—machinery and transport equipment, computers, crude oil and petroleum products, telecommunications equipment. Major suppliers—U.S. ($14 billion), Japan, China, Germany, U.K., China, New Zealand, Taiwan, and Singapore.

# PEOPLE

Australia's aboriginal inhabitants, a hunting-gathering people generally referred to as Aborigines, arrived about 40,000 years ago. Although their technical culture remained static—depending on wood, bone, and stone tools and weapons—their spiritual and social life was highly complex. Most spoke several languages, and confederacies sometimes linked widely scattered tribal groups. Aboriginal population density ranged

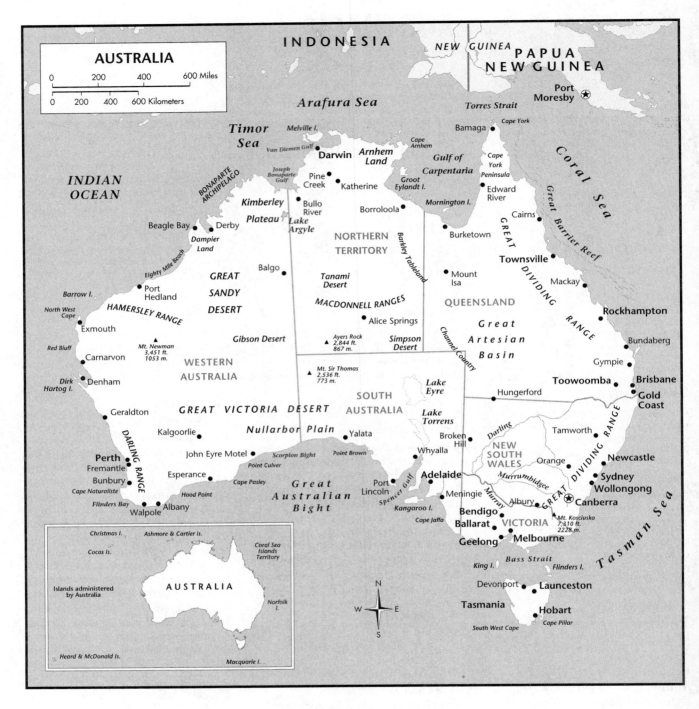

**AUSTRALIA**

0   200   400   600 Miles

0   200   400   600 Kilometers

INDONESIA

NEW GUINEA PAPUA NEW GUINEA

Arafura Sea

Torres Strait

Port Moresby ✪

Timor Sea

Melville I.

Van Diemen Gulf

Cape York

Bamaga

Cape York

Cape Arnhem

Coral Sea

INDIAN OCEAN

BONAPARTE ARCHIPELAGO

Joseph Bonaparte Gulf

Darwin

Arnhem Land

Gulf of Carpentaria

Cape York Peninsula

Pine Creek

Katherine

Groot Eylandt I.

Edward River

Kimberley Plateau

Bullo River

Borroloola

Mornington I.

Cairns

Great Barrier Reef

Beagle Bay

Derby

Lake Argyle

NORTHERN TERRITORY

Burketown

Townsville

Dampier Land

GREAT DIVIDING RANGE

Eighty Mile Beach

Balgo

Mount Isa

Mackay

Barrow I.

Port Hedland

Tanami Desert

QUEENSLAND

Rockhampton

North West Cape

HAMERSLEY RANGE

MACDONNELL RANGES

Great Artesian Basin

Bundaberg

Exmouth

Gibson Desert

Alice Springs

Gympie

Red Bluff

Mt. Newman 3,451 ft. 1053 m.

Ayers Rock 2,844 ft. 867 m.

Simpson Desert

Channel Country

Carnarvon

WESTERN AUSTRALIA

Mt. Sir Thomas 2,536 ft. 773 m.

Lake Eyre

Toowoomba

Brisbane

Dirk Hartog I.

Denham

SOUTH AUSTRALIA

Hungerford

Gold Coast

Geraldton

GREAT VICTORIA DESERT

Lake Torrens

Darling

Tamworth

Kalgoorlie

Nullarbor Plain

Yalata

Broken Hill

NEW SOUTH WALES

Orange

Newcastle

Perth

Fremantle

John Eyre Motel

Scorpion Bight

Point Brown

Whyalla

Murrumbidgee

Sydney

Bunbury

Point Culver

Adelaide

Wollongong

Cape Naturaliste

DARLING RANGE

Esperance

Cape Pasley

Port Lincoln

Spencer Gulf

Meningie

Murray

Albury

GREAT DIVIDING RANGE

Canberra ✪

Flinders Bay

Hood Point

Great Australian Bight

Kangaroo I.

Bendigo

Mt. Kosciusko 7,310 ft. 2228 m.

Walpole

Albany

Cape Jaffa

Ballarat

VICTORIA

Geelong

Melbourne

King I.

Bass Strait

Flinders I.

Tasman Sea

Devonport

Launceston

Tasmania

Hobart

South West Cape

Cape Pillar

N W E S

Christmas I.

Ashmore & Cartier Is.

Cocos Is.

Coral Sea Islands Territory

Islands administered by Australia

AUSTRALIA

Norfolk I.

Heard & McDonald Is.

Macquarie I.

---

from 1 person per square mile along the coasts to 1 person per 35 square miles in the arid interior. Food procurement was usually a matter for the nuclear family and was very demanding, since there was little large game, and they had no agriculture.

Australia may have been sighted by Portuguese sailors in 1601, and Capt. James Cook claimed it for Great Brit-

ain in 1770. At that time, the native population may have numbered 300,000 in as many as 500 tribes speaking many different languages. The aboriginal population currently numbers more than 300,000, representing about 1.7% of the population. Since the end of World War II, efforts have been made both by the government and by the public to be more responsive to aboriginal rights and needs.

Today, tribal aborigines lead a settled traditional life in remote areas of northern, central, and western Australia. In the south, where most aborigines are of mixed descent, movement to the cities is increasing.

Immigration has been essential to Australia's development since the beginning of European settlement in 1788. For generations, most settlers came from the British Isles, and the people of Australia are still predominantly of British or Irish origin, with a culture and outlook similar to those of Americans. However, since the end of World War II, the population has more than doubled; non-European immigration, mostly from the Middle East, Asia, and Latin America, has increased significantly since 1960 through an extensive, planned immigration program. From 1945 through 1996, nearly 5.5 million immigrants settled in Australia, and about 80% have remained; nearly one of every four Australians is foreign-born. Britain and Ireland have been the largest sources of post-war immigrants, followed by Italy, Greece, New Zealand, and the former Yugoslavia.

The 1970s saw progressive reductions in the size of the annual immigration program due to economic and employment conditions; in 1969-70, 185,000 persons were permitted to settle, but by 1975-76 the number had dropped to 52,700. Immigration has slowly risen since. In 1995-96, Australia accepted more than 99,000 regular immigrants. In 1999-2000, Australia will accept 82,000 new immigrants. In addition, since 1990 about 7,500 New Zealanders have settled in Australia each year.

Australia's refugee admissions of about 12,000 per year are in addition to the normal immigration program. In recent years, the government has given priority to refugees from the Former Yugoslavia, the Middle East, and Africa. In recent years, refugees from Indochina and the former Yugoslavia have comprised the largest single element in Australia's refugee program.

Although Australia has scarcely more than two persons per square kilometer, it is one of the world's most urbanized countries. Less than 15% of the population live in rural areas.

## Cultural Achievements

Much of Australia's culture is derived from European roots, but distinctive Australian features have evolved from the environment, aboriginal culture, and the influence of Australia's neighbors. The vigor and originality

of the arts in Australia—films, opera, music, painting, theater, dance, and crafts—are achieving international recognition.

Australia has had a significant school of painting since the early days of European settlement, and Australians with international reputations include Sidney Nolan, Russell Drysdale, and Arthur Boyd. Writers who have achieved world recognition include Thomas Keneally, Colleen McCullough, Nevil Shute, Morris West, Jill Ker Conway, and Nobel Prize winner Patrick White. Australian movies also are well known.

# HISTORY

Australia was uninhabited before stone-culture peoples arrived, perhaps by boat across the waters separating the island from the Indonesia archipelago about 40,000 years ago. Portuguese, Spanish, Dutch, and English explorers observed the island before 1770, when Captain Cook explored the east coast and claimed it for Great Britain (three American colonists were crew members aboard Cook's ship, the Endeavour).

On January 26, 1788 (now celebrated as Australia Day), the First Fleet under Capt. Arthur Phillip landed at Sydney, and formal proclamation of the establishment of the Colony of New South Wales followed on February 7. Many but by no means all of the first settlers were convicts, condemned for offenses that today would often be thought trivial. The mid-19th century saw the beginning of government policies to emancipate convicts and assist the immigration of free persons. The discovery of gold in 1851 led to increased population, wealth, and trade.

The six colonies that now constitute the states of the Australian Commonwealth were established in the following order: New South Wales, 1788; Tasmania, 1825; Western Australia, 1830; South Australia, 1836; Victoria, 1851; and Queensland, 1859.

Settlement had preceded these dates in most cases. Discussions between Australian and British representatives led to adoption by the British Government of an act to constitute the Commonwealth of Australia in 1900.

The first federal Parliament was opened at Melbourne in May 1901 by the Duke of York (later King George V). In May 1927, the seat of government was transferred to Canberra, a planned city designed by an American, Walter Burley Griffin. The first session of Parliament in that city was opened by another Duke of York (later King George VI). Australia passed the Statute of Westminster Adoption Act on October 9, 1942, which officially established Australia's complete autonomy in both internal and external affairs. Its passage formalized a situation that had existed for years. The Australia Act (1986) eliminated the last vestiges of British legal authority.

# GOVERNMENT

The Commonwealth government was created with a constitution patterned partly on the U.S. Constitution. The powers of the Commonwealth are specifically defined in the constitution, and the residual powers remain with the states. Australia is an independent nation within the Commonwealth. Queen Elizabeth II is the sovereign and since 1973 has been officially styled "Queen of Australia." The Queen is represented throughout Australia by a governor general and in each state by a governor.

The federal Parliament is bicameral, consisting of a 76-member Senate and a 148-member House of Representatives. Twelve senators from each state and two from each territory are elected for 6-year terms, with half elected every 3 years. The members of the House of Representatives are allocated among the states and territories roughly in proportion to population. In ordinary legislation, the two chambers have coordinate powers, but all proposals for appropriating revenue or imposing taxes must be introduced in the House of Representatives. Under the prevailing Westminster parliamentary system, the leader of the political party or coalition of parties that wins a majority of the seats in the House of Representatives is named prime minister. The prime minister and the cabinet wield actual power and are responsible to the Parliament, of which they must be elected members. General elections are held at least once every 3 years; the last general election was in October 1998.

Each state is headed by a premier, who is the leader of the party with a majority or a working minority in the lower house of the state legislature. Australia also has two self-governing territories, the Australian Capital Territory (where Canberra is located) and the Northern Territory, with political systems similar to those of the states.

At the apex of the court system is the High Court of Australia. It has general appellate jurisdiction over all other federal and state courts and possesses the power of constitutional review.

## Principal Government Officials

For up-to-date information on Principal Government Officials, see the Chiefs of State and Cabinet Members of Foreign Governments section starting on page 1.

Australia maintains an embassy in the United States at 1601 Massachusetts Avenue NW, Washington, DC 20036 (tel. 202-797-3000), and consulates general in New York (212-408-8400), San Francisco (415-362-6160), Honolulu (808-524-5050), Los Angeles (310-229-4800) and Atlanta (404-880-1700).

# POLITICAL CONDITIONS

Three political parties dominate the center of the Australian political spectrum: the Liberal Party (LP), nominally representing urban business-related groups; the National Party (NP), nominally representing rural interests; and the Australian Labor Party (ALP), nominally representing the trade unions and liberal groups. Although embracing some leftists, the ALP traditionally has been moderately socialist in its policies and approaches to social issues. All political groups are tied by tradition to domestic welfare policies, mostly enacted in the 1980s, which have kept Australia in the forefront of societies offering extensive social welfare programs. Australia's social welfare safety net has been reduced in recent years, however, in response to budgetary pressures and a changing political outlook. There is strong bipartisan sentiment on many international issues, including Australia's commitment to its alliance with the United States.

The Liberal Party/National Party coalition came to power in the March 1996 election, ending 13 years of ALP government and electing John Howard Prime Minister. Re-elected in October 1998, the coalition now holds 80 seats (64 Liberal/16 National) in the House of Representatives, against 68 for the ALP and 1 independent. In the Senate, the Liberal/ National coalition holds 34 seats, against 29 for the ALP, 9 for the Australian Democrats, 1 for the Greens, 1 for One Nation, 1 for the Country Labor Party, and 1 Independent. Lacking a majority in the Senate, the Liberal/National coalition has relied on the smaller parties and independents to enact legislation. Howard's conservative coalition has moved quickly to reduce Australia's government deficit and the influence of organized labor, placing more emphasis on workplace-based collective bargaining for wages.

The Howard government also has accelerated the pace of privatization,

beginning with the government-owned telecommunications corporation. The Howard government has continued the foreign policy of its predecessors, based on relations with four key countries: the United States, Japan, China, and Indonesia. The Howard government strongly supports U.S. engagement in the Asia-Pacific region.

# ECONOMY

Australia's developed market economy is dominated by its services sector (65% of GDP), yet it is the agricultural and mining sectors (7% of GDP combined) that account for the bulk (58%) of Australia's goods and services exports.

Australia's comparative advantage in primary products is a reflection of the natural wealth of the Australian Continent and its small domestic market; 19 million people occupy a continent the size of the contiguous United States. The relative size of the manufacturing sector has been declining for several decades, and now accounts for just under 12 percent of GDP.

Australia commenced a basic reorientation of its economy more than 16 years ago and has transformed itself from an inward looking, import-substitution country to an internationally competitive, export-oriented one. Key reforms include unilaterally reducing high tariffs and other protective barriers; floating the Australian dollar exchange rate; deregulating the financial services sector— including a decision in late 1992 to allow liberal access for foreign bank branches; rationalizing and reducing the number of trade unions; efforts to restructure the highly centralized system of industrial relations and labor bargaining; better integrating the State economies into a national federal system; improving and standardizing the national infrastructure; and privatizing many government-owned services and public utilities.

The ultimate goal is for Australia to become a competitive producer and exporter, not just of traditional farm and mineral commodities, but of a diversified mix of value-added manufactured products, services, and technologies. While progress has been made on this economic reform agenda—such as in opening the telecommunications market to competition—much remains to be done, particularly in the domestic arena.

While the near-term outlook is for continued economic expansion, Australia's longer term prospects depend heavily on continued fundamental economic reform. There is a general consensus among the major political parties, management, and labor on the necessary features of this reform but significant divergence of views on the methods, pace, and degree of change required.

Australia recorded economic growth over 1999 of 4.3%, founded for the third year running on strong domestic demand—thanks to a combination of low interest rates, low inflation, and rising asset prices. The economy is expected to downshift a gear over 2000-2001, as the composition of growth in gross domestic product moves away from domestic demand to exports and fiscal stimulus. The fiscal boost mentioned stems from the Australian Government's reform of the taxation system (to take effect in July 2000), granting substantial cuts in personal income tax in exchange for the introduction of a broad-based consumption tax.

# FOREIGN RELATIONS

Australia has been active in international affairs since World War II. Its first major independent foreign policy action was to conclude an agreement in 1944 with New Zealand dealing with the security, welfare, and advancement of the people of the independent territories of the Pacific (the ANZAC pact). After the war, Australia played a role in the Far Eastern Commission in Japan and supported Indonesian independence during that country's revolt against the Dutch (1945-49). Australia was one of the founders of both the United

Nations and the South Pacific Commission (1947), and in 1950, it proposed the Colombo Plan to assist developing countries in Asia. In addition to contributing to UN forces in Korea—it was the first country to announce it would do so after the United States—Australia sent troops to assist in putting down the communist revolt in Malaya in 1948-60 and later to combat the Indonesian-supported invasion of Sarawak in 1963-65. Australia also sent troops to assist South Vietnamese and U.S. forces in Vietnam and joined coalition forces in the Persian Gulf conflict in 1991. Australia has been active in the Australia-New Zealand-U.K. agreement and the Five-Power Defense Arrangement—successive arrangements with Britain and New Zealand to ensure the security of Singapore and Malaysia.

One of the drafters of the UN Charter, Australia has given firm support to the United Nations and its specialized agencies. It was a member of the Security Council in 1986-87, a member of the Economic and Social Council for 1986-89, and a member of the UN Human Rights Commission for 1994-96. Australia takes a prominent part in many other UN activities, including peacekeeping, disarmament negotiations, and narcotics control. Australia also is active in meetings of the Commonwealth Regional Heads of Government and the South Pacific Forum, and has been a leader in the Cairns Group—countries pressing for agricultural trade reform in the Uruguay Round of the General Agreement on Tariffs and Trade (GATT) negotiations—and in the APEC forum.

Australia has devoted particular attention to relations between developed and developing nations, with emphasis on the countries of the Association of South East Asian Nations (ASEAN)—Indonesia, Singapore, Malaysia, Thailand, the Philippines, and Brunei—and the island states of the South Pacific. Australia is an active participant in the ASEAN Regional Forum (ARF), which promotes regional cooperation on security issues. In September 1999, acting under a UN Security Council man-

date, Australia led an international coalition to restore order in East Timor upon Indonesia's withdrawal from that territory. Australia has a large bilateral aid program (about $1.3 billion for 1997-98, mostly in the form of grants) under which some 60 countries receive assistance.

Papua New Guinea (PNG), a former Australian trust territory, is the largest recipient of Australian assistance. In 1997, Australia contributed to the IMF program for Thailand and assisted Indonesia and PNG with regional environmental crises. From 1997-99 Australia contributed to IMF program for Thailand and assisted Indonesia and PNG with regional environmental crisis and drought relief efforts.

# ANZUS AND DEFENSE

The Australia, New Zealand, United States (ANZUS) security treaty was concluded at San Francisco on September 1, 1951, and entered into force on April 29, 1952. The treaty bound the signatories to recognize that an armed attack in the Pacific area on any of them would endanger the peace and safety of the others.

It committed them to consult in the event of a threat and, in the event of attack, to meet the common danger in accordance with their respective constitutional processes. The three nations also pledged to maintain and develop individual and collective capabilities to resist attack.

In 1985, the nature of the ANZUS alliance changed after the Government of New Zealand refused access to its ports by nuclear-weapons-capable and nuclear-powered ships of the U.S. Navy. The United States suspended defense obligations to New Zealand, and annual bilateral meetings between the U.S. Secretary of State and the Australian Foreign Minister replaced annual meetings of the ANZUS Council of Foreign Ministers. The first bilateral meeting was held in Canberra in 1985. At the second, in San Francisco in 1986, the United States and Australia announced that the United States was suspending its treaty security obligations to New Zealand pending the restoration of port access. Subsequent bilateral Australia-U.S. Ministerial (AUSMIN) meetings have alternated between Australia and the United States. The 12th AUSMIN meeting took place in Sydney in July 1998.

The U.S.-Australia alliance under the ANZUS Treaty remains in full force. Defense ministers of one or both nations often have joined the annual ministerial meetings, which are supplemented by consultations between the U.S. Commander in Chief Pacific and the Australian Chief of Defense Force. There also are regular civilian and military consultations between the two governments at lower levels.

Unlike NATO, ANZUS has no integrated defense structure or dedicated forces. However, in fulfillment of ANZUS obligations, Australia and the United States conduct a variety of joint activities. These include military exercises ranging from naval and landing exercises at the task-group level to battalion-level special forces training, assigning officers to each other's armed services, and standardizing, where possible, equipment and operational doctrine. The two countries also operate several joint defense facilities in Australia.

The Australian Defence Force numbers about 53,000 active duty personnel. This exceeds the current target of 50,000 personnel because of short-term increases necessary to fulfill Australia's commitment in East Timor. The Royal Australian Navy's front-line fleet currently comprises 3 guided-missile destroyers, 6 guided-missile frigates—including the first of the new Australian-built ANZAC class—1 destroyer escort and 4 submarines—2 of the older Oberon-class and 2 of the new, indigenous Collins class. Up to 6 Collins-class vessels are to be built. The F/A-18 fighter, built in Australia under license from the U.S. manufacturer, is the principal combat aircraft of the Royal Australian Air Force, backed by U.S.-built F-111 strike aircraft.

**Travel Notes**

**Travel Advice:** For up-to-date information from the U.S. State Department on possible inconvenient or hazardous situations, see the **Travel Warnings and Consular Information Sheets from the U.S. Government** section starting on page 1723. For the latest information on health requirements and conditions, see the **International Travelers' Health Information** section starting on page 1385. For further information dealing with non-urgent matter, see the **Tips for Travelers to...** section starting on page 1588.

# U.S.-AUSTRALIAN RELATIONS

The World War II experience, similarities in culture and historical background, and shared democratic values have made U.S. relations with Australia exceptionally strong and close. Ties linking the two nations cover the entire spectrum of international relations—from commercial, cultural, and environmental contacts to political and defense cooperation. Two-way trade totaled more than $19 billion in 1998. That same year, more than 200,000 Americans visited Australia, and nearly 53,000 resided there.

Traditional friendship is reinforced by the wide range of common interests and similar views on most major international questions. For example, both countries sent military forces to the Persian Gulf in support of UN Security Council resolutions relating to Iraq's occupation of Kuwait; both attach high priority to controlling and eventually eliminating chemical weapons, other weapons of mass destruction, and anti-personnel landmines; and both work closely on global environmental issues such as slowing climate change and preserving coral reefs. The Australian Government and opposition share the view that Australia's security depends on firm ties with the United States, and the ANZUS Treaty enjoys broad bipartisan support. Recent Presidential visits to Australia (in

1991 and 1996) and Australian Prime Ministerial visits to the United States (in 1995, 1997, 1999) have underscored the strength and closeness of the alliance.

Trade issues sometimes generate bilateral friction. In recent years, especially because of Australia's large trade deficit with the U.S., Australians have protested what they consider U.S. protectionist barriers against their exports of wool, meat, dairy products, lead, zinc, uranium, and fast ferries. Australia also opposes as "extraterritorial" U.S. sanctions legislation against Cuba, Iran, and Libya. Australia remains concerned that U.S. agricultural subsidies—although targeted against European subsidies—may undercut Australian markets for grain and dairy products in the Asia-Pacific region. For its part, the U.S. has concerns about Australian barriers to imports of cooked chicken, fresh salmon, and some fruits; changes in Australian law governing intellectual property protection; and Australian Government procurement practices. Both countries share a commitment to liberalizing global trade, however. They work together very closely in the World Trade Organization (WTO), and both are active members of the Asia-Pacific Economic Cooperation (APEC) forum.

A number of U.S. institutions conduct scientific activities in Australia because of its geographical position, large land mass, advanced technology, and, above all, the ready cooperation of its government and scientists. Under an agreement concluded in 1968 and since renewed, the U.S. National Aeronautics and Space Administration (NASA) maintains in Australia its largest and most important program outside the United States, including a number of tracking facilities vital to the U.S. space program. Indicative of the broadranging U.S.-Australian cooperation on other global issues, a Mutual Legal Assistance Treaty (MLAT) was concluded in 1997, enhancing already close bilateral cooperation on legal and counter-narcotics issues.

## Principal U.S. Officials

For up-to-date information on Principal U.S. Officials, see the U.S. Embassies, Consulates, and Foreign Service section starting on page 139.

The U.S. Embassy in Australia is located at Moonah Place, Yarralumla, Canberra, Australian Capital Territory 2600 (tel. (02) 6-214-5600; fax 6-214-5970).

Consulates General are in Sydney (tel. 2-9373-9200; fax 2-9373-9107), Melbourne (tel. 3-9526-5900; fax 3-9510-4646), and Perth (tel. 9-231-9400; fax. 9-231-9444).

For information on foreign economic trends, commercial development, production, trade regulations, and tariff rates, contact the International Trade Administration, U.S. Department of Commerce, Washington, DC 20230. This information also is available from any Commerce Department district office.

# AUSTRIA

July 2000

Official Name:
**Republic of Austria**

# PROFILE

## Geography

**Area:** 83,857 sq. km. (32,377 sq. mi.); slightly smaller than Maine.
**Cities:** Capital—Vienna (1998 pop. 1.6 million). Other cities—Graz, Linz, Salzburg, Innsbruck, Klagenfurt.
**Terrain:** Alpine (64%), northern highlands that form part of the Bohemian Massif (10%), lowlands to the east (26%).
**Climate:** Continental temperate.

## People

**Nationality:** Noun and adjective—Austrian(s).
**Population:** (1998) 8,078,449.
**Annual growth rate:** (1998) 0.07%.
**Ethnic Groups:** Germans 98%, Croats, Slovenes; other recognized minorities include Hungarians, Czechs, Slovaks, and Roma.
**Religion:** Roman Catholic 78%, Protestant 5%, Muslim and other 17%.
**Language:** German 92%.
**Education:** Years compulsory—9. Attendance—99%. Literacy—98%.
**Health:** (1998) Infant mortality rate—4.9 deaths/1,000. Life expectancy—men 74.7 years , women 80.9 years.
**Work force:** (1999, 3.7 million) Ser-

vices—67.2%; agriculture and forestry—0.8%.

## Government

**Type:** Parliamentary democracy.
**Constitution:** 1920; revised 1929 (reinstated May 1, 1945).
**Branches:** Executive—federal president (chief of state), chancellor (head of government), cabinet. Legislative—bicameral Federal Assembly (Parliament). Judicial—Constitutional Court, Administrative Court, Supreme Court.
**Political parties:** Social Democratic Party, People's Party, Freedom Party, Greens, Liberal Forum.
**Suffrage:** Universal over 19.
**Administrative subdivisions:** Nine Laender (federal provinces). Defense (2000) 0.8% of GDP.
**Flag:** Three horizontal bands—red, white, and red; flag also may have the national emblem (a black eagle centered in the white band).

## Economy

**GDP:** (1999) $207.9 billion.
**Real GDP growth rate:** (1999) 2.2%.
**Per capita income:** (1999) $25,655.
**Natural resources:** Iron ore, crude oil, natural gas, timber, tungsten, magnesite, lignite, cement.
**Agriculture:** (2.4% of 1999 GDP) Products—livestock, forest products, grains, sugarbeets, potatoes.

**Industry:** (30.0% of 1999 GDP) Types—iron and steel, chemicals, capital equipment, consumer goods.
**Services:** 67.6% of 1999 GDP.
**Trade:** (1999) Exports—$63.5 billion: iron and steel products, timber, paper, textiles, electrotechnical machinery, chemical products. Imports—$68.8 billion: machinery, vehicles, chemicals, iron and steel, metal goods, fuels, raw materials, foodstuffs. Principal trade partners—European Union, U.S., Hungary, and Switzerland.

# PEOPLE

Austrians are a homogeneous people; 92% are native German speakers. Only two numerically significant minority groups exist—30,000 Slovenes in Carinthia (south central Austria) and about 60,000 Croats in Burgenland (on the Hungarian border). The Slovenes form a closely knit community. Their rights as well as those of the Croats are protected by law and generally respected in practice. The present boundaries of Austria, once the center of the Habsburg Empire that constituted the second-largest state in Europe, were established in accordance with the Treaty of St. Germain in 1919. Some Austrians, particularly near Vienna, still have relatives in the Czech Republic, Slovakia, and Hungary. About 78% of

all Austrians are Roman Catholic. The church abstains from political activity; however, lay Catholic organizations are aligned with the conservative People's Party. The Social Democratic Party long ago shed its anticlerical stance. Small Lutheran minorities are located mainly in Vienna, Carinthia, and Burgenland.

# HISTORY

The Austro-Hungarian Empire played a decisive role in central European history. It occupied strategic territory containing the southeastern routes to western Europe and the north-south routes between Germany and Italy. Although present-day Austria is only a tiny remnant of the old empire, it retains this unique position.

Soon after the Republic of Austria was created at the end of World War I, it faced the strains of catastrophic inflation and of redesigning a government meant to rule a great empire into one that would govern only 6 million citizens. In the early 1930s, worldwide depression and unemployment added to these strains and shattered traditional Austrian society. Resultant economic and political conditions led in 1933 to a dictatorship under Engelbert Dollfuss. In February 1934, civil war broke out, and the Socialist Party was outlawed. In July, a coup d'etat by the National Socialists failed, but Dollfuss was assassinated by Nazis. In March 1938, Austria was incorporated into the German Reich, a development commonly known as the "Anschluss" (annexation).

At the Moscow conference in 1943, the Allies declared their intention to liberate Austria and reconstitute it as a free and independent state. In April 1945, both Eastern- and Western-front Allied forces liberated the country. Subsequently, Austria was divided into zones of occupation similar to those in Germany. Under the 1945 Potsdam agreements, the Soviets took control of German assets in their zone of occupation. These included 7% of Austria's manufacturing plants, 95% of its oil resources, and about 80% of its refinery capacity. The properties were returned to Austria under the Austrian State Treaty. This treaty, signed in Vienna on May 15, 1955, came into effect on July 27, and, under its provisions, all occupation forces were withdrawn by October 25, 1955. Austria became free and independent for the first time since 1938.

# GOVERNMENT

The Austrian president convenes and concludes parliamentary sessions and under certain conditions can dissolve Parliament. However, no Austrian president has dissolved Parliament in the Second Republic. The custom is for Parliament to call for new elections if needed. The president requests a party leader, usually the leader of the strongest party, to form a government. Upon the recommendation of the Federal Chancellor, the president also appoints cabinet ministers. No one can become a member of the government without the approval of the president. The Federal Assembly (Parliament) is composed of two houses—the National Council (Nationalrat), or lower house, and the Federal Council (Bundesrat), or upper house. Legislative authority is concentrated in the National Council. Its 183 members are elected for a maximum 4-year term in a three-tiered system, based on proportional representation. The National Council may dissolve itself by a simple majority vote or it may be dissolved by the president on the recommendation of the Chancellor. The 64 members of the Federal Council are elected by the legislatures of the nine provinces for 4- to 6-year terms. The Federal Council only reviews legislation passed by the National Council and can delay but not veto its enactment.

The highest courts of Austria's independent judiciary are the Constitutional Court; the Administrative Court, which handles bureaucratic disputes; and the Supreme Court, for civil and criminal cases. Cases in the Administrative and Supreme Courts concerning constitutional issues can be appealed to the Constitutional Court. Justices of the three courts are appointed by the president for specific terms.

The governors of Austria's nine Laender (provinces) are elected by the provincial legislatures. Although most authority, including that of the police, rests with the federal government, the provinces have considerable responsibility for welfare matters and local administration.

Strong provincial and local loyalties are based on tradition and history.

## Principal Government Officials

**For up-to-date information on Principal Government Officials, see the Chiefs of State and Cabinet Members of Foreign Governments section starting on page 1.**

Austria maintains an embassy in the United States at 3524 International Court, NW, Washington, DC 20008 (tel. 202-895-6700).

Consulates general are located in New York, Chicago, and Los Angeles, with honorary consulates in Atlanta, Boston, Buffalo, Cleveland, Denver, Honolulu, Houston, Miami, New Orleans, Newark, Philadelphia, St. Paul, San Francisco, San Juan, and Seattle.

# POLITICAL CONDITIONS

Since World War II, Austria has enjoyed political stability. A Socialist elder statesman, Dr. Karl Renner, organized an Austrian administration in the aftermath of the war, and general elections were held in November 1945. In that election, the conservative People's Party (OVP) obtained 50% of the vote (85 seats) in the National Council (lower house of Parliament), the Socialists won 45% (76 seats), and the communists won 5% (4 seats). The ensuing three-party government ruled until 1947, when the communists left the government and the OVP led a governing coalition with the socialists (now called the Social Democratic Party or SPO) that governed until 1966. Between 1970 and 1999, the SPO has ruled the country either alone or in conjunction with the OVP, except from 1983-86, when it governed in coalition with the Freedom Party. In 1999, the OVP formed a coalition with the right wing-populist Freedom Party (FPO).

The SPO, which was the strongest party in the 1999 elections, and the Greens now form the opposition. As a result of the inclusion of the FPO on the government, the EU imposed a series of sanctions on Austria. The U.S. and Israel, as well as various other countries, also reduced contacts with the Austrian Government.

The Social Democratic Party traditionally draws its constituency from blue- and white-collar workers. Accordingly, much of its strength lies in urban and industrialized areas. In the 1995 national elections, it garnered 38% of the vote. The SPO in the past advocated heavy state involvement in Austria's key industries, the extension of social security benefits, and a full-employment policy. Beginning in the mid-1980s, it shifted its focus to free market-oriented economic policies, balancing the federal budget, and European Union (EU) membership.

The People's Party advocates conservative financial policies and privatization of much of Austria's nationalized industry and finds support from farmers, large and small business owners, and lay Catholic groups, mostly in the rural regions of Austria. In 1995, it received 28% of the vote. The rightist Freedom Party attracts protest votes and those who desire no association with the other major parties. The party's mixture of populism and anti-establishment themes propagated by its aggressive leader Joerg Haider steadily gained support over the past years. It attracted about 27% of the vote in the 1999 elections. The Liberal Forum, founded on libertarian ideals, split from the Freedom Movement in February 1993. It received 5.5% of the vote in the 1999 election and, thus, failed to re-enter the national legislature. The Greens, a left-of-center party focusing on environmental issues, received 4.4% of the vote in 1999.

# ECONOMY

Austria has a well-developed social market economy with a high standard of living in which the government has played an important role. Many of the country's largest firms were nationalized in the early postwar period to protect them from Soviet takeover as war reparations. For many years, the government and its state-owned industries conglomerate played a very important role in the Austrian economy. However, starting in the early 1990s, the group was broken apart, state-owned firms started to operate largely as private businesses, and a great number of these firms were wholly or partially privatized. Although the government's privatization work in past years has been very successful, it still operates some firms, state monopolies, utilities, and services. The new government has presented an ambitious privatization program, which, if implemented, will considerably reduce government participation in the economy. Austria enjoys well-developed industry, banking, transportation, services, and commercial facilities.

Although some industries, such as several iron and steel works and chemical plants, are large industrial enterprises employing thousands of people, most industrial and commercial enterprises in Austria are relatively small on an international scale.

Austria has a strong labor movement. The Austrian Trade Union Federation (OGB) comprises constituent unions with a total membership of about 1.5 million—more than half the country's wage and salary earners. Since 1945, the OGB has pursued a moderate, consensus-oriented wage policy, cooperating with industry, agriculture, and the government on a broad range of social and economic issues in what is known as Austria's "social partnership." The OGB has announced tough opposition against the new government's program for budget consolidation, social reform, and improving the business climate, and indications are rising that Austria's peaceful social climate could become more confrontational.

Austrian farms, like those of other west European mountainous countries, are small and fragmented, and

production is relatively expensive. Since Austria's becoming a member of the EU in 1995, the Austrian agricultural sector has been undergoing substantial reform under the EU's common agricultural policy (CAP). Although Austrian farmers provide about 80% of domestic food requirements, the agricultural contribution to gross domestic product (GDP) has declined since 1950 to less than 3%.

Austria has achieved sustained economic growth. During the 1950s, the average annual growth rate was more than 5% in real terms and averaged about 4.5% through most of the 1960s. Following moderate real GDP growth of 1.7%, 2.0% and 1.2%, respectively, in 1995, 1996, and 1997, the economy rebounded and with real GDP expansion of 2.9% in 1998 and 2.2% in 1999.

Austria became a member of the EU on January 1, 1995. Membership brought economic benefits and challenges and has drawn an influx of foreign investors attracted by Austria's access to the single European market. Austria also has made progress in generally increasing its international competitiveness. As a member of the Economic and Monetary Union (EMU), Austria's economy is closely integrated with other EU member countries, especially with Germany. On January 1, 1999, Austria introduced the new Euro currency for accounting purposes. Starting January 2002, Euro notes and coins will be introduced and substitute for the Austrian schilling. Economists agree that the economic effects in Austria of using a common currency have been positive.s

Trade with other EU countries accounts for almost 66% of Austrian imports and exports. Expanding trade and investment in the emerging markets of central and eastern Europe is a major element of Austrian economic activity. Trade with these countries accounts for almost 14% of Austrian imports and exports, and Austrian firms have sizable investments in and continue to move labor-intensive, low-tech production to these countries. Although the big investment boom has waned, Austria

till has the potential to attract EU firms seeking convenient access to these developing markets.

Total trade with the United States in 1999 reached $6.6 billion. Imports from the United States amounted to $3.7 billion, constituting a U.S. market share in Austria of 5.4%. Austrian exports to the United States in 1999 were $2.9 billion or 4.6% of total Austrian exports.

# FOREIGN RELATIONS

The 1955 Austrian State Treaty ended the four-power occupation and recognized Austria as an independent and sovereign state. In October 1955, the Federal Assembly passed a constitutional law in which "Austria declares of her own free will her perpetual neutrality." The second section of this law stated that "in all future times Austria will not join any military alliances and will not permit the establishment of any foreign military bases on her territory." Since then, Austria shaped its foreign policy on the basis of neutrality.

In recent years, however, Austria began to reassess its definition of neutrality, granting overflight rights for the UN-sanctioned action against Iraq in 1991, and, since 1995, contemplating participation in the EU's evolving security structure. Also in 1995, it joined the Partnership for Peace, and subsequently participated in peacekeeping missions in Bosnia. Discussion of possible Austrian

NATO membership intensified during 1996. OVP and FPO aim at moving closer to NATO or a European defense arrangement. The SPO, in turn, believes continued neutrality is the cornerstone of Austria's foreign policy, and a majority of the population generally supports this stance.

Austrian leaders emphasize the unique role the country plays as East-West hub and as a moderator between industrialized and developing countries. Austria is active in the United Nations and experienced in UN peacekeeping efforts. It attaches great importance to participation in the Organization for Economic Cooperation and Development and other international economic organizations, and it has played an active role in the Organization for Security and Cooperation in Europe (OSCE).

Vienna hosts the Secretariat of the OSCE and the headquarters of the International Atomic Energy Agency, the UN Industrial Development Organization, and the UN Drug Control Program. Other international organizations based in Vienna include the Organization of Petroleum Exporting Countries and the International Institute for Applied Systems Analysis. Recently, Vienna added the Comprehensive Test Ban Treaty Organization and the Wassenaar Arrangement (a technology-transfer control agency) to the list of international organizations it hosts.

Austria traditionally has been active in "bridge-building to the east," increasing contacts at all levels with eastern Europe and the states of the former Soviet Union. Austrians maintain a constant exchange of business representatives, political leaders, students, cultural groups, and tourists with the countries of central and eastern Europe. Austrian companies are active in investing and trading with the countries of central and eastern Europe. In addition, the Austrian Government and various Austrian organizations provide assistance and training to support the changes underway in the region.

# U.S.-AUSTRIAN RELATIONS

Austria's political leaders and people recognize and appreciate the essential role played by U.S. economic assistance through the Marshall Plan in the reconstruction of their country after World War II, and by the U.S. in promoting the conclusion of the Austrian State Treaty. It is in the interest of the U.S. that the present friendly relations be maintained and strengthened and that Austria's political and economic stability be maintained.

## Principal U.S. Officials

For up-to-date information on Principal U.S. Officials, see the U.S. Embassies, Consulates, and Foreign Service section starting on page 139.

The U.S. embassy in Austria is located at Boltzmanngasse 16, Vienna 1091, tel. (43) (1) 313-39 (After office hours: (43) (1) 319-5523). The U.S. Consular Agency in Salzburg is located at Alte Markt 1, 5020 Salzburg, tel. (43) (662) 848-776.

# AZERBAIJAN

May 2001

Official Name:
**Republic of Azerbaijan**

# PROFILE

## Geography
**Area:** 33,774 sq. miles (includes Nakhchivan and Nagorno-Karabakh); slightly smaller than Maine.
**Cities:** Capital—Baku.
**Terrain:** Caucasus Mountains to the north, lowland in the central area through which the Kura River flows.
**Climate:** Dry, subtropical with hot summers and mild winters; forests, meadows and alpine tundra in the mountains.

## People
**Nationality:** Noun—Azerbaijani(s), Azeri. Adjective—Azerbaijani, Azeri.
**Population:** 8,082,000 (December 2000 est.).
**Population growth rate:** .27%.
**Net migration rate:** –5.92/1,000.
**Ethnic groups:** Azeri 90%, Dagestani Peoples 3.2%, Russian 2.5%, Armenians 2%, and other 2.3% (1998 est.).
**Religion:** Muslim 93.4% (majority Shia), Russian Orthodox 2.5%, Armenian Orthodox Church 2.3%, and other 1.8%.
**Languages:** Azerbaijani 89%, Russian 3%, Armenian 2%, and other 6%.
**Education:** Literacy—97%.
**Health:** Infant mortality rate–83.41/1,000 live births (2000 est.). Life

expectancy—62.87 years.
**Work force (3 million):** Agriculture and forestry—42.3%; industry—6.9%; construction—4.2%; other—46.6%.

## Government
**Type:** Republic.
**Constitution:** Approved in November 1995 referendum.
**Independence:** August 30, 1991 (from Soviet Union).
**Branches:** Executive—President (chief of state), Prime Minister (head of government), Council of Ministers (cabinet). Legislative—unicameral National Assembly (parliament). Judicial—Supreme Court.
**Administrative subdivisions:** 78 rayons, 11 cities, and 1 autonomous republic.
**Political parties:** New Azerbaijan Party, Popular Front Party, Musavat Party, National Independence Party, Civic Solidarity Party, Social Democratic Party, Communist Party, Liberal Party, Azerbaijan Democratic Independence Party, Islamic Party, plus 50 minor parties.
**Suffrage:** 18 years of age; universal.

## Economy
**GDP:** $4.8 billion (GOAJ–reported).
**GDP real growth rate:** 11.4%.
**Per capita GDP:** $600 (GOAJ–reported).
**Inflation rate:** 1.8%.

**Unemployment rate:** 20%. (GOAJ–reported).
**Natural resources:** Petroleum, natural gas, iron ore, nonferrous metals, and alumina.
**Agriculture:** Products—Cotton, tobacco, grain, rice, grapes, fruit, vegetables, tea; cattle, pigs, sheep and goats.
**Industry:** Types—Petroleum and natural gas, petroleum products, oilfield equipment; steel, iron ore, cement; chemicals and petrochemicals.
**Trade:** Exports—$1.7449 billion: oil and gas, chemicals, oilfield equipment, textiles, cotton. Imports—$1.1721 billion: machinery and parts, consumer durables, foodstuffs, textiles. Major trade partners: Italy, Russia, Turkey, Israel, U.S., Iran, other EU, and other NIS countries.

# HISTORY

Azerbaijan combines the heritage of two venerable civilizations—the Seljuk Turks of the Eleventh Century and the ancient Persians. Its name is thought to be derived from the Persian phrase "Land of Fire," referring both to its petroleum deposits, known since ancient times, and to its status as a former center of the Zoroastrian faith. The Azerbaijani Republic borders the Iranian provinces of East and West Azerbaijan, although they have not been united into a single state in modern times.

Little is known about Azerbaijan's history until its conquest and conversion to Islam by the Arabs in 642 AD. Centuries of prosperity as a province of the Muslim caliphate followed. After the decline of the Arab Empire, Azerbaijan was ravaged during the Mongol invasions but regained prosperity in the 13th–15th centuries under the Mongol II–Khans, the native Shirvan Shahs and under Persia's Safavid Dynasty.

Due to its location astride the trade routes connecting Europe to Central Asia and the Near East and on the shore of the Caspian Sea, Azerbaijan was fought over by Russia, Persia and the Ottomans for several centuries. Finally the Russians split Azerbaijan's territory with Persia in 1828 by the Treaty of Turkmenchay, establishing the present frontiers and extinguishing the last native dynasties of local Azerbaijani khans. The beginning of modern exploitation of the oil fields in the 1870s led to a period of unprecedented prosperity and growth in the years before World War I.

At the collapse of the Russian Empire in 1917, an independent republic was proclaimed in 1918 following an abortive attempt to establish a Transcaucasian Republic with Armenia and Georgia. Azerbaijan received de facto recognition by the Allies as an independent nation in January 1920, an independence terminated by the arrival of the Red Army in April.

Incorporated into the Transcaucasian Federated Soviet Socialist Republic in 1922, Azerbaijan became a union republic of the USSR in 1936. The late 1980s were characterized by increasing unrest, eventually leading to a violent confrontation when Soviet troops killed 190 nationalist demonstrators in Baku in January 1990. Azerbaijan declared its independence from the USSR on August 30, 1991.

# GOVERNMENT

The Government of Azerbaijan consists of three branches:

—The executive branch is made up of the President, his Apparat, a Prime Minister, and the Cabinet of Ministers;

—The legislative branch consists of the 125-member Parliament (Milli Majlis). Members are elected for 5-year terms, with 100 of them elected from territorial districts and 25 elected from party lists; and

—The judicial branch, headed by a Constitutional Court, is nominally independent.

Azerbaijan declared its independence from the former Soviet Union on August 30, 1991, with Ayaz Mutalibov, former First Secretary of the Azerbaijani Communist Party, becoming the country's first President. Following a massacre of Azerbaijanis at Khojali in Nagorno-Karabakh in March 1992, Mutalibov resigned and the country experienced a period of political instability. The old guard returned Mutalibov to power in May, 1992, but less than a week later his efforts to suspend scheduled presidential elections and ban all political activity prompted the opposition Popular Front Party (PFP) to organize a resistance movement and take power. Among its reforms, the PFP dissolved the predominantly Communist Supreme Soviet and transferred its functions to the 50-member upper house of the legislature, the National Council.

Elections in June 1992 resulted in the selection of PFP leader Abulfez Elchibey as the country's second president. The PFP-dominated government, however, proved incapable of either credibly prosecuting the Nagorno-Karabakh conflict or managing the economy, and many PFP officials came to be perceived as corrupt and incompetent. Growing discontent culminated in June 1993 in an armed insurrection in Ganja, Azerbaijan's second- largest city. As the rebels advanced virtually unopposed on

Baku, President Elchibey fled to his native province of Nakhchivan. The National council conferred presidential powers upon its new Speaker, Heydar Aliyev, former First Secretary of the Azerbaijani Communist Party (1969-81) and later a member of the USSR Politburo and USSR Deputy Prime Minister (until 1987). Elchibey was formally deposed by a national referendum in August 1993, and Aliyev was elected to a five-year term as President in October with only token opposition. Aliyev won re-election to another five year term in 1998, in an election marred by serious irregularities.

Azerbaijan's first Parliament was elected in 1995. The present 125-member unicameral Parliament was elected in November 2000 in an election that showed improvements in democratic processes, but still did not meet international standards as free and fair. A majority of parliamentarians are from the President's "New Azerbaijan Party." Opposition parties are represented in Parliament. According to the Constitution, the Speaker of Parliament stands next in line to the President. The current Speaker is Murtuz Aleskerov. Azerbaijan has a strong presidential system in which the legislative and judicial branches have only limited independence.

## Principal Government Officials

For up-to-date information on Principal Government Officials, see the Chiefs of State and Cabinet Members of Foreign Governments section starting on page 1.

Azerbaijan's embassy in the U.S. is at 927 Fifteenth Street, NW, Suite 700, Washington, D.C. 20005; tel: 202-842-0001; fax: 202-842-0004; www.azembassy.com.

## Defense And Military Issues

In July 1992, Azerbaijan ratified the Treaty on Conventional Armed Forces in Europe (CFE), which establishes comprehensive limits on key categories of conventional military equipment and provides for the destruction of weaponry in excess of those limits. Although Azerbaijan did not provide all data required by the treaty on its conventional forces at that time, it has accepted on-site inspections of forces on its territory. Azerbaijan approved the CFE flank agreement in May, 1997. It also has acceded to the nuclear Non-Proliferation treaty as a non-nuclear weapons state. Azerbaijan participates in NATO's Partnership for Peace.

# ECONOMY

Azerbaijan is an economy in transition in which the state continues to play a dominant role. It has important oil reserves and a significant agronomic potential based on a wide variety of climatic zones. Since 1995, in cooperation with the IMF, Azerbaijan has pursued a highly successful economic stabilization program, which has brought inflation down from 1,800% in 1994 to 1.8 percent in 2000. GDP in 2000 grew by more than 11%, the fifth consecutive increase. The national currency, the manat, was stable in 2000, depreciating 3.8 percent against the dollar. The budget deficit equaled a modest 1.3% of GDP in 2000.

Progress on economic reform has generally lagged behind macroeconomic stabilization. The government has undertaken regulatory reforms in some areas, including substantial opening of trade policy, but inefficient public administration in which commercial and regulatory interests are co-mingled limit the impact of these reforms. The government has largely completed privatization of agricultural lands and small and medium-sized enterprises. In August 2000, the government launched a second-stage privatization program, in which

many large state enterprises will be privatized.

For more than a century the backbone of the Azerbaijani economy has been petroleum. Now that western oil companies are able to tap deep-water oilfields untouched by the Soviets because of poor technology, Azerbaijan is considered one of the most important spots in the world for oil exploration and development. Proven oil reserves in the Caspian Basin, which Azerbaijan shares with Russia, Kazakhstan, and Turkmenistan, are comparable in size to the North Sea, although exploration is still in the early stages.

Azerbaijan has concluded twenty-one production-sharing agreements with various oil companies. Substantial progress has also occurred on plans for an export pipeline that would transport Caspian oil to the Mediterranean from Baku through Tbilisi, Georgia to Ceyhan, Turkey. Eastern Caspian producers in Kazakhstan have also expressed interest in accessing this pipeline to transport a portion of their production. In March 2001, Azerbaijan concluded a gas agreement with Turkey, providing a significant future export market for Azerbaijan.

## Environmental Issues

Azerbaijan faces serious environmental challenges. Soil throughout the region was contaminated by DDT and toxic defoliants used in cotton production during the Soviet era. Caspian petroleum and petrochemicals industries have also contributed to present air and water pollution problems. Several environmental organizations exist in Azerbaijan, yet few funds have been allocated to begin the necessary cleanup and prevention programs. Over- fishing by poachers is threatening the survival of Caspian sturgeon stocks, the source of most of the world's supply of caviar. The Convention on International Trade in Endangered Species (CITES) has listed as threatened all sturgeon species, including all commercial Caspian varieties.

# FOREIGN RELATIONS

Azerbaijan is a member of the United Nations; the Organization for Security and Cooperation in Europe; NATO's Partnership for Peace, and Euro-Atlantic Partnership; World Health Organization; CFE Treaty member state; the European Bank for Reconstruction and Development; the Council of Europe; the Community of Democracies; the International Monetary Fund; and the World Bank.

## Nagorno-Karabakh

The major domestic issue affecting Azerbaijan is the dispute over Nagorno-Karabakh, a predominantly ethnic Armenian region within Azerbaijan. The current conflict over Nagorno-Karabakh (NK) began in 1988 when Armenian demonstrations against Azerbaijani rule broke out in both N-K and Armenia and the N-K Supreme Soviet voted to secede from Azerbaijan. In 1990, after violent episodes in N-K, Baku and Sumgait, Moscow declared a state of emergency in N-K, sent troops to the region and forcibly occupied Baku. In April 1991, Azerbaijani militia and Soviet forces targeted Armenian paramilitaries operating in N-K; Moscow also deployed troops to Yere-

van. However, in September 1991, Moscow declared it would no longer support Azerbaijani military action in N-K. Armenian militants then stepped up the violence. In October 1991, a referendum in N-K approved independence.

Over 30,000 people were killed in the fighting from 1992 to 1994. In May 1992, Armenian and Karabakhi forces seized Susha (the historical, Azerbaijani-populated capital of N-K) and Lachin (thereby linking N-K to Armenia). By October 1993, Armenian and Karabakhi forces had succeeded in occupying almost all of N-K, Lachin and large areas in southwestern Azerbaijan. As Armenian and Karabakhi forces advanced, hundreds of thousands of Azerbaijani refugees fled to other parts of Azerbaijan. In 1993, the UN Security Council adopted resolutions calling for the cessation of hostilities, unimpeded access for international humanitarian relief efforts, and the eventual deployment of a peacekeeping force in the region. The UN also called for immediate withdrawal of all ethnic Armenian forces from the occupied territories of Azerbaijan. Fighting continued, however, until May 1994 when Russia brokered a cease-fire.

Negotiations to resolve the conflict peacefully have been ongoing since 1992 under the aegis of the Minsk Group of the OSCE. The Minsk Group is currently co-chaired by Russia, France and the United States and has representation from Turkey,

the U.S., several European nations, Armenia and Azerbaijan. Despite the 1994 cease-fire, sporadic violations, sniper-fire, and land-mine incidents continue to claim over a hundred lives each year.

Since 1997, the Minsk Group Co-Chairs have presented three proposals to serve as a framework for resolving the conflict. One side or the other rejected each of those proposals. Beginning in 1999, the Presidents of Azerbaijan and Armenia initiated a direct dialogue through a series of face-to-face meetings, often facilitated by the Minsk Group Co-Chairs. Most recently the OSCE sponsored a round of negotiations between the Presidents in Key West, Florida. U.S. Secretary of State Powell launched the talks on April 3, 2001 and the negotiations continued with mediation by the U.S., Russia and France until April 6, 2001. The Co-Chairs are continuing to work with the two Presidents in the hope of finding a lasting peace.

# U.S.-AZERBAIJAN RELATIONS

The dissolution of the Soviet Union in December 1991 brought an end to the Cold War and created the opportunity to build relations with the New Independent States (NIS) as they began a political and economic transformation. The United States opened an embassy in Azerbaijan's capital, Baku, in March 1992.

The United States has been actively engaged in international efforts to find a peaceful solution to the Nagorno-Karabakh conflict. The U.S. has played a leading role in the Minsk Group, which was created in 1992 by the Conference on Security and Cooperation in Europe—now the Organization for Security and Cooperation in Europe (OSCE)—to encourage a peaceful, negotiated resolution to the conflict between Azerbaijan and Armenia. In early 1997, the U.S. heightened its role by becoming a co-chair, along with Russia and France, of the Minsk Group.

The U.S. supports American investment in Azerbaijan. U.S. companies are involved in three offshore oil development projects with Azerbaijan and U.S. companies in other fields such as telecommunications have been exploring the emerging investment opportunities in Azerbaijan. The United States is committed to aiding Azerbaijan in its transition to democracy and formation of an open market economy. The Freedom Support Act (FSA), enacted in October 1992, has been the cornerstone of U.S. efforts to help Azerbaijan during this transition. While section 907 of the FSA prohibits most U.S. government assistance to the Government of Azerbaijan (until it "ceases all blockades and other offensive uses of force against Armenia and Nagorno-Karabakh"), subsequent legislation has allowed USG assistance in key areas including programs that support democracy, humanitarian assistance and nonproliferation. Under the FSA, the U.S. to date has provided approximately $165.92 million in humanitarian and developmental assistance to

Azerbaijan, including $32.18 million in FY 2000. The U.S. and Azerbaijan have signed a bilateral trade agreement and Azerbaijan has most favored nation status. A Bilateral Investment Treaty has also been signed.

## U.S. Humanitarian Assistance

Since 1992, the United States has disbursed over $140 million in humanitarian assistance to the IDP, refugee, and war-affected populations of Azerbaijan. United States assistance is provided principally through Private Voluntary Organizations (PVOs). The primary PVOs now implementing and coordinating USAID funded assistance programs are Mercy Corps International (MCI), Adventist Development and Relief Agency (ADRA), International Rescue Committee (IRC), Save the Children, and the Community Housing Foundation (CHF). Likewise Shore Bank LTD and the Foundation for International Community Assistance (FINCA) provide small and medium

scale loans to the IDP, refugee, and war-affected populations to increase their economic viability. USAID, USDA, as well as the State Department's Bureau of Population, Refugees and Migration (PRM) and the Office of the Coordinator for U.S. Assistance to the New Independent States (S/NIS/C) provide funds directed toward increased humanitarian assistance.

## Principal U.S. Embassy Officials

For up-to-date information on Principal U.S. Officials, see the U.S. Embassies, Consulates, and Foreign Service section starting on page 139.

The U.S. Embassy in Baku, Azerbaijan is at 83 Azadliq Prospect; tel: 9-9412-98-03-35; fax: 9-9412-98-37-55; www.usembassybaku.org.

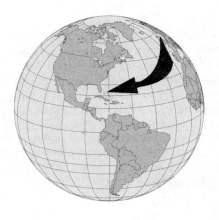

# THE BAHAMAS

April 2001

Official Name:
## The Commonwealth of The Bahamas

# PROFILE

## Geography

**Area:** 13,939 sq. km. (5,382 sq. mi.); slightly larger than Connecticut and Rhode Island combined.
**Cities:** Capital—Nassau, New Providence. Second-largest city—Freeport, Grand Bahama.
**Terrain:** Low and flat.
**Climate:** Semitropical.

## People

**Nationality:** Noun and adjective—Bahamian(s).
**Population:** (2000 est.) 304,913.
**Annual growth rate:** (1999 est.) 1.4%.
**Ethnic groups:** African 85%, European 12%, Asian and Hispanic 3%.
**Religious affiliation:** Baptist predominant (32%), Roman Catholic, Anglican, Evangelical Protestants, Methodist, Church of God.
**Language:** English; some Creole among Haitian groups.
**Education:** Years compulsory—through age 16. Attendance—95%. Literacy—93%.
**Health:** (1998) Infant mortality rate—17.0/1,000. Life expectancy—men 71. years, women 77.6. years.
**Work force:** (1999) 156,600; majority employed in the tourism, government, and financial services sectors.

## Government

**Type:** Constitutional parliamentary democracy.
**Independence:** July 10, 1973.
**Branches:** Executive—British monarch (nominal head of state), governor general (representative of the British monarch), prime minister (head of government), and cabinet. Legislative—bicameral Parliament (40-member elected House of Assembly, 16-member appointed Senate). Judicial—Privy Council in U.K., Court of Appeal, Supreme Court, and magistrates' courts.
**Political parties:** Free National Movement (FNM), Progressive Liberal Party (PLP), Bahamian Freedom Alliance (PFA), Coalition for Democratic Reform (CDR).
**Suffrage:** Universal over 18; (2000 est.) 140,000 registered voters.

## Economy

**GDP:** (1999) $4.56 billion.
**Growth rate:** (1999) 6%.
**Per capita GDP:** (1998) $14,492.
**Natural resources:** Salt, aragonite, timber.
**Agriculture and fisheries:** (1999; 5% of GDP) Products—vegetables, lobster, fish.
**Tourism:** (1999) 60% of GDP.
**Banking:** (1999) 15% of GDP.
**Manufacturing:** (1999)—3% of GDP products—pharmaceuticals, rum.
Trade: (1999)Exports ($380.1 million)—salt, aragonite, chemicals, lobster, fruits, vegetables. Major markets—U.S. (50%), U.K., other EU countries, Canada. Imports ($1.807 billion)—foodstuffs and manufactured goods; vehicles and automobile parts; hotel, restaurant, and medical supplies; computers and electronics. Major suppliers—U.S. (70%), U.K., other EU countries, Canada.
**Exchange rate:** Bahamian dollar 1=U.S. $1.
*Bahamas' export statistics do not include oil transhipments or the large transactions from the PFC Bahamas (formerly Syntex) pharmaceutical plant located in the Freeport free trade zone.

# PEOPLE

Eighty-five percent of the Bahamian population is of African heritage. About two-thirds of the population reside on New Providence Island (the location of Nassau). Many ancestors arrived in the Bahama Islands when they served as a staging area for the slave trade in the early 1800s. Others accompanied thousands of British loyalists who fled the American colonies during the Revolutionary War.

School attendance is compulsory between the ages of five and 16. The government fully operates 158 of the 210 primary and secondary schools in The Bahamas. The other 52 schools are privately operated. Enrollment for state and private primary and secondary schools amounts to more than 66,000 students. The College of The Bahamas, established in Nassau in 1974, provides programs leading to bachelors and associates degrees. The college is now converting from a 2-year to a 4-year institution. Several non-Bahamian colleges also offer higher education programs in The Bahamas.

# HISTORY

In 1492, Christopher Columbus made his first landfall in the Western Hemisphere in The Bahamas. Spanish slave traders later captured native Lucayan Indians to work in gold mines in Hispaniola, and within 25 years, all Lucayans perished. In 1647, a group of English and Bermudan religious refugees, the Eleutheran Adventurers, founded the first permanent European settlement in The Bahamas and gave Eleuthera Island its name. Similar groups of settlers formed governments in The Bahamas until the islands became a British Crown Colony in 1717.

The first Royal Governor, a former pirate named Woodes Rogers, brought law and order to The Bahamas in 1718, when he expelled the buccaneers who had used the islands as hideouts. During the American Civil War, The Bahamas prospered as a center of Confederate blockade-running. After World War I, the islands served as a base for American rum-runners. During World War II, the Allies centered their flight training and antisubmarine operations for the Caribbean in The Bahamas. Since then, The Bahamas has developed into a major tourist and financial services center.

Bahamians achieved self-government through a series of constitutional and political steps, attaining internal self-government in 1964 and full independence within the Commonwealth on July 10, 1973.

# GOVERNMENT AND POLITICAL CONDITIONS

The Bahamas is an independent member of the Commonwealth of Nations. It is a parliamentary democracy with regular elections. As a Commonwealth country, its political and legal traditions closely follow those of the United Kingdom. The Bahamas recognizes the British monarch as its formal head of state, while an appointed Governor General serves as the Queen's representative in The Bahamas. A bicameral legislature enacts laws under the 1973 constitution.

The House of Assembly consists of 40 members, elected from individual constituencies for 5-year terms. As under the Westminster system, the government may dissolve the parliament and call elections at any time. The House of Assembly performs all major legislative functions. The leader of the majority party serves as Prime Minister and head of government. The cabinet consists of at least nine members, including the Prime Minister and ministers of executive departments. They answer politically to the House of Assembly.

The Senate consists of 16 members appointed by the Governor General, including nine on the advice of the Prime Minister, four on the advice of the Leader of the Opposition, and three on the advice of the Prime Minister after consultation with the Leader of the Opposition.

The Governor General appoints the Chief Justice of the Supreme Court on the advice of the Prime Minister and the Leader of the Opposition. The Governor General appoints the other justices with the advice of a judicial commission. The Privy Council of the United Kingdom serves as the highest appellate court.

For decades, the white-dominated United Bahamian Party (UBP) ruled The Bahamas, then a dependency of the United Kingdom, while a group of influential white merchants, known as the "Bay Street Boys," dominated the local economy. In 1953, Bahamians dissatisfied with UBP rule formed the opposition Progressive Liberal Party (PLP). Under the leadership of Lynden Pindling, the PLP won control of the government in 1967 and led The Bahamas to full independence in 1973. A coalition of PLP dissidents and former UBP members formed the Free National Movement (FNM) in 1971. Former PLP cabinet minister and member of parliament Hubert Ingraham became leader of the FNM in 1990, upon the death of Sir Cecil Wallace-Whitfield. Under the leadership of Ingraham, the FNM won control of the government from the PLP in the August 1992 general elections. Winning again in March 1997, the ruling FNM controls 35 seats in the House of Assembly, while the PLP controls four seats and serves as the official opposition. A PLP member of Parliament split from the party and created the Coalition for Democratic Reform (CDR). The CDR holds one seat in Parliament.

The principal focus of the Ingraham administration has been economic development and job creation. Many of his government's policies are aimed at improving the image of The Bahamas and making it an attractive place for foreigners to invest. In 2000, in response to multilateral organizations concerns, the government passed stronger measures to prevent money laundering in the country's banking sector.

The FNM has made considerable progress in rebuilding the infrastructure, revitalizing the tourism industry, and attracting new investment to The Bahamas. A good start has been made to mitigate crime and provide for social needs.

Remaining challenges are to privatize The Bahamas' costly, inefficient national corporations, provide job retraining for hundreds of workers who will be affected by the change, and to continue creating jobs for new entries in the employment market. Currently, Bahamians do not pay income or sales taxes. Most government revenue is derived from high tariffs and import fees. A major challenge for Bahamians as the next century approaches will be to prepare for hemispheric free trade. Reduction of trade barriers will probably require some form of taxation to replace revenues when the country becomes a part of the Free Trade Area of the Americas (FTAA). The advantages may be hard for the government to sell since The Bahamas exports so little.

## Principal Government Officials

**For up-to-date information on Principal Government Officials, see the Chiefs of State and Cabinet Members of Foreign Governments section starting on page 1.**

The Bahamas maintains an embassy in the United States at 2220 Massachusetts Ave., NW, Washington, DC 20008 (tel: 202–319–2660) and Consulates General in New York at 767 Third Ave., 9th Floor, New York, NY 10017 (tel: 212–421–6925/27), and in Miami at Suite818, Ingraham Building, 25 SE Second Ave., Miami, FL 33131 (tel:305–373–6295/96).

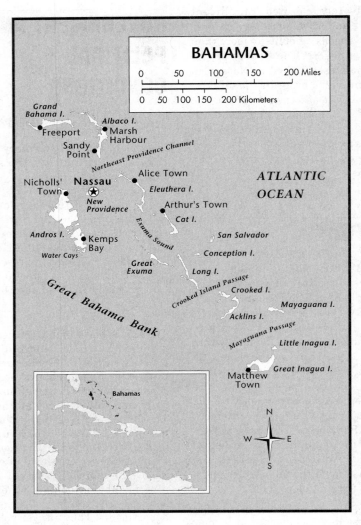

# ECONOMY

The Bahamian economy is almost entirely dependent on tourism and financial services to generate foreign exchange earnings. Tourism alone provides an estimated 60% of the gross domestic product (GDP) and employs about half the Bahamian work force. In 2000, over 4 million tourists visited The Bahamas, 83% of them from the United States.

A major contribution to the recent growth in the overall Bahamian economy is Sun International's Atlantis Resort and Casino, which took over the former Paradise Island Resort and has provided a much needed boost to the economy. In addition, the opening of Breezes Super Club and

Sandals Resort also aided this turnaround. The Bahamian Government also has adopted a proactive approach to courting foreign investors and has conducted major investment missions to the Far East, Europe, Latin America, and Canada. The primary purpose of the trips was to restore the reputation of The Bahamas in these markets.

Financial services constitute the second-most important sector of the Bahamian economy, accounting for up to 15% of GDP, due to the country's status as a tax haven and offshore banking center. As of December 1998, the government had licensed 418 banks and trust companies in The Bahamas. The Bahamas promulgated the International Business Companies (IBC) Act in January 1990 to enhance the country's status as a leading financial center. The act

served to simplify and reduce the cost of incorporating offshore companies in The Bahamas. Within 9 years, more than 84,000 IBC-type companies had been established. In February 1991, the government also legalized the establishment of Asset Protection Trusts in The Bahamas. In December 2000, the government enacted a legislative package to better regulate the financial sector, including creation of a Financial Intelligence Unit and enforcement of "know-your-customer" rules.

Agriculture and fisheries industry together account for 5% of GDP. The Bahamas exports lobster and some fish but does not raise these items commercially. There is no largescale agriculture, and most agricultural products are consumed domestically. The Bahamas imports more than $250 million in foodstuffs per year, representing about 80% of its food consumption. The government aims to expand food production to reduce imports and generate foreign exchange. It actively seeks foreign investment aimed at increasing agricultural exports, particularly specialty food items. The government officially lists beef and pork production and processing, fruits and nuts, dairy production, winter vegetables, and mariculture (shrimp farming) as the areas in which it wishes to encourage foreign investment.

The Bahamian Government maintains the value of the Bahamian dollar on a par with the U.S. dollar. The Bahamas is a beneficiary of the U.S.-Caribbean Basin Trade Partnership Act (CBTPA), Canada's CARIBCAN program, and the European Union's Lome IV Agreement. Although The Bahamas participates in the political aspects of the Caribbean Community (CARICOM), it has not entered into joint economic initiatives with other Caribbean states.

The Bahamas has a few notable industrial firms: the Freeport pharmaceutical firm, PFC Bahamas (formerly Syntex), which recently streamlined its production and was purchased by the Swiss pharmaceutical firm Roche; the BORCO oil facility, also in Freeport, which transships oil in the region; the Commonwealth Brewery in Nassau, which produces Heineken, Guinness, and Kalik beers; and Bacardi Corp., which distills rum in Nassau for shipment to the U.S. and European markets. Other industries include sun-dried sea salt in Great Inagua, a wet dock facility in Freeport for repair of cruise ships, and mining of aragonite—a type of limestone with several industrial uses— from the sea floor at Ocean Cay.

The Hawksbill Creek Agreement established a duty-free zone in Freeport, The Bahamas' second-largest city, with a nearby industrial park to encourage foreign industrial investment. The Hong Kong-based firm, Hutchison Whampoa, has opened a container port in Freeport. The Bahamian Parliament approved legislation in 1993 that extended most

## Travel Notes

**Travel Advice:** For up-to-date information from the U.S. State Department on possible inconvenient or hazardous situations, see the **Travel Warnings and Consular Information Sheets from the U.S. Government** section starting on page 1723. For the latest information on health requirements and conditions, see the **International Travelers' Health Information** section starting on page 1385. For further information dealing with non-urgent matter, see the **Tips for Travelers to...** section starting on page 1588.

Freeport tax and duty exemptions through 2054.

The Bahamas is largely an import, service economy. There are about 110 U.S.-affiliated businesses operating in The Bahamas, and most are associated with tourism and banking. With few domestic resources and little industry, The Bahamas imports nearly all its food and manufactured goods from the United States. American goods and services tend to be favored by Bahamians due to cultural similarities and heavy exposure to American advertising.

## Business Environment

The Bahamas offers attractive features to the potential investor: a stable democratic environment, relief from personal and corporate income taxes, timely repatriation of corporate profits, proximity to the U.S. with extensive air and telecommunications links, and a good pool of skilled professional workers. The Government of The Bahamas welcomes foreign investment in tourism and banking and has declared an interest in agricultural and industrial investments to generate local employment, particularly in white-collar or skilled jobs. Despite its interest in foreign investment to diversify the economy, the Bahamian Government responds to local concerns about foreign competition and tends to protect Bahamian business and labor interests. As a result of domestic resistance to foreign investment and high labor costs, growth

can stagnate in sectors which the government wishes to diversify.

The country's infrastructure is best developed in the principal cities of Nassau and Freeport, where there are relatively good paved roads and international airports. Electricity is generally reliable, although many businesses have their own backup generators. In Nassau, there are two daily newspapers, three weeklies, and several international newspapers available for sale. There also are five radio stations. Both Nassau and Freeport have a television station. Cable TV also is available locally and provides most American programs with some Canadian and European channels.

## Areas of Opportunity

The best U.S. export opportunities remain in the traditional areas of foodstuffs and manufactured goods: vehicles and automobile parts; hotel, restaurant, and medical supplies; and computers and electronics. Bahamian tastes in consumer products roughly parallel those in the U.S. With approximately 85% of the population of primarily African descent, there is a large and growing market in the Bahamas for "ethnic" personal care products. Merchants in southern Florida have found it profitable to advertise in Bahamian publications. Most imports in this sector are subject to high but nondiscriminatory tariffs.

# FOREIGN RELATIONS

The Bahamas has strong bilateral relationships with the United States and the United Kingdom, represented by an ambassador in Washington and High Commissioner in London. The Bahamas also associates closely with other nations of the Caribbean Community (CARICOM). The Bahamas has diplomatic relations with Cuba, although not with resident ambassadors. A repatriation agreement was signed with Cuba in1996, and there are commercial and cultural contacts between the two countries. The Commonwealth of

The Bahamas became a member of the United Nations (UN) in 1973 and the Organization of American States (OAS) in 1982.

The Bahamas holds membership in a number of international organizations: the UN and some specialized and related agencies, including Food and Agriculture Organization (FAO), International Civil Aviation Organization (ICAO), International Labor Organization (ILO), International Monetary Fund (IMF), International Telecommunication Union (ITU), World Bank, World Meteorological Organization (WMO), and World Health Organization (WHO); OAS and related agencies, including Inter-American Development Bank (IDB), Caribbean Development Bank(CDB), and Pan-American Health Organization (PAHO); the Caribbean Community (CARICOM), excluding its Common Market; the International Criminal Police Organization (INTERPOL); Universal Postal Union(UPU); the IMO (International Maritime Organization); and World Intellectual Property Organization (WIPO).

# U.S.-BAHAMIAN RELATIONS

The United States historically has had close economic and commercial relations with The Bahamas. Both countries share ethnic and cultural ties, especially in education, and The Bahamas is home to 7,000 American residents. In addition, there are about 110 U.S.-related businesses in The Bahamas and, in 2000, some 83% of the 4 million tourists visiting the country were American.

As a neighbor, The Bahamas and its political stability are especially important to the United States. The U.S. and the Bahamian Government have worked together on reducing crime and reforming the judiciary. With the closest island only 45 miles from the coast of Florida, The Bahamas often is used as a gateway for drugs and illegal aliens bound for the United States. The U.S. and The Bahamas cooperate closely to handle these threats. U.S. assistance and resources have been essential to Bahamian efforts to mitigate the persistent flow of illegal narcotics and migrants through the archipelago. The U.S. and The Bahamas also actively cooperate on law enforcement, civil aviation, marine research, meteorology, and agricultural issues. The U.S. Navy operates an underwater research facility on Andros Island.

In May 1997, Prime Minister Ingraham joined 14 other Caribbean leaders and President Clinton during the first-ever U.S.-regional summit in Bridgetown, Barbados. The summit strengthened the basis for regional cooperation on justice and counternarcotics issues , finance and development, and trade.

The Bahamas hosts U.S. preclearance facilities (U.S. Customs, Immigration, and Agriculture) for travelers to the U.S. at international airports in Nassau, Paradise Island, and Freeport.

## Principal U.S. Officials

For up-to-date information on Principal U.S. Officials, see the U.S. Embassies, Consulates, and Foreign Service section starting on page 139.

The U.S. embassy is located at 42 Queen Street, Nassau (tel. 242–322–1181;telex 20–138); the local postal address is P.O. Box N-8197, Nassau, The Bahamas.

## Other Contact Information

**U.S. Department of Commerce**
International Trade Administration
Office of Latin America and the Caribbean
14th and Constitution, NW
Washington, DC 20230
Tel: 202–482–0704; 800-USA-TRADE
Fax: 202–482–0464

**Caribbean/Latin American Action**
1818 N Street, NW, Suite 310
Washington, DC 20036
Tel: 202–466–7464
Fax: 202–822–0075

# BAHRAIN

October 1996

## Official Name:
## State of Bahrain

## PROFILE

### Geography

**Area:** 693 sq. km. (268 sq. mi.); about four times the size of Washington, DC. Bahrain is an archipelago consisting of 33 islands, only six of them inhabited.
**Cities:** Capital—Manama (pop. 145,000—1993 est.). Other city—Al Muharraq (81,000—1993 est.).
**Terrain:** Low interior plateau and hill on main island.
**Climate:** Hot and humid from May-September, temperate from October-April.

### People

**Nationality:** Noun and adjective—Bahraini(s).
**Population (1996 est.):** 586,000; 66% indigenous.
**Ethnic groups:** Bahraini 63%, Asian 19%, other Arab 10%, Iranian 8%.
**Religions:** Shi'a and Sunni Muslim.
**Languages:** Arabic (official), English, Farsi, Urdu.
**Education:** Attendance—73%. Literacy (1990 est.)—77% (male 82%, female 69%).
**Work force (1987 est.):** 197,000 (about 44% indigenous, 56% expatriate). Industry and commerce—74%. Services—19%. Agriculture—4%. Government—3%.

### Government

**Type:** Traditional emirate (cabinet—executive system).
**Independence:** August 15, 1971.
**Constitution:** May 26, 1973; suspended August 26, 1975.
**Branches:** Executive—Amir (chief of state), prime minister (head of government), Council of Ministers (cabinet). Judicial—independent judiciary with right of judicial review. Appointed Consultative Council (40 members) may review and propose legislation.
**Subdivisions:** Six towns and cities.
**Administrative divisions:** 12 districts.
**Political parties:** None.
**Suffrage:** None.

### Economy

**GDP (1995):** $5 billion.
**Growth rate (1995):** 4%.
**Per capita GDP (1995):** $8,262.
**Natural resources:** Oil, associated and non-associated natural gas, fish.
**Agriculture (1% of GDP):** Products—eggs, vegetables, dates, fish.
**Industry (39% of GDP):** Types—manufacturing (21% of GDP), oil (16%), aluminum, ship repair, natural gas, fish.
**Services (42% of GDP):** Banking, real estate, insurance.
Public administration (18% of GDP).
**Trade (1995):** Exports—$4 billion: petroleum and petroleum products (80%), aluminum (7%), fish. Major markets—Saudi Arabia, U.S., Japan. Imports—$3.6 billion: machinery, industrial equipment, motor vehicles, foodstuffs, clothing. Major suppliers—U.S., U.K., Japan.
**Official exchange rate:** 0.377 Bahraini dinar=U.S. $1 (fixed rate set in 1971).

## PEOPLE

Most of the population of Bahrain is concentrated in the two principal cities, Manama and Al Muharraq. The indigenous people—66% of the population—are from the Arabian Peninsula and Persia. The most numerous minorities are Europeans and South and East Asians.

Islam is the dominant religion. Though Shi'a Muslims make up more than two-thirds of the population, Sunni Islam is the prevailing belief held by those in the government, military, and corporate sectors. Roman Catholic and Protestant churches, as well as a tiny indigenous Jewish community, also exist in Bahrain.

Bahrain has traditionally boasted an advanced educational system. Schooling and related costs are entirely paid for by the government, and primary and secondary attendance rates are high. Bahrain also encourages institutions of higher learning, drawing on expatriate talent and the increasing pool of Bahrainis returning from abroad with advanced degrees. Bahrain University has been established for standard undergraduate and graduate study, and the College of Health Sciences—operating under the direction of the Ministry of Health—trains physicians, nurses, pharmacists, and paramedics.

# HISTORY

Bahrain was once part of the ancient civilization of Dilmun and served as an important link in trade routes between Sumeria and the Indus Valley as long as 5,000 years ago. Since the late 18th century, Bahrain has been governed by the Al Khalifa family, which created close ties to Britain by signing the General Treaty of Peace in 1820. A binding treaty of protection, known as the Perpetual Truce of Peace and Friendship, was concluded in 1861 and further revised in 1892 and 1951. This treaty was similar to those entered into by the British Government with the other Persian Gulf principalities. It specified that the ruler could not dispose of any of his territory except to the United Kingdom and could not enter into relationships with any foreign government other than the United Kingdom without British consent. The British promised to protect Bahrain from all aggression by sea and to lend support in case of land attack.

After World War II, Bahrain became the center for British administration of treaty obligations in the lower Persian Gulf. In 1968, when the British Government announced its decision (reaffirmed in March 1971) to end the treaty relationships with the Persian Gulf sheikdoms, Bahrain joined the other eight states (Qatar and the seven Trucial Sheikhdoms, which are now called the United Arab Emirates) under British protection in an effort to form a union of Arab emirates. By mid-1971, however, the nine sheikhdoms still had not agreed on terms of union. Accordingly, Bahrain sought independence as a separate entity and became fully independent on August 15, 1971, as the State of Bahrain.

# GOVERNMENT AND POLITICAL CONDITIONS

Bahrain is a hereditary emirate under the rule of the Al Khalifa family. The Amir, Sheikh Isa bin Sulman Al Khalifa, and his brother, Prime minister Khalifa bin Sulman Al Khalifa, govern Bahrain in consultation with a council of ministers. The government faces few judicial checks on its actions. Despite their minority status, the Sunnis predominate because the ruling family is Sunni and is supported by the armed forces, the security service, and powerful Sunni and Shi'a merchant families.

In 1973, the Amir enacted a new constitution, setting up an experimental parliamentary system and protecting individual liberties. But just two years later, in August 1975, the Amir disbanded the National Assembly. No date has been announced for the reintroduction of representative institutions, though a petition and other forms of protest have called for their return. In January 1993, the Amir appointed a 30-member Consultative Council to contribute "advice and opinion" on legislation proposed by the cabinet and, in certain cases, suggest new laws on its own. Political unrest broke out in December 1994 and included sporadic mass protests, skirmishes with local law enforcement, arson, and property attacks. In June 1995, the first Bahraini cabinet change in 20 years took place, producing mixed public response. In 1996, the Amir increased the membership of the Consultative Council to 40 and expanded its powers. The first session of the new Council began October 1, 1996.

Bahrain's six towns and cities are administered by one central municipal council, the members of which are appointed by the Amir. A complex system of courts, based on diverse legal sources including Sunni and Shi'a Sharia (religious law), tribal law, and other civil codes and regulation, was created with the help of British advisers in the early 20th century. This judiciary administers the legal code and reviews laws to ensure their constitutionality.

## Principal Government Officials

**For up-to-date information on Principal Government Officials, see the Chiefs of State and Cabinet Members of Foreign Governments section starting on page 1.**

Bahrain maintains an embassy in the United States at 3502 International Drive NW, Washington, DC 20008; tel: (202) 342-0741; fax: (202) 362-2192). The Bahraini UN Mission is located at 747 3rd Avenue, New York, NY 10017; tel: (212) 751-8805.

# U.S.-BAHRAINI RELATIONS

When Bahrain became independent, the traditionally excellent U.S.-Bahrain relationship was formalized with the establishment of diplomatic relations. The U.S. embassy at Manama was opened September 21, 1971, and a resident ambassador was sent in 1974. The Bahraini embassy in Washington, DC, opened in 1977. In October 1991, Amir Isa bin Sulman Al Khalifa made a state visit to Washington, after which he visited other parts of the U.S. as well.

In 1977, the agreement establishing Bahrain as the home port for the United States Navy's Middle East Force (MIDEASTFOR) was terminated. MIDEASTFOR was subsumed into NAVCENT, a part of U.S. Central Command in Tampa, Florida. Bahrain now is host to the Navy's Fifth Fleet.

The U.S. Department of Defense-sponsored Bahrain School remains, along with a small, administrative support unit. After the Gulf war, close cooperation between the two nations helped to stabilize the region. Bahrain has expressed a willingness for cooperation with plans for joint exercises, increased U.S. naval presence in the Gulf and cooperation on security matters.

U.S.-Bahraini economic ties have grown steadily since 1932, when Americans began to help develop Bahrain's oil industry. Currently, many American banks and firms use Bahrain as a base for regional operations. In 1986, the United States displaced Japan to become the top exporter to Bahrain.

## Principal U.S. Embassy Officials

For up-to-date information on Principal U.S. Officials, see the U.S. Embassies, Consulates, and Foreign Service section starting on page 139.

The U.S. embassy in Bahrain is located off Sheikh Isa Highway, Building 979, Road 3119 (next to the Al-Ahli Sports club), Block 331, Zinj, Manama, Bahrain. The mailing address is PO Box 26431, Manama, Bahrain; tel: (973) 273300, after hours 275126; fax: (973) 272594. The embassy's hours are 8:00 a.m.-4:00 p.m., Saturdays-Wednesdays.

# DEFENSE

Under the Ministry of Defense, the Bahrain Defense Force (BDF) numbers about 9,000 personnel and consists of army, navy, air force, air defense, and Amiri guard units. Separate from the BDF, the public security forces and the coast guard report to the Ministry of the Interior. Bahrain, in conjunction with its Gulf Cooperation Council (GCC) partners—Kuwait, Oman, Qatar, Saudi Arabia, and the United Arab Emirates—has moved to upgrade its defenses over the last 10 years in response to the threat posed by the Iran-Iraq and

**BAHRAIN**

0 2 4 6 8 Miles

0 2 4 6 8 Kilometers

Gulf wars. Defense spending has increased by as much as 30% each year since 1980. In 1982, the GCC gave Bahrain $1.7 billion to help improve its defenses.

In the wake of the Gulf war, Bahrain has received additional military support from the United States, including the sale of eight Apache helicopters in the summer of 1991, and subsequent sales of 54 M60A3 tanks, 12 F-16C/D aircraft, and 14 Cobra helicopters. Joint air and ground exercises have also been planned and executed to increase readiness throughout the Gulf. Bahrain and the United States signed an agreement in October 1991 granting U.S. forces access to Bahraini facilities and ensuring the right to pre-position material for future crises.

# ECONOMY

Bahrain has a mixed economy, with government control of many basic industries, including the important oil and aluminum industries. Between 1981 and 1993, Bahrain Government expenditures increased by 64%. During that same time, government revenues continued to be largely dependent on the oil industry and increased by only 4%. The country has run a deficit in nine out of the last 10 years. Bahrain has received significant budgetary support and project grants from Saudi Arabia, Kuwait, and the United Arab Emirates.

Bahrain's small economy is basically strong, despite the budget deficits. It is so small that it suffers from virtually any change in the region or world. Privatization, which could help reduce Bahrain's deficit, is moving ahead. Utilities, banks, financial services, telecommunications, and other areas will shortly come under the control of the private sector.

The government has used its modest oil revenues to build an advanced infrastructure in transportation and telecommunications. Bahrain is a regional financial and business center. Regional tourism is also a significant source of income. Bahrain benefited from the region's economic boom in the late 1970s and 1980s. During that time, the government emphasized infrastructure development and other projects to improve the standard of living; health, education, housing, electricity, water, and roads all received attention.

Petroleum and natural gas, the only significant natural resources in Bahrain, dominate the economy and provide about 60% of budget revenues. Bahrain was the first Persian Gulf state to discover oil. Because of limited reserves, Bahrain has worked to diversify its economy over the past decade. Bahrain has stabilized its oil production at about 40,000 barrels per day (b/d), and reserves are

## Travel Notes

**Travel Advice:** For up-to-date information from the U.S. State Department on possible inconvenient or hazardous situations, see the **Travel Warnings and Consular Information Sheets from the U.S. Government** section starting on page 1723. For the latest information on health requirements and conditions, see the **International Travelers' Health Information** section starting on page 1385. For further information dealing with non-urgent matter, see the **Tips for Travelers to...** section starting on page 1588.

expected to last 10-15 years. The Bahrain Oil Company refinery was built in 1935, has a capacity of about 250,000 b/d, and was the first in the Gulf. After selling 60% of the refinery to the state-owned Bahrain National Oil Company in 1980, Caltex, a U.S. company, now owns 40%. Saudi Arabia provides most of the crude for refinery operation via pipeline. Bahrain also receives a large portion of the net output and revenues from Saudi Arabia's Abu Saafa offshore oilfield.

The Bahrain National Gas Company operates a gas liquefaction plant that utilizes gas piped directly from Bahrain's oilfields. Gas reserves should last about 50 years at present rates of consumption.

The Gulf Petrochemical Industries Company is a joint venture of the petrochemical industries of Kuwait, the Saudi Basic Industries Corporation, and the Government of Bahrain. The plant, completed in 1985, produces ammonia and methanol for export.

Bahrain's other industries include Aluminum Bahrain, which operates an aluminum smelter—the largest in the world with an annual production of about 525,000 metric tons (mt)—and related factories, such as the Aluminum Extrusion Company and the Gulf Aluminum Rolling Mill. Other plants include the Arab Iron and Steel Company's iron ore pelletizing plant (4 million tons annually) and a shipbuilding and repair yard.

Bahrain's development as a major financial center has been the most widely heralded aspect of its diversi-

fication effort. In 1973, the Bahraini Monetary Agency was formed to provide oversight for the banking and financial sector. Since 1983, the regional economic climate in which these institutions operate has become less favorable because of the region's economic downturn. Banks, including some from the United States, have reacted by scaling back their operations or leaving the area. This decrease in business confidence was exacerbated by the Gulf war. Nevertheless, more than 100 offshore banking units and representative offices are located in Bahrain, as well as 65 American firms. Bahrain's international airport is one of busiest in the Gulf, serving 22 carriers. A modern, busy port offers direct and frequent cargo shipping connections to the U.S., Europe, and the Far East.

# FOREIGN RELATIONS

Bahrain plays a modest, moderating role in regional politics and adheres to the views of the Arab League on Middle East peace and Palestinian rights. Bahrain is a member of the GCC, established on May 26, 1981 with five other Gulf states. The country has fully complied with steps taken by the GCC to coordinate economic development and defense and security planning. However, Bahrain and fellow GCC member, Qatar, continue to argue over claims to the Hawar Islands.

Because of its small size and limited wealth, Bahrain has not taken a leading role in regional or international affairs. Rather, it generally pursues a policy of close consultation with neighboring states and works to narrow areas of disagreement. During the Gulf war, Bahraini pilots flew strikes in Iraq, and the island was used as a base for military operations in the Gulf.

Since achieving independence in 1971, Bahrain has maintained friendly relations with most of its neighbors and with the world community. In December 1994, it concurred with the GCC decision to drop secondary and tertiary boycotts against Israel. In many instances, it has established special bilateral trade agreements.

Bahrain-Iran relations have been strained since the Iranian revolution and the 1981 discovery of a planned Iran-sponsored coup in Bahrain. However, with the decline of Iraq as a regional power broker, Bahrain has begun taking steps to improve relations with Iran and increase regional harmony. These efforts have included encouraging Bahrain-Iran trade, although Bahraini suspicions of Iranian involvement in local unrest appear to have slowed these steps toward improved relations.

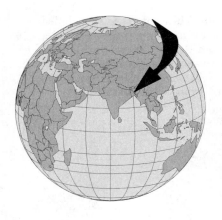

# BANGLADESH

March 2000

## Official Name:
## People's Republic of Bangladesh

# PROFILE

## Geography

**Area:** 143,998 sq. km. (55,813 sq. mi.); about the size of Wisconsin.
**Cities:** Capital—Dhaka (pop. 10 million). Other cities—Chittagong (2.8 million), Khulna (1.8 million), Rajshahi (1 million).
**Terrain:** Mainly flat alluvial plain, with hills in the northeast and southeast.
**Climate:** Semitropical, monsoonal.

## People

**Nationality:** Noun and adjective—Bangladeshi(s).
**Population:** Approximately 128 million.
**Annual growth rate:** 1.6%.
**Ethnic groups:** Bengali 98%, tribal groups, non-Bengali Muslims.
**Religions:** Muslim 88%; Hindu 11%; Christian, Buddhist, others 1%.
**Languages:** Bangla (official, also known as Bengali), English.
**Education:** Attendance—75.1% (primary school), 21.6% (secondary school). Literacy—50% for males; 27% for females, a total of 38.9% literacy.
**Health:** Infant mortality rate—81/1,000. Life expectancy—58 years (male), 58 years (female).
**Work force (54.6 million):** Agricul-

ture—63%; industry—12%; services—25%.

## Government

**Type:** Parliamentary democracy.
**Independence:** 1971, from Pakistan.
**Constitution:** 1972; amended 1974, 1979, 1986, 1988, 1991, 1996.
**Branches:** Executive—president (chief of state), prime minister (head of government), cabinet. Legislative—unicameral Parliament (330 members). Judicial—civil court system based on British model.
**Administrative subdivisions:** Divisions, districts, subdistricts, unions, villages.
**Political parties:** 30-40 active political parties.
**Suffrage:** Universal at age 18.

## Economy

**Annual GDP growth rate (1998-99):** 4.2%.
**Per capita GDP (2000 projected):** $354.
**Natural resources:** Natural gas, fertile soil, water.
**Agriculture (30% of GDP):** Products—rice, jute, tea, sugar, wheat. Land—cultivable area cropped at rate of 176% in 1997; largely subsistence farming dependent on monsoonal rainfall, but growing commercial farming and increasing use of irrigation.
**Industry (20% of GDP):** Types—

garments and knitwear, jute goods, frozen fish and seafood, textiles, fertilizer, sugar, tea, leather, shipbreaking for scrap, pharmaceuticals, ceramic tableware, newsprint.
**Trade (1999):** Merchandise exports—$5.4 billion: garments and knitwear, frozen fish, jute and jute goods, leather and leather products, tea, urea fertilizer, ceramic tableware. Exports to U.S. (1999)—$1.918. Merchandise imports—$8.6 billion: capital goods, foodgrains, petroleum, textiles, chemicals, vegetable oils. Imports from U.S. (1999)—$275 million.

# U.S.-BANGLADESH RELATIONS

Although the U.S. relationship with Bangladesh was initially troubled because of strong U.S. ties with Pakistan, U.S.-Bangladesh friendship and support developed quickly following Bangladesh's independence from Pakistan in 1971.

U.S.-Bangladesh relations are excellent, as demonstrated by the visits to Washington, DC in August 1980 by President Zia; in 1983, 1988, and 1990 by President Ershad; 1992 by Prime Minister Khaleda Zia; and in 1996, 1997, and 1999 by Prime Minister Sheikh Hasina. In 1995, First

Lady Hillary Rodham Clinton visited Bangladesh. U.S. policy has focused primarily on efforts to promote Bangladesh's economic development and the strength of its democratic institutions. The Government and people of Bangladesh are greatly looking forward to President Clinton's scheduled March 2000 visit to Bangladesh.

A centerpiece of the bilateral relationship is a large U.S. economic aid program, totaling about $153 million in 1999. U.S. economic and food aid programs, which began as emergency relief following the 1971 war for independence, now concentrate on long-term development. U.S. assistance objectives include stabilizing population growth, protecting human health, encouraging broad-based economic growth, and building democracy. In total, the United States has provided more than $4.2 billion in food and development assistance to Bangladesh. Food aid under Titles I, II, and III of PL-480 (congressional "food-for-peace" legislation) has been designed to help Bangladesh meet minimum food requirements, promote food production, and moderate fluctuation in consumer prices. Other U.S. development assistance emphasizes family planning and health, agricultural development, and rural employment. The United States works with other donors, and the Bangladesh Government, to avoid duplication and ensure that resources are used to maximum benefit.

In the late 1990s U.S. companies brought a new dimension to the bilateral relationship, bringing total U.S. investment at the end of the 1990s to a stock of about $750 million from only $25 million in 1995. This new investment, which should reach at least $1.2 billion by the end of 2002, has been almost entirely in natural gas exploration/production and power generation, came in response to the Government of Bangladesh's policy of opening those sectors to foreign participants.

Since 1986, with the exception of 1988-89, when an aircraft purchase made the trade balance even, the U.S. trade balance with Bangladesh has been negative, due largely to growing imports of ready-made garments. Jute carpetbacking is the other major U.S. import from Bangladesh; total imports from Bangladesh were about $1.846 billion in 1998. U.S. exports to Bangladesh (some $318 million in 1998) include wheat, fertilizer, cotton, communications equipment, aircraft, and medical supplies, a portion of which is financed by the U.S. Agency for International Development (USAID). A bilateral investment treaty was signed in 1989. Relations between Bangladesh and the United States were further strengthened by the participation of Bangladesh troops in the 1991 Gulf war coalition, and along side of U.S. forces in numerous UN Peacekeeping operations, as well as by the assistance of a U.S. Naval task force after a disastrous March 1991 cyclone in Bangladesh. The relief efforts of U.S. troops are credited with having saved as many as 200,000 lives. In response to Bangladesh's worst flooding of the century in 1998, the U.S. donated 700,000 metric tons of foodgrains, helping to mitigate shortages.

## Principal U.S. Embassy Officials

For up-to-date information on Principal U.S. Officials, see the U.S. Embassies, Consulates, and Foreign Service section starting on page 139.

# HISTORICAL AND CULTURAL HIGHLIGHTS

The area which is now Bangladesh has a rich historical and cultural past, combining Dravidian, Indo-Aryan, Mongol/Mughul, Arab, Persian, Turkic, and West European cultures. Residents of Bangladesh, about 98% of whom are ethnic Bengali and speak Bangla, are called Bangladeshis. Urdu-speaking, non-Bengali Muslims of Indian origin, and various tribal groups, mostly in the Chittagong Hill Tracts, comprise the remainder. Most Bangladeshis (about 88%) are Muslims, but Hindus constitute a sizable (11%) minority. There also are a small number of Buddhists, Christians, and animists. English is spoken in urban areas and among the educated.

About 1200 AD, Muslim invaders, under Sufi influence, supplanted existing Hindu and Buddhist dynasties in Bengal. This incursion led to the conversion to Islam of most of the population in the eastern areas of Bengal, and created a sizable Muslim minority in the western areas of Bengal. Since then, Islam has played a crucial role in the region's history and politics.

Bengal was absorbed into the Mughul Empire in the 16th century, and Dhaka, the seat of a nawab (the representative of the emperor), gained some importance as a provincial center. But it remained remote and thus a difficult to govern region—especially the section east of the Brahmaputra River—outside the mainstream of Mughul politics. Portuguese traders and missionaries were the first Europeans to reach Bengal in the latter part of the 15th century. They were followed by representatives of the Dutch, the French, and the British East India Companies. By the end of the 17th century, the British presence on the Indian subcontinent was centered in Calcutta. During the 18th and 19th centuries, the British gradually extended their commercial contacts and administrative control beyond Calcutta to Bengal. In 1859, the British Crown replaced the East India Company, extending British dominion from Bengal, which became a region of India, in the east to the Indus River in the west.

The rise of nationalism throughout British-controlled India in the late 19th century resulted in mounting animosity between the Hindu and Muslim communities. In 1885, the All-India National Congress was founded with Indian and British membership. Muslims seeking an organization of their own founded the

All-India Muslim League in 1906. Although both the League and the Congress supported the goal of Indian self-government within the British Empire, the two parties were unable to agree on a way to ensure the protection of Muslim political, social, and economic rights. The subsequent history of the nationalist movement was characterized by periods of Hindu-Muslim cooperation, as well as by communal antagonism. The idea of a separate Muslim state gained increasing popularity among Indian Muslims after 1936, when the Muslim League suffered a decisive defeat in the first elections under India's 1935 constitution. In 1940, the Muslim League called for an independent state in regions where Muslims were in the majority. Campaigning on that platform in provincial elections in 1946, the League won the majority of the Muslim seats contested in Bengal. Widespread communal violence followed, especially in Calcutta.

When British India was partitioned and the independent dominions of India and Pakistan were created in 1947, the region of Bengal was divided along religious lines. The predominantly Muslim eastern half was designated East Pakistan—and made part of the newly independent Pakistan—while the predominantly Hindu western part became the Indian state of West Bengal. Pakistan's history from 1947 to 1971 was marked by political instability and economic difficulties. Dominion status was rejected in 1956 in favor of an "Islamic republic within the Commonwealth." Attempts at civilian political rule failed, and the government imposed martial law between 1958 and 1962, and again between 1969 and 1972.

Almost from the advent of independent Pakistan in 1947, frictions developed between East and West Pakistan, which were separated by more than 1,000 miles of Indian territory. East Pakistanis felt exploited by the West Pakistan-dominated central government. Linguistic, cultural, and ethnic differences also contributed to the estrangement of East from West Pakistan. Bengalis strongly resisted

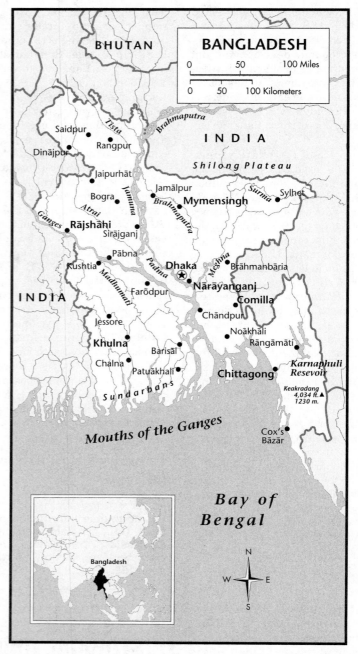

attempts to impose Urdu as the sole official language of Pakistan. Responding to these grievances, Sheikh Mujibur Rahman—known widely as "Mujib"—in 1949 formed the Awami League (AL), a party designed mainly to promote Bengali interests. Mujib became president of the Awami League and emerged as leader of the Bengali autonomy movement. In 1966, he was arrested for his political activities.

After the Awami League won all the East Pakistan seats of the Pakistan national assembly in 1970-71 elections, West Pakistan opened talks with the East on constitutional questions about the division of power between the central government and the provinces, as well as the formation of a national government headed by the Awami League. The talks proved unsuccessful, however, and on March 1, 1971, Pakistani President Yahya Khan indefinitely postponed the pending national assembly session, precipitating massive civil disobedience in East Pakistan. Mujib was arrested again; his party was banned, and most of his aides fled to India, where they organized a provisional government. On March 26, 1971, following a bloody crackdown by the Pakistan army, Bengali nationalists declared an independent People's Republic of Bangladesh. As fighting grew between the army and the Bengali mukti bahini ("freedom fighters"), an estimated 10 million Bengalis, mainly Hindus, sought refuge in the Indian states of Assam and West Bengal.

The crisis in East Pakistan produced new strains in Pakistan's troubled relations with India. The two nations had fought a war in 1965, mainly in the west, but the refugee pressure in India in the fall of 1971 produced new tensions in the east. Indian sympathies lay with East Pakistan, and in November, India intervened on the side of the Bangladeshis. On December 16, 1971, Pakistani forces surrendered, and Bangladesh—meaning "Bengal nation"—was born; the new country became a parliamentary democracy under a 1972 constitution.

# ECONOMY

Although one of the world's poorest and most densely populated countries, Bangladesh has made major strides to meet the food needs of its increasing population, through increased domestic production augmented by imports.. The land is devoted mainly to rice and jute cultivation, although wheat production has increased in recent years; the country is largely self-sufficient in rice production. Nonetheless, an estimated 10% to 15% of the population faces serious nutritional risk. Bangladesh's predominantly agricultural economy depends heavily on an erratic monsoonal cycle, with periodic flooding and drought. Although improving, infrastructure to support transportation, communications, and power supply is poorly developed. The country has large reserves of natural gas and limited reserves of coal and oil. While Bangladesh's industrial base is weak, unskilled labor is inexpensive and plentiful.

Since independence in 1971, Bangladesh has received more than $30 billion in grant aid and loan commitments from foreign donors, about $15 billion of which has been disbursed. Major donors include the World Bank, the Asian Development Bank, the UN Development Program, the United States, Japan, Saudi Arabia, and West European countries. Bangladesh has historically run a large trade deficit, financed largely through aid receipts and remittances from workers overseas. Foreign reserves dropped markedly in 1995 and 1996 but have now stabilized in the $1.5-$1.8 billion range (or about 2.2-2.5 monthly import cover).

## Land, Climate, and Demographics

Bangladesh is a low-lying, riverine country located in South Asia with a largely marshy jungle coastline of 710 kilometers (440 mi.) on the northern littoral of the Bay of Bengal. Formed by a deltaic plain at the confluence of the Ganges (Padma), Brahmaputra (Jamuna), and Meghna Rivers and their tributaries, Bangladesh's alluvial soil is highly fertile, but vulnerable to flood and drought. Hills rise above the plain only in the Chittagong Hill Tracts in the far southeast and the Sylhet division in the northeast. Straddling the Tropic of Cancer, Bangladesh has a subtropical monsoonal climate characterized by heavy seasonal rainfall, moderately warm temperatures, and high humidity. Natural calamities, such as floods, tropical cyclones, tornadoes, and tidal bores affect the country almost every year. Bangladesh also is affected by major cyclones—on average 16 times a decade.

Urbanization is proceeding rapidly, and it is estimated that only 30% of the population entering the labor force in the future will be absorbed into agriculture, although many will likely find other kinds of work in rural areas. The areas around Dhaka and Comilla are the most densely settled. The Sundarbans, an area of coastal tropical jungle in the southwest and last wild home of the Bengal Tiger, and the Chittagong Hill Tracts on the southeastern border with

Burma and India, are the least densely populated.

## Moves Toward a Market Economy

Following the violent events of 1971 during the fight for independence, Bangladesh—with the help of large infusions of donor relief and development aid—slowly began to turn its attention to developing new industrial capacity and rehabilitating its economy. The statist economic model adopted by its early leadership, however—including the nationalization of much of the industrial sector—resulted in inefficiency and economic stagnation. Beginning in 1975, the government gradually gave greater scope to private sector participation in the economy, a pattern that has continued. A few state-owned enterprises have been privatized, but many, including major portions of the banking and jute sectors, remain under government control. Population growth, inefficiency in the public sector, and limited natural resources and capital have continued to restrict economic growth. In the mid-1980s, there were encouraging, if halting, signs of progress. Economic policies aimed at encouraging private enterprise and investment, denationalizing public industries, reinstating budgetary discipline, and liberalizing the import regime were accelerated. From 1990-1993. In 1985 1989-1993, the government successfully followed an enhanced structural adjustment facility (ESAF) with the International Monetary Fund.

Although the Khaleda Zia Government (1991-96) initially took significant strides toward pro-market reform, including tax reform and allowing increased foreign direct investment in the gas and power sectors, preoccupation with its domestic political troubles stalled progress on this critical front in the last year of its tenure. The government of Prime Minister Sheikh Hasina, elected in June 1996, indicated that it would continue along the path toward privatization and open-market reform, but progress has been slow, especially in privatization. While the Awami League government has managed to maintain economic growth levels around 4%-5%, and single-digit inflation—except for a period of months after the 1998 floods—per capita income levels still remain distressingly low, at less than $1 per day.

Efforts to achieve Bangladesh's macroeconomic goals have been problematic. The privatization of public sector industries has proceeded at a slow pace, due in part to worker unrest in affected industries. The government also has proven unable to resist demands for wage hikes in government-owned industries. Economic growth has been further slowed by a largely dysfunctional banking system which has impeded access to capital-state-owned banks, which control about three-fourths of deposits and loans, and carry classified loan burdens of about 50%.

## Agriculture

Most Bangladeshis earn their living from agriculture. Although rice and jute are the primary crops, wheat is assuming greater importance. Tea is grown in the northeast. Because of Bangladesh's fertile soil and normally ample water supply, rice can be grown and harvested three times a year in many areas. Due to a number of factors, Bangladesh's labor-intensive agriculture has achieved steady increases in foodgrain production despite the often unfavorable weather conditions. These include better flood control and irrigation, a generally more efficient use of fertilizers, and the establishment of better distribution and rural credit networks. With 20.2 million metric tons produced in 1999, rice is Bangladesh's principal crop. By comparison, wheat output in 1999 was 1.9 million metric tons. Population pressure continues to place a severe burden on productive capacity, creating a food deficit, especially of wheat. Foreign assistance and commercial imports fill the gap. Underemployment remains a serious problem, and a growing concern for Bangladesh's agricultural sector will be its ability to absorb additional manpower. Finding alternative sources of employment will continue to be a daunting problem for future governments, par-

ticularly with the increasing numbers of landless peasants who already account for about half the rural labor force.

## Industry and Investment

Fortunately for Bangladesh, many new jobs—1.5 million, mostly for women—have been created by the country's dynamic private ready-made garment industry, which grew at double-digit rates through most of the 1990s. Despite the country's politically motivated general strikes, poor Infrastructure, and weak financial system, Bangladeshi entrepreneurs have shown themselves adept at competing in the global garments marketplace. Bangladesh's exports to the U.S. surpassed $1.9 billion in 1999. Bangladesh also exports significant amounts of garments and knitwear to the EU market. The country has done less well, however, in expanding its export base—garments account for more than three-fourths of all exports, dwarfing the country's historic cash crop, jute, along with leather, shrimp, pharmaceuticals and ceramics. Bangladesh has been a world leader in its efforts to end the use of child labor in garment factories. On July 4, 1995, the Bangladesh Garment Manufacturers Export Association, International Labor Organization, and UNICEF signed a memorandum of understanding on the elimination of child labor in the garment sector. Implementation of this pioneering agreement began in fall 1995, and by the end of 1999, child labor in the garment trade virtually had been eliminated.

The labor-intensive process of ship-breaking for scrap has developed to the point where it now meets most of Bangladesh's domestic steel needs. Other industries include sugar, tea, leather goods, newsprint, pharmaceutical, and fertilizer production.

The Bangladesh Government continues to court foreign investment, something it has done fairly successfully in private power generation and gas exploration and production, as well as in other sectors such as cellular telephony, textiles, and pharmaceuticals. In 1989, the same year it

signed a bilateral investment treaty with the United States, it established a Board of Investment to simplify approval and start-up procedures for foreign investors, although in practice the board has done little to increase investment. Bangladesh also has established successful export processing zones in Chittagong and Dhaka, and has given the private sector permission to build and operate competing EPZs-initial construction on a Korean EPZ started in 1999. In June 1999, the AFL-CIO petitioned the U.S. Government to deny Bangladesh access to U.S. markets under the Generalized System of Preferences (GSP), citing the country's failure to meet promises made in 1992 to allow freedom of association in EPZs.

# GOVERNMENT

The president, while chief of state, holds a largely ceremonial post; the real power is held by the prime minister, who is head of government. The president is elected by the legislature (Parliament) every 5 years. The president's normally circumscribed powers are substantially expanded during the tenure of a caretaker government. (Under the 13th Amendment, which the Parliament passed in March 1996, a caretaker government assumes power temporarily to oversee general elections after dissolution of the Parliament.) In the caretaker government, the president has control over the Ministry of Defense, the authority to declare a state of emergency, and the power to dismiss the Chief Advisor and other members of the caretaker government. Once elections have been held and a new government and Parliament are in place, the president's powers and position revert to their largely ceremonial role. The prime minister is appointed by the president; the prime minister must be a Member of Parliament (MP) who the president feels commands the confidence of the majority of other MPs. The cabinet is composed of ministers selected by the prime minister and appointed by the president. At least 90% of the ministers must be MPs. The other 10% may be non-MP experts or "technocrats" who are not otherwise disqualified from being elected MPs. According to the constitution, the president can dissolve Parliament upon the written request of the prime minister.

The legislature is a unicameral, 330-seat body. About 300 of its members are elected by universal suffrage at least every 5 years. The remaining 30 seats are reserved for women MPs, elected by the Parliament.

Bangladesh's judiciary is a civil court system based on the British model; the highest court of appeal is the Appellate Court of the Supreme Court. At the local government level, the country is divided into divisions, districts, subdistricts, unions, and villages. Local officials are elected at the union level. All larger administrative units are run by members of the civil service.

# DEFENSE

The Bangladesh Army, Navy, and Air Force are composed of regular military members. Some of the senior officers and noncommissioned officers served in the Pakistan military before the 1971 independence war. Senior officers include "repatriates" who were interned in Pakistan during the war, and "freedom fighters" who fought against Pakistan. The 110,000-member, seven-division army is modeled and organized along British lines, similar to other armies on the Indian subcontinent. However, it has adopted U.S. Army tactical planning procedures, training management techniques, and noncommissioned officer educational systems. It also is eager to improve its peacekeeping operations capabilities and is working with the U.S. military in that area. The Bangladesh Air Force is acquiring four U.S. C-130 B transport aircraft. These aircraft will improve the military's disaster response and peacekeeping capabilities. The Air Force also has recently procured eight MIG 29 fighters from Russia for $124 million. The Bangladesh Navy is mostly limited to coastal patrolling, but it is paying to have an ULSAN class frigate built in South Korea. It is supported by artillery, armored, and combat units.

In addition to traditional defense roles, the military has been called on to provide support to civil authorities for disaster relief and internal security. The Bangladesh Air Force and Navy, with about 7,000 personnel each, perform traditional military missions. A Coast Guard has been recently formed, under the Home Ministry, to play a stronger role in the area of anti-smuggling, anti-piracy, and protection of offshore resources. Recognition of economic and fiscal constraints has led to the establishment of several paramilitary and auxiliary forces, including the 40,000-member Bangladesh Rifles; the Ansars and Village Defense Parties Organization, which claims 64 members in every village in the country; and a 5,000-member specialized police unit known as the Armed Police. Bangladesh Rifles, under the authority of the Home Ministry are commanded by army officers who are seconded to the organization.

In addition to in-country military training, some advanced and technical training is done abroad, including grant aid training in the United States. China, Pakistan, and eastern Europe are is the major defense suppliers to Bangladesh, but military leaders are trying to find affordable alternatives to Chinese equipment.

In 1995 the Bangladesh Air Force made its largest purchase from the U.S to date—12 T-37 jet trainers. More recently, Bangladesh procured four C-130 transport aircraft. A 2,300-member Bangladesh Army contingent served with coalition forces during the 1991 Gulf war. Bangladesh is currently the second-leading contributor to UN peacekeeping operations, with an infantry battalion in UNIKOM (Kuwait), an engineer battalion in UNTAET, (East Timor) and another infantry battalion scheduled for Sierra Leone in May 2000.

# POLITICAL CONDITIONS SINCE INDEPENDENCE

The provisional government of the new nation of Bangladesh was formed in Dhaka with Justice Abu Sayeed Choudhury as President, and Sheikh Mujibur Rahman ("Mujib")—who was released from Pakistani prison in early 1972—as Prime Minister.

## Sheikh Mujibur Rahman, 1972-75

Mujib came to office with immense personal popularity, but had difficulty transforming this popular support into the political strength needed to function as head of government. The new constitution, which came into force in December 1972, created a strong executive prime minister, a largely ceremonial presidency, an independent judiciary, and a unicameral legislature on a modified Westminster model. The 1972 constitution adopted as state policy the Awami League's (AL) four basic principles of nationalism, secularism, socialism, and democracy.

The first parliamentary elections held under the 1972 constitution were in March 1973, with the Awami League winning a massive majority. No other political party in Bangladesh's early years was able to duplicate or challenge the League's broad-based appeal, membership, or organizational strength. Relying heavily on experienced civil servants and members of the Awami League, the new Bangladesh Government focused on relief, rehabilitation, and reconstruction of the economy and society. Economic conditions remained precarious, however. In December 1974, Mujib decided that continuing economic deterioration and mounting civil disorder required strong measures. After proclaiming a state of emergency, Mujib used his parliamentary majority to win a constitutional amendment limiting the powers of the legislative and judicial branches, establishing an executive presidency, and instituting a one-party system, the Bangladesh Krishak Sramik Awami League (BAKSAL), which all members of Parliament were obliged to join.

Despite some improvement in the economic situation during the first half of 1975, implementation of promised political reforms was slow, and criticism of government policies became increasingly centered on Mujib. In August 1975, Mujib, and most of his family, were assassinated by mid-level army officers. His daughter, Sheikh Hasina, happened to be out of the country. A new government, headed by former Mujib associate Khandakar Moshtaque, was formed.

## Ziaur Rahman, 1975-81

Successive military coups resulted in the emergence of Army Chief of Staff Gen. Ziaur Rahman ("Zia") as strongman. He pledged the army's support to the civilian government headed by President Chief Justice Sayem. Acting at Zia's behest, Sayem dissolved Parliament, promising fresh elections in 1977, and instituted martial law.

Acting behind the scenes of the Martial Law Administration (MLA), Zia sought to invigorate government policy and administration. While continuing the ban on political parties, he sought to revitalize the demoralized bureaucracy, to begin new economic development programs, and to emphasize family planning. In November 1976, Zia became Chief Martial Law Administrator (CMLA) and assumed the presidency upon Sayem's retirement 5 months later, promising national elections in 1978.

As President, Zia announced a 19-point program of economic reform and began dismantling the MLA. Keeping his promise to hold elections, Zia won a 5-year term in June 1978 elections, with 76% of the vote. In November 1978, his government removed the remaining restrictions on political party activities in time for parliamentary elections in February 1979. These elections, which were contested by more than 30 parties,

marked the culmination of Zia's transformation of Bangladesh's Government from the MLA to a democratically elected, constitutional one. The AL and the Bangladesh Nationalist Party (BNP), founded by Zia, emerged as the two major parties. The constitution was again amended to provide for an executive prime minister appointed by the president, and responsible to a parliamentary majority.

In May 1981, Zia was assassinated in Chittagong by dissident elements of the military. The attempted coup never spread beyond that city, and the major conspirators were either taken into custody or killed. In accordance with the constitution, Vice President Justice Abdus Sattar was sworn in as acting president. He declared a new national emergency and called for election of a new president within 6 months—an election Sattar won as the BNP's candidate. President Sattar sought to follow the policies of his predecessor and retained essentially the same cabinet, but the army stepped in once again.

## Hussain Mohammed Ershad, 1982-90

Army Chief of Staff Lt. Gen. H.M. Ershad assumed power in a bloodless coup in March 1982. Like his predecessors, Ershad suspended the constitution and—citing pervasive corruption, ineffectual government, and economic mismanagement—declared martial law. The following year, Ershad assumed the presidency, retaining his positions as army chief and CMLA. During most of 1984, Ershad sought the opposition parties' participation in local elections under martial law. The opposition's refusal to participate, however, forced Ershad to abandon these plans. Ershad sought public support for his regime in a national referendum on his leadership in March 1985. He won overwhelmingly, although turnout was small. Two months later, Ershad held elections for local council chairmen. Pro-government candidates won a majority of the posts, setting in motion the President's ambitious decentralization program. Political

life was further liberalized in early 1986, and additional political rights, including the right to hold large public rallies, were restored. At the same time, the Jatiya (People's) Party, designed as Ershad's political vehicle for the transition from martial law, was established.

Despite a boycott by the BNP, led by President Zia's widow, Begum Khaleda Zia, parliamentary elections were held on schedule in May 1986. The Jatiya Party won a modest majority of the 300 elected seats in the national assembly. The participation of the Awami League—led by the late Prime Minister Mujib's daughter, Sheikh Hasina Wajed—lent the elections some credibility, despite widespread charges of voting irregularities.

Ershad resigned as Army Chief of Staff and retired from military service in preparation for the presidential elections, scheduled for October. Protesting that martial law was still in effect, both the BNP and the AL refused to put up opposing candidates. Ershad easily outdistanced the remaining candidates, taking 84% of the vote. Although Ershad's government claimed a turnout of more than 50%, opposition leaders, and much of the foreign press, estimated a far lower percentage and alleged voting irregularities.

Ershad continued his stated commitment to lift martial law. In November 1986, his government mustered the necessary two-thirds majority in the national assembly to amend the constitution and confirm the previous actions of the martial law regime. The President then lifted martial law, and the opposition parties took their elected seats in the national assembly.

In July 1987, however, after the government hastily pushed through a controversial legislative bill to include military representation on local administrative councils, the opposition walked out of Parliament. Passage of the bill helped spark an opposition movement that quickly gathered momentum, uniting Bangladesh's opposition parties for the

## Travel Notes

**Travel Advice:** For up-to-date information from the U.S. State Department on possible inconvenient or hazardous situations, see the **Travel Warnings and Consular Information Sheets from the U.S. Government** section starting on page 1723. For the latest information on health requirements and conditions, see the **International Travelers' Health Information** section starting on page 1385. For further information dealing with non-urgent matter, see the **Tips for Travelers to...** section starting on page 1588.

first time. The government began to arrest scores of opposition activists under the country's Special Powers Act of 1974. Despite these arrests, opposition parties continued to organize protest marches and nationwide strikes. After declaring a state of emergency, Ershad dissolved Parliament and scheduled fresh elections for March 1988.

All major opposition parties refused government overtures to participate in these polls, maintaining that the government was incapable of holding free and fair elections. Despite the opposition boycott, the government proceeded. The ruling Jatiya Party won 251 of the 300 seats. The Parliament, while still regarded by the opposition as an illegitimate body, held its sessions as scheduled, and passed a large number of bills, including, in June 1988, a controversial constitutional amendment making Islam Bangladesh's state religion.

By 1989, the domestic political situation in the country seemed to have quieted. The local council elections were generally considered by international observers to have been less violent and more free and fair than previous elections. However, opposition to Ershad's rule began to regain momentum, escalating by the end of 1990 in frequent general strikes, increased campus protests, public rallies, and a general disintegration of law and order.

On December 6, 1990, Ershad offered his resignation. On February 27,

1991, after 2 months of widespread civil unrest, an interim government oversaw what most observers believed to be the nation's most free and fair elections to date.

## Khaleda Zia, 1991-96

The center-right BNP won a plurality of seats and formed a coalition government with the Islamic fundamentalist party Jamaat-I-Islami, with Khaleda Zia, widow of Ziaur Rahman, obtaining the post of Prime Minister. Only four parties had more than 10 members elected to the 1991 Parliament: The BNP, led by Prime Minister Begum Khaleda Zia; the AL, led by Sheikh Hasina; the Jamaat-I-Islami (JI), led by Golam Azam; and the Jatiyo Party (JP), led by acting chairman Mizanur Rahman Choudhury while its founder, former President Ershad, served out a prison sentence on corruption charges. The electorate approved still more changes to the constitution, formally re-creating a parliamentary system and returning governing power to the office of the prime minister, as in Bangladesh's original 1972 constitution. In October 1991, members of Parliament elected a new head of state, President Abdur Rahman Biswas.

In March 1994, controversy over a parliamentary by-election, which the opposition claimed the government had rigged, led to an indefinite boycott of Parliament by the entire opposition. The opposition also began a program of repeated general strikes to press its demand that Khaleda Zia's government resign and a caretaker government supervise a general election. Efforts to mediate the dispute, under the auspices of the Commonwealth Secretariat, failed. After another attempt at a negotiated settlement failed narrowly in late December 1994, the opposition resigned en masse from Parliament. The opposition then continued a campaign of marches, demonstrations, and strikes in an effort to force the government to resign. The opposition, including the Awami League's Sheikh Hasina , pledged to boycott national elections scheduled for February 15, 1996.

In February, Khaleda Zia was re-elected by a landslide in voting boycotted and denounced as unfair by the three main opposition parties. In March 1996, following escalating political turmoil, the sitting Parliament enacted a constitutional amendment to allow a neutral caretaker government to assume power conduct new parliamentary elections; former Chief Justice Mohammed Habibur Rahman was named Chief Advisor (a position equivalent to prime minister) in the interim government. New parliamentary elections were held in June 1996 and were won by the Awami League; party leader Sheikh Hasina became Prime Minister.

## Sheikh Hasina, 1996-Present

Sheikh Hasina formed what she called a "Government of National Consensus" in June 1996, which included one minister from the Jatiya Party and another from the Jatiyo Samajtantric Dal, a very small leftist party. The Jatiya Party never entered into a formal coalition arrangement, and party president H.M. Ershad withdrew his support from the government in September 1997. Only three parties had more than 10 members elected to the 1996 Parliament: The Awami League, BNP, and Jatiya Party. Jatiya Party president, Ershad, was released from prison on bail in January 1997.

Although international and domestic election observers found the June 1996 election free and fair, the BNP protested alleged vote rigging by the Awami League. Ultimately, however, the BNP party decided to join the new Parliament. The BNP soon charged that police and Awami League activists were engaged in large-scale harassment and jailing of opposition activists. At the end of 1996, the BNP staged a parliamentary walkout over this and other grievances but returned in January 1997 under a four-point agreement with the ruling party. The BNP asserted that this agreement was never implemented and later staged another walkout in August 1997. The BNP returned to

Parliament under another agreement in March 1998.

In June 1999, the BNP and other opposition parties again began to abstain from attending Parliament. Opposition parties have staged an increasing number of nationwide general strikes, rising from 6 days of general strikes in 1997 to 27 days in 1999. A four-party opposition alliance formed at the beginning of 1999 announced that it would boycott parliamentary by-elections and local government elections unless the government took steps demanded by the opposition to ensure electoral fairness. The government did not take these steps, and the opposition has subsequently boycotted all elections, including municipal council elections in February 1999, several parliamentary by-elections, and the Chittagong city corporation elections in January 2000. The opposition demands that the Awami League government step down immediately to make way for a caretaker government to preside over paliamentary and local government.

## Principal Government Officials

For up-to-date information on Principal Government Officials, see the Chiefs of State and Cabinet Members of Foreign Governments section starting on page 1.

# FOREIGN RELATIONS

Bangladesh pursues a moderate foreign policy that places heavy reliance on multinational diplomacy, especially at the United Nations.

## Participation in Multilateral Organizations

Bangladesh was admitted to the United Nations in 1974 and was elected to a Security Council term in 1978 and again for a 2000-2002 term.

Foreign Minister Choudhury served as president of the 41st UN General Assembly in 1986. Bangladesh is slated to become the next chairman of NAM at the summit scheduled for Dhaka 2001. Bangladesh is currently chairman of the Group of 8 Developing Countries. The government has participated in numerous international conferences, especially those dealing with population, food, development, and women's issues. In 1982-83, Bangladesh played a constructive role as chairman of the "Group of 77," an informal association encompassing most of the world's developing nations. In 1983, Bangladesh hosted the foreign ministers meeting of the Organization of the Islamic Conference (OIC). It has taken a leading role in the "Group of 48" developing countries.

Since 1975, Bangladesh has sought close relations with other Islamic states and a prominent role among moderate members of the OIC. The government also pursued the expansion of cooperation among the nations of South Asia, bringing the process—an initiative of former President Ziaur Rahman—through its earliest, most tentative stages to the formal inauguration of the South Asia Association for Regional Cooperation (SAARC) at a summit gathering of South Asian leaders in Dhaka in December 1985. Bangladesh has served in the chairmanship of SAARC and has participated in a wide range of ongoing SAARC regional activities.

In recent years, Bangladesh has played a significant role in international peacekeeping activities. Several thousand Bangladeshi military personnel are deployed overseas on peacekeeping operations. Under UN auspices, Bangladeshi troops have served or are serving in Somalia, Rwanda, Mozambique, Kuwait, Bosnia, and Haiti, and units are currently serving in Kuwait and East Timor. Bangladesh responded quickly to President Clinton's 1994 request for troops and police for the multinational force for Haiti and provided the largest non-U.S. contingent.

## Bilateral Relations with Other Nations

Bangladesh is bordered on the west, north, and east by a 2,400-kilometer land frontier with India, and on the southeast by a land and water frontier (193 kilometers) with Burma.

**India.** India is Bangladesh's most important neighbor. Geographic, cultural, historic, and commercial ties are strong, and both countries recognize the importance of good relations. During and immediately after Bangladesh's struggle for independence from Pakistan in 1971, India assisted refugees from East Pakistan, intervened militarily to help bring about the independence of Bangladesh, and furnished relief and reconstruction aid.

Indo-Bangladesh relations are often strained, and many Bangladeshis feel India likes to play "big brother" to smaller neighbors, including Bangladesh. Bilateral relations warmed in 1996, due to a softer Indian foreign policy and the new Awami League Government. A 30-year water-sharing agreement for the Ganges River was signed in December 1996, after an earlier bilateral water-sharing agreement for the Ganges River lapsed in 1988. Both nations also have cooperated on the issue of flood warning and preparedness. The government and tribal insurgents signed a peace accord in December 1997, which allowed for the return of tribal refugees who had fled into India, beginning in 1986, to escape violence caused by an insurgency in their homeland in the Chittagong Hill Tracts. The implementation of all parts of this agreement have stalled, and the army maintains a very strong presence in the area. The army is increasingly concerned about a growing problem of cultivation of illegal drugs.

**Pakistan.** Bangladesh enjoys warm relations with Pakistan, despite the strained early days of their relationship. Landmarks in their reconciliation are:

- An August 1973 agreement between Bangladesh and Pakistan on the repatriation of numerous individuals, including 90,000 Pakistani prisoners of war stranded in Bangladesh as a result of the 1971 conflict;

- A February 1974 accord by Bangladesh and Pakistan on mutual recognition, followed more than 2 years later by establishment of formal diplomatic relations;

- The organization by the UN High Commissioner for Refugees (UNHCR) of an airlift that moved almost 250,000 Bengalis from Pakistan to Bangladesh, and non-Bengalis from Bangladesh to Pakistan; and

- Exchanges of high-level visits, including a visit by Prime Minister Benazir Bhutto to Bangladesh in 1989 and visits by Prime Minister Zia to Pakistan in 1992 and in 1995.

Still to be resolved are the division of assets from the pre-1971 period and the status of more than 250,000 non-Bengali Muslims (known as "Biharis") remaining in Bangladesh but seeking resettlement in Pakistan.

**Burma.** Bilateral ties with Burma are good, despite occasional border strains and an influx of more than 270,000 Muslim refugees (known as "Rohingya") from predominantly Buddhist Burma. As a result of bilat-

eral discussions, and with the cooperation and assistance of the UNHCR, most of the Rohingya refugees have now returned to Burma. As of 2000, about 22,000 refugees remain in camps in southern Bangladesh.

**Former Soviet Union.** The former Soviet Union supported India's actions during the 1971 Indo-Pakistan war and was among the first to recognize Bangladesh. The U.S.S.R. initially contributed considerable relief and rehabilitation aid to the new nation. After Sheikh Mujib was assassinated in 1975 and replaced by military regimes, however, Soviet-Bangladesh relations cooled.

In 1989, the U.S.S.R. ranked 14th among aid donors to Bangladesh. The Soviets focused on the development of electrical power, natural gas and oil, and maintained active cultural relations with Bangladesh. They financed the Ghorasal thermal power station—the largest in Bangladesh. Recently, Russia has conducted an aggressive military sales effort in Dhaka and has succeeded with a $124 million deal for eight MIG-29 fighters. Bangladesh began to open diplomatic relations with the newly independent Central Asian states in 1992.

**China.** China traditionally has been more important to Bangladesh than the former U.S.S.R., even though China supported Pakistan in 1971.

As Bangladesh's relations with the Soviet Union and India cooled in the mid-1970s, and as Bangladesh and Pakistan became reconciled, China's relations with Bangladesh grew warmer. An exchange of diplomatic missions in February 1976 followed an accord on recognition in late 1975.

Since that time, relations have grown stronger, centering on trade, cultural activities, military and civilian aid, and exchanges of high-level visits, beginning in January 1977 with President Zia's trip to Beijing. The largest and most visible symbol of bilateral amity is the Bangladesh-China "Friendship Bridge," completed in 1989 near Dhaka, as well as the extensive military hardware in the Bangladesh inventory and warm military relations between the two countries. In the 1990s, the Chinese also built two 210 megawatt power plants outside of Chittagong; mechanical faults in the plants cause them to frequently shut down for days at a time, heightening the country's power shortage.

**Other countries in South Asia.** Bangladesh maintains friendly relations with Bhutan, Maldives, Nepal, and Sri Lanka and strongly opposed the Soviet invasion of Afghanistan. Bangladesh and Nepal recently agreed to facilitate land transit between the two countries.

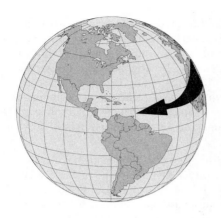

# BARBADOS

April 2001

Official Name:
**Barbados**

## PROFILE

### Geography

**Area:** 431 sq. km. (166 sq. mi.); about three times the size of Washington, DC.
**Cities:** Capital—Bridgetown.
**Terrain:** Generally flat, hilly in the interior.
**Climate:** Tropical.

### People

**Nationality:** Noun and adjective—Barbadian(s); also "Bajan(s)."
**Population (1999):** 267,000.
**Avg. annual growth rate (2000):** 3.7%.
**Ethnic groups:** African 80%, mixed 16%, European 4%.
**Religions:** Anglican 70%, Roman Catholic, Methodist, Baptist, and Moravian.
**Language:** English.
**Education:** Attendance—primary school 100%, secondary school 93%. Adult literacy—99%.
**Health:** Infant mortality rate (1998)—7.8/1,000. Life expectancy—75 yrs. men; 77 yrs. women.
**Work force (2000):** 140,000. Sectors—commerce, tourism, government, manufacturing, construction, mining, agriculture, and fishing.
**Unemployment (2000):** 9.3%.

### Government

**Type:** Parliamentary democracy; independent sovereign state within the Commonwealth.
**Independence:** November 30, 1966.
**Constitution:** 1966.
**Branches:** Executive—governor general (representing Queen Elizabeth II, head of state), prime minister (head of government), cabinet. Legislative—bicameral parliament. Judicial—magistrate's courts, Supreme Court (High Court and Court of Appeals), privy council in London.
**Subdivisions:** 11 parishes and the city of Bridgetown.
**Political parties:** Barbados Labor Party (BLP, incumbent), Democratic Labor Party (DLP), National Democratic Party (NDP).
**Suffrage:** Universal at 18. Economy
**GDP (est. 2000):** $2.43 billion.
**GDP growth rate (2000):** 3.7%.
**Per capita GDP (est. 2000):** US $9,100.
**Average inflation rate (2000):** 2.5%.
**Natural resources:** Petroleum, fishing, natural gas.
**Agriculture (4% of GDP):** Products—Sugar accounts for 2.4% of GDP and 80% of arable land.
**Industry:** Types—Manufacturing and construction (17% of GDP)—food, beverages, textiles, paper, chemicals, fabricated products.
**Services:** (76 % of GDP) Tourism, banking and other financial services,

Informatics (data processing).
**Trade (est. 2000):** Exports—$260.0 million. Major markets—U.S. 17%, CARICOM 45%, U.K. 14%, and Canada 3%. Imports—$800.3 million. Major suppliers—U.S. 42%, UK 8%, Canada 4%, CARICOM 15%.

## PEOPLE

About 80% of Barbados' population is of African descent, 4% European descent, and 16% mixed. About 70% of Barbadians are Anglican, and the rest mostly Roman Catholic, Methodist, Baptist, and Moravian. There also are small Jewish and Muslim communities. Barbados' population growth rate has been very low, less than 1% since the1960s, largely due to family planning efforts and a high emigration rate.

## HISTORY

British sailors who landed on Barbados in the 1620s at the site of present-day Holetown on the Caribbean coast found the island uninhabited. As elsewhere in the eastern Caribbean, Arawak Indians may have been annihilated by invading Caribs, who are believed to have subsequently abandoned the island.

From the arrival of the first British settlers in 1627-28 until independence in 1966, Barbados was under uninterrupted British control. Nevertheless, Barbados always enjoyed a large measure of local autonomy. Its House of Assembly, which began meeting in 1639, is the third-oldest legislative body in the Western Hemisphere, preceded only by Bermuda's legislature and the Virginia House of Burgesses.

As the sugar industry developed into the main commercial enterprise, Barbados was divided into large plantation estates which replace the small holdings of the early British settlers. Some of the displaced farmers relocated to British colonies in North America. To work the plantations, slaves were brought from Africa; the slave trade ceased a few years before the abolition of slavery throughout the British empire in 1834.

Local politics were dominated by plantation owners and merchants of British descent. It was not until the 1930s that a movement for political rights was begun by the descendants of emancipated slaves. One of the leaders of this movement, Sir Grantley Adams, founded the Barbados Labor Party in 1938. Progress toward more democratic government for Barbados was made in 1951, when universal adult suffrage was introduced. This was followed by steps toward increased self-government, and in 1961, Barbados achieved internal autonomy.

From 1958 to 1962, Barbados was one of 10 members of the West Indies Federation, and Sir Grantley Adams served as its first and only prime minister. When the federation was terminated, Barbados reverted to its former status as a self-governing colony. Following several attempts to form another federation composed of Barbados and the Leeward and Windward Islands, Barbados negotiated its own independence at a constitutional conference with the United Kingdom in June 1966. After years of peaceful and democratic progress, Barbados became an independent state within the British Commonwealth on November 30, 1966.

Under its constitution, Barbados is a parliamentary democracy modeled on the British system. The governor general represents the Monarch. Control of the government rests with the cabinet, headed by the prime minister and responsible to the Parliament.

The bicameral Parliament consists of the House of Assembly and Senate. The 28 members of the House are elected by universal suffrage to 5-year terms. Elections may be called at any time the government wishes to seek a new mandate or if the government suffers a vote of no-confidence in Parliament. The Senate's 21 members are appointed by the governor general—12 with the advice of the prime minister, two with the advice of the leader of the opposition, and seven at the governor general's discretion.

Barbados has an independent judiciary composed of magistrate courts, which are statutorily authorized, and a Supreme Court, which is constitutionally mandated. The Supreme Court consists of the high court and the court of appeals, each with four judges. The Chief Justice serves on both the high court and the court of appeals. The court of last resort is the Judicial Committee of Her Majesty's Privy Council in London, whose decisions are binding on all parties. Judges of the Supreme Court are appointed by the governor general on the recommendation of the prime minister after consultation with the leader of the opposition.

The island is divided into 11 parishes and the city of Bridgetown for administrative purposes. There is no local government. Barbados' defense expenditures account for about 2.5% of the government budget.

# GOVERNMENT

The three political parties—the Barbados Labor Party (BLP), the Democratic Labor Party (DLP), and the National Democratic Party (NDP)—are all moderate and have no major ideological differences; electoral contests and political disputes often have personal overtones. The major political problems facing Barbados today are in promoting economic growth: creating jobs, encouraging agricultural diversification, attracting small industry, and promoting tourism.

The ruling BLP was decisively returned to power in January 1999 elections, winning 26 seats in the Parliament with the DLP only winning two seats. The Prime Minister, Owen Arthur, who also serves as Minister of Finance, has given a high priority to economic development. The main opposition party, the DLP, is led by David Thompson.

## Principal Government Officials

**For up-to-date information on Principal Government Officials, see the Chiefs of State and Cabinet Members of Foreign Governments section starting on page 1.**

Barbados maintains an embassy in the United States located at 2144 Wyoming Avenue, NW, Washington, DC 20008 (tel. 202-939-9200), a consulate general in New York City at 800 2nd Avenue, 18th Floor, New York, NY 10017 (tel. 212-867-8435), and a consulate general in Miami at 150 Alhambra Circle, Suite 1270, Coral Gables, FL 33134 (tel. 305-442-1994).

# ECONOMY

Since independence, Barbados has transformed itself from a low-income economy dependent upon sugar production to a middle-income economy based on tourism. The economy went into a deep recession in 1990 after 3 years of steady decline brought on by fundamental macroeconomic imbalances. After a painful readjustment process, the economy began to grow again in 1993. Growth rates have averaged between 3%-5% since then.

The main factors responsible for the improvement in economic activity include an expansion in the number of tourist arrivals, an increase in manufacturing, and an increase in sugar production. Recently, offshore banking and financial services also have become an important source of foreign exchange and economic growth.

Economic growth has led to net increases in employment in the tourism sector, as well as in construction and other services sub-sectors of the economy. The public service remains Barbados' largest single employer. Total labor force has increased from 126,000 in 1993 to 140,000 persons in 2000, and unemployment has dropped significantly from over 20% in the early 1990s to 9.3% at the end of 2000.

# FOREIGN RELATIONS

As a small nation, the primary thrust of Barbados' diplomatic activity has been within international organizations. The island is a member of the Commonwealth and participates in its activities. Barbados was admitted to the United Nations in December 1966. Barbados joined the Organization of American States (OAS) in 1967.

On July 4, 1973, Barbados, Trinidad and Tobago, Guyana, and Jamaica signed a treaty in Trinidad to found the Caribbean Community and Common Market (CARICOM). In May 1974, most of the remaining English-speaking Caribbean states joined CARICOM, which now has 14 members. Barbados also is a member of the Caribbean Development Bank, established in 1970, with headquarters in Bridgetown. The eastern Caribbean's Regional Security System, which associates Barbados with six other island nations, also is headquartered in Barbados. In July 1994, Barbados joined the newly established Association of Caribbean States (ACS).

As a member of CARICOM, Barbados supported efforts by the United

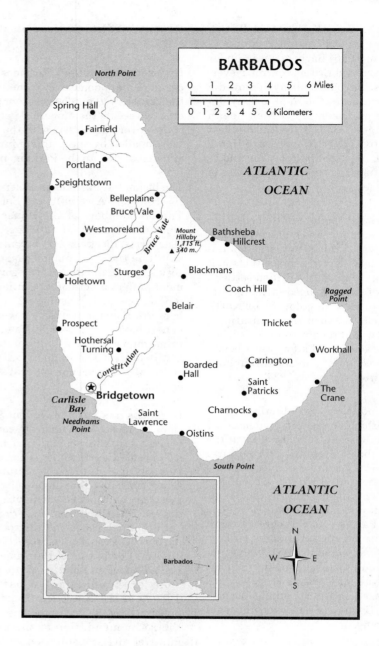

States to implement UN Security Council Resolution 940, designed to facilitate the departure of Haiti's de facto authorities from power. The country agreed to contribute personnel to the multinational force, which restored the democratically elected government of Haiti in October 1994.

In May 1997, Prime Minister Owen Arthur hosted President Clinton and 14 other Caribbean leaders during the first-ever U.S.-regional summit in Bridgetown, Barbados. The summit strengthened the basis for regional cooperation on justice and counterna-

rcotics issues, finance and development, and trade.

Barbados has diplomatic missions headed by resident ambassadors or high commissioners in Canada, the U.K., the U.S., and Venezuela, and at the European Union (Brussels) and the UN. It also has resident consuls general in Toronto, Miami, and New York City. Australia, Brazil, Cuba, Canada, Colombia, China, Guatemala, the U.K., the U.S., and Venezuela have ambassadors or high commissioners resident in Barbados.

# U.S.-BARBADIAN RELATIONS

In 1751, George Washington visited Barbados, making what is believed to have been his only trip abroad. The U.S. Government has been represented on Barbados since 1824. From 1956 to 1978, the U.S. operated a naval facility in Barbados.

The U.S. and Barbados have had friendly bilateral relations since Barbados's independence in 1966. The U.S. has supported the government's efforts to expand the country's economic base and to provide a higher standard of living for its citizens. Barbados is a beneficiary of the U.S. Caribbean Basin Initiative U.S. assistance is channeled primarily through multilateral agencies such as the Inter-American Development Bank, the World Bank, and the recently opened USAID satellite office in Bridgetown.

Barbados also receives counternarcotics assistance and is the beneficiary of the U.S. military's exercise-related and humanitarian assistance construction program.

## Travel Notes

**Travel Advice:** For up-to-date information from the U.S. State Department on possible inconvenient or hazardous situations, see the **Travel Warnings and Consular Information Sheets from the U.S. Government** section starting on page 1723. For the latest information on health requirements and conditions, see the **International Travelers' Health Information** section starting on page 1385. For further information dealing with non-urgent matter, see the **Tips for Travelers to...** section starting on page 1588.

Barbados and U.S. authorities cooperate closely in the fight against narcotics trafficking and other forms of transnational crime. In 1996, the U.S. and Barbados signed a mutual legal assistance treaty (MLAT) and an updated extradition treaty covering all common offenses, including conspiracy and organized crime. A maritime law enforcement agreement was signed in 1997. A popular tourist destination, Barbados had almost than 518,000 visitors in 2000. In addition, Barbados had nearly 433,000 cruise ship passenger arrivals, the majority of whom were U.S citizens. Approximately 3,000 Americans reside in the country.

## Principal U.S. Embassy Officials

For up-to-date information on Principal U.S. Officials, see the **U.S. Embassies, Consulates, and Foreign Service section starting on page 139.**

The U.S. embassy in Barbados is located in the Canadian Imperial Bank of Commerce Building, Broad Street, Bridgetown (tel: 246-436-4950; fax: 246-429-5246).

## Other Contact Information

**U.S. Department of Commerce**
International Trade Administration
Office of Latin America and the Caribbean
14th & Constitution Avenue, NW
Washington, DC 20230
Tel: 202-482-1658, 800-USA-Trade
Fax: 202-482-0464

**Caribbean/Latin American Action**
1818 N Street, NW
Suite 310
Washington, DC 20036
Tel: 202-466-7464
Fax: 202-822-0075

Background Notes

# BELARUS

March 1996

Official Name:
**Republic of Belarus**

# PROFILE

## Geography

**Area:** 207,600 sq. km. (80,100 sq. mi.); slightly smaller than Kansas.
**Cities:** Capital—Minsk.
**Terrain:** Generally flat and contains much marshland.
**Climate:** Cold winters, cool and moist summers, transitional between continental and maritime.

## People

**Nationality:** Noun—Belarusian(s). Adjective—Belarusian.
**Population:** 10.4 million.
**Population growth rate:** 0.3%.
**Ethnic groups:** Byelorussian (78%), Russian (13%), Polish, Ukrainian, other.
**Religions:** Eastern Orthodox, other.
Languages: Belarusian (official), Russian (predominant working language), other.
**Education:** Literacy—97%.
**Health:** Infant mortality rate—19/1,000. Life expectancy—71 years.
**Work force (4.9 million):** Industry and construction—40%. Agriculture and forestry—22%. Health, science, and education—16%. Other—22%.

## Government

**Type:** Republic.

**Constitution:** Adopted 1994.
**Independence:** 1991 (from Soviet Union).
**Branches:** Executive—president (head of state), prime minister (head of government), Council of Ministers (cabinet). Legislative—unicameral Supreme Soviet (parliament). Judicial—Supreme Court.
**Administrative subdivisions:** Six voblasti and one municipality.
**Political parties:** Belarusian Popular Front, Party of Popular Accord, Union of Belarusian Entrepreneurs, Belarusian Party of Communists, Belarus Peasant Party, Belarusian Socialist Party, Belarusian Social Democrat Party, Agrarian Party of Belarus, United Democratic Party of Belarus, Independent Trade Unions.
**Suffrage:** Universal at 18.

## Economy

**GDP (1994):** $53 billion.
**GDP growth rate (1994):** -20%.
**Per capita GDP (1994):** $5,100.
**Natural resources:** Forest land, peat deposits, small amounts of oil and natural gas.
**Agriculture:** Products—grain, potatoes and other vegetables, meat, milk.
**Industry:** Types—machinery and transport equipment, chemical products, fabrics, and consumer goods.
**Trade:** Exports—(about 60% go to CIS countries and 40% to non-CIS countries; for 1994, exports to countries outside the former Soviet Union were $968 million): machinery and transport equipment, chemicals, foodstuffs. Major markets—Russia, Ukraine, Poland, Bulgaria. Imports—(about 70% come from CIS countries and 30% from non-CIS countries; for 1994, imports from countries outside the former Soviet Union were $534 million): fuel, natural gas, industrial raw materials, textiles, sugar. Major suppliers—Russia, Ukraine, Poland.

**Exchange rate (March 1996):** 12,900 rubels=U.S.$1.

# U.S.-BELARUSIAN RELATIONS

The dissolution of the Soviet Union in December 1991 brought an end to the Cold War and created 15 new countries with which to establish bilateral relations. The United States opened an embassy in Belarus' capital, Minsk, in February 1992. The first U.S. Ambassador was David Heywood Swartz, who assumed his post on August 25, 1992—the first anniversary of Belarusian independence. Kenneth Spencer Yalowitz succeeded Ambassador Swartz in November 1994.

## U.S.-Belarusian Economic Relations

In February 1993, a bilateral trade treaty guaranteeing reciprocal most-favored-nation status entered into force. In January 1994, the U.S. and Belarus signed a bilateral investment treaty, which has been ratified by Belarus and is awaiting ratification by the U.S. Senate. In February 1996, a Mutual Legal Assistance Treaty was initialed. A formal signing and ratification by both countries' legislatures are pending.

Negotiations are continuing on a treaty for the avoidance of double taxation.

An Overseas Private Investment Corporation agreement was signed in June 1992 and is in force. Belarus is eligible for Export-Import Bank short-term financing insurance for U.S. investments. The International Monetary Fund (IMF) granted standby credit in September 1995, but Belarus has fallen off the program and did not receive the second tranche of funding, which had been scheduled for regular intervals throughout 1996.

Belarus welcomes joint ventures with American companies, particularly in computer software, electrical components, telecommunications equipment, and consumer goods. A 1991 foreign investment law provides protection from nationalization. However, rubel inconvertibility and other restrictions, such as on land ownership, continue to hamper investment opportunities.

## U.S. Assistance to Belarus

As of September 1995, the U.S. had provided about $73.8 million in humanitarian aid shipments, $229 million in U.S. Department of Agriculture (USDA) food assistance, and $19 million in technical assistance to Belarus. Current U.S. assistance priorities in Belarus are focused on programs that support defense industry conversion (see Defense and Military Issues), provide support for economic restructuring and small-scale democ-

racy-building efforts, and assist in social transition.

At its inception, the U.S. assistance program in Belarus was oriented toward providing humanitarian relief. In January 1992, the U.S. initiated the Coordinating Conference on Assistance to the New Independent States (NIS) in response to the humanitarian emergencies facing these states. The resulting Operation Provide Hope, coordinated by the Department of Defense, provided desperately needed food, fuel, medicine, and shelter. The U.S. shipped to Belarus pharmaceuticals and medical supplies for areas affected by the 1986 Chornobyl nuclear disaster, provided the country with Department of Defense excess medicines and supplies, and shipped components of a Department of Defense acute care hospital to several Minsk hospitals. Another significant shipment of aid—by airlift and by train transport—is scheduled for the 10th anniversary of Chornobyl in April 1996.

USDA has provided concessional loans to Belarus for the purchase of U.S. agricultural commodities and provided corn and other commodities through the Food for Progress program. In addition, the country has received soybean meal and feed wheat through the Food for Peace program and Section 416 (b) of the Agricultural Act, respectively.

The U.S. technical assistance program now targets areas of maximum impact in the promotion of a market

economy and a democratic society. U.S.-funded programs have helped carry out small-scale privatization in three cities in Belarus, where over 50% of communal enterprises have been privatized. (As of February 1996, however, less than 10% of all Belarusian firms had been privatized.) Technical assistance and training to selected Belarusian medical institutions through a hospital partnership program have improved the quality and availability of services to control and treat widespread, critical health problems. Advisers in areas as diverse as issuance of government securities to individual entrepreneurship to agribusiness have worked to introduce new, market-oriented concepts to their Belarusian counterparts.

The U.S. has provided rule-of-law and law enforcement assistance to Belarus. An advisor on rule-of-law issues has been resident in Minsk since 1992 and has provided advice on the drafting of legislation; development of a cadre of lawyers, targeting law students in particular; and other issues. On law enforcement, U.S. experts are training Belarusian counterparts in modern techniques of combating financial crimes, organized crime, and narcotics trafficking. In addition, Belarusian officials have participated in training and exchange programs on rule-of-law, copyright legislation, independent media, and educational reform.

## Principal U.S. Embassy Officials

**For up-to-date information on Principal U.S. Officials, see the U.S. Embassies, Consulates, and Foreign Service section starting on page 139.**

The U.S. embassy in Minsk, Belarus is at Starovilenskaya #46; tel: 375-172-31-5000; fax: 375-172-34-7853.

# HISTORICAL HIGHLIGHTS

Belarus has been inhabited since pre-historic times, and the first recorded settlements date back to the 6th century AD. The princes of Kiev ruled Belarus until the invasion of the Mongols in 1240, when most of its towns were destroyed.

The region came under the control of powerful Lithuanians and, in 1386, under the Lithuanian-Polish Jagiellonian Dynasty. For centuries, the Poles and the Muscovites struggled bitterly over Belarus. In 1772, Catherine the Great gained control over part of the country, and, by 1795, Russia ruled all of Belarus.

During the 19th and 20th centuries, the country again became a European battleground. Napoleon passed through Belarus—and fought there—in 1812, and the Germans fought the Soviets on Belarusian territory in World War I. Although a Soviet Socialist Republic was proclaimed in January 1919, fighting with Poland continued until 1921.

Belarus suffered heavy losses in World War II, when some 2.2 million inhabitants perished. The postwar period saw a significant rebirth—especially in the economic sphere. On August 25, 1991, Belarus declared its independence from the Soviet Union.

# ECONOMY

As part of the former Soviet Union, Belarus had a relatively well-developed industrial base; it retained this industrial base following the breakup of the U.S.S.R. The country also has a broad agricultural base and a high education level. Among the former republics of the Soviet Union, it has one of the highest standards of living. But Belarusians face the difficult challenge of moving from a state-run economy with high priority on military production to a civilian, free-market system.

The government is developing plans to privatize local and state enterprises through a voucher system, but progress has been slow. A Council of Ministers' decree allows privatization to proceed until Belarus' Supreme Soviet passes legislation. President Lukashenko signed the 1996 privatization plan in January of this year. The government has continued to subsidize foodstuffs and other basic goods to prevent social strife. The economy remains dependent on Russia for energy supplies and raw materials. About 80% of Belarus' products are exported to Russia.

Economic activity in Belarus has stagnated, as businesses have awaited the outcome of talks on a monetary union with Russia, including negotiations over an exchange rate between Belarusian rubels and Russian rubles. Belarus has sought to join the Russian ruble zone in order to stabilize its currency and boost its trade links with Russia.

The monthly rate of inflation in Belarus reached 40% in February 1994 but by May 1995 had dropped to 3.6%. An agreement on a monetary union will eventually be part of a planned April 1996 bilateral treaty that could bring about economic union between Belarus and Russia (see Foreign Relations).

## Environmental Issues

Belarus has established ministries of energy, forestry, land reclamation, and water resources and state committees to deal with ecology and safety procedures in the nuclear power industry. The most serious environmental issue in Belarus results from the accident at the 1986

Chernobyl nuclear power plant. About 70% of the nuclear fallout from the plant landed on Belarusian territory, and about 25% of the land is considered uninhabitable. But government restrictions on residence and use of contaminated land are not strictly enforced. As noted, the government receives U.S. assistance in its efforts to deal with the consequences of the radiation.

Belarus has long been a member of the UN Economic Commission for Europe (ECE) and has been active in its environmental meetings. The country has signed key ECE conventions on long-range transboundary environmental issues, but implementation has suffered from a lack of resources.

# GOVERNMENT AND POLITICAL CONDITIONS

Belarus is making gradual progress in establishing a democratic system. Under the planned April 1996 bilateral treaty (see Foreign Relations), Belarus' political structure may become joined in some form with that of Russia over the coming years, although no such changes appear imminent.

Following Belarus' declaration of independence from the Soviet Union in 1991, most power passed to the Council of Ministers (cabinet), whose decrees have the force of law. A new constitution took effect on March 30, 1994. It established for the first time a presidency and a constitutional court. Presidential elections in July 1994 resulted in the seating of Aleksander Lukashenko as Belarus' first president.

Belarus' Supreme Soviet (parliament) is technically the highest branch of government. Its then-chairman—elected to that post in January 1994 by the parliament following a vote of "no-confidence" in his predecessor—was considered head of state

until President Lukashenko's July 1994 election. Following a dormant period in 1995—during which it lacked the constitutionally mandated quorum because not enough deputies garnered the required percentage of votes—the Supreme Soviet was able to meet on January 9, 1996. Semyon Sharetsky, founder of the Agrarian Party, became chairman and parliamentary speaker on January 11, 1996.

Both Belarus' Council of Ministers and its Supreme Soviet are dominated by a coalition of former members of the Communist and Agrarian Parties. In February 1993, the Supreme Soviet repealed an August 1991 resolution that had temporarily suspended the activity of the Communist Party. The principal opposition party is the nationalist organization, the Belarusian Popular Front.

Government restrictions on freedom of speech and the press, peaceful assembly, religions, and movement all increased in 1995. Despite the passage of a press law in 1994 prohibiting the existence of a press monopoly, the government maintained a virtual monopoly over the press since it owns nearly all printing and broadcasting facilities and manages the distribution of all print media through official outlets.

There are, however, some private newspapers printed in Belarusian and Russian.

Freedom of assembly is restricted under former Soviet law, which is still valid. It requires an application at least 10 days in advance of the event. The local government must respond positively or negatively at least five days prior to the event. Public demonstrations occurred frequently in 1995, but always under government oversight.

The constitution provides for freedom of religion, and the government generally respects this right in practice. The majority of Belarusians are Eastern Orthodox Christians, and the church has been criticized by nationalists for its ties to the Russian Orthodox Church.

Citizens are free to travel within the country. But Belarusians must register their place of residence and may not move without official permission. The Ministry of the Interior has proposed legislation abolishing both regulations.

The constitution provides for the right of workers—except state security and military personnel—to voluntarily form and join independent unions and to carry out actions in defense of workers' rights, including the right to strike. In practice, however, these rights are limited. The two major independent trade unions are the Free Trade Union of Belarus and the Belarusian Independent Trade Union.

## Principal Government Officials

For up-to-date information on Principal Government Officials, see the Chiefs of State and Cabinet Members of Foreign Governments section starting on page 1.

Belarus' embassy in the U.S. is at 1619 New Hampshire Ave., NW, Washington, DC 20009; tel: 202-986-1604; fax: 202-986-1805.

# DEFENSE AND MILITARY ISSUES

In Lisbon on May 23, 1992, the United States signed a protocol to the Strategic Arms Reduction Treaty (START) with Belarus, Russia, Kazakstan, and Ukraine (those states on whose territory strategic nuclear weapons of the former Soviet Union are located). The protocol makes the four states party to the START Treaty and commits them to reductions in strategic nuclear weapons within the seven-year period provided for in the treaty.

On February 4, 1993, the Belarusian parliament ratified the START

**Editor's Update**      **Jan. 1997–June 2001**

*A report on important events that have taken place since the last State Department revision of this Background Note.*

Belarus fell under the control of President Aleksandr Lukashenka in November 1996, when a referendum gave the Communist hard-liner broad authority. Mr. Lukashenka disbanded Parliament and selected an Assembly of loyalist legislators following the vote.

The President also implemented a new Constitution, which gave him the power to hire and remove the heads of the Constitutional Court, the Supreme Court and the Central Bank.

In March 1997, Mr. Lukashenka banned opposition demonstrations, and ordered restrictions on the opposition National Front. Still, 10,000 anti-government dem-

onstrators who filled the streets of Minsk on March 15 were met with little resistance by police. With its reversion to authoritarian government, in 1997 Belarus was suspended from the Organization for Security and Cooperation in Europe (OSCE) and its observer status in the Council of Europe was withdrawn. Throughout 1999, Mr. Lukashenka continued to crack down on opposition to his rule. In July, opposition leader Semyon Sharetsky fled to Lithuania and declared himself as the leader of Belarus the following month. The Lithuanian government's decision to permit Mr. Sharetsky to establish residence there threatened to harm Belarus-Lithuanian relations.

Since 1998, Belarus has remained loyal to Russia and its president Vladimir Putin. Belarusan President Lukashenka has strongly supported a merger between Belarus and Russia, but Russia has been reluctant to take on the burden of its impoverished neighbor.

On June 5, 2001, Mr. Lukashenka denounced Russia for failing to follow through on a promised $100 million loan. The Belarusian president instead turned to Libya for financial aid. Only a few days later, the Russian embassy in Belarus suffered a bombing attack. No injuries were reported, but the attack may have political implications.

---

Treaty and voted to adhere to the nuclear Non-Proliferation Treaty (NPT) as a non-nuclear weapons state. The chairman of the Belarusian parliament deposited Belarus' instrument of accession to the NPT with President Clinton on July 22, 1993, at the White House.

The U.S. has signed six agreements with Belarus to provide more than $75 million in Nunn-Lugar assistance. These agreements call for providing Belarus with nuclear accident emergency response equipment; a government-to-government communications link for transmission of START and intermediate-range nuclear forces notifications; expanded military-to-military contacts; and assistance for defense conversion, environmental restoration, and establishment of an effective export control system.

On October 30, 1992, Belarus signed the Conventional Armed Forces in Europe (CFE) Treaty to reduce and numerically limit key categories of military equipment, such as tanks, artillery, armored combat vehicles, combat aircraft, and combat helicopters, and to provide for destruction of

weaponry in excess of those limits. Although Belarus did not comply with the CFE Treaty deadline of November 1995, destructions were proceeding in accordance with the treaty in early 1996. President Lukashenko pledged publicly in March 1996 that destruction would be complete by the end of 1996.

# FOREIGN RELATIONS

Belarus is actively working to become a full member of the international community. Under an arrangement with the former U.S.S.R., Belarus was an original member of the United Nations. It also is a member of the Commonwealth of Independent States (CIS—a group of 12 former Soviet republics) and its customs union, the Organization for Security and Cooperation in Europe (OSCE), NATO's Partnership for Peace, the North Atlantic Cooperation Council, the International Monetary Fund, and the World Bank.

The government has supported CIS and OSCE efforts to resolve regional

disputes. Minsk serves as the headquarters of the CIS, and President Lukashenko took an active role in the January 1996 CIS summit in Moscow.

On March 29, 1996, Belarus, Russia, Kazakstan, and Kyrgyzstan signed an accord calling for closer political, economic, trade, and cultural integration, along the lines of the EU. It envisions a common market of goods and services, unified transport, joint communications, and a common currency. The agreement is valid for five years and can be extended.

Belarus and Russia announced plans on March 23, 1996 to sign a treaty on April 2 to form a bilateral union. Such an arrangement would be the closest any former Soviet republic has come to merging again with Russia. Although the April 1996 treaty would tie them more closely together culturally, would include joint political bodies, and might mean economic union, each nation would retain its sovereignty.

Implementation of the treaty's provisions likely would take several years to complete.

# BELGIUM

June 2000

## Official Name:
## Kingdom of Belgium

# PROFILE

## Geography
**Area:** 30,528 square kilometers (11,800 sq. mi.), about the size of Maryland.
**Cities:** Capital—Brussels (pop. 954,460). Other cities—Antwerp (447,632); Ghent (224,074); Liege (187,538); Charleroi (202,020); Bruges (115,991); and Namur (104,994).

## People
**Population:** (1999) 10,213,752; urban—69%.
**Annual population growth rate:** 0.4%.
**Density:** 861 per sq. mi.
**Linguistic regions:** Dutch-speaking 58%; French-speaking 32%; legally bilingual (Brussels) 9.3%; German-speaking 0.7%.
**Religion:** Predominantly Roman Catholic (although 5%-20% practicing); Catholic, Protestant, Jewish, Islamic, Anglican, Greek and Russian Orthodox recognized, as well as secularism.
**Languages:** Dutch, French, German.
**Literacy:** 98%.

## Government
**Type:** Parliamentary democracy

under a constitutional monarch.
**Independence:** 1830.
**Constitution:** 1994 (revised).
**Branches:** Executive—King (head of state), Prime Minister (head of government), Cabinet. Legislative—bicameral parliament (Senate and House of Representatives). Flemish Parliament with the Flemish Government for regional, educational, and cultural affairs; Walloon Regional Council (legislator) and government for Walloon Regional Affairs; Francophone Community Council and government for Francophone cultural and educational affairs; Brussels Regional Council and government for Brussels regional affairs; and German language Community Council and government for cultural and educational affairs.
**Political parties:** Christian Democratic, Socialist, Liberal (conservative philosophy in American terminology), Green (ecologist).
**Suffrage:** Over 18, compulsory.
**Political subdivisions:** Ten provinces, three regions, three communities, 589 municipalities.
**Flag:** Three broad vertical bands—black, yellow, and red, from left to right
**Membership in International Organizations:** UN, NATO, EU, WEU, OSCE, WTO, OECD, G-10 (leading financial powers), BENELUX Customs Union, Schengen, and others.

## Economy
**GDP:** (1999) $266 billion.
**Annual real growth rate:** (1999) 2.2%.
**Per capita income:** (1999) $25,576.
**Natural resources:** Coal.
**Agriculture:** (1.4% of GDP) Products—livestock, including dairy cattle, grain, sugarbeets, nursery products, flax, tobacco, potatoes, and other fruits and vegetables.
**Industry:** (20% of GDP) Types—machinery, iron, coal, textiles, chemicals, glass, pharmaceuticals, manufactured goods.
**Trade:** (1999) Exports—$187.3 billion: Iron and steel, coal, transportation equipment, tractors, diamonds, petroleum products. Imports—$172.8 billion: Fuels, chemical products, grains, foodstuffs. Trading partners—EU 76%; United States 6%.

# PEOPLE

Belgium is located in Western Europe, bordered by the Netherlands, the Federal Republic of Germany, Luxembourg, France, and the North Sea.

Although generally flat, the terrain becomes increasingly hilly and forested in the southeast (Ardennes) region.

Climate is cool, temperate, and rainy; summer temperatures average 77°F,

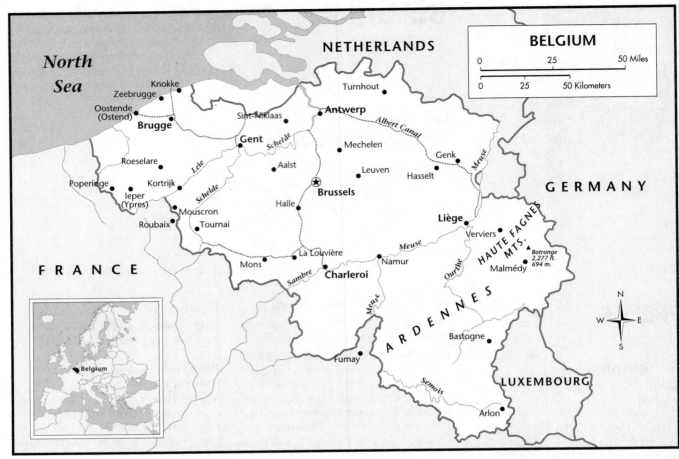

winters average 45°F. Annual extremes (rarely attained) are 10°F and 90°F.

Geographically and culturally, Belgium is at the crossroads of Europe, and during the past 2,000 years has witnessed a constant ebb and flow of different races and cultures. Consequently, Belgium is one of Europe's true melting pots with Celtic, Roman, Germanic, French, Dutch, Spanish, and Austrian cultures having made an imprint.

Today, the Belgians are divided ethnically into the Dutch-speaking Flemings and French-speaking Walloons, with a mixed population in Brussels representing the remainder. About 70,000 German speakers reside in the east.

The population density is the second-highest in Europe, after the Netherlands.

# HISTORY

Belgium derives its name from a Celtic tribe, the Belgae, whom Caesar described as the most courageous tribe of Gaul. However, the Belgae were forced to yield to Roman legions during the first century B.C. For some 300 years thereafter, what is now Belgium flourished as a province of Rome. But Rome's power gradually lessened. In about A.D. 300, Attila the Hun invaded what is now Germany and pushed Germanic tribes into northern Belgium. About 100 years later, the Germanic tribe of the Franks invaded and took possession of Belgium. The northern part of present-day Belgium became an overwhelmingly Germanized and Germanic-Frankish-speaking area, whereas in the southern part people continued to be Roman and spoke derivatives of Latin. After coming under the rule of the Dukes of Burgundy and, through marriage, passing into the possession of the

Hapsburgs, Belgium was occupied by the Spanish (1519-1713) and the Austrians (1713-1794).

Under these various rulers, and especially during the 500 years from the 12th to the 17th century, Ghent, Bruges, Brussels, and Antwerp took turns at being major European centers for commerce, industry (especially textiles) and art. Flemish painting—from Van Eyck and Breugel to Rubens and Van Dyck—became the most prized in Europe. Flemish tapestries hung on the walls of castles throughout Europe.

Following the French Revolution, Belgium was invaded and annexed by Napoleonic France in 1795. It was made a part of the Netherlands by the Congress of Vienna in 1815.

In 1830, Belgium wrested its independence from the Dutch as a result of an uprising of the Belgian people. A constitutional monarchy was established in 1831, with a monarch invited in from the House of Saxe-Coburg Gotha in Germany.

Belgium was invaded by the Germans in 1914 and again in 1940. This, plus disillusionment over postwar Soviet behavior, made Belgium one of the foremost advocates of collective security within the framework of European integration and the Atlantic partnership.

Since 1944, when Belgium was liberated by British, Canadian, and American armies, the nation has lived in security and at a level of increased well-being.

A parliamentary democracy, Belgium has been governed by successive coalitions of two or more political parties, with the centrist Flemish Christian Democratic Party providing the Prime Minister most of the time. Two major political controversies have marked the postwar years: a dispute over King Leopold III's conduct during World War II (which caused him to abdicate in 1951), and the insistence of the nation's majority linguistic community—the Flemish—upon a reorganization of the state into autonomous regions.

The last 30 years also have been marked by a rapid economic development of Flanders, which had been largely agricultural and, since the industrial revolution, had become the poorer half of Belgium. This Flemish resurgence has been accompanied by a corresponding shift of political power to the Flemings, who now constitute an absolute majority (58%) of the population.

# GOVERNMENT AND POLITICAL CONDITIONS

Belgium is a hereditary constitutional monarchy. The present King, Albert II, succeeded his brother, King Baudouin, who died July 31, 1993. Albert took the oath of office to become King on August 9, 1993.

As titular head of state, the King plays a ceremonial and symbolic role in the nation. A main political function is to designate a political leader to attempt to form a new cabinet after an election or the resignation of a cabinet. In conditions where there is a "constructive vote of no-confidence," the government has to resign and the Lower House of Parliament proposes a new Prime Minister to the King. The King also is seen as playing a symbolic unifying role, representing a common national Belgian identity.

The Belgian Parliament consists of a Senate and a House of Representatives (the Chamber). The House has 150 directly elected members. The Senate has 71 members. The executive branch of the government consists of ministers and secretaries of state (junior ministers) drawn from the political parties which form the government coalition. Formally, the ministers are appointed by the King. The number of ministers is limited to 15, and they have no seat in Parliament. The Cabinet is chaired by the Prime Minister. Ministers head executive departments of the government.

The allocation of powers between the Parliament and the Cabinet is somewhat similar to that of the United States—the Parliament enacts legislation and appropriates funds—but the Belgian Parliament does not have the same degree of independent power that the U.S. Congress has. Members of political parties represented in the government are expected to support all bills presented by the Cabinet.

The House of Representatives is the "political" chamber that votes on motions of confidence and budgets. The Senate deals with long-term issues and votes on an equal footing with the Chamber on a range of matters, including constitutional reform bills and international treaties.

The Prime Minister and his ministers administer the government and the various public services. As in Great Britain, ministers must defend their policies and performance in person before the Chamber.

## The Cabinet and the Ministries

At the federal level, executive power is wielded by the Cabinet. The Prime Minister is President of the Cabinet. Each minister heads a governmental department. The Cabinet reflects the weight of political parties that constitute the current governing coalition for the Chamber. No single party or party family across linguistic lines holds an absolute majority of seats in Parliament. The present Cabinet, the Guy Verhofstadt Cabinet, consists of the following members of the Flemish Liberal Party (VLD), the francophone Liberal Party (PRL), the Flemish Socialist Party (SP), the francophone Socialist Party (PS), the Flemish Green Party (AGALEV), and the francophone Green Party (ECOLO).

## Principal Government Officials

**For up-to-date information on Principal Government Officials, see the Chiefs of State and Cabinet Members of Foreign Governments section starting on page 1.**

The Belgian Embassy is located at 3330 Garfield Street NW, Washington, DC 20008 (tel. 202-333-6900; fax 202-333-3079).

## The Electoral System

The number of seats in the Chamber is constitutionally set at 150 elected from 20 electoral districts. Each district is given a number of seats proportional to its population (not number of voters) ranging from 3 for the Luxembourg district to 22 for Brussels. The districts are divided along linguistic lines: 10 Flemish, 9 Walloon, and the bilingual district of Brussels. Eligibility requirements for the Chamber are a minimum age of 21, citizenship, and residency in Belgium.

The Senate consists of 71 seats. For electoral purposes Senators are divided into three categories: directly elected; appointed by the community assemblies; and co-opted Senators. For the election of the 25 Flemish and 15 francophone directly elected Senators, the country is divided into three electoral districts. Of the Senators representing the communities, 10 are elected by the Flemish Council, 10 by the French Council, and 1 by the German-language Council. The remaining category, the co-opted Senators, consists of 10 representatives elected by the first two groups of Senators. Eligibility requirements for the Senate are identical to those for the Chamber. Under the electoral system, smaller parties rather easily attain the required quorum (minimum number of votes required in a given district) and have representation in the federal parliament.

In Belgium, there are no "national" parties operating on both sides of the linguistic border. Consequently, elections are a contest among Flemish parties on one side and Francophone parties on the other. Several months before an election, each party forms a list of candidates for each district. Parties are allowed to place as many candidates on their "ticket" as there are seats available. The formation of the list is an internal process that varies with each party. The number of seats each party receives and where on a list a candidate is placed determines whether a candidate is elected or not.

Political campaigns in Belgium are relatively short, lasting only about one month, and there are restrictions on the use of billboards. For all of their activities, campaigns included, the political parties have to rely on government subsidies and dues paid by their members. An electoral expenditures law restricts expenditures of political parties during an electoral campaign.

Since no single party holds an absolute majority, after the election the strongest party or party family will create a coalition with some of the other parties to form the government.

Voting is compulsory in Belgium; more than 90% of the population participates. Belgian voters are given four options when voting. They may:

Vote for a list as a whole, thereby showing approval of the order established by the party; Vote for one or more individual candidates, regardless of his/her ranking on the list. This is a "preference vote"; Vote for one or more of the "alternates"; or Vote for one or more candidates, and one or more alternates.

## 1999 Elections

General elections were last held on June 13, 1999. Driven in part by resentment over a mishandled dioxin food-contamination crisis in June 1999, Belgian voters rejected Jean Luc-Dehaene's longstanding coalition government of Christian Democrats and Socialists and voted into power a coalition put together by Flemish Liberal Leader Guy Verhofstadt. The Verhofstadt government is comprised of the Flemish and francophone Liberals, Flemish and francophone Socialists, and the Flemish and francophone Greens, the first Liberal-led coalition in generations, the first six-party coalition in 20 years, and the first Green participation ever in Belgium's federal government.

Belgium has 25 seats in the European Parliament in Strasbourg. Elections for the members of Belgium's municipal and provincial councils will be held in October 2000.

## Belgium's Linguistic Challenge

In the third century AD, Germanic Franks migrated into what is now Belgium. The less populated northern areas became Germanic, while in the southern part, where the Roman presence had been much stronger, Latin persisted despite the migrations of the Franks. This linguistic frontier has more or less endured.

The Industrial Revolution of the late 18th and the 19th century further accentuated the North-South division. Francophone Wallonia became an early industrial boom area, affluent and politically dominant. Dutch-speaking Flanders remained agricultural and was economically and politically outdistanced by Brussels and Wallonia. In the 20th century, and

particularly after the Second World War, Flanders saw an economic flowering while Wallonia became economically stagnant. As Flemings became more well off and sought a bigger share of political power, tension between the two communities rose.

Linguistic demonstrations in the early sixties led in 1962 to the establishment of a formal linguistic border and elaborate rules were made to protect minorities in linguistically mixed border areas. In 1970, the Constitution was amended. Flemish and francophone cultural councils were established with authority in matters relating to language and culture for the two language groups.

The 1970 constitutional revision did not finally settle the problem, however. A controversial amendment declared that Belgium consists of three economic regions—Flanders, Wallonia, and Brussels—each to be granted a significant measure of political autonomy. It was 1980, however, before an agreement could be reached on how to implement this new constitutional provision.

In August 1980, the Belgian Parliament passed a devolution bill and amended the Constitution, establishing:

A Flemish legislative assembly (council) and Flemish government competent for cultural and regional economic matters; A francophone community legislative council and government competent for cultural matters; and A Walloon regional legislative assembly and government competent for regional economic matters. Since 1984 the German language community of Belgium (in the eastern part of Liege Province) has had its own legislative assembly and executive, competent for cultural, language, and educational affairs.

In 1988-89 the Constitution was again amended to give additional responsibilities to the regions and communities. The most sweeping change was to devolve to the communities responsibilities for educational matters. Moreover, the regions and communities were provided additional revenue, and Brussels was given its own legislative assembly and executive.

Another important constitutional reform took place in the summer of 1993. It formally changed Belgium from a unitary to a federal state. It also reformed the bicameral parliamentary system and provided for the direct election of the members of the community and regional legislative councils. The bilingual Brabant province was split into separate Flemish Brabant and Walloon Brabant provinces.

## The Growing Power of Regional Governments

The new regional and community councils and governments have jurisdiction over transportation, public works, water policy, cultural matters, education, public health, environment, housing, zoning, and economic and industrial policy. They rely on a system of revenue-sharing for funds. They have the authority to levy taxes (mostly surcharges) and contract loans. Moreover, they have obtained exclusive treaty-making power for those issues coming under their respective jurisdictions.

Of total public spending (interest payments not considered), more than 40% is authorized by the regions and communities.

## Regional Executives

- President, Flemish Government—(VLD) Patrick Dewael

- President, Francophone Community Government—(PRL) Herve Hasquin

- President, Walloon Regional Government—(PS) Jean-Claude van Cauwenberghe

- President, Brussels Capital Government—(PRL) Jacques Simonet

- President, German Community Government—(PS) Karl-Heinz Lambertz

## Provincial and Local Government

In addition to three regions and three cultural communities, Belgium also is divided into 10 provinces and 589 municipalities.

The provincial governments are primarily administrative units and are politically weak. A governor appointed by the King presides over each province. He or she is supported by an elected Provincial Council of 47 to 84 members which sits only 4 weeks a year.

Municipal governments, on the other hand, are vigorous political entities with significant powers and a history of independence dating from medieval times. Many national politicians have a political base in a municipality, often doubling as mayor or alderman in their hometowns.

## Parliament

The Lower House is officially called Chambre des Representants (in French) or Kamer van Volksvertegenwoordigers (in Dutch). In English, it is often called the Chamber of Deputies or the House of Representatives. All are correct.

The major parties in the Lower House are the Flemish Liberal Party (VLD), 23 seats; the Flemish Social Christian Party (CVP), 22 seats; the Francophone Socialist Party (PS), 19 seats; the Francophone Liberal Party (PRL), 18 seats; the right-wing Vlaams Blok party, 15 seats; and the Flemish Socialist Party (SP), 14 seats.

The two Ecologist parties together have 20 seats. The moderate Flemish nationalist Volksunie has 8 seats. The President of the Lower House is Herman De Croo (VLD).

The Princes and Princesses of the royal line are full members of the Senate, but only Prince Philippe and Princess Astrid actually sit in the Senate. The President of the Senate is Armand De Decker (PRL).

From the creation of the Belgian state in 1830 and throughout most of the 19th century, two political parties dominated Belgian politics: the Catholic Party (Church-oriented and conservative) and the Liberal Party (anti-clerical and progressive). In the late 19th century the Socialist Party arose to represent the emerging industrial working class.

These three groups still dominate Belgian politics, but they have evolved substantially in character.

The Christian Democratic Parties. After World War II, the Catholic (now Christian Democratic) Party severed its formal ties with the Church. It became a mass party of the center, somewhat like a political party in the United States.

In 1968, the Christian Democratic Party, responding to linguistic tensions in the country, divided into two independent parties: the Parti Social Chretien (PSC) in French-speaking Belgium and the Christelijke Volkspartij (CVP) in Flanders. The two parties pursue the same basic policies but maintain separate organizations. The CVP is the larger of the two, getting more than twice as many votes as the PSC. CVP Party Chairman is Stefaan De Clerck. Deputy Joelle Milquet is president of the PSC. Following the 1999 general elections, the CVP and PSC were ousted from office, bringing an end to a 40-year term on the government benches.

The Socialist Parties. The modern Belgian Socialist parties have shed much of their early Marxist trappings. They are now primarily labor-based parties similar to the German Social Democratic Party and the French Socialist Party. The Socialists have headed several postwar governments and have produced some of the country's most distinguished statesmen. The Socialists also split along linguistic lines in 1978. Patrick Janssens is head of the Flemish Socialist Party (SP) and Deputy Elio Di Rupo is president of the Francophone Socialists (PS). In general, the Walloon Socialists tend to concentrate on domestic issues. In the eighties, the Flemish Socialists focused heavily on international issues, and on security in Europe in particular, where they frequently opposed U.S. policies. However, first with Willy Claes, then Frank Vandenbroucke and with Erik Derycke as Foreign Minister, all three Flemish Socialists, the party made a significant shift to the center adopting less controversial stances on foreign policy issues.

The francophone Socialists are mainly based in the industrial cities of Wallonia (Liege, Charleroi, and Mons). The Flemish Socialists' support is less regionally concentrated.

The Liberal Parties. The Liberal Parties chiefly appeal to businesspeople, property owners, shopkeepers, and the self-employed, in general. In American terms the Liberals' positions would be considered to reflect a traditionally conservative ideology.

There are two Liberal parties formed along linguistic lines: The Flemish Liberals and Democrats (VLD) who opened up their ranks to Volksunie defectors some years ago, are the largest political force in Belgium. The VLD is headed by Karl De Gucht, member of the Flemish regional parliament. The Party of Reform and Liberty (PRL) on the francophone side is headed by Euro-MP Daniel Ducarme. The PRL has formed an alliance with the Brussels-based FDF and is particularly strong in Brussels.

The Linguistic Parties. A postwar phenomenon in Belgium was the emergence of one-issue parties whose only reason for existence was the defense of the cultural, political, and economic interests of one of the linguistic groups or regions of Belgian society.

The most militant Flemish regional party in Parliament in the 1950s and 1960s, the Volksunie (VU), once drew nearly one-quarter of Belgium's Dutch-speaking electorate away from the traditional parties. The Volksunie was in the forefront of a successful campaign by the country's Flemish population for cultural and political parity with the nation's long dominant French-speaking population. However, in recent elections the

party has suffered severe setbacks and now is down to only 8 seats in the 150-seat House. The Volksunie's party chairman is Deputy Geert Bourgeois.

## Travel Notes

**Travel Advice:** For up-to-date information from the U.S. State Department on possible inconvenient or hazardous situations, see the **Travel Warnings and Consular Information Sheets from the U.S. Government** section starting on page 1723. For the latest information on health requirements and conditions, see the **International Travelers' Health Information** section starting on page 1385. For further information dealing with non-urgent matter, see the **Tips for Travelers to...** section starting on page 1588.

Another special-interest party is the Front Democratique des Bruxellois Francophones (FDF). Until 1982, the FDF dominated the capital's municipal politics. It is led by Deputy Olivier Maingain. In 1995, FDF and PRL decided on closer cooperation.

Others. The Flemish (AGALEV) and francophone (Ecolo) Ecologist parties made their Parliamentary breakthrough in 1981. They focus heavily on nuclear and environmental issues and are the most consistent critics of U.S. policy. Following significant gains made in the 1999 general elections, the two green parties joined a federal coalition cabinet for the first time in their history.

Another one-issue party is the ultra-right Vlaams Blok (VB—Flemish Bloc) which broke away from the Volksunie in 1976. The VB has replaced the VU as the most militant Flemish regional party and is strongly opposed to the presence of large numbers of immigrants in urban centers. Its ultra-nationalistic philosophy and anti-immigration positions are often tinged with xenophobia and racism. Long dismissed as a "fringe" party by mainstream politicians, the VB shocked observers when in the 1991 elections it posted respectable scores in much of Flanders, but especially in Antwerp,

and in 1995 and 1999 the VB did even better electorally. Party President is Euro-MP Frank Vanhecke.

Equally opposed to the presence of immigrants is the Brussels-based Francophone Front National.

## Labor Unions

Belgium is a highly unionized country, and organized labor is a powerful influence in politics. About 53% of all private sector and public service employees are labor union members. Not simply a "bread and butter" movement in the American sense, Belgian labor unions take positions on education, public finance, defense spending, environmental protection, women's rights, abortion, and other issues. They also provide a range of services, including the administration of unemployment benefits.

Belgium's three principal trade union organizations are the Confederation of Catholic Labor Unions (CSC/ACV), the Belgian Socialist Confederation of Labor (FGTB/ABVV) and the Confederation of Liberal Labor Unions (CGSLB/ACLVB) which has 213,000 members.

Until the fifties, the FGTB/ABVV was the largest confederation, since then, however, the CSC/ACV has become the leading trade union force. In the most recent works council elections held in 1995, the CSC/ACV garnered close to 52% of the vote, the Socialist confederation obtained 37.7%, and the Liberal confederation 8.2%.

The Confederation of Catholic Labor Unions (CSC/ACV). Organized in 1912, the CSC/ACV rejects the Marxist concept of "class struggle" and seeks to achieve a just social order based on Christian principles. The CSC/ACV is not formally linked to its party political counterparts, the Christian Democratic parties (CVP and PSC), but exercises great influence in their councils.

The CSC/ACV is the leading union in all Flemish provinces, in the Flemish part of Brabant, and in Wallonia's Luxembourg province. It has almost equal strength with the socialist confederation in the Brussels area. Its President is Luc Cortebeeck.

The Belgian Socialist Confederation of Labor (FGTB/ABVV). The FGTB/ABVV derives from the Socialist Trade Union Movement, established in the late 19th century in Walloon industrial areas, Brussels, and urban areas of Flanders. Today the FGTB/ABVV is the leading union in the Hainaut, Namur, and Liege provinces and matches the CSC/ACV in Brussels. The FGTB/ABVV is led by President Michel Nollet.

## Current Issues

By tight budgeting, the previous Dehaene II center-left coalition succeeded in qualifying the country for the Economic and Monetary Union. During its first year in office, the Verhofstadt cabinet has sought to implement justice and police reforms. While modernizing the judicial system is advancing according to plan, integrating the federal gendarmerie, judicial police, and local police into one single integrated force is meeting opposition from within the ranks.

Other priorities of the new cabinet are modernizing the civil service and adjusting the federal social security system to a rapidly aging population. Moreover, the cabinet has issued a blueprint for reforming the armed forces. The aim is to generate more outlays for new equipment by reducing staff.

With regard to Belgium's perennial institutional issues, the new cabinet has decided to discuss them within the framework of a government-sponsored "constitutional conference." The francophone parties demand additional financial means for francophone schools, while the Flemish parties are in favor of greater "fiscal autonomy" for the Flemish regional government.

Foreign Minister Louis Michel wants Belgium to play a more active role in Central Africa. Another of Michel's priorities is the combat against the far right in Europe. This has resulted in conflicts with the current Austrian Government. During the second half of 2001, Belgium will be in charge of the EU Presidency.

# ECONOMY

Belgium, a highly developed market economy, belongs to the Organization for Economic Cooperation and Development (OECD), a group of leading industrialized democracies. In recent years, with a geographic area about equal to that of Maryland, and a population of just over 10 million, Belgium's GDP level has placed it in the top 20 for all countries of the world. In 1999, the per capita income was $25,576.

Densely populated Belgium is located at the heart of one of the world's most highly industrialized regions. The first country to undergo an industrial revolution on the Continent of Europe in the early 1800s, Belgium developed an excellent transportation infrastructure of ports, canals, railways, and highways to integrate its industry with that of its neighbors. One of the founding members of the European Community (EC), Belgium strongly supports deepening the powers of the EC to integrate European economies. Belgium became a first-tier member of the European Monetary Union in January of 1999.

With exports equivalent to about two-thirds of GNP, Belgium depends heavily on world trade. Belgium exports twice as much per capita as Germany and five times as much as Japan. Belgium's trade advantages are derived from its central geographic location, and a highly skilled, multilingual, and productive work force.

The Belgian industrial sector can be compared to a complex processing machine: It imports raw materials and semifinished goods that are further processed and reexported. Except for its coal, which is no longer economical to exploit, Belgium has virtually no natural resources. Nonetheless, most traditional industrial sectors are represented in the economy, including steel, textiles, refin-

ing, chemicals, food processing, pharmaceuticals, automobiles, electronics, and machinery fabrication. Despite the heavy industrial component, services account for 72.5% of GDP. Agriculture accounts for only 1.4% of the GDP.

## Belgian Economy in the 20th Century

For 200 years through World War I, French-speaking Wallonia was a technically advanced, industrial region, while Dutch-speaking Flanders was predominantly agricultural. This disparity began to fade during the interwar period. When Belgium emerged from World War II with its industrial infrastructure relatively undamaged, the stage was set for a period of rapid development, particularly in Flanders. The postwar boom years, enhanced by the establishment of the EU and NATO headquarters in Brussels, contributed to the rapid expansion of light industry throughout most of Flanders, particularly along a corridor stretching between Brussels and Antwerp (now the second-largest port in Europe after Rotterdam), where a major concentration of petrochemical industries developed.

The older, traditional industries of Wallonia, particularly steelmaking, began to lose their competitive edge during this period, but the general growth of world prosperity masked this deterioration until the 1973 and 1979 oil price shocks and resultant shifts in international demand sent the economy into a period of prolonged recession. In the 1980s and 1990s, the economic center of the country continued to shift northwards to Flanders.

The early 1980s saw the country facing a difficult period of structural adjustment caused by declining demand for its traditional products, deteriorating economic performance, and neglected structural reform. Consequently, the 1980-82 recession shook Belgium to the core—unemployment mounted, social welfare costs increased, personal debt soared, the government deficit climbed to 13% of GDP, and the national debt, although mostly held domestically, mushroomed.

Against this grim backdrop, in 1982, Prime Minister Martens' center-right coalition government formulated an economic recovery program to promote export-led growth by enhancing the competitiveness of Belgium's export industries through an 8.5% devaluation.

Economic growth rose from 2% in 1984 to a peak of 4% in 1989. In May 1990, the government linked the franc to the German mark, primarily through closely tracking German interest rates. Consequently, as German interest rates rose after 1990, Belgian rates have increased and contributed to a decline in the economic growth rate.

In 1992-93, the Belgian economy suffered the worst recession since World War II, with the real GDP declining 1.7% in 1993. Growth improved in 1999, with real GDP growing by an estimated 2.2% (year-on-year) versus the 2% figure recorded in 1998.

Business investment (up 4.0% in real terms) and exports (up 4.4%) provided the economy's impetus. Private consumption, held back by weak consumer confidence and stagnant real wages, grew by 1% in real terms and public consumption by 0.9%.

## Foreign Investment

Foreign investment contributed significantly to Belgian economic growth in the 1960s. In particular, U.S. firms played a leading role in the expansion of light industrial and petrochemical industries in the 1960s and 1970s. The Belgian Government encourages new foreign investment as a means to promote employment. With regional devolution, Flanders, Brussels, and Wallonia are now courting potential foreign investors and offer a host of incentives and benefits.

More than 1,200 U.S. firms had invested a total of over $20 billion in Belgium by 1999. U.S. and other foreign companies in Belgium account for approximately 11% of the total work force, with the U.S. share at

about 5%. U.S. companies are heavily represented in chemical, automotive assembly, and petroleum refining. A number of U.S. service industries followed in the wake of these investments—banks, law firms, public relations, accounting and executive search firms. The resident American community in Belgium now exceeds 20,000. Attracted by the EU 1992 single-market program, many U.S. law firms and lawyers have settled in Brussels since 1989. Other foreign firms, particularly French ones, have invested locally for the same reason.

## Monetary Union

On May 1, 1998, Belgium became a first-tier member of the European Monetary Union. On January 1, 1999, the definitive exchange rate between the Euro and the BF was established at BF 40.33. Belgium will gradually shift from the use of the BF to the use of the Euro as its currency by January 1, 2002. To minimize confusion the old BF currency and the new Euro will only overlap for a period of 2 months. After that, the BF will be withdrawn from circulation and can only be changed into Euros at the local offices of the National Bank of Belgium.

## Trade

About 80% of Belgium's trade is with fellow EC member states. Given this high percentage, it seeks to diversify and expand trade opportunities with non-EC countries. Belgium ranks as the 10th-largest market for the export of U.S. goods and services. If goods in transit to other European countries are excluded, Belgium still ranks as the 12th-largest market for U.S. goods.

Bilaterally, there are few points of friction with the U.S. in the trade and economic area. The Belgian authorities are, as a rule, anti-protectionist and try to maintain a hospitable and open trade and investment climate. The U.S. Government focuses its market-opening efforts on the EC Commission and larger EC member states. In addition, the EC Commission negotiates on trade issues for all member states, which, in turn lessens

bilateral trade disputes with Belgium.

## Employment

The social security system, which expanded rapidly during the prosperous 1950s and 1960s, has numerous programs, including a medical system, unemployment insurance coverage, child allowances, invalid benefits and other benefits and pensions. With the onset of a recession in the 1970s, this system became an increasing burden on the economy and accounted for much of the government budget deficits. Unemployment, which declined from a high of 14.3% in 1984 to an average of 8.5% in 1999, has become less of a problem recently. However, more than 60% of the unemployed have been so for over 2 years and over 80% for at least one year.

The national unemployment figures mask considerable differences between Flanders and Wallonia. Unemployment in Wallonia is mainly structural, while in Flanders it is cyclical. Flanders' unemployment level equals only half that of Wallonia. In general, sunset industries (mainly coal and steel) dominate in Wallonia and sunrise industries (chemicals, high-tech and services) in Flanders.

From the second half of 1999 onward, Belgian unemployment figures declined substantially to 8.5%, one percentage point below the European average. Labor market participation also increased significantly from 54% in 1993 to 58.5% in 2000. In some sectors, labor shortages are already beginning to appear. To partly offset the increased labor costs which go with a tight labor market, the Belgian Government introduced stock option legislation for salaried employees in 1999.

## Budget

Although Belgium is a wealthy country, it overspent income and undercollected taxes for years. The Belgian Government reacted with poor macroeconomic policies to the 1973 and 1979 oil price hikes: it hired the redundant work force into the public sector and subsidized ailing industries—coal, steel, textiles, glass, and shipbuilding—in order to prop up the economy. As a result, cumulative government debt reached 121% by the end of the 1980s (versus a cumulative U.S. federal public debt/GNP ration of 31.2% in 1990). However, thanks to Belgium's high personal savings rate, the Belgian Government managed to finance the deficit from mainly domestic savings, which minimized the deleterious effects on the overall economy.

The main objective of Belgian Government economic policy in recent years has been to attain a budget deficit of 3% by the end of 1997, a goal that was successfully attained. This was one of the five criteria for membership into the first-tier group of Economic and Monetary Union (EMU) under the Maastricht treaty. Historically, Belgium has done relatively better on its budget in times of cyclical downswings. The total budget deficit in 1999 (federal, regional plus social security) amounted to 1.2% of GDP. This represents a substantial decrease from the 7.1% deficit recorded in 1992, as well as a significant difference from the expected figure of 2%, well within the Maastricht criterion.

Belgium cannot possibly bring its accumulated debt down from the 1999 level of 113% of GDP to the Maastricht target of 60%. In order to meet the "substantial progress" criterion" for its debt, Belgium has run a substantial primary surplus (excluding interest payments), reaching 6.2% of GDP in 1999.

# FOREIGN RELATIONS

The Concert of Nations sanctioned the creation of Belgium in 1830 on the condition that the country remain strictly neutral.

During the two World Wars Belgium tried, but was unable, to follow a policy of neutrality. In 1948, Belgium signed the Treaty of Brussels with Great Britain, France, the Netherlands, and Luxembourg, and one year later became one of the founding members of the Atlantic Alliance.

Belgium remains a strong proponent of NATO. It cooperates closely with the United States within the alliance framework, in addition to supporting European defense efforts through the Western European Union (WEU).

At the same time the Belgians, perceiving their diminutive role on the international scene, are strong advocates of strengthening economic and political integration within the EU. Recently, having federalized their own country, many Belgians view themselves as the ultimate "European federalists."

Both NATO (since 1966) and the EU have their headquarters in Brussels; SHAPE (Supreme Headquarters Allied Powers Europe) is in the south of the country, near Mons. Since January 1993, the WEU has been headquartered in Brussels.

Because of its location at the crossroads of Western Europe, Belgium has historically been the route of invading armies from its larger neighbors. With virtually defenseless borders, Belgium has traditionally sought to avoid domination by the more powerful nations which surround it through a policy of mediation.

Belgium actively seeks improved relations with the new democracies of central and eastern Europe through such fora as the Organization for Security and Cooperation in Europe, EU association agreements, and NATO's Partnership for Peace with the former Warsaw Pact countries and several others.

# U.S.-BELGIAN RELATIONS

Relations between the United States and Belgium are excellent. Good will and affection for Americans continues as a result of the U.S. role during and after the two World Wars. However, there also is a willingness to criticize U.S. policies and a tendency to adopt a more explicitly European viewpoint on many issues.

As an outward looking nation, Belgium works closely with the United States bilaterally and in international and regional organizations to encourage economic and political cooperation and assistance to developing countries. Belgium has welcomed hundreds of U.S. firms to its territory, many of which have their European headquarters here.

## Principal U.S. Officials

For up-to-date information on Principal U.S. Officials, see the U.S. Embassies, Consulates, and Foreign Service section starting on page 139.

The U.S. Embassy in Belgium is located at 27 Boulevard du Regent, 1000 Brussels (tel. 02/501-2111, fax 02/511-2725). The European Logistical Support Office (ELSO) is at Norrderlaan 147, Box 12A, 2030 Antwerp (tel. 03/542-4775, fax 03/542-6567).

The U.S. Mission to NATO (USNATO) is at NATO Headquarters, on the Autoroute de Zaventem, 1110 Brussels (tel. 02/724-3111, fax 02/726-5796). The U.S. Mission to the EU is located at 40 Boulevard du Regent, 1000 Brussels (tel. 02/508-2222, fax 02/502-8117).

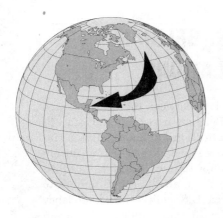

# BELIZE
April 2001

Official Name:
**Belize**

# PROFILE

## Geography
**Area:** 22,923 sq. km. (8,867 sq. mi.); slightly larger than Massachusetts.
**Cities:** Capital—Belmopan (2000 pop. est. 8,305) Other cities and towns—Belize City (54,125), Corozal (8,075), Orange Walk (13,795), San Ignacio & Santa Elena (13,545), Dangriga (9,020), Punta Gorda (4,425) and San Pedro (4,965).
**Terrain:** Flat and swampy coastline, low mountains in interior.
**Climate:** Subtropical (dry and wet seasons). Hot and humid. Rainfall ranges from 60 inches in the north to 200 inches in the south annually.

## People
**Nationality:** Noun and adjective—Belizean(s).
**Population:** (2000 est.): 249,800.
**Annual growth rate:** (2000 est.) 2.6%. Ethnic groups: Creole, Garifuna, Mestizo, Mayan.
**Religions:** Roman Catholic, Anglican, Methodist, other Protestant, Muslim, Hindu and Buddhist.
**Languages:** English (official), Creole, Spanish, Garifuna, Mayan.
**Education:** Years compulsory—9. Attendance—60%. Literacy—75.1%.years.
**Work force:** (April 2000–89,950)

Services—50.8%; agriculture, hunting, forestry, and fishing—27.2%; industry and commerce—17.8%; other—4.2%.

## Government
**Type:** Parliamentary.
**Independence:** September 21, 1981.
**Constitution:** September 21, 1981.
**Branches:** Executive—British monarch (head of state), represented by a governor general; prime minister (head of government, 5-year term). Legislative—bicameral National Assembly. Judicial—Supreme Court, Court of Appeal, district magistrates.
**Subdivisions:** Six districts.
**Political parties:** People's United Party (PUP), United Democratic Party (UDP), National Alliance for Belizean Rights (NABR), People's Liberation Front (PLF).
**Suffrage:** Universal adult.

## Economy
**GDP:** (2000) $727.5 million.
**Annual growth rate:** (2000) 8.2%; (1999): 6.4%.
**Per capita income:** (2000) $2,913.
**Avg. inflation rate:** (2000) 0.6%.
**Natural resources:** Arable land, timber, seafood, minerals.
**Agriculture:** (12.7% of GDP): Products—Sugar, citrus fruits and juices, bananas, mangoes, papayas, honey, corn, beans, rice, cattle.

**Industry:** (14% of GDP)Types—Clothing, fruit processing, beverages.
**Tourism:** (22% of GDP)Tourist arrivals (2000)—189,634.
**Trade:** (2000) Exports—$228.6 million: cane sugar, clothing, citrus concentrate, lobster, fish, banana, and farmed shrimp. Major markets—U.S. (48.5%), U.K., CARICOM. Imports—$446 million: food, consumer goods, building materials, vehicles, machinery, petroleum products. Major suppliers—U.S. (49.7%), Mexico, U.K.

# PEOPLE

Belize is the most sparsely populated nation in Central America. It is larger than El Salvador and compares in size to the State of Massachusetts. Slightly more than half of the people live in rural areas. About one-fourth live in Belize City, the principal port, commercial center, and former capital.

Most Belizeans are of multiracial descent. About 46.4% of the population is of mixed Mayan and European descent (Mestizo); 27.7% are of African and Afro-European (Creole) ancestry; about 10% are Mayan; and about 6.4% are Afro-Amerindian (Garifuna). The remainder, about 9.5%, includes European, East Indian, Chinese, Middle Eastern, and North American groups.

English, the official language, is spoken by virtually all except the refugees that arrived during the past decade. Spanish is the native tongue of about 50% of the people and is spoken as a second language by another 20%. The various Mayan groups still speak their original languages, and an English Creole dialect (or "Kriol" in the new orthography), similar to the Creole dialects of the English-speaking Caribbean Islands, is spoken by most. The rate of functional literacy is 75.1%. About 60% of the population is Roman Catholic; the Anglican Church and other Protestant Christian groups account for most of the remaining 40%. Mennonite settlers number about 7,160.

# HISTORY

The Mayan civilization spread into the area of Belize between 1500 BC and AD 300 and flourished until about AD 1200. Several major archeological sites, notably Caracol, Lamanai, Lubaantun, Altun Ha, and Xunantunich, reflect the advanced civilization and much denser population of that period. European contact began in 1502 when Christopher Columbus sailed along the coast. The first recorded European settlement was begun by shipwrecked English seamen in 1638. Over the next 150 years, more English settlements were established. This period also was marked by piracy, indiscriminate logging, and sporadic attacks by Indians and neighboring Spanish settlements.

Great Britain first sent an official representative to the area in the late 18th century but Belize was not formally termed the "Colony of British Honduras" until 1840. It became a crown colony in 1862. Subsequently, several constitutional changes were enacted to expand representative government. Full internal self-government under a ministerial system was granted in January 1964. The official name of the territory was changed from British Honduras to Belize in June 1973, and full independence was granted on September 21, 1981.

# GOVERNMENT AND POLITICAL CONDITIONS

Belize is a parliamentary democracy on the Westminster model and is a member of the Commonwealth. Queen Elizabeth II is head of state and is represented in the country by Governor General Dr. Colville N. Young, Sr., a Belizean and Belize's second governor general. The primary executive organ of government is the Cabinet led by a prime minister (head of government). Cabinet ministers are members of the majority political party in Parliament and usually hold elected seats in the National Assembly concurrently with their Cabinet positions.

The National Assembly consists of a House of Representatives and a Senate. The 29 members of the House are popularly elected to a maximum 5-year term. Of the Senate's eight members, five are elected by the prime minister, two by the leader of the opposition, and one by the governor general on the advice of the Belize Advisory Council. The Senate is headed by a president who is a non-voting member appointed by the governing party.

Currently, the Belize Government is controlled by the People's United Party (PUP) which won 26 of the 29 seats in the House of Representatives on August 27, 1998. The United Democratic Party (UDP) won the other three seats. Dean Barrow is the leader of the opposition. The UDP governed Belize from 1993–98; the PUP had governed from 1989–93; and the UDP from 1984–89. Before 1984, the PUP had dominated the electoral scene for more than 30 years and was the party in power when Belize became independent in 1981.

Prime Minister Said Musa has an ambitious plan to encourage economic growth while furthering social-sector development. Belize traditionally maintains a deep interest in the environment and sustainable development. A lack of government resources seriously hampers these goals. On other fronts the Government is working to improve its law enforcement capabilities. A long-running territorial dispute with Guatemala continues although cooperation between the two countries has increased in recent years across a wide spectrum of common interests, including trade and environment. Seeing itself as a bridge, Belize is actively involved with the Caribbean nations of CARICOM, and also has taken steps to work more closely with its Central American neighbors as a new member of SICA.

Members of the independent judiciary are appointed. The judicial system includes local magistrates, the Supreme Court, and the Court of Appeal. Cases may under certain circumstances be appealed to the Privy Council in London. However, in 2001, Belize joined with most members of CARICOM to campaign for the establishment of a "Caribbean Court of Justice." The country is divided into six districts: Corozal, Orange Walk, Belize, Cayo, Stann Creek, and Toledo.

The Belize Defense Force (BDF), established in January 1973, consists of a light infantry force of regulars and reservists along with small air and maritime wings. The BDF, currently under the command of Brig. Gen. Cedric Borland, assumed total defense responsibility from British Forces Belize (BFB) on January 1, 1994. The United Kingdom continues to maintain the British Army Training Support Unit Belize (BATSUB) to assist in the administration of the Belize Jungle School. The BDF receives military assistance from the United States and the United Kingdom.

## Principal Government Officials

**For up-to-date information on Principal Government Officials, see the Chiefs of State and Cabinet Members of Foreign Governments section starting on page 1.**

Belize maintains an embassy in the United States at 2535 Massachusetts Avenue NW, Washington, DC 20008 (Tel: 202–332–9636; Fax: 202–332–6888) and a consulate in Los Angeles. Belize travel information office in New York City: 800–624–0686.

# ECONOMY

Forestry was the only economic activity of any consequence in Belize until well into the 20th century when the supply of accessible timber began to dwindle. Cane sugar then became the principal export and recently has been augmented by expanded production of citrus, bananas, seafood, and apparel. The country has about 809,000 hectares of arable land, only a small fraction of which is under cultivation. To curb land speculation the government enacted legislation in 1973 that requires non-Belizeans to complete a development plan on land they purchase before obtaining title to plots of more than 10 acres of rural land or more than one-half acre of urban land.

Domestic industry is limited, constrained by relatively high-cost labor and energy and a small domestic market. The U.S. Embassy in Belize City knows of some 185 U.S. companies that have operations in Belize, including MCI, Duke Energy International, Archer Daniels Midland, Texaco, and Esso. Tourism attracts the most foreign direct investment although significant U.S. investment also is found in the energy, telecommunications, and agricultural sectors.

A combination of natural factors—climate, the longest barrier reef in the Western Hemisphere, numerous islands, excellent fishing, safe waters for boating, jungle wildlife, and Mayan ruins—support the thriving tourist industry. Development costs are high, but the Government of Belize has designated tourism as its second development priority after agriculture. In 2000, tourist arrivals totaled 189,634 (more than 110,000 from the U.S.) and tourist receipts amounted to $113.3 million.

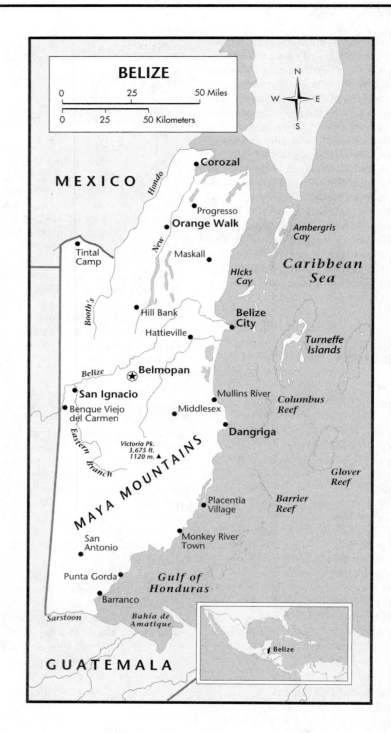

Belize's investment policy is codified in the Belize Investment Guide, which sets out the development priorities for the country. The "Country Commercial Guide" for Belize is available from the U.S. Embassy's Economic/Commercial section and on the Web at http://www.state.gov/www/about_state/business/com_guides/2001/wha/index.html.

## Infrastructure

A major constraint on the economic development of Belize continues to be the scarcity of infrastructure investments. Although electricity, telephone, and water utilities are all relatively good, Belize has the most expensive electricity in the region. Large tracts of land which would be suitable for development are inaccessible due to lack of roads. Some roads, including sections of major highways, are subject to damage or closure during the rainy season. Ports in Belize City, Dangriga, and Big Creek handle regularly scheduled shipping from the U.S. and the U.K. although draft is limited to a maximum of 10 feet in Belize City and 15 feet in southern ports. International air service is provided by American Airlines, Continental Airlines, and TACA to gateways in Dallas, Houston, Miami, and San Salvador.

Several capital projects are either currently underway or are programmed to start in fiscal year 2001/2002. The largest of these is a $15 million rural electrification program to be jointly implemented by the government and Belize Electricity Limited (BEL). In addition, the government will continue to implement an Inter-American Development Emergency Reconstruction Fund of $20 million aimed at restoring essential services such as health and education facilities and transportation networks to communities which were severely damaged by Hurricane Keith. The government will also invest close to $4.2 million in projects targeted at poverty alleviation across Belize. Initiated in 1999, the Ministry of Agriculture and Fisheries, through the Belize Agricultural Health Authority, will continue to implement the IDB-funded "Modernization of Agricultural Health Project." This $2.5 million project seeks to improve the competitiveness of Belize's agricultural products and thus enhance the ability of Belizean farmers and processors to maintain and expand the sale of their high-quality products to foreign markets. A $5 million soybean project, funded by the Brazilian Government, is scheduled to begin in 2001 and is intended to assist northern Belize farmers to diversify away from sugarcane cultivation.

The government also plans to invest $9.85 million to complete the rehabilitation of the Hummingbird Highway, as well as investing $9.5 million in its health-sector reform program. Another $9 million will be invested under the IDB-funded "Land Man-

agement Project" over the next 2 years. The Ministry of Tourism is confident that another IDB-funded project, the "Tourism Development Project," will make Belize the Mundo Maya centerpiece for travelers to Central America. The government will spend close to $1.4 million in improving access to archaeological sites in Belize, especially "Caracol." Using a generous soft loan from Taiwan, the government is funneling $50 million toward the construction of low-cost housing.

## Trade

Belize's economic performance is highly susceptible to external market changes. Although moderate growth has been achieved in recent years, the achievements are vulnerable to world commodity price fluctuations and continuation of preferential trading agreements, especially with the U.S. (cane sugar) and U.K. (bananas).

Belize continues to rely heavily on foreign trade with the United States as its number one trading partner. Total imports in 2000 totaled $446 million while total exports were only $228.6 million. In 2000, the U.S. accounted for 48.5% of Belize's total exports and provided 49.7% of all Belizean imports. Other major trading partners include the U.K., European Union, Canada, Mexico, and Caribbean Common Market (CARICOM) member states.

Belize aims to stimulate the growth of commercial agriculture through CARICOM. However, Belizean trade with the rest of the Caribbean is small compared to that with the United States and Europe. The country is a beneficiary of the Caribbean Basin Initiative (CBI), a U.S. Government program to stimulate investment in Caribbean nations by providing duty-free access to the U.S. market for most Caribbean products. Significant U.S. private investments in citrus and shrimp farms have been made in Belize under CBI. U.S. trade preferences allowing for duty-free reimport of finished apparel cut from U.S. textiles have significantly expanded the apparel industry. EU and U.K. preferences also have been

vital for the expansion and prosperity of the sugar and banana industries.

# FOREIGN RELATIONS

Belize's principal external concern has been the dispute involving the Guatemalan claim to Belizean territory. This dispute originated in imperial Spain's claim to all "New World" territories west of the line established in the Treaty of Tordesillas in 1494. Nineteenth-century efforts to resolve the problems led to later differences over interpretation and implementation of an 1859 British-Guatemalan treaty intended to establish the boundaries between Guatemala and Belize, then named British Honduras. Guatemala contends that the 1859 treaty is void because the British failed to comply with all of its economic assistance clauses. Neither Spain nor Guatemala ever exercised effective sovereignty over the area.

Negotiations proceeded for many years, including one period in the 1960s in which the U.S. Government sought unsuccessfully to mediate. A 1981 trilateral (Belize, Guatemala, and the United Kingdom) "Heads of Government Agreement" was not implemented due to disagreements. Thus, Belize became independent on September 21, 1981, with the territorial dispute unresolved. Significant negotiations between Belize and Guatemala, with the United Kingdom as an observer, resumed in 1988. Guatemala recognized Belize's independence in 1991 and diplomatic relations were established. Negotiations between Belize and Guatemala resumed on February 25, 2000, in Miami, Florida, but were suspended due to a border incident that occurred February 24, 2000. Further talks were held March 14, 2000, between the two countries at the Organization of American States (OAS) in Washington, DC, in the presence of the OAS Secretary General. Eventually the two parties agreed to establish an "adjacency zone" extending one kilometer on either side of the 1859 treaty line, now designated the "adjacency line," and to continue negotiations aimed at resolving their dispute. The Guatemalan claim remains unresolved, however.

In order to strengthen its potential for economic and political development Belize has sought to build closer ties with the Spanish-speaking countries of Central America to complement its historical ties to the English-speaking Caribbean states. Recent foreign policy initiatives include joining with the other Central American countries in signing the CONCAUSA Agreement on regional sustainable development and becoming a full member of the Central American Integration System (SICA) Belize is a member of CARICOM which was founded in 1973. In 1990, it became a member of the OAS. As a member of CARICOM Belize strongly backed efforts by the United States to implement UN Security Council Resolution 940 designed to facilitate the departure of Haiti's de facto authorities from power. The country agreed to contribute military personnel to the Multinational Task Force which restored the democratically elected Government of Haiti in October 1994 and to the United Nations Mission in Haiti (UNMIH).

# U.S.-BELIZEAN RELATIONS

The United States and Belize traditionally have had close and cordial relations. The United States is Belize's principal trading partner and major source of investment funds and also is home to the largest Belizean community outside Belize, estimated to be 70,000 strong. Because Belize's economic growth and accompanying democratic political stability are important U.S. objectives in a region successfully emerging from a prolonged period of civil strife, Belize benefits from the U.S.-Caribbean Basin Initiative.

International crime issues dominate the agenda of bilateral relations

## Travel Notes

**Travel Advice:** For up-to-date information from the U.S. State Department on possible inconvenient or hazardous situations, see the **Travel Warnings and Consular Information Sheets from the U.S. Government** section starting on page 1723. For the latest information on health requirements and conditions, see the **International Travelers' Health Information** section starting on page 1385. For further information dealing with non-urgent matter, see the **Tips for Travelers to...** section starting on page 1588.

between the U.S. and Belize. The U.S. is working closely with the Government of Belize to fight illicit narcotic trafficking. In 1996, the United States and Belize signed a stolen vehicle treaty, and in 2000 they signed an extradition treaty and a mutual legal assistance treaty (MLAT). Both governments seek to control the flow of illegal immigrants to the U.S. through Belize.

The United States is the largest provider of economic assistance to Belize, contributing approximately $4.17 million in various bilateral economic and military aid programs to Belize in FY 2000. The United States provided nearly $1 million in assistance to Belize to support its relief and recovery efforts following Hurricane Keith, which devastated much of the country in October 2000. The U.S. Agency for International Development (USAID) closed its Belize office in August 1996 after a 13-year program during which it provided $110 million worth of development assistance to Belize. In addition, during the past 34 years, almost 2,000 Peace Corps volunteers have served in Belize. In April 2001, the Peace Corps had 47 volunteers working in Belize. In Punta Gorda, the International Bureau of Broadcasting/Voice of America (IBB/VOA) operates a medium-wave radio relay station which broadcasts to the neighboring countries of Honduras, Guatemala, and El Salvador. The U.S. military

has a diverse and growing assistance program in Belize which included the construction of seven schools and four water wells by National Guard soldiers in Stann Creek District in 2000. Another "New Horizons" humanitarian assistance project is scheduled for 2003. Private American investors, who are responsible for some $250 million of investment in Belize, continue to play a key role in Belize's economy, particularly in the tourism sector.

## Principal U.S. Officials

**For up-to-date information on Principal U.S. Officials, see the U.S. Embassies, Consulates, and Foreign Service section starting on page 139.**

The U.S. Embassy is located in Belize City at the corner of Gabourel Lane and Hutson Street.
The mailing address is P. O. Box 286, Belize City, Belize, Central America. Tel: 011–501–2-77161 from the United States, or 77161 locally. Fax: 011–501–2-30802 Executive Office; 35321 Administrative Office; 71468 Economic/Commercial/Political Office; 35423 Consular Section. E-mail address: embbelize@belizwpoa.us-state.gov, Web Site address: http://www.usemb-belize.gov.

## Other useful contacts

**Caribbean/Latin American** Action
1818 N Street, NW
Washington, DC 20036
Tel: 202–466–7464
Fax: 202–822–0075

**U.S. Department of Commerce**
International Trade Administration
Office of Latin American and the Caribbean
14th & Constitution, NW
Washington, DC 20230
Tel: 202–482–1658; 202-USA-TRADE
Fax: 202–482–0464

# BENIN

March 1989

Official Name:
## The People's Republic of Benin

# PROFILE

## Geography

**Area:** 112,622 sq. km. (43,483 sq. mi.); slightly smaller than Pennsylvania.
**Cities:** Nominal capital—Porto Novo (pop.130,000). Political and economic capital—Cotonou (pop. 330,000).
**Terrain:** Generally flat.
**Climate:** Tropical.

## People

**Nationality:** Noun and adjective—Beninese (sing. and pl.).
**Population (1988):** 4 million.
**Annual growth rate (1988):** 3.6% (1980-85).
**Ethnic groups:** Fon, Adja, Bariba, Yoruba, others.
**Religions:** 65% traditional, 17% Christian, 12% Muslim.
**Language:** French (official).
**Education:** Years compulsory—6. Primary school enrollment (1983 est.)—67%. Adult literacy—11%.
**Health:** Infant mortality rate—116/1000. Life expectancy—49 yrs.
**Work force (1987 est.):** 1.9 million, 72% engaged in agriculture.

## Government

**Type:** Nominally Marxist-Leninist.
**Independence:** August 1, 1960.

**Constitution:** Adopted 1977.
**Branches:** Executive—President and National Executive Council (Cabinet). Legislative—National Revolutionary Assembly. Judicial—Peoples Central Court, prosecutor general, lower tribunals.
**Political party:** Peoples Revolutionary Party.
**Suffrage:** Universal.
**Administrative subdivisions:** 6 provinces, 84 districts.
**Central government operating budget (1987):** about $159.4 million; education 28.9%.
**Defense:** 21.6% of government budget.
**Flag:** Green with a red star at top left.

## Economy

**GDP (1987 prelim., current prices):** $1,497 million.
**Annual growth rate (1986-7):** 7.1% (-2.1% at constant 1980 prices).
**Per capita income (1987, current prices):** $374.
**Natural resources:** Small offshore oil deposits; no other known minerals in commercial quantity (other than unexploited deposits of high-quality marble).
**Agriculture (44.9% of GDP 1987 prelim.):** Products—cotton, oil palm products, groundnuts, food subsistence crops (cassava, yams, maize, beans, sorghum).
**Industry (13.8% of GDP 1987 pre-**lim.): Types—crude oil production, food processing, textiles, beverages, construction materials, steel reinforcing rods.
**Services:** 33.1% of GDP, 1987 prelim.
**Trade (1986):** Exports—$181.1 million: cotton, cement, palm oil products, cocoa, karite nut butter, and sea products. Estimate does not include value of 500,000 metric tons of petroleum exported. Major markets—Holland, France, other EC countries, Nigeria. Imports—$369.8 million: hydrocarbon products, construction materials, and consumer goods for re-export. Major suppliers—France, other EC countries, China, Japan, US ($16.9 million).
**Official exchange rate:** Floating; tied to French franc, 50 CFA francs=1 French franc.
**Economic aid received (1986):** Total—$79 million (grants and loans). US aid—$71 million (loans and grants) since 1953; $3.1 million in 1987.

## Membership in International Organizations

UN and some of its specialized and related agencies; Organization of African Unity (OAU); African, Malagasy, and Mauritanian Common Organization (OCAM); Entente Council; West African Monetary

311

Union; Economic Community of West Africa States (ECOWAS); Organization of the Islamic Conference (OIC); Communaute Economique de l'Afrique de l' Ouest (CEAO), INTEL-SAT.

# GEOGRAPHY

Located on the south side of the West Africa bulge, Benin is bounded by Nigeria, Niger Burkina Faso, Togo, and a 120-kilometer (75-mi.) coastline along the Gulf of Guinea. North of the coastal lagoons, the country is mostly flat and covered with dense vegetation. Although tempered by a sea breeze, the climate of the coastal region is hot and humid most of the year. Rainfall of 76-127 centimeters (30 in.) per year gradually diminishes toward the north until the climate and topography become Sahelian along the Niger River boundary with Niger. The south has two rainy seasons (April-July and October-November); the north has one (June-October).

While for historical and political reasons Porto Novo remains the nominal capital, the actual political and economic capital is Cotonou, where the presidency, National Revolutionary Assembly, most ministries, all embassies, and most of the country's commercial activities are located.

# PEOPLE

The population of the People's Republic of Benin comprises about 20 sociocultural groups. Four groups—the Fon, Aja (who are related), Bariba, and Yoruba—account for more than half of the population. Europeans constitute a very small fraction of the population, with French the most numerous. About 80% of the population is rural; 49% of the population is 15 years old or younger. Benin is not linguistically homogeneous. French is the official language, although it is spoken more in urban than rural areas.

## Travel Notes

**Climate and clothing:** Lightweight, washable clothing is appropriate in the hot, humid climate. The *harrnattan,* a dust-laden wind, blows in December and January. Shorts are generally not worn on the streets.

**Customs:** A visa and health certificate with a valid yellow fever inoculation are required for entry. Health requirements change; check latest information. Visas may be obtained from the Benin Embassy in Washington, DC, or from the Benin Mission to the United Nations in New York. Benin will not issue visas in passports containing Taiwanese, Israeli, or South African visas. Exit visas are required after stays in Benin. Benin has no restrictions on importation of currency, but there may be limits on taking out CFA francs. For full and current information on visas and other requirements, check with the Embassy of Benin.

**Health:** Water is generally not potable and must be boiled and filtered. Food must be prepared carefully. Malaria, including strains which resist the usual chloroquine prophylaxis, is endemic, and hepatitis is a hazard. Cotonou is latitude 6 north of the Equator; precaution against sun exposure is advised to avoid sunstroke and heat exhaustion. Limited quantities of French patent medicine are available.

**Telecommunications:** Telephone service from Cotonou is good but expensive. Cotonou is 6 hours ahead of eastern standard time.

**Transportation:** International air service to Benin is via Abidjan, Paris, and Brussels. UTA, Air Afrique, Sabena, Nigerian Airlines, Ghana Airways, Aeroflot, Air Burkina, Air Zaire, and Air Ivoire serve Cotonou. Air connections to Europe also can be made through Lome and Lagos. Two rail lines service the coast, and a third extends north to Parakou. Roads between Cotonou and Lagos and Lome are good. Many roads in Benin are in poor condition and, in the north, are often impassable during the rainy season. Spare parts and repair services are available for French cars. Both Honda and Toyota have dealerships in Cotonou, but models may differ from US models.

**Hotels:** Cotonou has an international class hotel, the Benin Sheraton, opened in 1982. The Hotel Aledjo, run by the French-PLM chain, also is first class. Less expensive is the Hotel de la Plage. In the north, the PLM runs an excellent hotel in Natitingou—the Tata-Somba. There is a good hotel in Parakou (Les Routiers). For trips to the Pendjari game park, there is a small (21-room) hotel in Porga. Abomey also has an adequate hotel.

**Tourist attractions:** Pendjari, a game reserve in northern Benin, is open from November to May. There are antelope, elephants, hippopotami, caymans, lions, cheetahs, baboons, and birds. A museum in Abomey, located in the old Royal Palace, is devoted to the Kingdom of Dahomey. In Ouidah, a museum has been established in the former Portuguese fort. Exhibits focus on the slave trade and Benin's links with Brazil and the Caribbean. The museum in Porto Novo has a small but good collection of traditional masks and statues. Another well-publicized tourist attraction is the village of Ganvie, one of the fishing villages built on stilts in the middle of a lagoon. One can visit Ganvie by motorcanoe run by the National Tourist Organization.

**Travel Advice:** For up-to-date information from the U.S. State Department on possible inconvenient or hazardous situations, see the **Travel Warnings and Consular Information Sheets from the U.S. Government** section starting on page 1723. For the latest information on health requirements and conditions, see the **International Travelers' Health Information** section starting on page 1385. For further information dealing with non-urgent matter, see the **Tips for Travelers to...** section starting on page 1588.

# HISTORY

In the precolonial era, Benin was a collection of small, often warring principalities, the most powerful of which was the Fon Kingdom of Dahomey (with its capital at Abomey), founded in the 17th century. In the 17th and 18th centuries, first the Portuguese and later other European powers established trading posts along the coast, notably at Porto Novo and Ouidah. They traded firearms and luxury items to the kings of Dahomey and other principalities for slaves, who were mostly prisoners taken in internecine wars. Thousands of slaves were shipped to the New World, primarily to Brazil and the Caribbean. This part of West Africa became known in the 18th and 19th centuries as the Slave Coast. Northern Benin traded primarily with other Africans and Arabs in the Sahel region and thus experienced limited European influence.

France led efforts to suppress the slave trade, beginning in the mid-19th century. These efforts, along with expansion into Africa by European colonial empires, led to alliances with some local groups and warfare with others. In 1892, the King of Dahomey was subjugated and the country organized as the French protectorate of Dahomey. Dahomey, in turn, became a territory of French West Africa, and it remained a French colony until independence in 1960, when it was called the Republic of Dahomey. The name was changed to the People's Republic of Benin in 1975.

In the early years of independence, the nation was plagued by political instability, including many coups and changes of government (nine in the first 12 years of independence). The last change took place on October 26, 1972, when a group of middle- and junior-grade officers seized control of the government. A military revolutionary government was established, with a Cabinet composed primarily of military officers. Then-Maj. Mathieu Kerekou was named chief of state, a position he has held since that time.

The Kerekou government, with the support of Benin's Marxist intellectuals, many of them French educated, soon began a process of revolutionary change, attempting to restructure the government, the economy, and the society along Marxist-Leninist lines. Close political ties were established with the Soviet Union and other socialist countries. Strained diplomatic relations prompted the United States to withdraw its ambassador to Benin in February 1976; although the United States continued to be represented in Cotonou by a charge d'affaires. Large private businesses were nationalized; a single political

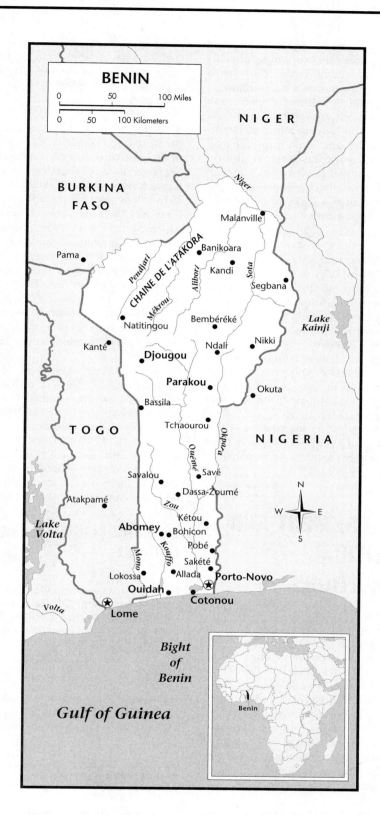

party was created; and institutions were established for the centralized direction of political and economic activity. Nevertheless, the thousands of small private commercial enterprises that are the lifeblood of Benin's

economy, continued to operate. Although some large-scale government agricultural projects were initiated, agriculture also is predominantly in the hands of individuals.

In 1977, a group of mercenaries landed at the Cotonou airport to carry out a coup d'etat. They were quickly repulsed after some minor fighting. Although the attempt may have been initiated by Beninese exile groups, the Government of Benin blamed "international imperialism." Relations with the West, including France and the United States, deteriorated markedly. Assistance provided by Libya in the wake of the attack encouraged closer Beninese-Libyan ties.

The government adopted a new constitution in 1977 to further institutionalize the revolution. Elections to the first National Revolutionary assembly were held in November 1979, and the assembly then elected Mathieu Kerekou president of the country in 1980. In August 1984, he was re-elected. Despite real and alleged plots against his government in 1973, 1975, and 1977, violence and demonstrations in 1978 and 1981, and pre-empted coup plots in 1988, Kerekou's 16 years of rule have been more stable than the politically turbulent 1960-72 period.

# GOVERNMENT AND POLITICAL CONDITIONS

In 1974, 2 years after Kerekou came into power Marxism-Leninism was declared the guiding philosophy of the new government. A single party, the People's Revolutionary Party, was established and modeled after those in communist countries. The party and its Central Committee play a primary role in government decision-making. The Central Committee makes all appointments to important positions and promulgates important government decisions.

Recently, President Kerekou has modified his government's attempts to apply strict Marxism-Leninism. Driven by heavy losses suffered by nationalized industries and the worsening economic situation, the government has shown an interest in privatizing many government-controlled sectors of the economy. In early 1986, Benin allowed a number of private foreign firms to begin operation in the transport sector.

Although no opposition parties are permitted, the people do have a voice in the political life of the country. Each elected level, starting at the village, chooses the next level of leadership. This process applies to the National Revolutionary Assembly, which, in turn, elects the president. While the party must approve all candidates, consideration is given to the selection of local leaders acceptable to their local communities. The process of elections to the Second National Revolutionary Assembly began in April 1984 and ended with the election of a new assembly in July 1984.

On July 29, 1988, the Cabinet was restructured. Cabinet ministers along with the six "prefets" (provincial governors), make up the National Executive Council. According to the constitution, the Council is the supreme administrative and executive organ of the country. In practice much of the work is done by the Permanent Committee of the Council.

## Principal Government Officials

For up-to-date information on Principal Government Officials, see the Chiefs of State and Cabinet Members of Foreign Governments section starting on page 1.

Benin maintains an embassy at 2737 Cathedral Avenue N.W., Washington, D.C. 20008 (tel. 202-232-6656).

# ECONOMY

The economy of Benin, heavily dependent upon regional trade and the export of cotton and crude oil, has been severely affected by ineffective government policies, regional recession, the collapse of world commodity prices heavy external debt, balance-of-payment deficits, and very low foreign exchange reserves and liquidity. Since 1985, the government has made considerable progress but, by November 1988, had still not reached an agreement with the International Monetary Fund (IMF) on economic reforms or a standby agreement that would pave the way for rescheduling Benin's external debt and the mobilization of new development resources.

The majority of Benin's population (about 80%) is engaged in subsistence agriculture. Benin, unlike many African states, is largely self-sufficient in food. The agricultural sector however has suffered from drought, poor infrastructure, insufficient and inefficient use of fertilizer and insecticides, and low producer prices. In addition to subsistence food crops (corn, sorghum, yams, cassava, beans, rice), Benin produces cash crops, including palm oil products, cotton, and peanuts. Recently, the government has encouraged cotton production through price supports and subsidies on fertilizers and insecticides. Cotton sales now represent a significant portion of Benin's agricultural exports (31% in 1987) even though the world price of cotton has dropped sharply since 1985. Although cotton exports have increased since 1985, the government can no longer afford its expensive cotton subsidy program and has begun to phase it out.

Benin's industrial sector produces textiles, beverages, processed food, and construction materials and is dominated by public enterprises. In 1982, in response to severe financial and economic problems, the government initiated steps to dissolve, merge, or reform many of its inefficient parastatals. Three major project—the Onigbolo cement plant, the Save sugar refinery, and the Seme oil field—have proved disappointing. Although the government-controlled Seme field produces approximately 5,500 barrels of crude oil per day, oil revenue is low due to high lifting costs, shortages of technical and managerial personnel, and low oil prices. Ashland Oil, however took over Seme operations in June 1988 and will carry out the planned Phase II expansion of the field that is expected to increase production and lower production costs. The inauguration of the joint Benin-Togo Nangbeto Hydroelectric Power Project, in May 1988, should meet 30% of Benin's electricity requirements and has reduced its need to import electricity from Ghana.

Benin has no refinery and imports petroleum products both for domestic consumption and for re-export. Traditionally, Benin's major source of export earnings has been re-exports to neighboring countries. The closure of the Nigerian border in April 1984 contributed to Benin's financial difficulties, since customs duties are the largest single source of government revenues. Although the border reopened in March 1986, the regional downturn in recorded trade persists. Nevertheless, customs duties continue to supply nearly half of government receipts. Informal imports, exports, and re-exports are considerable but difficult to document.

The government's 5-year plan (1983–88) emphasized the development of agriculture. The government wants to assure its own domestic needs, and to become a supplier of basic foodstuffs to the region. Recent government actions have reinforced the trend toward the privatization of government enterprises. Changes have been made in the investment laws to attract external investment to Benin.

# DEFENSE

Benin's Armed Forces number about 3,200 personnel (1985 estimate). In addition to the regular army, there is a small navy (100), air force (160), and militia. The president also retains a sizable and well-armed Presidential Guard Battalion (about 750). Equipment, supplies, and training have come from the Soviet Union, France, Libya, and Algeria.

# FOREIGN RELATIONS

Benin is a member of the Nonaligned Movement and the Organization of

## Further Information

These titles are provided as a general indication of material published on this country. The Department of State does not endorse unofficial publications.

Burton, Sir Richard F. *A Mission to Gelele, King of Dahome.* New York: Praeger 1966 (reprint).
Carter Gwendolen M. *Five African States.* Ithaca, N.Y.: Cornell University Press, 1963.
Chatwin, Bruce. *Viceroy of Ouidah.* New York: Summit Books, 1980.
Cornevin, Robert. *La Republique Populaire du Benin, des Origines dahomeenes a nos jours.* Paris: Academie des Sciences d'Outremer, 1984.
Decalo, Samuel. *Historical Dictionary for Dahomey* (African Historical Series, No.7). Metuchen, New Jersey: Scarecrow Press, 1976.
Herskovits, Melville J. *Dahomey.* Evanston, III.: Northwestern University Press, 1967.
Manning, Patrick. *Slavery, Colonialism, and Economic Growth in Dahomey, 1640-1960.* New Rochelle: Cambridge University Press, 1982.
Obichere, Boniface I. *West African States and European Expansion: The Dahomey-Niger Hinterland, 1885-1898.* New Haven: Yale University Press, 1971.
Ronen, Dov. *Dahomey: Between Tradition and Modernity.* Ithaca: Cornell University Press, 1975.

Available from the Superintendent of Documents, Government Printing Office, Washington, DC 20402:

U.S. Department of State. *Benin Post Report.* February 1984.

African Unity. In the United Nations its voting pattern is similar to those of other nonaligned nations. The People's Revolutionary Party maintains links with its counterparts in Cuba, North Korea, the Soviet Union, and Libya, although relations with Libya cooled in 1988. The United States, France, Federal Republic of Germany, Niger Nigeria, Chad, Ghana, Zaire, Egypt, China, Algeria, Soviet Union, Bulgaria, Cuba, North Korea, Libya, and Western Sahara (Polisario) maintain resident embassies in Cotonou.

Relations with France are important because of historical, cultural, economic, and aid links. In the period after the revolution, and particularly since 1977, these relations were strained. Many French citizens were expelled from Benin and their properties expropriated. Since 1981, and following the visit of President Francois Mitterrand in January 1983, relations with France have improved. The French Government and Embassy sponsor an active program of exchanges with Benin, including French naval ship visits and cultural events. The Federal Republic of Germany, Canada, and the European Community also have active aid programs in Benin.

Relations with Nigeria are particularly important to Benin because of the country's proximity and Nigeria's relative economic and military strength.

# U.S.-BENINESE RELATIONS

Relations between the United States and Benin were cordial in the years after independence, and the United States was an important bilateral aid donor as well as a major contributor to the international financial institutions assisting the country. After 1972, however relations became strained as Benin moved to strengthen its ties with the Soviet Union and other socialist countries and mounted harsh propaganda attacks on the United States. The U.S. Ambassador was withdrawn in 1976. Despite official tensions, diplomatic relations were never broken. The Embassy remained open, and the Peace Corps maintained its activities, although with fewer volunteers. Since the early 1980s, the Government of Benin has moved to improve relations with the United States. In November 1983, the United States appointed its first ambassador to Benin since 1976.

Although Benin's relations with Libya recently facilitated Libyan meddling in the region and prompted U.S. concerns, moves toward improved U.S.-Benin cooperation have continued. The U.S. Agency for International Development has a $6.5-million water and sanitation project in Zou Province and provides PL 480 food commodities. The Peace Corps maintains about 60 volunteers in the country.

There is no significant private U.S. investment in Benin currently, although a number of firms are actively exploring investment opportunities. U.S. exports to Benin totaled $16.9 million in 1986 and consisted mainly of tobacco, food, used clothing, and construction equipment. The Government of Benin adopted a more liberal investment code in 1982 in order to attract foreign investment; further modification of the code is anticipated.

However Benin's difficult economic situation and its traditional trading links, particularly with France and other European Community countries, may limit opportunities for U.S. exporters and investors.

About 250 U.S. citizens live in Benin, including embassy staff, missionaries, employees of international organizations, and their families.

## Principal U.S. Officials

For up-to-date information on Principal U.S. Officials, see the U.S. Embassies, Consulates, and Foreign Service section starting on page 139.

The U.S. Embassy in Benin is located at Rue Caporal Anani Bernard, Cotonou (tel. 30-06-50). The mailing address is Ambassade Americaine, B.P. 2012, Cotonou, Benin.

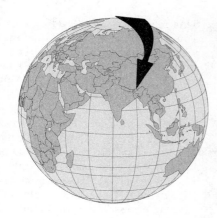

# BHUTAN

May 1990

## Official Name:
## Kingdom of Bhutan

# PROFILE

## Geography

**Area:** 46,620 sq. km. (18,000 sq. mi.); about the size of Vermont and New Hampshire combined.
**Cities:** Capital—Thimpu (population 20,000).
**Terrain:** Mostly mountainous—up to 7,000 m. (24,000 ft.), heavily forested; some arable land and savanna.
**Climate:** Subtropical in south, temperate in central region, alpine in north.

## People

**Nationality:** Noun and adjective—Bhutanese (sing. and pl.).
**Population (1989 est.):** 1.5 million.
**Annual growth rate:** 2.1%.
**Ethnic groups:** Ngalops and Sharchops 75%, Nepalese 25%.
**Religions:** Mahayana Buddhism (state religion) 75%, Hinduism 25%.
**Languages:** Dzongkha, a Tibetan dialect (official), Sharchop, Bumthap, Nepali, English (medium of instruction in schools), and a number of dialects.
**Education:** Years compulsory—none. Primary enrollment—25%. Adult literacy—15%.
**Health:** Life expectancy—47 yrs.

**Work force:** Agriculture, 90%; Industry and commerce, 1%; Other, 9%.

## Government

**Type:** Monarchy.
**Constitution:** None.
**Branches:** Executive—king (head of government and chief of state), Council of Ministers (cabinet), Royal Advisory Council. Legislative—Tshogdu (unicameral National Assembly, 150 members). Judicial—Supreme Court.
**Administrative subdivisions:** 18 districts.
**Political parties:** None.
**Suffrage:** One vote per family.
**Central government budget (1989-90):** $107 million.
**National holiday:** December 17.
**Flag:** Divided diagonally with yellow on the left over orange on the right; a white dragon in the center.

## Economy

**GDP (1988):** $297 million.
**Annual growth rate (1982-88):** 8.3%.
**Per capita income:** $217.
**Avg. inflation rate (1988):** 10%.
**Natural resources:** Timber, hydroelectric power.
**Agriculture and forestry (44% of GNP in 1988):** Products—rice, corn, wheat, buckwheat, barley, potatoes, oilseeds, cardamom, and timber.
**Industry (6% of GDP in 1988):**

Types—handicrafts, cement, calcium carbide production, food processing, wood milling, distilling.
**Trade (1988-89):** Exports—$70.9 million: cement, talc powder, fruit products, potatoes, alcoholic beverages, rosin, cardamom, sawn timber, pressboard, calcium carbide. Major market—India. Imports—$138.3 million: textiles, cereals, fuel, investment goods, including motor vehicles. Major source—India.
**Official exchange rate (Avg. FY 88–89):** 15.1 ngultrums=US$1. The ngultrum is set at par with the Indian rupee.
**Fiscal year:** July 1–June 30.

## Membership in International Organizations

UN and some of its specialized and related agencies, including the International Monetary Fund (IMF), the World Bank (IBRD), Economic and Social Commission for Asia and Pacific (ESCAP), Food and Agriculture Organization (FAO), UN Educational, Scientific, and Cultural Organization (UNESCO), World Health Organization (WHO), and the Universal Postal Union (UPU); Colombo Plan; Nonaligned Movement; Group of 77; Asian Development Bank (ADB), South Asian Association for Regional Cooperation (SAARC).

Bhutan

# PEOPLE

The people of Bhutan can be divided into three broad ethnic categories—Sharchops, Ngalops, and those of Nepali origin. The Sharchops, believed to be the earliest major group of inhabitants, live in eastern Bhutan and appear to be closely related to the inhabitants of northeast India and northern Burma. The Ngalops are said to be of Tibetan origin, arriving in Bhutan in the 8th century A.D. and bringing with them the culture and Buddhist religion that prevail in the northern two-thirds of Bhutan. The Nepalis, most of whom are Hindus, arrived in the late 19th and early 20th centuries. They farm Bhutan's southern foothill region.

The official language of Bhutan, Dzongkha, is related to classical Tibetan and is written partly in the classical Tibetan script, Choekay. Nepali predominates in southern Bhutan. As many as 11 other vernacular languages are spoken. English, the official working language and the medium of instruction in schools and colleges, is widely used. Population density is a relatively low 32 per sq. km. (83 per sq. mi.), contrasted with India's 255 per sq. km. (660 per sq. mi.). Communities are clustered in fertile valleys around dzongs, fortified monasteries that have served for centuries as administrative as well as religious centers.

# HISTORY

Bhutan's early history is obscure. The country may have been inhabited as early as 2,000 B.C., but not much is known about it until Tantric Buddhism was introduced in the 8th century A.D. The country's political history is intimately tied to its religious history and relations among the various monastic schools and monasteries.

The consolidation of Bhutan began 300 years ago. Ngawang Namgyal, a lama from Tibet, defeated three Tibetan invasions, subjugated rival

religious schools, codified an intricate and comprehensive system of laws, and established himself as ruler (shabdung) over a system of ecclesiastical and civil administrators.

After his death civil strife broke out, which, over the next 200 years, eroded shabdungs' power to the advantage of regional governors and local leaders. In 1885, the central authority recruited Chinese aid to crush the most powerful governors.

This move was countered by a local Tongsa leader, Ugyen Wangchuck, who arranged for a British presence in the area. In 1907, after the shabdung's death, Ugyen became Bhutan's first hereditary king.

In 1910, King Ugyen and the British signed the Treaty of Punakha, which provided that British India would not interfere in the internal affairs of Bhutan if the country accepted British advice in its external relations. Similar provisions were included in the 1949 Indo-Bhutan Treaty signed with independent India.

# GOVERNMENT AND POLITICAL CONDITIONS

Traditionally a decentralized theocracy, and since 1907 a monarchy, Bhutan is moving gradually toward representative government. The Tshogdu (National Assembly) is composed of not more than 150 members: 105 village elders or family heads, 12 representatives of regional monastic bodies, and 33 senior government administrators appointed by the king. Members are elected for 3-year terms. Any Bhutanese over 25 years of age can stand for election to the assembly.

The late King Jigme Dorji Wangchuck, who reigned from 1952 to 1972, guided his country toward constitutional monarchy and helped modernize public administration. He established the assembly in 1953, the Royal Advisory Council (Lodoi Tsokde) in 1965, and the Council of Ministers in 1968. The Lodoi Tsokde is responsible for advising the king and government ministers on important questions and for supervising the implementation of programs and policies legislated by the Tshogdu. It consists of a chairman appointed by the king, five representatives of the people, two of the monastic hierarchy, two southern Bhutanese representatives, and a women's representative. The Council of Ministers, composed of the ministers (lyonpos) of the government departments, is charged with implementing policy.

The present monarch, Jigme Singye Wangchuck, took the throne in 1972 and pledged to continue his father's progressive policies. Under Jigme Dorji the king was subject to a vote of confidence every 3 years, but this practice was dropped by Jigme Singye. Heads of government departments, however, are required to subject themselves and their policies to the scrutiny of the Tshogdu at least once a year.

The spiritual head of Bhutan, the Je Khempo—the only person besides the king who wears the saffron scarf, an honor denoting his authority over all religious institutions—is nominated by monastic leaders and appointed by the king. The monastic order is involved in government at many levels.

No political parties function within the Bhutanese governmental structure. Bhutan is divided into 18 districts, each headed by a district officer (dzongdad) appointed by the king. Each district is divided into subdistricts headed by an officer called a ramjam, who is assisted by a number of village leaders. Each leader (gup) controls several villages and is elected for 3 years by the villagers, who cast one vote per family. The gup convenes village meetings to discuss local issues.

## Principal Government Officials

**For up-to-date information on Principal Government Officials, see the Chiefs of State and Cabinet Members of Foreign Governments section starting on page 1.**

# ECONOMY

Bhutan's economy is largely rural-based. More than 90% of the work force is employed in subsistence farming and animal husbandry.

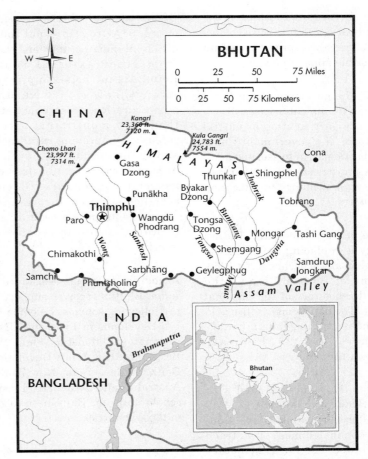

Although the United Nations identifies Bhutan as "least developed," economic welfare levels and nutrition are probably above the average for Asia. There is no shortage of land, and farmland generally is equitably distributed.

Once self-sufficient in food, Bhutan now imports about 7% of its foodgrains from India. Terrace agriculture is extensive; rice paddies can be found at elevations above 8,000 feet. Fruits grown in the inner valleys and on the plains are processed for local consumption and export.

The country has an abundance of untapped natural resources. These consist mainly of the vast forests, rivers with excellent hydroelectric potential, and various minerals in commercially exploitable quantities.

Bhutanese forest resources could sustain a net annual yield of about 400,000 cubic meters. In 1988, about 28,000 cubic meters were harvested. Preliminary estimates indicate that

Bhutan possesses a potential for generating 20,000 megawatts of hydro-electric power. The Jaldhaka River power project, a joint Bhutanese-Indian venture begun in September 1961, provides 18 megawatts to West Bengal and southwestern Bhutan. At Chukha, a modern hydroelectric facility, completed in 1988 with Indian assistance, now produces 336 megawatts.

Bhutan's mineral resources include dolomite, limestone, coal, graphite, gypsum, slate, marble, lead, zinc, and copper. Of these, only dolomite, limestone, slate, and coal have been mined.

Bhutan's industrial sector consists mainly of home-based handicrafts and some 60 privately owned small- or medium-scale factories producing mostly consumer goods. Cement, plastic pipe, and calcium carbide factories have been built recently. The cement factory, near Samchi, makes Bhutan self-sufficient in cement and produces a surplus for export.

Another factory produces plywood, particle board, and furniture components. A ferrosilicon production plant and a marble mine are planned.

In 1987, the government opened a number of public enterprises to private equity participation or partial divestiture. The government limits foreign participation to selected agro-industry projects or projects that generate foreign exchange and technology transfers.

The use of Bhutanese and Indian currency is replacing barter as the principal means of exchange. In 1968, the Bank of Bhutan became the principal repository of the national currency. The bank's main office is in Phuntsholing on the Indian border, and there are 23 branches throughout the country.

Traditionally, Bhutan traded with Tibet. Since the abortive 1959 Tibetan uprising against China, Bhutan has channeled most of its trade toward India. The Royal Monetary Authority provides the services needed to conduct foreign exchange operations. The country's largest source of convertible foreign exchange (1988–89: $1.8 million) is tourism. In 1988–89, Bhutan had a total trade deficit of about $67 million, of which $26 million was with India. In the same year, India provided foreign aid grants to Bhutan of almost $23 million. Other countries provided about $4 million.

In 1961, India agreed to finance Bhutan's first development plan. The outlay for Bhutan's fifth plan (1981–87) was $364 million (at the 1987 exchange rate). Of this amount, India provided $156 million in grants, and other foreign sources provided $76 million.

Bhutan's sixth plan (1981–87) envisaged a total outlay of $635 million (at the 1988 exchange rate).

Of this amount, Bhutan expects to obtain 31% from internal sources, 37% from Indian grants, and the rest from other external sources. Emphasis in the sixth plan is on strengthening government administration, preserving national identity, mobilizing internal resources, improving rural incomes and living standards, developing human resources, and promoting national self-reliance. Given the economy's increasing manpower requirements, primary education and technical training receive high priority.

In addition to foreign assistance from India, Bhutan receives support from the following sources: Colombo Plan, UN Development Program (UNDP), International Monetary Fund, World Bank, and the Asian Development Bank. India, Japan, New Zealand, Australia, and Switzerland provide scholarships for Bhutanese to study in those countries.

# DEFENSE

The Royal Bhutan Army was formed into a regular military force in the early 1950s, following the Chinese invasion of Tibet. The army consists of about 8,000 lightly armed troops. Conscript forces serve up to 15 years at the government's discretion. The officer corps is trained almost exclusively by the Indian army, and virtually all arms and equipment are manufactured in India. The Royal Bhutan Army assists the Royal Bhutan Police in internal security in addition to defending the country's frontiers.

# FOREIGN RELATIONS

Under the 1949 treaty between Bhutan and India, Bhutan agreed to "be guided by the advice" of India in foreign affairs. Bhutan does not interpret the treaty as binding. In 1971, Bhutan opened an office in New Delhi to handle diplomatic matters with other countries. In the same year, with Indian sponsorship, it became a UN member. In 1978, the Bhutanese mission in New Delhi was raised to embassy status. Bhutan is now a member of most Asian regional and international organizations, including the South Asian Association for Regional Cooperation, Asian Development Bank, Colombo Plan, Nonaligned Movement, World Bank, International Monetary Fund, and the Universal Postal Union.

Bhutan has full diplomatic relations with India, Pakistan, Bangladesh, Nepal, Maldives, Kuwait, Switzerland, Norway, Netherlands, Denmark, European Economic Community, Sweden, Japan, Sri Lanka, and Thailand. Only India, Bangladesh, and the UN Development Program have missions in Bhutan. Bhutan maintains embassies in India, Bangladesh, Kuwait, New York (UN), and Geneva. It also maintains honorary consuls general in Hong Kong, Macao, Singapore, and South Korea.

No formal diplomatic relations exist between the United States and Bhutan, although informal and friendly contact is maintained through the Bhutanese embassy at New Delhi, through occasional visits to Bhutan by US officials stationed in India, and by Bhutanese visitors to the United States such as the foreign minister. In 1986, the Bhutanese UN mission in New York (tel. 212-826-1919) was accorded consular jurisdiction in the United States. The US Embassy in New Delhi provides consular contact with Bhutan.

# BOLIVIA

April 2001

## Official Name:
## Republic of Bolivia

# PROFILE

## Geography
**Area:** 1.1 million sq. km. (425,000 sq. mi.); about the size of Texas and California combined.
**Cities:** Capital—La Paz (administrative—pop. 713,400); Sucre (constitutional—131,800). Other major cities—Santa Cruz (697,000), Cochabamba (407,800), El Alto (405,500).
**Terrain:** High plateau (altiplano), temperate and semitropical valleys, and the tropical lowlands.
**Climate:** Varies with altitude—from humid and tropical to semiarid and cold.

## People
**Nationality:** Noun and adjective—Bolivian(s).
**Population:** (1999 est.) 7.9 million. Annual growth rate: 1.96%.
**Ethnic groups:** 56%-70% indigenous (primarily Aymara, Quechua, and Guarani), 30%-42% European and mixed.
**Religions:** Predominantly Roman Catholic.
**Languages:** Spanish (official); Quechua, Aymara, Guarani.
**Education:** Years compulsory—ages 7–14. Literacy—83.1%.
**Health:** (1999) Infant mortality rate—62.02/1,000.

**Work force:** (2.5 million) Nonagricultural employment—1.26 million; services, including government—70%; industry and commerce—30%.

## Government
**Type:** Republic.
**Constitution:** 1967; revised 1994.
**Branches**: Executive—president and cabinet. Legislative—bicameral Congress. Judicial—five levels of jurisdiction, headed by Supreme Court.
**Subdivisions:** Nine departments.
**Major political parties:** Nationalist Democratic Action (ADN), Movement of the Revolutionary Left (MIR), Nationalist Revolutionary Movement (MNR), Conscience of the Fatherland (CONDEPA), Free Bolivia Movement (MBL), Civic Solidarity Union (UCS).
**Suffrage:** Universal adult, obligatory.

## Economy (1998)
**GDP:** $8.3 billion.
**Annual growth rate:** 2.5%
**Per capita income:** $1,036.
**Natural resources:** Hydrocarbons (natural gas, petroleum); mining (zinc, tungsten, antimony, silver, lead, gold, and iron). Agriculture (15% of GDP): Products—Soybeans, cotton, potatoes, corn, sugarcane, rice, wheat, coffee, beef, barley, and quinine. Arable land—27%.

**Industry:** Types—Mineral and hydrocarbon extraction, manufacturing, commerce, textiles, food processing, chemicals, plastics, mineral smelting, and petroleum refining.
**Trade:** Exports—$1.1 billion. Major products—natural gas, tin, zinc, coffee, silver, tungsten, wood, gold, jewelry, soybeans, and byproducts. Major markets—U.S. (12%), U.K. (16%), Argentina (10%), Peru (11%), Colombia (7%). Imports—$1.7 billion. Major products—machinery and transportation equipment, consumer products, construction and mining equipment. Major suppliers—U.S. (32%), Japan (24%), Brazil (12%), Argentina (12%), Chile (7%), Peru (4%), Germany (3%).

# PEOPLE

Bolivia's ethnic distribution is estimated to be 56%-70% indigenous people and 30%-42% European and mixed. The largest of the approximately three dozen indigenous groups are the Aymara, Quechua, and Guarani. There are small German, former Yugoslav, Asian, Middle Eastern, and other minorities, many of whose members descend from families that have lived in Bolivia for several generations.

Bolivia is one of the least-developed countries in South America. About two-thirds of its people, many of whom are subsistence farmers, live in poverty. Population density ranges from less than one person per square kilometer in the southeastern plains to about 10 per square km. (25 per sq. mi.) in the central highlands. Bolivia's high mortality rate restricts the annual population growth rate to around 1.96% (1999).

La Paz is at the highest elevation of the world's capital cities—3,600 meters (11,800 ft.) above sea level. The adjacent city of El Alto, at 4,200 meters above sea level, is one of the fastest-growing in the hemisphere. Santa Cruz, the commercial and industrial hub of the eastern lowlands, also is experiencing rapid population and economic growth.

The great majority of Bolivians are Roman Catholic (the official religion), although Protestant denominations are expanding strongly. Many indigenous communities interweave pre-Columbian and Christian symbols in their religious practices. About half of the people speak Spanish as their first language. Approximately 90% of the children attend primary school but often for a year or less. The literacy rate is low in many rural areas.

The cultural development of what is present-day Bolivia is divided into three distinct periods: pre-Columbian, colonial, and republican. Important archaeological ruins, gold and silver ornaments, stone monuments, ceramics, and weavings remain from several important pre-Columbian cultures. Major ruins include Tiwanaku, Samaipata, Incallajta, and Iskanwaya. The country abounds in other sites that are difficult to reach and hardly explored by archaeologists.

The Spanish brought their own tradition of religious art which, in the hands of local indigenous and mestizo builders and artisans, developed into a rich and distinctive style of architecture, painting, and sculpture known as "Mestizo Baroque." The colonial period produced not only the paintings of Perez de Holguin, Flores, Bitti, and others but also the works of skilled, but unknown, stonecutters,

woodcarvers, goldsmiths, and silversmiths. An important body of native baroque religious music of the colonial period was recovered in recent years and has been performed internationally to wide acclaim since 1994. Bolivian artists of stature in the 20th century include, among others, Guzman de Rojas, Arturo Borda, Maria Luisa Pacheco, and Marina Nunez del Prado.

Bolivia has rich folklore. Its regional folk music is distinctive and varied. The devil dances at the annual carnival of Oruro are one of the great folkloric events of South America, as is the lesser known carnival at Tarabuco.

# HISTORY

The Andean region probably has been inhabited for some 20,000 years. Beginning about the second century B.C., the Tiwanakan culture developed at the southern end of Lake Titicaca. This culture, centered around and named for the great city of Tiwanaku, developed advanced architectural and agricultural techniques before it disappeared around 1200 A.D., probably because of extended drought. Roughly contemporaneous with the Tiwanakan culture, the Moxos in the eastern lowlands and the Mollos north of present-day La Paz also developed advanced agricultural societies that had dissipated by the 13th century of our era. In about 1450, the Quechua-speaking Incas entered the area of modern highland Bolivia and added it to their empire. They controlled the area until the Spanish conquest in 1525.

During most of the Spanish colonial period, this territory was called "Upper Peru" or "Charcas" and was under the authority of the Viceroy of Lima. Local government came from the Audiencia de Charcas located in Chuquisaca (La Plata—modern Sucre). Bolivian silver mines produced much of the Spanish empire's wealth, and Potosi, site of the famed Cerro Rico—"Rich Mountain"—was, for many years, the largest city in the Western Hemisphere. As Spanish

royal authority weakened during the Napoleonic wars, sentiment against colonial rule grew. Independence was proclaimed in 1809, but 16 years of struggle followed before the establishment of the republic, named for Simon Bolivar, on August 6, 1825.

Independence did not bring stability. For nearly 60 years, coups and short-lived constitutions dominated Bolivian politics. Bolivia's weakness was demonstrated during the War of the Pacific (1879–83), when it lost its seacoast and the adjoining rich nitrate fields to Chile. An increase in the world price of silver brought Bolivia a measure of relative prosperity and political stability in the late 1800s. During the early part of the 20th century, tin replaced silver as the country's most important source of wealth. A succession of governments controlled by the economic and social elites followed laissez-faire capitalist policies through the first third of the century.

Living conditions of the indigenous peoples, who constituted most of the population, remained deplorable. Forced to work under primitive conditions in the mines and in nearly feudal status on large estates, they were denied access to education, economic opportunity, or political participation. Bolivia's defeat by Paraguay in the Chaco War (1932–35) marked a turning point. Great loss of life and territory discredited the traditional ruling classes, while service in the army produced stirrings of political awareness among the indigenous people. From the end of the Chaco War until the 1952 revolution, the emergence of contending ideologies and the demands of new groups convulsed Bolivian politics.

The Nationalist Revolutionary Movement (MNR) emerged as a broadly based party. Denied its victory in the 1951 presidential elections, the MNR lead the successful 1952 revolution. Under President Victor Paz Estenssoro, the MNR introduced universal adult suffrage, carried out a sweeping land reform, promoted rural education, and nationalized the country's largest tin mines. It also committed

many serious violations of human rights.

Twelve years of tumultuous rule left the MNR divided. In 1964, a military junta overthrew President Paz Estenssoro at the outset of his third term. The 1969 death of President Rene Barrientos, a former member of the junta elected President in 1966, led to a succession of weak governments. Alarmed by public disorder, the military, the MNR, and others

installed Col. (later General) Hugo Banzer Suarez as President in 1971. Banzer ruled with MNR support from 1971 to 1974. Then, impatient with schisms in the coalition, he replaced civilians with members of the armed forces and suspended political activities. The economy grew impressively during Banzer's presidency, but demands for greater political freedom undercut his support. His call for elections in 1978 plunged Bolivia into turmoil once again.

Elections in 1978, 1979, and 1980 were inconclusive and marked by fraud. There were coups, counter-coups, and caretaker governments. In 1980, Gen. Luis Garcia Meza carried out a ruthless and violent coup. His government was notorious for human rights abuses, narcotics trafficking, and economic mismanagement. Later convicted in absentia for crimes, including murder, Garcia Meza was extradited from Brazil and began serving a 30-year sentence in 1995.

After a military rebellion forced out Garcia Meza in 1981, three other military governments in 14 months struggled with Bolivia's growing problems. Unrest forced the military to convoke the Congress elected in 1980 and allow it to choose a new chief executive. In October 1982—22 years after the end of his first term of office (1956–60)—Hernan Siles Zuazo again became President. Severe social tension, exacerbated by economic mismanagement and weak leadership, forced him to call early elections and relinquish power a year before the end of his constitutional term.

In the 1985 elections, the Nationalist Democratic Action Party (ADN) of Gen. Banzer won a plurality of the popular vote, followed by former President Paz Estenssoro's MNR and former Vice President Jaime Paz Zamora's Movement of the Revolutionary Left (MIR). But in the congressional run-off, the MIR sided with MNR, and Paz Estenssoro was chosen for a fourth term as President. When he took office in 1985, he faced a staggering economic crisis. Economic output and exports had been declining for several years.

Hyperinflation had reached an annual rate of 24,000%. Social unrest, chronic strikes, and unchecked drug trafficking were widespread. In 4 years, Paz Estenssoro's administration achieved economic and social stability. The military stayed out of politics, and all major political parties publicly and institutionally committed themselves to democracy. Human rights violations, which badly tainted some governments earlier in the decade, were not a problem. However, his remarkable accomplishments were not won without sacrifice. The collapse of tin prices in October 1985, coming just as the government was moving to reassert its control of the mismanaged state mining enterprise, forced the government to lay off over 20,000 miners. The highly successful shock treatment that restored Bolivia's financial system also led to some unrest and temporary social dislocation.

Although the MNR list headed by Gonzalo Sanchez de Lozada finished first in the 1989 elections, no candidate received a majority of popular votes and so in accordance with the constitution, a congressional vote determined who would be president. The Patriotic Accord (AP) coalition between Gen. Banzer's ADN and Jaime Paz Zamora's MIR, the second- and third-place finishers, respectively, won out. Paz Zamora assumed the presidency, and the MIR took half the ministries. Banzer's center-right ADN took control of the National Political Council (CONAP) and the other ministries.

Paz Zamora was a moderate, center-left President whose political pragmatism in office outweighed his Marxist origins. Having seen the destructive hyperinflation of the Siles Zuazo administration, he continued the neoliberal economic reforms begun by Paz Estenssoro, codifying some of them. Paz Zamora took a fairly hard line against domestic terrorism, personally ordering the December 1990 attack on terrorists of the Nestor Paz Zamora Committee (CNPZ—named after his brother who died in the 1970 Teoponte insurgency) and authorizing the early 1992 crackdown against the Tupac Katari Guerrilla Army (EGTK).

Paz Zamora's regime was less decisive against narcotics trafficking. The government broke up a number of trafficking networks but issued a 1991 surrender decree giving lenient sentences to the biggest narcotics kingpins. Also, his administration was extremely reluctant to pursue net eradication of illegal coca. It did not agree to an updated extradition treaty with the U.S., although two traffickers have been extradited to the U.S. since 1992. Beginning in early 1994, the Bolivian Congress investigated Paz Zamora's personal ties to accused major trafficker Isaac Chavarria, who subsequently died in prison while awaiting trial. MIR deputy chief Oscar Eidwas was jailed in connection with similar ties in 1994; he was found guilty and sentenced to 4 years in prison in November 1996. Technically still under investigation,

Paz Zamora became an active presidential candidate in 1996.

The 1993 elections continued the tradition of open, honest elections and peaceful democratic transitions of power. The MNR defeated the ADN/MIR coalition by a 34% to 20% margin, and the MNR's Gonzalo "Goni" Sanchez de Lozada was selected as president by an MNR/MBL/UCS coalition in the Congress.

Sanchez de Lozada pursued an aggressive economic and social reform agenda. He relied heavily on successful entrepreneurs-turned-politicians like himself and on fellow veterans of the Paz Estenssoro administration (during which Sanchez de Lozada was planning minister). The most dramatic change undertaken by the Sanchez de Lozada government was the capitalization program, under which investors acquired 50% ownership and management control of public enterprises, such as the state oil corporation, telecommunications system, electric utilities, and others. The reforms and economic restructuring were strongly opposed by certain segments of society, which instigated frequent social disturbances, particularly in La Paz and the Chapare coca-growing region, from 1994 through 1996.

In the 1997 elections, Gen. Hugo Banzer, leader of the ADN, won 22% of the vote, while the MNR candidate won 18%. Gen. Banzer formed a coalition of the ADN, MIR, UCS, and CONDEPA parties which hold a majority of seats in the Bolivian Congress. The Congress elected him as president and he was inaugurated on August 6, 1997.

# GOVERNMENT AND POLITICAL CONDITIONS

The Banzer government has committed itself to shutting down illegal coca cultivation and narcotrafficking during its 5-year term. President Banzer has called for action against government and judicial corruption and has encouraged foreign investment as a means to stimulate economic growth and reduce poverty.

The 1967 constitution, revised in 1994, provides for balanced executive, legislative, and judicial powers. The traditionally strong executive, however, tends to overshadow the Congress, whose role is generally limited to debating and approving legislation initiated by the executive. The judiciary, consisting of the Supreme Court and departmental and lower courts, has long been riddled with corruption and inefficiency. Through revisions to the constitution in 1994, and subsequent laws, the government has initiated potentially far-reaching reforms in the judicial system and processes.

Bolivia's nine departments received greater autonomy under the Administrative Decentralization law of 1995, although principal departmental officials are still appointed by the central government. Bolivian cities and towns are governed by elected mayors and councils. The most recent municipal elections took place in December 1999. The Popular Participation Law of April 1994, which distributes a significant portion of national revenues to municipalities for discretionary use, has enabled previously neglected communities to make striking improvements in their facilities and services.

## Principal Government Officials

**For up-to-date information on Principal Government Officials, see the Chiefs of State and Cabinet Members of Foreign Governments section starting on page 1.**

Bolivia maintains an embassy in the U.S. at 3014 Massachusetts Ave., NW, Washington, DC 20008 (tel. 202–483–4410); consulates in Los Angeles, San Francisco, Miami, New Orleans, and New York; and honorary consulates in Atlanta, Chicago, Cincinnati, Houston, Mobile, Seattle, St. Louis, and San Juan.

# ECONOMY

Bolivia's 1998 gross domestic product (GDP) totaled $8.3 billion. Economic growth is 2.5% a year, and inflation declined from 6.7% in 1997 to 3.5% in 1999. The government's 2000 economic program has targeted GDP growth of 5% and an inflation rate below 6%. Since 1985, the Government of Bolivia has been implementing a far-reaching program of macroeconomic stabilization and structural reform aimed at restoring price stability, creating conditions for sustained growth, and alleviating poverty. Important components of these structural reform measures include the capitalization of state enterprises and strengthening of the country's financial system.

The most important recent structural changes in the Bolivian economy have involved the capitalization of numerous public sector enterprises. (Capitalization in the Bolivian context is a form of privatization where investors acquire a 50% stake and management control of public enterprises in return for a commitment to undertake capital expenditures equivalent to the enterprise's net worth). Parallel legislative reforms have locked into place market-oriented policies, especially in the hydrocarbon and mining sectors, that have encouraged private investment. Foreign investors are accorded national treatment, and foreign ownership of companies enjoys virtually no restrictions in Bolivia. As a consequence of these measures, 1996 private investment surged by 25% to an estimated $225 million, and in 1998 it exceeded $1 billion. The privatization program has generated commitments of $1.7 billion in foreign direct investment over the period 1996–2002.

In 1996, three units of the Bolivian state oil corporation (YPFB) involved in hydrocarbon exploration, production, and transportation were capitalized. The capitalization of YPFB allowed agreement to be reached on the construction of a gas pipeline to Brazil. A priority in the development strategy for the sector is the expansion of export markets for natural gas. The Brazil pipeline contract projects natural gas exports of 9 million metric cubic meters per day (mmcmd) by the end of 2000, increasing to over 30 mmcmd by 2004. The Bolivian Government has signed a financing contract for the Bolivian side of the gas pipeline with Petrobras, and the capitalization of YPFB's transportation company will facilitate the finance, construction, and operation of the pipeline. The government plans to position Bolivia as a regional hub for exporting hydrocarbons.

Six smaller public enterprises were sold during 1996, and the Government of Bolivia has taken steps to improve the efficiency of some public services through concession contracts with private sector managers. All three major airports were transferred to private managers in March 1997, and a water supply company was transferred to a private operator in June 1997.

By May 1996, three of the four Bolivian banks that had experienced difficulties in 1995 were recapitalized and restructured under new ownership with support from the Bolivian Government's Special Fund for Strengthening the Financial System (FONDESIF), which helped restore confidence in the banking system. In November 1996, the Bolivian Congress approved a comprehensive pension reform that replaces the old pay-as-you-go system by a system of privately managed, individually funded retirement accounts, and the new system began operations in May 1997. The reform represents a major step toward lasting fiscal consolidation in Bolivia. Bolivian exports were $1.1 billion in 1998, from a low of $652 million in 1991. Imports grew in 1998 to a level of $1.7 billion, with import growth facilitated by the gradual reduction of Bolivian tariffs to a flat 10% (except for capital equipment, which has a 5% rate). Bolivia's

## Travel Notes

**Travel Advice:** For up-to-date information from the U.S. State Department on possible inconvenient or hazardous situations, see the **Travel Warnings and Consular Information Sheets from the U.S. Government** section starting on page 1723. For the latest information on health requirements and conditions, see the **International Travelers' Health Information** section starting on page 1385. For further information dealing with non-urgent matter, see the **Tips for Travelers to...** section starting on page 1588.

trade deficit rose from $419 million in 1996 to $620 million in 1997.

Bolivia's trade with neighboring countries is growing, in part because of several regional preferential trade agreements it has negotiated. Bolivia is a member of the Andean Community and has free trade with other member countries—Peru, Ecuador, Colombia, and Venezuela. Bolivia began to implement an association agreement with MERCOSUR (Southern Cone Common Market) in March 1997. The agreement provides for the gradual creation of a free trade area covering at least 80% of the trade between the parties over a 10-year period. The U.S. Andean Trade Preference Act (ATPA) allows numerous Bolivian products to enter the United States free of duty on a unilateral basis. Tariffs have to be paid on clothing and leather products only.

The U.S. remains Bolivia's largest trading partner. In 1998, the U.S. exported $626 million of merchandise to Bolivia and imported $149 million, according to the World Trade Atlas of the Global Trade Information Service. Bolivia's major exports to the U.S. are tin, gold, jewelry, and wood products. Its major imports from the United States are computers, vehicles, wheat, and machinery. A Bilateral Investment Treaty has been signed but has not yet been ratified by the U.S.

Agriculture accounts for roughly 15% of Bolivia's GDP. The amount of land cultivated by modern farming techniques is increasing rapidly in the Santa Cruz area, where weather allows for two crops a year and soybeans are the major cash crop. The extraction of minerals and hydrocarbons accounts for another 10% of GDP. Bolivia exports natural gas to Brazil. Manufacturing represents less than 17% of GDP.

The Government of Bolivia remains heavily dependent on foreign assistance to finance development projects. At the end of 1998, the government owed $4.3 billion to its foreign creditors, with $1.6 billion of this amount owed to other governments and most of the balance owed to multilateral development banks. Most payments to other governments have been rescheduled on several occasions since 1987 through the Paris Club mechanism. External creditors have been willing to do this because the Bolivian Government has generally achieved the monetary and fiscal targets set by IMF programs since 1987. Rescheduling agreements granted by the Paris Club have allowed the individual creditor countries to apply very soft terms to the rescheduled debt. As a result, some countries have forgiven substantial amounts of Bolivia's bilateral debt. The U.S. Government reached an agreement at the Paris Club meeting in December 1995 which reduced by 67% Bolivia's existing debt stock. The Bolivian Government continues to pay its debts to the multilateral development banks on time and to receive soft loans. Bolivia has qualified for the Highly Indebted Poor Countries (HIPC) debt relief program.

# FOREIGN RELATIONS

Bolivia traditionally has maintained normal diplomatic relations with all hemispheric states except Chile. Relations with Chile, strained since Bolivia's defeat in the War of the Pacific (1879–83) and its loss of the coastal province of Atacama, were severed from 1962 to 1975 in a dispute over the use of the waters of the Lauca River. Relations were resumed in 1975 but broken again in 1978 over the inability of the two countries to reach an agreement that might have granted Bolivia a sovereign access to the sea. In the 1960s, relations with Cuba were broken following Castro's rise to power but resumed under the Paz Estenssoro Administration in 1985.

Bolivia pursues a foreign policy with a heavy economic component. Bolivia has become more active in the OAS, the Rio Group, and in MERCOSUR, with which it signed an association agreement in 1996. Bolivia promotes its policies on sustainable development and the empowerment of indigenous people. Bolivia is a member of the UN and some of its specialized agencies and related programs; Organization of American States (OAS); Andean Community; INTELSAT; Non-Aligned Movement; International Parliamentary Union; Latin American Integration Association (ALADI); World Trade Organization; Rio Treaty; Rio Group; MERCOSUR; and Uruguay, Paraguay, Bolivia (URUPABOL, restarted in 1993). As an outgrowth of the 1994 Summit of the Americas, Bolivia hosted a hemispheric summit conference on sustainable development in December 1996. A First Ladies' hemispheric summit was also hosted by Bolivia that same month.

# U.S.-BOLIVIAN RELATIONS

Relations between the United States and Bolivia are cordial and cooperative. The major issue in the bilateral relationship is control of illegal narcotics. Roughly one-third of the world's cocaine is made from coca grown in Bolivia: Bolivia's coca crop is third after Colombia's and Peru's in the production of the cocaine alkaloid, and the country is third after Colombia and Peru in the production of refined cocaine hydrochloride. For centuries, Bolivian coca leaf has been chewed and used in traditional rituals, but in the past few decades the emergence of the drug trade has led to a rapid expansion of coca cultivation, particularly in the tropical Chapare region. In 1988, a new law explicitly recognized that coca grown in the Chapare was not required to meet traditional demand for chewing or for tea, and the law called for the eradication, over time, of all "excess" coca. To accomplish that goal, the Bolivian Government instituted a program offering cash compensation to peasants who eradicated voluntarily, and the government began developing and promoting suitable alternative crops for the peasants to grow. Parallel efforts were undertaken by the police to interdict the smuggling of coca leaves, cocaine, and precursor chemicals. The U.S. Government has, in large measure, financed the alternative development program and the police effort.

Bolivian President Hugo Banzer has pledged to wipe out illicit coca production and drug trafficking in Bolivia by the end of his term in 2002. His administration unveiled its 5-year counternarcotics strategy in December 1997. The plan calls for significant funding from international donors. Former President Bill Clinton certified to the Congress in 2000 that Bolivia is cooperating fully with the U.S. on counternarcotics matters or has taken steps on its own to achieve full compliance with the 1988 UN Convention Against Illicit Traffic in Narcotic Drugs and Psychotropic Substances. The U.S. Government is seeking Bolivia's cooperation in achieving a net reduction in the amount of coca under cultivation and in enacting legislation to criminalize money laundering. In 1996, the United States and Bolivia ratified a new extradition treaty which makes it easier for both nations to more effectively prosecute drug traffickers and other criminals. It replaces the previous extradition treaty, which came into force in 1990. The new treaty is significant because, unlike its predecessor, it requires both countries to extradite their own nationals for serious criminal offenses.

In 1991, the U.S. Government forgave all of the debt owed by Bolivia to the U.S. Agency for International Development ($341 million) as well as 80% (or $31 million) of the amount owed to the Department of Agriculture for food assistance. Increased U.S. assistance since the late 1980s has been designed to reinforce democracy, to ensure sustainable economic development, and to make Bolivia less dependent on the cocaine industry. U.S. economic and development assistance totaled $53 million in FY 1999, in addition to military and counternarcotics assistance.

## U.S. Embassy Functions

In addition to working closely with Bolivian Government officials to strengthen our bilateral relationship, the U.S. Embassy provides a wide range of services to U.S. citizens and business. Political and economic officers deal directly with the Bolivian Government in advancing U.S. interests but also are available to provide information to American citizens on general conditions in the country. Commercial officers work closely with dozens of U.S. companies which operate direct subsidiaries in the country. These officers provide information on Bolivian trade and industry regulations and administer several programs intended to aid U.S. companies starting or maintaining business ventures in Bolivia.

The consular section of the embassy provides vital services to the estimated 14,000 American citizens resident in Bolivia. Among other services, the consular section assists Americans who wish to participate in U.S. elections while abroad and provides U.S. tax information. Besides the American citizens living in Bolivia, some 20,000 U.S. citizens visit annually. The consular section offers passport and emergency services to these tourists as needed during their stay in Bolivia.

## Principal U.S. Embassy Officials

**For up-to-date information on Principal U.S. Officials, see the U.S. Embassies, Consulates, and Foreign Service section starting on page 139.**

The U.S. Embassy is located at Avenida Arce #2780, La Paz (tel.591–2-430251). There are consular agents in the cities of Santa Cruz (tel. 591–3-330725) and Cochabamba (tel. 591–42–56714). Embassy Home Page: http://www/megalink.com/usembla-paz.

## Other Contact Information

**U.S. Department of Commerce International Trade Administration**
Trade Information Center 14th and Constitution Avenue, NW
Washington, D.C. 20230
Tel: 800-USA-TRADE
Home Page: http://www.ita.doc.gov

**American Chamber of Commerce in Bolivia**
Edificio Hilda, Oficina 3
Avenida 6 de Agosto
Apartado Postal 8268
La Paz, Bolivia Tel: (591) 2–43–25–73
Fax: (591) 2–43–24–72
Home Page: http://www.bolivi-anet.com/amcham

# BOSNIA AND HERZEGOVINA

December 2000

## Official Name:
**Bosnia and Herzegovina**

# PROFILE

## Geography

**Area:** 51,233 sq km, slightly smaller than West Virginia.
**Cities:** Capital—Sarajevo (est. pop 387,876); Banja Luka (220,407); Mostar (208,904); Tuzla (118,500); Bihac (49,544).
**Terrain:** Mountains in the central and southern regions, plains along the Sava River in the north.
**Climate:** Hot summers and cold winters; areas of high elevation have short, cool summers and long severe winters; mild, rainy winters along the coast.

## People

**Nationalities:** Bosnian; Herzegovinian.
**Population:** (July 1998 est.) 3,365,727.
**Population growth rate:** (1998 est.) 3.63%.
**Ethnic groups:** Bosniak 48.1%, Croat 14.3%, Serb 37.1%, others 0.5%. (Source: Bosnia-Herzegovina Agency for Statistics as of December 2000. Please note that the figure for Serbs includes some living in the FRY who lived on the territory of B-H before the war.)
**Religions:** Muslim (40%); Orthodox (31%); Catholic (15%); Protestant

(4%); other (10%).
**Languages:** Bosnian, Serbian, Croatian.
**Education:** Mandatory 8 years of primary school, 4 years in secondary school, and 4 years in universities and academies. In Bosnia and Herzegovina, there are 407 primary schools with 250,000 students, 171 secondary schools with 80,000 students, 6 universities in the major cities—Sarajevo, Mostar, Banja Luka, Tuzla, and Bihac—and 6 academies—4 pedagogic and 2 art academies.
**Health:** Infant mortality rate—30.8 deaths/1,000.
**Life expectancy:** male 69.2, female 74.6.
**Work force (total):** 1,026,254.

## Government

**Type:** Parliamentary democracy.
**Constitution:** The Dayton Agreement, signed December 14, 1995, included a new constitution now in force.
**Independence:** April 1992 (from Yugoslavia).
**Branches:** Executive—Chairman of the Presidency and 2 other members of three-member rotating presidency (chief of state), Cochairmen of the Council of Ministers (head of government), Council of Ministers (cabinet). Legislative—bicameral Parliamentary assembly, consisting of National House of Representatives and House of Peoples (parliament). Judicial—

Supreme Court, Constitutional Court, both supervised by the Ministry of Justice.
**Subdivisions:** Muslim/Croat Federation of Bosnia and Herzegovina (divided into 10 cantons), Republika Srpska.
**Political parties:** Party of Democratic Action (SDA); Croatian Democratic Union of BiH (HDZ-BiH); Serb Democratic Party (SDS); Party for Bosnia and Herzegovina (SBiH); Joint list (consisting of UBSD, RP, MBO, HSG, SPP); Civic Democratic Party (GDS); Croatian Peasants' Party of BiH (HSS); Independent Social Democratic Party (SNSD); Liberal Bosniak Organization (LBO); Liberal Party (LS); Muslim-Bosniac Organization (MBO); Republican Party of Bosnia and Herzegovina (RS); Serb Civic Council (SGV); Social Democratic Party (SDP); Socialist Party of Republika Srpska (SPRS); Social Democrats of Bosnia Herzegovina; Serb Radical Party of RS; Serb Party of Krojina and Posavina (SSKIP); National Democratic Union (DNZ); Serb National Alliance (SNS); Coalition for a United and Democratic BiH (coalition of SDA, SBiH, LS, and GDS).
**Suffrage:** Age 16 if employed, universal at age 18.

## Economy

GDP (1997 est.): purchasing power parity—$4.41 billion.

**GDP growth rate:** (1997 est.) 35%.
**Income per capita:** (1997 est.) purchasing power parity—$1,690.
**Inflation rate:** 5%.
**Natural resources:** Coal, iron, bauxite, manganese, forests, copper, chromium, lead, zinc. Agriculture: Wheat, corn, fruits, vegetables; livestock. Industry: Steel, minerals, vehicle assembly, textiles, tobacco products, wooden furniture, tank and aircraft assembly, domestic appliances, oil refining.
**Trade Exports:** (1995) $152 million. Major markets—NA Exchange rate: NA (strict currency board regime—convertible mark 1 KM=1 DEM).

## U.S.-Bosnian Relations

Bosnia's parliament declared the republic's independence on April 5, 1992. Full recognition of its independence by the U.S. and most European countries occurred soon after, on April 7, and Bosnia-Herzegovina was admitted to the United Nations on May 22. The war that then ensued was ended in 1995 with the crucial participation of the United States in brokering the Dayton Accords. After leading the diplomatic and military effort to secure the Dayton agreement, the U.S. has and must continue to lead the effort to ensure its implementation. A large contingent of U.S. troops participate in the Bosnia Peace-keeping force (SFOR), and the U.S. has poured billions of dollars into Bosnia to help with reconstruction, humanitarian assistance, economic development, and military reconstruction. USAID has played a large role in post-war Bosnia, including programs in economic development and reform, democratic reform (media, elections), infrastructure development, and training programs for Bosnian professionals, among others. NGOs such as Save the Children and CARE also have played a large role in the reconstruction of the republic.

## Principal U.S. Embassy Officials

**For up-to-date information on Principal U.S. Officials, see the U.S.**

**Embassies, Consulates, and Foreign Service section starting on page 139.**

# HISTORICAL HIGHLIGHTS

For the first centuries of the Christian era, Bosnia was part of the Roman Empire. After the fall of Rome, Bosnia was contested by Byzantium and Rome's successors in the West. Slavs settled the region in the 7th century, and the kingdoms of Serbia and Croatia split control of Bosnia in the 9th century. The 11th and 12th centuries saw the rule of the region by the kingdom of Hungary. The medieval kingdom of Bosnia gained its independence around 1200 A.D. Bosnia remained independent up until 1463, when Ottoman Turks conquered the region.

During Ottoman rule, many Bosnians dropped their ties to Christianity in favor of Islam. Bosnia was under Ottoman rule until 1878, when it was given to Austria-Hungary as a colony. While those living in Bosnia enjoyed the benefits of the Austro-Hungarian Empire, South Slavs in Serbia and elsewhere were calling for a South Slav state; World War I began when Serb nationalist Gavrilo Princip assassinated the Archduke Ferdinand in Sarajevo. Following the Great War, Bosnia became part of the South Slav state of Yugoslavia, only to be given to Nazi-puppet Croatia in World War II. The Cold War saw the establishment of the Communist Federal Republic of Yugoslavia under Tito, and the reestablishment of Bosnia as a republic with its medieval borders.

Yugoslavia's unraveling was hastened by the rise of Slobodan Milosevic to power in 1986. Milosevic's embrace of the Serb nationalist agenda led to intrastate ethnic strife. Slovenia and Croatia both declared independence in 1991, and Bosnia-Herzegovina soon followed. In February 1992, the Bosnian

Government held a referendum on independence, and Bosnian Serbs, supported by neighboring Serbia, responded with armed resistance in an effort to partition the republic along ethnic lines in an attempt to create a "greater Serbia." Muslims and Croats in Bosnia signed an agreement in March 1994 creating the Federation of Bosnia and Herzegovina. This narrowed the field of warring parties down to two.

The conflict continued through most of 1995, ending with the Dayton Peace Agreement signed on November 21, 1995 (the final version was signed December 14, 1995 in Paris). The Muslim/Croat Federation, along with the Serb-led Republika Srpska, make up Bosnia-Herzegovina.

# ECONOMY

Next to Macedonia, Bosnia and Herzegovina was the poorest republic in the old Yugoslav Federation. For the most part, agriculture has been in private hands, but farms have been small and inefficient, and food has traditionally been a net import for the republic. The centrally planned economy has resulted in some legacies in the economy. Industry is greatly overstaffed, reflecting the rigidity of the planned economy. Under Tito, military industries were pushed in the republic; Bosnia hosted a large share of Yugoslavia's defense plants. Three years of interethnic strife destroyed the economy and infrastructure in Bosnia, caused the death of about 200,000 people, and displaced half of the population.

However, considerable progress has been made since peace was reestablished in the republic. Due to Bosnia's strict currency board regime, inflation has remained low in the Federation and RS. However, growth has been uneven up until this point, with the Federation outpacing the RS; this is due to the disparity in economic assistance to the Federation as opposed to the RS. Bosnia's most immediate task remains economic revitalization to create jobs and income. In order to do this fully, the

environment must be conducive to a private sector, market-led economy. Bosnia faces a dual challenge: not only must the nation recover from the war, but it also must make the transition from socialism to capitalism. According to World Bank estimates, GDP growth was 62% in the Federation and 25% in the RS in 1996, 35% in the Federation and flat in the RS in 1997, and continued growth in the Federation in 1998. Growth in the RS should see dramatic increases following recent upsurges in donor investment. Support for Eastern European Democracy (SEED) assistance accounts for 20%-25% of economic growth in Bosnia. This kind of economic growth would not have been possible without both international assistance and the establishment of economic institutions and reforms. Movement has been slow, but progress has been made in economic reform. A Central Bank was established in late 1997, successful debt negotiations were held with the London Club in December 1997 and with the Paris Club in October 1998, and a new currency was introduced in mid-1998.

# GOVERNMENT AND POLITICAL CONDITIONS

## Principal Government Officials

**For up-to-date information on Principal Government Officials, see the Chiefs of State and Cabinet Members of Foreign Governments section starting on page 1.**

## President and Cabinet

The Presidency in Bosnia Herzegovina rotates among three members (Bosniak, Serb, Croat), each elected for a 4-year term. The three members of the Presidency are elected directly by the people (Federation votes for the Bosniak/Croat, RS for the Serb).

The Presidency is responsible for:

* Conducting the foreign policy of Bosnia and Herzegovina;

* Appointing ambassadors and other international representatives, no more than two thirds of which may come from the Federation;

* Representing Bosnia and Herzegovina in European and international organizations and institutions and seeking membership in such organizations and institutions of which it is not a member;

* Negotiating, denouncing, and, with the consent of the Parliamentary Assembly, ratifying treaties of Bosnia and Herzegovina;

* Executing decisions of the Parliamentary Assembly;

* Proposing, upon the recommendation of the Council of Ministers, an annual budget to the Parliamentary Assembly;

* Reporting as requested, but no less than annually, to the Parliamentary Assembly on expenditures by the Presidency;

* Coordinating as necessary with international and nongovernmental organizations in Bosnia and Herzegovina, and;

* Performing such other functions as may be necessary to carry out its duties, as may be assigned to it by the Parliamentary Assembly, or as may be agreed by the Entities.

The Chair of the Council of Ministers is nominated by the Presidency and approved by the House of Representatives. He is then responsible for appointing a Foreign Minister, Minister of Foreign Trade, and others as appropriate. The Council is responsible for carrying out the policies and decisions in the fields of foreign policy; foreign trade policy; customs policy; monetary policy; finances of the institutions and for the international obligations of Bosnia and Herzegovina; immigration, refugee, and asylum policy and regulation; international and inter-Entity criminal law enforcement, including relations with Interpol; establishment and operation of common and international communications facilities; regulation of inter-Entity transportation; air traffic control; facilitation of inter-Entity coordination; and other matters as agreed by the Entities.

## Legislature

The Parliamentary Assembly is the lawmaking body in Bosnia and Herzegovina. It consists of two houses: the House of Peoples and the House of Representatives. The House of Peoples includes 15 delegates, two-thirds of which come from the Federation (5 Croat and 5 Bosniaks) and one-third from the RS (5 Serbs). Nine members of the House of Peoples constitutes a quorum, provided that at least three delegates from each group are present. Federation representatives are selected by the House of Peoples of the Federation, and RS representatives are selected by the RS National Assembly. The House of Representatives is comprised of 42 Members, two-thirds elected from the Federation and one-third elected from the RS. Federation representatives are elected directly by the voters of the Federation, and RS representatives are selected by the RS National Assembly (the National Assembly is directly elected by RS voters).

The Parliamentary Assembly is responsible for enacting legislation as necessary to implement decisions of the Presidency or to carry out the responsibilities of the Assembly under the Constitution; deciding upon the sources and amounts of revenues for the operations of the institutions of Bosnia and Herzegovina and international obligations of Bosnia and Herzegovina; approving a budget for the institutions of Bosnia and Herzegovina; deciding whether to consent to the ratification of treaties; and other matters as are necessary to carry out its duties of as are assigned to it by mutual agreement of the Entities.

## Judiciary

The Constitutional Court of Bosnia and Herzegovina is the supreme, final arbiter of legal matters. It is composed of nine members: four members are selected by the House of Representatives of the Federation, two by the Assembly of the RS, and three by the President of the European Court of Human Rights after consultation with the Presidency. Terms of initial appointees are 5 years, unless they resign or are removed for cause by consensus of the other judges. Once appointed, judges are not eligible for reappointment. Judges subsequently appointed will serve until the age of 70, unless they resign or are removed for cause. Appointments made 5 years after the initial appointments may be governed by a different law of selection, to be determined by the Parliamentary Assembly.

Proceedings of the Court are public, and decisions will be published. Rules of court are adopted by a majority of the Court, and decisions are final and binding. The Constitutional Court's original jurisdiction lies in deciding any constitutional dispute that arises between the Entities or between Bosnia and Herzegovina and an Entity or Entities. Such disputes may be referred only by a member of the Presidency, by the Chair of the Council of Ministers, by the Chair or Deputy Chair of either chamber of the Parliamentary Assembly, or by one-fourth of the legislature of either Entity. The Court also has appellate jurisdiction within the territory of Bosnia and Herzegovina. Both the Federation and the RS government have established lower court systems for their territories.

Bosnian Embassy 43 Alipasina 71000 Sarajevo, Bosnia and Herzegovina tel: [387] (71) 445–700

# FOREIGN RELATIONS

The implementation of the Dayton Accords of 1995 has focused the efforts of policymakers in Bosnia and Herzegovina, as well as the international community, on regional stabilization in the former Yugoslavia. With the end of the conflict in Kosovo,

these efforts will continue to a larger extent. Within Bosnia and Herzegovina, relations with its neighbors of Croatia, Albania, and Serbia have been fairly stable since the signing of Dayton in 1995.

## Foreign aid

The U.S. role in the Dayton Accords and their implementation has been key to any of the successes in Bosnia. In the 3 years since the Dayton Accords were signed, over $4 billion in foreign aid has flown into Bosnia, about $800 million of it coming from SEED funds. As stated above, this support has been key to the growth and revitalization of the economy and infrastructure in the republic. However, most of this aid has been targeted at the Federation; the previous government of the RS was anti-Dayton and not assisted by the U.S. The election of the "Sloga" or "Unity" Coalition government, led by Prime Minister Dodik, has shifted the balance of power in the RS to a pro-Dayton stance and will result in an upsurge of funding to the RS from the international community.

## Travel Notes

**Travel Advice:** For up-to-date information from the U.S. State Department on possible inconvenient or hazardous situations, see the **Travel Warnings and Consular Information Sheets from the U.S. Government** section starting on page 1723. For the latest information on health requirements and conditions, see the **International Travelers' Health Information** section starting on page 1385. For further information dealing with non-urgent matter, see the **Tips for Travelers to...** section starting on page 1588.

In addition to SEED funding, USAID programs have been crucial to the redevelopment of Bosnia and Herzegovina. USAID has programing in the following areas: economic policy reform and restructuring; private sector development (the Business Development Program); infrastructure rebuilding; democratic reforms in the media, political process and elections, and rule of law/legal code formulation; and training programs for women and diplomats.

# BOTSWANA

February 2001

Official Name:
**Republic of Botswana**

# PROFILE

## Geography

**Area:** 582,000 sq. km. (224,710 sq. mi.), about the size of Texas.
**Cities:** Capital—Gaborone (pronounced ha-bo-ro-neh), pop. 213,017 (2000). Other towns—Francistown (101,805), Selebi-Phikwe (49,017), Molepolole (47,094), Kanye (36,877), Serowe (33,335), Mahalapye (32,407), Lobatse (32,075), Maun (31,260), Mochudi (30,671).
**Terrain:** Desert and savanna.
**Climate:** Mostly subtropical.

## People

**Nationality:** Noun and adjective—Motswana (sing.), Batswana (pl.).
**Population (1999):** 1.61 million.
**Annual population growth rate (1999):** 2.3%.
**Ethnic groups:** Tswana 55%-60%; Kalanga 25-30%; Kgalagadi, Herero, Basarwa ("Bushmen"), Khoi ("Hottentots"), whites 5-10%.
**Religions:** Christianity 60%, indigenous beliefs 40%.
**Languages:** English (official), Setswana, Ikalanga.
**Education:** Adult literacy (1993)—68.9%.
**Health (1999):** Life expectancy—39.9 years. Infant mortality rate—59/1,000.

**Work force (1999):** 255,618.

## Government

**Type:** Republic, parliamentary democracy.
**Independence:** September 30, 1966.
**Constitution:** March 1965.
**Branches:** Executive—president (chief of state and head of government), cabinet. Legislative—popularly elected National Assembly; advisory House of Chiefs. Judicial—High Court, Court of Appeal, local and customary courts, industrial labor court.
**Administrative subdivisions:** 5 town councils and 9 district councils.
**Major political parties:** Botswana Democratic Party (BDP)—37 seats, Botswana National Front (BNF)—6 seats, Botswana Congress Party (BCP)—1 seat, Botswana Peoples Party (BPP), Botswana Freedom Party (BFP).
**Suffrage:** Universal at 18.
**Flag:** Blue field with horizontal, white-edged black band in the center.

## Economy

**GDP (1999):** $5.2 billion.
**Annual growth rate (1998-99):** 4.5%.
**Per capita GDP (1999):** $3,200.
**Natural resources:** Diamonds, copper, nickel, coal, soda ash, salt, gold, potash.

**Agriculture (2.8% of GDP, 1998-99):** Products—livestock, sorghum, white maize, millet, cowpeas, beans.
**Industry:** Types—mining (35% of GDP): diamonds, copper, nickel, coal; textiles, construction, tourism, beef processing, chemical products production, food and beverage production.
**Trade (1995):** Exports—$4.5 billion: diamonds, nickel, copper, meat products, textiles, hides, skins, and soda ash. Partners—South Africa, Zimbabwe, UK. Imports—$1.8 billion: machinery, transport equipment, manufactured goods, food, chemicals, fuels. Major suppliers—South Africa, Zimbabwe, EU, U.S. Annual avg. economic aid: $25 million.

# PEOPLE AND HISTORY

The Batswana, a term also used to denote all citizens of Botswana, refers to the country's major ethnic group (the "Tswana" in South Africa), which came into the area from South Africa during the Zulu wars of the early 1880s. Prior to European contact, the Batswana lived as herders and farmers under tribal rule.

In the late 19th century, hostilities broke out between the Batswana and Boer settlers from the Transvaal.

After appeals by the Batswana for assistance, the British Government in 1885 put "Bechuanaland" under its protection. The northern territory remained under direct administration and is today's Botswana, while the southern territory became part of the Cape Colony and is now part of the northwest province of South Africa; the majority of Setswana-speaking people today live in South Africa.

Despite South African pressure, inhabitants of the Bechuanaland Protectorate, Basuotoland (now Lesotho), and Swaziland in 1909 asked for and received British assurances that they would not be included in the proposed Union of South Africa. An expansion of British central authority and the evolution of tribal government resulted in the 1920 establishment of two advisory councils representing Africans and Europeans. Proclamations in 1934 regularized tribal rule and powers. A European-African advisory council was formed in 1951, and the 1961 constitution established a consultative legislative council.

In June 1964, Britain accepted proposals for democratic self-government in Botswana. The seat of government was moved from Mafikeng, in South Africa, to newly established Gaborone in 1965. The 1965 constitution led to the first general elections and to independence in September 1966. Seretse Khama, a leader in the independence movement and the legitimate claimant to traditional rule of the Batswana, was elected as the first president, re-elected twice, and died in office in 1980. The presidency passed to the sitting vice president, Ketumile Masire, who was elected in his own right in 1984 and re-elected in 1989 and 1994. Masire retired from office in 1998. The presidency passed to the sitting vice president, Festus Mogae, who was elected in his own right in 1999.

# GOVERNMENT AND POLITICAL CONDITIONS

Botswana has a flourishing multi-party constitutional democracy. Each of the elections since independence has been freely and fairly contested and has been held on schedule. The country's small white minority and other minorities participate freely in the political process. There are two main rival parties and a number of smaller parties. In national elections in 1999, the Botswana Democratic Party (BDP) won 33 of 40 contested National Assembly seats, the Botswana National Front (BNF) won 6, and the Botswana Congress Party (BCP) won 1 seat. An additional 4 seats are held by individuals appointed by the President; all 4 are currently held by the ruling BDP. The opposition out-polled the ruling BDP in most urban areas. The openness of the country's political system has been a significant factor in Botswana's stability and economic growth. General elections are held at least every 5 years.

The president has executive power and is chosen by the National Assembly following country-wide legislative elections. The cabinet is selected by the president from the National Assembly; it consists of a vice president and a flexible number of ministers and assistant ministers, currently 12 and 3, respectively. The National Assembly has 40 elected and 4 appointed members; it is expanded following each census (every 10 years).

The advisory House of Chiefs represents the eight principal subgroups of the Batswana tribe, and four other members are elected by the subchiefs of four of the districts. A draft of any National Assembly bill of tribal concern must be referred to the House of Chiefs for advisory opinion. Chiefs and other leaders preside over customary, traditional courts, though all persons have the right to request that

their case be considered under the formal British-based legal system.

The roots of Botswana's democracy lie in Setswana traditions, exemplified by the Kgotla, or village council, in which the powers of traditional leaders are limited by custom and law. Botswana's High Court has general civil and criminal jurisdiction. Judges are appointed by the president and may be removed only for cause and after a hearing. The constitution has a code of fundamental human rights enforced by the courts, and Botswana has a good human rights record.

Local government is administered by nine district councils and five town councils. District commissioners have executive authority and are appointed by the central government and assisted by elected and nominated district councilors and district development committees. There has been ongoing debate about the political, social, and economic marginalization of the San (indigenous tribal population). The government's policies for remote area dwellers continue to spark controversy and to be revised in response to domestic and donor concerns.

## Principal Government Officials

**For up-to-date information on Principal Government Officials, see the Chiefs of State and Cabinet Members of Foreign Governments section starting on page 1.**

Botswana maintains an embassy at 1531-1533 New Hampshire Avenue NW, Washington DC 20036 (tel. 202-244-4990; fax 202-244-4164). Its mission to the United Nations is at 103 E. 37th Street, New York NY 10017 (tel. 212-889-2277; fax 212-725-5061).

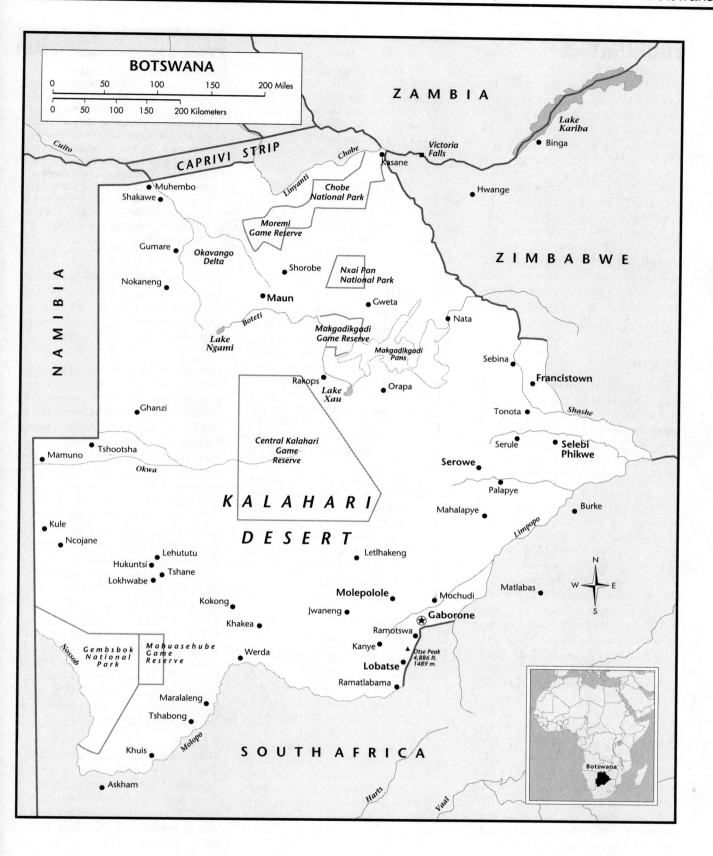

# ECONOMY

Since independence, Botswana has had the highest average economic growth rate in the world at about 9% per year from 1966 through 1999. Growth in formal sector employment has averaged about 10% per annum over Botswana's first 30 years of independence. The government has consistently maintained budget surpluses and has substantial foreign exchange reserves totaling about $6.2 billion in 1999. Botswana's impressive economic record has been built on a foundation of diamond mining, prudent fiscal policies, international financial and technical assistance, and a cautious foreign policy.

## Mining

Two large mining companies, Debswana (formed by the government and South Africa's DeBeers in equal partnership) and Bamangwato Concessions, Ltd. (BCL, also with substantial government equity participation) operate in the country.

Since the early 1980s, the country has been the world's largest producer of gem diamonds. Three large diamond mines have opened since independence. DeBeers prospectors discovered diamonds in northern Botswana in the early 1970s. The first mine began production at Orapa in 1972, followed by the smaller mine at Lethlakane. What has become the single-richest diamond mine in the world opened in Jwaneng in 1982. Botswana produced a total of 21.3 million carats of diamonds from the three Debswana mines in 1999. The Orapa 2000 Expansion of the existing Orapa mine was opened in 2000. BCL, which operates a copper-nickel mine at Selebi-Phikwe, has had a troubled financial history but remains an important employer. The soda ash operation at Sua Pan, opened in 1991 and supported by substantial government investment, has begun making a profit following significant restructuring.

## Tourism

Tourism is an increasingly important industry in Botswana, accounting for almost 12% of GDP. One of the world's unique ecosystems, the Okavango Delta, is located in Botswana. The country offers excellent game viewing and birding both in the Delta and in the Chobe Game Reserve—home to one of the largest herds of free-ranging elephants in the world. Botswana's Central Kalahari Game Reserve also offers good game viewing and some of the most remote and unspoiled wilderness in southern Africa.

## Agriculture

More than one-half of the population lives in rural areas and is largely dependent on subsistence crop and livestock farming. Agriculture meets only a small portion of food needs and contributes just 2.8% to GDP—primarily through beef exports—but it remains a social and cultural touchstone. Cattleraising in particular dominated Botswana's social and economic life before independence. The national herd was about 2.5 million in the mid-1990s, though the government-ordered slaughter of the entire herd in Botswana's northwest Kgamiland District in 1995 has reduced the number by at least 200,000. The slaughter was ordered to prevent the spread of "cattle lung disease" to other parts of the country.

## Private Sector Development and Foreign Investment

Botswana seeks to diversify its economy away from minerals, the earnings from which have leveled off. In 1998-99, nonmineral sectors of the economy grew at 8.9%, partially offsetting a slight 4.4% decline in the minerals sector. Foreign investment and management have been welcomed in Botswana. U.S. investment in Botswana is growing. In the early 1990s, two American companies, Owens Corning and H.J. Heinz, made major investments in production facilities in Botswana. In 1997, the St. Paul Group purchased Botswana

Insurance, one of the country's leading short-term insurance providers. An American Business Council (ABC), with over 30 member companies, was inaugurated in 1995.

Because of history and geography, Botswana has long had deep ties to the economy of South Africa. The Southern Africa Customs Union (SACU), comprised of Botswana, Namibia, Lesotho, Swaziland, and South Africa, dates from 1910. Under this arrangement, South Africa has collected levies from customs, sales, and excise duties for all five members, sharing out proceeds based on each country's portion of imports. The exact formula for sharing revenues and the decisionmaking authority over duties—held, until at least 1996, exclusively by the Government of South Africa—have been increasingly controversial, and the members began renegotiating the arrangement in 1995. Following South Africa's accession to the World Trade Organization (WTO—Botswana also is a member), many of the SACU duties are declining, making American products more competitive.

Botswana's currency—the pula—is fully convertible and is valued against a basket of currencies heavily weighted toward the South African rand. Profits and direct investment can be repatriated without restriction from Botswana. The Botswana Government has eliminated all exchange controls.

Gaborone is host to the headquarters of the 14-nation Southern African Development Community (SADC). A successor to the Southern Africa Development Coordination Conference (SADCC), which focused its efforts on freeing regional economic development from dependence on apartheid in South Africa, SADC embraced the newly democratic South Africa as a member in 1994 and has a broad mandate to encourage growth, development, and economic integration in Southern Africa. SADC's Trade Protocol, which was launched on September 1, 2000, calls for the elimination of all tariff and nontariff barriers to trade by 2012 among the 11 signatory countries. If successful, it will give Botswana companies free access to the far larger regional market. The Regional Center for Southern Africa (RCSA), which implements the U.S. Agency for International Development's (USAID) Initiative for Southern Africa (ISA), is headquartered in Gaborone as well.

## Transportation and Communications

A sparsely populated, arid country about the size of Texas, Botswana has nonetheless managed to incorporate much of its interior into the national economy. An "inner circle" highway connecting all major towns and district capitals is completely paved, and the all-weather Trans-Kalahari Highway connects the country (and, through it, South Africa's commercially dominant Gauteng Province) to Walvis Bay in Namibia. A fiber-optic telecommunications network has been completed in Botswana connecting all major population centers.

In addition to the government-owned newspaper and national radio network, there is an active, independent press (six weekly newspapers). Two privately owned radio stations began operations in 1999. At the end of July 2000, the government-owned Botswana Television (BTV) was launched, which is Botswana's first national television station. It began broadcasting with 3 hours of programming on weekdays and 5 on weekends, and offers news (Setswana and English), entertainment, and sports, with plans eventually to produce 60% of its programming locally. Foreign publications are sold without restriction in Botswana, and there are three commercial Internet service providers. Two cellular phone providers cover most of the country.

# DEFENSE

The president is commander in chief of the Botswana Defense Force (BDF). A defense council is presidentially appointed. The BDF was formed in 1977 and has approximately 8,000 members. The BDF is a capable and well-disciplined military force. Following positive political changes in South Africa and the region, the BDF's missions have increasingly focused on anti-poaching activities, disaster-preparedness, and foreign peacekeeping. The United States has been the largest single contributor to the development of the BDF, and a large segment of its officer corps has received U.S. training. It is considered an apolitical and professional institution.

# FOREIGN RELATIONS

Botswana has put a premium on economic and political integration in southern Africa. It has sought to make SADC a working vehicle for economic development, and it has promoted efforts to make the region self-policing in terms of preventative diplomacy, conflict resolution, and good governance. It has welcomed post-apartheid South Africa as a partner in these efforts. Botswana joins the African consensus on most major international matters and is a member of international organizations such as the United Nations and the Organization of African Unity (OAU).

# U.S.-BOTSWANA RELATIONS

The United States considers Botswana an advocate of and a model for stability in Africa and has been a major partner in Botswana's development since its independence. The U.S. Peace Corps closed out its presence in Botswana on December 1997, bringing to an end 30 years of well-regarded assistance in education, business, health, agriculture, and the environment.

Similarly, the USAID phased out a longstanding partnership with Botswana in 1996, after successful programs emphasizing education, training, entrepreneurship, environmental management, and reproductive health. Botswana, however, continues to benefit along with its neighbors in the region from USAID's Initiative for Southern Africa and the USAID Regional Center for Southern Africa is headquartered in Gaborone. The United States International Board of Broadcasters (IBB) operates a major Voice of America (VOA) relay station in Botswana serving most of the African Continent.

In 1995, the Centers for Disease Control (CDC) started the BOTUSA Project in collaboration with the Botswana Ministry of Health in order to generate information to improve TB control efforts in Botswana and elsewhere in the face of the TB and HIV/AIDS co-epidemics. Under the 1999 U.S. Government's Leadership and Investment in Fighting an Epidemic (LIFE) Initiative, CDC through the BOTUSA Project has undertaken many projects and has assisted many organizations in the fight against the HIV/AIDS epidemic in Botswana. The Governments of Botswana and the United States entered into an agreement in July 2000 to establish an International Law Enforcement Academy (ILEA) in Gaborone. The academy, jointly financed, managed and staffed by the two nations, will initially provide training to police and government officials from Southern Africa and eventually from across the continent. The academy is scheduled to begin operation in 2001.

## Principal U.S. Officials

**For up-to-date information on Principal U.S. Officials, see the U.S. Embassies, Consulates, and For-** **eign Service section starting on page 139.**

International Law Enforcement Agency—Appointment pending. The U.S. Embassy is on Embassy Drive off Khama Crescent—P. O. Box 90, Gaborone (tel. 267-353-982; fax 267-356-947).

USAID is located on Lebatlane Road. DAO and ODC are located at the embassy. CDC is located on Ditlhakore Way in Gaborone. ILEA is located in Otse, about 30 minutes outside of Gaborone. The IBB station is located in Selebi-Phikwe, about 400 kilometers northeast of Gaborone.

# BRAZIL

April 2001

Official Name:
**Federative Republic of Brazil**

# PROFILE

## Geography

**Area:** 8,511,965 sq. km. (3,290,000 sq. mi.); slightly smaller than the U.S.
**Cities:** Capital—Brasilia (pop. 2.0 million). Other cities—Sao Paulo (10.4 million), Rio de Janeiro (5.8 million), Belo Horizonte (2.2 million), Salvador (2.4 million), Fortaleza (2.1 million), Recife (1.4 million), Porto Alegre (1.4 million), Curitiba (1.6 million).
**Terrain:** Dense forests in northern regions including Amazon Basin; semiarid along northeast coast; mountains, hills, and rolling plains in the southwest, including Mato Grosso; and coastal lowland.
**Climate:** Mostly tropical or semitropical with temperate zone in the south.

## People

**Nationality:** Noun and adjective—Brazilian(s).
**Population:** (2000) 170 million.
**Annual growth rate:** 1.6%. Ethnic groups: Portuguese, Italian, German, Japanese, African, indigenous people.
**Religion:** Roman Catholic (80%).
**Language:** Portuguese.
**Education:** Literacy—81% of adult population.
**Health:** Infant mortality rate—44/1,000. Life expectancy—67 yrs.
**Work force:** (65 million) Services—40%; agriculture—35%; industry—25%.

## Government

**Type:** Federative republic.
**Independence:** September 7, 1822.
**Constitution:** Promulgated October 5, 1988.
**Branches**: Executive—president (chief of state and head of government popularly elected to no more than two 4-year terms). Legislative—Senate (81 members popularly elected to 8-year terms), Chamber of Deputies (513 members popularly elected to 4-year terms). Judicial—Supreme Federal Tribunal.
**Political parties:** Brazilian Democratic Movement Party (PMDB), Brazilian Social Democratic Party (PSDB), Liberal Front Party (PFL), Social Democratic Party (PSD), Democratic Workers Party (PDT), Workers Party (PT), Brazilian Labor Party (PTB), Liberal Party (PL), Brazilian Socialist Party (PSB), Communist Party of Brazil (PC do B), Brazilian Progressive Party (PPB), Popular Socialist Party (PPS), Green Party (PV), the Social Liberal Party (PSL), the National Mobilization Party (PMN), National Workers Party (PTN), Humanistic Solidarity Party (PHS).

## Economy (2000)

**GDP:** $588 billion.
**Annual real growth rate:** 4.2% (projected 4.5%, 2001).
**Per capita GDP:** $3,500.
**Natural resources:** Iron ore, manganese, bauxite, nickel, uranium, gemstones, oil, wood, and aluminum. Brazil has 12% of the world's fresh water.
**Agriculture:** (8% of GDP) Products—coffee, soybeans, sugarcane, cocoa, rice, beef, corn, oranges, cotton, wheat, and tobacco. Industry (34% of GDP): Types—steel, commercial aircraft, chemicals, petrochemicals, footware, machinery, motors, vehicles, and autoparts, consumer durables, cement, lumber.
**Trade:** Exports—$55 billion. Major markets—United States 24%, Argentina 11%, Netherlands 5%, Japan 5%, Germany 5%, Italy 4%, Belgium 3%, France 2%. Imports—$56 billion. Major suppliers—United States 23%, Argentina 12%, Germany 8%, Japan 5%, Italy 4%.

# PEOPLE AND HISTORY

With an estimated 170 million inhabitants, Brazil has the largest population in Latin America and ranks sixth in the world. The majority live in the south-central area, which includes the industrial cities of Sao Paulo, Rio de Janeiro, and Belo Horizonte. Urban growth has been rapid; by 2000, 81% of the total population were living in urban areas. Rapid growth has aided economic development but has also created serious social, environmental, and political problems for major cities.

Four major groups make up the Brazilian population: the Portuguese, who colonized Brazil in the 16th century; Africans brought to Brazil as slaves; various other European, Middle Eastern, and Asian immigrant groups who have settled in Brazil since the mid-19th century; and indigenous people of Tupi and Guarani language stock. Intermarriage between the Portuguese and indigenous people or slaves was common. Although the major European ethnic stock of Brazil was once Portuguese, subsequent waves of immigration have contributed to a diverse ethnic and cultural heritage.

From 1875 until 1960, about 5 million Europeans emigrated to Brazil, settling mainly in the four southern states of Sao Paulo, Parana, Santa Catarina, and Rio Grande do Sul. Immigrants have come mainly from Italy, Germany, Spain, Japan, Poland, and the Middle East. The largest Japanese community outside Japan is in Sao Paulo. Despite class distinctions, national identity is strong, and racial friction is a relatively new phenomenon. Indigenous full-blooded Indians, located mainly in the northern and western border regions and in the upper Amazon Basin, constitute less than 1% of the population. Their numbers are declining as contact with the outside world and commercial expansion into the interior increase. Brazilian Government programs to establish reservations and to provide other forms of assistance have existed for years but are controversial and often ineffective.

Brazil is the only Portuguese-speaking nation in the Americas. About 80% of all Brazilians belong to the Roman Catholic Church; most others are Protestant or follow practices derived from African religions.

Brazil was claimed for Portugal in 1500 by Pedro Alvares Cabral. It was ruled from Lisbon as a colony until 1808, when the royal family, having fled from Napoleon's army, established the seat of Portuguese Government in Rio de Janeiro. Brazil became a kingdom under Dom Joao VI, who returned to Portugal in 1821. His son declared Brazil's independence on September 7, 1822, and became emperor with the title of Dom Pedro I. His son, Dom Pedro II, ruled from 1831 to 1889, when a federal republic was established in a coup by Deodoro da Fonseca, Marshal of the army. Slavery had been abolished a year earlier by the Regent Princess Isabel while Dom Pedro II was in Europe.

From 1889 to 1930, the government was a constitutional democracy, with the presidency alternating between the dominant states of Sao Paulo and Minas Gerais. This period ended with a military coup that placed Getulio Vargas, a civilian, in the presidency; Vargas remained as dictator until 1945. From 1945 to 1961, Eurico Dutra, Vargas, Juscelino Kubitschek, and Janio Quadros were elected presidents. When Quadros resigned in 1961, he was succeeded by Vice President Joao Goulart.

Goulart's years in office were marked by high inflation, economic stagnation, and the increasing influence of radical political elements. The armed forces, alarmed by these developments, staged a coup on March 31, 1964. The coup leaders chose as president Humberto Castello Branco, followed by Arthur da Costa e Silva (1967–69), Emilio Garrastazu Medici (1968–74), and Ernesto Geisel (1974–79) all of whom were senior army officers. Geisel began a democratic opening that was continued by his successor, Gen. Joao Baptista de Oliveira Figueiredo (1979–85). Figueiredo not only permitted the return of politicians exiled or banned from political activity during the 1960s and 1970s, but also allowed them to run for state and federal offices in 1982.

At the same time, an electoral college consisting of all members of congress and six delegates chosen from each state continued to choose the president. In January 1985, the electoral college voted Tancredo Neves from the opposition Brazilian Democratic Movement Party (PMDB) into office as President. However, Neves became ill in March and died a month later. His Vice President, former Senator Jose Sarney, became President upon Neves' death. Brazil completed its transition to a popularly elected government in 1989, when Fernando Collor de Mello won 53% of the vote in the first direct presidential election in 29 years. In 1992, a major corruption scandal led to the impeachment and ultimate resignation of President Collor. Vice President Itamar Franco took his place and governed for the remainder of Collor's term culminating in the October 3, 1994 presidential elections, when Fernando Henrique Cardoso was elected President with 54% of the vote. He took office January 1, 1995 and was re-elected in October 1998 for a second 4-year term. Presidential elections will next be held in October 2002.

President Cardoso has sought to establish the basis for long-term stability and growth and to reduce Brazil's extreme socioeconomic imbalances. His proposals to Congress include constitutional amendments to open the Brazilian economy to greater foreign participation and to implement sweeping reforms—including social security, government administration, and taxation—to reduce excessive public sector spending and improve government efficiency.

# GOVERNMENT AND POLITICAL CONDITIONS

Brazil is a federal republic with 26 states and a federal district. The 1988 constitution grants broad powers to the federal government, made up of executive, legislative, and judicial branches. The president holds office for 4 years, with the right to re-election for an additional 4-year term, and appoints his own cabinet. There are 81 senators, three for each state and the Federal District, and 513 deputies. Senate terms are for 8 years, with election staggered so that two-thirds of the upper house is up for election at one time and one-third 4 years later. Chamber terms are for 4 years, with elections based on a complex system of proportional representation by states. Each state is eligible for a minimum of 8 seats; the largest state delegation (Sao Paulo's) is capped at 70 seats. The result is a system weighted in favor of geographically large but sparsely populated states.

Fifteen political parties are represented in Congress. Since it is common for politicians to switch parties, the proportion of congressional seats held by particular parties changes regularly. The following are the major political parties:

- PFL—Liberal Front Party (center-right)

- PMDB—Brazilian Democratic Movement Party (center)

- PSDB—Brazilian Social Democratic Party (center-left)

- PPB—Brazilian Progressive Party (center-right)

- PT—Workers Party (left)

- PDT—Democratic Labor Party (left)

- PTB—Brazilian Labor Party (center-right)

- PSB—Brazilian Socialist Party (left)

- PCdoB—Communist Party of Brazil (left)

- PL—Liberal Party (center-right)

President Cardoso was elected with the support of a heterodox alliance of his own center-left Social Democratic Party, the PSDB, and two center-right parties, the Liberal Front Party (PFL) and the Brazilian Labor Party (PTB). Brazil's largest party, the centrist Brazilian Democratic Movement Party (PMDB), joined Cardoso's governing coalition after the election, as did the center-right PPB, the Brazilian Progressive Party, in 1996. Party loyalty is weak, and deputies and senators who belong to the parties comprising the government coalition do not always vote with the government. As a result, President Cardoso has had difficulty, at times, gaining sufficient support for some of his legislative priorities, despite the fact that his coalition parties hold an overwhelming majority of congressional seats. Nevertheless, the Cardoso administration has accomplished many of its legislative and reform objectives.

States are organized like the federal government, with three government branches. Because of the mandatory revenue allocation to states and municipalities provided for in the 1988 constitution, Brazilian governors and mayors have exercised considerable power since 1989. Presidential, congressional, and gubernatorial elections last took place in October 1998. Fernando Henrique Cardoso won the presidential election with approximately 53% of the vote, while his closest challenger, Luiz Inacio Lula da Silva (PT), had about 32%. The next national elections will be held in October 2002.

## Principal Government Officials

**For up-to-date information on Principal Government Officials, see the Chiefs of State and Cabinet Members of Foreign Governments section starting on page 1.**

Brazil maintains an embassy in the United States at 3006 Massachusetts Avenue NW, Washington, DC 20008 (tel. 202–238–2700).
Brazil maintains consulates general in New York, Chicago, and Los Angeles; and consulates in Miami, Houston, Boston, San Francisco, and Orlando.

# ECONOMY

Brazil is the tenth-largest economy in the world, with 2000 GDP of $588 billion. It is a highly diversified economy with wide variations in levels of development. Most large industry is concentrated in the south and southeast. The northeast is traditionally the poorest part of Brazil, but it is beginning to attract new investment. Brazil embarked on a successful economic stabilization program, the Plano Real (named for the new currency, the real; plural: reais) in July 1994. Inflation, which had reached an annual level of nearly 5,000% at the end of 1993, fell sharply, reaching a low of 2.5% in 1998; it was 6% in 2000. Brazil successfully shifted from an essentially, fixed exchange rate regime to a floating regime in January 1999.

The Cardoso administration has introduced to Congress a series of constitutional reform proposals to replace a state-dominated economy with a market-oriented one and to restructure all levels of government on a sound fiscal sound basis. Congress has approved several amendments to open the economy to greater private sector participation, including foreign investors. By the end of last year, Brazil's privatization program, which included the sale of steel and telecommunications firms, had generated proceeds of more than $90 billion. Passage of the Fiscal Responsibility Law in mid-2000 improved fiscal discipline at all three levels—federal, state, and municipal—and all three branches of government. Some measures have been adopted to address large deficits in Brazil's pension programs, but more remains to be done. Tax reform—simplification—has been under debate for over 2 years, but there has not yet been sufficient closure for final legislative action. Despite fiscal austerity, the administration has acknowledged the need to invest more in education and health to redress social inequity.

Market opening and economic stabilization have significantly enhanced Brazil's growth prospects. Brazil's trade has almost doubled since 1990. U.S. direct foreign investment has increased from less than $19 billion in 1994 to an estimated $35 billion through 2000. The United States is the largest foreign investor in Brazil. Upcoming privatizations in the power and banking sectors will likely elicit strong interest from U.S. firms.

Brazil is endowed with vast agricultural resources. There are basically two distinct agricultural areas. The first, comprised of the southern one-half to two-thirds of the country, has a semi-temperate climate and higher rainfall, the better soils, higher technology and input use, adequate infrastructure, and more experienced farmers. It produces most of Brazil's grains and oilseeds and export crops.

The other, located in the drought-ridden northeast region and in the Amazon basin, lacks well-distributed rainfall, good soil, adequate infrastructure, and sufficient development capital. Although producing mostly for self-sufficiency, the latter regions are increasingly important as exporters of forest products, cocoa, and tropical fruits. Central Brazil contains substantial areas of grassland with only scattered trees. The Brazilian grasslands are less fertile than those of North America and are generally more suited for grazing.

Brazilian agriculture is well diversified, and the country is largely self-sufficient in food. Agriculture accounts for 8% of the country's GDP, and employs about one-quarter of the labor force in more than 6 million agricultural enterprises. Brazil is the world's largest producer of sugarcane and coffee, and a net exporter of cocoa, soybeans, orange juice, tobacco, forest products, and other tropical fruits and nuts. Livestock production is important in many sections of the country, with rapid growth in the poultry, pork, and milk industries reflecting changes in consumers tastes. On a value basis, production is 60% field crop and 40% livestock. Brazil is a net exporter of agricultural and food products, which account for about 35% of the country's exports.

Half of Brazil is covered by forests, with the largest rain forest in the world located in the Amazon Basin. Recent migrations into the Amazon and largescale burning of forest areas have placed the international spotlight on Brazil. The government has reduced incentives for such activity and is beginning to implement an ambitious environmental plan—and has just adopted an Environmental Crimes Law that requires serious penalties for infractions.

Brazil has one of the most advanced industrial sectors in Latin America. Accounting for one-third of GDP, Brazil's diverse industries range from automobiles, steel, and petrochemicals, to computers, aircraft, and consumer durables. With the increased economic stability provided by the

Plano Real, Brazilian firms and multinationals have invested heavily in new equipment and technology, a large share of which has been purchased from U.S. firms.

Brazil has a diverse and sophisticated services industry as well. During the early 1990s, the banking sector accounted for as much as 16% of GDP. Although undergoing a major overhaul, Brazil's financial services industry provides local firms a wide range of products and is attracting numerous new entrants, including U.S. financial firms. The Sao Paulo and Rio de Janeiro stock exchanges are undergoing a consolidation and the reinsurance sector is about to be privatized.

The Brazilian Government has undertaken an ambitious program to reduce dependence on imported oil. Imports previously accounted for more than 70% of the country's oil needs but now account for about 33%. Brazil is one of the world's leading producers of hydroelectric power, with a current capacity of about 58,000 megawatts. Existing hydroelectric power provides 92% of the nation's electricity. Two large hydroelectrical projects, the 12,600 megawatt Itaipu Dam on the Parana River—the world's largest dam—and the Tucurui Dam in Para in northern Brazil, are in operation. Brazil's first commercial nuclear reactor, Angra I, located near Rio de Janeiro, has been in operation for more than 10 years. Angra II is under construction and, after years of delays, is about to come

on line. An Angra III is planned. The three reactors would have combined capacity of 3,000 megawatts when completed.

Proven mineral resources are extensive. Large iron and manganese reserves are important sources of industrial raw materials and export earnings. Deposits of nickel, tin, chromite, bauxite, beryllium, copper, lead, tungsten, zinc, gold, and other minerals are exploited. High-quality coking-grade coal required in the steel industry is in short supply.

# FOREIGN RELATIONS

Traditionally, Brazil has been a leader in the inter-American community and has played an important role in collective security efforts, as well as in economic cooperation in the Western Hemisphere. Brazil supported the Allies in both World Wars. During World War II, its expeditionary force in Italy played a key role in the Allied victory at Monte Castello. It is a party to the Inter-American Treaty of Reciprocal Assistance (Rio Treaty) and a member of the Organization of American States (OAS). Recently, Brazil has given high priority to expanding relations with its South American neighbors and is a founding member of the Amazon Pact, the Latin American Integration Association (ALADI), and Mercosul (Mercosur in Spanish), an imperfect customs union including Argentina, Uruguay, Paraguay, and Brazil. Along with Argentina, Chile, and the United States, Brazil is one of the guarantors of the Peru-Ecuador peace process. Brazil is a charter member of the United Nations and participates in many of its specialized agencies. It has contributed troops to UN peacekeeping efforts in the Middle East, the former Belgian Congo, Cyprus, Mozambique, Angola, and most recently East Timor. Brazil has been a member of the UN Security Council four times, most recently 1998–2000.

As Brazil's domestic economy has grown and diversified, the country has become increasingly involved in international politics and economics. The United States, western Europe, and Japan are primary markets for Brazilian exports and sources of foreign lending and investment. Brazil has also bolstered its commitment to nonproliferation through ratification of the nuclear Non-Proliferation Treaty (NPT), signing a fullscale nuclear safeguard agreement with the International Atomic Energy Agency (IAEA), acceeding to the Treaty of Tlatelolco, and becoming a member of the Missile Technology Control Regime (MTCR) and the Nuclear Suppliers Group.

# U.S.-BRAZILIAN RELATIONS

The United States was the first country to recognize Brazil's independence in 1822. The two countries have traditionally enjoyed friendly, active relations encompassing a broad political and economic agenda.

With the inauguration of Brazil's internationally oriented, reformist President Fernando Henrique Cardoso on January 1, 1995, U.S.-Brazil engagement and cooperation have intensified. This is reflected in the unprecedented number of high-level contacts between the two governments, including President Cardoso's state visit to Washington in April 1995, visits to Brazil by former President Bill Clinton and First Lady Hillary Rodham Clinton, former Secretaries of State Madeleine Albright and Warren Christopher, former Secretaries of Commerce Ronald Brown and William Daley, former Secretary of Defense William S. Cohen, and many other exchanges between U.S. and Brazilian cabinet and subcabinet officials. Important topics of discussion and cooperation have included trade and finance; hemispheric economic integration; United Nations reform and peace-keeping efforts; nonproliferation and arms control; follow-up to the 1994 Miami Summit of the Americas; common efforts to help resolve the Peru-Ecuador border conflict; and support for Paraguay's democratic develop-

ment, human rights, counternarcotics, and environmental issues.

During former President Clinton's October 1997 visit to Brazil, several agreements were signed, including an Education Partnership Agreement, which enhances and expands cooperative initiatives in such areas as standards-based education reform, use of technology, and professional development of teachers; a Mutual Legal Assistance treaty—ratified in 2001; and agreements on cooperation in energy, the international space station, national parks, and government reform. In April 2000 the United States and Brazil signed a Technical Safeguards Agreement to permit U.S. commercial firms to participate in the development of the Alcantara spaceport. During a visit of then-Under Secretary of State Timothy Wirth to Brazil in October 1995, the two countries signed a Common Agenda on the Environment, laying the foundation for cooperative efforts in environmental protection. Brazil is a key player in hemispheric efforts to negotiate an FTAA by 2005, and hosted the May 1997 FTAA Trade Ministerial in Belo Horizonte.

President Cardoso has been willing to discuss race relations frankly. He instituted an Inter-Ministerial Task Force on Race in 1995 and strengthened the mandate of the government-funded Palmares Foundation, dedicated to the promotion of Afro-Brazilian heritage. U.S. embassy public diplomacy programs seek to support these efforts, which mirror former President Clinton's National Dialogue on Race.

Relations are advancing well in various aspects of scientific and technical work. During his 1996 visit, former Secretary of State Christopher signed a Space Cooperation agreement and initialed an agreement on Peaceful Uses of Nuclear Energy.

## U.S. Embassy and Consulate Functions

In addition to working closely with Brazilian Government officials to strengthen the bilateral relationship, the U.S. embassy and consulates in

Brazil provide a wide range of services to U.S. citizens and business. Political, economic, and science officers deal directly with the Brazilian Government in advancing U.S. interests but also are available to brief U.S. citizens on general conditions in the country. Attaches from the U.S. Commercial Service and Foreign Agriculture Service work closely with hundreds of U.S. companies that maintain offices in Brazil. These officers provide information on Brazilian trade and industry regulations and administer several programs to aid U.S. companies starting or maintaining business ventures in Brazil. The number of trade events and U.S. companies traveling to Brazil to participate in U.S. Commercial Service and Foreign Agriculture Service programs over the last 3 years has tripled.

The consular section of the embassy provides vital services to the estimated 50,000 U.S. citizens residing in Brazil. Among other services, the consular section assists Americans who wish to participate in U.S. elections while abroad and provides U.S. tax information. Besides the U.S. residents living in Brazil, some 150,000 U.S. citizens visit annually. The consular section offers passport and emergency services to U.S. tourists as needed during their stay in Brazil.

## Principal U.S. Embassy Officials

**For up-to-date information on Principal U.S. Officials, see the U.S. Embassies, Consulates, and Foreign Service section starting on page 139.**

The U.S. embassy in Brasilia is located at SES Avenida das Nacoes, quadra 801, lote 3, Brasilia, DF, CEP: 70.403–900 (tel. 55–61–321–7272), (fax 55–61–321–2833). Internet: http://www.embaixada-americana.org.br/
There are U.S. consulates general in Rio de Janeiro and Sao Paulo, and a consulate in Recife. Consular agents

are located in Manaus, Belem, Salvador, Fortaleza, and Porto Alegre. Branch offices of the U.S. Information Service.

(USIS) are located in Brasilia, Rio de Janeiro, and Sao Paulo. Branch offices of the U.S. Foreign Commercial Services are located in Brasilia, Sao Paulo, Rio de Janeiro, and Belo Horizonte.

## Other Business Contacts

**U.S. Department of Commerce Office of Latin America and the Caribbean**

International Trade Administration 14th and Constitution Avenue, NW Washington, DC 20230
Tel: 202–482–0428 1–800-U.S.A-TRADE
Fax: 202–482–4157
Automated fax service for trade-related info: 202–482–4464
Internet: http://www.ita.doc.gov

**American Chamber of Commerce of Sao Paulov**
Rua da Paz, no. 1431 04713–001 - Chacara Santo Antonio
Sao Paulo - SP, Brazil
Tel: 55–11–51–803–804

Fax: 55–11–51–803–777
E-mail: amhost@amcham.com.br
Home Page: http://www.amcham.com.br

**American Chamber of Commerce of Rio de Janeiro** (a branch also is in Salvador)
Praca Pio X-15, 5th Floor
Caixa Postal 916 20040 Rio de Janeiro—RJ-Brazil
Tel: 55–21–203–2477
Fax: 55–21–263–4477
E-mail:amchambr@unisys.com.br
Home Page: http://amchamrio.com.br

# BRUNEI

October 2000

Official Name:
**Brunei Darussalam**

# PROFILE

## Geography
**Area:** 5,769 sq. km. (2,227 sq. mi.), slightly larger than Delaware.
**Cities:** Capital—Bandar Seri Begawan.
**Terrain:** East—flat coastal plains with beaches; west—hilly with a few mountain ridges.
**Climate:** Equatorial; high temperatures, humidity, and rainfall.

## People
**Nationality:** Noun and adjective—Bruneian(s).
**Population:** (1999 est.) 330,700.
**Annual growth rate:** 2.4%.
**Ethnic Groups:** Malay, Chinese, other indigenous.
**Religion:** Islam.
**Languages:** Malay, English, Chinese; Iban and other indigenous dialects.
**Education:** Years compulsory—9. Literacy (1999)—92.5%.
**Health:** Life expectancy—74 yrs. Infant mortality rate (1998)—6.5/1,000.

## Government
**Type:** Malay Islamic Monarchy.
**Independence:** January 1, 1984.
**Constitution:** 1959.

**Branches:** Executive—Sultan is both head of state and prime minister, presiding over a nine-member cabinet. Judicial (based on Indian penal code and English common law)—magistrate's courts, High Court, Court of Appeals, Judicial Committee of the Privy Council (sits in London).
**Subdivisions:** Four districts—Brunei-Muara, Belait, Tutong, and Temburong.

## Economy
**GDP:** (1999 est.) $4.5 billion.
**Growth rate:** (1999 est.) 2.5%.
**Natural resources:** Oil and natural gas.
**Trade:** Exports—oil, liquefied natural gas, petroleum products, garments. Major markets—Japan, Korea, ASEAN, U.S. Imports—machinery and transport equipment, manufactured goods. Major suppliers—ASEAN, Japan, U.S., EU.

# PEOPLE

Many cultural and linguistic differences make Brunei Malays distinct from the larger Malay populations in nearby Malaysia and Indonesia, even though they are ethnically related and share the Muslim religion.

Brunei has a hereditary nobility with the title Pengiran. The Sultan can award to commoners the title Pehin, the equivalent of a life peerage awarded in the United Kingdom. The Sultan also can award his subjects the Dato, the equivalent of a knighthood in the United Kingdom, and Datin, the equivalent of a damehood. Bruneians adhere to the practice of using complete full names with all titles, including the title Haji (for men) or Hajjah (for women) for those who have made the Haj pilgrimage to Mecca. Many Brunei Malay women wear the tudong, a traditional head covering. Men wear the songkok, a traditional Malay cap. Men who have completed the Haj wear a white songkok.

The requirements to attain Brunei citizenship include passing tests in Malay culture, customs, and language. Stateless permanent residents of Brunei are given International Certificates of Identity, which allow them to travel overseas. The majority of Brunei's Chinese are permanent residents, and many are stateless.

Oil wealth allows the Brunei Government to provide the population with one of Asia's finest health care systems. The Brunei Medical and Health Department introduced the region's first government "flying doctor service" in early 1965. Malaria has been eradicated, and cholera is virtually nonexistent. There are three general hospitals—in Bandar Seri Begawan, Tutong, and Kuala Belait—and there are numerous health clinics throughout the country.

Education starts with preschool, followed by 6 years of primary education and up to 6 years of secondary education. Nine years of education are mandatory. Most of Brunei's college students attend universities and other institutions abroad, but approximately 2,542 study at the University of Brunei Darussalam. Opened in 1985, the university has a faculty of over 300 instructors and is located on a sprawling campus at Tungku, overlooking the South China Sea.

The official language is Malay, but English is widely understood and used in business. Other languages spoken are several Chinese dialects, Iban, and a number of native dialects. Islam is the official religion, but religious freedom is guaranteed under the constitution.

# HISTORY

Historians believe there was a forerunner to the present Brunei Sultanate, which the Chinese called Po-ni. Chinese and Arabic records indicate that this ancient trading kingdom existed at the mouth of the Brunei River as early as the seventh or eighth century A.D. This early kingdom was apparently conquered by the Sumatran empire of Srivijaya in the early ninth century and later controlled northern Borneo and the Philippines. It was subjugated briefly by the Java-based Majapahit Empire but soon regained its independence and once again rose to prominence.

The Brunei Empire had its golden age from the 15th to the 17th centuries, when its control extended over the entire island of Borneo and north into the Philippines. Brunei was particularly powerful under the fifth sultan, Bolkiah (1473-1521), who was famed for his sea exploits and even briefly captured Manila; and under the ninth sultan, Hassan (1605-19), who fully developed an elaborate

Royal Court structure, elements of which remain today.

After Sultan Hassan, Brunei entered a period of decline, due to internal battles over royal succession as well as the rising influences of European colonial powers in the region, that, among other things, disrupted traditional trading patterns, destroying the economic base of Brunei and many other Southeast Asian sultanates. In 1839, the English adventurer James Brooke arrived in Borneo and helped the Sultan put down a rebellion. As a reward, he became governor and later "Rajah" of Sarawak in northwest Borneo and gradually expanded the territory under his control.

Meanwhile, the British North Borneo Company was expanding its control over territory in northeast Borneo. In 1888, Brunei became a protectorate of the British Government, retaining internal independence but with British control over external affairs. In 1906, Brunei accepted a further measure of British control when executive power was transferred to a British resident, who advised the ruler on all matters except those concerning local custom and religion.

In 1959, a new constitution was written declaring Brunei a self-governing state, while its foreign affairs, security, and defense remained the responsibility of the United Kingdom. An attempt in 1962 to introduce a partially elected legislative body with limited powers was abandoned after the opposition political party, Partai Rakyat Brunei, launched an armed uprising, which the government put down with the help of British forces. In the late 1950s and early 1960s, the government also resisted pressures to join neighboring Sabah and Sarawak in the newly formed Malaysia. The Sultan eventually decided that Brunei would remain an independent state.

In 1967, Sultan Omar abdicated in favor of his eldest son, Hassanal Bolkiah, who became the 29th ruler. The former Sultan remained as Defense Minister and assumed the royal title Seri Begawan. In 1970, the

national capital, Brunei Town, was renamed Bandar Seri Begawan in his honor. The Seri Begawan died in 1986.

On January 4, 1979, Brunei and the United Kingdom signed a new treaty of friendship and cooperation. On January 1, 1984, Brunei Darussalam became a fully independent state.

# GOVERNMENT AND POLITICAL CONDITIONS

Under Brunei's 1959 constitution, the Sultan is the head of state with full executive authority, including emergency powers since 1962. The Sultan is assisted and advised by five councils, which he appoints. A Council of Ministers, or cabinet, which currently consists of nine members (including the Sultan himself), assists in the administration of the government. The Sultan presides over the cabinet as Prime Minister and also holds the positions of Minister of Defense and Minister of Finance. One of the Sultan's brothers, Prince Mohamed, serves as Minister of Foreign Affairs.

Brunei's legal system is based on English common law, with an independent judiciary, a body of written common law judgments and statutes, and legislation enacted by the sultan. Most cases are tried by the local magistrate's courts. More serious cases go before the High Court, which sits for about 2 weeks every few months. Brunei has an arrangement with the United Kingdom whereby United Kingdom judges are appointed as the judges for Brunei's High Court and Court of Appeal. Final appeal can be made to the Judicial Committee of the Privy Council in London in civil but not criminal cases.

The Government of Brunei assures continuing public support for the current form of government by providing economic benefits such as subsidized food, fuel and housing, free education and medical care, and low-interest loans for government employees. The Sultan said in a 1989 interview that he intended to proceed, with prudence, to establish more liberal institutions in the country and that he would reintroduce elections and a legislature when he "[could] see evidence of a genuine interest in politics on the part of a responsible majority of Bruneians." In 1994, a constitutional review committee submitted its findings to the Sultan, but these have not been made public.

Brunei's economy is almost totally supported by exports of crude oil and natural gas. The government uses its earnings in part to build up its foreign reserves, which at one time reportedly reached more than $30 billion. The country's wealth, coupled with its membership in the United Nations, Association of Southeast Asian Nations (ASEAN), the Asia Pacific Economic Cooperation (APEC) forum, and the Organization of the Islamic Conference give it an influence in the world disproportionate to its size.

## Principal Government Officials

**For up-to-date information on Principal Government Officials, see the Chiefs of State and Cabinet Members of Foreign Governments section starting on page 1.**

Brunei Darussalam maintains an embassy in the United States at 3520 International Court, NW, Washington, DC 20008, tel. 202-237-1838.

# ECONOMY

The Asian financial crisis in 1997 and 1998, coupled with fluctuations in the price of oil have created uncertainty and instability in Brunei's economy. In addition, the 1998 collapse of the AMEDEO Corporation, Brunei's largest construction firm whose projects helped fuel the domestic economy, caused the country to slip into a mild recession.

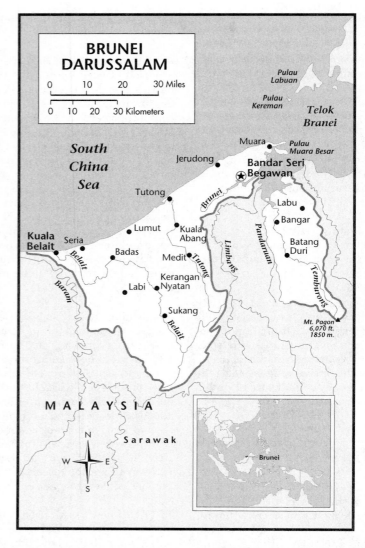

Brunei is the third-largest oil producer in Southeast Asia, averaging about 180,000 barrels a day. It also is the fourth-largest producer of liquefied natural gas in the world. Brunei's gross domestic product (GDP) soared with the petroleum price increases of the 1970s to a peak of $5.7 billion in 1980. It declined slightly in each of the next 5 years, then fell by almost 30% in 1986. This drop was caused by a combination of sharply lower petroleum prices in world markets and voluntary production cuts in Brunei. The GDP recovered somewhat since 1986, growing by 12% in 1987, 1% in 1988, and 9% in 1989. In recent years, GDP growth was 3.5% in 1996, 4.0% in 1997, 1.0% in 1998, and an estimated 2.5% in 1999. However, the 1999 GDP was still only about $4.5 billion, well below the 1980 peak.

In the 1970s, Brunei invested sharply increasing revenues from petroleum exports and maintained government spending at a low and constant rate. Consequently, the government was able to build its foreign reserves and invest them around the world to help provide for future generations. Part of the reserve earnings were reportedly also used to help finance the government's annual budget deficit. Since 1986, however, petroleum revenues have decreased, and government spending has increased. The government has been running a budget deficit since 1988. The disappearance of a revenue surplus has made Brunei's economy more vulnerable to petroleum price fluctuations.

Brunei Shell Petroleum (BSP), a joint venture owned in equal shares by the Brunei Government and the Royal

Dutch/Shell group of companies, is the chief oil and gas production company in Brunei. It also operates the country's only refinery. BSP and four sister companies constitute the largest employer in Brunei after the government. BSP's small refinery has a distillation capacity of 10,000 barrels per day. This satisfies domestic demand for most petroleum products.

The French oil company ELF Aquitaine, became active in petroleum exploration in Brunei in the 1980s. Known as Elf Petroleum Asia BV, it has discovered commercially exploitable quantities of oil and gas in three of the four wells drilled since 1987, including a particularly promising discovery announced in early 1990. Recently, UNOCAL, partnered with New Zealand's Fletcher Challenge has been granted concessions for oil exploration. Brunei is preparing to tender concessions for deep water oil and gas exploration.

Brunei's oil production peaked in 1979 at over 240,000 barrels per day. Since then it has been deliberately cut back to extend the life of oil reserves and improve recovery rates. Petroleum production is currently averaging 180,000 barrels per day. Japan has traditionally been the main customer for Brunei's oil exports, but its share dropped from 45% of the total in 1982 to 19% in 1998. In contrast, oil exports to South Korea increased from only 8% of the total in 1982 to 29% in 1998. Other major customers include Taiwan (6%), and the countries of ASEAN (27%). Brunei's oil exports to the United States accounted for 17% of the total exported.

Almost all of Brunei's natural gas is liquefied at Brunei Shell's Liquefied Natural Gas (LNG) plant, which opened in 1972 and is one of the largest LNG plants in the world. Over 82% of Brunei's LNG produced is sold to Japan under a long-term agreement renewed in 1993. The agreement calls for Brunei to provide over 5 million tons of LNG per year to three Japanese utilities. The Japanese company, Mitsubishi, is a joint venture partner with Shell and the Brunei Government in Brunei LNG,

**Travel Notes**

**Travel Advice:** For up-to-date information from the U.S. State Department on possible inconvenient or hazardous situations, see the **Travel Warnings and Consular Information Sheets from the U.S. Government** section starting on page 1723. For the latest information on health requirements and conditions, see the **International Travelers' Health Information** section starting on page 1385. For further information dealing with non-urgent matter, see the **Tips for Travelers to...** section starting on page 1588.

Brunei Coldgas, and Brunei Shell Tankers, which together produce the LNG and supply it to Japan. Since 1995, Brunei has supplied more than 700,000 tons of LNG to the Korea Gas Corporation as well. In 1999, Brunei's natural gas production reached 90 cargoes per day. A small amount of natural gas is used for domestic power generation. Brunei is the fourth-largest exporter of LNG in the Asia-Pacific region behind Indonesia, Malaysia, and Australia.

Brunei's proven oil and gas reserves are sufficient until at least 2015, and planned deep sea exploration is expected to find significant new reserves. The government sought in the past decade to diversify the economy with limited success. Oil and gas and government spending still account for most of Brunei's economic activity. Brunei's non-petroleum industries include agriculture, forestry, fishing, and banking.

The government regulates the immigration of foreign labor out of concern it might disrupt Brunei's society. Work permits for foreigners are issued only for short periods and must be continually renewed. Despite these restrictions, foreigners make up a significant portion of the work force. The government reported a total work force of 122,800 in 1999, with an unemployment rate of 5.5%.

Oil and natural gas account for almost all exports. Since only a few products other than petroleum are produced locally, a wide variety of

items must be imported. Brunei statistics show Singapore as the largest point of origin of imports, accounting for 25% in 1997. However, this figure includes some transshipments, since most of Brunei's imports transit Singapore. Japan and Malaysia were the second-largest suppliers. As in many other countries, Japanese products dominate local markets for motor vehicles, construction equipment, electronic goods, and household appliances. The United States was the third-largest supplier of imports to Brunei in 1998.

Brunei's substantial foreign reserves are managed by the Brunei Investment Agency (BIA), an arm of the Ministry of Finance. BIA's guiding principle is to increase the real value of Brunei's foreign reserves while pursuing a diverse investment strategy, with holdings in the United States, Japan, western Europe, and the Association of South East Asian Nations (ASEAN) countries.

The Brunei Government actively encourages more foreign investment. New enterprises that meet certain criteria can receive pioneer status, exempting profits from income tax for up to 5 years, depending on the amount of capital invested. The normal corporate income tax rate is 30%. There is no personal income tax or capital gains tax.

One of the government's most important priorities is to encourage the development of Brunei Malays as leaders of industry and commerce. There are no specific restrictions of foreign equity ownership, but local participation, both shared capital and management, is encouraged. Such participation helps when tendering for contracts with the government or Brunei Shell Petroleum. Companies in Brunei must either be incorporated locally or registered as a branch of a foreign company and must be registered with the Registrar of Companies. Public companies must have a minimum of seven shareholders. Private companies must have a minimum of two but not more than 50 shareholders. At least half of the directors in a company must be residents of Brunei.

The government owns a cattle farm in Australia that supplies most of the country's beef. At 2,262 square miles, this ranch is larger than Brunei itself. Eggs and chickens are largely produced locally, but most of Brunei's other food needs must be imported. Agriculture and fisheries are among the industrial sectors that the government has selected for highest priority in its efforts to diversify the economy.

Recently the government has announced plans for Brunei to become an International Offshore Financial Center as well as a Center for Islamic Banking. Brunei is keen on the development of Small and Medium Enterprises and also is investigating the possibility of establishing a "cyber park" to develop an information technology industry. Brunei also hopes to foster tourism through its "Visit Brunei 2001" campaign.

# DEFENSE

The Sultan is both Minister of Defense and Supreme Commander of the Armed Forces (RBAF). All infantry, navy, and air combat units are made up of volunteers. There are two infantry brigades, equipped with armored reconnaissance vehicles and armored personnel carriers and supported by Rapier air defense missiles and a flotilla of coastal patrol vessels armed with surface-to-surface missiles.

Brunei has a defense agreement with the United Kingdom, under which a British Armed Forces Ghurka battalion is permanently stationed in Seria, near the center of Brunei's oil industry. The RBAF has joint exercises, training programs, and other military cooperation with the United Kingdom and many other countries, including the United States.

# FOREIGN RELATIONS

Brunei joined ASEAN on January 7, 1984—1 week after resuming full independence —and gives its ASEAN membership the highest priority in its foreign relations. Brunei joined the UN in September 1984. It also is a member of the Organization of the Islamic Conference (OIC) and of the Asia-Pacific Economic Cooperation (APEC) forum. Brunei hosts the APEC Economic Leaders' Meeting in November 2000.

# U.S.-BRUNEI RELATIONS

Relations between the United States and Brunei date from the last century. On April 6, 1845, the U.S.S. Constitution visited Brunei. The two countries concluded a Treaty of Peace, Friendship, Commerce and Navigation in 1850, which remains in force today. The United States maintained a consulate in Brunei from 1865 to 1867.

The U.S. welcomed Brunei Darussalam's full independence from the United Kingdom on January 1, 1984, and opened an embassy in Bandar Seri Begawan on that date. Brunei opened its embassy in Washington in March 1984. Brunei's armed forces engage in joint exercises, training programs, and other military cooperation with the U.S. A memorandum of understanding on defense cooperation was signed on November 29, 1994.

## Principal U.S. Embassy Officials

For up-to-date information on Principal U.S. Officials, see the U.S. Embassies, Consulates, and Foreign Service section starting on page 139.

The U.S. Embassy in Bandar Seri Begawan is located on the third floor of Teck Guan Plaza, at the corner of Jalan Sultan and Jalan MacArthur; Tel: 673-2-229670; Fax: 673-2-225293; E-mail: amembsb@brunet.bn.

# BULGARIA
October 1999

## Official Name:
## Republic of Bulgaria

## PROFILE

### Geography

**Area:** 110,994 sq. km; slightly larger than Tennessee.
**Cities:** Capital—Sofia. Other cities—Plovdiv, Varna, Burgas, Ruse, Blago-evgrad.
**Terrain:** Mostly mountainous with large fertile valleys and plains; low-lands in the north and southeast; Black Sea coast on the east.
**Climate:** Temperate.

### People

**Nationality:** Noun and adjective—Bulgarian(s).
**Population (1998):** 8.2 million.
**Population growth rate (1998 est.):** −0.6%.
**Ethnic groups:** Bulgarian 85.6%; Turks 9.5%; Roma 4%; others 1%.
Religions: Bulgarian Orthodox 83.5%; Islam 13%; Roman Catholic 1.5%; others 0.5%. Languages: Bul-garian (official); Turkish; Roma.
**Education:** Literacy—98%.
**Health:** Infant mortality rate (1998)—14.4/1,000. Life expect-ancy—males 67 yrs., female 74 yrs.

### Government

**Type:** Parliamentary democracy.

**Constitution:** July 12, 1991.
**Independence:** March 3, 1887 (from the Ottoman Empire).
**Subdivisions:** 9 provinces (oblasti)—Sofia, Sofia City, Burgas, Haskovo, Lovech, Montana, Plovdiv, Ruse, Varna.
**Political parties:** Union of Demo-cratic Forces (UDF); People's Union (comprised of the Bulgarian Agrarian National Union, People's Union and the Democratic Party); Bulgarian Socialist Party (BSP); Alliance for National Salvation, comprised of the mainly ethnic Turkish Movement for Rights and Freedoms (MRF) and smaller partners; Bulgarian Busi-ness Bloc (BBB); and the Euroleft.
**Suffrage:** Universal at 18.

### Economy

**GDP (1998 est):** $12.3 billion. About 63.7% of GDP is contributed by the private sector.
**GDP growth rate (1998):** 3.5%.
**Per capita income:** $1,484.
**Inflation rate (1998):** 1%.
**Natural resources:** Copper, lead, zinc, lignite, iron, manganese, lime-stone and lumber.
**Agriculture (1998):** 21% of GDP. Products—grain crops (more than one–third of the arable land), oil-seeds, vegetables, fruits, tobacco (world's fourth–largest exporter); livestock.
**Industry (1998):** 28% of GDP. Types—machinery and metal prod-

ucts, food processing, textiles, chemi-cals, building materials, electronics.
**Services (1998):** 50% of GDP.
**Trade:** Imports—$4,609 million. Exports—$4,293 million.

## HISTORY

Long a crossroads of civilizations (archaeological finds date back to 4600 B.C.), Bulgaria was first recog-nized as an independent state in AD 681. Bulgarian Orthodox Christian-ity, which became a hallmark of national identity, was established in the 9th century. Bulgaria was ruled by the Byzantine Empire from 1018 to 1185 and the Ottoman Empire from 1396 to 1878. In 1879, Bulgaria adopted a democratic constitution and invited a German nobleman, Alexander of Battenburg, to be prince. When Alexander abdicated in 1885, Prince Ferdinand of Saxe–Coburg–Gotha became prince. In 1908 he proclaimed himself King.

In the early part of the 20th century, in an effort to gain Macedonian and other territories, Bulgaria engaged in two Balkan wars and become allied with Germany during World War I. It suffered disastrous losses as a result. The interwar period was dominated by economic and political instability and by terrorism as political factions, including monarchists and communists, struggled for influence. In World War II, Bulgaria ultimately allied again with Germany but protected its Jewish population of some 50,000 from the Holocaust. When King Boris III died in 1943, political uncertainty heightened. The Fatherland Front, an umbrella coalition led by the Communist Party, was established. This coalition backed neutrality and withdrawal from occupied territories. Bulgaria tried to avoid open conflict with the Soviet Union during the war, but the U.S.S.R. invaded in 1944 and placed the Fatherland Front in control of government.

After Bulgaria's surrender to the Allies, the Communist Party purged opposition figures in the Fatherland Front, exiled young King Simeon II, and rigged elections to consolidate power. In 1946, a referendum was passed overwhelmingly, ending the monarchy and declaring Bulgaria a people's republic. In a questionable election the next year, the Fatherland Front won 70% of the vote and Communist Party leader Georgi Dimitrov became Prime Minister. In 1947, the Allied military left Bulgaria, and the government declared the country a communist state. Forty–two years of heavy–handed totalitarian rule followed. All democratic opposition was crushed, agriculture and industry were nationalized, and Bulgaria became the closest of the Soviet Union's allies. Unlike other countries of the Warsaw Pact, however, Bulgaria did not have Soviet troops stationed on its territory.

Dimitrov died in 1949. Todor Zhivkov became Communist Party chief in 1956 and prime minister in 1962. Zhivkov held power until November 1989, when he was deposed by members of his own party, soon renamed the Bulgarian Socialist Party (BSP).

Bulgaria has been a parliamentary democracy since 1990. Four parliamentary and two presidential elections have been held since the fall of the communist dictatorship in November 1989, each followed by peaceful and orderly change.

# GOVERNMENT AND POLITICAL CONDITIONS

The president, elected for a 5–year term, is head of state and commander in chief of the armed forces. The president's main duties are to schedule elections and referenda, represent Bulgaria abroad, conclude international treaties, and head the Consultative Council for National Security. The president may return legislation to Parliament for further debate—a kind of veto—but the legislation can be passed again by a simple majority vote. Petar Stoyanov, the candidate of a united opposition coalition led by the Union of Democratic Forces (UDF), was nominated to run for president in the country's first primary election in June 1996. Stoyanov was elected in November and inaugurated in January 1997.

The legislative body is the unicameral National Assembly of 240 members elected to 4–year terms. Political parties must garner a minimum of 4% of the national vote in order to enter Parliament. Parliament is responsible for enactment of laws, approval of the budget, scheduling of presidential elections, selection and dismissal of the prime minister and other ministers, declaration of war and deployment of troops outside of Bulgaria, and ratification of international treaties and agreements.

The BSP won the first post–communist parliamentary elections in 1990 with a small majority. The BSP government formed at that time was brought down by a general strike in late 1990 and replaced by a transitional coalition government. Meanwhile, Zhelyu Zhelev, a communist–era dissident, was elected president by the Parliament in 1990 and later won Bulgaria's first direct presidential elections, in 1992. Zhelev served until early 1997. The country's first fully democratic parliamentary elections, in November 1991, ushered in another coalition government, which was led by the pro–reform UDF in

partnership with the Movement for Rights and Freedoms (MRF). This coalition collapsed in late 1992, however, and was succeeded by a technocratic team, put forward by the MRF, which governed at the sufferance of the BSP for 2 years. The BSP won pre–term elections in December 1994 and remained in office until February 1997, when a populace alienated by the BSP's failed, corrupt government demanded its resignation and called for new elections. A caretaker cabinet appointed by the President served until pre–term parliamentary elections in April 1997, which yielded a landslide victory for pro–reform forces led by the UDF in the United Democratic Forces coalition. Along with the UDF, there are five other parties represented in Parliament.

The Council of Ministers is the principal organ of the executive branch. It is usually formed by the majority party in Parliament, if one exists, or by the largest party in Parliament along with coalition partners. Chaired by the prime minister, it is responsible for carrying out state policy, managing the state budget, and maintaining law and order. The Council must resign if the National Assembly passes a vote of no confidence in the Council or the prime minister.

Bulgaria's judicial system is independent and is managed by the Supreme Judicial Council. Its principal elements are the Supreme Court of Administration and the Supreme Court of Cassation, which oversee application of all laws by the lower courts and judge the legality of government acts. There is a separate Constitutional Court, which interprets the Constitution and rules on the constitutionality of laws and treaties.

Six out of the 34 political parties and coalitions that fielded candidates in the last election are represented in Parliament. The UDF recaptured Parliament in April 1997 with 123 seats out of 240. Its electoral coalition partner, the People's Union, carried 14 seats. Also in that election, the BSP dropped from its 1994 majority of 125 seats to 58. The MRF formed

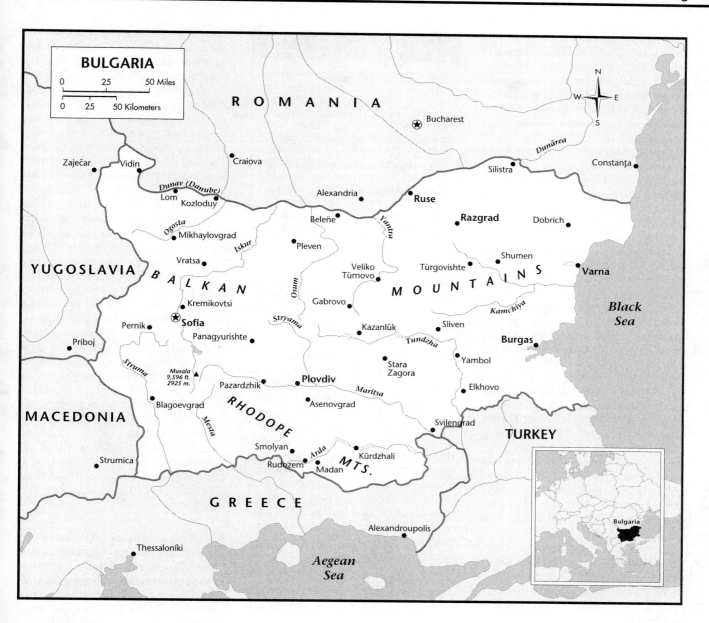

the Alliance for National Salvation with several smaller parties, taking 19 seats. The other party on the left is the Euroleft (comprised largely of defectors from the BSP with a social–democratic orientation), which holds 14 seats. The next parliamentary elections must take place no later than April 2001.

## Principal Government Officials

**For up-to-date information on Principal Government Officials, see the Chiefs of State and Cabinet Members of Foreign Governments section starting on page 1.**

The Embassy of the Republic of Bulgaria in the United States is located at 1621 22nd Street, NW, Washington, DC 20008; tel. 202–387–7969; fax. 202–123–7973.

# ECONOMY

Bulgaria's economy contracted dramatically after 1989 with the collapse of the COMECON system and the loss of the Soviet market, to which the Bulgarian economy had been closely tied. The standard of living fell by about 40%. In addition, UN sanctions against Serbia (1992–95) and Iraq took a heavy toll on the Bulgarian economy. First signs of recovery emerged when GDP grew 1.4% in 1994 for the first time since 1988, and 2.5% in 1995. Inflation, which surged in 1994 to 122%, fell to 32.9% in 1995. During 1996, however, the economy collapsed due to the BSP's go–slow, mismanaged economic reforms, its disastrous agricultural policy, and an unstable and decapitalized banking system, which led to inflation of 311% and the collapse of the lev. When pro–

reform forces come into power in spring 1997, an ambitious economic reform package, including introduction of a currency board regime, was agreed with the International Monetary Fund (IMF) and the World Bank, and the economy began to stabilize.

The government of Prime Minister Kostov, elected in April 1997, has made a clean break with the failed policies of the early and mid–1990s. In this, the Bulgarian Government received the backing of international financial institutions and committed itself to sound financial and structural policies as the only way out of crisis.

Since July 1997 the Bulgarian Government has been operating under a currency board as required by the International Monetary Fund's $510 million standby arrangement of March 1997. From July 1, 1997 to December 31, 1998 the Bulgarian lev (BGL) was tied to the German deutschmark (DM) at a rate of BGL 1000 to one deutschmark. Since January 1, 1999, the lev is tied to the euro at an exchange rate of 1,955.83 leva to one euro. Since July 5, 1999, BGL 1,000 was redenominated by the issuance of new currency and coins to be one lev (BGN). Thus BGN 1.00 equals DM 1.00.

The Currency Board rules provide that the Bulgarian National Bank (BNB) must hold sufficient foreign currency reserves to cover all the leva in circulation including the lev reserves of the banking system; the BNB can only refinance commercial banks in the event of systemic risk to the baking system; and the government is limited in taking on new financial liabilities or providing sovereign guarantees.

Under other IMF conditions for strict financial discipline, the Bulgarian government is pledged to close loss–making enterprises and to speed privatization, bank reform, and restructuring. The government established an isolation list of 70 state enterprises, accounting for half of the public sector losses, that do not have access to commercial credit unless they are privatized. The government

**Travel Notes**

**Travel Advice:** For up-to-date information from the U.S. State Department on possible inconvenient or hazardous situations, see the **Travel Warnings and Consular Information Sheets from the U.S. Government** section starting on page 1723. For the latest information on health requirements and conditions, see the **International Travelers' Health Information** section starting on page 1385. For further information dealing with non-urgent matter, see the **Tips for Travelers to...** section starting on page 1588.

succeeded in privatizing or beginning liquidation of all but one of the isolation list's commercial companies (Group B) by June 30, 1999.

The results have been very impressive. Inflation was reined in relatively quickly. Official reserves rebounded from $400 million in January 1997 to $2,964 million at the end of 1998. Moody's Investors Service upgraded Bulgaria's credit rating to B2. Foreign investment, including participation by American investors, has also revived as macroeconomic stabilization and a friendlier business climate have taken hold. The closure of 18 troubled banks also has helped to increase confidence in the banking system. Following declines in GDP in both 1996 and 1997, GDP increased from $10,200 million in 1997 to $12,257 million in 1998. In fact, some experts believe that official statistics underreport economic activity, and the active unofficial market statistics could represent an additional 20% to 40% of the official GDP. This means that there is more money flowing through the economy and higher actual disposable consumer income than is officially accounted for.

The private sector contributed between 25%–30% of GDP in 1995, 35%–40% in 1996, approximately 65% in 1997 and 1998, 62% in 1999; it should increase further with continuing privatization. Since the currency board constrains borrowing, the government needs to keep wage growth modest and focus on improving pro-

ductivity to generate revenues. The main threats to the Bulgarian economy's medium–term prospects are the effects of the Kosovo conflict and the threats of wider regional instability and turmoil in global financial markets affecting investments in emerging markets. This may adversely affect revenues to the government from privatizing large enterprises. Due to Bulgaria's geography, the Kosovo situation has interrupted Bulgaria's main highway and Danube River trade routes with western Europe through Serbia in Yugoslavia, which have increased transport costs and may reduce future economic growth and market potential over the short term. However, the Governments of the United States, European Union countries, and southeast European countries have committed to a Stability Pact aimed at developing prosperity and stability throughout the southeast Europe region. Washington is currently developing a major comprehensive plan for economic development in the region to be implemented in the aftermath of the Kosovo crisis. This should lead to new and expanded trade and investment opportunities in Bulgaria over the long term.

A second potential impediment to Bulgaria's economic transformation is the slow and less than fully transparent privatization process itself. The Bulgarian Government has relied heavily on controversial management–employee buyouts for smaller enterprises, and on use of foreign consultants to privatize pools of medium and large companies. The privatization framework has also included complex criteria for selecting buyers that has generated concerns about transparency and corruption. As a result, ownership transfer has been delayed and, in some cases, has provoked litigation.

However, the government completed a number of large privatization deals in mid-1999, meeting its commitment to sell or commence liquidation of a group of loss–making enterprises by June 30, 1999. These deals included sales of the Kremikovtsi Steelworks,

Balkan Bulgarian Airlines and DZU compact disk factory.

As a relatively small market in the Balkans, Bulgaria will have to make extra efforts to attract investors—by improving transparency, for example—as well as by more fully marketing its many advantages, including a highly skilled, low cost labor force and proximity to both European and Near Eastern markets.

# FOREIGN RELATIONS

Bulgaria has good relations with its neighbors and has proved to be a constructive force in the region under socialist and democratic governments alike. Promoting regional stability, Bulgaria hosted a Southeast European Foreign Ministers meeting in July 1996 and a Southeast European Defense Ministers conference in October 1997. Bulgaria also participated in the 1996 South Balkan Defense Ministerial in Albania and is active in the Southeast European Cooperative Initiative. In 1998, Bulgaria and FYROM solved their so-called language dispute and have developed closer bilateral relations.

With their close historical, cultural, and economic ties, Bulgaria seeks a mutually beneficial relationship with Russia, on which it is largely dependent for energy supplies. Negotiations are underway among Greece, Bulgaria, and Russia for construction of a gas pipeline from Burgas on the Black Sea to Alexandropolis to transport Caspian Sea oil.

Bulgaria's EU Association Agreement came into effect in 1994, and Bulgaria formally applied for full EU membership in December 1995. In 1996, Bulgaria acceded to the Wassenaar Arrangement controlling exports of weapons and sensitive technology to countries of concern and also was admitted to the World Trade Organization. Bulgaria is a member of the Zangger Committee and the Nuclear Suppliers Group.

After a period of equivocation under a socialist government, in March 1997 a UDF–led caretaker cabinet applied for full NATO membership, which the current government is pursuing as a priority.

Bulgaria joined NATO's Partnership for Peace in 1994 and applied for NATO membership in 1997. It is working toward NATO compatibility in communications and training, and has established a Peacekeeping Training Center. In 1999, Bulgaria inaugurated the headquarters of the Multinational Peacekeeping Force Southeast Europe.

# U.S.-BULGARIAN RELATIONS

U.S.–Bulgarian bilateral relations improved dramatically with the fall of communism in 1989. The United States moved quickly to encourage development of a multi–party democracy and a market economy. Initial progress was rapid, leading to full normalization of bilateral political and trade ties. A trade agreement was signed in 1991 and a bilateral investment treaty in 1992. The U.S. accorded Bulgaria unconditional most–favored–nation trade status in 1996. In 1998, the U.S. was Bulgaria's third–largest investor, with investments of $148 million. There is active bilateral military cooperation, including a linkage between the Bulgarian military and the Tennessee National Guard. Bulgaria hosts the only fully American university in the region, the American University of Bulgaria in Blagoevgrad, established in 1991 and drawing students from throughout southeast Europe and beyond. The American College of Sofia, a high school founded in the 1860s and closed under communism, reopened in 1992.

In 1989, the U.S. Congress passed the Support for East European Democracies Act (SEED), authorizing financial support to facilitate the development of democratic institu-

tions, political pluralism, and free market economies in the region. The U.S. Agency for International Development (USAID) administers the SEED programs in Bulgaria under the guidance of the U.S. ambassador. Bulgaria has received more than $290 million in SEED assistance as of 1999, along with an additional $60 million in food programs and a $15–million endowment for the American University in Bulgaria. Much of USAID's assistance focuses on strengthening non–governmental organizations and other grassroots initiatives, promoting the private sector, and enhancing local government effectiveness and accountability.

An additional $25 million has been pledged for budget support due to losses incurred during the Kosovo crisis.

In addition, the Peace Corps, with 106 volunteers in Bulgaria as of 1999, offers assistance in English–language instruction, small business centers, and environmental protection programs. The Department of Defense provides monetary and professional assistance through several programs, including the Joint Contact Team Program, Partnership for Peace, International Military Education and Training, Excess Defense Articles, Foreign Military Financing, and humanitarian assistance. Bulgaria serves as coordinator for the South Balkan Development Initiative, which is funded through the U.S. Trade and Development Agency to promote infrastructure development in Bulgaria, Albania, and The Former Yugoslav Republic of Macedonia.

## Principal U.S. Embassy Officials

**For up-to-date information on Principal U.S. Officials, see the U.S. Embassies, Consulates, and Foreign Service section starting on page 139.**

# BURKINA FASO

March 1998

Official Name:
**Burkina Faso**

# PROFILE

## Geography

**Area:** 274,200 sq. km. (106,000 sq. mi.); about the size of Colorado.
**Cities:** Capital—Ouagadougou (pop. 1 million). Other cities—Bobo-Dioulasso (450,000), Koudougou (90,000).
**Terrain:** Savanna; brushy plains, and scattered hills.
**Climate:** Sahelian; pronounced wet and dry seasons.

## People

**Nationality:** Noun and adjective—Burkinabe (accent on last "e").
**Population (1995):** 10.4 million.
**Annual growth rate:** 2.8%.
**Ethnic groups:** 63 ethnic groups among which are Mossi (almost half of the total population), Bobo, Mande, Lobi, Fulani, Gurunsi, and Senufo.
**Religions:** Traditional beliefs 40%, Muslim 40%, Christian 20%.
**Languages:** French (official), More, Dioula, others.
**Education:** Literacy (1997)—22%: male 29.5%; female 9.2%.
**Health:** Infant mortality rate (1995)—99/1,000. Life expectancy—49 years.
**Work force:** Agriculture—92%. Industry—2.1%. Commerce, services, and government—5.5%.

## Government

**Type:** Republic.
**Independence:** August 5, 1960.
**Constitution:** June 11, 1991.
**Branches:** Executive—president (chief of state) prime minister (head of government). Legislative—two chambers. Judicial—independent.
**Subdivisions:** 45 provinces.
**Political parties:** Congress for Democracy and Progress (CDP), Alliance for Democracy Federation (ADF), African Democratic Assembly (RDA), Party for Democracy and Progress (PDP), and numerous small opposition parties.
**Suffrage:** Direct universal.
**Central government budget (1996):** $394.5 million.
**Defense:** 16% of government budget.

## Economy

**GDP (1996):** $2.4 billion.
**Annual growth rate (1996):** 6.1%.
**Per capita income (1996):** $300.
**Avg. inflation rate (1996):** 6.1%.
**Natural resources (limited quantities):** manganese, gold, limestone, marble, phosphate, zinc. Agriculture (34% of GDP): Products—cotton, millet, sorghum, rice, livestock, peanuts, shea nuts, maize.
**Industry (27% of GDP):** Type—mining, agricultural processing plants, brewing and bottling, light industry.
**Trade (1995):** Exports—$306 million: cotton, gold, livestock, peanuts, shea nut products. Major markets—European Union, Taiwan. Imports—$731 million.
**Official exchange rate:** Floats with French franc. Communaute Financiere Africaine (CFA) francs 100=1 FF; CFA francs 595=US$1.

# GEOGRAPHY

Burkina Faso is a landlocked Sahel country that shares borders with six nations. It lies between the Sahara Desert and the Gulf of Guinea, south of the loop of the Niger River. The land is green in the south, with forests and fruit trees, and desert in the north. Most of central Burkina Faso lies on a savanna plateau, 198-305 meters (650-1,000 ft.) above sea level, with fields, brush, and scattered trees. Burkina Faso's game preserves—the most important of which are Arly, Nazinga, and W National Park—contain lions, elephants, hippopotamus, monkeys, warthogs, and antelopes. Tourism is not well developed.

Annual rainfall varies from about 100 centimeters (40 in.) in the south to less than 25 centimeters (10 in.) in the extreme north and northeast, where hot desert winds accentuate the dryness of the region. Burkina Faso has three distinct seasons: warm and dry (November-March), hot and dry (March-May), and hot and wet (June-October). Rivers are not navigable.

# PEOPLE

Burkina Faso's 10 million people belong to two major West African cultural groups—the Voltaic and the Mande. The Voltaic are far more numerous and include the Mossi, which make up about one-half of the population. The Mossi claim descent from warriors who migrated to present-day Burkina Faso and established an empire that lasted more than 800 years. Predominantly farmers, the Mossi are still bound by the traditions of the Mogho Naba, who hold court in Ouagadougou.

About 5,000 Europeans reside in Burkina Faso.

Most of Burkina's people are concentrated in the south and center of the country, sometimes exceeding 48 per square kilometer (125/sq. mi.). This population density, high for Africa, causes annual migrations of hundreds of thousands of Burkinabe to Cote d'Ivoire and Ghana for seasonal agricultural work. A plurality of Burkinabe adhere to traditional African religions. The introduction of Islam to Burkina Faso was initially resisted by the Mossi rulers. Christians, predominantly Catholics, are largely concentrated among the urban elite.

Few Burkinabe have had formal education. Schooling is free but not compulsory, and only about 29% of Burkina's primary school-age children receive a basic education. The University of Ouagadougou, founded in 1974, was the country's first institution of higher education. The Polytechnic University in Bobo-Dioulasso was opened in 1995.

# HISTORY

Until the end of the 19th century, the history of Burkina Faso was dominated by the empire-building Mossi,
who are believed to have come from central or eastern Africa sometime in the 11th century. For centuries, the Mossi peasant was both farmer and soldier, and the Mossi people were able to defend their religious beliefs and social structure against forcible attempts to convert them to Islam by Muslims from the northwest.

When the French arrived and claimed the area in 1896, Mossi resistance ended with the capture of their capital at Ouagadougou. In 1919, certain provinces from Cote d'Ivoire were united into a separate colony called the Upper Volta in the French West Africa federation. In 1932, the new colony was dismembered in a move to economize; it was reconstituted in 1937 as an administrative division called the Upper Coast. After World War II, the Mossi renewed their pressure for separate territorial status and on September 4, 1947, Upper Volta became a French West African territory again in its own right.

A revision in the organization of French Overseas Territories began with the passage of the Basic Law (Loi Cadre) of July 23, 1956. This act was followed by reorganizational measures approved by the French parliament early in 1957 that ensured a large degree of self-government for individual territories. Upper Volta became an autonomous republic in the French community on December 11, 1958.

Upper Volta achieved independence on August 5, 1960. The first president, Maurice Yameogo, was the leader of the Voltaic Democratic Union (UDV). The 1960 constitution provided for election by universal suffrage of a president and a national assembly for 5-year terms. Soon after coming to power, Yameogo banned all political parties other than the UDV. The government lasted until 1966 when after much unrest-mass demonstrations and strikes by students, labor unions, and civil servants-the military intervened.

The military coup deposed Yameogo, suspended the constitution, dissolved the National Assembly, and placed
Lt. Col. Aboukar Sangoule Lamizana at the head of a government of senior army officers. The army remained in power for 4 years, and on June 14, 1970, the Voltans ratified a new constitution that established a 4-year transition period toward complete civilian rule. Lamizana remained in power throughout the 1970s as president of military or mixed civil-military governments. After conflict over the 1970 constitution, a new constitution was written and approved in 1977, and Lamizana was reelected by open elections in 1978.

Lamizana's government faced problems with the country's traditionally powerful trade unions, and on November 25, 1980, Col. Saye Zerbo overthrew President Lamizana in a bloodless coup. Colonel Zerbo established the Military Committee of Recovery for National Progress as the supreme governmental authority, thus eradicating the 1977 constitution.

Colonel Zerbo also encountered resistance from trade unions and was overthrown two years later, on November 7, 1982, by Maj. Dr. Jean-Baptiste Ouedraogo and the Council of Popular Salvation (CSP). The CSP continued to ban political parties and organizations, yet promised a transition to civilian rule and a new constitution.

Factional infighting developed between moderates in the CSP and the radicals, led by Capt. Thomas Sankara who was appointed prime minister in January 1983. The internal political struggle and Sankara's leftist rhetoric led to his arrest and subsequent efforts to bring about his release, directed by Capt. Blaise Compaore. This release effort resulted in yet another military coup d'etat on August 4, 1983.

After the coup, Sankara formed the National Council for the Revolution (CNR), with himself as president. Sankara also established Committees for the Defense of the Revolution (CDRs) to "mobilize the masses" and implement the CNR's revolutionary programs. The CNR, whose exact membership remained secret until

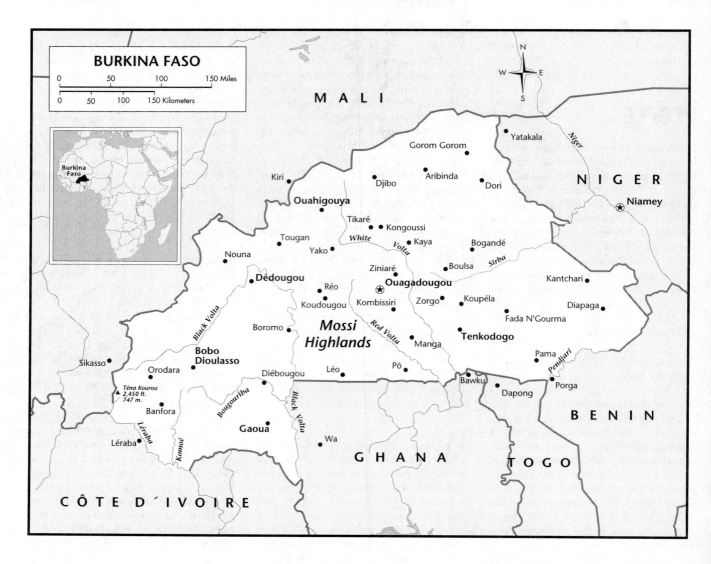

the end, contained two small intellectual Marxist-Leninist groups. Sankara, Compaore, Capt. Henri Zongo, and Maj. Jean-Baptiste Boukary Lengani-all leftist military officers-dominated the regime.

On August 4, 1984, Upper Volta changed its name to Burkina Faso, meaning "the country of honorable people." Sankara, a charismatic leader, sought by word, deed, and example to mobilize the masses and launch a massive bootstrap development movement. But many of the strict austerity measures taken by Sankara met with growing resistance and disagreement. Despite his initial popularity and personal charisma, problems began to surface in the implementation of the revolutionary ideals.

The CDRs, which were formed as popular mass organizations, deteriorated in some areas into gangs of armed thugs and clashed with several trade unions. Tensions over the repressive tactics of the government and its overall direction mounted steadily. On October 15, 1987, Sankara was assassinated in a coup which brought Capt. Blaise Compaore to power.

Compaore, Capt. Henri Zongo, and Maj. Jean-Baptiste Boukary Lengani formed the Popular Front (FP), which pledged to continue and pursue the goals of the revolution and to "rectify" Sankara's "deviations" from the original aims. The new government, realizing the need for popular support, tacitly moderated many of Sankara's policies. As part of a much-discussed

political "opening" process, several political organizations, three of them non-Marxist, were accepted under an umbrella political organization created in June 1989 by the FP.

Some members of the leftist Organisation pour le Democratie Populaire/Movement du Travail (ODP/MT) were against the admission of non-Marxist groups in the front. On September 18, 1989, while Compaore was returning from a two-week trip to Asia, Lengani and Zongo were accused of plotting to overthrow the Popular Front. They were arrested and summarily executed the same night. Compaore reorganized the government, appointed several new ministers, and assumed the portfolio of Minister of Defense and Security. On December 23, 1989, a presidential security detail arrested about 30 civilians and military personnel accused of plotting a coup in collaboration with the Burkinabe external opposition.

# GOVERNMENT AND POLITICAL CONDITIONS

In 1990, the Popular Front held its first National Congress, which formed a committee to draft a national constitution. The constitution was approved by referendum in 1991. In 1992, Compaore was elected president, running unopposed after the opposition boycotted the election because of Compaore's refusal to accede to demands of the opposition such as a sovereign National Conference to set modalities. The opposition did participate in the following year's legislative elections, in which the ODP/MT won a majority of seats.

The government of the Fourth Republic includes a strong presidency, a prime minister, a Council of Ministers presided over by the president, a two-chamber National Assembly, and the judiciary. The legislature and judiciary are independent but remain susceptible to outside influence.

In 1995, Burkina held its first multiparty municipal elections since independence. With minor exceptions, balloting was considered free and fair by the local human rights organizations which monitored the contest. The president's ODP/MT won over 1,100 of some 1,700 councillor seats being contested.

In February 1996, the ruling ODP/MT merged with several small opposition parties to form the Congress for Democracy and Progress (CDP). This effectively co-opted much of what little viable opposition to Compaore existed. The remaining opposition parties regrouped in preparation for 1997 legislative elections and the 1998 presidential election. The 1997 legislative elections, which international observers pronounced to be substantially free, fair, and transparent, resulted in a large CDP majority—101 to 111 seats.

## Principal Government Officials

**For up-to-date information on Principal Government Officials, see the Chiefs of State and Cabinet Members of Foreign Governments section starting on page 1.**

Burkina Faso maintains an embassy in the United States at 2340 Massachusetts Ave. NW, Washington, DC 20008 (tel. 202-332-5577).

# ECONOMY

Burkina Faso is one of the poorest countries in the world with per capita GNP of $300. More than 80% of the population relies on subsistence agriculture, with only a small fraction directly involved in industry and services. Drought, poor soil, lack of adequate communications and other infrastructure, a low literacy rate, and a stagnant economy are all longstanding problems. The export economy also remains subject to fluctuations in world prices.

Though hobbled by an extremely resource-deprived domestic economy, Burkina remains committed to the structural adjustment program it launched in 1991. It has largely recovered from the devaluation of the CFA in January 1994, with a 1996 growth rate of 5.9%.

Many Burkinabe migrate to neighboring countries for work, and their remittances provide a substantial contribution to the balance of payments. Burkina is attempting to improve the economy by developing its mineral resources, improving its infrastructure, making its agricultural and livestock sectors more productive and competitive, and stabilizing the supplies and prices of food grains.

## Travel Notes

**Travel Advice:** For up-to-date information from the U.S. State Department on possible inconvenient or hazardous situations, see the **Travel Warnings and Consular Information Sheets from the U.S. Government** section starting on page 1723. For the latest information on health requirements and conditions, see the **International Travelers' Health Information** section starting on page 1385. For further information dealing with non-urgent matter, see the **Tips for Travelers to...** section starting on page 1588.

The agricultural economy remains highly vulnerable to fluctuations in rainfall. The Mossi Plateau in north central Burkina faces encroachment from the Sahara. The resultant southward migration means heightened competition for control of very limited water resources south of the Mossi Plateau. Most of the population ekes out a living as subsistence farmers, living with problems of climate, soil erosion, and rudimentary technology. The staple crops are millet, sorghum, maize, and rice. The cash crops are cotton, groundnuts, karite (shea nuts), and sesame. Livestock, once a major export, has declined.

Industry, still in an embryonic stage, is located primarily in Bobo-Dioulasso, Ouagadougou, Banfora, and Koudougou. Manufacturing is limited to food processing, textiles, and other import substitution heavily protected by tariffs. Some factories are privately owned, and others are set to be privatized. Burkina's exploitable natural resources are limited, although a manganese ore deposit is located in the remote northeast. Gold mining has increased greatly since the mid-1980s and, along with cotton, is a leading export moneyearner.

A railway connects Burkina with the excellent deepwater port at Abidjan, Cote d'Ivoire, 1,150 kilometers (712 mi.) away. Burkina has over 13,000 kilometers (7,800 mi.) of roads, although only about 14% are paved.

# FOREIGN RELATIONS

Burkina has excellent relations with European—including the European Union—North African, and Asian donors, which are all active development partners. France, in particular, continues to provide significant aid and supports Compaore's developing role as a regional powerbroker. Compaore has mediated a political crisis in Togo and helped to resolve the Tuareg conflict in Niger. Several thousand Tuareg refugees from Mali, who sought protection in Burkina, will be repatriated by the end of 1997. Burkina maintains cordial relations with Libya.

# U.S.-BURKINA RELATIONS

U.S. relations with Burkina Faso, once strained because of Burkina's past involvement in Liberia's civil war, are improving. U.S. interests in Burkina are to promote continued democratization and greater respect for human rights.

U.S. trade with Burkina is still extremely limited—$14.5 million in U.S. exports in 1995—but investment possibilities exist, especially in the mining and communications sectors.

In response to the drought that plagued the Sahel countries from 1968 to 1974, the U.S. provided significant emergency food assistance to Burkina Faso. Following this, the United States and other international donors began to work with the Sahel countries to plan and implement long-term development assistance programs.

While the overall amount of U.S. assistance to Burkina dropped with the 1995 closure of the USAID mission in Ouagadougou, the U.S. contributes about $10 million to a feeding program managed by an American non-governmental organization. The embassy also maintains a variety of programs to support social and economic development projects throughout the country.

In 1995, the Peace Corps program resumed, after a 10-year absence, with volunteers working in rural health. In 1997, the program was expanded to include education.

## Principal U.S. Officials

For up-to-date information on Principal U.S. Officials, see the U.S. Embassies, Consulates, and Foreign Service section starting on page 139.

The U.S. Embassy in Burkina Faso is located on Avenue Raoul Follereau in Ouagadougou. Its mailing addresses are: (international mail) 01 B.P. 35, Ouagadougou 01, Burkina Faso; (US mail) Ouagadougou/DOS, Washington, D.C. 20521-2440, tel: (226) 30-67-23/24/25, fax: (226) 31-23-68 or (226) 30-38-90.

# BURMA
February 1989

## Official Name:
## Union of Burma

---

**Editor's Note: The Burmese Government was dissolved on September 18, 1988 in a military coup, and the nation was renamed Myanmar. Although this entry is dated 1989, the US does not presently recognize the current government of Myanmar and therefore continues to refer to the nation as Burma.**

# PROFILE

## Geography
**Area:** 678,576 sq. km. (262,000 sq. mi.); slightly smaller than Texas.
**Cities:** Capital—Rangoon (pop. 2.5 million). Other Cities—Mandalay, Moulmein.
**Terrain:** Varied.
**Climate:** Tropical, monsoon.

## People
**Nationality:** Noun and adjective—Burmese (sing. and pl.).
**Population (1987):** 37,900,000.
**Annual growth rate:** 2%.
**Ethnic groups:** Burman 68to, Shan 9%, Karen 7%, Rakhine 4%, Chinese 3%, Indian 2%.
**Religions:** Buddhist 85%; Muslim, traditional, Christian, other 13%.
**Languages:** Burmese, ethnic languages.
**Education:** Attendance—84%. Years compulsory—4. Literacy—66%.
**Health:** Infant mortality rate—96/1,000. Life expectancy—57 yrs.
**Work force (14.8 million est.):** Agriculture—66.1%. Industry—12%. Trade—9.7%. Government—10.6%.

## Government
With the military's assumption of governmental authority on September 18, 1988, all civil government activities were suspended, including the executive, legislative, and judicial branches. These functions are now exercised by the military authorities. Military State Law and Order Restoration Councils replaced the previous civilian Councils of State. As of December 1988, military government remained in effect pending promised national multiparty elections and eventual transfer of power to an elected civilian government.
**Type:** Interim military government.
**Independence:** Jan. 4, 1948.
**Constitution:** The previously applicable constitution was ratified on Jan. 3, 1974. It is not known which of the constitution's provisions are considered relevant by the governing military authorities.
**Subdivisions:** Seven divisions (ethnic Burman majority) and seven states (non-Burman majority).
**Political parties:** As of December 1988, there were more than 140 registered political parties. All have been created since the military takeover in September 1988.
**Central government budget (1986):** $4.368 billion, including expenditures of state economic enterprises.
**Defense (1985 est.):** 4.2% of GDP.
**Flag:** Red with blue canton; in the canton, a white cogwheel and rice stalk encircled with 14 white stars.
**National holiday:** Independence Day, Jan. 4.

## Economy
**GDP (Burmese FY 1985-86 in current dollars):** $8 billion.
**Annual growth rate:** 1%-4%.
**Per capita income:** $210.
**Avg. inflation rate (last 4 yrs.):** 6%.
**Natural resources:** Oil, timber, tin, tungsten, copper, lead, precious stones.
**Agriculture (27% of GDP):** Products—rice, beans and pulses, maize and oilseeds peanuts, sugarcane.
**Industry (10% of GDP):** Types—food, textiles, timber products, petroleum, construction materials.
**Trade (FY 1986):** Exports—$500 million f.o.b.: rice, teak and hardwoods, base metals and ores. Major market—Japan, Western Europe, ASEAN countries. Imports—$620 million f.o.b.: machinery, tools, transportation equipment, spare parts. Major suppliers—Japan, Western Europe, ASEAN.
**Official exchange rate:** 1 SDR=Kyat 8.551; 6.9 Kyat=US $1 (Mar. 1988).
**Fiscal year:** April 1-Mar. 31 (since April 1974).

## Membership in International Organizations
UN and some of its specialized and related agencies, including the World Bank, International Finance

Corporation (IFC), International Development Association (IDA), International Monetary Fund (IMF), General Agreement on Tariffs and Trade (GATT); Seabeds Committee; Asian Development Bank; Colombo Plan.

# GEOGRAPHY

Burma is the largest country on the southeast Asian mainland. Facing the Bay of Bengal and the Andaman Sea on the west and south, it shares borders with Thailand, Laos, China, India, and Bangladesh.

Burma is rimmed on the north, east, and west by mountain ranges, with elevations up to 4,570 meters (15,000 ft.) above sea level along the Chinese border and 2,400 meters (8,000 ft.) along the Indian border. The mountains have contributed to Burma's isolation from neighboring countries, and the rivers and dense forests have discouraged east-west movement. The Irrawaddy River is the country's economic lifeline and major transportation system, connecting Rangoon with Mandalay in the central area.

Located at about the same latitude as Mexico, Burma has a tropical monsoon climate. Annual rainfall varies from 500 centimeters (200 in.) in coastal areas to only 77 centimeters (30 in.) in the central "dry zone." Mean annual temperatures range from about 27°C (80°F) in southern Burma to around 24°C (75°F) in the northern lowlands. During the hot season, March-May, temperatures often exceed 38°C (100°F) in central Burma.

# PEOPLE

Burma's predominantly rural population is concentrated in the lower valleys of the Irrawaddy, Chindwin, and Sittang Rivers. The dominant ethnic group—the Burmans—number more than 25 million. More than 2 million Karens live throughout southern and eastern Burma. The Shans, who also number about 2 million, are ethni-cally related to the Thai and inhabit mainly the eastern plateau region. Other major indigenous groups are the Rakhines in the west, Chins in the northwest, and Kachins in the north—totaling more than 1 million. In addition, large ethnic Chinese, Indian, and Bangladeshi minorities live in Burma. Except for the diplomatic and UN, there are few Europeans. About 150 Americans reside there.

Theravada Buddhism—an older form of Buddhism prevalent in most of mainland Southeast Asia—is practiced by some 85% of the Burmese. Other religions include Islam, Christianity, and traditional practices.

Burma's ethnic groups speak numerous languages and subsidiary dialects. Burmese, related to Tibetan, is spoken by most of the people and is the official national language. English, the second language, is spoken among educated and official elements of society, but its use has declined recently. To reverse this trend, the government is expanding English-language instruction.

Government literacy campaigns have contributed to a rising literacy rate. Although education is free from primary through university level, all schools in Burma have been closed since the military takeover in September 1988. An estimated 84% of primary school children (ages attend school, usually in half-day sessions. Only a small percentage of older children attend middle and high schools. In rural areas, traditional Buddhist temple schools provide basic skills for primary school children.

Universities are located at Rangoon and Mandalay. In addition, there are four degree-granting colleges; three institutes of medicine; and additional institutes of dental medicine, animal husbandry and veterinary science, economics, technology, education, and foreign languages. Because recent college graduates are having difficulty finding employment, the government encourages students to attend technical schools that lead to wider employment opportunities.

# HISTORY

First unified during the 11th century by King Anawrahta, Burma remained independent until 1287, when Kublai Khan's Mongol hordes invaded the country and destroyed the political order. A second dynasty was established in 1486 but was plagued by internal disunity, compounded since the mid-16th century by intermittent wars with Siam (now Thailand). A new dynasty was established in 1752, and the country was reunited under King Alaungpaya. Under the rule of Alaungpaya and his successor, Burma repelled Chinese invasion and confronted the British, who were vying with the French for dominance in the area.

Burma was annexed to British India during the three Anglo-Burmese wars between 1824 and 1886. Thibaw, the last king, was exiled by the British, and the entire monarchical system was destroyed. During the colonial era, a large influx of Indians and Chinese, along with the British, came to control much of the country's economy. Burma was separated from India in 1937 and granted a constitution providing a limited measure of self-government. Until independence, the country's ethnic minorities were administered under a separate system.

During World War II, the Japanese occupied Burma and granted a fictitious independence under a puppet regime led by anti-British nationalists, who later turned against the Japanese and aided the Allied forces in retaking the country. A coalition of nationalist forces, the Anti-Fascist People's Freedom League (AFPFL), emerged as the principal political organization following the Japanese defeat in 1945 and the restoration of British authority. Under AFPFL leadership, various groups and regions within British Burma eventually joined to form the Union of Burma, which on January 4, 1948, became a fully independent nation outside the Commonwealth.

During the first decade of independence, the Burmese Government was controlled by the AFPFL, headed by Prime Minister U Nu, who had become president of that organization following the assassination in 1947 of Burma's great wartime and postwar hero, Gen. Aung San. The new government carried on the tradition of parliamentary democracy inherited from the British and was dedicated to the creation of a socialist welfare state.

During the early years of independence, the government vigorously consolidated its power and held the union together in the face of revolts by communists and other dissident groups as well as separatist movements among ethnic minorities. In 1958, the AFPFL split, precipitating a political crisis that led to an army takeover in September of that year led by the Chief of Staff, Gen. U Ne Win. Preserving constitutional forms, Gen. U Ne Win, acting as prime minister, set up a "caretaker" government with the limited objective of restoring order and stability necessary for new elections. U Nu and his faction of the AFPFL, renamed the Union Party, won an overwhelming majority in the 1960 elections.

Despite popular backing, the U Nu government proved ineffective and indecisive in coping with growing problems of internal security, national unity and economic development. Difficulties were compounded by factional disputes within the Union Party similar to those that split the AFPFL in 1958. U Nu's decision to move toward a federal system to placate minorities provoked fear among some that AFPFL would be destroyed. Gen. U Ne Win again deposed the AFPFL government in a March 1962 coup, suspended the constitution, and established a new revolutionary government.

On March 2, 1974, a constitutionally elected, single-party government was installed. Gen. U Ne Win assumed the presidency with the same basic group of military officers in control. Requirements that military officers in civilian positions resign reduced the military appearance of the government structure. However, candidates for top positions were recruited

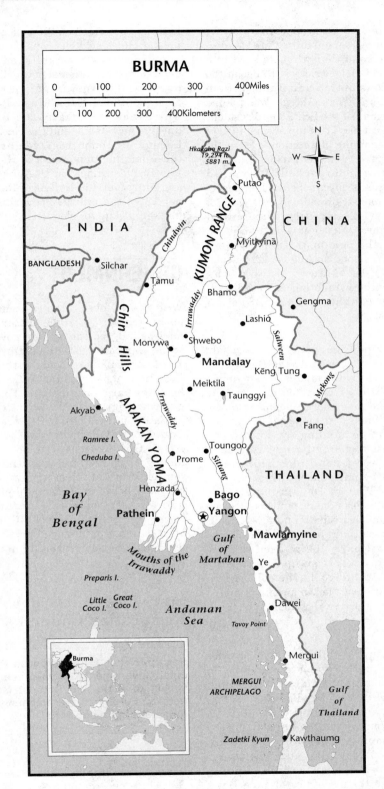

frequently from the military, which continued to play a key role in Burma's power structure.

U Ne Win retired in November 1981, upon election of his successor by the Council of State. Nevertheless, as

Chairman of the Central Executive Committee of the Burma Socialist Programme Party (BSPP) he continued to influence Burma's politics.

At an extraordinary congress of the BSPP in July 1988, U Ne Win resigned as party chairman, citing personal responsibility for the economic conditions that had led to a series of violent riots in Rangoon the previous March and June. U Sein Lwin, a Ne Win protege, was named Chairman of the BSPP and President of the country. His appointment led to the beginning of a nationwide revolt, with mass demonstrations in cities and towns throughout Burma. In Rangoon, army troops fired on peaceful demonstrators during the week of August 12 and killed substantial numbers, but they were unable to quell the demonstrations. U Sein Lwin resigned on August 12; his successor Dr. Maung Maung, was appointed by another extraordinary party congress of the BSPP on August 19.

Dr. Maung Maung was unable to halt popular opposition to the BSPP government. By the middle of September the BSPP virtually ceased functioning, and many party members joined the millions of demonstrators nationwide in demanding the immediate formation of an interim government of respected non-BSPP figures, followed by national multiparty elections. Though Dr. Maung Maung offered a formula for multiparty elections and decreed that no government employee could be a member of any political party, he refused to step down in favor of an interim government. In Rangoon, the collapse of civil authority led to a state of anarchy in many neighborhoods, and instances of looting were widespread.

The army formally took over governmental authority on September 18, deposing Maung Maung, abolishing the BSPP and the civilian Councils of State, and imposing strict military rule over the country. Large numbers of demonstrators were killed in Rangoon, Mandalay, and other cities, and open opposition was quelled through the use of brutal force. Several thousand students fled the cities and concentrated in insurgent-held areas near the Thai border where they hoped to acquire arms and training before returning to the cities to wage an urban guerrilla campaign against the army.

In taking power, the military pledged to hold multiparty elections once law and order was reestablished and allowed the formation of new political parties. Two principal parties emerged: the National Unity Party, which was essentially the BSPP under a new name, and the National League for Democracy, led by the three leading opponents of the Ne Win-BSPP regime, Tin U, Aung Gyi, and Aung San Suu Kyi. As of December 1988, the military government had set no date for elections.

# GOVERNMENT

With the takeover of the government on September 18, 1988, the armed forces abolished the civilian government apparatus established by the 1974 constitution and, with one exception, named military officers to head the various ministries. Formal governing authority is now vested in a State Law and Order Restoration Council (SLORC), headed by the Army Chief of Staff, Gen. Saw Maung. Gen. Saw Maung also named himself Prime Minister and retained the portfolios of the Defense Ministry and Ministry of Foreign Affairs. Other members of the SLORC have been assigned ministerial portfolios but have not been formally named ministers.

## State Law and Order Restoration Council

**For up-to-date information on Principal Government Officials, see the Chiefs of State and Cabinet Members of Foreign Governments section starting on page 1.**

Burma maintains an embassy in the United States at 2300 S Street NW., Washington, DC 20008 (tel. 202-3329044). The Burmese Consulate General in New York City and the Burmese Permanent Mission to the United Nations are located at 10 East 77th Street, New York, N.Y. 10021 (tel. 212-535-1310).

# POLITICAL CONDITIONS

With the military takeover of September 1988, the Burma Socialist Program Party was formally abolished, and all governing authority was concentrated in the hands of the military. In announcing the takeover, Gen. Saw Maung stated that military rule would be temporary and multiparty elections would be held once law and order was reestablished. The Commission on Elections, established by the Maung Maung government, shortly afterward published rules permitting the registration of new political parties. A trickle of new parties then applied for and received official registration; by October this trickle had become a flood, and by December 1988, more than 150 parties were officially in existence.

Underlying this veneer of democracy, however are the effects of military rule. The large number of demonstrators killed in the September takeover arrest and imprisonment of persons suspected of leading demonstrations, forced return to work of striking workers, and summary dismissal of thousands of government employees who had participated in demonstrations contribute to an atmosphere of fear and intimidation. Leaders of opposition parties have been able to campaign in various parts of Burma but at times have had campaign activities circumscribed by local military commands.

Two principal parties emerged from the September takeover: the National League for Democracy, led by several leading opponents of the regime, is generally acknowledged as the principal opposition party, while the National Union Party, made up mostly of former Burma Socialist Program Party members, is commonly viewed as a continuation of the BSPP.

Uncertainty presently surrounds the regime's stated intention to hold multiparty elections once law and order is reestablished. As of December 1988, the military government has not given a date for elections or indicated in general terms when an election might be held.

An additional unknown factor is U Ne Win. Though technically a private citizen, he is widely believed to retain a great deal of personal power and may well have substantial influence among the military leadership.

## Problems of Insurgency

The May 1980 amnesty while marking the end of most ethnic Burman opposition, did not significantly affect dissatisfaction and insurgency among Burma's ethnic minorities. From 1980 to 1981, secret negotiations were conducted with the Burmese Communist Party (BCP) and the Kachin Independence Organization, but both failed by May 1981. Kachin, Shan, Karen, and other ethnic insurgencies continue, motivated by demands for secession or autonomy within Burma.

Another factor in the insurgency is narcotics production and trafficking. Most insurgent groups depend largely on the narcotics trade for financial existence; and, for some, such as the Shan United Army, it is their primary reason for existence. Perhaps the most critical long-term problem facing the Burmese Government is how to combine political, economic, and military measures to harmonize relations between the central government and minorities.

The largest insurgency, that of the BCP dates to 1948. With the almost complete destruction of the old party leadership in an internal power struggle, followed by the 1968 Burmese Army capture of the party headquarters in the Pegu Yoma, the party organization was reconstructed under the Chinese-trained Thakin Ba Thein Tin. The current BCP military organization is concentrated in an area along the Sino-Burmese border east of the Salween River with its support restricted to local ethnic minorities without roots in the ethnic Burman center of the country. The BCP also has become increasingly involved in the narcotics trade. Since 1948, the communist and other insurgencies have seriously taxed the gov-

ernment's resources, but they currently pose no real threat to the government.

# ECONOMY

Burma is an agricultural country, although it has substantial mineral resources, including lead, zinc, tin, tungsten, and petroleum. Self-sufficient in almost all foodstuffs, it exports significant amounts of rice. Burma's industries include agricultural and wood processing, textiles, footwear mining, cement, and petroleum extraction and refining. Since the peak of the British colonial economy during the 1930s, Burma's economic progress has been hindered by the destruction of 50% of its capital base during World War II, widespread insurgencies independence, which delayed or prevented reconstruction and aspects of government policy, particularly after 1962, that discouraged capital formation required for development. Probably no other Southeast Asian country suffered such devastation during World War II as did Burma. After 1972, limited changes in government economic policy—including efforts to increase rice production with the introduction of new high-yield strains of rice and the acceptance of foreign aid improved economic performance. In the mid-1980s, weak markets for Burma's export commodities have contributed to a new slowdown in economic growth, which is unofficially estimated at between 1% and 4%.

In August 1987, Chairman U Ne Win, in a speech to the party, called for unspecified economic reforms. The first manifestation followed in October when trade in rice and other agricultural products was liberalized to allow private trade in these commodities. The government retained the monopoly on exports. In September however, the government withdrew from circulation the three largest denomination notes without compensation, effectively destroying 85% of the currency. This move sparked the first widespread anti-government demonstrations in 15 years.

The national insurrection against the BSPP regime from July to September 1988 included a general strike that lasted for about 2 months. Considerable damage resulted to factories, refineries, and other installations as a result of looting and sabotage. The military regime's use of coercion to force striking employees back to work also resulted in an apparent general drop in productivity. Although the government has left in place the liberalized rules on rice trading, it is evident that economic activity in general is substantially below that before the 1988 upheavals. The suspension of aid from Burma's main donors also has deprived the country of badly needed foreign exchange and has curtailed a number of development projects.

Burma's exports are dominated by commodities. Rice and teak have accounted for as much as 70% of total export earnings in recent years. Other major exports have included metallic ores, beans and pulses, seafood, and gems. Due primarily to a drop in rice export earnings, total exports fell 10% in 1984-85 and remained static in 1986.

Recent exports to the United States have averaged between $10 and $15 million and have included teak, shrimp and prawns, and tungsten ore. Imports from the United States have averaged $15 million per year and have included oil service equipment, agricultural chemicals, and heavy machinery.

## The Burmese Way to Socialism and its Legacy

Since independence, Burmese economic policies have been based on socialist ideas and the preservation of traditional Buddhist values. Socialism in Burma had its strongest roots in nationalist opposition to British colonial economic policy, which effectively handed the country's industry, finance, and trade over to British entrepreneurs and to ethnic Indian and Chinese businessmen. An early goal of Burma's leaders was to reduce the economic power of these elements through nationalization, that began in 1948 with the takeover of the

## Travel Notes

**Note:** The Burmese Government halted the issuance of tourist visas in August 1988. As of December 1988, the issuance of tourist visas has not resumed. The following information is provided for the benefit of future travel to Burma when tourism is resumed.

**Customs:** Tourist travel normally is restricted to major cultural centers and their vicinities, including Rangoon, Mandalay, Pagan, Pegu, and Taunggyi. Hotel and travel arrangements inside Burma for tourists must be handled by Tourist Burma, a branch of the official Hotel and Tourist Corporation. Tourist visas are readily available, but holders of such visas cannot extend stays beyond 7 days. Long-term visas for business trips can be obtained, but special arrangements must be made in advance and approved by the Burmese Government.

Because of internal security problems, travel to the border areas of Burma is prohibited. The import or export of Burmese currency—kyats—is forbidden, but foreign currency can be imported without limitation as long as it is declared. Travelers also are required to change $100 equivalent into kyat upon arrival in the country, which is not reconvertible. At departure, travelers must account for all currency and valuables brought into the country.

**Health:** Yellow fever inoculation certificates are required for entry of travelers who have been in an infected area within 6 days of arrival. Those leaving Burma will need a cholera inoculation certificate if going to countries requiring a certificate after travel through endemic cholera areas. Check the latest information. Boil all drinking water. Cholera, tuberculosis, plague, leprosy, and typhoid are endemic to Burma. Malaria, a serious problem in rural areas, is uncommon in Rangoon, but dengue fever is present. Although bacillary and amoebic dysenteries are prevalent, along with various other intestinal parasitic disorders, careful travelers can avoid exposure, at least in major cities.

**Telecommunications:** Telephone service within Rangoon is adequate; international service is available 24 hours a day, but connections may be delayed. Telegraphic service to and from Burma is often slow. Burma is 11½ hours ahead of eastern standard time.

**Transportation:** Rangoon is the only place in Burma where travelers are allowed to enter and exit the country. The Burma Air ways Corporation (UB) operates flights to and from Bangkok, Singapore, Calcutta, Dhaka, and Kathmandu, and Rangoon's international airport, Mingaladon. No US carriers fly to Burma. Internal UB flights connect Rangoon and the major cities where foreigners are permitted to travel freely. However, space on these flights is limited during the peak tourist season from October until April.

Schedules are often unreliable. Travel by car, train, or river steamer is possible but somewhat arduous. Public transportation in Rangoon and Mandalay is inadequate, unsafe, and overcrowded. Mini-pickups are used as taxis; many are uncomfortable and in poor condition.

**Travel Advice:** For up-to-date information from the U.S. State Department on possible inconvenient or hazardous situations, see the **Travel Warnings and Consular Information Sheets from the U.S. Government** section starting on page 1723. For the latest information on health requirements and conditions, see the **International Travelers' Health Information** section starting on page 1385. For further information dealing with non-urgent matter, see the **Tips for Travelers.**

famous Irrawaddy Flotilla Company and of British timber concessions. Further efforts were hindered by insurgencies.

U Ne Win's accession to power in 1962 revived the nationalization program. Steps taken in 1963 and 1964 included nationalization of all foreign and private banks, imposition of steep tax rates on private businesses, and nationalization of all foreign trade. By late 1965, the government had assumed control of all important industries. Several hundred other commercial and industrial enterprises were taken over in late 1968 and early 1969.

Although agriculture was not nationalized, government controls were imposed on processing and marketing of agricultural products; controls were partially lifted in October 1987. A direct result of the nationalization program has been the repatriation of many thousands of Indians and Chinese.

Economic policy after 1962 also emphasized self-reliant development and industrialization. Most foreign aid programs in Burma were eliminated. Imposition of centralized economic control complemented nationalization.

Economic difficulties resulting from these policies led to limited changes after 1972. Foreign aid again was encouraged; emphasis on heavy industry was modified to recognize the importance of agriculture, mining, and forestry; a role was acknowledged for material incentives to production; and tax reforms were instituted. The policies significantly affected the economy, especially agricultural production, and the growth rate improved.

At the August 1985 Party Congress, the government confirmed a willingness to enter into "mutually beneficial economic cooperation" arrangements, of limited duration, with foreign entities in cases where Burma lacked the necessary capital or technology to exploit its resources. Although this was a restatement of existing policy, in practice, Burma has moved extremely slow in this direction. In fall 1984, the government did form a joint venture for unspecified purposes with a partially government-owed West German company; the only example of "mutually beneficial economic cooperation" to date, it is unclear whether it will set a precedent for future foreign investment.

In July 1988, the BSPP's extraordinary party congress approved a number of changes to existing economic policy that would, in theory, have permitted a dramatic liberalization of the economy, including private foreign investment and joint ventures. The BSPP government did not have a chance to demonstrate its intent to deliver on these promises, as a general uprising paralyzed the regime and culminated with a military takeover in September. The military government pledged to follow through on a program of general economic liberalization. However, the first concrete proposal by the government to permit increased and private control in foreign trade was widely seen as excessively bureaucratic and restrictive. The regime declined to realign the exchange rate of the kyat to more accurately reflect its true value, a step many economists see as a prerequisite to attract foreign capital.

# FOREIGN RELATIONS

Strict neutralism has been the cornerstone of Burmese foreign policy under all governments since 1948. This policy entails avoiding international commitments, except through international organizations, and an impartial approach to issues between the major powers. Burma was a founding member of the Nonaligned Movement, although it withdrew after the 1979 Havana conference—protesting the violation of principles on which the movement had been organized—and has not rejoined. Burma maintains bilateral relations with the Association of South East Asian Nations but is not interested in joining ASEAN or other regional groupings.

After the 1962 military takeover, Burma's contacts with other countries were sharply reduced. Since 1972, the Burmese Government again has begun participating in the World Bank, the International Monetary Fund, and the Asian Development Bank and has entered into bilateral economic assistance agreements with individual countries, including the United States, Japan, and the Federal Republic of Germany. Nonetheless, Burma has maintained continuously its membership in the United Nations and many UN-associated organizations.

Burma was the first noncommunist country to recognize the People's Republic of China in 1949. Relations deteriorated during the mid-1960s, when support for the "Cultural Revolution" by some ethnic Chinese led to anti-Chinese riots. During 1970-71,

improved relations led to an exchange of ambassadors and a visit to Beijing by U Ne Win in August 1971. Sino-Burmese relations have continued to improve since that time and featured an exchange of presidential visits in 19845 and a trip to Beijing by U Ne Win in May 1985.

Burma maintains good relations with Japan. The Japanese economic assistance program was one of the few continued throughout the 1962-72 period. Until aid was halted in 1988 Japan was the largest aid donor to Burma and also the most active investor.

In 1983, Burma broke relations with North Korea and withdrew recognition of its government, following a North Korean terrorist bomb attack against a visiting presidential delegation from the Republic of Korea.

As a result of the military takeover in September 1988 and the violent suppression of antigovernment demonstrations, Japan, West Germany, and the United States halted all assistance to Burma. A number of countries have since taken steps to limit their contact with the regime.

# DEFENSE

Under the Ministry of Defense, the Burmese Armed Forces in 1987 totaled about 215,000 members- 198,000 army, 8,000 air force, and 9,000 navy. Paramilitary personnel include a People's Police Force of about 40,000 under the Ministry of Home and Religious Affairs and a People's Militia of about 35,000. Defense expenditures during Burmese fiscal year 1986 were $386 million, or 31% of the central government ministerial budget. Burma's strict neutrality, the absence of notable external threats, and persistent internal insurgencies have determined the character of the armed forces. In addition to counterinsurgency, their missions include internal security, territorial defense, assistance to national administration, and civic action.

Burma purchases small amounts of military equipment and training from various countries, including the United States and Western Europe. In addition to providing military training, the United States supplied arms and equipment valued at about $80 million to Burma from 1958 to 1971. These arrangements were gradually terminated by Burma after 1962, although military training resumed in 1980. However, following the September 1988 military takeover, the United States halted all military assistance to Burma.

# U.S.-BURMA RELATIONS

Historically, the United States and Burma have maintained friendly relations. The United States long has supported Burma's independence and neutral foreign policy. In the first two decades of Burmese independence, this support included substantial assistance to promote economic development and internal security. At Burma's request, aid was discontinued during the mid-1960s.

Bilateral relations are based on mutual understanding and cooperation. Specific U.S. interests in Burma include continued cooperation to suppress the illicit narcotics trade, assistance to Burmese economic development, commercial access, and improved educational and cultural contacts between Americans and Burmese. The United States wishes to see Burma's continued progress as an independent, stable country.

Since the early 1970s, the Burmese Government has attempted to control illicit drug traffic in its portion of the "Golden Triangle"—the opium-producing area of Burma, Thailand, and Laos. From 1974 to 1988, the United States provided the Burmese Government more than $7 1 million in antinarcotics equipment, primarily helicopters and fixed-wing aircraft. Because some 20% of the heroin reaching the United States originates as opium in the "Golden Triangle," use of this equipment in narcotics

*A report on important events that have taken place since the last State Department revision of this* Background Note.

The military government of Myanmar (Burma) continues to persecute its opponents, jailing thousands in 1996 and issuing threats through the controlled press. Placed on the defensive by pro-democracy leader Daw Aung San Suu Kyi and her supporters, the junta has also assembled thousands of people for pro-Government rallies. On May 29, 1996, Ms. Aung San Suu Kyi announced her intention to proceed with a strategy that is a direct challenge to the military regime.

Ms. Aung San Suu Kyi's National League for Democracy (NLD) planned to create a new draft constitution that would oust the ruling junta and begin to devise its own economic policies. Undaunted by the junta, Ms. Aung San Suu Kyi also intended more mass meetings.

But the Government returned Ms. Aung San Suu Kyi to house arrest in December 1996, reinstating a detention that had ended in 1995 after six years. In September 1997, the government permitted 800 NLD members to attend a congress at Ms. Aung San Suu Kyi's house. Government officials blamed her for student demonstrations that flared in early December 1996. The opposition leader claimed no ties to the student protesters, who were met in the streets by club-wielding police. The protests were the largest since 1988, when police killed hundreds in routing peaceful pro-democracy demonstrators.

The crackdown was seen as a setback for Burmese officials hopeful of full membership this year in the Association of Southeast Asian Nations (ASEAN), a political and economic union. In July 1997, Myanmar joined the ASEAN. The European Union protested Myanmar's inclusion in the association by canceling a November meeting between the two organizations.

There was trouble for the Government on other fronts as well. On April 22, 1997, the United States announced a ban on new American investment in the country, citing the human rights abuses of the Burmese military. In March, the European Union withdrew Myanmar's special trading privileges after receiving reports that the Government used forced labor to increase exports.

PepsiCo announced in April 1996 its plan to withdraw from a joint bottling venture in Burma (Myanmar), bending to criticism of its operations in the military dictatorship. The Asian bottler will continue to receive syrup concentrate from Pepsi and will continue to use the Pepsi trademark. In February 1996 a Coca-Cola representative announced that for "strictly business" reasons the Pepsi competitor will stay out of Burma. Coca-Cola's policy, she pointed out, is to remain apolitical. Other companies, primarily apparel producers that can more easily relocate operations from country to country, have withdrawn from Burma. Some companies cited concern for human rights; others cited business

reasons. These include Levi Strauss (which dropped its contract suppliers in Burma in 1993), Liz Claiborne, and Eddie Bauer, a unit of Spiegel Inc.

UNOCAL Corporation, which holds a 28% stake in a $1 billion natural-gas pipeline project in Myanmar, is proceeding, despite protests by human rights organizations. The company signed an agreement in January 1997 to expand exploration and development.

The Burmese military Government seized power in a harsh crackdown on pro-democracy organizations in September 1988. It voided the election of Ms. Aung San Suu Kyi and her party and placed her under house arrest. She has lived under house arrest on and off since that time. Burma continued to receive global condemnation for its human rights violations. In February 2001, the US State Department condemned the country for the repression of basic political and social freedoms. In June, the Coalition to Stop the Use of Child Soldiers reported that 50,000 minors, some as young as seven, were being used as soldiers, human shields, and minesweepers. Human Rights Watch condemned the country for its continued use of forced labor, despite a UN General Assembly ban on the practice.

The Burmese economy has been in steady decline due to economic sanctions and a marked decrease in international investment.

suppression was of direct benefit to the United States.

U.S. bilateral economic aid to Burma recommenced in 1980 after a hiatus of 15 years. Programs of the U.S. Agency for International Development (AID) in Burma concentrated on two sectors-agriculture and health. Economic assistance in FY 1987 totaled $8 million in grants. As a result of the September 1988 military takeover, all U.S. assistance to Burma, including development and antinarcotics assistance, was halted indefinitely.

Two U.S. companies signed Asian Development Bank-financed consultancy projects in Burma in 1985,

establishing the first U.S. business presence in the country since the 1970s. At the same time, however, U.S. exports to Burma have declined recently since, faced with declining export earnings, Burma has reduced imports.

Between 1962 and 1974, the educational and cultural exchange program was limited to occasional visits by American athletes. Since 1974, this program has gradually expanded to include educators, technical experts, artists, musicians, and cultural groups. In 1980 and 1983, the Fulbright and East-West Center educational exchange programs were reactivated, providing an opportunity for an increasing number of Burmese

scholars and professionals to study in the United States. The status of these exchange programs is presently undecided.

## Principal U.S. Officials

For up-to-date information on Principal U.S. Officials, see the U.S. Embassies, Consulates, and Foreign Service section starting on page 139.

The U.S. Embassy is located at 581 Merchant Street, Rangoon (tel. S2066).

# BURUNDI

August 2000

Official Name:
**Republic of Burundi**

## PROFILE

### Geography
**Location:** Central Africa. Bordering nations—Tanzania, the Democratic Republic of Congo, Rwanda.
**Area:** 27,830 sq. km. (10,747 sq. mi.); about the size of Maryland.
**Cities:** Capital—Bujumbura (pop. 300,000). Other cities—Cibitoke, Muyinga, Ngozi, Bubanza, Gitega, Bururi.
**Terrain:** Hilly, rising from 780 meters (2,600 ft.) at the Shore of Lake Tanganyika to mountains more than 2,700 meters (9,000 ft.) above sea level.
**Climate:** Warm but not uncomfortable in Bujumbura; cooler in higher regions.

### People
**Nationality:** Noun—Barundi (sing. and pl.); adjective—Burundian(s).
**Population:** (June 2000) 6.2 million.
**Annual growth rate:** (1999 est.) 3.54 %.
**Ethnic Groups:** Hutu 85%; Tutsi 14%; Twa 1.0%.
**Religion:** Roman Catholic 62%; Protestant 5%; traditional beliefs 32%; Muslim 1%.
**Languages:** Official—Kirundi, French; Other—Kiswahili, English.
**Education:** Years compulsory—6.

Attendance—55% male, 45% female. Literacy—35.3%.
**Health:** (1999 est.) Life expectancy—44 yrs. (men), 47 yrs. (women). Infant mortality rate—99/1,000.

### Government
**Type:** Republic—with power vested strongly in executive; transitional government (de facto military regime).
**Independence:** July 1, 1962 (from Belgium).
**Constitution:** A draft constitution was promulgated on March 13, 1992 and suspended following the July 1996 coup. A Transitional Constitutional Act, promulgated on June 6, 1998, legitimizes the authority of the president and establishes the political platform for the transitional regime.
**Branches:** Executive—president (chief of state, head of government) and 14-member presidential-appointed cabinet with two vice presidents. Legislative—121-member National Assembly (81 elected, 40 appointed). Judicial—Supreme Court and subsidiary courts.
**Administrative subdivisions:** 15 provinces with 114 communes.
**Political parties:** Multi-party system introduced after 1998. FRODEBU (the Front for Democracy in Burundi, predominantly Hutu with some Tutsi membership) and UPRONA (the National Unity

and Progress Party, predominantly Tutsi with some Hutu membership) are national, mainstream parties. Other Tutsi and Hutu opposition parties and groups include, among others, PARENA (the Party for National Redress, Tutsi), ABASA (the Burundi African Alliance for the Salvation, Tutsi), PRP (the People's Reconciliation Party, Tutsi), CNDD/FDD (the National Council for the Defense of Democracy/Front for the Defense of Democracy, now consisting of two groups, Hutu), PALIPE-HUTU (the Party for the Liberation of the Hutu People, Hutu) and FROL-INA/FAP (the Front for the National Liberation of Burundi/Popular Armed Forces, Hutu).
**Suffrage:** Universal adult; elections under transitional regime not yet held. Flag: White diagonal cross with two red and two green panels; white circle in center with three red stars.

### Economy
**GDP:** (1998 est.) $4.1 billion.
**Real growth rate:** (1998 est.) 2%.
**GDP per capita:** (1998 est.) $740.
**Inflation rate:** (1998) 17%.
**Central government budget:** (1999) Receipts—$138.7 million; spending—$186.8 million.
**Natural resources:** nickel, uranium, rare earth oxides, peat, cobalt, copper, platinum deposits not yet exploited, vanadium.
**Structure of production:** (1997

est.) Agriculture 58%, Industry 18%, Services 24%.

**Agriculture:** (1998 est., 49.4% of GDP). Products—coffee, tea, sugar, cotton fabrics and oil, corn, sorghum, sweet potatoes, bananas, manioc (tapioca), beef, milk, hides, livestock feed, rice. Arable land—44%.

**Industry:** (1998 est., 19.1% of GDP) Types—sugar refining, coffee processing, telecommunications, pharmaceuticals, food processing, chemicals (insecticides), public works construction, light consumer goods, assembly of imported components. Services (1998 est.) 31.5% of GDP.

**Mining:** Commercial quantities of alluvial gold, nickel, phosphates, rare earth, vanadium, and other; peat mining.

**Trade:** (1998) Exports—$49 million: coffee (88% of export earnings), tea, sugar, cotton fabrics, hides. Major markets: U.K., Germany, Benelux, Switzerland. Imports—$102 million: food, beverages, tobacco, chemicals, road vehicles, petroleum and products. Major suppliers—Benelux, France, Germany, Saudi Arabia, Japan.

**Total external debt:** (1997) $1.247 billion.

# PEOPLE

At 206.1 persons per sq. km., Burundi has the second-largest population density in Sub-Saharan Africa. Most people live on farms near areas of fertile volcanic soil. The population is made up of three major ethnic groups—Bahutu (Hutu), Batutsi or Watusi (Tutsi), and Batwa (Twa). Kirundi is the common language. Intermarriage takes place frequently between the Hutus and Tutsis. The terms "pastoralist" and "agriculturist," often used as ethnic designations for Watutsi and Bahutu, respectively, are only occupational titles which vary among individuals and groups. Although Hutus encompass the majority of the population, historically Tutsis have been politically and economically dominant.

# HISTORY

In the 16th century, Burundi was a kingdom characterized by a hierarchical political authority and tributary economic exchange. A king (mwani) headed a princely aristocracy (gwana) which owned most of the land and required a tribute, or tax, from local farmers and herders. In the mid-18th century, this Tutsi royalty consolidated authority over land, production, and distribution with the development of the ubugabire—a patron-client relationship in which the populace received royal protection in exchange for tribute and land tenure. Although European explorers and missionaries made brief visits to the area as early as 1856, it was not until 1899 that Burundi came under German East African administration. In 1916 Belgian troops occupied the area. In 1923, the League of Nations mandated to Belgium the territory of Ruanda-Urundi, encompassing modern-day Rwanda and Burundi. The Belgians administered the territory through indirect rule, building on the Tutsi-dominated aristocratic hierarchy. Following World War II, Ruanda-Urundi became a United Nations Trust Territory under Belgian administrative authority. After 1948, Belgium permitted the emergence of competing political parties. Two political parties emerged: the Union for National Progress (UPRONA), a multi-ethnic party led by Tutsi Prince Louis Rwagasore and the Christian Democratic Party (PDC) supported by Belgium. In 1961, Prince Rwagasore was assassinated following an UPRONA victory in legislative elections.

Full independence was achieved on July 1, 1962. In the context of weak democratic institutions at independence, Tutsi King Mwambutsa IV established a constitutional monarchy comprising equal numbers of Hutus and Tutsis. The 1965 assassination of the Hutu prime minister set in motion a series of destabilizing Hutu revolts and subsequent governmental repression. In 1966, King

Mwambutsa was deposed by his son, Prince Ntare IV, who himself was deposed by his prime minister Capt. Michel Micombero in the same year. Micombero abolished the monarchy and declared a republic, although a de facto military regime emerged. In 1972, an aborted Hutu rebellion triggered the flight of hundreds of thousands of Burundians. Civil unrest continued throughout the late 1960s and early 1970s. In 1976, Col. Jean-Baptiste Bagaza took power in a bloodless coup. Although Bagaza led a Tutsi-dominated military regime, he encouraged land reform, electoral reform, and national reconciliation. In 1981, a new constitution was promulgated. In 1984, Bagaza was elected head of state, as the sole candidate. After his election, Bagaza's human rights record deteriorated as he suppressed religious activities and detained political opposition members.

In 1987, Maj. Pierre Buyoya overthrew Colonel Bagaza. He dissolved opposition parties, suspended the 1981 constitution, and instituted his ruling Military Committee for National Salvation (CSMN). During 1988, increasing tensions between the ruling Tutsis and the majority Hutus resulted in violent confrontations between the army, the Hutu opposition, and Tutsi hardliners. During this period, an estimated 150,000 people were killed, with tens of thousands of refugees flowing to neighboring countries. Buyoya formed a commission to investigate the causes of the 1988 unrest and to develop a charter for democratic reform.

In 1991, Buyoya approved a constitution that provided for a president, nonethnic government, and a parliament. Burundi's first Hutu president, Melchior Ndadaye, of the Hutu-dominated FRODEBU Party, was elected in 1993. He was assassinated by factions of the Tutsi-dominated armed forces in October 1993. The country then plunged into civil war, which killed tens of thousands of people and displaced hundreds of thousands by the time the FRODEBU government regained control and elected Cyprien Ntaryamira president in January 1994. Nonetheless, the security situation continued to deteriorate. In April 1994, President Ntayamira and Rwandan President Juvenal Habyarimana died in a plane crash. This act marked the beginning of the Rwandan genocide, while in Burundi, the death of Ntaryamira exacerbated the violence and unrest. Sylvestre Ntibantunganya was installed to a 4-year presidency on April 8, but the security situation further declined. The influx of hundreds of thousands of Rwandan refugees and the activities of armed Hutu and Tutsi groups further destabilized the regime.

# GOVERNMENT AND POLITICAL CONDITIONS

In November 1995, the presidents of Burundi, Rwanda, Uganda, and Zaire announced a regional initiative for a negotiated peace in Burundi facilitated by former Tanzanian President Julius Nyerere. In July 1996, former Burundian President Buyoya returned to power in a bloodless coup. He declared himself president of a transitional republic, even as he suspended the National Assembly, banned opposition groups, and imposed a nationwide curfew. Widespread condemnation of the coup ensued, and regional countries imposed economic sanctions pending a return to a constitutional government. Buyoya agreed in 1996 to liberalize political parties. Nonetheless, fighting between the army and Hutu militias continued. In June 1998, Buyoya promulgated a transitional constitution and announced a partnership between the government and the opposition-led National Assembly. After Facilitator Julius Nyerere's death in October 1999, the regional leaders appointed Nelson Mandela as Facilitator of the Arusha peace process. Under Mandela the peace process has revived

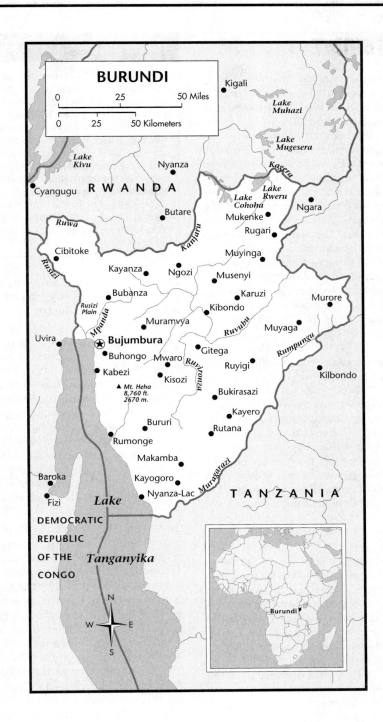

and important progress has taken place.

## Principal Government Officials

**For up-to-date information on Principal Government Officials, see the** **Chiefs of State and Cabinet Members of Foreign Governments section starting on page 1.**

Burundi maintains an embassy in the United States at Suite 212, 2233 Wisconsin Ave. NW, Washington, DC 20007 (tel. 202-342-2574).

# ECONOMY

The mainstay of the Burundian economy is agriculture, accounting for 58% of GDP in 1997. Agriculture supports more than 90% of the labor force, the majority of whom are subsistence farmers. Although Burundi is potentially self-sufficient in food production, the ongoing civil war, overpopulation, and soil erosion have contributed to the contraction of the subsistence economy by 25% in recent years. Large numbers of internally displaced persons have been unable to produce their own food and are largely dependent on international humanitarian assistance. Burundi is a net food importer, with food accounting for 17% of imports in 1997.

The main cash crop is coffee, which accounted for 78.5% of exports in 1997. This dependence on coffee has increased Burundi's vulnerability to seasonal yields and international coffee prices. Coffee is the largest state-owned enterprise. In recent years, the government has tried to attract private investment to this sector, with some success. Efforts to privatize other publicly held enterprises have stalled. Other principal exports include tea and raw cotton.

Little industry exists except the processing of agricultural exports. Although potential wealth in petrleum, nickel, copper, and other natural resources is being explored, the uncertain security situation has prevented meaningful investor interest. Industrial development also is hampered by Burundi's distance from the sea and high transport costs. Lake Tanganyika remains an important trading point. The trade embargo, lifted in 1999, negatively impacted trade and industry.

Burundi is heavily dependent on bilateral and multilateral aid, with external debt totaling $1.247 billion in 1997. A series of largely unsuccessful 5-year plans initiated in July 1986 in partnership with the World Bank and the International Monetary Fund attempted to reform the foreign exchange system, liberalize imports,

**Travel Notes**

**Travel Advice:** For up-to-date information from the U.S. State Department on possible inconvenient or hazardous situations, see the **Travel Warnings and Consular Information Sheets from the U.S. Government** section starting on page 1723. For the latest information on health requirements and conditions, see the **International Travelers' Health Information** section starting on page 1385. For further information dealing with non-urgent matter, see the **Tips for Travelers to...** section starting on page 1588.

reduce restrictions on international transactions, diversify exports, and reform the coffee industry.

IMF structural adjustment programs in Burundi were suspended following the outbreak of the crisis in 1993. The World Bank has identified key areas for potential growth, including the productivity of traditional crops and the introduction of new exports, light manufactures, industrial mining, and services. Other serious problems include the state's role in the economy, the question of governmental transparency, and debt reduction.

To protest the 1996 coup by President Buyoya, neighboring countries imposed an economic embargo on Burundi. Although the embargo was never officially ratified by the United Nations Security Council, most countries refrained from official trade with Burundi. Following the 1996 coup, the United States suspended all but humanitarian aid to Burundi. The regional embargo was lifted on January 23, 1999, based on progress by the government in advancing national reconciliation through the Burundi peace process.

# FOREIGN RELATIONS

Burundi's relations with its neighbors have often been affected by security concerns. Hundreds of thousands of Burundian refugees have at various times crossed to neighboring Rwanda, Tanzania, and the Demo-

cratic Republic of the Congo (DROC). Hundreds of thousands of Burundians are in neighboring countries as a result of the ongoing civil war. Most of them, more than 340,000 since 1993, are in Tanzania. Some Burundian rebel groups have used neighboring countries as bases for insurgent activities. The 1993 embargo placed on Burundi by regional states negatively impacted its diplomatic relations with its neighbors; relations have improved since the 1999 suspension of these sanctions. Burundi is a member of various international and regional organizations, including the United Nations, the Organization for African Unity, and the African Development Bank.

# U.S.-BURUNDI RELATIONS

Burundi is an important factor in regional stability in the Great Lakes region. The United States encourages political stability, democratic change, respect for human rights, and shared economic development in Burundi. The United States supports the Arusha/Tanzania peace process aimed at national reconciliation and the eventual formation of a constitutional government, and encourages a peaceful solution to the civil conflict in Burundi. In the long term, the U.S. seeks to strengthen the process of internal reconciliation and democratization within all the states of the region to promote a stable, democratic community of nations that will work toward mutual social, economic, and security interests on the continent.

The United States has provided financial support for the peace process. U.S. bilateral aid with the exception of humanitarian assistance was ended following the 1996 coup.

In view of progress in the peace talks, the U.S. and other international donors are reconsidering their policy of assistance. A State Department Travel Advisory was listed for Burundi in August 1999.

## Principal U.S. Officials

For up-to-date information on Principal U.S. Officials, see the U.S. Embassies, Consulates, and Foreign Service section starting on page 139.

The U.S. embassy is at Avenue des Etats Unis (Boite Postale 1720), Bujumbura (tel. [257] 22-34-54).

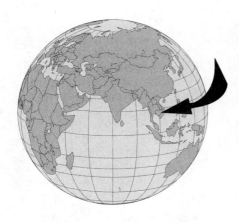

# CAMBODIA

January 1996

## Official Name:
## Kingdom of Cambodia

# PROFILE

## Geography

**Area:** 181,040 sq. km. (69,900 sq. mi.); about the size of Missouri.
**Cities:** Capital—Phnom Penh (pop. between 1 million and 1.2 million). Other cities—Battambang, Siem Reap, Kompong Cham, Kompong Speu, Kompong Thom.
**Terrain:** Central plain drained by the Tonle Sap (Great Lake) and Mekong and Bassac Rivers. Heavy forests away from the rivers and the lake, mountains in the southwest (Cardamom Mountains) and north (Dangrek Mountains) along the border with Thailand.
**Climate:** Tropical monsoon with rainy season June-Oct. and dry season Nov.-May.

## People

**Nationality:** Noun and adjective: Cambodian(s), Khmer.
**Population (1995):** 10.56 million.
**Avg. annual growth rate:** 4.1%. Births—44 births/1,000 population. Deaths—16 deaths/1,000 population.
**Health:** Infant mortality—108 deaths/1,000 live births. Life expectancy—48 years male/51 years female.
**Ethnic groups:** Cambodian 90%; Chinese and Vietnamese 5% each; small numbers of hill tribes, Chams, and Burmese.
**Religions:** Theravada Buddhism 95%; Islam; animism; atheism.
**Languages:** Khmer (official) spoken by more than 95% of the population, including minorities; some French still spoken; English increasingly popular as a second language.
**Literacy:** 35.2%.

## Government

The Royal Cambodian Government (RCG), a constitutional monarchy formed on the basis of elections internationally recognized as free and fair, was established on September 24, 1993. The RCG faces an armed threat from the Khmer Rouge (KR), also known as the Party of Democratic Kampuchea (PDK), who when they ruled Cambodia from 1975-1979 compiled one of the worst records of human rights abuse in this century.
**Administrative subdivisions:** 19 provinces and municipalities.
**Independence:** November 9, 1953.
**Constitution:** September 24, 1993.
**Elections:** Elections overseen by the UN in May 1993.
**National Legislature:** The National Assembly, consisting of 120 elected members.
**Political parties and leaders:** RCG Coalition: National United Front for an Independent, Neutral, Peaceful, and Cooperative Cambodia (FUNCINPEC) led by First Prime Minister Prince Ranariddh; Cambodian People's Party (CPP) led by Second Prime Minister Hun Sen; the Buddhist Liberal Democratic Party (BLDP); and the Liberal Democratic Party (Moulinaka). Outside the RCG: Party of Democratic Kampuchea (the Khmer Rouge), nominally led by Khieu Samphan.
**Diplomatic Relations:** The RCG has established diplomatic relations with most countries, including the United States. Cambodia does not have diplomatic relations with the Republic of Korea (ROK).
**Flag:** Two horizontal blue bands, divided by a wider red band on which is centered a white stylized representation of Angkor Wat.

## Economy

**GDP:** $2.92 billion (1995).
**Per capita GDP:** $275 (1995).
**Inflation (1995):** 6%.
**Natural resources:** Timber, gemstones, some iron ore, manganese and phosphate, hydroelectric potential from the Mekong River.
**Agriculture:** About 4,848,000 hectares (12 million acres) are unforested land; all are arable with irrigation but less than two million hectares are cultivated. Products—Rice, rubber, corn, meat, vegetables, dairy products, sugar, flour.
**Industry:** Types—rice milling, fishing, wood and wood products, tex-

tiles, cement, some rubber production.

**Central Government Budget (1995):** Revenues $223.5 million; Expenditure $407 million. Budget deficit 13.5% of GDP; capital expenditure 5% of GDP, 34% of budget; defense spending 5.4% of GDP, 29% of budget.

**Trade:** Exports: $358 million (1995 est.)—natural rubber, rice, pepper, wood; Major partners: Singapore, Japan, Thailand, Taiwan, Hong Kong, Indonesia; Imports: $720 million (1994)—vehicles, fuels, consumer goods, machinery; Major Partners: Singapore, Indonesia, Vietnam, Thailand, Hong Kong. Trade with the US: Cambodian imports from US (1995) $41 million; exports to US (1994) $1.2 million.

**Exchange rate:** Approximately 2,300 riels = $1 (June, 1995).

**Economic Aid:** $179 million in disbursements by official donors in fiscal year 1994/5. Major donors include Asian Development Bank (ADB), UN Development Program (UNDP), Australia, Canada, Denmark, France, Germany, Italy, Japan, Sweden, Thailand, the United Kingdom and the United States. Principle foreign commercial investors: Singapore, Hong Kong, Malaysia and Thailand.

## Membership in International Organizations

The RCG is a member of or is joining most major international organizations, including the UN and its specialized agencies such as the World Bank and International Monetary Fund. The RCG is an Asian Development Bank (ADB) member and is expected to obtain full membership in ASEAN by 1997.

## Principal Government Officials

For up-to-date information on Principal Government Officials, see the Chiefs of State and Cabinet Members of Foreign Governments section starting on page 1.

# MODERN HISTORY

Although Cambodia had a rich and powerful past under the Hindu state of Funan and the Kingdom of Angkor, by the mid-19th century the country was on the verge of dissolution. After repeated requests for French assistance, a protectorate was established in 1863. By 1884, Cambodia was a virtual colony; soon after it was made part of the Indochina Union with Annam, Tonkin, Cochin-China, and Laos.

France continued to control the country even after the start of World War II through its Vichy government. In 1945, the Japanese dissolved the colonial administration, and King Norodom Sihanouk declared an independent, anti-colonial government under Prime Minister Son Ngoc Thanh in March 1945. This government was deposed by the Allies in October. Many of Son Ngoc Thanh's supporters escaped and continued to fight for independence as the Khmer Issarak.

Although France recognized Cambodia as an autonomous kingdom within the French Union, the drive for total independence continued, resulting in a split between those who supported the political tactics of Sihanouk and those who supported the Khmer Issarak guerrilla movement. In January 1953, Sihanouk named his father as regent and went into self-imposed exile, refusing to return until Cambodia gained genuine independence.

## Full Independence

Sihanouk's actions hastened the French government's July 4, 1953 announcement of its readiness to perfect the independence and sovereignty of Cambodia, Laos, and Vietnam. Full independence came on November 9, 1953, but the situation remained uncertain until a 1954 conference was held in Geneva to settle the French-Indochina war.

All participants, except the United States and the State of Vietnam, associated themselves (by voice) with the final declaration. The Cambodian delegation agreed to the neutrality of the three Indochinese states but insisted on a provision in the ceasefire agreement that left the Cambodian government free to call for outside military assistance should the Viet Minh or others threaten its territory.

## Neutral Cambodia

Neutrality was the central element of Cambodian foreign policy during the 1950s and 1960s. By the mid-1960s, parts of Cambodia's eastern provinces were serving as bases for North Vietnamese Army and Viet Cong (NVA/VC) forces operating against South Vietnam, and the port of Sihanoukville was being used to supply them. As NVA/VC activity grew, the United States and South Vietnam became concerned, and in 1969, the United States began a series of air raids against NVA/VC base areas inside Cambodia.

Throughout the 1960s, domestic politics polarized. Opposition grew within the middle class and among leftists including Paris-educated leaders such as Son Sen, Ieng Sary, and Saloth Sar (later known as Pol Pot), who led an insurgency under the clandestine Communist Party of Kampuchea (CPK). Sihanouk called these insurgents the Khmer Rouge, literally the "Red Khmer." But the 1966 national assembly elections showed a significant swing to the right, and Gen. Lon Nol formed a new government, which lasted until 1967. During 1968 and 1969, the insurgency worsened. In August 1969, Gen. Lon Nol formed a new government. Prince Sihanouk went abroad for medical treatment in January 1970.

## The Khmer Republic and the War

In March 1970, Gen. Lon Nol deposed Prince Sihanouk and assumed power. Son Ngoc Thanh announced his support for the new government. On October 9, the Cambodian monarchy was abolished, and the country was renamed the Khmer Republic.

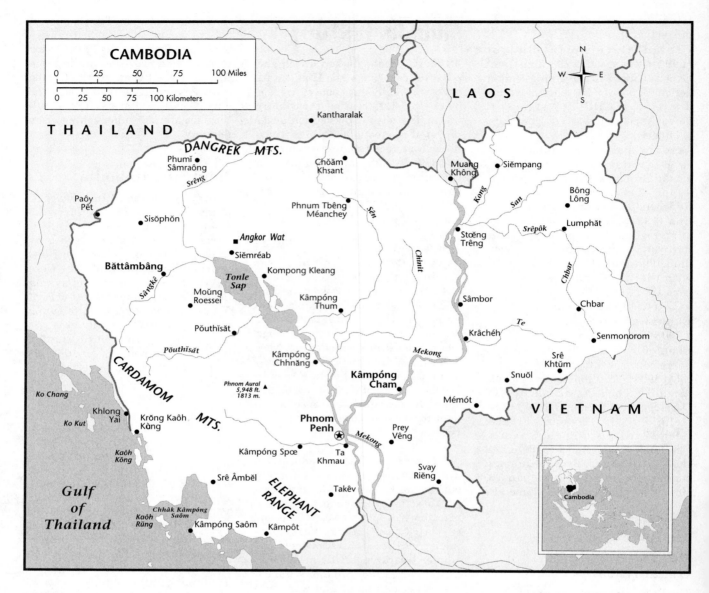

CAMBODIA

Hanoi rejected the new republic's request for the withdrawal of NVA/VC troops and began to reinfiltrate some of the 2,000-4,000 Cambodians who had gone to North Vietnam in 1954. They became a cadre in the insurgency.

The United States moved to provide material assistance to the new government's armed forces, which were engaged against both the Khmer Rouge insurgents and NVA/VC forces. In April 1970, US and South Vietnamese forces entered Cambodia in a campaign aimed at destroying NVA/VC base areas. Although a considerable quantity of equipment was seized or destroyed, NVA/VC forces proved elusive and moved deeper into

Cambodia. NVA/VC units overran many Cambodian army positions while the Khmer Rouge expanded their small-scale attacks on lines of communication.

The Khmer Republic's leadership was plagued by disunity among its three principal figures: Lon Nol, Sihanouk's cousin Sirik Matak, and National Assembly leader In Tam. Lon Nol remained in power in part because none of the others was prepared to take his place. In 1972, a constitution was adopted, a parliament elected, and Lon Nol became president. But disunity, the problems of transforming a 30,000-man army into a national combat force of more than 200,000 men, and spreading cor-

ruption weakened the civilian administration and army.

The insurgency continued to grow, with supplies and military support provided by North Vietnam. But inside Cambodia, Pol Pot and Ieng Sary asserted their dominance over the Vietnamese-trained communists, many of whom were purged. At the same time, the Khmer Rouge forces became stronger and more independent of their Vietnamese patrons. By 1973, the Khmer Rouge were fighting major battles against government forces on their own, and they controlled nearly 60% of Cambodia's territory and 25% of its population.

The government made three unsuccessful attempts to enter into negotiations with the insurgents, but by 1974, the Khmer Rouge were operating as divisions, and virtually all NVA/VC combat forces had moved into South Vietnam. Lon Nol's control was reduced to small enclaves around the cities and main transportation routes. More than 2 million refugees from the war lived in Phnom Penh and other cities.

On New Year's Day 1975, Communist troops launched an offensive which, in 117 days of the hardest fighting of the war, destroyed the Khmer Republic. Simultaneous attacks around the perimeter of Phnom Penh pinned down Republican forces, while other Khmer Rouge units overran fire bases controlling the vital lower Mekong resupply route. A US-funded airlift of ammunition and rice ended when Congress refused additional aid for Cambodia. Phnom Penh and other cities were subjected to daily rocket attacks causing thousands of civilian casualties. Phnom Penh surrendered on April 17—5 days after the US mission evacuated Cambodia.

## Democratic Kampuchea

Many Cambodians welcomed the arrival of peace, but the Khmer Rouge soon turned Cambodia—which it called Democratic Kampuchea (DK)—into a land of horror. Immediately after its victory, the new regime ordered the evacuation of all cities and towns, sending the entire urban population out into the countryside to till the land. Thousands starved or died of disease during the evacuation. Many of those forced to evacuate the cities were resettled in new villages, which lacked food, agricultural implements, and medical care. Many starved before the first harvest, and hunger and malnutrition—bordering on starvation—were constant during those years. Those who resisted or who questioned orders were immediately executed, as were most military and civilian leaders of the former regime who failed to disguise their pasts.

Within the CPK, the Paris-educated leadership—Pol Pot, Ieng Sary, Nuon Chea, and Son Sen—was in control. A new constitution in January 1976 established Democratic Kampuchea as a Communist People's Republic, and a 250-member Assembly of the Representatives of the People of Kampuchea (PRA) was selected in March to choose the collective leadership of a State Presidium, the chairman of which became the head of state.

Prince Sihanouk resigned as head of state on April 4. On April 14, after its first session, the PRA announced that Khieu Samphan would chair the State Presidium for a 5-year term. It also picked a 15-member cabinet headed by Pol Pot as prime minister. Prince Sihanouk was put under virtual house arrest.

The new government sought to restructure Cambodian society completely. Remnants of the old society were abolished and Buddhism suppressed. Agriculture was collectivized, and the surviving part of the industrial base was abandoned or placed under state control. Cambodia had neither a currency nor a banking system. The regime controlled every aspect of life and reduced everyone to the level of abject obedience through terror. Torture centers were established, and detailed records were kept of the thousands murdered there. Public executions of those considered unreliable or with links to the previous government were common. Few succeeded in escaping the military patrols and fleeing the country.

Solid estimates of the numbers who died between 1975 and 1979 are not available, but it is likely that hundreds of thousands were brutally executed by the regime. Hundreds of thousands more died of starvation and disease (both under the Khmer Rouge and during the Vietnamese invasion in 1978). Estimates of the dead range from 1 to 3 million, out of a 1975 population estimated at 7.3 million.

Democratic Kampuchea's relations with Vietnam and Thailand worsened rapidly as a result of border clashes and ideological differences. While communist, the CPK was fiercely anti-Vietnamese, and most of its members who had lived in Vietnam were purged. Democratic Kampuchea established close ties with China, and the Cambodian-Vietnamese conflict became part of the Sino-Soviet rivalry, with Moscow backing Vietnam. Border clashes worsened when Democratic Kampuchea's military attacked villages in Vietnam. The regime broke relations with Hanoi in December 1977, protesting Vietnam's attempt to create an Indochina Federation. In mid-1978, Vietnamese forces invaded Cambodia, advancing about 30 miles before the arrival of the rainy season.

In December 1978, Vietnam announced formation of the Kampuchean United Front for National Salvation (KUFNS) under Heng Samrin, a former DK division commander. It was composed of Khmer Communists who had remained in Vietnam after 1975 and officials from the eastern sector—like Heng Samrin and Hun Sen—who had fled to Vietnam from Cambodia in 1978. In late December 1978, Vietnamese forces launched a full invasion of Cambodia, capturing Phnom Penh on January 7 and driving the remnants of Democratic Kampuchea's army westward toward Thailand.

## The Vietnamese Occupation

On January 10, 1979, the Vietnamese installed Heng Samrin as head of state in the new People's Republic of Kampuchea (PRK). The Vietnamese army continued its pursuit of Pol Pot's Khmer Rouge forces. At least 600,000 Cambodians displaced during the Pol Pot era and the Vietnamese invasion began streaming to the Thai border in search of refuge. The international community responded with a massive relief effort coordinated by the United States through UNICEF and the World Food Program. More than $400 million was provided between 1979 and 1982, of which the United States contributed nearly $100 million. At one point, more than 500,000 Cambodians were living along the Thai-Cambodian border and more than 100,000 in holding centers inside Thailand.

## The Splendors of Angkor

Over a period of 300 years, between 900 and 1200 AD, the Khmer Kingdom of Angkor produced some of the world's most magnificent architectural masterpieces on the northern shore of the Tonle Sap, near the present town of Siem Reap. The Angkor area stretches 15 miles east to west and 5 miles north to south. Some 72 major temples or other buildings dot the area.

The principal temple, Angkor Wat, was built between 1112 and 1150 by Suryavarman II. With walls nearly one-half mile on each side, Angkor Wat portrays the Hindu cosmology with the central towers representing Mount Meru, home of the gods; the outer walls, the mountains enclosing the world; and the moat, the oceans beyond. Angkor Thom, the capital city built after the Cham sack of 1177, is surrounded by a 300-foot wide moat. Construction of Angkor Thom coincided with a change from Hinduism to Buddhism. Temples were altered to display images of the

Buddha, and Angkor Wat became a major Buddhist shrine.

During the 15th century, nearly all of Angkor was abandoned after Siamese attacks, except Angkor Wat, which remained a shrine for Buddhist pilgrims. The great city and temples remained largely cloaked by the forest until the late 19th century when French archaeologists began a long restoration process. France established the Angkor Conservancy in 1908 to direct restoration of the Angkor complex. For the next 64 years, the conservancy worked to clear away the forest, repair foundations, and install drains to protect the buildings from their most insidious enemy: water. After 1953, the conservancy became a joint project of the French and Cambodian Governments. Some temples were carefully taken apart stone by stone and reassembled on concrete foundations. Since the Royal Cambodian Government came to power in 1993, international tourism to Angkor has been on the increase.

Vietnam's occupation army of as many as 200,000 troops controlled the major population centers and most of the countryside from 1979 to September 1989. The Heng Samrin regime's 30,000 troops were plagued by poor morale and widespread desertion. Resistance to Vietnam's occupation continued, and there was some evidence that Heng Samrin's PRK forces provided logistic and moral support to the guerrillas.

A large portion of the Khmer Rouge's military forces eluded Vietnamese troops and established themselves in remote regions. The non-communist resistance, consisting of a number of groups which had been fighting the Khmer Rouge after 1975—including Lon Nol-era soldiers—coalesced in 1979-80 to form the Khmer People's National Liberation Armed Forces (KPNLAF), which pledged loyalty to former Prime Minister Son Sann, and Moulinaka (Movement pour la Liberation Nationale de Kampuchea), loyal to Prince Sihanouk. In 1979, Son Sann formed the Khmer People's National Liberation Front (KPNLF) to lead the political struggle for Cambodia's independence. Prince Sihanouk formed his own organization,

FUNCINPEC, and its military arm, the Armee Nationale Sihanoukienne (ANS) in 1981.

Warfare followed a wet season/dry season rhythm after 1980. The heavily-armed Vietnamese forces conducted offensive operations during the dry seasons, and the resistance forces held the initiative during the rainy seasons. In 1982, Vietnam launched a major offensive against the main Khmer Rouge base at Phnom Melai in the Cardamom Mountains. Vietnam switched its target to civilian camps near the Thai border in 1983, launching a series of massive assaults, backed by armor and heavy artillery, against camps belonging to all three resistance groups. Hundreds of civilians were injured in these attacks, and more than 80,000 were forced to flee to Thailand. Resistance military forces, however, were largely undamaged. In the 1984-85 dry season offensive, the Vietnamese again attacked base camps of all three resistance groups. Despite stiff resistance from the guerrillas, the Vietnamese succeeded in eliminating the camps in Cambodia and drove both the guerrillas and civilian refugees into neighboring

Thailand. The Vietnamese concentrated on consolidating their gains during the 1985-86 dry season, including an attempt to seal guerrilla infiltration routes into the country by forcing Cambodian laborers to construct trench and wire fence obstacles and minefields along virtually the entire Thai-Cambodian border.

Within Cambodia, Vietnam had only limited success in establishing its client Heng Samrin regime, which was dependent on Vietnamese advisors at all levels. Security in some rural areas was tenuous, and major transportation routes were subject to interdiction by resistance forces. The presence of Vietnamese throughout the country and their intrusion into nearly all aspects of Cambodian life alienated much of the populace. The settlement of Vietnamese nationals, both former residents and new immigrants, further exacerbated anti-Vietnamese sentiment. Reports of the numbers involved vary widely with some estimates as high as 1 million. By the end of this decade, Khmer nationalism began to reassert itself against the traditional Vietnamese enemy.

In 1986, Hanoi claimed to have begun withdrawing part of its occupation forces. At the same time, Vietnam continued efforts to strengthen its client regime, the PRK, and its military arm, the Kampuchean People's Revolutionary Armed Forces (KPRAF). These withdrawals continued over the next 2 years, although actual numbers were difficult to verify. Vietnam's proposal to withdraw its remaining occupation forces in 1989-90—the result of ongoing international pressure—forced the PRK to begin economic and constitutional reforms in an attempt to ensure future political dominance. In April 1989, Hanoi and Phnom Penh announced that final withdrawal would take place by the end of September 1989.

The military organizations of Prince Sihanouk (ANS) and of former Prime Minister Son Sann (KPNLAF) underwent significant military improvement during the 1988-89 period and both expanded their presence in

Cambodia's interior. These organizations provide a political alternative to the Vietnamese-supported People's Republic of Kampuchea [PRK] and the murderous Khmer Rouge. The last Vietnamese troops left Cambodia in September of 1989.

## Peace Efforts

From July 30 to August 30, 1989, representatives of 18 countries, the four Cambodian parties, and the UN Secretary General met in Paris in an effort to negotiate a comprehensive settlement. They hoped to achieve those objectives seen as crucial to the future of post-occupation Cambodia: a verified withdrawal of the remaining Vietnamese occupation troops, the prevention of the return to power of the Khmer Rouge, and genuine self-determination for the Cambodian people.

The Paris Conference on Cambodia was able to make some progress in such areas as the workings of an international control mechanism, the definition of international guarantees for Cambodia's independence and neutrality, plans for the repatriation of refugees and displaced persons, the eventual reconstruction of the Cambodia economy, and ceasefire procedures. However, complete agreement among all parties on a comprehensive settlement remained elusive until August 28, 1990, when after eight months of negotiations, a framework for comprehensive political settlement was agreed upon.

## Cambodia's Renewal

On October 23, 1991, the Paris Conference reconvened to sign a comprehensive settlement giving the UN full authority to supervise a ceasefire, repatriate the displaced Khmer along the border with Thailand, disarm and demobilize the factional armies, and to prepare the country for free and fair elections.

Prince Sihanouk, President of the Supreme National Council of Cambodia (SNC), and other members of the SNC returned to Phnom Penh in November, 1991, to begin the resettlement process in Cambodia. The

UN Advance Mission for Cambodia (UNAMIC) was deployed at the same time to maintain liaison among the factions and begin demining operations to expedite the repatriation of approximately 370,000 Cambodians from Thailand.

On March 16, 1992, the UN Transitional Authority in Cambodia (UNTAC), under UNSYG Special Representative Yasushi Akashi and Lt. General John Sanderson, arrived in Cambodia to begin implementation of the UN Settlement Plan. The UN High Commissioner for Refugees began full-scale repatriation in March, 1992. UNTAC grew into a 22,000 strong civilian and military peacekeeping force to conduct free and fair elections for a constituent assembly. Over four million Cambodians (about 90% of eligible voters) participated in the May 1993 elections, although the Khmer Rouge or Party of Democratic Kampuchea (PDK),

whose forces were never actually disarmed or demobilized, barred some people from participating in the 10-15 percent of the country (holding six percent of the population) it controls. Prince Ranariddh's FUNCINPEC Party was the top vote recipient with 45.5% vote followed by Hun Sen's Cambodian People's Party and the Buddhist Liberal Democratic Party, respectively. FUNCINPEC then entered into a coalition with the other parties that had participated in the election. The parties represented in the 120-member Assembly proceeded to draft and approve a new Constitution, which was promulgated September 24. It established a multiparty liberal democracy in the framework of a constitutional monarchy, with the former Prince Sihanouk elevated to King. Prince Ranariddh and Hun Sen became First and Second Prime Ministers, respectively, in the Royal Cambodian Government (RCG). The Constitution provides for a wide range of internationally recognized human rights.

# ECONOMY

In spite of recent progress, the Cambodian economy continues to suffer from the legacy of decades of war and internal strife. Per capita income, although rapidly increasing, is low compared with most neighboring countries. The main domestic activity on which most rural households depend is agriculture and its related sub-sectors. Manufacturing output is varied but is not very extensive and is mostly conducted on a small-scale and informal basis. The service sector is heavily concentrated in trading activities and catering-related services.

During 1995, the government implemented firm stabilization policies under difficult circumstances. Overall, macroeconomic performance was good. Growth in 1995 was estimated at 7% because of improved agricultural production (rice in particular). Strong growth in construction and services continued. Inflation dropped from 26% in 1994 to only 6% in 1995. Imports increased as a result of the

*A report on important events that have taken place since the last State Department revision of this* Background Note.

In October 1997, Pol Pot came out of seclusion for the first time in eighteen years. Between 1975 and 1978, Pol Pot's revolutionary Khmer Rouge regime controlled the country. Cities were emptied of their populations at gunpoint, religion was abolished, and schools were closed. The Khmer Rouge executed 200,000 people who were suspected opponents of the government. Forced collectivization and brutality caused many more to die of starvation or disease. As many as two million Cambodians died during Pol Pot's reign.

The death of Pol Pot came right as government forces closed in on the final Khmer Rouge strongholds in the north and west of the country.

On December 4, 1998, the surviving Khmer Rouge forces reached an agreement with the government whereby they would lay down their arms and accept the Phnom Phen government's authority. In return, the government promised them their own land, housing, food, and integration into the Cambodian armed forces. Three other senior Khmer Rouge leaders who did not sign the accord, Ta Mok, Khieu Samphan, and Nuon Chea, were ultimately arrested and awaited trial. The trial of Khmer Rouge leaders has yet to begin, however, due to disputes between Mr. Hun Sen and the United Nations. In January 2000, the Cambodian leader proposed a trial in Cambodia with a Cambodian majority on the judge's panel. The UN favors a trial outside Cambodia.

By mid–1999, the United Nations had resettled the almost 60,000 remaining refugees still in Cambodia following the peace settlement between the Khmer Rouge and the Cambodian government. These included internally displaced Cambodians, ethnic Vietnamese who live in Cambodia, and the nearly 36,000 repatriated Cambodians who had fled to Thailand from the fighting.

Violent street fighting and gun battles with government forces rocked Phnom Penh in November 2000. In all, 32 suspects were facing charges of terrorism, weapons possession, and membership in an armed group after a series of coordinated attacks in the Cambodian capital left at least eight people dead and seven injured. The clashes came as the country was enjoying its longest period of peace and stability in 30 years following the defection of the final remnants of the Khmer Rouge in late 1998. In June 2001, six lawyers (representatives of the non-profit Cambodian Defenders Project—CDP) for the alleged terrorists received phone calls threatening violence against themselves and their families. Unidentified individuals told them their lives were at risk if they continued with the two-day-old boycott. The boycott had been sparked by concerns about the fairness of the trial's conduct and restrictions on court access to relatives of the accused, media, and human rights observers.

availability of external financing. Exports also increased, due to an increase in log exports. With regard to the budget, both the current and overall deficits were lower than originally targeted.

Cambodia's emerging democracy has received strong international support. Under the mandate carried out by the United Nations Transitional Authority in Cambodia (UNTAC), $1.72 billion was spent in an effort to bring basic security, stability and democratic rule to the country. Regarding economic assistance, official donors had pledged $880 million at the Ministerial Conference on the Rehabilitation of Cambodia (MCRRC) in Tokyo in June 1992, to which pledges of $119 million were added in September 1993 at the meeting of the International Committee on the Reconstruction of Cambodia (ICORC) in Paris, and $643 million at the March 1994 ICORC meeting in Tokyo. To date, therefore, the total amount pledged for Cambodia's rehabilitation is approximately $1.6 billion.

# US-CAMBODIAN RELATIONS

The United States recognized Cambodia on February 7, 1950, and between 1955 and 1963 provided $409.6 million in economic grant aid and $83.7 million in military assistance. This aid was used primarily to repair damage caused by the first Indochina war, to support internal security forces, and for the construction of an all-weather road to the seaport of Sihanoukville, which gave Cambodia its first direct access to the sea and access to the southwestern hinterlands.

Relations deteriorated in the early 1960s. Diplomatic relations were broken by Cambodia in May 1965 but were reestablished on July 2, 1969. US relations continued after the establishment of the Khmer Republic until the US mission was evacuated on April 12, 1975. During the 1970-75 war, the United States provided $1.18 billion in military assistance and $503 million in economic assistance.

## Principal U.S. Officials

**For up-to-date information on Principal U.S. Officials, see the U.S. Embassies, Consulates, and Foreign Service section starting on page 139.**

The United States condemned the brutal character of the Khmer Rouge regime between 1975 and 1979. At the same time, the United States opposed the military occupation of Cambodia by Vietnam and supported ASEAN's efforts to achieve a comprehensive political settlement of the problem. This was accomplished on October 23, 1991, when the Paris Conference reconvened to sign a comprehensive settlement. The United States opened a Mission in Phnom Penh on November 11, 1991, headed by Mr. Charles H. Twining, Jr., designated U.S. Special Representative to the SNC. On January 3, 1992, the U.S. embargo was lifted, normalizing economic relations with Cambodia. The U.S. also ended blanket opposition to lending to Cambodia by international financial institutions. When the freely-elected Royal Cambodian Government was formed on September 24, 1993, the United States and the Kingdom of Cambodia immediately established full diplomatic relations. The United States continues to support efforts in Cambodia to build democratic institutions, promote human rights, foster economic development, eliminate corruption, improve security, achieve the fullest possible accounting for POW/MIAs, and to bring members of the Khmer Rouge to justice for their crimes.

# CAMEROON
December 1999

Official Name:
**Republic of Cameroon**

# PROFILE

## Geography

**Total Area:** 475,000 sq. km. (184,000) sq. mi.), about the size of California.
**Cities (1987 census):** Capital—Yaounde (pop. 900,000). Other major cities—Douala (1.4 million), Garoua (170,000), Maroua (150,000), Bafoussam (140,000), Bamenda (130,000), Nkongsamba (110,000), and Ngaoundere (100,000).
**Terrain:** Northern plains, central and western highlands, southern and coastal tropical forests. Mt. Cameroon (13,353 ft.) in the southwest is the highest peak in West Africa and the sixth in Africa.
**Climate:** Northern plains, the Sahel region—semiarid and hot (7–month dry season); central and western highlands where Yaounde is located—cooler, shorter dry season; southern tropical forest—warm, 4–month dry season; coastal tropical forest, where Douala is located—warm, humid year-round.

## People

**Nationality:** English noun and adjective—Cameroonian(s); French noun and adjective—Camerounais(e).

**Population (1998 est.):** 14.1 million (55% in rural areas).
**Annual growth rate:** 2.7%.
**Ethnic groups:** About 250.
**Religions:** Christian 40%, Muslim 20%, indigenous African 40%.
**Languages:** French and English (both official) and about 270 African languages and dialects, including Pidgin, Fulfulde, and Ewondo.
**Education:** Compulsory between ages 6 and 14. Attendance-more than 70%. Literacy—63%.
**Health:** Infant mortality rate—5.6%. Life expectancy—57 years.
**Work force:** Agriculture—70%. Industry and commerce—13%.

## Government

**Type:** Republic; strong central government dominated by president.
**Independence:** January 1, 1960 (for areas formerly ruled by France) and October 1, 1961 (for territory formerly ruled by Britain).
**Constitution:** June 2, 1972, last amended in January 1996.
**Branches:** Executive—president (chief of state) 7–yr. term, renewable once; appointed prime minister (head of government). Legislative—unicameral National Assembly (180 members, 5–yr. terms; meets briefly three times a year—March, June, November); a new Senate is called for under constitutional changes made in early 1996. Judicial—falls under the executive's Ministry of Justice.

**Administrative subdivisions:** 10 provinces, 56 departments or divisions, 276 subprefectures or subdivisions.
**Political parties:** Cameroon People's Democratic Movement (CPDM) or its predecessor parties have ruled since independence. Major opposition parties: the Social Democratic Front (SDF), the National Union of Democracy and Progress (NUDP), and the Cameroon Democratic Union (CDU).
**Suffrage:** Universal at 20.
**Flag:** Green, red, and yellow vertical bands with one yellow star in center.

## Economy

**GDP (1996):** $9.0 billion.
**Annual growth rate (1997):** 5%.
**Natural resources:** Oil, timber, hydroelectric power, natural gas, bauxite, gold, diamonds.
**Agriculture (1996):** 44.3% of GDP. Products—timber, coffee, tea, bananas, cocoa, rubber, palm oil and cotton. Arable land—3%.
**Manufacturing (1996):** 10.9% of GDP. Types (13.4% of GDP )—petroleum production and refining, food processing, aluminum and light consumer goods, textiles, finished wood products.
**Services (1996):** 31.5% of GDP.
**Trade (1997):** Exports—$1.7 billion: crude oil, timber and finished wood products, cotton, cocoa, aluminum and aluminum products, coffee, rubber and bananas. Major markets—

European Union, UDEAC/CEMAC, China, U.S., Nigeria (informal). Imports—$.56 million: crude oil, vehicle, pharmaceuticals, aluminum oxide, rubber, foodstuffs and grains, agricultural inputs, lubricants, and used clothing. Major suppliers—France, Nigeria, U.S., Germany, Belgium, Japan.

# PEOPLE

Cameroon's estimated 250 ethnic groups form five large regional-cultural groups: western highlanders (or grassfielders), including the Bamileke, Bamoun, and many smaller entities in the Northwest (est. 38% of population); coastal tropical forest peoples, including the Bassa, Douala, and many smaller entities in the Southwest (12%); southern tropical forest peoples, including the Beti, Bulu (subgroup of Beti), Fang (subgroup of Beti), and Pygmies (officially called Bakas) (18%); predominantly Islamic peoples of the northern semi-arid regions (the Sahel) and central highlands, including the Fulani, also known as Peuhl in French (14%); and the "Kirdi", non-Islamic or recently Islamic peoples of the northern desert and central highlands (18%).

The people concentrated in the southwest and northwest provinces—around Buea and Bamenda—use standard English and "pidgin," as well as their local languages. In the three northern provinces—Adamaoua, Garoua, and Maroua—either French or Fulfulde, the language of the Fulani, is widely spoken. Elsewhere, French is the principal second language, although pidgin and some local languages such as Ewondo, the dialect of a Beti clan from the Yaounde area, also are widely spoken.

Although Yaounde is Cameroon's capital, Douala is the largest city, main seaport, and main industrial and commercial center.

The western highlands are the most fertile in Cameroon and have a relatively healthy environment in higher altitudes. This region is densely populated and has intensive agriculture, commerce, cohesive communities, and historical emigration pressures. From here, Bantu migrations into eastern, southern, and central Africa are believed to have originated about 2,000 years ago. Bamileke people from this area have in recent years migrated to towns elsewhere in Cameroon, such as the coastal provinces, where they form much of the business community. About 14,000 non-Africans, including more than 6,000 French and 1,000 U.S. citizens, reside in Cameroon.

# HISTORY

The earliest inhabitants of Cameroon were probably the Bakas (Pygmies). They still inhabit the forests of the south and east provinces. Bantu speakers originating in the Cameroonian highlands were among the first groups to move out before other invaders.

During the late 1770s and early 1800s, the Fulani, a pastoral Islamic people of the western Sahel, conquered most of what is now northern Cameroon, subjugating or displacing its largely non-Muslim inhabitants.

Although the Portuguese arrived on Cameroon's coast in the 1500s, malaria prevented significant European settlement and conquest of the interior until the late 1870s, when large supplies of the malaria suppressant, quinine, became available. The early European presence in Cameroon was primarily devoted to coastal trade and the acquisition of slaves. The northern part of Cameroon was an important part of the Muslim slave trade network. The slave trade was largely suppressed by the mid-19th century. Christian missions established a presence in the late 19th century and continue to play a role in Cameroonian life.

Beginning in 1884, all of present-day Cameroon and parts of several of its neighbors became the German colony of Kamerun, with a capital first at Buea and later at Yaounde. After World War I, this colony was parti-

**Travel Notes**

**Travel Advice:** For up-to-date information from the U.S. State Department on possible inconvenient or hazardous situations, see the **Travel Warnings and Consular Information Sheets from the U.S. Government** section starting on page 1723. For the latest information on health requirements and conditions, see the **International Travelers' Health Information** section starting on page 1385. For further information dealing with non-urgent matter, see the **Tips for Travelers to...** section starting on page 1588.

tioned between Britain and France under a June 28, 1919 League of Nations mandate. France gained the larger geographical share, transferred outlying regions to neighboring French colonies, and ruled the rest from Yaounde. Britain's territory, a strip bordering Nigeria from the sea to Lake Chad, with an equal population was ruled from Lagos.

In 1955, the outlawed Union of Cameroonian Peoples (UPC), based largely among the Bamileke and Bassa ethnic groups, began an armed struggle for independence in French Cameroon. This rebellion continued, with diminishing intensity, even after independence. Estimates of death from this conflict vary from tens of thousands to hundreds of thousands.

French Cameroon achieved independence in 1960 as the Republic of Cameroon. The following year the largely Muslim northern two-thirds of British Cameroon voted to join Nigeria; the largely Christian southern third voted to join with the Republic of Cameroon to form the Federal Republic of Cameroon. The formerly French and British regions each maintained substantial autonomy. Ahmadou Ahidjo, a French-educated Fulani, was chosen president of the federation in 1961. Ahidjo, relying on a pervasive internal security apparatus, outlawed all political parties but his own in 1966. He successfully suppressed the UPC rebellion, capturing the last important rebel leader in 1970. In 1972, a new constitution replaced the federation with a unitary state.

Ahidjo resigned as president in 1982 and was constitutionally succeeded by his Prime Minister, Paul Biya, a career official from the Bulu-Beti ethnic group. Ahidjo later regretted his choice of successors, but his supporters failed to overthrow Biya in a 1984 coup. Biya won single-candidate elections in 1984 and 1983 and flawed multiparty elections in 1992 and 1997. His CPDM party holds a sizeable majority in the legislature.

# GOVERNMENT AND POLITICAL CONDITIONS

The 1972 constitution as modified by 1996 reforms provides for a strong central government dominated by the executive. The president is empowered to name and dismiss cabinet members, judges, generals, provincial governors, prefects, sub-prefects, and heads of Cameroon's parastatal (about 100 state-controlled) firms, obligate or disburse expenditures, approve or veto regulations, declare states of emergency, and appropriate and spend profits of parastatal firms. The president is not required to consult the National Assembly.

The judiciary is subordinate to the executive branch's Ministry of Justice. The Supreme Court may review the constitutionality of a law only at the president's request.

The 180-member National Assembly meets in ordinary session three times a year (March/April, June/July, and November/December), and has seldom, until recently, made major changes in legislation proposed by the executive. Laws are adopted by majority vote of members present or, if the president demands a second reading, of a total membership.

Following government pledges to reform the strongly centralized 1972 constitution, the National Assembly adopted a number of amendments in

December 1995 which were promulgated in January 1996. The amendments call for the establishment of a 100-member senate as part of a bicameral legislature, the creation of regional councils, and the fixing of the presidential term to 7 years, renewable once. One-third of senators are to be appointed by the President, and the remaining two-thirds are to be chosen by indirect elections. As of March 1998, the government has not established the Senate or regional councils.

All local government officials are employees of the central government's Ministry of Territorial Administration, from which local governments also get most of their budgets.

While the president, the minister of justice, and the president's judicial advisers (the Supreme Court) top the judicial hierarchy, traditional rulers, courts, and councils also exercise functions of government. Traditional courts still play a major role in domestic, property, and probate law. Tribal laws and customs are honored in the formal court system when not in conflict with national law. Traditional rulers receive stipends from the national government.

The government adopted legislation in 1990 to authorize the formation of multiple political parties and ease restrictions on forming civil associations and private newspapers. Cameroon' s first multiparty legislative and presidential elections were held in 1992 followed by municipal elections in 1996 and another round of legislative and presidential elections in 1997. Because the government refused to consider opposition demands for an independent election commission, the three major opposition parties boycotted the October 1977 presidential election, which Biya easily won. The leader of one of the opposition parties, Bello Bouba Maigari of the NUDP, subsequently joined the government.

Cameroon has a number of independent newspapers. Censorship was abolished in 1996, but the government sometimes seizes or suspends

newspapers and occasionally arrests journalists. Although a 1990 law authorizes private radio and television stations, the government has not granted any licenses as of March 1998.

The Cameroonian Government's human rights record has been improving over the years but remains flawed. There continue to be reported abuses, including beatings of detainees, arbitrary arrests, and illegal searches. The judiciary is frequently corrupt, inefficient, and subject to political influence.

## Principal Government Officials

For up-to-date information on Principal Government Officials, see the Chiefs of State and Cabinet Members of Foreign Governments section starting on page 1.

Cameroon maintains an embassy in the United States at 2349 Massachusetts Avenue N.W., Washington, D.C. 20008 (tel.: 202–265–8790).

# ECONOMY

For a quarter-century following independence, Cameroon was one of the most prosperous countries in Africa. The drop in commodity prices for its principal exports-oil, cocoa, coffee, and cotton-in the mid-1980s, combined with an overvalued currency and economic mismanagement, led to a decade-long recession. Real per capita GDP fell by more than 60% from 1986 to 1994. The current account and fiscal deficits widened, and foreign debt grew.

The government embarked upon a series of economic reform programs supported by the World Bank and IMF beginning in the late 1980s. Many of these measures have been painful; the government slashed civil service salaries by 65% in 1993. The CFA franc—the common currency of Cameroon and 13 other African

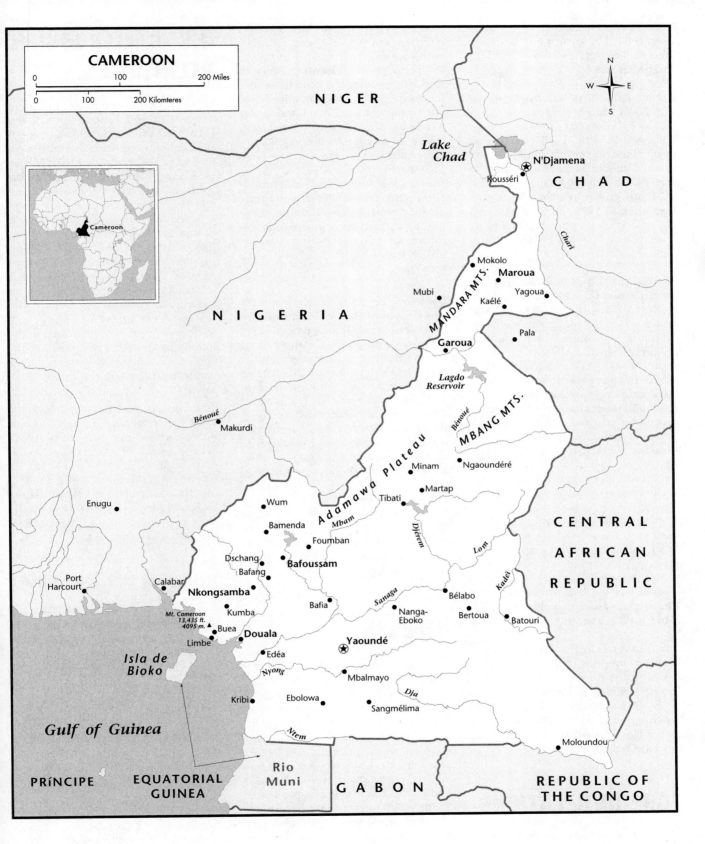

states—was devalued by 50% in January 1994. The government failed to meet the conditions of the first four IMF programs.

Recent signs, however, are encouraging. As of March 1998, Cameroon's fifth IMF program—a 3-year enhanced structural adjustment program approved in August 1997—is on track. Cameroon has rescheduled its Paris Club debt at favorable terms. GDP has grown by about 5% a year beginning in 1995. There is cautious optimism that Cameroon is emerging from its long period of economic hardship.

The Enhanced Structural Adjustment Facility (ESAF) signed recently by the IMF and Government of Cameroon calls for greater macroeconomic planning and financial accountability; privatization of most of Cameroon's nearly 100 remaining nonfinancial parastatal enterprises; elimination of state marketing board monopolies on the export of cocoa, certain coffees, and cotton; privatization and price competition in the banking sector; implementation of the 1992 labor code; a vastly improved judicial system; and political liberalization to boost investment.

France is Cameroon's main trading partner and source of private investment and foreign aid. Cameroon has an investment guaranty agreement and a bilateral accord with the United States. U.S. investment in Cameroon is about $1 million, most of it in the oil sector.

For further information on Cameroon's economic trends, trade, or investment climate, contact the International Trade Administration, U. S. Department of Commerce, Washington, D.C. 20230, and Commerce Department district office in any local federal building.

# FOREIGN RELATIONS

Cameroon's noncontentious, low-profile approach to foreign relations puts it squarely in the middle of other African and developing country states on major issues. It supports the principles of noninterference in the affairs of third countries and increased assistance to underdeveloped countries. Cameroon is an active participant in the United Nations, where its voting record demonstrates its commitment to causes that include international peacekeeping, the rule of law, environmental protection, and Third World economic development. In the UN and other human rights fora, Cameroon's nonconfrontational approach has generally led it to avoid criticizing other countries.

Cameroon enjoys good relations with the United States and other developed countries. It has particularly close ties with France, with whom it has numerous military, economic, and cultural agreements. China has a number of health and infrastructure projects underway in Cameroon. Cameroon enjoys generally good relations with its African neighbors, except for Nigeria, with whom it is engaged in a sporadic armed conflict in the oil-rich Bakassi Peninsula. Cameroon has repeatedly demonstrated its preference for resolving this conflict through peaceful legal means and has submitted its case to the International Court of Justice. It supports UN peacekeeping activities in Central Africa.

# DEFENSE

The Cameroonian military generally has been an apolitical force dominated by civilian control. Traditional dependence on the French defense capability, although reduced, continues to be the case as French military advisers remain closely involved in preparing the Cameroonian forces for deployment to the contested Bakassi Peninsula. The armed forces number 26,000–27,000 personnel in ground, air, and naval forces, the majority being the army and naval ground forces.

# U.S.-CAMEROONIAN RELATIONS

U.S.-Cameroonian relations have been affected by concerns over human rights abuses and the pace of political and economic liberalization, as well as U.S. budget realities. There is no longer a bilateral USAID program in Cameroon. However, some 135 Peace Corps volunteers continue to work successfully in agro-forestry, community development, education, and health. The United States Information Agency organizes and funds diverse cultural, educational, and information exchanges. It maintains a library in Yaounde and helps to foster the development of Cameroon's independent press by providing information in a number of areas, including U.S. human rights and democratization policies.

The United States and Cameroon work together in the United Nations and a number of other multilateral organizations. The U.S. Government continues to provide substantial funding for international financial institutions, such as the World Bank, IMF, and African Development Bank, that provide financial and other assistance to Cameroon.

## Principal U.S. Officials

For up-to-date information on Principal U.S. Officials, see the U.S. Embassies, Consulates, and Foreign Service section starting on page 139.

The U.S. Embassy in Cameroon is located on Rue Nachtigal, Yaounde (tel: 237–22–25–89/23–40–14; fax: 237–23–07–53, B. P. 817, Yaounde.

The U. S. mailing address is American Embassy Yaounde, Department of State, Washington, D.C. 20521-2520.

# CANADA

April 2001

### Official Name:
**Canada**

# PROFILE

## Geography

**Area:** 9.9 million sq. km. (3.8 million sq. mi.); second-largest country in the world.
**Cities:** Capital—Ottawa (pop. 1 million). Other cities—Toronto (4.5 million), Montreal (3.4 million), Vancouver (2.0 million).
**Terrain:** Mostly plains with mountains in the west and lowlands in the southeast.
**Climate:** Temperate to arctic.

## People

**Nationality:** Noun and adjective—Canadian(s).
**Population:** 31.0 million.
**Ethnic groups:** British 28%, French 23%, other European 15%, Asian/Arab/African 6%, indigenous Indian and Eskimo 2%, mixed background 26%.
**Religions:** Roman Catholic 42%, Protestant 40%.
**Languages:** English, French.
**Education:** Literacy—99% of population aged 15 and over have at least a ninth-grade education.
**Health:** Infant mortality rate—5.1/1000.
Life expectancy—76 yrs. male, 83 yrs. female.
**Work force:** (15 million) Trade—

17%. Manufacturing—15%. Transportation and communications—8%. Finance—6%. Public administration—6%. Construction—5%. Agriculture—4%. Forestry and mining—2%. Other services—37%.

## Government

**Type:** Confederation with parliamentary democracy.
**Independence:** July 1, 1867.
**Constitution:** The amended British North America Act of 1867 patriated to Canada on April 17, 1982, Charter of Rights and Freedoms, and unwritten custom.
**Branches:** Executive—Queen Elizabeth II (head of state represented by a governor general), prime minister (head of government), cabinet. Legislative—bicameral parliament (301-member House of Commons, 105-seat Senate). Judicial—Supreme Court.
**Political parties:** Liberal Party, Canadian Alliance, Bloc Quebecois, New Democratic Party, Progressive Conservative Party.
**Subdivisions:** 10 provinces, 3 territories.

## Economy

**Nominal GDP:** (2000) $675.42 billion.
**Real GDP growth rate:** (2000) 4.7%.
**Nominal per capita GDP:** (2000)

$21,788.
**Natural resources:** Petroleum and natural gas, hydroelectric power, metals and minerals, fish, forests, wildlife.
**Agriculture:** Products—wheat, livestock and meat, feed grains, oil seeds, dairy products, tobacco, fruits, vegetables. Industry: Types—motor vehicles and parts, machinery and equipment, aircraft and components, other diversified manufacturing, fish and forest products, processed and unprocessed minerals.
**Trade:** Merchandise exports (1999)—$242.7 billion: motor vehicles and spare parts, lumber, wood pulp and newsprint, crude and fabricated metals, natural gas, crude petroleum, wheat. 86% of 1999 Canadian exports went to the United States. Merchandise imports (1999)—$219.9 billion: motor vehicles and parts, industrial machinery, crude petroleum, chemicals, agricultural machinery. 76% of 1998 Canadian imports came from the United States.

# U.S.-CANADA RELATIONS

The bilateral relationship between the United States and Canada is perhaps the closest and most extensive in the world. It is reflected in the

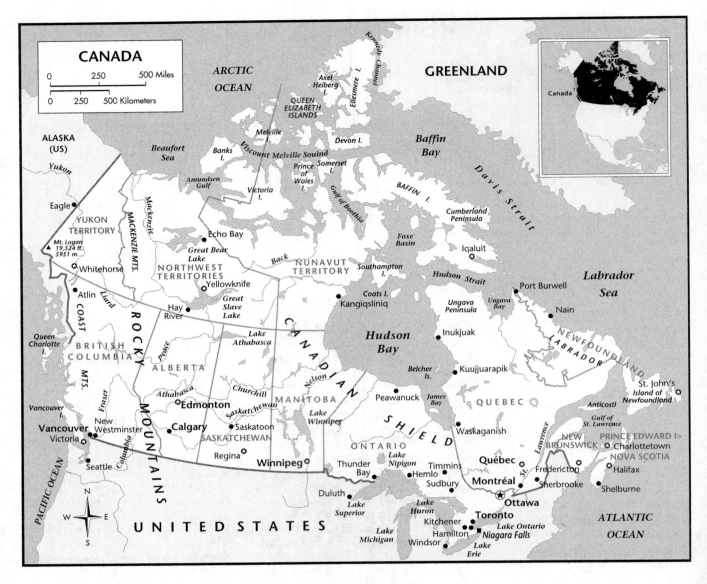

staggering volume of trade—over 1.3 billion a day—and people—over 200 million a year—crossing the U.S.-Canadian border. In fields ranging from environmental cooperation to free trade, the two countries have set the standard by which many other countries measure their own progress. In addition to their close bilateral ties, Canada and the U.S. also work closely through multilateral fora. Canada—a charter signatory to the United Nations and the North Atlantic Treaty Organization (NATO)—has continued to take an active role in the United Nations, including peacekeeping operations. Canada is also an active participant in discussions stemming from the Organization for Security and Coop-

eration in Europe (OSCE). Canada joined the Organization of American States (OAS) in 1990 and has been an active member, hosting the OAS General Assembly in Windsor in June of 2000. In 2001, Canada will host the third Summit of the Americas in Quebec City. Canada also seeks to expand its ties to Pacific Rim economies through membership in the Asia-Pacific Economic Cooperation forum (APEC)—of which the U.S. is also a member.

Although Canada views its relationship with the U.S. as crucial to a wide range of interests, it also occasionally pursues policies at odds with the United States. This is particularly true of Cuba, with regard to which

the U.S. and Canada have pursued divergent policies for nearly 40 years, even while sharing the common goal of a peaceful democratic transition.

U.S. defense arrangements with Canada are more extensive than with any other country. The Permanent Joint Board on Defense, established in 1940, provides policy-level consultation on bilateral defense matters. The United States and Canada share NATO mutual security commitments. In addition, U.S. and Canadian military forces have cooperated since 1958 on continental air defense within the framework of the North American Aerospace Defense Command (NORAD).

The two countries also work closely to resolve transboundary environmental issues, an area of increasing importance in the bilateral relationship. A principal instrument of this cooperation is the International Joint Commission (IJC), established as part of the Boundary Waters Treaty of 1909 to resolve differences and promote international cooperation on boundary waters. The Great Lakes Water Quality Agreement of 1972 is another historic example of joint cooperation in controlling transboundary water pollution. The two governments also consult semiannually on transboundary air pollution. Under the Air Quality Agreement of 1991, both countries have made substantial progress in coordinating and implementing their acid rain control programs and signed an annex on ground level ozone in 2000.

## Trade and Investment

Canada is by far our largest trading partner, with over 1.3 billion in trade a day. By comparison, in 1999 this was more than U.S. trade with all the countries of Latin America combined. Our exports to Canada exceed those to all members of the European Union combined. Just the two-way trade that crosses the Ambassador Bridge between Michigan and Ontario equals all U.S. exports to Japan. Canada's importance to the United States is not just a border-state phenomenon: Canada is the leading export market for 35 of our 50 states.

Bilateral trade increased by about 50% between 1989, when the U.S.-Canada Free Trade Agreement (FTA) went into effect, and 1994, when the North American Free Trade Agreement (NAFTA) superseded it. Trade has since increased by 40%. NAFTA continues the FTA's moves toward reducing trade barriers and establishing agreed upon trade rules. It also resolves some long-standing bilateral irritants and liberalizes rules in several areas, including agriculture, services, energy, financial services, investment, and government procurement. NAFTA forms the largest trading area in the world, embracing the 406 million people of the three North American countries.

The largest component of U.S.-Canadian trade is in the automotive sector. Under the 1965 U.S.-Canada Automotive Agreement (Auto Pact) which provided for free trade in cars, trucks, and auto parts, two-way trade in automotive products rose from $715 million in 1964 to $104.1 billion in 1999. Auto Pact benefits are incorporated into NAFTA.

The U.S. is Canada's leading agricultural market, taking nearly one-third of all food exports. Conversely, Canada is the second-largest U.S. agricultural market (after Japan), primarily importing fresh fruits and vegetables and livestock products. Nearly two-thirds of Canada's forest products, including pulp and paper, are exported to the United States; almost 75% of Canada's total newsprint production is also exported to the U.S.

At $21 billion in 1999, U.S.-Canada trade in energy is the largest U.S. energy trading relationship in the world. The primary components of our energy trade with Canada are oil, natural gas, and electricity. Canada is our largest oil supplier and the fifth-largest energy producing country in the world. Canada provides about 15% of U.S. oil imports and 14% of total U.S. consumption of natural gas. Our national electricity grids are linked and our two countries share hydropower facilities on the Western borders.

While 95% of U.S.-Canada trade flows smoothly, there are occasionally bilateral trade disputes over the remaining 5%, particularly in the agricultural and cultural fields. Usually, however, these issues are resolved through bilateral consultative forums or referral to WTO or NAFTA dispute resolution. In May 1999, the U.S. and Canadian governments negotiated an agreement on magazines that will provide increased access for the U.S. publishing industry to the Canadian market. The United States and Canada also have resolved several major issues involving fisheries. By common agreement, the two countries submitted a Gulf of Maine boundary dispute to the International Court of Justice in 1981; both accepted the Court's

October 12, 1984 ruling which demarcated the territorial sea boundary.

In 1990, the United States and Canada signed a bilateral Fisheries Enforcement Agreement, which has served to deter illegal fishing activity and reduce the risk of injury during fisheries enforcement incidents. The U.S. and Canada signed a Pacific Salmon Agreement in June 1999 that settled differences over implementation of the 1985 Pacific Salmon Treaty for the next decade.

Canada and the United States signed an aviation agreement during President Clinton's visit to Canada in February 1995, and air traffic between the two countries has increased dramatically as a result. The two countries also share in operation of the St. Lawrence Seaway, connecting the Great Lakes to the Atlantic Ocean.

The U.S. is Canada's largest foreign investor; at the end of 1999, the stock of U.S. direct investment was estimated at $116.7 billion, or about 72% of total foreign direct investment in Canada. U.S. investment is primarily in Canada's mining and smelting industries, petroleum, chemicals, the manufacture of machinery and transportation equipment, and finance.

Canada is the third-largest foreign investor in the United States. At the end of 1999, the stock of Canadian direct investment in the United States was estimated at $90.4 billion. Canadian investment in the United States— which includes investment from Canadian holding companies in the Netherlands —is concentrated in manufacturing, wholesale trade, real estate, petroleum, finance, and insurance and other services.

## Principal U.S. Embassy Officials

**For up-to-date information on Principal U.S. Officials, see the U.S. Embassies, Consulates, and Foreign Service section starting on page 139.**

The U.S. Embassy in Canada is located at 490 Sussex Drive, Ottawa, Ontario, K1N 1G8 (tel. 613–238–5335).

# GOVERNMENT

Canada is a constitutional monarchy with a federal system, a parliamentary government, and strong democratic traditions. Many of the country's legal practices are based on unwritten custom, but the federal structure resembles the U.S. system. The 1982 Charter of Rights guarantees basic rights in many areas.

Queen Elizabeth II, as Queen of Canada, serves as a symbol of the nation's unity. She appoints a governor general on the advice of the prime minister of Canada, usually for a five-year term. The prime minister is the leader of the political party in power and is the head of the cabinet. The cabinet remains in office as long as it retains majority support in the House of Commons on major issues.

Canada's parliament consists of an elected House of Commons and an appointed Senate. Legislative power rests with the 301-member Commons, which is elected for a period not to exceed 5 years. The prime minister may ask the governor general to dissolve parliament and call new elections at any time during that period. Federal elections were last held in November 2000. Vacancies in the 104-member Senate, whose members serve until the age of 75, are filled by the governor general on the advice of the prime minister. Recent constitutional initiatives have sought unsuccessfully to strengthen the Senate by making it elective and assigning it a greater regional representational role.

Criminal law, based largely on British law, is uniform throughout the nation and is under federal jurisdiction. Civil law is also based on the common law of England, except in Quebec, which has retained its own civil code patterned after that of France. Justice is administered by federal, provincial, and municipal courts.

Each province is governed by a premier and a single, elected legislative chamber. A lieutenant-governor appointed by the governor general represents the Crown in each province.

## Principal Government Officials

**For up-to-date information on Principal Government Officials, see the Chiefs of State and Cabinet Members of Foreign Governments section starting on page 1.**

Canada maintains an embassy in the United States at 501 Pennsylvania Avenue, NW, Washington, DC 20001 (tel. 202–682–1740).

# POLITICAL CONDITIONS

Prime Minister Jean Chretien's Liberal Party won a major victory in the November 2000 general elections. Chretien became the first Prime Minister to lead three consecutive majority governments since 1945, as the Liberals increased their majority in Parliament to 57% (172 of the 301 Parliamentary seats). The Canadian Alliance Party, which did well in western Canada but was unable to make significant inroads in the East, won the second-highest total of seats (66).

Federal-provincial interplay is a central feature of Canadian politics: Quebec wishes to preserve and strengthen its distinctive nature; western provinces desire more control over their abundant natural resources, especially energy reserves; industrialized central Canada is concerned with economic development; and the Atlantic provinces have resisted federal claims to fishing and mineral rights off their shores.

The Chretien Government has responded to these different regional needs by seeking to rebalance the Canadian confederation, giving up its spending power in areas of provincial jurisdiction, while attempting to strengthen the federal role in other areas. The federal government has reached agreement with a number of provinces returning to them authority over job training programs and is embarked on similar initiatives in other fields. Meanwhile, it has attempted to strengthen the national role on interprovincial trade, while also seeking national regulation of securities.

## National Unity

Key to the national unity debate is the ongoing issue of Quebec separatism. Following the failure of two constitutional initiatives in the past 14 years, Canada is still seeking a constitutional settlement that will satisfy the aspirations of the French-speaking province of Quebec. The issue has been a fixture in Canadian history, dating back to the 18th century rivalry between France and Britain. For more than a century, Canada was a French colony. Although New France came under British control in 1759, it was permitted to retain its religious and civil code.

The early 1960s brought a Quiet Revolution to Quebec, leading to a new assertiveness and heightened sense of identity among the French-speaking Quebecois, who make up about one-quarter of Canada's population. In 1976, the separatist Parti Quebecois won the provincial election and began to explore a course for Quebec of greater independence from the rest of Canada.

In a 1980 referendum, the Parti Quebecois sought a mandate from the people of Quebec to negotiate a new status of sovereignty-association, combining political independence with a continued economic association with the rest of Canada. Sixty percent of Quebec voters rejected the proposal. Subsequently, an agreement between the federal government and all provincial governments except Quebec, led to Canada in 1982 assuming from the United Kingdom full responsibility for its own constitution. Quebec objected to certain aspects of the new arrangement, including a constitutional amending formula that did not require consensus among all provinces. The 1987 Meech Lake Accord sought to address Quebec's concerns and bring it back into Canada's constitutional fold. Quebec's provincial government, then controlled by federalists, strongly endorsed the accord, but lack of support in Newfoundland and Manitoba prevented it from taking effect. Rejected in its bid for special constitutional recognition, Quebec's provincial government authorized a second sovereignty referendum.

Intense negotiations among Quebec, the federal government, and other provinces led to a second proposed constitutional accord in 1992—the

Charlottetown Accord. Despite near-unanimous support from the country's political leaders, this second

effort at constitutional reform was defeated in Quebec and the rest of Canada in an October 1992 nationwide referendum.

Tired of the country's constitutional deadlock, many Canadians prefer to focus on economic issues. Nonetheless, the election of the sovereigntist Bloc Quebecois as Canada's official opposition in 1993 and the subsequent election of the separatist Parti Quebecois as Quebec's provincial government in September 1994 kept national unity in the forefront of political debate and resulted in a second referendum on the issue.

This referendum, held in Quebec on October 30, 1995, resulted in a narrow 50.56% to 49.44% victory for federalists over sovereigntists. Quebec's status thus remains a serious political issue in Canada.

In December of 1999, the Chretien administration introduced the so-called "Clarity Bill", setting out the federal role in any future referendum on Quebec's status. Both houses of Parliament subsequently approved the legislation.

Bernard Landry, who succeeded Lucien Bouchard as Premier of Quebec in March of 2001, pledged to promote independence for Quebec.

**Background Notes**

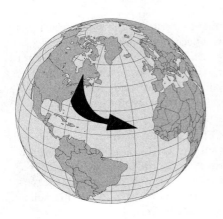

# CAPE VERDE

May 1998

Official Name:
**Republic of Cape Verde**

# PROFILE

## Geography

**Area:** 4,033 sq. km. (1,557 sq. mi.), slightly larger than Rhode Island.
**Cities:** Capital—Praia (pop. 78,675). Other city—Mindelo (pop. 53,300).
**Terrain:** Rugged volcanic islands.
**Climate:** Dry, temperate.

## People

**Nationality:** Noun and adjective—Cape Verdean (s).
**Population (1995):** 386,185.
**Annual growth rate (1994-2000):** 2.5%.
**Ethnic groups:** Creole (mixed African and Portuguese), African, European.
**Religions:** Roman Catholic, Protestant.
**Languages:** Portuguese (official); Crioulo (national).
**Education:** Literacy (1994)—69.9%.
**Health:** Infant mortality rate (1994)—48/1,000. Life expectancy (1994)—65.3 yrs.

## Government

**Type:** Republic.
**Independence:** July 5, 1975.
**Constitution:** 1982; revised 1992.
**Branches:** Executive—president (head of state), prime minister (head of government), Council of Ministers. Legislative—National Assembly. Judicial—Supreme Court, lower courts.
**Administrative subdivisions:** 16 administrative districts.
**Political parties:** Movement for Democracy (MpD); African Party for the Independence of Cape Verde (PAICV); Party for Democratic Convergence (PCD).
**Suffrage:** Universal over 18.
**Flag:** Broad horizontal blue bands at the top and bottom. Three horizontal bands (top white, middle red, bottom white) the middle third. A circle of 10 yellow five-pointed stars is centered on the hoist end of the red stripe and extends into the upper and lower blue bands.

## Economy

**GDP (1997):** $450 million.
**GDP per capita (1997):** $1,046.
**Annual growth rate (1997):** 4.5%.
**Natural resources:** Salt, pozzolana, limestone.
**Agriculture:** Products—bananas, corn, beans, sugarcane, coffee, fruits, vegetables, livestock products.
**Industry:** Types—fish and fish products, clothing, shoes, beverages, salt, construction, building materials, ship repair, furniture, metal products.
**Trade (1996):** Exports—$12.8 million: shoes, lobster, fish, garments, bananas, hides. Imports—$237 million: foodstuffs, consumer goods, industrial products, transport equipment, fuels. Major trading partners—Portugal, Netherlands, other EC, U.S.
**Fiscal year:** Calendar year.
**Economic aid received:** U.S. aid (1997)—$1.9 million.

# GEOGRAPHY

The Cape Verde Islands are located in the mid-Atlantic Ocean some 620 kilometers (385 mi.) off the west coast of Africa. The archipelago consists of 10 islands and 5 islets, divided into the windward (Barlavento) and leeward (Sotavento) groups. The six islands in the Barlavento group are Santo Antão, São Vicente, Santa Luzia, São Nicolau, Sal, and Boa Vista. The islands in the Sotavento group are Maio, Santiago, Fogo, and Brava. All but Santa Luzia are inhabited.

Three islands—Sal, Boa Vista, and Maio—generally are level and lack natural water supplies. Mountains higher than 1,280 meters (4,200 ft.) are found on Santiago, Fogo, Santo Antão, and São Nicolau.

Sand carried by high winds has caused erosion on all islands, especially the windward ones. Sheer, jagged cliffs rise from the sea on several of the mountainous islands. The lack of natural vegetation in the uplands and coast also contributes to soil erosion. Only the interior valleys support natural vegetation.

Rainfall is irregular, historically causing periodic droughts and famines. The average precipitation per year in Praia is 24 centimeters (9.5 in.). During the winter, storms blowing from the Sahara sometimes form dense dust clouds that obscure the sun; however, sunny days are the norm year round.

# PEOPLE

The Cape Verde archipelago was uninhabited until the Portuguese discovered it in 1456. African slaves were brought to the islands to work on Portuguese plantations. As a result, Cape Verdeans have mixed African and European origins. Vestiges of African culture are most pronounced on the island of Santiago, where 50% of the people live. Survival in a country with few natural resources historically has induced Cape Verdeans to emigrate. In fact, of the more than 1 million people of Cape Verdean ancestry in the world, only a little more than one-third actually live on the islands. Some 500,000 people of Cape Verdean ancestry live in the United States, mainly in New England. Portugal, Netherlands, Italy, France, and Senegal also have large communities.

Although the official language is Portuguese, most Cape Verdeans speak a Creole dialect—Crioulo—which consists of archaic Portuguese modified through contact with African and other European languages. Cape Verde has a rich tradition of Crioulo literature and music.

# HISTORY

In 1462, Portuguese settlers arrived at Santiago and founded Ribeira Grande (now Cidade Velha)—the first permanent European settlement city in the tropics. In the 16th century, the archipelago prospered from the transatlantic slave trade. Pirates occasionally attacked the Portuguese settlements. Sir Francis Drake sacked Ribeira Grande in 1585. After a French attack in 1712, the city declined in importance relative to Praia, which became the capital in 1770.

The archipelago has experienced recurrent drought and famine since the end of the 18th century, and, with the decline in the slave trade, its fragile prosperity slowly vanished. However, the islands' position astride mid-Atlantic shipping lanes made Cape Verde an ideal location for resupplying ships. Because of its excellent harbor, Mindelo (on the island of São Vicente) became an important commercial center during the 19th century.

Portugal changed Cape Verde's status from a colony to an overseas province in 1951 in an attempt to blunt growing nationalism. Nevertheless, in 1956, Amilcar Cabral, a Cape Verdean, and Rafael Barbosa organized (in Guinea-Bissau) the clandestine African Party for the Independence of Guinea-Bissau and Cape Verde (PAIGC), which demanded improvement in economic, social, and political conditions in Cape Verde and Portuguese Guinea and formed the basis of the two nations' independence movement. Moving its headquarters to Conakry, Guinea in 1960, the PAIGC began an armed rebellion against Portugal in 1961. Acts of sabotage eventually grew into a war in Portuguese Guinea that pitted 10,000 Soviet bloc-supported PAIGC soldiers against 35,000 Portuguese and African troops.

By 1972, the PAIGC controlled much of Portuguese Guinea despite the presence of the Portuguese troops. For logistical reasons, the organization did not attempt to disrupt Portuguese control in Cape Verde. Following the April 1974 revolution in Portugal, however, the PAIGC became an active political movement in Cape Verde.

In December 1974, the PAIGC and Portugal signed an agreement providing for a transitional government composed of Portuguese and Cape Verdeans. On June 30, 1975, Cape Verdeans elected a National Assembly, which received the instruments of independence from Portugal on July 5, 1975.

Immediately following a November 1980 coup in Guinea-Bissau (Portuguese Guinea declared independence in 1973 and was granted *de jure* independence in 1974), relations between the two countries became strained. Cape Verde abandoned its hope for unity with Guinea-Bissau and formed the African Party for the Independence of Cape Verde (PAICV). Problems have since been resolved, and relations between the countries are good. The PAICV and its predecessor established a one-party system and ruled Cape Verde from independence until 1990.

Responding to growing pressure for a political opening, the PAICV called an emergency congress in February 1990 to discuss proposed constitutional changes to end one-party rule. Opposition groups came together to form the Movement for Democracy (MpD) in Praia in April 1990. Together, they campaigned for the right to contest the presidential election scheduled for December 1990. The one-party state was abolished September 28, 1990, and the first multi-party elections were held in January 1991. The MpD won a majority of the seats in the National Assembly, and the MpD presidential candidate Mascarenhas Monteiro defeated the PAICV's candidate by 73.5% of the votes cast to 26.5%. Legislative elections in December 1995 increased the MpD majority in the National Assembly. The party now holds 50 of the National Assembly's 72 seats. A February 1996 presidential election returned President Mascarenhas Monteiro to office. The December 1995 and February 1996 elections were judged free and fair by domestic and international observers.

# GOVERNMENT

The constitution first approved in 1980 and substantially revised in 1992 forms the basis of government organization. It declares that the government is the "organ that defines, leads, and executes the general internal and external policy of the country" and is responsible to the National Assembly. The Prime Minister is the head of the government and as such proposes other ministers and secretaries of state. Members of the National Assembly are elected by popular vote for 5-year terms; the most recent elections were held in 1995. The Prime Minister is nominated by the National Assembly and appointed by the President. The President is the head of state and is elected by popular vote for a 5-year term; the most recent elections were held in February 1996.

The judicial system is comprised of a Supreme Court of Justice—whose members are appointed by the President, the National Assembly, and the Superior Board of the Magistrature—and regional courts. Separate courts hear civil and criminal cases. Appeal to the Supreme Court is possible.

## Principal Government Officials

**For up-to-date information on Principal Government Officials, see the Chiefs of State and Cabinet Members of Foreign Governments section starting on page 1.**

Cape Verde maintains an embassy in the United States at 3415 Massachusetts Avenue, NW., Washington, D.C. 20007 (tel. 202-965-6820) and a consulate in Boston (tel. 617-353-0014).

# POLITICAL CONDITIONS

Cape Verde enjoys a stable democratic system. The Movement for

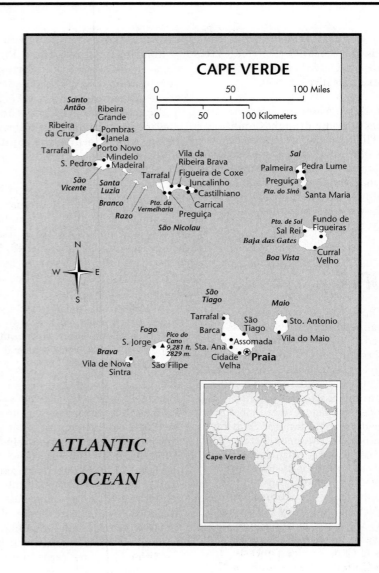

Democracy (MpD) captured a governing majority in the National Assembly in the country's first multi-party general elections in 1991. The MpD was returned to power with a larger majority in the general elections held in December 1995. Currently, there are three parties with seats in the National Assembly—MpD 50, PAICV 21, and PCD 1.

# ECONOMY

Cape Verde has few natural resources and suffers from inadequate rainfall and freshwater supplies. During periods of normal rainfall, only 4 of 10 islands (Santiago, Santo Antão, Fogo, and Brava) support significant agricultural production. Mineral resources are salt, pozzolana (a volcanic rock used in cement production), and limestone.

The economy of Cape Verde is service-oriented, with commerce, transport, and public services accounting for almost 70% of GDP.

Although nearly 70% of the population lives in rural areas, the share of agriculture in GDP in 1995 was only 8.9%, of which fishing accounts for only 1.5%. About 90% of food must be imported.

Since 1991, the government has pursued market-oriented economic policies, including an open welcome to foreign investors and a far-reaching privatization program. It established as top development priorities the promotion of market economy and of the private sector; the development of tourism, light manufacturing industries, and fisheries; and the development of transport, communications, and energy facilities. In 1994-95 Cape Verde received a total of about U.S.$50 million in foreign investments, of which 50% was in industry, 19% in tourism, and 31% in fisheries and services.

Fish and shellfish are plentiful, and small quantities are exported. Cape Verde has cold storage and freezing facilities as well as fish processing plants in Mindelo, Praia, and on Sal.

Cape Verde's strategic location at the crossroads of mid-Atlantic air and sea lanes has been enhanced by significant improvements at Mindelo's harbor (Porto Grande) and at Sal's international airport. Ship repair facilities at Mindelo were opened in 1983, and the harbors at Mindelo and Praia were recently renovated. The major ports are Mindelo and Praia, but all other islands have small port facilities, some of which are to be expanded in the near future. In addition to the international airport on Sal, airports are located on all of the inhabited islands. The archipelago has 3,050 kilometers (1,830 mi.) of roads, of which 1,010 kilometers (606 mi.) are paved. The airport of Praia is currently undergoing expansion.

# FOREIGN RELATIONS

Cape Verde follows a policy of non-alignment and seeks cooperative relations with all friendly states. Angola, Brazil, the People's Republic of China, Cuba, France, Germany, Portugal, Senegal, Russia, and the United States maintain embassies in Praia.

Cape Verde is actively interested in foreign affairs, especially in Africa. It has bilateral relations with other lusophone nations and holds membership in a number of international organizations. It also participates in most international conferences on economic and political issues.

# U.S.-CAPE VERDEAN RELATIONS

The cordial relations between the United States and Cape Verde have strong historical roots.

As early as the 18th century, U.S. whaling ships recruited crews from Brava and Fogo to hunt whales that were abundant in the waters surrounding Cape Verde. The tradition of emigration to the United States began at that time, continuing unabated until today. Both President Mascarenhas Monteiro and Prime Minister Carlos Veiga have visited the Cape Verdean communities in New England during official trips to the United States in 1995 and 1997, respectively.

Official ties between the United States and Cape Verde also date back to the early 19th century, when the first American consulate was established in Cape Verde in 1816. U.S. consular representation continued throughout the 19th century. The United States recognized Cape Verde on its independence day and supported its admission to the United Nations. Cape Verde assigned one of its first ambassadors to the United States, and a resident U.S. ambassador was assigned to Cape Verde in 1983.

**Travel Notes**

**Travel Advice:** For up-to-date information from the U.S. State Department on possible inconvenient or hazardous situations, see the **Travel Warnings and Consular Information Sheets from the U.S. Government** section starting on page 1723. For the latest information on health requirements and conditions, see the **International Travelers' Health Information** section starting on page 1385. For further information dealing with non-urgent matter, see the **Tips for Travelers to...** section starting on page 1588.

**Background Notes**

The United States promptly provided humanitarian aid and economic assistance to Cape Verde in the period immediately following Cape Verde's independence, as well as when a hurricane struck the island of Brava in 1982 and when Fogo's volcano erupted in 1995. The United States also ships 15,000 metric tons of corn or its equivalent in other grains yearly to Cape Verde.

The United States desires to expand and strengthen its present friendly relations with Cape Verde and wishes to encourage and participate in the country's economic and social development.

## Principal U.S. Officials

**For up-to-date information on Principal U.S. Officials, see the U.S. Embassies, Consulates, and Foreign Service section starting on page 139.**

The U.S. embassy is located at Rua Abílio Macedo, 81, Praia; C.P.201, tel. (238) 61 56 16, fax 61 13 55.

# CENTRAL AFRICAN REPUBLIC

November 1989

Official Name:
**Central African Republic**

# PROFILE

## Geography

**Area:** 623,000 sq. km (242,000 mi.); slightly smaller than Texas.
**Cities:** Capital—Bangui (pop. 500,000). Other cities—Berberati (39,000), Bouar (42,000), Bambari (45,000), Bangassou (31,000), Bossangoa (36,000), Mbaiki (25,000).
**Terrain:** Rolling plain 600-700 Meters (1,980-2,310 ft.) above sea level.
**Climate:** Tropical, ranging from humid equatorial in the south to Sahelo Sudanese in the north.

## People

**Nationality:** Noun and adjective—Central African(s).
**Population (1989):** 2.8 million.
**Annual rate:** 2.5%.
**Ethnic groups:** More than 80; Baya 34%, Banda 28%, Sara 10%, Mandja 9%, Mboum 9%, M'Baka 7%.
**Religions:** Traditional African 35%, Protestant 25%, Roman Catholic 25%, Muslim 15%.
**Languages:** French (official), Sangho (national).
**Education:** Year compulsory—6. Attendance—primary school 79%, secondary school 18%, higher education 1.4%. Literacy—40%.
**Health:** Infant mortality rate—143/1,000. Life expectancy—avg. 49 yrs.
**Work force (approx. 1 million est.):** Agriculture—72%. Industry—6%. Commerce and services—8.9%. Government—3%.

## Government

**Type:** Republic.
**Independence:** August 13, 1960.
**Constitution:** Adopted December, 1986.
**Branches:** Executive—president assisted by cabinet ministers. Legislative—National Assembly inaugurated October, 1987. Judicial—Supreme Court and regional courts.
**Administrative subdivisions:** 16 prefectures.
**Political parties:** Single government sponsored party—*Rassemblement Democratique Centrafricain*—formed in February 1987.
**Suffrage:** Universal over 21.
**Central government budget (1988):** $204 million.
**Defense (1988):** 5.6% of budget.
**National holidays:** August 13, Independence Day; December 1, National Day.
**Flag:** Blue, white, green, and yellow horizontal bands from top to bottom; vertical red band in center; yellow star at upper left on the blue band.

## Economy

**GDP (1988 est):** $1,118 million.
**Annual growth rate (1987):** 1.3%.
**Per capita income:** $376.
**Avg. inflation rate (1988):** 4%.
**Natural resources:** Diamonds, uranium, timber, gold, oil.
**Agriculture (40% of GNP):** Products—coffee, cotton, peanuts, tobacco, food crops, livestock. Cultivated land—15%.
**Industry (14.5% of GNP):** Types—beverages, textiles, soap.
**Trade (1988):** Exports—$138.3 million: diamonds, coffee, cotton, timber. Major markets—Belgium, France, Italy, F.R.G. Imports—$285.3 million: machinery and equipment, petroleum products, textiles. Major suppliers—France, other European Community countries, U.S.
**Official exchange rate (1988 avg.):** 300 *Communaute Financiere Africaine* (CFA) francs=U.S.$1.
**Fiscal year:** Calendar year.
**U.S. aid received (1988):** $2.5 million development assistance (includes $92,000 self-help funds). Peace Corps—78 volunteers. Military assistance—$250,000.

## Membership in International Organizations

UN and some of its specialized and related agencies, Organization for African Unity, Central African Customs and Economic Union (UDEAC), African Financial Community (Franc

Zone), Economic Community of Central African States (CEEAC).

# GEOGRAPHY

The Central African Republic (C.A.R.) is a landlocked country located approximately in the center of Africa, about 640 kilometers (400 mi.) from the nearest ocean. Its average elevation is about 600 meters (1,980 ft.). The terrain is mainly a vast, well watered plateau drained by two major river systems. The northerly system flows into the Chari Basin and eventually into Ice Chad. The southerly system drains into the Oubangui, a confluent of the Zaire River. Navigation is limited to the Oubangui and short sections of the Lobaye and the Sangha. These rivers produce several spectacular waterfalls; the best known are the Kotto River at Kembe and the Mbali River at Boali, which also is the source of the nation's hydroelectric energy.

Vegetation varies from tropical rainforest in the extreme southwest to semidesert in the northeastern tip. Most of the country is wooded. Wildlife abounds in the nearly uninhabited northeast and eastern sections. The Central African Republic has been considered as one of the last great refuges of the African elephant, but poaching has taken a severe toll. The elephant population is estimated to have dropped from 150,000 to 15,000 during the last 30 years. The government recently has, intensified conservation efforts and banned elephant hunting in 1985.

The Central African Republic has ample rainfall without the oppressive tropical climate found in many coastal areas. In the western highlands, the climate can be quite cool. Average monthly temperatures in Bangui range between 27°C and 32°C (80°F, 90°F). Annual rainfall in the Oubangui River valley is about 180 centimeters (70 in.). The river at Bangui normally rises about five meters (20 ft.) during the rainy season. In the extreme northeast, annual rainfall averages only 80 centimeters (31.5 in.). Much of the precipitation falls in June through November, although heavy rains occur intermittently throughout the year. Sunny skies and warm weather generally prevail from December through April.

# PEOPLE

More than 70% of the population of the Central African Republic live in rural areas. The chief agricultural areas arc around the prefectural centers of Bossangoa and Bambari.

There are more than 80 ethnic groups in the C.A.R., each with its own language. About 70% are Baya-Mandjia and Banda, and 7% are M'Baka. Sangho, the language of a small group along the Oubangui River, is the national language spoken by the majority of Central Africans. Only a small part of the population has more than an elemental knowledge of French, the official language.

# HISTORY AND POLITICAL CONDITIONS

Little is known of the successive waves of migration that occurred during the precolonial history of the C.A.R. However, it is believed that these migrations account for the complex ethnic and linguistic patterns in the area.

On April 19, 1887, a convention concluded with the Congo lee State granted France possession of the right bank of the Oubangui River. This convention and later international agreements established the boundaries of Oubangui-Chari.

In 1889, the French established an outpost at Bangui, located at the upper limit of the year-round navigable portion of the Oubangui River. In 1894, Oubangui-Chari became a territory; it was placed under a high commander and gradually given an administrative structure that began to be organized around 1900. United with Chad in 1906, it formed the Oubangui-ChariChad colony. In 1910, it became one of the four territories of the Federation of French Equatorial Africa (A.E.F.), along with Chad, Congo (Brazzaville), and Gabon.

In August 1940, the territory responded, with the rest of the A.E.F., to the call from Gen. Charles de Gaulle to fight for Free France. Alter World War II, the French Constitution of 1946 inaugurated the first of a series of reforms that led eventually to complete independence for all French territories in western and equatorial Africa. The 1946 rights granted French citizenship to all inhabitants and established local assemblies. The next landmark was the Basic La (Loi Cadre) of June 23, 1956, which eliminated all remaining voting inequalities and provided for creation of governmental organs to ensure a measure of sell government to individual territories. The constitutional referendum of September 1958 dissolved the A.E.F. and saw further expansion of the internal powers of the former overseas territories.

The nation became an autonomous republic within the newly established French Community on December 1, 1958, and acceded to complete independence as the Central African Republic on August 13, 1960. The first president, revered as the founder of the Central African Republic, was Barthelemy Boganda. He died in an airplane crash and was succeeded by his nephew David Dacko. On January 1, 1966, following a swift and almost bloodless coup, Col. Jean-Bedel Bokassa assumed power as president of the Republic. Bokassa abolished the constitution of 1959, dissolved the National Assembly, and issued a decree that placed all legislative and executive powers in the hands of the president On December 4, 1976, the republic became a monarchy with the promulgation of the imperial constitution and the proclamation of the president as Emperor Bokassa I.

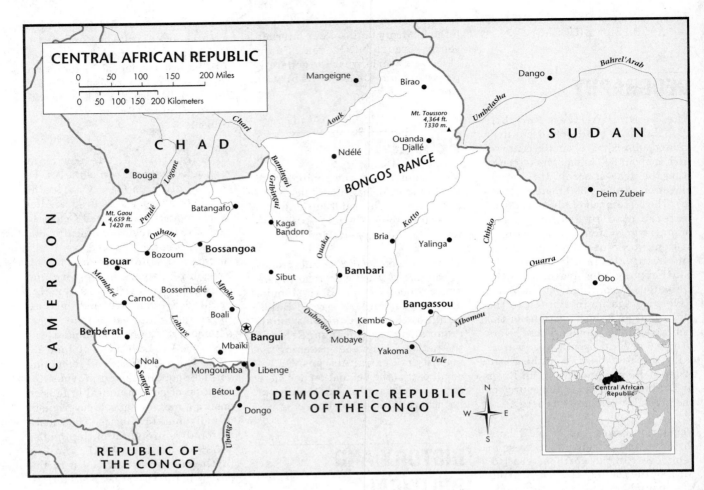

**CENTRAL AFRICAN REPUBLIC**

On September 20, 1979, former President Dacko led a successful and bloodless coup while Bokassa was out of the country. Gross human rights violations committed by Emperor Bokassa were largely responsible for his overthrow. Dacko's efforts to provide economic and political reforms proved ineffectual, and on September 20, 1981, he was overthrown in a bloodless coup by Gen. Andre Kolingba. Until September 21, 1985, Kolingba headed a predominantly military cabinet which composed the Military Committee for National Recovery (CRMN). On that date, the CRMN was dissolved, and Kolingba named a new cabinet with increased civilian participation, signaling the start of a return to civilian rule. In 1986, the process of democratization quickened with the creation of a new political patty, the *Rassemblement Democratique Centrafricain* (RDC), and the drafting of a new constitution that subsequently was ratified in a national referendum. The constitu-

tion established a parliament made up of a National Assembly, whose 52 deputies are elected, and an economic and regional council with 16 members elected by the National Assembly and 16 members appointed by the president Deputies to the assembly were elected in July 1987, and the assembly's first session was held later that year. During 1988, these institutions provided a forum for debate of public issues but had little substantive impact on government policy. In May 1988, the assembly passed legislation that lifted a ban on trade union activity in effect since 1981 and provided the legal basis for trade union freedom and the protection of union rights.

# GOVERNMENT

The government is formally a republic comprised of the executive branch (a president and a 21-member cabi-

net consisting of 16 ministers and 5 secretaries of state), the legislative branch (the National Assembly and the Economic and Regional Council), and the judicial branch (a Supreme Court, Court of Appeals, Criminal Court, and lower courts).

## Principal Government Officials

**For up-to-date information on Principal Government Officials, see the Chiefs of State and Cabinet Members of Foreign Governments section starting on page 1.**

For administrative purposes, the country is divided into 16 prefectures that are further divided into subprefectures. Each prefecture is represented in the National Assembly by three deputies, and the city of Bangui by four. Local elections held in mid-

## Travel Notes

**Climate and clothing:** Lightweight, washable clothing is recommended. Bring a jacket or sweater for the rainy season, May-October.

**Customs:** Visas are required of travelers carrying U.S. passports. Do not display or use photographic equipment without special permission of the Ministry of Information. A certificate of inoculation against yellow fever is required.

**Health:** Visitors are strongly urged to use malaria suppressants that provide protection against chloroquine-resistant strains of the parasite. Typhoid, polio, and hepatitis inoculations are recommended for travel to remote areas. Raw fruits and vegetables should be carefully prepared. and meats should be thoroughly cooked. Tapwater is not potable. Boiling and filtering are recommended. Local facilities are adequate for routine medical problems.

**Telecommunications:** International cable and telephone service is available. Bangui is six standard time zones ahead of eastern standard time.

**Transportation:** Bangui M'Poko International Airport has regular air service to Paris, Brazzaville, Douala, Libreville, N'djamena, and some West African capitals. The nearest railroad is in Cameroon.

Buses and taxis are available but not generally used by tourists. About 1,300 kilometers (810 mi.) of the east-west Trans-African Highway lie in the C.A.R. between Beloko on the Cameroon border and Bangassou bordering Zaire in the southeast. About 180 kilometers (113 mi.) of this road is paved. and most of the rest is of laterite. Roads often flood during the rainy season. There is no commercial transportation in the game areas.

**Tourist attractions:** Notable tourist sites include the falls at Boali and Kembe; the National Museum in Bangui; the Artisanal Center in Bangui, offering a variety of local and regional handicrafts; the tropical forest and Pygmy villages of southern Lobaye.

**Travel Advice:** For up-to-date information from the U.S. State Department on possible inconvenient or hazardous situations, see the **Travel Warnings and Consular Information Sheets from the U.S. Government** section starting on page 1723. For the latest information on health requirements and conditions, see the **International Travelers' Health Information** section starting on page 1385. For further information dealing with non-urgent matter, see the **Tips for Travelers to...** section starting on page 1588.

---

1988 created 176 municipal councils, each headed by a mayor. Suffrage is universal over the age of 21.

The Central African Republic maintains an embassy in the United States at 1618 - 22d Street, NW., Washington, D.C. (tel.202-483-7800 and 7801).

# ECONOMY

The Central African Republic is classified as one of the world's least developed countries, with an annual per capita income of $376. Sparsely populated and landlocked, the nation is an overwhelmingly agrarian society, with 75% of the population engaged in subsistence farming.

In the 28 years since independence, the C.A.R. has made only slow progress toward economic develop-

ment A long period of economic mismanagement, particularly during the Bokassa regime, combined with adverse external conditions, resulted in a decline in per capita GNP between 1966 and 1986. With the collaboration of the World Bank, International Monetary Fund (IMF), and other donors, the C.A.R. in 1986 embarked on phase one of a Structural Adjustment Program. Over a 2-year period, there was substantial progress in liberalizing prices and trade, introducing a more favorable investment code, curtailing growth in government spending, bringing order to the parapublic sector, and providing incentives for agriculture and forestry. In early 1988, the government initiated phase two of the reform program, which will concentrate on achieving real economic growth.

The economy is essentially agrarian: agricultural activities (including forestry) account for about 40% of the

gross national product (GNP). Nearly self-sufficient in food production with potential to become a regional exporter, the C.A.R.'s main food crops are manioc, corn, peanuts, sorghum, rice, and sesame. The principal agricultural export products are coffee, cotton, timber, and tobacco. livestock production, which currently accounts for one-third of agricultural gross domestic product (GDP), has the potential to double by the year 2000 and transform the C.A.R. into a meat exporter. Mining, manufacturing, and construction represent 14.5% of GDP, while services account for 41.5%. The large contribution of services is caused by an oversized bureaucracy and high transportation costs due to the country's landlocked position.

With the decline in recent years of coffee and cotton prices, diamonds now account for nearly one-half of the C.A.R.'s export earnings. In 1987, diamonds netted $50 million as opposed to $20.8 million for coffee, $9.1 million for cotton, $19.8 million for timber, and $3.7 for tobacco. The quantity and per carat value of diamonds extracted has been rising in recent years. The C.A.R. also produces a small amount of gold (205 kilograms in 1987). Like diamonds, the gold is produced by individual prospectors. Two American firms have established companies in the C.A.R. to recover diamonds and gold in a single, mechanized operation. Known uranium and petroleum deposits have gone unexploited for a variety of technical and economic reasons, including high start-up costs and transportation problems.

The C.A.R.'s industrial sector is limited. Processing of agricultural and forestry products represent the bulk of manufacturing. Other manufacturing activities include automobile and bicycle assembly factories, textiles, cigarettes, two French-owned breweries, and a soft drink bottling plant, all of which are geared toward import substitution as opposed to exports.

The main constraints to economic development in the C.A.R. are a poor transportation infrastructure and weak internal and international marketing systems. Multilateral and bilateral development assistance play a major role in providing capital for new investment.

France is the largest bilateral aid donor, providing nearly half of the $130 million in foreign aid received in 1987. The United States and West Germany have smaller programs. Multilateral assistance, which accounted for 38% of the 1987 aid influx, came primarily from the World Bank, International Development Agency, and the IMF, with lesser contributions from various UN agencies and the EC.

# FOREIGN RELATIONS

The Central African Republic maintains close ties with France and is a member of the French Community and the Franc Zone, as well as an associate member of the European Community. Although negotiations to form a confederation with the other states of former French Equatorial Africa failed in 1960, the four countries preserved features of their previous association, including cooperative arrangements in customs, transportation, and higher education. The Central African Customs and Economic Union—Comprising the C.A.R., Cameroon, Congo, Chad, Equatorial Guinea, and Gabon-came effective January 1, 1966. This union is supplemented by the Central African States Development Bank, which helps finance development projects in its member countries.

Successive governments have worked to expand diplomatic ties. Currently, 19 countries have resident diplomatic representatives in Bangui, and the C.A.R. maintains 17 diplomatic missions abroad. In an effort to reduce expenditures, other missions abroad have been closed. Formal diplomatic relations with the Soviet Union were suspended in 1980 but resumed in 1988. Since early 1989, the government recognizes both Israel and the Palestinian state.

# U.S.-C.A.R. RELATIONS

Bilateral relations are excellent U.S. policy seeks to encourage the Central African Republic's progress toward democratization efforts at implementing economic reforms, and advocacy of prudent and constructive policies at regional and international forums.

Although the bulk of U.S. development assistance to the C.A.R. is channeled through multilateral organizations such as the World Bank, IMF, and various UN organizations, the U.S. Government also maintains a bilateral assistance program through the Agency for International Development (AID). In 1988, AID grants to the C.A.R. totaled $2.5 million. Rural agricultural development was the principal focus, but AID also supported programs providing training in private sector management and postgraduate studies in various disciplines. In the health sector, AID funded programs to combat childhood communicable diseases, to foster family planning, and to assist the national campaign against acquired immune deficiency syndrome. In 1989, nearly 100 Peace Corps volunteers were active in education, health, and agriculture, often working closely with ongoing AID projects.

An active program of cultural and informational exchanges is managed by the U.S. Information Agency (USIA), which operates a cultural center and library adjacent to the embassy. Fourteen Central Africans were sent to the United States on exchange programs in fiscal year (FY) 1988. USIA also invites prominent speakers, conducts Worldnet satellite press interviews, and distributes a variety of informational publications.

The United States provides the C.A.R. with a modest amount of security assistance. In FY 1988, eight military students were trained in the United States under the International Military Education Training (IMET) program, and materials were donated for the construction of a bridge through the Military Civic Action Program, totaling $250,000.

Various U.S. nongovernmental organizations are active in the C.A.R. A number of American missionaries operate clinics and schools in remote parts of the country. The World Wildlife Fund, with support from AID, is assisting the C.A.R. Government in establishing the Dzanga-Sangha Dense Forest Reserve in southeastern C.A.R.

U.S. investment is limited to investments in diamond and gold mining that are expected to get underway in 1990. Exploratory drilling by Esso in 1985 revealed the presence of oil deposits in northern C.A.R., but further drilling is not economically feasible at current prices. Trade between the United States and C.A.R. also is minimal due to the cost of transportation, historical preference for European goods, and strong competition from Japanese goods. The C.A.R. does import U.S. logging, timber-handling, and cotton-ginning machinery in addition to food products, vaccines, and used clothing. The United States imports diamonds, tobacco, and cotton from the C.A.R.

## Principal U.S. Officials

For up-to-date information on Principal U.S. Officials, see the U.S. Embassies, Consulates, and Foreign Service section starting on page 139.

The U.S. Embassy is located at Avenue du President David Dacko, P.O. Box 924, Bangui (tel. 61-02 or 61-0210).

# CHAD
May 1992

Official Name:
**Republic of Chad**

# PROFILE

## Geography

**Area:** 1,284,634 sq. km. (496,000 sq. mi.); about the size of Texas, Oklahoma, and New Mexico combined.
**Cities:** Capital—N'Djamena (pop. 500,000 est.). Other major cities—Moundou (pop. 120,000), Abeche, Sarh.
**Terrain:** Desert, mountainous north, large arid central plain, fertile lowlands in extreme southern region.
**Climate:** Northern desert—very dry throughout the year; central plain—hot and dry, with brief rainy season mid-June to mid-September; southern lowlands—warm and more humid with seasonal rains from late May to early October.

## People

**Nationality:** Noun and adjective—Chadian(s).
**Population:** 5.5 million.
**Annual growth rate:** 2.5%.
**Density:** 4.2 per sq. km. (11 per sq. mi.)
**Health:** Life expectancy—46. Infant mortality rate—132/1,000.
**Ethnic groups:** 200 distinct groups—including Toubou (Gourane), Arabs, Fulbe, Kotoko, Hausa, Kanembou, Bagirmi, Boulala, Zaghawa, Hadjerai, and Maba—most

of whom are Muslim, in the north and center. Non-Muslims, Sara (Ngambaye, Mbaye, Goulaye), Moudang, Moussei, Massa—in the south. About 2,500 French citizens live in Chad.
**Religions:** Muslim, Christian, traditional.
**Languages:** French and Arabic (official); 200 indigenous Chadian languages.

## Government

**Type:** Republic.
**Independence:** August 11, 1960.
**Branches:** Executive—president (head of state, president of the council of ministers), council of ministers. Legislative—Provisional Council of the Republic. Judicial—court of appeals, several lower courts.
**Political party:** Six political parties as of May 18, 1992—Patriotic Salvation Movement (MPS), Rally for Democracy and Progress (RDP), Democratic Union for Progress in Chad (UDPT), National Rally for Democracy and Progress (VIVA-RNDP), Union for Democracy and the Republic (UDR), Chadian People's Assembly (RPT).
**Suffrage:** None.
**Administrative subdivisions:** 14 prefectures, 54 subprefectures, 27 administrative posts, and 9 municipalities.
**Flag:** Blue, yellow, and red vertical bands from left to right.

## Economy

**GDP (est.):** $1 billion.
**Per capita income (est.):** $200.
**Natural resources:** Petroleum (unexploited), natron (sodium carbonate), kaolin.
**Agriculture:** Products—cotton, gum arabic, livestock, fish, peanuts, millet, sorghum, rice, sweet potatoes, cassava, dates.
**Industry:** Types—agriculture and livestock processing plants, natron mining.
**Trade:** Exports—$155 million: cotton (46%), livestock, gum arabic. Imports—$250 million: petroleum, machinery, cement, motor vehicles, used clothing. Major trade partners—France and countries of the Customs and Economic Union of Central Africa. Chad enjoys preferential tariffs in France and other EC countries.
**Official exchange rate:** As of April 1992, the exchange rate was 255 CFA francs=US$1.
**Economic aid received (1990):** Economic, food relief—$312 million from all sources. US aid—$10.9 million (fiscal year ending 1990).

# PEOPLE

There are more than 200 ethnic groups in Chad. Those in the north and east are generally Muslim; most southerners are animists and

Christians. Through their long religious and commercial relationships with Sudan and Egypt, many of the peoples in Chad's eastern and central regions have become more or less Arabized, speaking Arabic and engaging in many other Arab cultural practices as well. Chad's southern peoples took more readily to European culture during the French colonial period.

# HISTORY

Chad has known human habitation since time immemorial. The oldest humanoid skull yet found in Chad (Borkou) is more than 1 million years old. Because in ancient times the Saharan area was not totally arid, Chad's population was more evenly distributed than it is today. For example, 7,000 years ago, the north central basin, now in the Sahara, was still filled with water, and people lived and farmed around its shores. The cliff paintings in Borkou and Ennedi depict elephants, rhinoceri, giraffes, cattle, and camels; only camels survive there today. The region was known to traders and geographers from the late Middle Ages. Since then, Chad has served as a crossroads for the Muslim peoples of the desert and savanna regions and the animist Bantu tribes of the tropical forests.

Sao people lived along the Chari River for thousands of years, but their relatively weak chiefdoms were overtaken by the powerful chiefs of what were to become the Kanem-Bornu and Baguirmi kingdoms. At their peak, these two kingdoms and the kingdom of Ouaddai controlled a good part of what is now Chad, as well as parts of Nigeria and Sudan. From 1500 to 1900, Arab slave raids were widespread. The French first penetrated Chad in 1891, establishing their authority through military expeditions primarily against the Muslim kingdoms. The first major colonial battle for Chad was fought in 1900 between the French Major Lamy and the African leader Rabah, both of whom were killed in the battle. Although the French won that battle, they did not declare the territory pacified until 1911; armed clashes between colonial troops and local bands continued for many years thereafter.

In 1905, administrative responsibility for Chad was placed under a governor general stationed at Brazzaville in what is now Congo. Although Chad joined the French colonies of Gabon, Oubangui-Charo, and Moyen Congo to form the Federation of French Equatorial Africa (AEF) in 1910, it did not have colonial status until 1920. The northern region of Chad was occupied by the French in 1914.

In 1959, the territory of French Equatorial Africa was dissolved, and four states—Gabon, the Central African Republic, Congo (Brazzaville), and Chad—became autonomous members of the French Community. In 1960, Chad became an independent nation under its first president, Francois Tombalbaye.

A long civil war began as a tax revolt in 1965 and soon set the Muslim north and east against the southern-led government. Even with the help of French combat forces, the Tombalbaye Government was never able to quell the insurgency. Tombalbaye's rule became more irrational and brutal, leading the military to carry out a coup in 1975 and to install Gen. Felix Malloum, a southerner, as head of state.

In 1978, Malloum's Government was broadened to include more northerners. Internal dissent within the government led the northern Prime Minister, Hissein Habre, to send his forces against the national army at N'Djamena in February 1979. This act led to intense fighting among the 11 factions that emerged. At this point, the civil war had become so widespread that regional governments decided there was no effective central government and stepped in.

A series of four international conferences held first under Nigerian and then Organization of African Unity (OAU) sponsorship attempted to bring the Chadian factions together. At the fourth conference, held in Lagos, Nigeria, in August 1979, the Lagos accord was signed. This accord established a transitional government pending national elections. In November 1979, the National Union Transition Government (GUNT) was created with a mandate to govern for 18 months. Goukouni Oueddei, a northerner, was named President; Col. Kamougue, a southerner, Vice President; and Habre, Minister of Defense.

This coalition proved fragile; in March 1980, fighting broke out again between Goukouni's and Habre's forces. The war dragged on inconclusively until Goukouni sought and obtained Libyan intervention. More than 7,000 Libyan troops entered Chad. Although Goukouni requested complete withdrawal of external forces in October 1981, the Libyans pulled back only to the Aozou Strip in northern Chad.

An OAU peacekeeping force of 3,500 troops replaced the Libyan forces in the remainder of Chad. The force, consisting of troops from Nigeria, Senegal, and Zaire, received funding from the United States. A special summit of the OAU ad hoc committee on the Chad/Libya dispute in February 1982 called for reconciliation among all the factions, particularly those led by Goukouni and Habre, who had resumed fighting in eastern Chad. Although Habre agreed to participate, Goukouni refused to negotiate with Habre on an equal basis. In the series of battles that followed, Habre's forces defeated the GUNT, and Habre occupied N'Djamena on June 7, 1982. The OAU force remained neutral during the conflict, and all of its elements were withdrawn from Chad at the end of June.

In the summer of 1983, GUNT forces launched an offensive against government positions in northern and eastern Chad. Following a series of initial defeats, government forces succeeded in stopping the rebels. At this point, Libyan forces directly intervened once again, bombing government forces at Faya Largeau. Ground attacks followed the bombings, forcing government troops to

abandon N'Djamena and withdraw to the south. In response to Libya's direct intervention, French and Zairian forces were sent to Chad to assist in defending the government. With the deployment of French troops, the military situation stabilized, leaving the Libyans and rebels in control of all Chad north of the 16th parallel.

In September 1984, the French and the Libyan Governments announced an agreement for the mutual withdrawal of their forces from Chad. By the end of the year, all French and Zairian troops were withdrawn. Libya did not honor the withdrawal accord, however, and its forces continued to occupy the northern third of Chad.

President Habre's efforts to deal with his opposition were aided by a number of African leaders, especially Gabon's President, Omar Bongo. During accords held in Libreville, Gabon, in 1985, two of the chief exile opposition groups, the Chadian Democratic Front and the Coordinating Action Committee of the Democratic Revolutionary Council, made peace with the Habre Government. By 1986, all of the rebel commando (CODO) groups in southern Chad came in from the forests, rallied to President Habre's side, and were re-integrated into the

Forces Armees Nationales Chadiennes (FANT).

In the fall of 1986, fighters loyal to Goukouni Oueddei, leader of the GUNT, began defecting to the FANT. Although Libyan forces were more heavily equipped than were the Chadians, Habre's FANT, with considerable assistance from ex-GUNT forces, began attacks against the Libyan occupiers in November 1986 and won victories at all the important cities. The Chadian offensive ended in August 1987, with the taking of Aozou Town, the principal village in the Aozou Strip. Chad Government forces held the village for a month but lost it to a heavy Libyan counterattack.

The OAU ad hoc committee continued to seek a peaceful solution to the Chad/Libya conflict, holding meetings over the years with heads of state or ministerial-level officials. In October 1988, Chad resumed formal diplomatic relations with Libya, in accordance with recommendations made by the OAU.

A month later, Habre's reconciliation efforts succeeded, and he took power in N'Djamena. In April 1989, Idriss Deby, one of Habre's leading generals, defected and fled to Darfur in Sudan, from which he mounted a series of attacks on the eastern region of Chad. In November 1990, he invaded; on December 2, 1990, his forces entered N'Djamena without a battle, President Habre and forces loyal to him having fled. After 3 months of provisional government, a national charter was approved by the Patriotic Salvation Movement (MPS) on February 28, 1991, with Deby as President.

# GOVERNMENT AND POLITICAL CONDITIONS

The Fundamental Act of the Republic, proclaimed on October 18, 1982, served as the constitutional basis for government until December 10, 1989, when it was replaced by a new consti-

tution. The latter was revoked by the MPS on December 4, 1990, after Habre's fall.

Until the December 1990 takeover of the government by the MPS, Chad's political structure comprised an executive office, a national assembly, and the National Union for Independence and Revolution (UNIR), the sole political party. The MPS embarked on an ambitious democratization program, which included authorization for multiple political parties in October 1991 and presidential, legislative, and local elections in 1993. The current government, self-described as a transitional or provisional government, is headed by President Idriss Deby. Prime Minister Jean Bawoyeu Alingue is charged with administration of government. A council of ministers, which the president heads, directs government policy. Authority for the current government structure comes from the national charter of March 1991. Until March 1992, the MPS was the only political organization permitted. Since then, the Rally for Democracy and Progress (headed by Lol Mahamat Choua), the Democratic Union for Progress in Chad (Elie Romba), the National Rally for Democracy and Progress (Kassire Joumakoye), the Union for Democracy and the Republic (Jean Bawoyeau Alingue), and the Chadian People's Assembly (Dangde Laobele Damaye), were authorized.

The MPS is composed of a 28-member executive committee and a 155-member national committee. Idriss Deby is the president of the MPS. Chad's politics are dominated by the democratization agenda, established by the MPS as a priority. Progress has been made in ameliorating Chad's human rights record and in liberalizing politics. Currently, an outspoken press, two trade unions, and two human rights organizations function openly.

Relations between Chad and Libya are important factors in Chad's political environment. Idriss Deby and the MPS have advocated a good-neighbor policy with all countries bordering Chad, including Libya. This has resulted in a lessening of the military tensions evident under the Habre

regime, but concerns remain as to Libya's political intentions in Chad, and the dispute over the Aozou Strip remains unresolved. The case was referred to the International Court of Justice for review.

## Principal Government Officials

**For up-to-date information on Principal Government Officials, see the Chiefs of State and Cabinet Members of Foreign Governments section starting on page 1.**

Chad maintains an embassy in the United States at 2002 R Street, NW, Washington, DC 20009 (tel: 202-462-4009).

# DEFENSE

The Chadian military under former President Hissein Habre was dominated by members of Gourane, Zaghawa, Kanembou, Hadjerai, and Massa groups. Idriss Deby, a member of a minority Zaghawa clan and a top military commander, revolted and fled to the Sudan, taking with him many Zaghawa and Hadjerai soldiers in 1989.

The forces Deby led into N'Djamena on December 1, 1990, and which overthrew Habre were mainly of Zaghawas, including a large number of

Sudanese Zaghawa. Many of these were recruited while Deby was in the bush. Deby's coalition also included a small number of Hadjerais and southerners.

Chad's armed forces numbered about 35,000 at the end of the Habre regime but swelled to an estimated 50,000 in the early days of Idriss Deby. The growth was a result of recruiting tribal members loyal to Deby and his principal commanders and of combining Habre's and Deby's armies into the new national Chadian army, FANT.

With French support, a reorganization of the armed forces was initiated early in 1991. The reorganization goal is to reduce the armed forces from 50,000 to 25,000 and to restructure it into a ground army of approximately 20,000, consisting of a republican guard, infantry regiments, and support battalions. Also included in the new structure is a gendarmerie of about 5,000 and an air force of about 400. Ethnic composition of the regiments is to reflect that of the country as a whole.

A key challenge for the national army of Chad is the reduction portion of the overall reorganization plan. Limited funds to pay mustering out bonuses and pensions and a lack of employment opportunities in the economy have inhibited efforts. However, a list of the initial reductions has been drafted and is being reviewed by government officials for implementation.

# ECONOMY

About 85% of Chadians make their living from subsistence agriculture, fishing, and stock raising. Cotton and livestock are the two major exports, accounting for 70% of Chad's export earnings. In years of adequate rainfall, Chad is self-sufficient in food. In years of drought, such as those that occurred in the mid-1970s, in 1984-85, and in 1990, large quantities of foodstuffs, primarily cereals, must be imported.

Cotton alone accounts for 10% of agricultural GDP. Primary markets include neighboring Cameroon and Nigeria and France, Germany, and Portugal. In 1986, cotton prices on the world market declined by more than 50%, and CotonTchad did not show a profit again until 1991. Rehabilitation of CotonTchad, the major cotton company, has been financed by France, the Netherlands, the European Economic Community (EC), and the International Bank for Reconstruction and Development (IBRD). Because of cotton's importance to the economy, the government excused the collection of export taxes until the company returned to profitability. CotonTchad is adhering to its agenda and is well on the road to recovery.

The other major export is livestock, herded to neighboring countries. Herdsmen in the Sudanic and Sahelian zones raise cattle, sheep, goats, and, among the non-Muslims, a few pigs. In the Saharan region, only camels and a few hardy goats can survive. Chad also sells smoked and dried fish to its neighbors and exports several million dollars worth of gum arabic to Europe each year. Other food crops include millet, sorghum, peanuts, rice, sweet potatoes, manioc, cassava, and yams.

In both the north and the south, industrial activity and minerals exploration peaked in 1978. The civil war and the Libyan intervention in 1980 devastated N'Djamena and destroyed most of the economic infrastructure there. Between the first outbreak of heavy fighting in N'Djamena in February 1979 and the withdrawal of Libyan forces from the capital in 1981, southern Chad became an autonomous area, not to be fully integrated into the country until 1983. The south continued to export cotton, but none of the economic benefits of that trade reached the rest of the country.

The effects of the war on foreign investment are still felt today, as investors who left Chad between 1979-82 have only recently begun to regain confidence in the country's future. By early 1983, the return of internal security and a successful

Geneva donors' conference had prompted a number of international business representatives to make exploratory visits to Chad.

An international consortium is conducting exploratory drilling for petroleum in the south. By mid-1991, seismic studies by an American oil company in the north-central desert area were completed. The World Bank has agreed to partially finance a pipeline/mini-refinery/power plant project in N'Djamena using small crude oil deposits found north of Lake Chad.

# FOREIGN RELATIONS

Chad is officially non-aligned but has close relations with France, the former colonial power, and other members of the Western community. It receives economic aid from countries of the European Community, the United States, and various international organizations. Libya supplies aid and has an ambassador resident in N'Djamena.

Other resident diplomatic missions in N'Djamena include the embassies of France, the United States, Egypt, Algeria, Iraq, Sudan, Germany, the Central African Republic, Zaire, Nigeria, China, Cameroon, and the European Economic Community. A number of other countries have non-resident ambassadors. In 1988, Chad decided to recognize the "State of Palestine," which maintains an "embassy" in N'Djamena. Chad has not recognized the State of Israel.

With the exception of Libya, whose expansionist policies have kept the two nations in conflict since 1980, Chad has generally good rapport with its neighbors. Although relations with Libya improved with the advent of the Deby Government, strains persist.

Chad has been an active champion of regional cooperation through the Central African Economic and Customs Union, the Lake Chad and Niger River Basin Commissions, and the Inter-state Commission for the

Fight Against the Drought in the Sahel.

# U.S.-CHAD RELATIONS

Relations between the United States and Chad are good. The American Embassy in N'Djamena, established at Chadian independence in 1960, was closed from the onset of the heavy fighting in the city in 1980 until the withdrawal of the Libyan forces at the end of 1981. It was reopened in January 1982. The US Agency for International Development (AID) and the US Information Service (USIS) offices resumed activities in Chad in September 1983.

The United States enjoyed close relations with the Habre regime, although strains over human rights abuses developed prior to Habre's fall. Cordial relations with the Deby Government continue. The USAID program is expanding, both in terms of project assistance and emergency aid. Approximately $15 million in emergency assistance was granted to combat a cholera epidemic and to prevent famine in 1991.

The US development program in Chad concentrates on the agricultural, health, and infrastructure sectors and includes projects in road repair and maintenance, maternal and child health, famine early warning systems, and agricultural marketing. USAID works with several American voluntary agencies such as CARE, AFRICARE, and VITA on some of its projects. The first Peace Corps volunteers of the post-war period arrived in Chad in September 1987, and about 40 are currently assigned.

Development assistance had increased from $3.3 million in 1982 to $15 million in 1991. Budget constraints have forced economic support funds cutbacks for FY 1992, however.

## Principal U.S. Officials

For up-to-date information on Principal U.S. Officials, see the U.S. Embassies, Consulates, and Foreign Service section starting on page 139.

The US Embassy in Chad is located on Avenue Felix Eboue, N'Djamena, (tel: 235-51-62-18 or 235-51-40-09).

# CHILE

April 2001

Official Name:
**Republic of Chile**

## PROFILE

### Geography

**Area:** 756,945 sq. km. (302,778 sq. mi.); nearly twice the size of California.

Cities: Capital—Santiago (metropolitan area est. 6 million). Other cities—Concepcion-Talcahuano (840,000), Vina del Mar-Valparaiso (800,000), Antofagasta (245,000), Temuco (230,000).

**Terrain:** Desert in north; fertile central valley; volcanoes and lakes toward the south, giving way to rugged and complex coastline; Andes Mountains on the eastern border.

**Climate:** Arid in north, Mediterranean in the central portion, cool and damp in south.

### People

**Nationality:** Noun and adjective—Chilean(s).

**Population:** (2000) 15.2 million.

**Annual population growth rate:** 1.2%.

**Ethnic groups:** Spanish-Native-American (mestizo), European, Native-American.

**Religions:** Roman Catholic 77%; Protestant 12%. Language: Spanish.

**Education:** Years compulsory—8. Attendance—3 million. Adult literacy rate—95%.

**Health:** Infant mortality rate—10/1,000. Life expectancy—75 yrs.

**Work force:** (5.8 million) Services and government—36%; industry and commerce—34%; agriculture, forestry, and fishing—14%; construction—7%; mining—2%.

### Government

**Type:** Republic.

**Independence:** September 18, 1810.

**Constitution:** Promulgated September 11, 1980; effective March 11, 1981; amended in 1989, 1993, and 1997.

**Branches:** Executive—president. Legislative—bicameral legislature. Judicial—Constitutional Tribunal, Supreme Court, court of appeals, military courts.

**Administrative subdivisions:** 12 numbered regions, plus Santiago metropolitan region, administered by appointed "intendentes," regions are divided into provinces, administered by appointed governors; provinces are divided into municipalities administered by elected mayors.

**Political parties:** Major parties are the Christian Democrat Party, the National Renewal Party, the Party for Democracy, the Socialist Party, the Independent Democratic Union, and the Radical Social Democratic Party. The Communist Party has not won a congressional seat in the last three elec-

tions.

**Suffrage:** Universal at 18, including foreigners legally resident for more than 5 years.

### Economy

**GDP:** $69.9 billion.

**Annual real growth rate:** 5.4%. Per capita GDP: $4,600.

**Commerce:** (18.8% of GDP) Sales, restaurants, hotels.

**Manufacturing:** (16.3% of GDP) Types—mineral refining, metal manufacturing, food processing, fish processing, paper and wood products, finished textiles.

**Financial services:** (15.2% of GDP) Insurance, leasing, consulting.

Mining (11.4% of GDP): Copper, iron ore, nitrates, precious metals, and molybdenum.

**Forestry, agriculture, and fisheries:** (8.3% of GDP) Products—wheat, potatoes, corn, sugarbeets, onions, beans, fruits, livestock, fish.

**Trade:** Exports—$18.2 billion: copper, fishmeal, fruits, wood products, paper products. Major markets—EU 25%, U.S. 17%, Japan 15%, U.K. 6%, Argentina 3%, Brazil 5%. Imports—$16.7 billion: petroleum, chemical products, capital goods, vehicles, electronic equipment, consumer durables, machinery. Major suppliers—U.S. 18%, EU 18%, Argentina 15%, Brazil 7%, China 5%, Japan 4%, Germany 4%.

# PEOPLE

About 85% of Chile's population live in urban centers with 40% living in greater Santiago. Most have Spanish ancestry. A small, yet influential number of Irish and English immigrants came to Chile during the colonial period. German immigration began in 1848 and lasted for 90 years; the southern provinces of Valdivia, Llanquihue, and Osorno show a strong German influence. Other significant immigrant groups are Italian, Croatian, French, and Middle Eastern. About 800,000 Native Americans, mostly of the Mapuche tribe, reside in the south-central area.

The northern Chilean desert contains great mineral wealth, primarily copper and nitrates. The relatively small central area dominates the country in terms of population and agricultural resources. This area also is the historical center from which Chile expanded until the late 19th century, when it incorporated its northern and southern regions. Southern Chile is rich in forests and grazing lands and features a string of volcanoes and lakes. The southern coast is a labyrinth of fjords, inlets, canals, twisting peninsulas, and islands. It also has small, rapidly declining petroleum reserves, which supplied about 8% of Chile's domestic requirements during 1996.

# HISTORY

About 10,000 years ago, migrating Indians settled in fertile valleys and along the coast of what is now Chile. The Incas briefly extended their empire into what is now northern Chile, but the area's remoteness prevented extensive settlement. In 1541, the Spanish, under Pedro de Valdivia, encountered hundreds of thousands of Indians from various cultures in the area that modern Chile now occupies. These cultures supported themselves principally through slash-and-burn agriculture and hunting. Although the Spanish did not find the extensive gold and silver they sought, they recognized the agricultural potential of Chile's central valley, and Chile became part of the Viceroyalty of Peru.

The drive for independence from Spain was precipitated by usurpation of the Spanish throne by Napoleon's brother Joseph. A national junta in the name of Ferdinand-heir to the deposed king-was formed on September 18, 1810. Spanish attempts to reimpose arbitrary rule during what was called the Reconquista led to a prolonged struggle under Bernardo O'Higgins, Chile's most renowned patriot. Chilean independence was formally proclaimed on February 12, 1818.

The political revolt brought little social change, however, and 19th century Chilean society preserved the essence of the stratified colonial social structure, family politics, and the influence of the Roman Catholic Church. The system of presidential power eventually predominated, but wealthy landowners continued to control Chile.

Toward the end of the 19th century, government in Santiago consolidated its position in the south by persistently suppressing the Mapuche Indians. In 1881, it signed a treaty with Argentina confirming Chilean sovereignty over the Strait of Magellan. As a result of the War of the Pacific with Peru and Bolivia (1879–83), Chile expanded its territory northward by almost one-third and acquired valuable nitrate deposits, the exploitation of which led to an era of national affluence.

Chile established a parliamentary style democracy in the late 19th century, which tended to protect the interests of the ruling oligarchy. By the 1920s, the emerging middle and working classes were powerful enough to elect a reformist president, whose program was frustrated by a conservative congress. Continuing political and economic instability resulted in the quasi-dictatorial rule of General Carlos Ibanez (1924–32).

When constitutional rule was restored in 1932, a strong middle-class party, the Radicals, emerged. It became the key force in coalition governments for the next 20 years. In the 1920s, Marxist groups with strong popular support developed. During the period of Radical Party dominance (1932–52), the state increased its role in the economy.

The 1964 presidential election of Christian Democrat Eduardo Frei-Montalva by an absolute majority initiated a period of major reform. Under the slogan "Revolution in Liberty," the Frei administration embarked on far-reaching social and economic programs, particularly in education, housing, and agrarian reform, including rural unionization of agricultural workers. By 1967, however, Frei encountered increasing opposition from leftists, who charged that his reforms were inadequate, and from conservatives, who found them excessive.

In 1970, Dr. Salvador Allende, a Marxist and member of Chile's Socialist Party, who headed the "Popular Unity" (UP) coalition of socialists, communists, radicals, and dissident Christian Democrats, was elected by a narrow margin. His program included the nationalization of most remaining private industries and banks, massive land expropriation, and collectivization. Allende's proposal also included the nationalization of U.S. interests in Chile's major copper mines. Elected with only 36% of the vote and by a plurality of only 36,000 votes, Allende never enjoyed majority support in the Chilean Congress or broad popular support. Domestic production declined; severe shortages of consumer goods, food, and manufactured products were widespread; and inflation reached 1,000% per annum. Mass demonstrations, recurring strikes, violence by both government supporters and opponents, and widespread rural unrest ensued in response to the general deterioration of the economy. By 1973, Chilean society had split into two hostile camps. A military coup overthrew Allende on September 11, 1973. As the armed forces bombarded the presidential palace,

Allende reportedly committed suicide.

# GOVERNMENT AND POLITICAL CONDITIONS

Following a coup in 1973, Chile was ruled by a military regime which lasted until 1990. The first years of the regime, headed by Gen. Augusto Pinochet, were marked by serious human rights violations. In its later years, the regime gradually permitted greater freedom of assembly, speech, and association, to include trade union activity.

In contrast to its authoritarian political rule, the military government pursued decidedly laissez faire economic policies. During its 16 years in power, Chile moved away from economic statism toward a largely free market economy that fostered an increase in domestic and foreign private investment.

General Pinochet was denied a second 8-year term as president in a national plebiscite in 1988. In December 1989, Christian Democrat Patricio Aylwin, running as the candidate of a multiparty, Concertación coalition, was elected president. In the 1993 election, Eduardo Frei Ruiz-Tagle of the Christian Democratic Party was elected president for a 6-year term leading the Concertación coalition, and took office in March 1994. Exceptionally close presidential elections in December 1999 required an unprecedented runoff election in January 2000. Ricardo Lagos Escobar of the Socialist Party and Party for Democracy led the Concertacion coalition to a narrow victory and took office in March 2000.

Chile's constitution was approved in a September 1980 national plebiscite. It entered into force in March 1981. After Pinochet's defeat in the 1988 plebiscite, the constitution was amended to ease provisions for future amendments to the constitution, cre-

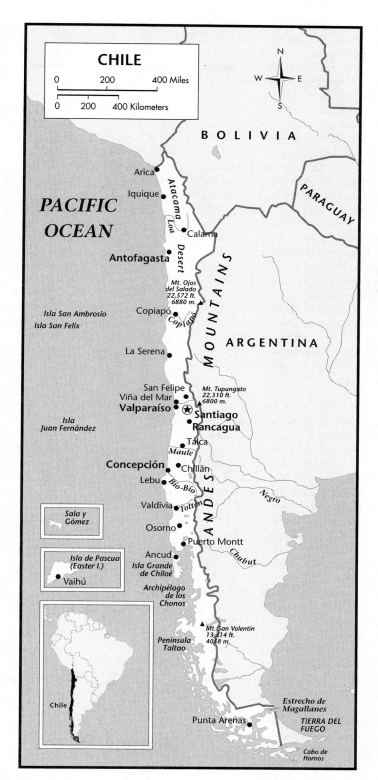

ate nine appointed or "institutional" senators, and diminish the role of the National Security Council by equalizing the number of civilian and military members—four members each. Many among Chile's political class consider these and other provisions

as "authoritarian enclaves" of the constitution and have begun to press for reform.

Chile's bicameral Congress has a 49-seat Senate—38 elected, 9 appointed, 2 for life—and a 120-member Chamber of Deputies. Deputies are elected every 4 years. Senators serve for 8 years with staggered terms. The current Senate contains 20 members from the center-left governing coalition, 18 from the rightist opposition. In March 1998, nine newly appointed institutional senators appointed in 1999, and two "senators for life," former Presidents Pinochet and Frei. (Chile's constitution provides that former presidents who have served at least 6 years shall be entitled to a lifetime senate seat.)

The last congressional elections were held in December 1997. The next congressional elections are scheduled for October 2001. The current lower house—the Chamber of Deputies—contains 70 members of the governing coalition and 50 from the rightist opposition. The Congress is located in the port city of Valparaiso, about 140 kilometers (84 mi.) west of the capital, Santiago.

Chile's congressional elections are governed by a unique binomial system that rewards coalition slates. Each coalition can run two candidates for the two Senate and two lower chamber seats apportioned to each chamber's electoral districts. Typically, the two largest coalitions split the seats in a district. Only if the leading coalition ticket out-polls the second-place coalition by a margin of more than 2-to-1 does the winning coalition gain both seats. The political parties with the largest representation in the current Chilean Congress are the centrist Christian Democrat Party and the center-right National Renewal Party. The Communist Party and the small Humanist Party failed to gain any seats in the 1997 elections.

Chile's judiciary is independent and includes a court of appeal, a system of military courts, a constitutional tribunal, and the Supreme Court.

# DEFENSE

Chile's armed forces are subject to civilian control exercised by the president through the Minister of Defense. Under the 1980 constitution, the services enjoy considerable autonomy, and the president cannot remove service commanders on his own authority.

Army. The Commander in Chief is Lt. Gen. Ricardo Izurieta. The 50,000-person army is organized into seven divisions and an air brigade.

Navy. Adm. Jorge Arancibia directs the 25,000-person navy, including 5,200 marines. Of the fleet of 29 surface vessels, only six are major combatant ships and they are based in Valparaíso. The navy operates its own aircraft for transport and patrol; there are no fighter or bomber aircraft. The Navy also operates three submarines based in Talcahuano. Air Force. Gen. Patricio Rios heads a force of 12,500. Air assets are distributed among five air brigades headquartered in Iquique, Antofagasta, Santiago, Puerto Montt, and Punta Arenas. The Air Force also operates an airbase on King George Island, Antarctica.

The Chilean police are comprised of a national, uniformed force (Carabineros) and a smaller, plainclothes investigations force. After the military coup in September 1973, the Chilean national police were incorporated into the Defense Ministry. With the return of democratic government, the police were placed under the operational control of the Interior Ministry but remain under the nominal control of the Defense Ministry. Gen. Manuel Ugarte Soto, who directs the national police force of 30,000, is responsible for law enforcement, traffic management, narcotics suppression, border control, and counter-terrorism throughout Chile.

# ECONOMY

After a decade of highly impressive growth rates, Chile experienced a moderate recession in 1999 brought on by the global economic slowdown. After averaging real GDP growth rates of around 7% in the 1990s, the economy grew 3.4% in 1998 and contracted 1.1% in 1999. The economy

has recovered in 2000, with Asian markets rebounding and copper prices edging up. GDP growth for 2001 is expected in the 5%-6% range.

The government's limited role in the economy, Chile's openness to international trade and investment, and the high domestic savings and investment rates that propelled Chile's economy to average growth rates of 8% during the decade before the recession are still in place. The 1973–90 military government sold many state-owned companies, and the three democratic governments since 1990 have continued privatization at a slower pace. Policy measures such as the privatization of the national pension system encourage domestic investment, contributing to an estimated total domestic savings rate of approximately 22% of GDP in 2000.

Unemployment peaked well above Chile's traditional 4%-6% range during the recession and is stubbornly remaining in the 8%-10% range well into the economic recovery. Despite recent labor troubles, wages have on average risen faster than inflation over the last several years as a result of higher productivity, boosting national living standards. The share of Chileans with incomes below the poverty line—roughly $4,000/year for a family of four—fell from 46% of the population in 1987 to 23% in 1998.

Maintaining a moderate inflation level is a foremost Central Bank objective. In 1996, December-to-December inflation stood at 8.2%, falling to 6.1% in 1997 and to 4.7% in 1998. The rate fell to only 2.3% during the 1999 recession. Most wage settlements and spending decisions are indexed, reducing inflation volatility. The rate for 2000 was 4.75%. The establishment of a compulsory private sector pension system in 1981 was an important step toward increasing domestic savings and the pool of investment capital. Under this system, most regular workers pay 10% of their salaries into privately managed funds. This large capital pool has been supplemented by substantial foreign investment.

Total public and private investment in the Chilean economy has remained high despite current economic difficulties. The government recognizes the necessity of private investment to boost worker productivity. The government also is encouraging diversification, including such nontraditional exports as fruit, wine, and fish to reduce the relative importance of basic traditional exports such as copper, timber, and other natural resources.

Chile's welcoming attitude toward foreign direct investment is codified in the country's Foreign Investment Law, which gives foreign investors the same treatment as Chileans. Registration is simple and transparent, and foreign investors are guaranteed access to the official foreign exchange market to repatriate their profits and capital. The Central Bank decided in May 1999 on the removal of the 1-year residency requirement on foreign capital entering Chile under Central Bank regulations, generally for portfolio investments. A modest capital control mechanism known as the "Encaje," which requires international investors to place a percentage of portfolio investment in noninterest-bearing accounts for up to 2 years, has been effectively suspended through reduction to zero of the applicable percentage; the mechanism could be resurrected depending on economic circumstances.

Total foreign direct investment flows in 2000 contracted to $3.6 billion , down from $9.2 billion in 1999, and $4.6 billion in 1998. The 2000 figure is about 13% of GDP. In 2000, Chile experienced an outflow of $1.4 billion, largely the result of diminished inward foreign investment and—for a second year running—elevated levels of Chilean direct investment abroad ($4.8 billion).

## Foreign Trade

Chile's economy is highly dependent on international trade. In 1999, exports increased to $18.3 billion from $15.6 billion in 1999, and imports increased to $16.9 billion from $14 billion the previous year. Exports accounted for about 25% of

GDP. Chile has traditionally been dependent upon copper exports; the state-owned firm CODELCO is the world's second-largest copper-producing company. Foreign private investment has developed many new mines, and the private sector now produces more copper than CODELCO. Copper output continued to increase in 2000. Nontraditional exports have grown faster than those of copper and other minerals. In 1975, nonmineral exports made up just over 30% of total exports, whereas now they account for about 60%. The most important nonmineral exports are forestry and wood products, fresh fruit and processed food, fishmeal and seafood, and other manufactured products.

Chile's export markets are fairly balanced among Europe, Asia, Latin America, and North America. The U.S., the largest-single market, takes in 17% of Chile's exports. Latin America has been the fastest-growing export market in recent years. The government actively seeks to promote Chile's exports globally. Since 1991, Chile has signed free trade agreements with several countries, including Canada, Mexico, Venezuela, Colombia, and Ecuador. An association agreement with MERCOSUR—Argentina, Brazil, Paraguay, and Uruguay—went into effect in October 1996. Chile, a member of the Asia-Pacific Economic Cooperation (APEC) organization, is seeking to boost commercial ties to Asian markets. Chile has begun free trade agreement discussions with the European Union.

In keeping with its trade-oriented development strategy, Chile is currently in negotiations with the U.S. on a free trade agreement; U.S. negotiating ability has been constrained in the absence of "fast-track" negotiating authority. Chile's 1996 free trade agreement with Canada was modeled largely on NAFTA in anticipation of an eventual trade pact with the United States; similarly, Chile broadened its bilateral free trade agreement with Mexico in August 1998. Chile has been a strong proponent of pressing ahead on negotiations for a Free Trade Area of the Americas (FTAA) agreement.

After growing for several years, imports were down in 1998 and 1999, reflecting reduced consumer demand and deferred investment. Imports have rebounded in 2000 and are up 19% over 1999; capital goods make up about 22% of total imports. The United States is Chile's largest-single supplier, supplying 18.5% of the country's imports in 2000, down from 21% in 1999. Chile unilaterally is lowering its across-the-board import tariff— for all countries with which it does not have a trade agreement—by a percentage point each year until it reaches 6% in 2003. Higher effective tariffs are charged only on imports of wheat, wheat flour, vegetable oils, and sugar as a result of a system of import price bands. Finance

Chile's financial sector has grown faster than other areas of the economy over the last few years; a banking law reform approved in 1997 broadened the scope of permissible foreign activity for Chilean banks. Domestically, Chileans have enjoyed the recent introduction of new financial tools such as home equity loans, currency futures and options, factoring, leasing, and debit cards.

The introduction of these new products has been accompanied by increased use of traditional instruments such as loans and credit cards. Chile's private pension system, with assets worth roughly $36 billion at the end of September 2000, has provided an important source of investment capital for the stock market. Chile has maintained one of the best credit ratings in Latin America despite the 1999 economic slump. In recent years, many Chilean companies have sought to raise capital abroad due to the relatively lower interest rates outside of Chile. There are three main ways Chilean firms raise funds abroad: bank loans, issuance of bonds, and the selling of stock on U.S. markets through American Depository Receipts (ADRs). Nearly all of the funds raised go to finance investment. The government is rapidly paying down its foreign debt. The combined public and private foreign debt was roughly 50% of GDP at the end of 2000, low by Latin American standards.

# FOREIGN RELATIONS

With its return to democracy in 1990, Chile became an active participant in the international political arena. It is an active member of the Rio Group, and it rejoined the Non-Aligned Movement. Chile was a driving force in the World Summit for Social Development held in Copenhagen in March 1995. Chile is an active member of the United Nations and the UN family of agencies, serving on the UN Security Council from 1995–97. Chile participates in UN peacekeeping activities.

The Chilean Government has diplomatic relations with most countries, including Cuba. Chile maintains only consular relations with Bolivia; Chile's acquisition of territory during the War of the Pacific (1879–83) continues adversely to influence its relations with Bolivia. Chile's association with the MERCOSUR countries in 1996 and its continuing interest in hemispheric free trade, as well as its membership in the Asia-Pacific Economic Cooperation grouping, auger well for even closer international economic ties in the future. Politically, Chile has been one of the most active countries in supporting the Summit of the Americas process, hosting the second Summit of the Americas in Santiago, April 1998.

## Principal Government Officials

For up-to-date information on Principal Government Officials, see the Chiefs of State and Cabinet Members of Foreign Governments section starting on page 1.

Chile maintains an embassy in the United States at: 1140 Connecticut Avenue, NW, Washington, DC 20036, Tel: 202–785–1746, Fax: 202–659–9624, Email: embassy@embassy-ofchile.org, Website: http://www.chile-usa.org

# U.S.-CHILEAN RELATIONS

Relations between the United States and Chile are better now than at any other time in history. The U.S. Government applauded the rebirth of democratic practices in Chile in the late 1980s and early 1990s and sees the maintenance of a vibrant democracy and a healthy and sustainable economy as among the most important U.S. interests in Chile. The two governments consult frequently on issues of mutual concern, and dialogue takes place in five major bilateral commissions—covering defense, agriculture, trade and investment, and bilateral issues.

Many other prominent Americans and senior U.S. officials visited Chile during the period 1995–2000, including Hillary Rodham Clinton; former-Presidents Carter, Bush, and Ford; former Secretary of State Christopher; Secretary of State Albright; Secretary of Defense Cohen; other Members of the Cabinet and Congress; and senior members of the U.S. military, addressing issues ranging from education to international trade.

## U.S. Embassy Functions

In addition to working closely with Chilean Government officials to strengthen our bilateral relationship, the U.S. Embassy in Santiago provides a wide range of services to U.S. citizens and businesses in Chile. (Please see the embassy's home page http://www.usembassy.cl/ for details of these services.) The embassy also is the locus for a number of American community activities in the Santiago area. Public Affairs works closely with universities and NGOs on a variety of programs of bilateral interest. Of special note are extensive U.S. Speaker, International Visitor, and Fulbright programs. Themes of particular interest include judicial reform, environmental concerns, and promotion of trade. Attaches at the embassy from the Foreign Commercial Service and Foreign Agriculture Service work closely with the hundreds of U.S. companies which maintain offices in Chile. These officers provide information on Chilean trade and industry regulations and administer several programs intended to support U.S. companies starting or maintaining business ventures in Chile.

The Consular section of the embassy provides vital services to the more than 10,000 U.S. citizens residing in Chile. Among other services, the Consular section assists Americans who wish to participate in U.S. elections while abroad and provides U.S. tax information. Besides the U.S. citizens residents in Chile, more than 120,000 U.S. citizens visit annually. The Consular section offers passport and emergency services to U.S. tourists as needed during their stay in Chile. It also issues over 60,000 visitors' visas annually to Chilean citizens who plan to travel to the U.S.

The Public Affairs Office works daily with Chilean media, which has a keen interest in bilateral and regional relations. It also assists visiting foreign media, including U.S. journalists, and is regularly involved in press events for high level visitors. Recent issues of great interest to the media include U.S. views on the evolving Pinochet case, and other cases associated with his regime.

## Principal U.S. Embassy Officials

**For up-to-date information on Principal U.S. Officials, see the U.S. Embassies, Consulates, and Foreign Service section starting on page 139.**

For up-to-date information on Principal U.S. Officials, see the U.S. Embassies, Consulates, and Foreign Service section starting on page 139.

The U.S. Embassy and Consulate in Santiago are located at 2800 Andres Bello
Avenue, Las Condes, (tel. 562–232–2600; fax: 562–330–3710).
The mailing address is Casilla 27-D, Santiago, Chile. The embassy's home page is at: http://www.usembassy.cl.

## Other Contact Information

### American Chamber of Commerce in Chile
Avenida Presidente Kennedy 5735, Oficina 201
El Torre Poniente, Las Condes
Santiago
Tel: 562–290–9700
Fax: 562–212–2620
Email: amcham@amchamchile.cl
Website: http://www.amchamchile.cl

### U.S. Department of Commerce
Trade Information Center
International Trade Administration
14th and Constitution Avenue, NW
Washington, DC 20230
Tel: 800-USA-TRADE
Fax: 202–482–4726
Home page: http://www.ita.doc.gov

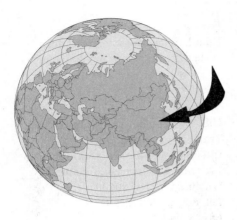

# CHINA
November 2000

Official Name:
## People's Republic of China

# PROFILE

## Geography

**Total Area:** 9,596,960 sq. km. (about 3.7 million sq. mi.).
**Cities:** Capital—Beijing. Other major cities—Shanghai, Tianjin, Shenyang, Wuhan, Guangzhou, Chongqing, Harbin, Chengdu.
**Terrain:** Plains, deltas, and hills in east; mountains, high plateaus, deserts in west.
**Climate:** Tropical in south to subarctic in north.

## People

**Nationality:** Noun and adjective—Chinese (singular and plural).
**Population:** (1998 est.) 1.251 billion.
**Population growth rate:** (1997 est.) 0.93%.
**Health:** (1997 est.) Infant mortality rate—37.9/1,000. Life expectancy—70.0 years (overall); 68.6 years for males, 71.5 years for females.
**Ethnic Groups:** Han Chinese—91.9%; Zhuang, Manchu, Hui, Miao, Uygur, Yi, Mongolian, Tibetan, Buyi, Korean, and other nationalities—8.1%.
**Religion:** Officially atheist; Taoism, Buddhism, Islam, Christianity.
**Language:** Mandarin (Putonghua), plus many local dialects.
**Education:** Years compulsory—9.

**Literacy rate:** 82%.
**Work force:** (699 million) Agriculture and forestry—60%; industry and commerce—25%; other—15%.

## Government

**Type:** Communist Party-led state.
**Constitution:** December 4, 1982.
**Independence:** Unification under the Qin (Ch'in) Dynasty 221 BC; Qing (Ch'ing or Manchu) Dynasty replaced by a republic on February 12, 1912; People's Republic established October 1, 1949.
**Branches:** Executive—president, vice president, State Council, premier. Legislative—unicameral National People's Congress. Judicial—Supreme People's Court.
**Administrative divisions:** 23 provinces (the P.R.C. considers Taiwan to be its 23rd province); 5 autonomous regions, including Tibet; 5 municipalities directly under the State Council.
**Political parties:** Chinese Communist Party, more than 58 million members; eight minor parties under communist supervision.
**Suffrage:** Universal at 18.

## Economy

**GDP:** (1999 est., based on 1999 IMF statistics) $991.2 billion (exchange rate based).
**Per capita GDP:** (1999 est.) $782.4 (exchange rate based).

**GDP real growth rate:** (1999) 7.1%.
**Natural resources:** Coal, iron ore, crude oil, mercury, tin, tungsten, antimony, manganese, molybdenum, vanadium, magnesite, aluminum, lead, zinc, uranium, hydropower potential (world's largest).
**Agriculture:** Products—Among the world's largest producers of rice, potatoes, sorghum, peanuts, tea, millet, barley; commercial crops include cotton, other fibers, and oilseeds; produces variety of livestock products.
**Industry:** Types—iron, steel, coal, machinery, light industrial products, armaments, petroleum.
**Trade:** (1999) Exports—$194.7 billion: mainly textiles, garments, electrical machinery, furniture, foodstuffs, chemicals, footwear, minerals. Main partners—Hong Kong, Japan, U.S., South Korea, Germany, Singapore, Netherlands. Imports—$158.5 billion: mainly industrial machinery, electrical equipment, chemicals, textiles, steel. Main partners—Japan, Taiwan, U.S., South Korea, Hong Kong, Germany, Russia.

# PEOPLE

## Ethnic Groups

The largest ethnic group is the Han Chinese, who constitute about 91.9%

of the total population. The remaining 8.1% are Zhuang (16 million), Manchu (10 million), Hui (9 million), Miao (8 million), Uygur (7 million), Yi (7 million), Mongolian (5 million), Tibetan (5 million), Buyi (3 million), Korean (2 million), and other ethnic minorities.

## Language
There are seven major Chinese dialects and many subdialects. Mandarin (or Putonghua), the predominant dialect, is spoken by more than 70% of the population. It is taught in all schools and is the medium of government. About two-thirds of the Han ethnic group are native speakers of Mandarin; the rest, concentrated in southwest and southeast China, speak one of the six other major Chinese dialects. Non-Chinese languages spoken widely by ethnic minorities include Mongolian, Tibetan, Uygur and other Turkic languages (in Xinjiang), and Korean (in the northeast).

## The Pinyin System of Romanization
On January 1, 1979, the Chinese Government officially adopted the pinyin system for spelling Chinese names and places in Roman letters. A system of Romanization invented by the Chinese, pinyin has long been widely used in China on street and commercial signs as well as in elementary Chinese textbooks as an aid in learning Chinese characters. Variations of pinyin also are used as the written forms of several minority languages.

Pinyin has now replaced other conventional spellings in China's English-language publications. The U.S. Government also has adopted the pinyin system for all names and places in China. For example, the capital of China is now spelled "Beijing" rather than "Peking."

## Religion
Religion plays a significant part in the lives of many Chinese. Buddhism is most widely practiced, with an estimated 100 million adherents. Traditional Taoism also is practiced.

Official figures indicate that there are 18 million Muslims, 4 million Catholics, and 10 million Protestants; unofficial estimates are much higher.

While the Chinese Constitution affirms religious toleration, the Chinese Government places restrictions on religious practice outside officially recognized organizations. Only two Christian organizations—a Catholic church without ties to Rome and the "Three-Self-Patriotic" Protestant church—are sanctioned by the Chinese Government. Unauthorized churches have sprung up in many parts of the country, and unofficial religious practice is flourishing. In some regions authorities have tried to control activities of these unregistered churches. In other regions registered and unregistered groups are treated similarly by authorities, and congregates worship in both types of churches.

China hosted a delegation of distinguished American religious leaders in February 1998. The religious leaders met with President Jiang Zemin, conveyed U.S. views on religious freedom, and traveled to numerous sites, including Tibet.

## Population Policy
With a population of more than 1.251 billion and an estimated growth rate of 0.93%, China is very concerned about its population growth and has attempted with mixed results to implement a strict family planning policy. The government's goal is one child per family, with exceptions in rural areas and for ethnic minorities. Official government policy opposes forced abortion or sterilization, but allegations of coercion continue as local officials strive to meet population targets. Recent international efforts, including those funded by the UN Population Fund (UNFPA), are demonstrating to government officials that a voluntary, noncoercive approach to family planning can be effective in promoting sustainable population growth. The government's goal is to stabilize the population early in the 21st century, although some current projections estimate a population of 1.6 billion by 2025.

# HISTORY

## Dynastic Period
China is the oldest continuous major world civilization, with records dating back about 3,500 years. Successive dynasties developed a system of bureaucratic control, which gave the agrarian-based Chinese an advantage over neighboring nomadic and hill cultures. Chinese civilization was further strengthened by the development of a Confucian state ideology and a common written language that bridged the gaps among the country's many local languages and dialects. Whenever China was conquered by nomadic tribes, as it was by the Mongols in the 13th century, the conquerors sooner or later adopted the ways of the "higher" Chinese civilization and staffed the bureaucracy with Chinese.

The last dynasty was established in 1644, when the nomadic Manchus overthrew the native Ming dynasty and established the Qing (Ch'ing) dynasty with Beijing as its capital. At great expense in blood and treasure, the Manchus over the next half-century gained control of many border areas, including Xinjiang, Yunnan, Tibet, Mongolia, and Taiwan. The success of the early Qing period was based on the combination of Manchu martial prowess and traditional Chinese bureaucratic skills.

During the 19th century, Qing control weakened, and prosperity diminished. China suffered massive social strife, economic stagnation, explosive population growth, and Western penetration and influence. The Taiping and Nian rebellions, along with a Russian-supported Muslim separatist movement in Xinjiang, drained Chinese resources and almost toppled the dynasty. Britain's desire to continue its illegal opium trade with China collided with imperial edicts prohibiting the addictive drug, and the First Opium War erupted in 1840. China lost the war; subsequently, Britain and other Western powers, including the United States, forcibly occupied "concessions" and gained

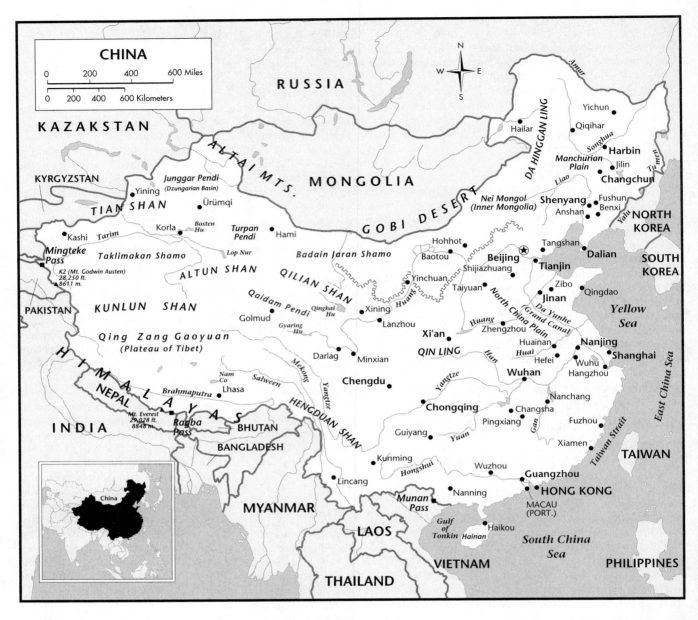

special commercial privileges. Hong
Kong was ceded to Britain in 1842
under the Treaty of Nanking, and in
1898, when the Opium Wars finally
ended, Britain executed a 99-year
lease of the New Territories, significantly expanding the size of the Hong
Kong colony.

As time went on, the Western powers,
wielding superior military technology, gained more economic and political privileges. Reformist Chinese
officials argued for the adoption of
Western technology to strengthen the
dynasty and counter Western
advances, but the Qing court played

down both the Western threat and
the benefits of Western technology.

## Early 20th Century China

Frustrated by the Qing court's resistance to reform, young officials, military officers, and students—inspired
by the revolutionary ideas of Sun Yat-
sen—began to advocate the overthrow of the Qing dynasty and creation of a republic. A revolutionary
military uprising on October 10,
1911, led to the abdication of the last
Qing monarch. As part of a compromise to overthrow the dynasty without a civil war, the revolutionaries

and reformers allowed high Qing officials to retain prominent positions in
the new republic. One of these figures, General Yuan Shikai, was chosen as the republic's first president.
Before his death in 1916, Yuan unsuccessfully attempted to name himself
emperor. His death left the republican government all but shattered,
ushering in the era of the "warlords"
during which China was ruled and
ravaged by shifting coalitions of competing provincial military leaders.

In the 1920s, Sun Yat-sen established
a revolutionary base in south China
and set out to unite the fragmented
nation. With Soviet assistance, he

organized the Kuomintang (KMT or "Chinese Nationalist People's Party"), and entered into an alliance with the fledgling Chinese Communist Party (CCP). After Sun's death in 1925, one of his protégés, Chiang Kai-shek, seized control of the KMT and succeeded in bringing most of south and central China under its rule. In 1927, Chiang turned on the CCP and executed many of its leaders. The remnants fled into the mountains of eastern China. In 1934, driven out of their mountain bases, the CCP's forces embarked on a "Long March" across China's most desolate terrain to the northwest, where they established a guerrilla base at Yan'an in Shaanxi Province.

During the "Long March," the communists reorganized under a new leader, Mao Zedong (Mao Tse-tung). The bitter struggle between the KMT and the CCP continued openly or clandestinely through the 14-year long Japanese invasion (1931-45), even though the two parties nominally formed a united front to oppose the Japanese invaders in 1937. The war between the two parties resumed after the Japanese defeat in 1945. By 1949, the CCP occupied most of the country.

Chiang Kai-shek fled with the remnants of his KMT government and military forces to Taiwan, where he proclaimed Taipei to be China's "provisional capital" and vowed to reconquer the Chinese mainland. The KMT authorities on Taiwan still call themselves the "Republic of China."

## The People's Republic of China

In Beijing, on October 1, 1949, Mao Zedong proclaimed the founding of the People's Republic of China. The new government assumed control of a people exhausted by two generations of war and social conflict, and an economy ravaged by high inflation and disrupted transportation links. A new political and economic order modeled on the Soviet example was quickly installed.

In the early 1950s, China undertook a massive economic and social recon-

struction. The new leaders gained popular support by curbing inflation, restoring the economy, and rebuilding many war-damaged industrial plants. The CCP's authority reached into almost every phase of Chinese life. Party control was assured by large, politically loyal security and military forces; a government apparatus responsive to party direction; and ranks of party members in labor, women's, and other mass organizations.

## The "Great Leap Forward" and the Sino-Soviet Split

In 1958, Mao broke with the Soviet model and announced a new economic program, the "Great Leap Forward," aimed at rapidly raising industrial and agricultural production. Giant cooperatives (communes) were formed, and "backyard factories" dotted the Chinese landscape. The results were disastrous. Normal market mechanisms were disrupted, agricultural production fell behind, and China's people exhausted themselves producing what turned out to be shoddy, unsalable goods. Within a year, starvation appeared even in fertile agricultural areas. From 1960 to 1961, the combination of poor planning during the Great Leap Forward and bad weather resulted in famine.

The already strained Sino-Soviet relationship deteriorated sharply in 1959, when the Soviets started to restrict the flow of scientific and technological information to China. The dispute escalated, and the Soviets withdrew all of their personnel from China in August 1960. In 1960, the Soviets and the Chinese began to have disputes openly in international forums.

## The Cultural Revolution

In the early 1960s, State President Liu Shaoqi and his protégé, Party General Secretary Deng Xiaoping, took over direction of the party and adopted pragmatic economic policies at odds with Mao's revolutionary vision. Dissatisfied with China's new direction and his own reduced

authority, Party Chairman Mao launched a massive political attack on Liu, Deng, and other pragmatists in the spring of 1966. The new movement, the "Great Proletarian Cultural Revolution," was unprecedented in communist history. For the first time, a section of the Chinese communist leadership sought to rally popular opposition against another leadership group. China was set on a course of political and social anarchy, which lasted the better part of a decade.

In the early stages of the Cultural Revolution, Mao and his "closest comrade in arms," National Defense Minister Lin Biao, charged Liu, Deng, and other top party leaders with dragging China back toward capitalism. Radical youth organizations, called Red Guards, attacked party and state organizations at all levels, seeking out leaders who would not bend to the radical wind. In reaction to this turmoil, some local People's Liberation Army (PLA) commanders and other officials maneuvered to outwardly back Mao and the radicals while actually taking steps to rein in local radical activity.

Gradually, Red Guard and other radical activity subsided, and the Chinese political situation stabilized along complex factional lines. The leadership conflict came to a head in September 1971, when Party Vice Chairman and Defense Minister Lin Biao reportedly tried to stage a coup against Mao; Lin Biao allegedly later died in a plane crash in Mongolia.

In the aftermath of the Lin Biao incident, many officials criticized and dismissed during 1966-69 were reinstated. Chief among these was Deng Xiaoping, who reemerged in 1973 and was confirmed in 1975 in the concurrent posts of Politburo Standing Committee member, PLA Chief of Staff, and Vice Premier. The ideological struggle between more pragmatic, veteran party officials and the radicals reemerged with a vengeance in late 1975. Mao's wife, Jiang Qing, and three close Cultural Revolution associates (later dubbed the "Gang of Four") launched a media campaign against Deng. In January 1976, Premier Zhou Enlai, a popular political figure, died of cancer. On April 5, Beijing citizens staged a spontaneous demonstration in Tiananmen Square in Zhou's memory, with strong political overtones in support of Deng. The authorities forcibly suppressed the demonstration. Deng was blamed for the disorder and stripped of all official positions, although he retained his party membership.

## The Post-Mao Era

Mao's death in September 1976 removed a towering figure from Chinese politics and set off a scramble for succession. Former Minister of Pubic Security Hua Guofeng was quickly confirmed as Party Chairman and Premier. A month after Mao's death, Hua, backed by the PLA, arrested Jiang Qing and other members of the "Gang of Four." After extensive deliberations, the Chinese Communist Party leadership reinstated Deng Xiaoping to all of his previous posts at the 11th Party Congress in August 1977. Deng then led the effort to place government control in the hands of veteran party officials opposed to the radical excesses of the previous two decades.

The new, pragmatic leadership emphasized economic development and renounced mass political movements. At the pivotal December 1978 Third Plenum (of the 11th Party Congress Central Committee), the leadership adopted economic reform policies aimed at expanding rural income and incentives, encouraging experiments in enterprise autonomy, reducing central planning, and establishing direct foreign investment in China. The plenum also decided to accelerate the pace of legal reform, culminating in the passage of several new legal codes by the National People's Congress in June 1979.

After 1979, the Chinese leadership moved toward more pragmatic positions in almost all fields. The party encouraged artists, writers, and journalists to adopt more critical approaches, although open attacks on party authority were not permitted. In late 1980, Mao's Cultural Revolution was officially proclaimed a catas-

trophe. Hua Guofeng, a protégé of Mao, was replaced as Premier in 1980 by reformist Sichuan party chief Zhao Ziyang and as party General Secretary in 1981 by the even more reformist Communist Youth League Chairman Hu Yaobang.

Reform policies brought great improvements in the standard of living, especially for urban workers and for farmers who took advantage of opportunities to diversify crops and establish village industries. Literature and the arts blossomed, and Chinese intellectuals established extensive links with scholars in other countries.

At the same time, however, political dissent as well as social problems such as inflation, urban migration, and prostitution emerged. Although students and intellectuals urged greater reforms, some party elders increasingly questioned the pace and the ultimate goals of the reform program. In December 1986, student demonstrators, taking advantage of the loosening political atmosphere, staged protests against the slow pace of reform, confirming party elders' fear that the current reform program was leading to social instability. Hu Yaobang, a protégé of Deng and a leading advocate of reform, was blamed for the protests and forced to resign as CCP General Secretary in January 1987. Premier Zhao Ziyang was made General Secretary and Li Peng, former Vice Premier and Minister of Electric Power and Water Conservancy, was made Premier.

## 1989 Student Movement and Tiananmen Square

After Zhao became the party General Secretary, the economic and political reforms he had championed came under increasing attack. His proposal in May 1988 to accelerate price reform led to widespread popular complaints about rampant inflation and gave opponents of rapid reform the opening to call for greater centralization of economic controls and stricter prohibitions against Western influence. This precipitated a political debate, which grew more heated through the winter of 1988-89.

The death of Hu Yaobang on April 15, 1989, coupled with growing economic hardship caused by high inflation, provided the backdrop for a large-scale protest movement by students, intellectuals, and other parts of a disaffected urban population. University students and other citizens in Beijing camped out at Tiananmen Square to mourn Hu's death and to protest against those who would slow reform. Their protests, which grew despite government efforts to contain them, called for an end to official corruption and for defense of freedoms guaranteed by the Chinese Constitution. Protests also spread through many other cities, including Shanghai and Guangzhou.

Martial law was declared on May 20, 1989. Late on June 3 and early on the morning of June 4, military units were brought into Beijing. They used armed force to clear demonstrators from the streets. There are no official estimates of deaths in Beijing, but most observers believe that casualties numbered in the hundreds. After June 4, while foreign governments expressed horror at the brutal suppression of the demonstrators, the central government eliminated remaining sources of organized opposition, detained large numbers of protesters, and required political reeducation not only for students but also for large numbers of party cadre and government officials.

Following the resurgence of conservatives in the aftermath of June 4, economic reform slowed until given new impetus by Deng Xiaoping's dramatic visit to southern China in early 1992. Deng's renewed push for a market-oriented economy received official sanction at the 14th Party Congress later in the year as a number of younger, reform-minded leaders began their rise to top positions. Deng and his supporters argued that managing the economy in a way that increased living standards should be China's primary policy objective, even if "capitalist" measures were adopted. Subsequent to the visit, the Communist Party Politburo publicly issued an endorsement of Deng's policies of economic openness. Though not completely eschewing political reform, China has consistently placed overwhelming priority on the opening of its economy.

## Third Generation of Leaders

Deng's health deteriorated in the years prior to his death in 1997. During that time, President Jiang Zemin and other members of his generation gradually assumed control of the day-to-day functions of government. This "third generation" leadership governs collectively with President Jiang at the center.

In March 1998, Jiang was re-elected President during the 9th National People's Congress. Premier Li Peng was constitutionally required to step down from that post. He was elected to the chairmanship of the National People's Congress. Zhu Rongji was selected to replace Li as Premier.

China is firmly committed to economic reform and opening to the outside world. The Chinese leadership has identified reform of state industries as a government priority. Government strategies for achieving that goal include largescale privatization of unprofitable state-owned enterprises. The leadership also has downsized the government bureaucracy.

# GOVERNMENT

## Chinese Communist Party

The more than 63 million member CCP, authoritarian in structure and ideology, continues to dominate government. Nevertheless, China's population, geographical vastness, and social diversity frustrate attempts to rule by fiat from Beijing. Central leaders must increasingly build consensus for new policies among party members, local and regional leaders, influential nonparty members, and the population at large.

In periods of relative liberalization, the influence of people and organiza-

tions outside the formal party structure has tended to increase, particularly in the economic realm. This phenomenon is apparent today in the rapidly developing coastal region. Nevertheless, in all-important government, economic, and cultural institutions in China, party committees work to see that party and state policy guidance is followed and that nonparty members do not create autonomous organizations that could challenge party rule. Party control is tightest in government offices and in urban economic, industrial, and cultural settings; it is considerably looser in the rural areas, where the majority of the people live.

Theoretically, the party's highest body is the Party Congress, which is supposed to meet at least once every 5 years. The primary organs of power in the Communist Party include:

The Politburo Standing Committee, which currently consists of seven members; The Politburo, consisting of 22 full members (including the members of the Politburo Standing Committee); The Secretariat, the principal administrative mechanism of the CCP, headed by the General Secretary; The Military Commission; and The Discipline Inspection Commission, which is charged with rooting out corruption and malfeasance among party cadres.

## State Structure

The Chinese Government has always been subordinate to the Chinese Communist Party (CCP); its role is to implement party policies. The primary organs of state power are the National People's Congress (NPC), the President, and the State Council. Members of the State Council include Premier Zhu Rongji, a variable number of vice premiers (now four), five state councilors (protocol equal of vice premiers but with narrower portfolios), and 29 ministers and heads of State Council commissions.

Under the Chinese Constitution, the NPC is the highest organ of state power in China. It meets annually for about 2 weeks to review and approve major new policy directions, laws, the

budget, and major personnel changes. These initiatives are presented to the NPC for consideration by the State Council after previous endorsement by the Communist Party's Central Committee. Although the NPC generally approves State Council policy and personnel recommendations, various NPC committees hold active debate in closed sessions, and changes may be made to accommodate alternate views.

When the NPC is not in session, its permanent organ, the Standing Committee, exercises state power.

## Principal Government and Party Officials

**For up-to-date information on Principal Government Officials, see the Chiefs of State and Cabinet Members of Foreign Governments section starting on page 1.**

# POLITICAL CONDITIONS

## Legal System

The government's efforts to promote rule of law are significant and ongoing. After the Cultural Revolution, China's leaders aimed to develop a legal system to restrain abuses of official authority and revolutionary excesses. In 1982, the National People's Congress adopted a new state constitution that emphasized the rule of law under which even party leaders are theoretically held accountable.

Since 1979, when the drive to establish a functioning legal system began, more than 300 laws and regulations, most of them in the economic area, have been promulgated. The use of mediation committees—informed groups of citizens who resolve about 90% of China's civil disputes and some minor criminal cases at no cost to the parties—is one innovative device. There are more than 800,000 such committees in both rural and urban areas.

Legal reform became a government priority in the 1990s. Legislation designed to modernize and professionalize the nation's lawyers, judges, and prisons was enacted. The 1994 Administrative Procedure Law allows citizens to sue officials for abuse of authority or malfeasance. In addition, the criminal law and the criminal procedures laws were amended to introduce significant reforms. The criminal law amendments abolished the crime of "counter-revolutionary" activity, while criminal procedures reforms encouraged establishment of a more transparent, adversarial trial process. The Chinese Constitution and laws provide for fundamental human rights, including due process, but these are often ignored in practice.

## Human Rights

China has acknowledged in principle the importance of protection of human rights and has taken steps to bring its human rights practices into conformity with international norms. Among these steps are signature in October 1997 of the International Covenant on Economic, Social, and Cultural Rights and signature in October 1998 of the International Covenant on Civil and Political Rights. These two covenants have been signed but not yet ratified. China also has expanded dialogue with foreign governments. These positive steps not withstanding, serious problems remain. The government restricts freedom of assembly, expression, and the press and represses dissent.

# ECONOMY

## Economic Reforms

Since 1979, China has been engaged in an effort to reform its economy. The Chinese leadership has adopted a pragmatic perspective on many political and socioeconomic problems and

has sharply reduced the role of ideology in economic policy. Consumer welfare, economic productivity, and political stability are considered indivisible. The government has emphasized raising personal income and consumption and introducing new management systems to help increase productivity.

The government also has focused on foreign trade as a major vehicle for economic growth. In the 1980s, China tried to combine central planning with market-oriented reforms to increase productivity, living standards, and technological quality without exacerbating inflation, unemployment, and budget deficits. China pursued agricultural reforms, dismantling the commune system and introducing the household responsibility system that provided peasants greater decisionmaking in agricultural activities. The government also encouraged nonagricultural activities such as village enterprises in rural areas, and promoted more self-management for state-owned enterprises, increased competition in the marketplace, and facilitated direct contact between Chinese and foreign trading enterprises. China also relied more upon foreign financing and imports.

During the 1980s, these reforms led to average annual rates of growth of 10% in agricultural and industrial output. Rural per capita real income doubled. China became self-sufficient in grain production; rural industries accounted for 23% of agricultural output, helping absorb surplus labor in the countryside. The variety of light industrial and consumer goods increased. Reforms began in the fiscal, financial, banking, price setting, and labor systems.

However, by the late 1980s, the economy had become overheated with increasing rates of inflation. At the end of 1988, in reaction to a surge of inflation caused by accelerated price reforms, the leadership introduced an austerity program.

China's economy regained momentum in the early 1990s. Deng Xiaoping's Chinese New Year's visit to

southern China in 1992 gave economic reforms new impetus. The 14th Party Congress later in the year backed up Deng's renewed push for market reforms, stating that China's key task in the 1990s was to create a "socialist market economy." Continuity in the political system but bolder reform in the economic system were announced as the hallmarks of the 10-year development plan for the 1990s.

During 1993, output and prices were accelerating, investment outside the state budget was soaring, and economic expansion was fueled by the introduction of more than 2,000 special economic zones (SEZs) and the influx of foreign capital that the SEZs facilitated. Fearing hyperinflation, Chinese authorities called in speculative loans, raised interest rates, and reevaluated investment projects. The growth rate was thus tempered, and the inflation rate dropped from over 17% in 1995 to 8% in early 1996. In 1996, the Chinese economy continued to grow at a rapid pace, at about 9.5%, accompanied by low inflation; the economy has been slowing since then, with official growth of 8.9% in 1997, 7.8% in 1998, and 7.1% for 1999.

Despite China's impressive economic development during the past two decades, reforming the state enterprise sector and modernizing the banking system remain major hurdles. More than half of China's large state-owned enterprises are inefficient and reporting losses. During the 15th National Congress of the Chinese Communist Party that met in September 1997, President Jiang Zemin announced plans to sell, merge, or close the vast majority of state-owned enterprises in his call for increased "public ownership" (privatization in euphemistic terms). The 9th National People's Congress endorsed the plans at its March 1998 session.

## Agriculture

Most of China's labor force is engaged in agriculture, even though only under 10% of the land is suitable for cultivation. There are 329 million

Chinese farmers—roughly half the work force—mostly laboring on small pieces of land relative to U.S. farmers. Virtually all arable land is used for food crops, and China is among the world's largest producers of rice, potatoes, sorghum, millet, barley, peanuts, tea, and pork. Major non-food crops, including cotton, other fibers, and oil seeds, furnish China with a large proportion of its foreign trade revenue. Agricultural exports, such as vegetables and fruits, fish and shellfish, grain and grain products, and meat and meat products, are exported to Hong Kong. Yields are high because of intensive cultivation, but China hopes to further increase agricultural production through improved plant stocks, fertilizers, and technology.

## Industry

Major state industries are iron, steel, coal, machine building, light industrial products, armaments, and textiles. These industries completed a decade of reform (1979-89) with little substantial management change. The 1999 industrial census revealed that there were 7,930,000 industrial enterprises at the end of 1999; total employment in state-owned industrial enterprises was approximately 24 million. The automobile industry is expected to grow rapidly in the coming decade, as is the petrochemical industry. Machinery and electronic products have become China's main exports.

## Energy and Mineral Resources

Over the past decade China has managed to keep its energy growth rate at just half the rate of GDP growth, a considerable achievement. Although energy consumption slumped in absolute terms and economic growth slowed during 1998, China's total energy consumption may double by 2020 according to some projections. China is expected to add approximately 15,000 megawatts of generating capacity a year, with 20% of that coming from foreign suppliers.

Beijing, due in large part to environmental concerns, would like to shift China's current energy mix from a heavy reliance on coal (which accounts for 75% of China's energy) toward greater reliance on oil, natural gas, renewable energy, and nuclear power. China has closed some 30,000 coal mines over the past 5 years to cut overproduction. This has reduced coal production by over 25%.

Since 1993, China has been a net importer of oil; today imported oil accounts for 20% of the processed crude in China. Net imports are expected to rise to 3.5 million barrels per day by 2010. China is interested in developing oil imports from Central Asia and has invested in Kazhakstan oil fields. Beijing is particularly interested in increasing China's natural gas production (currently just 10% of oil production) and is incorporating a natural gas strategy in its 10th 5-year plan (2001-2005) with the goal of expanding gas use from its current 2% share of China's energy production to 4% by 2005 (gas accounts for 25% of U.S. energy production).

Beijing also intends to continue to improve energy efficiency and promote the use of clean coal technology. Only one-fifth of the new coal power plant capacity installed from 1995 to 2000 included desulphurization equipment. Interest in renewable sources of energy is growing, but except for hydropower, their contribution to the overall energy mix is unlikely to rise above 1%-2% in the near future.

China's energy section continues to be hampered by difficulties in obtaining funding, including long-term financing, and by market balkanization due to local protectionism that prevents more efficient large plants from achieving economies of scale.

## Environment

A harmful by-product of China's rapid industrial development has been increased pollution. A 1998 World Health Organization report on air quality in 272 cities worldwide concluded that seven of the 10 most polluted cities were in China. According to Chinas own evaluation, two-thirds of the 338 cities for which air quality data are available are considered polluted—two-thirds of them moderately or severely so. Respiratory and heart diseases related to air pollution are the leading cause of death in China. Almost all of the nation's rivers are considered polluted to some degree, and half of the population lacks access to clean water. Ninety percent of urban water bodies are severely polluted. Water scarcity also is an issue; for example, severe water scarcity in Northern China has forced the government to plan a largescale diversion of water from the Yangtze to northern cities, including Beijing and Tianjin. Acid rain falls on 30% of the country. Various studies estimate pollution costs the Chinese economy about 7% of GDP each year.

China's leaders are increasingly paying attention to the country's severe environmental problems. In March 1998, the State Environmental Protection Administration (SEPA) was officially upgraded to a ministry-level agency, reflecting the growing importance the Chinese Government places on environmental protection. In recent years, China has strengthened its environmental legislation and made some progress in stemming environmental deterioration. In 1999, China invested more than 1% of GDP in environmental protection, a proportion that will likely increase in coming years. During the 10th 5-Year Plan China plans to reduce total emissions by 10%. Beijing, in particular, is investing heavily in pollution control as part of its campaign to host the 2008 Olympic Games.

China is an active participant in the climate change talks and other multilateral environmental negotiations. It is a signatory to the Basel Convention governing the transport and disposal of hazardous waste and the Montreal Protocol for the Protection of the Ozone Layer, as well as the Convention on International Trade in Endangered Species and other major environmental agreements.

The question of environmental impacts associated with the Three Gorges Dam project has generated controversy among environmentalists inside and outside China. Critics claim that erosion and silting of the Yangtze River threaten several endangered species, while Chinese officials say the hydroelectric power generated by the project will enable the region to lower its dependence on coal, thus lessening air pollution.

The U.S.-China Forum on Environment and Development, cochaired by the U.S. Vice President and the Chinese Premier, has been the principle vehicle of an active program of bilateral environmental cooperation since its inception in 1997. Despite positive reviews of the Forum's achievements from both sides, China has often compared the U.S. program, which lacks a foreign assistance component, with those of Japan and several EU countries that include generous levels of aid.

## Science and Technology

Science and technology have always preoccupied Chinas leaders; indeed, Chinas technocrats—both Jiang and Zhu were trained as electric power engineers—have a great reverence for science. Deng called it "the first productive force." Distortions in the economy and society created by Party rule have severely hurt Chinese science, according to some Chinese science policy experts. The Chinese Academy of Sciences, modeled on the Soviet system, puts much of China's greatest scientific talent in a large bureaucracy that remains largely isolated from industry and academia, although the reforms of the past decade have begun to address this problem.

Chinese science strategists see China's greatest opportunities in newly emerging fields such as biotechnology and computers where there is still a chance for China to become a significant competitor. Most Chinese students who went abroad have not returned, but they have built a dense network of transpacific contacts that will greatly facilitate U.S.-China scientific cooperation in the coming years. The United States is often held up as the standard of modernity in China. Indeed, photos of the Space Shuttle often appear in Chinese advertisements as a symbol of advanced technology. China's small space program, which will put a man in space within a few years, is a focus of national pride.

The U.S.-China Science and Technology Agreement remains the framework for U.S. China cooperation in this field. A 5-year agreement to extend the Science and Technology Agreement was signed in April 1996. There are currently more than 30 active protocols under the agreement, covering cooperation in areas such as marine conservation, renewable energy, and health. Japan and the European Union also have high profile science and technology cooperation with China.

## Trade and Investment

According to International Monetary Fund (IMF) statistics, China's global trade totaled $353 billion in 1999; the trade surplus stood at $36 billion. China's primary trading partners include Japan, Taiwan, the U.S., South Korea, Hong Kong, Germany, Singapore, Russia, and the Netherlands. According to U.S. statistics, China had a trade surplus with the U.S. of $68.7 billion in 1999.

China has experimented with decentralizing its foreign trading system and has sought to integrate itself into the world trading system. In November 1991, China joined the Asia Pacific Economic Cooperation (APEC) group, which promotes free trade and cooperation in economic, trade, investment, and technology issues. In 2001, China will serve as APEC chair, and Shanghai will host the annual APEC leaders meeting.

During his 1999 visit to the United States, Premier Zhu Rongji signed a bilateral Agricultural Cooperation Agreement, which lifted longstanding Chinese prohibitions on the import of citrus, grain, beef, and poultry. In November 1999, the United States and China reached a historic bilateral market-access agreement to pave the way for Chinas accession to the World Trade Organization (WTO). As part of the far-reaching trade liberalization agreement, China agreed to lower tariffs and abolish market impediments after it joins the world trading body. Chinese and foreign businessmen, for example, will gain the right to import and export on their own, and to sell their products without going through a government middleman. Average tariff rates on key U.S. agricultural exports will drop from 31% to 14% in 2004 and on industrial products from 25% to 9% by 2005. The agreement also opens new opportunities for U.S. providers of services like banking, insurance, and telecommunications. After reaching a bilateral WTO agreement with the European Union and other trading partners in summer 2000, China must now work on a multilateral WTO accession package before joining the world trade body.

To increase exports, China has pursued policies such as fostering the rapid development of foreign-invested factories, which assemble imported components into consumer goods for export. The U.S. is one of China's primary suppliers of power-generating equipment, aircraft and parts, computers and industrial machinery, raw materials, and chemical and agricultural products. However, U.S. exporters continue to have concerns about fair market access due to China's restrictive trade policies.

## Foreign Investment

Foreign investment stalled in late 1989 in the aftermath of Tiananmen. In response, the government introduced legislation and regulations designed to encourage foreigners to invest in high-priority sectors and regions. In 1990, the government eliminated time restrictions on the establishment of joint ventures, provided some assurances against nationalization, and allowed foreign partners to become chairs of joint venture boards. In 1991, China granted more preferential tax treatment for wholly foreign-owned businesses and contractual ventures and for foreign companies which invest in selected economic zones or in projects encouraged by the state, such as energy, communications, and transportation. It also authorized some foreign banks to open branches in Shanghai and allowed foreign investors to purchase special "B" shares of stock in selected companies listed on the Shanghai and Shenzhen Securities Exchanges. These "B" shares are sold to foreigners but carry no ownership rights in a company. In 1999, China received nearly $39 billion in foreign direct investment.

Opening to the outside remains central to China's development. Foreign-invested enterprises produce about 45% of China's exports, and China continues to attract large investment inflows. Foreign exchange reserves totaled about $155 billion in 1999.

# FOREIGN RELATIONS

Since its establishment, the People's Republic has worked vigorously to win international support for its position that it is the sole legitimate government of all China, including Hong Kong, Macao, and Taiwan. In the early 1970s, Beijing was recognized diplomatically by most world powers. Beijing assumed the China seat in the United Nations in 1971 and became increasingly active in multilateral organizations. Japan established diplomatic relations with China in 1972, and the U.S. did so in 1979. The number of countries that have established diplomatic relations with Beijing has risen to 156, while 28 have diplomatic relations with Taiwan.

After the founding of the P.R.C., China's foreign policy initially focused on solidarity with the Soviet Union and other communist countries. In 1950, China sent the People's Liberation Army into North Korea as "volunteers" to help North Korea halt the UN offensive that was approaching the Yalu River. After the conclusion of the Korean conflict, China sought to balance its identification as a member of the Soviet bloc by establishing friendly relations with Pakistan and Third World countries, particularly in Southeast Asia.

In the 1960s, Beijing competed with Moscow for political influence among communist parties and in the developing world generally. Following the 1968 Soviet invasion of Czechoslovakia and clashes in 1969 on the Sino-Soviet border, Chinese competition with the Soviet Union increasingly reflected concern over China's own strategic position.

In late 1978, the Chinese also became concerned over Vietnam's efforts to establish open control over Laos and Cambodia. In response to the Soviet-backed Vietnamese invasion of Cambodia, China fought a brief border war with Vietnam (February-March 1979) with the stated purpose of "teaching Vietnam a lesson." Chinese anxiety about Soviet strategic advances was heightened following the Soviet Union's December 1979 invasion of Afghanistan. Sharp differences between China and the Soviet Union persisted over Soviet support for Vietnam's continued occupation of Cambodia, the Soviet invasion of Afghanistan, and Soviet troops along the Sino-Soviet border and in Mongolia—the so-called "three obstacles" to improved Sino-Soviet relations.

In the 1970s and 1980s China sought to create a secure regional and global environment for itself and to foster good relations with countries that could aid its economic development. To this end, China looked to the West for assistance with its modernization drive and for help in countering Soviet expansionism—which it characterized as the greatest threat to its national security and to world peace.

China maintained its consistent opposition to "superpower hegemonism," focusing almost exclusively on the expansionist actions of the Soviet Union and Soviet proxies such as Vietnam and Cuba, but it also placed growing emphasis on a foreign policy independent of both the U.S. and the Soviet Union. While improving ties with the West, China continued to follow closely economic and other positions of the Third World nonaligned movement, although China was not a formal member.

In the immediate aftermath of Tiananmen crackdown in June 1989, many countries reduced their diplomatic contacts with China as well as their economic assistance programs. In response, China worked vigorously to expand its relations with foreign countries, and by late 1990, had reestablished normal relations with almost all nations. Following the collapse of the Soviet Union in late 1991, China also opened diplomatic relations with the republics of the former Soviet Union.

In recent years, Chinese leaders are regular travelers to all parts of the globe, and China has sought a higher profile in the UN through its permanent seat on the United Nations Security Council and other multilateral organizations. Closer to home, China seeks to reduce tensions in Asia; it has contributed to stability on the Korean Peninsula, cultivated a more cooperative relationship with members of the Association of Southeast Asian Nations (Brunei, Burma, Indonesia, Laos, Malaysia, Philippines, Singapore, Thailand, Vietnam), and participated in the ASEAN Regional Forum. The Chinese improved ties with Russia. President Yeltsin and President Jiang announced a "strategic partnership" during Yeltsin's 1997 visit to Beijing.

China has a number of border and maritime disputes, including with Vietnam in the Gulf of Tonkin, with a number of countries in the South

China Sea, as well as with Japan and India. Beijing has resolved many of these disputes, notably including a November 1997 agreement with Russia that resolved almost all outstanding border issues.

# DEFENSE

Establishment of a professional military force equipped with modern weapons and doctrine was the last of the "Four Modernizations" announced by Zhou Enlai and supported by Deng Xiaoping. In keeping with Deng's mandate to reform, the People's Liberation Army (PLA), which includes the strategic nuclear forces, army, navy, and air force, has demobilized millions of men and women since 1978 and has introduced modern methods in such areas as recruitment and manpower, strategy, and education and training.

Following the June 1989 Tiananmen crackdown, ideological correctness was temporarily revived as the dominant theme in Chinese military affairs. Reform and modernization appear to have since resumed their position as the PLA's priority objectives, although the armed forces' political loyalty to the CCP remains a leading concern. The Chinese military is trying to transform itself from a land-based power, centered on a vast ground force, to a smaller, mobile, high-tech military capable of mounting defensive operations beyond its coastal borders.

China's power-projection capability is limited. China has acquired some advanced weapons systems, including Sovremmeny destroyers, SU-27 aircraft, and Kilo-class diesel submarines from Russia. However, the mainstay of the air force continues to be the 1960s-vintage F-7, and naval forces still consist primarily of 1960s-era technology.

# NUCLEAR WEAPONS AND ARMS CONTROL POLICY

## Nuclear Weapons

In 1955, Mao Zedong's Chinese Communist Party decided to proceed with a nuclear weapons program; it was developed with Soviet assistance until 1960. After its first nuclear test in October 1964, Beijing deployed a modest but potent ballistic missile force, including land and sea-based intermediate-range and intercontinental ballistic missiles.

China became a major international arms exporter during the 1980s. Beijing joined the Middle East arms control talks, which began in July 1991 to establish global guidelines for conventional arms transfers, but announced in September 1992 that it would no longer participate because of the U.S. decision to sell F-16A/B aircraft to Taiwan. China was the first state to pledge "no first use" of nuclear weapons. It joined the International Atomic Energy Agency (IAEA) in 1984 and pledged to abstain from further atmospheric testing of nuclear weapons in 1986. China acceded to the nuclear Non-Proliferation Treaty (NPT) in 1992 and supported its indefinite and unconditional extension in 1995. In 1996, it signed the Comprehensive Test Ban Treaty and agreed to seek an international ban on the production of fissile nuclear weapons material.

In 1996, China committed not to provide assistance to unsafeguarded nuclear facilities. China attended the May 1997 meeting of the NPT Exporters (Zangger) Committee as an observer and became a full member in October 1997. The Zangger Committee is a group which meets to list items that should be subject to IAEA inspections if exported by countries which have, as China has, signed the Non-Proliferation Treaty. In September 1997, China issued detailed nuclear export control regulations.

China is implementing regulations establishing controls over nuclear-related dual-use items in 1998. China also has decided not to engage in new nuclear cooperation with Iran (even under safeguards) and will complete existing cooperation, which is not of proliferation concern, within a relatively short period. Based on significant, tangible progress with China on nuclear nonproliferation, President Clinton in 1998 took steps to bring into force the 1985 U.S.-China Agreement on Peaceful Nuclear Cooperation.

## Chemical Weapons

China is not a member of the Australia Group, an informal and voluntary arrangement made in 1985 to monitor developments in the proliferation of dual-use chemicals and to coordinate export controls on key dual-use chemicals and equipment with weapons applications. In April 1997, however, China ratified the Chemical Weapons Convention (CWC) and, in September 1997, promulgated a new chemical weapons export control directive.

## Missiles

While not formally joining the regime, in March 1992, China undertook to abide by the guidelines and parameters of the Missile Technology Control Regime (MTCR), the multinational effort to restrict the proliferation of missiles capable of delivering weapons of mass destruction. China reaffirmed this commitment in 1994 and pledged not to transfer MTCR-class ground-to-ground missiles.

# U.S.-CHINA RELATIONS

## From Liberation to the Shanghai Communiqué

As the PLA armies moved south to complete the communist conquest of China in 1949, the American embassy followed the Nationalist government headed by Chiang Kai-shek, finally moving to Taipei later that year. U.S. consular officials remained in mainland China. The new P.R.C. Government was hostile to this official American presence, and all U.S. personnel were withdrawn from the mainland in early 1950. Any remaining hope of normalizing relations ended when U.S. and Chinese communist forces fought on opposing sides in the Korean conflict.

Beginning in 1954 and continuing until 1970, the United States and China held 136 meetings at the ambassadorial level, first at Geneva and later at Warsaw. In the late 1960s, U.S. and Chinese political leaders decided that improved bilateral relations were in their common interest. In 1969, the United States initiated measures to relax trade restrictions and other impediments to bilateral contact. On July 15, 1971, President Nixon announced that his Assistant for National Security Affairs, Dr. Henry Kissinger, had made a secret trip to Beijing to initiate direct contact with the Chinese leadership and that he, the President, had been invited to visit China.

In February 1972, President Nixon traveled to Beijing, Hangzhou, and Shanghai. At the conclusion of his trip, the U.S. and Chinese Governments issued the "Shanghai Communiqué," a statement of their foreign policy views. (For the complete text of the Shanghai Communiqué, see the Department of State Bulletin, March 20, 1972).

In the Communiqué, both nations pledged to work toward the full normalization of diplomatic relations. The U.S. acknowledged the Chinese position that all Chinese on both sides of the Taiwan Strait maintain that there is only one China and that Taiwan is part of China. The statement enabled the U.S. and China to temporarily set aside the "crucial question obstructing the normalization of relations"—Taiwan—and to open trade and other contacts.

## Liaison Office, 1973-78

In May 1973, in an effort to build toward the establishment of formal diplomatic relations, the U.S. and China established the United States Liaison Office (USLO) in Beijing and a counterpart Chinese office in Washington, DC. In the years between 1973 and 1978, such distinguished Americans as David Bruce, George Bush, Thomas Gates, and Leonard Woodcock served as chiefs of the USLO with the personal rank of Ambassador.

President Ford visited China in 1975 and reaffirmed the U.S. interest in normalizing relations with Beijing. Shortly after taking office in 1977, President Carter again reaffirmed the interest expressed in the Shanghai Communiqué. The United States and China announced on December 15, 1978, that the two governments would establish diplomatic relations on January 1, 1979.

## Normalization

In the Joint Communiqué on the Establishment of Diplomatic Relations dated January 1, 1979, the United States transferred diplomatic recognition from Taipei to Beijing. The U.S. reiterated the Shanghai Communiqué's acknowledgment of the Chinese position that there is only one China and that Taiwan is a part of China; Beijing acknowledged that the American people would continue to carry on commercial, cultural, and other unofficial contacts with the people of Taiwan. The Taiwan Relations Act made the necessary changes in U.S. domestic law to permit such unofficial relations with Taiwan to flourish.

## U.S.-China Relations Since Normalization

Vice Premier Deng Xiaoping's January 1979 visit to Washington, DC initiated a series of important, high-level exchanges, which continued until the spring of 1989. This resulted in many bilateral agreements—especially in the fields of scientific, technological, and cultural interchange and trade relations. Since early 1979, the United States and China have initiated hundreds of joint research projects and cooperative programs under the Agreement on Cooperation in Science and Technology, the largest bilateral program.

On March 1, 1979, the United States and China formally established embassies in Beijing and Washington, DC. During 1979, outstanding private claims were resolved, and a bilateral trade agreement was concluded. Vice President Walter Mondale reciprocated Vice Premier Deng's visit with an August 1979 trip to China. This visit led to agreements in September 1980 on maritime affairs, civil aviation links, and textile matters, as well as a bilateral consular convention.

As a consequence of high-level and working-level contacts initiated in 1980, our dialogue with China broadened to cover a wide range of issues, including global and regional strategic problems, politico-military questions, including arms control, UN and other multilateral organization affairs, and international narcotics matters.

The expanding relationship that followed normalization was threatened in 1981 by Chinese objections to the level of U.S. arms sales to Taiwan. Secretary of State Alexander Haig visited China in June 1981 in an effort to resolve Chinese questions about America's unofficial relations with Taiwan. Eight months of negotiations produced the U.S.-China joint communiqué of August 17, 1982. In this third communiqué, the U.S. stated its intention to reduce gradually the level of arms sales to Taiwan, and the Chinese described as a fundamental policy their effort to strive for a peaceful resolution to the Taiwan question. Meanwhile, Vice President Bush visited China in May 1982.

High-level exchanges continued to be a significant means for developing U.S.-China relations in the 1980s. President Reagan and Premier Zhao Ziyang made reciprocal visits in 1984. In July 1985, President Li Xiannian traveled to the United States, the first such visit by a Chinese head of state. Vice President Bush visited China in October 1985 and opened the U.S. Consulate General in Chengdu, the U.S.'s fourth consular post in China. Further exchanges of cabinet-level officials occurred from 1985-89, capped by President Bush's visit to Beijing in February 1989.

In the period before the June 3-4, 1989 crackdown, a large and growing number of cultural exchange activities undertaken at all levels gave the American and Chinese peoples broad exposure to each other's cultural, artistic, and educational achievements. Numerous Chinese professional and official delegations visited the United States each month. Many of these exchanges continued after Tiananmen.

## Bilateral Relations After Tiananmen

Following the Chinese authorities' brutal suppression of demonstrators in June 1989, the U.S. and other governments enacted a number of measures to express their condemnation of Chinese action that violated the basic human rights of its citizens. The U.S. suspended high-level official exchanges with China and weapons exports from the U.S. to China. The U.S. also imposed a series of economic sanctions. In the summer of 1990, at the G-7 Houston summit, Western nations called for renewed political and economic reforms in China, particularly in the field of human rights.

The U.S.-China trade relationship was disrupted by Tiananmen, and U.S. investors' interest in China dropped dramatically. The U.S. Government also responded to the political repression by suspending certain trade and investment programs on June 5 and 20, 1989. Some sanctions were legislated; others were executive actions. Examples include:

The Trade and Development Agency (TDA) and Overseas Private Insurance Corporation (OPIC); New activities suspended since June 1989; Development Bank Lending/IMF Credits—the United States does not support development bank lending and will not support IMF credits to China except for projects that meet basic human needs; Munitions List Exports—subject to certain exceptions, no licenses may be issued for

the export of any defense article on the U.S. Munitions List. This restriction may be waived upon a Presidential national interest determination; Arms Imports—import of defense articles from China was banned after the imposition of the ban on arms exports to China. The import ban was subsequently waived by the Administration and reimposed on May 26, 1994. It covers all items on the Bureau of Alcohol, Tobacco, and Firearms' Munitions Import List. In 1996, the P.R.C. conducted military exercises in waters close to Taiwan in an apparent effort at intimidation. The United States dispatched two aircraft carrier battle groups to the region. Subsequently, tensions in the Taiwan Strait diminished, and relations between U.S. and China have improved, with increased high-level exchanges and progress on numerous bilateral issues, including human rights, nonproliferation, and trade. Chinese President Jiang Zemin visited the United States in the fall of 1997, the first state visit to the U.S. by a Chinese president since 1985.

In connection with that visit, the two sides reached agreement on implementation of their 1985 agreement on the Peaceful Uses of Nuclear Energy, as well as a number of other issues. President Clinton visited China in June 1998. He traveled extensively in China, and direct interaction with the Chinese people included live speeches and a radio show, allowing the President to convey first-hand to the Chinese people a sense of American ideals and values.

Relations between the U.S. and China were severely strained by the tragic accidental bombing of the Chinese Embassy in Belgrade in May 1999. By the end of 1999, relations began to gradually improve. In October 1999, the two sides reached agreement on humanitarian payments for families of those who died and those who were injured as well as payments for damages to respective diplomatic properties in Belgrade and China.

## U.S.-Chinese Economic Relations

U.S. direct investment in China covers a wide range of manufacturing sectors, several large hotel projects, and a heavy concentration in offshore oil and gas development in the South China Sea. U.S. companies have entered agreements establishing more than 20,000 equity joint ventures, contractual joint ventures, and wholly foreign-owned enterprises in China. More than 100 U.S.-based multinationals have projects, some with multiple investments. The 1999 trade deficit of $68.7 billion with China was the United States' second-largest. Some of the factors that influence the U.S. deficit with China include:

The strength of the U.S. economy; A shift of export industries to China from the newly industrialized economies (NIEs) in Asia. China has increasingly become the last link in a long chain of value-added production; China's restrictive trade practices, which include a wide array of barriers to foreign goods and services, often aimed at protecting state-owned enterprises. These practices include high tariffs, lack of transparency, requiring firms to obtain special permission to import goods, unevenness of application of laws and regulations, and leveraging technology from foreign firms in return for market access; China's domestic output of labor-intensive goods exceeds China's demand, while U.S. demand for labor-intensive goods exceeds domestic output. The increasingly important U.S. economic and trade relations with China are an important element of the Administration's engagement policy toward China. In economics and trade, there are two main elements to the U.S. approach:

First, the United States seeks to fully integrate China into the global, market-based economic and trading system. China's participation in the global economy will nurture the process of economic reform and increase China's stake in the stability and prosperity of East Asia; Second, the United States seeks to expand U.S. exporters' and investors' access to the Chinese market. As China grows and develops, its needs for imported goods and services will grow even more rapidly.

The United States and China maintain a very active dialogue on bilateral trade issues. The two countries have implemented or are considering agreements on IPR, textiles, and aviation, among others.

At the October 2000 Joint Economic Committee meeting in Washington, the U.S. continued dialogue with the Chinese on macroeconomic and finance issues. The meetings, following the bilateral WTO agreement signed in November 1999, discussed two main themes: global integration and structural reforms in China and the challenge of combating financial crime. The prospect of closer Chinese integration with the world economy will continue to spur state-owned enterprise and banking reform but also may witness an increase in illegitimate economic activities.

## Economic Relations With Hong Kong

Under the 1984 Sino-British Joint Declaration, Hong Kong became a Special Administrative Region (SAR) of the P.R.C. on July 1, 1997. Hong Kong has autonomy in its international trade and economic relations. The United States has substantial economic and social ties with Hong Kong, with an estimated $16 billion invested there. There are 1,100 U.S. firms and 50,000 American residents in Hong Kong. The United States was Hong Kong's second-largest market in 1997—the U.S. imported $10.2 billion. Hong Kong took $15.1 billion in U.S. exports in that year. (See separate Background Notes on Hong Kong for additional information.)

## China's Normal Trade Status

There has been debate in the U.S. regarding the extension of China's normal trade status, which allows nondiscriminatory tariff treatment for Chinese exports to the U.S. The reciprocal granting of normal trade treatment was the main pillar of the U.S.-China Trade Agreement signed

in 1979, which marked the beginning of normal commercial relations between the two countries. As a non-market-economy country, China's normal trade status had to be renewed annually by a U.S. presidential waiver stipulating that China meets the freedom of emigration requirements set forth in the Jackson-Vanik Amendment to the Trade Act of 1974. China had received the waiver routinely prior to 1989, but after Tiananmen, although the presidential waiver continued, Congress began to exert strong pressure to oppose normal trade status renewal. In 1991 and 1992, Congress voted to place conditions on normal trade status renewal for China, but those conditions were vetoed by the Bush administration, which stressed the importance of our relationship with China and the belief that normal trade status was not the correct tool to exert pressure on China and would only result in isolating it.

In 1994, President Clinton decided to delink the annual normal trade status process from China's human rights record. At the same time, the President decided to adopt a new human rights strategy, maintaining human rights concerns as an essential part of the U.S. engagement with China but in a broader context.

The President also ordered several additional steps to support those seeking to foster the rule of law and a more open civil society in China.

In May 2000, the U.S. House of Representatives, followed by the Senate in October, voted to approve Permanent Normal Trade Relations (PNTR—most-favored-nation-status) for China; President Clinton signed the bill into law in October. The law will go into effect after China joins the WTO.

## Chinese Diplomatic Representation in the U.S.

In addition to China's embassy in Washington, DC, there are Chinese Consulates General in Chicago, Houston, Los Angeles, New York, and San Francisco.

**Embassy of the People's Republic of China**
2300 Connecticut Avenue
NW Washington, DC 20008
Tel.: (202) 328-2500

**Consulate General of the People's Republic of China, New York**
520 12th Avenue
New York, New York 10036
Tel.: (212) 868-7752

**Consulate General of the People's Republic of China, San Francisco**
1450 Laguna Street
San Francisco, California 94115
Tel.: (415) 563-4885

**Consulate General of the People's Republic of China, Houston**
3417 Montrose Blvd.
Houston, Texas 77006
Tel.: (713) 524-4311

**Consulate General of the People's Republic of China, Chicago**
100 West Erie St.
Chicago, Illinois 60610
Tel.: (312) 803-0098

**Consulate General of the People's Republic of China, Los Angeles**
502 Shatto Place, Suite 300
Los Angeles, California 90020
Tel.: (213) 807-8088

## U.S. Diplomatic Representation in China

**For up-to-date information on Principal U.S. Officials, see the U.S. Embassies, Consulates, and Foreign Service section starting on page 139.**

In addition to the U.S. embassy in Beijing, there are U.S. Consulates General in Chengdu, Guangzhou, Shanghai, and Shenyang.

**American Embassy Beijing**
Xiu Shui Bei Jie 3
Beijing 100600
People's Republic of China
Tel.: (86) (10) 6532-3831
FAX: (86) (10) 6532-3178

# COLOMBIA

February 2001

Official Name:
**Republic of Colombia**

# PROFILE

## Geography

**Area:** 1.2 million sq. km. (440,000 sq. mi.); about the size of Texas, New Mexico, and Arkansas combined; fourth-largest country in South America.

**Cities:** Capital—Bogota (pop. about 6 million). Other major cities—Medellin, Cali, Barranquilla, Cartagena.

**Terrain:** Flat coastal areas, three rugged parallel mountain chains, central highlands, and flat eastern grasslands with extensive coastlines on the Pacific Ocean and Caribbean Sea.

**Climate:** Tropical on coast and eastern plains, cooler in highlands. Natural resources: Coal, petroleum, natural gas, iron ore, nickel, gold, silver, copper, platinum, emeralds.

## People

**Nationality:** Noun and adjective—Colombian(s).

**Population:** 42.8 million.

**Annual growth rate:** 1.8%.

**Religion:** Roman Catholic 90%. Language: Spanish.

**Education:** Years compulsory—9. Attendance—80% of children enter school. Only 5 years of primary school are offered in many rural areas. Literacy—93% in urban areas, 67% in rural areas.

**Health:** Infant mortality rate—25/1,000. Life expectancy—men 65 yrs., women 76 yrs.

## Government

**Type:** Republic.

**Independence:** July 20, 1810.

**Constitution:** 1991.

**Branches:** Executive—President (chief of state and head of government). Legislative—bicameral Congress. Judicial—Supreme Court, Constitutional Court, Council of State, Superior Judicial Council.

**Administrative divisions:** 32 departments; Bogota, capital district.

**Major political parties:** Conservative Party of Colombia, Liberal Party, and a score of small political movements (most of them allied with one or the other major party).

**Suffrage:** Universal, age 18 and over.

## Economy

**GDP:** $87.9 billion

**Annual growth rate:** 3.1%

**Per capita GDP:** $1,951

**Government:** 20.5 % of GDP. Manufacturing (13.6 % of GDP): Types—textiles and garments, chemicals, metal products, cement, cardboard containers, plastic resins and manufactures, beverages. Agriculture (14.7 % of GDP): Products—coffee, bananas, cut flowers, cotton, sugarcane, livestock, rice, corn, tobacco, potatoes, soybeans, sorghum. Cultivated land—8.2% of total area.

**Other sectors:** (by percentage of GDP) Financial services—17.7%; commerce—11.7%; Transportation and communications services—8.3%; mining and quarrying—4.7%; construction and public works—4.1%; electricity, gas, and water—3.3%.

**Trade:** Exports—$14.0 billion: petroleum, coffee, coal, ferronickel, bananas, flowers, chemicals and pharmaceuticals, textiles and garments, gold, sugar, cardboard containers, printed matter, cement, plastic resins and manufactures, emeralds. Major markets—U.S., Germany, Netherlands, Japan. Imports—$11.2 billion: machinery/equipment, grains, chemicals, transportation equipment, mineral products, consumer products, metals/metal products, plastic/rubber, paper products, aircraft, oil and gas industry equipment, and supplies. Major suppliers—U.S., Venezuela, Germany, Japan, Panama.

# PEOPLE

Colombia is the third-most populous country in Latin America, after Brazil and Mexico. Movement from rural to urban areas has been heavy. The urban population increased from 57%

of the total population in 1951 to about 74% by 1994. Thirty cities have a population of 100,000 or more. The nine eastern lowlands departments, constituting about 54% of Colombia's area, have less than 3% of the population and a density of less than one person per square kilometer (two persons per sq. mi.).

Ethnic diversity in Colombia is a result of the intermingling of indigenous Indians, Spanish colonists, and Africans. Today, only about 1% of the people can be identified as fully Indian on the basis of language and customs.

# HISTORY

During the pre-Colombian period, the area now known as Colombia was inhabited by indigenous peoples who were primitive hunters or nomadic farmers. The Chibchas, who lived in the Bogota region, dominated the various Indian groups.

The Spanish sailed along the north coast of Colombia as early as 1500, but their first permanent settlement, at Santa Marta, was not made until 1525. In 1549, the area was established as a Spanish colony with the capital at Santa fe de Bogota. In 1717, Bogota became the capital of the Viceroyalty of New Granada, which included what is now Venezuela, Ecuador, and Panama. The city became one of the principal administrative centers of the Spanish possessions in the New World, along with Lima and Mexico City. In August 2000 the capital's name was officially changed from "Santa Fe de Bogota" to the more usual "Bogota."

On July 20, 1810, the citizens of Bogota created the first representative council to defy Spanish authority. Full independence was proclaimed in 1813, and in 1819 the Republic of Greater Colombia was formed.

## The Republic

The new Republic of Greater Colombia included all the territory of the former Viceroyalty. Simon Bolivar was elected its first president and Francisco de Paula Santander, vice president. Two political parties grew out of conflicts between the followers of Bolivar and Santander and their political visions—the Conservatives and the Liberals—and have since dominated Colombian politics. Bolivar's supporters, who later formed the nucleus of the Conservative Party, sought strong centralized government, alliance with the Roman Catholic Church, and a limited franchise. Santander's followers, forerunners of the Liberals, wanted a decentralized government, state rather than church control over education and other civil matters, and a broadened suffrage.

Throughout the 19th and early 20th centuries, each party held the presidency for roughly equal periods of time. Colombia maintained a tradition of civilian government and regular, free elections. The military has seized power three times in Colombia's history: in 1830, when Ecuador and Venezuela withdrew from the republic (Panama became independent in 1903); again in 1854, and 1953–57. Civilian rule was restored within one year in the first two instances.

Notwithstanding the country's commitment to democratic institutions, Colombia's history has also been characterized by widespread, violent conflict. Two civil wars resulted from bitter rivalry between the Conservative and Liberal parties. The War of a Thousand Days (1899–1902) cost an estimated 100,000 lives, and up to 300,000 people died during "La Violencia" (The Violence) of the late 1940s and 1950s.

A military coup in 1953 brought Gen. Gustavo Rojas Pinilla to power. Initially, Rojas enjoyed considerable popular support, due largely to his success in reducing "La Violencia." When he did not restore democratic rule, however, he was overthrown by the military in 1957 with the backing of both political parties, and a provisional government was installed.

## The National Front

In July 1957, former Conservative President Laureano Gomez (1950–53) and former Liberal President Alberto Lleras Camargo (1945–46) issued the "Declaration of Sitges," in which they proposed a "National Front" whereby the Liberal and Conservative parties would govern jointly. The presidency would be determined by regular elections every 4 years; the two parties would have parity in all other elective and appointive offices.

The National Front ended "La Violencia," and National Front administrations instituted far-reaching social and economic reforms in cooperation with the Alliance for Progress.

Although the system established by the Sitges agreement was phased out by 1978, the 1886 Colombian constitution—in effect until 1991—required that the losing political party be given adequate and equitable participation in the government. The 1991 constitution does not have that requirement, but subsequent administrations have included members of opposition parties.

## Post-National Front Years

Between 1978 and 1982, the government focused on ending the limited, but persistent, Cuban-backed insurgencies that sought to undermine Colombia's traditional democratic system. The success of the government's efforts enabled it to lift the state-of-siege decree that had been in effect for most of the previous 30 years. In 1984, President Belisario Betancur, a Conservative who won 47% of the popular vote, negotiated a cease-fire that included the release of many guerrillas imprisoned during the effort to overpower the insurgents. The cease-fire ended when Democratic Alliance/M-19 (AD/M-19) guerrillas resumed fighting in 1985.

An attack on the Palace of Justice in Bogota by the AD/M-19 on November 6–7, 1985, and its violent suppression by the army, shocked Colombians. Of the 115 people killed, 11 were

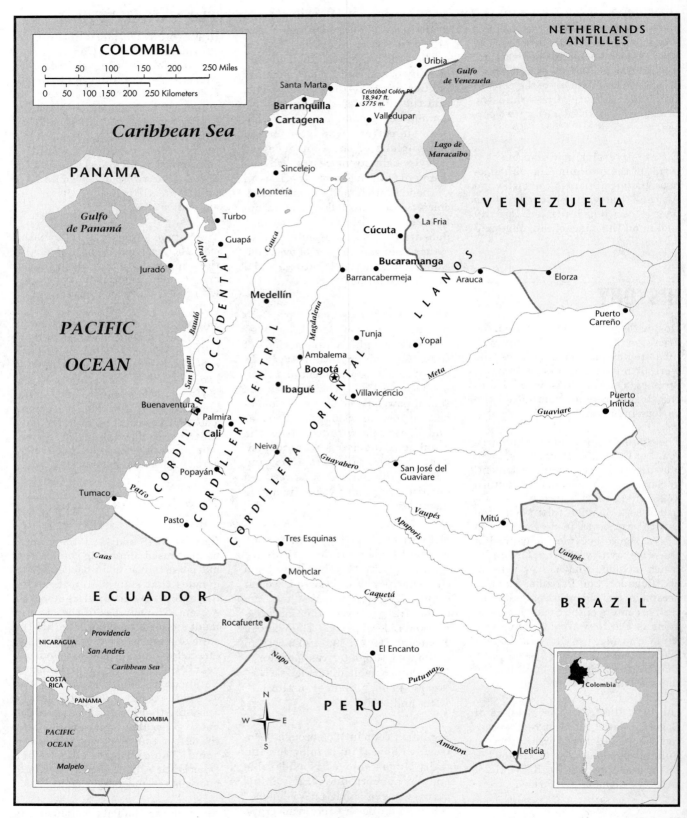

## COLOMBIA

0    50   100   150   200   250 Miles

0   50  100 150 200  250 Kilometers

**NETHERLANDS ANTILLES**

*Caribbean Sea*

PANAMA

*Gulfo de Panamá*

*Gulfo de Venezuela*

Uribia

Santa Marta

**Barranquilla**
**Cartagena**

*Cristóbal Colón Pk. 18,947 ft.*
▲ *5775 m.*

Valledupar

*Lago de Maracaibo*

Sincelejo

Montería

Turbo

Guapá

V E N E Z U E L A

**Cúcuta**

La Fria

**Bucaramanga**

Juradó

Barrancabermeja

Arauca

Elorza

**Medellín**

*Atrato*

*Cauca*

*Baudó*

Puerto Carreño

PACIFIC

OCEAN

*San Juan*

*Magdalena*

Tunja

Yopal

*Meta*

Ambalema

**Bogotá** ☆

Buenaventura

Palmira

**Ibagué**

Villavicencio

Puerto Inírida

**Cali**

Neiva

*Guaviare*

Popayán

*Guayabero*

San José del Guaviare

Tumaco

*Patío*

*Vaupés*

Mitú

Pasto

*Apaporis*

*Uaupés*

Tres Esquinas

*Caas*

Monclar

*Uaupés*

E C U A D O R

*Caquetá*

B R A Z I L

Rocafuerte

*Napo*

El Encanto

*Putumayo*

NICARAGUA

*Providencia*

*San Andrés*

*Caribbean Sea*

COSTA RICA

PANAMA

COLOMBIA

*PACIFIC OCEAN*

*Malpelo*

N
W   E
S

P E R U

*Amazon*

Leticia

Colombia

Supreme Court justices. Although the government and the Revolutionary Armed Forces of Colombia (FARC) renewed their truce in March 1986, peace with other revolutionary move-

ments, in particular the AD/M-19—then the largest insurgent group—and the National Liberation Army (ELN) was remote as Betancur left office.

The AD/M-19 and several smaller guerilla groups were successfully incorporated into a peace process during the late 1980s, which culminated in a national assembly to write a new constitution, which took effect in 1991. The FARC had declared a unilateral cease-fire under Betancur, which led to the establishment of the Union Patriotica (UP), a legal and non-clandestine political organization. After growing violence against its UP members, the truce with the FARC ended in 1990.

Following administrations had to contend with the guerrillas, paramilitaries, and narcotics traffickers. Narcoterrorists assassinated three presidential candidates before Cesar Gaviria Trujillo was elected in 1990. Since the death of Medellin cartel leader Pablo Escobar in a police shootout during December 1993, indiscriminate acts of violence associated with that organization have abated as the "cartels" have broken up into multiple, smaller and often-competing trafficking organizations. Nevertheless, violence continues as these drug organizations resort to violence as part of their operations but also to protest against government policies, including extradition.

President Ernesto Samper assumed office in August 1994. However, a political crisis relating to largescale contributions from drug traffickers to Samper's presidential campaign diverted attention from governance programs, thus slowing, and in many cases, halting progress on the nation's domestic reform agenda.

On August 7, 1998, Andres Pastrana was sworn in as the President of Colombia. A member of the Conservative Party, Pastrana defeated Liberal Party candidate Horacio Serpa in a run-off election marked by high voter turn-out and little political unrest. The new president's program was based on a commitment to bring about a peaceful resolution of Colombia's longstanding civil conflict and to cooperate fully with the United States to combat the trafficking of illegal drugs.

While early initiatives in the Colombian peace process gave reason for optimism, the Pastrana administration also has had to combat high unemployment and other economic problems, such as the fiscal deficit

and the impact of global financial instability on Colombia. During his administration, unemployment has risen to over 20%. Additionally, the growing severity of countrywide guerilla attacks by the FARC and ELN, and smaller movements, as well as the growth of drug production and the spread of paramilitary groups has made it difficult to solve the country's problems.

Although the FARC and ELN accepted participation in the peace process, they did not make explicit commitments to end the conflict. The FARC suspended talks in November 2000, to protest what it called "paramilitary terrorism" but returned to the negotiating table in February 2001, following 2 days of meetings between President Pastrana and FARC leader Mario Marulanda. The Colombian Government and ELN in early 2001 continued discussions aimed at opening a formal peace process.

No single explanation fully addresses the deep roots of Colombia's present-day troubles, but they include limited government presence in large areas of the interior, the expansion of illicit drug cultivation, endemic violence, and social inequities. In order to confront these challenges, the Pastrana administration unveiled its Plan Colombia in late 1999, an integrated strategy to deal with these longstanding, mutually reinforcing problems.

The main objectives of Plan Colombia are to promote peace, combat the narcotics industry, revive the Colombian economy, improve respect for human rights, and strengthen the democratic and social institutions of the country. Colombia plans to finance $4 billion of the estimated $7.5 billion overall cost. The United States approved a $1.3 billion assistance package, and the Colombian Government is seeking additional support from the IFIs, the European Union, and other countries.

# GOVERNMENT

## Constitutional Reforms

Colombia's present constitution, enacted on July 4, 1991, strengthened the administration of justice with the provision for introduction of an accusatorial system which ultimately is to replace entirely the existing Napoleonic Code. Other significant reforms under the new constitution provide for civil divorce, dual nationality, the election of a vice president, and the election of departmental governors. The constitution expanded citizens' basic rights, including that of "tutela," under which an immediate court action can be requested by an individual if he or she feels that their constitutional rights are being violated and if there is no other legal recourse.

The national government has separate executive, legislative, and judicial branches. The president is elected for a 4-year term and cannot be re-elected. The 1991 constitution reestablished the position of vice president, who is elected on the same ticket as the president. By law, the vice president will succeed in the event of the president's resignation, illness, or death.

Colombia's bicameral Congress consists of a 102-member Senate and a 161-member House of Representatives. Senators are elected on the basis of a nationwide ballot, while representatives are elected in multi-member districts co-located within the 32 national departments. The country's capital is a separate capital district and elects its own representatives. Members may be re-elected indefinitely, and, in contrast to the previous system, there are no alternate congressmen. Congress meets twice a year, and the president has the power to call it into special session when needed.

The civilian judiciary is a separate and independent branch of government. Guidelines and the general structure for Colombia's administration of justice are set out in Law 270 of March 7, 1996. Colombia's legal system has recently begun to incorporate some elements of an oral, accusatorial system. The judicial branch's general structure is composed of four distinct jurisdictions (civilian, administrative, constitutional, and special). Colombia's highest judicial organs include the Supreme Court, the Council of State, the Constitutional Court, and the Superior Judicial Council. This sometimes leads to conflicting opinions since there is no one court which clearly has authority over the decisions of the other three.

## Principal Government Officials

**For up-to-date information on Principal Government Officials, see the Chiefs of State and Cabinet Members of Foreign Governments section starting on page 1.**

Colombia maintains an embassy in the United States at 2118 Leroy Place NW, Washington, DC 20008 (tel. 202–387–8338).
Consulates are located in Atlanta, Boston, Chicago, Houston, Los Angeles, Miami, New Orleans, New ork, San Francisco, San Juan, and Washington.

# DEFENSE

Colombia's Ministry of Defense, charged with the country's internal and external defense and security, has an army, navy—which includes both marines and coast guard—air force, and national police under the leadership of a civilian Minister of Defense. In 1999, Colombia assigned 3.6% of its GDP to defense, according to the National Planning Department. The armed forces number about 250,000 uniformed personnel: 145,000 military and 105,000 police. Many Colombian military personnel have received training in the United States or in Colombia. The United States has provided equipment to the Colombian military and police through the military assistance pro-

gram, foreign military sales, and the international narcotics control program.

Narcotics decertification in 1996 forced a temporary halt to U.S. military assistance programs, except for those related to counternarcotics. On August 1, 1997, the U.S. and Colombia signed an End Use Monitoring (EUM) memorandum of understanding which stipulated that U.S. counternarcotics assistance to the Colombian military be conditioned on human rights screening of proposed recipient units. Once equipment is provided, it continues to be subject to end-use monitoring to ensure it is being used for counternarcotics purposes.

U.S. assistance to Colombian military and police forces is provided strictly in accordance with Section 564 of the Foreign Operations Appropriations Act (Public Law 106–113) and with Section 8098 of Department of Defense Appropriations Act Public Law 106–79). No assistance is provided to any unit of the security forces for which the U.S. Government has credible evidence of commission of gross violations of human rights, unless the Secretary of State is able to certify that the Government of Colombia has taken effective measures to bring those responsible to justice. End-use monitoring also is required in these cases.

# ECONOMY

Colombia is a free market economy with major commercial and investment ties to the United States. Transition from a highly regulated economy has been underway for more than a decade. In 1990, the administration of President Cesar Gaviria (1990–94) initiated economic liberalization or "apertura," and this has continued since then, with tariff reductions, financial deregulation, privatization of state-owned enterprises, and adoption of a more liberal foreign exchange rate. Almost all sectors became open to foreign investment although agricultural products remained protected.

Until 1997, Colombia had enjoyed a fairly stable economy. The first 5 years of liberalization were characterized by high economic growth rates of between 4% and 5%. The Samper administration (1994–98) emphasized social welfare policies which targeted Colombia's lower income population. However, these reforms led to higher government spending which increased the fiscal deficit and public sector debt, the financing of which required higher interest rates. An over-valued peso inherited from the previous administration was maintained.

The economy slowed, and by 1998 GDP growth was only 0.6 %. In 1999, the country fell into its first recession since the Great Depression. The economy shrank by 4.5 % with unemployment at over 20 %. While unemployment remained at 20% in 2000, GDP growth recovered to 3.1%.

The administration of President Andres Pastrana, when it took office on August 7, 1998, faced an economy in crisis, with the difficult internal security situation and global economic turbulence additionally inhibiting confidence. As evidence of a serious recession became clear in 1999, the government took a number of steps. It engaged in a series of controlled devaluations of the peso, followed by a decision to let it float. Colombia also entered into an agreement with the International Monetary Fund which provided a $2.7 billion guarantee (extended funds facility), while committing the government to budget discipline and structural reforms.

By early 2000 there had been the beginning of an economic recovery, with the export sector leading the way, as it enjoyed the benefit of the more competitive exchange rate, as well as strong prices for petroleum, Colombia's leading export product. Prices of coffee, the other principal export product, have been more variable.

Economic growth reached 3.1 % during 2000 and inflation was 9.0% although unemployment has yet to significantly improve. Colombia's international reserves have remained stable at around $8.35 billion, and Colombia has successfully remained in international capital markets. Colombia's total foreign debt at the end of 1999 was $34.5 billion with $14.7 billion in private sector and $19.8 billion in public sector debt. Major international credit rating organizations have dropped Colombian sovereign debt below investment grade, primarily as a result of large fiscal deficits, which current policies are seeking to close.

## Mining and Energy

Colombia is well-endowed with minerals and energy resources. It has the largest coal reserves in Latin America and is second to Brazil in hydroelectric potential. Estimates of oil reserves in 1995 were 3.1 billion barrels. It also possesses significant amounts of ferronickel, gold, silver, platinum, and emeralds.

The discovery of two billion barrels of high-quality oil at the Cusiana and Cupiagua fields, about 125 miles east of Bogota, has enabled Colombia to become a net oil exporter since 1986. Total crude oil production averages 620,000 b/d; about 184,000 b/d is exported. The Pastrana government has significantly liberalized its petroleum investment policies, leading to an increase in exploration activity. Refining capacity cannot satisfy domestic demand, so some refined products, especially gasoline, must be imported. Plans for the construction of a new refinery are under development.

The oil pipelines are a frequent target of extortion and bombing campaigns by the ELN and, more recently, the FARC. The bombings, which occur on average once every 5 days, have caused substantial environmental damage, often in fragile rainforests and jungles, as well as causing significant loss of life.

Colombia has 6.6 billion tons of proven coal reserves, and its coal production totaled 21.7 million metric tons (mt) in 1995. Production from El Cerrejon—the world's largest open-pit coal mine—located on Colombia's Guajira Peninsula, accounted for 65% of that amount. Colombia's exports of 18.4 million mt of steam coal in 1994 made it the world's fourth-largest exporter of this commodity. Private and public investments in Colombia's coal fields and related infrastructure projects are expected to enable the country's exports to grow to about 35 million mt.

While Colombia has vast hydroelectric potential, a prolonged drought in 1992 forced severe electricity rationing throughout the country until mid-1993. The consequences of the drought on electricity-generating capacity caused the government to commission the construction or upgrading of 10 thermoelectric power plants. Half will be coal-fired, and half will be fired by natural gas. The government also has begun awarding bids for the construction of a natural gas pipeline system that will extend from the country's extensive gas fields to its major population centers. Plans call for this project to make natural gas available to millions of Colombian households by the middle of the next decade.

## Trade

Colombia's estimated balance of trade showed a surplus $910 million in 1999, up from a $3.8 billion deficit in 1998. Total 1999 imports were $10.6 billion, while exports were $11.5 billion. Estimated 2000 imports were $11.2 billion with $14.0 imports. Colombia's major exports continue to be petroleum, coffee, coal, nickel, gold and nontraditional exports (e.g., cut flowers, semiprecious stones, sugar, and tropical fruits).

The United States remained Colombia's major trading partner in 1999, taking 48.5% of exports and providing 42.1% of imports. The EU and Japan also are important trading partners, as are Andean Pact countries.

## Foreign Investment

In 1991 and 1992, the government passed laws to stimulate foreign investment in nearly all sectors of the economy. The only activities closed to foreign direct investment are defense and national security, disposal of hazardous wastes, and real estate—the last of these restrictions is intended to hinder money laundering. Colombia established a special entity—CoInvertir—to assist foreigners in making investments in the country. Foreign investment flows for 1999 were $4.4 billion, down from $4.8 billion in 1998.

Major foreign investment projects underway include the $6 billion development of the Cusiana and Cupiagua oil fields, development of coal fields in the north of the country, and the recently concluded licensing for establishment of cellular telephone service. The United States accounted for 26.5% of the total $19.4 billion stock of nonpetroleum foreign direct investment in Colombia at the end of 1998.

On October 21, 1995, under the International Emergency Economic Powers Act (IEEPA), President Clinton signed an Executive Order barring U.S. entities from any commercial or financial transactions with four Colombian drug kingpins and with individuals and companies associated with the traffic in narcotics, as designated by the Secretary of the Treasury in consultation with the Secretary of State and the Attorney General. The list of designated individuals and companies is amended periodically and is maintained by the Office of Foreign Asset Control at the Department of the Treasury, tel. (202) 622–0077 (ask for Document #1900). The document also is available at the Department of Treasury web site www.ustreas.gov.

## Industry and Agriculture

The most industrially diverse member of the five-nation Andean Community, Colombia has four major industrial centers—Bogota, Medellin, Cali, and Barranquilla, each located in a distinct geographical region. Colombia's industries include textiles and clothing, leather products, processed foods and beverages, paper and paper products, chemicals and petrochemicals, cement, construction, iron and steel products, and metal-working. Its diverse climate and topography permit the cultivation of a wide variety of crops. In addition, all regions yield forest products, ranging from tropical hardwoods in the hot country to pine and eucalyptus in the colder areas.

Cacao, sugarcane, coconuts, bananas, plantains, rice, cotton, tobacco, cassava, and most of the nation's beef cattle are produced in the hot regions from sea level to 1,000 meters elevation. The temperate regions—between 1,000 and 2,000 meters—are better suited for coffee; certain flowers; corn and other vegetables; and fruits such as citrus, pears, pineapples, and tomatoes. The cooler elevations—between 2,000 and 3,000 meter—produce wheat, barley, potatoes, cold-climate vegetables, flowers, dairy cattle, and poultry.

## Narcotics Cultivation and Control

Colombia is the world's leading supplier of refined cocaine and a growing source for heroin. More than 90% of the cocaine that enters the United States is produced, processed, or transshipped in Colombia. The cultivation of coca more than doubled in 1999 to 302,500 acres from 125,700 acres in 1995, primarily in areas where government control is weak.

Despite the death of Medellin cartel drug kingpin Pablo Escobar in 1993 and the arrests of major Cali cartel leaders in 1995 and 1996, Colombian drug cartels remain among the most sophisticated criminal organizations in the world, controlling cocaine processing, international wholesale distribution chains, and markets. In 1999 Colombian police arrested over 30 narcotraffickers, most of them extraditable, in "Operation Millennium" involving extensive international cooperation. More arrests were made in a following "Operation Millennium II."

Colombia is engaged in a broad range of narcotics control activities. Through aerial spraying of herbicide and manual eradication, Colombia has attempted to keep coca, opium poppy, and cannabis cultivation from expanding. The government has committed itself to the eradication of all illicit crops, interdiction of drug shipments, and financial controls to prevent money laundering. Alternative development programs were introduced in 1999.

Corruption and intimidation by traffickers complicate the drug-control efforts of the institutions of government. Colombia passed revised criminal procedures code in 1993 that permits traffickers to surrender and negotiate lenient sentences in return for cooperating with prosecutors. In December 1996 and February 1997, however, the Colombian Congress passed legislation to toughen sentencing, asset forfeiture, and money-laundering penalties.

In November 1997, the Colombian Congress amended the constitution to permit the extradition of Colombian nationals, albeit not retroactively. In late 1999, President Pastrana authorized the first extradition in almost 10 years of a Colombian trafficker to stand trial for U.S. crimes. Three such extraditions to the United States have taken place, the most recent in August 2000, with cases against others pending in Colombian courts.

# FOREIGN RELATIONS

Colombia seeks diplomatic and commercial relations with all countries, regardless of their ideologies or political or economic systems. In 1969, it formed what is now the Andean Community along with Bolivia, Chile, Ecuador, and Peru (Venezuela joined in 1973, and Chile left in 1976). In the 1980s, Colombia broadened its bilateral and multilateral relations, joining the Contadora Group, the Group of Eight (now the Rio Group), and the Non-Aligned Movement, which it chaired from 1994 until September 1998. In addition, it has signed free trade agreements with Chile, Mexico, and Venezuela.

Colombia has traditionally played an active role in the United Nations and the Organization of American States and in their subsidiary agencies. Former President Gaviria became Secretary General of the OAS in September 1994 and was reelected in 1999. Colombia was a participant in the December 1994 and April 1998 Summits of the Americas and followed up on initiatives developed at the summit by hosting two post-summit, ministerial-level meetings on trade and science and technology.

Colombia regularly participates in international fora, including CICAD, the Organization of American States' body on money laundering, chemical controls, and drug abuse prevention. Although the Colombian Government ratified the 1988 UN Convention on Narcotics in 1994—the last of the Andean governments to do so—it took important reservations, notably to the anti-money-laundering measures, asset forfeiture and confiscation provisions, maritime interdiction, and extradition clauses. Colombia subsequently withdrew some of its reservations, most notably a reservation on extradition.

# U.S.-COLOMBIAN RELATIONS

In 1822, the United States became one of the first countries to recognize the new republic and to establish a resident diplomatic mission. Today, about 25,000 U.S. citizens are registered with the U.S. Embassy living in Colombia, most of them dual nationals. Currently there are about 250 American businesses.

Despite the strain which decertification and related issues placed on bilateral relations during the Samper administration, the U.S. and Colombian Governments continued to cooperate and consult. In 1995–96, the U.S. and Colombia signed important agreements on environmental protection and civil aviation. The two countries have signed agreements on asset sharing and chemical control. In 1997, the U.S. and Colombia signed an important maritime ship-boarding agreement to allow for search of suspected drug-running vessels. During the period 1988–96, the United States provided about $765 million in assistance to Colombia. In 1999, U.S. assistance exceeded $200 million. This funding supported Colombia's counternarcotics efforts, such as arresting drug traffickers, seizing drugs and illegal processing facilities, and eradicating coca and opium poppy.

Under the Pastrana administration, relations with the United States have improved significantly. The United States responded to the Colombian Government's request for international support to Plan Colombia by approving a $1.3 billion aid package in July 2000, in addition to previously programmed assistance of nearly $300 million for FY 2000. U.S. programs are a combination of military and police assistance to increase counternarcotics capabilities and also includes a package of nearly $230 million for human rights, humanitarian assistance, alternative development, and economic and judicial reforms. These programs are an integral component of our support for Plan Colombia's overall goals.

## Trade Development

Colombia is the United States' fifth-largest export market in Latin America—behind Mexico, Brazil, Venezuela, and Argentina—and the 26th-largest market for U.S. products

## Travel Notes

**Travel Advice:** For up-to-date information from the U.S. State Department on possible inconvenient or hazardous situations, see the **Travel Warnings and Consular Information Sheets from the U.S. Government** section starting on page 1723. For the latest information on health requirements and conditions, see the **International Travelers' Health Information** section starting on page 1385. For further information dealing with non-urgent matter, see the **Tips for Travelers to...** section starting on page 1588.

worldwide. The United States is Colombia's principal trading partner, with two-way trade from November 1999 through November 2000 exceeding $9.5 billion—$3.5 billion U.S. exports and $6.0 billion U.S. imports. Colombia benefits from duty-free entry—for a 10-year period, through 2001—for certain of its exports to the United States under the Andean Trade Preferences Act. Colombia improved protection of intellectual property rights through the adoption of three Andean Pact decisions in 1993 and 1994, but the U.S. remains concerned over deficiencies in licensing, patent regulations, and copyright protection.

The petroleum and natural gas coal mining, chemical, and manufacturing industries attract the greatest U.S.

investment interest. U.S. investment accounted for 37.8% ($4.2 billion) of the total $11.2 billion in foreign direct investment at the end of 1997, excluding petroleum and portfolio investment. Worker rights and benefits in the U.S.-dominated sectors are more favorable than general working conditions. Examples include shorter-than-average working hours, higher wages, and compliance with health and safety standards above the national average.

## Principal U.S. Embassy Officials

**For up-to-date information on Principal U.S. Officials, see the U.S. Embassies, Consulates, and Foreign Service section starting on page 139.**

The U.S. Embassy is located at Calle 22D Bis, No. 47–51, Bogota (tel: (571) 315–0811; fax: (571) 315–2196). The mailing address is APO AA 34038. Internet: http://www.usembassy.state.gov/posts/co1 (note: co number ONE and not co letter L). The U.S. Consular Agency in Baranquilla is located at Calle 77, No. 68–15 (tel: (575) 353–0970 or 0974; fax: (575) 353–5216).

# COMOROS

April 1997

Official Name:
**Federal Islamic Republic of Comoros**

## PROFILE

### Geography

**Area:** 2,171 sq. km. (838 sq. mi.); slightly less than half the size of Delaware. Major islands: Grande Comore (1,025 sq. km.), Anjouan (424 sq. km.), Mayotte (374 sq. km.), and Moheli (211 sq. km.).
**Cities:** Capital—Moroni (pop. 30,000). Mutsamudu (pop. 20,000).
**Terrain:** Rugged.
**Climate:** Tropical marine.

### People

**Nationality:** Noun and adjective—Comorian(s).
**Population (1995 est.):** 550,000. Mayotte (1990 est.)—70,000.
**Annual growth rate (1995 est.):** 3.56%.
**Ethnic groups:** Antalote, Cafre, Makoa, Oimatsaha, Sakalava.
**Religions:** Sunni Muslim 98%, Roman Catholic 2%.
**Languages:** Shikomoro (a Swahili-Arab), Malagasy, French.
**Education:** Attendance—62% primary, 32% secondary. Literacy—48%.
**Health:** Life expectancy—58 yrs. Infant mortality rate—77/1,000.
**Work force (1994):** 200,000. Agriculture—80%. Government—3%.

### Government

**Type:** Republic.
**Independence:** July 6, 1975 (Mayotte remains under French administration).
**Constitution:** Adopted by referendum in 1978 and since amended.
**Branches:** Executive—president. Legislative—National Assembly. Judicial—traditional Muslim and codified law from French sources.
**Political parties:** 17 political parties.
**Suffrage:** Universal adult.

### Economy (1994)

**GDP (purchasing power parity):** $370 million.
**Annual growth rate:** 2.5% between 1980 and 1993; 0.9% in 1994.
**Per capita income:** $770.
**Agriculture (40% of GDP):** Products—perfume essences, copra, coconuts, cloves, vanilla, cinnamon, yams, bananas.
**Services (25% of GDP):** commerce, tourism.
**Industry (6% of GDP):** Types—perfume distillation.
**Trade:** Exports (1993 est.)—$13.7 million: vanilla, cloves, perfume essences, copra. Major markets—United States 44%, France 40%, Germany 6%, Africa 5%. Imports (1993 est.)—$40.9 million: rice, petroleum, meat, wheat flour, cotton textiles, cement. Major suppliers—France 34%, South Africa 14%, Kenya 8%, Japan 4%.
**US Economic Aid:** FY96 assistance totaled $120,000: $20,000 in self-help, $25,000 in democracy/human rights funds and $75,000 in international military education and training (IMET). The Peace Corps ended its programs in Comoros in 1995.
**Exchange rate (1996):** 428 Comorian franc = U.S. $1.

## PEOPLE

The Comorians inhabiting Grande Comore, Anjouan, and Moheli (86% of the population) share African-Arab origins. Islam is the dominant religion, and Koranic schools for children reinforce its influence. Although Arab culture is firmly established throughout the archipelago, a substantial minority of the citizens of Mayotte (the Mahorais) are Catholic and have been strongly influenced by French culture.

The most common language is Shikomoro, a Swahili dialect. French and Malagasy are also spoken. About 48% of the population is literate.

## HISTORY

Over the centuries, the islands were invaded by a succession of diverse groups from the coast of Africa, the Persian Gulf, Indonesia, and Madagascar. Portuguese explorers visited the archipelago in 1505. "Shirazi" Arab migrants introduced Islam at about the same time. Between 1841 and 1912, France established colonial rule over Grande Comore, Anjouan, Mayotte, and Moheli and placed the islands under the administration of the governor general of Madagascar. Later, French settlers, French-owned companies, and wealthy Arab merchants established a plantation-based economy that now uses about one-third of the land for export crops. After World War II, the islands became a French overseas territory and were represented in France's National Assembly. Internal political autonomy was granted in 1961. Agreement was reached with France in 1973 for Comoros to become independent in 1978. On July 6, 1975, however, the Comorian parliament passed a resolution declaring unilateral independence. The deputies of Mayotte abstained. As a result, the Comorian Government has effective control over only Grande Comore, Anjouan, and Moheli. Mayotte remains under French administration.

# GOVERNMENT AND POLITICAL CONDITIONS

The present government of President Mohamed Taki Abdoulkarim was elected in March 1996 in internationally monitored elections that observers generally considered free and fair. Taki's election followed a short-lived coup by foreign mercenaries in October 1995 that ousted then-President Said Mohamed Djohar. French troops intervened, arresting the coup leaders and placing Djohar under virtual house arrest in the neighboring French territory of Reunion. An interim government ruled for five months prior to the March elections. The Taki government has taken several steps, including banning the sale of alcohol to Comorian residents, designed to appeal to the country's

**Travel Notes**

**Travel Advice:** For up-to-date information from the U.S. State Department on possible inconvenient or hazardous situations, see the **Travel Warnings and Consular Information Sheets from the U.S. Government** section starting on page 1723. For the latest information on health requirements and conditions, see the **International Travelers' Health Information** section starting on page 1385. For further information dealing with non-urgent matter, see the **Tips for Travelers to...** section starting on page 1588.

Islamic majority. The government has also indicated its desire to strengthen relations with the United States and France.

President Taki won an overwhelming majority in the March elections. He promptly replaced many ranking civil servants associated with the Djohar regime and believed to have been extremely corrupt. Their replacements have yet to establish a track record, but many observers believe widespread corruption continues. There were no reports of civil strife in the first nine months following the French intervention that ended the October 1995 coup; the March 1996 elections were conducted peacefully with no reports of violence. Civil unrest broke out in early 1997 as civil servants demanded payment of salary arrears. At President Taki's request, France agreed to maintain a small troop presence in Comoros. While Taki appears to be more popular and able than his predecessor, democratic institutions in Comoros are weak and political life will remain unstable until they are strengthened and the economy improves.

## National Security

The military resources of the Comoros consist of a small standing army and a 500-member police force, as well as a 500-member defense force. A defense treaty with France provides naval resources for protection of territorial waters, training of Comorian military personnel, and air surveillance. France maintains a small

troop presence in Comoros at government request. France maintains a small maritime base and a foreign legion contingent on Mayotte.

## Principal Government Officials

**For up-to-date information on Principal Government Officials, see the Chiefs of State and Cabinet Members of Foreign Governments section starting on page 1.**

Comoros maintains a mission to the United States at 336 E. 45th St., 2d floor, New York, NY 10017 (tel. 212-972-8010).

# ECONOMY

Comoros, with an estimated gross domestic product (GDP) per capita income of about $700, is among the world's poorest and least developed nations. Although the quality of the land differs from island to island, most of the widespread lava-encrusted soil formations are unsuited to agriculture. As a result, most of the inhabitants make their living from subsistence agriculture and fishing.

Agriculture, involving more than 80% of the population and 40% of the gross domestic product, provides virtually all foreign exchange earnings. Services including tourism, construction, and commercial activities constitute the remainder of the GDP. Plantations engage a large proportion of the population in producing the islands' major cash crops for export: vanilla, cloves, perfume essences, and copra. Comoros is the world's leading producer of essence of ylang-ylang, used in manufacturing perfume. It also is the world's second largest producer of vanilla. Principal food crops are coconuts, bananas, and cassava. Foodstuffs constitute 34% of total imports.

The country lacks the infrastructure necessary for development. Some villages are not linked to the main road system or at best are connected by tracks usable only by four-wheel-drive vehicles. The islands' ports are rudimentary, although a deep-water facility was recently completed on Anjouan. Only small vessels can approach the existing quays in Moroni on Grande Comore, despite recent improvements. Long-distance, ocean-going ships must lie offshore and be unloaded by smaller boats; during the cyclone season, this procedure is dangerous, and ships are reluctant to call at the island. Most freight is sent first to Mombasa or Reunion and transshipped from there.

France, Comoros' major trading partner, also provides direct budgetary support essential to the government's daily operations. The United States receives a growing percentage of Comoros' exports but supplies only a negligible fraction of its imports (less than 1%).

Comoros has an international airport at Hahaya on Grande Comore. It is a member of the franc zone (Communaute Financiere Africaine—CFA), with an exchange rate of 428 CFA francs = U.S. $1 (1991).

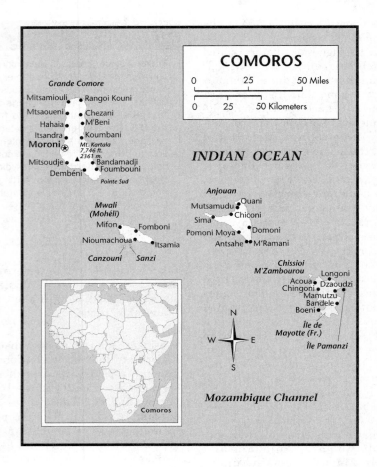

# FOREIGN RELATIONS

In November 1975, Comoros became the 143d member of the United Nations. The new nation was defined as consisting of the entire archipelago, despite the fact that France maintains control over Mayotte.

Comoros also is a member of the Organization of African Unity, the European Development Fund, the World Bank, the International Monetary Fund, the Indian Ocean Commission, and the African Development Bank.

# U.S.-COMORIAN RELATIONS

The United States recognized the Comorian Government in 1977. The two countries enjoy friendly relations. The United States closed its embassy in Moroni in 1993 and is now represented by a non-resident ambassador in neighboring Mauritius.

## Principal U.S. Embassy Officials

**For up-to-date information on Principal U.S. Officials, see the U.S. Embassies, Consulates, and Foreign Service section starting on page 139.**

The address of the United States embassy in Mauritius is Rogers House, John F. Kennedy Street, Port Louis. (tel: 230-208-2347; fax: 230-208-9534). The mailing address for the embassy is Department of State, Washington, DC 20521-2520.

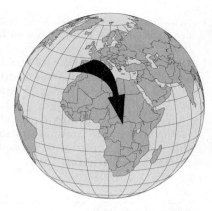

# CONGO

January 2000

## Official Name:
## Democratic Republic of the Congo

# PROFILE

## Geography

**Location:** Central Africa. Bordering nations—Angola, Burundi, Cameroon, Central African Republic, Republic of the Congo, Sudan, Rwanda, Tanzania, Uganda, Zambia.
**Area:** 2,345 square kilometers (905,063 sq. mi.; about the size of the U.S. east of the Mississippi).
**Cities:** Capital—Kinshasa (pop. 6.55 million). Regional Capitals—Bandundu, Bukavu, Goma, Kananga, Kindu, Kisangani, Lubumbashi, Matadi, Mbandaka, Mbuji-Mayi.
**Terrain:** Varies from tropical rainforests to mountainous terraces, plateau, savannas, dense grasslands, and mountains.
**Climate:** Equatorial; ranges from tropical rainforest in the Congo River basin, hot and humid in much of the north and west, cooler and drier in the south central area and the east.

## People

**Nationality:** Noun and adjective—Congolese.
**Population (1997):** 46.7 million.
**Annual growth rate (1997):** 3.1%.
**Ethnic groups:** More than 200 African ethnic groups; Bantu 80% of which Luba (18% of total population), Kongo (16.1%), and Mongo (13.5%)

are largest.
**Religions:** Roman Catholic 50%, Protestant 20%, Kimanguist 10%, Muslim 10%, other syncretic sects and traditional beliefs 10%.
**Language:** Official—French. Widely used—Lingala, Kingwana, Kikongo, Tshiluba.
**Education (1995 est.):** Literacy—77.3% in French or local language. Health (1998 est.): Infant mortality rate—101.6/1,000. Life expectancy—49 yrs.

## Government

**Type:** Republic—highly centralized with legislative and executive power vested in the president.
**Independence:** June 30, 1960 (from Belgium).
**Constitution:** June 24, 1967; amended August 1974; revised February 15, 1978; amended April 1990; transitional constitution promulgated April 1994; draft constitution proposed March 1998, not yet finalized.
**Branches:** Executive—(chief of state) head of government. Cabinet—National Executive Council, a 26-member executive dominated by the Alliance des Forces Democratiques pour la Liberation du Congo-Zaire (AFDL) and appointed by the president. There is no prime minister. Legislative—The legislature has been suspended pending constitutional reform. Judicial—Supreme

Court (Cour Supreme).
**Administrative subdivisions:** Ten provinces and the capital city, Kinshasa. A provincial governor, who is appointed and dismissed by the president, administers each province.
**Political parties:** Ruling AFDL is comprised of Alliance Democratique des Peuples (ADP), Parti Revolutionnaire du Peuple (PRP), Le Conseil National de la Resistance (CNR), and La Mouvement Revolutionnaire pour la Liberation du Congo-Zaire. The main opposition party is Union pour la Democratie et le Progres Social (UDPS). Militant rebel groups include the Rassemblement Congolais pour la Democratie (RCD) and La Movement pour La Liberation du Congo (MLC).
**Suffrage:** 18 years of age; universal and compulsory.
**Flag:** Light blue with gold star in center and six smaller gold stars vertically aligned on the left edge.

## Economy

**GDP (1997):** $6.1 billion.
**Annual GDP growth rate (1997):** -5.7%.
**Per capita GDP (1997):** $350.
**Natural resources:** copper, cobalt, diamonds, gold, other minerals; petroleum; wood; hydroelectric potential.
**Agriculture:** Cash crops—coffee, rubber, palm oil, quinquina, cocoa, sugar.

Food crops—manioc, corn, legumes, plantains, peanuts. Land use—agriculture 3%; pasture 7%; forest/woodland 77%; other 13% Industry: Types—processed and unprocessed minerals; consumer products, including textiles, plastics, footwear, cigarettes, metal products; processed foods and beverages, cement, timber. Currency: Congolese franc (FC).

**Trade:** Exports (1997)—$1.396 billion. Products—diamonds, cobalt, copper, coffee, petroleum. Partners—Belgium, France, Germany, Italy, Japan, South Africa, U.K., U.S. Imports (1997)—$1.022 billion. Products—Consumer goods (food, textiles), refined petroleum products. Partners—Belgium, China, France, Germany, Italy, South Africa, U.K., U.S.

**Total external debt (1997):** $14.384 billion.

# GEOGRAPHY

The Democratic Republic of the Congo (DROC), formerly Zaire, includes the greater part of the Congo River Basin, which covers an area of almost 1 million square kilometers (400,000 sq. mi.). The country's only outlet to the Atlantic Ocean is a narrow strip of land on the north bank of the Congo River.

The vast, low-lying central area is a basin-shaped plateau sloping toward the west and covered by tropical rainforest. This area is surrounded by mountainous terraces in the west, plateaus merging into savannas in the south and southwest, and dense grasslands extending beyond the Congo River in the north. High mountains are found in the extreme eastern region.

DROC lies on the Equator, with one-third of the country to the north and two-thirds to the south. The climate is hot and humid in the river basin and cool and dry in the southern highlands. South of the Equator, the rainy season lasts from October to May and north of the Equator, from April to November. Along the Equator, rainfall is fairly regular throughout the year. During the wet season, thunderstorms often are violent but seldom last more than a few hours. The average rainfall for the entire country is about 107 centimeters (42 in.).

# PEOPLE

The population of DROC was estimated at 46.7 million in 1997. As many as 250 ethnic groups have been distinguished and named. The most numerous people are the Kongo, Luba, and Mongo. Although 700 local languages and dialects are spoken, the linguistic variety is bridged both by the use of French and the intermediary languages Kikongo, Tshiluba, Swahili, and Lingala.

About 80% of the Congolese population are Christian, predominantly Roman Catholic. Most of the non-Christians adhere to either traditional religions or syncretic sects. Traditional religions embody such concepts as monotheism, animism, vitalism, spirit and ancestor worship, witchcraft, and sorcery and vary widely among ethnic groups; none is formalized. The syncretic sects often merge Christianity with traditional beliefs and rituals. The most popular of these sects, Kimbanguism, was seen as a threat to the colonial regime and was banned by the Belgians. Kimbanguism, officially "the church of Christ on Earth by the prophet Simon Kimbangu," now has about 3 million members, primarily among the Bakongo of Bas-Congo and Kinshasa. In 1969, it was the first independent African church admitted to the World Council of Churches.

Before independence, education was largely in the hands of religious groups. The primary school system was well-developed at independence; however, the secondary school system was limited, and higher education was almost nonexistent in most regions of the country. The principal objective of this system was to train low-level administrators and clerks. Since independence, efforts have been made to increase access to education, and secondary and higher education have been made available to many more Congolese. Despite the deterioration of the state-run educational system in recent years, about 80% of the males and 65% of females, ages 6-11, were enrolled in a mixture of state- and church-run primary schools in 1996. At higher levels of education, males greatly outnumber females. The elite continues to send their children abroad to be educated, primarily in Western Europe.

# HISTORY

The area known as the Democratic Republic of the Congo was populated as early as 10,000 years ago and settled in the 7th and 8th centuries A.D. by Bantus from present-day Nigeria. Discovered in 1482 by Portuguese navigator Diego Cao and later explored by English journalist Henry Morton Stanley, the area was officially colonized in 1885 as a personal possession of Belgian King Leopold II as the Congo Free State. In 1907, administration shifted to the Belgian Government, which renamed the country the Belgian Congo. Following a series of riots and unrest, the Belgian Congo was granted its independence on June 30, 1960. Parliamentary elections in 1960 produced Patrice Lumumba as prime minister and Joseph Kasavubu as president of the renamed Democratic Republic of the Congo.

Within the first year of independence, several events destabilized the country: the army mutinied; the governor of Katanga province attempted secession; a UN peacekeeping force was called in to restore order; Prime Minister Lumumba died under mysterious circumstances; and Col. Joseph Mobutu (later Mobutu Sese Seko) took over the government and ceded it again to President Kasavubu.

Unrest and rebellion plagued the government until 1965, when Lieutenant General Mobutu, by then commander in chief of the national army, again seized control of the country and declared himself president for 5 years. Mobutu quickly centralized power into his own hands and was elected unopposed as president in

## DEMOCRATIC REPUBLIC OF THE CONGO

0    100    200    300 Miles

0    100    200    300 Kilometers

CENTRAL AFRICAN REPUBLIC

SUDAN

CAMEROON

Zongo

Yakoma

Banda

Aba

Gemena

Bondo

Uélé

Isiro

Bomu

Ubangi

Congo

Lisala

Bumba

Lake Albert

MTS. BLEUS

Congo Basin

Yahuma

Kisangani

Margherita Pk. 16,762 ft. 5109 m.

UGANDA

Mbandaka

Ubundu

Lake Edward

REPUBLIC OF THE CONGO

Tshuapa

Aruwimi

Lomami

Lualaba

Goma
Lake Kivu

RWANDA

GABON

Inongo

Lac Mai-Ndombe

Lomela

Kindu

Bukavu

BURUNDI

Congo

Kwa

Kasai

Sankuru

Uvira

Kama

Brazzaville

Bandundu

Ilebo

Kampene

Lake Tanganyika

TANZANIA

Kinshasa

ANGOLA

Kikwit

Idiofa

Demba

Lukuga

Tshela

Kwango

Kananga

Kalemie

Banana

Matadi

Tshikapa

Mbuji-Mayi

Luvua

Soyo

Bumba

Mwene-Ditu

Quimele

Panzi

N'zeto

Kasai

CHAINE DES MITUMBA

Lake Mweru

Nchelenge

ANGOLA

Sandoa

Kolwezi

Luapula

Dilolo

Likasa

N
W    E
S

Cazombo

Lubumbashi

Democratic Republic of the Congo

ZAMBIA

1970. Embarking on a campaign of cultural awareness, Mobutu renamed the country the Republic of Zaire and required citizens to adopt African names. Relative peace and stability prevailed until 1977 and 1978 when Katangan rebels, staged in Angola, launched a series of invasions into the Katanga region. The rebels were driven out with the aid of Belgian paratroopers.

During the 1980s, Mobutu continued to enforce his one-party system of rule. Although Mobutu successfully maintained control during this period, opposition parties, most notably the Union pour la Democratie et le Progres Social (UDPS), were active. Mobutu's attempts to quell these groups drew significant international criticism.

As the Cold War came to a close, internal and external pressures on Mobutu increased. In late 1989 and early 1990, Mobutu was weakened by a series of domestic protests, by heightened international criticism of his regime's human rights practices, and by a faltering economy. In May 1990 Mobutu agreed to the principle of a multi-party system with elections and a constitution. As details of a reform package were delayed, soldiers in September 1991 began looting Kinshasa to protest their unpaid wages. Two thousand French and Belgian troops, some of whom were flown in on U.S. Air Force planes, arrived to evacuate the 20,000 endangered foreign nationals in Kinshasa.

In 1992, after previous similar attempts, the long-promised Sovereign National Conference was staged, encompassing over 2,000 representatives from various political parties. The conference gave itself a legislative mandate and elected Archbishop Laurent Monsengwo as its chairman, along with Etienne Tshisekedi, leader of the UDPS, as prime minister. By the end of the year Mobutu had created a rival government with its own prime minister. The ensuing stalemate produced a compromise merger of the two governments into the High Council of Republic-Parliament of Transition (HCR-PT) in 1994, with Mobutu as head of state and Kengo Wa Dondo as prime minister. Although presidential and legislative elections were scheduled repeatedly over the next 2 years, they never took place.

By 1996, tensions from the neighboring Rwanda war had spilled over to Zaire. Rwandan Hutu militia forces (Interahamwe), who had fled Rwanda following the ascension of a Tutsi-led government, had been using Hutu refugees camps in eastern Zaire as a basis for incursion against Rwanda. These Hutu militia forces soon allied with the Zairian armed forces (FAZ) to launch a campaign against Congolese ethnic Tutsis in eastern Zaire. In turn, these Tutsis formed a militia to defend themselves against attacks.

The Tutsi militia was soon joined by various opposition groups and supported by several countries, including Rwanda and Uganda. This coalition, led by Laurent-Desire Kabila, became known as the Alliance des Forces Democratiques pour la Liberation du Congo-Zaire (AFDL). The AFDL, now seeking the broader goal of ousting Mobutu, made significant military gains in early 1997. Following failed peace talks between Mobutu and Kabila in May 1997, Mobutu left the country, and Kabila marched unopposed to Kinshasa on May 20. Kabila named himself president, consolidated power around himself and the AFDL, and renamed the country the Democratic Republic of Congo.

# GOVERNMENT AND POLITICAL CONDITIONS

Despite President Kabila's claims that his was a transitional government leading to a new constitution and full elections by April 1999, these elections have not yet been held, and a 1998 draft constitution has not been finalized. All executive, legislative, and military powers are vested in the president. The judiciary is independent, with the president having the power to dismiss or appoint. The president is head of a 26-member cabinet dominated by the AFDL.

Despite some successes at improving internal security and lowering the inflation rate over his first year, Kabila was unable to control insurgent activities by various armed groups. Activities by Hutu ex-FAR/Interahamwe, Mai-Mai soldiers, and a February 1998 mutiny by Tutsi Banyamulenge destabilized the regime. In addition, Kabila's pledges to democratize the government over time contrasted with the reality of banned political parties and increasingly centralized power. Criticism of Kabila's government grew both domestically and within the international community.

In an attempt to stabilize the country and consolidate his control, President Kabila in August 1998 expelled the Rwandan troops remaining in DROC after his 1997 victory. This prompted army mutinies in Kinshasa and the Kivu provinces in the east. Although the Kinshasa mutiny was put down, the mutiny in the Kivus continued and mushroomed into a drive to topple the government. Opposing the Kabila government were factions of the Rally for Congolese Democracy (RCD), Rwanda, and Uganda. The Movement for the Liberation of Congo (MLC), another rebel group, emerged later. Defending the Kabila government were the former Rwandan army (ex-FAR)/Interahamwe militia, Angola, Namibia, Chad, Zimbabwe, and the Congolese army (FAC).

In July 1999 a cease-fire was proposed in Lusaka, Zambia. The Lusaka Peace Accord calls for a cease-fire, an international peacekeeping operation, and the beginning of a "national dialogue" on the future of the country. Signed by all major groups, the prospects for lasting peace remain uncertain.

## Principal Government Officials

**For up-to-date information on Principal Government Officials, see the Chiefs of State and Cabinet Members of Foreign Governments section starting on page 1.**

# ECONOMY

Sparsely populated in relation to its area, the Democratic Republic of the Congo is home to a vast potential of natural resources and mineral wealth. Agriculture is the mainstay of the economy, accounting for 57.9% of GDP in 1997. Main cash crops include coffee, palm oil, rubber, cotton, sugar, tea, and cocoa. Food crops include cassava, plantains, maize, groundnuts, and rice. In 1996, agriculture employed 66% of the work force.

Industry, especially mining, remains a great potential source of wealth for DROC. In 1997, industry accounted for 16.9% of GDP. The Congo was the world's fourth-largest producer of industrial diamonds during the 1980s, and diamonds continue to dominate exports, accounting for $717 million or 52% of exports in 1997. The Congo's main copper and cobalt interests are dominated by Gecamines, the state-owned mining giant. Gecamines production has faltered in recent years, due in part to a competitive world copper market.

Despite the country's vast potential, under the Mobutu regime widespread corruption, economic controls, and the diversion of public resources for personal gain thwarted economic growth. The unrecorded and illicit transactions of Zaire's unofficial economy were estimated in the early 1990s to be three times the size of official GDP.

The Congo's record with multilateral and bilateral donors has been uneven. Despite a succession of economic plans financed by the World Bank and the International Monetary Fund (IMF) since independence, budgetary imbalance, inflation, and debt consistently plagued the Mobutu government. In early 1990, both the World Bank and the IMF suspended most disbursements, and most bilateral aid was cut off. Unable to make debt payments, Zaire's borrowing rights with the IMF were cut off in February 1992; its World Bank credits were frozen in July 1993. Despite the introduction of a new currency, the New Zaire (NZ), currency issuance remained disorderly, and large-scale inflation rose to over 9,000% by early 1994.

In May 1997 the AFDL, led by Laurent Kabila, overthrew the regime of Mobutu Sese Seko. Under President Kabila the government and state enterprises began a program of reconstruction. The government began to reform the corrupt tax system, civilian police force, and repair the damaged road system.

In August 1998, a war broke out in the Democratic Republic of the Congo. At that time, some progress had been made in the economic reconstruction of the country, but major problems continued to exist in transportation infrastructure, customs administration, and the tax system. Government finances had not been put in order and relations with the IMF and World Bank were in disarray. Much of the government's revenue was kept "off book," and not included in published statistics on revenue and expenditure. Relations with the World Bank were on hold as a result of the government's failure to finalize an agreement for administration of the International Bank for Reconstruction and Development

## Travel Notes

**Travel Advice:** For up-to-date information from the U.S. State Department on possible inconvenient or hazardous situations, see the **Travel Warnings and Consular Information Sheets from the U.S. Government** section starting on page 1723. For the latest information on health requirements and conditions, see the **International Travelers' Health Information** section starting on page 1385. For further information dealing with non-urgent matter, see the **Tips for Travelers to...** section starting on page 1588.

The outbreak of war in the early days of August 1998 caused a major decline in economic activity that continues to the present. The country has been divided into rebel- and government-held territories, and commerce between them has stopped. The economic and commercial links among the various sections of the country are not strong, but they are important.

After a surge in inflation during August 1998, the government began enforcing price control laws. It also began regulating foreign exchange markets. Taken together, these measures have severely damaged the ability of businesses depending on imports to continue operations. The wide spread between the official rate for buying the new currency, Congo francs (FCs), and the black market rate for buying dollars has squeezed merchants forced to price their imported goods according to the official rate for buying local currency.

Faced with continued currency depreciation, the government resorted to more drastic measures and on January 1999 banned the widespread use of U.S. dollars for all domestic commercial transactions, a position it later adjusted. The government has been unable to provide foreign exchange for economic transactions, while it has resorted to printing money to finance its expenditure.

# FOREIGN RELATIONS

Its location in the center of Africa has made DROC a key player in the region since independence. Because of its size, mineral wealth, and strategic location, Zaire was able to capitalize on Cold War tensions to garner support from the West. In the early 1990s, however, in the face of growing evidence of human rights abuses, Western support waned as pressure for internal reform increased.

Relations with surrounding countries have often been driven by security concerns. Intricate and interlocking alliances have often characterized regional relations. Conflicts in Sudan, Uganda, Angola, Rwanda, and Burundi have at various times created bilateral and regional tensions. The current crisis in DROC has its roots both in the use of The Congo as a base by various insurgency groups attacking neighboring countries and in the absence of a broad-based political system in the Congo.

## Principal U.S. Officials

**For up-to-date information on Principal U.S. Officials, see the U.S. Embassies, Consulates, and Foreign Service section starting on page 139.**

# U.S.-CONGOLESE RELATIONS

Its dominating position in Central Africa makes stability in DROC an important part of overall stability in the region. The U.S. supports a resolution to the current conflict and encourages peace, prosperity, democracy, and respect for human rights in DROC. The U.S. remains a partner with DROC and other central African nations in their quest for stability and growth on the continent. From the start of the Congo crisis, the U.S. has pursued an active diplomatic strategy in support of these objectives. In the long term, the U.S. seeks to strengthen the process of internal reconciliation and democratization within all the states of the region to promote stable, economically self-reliant, and democratic nations with which it can work to address mutual economic and security interests on the continent.

The U.S. appointed an ambassador in November 1995. A charge had headed the Zaire/DROC since March 1993. There is no current U.S. bilateral aid to the Congo except for grants to NGOs in direct support for human rights and democratization projects. The Congo has been on the State Department's travel advisory list since 1977.

The United States maintains an embassy at 310 Avenue des Aviateurs, Kinshasa (tel. 243-12-21028; fax 243-88-43805). Mailing address is American Embassy Kinshasa, Box 31550, APO AE 09828.

# CONGO

February 2000

Official Name:
**Republic of Congo**

# PROFILE

## Geography

**Area:** 342,000 sq. km (132,000 sq. mi.); slightly larger than New Mexico.
**Cities:** *Capital*—Brazzaville (pop. 750,000). *Other cities*—Pointe- Noire (400,000), Dolisie (150,000).
**Climate:** Tropical.
**Terrain:** Coastal plains, fertile valleys, central plateau, forested flood plains.

## People

**Nationality:** *Noun and adjective*—Congolese (sing. and pl.).
**Population (1997 est.):** 2.6 million. Annual growth rate (1997 est.): 2.8%.
**Ethnic groups:** 15 principal Bantu groups, more than 70 subgroups; largest groups are Bacongo, Vili, Bateke, M'Bochi, and Sangha. Also present is a small population (less than 100,000) of Pygmies, ethnically unrelated to the Bantu majority.
**Religions:** Traditional beliefs 50%, Roman Catholic 35%, other Christian 15%, Muslim 2%.
**Languages:** French (official), Lingala and Munukutuba (national).
**Health:** *Infant mortality rate*—106/1,000. *Life expectancy*—46 yrs.
**Work force:** About 40% of population, two-thirds of whom work in agriculture.

## Government

**Type:** Republic.
**Independence:** August 15, 1960.
**Constitution:** February 16, 1992.(Suspended in October 1997.) A new constitution has been drafted but not yet adopted. Branches: *Executive*—President (chief of state), Council of Ministers (cabinet).*Legislative*—Transitional Advisory Council. *Judicial*—Supreme Court, Constitutional Council, High Court of Justice.
**Administrative subdivisions:** 10 regions, divided into districts, plus the capital district.
**Political parties:** More than 100 new parties formed since multi-party democracy was introduced in 1990. The largest are the Pan-African Union for Social Democracy (UPADS), Congolese Labor Party (PCT), Congolese Movement for Democracy and Integral Development (MCDDI), Coalition for Democracy and Social Progress (RDPS), Coalition for Democracy and Development (RDD), Union of Democratic Forces (UFD), Union of Democratic Renewal (URD), Union for Development and Social Progress (UDPS). However, following the June-October 1997 war, many parties, including UPADS and MCDDI, were left in disarray as their leadership fled the country.
**Suffrage:** Universal adult.

## Economy

**GDP (1995 est.):** $2.1 billion.
**Per capita income (1995):** $680.
**Natural resources:** Petroleum, wood, potassium, potash, lead, zinc, uranium, phosphates, natural gas.
**Structure of production:** Agriculture and forestry 12%, petroleum sector 38%, utilities and industry 15%, government and service 35%.
**Agriculture:** *Products*—manioc, plantains, bananas, peanuts, sugarcane, cocoa, coffee, and palm kernels. *Land*—less than 2% cultivated.
**Trade (1995):** *Exports*—$952 million: petroleum (84% of export earnings), tropical and other woods, diamonds, sugar, coffee, cocoa. *Imports*—$670 million: machines and appliances, construction materials, chemical products, transportation equipment, foodstuffs, textiles, and paper products.

# PEOPLE

Congo's sparse population is concentrated in the southwestern portion of the country, leaving the vast areas of tropical jungle in the north virtually uninhabited. Thus, Congo is one of the most urbanized countries in Africa, with 85% of its total population living in a few urban areas, namely in Brazzaville, Pointe-Noire, or one of the small cities or villages lining the 332-mile railway which connects the two cities. In rural areas, industrial and commercial activity has declined rapidly in recent years, leaving rural economies dependent on the government for support and subsistence. Before the 1997 war, about 9,000 Europeans and other non-Africans lived in Congo, most of whom were French. Only a fraction of this number remains.

# HISTORY

First inhabited by pygmies, Congo was later settled by Bantu groups that also occupied parts of present-day Angola, Gabon, and Zaire, forming the basis for ethnic affinities and rivalries among those states. Several Bantu kingdoms—notably those of the Kongo, the Loango, and the Teke—built trade links leading into the Congo River basin. The first European contacts came in the late 15th century, and commercial relationships were quickly established with the kingdoms—trading for slaves captured in the interior. The coastal area was a major source for the transatlantic slave trade, and when that commerce ended in the early 19th century, the power of the Bantu kingdoms eroded.

The area came under French sovereignty in the 1880s. Pierre Sauvignon de Brazza, a French empire builder, competed with agents of Belgian King Leopold's International Congo Association (later Zaire) for control of the Congo River basin. Between 1882 and 1891, treaties were secured with all the main local rulers on the river's right bank, placing their lands under French protection. In 1908, France organized French Equatorial Africa (AEF), comprising its colonies of Middle Congo (modern Congo), Gabon, Chad, and Oubangui-Chari (modern Central African Republic). Brazzaville was selected as the federal capital.

Economic development during the first 50 years of colonial rule in Congo

## Travel Notes

**Travel Advice:** For up-to-date information from the U.S. State Department on possible inconvenient or hazardous situations, see the **Travel Warnings and Consular Information Sheets from the U.S. Government** section starting on page 1723. For the latest information on health requirements and conditions, see the **International Travelers' Health Information** section starting on page 1385. For further information dealing with non-urgent matter, see the **Tips for Travelers to...** section starting on page 1588.

centered on natural resource extraction by private companies. In 1924-34, the Congo-Ocean Railway (CFCO) was built at a considerable human and financial cost, opening the way for growth of the ocean port of Pointe-Noire and towns along its route.

During World War II, the AEF administration sided with Charles DeGaulle, and Brazzaville became the symbolic capital of Free France during 1940-43. The Brazzaville Conference of 1944 heralded a period of major reform in French colonial policy, including the abolition of forced labor, granting of French citizenship to colonial subjects, decentralization of certain powers, and election of local advisory assemblies. Congo benefited from the postwar expansion of colonial administrative and infrastructural spending as a result of its central geographic location within AEF and the federal capital at Brazzaville.

The *Loi Cadre* (framework law) of 1956 ended dual voting roles and provided for partial self-government for the individual overseas territories. Ethnic rivalries then produced sharp struggles among the emerging Congolese political parties and sparked severe riots in Brazzaville in 1959. After the September 1958 referendum approving the new French constitution, AEF was dissolved. Its four territories became autonomous members of the French Community, and Middle Congo was renamed the Congo Republic. Formal independence was granted in August 1960.

Congo's first president was Fulbert Youlou, a former Catholic priest from the Pool region in the southeast. He rose to political prominence after 1956, and was narrowly elected president by the National Assembly at independence. Youlou's 3 years in power were marked by ethnic tensions and political rivalry. In August 1963, Youlou was overthrown in a 3-day popular uprising (*Les Trois Glorieuses*) led by labor elements and joined by rival political parties. All members of the Youlou government were arrested or removed from office. The Congolese military took charge of the country briefly and installed a civilian provisional government headed by Alphonse Massamba-Debat. Under the 1963 constitution, Massamba-Debat was elected President for a 5-year term and named Pascal Lissouba to serve as Prime Minister. However, President Massamba-Debat's term ended abruptly in August 1968, when Capt. Marien Ngouabi and other army officers toppled the government in a coup. After a period of consolidation under the newly formed National Revolutionary Council, Major Ngouabi assumed the presidency on December 31, 1968. One year later, President Ngouabi proclaimed Congo to be Africa's first "people's republic" and announced the decision of the National Revolutionary Movement to change its name to the Congolese Labor Party (PCT).

On March 16, 1977, President Ngouabi was assassinated. Although the persons accused of shooting Ngouabi were tried and some of them executed, the motivation behind the assassination is still not clear. An 11-member Military Committee of the Party (CMP) was named to head an interim government with Col. (later Gen.) Joachim Yhomby-Opango to serve as President of the Republic. Accused of corruption and deviation from party directives, Yhomby-Opango was removed from office on February 5, 1979, by the Central Committee of the PCT, which then simultaneously designated Vice President and Defense Minister Col. Denis Sassou-Nguesso as interim President. The Central Committee directed Sassou-Nguesso to take charge of preparations for the Third

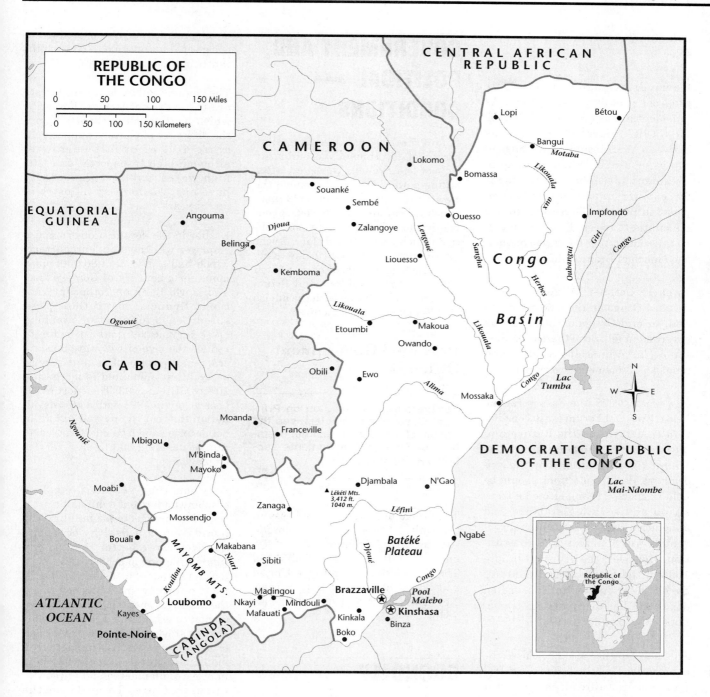

REPUBLIC OF
THE CONGO

0    50    100    150 Miles
0  50  100  150 Kilometers

CAMEROON

CENTRAL AFRICAN
REPUBLIC

EQUATORIAL
GUINEA

Lopi          Bétou

Bangui
Motaba

Lokomo

Bomassa

Souanké

Sembé                    Ouesso          Impfondo

Angouma

Zalangoye

Belinga        Djoua

Liouesso

Congo

Kemboma

Likouala

Etoumbi       Makoua         Basin

GABON                     Owando

Obili    Ewo

Lac
Tumba

Moanda                                  Mossaka

Franceville

DEMOCRATIC REPUBLIC
OF THE CONGO

Mbigou

M'Binda
Mayoko                    Djambala    N'Gao         Lac
                                                    Mai-Ndombe

Moabi           Lékéti Mts.
                3,412 ft.
Zanaga          1040 m.      Léfini

Mossendjo

Bouali                              Batéké
                                    Plateau
Makabana                                       Ngabé
MAYOMB MTS.
Sibiti                  Djoué
Madingou                        Congo
Loubomo   Nkayi  Mindouli   Brazzaville
Kayes          Mafauati              Pool
                        Kinkala      Malebo
ATLANTIC                             Kinshasa
OCEAN                    Boko   Binza

Pointe-Noire   CABINDA
               (ANGOLA)

Republic of
the Congo

N
W    E
S

Ngounié

Ogooué

Lengoué

Sangha

Herbes

Likouala aux

Oubangui

Giri

Congo

Congo

Altima

Niari

Kouilou

Extraordinary Congress of the PCT, which proceeded to elect him President of the Central Committee and President of the Republic. Under a congressional resolution, Yhomby-Opango was stripped of all powers, rank, and possessions and placed under arrest to await trial for high treason. He was released from house arrest in late 1984 and ordered back to his native village of Owando.

After decades of turbulent politics bolstered by Marxist-Leninist rheto-ric, and with the collapse of the Soviet Union, the Congolese gradually moderated their economic and political views to the point that, in 1992, Congo completed a transition to multi-party democracy. Ending a long history of one-party Marxist rule, a specific agenda for this transition was laid out during Congo's national conference of 1991 and culminated in August 1992 with multi-party presidential elections. Sassou-Nguesso conceded defeat and Congo's new

president, Prof. Pascal Lissouba, was inaugurated on August 31, 1992.

Congolese democracy experienced severe trials in 1993 and early 1994. The President dissolved the National Assembly in November 1992, calling for new elections in May 1993. The results of those elections were disputed, touching off violent civil unrest in June and again in November. In February 1994, the decisions of an international board of arbiters were accepted by all parties, and the risk of large-scale insurrection subsided.

However, Congo's democratic progress was derailed in 1997. As presidential elections scheduled for July 1997 approached, tensions between the Lissouba and Sassou camps mounted. When on June 5, President Lissouba's government forces surrounded Sassou's compound in Brazzaville, Sassou ordered his militia to resist. Thus began a 4-month conflict that destroyed or damaged much of Brazzaville.

In early October, Angolan troops invaded Congo on the side of Sassou and, in mid-October, the Lissouba government fell. Soon thereafter, Sassou declared himself President and named a 33-member government.

In January 1998, the Sassou regime held a National Forum for Reconciliation to determine the nature and duration of the transition period. The Forum, tightly controlled by the government, decided elections should be held in about 3 years, elected a transition advisory legislature, and announced that a constitutional convention will finalize a draft constitution. However, the eruption in late 1998 of fighting between Sassou's government forces and an armed opposition has disrupted the transitional return to democracy.

This new violence also has closed the economically vital Brazzaville-Pointe-Noire railroad; caused great destruction and loss of life in southern Brazzaville and in the Pool, Bouenza, and Niari regions; and displaced hundreds of thousands of persons. However, in November and December 1999, the government signed agreements with representatives of many, though not all, of the rebel groups. The December accord, mediated by President Omar Bongo of Gabon, calls for follow-on, inclusive political negotiations between the government and the opposition.

# GOVERNMENT AND POLITICAL CONDITIONS

Before the 1997 war, the Congolese system of government was similar to that of the French. However, after taking power, Sassou suspended the constitution approved in 1992 upon which this system was based. A convention has drafted a new constitution, which would provide for a 7-year presidential term. Until new elections are held in 2000 or later, Sassou will serve as President and Prime Minister and will rule with the advice of a 75-member parliament.

## Principal Government Officials

**For up-to-date information on Principal Government Officials, see the Chiefs of State and Cabinet Members of Foreign Governments section starting on page 1.**

The Congo maintains an embassy in the United States at 4891 Colorado Avenue, N.W., Washingt on, D.C. 20011 (tel: (202) 726-5500). The Congolese Mission to the United Nations is at 14 East 65th Street, New York, NY 10021 (tel: (212) 744-7840).

# ECONOMY

The Congo's economy is based primarily on its growing petroleum sector, which is by far the country's major revenue earner. The Congolese oil sector is dominated by the French parastatal oil company Elf-Aquitaine, which accounts for 70% of the country's annual oil production. In second position is the Italian oil firm Agip. Chevron, CMS Nomeko, and Exxon are among the American companies active in petroleum exploration or production. Following recent discoveries and oil fields currently under

development, Congo's oil production is expected to continue to rise significantly in the next few years.

The country's abundant rain forests are the source of timber. Forestry, which led Congolese exports before the discovery of oil, continues to generate 10% of export earnings, although high transportation costs, high wages, and low productivity have hurt the forestry industry in recent years.

Earlier in the decade, Congo's major employer was the state bureaucracy, which had a payroll of 80,000, enormous for a country of Congo's size. The World Bank and other international financial institutions pressured Congo to institute sweeping civil service reforms in order to reduce the size of the state bureaucracy and pare back a civil service payroll that amounted to more than 20% of GDP in 1993. The effort to cut back began in 1994 with a 50% devaluation that cut the payroll in half in dollar terms and by a mid-year reduction of nearly 8,000 in civil service employment.

Between 1994-96, the Congolese economy underwent a difficult transition. The prospects for building the foundation of a healthy economy, however, were better than at any time in the previous 15 years. Congo took a number of measures to liberalize its economy, including reforming the tax, investment, labor, and hydrocarbon codes. Planned privatizations of key parastatals, primarily telecommunications and transportation monopolies, were launched to help improve a dilapidated and unreliable infrastructure. To build on the momentum achieved during the 2-year period, the IMF approved a 3-year ESAF economic program in June 1996.

By the end of 1996, Congo had made substantial progress in various areas targeted for reform. It made significant strides toward macroeconomic stabilization through improving public finances and restructuring external debt. This change was accompanied by improvements in the structure of expenditures, with a reduction in personnel expenditures. Further, Congo benefited from debt restructuring from a Paris Club agreement in July 1996.

This reform program came to a halt, however, in early June 1997 when war broke out. Congo's economic prospects remain largely dependent on the country's ability to establish political stability and democratic rule. The World Bank is considering Congo for post-conflict assistance. Priorities will be in reconstruction, basic services, infrastructure, and utilities. President Sassou has publicly expressed interest in moving forward on economic reforms and privatization, as well as in renewing cooperation with international financial institutions. However, the return of armed conflict in 1998 hindered economic reform and recovery.

Congo and the United States ratified a bilateral investment treaty designed to facilitate and protect foreign investment. The country also adopted a new investment code intended to attract foreign capital. Despite this, Congo's investment climate is not considered favorable, offering few meaningful incentives. High costs for labor, energy, raw materials, and transportation; a restrictive labor code; low productivity and high production costs; militant labor unions; and an inadequate transportation infrastructure are among the factors discouraging investment. The recent political instability, war damage, and looting also will undermined investor confidence. As a result, Congo has little American investment outside of the oil sector.

# FOREIGN RELATIONS

For the two decades preceding Congo's 1991 National Conference, the country was firmly in the socialist camp, allied principally with the Soviet Union and other Eastern bloc nations. Educational, economic, and foreign aid links between Congo and its Eastern bloc allies were extensive, with the Congolese military and security forces receiving significant

Soviet, East German, and Cuban assistance.

France, the former colonial power, maintained a continuing but somewhat subdued relationship with Congo, offering a variety of cultural, educational, and economic assistance. The principal element in the French-Congolese relationship was the highly successful oil sector investment of the French petroleum parastatal Elf-Aquitaine, which entered the Congo in 1968 and has continued to grow since then.

After the worldwide collapse of communism and Congo's adoption of multi-party democracy in 1991, Congo's bilateral relations with its former socialist allies have become relatively less important. France is now by far Congo's principal external partner, contributing significant amounts of economic assistance, while playing a highly influential role.

Membership in international organizations includes the United Nations, Organization of African Unity, African Development Bank, GATT, Economic Commission for Central African States, Central African Customs and Economic Union, International Coffee Organization, Union of Central African States, INTELSAT, INTERPOL, Nonaligned Movement, and Group of 77.

# U.S.-CONGOLESE RELATIONS

Diplomatic relations between the U.S. and Congo were broken off during the most radical Congolese-Marxist period, 1965-77. The U.S. embassy was reopened in 1977 with the restoration of relations, which remained distant until the end of the socialist era. The late 1980s were marked by a progressive warming of Congolese relations with Western countries, including the United States. Congolese President Denis Sassou-Nguesso made a state visit to Washington in 1988, where he was received by President Bush.

## Principal U.S. Officials

**For up-to-date information on Principal U.S. Officials, see the U.S. Embassies, Consulates, and Foreign Service section starting on page 139.**

With the advent of democracy in 1991, Congo's relations with the U.S. have become cordial and cooperative. Congolese view the U.S. as the leader of the world's democracies and, as such, a model for democratic development. The U.S. has enthusiastically supported Congolese democratization efforts, contributing significant aid to the country's electoral process. The Congolese Government demonstrated an active interest in deepening and broadening its relations with the United States. Transition Prime Minister Andre Milongo made an official visit to Washington in 1992, where President Bush received him at the White House.

Then-presidential candidate Pascal Lissouba traveled to Washington in 1992, meeting with a variety of officials, including Assistant Secretary of State for African Affairs Herman J. Cohen. After his election in August 1992, President Lissouba expressed interest in expanding U.S.-Congo links, seeking increased U.S. development aid, university exchanges, and greater U.S. investment in Congo. The course of U.S.-Congolese relations following the 1997 war and deposing of Lissouba's government will be greatly affected by the current government's willingness to reestablish democratic procedures and institutions.

The U.S. embassy's operations in Brazzaville were suspended on June 18, 1997, because of the war. An office representing U.S. interests in Brazzaville is located at U.S. Embassy Kinshasa, 310 Avenue des Aviateurs, Kinshasa, Democratic Republic of the Congo. Its mailing address is Brazzaville Embassy Office, c/o American Embassy Kinshasa, Box 31550, APO AE 09828.

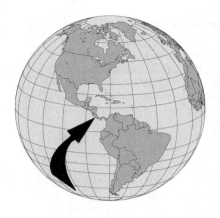

# COSTA RICA

April 2001

## Official Name:
## Republic of Costa Rica

# PROFILE

## Geography

**Area:** 51,032 sq. km. (19,652 sq. mi.); about twice the size of the state of Vermont.

**Cities:** Capital—San Jose (metropolitan area pop. 1.2 million). Other major cities—Puntarenas (300,000), Alajuela (250,000), Limon (150,000), Cartago (150,000).

**Terrain:** A rugged, central range separates the eastern and western coastal plains.

**Climate:** Mild in the central highlands, tropical and subtropical in coastal areas.

## People

**Nationality:** Noun and adjective—Costa Rican(s).

**Population:** (1999 est.) 3.67 million.

**Annual growth rate:** (1999 est., exclusive of immigration) 1.89%.

**Ethnic groups:** European and some mestizo 94%, African origin 3%, indigenous 1%.

**Religion:** Roman Catholic approx. 74%, Evangelical Protestant approx. 15%, none 8%, others 3%.

**Languages:** Spanish, with Jamaican dialect of English spoken around Puerto Limon.

**Education:** Years compulsory—9. Attendance—99% grades 1–6, 71%

grades 7–9. Literacy—94.8%.

**Health:** Infant mortality rate—13/1,000. Life expectancy—men 72 yrs., women 76 yrs.

**Work force:** (1995, 1.2 million) Services—45%; agriculture—22%; industry—17%; construction—6%; transportation—5%; banking and finance—4%.

## Government

**Type:** Democratic republic.

**Independence:** September 15, 1821.

**Constitution:** November 7, 1949.

**Branches**: Executive—president (head of government and chief of state) elected for one 4-year term, two vice presidents, Cabinet (15 ministers, one of whom also is vice president). Legislative—57-deputy unicameral Legislative Assembly elected at 4-year intervals. Judicial—Supreme Court of Justice (22 magistrates elected by Legislative Assembly for renewable 8-year terms). The offices of the Ombudsman, Comptroller General, and Procurator General assert autonomous oversight of the government.

**Subdivisions:** Seven provinces, divided into 81 cantons, subdivided into 421 districts.

**Political parties:** Social Christian Unity Party (PUSC), National Liberation Party (PLN), Democratic Force Party (PFD), National Integration Party (PIN), National Independent

Party (PNI), Agricultural Labor Action Party (PALA), Costa Rican Renovation Party (PRC), Libertarian Movement Party (PML).

**Suffrage:** Obligatory at 18.

## Economy

**GDP:** (1999) $15.2 billion.

**Inflation:** (1999) 10.1%.

**Real growth rate:** (2000) 1.4%.

**Per capita income:** (1999) $3,700.

**Natural resources:** Hydroelectric power, forest products, fisheries products.

**Agriculture** (13% of GDP): Products—bananas, coffee, beef, sugar cane, rice, dairy products, vegetables, fruits and ornamental plants.

**Industry:** (22% of GDP) Types—electronic components, food processing, textiles and apparel, construction materials, cement, fertilizer. Commerce and tourism (40% of GDP): Hotels, restaurants, tourist services, banks, and insurance.

**Foreign trade:** (1999) Exports—$6.6 billion (f.o.b., 1999): electronic components, bananas, coffee, textiles and apparel, fruits, jewelry, flowers and ornamental plants, small appliances, shrimp. Major markets—U.S. 51%, Europe 23%, Central America 11%, Japan 2%. Imports—$6.3 billion (c.i.f., 1999): electronic components, machinery, vehicles, consumer goods, chemicals, petroleum products, foods, and fertilizer. Major suppliers—U.S. 56%, Europe 10%,

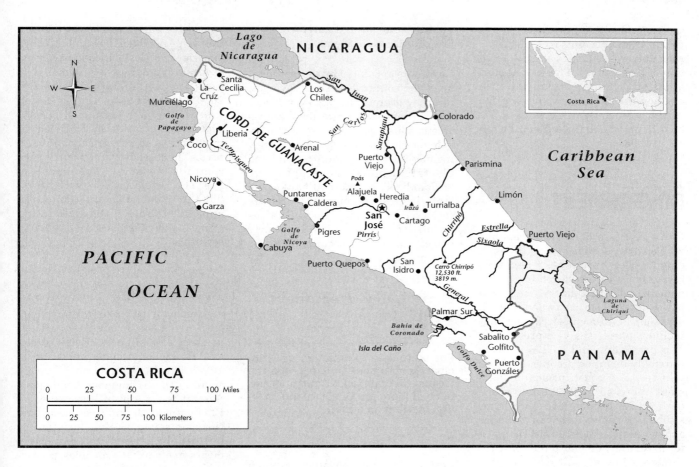

Mexico 5% Central America 5%, Japan 5%, Venezuela 4%.

**Currency exchange rate:** (May 2000) 305 colones=U.S.$1.

# PEOPLE AND HISTORY

Unlike many of their Central American neighbors, present-day Costa Ricans are largely of European rather than mestizo descent; Spain was the primary country of origin. Few of the native Indians survived European contact; the indigenous population today numbers about 29,000 or less than 1% of the population. Descendants of 19th century Jamaican immigrant workers constitute an English-speaking minority and—at 3% of the population—number about 96,000.

In 1502, on his fourth and last voyage to the New World, Christopher Columbus made the first European landfall in the area. Settlement of Costa Rica began in 1522. For nearly three centuries, Spain administered the region as part of the Captaincy General of Guatemala under a military governor. The Spanish optimistically called the country "Rich Coast." Finding little gold or other valuable minerals in Costa Rica, however, the Spanish turned to agriculture.

The small landowners' relative poverty, the lack of a large indigenous labor force, the population's ethnic and linguistic homogeneity, and Costa Rica's isolation from the Spanish colonial centers in Mexico and the Andes all contributed to the development of an autonomous and individualistic agrarian society. An egalitarian tradition also arose. This tradition survived the widened class distinctions brought on by the 19th-century introduction of banana and coffee cultivation and consequent accumulations of local wealth.

Costa Rica joined other Central American provinces in 1821 in a joint declaration of independence from Spain. Although the newly independent provinces formed a Federation, border disputes broke out among them, adding to the region's turbulent history and conditions. Costa Rica's northern Guanacaste Province was annexed from Nicaragua in one such regional dispute. In 1838, long after the Central American Federation ceased to function in practice, Costa Rica formally withdrew and proclaimed itself sovereign.

An era of peaceful democracy in Costa Rica began in 1899 with elections considered the first truly free and honest ones in the country's history. This began a trend continued until today with only two lapses: in 1917–19, Federico Tinoco ruled as a dictator, and, in 1948, Jose Figueres led an armed uprising in the wake of a disputed presidential election.

With more than 2,000 dead, the 44-day civil war resulting from this uprising was the bloodiest event in 20th century Costa Rican history, but

451

the victorious junta drafted a constitution guaranteeing free elections with universal suffrage and the abolition of the military. Figueres became a national hero, winning the first election under the new constitution in 1953. Since then, Costa Rica has held 11 presidential elections, the latest in 1998.

# GOVERNMENT

Costa Rica is a democratic republic with a strong system of constitutional checks and balances. Executive responsibilities are vested in a president, who is the country's center of power. There also are two vice presidents and a 15-member cabinet that includes one of the vice presidents. The president and 57 Legislative Assembly deputies are elected for 4-year terms. A constitutional amendment approved in 1969 limits presidents and deputies to one term, although a deputy may run again for an Assembly seat after sitting out a term. An amendment to the constitution to allow second presidential terms has been proposed. The constitutionality of the prohibition against a second presidential term also has been challenged in the courts.

The electoral process is supervised by an independent Supreme Electoral Tribunal—a commission of three principal magistrates and six alternates selected by the Supreme Court of Justice. Judicial power is exercised by the Supreme Court of Justice, composed of 22 magistrates selected for renewable 8-year terms by the Legislative Assembly, and subsidiary courts. A Constitutional Chamber of the Supreme Court, established in 1989, reviews the constitutionality of legislation and executive decrees and all habeas corpus warrants.

The offices of the Comptroller General of the Republic, the Procurator General of the Public, and the Ombudsman exercise autonomous oversight of the government. The Comptroller General's office has a statutory responsibility to scrutinize all but the smallest contracts of the public sector and strictly enforces procedural requirements.

Governors appointed by the president head the country's seven provinces, but they exercise little power. There are no provincial legislatures. Autonomous state agencies enjoy considerable operational independence; they include the telecommunications and electrical power monopoly, the nationalized commercial banks, the state insurance monopoly, and the social security agency. Costa Rica has no military and maintains only domestic police and security forces for internal security.

## Principal Government Officials

**For up-to-date information on Principal Government Officials, see the Chiefs of State and Cabinet Members of Foreign Governments section starting on page 1.**

Costa Rica maintains an embassy in the United States at 2114 S. Street NW, Washington, DC 20008 (tel. 202–328–6628).

# POLITICAL CONDITIONS

Costa Rica long has emphasized the development of democracy and respect for human rights. Until recently, the country's political system has contrasted sharply with many of its Central American and Caribbean neighbors; it has steadily developed and maintained democratic institutions and an orderly, constitutional scheme for government succession. Several factors have contributed to this tendency, including enlightened government leaders, comparative prosperity, flexible class lines, educational opportunities that have created a stable middle class, and high social indicators. Also, because Costa Rica has no armed forces, it has avoided the possibility of political intrusiveness by the military that some neighboring countries have experienced. Costa Rica experienced several unusual days of demonstrations and civil disturbance in early 2000 due to protests over legislation that would have permitted private sector participation in the telecommunications and electrical power sectors. These sectors currently are controlled by state-owned monopolies. The legislation was withdrawn, but the underlying question of the appropriate role of the state in the provision of public services remains sensitive.

In the February 1998 national election, Social Christian Unity Party (PUSC) candidate Miguel Angel Rodriguez won the presidency over National Liberation Party (PLN) nominee Jose Miguel Corrales. President Rodriguez assumed office May 8, 1998. The PUSC also obtained 27 seats in the 57-member Legislative Assembly, for a plurality, while the PLN gained 23, and five minor parties won seven. Social Christian in philosophy, the PUSC generally favors free-market principles, conservative fiscal policies, and government reform. President Rodriguez has pledged to reduce the country's large internal debt, privatize state-owned utilities, attract additional foreign investment, impose greater control over public-sector spending, and promote the creation of jobs with decent salaries.

# ECONOMY

Costa Rica's economy emerged from recession in 1997 and has shown strong aggregate growth since then. After 6.2% growth in 1998, GDP grew a substantial 8.3% in 1999, led by exports of the country's free trade zones and the tourism sector. The Central Bank attributes almost half of 1999 growth to the production of Intel Corporation's microprocessor assembly and testing plant. The strength in the nontraditional export and tourism sector is masking a relatively lackluster performance by traditional sectors, including agriculture. Inflation, as measured by the Consumer Price Index, was 10.1% in 1999, down from 11.2% the year before. The central government deficit decreased to 3.2% of GDP in 1999, down from 3.3% from the year before. On a consolidated basis, including Central Bank losses and parastatal enterprise profits, the public sector deficit was 2.3% of GDP. Controlling the budget deficit remains the single biggest challenge for the country's economic policymakers, as interest costs on the accumulated central government consumes the equivalent of 30% of the government's total revenues. This limits the resources available for investments in the country's deteriorated public infrastructure.

Costa Rica's major economic resources are its fertile land and frequent rainfall, its well-educated population, and its location in the Central American isthmus, which provides easy access to North and South American markets and direct ocean access to the European and Asian Continents. One-fourth of Costa Rica's land is dedicated to national forests, often adjoining picturesque beaches, which has made the country a popular destination for affluent retirees and ecotourists.

Costa Rica used to be known principally as a producer of bananas and coffee. In recent years, Costa Rica has successfully attracted important investments by such companies as Intel Corporation, which employs nearly 2,000 people at its $300 million microprocessor plant; Proctor and Gamble, which is establishing its administrative center for the Western Hemisphere; and Abbott Laboratories and Baxter Healthcare from the health care products industry. Manufacturing and industry's contribution to GDP overtook agriculture over the course of the 1990s, led by foreign investment in Costa Rica's free trade zone. Well over half of that investment has come from the U.S. Tourism also is booming, with the number of visitors up from 780,000 in 1996 to more than 1 million in 1999. Tourism now earns more foreign exchange than bananas and coffee combined.

## Travel Notes

**Travel Advice:** For up-to-date information from the U.S. State Department on possible inconvenient or hazardous situations, see the **Travel Warnings and Consular Information Sheets from the U.S. Government** section starting on page 1723. For the latest information on health requirements and conditions, see the **International Travelers' Health Information** section starting on page 1385. For further information dealing with non-urgent matter, see the **Tips for Travelers to...** section starting on page 1588.

The country has not discovered sources of fossil fuels—apart from minor coal deposits—but its mountainous terrain and abundant rainfall have permitted the construction of a dozen hydroelectric power plants, making it self-sufficient in all energy needs, except oil for transportation. Costa Rica exports electricity to Nicaragua and has the potential to become a major electricity exporter if plans for new generating plants and a regional distribution grid are realized. Mild climate and trade winds make neither heating nor cooling necessary, particularly in the highland cities and towns where some 90% of the population lives.

Costa Rica's infrastructure has suffered from a lack of maintenance and new investment. The country has an extensive road system of more than 30,000 kilometers, although much of it is in disrepair. Most parts of the country are accessible by road. The main highland cities in the country's Central Valley are connected by paved all-weather roads with the Atlantic and Pacific coasts and by the Pan American Highway with Nicaragua and Panama, the neighboring countries to the North and the South. Costa Rica's ports are struggling to keep pace with growing trade. They have insufficient capacity, and their equipment is in poor condition. The railroad does not function, with the exception of a couple of spurs reactivated by a U.S.-owned banana company. The government is expected to open both the ports and the railroads to competitive bidding opportunities

for private investment and management during the coming months. The government also hopes to bring foreign investment, technology, and management into the telecommunications and electrical power sectors, which are monopolies of the state. However, political opposition to opening these sectors to private participation has stalled the government's efforts. The poor state of public finances will continue to limit the state's ability to try to modernize these sectors in the absence of a political consensus to permit private investment. Failure to act soon on telecommunications could prove an obstacle to the government's desire to attract more world-class foreign investment.

Costa Rica has sought to widen its economic and trade ties, both within and outside the region. Costa Rica signed a bilateral trade agreement with Mexico in 1994, which was later amended to cover a wider range of products. Costa Rica joined other Central American countries, plus the Dominican Republic, in establishing a Trade and Investment Council with the United States in March 1998. Costa Rica is negotiating or seeking ratification of trade agreements with Chile, the Dominican Republic, Panama, and Trinidad and Tobago. It lobbied aggressively for enhancement of the U.S. Government's Caribbean Basin Initiative and has made clear its interest in joining the North American Free Trade Area (NAFTA) or signing a similar treaty with the U.S. Costa Rica is an active participant in the negotiation of the hemispheric Free Trade Area of the Americas, a process that the Costa Rican Government chaired in preparation for the April 1998 Summit of the Americas in Santiago, Chile. It also is a member of the so-called Cairns Group which is pursuing global agricultural trade liberalization in the World Trade Organization.

# FOREIGN RELATIONS

Costa Rica is an active member of the international community and, in 1993, proclaimed its permanent neutrality. Its record on the environment, human rights, and advocacy of peaceful settlement of disputes give it a weight in world affairs far beyond its size. The country lobbied aggressively for the establishment of the United Nations High Commissioner for Human Rights and became the first nation to recognize the jurisdiction of the Inter-American Human Rights Court, based in San Jose.

Then-President Oscar Arias authored a regional peace plan in 1987 that served as the basis for the Esquipulas Peace Agreement. Arias' efforts earned him the 1987 Nobel Peace Prize. Subsequent agreements, supported by the United States, led to the Nicaraguan election of 1990 and the end of civil war in Nicaragua. Costa Rica also hosted several rounds of negotiations between the Salvadoran Government and the Farabundo Marti National Liberation Front (FMLN), aiding El Salvador's efforts to emerge from civil war and culminating in that country's 1994 free and fair elections. Costa Rica has been a strong proponent of regional arms limitation agreements. President Rodriguez recently proposed the abolition of all Central American militaries and the creation of a regional counternarcotics police force in their stead.

With the establishment of democratically elected governments in all Central American nations by the 1990s, Costa Rica turned its focus from regional conflicts to the pursuit of democratic and economic development on the isthmus. It was instrumental in drawing Panama into the Central American development process and participated in the multinational Partnership for Democracy and Development in Central America.

Regional political integration has not proven attractive to Costa Rica. The country debated its role in the Central American integration process under former President Calderon. Costa Rica has sought concrete economic ties with its Central American neighbors rather than the establishment of regional political institutions, and it chose not to join the Central American Parliament. President

Figueres promoted a higher profile for Costa Rica in regional and international fora. Costa Rica gained election as President of the Group of 77 in the United Nations in 1995. That term ended in 1997 with the South-South Conference held in San Jose. Costa Rica occupied a nonpermanent seat in the Security Council from 1997 to 1999 and exercised a leadership role in confronting crises in the Middle East and Africa, as well as in the former Republic of Yugoslavia. It is currently a member of the United Nations Human Rights Commission.

Costa Rica broke relations with Cuba in 1961 to protest Cuban support of leftist subversion in Central America and has not renewed formal diplomatic ties with the Castro regime. In 1995, Costa Rica established a consular office in Havana. Cuba opened a consular office in Costa Rica in 2001.

Costa Rica strongly backed efforts by the United States to implement UN Security Council Resolution 940, which led to the restoration of the democratically elected Government of Haiti in October 1994. Costa Rica was among the first to call for a postponement of the May 22 elections in Peru when international observer missions found electoral machinery not prepared for the vote count.

# U.S.-COSTA RICAN RELATIONS

The United States and Costa Rica have a history of close and friendly relations based on respect for democratic government, human freedoms, and other shared values. During the crisis in Central America in the 1980s, Costa Rica and the United States worked for the restoration of peace and the establishment of democracy on the isthmus. Costa Rica works cooperatively with the United States and other nations in the international fight against narcotics trafficking.

The United States is Costa Rica's most important trading partner and more than 200 U.S. companies pro-

duce a variety of goods in Costa Rica. The two countries share growing concerns for the environment and want to use wisely Costa Rica's important tropical resources and prevent environmental degradation.

The United States responded to Costa Rica's economic needs in the 1980s with significant economic and development assistance programs. Through provision of more than $1.1 billion in assistance, the United States Agency for International Development (USAID) supported Costa Rican efforts to stabilize its economy and broaden and accelerate economic growth through policy reforms and trade liberalization. Assistance initiatives in the 1990s concentrated on democratic policies, modernizing the administration of justice, and sustainable development. For decades, Peace Corps volunteers have provided technical assistance in the areas of environmental education, natural resources, management, small business development, basic business education, urban youth, and community education. USAID recently launched a $9 million project to support refugees of Hurricane Mitch residing in Costa Rica.

As many as 35,000 American private citizens, mostly retirees, reside in the country, and an estimated 500,000 American citizens visit Costa Rica annually. There have been some vexing issues in the U.S.-Costa Rican relationship, principal among them longstanding expropriation and other U.S. citizen investment disputes, which have hurt Costa Rica's investment climate and produced bilateral tensions. Significant progress has been made in resolving some expropriation cases. However, several important cases remain outstanding. Land invasions from organized squatter groups who target foreign landowners also have occurred, and some have turned violent. The U.S. Government has made clear to Costa Rica its concern that Costa Rican inattention to these issues has left U.S. citizens vulnerable to harm and loss of their property.

The United States and Costa Rica signed the bilateral Maritime

Counter-Drug Agreement, the first of its kind in Central America, which entered into force in late 1999. The agreement permits bilateral cooperation on stopping drug trafficking through Costa Rican waters.

# Principal U.S. Embassy Officials

For up-to-date information on Principal U.S. Officials, see the U.S. Embassies, Consulates, and Foreign Service section starting on page 139.

The U.S. Embassy in Costa Rica is located in Pavas at Boulevard Pavas and Calle 120, San Jose, tel. (506) 220–3939.

# Other Contact Information

**U.S. Department of Commerce**
Trade Information Center

International Trade Administration
14th and Constitution Avenue, NW
Washington, DC 20320
Tel: 800-USA-TRADE
Home Page: http://www.ita.doc.gov

**Costa Rican American Chamber of Commerce c/o Aerocasillas**
P.O. Box 025216, Dept 1576
Miami, Florida 33102–5216
Tel: 506–22–0-22–00
Fax: 506–22–0-23–00
Email: Amchamcr@sol.racsa.co.cr

# CÔTE D'IVOIRE

July 1998

Official Name:
**Republic of Côte d'Ivoire**

## PROFILE

### Geography

**Area:** 322,500 sq. km. (124,500 sq. mi.); slightly larger than New Mexico.
**Cities:** Principal city-Abidjan. Capital-Yamoussoukro (official). Other cities-Bouake, Daloa, Gagnoa, Korhogo, Man, San Pedro.
**Terrain:** Undulating; hilly in the west.
**Climate:** Tropical.

### People

**Nationality:** Noun and adjective-Ivorian(s).
**Population (est):** 15 million, including immigrants.
**Annual growth rate:** 3.8%, with immigration.
**Ethnic groups:** More than 60.
**Religions:** Indigenous 25%-40%, Muslim 25%-40%, Christian 25%-40%.
**Language:** French (official); five principal language groups.
**Education:** Years compulsory-to age 16. Attendance-76%. Literacy-43%.
**Health:** Infant mortality rate-88/1,000. Life expectancy-56 years.

### Government

**Type:** Republic.
**Independence:** December 7, 1960.

**Branches:** Executive-president (chief of state and head of government). Legislative-unicameral National Assembly. Judicial-Supreme Court (4 chambers: constitutional, judicial, administrative, auditing).
**Administrative subdivisions:** 16 regions; 56 departments; 196 communes.
**Political parties:** Parti Democratique de la Côte d'Ivoire (PDCI) dominant party; Front Populaire Ivoirien (FPI); Rallie des Republicaines (RDR); numerous other smaller political parties operate in Côte d'Ivoire.
**Suffrage:** Universal at 21.

### Economy

**GDP (1997):** $10 billion.
**Annual real growth rate (1997):** 6%.
**Per capita income (1996):** $600.
**Natural resources:** Petroleum.
**Agriculture (33% of GDP):** Products—cocoa, coffee, timber, rubber, corn, rice, tropical foods.
**Industry (20% of GDP):** Types—food processing, textiles.
**Trade (1996):** Exports-$4.25 billion: cocoa, coffee, timber, rubber, cotton, palm oil, pineapples, bananas. Major markets—France, Germany, Netherlands. U.S. Imports—$2.5 billion: consumer goods, basic food stuffs (rice, wheat), capital goods. Major suppliers-France, Nigeria, U.S., EU, Japan.

## PEOPLE

Côte d'Ivoire has more than 60 ethnic groups, usually classified into five principal divisions: Akan (east and center, including Lagoon peoples of the southeast), Krou (southwest), Southern Mande (west), Northern Mande (northwest), Senoufo/Lobi (north center and northeast). The Baoules, in the the Akan division, probably comprise the largest single subgroup with 15%-20% of the population. They are based in the central region around Bouake and Yamoussoukro. The Betes in the Krou division, the Senoufos in the north, and the Malinkes in the northwest and the cities are the next largest groups, with 10%-15% of the national population. Most of the principal divisions have a significant presence in neighboring countries.

Of the more than 5 million non-Ivorian Africans living in Côte d'Ivoire, one-third to one-half are from Burkina Faso; the rest are from Ghana, Guinea, Mali, Nigeria, Benin, Senegal, Liberia, and Mauritania. The non-African expatriate community includes roughly 20,000 French and possibly 100,000 Lebanese. The number of elementary school-aged children attending classes increased from 22% in 1960 to 67% in 1995.

# HISTORY

The early history of Côte d'Ivoire is virtually unknown, although it is thought that a neolithic culture existed there. France made its initial contact with Côte d'Ivoire in 1637, when missionaries landed at Assinie near the Gold Coast (now Ghana) border. Early contacts were limited to a few missionaries because of the inhospitable coastline and settlers' fear of the inhabitants.

In the 18th century, the country was invaded by two related Akan groups-the Agnis, who occupied the southeast, and the Baoules, who settled in the central section. In 1843-44, Admiral Bouet-Williaumez signed treaties with the kings of the Grand Bassam and Assinie regions, placing their territories under a French protectorate. French explorers, missionaries, trading companies, and soldiers gradually extended the area under French control inland from the lagoon region. However, pacification was not accomplished until 1915.

## French Period

Côte d'Ivoire officially became a French colony in 1893. Captain Binger, who had explored the Gold Coast frontier, was named the first governor. He negotiated boundary treaties with Liberia and the United Kingdom (for the Gold Coast) and later started the campaign against Almany Samory, a Malinke chief, who fought against the French until 1898.

From 1904 to 1958, Côte d'Ivoire was a constituent unit of the Federation of French West Africa. It was a colony and an overseas territory under the Third Republic. Until the period following World War II, governmental affairs in French West Africa were administered from Paris. France's policy in West Africa was reflected mainly in its philosophy of "association," meaning that all Africans in Côte d'Ivoire were officially French "subjects" without rights to representation in Africa or France.

During World War II, the Vichy regime remained in control until

1943, when members of Gen. Charles De Gaulle's provisional government assumed control of all French West Africa. The Brazzaville conference in 1944, the first Constituent Assembly of the Fourth Republic in 1946, and France's gratitude for African loyalty during World War II led to far-reaching governmental reforms in 1946. French citizenship was granted to all African "subjects," the right to organize politically was recognized, and various forms of forced labor were abolished.

A turning point in relations with France was reached with the 1956 Overseas Reform Act (*Loi Cadre*), which transferred a number of powers from Paris to elected territorial governments in French West Africa and also removed remaining voting inequalities.

## Independence

In December 1958, Côte d'Ivoire became an autonomous republic within the French community as a result of a referendum that brought community status to all members of the old Federation of French West Africa except Guinea, which had voted against association. Côte d'Ivoire became independent on August 7, 1960, and permitted its community membership to lapse.

Côte d'Ivoire's contemporary political history is closely associated with the career of Felix Houphouet-Boigny, President of the republic and leader of the *Parti Democratique de la Côte d'Ivoire* (PDCI) until his death on December 7, 1993. He was one of the founders of the *Rassemblement Democratique Africain* (RDA), the leading pre-independence inter-territorial political party in French West African territories (except Mauritania).

Houphouet-Boigny first came to political prominence in 1944 as founder of the *Syndicat Agricole Africain*, an organization that won improved conditions for African farmers and formed a nucleus for the PDCI. After World War II, he was elected by a narrow margin to the first Constituent Assembly. Representing Côte d'Ivoire

in the French National Assembly from 1946 to 1959, he devoted much of his effort to inter-territorial political organization and further amelioration of labor conditions. After his 13-year service in the French National Assembly, including almost 3 years as a minister in the French Government, he became Côte d'Ivoire's first Prime Minister in April 1959, and the following year was elected its first President.

In May 1959, Houphouet-Boigny reinforced his position as a dominant figure in West Africa by leading Côte d'Ivoire, Niger, Upper Volta (Burkina), and Dahomey (Benin) into the Council of the Entente, a regional organization promoting economic development. He maintained that the road to African solidarity was through step-by-step economic and political cooperation, recognizing the principle of non-intervention in the internal affairs of other African states.

# GOVERNMENT

Côte d'Ivoire's 1959 constitution provides for strong presidency within the framework of a separation of powers. The executive is personified in the president, elected for a five-year term. The president is commander in chief of the armed forces, may negotiate and ratify certain treaties, and may submit a bill to a national referendum or to the National Assembly. According to the constitution, the President of the National Assembly assumes the presidency in the event of a vacancy, and he completes the remainder of the deceased president's term. The cabinet is selected by and is responsible to the president. Changes are being proposed to some of these provisions, to extend term of office to 7 years, establish a senate, and make president of the senate interim successor to the president.

The unicameral National Assembly is composed of 175 members elected by direct universal suffrage for a 5-year term concurrently with the president. It passes on legislation typically

# Côte d'Ivoire

introduced by the president although it also can introduce legislation.

The judicial system culminates in the Supreme Court. The High Court of Justice is competent to try government officials for major offenses.

For administrative purposes, Côte d'Ivoire is divided into 56 departments, each headed by a prefect appointed by the central government. There are 196 communes, each headed by an elected mayor, plus the city of Abidjan with 10 mayors.

## National Security

The 17,000-man Ivorian Armed Forces (FANCI) include an army, navy, air force, and gendarmerie. The Joint Staff is assigned to the FANCI Headquarters in Abidjan. A two-star officer serves as the chief of staff and commander of the FANCI. Côte d'Ivoire is broken down into five military regions, each commanded by a colonel.

The army has the majority of its forces in the First Military Region concentrated in and around Abidjan, its principal units there being a rapid intervention battalion (airborne), an infantry battalion, an armored battalion, and an air defense artillery battalion. The Second Military Region is located in Daloa and is assigned one infantry battalion. The Third Military Region is headquar-

**Travel Notes**

**Travel Advice:** For up-to-date information from the U.S. State Department on possible inconvenient or hazardous situations, see the **Travel Warnings and Consular Information Sheets from the U.S. Government** section starting on page 1723. For the latest information on health requirements and conditions, see the **International Travelers' Health Information** section starting on page 1385. For further information dealing with non-urgent matter, see the **Tips for Travelers to...** section starting on page 1588.

tered in Bouake and is home to an artillery, an infantry, and an engineer battalion. The Fourth Military Region maintains only a Territorial Defense Company headquartered in Korhogo. The fifth region is the Western Operational Zone, a temporary command created to respond to the security threat caused by the civil war in neighboring Liberia.

The gendarmerie is roughly equivalent in size to the army. It is a national police force which is responsible for territorial security, especially in rural areas. In times of national crisis the gendarmerie could be used to reinforce the army. The gendarmerie is commanded by a colonel-major and is comprised of four Legions, each corresponding to one of the four numbered military regions, minus the temporary military operational zone on the western border.

Côte d'Ivoire has a brown-water navy whose mission is coastal surveillance and security for the nation's 340-mile coastline. It has two fast-attack craft, two patrol crafts, and one light transport ship. It also has numerous smaller vessels used primarily for traffic, immigration, and contraband control within the lagoon system.

The Ivorian Air Force's mission is to defend the nation's airspace and provide transportation support to the other services. Within its inventory are 5 Alpha jets, 12 transport/utility aircraft, and 2 helicopters.

A mutual defense accord signed with France in 1961 provides for the stationing of French forces in Côte d'Ivoire. The 43rd Marine Infantry Battalion is based in Port Bouet adjacent to the Abidjan Airport and has more than 500 troops assigned.

## Principal Government Officials

**For up-to-date information on Principal Government Officials, see the Chiefs of State and Cabinet Members of Foreign Governments section starting on page 1.**

Côte d'Ivoire maintains an embassy at 2424 Massachusetts Avenue, NW, Washington, D.C. 20008 (202-483-2400).

# POLITICAL CONDITIONS

In a region whose political systems have otherwise been noted for lack of stability, Côte d'Ivoire has shown remarkable political stability since its independence from France in 1960. Its relations with the United States are excellent. When many other countries in the region were undergoing repeated military coups, experimenting with Marxism, and developing ties with the Soviet Union and China, Côte d'Ivoire-under Felix Houphouet-Boigny, president from independence until his death in December 1993-maintained a close political allegiance to the West. President Bedie is very familiar with the United States, having served as Côte d'Ivoire's first ambassador to this country.

Looking toward the country's future, the fundamental issue is whether its political system will maintain the stability which is the sine qua non for investor confidence and further economic development. Côte d'Ivoire evolved, with relatively little violence or dislocation, from a single-party state, beginning in 1990. Opposition parties, independent newspapers, and independent trades unions were made legal at that time. Since those major changes occurred, the country's pace of political change has been slow. Whether further democratic reform will take place, adequate to meet future challenges, is unknown. As is generally true in the region, the business environment is one in which personal contact and connections remain important, where rule of law does not prevail with assurance, and where the legislative and judicial branches of the government remain weak. The political system remains highly centralized with the president dominating both the ruling party and the legislature and judiciary. Côte d'Ivoire's efforts to break down central state control of the economy are undermined by the state's continued central control of the political system.

Côte d'Ivoire has a high population growth rate, a high crime rate (particularly in Abidjan), a high incidence of AIDS, a multiplicity of tribes, sporadic student unrest, a differential rate of in-country development according to region, and a dichotomy of religion associated with region and tribe. These factors put stress on the political system and will become more of a problem if the economy-not quite as dependent today on cocoa and coffee as it was some years ago but still dependent-takes a plunge similar to that of the 1980s.

The political system in Côte d'Ivoire is president-dominated. The Prime Minister concentrates principally on coordinating and implementing economic policy. The key decisions-political, military, or economic-continue to be made by President Bedie, as they were made by President Houphouet-Boigny. However, political dialogue is much freer today than prior to 1990, especially due to the opposition press, which vocalizes its criticism of the regime. The Ivorian Constitution affords the legislature some independence, but it has not been widely exercised. Until 1990, all legislators were from the PDCI. After the most recent elections (1995-96), the PDCI continues to hold 149 out of 175 seats. The PDCI's "core" region may be described as the terrain of the Baoule tribe in the country's center, home of both Houphouet-Boigny and Bedie; however, the PDCI is well-entrenched in all parts of Côte d'Ivoire.

The remaining 26 seats in the National Assembly are divided equally by the only two other parties of national scope-the FPI (Ivorian Popular Front) and RDR (Rally of Republicans). The oldest opposition party is the FPI, a moderate party which has a socialist coloration but which is more concerned with democratic reform than radical economic change; it is strongest in the terrain of its Bete tribe leader, Laurent Gbagbo. The non-ideological RDR was formed in September 1994 by former members of the PDCI's reformist wing who hoped that former Prime Minister Alassane Ouattara would run and prevail in the 1995 presidential election (but who was disqualified by subsequent legislation requiring 5-year residency); it is strongest in the Muslim north.

The presidential election of October 1995 was boycotted by the FPI and RDR because of Ouattara's disqualification and the absence of an independent electoral commission (among other grievances). Their "active boycott" produced a certain amount of violence and hundreds of arrests (with a number of the arrestees not tried for 2-1/2 years). These grievances remain unaddressed, with the next round of elections coming in the year 2000.

# ECONOMY

The Ivorian economy is largely market based and depends heavily on the agricultural sector. Almost 70% of the Ivorian people are engaged in some form of agricultural activity. The economy performed poorly in the 1980s and early 1990s, and high population growth coupled with economic decline resulted in a steady fall in living standards. Gross national product per capita, now rising again, was about U.S. $727 in 1996. (It was substantially higher two decades ago.) A majority of the population

remains dependent on smallholder cash crop production. Principal exports are cocoa, coffee, and tropical woods. Principal U.S. exports are rice and wheat, plastic materials and resins, Kraft paper, agricultural chemicals, telecommunications, and oil and gas equipment. Principal U.S. imports are cocoa and cocoa products, petroleum, rubber, and coffee.

## Foreign Direct Investment Statistics

Direct foreign investment (DFI) plays a key role in the Ivorian economy, accounting for between 40% and 45% of total capital in Ivorian firms. France is overwhelmingly the most important foreign investor. In recent years, French investment has accounted for about one-quarter of the total capital in Ivorian enterprises, and between 55% and 60% of the total stock of foreign investment capital.

## Infrastructure

By developing country standards, Côte d'Ivoire has an outstanding infrastructure. There is an excellent network of more than 8,000 miles of paved roads; good telecommunications services, including a public data communications network; cellular phones and Internet access; two active ports, one of which, Abidjan, is the most modern in West Africa; rail links-in the process of being upgraded-both within the country and to Burkina Faso; regular air service within the region and to and from Europe; and modern real estate developments for commercial, industrial, retail, and residential use. Côte d'Ivoire's location and easy, reliable connection to neighboring countries makes it a preferred platform from which to conduct West African operations. The city of Abidjan is one of the most modern and liveable cities in the region. Its school system is good by regional standards and includes an excellent international school based on a U.S. curriculum and several excellent French-based schools.

Côte d'Ivoire has stepped up public investment programs after the stagnation of the pre-devaluation era.

The government's public investment plan accords priority to investment in human capital, but it also will provide for significant spending on economic infrastructure needed to sustain growth. Continued infrastructure development also is expected to occur because of private sector activity. In the new environment of government disengagement from productive activities and in the wake of recent privatizations, anticipated investments in the petroleum, electricity, water, and telecommunications sectors, and in part in the transportation sector, will be financed without any direct government intervention.

## Major Trends and Outlooks

Since the colonial period, Côte d'Ivoire's economy has been based on the production and export of tropical products. Agriculture, forestry, and fisheries account for more than one-third of GDP and two-thirds of exports. Côte d'Ivoire produces 40% of the world's cocoa crop and is a major exporter of bananas, coffee, cotton, palm oil, pineapples, rubber, tropical wood products, and tuna. The 1994 devaluation of the CFA franc and accompanying structural adjustment measures generally favored the agricultural sector by increasing competitiveness. However, reliance on raw cocoa and coffee exports, which account for 40% of total exports, exposes the economy to sharp price swings on world markets for these commodities. The government encourages export diversification and intermediate processing of cocoa beans to reduce this exposure. Cocoa beans exports to the U.S. increased sharply in 1996 due to lower freight rates.

The four years following the January 12, 1994, devaluation of the CFA franc have seen Côte d'Ivoire return to the rapid economic growth it knew in the 1960s and 1970s. The spur provided by the devaluation, by increased aid flows, rigorous macroeconomic policies, and fortuitous international commodity prices yielded strong GDP growth in both 1996 and 1997. In addition to these factors, the long period of pre-devaluation stagnation, in which local businesses and potential outside investors put off capital expenditure, caused a boom in investment following the devaluation. Côte d'Ivoire has also begun to turn the corner on its daunting debt problem: first with a generous rescheduling of official bilateral debt at the Paris Club in March 1994; more recently, with a tentative London Club agreement in November 1996, and the April 1997 decision by the G-7 countries to include Côte d'Ivoire in the new IMF-World Bank debt forgiveness initiative for highly indebted poor countries.

Côte d'Ivoire's recent economic performance has been impressive, particularly in 1995 and 1996. Real GDP growth was 7% in 1995, 6.8% in 1996, and an estimated 6% in 1997. The country has been meeting its IMF targets for growth, inflation, government finance, and balance of payments. Traditional commodity exports were boosted both by the devaluation (though improved prices in local currency terms were only partially passed through to farmers) and by higher world prices for cocoa and coffee. At the same time, the devaluation and the generally favorable business environment produced growth in nontraditional crops, local processing of commodities, and the services sector.

In 1996 and 1997, inflation continued the downward trend begun after the devaluation, when the government kept a tight lid both on salary increases and on the size of the public sector work force. Inflation as measured by the increase in the consumer price index has fallen sharply, from 1994's post-devaluation 32.2% to 7.7% in 1995, 3.5% in 1996, and an estimated 5% in 1997.

Public sector finances are another bright spot: Government revenues are on a strongly rising trend since 1993, capped by a 15% increase from 1995 to 1996. The stronger revenue picture, when combined with restraint on the spending side, has resulted in three years of primary surpluses (i.e., receipts minus expenditure, excluding borrowing and debt service). Following a concerted government repayment effort, domestic arrears had been virtually eliminated by the end of 1996.

The outlook for the near and medium term in Côte d'Ivoire remains positive. The government hopes to attain double-digit real GDP growth, but this appears achievable only in a best-case scenario, including continued or enhanced investment flows, additional oil or mineral production, and no drop in world commodity prices; short of this optimistic scenario, a continuation of 6% or 7% growth seems likely for the near term.

# FOREIGN RELATIONS

Throughout the Cold War, Côte d'Ivoire's foreign policy was generally favorable toward the West. The country became a member of the United Nations in 1960 and participates in most of its specialized agencies. It maintains a wide variety of diplomatic contacts, and, in 1986, announced the reestablishment of diplomatic relations with Israel. Côte d'Ivoire sought change in South Africa through dialogue, and its ambassador was one of the first to be accredited to post-apartheid South Africa.

The Ivorian Government has traditionally played a constructive role in Africa. President Houphouet-Boigny was active in the mediation of regional disputes, most notably in Liberia and Angola, and had considerable stature throughout the continent. President Bedie has set in train a friendly neighbor policy with all contiguous states, having visited all of them. In 1996-97 Côte d'Ivoire sent a medical unit to participate in regional peacekeeping in Liberia, its first peacekeeping effort. President Bedie has announced that Côte d'Ivoire will expand its involvement in peacekeeping.

Côte d'Ivoire continues to maintain extremely close relations with France. President Houphouet, who was a minister in the French Government prior to independence, insisted that the connection remain unsevered. Concrete examples of Franco-Ivorian cooperation are numerous: French is Côte d'Ivoire's official language, Ivorian security is enhanced by a brigade of French marines stationed in Abidjan, some 20,000 French expatriates continue to make their home in Côte d'Ivoire, and the country's currency, the CFA franc, is tied to the French franc.

Côte d'Ivoire belongs to the UN and most of its specialized agencies, the Organization of African Unity (OAU), West African Economic and Monetary Union (UEMOA), African Mauritian Common Organization (OCAM), Council of Entente Communaute Financiere Africane (CFA), Economic Community of West African States (ECOWAS), Nonaggression and Defense Agreement (ANAD), INTELSAT, Nonaligned Movement, African Regional Satillite Organization (RASCOM), InterAfrican Coffee Organizations (IACO), International Cocoa Organization (ICCO), Alliance of Cocoa Producers, African, Caribbean and Pacific Countries (ACP), and Association of Coffee Producing Countries (ACPC). Côte d'Ivoire also belongs to the European Investment Bank (EIB) and the African Development Bank; it is an associate member of European Union.

## Principal U.S. Officials

For up-to-date information on Principal U.S. Officials, see the U.S. Embassies, Consulates, and Foreign Service section starting on page 139.

# U.S.-IVORIAN RELATIONS

U.S.-Ivorian relations are friendly and close. The United States is sympathetic to Côte d'Ivoire's program of rapid, orderly economic development as well as its moderate stance on international issues. Bilateral U.S. Agency for International Development (USAID) funding, with the exception of self-help and democratization funds, has been phased out.

The United States and Côte d'Ivoire maintain an active cultural exchange program, through which prominent Ivorian Government officials, media representatives, educators, and scholars visit the United States to become better acquainted with the American people and to exchange ideas and views with their American colleagues. This cooperative effort is furthered through frequent visits to Côte d'Ivoire by representatives of U.S. business and educational institutions, and by visits of Fulbright-Hays scholars and specialists in various fields.

The U.S. embassy is located at 5 Rue Jesse Owens, Abidjan, Côte d'Ivoire (tel. 21-09-79, telefax, 22-23-59); mailing address is 01 B.P. 1712, Abidjan 01, Côte d'Ivoire.

# CROATIA
January 2000

Official Name:
**Republic of Croatia**

# PROFILE

## Geography
**Area:** 56,538 sq. km. (slightly smaller than West Virginia).
**Cities:** Capital—Zagreb (est. pop. 706,770), Split (189,388), Osijek (104,761), Pula (62,378), Sisak (45,792).
**Terrain:** Geographically diverse, flat plains along Hungarian border, low mountains.
**Climate:** Continental in the north; Mediterranean in central regions and along the Adriatic coast.

## People
**Nationality:** Croatian(s) (Hrvat(i)).
**Population (July 1999 est.):** 4,676,865.
**Population growth rate (1999 est.):** .1%.
**Ethnic groups:** Croat 78%, Serb 12%, Muslim 0.9%, Hungarian 0.5%, Slovenian 0.5%, other 8.1%.
**Religions:** Catholic 76.5%, Orthodox 11.1%, Slavic Muslim 1.2%, Protestant 0.4%, others and unknown 10.8%.
**Language:** Croatian.
**Education:** Literacy—97%.
**Health:** Infant mortality rate—8/ 1,000. Life expectancy—male 70.43, female 77.28.
**Work force (1.4 million total):** Industry and mining—31.10%. Agri-

culture—4.3%. Government—19.1%. Other—45.5%.

## Government
**Type:** Parliamentary democracy.
**Constitution:** Adopted December 22, 1990, amended in 1992.
**Independence:** June 25,1991 (from Yugoslavia).
**Branches:** Executive—president (chief of state), prime minister (head of government), Council of Ministers (cabinet). Legislative—bicameral People's Assembly (parliament). Judicial—Supreme Court, Constitutional Court.
**Political parties:** Croatian Democratic Union (HDZ); Social Democratic Party (SDP); Croatian Social Liberal Party (HSLS); Liberal Party (LS); Istrian Democratic Congress (IDS); Croatian Peasant Party (HSS); Croatian National Party (HNS); Croatian Party of Rights (HSP); Croatian Democratic Union (HKDU); more than 20 other parties registered.
**Suffrage:** Universal at 18, 16 if employed.
**Flag:** The Croatian National flag is a red-white-blue tricolor (arranged horizontally in that order) with the coat of arms (13 red squares and 12 white squares arranged in a 5x5 checkerboard pattern). On top of the coat of arms is a crown composed of 5 regional symbols: the oldest known

Croatian coat of arms, Dubrovnik, Dalmatia, Istria, and Slavonia.

## Economy
**GDP:** $21.32 billion, 1998; $20.27 billion, 1997.
**Real GDP growth rate:** 2.7%, 1998; 6.5%, 1997.
**Income per capita (1998):** $ 4,663.
**Unemployment rate (June 1999):** 19.5%.
**Inflation rate:** 5.7%, 1998; 3.6%, 1997; 3.5%, 1996.
**Natural resources:** Oil, coal, bauxite, low-grade iron ore, calcium, natural asphalt, silica, mica, clays, salt.
**Agriculture (10% of GDP, 1996):** Wheat, corn, sugar, beets, sunflower seeds, alfalfa, olives, grapes.
**Industry (20% of GDP):** Chemicals and plastics, machine tools, electronics, textiles, aluminum, shipbuilding.
**Trade (1998):** Exports—$4.54 billion. Major markets—Italy, Germany, Bosnia and Herzegovina, Slovenia, Austria, Russia. Imports—$8.38 billion. Major suppliers—Germany, Italy, Slovenia, Austria, France, Russia.
**Services (55% of GDP):** Tourism, transport.

# U.S.-CROATIAN RELATIONS

Croatia declared its independence from the Federal Republic of Yugoslavia on June 25, 1991. The United States opposed the unilateral secession of Croatia and Slovenia, fearing it would lead to war. War broke out between Croatia and the Yugoslav People's Army in the fall of 1991. The European Union recognized Croatia several months later--on January 15, 1992. Largescale fighting ended later that month under a peace plan brokered by former U.S. Secretary of State Cyrus Vance.

Official relations between the United States and Croatia began on April 7, 1992, when the U.S. recognized Croatia, along with Slovenia and Bosnia-Herzegovina, the last of the major powers to do so. There was little substance to the relationship at first. Diplomatic relations were not established until August of 1992, and the first U.S. Ambassador to Croatia, Peter Galbraith, did not arrive until June 1993. The U.S. played a supporting role to the European-led peace process in the early 1990s.

The situation changed dramatically by 1997. The U.S. took the lead in negotiating and implementing the peaceful reintegration of Croatia's Danubian region (including Krajina, Eastern Slavonia, Baranja, and Western Sirmium). The U.S. and Croatian Governments were in close contact at all levels in an attempt to find a peaceful solution to the region's problems.

Lack of early U.S. involvement had upset Croats, but intense U.S. involvement in the implementation of the Dayton and Erdut Agreements led Croatians to complain of too much pressure. The U.S. has, however, continued to vigorously insist upon fulfillment of the terms of the agreements on all sides.

U.S. policy in Croatia and the area has centered on promoting the territorial integrity of existing states, the possibility for all refugees and displaced persons to return home, freedom from discrimination on ethnic or religious grounds, the sanctity of private property, and tolerance for democratic dissent. In February 1998, the U.S. presented a Partnership for Peace "road map" outlining specific

areas where improved performance was needed. The road map highlights Dayton implementation, democratization, and refugee returns and reconciliation as the main points on which progress must be made. Working to achieve these goals can pave the way to full integration of Croatia into Western political, security, and economic structures.

## Principal U.S. Embassy Officials

For up-to-date information on Principal U.S. Officials, see the U.S. Embassies, Consulates, and Foreign Service section starting on page 139.

# HISTORICAL HIGHLIGHTS

The Croats are believed to be a purely Slavic people who migrated from Ukraine, although newer theories hold they may have been nomadic Sarmatians. The Croats settled in present-day Croatia in the 6th century. They were Christianized in the 9th century, but preserved autonomy from Rome until the 1000s. The first King of Croatia, Tomislav, was crowned in 925, having created a sizeable state, including most of Croatia, Slavonia, Dalmatia, and Bosnia and Herzegovina. The state was destroyed by attacks from Bulgarians, Byzantines, Venetians, and Magyars. The 1102 pacta conventa recognized a common king for Croatia and Hungary. The two crowns would remain connected until the end of World War I.

After the 1526 Battle of Mohacs, the Hungarian dynasty was extinguished, and Croatian nobility elected the Austrian Ferdinand Habsburg king. During the next 200 years, the Ottoman Empire was a constant threat, and the Military Frontier was created in 1578, an area carved out of Croatia and ruled directly from Vienna. Austria encour-

aged settlement of Germans, Hungarians, Serbs, and other Slavs in the Military Frontier, creating an ethnic patchwork. The Ottoman Empire was driven out of Hungary and Croatia by the 1700s, and Austria brought the empire under central control.

As Austrians pushed germanization and Hungarians magyarization, Croatian nationalism emerged. The Croatian national revival began in the 1830s with the Illyrian Movement. By the 1840s, the movement had moved from cultural goals to resisting Hungarian political demands. In 1868, Croatia was given domestic autonomy, but the governor was appointed by Hungary. Croatian leadership divided between proponents of a South Slav union and supporters of a Greater Croatia. Croatian and Serbian parties began to cooperate in 1905, with the Croato-Serb Coalition.

Shortly before the end of World War I, on October 29, 1918, the Croatian Parliament proclaimed Croatia's administrative relations with Austria and Hungary void. The Kingdom of Serbs, Croats, and Slovenes was created December 1. The Croats were not happy with rule from Belgrade by a Serbian king, however. Croatia gained autonomy in 1939, but the Axis powers dismantled Yugoslavia in 1941. The Croatian radical-right Ustase was brought from Italy and installed as the government of the Independent State of Croatia. Antifascist and communist Croats joined Tito's Partisans.

Croatia became part of the Federal Republic of Yugoslavia in 1945. Decentralization in 1965 led to a resurgence of nationalism in the Croatian spring of 1970-71. In 1980, after Tito's death, political and economic difficulties mounted. The federal government began to crumble. Inflation soared, and reforms failed. In 1990, the Croatian Democratic Union won the first free postwar elections on a platform of nationalism, anticommunism, and privatization.

Conflict between Serbs and Croats in Croatia escalated, and 1 month after Croatia declared independence June 25, 1991, a civil war fueled by Serbian invasion broke out in Krajina. Janu-

ary 1992 brought a UN-sponsored cease-fire, but hostilities resumed the next year when Croatia fought to regain territory taken by Serbs. A second cease-fire was enacted in May 1993, and Croatia and Yugoslavia signed a joint declaration the next January. In September 1993, however, the Croatian Army led an offensive against the Serb-held "Republic of Krajina." A third cease-fire was signed in March 1994, but it was broken the next May when Croatian forces again attempted to reclaim lost

territory. In early August, Croatian forces recaptured Krajina with a major offensive, and some 150,000 Serbs fled the region, many to Serb-held areas in Bosnia and Herzegovina.

# ECONOMY

In an economy traditionally based on agriculture and livestock, peasants comprised more than half of the Croatian population until after World

War II. Pre-1945 industrialization was slow and centered on textile mills, sawmills, brickyards, and food-processing plants. Rapid industrialization and diversification occurred after World War II. Decentralization came in 1965, allowing growth of certain sectors, like the tourist industry. Profits from Croatian industry were used to develop poorer regions in the former Yugoslavia. This, coupled with austerity programs and hyperinflation in the 1980s, led to discontent in both Croatia and Slovenia that fueled the independence movement.

Privatization under the new Croatian Government had barely begun when war broke out. As a result of the Croatian war of independence, the economic infrastructure sustained massive damage in the period 1991-92.

In 1999, GDP growth has slowed after a period of expansion, and Croatia is facing a recession. This is due mainly to weak consumer demand and a decrease in industrial production.

Inflation and unemployment are rising, and the kuna has fallen, prompting the national bank to tighten fiscal policy. A new banking law passed in December 1998 will give the central bank more control over Croatia's 53 remaining commercial banks. Croatia is dependent on international debt to finance the deficit. A recently issued EURO-denominated bond was well received, selling $300 million, which will help offset economic losses from the Kosovo crisis. Despite the successful value-added tax program, planned privatization of state controlled businesses, and a revised budget with a 7% across that board cut in spending, the government still projects a $200 million deficit for 1999.

Low inflation and currency stability have been the main economic achievements of the Croatian Democratic Union (HDZ). Structural reform has been lagging, however, and problems of payment arrears and a lack of banking supervision continue. The upcoming elections may take HDZ focus off of economic policy. The party has promised two salary increases to public-sector employees before the end of the year which will increase the fiscal deficit.

# GOVERNMENT AND POLITICAL CONDITIONS

Croatian politics will be dominated by the legislative elections that will

occur at the end of this year. The ruling party, the Croatian Democratic Union (HDZ), has experienced a drop in its popularity, as evidenced by recent election polls. This has prompted President Franjo Tudjman to revive national issues. A period of political uncertainty may ensue as a result of HDZ's struggle to hold onto power. They have begun to tighten their reigns on the media and sow division among the opposition. Foreign relations could suffer as the HDZ targets the West in an attempt to reawaken nationalist feelings. This may be especially evident as the U.S. continues to put pressure on Croatia to accelerate the return of Serb refugees.

The President of the Republic of Croatia is the head of state and is elected by popular vote for a 5-year term. A president may not serve more than two terms. The presidency is strong, with an extensive veto. He also may issue decrees with the force of law. He appoints the prime minister and the cabinet, a council of ministers that is proposed by the prime minister. The president is the commander in chief of the armed forces. The next presidential election will be held February 7, 2000.

The Croatian legislature is the Sabor (Parliament), a bicameral body consisting of a Chamber of Deputies and a Chamber of Zupanije (counties). The Chamber of Deputies can have between 100 and 160 deputies, and the Chamber of Counties has 63 members (3 from each county). All representatives are elected for 4-year terms. The last parliamentary elections were held January 3, 2000. The Chambers meet in public sessions twice a year—January 15 to June 30 and September 15 to December 15. The powers of the legislature include enactment and amendment of the constitution; passage of laws; adoption of the state budget; declarations of war and peace; alteration of the boundaries of the Republic; calling referenda; carrying out elections, appointments, and relief of office; supervising the work of the Government of Croatia and other holders of public powers responsible to the Sabor; and granting amnesty. Deci-

sions are made based on a majority vote if more than half of the Chamber is present, except in cases of national rights and constitutional issues.

The Supreme Court of the Republic of Croatia is the highest court. Court hearings are open, and judgments are made publicly, except in issues of privacy of the accused. Judges are appointed for life. The High Judiciary Council of the Republic appoints judges. It is a body consisting of a president and 14 members proposed by the Chamber of Counties and elected by the Chamber of Deputies for 8-year terms.

The Constitutional Court of the Republic of Croatia decides on the constitutionality of laws and has the right to repeal a law it finds unconstitutional. It also can impeach the president. The body is made up of 11 judges proposed by the Chamber of Counties and elected by the Chamber of Deputies for 8-year terms. The president of the Constitutional Court is elected by the court for a 4-year term.

The country is composed of 21 counties (zupanijas). Three representatives from each county are elected to the Chamber of Zupanije.

Croatia's military consists of five branches: ground forces, naval forces, air and air defense forces, frontier guard, and home guard. Total active duty members of the armed forces number 56,180, including about 33,500 conscripts. Terms of service are 10 months. Reserves number 220,000. The Croatian military budget was approximately $1.1 billion in 1997 (a little more than 5% of GDP).

## Principal Government Officials

**For up-to-date information on Principal Government Officials, see the Chiefs of State and Cabinet Members of Foreign Governments section starting on page 1.**

The U.S. embassy is located at 2343 Massachusetts Ave. NW, Washington, DC 20008; Tel: 202-588-5899; Fax: 202-588-8936. Consulates are located in Cleveland, Los Angeles, New York.

# FOREIGN RELATIONS

Croatian foreign policy has focused on gaining access to European and transatlantic institutions, maintaining good relations with its neighbors, and securing close ties with the United States. Relations with the U.S. and the European Union (EU) focus on implementation of the Dayton Accords, Erdut Agreement, ethnic reconciliation, nondiscriminatory facilitation of the return of refugees and displaced persons, and democratization. Croatia has had an uneven record in these areas since 1996, inhibiting its relations with the U.S. and Europe. Improvement in these areas will be necessary to advance Croatia's prospects for further Euro-Atlantic integration.

Progress in the areas of Dayton, Erdut, and refugee returns were evident in 1998, but progress was slow and requires intensive international engagement. Thus far, refugee returns have accelerated in 1999. However, unsatisfactory performance, in 1998, in implementing broader democratic reforms still raises questions about the ruling party's commitment to basic democratic principles and norms. Areas that are of concern today include restrictions on freedom of speech, one-party control of public TV and radio, repression of independent media, unfair electoral regulations, a judiciary that is not fully independent, and lack of human and civil rights protection.

Relations with neighboring states have normalized somewhat since the breakup of Yugoslavia. Work has begun—bilaterally and within the new Stability Pact for Southeastern Europe—on political and economic cooperation in the region. Outstanding issues with neighboring countries include border disputes with Bosnia and Herzegovina, Slovenia, and Montenegro.

U.S. support to Croatia comes through the Southeastern European Economic Development Program (SEED). In 1998, SEED funding in Croatia totaled $23.25 million. More than half of that money was used to fund programs encouraging sustainable returns of refugees and displaced persons. About one-third of the assistance was used for democratization efforts, and another 5% funded financial sector restructuring.

# CUBA
April 1998

Official Name:
**Republic of Cuba**

# PROFILE

## Geography

**Area:** 110,860 sq. km. (44,200 sq. mi.); about the size of Pennsylvania.
**Cities:** Capital—Havana (pop. 2 million). Other major cities—Santiago de Cuba, Camaguey, Santa Clara, Holguin, Guantanamo, Matanzas, Cienfuegos, Pinar del Rio.
**Terrain:** Flat or gently rolling plains, hills, mountains up to 2,000 meters (6,000 ft.) in the southeast.
**Climate:** Tropical, moderated by trade winds; dry season (November-April); rainy season (May-October).

## People

**Nationality:** Noun and adjective—Cuban(s).
**Population:** 11 million; 70% urban, 30% rural.
**Avg. annual growth rate:** 0.41%.
**Ethnic groups:** Spanish-African mixture.
**Language:** Spanish.
**Education:** Years compulsory-6. Attendance—92% (ages 6-16). Literacy—95%.
**Health:** Infant mortality rate—7.2/1,000. Life expectancy—78 yrs. for women, 73 yrs. for men.
**Work force (4.5 million):** Government and services—30%. Industry—22%. Agriculture—20%. Commerce—11%. Construction—11%. Transportation and communications—6%.

## Government

**Type:** Communist state; current government assumed power January 1, 1959.
**Independence:** May 20, 1902.
**Constitution:** February 24, 1976.
**Branches:** Executive—president, council of ministers. Legislative—National Assembly of People's Government. Judicial—People's Supreme Court.
**Political party:** Cuban Communist Party (PCC).
**Suffrage:** All citizens age 16 and older, except those who have applied for permanent emigration. National Assembly elections were held in 1998.
**Administrative subdivisions:** 14 provinces, including the city of Havana, and one special municipality (Isle of Youth).

## Economy

**GDP (1997 est.):** Purchasing power parity $16.9 billion.
**Real annual growth rate (1997):** 2.5%.
**Per capita income:** $1,540.
**Natural resources:** Nickel, cobalt, iron ore, copper, manganese, salt, timber.
**Agriculture:** Products—sugar, citrus and tropical fruits, tobacco, coffee, rice, beans, meat, and vegetables.
**Industry:** Types—sugar and food processing, oil refining, cement, electric power, light consumer and industrial products.
**Trade:** Exports—$1.9 billion (FOB, 1997 est.): Sugar and its by-products, nickel, seafood, citrus, tobacco products, rum. Major markets—Russia 25%, Canada 15%, Netherlands 11%. Imports—$3.3 billion (CIF, 1997 est.): petroleum, food, machinery, chemicals. Major suppliers—Spain 14%, Russia 12%, Mexico 9%.
**Official exchange rate:** 1 Cuban peso=U.S.$1 (official rate). 23 Cuban pesos=U.S.$1 (internal exchange rate).

# PEOPLE

Cuba is a multiracial society with a population of mainly Spanish and African origins. The largest organized religion is the Roman Catholic Church. Santeria, a blend of native African religions and Roman Catholicism, is the most widely practiced religion in Cuba. Officially, Cuba has been an atheist state for most of the Castro era. However, a constitutional amendment adopted on July 12, 1992 changed the nature of the Cuban state from atheist to secular, enabling religious believers to belong to the Cuban Communist Party (PCC).

# HISTORY

Spanish settlers established sugar cane and tobacco as Cuba's primary products. As the native Indian population died out, African slaves were imported to work the plantations. Slavery was abolished in 1886.

Cuba was the last major Spanish colony to gain independence, following a 50-year struggle begun in 1850. The final push for independence began in 1895, when Jose Marti, Cuba's national hero, announced the "Grito de Baire" ("Call to arms from Baire"). In 1898, after the USS *Maine* sunk in Havana Harbor on February 15 due to an explosion of undetermined origin, the United States entered the conflict. In December of that year Spain relinquished control of Cuba to the United States with the Treaty of Paris. On May 20, 1902, the United States granted Cuba its independence, but retained the right to intervene to preserve Cuban independence and stability under the Platt Amendment. In 1934, the amendment was repealed and the United States and Cuba reaffirmed the 1903 agreement which leased the Guantanamo Bay naval base to the United States. The treaty remains in force and can only be terminated by mutual agreement or abandonment by the United States.

Until 1959, Cuba was often ruled by military figures, who either obtained or remained in power by force. Fulgencio Batista, an army sergeant who established himself as Cuba's dominant leader for more than 25 years, fled on January 1, 1959, as Castro's "26th of July Movement" gained control. Castro had established the movement in Mexico, where he was exiled after the failed July 26, 1953, attack on the Moncada army barracks at Santiago de Cuba. Within months of taking power, Castro moved to consolidate his power by imprisoning or executing opponents. Hundreds of thousands of Cubans fled the island.

Castro declared Cuba a socialist state on April 16, 1961. For the next 30 years, Castro pursued close relations with the Soviet Union until the advent of *perestroika* and the subsequent demise of the U.S.S.R. During that time Cuba received substantial economic and military assistance from the U.S.S.R.—generally estimated at $5.6 billion annually—which kept its economy afloat and enabled it to maintain an enormous military establishment. In 1962, Cuban-Soviet ties led to a direct confrontation between the United States and the Soviet Union over the installation of nuclear-equipped missiles in Cuba, resolved only when the U.S.S.R. agreed to withdraw the missiles and other offensive weapons. Soviet subsidies ended in 1991 with the end of the Soviet Union. Former Soviet military personnel in Cuba—numbering around 15,000 in 1990—were withdrawn by 1993.

Russia still maintains a signal intelligence-gathering facility at Lourdes and has provided funding to preserve the still uncompleted thermonuclear plant at Juragua.

# GOVERNMENT

Cuba is a totalitarian state controlled by President Fidel Castro, who is Chief of State, Head of Government, First Secretary of the Communist Party (PCC), and commander in chief of the armed forces. Castro exercises control over all aspects of Cuban life through the Communist Party and its affiliated mass organizations, the government bureaucracy, and the state security apparatus. The Ministry of Interior is the principal organ of state security and control. In addition to the routine law enforcement functions of regulating migration, controlling the Border Guard and the regular police forces, the Ministry's Department of State Security investigates and actively suppresses organized opposition and dissent.

From January 1959 until December 1976, Castro ruled by decree. The 1976 constitution, extensively revised in 1992, enshrines the PCC as "the highest leading force of the society and state." In addition to Fidel Castro and his brother Raul Castro, the cen-ter of party power is the 24-member Politburo. There are 149 members in the Central Committee.

Executive and administrative power is vested in the Council of State and the subordinate Council of Ministers, over which Fidel Castro presides, supported by six vice presidents. Legislative authority rests with the National Assembly of People's Power, which meets annually for about five days, and is state-controlled. When not in session, the Assembly is represented by the Council of State. Fidel Castro is president of the Council of State, and his brother, Raul Castro, is first vice president, which places him first in the line of succession. Raul Castro is also the Minister of the Revolutionary Armed Forces.

The Communist Party is constitutionally recognized as Cuba's only legal political party. The party's Politburo and Central Committee together include most of the country's military and civilian leaders. The party monopolizes all government positions, including judicial offices. Though not a formal requirement, party membership is a de facto prerequisite for high-level official positions and professional advancement in most areas, although non-party members are sometimes allowed to serve in the National Assembly.

In 1992, the National Assembly amended the 1976 constitution, abolishing references to the former Soviet bloc, outlawing discrimination for religious beliefs, permitting foreign investment, giving Fidel Castro new emergency powers, and allowing direct elections to the National Assembly of candidates approved by "mass organizations" controlled by the Communist Party.

Although the constitution grants limited rights of assembly and association, these rights are subject to the requirement that they may not be "exercised against...the existence and objectives of the socialist State." The government denies citizens the freedom of association. The Penal Code specifically outlaws "illegal or unrecognized groups." Cubans do not have the right to change their govern-

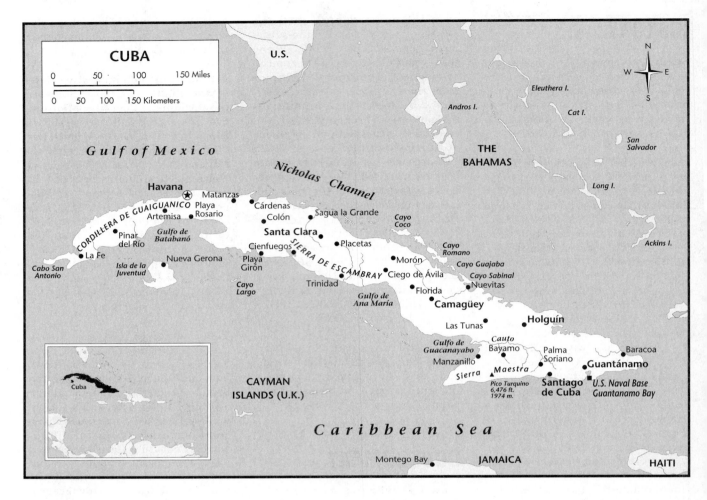

ment, to freedom of expression, or freedom to travel to and from Cuba without restriction. The government and party control all electronic and print media. Since 1992, the Cuban Government has eased the harsher aspects of its repression of religious freedom. In preparation for the visit of Pope John Paul II in January 1998, the government further relaxed its restrictions on religion, especially toward the Roman Catholic Church.

Although the constitution theoretically provides for independent courts, it explicitly subordinates them to the National Assembly and to the Council of State. The People's Supreme Court is the highest judicial body. Due process is routinely denied to Cuban citizens, especially in cases involving political offenses. The constitution states that all legally recognized civil liberties can be denied to anyone who opposes the "decision of the Cuban people to build socialism."

The Cuban Government's human rights record is abysmal. It systematically violates fundamental civil and political rights of its citizens. The government uses incessant harassment in the form of detention, threat of long-term imprisonment, exile, physical injury, and search and seizure of private property to intimidate pro-democracy and human rights activists. There are hundreds of political prisoners. Since 1994, when it invited the UN High Commissioner for Human Rights to visit, the Cuban Government has refused permission for international human rights monitors, including the UN Special Rapporteur for Human Rights, to visit Cuba.

## National Security

Under Castro, Cuba became a highly militarized society. From 1975 until the late 1980s, massive Soviet military assistance enabled Cuba to

upgrade its military capabilities and project power abroad. The tonnage of Soviet military deliveries to Cuba throughout most of the 1980s exceeded deliveries in any year since the military build-up during the 1962 missile crisis. In 1990, Cuba's air force, with about 150 Soviet-supplied fighters, including advanced MiG-23 Floggers and MiG-29 Fulcrums, was probably the best equipped in Latin America. In 1994, Cuba's armed forces were estimated to have 235,000 active duty personnel.

Cuban military power has been sharply reduced by the loss of Soviet subsidies. Lack of fuel has resulted in reduced training and military exercises. Lack of spare parts and new material has resulted in the mothballing of planes, tanks, and other military equipment. Today, the Revolutionary Armed Forces number about 60,000 regular troops. The country's two paramilitary organizations, the Territorial Militia Troops and the Youth Labor Army, have a reduced training capability. Cuba also adopted a "war of the people" strategy that highlights the defensive nature of its capabilities. The government has, however, maintained a large state security apparatus, under the Ministry of Interior, to repress dissent within Cuba.

## Principal Government Officials

**For up-to-date information on Principal Government Officials, see the Chiefs of State and Cabinet Members of Foreign Governments section starting on page 1.**

# ECONOMY

Under the slogan "Socialism or Death," the Cuban Government continues to proclaim Cuba a socialist or communist nation with an economy organized under Marxist-Leninist precepts. Most means of production are owned and run by the government. About 75% of the labor force is employed directly by the state.

Responsibility for running the economy and for economic policy rests with the Council of State, although the government has devolved some authority to ministries and enterprises in recent years.

Minimal public services are provided by the state, either free of charge or for nominal fees. Access to education generally is adequate, but urban housing and medical facilities have deteriorated, as has transportation.

In 1997, the Cuban Government created the Cuban Central Bank to play a role in monetary policy similar to that of a central bank in a market economy. The National Bank of Cuba continued as a commercial bank, and the Cuban Government is creating additional commercial banks. Some foreign banks have begun limited operations in Cuba.

The major sectors of the Cuban economy are tourism, nickel mining, and agriculture, especially sugar and tobacco. Sugar, long the mainstay of the Cuban economy, was surpassed by tourism in the late 1990s as the main source of foreign exchange. Remittances from abroad, estimated at $500–800 million annually, are a major source of income in Cuba, and help sustain many families. An estimated 40% of the population have access to dollars. The Cuban Government stopped producing its annual statistical survey on the Cuban economy in 1990.

The Cuban Government defaulted on most of its international debt in 1986, and remains outside of international financial institutions such as the World Bank. To finance imports, the government relies heavily on short-term loans. Because of its poor credit rating, an $11 billion hard currency debt, and the risks associated with Cuban investment, interest rates have reportedly been as high as 22%.

The Cuban economy suffered a 35% decline in gross domestic product between 1989 and 1993 because of the loss of Soviet subsidies. In October 1990, Castro announced that Cuba had entered a "special period in time of peace" and that the economy would function as if in time of war until the crisis had passed. Most goods are now rationed, and many previously imported from the Soviet Union simply have disappeared.

Economic growth resumed in the mid-1990s after the Cuban Government launched a concerted program to attract foreign tourism and investment. The Cuban Government estimated growth in 1997 at 2.5%. Estimated per capita income in 1997 was $1,540. Living conditions in 1998 are well below the 1990 level.

To deal with the severe shortages brought on by the end of Soviet subsidies and the failure of socialist economic policies, the Cuban Government in the mid-1990s permitted Cubans to offer certain services privately under strict government regulation and scrutiny. It appears that employment in this sector peaked in 1996 at around 206,000 and fell in 1997 to about 170,000. In 1997, the Cuban Government introduced heavy taxes on this sector which forced many out of business. In 1994, the government introduced agricultural markets at which state and private farmers could sell at market prices what they have produced above the quota required by the state. This has helped to alleviate grave food shortages and nutritional problems.

A popular example of this kind of venture has been small restaurants in private homes, known as "paladares." These seek to serve international visitors, but are subject to rules limiting employment of anyone outside of the owner's immediate family and forbidding sales of lobster or shrimp. Such rules are frequently violated, but restaurants and other entities are often closed for minor infractions.

While continuing to limit private investment by Cuban citizens, the Cuban Government is actively courting international investment. It has attracted investment from Canada, Italy, the United Kingdom, Mexico, Spain, France, and other countries. Foreign entities cannot own 100% of the equity of an investment, and must include a Cuban Government entity as a majority partner in the venture. Estimates of the amount of international investment paid in vary widely, but it is thought to be between $1.1 billion to $1.4 billion since 1990.

Cuban officials said early in 1998, there were a total of 332 joint ventures. Many of these are loans or contracts for management, supplies or services, normally not considered equity investment in Western economies. Nevertheless, Cuban officials said in early 1998, that they intend to be more selective in the investment they permit in Cuba. Investors are constrained by the U.S. Cuban Liberty and Democratic Solidarity Act (also known as the Libertad or Helms-Burton Act) which provides for sanctions for those who "traffic" in property expropriated from U.S. citizens. As of March 1998, 15 executives of three foreign companies have been excluded from entry into the U.S.

Over a dozen companies had pulled out of Cuba or altered their plans to invest there due to the threat of action under the Libertad Act.

Tourism, a top Cuban official said, is the "heart of the economy." The Cuban Government is stressing its beaches and has actively encouraged sex tourism to attract Europeans, Canadians, and Latin Americans. Cuban officials expect 1.4 million tourists in 1998, an increase of 20% over 1997. The Cuban Government forecasts 1998 gross revenue from tourism as $1.8 billion.

In 1993, the Cuban Government made it legal for its people to possess and use the U.S. dollar. Since then, the dollar has become the major currency in use. Many businesses, including many run by the Cuban Government, and individuals do not accept Cuban pesos.

Those with access to dollars can purchase imported goods at government-run dollar stores that are not accessible to average Cubans with pesos who must shop in understocked peso stores. Thus, those jobs that can earn dollar tips from foreign tourists and business travelers have become highly desirable. It is not uncommon to meet skilled doctors, teachers, engineers, and scientists working in restaurants or as taxi drivers.

Sugar remains an important part of the Cuban economy, with large amounts of land, labor, and other resources dedicated to its production. Sugar production in 1989 was over 8 million tons, but fell to about 3.5 million tons in the 1994-1995 sugar harvest, one of the worst on record. With increased fertilizers and management attention, the 1995-1996 harvest improved, according to official Cuban estimates, to about 4.4 million tons. Cuba was unable to sustain this level of output, however, and the 1996-1997 harvest declined. The threat of U.S. actions against those who finance the sugar harvest—where there are extensive numbers of confiscated properties—had a major impact on the 1996-97 harvest. Prospects for future harvests are considered poor unless the Cuban

Government undertakes substantial reform of the sugar industry, something it has not been willing to do.

Cuba is not a party to the Nuclear Non-Proliferation Treaty (NPT). It signed the Treaty of Tlatelolco, a Latin American regional non-proliferation regime, but has not ratified the treaty and brought it into force. Cuba has entered into an agreement with the IAEA to apply safeguards to individual nuclear facilities, including the partially completed Juragua nuclear power plant. The reactors that would be installed are of the VVER-400 type, an advanced model of the Soviet pressurized water reactor. There are serious concerns about the safety of the plant. However, since the plant does not appear to be economically viable, no international investors have been willing to provide funds for completion of the facility.

Cuban failure to launch serious economic reforms has led to the development of a large black market and growing corruption.

# FOREIGN RELATIONS

Cuba's once-ambitious foreign policy has been scaled back and redirected as a result of economic hardship and the end of the Cold War.

Cuba aims to find new sources of trade, aid, and foreign investment, and to promote opposition to U.S. policy, especially the trade embargo and the 1996 Libertad Act. Cuba has relations with over 160 countries and has civilian assistance workers—principally medical—in more than 20 nations.

Cuba has largely abandoned the support for guerrilla movements that typified its involvement in regional politics in Latin America and Africa. In 1959, Cuba aided armed expeditions against Panama, the Dominican Republic, and Haiti. During the 1960s and 1970s, Guatemala, Colombia, Venezuela, Peru, and Bolivia faced Cuban-backed guerrilla insurgencies. Although these movements failed to take control of governments,

they inflicted heavy loss of life and economic damage in each of the countries. Cuba's support for Latin guerrilla movements, its Marxist-Leninist government, and its alignment with the U.S.S.R., contributed to its isolation in the hemisphere. In January 1962, the Organization of American States (OAS) suspended Cuba. Cuba now has diplomatic or commercial relations with most countries in Latin American and the Caribbean.

Throughout the 1970s and 1980s, Cuba expanded its military presence abroad—deployments reached 50,000 troops in Angola, 24,000 in Ethiopia, 1,500 in Nicaragua, and hundreds more elsewhere. In Angola, Cuban troops, supported logistically by the U.S.S.R., backed the Popular Movement for the Liberation of Angola (MPLA) in its effort to take power after Portugal granted Angola its independence. Cuban forces played a key role in Ethiopia's war against Somalia, and remained there in substantial numbers as a garrison force for a decade. Cubans served in a non-combat advisory role in Mozambique and the Congo. Cuba also used the Congo as a logistical support center for Cuba's Angola mission.

In the late 1980s, Cuba began to pull back militarily. Cuba unilaterally removed its forces from Ethiopia; met the timetable of the 1988 Angola-Namibia accords by completing the withdrawal of its forces from Angola before July 1991; and ended military assistance to Nicaragua following the Sandinistas' 1990 electoral defeat. In January 1992, following the peace agreement in El Salvador, Castro stated that Cuban support for insurgents was a thing of the past.

# U.S.-CUBAN RELATIONS

The United States recognized the new Cuban Government on January 7, 1959. However, bilateral relations deteriorated rapidly as the regime expropriated U.S. properties and moved toward adoption of a one-party Communist system. In response, the

United States began imposing economic sanctions in 1960, culminating with a comprehensive economic embargo in 1962. The United States broke diplomatic relations on January 3, 1961. Tensions between the two governments peaked during the abortive "Bay of Pigs" invasion by anti-Castro Cubans supported by the United States on April 7, 1961, and the October 1962 missile crisis.

In 1975, U.S.-Cuban normalization talks ended when Cuba launched a large-scale intervention in Angola. However, the U.S. and Cuba established interests sections in their respective capitals on September 1, 1977. Currently, the U.S. interests section in Havana and the Cuban interests section in Washington, DC, are under the protection of the Swiss embassy.

The deployment of Cuban troops to Ethiopia and the discovery of Soviet troops in Cuba in 1979 led President Carter to establish the Caribbean Joint Task Force Headquarters in Florida and warned that Cuban troops would not be allowed to move against neighboring countries.

In April 1980, 10,000 Cubans stormed the Peruvian embassy in Havana seeking political asylum. Eventually, the Cuban Government allowed 125,000 Cubans to illegally take to boats to go to the United States from the port of Mariel, or the "Mariel boatlift." Quiet efforts to explore the prospects for improving relations were initiated by the United States in 1981-82, but ceased as Cuba continued to intervene in the Latin region. In 1983, the United States and regional allies liberated Grenada, forcing the withdrawal of Cuban forces stationed there.

In 1984, the United States and Cuba negotiated an agreement to resume normal immigration, interrupted in the wake of the 1980 Mariel boatlift, and to return to Cuba persons who had arrived during the boatlift who were "excludable" under U.S. law. Cuba suspended this agreement in May 1985 following the U.S. initiation of Radio Marti broadcasts to Cuba, but it was reinstated in

November 1987. In March 1990, TV Marti transmissions began to Cuba. Since its inception, Cuba has jammed TV Marti and blocked Radio Marti on the AM band. Radio Marti on short wave has a large audience.

The principal U.S. concerns regarding Cuba are its undemocratic system and lack of respect for human rights, and the potential danger of future mass exoduses. The principal objective of U.S. policy toward Cuba is to promote a peaceful transition to democracy and respect for human rights. U.S. policy seeks to do this by maintaining pressure on the Cuban Government; supporting the Cuban people; forging a multilateral effort to press for democratic change; and keeping migration in safe, legal, and orderly channels. President Bush set free and fair elections under international supervision, respect for human rights, and an end to efforts to subvert its neighbors as the conditions for improving relations with Cuba. In October 1992, the Cuban Democracy Act (CDA) was enacted, codifying portions of the embargo and providing for measures in support of the Cuban people and for improved telecommunications with Cuba and sale of medicines. Other provisions ban most U.S. subsidiary trade with Cuba and exclude any vessel which stops in Cuba from entering U.S. ports for 180 days. It provides for humanitarian donations by U.S. non-governmental organizations to Cuba. Since its enactment, more than $2 billion worth of humanitarian assistance for Cuba has been licensed, including $275 million in medical items. Since 1992, 50 licenses have been issued for sale of medicines or travel to Cuba by representatives of pharmaceutical companies. The U.S. Federal Communications Commission (FCC) approved five U.S. carriers to provide direct telecommunications service between the U.S. and Cuba.

In 1994, regular immigration talks were initiated between the United States and Cuba, prompted by another mass exodus of Cubans that summer. The two governments agreed in September 1994 to direct Cuban migration into safe, legal, and orderly channels. The U.S. committed

itself to admit a minimum of 20,000 Cuban immigrants each year, and Cuba pledged to discourage irregular and unsafe departures. Under a May 1995 agreement, the United States began returning Cubans interdicted at sea or entering the U.S. Naval Base at Guantanamo Bay, and Cuba agreed to reintegrate the returnees into Cuban society, with no action to be taken against the returned migrants as a consequence of their attempt to immigrate illegally. The U.S. Interests Section verifies Cuban compliance with that provision through regular visits to the homes of returnees throughout Cuba. Interdicted Cubans who can demonstrate a well-founded fear of persecution in Cuba are resettled in third countries, rather than returned to Cuba.

While the United States engaged in efforts to promote democratic change, the development of an independent civil society, and support for the Cuban people, in February 1996 the Cuban Government moved aggressively against 140 groups of pro-democracy and human rights activists who were seeking to hold a meeting under the auspices of their umbrella organization "Concilio Cubano." The Cuban Government never responded to Concilio's request to legally hold a meeting, and in mid-February began an island-wide crackdown against dissidents—arresting, interrogating, and harassing them. On February 24, 1996, the day the meeting was to be held, the Cuban Government ordered the shootdown of two unarmed civilian aircraft in international airspace. Three U.S. citizens and one legal permanent resident, all members of the Miami-based exile organization Brothers to the Rescue, were killed when their planes were shot down by Cuban MiGs.

On February 26, 1996, President Clinton ordered five punitive measures in response to the shootdown. He suspended direct charter flights to Cuba; sought to obtain international condemnation of Cuba's actions; committed to reach agreement with Congress on the pending Helms-Burton legislation; announced that some form of justice was due to the families of the victims and ordered that funds be transferred from the Cuban Government's blocked accounts in the United States to the families; and set restrictions on the movement of Cuban diplomats in the U.S.

On March 12, 1996, President Clinton signed into law the Cuban Liberty and Democratic Solidarity Act (also known as the Libertad or Helms-Burton Act). The Libertad Act has four main parts:

- Title I codifies and tightens enforcement of the U.S. embargo;

- Title II states U.S. policy toward a transition or democratic government in Cuba;

- Title III creates a cause of action and authorizes U.S. nationals with claims to confiscated property in Cuba to file suit in U.S. courts against persons "trafficking" in such property; and

- Title IV requires the Executive Branch to deny visas to, and exclude from the United States,

foreign nationals determined to have confiscated or "trafficked" in confiscated property, claimed by a U.S. national.

In accordance with the provisions of the Act, the President suspended the Title III lawsuit provisions because he determined suspension to be necessary and in the national interest and that it will expedite a transition to democracy in Cuba.

On March 20, 1998, President Clinton announced measures intended to respond to the historic visit of Pope John Paul II to Cuba in January and to support the Cuban people. The measures include: resuming direct humanitarian charter cargo and passenger flights to Cuba; reinstituting legal remittances by Cuban Americans and Cuban families living in the United States to their close relatives in Cuba at the level of $300 per quarter (such remittances were suspended in August 1994 in response to the migration crisis); simplifying and expediting the issuance of licenses for the sale of medicines and medical supplies to Cuba. The President also said he would work with Congress to develop bipartisan legislation on the transfer of food and expansion of humanitarian assistance to the Cuban people.

Support for the Cuban people has been a key element of U.S. policy beginning with the CDA and strengthened by President Clinton's initiatives in October 1995 to encourage groups in the U.S. to develop contacts on the island. The 1995 initiatives included licensing U.S. non-governmental organizations (NGOs) to assist Cuban NGOs; allowing sales and donations of communi-

cations equipment to Cuban NGOs; establishing news bureaus; increasing academic, cultural, and educational exchanges; and allowing under a general Treasury license once-a-year visits to relatives in Cuba in cases of humanitarian emergencies.

The measures announced March 20 enhance this policy of support for the Cuban people. They support the religious opening, expand humanitarian assistance, and assist development of independent civil society. The measures are in response to the Cuban people, not to anything the Cuban Government has done. Hundreds of political prisoners remain in Cuban jails, including the four leaders of the Dissident Working Group. The U.S. Government has repeatedly made clear, however, that it will consider responding reciprocally if the Cuban Government initiates fundamental democratic change.

## Interests Sections

*Havana:* U.S. Interests Section Calzada between L and M, Vedado (tel. (53) (7) 33-3551 through 33-3559).

*Washington, DC:* Cuban Interests Section 2630 16th Street, NW, Washington, DC 20009 (tel. 202-797-8518).

## Principal U.S. Officials

**For up-to-date information on Principal U.S. Officials, see the U.S. Embassies, Consulates, and Foreign Service section starting on page 139.**

# CYPRUS

October 1998

Official Name:
**Republic of Cyprus**

# PROFILE

## Geography

**Area:** 9,251 sq. km. (3,572 sq. mi.); about the size of Connecticut.
**Cities:** Capital—Nicosia (pop. 164,400). Other cities—Limassol, Larnaca, Famagusta, Paphos, Kyrenia, Morphou.
**Terrain:** Central plain with mountain ranges to the north and south.
**Climate:** Mediterranean with hot, dry summers and cool, wet winters.

## People

**Nationality:** Noun and adjective—Cypriot(s).
**Population (1997 est.):** 837,000. Greek area: 655,000; Turkish area: 182,000.
**Annual growth rate:** 1%.
**Ethnic groups:** Greek (78%), Turkish (18%), Armenian and other (4%).
**Religions:** Greek Orthodox, Muslim, Maronite, Roman Catholic, Armenian Orthodox.
**Languages:** Greek, Turkish, English.
**Education:** Years compulsory—6 in elementary; 3 in high school. Attendance—almost 100%. Literacy—about 99%.
**Health:** Infant mortality rate—9/1,000. Life expectancy—73 yrs. males; 78 yrs. females.
**Work force (1997):** Greek area—

285,000. Business and social services—31%; trade and tourism—26%; agriculture—12%; manufacturing and utilities—16%; construction and mining—9%; other—6%. Turkish area—19,000. Agriculture—22%; public services—22%; industry—11%; trade and tourism—11%; other—34%.

## Government

**Type:** Republic.
**Independence:** August 16, 1960.
**Constitution:** August 16, 1960.
**Branches:** Executive—president elected to 5-yr. term. Legislative—unicameral House of Representatives, members elected to 5-yr. terms. Judicial—Supreme Court; six district courts.
**Administrative subdivisions:** six.
**Political parties:** Greek Cypriot Community—Democratic Rally (right); Democratic Party (center-right); AKEL (communist); EDEK (socialist); United Democrats (center-left). Turkish Cypriot Community—National Unity (right); Democratic party (center-right); Republican Turkish (left); Communal Liberation (center-left); National Revival (center-right); Patriotic Unity Movement (left), National Justice Party (ultra-nationalist).
**Suffrage:** Universal at age 18.
**Flag:** Against a white background, island's shape in gold above two crossed olive branches.

## Economy

**GDP (1997):** $8.5 billion.
**Annual real growth rate (1997):** 2.3%.
**Per capita GDP income (1997):** Greek Cypriots—$13,000; Turkish Cypriots—about $3,600.
**Agriculture and natural resources (6.0% of GDP):** Products—Potatoes and other vegetables, citrus fruits, olives, grapes, wheat, carob seeds. Resources—Pyrites, copper, asbestos, gypsum, lumber, salt, marble, clay, earth pigment.
**Industry and construction (24.3% of GDP):** Types—mining, cement, construction, utilities, manufacturing, chemicals, non-electric machinery, textiles, footwear, food, beverages, tobacco.
**Services and tourism (69.7% of GDP):** Trade, restaurants, and hotels 21.6%; banking, insurance, real estate, and business 17.5%; transport and communication 11%; government services 12%; social and personal services 8%.
**Trade (1997):** Exports—$1.2 billion: citrus, grapes, wine, potatoes, clothing, footwear. Major markets—EU (especially the U.K.), Middle East. Imports—$3.3 billion: consumer goods, raw materials for industry, petroleum and lubricants, food and feed grains. Major suppliers—EU, U.S., Japan. (U.S. trade surplus $700 million.)

# PEOPLE AND HISTORY

Greek and Turkish Cypriots share many customs but maintain distinct identities based on religion, language, and close ties with their respective motherlands. Greek is predominantly spoken in the south, Turkish in the north. English is widely used. Cyprus has a well-developed system of primary and secondary education. The majority of Cypriots earn their higher education at Greek, Turkish, British, or American universities. Private colleges and state-supported universities have been developed by both the Turkish and Greek communities.

Cypriot culture is among the oldest in the Mediterranean. By 3700 BC, the island was well-inhabited, a crossroads between East and West. The island fell successively under Assyrian, Egyptian, Persian, Greek, and Roman domination. For 800 years, beginning in AD 364, Cyprus was ruled by Byzantium. After brief possession by Richard the Lion-Hearted during the Crusades, the island came under Frankish control in the late 12th century. It was ceded to the Venetian Republic in 1489 and conquered by the Ottoman Turks in 1571. The Ottomans applied the millet system to Cyprus, which allowed religious authorities to govern their own non-Muslim minorities. This system reinforced the position of the Orthodox Church and the cohesion of the ethnic Greek population. Most of the Turks who settled on the island during the 3 centuries of Ottoman rule remained when control of Cyprus—although not sovereignty—was ceded to Great Britain in 1878. Many, however, left for Turkey during the 1920s. The island was annexed formally by the U.K. in 1914 at the outbreak of World War I and became a crown colony in 1925.

Cyprus gained its independence from the U.K. in 1960, after an anti-British campaign by the Greek Cypriot EOKA (National Organization of Cypriot Fighters), a guerrilla group which desired political union with Greece, or *enosis*. Archbishop Makarios, a charismatic religious and political leader, was elected president.

Shortly after the founding of the republic, serious differences arose between the two communities about the implementation and interpretation of the constitution. The Greek Cypriots argued that the complex mechanisms introduced to protect Turkish Cypriot interests were obstacles to efficient government. In November 1963, President Makarios advanced a series of constitutional amendments designed to eliminate some of these special provisions. The Turkish Cypriots opposed such changes. The confrontation prompted widespread intercommunal fighting in December 1963, after which Turkish Cypriot participation in the central government ceased. UN peacekeepers were deployed on the island in 1964. Following another outbreak of intercommunal violence in 1967-68, a Turkish Cypriot provisional administration was formed.

In July 1974, the military junta in Athens sponsored a coup led by extremist Greek Cypriots hostile to Makarios for his alleged pro-communist leanings and for his perceived abandonment of *enosis*. Turkey, citing the 1960 Treaty of Guarantee, intervened militarily to protect Turkish Cypriots.

In a two-stage offensive, Turkish troops took control of 38% of the island. Many Greek Cypriots fled south while many Turkish Cypriots fled north. Since then, the southern part of the country has been under the control of the Government of Cyprus and the northern part under an autonomous Turkish-Cypriot administration supported by the presence of Turkish troops. In 1983, that administration proclaimed itself the "Turkish Republic of Northern Cyprus," recognized only by Turkey. UN peacekeeping forces maintain a buffer zone between the two sides. Except for occasional demonstrations or infrequent incidents between soldiers in the buffer zone, there had been no violent conflict since 1974 until August 1996, when violent clashes led to the death of two demonstrators and escalated tension. There is little movement of people and essentially no movement of goods or services between the two parts of the island. Efforts to reunite the island under a federal structure continue, however, under the auspices of the United Nations.

# GOVERNMENT

Since 1974, Cyprus has been divided de facto into the government-controlled southern two-thirds of the island and the Turkish-Cypriot northern one-third. The Government of the Republic of Cyprus has continued as the internationally recognized authority; in practice, its power extends only to the Greek Cypriot-controlled areas.

The 1960 Cypriot Constitution provided for a presidential system of government with independent executive, legislative, and judicial branches, as well as a complex system of checks and balances, including a weighted power-sharing ratio designed to protect the interests of the Turkish Cypriots. The executive, for example, was headed by a Greek Cypriot president and a Turkish Cypriot vice president, elected by their respective communities for 5-year terms and each possessing a right of veto over certain types of legislation and executive decisions.

Following the 1974 hostilities, the Turkish Cypriots formally set up their own institutions with a popularly elected president and a prime minister responsible to the National Assembly exercising joint executive powers. In 1983, the Turkish Cypriots declared an independent "Turkish Republic of Northern Cyprus" (T.R.N.C.). In 1985, they adopted a constitution and held elections—an arrangement recognized only by Turkey.

# POLITICAL CONDITIONS

In February 1998, Greek Cypriots narrowly re-elected Glafcos Clerides, a seasoned politician from the conservative Democratic Rally Party, as president of the Republic of Cyprus.

Following his re-election, Clerides formed a government of national unity, with open invitations for participation of all political parties. His cabinet includes six ministers from Clerides' Democratic Rally party, two ministers from the EDEK (socialist) party, three from the Democratic Party (who broke ranks with party leader Spyros Kyprianou) and one from the United Democrats. None of the Greek Cypriot parties has been able to elect a president by itself or dominate the 56-seat House of Representatives. The 165,000 Greek Cypriot refugees are also a potent political force, along with the independent Orthodox Church of Cyprus, which has some influence in temporal as well as ecclesiastical matters.

Turkish Cypriots held multi-party "parliamentary" elections in 1993, removing the long-ruling National Unity Party in favor of a coalition of the Democratic and Republican Turkish parties. However, in August 1996, a new coalition was formed between the two main rightist parties, the National Unity Party and the Democratic Party. The next "parliamentary" elections will take place in the fall of 1998. "T.R.N.C. President" Rauf Denktash won re-election in 1995 after an unprecedented second round of voting. He defeated the incumbent "Prime Minister," Dr. Dervis Eroglu.

## Principal Government Officials

For up-to-date information on Principal Government Officials, see the Chiefs of State and Cabinet Members of Foreign Governments section starting on page 1.

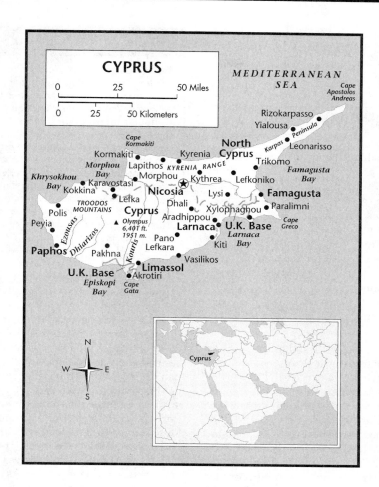

UN-sponsored negotiations to develop institutional arrangements acceptable to both communities began in 1968; several sets of negotiations and other initiatives followed. Turkish Cypriots focus on bi-zonality, security guarantees, and political equality between the two communities. Greek Cypriots emphasize the rights of movement, property, settlement, and the return of territory. Turkish Cypriots favor a federation of two nearly autonomous societies living side by side with limited contact, while Greek Cypriots envision a more integrated structure.

The last face-to-face meeting between the leaders of the two communities, President Clerides and Mr. Denktash, took place when the two were invited in June 1997 by the UN Secretary General to engage again in face-to-face negotiations. The two leaders met July 9-13, 1997, in Troutbeck, New York, to resume discus-

sions to resolve intercommunal strife and reunite the island. They met for a second round in Switzerland, August 11-15, 1997. The U.S. also brokered two direct meetings between the two leaders, including one meeting in September 1997 to discuss security issues and a second meeting in November 1997 under the auspices of U.S. Special Presidential Emissary Richard C. Holbrooke to review informally the core issues of a settlement agreement. International efforts to promote a settlement to the Cyprus dispute began again in earnest following the February 1998 presidential election.

Cyprus maintains an embassy in the United States at 2211 R Street NW, Washington, DC 20008 (tel. 202-462-5772) and a Consulate General in New York City. Cyprus also maintains a trade center at 13 East 40th Street, New York, NY 10016 (tel. 212-686-6016). Turkish Cypriots maintain offices in Washington (tel. 202-887-6198) and at the Republic of Turkey's Mission to the UN.

# ECONOMY

Cyprus has an open, free-market, serviced-based economy with some light manufacturing. The Cypriots are among the most prosperous people in the Mediterranean region. Internationally, Cyprus promotes its geographical location as a "bridge" between West and East, along with its educated English-speaking population, moderate local costs, good airline connections, and telecommunications.

In the past 20 years, the economy has shifted from agriculture to light manufacturing and services. The service sector, including tourism, contributes 70% to the GDP and employs 62% of the labor force. Industry and construction contribute 24% and employ 25% of labor. Manufactured goods account for approximately 69% of domestic exports. Agriculture is responsible for 6% of GDP and 12% of the labor force. Potatoes and citrus are the principal export crops.

After robust growth rates in the 1980s (average annual growth was 6.1%), economic performance in the 1990s has been mixed: Real GDP growth was 9.7% in 1992, 1.7% in 1993, 6.0% in 1994, 6.0% in 1995, 1.9% in 1996 and 2.3% in 1997. This pattern underlines the economy's vulnerability to swings in tourist arrivals (i.e., to economic and political conditions in Cyprus, Western Europe, and the Middle East) and the need to restructure the economy. Declining competitiveness in tourism and especially in manufacturing will act as a drag on growth until structural changes are effected. Overvaluation of the Cypriot pound has kept inflation in check in recent years (3.5% in 1997) and is forecast to continue to do so in the foreseeable future. Economic prospects are good over the long term, and real growth in 1998 is expected to reach 3.0%.

**Travel Notes**

**Travel Advice:** For up-to-date information from the U.S. State Department on possible inconvenience or hazardous situations, see the **Travel Warnings and Consular Information Sheets from the U.S. Government** section starting on page 1723. For the latest information on health requirements and conditions, see the **International Travelers' Health Information** section starting on page 1385. For further information dealing with non-urgent matter, see the **Tips for Travelers to...** section starting on page 1588.

Trade is vital to the Cypriot economy—the island is not self-sufficient in food and has few natural resources—and the trade deficit continues to grow. Exports rose by 1.3% in 1997, while imports rose by 2.2%, resulting in a trade deficit of $2.1 billion (2.7% higher than the previous year). Cyprus must import fuels, most raw materials, heavy machinery, and transportation equipment. More than 50% of its trade is with the European Union (especially the U.K.); the Middle East receives 20% of exports. Cyprus signed an Association Agreement with the European Union (EU) in 1972, which resulted in the establishment of a Customs Union between the two sides. Cyprus applied for full EU membership in 1990 and has since linked the Cyprus pound to the European Monetary Unit (ECU). EU accession negotiations started on March 31, 1998. In 1991, Cyprus introduced a Value Added Tax (VAT), which is currently 8%. Cyprus ratified the new world trade agreement (GATT) in 1995 and began implementing it fully on January 1, 1996.

Cyprus has the fourth-largest ship registry in the world, with 2,758 ships and 25.5 million gross registered tons (GRTs). It is an open registry and includes ships from more than 43 countries, including Greece, Germany, and Russia.

## Export Opportunities

Cyprus has been liberalizing its trade regime by eliminating import quotas and licenses and lowering tariffs on most products as a result of its obligations under the new world trade agreement and its Customs Union agreement with the European Union. As a result, U.S. products are becoming more competitive in Cyprus and prospects for further expansion of bilateral trade ties are excellent.

Government computerization and telecommunications development, two of the priorities of the government's 5-year development plan (1994-1998), provide excellent opportunities for U.S. exports. Sales of computer-assisted design systems, new capital equipment for textile, clothing, footwear production, medical equipment, environmental equipment, and services are also expected to grow. U.S. pressure resulted in the adoption of a new copyright law in 1994 and a new patent law in 1998.

## Investment Climate

In February 1997, the government revised its policy on foreign direct investment, permitting 100% foreign ownership in certain cases. Regulations on foreign portfolio investment in the Cyprus Stock Exchange also have been liberalized. Additionally, Cyprus passed a modern banking law in July 1997, incorporating all the provisions and directives of the EU for the prudential supervision of credit institutions.

Cyprus has concluded treaties on double taxation with 26 countries, including the U.S., and has removed exchange restrictions on current international transactions. Non-residents and foreign investors may freely repatriate proceeds from investments in Cyprus.

## Offshore Sector

The 1,049 full-fledged offshore companies—which are located in Cyprus but conduct business abroad only—qualify for various tax- and duty-free concessions. Foreign exchange earnings from offshore companies rose to $346 million in 1997. There are about 40 U.S.-owned firms in Cyprus; about half operate exclusively on an offshore basis.

U.S. firms are mainly engaged in the regional marketing of computers, computer graphics, telecommunications, printing equipment, household products, and soft drinks. Since 1994, re-entry visa provisions have been streamlined and 3-year work permits have been introduced for offshore employees.

## Trade Between Cyprus and the United States

The U.S. embassy in Nicosia sponsors a popular pavilion for American products at the annual Cyprus International State Fair, hosts the Commercial Awards dinner, and organizes other events to promote U.S. products throughout the year. Total U.S. exports to Cyprus were about $700 million in 1997 (compared with $670 million in 1996), making the U.S. Cyprus' number-one supplier of total imports for the third year in a row. Exports include American tobacco and tobacco products, automatic data processing and other machinery, and cereals. Principal U.S. imports from Cyprus consist of clothing, footwear, steel tubes and pipes, dairy products, and various food items.

## Turkish Cypriot Economy

The economic disparity between the two communities is pronounced. Although the Turkish Cypriot area operates on a free-market basis, the lack of private and governmental investment, shortages of skilled labor and experienced managers, plus inflation and the devaluation of the Turkish lira (which the Turkish Cypriots use as their currency) continue to plague the economy. A Greek-Cypriot-organized economic boycott of the Turkish Cypriot region also has negatively affected the Turkish Cypriot economy.

Turkey is, by far, the main trading partner of the "T.R.N.C.," supplying 55% of imports and absorbing 48% of exports. In a landmark case, the European Court of Justice (ECJ) ruled on July 5, 1994, against the British practice of importing produce from Northern Cyprus based on certificates of origin and phytosanitary certificates granted by "T.R.N.C." authorities. The ECJ decision stated that only goods bearing certificates of origin from the Government of Cyprus could be recognized for trade by EU member countries. That decision resulted in a considerable decrease of Turkish Cypriot exports to the EU: from $36.4 million (or 66.7% of total Turkish Cypriot exports) in 1993 to $24.7 million in 1996 (or 35% of total exports) in 1996. Even so, the EU continues to be the "T.R.N.C.'s" second-largest trading partner, with a 24.7% share of total imports and 35% share of total exports.

Assistance from Turkey is the mainstay of the Turkish Cypriot economy. Under the latest economic protocol (signed January 3, 1997), Turkey undertakes to provide Turkish Cypriots loans totaling $250 million for the purpose of implementing projects included in the protocol related to public finance, tourism, banking, and privatization. Fluctuation in the Turkish lira, which loses about 50% of its value against the U.S. dollar every year, continues to exert downward pressure on the Turkish Cypriot standard of living.

Turkish Cypriot authorities have instituted a free market in foreign exchange and authorize residents to hold foreign-currency denominated bank accounts. This encourages transfers from Turkish Cypriots living abroad.

# FOREIGN RELATIONS

The Government of Cyprus has historically followed a non-aligned foreign policy, although it increasingly identifies with the West in its cultural affinities and trade patterns and maintains close relations with Greece.

Since 1974, the foreign policy of the Government of Cyprus has sought the withdrawal of Turkish forces and the most favorable constitutional and territorial settlement possible. This campaign has been pursued primarily through international forums such as the United Nations and the Non-aligned Movement. Turkey does not recognize the Government of Cyprus.

Cyprus' 1990 application for full EU membership caused a storm in the Turkish Cypriot community, which argued that the move required their consent. Following the December 1997 EU Summit decisions on EU enlargement, accession negotiations began March 31, 1998.

The Government of Cyprus enjoys close relations with Greece. Cyprus is expanding relations with Russia, Israel, and Syria, from which it purchases most of its oil.

Cyprus is a member of the UN and most of its agencies as well as the World Bank, International Monetary Fund, Council of Europe, and the Commonwealth.

In addition, the country has signed the General Agreement on Tariffs and Trade (GATT) and the Multilateral Investment Guarantee Agency Agreement (MIGA).

# U.S.-CYPRUS RELATIONS

The United States regards the status quo on Cyprus as unacceptable. Successive administrations have viewed UN-led intercommunal negotiations as the best means to achieve a fair and permanent settlement. The United States will continue actively to support and aid the UN Secretary General's efforts. In June 1997, the U.S. appointed Ambassador Richard C. Holbrooke as Special Presidential Emissary for Cyprus.

The United States has channeled $305 million in assistance to the two communities through the UN High Commissioner for Refugees and the Cyprus Red Cross since the mid-1970s. The United States now provides $15 million annually to promote bicommunal projects and finance U.S.

scholarships for Greek and Turkish Cypriots.

The U.S. Embassy in Cyprus is located at the corner of Metochiou and Ploutarchou Streets in Engomi, Nicosia, Cyprus mailing address: PO Box 4536, Nicosia Cyprus. U.S. mailing address: PSC 815, FPO-AE 09836-0001. Tel. [357](2)776-400; Telex: 4160 AMEMY CY; Fax: [357](2)780-944; Consular Fax: [357](2)776-841; Web Page: http://www.americanembassy.org.cy/index.html

## Principal U.S. Officials

For up-to-date information on Principal U.S. Officials, see the U.S. Embassies, Consulates, and Foreign Service section starting on page 139.

# CZECH REPUBLIC

March 1999

Official Name:
**Czech Republic**

# PROFILE

## Geography

**Area:** 78,864 sq. kilometers; about the size of Virginia.
**Cities:** Capital—Prague (pop. 1.2 million). Other cities—Brno (387,000), Ostrava (324,000), Plzen (175,000).
**Terrain:** Low mountains to the north and south, hills in the west.
**Climate:** Temperate.

## People

**Nationality:** Noun and adjective—Czech(s).
**Population (est.):** 10.5 million.
**Annual growth rate:** 0.1%.
**Ethnic groups:** Czech (95%), Germans, Roma, Poles, Silesians, Slovaks.
**Religions:** Roman Catholic, Protestant.
**Language:** Czech.
**Education:** Literacy—99%.
**Health:** Life expectancy—males 68 yrs., females 75 yrs.
**Work force (5.2 million):** Industry, construction and commerce—47%. Government and other services—41%. Agriculture—11%.

## Government

**Type:** Parliamentary republic.

**Independence:** The Czech Republic was established January 1, 1993 (former Czechoslovak state established 1918).
**Constitution:** Signed December 16, 1992.
**Branches:** Executive—president (chief of state), prime minister (head of government), cabinet. Legislative—Chamber of Deputies, Senate. Judicial—Supreme Court, Constitutional Court.
**Political parties (June 1998 election):** Czech Social Democratic Party (CSSD), 74 seats; Civic Democratic Party (ODS), 63 seats; Communist Party of Bohemia and Moravia [KSCM], 24 seats; Christian Democratic Union–Czechoslovak Peoples Party (KDU–CSL), 20 seats; Freedom Union (US), 19 seats. Suffrage: Universal at 18.
**Administrative subdivisions:** Two regions—Bohemia and Moravia; seven administrative districts and Prague.
**Flag:** Blue triangle on staff side; upper white band, lower red band.

## Economy

**GDP (1998 est.):** $54.54 billion.
**Per capita income (1998 est.):** $5,454.
**Natural resources:** Coal, coke, timber, lignite, uranium, magnesite.
**Agriculture:** Products—wheat, rye, oats, corn, barley, hops, potatoes, sugarbeets, hogs, cattle, horses.

**Industry:** Types—iron, steel, machinery and equipment, cement, sheet glass, motor vehicles, armaments, chemicals, ceramics, wood, paper products, and footwear.
**Trade (1997):** Exports—$21.850 billion: machinery, iron, steel, chemicals, raw materials, consumer goods. Trading partners—Austria, Belgium, Commonwealth of Independent States, France, Germany, Hungary, Poland, Slovakia, Switzerland, United States.

# PEOPLE

The majority of the 10.5 million inhabitants of the Czech Republic are ethnically and linguistically Czech (95%). Other ethnic groups include Germans, Roma, and Poles. After the 1993 division, some Slovaks remained in the Czech Republic and comprise roughly 3% of the current population. The border between the Czech Republic and Slovakia is open for former citizens of Czechoslovakia. Laws establishing religious freedom were passed shortly after the revolution of 1989, lifting oppressive regulations enacted by the former communist regime. Major denominations and their estimated percentage populations are Roman Catholic (39%) and Protestant (3%). A large percentage of the Czech population claim to be atheists (40%), and 16%

describe themselves as uncertain. The Jewish community numbers a few thousand today; a synagogue in Prague memorializes the names of more than 80,000 Czechoslovak Jews who perished in World War II.

# HISTORY

The Czech Republic was the western part of the Czech and Slovak Federal Republic. Formed into a common state after World War I (October 18, 1918), the Czechs, Moravians, and Slovaks remained united for almost 75 years. On January 1, 1993, the two republics split to form two separate states.

The Czechs lost their national independence to the Austro–Hungarian Empire in 1620 at the Battle of White Mountain and, for the next 300 years, were ruled by the Austrian Monarchy. With the collapse of the monarchy at the end of World War I, the independent country of Czechoslovakia was formed, encouraged by, among others, U.S. President Woodrow Wilson.

Despite cultural differences, the Slovaks shared with the Czechs similar aspirations for independence from the Hapsburg state and voluntarily united with the Czechs. The Slovaks were not at the same level of economic and technological development as the Czechs, but the freedom and opportunity found in Czechoslovakia enabled them to make strides toward overcoming these inequalities. However, the gap never was fully bridged, and the discrepancy played a continuing role throughout the 75 years of the union.

Although Czechoslovakia was the only east European country to remain a parliamentary democracy from 1918 to 1938, it was plagued with minority problems, the most important of which concerned the country's large German population. Constituting more than 22% of the interwar state's population and largely concentrated in the Bohemian and Moravian border regions (the Sudetenland), members of this

minority, including some who were sympathetic to Nazi Germany, undermined the new Czechoslovak state. Internal and external pressures culminated in September 1938, when France and the United Kingdom yielded to Nazi pressures at Munich and agreed to force Czechoslovakia to cede the Sudetenland to Germany.

Fulfilling Hitler's aggressive designs on all of Czechoslovakia, Germany invaded what remained of Bohemia and Moravia in March 1939, establishing a German "protectorate." By this time, Slovakia had already declared independence and had become a puppet state of the Germans.

At the close of World War II, Soviet troops overran all of Slovakia, Moravia, and much of Bohemia, including Prague. In May 1945, U.S. forces liberated the city of Plzen and most of western Bohemia. A civilian uprising against the German garrison took place in Prague in May 1945. Following Germany's surrender, some 2.9 million ethnic Germans were expelled from Czechoslovakia with Allied approval under the Benes Decrees.

Reunited after the war, the Czechs and Slovaks set federal and national elections for the spring of 1946. The democratic elements, led by President Eduard Benes, hoped the Soviet Union would allow Czechoslovakia the freedom to choose its own form of government and aspired to a Czechoslovakia that would act as a bridge between East and West. The Czechoslovak Communist Party, which won 38% of the vote, held most of the key positions in the government and gradually managed to neutralize or silence the anti–communist forces. Although the communist–led government initially intended to participate in the Marshall Plan, it was forced by Moscow to back out. Under the cover of superficial legality, the Communist Party seized power in February 1948.

After extensive purges modeled on the Stalinist pattern in other east European states, the Communist Party tried 14 of its former leaders in November 1952 and sentenced 11 to

death. For more than a decade thereafter, the Czechoslovak communist political structure was characterized by the orthodoxy of the leadership of party chief Antonin Novotny.

## The 1968 Soviet Invasion

The communist leadership allowed token reforms in the early 1960s, but discontent arose within the ranks of the communist party central committee, stemming from dissatisfaction with the slow pace of the economic reforms, resistance to cultural liberalization, and the desire of the Slovaks within the leadership for greater autonomy for their republic. This discontent expressed itself with the removal of Novotny from party leadership in January 1968 and from the presidency in March. He was replaced as party leader by a Slovak, Alexander Dubcek.

After January 1968, the Dubcek leadership took practical steps toward political, social, and economic reforms. In addition, it called for politico-military changes in the Soviet-dominated Warsaw Pact and Council for Mutual Economic Assistance. The leadership affirmed its loyalty to socialism and the Warsaw Pact but also expressed the desire to improve relations with all countries of the world regardless of their social systems.

A program adopted in April 1968 set guidelines for a modern, humanistic socialist democracy that would guarantee, among other things, freedom of religion, press, assembly, speech, and travel; a program that, in Dubcek's words, would give socialism "a human face." After 20 years of little public participation, the population gradually started to take interest in the government, and Dubcek became a truly popular national figure.

The internal reforms and foreign policy statements of the Dubcek leadership created great concern among some other Warsaw Pact governments. On the night of August 20, 1968, Soviet, Hungarian, Bulgarian, East German, and Polish troops invaded and occupied Czechoslovakia. The Czechoslovak Government

immediately declared that the troops had not been invited into the country and that their invasion was a violation of socialist principles, international law, and the UN Charter.

The principal Czechoslovak reformers were forcibly and secretly taken to the Soviet Union. Under obvious Soviet duress, they were compelled to sign a treaty that provided for the "temporary stationing" of an unspecified number of Soviet troops in Czechoslovakia. Dubcek was removed as party First Secretary on April 17, 1969, and replaced by another Slovak, Gustav Husak. Later, Dubcek and many of his allies within the party were stripped of their party positions in a purge that lasted until 1971 and reduced party membership by almost one–third.

The 1970s and 1980s became known as the period of "normalization," in which the apologists for the 1968 Soviet invasion prevented, as best they could, any opposition to their conservative regime. Political, social, and economic life stagnated. The population, cowed by the "normalization," was quiet.

At the time of the communist takeover, Czechoslovakia had a balanced economy and one of the higher levels of industrialization on the continent. In 1948, however, the government began to stress heavy industry over agricultural and consumer goods and services. Many basic industries and foreign trade, as well as domestic wholesale trade, had been nationalized before the communists took power. Nationalization of most of the

retail trade was completed in 1950–51.

Heavy industry received major economic support during the 1950s, but central planning resulted in waste and inefficient use of industrial resources. Although the labor force was traditionally skilled and efficient, inadequate incentives for labor and management contributed to high labor turnover, low productivity, and poor product quality. Economic failures reached a critical stage in the 1960s, after which various reform measures were sought with no satisfactory results.

Hope for wide–ranging economic reform came with Alexander Dubcek's rise in January 1968. Despite renewed efforts, however, Czechoslovakia could not come to grips with inflationary forces, much less begin the immense task of correcting the economy's basic problems.

The economy saw growth during the 1970s but then stagnated between 1978–82. Attempts at revitalizing it in the 1980s with management and worker incentive programs were largely unsuccessful. The economy grew after 1982, achieving an annual average output growth of more than 3% between 1983–85. Imports from the West were curtailed, exports boosted, and hard currency debt reduced substantially. New investment was made in the electronic, chemical, and pharmaceutical sectors, which were industry leaders in eastern Europe in the mid–1980s.

## The Velvet Revolution

The roots of the 1989 Civic Forum movement that came to power during the "Velvet Revolution" lie in human rights activism. On January 1, 1977, more than 250 human rights activists signed a manifesto called the Charter 77, which criticized the government for failing to implement human rights provisions of documents it had signed, including the state's own constitution; international covenants on political, civil, economic, social, and cultural rights; and the Final Act of the Conference for Security and Cooperation in Europe. Although not organized in any real sense, the signatories of Charter 77 constituted a citizens' initiative aimed at inducing the Czechoslovak Government to observe formal obligations to respect the human rights of its citizens.

On November 17,1989, the communist police violently broke up a peaceful pro–democracy demonstration, brutally beating many student participants. In the days which followed, Charter 77 and other groups united to become the Civic Forum, an umbrella group championing bureaucratic reform and civil liberties. Its leader was the dissident playwright Vaclav Havel. Intentionally eschewing the label "party," a word given a negative connotation during the previous regime, Civic Forum quickly gained the support of millions of

Czechs, as did its Slovak counterpart, Public Against Violence.

Faced with an overwhelming popular repudiation, the Communist Party all but collapsed. Its leaders, Husak and party chief Milos Jakes, resigned in December 1989, and Havel was elected President of Czechoslovakia on December 29. The astonishing quickness of these events was in part due to the unpopularity of the communist regime and changes in the policies of its Soviet guarantor as well as to the rapid, effective organization of these public initiatives into a viable opposition.

A coalition government, in which the Communist Party had a minority of ministerial positions, was formed in December 1989. The first free elections in Czechoslovakia since 1946 took place in June 1990 without incident and with more than 95% of the population voting. As anticipated, Civic Forum and Public Against Violence won landslide victories in their respective republics and gained a comfortable majority in the federal parliament. The parliament undertook substantial steps toward securing the democratic evolution of Czechoslovakia. It successfully moved toward fair local elections in November 1990, ensuring fundamental change at the county and town level.

Civic Forum found, however, that although it had successfully completed its primary objective—the overthrow of the communist regime—it was ineffectual as a governing party. The demise of Civic Forum was viewed by most as necessary and inevitable.

By the end of 1990, unofficial parliamentary "clubs" had evolved with distinct political agendas. Most influential was the Civic Democratic Party, headed by former Prime Minister Vaclav Klaus. Other notable parties that came into being after the split were the Czech Social Democratic Party, Civic Movement, and Civic Democratic Alliance.

By 1992, Slovak calls for greater autonomy effectively blocked the

daily functioning of the federal government. In the election of June 1992, Klaus's Civic Democratic Party won handily in the Czech lands on a platform of economic reform. Vladimir Meciar's Movement for a Democratic Slovakia emerged as the leading party in Slovakia, basing its appeal on fairness to Slovak demands for autonomy. Federalists, like Havel, were unable to contain the trend toward the split. In July 1992, President Havel resigned. In the latter half of 1992, Klaus and Meciar hammered out an agreement that the two republics would go their separate ways by the end of the year.

Members of the federal parliament, divided along national lines, barely cooperated enough to pass the law officially separating the two nations. The law was passed on December 27, 1992. On January 1, 1993, the Czech Republic and the Republic of Slovakia were simultaneously and peacefully founded.

Relationships between the two states, despite occasional disputes about the division of federal property and governing of the border have been peaceful, Both states attained immediate recognition from the U.S. and their European neighbors.

# GOVERNMENT AND POLITICAL CONDITIONS

The Czech political scene supports a broad spectrum of parties ranging from the semi–reformed Communist Party on the far left to the nationalistic Republican Party on the extreme right. Czech voters returned a split verdict in the June 1998 parliamentary elections, giving the left–of–center Social Democrats (CSSD) a plurality but the right–of–center parties a majority. The results produced a CSSD minority government tolerated by the largest right–of–center party in parliament, former Prime Minister Klaus' Civic Democrats (ODS). Prime Minister Milos Zeman is the head of government and wields considerable powers, including the right to set the agenda for most foreign and domestic policy, mobilize the parliamentary majority, and choose governmental ministers.

Vaclav Havel, now President of the Czech Republic, is not affiliated with any party but remains one of the country's most popular politicians. As formal head of state, he is granted specific powers such as the right to nominate Constitutional Court judges, dissolve parliament under certain conditions, and enact a veto on legislation.

The legislature is bicameral, with a Chamber of Deputies and a Senate. With the split of the former Czechoslovakia, the powers and responsibilities of the now defunct federal parliament were transferred to the Czech National Council, which renamed itself the Chamber of Deputies. Chamber delegates are elected from seven districts and the capital, Prague, for 4–year terms, on the basis of proportional representation. The Czech Senate is patterned after the U.S. Senate and was first elected in 1996; its members serve for 6–year terms with one–third being elected every 2 years.

The country's highest court of appeals is the Supreme Court. The Constitutional Court, which rules on constitutional issues, is appointed by the president, and its members serve 10–year terms.

# NATIONAL SECURITY ISSUES

The Czech Republic became a member of NATO on March 12, 1999. A major overhaul of the Czechoslovak defense forces began in 1990 and continues in the Czech Republic. Czech forces are being downsized from 200,000 to 55,000 and at the same time reoriented toward a more defensive posture. The Czechs have made good progress in reforming the military personnel structure, and a strong commitment to English lan-

guage training is paying off. Public support for NATO membership remains around 50%–60%. The Czech Government committed itself in 1996 to increase defense spending by 0.1% of GDP annually until the year 2000, when military spending will reach or exceed 2% of GDP. This will put Czech defense spending on a level proportionately comparable with other NATO allies.

The Czech Republic has friendly relations with all of its neighbors, and none of its borders are in question. The Czech Republic is a member of the UN and OSCE and has contributed to numerous peacekeeping operations, including IFOR/SFOR in Bosnia as well as Desert Shield/Desert Storm.

## Principal Government Officials

For up-to-date information on Principal Government Officials, see the Chiefs of State and Cabinet Members of Foreign Governments section starting on page 1.

The Czech Republic maintains an embassy at 3900 Spring of Freedom Street, NW, Washington, DC 20008, (tel. 202–274–9101).

# ECONOMY

Of the emerging democracies in central and eastern Europe, the Czech Republic has one of the most developed industrialized economies. Its strong industrial tradition dates to the 19th century, when Bohemia and Moravia were the economic heartland of the Austro–Hungarian Empire. Today, this heritage is both an asset and a liability. The Czech Republic has a well–educated population and a well– developed infrastructure, but its industrial plants and much of its industrial equipment are obsolete.

According to the Stalinist development policy of planned interdepen-

dence, all the economies of the socialist countries were linked tightly with that of the Soviet Union. With the disintegration of the communist economic alliance in 1991, Czech manufacturers lost their traditional markets among former communist countries to the east, some of which still owe the former Czechoslovakia sizable debts.

The Czech Republic is reducing its dependence on highly polluting low–grade brown coal as a source of energy. Nuclear energy presently provides about 25% of total power needs, and its share is projected to increase to 40%. Norway (via pipelines through Germany) and Russia also supply the Czech Republic with liquid and natural gas.

The principal industries are heavy and general machine–building, iron and steel production, metalworking, chemicals, electronics, transportation equipment, textiles, glass, brewing, china, ceramics, and pharmaceuticals. Its main agricultural products are sugarbeets, fodder roots, potatoes, wheat, and hops.

The "Velvet Revolution" in 1989 offered a chance for profound and sustained economic reform. Signs of economic resurgence began to appear in the wake of the shock therapy that the International Monetary Fund (IMF) labeled the "big bang" of January 1991. Since then, astute economic management has led to the liberalization of 95% of all price controls, annual inflation in the 10% range, modest budgetary deficits, low unemployment, a positive balance–of–payments position, a stable exchange rate, a shift of exports from former communist economic bloc markets to Western Europe, and relatively low foreign debt.

Particularly impressive have been the Republic's strict fiscal policies. Following a series of currency devaluations, the crown has remained stable in relation to the U.S. dollar. The Czech crown became fully convertible for most business purposes in late 1995.

In addition, the government has revamped the legal and administrative structure governing investment in order to stimulate the economy and attract foreign partners. Shifting emphasis from the East to the West has necessitated restructuring existing facilities in banking and telecommunications as well as adjusting commercial laws and practices to fit Western standards. The republic has made progress toward creating a stable investment climate.

This success has enabled the Czech Republic to become the first post–communist country to receive an investment–grade credit rating by international credit institutions. Successive Czech governments have welcomed U.S. investment, in particular, as a counter–balance to the strong economic influence of Western Europe, especially of their powerful neighbor, Germany. Although foreign direct investment (FDI) runs in uneven cycles, with a 12.9% share of total FDI between 1990 and March 1998, the U.S. was the third–largest foreign investor in the Czech economy, behind Germany and the Netherlands.

The republic boasts a flourishing consumer production sector and has privatized most state–owned heavy industries through the voucher privatization system. Under the system, every citizen was given the opportunity to buy, for a moderate price, a book of vouchers that represents potential shares in any state–owned company. The voucher holders could then invest their vouchers, infusing the chosen company with valuable capital. State ownership of businesses was estimated to be about 97% under communism. In 1998, more than 80% of enterprises are in private hands. When the voucher privatization process is complete, Czechs will own shares of each of the Czech companies, making them one of the highest per capita share owners in the world. Privatization through restitution of real estate to the former owners was largely completed in 1992.

The republic's economic transformation is far from complete. A recession in 1998 revealed that the government

## Travel Notes

**Travel Advice:** For up-to-date information from the U.S. State Department on possible inconvenient or hazardous situations, see the **Travel Warnings and Consular Information Sheets from the U.S. Government** section starting on page 1723. For the latest information on health requirements and conditions, see the **International Travelers' Health Information** section starting on page 1385. For further information dealing with non-urgent matter, see the **Tips for Travelers to...** section starting on page 1588.

still faces serious challenges in completing industrial restructuring, increasing transparency in capital market transactions, fully privatizing the banking sector, transforming the housing sector, privatizing the health care system, and solving serious environmental problems.

# FOREIGN RELATIONS

Until 1989, the foreign policy of Czechoslovakia had followed that of the Soviet Union. Since independence, the Czechs have made integration into Western institutions their chief foreign policy objective.

Fundamental to this objective is Czech membership in the European Union. The government hopes to achieve full membership in the EU by 2003. Relations are currently governed under an association agreement which came into force in 1993. Although there have been disagreements over some economic issues, such as agricultural quotas and a recent amendment to the gaming law, relations are good, and negotiations toward full membership are proceeding smoothly.

The Czech Republic is a member of the United Nations and participates in its specialized agencies. It is a member of the General Agreement on Trade and Tariffs. It maintains diplomatic relations with more than 85 countries, of which 63 have permanent representation in Prague.

The Czech Republic became a member of the North Atlantic Treaty Organization, along with Poland and Hungary on March 12, 1999. This membership represents a milestone in the country's foreign policy and security orientation.

# U.S.-CZECH RELATIONS

Millions of Americans have their roots in Bohemia and Moravia, and a large community in the United States has strong cultural and familial ties with the Czech Republic. President Woodrow Wilson and the United States played a major role in the establishment of the original Czechoslovak state on October 28, 1918. President Wilson's 14 Points, including the right of ethnic groups to form their own states, were the basis for the union of the Czechs and Slovaks. Tomas Masaryk, the father of the state and its first President, visited the United States during World War I and worked with U.S. officials in developing the basis of the new country. Masaryk used the U.S. Constitution as a model for the first Czechoslovak constitution.

After World War II, and the return of the Czechoslovak Government in exile, normal relations continued until 1948, when the communists seized power. Relations cooled rapidly. The Soviet invasion of Czechoslovakia in August 1968 further complicated U.S.–Czechoslovak relations. The United States referred the matter to the UN Security Council as a violation of the UN Charter, but no action was taken against the Soviets.

Since the "Velvet Revolution" of 1989, bilateral relations have improved immensely. Dissidents once sustained by U.S. encouragement and human rights policies reached high levels in the government. President Havel, in his first official visit as head of Czechoslovakia, addressed the U.S. Congress and was interrupted 21 times by standing ovations. In 1990, on the first anniversary of the revolution, President Bush, in front of an enthusiastic crowd on Prague's Wenceslas Square, pledged U.S. support in building a democratic Czechoslovakia. Toward this end, the U.S. Government has actively encouraged political and economic transformation.

The U.S. Government was originally opposed to the idea of Czechoslovakia forming two separate states, because of concerns that a split might aggravate existing regional political tensions. However, the U.S. recognized both the Czech Republic and Slovakia on January 1, 1993. Since then, U.S.–Czech relations have remained strong economically, politically, and culturally.

Relations between the U.S. and the Czech Republic are excellent and reflect the common approach both have to the many challenges facing the world at present. The U.S. looks to the Czech Republic as a partner in issues ranging from the Middle East to the Balkans, and seeks opportunities to continue to deepen this relationship.

## Principal U.S. Officials

**For up-to-date information on Principal U.S. Officials, see the U.S. Embassies, Consulates, and Foreign Service section starting on page 139.**

# DENMARK

March 1997

Official Name:
**Kingdom of Denmark**

# PROFILE

## Geography*

**Area:** 43,094 sq. km. (16,640 sq. mi.); slightly smaller than Vermont and New Hampshire combined.
**Cities:** Capital—Copenhagen (pop. 1.4 million in Greater Copenhagen). Other cities—Aarhus (281,000), Odense (184,000), Aalborg (160,000).
**Terrain:** Low and flat or slightly rolling; highest elevation is 173 m. (568 ft.).
**Climate:** Temperate. The terrain, location, and prevailing westerly winds make the weather changeable.

## People

**Nationality:** Noun—Dane(s). Adjective—Danish.
**Population (1996):** 5.3 million.*
**Annual growth rate:** 0.6%.
**Ethnic groups:** Scandinavian, Inuit, Faroese, German.
**Religion:** Evangelical Lutheran (about 97%).
**Languages:** Danish, Faroese, Greenlandic (an Inuit dialect), some German. English is the predominant second language.
**Education:** Years compulsory—9. Attendance—100%. Literacy—100%.

*Excluding Greenland and the Faroe Islands.

**Health:** Infant mortality rate (1996, est.)—5.5/1,000. Life expectancy—men 72 yrs., women 78 yrs.
**Work force (1996):** 2.8 million. Industry and construction—25%. Government—31%. Services—38%. Agriculture and fisheries—5%. Other—1%.

## Government

**Type:** Constitutional monarchy.
**Constitution:** June 5, 1953.
**Branches:** Executive—queen (chief of state), prime minister (head of government), cabinet. Legislative—unicameral parliament (Folketing). Judicial—appointed Supreme Court.
**Political parties:** Social Democratic, Venstre (Liberal), Konservative, Socialist People's, Progress, Radikale, Unity List, Center Democratic, Danish People's.
**Suffrage:** Universal adult.
**Administrative subdivisions:** 14 counties and 275 municipalities.

## Economy

**GDP (1996):** $174 billion.
**Annual growth rate:** 2.2%.
**Per capita income:** $33,000.
**Agriculture (and related production, 4% of GDP):** Products—meat, dairy products, fish.
**Industry (20% of GDP):** Types—industrial and construction equipment, electronics, chemicals, pharmaceuticals, furniture, textiles, ships.

**Natural resources:** North Sea—oil and gas, fish. Greenland—fish, zinc, lead, molybdenum, uranium, gold, platinum. The Faroe Islands—fish.
**Trade (1996):** Exports—$49 billion: machinery and instruments 25%; meat and meat products 9%; chemical, medical, and pharmaceutical products 11%; fish and fish products 4%; transport equipment 4%; textiles and apparel 5%; furniture 4%. Imports—$43 billion: machinery and computers 24%; iron, steel, and metals 8%; transport equipment (excluding ships) 8%; paper and paperboard 4%; fish and fish products 3%. Partners—Germany 22%, Sweden 11%, U.K. 8%, U.S. 5%, Eastern European countries 5%.

**Official exchange rate (1996 avg.):** 5.79 kroner=U.S. $1.

# PEOPLE AND HISTORY

The Danes, a homogenous Gothic-Germanic people, have inhabited Denmark since prehistoric times. Danish is the principal language. A small German-speaking minority lives in southern Jutland; a mostly Inuit population inhabits Greenland; and the Faroe Islands have a Nordic population with its own language. Education is compulsory from ages seven to 16 and is free through the university level.

The Evangelical Lutheran Church is state supported and accounts for about 97% of Denmark's religious affiliation. Denmark has religious freedom, however, and several other Protestant denominations and other religions exist.

During the Viking period (9th-11th centuries), Denmark was a great power based on the Jutland Peninsula, the Island of Zealand, and the southern part of what is now Sweden. In the early 11th century, King Canute united Denmark and England for almost 30 years.

Viking raids brought Denmark into contact with Christianity, and in the 12th century, crown and church influence increased. By the late 13th century, royal power had waned, and the nobility forced the king to grant a charter, considered Denmark's first constitution. Although the struggle between crown and nobility continued into the 14th century, Queen Margrethe I succeeded in uniting Denmark, Norway, Sweden, Finland, the Faroe Islands, Iceland, and Greenland under the Danish crown. Sweden and Finland left the union in 1520; however, Norway remained until 1814. Iceland, in a "personal union" under the king of Denmark after 1918, became independent in 1944.

The Reformation was introduced in Denmark in 1536. Denmark's provinces in today's southwestern Sweden were lost in 1658, and Norway was transferred from the Danish to the Swedish crown in 1814, following the defeat of Napoleon, with whom Denmark was allied.

The Danish liberal movement gained momentum in the 1830s, and in 1849 Denmark became a constitutional monarchy. After the war with Prussia and Austria in 1864, Denmark was forced to cede Schleswig-Holstein to Prussia and adopt a policy of neutrality. Toward the end of the 19th century, Denmark inaugurated important social and labor market

## Travel Notes

**Travel Advice:** For up-to-date information from the U.S. State Department on possible inconvenient or hazardous situations, see the **Travel Warnings and Consular Information Sheets from the U.S. Government** section starting on page 1723. For the latest information on health requirements and conditions, see the **International Travelers' Health Information** section starting on page 1385. For further information dealing with non-urgent matter, see the **Tips for Travelers to...** section starting on page 1588.

reforms, laying the basis for the present welfare state.

Denmark remained neutral during World War I. Despite its declaration of neutrality at the beginning of World War II, it was invaded by the Germans in 1940 and occupied until it was liberated by the Allied forces in May 1945. Denmark became a charter member of the United Nations and was one of the original signers of the North Atlantic Treaty.

## Cultural Achievements

Denmark's rich intellectual heritage contributes to the cultural achievements of the modern world. The astronomical discoveries of Tycho Brahe (1546-1601) and the brilliant contributions to atomic physics of Niels Bohr (1885-1962) indicate the range of Danish scientific achievement. The fairy tales of Hans Christian Andersen (1805-75), the philosophical essays of Soren Kierkegaard (1813-55), and the short stories of Karen Blixen (penname Isak Dinesen, 1885-1962) have earned international recognition, as have the symphonies of Carl Nielsen (1865-1931). Danish applied art and industrial design have won awards for excellence. The name of Georg Jensen (1866-1935) is known worldwide for outstanding modern design in silver, and "Royal Copenhagen" is among the finest porcelains.

Visitors to Denmark will discover a wealth of cultural activity. The Royal Danish Ballet, an exceptional company, specializes in the work of the great Danish choreographer August Bournonville (1805-79). Danes have distinguished themselves as jazz musicians, and the Copenhagen Jazz Festival has acquired an international reputation. International collections of modern art enjoy unusually attractive settings at the Louisiana Museum north of Copenhagen and at the North Jutland Art Museum in Aalborg. The State Museum of Art and the Glyptotek, both in Copenhagen, contain treasures of Danish and international art. The Museum of Applied Art and Industrial Design in Copenhagen exhibits the best in Danish design. The Royal Danish Porcelain Factory and Bing & Grondahl, renowned for the quality of their porcelain and ceramics, export their products worldwide. Ceramic designs by Bjorn Wiinblad also are well known and popular.

Among today's Danish writers, probably the most well-known to American readers is Peter Hoeg (*Smilla's Sense of Snow; Borderliners*), and the most prolific is Klaus Rifbjerg—poet, novelist, playwright, and screenwriter. Benny Andersen writes poems, short stories, and music. Poems by both writers have been translated into English by the Curbstone Press. Kirsten Thorup's *Baby*, winner of the 1980 Pegasus Prize, is printed in English by the University of Louisiana Press. The psychological thrillers of Anders Bodelsen also appear in English. Suzanne Brogger and Vita Andersen focus largely on the changing roles of women in society. In music, Hans Abrahamsen and Per Norgaard are the two most famous living composers. Hans Abrahamsen's works have been performed by the National Symphony Orchestra in Washington, DC.

## Cultural Policy

The Ministry of Cultural Affairs was created in 1961. Cultural life and meaningful leisure time were then and remain subjects of debate by politicians and parliament as well as the general public. The democratization of cultural life promoted by the government's 1960s cultural policy

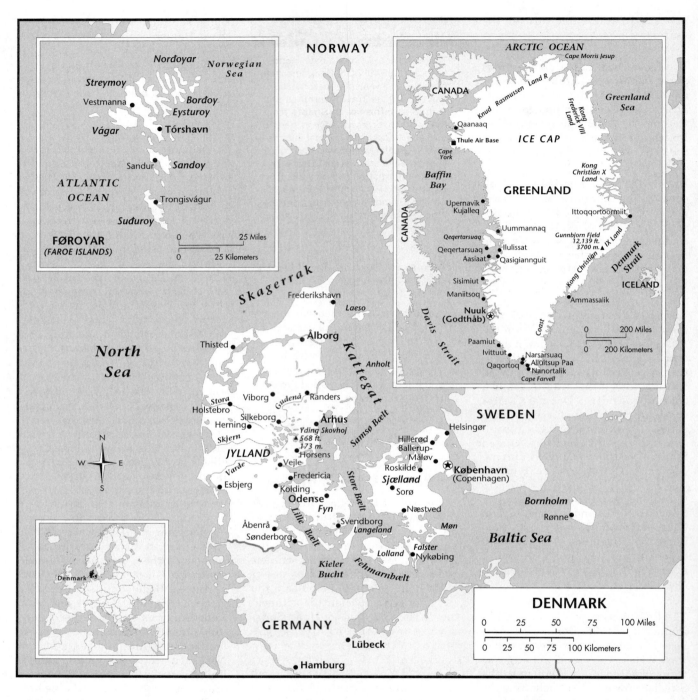

recently has come to terms with the older "genteel culture;" broader concepts of culture now generally accepted include amateur and professional cultural, media, sports, and leisure-time activities.

Denmark's cultural policy is characterized by decentralized funding, program responsibility, and institutions. Danish cultural direction differs from other countries with a Ministry of Culture and a stated policy in that special laws govern each cultural field—e.g., the New Theater Act of 1990 and the Music Law of 1976.

The Ministry of Cultural Affairs includes among its responsibilities international cultural relations; training of librarians and architects; copyright legislation; and subsidies to archives, libraries, museums, literature, music, arts and crafts, theater, and film production. During 1970-82, the Ministry also recognized protest movements and street manifestations as cultural events, because social change was viewed as an important goal of Danish cultural policy. The current government exercises caution in moderating this policy and practice. Radio and broadcasting also fall under the Ministry of Culture.

Government contributions to culture have increased steadily in recent years, but viewed against the present government's firm objective to limit public expenditures, contributions will stabilize in the future. Municipal and county governments assume a relatively large share of the costs for cultural activities in their respective districts. In 1996, government expenditures for culture totaled about 1.0% of the budget. Most support went to libraries and archives, theater, museums, arts and crafts training, and films.

# GOVERNMENT

Denmark is a constitutional monarchy. Queen Margrethe II has largely ceremonial functions; probably her most significant formal power lies in her right to appoint the prime minister and cabinet ministers, who are responsible for administration of the government. However, she must consult with parliamentary leaders to determine the public's will, since the cabinet may be dismissed by a vote of no confidence in the Folketing (parliament). Cabinet members are occasionally recruited from outside the Folketing.

## Principal Government Officials

**For up-to-date information on Principal Government Officials, see the Chiefs of State and Cabinet Members of Foreign Governments section starting on page 1.**

The 1953 constitution established a unicameral Folketing of not more than 179 members, of whom two are elected from the Faroe Islands and two from Greenland. Elections are held at least every four years, but the prime minister can dissolve the Folketing at any time and call for new elections. Folketing members are elected by a complicated system of proportional representation; any party receiving at least 2% of the total national vote receives represen-

tation. The result is a multiplicity of parties (nine currently in parliament), none of which holds a majority. Electorate participation normally is more than 85%.

The judicial branch consists of about 100 local courts, two high courts, several special courts (e.g., arbitration and maritime), and a supreme court of 15 judges appointed by the crown on the government's recommendation.

Denmark is divided into 14 counties (Amter) and 275 municipalities (Kommuner). The chief official of the Amt, the county mayor (Amtsborgmester), is elected by the county council from among its members, according to the municipal reform of 1970. The cities of Copenhagen and Frederiksborg function as both counties and municipalities.

The Faroe Islands and Greenland enjoy home rule, with the Danish Government represented locally by high commissioners. These home-rule governments are responsible for most domestic affairs, with foreign relations, monetary affairs, and defense falling to the Danish Government.

## National Security

Although Denmark remained neutral during the First World War, its rapid occupation by Nazi Germany in 1940 persuaded most Danes that neutrality was no longer a reliable guarantee of Danish security. Danish security policy is founded on its membership in NATO. Since 1988, Danish defense budgets and security policy have been set by multi-year agreements supported by a wide parliamentary majority including government and opposition parties. However, public opposition to increases in defense spending—during a period when economic constraints require reduced spending for social welfare—has created differences among the political parties regarding a broadly acceptable level of new defense expenditure. Current resource plans are based on the 1995 defense agreement covering the period 1995-1999. The average percentage of Danish GDP absorbed by defense in 1996 was about 1.5%.

Denmark maintains an embassy at 3200 Whitehaven Street NW, Washington, DC 20008 (tel. 202-234-4300). Consulates general are in Chicago, Los Angeles, and New York.

# POLITICAL CONDITIONS

Political life in Denmark is orderly and democratic. Political changes occur gradually through a process of consensus, and political methods and attitudes are generally moderate.

The Social Democratic Party, Denmark's largest and closely identified with a large, well-organized labor movement, has held power either alone or in coalition for most of the postwar period except from 1982 to 1993. Since the parliamentary elections in September 1994, Prime Minister Poul Nyrup Rasmussen and his Social Democratic Party have led a minority coalition government, which at first included the centrist Radikales and the Center Democrats. The Center Democrats left the government in December 1996; the present SDP-Radikales coalition controls 71 of 179 seats in the Folketing.

The vulnerability implicit in a minority coalition has been evidenced in recent coalition failure to achieve consensus on issues such as extensive labor, tax, and welfare reforms. Consensus decision-making is the most prominent feature of Danish politics. It often allows the small centrist parties to play a larger role than their size suggests. Although the centrist Radikale party sometimes shows traces of its pacifist past, particularly on defense spending, most major legislation is passed by sizeable majorities.

Since the 1988 elections, which led to a domestic truce on North Atlantic Treaty Organization (NATO) and security questions, Denmark's role in the European Union (EU) has come to be a key political issue. Denmark emerged from two referendums (June 2, 1992, and May 18, 1993) with four important exemptions (or "opt-outs") to the Maastricht Treaty on the European Union: common defense, common currency, EU citizenship, and certain aspects of legal cooperation, including law enforcement. Fear of losing Denmark's identity in an integrating Europe runs deep in the public, especially among key Social Democratic voters. (Denmark's electorate voted to join the EEC in 1973 for economic reasons.) Any government push to remove some or all of the Danish exemptions would require at least one other referendum to be held sometime after the EU's Intergovernmental Conference to review the Maastricht Treaty.

# ECONOMY

Denmark's industrialized market economy depends on imported raw materials and foreign trade. Within the European Union, Denmark advocates a liberal trade policy. Its standard of living is among the highest in the world, and the Danes devote 1% of GDP to foreign aid.

Denmark is almost self-sufficient in energy. Its principal exports are machinery, instruments, and food products. The U.S. is Denmark's largest non-European trading partner, accounting for about 5% of total Danish merchandise trade. Aircraft, computers, machinery, and instruments are among the major U.S. exports to Denmark. There are some 250 U.S.-owned companies in Denmark. Among major Danish exports to the U.S. are industrial machinery, chemical products, furniture, pharmaceuticals, and canned ham and pork.

From 1982, a center-right government corrected accumulated economic pressures, mainly inflation and balance-of-payments deficits, but lost power in 1993 to a Social Democratic coalition government led by Poul Nyrup Rasmussen. The current government has had success in cutting official unemployment, which peaked at 12.5% and is now 8%. Average annual growth rates are now 2-3%.

Danes are proud of their highly developed welfare safety net, which ensures that all Danes receive basic health care and need not fear real poverty. Over the last 20 years, however, the number of Danes living on transfer payments has grown to about 1 million working-age persons (roughly 20% of the population), and the system is beginning to show strains. Health care and care for the elderly particularly have suffered, and the need for welfare reform is increasingly discussed. More than one-quarter of the labor force is employed in the public sector.

## Greenland and the Faroe Islands

Greenland suffered negative economic growth in the early 1990s, but since 1993 the economy has improved. A tight fiscal policy by the Greenland Home Rule Government since the late 1980s helped create surpluses in the public budget and a low inflation rate. Since 1990, Greenland has registered a foreign trade deficit.

Following the closure of Greenland's last lead and zinc mine in 1989, Greenland's economy is solely dependent on the fishing industry and Danish grants. Despite resumption of several interesting hydrocarbon and mineral exploration activities, it will take several years before production may materialize. Greenland's shrimp fishery is by far the largest income earner, since cod catches have dropped to historically low levels. Tourism is the only sector offering any near-term potential, and even this is limited due to the short season and high costs. The public sector plays a dominant role in Greenland's economy. Grants from mainland Denmark and EU fisheries payments make up about one-half of the home-rule government's revenues.

The Faroe Islands also depend almost entirely on fisheries and related exports. Without Danish Government bailouts in 1992 and 1993, the Faroese economy would have gone bankrupt. The Faroese economy in 1995 and 1996 saw a noticeable upturn again, but remains extremely vulnerable. Recent off-shore oil finds close to the Faroese area give hope for Faroese deposits, too, which may lay the basis for an economic rebound over the longer term.

# FOREIGN RELATIONS

Danish foreign policy is founded upon four cornerstones: the United Nations, NATO, the EU, and Nordic cooperation. Denmark also is a member of the World Bank and the International Monetary Fund; the World Trade Organization (WTO); the Organization for Security and Cooperation in Europe (OSCE); the Organization for Economic Cooperation and Development (OECD); the Council of Europe; the Nordic Council; the Baltic Council; and the Barents Council. Denmark emphasizes its relations with developing nations and is one of the few countries to exceed the UN goal of contributing 1% of GNP to development assistance.

In the wake of the Cold War, Denmark has been active in international efforts to integrate the countries of Central and Eastern Europe into the West. It has played a leadership role in coordinating Western assistance to the Baltic states (Estonia, Latvia, and Lithuania). The country is a strong supporter of international peacekeeping. Danish forces were heavily engaged in the former Yugoslavia in the UN Protection Force (UNPROFOR), with 900 in IFOR in 1996.

Denmark has been a member of NATO since its founding in 1949, and membership in NATO remains highly popular. There were several serious confrontations between the U.S. and Denmark on security policy in the so-called "footnote era" (1982-88), when a hostile parliamentary majority forced the government to adopt specific national positions on nuclear and arms control issues. With the end of the Cold War, however, Denmark has been supportive of U.S. policy objectives in the Alliance. Denmark is not a member of the Western European Union but does hold observer status.

Danes always have enjoyed a reputation as "reluctant" Europeans. When they rejected ratification of the Maastricht Treaty on June 2, 1992, they put the EC's plans for the European Union on hold. In December 1992, the rest of the EC agreed to exempt Denmark from certain aspects of the European Union, including a common defense, a common currency, EU citizenship, and certain aspects of legal cooperation. On this revised basis, a clear majority of Danes approved continued participation in the EU in a second referendum on May 18, 1993. Denmark will have to review its exemptions as the EU's Intergovernmental Conference proposes changes in the Maastricht Treaty.

# U.S.-DANISH RELATIONS

Denmark is a close NATO ally, and overall U.S.-Danish relations are excellent. Active in Bosnia, OSCE Chairman-in-Office for 1997, and a leader in the Baltic region, Denmark and the U.S. consult closely on European political and security matters. Denmark shares U.S. views on the positive ramifications of NATO enlargement. Danish and U.S. troops serve side by side in Bosnia in an effort to bring peace to the region.

Denmark's active liberal trade policy in the EU, OECD, and WTO largely coincides with U.S. interests; the U.S. is Denmark's largest non-European trade partner with about 5% of Danish merchandise trade. Denmark's role in European environmental and agricultural issues and its strategic location at the entrance to the Baltic Sea have made Copenhagen a center for U.S. agencies and the private sector dealing with the Nordic/Baltic region.

American culture—and particularly popular culture, from jazz, rock, and rap to television shows and literature—is very popular in Denmark. Some 350,000 U.S. tourists visit the country annually.

The U.S. Air Force (USAF) base and early warning radar at Thule, Greenland—a Danish self-governing territory—serve as a vital link in Western defenses. The role of the USAF base in Greenland has sparked a degree of domestic controversy vis-a-vis U.S.-Danish cooperation at Thule. The U.S. and Denmark in 1994 agreed to allow use of the Thule Air Base for limited tourist transit, to assist Greenland's economic development. The U.S. and Denmark continue to cooperate closely on matters related to the air base.

## Principal U.S. Officials

**For up-to-date information on Principal U.S. Officials, see the U.S. Embassies, Consulates, and Foreign Service section starting on page 139.**

The U.S. embassy is located at Dag Hammarskjolds Alle 24, 2100 Copenhagen O, Denmark (tel. 31/42-31-44).

# DJIBOUTI

March 1996

Official Name:
**Republic of Djibouti**

---

# PROFILE

## Geography

**Area:** 23,200 sq. km. (9,000 sq. mi.); about the size of New Hampshire.

**Cities:** Capital—Djibouti. Other cities—Dikhil, Ali-Sabieh, Obock, Tadjoura.

**Terrain:** Coastal desert.

**Climate:** Torrid and dry.

## People

**Nationality:** Noun and adjective—Djiboutian(s).

**Population (est.):** 560,000.

**Annual growth rate:** 4.5%.

**Ethnic groups:** Somalis (Issaks, Issas, and Gadaboursis), Ethiopian (Issas and Afars), Arab, French, and Italian.

**Religions:** Muslim 94%, Christian 6%.

**Languages:** French and Arabic (official); Somali and Afar widely used.

**Education:** Literacy—42%.

**Health:** Infant mortality rate—114/1,000. Life expectancy—50 yrs.

**Work force:** Small number of semi-skilled laborers at port, 3,000 railway workers organized. The majority of the population is not formally employed.

## Government

**Type:** Republic.

**Constitution:** Ratified September 1992 by referendum.

**Independence:** June 27, 1977.

**Branches:** Executive—president. Legislative—65-member parliament, cabinet, prime minister. Judicial—based on French civil law system, traditional practices, and Islamic law.

**Administrative subdivisions:** 5 cercles (districts)—Ali-Sabieh, Dikhil, Djibouti, Obock, and Tadjoura.

**Political parties:** People's Rally for Progress (RPP) established in 1981; New Democratic Party (PRD) and the National Democratic Party (PND) were both established in 1992; and the Front For The Restoration of Unity and Democracy (FRUD) established in 1996.

**Suffrage:** Universal at 18.

**National holiday:** June 27.

**Flag:** A white triangle, with a five-pointed red star within, extending on the staff side. The remaining area has a light blue zone above a light green zone.

## Economy

**GNP (1994 est.):** $450 million.

**Adjusted per capita income:** $10,000 per capita for expatriates, $700 for Djiboutians.

**Natural resources:** Minerals (salt, perlite, gypsum, limestone) and energy resources (geothermal and solar).

**Agriculture (less than 3% of GDP):** Products—livestock, fishing, and limited commercial crops, including fruits and vegetables.

**Industry:** Types—banking and insurance (40% of GDP), public administration (34% of GDP), construction and public works, manufacturing, commerce, and agriculture.

**Trade (1994 est.):** Imports $240.9 million, consists of basic commodities, pharmaceutical drugs, durable and non-durable goods; exports, $19.3 million, consists of everyday personal effects, household effects, hides and skins, and coffee. Major markets—France, Ethiopia, Somalia and Arabian peninsula countries.

**Official exchange rate:** Pegged at 177.721 Djibouti francs = U.S.$1 since 1973.

**Able-bodied unemployed population:** 50%.

# PEOPLE

More than half of the Republic of Djibouti's 560,000 inhabitants live in the capital city. The indigenous population is divided between the majority Somalis (predominantly of the Issa tribe, with minority Issak and Gadaboursi representation) and the Afars (Danakils). All are Cushitic-speaking peoples, and nearly all are Muslim. Among the 15,000 foreigners residing in Djibouti, the French are the most numerous. Among the French are 3,400 troops.

# HISTORY

The Republic of Djibouti gained its independence on June 27, 1977. It is the successor to the French Territory of the Afars and Issas, which was created in the first half of the 19th century as a result of French interest in the Horn of Africa.

However, the history of Djibouti, recorded in poetry and songs of its nomadic peoples, goes back thousands of years to a time when Djiboutians traded hides and skins for the perfumes and spices of ancient Egypt, India, and China. Through close contacts with the Arabian peninsula for more than 1,000 years, the Somali and Afar tribes in this region became the first on the African continent to adopt Islam.

It was Rochet d'Hericourt's exploration into Shoa (1839-42) that marked the beginning of French interest in the African shores of the Red Sea. Further exploration by Henri Lambert, French Consular Agent at Aden, and Captain Fleuriot de Langle led to a treaty of friendship and assistance between France and the sultans of Raheita, Tadjoura, and Gobaad, from whom the French purchased the anchorage of Obock (1862).

Growing French interest in the area took place against a backdrop of British activity in Egypt and the opening of the Suez Canal in 1869. In 1884-85, France expanded its protectorate to include the shores of the Gulf of Tadjoura and the Somaliland. Boundaries of the protectorate, marked out in 1897 by France and Emperor Menelik II of Ethiopia, were affirmed further by agreements with Ethiopian Emperor Haile Selassie I in 1945 and 1954.

The administrative capital was moved from Obock to Djibouti in 1896. Djibouti, which has a good natural harbor and ready access to the Ethiopian highlands, attracted trade

caravans crossing East Africa as well as Somali settlers from the south. The Franco-Ethiopian railway, linking Djibouti to the heart of Ethiopia, was begun in 1897 and reached Addis Ababa in June 1917, further facilitating the increase of trade.

During the Italian invasion and occupation of Ethiopia in the 1930s and during World War II, constant border skirmishes occurred between French and Italian forces. The area was ruled by the Vichy (French) government from the fall of France until December 1942, when French Somaliland forces broke a Vichy blockade to join the Free French and the Allied forces. A local battalion from Djibouti participated in the liberation of France in 1944.

On July 22, 1957, the colony was reorganized to give the people considerable self-government. On the same day, a decree applying the Overseas Reform Act (Loi Cadre) of June 23, 1956, established a territorial assembly that elected eight of its members to an executive council. Members of the executive council were responsible for one or more of the territorial services and carried the title of minister. The council advised the French-appointed governor general.

In a September 1958 constitutional referendum, French Somaliland opted to join the French community as an overseas territory. This act entitled the region to representation by one deputy and one senator in the French Parliament, and one counselor in the French Union Assembly.

The first elections to the territorial assembly were held on November 23, 1958, under a system of proportional representation. In the next assembly elections (1963), a new electoral law was enacted. Representation was abolished in exchange for a system of straight plurality vote based on lists submitted by political parties in seven designated districts. Ali Aref Bourhan, allegedly of Turkish origin, was selected to be the president of the executive council.

French President Charles de Gaulle's August 1966 visit to Djibouti was

marked by 2 days of public demonstrations by Somalis demanding independence. On September 21, 1966, Louis Saget, appointed governor general of the territory after the demonstrations, announced the French Government's decision to hold a referendum to determine whether the people would remain within the French Republic or become independent. In March 1967, 60% chose to continue the territory's association with France.

In July of that year, a directive from Paris formally changed the name of the region to the French Territory of Afars and Issas. The directive also reorganized the governmental structure of the territory, making the senior French representative, formerly the governor general, a high commissioner. In addition, the executive council was redesignated as the council of government, with nine members.

In 1975, the French Government began to accommodate increasingly insistent demands for independence. In June 1976, the territory's citizenship law, which favored the Afar minority, was revised to reflect more closely the weight of the Issa Somali. The electorate voted for independence in a May 1977 referendum, and the Republic of Djibouti was established on June 27, 1977.

# GOVERNMENT

In 1981, Hassen Gouled Aptidon was elected as President of Djibouti. He was re-elected, unopposed, to a second 6-year term in April 1987 and to a third 6-year term in May 1993 multiparty elections. The electorate approved the current constitution in September 1992. Many laws and decrees from before independence remain in effect.

In early 1992, the government decided to permit multiple party politics and agreed to the registration of four political parties. By the time of the national assembly elections in December 1992, only three had qualified. They are the Rassemblement

Populaire Pour le Progres (People's Rally for Progress) (RPP) which was the only legal party from 1981 until 1992, the Parti du Renouveau Democratique (The Party for Democratic Renewal) (PRD), and the Parti National Democratique (National Democratic Party) (PND). Only the RPP and the PRD contested the national assembly elections, and the PND withdrew, claiming that there were too many unanswered questions on the conduct of the elections and too many opportunities for government fraud. The RPP won all 65 seats in the national assembly, with a turnout of less than 50% of the electorate on a winner-take-all basis.

Currently, political power is shared by a Somali president and an Afar prime minister, with cabinet posts roughly divided. However, it is the Issas who presently dominate the government, civil service, and the ruling party, a situation that has bred resentment and political competition between the Somali Issas and the Afars.

In early November 1991, civil war erupted in Djibouti between the government and a predominantly Afar rebel group (Front for the Restoration of Unity and Democracy). The conflict concluded with a peace accord in December 1994. The Afars won few concessions, the most noteworthy of which was the appointment of two additional Afars to cabinet posts.

Djibouti has its own armed forces, including a small army, which has grown significantly since the start of the civil war. The country's security also is assured by the continued presence of some 3,400 French troops, which includes a unit of the French Foreign Legion of about 800 men.

The right to own property is respected in Djibouti, as are freedom of religion and organized labor.

Although women in Djibouti enjoy a higher public status than in many other Islamic countries, women's rights and family planning are not high priorities. Few women hold senior positions. However, a women's

organization (Union Nationale Aicha Bogoreh) is active.

## Principal Government Officials

**For up-to-date information on Principal Government Officials, see the Chiefs of State and Cabinet Members of Foreign Governments section starting on page 1.**

Djibouti's mission to the UN is located at 866 UN Plaza, Suite 4011, New York, NY 10017 (tel. 212-753-3163). Djibouti's embassy in Washington is located at Suite 515, 1156 15th Street, NW, Washington, DC 20005 (tel. 202-331-0270) (fax 202-331-0302).

# ECONOMY

Djibouti's fledgling economy depends on a large foreign expatriate community, the maritime and commercial activities of the Port of Djibouti, its airport, and the operation of the Addis Ababa-Djibouti railroad. During the civil war (1991-1994), there was a significant diversion of government budgetary resources from developmental and social services to military needs. France is insisting that future aid be conditional on an overhaul of Djibouti's dilapidated state finances in conjunction with the International Monetary Fund. Agriculture and industry are little developed, in part due to the harsh climate, high production costs, unskilled labor, and limited natural resources. Only a few mineral deposits exist in the country, and the arid soil is unproductive—89% is desert wasteland, 10% is pasture, and 1% is forested. Services and commerce provide most of the gross domestic product.

Djibouti's most important economic asset is its strategic location on the shipping routes between the Mediterranean Sea and the Indian Ocean—the republic lies on the west side of the Bab-el-Mandeb, which connects the Red Sea and the Gulf of Aden. Its port remains an important container shipment and transshipment point on the shipping lanes transiting the Red Sea and the Suez Canal. It also functions as a bunkering port and a small French naval facility. The decision by the Saudi Arabian Government to improve its own port facilities in Jeddah and Ethiopia's decision to promote its port at Assab recently have decreased the volume of economic activity for the Port of Djibouti.

The Addis Ababa-Djibouti railroad is the only line serving central and southeastern Ethiopia. The single-track railway—a prime source of employment—occupies a prominent place in Ethiopia's internal distribution system for domestic commodities such as cement, cotton textiles, sugar, cereals and charcoal.

Principal exports from the region transiting Djibouti are coffee, salt, hides, dried beans, cereals, other agricultural products, wax and salt. Djibouti itself has few exports, and the majority of its imports come from France. Most imports are consumed in Djibouti, and the remainder goes to Ethiopia and northwestern Somalia. Djibouti's unfavorable balance of trade is offset partially by invisible earnings such as transit taxes and harbor dues. In 1995, U.S. exports to

Djibouti totaled $8.5 million while U.S. imports from Djibouti were less than $50,000.

The city of Djibouti has the only paved airport in the republic. Djibouti has one of the most liberal economic regimes in Africa, with almost unrestricted banking and commerce sectors.

# FOREIGN RELATIONS

Military and economic agreements with France provide continued security and economic assistance. Links with Arab states and east Asian states, Japan and China in particular, are also welcome.

Because Djibouti is greatly affected by events that occur in Somalia and Ethiopia, and vice versa, relations are delicate. With the fall of the Siad Barre and Mengistu Governments in Somalia and Ethiopia in 1991, Djibouti found itself faced with

national security threats due to neighboring instability and a massive influx of refugees estimated at 100,000. In 1991, Djibouti hoped to play a key role in the transition process toward peace in Somalia by hosting the Somali National Reconciliation Conference, and the republic's role in assisting Ethiopia's redevelopment will likely increase in the near future. As a result of such regional conflicts, ties to other states and organizations more removed from tensions of the Horn of Africa are particularly valued.

# U.S.-DJIBOUTIAN RELATIONS

In April 1977, the United States established a Consulate General in Djibouti and at independence several months later raised its status to Embassy. The first U.S. Ambassador to the Republic of Djibouti arrived in October 1980. The United States provides less than $500,000 in economic support funds and military aid annually.

Djibouti has permitted the U.S. Navy access to its sea- and airports. The importance of that access to the U.S. has grown, with an increased U.S. naval presence in the Indian Ocean. The Djiboutian Government has generally been supportive of U.S. and Western interests, as was demonstrated during the Gulf crisis of 1990-1991.

## Principal U.S. Officials

**For up-to-date information on Principal U.S. Officials, see the U.S. Embassies, Consulates, and Foreign Service section starting on page 139.**

The U.S. Embassy in Djibouti is located at Villa Plateau du Serpent, Blvd. Marechal Joffre (Boite Postal 185), Djibouti (tel. 253 35-39-95; fax 253 35-39-40).

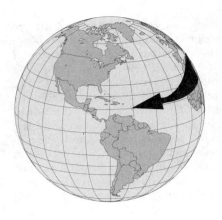

# DOMINICA
March 1998

Official Name:
**Commonwealth of Dominica**

## PROFILE

### Geography
**Area:** 754 sq. km. (290 sq. mi.).
**Cities:** Capital—Roseau.
**Terrain:** Mountainous volcanic island with rainforest cover.
**Climate:** Tropical.

### People
**Nationality:** Noun and adjective—Dominican (Dom-i-nee-can).
**Population (1996):** 74,900.
**Annual growth rate:** 0.4%.
**Ethnic groups:** Mainly African descent, some Carib Indians.
**Religions:** Roman Catholic (80%), Anglican, other Protestant denominations.
**Languages:** English (official); a French patois is widely spoken.
**Education:** Years compulsory—to age 14. Literacy—about 95%.
**Health:** Infant mortality rate—10/1,000. Life expectancy—71 yrs. (men); 74 yrs. (women).
**Work force (1994) (30,600):** Agriculture—37%. Services—30%. Commerce—20%. Unemployment—exceeds 20% (official 1994 figure—9.7%).

### Government
**Type:** Parliamentary Democracy; republic within commonwealth.
**Independence:** November 3, 1978.
**Constitution:** November 1978.
**Branches:** Executive—president (head of state), prime minister (head of government), cabinet. Legislative—unicameral house of assembly. Judicial—magistrate and jury courts, Eastern Caribbean supreme court (high court and court of appeals), privy council.
**Subdivisions:** 10 parishes.
**Political parties:** Dominica United Workers Party (ruling), Dominica Labor Party (opposition), and Dominica Freedom Party (opposition).
**Suffrage:** Universal adult.

### Economy (1996)
**GDP:** $234 million.
**GDP growth rate:** 3.7%.
**Per capita GDP:** $3,120.
**Natural resources:** timber, water (hydropower), copper.
**Agriculture (20% of GDP):** Products—bananas, citrus, coconuts, cocoa, herbal oils and extracts.
**Manufacturing (7.3% of GDP):** Types—agricultural processing, soap and other coconut-based products, apparel.
**Trade:** Exports—$52.7 million: bananas, citrus fruits, soap, cocoa. Major markets—European Union (EU), CARICOM, U.S. (16%). Imports—$100.5 million: machinery and equipment, foodstuffs, manufactured articles, cement. Major suppliers—CARICOM, U.S. (35%), EU, Japan.
**Exchange rate:** Eastern Caribbean dollare 2.70=U.S. $1.

## PEOPLE

Almost all Dominicans are descendants of African slaves brought in by colonial planters in the 18th century. Dominica is the only island in the eastern Caribbean to retain some of its pre-Columbian population—the Carib Indians—about 3,000 of whom live on the island's east coast.

The population growth rate is very low, due primarily to emigration to more prosperous Caribbean Islands, the United Kingdom, the United States, and Canada.

English is the official language; however, because of historic French domination, the most widely spoken dialect is a French patois. About 80% of the population is Catholic. In recent years, a number of Protestant churches have been established.

## HISTORY

The island's indigenous Arawak people were expelled or exterminated by Caribs in the 14th century. Columbus landed there in November 1493. Spanish ships frequently landed on Dominica during the 16th century, but fierce resistance by the Caribs discouraged Spain's efforts at settlement.

In 1635, France claimed Dominica. Shortly thereafter, French missionaries became the first European inhabitants of the island. Carib incursions continued, though, and in 1660, the French and British agreed that both Dominica and St. Vincent should be abandoned. Dominica was officially neutral for the next century, but the attraction of its resources remained; rival expeditions of British and French foresters were harvesting timber by the start of the 18th century.

Largely due to Dominica's position between Martinique and Guadeloupe, France eventually became predominant, and a French settlement was established and grew. As part of the 1763 Treaty of Paris that ended the seven years' war, the island became a British possession. In 1778, during the American Revolutionary War, the French mounted a successful invasion with the active cooperation of the population, which was largely French. The 1783 Treaty of Paris, which ended the war, returned the island to Britain. French invasions in 1795 and 1805 ended in failure.

In 1763, the British established a legislative assembly, representing only the white population. In 1831, reflecting a liberalization of official British racial attitudes, the brown privilege bill conferred political and social rights on free nonwhites. Three Blacks were elected to the legislative assembly the following year. Following the abolition of slavery, in 1838 Dominica became the first and only British Caribbean colony to have a Black-controlled legislature in the 19th century. Most Black legislators were smallholders or merchants who held economic and social views diametrically opposed to the interests of the small, wealthy English planter class. Reacting to a perceived threat, the planters lobbied for more direct British rule.

## Travel Notes

**Travel Advice:** For up-to-date information from the U.S. State Department on possible inconvenient or hazardous situations, see the **Travel Warnings and Consular Information Sheets from the U.S. Government** section starting on page 1723. For the latest information on health requirements and conditions, see the **International Travelers' Health Information** section starting on page 1385. For further information dealing with non-urgent matter, see the **Tips for Travelers to...** section starting on page 1588.

In 1865, after much agitation and tension, the colonial office replaced the elective assembly with one comprised of one-half elected members and one-half appointed. The elected legislators were outmaneuvered on numerous occasions by planters allied with colonial administrators. In 1871, Dominica became part of the Leeward Island Federation. The power of the Black population progressively eroded. Crown Colony government was re-established in 1896. All political rights for the vast majority of the population were effectively curtailed. Development aid, offered as compensation for disenfranchisement, proved to have a negligible effect.

Following World War I, an upsurge of political consciousness throughout the Caribbean led to the formation of the representative government association. Marshaling public frustration with the lack of a voice in the governing of Dominica, this group won one-third of the popularly elected seats of the legislative assembly in 1924 and one-half in 1936. Shortly thereafter, Dominica was transferred from the Leeward Island Administration and was governed as part of the Windwards until 1958, when it joined the short-lived West Indies Federation.

After the federation dissolved, Dominica became an associated state of the United Kingdom in 1967 and formally took responsibility for its internal affairs. On November 3, 1978, the Commonwealth of Dominica was granted independence by the United Kingdom.

Independence did little to solve problems stemming from centuries of economic underdevelopment, and in mid-1979, political discontent led to the formation of an interim government. It was replaced after the 1980 elections by a government led by the Dominica Freedom Party under Prime Minister Eugenia Charles, the Caribbean's first female prime minister. Chronic economic problems were compounded by the severe impact of hurricanes in 1979 and in 1980. By the end of the 1980's, the economy had made a healthy recovery, which weakened in the 1990's due to a decrease in banana prices.

In June 1995 elections, Edison James, leader of the United Workers Party, became Prime Minister, replacing Dame Eugenia Charles.

# GOVERNMENT

Dominica has a Westminster-style parliamentary government, and there are three political parties: The Dominica United Workers Party (the majority party), the Dominica Labor Party, and the Dominica Freedom Party. A president and prime minister make up the executive branch. Nominated by the prime minister in consultation with the leader of the opposition party, the president is elected for a five-year term by the parliament. The president appoints as prime minister the leader of the majority party in the parliament and also appoints, on the prime minister's recommendation, members of the parliament from the ruling party as cabinet ministers. The prime minister and cabinet are responsible to the parliament and can be removed on a no-confidence vote.

The unicameral parliament, called the House of Assembly, is composed of 21 regional representatives and nine senators. The regional representatives are elected by universal suffrage and, in turn, decide whether senators are to be elected or appointed. If appointed, five are chosen by the president with the advice of the prime minister and four with the advice of the opposition leader. If elected, it is by vote of the regional representatives. Elections for representatives and senators must be held at least every five years, although the prime minister can call elections any time.

Dominica's legal system is based on English common law. There are three magistrate's courts, with appeals made to the Eastern Caribbean court of appeal and, ultimately, to the Privy Council in London.

Councils elected by universal suffrage govern most towns. Supported largely by property taxation, the councils are responsible for the regulation of markets and sanitation and the maintenance of secondary roads and other municipal amenities. The island is also divided into 10 parishes, whose governance is unrelated to the town governments.

## Principal Government Officials

**For up-to-date information on Principal Government Officials, see the Chiefs of State and Cabinet Members of Foreign Governments section starting on page 1.**

Although the Dominican ambassador to the United States has customarily been resident in Dominica, the country maintains an embassy in the U.S. at 3216 New Mexico Ave., NW, Washington, DC 20016 (tel. 202-364-6781). Dominica also has a consulate general co-located with its UN mission in New York at Suite 900, 820 Second Avenue, New York, NY 10017 (tel: 212-599-8478).

# ECONOMY

Agriculture, with bananas as the principal crop, is still the economic mainstay. Banana production employs, directly or indirectly, upwards of one-third of the work force. Banana exports to the United Kingdom account for approximately 50% of merchandise trade earnings. This sector is highly vulnerable to weather conditions and to external events affecting commodity prices.

In view of the EU's announced phase-out of preferred access of bananas to its markets, agricultural diversification is a priority. Dominica has made some progress toward it, with the export of small quantities of citrus fruits and vegetables and the introduction of coffee, patchouli, aloe vera, cut flowers, and exotic fruits such as mangoes, guavas, and papayas.

Because Dominica is mostly volcanic and has few beaches, development of tourism has been slow compared with that on neighboring islands. Nevertheless, Dominica's high, rugged mountains, rainforests, freshwater lakes, hot springs, waterfalls, and diving spots make it an attractive

DOMINICA

0   2   4   6   8 Miles
0 2 4 6   8 Kilometers

Dominica Passage

Caribbean Sea

Vielle Case
Portsmouth
Glanvillia
Wesley
Marigot
Toulaman
Morne Diablatins 4,747 ft. 1447 m.
Salibia
Colihaut
Morne Raquette
Castle Bruce
Salisbury
Layou
Saint Joseph
Pont Cassé
Rosalie
Massacre
Laudat
La Plaine
Roseau
Roseau
Pointe Michel
Berekua
Soufrière
Grand Bay
Caribbean Sea

Dominica

destination. Cruise ship stopovers have increased following the development of modern docking and waterfront facilities in the capital. Ecotourism also is a growing industry on the island.

Dominica is a member of the Eastern Caribbean Central Bank, which issues a common currency. Dominica is a beneficiary of the U.S. Caribbean Basin Initiative (CBI). Its 1996 exports to the U.S. were $7.7 million, and its U.S. imports were $34 million. Dominica is also a member of the 14-member Caribbean Community and Common Market (CARICOM).

# FOREIGN RELATIONS

Like its Eastern Caribbean neighbors, the main priority of Dominica's foreign relations is economic development. The country maintains missions in Washington, New York, London, and Brussels and is represented jointly with other organization of Eastern Caribbean states (OECS) members in Canada. Dominica is also a member of the Caribbean Development Bank (CDB), and the British Commonwealth. It became a member of the United Nations and the International Monetary Fund (IMF) in 1978 and of the World Bank and Organization of American States (OAS) in 1979.

As a member of CARICOM, in July 1994 Dominica strongly backed efforts by the United States to implement UN Security Council Resolution 940, designed to facilitate the departure of Haiti's de facto authorities from power. The country agreed to contribute personnel to the multinational force, which restored the democratically elected government of Haiti in October 1994.

In May 1997, Prime Minister James joined 14 other Caribbean leaders, and President Clinton, during the first-ever U.S.-regional summit in Bridgetown, Barbados. The summit strengthened the basis for regional cooperation on justice and counternarcotics issues, finance and development, and trade.

# U.S.-DOMINICAN RELATIONS

The United States and Dominica have friendly bilateral relations. The United States supports the Dominican Government's efforts to expand its economic base and to provide a higher standard of living for its citizens. Following the closure in July 1996 of USAID's Eastern Caribbean regional office, U.S. assistance is primarily channeled through multilateral agencies such as the Inter-American Development Bank, the World Bank, and the Caribbean Development Bank (CDB). Technical assistance is also provided by the Peace Corps, which has about 20 volunteers in Dominica, working primarily in education, youth development, and health.

In addition, the United States and Dominica work together in the battle against illegal drugs. Dominica cooperates with U.S. agencies and participates in counternarcotics programs in an effort to curb narco-trafficking and marijuana cultivation. In 1995, the Dominican Government signed a maritime law enforcement agreement with the U.S. to strengthen counternarcotics coordination, and in 1996, the government signed mutual legal assistance and extradition treaties to enhance joint efforts in combating international crime.

As a popular tourist destination for Americans, Dominica had nearly 188,000 cruise ship passenger arrivals in 1996, the majority of whom were U.S. citizens. In addition, there were more than 13,500 other U.S. visitors in 1996. It is estimated that 4,500 Americans reside in the country.

## Principal U.S. Embassy Officials

**For up-to-date information on Principal U.S. Officials, see the U.S. Embassies, Consulates, and Foreign Service section starting on page 139.**

The United States maintains no official presence in Dominica. The ambassador and embassy officers are resident in Barbados and frequently travel to Dominica.

The U.S. Embassy in Barbados is located in the Canadian Imperial Bank of Commerce Building, Broad Street, Bridgetown (Tel: 246-436-4950; Fax: 246-429-5246).

## Other Contact Information

U.S. Department of Commerce International Trade Administration Trade Information Center 14th and Constitution, NW Washington, DC 20230 Tel: 1-800-USA-TRADE

Caribbean/Latin America Action 1818 N Street, NW, Suite 310 Washington, DC 20036 Tel: 202-466-7464 Fax: 202-822-0075

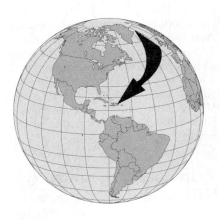

# DOMINICAN REPUBLIC

October 2000

Official Name:
**Dominican Republic**

## PROFILE

### Geography

**Area:** 48,442 sq. km. (18,704 sq. mi.), about the size of Vermont and New Hampshire combined.
**Cities:** Capital—Santo Domingo (pop. 2.4 million). Other city—Santiago de los Caballeros (500,000).
**Terrain:** Mountainous.
**Climate:** Maritime tropical.

### People

**Nationality:** Noun and adjective—Dominican(s).
**Population:** (1997) 8 million.
**Annual growth rate:** 2.6%.
**Ethnic Groups:** European 16%, African origin 11%, mixed 73%.
**Religion:** Roman Catholic 95%.
**Language:** Spanish.
**Education:** Years compulsory—6. Attendance—70%. Literacy—83%.
**Health:** Infant mortality rate—54/1,000. Life expectancy—65 years for men, 70 years for women.
**Work force:** Services and government—31% (includes parastatal corporations); agriculture—28%; industry—12%. Unemployment—approximately 16%.

### Government

**Type:** Representative democracy.
**Independence:** February 27, 1844.

**Constitution:** November 28, 1966.
**Branches:** Executive—president (chief of state and head of government, vice president, cabinet. Legislative—bicameral Congress (Senate and Chamber of Deputies). Judicial—Supreme Court of Justice.
**Subdivisions:** 29 provinces and the National District of Santo Domingo.
**Political parties:** Social Christian Reformist Party (PRSC), Dominican Revolutionary Party (PRD), Dominican Liberation Party (PLD), and several others.
**Suffrage:** Universal and compulsory, over 18 or married.

### Economy

**Year:** 1997.
**GDP:** $14.9 billion.
**Growth rate:** (1997) 8.3%.
**Per capita GDP:** $1,860.
**Non-fuel minerals:** (3% of GDP) Nickel, gold, silver.
**Agriculture:** (13% of GDP) Products—sugar, coffee, cocoa, bananas, tobacco, rice, plantains, beef, flowers.
**Industry:** (17% of GDP) Types—sugar refining, pharmaceuticals, cement, light manufacturing, construction; services, including offshore assembly operations (esp. textiles); and transportation—60% of GDP.
**Trade:** Exports ($4.8 billion, excluding processing zones)—$661 million: sugar, coffee, gold, silver, ferronickel, cacao, tobacco, meats. Markets—U.S. (45%), Netherlands. Imports—$6.6

billion: food stuffs, petroleum, industrial raw materials, capital goods. Suppliers—U.S. (44%), Japan, Germany, Venezuela, Mexico.

## PEOPLE

About half of Dominicans live in rural areas; many are small landholders. Haitians form the largest foreign minority group. All religions are tolerated; the state religion is Roman Catholicism.

## HISTORY

The island of Hispaniola, of which the Dominican Republic forms the eastern two-thirds and Haiti the remainder, was originally occupied by Tainos, an Arawak-speaking people. The Tainos welcomed Columbus in his first voyage in 1492, but subsequent colonizers were brutal, reducing the Taino population from about 1 million to about 500 in 50 years. To ensure adequate labor for plantations, the Spanish brought African slaves to the island beginning in 1503.

In the next century, French settlers occupied the western end of the island, which Spain ceded to France in 1697, and which, in 1804, became the Republic of Haiti. The Haitians

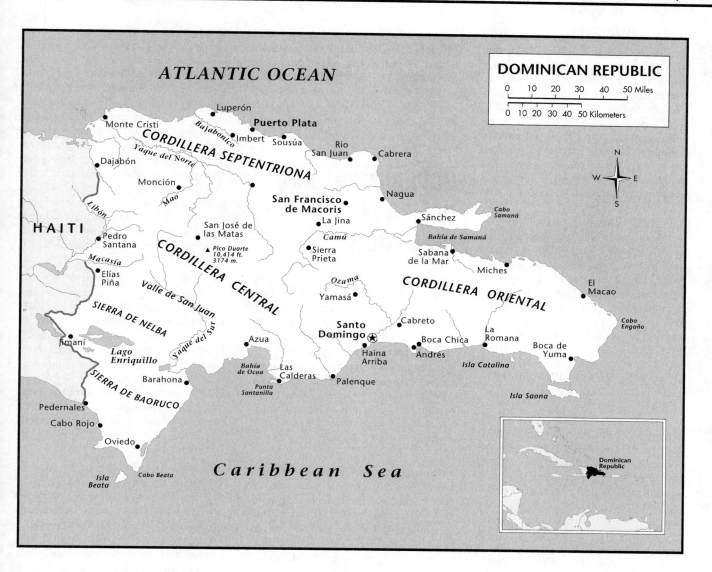

conquered the whole island in 1822 and held it until 1844, when forces led by Juan Pablo Duarte, the hero of Dominican independence, drove them out and established the Dominican Republic as an independent state. In 1861, the Dominicans voluntarily returned to the Spanish Empire; in 1865, independence was restored. Economic difficulties, the threat of European intervention, and ongoing internal disorders led to a U.S. Occupation in 1916 and the establishment of a military government in the Dominican Republic. The occupation ended in 1924, with a democratically elected Dominican Government.

In 1930, Rafael L. Trujillo, a prominent army commander, established absolute political control. Trujillo promoted economic development—

from which he and his supporters benefited—and severe repression of domestic human rights. Mismanagement and corruption resulted in major economic problems. In August 1960, the Organization of American States (OAS) imposed diplomatic sanctions against the Dominican Republic as a result of Trujillo's complicity in an attempt to assassinate President Romulo Betancourt of Venezuela. These sanctions remained in force after Trujillo's death by assassination in May 1961. In November 1961, the Trujillo family was forced into exile.

In January 1962, a council of state that included moderate opposition elements with legislative and executive powers was formed. OAS sanctions were lifted January 4, and, after

the resignation of President Joaquin Balaguer on January 16, the council under President Rafael E. Bonnelly headed the Dominican government. In 1963, Juan Bosch was inaugurated President. Bosch was overthrown in a military coup in September 1963. Another military coup, on April 24, 1965, led to violence between military elements favoring the return to government by Bosch and those who proposed a military junta committed to early general elections. On April 28, U.S. military forces landed to protect U.S. citizens and to evacuate U.S. and other foreign nationals. Additional U.S. forces subsequently established order.

In June 1966, President Balaguer, leader of the Reformist Party (now called the Social Christian Reformist

Party—PRSC), was elected and then re-elected to office in May 1970 and May 1974, both times after the major opposition parties withdrew late in the campaign. In the May 1978 election, Balaguer was defeated in his bid for a fourth successive term by Antonio Guzman of the PRD. Guzman's inauguration on August 16 marked the country's first peaceful transfer of power from one freely elected president to another.

The PRD's presidential candidate, Salvador Jorge Blanco, won the 1982 elections, and the PRD gained a majority in both houses of Congress. In an attempt to cure the ailing economy, the Jorge administration began to implement economic adjustment and recovery policies, including an austerity program in cooperation with the International Monetary Fund (IMF). In April 1984, rising prices of basic foodstuffs and uncertainty about austerity measures led to riots.

Balaguer was returned to the presidency with electoral victories in 1986 and 1990. Upon taking office in 1986, Balaguer tried to reactivate the economy through a public works construction program. Nonetheless, by 1988 the country slid into a 2-year economic depression, characterized by high inflation and currency devaluation. Economic difficulties, coupled with problems in the delivery of basic services—e.g., electricity, water, transportation—generated popular discontent that resulted in frequent protests, occasionally violent, including a paralyzing nationwide strike in June 1989. In 1990, Balaguer instituted a second set of economic reforms. After concluding an IMF agreement, balancing the budget, and curtailing inflation, the Dominican Republic is experiencing a period of economic growth marked by moderate inflation, a balance in external accounts, and a steadily increasing GDP.

The voting process in 1986 and 1990 was generally seen as fair, but allegations of electoral board fraud tainted both victories. The elections of 1994 were again marred by charges of fraud. Following a compromise call-

ing for constitutional and electoral reform, President Balaguer assumed office for an abbreviated term. In June 1996, Leonel Fernandez Reyna was elected to a 4-year term as president. In May 2000 Hipolito Mejia was elected to a 4-year term as president.

# GOVERNMENT AND POLITICAL CONDITIONS

The Dominican Republic is a representative democracy whose national powers are divided among independent executive, legislative, and judicial branches. The president appoints the cabinet, executes laws passed by the legislative branch, and is commander in chief of the armed forces. The president and vice president run for office on the same ticket and are elected by direct vote for 4-year terms.

Legislative power is exercised by a bicameral congress—the senate (30 members), and the chamber of deputies (120 members). Presidential elections are held in years evenly divisible by four. Congressional and municipal elections are held in even numbered years not divisible by four.

Under the constitutional reforms negotiated after the 1994 elections, the 16-member Supreme Court of Justice is appointed by a National Judicial Council, which is nominated by the three major political parties. The Court has sole jurisdiction over actions against the president, designated members of his cabinet, and members of Congress.

The Supreme Court hears appeals from lower courts and chooses members of lower courts. Each of the 29 provinces is headed by a presidentially appointed governor. Elected mayors and municipal councils administer the National District (Santo Domingo) and the 103 municipal districts.

The Dominican Republic has a multiparty political system with national elections every 4 years. In two rounds of presidential elections in 1996, nearly 80% of eligible Dominican voters went to the polls. The leading parties in 1994 were the PRSC, linked to the International Christian Democratic political movement, whose candidate was President Joaquin Balaguer; the PRD, affiliated with the Socialist International, whose candidate was Jose Francisco Pena Gomez; and the Dominican Liberation Party (PLD), whose candidate was former President Juan Bosch.

On election day, international observers noted many irregularities in the voter lists, and the opposition PRD immediately charged the Central Electoral Board and the PRSC with fraud. A Verification Commission appointed by the Central Electoral Board, however, did not accept the PRD's charges. By all estimates, total disenfranchised voters far exceeded the 22,281-vote margin of victory in favor of President Balaguer on August 2, 1994.

Following an intense period of political activity, the competing political parties signed a Pact for Democracy on August 10, reducing President Balaguer's term of office from 4 to 2 years, setting early elections, and reforming the constitution. A new Central Electoral Board was named to work on electoral reform. The main candidates in 1996 were Vice President Jacinto Peynado (PRSC), Jose Francisco Pena Gomez (PRD), and Leonel Fernandez (PLD).

Domestic and international observers saw the 1996 election as transparent and fair. After the first round in which Jacinto Peynado (PRSC) was eliminated, President Balaguer endorsed the PLD candidate. Results in the second round, 45 days later on June 30, were tabulated quickly, and although the victory margin was narrow (1.5%), it was never questioned. The transition from incumbent administration to incoming administration was smooth and ushered in a new, modern era in Dominican political life.

Fernandez' political agenda was one of economic and judicial reform. He helped enhance Dominican participation in hemispheric affairs, such as the Organization of American States and the follow up to the Miami Summit. On May 16, 2000, Hiploito Mejia, the Revolutionary Democratic Party candidate, was elected president in another free and fair election. He defeated Dominican Liberation Party candidate Danilo Medina 49.8% to 24.84%. Former President Balaguer garnered 24.68% of the vote. Mejia entered office on August 16 with four priorities: education reform, economic development, increased agricultural production, and poverty alleviation. Mejia also champions the cause of Central American and Caribbean economic integration and migration, particularly as it relates to Haiti.

The military consists of about 24,000 active duty personnel, commanded by the president. Its principal mission is to defend the nation, but it serves more as an internal security force. The army, twice as large as the other services combined, consists of four infantry brigades and a combat support brigade; the air force operates three flying squadrons; and the navy maintains 30 aging vessels. The Dominican Republic's military is second in size to Cuba's in the Caribbean.

The armed forces participate fully in counter-narcotics efforts. They also are active in efforts to control contraband and illegal immigration from Haiti to the Dominican Republic and from the Dominican Republic to the United States.

## Principal Government Officials

**For up-to-date information on Principal Government Officials, see the Chiefs of State and Cabinet Members of Foreign Governments section starting on page 1.**

The Dominican Republic maintains an embassy in the United States at 1715 22d Street NW, Washington, DC 20008 (tel. 202-332-6280).

# ECONOMY

The Dominican Republic is a middle-income developing country primarily dependent on agriculture, trade, and services, especially tourism. Although the service sector has recently overtaken agriculture as the leading employer of Dominicans (due principally to growth in tourism and Free Trade Zones), agriculture remains the most important sector in terms of domestic consumption and is in second place (behind mining) in terms of export earnings. Tourism accounts for more than $1 billion in annual earnings. Free Trade Zone earnings and tourism are the fastest-growing export sectors. Remittances from Dominicans living in the United States are estimated to be about $1.5 billion per year.

Following economic turmoil in the late 1980s and 1990, during which the GDP fell by up to 5% and consumer price inflation reached an unprecedented 100%, the Dominican Republic entered a period of moderate growth and declining inflation. GDP in 1999 grew by 8.3% while the inflation rate was 5%.

Despite a widening merchandise trade deficit, tourism earnings and remittances have helped build foreign exchange reserves. The Dominican Republic is current on foreign private debt, and has agreed to pay arrears of about $130 million to the U.S. Department of Agriculture's Commodity Credit Corporation.

The government faces several economic policy challenges—high real interest rates, fiscal imbalances caused by money-losing public enterprises and poor tax-collection rates, and reducing dependence on taxes on international trade. Years of tariff protection for domestic production have left the economy vulnerable in a rapidly integrating global economy. The deteriorating non-free trade zone merchandise trade balance is in part due to the failure of the exchange rate to reflect inflationary trends in the 1993-95 period.

# FOREIGN RELATIONS

The Dominican Republic has a close relationship with the United States and with the other states of the Inter-American system. It has accredited diplomatic missions in most Western Hemisphere countries and in principal European capitals. The Dominican Republic and Cuba recently established consular relations, and there is contact in fields such as commerce, culture, and sports. Although Dominican relations with its closest neighbor, the Republic of Haiti, have never been extensive, there are signs this will change with the new government of President Mejia. Growing immigration from and political instability in Haiti have forced the Dominican Republic to take a closer look at relations with its neighbor both country-to-country and in international fora. There is a sizeable Haitian migrant community in the Dominican Republic.

The Dominican Republic belongs to the UN and many of its specialized and related agencies, including the World Bank, International Labor Organization, International Atomic Energy Agency, and International Civil Aviation Organization. It also is a member of the OAS, the Inter-American Development Bank, and INTELSAT.

# U.S.-DOMINICAN REPUBLIC RELATIONS

The U.S. has a strong interest in a democratic, stable, and economically healthy Dominican Republic. Its standing as the largest Caribbean economy, the second-largest in terms of population and land mass, and its proximity to the United States and other smaller Caribbean nations make the Dominican Republic an important partner in hemispheric affairs. This close relationship was underscored when President Fernandez joined President Clinton at the summit with Central American leaders in May 1997 in Costa Rica.

U.S. relations with the Dominican Republic are excellent, and the U.S. has been an outspoken supporter of that country's democratic and economic development. In addition, the Dominican Government has been supportive of many U.S. initiatives in the United Nations and related agencies. The two governments cooperate in the fight against the traffic in illegal substances. The Dominican Republic has worked closely with U.S. law enforcement officials on issues such as the return of stolen cars to the U.S. and reducing illegal migration. The U.S. also supports the current administration's efforts to open the economy to more trade, increase foreign private investment, privatize state-owned firms, and modernize the tax system.

Bilateral trade is important to both countries, and U.S. firms—mostly apparel, footwear, and light electronics manufacturers—account for much of the foreign private investment in the Dominican Republic. U.S. exports to the Dominican Republic in 1996 totaled $3.8 billion and constituted 65% of that country's imports. The Dominican Republic exported $3.7 million to the U.S. in 1996, equaling some 65% of its exports. NAFTA has not caused any profound changes in Dominican trade with the U.S. The U.S. embassy works closely with U.S. business firms and Dominican trade groups, both of which can take advantage of the new opportunities in this growing market. At the same time the embassy is working with the Dominican Government to resolve

## Travel Notes

**Travel Advice:** For up-to-date information from the U.S. State Department on possible inconvenient or hazardous situations, see the **Travel Warnings and Consular Information Sheets from the U.S. Government** section starting on page 1723. For the latest information on health requirements and conditions, see the **International Travelers' Health Information** section starting on page 1385. For further information dealing with non-urgent matter, see the **Tips for Travelers to...** section starting on page 1588.

outstanding disputes U.S. firms have with the government as result of actions by previous administrations.

The embassy counsels U.S. firms through its written <a href=http://www.state.gov/www/about_state/business/com_guides/2001/wha/index.html> Country Commercial Guide and informally via meetings with business persons planning to or already investing in the Dominican Republic. It is a challenging business environment for U.S. firms, although agile exporters and investors can profit doing business in the Dominican Republic.

The U.S. Agency for International Development (USAID) mission is focused on four areas: availability of health care, increasing economic opportunity, improving participation in democratic processes, and environmentally sound energy production. About 90% of USAID resources are channeled through nongovernmental organizations for reasons of efficiency.

The embassy estimates that 60,000 U.S. citizens live in the Dominican Republic, although precise figures are unavailable; many are dual nationals. An important element of

the relationship between the two countries is the more than 1 million Dominicans residing in the U.S. The majority of Dominicans live in metropolitan New York City.

## Principal U.S. Officials

**For up-to-date information on Principal U.S. Officials, see the U.S. Embassies, Consulates, and Foreign Service section starting on page 139.**

AThe U.S. Embassy is located at Calle Cesar Nicolas Penson and Calle Leopoldo Navarro, Santo Domingo (tel. 809-221-2171).

## Other Contact Information

**U.S. Department of Commerce**
International Trade Administration
Trade Information Center
14th and Constitution, NW
Washington, DC 20230
Tel: 1-800-USA-TRADE
Internet: http://www.doc.gov

**Caribbean/Latin American Action** 1818 N. Street, NW, Suite 310
Washington, DC 20036
Tel: (202) 466-7464
Fax: (202) 822-0075

**American Chamber of Commerce in the Dominican Republic**
Torre B.H.D.
Avenida Winston Churchill
P.O. Box 95-2
Santo Domingo, Dominican Republic
Tel: (809) 544-2222
Fax: (809) 544-0502
E-mail: amchamcodetel.net.do
Home Page: http://www.code-tel.net.do/amcham

# ECUADOR

March 2001

## Official Name:
## Republic of Ecuador

# PROFILE

## Geography

**Area:** 256,370 sq. km.; about the size of Colorado.
**Cities:** Capital—Quito (pop. 1.5 million). Other cities—Guayaquil (2.0 million).
**Terrain:** Jungle east of the Andes, a rich agricultural coastal plain west of the Andes, and high-elevation valleys through the mountainous center of the country.
**Climate:** Varied, mild year-round in the mountain valleys; hot and humid in coastal and Amazonian jungle lowlands.

## People

**Nationality:** Noun and adjective—Ecuadorian(s).
**Population:** (2000 est.) 12,646,095.
**Annual growth rate:** 1.72%.
**Ethnic groups:** Indigenous 25%, mestizo (mixed Indian and Spanish) 55%, Caucasian and others 10%, African 10%.
**Religion:** Predominantly Roman Catholic, but religious freedom recognized.
**Languages:** Spanish (official), indigenous languages, especially Quichua, the Ecuadorian dialect of Quechua.
**Education:** Years compulsory—ages 6–14, but enforcement varies. Atten-

dance (through 6th grade)—76% urban, 33% rural. Literacy—90%.
**Health:** Infant mortality rate-32.2/1,000. Life expectancy—70.8 yrs.
**Work force:** (4.8 million) Agriculture—42%. Commerce—20%. Services—19%. Manufacturing—11%. Other—8%.

## Government

**Type:** Republic.
**Constitution:** August 11, 1998.
**Independence:** May 24, 1822 (from Spain).
**Branches**: Executive—president and 14 cabinet ministers. Legislative—123-member unicameral Congress. Judicial—Supreme Court, Provincial Courts, and ordinary civil and criminal judges.
**Administrative subdivisions:** 22 provinces.
**Political parties:** 11 political parties; none predominates.
**Suffrage:** Obligatory for literate citizens 18–65 yrs. of age; optional for other eligible voters; active duty military personnel may not vote.

## Economy

**GDP** (2000): $13.9 billion.
**Real annual growth rate:** 1996, 2.0%; 1997, 3.4%; 1998, 0.4%; 1999, -7.3%; 2000, 1.9%.
**Per capita GDP:** $1,100
**Natural resources:** Petroleum, fish, shrimp, timber, gold.

**Agriculture:** (10.5% of GDP) Bananas, seafood, coffee, cacao, sugar, rice, corn, and livestock.
**Industry:** (19.0% of GDP-oil and mining 17.4%) Petroleum extraction, food processing, wood products, textiles, chemicals, and pharmaceuticals.
**Trade:** Exports—$4,845 million: petroleum , bananas, shrimp, coffee, cacao, hemp, wood, fish, cut flowers. Major markets—U.S. 38%, Latin America 32%, European Union (EU) 12%, and Asia 12%. Imports—$3,465 million: industrial materials, non-durable consumer goods, agricultural products, Major suppliers—Latin America 46%, U.S. 26%, EU 12%, and Asia 11%.
Note: Central Bank of Ecuador official data

# PEOPLE

Ecuador's population is ethnically mixed. The largest ethnic groups are indigenous and mestizo (mixed Indian-Caucasian). Although Ecuadorians were heavily concentrated in the mountainous central highland region a few decades ago, today's population is divided about equally between that area and the coastal lowlands. Migration toward cities—particularly larger cities—in all regions has increased the urban population to about 55%. The tropical forest region to the east of the mountains remains sparsely populated and contains only about 3% of the population. The public education system is tuition-free, and attendance is mandatory from ages 6 to 14. In practice, however, many children drop out before age 15, and, in rural areas only about one-third complete sixth grade. The government is striving to create better programs for the rural and urban poor, especially in technical and occupational training. In recent years, it has also been successful in reducing illiteracy. Enrollment in primary schools has been increasing at an annual rate of 4.4%—faster than the population growth rate. According to the 1979 constitution, the central government must allocate at least 30% of its revenue to education; in practice, however, it allots a much smaller percentage. Public universities have an open admissions policy. In recent years, however, large increases in the student population, budget difficulties, and extreme politicization of the university system have led to a decline in academic standards.

# HISTORY

Advanced indigenous cultures flourished in Ecuador long before the area was conquered by the Inca empire in the 15th century. In 1534, the Spanish arrived and defeated the Inca armies, and Spanish colonists became the new elite. The indigenous population was decimated by disease in the first decades of Spanish rule—a time when the natives were also forced into the "encomienda" labor system for Spanish landlords. In 1563, Quito became the seat of a royal "audiencia" (administrative district) of Spain. After independence forces defeated the royalist army in 1822, Ecuador joined Simon Bolivar's Republic of Gran Colombia, only to become a separate republic in 1830. The 19th century was marked by instability, with a rapid succession of rulers. The conservative Gabriel Garcia Moreno unified the country in the 1860s with the support of the Catholic Church. In the late 1800s, world demand for cocoa tied the economy to

commodity exports and led to migrations from the highlands to the agricultural frontier on the coast. A coastal-based liberal revolution in 1895 under Eloy Alfaro reduced the power of the clergy and opened the way for capitalist development. The end of the cocoa boom produced renewed political instability and a military coup in 1925. The 1930s and 1940s were marked by populist politicians such as five-time president Jose Velasco Ibarra.

In January 1942, Ecuador signed the Rio Protocol to end a brief war with Peru the year before; Ecuador agreed to a border that conceded to Peru much territory Ecuador previously had claimed in the Amazon. After World War II, a recovery in the market for agricultural commodities and the growth of the banana industry helped restore prosperity and political peace. From 1948–60, three presidents— beginning with Galo Plaza— were freely elected and completed their terms. Recession and popular unrest led to a return to populist politics and domestic military interventions in the 1960s, while foreign companies developed oil resources in the Ecuadorian Amazon. In 1972, a nationalist military regime seized power and used the new oil wealth and foreign borrowing to pay for a program of industrialization, land reform, and subsidies for urban consumers. With the oil boom fading, Ecuador returned to democracy in 1979, but by 1982, the government faced a chronic economic crisis— including inflation, budget deficits, a falling currency, mounting debt service, and uncompetitive industries.

The 1984 presidential elections were narrowly won by Leon Febres-Cordero of the Social Christian Party (PSC). During the first years of his administration, Febres-Cordero introduced free-market economic policies, took strong stands against drug trafficking and terrorism, and pursued close relations with the United States. His tenure was marred by bitter wrangling with other branches of government and his own brief kidnaping by elements of the military. A devastating earthquake in March 1987 interrupted oil exports and

worsened the country's economic problems. Rodrigo Borja of the Democratic Left (ID) party won the presidency in 1988. His government was committed to improving human rights protection and carried out some reforms, notably an opening of Ecuador to foreign trade. The Borja Government concluded an accord leading to the disbanding of the small terrorist group, "Alfaro Lives." However, continuing economic problems undermined the popularity of the ID, and opposition parties gained control of Congress in 1990.

In 1992, Sixto Duran-Ballen won in his third run for the presidency. His government's popularity suffered from tough macroeconomic adjustment measures, but it succeeded in pushing a limited number of modernization initiatives through Congress. Duran-Ballen's vice president, Alberto Dahik, was the architect of the administration's economic policies, but in 1995, Dahik fled the country to avoid prosecution on corruption charges following a heated political battle with the opposition. A war with Peru erupted in January-February 1995 in a small, remote region where the boundary prescribed by the 1942 Rio Protocol was in dispute.

Abdala Bucaram, from the Guayaquil-based Ecuadorian Roldosista Party (PRE), won the presidency in 1996 on a platform that promised populist economic and social reforms and the breaking of what Bucaram termed as the power of the nation's oligarchy. During his short term of office, Bucaram's administration drew criticism for corruption. Bucaram was deposed by the Congress in February 1997 on grounds of alleged mental incompetence. In his place, Congress named interim President Fabian Alarcon, who had been President of Congress and head of the small Radical Alfarist Front party. Alarcon's interim presidency was endorsed by a May 1997 popular referendum. Congressional and first-round presidential elections were held on May 31, 1998. No presidential candidate obtained a majority, so a run-off election between the top two candidates—Quito Mayor Jamil Mahuad of the Popular Democracy party and Social Christian Alvaro Noboa—was held on July 12, 1998. Mahuad won by a narrow margin. He took office on August 10, 1998. On the same day, Ecuador's new constitution came into effect.

Mahuad concluded a well-received peace with Peru on October 26, 1998, but increasing economic, fiscal, and financial difficulties drove his popularity steadily lower. On January 21, 2000, during demonstrations in Quito by indigenous groups, the military and police refused to enforce public order. Demonstrators entered the National Assembly building and declared a three-person "junta" in charge of the country. Field grade military officers declared their support for the concept. During a night of confusion and negotiations President Mahuad was obliged to flee the presidential palace for his own safety. Vice President Gustavo Noboa took charge; Mahuad went on national television in the morning to endorse Noboa as his successor. Congress met in emergency session in Guayaquil the same day, January 22, and ratified Noboa as President of the Republic in constitutional succession to Mahuad.

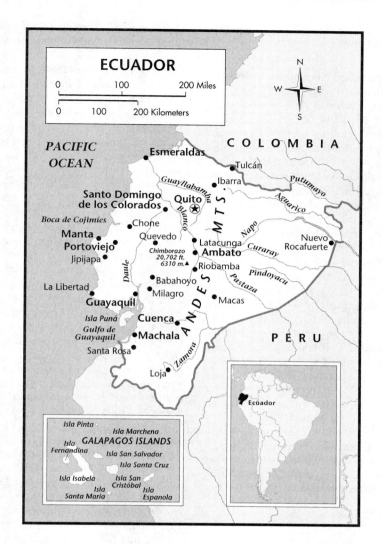

# GOVERNMENT

The constitution provides for concurrent 4-year terms of office for the president, vice president, and Members of Congress. Presidents may be re-elected after an intervening term, while legislators may be re-elected immediately.

The executive branch includes 15 ministries. Provincial governors and councilors, like mayors and aldermen and parrish boards, are directly elected. Each 2 years, legislators are elected from the majority party. Congress meets throughout the year except for recess in July and December. There are twenty 7-member Congressional committees. Justices of the Supreme Court are appointed by the Congress for indefinite terms.

## Principal Government Officials

**For up-to-date information on Principal Government Officials, see the Chiefs of State and Cabinet Members of Foreign Governments section starting on page 1.**

Ecuador maintains an embassy in the United States at 2535 - 15th Street NW, Washington, DC 20009 (tel. 202–234–7200) and consulates in Chicago, Dallas, Houston, Los Angeles, Miami, New Orleans, New York, and San Francisco.

## Legislative Branch

Unicameral National Congress or Congreso Nacional (123 seats; 20 members popularly elected at large nationally, 103 members popularly elected by province.)

## Political Conditions

Ecuador's political parties have historically been small, loose organizations that depended more on populist, often charismatic, leaders to retain support than on programs or ideology. Frequent internal splits have produced extreme factionalism. However, a pattern has emerged in which administrations from the center-left alternate with those from the center-right. Although Ecuador's political elite is highly factionalized along regional, ideological, and personal lines, a strong desire for consensus on major issues often leads to compromise. Opposition forces in Congress are loosely organized, but historically they often unite to block the administration's initiatives and to remove cabinet ministers.

Constitutional changes enacted by a specially elected National Constitutional Assembly in 1998 took effect on August 10, 1998. The new constitution strengthens the executive branch by eliminating mid-term congressional elections and by circumscribing Congress' power to challenge cabinet ministers. Party discipline is traditionally weak, and routinely many deputies switch allegiance during each Congress. However, after the new Constitution took effect, the Congress passed a code of ethics which imposes penalties on members who defy their party leadership on key votes. Beginning with the 1996 election, the indigenous population abandoned its traditional policy of shunning the official political system and participated actively. The indigenous population has established itself as a significant force in Ecuadorian politics, as shown by the selection of indigenous representative Nina Pacari, who led the indigenous political party, Pachakutik, as second vice president of the 1998 Congress. The next presidential and Congressional elections are currently scheduled for 2002.

# ECONOMY

The Ecuadorian economy is based on petroleum production and exports of bananas, shrimp and other primary agricultural products. Industry is largely oriented to servicing the domestic market. Deteriorating economic performance in 1997–1998 culminated in a severe economic and financial crisis in 1999. The crisis was precipitated by a number of external shocks, including the El Nino weather phenomenon in 1997, a sharp drop in global oil prices in 1997–1998, and international emerging market instability in 1997–1998. These factors highlighted the Government of Ecuador's unsustainable economic policy mix of large fiscal deficits and expansionary money policy and resulted in an 7.3% contraction of GDP, annual year-on-year

inflation of 52.2% and a 65% devaluation of the national currency in 1999.

On January 9, 2000, the Administration of President Jamil Mahuad announced its intention to adopt the U.S. dollar as the official currency of Ecuador to address the ongoing economic crisis. Subsequent protest led to the removal of Mahuad from office and the elevation of Vice President Gustavo Noboa to the Presidency.

The Noboa Government confirmed its commitment to dollarize as the centerpiece of its economic recovery strategy. The Government also entered into negotiations with the International Monetary Fund (IMF), culminating in the negotiation of a 12-month Stand-by Arrangement with the Fund. Additional policy initiatives include efforts to reduce the Government's fiscal deficit, implement structural reforms to strengthen the banking system and regain access to private capital markets.

Buoyed by high oil prices, the Ecuadorian economy experienced a modest recovery in 2000, with GDP rising 1.9%. However, 70% of the population lives below the poverty line, more than double the rate of five years ago. Inflation in 2000 remained high at 96.1%, but the rate of inflation continues to fall. Monthly inflation in February 2001 was 2.9%.

# FOREIGN RELATIONS

Ecuador always has placed great emphasis on multilateral approaches to international problems. Ecuador is a member of the United Nations (and most of its specialized agencies) and the Organization of American States and is also a member of many regional groups, including the Rio Group, the Latin American Economic System, the Latin American Energy Organization, the Latin American Integration Association, and the Andean Pact. Ecuador's border dispute with Peru, festering since the independence era, has been the nation's principal foreign policy issue. For more than 50 years, Ecuador

maintained that the 1942 Rio Protocol of Peace, Friendship and Boundaries left several issues unresolved. For example, it asserted that geographic features in the area of the Cenepa River Valley did not match the topographical descriptions in the Protocol, thus making demarcation of the boundary there "inexecutable." This long-running border dispute occasionally erupted into armed hostility along the undemarcated sections. The most serious conflict since the 1941 war occurred in January-February 1995, when thousands of soldiers from both sides fought an intense but localized war in the disputed territory in the upper Cenepa valley. A peace agreement brokered by the four Guarantors of the Rio Protocol (Argentina, Brazil, Chile, and the United States) in February 1995 led to the cessation of hostilities and the establishment of the Military Observers Mission to Ecuador-Peru (MOMEP) to monitor the zone.

In 1996, Ecuador and Peru began a series of meetings intended to set the stage for substantive negotiations to resolve the dispute. Those talks were successful. In January 1998, Ecuador and Peru initialed a historic agreement in Rio de Janeiro, Brazil, which provided a framework to resolve the major outstanding issues between the two countries through four commissions. The commissions were to prepare a Treaty of Commerce and Navigation and a Comprehensive Agreement on Border Integration, to fix on the ground the common land boundary, and to establish a Binational Commission on Mutual Confidence Measures and Security. The commissions began work in February, with the intention of reaching a definitive agreement by May 30, 1998. The commissions on border integration and mutual confidence measures successfully concluded their work, and the commission working on a treaty of commerce and navigation produced a draft treaty text, but the commission on border demarcation failed to produce agreement by May 30.

A flare-up in military tensions in the disputed region in August 1998 led to the creation of a temporary second MOMEP-patrolled demilitarized zone just south of the first demilitarized zone. Presidents Mahuad and Fujimori established direct communication by meetings and phone calls in an effort to overcome the two countries' remaining differences. In October 1998, after asking for and receiving a boundary determination from the guarantors, the two presidents reached agreement. On October 26, 1998, at a ceremony in Brasilia, Presidents Fujimori and Mahuad and their Foreign Ministers signed a comprehensive settlement.

# U.S.-ECUADORIAN RELATIONS

The United States and Ecuador have maintained close ties based on mutual interests in maintaining democratic institutions; combating narcotrafficking; building trade, investment, and financial ties; cooperating in fostering Ecuador's economic development; and participating in inter-American organizations. Ties are further strengthened by the presence of an estimated 150,000–200,000 Ecuadorians living in the United States and by 24,000 U.S. citizens visiting Ecuador annually, and by approximately 15,000 U.S. citizens residing in Ecuador.

The United States assists Ecuador's economic development directly through the Agency for International Development (USAID) program in Ecuador and through multilateral organizations such as the Inter-American Development Bank and the World Bank. In addition, the U.S. Peace Corps operates a sizable program in Ecuador. Over 100 U.S. companies are doing business in Ecuador. Both nations are signatories of the Rio Treaty of 1947, the Western Hemisphere's regional mutual security treaty.

Ecuador shares U.S. concern over increasing narcotrafficking and international terrorism, and has energetically condemned terrorist actions, whether directed against government officials or private citizens. The government has maintained Ecuador virtually free of coca production since

the mid-1980s and is working to combat money laundering and the transshipment of drugs and chemicals essential to the processing of cocaine. Ecuador and the U.S. agreed in 1999 to a 10-year arrangement whereby U.S. military surveillance aircraft could use the airbase at Manta, Ecuador, as a Forward Operating Location to detect drug trafficking flights through the region.

In fisheries issues, the United States claims jurisdiction for the management of coastal fisheries up to 320 kilometers (200 mi.) from its coast, but excludes highly migratory species; Ecuador, on the other hand, claims a 320-kilometer-wide (200-mi.) territorial sea, and imposes license fees and fines on foreign fishing vessels in the area, making no exceptions for catches of migratory species. In the early 1970s, Ecuador seized about 100 foreign-flag vessels (many of them U.S.) and collected fees and fines of more than $6 million. After a drop-off in such seizures for some years, several U.S. tuna boats were again detained and seized in 1980 and 1981. The U.S. Magnuson Fishery Conservation and Management Act then triggered an automatic prohibition of U.S. imports of tuna products from Ecuador. The prohibition was lifted in 1983, and although fundamental differences between U.S. and Ecuadorian legislation still exist, there is no current conflict. During the period that has elapsed since seizures which triggered the tuna import ban, successive Ecuadorian governments have declared their willingness to explore possible solu-

tions to this problem with mutual respect for long-standing positions and principles of both sides.

## Principal U.S. Embassy Officials

**For up-to-date information on Principal U.S. Officials, see the U.S. Embassies, Consulates, and Foreign Service section starting on page 139.**

The U.S. Embassy in Ecuador is located at Avenida Patria 120, Quito (tel. (593)(2) 562–890/561–634). Embassy Internet Home Page: http://www.usis.org.ec.
The Consulate General is at 9 de Octubre and Garcia Moreno, Guayaquil (tel. (593)(4) 323–570).

## Other Contact Information

**U.S. Department of Commerce**
International Trade Administration
Trade Information Center
14th and Constitution Avenue, NW
Washington, DC 20230
Tel: 1–800-USA-TRADE
Internet: http://www.ita.doc.gov

**Ecuadorian-American Chamber of Commerce—Quito**
Edificio Multicentro, 4 Piso
La Nina y Avenida 6 de Diciembre
Quito, Ecuador
Tel: (5932) 507–450
Fax: (5932) 504–571
E-Mail: CCEA1@ACCEA.ORG.EC or CCEA2@ACCEA.ORG.EC
Branches: Ambato, Cuenca & Manta)

**Ecuadorian-American Chamber of Commerce—Guayaquil G. Cordova**
812, Piso 3, Oficina 1
Edificio Torres de la Merced
Guayaquil, Ecuador
Tel: (5934) 566–481 or 565–761
Fax: (5934) 563–259
E-Mail: caecam1@caecam.org.ec
(Branch: Manchala)

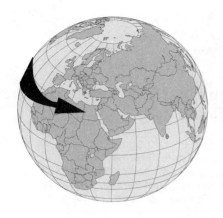

# EGYPT

March 1995

Official Name:
**Arab Republic of Egypt**

# PROFILE

## Geography

**Area:** 1 million sq. km. (386,000 sq. mi.); slightly smaller than Texas, Oklahoma, and Arkansas combined.
**Cities:** Capital—Cairo (pop. over 14 million). Other cities—Alexandria (6 million), Aswan, Asyut, Port Said, Suez, Ismailia.
**Terrain:** Desert, except Nile valley and delta.
**Climate:** Dry, hot summers; moderate winters.

## People

**Nationality:** Noun and adjective—Egyptian(s).
**Population (1993):** 56.4 million.
**Annual growth rate:** 2.2%.
**Ethnic groups:** Egyptian, Bedouin Arab, Nubian.
**Religions:** Sunni Muslim 90%, Coptic Christian.
**Languages:** Arabic (official), English, French.
**Education:** Years compulsory—ages 6-12. Literacy—48%.
**Health:** Infant mortality rate (1992)—80/1,000. Life expectancy—58 yrs. male, 62 yrs. female.
**Work force:** Agriculture—39%. Government, public services, and armed forces—32%. Privately owned service and manufacturing enterprises—29%.

## Government

**Type:** Republic.
**Independence:** 1922.
**Constitution:** 1971.
**Branche:** Executive—president, prime minister, cabinet. Legislative—People's Assembly (444 elected and 10 presidentially appointed members) and Shura (consultative) Council (172 elected members, 86 presidentially appointed). Judicial—Supreme Constitutional Court.
**Administrative subdivisions:** 26 governorates.
**Political parties:** National Democratic Party (ruling), New Wafd Party, Socialist Labor Party, Liberal Party, National Progressive Unionist Grouping, Umma Party, Misr Al-Fattah Party, Green Party, Democratic Nasserite Party, and Unionist Democratic Party.
**Suffrage:** Universal at 18.

## Economy

**GDP (FY 1992-93):** $40.3 billion.
**Annual growth rate:** 2.4%.
**Per capita GDP:** $715.
**Natural resources:** Petroleum and natural gas, iron ore, phosphates, manganese, limestone, gypsum, talc, asbestos, lead, zinc.
**Agriculture:** Products—cotton, rice, onions, beans, citrus fruits, wheat, corn, barley, sugar.
**Industry:** Types—food processing, textiles, chemicals, petrochemicals, construction, light manufacturing, iron and steel products, aluminum, cement, military equipment.
**Trade (FY 1992-93):** Exports—$3.4 billion: petroleum, cotton, manufactured goods. Major markets—Japan, Italy, Germany, France, U.K.
**Imports—$10.7 billion:** foodstuffs, machinery and transport equipment, paper and wood products. Major suppliers—U.S., Germany, France, Japan, Netherlands, U.K., Italy.
**Exchange rate (August 1994):** 3.39 Egyptian pounds=U.S. $1.

# PEOPLE AND HISTORY

Egypt is the most populous country in the Arab world and the second-most populous on the African Continent. Nearly 100% of the country's 58 million people live in Cairo and Alexandria; elsewhere on the banks of the Nile; in the Nile delta, which fans out north of Cairo; and along the Suez Canal. These regions are among the world's most densely populated, containing an average of over 1,540 person per square kilometer (3,820 per sq. mi.).

Small communities spread throughout the desert regions of Egypt are clustered around oases and historic trade and transportation routes. The government has tried with mixed success to encourage migration to newly irrigated land reclaimed from the desert. However, the proportion of the population living in rural areas has continued to decrease as people move to the cities in search of employment and a higher standard of living.

The Egyptians are a fairly homogeneous people of Hamitic origin. Mediterranean and Arab influences appear in the north, and there is some mixing in the south with the Nubians of northern Sudan. Ethnic minorities include a small number of Bedouin Arab nomads in the eastern and western deserts and in the Sinai, as well as some 50,000-100,000 Nubians clustered along the Nile in upper Egypt.

The literacy rate is about 48% of the adult population. Education is free through university and compulsory from ages six through 12. About 87% of children enter primary school; half drop out after their sixth year. There are 20,000 primary and secondary schools with some 10 million students, 12 major universities with about 500,000 students, and 67 teacher colleges. Major universities include Cairo University (100,000 students), Alexandria University, and the 1,000-year-old Al-Azhar University, one of the world's major centers of Islamic learning.

Egypt's vast and rich literature constitutes an important cultural element in the life of the country and in the Arab world as a whole. Egyptian novelists and poets were among the first to experiment with new styles of Arabic literature, and the forms they developed have been widely imitated. Egyptian novelist Naguib Mahjfouz was the first Arab to win the Nobel prize for literature. Egyptian books and films are available throughout the Middle East.

Egypt has endured as a unified state for more than 5,000 years, and archeological evidence indicates that a developed Egyptian society has existed for much longer. Egyptians take pride in their "pharaonic heritage" and in their descent from what they consider mankind's earliest civilization. The Arabic word for Egypt is Misr, which originally connoted "civilization" or "metropolis."

Archeological findings show that primitive tribes lived along the Nile long before the dynastic history of the pharaohs began. By 6000 B.C., organized agriculture had appeared.

In about 3100 B.C., Egypt was united under a ruler known as Mena, or Menes, who inaugurated the 30 pharaonic dynasties into which Egypt's ancient history is divided—the Old and the Middle Kingdoms and the New Empire. For the first time, the use and managements of vital resources of the Nile River came under one authority.

The pyramids at Giza (near Cairo) were built in the fourth dynasty, showing the power of the pharaonic religion and state. The Great Pyramid, the tomb of Pharaoh Khufu (also known as Cheops), is the only surviving example of the Seven Wonders of the Ancient World. Ancient Egypt reached the peak of its power, wealth, and territorial extent in the period called the New Empire (1567-1085 B.C.). Authority was again centralized, and a number of military campaigns brought Palestine, Syria, and northern Iraq under Egyptian control.

## Persian, Greek, Roman, and Arab Conquerors

In 525 B.C., Cambyses, the son of Cyrus the Great, led a Persian invasion force that dethroned the last pharaoh of the 26th Dynasty. The country remained a Persian province until Alexander the Great. The Roman/Byzantine rule of Egypt lasted for nearly 700 years.

Following a brief Persian reconquest, Egypt was invaded and conquered by Arab forces in 642. A process of Arabization and Islamization ensued. Although a Coptic Christian minority remained—and remains today, constituting about 10% of the population—the Arab language inexorably supplanted the indigenous Coptic tongue. Ancient Egyptian ways—passed from pharaonic times through the Persian, Greek, and Roman periods and Egypt's Christian era—were gradually melded with or supplanted by Islamic customs. For the next 1,300 years, a succession of Turkish, Arabic, Mameluke, and Ottoman caliphs, beys, and sultans ruled the country.

## European Influence

Napoleon Bonaparte arrived in Egypt in 1798. The three-year sojourn in Egypt (1798-1801) of his army and a retinue of French scientists opened Egypt to direct Western influence. Napoleon's adventure awakened Great Britain to the importance of Egypt as a vital link with India and the Far East and launched 150 years of Anglo-French rivalry over the region.

An Anglo-Ottoman invasion force drove out the French in 1801, and, following a period of chaos, the Albanian Mohammed Ali obtain control of the country. Ali ruled until 1849, and his successors retained at least nominal control of Egypt until 1952. He imported European culture and technology, introduced state organization of Egypt's economic life, improved education, and fostered training in engineering and medicine. His authoritarian rule was also marked by a series of foreign military adventures. Ali's successors granted to the French Promoter, Ferdinand de Lesseps, a concession for construction of the Suez Canal—begun in 1859 and opened 10 years later.

Their regimes were characterized by financial mismanagement and personal extravagance that reduced Egypt to bankruptcy. These developments led to rapid expansion of British and French financial oversight. This produced popular resentment, which, in 1879, led to revolt.

In 1882, British expeditionary forces crushed this revolt, marking the beginning of British occupation and the virtual inclusion of Egypt within the British Empire. During the rule

of three successive British High Commissioners between 1883 and 1914, the British agency was the real source of authority. It established special courts to enforce foreign laws for foreigners residing in the country. These privileges for foreigners generated increasing Egyptian resentment. To secure its interests during World War I, Britain declared a formal protectorate over Egypt on December 18, 1914. This lasted until 1922, when, in deference to growing

nationalism, the U.K. unilaterally declared Egyptian independence. British influence, however, continued to dominate Egypt's political life and fostered fiscal, administrative, and governmental reforms.

In the post-independence period, three political forces competed with one another: the Wafd, a broadly based nationalist political organization strongly opposed to British influence; King Fuad, whom the British

had installed during the war; and the British themselves, who were determined to maintain control over the canal.

Although both the Wafd and the King wanted to achieve independence from the British, they competed for control of Egypt. Other political forces emerging in this period included the communist party (1925) and the Muslim Brotherhood (1928), which eventually became a potent political and religious force.

During World War II, British troops used Egypt as a base for Allied operations throughout the region. British troops were withdrawn to the Suez Canal area in 1947, but nationalist, anti-British feelings continued to grow after the war. Violence broke out in early 1952 between Egyptians and British in the canal area, and anti-Western rioting in Cairo followed.

On July 22-23, 1952, a group of disaffected army officers led by Lt. Col. Gamal Abdel Nasser overthrew King Farouk, whom the military blamed for Egypt's poor performance in the 1948 war with Israel. Following a brief experiment with civilian rule, they abrogated the 1923 constitution and declared Egypt a republic on June 19, 1953. Nasser evolved into a charismatic leader, not only of Egypt but of the Arab world.

Nasser and his "free officer" movement enjoyed almost instant legitimacy as liberators who had ended 2,500 years of foreign rule. They were motivated by numerous grievances and goals but wanted especially to break the economic and political power of the land-owning elite, to remove all vestiges of British control, and to improve the lot of the people, especially the fellahin (peasants).

A secular nationalist, Nasser developed a foreign policy characterized by advocacy of pan-Arab socialism, leadership of the "nonaligned" of the "Third World," and close ties with the Soviet Union. He sharply opposed the Western-sponsored Baghdad Pact. When the United States held up military sales in reaction to Egyptian neutrality vis-a-vis Moscow, Nasser concluded an arms deal with Czechoslovakia in September 1955.

When the U.S. and the World Bank withdrew their offer to help finance the Aswan High Dam in mid-1956, he nationalized the privately owned Suez Canal Company. The crisis that followed, exacerbated by growing tensions with Israel over guerrilla attacks from Gaza and Israeli reprisals, resulted in the invasion of Egypt

that October by France, Britain, and Israel.

While Egypt was defeated, the invasion forces were quickly withdrawn under heavy pressure from the U.S. The Suez war (or, as the Egyptians call it, the Tripartite Aggression) accelerated Nasser's emergence as an Egyptian and Arab hero.

He soon after came to terms with Moscow for the financing of the Aswan High Dam—a step that enormously increased Soviet involvement in Egypt and set Nasser's Government on a policy of close ties with the Soviet Union.

In 1958, pursuant to his policy of pan-Arabism, Nasser succeeded in uniting Egypt and Syria into the United Arab Republic. Although this union had failed by 1961, it was not officially dissolved until 1984.

Nasser's domestic policies were arbitrary, frequently oppressive, and yet generally popular. All opposition was stamped out, and opponents of the regime frequently were imprisoned without trial. Nasser's foreign and military policies, among other things, helped provoke the Israeli attack of June 1967 that virtually destroyed Egypt's armed forces along with those of Jordan and Syria. Israel also occupied the Sinai peninsula, the Gaza Strip, the West Bank, and the Golan Heights. Nasser, nonetheless, was revered by the masses in Egypt and elsewhere in the Arab world until his death in 1970.

After Nasser's death, another of the original "free officers," Vice President Anwar el-Sadat, was elected President. In 1971, Sadat concluded a treaty of friendship with the Soviet Union but, a year later, ordered Soviet advisers to leave. In 1973, he launched the October war with Israel, in which Egypt's armed forces achieved initial successes but were defeated in Israeli counterattacks.

## Camp David and the Peace Process

In a momentous change from the Nasser era, President Sadat shifted Egypt from a policy of confrontation with Israel to one of peaceful accommodation through negotiations. Following the Sinai Disengagement Agreements of 1974 and 1975, Sadat created a fresh opening for progress by his dramatic visit to Jerusalem in November 1977. This led to President Jimmy Carter's invitation to President Sadat and Prime Minister Begin to join him in trilateral negotiations at Camp David.

The outcome was the historic Camp David accords, signed by Egypt and Israel and witnessed by the U.S. on September 17, 1978. The accords led to the March 26, 1979, signing of the Egypt-Israel peace treaty, by which Egypt regained control of the Sinai in May 1982. Throughout this period, U.S.-Egyptian relations steadily improved, but Sadat's willingness to break ranks by making peace with Israel earned him the enmity of most other Arab states.

In domestic policy, Sadat introduced greater political freedom and a new economic policy, the most important aspect of which was the infitah or "open door." This relaxed government controls over the economy and encouraged private investment. Sadat dismantled much of the policy apparatus and brought to trial a number of former government officials accused of criminal excesses during the Nasser era.

Liberalization also included the reinstitution of due process and the legal banning of torture. Sadat tried to expand participation in the political process in the mid-1970s but later abandoned this effort. In the last years of his life, Egypt was racked by violence arising from discontent with Sadat's rule and sectarian tensions, and it experienced a renewed measure of repression.

On October 6, 1981, President Sadat was assassinated by Islamic extremists. Hosni Mubarak, Vice President since 1975 and air force commander during the October 1973 war, was elected President later that month. He was re-elected to a second term in October 1987 and to a third term in October 1993. Mubarak has maintained Egypt's commitment to the Camp David peace process, while at the same time re-establishing Egypt's position as an Arab leader. Egypt was readmitted to the Arab League in 1989. Egypt has also played a moderating role in such international fora as the UN and the Nonaligned Movement.

Mubarak was elected chairman of the Organization of African Unity in 1989, and again at the OAU summit in Cairo in June 1993. Domestically, since 1991, Mubarak has undertaken an ambitious reform program to reduce the size of the public sector and expand the role of the private sector. There has also been a democratic opening and increased participation in the political process by opposition groups. The November 1990 National Assembly elections saw 61 members of the opposition win seats in the 454-seat assembly, despite a boycott by several opposition parties citing possible manipulation by Mubarak's National Democratic Party (NDP). The opposition parties have been weak and divided and are not yet credible alternatives to the NDP.

Freedom of the press has increased greatly. While concern remains that economic problems could promote increasing dissatisfaction with the government, President Mubarak enjoys broad support.

For several years, domestic political debate in Egypt has been concerned with the phenomenon of "Political Islam," a movement which seeks to establish a state and society governed strictly by Islamic doctrine. The Muslim Brotherhood, founded in Egypt in 1928, is legally proscribed but operates more or less openly. Egyptian law, however, prohibits the formation of religion-based political parties. Members of the Brotherhood have been elected to the People's Assembly as independents and have been elected to local councils as candidates on the Socialist Labor Party ticket.

# GOVERNMENT AND POLITICAL CONDITIONS

The Egyptian constitution provides for a strong executive. Authority is vested in an elected president who can appoint one or more vice presidents, a prime minister, and a cabinet. The president's term runs for six years. Egypt's legislative body, the People's Assembly, has 454 members—444 popularly elected and 10 appointed by the president. The constitution reserves 50% of the assembly seats for "workers and peasants." The assembly sits for a five-year term but can be dissolved earlier by the president. There is also a 258-member National Shura (consultative) Council, in which 86 members are appointed and 172 elected for six-year terms. Below the national level, authority is exercised by and through governors and mayors appointed by the central government and by popularly elected local councils.

Although power is concentrated in the hands of the president and the National Democratic Party majority in the People's Assembly, opposition party organizations make their views public and represent their followers at various levels in the political system.

In addition to the ruling National Democratic Party, there are nine other recognized parties. Since 1990, the number of recognized parties has doubled from five to 10. The law prohibits the formation of parties along class lines, thereby making it illegal for communist groups to organize formally as political parties.

Egyptians now enjoy considerable freedom of the press, and recognized opposition political parties operate freely. Although the November 1990 elections are generally considered to have been fair and free, there are significant restrictions on the political process and freedom of association for non-governmental organizations. Opposition parties continue to make credible complaints about electoral manipulation by the government. For example, in the 1989 Shura Council elections, the ruling NDP won 100% of the seats.

The process of gradual political liberalization begun by Sadat and continued under Mubarak is now on hold. A terrorist campaign that the government has been battling since 1992 has slowed the progress of democracy. Egyptian security services and terrorist groups remain locked in a cycle of violence. Groups seeking to overthrow the government have bombed banks and attacked and killed government officials, security forces, Egyptian Christians, secular intellectuals, and foreign tourists. They were responsible for the majority of civilian deaths in 1994. Some attacks have occurred in Cairo, but most of the violent incidents have taken place in the southern provinces of Assiyut, Minya, and Qena, which are located between Cairo and Luxor. A series of successful police counterterrorist operations since the beginning of 1994 has reduced terrorist capabilities and operations, particularly in Cairo; however, terrorists stepped up their activity in Minya in January 1995.

Egypt's judicial system is based on European (primarily French) legal concepts and methods. Under the Mubarak Government, the courts have demonstrated increasing independence, and the principles of due process and judicial review have gained greater respect. The legal code is derived largely from the Napoleonic Code. Marriage and personal status (family law) are primarily based on the religious law of the individual concerned, which for most Egyptians is Islamic Law (Sharia).

## National Security

Egypt's armed forces are among the largest in the region, and include the army (290,000), air defense (70,000), air force (30,000), and navy (20,000). The armed forces inventory includes equipment from the United States, France, Italy, the United Kingdom, the former Soviet Union, and China. Most of the equipment from the former Soviet Union is being replaced by more modern American, French, and British equipment, of which significant amounts are being built under license in Egypt. To bolster stability and moderation in the region, Egypt has provided military assistance and training to a number of African and Arab states.

## Principal Government Officials

For up-to-date information on Principal Government Officials, see the Chiefs of State and Cabinet Members of Foreign Governments section starting on page 1.

Egypt maintains an embassy in the United States at 3521 International Court NW, Washington, DC 20008 (tel. 202-895-5400). The Washington consulate has the same address (tel. 202-966-6342). The Egyptian mission to the United Nations is located at 36 East 67th Street, New York, NY (tel. 212-879-6300). Egyptian consulates general are located at: 1110 Second Avenue, New York, NY 10022 (tel. 212-759-7120); 2000 West Loop South, Suite 1750, Control Data Building, Houston, TX 77027 (tel. 713-961-4915); 505 N. Lake Shore Drive, Suite 4902, Chicago, IL 60611 (tel. 312-670-2655); and 3001 Pacific Avenue, San Francisco, CA 94115 (tel. 415-346-9700).

# ECONOMY

Under comprehensive economic reforms initiated in 1991, Egypt has relaxed many price controls, reduced subsidies, and partially liberalized trade and investment. Manufacturing is still dominated by the public sector, which controls virtually all heavy industry. A process of public sector reform and privatization has begun, however, which could enhance opportunities for the private sector. Agriculture, mainly in private hands, has been largely deregulated, with the exception of cotton and sugar production. Construction, non-financial

---

## Travel Notes

**Climate and clothing:** Clothing should be suitable for hot summers and temperate winters. Modest attire is required.

**Customs:** Visas are required. Travelers are advised to obtain visas through any Egyptian embassy or consulate prior to travel, although visas can also usually be obtained on arrival at Cairo Airport. Shots are not required for visitors coming from the United States or Europe, but yellow fever immunizations are required of travelers coming from infected areas. The Department of State Medical Division recommends that visitors to Egypt obtain typhoid, tetanus, polio, meningitis, gamma globulin, hepatitis B, measles-mumps-rubella, and rabies immunizations; however, travelers should consult their physicians.

**Health:** Travelers should be aware of prevalent rabies hazards, and, in some outlying areas, malaria.

**Telecommunications:** Telephone service is good and international direct dialing is available. Telegrams can be sent from the main post office and hotels, and telex service is available.

**Transportation:** Several international airlines serve Cairo. There is domestic air service between Cairo, Alexandria, Aswan, Luxor, Hurghada, the Sinai, and the New Valley. Rail service is available from Cairo to Aswan in the south and to Alexandria in the north. Taxis are often shared with other customers. Settle on a price before entering a taxi.

**Travel Advice:** For up-to-date information from the U.S. State Department on possible inconvenient or hazardous situations, see the **Travel Warnings and Consular Information Sheets from the U.S. Government** section starting on page 1723. For the latest information on health requirements and conditions, see the **International Travelers' Health Information** section starting on page 1385. For further information dealing with non-urgent matter, see the **Tips for Travelers to...** section starting on page 1588.

---

services, and domestic marketing are largely private.

## Agriculture

More than one-third of Egyptian labor is engaged directly in farming, and many others work in the processing or trading of agricultural products. Practically all Egyptian agriculture takes place in some 2.5 million hectares (6 million acres) of fertile soil in the Nile Valley and Delta. Some desert lands are being developed for agriculture, but other fertile lands in the Nile Valley and Delta are being lost to urbanization and erosion.

Warm weather and plentiful water permit several crops a year. Further improvement is possible, but agricultural productivity is already high, considering the traditional methods used. Egypt has little subsistence farming. Cotton, rice, onions, and beans are the principal crops. Cotton is the largest agricultural export earner.

The United States is a major supplier of wheat to Egypt, through commer-

cial sales and the PL 480 (Food for Peace) program. Other Western countries have also supplied food on concessional terms.

"Egypt," wrote the Greek historian Herodotus 25 centuries ago, "is the gift of the Nile." The land's seemingly inexhaustible resources of water and soil carried by this mighty river created in the Nile Valley and Delta the world's most extensive oasis. Without the Nile, Egypt would be little more than a desert wasteland.

The river carves a narrow, cultivated floodplain, never more than 20 kilometers wide, as it travels northward from Sudan to form Lake Nasser, behind the Aswan High Dam. Below the dam, just north of Cairo, the Nile spreads out over what was once a broad estuary that has been filled by riverine deposits to form a fertile delta about 250 kilometers wide (150 mi.) at the seaward base and about 160 kilometers (96 mi.) from south to north.

Before the construction of dams on the Nile, particularly the Aswan High Dam, the fertility of the Nile Valley was sustained by the water flow and the silt deposited by the annual flood. Sediment is now obstructed by the Aswan High Dam and retained in Lake Nasser. The interruption of yearly, natural fertilization and the increasing salinity of the soil have detracted somewhat from the high dam's value. Nevertheless, the benefits remain impressive: more intensive farming on millions of acres of land made possible by improved irrigation, prevention of flood damage, and the generation of billions of low-cost kilowatt hours of electricity.

The Western Desert accounts for about two-thirds of the country's land area. For the most part, it is a massive sandy plateau marked by seven major depressions. One of these, Fayoum, was connected about 3,600 years ago to the Nile by canals. Today, it is an important irrigated agricultural area.

## Natural Resources

In addition to the agricultural capacity of the Nile Valley and delta, Egypt's natural resources include petroleum, natural gas, phosphates, and iron ore. Petroleum deposits are found primarily in the Gulf of Suez, the Nile delta, and the Western Desert. The petroleum and natural gas sector accounted for approximately 10% of GDP in FY 1991.

Petroleum products represented about 45% of export earnings during that period. The fall in world oil prices after the 1991 Gulf war pushed Egypt's benchmark "Suez Blend" to an average price of $15 per barrel in 1991, compared with $20 per barrel in 1990. Thus, the value of Egyptian crude oil exports dropped to $1.2 billion in 1991 versus $1.5 billion in 1990.

Petroleum production dropped slightly in 1991 to 44 million tons at 870,000 barrels per day. To limit the domestic consumption of oil, Egypt is encouraging the production of natural gas. Natural gas output continues to increase and reached 7.2 million metric tons equivalent in 1991.

Twelve petroleum exploration agreements were signed in 1992, under which six companies are expected to spend over $90 million to drill 24 wells.

Since 1991, the government has tried to attract enough foreign investment to maintain existing exploration and production and attract new investment. In October 1991, the government adopted a market-determined petroleum export pricing formula.

## Transport and Communication

Transportation facilities in Egypt are centered on Cairo and largely follow the pattern of settlement along the Nile. The major line of the nation's 4,800-kilometer (2,800-mi.) railway network runs from Alexandria to Aswan. The well-maintained road network has expanded rapidly to over 21,000 miles, covering the Nile valley and delta, Mediterranean and Red Sea coasts, the Sinai, and the Western oases.

Egyptair provides reliable domestic air services to major tourist destinations from its Cairo hub (in addition to overseas routes). The Nile River system (about 1,600 km. or 1,000 mi.) and the principal canals (1,600 km.) are important locally for transportation. The Suez Canal is a major waterway of international commerce and navigation, linking the Mediterranean and Red Seas. Major ports are Alexandria, Port Said, and Damietta on the Mediterranean, and Suez and Safraga on the Red Sea.

Egypt has long been the cultural and informational center of the Arab world, and Cairo is the region's largest publishing and broadcasting center. There are eight daily newspapers with a total circulation of more than 2 million, and a number of monthly newspapers, magazines, and journals. The majority of political parties have their own newspapers, and these papers conduct a lively, often highly partisan, debate on public issues.

Radio and television are owned and controlled by the government through the Egyptian Radio and Television Federation. The federation operates two national television networks and three regional stations in Cairo, Alexandria, and Ismailia. The government also beams daily satellite programming to the rest of the Arab world, the U.K., and the U.S.

# FOREIGN RELATIONS

Egypt was readmitted to the Arab League in May 1989, and the Arab League headquarters has returned to Cairo from Tunis. Former Egyptian Foreign Minister Abdel Meguid is the present Secretary General of the Arab League. President Mubarak chaired the Organization of African Unity from 1989 to 1990 and again in 1993. In 1991, Egyptian Deputy Prime Minister Boutros Boutros-Ghali was elected Secretary General of the United Nations.

Egypt played a key role during the 1990-91 Gulf crisis. President Mubarak helped assemble the international coalition and deployed 35,000 Egyptian troops against Iraq to liberate Kuwait. The Egyptian contingent was the second largest in the coalition forces. In the aftermath of the Gulf war, Egypt signed the Damascus declaration with Syria and the Gulf states to strengthen Gulf security.

Egypt also played an important role in the negotiations leading to the Madrid Peace Conference in 1991, which, under U.S. and Russian sponsorship, brought together all parties in the region to discuss Middle East peace. Since then, Egypt has been an active participant in the peace process and has been a strong supporter of the bilateral discussions leading to the 1993 "declaration of principles" and the October 1994 signing of the Jordan-Israel peace treaty.

Egyptian-Israeli relations improved after Labor's 1992 victory in Israeli national elections, and Egypt and Israel are committed to improving their bilateral relationship. By mid-1993, President Mubarak and Prime Minister Rabin had met twice, and other senior-level bilateral contacts have increased. There has also been progress on the return of Sinai antiquities to Egypt and on issues relating to military personnel missing in action. Agricultural cooperation continues to be the most active area of Egyptian-Israeli technical cooperation.

# U.S.-EGYPTIAN RELATIONS

President Mubarak has long been a supporter of a strong U.S.-Egyptian relationship based on shared interests in regional security and stability and the peaceful resolution of international disputes. President Mubarak was the first Arab leader to visit the U.S. after President Clinton's inauguration. President Clinton visited Egypt in October 1994 enroute to Jordan for the signing of the Jordan-Israel peace treaty. The two countries have worked closely together to promote a peaceful settlement of the Arab-Israeli conflict and to resolve conflicts in Africa—including most recently participation by Egyptian soldiers in UN peace-keeping efforts in Somalia.

An important pillar of the bilateral relationship remains U.S. security and economic assistance to Egypt, which expanded significantly in the wake of the Egyptian-Israeli Peace Treaty in 1979. In FY 1993, total U.S. assistance levels to Egypt were $1.3 billion in foreign military sales (FMS) grants and $815 million in economic support fund grants. The Egyptians

have used FMS to support their military modernization program. PL 480 food aid in FY 1993 amounted to $50 million, down from $150 million annually in previous years, due to Egypt's increased commercial purchases.

U.S. assistance promotes Egypt's economic development, supports U.S.-Egyptian cooperation, and enhances regional stability. U.S. economic aid stimulates economic growth by funding major projects in electric power generation, telecommunications, housing and transport, and the financing of commodity imports such as raw materials and capital equipment. Power plants built with U.S. assistance generate more electricity than the Aswan High Dam.

Vice President Gore and President Mubarak launched in September 1994 a bilateral partnership for economic growth and development, designed to foster high-level economic policy dialogue between the two governments. The Gore-Mubarak initiative will encourage and facilitate private sector contacts, strengthen technology cooperation, and promote economic growth and development. It will also foster job growth and technological development of Egyptian firms. In addition, it will enhance the environment for the development of the Egyptian private sector and increase the impact of existing U.S. assistance on Egyptian economic growth.

Since 1975, the United States has provided $2.2 billion to improve and expand water and sewage systems in

Cairo, Alexandria, and other Egyptian cities. U.S. military cooperation has helped Egypt modernize its armed forces and strengthen regional security and stability. Under FMS programs, the U.S. has provided F-4 jet aircraft, F-16 jet fighters, M- 60A3 and M1A1 tanks, armored personnel carriers, Apache helicopters, antiaircraft missile batteries, aerial surveillance aircraft, and other equipment.

The U.S. and Egypt also participate in combined military exercises, including deployment of U.S. troops to Egypt. Units of the U.S. 6th Fleet are regular visitors to Egyptian ports.

## Principal U.S. Embassy Officials

**For up-to-date information on Principal U.S. Officials, see the U.S. Embassies, Consulates, and Foreign Service section starting on page 139.**

The U.S. embassy in Cairo is located on Lazoughli Street, Garden City, near downtown Cairo. The mailing address for the embassy from the U.S. is American Embassy, APO AE 09839-4900; from Egypt, it is 8 Sharia Kamal El-Din Salah, Garden City, Cairo. The telephone number is (20) (2)355- 7371; fax (20) (2)355-7375; telex 93773 Amemb UN. The embassy is closed on all U.S. federal holidays and some Egyptian holidays.

# EL SALVADOR

April 2001

## Official Name:
## Republic of El Salvador

# PROFILE

## Geography

**Area:** 21,476 sq. km. (8,260 sq. mi.); about the size of Massachusetts.
**Cities:** Capital—San Salvador (pop. 1.7 million). Other cities—San Miguel, Ahuachapan, Santa Ana, Sonsonate.
**Terrain:** Mountains separate country into three distinct regions—southern coastal belt, central valleys and plateaus, and northern mountains.
**Climate:** Semitropical, distinct wet and dry seasons.

## People

**Nationality:** Noun and adjective—Salvadoran(s).
**Population:** (1999) 6.2 million.
**Annual growth rate:** (1999) 2%.
**Ethnic groups:** Mestizo 90%, indigenous 1%, Caucasian 9%.
**Religion:** Largely Roman Catholic, with growing Protestant groups throughout the country.
**Language:** Spanish.
**Education:** Free through ninth grade. Attendance (grades 1–9)—82%. Literacy—72% among adults.
**Health:** Infant mortality rate (1999)—28/1,000. Life expectancy (1999)—males 67 yrs., females 74 yrs.

**Work force:** (approximately 2.4 million) Agriculture—25%; services—21%; commerce—22%; manufacturing—19%; construction—7%; transportation and communication—4% other—2%.

## Government

**Type:** Republic.
**Constitution:** December 20, 1983.
**Independence:** September 15, 1821.
**Branches**: Executive—president and vice president. Legislative—84-member Legislative Assembly. Judicial—independent (Supreme Court). Administrative subdivisions: 14 departments.
**Political parties:** (represented in the Legislature) Farabundo Marti National Liberation Front (FMLN), Nationalist Republican Alliance (ARENA), National Conciliation Party (PCN), Christian Democratic Party (PDC), and the National Action Party (PAN).
**Suffrage:** Universal at 18.

## Economy (1999)

**GDP:** $12.4 billion.
**Annual growth rate:** 2.6%.
**Per capita income:** $2,013.
**Agriculture:** (12% of GDP) Products—coffee, sugar, livestock, corn, poultry, sorghum. Arable, cultivated, or pasture land—64%.

**Industry:** (22% of GDP) Types—food and beverage processing, textiles, footwear and clothing, chemical products, petroleum products, electronics. Trade: Exports—$2.5 billion: coffee, sugar, textiles, shrimp. Major markets—U.S. 64%, Central American Common Market (CACM) 25%, European Union (EU) 4%. Imports—$4.1 billion: consumer goods, foodstuffs, capital goods, raw industrial materials, petroleum. Major suppliers—U.S. 51.7%, CACM 16%, Mexico 5%, EU 2%, Japan 3%.

# PEOPLE

El Salvador's population numbers about 6.2 million; almost 90% is of mixed Indian and Spanish extraction. About 1% is indigenous; very few Indians have retained their customs and traditions.

The country's people are largely Roman Catholic—though Protestant groups are growing—and Spanish is the language spoken by virtually all inhabitants. The capital city of San Salvador has about 1.7 million people; an estimated 42% of El Salvador's population live in rural areas.

# HISTORY

Before the Spanish conquest, the area that is now El Salvador was made up of two large Indian states and several principalities. The indigenous inhabitants were the Pipils, a tribe of nomadic Nahua people long established in Central Mexico. Early in their history, they became one of the few Mesoamerican Indian groups to abolish human sacrifice. Otherwise, their culture was similar to that of their Aztec neighbors. Remains of Nahua culture are still found at ruins such as Tazumal (near Chalchuapa), San Andres (northeast of Armenia), and Joya De Ceren (north of Colón). The first Spanish attempt to subjugate this area failed in 1524, when Pedro de Alvarado was forced to retreat by Pipil warriors. In 1525, he returned and succeeded in bringing the district under control of the Captaincy General of Guatemala, which retained its authority until 1821, despite an abortive revolution in 1811.

## Independence

In 1821, El Salvador and the other Central American provinces declared their independence from Spain. When these provinces were joined with Mexico in early 1822, El Salvador resisted, insisting on autonomy for the Central American countries. Guatemalan troops sent to enforce the union were driven out of El Salvador in June 1822. El Salvador, fearing incorporation into Mexico, petitioned the U.S. Government for statehood. But in 1823, a revolution in Mexico ousted Emperor Augustin Iturbide, and a new Mexican congress voted to allow the Central American provinces to decide their own fate. That year, the United Provinces of Central America was formed of the five Central American states under Gen. Manuel Jose Arce. When this federation was dissolved in 1838, El Salvador became an independent republic. El Salvador's early history as an independent state—as with others in Central America—was marked by frequent revolutions; not until the period 1900–30 was relative stability achieved. The economic elite ruled

the country in conjunction with the military, and the power structure was controlled by a relatively small number of wealthy landowners, known as the 14 Families. The economy, based on coffee-growing, prospered or suffered as the world coffee price fluctuated. From 1932—the year of Gen. Maximiliano Hernandez Martinez's coup following his brutal suppression of rural resistance—until 1980, all but one Salvadoran temporary president was an army officer. Periodic presidential elections were seldom free or fair.

## From Military to Civilian Rule

From the 1930s to the 1970s, authoritarian governments employed political repression and limited reform to maintain power, despite the trappings of democracy. During the 1970s, the political situation began to unravel. In the 1972 presidential election, the opponents of military rule united under Jose Napoleon Duarte, leader of the Christian Democratic Party (PDC). Amid widespread fraud, Duarte's broad-based reform movement was defeated. Subsequent protests and an attempted coup were crushed and Duarte exiled. These events eroded hope of reform through democratic means and persuaded those opposed to the government that armed insurrection was the only way to achieve change. As a consequence, leftist groups capitalizing upon social discontent gained strength. By 1979, leftist guerrilla warfare had broken out in the cities and the countryside, launching what became a 12-year civil war. A cycle of violence took hold as rightist vigilante death squads in turn killed thousands. The poorly trained Salvadoran Armed Forces (ESAF) also engaged in repression and indiscriminate killings.

After the collapse of the Somoza regime in Nicaragua that year, the new Sandinista Government provided large amounts of arms and munitions to five Salvadoran guerrilla groups. On October 15, 1979, reform-minded military officers and civilian leaders ousted the right-wing government of Gen. Carlos Humberto

Romero (1977–79) and formed a revolutionary junta. PDC leader Duarte joined the junta in March 1980, leading the provisional government until the elections of March 1982. The junta initiated a land reform program and nationalized the banks and the marketing of coffee and sugar. Political parties were allowed to function again, and on March 28, 1982, Salvadorans elected a new constituent assembly. Following that election, authority was peacefully transferred to Alvaro Magana, the provisional president selected by the assembly.

The 1983 constitution, drafted by the assembly, strengthened individual rights, established safeguards against excessive provisional detention and unreasonable searches, established a republican, pluralistic form of government, strengthened the legislative branch, and enhanced judicial independence. It also codified labor rights, particularly for agricultural workers. The newly initiated reforms, though, did not satisfy the guerrilla movements, which had unified under Cuban auspices—while each retained their autonomous status—as the Farabundo Marti National Liberation Front (FMLN). Duarte won the 1984 presidential election against rightist Roberto D'Aubuisson of the Nationalist Republican Alliance (ARENA) with 54% of the vote and became the first freely elected president of El Salvador in more than 50 years. In 1989, ARENA's Alfredo Cristiani won the presidential election with 54% of the vote. His inauguration on June 1, 1989, marked the first time that power had passed peacefully from one freely elected civilian leader to another.

## Ending the Civil War

Upon his inauguration in June 1989, President Cristiani called for direct dialogue to end the decade of conflict between the government and guerrillas. An unmediated dialogue process involving monthly meetings between the two sides was initiated in September 1989, lasting until the FMLN launched a bloody, nationwide offensive in November of that year. In early 1990, following a request from the Central American presidents, the United Nations became involved in an effort to mediate direct talks between the two sides. After a year of little progress, the government and the FMLN accepted an invitation from the UN Secretary General to meet in New York City. On September 25, 1991, the two sides signed the New York City Accord. It concentrated the negotiating process into one phase and created the Committee for the Consolidation of the Peace (COPAZ), made up of representatives of the government, FMLN, and political parties, with

Catholic Church and UN observers. On December 31, 1991, the government and the FMLN initialed a peace agreement under the auspices of then Secretary General Perez de Cuellar. The final agreement, called the Accords of Chapultepec, was signed in Mexico City on January 16, 1992. A 9-month cease-fire took effect February 1, 1992, and was never broken. A ceremony held on December 15, 1992, marked the official end of the conflict, concurrent with the demobilization of the last elements of the FMLN military structure and the FMLN's inception as a political party.

# GOVERNMENT AND POLITICAL CONDITIONS

El Salvador is a democratic republic governed by a president and an 84-member unicameral Legislative Assembly. The president is elected by universal suffrage and serves for a 5-year term by absolute majority vote. A second round runoff is required in the event that no candidate receives more than 50% of the first round vote. Members of the assembly, also elected by universal suffrage, serve for 3-year terms. The country has an independent judiciary and Supreme Court.

The most recent presidential election, in March 1999, was free and fair, but voter turnout was low (39%). ARENA presidential candidate Francisco

Guillermo Flores Perez faced Facundo Guardado of the CC party and won with 52% of the votes. Since Flores received just over 50% of the votes, a runoff was not required. Francisco Guillermo Flores Perez of the ARENA party began his 5-year term as president in June 1999, and cannot succeed himself. In the March 2000 legislative races, FMLN won 31 seats in the Legislative Assembly, the ARENA won 29, the National Conciliation Party (PCN) 14, the PDC five, and the Coalition Democratic United Center (CDU) and National Action Party (PAN) winning 3 and 2 seats, respectively.

Although the FMLN is now the majority seat holder in the Legislative Assembly in El Salvador, ARENA's 31 seats and the PCN's 14 seats guarantee the rightwing block a bare majority (43 out of 84) in the Legislative Assembly. A post-electoral controversy over the Fifth District in La Libertad, which the PDC claimed to have won, was ultimately decided in favor of the PCN. The FMLN retained the capital city of San Salvador as incumbent Hector Silva was re-elected. Unfortunately voter turnout was low. Only 35% of eligible voters cast ballots.

## Political Parties

ARENA is El Salvador's leading political party. It was created in 1982 by Roberto D'Aubuisson and other ultra-rightists, including some members of the military. His electoral fortunes were diminished by credible reports that he was involved in organized political violence. Following the 1984 presidential election, ARENA began reaching out to more moderate individuals and groups, particularly in the private sector. By 1989, ARENA had attracted the support of business groups, and Alfredo Cristiani won the presidency. Despite sincere efforts at reform, Duarte's PDC administration had failed to either end the insurgency or improve the economy. Allegations of corruption, poor relations with the private sector, and historically low prices for the nation's main agricultural exports also contributed to ARENA victories in the 1988 legislative and 1989 presidential elec-

tions. The 1989-94 Cristiani administration's successes in achieving a peace agreement to end the civil war and in improving the nation's economy helped ARENA, led by standard-bearer Calderon Sol, keep both the presidency and a working majority in the Legislative Assembly in the 1994 elections. ARENA's legislative position was weakened in the 1997 elections, but it recovered its strength, helped by divisions in the opposition, in time for another victory in the 1999 presidential race that brought President Flores to office.

In the March 2000 legislative and municipal elections, ARENA won 29 seats in the Legislative Assembly and 127 mayoral races. In December 1992, the FMLN became a political party, composed of the political factions of the wartime guerrilla movement, and maintained a united front during the 1994 electoral campaign. The FMLN also came in second in the legislative assembly races. Internal political differences, however, among the FMLN's constituent parties led to the breakaway of two of the FMLN's original five factions after the 1994 elections. Despite the defections, the FMLN was able to consolidate its remaining factions and present itself as a viable option to ARENA in the 1997 elections. Divisions between "orthodox" and "reformist" wings of the FMLN crippled the party in the 1999 elections. In the March 2000 legislative and municipal elections, FMLN received 31 seats on the Legislative Assembly, which is three more than rival party ARENA. FMLN also won 77 mayorships and won 10 municipalities in coalition with other parties. The right wing of the National Conciliation Party (PCN), which ruled the country in alliance with the military from the 1960s until 1979, maintains a small electoral base, and gained 10 seats in the March 2000 legislative election. Several smaller parties have in recent years fought for space in the political center with limited success. The PDC, which won more municipal elections in 1994 than did the FMLN, is now down to five seats in the Legislative Assembly and is no longer a significant electoral force.

## Compliance With the Peace Accords

While most aspects of the accords have been largely implemented, important components such as judicial reform remain incomplete. The peace process set up under the Chapultepec Accords was monitored by the United Nations from 1991 until June 1997 when it closed its special monitoring mission in El Salvador.

## Human Rights

During the 12-year civil war, human rights violations by both left- and right-wing forces were rampant. The accords established a Truth Commission under UN auspices to investigate the most serious cases. The commission reported its findings in 1993. It recommended that those identified as human rights violators be removed from all government and military posts, as well as recommending judicial reforms. Thereafter, the Legislative Assembly granted amnesty for political crimes committed during the war. Among those freed as a result were the ESAF officers convicted in the November 1989 Jesuit murders and the FMLN ex-combatants held for the 1991 murders of two U.S. servicemen. The peace accords also required the establishment of the Ad Hoc Commission to evaluate the human rights record of the ESAF officer corps.

In 1993, the last of the 103 officers identified by this commission as responsible for human rights violations were retired, and the UN observer mission declared the government in compliance with the Ad Hoc Commission recommendations. Also in 1993, the Government of El Salvador and the UN established the Joint Group to investigate whether illegal, armed, politically motivated groups continued to exist after the signing of the peace accords. The group reported its findings in 1994 stating that death squads were no longer active but that violence was still being used to obtain political ends. The group recommended a special National Civilian Police (PNC) unit be created to investigate political

and organized crime and that further reforms be made in the judicial system. Not all the group's recommendations were implemented. The peace accords provided for the establishment of a Human Rights Ombudsman's Office.

## Military Reform

In accordance with the peace agreements, the constitution was amended to prohibit the military from playing an internal security role except under extraordinary circumstances. Demobilization of Salvadoran military forces generally proceeded on schedule throughout the process. The Treasury Police and National Guard were abolished, and military intelligence functions were transferred to civilian control. By 1993—9 months ahead of schedule—the military had cut personnel from a wartime high of 63,000 to the level of 32,000 required by the peace accords. By 1999, ESAF strength stood at less than 15,000, including uniformed and non-uniformed personnel, consisting of personnel in the army, navy, and air force. A purge of military officers accused of human rights abuses and corruption was completed in 1993 in compliance with the Ad Hoc Commission's recommendations.

## National Civilian Police

The new civilian police force, created to replace the discredited public security forces, deployed its first officers in March 1993, and was present throughout the country by the end of 1994. As of 1999, the PNC had over 18,000 officers. The United States, through the Department of Justice's International Criminal Investigative Training Assistance Program (ICITAP), has led international support for the PNC and the National Public Security Academy (ANSP), providing more than $30 million in nonlethal equipment and training since 1992. The Justice Department's ICITAP program plans to spend $1.5 million on assistance to the PNC in 2000. The ICITAP mission is to help the ANSP and the PNC to develop more experience in police techniques and procedures and assist with the

development of an efficient operation and administration.

The PNC faces many challenges in building a completely new police force. With common crime rising dramatically since the end of the war, over 500 PNC officers had been killed in the line of duty by late 1998. PNC officers also have arrested a number of their own in connection with various high-profile crimes, and a "purification" process to weed out unfit personnel from throughout for force was undertaken late in 2000. U.S. assistance—about $1.2 million—is critical in helping start innovative community policing programs that attack the gang problem head-on, training criminal investigators and improving the training of police supervisors.

## Judiciary

Both the Truth Commission and the Joint Group identified weaknesses in the judiciary and recommended solutions, the most dramatic being the replacement of all the magistrates on the Supreme Court. This recommendation was fulfilled in 1994 when an entirely new court was elected. The process of replacing incompetent judges in the lower courts, and of strengthening the attorney general's and public defender's offices, has moved more slowly. The government continues to work in all of these areas with the help of international donors, including the United States. Action on peace-accord driven constitutional reforms designed to improve the administration of justice was largely completed in 1996 with legislative approval of several amendments and the revision of the Criminal Procedure Code—with broad political consensus.

## Land Transfers

More than 35,000 eligible beneficiaries from among the former guerrillas and soldiers who fought the war received land under the Peace Accord-mandated land transfer program which ended in January 1997. The majority of them also have received agricultural credits. The international community, the Salvadoran Government, the former rebels, and the various financial institutions involved in the process continue to work closely together to deal with follow-on issues resulting from the program.

## Principal Government Officials

For up-to-date information on Principal Government Officials, see the Chiefs of State and Cabinet Members of Foreign Governments section starting on page 1.

El Salvador maintains an embassy in the United States at 2308 California Street NW, Washington, DC 20008 (tel: (202) 265–9671).
There are consulates in Chicago, Houston, Los Angeles, Miami, New Orleans, New York, and San Francisco.

# ECONOMY

The Salvadoran economy continues to benefit from a commitment to free markets and careful fiscal management. The impact of the civil war on El Salvador's economy was devastating; from 1979–90, losses from damage to infrastructure and means of production due to guerrilla sabotage as well as from reduced export earnings totaled about $2.2 billion. But since attacks on economic targets ended in 1992, improved investor confidence has led to increased private investment.

Rich soil, moderate climate, and a hard-working and enterprising labor pool comprise El Salvador's greatest assets. Much of the improvement in El Salvador's economy is due to free market policy initiatives carried out by the Cristiani and Calderon Sol governments, including the privatization of the banking system, telecommunications, public pensions, electrical distribution and some electrical generation, reduction of import duties, elimination of price controls on virtually all consumer products,

and enhancing the investment climate through measures such as improved enforcement of intellectual property rights.

The post-war boom in the Salvadoran economy began to fade in July 1995 after an abrupt shift in monetary policy was followed by a June increase in the value added tax (VAT) and price hikes in basic public services. The slowdown lingered into 1996. Growth in GDP in 1996 was a mere 2.1%, but by 1997 it had picked up to 4%. In 1998, El Salvador's economy grew by 3.2% compared to the 4.2% growth posted in 1997. The damage caused by Hurricane Mitch to infrastructure and to agricultural production reduced 1998 growth by an estimated .5%. Growth weakened further (to 2.6%) in 1999 due to poor international prices for El Salvador's principal export commodities, weak exports to Central American neighbors recovering from Hurricane Mitch, and an investment slowdown caused by the March 1999 presidential elections and delays in legislative approval of a national budget. It picked up slightly to 3% in 2000. Because of the earthquakes that struck the country in January and February, prospects for any growth in 2001 are dim. Inflation for 1998 was 4%, and remained stable in 1999–2000.

Fiscal policy has been the biggest challenge for the Salvadoran Government. The 1992 peace accords committed the government to heavy expenditures for transition programs and social services. Although international aid was generous, the government has focused on improving the collection of its current revenues. A 10% value-added tax, implemented in September 1992, was raised to 13% in July 1995. The VAT is estimated to have contributed 51% of total tax revenues in 1999, due mainly to improved collection techniques. A multiple exchange rate regime that had been used to conserve foreign exchange was phased out during 1990 and replaced by a free-floating rate. The colón depreciated from five to the dollar in 1989 to eight in 1991, and in 1993, was informally pegged at 8.73 colónes to the dollar, later adjusted to 8.79. Large inflows of dol-

lars in the form of family remittances from Salvadorans working in the United States offset a substantial trade deficit and support the exchange rate. The monthly average of remittances reported by the Central Bank is around $117 million, with the total estimated at more than $1.4 billion for 1999. As of December 1999, net international reserves equaled $1.8 billion or roughly 5 months of imports. Having this hard currency buffer to work with, the Salvadoran Government undertook a "monetary integration plan" beginning January 1, 2001, by which the dollar became legal tender alongside the colón. No more colónes are to be printed, the economy is expected to be, in practice, fully dollarized, and the Central Reserve Bank dissolved, by late 2003. The FMLN is strongly opposed to the plan, regarding it as unconstitutional, and plans to make it an issue in the 2003 legislative elections.

## Foreign Debt and Assistance

El Salvador's external debt decreased sharply in 1993, chiefly as a result of an agreement under which the United States forgave about $461 million of official debt. As a result, total debt service decreased by 16% over 1992. External debt stood at $2.8 billion at the end of 1999. Debt service amounted to 2.5% of GDP in 1998 and is considered moderate. The Government of El Salvador has been successful in obtaining significant new credits from the international financial institutions. Among the most significant loans are a second structural adjustment loan from the World Bank for $52.5 million, another World Bank loan of $40 million for agricultural reform, a $20 million loan from the Central American Bank for Economic Integration to be used to repair roads, and a $60 million Inter-American Development Bank loan for poverty alleviation projects. Total non-U.S. Government aid, excluding NGO assistance and bilateral loan programs, reached $38 million in1999. Although official figures show relatively small and diminishing aid flows, the total is probably larger. Significant amounts come in

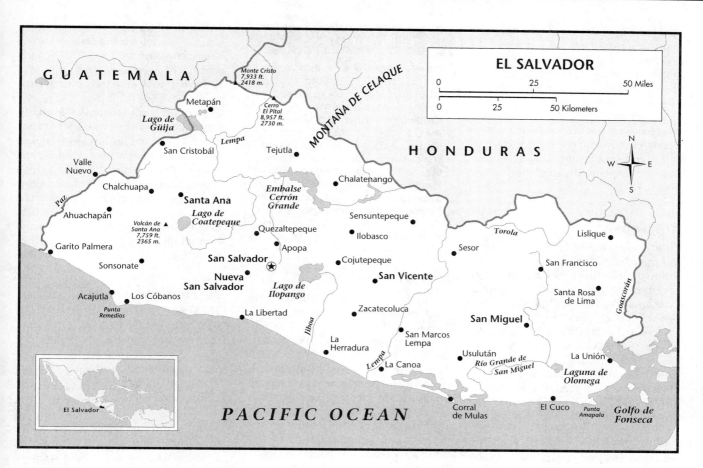

through nongovernmental organizations and are channeled to groups not generally included in official statistics, such as political parties, unions, and churches. Some $300 million has been contracted from international institutions and governments for infrastructure works and social programs to be undertaken. The debt profile is expected to increase over the next several years as the international donor community has pledged $1.26 billion to finance El Salvador's reconstruction and modernization. Large loans now being sought to finance reconstruction from the 2001 earthquakes will further alter the country's debt profile.

## Natural Disasters: Hurricane Mitch (1998) and the Earthquakes (2001)

Hurricane Mitch hit El Salvador in late October 1998, generating extreme rainfall of which caused widespread flooding and landslides. Roughly 65,200 hectares were flooded, and the Salvadoran Government pronounced 374 people dead or missing. In addition, approximately 55,864 people were rendered homeless. The areas that suffered the most were the low-lying coastal zones, particularly in the floodplain of the Lempa and Sam Miguel Grande rivers. Three major bridges that cross the Lempa were swept away, restricting access to the eastern third of the country and forcing the emergency evacuation of many communities. The heavy rainfall, flooding, and mudslides caused by Hurricane Mitch also severely damaged El Salvador's road network. Along with the three major bridges over the Lempa River, 12 other bridges were damaged or destroyed by the Mitch flooding.

The largest single-affected sector was El Salvador's agriculture. Nearly 18% of the total 1998–99 basic grain harvest was lost. Coffee production was hit particularly hard; 3% of the harvest was lost in addition to 8.2% that was lost earlier in the year due to El Nino. Major losses of sugarcane, totaling 9% of the estimated 1998–99 production, were sustained primarily in the coastal regions. Livestock losses amounted to $1 million, including 2,992 head of cattle. In addition to these losses, El Salvador also had to face the threat of disease outbreak. The Ministry of Health recorded a total of 109,038 medical cases related to Hurricane Mitch between October 31 and November 18, 1998; 23% of these cases were respiratory infections, followed by skin ailments, diarrhea, and conjunctivitis.

Reconstruction from Mitch was still underway when, in early 2001, the country experienced a series of devastating earthquakes that left nearly 2,000 people dead or missing, 8,000 injured, and caused severe dislocations across all sectors of Salvadoran society. Nearly 25% of all private homes in the country were either destroyed or badly damaged, and 1.5 million persons were left without housing. Hundreds of public buildings were damaged or destroyed, and sanitation and water systems in many communities put out service. The total cost of the damage was estimated at between $1.5 billion and $2 billion, and the devastation thought to equal or surpass that of the 1986 quake that struck San Salvador. Given the magnitude of the disaster, reconstruction and economic recovery will remain the primary focus of the Salvadoran Government for some time to come.

## Response

The Hurricane Mitch disaster prompted a tremendous response from the international community governments, nongovernmental organizations (NGOs), and private citizens alike. Sixteen foreign governments—including the U.S., 19 international NGOs, 20 Salvadoran embassies and consulates, and 20 private firms and individuals provided El Salvador with in-kind assistance. The Government of El Salvador reports that 961 tons of goods and food were received. The Ministry of Foreign Affairs estimates that contribution in cash given directly to the Salvadoran Government totaled $4.3 million. The U.S. Government has provided $37.7 million in assistance through USAID and the U.S. Departments of Agriculture and Defense.

Following the 2001 earthquakes, the U.S. Embassy assumed a leading role in implementing U.S. sponsored assistance. The U.S. Government responded immediately to the emergency, with military helicopters active in initial rescue operations, delivering emergency supplies, rescue workers, and damage assessment teams to stricken communities all over the country. USAID's Office of Foreign Disaster Assistance had a team of experts working with Salvadoran relief authorities immediately after both quakes, and provided assistance totaling more than $14 million. In addition, the Department of Defense provided an initial response valued at more than $11 million. For long-term reconstruction, the international community offered a total aid package of $1.3 billion, over $110 million of it from the United States.

**Travel Notes**

**Travel Advice:** For up-to-date information from the U.S. State Department on possible inconvenient or hazardous situations, see the **Travel Warnings and Consular Information Sheets from the U.S. Government** section starting on page 1723. For the latest information on health requirements and conditions, see the **International Travelers' Health Information** section starting on page 1385. For further information dealing with non-urgent matter, see the **Tips for Travelers to...** section starting on page 1588.

## Manufacturing

El Salvador historically has been the most industrialized nation in Central America, though a decade of war eroded this position. In 1999, manufacturing accounted for 22% of GDP. The industrial sector has shifted since 1993 from a primarily domestic orientation to include free zone (maquiladora) manufacturing for export. Maquila exports have led the growth in the export sector and in the last 3 years have made an important contribution to the Salvadoran economy.

## Trade

El Salvador's balance of payments continued to show a net surplus. Exports in 1999 grew 1.9% while imports grew 3%, narrowing El Salvador's trade deficit. As in the previous year, the large trade deficit was offset by foreign aid and family remittances. Remittances are increasing at an annual rate of 6.5%, and an estimated $1.35 billion will enter the national economy during 1999. Private foreign capital continued to flow in, though mostly as short-term import financing and not at the levels of previous years. The Central American Common Market continued its dynamic reactivation process, now with most regional commerce duty-free. In September 1996, El Salvador, Guatemala, and Honduras opened free trade talks with Mexico. Although tariff cuts that were expected in July 1996 were delayed until 1997, the Government of El Salvador is committed to a free and open economy. Total U.S. exports to El Sal-

vador reached $2.1 billion in 1999, while El Salvador exported $1.6 billion to the United States. U.S. support for El Salvador's privatization of the electrical and telecommunications markets has markedly expanded opportunities for U.S. investment in the country. More than 300 U.S. companies have established either a permanent commercial presence in El Salvador or work through representative offices in the country. The Department of State maintains a Country Commercial Guide for U.S. businesses seeking detailed information on business opportunities in El Salvador.

## Agriculture and Land Reform

Before 1980, a small economic elite owned most of the land in El Salvador and controlled a highly successful agricultural industry. About 70% of farmers were sharecroppers or laborers on large plantations. Many farm workers were under- or unemployed and impoverished. The civilian-military junta, which came to power in 1979, instituted an ambitious land reform program to redress the inequities of the past, respond to the legitimate grievances of the rural poor, and promote more broadly based growth in the agricultural sector. The ultimate goal was to develop a rural middle class with a stake in a peaceful and prosperous future for El Salvador. At least 525,000 people—more than 12% of El Salvador's population at the time and perhaps 25% of the rural poor—benefited from agrarian reform, and more than 22% of El Salvador's total farmland was transferred to those who previously worked the land but did not own it. But when agrarian reform ended in 1990, about 150,000 landless families still had not benefited from the reform actions. The 1992 peace accords made provisions for land transfers to all qualified ex-combatants of both the FMLN and ESAF, as well as to landless peasants living in former conflict areas. The United States undertook to provide $300 million for a national reconstruction plan. This included $60 million for land purchases and $17 million for agricultural credits. USAID remains actively involved in providing technical training, access to credit, and other financial services for many of the land beneficiaries.

# FOREIGN RELATIONS

In March, 2001, President Flores met with President Bush in Washington, D.C., to discuss the disastrous earthquakes that had recently struck El Salvador, and U.S. support for the process of recovery and reconstruction. Salvador is a member of the United Nations and several of its specialized agencies, the Organization of American States (OAS), the Central American Common Market (CACM), the Central American Parliament (PARLACEN), and the Central American Integration System (SICA). It actively participates in the Central American Security Commission (CASC), which seeks to promote regional arms control. El Salvador also is a member of the World Trade Organization and is pursuing regional free trade agreements. An active participant in the Summit of the Americas process, El Salvador chairs a working group on market access under the Free Trade Area of the Americas initiative. El Salvador has joined its six Central American neighbors in signing the Alliance for Sustainable Development, known as the Conjunta Centroamerica-USA or CONCAUSA to promote sustainable economic development in the region.

In July 1969, El Salvador and Honduras fought the 100-hour Soccer War over disputed border areas and friction resulting from the 300,000 Salvadorans who had emigrated to Honduras in search of land and employment. The catalyst was nationalistic feelings aroused by a series of soccer matches between the two countries. The two countries formally signed a peace treaty on October 30, 1980, which put the border dispute before the International Court of Justice. In September 1992, the court issued a 400-page ruling, awarding much of the disputed land to Honduras. Although there have been tensions between citizens on both sides of the border, the two countries have worked to maintain stability and signed an agreement in November 1996 to establish a framework for negotiating the final disposition of citizens and property in the affected areas. El Salvador and Honduras share normal diplomatic and trade relations.

# U.S.-SALVADORAN RELATIONS

U.S.-Salvadoran relations remain close and cordial. U.S. policy toward El Salvador seeks to promote the strengthening of El Salvador's democratic institutions, rule of law, judicial reform, and civilian police and national reconciliation and reconstruction, economic opportunity, and growth.

Bilateral aid in general has declined since the end of the war with FY 1999 total economic assistance projected at $38 million. The Salvadoran Government relies increasingly on loans from international lending institutions to finance special projects.

## Private Sector

U.S. ties to El Salvador are dynamic and growing. More than 9,000 American citizens live and work full-time in El Salvador. Most are private businesspersons and their families, but a small number of American citizen retirees have been drawn to El Salvador by favorable tax conditions. The embassy's consular section provides the full range of visa, passport, federal benefit, absentee voting, and related citizenship services to this community. The American Chamber of Commerce in El Salvador is located at 87 Avenida Norte No. 720, Apto. A, Colónia Escalon, San Salvador, El Salvador (tel: 011–503–223–3292; fax: 011–503–224–6856).

## Principal U.S. Embassy Officials

For up-to-date information on Principal U.S. Officials, see the U.S. Embassies, Consulates, and Foreign Service section starting on page 139.

The U.S. embassy in El Salvador is located at Final Blvd. Santa Elena, Antiguo Cuscatlán, La Libertad (tel: 011–503–278–4444; fax: 011–503–278–6011).

## Other Contact Information

**U.S. Department of Commerce**
International Trade Administration
Office of Latin America and the Caribbean
14th and Constitution Avenue, NW
Washington, DC 20230
Tel: (202)482–1658; 1-(800)USA-TRADE
Fax: (202)482–0464

**Caribbean/Latin American Action**
1818 N Street, NW
Suite 310
Washington, DC 20036 Tel: (202)466–7464
Fax: (202)822–0075

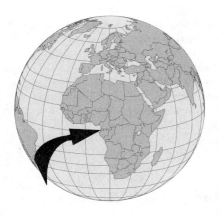

# EQUATORIAL GUINEA

March 1989

Official Name:
**Republic of Equatorial Guinea**

# PROFILE

## Geography

**Area:** 28,023 sq. km. (10,820 sq. mi.), slightly larger than Maryland.
**Cities:** Capital—Malabo (pop.) 38,000 (also capital of Bioko Norte Province). Other city—Bata (also capital of Litoral Province).
**Terrain:** Varies. Bioko Island is volcanic, rising to 10,190 ft. Mainland provinces are hilly at a level of about 2,000 ft. behind the coastal plain with some 4,000 ft. peaks. Highest point on Bioko: 9,980 ft.
**Climate:** Tropical with heavy rainfall on Bioko; annual avg.—200 cm. (80 in.). Bata is somewhat drier and cooler.

## People

**Nationality:** Noun—Equatorial Guinea. Adjective—Equatorial Guinean, Equatoguinean.
**Population (1988 est.):** 350,000.
**Annual growth rate:** 2.5% (1987-91 est.).
**Ethnic groups:** Fang 80%, Bubi 15%, other 5%.
**Religions:** Roman Catholic 83%, Protestant, traditional.
**Languages:** Spanish (official), Fang, Bubi, other African vernaculars, pidgin, English, French.
**Education:** Years compulsory—primary. Attendance—65%-70%. Literacy—est. 55%.
**Health:** Infant mortality rate—approx. 155/1,000. Life expectancy (1986 est.)—male 43.3 yrs.; female 46.6 yrs.
**Workforce (20,000):** Agriculture and forestry—50%. Public sector—40%. Commerce and industry—10%.

## Government

**Type:** Unitary Republic.
**Constitution:** August 16, 1982.
**Independence:** October 12, 1968.
**Branches:** Executive—president. Legislative—Peoples' Representative Chamber (60 members). Judicial—Supreme Court.
**Administrative subdivisions:** Provincial governments of the provinces of Bioko Norte, Bioko Sur (on Bioko Island); Litoral, Centro-Sur, Kie-Ntem, Wele Nzas (on mainland); and Annobon and 18 municipalities.
**Political parties:** Single legal political party—the Democratic Party for Equatorial Guinea formed July 30, 1987.
**Suffrage:** Universal adult.
**Central government budget (1987):** $29.1 million.
**Defense (1982):** 17% government budget.
**Flag:** Three horizontal stripes-green, white, red, joined by blue triangle on staff side.

## Economy

**GNP (1987 est.):** $130 million.
**Annual growth rate:** 3.5%.
**Per capita income:** $300.
**Avg. inflation rate (1987 est.):** 2%.
**Natural resources:** Timber, petroleum, minerals.
**Agriculture (greater than 50% of GDP):** Products—cacao, wood, coffee.
**Industry (negligible percentage of GNP):** Types—furniture, cementblock, wood processing, coffee, milling.
**Trade (1985):** Exports—$24.8 million: cacao, wood, coffee. Major markets—Spain, France, Germany, Italy, the Netherlands. Imports—$34 million: foodstuffs, beverages, textiles, machinery, vehicles, agricultural products, fuels, tobacco. Major suppliers—Spain, France, Italy, the Netherlands, EEC, USSR, PRC, FRG, and UK.
**Official exchange rate:** Varies; 32 1.5 *Communate Financiere Africaine* (CFA) francs US$1 (Aug. 1988).
**Economic aid received:** Spain is the largest aid donor. Equatorial Guinea enjoys certain trade privileges and price support from Spain. It also receives increasing assistance from France. Other donors include EEC, FRG, US, Italy, Kuwait, PRC, North Korea, Cuba, USSR, Argentina, UN Development Program, World Bank, and the International Monetary Fund.

## Membership in International Organizations

UN and some of its specialized and related agencies, including the International Monetary Fund (IMF), World Bank (IBRD); Organization of African Unity (OAU); Customs and Economic Union of Central Africa (UDEAC); African Timber Organization (ATO); International Coffee Organization (ICO).

# GEOGRAPHY

The Republic of Equatorial Guinea is located in west central Africa. The Insular Region includes Bioko Island, about 32 kilometers (20 mi.) from Cameroon, the adjacent islets, and Annobón Island, about 595 kilometers (370 mi.) southwest of the main island. The Continental Region lies between Cameroon and Gabon on the mainland, and includes the islands of Corisco, Elobey Grande, Elobey Chico, and adjacent islets.

Bioko Island, once called Fernando Po, is the largest island in the Gulf of Guinea—2,020 square kilometers (780 sq. mi.). It is shaped like a boot, with two large volcanic formations separated by a valley that bisects the island at its narrowest point. The 195-kilometer (120-mi.) coastline is high and rugged in the south but lower and more accessible in the north, with an excellent harbor at Malabo, and several scenic beaches between Malabo and Luba. The Continental Region, unofficially still Rio Muni—26,003 square kilometers (10,040 sq. mi.Whas a coastal plain that gives way to a succession of valleys separated by low hills and spurs of the Crystal Mountains. The main river the Rio Benito (Mbini), is unnavigable except for a 20-kilometer stretch; it divides Rio Muni in two. Temperatures and humidity on Bioko Island are generally higher than on Rio Muni. Annobón Island—18 square kilometers (7 sq. mi.)—has a volcanic peak with four summits; its coastline is abrupt except in the north. Most of its 1,900 inhabitants are fishermen specializing in traditional, small-scale tuna fishing and whaling. The climate is tropical—heavy rainfall, high humidity, and frequent seasonal changes with violent windstorms.

# PEOPLE

The majority of the Equatoguinean people are of Bantu origin. The largest tribe, the Fang, is indigenous to the mainland, although many now also live on Bioko Island. The Fang constitute 80% of the population and are divided into about 67 clans. Those to the north of Rio Benito on Rio Muni speak Fang-Ntumu, and those to the south speak Fang-Okak, two mutually intelligible dialects. The Bubi, who form 15% of the population, are indigenous to Bioko Island. In addition, there are coastal tribes, sometimes referred to as "Playeros": Ndowes, Bujebas, Balengues, and Bengas on the mainland and small islands, and Fernandinos, a Creole community, on Bioko. These groups comprise 5% of the population. There also are approximately 1,500 foreigners, of which half are from the neighboring countries of Cameroon, Gabon, Ghana, and Nigeria. Spanish is the official language. The Roman Catholic Church has greatly influenced both religion and education.

## Cultural Achievements

The Bantu culture is predominant in Equatorial Guinea. Traditional dances and folk songs are performed. In each village throughout Equatorial Guinea, it is a custom for a group of women to chant songs of praise and dance at each important event or local celebration. In 1982, the Spanish/Guinean Cultural Center opened with local and international art exhibits on display. There also are occasional lectures as well as poetry readings and dance performances. The center houses two libraries: Spanish and Equatoguinean. Local plays are performed from time to time in the theater in Malabo. In Bata, there is a museum of art containing, among other works, the sculpture and paintings of the internationally acclaimed Equatoguinean artist, Leandro Mbomio. It is not open to the public. There are Spanish and French cultural centers in both Malabo and Bata.

# HISTORY

The first inhabitants of the region that is now Equatorial Guinea are believed to have been Pygmies, of whom only isolated pockets remain in northern Rio Muni. Bantu migrations between the 17th and 19th centuries brought the coastal tribes and later the Fang. Elements of the latter may have generated the Bubi, who emigrated to Bioko from Cameroon and Rio Muni in several waves and succeeded former neolithic populations. The Annobon population, native to Angola, was introduced into Bioko by the Portuguese via Sao Tome.

The Portuguese explorer, Fernanda Po, seeking a route to India, is credited with having discovered the island of Bioko in 1471. The Portuguese retained control until 1778, when the island, adjacent islets, and commercial rights to the mainland between the Niger and Ogooue Rivers were ceded to Spain. From 1827 to 1843, Britain established a base on the island to combat the slave trade. Conflicting claims to the mainland were settled in 1900 by the Treaty of Paris, and periodically, the mainland territories were united administratively.

Spain lacked the wealth and the interest to develop an extensive economic infrastructure in Equatorial Guinea during the first half of this century; however, through a paternal system, particularly on Bioko Island, Spain developed large cacao plantations for which thousands of Nigerian workers were imported as laborers. At independence in 1968, largely as a result of this system, Equatorial Guinea had one of the highest per capita incomes in Africa. The Spanish also helped Equatorial Guinea achieve one of the continent's highest literacy rates and developed a good network of health care facilities.

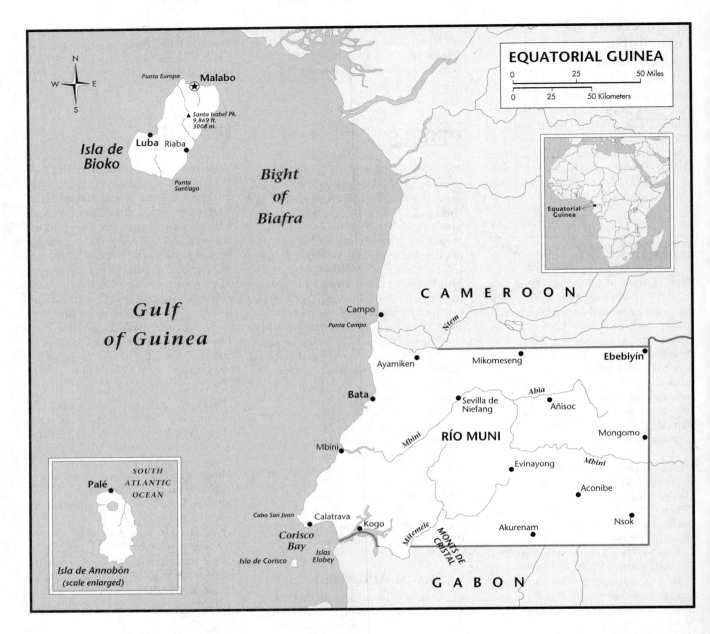

In 1959, the Spanish territory of the Gulf of Guinea was established with status similar to the provinces of metropolitan Spain. As the Spanish Equatorial region, it was ruled by a governor general exercising military and civilian powers. The first local elections were held in 1959, and the first Equatoguinean representatives were seated in the Spanish Parliament. Under the Basic Law of December 1963, limited autonomy was authorized under a joint legislative body for the territory's two provinces. The name of the country was changed to Equatorial Guinea. Although Spain's Commissioner General had

extensive powers, the Equatorial Guinean General Assembly had considerable initiative in formulating laws and regulations.

In March 1968, under pressure from Equatoguinean nationalists and the United Nations, Spain announced that it would grant independence to Equatorial Guinea. A constitutional convention produced an electoral law and draft constitution. In the presence of a U.N. observer team, a referendum was held on August 11, 1968, and 63% of the electorate voted in favor of the constitution, which provided for a government with a gen-

eral assembly and presidentially appointed judges in the Supreme Court.

In September 1968, Francisco Macias Nguema was elected first president of Equatorial Guinea, and independence was granted in October. In July 1970, Macias created a single-party state, and by May 1971, key portions of the constitution were abrogated. In 1972, the president assumed complete control of the government and the title of President-for-Life. The Macias regime was characterized by abandonment of all government functions except internal security, which was accomplished by terror; this led to the death or exile of up to one-third of the country's population. Due to pilferage, ignorance, and neglect, the country's infrastructure—electrical, water road, transportation, and health—fell into ruin. Religion was repressed, and education ceased. The private and public sectors of the economy were devastated. Nigerian contract laborers on Bioko, who left en masse in early 1976, have not returned. The economy collapsed, and skilled citizens and foreigners left. In August 1979, Lt. Col. Teodoro Obiang Nguema Mbasogo (effective December 1987 addressed only by his African name, Obiang Nguema Mbasogo) led a successful coup d'etat; Macias was executed after a trial attended by international observers.

# GOVERNMENT

After the August 1979 coup, power was transferred to a Supreme Military Council with the president having the power to rule by decree, upon approval by the cabinet. In 1981, the president appointed a number of civilian commissioners. A new constitution was drafted with the assistance of representatives of the UN Commission on Human Rights. The new constitution came into effect after a popular vote on August 15,1982, which abolished the Supreme Military Council. The president was not elected but took office on the basis of the ratification of the constitution. Although political rights are not freely exercised, a single political party to which all adults must pay dues, the Democratic Party for Equatorial Guinea, was formed July 30, 1987; its leader is undetermined. The country's second presidential election, to be held under the party's auspices, is scheduled for 1989.

Under the terms of the constitution, the president is given extensive powers, including naming and dismissing members of the cabinet, making decree laws, dissolving the Chamber of Representatives, negotiating and ratifying treaties, and calling parliamentary elections. Although several former military officers remained in

the cabinet, the government assumed a more civilian character, the few remaining military members having, for the most part, severed officially their ties with the armed forces. The president remains commander in chief of the armed forces and minister of defense, and he maintains close supervision of military activity. The position of prime minister w as created to coordinate government activities in areas other than foreign affairs, national defense, and security. The prime minister operates under powers designated by the president, who appoints and dismisses the prime minister and all other members of the government.

In mid-1983, a 60-member unicameral "Chamber of Representatives of the People" was formed, comprising 15 leaders appointed by the president and 45 members chosen by indirect elections. At the conclusion of their 5year terms, legislators were again chosen in the same fashion, with approximately half of these individuals retaining their positions. All adult citizens elected officials by secret ballot in their towns and villages. These officials then became electors who chose 45 representatives out of their own number, one per district, to serve in the national Parliament. The Parliament, however is not independent and is unable to act without presidential approval or direction.

Each of the seven provincial governments consists of a governor appointed by the president and an administrative staff. Each province is divided administratively into districts and municipalities. The internal administrative system falls under the Ministry of Territorial Administration; several other ministries also are represented at the provincial and district levels.

The judicial system follows the same administrative levels. At the top are the president and his judicial advisers (Supreme Court). In descending rank are the appeals courts, chief judges for the divisions, and local magistrates. Tribal laws and customs are honored in the formal court system when not in conflict with national law. The current court sys-

tem, which often uses local customary law, is a combination of traditional, civil, and military Justice, and operates in an ad hoc manner for lack of established procedures and experienced judicial personnel.

The other official branch of the government is the State Council. The State Council's main function is to serve as caretaker in case of death or physical incapacity of the president. It comprises the following members who are appointed by virtue of their position: the president of the republic, the prime minister, the minister of defense, the president of the National Assembly, and the chairman of the Social and Economic Council.

Since its creation in 1979, the current government has made very little progress in stimulating the economy. Extremely serious health and sanitary conditions persist, and the education system remains in desperate condition. The abuses and atrocities that characterized the Macias years have been eliminated, but an effective rule of law does not exist. Religious freedom existed until early 1986 when the government closed Jehovah's Witnesses meeting halls and meeting places of other religious denominations.

## Principal Government Officials

**For up-to-date information on Principal Government Officials, see the Chiefs of State and Cabinet Members of Foreign Governments section starting on page 1.**

Equatorial Guinea maintains an embassy in the United States, which also is the UN Mission, at 801 Second Avenue, Suite 1403, New York, N.Y. 10017 (tel. 212-599-1523).

# POLITICAL CONDITIONS

Only after local autonomy was granted in 1963 was there much political party activity in Equatorial Guinea. Ethnically based political parties on Rio Muni favored independence of the two provinces as a single political entity and won out over the Bubi and Fernandino parties on Bioko Island, who preferred separation from Rio Muni or a loose federation. Offshoots of these parties exist in exile today. Their leaders have yet to reconcile themselves to the new government. However they have strength only among the exile community (Spain, Cameroon, and Gabon) and have had little influence or following in Equatorial Guinea.

In August 1979, Obiang Nguema Mbasogo led a coup d'etat and pledged to restore human rights, resume economic development of the country, and reestablish good relations with traditionally friendly nations. A constitution was approved in 1983, and President Obiang Nguema Mbasogo began a 7-year term of office which ends in 1989. The Democratic Party for Equatorial Guinea, formed in 1987, is the nation's sole legal political party.

Once the chaotic situation in the country was brought under control and public administration reestablished, politics became the province of Cabinet ministers, presidential advisers, and mid-level government officials, the latter functioning in an advisory capacity to the president. With local and parliamentary elections in 1981 and 1982, normal political life is gradually returning to the country.

Since 1979, the president has been the country's dominant political force. So far he has been constrained only by a need to maintain a consensus among his advisers and political supporters—most, but not all, of whom are drawn from the majority Fang tribe. Many factors—including discontent among military personnel displaced by civilian, intratribal and

## Travel Notes

**Customs:** Visas are required for American diplomatic personnel and for all other Americans. Applications should be made to the Equatorial Guinea Mission to the UN at least 3 weeks prior to departure and should be secured for entire length of stay. Visas also may be obtained at Equatorial Guinea embassies in Spain, France, Cameroon, Nigeria, and Gabon.

**Climate and clothing:** Hot and humid most of the year with 200 cm. (80 in.) of rain. Average temperature is 80°F. Bring lightweight summer apparel, rainwear, and a sweater for the mountains. Long sleeves and long pants are recommended as protection against insect bites.

**Health:** There is no adequate hospital in Equatorial Guinea and few trained physicians. Medicines and equipment are limited. Immunization against yellow fever is required. Immunizations against polio, typhoid, tetanus, and measles also are recommended. Malaria is endemic, and malaria suppressants must be taken regularly. Tapwater is not potable and often unavailable-many people bring bottled water. There are no dentists or opticians in the country. Bring a supply of basic medicines.

**Telecommunications:** Poor system (about 2,000 telephones) with adequate government services. Daytime incoming long-distance telephone service via Madrid is sometimes available as is outgoing via Yaounde. Sound quality is poor. Equatorial Guinea currently has a single telex line, located in the telecommunications company, which serves as an international telegram service. Telegraph rates are considerably higher than in the US. There are two AM radio stations (no FM) and one television station.

**Transportation:** Bus service is available from Malabo to Luba and Riaba. Few taxis are available. Malabo is served by international airlines: four times weekly from Douala; once weekly from and to Madrid via Lagos; once weekly to and from Lagos

via Calabar; weekly to and from Morocco via Libreville; and monthly from Moscow via Cotonou and Valletta. Air transport to Bata is irregular. Charter flights to Douala and Bata can be arranged. Maritime transport is irregular.

**Hotels:** Accommodations in the four hotels in Malabo and the one in Bata are extremely difficult to obtain. None of the hotels has restaurant facilities. Utilities are occasionally interrupted; flashlights with batteries or candles and matches are recommended. None of the hotels are screened; mosquito netting or insect repellent is recommended. The markets in Malabo have most staples except dairy products, but visitors may wish to carry with them a small supply of any special needs, such as dietetic or sodium-free foods.

**Tourist attractions:** The Island of Bioko with its varied vegetation and topography is quite attractive. There are several scenic beaches on Bioko and Rio Muni. Snorkeling, boating, and fishing are enjoyed; bring equipment. Spanish-Guinean and French cultural centers are in Malabo and Bata.

**National holidays:** January 1, New Year's Day; Good Friday; May 1, International Labor Day; Corpus Christi; June 5, President's birthday; August3, Armed Forces Day; August 15, Constitution Day; October 12, Independence Day; December 8, Immaculate Conception Day; December 25, Christmas Day.

**Travel Advice:** For up-to-date information from the U.S. State Department on possible inconvenient or hazardous situations, see the **Travel Warnings and Consular Information Sheets from the U.S. Government** section starting on page 1723. For the latest information on health requirements and conditions, see the **International Travelers' Health Information** section starting on page 1385. For further information dealing with nonurgent matter, see the **Tips for Travelers to...** section starting on page 1588.

ethnic rivalries, and personal ambitions among those who regarded themselves as an alternative leadership for the country—led to two abortive coups in 1981 and 1983. Neither coup attempt had any popular or appreciable military support.

The government, which is credited with restoring greater personal freedoms—reopening the schools and expanding primary education, improving public utilities and roads, as well as attracting considerable foreign aid—is regarded favorably by the populace. However, it has been criticized for not reducing petty corruption, halting inflation, eliminating the black market, or effectively sharing power with a more nationally representative group of Fang, Playero, and Bubi leaders. The Parliament is, however representative of the nation as a whole ana eventually may remedy this politically unbalanced situation if it develops along the lines set out for it by the constitution and receives a real share of power.

Although Equatorial Guinea lacks a well-established democratic tradition comparable to the developed democracies of the West, it has progressed toward developing a participatory political system out of the anarchic, chaotic, and repressive conditions of the Macias years.

# ECONOMY

Equatorial Guinea's economy is based on three products—cacao, wood, and coffee—which are exported to Spain and other European countries. Cacao exports of 7,905 metric tons were reported for 1987; significantly below the 1968 production of 36,000 metric tons. The continued low volume of exports is due partly to the exodus of Nigerian contract workers in 1976 but also to governmental exercise of its control over production.

The government's internal pricing policy and its inability to effectively supply producers with materials or incentive to produce cacao are chief among the problems. Cacao and coffee also are smuggled to Equatorial Guinea's neighbors, where prices have been, until recently, from two to three times higher making any production figures inexact. Yield and quality of Equatoguinean cacao are normally quite high and exceed those of other African countries. Foreign-exchange earnings for cacao in 1987 were $9.9 million.

Cacao is grown on plantations; coffee is grown mainly on small farms on Rio Muni. Rio Muni and Gabon have a virtual monopoly of the world pro-

duction of okoume, from which plywood is made. French and Italian firms harvest the timber. Foreign-exchange earnings for timber in 1987 are reported to have been about $13.5 million for 127,500 metric tons exported.

There is little industry in the country, and the local market for industrial products is small. The government seeks to expand the role of free enterprise and to promote foreign investment, but has had little success in creating an atmosphere conducive to investor interest. French and U.S. firms have concessions to drill for oil in Equatorial Guinean waters, and a joint Spanish-Equatoguinean firm is reported to have found gas and oil in the waters north of Bioko near the present Cameroonian and Nigerian offshore oil fields. However a maritime border dispute with Gabon has delayed exploration. Preliminary geological surveys have been conducted by French and Spanish aid personnel who have confirmed traces of petroleum, iron ore, and radioactive materials on continental Rio Muni.

The population engages in subsistence agriculture; traditional, small-scale fishing; and raising goats, chickens, pigs, and cattle in some higher areas free of tsetse flies. No desperate hunger exists, but there is some malnutrition. The potential exists in Equatorial Guinea for a viable agriculture-based, export-oriented economy, provided the government can repair the damage to the nation's economic and social fabric that occurred during the Macias regime. To this end, with the assistance of the UN Development Program (UNDP), the government proposed a plan for economic reconstruction through which a large number of friendly nations and international organizations-including Spain, France, the European Economic Community the World Bank, the Central African Economic and Customs Union (UDEAC), the Bank of Central African States (BEAC), and its African neighbors, especially Gabon and Cameroon-are coordinating their development assistance to the country. A UN-sponsored Interna-

tional Donors' Conference was held in Geneva in late November 1988.

The country is still struggling to close the serious gap in its balance of payments and to bring its budget under control. It has joined the UDEAC and the BEAC and as of January 1985, has had a hard convertible currency-the CFA (*Communaute Financiere Africaine*) franc—which is pegged to the French franc. As a result of some of these measures, the inflation picture in Equatorial Guinea has stabilized. It also is currently engaged with the International Monetary Fund and foreign donors in negotiating and implementing foreign financial and technical assistance programs. In 1986, the World Bank approved a $10.6 million import credit to assist the government in financing vitally needed inputs for-agricultural production. Equatoguinean cacao and wood products are competitive in world markets. There is potential to diversify the economy into other agricultural products, and petroleum may be found either offshore or onshore. Now that Equatorial Guinea is able to enjoy the benefits of a convertible currency, the country's economic prospects have improved. Adherence to its economic policy reforms will be essential, however and the transition to economic good health is likely to take several years.

# FOREIGN RELATIONS

A transitional agreement, signed in October 1968, implemented a Spanish preindependence decision to assist Equatorial Guinea and provided for the temporary maintenance of Spanish forces there. A dispute with President Macias in 1969 led to a request that all Spanish troops immediately depart, and a large number of civilians left at the same time. Diplomatic relations between the two countries were never broken but were suspended by Spain in March 1977 in the wake of renewed disputes. After Macias' fall in 1979, President Obiang asked for Spanish assistance, and since then, Spain has regained its historical preeminence in Equatorial Guinea's diplomatic relations. Permanent agreements for economic and technical cooperation, private concessions, and trade relations have recently been signed. Following negotiations in November 1985, a Spanish Mixed Commission signed agreements calling for about $10 million in annual economic and technical cooperation over a 4-year period.

Since 1979, Cameroon and Gabon have provided significant political and economic support to Equatorial Guinea. The latter in turn, by joining UDEAC, has taken the first steps toward integration into the economy and politics of the central African region. Parallel to the Equatoguinean rapprochement with its francophone neighbors, France has taken a greater interest in Equatorial Guinea and has augmented its aid programs in the country. In 1984, France became Equatorial Guinea's leading trade partner and France's role has significantly increased following Equatorial Guinea's entry into the CFA franc zone and the BEAC. French technical advisers work in the Finance and Planning Ministries, and agreements have been signed for infrastructure development projects.

Equatorial Guinea's relations with the Soviet bloc have cooled considerably since 1979. The fishing treaty giving Soviet fleets access to the Port of Luba was abrogated shortly after Obiang came into power. The number of Soviet and Eastern-bloc citizens in the country has been reduced, as have Soviet and Cuban activities in the military and economic spheres. In January 1981, the Libyan Embassy was closed and all its staff expelled.

The government's official policy is one of nonalignment. In its search for assistance to meet the goal of national reconstruction, the Government of Equatorial Guinea has established diplomatic relations with numerous European and Third World countries, many of which provide it with some economic assistance. Having achieved independence under UN sponsorship, Equatorial Guinea feels a special kinship with that organization, from which it derives important

economic assistance. It became the 126th UN member on November 12, 1968.

# DEFENSE

The Equatorial Guinean police and military, with substantial assistance from Spain, have been totally reorganized since 1979. Spain has trained hundreds of Equatoguineans, including officers, noncommissioned officers, and enlisted men. France and the United States also have provided modest military training assistance. France, Morocco, and Spain have provided jeeps and similar vehicles to the police. Provincial governors and prefects (delegados) have reestablished central government authority in the outlying provinces. Arbitrary acts by security forces, which were daily occurrences under the Macias regime, are now the exception rather than the rule. The Equatorial Guinean Army has sufficient small arms and light vehicles to guarantee internal security. Equatorial Guinea has 73,000 males between the ages of 15 and 49, of which 36,000 would be fit for military service. In 1982, the military budget comprised 17% of the central government budget. A 300-man guard force provided by Morocco assists in protecting the president. Equatorial Guinea also has a navy and possibly an air force. In June 1988, the United States donated a 68-foot patrol boat to the Equatorial Guinean Navy so it could patrol its exclusive economic zone better.

# U.S.-EQUATORIAL GUINEA RELATIONS

The United States recognized Equatorial Guinea upon its independence on October 12, 1968. A small embassy, headed by a charge d'affaires, was established in Malabo, and the U.S. Ambassador in Cameroon also was accredited to Equatorial Guinea. In suspended relations following a dispute with the Macias government. After the coup d'etat in August 1979, the United States rees-

tablished relations, and the U.S. Ambassador in Cameroon again was accredited. In June 1981, the first officer arrived in Malabo to open the new U.S. Embassy, and on November 19, 1981, the first resident U.S. Ambassador presented his credentials to President Obiang.

The United States provides nearly $1 million annually in economic assistance, primarily in agricultural development and training to assist in production of cash and food crops, and nearly $75,000 for the International Military Education and Training Program that has been instituted. The United States donated a 68-foot patrol boat to the Equatorial Guinean Navy in June 1988 under the military assistance program. During the past 5 years, more than 40 Equatoguineans have visited the United States under various programs of study and cultural exchange. Self-help projects have aided villages in the repair of health centers schools, water supply, and roads. In addition, the United States was an active participant in the Conference on the Reconstruction of Equatorial Guinea, held in Geneva in April 1982 under the auspices of the UNDP and contributes substantially to Equatorial Guinean development through its contributions the UNDP, World Health Organization, World Food Program, World Bank, and African Development Bank.

## Principal U.S. Officials

For up-to-date information on Principal U.S. Officials, see the U.S. Embassies, Consulates, and Foreign Service section starting on page 139.

The U.S. Embassy in Equatorial Guinea is located at Calle de los Ministros, Malabo P. O. Box 597, Malabo Equatorial Guinea (tel. 2507 or 2406).

# ERITREA

March 1998

Official Name:
**State of Eritrea**

# PROFILE

## Geography

**Area:** 125,000 sq. km. (48,000 sq. mi.); about the size of Pennsylvania.
**Cities:** Capital—Asmara (est. pop. 435,000). Other cities—Keren (57,000); Assab (28,000); Massawa (25,000); Afabet (25,000); Tessenie (25,000); Mendefera (25,000); Dekemhare (20,000); Adekeieh (15,000); Barentu (15,000); Ghinda (15,000).
**Terrain:** Central highlands straddle escarpment associated with Rift Valley, dry coastal plains, and western lowlands.
**Climate:** Temperate in the highlands, hot in the lowlands.

## People

**Nationality:** Noun and adjective—Eritrean(s).
**Population (1997 est.):** 3.75 million.
**Annual growth rate:** 2.6%.
**Ethnic groups:** Tigrinya 50%, Tigre 31.4%, Saho 5%, Afar 5%, Begia 2.5%, Bilen 2.1%, Kunama 2%, Nara 1.5%, and Rashaida 0.5%.
**Religions:** Christian 50%, mostly Orthodox, Muslim 48%, indigenous beliefs 2%.
**Education:** Years compulsory—none. Attendance—elementary 26%; secondary 17%.

**Health:** Infant mortality rate—135/1,000. Life expectancy—46 yrs.
**Work force:** Agriculture—80%. Industry and commerce—20%.

## Government

**Type:** Transition government.
**Constitution:** Ratified May 24, 1997, but not yet implemented.
**Branches:** Executive—President, Cabinet. Legislative—National Assembly. Judicial—Supreme Court.
**Administrative subdivisions:** 6 administrative regions.
**Political parties:** People's Front for Democracy and Justice (name adopted by the Eritrean People's Liberation Front when it established itself as a political party).
**Suffrage:** Universal, age 18 and above.
**Central government budget (1997):** $345 million.
**Defense:** 39% of total government expenditure.
**National holiday:** May 24 (Liberation Day).
**Flag:** green, red, and blue with a gold laurel wreath and olive branch.

## Economy

Statistics prior to 1992 are extrapolated from Ethiopian data.
**Real GDP (1997 est.):** $800 million.
**Annual growth rate (1995 est.):** 3%.
**Per capita income:** Less than $300 per year.

**Avg. inflation rate (last 2 years):** 11%-12%.
**Mineral resources:** Gold, copper, iron ore, potash, oil.
**Agriculture (22.1% of GDP in 1990):** Products—millet, sorghum, teff, wheat, barley, flax, cotton, coffee, papayas, citrus fruits, bananas, beans and lentils, potatoes, vegetables, fish, dairy products, meat, and skins. Cultivated land—10% of arable land.
**Industry (29.6% of GDP in 1990):** Processed food and dairy products, alcoholic beverages, leather goods, textiles, chemicals, cement and other construction materials, salt, paper, and matches.
**Trade:** Exports (1996)—$48 million: skins, meat, live sheep and cattle, gum arabic. Major markets—Ethiopia, Saudi Arabia, Italy. Imports (1994)—$360 million: food, manufactured goods, machinery and transportation equipment. Major suppliers—Saudi Arabia, Ethiopia, Italy, UAE.
**Official exchange rate:** 7.2 nakfa=U.S.$1.

# GEOGRAPHY

Eritrea is located in the Horn of Africa and is bordered on the northeast and east by the Red Sea, on the west and northwest by Sudan, on the south by Ethiopia, and on the southeast by Djibouti. The country has a high central plateau that varies from 1,800 to 3,000 meters (6,000-8,000 feet) above sea level. A coastal plain, western lowlands, and some 300 islands comprise the remainder of Eritrea's land mass. Eritrea has no year-round rivers.

The climate is temperate in the mountains and hot in the lowlands. Asmara, the capital, is about 3,000 meters (8,000 ft.) above sea level. Maximum temperature is 26° C (80° F). The weather is usually sunny and dry, with the short or belg rains occurring February-April and the big or meher rains beginning in late June and ending in mid-September.

# PEOPLE

Eritrea's population comprises nine ethnic groups, most of which speak Semitic or Cushitic languages. The Tigrinya and Tigre make up four-fifths of the population and speak different, but related and somewhat mutually intelligible, Semitic languages. In general, most of the Christians live in the highlands, while Muslims and adherents of traditional beliefs live in the lowland regions. Tigrinya and Arabic are the most frequently used languages for commercial and official transactions, but English is widely spoken and is the language used for secondary and university education.

# HISTORY

Eritrea officially celebrated its independence on May 24, 1993, becoming the world's newest nation. Prior to Italian colonization in 1885, what is now Eritrea had been ruled by the various local or international powers that successively dominated the Red Sea region. In 1896, the Italians used Eritrea as a springboard for their disastrous attempt to conquer Ethiopia. Eritrea was placed under British military administration after the Italian surrender in World War II. In 1952, a UN resolution federating Eritrea with Ethiopia went into effect.

**Travel Notes**

**Travel Advice:** For up-to-date information from the U.S. State Department on possible inconvenient or hazardous situations, see the **Travel Warnings and Consular Information Sheets from the U.S. Government** section starting on page 1723. For the latest information on health requirements and conditions, see the **International Travelers' Health Information** section starting on page 1385. For further information dealing with non-urgent matter, see the **Tips for Travelers to...** section starting on page 1588.

The resolution ignored Eritrean pleas for independence but guaranteed Eritreans some democratic rights and a measure of autonomy. Almost immediately after the federation went into effect, however, these rights began to be abridged or violated.

In 1962, Emperor Haile Sellassie unilaterally dissolved the Eritrean parliament and annexed the country, sparking the Eritrean fight for independence that continued after Haile Sellassie was ousted in a coup in 1974. The new Ethiopian Government, called the Derg, was a Marxist military junta led by strongman Mengistu Haile Miriam.

During the 1960s, the Eritrean independence struggle was led by the Eritrean Liberation Front (ELF). In 1970, members of the group had a falling out, and a group broke away from the ELF and formed the Eritrean People's Liberation Front (EPLF). By the late 1970s, the EPLF had become the dominant armed Eritrean group fighting against the Ethiopian Government, and Isaias Afwerki had emerged as its leader. Much of the materiel used to combat Ethiopia was captured from the Ethiopian Army.

By 1977 the EPLF was poised to drive the Ethiopians out of Eritrea. That same year, however, a massive airlift of Soviet arms to Ethiopia enabled the Ethiopian Army to regain the initiative and forced the EPLF to retreat to the bush. Between 1978 and 1986, the Derg launched eight major offen-

sives against the independence movement—all failed. In 1988, the EPLF captured Afabet, headquarters of the Ethiopian Army in northeastern Eritrea, prompting the Ethiopian Army to withdraw from its garrisons in Eritrea's western lowlands. EPLF fighters then moved into position around Keren, Eritrea's second-largest city. Meanwhile, other dissident movements were making headway throughout Ethiopia. At the end of the 1980s, the Soviet Union informed Mengistu that it would not be renewing its defense and cooperation agreement. With the withdrawal of Soviet support and supplies, the Ethiopian Army's morale plummeted, and the EPLF—along with other Ethiopian rebel forces—began to advance on Ethiopian positions.

The United States played a facilitative role in the peace talks in Washington during the months leading up to the May 1991 fall of the Mengistu regime. In mid-May, Mengistu resigned as head of the Ethiopian Government and went into exile in Zimbabwe, leaving a caretaker government in Addis Ababa. Having defeated the Ethiopian forces in Eritrea, EPLF troops took control of their homeland. Later that month, the United States chaired talks in London to formalize the end of the war. These talks were attended by the four major combatant groups, including the EPLF.

A high-level U.S. delegation also was present in Addis Ababa for the July 1-5, 1991 conference that established a transitional government in Ethiopia. The EPLF attended the July conference as an observer and held talks with the new transitional government regarding Eritrea's relationship to Ethiopia. The outcome of those talks was an agreement in which the Ethiopians recognized the right of the Eritreans to hold a referendum on independence.

Although some EPLF cadres at one time espoused a Marxist ideology, Soviet support for Mengistu had cooled their ardor. The fall of communist regimes in the former Soviet Union and the Eastern Bloc convinced them it was a failed system.

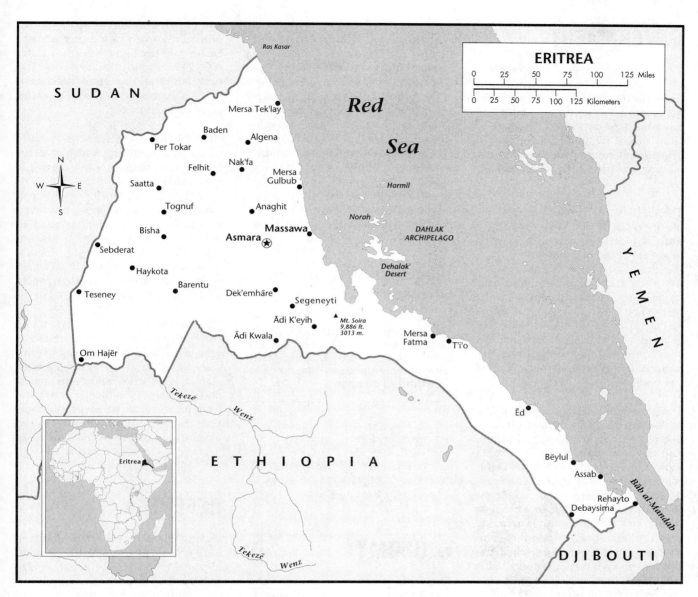

The EPLF now says it is committed to establishing a democratic form of government and a free-market economy in Eritrea. The United States agreed to provide assistance to both Ethiopia and Eritrea, conditional on continued progress toward democracy and human rights.

In May 1991, the EPLF established the Provisional Government of Eritrea (PGE) to administer Eritrean affairs until a referendum was held on independence and a permanent government established. EPLF leader Isaias became the head of the PGE, and the EPLF Central Committee served as its legislative body.

On April 23-25, 1993, Eritreans voted overwhelmingly for independence from Ethiopia in a UN-monitored free and fair referendum. The Eritrean authorities declared Eritrea an independent state on April 27. The government was reorganized and after a national, freely contested election, the National Assembly, which chose Isaias as President of the PGE, was expanded to include both EPLF and non-EPLF members. The EPLF established itself as a political party, the People's Front for Democracy and Justice (PFDJ), and is now in the process of drafting a new constitution and setting up a permanent government.

Meanwhile, Sudan's aggressiveness toward its neighbors, its goal of spreading Islamic fundamentalism throughout the region, and its unwillingness to play a constructive role in regional development have raised security concerns along Eritrea's border with Sudan. Khartoum gives support and safehaven to a small, relatively ineffectual Eritrean insurgent group, the Eritrean Islamic Jihad (EIJ). Eritrea, in turn, supports the Sudanese opposition, which has coalesced in the National Democratic Alliance (NDA). The NDA has the stated objective of overturning the current National Islamic Front (NIF)-dominated government in Khartoum.

# GOVERNMENT

The new government faces formidable challenges. Beginning with no constitution, no judicial system, and an education system in shambles, it has been forced to build the institutions of government from scratch. The present government includes legislative, executive, and judicial bodies.

The legislature, the National Assembly, includes 75 members of the PFDJ and 75 additional popularly elected members. The National Assembly is the highest legal power in the government until the establishment of a democratic, constitutional government. The legislature sets the internal and external policies of the government, regulates implementation of those policies, approves the budget, and elects the president of the country.

The president nominates individuals to head the various ministries, authorities, commissions, and offices, and the National Assembly ratifies those nominations. The cabinet is the country's executive branch. It is composed of 16 ministers and chaired by the president. It implements policies, regulations, and laws and is accountable to the National Assembly. The ministries are agriculture; construction; defense; education; energy, mining, and water; finance and development; foreign; health; information and culture; internal affairs; justice; local government; marine resources; transport; trade and industry; and tourism.

The judiciary operates independently of both the legislative and executive bodies, with a court system that extends from the village through to the district, provincial, and national levels. On May 19, 1993, the PGE issued a proclamation regarding the reorganization of the government. It declared that during a four-year transition period, and sooner if possible, it would draft and ratify a constitution, prepare a law on political parties, prepare a press law, and carry out elections for a constitutional government. In March 1994, the PGE created a constitutional commission charged with drafting a constitution flexible enough to meet the current needs of a population suffering from 30 years of civil war as well as those of the future, when stability and prosperity change the political landscape. Commission members have traveled throughout the country and to Eritrean communities abroad holding meetings to explain constitutional options to the people and to solicit their input. A new constitution was promulgated in 1997 but has not yet been implemented, and general elections have been postponed.

## Principal Government Officials

**For up-to-date information on Principal Government Officials, see the Chiefs of State and Cabinet Members of Foreign Governments section starting on page 1.**

Eritrea maintains an embassy in the United States at 1708 New Hampshire Ave., NW, Washington, DC 20009 (tel. 202-319-1991) headed by Ambassador Semere Rossom.

# ECONOMY

The Government of Eritrea states that it is committed to a market economy and privatization, and it has made development and economic recovery its priorities. The economy was devastated by war and the misguided policies of the Derg, which disrupted agriculture and industry. Much of the transportation and communications infrastructure that was not destroyed by the war is outmoded and deteriorating. As a result, the government has sought international assistance for a variety of development projects and has mobilized young Eritreans serving in the National Youth Service to repair crumbling roads and dams. Small businesses, such as restaurants, bars, stores, auto repair, and crafts continue to thrive in the Asmara area. A brewery, cigarette factory, small glass and plastics producers, several companies involved in making leather goods, and textile and sweater factories operate in the Asmara area. The textile and leather industries have made a particularly robust recovery since independence.

The Eritrean economy is largely based on agriculture, which employs 80% of the population but currently may contribute as little as 22% to GDP. Export crops include coffee, cotton, fruit, hides, and meat, but farmers are largely dependent on rain-fed agriculture, and growth in this and other sectors is hampered by lack of a dependable water supply. Worker remittances from abroad currently contribute 40%-50% of GDP.

The Port of Massawa, destroyed by the Ethiopian Army during the final year of the war, is on its way to complete rehabilitation. With political stability and a liberal investment climate, Eritrea has begun to attract international businesses. Various U.S. and other Western concerns are planning to invest in tourism, mining, and offshore oil exploration.

# DEFENSE

During the war, the EPLF fighting force grew to almost 110,000 fighters, almost 3% of the total population of Eritrea. The fragile peace-time economy cannot sustain such a large army, and in 1993, Eritrea embarked on a phased program to demobilize 50%-60% of the army, which had by then shrunk to about 95,000. During the first phase of demobilization in 1993, some 26,000 soldiers—most of whom enlisted after 1990—were demobilized. They received cash bonuses and six-month food rations, and many also took advantage of government loans, grants of farm land in western Eritrea, or vocational training courses. The second phase of demobilization, which occurred the following year, demobilized more than 17,000 soldiers who had joined the EPLF before 1990 and in many cases had seen considerable combat experience. Many of these fighters had spent their entire adult lives in the EPLF and lacked the social, personal, and vocational skills to become competitive in the work place. As a result, they received higher compensation, more intensive training, and more psychological counseling than the first group. Special attention has been given to women fighters, who made up some 30% of the EPLF's combat troops. By 1998, the army had shrunk to 47,000.

In order to fund the demobilization program, the government cut other expenditures, campaigned to raise voluntary contributions, took its first loans, and sought external aid. Germany, Italy, Israel, and the U.S. have provided help.

Although committed to demobilization, the Government of Eritrea has some legitimate security concerns and seeks U.S. assistance to upgrade its equipment and training with a goal of producing a smaller, more professional, and more efficient army. United States military assistance so far has included deploying in-country training teams, establishing a demining training program, ship visits during which U.S. service personnel contribute labor and materials for various community relations projects, and the training of Eritrean military officers in the United States.

The Eritrean Army is equipped with a hodgepodge of captured Ethiopian equipment, mostly of Soviet origin. Eritreans have proven particularly adept at maintenance, and in many cases have improved on Soviet designs.

# FOREIGN RELATIONS

Eritrea is a member in good standing of the OAU. It has a close relationship with the United States, Italy, and a number of other European nations, including the United Kingdom, Germany, and Norway, which have become important aid donors. Within the region, it is particularly close to Ethiopia, its largest trading partner and fellow IGADD member, and

Uganda, also an IGADD member. In the Middle East, Eritrea has close ties with Yemen. Relations with Israel, Saudi Arabia, and Dubai are likely to become closer as their aid programs increase.

Eritrea broke diplomatic relations with the Sudan in December 1994. This action was taken after a long period of increasing tension between the two countries due to a series of cross-border incidents involving the extremist group the Eritrean Islamic Jihad (EIJ). Although the attacks did not pose a threat to the stability of the Government of Eritrea (the infiltrators have generally been killed or captured by government forces), the Eritreans believe the National Islamic Front (NIF) in Khartoum supported, trained, and armed the insurgents. After many months of negotiations with the Sudanese to try and end the incursions, the Government of Eritrea concluded that the NIF did not intend to change its policy and broke relations. Subsequently, the Government of Eritrea hosted a conference of Sudanese opposition leaders in June 1995 in an effort to help the opposition unite and to provide a credible alternative to the present government in Khartoum.

# U.S.-ERITREAN RELATIONS

The U.S. consulate in Asmara was first established in 1942. In 1953, the United States signed a mutual defense treaty with Ethiopia. The treaty granted the United States control and expansion of the highly important British military communications base at Kagnew near Asmara. In the 1960s, as many as 4,000 U.S. military personnel were stationed at Kagnew. In the 1970s, technological advances in the satellite and communications fields were making the communications station at Kagnew increasingly obsolete. Early in 1977, the United States informed the Ethiopian Government that it intended to

close Kagnew Station by September 30, 1977. In the meantime, U.S. relations with the Mengistu regime were worsening. In April 1977, Mengistu abrogated the 1953 mutual defense treaty and ordered a reduction of U.S. personnel in Ethiopia, including the closure of Kagnew Communications Center and the consulate in Asmara.

In August 1992, the United States reopened its consulate in Asmara, staffed with one officer. The PGE returned consulate property, confiscated by Mengistu, and the U.S. is in the process of renovating it—Kagnew Station and other facilities used by the U.S. military in Eritrea had been leased. On April 27, 1993, the U.S. recognized Eritrea as an independent state, and on June 11, diplomatic relations were established, with a charge d'affaires.

The United States has provided substantial assistance to Eritrea, including food aid, development assistance, and election assistance. In FY 1995, USAID programs provided almost $16 million in direct assistance in the areas of health, demobilization, refugee resettlement, and government and university training programs. An additional $4 million in food assistance was provided to U.S. private volunteer organizations.

Ongoing U.S. interests in Eritrea include encouraging the growth of a democratic political culture, supporting Eritrean efforts to become constructively involved in solving regional problems, and assisting Eritrea in filling its humanitarian needs.

## Principal U.S. Officials

For up-to-date information on Principal U.S. Officials, see the U.S. Embassies, Consulates, and Foreign Service section starting on page 139.

The address of the U.S. Embassy in Eritrea is 34 Zera Yacob St., P.O. Box 211, Asmara (tel 291-1-120004).

# ESTONIA

June 1997

Official Name:
**Republic of Estonia**

# PROFILE

## Geography

**Area:** 45,226 sq. km. (18,086 sq. miles); about the size of New Hampshire and Vermont.
**Cities:** Capital—Tallinn (pop. 434,763); Tartu (115,400); Narva (77,770); Kohtla-Jarve (71,066); Parnu (54,200); Sillamae (19,804); Rakvere (20,100).
**Terrain:** Flat, with an average elevation of 50m. Elevation is slightly higher in the east and southeast. Steep limestone banks and 1,520 islands mark the coastline.
**Land use:** 22% arable land, 11% meadows and pasture, 31% forest and woodland, 21% other, 15% swamps and lakes. Coastal waters are largely polluted.
**Climate:** Temperate, with four seasons of near-equal length. January temperatures average -3–7°C (20–27°F); July, 15–18°C (60–65°F). Annual precipitation averages 61–71 cm. (28 in.).

## People

**Nationality:** Noun and adjective—Estonian(s).
**Population:** 1.49 million.
**Annual growth rate:** .7%. Birth Rate: 6/1,000. Death Rate: 12/1,000.
**Migration Rate:** 3/1,000.

**Density:** 35/sq. km. (90.4/sq. mi.). Urban dwellers: 71%.
**Ethnic groups:** Estonians 64%, Russians 29%, Ukrainians 3%, Belarusians 2%.
**Religions:** Predominantly Lutheran; minorities of Russian Orthodox, Baptist.
**Language:** Estonian. Most people also speak Russian.
**Education:** Years compulsory—12. By 1989, 12% of the adult populace completed college. Attendance—214,000 students at 561 schools, plus 24,000 university students. Literacy—100%.
**Health:** Infant mortality rate—9/1,000 births. Life expectancy—65 years for men, 74 for women.
**Work force (785,500 people):** Agriculture—12%. Industry—32%. Housing—5%. Health care—6%. Education, culture—12%. Trade—9%. Transport—8%. Construction—10%. Other—4%. Government—2%.

## Government

**Type:** Parliamentary democracy.
**Constitution:** On June 28, 1992 Estonians ratified a constitution based on the 1938 model, offering legal continuity to the Republic of Estonia prior to Soviet occupation.
**Branches:** Executive—President (Chief of State), elected by Parliament every five years; Prime Minister (Head of Government). Legislative—Riigikogu (Parlia-

ment—101 members, 4-year term). Judicial—Supreme Court.
**Administrative regions:** 15 counties and 6 independent towns.
**Principal Political Parties/Coalitions:** Coalition/Rural Union (PM Siiman/ex-Pres. Ruutel)—19/22 seats; Reform Party (ex-FM Kallas, Riigikogu Chair Savi)—19 seats; Center Party (ex-PM Savisaar, Rein Veidemann)—15 seats; Pro Patria/Nat'l. Independence (ex-PM Laar, Kelam)—8 seats; Moderates (ex-PM Andres Tarand, Lauristin)—6 seats; "Our Home is Estonia;" ("Russian"; faction, Andrejev)—6 seats; Right-Wing (ex-Parliament Chairman Ulo Nugis)—5 seats Suffrage: 18 years-universal; non-citizen residents may vote in municipal elections.
**Government budget:** $790 million.
**National holidays:** February 24 (Independence Day), June 23 (Victory Day—anniversary of Battle of Vonnu in 1919).
**Flag:** Horizontal tricolor—blue, black and white.

## Economy

**GDP (1995):** $5 billion 1994–96 growth rates: 5% annually.
**Per capita income:** $3,000.
**1996 inflation rate:** 26%.
**Unemployment:** 8%.
**Natural resources:** Oil shale, phosphorite, limestone, blue clay.
**Agriculture/Forestry (10% of 1995 GDP):** milk and dairy products,

meat, cereals, potatoes. Cultivable land—1.36 million hectares (60% arable, 18% meadow, 13% pasture).

**Manufacturing/Mining/Energy (45% of GDP):** electricity, oil shale, chemical products, electric motors, textiles, furniture, cellulose/paper products, building materials, processed foods. Trade, Hotel/Dining: 15% of GDP.

**Construction:** 8% of GDP.

**Public Services:** 7% of GDP.

**Transport/Communication:** 8% of GDP.

**Exports ($1.6 billion):** textiles/clothes 15%, machinery/equipment 12%, food 10%, wood/wood products 8%, chemicals 8%. Major markets—Finland (32%), Russia (16%), Sweden (9%), Germany (10%), USA (2%). 1995 Imports ($2.2 billion): machinery/equipment 20%, minerals 13%, vehicles 10%, textiles/clothes 10%, food 8%. Partners—Finland (21%), Russia (18%), Sweden (11%), Latvia (8%), Germany (7%), USA (2%).

**Official exchange rate:** 8 kroon (EEK) = 1 Deutschmark (DM). 12.5 kroon = US$1.

**Foreign Capital Investment:** 6,000-plus foreign enterprises with investment of $230 million. Finland 52% of firms with 22% of capital; Sweden 11% of firms with 27% of capital; Russia 13% with 12% of capital; Germany 4% with 4% of capital; USA 4% with 7% of capital.

# GEOGRAPHY

Between 57.3 and 59.5 latitude and 21.5 and 28.1 longitude, Estonia lies on the eastern shores of the Baltic Sea on the level northwestern part of the rising East European platform. Average elevation reaches only 50 m (160 ft.). The climate resembles New England's. Shale and limestone deposits, along forests which cover 40% of the land, play key economic roles in this resource-poor country. Estonia boasts over 1,500 lakes, numerous bogs, and 3,794 km of coastline marked by numerous bays, straits and inlets. Tallinn's Muuga port offers one of Europe's finest warm-water harbor facilities.

Today, Estonia is slightly larger than Denmark, the Netherlands and Switzerland. Estonia's strategic location has precipitated many wars that were fought on its territory between two other rival powers at its expense. In 1944 the U.S.S.R. granted Russia the trans-Narva and Petseri regions on Estonia's eastern frontier, which still remain contested bilaterally.

# PEOPLE

The name "Eesti," or Estonia, is derived from the word "Aisti," the name given by the ancient Germans to the peoples living northeast of the Vistula River. The Roman historian Tacitus in the first century A.D. was the first to mention the Aisti, and early Scandinavians called the land south of the Gulf of Finland "Eistland," and the people "aistr." Estonians belong to the Baltic-Finnic group of the Finno-Ugric peoples, as do the Finns and Hungarians. Archaeological research supports the existence of human activity in the region as early as 8,000 BC but by 3,500 BC the principal ancestors of the Estonians had arrived from the east.

Estonians look like, and consider themselves, Nordics, evidenced through the strong cultural and religious influences gained over centuries during Germanic and Scandinavian colonization and settlement. This highly literate society places strong emphasis upon education, which is free and compulsory until age 16. The first book in Estonian was printed in 1525. Most Estonians belong to the Evangelical Lutheran Church, but a sizable minority are Russian Orthodox.

From 1945–1989 the percentage of ethnic Estonians in Estonia dropped from 94% to 61%, caused primarily by the Soviet program promoting mass immigration of urban industrial workers from Russia, Ukraine and Belarus; as well as by wartime emigration and Stalin's mass deportations and executions. Estonia's citizenship law and constitution meet international and CSCE standards,

guaranteeing universal human and civil rights.

Written with the Latin alphabet, Estonian is the language of the Estonian people and the official language of the country. One-third of the standard vocabulary is derived from adding suffixes to root words. The oldest known examples of written Estonian originate in thirteenth century chronicles. The Soviet era had imposed the official use of Russian, so most Estonians speak Russian as a second language while the resident Slavic populace speaks Russian as a first language.

# HISTORY

Estonians are one of the longest settled European peoples, whose forebears, known as the "comb pottery" people, lived on the southeastern shores of the Baltic Sea over 5,000 years ago. Like other early agricultural societies, Estonians were organized into economically self-sufficient, male-dominated clans with few differences in wealth or social power. By the early Middle Ages most Estonians were small landholders, with farmsteads primarily organized by village. Estonian government remained decentralized, with local political and administrative subdivisions emerging only during the first century A.D. By then, Estonia had a population of over 150,000 people and remained the last corner of medieval Europe to be Christianized.

Estonia also managed to remain nominally independent from the Vikings to the west and Kievan Rus to the east, subject only to occasional forced tribute collections.

However, the Danes conquered Toompea, the hilled fortress at what is now the center of Tallinn, and in 1227 the German crusading order of the Sword Brethren defeated the last Estonian stronghold; the people were Christianized, colonized and enserfed. Despite attempts to restore independence, Estonia was divided among three domains and small states were formed. Tallinn joined the Hanseatic League in 1248.

By 1236, the Sword Brethren allied with the Order of the Teutonic Knights and became known as the Livonian Order of the Teutonic Knights. Finding upkeep of the distant colony too costly, the Danes in 1346 sold their part of Estonia to the Livonian Order. Despite successful Russian raids and invasions in 1481 and 1558, the local German barons continued to rule Estonia and who since 1524 preserved Estonian commitment to the Protestant Reformation. Northern Estonia submitted to Swedish control in 1561 during the Livonian Wars, and in 1582/3 southern Estonia (Livonia) became part of Poland's Duchy of Courland.

In 1625, mainland Estonia came entirely under Swedish rule, and in 1645, Sweden bought the island of Saaremaa from Denmark. In 1631, the Swedish king Gustav II Adolf granted the peasantry greater autonomy, opened the first known Estonian-language school in Tallinn, and in 1632, established a printing press and university in the city of Tartu. The Swedish defeat resulting in the 1721 Treaty of Nystad imposed Russian rule in what became modern Estonia. Nonetheless, the legal system, Lutheran church, local and town governments, and education remained mostly German until the late 19th century and partially until 1918.

By 1819, the Baltic provinces were the first in the Russian empire in which serfdom was abolished, spurring the peasants to own their own land or move to the cities. These moves created the economic foundation for the Estonian national cultural awakening that had lain dormant for some 600 years of foreign rule. Estonia was caught in a current of national awakening that began sweeping through Europe in the mid-1800s.

A cultural movement sprang forth to adopt the use of Estonian as the language of instruction in schools, all-Estonian song festivals were held regularly after 1869, and a national

literature in Estonia developed. Kalevipoeg, Estonia's epic national poem, was published in 1861 in both Estonian and German.

More importantly, activists who agitated for a modern national culture also agitated for a modern national state.

As the 1905 Revolution swept through Estonia, the Estonians called for freedom of the press and assembly, for universal franchise, and for national autonomy. The 1905 uprisings were brutally suppressed and Estonian gains were minimal, but the tense stability that prevailed between 1905 and 1917 allowed Estonians to advance the aspiration of national statehood.

With the collapse of the Russian empire in World War I, Russia's Provisional Government granted national autonomy to Estonia. A popularly elected assembly (Maapaev) was formed but was quickly forced underground by opposing extremist political forces. The Committee of Elders of the underground Maapaev

announced the Republic of Estonia on 24 February 1918, one day before German troops invaded. After the withdrawal of German troops in November 1918, fighting broke out between Bolshevik and Estonian troops. On February 2, 1920 the Treaty of Tartu—the Soviet Union's first foreign peace treaty—was signed by the Republic of Estonia and Soviet Russia. The terms of the treaty stated that Soviet Russia renounced in perpetuity all rights to the territory of Estonia.

Independence lasted twenty-two years. Estonia underwent a number of economic, social, and political reforms necessary to come to terms with its new status as a sovereign state. Economically and socially, land reform in 1919 was the most important step. Large estate holdings belonging to the Baltic nobility were redistributed among the peasants and especially among volunteers in the War of Independence. Loss of markets in the east led to considerable hardships until Estonia developed an export-based economy and domestic industries. Estonia's principal markets became Scandinavia, Great Britain and Western Europe, with some exports to the United States and Soviet Union.

During its early independence Estonia operated under a liberal democratic constitution patterned on the Swiss model. However, with nine to fourteen politically divergent parties Estonia experienced twenty different parliamentary governments between 1919–1933. The Great Depression spawned the growth of powerful, far-rightist parties which successfully pushed popular support in 1933 for a new constitution granting much stronger executive powers. In a preemptive move against the far right, Estonia's first and also then-president, Konstantin Pats, dissolved parliament and governed the country by decree. By 1938 Estonia ratified a third, more balanced and very liberal constitution, and elected a new parliament the following year.

The independence period was one of great cultural advancement. Estonian language schools were established, and artistic life of all kinds flourished. One of the more notable cultural acts of the independence period, unique in Western Europe at the time of its passage in 1925, was a guarantee of cultural autonomy to minority groups comprising at least 3,000 persons, and to Jews.

Estonia had pursued a policy of neutrality, but the signing of the Molotov-Ribbentrop Non-aggression Pact on August 23, 1939 signaled the end of independence. The agreement provided for the Soviet occupation of Estonia, Latvia, part of Finland and later, Lithuania, in return for Nazi Germany's assuming control over most of Poland. After extensive diplomatic intrigue, the Estonian Soviet Socialist Republic was proclaimed on July 21, 1940, one month after Estonia was occupied by Soviet troops. The ESSR was formally accepted into the Soviet Union on August 6.

Soviet occupation was accompanied by expropriation of property, Sovietization of cultural life and the installation of Stalinist communism in political life. Deportations also

quickly followed, beginning on the night of June 14, 1941.

That night, more than 10,000 people, most of them women, children and the elderly, were taken from their homes and sent to Siberia in cattle cars. When Nazi Germany attacked the Soviet Union on June 22, most Estonians greeted the Germans with relatively open arms.

Two and a half years of Nazi occupation amply demonstrated that German intentions were nearly as harsh as Soviet aggression: Estonia became a part of "Ostland," and about 5,500 Estonians died in concentration camps. However, few Estonians welcomed the Red Army's return to the frontier in January 1944. Without much support from retreating German troops, Estonian conscripts engaged the Soviets in a slow, bloody, nine-month battle. Some ten percent of the population fled to the West between 1940 and 1944. By late September, Soviet forces expelled the last German troops from Estonia, ushering in a second phase of Soviet rule. That year, Moscow also moved to transfer the Estonian Narva and Petseri border districts, which held a large percentage of ethnic Russians, to Russian control.

For the next decade in the countryside, an anti-Soviet guerrilla movement known as "the Forest Brethren" existed in the countryside. Composed of formerly conscripted Estonian soldiers from the German Army, fugitives from the Soviet military draft or security police arrest, and those seeking revenge for mass deportations the Forest Brethren used abandoned German and Soviet equipment and worked in groups or alone. In the hope that protracted resistance would encourage Allied intervention for the restoration of Estonian independence, the movement reached its zenith in 1946–48 with an estimated 5,000–30,000 followers and held effective military control in some rural areas.

After the war the Estonian Communist Party (ECP) became the pre-eminent organization in the republic. Most of these new members were

Russified Estonians who had spent most of their lives in the Soviet Union. Not surprisingly, Estonians were reluctant to join the ECP and thus take part in the Sovietization of their own country. The ethnic Estonian share in the total ECP membership went from 90% in 1941 to 48% in 1952.

After Stalin's death, Party membership vastly expanded its social base to include more ethnic Estonians. By the mid-1960s, the percentage of ethnic Estonian membership stabilized near 50%. On the eve of perestroika the ECP claimed about 100,000 members; less than half were ethnic Estonians and comprised less than two percent of the country's population. Russians or Russified Estonians continued to dominate the party's upper echelons.

A positive aspect of the post-Stalin era in Estonia was a re-opening in the late 1950s of citizens' contacts with foreign countries. Ties were also reactivated with Finland, boosting a flourishing black market. In the mid-1960s, Estonians began watching Finnish television. This electronic "window on the West" afforded Estonians more information on current affairs and more access to Western culture and thought than any other group in the Soviet Union. This heightened media environment was important in preparing Estonians for their vanguard role in extending perestroika during the Gorbachev era.

By the 1970s, national concerns, including worries about ecological ruin, became the major theme of dissent in Estonia. In the late 1970s, Estonian society grew increasingly concerned about the threat of cultural Russification to the Estonian language and national identity. By 1981, Russian was taught in the first grade of Estonian language schools and was also introduced into the Estonian pre-school teaching. These acts prompted forty established intellectuals to write a letter to Moscow and the republic authorities. This "Letter of the Forty" spoke out against the use of force against protesters and the increasing threat to the Estonian language and culture.

In October of 1980, the youth of Tallinn also demonstrated against toughened Russification policies, particularly in education.

By the beginning of the Gorbachev era, concern over the cultural survival of the Estonian people had reached a critical point. Although these complaints were first couched in environmental terms, they quickly became the grist of straightforward political national feelings. In this regard the two decades of independent statehood were pivotal.

The ECP remained stable in the early perestroika years and appeared strong at its 19th Congress in 1986. By 1988, however, the ECP's weakness had become clear when it was unable to assume more than a passive role and was relegated to a reactive position.

Praising the 1980 "Letter of the Forty" Vaino Valjas replaced Karl Vaino as Party Chief and thereby temporarily enhanced the ECP's reputation along with his own. Nevertheless, the Party continued its downward spiral of influence in 1989 and 1990. In November 1989, the Writers' Union Party Organization voted to suspend its activity and the Estonian Komsomol disbanded.

In February 1990, Estonia's Supreme Soviet eliminated paragraph 6 of the republic's constitution which had guaranteed the Party's leading role in society. The final blow came at the ECP's 20th Congress in March 1990 when it voted to break with the CPSU. The Party splintered into three branches, then consolidated into a pro-CPSU (Moscow) and an independent ECP.

As the ECP waned, other political movements, groupings and parties moved to fill the power vacuum. The first and most important was the Estonian Popular Front, established in April 1988 with its own platform, leadership and broad constituency. The Greens and the dissident-led Estonian National Independence Party soon followed. By 1989, the political spectrum widened and new parties were formed and re-formed almost daily.

A number of changes in the republic's government brought about by political advances in the late 1980s played a major role in forming a legal framework for political change. This involved the republic's Supreme Soviet being transformed into an authentic regional law-making body. This relatively conservative legislature managed to pass a number of laws, notably a package of laws that addressed the most sensitive ethnic concerns. These laws included the early declaration of sovereignty (November 1988); a law on economic independence (May 1989) confirmed by the U.S.S.R. Supreme Soviet that November; a language law making Estonian the official language (January 1989); and local and republic election laws stipulating residency requirements for voting and candidacy (August, November 1989).

Although not all non-Estonians supported full independence, they were divided in their goals for the republic. In March 1990 some 18% of Russian speakers supported the idea of fully independent Estonia, up from 7% the previous autumn, and only a small group of Estonians were opposed to full independence in early 1990. Estonia held free elections for the 105-member Supreme Council on March 18, 1990. All residents of Estonia were eligible to participate in the elections, including the approximately 50,000 Soviet troops stationed there. The Popular Front coalition, composed of left and centrist parties and led by former Central Planning Committee official Edgar Savisaar, held a parliamentary majority.

Despite the emergence of the new lawmaking body, an alternative legislature developed in Estonia. In February 1990, a body known as the Congress of Estonia was elected in unofficial and unsanctioned elections. Supporters of the Congress argued that the inter-war republic continued to exist de jure: since Estonia was forcibly annexed by the U.S.S.R., only citizens of that republic and their descendants could decide Estonia's future.

Through a strict, nonconfrontational policy in pursuing independence, Estonia managed to avoid the violence which Latvia and Lithuania incurred in the bloody January 1991 crackdowns and in the border-customs post guard murders that summer. During the August coup in the U.S.S.R., Estonia was able to maintain constant operation and control of its telecommunications facilities, thereby offering the West a clear view into the latest coup developments and serving as a conduit for swift Western support and recognition of Estonia's redeclaration of independence on August 20. Following Europe's lead, the U.S. formally reestablished diplomatic relations with Estonia on September 2, and the USSR Supreme Soviet offered recognition on September 6.

During the subsequent cold winter which compounded Estonia's economic restructuring problems, Prime Minister Edgar Savisaar demanded emergency powers to deal with the economic and fuel crises. A consequent no-confidence vote by the Supreme Council caused the Popular Front leader to resign, and a new government led by former Transportation Minister Tiit Vahi took office.

After more than three years of negotiations, on August 31, 1994, the armed forces of the Russian Federation withdrew from Estonia. Several hundred civilian-clad Russian military will remain at the nuclear submarine training reactor facility at Paldiski until September 30, 1995, in order to remove equipment and help decommission the facility. Estonia also maintains that in the absence of any other agreements, Russia must recognize the interstate border established by the 1920 Treaty of Tartu as the official negotiating position for any new border agreement.

# GOVERNMENT AND POLITICAL CONDITIONS

On June 28, 1992, Estonian voters approved the constitutional assembly's draft constitution and implementation act, which established a parliamentary government with a President as chief of State and with a government headed by a Prime Minister.

The Riigikogu, a unicameral legislative body, is the highest organ of state authority. It initiates and approves legislation sponsored by the Prime Minister. The Prime Minister has full responsibility and control over his cabinet.

Free and fair parliamentary and presidential elections were held on September 20, 1992. Approximately 68% of the country's 637,000 registered voters cast ballots. The leading presidential contenders, President Ruutel and former Foreign Minister Lennart Meri, faced a secret parliamentary vote to determine the winner. Ruutel's former association with the ruling Communist Party probably helped Meri win on the first ballot. Meri chose 32-year old historian and Christian Democratic Party founder Mart Laar as prime minister.

In February 1992, and with amendments in January 1995, the Riigikogu renewed Estonia's liberal 1938 citizenship law, which also provides equal civil protection to resident aliens. Dual citizenship is allowed for Estonians and their families who fled the Soviet occupation. Accordingly, those who were citizens in 1940 are citizens now. Those who arrived subsequently can become citizens one year following a four year residence retroactive to March 30, 1990 and demonstrate comprehension of Estonian. Most non-citizen ethnic Slavs (35% of the populace) became eligible for naturalization in March, 1993. The Government funds Estonian language training.

In nationwide municipal elections held on October 17, 1993, opposition party and ethnic Russian candidates gained a majority in most areas, especially in Tallinn and the Northeast. After having survived a number of government scandals and controversies (over his handling of an Israeli arms deal, bank failures, ruble sales, and alleged misconduct of certain

ministers), Mart Laar resigned in August 1994, after losing a parliamentary vote of confidence. The popular, nonpartisan former Minister of Environment, Andres Tarand, was appointed as Laar's successor.

Nearly 70% of the electorate voted in parliamentary elections held March 5, 1995. The Coalition Party (former PM Vahi) and the Rural Union (ex-ESSR Chairman Ruutel)-"KMU"—garnered 1/3 of the vote for a plurality. The Reform Party (Estonian Bank Director Siim Kallas) got 16% of the vote, and the Centrist Party (former PM Savisaar) 14%. Pro Patria (former PM Laar) and the National Independence Party received 7%, the Moderates (acting PM Tarand) 6%, "Our Home is Estonia" (Russians) 6%, and the right-wingers Riigikogu chairman Nugis) 5%. The new government, led once again by Tiit Vahi, has continued to pursue the same style of economic reform and Western integration that characterized Estonia since 1992.

With the August 1995 discovery that some Estonian politicians had been subjected to illegal surveillance, including wiretaps (referred to as Estonia's "Watergate"), the country faced its most severe political and constitutional test since regaining independence in 1991. After dismissing Interior Minister Edgar Savisaar for his implication in the scandal, Prime Minister Vahi submitted his cabinet's resignation. President Meri subsequently tapped Vahi to form a new coalition, which resulted in Vahi's alliance with the Reform Party. In meeting that test, Estonia again demonstrated that it is a normal democratic country based on rule of law and with a vibrant free press.

In 1996, Estonia ratified a border agreement with Latvia and completed work with Russia on a technical border agreement that Estonia is ready to sign. President Meri was re-elected in free and fair indirect elections in August and September. Free and fair nationwide municipal elections were held in October. In November, the Reform Party pulled out of the government when its majority partner, the Coalition Party, signed

an agreement with the rival Center Party to cooperate in the municipal government councils. The Coalition Party survived the cabinet crisis as a minority government when the Prime Minister appointed several popular non-partisan candidates in ministerial posts.

## Government Officials

For up-to-date information on Principal Government Officials, see the Chiefs of State and Cabinet Members of Foreign Governments section starting on page 1.

Estonia maintains an embassy in the United States at 2131 Massachusetts Avenue, NW; Washington DC 20005 (tel: 202-588-0101). It operates a consulate at 630 Fifth Ave., Suite 2415, New York, NY 10020 (tel: 212-247-7634).

# ECONOMY

For centuries until 1920, Estonian agriculture consisted of native peasants working large feudal-type estates held by ethnic German landlords. In the previous decades, centralized Czarist rule had contributed a rather large industrial sector dominated by the world's largest cotton mill, a ruined post-war economy, and an inflated ruble currency.

By the early 1930s, Estonia entirely transformed its economy, despite considerable hardship, dislocation and unemployment. Compensating the German landowners for their holdings, the Government confiscated the estates and divided them into small farms which subsequently formed the basis of Estonian prosperity.

By 1929, a stable currency, the kroon (or crown), was established, and by 1939, Estonia's living standard compared well with Sweden's. Trade focused on the local market and the West, particularly Germany and the United Kingdom. Only 3% of all commerce was with the USSR.

The U.S.S.R.'s forcible annexation of Estonia in 1940 and the ensuing Nazi and Soviet destruction during World War II crippled the Estonian economy. Post-war Sovietization of life continued with the integration of Estonia's economy and industry into the U.S.S.R.'s centrally-planned structure. Over 56% of Estonian farms were collectivized in the month of April, 1949 alone. Moscow expanded on those Estonian industries which had locally available raw materials, such as oil-shale mining and phosphorites. As a laboratory for economic experiments, especially in industrial management techniques, Estonia enjoyed more success and greater prosperity than other regions under Soviet rule. As the author of the then-radical "Self-Accounting Estonia" plan in 1988, Prime Minister Savisaar succeeded by early 1992 in freeing most prices and encouraging privatization and foreign investment far earlier than other former Soviet-bloc countries. This experimentation with Western capitalism has promoted Estonia's clear advantage in reorienting to Western markets and business practice.

Upon re-establishing independence, Estonia has styled itself as the gateway between East and West and aggressively pursued economic reform and integration with the West. Estonia's market reforms put it among the economic leaders in the former COMECON area. A balanced budget, flat-rate income tax, free trade regime, fully convertible currency, competitive commercial banking sector, and hospitable environment for foreign investment helped Estonia sign an EU Europe Agreement in June 1995 without transition period. These policies have also helped reduce inflation from 90% a month in early 1992 to less than 3% a month in 1995 and 1996.

Estonia has also made excellent progress in regard to structural adjustment. Since late 1995, more than 90% of small- and medium-scale privatization was complete, and the national privatization agency had privatized over 50% of large enterprises, including engineering, sea, air, and railway transport, health-care, and insurance sectors. The privatization law provides equal opportunities for domestic and foreign individuals as well as corpora-

tions. The constitution requires a balanced budget, and Estonia's intellectual property protection laws are among Europe's strongest. In early

## Travel Notes

**Customs:** Estonia does not require visas for American, Canadian or British citizens. Visitors are encouraged to register at the U.S. Embassy.

Hard currency exceeding 1,000 DM must be declared upon entry; foreigners need not declare hard currency exports less than this sum but may not export more currency than what they declared upon arrival. Articles with a total value of less than 5,000 kroons, either already declared or purchased in Estonia, are duty-free upon departure. A 100% export duty exists on items of greater total value, and 10–100% export duties can be levied on tobacco, alcohol, gasoline, precious metals and jewelry, furs and cultural objects.

**Climate and clothing:** Estonia's climate enjoys seasons of almost equal length. Tallinn and the coast is temperate, with pleasant, cool summers and damp winters; eastern Estonia is continental, with warmer summers and harsher winters.

**Health:** Medical care does not meet Western standards, but is constantly improving. Raw fruits and vegetables are safe to eat, and the water is potable. Heat and hot water are readily available.

**Transportation:** SAS, Finnair, KLM, Lufthansa and Estonia Airlines provide service between European cities and Tallinn Airport. Train service is available via Moscow, St. Petersburg and Warsaw/Frankfurt, and a bus line connects the Baltic capitals with Poland and Germany. Bus and taxi services within the capital and its environs are good. Excellent Tallinn-Helsinki and Tallinn-Stockholm ferry links exist year-round. Taxis are inexpensive and available at stands or may be ordered by phone. Rental cars are available, and gasoline prices are at market rates.

**Telecommunications:** Telephone and telegraph services are readily available at standard international rates. Tallinn is 7 hours ahead of eastern standard time.

**Work week:** 41 hours for blue-collar, 40 hours white-collar. Most stores and shops are closed on Sunday, open Monday-Friday from 10:00am - 6:00pm and on Saturday from 9:00am - 1:00pm.

**National holidays:** Businesses and the U.S. Embassy may be closed on the following Estonian holidays: January 1—New Year's Day; February 24—Independence Day; Good Friday; Easter Sunday; May 1—Labor Day; June 23—Victory Day (commemoration of Battle of Vonnu in 1919 during the War of Independence); June 21, 22—Midsummer; December 25—Christmas; December 26—Second Day of Christmas. The U.S. Embassy also is closed on U.S. federal holidays.

**Tourist attractions:** Estonia carries a 150-year history in tourism and witnessed over 200,000 visitors in 1990. Tallinn is the country's leading attraction, with its beautiful, Hanseatic, architecturally intact "Old Town." The island of Saaremaa holds deep cultural and traditional roots. Estonia offers verdant landscapes and nature reserves, numerous manors and medieval ruins, fascinating museums, tradition-rich folk music and folk dance festivals, and excellent sailing opportunities.

**Currency, weights and measures:** The freely convertible kroon is pegged to 1/8 the value of the German deutschmark. Traveler's checks and major credit cards can be used at most banks, hotels, and stores. Estonia uses the metric system and 220v current.

**Crime:** By U.S. standards, Estonia has a low rate of violent crime. However, the introduction of a market-oriented economy has resulted in an increase in street crime, especially at night near major hotels and restaurants frequented by foreigners. Penalties for possession, use and dealing in illegal drugs are strict, and convicted offenders can expect jail sentences and fines.

**Travel Advice:** For up-to-date information from the U.S. State Department on possible inconvenient or hazardous situations, see the **Travel Warnings and Consular Information Sheets from the U.S. Government** section starting on page 1723. For the latest information on health requirements and conditions, see the **International Travelers' Health Information** section starting on page 1385. For further information dealing with non-urgent matter, see the **Tips for Travelers to...** section starting on page 1588.

1992, both liquidity problems and structural weakness stemming from the communist period precipitated a banking crisis. As a result, effective bankruptcy legislation was enacted and privately owned, well-managed banks emerged as market leaders. Today, near-ideal conditions for the banking sector exist. Foreigners are not restricted from buying bank shares or acquiring majority holdings. Tallinn Stock Exchange opened in early 1996, and is fully electronic.

Trade has continued to expand since 1994; the current account deficit reflects continuing imports of capital goods. Estonia supplies 60% of its own energy converted from peat, wood, hydroelectric plants, and oil shale. Estonia has no domestic capacity to refine crude oil, and thus depends heavily on exports from Western Europe and Russia. Energetics, telecommunications, textiles, chemical products, banking, services, food and fishing, timber, shipbuilding, electronics, and transportation are key sectors of the economy. The ice-free port of Muuga, near Tallinn, is an underutilized modern facility featuring good transshipment capability, a high-capacity grain elevator, chill/frozen storage and brand-new oil tanker offloading capabilities.

Yet Estonia still faces challenges, including a slow pace of establishing and putting into effect a legal framework compatible with a market economy. Laws to streamline the privatization process, facilitate the transfer of real property, privatize housing and establish a commission for the enforcement of competition and anti-monopoly laws were enacted in late 1993, but have not yet been fully implemented. Housing privatization is moving relatively slowly. The same circumstances apply in regard to agricultural privatization, which has caused severe problems for farmers needing collateral to be eligible for loans.

Estonia has paid a price in terms of eroded standards of living, especially for the large portion of the population on fixed pensions. However, it is reaping the macroeconomic dividends from its "shock therapy", and is the first country from the former Soviet

area to experience such a spectacular turnaround. After having declined for four consecutive years by a cumulative total of more than 50%, Estonia's GDP increased by nearly 6% in 1994, and has remained around 5% ever since. During that four-year period overall, employment declined 15% and average real wages and real disposable income declined 60%. Since 1994, by contrast, real wages have increased by about 5% annually and unemployment has stabilized.

Estonia has made a determined effort to reorient its trade toward the West. Trade with Russia, which once accounted for the overwhelming majority of Estonia's imports and exports, now accounts for only one-fifth of all trade; almost 80% of Estonia's trade now is directed toward the West. This reorientation of trade helped Estonia to conclude a Europe Agreement with the European Union in June 1995 which foresees no transition period to associated member status. With the United States in 1994, Estonia signed agreements on trade and intellectual property protection, investment, and science and technology cooperation. Given this base and Estonia's associate status with the EU, U.S. firms should consider Estonia for significant investment and re-export opportunities.

Estonia's graduation from USAID's assistance programs, completed in September 1996, recognizes Estonia's position as a leading economic reformer in all of Central and Eastern Europe.

# DEFENSE

Estonia's defense system is based upon the Swedish-Finnish concept of a rapid response force composed of a mobilization base and a small group of career professionals. The army consists of three battalions of 714 men each, and there is a mandatory one year draft period of active duty. Alternative conscription for eighteen months for conscientious objectors is available. The fledgling navy and air force are still rudimentary.

Border guards fall under the Interior Ministry's supervision. Comprised of 250–300 men each, the seven border guard districts, including a "coast guard," are responsible for border protection and passport and customs duties, as well as smuggling and drug trafficking interdiction. A volunteer paramilitary organization, "kaitseliit," serves as a type of national guard.

# FOREIGN RELATIONS

Estonia joined the United Nations on September 18, 1991, and is a signatory to a number of UN organizations and other international agreements. It also is a member of the Organization on Security and Cooperation in Europe, Partnership for Peace, the North Atlantic Coordinating Council, and the Council of Europe, which presidency it held in 1996. Estonia is unaffiliated directly with any political alliance but welcomes further cooperation and integration with NATO, the EU, and other Western organizations.

Estonia maintains embassies in the United States, Austria, Argentina, Australia, Belarus, Belgium, Brazil, Chile, Denmark, Finland, France, Germany, India, Israel, Korea, Latvia, Lithuania, Pakistan, Poland, Russia, South Africa, Sweden, Switzerland, Turkey, Ukraine, and United Kingdom. It operates missions in Canada, Hungary, Norway, the Netherlands, to the United Nations, and a Consulate General in Toronto, Canada. Honorary consuls are located in Australia, Austria, Switzerland, and in Seattle.

## Principal U.S. Officials

**For up-to-date information on Principal U.S. Officials, see the U.S. Embassies, Consulates, and Foreign Service section starting on page 139.**

The United States established diplomatic relations with Estonia on July 28, 1922. U.S. representation accredited to Estonia served from the U.S. Legation in Riga, Latvia, until June 30, 1930, when a legation was established with a non-resident minister. The Soviet invasion forced the closure of Legation Tallinn on September 5, 1940, but Estonian representation in the United States has continued uninterrupted for over seventy years. The U.S. never recognized the forcible incorporation of Estonia into the USSR, and views the present Government of Estonia as a legal continuation of the inter-war republic. Estonia has enjoyed Most-Favored-Nation (MFN) treatment with the U.S. since December, 1991. Through 1994, the U.S. committed over $45 million to assist Estonia's economic and political transformation and to address humanitarian needs. In 1994, Estonian exports to the United States amounted to $23.4 million while U.S. imports accrued to $25.5 million. In 1994, U.S. investment, consisting of over 145 firms, made up over $50 million of $185 million in foreign investment in Estonia.

The U.S. Embassy in Estonia is located at Kentmanni 20, Tallinn [tel. (372-6)312-021/4].

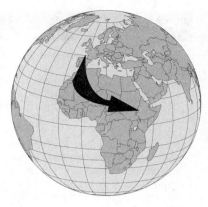

# ETHIOPIA

March 1998

Official Name:
**Federal Democratic Republic of Ethiopia**

# PROFILE

## Geography

**Area:** 1.1 million sq. km (472,000 sq. mi.); about the size of Texas, Oklahoma, and New Mexico combined.
**Cities:** Capital—Addis Ababa (pop. 2.3 million). Other cities—Dire Dawa (180,000), Harar (138,000), Dessie (105,000), Nazret (100,000), Bahir Dar (95,000), Awassa (90,000).
**Terrain:** High plateau, mountains, dry lowland plains.
**Climate:** Temperate in the highlands; hot in the lowlands.

## People

**Nationality:** Noun and adjective—Ethiopian(s).
**Population (1997 est.):** 58 million.
**Annual growth rate:** 3%.
**Ethnic groups (est.):** Oromo 35%, Amhara 30%, Tigre 6%-8%, Somali 6%.
**Religions:** Muslim 40%, Ethiopian Orthodox Christian 45%-50%, Protestant 5%, indigenous beliefs, remainder.
**Languages:** Amharic (official), Tigrinya, Oromifa, English, Somali.
**Education:** Years compulsory—none. Attendance (elementary) 46%. Literacy—25%. Health: Infant mortality rate—112/1,000 live births.
**Work force:** Agriculture—80%. Industry and commerce—20%.

## Government

**Type:** Federal Republic.
**Constitution:** Ratified 1994.
**Branches:** Executive—President, Council of State, Council of Ministers. Executive power resides with the prime minister. Legislative—bicameral parliament. Judicial—divided into Federal and Regional Courts.
**Administrative subdivisions:** 10 regions.
**Political parties:** Ethiopian People's Revolutionary Democratic Front (EPRDF) and 50 other registered parties, most of which are small and ethnically based.
**Suffrage:** Universal.
**Central government budget:** $1.76 billion.
**Defense:** $128 million (7.3%).
**National holiday:** May 28.
**Flag:** Green, yellow and red horizontal stripes from top to bottom, with gold five-pointed star and rays on a blue circular background.

## Economy

**Real GDP:** $6.1 billion.
**Annual growth rate (last 5 years):** 8%.
**Per capita income:** $110.
**Average inflation rate (last 3 years):** 3.5%.
**Natural resources:** Potash, salt, gold, copper, platinum, natural gas (unexploited).
**Agriculture (40% of GDP):** Products—coffee, cereals, pulses, oilseeds, khat, meat, hides and skins. Cultivated land—67%.
**Industry (13.7% of GDP):** Types—textiles, processed foods, construction, cement, hydroelectric power.
**Trade (1996):** Exports—$783 million. Imports—$1.65 billion.
**Official exchange rate (Feb. 1998):** 6.92 Ethiopian Birr=U.S.$1.
**Fiscal year:** July 8-July 7.

# GEOGRAPHY

Ethiopia is located in the Horn of Africa and is bordered on the north and northeast by Eritrea, on the east by Djibouti and Somalia, on the south by Kenya, and on the west and southwest by Sudan. The country has a high central plateau that varies from 1,800 to 3,000 meters (6,000-10,000 ft.) above sea level, with some mountains reaching 4,620 meters (15,158 ft.). Elevation is generally highest just before the point of descent to the Great Rift Valley, which splits the plateau diagonally. A number of rivers cross the plateau—notably the Blue Nile rising from Lake Tana. The plateau gradually slopes to the lowlands of the Sudan on the west and the Somali-inhabited plains to the southeast.

The climate is temperate on the plateau and hot in the lowlands. At

Addis Ababa, which ranges from 2,200 to 2,600 meters (7,000-8,500 ft.), maximum temperature is 26° C (80° F) and minimum 4° C (40° F). The weather is usually sunny and dry with the short (belg) rains occurring February-April and the big (meher) rains beginning in mid-June and ending in mid-September.

# PEOPLE

Ethiopia's population is highly diverse. Most of its people speak a Semitic or Cushitic language. The Oromo, Amhara, and Tigreans make up more than three-fourths of the population, but there are more than 80 different ethnic groups within Ethiopia. Some of these have as few as 10,000 members. In general, most of the Christians live in the highlands, while Muslims and adherents of traditional African religions tend to inhabit lowland regions. English is the most widely spoken foreign language and is taught in all secondary schools. Amharic was the language of primary school instruction but has been replaced in many areas by local languages such as Oromifa and Tigrinya.

# HISTORY

Ethiopia is the oldest independent country in Africa and one of the oldest in the world. Herodotus, the Greek historian of the fifth century B.C. describes ancient Ethiopia in his writings. The Old Testament of the Bible records the Queen of Sheba's visit to Jerusalem. According to legend, Menelik I, the son of King Solomon and the Queen of Sheba, founded the Ethiopian Empire. Missionaries from Egypt and Syria introduced Christianity in the fourth century A.D. Following the rise of Islam in the seventh century, Ethiopia was gradually cut off from European Christendom. The Portuguese established contact with Ethiopia in 1493, primarily to strengthen their hegemony over the Indian Ocean and to convert Ethiopia to Roman Catholicism. There followed a century of

conflict between pro- and anti-Catholic factions, resulting in the expulsion of all foreign missionaries in the 1630s. This period of bitter religious conflict contributed to hostility toward foreign Christians and Europeans, which persisted into the 20th century and was a factor in Ethiopia's isolation until the mid-19th century.

Under the Emperors Theodore II (1855-68), Johannes IV (1872-89), and Menelik II (1889-1913), the kingdom began to emerge from its medieval isolation. When Menelik II died, his grandson, Lij Iyassu, succeeded to the throne but soon lost support because of his Muslim ties. He was deposed in 1916 by the Christian nobility, and Menelik's daughter, Zewditu, was made empress. Her cousin, Ras Tafari Makonnen (1892-1975), was made regent and successor to the throne.

In 1930, after the empress died, the regent, adopting the throne name Haile Selassie, was crowned emperor. His reign was interrupted in 1936 when Italian Fascist forces invaded and occupied Ethiopia. The emperor was forced into exile in England despite his plea to the League of Nations for intervention. Five years later, the Italians were defeated by British and Ethiopian forces, and the emperor returned to the throne.

After a period of civil unrest which began in February 1974, the aging Haile Selassie I was deposed on September 12, 1974, and a provisional administrative council of soldiers, known as the Derg ("committee") seized power from the emperor and installed a government which was socialist in name and military in style. The Derg summarily executed 59 members of the royal family and ministers and generals of the emperor's government; Emperor Haile Selassie was strangled in the basement of his palace on August 22, 1975.

Lt. Col. Mengistu Haile Mariam assumed power as head of state and Derg chairman, after having his two predecessors killed. Mengistu's years in office were marked by a totalitarian-style government and the coun-

try's massive militarization, financed by the Soviet Union and the Eastern Bloc, and assisted by Cuba. From 1977 through early 1978 thousands of suspected enemies of the Derg were tortured and/or killed in a purge called the "red terror." Communism was officially adopted during the late 1970s and early 1980s with the promulgation of a Soviet-style constitution, Politburo, and the creation of the Workers' Party of Ethiopia (WPE).

In December 1976, an Ethiopian delegation in Moscow signed a military assistance agreement with the Soviet Union. The following April, Ethiopia abrogated its military assistance agreement with the United States and expelled the American military missions. In July 1977, sensing the disarray in Ethiopia, Somalia attacked across the Ogaden Desert in pursuit of its irredentist claims to the ethnic Somali areas of Ethiopia. Ethiopian forces were driven back far inside their own frontiers but, with the assistance of a massive Soviet airlift of arms and Cuban combat forces, they stemmed the attack. The major Somali regular units were forced out of the Ogaden in March 1978. Twenty years later, the Somali region of Ethiopia remains under-developed and insecure.

The Derg's collapse was hastened by droughts and famine, as well as by insurrections, particularly in the northern regions of Tigray and Eritrea. In 1989, the Tigrayan People's Liberation Front (TPLF) merged with

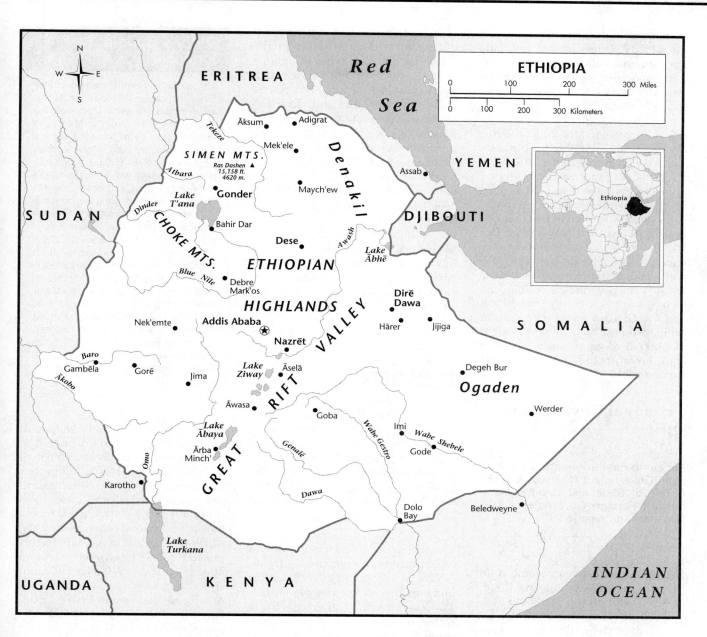

other ethnically based opposition movements to form the Ethiopian Peoples' Revolutionary Democratic Front (EPRDF). In May 1991, EPRDF forces advanced on Addis Ababa. Mengistu fled the country and was granted asylum in Zimbabwe, where he still resides.

In July 1991, the EPRDF, the Oromo Liberation Front (OLF), and others established the Transitional Government of Ethiopia (TGE) which was comprised of an 87-member Council of Representatives and guided by a national charter that functioned as a transitional constitution. In June

1992 the OLF withdrew from the government; in March 1993, members of the Southern Ethiopia Peoples' Democratic Coalition left the government.

In May 1991, the Eritrean People's Liberation Front (EPLF), led by Isaias Afwerki, assumed control of Eritrea and established a provisional government. This provisional government independently administered Eritrea until April 23-25, 1993, when Eritreans voted overwhelmingly for independence in a UN-monitored free and fair referendum. Eritrea was declared independent on April 27,

and the U.S. recognized Eritrean independence on April 28.

In Ethiopia, President Meles Zenawi and members of the TGE pledged to oversee the formation of a multi-party democracy. The election for a 547-member constituent assembly was held in June 1994, and this assembly adopted the constitution of the Federal Democratic Republic of Ethiopia in December 1994. The elections for Ethiopia's first popularly chosen national parliament and regional legislatures were held in May and June 1995. Most opposition parties chose to boycott these elections, ensuring a landslide victory for the EPRDF. International and non-governmental observers concluded that opposition parties would have been able to participate had they chosen to do so.

The Government of the Federal Democratic Republic of Ethiopia was installed in August 1995. The EPRDF-led government of Prime Minister Meles has promoted a policy of ethnic federalism, devolving significant powers to regional, ethnically based authorities. Ethiopia today has 10 semi-autonomous administrative regions which have the power to raise and spend their own revenues. Under the present government, Ethiopians enjoy greater political participation and freer debate than ever before in their history, although some fundamental freedoms, including freedom of the press, are in practice somewhat circumscribed.

## Principal Government Officials

For up-to-date information on Principal Government Officials, see the Chiefs of State and Cabinet Members of Foreign Governments section starting on page 1.

Ethiopia maintains an embassy in the U.S. at 2134 Kalorama Road, N.W., Washington, D.C. 20008 (tel. 202/234-2281) headed by Ambassador Berhane Gebre-Christos. A separate trade and commercial office is located at 1800 K Street, N.W., Suite 824, Washington, D.C. 20006 (tel. 202/452-1272).

# DEFENSE

The Ethiopian National Defense Force (ENDF) has approximately 100,000 personnel, which makes it one of the largest military forces in Africa. This number is significantly smaller than the 250,000 plus troops that existed during the Derg regime that fell to the rebel forces in 1991. The U.S. was Ethiopia's major arms supplier from the end of World War until 1977, when Ethiopia began receiving massive arms shipments from the Soviet Union. These shipments, including armored patrol boats, transport and jet fighter aircraft, helicopters, tanks, trucks, missiles, artillery, and small arms have incurred an unserviced Ethiopian debt to the former Soviet Union estimated at more than $3.5 billion. Since the early 1990s, the ENDF has been in transition from a rebel force to a professional military organization with the aid of the U.S. and other countries. Training in demining, humanitarian and peace-keeping operations, professional military education, and military justice are among the major programs sponsored by the U.S.

# ECONOMY

The current government has embarked on a program of economic reform, including privatization of state enterprises and rationalization of government regulation. While the process is still ongoing, the reforms have begun to attract much-needed foreign investment.

The Ethiopian economy is based on agriculture, which contributes 45% to GNP and more than 80% of exports and employs 85% of the population. The major agricultural export crop is coffee, providing 65%-75% of Ethiopia's foreign exchange earnings. Other traditional major agricultural exports are hides and skins, pulses, oilseeds, and the traditional "khat," a leafy shrub which has psychotropic qualities when chewed.

Ethiopia's agriculture is plagued by periodic drought, soil degradation caused by overgrazing, deforestation, high population density, and poor infrastructure, making it difficult and expensive to get goods to market. Yet it is the country's most promising resource. A potential exists for self-sufficiency in grains and for export development in livestock, grains, vegetables, and fruits.

## Editor's Update June 2001

The border war with Eritrea dominates Ethiopian foreign relations. Hostilities, which began with skirmishes along the poorly defined frontier in May 1998 erupted again in full force in February 1999. In January 2001, Meles Zenawi, Prime Minister of Ethiopia, signed a peace agreement with Eritrea, ending a three-year bloody and costly war. Mr. Meles is a reformer, yet a faction within his Party is very committed to Marxist–Leninist dogma. This faction nearly unseated Mr. Meles in March 2001, accusing him of being a puppet for American imperialism and too precipitous in signing the peace agreement with Eritrea. The fact that Mr. Meles survived this political onslaught does not mean that his troubles with his opposition are over. Territorial disputes, civilian detainees, and demobilization are important issues, all tied to colonial imperatives on both sides of this conflict.

Gold, marble, limestone, and small amounts of tantalum are mined in Ethiopia. Other resources with potential for commercial development include large potash deposits, natural gas, iron ore, and possibly oil and geothermal energy. Although Ethiopia has good hydroelectric resources, which power most of its manufacturing sector, it is totally dependent on imports for its oil. A landlocked country, Ethiopia uses the seaports of Assab and Massawa in Eritrea. Ethiopia also uses the port of Djibouti, connected to Addis Ababa by rail, for international trade. Of the 23,812 kilometers of Ethiopia's all-weather roads, 15% are asphalt. Mountainous terrain and the lack of good roads and sufficient vehicles make land transportation difficult. However, the government-owned airline is excellent. Ethiopian Airlines serves 38 domestic airfields and has 42 international destinations.

Dependent on a few vulnerable crops for its foreign exchange earnings and reliant on imported oil, Ethiopia lacks sufficient foreign exchange. The financially conservative government has taken measures to solve this problem, including stringent import controls and sharply reduced subsidies on retail gasoline prices. Nevertheless, the largely subsistence economy is incapable of supporting high military expenditures, drought relief, an ambitious development plan, and indispensable imports such as oil and, therefore, must depend on foreign assistance.

# FOREIGN RELATIONS

Ethiopia was relatively isolated from major movements of world politics until the 1895 and 1935 Italian invasions. Since World War II, it has played an active role in world and African affairs. Ethiopia was a charter member of the United Nations and took part in UN operations in Korea in 1951 and the Congo in 1960. Former Emperor Haile Selassie was a founder of the Organization of African Unity (OAU). Addis Ababa is the host capital for the UN Economic Commission for Africa and the OAU.

Although nominally a member of the Non-Aligned Movement, after the 1974 revolution, Ethiopia moved into a close relationship with the Soviet Union and its allies and supported their international policies and positions until the change of government in 1991. Today, Ethiopia has very good relations with the U.S. and the West, especially in responding to regional instability and, increasingly, through economic involvement. Ethiopia's relations with Eritrea are extremely close, reflecting the shared revolutionary struggle against the Derg. Continuing instability along Ethiopia's borders with Sudan and Somalia contributes to tension with the National Islamic Front regime in Sudan and several groups in Somalia.

# U.S.-ETHIOPIA RELATIONS

U.S.-Ethiopian relations were established in 1903 and were good throughout the period prior to the Italian occupation in 1935. After World War II, these ties strengthened, on the basis of a September 1951 treaty of amity and economic relations. In 1953, two agreements were signed: a mutual defense assistance agreement, under which the U.S. agreed to furnish military equipment and training, and an accord regularizing the operations of a U.S. communication facility at Asmara. Through fiscal year 1978, the U.S. provided Ethiopia with $282 million in military assistance and $366 million in economic assistance in agriculture, education, public health, and transportation. A Peace Corps program emphasized education, and United States Information Service educational and cultural exchanges were numerous.

After Ethiopia's revolution, the bilateral relationship began to cool as a result of the Derg's identification with international communism and U.S. revulsion at the Derg's murderous means of maintaining itself in power. The U.S. rebuffed Ethiopia's request for increased military assistance to intensify its fight against the Eritrean secessionist movement and to repel the Somali invasion. The International Security and Development Act of 1985 prohibited all U.S. economic assistance to Ethiopia with the exception of humanitarian disaster and emergency relief. In July 1980, the U.S. Ambassador to Ethiopia was recalled at the request of the Ethiopian Government, and the U.S.

Embassy in Ethiopia and the Ethiopian Embassy in the U.S. were headed by Charges d'Affaires.

With the downfall of the Mengistu regime, U.S.-Ethiopian relations improved dramatically. Legislative restrictions on assistance to Ethiopia other than humanitarian assistance were lifted. Diplomatic relations were upgraded to the ambassadorial level in 1992. During FY 1997, the U.S. provided about $77.2 million in assistance to Ethiopia, of which $39.9 million was food aid ($6.4 million in emergency food assistance). U.S. development assistance to Ethiopia is conditional on progress in democracy and human rights as well as economic reforms. Some in military training funds, including training in such issues as the laws of war and observance of human rights, also are provided. The Peace Corps returned about 3 years ago to Ethiopia where, in the past, it had one of its largest programs. In FY 1999, the Peace Corps expects to have more than 100 volunteers in-country.

## Principal U.S. Officials

**For up-to-date information on Principal U.S. Officials, see the U.S. Embassies, Consulates, and Foreign Service section starting on page 139.**

The address and telephone/fax numbers for the U.S. Embassy in Ethiopia are P.O. Box 1014, Entoto Street, Addis Ababa, Ethiopia. Tel: 251/1/550-666; fax: 251/1/552-191.

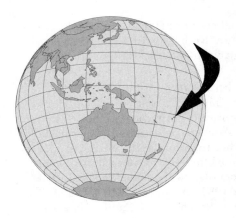

# FIJI

February 2001

Official Name:
**Republic of Fiji**

# PROFILE

## Geography
**Area:** 18,376 sq. km (7,056 sq. mi.).
**Cities:** Capital—Suva (pop. 167,000), Lautoka, Nadi.
**Terrain:** Mountainous or varied.
**Climate:** Tropical maritime.

## People
**Nationality:** noun—Fiji Islander; adjective—Fiji or Fijian. **Population:** 807,000.
**Age structure:** 33% under 15, 4% over 65.
**Growth rate:** 1.4%.
**Ethnic groups:** Indigenous Fijian 51%, Indo-Fijian 44%.
**Religion:** Christian 52% (Methodist and Roman Catholic), Hindu 35%, Muslim 7%.
**Languages:** English (official), Fijian, Hindi.
**Education:** Literacy—91%.
**Health:** Life expectancy—male 65.5 yrs.; female 70.5 yrs.
**Infant mortality rate:** 14.5/1,000.
**Work force:** Agriculture—67%.

## Government
**Type:** Interim civil government.
Independence (from U.K.): October 10, 1970.
**Constitution:** July 1997 (suspended May 2000).
**Branches:** Executive—President (head of state), Prime Minister (head of government), Cabinet. Legislative—bicameral parliament; upper house is appointed, lower house is elected. Judicial—Supreme Court and supporting hierarchy.

**Major political parties:** Fiji Labor Party (FLP), Fijian Association Party (FAP), Fijian Political Party (SVT).

## Economy
**GDP:** $2.01 billion.
**GDP per capita** (nominal): $2,470.
**GDP per capita** (purchasing power parity): $7,800.
**GDP composition by sector:** Services 58%, industry 25.5%, agriculture 16.5%.
**Industry:** Types—tourism, sugar, garments.
**Trade:** Exports—$494.5 million; sugar, garments, gold, timber. Export markets—Australia, U..K., New Zealand, U.S., Japan. Imports—$721 million; basic manufactures, machinery and transport equipment. Import sources—Australia, New Zealand, U.S. ($91.8 million).
**External debt:** (1997) $213 million.
**Currency:** Fijian dollar (F$).
**Exchange rate:** (Jan 2001) F$2.16 = $US1.

# GEOGRAPHY AND PEOPLE

Fiji comprises a group of volcanic islands in the South Pacific lying about 4,450 km (2,775 mi.) southwest of Honolulu and 1,770 km (1,100 mi.) north of New Zealand. Its 322 islands range in size from the large—Vitu Levu (where Suva and 70% of the population are located) and Vanua Levu—to much smaller islands, of which just over 100 are inhabited. The larger islands contain mountains as high as 1,200 meters (4,000 ft) rising abruptly from the shore. Heavy rains (up to 304 cm or 120 inches annually) fall on the windward (southeastern) side, covering these sections of the islands with dense tropical forest. Lowlands on the western portions of each of the main islands are sheltered by the mountains and have a well-marked dry season favorable to crops such as sugarcane.

More than half of Fiji's population lives on the island coasts, either in Suva or in smaller urban centers. The interior is sparsely populated due to its rough terrain.

Indigenous Fijians are a mixture of Polynesian and Melanesian, resulting from the original migrations to the South Pacific many centuries ago.

The Indo-Fijian population has grown rapidly from the 60,000 indentured laborers brought from India between 1879 and 1916 to work in the sugarcane fields. Thousands more Indians migrated voluntarily in the 1920s and 1930s and formed the core of Fiji's business class. The native Fijians live throughout the country, while the Indo-Fijians reside primarily near the urban centers and in the cane-producing areas of the two main islands. Nearly all of the indigenous Fijians are Christian, with more than three-quarters being Methodist. About 80% of the Indo-Fijians are Hindu, 15% are Muslim, and the rest mostly Sikh, with a few Christians.

# HISTORY

Melanesian and Polynesian peoples settled the Fijian islands some 3,500 years ago. European traders and missionaries arrived in the first half of the 19th century, and the resulting disruption led to increasingly serious wars among the native Fijian confederacies. One ratu (chief), Cakobau, gained limited control over the western islands by the 1850s, but the continuing unrest led a convention of chiefs to cede Fiji unconditionally to the British in 1874.

The pattern of colonialism in Fiji during the following century was similar to that in other British possessions: the pacification of the countryside, the spread of plantation agriculture, and the introduction of Indian indentured labor. Many traditional institutions, including the system of communal land ownership, were maintained.

Fiji soldiers fought alongside the Allies in the Second World War, gaining a fine reputation in the tough Solomon Islands campaign. The United States and other allied countries maintained military installations in Fiji during the war, but Fiji itself never came under attack.

In April 1970, a constitutional conference in London agreed that Fiji should become a fully sovereign and independent nation within the Commonwealth. Fiji became independent on October 10, 1970.

Post-independence politics came to be dominated by the Alliance Party of Ratu Sir Kamisese Mara. The Indian-led opposition won a majority of House seats in 1977, but failed to form a government out of concern that indigenous Fijians would not accept Indo-Fijian leadership. In April 1987, a coalition led by Dr. Timoci Bavadra, an ethnic Fijian supported by the Indo-Fijian community, won the general election and formed Fiji's first majority Indian government, with Dr. Bavadra serving as Prime Minister. Less than a month later, Dr. Bavadra was forcibly removed from power during a military coup led by Lt. Col. Sitiveni Rabuka on May 14, 1987.

After a period of continued jockeying and negotiation, Rabuka staged a second coup on September 25, 1987. The military government revoked the constitution and declared Fiji a republic on October 10. This action, coupled with protests by the Government of India, led to Fiji's expulsion from the Commonwealth and official nonrecognition of the Rabuka regime from foreign governments, including Australia and New Zealand. On December 6, Rabuka resigned as head of state and Governor-General Ratu Sir Penaia Ganilau was appointed the first President of the Fijian Republic. Mara was reappointed Prime Minister, and Rabuka became Minister of Home Affairs.

The new government drafted a new constitution that went into force in July 1990. Under its terms, majorities were reserved for ethnic Fijians in both houses of the legislature. Previously, in 1989, the government had released statistical information showing that for the first time since 1946, ethnic Fijians were a majority of the population. More than 12,000 Indo-Fijians and other minorities had left the country in the 2 years following the 1987 coups. After resigning from the military, Rabuka became Prime Minister under the new constitution in 1993.

Ethnic tensions simmered in 1995–96 over the renewal of Indo-Fijian land leases and political maneuvering surrounding the mandated 7-year review of the 1990 constitution. The Constitutional Review Commission produced a draft constitution which expanded the size of the legislature, lowered the proportion of seats reserved by ethnic group, reserved the presidency for ethnic Fijians but opened the position of prime minister to all races. Prime Minister Rabuka and President Mara supported the proposal, while the nationalist indigenous Fijian parties opposed it. The reformed constitution was approved in July 1997. Fiji was readmitted to the Commonwealth in October.

The first legislative elections held under the new constitution took place in May 1999. Rabuka's coalition was defeated by Indo-Fijian parties led by Mahendra Chaudhry, who became Fiji's first Indo-Fijian prime minister. One year later, in May 2000, Chaudhry and most other members of parliament were taken hostage in the House of Representatives by gunmen led by ethnic Fijian nationalist George Speight. The standoff dragged on for 8 weeks—during which time Chaudhry was removed from office by the then-president due to his incapacitation—before the Fijian military seized power and brokered a negotiated end to the situation, then arrested Speight when he violated its terms. Former banker Laisenia Qarase was named interim prime minister and head of the interim civilian government by the military and Great Council of Chiefs in July. A constitutional review commission is in the process of drafting a new constitution. The timetable for elections to replace the interim government is still under discussion.

# GOVERNMENT

The president (head of state) is appointed for a 5-year term by the Great Council of Chiefs, a traditional ethnic Fijian leadership body. The president in turn appoints the prime minister (head of government) and cabinet from among the members of parliament. Both houses of the legislature have seats reserved by ethnicity. The Senate is appointed; the House of Representatives is elected.

Fiji maintains an independent judiciary consisting of a Supreme Court, a Court of Appeals, a High Court, and magistrate courts. The judiciary remained independent through the coups and the consequent absence of an elected government.

There are four administrative divisions (central, eastern, northern and western), each under the charge of a commissioner. Ethnic Fijians have their own administration in which councils preside over a hierarchy of provinces, districts, and villages. The councils deal with all matters affecting ethnic Fijians. The Great Council of Chiefs (Bose Levu Vakaturaga) contains every hereditary chief, or Ratu, of a Matagali, or Fijian clan.

## Principal Government Officials

**For up-to-date information on Principal Government Officials, see the Chiefs of State and Cabinet Members of Foreign Governments section starting on page 1.**

Fiji maintains an embassy at Suite 240, 2233 Wisconsin Avenue NW, Washington, DC 20007 (tel: 202–337–8320).

# POLITICAL CONDITIONS

For 17 years after independence, Fiji was a parliamentary democracy. During that time, political life was dominated by Ratu Sir Kamisese Mara and the Alliance Party, which combined the traditional Fijian chiefly system with leading elements of the European, part-European, and Indian communities. The main parliamentary opposition, the National Federation Party, represented mainly

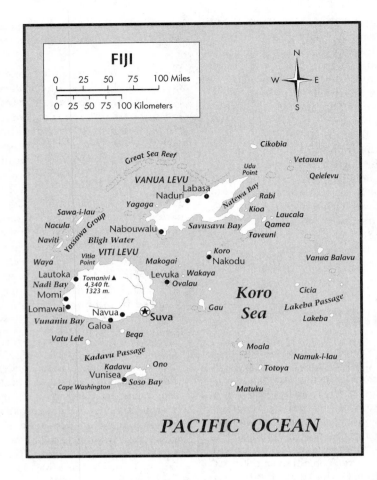

rural Indo-Fijians. Intercommunal relations were managed without serious confrontation. However, when Dr. Bavadra's coalition democratically installed a cabinet with substantial ethnic Indian representation after the April 1987 election, extremist elements played on ethnic Fijian fears of domination by the Indo-Fijian community. The racial situation took a turn for the worse from which it has yet to fully recover. Three coups, two discarded constitutions, and tens of thousands of outward emigrants have been the result.

One of the main issues of contention is land tenure. Indigenous Fijian communities very closely identify themselves with their land. In 1909 near the peak of the inflow of indentured Indian laborers, the land ownership pattern was frozen and further sales prohibited. Today over 80% of the land is held by indigenous Fijians, under the collective ownership of the traditional Fijian clans. Indo-Fijians produce over 90% of the

sugar crop but must lease the land they work from its ethnic Fijian owners instead of being able to buy it outright. The leases have been generally for 10 years, although they are usually renewed for two 10-year extensions. Many Indo-Fijians argue that these terms do not provide them with adequate security and have pressed for renewable 30-year leases, while many ethnic Fijians fear that an Indo-Fijian government would erode their control over the land.

The Indo-Fijian parties' major voting bloc is made up of sugarcane farmers. The farmers' main tool of influence has been their ability to galvanize widespread boycotts of the sugar industry, thereby crippling the economy.

Prior to the 1987 coups, Fiji was often cited as a model of human rights and multiracial democracy. Despite the difficulties that have arisen in the decade and a half since then, Fiji has maintained at least a certain degree of restraint.

# ECONOMY

Fiji is one of the most developed of the Pacific island economies, although it remains a developing country with a large subsistence agriculture sector. The effects of the Asian financial crisis contributed to substantial drops in GDP in 1997 and 1998, with a return to positive growth in 1999 aided by a 20% devaluation of the Fijian dollar. The economy is estimated to have contracted by about 10% due to the disruptions from the 2000 political turmoil.

Tourism has expanded rapidly since the early 1980s and is the leading economic activity in the islands. More than 409,000 people visited Fiji in 1999 (excluding cruise ship passengers). About one-quarter came from Australia, with large contingents also coming from New Zealand, Japan, the U.S. and U.K. Over 62,000 of the tourists were American, a number that has steadily increased since the start of regularly scheduled nonstop air service from Los Angeles. Tourism earned more than $300 million in foreign exchange for Fiji in 1998, an amount exceeding the revenue from its two largest goods exports (sugar and garments).

Fiji runs a persistently large trade deficit, although its tourism revenue yields a services surplus which keeps the current account of its balance of payments roughly in balance. Australia accounts for between 35% and 45% of Fiji's trade, with New Zealand, the U.S., the U.K., and Japan varying year-by-year between 5% and 15% each.

Fiji's two largest exports are sugar and garments, which each accounted for approximately one-quarter of export revenue in 1998 (roughly $122 million each). The sugar industry suffered in 1997 due to low world prices and rent disputes between farmers and landowners, and again in 1998 from drought, but recovered in 1999. The Fijian garment industry has

## Travel Notes

**Travel Advice:** For up-to-date information from the U.S. State Department on possible inconvenient or hazardous situations, see the **Travel Warnings and Consular Information Sheets from the U.S. Government** section starting on page 1723. For the latest information on health requirements and conditions, see the **International Travelers' Health Information** section starting on page 1385. For further information dealing with non-urgent matter, see the **Tips for Travelers to...** section starting on page 1588.

developed rapidly since the introduction of tax exemptions in 1988. The industry's output has increased nearly ten-fold since that time.

Other important export crops include coconuts and ginger, although production levels of both are declining. Fiji has extensive timber reserves, but forestry has become important as an export trade only since the mid-1980s. Fishing is important as an export sector and for domestic consumption. In the mining and manufacturing sectors, gold and silver are exported, with the most important manufacturing activities being the processing of sugar and fish.

Since 1987, Fiji has suffered a very high rate of emigration, particularly of skilled and professional personnel. More than 70,000 people left the country in the aftermath of the 1987 coup, some 90% of which were Indo-Fijians. With the continued expiration of land leases and the instability surrounding the 2000 coup, an outflow of skilled workers is again being reported.

Other long-term economic problems include low investment rates and uncertain property rights. Investment laws are being reviewed to make them more business friendly, including a relaxation of work permit requirements. But investor confidence in Fiji has dropped significantly due to the recurrence of political instability. Beyond investor and tourist unease, the fallout from Chaudhry's removal and the poten-

tial return to a racially biased constitution also could cost Fiji the preferential price and access arrangements its sugar enjoys with the European Union and the preferential treatment Australia affords the Fijian garment industry.

# FOREIGN RELATIONS

Fiji maintains an independent, but generally pro-Western, foreign policy. It has traditionally had close relations with its major trading partners Australia and New Zealand, although these relations cooled after both the 1987 and 2000 coups.

Since independence, Fiji has been a leader in the South Pacific region. Other Pacific Island governments have generally been sympathetic to Fiji's internal political problems and have declined to take public positions.

Fiji became the 127th member of the United Nations on October 13, 1970, and participates actively in the organization. Fiji's contributions to UN peacekeeping are unique for a nation of its size. It maintains nearly 1,000 soldiers overseas in UN peacekeeping missions, mainly in the Middle East.

## Principal U.S. Officials

**For up-to-date information on Principal U.S. Officials, see the U.S. Embassies, Consulates, and Foreign Service section starting on page 139.**

The U.S. embassy in Fiji is located at 31 Loftus Street, Suva. Internet: www.amembassy-fiji.gov. Telephone: 679–314–466. Fax: 679–300–081. The mailing address is U.S. Embassy, P.O. Box 218, Suva, Fiji.

# FINLAND

June 1999

Official Name:
**Republic of Finland**

# PROFILE

## Geography

**Area:** 337,113 sq. km. (130,160 sq. mi.); about the size of New England, New Jersey, and New York combined.
**Cities:** Capital—Helsinki (pop. 525,000). Other cities—Tampere (182,700), Turku (164,700).
**Terrain:** Low but hilly, more than 70% forested, with more than 60,000 lakes.
**Climate:** Northern temperate.

## People

**Nationality:** Noun—Finn(s). Adjective—Finnish.
**Population:** 5.13 million.
**Population growth rate:** 0.3%.
**Ethnic groups:** Finns, Swedes, Lapps, Roma, Tartars.
**Religions:** Lutheran 89%, Orthodox 1%.
**Languages:** Finnish 93%, Swedish 6% (both official); small Lapp– and Russian–speaking minorities.
**Education:** Years compulsory—9. Attendance—almost 100%. Literacy—almost 100%.
**Health:** Infant mortality rate—3.8/1,000. Life expectancy—males 72 yrs., females 80 yrs.
**Work force (2.5 million; of which 2 million are employed):** Public services—32%. Industry—22%. Commerce—14%. Finance, insurance,
and business services—10%. Agriculture and forestry—8%. Transport and communications—8%. Construction—6%.

## Government

**Type:** Constitutional republic.
**Constitution:** July 17, 1919.
**Independence:** December 6, 1917.
**Branches:** Executive—president (chief of state), prime minister (head of government), Council of State (cabinet). Legislative—unicameral parliament. Judicial—Supreme Court, regional appellate courts, local courts.
**Subdivisions:** 12 provinces, provincial self–rule for the Aland Islands.
**Political parties:** Social Democratic Party, Center Party, National Coalition (Conservative) Party, Leftist Alliance, Swedish People's Party, Green Party.
**Suffrage:** Universal at 18.

## Economy (1999)

**GDP:** $124 billion.
**GDP growth rate:** 3.2%.
**Per capita income:** $16,000.
**Inflation rate:** 0.6%.
**Natural resources:** Forests, minerals (copper, zinc, iron), farmland.
**Agriculture (3% of GDP):** Products—meat (pork and beef), grain (wheat, rye, barley, oats), dairy products, potatoes, grapeseed.
**Industry (31% of GDP):** Types—metal and steel, forest products,
chemicals, shipbuilding, foodstuffs, textiles and clothing.
**Trade:** Exports—$40 billion. Major markets—EU 58%, U.S. 7%, Russia 5%, Japan 2.5%. Imports—$29 billion. Major suppliers—EU 60%, U.S. 7%, Russia 7%, Japan 6%.

# HISTORY

The origins of the Finnish people are still a matter of conjecture, although many scholars argue that their original home was in what is now west–central Siberia. The Finns arrived in their present territory thousands of years ago, pushing the indigenous Lapps into the more remote northern regions. Finnish and Lappish—the language of Finland's small Lapp minority—both are Finno–Ugric languages and are in the Uralic rather than the Indo–European family.

Finland's nearly 700–year association with the Kingdom of Sweden began in 1154 with the introduction of Christianity by Sweden's King Eric. During the ensuing centuries, Finland played an important role in the political life of the Swedish–Finnish realm, and Finnish soldiers often predominated in Swedish armies. Finns also formed a significant proportion of the first "Swedish" settlers in 17th–century America.

Following Finland's incorporation into Sweden in the 12th century, Swedish became the dominant language, although Finnish recovered its predominance after a 19th–century resurgence of Finnish nationalism. Publication in 1835 of the Finnish national epic, *The Kalevala*—a collection of traditional myths and legends—first stirred the nationalism that later led to Finland's independence from Russia.

In 1809, Finland was conquered by the armies of Czar Alexander I and thereafter remained an autonomous grand duchy connected with the Russian Empire until the end of 1917. On December 6, 1917, shortly after the Bolshevik Revolution in Russia, Finland declared its independence. In 1918, the country experienced a brief but bitter civil war that colored domestic politics for many years. During World War II, Finland fought the Soviet Union twice—in the Winter War of 1939–40 and again in the Continuation War of 1941–44. This was followed by the Lapland War of 1944–45, when Finland fought against the Germans as they withdrew their forces from northern Finland.

Treaties signed in 1947 and 1948 with the Soviet Union included obligations and restraints on Finland vis–a–vis the U.S.S.R. as well as territorial concessions by Finland; both have been abrogated by Finland since the 1991 dissolution of the Soviet Union (see Foreign Relations).

# GOVERNMENT AND POLITICAL CONDITIONS

Finland has a mixed presidential/parliamentary system with executive powers divided between the president, who has primary responsibility for national security and foreign affairs, and the prime minister, who has primary responsibility for all other areas. Constitutional changes made in the late 1980s strengthened

the prime minister—who must enjoy the confidence of the parliament (Eduskunta)—at the expense of the president. Finland's 1995 accession to the European Union has blurred the line between foreign and domestic policy; the respective roles of the president and prime minister are evolving, and plans are under consideration to rewrite the constitution to clarify these and other issues.

Finns enjoy individual and political freedoms, and suffrage is universal at 18. The country's population is ethnically homogeneous with no sizable immigrant population. Few tensions exist between the Finnish–speaking majority and the Swedish–speaking minority.

Elected for a 6–year term, the president:

- Handles foreign policy, except for certain international agreements and decisions of peace or war, which must be submitted to the parliament;

- Is commander–in–chief of the armed forces and has wide decree and appointive powers;

- May initiate legislation, block legislation by pocket veto, and call extraordinary parliamentary sessions; and

- Appoints the prime minister and the rest of the cabinet (Council of State).

The Council of State is made up of the prime minister and ministers for the various departments of the central government as well as an ex–officio member, the Chancellor of Justice. Ministers are not obliged to be members of the Eduskunta and need not be formally identified with any political party.

Constitutionally, the 200–member unicameral Eduskunta is the supreme authority in Finland. It may alter the constitution, bring about the resignation of the Council of State, and override presidential vetoes; its acts are not subject to judicial review. Legislation may be initiated by the

president, the Council of State, or one of the Eduskunta members.

The Eduskunta is elected on the basis of proportional representation. All persons 18 or older, except military personnel on active duty and a few high judicial officials, are eligible for election. The regular parliamentary term is four years; however, the president may dissolve the Eduskunta and order new elections at the request of the prime minister and after consulting the speaker of parliament.

The judicial system is divided between courts with regular civil and criminal jurisdiction and special courts with responsibility for litigation between the public and the administrative organs of the state. Finnish law is codified. Although there is no writ of habeas corpus or bail, the maximum period of pre–trial detention has been reduced to four days. The Finnish court system consists of local courts, regional appellate courts, and a Supreme Court.

Finland has 12 provinces. Below the provincial level, they are divided into cities, townships, and communes administered by municipal and communal councils elected by proportional representation once every four years. At the provincial level, the 11 mainland provinces are administered by provincial boards composed of civil servants, each headed by a presidentially appointed governor. The boards are responsible to the Ministry of the Interior and play a supervisory and coordinating role within the provinces.

The island province of Aland is located near the 60th parallel between Sweden and Finland. It enjoys local autonomy by virtue of an international convention of 1921, implemented most recently by the Act on Aland Self–Government of 1951. The islands are further distinguished by the fact that they are entirely Swedish–speaking. Government is vested in the provincial council, which consists of 30 delegates elected directly by Aland's citizens.

Finland's defense forces consist of 34,700 persons in uniform (27,300 army; 3,000 navy; and 4,400 air force); the country's defense budget equals about 2% of GDP. There is universal male conscription under which all men serve from eight to 11 months. As of 1995, women were permitted to serve as volunteers. A reserve force ensures that Finland can field 500,000 trained military personnel in case of need.

Finland's proportional representation system encourages a multitude of political parties and has resulted in many coalition governments. Political activity by communists was legalized in 1944, and although four major parties have dominated the postwar political arena, none now has a majority position. The Social Democratic Party (SDP) gained a plurality in Finland's parliament in the general election of March 1995. But it won far less than an overall majority and so formed a five–party governing coalition.

The SDP won 28% of the vote in 1995, mainly among the urban working class but also with some support among small farmers, white–collar workers, and professionals. The Leftist Alliance (LA)—the SDP's rival on the left—gained 11% of the vote in 1995 and joined the SDP–led government. The LA was formed in May 1990 and replaced the People's Democratic League, the group that represented the Finnish Communist Party in the Eduskunta.

## Principal Government Officials

**For up-to-date information on Principal Government Officials, see the Chiefs of State and Cabinet Members of Foreign Governments section starting on page 1.**

Finland's two other major parties are the Center Party, traditionally representing rural interests, and the National Coalition—or Conservative—Party, which draws its major support from the business commu-

nity and urban professionals. The Center won nearly 20% and the Conservatives 18% of the vote in 1995. The Conservatives are the second–largest party in the SDP–led coalition, which is rounded out by the Swedish People's Party and the Green Party. The Center Party leads the opposition in Parliament.

Finland's embassy in the United States is at 3301 Massachusetts Ave-

nue, NW, Washington, DC 20008; tel: 202–298–5800; fax: 202–298–6030.

# ECONOMY

Finland has a dynamic industrial economy based on abundant forest resources, capital investments, and technology. Traditionally, Finland has been a net importer of capital to finance industrial growth. In the 1980s, Finland's economic growth rate was one of the highest of industrialized countries.

In 1991, Finland fell into a deep recession caused by economic overheating, depressed foreign markets, and the dismantling of the barter system between Finland and the former Soviet Union. The same year, Finland devalued the markka to promote export competitiveness. This helped stabilize the economy, and the recession bottomed out in 1993.

Exports of goods contribute more than 20% of Finland's GDP; combined exports of goods and services amount to at least 25% of GDP. Exports and imports of goods equal about 40% of GDP. Timber and metalworking are Finland's main industries, but other industries produce manufactured goods ranging from electronics to motor vehicles. Finnish-designed consumer products such as textiles, porcelain, and glassware are world-famous.

Except for timber and several minerals, Finland depends on imported raw materials, energy, and some components for its manufactured products. Farms tend to be small, but sizable timber stands are harvested for supplementary income in winter. The country's main agricultural products are dairy, meat, and grains. Finland's EU accession has accelerated the process of restructuring and downsizing of this sector.

An extensive social welfare system, constituting about one-fifth of the national income, includes a variety of pension and assistance programs and a comprehensive health insurance program. Although free education through the university level also is available, only about one child in four receives a higher education in the highly competitive system. In the mid-1970s, the educational system was reformed with the goal of equalizing educational opportunities. Beginning at age seven, all Finnish children are required to attend a "basic school" of nine grade levels. After this, they may elect to continue along an academic (lukio) or voca-

tional (ammat-tikoulu) line. But most pursue vocational studies, since the number of openings in higher educational institutions is less than the demand.

# FOREIGN RELATIONS

Finland's basic foreign policy goal from the end of the Continuation War with the U.S.S.R. in 1944 until 1991 was to avoid great-power conflicts and to build mutual confidence with the Soviet Union. Although the country was culturally, socially, and politically Western, Finns realized they must live in peace with the U.S.S.R. and take no action that might be interpreted as a security threat. The dissolution of the Soviet Union in 1991 opened up dramatic new possibilities for Finland and has resulted in the Finns actively seeking greater participation in Western political and economic structures.

## Relations With the Soviet Union and With Russia

The principal architect of the post-1944 foreign policy of neutrality was J.K. Paasikivi, who was President from 1946 to 1956. Urho Kekkonen, President from 1956 until 1981, further developed this policy, stressing that Finland should be an active rather than a passive neutral. This policy is now popularly known as the "Paasikivi-Kekkonen Line."

Finland and the U.S.S.R. signed a peace treaty at Paris in February 1947 limiting the size of Finland's defense forces and providing for the cession to the Soviet Union of the Petsamo area on the Arctic coast, the Karelian Isthmus in southeastern Finland, and other territory along the former eastern border. Another provision, terminated in 1956, leased the Porkkala area near Helsinki to the U.S.S.R. for use as a naval base and gave free access to this area across Finnish territory.

The 1947 treaty also called for Finland to pay to the Soviet Union reparations of 300 million gold dollars

(amounting to an estimated $570 million in 1952, the year the payments ended). Although an ally of the Soviet Union in World War II, the United States was not a signatory to this treaty because it had not been at war with Finland.

In April 1948, Finland signed an Agreement of Friendship, Cooperation, and Mutual Assistance with the Soviet Union. Under this mutual assistance pact, Finland was obligated—with the aid of the Soviet Union, if necessary—to resist armed attacks by Germany or its allies against Finland or against the U.S.S.R. through Finland. At the same time, the agreement recognized Finland's desire to remain outside great-power conflicts. This agreement was renewed for 20 years in 1955, in 1970, and again in 1983 to the year 2003.

The Finns responded cautiously in 1990-91 to the decline of Soviet power and the U.S.S.R.'s subsequent dissolution. They unilaterally abrogated restrictions imposed by the 1947 and 1948 treaties, joined in voicing Nordic concern over the coup against Soviet leader Mikhail Gorbachev, and gave increasing unofficial encouragement to Baltic independence.

At the same time, by replacing the Soviet-Finnish mutual assistance pact with treaties on general cooperation and trade, Finns put themselves on an equal footing while retaining a friendly bilateral relationship. Finland now is boosting cross-border commercial ties and touting its potential as a commercial gateway to Russia. It has reassured Russia that it will not raise claims for Finnish territory seized by the U.S.S.R., and continues to reaffirm the importance of good bilateral relations.

## Multilateral Relations

Finnish foreign policy emphasizes its participation in multilateral organizations. Finland joined the United Nations in 1955 and the EU in 1995. As noted, the country also is a member of NATO's Partnership for Peace as well as an observer in the North

## Travel Notes

**Travel Advice:** For up-to-date information from the U.S. State Department on possible inconvenient or hazardous situations, see the **Travel Warnings and Consular Information Sheets from the U.S. Government** section starting on page 1723. For the latest information on health requirements and conditions, see the **International Travelers' Health Information** section starting on page 1385. For further information dealing with non-urgent matter, see the **Tips for Travelers to...** section starting on page 1588.

Atlantic Cooperation Council and the Western European Union.

Finland is well represented in the UN civil service in proportion to its population and belongs to several of its specialized and related agencies. Finnish troops have participated in UN peacekeeping activities since 1956, and the Finns continue to be one of the largest per capita contributors of peacekeepers in the world. Finland is an active participant in the Organization for Security and Cooperation in Europe (OSCE).

Cooperation with the other Scandinavian countries also is important to Finland, and it has been a member of the Nordic Council since 1955. Under the council's auspices, the Nordic countries have created a common labor market and have abolished immigration controls among themselves. The council also serves to coordinate social and cultural policies of the participating countries and has promoted increased cooperation in many fields.

In addition to the organizations already mentioned, Finland is a member of the International Bank for Reconstruction and Development, the International Monetary Fund, the World Trade Organization, the International Finance Corporation, the International Development Association, the Bank for International Settlements, the Asian Development Bank, the Inter–American Development Bank, the Council of Europe, the Organization for Economic Cooperation and Development, and INTELSAT.

# U.S.-FINLAND RELATIONS

Relations between the United States and Finland are warm. Some 200,000 U.S. citizens visit Finland annually, and about 3,000 U.S. citizens are resident there. The U.S. has an educational exchange program in Finland which is comparatively large for a Western European country of Finland's size. It is financed in part from a trust fund established in 1976 from Finland's final repayment of a U.S. loan made in the aftermath of World War I.

Finland is bordered on the east by Russia and, as one of the former Soviet Union's neighbors, has been of particular interest and importance to the U.S. both during the Cold War and in its aftermath. Before the U.S.S.R. dissolved in 1991, longstanding U.S. policy was to support Finnish neutrality while maintaining and reinforcing Finland's historic, cultural, and economic ties with the West. The U.S. has welcomed Finland's increased participation since 1991 in Western economic and political structures.

Following the dissolution of the Soviet Union, Finland has moved steadily toward integration into Western institutions and abandoned its formal policy of neutrality, which has been recast as a policy of military nonalliance coupled with the maintenance of a credible, independent defense. Finland's 1994 decision to buy 64 F–18 fighter planes from the United States signaled the abandonment of the country's policy of balanced arms purchases from East and West.

In 1994, Finland joined NATO's Partnership for Peace; the country also is an observer in the North Atlantic Cooperation Council. Finland became a full member of the European Union (EU) in January 1995, at the same time acquiring observer status in the EU's defense arm, the Western European Union.

Economic and trade relations between Finland and the United States are active and were bolstered by the F–18 purchase. U.S.–Finland trade totals almost $5 billion annually. The U.S. receives about 7% of Finland's exports—mainly pulp and paper, ships, and machinery—and provides about 7% of its imports—principally computers, semiconductors, aircraft, and machinery.

Finland generally welcomes foreign investment. Areas of particular interest for U.S. investors are specialized high–tech companies and investments that take advantage of Finland's position as a gateway to Russia and the Baltic countries.

## Principal U.S. Embassy Officials

**For up-to-date information on Principal U.S. Officials, see the U.S. Embassies, Consulates, and Foreign Service section starting on page 139.**

The U.S. embassy in Finland is at Itainen Puistotie 14, Helsinki 00140; tel: 358–9–171931; fax: 358–9–174681.

# FRANCE

October 1999

## Official Name:
## French Republic

# PROFILE

## Geography

**Area:** 551,670 sq. km. (220,668 sq. mi.); largest west European country, about four–fifths the size of Texas.
**Cities:** Capital—Paris. Other cities—Marseille, Lyon, Toulouse, Strasbourg, Nice, Bordeaux. Terrain: Varied.
**Climate:** Temperate; similar to that of the eastern U.S.

## People

**Nationality:** Adjective—French.
**Population:** 58 million.
**Annual growth rate:** 0.5%.
**Ethnic groups:** Celtic and Latin with Teutonic, Slavic, North African, Indochinese, and Basque minorities.
**Religion:** Roman Catholic 90%.
**Language:** French.
**Education:** Years compulsory—10. Literacy—99%.
**Health:** Infant mortality rate—7/1,000.
**Work force (25 million):** Services—66%. Industry and commerce—28%. Agriculture—6%.

## Government

**Type:** Republic.
**Constitution:** September 28, 1958.
**Branches:** Executive—president

(chief of state); prime minister (head of government). Legislative—bicameral Parliament (577–member National Assembly, 319–member Senate). Judicial—Court of Cassation (civil and criminal law), Council of State (administrative court), Constitutional Council (constitutional law).
**Subdivisions:** 22 administrative regions containing 96 departments (metropolitan France). Four overseas departments (Guadeloupe, Martinique, French Guiana, and Reunion); five overseas territories (New Caledonia, French Polynesia, Wallis and Futuna Islands, and French Southern and Antarctic Territories); and two special status territories (Mayotte and St. Pierre and Miquelon).
**Political parties:** Rally for the Republic (Gaullists/conservatives); Union for French Democracy (a center–right conglomerate of 5 parties: Democratic Force, Republican Party, and Radical Party are the three major components.) Socialist Party; Communist Party; National Front; Greens; Ecology Generation; various minor parties.
**Suffrage:** Universal at 18.

## Economy

**GDP:** $1.4 trillion.
**Avg. annual growth rate:** 3.2%.
**Per capita GDP:** $23,000.
**Agriculture:** Products—grains

(wheat, barley, corn); wines and spirits; dairy products; sugarbeets; oilseeds; meat and poultry; fruits and vegetables.
**Industry:** Types—aircraft, electronics, transportation, textiles, clothing, food processing, chemicals, machinery, steel.
**Trade (est.):** Exports—$305 billion: chemicals, electronics, automobiles, automobile spare parts, machinery, aircraft, foodstuffs. Imports—$286 billion: crude petroleum, electronics, machinery, chemicals, automobiles, automobile spare parts. Major trading partners—EU, U.S., Japan.

# PEOPLE

Since prehistoric times, France has been a crossroads of trade, travel, and invasion. Three basic European ethnic stocks—Celtic, Latin, and Teutonic (Frankish)—have blended over the centuries to make up its present population. France's birth rate was among the highest in Europe from 1945 until the late 1960s. Since then, its birth rate has fallen but remains higher than that of most other west European countries. Traditionally, France has had a high level of immigration. About 90% of the people are Roman Catholic, less than 2% are Protestant, and about 1% are Jewish. More than 1 million Muslims immigrated in the 1960s and early 1970s

563

from North Africa, especially Algeria. At the end of 1994, there were about 4 million persons of Muslim descent living in France.

Education is free, beginning at age 2, and mandatory between ages 6 and 16. The public education system is highly centralized. Private education is primarily Roman Catholic. Higher education in France began with the founding of the University of Paris in 1150. It now consists of 69 universities and special schools, such as the Grandes Ecoles, technical colleges, and vocational training institutions.

The French language derives from the vernacular Latin spoken by the Romans in Gaul, although it includes many Celtic and Germanic words. French has been an international language for centuries and is a common second language throughout the world. It is one of five official languages at the United Nations. In Africa, Asia, the Pacific, and the West Indies, French has been a unifying factor, particularly in those countries where it serves as the only common language among a variety of indigenous languages and dialects.

# HISTORY

France was one of the earliest countries to progress from feudalism into the era of the nation–state. Its monarchs surrounded themselves with capable ministers, and French armies were among the most innovative, disciplined, and professional of their day.

During the reign of Louis XIV (1643–1715), France was the dominant power in Europe. But overly ambitious projects and military campaigns of Louis and his successors led to chronic financial problems in the 18th century. Deteriorating economic conditions and popular resentment against the complicated system of privileges granted the nobility and clerics were among the principal causes of the French Revolution (1789–94).

Although the revolutionaries advocated republican and egalitarian principles of government, France reverted to forms of absolute rule or constitutional monarchy four times— the Empire of Napoleon, the Restoration of Louis XVIII, the reign of Louis–Philippe, and the Second Empire of Napoleon III. After the Franco–Prussian War (1870), the Third Republic was established and lasted until the military defeat of 1940.

World War I (1914–18) brought great losses of troops and materiel. In the 1920s, France established an elaborate system of border defenses (the Maginot Line) and alliances to offset resurgent German strength.

France was defeated early in World War II, however, and occupied in June 1940. The German victory left the French groping for a new policy and new leadership suited to the circumstances. On July 10, 1940, the Vichy government was established. Its senior leaders acquiesced in the plunder of French resources, as well as the sending of French forced labor to Germany; in doing so, they claimed they hoped to preserve at least some small amount of French sovereignty.

The German occupation proved quite costly, however, as a full one–half of France's public sector revenue was appropriated by Germany. After 4 years of occupation and strife, Allied forces liberated France in 1944. A bitter legacy carries over to the present day.

France emerged from World War II to face a series of new problems. After a short period of provisional government initially led by Gen. Charles de Gaulle, the Fourth Republic was set up by a new constitution and established as a parliamentary form of government controlled by a series of coalitions. The mixed nature of the coalitions and a consequent lack of agreement on measures for dealing with Indochina and Algeria caused successive cabinet crises and changes of government.

Finally, on May 13, 1958, the government structure collapsed as a result

of the tremendous opposing pressures generated in the divisive Algerian issue. A threatened coup led the Parliament to call on General de Gaulle to head the government and prevent civil war. He became prime minister in June 1958 (at the beginning of the Fifth Republic) and was elected president in December of that year.

Seven years later, in an occasion marking the first time in the 20th century that the people of France went to the polls to elect a president by direct ballot, de Gaulle won re–election with a 55% share of the vote, defeating Francois Mitterrand. In April 1969, President de Gaulle's government conducted a national referendum on the creation of 21 regions with limited political powers. The government's proposals were defeated, and de Gaulle subsequently resigned.

Succeeding him as president of France have been Gaullist Georges Pompidou (1969–74), Independent Republican Valery Giscard d'Estaing (1974–81), Socialist Francois Mitterrand (1981–95), and neo–Gaullist Jacques Chirac (elected in spring 1995).

While France continues to revere its rich history and independence, French leaders are increasingly tying the future of France to the continued development of the European Union. During President Mitterrand's tenure, he stressed the importance of European integration and advocated the ratification of the Maastricht Treaty on European economic and political union, which France's electorate narrowly approved in September 1992.

Current President Jacques Chirac assumed office May 17, 1995, after a campaign focused on the need to combat France's stubbornly high unemployment rate. The center of domestic attention soon shifted, however, to the economic reform and belt–tightening measures required for France to meet the criteria for Economic and Monetary Union (EMU) laid out by the Maastricht Treaty. In late 1995, France experienced its worst labor unrest in at least a decade, as

employees protested government cutbacks. On the foreign and security policy front, Chirac took a more assertive approach to protecting French peacekeepers in the former Yugoslavia and helped promote the peace accords negotiated in Dayton and signed in Paris in December 1995. The French have been one of the strongest supporters of NATO and EU policy in Kosovo and the Balkans.

# GOVERNMENT

The constitution of the Fifth Republic was approved by public referendum on September 28, 1958. It greatly strengthened the authority of the executive in relation to parliament. Under the constitution, the president is elected directly for a 7–year term. Presidential arbitration assures regular functioning of the public powers and the continuity of the state. The president names the prime minister, presides over the cabinet, commands the armed forces, and concludes treaties.

The president may submit questions to a national referendum and can dissolve the National Assembly. In certain emergency situations, the president may assume full powers. Besides the president, the other main component of France's executive branch is the cabinet. Headed by the prime minister, who is the nominal head of government, the cabinet is composed of a varying number of ministers, ministers–delegates, and secretaries of state. Parliament meets for one 9–month session each year. Under special circumstances an additional session can be called by the president. Although parliamentary powers are diminished from those existing under the Fourth Republic, the National Assembly can still cause a government to fall if an absolute majority of the total Assembly membership votes to censure.

The National Assembly is the principal legislative body. Its deputies are directly elected to 5–year terms, and all seats are voted on in each election. Senators are chosen by an electoral college for 9–year terms, and one–third of the Senate is renewed every 3 years. The Senate's legislative powers are limited; the National Assembly has the last word in the event of a disagreement between the two houses. The government has a strong influence in shaping the agenda of Parliament. The government also can link its life to any legislative text, and unless a motion of censure is introduced and voted, the text is considered adopted without a vote.

The most distinctive feature of the French judicial system is that it is divided into the Constitutional Council and the Council of State. The Constitutional Council examines legislation and decides whether it conforms to the constitution. Unlike the U.S. Supreme Court, it considers only legislation that is referred to it by Parliament, the prime minister, or the president; moreover, it considers legislation before it is promulgated. The Council of State has a separate function from the Constitutional Council and provides recourse to individual citizens who have claims against the administration.

Traditionally, decisionmaking in France has been highly centralized, with each of France's departments headed by a prefect appointed by the central government. In 1982, the national government passed legislation to decentralize authority by giving a wide range of administrative and fiscal powers to local elected officials. In March 1986, regional councils were directly elected for the first time, and the process of decentralization continues, albeit at a slow pace.

## Principal Government Officials

For up-to-date information on Principal Government Officials, see the Chiefs of State and Cabinet Members of Foreign Governments section starting on page 1.

France maintains an embassy in the U.S. at 4101 Reservoir Rd. NW, Washington, DC 20007 (tel. 202–944–6000).

# POLITICAL CONDITIONS

During his first 2 years in office, President Chirac's prime minister was Alain Juppe, who served contemporaneously as leader of Chirac's neo–Gaullist Rally for the Republic (RPR) Party. Chirac and Juppe benefited from a very large, if rather unruly, majority in the National Assembly (470 out of 577 seats). Mindful that the government might have to take politically costly decisions in advance of the legislative elections planned for spring 1998 in order to ensure France met the Maastricht criteria for the single European currency, Chirac decided in April 1997 to call early elections. The Left, however, led by Socialist Party leader Lionel Jospin, whom Chirac defeated in the 1995 presidential race, unexpectedly won a solid National Assembly majority (319 seats, with 289 required for an absolute majority) in

the two rounds of balloting, which took place May 25 and June 1, 1997. President Chirac named Jospin prime minister on June 2, and Jospin went on to form a government composed primarily of Socialist ministers, along with some ministers from allied parties of the Left, such as the Communist and the Greens. Jospin stated his support for continued European integration and his intention to keep France on the path of toward Economic and Monetary Union, albeit with greater attention to social concerns.

The tradition in periods of "cohabitation" (president of one party, prime minister of another) is for the president to exercise the primary role in foreign and security policy, with the dominant role in domestic policy falling to the prime minister and his government. Jospin stated, however, that he would not a priori leave any domain exclusively to the president.

Chirac and Jospin have worked together, for the most part, in the foreign affairs field with representatives of the presidency and the government pursuing a single, agreed French policy. The current "cohabitation" arrangement is the longest–lasting in the history of the Fifth Republic.

# ECONOMY

With a GDP of $1.4 trillion, France is the fourth–largest Western industrialized economy. It has substantial agricultural resources, a large industrial base, and a highly skilled work force. A dynamic services sector accounts for an increasingly large share of economic activity (72% in 1997) and is responsible for nearly all job creation in recent years. GDP growth averaged 2% between 1994 and 1998, with 3.2% recorded in 1998.

Government economic policy aims to promote investment and domestic growth in a stable fiscal and monetary environment. Creating jobs and reducing the high unemployment rate (11.5% in 1998) is a top priority. France joined 10 other European

## Travel Notes

**Travel Advice:** For up-to-date information from the U.S. State Department on possible inconvenient or hazardous situations, see the **Travel Warnings and Consular Information Sheets from the U.S. Government** section starting on page 1723. For the latest information on health requirements and conditions, see the **International Travelers' Health Information** section starting on page 1385. For further information dealing with non-urgent matter, see the **Tips for Travelers to...** section starting on page 1588.

Union countries in adopting the euro as its currency in January 1999. Henceforth, monetary policy will be set by the European Central Bank in Frankfurt.

Despite significant reform and privatization over the past 15 years, the government continues to control a large share of economic activity: Government spending, at 54.2% of GDP in 1998, is the highest in the G–7. Regulation of labor and product markets is pervasive. The government continues to own shares in corporations in a range of sectors, including banking, energy production and distribution, automobiles, transportation, and telecommunications.

Legislation passed in 1998 will shorten the legal workweek from 39 to 35 hours effective January 1, 2000. A key objective of the legislation is to encourage job creation, for which significant new subsidies will be made available. It is difficult to assess the impact of workweek reduction on growth and jobs since many of the key economic parameters (such as the impact on labor costs and company's ability to reorganize work schedules) will depend on the outcome of labor–management negotiations which should extend through 2000 and beyond.

France has been very successful in developing dynamic telecommunications, aerospace, and weapons sectors. With virtually no domestic oil production, France has relied heavily on the development of nuclear power, which now accounts for about 80% of the country's electricity production. Nuclear waste is stored on site at reprocessing facilities.

Membership in France's labor unions accounts for less than 10% of the private sector workforce and is concentrated in the manufacturing, transportation, and heavy industry sectors. Most unions are affiliated with one of the competing national federations, the largest and most powerful of which are the communist–dominated General Labor Confederation, the Workers' Force, and the French Democratic Confederation of Labor.

## Trade

France is the second–largest trading nation in Western Europe (after Germany). Its foreign trade balance for goods has been in surplus since 1992, reaching $25.4 billion in 1998. Total trade for 1998 amounted to $730 billion, or 50% of GDP (imports plus exports of goods and services). Trade with European Union (EU) countries accounts for 60% of French trade.

In 1998, U.S.–France trade totaled about $47 billion (goods only). According to French trade data, U.S. exports accounted for 8.7% (about $25 billion) of France's total imports. U.S. industrial chemicals, aircraft and engines, electronic components, telecommunications, computer software, computers and peripherals, analytical and scientific instrumentation, medical instruments and supplies, broadcasting equipment, and programming and franchising are particularly attractive to French importers.

Principal French exports to the United States are aircraft and engines, beverages, electrical equipment, chemicals, cosmetics, and luxury products.

## Agriculture

France is the European Union's leading agricultural producer, accounting for about one–third of all agricultural land within the EU. Northern France is characterized by large wheat farms. Dairy products, pork, poultry, and apple production are concentrated in the Western region. Beef production is located in central France, while the production of fruits, vegetables, and wine ranges from central to southern France. France is a large producer of many agricultural products and is currently expanding its forestry and fishery industries. The implementation of the Common Agricultural Policy (CAP) and the Uruguay Round of the GATT Agreement have resulted in reforms in the agricultural sector of the economy.

France is the world's second–largest agricultural producer, after the United States. However, the destination of 70% of its exports are other EU member states. Wheat, beef, pork, poultry, and dairy products are the principal exports. The United States, although the second–largest exporter to France, faces stiff competition from domestic production, other EU member states, and other third countries. U.S. agricultural exports to France, totaling some $600 million annually, consist primarily of soybeans and products, feeds and fodders, seafood, and consumer oriented products, especially snack foods and nuts. French exports to the United States are mainly cheese, processed products and wine. They amount to more than $900 million annually.

# FOREIGN RELATIONS

A charter member of the United Nations, France holds one of the permanent seats in the Security Council and is a member of most of its specialized and related agencies.

## Europe

France is a leader in Western Europe because of its size, location, strong economy, membership in European organizations, strong military posture, and energetic diplomacy. France generally has worked to strengthen the global economic and political influence of the EU and its role in common European defense. It views Franco–German cooperation and the development of a European Security and Defense Identity (ESDI) as the foundation of efforts to enhance European security.

## Middle East

France supports the Middle East Peace Process as revitalized by the 1991 Madrid peace conference. In this context, France backed the establishment of a Palestinian homeland and the withdrawal of Israel from all occupied territories. Recognizing the need for a comprehensive peace agreement, France supports the involvement of all Arab parties and Israel in a multilateral peace process. France has been active in promoting a regional economic dialogue and has played an active role in providing assistance to the Palestinian Authority.

## Africa

France plays a significant role in Africa, especially in its former colonies, through extensive aid programs, commercial activities, military agreements, and cultural impact. In those former colonies where the French presence remains important, France contributes to political, military, and social stability.

## Asia

France has extensive political and commercial relations with Asian countries, including China, Japan and Southeast Asia as well as an increasing presence in regional fora. France was instrumental in launching the Asia–Europe Meeting (ASEM) process which could eventually emerge as a competitor to APEC. France is seeking to broaden its commercial presence in China and will pose a competitive challenge to U.S. business, particularly in aerospace, high–tech and luxury markets. In Southeast Asia, France was an architect of the Paris Accords, which ended the conflict in Cambodia.

## Latin America

France supports strengthening democratic institutions in Latin America. It supports the ongoing efforts to restore democracy to Haiti and seeks to expand its trade relations with all of Latin America.

## Security Issues

French military doctrine is based on the concepts of national independence, nuclear deterrence, and military sufficiency. France is a founding member of the North Atlantic Treaty Organization (NATO), and has worked actively with Allies to adapt NATO—internally and externally—to the post–Cold War environment. In December 1995, France announced that it would increase its participation in NATO's military wing, including the Military Committee (the French withdrew from NATO's military bodies in 1966 while remaining full participants in the alliance's political councils). France remains a firm supporter of the Organization for Security and Cooperation in Europe and other efforts at cooperation. Paris hosted the May 1997 NATO–Russia Summit for the signing of the Founding Act on Mutual Relations, Cooperation and Security.

Outside of NATO, France has actively and heavily participated in recent peacekeeping/coalition efforts in Africa, the Middle East, and the Balkans, often taking the lead in these operations.

France has undertaken a major restructuring to develop a professional military which will be smaller, more rapidly deployable and better tailored for operations outside of mainland France. Key elements of the restructuring include reducing personnel, bases, and headquarters, and rationalizing equipment and the armament industry. French active–duty military at the beginning of 1997 numbered approximately 475,000, of which nearly 60,000 were assigned outside of metropolitan France. The overall force is expected to decline by approximately 25,000 per year through 2002.

France places a high priority on arms control and non–proliferation. It supported the indefinite extension of the Non–Proliferation Treaty in 1995. After conducting a final series of six nuclear tests, the French signed the Comprehensive Test Ban Treaty in 1996. France has implemented a moratorium on the production, export, and use of anti–personnel landmines and supports negotiations leading toward a universal ban. The French

are key players in the adaptation of the Treaty on Conventional Armed Forces in Europe to the new strategic environment.

France is an active participant in the major supplier regimes designed to restrict transfer of technologies that could lead to proliferation of weapons of mass destruction: the Nuclear Suppliers Group, the Australia Group (for chemical and biological weapons), and the Missile Technology Control Regime. France has signed and ratified the Chemical Weapons Convention.

# U.S.-FRENCH RELATIONS

Relations between the United States and France are active and cordial. Mutual visits by high–level officials are conducted on a regular basis. Bilateral contact at the cabinet level has traditionally been active. France and the United States share common values and have parallel policies on most political, economic, and security issues. Differences are discussed frankly and have not been allowed to impair the pattern of close cooperation that characterizes relations between the two countries.

## Principal U.S. Embassy Officials

**For up-to-date information on Principal U.S. Officials, see the U.S. Embassies, Consulates, and Foreign Service section starting on page 139.**

The U.S. embassy in France is located at 2 Avenue Gabriel, Paris 8 (tel. [33] (1) 4312–2222).
The United States also is represented in Paris by its mission to the Organization for Economic Cooperation and Development.

# FRENCH ANTILLES AND GUIANA

January 1989

## Official Name:
## Martinique; Guadeloupe; French Guiana

# PROFILE

## MARTINIQUE

### Geography

**Area:** 1,100 sq. km. (425 sq. mi.); about one-third the size of Rhode Island.
**Cities:** Capital—Fort-de-France (pop. 117,438). Other cities—Lamentin (26,367); Sainte Marie (18,526).
**Terrain:** Volcanic mountains in north (elev. 1,397 m.); a central plain and descending hills in the south.
**Climate:** Tropical.

### People

**Nationality:** Noun and adjective—Martiniquais (sing. and pl.).
**Population (1988):** 351,105.
**Annual growth rate (1988):** 1.71%.
**Ethnic groups:** Afro-European, Afroindian, European.
**Religions:** Roman Catholic 95%; Baptist, Seventh-day Adventist, Jehovah Witness, Pentecostal, Hindu, traditional African, others 5%.
**Education:** Literacy—more than 70%. Years compulsory—through age 16. Attendance (1987-88)—100,152.
**Health:** Infant mortality rate (1986)—10.1/1,000. Life expectancy—male 71 yrs.; female 76 yrs.

**Work force (1984-125,987):** Agricultural—10.7%. Industry—16%. Services, government, commerce 47.6%.
**Unemployment (1987):** 28.4%.

### Government

**Type:** Overseas department (1946) and region (1977) of France. Prefect appointed by Ministry of Interior, Paris. Locally elected general and regional councils.
**Subdivisions:** 2 subprefectures, Trinite and Marin; 45 cantons and 34 municipalities.
**Political parties:** Progressive Party of Martinique (PPM), Socialists (PS), Communists (PCM), Union for French Democracy (UDF), Rally for the Republic (RPR), Movement for Martinique Independence (MIM), and several small radical left parties.
**Departmental budget (1987):** 1.35 billion francs.
**Flag:** French tricolor-blue, white, and red vertical stripes.

### Economy

**GDP (1985):** $1.3 billion.
**Growth rate (1984-85):** 14.1%.
**Per capita income (1985):** $3,650.
**Inflation rate (1987):** 3.6%.
**Natural resources:** Scenery and cultivable land.
**Agriculture:** Products-bananas, pineapples, sugarcane (for rum), avocados, tropical fruits, vegetables, flowers.
**Industry:** Types—construction, rum, cement, oil refining, canning, light industry.
**Trade (1985):** Exports—$145 million: bananas 48%, refined oil 20%, rum 9.4%, pineapples 3.1%, cement 1%. Major markets—Franc Zone 93.5%; US, less than 1%. Imports—$683 million: food and household goods 50%; fuels and chemicals 20%; machines, equipment, and building supplies 20%; vehicles and transport 10%. Major suppliers—Franc Zone 66%, EEC 18%, US 3%, non-French Caribbean 1%, other 15%.

## GUADELOUPE

### Geography

**Area:** 1,709 sq. km. (660 sq. mi.); about one-half the size of Rhode Island.
**Cities:** Capital—BasseTerre (1982 pop. 13,796). Other cities—Pointe-a-Pitre/Abymes (81,549).
**Terrain:** An archipelago, consisting of two islands (Grand-Terre and Ilasse Terre) separated by a stream and several smaller islands, including Marie Galante, Desirade, and The Saints. The northern island of Grand-Terre consists of hills and plains; the southern island of Basse-Terre is volcanic and mountainous (elev. 1,467 m.).
**Climate:** Tropical.

## People

**Nationality:** Noun and adjective Guadeloupean(s).
**Population (Jan. 1988):** 337,524.
**Annual growth rate (1987):** 1.2%.
**Ethnic groups:** Afro-European, European, Afro-East Asian, East Asian.
**Religion:** Predominantly Roman Catholic, some Hindu and traditional African.
**Education:** Compulsory through age 16. Literacy—more than 70to.
**Health:** Infant mortality rate (1986)—15.5/1,000. Life expectancy—male 69 yrs.; female 77 yrs.
**Work force (1986, 116,842):** Agriculture—11.12%. Industry—8.56%. Building trades—7%. Services, government, commerce, transportation—70%.
**Unemployment (1986):** 26%.

## Government

**Type:** Overseas department (1946) and region (1977) of France.
**Branches:** Executive—prefect appointed by Ministry of Interior, Paris. Legislative—locally elected general and regional councils. Judicial—French jurisdiction.
**Subdivisions:** 2 subprefectures, Pointe-a-Pitre and Saint Martin; 42 cantons and 32 municipalities. St. Barthelemy and French St. Martin fall under the jurisdiction of the Department of Guadeloupe.
**Political parties:** Socialists(PS), Communists (PCG), Union for French Democracy (UDF), Rally for the Republic (RPR), Union for the Liberation of Guadeloupe (UPLG), and several small radical left parties.
**Suffrage:** Universal over 18.
**Departmental budget (1985):** $380.5 million.
**Flag:** French tricolor-blue, white, and red vertical stripes.

## Economy

**GDP (1984):** $998 million.
**Growth rate (1982-83 avg):** 10.9%.
**Per capita income (1986):** $3,630.
**Inflation rate (1987):** 3.5%.
**Natural resources:** Scenery, cultivable land, an underwater park.
**Agriculture:** Products—sugarcane, bananas, pineapples, tropical fruits and vegetables, coffee, flowers.
**Industry:** Types—construction, cement, rum, various light industry.
**Trade (1985):** Exports—approx. $75 million: bananas 48%, sugar 20%, rum 6%, flour 6%. Major markets—Franc Zone 89%, non-French Caribbean 5%, US 2%, EEC 1%. Imports—approx. $647 million: food and household goods 48%; machinery, equipment, and building supplies 22%; fuels and chemicals 18%; vehicles and transport 9%. Major suppliers (1986)—Franc Zone 70%, EEC 12.5%, US 2%, non French Caribbean 3%, other 12.5%.

# FRENCH GUIANA

## Geography

**Area:** 89,941 sq. km. (43,740 sq. mi.); about the size of Indiana.
**Cities:** Capital—Cayenne (pop. 38,135). Other cities—Kourou (12,000); St. Laurent du Maroni (1982-6,984).
**Terrain:** Low-lying coastal plains, tropical forest rising to hills (elev. 700 m.).

## People

**Nationality:** Noun and adjective—French Guianese.
**Population (Jan. 1988):** 90,240.
**Annual growth rate (1986-87):** 3.6%.
**Ethnic groups:** African and Afro-European 66%; European 18%; East Asian, Chinese, Amerindian, Brazilian 16%.
**Religion:** Predominantly Roman Catholic, some Protestant sects, Hindu, traditional African.
**Education:** Years compulsory—through age 16. Attendance (1985)—3,783.
**Health:** Infant mortality rate (1984)—25.7/1,000. Life expectancy (1983)—male 66 yrs.; female 74 yrs.
**Work force (1982, 47,702):** Agriculture—15.18%. Industry—19.41%. Services, government, commerce—65.40%.
**Unemployment (1986):** 15%.

## Government

**Type:** Overseas department (1946) and region (1977) of France.
**Branches:** Executive—prefect appointed by Ministry of Interior, Paris. Legislative—locally elected general and regional councils.
**Subdivision:** 1 subprefecture, St. Laurent du Maroni; 16 cantons or municipalities.
**Political parties:** Socialist (PSG), RPR, UDF, several small radical left parties; Communist Party membership is negligible.
**Departmental budget (1987):** 847 million francs.
**Flag:** French tricolor-blue, white, and red vertical stripes.

## Economy

**Inflation rate (1987):** 4%.
**Natural resources:** Fisheries (shrimp), forestry products, gold, unexploited kaolin and bauxite, agriculture, aquaculture.
**Agriculture:** Products—rice, fruits, and vegetables for local consumption.
**Industry:** Types—construction, shrimp and fish processing, lumber, aerospace.
**Trade (1985):** Exports—approx. $37.5 million: shrimp 59%, lumber 7%, rice 3%. Major markets—Franc Zone 45%; US 36%; Japan 16%. Imports—$257.0 million: food and household goods 27%; machinery, equipment, building supplies 30%; fuels and chemicals 17%; vehicles and transport 26%. Major suppliers—Franc Zone 65%, EEC 11%, Trinidad 8%, US 5%.

# GEOGRAPHY

Martinique is the northernmost of the Windward Islands, which are part of the Lesser Antilles chain in the Caribbean Sea southeast of Puerto Rico. This volcanic island is characterized by an indented coastline and mountainous terrain. The highest point is Mt. Pelee, with an altitude of 1,417 meters (4,650 ft.) above sea level. December to May are generally the coolest, driest, and most comfortable months. The mean temperature varies from a low of 24°C (75.7°F) to a high of 26°C (79.9°F). Average relative humidity ranges from 77% to 85%.

Guadeloupe comprises two of the Leeward Islands, which also are part of the Lesser Antilles chain. Volcanic Basse-Terre lies to the west and is separated from the flatter limestone formation of Grande-Terre by a narrow saltwater stream, Riviere Salee. The highest point, about 1,478 meters (4,850 ft.) above sea level, is the dormant volcano of Soufriere in BasseTerre. Although Pointe-a-Pitre is the principal city and commercial center of the is land, the prefecture is located in BasseTerre.

Several smaller islands in the region are administratively part of Guadeloupe: Marie-Galante, La Desirade, and the Iles-des-Saintes, which are quite close to Guadeloupe, and the islands of St. Barthelemy and St. Martin (two-thirds of which is French; the other one-third is Dutch), which are located 240 Kilometers (150 mi.) north and east of Guadeloupe. November to April are generally the coolest and driest months. At Pointe-a-Pitre, mean temperatures vary from 23 °C (74° F) in January to 30° C (87°F) in August; the average monthly humidity varies from 77% in March and April to 85% in October.

French Guiana is located on the northern coast of South America a few degrees north of the Equator. The coast has fertile, rolling plains occasionally broken by hills that gradually rise to the Tumuc-Humac Mountains along the Brazilian border in the south. Most of the country is unsettled, covered by a dense tropical rain forest of the Amazon Basin. The climate is subequatorial; the temperature averages about 26°C (80°F) throughout the year. Annual rainfall averages more than 250 centimeters (100 in.); the wet season extends from December through June.

# PEOPLE

About 95% of the people of Martinique are of Afro-European or Afro-European-Indian descent. The rest are traditional white planter families, commonly referred to as bekes or white creoles, and a sizable number of metropolitan French working in

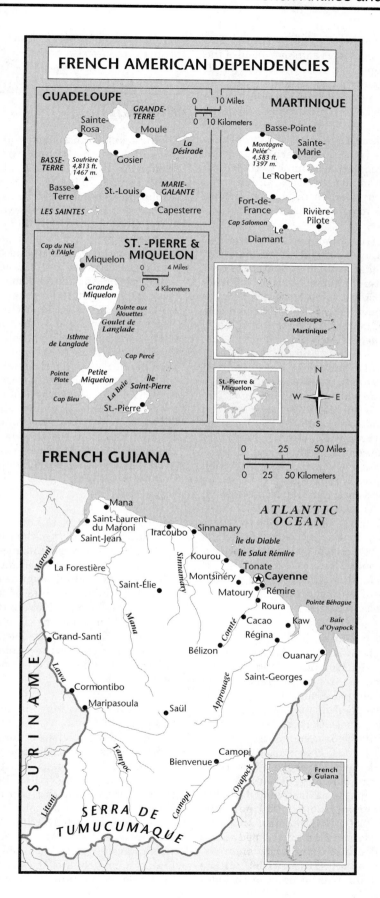

administration and business. The island possesses a unique blend of the cosmopolitan and the traditional, with many people in and around the bustling capital of Fort-de-France employed in commerce and administration, while the rural areas retain the island's agricultural flavor. Dress varies from the latest in European and American fashion to the traditional madras dresses and scarves worn by women in the rural communes and open markets.

Most Guadeloupeans are of mixed Afro-European and Afro-Indian (i.e., descendants of laborers brought over from the Indian subcontinent during the l9th century) ancestry. Several thousand metropolitan French reside there; most are civil servants, business people, and their dependents. Iles-des Saints and St. Barthelemy are still inhabited by descendants of the Normans and Bretons who arrived three centuries ago. The islands of MarieGalante and La Desirade are inhabited by Antilleans of African descent, primarily employed in agriculture and administration. French St. Martin, which occupies about two-thirds of the hybrid island of St. Martin/Dutch St. Maarten, is the only French-administered area in the Caribbean where English is widely spoken. The island has a varied population, including St. Martiners, Haitians, Anguillans, Virgin Islanders, and growing populations of metropolitan French and American retirees.

About two-thirds of the population of French Guiana are Afro-European Creoles or Guianese. The remainder includes metropolitan French (about 12%) serving in military or administrative positions or working at the Kourou Space Center; Asians primarily involved in commerce and the retail trades; Haitians, Brazilians, and St. Lucians involved in agriculture; two Hmong (Laotian) resettlement villages at Cacao and Javouhey numbering some 1,200 persons; about 3,000 Amerindians; and some 4,000 descendants of escaped slaves who fled into the interior and reestablished an African tribal village way of life. This latter group includes Bonis, Saramacas, and Bosch I who

are primarily hunters, fishermen farmers, and woodworkers.

# HISTORY

The first known indigenous inhabitants of French Guiana and the French Antilles were Arawak and Carib Indians. The Arawaks were among the dominant Indian nations in French Guiana and migrated to Martinique at the beginning of the Christian era. A peaceful people known for their pottery and other crafts, the Arawaks lived tranquilly in the French Antilles for some 1,000 years. Only about 100 Arawaks currently remain in French Guiana. They were supplanted by the warlike Caribs, whose migrations took them from the Amazon to the northeast shoulder of South America and on to the Antilles, where they were still arriving during the voyages of Christopher Columbus. Columbus sighted Guadeloupe in 1493, Martinique in 1493 or 1502, and the Guiana coast probably during his third voyage in 1498. The area was permanently settled by the French in the 17th century.

The Caribs fled or were killed by the first European settlers of the Antilles in the 17th century. No Indian settlements remain in the French Antilles, and the Amerindian population in French Guiana consists of about 3,000 people belonging to six tribes. The term "Amerindians" is used to distinguish them from the East Indians who came to work the plantations following the abolition of slavery in 1848.

The name "Martinique" is derived from an old Carib word meaning "island of flowers." Except for three short periods of British occupation, Martinique has been a French possession since 1635, when Belain D'Esnambuc took the island for France. The American colonies had close relations with Martinique and the French Antilles. With the advent of the Revolutionary War, Benjamin Franklin, on behalf of the Continental Congress on June 3, 1776, commissioned William Bingham of New

York to represent the fledgling American Government in Martinique. In 1781, a French fleet, under the command of Admiral Comte de Grasse, sailed from Martinique to blockade the British forces at Yorktown, thereby ensuring the victory of General Washington. Overlooking the bay from which de Grasse sailed was the plantation of the Tashcer de la Pagerie family, whose daughter Josephine, was to become the first wife of Napoleon I and Empress of France.

In 1902, Mt. Pelee erupted in the north of the island and, in a matter of minutes, killed 30,000 people. The eruption destroyed Saint-Pierre, the "Pearl of the Antilles," which was the island's largest town and commercial and cultural capital. U.S. Consul Thomas T. Prentis and his family were among those who perished in the disaster. Obtaining an emergency grant from the U.S. Congress, President Theodore Roosevelt immediately sent two U.S. Navy ships to provide relief, but there were few survivors. Today Saint-Pierre is a quiet tourist center with fewer than 7,000 residents.

In 1940, following the Franco German armistice, Martinique became semiautonomous under a high commission from Vichy France until 1943 when the Free French took control.

Guadeloupe was known to its Indian inhabitants as Karukera, or aisle of good waters." Columbus named the island after the saint, Santa Maria de Guadeloupe de Estremadura; it was soon shortened to Guadeloupe. In 1635, Jean de Plessis and Charles Lienard took possession of the island in the name of the Compagnie des Iles d'Amerique. The first slaves were brought from Africa to work the plantations around 1650, and the first slave rebellion occurred in 1656. Guadeloupe was poorly administered in its early days and was a dependency of Martinique until 1775. In 1794, following a slave revolt and a short period of British occupation, Victor Hugues (nick named "The Terrible") arrived from the revolutionary government in Paris complete with portable guillotine, which he used on a number of white planters, and proclaimed the abolition of slavery. In 1802, Napoleon re-established slavery until 1848, when slavery was finally abolished in all French possessions, due in large measure to the work of the abolitionist National Assembly deputy from Guadeloupe and Martinique, Victor Schoelcher. Schoelchers memory is commemorated by monuments, street names, and public parks in all corners of the French Antilles.

Following the Napoleonic wars, Guadeloupe again settled into a plantation economy, but a significant portion of its agricultural economy was owned by large firms or absentee landlords. Unlike Martinique, where the white planting class had been preserved in part by the British occupation, many Guadeloupean planters had been killed or had fled from the revolutionary terror.

The first French settlement in French Guiana was established in 1604, but the settlers fled the enervating climate and the terror of the Indians the following year. The first permanent settlement began in 1634, and in 1664, the town of Cayenne was established. Agricultural Jesuit settlements flourished in the succeeding years until the order was expelled from France in 1767. A badly planned and organized settlement in the region of Kourou perished in 1763. Following the abolition of slavery in 1848, the fragile plantation economy declined precipitously. The penal colony known as "Devils Island" was established at Kourou in 1852, and some 70,000 prisoners were shipped to French Guiana before the colony's abolition in 1947.

In 1964, Kourou was chosen as the site of the French (now Euro-French) space center which has brought a substantial increase in population and relative prosperity to the immediate area. In 1977, the first of two settlements of Hmong (Meo) refugees from Indochina was established in the hilly forests at Cacao, southwest of Cayenne. A second Hmong settlement was started in 1979, in Javouhey near coastal Mana in the northern tip of the department.

# GOVERNMENT

French Guiana, Guadeloupe, and Martinique, as overseas departments of France since 1946, are integral parts of the French Republic. Their relationship is somewhat similar to that of Alaska and Hawaii to the conterminous United States. Each department has a general council composed of one representative elected by popular vote from each canton (42 in Guadeloupe, 45 in Martinique, and 16 in French Guiana). The general council is responsible for the day-to-day management on behalf of the French central government the departmental budget, including the distribution of transfer payments for health care, social security, child care, and other social welfare programs. The general council also is responsible for the distribution and supervision of funds for roads, transportation, and public works programs; school transportation; the construction and maintenance of professional and secondary schools; sports and cultural programs; public housing; and public health and economic development, including the allocation of public funds to private sector projects.

In 1972, the metropolitan departments of France were combined into 22 regions, with an elected regional council for each region. Since the three French overseas departments in the Caribbean could not agree upon a single regional council to represent them, it was determined that each department would also be designated a region. New regional councils were elected in Martinique, Guadeloupe, and French Guiana in February 1983. Unlike the canton or district elections held for the general council, regional councilors are elected by proportional representation; each political party presents a list and elects representatives to the regional council in proportion to the number of region-wide votes received by each party. Only those parties receiving at least 5% of the vote are apportioned seats. There are 41 regional councilors in Martinique and Guadeloupe and 31 in French Guiana.

Although it shares many overlap ping functions with the general council, the regional council is responsible for long-range planning in housing, energy, public works, economic development including tourism, air transport, preservation of the region's cultural and ethnic heritage, sports and educational programs, and public assistance to private sector development. The new system was created as part of the political de centralization policy of the socialist administration of President Francois Mitterrand, a program that has sought to transfer many reponsibilities to locally elected officials.

The greatest change has been in diminishing the role and powers of the prefect, the senior central government official in each overseas department/region. The prefect is appointed from Paris for an indefinite period, usually years, and is normally a career civil servant. Although it oversees the departmental offices of most central government agencies such as the national police, gendarmes, customs, immigration, and the military, many other bud get, economic, and social planning responsibilities have been turned over to local officials. The French Caribbean departments also are represented in the national legislature, with Guadeloupe and Martinique each electing four deputies to the National Assembly and two senators to the French Senate. French Guiana elects two deputies and one senator.

## Principal Government Officials

---

**For up-to-date information on Principal Government Officials, see the Chiefs of State and Cabinet Members of Foreign Governments section starting on page 1.**

---

The French Embassy in the United States is at 4101 Reservoir Road, NW., Washington, D.C. 20007 (tel. 202-944-6000).

# POLITICAL CONDITIONS

As integral parts of the French Republic, the political systems of the three French Caribbean departments essentially are extensions of those of metropolitan France. Just as each state in the United States will have a local branch of the Republican or Democratic Party, so each department has active arms of the French Socialist Party, the Gaullist RPR (Rassemblernent pour la Republique), and the centrist UDF (Union de la Democratie Francaise). But politics in the French Caribbean departments also has a distinctly local flavor, and one finds indigenous political movements supporting everything from increased autonomy for the overseas departments to immediate independence from France. Although those political movements urging an immediate rupture with France garner only a small percentage of the vote in local elections, those parties favoring decentralization and greater recognition of the cultural and social specificity of the French Caribbean departments have enjoyed much greater electoral success.

The political decentralization policies of the Mitterrand presidency have proven popular in the French Caribbean departments. These policies—which have led to increased local control over the departmental budget, long-term planning in areas of economic development and social allocations, and greater recognition of local cultural and social institutions, including "Antille anization" of the local media—have relegated radical leftwing parties calling for immediate independence from France to the political sidelines. The extreme right National Front enjoys little support in the French Caribbean departments.

In Martinique, elections are highly competitive, with the left and right each sending two deputies to the National Assembly. Aime Cesaire— the well-known poet, playwright, and leader of the Negritude movement, who broke with the Communist Party in 1950s among the island's most respected political figures. He has served as mayor of Fort-de-France and deputy since 1946 and also is president of the regional council. His indigenous political movement, the PPM (Parti Progressiste Martiniquais), advocates political autonomy to counter growing economic and social assimilation of Martinique into France and is the most influential party on the island. With its power base in Fort-de-France, where one-third of the island's population lives, the PPM has forged a political alliance with the Socialist and Communist Parties. This has enabled the left to capture the regional council, where candidates are chosen by proportional representation, and elect the island's first PPM senator (Rudolph Desire).

The older, more established general council, whose members are chosen in cantonal elections, is in the hands of the right, resulting in an uneasy marriage between the island's two elective bodies. The radical pro-independence parties, which urge their adherents to boycott the French national elections, nonetheless campaign actively for the local legislative bodies. Although two of their leaders have been elected to the general council, none of the extreme left movements was able to garner the necessary 5% of the vote for representation on the regional council. Only 55% of Martinique's eligible voters participate in national and local elections—considerably below the 80% participation rate in metropolitan France.

Politics in Guadeloupe often has taken a more violent twist, with radical pro-independence groups using bombs, not ballots, to make their point. After a series of terrorist incidents in the fall of 1986, leaders of the Caribbean Revolutionary Alliance (ARC) were arrested and sentenced to prison in Paris. Since those arrests, the island's major aboveground pro-independence movement-the UPLG (Union pour Ia Liberation de Ia Guadeloupehas announced its intention to join the political fray, with plans to contest regional and general council elections. Previously, the party had urged supporters to abstain from voting. Although the island voted overwhelmingly for the right in the 1981 presidential elections, the general and regional councils are now firmly in the hands of the left. The Communist Party of Guadeloupe—whose adherents include the mayors of the capital, Basse Terre, and the largest town and commercial center, Pointe-a-Pitre—has elected one deputy and one of the is land's two senators. Socialist leader Frederic Jalton holds another seat as deputy, while the right, led by Secretary of State for French-speaking Communities Lucette Michaux-Chevry (RPR), sends two deputies to Paris. The department's political anomalies, French St. Martin and St. Barthelemy, generally send right-of-center officials to the legislative councils. While there has been talk of greater political autonomy for French St. Martin, there is little visible movement in that direction.

Politics in French Guiana has a distinctly ethnic flair; the local Guianese Creole population, which holds power, expresses concern about the influx of Asians, Europeans, Brazilians, Surinamese, Haitians, and others who add to the department's colorful cultural mix. The newcomers—some legal, many others illegal—do not participate in the political process. Only 26,000 of approximately 90,000 residents are registered to vote. Of these, only about 15,000 cast their vote in legislative elections. Socialists control the general and regional councils and the mayor's office in the capital, Cayenne. The department's two deputies are split between the right (Paulin Brune, RPR) and the left (Elie Castor, PS). Although pro-independence forces captured three seats on the regional council in the 1983 elections, they faired poorly in the 1986 contests. The pro-independence PNPG (Parti National Populaire Guyanais) captured only 3% of the vote, finishing behind the National Front-the ultra-rightwing party that enjoys some support among metropolitan French working at the space center. A dissident socialist group, Action Democratique Guyanais, captured four seats on the regional council in

1986, beating the UDF ticket led by Claude Ho-A-Chuck, which captured three spots. The Communist Party does not compete in local elections and won only 1% of the vote in the last presidential election.

# ECONOMY

Guadeloupe and Martinique owed their colonial prosperity to agriculture, principally sugar produced in self-contained plantations known as habitations on which food and commercial crops were grown, animals raised, and slaves or indentured servants housed and fed. But sugar is no longer king in the French West Indies; although Martinique had more than 450 sugar refineries in the 17th century, it now has only one and no longer exports sugar. Guadeloupe has retained three refineries, and sugar still accounts for 20% of its export earnings. Much of the sugar grown in Martinique and Guadeloupe is used in the production of rum.

In Martinique, sugar has been replaced as an export crop by bananas and pineapples. Bananas now account for almost 50% of Guadeloupe's total ex-port earnings. Growers in both departments have diversified their crops and experimented with new agricultural processes such as hydroponics. Martinique also exports large quantities of avocados, limes, eggplants, and tropical flowers, primarily to metropolitan France. Guadeloupe has doubled its exports of melons and tropical flowers and has resumed coffee growing, primarily for local consumption, producing some 26 tons in 1986. Both islands produce a wide array of fruits, vegetables, and tubers for local consumption, and market days in the capitals of Fort-de-France and Basse Terre are resplendent with a wide selection of locally grown foods.

In French Guiana, the impact of the French National Space Agency's Guiana Space Center has been immense. Kourou has grown from a sleepy town of 3,500 into a busy European community of some 12,000 people and the center of some of the world's most

advanced space technology. The center is now the second-largest employer in French Guiana, with important links to virtually all sectors of the local economy, including roads, communications, transport, the building trades, and services sectors. Many commercial enterprises, from hotels to bakeries have benefited from the space program. With firm contracts for 45 additional satellite launches on Ariane rockets, French Guiana will continue this space-related development.

Shrimp production, in which American firms have played an important role, accounts for some 60% of export earnings in French Guiana. Lumber production, including Guiana's prized hardwoods, accounts for 7% of export revenue. In recent years, rice cultivation, aquaculture, and commercial fishing also have improved. Rice exports now account for 3% of export earnings, while crayfish production, including exports to the French Caribbean departments and the metropole, more than doubled between 1985 and 1986. New fish processing facilities in the Port of Larivot near Cayenne have resulted in renewed French interest in commercial fishing in French Guianese waters and a net increase of almost 100% in catches of red snapper and other commercial varieties. Gold mining yielded some 300 kilos of ore in 1986, while kaolin deposits remain largely unexploited.

The overall importance of agriculture in export earnings has decreased in all the French Caribbean departments; agriculture now accounts for about 10%-15% of national income in Martinique and Guadeloupe. With modern European tastes and a highly developed infrastructure of roads, ports, schools, and hospitals, the French Caribbean departments are heavily dependent on French Government transfers. In Martinique, exports pay only 25% of the import bill; in Guadeloupe and French Guiana, exports cover even less—14% and 12%, respectively. More than 70% of the national income of Martinique and Guadeloupe derives from the services and government sectors of the economy, mainly from government transfers.

Although not as dependent on tourism as many of its English- and Dutch-speaking neighbors, the French Caribbean departments have begun to place new emphasis on tourism and related sectors of the economy. With liberalized air service to Europe and strong promotional campaigns producing a 30% increase in European visitors, the islands of Martinique and Guadeloupe are enjoying good tourist seasons. Martinique experienced a 40% rise in cruise ship visits in 1987-88, with 600 vessels bringing more than 450,000 visitors to the island, mainly from North America. Hotel tourism from the United States and Canada, however, is down 20%-25% due to the weak dollar and stiff competition from other sunny climates where English is more widely spoken.

The French Government extends to the overseas departments and territories essentially the same benefits and services enjoyed by its citizens in Franc-including similar minimum wages, family allowances, and unemployment compensation. Government employees serving in the French Caribbean departments earn salary premiums totaling 40% of wages and enjoy a 39-hour workweek and 5-week annual vacations. Consequently, Martinique and Guadeloupe rank just behind Puerto Rico, the Virgin Islands, and the Netherlands Antilles in regional per capita income and substantially above many developing nations in the region. Per capita income and house hold consumption still lag substantially behind that of metropolitan France, but the gap is decreasing.

Nonetheless, high unemployment and meager job opportunities for well educated Antilleans have led many to emigrate to metropolitan France in search of employment. This contributes to political, social, and economic problems as the region loses many of its brightest and most highly motivated young people. On the other hand, the better standard of living in the French Caribbean departments attracts legal and illegal emigration from less developed Caribbean neighbors.

France recognizes that improving economic conditions throughout the region creates new markets for French products and expertise as well as new jobs and opportunities in the French Caribbean departments. French investors have been encouraged to investigate investment opportunities in neighboring Caribbean countries with privileged access to the European market under the Lome accords and the American market via the Caribbean Basin Initiative. Although high labor costs in the French Caribbean departments have proved a disincentive to investment, some light manufacturing industries, often with a high-technology component, have located there.

# U.S. RELATIONS

As the overseas departments are integral parts of France, U.S. policy toward them is inseparable from its overall policy of friendly relations with France. In addition, as neighbors in the Western Hemisphere that share historical ties, the United States seeks to maintain good relations with the people of the three departments and to encourage strong and stable economies in these areas.

The United States maintains no resident representation in Guadeloupe or French Guiana. The departments and their dependencies are within the consular district of the U.S. Consulate General at Fort-de-France, Martinique.

## Principal U.S. Officials

For up-to-date information on Principal U.S. Officials, see the U.S. Embassies, Consulates, and Foreign Service section starting on page 139.

For up-to-date information on Principal U.S. Officials, see the U.S. Embassies, Consulates, and Foreign Service section starting on page 139.

# TRAVEL NOTES

The Consulate General in Martinique is at 14 Rue Blenac, B.P. 561, 97206 Fort-de-France CEDEX, Martinique, F.W.I. (tel. 63-13-03; telex 912670 or 912315).

# French Guiana

The capital, Cayenne, has a quiet charm, with occasional public parks and buildings recalling the colonial era. The second city of French Guiana, Kourou, is the home of the French National Space Agency's Guiana Space Center, from which the European Space Agency's Ariane rockets are launched. Not far from Kourou, one can also visit the offshore islands housing the Devil's Island prison. French Guiana's third city, St. Laurent de Maroni on the banks of the Maroni River bordering Suriname, was the administrative center of the French Guiana penal colony until 1947. It is here that one finds most of the decaying cell blocks and other prison facilities popularized by the film "Papillon." In town, one can still encounter a few 90-year-old former convicts tending their small shops alongside Bosch tribesmen selling fine wood carvings.

In Javouhey and Cacao at opposite ends of French Guiana, two Hmong villages contain some 1,200 Meo tribesmen, resettled in areas resembling their former villages in Laos. Open to tourists, the villages offer a wide array of colorful tapestries woven by the Hmong women and traditional Southeast Asian vegetables.

With a small population and a vast unexplored interior, French Guiana has a frontier air, disturbed only by the roar of a 21st-century rocket occasionally zooming overhead. The interior, accessible only by air or motorized dugout canoe, offers spectacular scenery and an array of bird and animal life that attracts a growing number of sportsmen and nature lovers hearty enough to withstand the primitive and sometimes dangerous travel conditions. At many of the inland stops along the Maroni and Oyapock Rivers, one can still encounter villages of Amerindians living in traditional lean-tos and hunting with spears and blow darts.

# Martinique

There is wide variety of scenery—rain forests covering the spiny central ridge of hills, palm-lined white beaches in the south, black volcanic sand beaches in the north, pineapple and banana groves that descend the steep eastern coast, fields of sugarcane in the central plain, and flowers everywhere, especially at the newly created Botanical Garden in Balata. Hiking trails are numerous and well marked for those who wish to enjoy the natural beauty of the island. The site of St. Pierre and its museum tracing the eruption of Mt. Pelee in 1902 is a must.

A sense of history is everywhere in Martinique, from the small museum and plantation ruins that mark the birthplace of France's Empress Josephine and the museum of sugarcane in TFois Islets, to Diamond Rock off the southwest coast, which was defended so bravely by British marines in the Napoleonic wars that it was commissioned in the Royal Navy as a ship of the line—H.M.S. Diamond. The boutiques of Fort-de-France, offering luxurious French goods, from perfumes to designer accessories, and the island's modern supermarkets, with fresh cheeses, meats, wines, and pastries produced locally or flown in from France, contribute to Martinique's reputation as one of the most sophisticated islands of the Caribbean. Modern roadways carry visitors to all parts of the island, and numerous taxis, buses, and collective cabs are available for the independent traveler. Tourist facilities include deluxe, modern resort hotels, converted but still elegant plantation hotels, small seaside pensions, and inns that rim the volcano. Martinique has excellent restaurants featuring French and Creole cooking with local vegetables and seafood.

# Guadeloupe

Guadeloupe has many natural features to delight the tourist: fine beaches and secluded, tranquil bays with clear, blue waters; tropical forests in the mountainous southern half, with the recently active volcano,

## Travel Notes

**Travel Advice:** For up-to-date information from the U.S. State Department on possible inconvenient or hazardous situations, see the **Travel Warnings and Consular Information Sheets from the U.S. Government** section starting on page 1723. For the latest information on health requirements and conditions, see the **International Travelers' Health Information** section starting on page 1385. For further information dealing with non-urgent matter, see the **Tips for Travelers to...** section starting on page 1588.

Soufriere (which can be climbed); warm-water springs; and the high cliffs of the northern extremities, dotted with ruined sugar mills. Good tourist facilities, from luxury hotels and casinos to quiet inns dot the island, and restaurants abound, serving excellent French and Creole food. Bustling marinas in St. Francois and Bas du Fort serve the growing pleasure-craft industry. The sunny weather and fine beaches of the northern dependencies of Guadeloupe-St. Martin (which shares the small island with Dutch St. Maarten) and the lesser-known, small, quiet island of St. Barthelemy-are highly popular with North American tourists. Closer to the main island of Guadeloupe are the charming, tiny islands of the lles-des-Saintes (favored by pleasure-craft sailors), where, in 1782, the British Admiral Rodney defeated and captured the French Admiral, Comte de Grasse, whose fleet had helped to ensure the American colonists' victory over the British at Yorktown the previous year. Almost undiscovered by the average tourist, the two small islands of Marie Galante and La Desirade offer tranquility, fine empty beaches,

lovely countryside, and friendly people. Hotel facilities on these islands are varied but adequate for tourists desiring a simple, different Caribbean vacation where little, if any, English is spoken.

**Health:** No inoculations are required for North American travelers to Martinique and Guadeloupe. A valid certificate of vaccination against yellow fever is required for entry into French Guiana. Visitors to French Guiana also should consult a physician to begin a malaria suppressant medication several weeks before their trip. Water is safe for drinking in Guadeloupe and Martinique and in major towns in French Guiana. Medical facilities are modern and clean, although few medical personnel speak English. American pharmaceuticals are not commonly available, but there is almost always a French equivalent. A ready supply of mosquito repellant is useful for travel in all three French departments. Swimming is safe at most beaches, although some areas on the Atlantic side may be very turbulent; as a rule, ask around before venturing in the water at a beach that appears deserted. If unusual quantities of prescription medicines are required, bring a physician's prescription or certification to avoid queries by customs or other officials, who strictly enforce the strong French narcotics abuse laws.

**Tourist documentation:** Although a valid French visa is required for travel to France, US citizens may obtain French visas at ports of entry in the French Caribbean departments. Travelers should possess a valid US passport or a birth certificate accompanied by valid photo identification. Cruise ship visitors are exempt from the visa require-

ment and generally are not asked to produce identification; however, it is wise for cruise ship visitors to be in possession of valid identification, should any problems arise. French immigration laws are strictly enforced, and there are restrictions on the amount of French currency that can be exported. Before traveling, check with the nearest French consular office to determine current requirements.

**Other information:** The three French departments do not observe daylight saving time. Guadeloupe and Martinique correspond to eastern daylight time during the spring and summer; in the fall and winter, they are 1 hour later. French Guiana is 1 hour later than eastern daylight time in spring and summer and 2 hours later in fall and winter.

All three French Caribbean departments have modern roads and communications facilities. Local transportation, including taxis and rental vehicles, is good, and most well-known credit cards are accepted in hotels, restaurants, and shops.

**Local holidays:** Businesses may be closed on the following holidays in Martinique, Guadeloupe, French Guiana, and their dependencies: New Year's Day (January 1), Ash Wednesday (and two preceding days, Lundi Gras and Mardi Gras—see note)*, Good Friday*, Easter Monday*, Ascension Day (May 12), Emancipation Day (Martinique-May 22), Pentecost*, Bastille Day (July 14), Assumption Day (August 15), All Saints' Day (November 1), All Souls' Day (November 2), Armistice (1914)-November 11, Christmas Day (December 25). *Date varies.

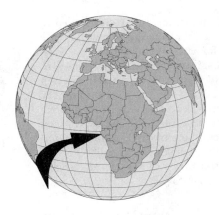

# GABON

August 2000

## Official Name:
## Gabonese Republic

# PROFILE

## Geography

**Area:** 267,667 sq. km. (103,347 sq. mi.); about the size of Colorado
**Cities:** Capital—Libreville (pop. 300,000). Other cities—Port-Gentil, Franceville.
**Terrain:** Narrow coastal plain; hilly, heavily forested interior (about 80% forested); some savanna regions in east and south.
**Climate:** Hot and humid all year with two rainy and two dry seasons.

## People

**Nationality:** Noun and adjective—Gabonese (sing. and pl.).
**Population:** (UN/World Bank 1997 est.) 1.1 million (figs. disputed).
**Annual growth rate:** (1995 UN est.) 2.4%.
**Ethnic Groups:** Fang (largest), Myene, Bapounou, Eschira, Bandjabi, Bateke/ Obamba.
**Religion:** Christian, Muslim, indigenous.
**Languages:** French (official), Fang, Myene, Bateke, Bapounou/Eschira, Bandjabi.
**Education:** Years compulsory—to age 16. Attendance—60%. Literacy—63%.
**Health:** Infant mortality rate—87/1,000. Life expectancy—54 yrs.

**Work force:** (500,000) Agriculture—52%; industry and commerce—16%; services and government—33%.

## Government

**Type:** Republic.
**Independence:** August 17, 1960.
**Constitution:** February 21, 1961 (revised April 15, 1975; rewritten March 26, 1991).
**Branches:** Executive—president (head of state). Legislative—bicameral legislature (National Assembly and Senate). Government—prime minister and appointed Council of Ministers (current government of 32 appointed December 1999). Judicial—Supreme Court.
**Administrative subdivisions:** 9 provinces, 37 prefectures, and 9 subprefectures.
**Political parties:** (including number of seats in 120-member Assembly elected in 1996-97: Parti Democratique Gabonais (PDG-88), Parti Gabonais Du Progres (PGP-9), Rassemblement National Des Bucherons (RNB-5), Independents and other parties-18.
**Suffrage:** Universal, direct.
**Central government budget:** (1999 rev.) Receipts—$0.9 billion (based on low oil prices); expenses—$2.5 billion (including projected debt arrears); defense (1999)—3.0% of government budget.
**Flag:** From top, blue, yellow, and green horizontal bands.

## Economy

**GDP:** (1998 est.) $4.7 billion.
**Annual real growth rate:** (1998 official est.) 1.7%.
**Per capita income:** (1998 est.) $4,200.
**Avg. inflation rate:** (1998) 2%.
**Natural resources:** Petroleum (40% of GDP), manganese, uranium, timber.
**Agriculture and forestry:** (8% of GDP) Products—cocoa, coffee, rubber, sugar, and pineapples. Cultivated land—1%.
**Industry:** (10% of GDP) Types—petroleum related, wood processing, food and beverage processing.
**Trade:** (1998 est.) Exports—$3.4 billion: petroleum, wood, manganese. Major markets—U.S., France. Imports—$1.5 billion: construction equipment, machinery, food, automobiles, manufactured goods. Major suppliers—France, Germany, Japan, U.S.

# PEOPLE

Almost all Gabonese are of Bantu origin. Gabon has at least 40 ethnic groups, with separate languages and cultures. The largest is the Fang. Other ethnic groups include the Myene, Bandjabi, Eshira, Bapounou, Bateke/Obamba, and Okande.

Ethnic group boundaries are less sharply drawn in Gabon than elsewhere in Africa. French, the official language, is a unifying force. More than 10,000 French people live in Gabon, and France predominates foreign cultural and commercial influences. Historical and environmental factors caused Gabon's population to decline between 1900 and 1940. It is one of the least-densely inhabited countries in Africa, and a labor shortage is a major obstacle to development and a draw for foreign workers. The population is generally accepted to be just over 1 million but remains in dispute.

# HISTORY

During the last seven centuries, Bantu ethnic groups arrived in the area from several directions to escape enemies or find new land. Little is known of tribal life before European contact, but tribal art suggests rich cultural heritages.

Gabon's first European visitors were Portuguese traders who arrived in the 15th century and named the country after the Portuguese word "gabao," a coat with sleeve and hood resembling the shape of the Komo River estuary. The coast became a center of the slave trade. Dutch, British, and French traders came in the 16th century. France assumed the status of protector by signing treaties with Gabonese coastal chiefs in 1839 and 1841. American missionaries from New England established a mission at Baraka (now Libreville) in 1842. In 1849, the French captured a slave ship and released the passengers at the mouth of the Komo River. The slaves named their settlement Libreville-"free town." French explorers penetrated Gabon's dense jungles between 1862 and 1887. The most famous, Savorgnan de Brazza, used Gabonese bearers and guides in his search for the headwaters of the Congo River. France occupied Gabon in 1885 but did not administer it until 1903. In 1910, Gabon became one of the four territories of French Equatorial Africa, a federation that survived until 1959. The territories became

independent in 1960 as the Central African Republic, Chad, Congo (Brazzaville), and Gabon.

# GOVERNMENT

Under the 1961 constitution (revised in 1975 and rewritten in 1991), Gabon became a republic with a presidential form of government. The National Assembly has 120 deputies elected for a 5-year term. The president is elected by universal suffrage, for a 7-year term. The president appoints the prime minister, the cabinet, and judges of the independent Supreme Court. The government in 1990 made major changes in the political system. A transitional constitution was drafted in May as an outgrowth of a national political conference in March-April and later revised by a constitutional committee. Among its provisions were a Western-style bill of rights; creation of a National Council of Democracy, which oversees the guarantee of those rights; a governmental advisory board on economic and social issues; and an independent judiciary. After approval by the National Assembly, the PDG Central Committee, and the president, the Assembly unanimously adopted the constitution in March 1991. Multi-party legislative elections were held in 1990-91, despite the fact that opposition parties had not been declared formally legal.

After a peaceful transition, the elections produced the first representative, multi-party, National Assembly. In January 1991, the Assembly passed by unanimous vote a law governing the legalization of opposition parties. The president was re-elected in a disputed election in 1993 with 51% of votes cast.

Social and political disturbances led to the 1994 Paris Conference and Accords, which provided a framework for the next elections. Local and legislative elections were delayed until 1996-97. In 1997 constitutional amendments were adopted to create an appointed Senate, the position of vice president, and to extend the

president's term to 7 years. Facing a divided opposition, President Bongo was re-elected in December 1998, with 66% of the votes cast. Although the main opposition parties claimed the elections had been manipulated, there was none of the civil disturbance that followed the 1993 election. The president retains strong powers, such as authority to dissolve the National Assembly, declare a state of siege, delay legislation, conduct referenda, and appoint and dismiss the prime minister and cabinet members. For administrative purposes, Gabon is divided into 9 provinces, which are further divided into 36 prefectures and 8 separate subprefectures. The president appoints the provincial governors, the prefects, and the subprefects.

## Principal Government Officials

For up-to-date information on Principal Government Officials, see the Chiefs of State and Cabinet Members of Foreign Governments section starting on page 1.

Gabon maintains an embassy in the United States at 2034 - 20th Street NW, Washington, DC 20009 (tel. 202-797-1000).

# POLITICAL CONDITIONS

At the time of Gabon's independence in 1960, two principal political parties existed: the Bloc Democratique Gabonais (BDG), led by Leon M'Ba, and the Union Democratique et Sociale Gabonaise (UDSG), led by J.H. Aubame. In the first post-independence election, held under a parliamentary system, neither party was able to win a majority. The BDG obtained support from three of the four independent legislative deputies, and M'Ba was named prime minister. Soon after concluding that Gabon had an insufficient number of people for a two-party system, the two party leaders agreed on a single list of candidates. In the February 1961 election, held under the new presidential system, M'Ba became president and Aubame foreign minister.

This one-party system appeared to work until February 1963, when the larger BDG element forced the UDSG members to choose between a merger of the parties or resignation. The UDSG cabinet ministers resigned, and M'Ba called an election for February 1964 and a reduced number of National Assembly deputies (from 67 to 47). The UDSG failed to muster a list of candidates able to meet the requirements of the electoral decrees. When the BDG appeared likely to win the election by default, the Gabonese military toppled M'Ba in a bloodless coup on February 18, 1964. French troops re-established his government the next day.

Elections were held in April with many opposition participants. BDG-supported candidates won 31 seats and the opposition 16. Late in 1966, the constitution was revised to provide for automatic succession of the vice president should the president die in office. In March 1967, Leon M'Ba and Omar Bongo (then Albert Bongo) were elected president and vice president. M'Ba died later that year, and Omar Bongo became president.

In March 1968, Bongo declared Gabon a one-party state by dissolving the BDG and establishing a new party—the Parti Democratique Gabonais. He invited all Gabonese, regardless of previous political affiliation, to participate. Bongo was elected president in February 1975 and re-elected in December 1979 and November 1986 to 7-year terms. In April 1975, the office of vice president was abolished and replaced by the office of prime minister, who has no right to automatic succession. Under the 1991 constitution, in the event of the president's death, the prime minister, the National Assembly president, and the defense minister share power until a new election is held. Using the PDG as a tool to submerge the regional and tribal rivalries that have

divided Gabonese politics in the past, Bongo sought to forge a single national movement in support of the government's development policies.

Opposition to the PDG continued, however, and in September 1990, two coup attempts were uncovered and aborted. Economic discontent and a desire for political liberalization provoked violent demonstrations and strikes by students and workers in early 1990. In response to grievances by workers, Bongo negotiated with

them on a sector-by-sector basis, making significant wage concessions. In addition, he promised to open up the PDG and to organize a national political conference in March-April 1990 to discuss Gabon's future political system. The PDG and 74 political organizations attended the conference. Participants essentially divided into two loose coalitions, the ruling PDG and its allies and the United Front of Opposition Associations and Parties, consisting of the breakaway

Morena Fundamental and the Gabonese Progress Party.

The April conference approved sweeping political reforms, including creation of a national senate, decentralization of the budgetary process, freedom of assembly and press, and cancellation of the exit visa requirement. In an attempt to guide the political system's transformation to multi-party democracy, Bongo resigned as PDG chairman and created a transitional government headed by a new Prime Minister, Casimir Oye-Mba. The Gabonese Social Democratic Grouping (RSDG), as the resulting government was called, was smaller than the previous government and included representatives from several opposition parties in its cabinet. The RSDG drafted a provisional constitution that provided a basic bill of rights and an independent judiciary but retained strong executive powers for the president. After further review by a constitutional committee and the National Assembly, this document came into force in March 1991.

Despite further anti-government demonstrations after the untimely death of an opposition leader, the first multi-party National Assembly elections in almost 30 years took place in September-October 1990, with the PDG garnering a large majority. Following President Bongo's re-election in December 1993 with 51% of the vote, opposition candidates refused to validate the election results. Serious civil disturbances led to an agreement between the government and opposition factions to work toward a political settlement. These talks led to the Paris Accords in November 1994 in which several opposition figures were included in a government of national unity. This arrangement soon broke down, and the 1996 and 1997 legislative and municipal elections provided the background for renewed partisan politics. The PDG won a landslide victory in the legislative election, but several major cities, including Libreville, elected opposition mayors during the 1997 local election. President Bongo coasted to an easy re-election in December 1998 with 66% of the vote against a divided

**Travel Advice:** For up-to-date information from the U.S. State Department on possible inconvenient or hazardous situations, see the **Travel Warnings and Consular Information Sheets from the U.S. Government** section starting on page 1723. For the latest information on health requirements and conditions, see the **International Travelers' Health Information** section starting on page 1385. For further information dealing with non-urgent matter, see the **Tips for Travelers to...** section starting on page 1588.

opposition. While Bongo's major opponents rejected the outcome as fraudulent, international observers characterized the result as representative even if the election suffered from serious administrative problems. There was no serious civil disorder or protests following the election in contrast to the 1993 election.

# ECONOMY

Gabon's economy is dominated by oil. Oil revenues have comprised 60% of the Government of Gabon budget, 40% of GDP, and 80% of exports. Oil production is now declining from its apogee of 370,000 barrels per day in 1997. The 1998 fall-off in oil prices had a negative impact on government revenues and the economy. Little thought or plans have been made for an after-oil scenario. Gabon public expenditures from the years of significant oil revenues have not been spent efficiently. Overspending on the Transgabonais railroad, the oil price shock of 1986, and the franc CFA devaluation of 1994 have caused debt problems. Gabon has earned a poor reputation with the Paris Club and the IMF for poor management of its debt and revenues. IMF missions (related to the now lapsed EFF program) have criticized the government for over-spending on off-budget items (in good years and bad), over-borrowing from the Central Bank, and slipping on the schedule for privatization and administrative reform.

Gabon's oil revenues have given it a strong per capita GDP of more than $4,000, extremely high for the region. On the other hand, a skewed income distribution and poor social indicators are evident. The economy is highly dependent on extraction of abundant primary materials. After oil, timber and manganese mining are the other major sectors. Foreign and Gabonese observers have consistently lamented the lack of transformation of primary materials in the Gabonese economy. Various factors have so far stymied more diversification (small market of 1 million people, dependence on French imports, inability to capitalize on regional markets, lack of entrepreneurial zeal among the Gabonese, and the fairly regular stream of oil "rent"). The small processing and service sectors are largely dominated by just a few prominent local investors. At World Bank and IMF insistence, the government has embarked on a program of privatization of its state-owned companies and administrative reform, including reducing public sector employment and salary growth. The government has been slipping on its targets.

# DEFENSE

Gabon has a small, professional military of about 5,000 personnel, divided into army, navy, air force, gendarmerie, and national police. Gabonese forces are oriented to the defense of the country and have not been trained for an offensive role. A well-trained, well-equipped 1,800-member guard provides security for the president.

# FOREIGN RELATIONS

Gabon has followed a nonaligned policy, advocating dialogue in international affairs and recognizing both parts of divided countries. Since 1973, the number of countries establishing diplomatic relations with Gabon has doubled. In inter-African affairs, Gabon espouses development by evolution rather than revolution and favors regulated free enterprise as the system most likely to promote rapid economic growth. Concerned about stability in Central Africa and the potential for intervention, Gabon has been directly involved with mediation efforts in Chad, Central African Republic, Congo/Brazzaville, Angola, and former Zaire. In December 1999, through the mediation efforts of President Bongo, a peace accord was signed in Congo/Brazzaville between the government and most leaders of an armed rebellion. President Bongo has remained involved in the continuing Congolese peace process. Gabon has been a strong proponent of regional stability, and Gabonese armed forces played an important role in the UN Peacekeeping Mission to the Central African Republic (MINURCA).

Gabon is a member of the UN and some of its specialized and related agencies, including the World Bank; Organization of African Unity (OAU); Central African Customs Union (UDEAC/CEMAC); EC association under Lome Convention; Communaute Financiere Africaine (CFA); Organization of the Islamic Conference (OIC); Nonaligned Movement; withdrew from the Organization of Petroleum Exporting Countries (OPEC).

# U.S.-GABONESE RELATIONS

Relations between the United States and Gabon are excellent. In 1987, President Bongo made an official visit to Washington, DC. The United States imports a considerable percentage of Gabonese crude oil and manganese and exports heavy construction equipment, aircraft, and machinery to Gabon. The major U.S. assistance program in Gabon is a Peace Corps contingent of about 80 volunteers who teach math and science, promote health programs and agro-fish-forestry projects, and build rural schools. Through a modest International Military Education and Training program, the United States provides military training to members of the Gabonese armed forces each year. U.S. private capital has been attracted to Gabon since before its independence.

## Principal U.S. Officials

**For up-to-date information on Principal U.S. Officials, see the U.S. Embassies, Consulates, and Foreign Service section starting on page 139.**

The U.S. Embassy is located on the Blvd. de la Mer, B.P. 4000, Libreville, Gabon (tel: 241-762-003/004; fax: 241- 745-507).

# THE GAMBIA

July 1996

Official Name:
**Republic of The Gambia**

## PROFILE

### Geography
**Area:** 11,300 sq. km. (4,361 sq. mi.) slightly more than twice the size of Delaware.
**Cities:** Capital—Banjul (pop. 42,326).
**Terrain:** Flood plain of the Gambia River flanked by low hills.
**Climate:** Tropical; hot rainy season (June to November); cooler, dry season (November to May).

### People
**Nationality:** Noun and adjective—Gambian(s).
**Population (1993 est.):** 1.014 million.
**Annual growth rate (1993 est.):** 4.1 percent.
**Ethnic groups:** Mandinka 42 percent, Fula 18 percent, Wolof 16 percent, Jola 10 percent, Serahuli 9 percent, other 4 percent, non-Gambian 1 percent.
**Religions:** Muslim 90 percent, Christian 9 percent, and animist 1 percent.
**Languages:** English (official), Mandinka, Wolof, Fula, other indigenous languages.
**Education:** Years compulsory—none. Attendance—68.7 percent primary, 20 percent secondary. Literacy—25 percent.

**Health:** Infant mortality rate—85/1,000. Life expectancy—men 47 yrs., women 51 yrs.
**Work force:** 400,000. Agriculture—75 percent, Industry, commerce, and services—19 percent, Government—7 percent.

### Government
**Type:** Military.
**Independence:** February 18, 1965.
**Constitution:** April 24, 1970 (suspended after July 1994).
**Branches:** Parliament suspended since July 1994, court system functioning but country ruled primarily through government decree.
**Subdivisions:** capital and 5 divisions.
**Political parties:** currently banned.
**Flag:** three horizontal bands of red, blue, and green, with blue center bordered by two white stripes.

### Economy
**GDP (1994):** $310 million.
**Annual growth rate:** 2 percent.
**Per capita income:** $309.
**Natural resources:** Seismic studies show that oil may be present.
**Agriculture (23 percent of GDP):** Products—peanuts, rice, millet, sorghum, fish, palm kernels, vegetables, livestock, forestry.
**Industry (11 percent of GDP):** Types—peanut products, construction, brewing, soft drinks, agricul-

tural machinery assembly, small woodworking and metal working, clothing.
**Trade (1994 est.):** Exports—$120 million, including re-export of various goods (83 percent), peanuts (8 percent), palm kernels, fish, and other domestic products. Major markets—UK, other EU countries, and Senegal. Imports—$174 million, including textiles, foodstuffs, machinery, transportation equipment, 62 percent for domestic consumption, 38 percent for re-export. Major suppliers—UK, other EU countries, China, Japan, and other Asian countries, West African neighbors.
**Official exchange rate (1996 est.):** 9.85 Dalasis=US$1.

**US economic aid received (FY1995):** $1 million in the form of assistance to democracy and human rights programs and food and health aid.

## PEOPLE AND HISTORY

A wide variety of ethnic groups live side by side in The Gambia with a minimum of inter-tribal friction, each preserving its own language and traditions. The Mandinka tribe is the largest, followed by the Fula, Wolof, Jola, and Serahuli. Approximately 2,500 non-Africans live in The Gambia, including Europeans and many families of Lebanese origin.

Muslims constitute over 95 percent of the population. Christians of different denominations account for most of the remainder. Gambians officially observe the holidays of both religions and practice religious tolerance.

More than 80 percent of Gambians live in rural villages, although more and more young people come to the capital in search of work and education. While urban migration, development projects, and modernization are bringing more and more Gambians into contact with Western habits and values, the traditional emphasis on the extended family, as well as indigenous forms of dress and celebration, remain integral parts of everyday life.

The Gambia was once part of the Empire of Ghana and the Kingdom of the Songhais. The first written accounts of the region come from records of Arab traders in the 9th and 10th centuries A.D. Arab traders established the trans-Saharan trade route for slaves, gold, and ivory. In the 15th century, the Portuguese took over this trade using maritime routes. At that time, The Gambia was part of the Kingdom of Mali.

In 1588, the claimant to the Portuguese throne, Antonio, Prior of Crato, sold exclusive trade rights on The Gambia River to English merchants; this grant was confirmed by letters patent from Queen Elizabeth I. In 1618, James I granted a charter to a British company for trade with The Gambia and the Gold Coast (now Ghana).

During the late 17th century and throughout the 18th, England and France struggled continuously for political and commercial supremacy in the regions of the Senegal and Gambia rivers. The 1783 Treaty of Versailles gave Great Britain possession of The Gambia, but the French retained an enclave at Albreda on the north bank of the river (ceded to the United Kingdom in 1857).

As many as 3 million slaves may have been taken from the region during the 3 centuries that the trade operated. It is not known how many were taken by Arab traders. Most of those taken were sold to Europeans by other Africans; some were prisoners of inter-tribal wars, some were sold because of unpaid debts, while others were kidnapped. Slaves were initially sent to Europe to work as servants until the market for labor expanded in the West Indies and North America in the 18th century. In 1807, slave trading was abolished throughout the British empire, and the British tried unsuccessfully to end the slave traffic in The Gambia. They established the military post of Bathurst (now Banjul) in 1816. In the ensuing years, Banjul was at times under the jurisdiction of the governor general in Sierra Leone. In 1888, The Gambia became a separate entity again.

An 1889 agreement with France established the present boundaries, and The Gambia became a British Crown Colony, divided for administrative purposes into the colony (city of Banjul and the surrounding area) and the protectorate (remainder of the territory). The Gambia received its own executive and legislative councils in 1901 and gradually progressed toward self-government. A 1906 ordinance abolished slavery.

During World War II, Gambian troops fought with the Allies in Burma, and Banjul served as an air stop for the US Army Air Corps and a port of call for allied naval convoys. US President Franklin D. Roosevelt stopped overnight in Banjul en route to and from the Casablanca Conference in 1943, marking the first visit to the African continent by an American president in office.

After World War II, the pace of constitutional advance quickened, and following general elections in 1962, full internal self-government was granted in 1963.

The Gambia achieved independence on February 18, 1965, as a constitutional monarchy within the British Commonwealth. Shortly thereafter, the government proposed conversion

from a monarchy to a republic with an elected president replacing the British monarch as chief of state. The proposal failed to receive the two-thirds majority required to amend the constitution, but the results won widespread attention abroad as testimony to The Gambia's observance of secret balloting, honest elections, and civil rights and liberties. On April 24, 1970, The Gambia became a republic following a majority-approved referendum.

Until a military coup in July 1994, The Gambia was led by President Dawda Kairaba Jawara, who was re-elected five times. The relative stability of the Jawara era was broken first in a violent coup attempt in 1981. The coup was led by Kukoi Samba Sanyang, who, on two occasions, had unsuccessfully sought election to parliament. After a week of violence which left several hundred dead, Jawara, in London when the attack began, appealed to Senegal for help. Senegalese troops defeated the rebel force.

In the aftermath of the attempted coup, Senegal and The Gambia signed the 1982 Treaty of Confederation. The result, the Senegambia Confederation, aimed eventually to combine the armed forces of the two nations and unify economies and currencies. The Gambia withdrew from the confederation in 1989.

In July 1994, the Armed Forces Provisional Ruling Council (AFPRC) seized power in a military coup d'etat. The AFPRC deposed the democratically elected government of Sir Dawda Jawara. Captain Yahya A.J.J. Jammeh, chairman of the AFPRC, became head of state.

The AFPRC has announced a transition schedule for return to democratic, civilian government before the end of 1996. It has denied its intention to stay in power and, although delayed, has proceeded with the transition timetable. Presidential elections are scheduled for September 11, 1996.

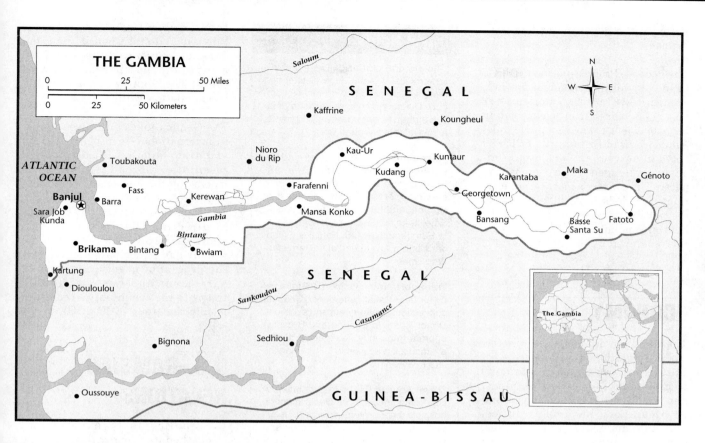

THE GAMBIA

0    25    50 Miles

0    25    50 Kilometers

# GOVERNMENT

The 1970 constitution, which divided the government into independent executive, legislative, and judicial branches, was suspended after the 1994 military coup. As part of its announced transition process, the AFPRC established the Constitution Review Commission (CRC) through decree in March 1995. In accordance with the timetable for the transition to a democratically elected government, the commission has drafted a new constitution for The Gambia to be approved or disapproved in a referendum to be held August 7, 1996. The draft provides for a strong presidential government, a unicameral legislature, an independent judiciary, and protection of human rights.

Local government in The Gambia varies. Banjul has an elected town council. Five rural divisions exist, each with a council containing a majority of elected members. Each council has its own treasury and is responsible for local government services. The tribal chiefs retain traditional powers authorized by customary law.

## Principal Government Officials

**For up-to-date information on Principal Government Officials, see the Chiefs of State and Cabinet Members of Foreign Governments section starting on page 1.**

The Gambia maintains an embassy at 1155 15th Street, NW, Suite 1000, Washington, DC 20005. Tel. 202-785-1399. Its UN Mission is located at 820 2nd Avenue, Suite 900-C , New York, NY 10017. Tel. 212-949-6640.

# DEFENSE

The Gambian national army numbers approximately 900. The Gambian army had received technical assistance and training from the United States and United Kingdom prior to the coup. With the withdrawal of this aid, the army has sought assistance from other African countries.

Members of the force have participated in the monitoring group of the peace-keeping force (ECOMOG) deployed during the Liberian civil war beginning in 1990. Responsibilities for internal security and law enforcement rest with the Gambian police/gendarme force under the Inspector General of Police and the Ministry of Interior.

# POLITICAL CONDITIONS

Prior to the coup d'etat in July 1994, The Gambia had been one of the oldest existing multi-party democracies in Africa. It had conducted freely-contested elections every 5 years. Since the military coup, freedom of speech has been severely restricted and the right to form political parties in opposition to the government has been banned.

The People's Progressive Party (PPP), headed by former president Jawara, dominated Gambian politics for nearly 30 years. After spearheading the movement toward complete independence from Britain, the PPP was voted into power and was never seriously challenged by any opposition party. The country's most recent elections were held in April 1992. Presidential elections are scheduled to be held on September 11, 1996 and legislative elections on December 11, 1996.

# ECONOMY

The Gambian economy is characterized by traditional subsistence agriculture, historic reliance on peanuts or groundnuts for export earnings, and a re-export trade built up around its ocean port, low import duties, minimal administrative procedures, and a fluctuating exchange rate with no exchange controls. Three sectors of the economy—horticulture, fisheries, and tourism—have experienced significant growth during recent years, and are expected to be the focus of export-oriented investment.

Agriculture accounts for 23 percent of gross domestic product (GDP) and employs 75 percent of the labor force. Within agriculture, peanut production accounts for 5.3 percent of GDP, other crops 8.3 percent, livestock 4.4 percent, fishing 1.8 percent and forestry 0.5 percent. Industry accounts for 12 percent of GDP and forestry .5 percent. Manufacturing accounts for 6 percent of the industry share of GDP. The limited amount of manufacturing is primarily agriculturally-based (e.g., peanut processing, bakeries, a brewery, and a tannery). Other manufacturing activities include soap, soft drinks, and clothing. Services account for the remaining 19 percent of GDP.

In FY 1995, the U.K. was The Gambia's major export market, accounting for 26 percent total, followed by Senegal with 22 percent and France

## Travel Notes

**Climate and clothing:** The Gambia's sub-tropical climate has a distinct hot, rainy season (mid-May to mid-November). During the cold, dry season (mid-November to mid-May), light jackets and sweaters are often worn.

**Telecommunications:** Telex and fax services are available to the US, Europe, and Dakar. Radiotelephone service operates to the UK, most of Europe, and the west coast of Africa. Satellite-telephone service is available to Europe and the US. Banjul is 5 standard time zones ahead of eastern standard time.

**Transportation:** Banjul is 25 minutes by air from Dakar, where worldwide air connections are frequent and excellent. Direct flights to London and Brussels operate frequently. Taxis are available at stands; it is advisable to agree on the fare in advance.

**Travel Advice:** For up-to-date information from the U.S. State Department on possible inconvenient or hazardous situations, see the **Travel Warnings and Consular Information Sheets from the U.S. Government** section starting on page 1723. For the latest information on health requirements and conditions, see the **International Travelers' Health Information** section starting on page 1385. For further information dealing with non-urgent matter, see the **Tips for Travelers to...** section starting on page 1588.

with 21 percent. The U.K. was the major source of imports, accounting for 14 percent followed by Belgium, the Netherlands and Cote D'Ivoire. The Gambia reports 3 percent of its exports going to and 5 percent of its imports coming from the United States.

# FOREIGN RELATIONS

The Gambia followed a formal policy of non-alignment throughout most of former president Jawara's reign. It maintains particularly close relations with the United Kingdom, Senegal, and other African countries.

In November 1995, Armed Forces Provisional Ruling Council Chairman Jammeh announced the establishment of diplomatic relations with Libya. The country has also established relations with Taiwan.

The Gambia takes an active interest in international—especially African and Arab—affairs, although its representation abroad is limited. As member of the Economic Community of West African States (ECOWAS), The Gambia has played an active role in directing that organization's efforts to resolve the Liberian civil war. It has participated actively in the process of negotiating a peace agreement and has contributed troops to the community's cease-fire monitoring group (ECOMOG).

# U.S.-GAMBIAN RELATIONS

U.S. policy is to expand and strengthen its friendly ties with The Gambia through promotion of the return to democratic rule and respect for human rights. The U.S. development effort in The Gambia continues in the form of such programs as food aid (through Catholic Relief Services) assistance in the transition to democracy and the work of the peace corps. The Peace Corps program involves about 75 volunteers mainly engaged in forestry, agriculture, and secondary school teaching.

## Principal U.S. Officials

**For up-to-date information on Principal U.S. Officials, see the U.S. Embassies, Consulates, and Foreign Service section starting on page 139.**

The US Embassy in The Gambia is in Fajara on Pipeline Road (Kairaba Avenue). (Tel. [220] 392856; Fax [220] 392475). The Peace Corps office (Tel. [220] 392466) is on Pipeline Road (Kairaba Avenue), one city block from the Embassy.

# GEORGIA

November 1998

Official Name:
**Georgia**

# PROFILE

## Geography

**Area:** 70,000 sq km; slightly larger than South Carolina.
**Cities:** Capital—Tbilisi (pop 1.3 million 1994).
**Terrain:** Mostly rugged and mountainous.
**Climate:** Generally moderate; mild on the Black Sea coast with cold winters in the mountains.

## People

**Nationality:** Noun and adjective—Georgian(s).
**Population (1997 est.):** 5.16 million.
**Population growth rate:** -1.09%
**Ethnic groups:** Georgian 70.1%, Armenian 8.1%, Russian 6.3%, Azerbaijan 5.7%, Ossetian 3%, Abkhaz 1.8%, other 5%.
**Religion:** Georgian Orthodox 65%, Muslim 11%, Russian Orthodox 10%, Armenian Apostolic 8%.
**Language:** Georgian (official), Abkhaz also official language in Abkhazia.
**Education:** Years compulsory—11 . Literacy—99%.
**Health:** Infant mortality rate—22.5 deaths/1,000 live births. Life expectancy—68 years.

## Government

**Type:** Republic.
**Constitution:** October 17, 1995.
**Branches:** Executive—president with State Chancellery. Legislative—unicameral parliament, 235 members. Judicial—supreme court, prosecutor general, and local courts.
**Subdivisions:** 63 districts, including those within the two autonomous republics (Abkhazia and Ajaria ) and seven cities.
**Political parties:** Citizens Union of Georgia, National Democratic Party, People's National Democratic Party, United Republican Party, Georgian Popular Front, Georgian Social Democratic Party, All Georgia Revival Union, Greens Party, Agrarian Party, United Communist Party of Georgia Socialist Party, and others.
**Suffrage:** Universal over 18.

## Economy (1997)

**GDP:** $4.9 billion.
**Per capita income:** $980.
**GDP growth:** 11.3%.
**Inflation rate:** 7%.
**Natural resources:** Citrus fruits, tea, wine, nonferrous metals, textiles, chemicals and fuel re-exports.
**Industry:** Steel, aircraft, machine tools, foundry equipment (automobiles, trucks, and tractors), tower cranes, electric welding equipment, machinery for food packing, electric motors, textiles, shoes, chemicals, wood products, bottled water, and wine.
**Trade (1996):** Exports—$199.4 million; Partners—Russia, Turkey, Azerbaijan, Armenia. Imports—$656.6 million; Partners—Russia, Turkey, Azerbaijan, U.S.
**Work force ( 2.4 million):** Agriculture—23.8%, trade—23.2%, transport and communications—10.5%, industry—10.2%, construction—5%, unemployment (1996 est.)—21%.

# PEOPLE AND HISTORY

Georgian history dates back more than 2,500 years, and Georgian is one of the oldest living languages in the world. Tbilisi, located in a picturesque valley divided by the Mtkvari River, is more than 1,500 years old. Much of Georgia's territory was besieged by its Persian and Turkish neighbors along with Arabs and Mongols over the course of the 7th to the 18th centuries. After 11 centuries of mixed fortunes of various Georgian kingdoms, including a golden age from the 11th to 12th centuries, Georgia turned to Russia for protection. Russia essentially annexed Georgia and exiled the royalty in 1801. Pockets of Georgian resistance to foreign rule continued, and the first Republic of Georgia was established on May

26, 1918 after the collapse of Tsarist Russia. By March 1921, the Red army had reoccupied the country and Georgia became part of the Soviet Union. On April 9, 1991, the Supreme Council of the Republic of Georgia declared independence from the U.S.S.R.

Beset by ethnic and civil strife from independence in 1991, Georgia began to stabilize in 1995. However, more than 230,000 internally displaced persons present an enormous strain on local politics. Peace in the separatist areas of Abkhazia and south Ossetia, overseen by Russian peacekeepers and international organizations, will continue to be fragile, requiring years of economic development and negotiation to overcome local enmities. Considerable progress has been made in negotiations on the Ossetian-Georgian conflict, and negotiations are continuing in the Georgia-Abkhazia conflict.

The Georgian Government is committed to economic reform in cooperation with the IMF and World Bank, and stakes much of its future on the revival of the ancient Silk Road as the Eurasian corridor, using Georgia's geography as a bridge for transit of goods between Europe and Asia.

Georgians are renowned for their hospitality and artistry in dance, theater, music, and design.

# GOVERNMENT

Georgia has been a democratic republic since the presidential elections and constitutional referendum of October 1995. The President is elected for a term of 5 years; his constitutional successor is the Chairman of the Parliament.

The Georgian state is highly centralized, except for the autonomous regions of Abkhazia and Ajaria, which are to be given special autonomous status once Georgia's territorial integrity is restored. Those regions were subjects of special autonomies during Soviet rule and the legacy of that influence remains. In most locations local elections took place on November 15, 1998, marking the first elections under the 1995 constitution. Candidates from 11 political parties and two political blocks presented candidates.

## Principal Government Offcials

For up-to-date information on Principal Government Officials, see the Chiefs of State and Cabinet Members of Foreign Governments section starting on page 1.

Georgia maintains an embassy in the United States at Suite 424, 1511 K Street, N.W., Washington, D.C. 20005, telephone (202) 393-5959, fax (202) 393-4532.

# POLITICAL CONDITIONS

Since surviving assassination attempts in August 1995 and February 1998 by reactionary forces opposed to reform, President Shevardnadze has consolidated his leadership and moved ahead with an ambitious and courageous reform agenda. Elections on November 5, 1995, described as the freest and fairest in the Caucasus or Central Asia, gave him the presidency and resulted in a progressive parliament led by sophisticated reformers.

The Abkhaz separatist dispute absorbs much of the government's attention. While a cease-fire is in effect, more than 230,000 internally displaced persons (IDPs) who were driven from their homes during the conflict constitute a vocal lobby. The government has offered the region considerable autonomy in order to encourage a settlement that would allow the IDPs, the majority of whom are ethnic Georgians from the Gali region, to return home, but the Abkhaz insist on virtual independence.

Currently, Russian peacekeepers, under the authority of the Commonwealth of Independent States, are stationed in Abkhazia, along with UN observers, but both groups have recently had to restrict their activities due to increased mining and guerrilla activity. Negotiations have not resulted in movement toward a settlement. Working with France, U.K., Germany, and Russia and through the UN and the OSCE, the U.S. continues to encourage a comprehensive settlement consistent with Georgian independence, sovereignty, and territorial integrity. The UN observer force and other organizations are quietly encouraging grassroots cooperative and confidence-building measures in the region.

The parliament has instituted wide-ranging political reforms supportive of higher human rights standards, but problems persist, largely as a result of the unwillingness of certain law enforcement and criminal justice officials to support constitutionally mandated changes. Mistreatment of detainees is a significant and continuing problem, as is corruption within certain state agencies and monopolies. In 1998, increased citizen awareness of civil rights and democratic values has provided an increasingly effective check on the excesses of law enforcement agencies.

## Political Parties

There are 11 main political parties and two political blocks in Georgia. Of these, four are pro-government and seven are opposition parties. The Citizens Union of Georgia (CUG), a pro-government party formed in late 1993, is dominated by young reformers but also includes Soviet bureaucrats connected to Shevardnadze from his days as leader of Soviet Georgia. The CUG's name recognition, financial support, and organization give it a distinct advantage over the other political parties.

The National Democratic Party represents the opposition in parliament. The party was formed in 1981 and has strong name recognition throughout most of the country. The Union of Democratic Revival is a vehicle in Tbilisi for political representation of

the Ajarian region. The Abkhaz faction remains vocal and influential in pushing for resolution for the Abkhaz conflict.

# ECONOMY

Georgia's economic recovery has been hampered by the separatist disputes in Abkhazia and South Ossetia, a persistently weak economic infrastructure, resistance to reform on the part of some corrupt and reactionary factions, and the Russian and Asian economic crises. Under President Shevardnadze's leadership, the government has nonetheless guided the economy to impressive gains: slashing inflation, meeting most IMF targets through its July 1998 review, and qualifying for economic structural adjustment facility credit status, introducing a stable national

currency (the lari), introducing free market prices of bread products, preparing for the second stage of accession to the World Trade Organization (the first stage has already been met), signing agreements that allow for development of a pipeline to transport Caspian oil across Georgia to the Black Sea, and passing laws on commercial banking, land, and tax reform. However, as a result of the fallout from the Russian and Asian economic crises, Georgia has been unable to meet IMF conditions recently.

Georgia's deficit fell from the 1996 rate of 6.2% to 3.6% in 1997. The Government expects to continue reducing the country's deficit to 3% in 1998. President Shevardnadze recently announced that tax revenues have risen dramatically, and recent tax reform, encouraged by the IMF, should lead to further increases.

However, Georgia needs to implement its tax legislation and take concrete steps to meet IMF programs. Although total revenue increased from 1996 to 1997, these increases were lower than expected. International financial institutions continue to play a critical role in Georgia's budgetary calculations. Multilateral and bilateral grants and loans totaled 116.4 million lari in 1997 and are expected to total 182.8 million lari in 1998.

There has been strong progress on structural reform. All prices and most trade have been liberalized, legal-framework reform is on schedule, and massive government downsizing is underway. More than 10,500 small enterprises have been privatized, and although privatization of medium- and large-sized firms has been slow, more than 1,200 medium- and large-sized companies have been set up as joint stock companies. A law and a decree establishing the legal basis and procedures for state property privatization should continue to reduce the number of companies controlled by the state.

Due to a lack of investment, Georgia's transportation and communication infrastructure remains in very poor condition. Parliament has set an agenda to start the privatization of the telecommunications industry, although there is still resistance to the plan and Parliament needs to draft implementing legislation.

Georgia's electrical energy sector is in critical condition. Shortages of electricity have resulted in public unrest. In 1998, Georgia began to privatize its energy distribution system and expects to privatize its energy generation system by 2000. Privatization is the only means to generate the capital needed to rehabilitate the sector.

To encourage and support the reform process, the U.S. is joining other donors in shifting the focus of assistance from humanitarian to technical and institution-building programs. Provision of legal and technical advisors is complemented by training opportunities for parliamentarians, law enforcement officials, and economic advisors. The U.S. is increasingly willing to impose conditions on assistance in order to encourage improved performance on key issues and privatization of key sectors, including energy. Georgia continues to depend on humanitarian aid,

which is increasingly targeted to most-needy groups.

Georgian agricultural production is beginning to recover following the devastation caused by the civil unrest and the restructuring necessary following the breakup of the Soviet Union. Livestock production is beginning to rebound, although it faces periodic disease. Domestic grain production is increasing, and will require sustained political and infrastructure improvements to ensure appropriate distribution and return to farmers. Tea, hazelnut, and citrus production have suffered greatly as a result of the conflict in Abkhazia, an especially fertile area.

While approximately 30% of the Georgian economy is agricultural, crops spoil in the field because farmers either cannot get their produce to market or must pay costs that drive market prices above those for imported goods. In concert with European assistance, Georgia has taken steps to control the quality of and appropriately market its natural spring water. Georgian viniculture, well supported during Soviet times, is internationally acclaimed and has absorbed some new technologies and financing since 1994.

# FOREIGN RELATIONS

Georgia's location, nestled between the Black Sea, Russia, and Turkey, gives it strategic importance far beyond its size. It is developing as the gateway from the Black Sea to the Caucasus and the larger Caspian region, but also serves as a buffer between Russia and Turkey. Georgia has a long and close relationship with Russia, but it is reaching out to its other neighbors and looking to the West in search of alternatives and opportunities. It signed a partnership and cooperation agreement with the EU, participates in the Partnership for Peace, and encourages foreign investment. France, Germany, and the U.K. all have embassies in Tbilisi, and Germany is a significant donor.

Georgia is a member of the UN, the OSCE, and the CIS. It is an observer in the Council of Europe.

# U.S.-GEORGIA RELATIONS

U.S.-Georgia relations have been and continue to be excellent. Georgian leaders note that U.S. humanitarian assistance was critical to Georgia's recovery from civil war and economic difficulties following independence. U.S. assistance currently is targeted to support Georgia's economic and political reform programs, with emphasis on institution-building. The U.S. is working with the Georgian parliament on draft laws and establishing procedures and standards consistent with the country's 1995 constitution. The U.S. also provides Georgia with bilateral security assistance, including through the International Military Education and Training (IMET) program. Evolving U.S.-Georgia partnerships include programs by the Georgia (U.S.) National Guard, visits by the Sixth Fleet and the Coast Guard to Georgia, and the Bilateral Working Group on Defense and Military Cooperation.

## Principal U.S. Officials

**For up-to-date information on Principal U.S. Officials, see the U.S. Embassies, Consulates, and Foreign Service section starting on page 139.**

The U.S. embassy in Georgia is located at 25 Antoneli Street, Tbilisi 380026, telephone 995-32-98-99-67, fax 995-32-93-37-59.

The U.S. embassy's home page address is: http://www.sanet.ge/usis/usistbl.html

# GERMANY

May 2000

## Official Name:
## Federal Republic of Germany

# PROFILE

## Geography

**Area:** 357,000 sq. km. (137,821 sq. mi.); about the size of Montana.
**Cities:** Capital—Berlin (population about 3.5 million). Other cities—Hamburg (1.7 million), Munich (1.2 million), Cologne (964,000), Frankfurt (647,000), Essen (612,000), Dortmund (597,000), Stuttgart (585,000), Dusseldorf (571,000), Bremen (549,000), Hannover (523,000).
**Terrain:** Low plain in the north; high plains, hills, and basins in the center and east; mountainous alpine region in the south.
**Climate:** Temperate; cooler and rainier than much of the U.S.

## People

**Nationality:** Noun and adjective—German(s).
**Population:** (1998 est.) 82 million.
**Ethnic Groups:** Primarily German; Danish minority in the north, Sorbian (Slavic) minority in the east, 7.3 million noncitizens.
**Religion:** Protestants slightly outnumber Roman Catholics.
**Language:** German.
**Education:** Years compulsory—10. Attendance—100%. Literacy—99%.
**Health:** Infant mortality rate (1998 est.)—5.2/1,000. Life expectancy

(1998 est.) Women 80 yrs., men 74 yrs.
**Persons employed:** (1998 avg.) 34.1 million. Persons unemployed (Feb. 1999) 4.5 million—11.6% of labor force.

## Government

**Type:** Federal republic.
**Founded:** 1949 (Basic Law, i.e., constitution, promulgated on May 23, 1949). On October 3, 1990, the Federal Republic of Germany and the German Democratic Republic unified in accordance with Article 23 of the F.R.G. Basic Law.
**Branches:** Executive—president (titular chief of state), chancellor (executive head of government). Legislative—bicameral parliament. Judicial—independent, Federal Constitutional Court. Administrative divisions: 16 Laender (states).
**Major political parties:** Social Democratic Party (SPD); Christian Democratic Union (CDU); Christian Social Union (CSU); Alliance 90/Greens; Free Democratic Party (FDP); Party of Democratic Socialism (PDS).
**Suffrage:** Universal at 18.

## Economy

**GDP:** (1998) $2.1 trillion.
**Annual growth rate:** (1998) 2.8%.
**Per capita income:** $25,000.
**Inflation rate:** cost of living index

(1998/97) 0.9%.
**Natural resources:** Iron, hard coal, lignite, potash, natural gas.
**Agriculture:** Accounts for 1% of GDP. Products—corn, wheat, potatoes, sugar, beets, barley, hops, viticulture, forestry, fisheries.
**Industry:** (35% of GDP) Types—iron and steel, coal, chemicals, electrical products, ships, vehicles, construction.
**Trade:** (1998) Exports—$539 billion: chemicals, motor vehicles, iron and steel products, manufactured goods, electrical products. Major markets—France, U.S., U.K. Imports—$467 billion: food, petroleum products, manufactured goods, electrical products, automobiles, apparel. Major suppliers—France, U.S., Netherlands.

# PEOPLE

The population of Germany is primarily German. There are more than 7 million foreign residents, including those granted asylum, guest workers, and their dependents. Germany is a prime destination for political and economic refugees from many developing countries. An ethnic Danish minority lives in the north, and a small Slavic minority, known as the Sorbs, lives in eastern Germany.

Germany has one of the world's highest levels of education, technological development, and economic productivity. Since the end of World War II, the number of youths entering universities has more than tripled, and the trade and technical schools of the Federal Republic of Germany (F.R.G.) are among the world's best. With a per capita income level of more than $25,000, Germany is a broadly middle class society. A generous social welfare system provides for universal medical care, unemployment compensation, and other social needs. Germans also are mobile; millions travel abroad each year.

With unification on October 3, 1990, Germany began the major task of bringing the standard of living of Germans in the former German Democratic Republic (G.D.R.) up to that of western Germany. This will be a lengthy and difficult process due to the relative inefficiency of industrial enterprises in the former G.D.R., difficulties in resolving property ownership in eastern Germany, and the inadequate infrastructure and environmental damage that resulted from years of mismanagement under communist rule.

Drastic changes in the socioeconomic landscape brought about by reunification have resulted in troubling social problems. Economic uncertainty in eastern Germany is often cited as one factor contributing to extremist violence, primarily from the political right. Confusion about the causes of the current hardships and a need to place blame have found expression in harassment and violence by some Germans directed toward foreigners, particularly non-Europeans. The vast majority of Germans condemn such violence.

# HISTORY

The rise of Prussian power in the 19th century, supported by growing German nationalism, eventually ended interstate fighting and resulted in the formation of the German empire in 1871 under the chancellorship of Otto von Bismarck. Although authoritarian in many respects, the empire eventually permitted the development of political parties, and Bismarck was credited with passing the most advanced social welfare legislation of the age. Dynamic expansion of military power, however, contributed to tensions on the continent. The fragile European balance of power broke down in 1914, and World War I and its aftermath, including the Treaty of Versailles, led to the collapse of the German empire.

## Fascism's Rise and Defeat

The postwar Weimar Republic (1919-33) was an attempt to establish a peaceful, liberal democratic regime in Germany. This government was severely handicapped and eventually doomed by economic problems and the inherent weakness of the Weimar state. The inflation of the early 1920s, the world depression of the 1930s, and the social unrest stemming from the draconian conditions of the Versailles Treaty worked to destroy the Weimar government from inside and out.

The National Socialist (Nazi) Party, led by Adolf Hitler, stressed nationalistic themes and promised to put the unemployed back to work. The party blamed many of Germany's ills on alleged Jewish conspiracies. Nazi support expanded rapidly in the early 1930s. Hitler was asked to form a government as Reich Chancellor in January 1933. After President Paul von Hindenburg died in 1934, Hitler assumed that office as well. Once in power, Hitler and his party first undermined then abolished democratic institutions and opposition parties. The Nazi leadership attempted to remove or subjugate the Jewish population in Germany and later, in the occupied countries, forced emigration and, ultimately, genocide. Hitler restored Germany's economic and military strength, but his ambitions led Germany into World War II. For Germany, World War II resulted in the destruction of its political and economic infrastructures, led to its division, and left a humiliating legacy.

After Germany's unconditional surrender on May 8, 1945, the United States, the United Kingdom, and the U.S.S.R. occupied the country and assumed responsibility for its administration. The commanders in chief exercised supreme authority in their respective zones and acted in concert on questions affecting the whole country. France was later given a separate zone of occupation.

Although the United States, the United Kingdom, and the Soviet Union agreed at Potsdam in August 1945 to a broad program of decentralization, treating Germany as a single economic unit with some central administrative departments, these plans failed. The turning point came in 1948, when the Soviets withdrew from the Four Power governing bodies and blockaded Berlin. Until May 1949, West Berlin was kept supplied only by an Allied airlift.

## Political Developments in West Germany

The United States and the United Kingdom moved to establish a nucleus for a future German government by creating a central Economic Council for their two zones. The program later provided for a West German constituent assembly, an occupation statute governing relations between the Allies and the German authorities, and the political and economic merger of the French with the British and American zones.

On May 23, 1949, the Basic Law, the constitution of the Federal Republic of Germany, was promulgated. The first federal government was formed by Konrad Adenauer on September 20, 1949. The next day, the occupation statute came into force, granting powers of self-government with certain exceptions.

The F.R.G. quickly progressed toward fuller sovereignty and association with its European neighbors and the Atlantic community. The London and Paris agreements of 1954 restored full sovereignty (with some exceptions) to the F.R.G. in May 1955 and opened the way for German membership in the North Atlantic Treaty Organization (NATO) and the Western European Union (WEU).

The three Western Allies retained occupation powers in Berlin and certain responsibilities for Germany as a whole. Under the new arrangements, the Allies stationed troops within the F.R.G. for NATO defense, pursuant to stationing and status-of-forces agreements. With the exception of 45,000 French troops, Allied forces were under NATO's joint defense command. (France withdrew from the collective military command structure of NATO in 1966.)

Political life in the F.R.G. was remarkably stable and orderly. The Adenauer era (1949-63) was followed by a brief period under Ludwig Erhard (1963-66) who, in turn, was replaced by Kurt Georg Kiesinger (1966-69). All governments between 1949 and 1966 were formed by the united caucus of the Christian Democratic Union (CDU) and Christian Social Union (CSU), either alone or in coalition with the smaller Free Democratic Party (FDP). Kiesinger's 1966-69 "Grand Coalition" included the F.R.G.'s two largest parties, CDU/

CSU and the Social Democratic Party (SPD). In the 1969 election, the SPD—headed by Willy Brandt—gained enough votes to form a coalition government with the FDP. Chancellor Brandt remained head of government until May 1974, when he resigned after a senior member of his staff was uncovered as a spy for the East German intelligence service.

Finance Minister Helmut Schmidt (SPD) formed a government and received the unanimous support of coalition members. He served as Chancellor from 1974 to 1982. Hans-Dietrich Genscher, a leading FDP official, became Vice Chancellor and Foreign Minister. Schmidt, a strong supporter of the European Community (EC) and the Atlantic alliance, emphasized his commitment to "the political unification of Europe in partnership with the U.S.A."

In October 1982, the SPD-FDP coalition fell apart when the FDP joined forces with the CDU/CSU to elect CDU Chairman Helmut Kohl as Chancellor. Following national elections in March 1983, Kohl emerged in firm control of both the government and the CDU. The CDU/CSU fell just short of an absolute majority, due to the entry into the Bundestag of the Greens, who received 5.6% of the vote.

In January 1987, the Kohl-Genscher government was returned to office, but the FDP and the Greens gained at the expense of the larger parties. Kohl's CDU and its Bavarian sister party, the CSU, slipped from 48.8% of the vote in 1983 to 44.3%. The SPD fell to 37%; long-time SPD Chairman Brandt subsequently resigned in April 1987 and was succeeded by Hans-Jochen Vogel. The FDP's share rose from 7% to 9.1%, its best showing since 1980. The Greens' share rose to 8.3% from their 1983 share of 5.6%.

## Political Developments in East Germany

In the Soviet zone, the Social Democratic Party was forced to merge with the Communist Party in 1946 to form a new party, the Socialist Unity Party (SED). The October 1946 elections resulted in coalition governments in the five Land (state) parliaments with the SED as the undisputed leader.

A series of people's congresses were called in 1948 and early 1949 by the SED. Under Soviet direction, a constitution was drafted on May 30, 1949, and adopted on October 7, which was celebrated as the day when the German Democratic Republic was proclaimed. The People's Chamber (Volkskammer)—the lower house of the G.D.R. Parliament—and an upper house—the States Chamber (Laenderkammer)—were created. (The Laenderkammer was abolished in 1958.) On October 11, 1949, the two houses elected Wilhelm Pieck as President, and a SED government was set up. The Soviet Union and its east European allies immediately recognized the G.D.R., although it remained largely unrecognized by non-communist countries until 1972-73.

The G.D.R. established the structures of a single-party, centralized, communist state. On July 23, 1952, the traditional Laender were abolished and, in their place, 14 Bezirke (districts) were established. Effectively, all government control was in the hands of the SED, and almost all important government positions were held by SED members.

The National Front was an umbrella organization nominally consisting of the SED, four other political parties controlled and directed by the SED, and the four principal mass organizations (youth, trade unions, women, and culture). However, control was clearly and solely in the hands of the SED. Balloting in G.D.R. elections was not secret. As in other Soviet bloc countries, electoral participation was consistently high, with nearly unanimous candidate approval.

## Inter-German Relations

The constant stream of east Germans fleeing to West Germany placed great strains on F.R.G.-G.D.R. relations in the 1950s. On August 13, 1961, the G.D.R. began building a wall through the center of Berlin to divide the city and slow the flood of refugees to a trickle. The Berlin Wall became the symbol of the east's political debility and the division of Europe.

In 1969, Chancellor Brandt announced that the F.R.G. would remain firmly rooted in the Atlantic alliance but would intensify efforts to improve relations with eastern Europe and the G.D.R. The F.R.G. commenced this Ostpolitik by negotiating nonaggression treaties with the Soviet Union, Poland, Czechoslovakia, Bulgaria, and Hungary.

The F.R.G.'s relations with the G.D.R. posed particularly difficult questions. Though anxious to relieve serious hardships for divided families and to reduce friction, the F.R.G. under Brandt was intent on holding to its concept of "two German states in one German nation." Relations improved, however, and in September 1973, the F.R.G. and the G.D.R. were admitted to the UN. The two Germanys exchanged permanent representatives in 1974, and, in 1987, G.D.R. head of state Erich Honecker paid an official visit to the F.R.G.

## German Unification

During the summer of 1989, rapid changes took place in the G.D.R., which ultimately led to German unification. Growing numbers of east Germans emigrated to the F.R.G. via Hungary after the Hungarians decided not to use force to stop them. Thousands of east Germans also tried to reach the west by staging sit-ins at F.R.G. diplomatic facilities in other east European capitals. The exodus generated demands within the G.D.R. for political change, and mass demonstrations in several cities—particularly in Leipzig—continued to grow. On October 7, Soviet leader Mikhail Gorbachev visited Berlin to celebrate the 40th anniversary of the establishment of the G.D.R. and urged the east German leadership to pursue reform.

On October 18, Erich Honecker resigned as head of the SED and as head of state and was replaced by Egon Krenz. But the exodus continued unabated and pressure for political reform mounted. On November 4, a demonstration in East Berlin drew as many as 1 million east Germans. Finally, on November 9, the Berlin Wall was opened, and east Germans were allowed to travel freely. Thousands poured through the wall into the western sectors of Berlin, and on November 12, the G.D.R. began dismantling it.

On November 28, F.R.G. Chancellor Kohl outlined a 10-point plan for the peaceful unification of the two Germanys based on free elections in the G.D.R. and a unification of their two economies. In December, the G.D.R. Volkskammer eliminated the SED monopoly on power, and the entire Politburo and Central Committee, including Krenz, resigned. The SED changed its name to the Party of Democratic Socialism (PDS), and the formation and growth of numerous political groups and parties marked the end of the communist system. Prime Minister Hans Modrow headed a caretaker government that shared power with the new, democratically oriented parties. On December 7, 1989, agreement was reached to hold free elections in May 1990 and rewrite the G.D.R. constitution. On January 28, all the parties agreed to advance the elections to March 18, primarily because of an erosion of state authority and because the east German exodus was continuing apace; more than 117,000 left in January and February 1990.

In early February 1990, the Modrow government's proposal for a unified, neutral German state was rejected by Chancellor Kohl, who affirmed that a unified Germany must be a member of NATO. Finally, on March 18, the first free elections were held in the G.D.R., and a government led by Lothar de Maiziere (CDU) was formed under a policy of expeditious unification with the F.R.G. The freely elected representatives of the Volkskammer held their first session on April 5, and the G.D.R. peacefully evolved from a communist to a democratically elected government. Free and secret communal (local) elections were held in the G.D.R. on May 6, and the CDU again won. On July 1, the

two Germanys entered into an economic and monetary union.

## Four Power Control Ends

During 1990, in parallel with internal German developments, the Four Powers—the United States, U.K., France, and the Soviet Union—together with the two German states negotiated to end Four Power reserved rights for Berlin and Germany as a whole. These "Two-plus-Four" negotiations were mandated at the Ottawa Open Skies conference on February 13, 1990. The six foreign ministers met four times in the ensuing months in Bonn (May 5), Berlin (June 22), Paris (July 17), and Moscow (September 12). The Polish Foreign Minister participated in the part of the Paris meeting that dealt with the Polish-German borders.

Of key importance was overcoming Soviet objections to a united Germany's membership in NATO. This was accomplished in July when the alliance, led by President Bush, issued the London Declaration on a transformed NATO. On July 16, President Gorbachev and Chancellor Kohl announced agreement in principle on a united Germany in NATO. This cleared the way for the signing of the Treaty on the Final Settlement With Respect to Germany in Moscow on September 12. In addition to terminating Four Power rights, the treaty mandated the withdrawal of all Soviet forces from Germany by the end of 1994, made clear that the current borders were final and definitive, and specified the right of a united Germany to belong to NATO. It also provided for the continued presence of British, French, and American troops in Berlin during the interim period of the Soviet withdrawal. In the treaty, the Germans renounced nuclear, biological, and chemical weapons and stated their intention to reduce German armed forces to 370,000 within 3 to 4 years after the Conventional Armed Forces in Europe (CFE) Treaty, signed in Paris on November 19, 1990, entered into force.

Conclusion of the final settlement cleared the way for unification of the F.R.G. and G.D.R. Formal political union occurred on October 3, 1990, with the accession (in accordance with Article 23 of the F.R.G.'s Basic Law) of the five Laender which had been reestablished in the G.D.R. On December 2, 1990, all-German elections were held for the first time since 1933.

# GOVERNMENT AND POLITICAL CONDITIONS

The government is parliamentary and based on a democratic constitution that emphasizes the protection of individual liberty and division of powers in a federal structure. The chancellor (prime minister) heads the executive branch of the federal government. The duties of the president (chief of state) are largely ceremonial; power is exercised by the chancellor. Elected by and responsible to the Bundestag (lower and principal chamber of the parliament), the chancellor cannot be removed from office during a 4-year term unless the Bundestag has agreed on a successor. The President is elected every 5 years on May 23 by the Federal Assembly, a body convoked only for this purpose, comprising the entire Bundestag (federal legislative lower house) and an equal number of state delegates. In the 1999 election, Johannes Rau of the Social Democratic Party was elected.

The Bundestag, also elected for a 4-year term, consists of at least twice the number of electoral districts in the country. (More deputies may be admitted when parties' directly elected seats exceed their proportional representation.) Elections for an all-German Bundestag were first held on December 2, 1990, and again on October 16, 1994 and September 27, 1998. 669 deputies were seated after the 1998 national elections. The Bundesrat (upper chamber or Federal Council) consists of 69 members who are delegates of the 16 Laender (states). The legislature has powers of exclusive jurisdiction and concurrent jurisdiction with the Laender in areas specifically enumerated by the Basic Law. The Bundestag bears the major responsibility. The necessity for the Bundesrat to concur on legislation is limited to bills treating revenue shared by federal and state governments and those imposing responsibilities on the states.

Germany has an independent federal judiciary consisting of a constitutional court, a high court of justice, and courts with jurisdiction in administrative, financial, labor, and social matters. The highest court is the Federal Constitutional Court, which ensures a uniform interpretation of constitutional provisions and protects the fundamental rights of the individual citizen as defined in the Basic Law.

### Social Democratic Party (SPD).

The SPD, one of the oldest organized political parties in the world, emerged as the winner in the September 1998 elections with 40.9% of the votes cast. Historically, it advocated Marxist principles, but in the Godesberg Program, adopted in 1959, the SPD abandoned the concept of a class party while continuing to stress social welfare programs. Although the SPD originally opposed West Germany's 1955 entry into NATO, it now strongly supports German ties with the alliance. Gerhard Schroeder led the party to victory in 1998 on a moderate platform emphasizing the need to reduce unemployment. The SPD has a powerful base in the bigger cities and industrialized Laender. Oskar Lafontaine, SPD chairman since November 1995, resigned from his party and government positions in March, 1999. Schroeder succeeded Lafontaine as party chairman.

### Christian Democratic Union/ Christian Social Union (CDU/ CSU).

An important aspect of postwar German politics was the emergence of a moderate Christian party—the Christian Democratic Union—operating with a related Bavarian party, the Christian Social Union. Although each party main-

## Travel Notes

**Travel Advice:** For up-to-date information from the U.S. State Department on possible inconvenient or hazardous situations, see the **Travel Warnings and Consular Information Sheets from the U.S. Government** section starting on page 1723. For the latest information on health requirements and conditions, see the **International Travelers' Health Information** section starting on page 1385. For further information dealing with non-urgent matter, see the **Tips for Travelers to...** section starting on page 1588.

tains its own structure, the two form a common caucus in the Bundestag and do not run opposing campaigns. The CDU/CSU has adherents among Catholics, Protestants, rural interests, and members of all economic classes. It is generally conservative on economic and social policy and more identified with the Roman Catholic and Protestant churches than are the other major parties, although its programs are pragmatic rather than ideological. Helmut Kohl served as chairman of the CDU from 1973 until the party's electoral defeat in 1998 when he was succeeded by Wolfgang Schaeuble; Early in 1999, as a result of a CDU financial scandal, Schaeuble stepped down. During this time Edmund Stoiber took over the CSU chairmanship. Angela Merkel, succeeding Schaeuble, currently serves as the CDU chairperson. In the 1998 general election, the CDU polled 28.4% and the CSU 6.7% of the national vote.

### Alliance 90/Greens.

In the late 1970s, environmentalists organized politically as the Greens. Opposition to expanded use of nuclear power, to NATO strategy, and to certain aspects of highly industrialized society were principal campaign issues. The Greens received 8.3% of the vote in the January 1987 west German national election. However, in the December 1990 all-German elections, the Greens in western Germany were not able to clear the 5% hurdle required to win seats in the Bundestag. It was only in the territory of the former G.D.R. that the Greens, in a

merger with Alliance 90 (a loose grouping civil rights activists with diverse political views), were able to clear the 5% hurdle and win Bundestag seats. In 1994, Greens from east and west returned to the Bundestag with 7.3% and 49 seats in 1998; despite a slight fall in percentage of the vote (6.7%), the Greens retained 47 seats and joined of the federal government for the first time in coalition with the SPD. Joschka Fischer became vice chancellor and foreign minister in the new government, which has two other Greens ministers.

### Free Democratic Party (FDP).

The FDP has traditionally been composed mainly of middle and upper-class Protestants, who consider themselves "independents" and heirs to the European liberal tradition. Although the party is weak on the state level, it has participated in all but three postwar federal governments and has spent only 8 years out of government in the 50-year history of the Federal Republic. The party took 6.2% of the vote and returned 43 deputies to the Bundestag in 1998. Wolfgang Gerhardt has been party chairman since 1995.

### Party of Democratic Socialism (PDS).

Under chairman Lothar Bisky and Bundestag caucus leader Gregor Gysi, the PDS is the successor party to the SED (the communist party of the G.D.R.). Established in December 1989, it renounced most of the extreme aspects of SED policy but has retained much of the ideology. In the December 1990 all-German elections, the PDS gained 10% of the vote in the former G.D.R. and 17 seats in the Bundestag. In October 1994, the PDS won four directly elected seats, to reenter parliament with a total caucus of 30 seats despite staying below the 5% hurdle for proportional representation. In 1998, the party improved its result slightly to 5.1% of the national vote and 36 deputies.

### Other parties.

In addition to those parties that won representation in the Bundestag in 1998, a variety of minor parties won a cumulative total of 5.9% of the vote, up from 3.5% in 1994. Sixteen other parties were on the ballot in one or more states but not qualified for representation in the Bundestag. The right-wing parties remained fragmented and ineffectual at the national level.

## Recent Election Issues

The SPD in the 1998 election emphasized commitment to reducing persistently high unemployment and appealed to voters' desire for new faces after 16 years of Kohl government. Schroeder positioned himself as a centrist "Third Way" candidate in the mold of Britain's Tony Blair. The CDU/CSU stood on its record of economic performance and experience in foreign policy. The Kohl government was hurt at the polls by slower growth in the east in the past 2 years, widening the economic gap between east and west. The final margin of victory was sufficiently high to permit a "red-green" coalition of the SPD with the Greens, bringing the Greens into a national government for the first time.

## Principal Government Officials

**For up-to-date information on Principal Government Officials, see the Chiefs of State and Cabinet Members of Foreign Governments section starting on page 1.**

Germany maintains an embassy in the United States at 4645 Reservoir Road NW, Washington, DC 20007 (tel. 202-298-4000).
Consulates general are located in Atlanta, Boston, Chicago, Detroit, Houston, Los Angeles, Miami, New York, San Francisco, and Seattle. Germany has honorary consuls in over 30 U.S. cities.

# ECONOMY

Germany ranks among the world's most important economic powers, witnessed by its presence among the G7. From the 1948 currency reform until the early 1970s, west Germany experienced almost continuous economic expansion, but real growth in gross national product slowed and even declined from the mid-1970s through the recession of the early 1980s. The economy then experienced 8 consecutive years of growth that ended with a downturn beginning in late 1992.

After national unification, eastern German industrial output collapsed to about 40% of its 1989 level, leading to high unemployment in the new states. Reunification strained German public finance, hurt the labor market, and eventually exposed structural weaknesses in the economy. Following a reunification-induced western German economic boom during 1990-92 fueled by explosive consumer demand and capital spending, growth stalled while transfer payments to the eastern states rose to $90 billion per year. In an effort to contain the inflationary pressures of these transfers, the Central Bank (Bundesbank) maintained a high (short-term) interest rate policy that further dampened economic activity. In 1994, the German economy began to recover, and the 10% growth rate in the eastern states was the highest of any region in Europe. Although eastern Germany maintained growth of more than 5%, 1995 growth was unexpectedly low at 1.9%. GDP growth was an even lower in 1996—1.4%—due mainly to a drop in construction investment and lower private consumption. Growth strengthened in 1997, continued through 1998, and is forecasted at 2.5 % for 2000.

Germans often describe their economic system as a "social market economy." The German Government provides an extensive array of social services. Although the state intervenes in the economy through the provision of subsidies to selected sectors and the ownership of some segments of the economy, competition and free enterprise are promoted as a matter of government policy. The government has restructured the railroad system on a corporate basis and is privatizing the national airline, energy sectors (gas and electric), and postal service. Germany also has privatized its telecommunication giant Deutsche Telekom. Changes to the German "social compact" have met with strong resistance from labor and management alike, leaving the labor market highly regulated and inflexible.

The German economy is heavily export oriented, with one-third of national output going to the external sector. As a result, exports traditionally have been a key element in German acroeconomic expansion. Germany is a strong advocate of closer European economic integration, and its economic and commercial policies are increasingly determined by agreements among European Union (EU) members.

Outside the EU, the United States and Japan are Germany's major trading partners. U.S.- German trade has continued to grow strongly. Two-way U.S.-German trade is more than $80 billion. The United States continued to run trade deficits with Germany; U.S. exports in 1998 were $37.6 billion, while German exports expanded to $49.9 billion. Major U.S. export categories include aircraft, electrical equipment, telecommunications equipment, data processing equipment, and motor vehicles and parts. German export sales are concentrated in motor vehicles, machinery, chemicals, and heavy electrical equipment. In services, the United States consistently shows a surplus in trade with Germany.

Germany follows a liberal policy toward foreign investment. About 65% of U.S. capital invested in Germany is in manufacturing. In 1997, total U.S. direct investment in Germany was $44 billion, making the U.S. Germany's leading source of foreign investment. Total German investment in the United States in 1998 was $95 billion.

Eleven years after the unification of the two German states, great strides have been made, and the complex task of introducing a market economy in the east is well-advanced. Overall productivity in the former G.D.R., which was less than half that in the F.R.G., is now increasing, narrowing the gap in productivity rates. The challenge is to close the productivity gap altogether. The poor condition of the basic infrastructure, widespread environmental damage, and lower-than-expected levels of private investment in the east have complicated the process of economic integration. Private investment in eastern Germany has been slower than expected in large part because the issue of property ownership in the former G.D.R. has proven difficult to resolve. Public net transfers from west to east from 1991-97 are estimated at $488 billion, or an annual average of over 4% of the GDP of the former west Germany. After several years of exceptionally rapid growth, growth in the east lagged the national rate in 1997 and 1998. Unemployment in the east has remained high: in February 1999 it was 19.1% in east Germany compared to 10.4% in west Germany.

Germany's greatest economic problem is its persistently high unemployment rate. Solid growth in 1998 brought the national, nonseasonally adjusted unemployment rate down only to 11.1% in March 1999 from 12.1% a year earlier. Although the new government elected in September 1998 made employment creation its central theme, there is no national consensus on how to achieve this. Some of the modest reforms designed to loosen structural rigidities introduced near the end of the Kohl government have been reversed since the election.

Despite persistence of structural rigidities in the labor market and extensive government regulation, the economy remains strong and internationally competitive. Although production costs are very high, Germany is still an export powerhouse. Germany competes successfully in highly engineered, quality products backed by excellent service. German firms are somewhat less successful in high-tech electronic goods. In 1998, Germany ran a trade surplus of $73 billion and a current account deficit of about $9 billion. Imports and exports were both down in the last months of 1998 and in January 1999, in part reflecting continued problems in

emerging country markets. Abundant personnel, low corporate debt burdens, and cooperative industrial relations continue to characterize the German economy. Additionally, Germany is strategically placed to take advantage of the rapidly growing central European countries. Although the Germans face fundamental economic adjustments, they have the discipline and the resources to meet the challenges ahead.

# FOREIGN RELATIONS

Germany continues to emphasize close ties with the United States, membership in NATO, the "deepening" of integration among current members of the EU, and expansion of union membership to include central and southern European neighbors. The F.R.G. took part in all of the joint postwar efforts aimed at closer political, economic, and defense cooperation among the countries of Western Europe. Germany has been a large net contributor to the EU budget; the Schroeder government is seeking to limit the growth of these net payments before the next round of enlargement. Germany also is a strong supporter of the United Nations and of the Organization for Security and Cooperation in Europe (OSCE), which seeks to reduce tensions and improve relations among the European nations, the U.S., and Canada.

During the postwar era, the F.R.G. also sought to improve its relationship with the countries of eastern Europe, first establishing trade agreements and, subsequently, diplomatic relations. With unification, German relations with the new democracies in central and eastern Europe intensified. On November 14, 1990, Germany and Poland signed a treaty confirming the Oder-Neisse border. They also concluded a cooperation treaty on June 17, 1991. Germany concluded four treaties with the Soviet Union covering the overall bilateral relationship, economic relations, the withdrawal of Soviet troops from the territory of the former G.D.R., and German support for those

troops. Russia accepted obligations under these treaties as successor to the Soviet Union. Germany continues to be active economically in the states of central and eastern Europe, and to actively support the development of democratic institutions.

## Berlin

Shortly after World War II, Berlin became the seat of the Allied Control Council, which was to have governed Germany as a whole until the conclusion of a peace settlement. In 1948, however, the Soviets refused to participate any longer in the quadripartite administration of Germany. They also refused to continue the joint administration of Berlin and drove the government elected by the people of Berlin out of its seat in the Soviet sector and installed a communist regime in its place. From then until unification, the Western Allies continued to exercise supreme authority—effective only in their sectors—through the Allied Kommandatura. To the degree compatible with the city's special status, however, they turned over control and management of city affairs to the Berlin Senate (executive) and House of Representatives, governing bodies established by constitutional process and chosen by free elections. The Allies and German authorities in the F.R.G. and West Berlin never recognized the communist city regime in East Berlin or G.D.R. authority there.

During the years of Berlin's isolation—176 kilometers (110 mi.) inside the former G.D.R.—the Western Allies encouraged a close relationship between the Government of West Berlin and that of the F.R.G. representatives of the city participated as nonvoting members in the F.R.G. Parliament; appropriate West German agencies, such as the supreme administrative court, had their permanent seats in the city; and the governing mayor of Berlin took his turn as President of the Bundesrat. In addition, the allies carefully consulted with the F.R.G. and Berlin Governments on foreign policy questions involving unification and the status of Berlin.

Between 1948 and 1990, major events such as fairs and festivals were sponsored in West Berlin, and investment in commerce and industry was encouraged by special concessionary tax legislation. The results of such efforts, combined with effective city administration and the Berliners' energy and spirit, were encouraging. Berlin's morale was sustained, and its industrial production considerably surpassed the prewar level.

The Final Settlement Treaty ended Berlin's special status as a separate area under Four Power control. Under the terms of the treaty between the F.R.G. and the G.D.R., Berlin became the capital of a unified Germany. The Bundestag voted in June 1991 to make Berlin the seat of government. The Government of Germany asked the allies to maintain a military presence in Berlin until the complete withdrawal of the Western Group of Forces (ex-Soviet) from the territory of the former G.D.R. The Russian withdrawal was completed August 31, 1994. Ceremonies were held on September 8, 1994, to mark the final departure of Western Allied troops from Berlin.

In 1999, Berlin became the formal seat of the German federal government.

# U.S.-GERMAN RELATIONS

U.S.-German relations have been a focal point of American involvement in Europe since the end of World War II. Germany stands at the center of European affairs and is a key partner in U.S. relations with Europeans in NATO and the European Union.

But German-American ties extend back to the colonial era. More than 7 million Germans have immigrated over the last three centuries, and today nearly 25% of U.S. citizens can claim some German ancestry. In recognition of this heritage and the importance of modern-day U.S.-German ties, the U.S. Congress annually

has declared October 6 to be "German-American Day."

The U.S. objective in Germany remains the preservation and consolidation of a close and vital relationship with Germany not only as friends and trading partners but also as allies sharing common institutions. During the 45 years in which Germany was divided, the U.S. role in Berlin and the large American military presence in West Germany served as symbols of the U.S. commitment to the preservation of peace and security in Europe. Since German unification, the U.S. commitment to these goals has not changed. The U.S. made significant reductions in its troop levels in Germany after the Cold War ended, and, on July 12, 1994, President Clinton "cased the colors" at the Berlin Brigade's deactivation ceremony. American policies, however, continue to be shaped by the awareness that the security and prosperity of the United States and Germany depend—to a major extent—on each other. Over 80,000 U.S. military personnel remain in Germany to protect these common interests.

As allies in NATO, the United States and Germany work side by side to maintain peace and freedom. This unity and resolve made possible the successful conclusion of the 1987 U.S.-U.S.S.R. Intermediate-Range Nuclear Forces Treaty (INF), the Two-plus-Four process, which led to the Final Settlement Treaty, and the November 1990 Conventional Armed Forces in Europe (CFE) Treaty. More recently, the two allies have cooperated closely in peacekeeping efforts in the Balkans and have worked together to encourage the evolution of open and democratic states throughout central and eastern Europe.

As two of the world's leading trading nations, the United States and Germany share a common, deep-seated commitment to an open and expanding world economy. Germany is the world's second-leading trading nation. It is the fifth-largest trading partner of the United States.

Personal ties between the United States and Germany extend beyond

immigration to include lively foreign exchange programs, booming tourism in both directions, and the presence in Germany of large numbers of American military personnel and their dependents. In the commercial sphere, more than 600,000 Germans work for U.S. companies in Germany while Americans employed by German firms here number over 500,000.

The United States and Germany have built a solid foundation of bilateral cooperation in a relationship that has changed significantly over five decades. The historic unification of Germany and the role played by the United States in that process have served to strengthen ties between the two countries. The relationship is now a mature partnership but remains subject to occasional misunderstandings and differences. These strains tend to reflect the importance, variety, and intensity of U.S.-German ties and respective interests rather than fundamental differences.

German-American political, economic, and security relationships continue to be based on close consultation and coordination at the most senior levels. High-level visits take place frequently, and the United States and Germany cooperate actively in international forums.

## Principal U.S. Embassy Officials

**For up-to-date information on Principal U.S. Officials, see the U.S. Embassies, Consulates, and Foreign Service section starting on page 139.**

The U.S. Embassy, in Berlin, is located at Neustaedtische Kirchstrasse 4-5, 10117 Berlin, Tel: (030) 238-5174.
Consulates general are in Frankfurt, Hamburg, Munich, Leipzig, and Dusseldorf. Mission Germany maintains an informative web site at: http://www.usembassy.de.

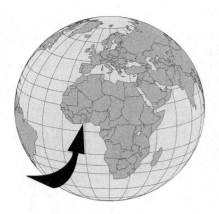

# GHANA

February 1998

## Official Name:
## Republic of Ghana

# PROFILE

## Geography

**Area:** 238,538 sq. km. (92,100 sq. mi.); about the size of Illinois and Indiana combined.
**Cities:** Capital—Accra (metropolitan area pop. 3 million est.). Other cities—Kumasi (1 million est.), Tema (250,000 est.), Sekondi-Takoradi (200,000 est.).
**Terrain:** Plains and scrubland, rain forest, savanna.
**Climate:** Tropical.

## People

**Nationality:** Noun and adjective—Ghanaian(s).
**Population (1997 est.):** 17.7 million.
**Density:** 74/sq. km. (192/sq. mi.).
**Annual growth rate (1996 est.):** 2.3%.
**Ethnic groups:** Akan, Ewe, Ga.
**Religions:** Christian 35%, indigenous beliefs 31%, Muslim 27%, other 7%.
**Languages:** English (official), Akan 44%, Mole-Dagbani 16%, Ewe 13%, Ga-Adangbe 8%.
**Education:** Years compulsory—9. Literacy—64.5%.
**Health:** Infant mortality rate (1996 est.)—80/1,000. Life expectancy—56 yrs.

**Work force:** 4 million: Agriculture and fishing—54.7%. Industry—18.7%. Sales and clerical—15.2%. Services, transportation, and communications—7.7%. Professional—3.7%.

## Government

**Type:** Democracy.
**Independence:** March 6, 1957.
**Constitution:** Entered into force January 7, 1993.
**Branches:** Executive—President popularly elected for a maximum of two four-year terms. Legislative—unicameral Parliament popularly elected for four-year terms. Judicial—Independent, Supreme Court Justices nominated by President with approval of Parliament. Subdivisions: 10 regions.
**Political parties:** National Democratic Congress, New Patriotic Party, People's Convention Party, National Convention Party, People's National Convention, et alia. Names, slogans, and symbols of parties existing prior to 1992 are banned by law.
**Suffrage:** Universal at 18.
**Flag:** Three horizontal stripes of red, gold, and green, with a black star in the center of the gold stripe.

## Economy

**GDP (1997):** $6.01 billion.
**Real GDP growth rate (1997):** 5.5%.

**Per capita GDP (1997):** $340.
**Inflation rate (1997):** 27%.
**Natural resources:** Gold, timber, diamonds, bauxite, manganese, fish.
**Agriculture:** Products—cocoa, coconuts, coffee, pineapples, cashews, pepper, other food crops, rubber. Land—70% arable and forested.
**Business and industry:** Types—mining, lumber, light manufacturing, fishing, aluminum, tourism. Trade (1997): Exports—$1.6 billion: cocoa ($600 million), aluminum, gold, timber, diamonds, manganese. Imports—$1.9 billion: petroleum ($272 million), food, industrial raw materials, machinery, equipment. Major trade partners—U.K., Germany, U.S., Nigeria.
**Official exchange rate (Dec. 1997):** 2,295 cedis=US$1.
**Fiscal year:** Calendar year.

# GEOGRAPHY

Ghana is located on West Africa's Gulf of Guinea only a few degrees north of the Equator. Half of the country lies less than 152 meters (500 ft.) above sea level, and the highest point is 883 meters (2,900 ft.). The 537-kilometer (334-mi.) coastline is mostly a low, sandy shore backed by plains and scrub and intersected by several rivers and streams, most of which are navigable only by canoe. A tropical rain forest belt, broken by heavily forested hills and many streams and rivers, extends northward from the shore, near the Cote d'Ivoire frontier. This area, known as the "Ashanti," produces most of the country's cocoa, minerals, and timber. North of this belt, the country varies from 91 to 396 meters (300-1,300 ft.) above sea level and is covered by low bush, park-like savanna, and grassy plains.

The climate is tropical. The eastern coastal belt is warm and comparatively dry; the southwest corner, hot and humid; and the north, hot and dry. There are two distinct rainy seasons in the south—May-June and August-September; in the north, the rainy seasons tend to merge. A dry, northeasterly wind, the Harmattan, blows in January and February. Annual rainfall in the coastal zone averages 83 centimeters (33 in.).

Volta Lake, the largest man-made lake in the world, extends from the Akosombo Dam in southeastern Ghana to the town of Yapei, 520 kilometers (325 mi.) to the north. The lake generates electricity, provides inland transportation, and is a potentially valuable resource for irrigation and fish farming.

# PEOPLE

Ghana's population is concentrated along the coast and in the principal cities of Accra and Kumasi. Most Ghanaians descended from migrating tribes that probably came down the Volta River valley at the beginning of the 13th century. Ethnically, Ghana is divided into small groups speaking more than 50 languages and dialects. Among the more important linguistic groups are the Akans, which include the Fantis along the coast and the Ashantis in the forest region north of the coast; the Guans, on the plains of the Volta River; the Ga- and Ewe-speaking peoples of the south and southeast; and the Moshi-Dagomba-speaking tribes of the northern and upper regions. English, the official and commercial language, is taught in all the schools.

Drying groundnuts and other grains, Fihini Village, Ghana.

Photo credit: Corel Corporation.

Primary and junior secondary school education is tuition-free and mandatory. The Government of Ghana support for basic education is unequivocal. Article 39 of the Constitution mandates the major tenets of the free, compulsory, universal basic education (FCUBE) initiative. Launched in 1996, it is one of the most ambitious pre-tertiary education programs in West Africa. Since 1987, the Government of Ghana has increased its education budget by 700%. Basic education's share has grown from 45% to 60% of that total.

Students begin their 6-year primary education at age six. Under educational reforms implemented in 1987, they pass into a junior secondary school system for 3 years of academic training combined with technical and vocational training. Those continuing move into the 3-year senior secondary school program. Entrance to one of the five Ghanaian universities is by examination following completion of senior secondary school. School enrollment totals almost 3 million.

# HISTORY

The history of the Gold Coast before the last quarter of the 15th century is derived primarily from oral tradition that refers to migrations from the ancient kingdoms of the western Soudan (the area of Mauritania and Mali). The Gold Coast was renamed Ghana upon independence in 1957 because of indications that present-day inhabitants descended from migrants who moved south from the ancient kingdom of Ghana.

The first contact between Europe and the Gold Coast dates from 1470, when a party of Portuguese landed. In 1482, the Portuguese built Elmina Castle as a permanent trading base. The first recorded English trading voyage to the coast was made by Thomas Windham in 1553. During the next three centuries, the English, Danes, Dutch, Germans, and Portuguese controlled various parts of the coastal areas.

In 1821, the British Government took control of the British trading forts on the Gold Coast. In 1844, Fanti chiefs in the area signed an agreement with the British that became the legal steppingstone to colonial status for the coastal area.

From 1826 to 1900, the British fought a series of campaigns against the Ashantis, whose kingdom was located inland. In 1902, they succeeded in establishing firm control over the Ashanti region and making the northern territories a protectorate. British Togoland, the fourth territorial element eventually to form the nation, was part of a former German colony administered by the United Kingdom from Accra as a League of Nations mandate after 1922. In December 1946, British Togoland became a UN Trust Territory, and in 1957, following a 1956 plebiscite, the United Nations agreed that the territory would become part of Ghana when the Gold Coast achieved independence.

The four territorial divisions were administered separately until 1946, when the British Government ruled them as a single unit. In 1951, a constitution was promulgated that called for a greatly enlarged legislature composed principally of members elected by popular vote directly or indirectly. An executive council was responsible for formulating policy, with most African members drawn from the legislature and including three ex officio members appointed by the governor. A new constitution, approved on April 29, 1954, established a cabinet comprising African ministers drawn from an all-African legislature chosen by direct election. In the elections that followed, the Convention People's Party (CPP), led by Kwame Nkrumah, won the majority of seats in the new Legislative Assembly. In May 1956, Prime Minister Nkrumah's Gold Coast government issued a white paper containing proposals for Gold Coast independence. The British Government stated it would agree to a firm date for independence if a reasonable majority for such a step were obtained in the Gold Coast Legislative Assembly after a general election. This election, held in 1956, returned the CPP to power with 71 of the 104 seats in the Legislative Assembly. Ghana became an independent state on March 6, 1957, when the United Kingdom relinquished its control over the Colony of the Gold Coast and Ashanti, the Northern Territories Protectorate, and British Togoland.

In subsequent reorganizations, the country was divided into 10 regions, which currently are subdivided into 110 districts. The original Gold Coast Colony now comprises the Western, Central, Eastern, and Greater Accra Regions, with a small portion at the mouth of the Volta River assigned to the Volta Region; the Ashanti area was divided into the Ashanti and Brong-Ahafo Regions; the Northern Territories into the Northern, Upper East, and Upper West Regions; and British Togoland essentially is the same area as the Volta Region.

## Post-Independence Politics

After independence, the CPP government under Nkrumah sought to develop Ghana as a modern, semi-industrialized, unitary socialist state. The government emphasized political and economic organization, endeavoring to increase stability and productivity through labor, youth, farmers, cooperatives, and other organizations integrated with the CPP. The government, according to Nkrumah, acted only as "the agent of the CPP" in seeking to accomplish these goals.

The CPP's control was challenged and criticized, and Prime Minister Nkrumah used the Preventive Detention Act (1958), which provided for detention without trial for up to 5 years (later extended to 10 years). On July 1, 1960, a new constitution was adopted, changing Ghana from a parliamentary system with a prime minister to a republican form of government headed by a powerful president. In August 1960, Nkrumah was given authority to scrutinize newspapers and other publications before publication. This political evolution continued into early 1964, when a constitutional referendum changed the country to a one-party state.

On February 24, 1966, the Ghanaian Army and police overthrew Nkrumah's regime. Nkrumah and all his ministers were dismissed, the CPP and National Assembly were dissolved, and the constitution was suspended. The new regime cited

Nkrumah's flagrant abuse of individual rights and liberties, his regime's corrupt, oppressive, and dictatorial practices, and the rapidly deteriorating economy as the principal reasons for its action.

## Post-Nkrumah Politics

The leaders of the February 24 coup established the new government around the National Liberation Council (NLC) and pledged an early return to a duly constituted civilian government. Members of the judiciary and civil service remained at their posts and committees of civil servants were established to handle the administration of the country.

Ghana's government returned to civilian authority under the Second Republic in October 1969 after a parliamentary election in which the Progress Party, led by Kofi A. Busia, won 105 of the 140 seats. Until mid-1970, the powers of the chief of state were held by a presidential commission led by Brigadier A.A. Afrifa. In a special election on August 31, 1970, former Chief Justice Edward Akufo-Addo was chosen president, and Dr. Busia became prime minister.

Faced with mounting economic problems, Prime Minister Busia's government undertook a drastic devaluation of the currency in December 1971. The government's inability to control the subsequent inflationary pressures stimulated further discontent, and military officers seized power in a bloodless coup on January 13, 1972.

The coup leaders, led by Col. I.K. Acheampong, formed the National Redemption Council (NRC) to which they admitted other officers, the head of the police, and one civilian. The NRC promised improvements in the quality of life for all Ghanaians and based its programs on nationalism, economic development, and self-reliance. In 1975, a government reorganization resulted in the NRC's replacement by the Supreme Military Council (SMC), also headed by now-General Acheampong.

Unable to deliver on its promises, the NRC/SMC became increasingly

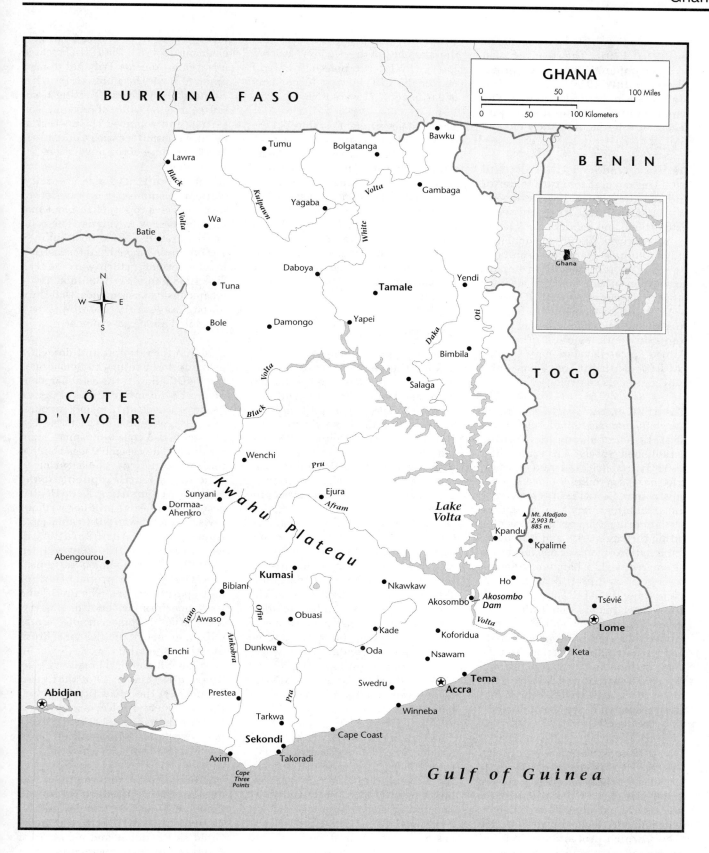

marked by mismanagement and rampant corruption. In 1977, General Acheampong brought forward the concept of union government (UNIGOV), which would make Ghana a non-party state. Perceiving this as a ploy by Acheampong to retain power, professional groups and students launched strikes and demonstrations against the government in 1977 and 1978. The steady erosion in Acheampong's power led to his arrest in July 1978 by his chief of staff, Lt. Gen. Frederick Akuffo, who replaced him as head of state and leader of what became known as the SMC-2.

Akuffo abandoned UNIGOV and established a plan to return to constitutional and democratic government. A Constitutional Assembly was established, and political party activity was revived. Akuffo was unable to solve Ghana's economic problems, however, or to reduce the rampant corruption in which senior military officers played a major role. On June 4, 1979, his government was deposed in a violent coup by a group of junior and non-commissioned officers—Armed Forces Revolutionary Council (AFRC)—with Flt. Lt. Jerry John Rawlings as its chairman.

The AFRC executed eight senior military officers, including former chiefs of state Acheampong and Akuffo; established Special Tribunals that, secretly and without due process, tried dozens of military officers, other government officials, and private individuals for corruption, sentencing them to long prison terms and confiscating their property; and, through a combination of force and exhortation, attempted to rid Ghanaian society of corruption and profiteering. At the same time, the AFRC accepted, with a few amendments, the draft constitution that had been submitted, permitted the scheduled presidential and parliamentary elections to take place in June and July, promulgated the constitution, and handed over power to the newly elected president and parliament of the Third Republic on September 24, 1979.

The 1979 constitution was modeled on those of Western democracies. It provided for the separation of powers among an elected president and a unicameral parliament, an independent judiciary headed by a Supreme Court, which protected individual rights, and other autonomous institutions, such as the Electoral Commissioner and the Ombudsman. The new president, Dr. Hilla Limann, was a

career diplomat from the north and the candidate of the People's National Party (PNP), the political heir of Nkrumah's CPP. Of the 140 members of parliament, 71 were PNP.

The PNP government established the constitutional institutions and generally respected democracy and individual human rights. It failed, however, to halt the continuing decline in the economy; corruption flourished, and the gap between rich and poor widened. On December 31, 1981, Flight Lt. Rawlings and a small group of enlisted and former soldiers launched a coup that succeeded against little opposition in toppling President Limann.

## The PNDC Era

Rawlings and his colleagues suspended the 1979 constitution, dismissed the president and his cabinet, dissolved the parliament, and proscribed existing political parties. They established the Provisional National Defense Council (PNDC), initially composed of seven members with Rawlings as chairman, to exercise executive and legislative powers. The existing judicial system was preserved, but alongside it the PNDC created the National Investigation Committee to root out corruption and other economic offenses, the anonymous Citizens' Vetting Committee to punish tax evasion, and the Public Tribunals to try various crimes. The PNDC proclaimed its intent to allow the people to exercise political power through defense committees to be established in communities, workplaces, and in units of the armed forces and police. Under the PNDC, Ghana remained a unitary government.

In December 1982, the PNDC announced a plan to decentralize government from Accra to the regions, the districts, and local communities, but it maintained overall control by appointing regional and district secretaries who exercised executive powers and also chaired regional and district councils. Local councils, however, were expected progressively to take over the payment of salaries, with regions and districts assuming

more powers from the national government. In 1984, the PNDC created a National Appeals Tribunal to hear appeals from the public tribunals, changed the Citizens' Vetting Committee into the Office of Revenue Collection and replaced the system of defense committees with Committees for the Defense of the Revolution.

In 1984, the PNDC also created a National Commission on Democracy to study ways to establish participatory democracy in Ghana. The commission issued a "Blue Book" in July 1987 outlining modalities for district-level elections, which were held in late 1988 and early 1989, for newly created district assemblies. One-third of the assembly members are appointed by the government.

Under international and domestic pressure for a return to democracy, the PNDC allowed the establishment of a 258-member Consultative Assembly made up of members representing geographic districts as well as established civic or business organizations. The assembly was charged to draw up a draft constitution to establish a fourth republic, using PNDC proposals. The PNDC accepted the final product without revision, and it was put to a national referendum on April 28, 1992, in which it received 92% approval. On May 18, 1992, the ban on party politics was lifted in preparation for multi-party elections. The PNDC and its supporters formed a new party, the National Democratic Congress (NDC), to contest the elections. Presidential elections were held on November 3 and parliamentary elections on December 29 of that year. Members of the opposition boycotted the parliamentary elections, however, which resulted in a 200 seat Parliament with only 17 opposition party members and two independents.

The Constitution entered into force on January 7, 1993, to found the Fourth Republic. On that day, Flt. Lt. Jerry John Rawlings was inaugurated as President and members of Parliament swore their oaths of office. In 1996, the opposition fully contested the presidential and parliamentary elections, which were described as peaceful, free, and transparent by domestic and international observers. In that election, President Rawlings was re-elected with 57% of the popular vote. In addition, Rawlings' NDC party won 133 of the Parliament's 200 seats, just one seat short of the two-thirds majority needed to amend the Constitution, although the election returns of two parliamentary seats face legal challenges.

# GOVERNMENT

The Constitution that established the Fourth Republic provided a basic charter for republican democratic government. It declares Ghana to be a unitary republic with sovereignty residing in the Ghanaian people. Intended to prevent future coups, dictatorial government, and one-party states, it is designed to establish the concept of powersharing. The document reflects lessons learned from the abrogated constitutions of the 1957, 1960, 1969, and 1979, and incorporates provisions and institutions drawn from British and American constitutional models. One controversial provision of the Constitution indemnifies members and appointees of the PNDC from liability for any official act or omission during the years of PNDC rule. The Constitution calls for a system of checks and balances, with power shared between a president, a unicameral parliament, a council of state, and an independent judiciary.

Executive authority is established in the Office of the Presidency, together with his Council of State. The president is head of state, head of government, and commander in chief of the armed forces. He also appoints the vice president. According to the Constitution, more than half of the presidentially appointed ministers of state must be appointed from among members of Parliament.

Legislative functions are vested in Parliament, which consists of a unicameral 200-member body plus the Speaker. To become law, legislation must have the assent of the presi-

dent, who has a qualified veto over all bills except those to which a vote of urgency is attached. Members of Parliament are popularly elected by universal adult suffrage for terms of four years, except in war time, when terms may be extended for not more than 12 months at a time beyond the four years.

The structure and the power of the judiciary are independent of the two other branches of government. The Supreme Court has broad powers of judicial review. It is authorized by the Constitution to rule on the constitutionality of any legislation or executive action at the request of any aggrieved citizen. The hierarchy of courts derives largely from British juridical forms. The hierarchy, called the Superior Court of Judicature, is composed of the Supreme Court of Ghana, the Court of Appeal, the High Court of Justice, regional tribunals, and such lower courts or tribunals as Parliament may establish. The courts have jurisdiction over all civil and criminal matters.

## Principal Government Officials

For up-to-date information on Principal Government Officials, see the Chiefs of State and Cabinet Members of Foreign Governments section starting on page 1.

Ghana maintains an embassy in the United States at 3512 International Drive, NW., Washington, D.C. 20008 (tel. 202-686-4500). Its permanent mission to the United Nations is located at 19 E. 47th Street., New York, N.Y. 10017 (tel. 212-832-1300).

# ECONOMY

By West African standards, Ghana has a diverse and rich resource base. The country is mainly agricultural, however, with a majority of its workers engaged in farming. Cash crops consist primarily of cocoa and cocoa products, which typically provide

about two-thirds of export revenues, timber products, coconuts and other palm products, shea nuts, which produce an edible fat, and coffee. Ghana also has established a successful program of nontraditional agricultural products for export, including pineapples, cashews, and pepper. Cassava, yams, plantains, corn, rice, peanuts, millet, and sorghum are the basic foodstuffs. Fish, poultry, and meat also are important dietary staples.

Minerals—principally gold, diamonds, manganese ore, and bauxite—are produced and exported. The only commercial oil well has been closed after producing 3.5 million barrels over its seven-year life, but signs of natural gas are being studied for power generation, while exploration continues for other oil and gas resources.

Ghana's industrial base is relatively advanced compared to many other African countries. Import-substitution industries include textiles; steel (using scrap); tires; oil refining; flour milling; beverages; tobacco; simple consumer goods; and car, truck, and bus assembly.

Tourism has become one of Ghana's largest foreign income earners (ranking third in 1997), and the Ghanaian Government has placed great emphasis upon further tourism support and development.

## Economic Development

At independence, Ghana had a substantial physical and social infrastructure and $481 million in foreign reserves. The Nkrumah government further developed the infrastructure and made important public investments in the industrial sector. With assistance from the United States, the World Bank, and the United Kingdom, construction of the Akosombo Dam was completed on the Volta River in 1966. Two U.S. companies built Valco, Africa's largest aluminum smelter, to use power generated at the dam. Aluminum exports from Valco are a major source of foreign exchange for Ghana.

Many Nkrumah-era investments were monumental public works projects and poorly conceived, badly managed agricultural and industrial schemes. With cocoa prices falling and the country's foreign exchange reserves fast disappearing, the government resorted to supplier credits to finance many projects. By the mid-1960s, Ghana's reserves were gone, and the country could not meet repayment schedules. To rationalize, the National Liberation Council abandoned unprofitable projects, and some inefficient state-owned enterprises were sold to private investors. On three occasions, Ghana's creditors agreed to reschedule repayments due on Nkrumah-era supplier credits. Led by the United States, foreign donors provided import loans to enable the foreign exchange-strapped government to import essential commodities.

Prime Minister Busia's government (1969-72) liberalized controls to attract foreign investment and to encourage domestic entrepreneurship. Investors were cautious, however, and cocoa prices began declining again while imports surged, precipitating a serious trade deficit. Despite considerable foreign assistance and some debt relief, the Busia regime also was unable to overcome the inherited restraints on growth posed by the debt burden, balance-of-payments imbalances, foreign exchange shortages, and mismanagement.

Although foreign aid helped prevent economic collapse and was responsible for subsequent improvements in many sectors, the economy stagnated in the 10-year period preceding the NRC takeover in 1972. Population growth offset the modest increase in gross domestic product, and real earnings declined for many Ghanaians.

To restructure the economy, the NRC, under General Acheampong (1972-78), undertook an austerity program that emphasized self-reliance, particularly in food production. These plans were not realized, however, primarily because of post-1973 oil price increases and a drought in 1975-77 that particularly affected northern Ghana. The NRC, which had inherited foreign debts of almost $1 billion, abrogated existing rescheduling arrangements for some debts and rejected other repayments. After creditors objected to this unilateral action, a 1974 agreement rescheduled the medium-term debt on liberal terms. The NRC also imposed the Investment Policy Decree of 1975—effective on January 1977—that required 51% Ghanaian equity participation in most foreign firms, but the government took 40% in specified industries. Many shares were sold directly to the public.

Continued mismanagement of the economy, record inflation (more than 100% in 1977), and increasing corruption, notably at the highest political levels, led to growing dissatisfaction. The post-July 1978 military regime led by General Akuffo attempted to deal with Ghana's economic problems by making small changes in the overvalued cedi and by restraining government spending and monetary growth. Under a one-year standby agreement with the International Monetary Fund (IMF) in January 1979, the government promised to undertake economic reforms, including a reduction of the budget deficit, in return for a $68 million IMF support program and $27 million in IMF Trust Fund loans. The agreement became inoperative, however, after the June 4 coup that brought Flight Lieutenant Rawlings and the AFRC to power for 4 months.

In September 1979, the civilian government of Hilla Limann inherited declining per capita income; stagnant industrial and agricultural production due to inadequate imported supplies; shortages of imported and locally produced goods; a sizable budget deficit (almost 40% of expenditures in 1979); high inflation, "moderating" to 54% in 1979; an increasingly overvalued cedi; flourishing smuggling and other black-market activities; unemployment and underemployment, particularly among urban youth; deterioration in the transport network; and continued foreign exchange constraints.

Limann's PNP government announced yet another (2-year) reconstruction program, emphasizing increased food production and productivity, exports, and transport improvements. Import austerity was imposed and external payments arrears cut. However, declining cocoa production combined with falling cocoa prices, while oil prices soared. No effective measures were taken to reduce rampant corruption and black marketing.

When Rawlings again seized power at the end of 1981, cocoa output had fallen to half the 1970-71 level and its world price to one-third the 1975 level. By 1982, oil would constitute half of Ghana's imports, while overall trade contracted greatly. Internal transport had slowed to a crawl, and inflation remained high. During Rawlings' first year, the economy was stagnant. Industry ran at about 10% of capacity due to the chronic shortage of foreign exchange to cover the importation of required raw materials and replacement parts. Economic conditions deteriorated further in early 1983 when Nigeria expelled an estimated 1 million Ghanaians who had to be absorbed by Ghana.

In April 1983, in coordination with the IMF, the PNDC launched an economic recovery program, perhaps the most stringent and consistent of its day in Africa, aimed at reopening infrastructural bottlenecks and reviving moribund productive sectors—agriculture, mining, and timber. The largely distorted exchange rate and prices were realigned to encourage production and exports. Increased fiscal and monetary discipline was imposed to curb inflation and to focus on priorities. Through November 1987, the cedi was devalued by more than 6,300%, and widespread direct price controls were substantially reduced.

The economy's response to these reforms was initially hampered by the absorption of one million returnees from Nigeria, the onset of the worst drought since independence, which brought on widespread bushfires and forced closure of the aluminum smelter and severe power cuts for industry and decline in foreign aid. In 1985, the country absorbed an additional 100,000 expellees from Nigeria. In 1987, cocoa prices began declining again; however, initial infrastructural repairs, improved weather, and producer incentives and support revived output in the early 1990s. During 1984-88 the economy experienced solid growth for the first time since 1978. Renewed exports, aid inflows, and a foreign exchange auction have eased hard currency constraints.

Since an initial August 1983 IMF standby agreement, the economic recovery program has been supported by three IMF standbys and two other credits totaling $611 million, $1.1 billion from the World Bank, and hundreds of millions of dollars more from other donors. In November 1987, the IMF approved a $318-million, 3-year extended fund facility. The second phase (1987-90) of the recovery program concentrated on economic restructuring and revitalizing social services. The third phase, focused on financial transparency and macroeconomic stability is scheduled for March 1998.

Ghana intends to achieve its goals of accelerated economic growth, improved quality of life for all Ghanaians, and reduced poverty through macroeconomic stability, higher private investment, broad-based social and rural development, as well as direct poverty-alleviation efforts. These plans are fully supported by the international donor community and have been forcefully reiterated in the 1995 government report, Ghana: Vision 2020. Privatization of state-owned enterprises continues, with about two-thirds of 300 parastatal enterprises sold to private owners. Other reforms adopted under the government's structural adjustment program include the elimination of exchange rate controls and the lifting of virtually all restrictions on imports. The establishment of an interbank foreign exchange market has greatly expanded access to foreign exchange.

The medium-term macroeconomic forecast assumes political stability,

## Travel Notes

**Travel Advice:** For up-to-date information from the U.S. State Department on possible inconvenient or hazardous situations, see the **Travel Warnings and Consular Information Sheets from the U.S. Government** section starting on page 1723. For the latest information on health requirements and conditions, see the **International Travelers' Health Information** section starting on page 1385. For further information dealing with non-urgent matter, see the **Tips for Travelers to...** section starting on page 1588.

successful economic stabilization, and the implementation of a policy agenda for private sector growth, and adequate public spending on social services and rural infrastructure. The ninth Consultative Group Meeting for Ghana ended November 5, 1997 after deliberations in Paris. Twenty-four countries and donor entities were represented at this meeting called by the World Bank on behalf of the Ghanaian Government. The World Bank announced that, of the targeted disbursement level of $1.6 billion sought from the donor community for 1998-99, they foresaw only a $150 million shortfall in commitments, and that this shortfall would be easily realized should Ghana rapidly enact its macroeconomic program.

The government repealed a 17.% value-added tax (VAT) shortly after its introduction in 1995, which resulted in wide-spread public protests. The government reverted to several previously imposed taxes, including a sales tax. The government has set in motion a program to reintroduce a VAT bill, with implementation in 1998 after an extensive public education campaign.

## FOREIGN RELATIONS

Ghana is active in the United Nations and many of its specialized agencies (including the World Trade Organization), the Nonaligned Movement, the Organization of African Unity (OAU), and the Economic Community of

West African States. Generally, it follows the consensus of the Nonaligned Movement and the OAU on economic and political issues not directly affecting its own interests. Ghana has been extremely active in international peacekeeping activities under UN auspices in Lebanon, Afghanistan, Rwanda, the Balkans, and Pakistan, in addition to an eight-year subregional initiative with its ECOWAS partners to develop and then enforce a cease-fire in Liberia. Ghana maintains friendly relations with all states, regardless of ideology.

## U.S.-GHANAIAN RELATIONS

The United States has enjoyed good relations with Ghana at the nonofficial, personal level since Ghana's independence. Thousands of Ghanaians have been educated in the United States. Close relations are maintained between educational and scientific institutions, and cultural links, particularly between Ghanaians and African-Americans, are strong.

After a period of strained relations in the mid-1980s, U.S.-Ghanaian official relations are stronger than at any other time in recent memory. Ghanaian parliamentarians and other government officials have through the U.S. International Visitor Program acquainted themselves with U.S. Congressional and state legislative practices and participated in programs designed to address other issues of interest. The U.S. and Ghanaian militaries have cooperated in numerous joint training exercises, culminating with Ghanaian participation in the African Crisis Response Initiative, an international activity in which the U.S. is facilitating the development of an interoperable peacekeeping capacity among African nations. In addition, there is an active bilateral international military and educational training program. The Office of the President of Ghana worked closely with the U.S. Embassy in Accra to establish an American Chamber of Commerce to continue to develop closer economic ties in the private sector.

The United States is among Ghana's principal trading partners. The American privately owned VALCO aluminum smelter imports many of its supplies from, and exports almost all the aluminum ingots to, the United States. With a replacement value of more than $600 million, U.S. investments in Ghana form one of the largest stocks of foreign capital. VALCO—90% owned by Kaiser, and 10% by Reynolds—is by far the biggest investment, but other important U.S. companies operating in the country include Mobil, Coca Cola, S.C. Johnson, Ralston Purina, Star-Kist, A.H. Robins, Sterling, Pfizer, IBM, Carson Products, 3M, Pioneer Gold, Stewart & Stevenson, Price Waterhouse, Great Lakes Shipping, and National Cash Register (NCR). Several U.S. firms recently made or are considering investments in Ghana, primarily in gold mining, wood products, and petroleum. In late 1997, Nuevo Petroleum concluded an oil exploration agreement accounting for the last of Ghana's offshore mineral rights zones. Two other U.S. oil companies, Sante Fe and Hunt, are also engaged in offshore exploration.

## Principal U.S. Officials

**For up-to-date information on Principal U.S. Officials, see the U.S. Embassies, Consulates, and Foreign Service section starting on page 139.**

U.S. development assistance to Ghana in fiscal year 1997 totaled $52 million, divided between small business enterprise, health, education, and democracy/governance programs. Ghana was the first country in the world to accept Peace Corps volunteers, and the program remains one of the largest. Currently, there are more than 150 volunteers in Ghana. Almost half work in education, and the others in various fields such as agroforestry, small business development, health education and water sanitation, as well as youth development.

The U.S. Embassy is located on Ring Road East, near Danquah Circle, Accra (tel. 233-21-775347/8/9). The mailing address is P.O. Box 194, Accra, Ghana. For American citizen services and visa questions, the Embassy Consular Section telephone number is 233-21-776602.

# GREECE

October 1999

## Official Name:
## Hellenic Republic

# PROFILE

## Geography

**Area:** 131,957 sq. km. (51,146 sq. mi.; roughly the size of Alabama).
**Major cities:** Capital—Athen (pop. greater Athens 3,096,775, municipality of Athens 748,110). Other cities—Thessaloniki (377,951), Piraeus (169,622), Greater Piraeus (880,529), Patras (172,763), Larissa (113,426), Iraklion (117,167).
**Terrain:** Mountainous interior with coastal plains; many islands.
**Climate:** Mediterranean; mild winter and hot, dry summer.

## People

**Population:** 11.5 million.
**Growth rate:** 0.4%.
**Languages:** Greek 99%; other 1%.
**Religions:** Greek Orthodox 98%, Muslim 1%, other 1%.
**Education:** Years compulsory—9. Literacy—93%. All levels are free.
**Health:** Infant mortality rate—8/1,000. Life expectancy—male 74 yrs.; female 79 yrs.
**Work force:** 4.85 million.

## Government

**Type:** Presidential parliamentary republic.
**Independence:** 1830.

**Constitution:** June 11, 1975, amended March 1986.
**Branches:** Executive—president (head of state), prime minister (head of government). Legislative—300–seat unicameral Vouli (parliament). Judicial—Supreme Court.
**Political parties:** Panhellenic Socialist Movement (PASOK), New Democracy (ND), Political Spring, Communist Party of Greece (KKE), Coalition of the Left (SYNASPIS-MOS).
**Suffrage:** Universal at 18.
**Administrative subdivisions:** 13 peripheries (regional districts), 51 nomi (prefectures).

## Economy (1998)

**GDP:** $120.25 billion.
**Per capita GDP:** $11,305.
**Growth rate:** 3.5%.
**Inflation rate:** 4.7%.
**Unemployment rate:** 10.1%.
**Natural resources:** Bauxite, lignite, magnesite, oil, marble.
**Agriculture (10% of GDP):** Products—Sugar, beets, wheat, maize, tomatoes, olives, olive oil, grapes, raisins, wine, oranges, peaches, tobacco, cotton, livestock, dairy products.
**Manufacturing (14% of GDP):** Types—Processed foods, shoes, textiles, metals, chemicals, electrical equipment, cement, glass, transport equipment, petroleum products, construction, electrical power.
**Services (66.5% of GDP):** Trans-

portation, tourism, communications, trade, banking, public administration, defense.

**Trade:** Exports—$10.5 billion: manufactured goods, food and beverages, petroleum products, cement, chemicals. Major markets—Germany, Italy, France, U.S., U.K. Imports—$27 billion: basic manufactures, food and animals, crude oil, chemicals, machinery, transport equipment. Major suppliers—Germany, Italy, France, Japan, Netherlands, U.S.

# GEOGRAPHY

Greece is located in southeastern Europe on the southern tip of the Balkan Peninsula. The Greek mainland is bounded on the north by Bulgaria, The Former Yugoslav Republic of Macedonia, and Albania; on the east by the Aegean Sea and Turkey; and on the west and south by the Ionian and Mediterranean Seas. The country consists of a large mainland; the Peloponnesus Peninsula, connected to the mainland by the Isthmus of Corinth; and more than 1,400 islands, including Crete, Rhodes, Corfu, and the Dodecanese and Cycladic groups. Greece has more than 14,880 kilometers (9,300 mi.) of coastline and a land boundary of 1,160 kilometers (726 mi.).

About 80% of Greece is mountainous or hilly. Much of the country is dry and rocky; only 28% of the land is arable. Greece has mild, wet winters and hot, dry summers. Temperatures are rarely extreme, although snowfalls do occur in the mountains and occasionally even in Athens in the winter.

Greece is located at the junction of three continents: Europe, Asia, and Africa. Greece's foreign policy, despite its joining NATO in 1952 and its accession to the European Community in 1981, has remained focused on the Balkans and the eastern Mediterranean region.

Greece maintains full diplomatic, political, and economic relations with its south–central European neighbors. It provided a 250–man military contingent to IFOR/ SFOR in Bosnia and assigned a 1,200–man unit to KFOR in Kosovo. Diplomatic relations with Bulgaria were restored in 1965—after a 24–year break—when Bulgaria renounced its claim to Greek territory in Thrace and Macedonia. Since the breakup of the Soviet Union, Greece has had good relations with Russia and has opened embassies in a number of the former Soviet republics, which it sees as potentially important trading partners.

# PEOPLE

Greece was inhabited as early as the Paleolithic period and by 3000 BC had become home, in the Cycladic Islands, to a culture whose art remains among the most evocative in world history. Early in the 2nd millennium BC, the island of Crete nurtured the sophisticated maritime empire of the Minoans, whose trade reached from Egypt to Sicily. The Minoans were challenged and eventually supplanted by the Mycenaeans of the Greek mainland, who spoke a dialect of ancient Greek. Initially, Greece's mosaic of small city–states were ethnically similar. During the Roman, Byzantine, and Ottoman Empires (1st–19th centuries), Greece's ethnic composition became more diverse. Since independence in

1830 and an exchange of populations with Turkey in 1923, Greece has forged a national state which claims roots reaching back 3,000 years.

The Greek language dates back at least 3,500 years, and modern Greek preserves many elements of its classical predecessor. In the 19th century, after Greece's War of Independence, an effort was made to rid the language of Turkish and Arabic words and expressions. The resulting version was considered to be closer to the classical Greek language of Homer and was called Katharevousa. However, Katharevousa was never adopted by most Greeks in daily speech. The commonly spoken language, called Demotiki, became the official language in 1976.

Greek education is free and compulsory for children between the ages of 5 and 15. English language study is compulsory from 5th grade through high school. University education, including books, is also free, contingent upon the student's ability to meet stiff entrance requirements. Recent statistics indicate progressively poorer results in the annual entrance examinations. Low salaries and status of teachers; lack of books, supplies, labs, and computers; frequent strikes; and continuing reliance on rote memorization methods are all matters of concern for Greek educators.

A high percentage of the student population seeks higher education. About 100,000 students are registered at Greek universities, and 15% of the population currently holds a university degree. Entrance to a university is determined by state–administered exams, the candidate's grade–point average from high school, and his/her priority choices of major. About one in four candidates gains admission to Greek universities.

Since Greek law does not permit the operation of private universities in Greece, a large and growing number of students are pursuing higher education abroad. The Greek Government decides through an evaluation procedure whether to recognize

degrees from specific foreign universities as qualification for public sector hiring. Other students attend private, post–secondary educational institutions in Greece that are not recognized by the Greek Government.

The number of Greek students studying at European institutions is increasing along with EU support for educational exchange. In addition, nearly 5,000 Greeks are studying in the United States, about half of whom are in graduate school. Greek per capita student representation in the U.S. is the highest of any European country.

Orthodox Christianity is the dominant religion in Greece. During the centuries of Ottoman domination, the Greek Orthodox Church preserved Greek language, values, and national identity and was an important rallying point in the struggle for independence. There is a Muslim minority concentrated in Thrace. Other religious communities in Greece include Catholics, Jews, Old Calendar Orthodox, Jehovah's Witnesses, Mormons, and Protestants.

# HISTORY

The Greek War of Independence from the Ottoman Empire began in 1821 and concluded with the winning of independence in 1830. With the support of England, France, and Russia, a monarchy was established. A Bavarian prince, Otto, was named king in 1833. He was deposed 30 years later, and the Great Powers chose a prince of the Danish House of Glucksberg as his successor. He became George I, King of the Hellenes.

The Megali Idea (Great Idea), a vision of uniting all Greeks of the declining Ottoman Empire within the newly independent Greek State, exerted strong influence on the early Greek state. At independence, Greece had an area of 47,515 square kilometers (18,346 square mi.), and its northern boundary extended from the Gulf of Volos to the Gulf of Arta. The Ionian Islands were added in 1864;

### GREECE

| | | | | |
|---|---|---|---|---|
| 0 | 25 | 50 | 75 | 100 Miles |
| 0 | 25 | 50 | 75 | 100 Kilometers |

BULGARIA

Black Sea

MACEDONIA

*Ohridsko Jezero*

*Prespansko Jezero*

RHODOPE MTS.

Serrai · Dráma · Xánthi · Souflíon ·

*Struma*

ALBANIA

Flórina · Giannitsá

Kilkís ·

Kavála · Alexandroúpolis ·

*Marmara Denizi*

*Axios*

Borovë · Véroia

*ÓROS GRÁMMOS*

Thessaloníki

*Thásos*

*Samothráki*

Libohovë · Kozáni ·

*Chalkidhikí Peninsula*

Çanakkale ·

Kateríni ·

*Aliákman*

*Thermaïkós Kólpos*

*Áthos 6,670 ft. 2033 m.*

*PINDUS*

▲ *Óros Ólimbos 9,570 ft. 2917 m.*

Koufós ·

Myrina · *Límnos*

Burhaniye ·

Kérkyra · Ioánnina

Tríkala · Lárisa

Sklíthron ·

*Corfu*

Párga

*Akhelóös*

Vólos ·

*Pélagos*

*Lésvos*

TURKEY

*Paxoí*

Árta

*MTS.*

Áno Vasiliká ·

*Skópelos*

Vrissá ·

Prévaza

Pálairos ·

Halus ■

Lamía ·

Strofyliá ·

*Skíros*

▲ *Timfristós 7,595 ft. 2315 m.*

*Levkás*

Agrínion · Mólos ·

*ÉVVOIA*

Izmir ·

*Lúmní Trikonís*

Delphi ■ Thebes · Khalkís ·

*Chíos*

*Kefallinía* *Itháki*

*Ákra Áraxos*

*Korinthiakós Kólpos*

Pátrai

Mégara ·

Athens ☆

*Ákra Kafirévs*

*Ionian Sea*

Chionáta ·

PELOPONNESUS

Peiraiéfs ·

*Ándros*

*Sámos*

*Zákinthos*

Olympia ■

Kórinthos ·

Náfplion ·

*Tínos*

*Ikaría*

*SPORADES*

Katákolon ·

Árgos

Galatás ·

▲ *Likaion Óros 4,662 ft. 1421 m.*

Trípolis ·

*Ydra*

KYKLÁDES

*Mýkonos*

Filiatrá ·

*Alfiós*

*Spetsopoúla*

*Náxos*

*Kos*

Kalámai ·

Spárti ·

*PÁRNON ÓROS*

*Páros*

*TAÏYETOS ÓROS*

Pylos ■

Moláoi ·

DODEKANISOS

Ródhos ·

*Schíza*

*Messiniakós Kólpos*

*Ákra Taínaron*

*Lakonikós Kólpos*

Neápolis ·

*Ródhos*

Mitáta · *Kíthira*

Apolakkiá ·

*Sea of Crete*

*Karpathos*

*Ákra Voúxa*

Chaniá ·

Pánormos ·

Irâklion ·

*Ákra Sídheros*

Kámbos ·

Elyrus ■

Cnossus ■

Zákros ·

*Ákra Kriós*

*CRETE*

Myrtos ·

MEDITERRANEAN SEA

Chóra Sfakion ·

*Ákra Lithínon*

*Gávdos*

*Greece*

Thessaly and part of Epirus in 1881; Macedonia, Crete, Epirus, and the Aegean Islands in 1913; Western Thrace in 1918; and the Dodecanese Islands in 1947.

Greece entered World War I in 1917 on the side of the Allies. After the war, Greece took part in the Allied occupation of Turkey, where many Greeks still lived. In 1921, the Greek army attacked from its base in Smyrna (now Izmir), and marched toward Ankara. The Greeks were defeated by Turkish forces led by Mustafa Kemal (later Ataturk) and were forced to withdraw in the summer of 1922. Smyrna was sacked by the Turks, and more than 1.3 million Greek refugees from Turkey poured into Greece, creating enormous challenges for the Greek economy and society and effectively ending the Megali Idea.

Greek politics, particularly between the two World Wars, involved a struggle for power between monarchists and republicans. Greece was proclaimed a republic in 1924, but

George II returned to the throne in 1935, and a plebiscite in 1946 upheld the monarchy. It was finally abolished, however, by referendum on December 8, 1974, when more than two–thirds of the voters supported the establishment of a republic.

Greece's entry into World War II was precipitated by the Italian invasion on October 28, 1940. That date is celebrated in Greece by the one–word reply—ochi ("no")—symbolizing the Greek Prime Minister's rejection of the surrender demand made by Mussolini. Despite Italian superiority in numbers and equipment, determined Greek defenders drove the invaders back into Albania. Hitler was forced to divert German troops to protect his southern flank and attacked Greece in early April 1941. By the end of May, the Germans had overrun most of the country, although Greek resistance was never entirely suppressed. German forces withdrew in October 1944, and the government in exile returned to Athens.

After the German withdrawal, the principal Greek resistance movement, which was controlled by the communists, refused to disarm. A banned demonstration by resistance forces in Athens in December 1944 ended in violence and was followed by an intense, house–to–house battle with Greek Government and British forces. After 3 weeks, the communists were defeated, and an unstable coalition government was formed. Continuing tensions led to the dissolution of that government and the outbreak of full–fledged civil war in 1946. First the United Kingdom and later the United States gave extensive military and economic aid to the Greek Government.

Communist successes in 1947–48 enabled them to move freely over much of mainland Greece, but with extensive reorganization and American material support, the Greek National Army was slowly able to regain control over most of the countryside. Yugoslavia closed its borders to the insurgent forces in 1949, after Marshal Tito of Yugoslavia broke with Stalin and the Soviet Union.

In August 1949, the National Army under Marshal Alexander Papagos launched a final offensive that forced the remaining insurgents to surrender or flee across the northern border into the territory of Greece's communist neighbors. The insurgency resulted in 100,000 killed and caused catastrophic economic disruption. In addition, at least 25,000 Greeks were either voluntarily or forcibly evacuated to Eastern bloc countries, while 700,000 became displaced persons inside the country.

After the 1944–49 Greek civil war, Greece sought to join the Western democracies and became a member of NATO in 1952. From 1952 to late 1963, Greece was governed by conservative parties—the Greek Rally of Marshal Alexandros Papagos and its successor, the National Radical Union (ERE) of Constantine Karamanlis. In 1963, the Center Union Party of George Papandreou was elected and governed until July 1965. It was followed by a succession of unstable coalition governments.

On April 21, 1967, just before scheduled elections, a group of colonels led by Col. George Papadopoulos seized power in a coup d'etat. Civil liberties were suppressed, special military courts were established, and political parties were dissolved. Several thousand political opponents were imprisoned or exiled to remote Greek islands. In November 1973, following an uprising of students at the Athens Polytechnic University, Gen. Dimitrios Ioannides replaced Papadopoulos and tried to continue the dictatorship.

Gen. Ioannides' attempt in July 1974 to overthrow Archbishop Makarios, the President of Cyprus, brought Greece to the brink of war with Turkey, which invaded Cyprus and occupied part of the island. Senior Greek military officers then withdrew their support from the junta, which toppled. Leading citizens persuaded Karamanlis to return from exile in France to establish a government of national unity until elections could be held. Karamanlis' newly organized party, New Democracy (ND), won

elections held in November 1974, and he became prime minister.

Following the 1974 referendum which resulted in the rejection of the monarchy, a new constitution was approved by parliament on June 19, 1975, and parliament elected Constantine Tsatsos as President of the republic. In the parliamentary elections of 1977, New Democracy again won a majority of seats. In May 1980, Prime Minister Karamanlis was elected to succeed Tsatsos as president. George Rallis was then chosen party leader and succeeded Karamanlis as Prime Minister.

On January 1, 1981, Greece became the 10th member of the European Community (now the European Union). In parliamentary elections held on October 18, 1981, Greece elected its first socialist government when the Panhellenic Socialist Movement (PASOK), led by Andreas Papandreou, won 172 of 300 seats. On March 29, 1985, after Prime Minister Papandreou declined to support President Karamanlis for a second term, Supreme Court Justice Christos Sartzetakis was elected president by the Greek parliament.

Greece had two rounds of parliamentary elections in 1989; both produced weak coalition governments with limited mandates. Party leaders withdrew their support in February 1990, and elections were held on April 8. In the April 1990 election, ND won 150 seats and subsequently gained 2 others. After Mitsotakis fired his first Foreign Minister—Andonis Samaras—in 1992, Samaras formed his own political party, Political Spring. A split between Mitsotakis and Samaras led to the collapse of the ND government and new elections in September 1993.

On January 17, 1996, following a protracted illness, Prime Minister Papandreou resigned and was replaced as Prime Minister by former Minister of Industry Constantine Simitis. In elections held in September 1996, Constantine Simitis was elected Prime Minister. PASOK won 162 seats, New Democracy, 108.

# GOVERNMENT

The 1975 constitution, which describes Greece as a "presidential parliamentary republic," includes extensive specific guarantees of civil liberties and vests the powers of the head of state in a president elected by parliament and advised by the Council of the Republic. The Greek governmental structure is similar to that found in many Western democracies and has been described as a compromise between the French and German models. The prime minister and cabinet play the central role in the political process, while the president performs some governmental functions in addition to ceremonial duties.

The president is elected by parliament to a 5–year term and can be reelected once. The president has the power to declare war and to conclude agreements of peace, alliance, and participation in international organizations; upon the request of the government a three–fifths parliamentary majority is required to ratify such actions, agreements, or treaties. The president also can exercise certain emergency powers, which must be countersigned by the appropriate cabinet minister. Changes to the constitution in 1986 limited the president's political powers. As a result, the president may not dissolve parliament, dismiss the government, suspend certain articles of the constitution, or declare a state of siege. To call a referendum, he must obtain approval from parliament.

Parliamentary deputies are elected by secret ballot for a maximum of 4 years, but elections can be called earlier. Greece uses a complex reinforced proportional representation electoral system which discourages splinter parties and makes a parliamentary majority possible even if the leading party falls short of a majority of the popular vote. A party must receive 3% of the total national vote to qualify for parliamentary seats.

Greece is divided into 51 prefectures, each headed by a prefect, who is elected by direct popular vote. There are also 13 regional administrative districts (peripheries), each including a number of prefectures and headed by a regional governor (periferiarch), appointed by the Minister of the Interior. In northern Greece and in greater Athens, three areas have an additional administrative position between the nomarch and periferiarch. This official, known as the president of the prefectural local authorities or "super nomarch," is elected by direct popular vote. Although municipalities and villages have elected officials, they do not have an adequate independent tax base and must depend on the central government for a large part of their financial needs. Consequently they are subject to numerous central government controls.

## The Government and Education, Religion, and the Media

**Education.** Under the Greek constitution, education is the responsibility of the state. Most Greeks attend public primary and secondary schools. There are a few private schools, which must meet the standard curriculum of and be supervised by the Ministry of Education. The Ministry of Education oversees and directs every aspect of the public education process at all levels, including hiring all teachers and professors and producing all required textbooks.

**Religion.** The Greek Orthodox Church is under the protection of the state, which pays the clergy's salaries, and Orthodox Christianity is the "prevailing" religion of Greece according to the constitution. The Greek Orthodox Church is self–governing but under the spiritual guidance of the Ecumenical Patriarch in Istanbul.

The Muslim minority, concentrated in Thrace, was given legal status by provisions of the Treaty of Lausanne in 1923 and is Greece's only officially recognized minority.

**Media.** The Greek media, collectively, is a very influential institution—usually aggressive, sensationalist, and frequently irre-sponsible with regard to content. Objectivity as known to the U.S. media on the whole does not exist in the Greek media. Most of the media are owned by businessmen with extensive commercial interests in other sectors of the economy. They use their newspapers, magazines, and radio and TV channels to promote their commercial enterprises as well as to seek political influence.

In 1994, the Ministry of Press and Information was established to deal with media and communication issues. ERT S.A.—a public corporation supervised by the Minister of Press—operates three national television channels and five national radio channels. The Minister of Press also serves as the primary government spokesman.

The Secretary General of Press and Information prepares the Athens News Agency (ANA) Bulletin, which is used, with AP and Reuters, as a primary source of information by the Greek press. The Ministry of Press and Information also issues the Macedonian News Agency (MPE) Bulletin, which is distributed throughout the Balkan region. For international news, CNN is a particular influence in the Greek market; the major TV channels often use it as a source. State and private TV stations also use "Eurovision" and "Visnews" as sources. While few papers and stations have overseas correspondents, those few correspondents abroad can be very influential.

In 1988, a new law provided the legal framework for the establishment of private radio stations and, as of 1989, private TV stations. According to the law, supervision of radio and television is exercised by the National Radio and Television Council. In practice, however, official licensing has been delayed for many years. Because of this, there has been a proliferation of private radio and TV stations, as well as European satellite channels, including Euronews; more than 1,000 radio stations are currently operating in Greece. The Greek Government is now implementing its plans to reallocate TV frequencies and issue licenses, authorized by the 1993 Media Law.

## Principal Government Officials

**For up-to-date information on Principal Government Officials, see the Chiefs of State and Cabinet Members of Foreign Governments section starting on page 1.**

Greece's embassy in the U.S. is located at 2221 Massachusetts Ave., NW, Washington, DC 20008; tel: (202) 939–5800; fax: (202) 939–5824.

# ECONOMY

The Greek economy is slowly coming out of a slump caused by a drop in investment and the implementation of stabilization policies in recent years. Greece remains a net importer of industrial and capital goods, foodstuffs, and petroleum. Leading exports are manufactured goods, food and beverages, petroleum products, cement, chemicals, and pharmaceuticals.

## Recent Economic History

The development of the modern Greek economy began in the late 19th and early 20th centuries with the adoption of social and industrial legislation and protective tariffs and the creation of the first industrial enterprises. Industry at the turn of the century consisted primarily of food processing, shipbuilding, and the manufacture of textiles and simple consumer products.

Greece achieved high rates of growth in the late 1960s and early 1970s due to large foreign investments. In the mid–1970s, Greece suffered declines in its GDP growth rate, ratio of investment to GDP, and productivity, and real labor costs and oil prices rose. In 1981, protective barriers were removed when Greece joined the

European Community. The government pursued expansionary policies, which fueled inflation and caused balance–of–payment difficulties. Growing public sector deficits were financed by borrowing. In October 1985, supported by a 1.7–billion European Currency Unit (ECU) loan from the European Union (EU), the government implemented a 2–year "stabilization" program with limited success. Public sector inefficiency and excessive spending caused government borrowing to increase; by the end of 1992, general government debt exceeded 100% of GDP.

Greece continued to rely on foreign borrowing to finance its deficits. Public sector external debt was $32 billion at the end of 1998. The general government debt was $119 billion at the end of 1998, or 105.5% of GDP. Greece's external debt was $32 billion at the end of 1998.

Greece, as a member of the EU, is currently striving to reduce its budget deficit and inflation rate in order to meet the prerequisites for the European monetary union. Although growth remained above the convergence program guidelines, high budget deficits and deficient infrastructure continue to dampen the economy's long–term potential growth rate.

In May 1994, the Bank of Greece successfully managed a currency crisis triggered by the lifting of currency restrictions on short–term capital movements. The bank contained speculative attacks on the drachma by tightening its monetary policy and raising interest rates dramatically: For a few days, interest rates pushed as high as 180%. In less than 2 months, with speculation on the drachma no longer a threat, interest rates returned to normal levels. A similar wave of speculation was beaten back in fall 1997, following the Asian financial crisis.

One of the successes of recent Greek economic policy has been the reduction of inflation rates. For more than 20 years, inflation hovered in the double digits, but a combination of fiscal consolidation, wage restraint,

and strong drachma policies resulted in lowered inflation. Inflation fell to 2.0% by mid–1999. High interest rates have been a significant problem, despite recent cuts in both treasury bill and bank rates for savings and loans. The government's strong drachma policy and Public Sector Borrowing Requirement (PSBR) make the lowering of interest rates difficult, but progress was made in 1997–99 and rates are gradually declining in line with inflation.

## Principal Sectors

Services, including tourism, make up the largest and fastest–growing sector of the Greek economy, accounting for about 62.7% of GDP in 1998.

Tourism is a major source of foreign exchange earnings. Although it is one of the country's most important industries, it has been slow to expand and suffers from poor infrastructure. With more than 10 million tourists visiting Greece in 1996, the tourist industry faced declining revenues, partly due to the strong drachma. Revenue from tourism exceeded $5.2 billion in 1998, having increased somewhat as Greek tourism benefited from problems in neighboring countries and an economic recovery in the European Union.

The manufacturing sector accounts for about 14% of GDP. The food industry is one of the most profitable and fastest–growing areas of manufacturing with significant export potential. High–technology equipment production, especially for telecommunications, is also a fast–growing sector. Other important areas include textiles, building materials, machinery, transport equipment, and electrical appliances.

Greece is traditionally a seafaring nation and has built an impressive shipping industry based on its geographic location and the entrepreneurial ability of its ship owners. The Greek–owned fleet (all flags) totaled 3,358 ships (134 million DWT) in 1998.

Construction activity (about 7.5% of GDP) is expected to increase due to infrastructure projects partially financed by European Union structural funds. Through 1999, about $20 billion will go to projects to modernize and develop Greece's transportation network. The centerpiece of this effort will be the construction of a new international airport near Athens. In addition, the Athens subway system is being greatly expanded, and construction or expansion of roads, railway lines, and bridges is either underway or planned.

## EU Membership

Greece must realign its economy as part of an extended transition to full EU membership that began in 1981. Greek businesses are adjusting to competition from EU firms and the government has had to liberalize its economic and commercial regulations and practices. However, Greece has been granted waivers from certain aspects of the EU's 1992 single market program.

Historically, Greece has been a net beneficiary of the EU budget. Net payments to Greece totaled $4.9 billion in 1998, representing 4.2% of GDP. Net inflows were estimated at about $5 billion in 1998. These funds contribute significantly to Greece's current accounts balance and reduce the state budget deficit.

Greece is receiving additional substantial support from the EU through the Delors II package. In July 1994, the Greek Government and the EU agreed on a final plan which provided Greece 16.6 billion ecu ($17.1 billion at current exchange rates) for the period 1994–98 of which 14 billion ecu was from the Community Support Framework and 2.6 billion ecu was from the Cohesion Fund. This level of assistance was continued in 1999 and finances major public works and economic development projects, upgrades competitiveness and human resources, improves living conditions, and addresses disparities between poorer and more developed regions of the country.

# FOREIGN RELATIONS

Prominent issues in Greek foreign policy include a dispute over the name of The Former Yugoslav Republic of Macedonia (F.Y.R.O.M.), the enduring Cyprus problem, Greek–Turkish differences over the Aegean, and Greek–American relations.

## The Former Yugoslav Republic of Macedonia (F.Y.R.O.M.)

Greek refusal to recognize F.Y.R.O.M. under the name "Republic of Macedonia" has been an important issue in Greek politics since 1992. Greece was adamantly opposed to the use of the name "Macedonia" by the government in Skopje, claiming that the name is intrinsically Greek and should not be used by a foreign country.

Furthermore, Greece believes that an independent "Republic of Macedonia" bordering the Greek region of Macedonia would fuel irredentist tensions in F.Y.R.O.M. The dispute led to a Greek trade embargo against F.Y.R.O.M. in February 1994. Mediation efforts by the UN, U.S., and EU brokered an interim solution to some of these differences in September 1995, leading to the lifting of the Greek embargo. Since the signing of these interim accords, the two governments have concluded agreements designed to facilitate the movement of people and goods across their common border and improve bilateral relations. Talks on remaining issues are still being held under UN auspices in New York.

## Albania

Greece restored diplomatic relations with Albania in 1971, but the Greek Government did not formally lift the state of war, declared during World War II, until 1987. After the fall of the Albanian communist regime in 1991, relations between Athens and Tirana became increasingly strained because of widespread allegations of mistreatment by Albanian authorities of the Greek ethnic minority in southern Albania. A wave of Albanian illegal economic migrants to Greece exacerbated tensions. The crisis in Greek–Albanian relations reached its peak in the summer of 1994, when an Albanian court sentenced five members (a sixth member was added later) of the ethnic Greek organization "Omonia" to prison terms on charges of undermining the Albanian state. Greece responded by freezing all EU aid to Albania and deporting tens of thousands of illegal Albanians. In December 1994, however, Greece began to permit limited EU aid to Albania, while Albania released two of the Omonia defendants and reduced the sentences of the remaining four.

Today, relations between the two countries are good, and, at the Albanian Government's request, about 250 Greek military personnel are stationed in Albania to assist with training and restructuring the Albanian armed forces.

## Greece–Turkey Relations

Greece and Turkey enjoyed good relations in the 1930s, but relations began to deteriorate in the mid–1950s, sparked by the Cyprus independence struggle and Turkish violence directed against the Greek minority in Istanbul. The July 1974 coup against Cyprus President Makarios—inspired by the Greek military junta in Athens—and the subsequent Turkish military intervention in Cyprus helped bring about the fall of the Greek military dictatorship. It also led to the de facto division of Cyprus. Since then, Greece has strongly supported Greek–Cypriot efforts, calling for the removal of Turkish troops and the restoration of a unified state. The Republic of Cyprus has received strong support from Greece in international forums. Greece has a military contingent on Cyprus, and Greek officers fill some key positions in the Greek Cypriot National Guard, as permitted by the constitution of Cyprus.

Other issues dividing Greece and Turkey involve the delimitation of the continental shelf in the Aegean Sea, territorial waters and airspace, and the condition of the Greek minority in Turkey and the Muslim minority in Greece. Greek and Turkish officials held meetings in the 1970s to discuss differences on Aegean questions, but Greece discontinued these discussions in the fall of 1981. In 1983, Greece and Turkey held talks on trade and tourism, but these were suspended by Greece when Turkey recognized the Turkish–Cypriot declaration of an independent state in northern Cyprus in November 1983.

After a dangerous dispute in the Aegean in March 1987 concerning oil drilling rights, the Prime Ministers of Greece and Turkey exchanged messages exploring the possibility of resolving the dispute over the continental shelf. Greece wanted the dispute to be decided by the International Court of Justice. Turkey preferred bilateral political discussions. In early 1988, the Turkish and Greek Prime Ministers met at Davos, Switzerland, and later in Brussels. They agreed on various measures to reduce bilateral tensions and to encourage cooperation. New tensions over the Aegean surfaced in November 1994, precipitated by Greece's ratification of the Law of the Sea Treaty and its ensuing statement that it reserved the right to declare a 12–mile territorial sea boundary around its Aegean islands as permitted by the treaty. Turkey stated that it would consider any such action a cause for war. New technical–level bilateral discussions began in 1994 but quickly fizzled.

In January 1996, Greece and Turkey came close to an armed confrontation over the question of which country had sovereignty over an islet in the Aegean. In July 1997, on the sidelines of the NATO summit in Madrid, Greek and Turkish leaders reached agreement on six principles to govern their bilateral relations. Within a few months, however, the two countries were again at odds over Aegean airspace and sovereignty issues. Tensions remain high. However, the two countries are discussing, under the auspices of the NATO Secretary General, various confidence–building measures to reduce the risk of military accidents or conflict in the Aegean.

## The Middle East

Greece has a special interest in the Middle East because of its geographic position and its economic and historic ties to the area. Greece cooperated with allied forces during the 1990–91 Persian Gulf war. Since 1994, Greece has signed defense cooperation agreements with Israel and Egypt. In recent years, Greek leaders have made numerous trips to the region in order to strengthen bilateral ties and encourage the Middle East Peace Process. In July and December 1997, Greece hosted meetings of Israeli and Palestinian politicians to contribute to the peace process. Greece hosted another such meeting in July 1998.

# U.S.-GREECE RELATIONS

The U.S. and Greece have long–standing historical, political, and cultural ties based on a common heritage, shared democratic values, and participation as Allies during World War II, the Korean conflict, and the Cold War. The U.S. is the largest foreign investor in Greece; U.S. foreign investment in Greece was about $1.5 billion in 1994.

About 1.1 million Americans are of Greek origin. The large, well–orga-

nized Greek–American community in the U.S. cultivates close political and cultural ties with Greece. Greece has the seventh–largest population of U.S. Social Security beneficiaries in the world.

During the Greek civil war of 1946–49, the U.S. proclaimed the Truman Doctrine, promising assistance to governments resisting communist subjugation, and began a period of substantial financial and military aid. The U.S. has provided Greece with more than $11.1 billion in economic and security assistance since 1946. Economic programs were phased out by 1962, but military assistance has continued. In fiscal year 1995, Greece was the fourth–largest recipient of U.S. security assistance, receiving loans totaling $255.15 million in foreign military financing.

In 1953, the first defense cooperation agreement between Greece and the United States was signed, providing for the establishment and operation of American military installations on Greek territory. The current mutual defense cooperation agreement (MDCA) provides for continued U.S. military assistance to Greece and the operation by the U.S. of a major military facility at Souda Bay, Crete.

## Principal U.S. Embassy Officials

**For up-to-date information on Principal U.S. Officials, see the U.S. Embassies, Consulates, and Foreign Service section starting on page 139.**

The U.S. embassy in Greece is located at 91 Vasilissis Sophias Blvd., 10160 Athens; tel: [30] (1) 721–2951 or 721–8401, after hours 722–3652; fax: [30] (1) 645–6282.

# GRENADA

April 2001

Official Name:
**Grenada**

## PROFILE

### Geography

**Area:** 344 sq. km. (133 sq. mi.); about twice the size of Washington, DC.
**Cities:** Capital—St. George's (est. pop. 33,734).
**Terrain:** Volcanic island with mountainous rainforest.
**Climate:** Tropical.

### People

**Nationality:** Noun and adjective—Grenadian(s).
**Population:** (1999 est.) 100,700.
**Annual growth rate:** (1999) 0.6%.
**Ethnic Groups:** African descent (82%), some South Asians (East Indians) and Europeans, trace Arawak/Carib Indian.
**Religion:** Roman Catholic, Anglican, various Protestant denominations.
**Languages:** English (official).
**Education:** Years compulsory—6. Literacy—95% of adult population.
**Health:** Infant mortality rate—19.5/1,000. Life expectancy—72 yrs.
**Work force:** (1999—41,017) Services/tourism—50.1%; industry—23.9%; agriculture—13.8%; other—12.2%; unemployment (1999)—14%.

### Government

**Type:** Constitutional monarchy with Westminster-style Parliament.

**Independence:** February 7, 1974.
**Constitution:** December 19, 1975.
**Branches:** Executive—governor general (appointed by and represents British monarch, head of state); prime minister (head of government, leader of majority party) and Cabinet direct an apolitical career civil service in the administration of the government. Legislative – Parliament composed of 15 directly elected members in the House of Representatives and a 13-seat Senate appointed by the governor general on the advice of the majority party and opposition. Judicial—magistrate's courts, Eastern Caribbean Supreme Court (high court and court of appeals), final appeal to privy council in London.
**Subdivisions:** Six parishes and one dependency (Carriacou and Petit Martinique).
**Major political parties:** New National Party (NNP), incumbent; National Democratic Congress (NDC); Grenada United Labor Party (GULP).
**Suffrage:** Universal at 18.

### Economy

**GDP:** (1999 est.) $310 million.
**GDP growth rate:** 8.16%.
**Per capita GDP:** (1999) $3,080.
**Agriculture:** Products—nutmeg, mace, cocoa, bananas, other fruits, vegetables.
**Industry:** Types—manufacturing, hotel/restaurant, construction.
**Trade:** (1999) Merchandise exports—$49.92 million: nutmeg, mace, cocoa, bananas, other fruits, vegetables, fish. Major markets—U.K., U.S., CARICOM countries, Germany, Netherlands. Merchandise imports—$231.4 million: food, machinery, transport, manufactured goods, fuel. Major suppliers—U.S. (36.6%), CARICOM countries, U.K., Japan.

## PEOPLE

Most of Grenada's population is of African descent; there is some trace of the early Arawak and Carib Indians. A few East Indians and a small community of the descendants of early European settlers reside in Grenada. About 50% of Grenada's population is under the age of 30. English is the official language; only a few people still speak French patois. A more significant reminder of Grenada's historical link with France is the strength of the Roman Catholic Church to which about 60% of Grenadians belong. The Anglican Church is the largest Protestant denomination.

## HISTORY

Before the arrival of Europeans, Grenada was inhabited by Carib Indians who had driven the more peaceful Arawaks from the island.

Columbus landed on Grenada in 1498 during his third voyage to the new world. He named the island "Concepcion." The origin of the name Grenada is obscure, but it is likely that Spanish sailors renamed the island for the city of Granada. By the beginning of the 18th century, the name "Grenada" or "la Grenade" in French, was in common use.

Partly because of the Caribs, Grenada remained uncolonized for more than 100 years after its discovery; early English efforts to settle the island were unsuccessful. In 1650, a French company founded by Cardinal Richelieu purchased Grenada from the English and established a small settlement. After several skirmishes with the Caribs, the French brought in reinforcements from Martinique and defeated the Caribs the last of whom leaped into the sea rather than surrender.

The island remained under French control until its capture by the British in 1762, during the Seven Years' War. Grenada was formally ceded to Great Britain in 1763 by the Treaty of Paris. Although the French regained control in 1779, the island was restored to Britain in 1783 by the Treaty of Versailles. Although Britain was hard pressed to overcome a pro-French revolt in 1795 Grenada remained British for the remainder of the colonial period.

During the 18th century, Grenada's economy underwent an important transition. Like much of the rest of the West Indies it was originally settled to cultivate sugar which was grown on estates using slave labor. But natural disasters paved the way for the introduction of other crops. In 1782, Sir Joseph Banks, the botanical adviser to King George III, introduced nutmeg to Grenada. The island's soil was ideal for growing the spice and because Grenada was a closer source of spices for Europe than the Dutch East Indies the island assumed a new importance to European traders.

The collapse of the sugar estates and the introduction of nutmeg and cocoa encouraged the development of smaller land holdings, and the island developed a land-owning yeoman farmer class. Slavery was outlawed in 1834. In 1833, Grenada became part of the British Windward Islands Administration. The governor of the Windward Islands administered the island for the rest of the colonial period. In 1958, the Windward Islands Administration was dissolved, and Grenada joined the Federation of the West Indies. After that federation collapsed in 1962, the British Government tried to form a small federation out of its remaining dependencies in the Eastern Caribbean.

Following the failure of this second effort, the British and the islands developed the concept of associated statehood. Under the Associated Statehood Act of 1967 Grenada was granted full autonomy over its internal affairs in March 1967. Full independence was granted on February 7, 1974.

After obtaining independence, Grenada adopted a modified Westminster parliamentary system based on the British model with a governor general appointed by and representing the British monarch (head of state) and a prime minister who is both leader of the majority party and the head of government. Sir Eric Gairy was Grenada's first prime minister.

On March 13, 1979, the new joint endeavor for welfare, education, and liberation (New Jewel) movement ousted Gairy in a nearly bloodless coup and established a people's revolutionary government (PRG), headed by Maurice Bishop who became prime minister. His Marxist-Leninist government established close ties with Cuba, the Soviet Union, and other communist bloc countries.

In October 1983, a power struggle within the government resulted in the arrest and subsequent murder of Bishop and several members of his cabinet by elements of the people's revolutionary army. Following a breakdown in civil order, a U.S.-Caribbean force landed on Grenada on October 25 in response to an appeal from the governor general and to a request for assistance from the Organization of Eastern Caribbean States. U.S. citizens were evacuated, and order was restored.

An advisory council named by the governor general administered the country until general elections were held in December 1984. The New National Party (NNP) led by Herbert Blaize won 14 out of 15 seats in free and fair elections and formed a democratic government. Grenada's constitution had been suspended in 1979 by the PRG but it was restored after the 1984 elections.

The NNP continued in power until 1989 but with a reduced majority. Five NNP parliamentary members, including two cabinet ministers, left the party in 1986-87 and formed the National Democratic Congress (NDC) which became the official opposition.

In August 1989, Prime Minister Blaize broke with the NNP to form another new party, The National Party (TNP), from the ranks of the NNP. This split in the NNP resulted in the formation of a minority government until constitutionally scheduled elections in March 1990. Prime Minister Blaize died in December 1989 and was succeeded as prime minister by Ben Jones until after the elections.

The NDC emerged from the 1990 elections as the strongest party, winning seven of the 15 available seats. Nicholas Brathwaite added two TNP members and one member of the Grenada United Labor Party (GULP) to create a 10-seat majority coalition. The governor general appointed him to be prime minister.

In parliamentary elections on June 20, 1995, the NNP won eight seats and formed a government headed by Dr. Keith Mitchell. The leader of the opposition in parliament is NDC leader George Brizan.

# GOVERNMENT AND POLITICAL CONDITIONS

Grenada is governed under a parliamentary system based on the British model; it has a governor general, a prime minister and a cabinet, and a bicameral Parliament with an elected House of Representatives and an appointed Senate.

Citizens enjoy a wide range of civil and political rights guaranteed by the constitution. Grenada's constitution provides citizens with the right to change their government peacefully. Citizens exercise this right through periodic, free, and fair elections held on the basis of universal suffrage.

Grenada's political parties range from the moderate TNP, NNP, and NDC to the left-of-center Maurice Bishop Patriotic Movement (MBPM—organized by the pro-Bishop survivors of the October 1983 anti-Bishop coup) and the populist GULP of former Prime Minister Gairy.

Security in Grenada is maintained by the 650 members of the Royal Grenada Police Force (RGPF), which included an 80-member paramilitary special services unit (SSU) and a 30-member coast guard. The U.S. Army and the U.S. Coast Guard provide periodic training and material support for the SSU and the coast guard.

# ECONOMY

The economy of Grenada is based upon agricultural production (nutmeg, mace, cocoa, and bananas) and tourism. Agriculture accounts for over half of merchandise exports, and a large portion of the population is employed directly or indirectly in agriculture. Recently the performance of the agricultural sector has not been good. Grenada's banana exports declined markedly in volume and quality in 1996, and it is a ques-

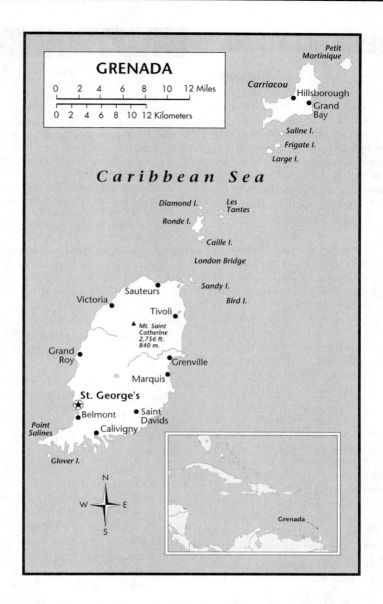

tion to what extent the country will remain a banana exporter. Tourism remains the key earner of foreign exchange.

Grenada is a member of the Caribbean Community and Common Market (CARICOM). Most goods can be imported into Grenada under open general license but some goods require specific licenses. Goods that are produced in the Eastern Caribbean receive additional protection; in May 1991, the CARICOM common external tariff (CET) was implemented. The CET aims to facilitate economic growth through intraregional trade by offering duty-free trade among CARICOM members

and duties on goods imported from outside CARICOM.

## Principal Government Officials

**For up-to-date information on Principal Government Officials, see the Chiefs of State and Cabinet Members of Foreign Governments section starting on page 1.**

Grenada maintains an embassy in the United States at 1701 New Hampshire Avenue, NW, Washington, DC 20009 Tel: 202-265-2561.

# FOREIGN RELATIONS

The United States, Venezuela, and Taiwan have embassies in Grenada. The United Kingdom is represented by a resident commissioner (as opposed to the governor general who represents the British monarch). Grenada has been recognized by most members of the United Nations and maintains diplomatic missions in the United Kingdom, the United States, Venezuela, and Canada.

Grenada is a member of the Caribbean Development Bank, CARICOM, the Organization of Eastern Caribbean States (OECS), and the Commonwealth of Nations. It joined the United Nations in 1974, and the World Bank, the International Monetary Fund, and the Organization of American States in 1975. Grenada also is a member of the Eastern Caribbean's Regional Security System (RSS).

As a member of CARICOM Grenada strongly backed efforts by the United States to implement UN Security Council Resolution 940, designed to facilitate the departure of Haiti's de facto authorities from power. Grenada subsequently contributed personnel to the multinational force which restored the democratically elected government of Haiti in October 1994.

Prime Minister Mitchell joined President Clinton, in May 1997, for a meeting with 14 other Caribbean leaders during the first-ever U.S.-regional summit in Bridgetown, Barbados. The summit strengthened the basis for regional cooperation on justice and counter-narcotics issues, finance and development, and trade.

# U.S.-GRENADIAN RELATIONS

The U.S. Government established an embassy in Grenada in November

## Travel Notes

**Travel Advice:** For up-to-date information from the U.S. State Department on possible inconvenient or hazardous situations, see the **Travel Warnings and Consular Information Sheets from the U.S. Government** section starting on page 1723. For the latest information on health requirements and conditions, see the **International Travelers' Health Information** section starting on page 1385. For further information dealing with non-urgent matter, see the **Tips for Travelers to...** section starting on page 1588.

1983. The U.S. ambassador to Grenada is resident in Bridgetown, Barbados. The embassy in Grenada is staffed by a charge d'affaires who reports to the ambassador in Bridgetown.

The U.S. Agency for International Development (USAID) has played a major role in Grenada's development providing more than $120 million in economic assistance from 1984 to 1993. Following the closure in July 1996 of the USAID regional mission for the Eastern Caribbean, U.S. assistance is channeled primarily through multilateral agencies such as the World Bank. About 10 Peace Corps volunteers in Grenada teach remedial reading, English-language skills, and vocational training. Grenada also is a beneficiary of the U.S. Caribbean Basin Initiative. In addition Grenada receives counter-narcotics assistance from the U.S. and benefits from U.S. military exercise-related construction and humanitarian civic action projects.

Grenada and the U.S. cooperate closely in fighting narcotics smuggling and other forms of transnational crime. In 1995, the U.S. and Grenada signed a maritime law enforcement treaty. In 1996, they signed a mutual legal assistance treaty and an extradition treaty as well as an over-flight/order-to-land amendment to the maritime law enforcement treaty. Some U.S. mili-

tary training is given to Grenadian security and defense forces.

Grenada continues to be a popular destination for Americans. Of the nearly 267,000 cruise ship passengers arriving in 1996, the majority were U.S. citizens. In addition, there were more than 30,000 other U.S. visitors in 1996. It is estimated that some 2,600 Americans reside in the country, plus the 800 U.S. medical students who study at the St. George's University School of Medicine. (Those students are not counted as residents for statistical purposes.)

## Principal U.S. Embassy Officials

**For up-to-date information on Principal U.S. Officials, see the U.S. Embassies, Consulates, and Foreign Service section starting on page 139.**

The U.S. Embassy in Grenada is located on the Lance-aux-Epines Stretch, St. George's, Grenada Tel: 1-(473)-444-1173; Fax: 1-(473)-444-4820). The mailing address is P.O. Box 54, St. George's, Grenada, West Indies.

## Other Contact Information

**U.S. Department of Commerce**
International Trade Administration
Trade Information Center
14th and Constitution, NW
Washington, DC 20230
Tel: 1-800-USA-TRADE

**Caribbean/Latin America Action**
1818 N Street, NW; Suite 310
Washington, DC 20036
Tel: 202-466-7464
Fax: 202-822-0075

# GUATEMALA

May 2000

Official Name:
**Republic of Guatemala**

# PROFILE

## Geography

**Area:** 108,780 sq. km. (42,000 sq. mi.); about the size of Tennessee.
**Cities:** Capital—Guatemala City (metro area pop. 2 million). Other major cities—Quetzaltenango, Escuintla.
**Terrain:** Mountainous, with fertile coastal plain.
**Climate:** Temperate in highlands; tropical on coasts.

## People

**Nationality:** Noun and adjective—Guatemalan(s).
**Population (1999 est. by INE):** 11.1 million.
**Annual population growth rate:** 2.68%.
**Ethnic groups:** Mestizo (mixed Spanish-Indian), indigenous.
**Religions:** Roman Catholic, Protestant, traditional Mayan.
**Languages:** Spanish, 24 indigenous languages (principally K'iche', Kakchiquel, K'ekchi, and Mam).
**Education:** Years compulsory—6. Attendance—41%. Literacy—55.6%
**Health:** Infant mortality rate—79/1,000. Life expectancy—66.45 yrs.
**Work force:** 50% of the population engages in some form of agriculture, often at the subsistence level outside the monetized economy. Salaried

work force breakdown: services—36%; industry and commerce—29%; agriculture—28%; construction, mining, utilities—4%.

## Government

**Type:** Constitutional Democratic Republic.
**Constitution:** May 1985; amended January 1994.
**Independence:** September 15, 1821.
**Branches:** Executive—president (4-year term). Legislative—unicameral 113-member Congress (4-year term). Judicial—13-member Supreme Court of Justice (5-year term).
**Subdivisions:** 22 departments (appointed governors). 331 municipalities with elected mayors and city councils.
**Major political parties:** Guatemalan Republican Front (FRG), National Advancement Party (PAN), New Nation Alliance (ANN), Guatemalan Christian Democracy (DCG).
**Suffrage:** Universal for adults 18 and over who are not serving on active duty with the armed forces or police. A variety of procedural obstacles have historically reduced participation by poor, rural and indigenous people.

## Economy

**GDP (1999 est.):** $18.07 billion.
Annual growth rate (1999 est.): 3.5%.
**Per capita GDP** (1999 est.): $1,570.

Natural resources: Oil, timber, nickel.
**Agriculture** (23% of GDP): Products— coffee , sugar, bananas, cardamom, vegetables, flowers and plants, timber, rice, rubber.
**Manufacturing** (13% of GDP): Types—prepared food, clothing and textiles, construction materials, tires, pharmaceuticals.
**Trade (1999):** Exports— $2.5 billion: coffee, sugar, cardamom, bananas, fruits and vegetables, petroleum, apparel. Major markets—U.S. 34%, Central American Common Market(CACM) 32%. Imports— $4.6 billion: fuels and lubricants, industrial machinery, motor vehicles, iron, and steel. Major suppliers—U.S. 41%, CACM 11%, Mexico 11%.

# HISTORICAL HIGHLIGHTS

More than half of Guatemalans are descendants of indigenous Mayan nations. Westernized Mayans and mestizos (mixed European and indigenous ancestry) are known as Ladinos. Most of Guatemala's population is rural, though urbanization is accelerating. The predominant religion is Roman Catholicism, into which many indigenous Guatemalans have incorporated traditional forms of worship. Protestantism and traditional Mayan religions are practiced by an estimated 40% and 1% of the population, respectively. Though the official language is Spanish, it is not universally understood among the indigenous population. However, the Peace Accords signed in December 1996 provide for the translation of some official documents and voting materials into several indigenous languages (see summary of main substantive accords).

The Mayan civilization flourished throughout much of Guatemala and the surrounding region long before the Spanish arrived, but it was already in decline when the Mayans were defeated by Pedro de Alvarado in 1523-24. During Spanish colonial rule, most of Central America came under the control of the Captaincy General of Guatemala.

The first colonial capital, Ciudad Vieja, was ruined by floods and an earthquake in 1542. Survivors founded Antigua, the second capital, in 1543. In the 17th century, Antigua became one of the richest capitals in the New World. Always vulnerable to volcanic eruptions, floods, and earthquakes, Antigua was destroyed by two earthquakes in 1773, but the remnants of its Spanish colonial architecture have been preserved as a national monument. The third capital, Guatemala City, was founded in 1776, after Antigua was abandoned.

Guatemala gained independence from Spain on September 15, 1821; it briefly became part of the Mexican Empire and then for a period belonged to a federation called the United Provinces of Central America. From the mid-19th century until the mid-1980s, the country passed through a series of dictatorships, insurgencies (particularly beginning in the 1960s), coups, and stretches of military rule with only occasional periods of representative government.

## 1944 to 1986

In 1944, General Jorge Ubico's dictatorship was overthrown by the "October Revolutionaries"—a group of dissident military officers, students, and liberal professionals. A civilian

president, Juan Jose Arevalo, was elected in 1945 and held the presidency until 1951. Social reforms initiated by Arevalo were continued by his successor, Col. Jacobo Arbenz. Arbenz permitted the communist Guatemalan Labor Party to gain legal status in 1952. By the mid-point of Arbenz's term, communists controlled key peasant organizations, labor unions, and the governing political party, holding some key government positions. Despite most Guatemalans' attachment to the original ideals of the 1944 uprising, some private sector leaders and the military viewed Arbenz's policies as a menace. The army refused to defend the Arbenz government when a U.S.-backed group led by Col. Carlos Castillo Armas invaded the country from Honduras in 1954 and quickly took over the government.

In response to the increasingly autocratic rule of Gen. Ydigoras Fuentes, who took power in 1958 following the murder of Colonel Castillo Armas, a group of junior military officers revolted in 1960. When they failed, several went into hiding and established close ties with Cuba. This group became the nucleus of the forces that were in armed insurrection against the government for the next 36 years.

Four principal left-wing guerrilla groups—the Guerrilla Army of the Poor (EGP), the Revolutionary Organization of Armed People (ORPA), the Rebel Armed Forces (FAR), and the Guatemalan Labor Party (PGT)—conducted economic sabotage and targeted government installations and members of government security forces in armed attacks. These organizations combined to form the Guatemalan National Revolutionary Unity (URNG) in 1982. At the same time, extreme right-wing groups of self-appointed vigilantes, including the Secret Anti-Communist Army (ESA) and the White Hand, tortured and murdered students, professionals, and peasants suspected of involvement in leftist activities.

Shortly after President Julio Cesar Mendez Montenegro took office in 1966, the army launched a major

counterinsurgency campaign that largely broke up the guerrilla movement in the countryside. The guerrillas then concentrated their attacks in Guatemala City, where they assassinated many leading figures, including U.S. Ambassador John Gordon Mein in 1968. Between 1966 and 1982, there were a series of military or military-dominated governments.

In March 1982, army troops commanded by junior officers staged a coup to prevent the assumption of power by former Defense Minister Gen. Anibal Guevara, whose electoral victory was marred by fraud. The coup leaders asked Brig. Gen. Efrain Jose Rios Montt to negotiate the departure of presidential incumbent Gen. Lucas Garcia. Rios Montt had been the candidate of the Christian Democratic Party in the 1974 presidential elections and was also widely believed to have lost by fraud. Rios Montt formed a three-member junta that annulled the 1965 constitution, dissolved the Congress, suspended political parties, and canceled the election law. Shortly thereafter, Rios Montt assumed the title of President of the Republic. Responding to a wave of violence, the government imposed a state of siege, while at the same time forming an advisory Council of State to guide a return to democracy. In 1983, electoral laws were promulgated, the state of siege was lifted, political activity was once again allowed, and constituent assembly elections scheduled.

Guerrilla forces and their leftist allies then denounced the new government and stepped up attacks. Rios Montt sought to combat the threat with military actions and economic reforms, in his words, "rifles and beans." The government formed civilian defense forces, which, along with the army, successfully contained the insurgency, although there were widespread reports of human rights abuses and violence against noncombatant rural populations. However, on August 8, 1983, Rios Montt was deposed by the Guatemalan Army, and Minister of Defense, Gen. Oscar Humberto Mejia Victores, was proclaimed head of state. General Mejia claimed that certain "religious fanat-

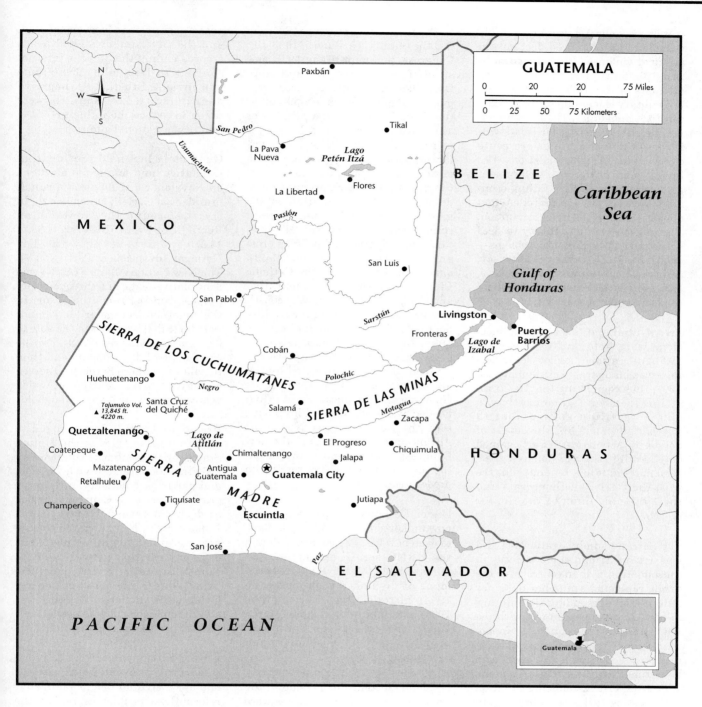

### GUATEMALA

ics" were abusing their positions in the government and that corruption had to be weeded out. Constituent Assembly elections were held on July 1, 1984.

On May 30, 1985, after 9 months of debate, the Constituent Assembly finished drafting a new constitution, which took immediate effect. Mejia called general elections. The Christian Democratic Party (DCG) candidate, Vinicio Cerezo, won the presidency with almost 70% of the vote and took office in January 1986.

## 1986 to 2000

Upon its inauguration in January 1986, President Cerezo's civilian government announced that its top priorities would be to end the political violence and establish the rule of law. Reforms included new laws of habeas corpus and amparo (court-ordered protection), the creation of a legislative human rights committee, and the establishment in 1987 of the Office of Human Rights Ombudsman. The Supreme Court also embarked on a series of reforms to fight corruption and improve legal system efficiency.

With Cerezo's election, the military moved away from governing and returned to the more traditional role of providing internal security, specifically by fighting armed insurgents. The first 2 years of Cerezo's administration were characterized by a stable economy and a marked decrease in political violence. Dissatisfied military personnel made two coup attempts in May 1988 and May 1989, but military leadership supported the constitutional order. The government was heavily criticized for its unwillingness to investigate or prosecute cases of human rights violations. The final 2 years of Cerezo's government also were marked by a failing economy, strikes, protest marches, and allegations of widespread corruption. The government's inability to deal with many of the nation's problems— such as infant mortality, illiteracy, deficient health and social services, and rising levels of violence—contributed to popular discontent.

Presidential and congressional elections were held on November 11, 1990. After a runoff ballot, Jorge Serrano was inaugurated on January 14, 1991, thus completing the first transition from one democratically elected civilian government to another. Because his Movement of Solidarity Action (MAS) Party gained only 18 of 116 seats in Congress, Serrano entered into a tenuous alliance with the Christian Democrats and the National Union of the Center (UCN).

The Serrano administration's record was mixed. It had some success in consolidating civilian control over the army, replacing a number of senior officers and persuading the military to participate in peace talks with the URNG. He took the politically unpopular step of recognizing the sovereignty of Belize. The Serrano government reversed the economic slide it inherited, reducing inflation and boosting real growth from 3% in 1990 to almost 5% in 1992. On May 25, 1993, Serrano illegally dissolved Congress and the Supreme Court and tried to restrict civil freedoms, allegedly to fight corruption. The "autogolpe" (or autocoup) failed due to unified, strong protests by most elements of Guatemalan society, international pressure, and the army's enforcement of the decisions of the Court of Constitutionality, which ruled against the attempted takeover.

In the face of this pressure, Serrano fled the country. On June 5, 1993, the Congress, pursuant to the 1985 constitution, elected the Human Rights Ombudsman, Ramiro De Leon Carpio, to complete Serrano's presidential term. De Leon, not a member of any political party and lacking a political base, but with strong popular support, launched an ambitious anticorruption campaign to "purify" Congress and the Supreme Court, demanding the resignations of all members of the two bodies. Despite considerable congressional resistance, presidential and popular pressure led to a November 1993 agreement brokered by the Catholic Church between the administration and Congress. This package of constitutional reforms was approved by popular referendum on January 30, 1994. In August 1994, a new Congress was elected to complete the unexpired term. Controlled by the anti-corruption parties—the populist Guatemalan Republican Front (FRG) headed by ex-Gen. Efrain Rios Montt, and the center-right National Advancement Party (PAN)—the new Congress began to move away from the corruption that characterized its predecessors.

Under De Leon, the peace process, now brokered by the United Nations, took on new life. The government and the URNG signed agreements on human rights (March 1994), resettlement of displaced persons (June 1994), historical clarification (June 1994), and indigenous rights (March 1995). They also made significant progress on a socioeconomic and agrarian agreement.

National elections for president, the Congress, and municipal offices were held in November 1995. With almost 20 parties competing in the first round, the presidential election came down to a January 7, 1996 runoff in which PAN candidate Alvaro Arzu defeated Alfonso Portillo of the FRG by just over 2% of the vote. Arzu won because of his strength in Guatemala City, where he had previously served as mayor, and in the surrounding urban area. Portillo won all of the rural departments except Peten. Under the Arzu administration,

peace negotiations were concluded, and the government signed peace accords ending the 36-year internal conflict in December 1996. The human rights situation also improved during Arzu's tenure, and steps were taken to reduce the influence of the military in national affairs.

Guatemala last held presidential, legislative, and municipal elections on November 7, 1999, and a runoff presidential election December 26. In the first round the Guatemalan Republican Front (FRG) won 63 of 113 legislative seats, while The National Advancement Party won 37. The New Nation Alliance (ANN) won 9 legislative seats, and three minority parties won the remaining four. In the runoff on December 26, Alfonso Portillo (FRG) won 68% of the vote to 32% for Oscar Berger (PAN). Portillo carried all 22 departments and Guatemala City, where Berger had served as mayor until recently and which was considered the PAN's stronghold.

President Portillo has pledged to maintain strong ties to the United States, further enhance Guatemala's growing cooperation with Mexico, and participate actively in the integration process in Central America and the Western Hemisphere. Domestically, he has vowed to support continued liberalization of the economy, increase investment in human capital and infrastructure, establish an independent central bank, and increase revenue by stricter enforcement of tax collections rather than increasing taxation.

During his campaign, Portillo promised to continue the peace process, appoint a civilian defense minister, reform the armed forces, replace the military presidential security service with a civilian one, and strengthen protection of human rights. During the campaign, Portillo was criticized for his relationship with the party's chairman, former Gen. Efrain Rios Montt, the de facto president of Guatemala in 1982-83. Many charge that some of the worst human rights violations of the internal conflict were committed under Rios Montt's rule. Nonetheless, Portillo's impressive electoral triumph, with two-thirds of the vote in the second round, gives him a claim to a mandate from the people to carry out his reform program.

# GOVERNMENT

Guatemala's 1985 constitution provides for a separation of powers among the executive, legislative, and judicial branches of government. The 1993 constitutional reforms included an increase in the number of Supreme Court justices from 9 to 13. The terms of office for president, vice president, and congressional representatives were reduced from 5 years to 4 years; for Supreme Court justices from 6 years to 5 years, and increased the terms of mayors and city councils from 2½ to 4 years.

The president and vice president are directly elected through universal suffrage and limited to one term. A vice president can run for president after 4 years out of office. Supreme Court justices are elected by the Congress from a list submitted by the bar association, law school deans, a university rector, and appellate judges. The Supreme Court and local courts handle civil and criminal cases. There also is a Constitutional Court.

Guatemala has 22 administrative subdivisions (departments) administered by governors appointed by the president. Guatemala City and 330 other municipalities are governed by popularly elected mayors or councils.

## National Security

Guatemala is a signatory to the Rio Pact and is a member of the Central American Defense Council (CONDECA). The president is commander in chief. The Defense Minister is responsible for policy. Day-to-day operations are the responsibility of the military chief of staff and the national defense staff. An agreement signed in September 1996, which is one of the substantive Peace Accords, mandated that the mission of the armed forces change to focus exclusively on external threats, although President Arzu subsequently used a

constitutional power to order the army on a temporary basis to support the police in response to a nationwide wave of violent crime. The accord calls for a one-third reduction in the army's authorized strength and budget (already achieved), and for a constitutional amendment to permit the appointment of a civilian Minister of Defense. A constitutional amendment to this end was defeated as part of a May 1999 plebiscite.

The army has met its accord-mandated target of 28,000, including subordinate air force (1,000) and navy (1,000) elements. It is equipped with armaments and materiel from the United States, Israel, Yugoslavia, Taiwan, Argentina, Spain, and France. As part of the army downsizing, the operational structure of 19 military zones and three strategic brigades are being recast as several military zones are eliminated and their area of operations absorbed by others. The air force operates three air bases; the navy has two port bases.

## Principal Government Officials

**For up-to-date information on Principal Government Officials, see the Chiefs of State and Cabinet Members of Foreign Governments section starting on page 1.**

The Guatemalan Embassy is at 2220 R Street, NW, Washington, DC20008 (tel. 202-745-4952).
Consulates are in New York, Miami, Chicago, Houston, and Los Angeles, and honorary consuls in Montgomery, San Diego, Ft. Lauderdale, Atlanta, Leavenworth, Lafayette, New Orleans, Minneapolis, Philadelphia, Pittsburgh , San Juan, Providence, Memphis, San Antonio and Seattle. [See the State Department Web Page: www.state.gov under Foreign Consular Offices in the U.S.]

# POLITICAL CONDITIONS

Upon taking office, the Arzu administration made resolution of the 36-year internal conflict before the end of 1996 its highest priority. The final agreement, signed on December 29, 1996, contributed significantly to an improvement in Guatemala's human rights (see last page for summary of main substantive accords). Within 2 weeks of taking office, President Alvaro Arzu initiated a major shakeup of the military high command and oversaw the firing of almost 200 corrupt police officials.

The Arzu administration also began a series of actions to boost the economy, including a reform of the tax system and privatization of the electricity and telecommunication sectors. President Arzu strongly and publicly condemned human rights abuses. Positive political developments and the demobilization of 200,000 members of the Civilian Defense Patrols were major factors in the positive change. In contrast to past years, there was a marked decline in new cases of human rights abuse, but problems remain in some areas. Common crime, aggravated by a legacy of violence and vigilante justice, presents a serious challenge to the government. Impunity remains a major problem, primarily because democratic institutions, including those responsible for the administration of justice, have developed only a limited capacity to cope with this legacy. Although making some progress, the government has stated it will require 4 more years (to the year 2004) to meet the target of increasing its tax burden (currently at 10% of GDP, lowest in the hemisphere) to 12% of GDP. Fifty proposed constitutional amendments meant to institutionalize the peace process or otherwise make Guatemala a fairer and more open society were rejected in a May 1999 plebiscite, with voting following ethnic lines.

President Alfonso Portillo began his 4-year term of office on January 14, 2000. Portillo, who was elected to

Congress as a member of the Christian Democratic Party in 1993, has only been a member of the Guatemalan Republican Front (FRG) since 1995. The FRG has diverse factions, unified primarily by populism. FRG founder Efrain Rios Montt serves as the President of Congress. With the continuing development of democracy and participation in Guatemala, President Portillo has shown more deference to Congress than have previous presidents. Under the Guatemalan Constitution of 1985, passage of many kinds of legislation requires a two-thirds vote. Passage of such legislation is not possible with FRG votes alone.

# ECONOMY

Guatemala's GDP for 1999 was estimated at $18.07 billion, with real growth of approximately 3.5%. After the signing of the final peace accord in December 1996, Guatemala was well-positioned for rapid economic growth over the next several years.

Guatemala's economy is dominated by the private sector, which generates about 85% of GDP. Agriculture contributes 23% of GDP and accounts for 75% of exports. Most manufacturing is light assembly and food processing, geared to the domestic, U.S., and Central American markets. Over the past several years, tourism and exports of textiles, apparel, and nontraditional agricultural products such as winter vegetables, fruit, and cut flowers have boomed, while more traditional exports such as sugar, bananas, and coffee continue to represent a large share of the export market. The United States is the country's largest trading partner, providing 41% of Guatemala's imports and receiving 34% of its exports. The government sector is small and shrinking, with its business activities limited to public utilities (some of which have been privatized) ports and airports and several development-oriented financial institutions.

Current economic priorities include:

- Liberalizing the trade regime;

- Financial services sector reform;

- Overhauling Guatemala's public finances;

- Simplifying the tax structure, enhancing tax compliance, and broadening the tax base. At about 10% of GDP, Guatemala's tax burden is among the lowest in the Western Hemisphere; and

- Improving the investment climate through procedural and regulatory simplification and adopting a goal of concluding treaties to protect investment and intellectual property rights.

Import tariffs have been lowered in conjunction with Guatemala's Central American neighbors so that most now fall between 0% and 15%, with further reductions planned. Responding to Guatemala's changed political and economic policy environment, the international community has mobilized substantial resources to support the country's economic and social development objectives. The United States, along with other donor countries—especially France, Italy, Spain, Germany, Japan, and the international financial institutions—have increased development project financing. Donors' response to the need for international financial support funds for implementation of the Peace Accords is, however, contingent upon Guatemalan Government reforms and counterpart financing.

Problems hindering economic growth include illiteracy and low levels of education; inadequate and underdeveloped capital markets; and lack of infrastructure, particularly in the transportation, telecommunications, and electricity sectors, although the state telephone company and electricity distribution were privatized in 1998. The distribution of income and wealth remains highly skewed. The wealthiest 10% of the population receives almost one-half of all income; the top 20% receives two-thirds of all income. As a result, approximately 75% of the population lives in poverty, and two-thirds of that number live in extreme poverty. Guatemala's social indicators, such as infant mortality and illiteracy, are among the worst in the hemisphere.

# FOREIGN RELATIONS

Guatemala's major diplomatic interests are regional security and, increasingly, regional development and economic integration. The Central American Ministers of Trade meet on a regular basis to work on regional approaches to trade issues. In March 1997, Guatemala hosted the second annual Trade and Investment Forum, under the sponsorship of the U.S. Department of Commerce. The 2-day event highlighted the growing relationship that Guatemala has with its closest trading partners and offer regional opportunities to foreign investors. In March 1998, Guatemala joined its Central American neighbors in signing a Trade and Investment Framework Agreement (TIFA). Guatemala also originated the idea for, and is the seat of, the Central American Parliament (PARLACEN).

Guatemala participates in several regional groups, particularly those related to the environment and trade. For example, President Clinton and the Central American presidents signed the CONCAUSA (*Conjunto Centroamerica*-USA) agreement at the Summit of the Americas in December 1994. CONCAUSA is a cooperative plan of action to promote clean, efficient energy use; conserve the region's biodiversity; strengthen legal and institutional frameworks and compliance mechanisms; and improve and harmonize environmental protection standards.

Guatemala long laid claim to Belize; the territorial dispute caused problems with the United Kingdom and later with Belize following its 1981 independence from the U.K. Relations have had their ups and downs but are strained at present. In 1986, Guatemala and the U.K. re-established commercial and consular relations; in 1987, they re-established full diplomatic relations. In December 1989, Guatemala sponsored Belize for permanent observer status in the

Organization of American States (OAS). In September 1991, Guatemala recognized Belize's independence and established diplomatic ties, while acknowledging that the boundaries remained in dispute. Although Belize has recognized Guatemalan diplomatic representation at the ambassadorial level for several years, the Guatemalan Government did not accredit the first ambassador from Belize until December 1996. In early 2000, the Guatemalan Foreign Ministry proposed a border settlement that would transfer more than half of Belize's territory to Guatemala.

While Belize continues to be a difficult domestic political issue in Guatemala, the two governments have quietly maintained constructive relations. The Portillo administration has indicated its intent to resolve the dispute with Belize, making it the number one priority now that the final peace accord has been signed. In anticipation of an effort to bring the border dispute to an end, in early 1996, the Guatemalan Congress ratified two long-pending international agreements governing frontier issues and maritime rights.

# U.S.-GUATEMALAN RELATIONS

Relations between the United States and Guatemala traditionally have been close, although at times strained by human rights and civil/military issues in earlier periods. U.S. policy objectives in Guatemala include:

- Supporting the institutionalization of democracy and implementation of the peace accords;

- Encouraging respect for human rights and the rule of law;

- Supporting broad-based economic growth and sustainable development and maintaining mutually beneficial trade and commercial relations;

- Cooperating to combat narcotics

trafficking; and

- Supporting Central American integration.

The United States, as a member of "the Friends of Guatemala," along with Colombia, Mexico, Spain, Norway, and Venezuela, played an important role in the UN-moderated Peace Accords, providing public and behind-the-scenes support. The U.S. strongly supports the six substantive and three procedural accords, which, along with the signing of the December 29, 1996 final accord, form the blueprint for profound political, economic, and social change.

In Costa Rica in May 1997 and in Guatemala in 1999, President Clinton met with President Arzu and other Central American presidents, the President of the Dominican Republic, and the Prime Minister of Belize to celebrate the remarkable democratic transformation in the region and reaffirm support for strengthening democracy; good governance; and promoting prosperity through economic integration, free trade, and investment. The leaders also expressed their commitment to the continued development of just and equitable societies and responsible environmental policies as integral elements of sustainable development.

Although almost all of the 180,000 U.S. tourists who visit Guatemala annually do so without incident, in recent years, the number of violent crime reported by U.S. citizens has steadily increased. In 1997, 46 U.S. citizens reported to the U.S. Embassy that they were victims of violent crime. In 1998, the number climbed to 52 and in 1999 to 79. Increases in the number of Americans reported as victims of violent crime may be the result of any combination of factors: increased numbers of Americans traveling to Guatemala; increased accuracy in the embassy's reporting of crime; more Americans traveling to higher risk areas of Guatemala; or more crime.

Guatemala-Central American Program (USAID/G-CAP) plays a key role in implementing priority U.S. for-

## Travel Notes

**Travel Advice:** For up-to-date information from the U.S. State Department on possible inconvenient or hazardous situations, see the **Travel Warnings and Consular Information Sheets from the U.S. Government** section starting on page 1723. For the latest information on health requirements and conditions, see the **International Travelers' Health Information** section starting on page 1385. For further information dealing with non-urgent matter, see the **Tips for Travelers to...** section starting on page 1588.

eign policy objectives in Guatemala. USAID's program seeks to aid the financial stability and long-term growth of Guatemala, working primarily with the socially and economically disadvantaged persons living in poverty, with special emphasis on the rural indigenous poor whose lives have been most seriously affected by the internal civil conflict. In addition to low incomes, these populations have limited economic opportunities for economic advancement, lack access to social services, and have limited access to, or influence over, the policymaking processes.

Providing $60-$70 million in annual assistance, USAID/Guatemala is working to address limitations to Guatemalan development pursuing seven objectives. These are:

- Support the implementation of the 1996 Peace Accords;

- Provide agricultural recovery assistance to victims of Hurricane Mitch and help Guatemala prepare for future disasters;

- Aid in the improvement of the legal system and assist citizens in its use;

- Increase educational access and quality for all Guatemalans;

- Improve the health of Guatemalan women, children, and rural families; and,

**Background Notes**

- Increase the earning capacity of poor rural families; and

- Expand natural resources management and conservation of biodiversity.

USAID/Guatemala's largest program is the support of the peace accords. The Guatemalan Peace Accords are more than a formal ending to 36 years of armed conflict. The accords require major investments in health, education, and other basic services to reach the rural indigenous poor and require the full participation of the indigenous people in local and national decisionmaking. In addition, the accords call for a profound restructuring of the state, affecting some of its most fundamental institutions—the military, the national police and the system of justice—in order to end impunity and confirm the rule of law. They also require basic changes in tax collection and expenditure and improved financial management.

In 1998, Hurricane Mitch caused human and property damage on a massive scale. In Guatemala vast economic and social damage diverted resources away from the implementation of the Peace Accords and development priorities. It is estimated that 1999 exports dropped $365 million, which translates into the loss of jobs for 35,000 people. USAID/Guatemala's Special Mitch Objective is helping agricultural productivity recover, improving disease control and community sanitation, and supporting national and community level disaster preparedness.

USAID's regional Central American Program is also based in Guatemala. Providing between $15-$20 million in annual assistance, USAID's regional program in coordination with the U.S. embassies in the region and bilateral USAID Missions in Nicaragua, Honduras, El Salvador, and Panama supports four key objectives. These are:

- Promotion of free trade;
- Expansion of Central American natural resources management and conservation;
- Advancement of regional HIV/AIDS services and information; and

- Post-Mitch assistance for Central America in preparing for future weather-related disasters.

## Principal U.S. Embassy Officials

**For up-to-date information on Principal U.S. Officials, see the U.S. Embassies, Consulates, and Foreign Service section starting on page 139.**

The U.S. Embassy in Guatemala is located at Avenida la Reforma 7-01, Zone 10, Guatemala City (tel. [502] 331-1541); fax [502] 331-8885)

## Other Contact Information

**U.S. Department of Commerce**
International Trade Administration
Trade Information Center
14th & Constitution, NW
Washington, DC 20230
Tel: 800-USA-TRADE
Internet: http://www.ita.doc.gov

**American Chamber of Commerce in Guatemala**
6a, Avenida 14-77, Zona 10
Apartado Postal 832
Guatemala City, Guatemala
Tel.: 502-366-4822/4716
Fax: 502-368-3106
E-mail: guamcham@ns.guate.net

**Caribbean/Latin American Action (C/LAA)**
1818 N Street, NW, Suite 310
Washington, DC 20036
Tel.: 202-466-7464
Fax: 202-822-0075

## The Guatemalan Peace Process

On December 29, 1996, the Government of Guatemala and representatives of the URNG—an umbrella organization grouping four insurgency movements—signed the last of a number of Peace Accords, which brought to a close a 36-year long internal conflict, the longest in Latin America. Six of the accords are "sub-

stantive." Others focus on procedural matters.

The main substantive accords are:

- **Human Rights.** Signed in March 1994: Aimed at strengthening human rights organizations and ending impunity. It established MINUGUA, the UN human rights monitoring entity, which has been a key element in the restoration of peace, and called for the disbanding of clandestine security forces.

- **Resettlement.** Signed in June 1994: Established objectives for the resettlement and economic integration of displaced peoples into Guatemalan society.

- **Historical Clarification.** Signed in June 1994: Establishes a commission to report on human rights violations committed during the conflict.

- **Indigenous Rights.** Signed in March 1995: Calls for recognition of Guatemala's ethnic, cultural, and linguistic diversity and for the rights of indigenous people to live by their own cultural norms.

- **Socioeconomic and Agrarian issues.** Signed in May 1996: Promotes decentralization and regionalization of government services, urges land reform, protection of the environment, and a more equitable budgetary and taxation policy.

- **Strengthening Civil Authority and the Role of the Military in a Democratic Society.** Signed in September 1996: Calls for improvement, modernization, and strengthening of all three branches of the state. It contains an agreed list of constitutional reforms which the government will propose and limits the armed forces' role to defense of national sovereignty and territorial integrity.

# GUINEA

December 1999

Official Name:
## Republic of Guinea (République de Guinée)

# PROFILE

## Geography

**Area:** 245,860 sq. km. (95,000 sq. mi.), about the size of Oregon.
**Capital:** Conakry; Other Cities: Guéckédou, Boké, Kindia, N'Zérékoré, Macenta, Mamou, Kankan, Faranah, Siguiri, Dalaba, Labe, Pita, Kamsar.
**Terrain:** Generally flat along the coast and mountainous in the interior. The country's four geographic regions include a narrow coastal belt; pastoral highlands (the source of West Africa's major rivers); the northern savanna; and the southeastern rain forest.
**Climate:** Tropical.

## People

**Nationality:** Noun and adjective—Guinean(s).
**Population (1996 census):** 7.2 million (including refugees and foreign residents). Refugee population (June 1998 est.): 548,000.
**Cities:** Conakry (pop. 1.1 million). Population of largest prefectures—Guéckédou (348,053), Boké (294,314), Kindia (288,007), N'Zérékoré (282,903), Macenta (281,053).

**Annual growth rate (1996 census):** 2.8%.
**Ethnic groups:** Peuhl 40%, Malinke 30%, Soussou 20%, other ethnic groups 10%.
**Religions:** Muslim 85%, Christian 8%, traditional beliefs 7%.
**Languages:** French (official), national languages.
**Education:** Years compulsory—8. Enrollment—primary school, 51% (male 66%, female 35%); secondary, 15%; and post secondary, 3%. Literacy (Total population over age 15 that can read and write, 1996 est.)—36% (male 50%, female 22%).
**Health (1996 est.):** Life expectancy—total population 45 years (female 47 years, male 43 years). Infant mortality rate (1995 UNDP)—229/1,000.
**Work force (1995 Min of Plan):** 3.4 million. Agriculture 76%. Industry and commerce 18%. Services 6%.

## Government

**Type:** Republic.
**Independence:** October 2, 1958. Anniversary of the Second Republic, April 3, 1984. Government based on ordinances, decrees, and decisions issued by a president and his ministers or through legislation produced by the National Assembly and approved by the president.
**Branches:** Executive —Elected President (chief of state); 25 appointed civilian ministers. Legisla-

tive—Elected National Assembly (114 seats). Judicial—Supreme Court.
**Administrative subdivisions:** Region, prefecture, subprefecture, rural district.
**Political parties:** Legalized on 1 April 1992. Seven parties, of the more than 40 with legal status, won seats in the June 1995 legislative elections. Pro-government—Party for Unity and Progress (PUP) and DJAMA. Opposition —Rally for the Guinean People (RPG), Union for a New Republic (UNR), Party for Renewal and Progress (PRP), Union for Progress of Guinea (UPG), Democratic Party of Guinea (PDG).
**Suffrage:** Universal over age 18.
**Central government budget (1998):** $328 million.
**Flag:** Red, yellow, and green vertical stripes.

## Economy

**GDP (1998 est.):** $3.3 billion.
**Annual economic growth rate (1997):** 5%.
**Per capita GDP (1997 est.):** $750.
**Average inflation rate (1997):** 2.1%.
**Natural resources:** Bauxite, iron ore, diamonds, gold, water power, uranium, fisheries.
**Industry (28.4% of GDP):** Types—mining, light manufacturing, construction.
**Trade (28.2% of GDP):** Exports—$793 million: bauxite, alumina, dia-

monds, gold, coffee, pineapples, bananas, palm products, coffee.

**Agriculture (20.4% of GDP):** Products—rice, cassava, fonio, millet, corn, coffee, cocoa, bananas, palm products, pineapples, livestock, forestry. Arable land—30%. Cultivated land—4%. Major markets—European Union, U.S., Commonwealth of Independent States, China, Eastern Europe, Japan, Saudi Arabia, Morocco.

# GEOGRAPHY

Guinea is located on the Atlantic Coast of West Africa and is bordered by Guinea-Bissau, Senegal, Mali, Côte d'Ivoire, Liberia, and Sierra Leone. The country is divided into four geographic regions: A narrow coastal belt (Lower Guinea); the pastoral Fouta Djallon highlands (Middle Guinea); the northern savannah (Upper Guinea); and a southeastern rain-forest region (Forest Guinea). The Niger, Gambia, and Senegal Rivers are among the 22 West African rivers that have their origins in Guinea.

The coastal region of Guinea and most of the inland have a tropical climate, with a rainy season lasting from April to November, relatively high and uniform temperatures, and high humidity. Conakry's year-round average high is 29 degrees C (85 degrees F), and the low is 23 degrees C (74 degrees F); its average annual rainfall is 430 centimeters (169 inches). Sahelian Upper Guinea has a shorter rainy season and greater daily temperature variations.

# PEOPLE

Guinea has four main ethnic groups:

- Peuhl (Foula or Foulani), who inhabit the mountainous Fouta Djallon;

- Malinke (or Mandingo), in the savannah and forest regions;

- Soussous in the coastal areas; and

- several small groups (Gerzé, Toma, etc.) in the forest region.

West Africans make up the largest non-Guinean population. Non-Africans total about 10,000 (mostly Lebanese, French, and other Europeans). Seven national languages are used extensively; major written languages are French, Peuhl, and Arabic.

# HISTORY

The area occupied by Guinea today was included in several large West African political groupings, including the Ghana, Mali, and Songhai empires, at various times from the 10th to the 15th century, when the region came into contact with European commerce. Guinea's colonial period began with French military penetration into the area in the mid-19th century. French domination was assured by the defeat in 1898 of the armies of Almamy Samory Touré, warlord and leader of Malinke descent, which gave France control of what today is Guinea and adjacent areas.

France negotiated Guinea's present boundaries in the late 19th and early 20th centuries with the British for Sierra Leone, the Portuguese for their Guinea colony (now Guinea-Bissau), and the Liberia. Under the French, the country formed the Territory of Guinea within French West Africa, administered by a governor general resident in Dakar. Lieutenant governors administered the individual colonies, including Guinea.

Led by Ahmed Sékou Touré, head of the Democratic Party of Guinea (PDG), which won 56 of 60 seats in 1957 territorial elections, the people of Guinea in a September 1958 plebiscite overwhelmingly rejected membership in the proposed French Community. The French withdrew quickly, and on October 2, 1958, Guinea proclaimed itself a sovereign and independent republic, with Sékou Touré as president.

Under Touré, Guinea became a one-party dictatorship, with a closed, socialized economy and no tolerance for human rights, free expression, or political opposition, which was ruthlessly suppressed. Originally credited for his advocacy of cross-ethnic nationalism, Touré gradually came to rely on his own Malinke ethnic group to fill positions in the party and government. Alleging plots and conspiracies against him at home and abroad, Touré's regime targeted real and imagined opponents, imprisoning many thousands in Soviet-style prison gulags, where hundreds perished. The regime's repression drove more than a million Guineans into exile, and Touré's paranoia ruined relations with foreign nations, including neighboring African states, increasing Guinea's isolation and further devastating its economy.

Sékou Touré and the PDG remained in power until his death on April 3, 1984, when a military junta headed by then-Lt. Col. Lansana Conte power.

# GOVERNMENT

The president governs Guinea, assisted by a council of 25 civilian ministers appointed by him. The government administers the country through eight regions, 33 prefectures, over 100 subprefectures, and many districts (known as communes in Conakry and other large cities and villages or "quartiers" in the interior). District-level leaders are elected; the president appoints officials to all other levels of the highly centralized administration.

## Principal Government Officials

**For up-to-date information on Principal Government Officials, see the Chiefs of State and Cabinet Members of Foreign Governments section starting on page 1.**

Guinea maintains an embassy in the United States at 2112 Leroy Place, NW, Washington, DC 20008 (tel. 202–

483–9420) and a mission to the United Nations at 140 E. 39th St., New York, NY 10016 (tel. 212–687–8115/16/17).

# POLITICAL CONDITIONS

A military junta, led by then-Lt. Col. Lansana Conte and styling itself the Military Committee of National Recovery (CMRN), took control of Guinea in April 1984, shortly after the death of independent Guinea's

first president, Sékou Touré. With Conte as president, the CMRN set about dismantling Touré's oppressive regime, abolishing the authoritarian constitution, dissolving the sole political party and its mass youth and women's organizations, and announcing the establishment of the Second Republic. The new government also released all political prisoners and committed itself to the protection of human rights. The CMRN also reorganized the judicial system, decentralized the administration, and began to liberalize the economy, promote private enterprise, and encourage foreign investment in order to reverse the steady economic decline

under Touré's rule by developing the country's natural resources.

In 1990, Guineans approved by referendum a new constitution that inaugurated the Third Republic, and a Supreme Court was established. In 1991, the CMRN was replaced by a mixed military and civilian body, the Transitional Council for National Recovery (CTRN), with Conte as president and a mandate to manage a 5-year transition to full civilian rule. The CTRN drafted "organic" laws to create republican institutions and to provide for independent political parties, national elections, and freedom of the press. Political party activity was legalized in 1992, when more than 40 political parties were officially recognized.

In December 1993, Conté was elected to a 5-year term as president in the country's first multi-party elections, which were marred by irregularities and lack of transparency on the part of the government. In 1995, Conte's ruling PUP party won 76 of 114 seats in elections for the National Assembly amid opposition claims of irregularities and government tampering. In 1996, President Conté reorganized the government, appointing Sidya Touré to the revived post of Prime Minister and charging him with special responsibility for leading the government's economic reform program.

Guinea's second presidential election, scheduled for December 1998, will be a crucial test of the country's commitment to fulfilling its transition to democracy.

# ECONOMY

Guinea is richly endowed with minerals, possessing an estimated one-third of the world's proven reserves of bauxite, more than 1.8 billion metric tons (MT) of high-grade iron ore, significant diamond and gold deposits, and undetermined quantities of uranium. Guinea also has considerable potential for growth in the agricultural and fishing sectors. Land, water, and climatic conditions provide opportunities for largescale irrigated farming and agroindustry.

Bauxite mining and alumina production provide about 80% of Guinea's foreign exchange. Several U.S. companies are active in this sector. Diamonds and gold also are mined and exported on a large scale, providing additional foreign exchange. Concession agreements have been signed for future exploitation of Guinea's extensive iron ore deposits. Remittances from Guineans living and working abroad and coffee exports account for the rest of Guinea's foreign exchange.

Since 1985, the Guinean Government has adopted policies to return com-

mercial activity to the private sector, promote investment, reduce the role of the state in the economy, and improve the administrative and judicial framework. The government has eliminated restrictions on agricultural enterprise and foreign trade, liquidated many parastatals, increased spending on education, and vastly downsized the civil service. The government also has made major strides in restructuring the public finances. The IMF and the World Bank are heavily involved in the development of Guinea's economy, as are many bilateral donor nations, including the United States. Guinea's economic reforms have had recent notable success, improving the rate of economic to 5% and reducing the rate of inflation to about 2%, as well as increasing government revenues while restraining official expenditures. Although Guinea's external debt burden remains high, the country is now current on external debt payments.

The government revised the private investment code in 1998 to stimulate economic activity in the spirit of a free enterprise. The code does not discriminate between foreigners and nationals and provides for repatriation of profits. Foreign investments outside Conakry are entitled to especially favorable conditions. A national investment commission has been formed to review all investment proposals. The United States and Guinea have signed an investment guarantee agreement that offers political risk insurance to American investors through OPIC. Guinea plans to inaugurate an arbitration court system to allow for the quick resolution of commercial disputes.

Guinea is richly endowed with minerals, possessing an estimated one-third of the world's proven reserves of bauxite, more than 1.8 billion metric tons (MT) of high-grade iron ore, significant diamond and gold deposits, and undetermined quantities of uranium. Guinea also has considerable potential for growth in the agricultural and fishing sectors. Land, water, and climatic conditions provide opportunities for largescale irrigated farming and agroindustry.

Possibilities for investment and commercial activities exist in all these areas, but Guinea's poorly developed infrastructure continues to present obstacles to investment projects.

See the comprehensive Country Commercial Guide for Guinea at the U.S. Embassy's web site or at the Department of State's web site.

# DEFENSE

Guinea's armed forces are divided into four branches—army, navy, air force, and gendarmerie—whose chiefs report to the Chairman of the Joint Chiefs of Staff, who is subordinate to the Minister of Defense. President Conté appointed his first civilian Minister of Defense in 1997. The 10,000-member army is the largest of the four services. The navy has about 900 personnel and operates several small patrol craft and barges. Air force personnel total about 700; its equipment includes several Russian-supplied fighter planes and transport planes. Several thousand gendarmes are responsible for internal security.

# FOREIGN RELATIONS

Guinea's relations other countries, including with West African neighbors, have improved steadily since 1985. Guinea reestablished relations with France and Germany in 1975, and with neighboring Côte d'Ivoire and Senegal in 1978. Guinea has been active in efforts toward regional integration and cooperation, especially regarding the Organization of African Unity and the Economic Organization of West African States (ECOWAS). Guinea takes its role in a variety of international organizations seriously and participates actively in their deliberations and decisions.

Guinea has participated in both diplomatic and military efforts to resolve conflicts in Liberia, Sierra Leone, and Guinea-Bissau, and contributed contingents of troops to peacekeeping operations in all three countries as part of ECOMOG, the Military Observer Group of ECOWAS. Guinea has offered asylum to over 700,000 Liberian, Sierra Leonean, and Bissauan refugees since 1990, despite the economic and environmental costs involved.

# U.S.-GUINEAN RELATIONS

The United States maintains close relations with Guinea. U.S. policy seeks to encourage Guinea's sustainable economic and social development, and its full integration into regional cooperative institutions, to achieve economic, social, political, and environmental objectives. The U.S. also seeks to promote increased U.S. private investment in Guinea's emerging economy.

The U.S. Mission in Guinea is composed of six agencies—Department of State, USAID, Peace Corps, USIS, the Centers for Disease Control, and the Department of Defense. In addition to the providing the full range of diplomatic functions, the embassy will disburse in FY 1998 $57,000 for Self-Help projects and $55,000 for Democracy and Human Rights projects. The Embassy also manages a military assistance program that provides $150,000 per year in military education and language training, as well as modest humanitarian assistance programs. In FY 1997 and FY 1998, U.S. military personnel deployed to Guinea to conduct disaster management training and a joint medical exercise.

USAID Guinea is now one of only five sustainable development missions in West Africa, with current core program areas in primary education, family health, democracy and governance, and natural resources management. The total FY 1998 budget for Guinea alone is $16.9 million.

The Peace Corps has about 110 volunteers throughout the country. Volunteers teach English and mathematics in high schools, assist in village development and health education, and collaborate with USAID on a natural resources management project. Guinea was the first country to inaugurate a full-fledged Crisis Corps program, a new Peace Corps initiative developed to address natural and man-made disasters.

## Principal U.S. Officials

**For up-to-date information on Principal U.S. Officials, see the U.S. Embassies, Consulates, and Foreign Service section starting on page 139.**

The U.S. Embassy is located at 2d Blvd. and 9th Avenue, Conakry. The mailing address is B.P. 603, Conakry, Guinea (Tel: 41–15–20/21/23. Fax: 41–15–22).

For further information on the U.S. Mission to Guinea, see U.S. Embassy Conakry's web site.

See the U.S. State Department's annual Country Report on Human Rights Practices in Guinea.

See also the comprehensive Country Commercial Guide for Guinea at the U.S. Embassy's web site or at the Department of State's web site.

# GUINEA-BISSAU

April 1994

Official Name:
**Republic of Guinea-Bissau**

# PROFILE

## Geography

**Area (including Bijagos Archipelago):** 36,260 sq. km. (14,000 sq. mi.), about the size of Indiana.
**Cities:** Capital—Bissau (pop. 200,000 est.) Other cities—Bafata, Gabu, Canchungo.
**Terrain:** Coastal plain; savanna in the east.
**Climate:** Tropical.

## People

**Nationality:** Noun and adjective—Guinean(s).
**Population (est.):** 1 million.
**Annual Growth Rate (est.):** 2.3%.
**Ethnic Groups:** Balanta 27%, Fula 23%, Mandinka 12%, Manjaco 11%, Papel 10%.
**Religions:** Indigenous beliefs 65%, Muslim 30%, Christian 5%.
**Languages:** Portuguese (official), Criolo, French, many indigenous languages, including Mandinka and Fula.
**Education:** Years compulsory—4. Literacy—30% of adults.
**Health:** Infant mortality rate—140/1,000. Life expectancy—43 years.
**Work Force (454,000):** Agriculture—78%. Industry, services and commerce—14%. Government—8%

## Government

**Type:** Republic.
**Independence:** September 24, 1973 (proclaimed unilaterally); September 10, 1974 (de jure from Portugal).
**Constitution:** Adopted 1984; amended 1991.
**Branches:** Executive—president (chief of state and head of government), prime minister and council of state, ministers and secretaries of state. Legislature—People's National Assembly (ANP), 150 members indirectly elected in 1989. Judicial—Supreme Court and lower courts. Administrative Subdivisions: Autonomous sector of Bissau and eight regions.
**Political parties:** African Party for the Independence of Guinea-Bissau and Cape Verde is the ruling party; 11 other political parties were legalized during 1991-93.
**Suffrage:** Universal at 18.
**Flag:** Vertical red band with black star on the staff side, yellow upper horizontal band, green lower horizontal band.

## Economy

**GDP (1993 est):** $190 million
**Annual growth rate:** 3%.
**Per Capita Income (1993):** $200.
**Natural resources:** Fish and timber. Bauxite and phosphate deposits are not exploited; possible off-shore petroleum.
**Agriculture (50% of GDP):** Prod-ucts—cashews, rice, peanuts, cotton, palm oil, sugar. Arable land—43%.
**Industry (16% of GDP):** Products—agricultural processing, fish processing, light construction, soft drinks.
**Trade (1991):** Exports—$20.4 million: cashews, cotton, wood, fish and shellfish, coconuts. Major markets—Portugal, India, Spain, France. Imports $67.5 million—rice and other foodstuffs, transportation equipment, machinery and spare parts, construction equipment, petroleum products. Major suppliers—Portugal, Germany, Netherlands, Taiwan, Senegal, France.
**Exchange Rate:** (March 1994) 12,300 Guinea-Bissau Pesos=U.S.$1. Rate fluctuates daily; pesos not convertible abroad.

# PEOPLE

The population of Guinea-Bissau is ethnically diverse with distinct languages, customs, and social structures. Most people are agriculturalists, with traditional religious beliefs (animism); 30% percent are Muslim, principally Fula and Mandinka-speaker concentrated in the north and northeast. Other important groups are the Balanta and Papel, living in the southern coastal regions, and the Manjaco and Mancanha, occupying the central and northern coastal areas. The various groups mix easily in urban areas, where there is a notable lack of tribal tensions.

# HISTORY

The rivers of Guinea and the islands of Cape Verde were among the first areas in Africa explored by the Portuguese in the 15th century. Portugal claimed Portuguese Guinea in 1446, but few trading posts were established before 1600. In 1630, a "captaincy-general" of Portuguese Guinea was established to administer the territory. With the cooperation of some local tribes, the Portuguese entered the slave trade and exported large numbers of Africans to the Western Hemisphere via the Cape Verde Islands. Cacheu became one of the major slave centers, and a small fort still stands in the town. The slave trade declined in the 19th century, and Bissau, originally founded as a military and slave-trading center in 1765, grew to become the major commercial center.

Portuguese conquest and consolidation of the interior did not begin until the latter half of the 19th century. Portugal lost part of Guinea to French West Africa (including the center of earlier Portuguese commercial interest, the Casamance River region). A dispute with Great Britain over the island of Bolama was settled in Portugal's favor with the involvement of U.S. President Ulysses S. Grant.

Before World War I, Portuguese forces under Maj. Teixeira Pinto, with some assistance from the Muslim population, subdued animist tribes and eventually established the territory's borders. The interior of Portuguese Guinea was brought under control after more than 30 years of fighting; final subjugation of the Bijagos Islands did not occur until 1936. The administrative capital was moved from Bolama to Bissau in 1941, and in 1952, by constitutional amendment, the colony of Portuguese Guinea became an overseas province of Portugal.

In 1956, the African Party for the Independence of Guinea and Cape Verde (PAIGC) was organized clandestinely by Amilcar Cabral and Raphael Barbosa. The PAIGC moved its headquarters to Conakry, Guinea, in 1960 and started an armed rebellion against the Portuguese in 1961.

Despite the presence of Portuguese troops, which grew to more than 35,000, the PAIGC steadily expanded its influence until, by 1968, it controlled most of the country. It established civilian rule in the territory under its control and held elections for a National Assembly. Portuguese forces and civilians increasingly were confined to their garrisons and larger towns. The Portuguese Governor and Commander-in-Chief from 1968 to 1973, Gen. Antonio de Spinola, returned to Portugal and led the movement which brought democracy to Portugal and independence for its colonies.

Amilcar Cabral was assassinated in Conakry in 1973, and party leadership fell to Aristides Pereira, who later became the first president of the Republic of Cape Verde. The PAIGC National Assembly met at Boe in the southeastern region and declared the independence of Guinea-Bissau on September 24, 1973. Following Portugal's April 1974 revolution, it granted independence to Guinea-Bissau on September 10, 1974. The United States recognized the new nation that day. Luis Cabral, Amilcar Cabral's half-brother, became President of Guinea-Bissau. In late 1980, the government was overthrown in a relatively bloodless coup led by Prime Minister and former armed forces commander Joao Bernardo Vieira.

From November 1980 to May 1984, power was held by a provisional government responsible to a Revolutionary Council headed by President Joao Bernardo Vieira. In 1984, the council was dissolved, and the 150-member National Popular Assembly (ANP) was reconstituted. The single-party assembly approved a new constitution, elected President Vieira to a new 5-year term, and elected a Council of State, which is the executive agent of the ANP. Under this system,

the president presides over the Council of State and serves as head of state and government. The president is also head of the PAIGC and commander in chief of the armed forces.

There were alleged coup plots against the Vieira Government in 1983, 1985, and 1993. In 1986, first Vice President Paulo Correia and five others were executed for treason.

# GOVERNMENT AND POLITICAL CONDITIONS

In 1989, the ruling PAIGC under the direction of President Vieira began to outline a political liberalization program which the ANP approved in 1991. Reforms which paved the way for multi-party democracy included the repeal of articles of the constitution which had enshrined the leading role of the PAIGC. Laws were ratified to allow the formation of other political parties, a free press, and independent trade unions with the right to strike.

By late 1993, there were 12 legal political parties in the country. A national elections law was approved in February 1993, and a month later a national elections commission was established. Guinea-Bissau's first multi-party elections for president and parliament are tentatively planned for 1994, following a nationwide voter registration process.

## Principal Government Officials

**For up-to-date information on Principal Government Officials, see the Chiefs of State and Cabinet Members of Foreign Governments section starting on page 1.**

The embassy of the Republic of Guinea-Bissau is located at 918 16th Street, NW, Washington, DC 20006 (tel. 202-872-4222). The Mission of

Guinea-Bissau to the United Nations is located at 211 East 43rd Street, Suite 604, New York, NY 10017 (tel. 212-611-3977).

# ECONOMY

Guinea-Bissau is among the world's least developed nations. The principal economic activity is agriculture. Cashew crops have increased in recent years, and the country now ranks sixth in cashew production. Guinea-Bissau exports some fish and seafood, along with small amounts of peanuts, palm kernels, and timber. License fees for fishing provided the government with revenues of $13.5 million in 1992. Rice is the major crop and staple food. Rice production has increased by more than 10% per year since 1983, largely because of improved economic incentives. However, rice imports remain high—up to 80,000 tons per year.

In 1987, the government launched a program of economic reform and signed an agreement for a structural adjustment program with the World Bank. A second structural adjustment credit, worth about $18 million, was negotiated in 1989.

Trade reform and price liberalization are the most successful areas of the country's structural adjustment program. While institutional weaknesses in the public and private sectors persist, reforms and the development of the private sector have begun to invigorate the economy. Real gross domestic product has grown steadily at 3%-to-6% per annum.

Inflation decreased from 70% in 1992 to 30% in 1993. There were major reforms in tax revenue and customs collections. Monetary expansion was reduced from 118% in 1992 to 40% in 1993. However, with an external debt of $600 million, the country has a debt-to-GDP ratio of 300% and an annual debt service more than twice the value of exports.

At independence, Guinea-Bissau had little infrastructure and its industry

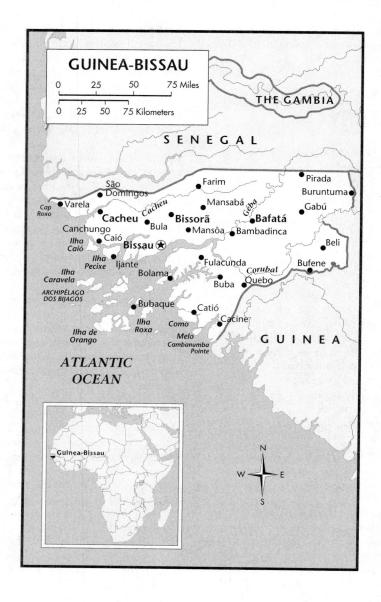

consisted of one factory—a brewery. A socialist-statist program for light industries during the late 1970s resulted in extensive foreign debt and failed enterprises. A corrective program has been established to privatize parastatal organizations. The country plans to develop its timber resources and rich offshore fish and shellfish production.

Mineral deposits have proved difficult to develop, and any potential offshore petroleum reserves may lie in the area which the International Court of Justice declared in 1991 to be Senegalese maritime territory. Bissau's port facilities have been expanded and improved in recent

years, with better shipping connections to European ports. The city's international airport can accommodate any type of jet aircraft; a new passenger terminal is under construction. The country has 2,600 kilometers (1,600 mi.) of roads, of which 550 (350 mi.) kilometers are paved.

# FOREIGN RELATIONS

Guinea-Bissau follows a non-aligned foreign policy and seeks friendly and cooperative relations with a wide variety of states and organizations. France, Portugal, Brazil, Egypt, Nigeria, Taiwan, Libya, Cuba, Sweden, the Palestine Liberation Organization, Russia, and the U.S. have diplomatic offices in Bissau.

Guinea-Bissau is a member of the UN and many of its specialized and related agencies, including the World Bank and the International Monetary Fund (IMF); African Development Bank (AFDB), Economic Community of West African States (ECOWAS), West African Economic Community (CEDAO), Organization of the Islamic Conference (OIC), Organization of African Unity (OAU), and permanent Interstate Committee for drought control in the Sahel (CILSS).

# U.S.-GUINEA-BISSAU RELATIONS

The United States and Guinea-Bissau enjoy excellent bilateral relations. The U.S. recognized the independence of Guinea-Bissau on September 10, 1974. Guinea-Bissau's ambassador to the United States and the United Nations was one of the first that the new nation sent abroad. The U.S. opened an embassy in Bissau in 1976, and the first U.S. ambassador presented credentials later that year.

U.S. assistance began in 1975 with a $1 million grant to the UN High Commissioner for Refugees for resettlement of refugees returning to Guinea-Bissau and for 25 training grants at African technical schools for Guinean students. Emergency food was a major element in U.S. assistance to Guinea-Bissau in the first years after independence. Since 1975, the U.S. has provided more than $65 million in grant aid and other assistance.

Currently U.S. Agency for International Development assistance to the country is about $5.5 million per year. It is designed to increase sustainable private sector economic activity in Guinea-Bissau's critical growth sec-

## Travel Notes

**Clothing:** Lightweight, loose-fitting, washable clothing is recommended. Dress is casual.

**Currency:** The Guinea-Bissau peso is not convertible outside the country. Dollars and travelers checks can be exchanged at banks. Some hotels and stores accept only hard currency or international credit cards.

**Customs:** U.S. citizens must obtain visas before arrival; airport visas are not issued. Immunization against yellow fever is required.

**Health:** Sanitation is poor, and tap water is not potable. Hospitals are inadequately staffed, and medicines often are in short supply. Although the Guinea-Bissau Government only requires immunization for yellow fever, immunization against typhus, typhoid, cholera, rabies, hepatitis, and tetanus is strongly recommended. Malaria is prevalent, and visitors should begin a regimen of malaria prophylaxis prior to arrival. Gastrointestinal infections, bilharzia, HIV infection, and tuberculosis are endemic. Medical air evacuation insurance coverage is highly recommended for all visitors.

**Transportation:** There are weekly flights between Bissau, Lisbon, and Paris. Regular air service also links Bissau with Dakar, Banjul, and Praia. Unreliable ferry service in northern areas makes travel by road between Guinea-Bissau and Senegal difficult. Land transportation between Bissau and Conakry is very difficult and usually takes at least two days in the dry season (longer in the rainy season).

**Telecommunications:** International telephone calls can be dialed direct, and connections with the U.S. are good. Internal telephone service is adequate. Telegraphic communications generally are reliable. Bissau is five time zones ahead of eastern standard time, in the Greenwich mean zone.

**Travel Advice:** For up-to-date information from the U.S. State Department on possible inconvenient or hazardous situations, see the **Travel Warnings and Consular Information Sheets from the U.S. Government** section starting on page 1723. For the latest information on health requirements and conditions, see the **International Travelers' Health Information** section starting on page 1385. For further information dealing with nonurgent matter, see the **Tips for Travelers to...** section starting on page 1588.

tors—the production, processing, and marketing of cashews, rice, fruits, and vegetables as well as fish and forest products. Removing legal, regulatory, and judicial constraints to private sector activity is also a goal of U.S. assistance. Direct private sector assistance is offered to help the country respond quickly to emerging market opportunities.

The United States and Guinea-Bissau signed an international military training agreement (IMET) in 1986, and the U.S. has provided English-language teaching facilities as well as communications and navigational equipment to support the navy's costal surveillance program.

Beginning in 1988, Peace Corps volunteers began working as English teachers, teacher trainers, health

workers, and agricultural extension agents. The Peace Corps now has about 40 volunteers throughout the country.

## Principal U.S. Embassy Officials

For up-to-date information on Principal U.S. Officials, see the U.S. Embassies, Consulates, and Foreign Service section starting on page 139.

The U.S. embassy in Bissau is located at Bairro de Penha, tel (245) 25-2273/74/75/76. The USAID telephone is (245) 20-1800; Peace Corps is (245) 25-2127.

# GUYANA

April 2001

## Official Name:
## Co-operative Republic of Guyana

# PROFILE

## Geography

**Area:** 214,970 sq. km. (82,980 sq. mi.); about the size of Idaho.
**Cities:** Capital—Georgetown (pop. 250,000). Other cities—Linden (29,000) and New Amsterdam (18,000).
**Terrain:** Coastal plain, inland highlands, rain forest, savanna.
**Climate:** Tropical.

## People

**Nationality:** Noun and adjective—Guyanese (sing. and pl.).
**Population:** (last census 1991) 723,673; (2000 est.) 700,000.
**Ethnic groups:** East Indian origin 49%, African origin 32%, mixed 12%, Amerindian 6%, White and Chinese 1%.
**Religions:** Christian 57%, Hindu 33%, Muslim 9%, other 1%.
**Languages:** English, Guyanese Creole, Amerindian languages (primarily Carib and Arawak).
**Education:** Years compulsory—ages 5 1/2–14 1/2. Attendance—primary 78.6%, secondary 80.5%. Literacy—96.5% of adults who have attended school.
**Health:** Infant mortality rate—49/1,000. Life expectancy—men 59 yrs., women 64 yrs. Work force (278,000):

Industry and commerce—36.4%; agriculture—30.2%; services—30.2%; other—3.2%.

## Government

**Type:** Republic within the Commonwealth.
**Independence:** May 26, 1966; Republic, February 23, 1970. Constitution: 1980.
**Branches:** Executive—executive president (chief of state and head of government), prime minister. Legislative—unicameral National Assembly (53 directly, 12 indirectly elected members for 5-year term. Judicial—Judicial Court of Appeal, High Court.
**Subdivisions:** 10 regions. Political parties (voting seats in the National Assembly): People's Progressive Party/Civic (PPP/C) 36; People's National Congress (PNC) 25; Alliance for Guyana (AFG) 2; The United Force (TUF) 2. Total seats: 65.
**Suffrage:** Universal at 18.

## Economy (1999)

**GDP:** $577 million. Real annual growth rate: (1999) 3.0%., (2000) 0.5%.
**Per capita GDP:** $824.
**Agriculture:** Products—sugar, rice.
**Natural resources:** Gold, bauxite, diamonds, timber, shrimp, fish.
**Industry:** Types—gold and bauxite mining, rice milling, beverage, food stuff processing, apparel, footwear

assembly.
**Trade:** (1999) Exports—$525 million, $360 million (through third quarter 2000): gold, sugar, bauxite, shrimp, rice, timber. Major markets—U.S. (24.5%), U.K., CARICOM countries, Canada. Imports—$550 million, $437 million (through third quarter 2000). Major suppliers—U.S. (37.7%), U.K., Venezuela, CARICOM, Canada.

# PEOPLE

Guyana's population is made up of five main ethnic groups—East Indian, African, Amerindian, Chinese, and Portuguese. Ninety percent of the inhabitants live on the narrow coastal plain, where population density is more than 115 persons per square kilometer (380 per sq. mi.). The population density for Guyana as a whole is low—less than four persons per square kilometer. Although the government has provided free education from nursery school to the university level since 1975, it has not allocated sufficient funds to maintain the standards of what had been considered the best educational system in the region. Many school buildings are in poor condition, there is a shortage of text and exercise books, the number of teachers has declined, and fees are being charged at the university level for some courses of study for the first time.

# HISTORY

Before the arrival of Europeans, the region was inhabited by both Carib and Arawak tribes, who named it Guiana, which means land of many waters. The Dutch settled in Guyana in the late 16th century, but their control ended when the British became the de facto rulers in 1796. In 1815, the colonies of Essequibo, Demerara, and Berbice were officially ceded to Great Britain at the Congress of Vienna and, in 1831, were consolidated as British Guiana. Following the abolition of slavery in 1834, thousands of indentured laborers were brought to Guyana to replace the slaves on the sugarcane plantations, primarily from India but also from Portugal and China. The British stopped the practice in 1917. Many of the Afro-Guyanese former slaves moved to the towns and became the majority urban population, whereas the Indo-Guyanese remained predominantly rural. A scheme in 1862 to bring black workers from the United States was unsuccessful. The small Amerindian population lives in the country's interior.

The people drawn from these diverse origins have coexisted peacefully for the most part. Slave revolts, such as the one in 1763 led by Guyana's national hero, Cuffy, demonstrated the desire for basic rights but also a willingness to compromise. Politically inspired racial disturbances between Indo-Guyanese and Afro-Guyanese erupted in 1962–64. However, the basically conservative and cooperative nature of Guyanese society contributed to a cooling of racial tensions.

Guyanese politics, nevertheless, occasionally has been turbulent. The first modern political party in Guyana was the People's Progressive Party (PPP), established on January 1, 1950, with Forbes Burnham, a British-educated Afro-Guyanese, as chairman; Dr. Cheddi Jagan, a U.S.-educated Indo-

Guyanese, as second vice chairman; and his American-born wife, Janet Jagan, as secretary general. The PPP won 18 out of 24 seats in the first popular elections permitted by the colonial government in 1953, and Dr. Jagan became leader of the house and minister of agriculture in the colonial government. Five months later, on October 9, 1953, the British suspended the constitution and landed troops because, they said, the Jagans and the PPP were planning to make Guyana a communist state. These events led to a split in the PPP, in which Burnham broke away and founded what eventually became the People's National Congress (PNC).

Elections were permitted again in 1957 and 1961, and Cheddi Jagan's PPP ticket won on both occasions, with 48% of the vote in 1957 and 43% in 1961. Cheddi Jagan became the first premier of British Guiana, a position he held for 7 years. At a constitutional conference in London in 1963, the U.K. Government agreed to grant independence to the colony but only after another election in which proportional representation would be introduced for the first time. It was widely believed that this system would reduce the number of seats won by the PPP and prevent it from obtaining a clear majority in Parliament. The December 1964 elections gave the PPP 46%, the PNC 41%, and the United Force (TUF), a conservative party, 12%. TUF threw its votes in the legislature to Forbes Burnham, who became prime minister.

Guyana achieved independence in May 1966, and became a republic on February 23, 1970—the anniversary of the Cuffy slave rebellion. From December 1964 until his death in August 1985, Forbes Burnham ruled Guyana in an increasingly autocratic manner, first as prime minister and later, after the adoption of a new constitution in 1980, as executive president. During that time- frame, elections were viewed in Guyana and abroad as fraudulent. Human rights and civil liberties were suppressed, and two major political assassinations occurred: the Jesuit Priest and journalist Bernard Darke in July 1979, and the distinguished historian

and WPA Party leader Walter Rodney in June 1980. Agents of President Burnham are widely believed to have been responsible for both deaths.

Following Burnham's own death in 1985, Prime Minister Hugh Desmond Hoyte acceded to the presidency and was formally elected in the December 1985 national elections. Hoyte gradually reversed Burnham's policies, moving from state socialism and one-party control to a market economy and unrestricted freedom of the press and assembly. On October 5, 1992, a new National Assembly and regional councils were elected in the first Guyanese election since 1964 to be internationally recognized as free and fair. Cheddi Jagan was elected and sworn in as president on October 9, 1992.

When President Jagan died in March 1997, Prime Minister Samuel Hinds replaced him in accordance with constitutional provisions. President Jagan's widow, Janet Jagan, was elected president in December 1997. She resigned in August 1999 due to ill health and was succeeded by Finance Minister Bharrat Jagdeo, who had been named prime minister a day earlier. National elections were held March 2001, but results are not final.

# GOVERNMENT

Legislative power rests in a unicameral National Assembly, with 53 members chosen on the basis of proportional representation from national lists named by the political parties. An additional 12 members are elected by regional councils at the same time as the National Assembly. The elections system was revised for the 2001 elections. The president may dissolve the assembly and call new elections at any time, but no later than 5 years from its first sitting.

Executive authority is exercised by the president, who appoints and supervises the prime minister and other ministers. The president is not directly elected; each party presenting a slate of candidates for the assembly must designate in advance a leader who will become president if that party receives the largest number of votes. Any dissolution of the assembly and election of a new assembly can lead to a change in the assembly majority and consequently a change in the presidency. Only the prime minister is required to be a member of the assembly. In practice, most other ministers also are members. Those who are not serve as non-elected members, which permits them to debate but not to vote.

The highest judicial body is the Court of Appeal, headed by a chancellor of the judiciary. The second level is the High Court, presided over by a chief justice. The chancellor and the chief justice are appointed by the president.

For administrative purposes, Guyana is divided into 10 regions, each headed by a chairman who presides over a regional democratic council. Local communities are administered by village or city councils.

## Principal Government Officials

**For up-to-date information on Principal Government Officials, see the Chiefs of State and Cabinet Members of Foreign Governments section starting on page 1.**

Guyana maintains an embassy in the United States at 2490 Tracy Place NW, Washington, DC 20008 (tel. 202–265–6900).

# POLITICAL CONDITIONS

Race and ideology have been the dominant political influences in Guyana. Since the split of the multiracial PPP in 1955, politics has been based more on ethnicity than on ideology. From 1964 to 1992, the PNC dominated Guyana's politics. The PNC draws its support primarily from urban Blacks, and for many years declared itself a

GUYANA

socialist party whose purpose was to make Guyana a nonaligned socialist state, in which the party, as in communist countries, was above all other institutions.

The overwhelming majority of Guyanese of East Indian extraction traditionally have backed the People's Progressive Party, headed by the

Jagans. Rice farmers and sugar workers in the rural areas form the bulk of PPP's support, but Indo-Guyanese who dominate the country's urban business community also have provided important support.

Following independence, and with the help of substantial foreign aid, social benefits were provided to a broader section of the population, specifically in health, education, housing, road and bridge building, agriculture, and rural development. However, during Forbes Burnham's last years, the government's attempts to build a socialist society caused a massive emigration of skilled workers, and, along with other economic factors, led to a significant decline in the overall quality of life in Guyana.

After Burnham's death in 1985, President Hoyte took steps to stem the economic decline, including strengthening financial controls over the parastatal corporations and supporting the private sector. In August 1987, at a PNC Congress, Hoyte announced that the PNC rejected orthodox communism and the one-party state.

As the elections scheduled for 1990 approached, Hoyte, under increasing pressure from inside and outside Guyana, gradually opened the political system. After a visit to Guyana by former U.S. President Jimmy Carter in 1990, Hoyte made changes in the electoral rules, appointed a new chairman of the Elections Commission, and endorsed putting together new voters' lists, thus delaying the election. The elections, which finally took place in 1992, were witnessed by 100 international observers, including a group headed by Mr. Carter and another from the commonwealth of nations. Both groups issued reports saying that the elections had been free and fair, despite violent attacks on the Elections Commission building on election day and other irregularities.

Cheddi Jagan served as Premier (1957–64) and then minority leader in Parliament until his election as President in 1992. One of the Caribbean's most charismatic and famous leaders, Jagan was a founder of the PPP which led Guyana's struggle for independence. Over the years, he moderated his Marxist-Leninist ideology. After his election as President, Jagan demonstrated a commitment to democracy, followed a pro-Western foreign policy, adopted free market policies, and pursued sustainable development for Guyana's environment. Nonetheless, he continued to

press for debt relief and a new global human order in which developed countries would increase assistance to less developed nations. Jagan died on March 6, 1997, and was succeeded by Samuel A. Hinds, whom he had appointed Prime Minister. President Hinds then appointed Janet Jagan, widow of the late President, to serve as Prime Minister.

In national elections on December 15, 1997, Janet Jagan was elected President, and her PPP party won a 55% majority of seats in Parliament. She was sworn in on December 19. Mrs. Jagan is a founding member of the PPP and was very active in party politics. She was Guyana's first female prime minister and vice president, two roles she performed concurrently before being elected to the presidency.

The PNC, which won just under 40% of the vote, disputed the results of the 1997 elections, alleging electoral fraud. Public demonstrations and some violence followed, until a CARICOM team came to Georgetown to broker an accord between the two parties, calling for an international audit of the election results, a redrafting of the constitution, and elections under the constitution within 3 years. Elections were held in March 2001, but results are not final.

# ECONOMY

With a per capita gross domestic product of only $824 in 1999, Guyana is one of the poorest countries in the Western Hemisphere. The economy made dramatic progress after President Hoyte's 1989 economic recovery program (ERP). As a result of the ERP, Guyana's GDP increased 6% in 1991 following 15 years of decline. Growth was consistently above 6% until 1995 when it dipped to 5.1%. The government reported that the economy grew at a rate of 7.9% in 1996, 6.2% in 1997, and fell 1.3% in 1998. The 1999 growth rate was 3%. The unofficial growth rate in 2000 was 0.5%.

Developed in conjunction with the World Bank and the International Monetary Fund (IMF), the ERP significantly reduced the government's role in the economy, encouraged foreign investment, enabled the government to clear all its arrears on loan repayments to foreign governments and the multilateral banks, and brought about the sale of 15 of the 41 government-owned (parastatal) businesses. The telephone company and assets in the timber, rice, and fishing industries also were privatized. International corporations were hired to manage the huge state sugar company, GUYSUCO, and the largest state bauxite mine. An American company was allowed to open a bauxite mine, and two Canadian companies were permitted to develop the largest open-pit gold mine in Latin America. However, efforts to privatize the two state-owned bauxite mining companies, Berbice Mining Company and Linden Mining Company have so far been unsuccessful.

Most price controls were removed, the laws affecting mining and oil exploration were improved, and an investment policy receptive to foreign investment was announced. Tax reforms designed to promote exports and agricultural production in the private sector were enacted.

Agriculture and mining are Guyana's most important economic activities, with sugar, bauxite, rice, and gold accounting for 70%-75% of export earnings. However, the rice sector experienced a decline in 2000, with export earnings down 27% through the third quarter 2000. Ocean shrimp exports, which were heavily impacted by a 1-month import ban to the United States in 1999, accounted for only 3.5% of total export earnings that year. Shrimp exports rebounded in 2000, representing 11% of export earnings through the third quarter 2000. Other exports include timber, diamonds, garments, rum, and pharmaceuticals. The value of these other exports is increasing.

Since 1986, Guyana has received its entire wheat supply from the United States on concessional terms under a PL 480 Food for Peace program. It is now supplied on a grant basis. The Guyanese currency generated by the sale of the wheat is used for purposes agreed upon by the U.S. and Guyana Governments. As with many developing countries, Guyana is heavily indebted. Reduction of the debt burden has been one of the present administration's top priorities. In 1999, through the Paris Club "Lyons terms" and the heavily indebted poor countries initiative (HIPC) Guyana managed to negotiate $256 million in debt forgiveness.

In qualifying for HIPC assistance, for the first time, Guyana became eligible for a reduction of its multilateral debt. About half of Guyana's debt is owed to the multilateral development banks and 20% to its neighbor Trinidad and Tobago, which until 1986 was its principal supplier of petroleum products. Almost all debt to the U.S. Government has been forgiven. In late 1999, net international reserves were at $123.2 million, down from $254 million in 1994. However, net international reserves had rebounded to $174.1 million by January 2001.

Guyana's extremely high debt burden to foreign creditors has meant limited availability of foreign exchange and reduced capacity to import necessary raw materials, spare parts, and equipment, thereby further reducing production. The increase in global fuel costs also contributed to the country's decline in production and growing trade deficit. The decline of production has increased unemployment. Although no reliable statistics exist, combined unemployment and underemployment are estimated at about 30%.

Emigration, principally to the U.S. and Canada, remains substantial. Net emigration in 1998 was estimated to be about 1.4% of the population, and in 1999, this figure totaled 1.2%. After years of a state-dominated economy, the mechanisms for private investment, domestic or foreign, are still evolving. The shift from a state-controlled economy to a primarily free market system began under Desmond Hoyte and continued

## Travel Notes

**Travel Advice:** For up-to-date information from the U.S. State Department on possible inconvenient or hazardous situations, see the **Travel Warnings and Consular Information Sheets from the U.S. Government** section starting on page 1723. For the latest information on health requirements and conditions, see the **International Travelers' Health Information** section starting on page 1385. For further information dealing with non-urgent matter, see the **Tips for Travelers to...** section starting on page 1588.

under PPP/CIVIC governments. The current PPP/C administration recognizes the need for foreign investment to create jobs, enhance technical capabilities, and generate goods for export.

The foreign exchange market was fully liberalized in 1991, and currency is now freely traded without restriction. The rate is subject to change on a daily basis, but the Guyana dollar has depreciated 17.6% from 1998 to 2000 and may depreciate further pending the stability of the post-election period.

# FOREIGN RELATIONS

After independence in 1966, Guyana sought an influential role in international affairs, particularly among Third World and nonaligned nations. It served twice on the UN Security Council (1975–76 and 1982–83). Former Vice President, Deputy Prime Minister, and Attorney General Mohamed Shahabuddeen served a 9-year term on the International Court of Justice (1987–96).

Guyana has diplomatic relations with a wide range of nations. The European Union (EU), the Inter-American Development Bank (IDB), the UN Development Program (UNDP), the World Health Organization (WHO), and the Organization of American States (OAS) have offices in Georgetown.

Guyana strongly supports the concept of regional integration. It played an important role in the founding of the Caribbean Community and Common Market (CARICOM), but its status as the organization's poorest member limits its ability to exert leadership in regional activities. Guyana has sought to keep foreign policy in close alignment with the consensus of CARICOM members, especially in voting in the UN, OAS, and other international organizations. In 1993, Guyana ratified the 1988 Vienna Convention on illicit traffic in narcotic drugs and cooperates with U.S. law enforcement agencies on counter-narcotics efforts.

Two neighbors have longstanding territorial disputes with Guyana. Since the 19th century, Venezuela has claimed all of Guyana west of the Essequibo River—62% of Guyana's territory. At a meeting in Geneva in 1966, the two countries agreed to receive recommendations from a representative of the UN Secretary General on ways to settle the dispute peacefully. Diplomatic contacts between the two countries and the Secretary General's representative continue. Neighboring Suriname also claims the territory east of Guyana's new river, a largely uninhabited area of some 15,000 square kilometers (6,000 sq. mi.) in southeast Guyana. Guyana and Suriname also dispute their offshore maritime boundries. This dispute flared up in June 2000 in response to an effort by a Canadian company to drill for oil under a Guyanese concession. Guyana regards its legal title to all of its territory as sound.

# U.S.-GUYANESE RELATIONS

U.S. policy toward Guyana seeks to promote democracy, sustainable development, and human rights. During the last years of his administration, President Hoyte sought to improve relations with the United States as part of a decision to move his country toward genuine political nonalignment. Relations also were improved by Hoyte's efforts to respect human rights, invite international observers for the 1992 elections, and reform electoral laws. The United States also welcomed the Hoyte government's economic reform and efforts, which stimulated investment and growth. The 1992 democratic elections and Guyana's reaffirmation of sound economic policies and respect for human rights have placed U.S.-Guyanese relations on an excellent footing. Under successive PPP governments, the United States and Guyana continued to improve relations. President Cheddi Jagan was committed to democracy, adopted more free market policies, and pursued sustainable development for Guyana's environment.

President Hinds joined President Clinton and 14 other Caribbean leaders in May 1997, during the first-ever US.-regional summit in Bridgetown, Barbados. The meeting strengthened the basis for regional cooperation on justice and counternarcotics, finance and development, and trade. The U.S.

maintains positive relations with the current government.

Following the 1992 elections, Canada, the United Kingdom, and the United States increased their aid to Guyana. U.S. assistance had ceased in 1982 due to economic and political differences with the Burnham regime, but in 1986, the United States began to supply humanitarian food aid to the country, to a total value of nearly $500 million in the years 1986–93. All together, since 1955, the United States has provided Guyana with more than $171 million in assistance.

U.S. military medical and engineering teams have conducted training exercises in Guyana, digging wells, building schools and clinics, and providing medical treatment.

## Principal U.S. Embassy Officials

**For up-to-date information on Principal U.S. Officials, see the U.S.**

**Embassies, Consulates, and Foreign Service section starting on page 139.**

The U.S. embassy in Guyana is located at the corner of Duke and Young Streets, Georgetown (tel. 592–2-54900/9; fax: 592–2-58497).

## Other Contact Information

**U.S. Department of Commerce**
International Trade Administration
Trade Information Center
14th & Constitution, NW
Washington, DC 20230
Tel: 800-USA-TRADE

**Caribbean/Latin American Action**
1818 N Street, NW, Suite 310
Washington, DC 20036
Tel: (202) 466–7464
Fax: (202) 822–0075

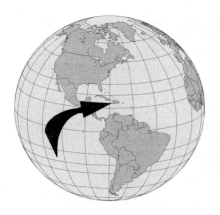

# HAITI

April 2001

Official Name:
**Republic of Haiti**

# PROFILE

## Geography

**Area:** 27,750 sq. km. (10714 sq. mi.); about the size of Maryland. Isle de la Gonave and Isle de la Tortue comprise Haiti's principal offshore territories.

**Cities:** Capital—Port-au-Prince (pop. 1,220,000). Other cities—Cap Haitien (pop. 600,000).

**Terrain:** Rugged mountains with small coastal plains and river valleys, and a large east-central elevated plateau.

**Climate:** Warm, semiarid, high humidity in many coastal areas.

## People

**Nationality:** Noun and adjective—Haitian(s).

**Population:** (1999 est.) 7,771,000.

**Annual population growth rate:** (1999 est.) 2.0%.

**Ethnic groups:** African descent 95%, African and European descent 5%.

**Religions:** Roman Catholic 80%, Protestant 16%, voodoo practices pervasive.

**Languages:** French (official), Creole (official).

**Education:** Years compulsory—6. Adult literacy (1999 est.)—46%.

**Health:** Infant mortality rate—71/ 1,000. Life expectancy—54 yrs.

## Government

**Type:** Republic

**Independence:** 1804. **Constitution:** 1987.

**Branches:** Executive—President. Legislative—Senate (27 Seats), Chamber of Deputies (83 seats). Judicial—Court of Cassation.

**Administrative subdivisions:** Nine departments.

**Political parties and coalitions:** Lavalas Family (FL), Struggling People's Organization (OPL), Open the Gate Party (PLB), Christian Movement for a New Haiti (MOCHRENHA), Democratic Consultation Group (ESPACE), Popular Solidarity Alliance (ESKANP), several others. The Democratic Convergence is a coalition of parties formed to protest the results of the May 2000 elections.

**Suffrage:** Universal at 18.

## Economy

**GDP:** (1999) $3.0 billion.

**GDP growth rate:** (est. 2000) 1.2%.

**Per capita GNP:** (1999) $460

**GDP by sector:** (1999) Agriculture—31%. Industry—21%. Services—45%.

**Inflation:** (2000 year-end) 12.6%.

**Natural resources:** Bauxite, copper, calcium carbonate, gold, marble. Agriculture (31% of GDP): Coffee, mangoes, sugarcane, rice, corn, cacao, sorghum, pulses, other fruits and vegetables.

**Industry:** (21% of GDP) Apparel, handicrafts, electronics, food processing, beverages, tobacco products, furniture, printing, chemicals, steel. Services (45% of GDP): Commerce, government, tourism.

**Trade:** (1999) Total exports F.O.B.—$352 million: apparel, mangoes, leather and raw hides, seafood, electrical. Major market—U.S. ($301 million). Imports—$1.0 billion C.I.F. From U.S. $599 million—grains, soybean oil, motor vehicles, machinery, meat, vegetables, plastics, petroleum.

**Exchange rate:** Approx. 24 Haitian gourdes=U.S.$1.00.

**Note:** There are serious problems with national accounts in Haiti, including incomplete coverage and the questionable accuracy of raw data.

# PEOPLE

Although Haiti averages approximately 250 people per square kilometer (650 per sq. mi.), its population is concentrated most heavily in urban areas, coastal plains, and valleys. About 95% of Haitians are of African descent. The rest of the population is mostly of mixed Caucasian-African ancestry. A few are of European or

Levantine heritage. About two thirds of the population live in rural areas.

French is one of two official languages, but it is spoken by only about 10% of the people. All Haitians speak Creole, the country's other official language. English is increasingly spoken among the young and in the business sector.

The state religion is Roman Catholicism, which most of the population professes. Some Haitians have converted to Protestantism through the work of missionaries active throughout the country. Much of the population also practices voodoo traditions. Haitians tend to see no conflict in these African-rooted beliefs co-existing with Christian faiths.

Although public education is free, private and parochial schools provide around 75% of educational programs offered and less than 65% of those eligible for primary education are actually enrolled. At the secondary level, the figure drops to 15%. Only 63% of those enrolled will complete primary school. On average it takes 16 years to produce a single graduate of the 6-year cycle. Though Haitians place a high value on education, few can afford to send their children to secondary school. Remittances sent by Haitians living abroad are important in paying educational costs.

Large-scale emigration, principally to the U.S.—but also to Canada, the Dominican Republic, the Bahamas, and other Caribbean neighbors—has created what Haitians refer to as the Tenth Department or the Diaspora. About one of every six Haitians live abroad.

# HISTORY

The Spaniards used the island of Hispaniola (of which Haiti is the western part and the Dominican Republic the eastern) as a launching point from which to explore the rest of the Western Hemisphere. French buccaneers later used the western third of the island as a point from which to harass English and Spanish ships. In 1697, Spain ceded the western third of Hispaniola to France. As piracy was gradually suppressed, some French adventurers became planters, making San Domingue, as the French portion of the island was known, the "pearl of the Antilles"—one of the richest colonies in the 18th century French empire.

During this period, African slaves were brought to work on sugarcane and coffee plantations. In 1791, the slave population revolted—led by Haitian heroes Toussaint L'Ouverture, Jean Jacques Dessalines, and Henri Christophe—and gained control of the northern part of the French colony, waging a war of attrition against the French.

By January 1804, local forces defeated an army sent by Napoleon Bonaparte, established independence from France, and renamed the area Haiti. The impending defeat of the French in Haiti is widely credited with contributing to Napoleon's decision to sell the Louisiana territory to the United States in 1803. Haiti is the world's oldest black republic and the second-oldest republic in the Western Hemisphere, after the United States. Although Haiti actively assisted the independence movements of many Latin American countries, the independent nation of former slaves was excluded from the hemisphere's first regional meeting of independent nations, in Panama in 1826, and did not receive U.S. diplomatic recognition until 1862.

Two separate regimes (north and south) emerged after independence, but were unified in 1820. Two years later, Haiti occupied Santo Domingo, the eastern, Spanish speaking part of Hispaniola. In 1844, however, Santo Domingo broke away from Haiti and became the Dominican Republic. With 22 changes of government from 1843 to 1915, Haiti experienced numerous periods of intense political and economic disorder, prompting the United States military intervention of 1915. Following a 19-year occupation, U.S. military forces were withdrawn in 1934 and Haiti regained sovereign rule.

From February 7, 1986—when the 29-year dictatorship of the Duvalier family ended—until 1991, Haiti was ruled by a series of provisional governments. In 1987, a constitution was ratified that provides for an elected, bicameral parliament, an elected president that serves as head of state, and a prime minister, cabinet, ministers, and supreme court appointed by the president with parliament's consent. The Haitian Constitution also provides for political decentralization through the election of mayors and administrative bodies responsible for local government.

## The 1991 Coup

In December 1990, Jean-Bertrand Aristide, a charismatic Roman Catholic priest, won 67% of the vote in a presidential election that international observers deemed largely free and fair. Aristide took office on February 7, 1991, but was overthrown that September in a violent coup led by dissatisfied elements of the army and supported by many of the country's economic elite. Following the coup, Aristide began what became a 3-year period of exile. An estimated 3,000–5,000 Haitians were killed during the period of de facto military rule. The coup created a large-scale exodus of boat people. The U.S. Coast Guard rescued a total of 41,342 Haitians during 1991 and 1992, more than the number of rescued refugees from the previous 10 years combined.

From October 1991 to September 1994 an unconstitutional military de facto regime governed Haiti. Various OAS and the UN initiatives to end the political crisis through the peaceful restoration of the constitutionally elected government, including the Governors Island Agreement of July 1993, failed when the military refused to uphold its end of the agreements. The de facto authorities chose to ignore the impact of international sanctions imposed after the coup allowing Haiti's already weak economy to collapse and the country's infrastructure to deteriorate from neglect.

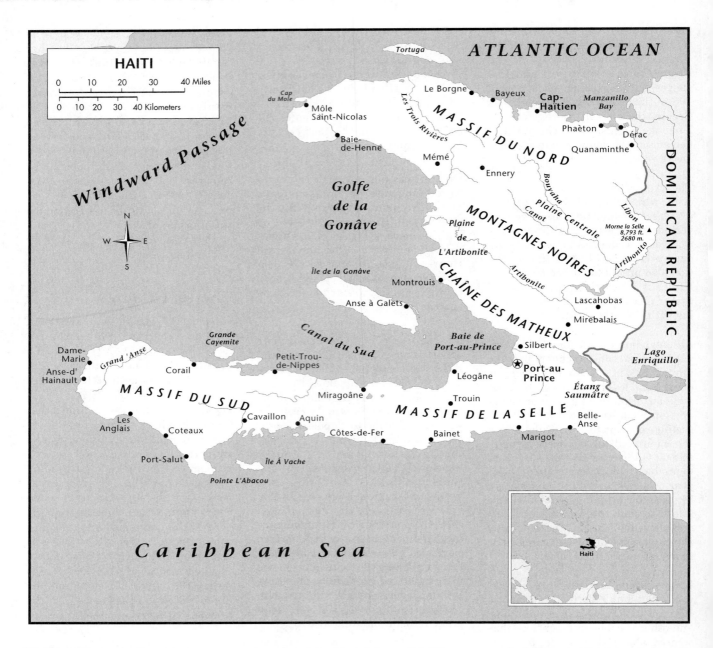

## HAITI

| | | | | |
|---|---|---|---|---|
| 0 | 10 | 20 | 30 | 40 Miles |
| 0 | 10 | 20 | 30 | 40 Kilometers |

ATLANTIC OCEAN

Tortuga

Windward Passage

Cap du Mole

Môle Saint-Nicolas

Baie-de-Henne

Le Borgne

Bayeux

Cap-Haïtien

Manzanillo Bay

Les Trois Rivières

MASSIF DU NORD

Phaèton

Dérac

Quanaminthe

Mémé

Ennery

Bouyaha

Plaine Centrale

Canot

Libon

DOMINICAN REPUBLIC

Golfe de la Gonâve

MONTAGNES NOIRES

Plaine de L'Artibonite

Morne la Selle 8,793 ft. 2680 m.

Artibonito

Île de la Gonâve

Montrouis

Artibonite

Lascahobas

Anse à Galets

CHAÎNE DES MATHEUX

Mirebalais

Grande Cayemite

Canal du Sud

Baie de Port-au-Prince

Silbert

Lago Enriquillo

Dame-Marie

Grand 'Anse

Petit-Trou-de-Nippes

Léogâne

Port-au-Prince

Anse-d' Hainault

Corail

Étang Saumâtre

MASSIF DU SUD

Miragoâne

Trouin

MASSIF DE LA SELLE

Belle-Anse

Les Anglais

Cavaillon

Aquin

Coteaux

Côtes-de-Fer

Bainet

Marigot

Port-Salut

Île Á Vache

Pointe L'Abacou

Caribbean Sea

Haiti

## Transition to Democracy

On July 31, 1994, as repression mounted in Haiti and a UN/OAS civilian human rights monitoring mission (MICIVIH) was expelled from the country, the UN Security Council adopted Resolution 940. UNSC Resolution 940 authorized member states to use all necessary means to facilitate the departure of Haiti's military leadership and to restore Haiti's constitutionally elected government to power.

In the weeks that followed, the United States took the lead in form-

ing a multinational force (MFN) to carry out the UN's mandate by means of a military intervention. In mid-September, with U.S. troops prepared to enter Haiti by force, President Clinton dispatched a negotiating team led by former President Jimmy Carter to persuade the de facto authorities to step aside and allow for the return of constitutional rule. With intervening troops already airborne, General Raoul Cedras and other top leaders agreed to step down and accept the unopposed intervention of the MNF. On September 19, 1994, the first contingents of what became a 21,000 international force

touched down in Haiti to oversee the end of military rule and the restoration of the constitutional government. By early October, the three de facto leaders—Cedras, General Philippe Biamby, and Police Chief Lt. Colonel Michel Francois—had departed Haiti. President Aristide and other elected officials returned on October 15.

Under the watchful eyes of international peacekeepers, restored Haitian authorities organized nationwide local and parliamentary elections in June 1995. A pro-Aristide, multiparty coalition called the Lavalas

Political Organization (OPL) swept into power at all levels. With his term ending in February 1996 and barred by the constitution from succeeding himself, President Aristide agreed to step aside and support a presidential election in December 1995. Rene Preval, a prominent Aristide political ally, who had been Aristide's Prime Minister in 1991, took 88% of the vote, and was sworn in to a 5-year term on February 7, 1996 during what was Haiti's first-ever transition between two democratically elected presidents.

## Political Gridlock

In late 1996, former President Aristide broke from the OPL and created a new political party, the Lavalas Family (FL). The OPL, holding the majority of the parliament, renamed itself the Struggling People's Party, maintaining the OPL acronym. Elections in April 1997 for the renewal of one-third of the Senate and creation of commune-level assemblies and town delegations provided the first opportunity for the former political allies to compete for elected office. Although preliminary results indicated victories for FL candidates in most races, the elections, which drew only about 5% of registered voters, were plagued with allegations of fraud and not certified by most international observers as free and fair. Under pressure, the Preval government refused to accept the results, but did little to remedy the situation. Partisan rancor from the election dispute led to deep divisions within Parliament and between the legislative and executive branches, resulting in almost total governmental gridlock. In June 1997, Prime Minister Rosny Smarth resigned. Two successors proposed by President Preval thereafter were rejected by the legislature. Eventually, in December 1998, Jacques Alexis was confirmed as Prime Minister.

During this gridlock period, the government was unable to organize the local and parliamentary elections due in late 1998. In early January 1999, President Preval dismissed legislators whose terms had expired—the entire Chamber of Deputies and all

but nine members of the Senate—and converted local elected officials into state employees. The President and Prime Minister then ruled by decree, establishing a cabinet composed almost entirely of FL partisans. Under pressure from a new political coalition called the Democratic Consultation Group (ESPACE), the government allocated three seats of the nine-member Provisional Electoral Council (CEP) to opposition groups and mandated the CEP to organize the overdue elections for the end of 1999. Following several delays, the first round of elections for local councils (ASEC and CASEK), municipal governments, town delegates, the Chamber of Deputies, and two-thirds of the Senate took place on May 21, 2000. The election drew the participation of a multitude of candidates from a wide array of political parties and a voter turnout of more than 60%.

## The Electoral Crisis

Controversy mired the good start, however, when the CEP used a flawed methodology to determine the winners of the Senate races, thus avoiding run-off elections and giving the FL a virtual sweep in the first round. The flawed vote count, combined with the lack of CEP follow-up of investigations of alleged irregularities and fraud, undercut the credibility of that body, whose President fled Haiti and two members eventually resigned rather than accede to government pressure to release the erroneous results. This electoral manipulation and the subsequent intransigence of Haitian authorities toward international efforts led by the OAS to assist them take corrective measures, led to sharp criticism of the Government of Haiti from the international community. On August 28, 2000, Haiti's new parliament, including 10 Senators accorded victory under the flawed vote count, was convened.

Concurrently, most opposition parties regrouped in a tactical alliance that eventually became the Democratic Convergence. It was the position of the Convergence that the May elections were so fraudulent that they should be annulled and held again

under a new CEP, but only after then President Preval had stood down and replaced by a provisional government. In the meantime, the opposition announced it would boycott the November presidential and senatorial elections.

Through a number of diplomatic missions by the OAS, the Caribbean Community (CARICOM), and the United States, the international community had sought to delay Parliament's seating until the electoral problems could be rectified. When these efforts were rebuffed and Parliament was seated, Haiti's main bilateral donors announced the end of "business as usual." They moved to re-channel Haitian assistance away from the government, and announced they would not support or send observers to the November elections.

>From September through late October, the international community attempted unsuccessfully to bridge the differences between the Fanmi Lavalas government and the Democratic Convergence. In the absence of a solution and in keeping with the timetable established by the Haitian Constitution, elections for President and nine Senators took place on November 26, 2000. All major opposition parties boycotted these elections in which voter participation was very low. Jean-Bertrand Aristide emerged as the victor of these elections and the candidates of his Fanmi Lavalas swept all nine contested Senate seats.

On December 14, 2000 the Democratic Convergence announced it was taking steps toward creating a provisional government that would assume "office" on February 7—the day of president-elect Aristide's inauguration. The primary objective of this "government" would be to organize new elections. To forestall a more serious crisis, a United States diplomatic mission in late December obtained Mr. Aristide's commitment to an eight-point plan that among others things would rectify the May elections and create a credible new electoral council.

In early February 2001, a group of prominent Haitians, known as the

Commission of Facilitation of the Civil Society Initiative and a representative of the OAS brought together for face-to-face negotiations representatives of the Fanmi Lavalas and the Democratic Convergence. The talks collapsed February 6 on the eve of the presidential inauguration. The Fanmi Lavalas would not moved beyond its eight-point commitment of December. The Democratic Convergence insisted on the annulment of the May 21 and the November 6, 2000 elections as well as on broad power-sharing arrangements for the Convergence in the government.

On February 7, 2001, Jean-Bertrand Aristide was sworn in as the new Haitian president. That same day, the Democratic Convergence sworn in Gerard Gourgue "Provisional President of the Government of Consensus and National Union." As of the date of this report, no further direct talks between the Fanmi Lavalas and the Democratic Convergence have occurred.

## International Military Presence

Since the transition of the 21,000 strong MNF into a peacekeeping force on March 31, 1995, the presence of international military forces that helped restore constitutional government to power was gradually ended. Initially, the U.S.-led UN peacekeeping force numbered 6,000 troops, but that number was scaled back progressively over the next 4 years as a series of UN technical missions succeeded the peacekeeping force. By January 2000, all U.S. troops stationed in Haiti had departed. In March 2000, the UN peacekeeping mission transitioned into a peace building mission, the International Civilian Support Mission in Haiti (MICAH). MICAH consisted of some 80 non-uniformed UN technical advisors providing advice and material assistance in policing, justice, and human rights to the Haitian Government. MICAH's mandate ended on February 7, 2001, coincidentally with the end of the Preval administration. Between February and September, 2000, U.S. military civil engineering and medical training missions visited

Haiti for 6-week periods under the auspices of the Department of the Army's Southern Command's New Horizons program.

## Principal Government Officials

**For up-to-date information on Principal Government Officials, see the Chiefs of State and Cabinet Members of Foreign Governments section starting on page 1.**

The Embassy of Haiti is located at 2311 Massachusetts Ave., NW, Washington, DC 20008 (tel. 202–332–4090).

# ECONOMY

Since the demise of the Duvalier dictatorship in 1986, international economists have urged Haiti to reform and modernize its economy. Under President Preval, the country's economic agenda has included trade/tariff liberalization, measures to control government expenditure and increase tax revenues, civil service downsizing, financial sector reform, and the modernization of state-owned enterprises through their sale to private investors, the provision of private sector management contracts, or joint public-private investment. Structural adjustment agreements with the International Monetary Fund, World Bank, Inter-American Development Bank, and other international financial institutions are aimed at creating necessary conditions for private sector growth, have proved only partly successful.

In the aftermath of the 1994 restoration of constitutional governance, Haitian officials have indicated their commitment to economic reform through the implementation of sound fiscal and monetary policies and the enactment of legislation mandating the modernization of state-owned enterprises. A council to guide the modernization program (CMEP) was established and a timetable was

drawn up to modernize nine key parastatals. Although the state-owned flour mill and cement plants have been transferred to private owners, progress on the other seven parastatals has stalled. The modernization of Haiti's state-enterprises remains a controversial political issue in Haiti.

External aid is essential to the future economic development of Haiti, the least-developed country in the Western Hemisphere and one of the poorest in the world. Comparative social and economic indicators show Haiti falling behind other low-income developing countries (particularly in the hemisphere) since the 1980s. Haiti's economic stagnation is the result of earlier inappropriate economic policies, political instability, a shortage of good arable land, environmental deterioration, continued use of traditional technologies, undercapitalization and lack of public investment in human resources, migration of large portions of the skilled population, and a weak national savings rate.

Haiti continues to suffer the consequences of the 1991 coup and the irresponsible economic and financial policies of the de facto authorities greatly accelerated Haiti's economic decline. Following the coup, the United States adopted mandatory sanctions, and the OAS instituted voluntary sanctions aimed at restoring constitutional government. International sanctions culminated in the May 1994 UN embargo of all goods entering Haiti except humanitarian supplies, such as food and medicine. The assembly sector, heavily dependent on U.S. markets for its products, employed nearly 80,000 workers in the mid-1980s. During the embargo, employment fell from 33,000 workers in 1991 to 400 in October 1994. Private domestic and foreign investment has been slow to return to Haiti. Since the return of constitutional rule, assembly sector employment has gradually recovered with over 20,000 now employed, but further growth has been stalled by investor concerns over safety and supply reliability.

If the political situation stabilizes, high crime levels reduce, and new investment increases, tourism could take its place next to export-oriented manufacturing (the assembly sector) as a potential source of foreign exchange. Remittances from abroad now constitute a significant source of financial support for many Haitian households.

Workers in Haiti are guaranteed the right of association. Unionization is protected by the labor code. A legal minimum wage of 36 gourds a day (about U.S. $1.80) applies to most workers in the formal sector.

# FOREIGN RELATIONS AND INTERNATIONAL SUPPORT

Haiti is one of the original members of the United Nations and several of its specialized and related agencies, as well as a member of the Organization of American States (OAS). It maintains diplomatic relations with 37 countries.

The international community rallied to Haiti's defense during the 1991–94 period of illegal military rule. Thirty-one countries participated in the U.S.-led Multinational Force (MNF) which, acting under UN auspices, intervened in September 1994 to help restore the legitimate government and create a secure and stable environment in Haiti. At its peak, the MNF included roughly 21,000 troops, mostly Americans, and more than 1,000 international police monitors. Within six months, the troop level was gradually reduced as the MNF transitioned to a 6,000 strong peacekeeping force, the UN Mission in Haiti (UNMIH). UNMIH was charged with maintaining the secure environment, which the MNF had helped establish, as well as nurturing Haiti's new police force through the presence of 900 police advisors. A total of 38 countries participated in UNMIH.

**Travel Notes**

**Travel Advice:** For up-to-date information from the U.S. State Department on possible inconvenient or hazardous situations, see the **Travel Warnings and Consular Information Sheets from the U.S. Government** section starting on page 1723. For the latest information on health requirements and conditions, see the **International Travelers' Health Information** section starting on page 1385. For further information dealing with non-urgent matter, see the **Tips for Travelers to...** section starting on page 1588.

In order to spur Haiti's social and economic recovery from 3 years of de facto military rule and decades of misrule before that, international development banks and donor agencies pledged in 1994 to provide over $2 billion in assistance by 1999. Disbursements were largely conditioned on progress in economic reform. Parliamentary inaction, principally as a result of the political struggles and gridlock that plagued Haiti since 1996, resulted in the blockage of much of this assistance as disbursement conditions were not met. The electoral crisis that has brewed in the aftermath of the May 21, 2000 local and parliamentary elections has resulted in the blockage of most multilateral and bilateral assistance. Major donors are led by the United States, with the largest bilateral assistance program, and also include Canada, France, Germany, Japan and Taiwan. Multilateral aid is coordinated through an informal grouping of major donors under the auspices of the World Bank which, in addition to the Inter-American Development Bank (IDB) and the European Union, is also a major source of Haitian development assistance.

# U.S.-HAITI RELATIONS

U.S. policy toward Haiti is designed to foster and strengthen democracy; help alleviate poverty, illiteracy, and malnutrition, promote respect for human rights; and counter illegal migration and drug trafficking. U.S. policy goals are met through direct bilateral action and by working with the international community. The United States has taken a leading role in organizing international involvement with Haiti. In particular, the U.S. works with the United Nations, particularly through the Secretary General's "Friends of Haiti" group (the U.S., Canada, France, Venezuela, Chile, Argentina), and with the Organization of American States, the Caribbean Community (CARICOM), and individual countries to achieve policy goals.

Maintaining good relations with and fostering democracy in Haiti are important for many reasons, not the least of which is the country's geographical proximity to the continental United States. In addition to the approximately 16,000 Haitians who receive visas to enter the U.S. annually, there is a flow of undocumented and illegal migrants. Tens of thousands of undocumented Haitian migrants have been intercepted at sea by the U.S. Coast Guard in the past two decades, particularly during the 1991–94 period of illegal military rule when more than 67,000 migrants were interdicted. Since the return of the legitimate government in 1994, the interdiction of illegal migrants has decreased dramatically, averaging fewer than 1,500 annually. The prospect remains, however, for the renewal of higher flows of illegal migrants, particularly under conditions of political unrest or further economic downturn.

## U.S. Economic and Development Assistance

Political insecurity and the failure of Haiti's governments to invest in developing the country's natural and human resources attribute significantly to the country's current state of underdevelopment. U.S. efforts to strengthen democracy and to rebuild Haiti's economy aim to rectify this condition. The U.S. has been Haiti's largest donor since 1973. Between FY 95 and FY 99, the U.S. has contributed roughly $884 million in assistance to Haiti. These funds have been used to support programs that have addressed a variety of problems. Among the initiatives funds have supported are:

* Food assistance programs that include a school lunch program that feeds around 500,000 children daily.

* Agricultural development programs that have endeavored to revitalize.

Haiti's coffee sector and to help thousands of Haitian farmers adopt sustainable agricultural practices and protect the environment.

* Teacher training programs that have included 6,000 educators at the primary and secondary level.

* Population programs that have expanded modern family planning practices in many rural areas.

* Health care programs that have supported child immunization and have helped provide primary care to nearly half of the Haitian population.

In addition to financial support, the U.S. provides human resources. U.S. Peace Corps volunteers returned to Haiti in 1995, largely focusing their efforts on income generation programs in Haiti's rural areas. Many private U.S. citizens travel regularly to Haiti or reside there for extended periods to work in humanitarian projects.

Haiti has been plagued for decades by extremely high unemployment and underemployment. The precipitous decline in urban assembly sector jobs, from a high of 80,000 in 1986 to fewer than 17,000 in 1994, exacerbated the scarcity of jobs. To revitalize the economy, U.S. assistance has attempted to create opportunities for stable sustainable employment for the growing population, particularly those who comprise the country's vast informal economy. A post-intervention transitional program of short-term job creation principally in small towns and rural areas provided employment to as many as 50,000 workers per day throughout the country. More recently, programs that help to

increase commercial bank lending to small- and medium-scale entrepreneurs, especially in the agricultural sector, have helped to create jobs and foster economic growth.

Additional U.S. efforts in economic revitalization include the establishment of the U.S.-Haiti Business Development Council, an Overseas Private Investment Corporation commercial loan program, and inclusion of Haiti within the Caribbean Basin Initiative. These efforts all provide greater market opportunities for American and Haitian businesses. Current Congressional prohibitions on providing assistance to or through the Haitian Government has accelerated the move to private voluntary agencies as contractors to oversee use of U.S. aid funds.

## Security Assistance

A major focus of American assistance in Haiti since the restoration of democracy has been to improve public security, rule of law, and respect for human rights through bolstering the capacities of the newly created Haitian National Police (HNP) and the Haitian judiciary. Since 1995, when the HNP was created to bring public security under civilian control as mandated in Haiti's constitution, more than 6,000 police officers have completed training in modern law enforcement. U.S. instructors from the International Criminal Investigative Training Assistance Program (ICITAP) have provided much of that general training. Specialized training in such areas as crowd control, operation of firearms, and VIP protection has been provided by ICITAP, whose experts have also worked closely with the Haitian Government in meeting the material needs of the new force; ICITAP closed in September 2000.

Through its Administration of Justice (AOJ) program, the U.S. has helped support the independence and competency of Haiti's judicial branch through the training of hundreds of Haitian judges and prosecutors, particularly at the Magisterial Training School established in 1995. The AOJ program ended in July 2000, upon

expiration of a bilateral assistance agreement between the United States and the Government of Haiti. During its tenure, the AOJ program also provided free legal assistance for thousands of impoverished Haitians, and has helped obtain the release of hundreds of people detained without trial. U.S. reform programs have included the participation of non-governmental organizations, particularly to encourage conflict resolution and mediation programs that alleviate pressure on the still-overmatched judicial system. In spite of these initiatives, Haiti's judicial system remains severely troubled—lacking the modern facilities, properly trained officials, and resources it requires to be able to meet the demands placed upon it. The Carrefour Feuilles trial in September 2000 and the Raboteau trial in November 2000 evidenced significant improvements in the judicial system's capacity. Nevertheless, Haiti's system remains in need of continued reform and strengthening.

## Combating Drug Trafficking

In recent years, Haiti has become a major transshipment point for South American narcotics being sent to the United States, with as much as 9% of cocaine entering the U.S. in 2000 transiting Haiti. To counter this threat, the U.S. has taken a number of steps, including bolstering the number of U.S. drug enforcement personnel in Haiti, training the counternarcotics division of the Haitian National Police, providing material assistance and training to the Haitian Coast Guard for drug and migrant interdiction, and pressing for extradition or expulsion of traffickers under indictment in the United States detained in Haiti. Although Haiti did not meet counternarcotics certification criteria the past 2 years, the country was certified on grounds of vital national security interest.

## Principal U.S. Officials

**For up-to-date information on Principal U.S. Officials, see the U.S.**

Embassies, Consulates, and Foreign Service section starting on page 139.

The U.S. embassy in Haiti is located on Harry Truman Blvd., Port-au-Prince.

## U.S. Business Opportunities

The U.S. remains Haiti's largest trading partner. Port-au-Prince is less than two hours by air from Miami, with several daily direct flights. A daily flight also connects Port-au-Prince with New York. Both Port-au-Prince and Cap Haitien on the north coast have deep water port facilities. U.S. development assistance has been instrumental in stimulating efforts that have been made in recent years to improve the prospects for secondary cities, especially Jacmel, for attracting business investment. Increasingly, Haitian entrepreneurs conduct business in English. U.S. currency circulates freely in Haiti. A number of U.S. firms, including commercial banks, telecommunications, airlines, oil and agribusiness companies, and U.S.-owned assembly plants are present in Haiti.

Further opportunities for U.S. businesses include the development and trade of medical supplies and equipment, rebuilding and modernizing Haiti's depleted infrastructure, developing tourism and allied sectors—including arts and crafts—and improving capacity in waste disposal, transportation, energy, telecommunications, and export assembly operations. Because of the assembly sector's capacity to create employment quickly, priority is placed on providing opportunities for U.S. investors and exporters to become involved in this sector. Haiti's primary assembly sector inputs include textiles, electronics components, packaging materials, and raw materials used in the manufacture of toys and sporting goods. Other U.S. export prospects include construction materials, plumbing fixtures, hardware, and lumber. Benefits for both Haitian and American importers and exporters are available under the 806 and 807/HTSUS Programs (U.S. Customs laws on products assembled from U.S. components or materials), and under the Caribbean Basin Initiative.

Markets exist for four-wheel-drive vehicles, consumer electronics, rice, wheat, flour, sugar, and processed foodstuffs. The Government of Haiti seeks to reactivate and develop agricultural industries where Haiti enjoys considerable comparative advantages, among which are essential oils, spices, fruits and vegetables, and sisal. The government encourages the inflow of new capital and technological innovations.

Additional information on business opportunities in Haiti can be found at www.usatrade.gov, then to market research, then country commercial guide.

## Establishing a Business

Foreigners seeking to establish a business in Haiti must obtain a residence visa. Non-resident entrepreneurs must have a locally licensed agent to conduct business transactions within the country. Individuals wishing to practice a trade in Haiti must obtain an immigrant visa from a Haitian Consulate and, in most cases, a government work permit. Transient and resident traders must also have a professional ID card.

Property restrictions still exist for foreign individuals. Property rights of foreigners are limited to 1.29 hectares in urban areas and 6.45 hectares in rural areas. No foreigner may own more than one residence in the same district, or own property or buildings near the border. To own real estate, authorization from the Ministry of Justice is necessary.

Hurdles for businesses in Haiti include poor infrastructure, a high-cost port, an irregular supply of electricity, and customs delays. The government places a 30% withholding tax on all profits received. There is little direct investment, though more is incoming than outgoing (see Economy).

Foreign investment protection is provided by the constitution of 1987, which permits expropriation of private property for public use or land reform with payment in advance. American firms enjoy free transfer of interest, dividends, profits, and other revenues stemming from their investments, and are guaranteed just compensation paid in advance of expropriation, as well as compensation in case of damages or losses caused by war, revolution, or insurrection.

Additional information on establishing a business in Haiti can be found at www.usatrade.gov, then to market research, then country commercial guide.

## Other Contact Information

**U.S. Commercial Service**
111 Rue Faubert
Petionville
Republic of Haiti
Tel: (509) 256–5778
Fax: (509) 256–5779
Cell: (509) 401–0953 (Commercial Attaché)

**Overseas Private Investment Corporation (OPIC)**
1615 M Street, NW
Washington, DC 20527
Tel: (202) 457–7200
Fax: (202) 331–4234

**U.S. Department of Commerce**
14th and Constitution Ave., NW
Washington, DC 20230
Haiti Hotline (202) 482–4302
Haiti Telefax (202) 482–2521

**Office of Latin America and the Caribbean**
Tel: (202) 482–0704
Fax: (202) 482–0464

**Caribbean/Latin American Action**
1818 N Street, NW, Suite 310
Washington, DC 20036
Tel: (202) 466–7464
Fax: (202) 822–0075

**Association des Industries d'Haiti (ADIH)**
Bldg. Le Triangle Delmas 31, #139

Port-au-Prince
Tel: (509) 246–4509/4510 or 2211

**Centre Pour la Livre Entreprise et la Democratie (CLED)**
37, Avenue Marie-Jeanne
No. 8 B.P. 1316
Port-au-Prince
Tel: (509) 222–9720 or (509) 222–9721
Fax: (509) 222–8252

**Chambre de Commerce et d'Industrie d'Haiti**
P.O. Box 982
Port-au-Prince
Tel: (509) 222–0281 or (509) 222–2475

**Haitian American Chamber of Commerce and Industry (HAM-CHAM)**
Rue Oge, A-5
Petionville
Republic of Haiti
Tel: (509) 511–3024, fax not available.

# THE HOLY SEE

July 2000

Official Name:
**The Holy See**

# PROFILE

## Geography

**Area:** (Vatican City) 0.439 sq. km. (109 acres).
**Cities:** Vatican City.
**Terrain:** low hill.
**Climate:** temperate, mild, rainy winters with hot, dry summers.

## People

**Population:** 813.
**Ethnic Groups:** Italian, Swiss, other.
**Religion:** Catholic.
**Language:** Latin.
**Literacy:** 100%.
**Work force:** About 3,000 lay workers (mostly resident outside the Vatican).

## Government

**Type:** Papacy; ecclesiastical governmental and administrative capital of the Roman Catholic Church.
**Independence:** Lateran Pacts regulating independence and sovereignty of the Holy See signed with Italy on February 11, 1929, and revised in 1984.
**Suffrage:** The Pope is elected for life by members of the College of Cardinals who are less than 80 years old.

# PEOPLE AND HISTORY

Almost all of Vatican City's 813 citizens live inside the Vatican City walls. The Vatican includes Vatican government officials, Roman Catholic Church dignitaries, priests, nuns, and guards as well as approximately 3,000 lay workers who comprise the majority of the work force.

The Holy See's diplomatic history began in the fourth century, but the boundaries of the papacy's temporal power have shifted over the centuries. In the middle of the 19th century, the Popes ruled the Papal States, including a broad band of territory across central Italy. In 1860, after prolonged civil and regional unrest, Victor Emmanuel's army seized the Papal States, leaving only Rome and surrounding coastal regions under papal control.

In 1870, the forces of Victor Emmanuel captured Rome itself and declared it the new capital of Italy. Pope Pius IX and his successors disputed the legitimacy of these acts and proclaimed themselves to be "prisoners" in the Vatican. Finally, in 1929, the Italian Government and the Holy See signed three agreements resolving the dispute: A treaty recognizing the independence and sovereignty of the Holy See and creating the State of Vatican City; A concordat defining the relations between the government and the church within Italy; and A financial convention providing the Holy See with compensation for its losses in 1870. In 1984 a revised concordat, altering the terms of church-state relations, was signed.

# GOVERNMENT AND INSTITUTIONS

The Pope exercises supreme legislative, executive, and judicial power and sends and receives diplomatic representatives. The Holy See is recognized under international law and enters into international agreements. It has formal diplomatic relations with 172 nations, including the United States. The State of Vatican City was established in 1929 as a political and territorial entity to ensure the Holy See "absolute and visible independence and to guarantee it indisputable international sovereignty."

## Administration of the Vatican

The Pope delegates the internal administration of Vatican City to the Pontifical Commission for the State of Vatican City. The legal system is

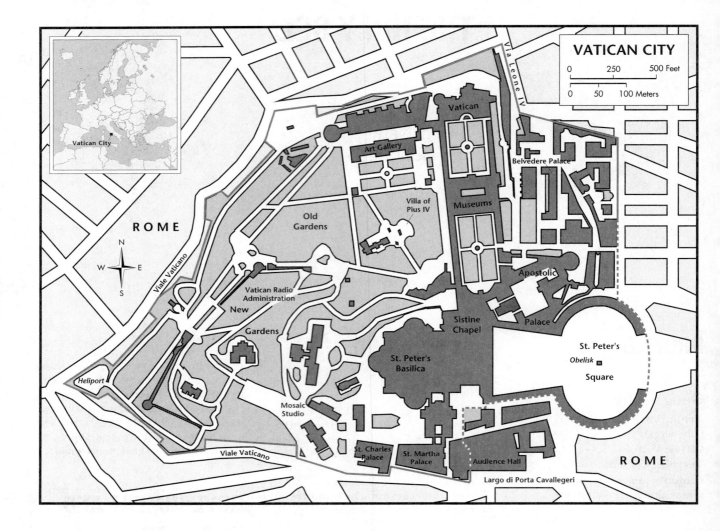

based on canon, or ecclesiastical, law, and the state has civil and criminal law codes. Vatican City maintains the Swiss Guards, a voluntary military force, as well as a modern security corps. It has its own post office, commissary, bank, railway station, electrical generating plant, and publishing house, and it administers a comprehensive health care and pension scheme for its employees. The Vatican operates a medical clinic, pharmacy, supermarket, clothing store, gas stations, and other services. The Vatican also issues its own coins, stamps, and passports. Radio Vatican, the official radio station, is one of the most influential in Europe. L'Osservatore Romano is the semi-official newspaper, published daily in Italian, and weekly in English, Spanish, Portuguese, German, and French (plus a monthly edition in Polish). It is published by Catholic laymen but

carries official information. There is an official Vatican website at www.vatican.va.

## Administration of the Holy See

The Pope governs with the assistance of the Roman Curia and the Papal Civil Service. The Roman Curia consists of the Secretariat of State, six Congregations, three Tribunals, 12 Pontifical Councils, and a complex of offices that administer church affairs at the highest level. The Secretariat of State, under the Cardinal Secretary of State, directs and coordinates the Curia. The current incumbent, Cardinal Angelo Sodano, is the Holy See equivalent of a prime minister. Archbishop Jean-Louis Tauran, Secretary of the Section for Relations With States of the Secretariat of

State, is the Holy See equivalent of a foreign minister.

Among the most active of the major Curial institutions are the Congregation for the Doctrine of the Faith, which oversees church doctrine; the Congregation for Bishops, which coordinates the appointment of bishops worldwide; the Congregation for the Evangelization of Peoples, which oversees all missionary activities; and the Pontifical Council for Justice and Peace, which deals with international peace and social issues.

Three tribunals are responsible for judicial power. The Apostolic Penitentiary deals with matters of conscience; the Roman Rota is responsible for appeals, including annulments of marriage; and the Apostolic Signatura is the final court of appeal. Three other tribunals are responsible for civil and criminal matters within Vatican City.

The Prefecture for Economic Affairs coordinates the finances of the Holy See departments and supervises the administration of the Patrimony of the Holy See, an investment fund dating back to the Lateran Pacts. A committee of 15 cardinals, chaired by the Secretary of State, has final oversight authority over all financial matters of the Holy See, including those of the Institute for Works of Religion, the Vatican bank.

## Papal Audiences

The North American College in Rome, owned and operated by the U.S. Catholic hierarchy for training American priests, handles requests for papal audiences. The address is Casa Santa Maria dell'Umilta, Via dell'Umilta 30, 00187, Rome, Italy (tel. +39-06-690-0189).

## Principal Government Officials

Head of State—Pope John Paul II
Secretary of State (Prime Minister)—
Cardinal Angelo Sodano Deputy Secretary of State (Interior Minister)—
Archbishop Giovanni Battista Re
Secretary of the Section for Relations With States (Foreign Minister)—
Archbishop Jean-Louis Tauran Apostolic Nuncio (equivalent to ambassador) to the United States—
Archbishop Gabriel Montalvo

The Holy See maintains an Apostolic Nuniciature, the equivalent of an embassy, in the U.S. at 3339 Massachusetts Ave. NW, Washington, DC 20008; tel. (202) 333-7121.

# FOREIGN RELATIONS

The Holy See maintains formal diplomatic relations with 172 nations; 71 of these maintain permanent resident diplomatic missions accredited to the Holy See in Rome. The rest have missions located outside Italy with dual accreditation. The Holy See maintains permanent diplomatic

## Travel Notes

**Travel Advice:** For up-to-date information from the U.S. State Department on possible inconvenient or hazardous situations, see the **Travel Warnings and Consular Information Sheets from the U.S. Government** section starting on page 1723. For the latest information on health requirements and conditions, see the **International Travelers' Health Information** section starting on page 1385. For further information dealing with non-urgent matter, see the **Tips for Travelers to...** section starting on page 1588.

missions to 197 countries and international organizations.

The Holy See is especially active in international organizations. It has permanent observer status at the United Nations in New York, the Office of the United Nations in Geneva and specialized institutes, the UN Food and Agriculture Organization in Rome, and the UN Educational, Scientific and Cultural Organization in Paris. The Holy See also has a member delegate at the International Atomic Energy Agency and at the UN Industrial Development Organization in Vienna. It maintains permanent observers at the Organization of American States in Washington, DC, and the Council of Europe. In addition, the Holy See has diplomatic relations with the European Union in Brussels. In 1997 the Holy See became a member of the World Trade Organization.

In 1971, the Holy See announced the decision to adhere to the nuclear Non-Proliferation Treaty in order to "give its moral support to the principles that form the base of the treaty itself." The Holy See also is a participating state in the Organization for Security and Cooperation in Europe.

# U.S.-HOLY SEE RELATIONS

The United States maintained consular relations with the Papal States

from 1797 to 1870 and diplomatic relations with the Pope, in his capacity as head of the Papal States, from 1848 to 1868. These relations lapsed with the loss of all papal territories in 1870.

From 1870 to 1984, the United States did not have diplomatic relations with the Holy See. Until the establishment of formal relations, some U.S. presidents designated personal envoys who visited with the Holy See periodically for discussions on international humanitarian and political issues. Myron C. Taylor was the first of these representatives, serving from 1939 to 1950. Presidents Nixon, Ford, Carter, and Reagan also appointed personal envoys to the Pope. The United States and Holy See announced the establishment of diplomatic relations in January 1984. On March 7, 1984, the Senate confirmed William A. Wilson as the first U.S. Ambassador to the Holy See. Establishment of diplomatic relations has bolstered the frequent contact and consultation between the United States and the Holy See on many important international issues of mutual interest. The United States values the Holy See's significant contributions to international peace and human rights.

## Principal U.S. Embassy Officials

For up-to-date information on Principal U.S. Officials, see the U.S. Embassies, Consulates, and Foreign Service section starting on page 139.

The U.S. Embassy to the Holy See is located in the Villa Domiziana, Via delle Terme Deciane 26, 00153 Rome, Italy. Tel: (39) 06-4674-3428. Fax: (39) 06-575-8346. Within the United States: PSC 59, Box 66, APO AE 09624.

# HONDURAS

April 2001

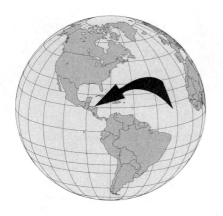

Official Name:
**Republic of Honduras**

## PROFILE

### Geography

**Area:** 112,100 sq. km. (43,270 sq. mi.); about the size of Louisiana.
**Cities:** Capital—Tegucigalpa (850,000); San Pedro Sula (500,000); metropolitan area of each city over 1 million.
**Terrain:** Mountainous.
**Climate:** Tropical to subtropical, depending on elevation.

### People

**Nationality:** Noun and adjective—Honduran(s).
**Population:** (1998 est.) 6 million.
**Growth rate:** 2.8%.
**Ethnic groups:** 90% mestizo (mixed Indian and European); others of European, Arab, African, or Asian ancestry; and indigenous Indians.
**Religions:** Roman Catholic, Protestant minority.
**Language:** Spanish.
**Education:** Years compulsory—6. Attendance—70% overall, but less than 16% at junior high level. Literacy—78.5%.
**Health:** Infant mortality rate—42/1,000. Life expectancy—68 yrs.
**Work force:** Services—42%. Natural resources/agriculture—39%. Manufacturing—12%. Construction/housing—7%.

### Government

**Type:** Democratic constitutional republic.
**Independence:** September 15, 1821.
**Constitution:** 1982.
**Branches:** Executive—president, directly elected to 4-year term. Legislative—unicameral National Congress, elected for 4-year term. Judicial—Supreme Court of Justice (appointed by Congress and confirmed by the president); several lower courts.
**Political parties:** Liberal Party, National Party, Innovation and Unity Party, Christian Democratic Party, and the Democratic Unification Party.
**Suffrage:** Universal adult.
**Administrative subdivisions:** 18 departments.

### Economy (1998 preliminary data)

**GDP:** $4.7 billion.
**Growth rate:** 4.8%.
**Per capita GDP:** $810.
**Natural resources:** Arable land, forests, minerals, fisheries. Agriculture (22% of GDP): Products—coffee, bananas, shrimp and lobster, sugar, fruits, basic grains, livestock.
**Manufacturing:** (15% of GDP) Types—textiles and apparel, cement, wood products, cigars, foodstuffs.
**Trade:** Exports—$1.3 billion: coffee, shrimp, bananas, zinc/lead concentrates, soap/detergents, melons, lobster, pineapple, lumber, tobacco. Major market—U.S. (40%). Imports—$2.9 billion: machinery, chemicals, petroleum, vehicles, processed foods, metals, agricultural products, plastic articles, paper articles. Major source—U.S. (46%).
**Exchange rate:** (March 2001) 15.2 lempiras=U.S.$1.

## PEOPLE AND HISTORY

About 90% of the population is mestizo. There also are small minorities of European, African, Asian, Arab, and indigenous Indian descent. Most Hondurans are Roman Catholic, but Protestant proselytization has resulted in significant numbers of converts. Spanish is the predominant language, although some English is spoken along the northern coast and on the Caribbean Bay Islands. Indigenous Indian dialects and the Garifuna dialect also are spoken. The restored Mayan ruins near the Guatemalan border in Copan reflect the great Mayan culture that flourished there for hundreds of years until the early 9th century. Mayan artifacts also can be found at the National Museum in Tegucigalpa. Columbus landed at mainland Honduras

(Trujillo) in 1502. He named it "Honduras" (meaning "depths") for the deep water off the coast. Spaniard Hernan Cortes arrived in 1524. The Spanish began founding settlements along the coast and Honduras came under the control of the Captaincy General of Guatemala. The cities of Comayagua and Tegucigalpa developed as early mining centers.

## Independence

Honduras, along with the other Central American provinces, gained independence from Spain in 1821; it then briefly was annexed to the Mexican Empire. In 1823, Honduras joined the newly formed United Provinces of Central America. Before long, social and economic differences between Honduras and its regional neighbors exacerbated harsh partisan strife among Central American leaders and brought on the federation's collapse in 1838. Gen. Francisco Morazan—a Honduran national hero—led unsuccessful efforts to maintain the federation, and restoring Central American unity remained the chief aim of Honduran foreign policy until after World War I.

Since independence, Honduras has been plagued with nearly 300 internal rebellions, civil wars, and changes of government—more than half occurring during this century. The country traditionally lacked both an economic infrastructure and social and political integration. Its agriculturally based economy came to be dominated in this century by U.S. companies that established vast banana plantations along the north coast. Foreign capital, plantation life, and conservative politics held sway in Honduras from the late 19th until the mid-20th century. During the relatively stable years of the Great Depression, authoritarian Gen. Tiburcio Carias Andino controlled Honduras. His ties to dictators in neighboring countries and to U.S. banana companies helped him maintain power until 1948. By then, provincial military leaders had begun to gain control of the two major parties, the Nationalists and the Liberals.

## From Military to Civilian Rule

In October 1955—after two authoritarian administrations and a general strike by banana workers on the north coast in 1954—young military reformists staged a palace coup that installed a provisional junta and paved the way for constituent assembly elections in 1957. This assembly appointed Dr. Ramon Villeda Morales as president and transformed itself into a national legislature with a 6-year term. The Liberal Party ruled during 1957–63. At the same time, the military took its first steps to become a professional institution independent of leadership from any one political party, and the newly created military academy graduated its first class in 1960. In October 1963, conservative military officers preempted constitutional elections and deposed Villeda in a bloody coup. These officers exiled Liberal Party members and took control of the national police. The armed forces, led by Gen. Lopez Arellano, governed until 1970. A civilian president—Ramon Cruz of the National Party—took power briefly in 1970 but proved unable to manage the government. Popular discontent had continued to rise after a 1969 border war with El Salvador; in December 1972, Gen. Lopez staged another coup. Lopez adopted more progressive policies, including land reform, but his regime was brought down in the mid-1970s by scandals.

Gen. Lopez' successors continued armed forces modernization programs, building army and security forces, and concentrating on Honduran air force superiority over its neighbors. The regimes of Gen. Melgar Castro (1975–78) and Gen. Paz Garcia (1978–83) largely built the current physical infrastructure and telecommunications system of Honduras. The country also enjoyed its most rapid economic growth during this period, due to greater international demand for its products and the availability of foreign commercial lending.

Following the overthrow of Anastasio Somoza in Nicaragua in 1979 and general instability in El Salvador at the time, the Honduran military accelerated plans to return the country to civilian rule. A constituent assembly was popularly elected in April 1980 and general elections were held in November 1981. A new constitution was approved in 1982 and the Liberal Party government of President Roberto Suazo Cordoba assumed power.

Suazo relied on U.S. support to help with a severe economic recession and with the threat posed by the revolutionary Sandinista government in Nicaragua amid a brutal civil war in El Salvador. Close cooperation on political and military issues with the United States was complemented by ambitious social and economic development projects sponsored by the U.S. Agency for International Development (USAID). Honduras became host to the largest Peace Corps mission in the world and non-governmental and international voluntary agencies proliferated.

As the November 1985 election approached, the Liberal Party had difficulty settling on a candidate and interpreted election law as permitting multiple presidential candidates from one party. The Liberal Party claimed victory when its presidential candidates collectively outpolled the National Party candidate, Rafael Leonardo Callejas, who received 42% of the vote. Jose Azcona Hoyo, the candidate receiving the most votes 27% among the Liberals, assumed the presidency in January 1986. With strong endorsement and support from the Honduran military, the Suazo Administration had ushered in the first peaceful transfer of power between civilian presidents in more than 30 years. Four years later, Rafael Callejas won the presidential election, taking office in January 1990. Callejas concentrated on economic reform, reducing the deficit, and taking steps to deal with an overvalued exchange rate and major structural barriers to investment. He began the movement to place the military under civilian control and laid the groundwork for the creation of the public ministry (Attorney General's office).

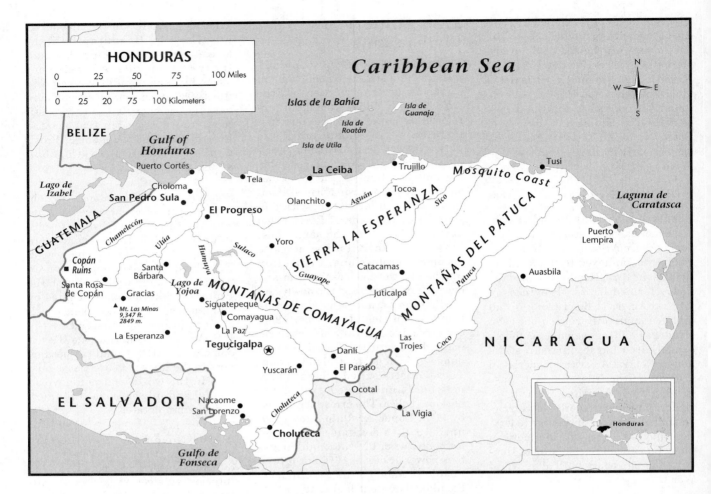

Despite the Callejas Administration's economic reforms, growing public dissatisfaction with the rising cost of living and with seemingly widespread government corruption led voters in 1993 to elect Liberal Party candidate Carlos Roberto Reina over National Party contender Oswaldo Ramos Soto, with Reina winning 56% of the vote.

President Reina, elected on a platform calling for a "Moral Revolution," actively prosecuted corruption and pursued those responsible for human rights abuses in the 1980s. He created a modern attorney general's office and an investigative police force. As a result, a notable start was made in institutionalizing the rule of law in Honduras.

A hallmark of the Reina Administration was his successful efforts to increase civilian control over the armed forces, making his time in office a period of fundamental change

in civil-military relations in Honduras. Important achievements—including the abolition of the military draft and passage of legislation transferring the national police from military to civilian authority—have brought civil-military relations closer to the kind of balance normal in a constitutional democracy. Additionally, President Reina in 1996 named his own defense minister, breaking the precedent of accepting the nominee of the armed forces leadership.

Reina restored national fiscal health. After a rough start in 1994–95, the Reina administration substantially increased Central Bank net international reserves, reduced inflation to 12.8% a year, restored a healthy pace of economic growth (about 5% in 1997), and, perhaps most important, held down spending to achieve a 1.1% non-financial public sector deficit in 1997.

Carlos Roberto Flores Facusse took office on January 27, 1998, as Honduras' fifth democratically elected President since free elections were restored in 1981. Like three of his four predecessors, including his immediate predecessor, Flores is a member of the Liberal Party. He was elected with a 10% margin over his main opponent—National Party nominee Nora de Melgar —in free, fair, and peaceful elections on November 30, 1997. These elections, probably the cleanest in Honduran history, reflected the maturing of Honduras' democratic institutions. Upon taking office on January 27, 1998, Flores inaugurated programs of reform and modernization of the Honduran Government and economy, with emphasis on helping Honduras' poorest citizens while maintaining the country's fiscal health and improving international competitiveness.

In October 1998, Hurricane Mitch devastated Honduras, leaving more than 5,000 people dead and 1.5 million displaced. Damages totaled nearly $3 billion. International donors came forward to assist in rebuilding infrastructure, and the Honduran Government has been fairly transparent in the management of relief funds.

# GOVERNMENT

The 1982 constitution provides for a strong executive, a unicameral National Congress, and a judiciary appointed by the National Congress. The president is directly elected to a 4-year term by popular vote. The congress also serves a 4-year term; congressional seats are assigned the parties' candidates in proportion to the number of votes each party receives. The judiciary includes a Supreme Court of Justice, courts of appeal, and several courts of original jurisdiction—such as labor, tax, and criminal courts. For administrative purposes, Honduras is divided into 18 departments, with departmental and municipal officials selected for 2-year terms.

# NATIONAL SECURITY

Events during the 1980s in El Salvador and Nicaragua led Honduras—with U.S. assistance—to expand its armed forces considerably, laying particular emphasis on its air force, which came to include a squadron of U.S.-provided F-5s. The resolution of the civil wars in El Salvador and Nicaragua and across-the-board budget cuts made in all ministries has brought reduced funding for the Honduran armed forces. The abolition of the draft has created staffing gaps in the now all-volunteer armed forces. The military now is far below its authorized strength, and further reductions are expected. In January 1999, the Constitution was amended to abolish the position of military commander-in-chief of the armed forces, thus codifying civilian authority over the military. President Flores also named the first civilian minister of defense in the country's history.

# POLITICAL CONDITIONS

Reinforced by the media and several political watchdog organizations, human rights and civil liberties are reasonably well protected. There are no known political prisoners in Honduras and the privately owned media frequently exercises its right to criticize without fear of reprisals. Organized labor now represents less than 15% of the work force and its economic and political influence has declined. Honduras held its fifth consecutive democratic elections in November 1997, to elect a new President, unicameral Congress, and mayors; for the first time, voters were able to cast separate ballots for each office.

## Political Parties

The two major parties—the Liberal Party and the National Party—run active campaigns throughout the country. Their ideologies are mostly centrist, with diverse factions in each centered on personalities. The three smaller registered parties—the Christian Democratic Party, the Innovation and Unity Party, and the Democratic Unification Party—remain marginal, slightly left-of-center groupings with few campaign resources and little organization. Despite significant progress in training and installing more skillful advisers at the top of each party ladder, electoral politics in Honduras remain traditionalist and paternalistic. Honduras will hold its next general elections—which will choose the nation's next President, Congress, and mayors—in November 2001.

## Principal Government Officials

**For up-to-date information on Principal Government Officials, see the Chiefs of State and Cabinet Members of Foreign Governments section starting on page 1.**

Honduras maintains an embassy in the United States at 3007 Tilden Street NW, Washington, DC 20008 (tel. 202–966–7702).

# ECONOMY

Honduras is one of the poorest and least developed countries in Latin America. The economy is based mostly on agriculture, which accounted for 22% of GDP in 1999. Leading export coffee ($340 million) accounted for 22% of total Honduran export revenues. Bananas, formerly the country's second-largest export until being virtually wiped out by 1998's Hurricane Mitch, recovered in 2000 to 57% of pre-Mitch levels. Cultivated shrimp are another important export sector. Honduras has extensive forest, marine, and mineral resources, although widespread slash-and-burn agricultural methods continue to destroy Honduran forests. Unemployment is estimated at around 4.0%, though underemployment is much higher. The Honduran economy grew 4.8% in 2000, recovering from the Mitch-induced recession (-1.9%) of 1999. The economy is expected to grow 4–5% in 2001, led by continuation of foreign-funded reconstruction projects. The Honduran maquiladora sector, the second-largest in the world, continued its strong performance in 2000, providing employment to over 120,000 and generating more than $528 million in foreign exchange for the country. Inflation, as measured by the consumer price index, was 10.1% in 2000, down slightly from the 10.9% recorded in 1999. The country's international reserve position continued to be strong in 2000, at slightly over $1 billion. Remittances from Hondurans living abroad (mostly in the U.S.) rose 28% to $410 million in 2000. The currency (lempira) has only moderately devalued.

The country signed an Enhanced Structural Adjustment Facility (ESAF)— later converted to a Poverty Reduction and Growth Facility (PRGF) with the International Monetary Fund in March 1999. While Honduras continues to maintain stable macroeconomic policies, it has lagged in implementing structural reforms, such as privatization of the publicly-owned telephone and energy distribution companies. Honduras received significant debt relief in the aftermath of Hurricane Mitch, including the suspension bilateral debt service payments and bilateral debt reduction by the Paris Club—including the U.S.—worth over $400 million. In July 2000, Honduras reached its decision point under the Highly Indebted Poor Countries Initiative (HIPC), qualifying the country for interim multilateral debt relief.

# FOREIGN RELATIONS

Honduras is a member of the United Nations, the World Trade Organization (WTO), the Organization of American States (OAS), the Central American Parliament (PARLACEN), the Central American Integration System (SICA), and the Central American Security Commission (CASQ). During 1995–96, Honduras, a founding member of the United Nations, for the first time served as a non-permanent member of the UN Security Council.

President Flores consults frequently with the other Central American presidents on issues of mutual interest. He has continued his predecessor's strong emphasis on Central American cooperation and integration, which resulted in an agreement easing border controls and tariffs among Honduras, Guatemala, Nicaragua, and El Salvador. Honduras also joined its six Central American neighbors at the 1994 Summit of the Americas in signing the Alliance for Sustainable Development, known as the Conjunta Centroamerica-USA, or CONCAUSA, to promote sustainable economic development in the region. Honduras held the 6-month SICA presidency during the second half of 1998.

In 1969, El Salvador and Honduras fought the brief "Soccer War" over disputed border areas and friction resulting from the 300,000 Salvadorans who had emigrated to Honduras

in search of land and employment. The catalyst was nationalistic feelings aroused by a series of soccer matches between the two countries. The two countries formally signed a peace treaty on October 30, 1980, which put the border dispute before the International Court of Justice (ICJ). In September 1992, the court awarded most of the disputed territory to Honduras. In January 1998, Honduras and El Salvador signed a border demarcation treaty that will implement the terms of the ICJ decree. The treaty awaits legal ratification in both countries. Honduras and El Salvador maintain normal diplomatic and trade relations.

Honduras and Nicaragua had tense relations throughout 2000 and early 2001 due to a boundary dispute off the Atlantic coast. Nicaragua imposed a 35% tariff against Honduras due to the dispute, and the matter is currently awaiting a decision from the ICJ.

At the 17th Central American Summit in 1995, hosted by Honduras in the northern city of San Pedro Sula, the region's six countries (excluding Belize) signed treaties creating confidence- and security-building measures and combating the smuggling of stolen automobiles in the isthmus. In subsequent summits (held every 6 months), Honduras has continued to work with the other Central American countries on issues of common concern.

In Costa Rica in May 1997, former President Reina met with former President Clinton, his Central American counterparts, and the President of the Dominican Republic to reaffirm support for strengthening democracy, good governance, and promoting prosperity through economic integration, free trade, and investment. The leaders also expressed their commitment to the continued development of just and equitable societies and responsible environmental policies as an integral element of sustainable development.

# U.S.-HONDURAN RELATIONS

The United States and Honduras have close and friendly relations. Honduras is supportive of U.S. policy in the UN and other fora. I n 1996, Honduras' overall voting coincidence with the United States in the United Nations was 44.3% and in 1997, it was 40.3%. As a non-permanent member of the UN Security Council, Honduras played a very helpful role in 1996, most notably in advancing the process of selecting a new UN Secretary General during its October presidency of the Council. The U.S. also continued to be able to count on Honduras' strong support against Iraq.

The U.S. favors stable, peaceful relations between Honduras and its Central American neighbors. During the 1980s, Honduras supported U.S. policy in Central America opposing a revolutionary Marxist government in Nicaragua and an active leftist insurgency in El Salvador. The Honduran Government also played a key role in negotiations that culminated in the 1990 Nicaraguan elections. Honduras contributed troops for the UN peacekeeping mission in Haiti and continues to participate in the UN observers mission in the Western Sahara.

The U.S. works with Honduras for sustained economic, political, and social development and to combat drug trafficking in the region. Because of economic needs and security concerns, U.S. material assistance and political support are important to Honduras. The U.S. Agency for International Development (USAID) is active in Honduras, although official U.S. assistance to the country was reduced—from $51 million in 1993 to $29 million in 1997—due to worldwide reductions in U.S. bilateral assistance. The U.S. increased its assistance to Honduras to over $300 million for 1999 through 2001 and is working with international lenders such as the World Bank and the private sector to promote economic recovery from Hurricane Mitch.

The United States is Honduras' chief trading partner, supplying 46% of its imports and purchasing 40% of its exports. Leading Honduran exports to the United States have included coffee, bananas, seafood (particularly shrimp), minerals (including zinc, lead, gold, and silver), and other fruits and vegetables. The United States encourages U.S. investment that contributes to Honduran development and bilateral trade. The United States' direct investment in Honduras is an estimated $840 million, about two thirds of the total foreign direct investment in the country. The largest U.S. investments in Honduras are in the maquila (garment assembly) sector, fruit production—particularly bananas, melons, and pineapple—tourism, energy generation, shrimp culture, animal feed production, telecommunications, fuel distribution, cigar manufacturing, insurance, brewing, leasing, food processing, and furniture manufacturing. U.S. maquilas are responsible for the majority of the approximately 120,000 jobs in that sector. Many U.S. franchises, particularly in the restaurant sector, operate in Honduras.

The U.S. maintains a small presence at a Honduran military base; the two countries conduct joint counternarcotics, humanitarian, and civic action exercises. U.S. troops conduct and provide logistics support for a variety of exercises (medical, engineering, peacekeeping, counternarcotics, and disaster relief) for the benefit of the Honduran people and their Central American neighbors. U.S. forces—regular, reserve, and National Guard— benefit greatly from the training and exercises.

U.S. troops—in collaboration with counterparts from Brazil and Colombia —since 1994 have assisted Honduran soldiers in clearing land mines from the country's border with Nicaragua. As of early 2001, the U.S.-trained Honduran demining unit had cleared nine major minefields measuring approximately 333,000 square meters and more than 2,200 mines had been destroyed.

## Principal U.S. Embassy Officials

**For up-to-date information on Principal U.S. Officials, see the U.S. Embassies, Consulates, and Foreign Service section starting on page 139.**

The U.S. embassy in Honduras is located on Avenida La Paz, Tegucigalpa (tel.: 011–504–2369320; faxes: general—011–504–236–9037, USAID-011–504–236–7776, USIS—011–504–236–9309, Military Group—011–504–233–6171, Commercial Section—011–504–238–2888, Consulate-011–504–237–1792). Internet: http://www.usia.gov/abtusia/posts/HO1/wwwhmain.html

## U.S. Policy Toward Honduras

U.S. policy toward Honduras is aimed at consolidating stable democracy with a justice system that protects human rights and is fair and effective. U.S. Government programs are aimed at promoting a healthy and more open economy capable of sustainable growth, improving the climate for business and investment while protecting U.S. citizen and corporate rights, and promoting the well-being of the Honduran people. The U.S. also works with Honduras to meet transnational challenges, including the fight against narcotics trafficking, and encourages and supports Honduran efforts to protect the environment. The goals of strengthening democracy and promoting viable economic growth are especially important given the geographical proximity of Honduras to the United States.

A top priority is to assist Honduras and its Central American neighbors in recovering from Hurricane Mitch, which brought unprecedented destruction to the region in October 1998. In Honduras alone, an estimated $3 billion in damage to infrastructure and productive capacity was sustained. To the extent U.S. policy is successful in helping democracy

and economic opportunity to flourish in Honduras, we contribute to a better quality of life for Hondurans and reduce the pressures that compel many Hondurans to attempt to migrate illegally to the U.S.

U.S.-Honduran ties are further strengthened by numerous private sector contacts, with an average of 110,000 U.S. citizens visiting Honduras annually and about 10,500 Americans residing there. In recent years, more than 100 American companies have been operating in Honduras.

## U.S. Economic and Development Assistance

In order to help strengthen Honduras' democratic institutions and improve living conditions, the U.S. has provided substantial economic assistance. The U.S. has historically been the largest bilateral donor to Honduras. USAID obligations to Honduras totaled $19.6 million for development assistance and $12.7 million for foodstuffs in 2000. Over the years, such appropriations have been used to achieve such objectives as fostering democratic institutions, increasing private sector employment and income, helping Honduras fund its arrears with international financial institutions, providing humanitarian aid, increasing agricultural production, and providing loans to micro-businesses.

However, Hurricane Mitch—the worst natural disaster ever to strike the Western Hemisphere—brought massive rains to Honduras that killed thousands of people, left hundreds of thousands homeless, devastated the road network and other public infrastructure, and crippled certain key sectors of the economy. Estimates are that Hurricane Mitch caused $8.5 billion in damages to homes, hospitals, schools, roads, farms, and businesses throughout Central America, including more than $3 billion in Honduras alone. Throughout the country, damage-affected highways, bridges, ports and airports; the electrical power system, the telephone, water, and sewage systems; hospitals and health centers; more than 3,000 schools; almost

83,000 houses; private agricultural infrastructure; and the non-agricultural private sector. Estimates of lost future productive capacity vary.

In response to this disaster, the U.S. provided more than $300 million in humanitarian aid spread over the years 1999–2001. This supplemental assistance is designed to help repair water and sanitation systems; housing, schools, and roads; provide agricultural inputs; local government crisis management training; debt relief for Honduras and Nicaragua; and environmental management expertise. Additional resources have been proposed to maintain anti-crime and drug assistance programs.

New and existing U.S. economic programs—some with proposed enhancements that have taken on even greater importance since the hurricane—include the Caribbean Basin Economic Recovery Act, Overseas Private Investment Corporation financing for private investment and insurance against risks of war and expropriation, U.S. Trade Development Agency grant loans for pre-feasibility studies of projects with U.S. product and services export potential, and U.S. Export-Import Bank short- and medium-term financing for U.S. exports to Honduran importers. All of these provide greater economic opportunity for U.S. and Honduran businessmen and women.

The Peace Corps has been active in Honduras since 1962, and at one time the program there was the largest in the world. During that time some 5,000 American women and men, ranging in age from 22 to 65, have helped the people of Honduras. In 2001, there were 200 Peace Corps Volunteers working in the poorest parts of Honduras.

The government of President Flores is committed to the full implementation of a civilian police force and the Congress has taken essential constitutional steps to effect that. The U.S. Government strongly supports this action. The American embassy in Tegucigalpa provides specialized training to police officers through the

International Criminal Training Assistance Program (ICITAP).

## Security Assistance

The role of the Honduran armed forces has changed significantly in recent years as many institutions formerly controlled by the military are now under civilian authority. The defense and police budgets have hovered at around $35 million during the past few years. The abolition of conscription resulted in a decrease in the size of the armed forces. The volunteer system has helped to increase troop strength somewhat, but many military units are still significantly below authorized strength levels. Formal U.S. security assistance has declined from over $500 million provided between 1982 and 1993 to $500,000 annually in International Military Education and Training (IMET) courses. Some residual credits are still available from previous military aid, but will be exhausted within the next few years.

In the absence of a large security assistance program, defense cooperation has taken the form of increased participation by the Honduran armed forces in military-to-military contact programs and bilateral and multilateral combined exercises oriented toward peacekeeping, disaster relief, humanitarian/civic assistance, and counternarcotics. The U.S. Joint Task Force (JTF) stationed at the Honduran Soto Cano Air Base plays a vital role in supporting combined exercises in Honduras and in neighboring Central American countries. While JTF-

Bravo has been involved in several multilateral exercises and numerous smaller humanitarian deployments, it played an absolutely critical role in helping the U.S. to respond to Hurricane Mitch, Hurricane Keith, and the earthquakes in El Salvador by saving lives, repairing roads and critical infrastructure, and meeting high priority health and sanitation needs. U.S. forces also delivered millions of dollars worth of privately donated goods to those in need.

## U.S. Business Opportunities

The United States historically has been, and remains today, Honduras' largest trading partner. U.S. Department of Commerce trade data show that bilateral trade between the two nations reached $1.86 billion in 2000. American businesses exported $1.3 billion in goods and services to Honduras in 2000.

U.S. investors account for nearly two-thirds of the estimated $1.3 billion in foreign direct investment in Honduras, and more than 150 American companies operate there. The largest U.S. investment in Honduras is in the agribusiness sector. Other important sectors include petroleum products, marketing, maquiladoras (in bond assembly plants), electric power generation, banking, insurance, and tobacco. U.S. franchises have taken off in recent years, mostly in the fast food sector.

Opportunities for U.S. businesses include textile machinery, construction equipment, telecommunications equipment, pollution control/water resources equipment, agricultural machinery, hotel and restaurant equipment, computers and software, franchising, and household consumer goods. Best prospects for agricultural products are corn, milled rice, wheat, soybean meal, and consumer-ready products.

U.S. citizens contemplating investment in real estate in Honduras should proceed with caution, especially in coastal areas or on the Bay Islands, because of frequently conflicting legislation and problems with land titles. Such investors, or their attorneys, should check property titles not only with the property registry office having jurisdiction in the area in which the property is located (being especially observant of marginal annotations on the deed and that the property is located within the area covered by the original title), but also with the National Agrarian Institute (INA) and the National Forestry Administration (COHDEFOR).

## Other Contact Information

**American Chamber of Commerce**
Hotel Honduras Maya Apartado

Postal 1838
Tegucigalpa, Honduras
Tel: (504) 232–7043/232–6035
Fax: (504) 232–9959

**Branch office in San Pedro Sula**
Tel: (504) 558–0164/66
Fax: (504) 552–2401
**Caribbean/Latin American Action**
1818 N Street, N.W. Suite 310
Washington, D.C. 20036
Tel: 202–466–7464
Fax: 202–822–0075
Internet: http://www.claa.org

**U.S. Department of Commerce**
International Trade Administration
Office of Latin America and the Caribbean
14th and Constitution Avenue, N.W.
Washington, D.C. 20230
Tel: 202–482–0057 800-USA-TRADE
Fax: 202–482–0464
Internet: http://www.ita.doc.gov

**U.S. Agency for International Development**
1300 Pennsylvania Avenue, N.W.
Washington, D.C. 20523–0001
Tel: 202–712–4810
Fax: 202–216–3524

Hurricane Relief Website: http://hurricane.info.usaid.gov

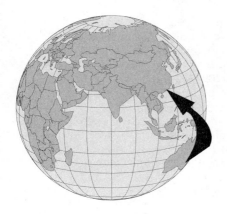

# HONG KONG

November 2000

Official Name:
**Hong Kong Special Administrative Region**

# PROFILE

## Geography

**Area:** 1,092 sq. km.; Hong Kong comprises Hong Kong Island, Kowloon, the New Territories, and numerous small islands.
**Terrain:** Hilly to mountainous, with steep slopes and natural harbor.
**Climate:** Tropical monsoon. Cool and humid in winter, hot and rainy from spring through summer, warm and sunny in fall.

## People

**Population:** (mid-2000) 6.782 million.
**Population growth rate:** (1999) 2.5%.
**Ethnic Groups:** Chinese—95%, other—5%.
**Religion:** Approximately 43% participate in some form of religious practice. Christian—about 8%.
**Languages:** Cantonese (a dialect of Chinese) and English are official.
**Literacy:** 92% (96% male, 88% female).
**Health:** (1999) Infant mortality rate—3.1/1,000. Life expectancy—79.8 yrs. (overall); 77.2 yrs. males, 82.4 yrs. females.
**Work force:** (1999) 3.5 million. Wholesale, retail, and import/export trades and restaurants and hotels—

45%; manufacturing—11%; finance, insurance, real estate, and business services—18%.

## Government

**Type:** Special Administrative Region (SAR) of China, with its own mini-constitution (the Basic Law).
**Branches:** Executive—Executive Council, serving in an advisory role for the Chief Executive. Legislative—Legislative Council elected in September 2000. Judicial—Court of Final Appeal.
**Subdivisions:** Hong Kong, Kowloon, New Territories.
**Suffrage:** Universal at 18 years of age for permanent residents living in Hong Kong for the past 7 years.

## Economy

**GDP:** (1999) $158 billion.
**GDP real growth rate:** (1999) 3.1%.
**Per capita income:** (1999) $23,068.
**Natural resources:** Outstanding deepwater harbor, feldspar.
**Agriculture:** Products—vegetables, poultry.
**Industry:** Types—textiles, clothing, tourism, electronics, plastics, toys, watches, clocks.
**Trade:** Exports—$173 billion: clothing, electronics, textiles, watches and clocks, office machinery. Main partners—China, U.S., Japan, Germany, United Kingdom, Taiwan. Imports—

$178.6 billion: consumer goods, raw materials and semi-manufactures, capital goods, foodstuffs, fuels. Main partners—China, Japan, Taiwan, U.S., Singapore, South Korea.

# PEOPLE

Hong Kong's population has increased steadily over the past decade, reaching about 6.8 million by 1999. Hong Kong is one of the most densely populated areas in the world, with an overall density of some 6,300 people per square kilometer. Cantonese, the official Chinese dialect, is spoken by most of the population. English, also an official language, is widely understood; it is spoken by more than one-third of the population. Every major religion is practiced in Hong Kong; ancestor worship is predominant due to the strong Confucian influence.

All children are required by law to be in full-time education between the ages of 6 and 15. Preschool education for most children begins at age 3. Primary school begins normally at the age of 6 and lasts for 6 years. At about age 12, children progress to a 3-year course of junior secondary education. Most stay on for a 2-year senior secondary course, while others join full-time vocational training. More than 90% of children complete upper secondary education or equivalent vocational education.

# HISTORY

According to archaeological studies initiated in the 1920s, human activity on Hong Kong dates back over five millennia. Excavated Neolithic artifacts suggest an influence from northern Chinese Stone-Age cultures, including the Longshan. The territory was settled by Han Chinese during the seventh century, A.D., evidenced by the discovery of an ancient tomb at Lei Cheung Uk in Kowloon. The first major migration from northern China to Hong Kong occurred during the Ching Dynasty (960-1279). The British East India Company made the first successful sea venture to China in 1699, and Hong Kong's trade with British merchants developed rapidly soon after. After the Chinese defeat in the First Opium War (1839-1842), Hong Kong was ceded to Britain in 1842 under the Treaty of Nanking. Britain was granted a perpetual lease on the Kowloon Peninsula under the 1860 Convention of Beijing, which formally ended hostilities in the Second Opium War (1856-1858). The United Kingdom, concerned that Hong Kong could not be defended unless surrounding areas were also under British control, executed a 99-year lease of the New Territories in 1898, significantly expanding the size of the Hong Kong colony.

In the late 19th century and early 20th centuries, Hong Kong developed as a warehousing and distribution center for U.K. trade with southern China. After the end of World War II and the communist takeover of Mainland China in 1949, hundreds of thousands of people emigrated from China to Hong Kong. This helped Hong Kong become an economic success and a manufacturing, commercial, and tourism center. High life expectancy, literacy, per capita income, and other socioeconomic measures attest to Hong Kong's

achievements over the last four decades.

# GOVERNMENT

The Hong Kong Special Administrative Region (SAR) is headed by Chief Executive Tung Chee Hwa. Mr. Tung assumed office on July 1, 1997, following his selection by a 400-member committee appointed by Beijing. Legislative Council elections were held in May 1998 and again in September 2000. According to The Basic Law, Hong Kong's "Mini-constitution," the Legislative Council has 24 directly elected members—30 members elected by functional (occupational) constituencies and 6 elected by an Election Committee. The 1998 and 2000 elections were seen as free, open, and widely contested, despite discontent among mainly prodemocracy politicians that the functional constituency and Election Committee elections are essentially undemocratic because so few voters are eligible to vote. The Civil Service maintains its quality and neutrality, operating without discernible direction from Beijing.

## Principal Government Officials

**For up-to-date information on Principal Government Officials, see the Chiefs of State and Cabinet Members of Foreign Governments section starting on page 1.**

# POLITICAL CONDITIONS

On July 1, 1997, China resumed the exercise of sovereignty over Hong Kong, ending more than 150 years of British colonial control. Hong Kong is a Special Administrative Region of the People's Republic of China with a high degree of autonomy in all mat-

ters except foreign and defense affairs. According to the Sino-British Joint Declaration (1984) and the Basic Law—Hong Kong's mini-constitution—for 50 years after reversion Hong Kong will retain its political, economic, and judicial systems and unique way of life and continue to participate in international agreements and organizations under the name, "Hong Kong, China."

Although concerns about the continued independence of the judiciary arose when the Hong Kong Government sought interpretation of the Basic Law from the National People's Congress following a controversial Court of Final Appeal ruling (the Right of Abode case), Hong Kong's courts remain independent and the rule of law is respected. Hong Kong remains a free and open society where human rights are generally respected.

# ECONOMY

After a slump caused by the region-wide Asian financial crisis that began in 1997, Hong Kong's economy is on the rebound. Real GDP growth was 3.1% in 1999 and reached double digits in the first half of 2000. After peaking at 6.3% in 1999, the unemployment rate eased back to 4.8% in mid-2000. In August 1998, the government intervened in the stock, futures, and currency markets to fend off "manipulators," terming the move a one-time divergence from its usual adherence to noninterventionist, market-oriented policies. The banking sector remains solid, and the government is committed to the U.S.-Hong Kong dollar link.

Hong Kong has little arable land and virtually no natural resources, including water for agriculture. Agriculturally, it is less than 20% self-sufficient. However, its magnificent harbor has facilitated rapid development of foreign trade. Hong Kong's principal trading partners include China, the United States, Japan, Taiwan, Germany, Singapore, and South Korea. Hong Kong enjoyed economic growth in the past because of its strong manufacturing sector, but in recent years the service sector has surpassed it in importance and now accounts for 85% of GDP. The major components of Hong Kong's service trade are shipping, civil aviation, tourism, and various financial services. Hong Kong has one of the world's most sophisticated telecommunications and information technology infrastructures and functions as a major regional and international financial and commercial center. In 1999, Hong Kong's gross domestic product (GDP) was $158 billion.

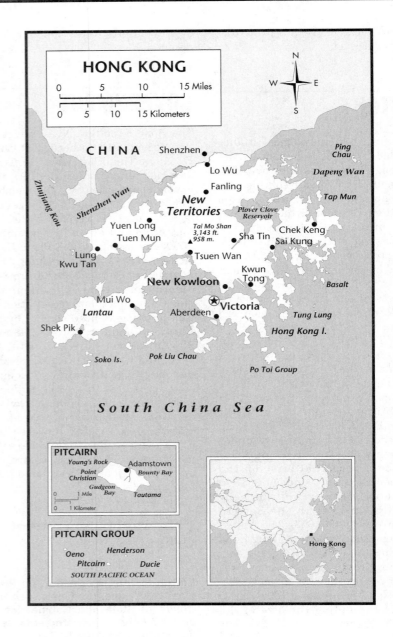

# FOREIGN RELATIONS

Hong Kong's foreign relations and defense are the responsibility of China. China has granted Hong Kong considerable autonomy in economic and commercial relations. Hong Kong continues to be an active, independent member of the World Trade Organization (WTO) and the Asia-Pacific Economic Cooperation (APEC) forum.

# U.S.-HONG KONG RELATIONS

U.S. policy toward Hong Kong, grounded in a determination to help preserve Hong Kong's prosperity, autonomy, and way of life, is stated in the Hong Kong Policy Act of 1992. The United States encourages high-level visits to Hong Kong as evidence of close ties and the importance of Hong Kong to U.S. interests.

The United States has substantial economic and social ties with Hong Kong. There are some 1,100 U.S. firms, including more than 400 regional operations, and 50,000 American residents in Hong Kong. According to U.S. Government statistics, U.S. exports to Hong Kong totaled U.S.$12.6 billion in 1999 and two-way trade totaled U.S.$23.1 billion, making Hong Kong the United States' 15th-largest trading partner. U.S. direct investment in Hong Kong at the end of 1999 totaled approximately U.S.$20.8 billion, making the United States one of Hong Kong's largest investors, along with the U.K., China, and Japan.

The Hong Kong Government maintains three Economic and Trade

Offices in the United States. Addresses and telephone numbers for these offices are listed below:

1520 - 18th Street NW
Washington, DC 20036
Tel: (202) 331-8947
Fax: (202) 331-8958

115 East 54th Street
New York, NY 10022
Tel: (212) 752-3320
Fax: (212) 752-3395

130 Montgomery Street
San Francisco, CA 94104
Tel: (415) 835-9300
Fax: (415) 421-0646

## Principal U.S. Officials

**For up-to-date information on Principal U.S. Officials, see the U.S. Embassies, Consulates, and Foreign Service section starting on page 139.**

The U.S. Consulate General is located at 26 Garden Road, Hong Kong. Tel: (852) 2523-9011 (general). FAX: (852) 2845-1598 (general) (852) 2147-5790 (consular); (852) 2845-9800 (commercial).

## Web Sites

U.S. Consulate General web site: http://www.usconsulate.org.hk The following sites are not U.S. Government web sites: Hong Kong homepage: http://www.info.gov.hk Hong Kong Tourist Association: http://www.hkta.org Hong Kong Trade Development Council: http://www.tdctrade.com.hk For more information regarding visa requirements for Hong Kong, refer to the Hong Kong immigration web site: http://www.info.gov.hk/immd/english/topical/e/1.htm

# HUNGARY

August 1999

Official Name:
**Republic of Hungary**

## PROFILE

### Geography

**Area:** 93,030 sq. km. (35,910 sq. mi.); about the size of Indiana.
**Cities:** Capital—Budapest (est. pop. 2 million). Other cities—Debrecen (220,000); Miskolc (208,000); Szeged (189,000); Pecs (183,000).
**Terrain:** Mostly flat, with low mountains in the north and northeast and north of Lake Balaton.
**Climate:** Temperate.

### People

**Nationality:** Noun and adjective—Hungarian(s).
**Population (est.):** 10.1 million.
**Ethnic groups:** Magyar 92%, Romany 4% (est.), German 2%, Slovak 1%, others 1%.
**Religions:** Roman Catholic 68%, Calvinist 21%, Lutheran 4%, Jewish 1%, others, including Baptist Adventist, Pentecostal, Unitarian 3%.
**Languages:** Magyar 98%, other 2%.
**Education:** Compulsory to age 16. Attendance—96%. Literacy—99%.
**Health:** Infant mortality rate—15/1,000. Life expectancy—men 66 yrs., women 75 yrs.
**Work force (4 million):** Agriculture—8%. Industry and commerce—42%. Services—32%. Government— 7%.

### Government

**Type:** Republic.
**Constitution:** August 20, 1949. Substantially rewritten in 1989, amended in 1990.
**Branches:** Executive—president of the Republic (head of state), prime minister (head of government), Council of Ministers. Legislative—National Assembly (386 members, 4–year term). Judicial—Supreme Court and Constitutional Court.
**Administrative regions:** 19 counties plus capital region of Budapest.
**Principal political parties:** Fidesz–Hungarian Civic Parry—center–right; Hungarian Socialist Party (MSZP)—center–left; Independent Smallholders' Party (FKGP)—populist–agrarian right; Alliance of Free—center–right; Hungarian Justice and Life Party (MIEP)—far right, Hungarian Democratic People's Party (MDNP)— center–right. Christian Democratic People's Party (KDNP)—Christian center–right.

### Economy

**GDP (1998):** $45.5 billion.
**Annual growth rate:** 4.4%; 5.5%–6.0% forecast through 2001.
**Per capita GDP (1997):** $4,500.
**Natural resources (1998):** Fertile land, bauxite, brown coal.
**Agriculture/forestry (7% of 1997 GDP):** Products—meat, corn, wheat, potatoes, sugarbeets, vegetables, fruits, sunflower seeds.
**Industry/construction (26% of 1997 GDP):** Types—machinery, vehicles, chemicals, precision and measuring equipment, computer products, medical instruments, pharmaceuticals.
**Trade (1998):** Exports—$19.1 billion: machinery, vehicles, medical instruments: food and beverages, agricultural products. Major markets—EU (Germany, Austria, Italy), CEFTA, CIS, U.S. Imports—$21.1 billion: machinery, vehicles, consumer manufactures, energy, food and beverages. Major suppliers—EU (Germany, Austria, Italy, France), CIS, CEFTA, U.S.
**Exchange rate (1998):** About 220 forint=US$1.

## HISTORY

Since its conversion to Western Christianity before AD 1000, Hungary has been an integral part of Europe. Although Hungary was a monarchy for nearly 1,000 years, its constitutional system preceded by several centuries the establishment of Western–style governments in other European countries. Following the defeat of the Austro–Hungarian Dual Monarchy (1867–1918) at the end of World War I, Hungary lost two–thirds of its territory and nearly as much of its population. It experienced a brief but bloody communist dictatorship and counterrevolution in 1919, followed by a 25–year regency under Adm. Miklos Horthy. Although Hungary fought in most of World War II as a German ally, it fell under German military occupation following an unsuccessful attempt to switch sides on October 15, 1944. In January 1945, a provisional government concluded an armistice with the Soviet Union and established the Allied Control Commission, under which Soviet, American, and British representatives held complete sovereignty over the country. The Commission's chairman was a member of Stalin's inner circle and exercised absolute control.

## Communist Takeover

The provisional government, dominated by the Hungarian Communist Party (MKP), was replaced in November 1945 after elections which gave majority control of a coalition government to the Independent Smallholders' Party. The government instituted a radical land reform and gradually nationalized mines, electric plants, heavy industries, and some large banks. The communists ultimately undermined the coalition regime by discrediting leaders of rival parties and through terror, blackmail, and framed trials. In elections tainted by fraud in 1947, the leftist bloc gained control of the government. Postwar cooperation between the U.S.S.R. and the West collapsed, and the Cold War began. With Soviet support, Moscow-trained Matyas Rakosi began to establish a communist dictatorship.

By February 1949, all opposition parties had been forced to merge with the MKP to form the Hungarian Workers' Party. In 1949, the communists held a single–list election and adopted a Soviet–style constitution which created the Hungarian People's Republic. Rakosi became Prime Minister in 1952. Between 1948 and 1953, the Hungarian economy was

reorganized according to the Soviet model. In 1949, the country joined the Council for Mutual Economic Assistance (CMEA, or Comecon), a Soviet–bloc economic organization. All private industrial firms with more than 10 employees were nationalized. Freedom of the press, religion, and assembly were strictly curtailed. The head of the Roman Catholic Church, Cardinal Jozsef Mindszenty, was sentenced to life imprisonment.

Forced industrialization and land collectivization soon led to serious economic difficulties, which reached crisis proportions by mid–1953, the year Stalin died. The new Soviet leaders blamed Rakosi for Hungary's economic situation and began a more flexible policy called the "New Course." Imre Nagy replaced Rakosi as prime minister in 1953 and repudiated much of Rakosi's economic program of forced collectivization and heavy industry. He also ended political purges and freed thousands of political prisoners. However, the economic situation continued to deteriorate, and Rakosi succeeded in disrupting the reforms and in forcing Nagy from power in 1955 for "right–wing revisionism." Hungary joined the Soviet–led Warsaw Pact Treaty Organization the same year. Rakosi's attempt to restore Stalinist orthodoxy then foundered as increasing opposition developed within the party and among students and other organizations after Khrushchev's 1956 denunciation of Stalin. Fearing revolution, Moscow replaced Rakosi with his deputy, Erno Gero, in order to contain growing ideological and political ferment.

## 1956 Revolution

Pressure for change reached a climax on October 23, 1956, when security forces fired on Budapest students marching in support of Poland's confrontation with the Soviet Union. The ensuing battle quickly grew into a massive popular uprising. Gero called on Soviet troops to restore order on October 24. Fighting did not abate until the Central Committee named Imre Nagy as prime minister on October 25, and the next day Janos Kadar

replaced Gero as party first secretary. Nagy dissolved the state security police, abolished the one–party system, promised free elections, and negotiated with the U.S.S.R. to withdraw its troops. Faced with reports of new Soviet troops pouring into Hungary despite Soviet Ambassador Andropov's assurances to the contrary, on November 1 Nagy announced Hungary's neutrality and withdrawal from the Warsaw Pact. He appealed to the United Nations and the Western powers for protection of its neutrality. Preoccupied with the Suez Crisis, the UN and the West failed to respond, and the Soviet Union launched a massive military attack on Hungary on November 3. Some 200,000 Hungarians fled to the West. Nagy and his colleagues took refuge in the Yugoslav Embassy. Kadar, after delivering an impassioned radio address on November 1 in support of "our glorious revolution" and vowing to fight the Russians with his bare hands if they attacked Hungary, defected from the Nagy cabinet; he fled to the Soviet Union and on November 4 announced the formation of a new government. He returned to Budapest and, with Soviet support, carried out severe reprisals; thousands of people were executed or imprisoned. Despite a guarantee of safe conduct, Nagy was arrested and deported to Romania. In June 1958, the government announced that Nagy and other former officials had been executed.

## Reform Under Kadar

In the early 1960s, Kadar announced a new policy under the motto of "He who is not against us is with us." He declared a general amnesty, gradually curbed some of the excesses of the secret police, and introduced a relatively liberal cultural and economic course aimed at overcoming the post–1956 hostility toward him and his regime. In 1966, the Central Committee approved the "New Economic Mechanism," through which it sought to overcome the inefficiencies of central planning, increase productivity, make Hungary more competitive in world markets, and create prosperity to ensure political stabil-

**HUNGARY**

ity. However, the reform was not as comprehensive as planned, and basic flaws of central planning produced economic stagnation. Over the next two decades of relative domestic quiet, Kadar's government responded to pressure for political and economic reform and to counterpressures from reform opponents, By the early 1980s, it had achieved some lasting economic reforms and limited political liberalization and pursued a foreign policy which encouraged more trade with the West. Nevertheless, the New Economic Mechanism led to mounting foreign debt incurred to share up unprofitable industries.

## Transition to Democracy

Hungary's transition to a Western—style parliamentary democracy was the first and the smoothest among the former Soviet bloc, inspired by a nationalism that long had encouraged Hungarians to control their own destiny. By 1987, activists within the party and bureaucracy and Budapest–based intellectuals were increasing pressure for change. Some of these became reform socialists, while others began movements which were to develop into parties. Young liberals formed the Federation of Young Democrats (Fidesz); a core from the so–called Democratic Opposition formed the Association of Free Democrats (SZDSZ), and the neopopulist national opposition established the Hungarian Democratic Forum (MDF). Civic activism intensified to a level not seen since the 1956 revolution.

In 1988, Kadar was replaced as General Secretary of the Communist Party, and reform communist leader Imre Pozsgay was admitted to the Politburo. That same year, the Parliament adopted a "democracy package," which included trade union pluralism; freedom of association, assembly, and the press; a new electoral law; and a radical revision of the constitution, among others. A Central Committee plenum in February 1989 endorsed in principle the multiparty political system and the characterization of the October 1956 revolution as a "popular uprising," in the words of Pozsgay, whose reform movement had been gathering strength as Communist Party membership declined dramatically. Kadar's major political rivals then cooperated to move the country gradually to democracy. The Soviet Union reduced its involvement by signing an agreement in April 1989 to withdraw Soviet forces by June 1991.

## Travel Notes

**Travel Advice:** For up-to-date information from the U.S. State Department on possible inconvenient or hazardous situations, see the **Travel Warnings and Consular Information Sheets from the U.S. Government** section starting on page 1723. For the latest information on health requirements and conditions, see the **International Travelers' Health Information** section starting on page 1385. For further information dealing with non-urgent matter, see the **Tips for Travelers to...** section starting on page 1588.

National unity culminated in June 1989 as the country reburied Imre Nagy, his associates, and, symbolically, all other victims of the 1956 revolution. A national roundtable, comprising representatives of the new parties and some recreated old parties—such as the Smallholders and Social Democrats—the Communist Party, and different social groups, met in the late summer of 1989 to discuss major changes to the Hungarian constitution in preparation for free elections and the transition to a fully free and democratic political system.

In October 1989, the communist party convened its last congress and re-established itself as the Hungarian Socialist Party (MSZP). In a historic session an October 16–20, 1989, the Parliament adopted legislation providing for multiparty parliamentary elections and a direct presidential election. The legislation transformed Hungary from a people's republic into the Republic of Hungary, guaranteed human and civil rights, and created an institutional structure that ensures separation of powers among the judicial, executive, and legislative branches of government. But because the national roundtable agreement was the result of a compromise between communist and noncommunist parties and societal forces, the revised constitution still retained vestiges of the old order. It championed the "values of bourgeois democracy and democratic socialism" and gave equal status to public and private property. Such pro-

visions were erased in 1990 as the need for compromise solutions was obviated by the poor performance of the MSZP in the first free elections.

## Free Elections and a Democratic Hungary

The first free parliamentary election, held in May 1990, was a plebiscite of sorts on the communist past. The revitalized and reformed communists performed poorly despite having more than the usual advantages of an "incumbent" party. Populist, center-right, and liberal parties fared best, with the Democratic Forum (MDF) winning 43% of the vote and the Free Democrats (SZDSZ) capturing 24%. Under Prime Minister Jozsef Antall, the MDF formed a center-right coalition government with the Independent Smallholders' Party (FKGP) and the Christian Democratic People's Party (KDNP) to command a 60% majority in the parliament. Parliamentary opposition parties included SZDSZ, the Socialists (MSZP), and the Alliance of Young Democrats (Fidesz). Peter Boross succeeded as Prime Minister after Antall died in December 1993. The Antall/Boross coalition governments achieved a reasonably well-functioning parliamentary democracy and laid the foundation for a free market economy.

In May 1994, the socialists came back to win a plurality of votes and 54% of the seats after an election campaign focused largely on economic issues and the substantial decline in living standards since 1990. A heavy turnout of voters swept away the right-of-center coalition but soundly rejected extremists on both right and left. Despite its neocommunist pedigree, the MSZP continued economic reforms and privatization, adopting a painful but necessary policy of fiscal austerity (the "Bokros plan") in 1995. The government pursued a foreign policy of integration with Euro-Atlantic institutions and reconciliation with neighboring countries. But neither an invitation to join NATO nor improving economic indicators guaranteed the MSZP's re-election; dissatisfaction with the pace of economic recovery, rising crime, and

cases of government corruption convinced voters to propel center-right parties into power following national elections in May 1998. The Federation of Young Democrats (renamed Fidcsz–Hungarian Civic Party (MPP) in 1995) captured a plurality of parliamentary seats and forged a coalition with the Smallholders and the Democratic Forum. The new government, headed by 35-year-old Prime Minister Viktor Organ, promised to stimulate faster growth, curb inflation, and lower taxes. Although the Orban administration also pledged continuity in foreign policy, and has continued to pursue Euro-Atlantic integration as its first priority, it has been a more vocal advocate of minority rights for ethnic Hungarians abroad than the previous government.

# GOVERNMENT

The President of the Republic, elected by the National Assembly every 5 years, has a largely ceremonial role but powers also include appointing the prime minister. The prime minister selects cabinet ministers and has the exclusive right to dismiss them. Each cabinet nominee appears before one or more parliamentary committees in consultative open hearings and must be formally approved by the president. The unicameral, 386-member National Assembly is the highest organ of state authority and initiates and approves legislation sponsored by the prime minister. A party must win at least 5% of the national vote to form a parliamentary faction. National parliamentary elections are held every 4 years (the last in May 1998). A 15-member Constitutional Court has power to challenge legislation on grounds of unconstitutionality.

## Principal Government Officials

**For up-to-date information on Principal Government Officials, see the Chiefs of State and Cabinet Mem-**

bers of Foreign Governments section starting on page 1.

The Hungarian Embassy is located at 3910 Shoemaker St. NW, Washington, DC 20008 (tel. 202–362–6730). Hungary has consulates in New York City and Los Angeles.

# NATIONAL SECURITY

Hungary spearheaded the movement to dissolve the Warsaw Pact Treaty Organization in 1990 and has since worked to modernize and Westernize its armed forces. The prospect of imminent NATO membership has led the government to focus on assuring the interoperability of the Hungarian Home Defense Forces (Honvedseg) with those of its future allies. This requires not only a slow, expensive overhaul of military hardware but also a major restructuring of organization, military doctrine, and training. Hungary has been an active participant in the Partnership for Peace since 1994, as well as the NATO–led IFOR/SFOR operations in Bosnia, and regularly contributes to UN peacekeeping missions.

The Honvedseg's largest service is the army, followed by the air force and a small naval contingent that patrols the Danube River. The size of the armed forces is now 58,000, down from over 130,000 in 1989. The current mandatory conscription period for Hungarian males is 9 months, although the new government has declared that it wants to reduce this to 6 months as part of a plan to professionalize the army. The Orban administration also has pledged to increase defense spending by 0.1% of GDP for the next 4 years to bring Hungary's military budget in line with those of NATO countries. In 1997, Hungary spent about 123 billion HUF ($560 million) on defense. Hungary became a member of NATO on March 12, 1999. Hungary provided airbases and support for NATO's air campaign against Serbia and has provided military units to serve in Kosovo as part of the NATO–led KFOR operation.

# ECONOMY

The Hungarian economy prior to WWII was primarily oriented toward agriculture and small–scale manufacturing. Hungary's strategic position in Europe and its relative lack of natural resources also have dictated a traditional reliance on foreign trade. In the early 1950s, the communist government forced rapid industrialization after the standard Stalinist pattern in an effort to encourage a more self–sufficient economy. Most economic activity was conducted by state–owned enterprises or cooperatives and state farms. In 1968, Stalinist self–sufficiency was replaced by the "New Economic Mechanism," which reopened Hungary to foreign trade, gave limited freedom to the workings of the market, and allowed a limited number of small businesses to operate in the services sector.

Although Hungary enjoyed one of the most liberal and economically advanced economies of the former Eastern bloc, both agriculture and industry began to suffer from a lack of investment in the 1970s, and Hungary's net foreign debt rose significantly—from $1 billion in 1973 to $15 billion in 1993—due largely to consumer subsidies and unprofitable state enterprises. In the face of economic stagnation, Hungary opted to try further liberalization by passing a joint venture law, enstating an income tax, and joining the International Monetary Fund (IMF) and the World Bank. By 1988, Hungary had developed a two–tier banking system and had enacted significant corporate legislation which paved the way for the ambitious market–oriented reforms of the post–communist years.

The Antall government of 1990–94 began market reforms with price and trade liberation measures, a revamped tax system, and a nascent market–based banking system. By 1994, however, the costs of government overspending and hesitant privatization had become clearly visible. Cuts in consumer subsidies led to increases in the price of food, medicine, transportation services, and energy. Reduced exports to the former Soviet bloc and shrinking industrial output contributed to a sharp decline in GDP. Unemployment rose rapidly—to about 12% in 1993. The external debt burden, one of the highest in Europe, reached 250% of annual export earnings, while the budget and current account deficits approached 10% of GDP. In March 1995, the government of Prime Minister Gyula Horn implemented an austerity program, coupled with aggressive privatization of state–owned enterprises and an export–promoting exchange raw regime, to reduce indebtness, cut the current account deficit, and shrink public spending. By the end of 1997 the consolidated public sector deficit decreased to 4.6% of GDP— with public sector spending falling from 62% of GDP to below 50%—the current account deficit was reduced to 2% of GDP, and government debt was paid down to 94% of annual export earnings.

The Government of Hungary no longer requires IMF financial assistance and has repaid all of its debt to the fund. Consequently, Hungary enjoys favorable borrowing terms, and its sovereign foreign currency debt issuances carry investment–grade ratings with positive outlooks from all major credit–rating agencies. In 1995 Hungary's currency, the forint (HUF), became convertible for all current account transactions, and subsequent to OECD membership in 1996, for almost all capital account transactions as well. Since 1995, Hungary has pegged the forint against a basket of currencies (in which the German mark is 70% and the U.S. dollar 30%), and the central rate against the basket is devalued at a preannounced rate, currently set at 0.8% per month. The government privatization program will end on schedule in 1998: 80% of GDP is now produced by the private sector, and foreign owners control 70% of financial institutions, 66% of industry, 90%

of telecommunications, and 50% of the trading sector.

After Hungary's GDP declined about 18% from 1990 to 1993 and grew only 1%–1.5% up to 1996, strong export performance has propelled GDP growth to 4.4% in 1997, with other macroeconomic indicators similarly improving. These successes allowed the government to concentrate in 1996 and 1997 on major structural reforms such as the implementation of a fully funded pension system, reform of higher education, and the creation of a national treasury. Remaining economic challenges include reducing fiscal deficits and inflation (expected to fall to 13% by the end of 1998), maintaining stable external balances, and completing structural reforms of the tax system, health care, and local government financing. The overriding goal of Hungarian economic policy, however, will be to prepare the country for accession to the European Union at the earliest possible date. Although many challenges remain, the prospects of EU membership with the next decade are excellent.

Prior to the change of regime in 1989, 65% of Hungary's trade was with Comecon countries. By the end of 1997, Hungary had shifted much of its trade to the West. Trade with EU countries and the OECD now comprises over 70% and 80% of the total, respectively. Germany is Hungary's single most important trading partner. The U.S. has become Hungary's sixth–largest export market, while Hungary is ranked as the 72d largest export market for the U.S. Bilateral trade between the two countries increased 46% in 1997 to more than $1 billion. The U.S. has extended to Hungary most–favored–nation status, the Generalized System of Preferences, Overseas Private Investment Corporation insurance, and access to the Export/Import Bank.

With about $18 billion in foreign direct investment (FDI) since 1989, Hungary has attracted over one–third of all FDI in central and eastern Europe, including the former Soviet Union. Of this, about $6 billion came from American companies. Foreign capital is attracted by skilled and relatively inexpensive labor, tax incentives, and a good telecommunications system.

# FOREIGN RELATIONS

Except for the short–lived neutrality declared by Imre Nagy in November 1956, Hungary's foreign policy generally followed the Soviet lead from 1947 to 1989. During the communist period, Hungary maintained treaties of friendship, cooperation, and mutual assistance with the Soviet Union, Poland, Czechoslovakia, the German Democratic Republic, Romania, and Bulgaria. It was one of the founding members of the Soviet–led Warsaw Pact and Comecon, and it was the first central European country to withdraw from those organizations, now defunct.

As with any country, Hungarian security attitudes are shaped largely by history and geography. For Hungary, this is a history of more than 400 years of domination by great powers—the Ottomans, the Habsburgs, the Germans during World War II, and the Soviets during the Cold War—and a geography of regional instability and separation from Hungarian minorities living in neighboring countries. Hungary's foreign policy priorities, largely consistent since 1990, represent a direct response to these factors. Since 1990, Hungary's top foreign policy goal has been achieving integration into Western economic and security organizations. Hungary joined the Partnership for Peace program in 1994 and has actively supported the IFOR and SFOR missions in Bosnia. The Horn government achieved Hungary's most important foreign policy successes of the post–communist era by securing invitations to join both NATO and the European Union in 1997.

Hungary also has improved its often–chilled neighborly relations by signing basic treaties with Romania, Slovakia, and Ukraine. These renounce all outstanding territorial claims and lay the foundation for constructive relations. However, the issue of ethnic Hungarian minority rights in Slovakia and Romania periodically causes bilateral tensions to flare. Hungary was a signatory to the Helsinki Final Act in 1975, has signed all of the CSCE/OSCE follow–on documents since 1989, and served as the OSCE's Chairman–in–Office in 1997. Hungary's record of implementing CSCE Helsinki Final Act provisions, including those on reunification of divided families, remains among the best in eastern Europe. Hungary has been a member of the United Nations since December 1955.

# U.S.-HUNGARIAN RELATIONS

Relations between the United States and Hungary following World War II were affected by the Soviet armed forces' occupation of Hungary. Full diplomatic relations were established at the legation level on October 12, 1945, before the signing of the Hungarian peace treaty on February 10, 1947. After the communist takeover in 1947–48, relations with Hungary became increasingly strained by the nationalization of U.S.–owned property, unacceptable treatment of U.S. citizens and personnel, and restrictions on the operations of the American legation. Though relations deteriorated further after the suppression of the Hungarian national uprising in 1956, an exchange of ambassadors in 1966 inaugurated an era of improving relations. In 1972, a consular convention was concluded to provide consular protection to U.S. citizens in Hungary.

In 1973, a bilateral agreement was reached under which Hungary settled the nationalization claims of American citizens. In January 1978, the United States returned to the people of Hungary the historic Crown of Saint Stephen, which had been safeguarded by the United States since the end of World War II. Symbolically and actually, this event marked the beginning of excellent relations between the two countries. A 1978 bilateral trade agreement included extension of most–favored–nation status to Hungary. Cultural and scientific exchanges were expanded. As Hungary began to pull away from the Soviet orbit, the United States offered assistance and expertise to help establish a constitution, a democratic political system, and a plan for a free market economy.

Between 1989 and 1993, the Support for East European Democracy (SEED) Act provided more than $136 million for economic restructuring and private sector development. The Hungarian–American Enterprise Fund offers loans, equity capital and technical assistance to promote private–sector development. The U.S. Government has provided expert and financial assistance for the development of modern and Western institutions in many policy areas, including national security, law enforcement, free media, environmental regulations, education, and health care. Direct investment in Hungary by American companies is rising rapidly. When Hungary acceded to NATO in April 1999, it became a formal ally of the United States. This move has been consistently supported by the 1.5 million–strong Hungarian–American community.

## Principal U.S. Embassy Officials

**For up-to-date information on Principal U.S. Officials, see the U.S. Embassies, Consulates, and Foreign Service section starting on page 139.**

The U.S. Embassy in Hungary is located at Szabadsag Ter 12, Budapest 1054 (tel. (36) 1–475–4400).

# ICELAND

October 1999

Official Name:
**Republic of Iceland**

# PROFILE

## Geography

**Area:** 102,845 sq. km. (39,709 sq. miles); about the size of Virginia or twice the size of Ireland.
**Cities:** Capital— Reykjavik (pop. 167,596). Other towns—Kopavogur (16,186), Hafnarfjordur (15,151) Akureyri (14,174).
**Terrain:** Rugged.
**Climate:** Maritime temperate.
**Highest elevation:** Vatnajokull Glacier, at 2,119 meters (6,952 ft.).

## People

**Nationality:** Noun—Icelander(s). Adjective—Icelandic.
**Population:** 275,264.
**Annual growth rate:** 1.18%.
**Ethnic group:** Homogenous mixture of descendants of Norwegians and Celts.
**Religion:** Evangelical Lutheran, 91%.
**Language:** Icelandic.
**Education:** Compulsory up to age 16. Attendance—99%. Literacy—99.9%.
**Health:** Infant mortality rate—6/1,000. Life expectancy—men 76.3 yrs., women 80.8 yrs.
**Work force (1998, 131,038):** Commerce—14.9%. Manufacturing—12.9%. Fishing/fish processing—11.8%. Construction—10.7%. Transportation and communications—6.8%. Agriculture—5.1%. Unemployment: 1.5%.

## Government

**Type:** Constitutional republic.
**Independence:** 1944.
**Constitution:** 1874.
**Branches:** Executive—president (chief of state), prime minister (head of government), Cabinet (9 ministers). Legislative—63 member unicameral parliament (Althingi). Judicial—Supreme Court, district court, special courts.
**Subdivisions:** 23 Syslur (counties).
**Major political parties:** Independence (IP), Progressive (PP), Alliance (A), Left–Green (G), Liberal Party (L).
**Suffrage:** Universal over 18.
**National holiday:** June 17, anniversary of the establishment of the republic.
**Flag:** Red cross edged in white on a blue field.

## Economy

**GNP:** $8.5 billion.
**GNP growth rate:** 4.2%.
**Per capita GDP (1998):** $31,406.
**Inflation rate (1999):** 4%.
**Budget:** $3 billion.
**Annual budget deficit (1998):** None.
**Net public debt:** $2.6 billion.
**Foreign aid as part of budget:** 0.15%.
**Natural resources:** Marine products, hydroelectric and geothermal power, diatomite.
**Agriculture:** Products—potatoes, turnips, livestock.
**Industry:** Types—aluminum smelting, fish processing, ferro–silicon production, geothermal power.
**Trade:** Exports—$1.9 billion: marine products 71%, other manufacturing products 22%, miscellaneous 5%, agriculture 2%. Partners—EU 65% (U.K. 19%, Germany 15%, France 7%, Denmark 5%); U.S. 13% ($247 million); EFTA 9%; Japan 5%. Imports (1998)—$2.4 billion: industrial supplies 26%; capital goods, parts, accessories 24%; consumer goods 20%; transport equipment 14%; food and beverages 9%; fuels and lubricants 7%. Partners—EU 56% (Germany 11%, U.K. 10%, Denmark 8%, Sweden 6%, Netherlands 6%); U.S. 11% ($268 million); EFTA 11%; Japan 5%.

# GEOGRAPHY

Iceland is a volcanic island in the North Atlantic Ocean east of Greenland and immediately south of the Arctic Circle. It lies about 4,200 kilometers (2,600 mi.) from New York and 830 kilometers (520 mi.) from Scotland.

About 79% of Iceland's land area, which is of recent volcanic origin, consists of glaciers, lakes, a mountainous lava desert (highest elevation 2,000 meters—6,590 ft. —above sea level), and other wasteland. Twenty percent of the land is used for grazing, and 1% is cultivated. The inhabited areas are on the coast, particularly in the southwest.

Because of the Gulf Stream's moderating influence, the climate is characterized by damp, cool summers and relatively mild but windy winters. In Reykjavik, the average temperature is 11°C (52°F) in July and −1°C (30°F) in January.

# PEOPLE

Most Icelanders are descendants of Norwegian settlers and Celts from the British Isles, and the population is remarkably homogeneous. According to Icelandic Government statistics, 99% of the nation's inhabitants live in urban areas (localities with populations greater then 200) and 60% live in Reykjavik and the surrounding area. Of the Nordic languages, the Icelandic language is closest to the Old Norse language and has remained relatively unchanged since the 12th century.

About 91% of the population belong to the state church, the Evangelical Lutheran Church, or other Lutheran Churches. However, Iceland has complete religious liberty, and other Protestant and Roman Catholic congregations are present.

Most Icelandic surnames are based on patronymy, or the adoption of the father's first given name. For example, Magnus and Anna, children of a man named Petur, would hold the surname Petursson and Petursdottir, respectively. Magnus' children, in turn, would inherit the surname Magnusson, while Anna's children would claim their father's first given name as their surname. Women nor-

mally maintain their original surnames after marriage. This system of surnames is required by law, except for the descendants of those who had acquired family names before 1913. Most Icelanders, while reserved by nature, rarely call each other by their surnames, and even phone directories are based on first names. Because of its small size and relative homogeneity, Iceland holds all the characteristics of a very close–knit society.

## Cultural Achievements

The Sagas, almost all written between 1180–1300 A.D., remain Iceland's best known literary accomplishment, and they have no surviving counterpart anywhere in the Nordic world. Based on Norwegian and Icelandic histories and genealogies, the Sagas present views of Nordic life and times up to 1100 A.D. The Saga writers sought to record their heroes' great achievements and to glorify the virtues of courage, pride, and honor, focusing in the later Sagas on early Icelandic settlers.

Unlike its literature, Iceland's fine arts did not flourish until the 19th century because the population was small and scattered. Iceland's most famous painters are Asgrimur Jonsson, Jon Stefansson, and Johannes Kjarval, all of whom worked during the first half of the 20th century. The best–known modern sculptor, Asmundur Sveinsson (1893–1982), drew his inspiration from Icelandic folklore and the Sagas for many of his works.

The best known Icelandic writer in this century is the Nobel Prize winner Halldor Laxness. The literacy rate is 100%, and literature and poetry are a passion with the population. Per capita publication of books and magazines is the highest in the world. In a population of 265,000 people, 1993 data show five daily newspapers, 78 other newspapers, and 629 periodicals.

Kristjan Johannsson is Iceland's most famous opera singer, while pop

singer Bjork is probably its best known artist in this century.

# HISTORY

Iceland was settled in the late 9th and early 10th centuries, principally by people of Norse origin. In 930 A.D., the ruling chiefs established a republican constitution and an assembly called the Althingi—the oldest parliament in the world. Iceland remained independent until 1262, when it entered into a treaty which established a union with the Norwegian monarchy. It passed to Denmark in the late 14th century when Norway and Denmark were united under the Danish crown.

In the early 19th century, national consciousness revived in Iceland. The Althingi had been abolished in 1800 but was reestablished in 1843 as a consultative assembly. In 1874, Denmark granted Iceland home rule, which again was extended in 1904. The constitution, written in 1874, was revised in 1903, and a minister for Icelandic affairs, residing in Reykjavik, was made responsible to the Althingi. The Act of Union, a 1918 agreement with Denmark, recognized Iceland as a fully sovereign state united with Denmark under a common king. Iceland established its own flag and asked that Denmark represent its foreign affairs and defense interests.

German occupation of Denmark in 1940 severed communications between Iceland and Denmark. In May 1940, British military forces occupied Iceland. In July 1941, responsibility for Iceland's defense passed to the United States under a U.S. – Icelandic defense agreement. Following a plebiscite, Iceland formally became an independent republic on June 17, 1944.

In October 1946, the Icelandic and U.S. Governments agreed to terminate U.S. responsibility for the defense of Iceland, but the United States retained certain rights at Keflavik. Iceland became a charter member of the North Atlantic Treaty

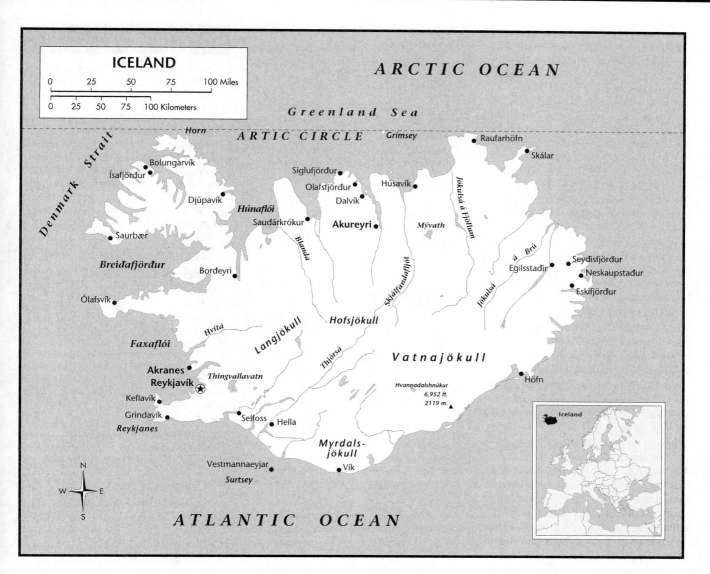

ICELAND

| | | | | |
|---|---|---|---|---|
| 0 | 25 | 50 | 75 | 100 Miles |
| 0 | 25 | 50 | 75 | 100 Kilometers |

Background Notes

Organization (NATO) in 1949. After the outbreak of hostilities in Korea in 1950, and pursuant to the request of NATO military authorities, the United States and Iceland agreed that the United States should again be responsible for Iceland's defense. This agreement, signed on May 5, 1951, is the authority for U.S. military presence in Iceland. Iceland is the only NATO country with no military forces.

# GOVERNMENT

The president, elected to a 4–year term, has limited powers. The prime minister and cabinet exercise most executive functions. The Althingi is composed of 63 members, elected every 4 years unless it is dissolved sooner. Suffrage for presidential and parliamentary elections is universal, and members of the Althingi are elected on the basis of proportional representation from eight constituencies. The judiciary consists of the Supreme Court, district courts, and various special courts. The constitution protects the judiciary from infringement by the other two branches.

## Principal Government Officials

**For up-to-date information on Principal Government Officials, see the Chiefs of State and Cabinet Members of Foreign Governments section starting on page 1.**

Iceland maintains an embassy in the United States at 1156 – 15th Street, NW, Suite 1200, Washington, DC 20005 [tel. (202)265–6653], and a consulate general at 800 Third Ave, 36th floor, New York, NY 10022 [tel. (212)593–2700]. Iceland also has 20 honorary consulates in major U.S. cities.

# POLITICAL CONDITIONS

In nationwide town council elections in 1994, government coalition partners, the conservative Independence Party (IP), and the Social Democrat Party (SDP) lost support throughout the country, including the capital Reykjavik, which the IP had controlled for more than a half–century. In losing four seats in the April 1995 parliamentary elections, the IP and SDP mustered a simple majority in the 63–seat Althingi. However, Prime Minister and IP leader Oddsson chose the resurgent Progressive Party as a more conservative partner to form a stronger and more stable majority with 40 seats. Splintered by factionalism over the economy and Iceland's role in the European Union (EU), the SDP also suffered from being the only party to support Iceland's EU membership application. Nonetheless, Icelandic policy toward the U.S. has remained unchanged.

After four 4–year terms as the world's first and only elected woman president, the widely popular Vigdis Finnbogadottir chose not to run for re-election in 1996. More than 86% of voters turned out in the June 29, 1997 presidential elections to give former leftist party chairman Olafur Ragnar Grimsson a 41% plurality and relatively comfortable 12% victory margin over the closest of three other candidates. Traditionally limited to 6–12 weeks, Iceland's campaign season was marked by several intensely personal attacks on Grimsson, a former finance minister who tried to erase memories of his controversial support of inflationary policies and opposition to the U.S. military presence at the NATO base in Keflavik. Grimsson successfully has used his largely ceremonial office to promote Icelandic trade abroad and family values at home.

In May 8 parliamentary elections, the ruling, conservative Independence Party gained one seat for a total of 26 of 63 seats in the Althingi. Its continued coalition partner, the Progressive Party, lost three seats for a total of 12. The newly established United Left took 17 seats, and the Left–Green alliance garnered six. In a surprise, the Liberal Party won two seats. More than 84% of the electorate came out to vote, which actually fell from over 87% in the

1995 election. Women now hold three ministries and account for 22 of 63 parliamentarians.

## Parties in Government

Independence Party (IP) 26
Progressive Party (PP) 12

## Parties in Opposition

Liberal Party (WL) 02
United Left (UL) 17
Left–Green Alliance (LG) 06

**Total: 63**

# ECONOMY

Marine products account for more than 70% of Iceland's total export earnings. Other important exports include aluminum, ferro–silicon, equipment and electronic machinery for fishing and fish processing, and woolen goods. Foreign trade plays an important role in the Icelandic economy. Exports and imports each account for one–third of GDP. Most of Iceland's exports go to the EU and EFTA countries, the United States, and Japan.

Iceland's relatively liberal trading policy has been strengthened by accession to the European Economic Area in 1993 and by the Uruguay Round agreement, which also brought significantly improved market access for Iceland's exports, particularly seafood products. However, the agricultural sector remains heavily subsidized and protected; some tariffs range as high as 700%.

Iceland's economy is prone to inflation but remains rather broad–based and highly export–driven. During the 1970s the oil shocks hit Iceland hard. Inflation rose to 43% in 1974 and 59% in 1980, falling to 15% in 1987 but rising to 30% in 1988. Since then, inflation has dramatically fallen, and the current government is committed to tight fiscal measures. The current unemployment rate stands at a record low 1%. Iceland's economy has experienced moderately strong GDP growth (3%) for the past 3 years.

## Travel Notes

**Travel Advice:** For up-to-date information from the U.S. State Department on possible inconvenient or hazardous situations, see the **Travel Warnings and Consular Information Sheets from the U.S. Government** section starting on page 1723. For the latest information on health requirements and conditions, see the **International Travelers' Health Information** section starting on page 1385. For further information dealing with non-urgent matter, see the **Tips for Travelers to...** section starting on page 1588.

Inflation averaged merely 1.5% from 1993–94, and only 1.7% from 1994–95. Increasing economic activity is predicted again for 2000, and inflation is projected to increase to about 3% for 1999.

Iceland has few proven mineral resources, although deposits of diatomite (skeletal algae) are being developed. Abundant hydroelectric and geothermal power sources are gradually being harnessed, and in 1991 80% of the population enjoyed geothermal heating. The Burfell hydroelectric project is the largest single station with capacity of 240 mw. The other major hydroelectric stations are at Hrauneyjarfoss (210 mw) and Sigalda (150 mw). Iceland is exploring the feasibility of exporting hydroelectric energy via submarine cable to mainland Europe and also actively seeks to expand its power–intensive industries, including aluminum and ferro–silicon smelting plants. Nordural Aluminum is a wholly owned $180 million investment by Columbia Ventures of Washington State. The plant employs over 150 people and accounted for a 1% growth rate in Iceland's 1998 GDP.

Iceland has no railroads. Organized road building began about 1900 and has greatly expanded in the past decade. The current national road system connecting most of the population centers is largely in the coastal areas and consists of about 12,177 kilometers (7,565 mi.) of dirt and gravel roads and about 1,150 kilometers (714 mi.) of hard–surfaced roads. Regular air and sea service connects

Reykjavik with the other main urban centers. In addition, airlines schedule flights from Iceland to Europe and North America. The national airline, Icelandair, is one of the country's largest employers. Iceland became a full European Free Trade Association member in 1970 and entered into a free trade agreement with the European Community in 1973. Under the agreement on a European Economic Area, effective January 1, 1994, there is basically free cross–border movement of capital, labor, goods, and services between Iceland, Norway, and the EU countries.

# FOREIGN RELATIONS

Iceland maintains diplomatic and commercial relations with practically all nations, but its ties with other Nordic states, with the U.S., and with the other NATO nations are particularly close. Icelanders remain especially proud of the role Iceland played in hosting the historic 1986 Reagan–Gorbachev summit in Reykjavik, which set the stage for the end of the Cold War.

Iceland's principal historical international dispute involved disagreements with Norway and Russia over fishing rights in the Barents Sea, which the parties successfully resolved this year. Certain environmentalists are concerned that Iceland left the International Whaling Commission (IWC) in June 1992 in protest of an IWC decision to refuse to lift the ban on whaling, after the IWC Scientific Committee had determined that the taking of certain species could safely be resumed. That year, Iceland established its own commission—which the U.S. does not recognize—along with Norway, Greenland, and the Faroes for the conservation, management, and study of marine mammals. Since then, Iceland has not resumed whaling but has asserted the right to do so.

Icelanders have a strong emotional bond toward the Baltic States, and Iceland prides itself on being the first country to recognize their independence. Iceland also is the greatest Nordic contributor per capita to NATO-led troops in Bosnia and Kosovo, to police in Bosnia, and to Bosnia/Kosovo reconstruction, resettlement, and relief.

## Membership in International Organizations

Iceland is a member of the following organizations: North Atlantic Treaty Organization; Organization on Security and Cooperation in Europe; Western European Union (associate member); International Bank for Reconstruction and Development; International Development Association; International Finance Corporation; Organization for Economic Cooperation and Development; European Economic Area; European Free Trade Organization; Council of Europe; International Criminal Police Organization; and the United Nations and most of its specialized agencies, including the International Monetary Fund, World Trade Organization, Food and Agricultural Organization, International Atomic Energy Agency, International Civil Aviation Organization, International Labor Organization, International Maritime Organization, International Telecommunications Union, UN Educational, Scientific, and Cultural Organization, Universal Postal Union, World Health Organization, and World Meteorological Organization.

# U.S.-ICELANDIC RELATIONS

U.S. policy aims to maintain close, cooperative relations with Iceland, both as a NATO ally and as a friend interested in the shared objectives of enhancing world peace, respect for human rights, arms control, and economic development. Moreover, the United States endeavors to strengthen bilateral economic and trade relations. A consistently reliable ally, Iceland has voted with the United States on virtually all major UN, NATO, and environmental issues.

In celebration of the 1000th anniversary in the Year 2000 of Leif Eriksson's voyage to North America, the United States has established a volunteer binational working group to coordinate a number of millennium activities with the Government of Iceland and interested parties. These activities will highlight, among other areas, shared culture, scholarship and research, scientific discovery and exploration, pioneer legacy, and the strong defense relationship between the countries.

## Principal U.S. Officials

For up-to-date information on Principal U.S. Officials, see the U.S. Embassies, Consulates, and Foreign Service section starting on page 139.

The U.S. embassy in Iceland is located at Laufasvegur 21, Reykjavik [tel. (354) 562–9100].

# DEFENSE

When Iceland became a founding member of NATO in 1949, it did so on the explicit understanding that Iceland, which has never had a military, would not be expected to establish an indigenous force. Iceland's main contribution to the common defense effort has been the rent–free provision of the "agreed areas"—sites for military facilities. By far the largest and most important of these is the NATO Naval Air Station at Keflavik. Although this base is manned primarily by U.S. forces, it also has a permanently stationed Dutch P–3 aircraft and crew, as well as officers from Canada, Denmark, Norway, and the United Kingdom. Units from these and other NATO countries also are deployed temporarily to Keflavik, and they stage practice operations, mainly anti–submarine warfare patrols. Iceland and the United

States regard the ongoing U.S. military presence since World War II as a cornerstone to bilateral foreign/security policy. Bilateral negotiations regarding implementation of a new "Agreed Minute" governing force structure and deployment for the defense of Iceland will be renewed in 2001.

In addition to providing the "agreed areas," the Government of Iceland contributes financially to NATO's international overhead costs and recently has taken a more active role in NATO deliberations and planning. Iceland hosted the NATO Foreign Minister Meeting in Reykjavik in June 1987 and participates in biennial NATO exercises entitled "Northern Viking" in Iceland; the next exercises will be held in 2001. In 1997 Iceland hosted its first Partnership for Peace (PfP) exercise, "Cooperative Safeguard," which is the only multilateral PfP exercise so far in which Russia has participated. It will host another major PfP exercise in 2000.

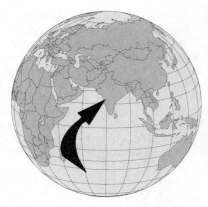

# INDIA

March 2000

Official Name:
**Republic of India**

# PROFILE

## Geography

**Area:** 3.3 million sq. km. (1.3 million sq. mi.); about one-third the size of the U.S.
**Cities:** Capital—New Delhi (pop. 11 million). Other major cities—Mumbai, formerly Bombay (15 million); Calcutta (12 million); Chennai, formerly Madras (6 million); Bangalore (5 million); Hyderabad (5 million); Ahmedabad (3.7 million).
**Terrain:** Varies from Himalayas to flat river valleys.
**Climate:** Temperate to subtropical monsoon.

## People

**Nationality:** Noun and adjective—Indian(s).
**Population (1999 est.):** one billion; urban 32%.
**Annual growth rate:** 1.8%.
**Density:** 311/sq. km.
**Ethnic groups:** Indo-Aryan 72%, Dravidian 25%, Mongoloid 2%, others. Religions: Hindu 81.3%, Muslim 12%, Christian 2.3%, Sikh 1.9%, other groups including Buddhist, Jain, Parsi 2.5%.
**Languages:** Hindi, English, and 16 other official languages.
**Education:** Years compulsory—9 (to age 14). Literacy—54%. Health:

Infant mortality rate—71/1,000. Life expectancy—63 years.
**Work force (est.):** 416 million. Agriculture—63%; industry and commerce—22%; services and government—11%; transport and communications—4%.

## Government

**Type:** Federal republic.
**Independence:** August 15, 1947.
**Constitution:** January 26, 1950.
**Branches:** Executive—president (chief of state), prime minister (head of government), Council of Ministers (cabinet). Legislative—bicameral parliament (Rajya Sabha or Council of States and Lok Sabha or House of the People). Judicial—Supreme Court.
**Political parties:** Bharatiya Janata Party, Congress (I), Janata Dal (United), Communist Party of India, Communist Party of India-Marxist, and numerous regional and small national parties.
**Political subdivisions:** 25 states, 7 union territories.
**Suffrage:** Universal over 18.

## Economy

**GDP:** $390 billion.
**Real growth rate (1998-99):** 6.8%.
**Per capita GDP:** $420.
**Natural resources:** Coal, iron ore, manganese, mica, bauxite, chromite, thorium, limestone, barite, titanium

ore, diamonds, crude oil.
**Agriculture (25% of GDP):** Products—wheat, rice, coarse grains, oilseeds, sugar, cotton, jute, tea.
**Industry (29% of GDP):** Products—textiles, jute, processed food, steel, machinery, transport equipment, cement, aluminum, fertilizers, mining, petroleum, chemicals, computer software.
**Trade:** Exports—$34 billion: agricultural products, engineering goods, precious stones, cotton apparel and fabrics, handicrafts, tea. Imports—$42 billion: petroleum, machinery and transport equipment, edible oils, fertilizer, jewelry, iron and steel. Major trade partners—U.S., EU, Russia, Japan, Iraq, Iran, central and eastern Europe.

# PEOPLE

Although India occupies only 2.4% of the world's land area, it supports over 15% of the world's population. Only China has a larger population. Almost 40% of Indians are younger than 15 years of age. About 70% of the people live in more than 550,000 villages, and the remainder in more than 200 towns and cities. Over thousands of years of its history, India has been invaded from the Iranian plateau, Central Asia, Arabia, Afghanistan, and the West; Indian people and culture have absorbed and changed these influences to produce a remarkable racial and cultural synthesis.

Religion, caste, and language are major determinants of social and political organization in India today. The government has recognized 18 languages as official; Hindi is the most widely spoken.

Although 83% of the people are Hindu, India also is the home of more than 120 million Muslims—one of the world's largest Muslim populations. The population also includes Christians, Sikhs, Jains, Buddhists, and Parsis.

The caste system reflects Indian occupational and religiously defined hierarchies. Traditionally, there are four broad categories of castes (varnas), including a category of outcastes, earlier called "untouchables" but now commonly referred to as "dalits." Within these broad categories there are thousands of castes and subcastes , whose relative status varies from region to region. Despite economic modernization and laws countering discrimination against the lower end of the class structure, the caste system remains an important source of social identification for most Hindus and a potent factor in the political life of the country.

# HISTORY

The people of India have had a continuous civilization since 2500 B.C., when the inhabitants of the Indus River valley developed an urban culture based on commerce and sustained by agricultural trade. This civilization declined around 1500 B.C., probably due to ecological changes.

During the second millennium B.C., pastoral, Aryan-speaking tribes migrated from the northwest into the subcontinent. As they settled in the middle Ganges River valley, they adapted to antecedent cultures.

The political map of ancient and medieval India was made up of myriad kingdoms with fluctuating boundaries. In the 4th and 5th centuries A.D., northern India was unified under the Gupta Dynasty. During this period, known as India's Golden Age, Hindu culture and political administration reached new heights.

Islam spread across the subcontinent over a period of 500 years. In the 10th and 11th centuries, Turks and Afghans invaded India and established sultanates in Delhi. In the early 16th century, descendants of Genghis Khan swept across the Khyber Pass and established the Mughal (Mogul) Dynasty, which lasted for 200 years. From the 11th to the 15th centuries, southern India was dominated by Hindu Chola and Vijayanagar Dynasties. During this time, the two systems—the prevailing Hindu and Muslim—mingled, leaving lasting cultural influences on each other.

The first British outpost in South Asia was established in 1619 at Surat on the northwestern coast. Later in the century, the East India Company opened permanent trading stations at Madras, Bombay, and Calcutta, each under the protection of native rulers.

The British expanded their influence from these footholds until, by the 1850s, they controlled most of present-day India, Pakistan, and Bangladesh. In 1857, a rebellion in north India led by mutinous Indian soldiers caused the British Parliament to transfer all political power from the East India Company to the Crown. Great Britain began administering most of India directly while controlling the rest through treaties with local rulers.

In the late 1800s, the first steps were taken toward self-government in British India with the appointment of Indian councilors to advise the British viceroy and the establishment of provincial councils with Indian members; the British subsequently widened participation in legislative councils. Beginning in 1920, Indian leader Mohandas K. Gandhi transformed the Indian National Congress political party into a mass movement to campaign against British colonial rule. The party used both parliamentary and nonviolent resistance and noncooperation to achieve independence.

On August 15, 1947, India became a dominion within the Commonwealth, with Jawaharlal Nehru as Prime Minister. Enmity between Hindus and Muslims led the British to partition British India, creating East and West Pakistan, where there were Muslim majorities. India became a republic within the Commonwealth after promulgating its constitution on January 26, 1950.

After independence, the Congress Party, the party of Mahatma Gandhi and Jawaharlal Nehru, ruled India under the influence first of Nehru and then his daughter and grandson, with the exception of two brief periods in the 1970s and 1980s.

Prime Minister Nehru governed the nation until his death in 1964. He was succeeded by Lal Bahadur Shastri, who also died in office. In 1966, power passed to Nehru's daughter, Indira Gandhi, Prime Minister from 1966 to 1977. In 1975, beset with deepening political and economic problems, Mrs. Gandhi declared a state of emergency and suspended many civil liberties. Seeking a mandate at the polls for her policies, she called for elections in 1977, only to be defeated by Moraji Desai, who headed the Janata Party, an amalgam of five opposition parties.

In 1979, Desai's Government crumbled. Charan Singh formed an interim government, which was followed by Mrs. Gandhi's return to power in January 1980. On October 31, 1984, Mrs. Gandhi was assassinated, and her son, Rajiv, was chosen by the Congress (I)—for "Indira"—Party to take her place. His government was brought down in 1989 by allegations of corruption and was followed by V.P. Singh and then Chandra Shekhar.

In the 1989 elections, although Rajiv Gandhi and Congress won more seats in the 1989 elections than any other single party, he was unable to form a government with a clear majority. The Janata Dal, a union of opposition parties, was able to form a government with the help of the Hindu-nationalist Bharatiya Janata Party (BJP) on the right and the communists on the left. This loose coalition collapsed in November 1990, and the

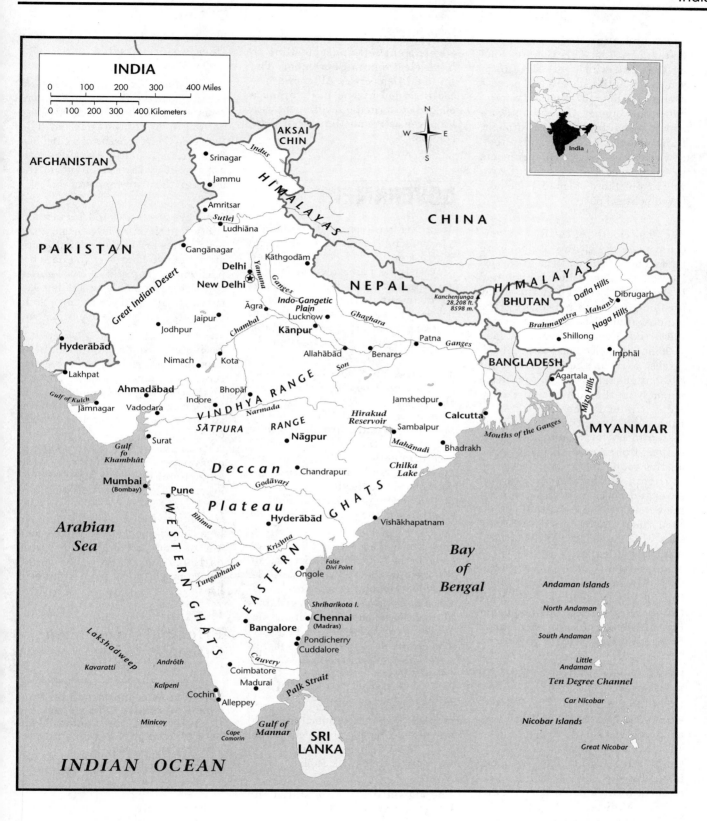

**INDIA**

0   100   200   300   400 Miles

0   100   200   300   400 Kilometers

government was controlled for a short period by a breakaway Janata Dal group supported by Congress (I), with Chandra Shekhar as Prime Minister. That alliance also collapsed, result-ing in national elections in June 1991.

On May 27, 1991, while campaigning in Tamil Nadu on behalf of Congress (I), Rajiv Gandhi was assassinated, apparently by Tamil extremists from Sri Lanka. In the elections, Congress (I) won 213 parliamentary seats and put together a coalition, returning to

683

power under the leadership of P.V. Narasimha Rao. This Congress-led government, which served a full 5-year term, initiated a gradual process of economic liberalization and reform, which has opened the Indian economy to global trade and investment. India's domestic politics also took new shape, as traditional alignments by caste, creed, and ethnicity gave way to a plethora of small, regionally based political parties.

The final months of the Rao-led government in the spring of 1996 were marred by several major political corruption scandals, which contributed to the worst electoral performance by the Congress Party in its history. The Hindu-nationalist Bharatiya Janata Party (BJP) emerged from the May 1996 national elections as the single-largest party in the Lok Sabha but without enough strength to prove a majority on the floor of that Parliament. Under Prime Minister Atal Bihari Vajpayee, the BJP coalition lasted in power 13 days. With all political parties wishing to avoid another round of elections, a 14-party coalition led by the Janata Dal emerged to form a government known as the United Front, under the former Chief Minister of Karnataka, H.D. Deve Gowda. His government lasted less than a year, as the leader of the Congress Party withdrew his support in March 1997. Inder Kumar Gujral replaced Deve Gowda as the consensus choice for Prime Minister of a 16-party United Front coalition.

In November 1997, the Congress Party again withdrew support for the United Front. New elections in February 1998 brought the BJP the largest number of seats in Parliament—182—but fell far short of a majority. On March 20, 1998, the President inaugurated a BJP-led coalition government with Vajpayee again serving as Prime Minister. On May 11 and 13, 1998, this government conducted a series of underground nuclear tests forcing U.S. President Clinton to impose economic sanctions on India pursuant to the 1994 Nuclear Proliferation Prevention Act.

In April 1999, the BJP-led coalition government fell apart, leading to fresh elections in September. The National Democratic Alliance-a new coalition led by the BJP-gained a majority to form the government with Vajpayee as Prime Minister in October 1999.

# GOVERNMENT

According to its constitution, India is a "sovereign, socialist, secular, democratic republic." Like the United States, India has a federal form of government. However, the central government in India has greater power in relation to its states, and its central government is patterned after the British parliamentary system.

The government exercises its broad administrative powers in the name of the president, whose duties are largely ceremonial. The president and vice president are elected indirectly for 5-year terms by a special electoral college. Their terms are staggered, and the vice president does not automatically become president following the death or removal from office of the president.

Real national executive power is centered in the Council of Ministers (cabinet), led by the prime minister. The president appoints the prime minister, who is designated by legislators of the political party or coalition commanding a parliamentary majority. The president then appoints subordinate ministers on the advice of the prime minister.

India's bicameral parliament consists of the Rajya Sabha (Council of States) and the Lok Sabha (House of the People). The Council of Ministers is responsible to the Lok Sabha.

The legislatures of the states and union territories elect 233 members to the Rajya Sabha, and the president appoints another 12. The elected members of the Rajya Sabha serve 6-year terms, with one-third up for election every 2 years. The Lok Sabha consists of 545 members; 543 are directly elected to 5-year terms. The other two are appointed.

India's independent judicial system began under the British, and its concepts and procedures resemble those of Anglo-Saxon countries. The Supreme Court consists of a chief justice and 25 other justices, all appointed by the president on the advice of the prime minister.

India has 25 states* and 7 union territories. At the state level, some of the legislatures are bicameral, patterned after the two houses of the national parliament. The states' chief ministers are responsible to the legislatures in the same way the prime minister is responsible to parliament.

Each state also has a presidentially appointed governor who may assume certain broad powers when directed by the central government. The central government exerts greater control over the union territories than over the states, although some territories have gained more power to administer their own affairs. Local governments in India have less autonomy than their counterparts in the United States. Some states are trying to revitalize the traditional village councils, or panchayats, which aim to promote popular democratic participation at the village level, where much of the population still lives.

## Principal Government Officials

**For up-to-date information on Principal Government Officials, see the Chiefs of State and Cabinet Members of Foreign Governments section starting on page 1.**

India maintains an embassy in the United States at 2107 Massachusetts Avenue NW, Washington, DC 20008 (tel. 202-939-7000, fax 202-265-4351, email indembwash@indiagov.org) and consulates general in New York, Chicago, Houston, and San Francisco.

# POLITICAL CONDITIONS

Prime Minister Atal Bihari Vajpayee took office in October 1999 after a general election in which a BJP-led coalition of 13 parties called the National Democratic Alliance emerged with an absolute majority. The coalition reflects the ongoing transition in Indian politics away from the historically dominant and national-based Congress Party toward smaller, narrower-based regional parties. This process has been underway throughout much of the past decade and is likely to continue in the future.

The Bharatiya Janata Party emerged as the single-largest party in the Lok Sabha (lower house of Parliament) elections in September 1999. The BJP currently leads a coalition government under Prime Minister A.B. Vajpayee. Party President Kushabhhau Thakre was elected by the Party National Executive in April 1998. The Hindu-nationalist BJP draws its political strength mainly from the "Hindi belt" in the northern and western regions of India. The party holds power in the states of Gujarat, Uttar Pradesh (in coalition with several small parties), Himachal Pradesh (in coalition with Himachal Vikas Congress) Punjab (in coalition with Akali Dal) and in Haryana (in coalition with the Indian National Lok Dal). Popularly viewed as the party of the upper caste and trading communities, the BJP has made strong inroads into the lower caste vote bank in recent national and state assembly elections.

The Congress (I) Party, led by Sonia Gandhi (widow of the late Prime Minister Rajiv Gandhi), holds the second-largest number of seats in the Lok Sabha. Priding itself as a secular, centrist party, the Congress has been the historically dominant political party in India. Its performance in national elections has steadily declined during the last decade. The Congress still rules in the states of Madhya Pradesh, Rajasthan, Maharashtra (in coalition with the National Congress Party), Karnataka, and three of the smaller states in the northeast. The political fortunes of the Congress have suffered badly as major groups in its traditional vote bank have been lost to emerging regional and caste-based parties, such as the Bahujan Samaj Party and the Samajwadi Party.

The Janata Dal (United) Party claims to be a national party but currently holds significant strength only in Karnataka and Bihar. It advocates a secular and socialist ideology and draws much of its popular support from Muslims, lower castes, and tribals.

# ECONOMY

India's population continues to grow at about 1.8% per year and is estimated at one billion. While its GDP is low in dollar terms, India has the world's 13th-largest GNP. About 62% of the population depends directly on agriculture.

Industry and services sectors are growing in importance and account for 26% and 48% of GDP, respectively, while agriculture contributes about 25.6% of GDP. More than 35% of the population live below the poverty line, but a large and growing middle class of 150-200 million has disposable income for consumer goods.

India embarked on a series of economic reforms in 1991 in reaction to a severe foreign exchange crisis. Those reforms have included liberalized foreign investment and exchange regimes, significant reductions in tariffs and other trade barriers, reform and modernization of the financial sector, and significant adjustments in government monetary and fiscal policies.

The reform process has had some very beneficial effects on the Indian economy, including higher growth rates, lower inflation, and significant increases in foreign investment. Real GDP growth was 6.8% in 1998-99, up from 5% in the 1997-98 fiscal year. Growth in 1999-2000 is expected to be around 6%. Foreign portfolio and direct investment flows have risen significantly since reforms began in 1991 and have contributed to healthy foreign currency reserves ($32 billion in February 2000) and a moderate current account deficit of about 1% (1998-99). India's economic growth is constrained, however, by inadequate infrastructure, cumbersome bureaucratic procedures, and high real interest rates. India will have to address these constraints in formulating its economic policies and by pursuing the second generation reforms to maintain recent trends in economic growth.

India's trade has increased significantly since reforms began in 1991, largely as a result of staged tariff reductions and elimination of nontariff barriers. The outlook for further trade liberalization is mixed. India has agreed to eliminate quantitative restrictions on imports of about 1,420 consumer goods by April 2001 to meet its WTO commitments. On the other hand, the government has imposed "additional" import duties of 5% on most products plus a surcharge of 10% over the past 2 years. The U.S. is India's largest trading partner; bilateral trade in 1998-99 was about $10.9 billion. Principal U.S. exports to India are aircraft and parts, advanced machinery, fertilizers, ferrous waste and scrap metal, and computer hardware. Major U.S. imports from India include textiles and ready-made garments, agricultural and related products, gems and jewelry, leather products, and chemicals.

Significant liberalization of its investment regime since 1991 has made India an attractive place for foreign direct and portfolio investment. The U.S. is India's largest investment partner, with total inflow of U.S. direct investment estimated at $2 billion (market value) in 1999. U.S. investors also have provided an estimated 11% of the $18 billion of foreign portfolio investment that has entered India since 1992. Proposals for direct foreign investment are considered by the Foreign Investment Promotion Board and generally receive government approval. Automatic approvals are available for investments involving up to 100% foreign equity, depending on the kind of industry. Foreign investment is particularly sought after in power generation, telecommunications, ports, roads, petroleum exploration and processing, and mining.

India's external debt was up to $98 billion in March 1999, compared to $94 billion in March 1998. The country's debt service ratio has fallen to about 20%. Bilateral assistance has been about $1 billion annually in recent years, with the U.S. providing about $150 million in development assistance in Fiscal Year 1999. The World Bank had approved loans worth about $1.05 billion for India in 1999.

# FOREIGN RELATIONS

India's size, population, and strategic location give it a prominent voice in international affairs, and its growing industrial base, military strength, and scientific and technical capacity give it added weight. It collaborates closely with other developing countries on issues from trade to environmental protection. The end of the Cold War dramatically affected Indian foreign policy. India remains a leader of the developing world and the Non-Aligned Movement (NAM), and hosted the NAM Heads of State Summit in 1997. India is now also seeking to strengthen its political and commercial ties with the United States, Japan, the European Union, Iran, China, and the Association of Southeast Asian Nations. India is an active member of the South Asia Association for Regional Cooperation (SAARC) and the Indian Ocean Rim Association for Regional Cooperation (IORARC).

India has always been an active member of the United Nations and now seeks a permanent seat on the UN Security Council. India has a long tradition of participating in UN peacekeeping operations and most recently contributed personnel to UN operations in Somalia, Cambodia, Mozambique, Kuwait, Bosnia, Angola, and El Salvador.

## Bilateral and Regional Relations

**Pakistan.** India's relations with Pakistan are influenced by the centuries-old rivalry between Hindus and Muslims which led to partition of British India in 1947. The principal source of contention has been Kashmir, whose Hindu Maharaja chose in 1947 to join India, although a majority of his subjects were Muslim. India maintains that his decision and the subsequent elections in Kashmir have made it an integral part of India. Pakistan asserts Kashmiris' rights to self-determination through a plebiscite in accordance with an earlier Indian pledge and a UN resolution. This dispute triggered wars between the two countries in 1947 and 1965.

In December 1971, following a political crisis in what was then East Pakistan and the flight of millions of Bengali refugees to India, Pakistan and India again went to war. The brief conflict left the situation largely unchanged in the west, where the two armies reached an impasse, but a decisive Indian victory in the east resulted in the creation of Bangladesh.

Since the 1971 war, Pakistan and India have made only slow progress toward normalization of relations. In July 1972, Indian Prime Minister Indira Gandhi and Pakistani President Zulfikar Ali Bhutto met in the Indian hill station of Simla. They signed an agreement by which India would return all personnel and captured territory in the west and the two countries would "settle their differences by peaceful means through bilateral negotiations." Diplomatic and trade relations were re-established in 1976.

After the 1979 Soviet invasion of Afghanistan, new strains appeared in India-Pakistan relations; Pakistan supported the Afghan resistance, while India implicitly supported Soviet occupation. In the following eight years, India voiced increasing concern over Pakistani arms purchases, U.S. military aid to Pakistan, and Pakistan's nuclear weapons pro-

gram. In an effort to curtail tensions, the two countries formed a joint commission. In December 1988, Prime Ministers Rajiv Gandhi and Benazir Bhutto concluded a pact not to attack each other's nuclear facilities. Agreements on cultural exchanges and civil aviation also were initiated.

In 1997, high-level Indo-Pakistani talks resumed after a 3-year pause. The Prime Ministers of India and Pakistan met twice and the foreign secretaries conducted three rounds of talks. In June 1997, the foreign secretaries identified eight "outstanding issues" around which continuing talks would be focused. The dispute over the status of Jammu and Kashmir, an issue since partition, remains the major stumbling block in their dialogue. India maintains that the entire former princely state is an integral part of the Indian union, while Pakistan insists that UN resolutions calling for self-determination of the people of the state must be taken into account.

In September 1997, the talks broke down over the structure of how to deal with the issues of Kashmir and peace and security. Pakistan advocated that the issues be treated by separate working groups. India responded that the two issues be taken up along with six others on a simultaneous basis. In May 1998 India, and then Pakistan, conducted nuclear tests. Attempts to restart dialogue between the two nations were given a major boost by the February 1999 meeting of both Prime Ministers in Lahore and their signing of three agreements. These efforts have since been stalled by the intrusion of Pakistani-backed forces into Indian-held territory near Kargil in May 1999, and by the military coup in Pakistan that overturned the Nawaz Sharif government in October the same year.

**SAARC.** Certain aspects of India's relations within the subcontinent are conducted through the South Asia Association for Regional Cooperation (SAARC). Its members are Bangladesh, Bhutan, India, Maldives, Nepal, Pakistan, and Sri Lanka. Established in 1985, SAARC encourages cooperation in agriculture, rural development, science and technology, culture, health, population control, narcotics, and terrorism.

SAARC has intentionally stressed these "core issues" and avoided more divisive political issues, although political dialogue is often conducted on the margins of SAARC meetings. In 1993, India and its SAARC partners signed an agreement gradually to lower tariffs within the region. Forward movement in SAARC has come to a standstill because of the tension between India and Pakistan, and the SAARC Summit originally scheduled for, but not held in, November 1999 has not been rescheduled.

**China.** Despite suspicions remaining from the 1962 border conflict between India and China and continuing territorial/boundary disputes, Sino-Indian relations have improved gradually since 1988. Both countries have sought to reduce tensions along the frontier, expand trade and cultural ties, and normalize relations.

A series of high-level visits between the two nations has helped to improve relations. In December 1996, Chinese President Jiang Zemin visited India on a tour of South Asia. While in New Delhi, he signed, with the Indian Prime Minister, a series of confidence-building measures along the disputed border, including troop reductions and weapons limitations.

Sino-Indian relations received a setback in May 1998 when India justified its nuclear tests by citing potential threats from China. These accusations followed criticism of Chinese "aggressive actions" in Pakistan and Burma by Indian Defense Minister George Fernandes. However, in June 1999, during the Kargil crisis, External Affairs Minister Jaswant Singh visited Beijing and stated that India did not consider China a threat. Relations between India and China are on the mend, and the two sides handled the move from Tibet to India of the Karmapa Lama in January 2000 with delicacy and tact.

**New Independent States of the Former Soviet Union.** The collapse of

**Travel Notes**

**Travel Advice:** For up-to-date information from the U.S. State Department on possible inconvenient or hazardous situations, see the **Travel Warnings and Consular Information Sheets from the U.S. Government** section starting on page 1723. For the latest information on health requirements and conditions, see the **International Travelers' Health Information** section starting on page 1385. For further information dealing with non-urgent matter, see the **Tips for Travelers to...** section starting on page 1588.

the Soviet Union and the emergence of the Commonwealth of Independent States (CIS) had major repercussions for Indian foreign policy. Substantial trade with the former Soviet Union plummeted after the Soviet collapse and has yet to recover. Longstanding military supply relationships were similarly disrupted due to questions over financing, although Russia continues to be India's largest supplier of military systems and spare parts.

Russia and India have decided not to renew the 1971 Indo-Soviet Peace and Friendship Treaty and have sought to follow what both describe as a more pragmatic, less ideological relationship. Russian President Yeltsin's visit to India in January 1993 helped cement this new relationship. The pace of high-level visits has since increased, as has discussion of major defense purchases.

# DEFENSE

Supreme command of India's armed forces—the third-largest in the world— rests with the president, but actual responsibility for national defense lies with the cabinet committee for political affairs under the chairmanship of the prime minister. The minister of defense is responsible to parliament for all defense matters. India's military command structure has no joint defense staff or unified command apparatus. The ministry of defense provides administrative and operational control over the three ser-

vices through their respective chiefs of staff. The armed forces have always been loyal to constitutional authority and maintain a tradition of non-involvement in political affairs.

The army numbers about 1.1 million personnel and fields 34 divisions. Designed primarily to defend the country's frontiers, the army has become heavily committed to internal security duties in Kashmir and the Northeast.

The navy is much smaller, but it is relatively well-armed among Indian Ocean navies, operating one aircraft carrier, 41 surface combatants, and 18 submarines. The fleet is aging, and replacement of ships and aircraft has not been adequately funded. India's coast guard is small and is organized along the lines of the U.S. Coast Guard. With India's long coastline and extensive Exclusive Economic Zone, the navy and coast guard work hard to patrol the waters dictated by India's economic and strategic interests.

The air force, the world's fourth largest, has over 600 combat aircraft and more than 500 transports and helicopters. The air force takes pride in its ability to fly low and fast, as well as to operate in the extremes of temperature and altitude ranging from the Thar Desert to the Siachen Glacier. The air force has enhanced the capability of its fighter force with the addition of the multi-role Sukhoi 30, and it hopes to replace much of its MIG-21 fleet with the indigenous Light Combat Aircraft currently under development.

# U.S.-INDIA RELATIONS

India's nuclear tests in May 1998 seriously damaged Indo-American relations. President Clinton imposed wideranging sanctions pursuant to the 1994 Nuclear Proliferation Prevention Act. The United States encouraged India to sign the Comprehensive Nuclear Test Ban Treaty (CTBT) immediately and without condition. The U.S. also called for restraint in missile and nuclear testing and deployment in both India and Pakistan. The nonproliferation dialogue initiated after the 1998 nuclear tests has bridged many of the gaps in understanding between the countries. However, India has yet to sign the CTBT, agree to a fissile material production moratorium, or define its intentions on acquiring a nuclear deterrent clearly. U.S. sanctions on Indian entities involved in the nuclear industry and opposition to international financial institution loans for non-humanitarian assis-

tance projects in India remain sources of friction.

*This number includes the Indian state of Jammu and Kashmir. The United States considers all of the former princely state of Kashmir to be disputed territory. India, Pakistan, and China each control parts of Kashmir.

The U.S. embassy in India is located on Shantipath, Chanakyapuri, New Delhi 110021 (tel. 91-11-419-8000) (fax: 91-11-4190017). Embassy and consulate working hours are Monday

to Friday, 8:30 a.m. to 5:30 p.m. Visa application hours are Monday to Friday, 8:30 a.m. to 10:00 a.m.

## Principal U.S. Embassy Officials

For up-to-date information on Principal U.S. Officials, see the U.S. Embassies, Consulates, and Foreign Service section starting on page 139.

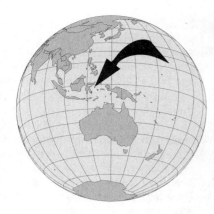

# INDONESIA

October 2000

## Official Name:
## Republic of Indonesia

# PROFILE

## Geography

**Area:** 2 million sq. km. (736,000 sq. mi.), about three times the size of Texas; maritime area: 7,900,000 sq. km.
**Cities:** Capital—Jakarta (est. 8.8 million). Other cities—Surabaya 3.0 million, Medan 2.5 million, Bandung 2.5 million plus an additional 3 million in the surrounding area.
**Terrain:** More than 17,000 islands; 6,000 are inhabited; 1,000 of which are permanently settled. Large islands consist of coastal plains with mountainous interiors.
**Climate:** Equatorial but cooler in the highlands.

## People

**Nationality:** Noun and adjective—Indonesian(s).
**Population:** (1997) 201 million.
**Annual growth rate:** 1.5%.
**Ethnic Groups:** Javanese 45%, Sundanese 14%, Madurese 7.5%, coastal Malays 7.5%, others 26%.
**Religion:** Islam 87%, Protestant 6%, Catholic 3%, Hindu 2%, Buddhist and other 1%.
**Languages:** Indonesian (official), local languages, the most important of which is Javanese.
**Education:** Years compulsory—9.

Enrollment—92% of eligible primary school age children. Literacy—85%.
**Health:** Infant mortality rate—63/1,000 live births. Life expectancy at birth—men 60 years, women 64 years.
**Work force:** 90 million. Agriculture—41.2%, trade and restaurants—19.8%, public services—13.7%, manufacturing—12.9% (1997 data).

## Government

**Type:** Independent republic.
**Independence:** August 17, 1945 proclaimed.
**Constitution:** 1945. Embodies five principles of the state philosophy, called Pancasila, namely monotheism, humanitarianism, national unity, representative democracy by consensus, and social justice.
**Branches:** Executive—president (head of government and chief of state) chosen for a 5-year term by the 700-member People's Consultative Assembly (MPR). Legislature—500-member House of Representatives (DPR) elected for a 5-year term. Judicial—Supreme Court.
**Suffrage:** 17 years of age universal and married persons regardless of age.

## Economy

**GDP (1999):** $142 billion.
**Annual growth rate:** 1999 0.2%.

**Per capita income:** 1999 $684.
**Natural resources:** (8.4% of GDP) Oil and gas, bauxite, silver, tin, copper, gold, coal.
**Agriculture:** (17.2% of GDP) Products—timber, rubber, rice, palm oil, coffee. Land—17% cultivated.
**Manufacturing:** (25.3% of GDP) Garments, footwear, electronic goods, furniture, paper products.
**Trade:** Exports (1999)—$48.7 billion including oil, natural gas, plywood, manufactured goods. Major markets—Japan, Singapore, Taiwan. Korea, EU, U.S. Imports (1999)—$24 billion including food, chemicals, capital goods, consumer goods. Major suppliers—Japan, U.S., Thailand.

# PEOPLE

Indonesia's 201 million people make it the world's fourth-most populous nation. The island of Java is one of the most densely populated areas in the world, with more than 107 million people living in an area the size of New York State. Indonesia includes numerous related but distinct cultural and linguistic groups, many of which are ethnically Malay. Since independence, Bahasa Indonesia (the national language, a form of Malay) has spread throughout the archipelago and has become the language of most written communication, education, government, and business. Many local languages are still important in many areas, however. English is the most widely spoken foreign language.

Education is free and compulsory for children through grade 9. Although about 92% of eligible children are enrolled in primary school, a much smaller percentage attend full time. About 44% of secondary school-age children attend junior high school, and some others of this age group attend vocational schools.

Constitutional guarantees of religious freedom apply to the five religions recognized by the state, namely Islam (87%), Protestantism (6%), Catholicism (3%), Buddhism (2%), and Hinduism (1%). In some remote areas, animism is still practiced.

# HISTORY

By the time of the Renaissance, the islands of Java and Sumatra had already enjoyed a 1,000-year heritage of advanced civilization spanning two major empires. During the 7th-14th centuries, the Buddhist kingdom of Srivijaya flourished on Sumatra. At its peak, the Srivijaya Empire reached as far as West Java and the Malay Peninsula. Also by the 14th century, the Hindu Kingdom of Majapahit had risen in eastern Java. Gadjah Mada, the empire's chief minister from 1331 to 1364, succeeded in gaining allegiance from most of what is now modern Indonesia and much of the Malay archipelago as well. Legacies from Gadjah Mada's time include a codification of law and an epic poem. Islam arrived in Indonesia sometime during the 12th century and, through assimilation, supplanted Hinduism by the end of the 16th century in Java and Sumatra. Bali, however, remains overwhelmingly Hindu. In the eastern archipelago, both Christian and Islamic proselytizing took place in the 16th and 17th centuries, and, currently, there are large communities of both religions on these islands.

Beginning in 1602, the Dutch slowly established themselves as rulers of present-day Indonesia, exploiting the weakness of the small kingdoms that had replaced that of Majapahit. The only exception was East Timor, which remained under Portugal until 1975. During 300 years of Dutch rule, the Dutch developed the Netherlands East Indies into one of the world's richest colonial possessions.

During the first decade of the 20th century, an Indonesian independence movement began and expanded rapidly, particularly between the two World Wars. Its leaders came from a small group of young professionals and students, some of whom had been educated in the Netherlands. Many, including Indonesia's first president, Sukarno (1945-67), were imprisoned for political activities.

The Japanese occupied Indonesia for 3 years during World War II. On August 17, 1945, 3 days after the Japanese surrender to the Allies a small group of Indonesians, led by Sukarno and Mohammad Hatta, proclaimed independence and established the Republic of Indonesia. They set up a provisional government and adopted a constitution to govern the republic until elections could be held and a new constitution written. Dutch efforts to reestablish complete control met strong resistance. After 4 years of warfare and negotiations, the Dutch transferred sovereignty to a federal Indonesian Government. In 1950, Indonesia became the 60th member of the United Nations.

Shortly after hostilities with the Dutch ended in 1949, Indonesia adopted a new constitution providing for a parliamentary system of government in which the executive was chosen by and made responsible to parliament. Parliament was divided among many political parties before and after the country's first nationwide election in 1955, and stable governmental coalitions were difficult to achieve. The role of Islam in Indonesia became a divisive issue. Sukarno defended a secular state based on Pancasila while some Muslim groups preferred either an Islamic state or a constitution which included pream-

bular provision requiring adherents of Islam to be subject to Islamic law. At the time of independence, the Dutch retained control over the western half of New Guinea, and permitted steps toward self-government and independence.

Negotiations with the Dutch on the incorporation of the territory into Indonesia failed, and armed clashes broke out between Indonesian and Dutch troops in 1961. In August 1962, the two sides reached an agreement, and Indonesia assumed administrative responsibility for Irian Jaya on May 1, 1963. The Indonesian Government conducted an "Act of Free Choice" in Irian Jaya under UN supervision in 1969, in which 1,025 Irianese representatives of local councils agreed by consensus to remain a part of Indonesia. A subsequent UN General Assembly resolution confirmed the transfer of sovereignty to Indonesia. Opposition to Indonesian administration of Irian Jaya, also known as Papua or West Papua, gave rise to smallscale guerrilla activity in the years following Jakarta's assumption of control. In the more open atmosphere since 1998, there have been more explicit expressions within Irian Jaya of a desire for independence from Indonesia.

From 1524 to 1975, East Timor was a Portuguese colony on the island of Timor, separated from Australia's north coast by the Timor Sea. As a result of political events in Portugal, Portuguese authorities abruptly withdrew from Timor in 1975, exacerbating power struggles among several Timorese political factions. An avowedly Marxist faction called "Fretilin" achieved military superiority. Fretilin's ascent in an area contiguous to Indonesian territory alarmed the Indonesian Government, which regarded it as a threatening movement. Following appeals from some of Fretilin's Timorese opponents, Indonesian military forces intervened in East Timor and overcame Fretilin's regular forces in 1975-76. Smallscale guerrilla activity persisted after Indonesia declared East Timor its 27th province in 1976, following a petition by a provisional government

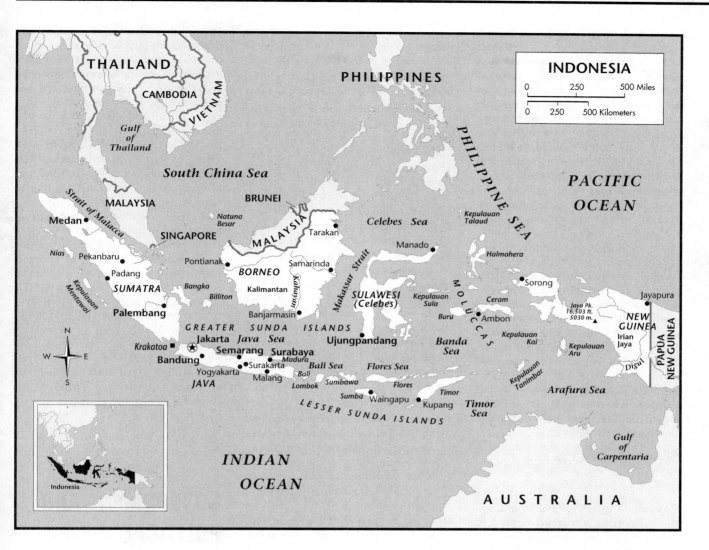

for incorporation into Indonesia. The UN never recognized Indonesia's incorporation of East Timor and later brokered negotiations between Indonesia and Portugal on the territory's status. In January 1999, the Indonesian Government agreed to a process, with UN involvement, under which the people of East Timor would be allowed to choose between autonomy and independence through a direct ballot.

The direct ballot was held on August 30, 1999. Some 98% of registered voters cast their ballots, and 78.5% of the voters chose independence over continued integration with Indonesia. Many persons were killed in a wave of violence and destruction after the announcement of the pro-independence vote. In October 1999, the People's Consultative Assembly (MPR) revoked the 1978 decree that

annexed East Timor, and the United Nations Transitional Authority in East Timor (UNTAET) assumed responsibility for administering East Timor until it becomes independent.

Unsuccessful rebellions on Sumatra, Sulawesi, West Java, and other islands beginning in 1958, plus a failure by the constituent assembly to develop a new constitution, weakened the parliamentary system. Consequently, in 1959, when President Sukarno unilaterally revived the provisional 1945 constitution, which gave broad presidential powers, he met little resistance.

From 1959 to 1965, President Sukarno imposed an authoritarian regime under the label of "Guided Democracy." He also moved Indonesia's foreign policy toward nonalignment, a foreign policy stance

supported by other prominent leaders of former colonies who rejected formal alliances with either the Western or Soviet blocs. Under Sukarno's auspices, these leaders gathered in Bandung, West Java, 1955, to lay the groundwork for what became known as the Non-Aligned Movement. In the late 1950s and early 1960s, President Sukarno moved closer to Asian communist states and toward the Indonesian Communist Party (PKI) in domestic affairs. Though the PKI represented the largest communist party outside the Soviet Union and China, its mass support base never demonstrated an ideological adherence typical of communist parties in other countries.

By 1965, the PKI controlled many of the mass civic and cultural organizations that Sukarno had established to mobilize support for his regime and,

Indonesia

with Sukarno's acquiescence, embarked on a campaign to establish a "Fifth Column" by arming its supporters. Army leaders resisted this campaign. Under circumstances that have never been fully explained, on October 1, 1965, PKI sympathizers within the military, including elements from Sukarno's palace guard, occupied key locations in Jakarta and kidnapped and murdered six senior generals. Major General Soeharto, the commander of the Army Strategic Reserve, rallied army troops opposed to the PKI to reestablish control over the city. Violence swept throughout Indonesia in the aftermath of the October 1 events, and unsettled conditions persisted through 1966. Rightist gangs killed tens of thousands of alleged communists in rural areas. Estimates of the number of deaths range between 160,000 and 500,000. The violence was especially brutal in Java and Bali. During this period, PKI members by the tens of thousands turned in their membership cards. The emotions and fears of instability created by this crisis persisted for many years; the communist party remains banned from Indonesia.

Throughout the 1965-66 period, President Sukarno vainly attempted to restore his political position and shift the country back to its pre-October 1965 position. Although he remained president, in March 1966, Sukarno had to transfer key political and military powers to General Soeharto, who by that time had become head of the armed forces. In March 1967, the Provisional People's Consultative Assembly (MPRS) named General Soeharto acting president. Sukarno ceased to be a political force and lived under virtual house arrest until his death in 1970.

President Soeharto proclaimed a "New Order" in Indonesian politics and dramatically shifted foreign and domestic policies away from the course set in Sukarno's final years. The New Order established economic rehabilitation and development as its primary goals and pursued its policies through an administrative structure dominated by the military but

with advice from Western-educated economic experts.

In 1968, the People's Consultative Assembly (MPR) formally selected Soeharto to a full 5-year term as president, and he was re-elected to successive 5-year terms in 1973, 1978, 1983, 1988, 1993, and 1998. In mid-1997, Indonesia was afflicted by the Asian financial and economic crisis, accompanied by the worst drought in 50 years and falling prices for oil, gas, and other commodity exports. The rupiah plummeted, inflation soared, and capital flight accelerated. Demonstrators, initially led by students, called for Soeharto's resignation. Amidst widespread civil unrest, Soeharto resigned on May 21, 1998, 3 months after the MPR had selected him for a seventh term. Soeharto's hand-picked Vice President, B. J. Habibie, became Indonesia's third president.

President Habibie quickly assembled a cabinet. One of its main tasks was to reestablish International Monetary Fund and donor community support for an economic stabilization program. He moved quickly to release political prisoners and lift controls on freedom of speech and association. Elections for the national, provincial, and sub-provincial parliaments were held on June 7, 1999. For the national parliament, Parti Demokrasi Indonesia Perjuangan (PDI-P, Indonesian Democratic Party of Struggle led by Sukarno's daughter Megawati Soekarnoputri) won 34% of the vote; Golkar ("functional groups" party of the government) 22%; Partai Persatuan Pembangunan (PPP, United Development Party led by Hamzah Haz) 12%, and Partai Kebangkitan Bangsa (PKB, National Awakening Party led by Abdurrahman Wahid) 10%. In October 1999, the People's Consultative Assembly, which consists of the 500-member Parliament plus 200 appointed members, elected Abdurrahman Wahid as President, and Megawati Soekarnoputri as Vice President, for 5-year terms. Wahid named his first Cabinet in early November 1999 and a reshuffled, second Cabinet in August 2000.

President Wahid's government has continued to pursue democratization and to encourage renewed economic growth under challenging conditions. In addition to continuing economic malaise, his government has faced regional, interethnic, and interreligious conflict, particularly in Aceh, the Moluccas, and Irian Jaya. In West Timor, the problems of displaced East Timorese and violence by pro-Indonesian East Timorese militias have caused considerable humanitarian and social problems. An increasingly assertive Parliament has frequently challenged President Wahid's policies and prerogatives, contributing to a lively and sometimes rancorous national political debate. During the People's Consultative Assembly's first annual session in August 2000, President Wahid gave an account of his government's performance. Under pressure from the Assembly to improve management and coordination within the government, he issued a presidential decree giving Vice President Megawati control over the day-to-day administration of government.

# GOVERNMENT AND POLITICAL CONDITIONS

Indonesia is a republic based on the 1945 constitution providing for a limited separation of executive, legislative, and judicial power. The governmental system has been described as "presidential with parliamentary characteristics." A constitutional reform process has been underway since 1999, and has already produced several important changes. Among these are two 5-year term limits for the President and Vice President and measures to institute checks and balances. The highest state institution is the People's Consultative Assembly (MPR), whose functions include electing the president and vice president, establishing broad guidelines of state policy, and amending the constitution. The 695-member MPR includes all 500 members of the House of Representatives (DPR) plus 130 "regional representatives" elected by the 26 provincial parliaments and 65 appointed members from societal groups. The DPR, which is the premier legislative institution, includes 462 members elected through a mixed proportional/district representation system and 38 appointed members of the armed forces (TNI) and police (POLRI). During the authoritarian Soeharto era, the armed forces played a central political role under a doctrine known as "dual function," with the DPR and MPR comprising a substantially higher proportion of appointed TNI/POLRI and societal group members than at present. Under existing agreements, TNI/POLRI representation in the DPR will end at the time of the next general election in 2004 and will end in the MPR in 2009. Societal group representation in the MPR is expected to be eliminated in 2004 through further constitutional change. Military domination of regional administration is gradually breaking down, with new regulations prohibiting active-duty officers from holding political office.

A general election in June 1999 produced the first freely elected national, provincial, and regional parliaments in over 40 years. In October 1999 the MPR elected a compromise candidate, Abdurrahman Wahid (a.k.a Gus Dur), as the country's fourth president, and Megawati Sukarnoputri, a daughter of the country's first president, as the vice president. Megawati's PDI-P party had won the largest share of the vote (34%) in the general election, while Golkar, the dominant party during the Soeharto era, came in second (22%). Several other, mostly Islamic parties won shares large enough to be seated in the DPR. Having served as rubber-stamp bodies in the past, the DPR and MPR have gained considerable power and are increasingly assertive in oversight of the executive branch. In part, this reflects a desire to prevent the presidential excesses of the past and, in part, to restrain Wahid, who is seen as at times dangerously unpredictable. Through his appointed cabinet, the president retains the authority to conduct the administration of the government, but some observers believe the balance of power has shifted too far in the direction of the legislature.

## Principal Government Officials

For up-to-date information on Principal Government Officials, see the Chiefs of State and Cabinet Members of Foreign Governments section starting on page 1.

**Consulates General are in:** New York (5 East 68th Street, New York, NY 10021, tel. 212-879-0600/0615; FAX: 212-570-6206); Los Angeles(3457 Wilshire Blvd., Los Angeles, CA 90010; tel. 213-383-5126; FAX: 213-487-3971); Houston (10900 Richmond Ave., Houston, TX 77042; tel. 713-785-1691; FAX: 713-780-9644).
**Consulates are in:** San Francisco (1111 Columbus Avenue, San Francisco, CA 94133; tel. 415-474-9571; FAX: 415-441-4320); and Chicago (2 Illinois Center, Suite 1422233 N. Michigan Avenue, Chicago, IL 60601; tel. 312-938-0101/4; 312-938-0311/0312; FAX: 312-938-3148).

# ECONOMY

Indonesia has a market-based economy in which the government plays a significant role. It owns more than 164 state-owned enterprises and administers prices on several basic goods, including fuel, rice, and electricity. In the aftermath of the financial and economic crisis that began in mid-1997, the government took custody of a significant portion of private sector assets through acquisition of nonperforming bank loans and corporate assets through the debt restructuring process.

During the 30 years of Soeharto's "New Order" government, Indonesia's economy grew from a per capita GDP of $70 to more than $1,000 by 1996. Through prudent monetary and fiscal policies, inflation was held in the 5%-10% range, the rupiah was stable and predictable, and the government avoided domestic financing of budget deficits. Much of the development budget was financed by concessional foreign aid.

In the mid-1980s, the government began eliminating regulatory obstacles to economic activity. The steps were aimed primarily at the external and financial sectors and were designed to stimulate employment and growth in the non-oil export sector. Annual real GDP growth averaged nearly 7% from 1987-97, and most analysts recognized Indonesia as a newly industrializing economy and emerging major market.

High levels of economic growth from 1987-97 masked a number of structural weaknesses in Indonesia's economy. The legal system was very weak, and there was and is no effective way to enforce contracts, collect debts, or sue for bankruptcy. Banking practices were very unsophisticated, with collateral-based lending the norm and widespread violation of prudential regulations, including limits on connected lending. Non-tariff barriers, rent-seeking by state-owned enterprises, domestic subsidies, barriers to domestic trade, and export restrictions all created economic distortions.

The regional financial problems that swept into Indonesia in late 1997 quickly became an economic and political crisis. Indonesia's initial response was to float the rupiah, raise key domestic interest rates, and tighten fiscal policy. In October 1997, Indonesia and the International Monetary Fund (IMF) reached agreement on an economic reform program aimed at macroeconomic stabilization and elimination of some of the country's most damaging economic policies, such as the National Car Program and the clove monopoly, both involving family members of President Soeharto. The rupiah failed to stabilize for any significant period of time, however, and President Soeharto was forced to resign in May 1998. In August 1998, Indonesia and the IMF agreed on an Extended Fund Facility (EFF) under President Habibie that included significant structural reform targets. President Abdurrahman Wahid took office in October 1999, and Indonesia and the IMF signed another EFF in January 2000. The new program also has a range of economic, structural reform, and governance targets.

The effects of the financial and economic crisis were severe. In 1998, real GDP contracted by an estimated 13.7%. The economy bottomed out in mid-1999, and real GDP growth for the year was an anemic 0.3%. Inflation reached 77% in 1998 but slowed to 2% in 1999. The rupiah, which had been in the Rp 2,400/USD1 range in 1997 reached Rp 17,000/USD1 at the height of the 1998 violence, returned to the Rp 6,500-8,000/USD1 range in late 1998. It has traded in the Rp 6,500-9,000/USD1 range since, with significant volatility. Although a severe drought in 1997-98 forced Indonesia to import record amounts of rice, overall imports dropped precipitously in the early stage of the crisis in response to the unfavorable exchange rate, reduced domestic demand, and absence of new investment. Although reliable unemployment data are not available, formal sector employment contracted significantly.

As of September 2000, Indonesia's economic outlook is mixed. Recently released economic data provide evidence that the economic turnaround that began in the second quarter of 1999 has continued and accelerated. According to the Central Bureau of Statistics (BPS), year-on-year real GDP growth reached 4.13% in August 2000. Driving this higher than expected GDP growth are record exports, solid manufacturing growth, and continued strong levels of household consumption. At the same time, high petroleum prices are increasing the value of Indonesia's oil exports. As the economy has picked up, there has been a significant increase in corporate debt restructuring, although questions remain about the viability of some deals.

Less positively, foreign investment still lags far below its pre-crisis levels; the rupiah has lost more than 22% of its value since President

Wahid was elected, and the stock market is in record low territory. Indonesia's banking and corporate sectors are still extremely weak. Asset sales by the Indonesian Bank Restructuring Agency have slowed amidst turmoil in the agency's senior leadership. Banking sector reform has stalled. Progress on corruption cases against is excruciatingly slow and capricious. These developments have shaken most analysts' faith in the reform credentials of the Wahid administration.

Indonesia's public sector external debt rose from $54.2 billion in March 1998 to about $80 billion by mid-2000. Private sector external debt stood at approximately $82 billion.

## Oil and Minerals Sector

Indonesia, the only Asian member of the Organization of Petroleum Exporting Countries (OPEC), ranks 15th among world oil producers, with about 2.4% of world production. Crude and condensate output averaged 1.5 million barrels per day (b/d) in 1999. In the 1998 calendar year the oil and gas sector, including refining, contributed approximately 9% to GDP and, in FY 1999-00, provided 28% to domestic revenues. The sector's share of export earnings was 20% in 1999, a greater percentage than recent years due to high world oil prices. U.S. companies have invested heavily in the petroleum sector. With domestic demand for petroleum fuels expanding, Indonesia will become a net importer of oil by

the next decade unless new reserves are found. In 1999, Indonesian imports of crude oil and petroleum products totaled $3.2 billion while Indonesian exports of crude oil and oil products totaled $10.7 billion.

The state owns all oil and mineral rights. Foreign firms participate through production-sharing and work contracts. Oil and gas contractors are required to finance all exploration, production, and development costs in their contract areas; they are entitled to recover operating, exploration, and development costs out of the oil and gas produced.

Although minerals production traditionally centered on bauxite, silver, and tin production, Indonesia is expanding its copper, nickel, gold, and coal output for export markets. In mid-1993, the Department of Mines and Energy reopened the coal sector to foreign investment, with the result that the leading Indonesian coal producer now is a joint venture between U.K. firms BP and Rio Tinto. Total coal production reached 74 million metric tons in 1999, including exports of 55 million tons. The Indonesian Government hopes to surpass 100 million metric tons of coal production in 2002. Two U.S. firms operate three copper/gold mines in Indonesia, with a Canadian and U.K. firm holding significant other investments in nickel and gold, respectively. In 1998, the value of Indonesian gold production was $1 billion and copper, $843 million. Receipts from gold, copper, and coal comprised 84% of the $3 billion earned in 1998 by the mineral mining sector.

## Investment

Since the late 1980s, Indonesia has made significant changes to its regulatory framework to encourage economic growth. This growth was financed largely from private investment, both foreign and domestic. U.S. investors dominated the oil and gas sector and undertook some of Indonesia's largest mining projects. In addition, the presence of U.S. banks, manufacturers, and service providers expanded, especially after the industrial and financial sector reforms of the 1980s. Other major foreign investors included Japan, the United Kingdom, Singapore, the Netherlands, Hong Kong, Taiwan, and South Korea.

The economic crisis made continued private financing imperative but problematic. New foreign investment approvals fell by almost two-thirds between 1997 and 1999. The crisis further highlighted areas where additional reform was needed. Frequently cited areas for improving the investment climate were establishment of a well- functioning legal and judicial system, adherence to competitive processes, and adoption of internationally acceptable accounting and disclosure standards. Despite improvements in the laws in recent years, Indonesia's intellectual property rights regime remains weak; lack of effective enforcement is a major concern. Under Soeharto, Indonesia had moved toward private provision of public infrastructure, including electric power, tollroads, and telecommunications. The financial crisis brought to light serious weaknesses in the process of dispute resolution, however, particularly in the area of private infrastructure projects. Although Indonesia continued to have the advantages of a large labor force, abundant natural resources and modern infrastructure, private investment in new projects largely ceased during the crisis.

# FOREIGN RELATIONS

Since independence, Indonesia has espoused a "free and active" foreign policy, seeking to play a role in regional affairs commensurate with its size and location but avoiding involvement in conflicts among major powers. Indonesian foreign policy under the "New Order" government of President Soeharto moved away from the stridently anti-Western, anti-American posturing that characterized the latter part of the Sukarno era. Following Soeharto's ouster in 1998, Presidents Habibie and Wahid have preserved the broad outlines of

Soeharto's independent, moderate foreign policy. Preoccupation with domestic problems has not prevented President Wahid from frequently traveling abroad and continuing to participate vigorously, though peripatetically, in many international fora. The traumatic separation of East Timor from Indonesia after an August 1999 East Timor referendum, and subsequent events in East and West Timor, strained Indonesia's relations with the international community.

A cornerstone of Indonesia's contemporary foreign policy is its participation in the Association of Southeast Asian Nations (ASEAN), of which it was a founding member in 1967 with Thailand, Malaysia, Singapore, and the Philippines. Since then, Brunei, Vietnam, Laos, Burma, and Cambodia also have joined ASEAN. While organized to promote common economic, social, and cultural goals, ASEAN acquired a security dimension after Vietnam's invasion of Cambodia in 1979; this aspect of ASEAN expanded with the establishment of the ASEAN Regional Forum in 1994, which comprises 22 countries, including the U.S. Indonesia's continued domestic troubles have distracted it from ASEAN matters and consequently lessened its influence within the organization.

Indonesia also was one of the founders of the Non-Aligned Movement (NAM) and has taken moderate positions in its councils. As NAM Chairman in 1992-95, it led NAM positions away from the rhetoric of North-South confrontation, advocating instead the broadening of North-South cooperation in the area of development. Indonesia continues to be a prominent, and generally helpful, leader of the Non-Aligned Movement.

Indonesia has the world's largest Muslim population, though it is a secular state, and is a member of the Organization of the Islamic Conference (OIC). It carefully considers the interests of Islamic solidarity in its foreign policy decisions but generally has been an influence for moderation

in the OIC. President Wahid has pursued better relations with Israel, and in August 2000 he met with former Israeli Prime Minister Peres.

After 1966, Indonesia welcomed and maintained close relations with the donor community, particularly the United States, western Europe, Australia, and Japan, through the Intergovernmental Group on Indonesia (IGGI) and its successor, the Consultative Group on Indonesia (CGI), which have provided substantial foreign economic assistance. Problems in Timor and Indonesia's reluctance to implement economic reform, have complicated Indonesia's relationship with donors.

Indonesia has been a strong supporter of the Asia-Pacific Economic Cooperation (APEC) forum. Largely through the efforts of President Soeharto at the 1994 meeting in Bogor, Indonesia, APEC members agreed to implement free trade in the region by 2010 for industrialized economies and 2020 for developing economies.

# NATIONAL SECURITY

Indonesia's armed forces (Tentara Nasional Indonesia, or TNI, formerly ABRI) total about 250,000 members, including the army, navy, marines, and air force. The army is by far the largest, with about 196,000 active-duty personnel. Defense spending in the national budget is only 1.8% of GDP but is supplemented by revenue from many military businesses and foundations.

The Indonesian National Police were for many years a branch of the armed forces. The police were formally separated from the military in April 1999, a process which was formally completed in July 2000. With 150,000 personnel, the police form a much smaller portion of the population than in most nations.

Indonesia is at a relative peace with its neighbors, although competing South China Sea claims, where Indonesia has large natural gas reserves, concern the Indonesian Government. Without a credible external threat in the region, the military historically viewed its prime mission as assuring internal security. Military leaders now say they wish to transform the military to a professional, external security force but acknowledge that the armed forces will continue to play an internal security role for some time.

Throughout Indonesian history the military maintained a prominent role in the nation's political and social affairs. Traditionally a significant number of cabinet members had military backgrounds, while active duty and retired military personnel occupied a large number of seats in the parliament. Commanders of the various territorial commands played influential roles in the affairs of their respective regions. In the post-Soeharto period, civilian and military leaders have advocated removing the military from politics (for example, the military's representatives in parliament have been much reduced), but the military's political influence remains extensive.

# U.S.-INDONESIAN RELATIONS

The United States has important economic, commercial, and security interests in Indonesia. Indonesia remains a linchpin of regional security due to its strategic location astride a number of key international maritime straits. Relations between Indonesia and the U.S. are good. The U.S. played an important role in Indonesian independence in the late 1940s and appreciated Indonesia's role as a staunch anti-communist bulwark during the Cold War. Cordial and cooperative relations are maintained today, although the two countries are not bound by any formal security treaties. The United States and Indonesia share the common goal of maintaining peace, security, and stability in the region and engaging in a dialogue on threats to regional

security. The United States has welcomed Indonesia's contributions to regional security, especially its leading role in helping restore democracy in Cambodia and in mediating among the many territorial claimants in the South China Sea.

The U.S. is committed to assisting Indonesia's democratic transition and supports the territorial integrity of the country. There are, nonetheless, friction points in the bilateral political relationship. These have centered primarily on East Timor and human rights, as well as on differences in our respective foreign policy orientations. The U.S. Congress cut off grant military training assistance (IMET) to Indonesia in 1992 in response to a November 12, 1991, incident in East Timor in which Indonesian security forces shot and killed East Timorese demonstrators. This restriction was partially lifted in 1995. Military assistance programs were again suspended, however, in the aftermath of the violence and destruction in East Timor following the August 30, 1999 referendum favoring separation from Indonesia. Indonesia continues to align itself with Non-Aligned Movement and G-77 foreign policy views, often taking unhelpful positions on issues of international human rights concern.

On worker rights, Indonesia was the target of several petitions filed under the Generalized System of Preferences (GSP) legislation arguing that Indonesia did not meet internationally recognized labor standards. A formal GSP review was suspended in February 1994 without terminating GSP benefits for Indonesia. Since 1998, Indonesia has ratified all eight International Labor Organization core conventions on protecting internationally recognized worker rights and allowed trade unions to organize. However, enforcement of labor laws and protection of workers rights remains inconsistent and weak in some areas. Continuing economic malaise has increased difficulties for workers and caused an increase in child labor (10-14 years old).

# Economic Relations with the United States

U.S. exports to Indonesia in 1999 totaled $2.0 billion, down significantly from $4.5 billion in 1997. The main exports were construction equipment, machinery, aviation parts, chemicals, and agricultural products. U.S. imports from Indonesia in 1999 totaled $9.5 billion and consisted primarily of clothing, machinery and transportation equipment, petroleum, natural rubber, and footwear. Economic assistance to Indonesia is coordinated through the Consultative Group on Indonesia (CGI), formed in 1989. It includes 19 donor countries and 13 international organizations that meet annually to coordinate donor assistance. The 2000 CGI meeting is to be held October 17-18 in Tokyo.

The U.S. Agency for International Development (USAID) has provided development assistance to Indonesia since 1950. Initial assistance focused on the most urgent needs of the new republic, including food aid, infrastructure rehabilitation, health care, and training. Through the 1970s, a time of great economic growth in Indonesia, USAID played a major role in helping the country achieve self-sufficiency in rice production and in reducing the birth rate.

USAID's current program aims to support Indonesia as it recovers from the financial crisis by providing food aid, employment generating activities, and maintaining critical public health services. USAID is also providing technical advisers to help the Indonesian Government implement economic reforms and fiscal decentralization and is supporting democratization and civil society development activities through nongovernmental organizations.

## Principal U.S. Embassy Officials

**For up-to-date information on Principal U.S. Officials, see the U.S. Embassies, Consulates, and For-**

eign Service section starting on page 139.

The U.S. Embassy in Indonesia is located at Jalan Medan Merdeka Selatan 3-5, Jakarta (tel. (62-021) 344-2211). U.S. mail to the embassy may be addressed to FPO AP 96520. The U.S. Consulate General in Surabaya is located at Jalan Dr. Sutomo 33, Surabaya East Java (tel. (62-31) 568-2287). Principal Officer—Robert Pollard.

The U.S. Consular Agency in Bali is located at Jalan Hayam Wuruk 188, Bali (tel. (62-361) 233-605. Consular Agent—Andrew Toth.

For information on economic trends, commercial development, production, trade regulations, and tariff rates, contact the International Trade Administration, U.S. Department of Commerce, Washington, DC 20230.

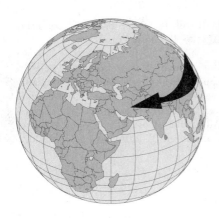

# IRAN

July 1994

Official Name:
**Islamic Republic of Iran**

## PROFILE

### Geography
**Area:** 1.6 million sq. km. (636, 294 sq. mi.); slightly larger than Alaska.
**Cities:** Capital—Tehran. Other cities—Isfahan, Tabriz, Mashhad.
**Terrain:** Desert and mountains.
**Climate:** Semiarid; subtropical along the Caspian coast.

### People
**Nationality:** Noun and adjective—Iranian(s).
**Population (1992):** 61 million.
**Annual growth rate (1992):** 3.5%.
**Ethnic groups (1992):** Persian; Azeri Turks; Kurds; Arabs; Turkomans and Baluchis; and Lur, Bakhtiari, and Qashqai tribes.
**Religions:** Shi'a Muslim 95%; Sunni Muslim 4%; Zoroastrian, Jewish, Christian, and Baha'i 1%.
**Languages:** Persian, Turkish dialects, Kurdish, Luri, Gilaki, Arabic.
**Education (1992):** Literacy—50%.
**Health (1992):** Infant mortality rate—64/1,000. Life expectancy—65 years.
**Work force:** Agriculture 33%, manufacturing 21%.

### Government
**Type:** Islamic republic.

**Constitution:** Ratified December 1979, revised 1989.
**Branches:** Executive—"Leader of the Islamic Revolution" (head of state); president and Council of Ministers. Legislative—270-member National Consultative Assembly (Majles). Judicial—Supreme Court.
**Political parties:** None.
**Suffrage:** Universal at 15.
**Administrative subdivisions:** 25 provinces.
**Flag:** Three horizontal bands of green, white, and red, with the national emblem, a stylized representation of the word Allah, in the center.

### Economy
**GDP (est.):** $90 billion.
**Annual growth rate (est.):** 5%.
**Per capita income (est.):** $1,500.
**Natural resources:** Petroleum, natural gas, and some mineral deposits.
**Agriculture:** Principal products—wheat, rice, other grains, sugar beets, fruits, nuts, cotton, dairy products, wool, caviar; not self-sufficient in food.
**Industry:** Types—petroleum, petrochemicals, textiles, cement and building materials, food processing (particularly sugar refining and vegetable oil production), metal fabricating (steel and copper).
**Trade:** Exports—$18 billion: petroleum 90%, carpets, fruits, nuts, hides. Imports—$28 billion: food, machin-

ery, and medical products. Major markets/suppliers: Germany, Japan, Italy, U.K., France.
**Exchange rate (1994, unofficial):** 2,600 rials=U.S. $1.

## PEOPLE

Almost two-thirds of Iran's people are of Aryan origin—their ancestors migrated from Central Asia. The major groups in this category include Persians, Kurds, Lurs, and Baluchi. The remainder are primarily Turkic but also include Arabs, Armenians, Jews, and Assyrians.

The 1979 Islamic revolution and the war with Iraq transformed Iran's class structure politically, socially, and economically. In general, however, Iranian society remains divided into urban, market-town, village, and tribal groups. Clerics, called mullahs, dominate politics and nearly all aspects of Iranian life, both urban and rural. After the fall of the Pahlavi regime in 1979, much of the urban upper class of prominent merchants, industrialists, and professionals, favored by the former Shah, lost standing and influence to the senior clergy and their supporters. Bazaar merchants, who were allied with the clergy against the Pahlavi shahs, have also gained political and economic power since the revolution.

The urban working class has enjoyed somewhat enhanced status and economic mobility, spurred in part by opportunities provided by revolutionary organizations and the government bureaucracy.

Unemployment, a major problem even before the revolution, has many causes, including population growth, the war with Iraq, and shortages of raw materials and trained managers. Farmers and peasants received a psychological boost from the attention given them by the Islamic regime but appear to be hardly better off in economic terms. The government has made progress on rural development, including electrification and road building but has not yet made a commitment to land redistribution.

Most Iranians are Muslims; 95% belong to the Shi'a branch of Islam, the official state religion, and about 4% belong to the Sunni branch, which predominates in neighboring Muslim countries. Non-Muslim minorities include Zoroastrians, Jews, Baha'is, and Christians.

# HISTORY

The ancient nation of Iran, historically known to the West as Persia and once a major empire in its own right, has been overrun frequently and has had its territory altered throughout the centuries. Invaded by Arabs, Seljuk Turks, Mongols, and others—and often caught up in the affairs of larger powers—Iran has always reasserted its national identity and has developed as a distinct political and cultural entity.

Archeological findings have placed knowledge of Iranian prehistory at middle paleolithic times (100,000 years ago). The earliest sedentary cultures date from 18,000–14,000 years ago. The sixth millennium B.C. saw a fairly sophisticated agricultural society and proto-urban population centers. Many dynasties have ruled Iran, the first of which was under the Achaemenians (559–330 B.C.), a dynasty founded by Cyrus the Great. After the Hellenistic period

(300–250 B.C.) came the Parthian (250 B.C.–226 A.D.) and the Sassanian (226–651) dynasties.

The seventh-century Arab-Muslim conquest of Iran was followed by conquests by the Seljuk Turks, the Mongols, and Tamerlane. Iran underwent a revival under the Safavid dynasty (1502–1736), the most prominent figure of which was Shah Abbas. The conqueror Nadir Shah and his successors were followed by the Zand dynasty, founded by Karim Kahn, and later the Qajar (1795–1925) and the Pahlavi dynasties (1925–1979).

Modern Iranian history began with a nationalist uprising against the Shah (who remained in power) in 1905, the granting of a limited constitution in 1906, and the discovery of oil in 1908. In 1921, Reza Khan, an Iranian officer of the Persian Cossack Brigade, seized control of the government. In 1925, he made himself Shah, ruling as Reza Shah Pahlavi for almost 16 years and installing the new Pahlavi dynasty.

Under his reign, Iran began to modernize and to secularize politics, and the central government reasserted its authority over the tribes and provinces. In September 1941, following the Allies' (U.K.-Soviet Union) occupation of western Iran, Reza Shah was forced to abdicate. His son, Mohammad Reza Pahlavi, became Shah and ruled until 1979.

During World War II, Iran was a vital link in the Allied supply line for lend-lease supplies to the Soviet Union. After the war, Soviet troops stationed in northwestern Iran not only refused to withdraw but backed revolts that established short-lived, pro-Soviet separatist regimes in the northern regions of Azerbaijan and Kurdistan. These were ended in 1946. The Azerbaijan revolt crumbled after U.S. and UN pressure forced a Soviet withdrawal and Iranian forces suppressed the Kurdish revolt.

In 1951, Premier Mohammed Mossadeq, a militant nationalist, forced the parliament to nationalize the British-owned oil industry. Mossadeq was opposed by the Shah and was

removed, but he quickly returned to power. The Shah fled Iran but returned when supporters staged a coup against Mossadeq in August 1953. Mossadeq was then arrested by pro-Shah army forces.

In 1961, Iran initiated a series of economic, social, and administrative reforms that became known as the Shah's White Revolution. The core of this program was land reform. Modernization and economic growth proceeded at an unprecedented rate, fueled by Iran's vast petroleum reserves, the third-largest in the world.

In 1978, domestic turmoil swept the country as a result of religious and political opposition to the Shah's rule and programs—especially SAVAK, the hated internal security and intelligence service. In January 1979, the Shah left Iran; he died abroad several years after.

On February 1, 1979, exiled religious leader Ayatollah Ruhollah Khomeini returned from France to direct a revolution resulting in a new, theocratic republic guided by Islamic principles. Back in Iran after 15 years in exile in Turkey, Iraq, and France, he became Iran's national religious leader. Following Khomeini's death on June 3, 1989, the Assembly of Experts—an elected body of senior clerics—chose the outgoing president of the republic, Ali Khamenei, to be his successor as national religious leader in what proved to be a smooth transition.

In August 1989, Ali Akbar Hashemi-Rafsanjani, the speaker of the National Assembly, was elected President by an overwhelming majority. He was re-elected June 11, 1993, with a more modest majority of about 63%; some Western observers attributed the reduced voter turnout to disenchantment with the deteriorating economy.

# GOVERNMENT

The December 1979 Iranian constitution defines the political, economic, and social order of the Islamic repub-

ARMENIA  AZERBAIJAN

TURKEY

*Aras*

Tabriz
Orūmīyeh
Ardebil

*Daryācheh-ye Orūmīyeh*

Rasht

*Caspian Sea*

Atrak

KOPET MTS.

TURKMENISTAN

Saqqez

Qazvin

RESHTEH-YE ALBORZ

Sāri    Gorgān

Qūchān

Sabezevār    Mashhad

*Qezel Owzan*

Sanandaj

Tehrān ✪

▲ *Qolleh-ye Damāvand 18,605 ft. 5671 m.*

Torbat-e Ḥeydariyeh

Kāshmar

Hamadān

*Qareh Chāy*

Qom

*Dasht-e Kavōr (Salt Desert)*

Kermānshāh

Arāk

Khorramābād

Birjand

AFGHANISTAN

Herāt

Baghdad ✪

KŪHHĀ-YE ZAGROS

Dezfūl

Esfahān
Qomsheh

*Kārūn*

Yazd

*Dasht-e Lūt*

I R A Q

Ahvāz
Khorramshahr

*Namakzār-e Shahdād*

Zābol

Ābādān

Behbehān

Marv Dasht  *Persepolis*

KUWAIT

*Khārk*

Shirāz

Kermān

Bām

Zāhedān

PAKISTAN

Kuwait ✪

SAUDI ARABIA

Bandar-e Būshehr

Neyriz

*Halil*

Zāhedān

*Mand*

Deyyer

*Kul*

*Hāmūn-e Jaz Mūriān*

Gazak

Kuhak

Bastak

Bandar-e 'Abbās

*Persian Gulf*

*Qeshm I.*

*Strait of Hormuz*

Jāsk

Hūmedān

QATAR

✪ Doha

UNITED ARAB EMIRATES

OMAN

*Gulf of Oman*

Iran

IRAN

0    50   100   150   200 Miles

0  50 100 150 200 Kilometers

lic. It declares that Shi'a Islam of the Twelver (Jaafari) sect is Iran's official religion. The country is governed by secular and religious leaders and governing bodies, and duties often overlap. The chief ruler is a religious leader or, in the absence of a single leader, a council of religious leaders. The constitution stipulates that this national religious leader or members of the council of leaders are to be chosen from the clerical establishment on the basis of their qualifications and the high esteem in which they are held by Iran's Muslim population. This leader or council appoints the six religious members of the Council of Guardians (the six lay members— lawyers—are named by the National Consultative Assembly, or Majles);

appoints the highest judicial authorities, who must be religious jurists; and is commander-in-chief of the armed forces. The Council of Guardians, in turn, certifies the competence of candidates for the presidency and the National Assembly.

The president of the republic is elected by universal suffrage to a four-year term by an absolute majority of votes and supervises the affairs of the executive branch. The president appoints and supervises the Council of Ministers (members of the cabinet), coordinates government decisions, and selects government policies to be placed before the National Assembly.

The National Assembly consists of 270 members elected to a four-year term. The members are elected by direct and secret ballot. All legislation from the assembly must be reviewed by the Council of Guardians. The Council's six lawyers vote only on limited questions of the constitutionality of legislation; the religious members consider all bills for conformity to Islamic principles.

In 1988, Ayatollah Khomeini created the Council for Expediency, which resolves legislative issues on which the Majles and the Council of Guardians fail to reach an agreement. Since 1989, it has been used to advise the national religious leader on matters of national policy as well. It is composed of the heads of the three branches of government, the clerical members of the Council of Guardians, and members appointed by the national religious leader for three-year terms. Cabinet members and Majles committee chairs also serve as temporary members when issues under their jurisdictions are considered.

Judicial authority is constitutionally vested in the Supreme Court and the four-member High Council of the Judiciary; these are two separate groups with overlapping responsibilities and one head. Together, they are responsible for supervising the enforcement of all laws and for establishing judicial and legal policies.

The military is charged with defending Iran's borders, while the Revolutionary Guard Corps is charged mainly with maintaining internal security. Iran has 25 provinces, each headed by a governor general. The provinces are further divided into counties, districts, and villages.

## Principal Government Officials

For up-to-date information on Principal Government Officials, see the Chiefs of State and Cabinet Members of Foreign Governments section starting on page 1.

# POLITICAL CONDITIONS

Iran's post-revolution difficulties have included an eight-year war with Iraq, internal political struggles and unrest, and economic disorder. The early days of the regime were characterized by severe human rights violations and political turmoil, including the seizure of the U.S. embassy compound and its occupants on November 4, 1979, by Iranian militants.

By mid-1982, a succession of power struggles eliminated first the center of the political spectrum and then the leftists, leaving only the clergy. There has been some moderation of excesses both internally and internationally, although Iran remains a significant sponsor of terrorism.

The Islamic Republican Party (IRP) was Iran's dominant political party until its dissolution in 1987; Iran now has no functioning political parties. The Iranian Government is opposed by a few armed political groups including the Mojahedin-e-Khalq (People's Mojahedin of Iran), the People's Fedayeen, and the Kurdish Democratic Party.

# ECONOMY

Pre-revolutionary Iran's economic development was rapid. Traditionally an agricultural society, by the 1970s, Iran had achieved significant industrialization and economic modernization. However, the pace of growth had slowed dramatically by 1978, just before the Islamic revolution.

Since the revolution, increased government involvement in the economy has further stunted growth. Iran's current difficulties can be traced to a combination of factors. Economic activity, severely disrupted by the revolution, was further depressed by the war with Iraq and by the decline of oil prices beginning in late 1985. After the war with Iraq ended, the situation began to improve: Iran's GDP grew for two years running, partly from an oil windfall in 1990, and there was a substantial increase in imports.

A decrease in oil revenues in 1991 and growing external debt, though, dampened optimism. In March 1989, Khomeini had approved Rafsanjani's five-year plan for economic development, which allowed Iran to seek foreign loans. But mismanagement and inefficient bureaucracy, as well as political and ideological infighting, have hampered the formulation and execution of coherent economic policies.

All major business and industrial growth indicators are significantly below pre-revolutionary levels; unemployment was estimated to be 30% for 1993. Although Islam guarantees the right to private ownership, banks and some industries—including the petroleum, transportation, utilities, and mining sectors—have been nationalized. The import-dependent industrial sector is further plagued by low labor productivity, lack of foreign exchange, and shortages of raw materials and spare parts.

Agriculture also has suffered from shortages of capital, raw materials, and equipment, as well as from the war with Iraq; in addition, a major area of dissension within the regime has been how to proceed with land reform.

Oil revenues have been affected by the decline of oil prices. Oil accounts for about 90% of Iran's exports; because of reduced revenues, the government has imposed austerity measures, adding to the hardships of the Iranian people. In 1993, Iran's OPEC quota was about 3.4 million barrels per day, and estimated production was 3.5 million barrels per day.

Iran was unable to meet its obligations on short-term debt in 1993; by the end of the year, it was more than $9 billion in arrears on payments. Early in 1994, estimates of Iran's debt ranged from $16 billion to $30 billion.

# FOREIGN RELATIONS

Khomeini's revolutionary regime initiated sharp changes from the foreign policy pursued by the Shah, particularly in reversing the country's orientation toward the West. In the Middle East, Iran's only significant ally has been Syria. Iran's regional goals are dominated by wanting to establish a leadership role, curtail the presence of the U.S. and other outside powers, and build trade ties.

In broad terms, Iran's "Islamic foreign policy" emphasizes:

- Vehement anti-U.S. and anti-Israel stances;

- Eliminating outside influence in the region;

- Exporting the Islamic revolution;

- Support for Muslim political movements abroad; and

- A great increase in diplomatic contacts with developing countries.

Despite these guidelines, however, bilateral relations are frequently confused and contradictory due to Iran's oscillation between pragmatic and ideological concerns.

The country's foreign relations since the revolution have been tumultuous. In addition to the U.S. hostage crisis, tension between Iran and Iraq escalated in September 1980, when Iraq invaded Iran. Much of the dispute centered around sovereignty over the waterway between the two countries, the Shatt al-Arab, although underlying causes included each nation's overt desire for the overthrow of the other's government. Iran demanded the withdrawal of Iraqi troops from Iranian territory and the return to the status quo ante for the Shatt al-Arab as established under the 1975 Algiers Agreement signed by Iraq and Iran. After eight punishing years of war, in July 1988, Iran agreed to UN Security Council Resolution 598, which called for a cease-fire. The cease-fire was implemented on August 20, 1988; neither nation had made any real gains in the war.

Iran's relations with many of its Arab neighbors have been strained by Iranian attempts to spread its Islamic revolution. In 1981, Iran supported a plot to overthrow the Bahraini Government. In 1983, Iran expressed support for Shi'ites who bombed Western embassies in Kuwait, and in 1987, Iranian pilgrims rioted during the Hajj (pilgrimage) in Mecca, Saudi Arabia. Nations with strong fundamentalist movements, such as Egypt and Algeria, also mistrust Iran. Iran backs Hizballah, Hamas, the Palestinian Islamic Jihad, and the Popular Front for the Liberation of Palestine-General Command—all groups violently opposed to the Arab-Israeli peace process.

Relations with Western European nations have alternated between improvements and setbacks. French-Iranian relations were badly strained by the sale of French arms to Iraq. Since the war, relations have improved commercially but periodically are worsened by Iranian-sponsored terrorist acts committed in France.

Another source of tension has been Ayatollah Khomeini's 1989 call for all Muslims to kill Salman Rushdie, British author of The Satanic Verses, a novel many Muslims consider blasphemous. The United Kingdom has sheltered Rushdie, and strains over this issue persist.

Iran maintains regular diplomatic and commercial relations with Russia and the other Newly Independent States of the former Soviet Union. Both Iran and Russia feel they have important national interests at stake in developments in Central Asia and the Transcaucasus. Russian and other sales of military equipment and technology concern Iran's neighbors and the United States.

Iran spends about 14%–15% of its GDP on its military. Branches of its military include ground forces, a navy, an air force, and Revolutionary Guard Corps. The Iran-Iraq war took a heavy toll on these military forces. Iran is trying to modernize its military and acquire weapons of mass destruction; it does not yet have, but continues to seek, nuclear capabilities.

# U.S.-IRANIAN RELATIONS

On November 4, 1979, militant Iranian students occupied the American embassy in Tehran with the support of Ayatollah Khomeini. Fifty-two Americans were held hostage for 444 days. On April 7, 1980, the United States broke diplomatic relations with Iran, and on April 24, 1981, the Swiss Government assumed representation of U.S. interests in Tehran. Iranian interests in the United States are represented by the Pakistani Government.

In accordance with the Algiers declaration of January 20, 1981, the Iran-U.S. Claims Tribunal (located in The Hague, Netherlands) was established for the purpose of handling claims of U.S. nationals against Iran and of Iranian nationals against the United States. U.S. contact with Iran through The Hague covers only legal matters.

Commercial relations between Iran and the United States consist mainly of Iranian purchases of food and manufactured products. The U.S. Government prohibits the export of military and dual-use items to Iran as well as items forbidden under anti-terrorism legislation; it prohibits all imports from Iran.

There are serious obstacles to improved relations between the two countries. The U.S. Government defines five areas of objectionable Iranian behavior: Iranian efforts to acquire nuclear weapons and other weapons of mass destruction, its involvement in international terrorism, its support for violent opposition to the Arab-Israeli peace process, its

## Editor's Update

*A report on important events that have taken place since the last State Department revision of this* Background Note.

In early 1997, the split between Iran and the United States widened as Iran continued a military build-up in the Persian Gulf, and the US accused the Islamic Government of continued state sponsorship of terrorism.

In April 1998, the mayor of Teheran, Gholamhossein Karabaschi, was denounced by political conservatives and arrested on corruption charges. Mr. Karabaschi is politically allied with the moderate President Khatami. Protesters demonstrated against the arrest, which revealed the division between the moderates that won elections in 1997 and the conservatives that have controlled Iran since 1979.

Tensions between Tehran and Taliban-dominated Afghanistan intensified during the late summer of 1998 following the pillaging of Shia towns (including the slaying of several Iranian diplomats) by Taliban forces. In response to the Taliban violence, Iran massed forces on its border with Afghanistan and war threatened for a time.

On the domestic front, President Khatami continued to spar with his conservative opponents over the pace of reform. With the revelation of the intelligence ministry's involvement in the murders in 1998 of four dissidents, many hoped that Khatami would encourage the judiciary to expand the search for the conservative politicians and judges behind the assassinations. It appears that President Khatami's aim was to disgrace the intelligence ministry and rid it of his opponents, and not to widen the investigation beyond that point.

An electoral sweep by Mr. Khatami's supporters in local elections held on February 26, 1999, set the stage appeared for a showdown between the conservatives and the forces of Mr. Khatami and his support-

ers in the 2000 parliamentary elections. When the votes were counted, Mr. Khatami and the reformists won big, taking 136 of parliament's 290 seats. On June 6, 2001, President Mohammed Khatami was reelected to his second term with 77% of the vote. Faced with a recession and high unemployment, businessmen are urging the president to speed up market reforms. Khatami hopes to deepen democratic reforms, but knows that his greatest impediment is the hard–line Muslim clerics who still have a strong influence on social and political movements in the country.

President Khatami has plans to visit Russian President Vladimir Putin in March 2001 to seal the terms on what both countries are calling a "strategic partnership." The cornerstone of the agreement is arms trade.

threats and subversive activities against its neighbors, and its dismal human rights record. The U.S. believes that normal relations are impossible until Iran's behavior changes. However, the United States has offered to enter into dialogue with authorized representatives of the Iranian Government without preconditions. The Iranian Government has not accepted this offer. The United States has made clear that it does not seek to overthrow the Iranian Government but will continue to pressure Iran to change its behavior.

# IRAQ

October 1987

Official Name:

## Republic of Iraq

UPDATE NOTE: This entry has not yet been rewritten since the August 20, 1990 Iraqi invasion of Kuwait, the subsequent withdrawal of Iraqi troops as a result of a multi-national military attack (which was sponsored by the United Nations and included the U.S.), and the restoration to power of the Kuwaiti government. Hostilities in the Gulf region ceased on February 27, 1991; however, conditions in Iraq remain unsettled and regional conflicts continue in northern Iraq. This entry should, therefore, be read with awareness of its limits. Additional information can be found in the Travel Warning and Consular Information Sheet section in this Yearbook; please see CONTENTS for location.

# PROFILE

## Geography

**Area:** 434,934 sq. km. (167,924 sq. mi.); about the size of California.
**Cities:** Capital—Baghdad (pop. 3.8 million). Other cities—Basra, Mosul, Kirkuk.
**Terrain:** Alluvial plains, mountains, and desert.
**Climate:** Mostly hot and dry.

## People

**Nationality:** Noun and adjective—Iraqi(s).
**Population (1986 est.):** 16 million.
**Annual growth rate:** 3.3%.
**Ethnic groups:** Arab 75%, Kurd 1520%.
**Religions:** Shi'a Muslim 55%, Sunni Muslim 40%, Christian 5%.
**Languages:** Arabic, Kurdish, Assyrian, Armenian.
**Education:** Years compulsory—primary school (age 6 through grade 6). Literacy—70%.
**Health:** Infant mortality rate—25/1,000. Life expectancy—56.1 yrs.
**Work force (1980):** 3.5 million. Agriculture—44%. Industry—26%. Services—31%.

## Government

**Type:** Ruling Council.
**Independence:** 1932.
**Interim constitution:** 1970.
**Branches:** Executive—Revolutionary Command Council (RCC); President and Council of Ministers appointed by RCC. Legislative—National Assembly of 250 members elected in 1980 and 1984. Judicial—Civil, religious, and special courts.
**Administrative subdivisions:** 18 provinces.
**Political parties:** Ba'ath Party dominates; Kurdish Democratic Party and Kurdish Republican Party (legal parties).
**Suffrage:** Universal adult.
**National holidays:** Anniversaries of the 1958 and 1968 revolutions-July 14 and July 17.
**Flag:** Three horizontal bands of red white, and black, with three green stars on center white band.

## Economy

**GDP (1984):** $27 billion.
**Annual growth rate (1984 est.):** 0.6%.
**Per capita income:** $1,740.
**Inflation rate (1984 est.):** 15%.
**Natural resources:** Oil, natural gas, phosphates, sulfur.
**Agriculture (less than 10% of GNP):** Products—wheat, barley, rice, cotton, dates, poultry.
**Industry:** Types—petroleum, petrochemical, textile, cement.
**Trade (1984):** Exports—$10.7 billion: crude oil, dates. Major markets—Western Europe, Brazil, Japan. Imports—$12.3 billion: construction equipment, machinery, motor vehicles, agricultural commodities. Major suppliers—Japan, Western Europe, US.
**Official exchange rate (floats with US dollar):** 0.311 Iraqi dinar=US$1; 1 dinar=US$3.22.

## Membership in International Organizations

UN and some of its specialized agencies, including the World Bank, International Monetary Fund (IMF), International Atomic Energy Agency (IAEA); Nonaligned Movement; Organization of the Islamic Conference (OIC); Arab League; Organization of Petroleum Exporting Countries (OPEC); Organization of Arab Petroleum Exporting Countries (OAPEC); INTELSAT.

# GEOGRAPHY

Iraq is bordered by Kuwait, Iran, Turkey, Syria, Jordan, and Saudi Arabia. The country slopes from mountains 3,000 meters (10,000 ft.) above sea level along the border with Iran and Turkey to reedy marshes in the southeast. Much of the land is desert or wasteland.

The mountains in the northeast are an extension of the alpine system that runs eastward from the Balkans into southern Turkey, northern Iraq, Iran, and Afghanistan, terminating in the Himalayas.

Average temperatures range from higher than 48°C (120°F) in July and August to below freezing in January. Most of the rainfall occurs from December through April and averages between 10 and 18 centimeters (4-7 in.) annually.

# PEOPLE

Almost 75% of Iraq's population live in the flat, alluvial plain stretching southeast toward Baghdad and Basra to the Persian Gulf. The Tigris and Euphrates Rivers carry about 70 million cubic meters of silt annually to the delta. Known in ancient times as Mesopotamia, the region is the legendary locale of the Garden of Eden. The ruins of Ur, Babylon, and other ancient cities are here.

Iraq's two largest ethnic groups are Arabs and Kurds. Other distinct groups are Assyrians, Turkomans Iranians, Lurs, and Armenians. Arabic is the most commonly spoken language. Kurdish is spoken in the north and English is the most commonly spoken Western language.

Most Iraqi Muslims are members of the Shi'a sect, but there is a large Sunni population as well, made up of both Arabs and Kurds. Small communities of Christians Jews, Bahais, Mandaeans, and Yezidis also exist. Most Kurds are Sunni Muslim but differ from their Arab neighbors in language, dress, and customs.

# HISTORY

Once known as Mesopotamia, Iraq was the site of flourishing ancient civilizations, including the Sumerian, Babylonian, and Parthian cultures. Muslims conquered Iraq in the seventh century A.D. In the eighth century, the Abassid caliphate established its capital at Baghdad, which became a famous center of learning and the arts. By 1638, Baghdad had become a frontier outpost of the Ottoman Empire.

At the end of World War I, Iraq became a British-mandated territory. When it was declared independent in 1932, the Hashemite family, which also ruled in Jordan, ruled as a constitutional monarchy. In 1945, Iraq joined the United Nations and became a founding member of the Arab League. In 1956, the Baghdad pact allied Iraq, Turkey, Iran, Pakistan, and the United Kingdom, and established its headquarters in Baghdad.

Gen. Abdul Karim Qasim took power in a July 1958 coup, during which King Faysal II and Prime Minister Nuri as-Said were killed. Qasim ended Iraq's membership in the Baghdad Pact (later reconstituted as the Central Treaty Organization— CENTO) in 1959. Qasim was assassinated in February 1963, when the Arab Socialist Renaissance Party (Ba'ath Party) took power under the leadership of Gen. Ahmad Hasan alBakr as prime minister and Col. Abdul Salam Arif as president.

Nine months later, Arif led a coup ousting the Ba'ath government. In April 1966, Arif was killed in a plane crash and was succeeded by his brother, Gen. Abdul Rahman Mohammad Arif. On July 17, 1968, a group of Ba'athists and military elements overthrew the Arif regime. Ahmad Hasan al-Bakr reemerged as President of Iraq and Chairman of the Revolutionary Command Council (RCC). In July 1979, Bakr resigned, and his chosen successor, Saddam Hussein, assumed both offices.

# GOVERNMENT

The Ba'ath Party rules Iraq through the nine-member RCC, which enacts legislation by decree. The RCC's president (chief of state and supreme commander of the armed forces) is elected by a two thirds majority of the RCC. A Council of Ministers (cabinet), appointed by the RCC, has administrative and some legislative responsibilities.

A 250-member National Assembly was elected on June 20, 1980, in the first elections since the end of the monarchy. Another National Assembly election was held in October 1984. Iraq is divided into 18 provinces, each headed by a governor with extensive administrative powers.

Iraq's judicial system is based on the French model introduced during Ottoman rule and has three types of lower courts-civil, religious, and special. Special courts try broadly defined national security cases. An appellate court system and the court of cassation (court of last recourse) complete the judicial structure.

## Principal Government Officials

**For up-to-date information on Principal Government Officials, see the Chiefs of State and Cabinet Members of Foreign Governments section starting on page 1.**

# POLITICAL CONDITIONS

The Ba'ath Party controls the government. The Kurdish Democratic Party and the Kurdish Republican Party have nominally participated in a coalition government with the Ba'ath Party under the Popular Progressive National Front, but the Ba'ath Party carefully circumscribed their political activities, and are, often as not, in open rebellion against the govern-

ment. Several senior government officials are Kurds.

The Iraqi regime does not tolerate
opposition. The Communist Party
was removed from the coalition and
declared illegal in 1979. Since then,
its activities have been conducted pri-

marily in exile. The leaders of the
outlawed Da'wa (Islamic Call) Party,
which seeks to establish an Islamic
republic in Iraq, operate from exile in
Iran and other countries.

A large-scale rebellion by elements of
the Kurdish population against the

Ba'ath government ended in 1975 following the Algiers agreement
between Iraq and Iran. The Iraq-Iran
war has, sparked renewed but limited
antiregime insurgency in the Kurdish
areas of northern Iraq since 1980.
The two principal Kurdish opposition
parties are the Kurdish Democratic

Party, led by the remaining son of the late Mustafa Barzani, and the Patriotic Union of Kurdistan of Jalal Talabani.

# ECONOMY

Iraq's economy is characterized by a heavy dependence on oil exports and an emphasis on development through central planning. Prior to the outbreak of war with Iran in September 1980, Iraq's economic prospects brightened. Oil production had reached a level of 3.5 million barrels per day (b/d), and oil revenues were $21 billion in 1979 and $27 billion in 1980. At the outbreak of the war with Iran, Iraq had amassed an estimated $35 billion in foreign exchange reserves. Prewar projections of expenditures on Iraq's 1981-85 economic development plan were as high as $75 billion.

During the first weeks of the war, Iran destroyed Iraq's oil export terminals on the Persian Gulf, cutting export capacity to under 1 million b/d. Nevertheless, the Iraqi leadership initially attempted to continue its ambitious development programs while prosecuting the war. By 1983, however, reduced export earnings and the unexpectedly high cost of the war had depleted Iraq's foreign exchange reserves, despite massive infusions of aid from Arab gulf states. The government was forced to cut expenditures, restrict imports, defer payments to contractors, and seek out foreign credits and loans. By 1984, Iraq's strict austerity program, foreign government subsidies and trade credits, improved oil exports, and foreign suppliers' agreements to defer Iraq's payments had brought relative stability to the economy.

Iraq has four existing oil export pipelines: northward, via Turkey; south, via offshore terminals in the gulf; south, via Saudi Arabia; and west, via Syria. The Iran-Iraq war and Syria's alignment with Iran have prevented use of the pipelines via Syria and via offshore gulf terminals in recent years. New pipelines are planned via Turkey and Saudi Arabia.

---

## Travel Notes

**Climate and clothing:** The climate is similar to that of Arizona. Temperatures may exceed 48°C (120°F) in summer. Western clothing and shoes are not readily available. Dress conservatively in public.

**Customs:** All foreigners must have a visa. Check requirements with the Iraqi Embassy, 1801 P St. NW., Washington, DC 20036, tel. 202-483-7500. Yellow fever inoculations are required of travelers coming from infected areas. Health requirements and currency import restrictions may change; check latest information.

**Health:** Baghdad's facilities suffice for uncomplicated medical and surgical problems. Doctors are generally overworked and facilities overcrowded. Malaria suppressants are recommended.

**Telecommunications:** Long-distance calls within Iraq and to points abroad can sometimes be made but with considerable difficulty. Telex service is available, but prolonged outrages are common. Iraq is eight time zones ahead of eastern standard time, except during brief periods between US and Iraqi conversion dates to daylight or standard time.

All communications media are controlled or owned by the government. Two television stations are located in Baghdad but carry few English-language programs. The Baghdad Observer is a daily English-language newspaper.

**Transportation:** International flight schedules change without notice. AlBasrah and Umm Qasr Seaports are closed because of proximity to the war zone. A railroad connects Al-Basrah to Baghdad, but the Syrian segment of the railroad linking Iraq to Turkey and Europe has been closed since 1982. Border crossing points between Iraq and Syria and Iraq and Iran are closed. Paved highways connect mayor cities and neighboring countries. Some highways have severely deteriorated due to increased use by heavy military and commercial vehicles.

Buses and taxis provide good local transportation; taxi fares are negotiable. All vehicles must be covered by third-party personal injury insurance.

**Hotel accommodations:** Baghdad has modern, world-class hotels.

**Travel Advice:** For up-to-date information from the U.S. State Department on possible inconvenient or hazardous situations, see the **Travel Warnings and Consular Information Sheets from the U.S. Government** section starting on page 1723. For the latest information on health requirements and conditions, see the **Health Information for International Travel** section starting on page 1385. For further information dealing with nonurgent matter, see the **Tips for Travelers to...** section starting on page 1588.

---

Economic performance deteriorated again in 1986 because of the sharp decline in world oil prices. Although completion in 1985 of an oil pipeline through Saudi Arabia raised oil export capacity, oil revenues decreased due to lower prices. Estimates of Iraq's 1986 oil revenues are as low as $8.8 billion. The Iraqi Government has responded by implementing additional austerity measures and seeking agreements to reschedule foreign debt payments.

## Petroleum

The petroleum sector dominates the Iraqi economy. Iraq claimed proven oil reserves of 79.5 billion barrels at the end of 1986 and estimated natural gas reserves of 28.8 trillion cubic feet. Petroleum accounts for 32% of nominal GNP and represents 99% of Iraq's merchandise exports. Production capacity has remained virtually intact despite the war, but actual production was cut sharply early in the war because of damage to Iraq's export facilities. Iran's destruction of Iraqi oil export platforms in late 1980 reduced Iraq's export capacity by almost 3 million b/d. Syria closed another Iraqi export pipeline in April 1982, further reducing exports to about one-Fifth of prewar levels, or 650,000 b/d.

Wartime production levels have increased gradually since 1982 to around 1.8 million b/d in 1986. Iraq's first—and until 1985 its only—functioning oil export pipeline (through Turkey) was upgraded in 1984, and exports recovered to about 1.1 million b/d. In September 1985, work was completed on a spur line connecting

Iraq's oil fields with Saudi Arabia's pipeline to the Red Sea. This line (Phase I of the Iraqi-Saudi pipeline) boosted the country's export capacity to 1.5 million b/d. Phase II of the Saudi pipeline, under construction, will consist of an independent pipeline running to the Red Sea. In 1990, when Phase II is completed, Iraq's oil export capacity through Saudi Arabia should increase to 1.5 million b/d. The inauguration of a second Turkish pipeline in August 1987 is expanding export capacity through Turkey to 1.5 million b/d.

The recent weakness in the oil market and the uncertainty surrounding future demand for oil cast a shadow over Iraq's plans for increased production. At the 1982 London OPEC (Organization of Petroleum Exporting Countries) meeting, Iraq accepted a production quota of 1.2 million b/d. This figure was revised to more than 2 million b/d in 1985. More recently, Iraq was allocated a quota of 1.466 million b/d at the December 1986 OPEC meeting. However, the Iraqis have said that they recognize no quota restraints and that they will produce whatever amount best serves their national interest.

Oil refining capacity has expanded during the war to exceed 400,000 b/d, although actual refinery output is probably no higher than 350,000 b/d. With domestic consumption estimated at only 300,000 b/d, Iraq was able to begin exporting refined products, primarily fuel oils, in 1983.

The Iraq Petroleum Company (IPC), a consortium of Western companies that first discovered oil in Iraq in 1927, was nationalized in 1972 after a decade of disputes over concession rights. The March 1973 IPC agreement resolved the major problems between Iraq and Western oil companies. After the October 1973 Arab-Israeli war, Iraq nationalized part of the only remaining Western-owned petroleum interest, the Basra Petroleum Company (BPC). Nationalization of the BPC-and thus of all foreign oil interests in Iraq-was completed on December 8, 1975, when the remaining French and British holdings were taken over. Final agreement on com-

## Further Information

These titles are provided as a general indication of material published on this country. The Department of State does not endorse unofficial publications.

Abu Jaber, Kamel S. *The Arab Ba'th Socialist Party: History, Ideology & Organization*. Syracuse: Syracuse University Press, 1966.

Batatu, Hanna. *The Old Social Classes and the Revolutionary Movement of Iraq*. Princeton: Princeton University Press, 1978.

Fernea, Elizabeth Warnock. *Guest of the Sheikh*. Garden City, N.Y.: Doubleday, 1969.

Ghareeb, Edmund. *The Kurdish Question in Iraq*. Syracuse: Syracuse University Press, 1981.

Grummon, Stephen R. *The Iran-Iraq War: Islam Embattled*. New York: Praeger Publishers, 1982.

Helms, Christine Moss. *Iraq: Eastern Flank of the Arab World*. Washington, D.C.: Brookings Institute, 1984.

Khadduri, Majid. *Independent Iraq 1932-1958*. New York: Oxford University Press, 1960.

___. *Republican Iraq*. New York: Oxford University Press, 1969.

___. *Socialist Iraq*. Washington, D.C.: The Middle East Institute, 1978.

Marr, Phebe. *The Modem History of Iraq*. Boulder: Westview Press, 1985.

Penrose, Edith and E.F. *Iraq, International Relations and National Development*. Boulder: Westview Press, 1978.

Thesiger, Wilfred. *The Marsh Arabs*. New York: Penguin, 1967.

*War in the Gulf*. United States Senate Foreign Relations Committee Staff Report. Washington, D.C.: August 1984.

Young, Gavin. *Land of Two Rivers*. London: Collins, 1980.

Available from the Superintendent of Documents, US Government Printing Office, Washington, DC 20402:

American University: *Iraq, A Country Study*. Richard 8. Nyrop, ed. 1979.

pensation for these interests was reached in 1979.

The Ba'ath Party makes ultimate petroleum policy decisions, while the Ministry of Oil manages routine operations and marketing. The Minister of Oil also heads the Iraq National Oil Company, created in 1964 to operate in areas confiscated from the IPC.

Iraq uses primarily Western technology in its petroleum-related projects. Under service contracts, foreign companies are involved in exploration and other technical operations and in construction of new facilities. Recent projects have included refinery expansion, construction of pipelines and storage facilities, and gas-gathering and utilization projects designed to make use of large quantities of petroleum-associated gas, 75% of which is currently flared.

## Agriculture

Despite its abundant land and water resources, Iraq is a net food importer. It exports limited quantities of fruits, such as dates, but imports large quantities of grains, meat, poultry, and dairy products. The government abolished its farm collectivization program in 1981, allowing a greater role for private enterprise in agriculture. The Agricultural Cooperative Bank, capitalized at nearly $1 billion by 1984, targets its low-interest, low-collateral loans to private farmers for mechanization, poultry projects, and orchard development. Large modern cattle, dairy, and poultry farms are under construction. Obstacles to agricultural development include labor shortages, inadequate management and maintenance, salinization, urban migration, and dislocations resulting from previous land reform and collectivization programs. Importation of foreign workers and increased entry of women into traditionally male labor roles have helped compensate for agricultural and industrial labor shortages exacerbated by the war.

# TRADE

The Iran-Iraq war reversed Iraq's foreign trade balance from a large surplus into a severe deficit, which topped $7 billion in 1982. In 1983, reducing the trade deficit became Iraq's primary goal. Under strict austerity, Iraqi imports fell to $10-$11 billion annually in 1983-85, about half the 1982 figure. The sharp

**Babylon Wall. The ancient Babylonians ruled Mesopotamia (the ancient name of Iraq) until 1550 B.C. when Babylon was destroyed.**

decline in imports, combined in a steady rise in oil exports in 1984-85, reduced the trade deficit to about $1 billion by the end of 1985. However, the sharp drop in oil prices in 1985-86 had severely affected Iraq's terms of trade, once again producing a large trade deficit.

The dollar volume in U.S. exports to Iraq peaked in 1981 at $916 million. Exports fell to $511 million in 1983, and after recovering to $664 million in 1984, dropped to $427 million in 1985. Agricultural sales, boosted by a sizable Commodity Credit Corporation (CCC) program of credits and guarantees beginning in 1983-84, have dominated U.S. exports to Iraq. The Iraqis used nearly $400 million in credit guarantees under the CCC program during FY 1986, and were extended $700 million in credit guarantees under the program in 1987.

# DEFENSE

The war with Iran has caused the Iraqi Government to expand significantly the size of its armed forces and the paramilitary "People's Army" affiliated with the Ba'ath Party. President Saddam Hussein, commander in chief of the Iraqi Armed Forces, assumed the rank of field marshal in 1980, following the outbreak of the war. However, Defense Minister Adnan Khairallah directly administers the armed forces, and First Deputy Prime Minister Taha Yassin Ramadan commands the People's Army. The regular armed forces are deployed almost entirely against Iran. The People's Army also has been used at the front but performs primarily internal security functions or rear-echelon military tasks. Formerly dependent upon the Soviet bloc for its arms supplies, in the mid-1970s Iraq began to seek Western suppliers in order to diversify its sources. In recent years, France has become Iraq's leading source of arms after the Soviet Union.

# FOREIGN RELATIONS

Iraqi-Iranian relations improved following the March 1975 Algiers agreement that ended the Kurdish rebellion and provided for border adjustments. Iraq claims that the Shah never fully implemented the agreement, and it initially welcomed the accession of Iran's revolutionary government in 1979. However, Ira-

nian Shi'ite fundamentalist leader Ayatollah Khomeini, bitter over years of confined exile in Iraq, attempted to incite opposition to Baghdad's secular government. Iraq claims that its September 1980 invasion of Iran was in response to a series of border incidents, Iranian-backed assassination attempts, and Iran's failure to honor its 1975 treaty commitments on border adjustments and the Shatt al-Arab waterway. The outbreak of the war stopped all Iraqi shipping and oil exports via the gulf. From June 1982, when Iraqi forces withdrew from substantially all undisputed Iranian territory, through spring 1987, successive bloody land engagements led to limited territorial losses for Iraq but have not changed the larger strategic stalemate.

Iraq accepted UN Security Council Resolution 540 of October 1983, subject to Iranian acceptance. After Iran rejected this resolution, which called among other things for a cease-fire against shipping and ports, Iraq stepped up attacks on Iranian ports and ships serving them. Iran retaliated against ships serving neutral ports. The resulting "tanker war" persisted with increasing intensity during 1986. In March 1984 and repeatedly thereafter, the United States condemned Iraq's use of chemical weapons, which Iraq continued to deny. Major Iranian campaigns against Iraqi forces took place in 1984, 1985, and 1986. In February 1986, Iran seized a segment of Iraqi territory around the abandoned peninsular port city of al-Faw. In 1985-86, Iran launched occasional missile attacks on Baghdad in response to Iraqi air strikes on targets inside Iran. From July to October 1986, Iraq conducted its first sustained campaign of air attacks on Iranian oil export facilities, refineries, and electrical power installations. In January 1987, Iran launched an attack east of Basra that brought Iranian forces to within close artillery range of that city, Iraq's second largest.

Iraq has accepted all UN cease-fire resolutions, including UN Security Council Resolution 582 of February 1986, as well as all mediation efforts and other peace initiatives by the

Nonaligned Movement, the Organization of the Islamic Conference (OIC), and others. Through mid 1987, Iran regime continued to reject all such mediation initiatives, demanding the ouster of the Government of Iraq as a precondition for a settlement. Despite future changes in regimes or an eventual end to hostilities, antagonisms probably will persist, and the two countries are likely to maintain their historic rivalry for regional influence.

Iraq participated in the Arab-Israeli wars of 1948, 1967 and 1973, and traditionally has opposed all attempts to reach a peaceful settlement between Israel and the Arab states. Israel attacked Iraq's nuclear research reactor under construction near Baghdad in July 1981. In recent years, however, Iraq has modified its stance significantly. In August 1982, President Hussein stated to a visiting U.S. Congressman that "a secure state is necessary for both Israel and the Palestinians." Iraq did not oppose President Reagan's September 1, 1982, Arab-Israeli peace initiative, and it supported the moderate Arab position at the Fez summit that same month. Since 1982, Iraq has reiterated that it will support whatever settlement is found acceptable by the Palestinians, adding that it views a Palestinian relationship with Jordan as both a natural and necessary." In recent years, declaring a national interest in regional stability, Iraq has called for the withdrawal of all foreign forces from Lebanon and for normalization of Egyptian-Arab relations despite Egypt's peace treaty with Israel. Although the Iran-Iraq war has preoccupied Iraq since 1980, the Arab-Israeli conflict will continue to exercise an important influence on Iraq's international orientation.

Iraq's relations within the Arab world have been extremely varied. Egypt broke relations with Iraq in 1977, following Iraq's criticism of President Anwar Sadat's peace initiatives. In 1978, Baghdad hosted an Arab League summit that condemned and ostracized Egypt for accepting the Camp David accords. However, Egypt's strong material and diplomatic support for Iraq in the war with

Iran has led to warmer relations and numerous contacts between senior officials, despite the continued absence of ambassadorial-level representation. Since 1983, Iraq has repeatedly called for restoration of Egypt's "natural role" among Arab countries. In January 1984, Iraq successfully led Arab efforts within the OIC to restore Egypt's membership.

Relations with Syria have been marred by traditional rivalry for preeminence in Arab affairs, allegations of involvement in each other's internal politics, and disputes over the waters of the Euphrates River, oil transit fees, and stances toward Israel. Relations with Syria and Libya have been even more antagonistic since the wartime alignment of those countries with Iran though Iraq and Libya have recently taken steps to improve relations.

Iraq's relations with Jordan have improved significantly since 1980, when Jordan declared its support for Iraq at the outset of the Iran-Iraq war. Relations with Saudi Arabia, Kuwait, and other Arab states of the gulf also have become closer.

Iraq has diplomatic relations with almost all communist countries except North Korea, which is a leading supplier of arms to Iran. In April 1972, Iraq and the Soviet Union signed a treaty of friendship and cooperation that was renewed in 1987. The scope of Soviet-Iraqi relations has been limited, however, by the increasing diversification of Iraq's arms suppliers, intense Iraqi nationalism and adherence to the concept of nonalignment, and the anti-government activities of the outlawed, Soviet-backed Communist Party of Iraq.

Iraq has diplomatic relations with Japan and with all West European countries. Its commercial and political relations with the industrialized democracies are generally extensive. Iraq also has developed a major military supply relationship with France.

The war forced postponement and transfer of the summit conference of nonaligned states scheduled for

Baghdad in September 1982, frustrating Iraq's expectation to become leader of the Nonaligned Movement. Nevertheless, Iraq continues to play an active role among those countries.

# U.S.-IRAQI RELATIONS

Iraq broke diplomatic relations with the United States during the June 1967 Arab-Israeli war. In November 1984, President Reagan and visiting Iraqi Deputy Prime Minister Tariq Aziz announced the resumption of full diplomatic relations between their two countries, and the U.S. Interests Section in Baghdad, under the Belgian flag since its establishment in 1972, was upgraded to embassy status. The Iraqi Embassy, which had functioned as an Interests Section under the protection of India, simultaneously reverted to its former status.

## Principal U.S. Officials

**For up-to-date information on Principal U.S. Officials, see the U.S. Embassies, Consulates, and Foreign Service section starting on page 139.**

The U.S. Embassy is located in the Masbah Quarter, Baghdad, opposite the Foreign Ministry Club (tel. 7196138/6139). The work week is Sunday through Thursday.

## EDITOR'S UPDATE
## Dec. 1994–May 2000

*A report on important events that have taken place since the last State Department revision of this Background Note.*

Iraqi courts moved quickly and severely for two Americans working in Kuwait who blundered over the border into Iraq.

On March 17, 1995, Iraqi forces arrested the men, who wandered over the border while trying to visit friends nearby in Kuwait. The McDonnell Douglas Corp. employees, David Daliberti and Bill Barloon, said they got lost and crossed the border by accident.

Since the United States and Iraq have no diplomatic ties, America had to work through officials of the United Nations and Poland to petition for the men's release. The efforts went for naught, however, and on March 23, an Iraqi court sentenced the men to eight years in prison on charges of entering Iraq illegally. The Clinton Administration condemned the severity of the sentences.

The United States said it would take diplomatic channels in pressing for the men's release. It denied an allegation that they had entered Iraq as saboteurs or spies. The Polish diplomat representing the United States in Iraq was allowed weekly visits with the men to check on their welfare.

Iraq and the United Nations temporarily halted negotiations on April 24, 1996 on a plan that would permit Iraq to sell a limited quantity of oil in order to purchase food and supplies for Iraqi citizens. American and British envoys reiterated their desire for an agreement on the issue, but said they want to avoid weakening current economic sanctions against Iraq or allowing Iraqi President Saddam Hussein to advance his goals.

Specifically, the United States and Britain want money earmarked for Iraq's Kurdish provinces funneled through the existing United Nations assistance program there. They raised the issue of equity with respect to Iraq's existing rationing system, which handles food distribution. The United States and Britain are also opposed to Iraq's selecting the bank into which oil payments are made and from which letters of credit would be issued to pay for essential supplies.

Jordan disclosed on March 7, 1996 that it had seized aircraft spare parts and other supplies destined for Iraq in violation of United Nations sanctions. According to acting Information Minister, Mohammed Daoudiyeh, the 450-pound shipment, tagged as "agricultural equipment," arrived from Warsaw, was confiscated at Queen Alia International Airport in Amman and handed over to a private Jordanian-Iraqi company. He did not elaborate. An Iraqi representative of the company, Mohammed Abdul-Salam, claimed the shipment did not include military equipment. The Iraqi Embassy refused to discuss the matter. Baghdad claims it is cooperating with United Nations resolutions mandating dismantling of certain Iraqi weapons and missile programs.

The announcement came as the United Nations Security Council convened on March 7 in New York and extended economic sanctions against Iraq following a two-month review. However, the UN agreed late last year to allow Iraq to export $2 billion in oil to buy food and medical supplies. Iraq began receiving 400,000 tons of wheat in the spring of 1997.

Also in 1997, the UN took no action against Iraq for flying religious pilgrims to and from Saudi Arabia in defiance of UN-imposed "no-fly" zones. Saddam Hussein's order that planes and helicopters ferry 100 pilgrims to the Saudi border was not seen as a serious breach of UN sanctions.

In an effort to boost morale in Iraq and bolster its image abroad, Iraq conducted its first parliamentary elections since 1989. However, only candidates loyal to Saddam Hussein were allowed to run.

The 250-seat Parliament is essentially impotent and invariably supports Hussein. A Government screening committee reviewed and approved all 689 candidates who either belonged to Hussein's Baath Party or were independents who supported the 1968 coup that brought the party to power.

The United Nations commenced a fourth round of talks May 6, 1996 on a deal that would permit Iraq to sell a limited quantity of oil to pay for critical civilian needs.

The talks began shortly after the United Nations Security Council extended for sixty days blanket sanctions that have seriously damaged the Iraq economy. The two issues are not directly related but diplomats said the strong consensus on the sanctions' renewal should dissuade the Iraqis from allowing the oil-for-food negotiations to fall through, since it is unlikely that the unrestricted sale of Iraqi oil will be possible in the near term. The plan, proposed by the Security Council in 1995 in response to criticism that sanctions were hurting the poorest and most vulnerable Iraqis, would allow Iraq to sell $1 billion in oil in renewable 90-day periods. The sanctions have prohibited Iraq from selling oil on the global market in major transactions since its invasion of Kuwait in 1990. Current restrictions permit Iraq to export some oil for food and medicine.

US and other forces in the Persian Gulf region currently keep a close eye on Iraq. According to US and United Nations officials, some oil is transported secretly to markets with the assistance of Iran but the quantity does not come close to violating the 1990 sanctions. A report recently delivered by the Clinton Administration to Congress reported that ships transporting $1.1 million in petroleum products and $1.4 million in dates had been intercepted in recent months.

The White House regularly updates Congress on Iraqi adherence with sanctions.

The Security Council cannot drop broader sanctions against Iraq until Iraq has destroyed or otherwise accounted for all of its weapons of mass annihilation. Recent revelations that Iraq had consistently provided falsified its accounting, and numerous incidents of non-cooperation with United Nations arms inspectors in 1996 have fueled further distrust of Iraq in the Security Council.

In late 1997, Mr. Hussein banned ten American citizens from conducting weapons inspections mandated by the United Nations. The Americans were members of the UN weapons-inspection team (UNSCOM) operating in Iraq. By authority of the UN, the inspectors were entitled to immediate access to any site suspected of containing chemical, biological, or nuclear materials that could be used to construct offensive weapons. In January 1998, the United States responded to the impasse by sending 20 ships and 30,000 troops to the Persian Gulf to prompt Mr. Hussein to comply to the UN Security Council's resolutions. Tensions mounted between the two countries, and a military strike seemed imminent. In February 1998 the secretary-general of the UN, Kofi Annan, went to Iraq and was able to persuade the Iraqi government to comply with the UN Security Council's resolutions. By April, however, the UN reported that Iraq had not made any progress in meeting the requirements to verify disarmament.

Throughout 1998, Iraqi officials continued to thwart the arms inspections efforts of UNSCOM. In late December, following a report by UNSCOM chief Richard Butler which cited continuing Iraqi violations, the United States and Great Britain mounted air strikes against Iraqi installations. Air strikes resumed in early 1999 as Iraq continued to violate the no-fly zone on almost a daily basis.

Iraqi opposition to Mr. Hussein's regime also expressed itself in February 1999 following the assassination of popular Shia cleric, Grand Ayatollah Muhammad el Sadr. Demonstrations by Shias ensued and garnered the support of numbers of Sunnis in the north. However, forces loyal to President Hussein soon stamped out the demonstrations, thus indicating the regime's continuing reliance upon repression to remain in power.

By April 2000 the trade sanctions imposed by the UN Security Council had reduced Iraq's economy to a shambles. The oil for food program has failed to provide Iraq with sufficient resources to provide for its people. UNICEF estimates are that 500,000 children under five have died since 1991. Factories and businesses have shut down, the power supply is intermittent, telephone service is unreliable, and food and medical supplies are severely limited. The Iraqi authorities estimate that over a million people have died because of the embargo, a number that has been questioned by western authorities.

# IRELAND
July 2000

**Official Name:**
**Ireland**

## PROFILE

### Geography

**Area:** 70,282 sq. km. (27,136 sq. mi.); slightly larger than West Virginia.
**Cities:** Capital—Dublin (pop. 1,058,264—somewhat less than one-third the total population). Other cities—Cork (127,187), Galway (57,241), Limerick (52,039), Waterford, (42,540).
**Terrain:** Arable 10%, meadows and pastures 77%, rough grazing in use 11%, inland water 2%.
**Climate:** Temperate maritime.

### People

**Nationality:** Noun—Irishman, Irishwoman. Adjective—Irish.
**Population:** 3.7 million.
**Ethnic Groups:** Irish, with English minority.
**Religion:** Roman Catholic 91.6%; Church of Ireland 2.3%; other 6.1%.
**Languages:** English, Irish (Gaelic).
**Education:** Compulsory up to age 16. Enrollment rates—5-14 year olds—100%; 15 year olds, 96%; 16 year olds, 92%. Literacy—98%-99%.
**Health:** Infant mortality rate—5.5/1,000. Life expectancy at birth—male 73.0 yrs., female 78.7 yrs.
**Work force:** Services—56%; industry—29%; agriculture—10%; government—5%.

### Government

**Type:** Parliamentary republic.
**Independence:** 1921.
**Constitution:** December 29, 1937.
**Branches:** Executive—president, chief of state; prime minister (Taoiseach—pronounced "TEE-shock"), head of government. Legislative—bicameral National Parliament (Oireachtas—pronounced "o-ROCK-tas") House of Representatives (Dail—pronounced "DOIL") and Senate (Seanad—pronounced "SHAN-ad"). Judicial—Supreme Court.
**Administrative subdivisions:** 26 counties, 34 local authorities.
**Major political parties:** Fianna Fail, Fine Gael, Labor, Progressive Democrats, Green Party, Sinn Fein.
**Suffrage:** Universal over 18.

### Economy

**GNP at market prices:** (2000) $81.97 billion (estimate).
**Annual growth rate:** (2000) 7.0% (estimate). Per capita income: $21,887 (estimate).
**Natural resources:** Zinc, lead, natural gas, barite, copper, gypsum, limestone, dolomite, peat.
**Agriculture:** (8% of GNP) Products—cattle, meat, and dairy products; potatoes; barley; sugarbeets; hay; silage; wheat.
**Industry:** (43% of GNP) Types—food processing, beverages, engineering, computer equipment, textiles and clothing, chemicals, pharmaceuticals, construction.
**Trade:** (1999) Exports—$70.2 billion (excluding services) computer equipment, chemicals, meat, dairy products, machinery. Major markets—U.K. 22%, other EU countries 43%, U.S. 15.2%. Imports—$46.3 billion (excluding services) grains, petroleum products, machinery, transport equipment, chemicals, textile yarns. Major suppliers—U.K. 32%, other EU countries 22%, U.S. 15.8%.

## PEOPLE AND HISTORY

The Irish people are mainly of Celtic origin, with the country's only significant sized minority having descended from the Anglo-Normans. English is the common language, but Irish (Gaelic) also is an official language and is taught in the schools.

A national literature in Irish is reemerging. Anglo-Irish writers, including Swift, Sheridan, Goldsmith, Burke, Wilde, Joyce, Yeats, Shaw, and Beckett, have made a major contribution to world literature over the past 300 years. What little is known of pre-Christian Ireland comes from a few references in Roman writings, Irish poetry and myth, and archaeology. The earliest inhabitants—people of a mid-Stone Age culture—arrived about 6000 BC, when the climate had become hospitable following the retreat of the polar icecaps. About 4,000 years later, tribes from southern Europe arrived and established a high Neolithic culture, leaving behind gold ornaments and huge stone monuments for archaeologists. This culture apparently prospered, and the island became more densely populated. The Bronze Age people, who arrived during the next 1,000 years, produced elaborate gold and bronze ornaments and weapons.

The Iron Age arrived abruptly in the fourth century BC with the invasion of the Celts, a tall, energetic people who had spread across Europe and Great Britain in the preceding centuries. The Celts, or Gaels, and their more numerous predecessors divided into five kingdoms in which, despite constant strife, a rich culture flourished. This pagan society was dominated by druids—priests who served as educators, physicians, poets, diviners, and keepers of the laws and histories.

But the coming of Christianity from across the Irish Sea brought major changes and civilizing influences. Tradition maintains that in 432 AD, St. Patrick arrived on the island and, in the years that followed, worked to convert the Irish to Christianity. Probably a Celt himself, St. Patrick preserved the tribal and social patterns of the Irish, codifying their laws and changing only those that conflicted with Christian practices. He also introduced the Roman alphabet, which enabled Irish monks to preserve parts of the extensive Celtic oral literature.

The pagan druid tradition collapsed in the face of the spread of the new faith, and Irish scholars excelled in the study of Latin learning and Christian theology in the monasteries that shortly flourished. Missionaries from Ireland to England and the continent spread news of the flowering of learning, and scholars from other nations came to Irish monasteries. The excellence and isolation of these monasteries helped preserve Latin learning during the Dark Ages. The arts of manuscript illumination, metalworking, and sculpture flourished and produced such treasures as

## Travel Notes

**Travel Advice:** For up-to-date information from the U.S. State Department on possible inconvenient or hazardous situations, see the **Travel Warnings and Consular Information Sheets from the U.S. Government** section starting on page 1723. For the latest information on health requirements and conditions, see the **International Travelers' Health Information** section starting on page 1385. For further information dealing with non-urgent matter, see the **Tips for Travelers to...** section starting on page 1588.

the Book of Kells, ornate jewelry, and the many carved stone crosses that dot the island.

This golden age of culture was interrupted by 200 years of intermittent warfare with waves of Viking raiders who plundered monasteries and towns. The Vikings established Dublin and other seacoast towns but were eventually defeated. Although the Irish were subsequently free from foreign invasion for 150 years, internecine clan warfare continued to drain their energies and resources.

In the 12th century, Pope Adrian IV granted overlordship of the island to Henry II of England, who began an epic struggle between the Irish and the English which not only burned intermittently for 800 years but which continues to affect Irish politics and bilateral relations to this day. The Reformation exacerbated the oppression of the Roman Catholic Irish, and, in the early 17th century, Scottish and English Protestants were sent as colonists to the north of Ireland and the Pale around Dublin.

From 1800 to 1921, Ireland was an integral part of the United Kingdom. Religious freedom was restored in 1829. But this victory for the Irish Catholic majority was overshadowed by severe economic depression and mass famine from 1846-48 when the potato crop failed. The famine spawned the first mass wave of Irish emigration to the United States. A decade later, in 1858, the Irish Republican Brotherhood (IRB—also known as the Fenians) was founded

as a secret society dedicated to armed rebellion against the British. An above-ground political counterpart, the Home Rule Movement, was created in 1874, advocating constitutional change for independence. Galvanized by the leadership of Charles Stewart Parnell, the party was able to force British governments after 1885 to introduce several home rule bills. The turn of the century witnessed a surge of interest in Irish nationalism, including the founding of Sinn Fein ("Ourselves Alone") as an open political movement.

Nationalism was and is a potent populist force in Irish politics. The outbreak of war in Europe in 1914 put home rule efforts on hold, and, in reaction, Padraic Pearse and James Connolly led the unsuccessful Easter Rising of 1916. The decision by the British-imposed court structure to execute the leaders of the rebellion, coupled with the British Government's threat of conscription, alienated public opinion and produced massive support for Sinn Fein in the 1918 general election. Under the leadership of Eamon de Valera, the elected Sinn Fein deputies constituted themselves as the first Dail. Tensions only increased: British attempts to smash Sinn Fein ignited the Anglo-Irish War of 1919-1921.

The end of the war brought the Anglo-Irish treaty of 1921, which established the Irish Free State of 26 counties within the British Commonwealth and recognized the partition of the island into Ireland and Northern Ireland, though supposedly as a temporary measure. The six predominantly Protestant counties of northeast Ulster—Northern Ireland—remained a part of the United Kingdom with limited self-government. A significant Irish minority repudiated the treaty settlement because of the continuance of subordinate ties to the British monarch and the partition of the island. This opposition led to further hostilities—a civil war (1922-23), which was won by the pro-treaty forces.

In 1932, Eamon de Valera, the political leader of the forces initially opposed to the treaty, became prime minister, and a new Irish constitution was enacted in 1937. The last British military bases were soon withdrawn, and the ports were returned to Irish control. Ireland was neutral in World War II. The government formally declared Ireland a republic in 1948; however, it does not normally use the term "Republic of Ireland," which tacitly acknowledges the partition but refers to the country simply as "Ireland."

# U.S.-IRISH RELATIONS

U.S. relations with Ireland have long been based on common ancestral ties and on similar values and political views. These relations, however, have now broadened and matured, given the substantial U.S. corporate involvement in the Irish economy. The United States seeks to maintain and strengthen the traditionally cordial relations between the people of the United States and Ireland.

Economic and trade relations are an important element of the bilateral relationship. U.S. investment has been a major factor in the growth of the Irish economy, and Irish membership in the European Union (EU) means that discussion of EU trade and economic policies, as well as other aspects of EU policy, are a key element in exchanges between the two countries.

Emigration, long a vital element in the U.S.-Irish relationship, has declined significantly with Ireland's economic boom in the 1990s. For the first time in its modern history, immigration to Ireland, especially of non-Europeans, is a growing phenomenon with political, economic, and social consequences. However, Irish citizens do continue the common practice of taking temporary residence overseas for work or study, mainly in the U.S., U.K., and elsewhere in Europe, before returning to establish careers in Ireland.

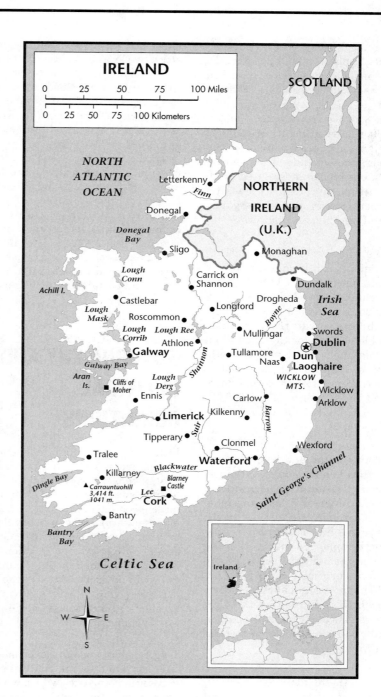

## Principal U.S. Officials

**For up-to-date information on Principal U.S. Officials, see the U.S. Embassies, Consulates, and Foreign Service section starting on page 139.**

The U.S. embassy in Ireland is located at 42 Elgin Road, Ballsbridge,

Dublin 4 (tel. 668-7122; fax 668-9946).

# ECONOMY

In 1999, trade between Ireland and the United States was worth around $18.5 billion, a 24% increase over 1998. U.S. exports to Ireland were valued at $7.72 billion, an increase of about 8% over 1998 and 16% of Ireland's total imports. The range of

U.S. products includes electrical components, computers and peripherals, drugs and pharmaceuticals, electrical equipment, and livestock feed. Irish exports to the United States grew by almost 32% over 1998 to $10.8 billion in 1999, representing about 15.5% of all Irish exports. Exports to the United States include alcoholic beverages, chemicals and related products, electronic data processing equipment, electrical machinery, textiles and clothing, and glassware.

In 1999, the recent trend of a U.S. trade deficit with Ireland continued. Overall, the value of U.S. imports from Ireland exceeded the value of U.S. exports to Ireland by $3.3 billion. Nonetheless, given the continued favorable outlook for the Irish economy, sales opportunities for U.S. producers in Ireland are expected to improve. Export-Import Bank financing and the presence of major U.S. banks in Ireland facilitate marketing by U.S. suppliers.

President Clinton and Irish Government officials have noted the important contribution toward economic and social progress American industrial investment in Ireland—north and south—has made. President Clinton has pledged to maintain the U.S. commitment to facilitate the growth of such job-creating investment. The International Fund for Ireland, which is funded by the U.S. Congress, has contributed $5 million annually to Ireland to support cross-border initiatives.

U.S. investment has been particularly important to the growth and modernization of Irish industry over the past 25 years, providing new technology, export capabilities, and employment opportunities. The stock of U.S. investment in Ireland at end-1998 was valued at $16.1 billion. Currently, there are more than 580 U.S. subsidiaries, employing almost 86,000 people and spanning activities from manufacturing of high-tech electronics, computer products, medical supplies, and pharmaceuticals to retailing, banking and finance, and other services.

Many U.S. businesses find Ireland an attractive location to manufacture for the EU market, since it is inside the EU customs area. Government policies are generally formulated to facilitate trade and inward direct investment. The availability of an educated, well-trained, English-speaking work force and relatively moderate wage costs have been important factors. Ireland offers good long-term growth prospects for U.S. companies under an innovative financial incentive program, including capital grants and favorable tax treatment, such as a low corporation income tax rate for manufacturing firms and certain financial services firms.

# GOVERNMENT AND POLITICAL CONDITIONS

Ireland is a sovereign, independent, democratic state with a parliamentary system of government. The president, who serves as chief of state in a largely ceremonial role, is elected for a 7-year term and can be re-elected only once. In carrying out certain constitutional powers and functions, the president is aided by the Council of State, an advisory body. On the Taoiseach's (prime minister's) advice, the president also dissolves the Oireachtas (Parliament).

The president appoints as prime minister the leader of the political party, or coalition of parties, which wins the most seats in the Dail (house of representatives). Executive power is vested in a cabinet whose ministers are nominated by the Taoiseach and approved by the Dail.

The bicameral Oireachtas (parliament) consists of the Seanad Eireann (senate) and the Dail Eireann (house of representatives). The Seanad is composed of 60 members—11 nominated by the prime minister, 6 elected by the national universities, and 43 elected from panels of candidates established on a vocational basis. The

Senate has the power to delay legislative proposals and is allowed 90 days to consider and amend bills sent to it by the Dail, which wields greater power in parliament. The Dail has 166 members popularly elected to a maximum term of 5 years under a complex system of proportional representation.

Judges are appointed by the president on nomination by the government and can be removed from office only for misbehavior or incapacity and then only by resolution of both houses of parliament. The ultimate court of appeal is the Supreme Court, consisting of the Chief Justice and five other justices. The Supreme Court also can decide upon the constitutionality of legislative acts if the president asks for an opinion.

Local government is by elected county councils and—in the cities of Dublin, Cork, Limerick, and Waterford—by county borough corporations. In practice, however, authority remains with the central government.

Irish politics remain dominated by the two political parties that grew out of Ireland's bitter 1922-23 civil war. Fianna Fail was formed by those who opposed the 1921 treaty that partitioned the island. Although treaty opponents lost the civil war, Fianna Fail soon became Ireland's largest political party. Fine Gael, representative of the pro-treaty forces, remains the country's second-largest party.

In recent years, however, there have been signs that this largely two-party structure is evolving. Mary Robinson of the Labour Party shocked the political establishment by winning the 1990 presidential election. Articulating a progressive agenda for Ireland's future and outspoken on social issues, Robinson represented a distinct break from the traditional politics of the two major parties. The November 1992 general election confirmed this trend. The two main parties lost ground as the Labour Party scored an historic breakthrough, winning 19% of the vote and 33 seats in the House. As a result of the election, Labour held the balance of power between the two largest parties and initially chose to go into coalition with Fianna Fail. That government collapsed in November 1994, and Labour again demonstrated its new role when it dictated the terms of a new "rainbow" government coalition with Fine Gael and the Democratic Left.

The year 1997, however, saw a return to a more traditional model. In the June general election, Labour lost heavily and was reduced to 18 seats in the Dail. Though Fianna Fail did not win an outright majority, it increased its seats to 76 (currently 75) and was able to form a coalition with the much smaller (4 seats) Progressive Democrats. Fine Gael also picked up seats but was unable to form a coalition with the much-reduced Labour party. In the November 1997 presidential election, Fianna Fail candidate Mary McAleese, a lawyer from Northern Ireland, won a record victory over four other candidates.

As a result of the 1997 elections, a minority government led by Taoiseach (prime minister) Bertie Ahern of Fianna Fail took office. Mary Harney, who heads the Progressive Democrats Party, serves as the Tanaiste (deputy prime minister) and Minister for Enterprise, Employment, and Trade. The coalition relies on the support of four independent members to give it a governing majority. In 1999, the Labour Party absorbed the smaller party of the Democratic Left, bringing its total number of seats in the Dail to 21 (currently 20).

Since coming to power, the government of Prime Minister Ahern has presided over a strong economy. Ireland boasts the highest growth rate of any country in the OECD over the last 3 years, low unemployment, and a surplus in the country's finances. However, the "Celtic Tiger's" inflation rate has edged up over the past year. To address this concern, Prime Minister Ahern has pledged action to curb inflation and, thereby, sustain sound economic growth. On the diplomatic front, the government has played a key role in brokering a lasting peace in Northern Ireland, in bolstering

Ireland's role in the European Union, and in leading Ireland to join NATO's Partnership for Peace in 1999.

Most recently, allegations of political corruption related to property development schemes, tax avoidance by business and political leaders, as well as other scandals dating back to the late 1980s and early 1990s have surfaced. The Dail has established two tribunals—the Flood Tribunal and the Moriarty Tribunal—to investigate these various scandals, and the work of the two tribunals will likely continue until 2001. Although several senior political leaders and members of parliament have been named in connection with the scandals, the government of Prime Minister Ahern remains stable, and most observers think it unlikely new general elections will be held before spring 2001.

# NORTHERN IRELAND

Resolving the Northern Ireland problem remains a leading political issue in Ireland and is a major priority in U.S. relations with Ireland. The U.S. Government is engaged with both the Irish and British Governments on ways that the U.S. can play a constructive role in supporting the peace process in the North.

The conflict in Northern Ireland stems from the division between "Nationalist" and Unionist" segments of the Northern Ireland Nationalists in Northern Ireland want unification with Ireland, while Unionists want Northern Ireland to continue its union with Great Britain.

Since the 1985 Anglo-Irish Agreement granting Ireland a formal voice in Northern Ireland affairs, there has been an extensive dialogue between the two governments on how to bring about a peaceful, democratic resolution of the conflict. In December 1993, the "Downing Street Declaration," holding out the promise of inclusive political talks on the future of Northern Ireland, was issued. This led the Irish Republican Army (IRA) to call a "total cessation" of military operations on August 31, 1994. This was

followed 6 weeks later by a similar cease-fire by the loyalist paramilitaries.

Following up on the cease-fires, the two governments in February 1995 issued a "frameworks" document, which proposed a basis for negotiations. Generally welcomed by Nationalists, it was rejected by Unionists, who disparaged it as a "blueprint for a united Ireland." Despite the negative Unionist reaction, the two governments tried to launch the negotiating process by announcing that they would hold a series of bilaterals with all the constitutional parties in the north.

The process stalled in 1995 due to disagreements between the British Government and Sinn Fein, the political arm of the IRA, about the decommissioning of IRA weapons. President Clinton's visit to Ireland in December 1995 led to the establishment later the same month of an International Commission, chaired by former U.S. Senator George Mitchell, to recommend a solution to this impasse.

The January 1996 "Mitchell Report" recommended decommissioning during a talks process and was widely praised. However, the British Government decision to hold elections for a negotiating body was seen as a step backwards, and in February 1996 the IRA officially ended its cease-fire with a bomb attack in London that killed two. At the end of February the two governments announced that all-party talks would begin in June and be open to all parties disavowing violence. In May 1996 the elections were held, with Sinn Fein doing particularly well. However, the party was turned away from the negotiations, chaired by Sen. Mitchell, when they began on June 10 because of the IRA's continued campaign of violence.

Throughout the latter half of 1996 and early 1997 the negotiations made little progress. The May 1997 election of Tony Blair and the Labour Party Government in the U.K., however, re-energized the process and led to increasing pressure on the IRA/Sinn Fein to restore the cease-fire. After gaining assurances that the negotiations process would be time-limited and that decommissioning would not again become a stumbling block, the IRA did restore its cease-fire in July 1997, and Sinn Fein was admitted to the talks process in September 1997. The negotiations moved from process into substance in October 1997. In a final marathon push in April 1998, which included the personal intervention of President Clinton, all parties, on April 10, signed an agreement. The "Good Friday" (April 10 happened to be Good Friday) Agreement was put to a vote, and strong majorities in Northern Ireland and the Republic of Ireland approved it in simultaneous referendums on May 22, 1998.

The agreement provides for a 108-member Northern Ireland elected assembly to be overseen by a 12-minister executive committee in which Unionists and Nationalists would share responsibility for governing. The agreement, which is now being implemented, also will institutionalize the cross-border cooperation with the Republic of Ireland and will create mechanisms to guarantee the rights of all. Members of the 108-seat assembly were elected on June 25. The results of the election confirm that four parties will play a dominant role in the new legislative body: the Ulster Unionist Party (UUP) won 28 seats, and the Democratic Unionist Party (DUP) won 20 seats on the Unionist side. On the Nationalist side, the Social Democratic and Labour Party (SDLP) won 24 seats and Sinn Fein, 18. Assembly members met in "shadow" mode while they prepared the procedures and modalities of the new legislative body, which assumed governing responsibilities in 1999. Following the election, the Northern Ireland Executive was created, headed by First Minister David Trimble (UUP), and Deputy

Minister Seamus Mallon (SDLP) emerged in December 1999.

The issue of decommissioning has proven to be a stumbling block that, for a time, thwarted effective implementation of the Good Friday Agreement. When the UUP threatened to pull out of the powersharing Executive in February 2000 over what the UUP charged was the IRA's failure to disarm in accordance with the commitments made in the Belfast Agreement, the British Government suspended Northern Ireland's local governing body. In so doing, it sought to prevent both sides from renouncing the 1998 Good Friday Agreement altogether. Nevertheless, a substantial majority of Catholics and Protestants in Northern Ireland and in the Republic of Ireland continued to support the peace process throughout the 72-day impasse.

British Prime Minister Tony Blair and Irish Prime Minister Bertie Ahern mediated a series of talks aimed at the restoration of the Northern Ireland Executive, as high-level engagement on the part of Ireland, the United Kingdom, and the United States continued. Finally, on May 6, 2000, the IRA pledged to put its arms completely and verifiably "beyond use" in a groundbreaking statement on decommissioning. David Trimble, as leader of the Ulster Unionist Party (UUP), welcomed the statement and rallied support for his party's return to the Executive. In a divided vote, 459 in favor to 403 against, the UUP decided to resume its involvement. On May 29, 2000, the British Government restored direct rule to Northern Ireland. President Clinton hailed the resumption of Northern Ireland's home rule as an important step toward the "promise of peace."

Although the reestablishment of the Executive has further reinforced pop-

ular and political support for the Good Friday Agreement, significant challenges persist. Splinter groups opposed to the peace process have committed terrorist attacks in Northern Ireland and in mainland Britain on several occasions since the Belfast Agreement was signed. The worst of these attacks took place in Omagh, Co. Tyrone in August 1998 when 29 people were killed and hundreds seriously injured. Other divisive issues that have yet to be resolved include carrying out the Patten Commission's recommendations on reform of the Royal Ulster Constabulary (Northern Ireland's police force), as well as the emotive issue of flying British and Irish flags over public buildings on holidays and special occasions. U.S. Government policy on Northern Ireland condemns all acts of terrorism and violence, perpetrated by any party on either side. It also cautions all Americans to question closely any appeal for financial or other aid from groups involved in the Northern Ireland conflict to ensure that contributions do not end up in the hands of those who support violence, either directly or indirectly.

## Principal Government Officials

**For up-to-date information on Principal Government Officials, see the Chiefs of State and Cabinet Members of Foreign Governments section starting on page 1.**

The Irish Embassy in the United States is at 2234 Massachusetts Ave. NW, Washington, DC 20008 (tel. 202-462-3939/40/41/42). Irish Consulates are located in New York, Chicago, Boston, and San Francisco.

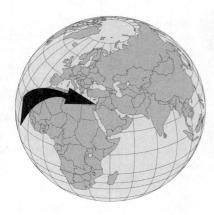

# ISRAEL
December 1998

Official Name:
**State of Israel**

# PROFILE

## Geography
**Area:** *20,325 sq. km. (7,850 sq. mi.); about the size of New Jersey.
**Cities:** Capital—**Jerusalem. Other cities—Tel Aviv, Haifa.
**Terrain:** Plains, mountains, desert, and coast.
**Climate:** Temperate, except in desert areas.

## People
**Population (1997):** 5.9 million.
**Annual growth rate (1997):** 1.9%.
**Ethnic groups (1997):** Jewish 4.7 million; non-Jewish 1.2 million.
**Religions:** Judaism, Islam, Christianity, Druze.
**Languages:** Hebrew, Arabic, Russian, English.
**Education:** Years compulsory—11; Literacy—Jewish 97%, Arab 90%.
**Health (1995):** Infant mortality rate—7.4/1,000. Life expectancy—79.5 years (female), 75.5 years (male).
**Work force (2.1 million):** Manufacturing—20%. Commerce—13%. Education—12%. Other business services—10%. Health and social services—9%. Construction—7%. Other—6%. Transportation—6%. Public Administration—6%. Hotels and restaurants—4%. Banking and finance—4%. Agriculture—2%. Electricity and water—1%.

## Government
**Type:** Parliamentary democracy.
**Independence:** May 14, 1948.
**Constitution:** None.
**Branches:** Executive—president (chief of state); prime minister (head of government). Legislative—unicameral, Knesset. Judicial—Supreme Court.
**Political parties:** Likud-led bloc, Labor Party, and various other secular and religious parties, including some wholly or predominantly supported by Israel's Arab citizens. A total of 13 parties—constituting blocs of smaller parties—are represented in the 14th Knesset, elected May 29, 1996.
**Suffrage:** Universal at 18.

## Economy (1997)
**GDP:** $98 billion.
**Annual growth rate:** 1.9%.
**Per capita GDP:** $16,800.
**Natural resources:** Copper, phosphate, bromide, potash, clay, sand, sulfur, bitumen, manganese.
**Agriculture:** Products—citrus and other fruits, vegetables, beef, dairy, poultry products.
**Industry:** Types—food processing, diamond cutting and polishing, textiles and clothing, chemicals, metal products, transport equipment, electrical equipment, high technology electronics.
**Trade:** Exports—$22.5 billion: polished diamonds, citrus and other fruits, chemical and oil products, electrical and electronic products, textiles and clothing, processed foods. Tourism is also an important foreign exchange earner. Imports—$29.0 billion: military equipment, rough diamonds, oil, chemicals, machinery, iron and steel, textiles, vehicles, ships and aircraft. Major partners—U.S., EU, India, Hong Kong, Japan, South Korea.

# PEOPLE

Of the approximately 5.9 million Israelis in 1997, about 4.7 million were Jewish. While the non-Jewish minority grows at an average rate of 4.9% per year, the Jewish population has increased by more than 27% since 1989 as a result of massive immigration to Israel, primarily from the republics of the former Soviet Union. Since 1989, nearly 841,000 such immigrants have arrived in Israel, making this the largest wave of immigration since independence. In addi-

*Including Jerusalem.
**Israel proclaimed Jerusalem as its capital in 1950. The United States, like nearly all other countries, maintains its embassy in Tel Aviv.

tion, almost 20,000 members of the Ethiopian Jewish community have immigrated to Israel, 14,000 of them during the dramatic May 1991 Operation Solomon airlift.

The three broad Jewish groupings are: the Ashkenazim, or Jews who came to Israel mainly from Europe, North and South America, South Africa, and Australia; the Sephardim, who trace their origin to Spain, Portugal, and North Africa; and Eastern or Oriental Jews, who descend from ancient communities in Islamic lands. Of the non-Jewish population, about 75% are Muslims, 16% are Christian, and about 9% are Druze and others.

Education between ages 5 and 16 is free and compulsory. The school system is organized into kindergartens, 6-year primary schools, 3-year junior secondary schools, and 3-year senior secondary schools, after which a comprehensive examination is offered for university admissions. There are seven university-level institutions in Israel.

With a population drawn from more than 100 countries on 5 continents, Israeli society is rich in cultural diversity and artistic creativity. The arts are actively encouraged and supported by the government. The Israeli Philharmonic Orchestra performs throughout the country and frequently tours abroad. The Jerusalem Symphony, the orchestra of the Israeli Broadcasting Authority, also tours frequently as do other musical ensembles. Almost every municipality has a chamber orchestra or ensemble, many boasting the talents of gifted performers recently arrived from the countries of the former Soviet Union.

Folk dancing, which draws upon the cultural heritage of many immigrant groups, is very popular. Israel also has several professional ballet and modern dance companies. There is great public interest in the theater; the repertoire covers the entire range of classical and contemporary drama in translation, as well as plays by Israeli authors. Of the three major repertory companies, the most

famous, Habimah, was founded in 1917.

Active artist colonies thrive in Safed, Jaffa, and Ein Hod, and Israeli painters and sculptors exhibit and sell their works worldwide. Haifa, Tel Aviv, and Jerusalem have excellent art museums, and many towns and kibbutzim have smaller high-quality museums. The Israel Museum in Jerusalem houses the Dead Sea Scrolls along with an extensive collection of Jewish religious and folk art. The Museum of the Diaspora is located on the campus of Tel Aviv University. Israelis are avid newspaper readers. Israeli papers have an average daily circulation of 600,000 copies. Major daily papers are in Hebrew; others are in Arabic, English, French, Polish, Yiddish, Russian, Hungarian, and German.

# HISTORY

The creation of the State of Israel in 1948 was preceded by more than 50 years of efforts by Zionist leaders to establish a sovereign nation as a homeland for Jews. The desire of Jews to return to what they consider their rightful homeland was first expressed during the Babylonian exile and became a universal Jewish theme after the destruction of Jerusalem by the Romans in 70 A.D. and the dispersal that followed.

It was not until the founding of the Zionist movement by Theodore Herzl at the end of the 19th century that practical steps were taken toward securing international sanction for large-scale Jewish settlement in Palestine—then a part of the Ottoman Empire.

The Balfour declaration in 1917 asserted the British Government's support for the creation of a Jewish homeland in Palestine. This declaration was supported by a number of other countries, including the United States, and became more important following World War I, when the United Kingdom was assigned the Palestine mandate by the League of Nations.

Jewish immigration grew slowly in the 1920s; it increased substantially in the 1930s, due to political turmoil in Europe and Nazi persecution, until restrictions were imposed by the United Kingdom in 1939. After the end of World War II, and the near-extermination of European Jewry by the Nazis, international support for Jews seeking to settle in Palestine overcame British efforts to restrict immigration.

International support for establishing a Jewish state led to the adoption in November 1947 of the UN partition plan, which called for dividing the Mandate of Palestine into a Jewish and an Arab state and for establishing Jerusalem separately as an international city under UN administration.

Violence between Arab and Jewish communities erupted almost immediately. Toward the end of the British mandate, the Jews planned to declare a separate state, a development the Arabs were determined to prevent. On May 14, 1948, the State of Israel was proclaimed. The following day, armies from neighboring Arab nations entered the former Mandate of Palestine to engage Israeli military forces.

In 1949, under UN auspices, four armistice agreements were negotiated and signed at Rhodes, Greece, between Israel and its neighbors Egypt, Jordan, Lebanon and Syria. The 1948-49 war of independence resulted in a 50% increase in Israeli territory, including western Jerusalem. No general peace settlement was achieved at Rhodes, however, and violence along the borders continued for many years.

In October 1956, Israel invaded the Gaza Strip and the Sinai Peninsula at the same time that operations by French and British forces against Egypt were taking place in the Suez Canal area. Israeli forces withdrew in March 1957, after the United Nations established the UN Emergency Force (UNEF) in the Gaza Strip and Sinai. In 1966-67, terrorist incidents and retaliatory acts across the armistice demarcation lines increased.

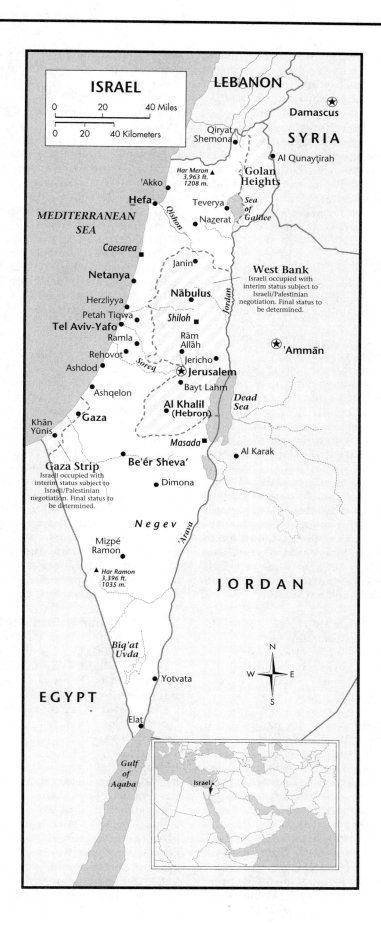

In May 1967, after tension had developed between Syria and Israel, Egyptian President Nasser moved armaments and about 80,000 troops into the Sinai and ordered a withdrawal of UNEF troops from the armistice line and Sharm El Sheikh. Nasser then closed the Strait of Tiran to Israeli ships, blockading the Israeli port of Eilat at the northern end of the Gulf of Aqaba. On May 30, Jordan and Egypt signed a mutual defense treaty.

In response to these events, Israeli forces struck targets in Egypt, Jordan, and Syria on June 5. After 6 days of fighting, by the time all parties had accepted the cease-fire called for by UN Security Council Resolutions 235 and 236, Israel controlled the Sinai Peninsula, the Gaza Strip, the Golan Heights, and the formerly Jordanian-controlled West Bank of the Jordan River, including East Jerusalem. On November 22, 1967, the Security Council adopted Resolution 242, the "land for peace" formula, which called for the establishment of a just and lasting peace based on Israeli withdrawal from territories occupied in 1967 in return for the end of all states of belligerency, respect for the sovereignty of all states in the area, and the right to live in peace within secure, recognized boundaries.

In the 1969-70 war of attrition, Israeli planes made deep strikes into Egypt in retaliation for repeated Egyptian shelling of Israeli positions along the Suez Canal. In early 1969, fighting broke out between Egypt and Israel along the Suez Canal. The United States helped end these hostilities in August 1970, but subsequent U.S. efforts to negotiate an interim agreement to open the Suez Canal and achieve disengagement of forces were unsuccessful.

On October 6, 1973—Yom Kippur (the Jewish Day of Atonement)—Syrian and Egyptian forces attacked Israeli positions in Golan and along the Suez Canal. Initially, Syria and Egypt made significant advances against Israeli forces. However, Israel recovered on both fronts, pushed the Syrians back beyond the

1967 cease-fire lines, and recrossed the Suez Canal to take a salient on its west bank, isolating Egyptian troops, who eventually surrendered.

The United States and the Soviet Union helped bring about a cease-fire between the combatants. In the UN Security Council, the United States supported Resolution 338, which reaffirmed Resolution 242 as the framework for peace and called for peace negotiations between the parties.

The cease-fire did not end the sporadic clashes along the cease-fire lines nor did it dissipate military tensions. The United States tried to help the parties reach agreement on cease-fire stabilization and military disengagement. On March 5, 1974, Israeli forces withdrew from the canal, and Egypt assumed control. Syria and Israel signed a disengagement agreement on May 31, 1974, and the UN Disengagement and Observer Force (UNDOF) was established as a peace-keeping force in the Golan.

Further U.S. efforts resulted in an interim agreement between Egypt and Israel in September 1975, which provided for another Israeli withdrawal in the Sinai, a limitation of forces, and three observation stations staffed by U.S. civilians in a UN-maintained buffer zone between Egyptian and Israeli forces.

In November 1977, Egyptian President Anwar Sadat broke 30 years of hostility with Israel by visiting Jerusalem at the invitation of Israeli Prime Minister Menachem Begin. During a 2-day visit, which included a speech before the Knesset, the Egyptian leader created a new psychological climate in the Middle East in which peace between Israel and its Arab neighbors seemed a realistic possibility. Sadat recognized Israel's right to exist and established the basis for direct negotiations between Egypt and Israel.

In September 1978, U.S. President Jimmy Carter invited President Sadat and Prime Minister Begin to meet with him at Camp David, where they agreed on a framework for peace

between Israel and Egypt and a comprehensive peace in the Middle East. It set out broad principles to guide negotiations between Israel and the Arab states. It also established guidelines for a West Bank-Gaza transitional regime of full autonomy for the Palestinians residing in the occupied territories and for a peace treaty between Egypt and Israel.

The treaty was signed on March 26, 1979, by Begin and Sadat, with President Carter signing as witness. Under the treaty, Israel returned the Sinai to Egypt in April 1982. In 1989, the Governments of Israel and Egypt concluded an agreement that resolved the status of Taba, a resort area on the Gulf of Aqaba.

In the years following the 1948 war, Israel's border with Lebanon was quiet, compared to its borders with other neighbors. After the expulsion of the Palestinian fedayeen (fighters) from Jordan in 1970—and their influx into southern Lebanon, however, hostilities on Israel's northern border increased. In March 1978, after a series of clashes between Israeli forces and Palestinian guerrillas in Lebanon, Israeli forces crossed into Lebanon. After passage of Security Council Resolution 425, calling for Israeli withdrawal and the creation of the UN Interim Force in Lebanon peace-keeping force (UNIFIL), Israel withdrew its troops.

In July 1981, after additional fighting between Israel and the Palestinians in Lebanon, President Reagan's special envoy, Philip C. Habib, helped secure a cease-fire between the parties. However, in June 1982, Israel invaded Lebanon to fight the forces of the Palestine Liberation Organization (PLO).

In August 1982, the PLO withdrew its forces from Lebanon. With U.S. assistance, Israel and Lebanon reached an accord in May 1983 that set the stage to withdraw Israeli forces from Lebanon. The instruments of ratification were never exchanged, however, and in March 1984, under pressure from Syria, Lebanon canceled the agreement. In June 1985, Israel withdrew most of

its troops from Lebanon, leaving a small residual Israeli force and an Israeli-supported militia in southern Lebanon in a "security zone," which Israel considers a necessary buffer against attacks on its northern territory.

By the late 1980s, the spread of non-conventional weaponry—including missile technology—in the Middle East began to pose security problems for Israel from further afield. This was evident during the Gulf crisis that began with Iraq's August 1990 invasion of Kuwait.

When allied coalition forces moved to expel Iraqi forces from Kuwait in January 1991, Iraq launched a series of missile attacks against Israel. Despite the provocation, Israel refrained from entering the Gulf war directly, accepting U.S. assistance to deflect continued Iraqi missile attacks.

The coalition's victory in the Gulf war opened new possibilities for regional peace, and in October 1991, the Presidents of the United States and the Soviet Union jointly convened an historic meeting in Madrid of Israeli, Lebanese, Jordanian, Syrian, and Palestinian leaders which became the foundation for ongoing bilateral and multilateral negotiations designed to bring lasting peace and economic development to the region.

On September 13, 1993, Israel and the PLO signed a Declaration of Principles (DOP) on the South Lawn of the White House. The declaration was a major conceptual breakthrough achieved under the Madrid framework. It established an ambitious set of objectives relating to a transfer of authority from Israel to an interim Palestinian authority. The DOP established May 1999 as the date by which a permanent status agreement for the West Bank and Gaza Strip would take effect. Israel and the PLO subsequently signed the Gaza-Jericho Agreement on May 4, 1994, and the Agreement on Preparatory Transfer of Powers and Responsibilities on August 29, 1994, which began the process of transferring authority from Israel to the Palestinians.

Prime Minister Rabin and PLO Chairman Arafat signed the historic Israeli-Palestinian Interim Agreement on the West Bank and the Gaza Strip on September 28, 1995, in Washington. The agreement, witnessed by the President on behalf of the United States and by Russia, Egypt, Norway, and the European Union, incorporates and supersedes the previous agreements and marked the conclusion of the first stage of negotiations between Israel and the PLO.

The accord broadens Palestinian self-government by means of a popularly elected legislative council. It provides for election and establishment of that body, transfer of civil authority, Israeli redeployment from major population centers in the West Bank, security arrangements, and cooperation in a variety of areas. Negotiations on permanent status began on May 5, 1996 in Taba, Egypt. As agreed in the 1993 DOP, those talks will address the status of Jerusalem, Palestinian refugees, Israeli settlements in the West Bank and Gaza Strip, final security arrangements, borders, relations and cooperation with neighboring states, and other issues of common interest.

Israel signed a non-belligerency agreement with Jordan (the Washington Declaration) in Washington, DC, on July 25, 1994. Jordan and Israel signed a historic peace treaty at a border post between the two countries on October 26, 1994, witnessed by President Clinton, accompanied by Secretary Christopher.

The assassination of Prime Minister Rabin by a right-wing Jewish radical on November 4, 1995 climaxed an increasingly bitter national debate over where the peace process was leading. Rabin's death left Israel profoundly shaken, ushered in a period of national self-examination, and produced a new level of national consensus favoring the peace process. In February 1996 Rabin's successor, Shimon Peres, called early elections. Those elections, held in May 1996 and the first featuring direct election of the prime minister, resulted in a narrow election victory for Likud

Party leader Binyamin Netanyahu and his center-right National Coalition and the defeat of Peres and his left-of-center Labor/Meretz government. Despite his stated differences with the Oslo Accords, Prime Minister Netanyahu continued its implementation, signing the Hebron Protocol with the Palestinians on January 15, 1997. The Protocol resulted in the redeployment of Israeli forces in Hebron and the turnover of civilian authority in much of the area to the Palestinian Authority. Since that agreement, there has been little progress in the Israeli-Palestinian negotiations. A crisis of confidence developed between the parties as the parties had difficulty responding to each other and addressing each other's concerns. Israel and the Palestinians did agree, however, in September 1997, to a four-part agenda to guide further negotiations: security cooperation in the fight against terror; further redeployments of Israeli forces; a "time-out" on unilateral actions that may prejudge the outcome of the permanent status talks; and acceleration of these talks. The U.S. sought to marry continued implementation of the 1995 Interim Agreement with the start of the accelerated permanent status talks. In order to overcome the crisis of confidence and break the negotiating impasse, President Clinton presented U.S. ideas for getting the peace process back on track to Prime Minister Netanyahu and Chairman Arafat in Washington in January 1998. Those ideas included all aspects of the September 1997 four-part agenda and would allow for the start of accelerated permanent status negotiations. The Palestinians agreed in principle to the U.S. ideas.

The U.S. continued working intensively with the parties to reach agreement on the basis of U.S. ideas. After a 9-day session at the Wye River Conference Center in Maryland, agreement was reached on October 23, 1998. The Wye agreement is based on the principle of reciprocity and meets the essential requirements of both the parties, including unprecedented security measures on the part of the Palestinians and the further redeployment of Israeli troops in the West

Bank. The agreement also permits the launching of the permanent status negotiations as the May 4, 1999 expiration of the period of the Interim Agreement.

# GOVERNMENT

Israel is a parliamentary democracy. Its governmental system is based on several basic laws enacted by its unicameral parliament, the Knesset. The president (chief of state) is elected by the Knesset for a 5-year term.

The prime minister (head of government) exercises executive power and has in the past been selected by the president as the party leader most able to form a government. In the May 1996 elections, Israelis for the first time voted for the prime minister directly, in accordance with recent legislation. The members of the cabinet must be collectively approved by the Knesset.

The Knesset's 120 members are elected by secret ballot to 4-year terms, although the prime minister may decide to call for new elections before the end of the 4-year term. Voting is for party lists rather than for individual candidates, and the total number of seats assigned each party reflects that party's percentage of the vote. Successful Knesset candidates are drawn from the lists in order of party-assigned rank. Under the present electoral system, all members of the Knesset are elected at large.

The independent judicial system includes secular and religious courts. The courts' right of judicial review of the Knesset's legislation is limited. Judicial interpretation is restricted to problems of execution of laws and validity of subsidiary legislation. The highest court in Israel is the Supreme Court, whose judges are approved by the president.

Israel is divided into six districts, administration of which is coordinated by the Ministry of Interior. The Ministry of Defense is responsible for the administration of the occupied territories.

## Principal Government Officials

**For up-to-date information on Principal Government Officials, see the Chiefs of State and Cabinet Members of Foreign Governments section starting on page 1.**

Israel maintains an embassy in the United States at 3514 International Drive NW, Washington DC, 20008 (tel. 202-364-5500). There are also consulates general in Atlanta, Boston, Chicago, Houston, Los Angeles, Miami, New York, Philadelphia, and San Francisco.

# POLITICAL CONDITIONS

From the founding of Israel in 1948 until the election of May 1977, Israel was ruled by successive coalition governments led by the Labor alignment or its constituent parties. From 1967-70, the coalition government included all of Israel's parties except the communist party. After the 1977 election, the Likud bloc, then composed of Herut, the Liberals, and the smaller La'am Party, came to power forming a coalition with the National Religious Party, Agudat Israel, and others.

As head of Likud, Menachem Begin became Prime Minister. The Likud retained power in the succeeding election in June 1981, and Begin remained Prime Minister. In the summer of 1983, Begin resigned and was succeeded by his Foreign Minister, Yitzhak Shamir. After losing a Knesset vote of confidence early in 1984, Shamir was forced to call for new elections, held in July of that year.

The vote was split among numerous parties and provided no clear winner leaving both Labor and Likud considerably short of a Knesset majority.

Neither Labor nor Likud was able to gain enough support from the small parties to form even a narrow coalition. After several weeks of difficult negotiations, they agreed on a broadly based government of national unity. The agreement provided for the rotation of the office of prime minister and the combined office of vice prime minister and foreign minister midway through the government's 50-month term.

During the first 25 months of unity government rule, Labor's Shimon Peres served as prime minister, while Likud's Yitzhak Shamir held the posts of vice prime minister and foreign minister. Peres and Shamir switched positions in October 1986. The November 1988 elections resulted in a similar coalition government. Likud edged Labor out by one seat but was unable to form a coalition with the religious and right-wing parties. Likud and Labor formed another national unity government in January 1989 without providing for rotation. Yitzhak Shamir became Prime Minister, and Shimon Peres became Vice Prime Minister and Finance Minister.

The national unity government fell in March 1990, in a vote of no-confidence precipitated by disagreement over the government's response to U.S. Secretary of State Baker's initiative in the peace process.

Labor Party leader Peres was unable to attract sufficient support among the religious parties to form a government. Yitzhak Shamir then formed a Likud-led coalition government including members from religious and right-wing parties.

Shamir's government took office in June 1990, and held power for 2 years. In the June 1992 national elections, the Labor Party reversed its electoral fortunes, taking 44 seats. Labor Party leader Yitzhak Rabin formed a coalition with Meretz (a group of three leftist parties) and Shas (an ultra-Orthodox religious party). The coalition included the support of two Arab-majority parties. Rabin became Prime Minister in July 1992. Shas subsequently left the coa-

lition, leaving Rabin with a minority government dependent on the votes of Arab parties in the Knesset.

Rabin was assassinated by a right-wing Jewish radical on November 4, 1995. Peres, then Deputy Prime Minister and Foreign Minister, once again became Prime Minister and immediately proceeded to carry forward the peace policies of the Rabin government and to implement Israel's Oslo commitments (including military redeployment in the West Bank and the holding of historic Palestinian elections on January 20, 1996).

Enjoying broad public support and anxious to secure his own mandate, Peres called for early elections after just 3 months in office. (They would have otherwise been held by the end of October 1996.) In late February and early March, a series of suicide bombing attacks by Palestinian terrorists took some 60 Israeli lives, seriously eroding public support for Peres and raising concerns about the peace process. Increased fighting in southern Lebanon, which also brought Katyusha rocket attacks against northern Israel, also raised tensions and weakened the government politically just a month before the May 29 elections.

In those elections—the first direct election of a prime minister in Israeli history—Likud leader Binyamin Netanyahu won by a narrow margin, having sharply criticized the government's peace policies for failing to protect Israeli security. Netanyahu subsequently formed a predominantly right-wing coalition government publicly committed to pursuing the peace process, but with an emphasis on security first and reciprocity. His coalition included the Likud party, allied with the Tsomet and Gesher parties in a single list; three religious parties (Shas, the National Religious Party, and the United Torah Judaism bloc); and two centrist parties, The Third Way and Yisrael b'Aliyah. The latter is the first significant party formed expressly to represent the interests of Israel's new immigrants. The Gesher party withdrew from the coalition in

January 1998 upon the resignation of its leader, David Levy, from the position of Foreign Minister.

# ECONOMY

Israel has a diversified modern economy with substantial government ownership and a rapidly developing high-tech sector. Poor in natural resources, Israel depends on imports of oil, coal, food, uncut diamonds, other production inputs, and military equipment. Its GDP in 1997 reached $98 billion, or $16,800 per person. The major industrial sectors include metal products, electronic and bio-medical equipment, processed foods, chemicals, and transport equipment. Israel possesses a substantial service sector and is one of the world's centers for diamond cutting and polishing. It is also a world leader in software development and is a major tourist destination.

Israel's strong commitment to economic development and its talented work force led to economic growth rates during the nation's first two decades that frequently exceeded 10% annually. The years after the 1973 Yom Kippur War were a lost decade economically, as growth stalled and inflation reached triple-digit levels. The successful economic stabilization plan implemented in 1985 and the subsequent introduction of market-oriented structural reforms reinvigorated the economy and paved the way for its rapid growth in the 1990s.

Two developments have helped to transform Israel's economy since the beginning of the decade. The first is the wave of Jewish immigration, predominantly from the countries of the former U.S.S.R., that has brought some 841,000 new citizens to Israel. These new immigrants, many of them highly educated, now constitute some 16% of Israel's 5.9 million population. Their successful absorption into Israeli society and its labor force forms a remarkable chapter in Israeli history. The skills brought by the new immigrants and their added demand as consumers have given the Israeli economy a strong upward push.

The second development benefiting the Israeli economy is the Mideast peace process begun at the Madrid conference of October 1991, which led to the signing of accords between Israel and the Palestinians and a peace treaty between Israel and Jordan. The peace process has helped to erode Israel's economic isolation from its neighbors and has begun a process of regional economic integration that will help to stabilize the region. It has also opened up new markets to Israeli exporters farther afield, such as in the rapidly growing countries of East Asia. The peace process has stimulated an unprecedented inflow of foreign investment in Israel, as companies that formerly shunned the Israeli market now see its potential contribution to their global strategies.

Israeli companies, particularly in the high-tech area, have recently enjoyed considerable success raising money on Wall Street and other world financial markets; Israel now ranks second among foreign countries in the number of its companies listed on U.S. stock exchanges.

Economic growth slowed considerably over the last 2 years, to 4.4% in 1996 and only 1.9% in 1997. Per capita income fell slightly in 1997 for the first time in the previous 10 years. The slowdown is generally attributed to setbacks in the peace process, the waning of the beneficial effects of immigration, labor shortages in high-tech industries, tighter fiscal and monetary policy, and the Asian financial crisis which began in late 1997.

The United States is Israel's largest trading partner; two-way trade totaled some $12.6 billion in 1997. The principal U.S. exports to Israel include computers, integrated circuits, aircraft parts and other defense equipment, wheat, and automobiles. Israel's chief exports to the U.S. include diamonds, jewelry, integrated circuits, printing machinery, and telecommunications equipment. The two countries signed a free trade agreement (FTA) in 1985 that progres-sively eliminated tariffs on most goods traded between the two countries over the following ten years. An agricultural trade accord was signed in November 1996, which addressed the remaining goods not covered in the FTA. Some non-tariff barriers and tariffs on goods remain, however. Israel also has trade and cooperation agreements in place with the European Union and Canada, and is seeking to conclude such agreements with a number of other countries, including Turkey and several countries in Eastern Europe.

# FOREIGN RELATIONS

In addition to seeking an end to hostilities with Arab forces, against which it has fought five wars since 1948, Israel has given high priority to gaining wide acceptance as a sovereign state with an important international role. Before 1967, it had established diplomatic relations with a majority of the world's nations, except for the Arab states and most other Muslim countries. While the Soviet Union and the communist states of Eastern Europe (except Romania) broke diplomatic relations with Israel in the 1967 war, those relations were restored by 1991.

Today, Israel has diplomatic relations with some 153 states. Following the Madrid conference in 1991, and as a direct result of the peace process, Israel established or renewed diplomatic relations with 62 countries. Most important are its ties with Arab states. In addition to full diplomatic relations with Egypt and Jordan, Israel now has ties of one kind or another with Morocco, Tunisia, Oman, Qatar, and Bahrain.

On October 1, 1994, the Gulf States publicly announced their support for a review of the Arab boycott, in effect abolishing the secondary and tertiary boycotts against Israel. Israel has diplomatic relations with 9 non-Arab Muslim states and with 32 of the 43 Sub-Saharan states that are not members of the Arab League. Israel established relations with China and India in 1992.

# DEFENSE

Israel's ground, air, and naval forces, known as the Israel Defense Force (IDF), fall under the command of a single general staff. Conscription is universal for Jewish men and women over the age of 18, although exemptions may be made on religious grounds. Druze, members of a small Islamic sect living in Israel's mountains, also serve in the IDF. Israeli Arabs, with few exceptions, do not serve. During 1950-66, Israel spent an average of 9% of GDP on defense. Real defense expenditures increased dramatically after both the 1967 and 1973 wars. In 1996, the military budget reached 10.6% of GDP and represented about 21.5% of the total 1996 budget.

In 1983, the United States and Israel established the Joint Political Military Group, which meets twice a year. Both the U.S. and Israel participate in joint military planning and combined exercises, and have collaborated on military research and weapons development.

# U.S.-ISRAELI RELATIONS

Commitment to Israel's security and well-being has been a cornerstone of U.S. policy in the Middle East since Israel's creation in 1948, in which the United States played a key supporting role. Israel and the United States are bound closely by historic and cultural ties as well as by mutual interests. Continuing U.S. economic and security assistance to Israel acknowledges these ties and signals U.S. commitment. The broad issues of Arab-Israeli peace have been a major focus in the U.S.-Israeli relationship. U.S. efforts to reach a Middle East peace settlement are based on UN Security Council Resolutions 242 and 338 and, under the Clinton Administration,

## Travel Notes

**Travel Advice:** For up-to-date information from the U.S. State Department on possible inconvenient or hazardous situations, see the **Travel Warnings and Consular Information Sheets from the U.S. Government** section starting on page 1723. For the latest information on health requirements and conditions, see the **International Travelers' Health Information** section starting on page 1385. For further information dealing with non-urgent matter, see the **Tips for Travelers to...** section starting on page 1588.

have been based on the premise that as Israel takes calculated risks for peace, it is the role of the United States to help minimize those risks.

UNSC resolutions provided the basis for cease-fire and disengagement agreements concerning the Sinai and the Golan Heights between Israel, Egypt, and Syria and for promoting the Camp David accords and the Egyptian-Israeli Peace Treaty. They were also the foundation for President Reagan's September 1982 peace initiative and Secretary Shultz's January 1988 initiative aimed at stimulating conditions to bring Jordan and representative Palestinians into the Middle East peace process.

The landmark October 1991 Madrid conference also recognized the importance of Security Council Resolutions 242 and 338 in resolving regional disputes, and brought together for the first time Israel, the Palestinians, and the neighboring Arab countries, launching a series of direct bilateral and multilateral negotiations. These talks were designed to finally resolve outstanding security, border, and other issues between the parties while providing a basis for mutual cooperation on issues of general concern, including the status of refugees, arms control and regional security, water and environmental concerns, and economic development.

On a bilateral level, relations between the United States and Israel have been strengthened in recent years by the establishment of cooperative institutions in many fields. Bilateral foundations in the fields of science and technology include the Binational Science Foundation and the Binational Agricultural Research and Development Foundation. The U.S.-Israeli Education Foundation sponsors educational and cultural programs.

In addition, the Joint Economic Development Group maintains a high-level dialogue on economic issues. In early 1993, the United States and Israel agreed to establish a Joint Science and Technology Commission. In 1983, the United States and Israel established the Joint Political Military Group, which includes joint military planning and combined exercises. In 1996, reflecting heightened concern about terrorism, the United States and Israel established a Joint Counterterrorism Group designed to enhance cooperation in fighting terrorism.

## Principal U.S. Officials

**For up-to-date information on Principal U.S. Officials, see the U.S. Embassies, Consulates, and Foreign Service section starting on page 139.**

The U.S. embassy in Israel is located at 71 Hayarkon Street, Tel Aviv (tel. 03-519-7575).

The U.S. consulate general in Jerusalem has offices at 18 Agron Road (tel. 02-622-7230) and on Nablus Road (tel. 02-622-7230). The consulate general in Jerusalem is an independent U.S. mission, established in 1928, whose members are not accredited to a foreign government.

# ITALY

July 2000

Official Name:
**Republic of Italy**

# PROFILE

## Geography

**Area:** 301,225 sq. km. (116,303 sq. mi.); about the size of Georgia and Florida combined.
**Cities:** Capital—Rome (pop. 2.7 million). Other cities—Milan, Naples, Turin.
**Terrain:** Mostly rugged and mountainous.
**Climate:** Generally mild Mediterranean; cold northern winters.

## People

**Nationality:** Noun and adjective—Italian(s).
**Population:** 56.9 million.
**Annual growth rate:** 1.4%.
**Ethnic Groups:** Primarily Italian, but there are small groups of German-, French-, Slovene-, and Albanian-Italians.
**Religion:** Roman Catholic (majority).
**Language:** Italian (official).
**Education:** Years compulsory—14. Literacy—98%.
**Health:** Infant mortality rate—8/1,000 live births. Life expectancy—74 yrs.
**Work force:** (23 million) Services—61%. Industry and commerce—32%. Unemployed—11%. Agriculture—7%.

## Government

**Type:** Republic since June 2, 1946.
**Constitution:** January 1, 1948.
**Branches:** Executive—president (chief of state), Council of Ministers (cabinet), headed by the president of the council (prime minister). Legislative—bicameral Parliament: 630-member Chamber of Deputies, 325-member Senate. Judicial—independent constitutional court and lower magistracy.
**Subdivisions:** 94 provinces, 20 regions.
**Political parties:** Christian Democratic Center, Communist Renewal, Democrats, Democratic Party of the Left, Forza Italia, Greens, Italian People's Party, Italian Communists, Italian Renewal, National Alliance, Northern League, Republican, Socialist.
**Suffrage:** Universal over 18.

## Economy

**GDP:** (1999) $1.17 trillion.
**Per capita income:** (1999 est.) $20,000.
**GDP growth:** (1999 est.) 1.4%.
**Natural resources:** Fish, natural gas.
**Agriculture:** Products—wheat, rice, grapes, olives, citrus fruits.
**Industry:** Types—automobiles, machinery, chemicals, textiles, shoes.
**Trade:** (1999) Exports—$229 billion: mechanical products, textiles and apparel, transportation equip-ment, metal products, chemical products, food and agricultural products. Partners—EU 55%, U.S. 7%, OPEC 3%. Imports—$215 billion: machinery and transport equipment, foodstuffs, ferrous and nonferrous metals, wool, cotton, energy products. Partners—EU 61%, OPEC 6%, U.S. 5%.

# HISTORY

Italy is largely homogeneous linguistically and religiously but is diverse culturally, economically, and politically. Italy has the fifth-highest population density in Europe—about 200 persons per square kilometer (490/sq. mi.). Minority groups are small, the largest being the German-speaking people of Bolzano Province and the Slovenes around Trieste. Other groups comprise small communities of Albanian, Greek, Ladino, and French origin. Although Roman Catholicism is the majority religion—85% of native-born citizens are nominally Catholic—all religious faiths are provided equal freedom before the law by the constitution. Greeks settled in the southern tip of the Italian Peninsula in the eighth and seventh centuries B.C.; Etruscans, Romans, and others inhabited the central and northern mainland. The peninsula subsequently was unified under the Roman Republic. The neighboring

islands also came under Roman control by the third century B.C.; by the first century A.D., the Roman Empire effectively dominated the Mediterranean world. After the collapse of the Roman Empire in the west in the fifth century A.D., the peninsula and islands were subjected to a series of invasions, and political unity was lost. Italy became an oft-changing succession of small states, principalities, and kingdoms which fought

among themselves and were subject to ambitions of foreign powers. Popes of Rome ruled central Italy; rivalries between the popes and the Holy Roman Emperors, who claimed Italy as their domain, often made the peninsula a battleground.

The commercial prosperity of northern and central Italian cities, beginning in the 11th century, and the influence of the Renaissance miti-

gated somewhat the effects of these medieval political rivalries. Although Italy declined after the 16th century, the Renaissance had strengthened the idea of a single Italian nationality. By the early 19th century, a nationalist movement developed and led to the reunification of Italy—except for Rome—in the 1860s. In 1861, Victor Emmanuel II of the House of Savoy was proclaimed King of Italy. Rome was incorporated in

1870. From 1870 until 1922, Italy was a constitutional monarchy with a parliament elected under limited suffrage.

## 20th-Century History

During World War I, Italy renounced its standing alliance with Germany and Austria-Hungary and, in 1915, entered the war on the side of the Allies. Under the postwar settlement, Italy received some former Austrian territory along the northeast frontier. In 1922, Benito Mussolini came to power and, over the next few years, eliminated political parties, curtailed personal liberties, and installed a fascist dictatorship termed the Corporate State. The king, with little or no effective power, remained titular head of state.

Italy allied with Germany and declared war on the United Kingdom and France in 1940. In 1941, Italy—with the other Axis powers, Germany and Japan—declared war on the United States and the Soviet Union. Following the Allied invasion of Sicily in 1943, the King dismissed Mussolini and appointed Marshal Pietro Badoglio as premier. The Badoglio government declared war on Germany, which quickly occupied most of the country and freed Mussolini, who led a brief-lived regime in the north. An anti-fascist popular resistance movement grew during the last 2 years of the war, harassing German forces before they were driven out in April 1945. The monarchy was ended by a 1946 plebiscite, and a constituent assembly was elected to draw up plans for the republic.

Under the 1947 peace treaty, minor adjustments were made in Italy's frontier with France. The eastern border area was transferred to Yugoslavia, and the area around the city of Trieste was designated a free territory. In 1954, the free territory, which had remained under the administration of U.S.-U.K. forces (Zone A, including the city of Trieste) and Yugoslav forces (Zone B), was divided between Italy and Yugoslavia, principally along the zonal boundary. This arrangement was made permanent by the Italian-Yugoslav Treaty of

Osimo, ratified in 1977 (currently being discussed by Italy, Slovenia, and Croatia). Under the 1947 peace treaty, Italy also gave up its overseas territories and certain Mediterranean islands.

The Roman Catholic Church's status in Italy has been determined, since its temporal powers ended in 1870, by a series of accords with the Italian Government. Under the Lateran Pacts of 1929, which were confirmed by the present constitution, the state of Vatican City is recognized by Italy as an independent, sovereign entity. While preserving that recognition, in 1984, Italy and the Vatican updated several provisions of the 1929 accords. Included was the end of Roman Catholicism as Italy's formal state religion.

## Italy's Cultural Contributions

Europe's Renaissance period began in Italy during the 14th and 15th centuries. Literary achievements—such as the poetry of Petrarch, Tasso, and Ariosto and the prose of Boccaccio, Machiavelli, and Castiglione—exerted a tremendous and lasting influence on the subsequent development of Western civilization, as did the painting, sculpture, and architecture contributed by giants such as da Vinci, Raphael, Botticelli, Fra Angelico, and Michelangelo.

The musical influence of Italian composers Monteverdi, Palestrina, and Vivaldi proved epochal; in the 19th century, Italian romantic opera flourished under composers Gioacchino Rossini, Giuseppe Verdi, and Giacomo Puccini. Contemporary Italian artists, writers, filmmakers, architects, composers, and designers contribute significantly to Western culture.

# GOVERNMENT

Italy has been a democratic republic since June 2, 1946, when the monarchy was abolished by popular referendum. The constitution was promulgated on January 1, 1948.

The Italian state is highly centralized. The prefect of each of the provinces is appointed by and answerable to the central government. In addition to the provinces, the constitution provides for 20 regions with limited governing powers. Five regions—Sardinia, Sicily, Trentino-Alto Adige, Valle d'Aosta, and Friuli-Venezia Giulia—function with special autonomy statutes. The other 15 regions were established in 1970 and vote for regional "councils." The establishment of regional governments throughout Italy has brought some decentralization to the national governmental machinery.

The 1948 constitution established a bicameral Parliament (Chamber of Deputies and Senate), a separate judiciary, and an executive branch composed of a Council of Ministers (cabinet) which is headed by the president of the council (prime minister). The president of the republic is elected for 7 years by the Parliament sitting jointly with a small number of regional delegates. The president nominates the prime minister, who chooses the other ministers. The Council of Ministers—in practice composed mostly of members of Parliament—must retain the confidence of both houses.

The houses of Parliament are popularly and directly elected by a mixed majoritarian and proportional representation system. Under 1993 legislation, Italy has single-member districts for 75% of the seats in Parliament; the remaining 25% of seats are allotted on a proportional basis. The Chamber of Deputies has 630 members. In addition to 315 elected members, the Senate includes former presidents and several other persons appointed for life according to special constitutional provisions. Both houses are elected for a maximum of 5 years, but either may be dissolved before the expiration of its normal term. Legislative bills may originate in either house and must be passed by a majority in both.

The Italian judicial system is based on Roman law modified by the Napoleonic code and subsequent statutes. There is only partial judicial review of legislation in the American sense. A constitutional court, which passes on the constitutionality of laws, is a post-World War II innovation. Its powers, volume, and frequency of decisions are not as extensive as those of the U.S. Supreme Court.

## Principal Government Officials

For up-to-date information on Principal Government Officials, see the Chiefs of State and Cabinet Members of Foreign Governments section starting on page 1.

Italy maintains an embassy in the United States at 3000 Whitehaven Street NW, Washington, DC 20008 (tel. 202-328-5500).

# POLITICAL CONDITIONS

There have been frequent government turnovers since 1945. The dominance of the Christian Democratic (DC) Party during much of the postwar period lent continuity and comparative stability to Italy's political situation. From 1992 to 1997, Italy faced significant challenges as voters— disenchanted with past political paralysis, massive government debt, extensive corruption, and organized crime's considerable influence— demanded political, economic, and ethical reforms. In 1993 referendums, voters approved substantial changes, including moving from a proportional to a largely majoritarian electoral system and the abolishment of some ministries.

Major political parties, beset by scandal and loss of voter confidence, underwent far-reaching changes. New political forces and new alignments of power emerged in March 1994 national elections: There was a major turnover in the new parliament, with 452 out of 630 deputies and 213 out of 315 senators elected

for the first time. The 1994 elections also swept media magnate Silvio Berlusconi—and his "Freedom Pole" coalition—into office as Prime Minister. However, Berlusconi was forced to step down in January 1995 when one member of his coalition withdrew support. The Berlusconi government was succeeded by a technical government headed by Prime Minister Lamberto Dini, which fell in early 1996.

In April 1996, national elections were again held and led to the victory of a center-left coalition (the Olive Tree) led by Romano Prodi. Prodi's government became the third-longest to stay in power before he narrowly lost a vote of confidence (by three votes) in October 1998. A new government was formed by Democratic Party of the Left leader and former-communist Massimo D'Alema. Like Prodi's government, D'Alema's coalition included the Democratic Party of the Left (DS), the Italian People's Party (PPI), the newly created Italian Communist Party (split from the Communist Renewal in October 1998) and other small, center-left groups. D'Alema resigned following the center-left losses in regional elections and was succeeded in April 2000 by Giuliano Amato. In May 1999, the Parliament selected Carlo Azeglio Ciampi as the new Italian President (replacing Oscar Luigi Scalfaro). Ciampi, a former Prime Minister, and serving Minister of Treasury, was elected on the first ballot with an easy margin over the required two-thirds votes.

Italy's dramatic self-renewal transformed the political landscape between 1992 and 1997. Scandal investigations touched thousands of politicians, administrators, and businessmen; the shift from a proportional to majoritarian voting system—with the requirement to obtain a minimum of 4% of the national vote to obtain representation—also altered the political landscape. Party changes were sweeping. The Christian Democratic party dissolved; the Italian People's Party and the Christian Democratic Center emerged. Other major parties, such as the Socialists, saw support plummet. New movements such as Forza

Italia, led by former Prime Minister Berlusconi, gained wide support. The National Alliance broke from the neofascist Italian Social Movement. A trend toward two large coalitions— one on the center-left and the other on the center-right—emerged from the April 1995 regional elections. For the 1996 national elections, the center-left parties created the Olive Tree coalition while the center right united again under the Freedom Pole. This emerging bipolarity represents a major break from the fragmented, multiparty political landscape of the postwar era, but attempts were defeated in 1999 and again in 2000 to remove the last vestiges of the proportional system of representation. The three largest parties in the Chamber are Democratic Party of the Left, Forza Italia, and the National Alliance. The same rankings generally apply in the Senate.

# ECONOMY

The Italian economy has changed dramatically since the end of World War II. From an agriculturally based economy, it has developed into an industrial state ranked as the world's fifth-largest industrial economy. Italy belongs to the Group of Eight (G-8) industrialized nations; it is a member of the European Union and the OECD.

Italy has few natural resources. With much of the land unsuited for farming, it is a net food importer. There are no substantial deposits of iron, coal, or oil. Proven natural gas reserves, mainly in the Po Valley and offshore Adriatic, have grown in recent years and constitute the country's most important mineral resource. Most raw materials needed for manufacturing and more than 80% of the country's energy sources are imported. Italy's economic strength is in the processing and the manufacturing of goods, primarily in small and medium-sized family-owned firms. Its major industries are precision machinery, motor vehicles, chemicals, pharmaceuticals, electric goods, and fashion and clothing. Italy is in the midst of a slow economic recovery but lags behind most of its west European neighbors. Italy's economy accelerated from anemic 0.7% growth in 1996 to 1.4% in 1999, still one of the lowest growth rates among industrialized economies. Domestic demand and exports were the dominant factors in GDP growth. Most economic forecasters expect GDP growth to increase to around 2.8% in 2000. While exports declined during 1999, imports grew, resulting in a trade surplus of $14 billion in 1999, down from $27 billion in 1998, and $47.1 billion in 1997. Italy has continued to build foreign exchange reserves to $80 billion in 1998, a record high.

On inflation, Italy is now firmly within norms specified for Economic and Monetary Union (EMU), a major achievement for this historically inflation-prone country. Consumer inflation fell from 3.9% in 1996 to 1.5% in 1997, but rose gradually to 1.9% in 1999. The 2000 target of 1.5% seems well within reach. The 1992 agreement on wage adjustments, which has helped keep wage pressures on inflation low, remains in effect. Tight monetary policy by the Bank of Italy also has helped bring inflation expectations down.

Since 1992, economic policy in Italy has focused primarily on reducing government budget deficits and reining in the national debt. Successive Italian governments have adopted annual austerity budgets with cutbacks in spending, as well as new revenue raising measures. Italy has enjoyed a primary budget surplus, net of interest payments, for the last 7 years. The deficit in public administration is expected to decline to 1.5% of GDP in 2000, down from 7% in 1995. Italy joined the European Monetary Union in May 1998.

The national debt should continue to decline slowly. It stabilized in 1995 at roughly 124% of GDP and is expected to decline to 111% of GDP in 2000. Given the heavy weight of interest payments in government expenditures, public finances remain susceptible to international capital market developments, as well as domestic political developments.

## Travel Notes

**Travel Advice:** For up-to-date information from the U.S. State Department on possible inconvenient or hazardous situations, see the **Travel Warnings and Consular Information Sheets from the U.S. Government** section starting on page 1723. For the latest information on health requirements and conditions, see the **International Travelers' Health Information** section starting on page 1385. For further information dealing with non-urgent matter, see the **Tips for Travelers to...** section starting on page 1588.

Italy's closest trade ties are with the other countries of the European Union, with whom it conducts about 59% of its total trade. Italy's largest EU trade partners, in order of market share, are Germany (18%), France (13%), and the United Kingdom (7%).

## U.S.-Italy Economic Relations

The U.S.-Italian bilateral relationship is strong and growing. The U.S. and Italy cooperate closely on major economic issues, including within the G-8. With a large population and a high per capita income, Italy is one of the United States' most important trade partners. In 1999, the United States was the fourth-largest foreign supplier of the Italian market (with a market share of 5.6%) and the largest supplier outside the EU. Total trade between the United States and Italy exceeded $30 billion in 1999. The U.S. ran more than a $6 billion deficit with Italy.

Significant changes are occurring in the composition of this trade which could narrow the gap. More value-added products such as office machinery and aircraft are becoming the principal U.S. exports to Italy. The change reveals the growing sophistication of the Italian market, and bilateral trade should expand further. During 1998, the United States imported about $19 billion in Italian goods while exporting about $11.3 billion in U.S. goods to Italy. U.S. foreign direct investment in Italy at the end of 1998 exceeded $14.3 billion; Italian

investment in the U.S. was roughly $9 billion.

## Labor

Unemployment remains high (a 12.2% high in 1998 declined to 10.7% by mid-year 2000). It is especially severe in the south where average unemployment for the year was more than 22%. Women and youth have significantly higher rates of unemployment than men. A rigid labor market has served as a disincentive to job creation. There is a significant underground economy absorbing substantial numbers of people, but they work for low wages and without standard social benefits and protections.

Unions claim to represent some 35% of the work force. Most Italian unions are grouped in four major confederations: the Confederation of Labor (CGIL), the Italian Confederation of Workers' Unions (CISL), the Italian Union of Labor (UIL), and the General Union of Labor (UGL). These confederations formerly were associated with important political parties or currents, but they have formally terminated such ties. Nowadays, the four often coordinate their positions before confronting management or lobbying the government. The confederations have an important consultative role on national social and economic issues. Among their major agreements are a 4-year wage moderation agreement signed in 1993, a reform of the pension system in 1995, an employment pact, introducing steps for labor market flexibility in economically depressed areas, in 1996, and a 1998 "Christmas Pact" that renewed previous social accords and introduced tax reductions for workers and employers. The CGIL, CISL, and UIL are affiliates of the International Confederation of Free Trade Unions, affiliated with the World Confederation of Labor (WCL).

## Agriculture

Italy's agriculture is typical of the division between the agricultures of the northern and southern countries of the European Union. The northern part of Italy produces primarily grains, sugarbeets, soybeans, meat, and dairy products, while the south specializes in producing fruits, vegetables, olive oil, wine, and durum wheat.

Even though much of its mountainous terrain is unsuitable for farming, Italy has a large work force (1.4 million) employed in farming. Most farms are small, with the average farm only seven hectares.

For further economic and commercial information, please refer to the "Country Commercial Guide" for Italy, available on the State Department web page at www.state.gov.

# FOREIGN RELATIONS

Italy was a founding member of the European Community—now the European Union (EU). Italy was admitted to the United Nations in 1955 and is a member and strong supporter of the North Atlantic Treaty Organization (NATO), the Organization for Economic Cooperation and Development (OECD), the General Agreement on Tariffs and Trade/World Trade Organization (GATT/WTO), the Organization for Security and Cooperation in Europe (OSCE), the Western European Union (WEU), and the Council of Europe. It chaired the CSCE and the G-7 in 1994 and the EU in 1996. Italy firmly supports the United Nations and its international security activi-

ties. Italy actively participated in and deployed troops in support of UN peacekeeping missions in Somalia, Mozambique, and Cambodia and provides critical support for NATO and UN operations in Bosnia, Kosovo, and Albania.

The Italian Government seeks to obtain consensus with other European countries on various defense and security issues within the WEU as well as NATO. European integration and the development of common defense and security policies will continue to be of primary interest to Italy.

# U.S.-ITALY RELATIONS

The United States enjoys warm and friendly relations with Italy. The two are NATO allies and cooperate in the United Nations; in various regional organizations; and bilaterally for peace, prosperity, and defense. Italy has worked closely with the United States and others on such issues as NATO and UN operations in Bosnia and Kosovo; sanctions against the former Yugoslavia; assistance to Russia and the New Independent States (NIS); Middle East peace process multilateral talks; Somalia and Mozambique peacekeeping; and combating drug trafficking, trafficking in women and children, and terrorism.

Under longstanding bilateral agreements flowing from NATO membership, Italy hosts important U.S. military forces at Vincenza and Livorno (Army); Aviano (Air Force); and Sigonella, Gaeta, and Naples—home port for the U.S. Navy Sixth Fleet. The United States has about 17,000 military personnel stationed in Italy. Italy hosts the NATO War College in Rome.

Italy remains a strong and active transatlantic partner which, along with the United States, has sought to foster democratic ideals and international cooperation in areas of strife and civil conflict. Toward this end, the Italian Government has cooperated with the U.S. in the formulation of defense, security, and peacekeeping policies.

## Principal U.S. Officials

**For up-to-date information on Principal U.S. Officials, see the U.S. Embassies, Consulates, and Foreign Service section starting on page 139.**

The U.S. embassy in Italy is located at Via Veneto 119, Rome (tel. (39)(06) 46741 The URL for the embassy web page is: http://www.usis. it/mission/

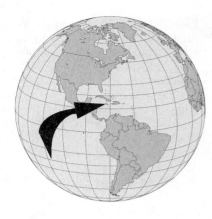

# JAMAICA

April 2001

Official Name:
**Jamaica**

# PROFILE

## Geography

**Area:** 10,991 sq. km. (4,244 sq. mi.).
**Cities:** Capital—Kingston metro area (pop. 628,000). Other cities—Montego Bay (96,600), Spanish Town (122,700).
**Terrain:** Mountainous, coastal plains.
**Climate:** Tropical.

## People

**Nationality:** Noun and adjective—Jamaican(s).
**Population:** (2000 est.) 2.65 million.
**Annual growth rate:** (1993–99) 1.0%.
**Ethnic groups:** African 90.9 %, East Indian 1.3%, Chinese 0.2%, White 0.2%, mixed 7.3%, other 0.1%. Religious affiliation: Anglican, Baptist and other Protestant, Roman Catholic, Rastafarian, Jewish.
**Languages:** English. Patois.
**Education:** Years compulsory—to age 14. Literacy (age 15 and over)—75.4%.
**Health:** (1999) Infant mortality rate—25/1,000. Life expectancy—female 72 yrs., male 69 yrs.
**Work force:** (1999 1,119.1 million) Industry—17.8%. Agriculture—21.4%. Services—60.8 %.

## Government

**Type:** Constitutional parliamentary democracy.
**Independence:** August 6, 1962.
**Constitution:** August 6, 1962.
**Branches**: Executive—Governor General (chief of state, representing British monarch), prime minister, cabinet. Legislative—bicameral Parliament (21 appointed senators, 60 elected representatives). Judicial—Court of Appeal and courts of original jurisdiction.
**Subdivisions:** 14 parishes, 60 electoral constituencies.
**Political parties:** People's National Party (PNP), Jamaica Labour Party (JLP), National Democratic Movement (NDM).
**Suffrage:** Universal at 18.

## Economy

**GDP:** (2000 est.) $6.6 billion.
**Real growth rate:** (1999) -0.4%.
**Per capita GDP:** (1999) $2,531.
**Natural resources:** Bauxite, gypsum, limestone.
**Agriculture:** Products—sugar, bananas, coffee, citrus fruits, allspice.
Industry: Types—tourism, bauxite and alumina, garment assembly, processed foods, sugar, rum, cement, metal, paper, chemical products.
**Trade:** (1999) Exports—$1.24 billion: alumina, bauxite, sugar, bananas, garments, citrus fruits and products, rum, cocoa. Major markets (1998 data)—U.S. 37.8%, U.K. 12.5%, Canada 11.9%, Netherlands 9.7%, Russian Federation 7.2%, Norway 6.1%, CARICOM 3.4%, Japan 1.3%. Imports (1999)—$2.9 billion : machinery, transportation and electrical equipment, food, fuels, fertilizer. Major suppliers (1998)—U.S. 50.9%, Trinidad and Tobago 7.7%, Japan 6.7%, U.K. 3.9%, Canada 3.2%, Mexico 2.6%, China 1.6%, Venezuela 1.5%, Brazil 1.1%.

# U.S.-JAMAICAN RELATIONS

The United States maintains close and productive relations with the Government of Jamaica. Prime Minister Patterson has visited Washington, DC, several times since assuming office in 1992. In May 1997, Prime Minister Patterson joined President Clinton and 14 other Caribbean leaders during the first-ever U.S.-regional summit in Bridgetown, Barbados. The summit strengthened the basis for regional cooperation on justice and counternarcotics issues, finance and development, and trade. The United States is Jamaica's most important trading partner: The bilateral trade in goods in 1999 amounted to about $2 billion. Jamaica is a popular destination for American tourists—more than 800,000 Americans visited in 1999, and the Jamaican Government hopes to increase that number. In addition, some 10,000 American citizens, including many dual-nationals born on the island, permanently reside in Jamaica.

The Government of Jamaica also seeks to attract U.S. investment. An active participant in the Summit of the Americas and its follow-on activities, the Government of Jamaica supports efforts to create a Free Trade Area of the Americans (FTAA). More than 80 U.S. firms have operations in Jamaica, and total U.S. investment is estimated at more than $1 billion. An office of the U.S. and Foreign Commercial Service, located in the embassy, actively assists American businesses seeking trade opportunities in Jamaica. The "807A" program, which guarantees access in the United States for garments made in Caribbean Basin Initiative (CBI) countries from textiles woven and cut in the United States, has opened new opportunities for investment and expansion in Jamaica. The American Chamber of Commerce, which also is available to assist U.S. businesses interested in Jamaica, has offices in Kingston and Montego Bay.

U.S. Agency for International Development (USAID) assistance to Jamaica since its independence in 1962 has contributed to reducing the population growth rate, the attainment of First World standards in a number of critical health indicators, and the diversification and expansion of Jamaica's export base. USAID's primary objective is promoting economic growth and reinforcing Jamaica's commitment to the private sector. Other key objectives are improved environmental quality and natural resource protection, as well as smaller, better-educated families. In FY 2000, the USAID mission in Jamaica operated a $11.8 million program.

The Peace Corps has been in Jamaica continuously since 1962. Since then, over 3,300 volunteers have served in the country. Today, the Peace Corps works in the following projects: Youth-at-Risk, which includes adoles-

cent reproductive health, HIV/AIDS education, and the needs of marginalized males; water sanitation, which includes rural waste water solutions and municipal waste water treatment; and environmental education, which helps address low levels of awareness and strengthens environmental nongovernmental organizations. The Peace Corps in Jamaica fields about 100 volunteers who work in every parish on the island, including some inner-city communities in Kingston.

Jamaica is a producer of marijuana and an increasingly significant cocaine transshipment country. U.S. assistance has played a vital role in stemming the flow of these drugs to the United States. In 2000, Jamaica eradicated 517 hectares of cannabis, seized 55.9 metric tons of marijuana, and seized 1,624 kilograms of cocaine. Effective cooperation between the DEA's Kingston country office and Jamaican law enforcement contributed to more than 8,659 drug arrests in 2000. In March 1998, the U.S. and Jamaica exchanged diplomatic notes bringing into effect a maritime counternarcotics agreement that facilitates U.S.-Jamaican counternarcotics operations.

# HISTORY

Arawaks from South America had settled in Jamaica prior to Christopher Columbus' first arrival to the island in 1494. During Spain's occupation of the island, starting in 1510, the Arawaks were exterminated by disease, slavery, and war. Spain brought the first African slaves to Jamaica in 1517. In 1655, British forces seized the island, and in 1670, Great Britain gained formal possession. Sugar and slavery made Jamaica one of the most valuable possessions in the world for more than 150 years. The British Parliament abolished slavery as of August 1, 1834.

After a long period of direct British colonial rule, Jamaica gained a degree of local political control in the

late 1930s, and held its first election under full universal adult suffrage in 1944. Jamaica joined nine other U.K. territories in the West Indies Federation in 1958 but withdrew after Jamaican voters rejected membership in 1961. Jamaica gained independence in 1962, remaining a member of the Commonwealth.

Historically, Jamaican emigration has been heavy. Since the United Kingdom restricted emigration in 1967, the major flow has been to the United States and Canada. About 20,000 Jamaicans emigrate to the United States each year; another 200,000 visit annually. New York, Miami, Chicago, and Hartford are among the U.S. cities with a significant Jamaican population. Remittances from the expatriate communities in the United States, United Kingdom, and Canada make increasingly significant contributions to Jamaica's economy.

# GOVERNMENT

The 1962 Constitution established a parliamentary system based on the U.K. model. As chief of state, Queen Elizabeth II appoints a governor general, on the advice of the prime minister, as her representative in Jamaica. The governor general's role is largely ceremonial. Executive power is vested in the cabinet, led by the prime minister.

Parliament is composed of an appointed Senate and an elected House of Representatives. Thirteen Senators are nominated on the advice of the prime minister and eight on the advice of the leader of the opposition. General elections must be held within 5 years of the forming of a new government. The prime minister may ask the governor general to call elections sooner, however. The Senate may submit bills, and it also reviews legislation submitted by the House. It may not delay budget bills for more than 1 month or other bills for more than 7 months. The prime minister and the Cabinet are selected from the Parliament. No fewer than two nor more than four members of the Cabinet must be selected from the Senate.

The judiciary also is modeled on the U.K. system. The Court of Appeals is the highest appellate court in Jamaica. Under certain circumstances, cases may be appealed to the Privy Council of the United Kingdom. Jamaica's parishes have elected councils that exercise limited powers of local government.

## Principal Government Officials

**For up-to-date information on Principal Government Officials, see the Chiefs of State and Cabinet Members of Foreign Governments section starting on page 1.**

Jamaica maintains an embassy in the United States at 1520 New Hampshire Avenue NW, Washington, DC 20036 (tel. 202–452–0660). It also has consulates in New York at 767 3rd Avenue, New York, NY 10017 (tel. 212–935–9000); and in Miami in the Ingraham Building, Suite 842, 25 SE 2nd Avenue, Miami, FL 33131 (tel. 305–374–8431/2).

# POLITICAL CONDITIONS

Jamaica's political system is stable. However, the country's serious economic problems have exacerbated social problems and have become the subject of political debate. High unemployment—averaging 15.7% in 1999—rampant underemployment, growing debt, high interest rates, and labor unrest are the most serious economic problems. The migration of unemployed people to urban areas, coupled with an increase in the use and trafficking of narcotics—crack cocaine and ganja (marijuana)—contribute to a high level of violent crime, especially in Kingston.

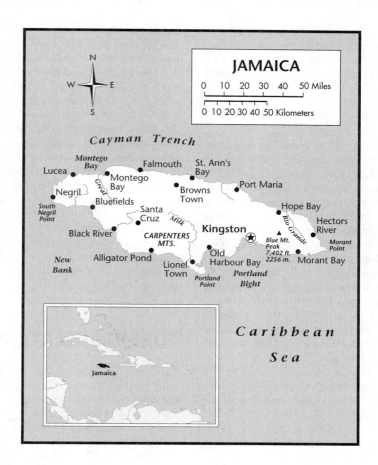

The two long-established political parties have historical links with two major trade unions—the Jamaica Labour Party (JLP) with the Bustamante Industrial Trade Union (BITU) and the People's National Party (PNP) with the National Workers Union (NWU). A third party, the National Democratic Movement (NDM), was created in October 1995; it does not have links with any particular trade union.

For health reasons, Michael Manley stepped down as Prime Minister in March 1992 and was replaced by P.J. Patterson. Patterson subsequently led the PNP to victory in general elections in 1993 and in December 1997. The 1997 victory marked the first time any Jamaican political party has won three consecutive general elections since the introduction of universal suffrage to Jamaica in 1944. The current composition of the lower house of Jamaica's Parliament is 49 PNP and 11 JLP. The JLP won a long-held PNP parliamentary seat in a

March 2001 by-election. The NDM, a breakaway faction of the JLP, failed to win any seats in the 1997 election.

Since the 1993 elections, the Jamaican Government, political parties, and Electoral Advisory Committee have worked to enact electoral reform, with limited success. In the 1997 general elections, grass-roots Jamaican efforts, supplemented by international observers, helped reduce the violence that has tended to mar Jamaican elections. Local elections were held in 1998, when the PNP won a decisive victory. Jamaican law requires that local elections be held every 3 years; elections may be delayed through legislation.

# ECONOMY

Jamaica has natural resources, primarily bauxite, and an ideal climate conducive to agriculture and tourism. The discovery of bauxite in the 1940s and the subsequent establishment of the bauxite-alumina industry shifted Jamaica's economy from sugar and bananas. By the 1970s, Jamaica had emerged as a world leader in export of these minerals as foreign investment increased.

The country faces some serious problems but has the potential for growth and modernization. The Jamaican economy suffered its fourth consecutive year of negative growth (0.4%) in 1999. In 2000, Jamaica may have experienced its first year of positive growth since 1995. All sectors excepting bauxite/alumina, energy, and tourism shrank in 1998 and 1999. This reduction in aggregate demand and output is the result of the government's continued tight macroeconomic policies. In part, these policies have been successful. Inflation has fallen from 25% in 1995 to 6.1% in 2000. Through periodic intervention in the market, the central bank also has prevented any abrupt drop in the exchange rate. The Jamaican dollar has been slipping, despite intervention, resulting in an average exchange rate of J$43.5 to the US$1.00 (2000).

Weakness in the financial sector, speculation, and lower levels of investment erode confidence in the productive sector. The government continues its efforts to raise new sovereign debt in local and international financial markets in order to meet its U.S. dollar debt obligations, to mop up liquidity to maintain the exchange rate and to help fund the current budget deficit.

Jamaican Government economic policies encourage foreign investment in areas that earn or save foreign exchange, generate employment, and use local raw materials. The government provides a wide range of incentives to investors, including remittance facilities to assist them in repatriating funds to the country of origin; tax holidays which defer taxes for a period of years; and duty-free access for machinery and raw materials imported for approved enter-

prises. Free trade zones have stimulated investment in garment assembly, light manufacturing, and data entry by foreign firms. However, over the last 5 years, the garment industry has suffered from reduced export earnings, continued factory closures, and rising unemployment. This may be attributed to intense competition, absence of NAFTA parity, drug contamination delaying deliveries, and the high cost of operation, including security costs. The Government of Jamaica hopes to encourage economic activity through a combination of privatization, financial sector restructuring, reduced interest rates, and by boosting tourism and related productive activities.

# FOREIGN RELATIONS

Jamaica has diplomatic relations with most nations and is a member of the United Nations and the Organization of American States. In the follow-on meetings to the December 1994 Summit of the Americas, Jamaica—together with Uruguay—was given the responsibility of coordinating discussions on invigorating society. Jamaica also chairs the Working Group on Smaller Economies.

Jamaica is an active member of the British Commonwealth and the Non-Aligned Movement (G-77). Jamaica is a beneficiary of the Lome Conventions, through which the European Union (EU) grants trade preferences to selected states in Asia, the Caribbean, and the Pacific, and has played a leading role in the negotiations of the successor agreement in Fiji in 2000.

Historically, Jamaica has had close ties with the U.K., but trade, financial, and cultural relations with the United States are now predominant. Jamaica is linked with the other countries of the English-speaking Caribbean through the Caribbean Community (CARICOM), and more broadly through the Association of Caribbean States (ACS). In January

2000, Jamaica began serving a 2-year term on the United Nations Security Council.

## Travel Notes

**Travel Advice:** For up-to-date information from the U.S. State Department on possible inconvenient or hazardous situations, see the **Travel Warnings and Consular Information Sheets from the U.S. Government** section starting on page 1723. For the latest information on health requirements and conditions, see the **International Travelers' Health Information** section starting on page 1385. For further information dealing with non-urgent matter, see the **Tips for Travelers to...** section starting on page 1588.

Prime Minister Patterson visited Cuba at the end of May 1997. In the fall of 1997, Jamaica upgraded its consulate in Havana to an embassy, and the nonresident Jamaican ambassador to Cuba was replaced by a resident ambassador.

## Principal U.S. Officials

**For up-to-date information on Principal U.S. Officials, see the U.S. Embassies, Consulates, and Foreign Service section starting on page 139.**

The U.S. Embassy in Jamaica is at 2 Oxford Road, Jamaica Mutual Life Center, Kingston (tel. 876- 929–4850).
The Consular section is at 16 Oxford Road, Kingston (tel. 876–929–4850). The USAID Mission is at 2 Haining Road, Kingston (tel. 876–926–3645). The Peace Corps is at 1A Holborn Road, Kingston (tel. 876–929–0495). Log on the internet to: http://www.usembassy.state.gov/kingston for more information about Jamaica, the U.S. embassy and its activities, and current contact information.

## Other Contact Information

### U.S. Department of Commerce

International Trade Administration
Trade Information Center 14th and
Constitution Avenue, NW
Washington, DC 20230
Tel: 800-USA-TRADE or 800–872–8723
Web site: www.ita.doc.gov/tic

### American Chamber of Commerce of Jamaica

The Hilton Hotel 77 Knutsford Boulevard
Kingston 5, Jamaica Tel: (876) 929–7866/67
Fax: (876) 929–8597
E-Mail: amcham@cwjamaica.com
(Branch in Montego Bay)

### Caribbean/Latin American Action

1818 N Street, NW Suite 500
Washington, DC 20036
Tel: (202) 466–7464
Fax: (202) 822–0075
E-mail: info@claa.org
Web site: www.claa.org

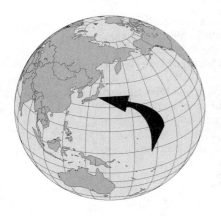

# JAPAN

July 2000

Official Name:
**Japan**

# PROFILE

## Geography

**Area:** 377,765 sq. km. (145,856 sq. mi.); slightly smaller than California.
**Cities:** Capital—Tokyo. Other cities—Yokohama, Osaka, Nagoya, Sapporo, Kobe, Kyoto, Fukuoka.
**Terrain:** Rugged, mountainous islands.
**Climate:** Varies from subtropical to temperate.

## People

**Nationality:** Noun and adjective—Japanese.
**Population:** (1998) 126.2 million.
**Population growth rate:** (1997) 0.23%.
**Ethnic Groups:** Japanese; Korean (0.6%).
**Religion:** Shinto and Buddhist; Christian (about 1%).
**Language:** Japanese.
**Education:** Literacy—99%.
**Health:** (1997) Infant mortality rate—4/1,000. Life expectancy—males 77 yrs., females 83 yrs.
**Work force:** (67 million, 1997) Services—23%; trade, manufacturing, mining, and construction—56%; agriculture, forestry, fisheries—6%; government—3%.

## Government

**Type:** Constitutional monarchy with a parliamentary government.
**Constitution:** May 3, 1947.
**Branches:** Executive—prime minister (head of government). Legislative—bicameral Diet (House of Representatives and House of Councillors). Judicial—civil law system based on the model of Roman law.
**Administrative subdivisions:** 47 prefectures.
**Political parties:** Liberal Democratic Party (LDP), Democratic Party of Japan (DPJ), Komeito, Liberal Party, Conservative Party, Japan Communist Party (JCP), Social Democratic Party (SDP).
**Suffrage:** Universal at 20.

## Economy

**GDP:** (1998) $3.797 trillion.
**Real growth rate:** (1998) -2.8%.
**Per capita GDP:** (1998) $30,100.
**Natural resources:** Negligible mineral resources, fish.
**Agriculture:** Products—rice, vegetables, fruits, milk, meat, silk.
**Industry:** Types—machinery and equipment, metals and metal products, textiles, autos, chemicals, electrical and electronic equipment. Japan's industrialized, free market economy is the second-largest in the world. Its economy is highly efficient and competitive in areas linked to international trade, but productivity is far lower in areas such as agriculture, distribution, and services. After achieving one of the highest economic growth rates in the world from the 1960s through the 1980s, the Japanese economy slowed dramatically in the early 1990s, when the "bubble economy" collapsed. For 2000, the economy is projected to grow at a rate of 0.9% (IMF fig.).

# PEOPLE

Japan is one of the most densely populated nations in the world, with some 330 persons per square kilometer (almost 860 persons per sq. mi.). For 1997, the population growth rate was about 0.23%. Japan's low population growth rate in recent years has raised concerns about the social implications of an aging population.

The Japanese are a Mongoloid people, closely related to the major groups of East Asia. However, some evidence also exists of a mixture with Malayan and Caucasoid strains. About 750,000 Koreans and much smaller groups of Chinese and Caucasians reside in Japan.

Buddhism is important in Japan's religious life and has strongly influenced fine arts, social institutions, and philosophy. Most Japanese consider themselves members of one of the major Buddhist sects.

Shintoism is an indigenous religion founded on myths, legends, and ritual practices of the early Japanese. Neither Buddhism nor Shintoism is an exclusive religion. Most Japanese observe both Buddhist and Shinto rituals: the former for funerals and the latter for births, marriages, and other occasions. Confucianism, primarily an ethical system, profoundly influences Japanese thought as well. About 1.3 million people in Japan are Christians, of whom 60% are Protestant and 40% Roman Catholic.

Japan provides free public schooling for all children through junior high school. Ninety-four percent of students go on to 3-year senior high schools, and competition is stiff for entry into the best universities. Japan enjoys one of the world's highest literacy rates (99%), and nearly 90% of Japanese students complete high school.

# HISTORY

Traditional Japanese legend maintains that Japan was founded in 600 BC by the Emperor Jimmu, a direct descendant of the sun goddess and ancestor of the present ruling imperial family. About AD 405, the Japanese court officially adopted the Chinese writing system. During the sixth century, Buddhism was introduced. These two events revolutionized Japanese culture and marked the beginning of a long period of Chinese cultural influence. From the establishment of the first fixed capital at Nara in 710 until 1867, the emperors of the Yamato dynasty were the nominal rulers, but actual power was usually held by powerful court nobles, regents, or "shoguns" (military governors).

## Contact With the West

The first contact with the West occurred about 1542, when a Portuguese ship, blown off its course to China, landed in Japan. During the next century, traders from Portugal, the Netherlands, England, and Spain arrived, as did Jesuit, Dominican, and Franciscan missionaries. During the early part of the 17th century, Japan's shogunate suspected that the traders and missionaries were actually forerunners of a military conquest by European powers. This caused the shogunate to place foreigners under progressively tighter restrictions. Ultimately, Japan forced all foreigners to leave and barred all relations with the outside world except for severely restricted commercial contacts with Dutch and Chinese merchants at Nagasaki. This isolation lasted for 200 years, until Commodore Matthew Perry of the U.S. Navy forced the opening of Japan to the West with the Convention of Kanagawa in 1854.

Within several years, renewed contact with the West profoundly altered Japanese society. The shogunate was forced to resign, and the emperor was restored to power. The "Meiji restoration" of 1868 initiated many reforms. The feudal system was abolished, and numerous Western institutions were adopted, including a Western legal system and constitutional government along quasi-parliamentary lines.

In 1898, the last of the "unequal treaties" with Western powers was removed, signaling Japan's new status among the nations of the world. In a few decades, by creating modern social, educational, economic, military, and industrial systems, the Emperor Meiji's "controlled revolution" had transformed a feudal and isolated state into a world power.

## Wars With China and Russia

Japanese leaders of the late 19th century regarded the Korean Peninsula as a "dagger pointed at the heart of Japan." It was over Korea that Japan became involved in war with the Chinese Empire in 1894-95 and with Russia in 1904-05. The war with China established Japan's dominant interest in Korea, while giving it the Pescadores Islands and Formosa (now Taiwan). After Japan defeated Russia in 1905, the resulting Treaty of Portsmouth awarded Japan certain rights in Manchuria and in southern Sakhalin, which Russia had received in 1875 in exchange for the Kurile Islands. Both wars gave Japan a free hand in Korea, which it formally annexed in 1910.

## World War I to 1952

World War I permitted Japan, which fought on the side of the victorious Allies, to expand its influence in Asia and its territorial holdings in the Pacific. The postwar era brought Japan unprecedented prosperity. Japan went to the peace conference at Versailles in 1919 as one of the great military and industrial powers of the world and received official recognition as one of the "Big Five" of the new international order. It joined the League of Nations and received a mandate over Pacific islands north of the Equator formerly held by Germany. During the 1920s, Japan progressed toward a democratic system of government. However, parliamentary government was not rooted deeply enough to withstand the economic and political pressures of the 1930s, during which military leaders became increasingly influential.

Japan invaded Manchuria in 1931 and set up the puppet state of Manchukuo. In 1933, Japan resigned from the League of Nations. The Japanese invasion of China in 1937 followed Japan's signing of the "anti-Comintern pact" with Nazi Germany the previous year and was part of a chain of developments culminating in the Japanese attack on the United States at Pearl Harbor, Hawaii on December 7, 1941.

After almost 4 years of war, resulting in the loss of 3 million Japanese lives and the atomic bombings of Hiroshima and Nagasaki, Japan signed an instrument of surrender on the U.S.S. Missouri in Tokyo Harbor on September 2, 1945. As a result of World War II, Japan lost all of its overseas possessions and retained only the home islands. Manchukuo was dissolved, and Manchuria was returned to China; Japan renounced all claims to Formosa; Korea was granted independence; southern Sakhalin and the Kuriles were occupied by the U.S.S.R.; and the United States became the sole administering

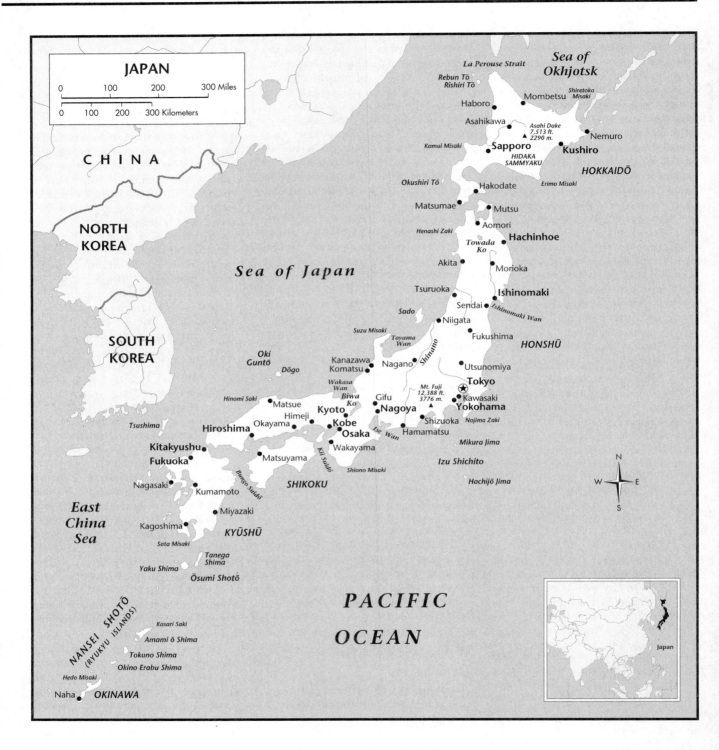

**JAPAN**

| 0 | 100 | 200 | 300 Miles |
| 0 | 100 | 200 | 300 Kilometers |

authority of the Ryukyu, Bonin, and Volcano Islands. The 1972 reversion of Okinawa completed the United States' return of control of these islands to Japan.

After the war, Japan was placed under international control of the Allies through the Supreme Com-mander, Gen. Douglas MacArthur. U.S. objectives were to ensure that Japan would become a peaceful nation and to establish democratic self-government supported by the freely expressed will of the people. Political, economic, and social reforms were introduced, such as a freely elected Japanese Diet (legisla-ture). The country's constitution took effect on May 3, 1947. The United States and 45 other Allied nations signed the Treaty of Peace with Japan in September 1951. The U.S. Senate ratified the treaty in March 1952, and under the terms of the treaty, Japan regained full sover-eignty on April 28, 1952.

## Recent Political Developments

The post-World War II years saw tremendous economic growth in Japan, with the political system dominated by the Liberal Democratic Party (LDP). That total domination lasted until the Diet Lower House elections on July 18, 1993 in which the LDP, in power since the mid-1950s, failed to win a majority and saw the end of its four-decade rule. A coalition of new parties and existing opposition parties formed a governing majority and elected a new prime minister, Morihiro Hosokawa, in August 1993. His government's major legislative objective was political reform, consisting of a package of new political financing restrictions and major changes in the electoral system. The coalition succeeded in passing landmark political reform legislation in January 1994.

Under the 1994 legislation, the Lower House electoral system was changed to one in which 300 members are elected in single-member districts and another 200 members on proportional slates in 11 regions. The new electoral system also reduced the number of seats in overly represented rural areas and shifted them to some urban areas. The overall number of seats was reduced to 480 total as of the June 2000 elections.

In April 1994, Prime Minister Hosokawa resigned. Prime Minister Tsutomu Hata formed the successor coalition government, Japan's first minority government in almost 40 years. Prime Minister Hata resigned less than 2 months later. Prime Minister Tomiichi Murayama formed the next government in June 1994, a coalition of his Japan Socialist Party (JSP), the LDP, and the small Sakigake Party. The advent of a coalition containing the JSP and LDP shocked many observers because of their previously fierce rivalry. Prime Minister Murayama served from June 1994 to January 1996. He was succeeded by Prime Minister Ryutaro Hashimoto, who served from January 1996 to July 1998. Prime Minister Hashimoto headed a loose coalition of three parties until the July 1998 Upper House election, when the two smaller parties cut ties with the LDP. Hashimoto resigned due to a poor electoral showing by the LDP in those Upper House elections. He was succeeded as party president of the LDP and prime minister by Keizo Obuchi, who took office on July 30, 1998.

The LDP formed a governing coalition with the Liberal Party in January 1999, and Keizo Obuchi remained prime minister. The LDP-Liberal coalition expanded to include the Komeito Party in October 1999. Prime Minister Obuchi suffered a stroke in April 2000 and was replaced by Yoshiro Mori, who retained all of his predecessor's cabinet members. After the Liberal Party left the coalition in April 2000, Prime Minister Mori welcomed a Liberal Party splinter group, the Conservative Party, into the ruling coalition. In June 2000 Lower House elections, Prime Minister Mori's three-party coalition of the LDP, Komeito, and the Conservative Party maintained its majority in the Diet.

# GOVERNMENT AND POLITICAL CONDITIONS

Japan is a constitutional monarchy with a parliamentary government. There is universal adult suffrage with a secret ballot for all elective offices. The executive branch is responsible to the Diet, and the judicial branch is independent. Sovereignty, previously embodied in the emperor, is vested in the Japanese people, and the emperor is defined as the symbol of the state. Japan's Government is a parliamentary democracy, with a House of Representatives and a House of Councillors. Executive power is vested in a cabinet composed of a prime minister and ministers of state, all of whom must be civilians. The prime minister must be a member of the Diet and is designated by his colleagues. The prime minister has the power to appoint and remove ministers, a majority of whom must be Diet members.

Japan's judicial system, drawn from customary law, civil law, and Anglo-American common law, consists of several levels of courts, with the Supreme Court as the final judicial authority. The Japanese constitution includes a bill of rights similar to the U.S. Bill of Rights, and the Supreme Court has the right of judicial review. Japanese courts do not use a jury system, and there are no administrative courts or claims courts. Because of the judicial system's basis, court decisions are made in accordance with legal statutes. Only Supreme Court decisions have any direct effect on later interpretation of the law.

Japan does not have a federal system, and its 47 prefectures are not sovereign entities in the sense that U.S. States are. Most depend on the central government for subsidies. Governors of prefectures, mayors of municipalities, and prefectural and municipal assembly members are popularly elected to 4-year terms.

## Principal Government Officials

**For up-to-date information on Principal Government Officials, see the Chiefs of State and Cabinet Members of Foreign Governments section starting on page 1.**

Japan maintains an embassy in the United States at 2520 Massachusetts Avenue NW, Washington, DC (tel. 202-238-6700).
Consulates General are in Anchorage, Atlanta, Boston, Chicago, Detroit, Guam, Honolulu, Houston, Kansas City, Los Angeles, New Orleans, New York City, Portland, San Francisco, and Seattle.
Honorary consulates general are in Buffalo, Cleveland, Dallas, Denver, Nashville, Miami, Minneapolis, Mobile, Phoenix, St. Louis, San Diego, and San Juan; and an honorary consulate is in American Samoa.
The Japan National Tourist Organi-

zation is at 630 Fifth Avenue, New York, NY, 10111.

# ECONOMY

Japan is the second-largest economy in the world after the United States. Its reservoir of industrial leadership and technicians, well-educated and industrious work force, high savings and investment rates, and intensive promotion of industrial development and foreign trade have produced a mature industrial economy. Along with North America and western Europe, Japan is one of the three major industrial complexes among the market economies. Japan has few natural resources, and trade helps it earn the foreign exchange needed to purchase raw materials for its economy. In 1997, the country's exports amounted to about 12% of its GDP.

While Japan's long-term economic prospects are considered good, Japan is currently in its worst recession since World War II. Plummeting stock and real estate prices marked the end of the "bubble economy" of the late 1980s. The impact of the Asian financial crisis also has been substantial. Real GDP in Japan grew at an average of roughly 1.25% yearly between 1991-98, compared to growth in the 1980s of about 4% per year. Growth in Japan in this decade has been slower than growth in other major industrial nations. The Government of Japan has forecast growth in Japan fiscal year 1999 at 0.5%. A number of economic indicators remain in negative territory, but Japan announced strong growth (1.9%) for first quarter 1999.

## Agriculture, Energy, and Minerals

Only 15% of Japan's land is suitable for cultivation. The agricultural economy is highly subsidized and protected. With per hectare crop yields among the highest in the world, Japan maintains an overall agricultural self-sufficiency rate of about 50% on fewer than 5.6 million cultivated hectares (14 million acres). Japan normally produces a slight

**Travel Notes**

**Travel Advice:** For up-to-date information from the U.S. State Department on possible inconvenient or hazardous situations, see the **Travel Warnings and Consular Information Sheets from the U.S. Government** section starting on page 1723. For the latest information on health requirements and conditions, see the **International Travelers' Health Information** section starting on page 1385. For further information dealing with non-urgent matter, see the **Tips for Travelers to...** section starting on page 1588.

surplus of rice but imports large quantities of wheat, sorghum, and soybeans, primarily from the United States. As part of the General Agreement on Tariffs and Trade (GATT) Uruguay Round, Japan agreed to open its agricultural markets further, including partial liberalization of the rice market.

Given its heavy dependence on imported energy, Japan has aimed to diversify its sources. Since the oil shocks of the 1970s, Japan has reduced dependence on petroleum as a source of energy from more than 75% in 1973 to about 57% at present. Other important energy sources are coal, liquefied natural gas, nuclear power, and hydropower.

Deposits of gold, magnesium, and silver meet current industrial demands, but Japan is dependent on foreign sources for many of the minerals essential to modern industry. Iron ore, coke, copper, and bauxite must be imported, as must many forest products.

## Transportation

Japan has a well-developed international and domestic transportation system, although highway development still lags. Tokyo and Osaka International Airports and the ports of Yokohama, Osaka, Kobe, and Nagoya are important terminals for air and sea traffic in the western Pacific. However, greatly increased traffic in the Pacific markets is put-

ting a severe strain on Japan's airports.

The domestic transportation system depends on a recently privatized rail network. National rail transportation is supplemented by private railways in metropolitan areas, a developing highway system, coastal shipping, and several airlines. The rail system is efficient and well-distributed and is maintained throughout the country. The super express "bullet trains" take as little as 3 hours between Tokyo and Osaka, a distance of 520 kilometers (325 mi.).

## Labor

Japan's labor force consists of some 67 million workers, 40% of whom are women. Labor union membership is about 12 million. The unemployment rate is currently at a record high 4.9%. In 1989, the predominantly public sector union confederation, SOHYO (General Council of Trade Unions of Japan), merged with RENGO (Japanese Private Sector Trade Union Confederation) to form the Japanese Trade Union Confederation, also called RENGO, which has more than 7 million members.

# FOREIGN RELATIONS

Despite its current slow economic growth, Japan remains a major economic power both in the region and globally. Japan has diplomatic relations with nearly all independent nations and has been an active member of the United Nations since 1956. Japanese foreign policy has aimed to promote peace and prosperity for the Japanese people by working closely with the West and supporting the United Nations.

After World War II, the Allies disarmed and occupied Japan. Article IX of the Japanese constitution provides that "land, sea, and air forces, as well as other war potential, will never be maintained." During the 1950-53 Korean war, a national police reserve force was established. Before the end of the U.S. occupation of Japan in 1952, the first steps had been taken

Photo credit: Corel Corporation.

**Farmer planting rice. Japan's per-hectare crop yields are among the highest in the world.**

to expand and transform the force into the Self-Defense Force (SDF). At the same time, the Japanese Government accepted Article 51 of the UN Charter that each nation has the right of self-defense against armed attack. This doctrine was consistent with Article IX of the Japanese constitution.

In 1954, the Japan Defense Agency was created with the specific mission of defending Japan against external aggression. Ground, maritime, and air self-defense forces were established.

In recent years, the Japanese public has shown a substantially greater awareness of security issues and increasing support for the SDF. This is in part due to its success in disaster relief efforts at home and its participation in peacekeeping operations in Cambodia in the early 1990s. However, there are still significant political and psychological constraints on strengthening Japan's defense.

Although a military role for Japan in international affairs is precluded by its constitution and government policy, Japanese cooperation with the United States through the 1960 U.S.-Japan security treaty has been important to the peace and stability of East Asia. All postwar Japanese governments have relied on a close

relationship with the United States as the foundation of their foreign policy and have depended on the mutual security treaty for strategic protection.

While maintaining its relationship with the United States, Japan has diversified and expanded its ties with other nations. Good relations with its neighbors continue to be of vital interest. After the signing of a peace and friendship treaty with China in 1978, ties between the two countries developed rapidly. The Japanese extend significant economic assistance to the Chinese in various modernization projects. At the same time, Japan has maintained economic but not diplomatic relations with Taiwan, where a strong bilateral trade relationship thrives.

Japanese ties with South Korea have improved since an exchange of visits in the mid-1980s by their political leaders. R.O.K. President Kim Dae-jung had a very successful visit to Japan in October 1998. Japan has limited economic and commercial ties with North Korea. Japanese normalization talks halted when North Korea refused to discuss a number of issues with Japan. Japan strongly supports the U.S. in its efforts to encourage Pyongyang to abide by the nuclear Non-Proliferation Treaty and its agreements with the International

Atomic Energy Agency (IAEA). Despite the August 31, 1998 North Korean missile test which overflew the Home Islands, Japan has repeated its support for the Korean Energy Development Organization (KEDO) and the Agreed Framework, which seek to freeze the North Korean nuclear program.

Russo-Japanese relations have warmed considerably since 1996, despite the fact that Russia continues to claim and occupy the Northern Territories, small islands off the coast of Hokkaido occupied by the U.S.S.R. at the end of World War II. But recent summits in 1997 and 1998 between former PM Hashimoto and President Yeltsin have accelerated work on a peace treaty that would settle the Northern Territories dispute and normalize bilateral relations. To further mutual confidence and trust, Japan has pledged about $4 billion to various programs designed to bolster Russian democracy and economic reform.

Beyond its immediate neighbors, Japan has pursued a more active foreign policy in recent years, recognizing the responsibility that accompanies its economic strength. It has expanded ties with the Middle East, which provides most of its oil. Japan increasingly is active in Africa and Latin America and has extended significant support to development projects in both regions. And a Japanese-conceived peace plan became the foundation for nationwide elections in Cambodia in 1998.

After the Iraqi invasion of Kuwait in August 1990, Japan adopted tough sanctions against Iraq and strongly supported the UN effort against the aggression. Japanese financial support for the Gulf war reached $14 billion. Japan actively supported the Israel-Palestine peace framework. From October 1993, Japan has contributed $300 million to Palestinian reconstruction. Under the framework of the Middle East Peace Process, Japan chairs the multilateral working group on environment and participates in other working groups.

In the 1990s, Japanese military and police forces as well as civilians have participated in a wide variety of UN peacekeeping missions. These have included Cambodia (two Japanese citizens were killed in that effort), Mozambique, the Golan Heights, and relief efforts for Rwandan refugees in what was then Zaire (now Congo). Japan did not send any Self-Defense Force units to Somalia but financed much of the effort there with a $100 million contribution. In 1998, the Japanese Self-Defense Forces conducted its first-ever overseas military relief operation. The Japanese military dispatched 105 personnel to Central America to provide humanitarian disaster relief in Honduras and Nicaragua in the wake of Hurricane Mitch.

Development assistance is a major tool of Japan's foreign policy. Japan has been the world's largest aid donor since 1989, with aid levels of $9 billion. Japanese aid to other Asian countries exceeds that of the United States, and Japan also is a major donor to central and eastern Europe, Latin America, and the Middle East. Japan and the United States hold regular consultations to coordinate foreign assistance programs. The United States supports Japan's efforts to open its markets to developing nations' products.

# U.S.-JAPAN RELATIONS

The United States' close and cooperative relationship with Japan is the cornerstone of U.S. policy in Asia and the basis of a strong, productive partnership in addressing global issues. Despite different social and cultural traditions, Japan and the United States have much in common. Both have open, democratic societies, high literacy rates, freedom of expression, multiparty political systems, universal suffrage, and open elections. Both have highly developed free-market industrial economies and favor an open and active international trading system. As noted, Japan is one of the three major industrial complexes among the market economies, along with North America and western Europe. The U.S. supports Japan's goal of obtaining a permanent seat on the United Nations Security Council.

Because of the two countries' combined economic and technological impact on the world (together accounting for a little more than 30% of world GDP and 60% of the Western industrialized nations' GDP), the U.S.-Japan relationship has become global in scope. The two governments have developed a partnership to address shared priorities. An example of that partnership is the U.S.-Japan "Common Agenda for Global Issues," a set of initiatives in areas such as the environment, technology development, and health. Under the Common Agenda, the United States and Japan are coordinating $12 billion in population and HIV/AIDS assistance to developing countries and are conducting joint research on advanced transportation and environmental technologies. The two governments also are cooperating closely on issues as diverse as ocean pollution, children's vaccines, narcotics demand reduction, the role of women in development, and the protection of forests and coral reefs.

## Security Relations

The U.S.-Japan security alliance remains indispensable to the defense of Japan and to U.S. security strategy in East Asia. The U.S.-Japan Treaty of Mutual Cooperation and Security came into force on June 23, 1960. Under the treaty, Japan hosts a carrier battle group, the III Marine Expeditionary Force, the 5th Air Force, and elements of the Army's I Corps. At the end of U.S. occupation in 1952, U.S. military forces in Japan numbered around 260,000. The U.S. currently maintains over 40,000 forces in Japan, more than half of whom are stationed in Okinawa. Japan's Host Nation Support (HNS) helps to defray about 75% of the costs of maintaining these forces in Japan. In Okinawa, initiatives begun under the U.S.-Japan Special Action Committee on Okinawa (SACO) are returning tracts of military base land to Okinawans, as well as making U.S. military activity on the island less intrusive to Okinawan residents.

Japan's Self-Defense Force has gradually expanded its capabilities and assumed primary responsibility for the immediate conventional national defense. The SDF mission, which the United States supports, is the defense of Japan's homeland, territorial seas and skies, and sea lines of communication out to 1,000 nautical miles. As a matter of policy, Japan has forsworn nuclear armaments and forbids arms sales abroad. A bilateral agreement signed in 1983, however, allows the export of Japanese defense and dual-use technology to the United States. Despite the changes in the post-Cold War strategic landscape, the U.S.-Japan alliance continues to be based on shared vital interests. These include stability in the Asia-Pacific region, the preservation and promotion of political and economic freedoms, support for human rights and democratic institutions, and securing of prosperity for our people and other people of the region.

## Economic Relations

U.S. economic policy toward Japan is aimed at increasing access to Japan's markets, stimulating domestic demand-led economic growth, and raising the standard of living in both the U.S. and Japan. The U.S.-Japan bilateral economic relationship is strong, mature, and increasingly interdependent. It is based on enormous flows of trade, investment, and finance. It is firmly rooted in the shared interest and responsibility of the U.S. and Japan to promote global growth, open markets, and a vital world trading system.

In addition to bilateral economic ties, the U.S. and Japan cooperate closely in multilateral fora such as the World Trade Organization (WTO), Organization for Economic Cooperation and Development, the World Bank, and the International Monetary Fund, and regionally in the Asia-Pacific Economic Cooperation forum (APEC).

Japan is a major market for many U.S. manufactured goods, including chemicals, pharmaceuticals, photo supplies, commercial aircraft, nonferrous metals, plastics, and medical and scientific supplies. Japan also is the largest foreign market for U.S. agricultural products, with total agricultural imports valued at close to $17 billion in 1996.

Bilateral trade has increased dramatically over the decade. U.S. exports to Japan reached $57.8 billion in 1998, down, due to Japan's recession, from $67.6 billion in 1996 but up from $47.9 billion in 1993. U.S. imports from Japan were $121.8 billion in 1998, up from $102.2 billion in 1993.

However, U.S. businesses continue to face structural obstacles in Japan, ranging from time-consuming customs clearance to anticompetitive practices to government regulation. The U.S. Government shares the view of many in Japan who believe that Japanese deregulation is crucial for Japan's long-term economic growth. The U.S. Government is addressing the sectoral, structural, and macroeconomic issues in the bilateral economic relationship through the "Framework for a New Economic Partnership," signed in June 1993 by President Clinton and then-Prime Minister Miyazawa and renewed in June 1995. Under the Framework, the U.S. has concluded with Japan the Enhanced Initiative on Deregulation, as well as agreements to expand market access in such important sectors as telecommunications, medical and pharmaceutical products, autos and parts, agricultural products, insurance, flat glass, financial services, and civil aviation.

The U.S. also has successfully pursued WTO cases against Japan to increase market access for distilled spirits and for agricultural products. Building on research that demonstrates that trade follows investment, the U.S. also has held discussions with Japan to address the structural features of the Japanese economy that impede the inflow of foreign direct investment. Japan continues to host a far smaller share of global foreign direct investment than any of its G-7 counterparts. U.S. discussions with Japan aim to improve the environment for mergers and acquisitions so that U.S. firms can establish a presence in Japan without having to build one from the ground up; to recruit qualified Japanese employees; and to cut entry costs for U.S. firms by promoting the efficiency of the land market.

U.S. foreign direct investment in Japan reached $38.2 billion in 1998, up from $31.1 billion in 1993. New U.S. investment was especially significant in financial services, internet services, and software, generating new export opportunities for U.S. firms and employment for U.S. workers.

## Principal U.S. Embassy Officials

**For up-to-date information on Principal U.S. Officials, see the U.S. Embassies, Consulates, and Foreign Service section starting on page 139.**

The street address and the international mailing address of the U.S. embassy in Japan is 10-5 Akasaka 1-chome, Minato-ku, Tokyo (107); tel. 81-3-3224-5000; fax 81-3-3505-1862. The APO mailing address is American Embassy Tokyo, Unit 45004, Box 258, APO AP 96337-5004. U.S. consulates general are in Osaka, Sapporo, and Naha, and consulates are in Fukuoka and Nagoya. The American Chamber of Commerce in Japan is at 7th floor, Fukide No. 2 Bldg., 1-21 Toranomon 4-chome, Minato-ku, Tokyo (105).

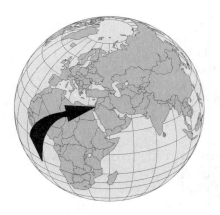

# JORDAN

August 2000

## Official Name:
## Hashemite Kingdom of Jordan

# PROFILE

## Geography

**Area:** 89,544 sq. km. (34,573 sq. mi.).
**Cities:** Capital—Amman (pop. 1 million). Other cities—Irbid (281,000), Az-Zarqa (421,000).

## People

**Nationality:** Noun and adjective—Jordanian(s).
**Population:** (est.) 4.7 million.
**Religions:** (est.) Sunni Muslim 96%, Christian 4%.
**Languages:** Arabic (official), English.
**Education:** (1995) Literacy—87%.
**Health:** Infant mortality rate (1999)—33/1,000. Life expectancy (1992)—71 yrs.
**Ethnic Groups:** Mostly Arab but small communities of Circassians, Armenians, and Kurds.
**Work force:** (1.15 million) Services—64%; industry—30%; agriculture—6%.

## Government

**Type:** Constitutional monarchy.
**Independence:** May 25, 1946.
**Constitution:** January 8, 1952.
**Branches:** Executive—king (chief of state), prime minister (head of government), council of ministers (cabinet). Legislative—bicameral National Assembly (appointed Senate, elected Chamber of Deputies). Judicial—civil, religious, special courts.
**Political parties:** Wide spectrum of parties legalized in 1992.
**Suffrage:** Universal at 20.
**Administrative subdivisions:** Twelve governorates—Irbid, Jarash, Ajloun, al-'Aquaba, Madaba al-Mafraq, al-Zarqa, Amman, al-Balqa, al-Karak, al-Tafilah, and Ma'an.

## Economy

**GDP:** (2000 est.) $16 billion.
**Annual growth rate:** (2000 est.) 3.2%.
**Per capita GDP:** (2000 est.) $3,400.
**Natural resources:** Phosphate, potash.
**Agriculture:** Products—fruits, vegetables, wheat, olive oil. Land—4% arable.
**Industry:** (30% of GDP) Types—phosphate mining, manufacturing, and cement and petroleum production.
**Trade:** (1997 est.) Exports—$1.5 billion: phosphates, fertilizers, potash, agricultural products, manufactures. Major markets—Iraq, Saudi Arabia, U.S., India, EU, Asia, UAE, Syria, Ethiopia, Indonesia. Imports—$3.9 billion: machinery, transportation equipment, food, live animals, petroleum products. Major suppliers—U.S., Iraq, Japan, U.K., Syria, Turkey, Malaysia, China.

Note: From 1949 to 1967, Jordan administered that part of former mandate Palestine west of the Jordan River known as the West Bank. Since the 1967 war, when Israel took control of this territory, the United States has considered the West Bank to be territory occupied by Israel. The United States believes that the final status of the West Bank can be determined only through negotiations among the parties concerned on the basis of Security Council Resolutions 242 and 338.

# PEOPLE

Jordanians are Arabs, except for a few small communities of Circassians, Armenians, and Kurds which have adapted to Arab culture. The official language is Arabic, but English is used widely in commerce and government. About 70% of Jordan's population is urban; less than 6% of the rural population is nomadic or seminomadic. Most people live where the rainfall supports agriculture. About 1.5 million Palestinian Arabs registered as refugees and displaced persons reside in Jordan, most as citizens.

# HISTORY

The land that became Jordan is part of the richly historical Fertile Crescent region. Its history began around 2000 B.C., when Semitic Amorites settled around the Jordan River in the area called Canaan. Subsequent invaders and settlers included Hittites, Egyptians, Israelites, Assyrians, Babylonians, Persians, Greeks, Romans, Arab Muslims, Christian Crusaders, Mameluks, Ottoman Turks, and, finally, the British. At the end of World War I, the territory now comprising Israel, Jordan, the West Bank, Gaza, and Jerusalem was awarded to the United Kingdom by the League of Nations as the mandate for Palestine and Transjordan. In 1922, the British divided the mandate by establishing the semiautonomous Emirate of Transjordan, ruled by the Hashemite Prince Abdullah, while continuing the administration of Palestine under a British High Commissioner. The mandate over Transjordan ended on May 22, 1946; on May 25, the country became the independent Hashemite Kingdom of Transjordan. It ended its special defense treaty relationship with the United Kingdom in 1957.

Transjordan was one of the Arab states which moved to assist Palestinian nationalists opposed to the creation of Israel in May 1948, and took part in the warfare between the Arab states and the newly founded State of Israel. The armistice agreements of April 3, 1949 left Jordan in control of the West Bank and provided that the armistice demarcation lines were without prejudice to future territorial settlements or boundary lines.

In 1950, the country was renamed the Hashemite Kingdom of Jordan to include those portions of Palestine annexed by King Abdullah. While recognizing Jordanian administration over the West Bank, the United States maintained the position that ultimate sovereignty was subject to future agreement.

Jordan signed a mutual defense pact in May 1967 with Egypt, and it participated in the June 1967 war between Israel and the Arab states of Syria, Egypt, and Iraq. During the war, Israel gained control of the West Bank and all of Jerusalem. In 1988, Jordan renounced all claims to the West Bank but retained an administrative role pending a final settlement, and its 1994 treaty with Israel allowed for a continuing Jordanian role in Muslim holy places in Jerusalem. The U.S. Government considers the West Bank to be territory occupied by Israel and believes that its final status should be determined through direct negotiations among the parties concerned on the basis of UN Security Council Resolutions 242 and 338.

The 1967 war led to a dramatic increase in the number of Palestinians living in Jordan. Its Palestinian refugee population—700,000 in 1966—grew by another 300,000 from the West Bank. The period following the 1967 war saw an upsurge in the power and importance of Palestinian resistance elements (fedayeen) in Jordan. The heavily armed fedayeen constituted a growing threat to the sovereignty and security of the Hashemite state, and open fighting erupted in June 1970.

Other Arab governments attempted to work out a peaceful solution, but by September, continuing fedayeen actions in Jordan—including the destruction of three international airliners hijacked and held in the desert east of Amman—prompted the government to take action to regain control over its territory and population. In the ensuing heavy fighting, a Syrian tank force took up positions in northern Jordan to support the fedayeen but were forced to retreat. By September 22, Arab foreign ministers meeting at Cairo had arranged a cease-fire beginning the following day. Sporadic violence continued, however, until Jordanian forces won a decisive victory over the fedayeen in July 1971, expelling them from the country.

No fighting occurred along the 1967 Jordan River cease-fire line during the October 1973 Arab-Israeli war, but Jordan sent a brigade to Syria to fight Israeli units on Syrian territory.

Jordan did not participate in the Gulf war of 1990-91. In 1991, Jordan agreed, along with Syria, Lebanon, and Palestinian representatives, to participate in direct peace negotiations with Israel sponsored by the U.S. and Russia. It negotiated an end to hostilities with Israel and signed a peace treaty in 1994. Jordan has since sought to remain at peace with all of its neighbors.

# GOVERNMENT

Jordan is a constitutional monarchy based on the constitution promulgated on January 8, 1952. Executive authority is vested in the king and his council of ministers. The king signs and executes all laws. His veto power may be overridden by a two-thirds vote of both houses of the National Assembly. He appoints and may dismiss all judges by decree, approves amendments to the constitution, declares war, and commands the armed forces. Cabinet decisions, court judgments, and the national currency are issued in his name. The council of ministers, led by a prime minister, is appointed by the king, who may dismiss other cabinet members at the prime minister's request. The cabinet is responsible to the Chamber of Deputies on matters of general policy and can be forced to resign by a two-thirds vote of "no confidence" by that body.

Legislative power rests in the bicameral National Assembly. The 80-member Chamber of Deputies, elected by universal suffrage to a 4-year term, is subject to dissolution by the king. Of the 80 seats, 71 must go to Muslims and nine to Christians. The 40-member Senate is appointed by the king for an 8-year term. The constitution provides for three categories of courts—civil, religious, and special. Administratively, Jordan is divided into eight governorates, each headed by a governor appointed by the king. They are the sole authorities for all government departments and development projects in their respective areas.

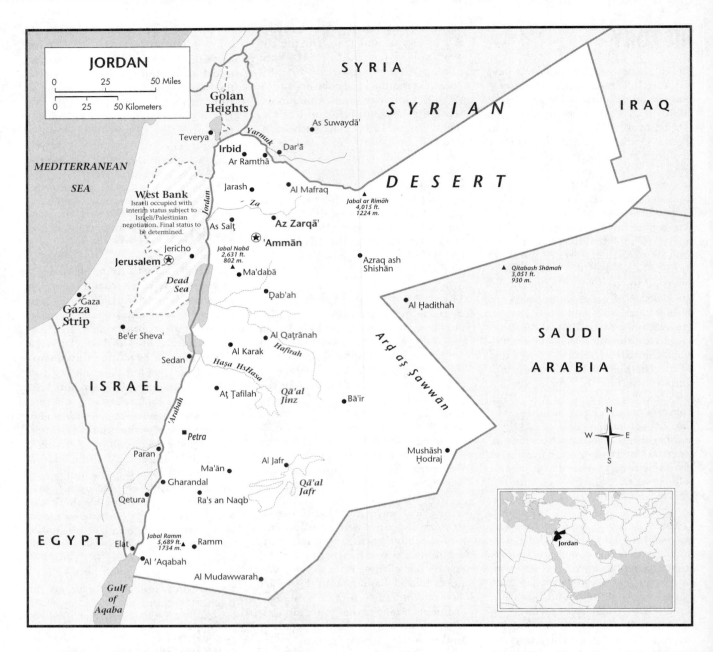

## Principal Government Officials

**For up-to-date information on Principal Government Officials, see the Chiefs of State and Cabinet Members of Foreign Governments section starting on page 1.**

Jordan maintains an embassy in the United States at 3504 International Drive NW, Washington, DC 20008 (tel. 202-966-2664).

# POLITICAL CONDITIONS

King Hussein ruled Jordan from 1953 to 1999, surviving a number of challenges to his rule, drawing on the loyalty of his military, and serving as a symbol of unity and stability for both the East Bank and Palestinian communities in Jordan. In 1989 and 1993, Jordan held free and fair parliamentary elections. Controversial changes in the election law led Islamist parties to boycott the 1997 elec-

tions. King Hussein ended martial law in 1991 and legalized political parties in 1992.

King Abdullah II succeeded his father Hussein following the latter's death in February 1999. Abdullah moved quickly to reaffirm Jordan's peace treaty with Israel and its relations with the U.S. Abdullah, during the first year in power, refocused the government's agenda on economic reform.

Jordan's continuing structural economic difficulties, burgeoning population, and more open political environment led to the emergence of a variety of political parties. Moving toward greater independence, Jordan's parliament has investigated corruption charges against several regime figures and has become the major forum in which differing political views, including those of political Islamists, are expressed. While King Abdullah remains the ultimate authority in Jordan, the parliament plays an important role.

# ECONOMY

Jordan is a small country with limited natural resources. Just over 10% of its land is arable, and even that is subject to the vagaries of a limited water supply. Rainfall is low and highly variable, and much of Jordan's available ground water is not renewable. Jordan's economic resource base centers on phosphates, potash, and their fertilizer derivatives; tourism; overseas remittances; and foreign aid. These are its principal sources of hard currency earnings. Lacking forests, coal reserves, hydroelectric power, or commercially viable oil deposits, Jordan relies on natural gas for 10% of its domestic energy needs. Jordan depends on Iraq for most of its oil.

Although the population is highly educated, its high growth rate (3.4%) and relative youth (more than 50% of Jordanians are under 16) make it difficult for the economy to generate jobs and sustain living standards. Jordan's distance from other markets makes its exports less competitive outside the region, and political disputes among its traditional trading partners—Iraq, Saudi Arabia, and the Gulf states—frequently restrict regional trade and development. King Abdullah has encouraged his government to liberalize the economy, improve economic ties in the region, and seek opportunities in the global information economy.

Since 1987, Jordan has struggled with a substantial debt burden, lower per capita income, and rising unemployment. In 1989, efforts to increase

revenues by raising prices of certain commodities and utilities triggered riots in the south. The mood of political discontent that swept the country in the wake of the riots helped set the stage for Jordan's moves toward democratization. Jordan also suffered adverse economic consequences from the 1990-91 Gulf war.

While tourist trade plummeted, the Gulf states' decision to limit economic ties with Jordan deprived it of worker remittances, traditional export markets, a secure supply of oil, and substantial foreign aid revenues. UN sanctions against Iraq—Jordan's largest pre-war trading partner—caused further hardships, including higher shipping costs due to inspections of cargo shipments entering the Gulf of Aqaba. Finally, absorbing up to 300,000 returnees from the Gulf countries exacerbated unemployment and strained the government's ability to provide essential services.

Since 1995, economic growth has been low. Real GDP has grown at only about 1.5% annually, while the official unemployment has hovered at 14% (unofficial estimates are double this number). The budget deficit and public debt have remained high, yet during this period inflation has remained low, and exports of manufactured goods have risen at an annual rate of 9%. Monetary stability has been reinforced, even when tensions were renewed in the region during 1998, and during the illness and ultimate death of King Hussein in 1999.

Expectations of increased trade and tourism as a consequence of Jordan's peace treaty with Israel have been disappointing. Security-related restrictions to trade with the West Bank and Gaza have led to a substantial decline in Jordan's exports there. Following his ascension, King Abdullah improved relations with Arab Gulf states and Syria, but this brought few real economic benefits. Most recently the Jordanians have focused on WTO membership and a Free Trade Agreement with the U.S. as means to encourage export-led growth.

# FOREIGN RELATIONS

Jordan has consistently followed a pro-Western foreign policy and traditionally has had close relations with the United States and the United Kingdom. These relations were damaged by support in Jordan for Iraq during the Gulf war. Although the Government of Jordan stated its opposition to the Iraqi occupation of Kuwait, popular support for Iraq was driven by Jordan's Palestinian community, which favored Saddam as a champion against Western supporters of Israel. Publicly, Jordan continues to call for the lifting of UN sanctions against Iraq within the context of implementing UNIC resolutions.

Since the end of the war, Jordan has largely restored its relations with Western countries through its participation in the Middle East peace process and enforcement of UN sanctions against Iraq. Relations between Jordan and the Gulf countries improved substantially after King Hussein's death.

Jordan signed a nonbelligerency agreement with Israel (the Washington Declaration) in Washington, DC, on July 25, 1994. Jordan and Israel signed a historic peace treaty on October 26, 1994, witnessed by President Clinton, accompanied by Secretary Christopher. The U.S. has participated with Jordan and Israel in trilateral development discussions in which key issues have been water-sharing and security; cooperation on Jordan Rift Valley development; infrastructure projects; and trade, finance, and banking issues. Jordan also participates in the multilateral peace talks. Jordan belongs to the UN and several of its specialized and related agencies, including the Food and Agriculture Organization (FAO), International Atomic Energy Agency (IAEA), and World Health Organization (WHO). Jordan also is a member of the World Bank, International Monetary Fund (IMF), Organization of the Islamic Conference (OIC), INTELSAT, Nonaligned Movement, and Arab League.

# U.S.-JORDANIAN RELATIONS

Relations between the U.S. and Jordan have been close for four decades. A primary objective of U.S. policy, particularly since the end of the Gulf war, has been the achievement of a comprehensive, just, and lasting peace in the Middle East. Jordan's constructive participation in the Madrid peace process is key in achieving peace.

U.S. policy seeks to reinforce Jordan's commitment to peace, stability, and moderation. The peace process and Jordan's opposition to terrorism parallel and indirectly assist wider U.S. interests. Accordingly, through economic and military assistance and through close political cooperation, the United States has helped Jordan maintain its stability and prosperity.

Since 1952, the United States has provided Jordan with economic assistance totaling more than $2 billion, including funds for development projects, health care, support for macroeconomic policy shifts toward a more completely free market system, and both grant and loan acquisition of U.S. agricultural commodities. These programs have been successful and have contributed to Jordanian stability while strengthening the bilateral relationship. U.S. military assistance—provision of materiel and training—is designed to meet Jordan's legitimate defense needs, including preservation of border integrity and regional stability.

## Principal U.S. Officials

For up-to-date information on Principal U.S. Officials, see the U.S. Embassies, Consulates, and Foreign Service section starting on page 139.

The U.S. embassy in Jordan is located in Abdoun, Amman (tel. 962-6-592-0101) and is closed on all U.S. federal holidays and some Jordanian holidays.

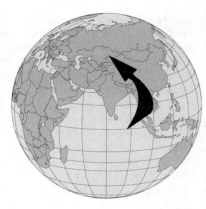

# KAZAKSTAN

February 1993

Official Name:

**Republic of Kazakstan**

---

**Editor's Note: The U.S. State Department has not yet issued a _Background Note_ on this nation. The information presented here is from the Congressional Research Service of the Library of Congress; it is the latest material available about this nation.**

---

## BACKGROUND

### Area and Population

Land area is 1,059,750 sq. mi., 12 percent of the former U.S.S.R. and the second largest republic after the Russian Republic; about four times the size of Texas. Population is 16.5 million (1989 census); 5.8 percent of the total for the former U.S.S.R. Kazakstan and Uzbekistan are by far the most populous of the Central Asian states. Administrative subdivisions include regions, districts, cities, and towns. There are no ethnically based subdivisions. Most Kazakhs are Sunni Moslems.

### History

The Kazakh nation emerged in the fifteenth century from Turkic Moslem peoples and Mongols living in the area of modern Kazakstan. Contact with Russia began in the sixteenth century. By the nineteenth century, vast areas of the steppes had been taken over by Russian and other settlers. After the Russian revolution in 1917, Kazakstan declared itself independent, but came under Bolshevik power in 1919. It became a separate republic within the Soviet Union in 1936. During Stalin's forced collectivization campaign in the 1930s, as much as one-third of the population

and most livestock perished. There were major boosts in industrialization during World War II and in grain and livestock production during the "Virgin Lands" campaign of the 1950s, but these also resulted in environmental degradation and human suffering. In December 1986, riots broke out in the capital, Alma-Ata, and other cities after Gorbachev appointed an ethnic Russian as Kazakh Communist Party (KCP) leader and accused the previous Kazakh leadership of widespread corruption. Not repeating his earlier mistake, Gorbachev appointed a Kazakh—Nursultan Nazarbayev—to head the KCP in 1989. Hoping to maintain economic links with the Slavic republics, to serve as a "window on the west," and to assuage the large Russian minority in the republic, Nazarbayev insisted in December 1991 that Kazakstan and other Central Asian states be considered "founding members" of the new Commonwealth of Independent States (CIS).

### Republic Ethnic Divisions and Tensions

6.5 million (39.7%) are Kazakh, 6.2 million Russian (37.8%), 958 thousand German (5.8%), 896 thousand Ukrainian (5.4%), 332 thousand Uzbeks (2.0%), 328 thousand Tatars (2.1%), 185 thousand Uighurs (1.1%), and others (1989 census). The Rus-

sian population is heavily concentrated in northern Kazakstan. Many ethnic groups were also deported by Stalin to Kazakstan. Because of earlier in-migration by Russians and deported nationalities, and deaths of Kazakhs during collectivization and the purges, Kazakhs became a minority in their own republic. Kazakstan is now encouraging in-migration of Kazakhs from Mongolia and elsewhere. Tensions between Russians and Kazakhs led to major riots in December 1986, increased again in 1989 after passage of a law declaring Kazakh the state language, and were exacerbated in August 1991 after Yeltsin called for a review of Russia's borders, leading to fears of designs on northern Kazakstan. As a political concession to Slavs in Kazakstan, the Kazakh Prime Minister has been an ethnic Russian-Ukrainian who speaks nationalist demands on language and other issues led Nazarbayev in late November 1992 to urge continued "civil peace" in Kazakstan, arguing that Russians play "a stabilizing role" in Kazakstan and claiming that the exodus of Russians from Tajikistan contributed to the chaos there.

Nazarbayev, born in 1940 and a Kazakh, received a degree in metallurgy and a correspondence degree from the Soviet Communist Party Higher Party School. In 1977, he became a Secretary, then Second Sec-

Kazakstan

retary, of the Karaganda Regional Committee of the KCP. In 1979, he became a Secretary of the KCP Central Committee, and, in 1984-1989, also was Chairman of the Kazakh Cabinet of Ministers (Prime Minister). In 1989, he became First Secretary of the KCP, and, in 1990, was also selected by the Kazakh legislature as President. After the failed Soviet coup attempt in August 1991, he resigned as First Secretary and member of the KCP. He was popularly elected in an unopposed election as President in December 1991. Despite economic problems in Kazakstan, polls show that he remains popular.

## Political Parties and Groups

By one Kazakh report, there are over 120 political parties in Kazakstan, though only the Socialist Party, the "Azat" Republican Party, and the Social-Democratic Party have been allowed to legally register. The largest is the Socialist Party (former KCP), consisting of at least 30,000 members. Nazarbayev was instrumental, in September 1991, in getting the KCP to change its name and ostensibly embrace democratic reforms, though he eschewed leading or joining the new party. The Azat Republican Party (composed mostly of Kazakhs) calls for creation of a multiethnic multiparty democracy that will elevate Kazakh culture and "decolonize" Kazakstan. Some Russian and intellectuals belong to a Social-Democratic Party which broke away from the KCP in 1991. Other parties include "Alash" and "Zheltoqsan." Both Alash and Zheltoqsan are Kazakh nationalist parties that have been refused registration. Alash, taking its name from a party repressed by Stalin, advocates de-collectivization of agriculture, enlarging borders to incorporate traditional Kazakh lands, and Turkic and Moslem solidarity. Zheltoqsan leaders announced in October 1992 that they would merge with the Azat Republican Party. A new party called National Unity of Kazakstan, headed by a former Komsomol chief, was formed in October 1992, dedicated to multi-ethnic harmony and support for Naz-

arbayev. Russian nationalist parties and groups include the "afedinstvo" Society and Cossack Movement. Yedinstvo's appeal for registration as a party was rejected by the Kazakh Supreme Court in November 1992.

## Political Institutions and Policies

A 360-member unicameral Supreme Soviet (now called Supreme Council) was elected in March 1990, in an electoral contest dominated by the KCP, though some KCP and government candidates were defeated. In April 1990, the Supreme Soviet selected Nazarbayev to the new post of president of Kazakstan. In uncontested presidential elections held on December 1, 1991, Nazarbayev won over 98 percent of the popular vote. Opposition parties denounced a requirement that they obtain 100,000 signatures on a petition in order to register a candidate. In October 1990, Kazakstan adopted a declaration of sovereignty, and, in December 1991, declared its independence. In January 1992, Nazarbayev decreed direct presidential rule in the localities, replacing executives of local Supreme Soviets with presidential administrators. In December 1992, he announced the creation of a presidential inspectorate to insure that decrees were being implemented at the local level. In late 1992, after stormy debate in the Supreme Council, a proposal to allow greater local self-management was defeated, reportedly because of officials' concerns that this might encourage separatism in Russian-dominated northern areas of Kazakstan. Opposition forces have called for forming a coalition government, disbanding the former Communist-dominated Supreme Council, and holding new elections, proposals rejected by Nazarbayev.

On January 28, 1993, the Kazakh Supreme Council almost unanimously approved a new constitution after a lengthy period of public discussion and debate. It proclaims Kazakstan as an independent, democratic, secular, and unitary state, designates Kazakh as the official language and Russian as the "lan-

guage of interethnic communication," and establishes a strong presidential system. The president, who must be a citizen who speaks Kazakh fluently, is the head of state and administration. He appoints the prime minister and foreign, defense, finance, and interior ministers, among others, who must be approved by the Supreme Council. Local administrators are direct representatives of the president. There is a long list of human rights guarantees of speech, association, religion, travel, place of residence, and others. However, these rights are liable to constraint by the stated need to ensure "law and order and legality."

## Principal Government Officials

**For up-to-date information on Principal Government Officials, see the Chiefs of State and Cabinet Members of Foreign Governments section starting on page 1.**

## Human Rights and Freedoms

Although Nazarbayev's rule has been somewhat authoritarian, many Western analysts characterize his regime as committing fewer human rights violations than some other Central Asian states. Some political party and opposition group activities are tolerated, though meeting and demonstrations are restricted. Also, parties must register with authorities and provide lists of members. Nazarbayev has termed the Alash and Zheltoqsan parties and the Cossack Movement as "destabilizing" and called for their leaders to "be dealt with by law-enforcement bodies." The practice of Islamic religion is upheld. Alash protests led to the arrest of its leaders in December 1991, several of whom were held without trial for several months. During mass demonstrations in mid-1992 outside of the Supreme Council calling for the holding of new elections, the Zheltoqsan leader was arrested, and the demonstrations forcibly suppressed. Myriad

independent and some party publications have appeared since independence. All publications must be registered with the state, however, and a few have been banned or restricted. The state also exercises media influence through its control over newsprint and distribution, and through laws against insulting the president. Nazarbayev has called for creation of an independent, though "socially responsible," media. Some local leaders continue to adhere to authoritarian controls over citizenry.

## Relations with Commonwealth of Independent States

Kazakhstan and other Central Asian states were admitted as "founding members" of the Commonwealth of Independent States (CIS) on December 21, 1991. Kazakstan, along with Russia, advocated close policy coordination among the CIS countries, but in recent months Nazarbayev has explored extra-CIS bilateral and multilateral ties with former Soviet republics. At the Bishkek Summit in October 1992, he strongly urged the creation of CIS economic coordination bodies. Although agreed to, delays in forming these bodies sparked Nazarbayev to pursue other regional economic initiatives. At a Central Asian Summit in Tashkent in January 1993, Kazakstan joined Kyrgyzstn, Tajikistan, Turkmenistan, and Uzbekistan in proclaiming a potential common market, with details to be worked out at a future summit. At the Minsk Summit of CIS Heads of

State in January 1993, an agreement on Nazarbayev's proposed interstate bank was reached. Nazarbayev also signed the CIS Charter and supported creation of a five-nation CIS peace keeping force to help restore order in Tajikistan. In August-September 1992, Nazarbayev unsuccessfully tried to mediate a cease-fire in the Armenian-Azerbaijani conflict.

The Kazakh government has been apprehensive about possible Russian territorial ambitions in northern Kazakstan, though Nazarbayev also has pursued close relations with Russia for economic and security reasons. On May 25, 1992, Kazakstan and Russia concluded a bilateral treaty of friendship, cooperation, and mutual aid, the first of several such treaties Russia signed with former Soviet republics. The treaty affirms existing borders and creates "a united military and strategic zone," including joint use of military bases and test sites. Nazarbayev has described Kazakstan as under "Russia's nuclear umbrella." New Russian Prime Minister Viktor Chernomyrdin hurriedly visited Kazakstan in December 1992 to arrange purchase of much-needed grain and oil and discuss mutual debt repayments.

## Foreign Policy and Defense

In early 1993, the Kazakh foreign minister reported that Kazakstan had established diplomatic relations with 70 countries and 19 foreign diplomatic missions had been set up in Alma-Ata. Kazakstan is a member of the United Nations, Conference on Security and Cooperation in Europe (CSCE), World Bank, the International Monetary Fund (IMF), European Bank for Reconstruction and Development (EBRD), the North Atlantic Coordination Council, and the Economic Cooperation Organization, among others. Nazarbayev has stated that the geographic location of Kazakstan and its ethnic makeup dictate its "multipolar orientation toward both the West and the East." He has also called for extending the CSCE process to Asia with Kazakstan acting as a "bridge" between East and West. Nazarbayev, in December 1992, noted the priority of good relations with the United States, China, and Turkey, as well as Russia and the other Central Asian states. Kazakstan has direct railway and air links with China and extensive trade ties with Xinjiang Province, where many ethnic Kazakhs and Uighurs reside. Economic agreements have been concluded with South Korea. Nazarbayev has repeatedly visited Turkey and, in November 1992, visited Iran. In his October 1992 visit to Turkey, Nazarbayev endorsed the Ankara Declaration calling for multilateral cooperation, though he reportedly balked at language that might imply the creation of an ethnic Turkic regional grouping. During his Iranian visit, Iran agreed to help in rebuilding Kazakh port facilities on the Capsian Sea to facilitate increased trade, among other agreements. India and Pakistan have agreed to train Kazakhs in banking, management, diplomacy, and agriculture.

A Kazakh Ministry of Defense and armed forces were created by decrees in May 1992. According to some reports, Kazakh armed forces will number 80,000-90,000 by the end of 1993. In January 1992, a decision was made to form a 2,000-member national guard. Border troops were placed under Kazakh jurisdiction in August.

1992. At the meeting of the Heads of State of CIS Countries held in Tashkent on May 15, 1992, Russia, Armenia, and the Central Asian states signed a collective security agreement pledging the parties to provide military assistance, if necessary, in case of aggression against anyone of them. It was ratified by the Kazakh Supreme Council in late December 1992. The Russian-Kazakh treaty of May 1992, said to form the basis of Kazakstan's draft defense doctrine, calls for Russia to assist Kazakstan in case of aggression. Kazakstan pledged, in joining the CIS, that its strategic nuclear forces would be placed under CIS joint control. Kazakstan also agreed to the removal of all tactical nuclear weapons from Kazakh soil to Russia; they had been removed by mid-1992. In May 1992, Kazakstan signed a protocol to START I that it would relinquish all strategic nuclear missiles before the year 2000 and would accede to the Nuclear Non-Proliferation Treaty (NPT) as a non-nuclear weapons state "in the shortest possible time." The Supreme Council ratified START I on July 2, 1992, and the Conventional Armed Forces in Europe (CFE) Treaty earlier in the year.

## Economy

Kazakstan had an estimated GNP in 1991 of 81.2 billion rubles, about 4.6 percent of the total for the former Soviet Union. Per capita income is 4,822 rubles (1991 estimate), the highest among the former Soviet Central Asian republics but below that of the former Slavic and Baltic republics. Rich in natural resources, Kazakstan is a major world source of copper, zinc, titanium, magnesium, and chromium. There are sizable oil reserves. Uranium is mined and fabricated, and there are nuclear facilities such as the research center at the Semipalatinsk nuclear test site. Coal exports to the former Soviet republics were a major source of earnings. A good 1992 grain harvest—following two years of bad harvests—allowed Kazakstan to renew or boost grain exports to CIS states and foreign countries. Kazakstan continues to belong to Russia's ruble zone. Efforts to attract foreign investment include joint ventures in oil exploitation concluded with the U.S. corporation Chevron in May 1992, with joint production reported to begin in April 1993, and with Turkey in late 1992. Environmental damage around the Aral and Caspian Seas, at Semipalatinsk, and other areas has contributed to high rates of infant mortality and illness.

As a reaction to deepening economic distress, Nazarbayev directed the creation of a Kazakh "anti-crisis" program in late 1992. Somewhat conservative, it calls for strengthening presidential control over the economy, slowing the growth of wages, controlling price rises, increasing state-owned industrial production and social protections, and temporarily halting "uncontrolled" and government-sponsored privatization of enterprises and housing until new

## Travel Notes

**Travel Advice:** For up-to-date information from the U.S. State Department on possible inconvenient or hazardous situations, see the **Travel Warnings and Consular Information Sheets from the U.S. Government** section starting on page 1723. For the latest information on health requirements and conditions, see the **International Travelers' Health Information** section starting on page 1385. For further information dealing with non-urgent matter, see the **Tips for Travelers to...** section starting on page 1588.

## Editor's Update                    Dec. 1995–June 2001

*A report on important events that have taken place since the last State Department revision of this* Background Note.

Kazakstan is the most economically developed of the former Soviet Central Asian republics. Problems abound within Kazakstan, but observers have reasons to be cautiously optimistic. In 1996, GDP grew by 1.1% and again in 1997 by 1.7%. Although inflation peaked at 2,000% in 1993, it declined to just 7% in 1998. The region holds the old Soviet empire's largest reserve of oil, natural gas and iron. Kazakstan has also attracted US and other foreign investment. Analysts forecasted foreign investment in the republic to total $15 billion by the end of the 1990s. In a $1.1 billion transaction, Mobil Oil acquired a 25 percent stake in the huge Tengiz oil field in Kazakstan. In 1996, Kazakstan signed an agreement with the Caspian Pipeline Consortium to build a pipeline from the Tenzig oil field to the Black Sea, promising even further growth in the oil sector of the economy.

Between 1989 and 1997, about two-thirds of the one million ethnic Germans living in Kazakstan left the country, many to Germany (Germany's constitution allows any ethnic German to immigrate). About half of the 300,000 ethnic Germans still living in Kazakstan are expected to emigrate by the end of the decade. Some communities that were once heavily populated by ethnic Germans have almost become ghost towns.

As of 1996, nearly 42,000 Kazaks were displaced internally because of environmental problems with the Aral Sea, and an additional 160,000 because of the above-ground nuclear testing of the Semipalatinsk site. As of September 1999, there were an estimated 35,000 refugees and asylum seekers in Kazakstan, many in the former capital of Almaty. The refugees were from other former Soviet regions, China, and Africa.

In November 1996, 349 passengers died when a Kazakstan Airlines jetliner collided in midair with a Saudi Arabian Airlines Boeing 747. The collision, the world's worst midair accident, occurred minutes after the Saudi aircraft took off from New Delhi, India. Both airlines claimed that problems with Indian air traffic control contributed to the collision.

In September 1997, Kazakstan and China signed an agreement providing for the construction of an oil pipeline through China's Xinjiang province in return for Chinese help in developing Kazakstan's oilfields. In spite of President Nazarbaev's continuing efforts to improve Kazakstan's economy, significant problems remain as over half of the population lives in poverty.

On June 10, 1998, the Kazak government officially transferred the country's capital from Almaty in the south to Astana (formerly Akmola, or Tselinograd) in the north. Astana, which means capital, is a rapidly growing city of 300,000. Foreign companies provide the largest portion of capital infusion for the new capital's development.

In elections held on January 10, 1999, President Nazarbaev won a resounding victory with 82 percent of the vote. Foreign governments, including the United States, noted the unfair nature of Mr. Nazarbaev's triumph. Elections had been moved up a year and opponents were given only three months to organize. In addition, two opponents were banned from participating while President Nazarbaev monopolized all advertising media.

Parliamentary elections held in October 1999 confirmed a resurgence in communist influence, as no candidate nominated by a non–communist for the legislative chamber gained a single constituent seat.

The Kazak government is showing greater assertiveness internationally, as evidenced by their public rejection of the US report on human rights in early 2001.

means of transfer can be worked out. Nevertheless, Nazarbayev maintains that the program will result in the creation of a basic social market economy by 1995.

## U.S. POLICY

On December 25, the United States offered to establish diplomatic relations with Kazakstan after receiving assurances that Kazakstan would follow responsible nuclear security policies, democratize, and uphold human rights, according to the U.S. State Department. Formal relations were established in early 1992, and a U.S.

mission was opened in early February. A Kazakh mission has been set up in Washington. The United States is providing humanitarian and technical assistance to Kazakstan. A U.S.-Kazakh Trade Agreement was signed during Nazarbayev's May 1992 state visit to the United States and was approved in late December 1992 by the Kazakh legislature. It will come into force with the exchange of notes.

An Overseas Private Investment Corporation (OPIC) agreement was also signed in May 1992. The Agency for International Development (AID) opened a regional Central Asian Office in Alma Ata, Kazakstan, in

mid1992. In October 1992, Kazakstan and other former Soviet republics signed an agreement with the United States to halt the dumping of uranium on the U.S. market, at least temporarily closing this avenue for trade earnings. An agreement on Peace Corps activity in Kazakstan was signed in December 1992.

### Principal U.S. Officials

**For up-to-date information on Principal U.S. Officials, see the U.S. Embassies, Consulates, and Foreign Service section starting on page 139.**

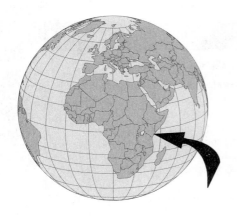

# KENYA

May 2001

## Official Name:
## Republic of Kenya

# PROFILE

## Geography

**Area:** 582,646 sq. km. (224,960 sq mi.); slightly smaller than Texas.
**Cities:** Capital—Nairobi (pop. 2.1 million). Other cities—Mombasa (665,000), Kisumu (504,000), Nakuru (1.2 million).
**Terrain:** Kenya rises from a low coastal plain on the Indian Ocean in a series of mountain ridges and plateaus which stand above 3,000 meters (9,000 ft.) in the center of the country. The Rift Valley bisects the country above Nairobi, opening up to a broad arid plain in the north. Mountain plains cover the south before descending to the shores of Lake Victoria in the west.
**Climate:** Varies from the tropical south, west, and central regions to arid and semi-arid in the north and the northeast.

## People

**Nationality:** Noun and adjective—Kenyan(s).
**Population (1999 est.):** 28.7 million.
**Annual growth rate (1996 est.):** 2.4%.
**Ethnic groups:** African—Kikuyu 21%, Luhya 14%, Luo 13%, Kalenjin 11%, Kamba 11%, Kisii 6%, Meru 5%. Non-African—Asian, European,

Arab 1%.
**Religions:** Indigenous beliefs 10%, Protestant 40%, Roman Catholic 30%, Muslim 20%.
**Languages:** English, Swahili, more than 40 local ethnic languages.
**Education:** Years compulsory—none, but first 8 yrs. of primary school are provided through cost-sharing between government and parents. Attendance—73% for primary grades. Literacy (in English)—59%.
**Health:** Infant mortality rate—115/1,000. Life expectancy—49 yrs.
**Work force (1.7 million wage earners):** Public sector—30%. Private sector—70%. Informal sector workers—3.7 million.
**Formal sector breakdown:** Services—445%; industry and commerce—35%; agriculture—20%.

## Government

**Type:** Republic.
**Independence:** December 12, 1963.
**Constitution:** 1963.
**Branches:** Executive—president (chief of state, head of government, commander in chief of armed forces). Legislative—unicameral National Assembly (parliament). Judicial—Court of Appeal, High Court, various lower courts.
**Administrative subdivisions:** 63 districts, joined to form 7 rural provinces. Nairobi area has special status.
**Political parties:** 41 registered

political parties. Ruling party, Kenya African National Union.
**Suffrage:** Universal at 18.

## Economy

**GDP (2000):** $9.7 billion.
**Annual growth rate (1996):** -0.4%.
**Per capita income:** $271.
**Natural resources:** wildlife, land.
**Agriculture:** Products—tea, coffee, sugarcane, horticultural products, corn, wheat, rice, sisal, pineapples, pyrethrum, dairy products, meat and meat products, hides, skins. Arable land—5%.
**Industry:** Types—petroleum product, grain and sugar milling, cement, beer, soft drinks, textiles, paper and light manufacturing.
**Trade (2000):** Exports—$1.8 billion: tea, coffee, horticultural products, petroleum products, cement, pyrethrum, soda ash, sisal, hides and skins, fluorspar. Major markets—Uganda, Tanzania, United Kingdom, Germany, Netherlands, Ethiopia, Rwanda, Egypt, South Africa, United States.
**Imports—$3.3 billion:** machinery, vehicles, crude petroleum, iron and steel, resins and plastic materials, refined petroleum products, pharmaceuticals, paper and paper products, fertilizers, wheat. Major suppliers—U.K., Japan, South Africa, Germany, United Arab Emirates, Italy, India, France, United States, Saudi Arabia.

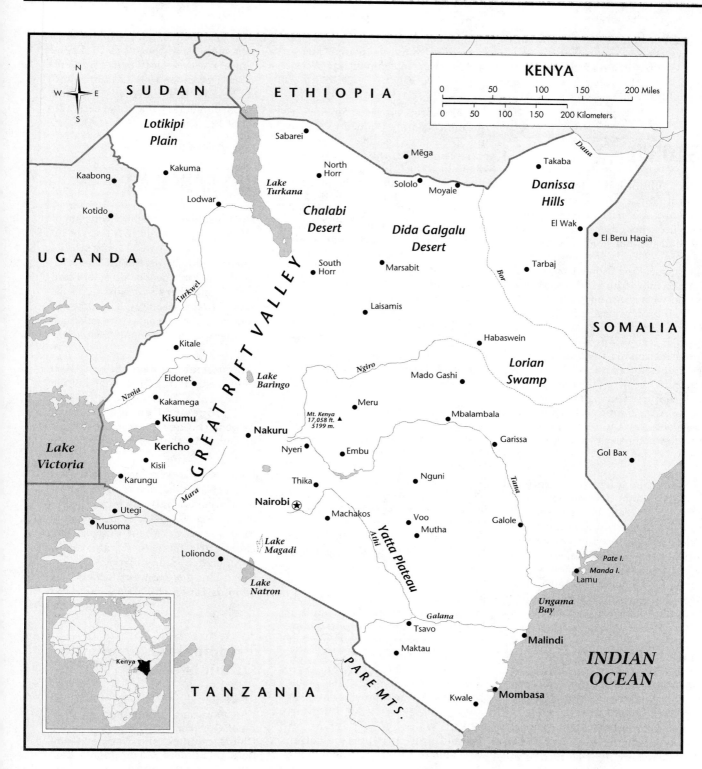

# PEOPLE

Kenya has a very diverse population that includes most major language groups of Africa. Traditional pastoralists, rural farmers, Muslims, and urban residents of Nairobi and other cities contribute to the cosmopolitan culture. The standard of living in major cities, once relatively high compared to much of Sub-Saharan Africa, has been declining in recent years. Most city workers retain links with their rural, extended families and leave the city periodically to help work on the family farm. About 75% of the work force is engaged in agriculture, mainly as subsistence farmers. The national motto of Kenya is harambee, meaning "pull together." In that spirit, volunteers in hundreds of communities build schools, clinics, and other facilities each year and collect funds to send students abroad. The five state universities enroll about 38,000 students, representing some 25% of the Kenyan students who qualify for admission.

# HISTORY

Fossils found in East Africa suggest that protohumans roamed the area more than 20 million years ago. Recent finds near Kenya's Lake Turkana indicate that hominids lived in the area 2.6 million years ago. Cushitic-speaking people from northern Africa moved into the area that is now Kenya beginning around 2000 BC. Arab traders began frequenting the Kenya coast around the first century A.D. Kenya's proximity to the Arabian Peninsula invited colonization, and Arab and Persian settlements sprouted along the coast by the eighth century. During the first millennium A.D., Nilotic and Bantu peoples moved into the region, and the latter now comprises three-quarters of Kenya's population.

The Swahili language, a mixture of Bantu and Arabic, developed as a lingua franca for trade between the different peoples. Arab dominance on the coast was eclipsed by the arrival in 1498 of the Portuguese, who gave way in turn to Islamic control under the Imam of Oman in the 1600s. The United Kingdom established its influence in the 19th century.

The colonial history of Kenya dates from the Berlin Conference of 1885, when the European powers first partitioned East Africa into spheres of influence. In 1895, the U.K. Government established the East African Protectorate and, soon after, opened the fertile highlands to white settlers. The settlers were allowed a voice in government even before it was officially made a U.K. colony in 1920, but Africans were prohibited from direct political participation until 1944.

From October 1952 to December 1959, Kenya was under a state of emergency arising from the "Mau Mau" rebellion against British colonial rule. During this period, African participation in the political process increased rapidly.

The first direct elections for Africans to the Legislative Council took place in 1957. Kenya became independent on December 12, 1963, and the next year joined the Commonwealth. Jomo Kenyatta, a member of the predominant Kikuyu tribe and head of the Kenya African National Union (KANU), became Kenya's first president. The minority party, Kenya African Democratic Union (KADU), representing a coalition of small tribes that had feared dominance by larger ones, dissolved itself voluntarily in 1964 and joined KANU. A small but significant leftist opposition party, the Kenya People's Union (KPU), was formed in 1966, led by Jaramogi Oginga Odinga, a former vice president and Luo elder. The KPU was banned and its leader detained after political unrest related to Kenyatta's visit to Nyanza Province. No new opposition parties were formed after 1969, and KANU became the sole political party. At Kenyatta's death in August 1978, Vice President Daniel arap Moi became interim President. On October 14, Moi became President formally after he was elected head of KANU and designated its sole nominee.

In June 1982, the National Assembly amended the constitution, making Kenya officially a one-party state, and parliamentary elections were held in September 1983. The 1988 elections reinforced the one-party system. However, in December 1991, parliament repealed the one-party section of the constitution. By early 1992, several new parties had formed, and multiparty elections were held in December 1992.

President Moi was reelected for another 5-year term. Opposition parties won about 45% of the parliamentary seats, but President Moi's KANU Party obtained the majority of seats. Parliamentary reforms in November 1997 enlarged the democratic space in Kenya, including the expansion of political parties from 11 to 26. President Moi won re-election as President in the December 1997 elections, and his KANU Party narrowly retained its parliamentary majority, with 109 out of 122 seats.

# GOVERNMENT

The unicameral assembly consists of 210 members elected to a term of up to 5 years, plus 12 members appointed by the president. The president appoints the vice president and cabinet members from among those elected to the assembly. The attorney general and the speaker are ex-officio members of the National Assembly.

The judiciary is headed by a High Court, consisting of a chief justice and at least 30 High Court judges and judges of Kenya's Court of Appeal (no associate judges), all appointed by the president.

Local administration is divided among 63 rural districts, each headed by a presidentially appointed commissioner. The districts are joined to form seven rural provinces. The Nairobi area has special status and is not included in any district or province. The government supervises administration of districts and provinces.

## Principal Government Officials

**For up-to-date information on Principal Government Officials, see the Chiefs of State and Cabinet Members of Foreign Governments section starting on page 1.**

Kenya maintains an embassy in the United States at 2249 R Street NW, Washington, DC 20008 (Tel. 202-387-6101).

# POLITICAL CONDITIONS

Since independence, Kenya has maintained remarkable stability despite changes in its political system and crises in neighboring countries. Particularly since the re-emergence of multiparty democracy, Kenyans have enjoyed an increased degree of freedom. A bipartisan parliamentary reform initiative in the fall of 1997 revised some oppressive laws inherited from the colonial era that had been used to limit freedom of speech and assembly. This significantly improved public freedoms and assembly and made for generally credible national elections in December 1997.

Kenya is now focusing on the succession of President Moi, whose current term expires in December 2002. The government has restricted opposition party activities as the 2002 elections draw near. The elections have been complicated by a stalled constitutional review process and ambiguity about President Moi's intentions regarding a third term in office.

# ECONOMY

After independence, Kenya promoted rapid economic growth through public investment, encouragement of smallholder agricultural production, and incentives for private (often foreign) industrial investment. Gross domestic product (GDP) grew at an annual average of 6.6% from 1963 to 1973. Agricultural production grew by 4.7% annually during the same period, stimulated by redistributing estates, diffusing new crop strains, and opening new areas to cultivation.

Between 1974 and 1990, however, Kenya's economic performance declined. Inappropriate agricultural policies, inadequate credit, and poor international terms of trade contributed to the decline in agriculture. Kenya's inward-looking policy of import substitution and rising oil prices made Kenya's manufacturing

Photo credit: Brian Mantrop and Pierre St. Jacques.

**Married Samburu man, Marala.**

Background Notes

sector uncompetitive. The government began a massive intrusion in the private sector. Lack of export incentives, tight import controls, and foreign exchange controls made the domestic environment for investment even less attractive.

From 1991 to 1993, Kenya had its worst economic performance since independence. Growth in GDP stagnated, and agricultural production shrank at an annual rate of 3.9%. Inflation reached a record 100% in August 1993, and the government's budget deficit was over 10% of GDP. As a result of these combined problems, bilateral and multilateral

donors suspended program aid to Kenya in 1991.

In 1993, the Government of Kenya began a major program of economic reform and liberalization. A new minister of finance and a new governor of the central bank undertook a series of economic measures with the assistance of the World Bank and the International Monetary Fund (IMF). As part of this program, the government eliminated price controls and import licensing, removed foreign exchange controls, privatized a range of publicly owned companies, reduced the number of civil servants, and introduced conservative fiscal and monetary policies. From 1994-96, Kenya's real GDP growth rate averaged just over 4% a year.

In 1997, however, the economy entered a period of slowing or stagnant growth, due in part to adverse weather conditions and reduced economic activity prior to general elections in December 1997. In 2000, GDP growth was negative.

In July 1997, the Government of Kenya refused to meet commitments made earlier to the IMF on governance reforms. As a result, the IMF suspended lending for 3 years, and the World Bank also put a $90 million structural adjustment credit on hold. Although many economic reforms put in place in 1993-94 remained, Kenya needed further reforms, particularly in governance, in order to increase GDP growth and combat poverty among the majority of its population.

The Government of Kenya took some positive steps on reform, including the 1999 establishment of the Kenyan Anti-Corruption Authority, and measures to imporve the transparency of government procurements and reduce the government payroll. In July 2000, the IMF signed a $150 million Poverty Reduction and Growth Facility, and the World Bank followed suit shortly after with a $157 million Economic and Public Sector Reform credit. By early 2001, however, the pace of reform appeared to be slowing again, and the IMF and World Bank programs were in abeyance as the government failed to meet its commitments under the programs.

Nairobi continues to be the primary hub of East Africa. It enjoys the region's best transportation linkages, communications infrastructure, and trained personnel. A wide range of foreign firms maintain regional branch or representative offices in the city. In March 1996, the Presidents of Kenya, Tanzania, and Uganda re-established the East African Cooperation (EAC). The EAC's objectives include harmonizing tariffs and customs regimes, free movement of people, and improving regional infrastructures.

# FOREIGN RELATIONS

Despite internal tensions in Sudan and Ethiopia, Kenya has maintained good relations with its northern neighbors. Recent relations with Uganda and Tanzania have improved as the three countries work for mutual economic benefit. The lack of a cohesive government in Somalia prevents normal contact with that country. Kenya serves as the major host for refugees from turmoil in Somalia.

Kenya maintains a moderate profile in Third World politics. Kenya's relations with Western countries are generally friendly, although current political and economic instabilities are often blamed on Western pressures. Kenya serves as a major host for refugees from Somalia and Sudan and currently has troops in three UN peacekeeping operations.

# U.S.-KENYAN RELATIONS

The United States and Kenya have enjoyed cordial relations since Kenya's independence. More than 7,000 U.S. citizens live in Kenya, and as many as 25,000 Americans visit Kenya annually. About two-thirds of the resident Americans are missionaries and their families. U.S. business investment is estimated to be more than $285 million, primarily in commerce, light manufacturing, and the tourism industry.

## Travel Notes

**Travel Advice:** For up-to-date information from the U.S. State Department on possible inconvenient or hazardous situations, see the **Travel Warnings and Consular Information Sheets from the U.S. Government** section starting on page 1723. For the latest information on health requirements and conditions, see the **International Travelers' Health Information** section starting on page 1385. For further information dealing with non-urgent matter, see the **Tips for Travelers to...** section starting on page 1588.

U.S. assistance to Kenya promotes broadbased economic development as the basis for continued progress in political, social, and related areas of national life. U.S. aid strategy is designed to achieve four major objectives—health care, including family planning and AIDS prevention; increasing rural incomes by assisting small enterprises and boosting agricultural productivity; sustainable use of natural resources; and strengthening democratic institutions. The U.S. also is helping the Kenyan victims of the August 7, 1998 bombing of the American Embassy to recover and rebuild. The U.S. Peace Corps has more than 111 volunteers in Kenya.

## Principal U.S. Officials

For up-to-date information on Principal U.S. Officials, see the U.S. Embassies, Consulates, and Foreign Service section starting on page 139.

The U.S. Embassy in Kenya is located at Haile Selassie and Moi Avenues, Nairobi, P.O. Box 30137 (Tel. 334141; Fax 340838).

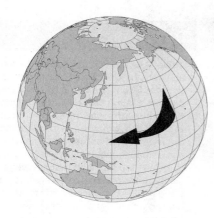

# KIRIBATI

February 2001

Official Name:
**Republic of Kiribati**

## PROFILE

### Geography

**Area:** 719 sq. km (266 sq. mi.) in one island and 32 atolls.
**Cities:** Capital—Tarawa (pop. 25,000).
**Terrain:** Archipelago of low-lying coral atolls surrounded by extensive reefs.
**Climate:** Maritime equatorial or tropical.

### People

**Nationality:** Noun and adjective—I-Kiribati (singular and plural).
**Population:** 86,000. Age structure—41% under 15; 3% over 65. Growth rate: 2%.
**Ethnic groups:** Micronesian 98%.
**Religion:** Roman Catholic 53%, Kiribati Protestant 39%.
**Languages:** English (official), Gilbertese/I-Kiribati.
**Health:** Life expectancy—male 57 yrs., female 63 yrs. Infant mortality rate—55.3/1,000.
**Work force:** Majority engaged in subsistence activities.

### Government

**Type:** Republic
**Independence (from UK):** July 12, 1979.
**Constitution:** July 12, 1979.
**Branches:** Executive—president (head of state and government), vice president, cabinet. Legislative—unicameral House of Assembly. Judicial—High Court, Court of Appeal, Magistrates' Courts.
**Major political parties:** Parties are only very loosely organized: Maneaban Te Mauri (Protect the Maneaba), National Progressive Party, Liberal Party.

### Economy

**GDP:** $48.3 million.
**GNP** (GDP + investment income, fishing license fees and seamen's remittances): $81.2 million.
**GNP per capita:** $950.
**GDP composition by sector:** Services 79%, agriculture 14%, industry 7%.
**Industry:** Types—tourism, copra, fish.
**Trade:** Exports ($5.9 million)—copra, pet fish, seaweed. Export markets—Australia, U.S. Imports ($41.7 million)—food, manufactured goods. Import sources—Australia, Fiji, Japan, New Zealand.
**External debt:** $20 million.
**Currency:** Australian dollar (A$).

## GEOGRAPHY AND PEOPLE

Kiribati (pronounced "keer-ih-bahs") consists of 32 atolls and one island scattered over an expanse of ocean equivalent in size to the continental United States. The islands lie roughly halfway between Hawaii and Australia in the Micronesian region of the South Pacific. The three main groupings are the Gilbert Islands, Phoenix Islands, and Line Islands. On January 1, 1995 Kiribati unilaterally moved the International Date Line to include its easternmost islands and make it the same day throughout the country.

Kiribati contains Kiritimati (Christmas Island), the largest coral atoll in the world, and Banaba (Ocean Island), one of the three great phosphate rock islands in the Pacific.

Most of the land is less than two meters above sea level. A 1989 United Nations report identified Kiribati as one of the countries that would completely disappear in the 21st century if steps were not taken to address global climate change. In mid-1999 it was announced that two uninhabited coral reefs had sunk beneath the sea.

Owing to a population growth rate of more than 2% and the overcrowding around the capital, a program of migration was begun in 1989 to move nearly 5,000 inhabitants to outlying atolls, mainly in the Line Islands. A further program of resettlement to the Phoenix Islands was begun in 1995.

# HISTORY

The I-Kiribati people settled what would become known as the Gilbert Islands between 1000 and 1300 AD. Subsequent invasions by Fijians and Tongans introduced Polynesian elements to the Micronesian culture, but extensive intermarriage produced a population reasonably homogeneous in appearance and traditions.

European contact began in the 16th century. Whalers, slave traders, and merchant vessels arrived in great numbers in the 1800s, and the resulting upheaval fomented local tribal conflicts and introduced damaging European diseases. In an effort to restore a measure of order, the Gilbert and Ellice Islands (now Tuvalu) consented to becoming British protectorates in 1892. Banaba (Ocean Island) was annexed in 1900 after the discovery of phosphate-rich guano deposits, and the entire collection was made a British colony in 1916. The Line and Phoenix Islands were incorporated piecemeal over the next 20 years.

Japan seized the islands during World War II to form part of their island defenses. In November 1943, allied forces threw themselves against Japanese positions at Tarawa Atoll in the Gilberts, resulting in some of the bloodiest fighting of the Pacific campaign. The battle was a major turning point in the war for the Allies.

Britain began expanding self-government in the islands during the 1960s. In 1975 the Ellice Islands separated from the colony to form the independent state of Tuvalu. The Gilberts obtained internal self-government in 1977, and formally became an independent nation on July 12, 1979 under the name of Kiribati.

Post-independence politics were initially dominated by Ieremia Tabai, Kiribati's first president, who served from 1979 to 1991. Teburoro Tito has been President since 1994, and was most recently reelected in 1998.

# GOVERNMENT

The constitution promulgated at independence on July 12, 1979, establishes Kiribati as a sovereign democratic republic and guarantees the fundamental rights of its citizens.

The unicameral House of Assembly (Maneaba) has 41 members: 39 elected representatives; one appointed member from Banaba, and the Attorney General on an ex officio basis. All of the members of the Maneaba serve 4-year terms. The speaker for the legislature is elected by the Maneaba from outside of its membership.

After each general election, the new Maneaba nominates three or four of its members to stand as candidates for president (Beretitenti). The voting public then elects the president from among these candidates. A cabinet of up to 10 members is appointed by the president from among the members of the Maneaba.

The judicial system consists of the High Court, a court of appeal, and magistrates' courts. All judicial appointments are made by the president.

## Principal Government Officials

For up-to-date information on Principal Government Officials, see the Chiefs of State and Cabinet Members of Foreign Governments section starting on page 1.

Kiribati does not have an embassy in the United States. It offers consular services in Hawaii.

# POLITICAL CONDITIONS

Political parties exist but are more similar to informal coalitions in behavior. They do not have official platforms or party structures. Most candidates formally present themselves as independents.

A major source of conflict has been the protracted bid by the residents of Banaban Island to secede and have their island placed under the protection of Fiji. The government's attempts to placate the Banabans include several special provisions in the constitution, such as the designation of a Banaban seat in the legislature and the return of land previously acquired by the government for phosphate mining.

The most recent parliamentary elections were held in September 1998. New elections will be held no later than September 2002.

# ECONOMY

Kiribati's per capita GNP of less than $1,000 makes it one of the poorest countries in the world. Phosphates had been profitably exported from Banaban Island since the turn of the century, but the deposits were exhausted in 1979. The economy now depends on foreign assistance and revenue from fishing licenses to finance its needed imports and development budget.

The expiration of phosphate deposits in 1979 had a devastating impact on the economy. Receipts from phosphates had accounted for roughly 80% of export earnings and 50% of government revenue. Per capita GDP was more than cut in half between 1979 and 1981. A trust fund financed by phosphate earnings over the years—the Revenue Equalization Reserve Fund—does still exist, and contained more than $350 million in 1999. Prudent management of the Reserve Fund will be vital for the long-term welfare of the country.

In one form or another, Kiribati gets a large portion of its income from abroad. Examples include fishing licenses, development assistance, worker remittances, and tourism. Given Kiribati's limited domestic production ability, it must import nearly all of its essential foodstuffs and manufactured items; it depends on these external sources of income for financing.

Fishing fleets from South Korea, Japan, Taiwan, and the United States pay a licensing fee in order to operate in Kiribati's territorial waters. These licenses produce over $20 million annually, with a surge in 1998 to nearly $30 million when El Nino climatic conditions boosted the local catch. Due to its small size and spread-out nature, however, Kiribati also loses untold millions of income per year from illegal, unlicensed fishing in its exclusive economic zone.

Another $20 million to $25 million of external income takes the form of direct financial transfers. Official development assistance amounts to between $15 million and $20 million per year. The largest donors are Japan, the UK, Australia, and New Zealand. Remittances from Kiribati workers living abroad provide another $5 million.

Tourism is one of the largest domestic activities. Between 3,000 and 4,000 visitors per year provide $5-$10 million in revenue. Attractions include World War II battle sites, game fishing, ecotourism, and the Millennium Islands, situated just inside the International Date Line and the first place on earth to celebrate every New Year.

Most islanders engage in subsistence activities ranging from fishing to the growing of food crops like bananas,

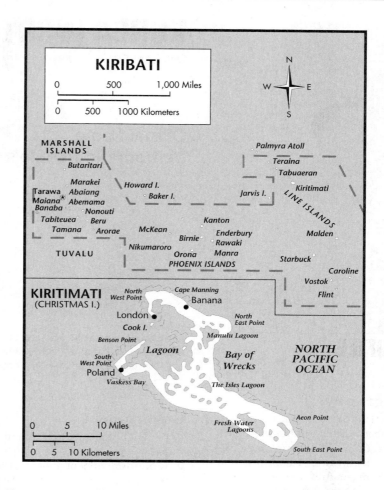

breadfruit, and papaya. The leading export is the coconut product copra, which accounts for about two-thirds of export revenue. Other exports include pet fish, shark fins, and seaweed. Kiribati's principal trading partner is Australia.

# FOREIGN RELATIONS

Kiribati maintains good relations with most countries and has particularly close ties to its Pacific neighbors—Japan, Australia, New Zealand, and China. Kiribati suspended its relations with France in 1995 over that country's decision to renew nuclear testing in the South Pacific.

Kiribati signed a treaty of friendship with the United States in 1979. The U.S. has no consular or diplomatic facilities in the country. Officers of the American Embassy in Majuro, Republic of the Marshall Islands, are

concurrently accredited to Kiribati and make periodic visits.

Kiribati hosted the Thirty-First Pacific Islands Forum in October 2000. The country became a member of the United Nations in 1999.

## Principal U.S. Officials

**For up-to-date information on Principal U.S. Officials, see the U.S. Embassies, Consulates, and Foreign Service section starting on page 139.**

Ambassador (accredited to both the Marshall Islands and Kiribati; resident in Majuro)—Michael J. Senko

The U.S. Embassy responsible for Kiribati is located in Majuro, Republic of the Marshall Islands. Its location is Lagoon Road, Majuro. Mailing address: P.O. Box 1379, Majuro, MH 96960–1379. Tel: 692–247–4011.

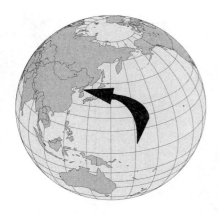

# KOREA (NORTH)

October 2000

## Official Name:
## Democratic People's Republic of Korea

# PROFILE

## Geography
**Area:** 120,410 sq. km. (47,000 sq. mi.), about the size of Mississippi.
**Cities:** Capital—Pyongyang. Other cities—Hamhung, Chongjin, Wonsan, Nampo, and Kaesong.
**Terrain:** About 80% of land area is moderately high mountains separated by deep, narrow valleys and small, cultivated plains. The remainder is lowland plains covering small, scattered areas.
**Climate:** Long, cold, dry winters; short, hot, humid, summers.

## People
**Nationality:** Noun and adjective—Korean(s).
**Population:** (1998) 21.2 million.
**Annual growth rate:** About -0.03%.
**Ethnic Groups:** Korean; small Chinese and Japanese populations.
**Religion:** Buddhism, Shamanism, Chongdogyo, Christian; religious activities have been virtually nonexistent since 1945.
**Language:** Korean.
**Education:** Years compulsory—11. Attendance—3 million (primary, 1.5 million; secondary, 1.2 million; tertiary, 0.3 million). Literacy—99%.
**Health:** (1998) Medical treatment is free; one doctor for every 700 inhabitants; one hospital bed for every 350. Infant mortality rate—88/1,000. Life expectancy—males 49 yrs., females 54 yrs.

## Government
**Type:** Highly centralized communist state.
**Independence:** September 9, 1948.
**Constitution:** 1948; 1972, revised in 1992.
**Branches:** Executive—president (chief of state); premier (head of government). Legislative—Supreme People's Assembly. Judicial—Supreme Court; provincial, city, county, and military courts.
**Subdivisions:** Nine provinces; four province-level municipalities (Pyongyang, Kaesong, Chongjin, Nampo); one free trade zone (Najin-Sonbong FTZ).
**Political party:** Korean Workers' Party (communist).
**Suffrage:** Universal at 17.

## Economy
**GDP:** (1997) $21.8 billion; 25% is agriculture, 60% is mining and manufacturing, and 15% is services and other.
**Per capita GDP:** (1997) $900 purchasing power parity.
**Agriculture:** Products—rice, corn, potatoes, fruits, vegetables, tobacco.
**Mining and manufacturing:** Types—steel, cement, textiles, petro-chemicals, machines, military equipment.
**Trade:** (1996) Exports—$912 billion; machinery and equipment, military hardware, iron, steel, metal ores, nonferrous metals, nonmetallic minerals, textile fibers. Imports—$1.95 billion: textiles, petroleum, coking coal, grain. Major partners—Russia, China, Japan, Hong Kong, European countries. These figures do not include trade with South Korea.
*In most cases, the figures used above are estimates based upon incomplete data and projections.

# U.S. POLICY TOWARD NORTH KOREA

## The Perry Process
On November 12, 1998, President Clinton named former Secretary of Defense William J. Perry to conduct a comprehensive review of U.S. policy toward North Korea. The President's decision rose out of North Korea's August 31, 1998 launching of a "Taepodong-1" ballistic missile, which was widely perceived as a destabilizing act.

The U.S. seeks progress from North Korea in the following areas as being necessary for improved bilateral relations: credible condemnation and forswearing of terrorism, continued dialogue between North and South Korea on the future and possible reunification of the Korean Peninsula, nuclear matters, restraints on the development of long-range missiles, return of the remains of U.S. military personnel missing in action during the Korean war, and greater respect for human rights. The U.S. also has expressed concern about North Korea's export of ballistic missiles and related technology and the North Korean conventional military threat.

After a comprehensive review of U.S. policy, a May 25-28, 1999 trip to Pyongyang, and extensive international coordination, especially with the Governments of South Korea and Japan, Dr. Perry issued his report, "Review of United States Policy Toward North Korea: Findings and Recommendations" on October 12, 1999. The report recommended a two-path strategy. If North Korea would address areas of concern, the U.S. (and U.S. allies) would "in a step-by-step and reciprocal fashion, move to reduce pressures on the D.P.R.K. that it perceives as threatening.... If the D.P.R.K. moved to eliminate its nuclear and long-range missile threats, the United States would normalize relations with the D.P.R.K., relax sanctions that have long constrained trade with the D.P.R.K. and take other positive steps..."If, however, North Korea refused to go down this 'positive path,' "the United States and its allies would have to take other steps to assure their security and contain the threat."

As part of the process begun by Dr. Perry, the U.S., South Korea, and Japan established a high-level Trilateral Coordination and Oversight Group (TCOG) to coordinate North Korea policy. The TCOG's creation was announced jointly by representatives of the three governments on April 25, 1999, after a meeting in Hawaii. There were six TCOG meetings in 1999, including a summit in Auckland on September 12 and a ministerial level meeting in Singapore on July 27. A 12th TCOG

meeting was held on October 7, 2000, in Washington.

On September 25, 2000, the State Department announced that Dr. William Perry was stepping down from his duties as North Korea Policy Coordinator. Ambassador Wendy R. Sherman, the Counselor of the Department, succeeded Dr. Perry as North Korea Policy Coordinator and Special Adviser to the President and the Secretary of State.

From October 8-12, 2000, North Korean Vice Marshal Jo Myong Rok, the First Vice Chairman of the National Defense Commission, visited the U.S. as the Special Envoy of Chairman Kim Jong Il. At the conclusion of his visit, the two countries issued a Joint Communique in which the two sides stated that neither government would have hostile intent toward the other and confirmed the commitment of both governments to make every effort in the future to build a new relationship free from past enmity. Among other issues, the communique mentioned missile issues and the Agreed Framework, and it noted that Secretary of State Madeleine Albright would visit the D.P.R.K. "to convey the views of U.S. President William Clinton directly to Chairman Kim Jong Il... and to prepare for a possible visit by the President of the United States."

The United States does not maintain any diplomatic, consular, or trade relations with the Democratic People's Republic of Korea (D.P.R.K., or North Korea). Negotiations are ongoing to implement a provision of the 1994 Agreed Framework between the U.S. and D.P.R.K. for an exchange of diplomatic missions at the liaison office level.

On September 20, 1995, a consular protecting power arrangement was implemented, allowing for consular protection by the Swedish Embassy of U.S. citizens traveling in North Korea. The Swedish Embassy in Pyongyang is not authorized to issue U.S. visas. U.S. citizens and residents wishing to travel to North Korea must obtain visas in third countries.

There are no U.S. Government restrictions on travel by private U.S. citizens to North Korea. However, they may spend money in North Korea only to purchase items related to travel, e.g. plane and train tickets, accommodations, meals, guide and admission fees. In addition, $100 worth of merchandise for personal use may be brought back into the United States as unaccompanied baggage. (Also see Travel and Business Information.)

## U.S. Support for North-South Dialogue and Reunification

The United States supports the peaceful reunification of Korea—divided following World War II—on terms acceptable to the Korean people and recognizes that the future of the Korean Peninsula is primarily a matter for them to decide. The U.S. believes that a constructive and serious dialogue between the authorities of North and South Korea is necessary to resolve the issues on the peninsula, and that concrete steps to promote greater understanding and reduce tension are needed to pave the way for reunifying the Korean nation. The U.S. remains prepared to participate in negotiations between North and South Korea if so desired by the two Korean Governments and provided that both are full and equal participants in any such talks.

On the basis of these principles, on April 16, 1996, President Clinton and South Korean President Kim Young Sam proposed to convene a "Four Party Meeting" of representatives of South Korea, North Korea, the United States, and the People's Republic of China as soon as possible, without preconditions. The purpose of these "Four Party Talks" has been to initiate a process aimed at replacing the current military armistice agreement with a permanent peace. Six plenary sessions of the Four Party Talks were held in Geneva from December 1997 through August 1999. Two subcommittees have been created to discuss armistice replacement and tension reduction.

On his inauguration in February 1998, R.O.K. President Kim Dae-jung enunciated a new policy of engagement with North Korea dubbed "The Sunshine Policy." The policy had three fundamental principles: no tolerance of provocations from the North, no intention to absorb the North, and the separation of political cooperation from economic cooperation. Private sector overtures would be based on commercial and humanitarian considerations. The use of government resources would entail reciprocity. President Kim's consistent application of this policy eventually set the stage for the inter-Korean summit held in Pyongyang June 13-15, 2000.

The U.S. has strongly supported R.O.K. President Kim Dae-jung's engagement policy and welcomed the active phase of North-South dialogue that began with the inter-Korean summit. That summit produced a Joint Declaration noting that the two governments "have agreed to resolve the question of reunification independently and through the joint efforts of the Korean people. . . ." Following the summit, the two Koreas held ministerial-level meetings July 29-31 in Seoul and August 29-September 1 in Pyongyang. They also held Defense Minister talks on Cheju Island (South Korea) September 25-26. Also, on September 14, following a visit to South Korea by Kim Yong Sun (Chairman of the Korean Workers' Party's Asia-Pacific Peace Committee), the R.O.K. and D.P.R.K. announced that Chairman Kim Jong Il would visit South Korea in the near future, following a visit by Supreme People's Assembly (SPA) Presidium President Kim Yong Nam. This dialogue led the two governments to open liaison offices in the truce village of Panmunjom on August 14. On August 15, in accordance with the summit's Joint Declaration, the two sides sent delegations of 100 members of separated families to each other's capitals for reunion meetings. On September 18, R.O.K. President Kim Dae-jung presided over a groundbreaking ceremony for the planned re-linking of the Seoul-Sinuiju railway line, which crosses

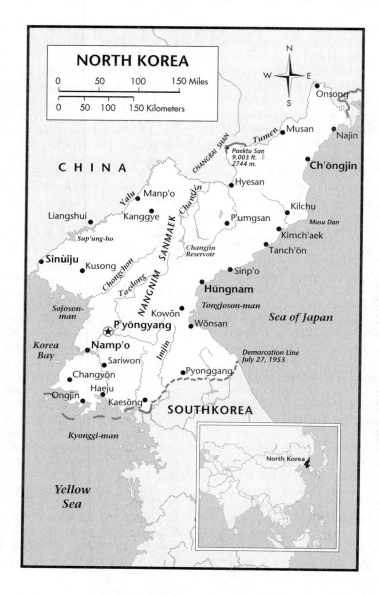

through the Demilitarized Zone (DMZ).

## U.S. Efforts on Denuclearization

North and South Korea had begun talks in 1990, which resulted in a 1991 denuclearization accord (see, under Foreign Relations, Reunification Efforts Since 1971). Lack of progress on implementation of this accord triggered actions on both sides that led to North Korea's March 12, 1993, announcement of its withdrawal from the nuclear Non-Proliferation Treaty (NPT). The UN Security Council on May 11 passed a resolution urging the D.P.R.K. to cooperate with the International Atomic Energy Agency (IAEA) and to implement the 1991 North-South denuclearization accord. It also urged all member states to encourage the D.P.R.K. to respond positively to this resolution and to facilitate a solution.

The U.S. responded by holding political-level talks with the D.P.R.K. in early June 1993 that led to a joint statement outlining the basic principles for continued U.S.-D.P.R.K. dialogue and North Korea's "suspending" its withdrawal from the NPT. A second round of talks was held July 14-19, 1993, in Geneva. The talks set the guidelines for resolving the nuclear issue, improving U.S.-North Korean relations, and restarting inter-Korean talks, but further negotiations deadlocked.

Following the D.P.R.K.'s spring 1994 unloading of fuel from its five-megawatt nuclear reactor, the resultant U.S. push for UN sanctions, and former U.S. President Carter's June 1994 visit to Pyongyang, a third round of talks between the U.S. and the D.P.R.K. opened in Geneva on July 8, 1994. The talks were recessed upon news of the July death of North Korean President Kim Il Sung, then resumed in August. On October 21, 1994, representatives of the United States and the D.P.R.K. signed an Agreed Framework for resolving the nuclear issue.

The 1994 Agreed Framework calls for the following steps.

North Korea agreed to freeze its existing nuclear program to be monitored by the IAEA. Both sides agreed to cooperate to replace the D.P.R.K.'s graphite-moderated reactors for related facilities with light-water (LWR) power plants, to be financed and supplied by an international consortium (later identified as KEDO). The U.S. and D.P.R.K. will work together to store safely the spent fuel from the five-megawatt reactor and dispose of it in a safe manner that does not involve reprocessing in the D.P.R.K. The two sides agreed to move toward full normalization of political and economic relations. Both sides will work together for peace and security on a nuclear-free Korean Peninsula. Both sides agreed to work together to strengthen the international nuclear non-proliferation regime. In accordance with the terms of the 1994 Framework, the U.S. Government in January 1995 responded to North Korea's decision to freeze its nuclear program and cooperate with U.S. and IAEA verification efforts by easing economic sanctions against North Korea in four areas through:

Authorizing transactions related to telecommunications connections, credit card use for personal or travel-related transactions, and the opening of journalists' offices; Authorizing D.P.R.K. use of the U.S. banking system to clear transactions not origi-

nating or terminating in the United States and unblocking frozen assets where there is no D.P.R.K. Government interest; Authorizing imports of magnesite, a refractory material used in the U.S. steel industry—North Korea and China are the world's primary sources of this raw material; and Authorizing transactions related to future establishment of liaison offices, case-by-case participation of U.S. companies in the light-water reactor project, supply of alternative energy, and disposition of spent nuclear fuel as provided for by the Agreed Framework, in a manner consistent with applicable laws. North Korea agreed to accept the decisions of the Korean Peninsula Energy Development Organization (KEDO), the financier and supplier of the LWRs, with respect to provision of the reactors. KEDO subsequently identified Sinpo as the LWR project site and held a groundbreaking ceremony in August 1987. In December 1999, KEDO and KEPCO signed the Turnkey Contract (TKC), permitting full-scale construction of the LWRs.

In January 1995, as called for in the 1994 Geneva Agreed Framework, the U.S. and D.P.R.K. negotiated a method to store safely the spent fuel from the five-megawatt reactor. According to this method, U.S. and D.P.R.K. operators would work together to can the spent fuel and store the canisters in the spent fuel pond. Actual canning began in 1995. In April 2000, canning of all accessible spent fuel rods and rod fragments was declared complete.

In 1998, the U.S. identified an underground site in Kumchang-ni, D.P.R.K., which it suspected of being nuclear-related. In March 1999, after several rounds of negotiations, the U.S. and D.P.R.K. agreed that the U.S. would be granted "satisfactory access" to the underground site at Kumchang-ni. In October 2000, during Special Envoy Jo Myong Rok's visit to Washington, the U.S. announced in a Joint Communique with the D.P.R.K. that U.S. concerns about the site had been resolved.

As called for in Dr. William Perry's review of U.S. policy toward North

Korea (see under U.S. Policy Toward North Korea) the U.S. and D.P.R.K. launched new negotiations in May 2000 called the Agreed Framework Implementation Talks.

# HISTORICAL AND CULTURAL HIGHLIGHTS

The Korean Peninsula was first populated by peoples of a Tungusic branch of the Ural-Altaic language family who migrated from the northwestern regions of Asia. Some of these peoples also populated parts of northeast China (Manchuria); Koreans and Manchurians still show physical similarities.

Koreans are racially and linguistically homogeneous. Although there are no indigenous minorities in North Korea, there is a small Chinese community (about 50,000) and some 1,800 Japanese wives who accompanied the roughly 93,000 Koreans returning to the North from Japan during 1959-62. Korean is a Ural-Altaic language and is related to Japanese and remotely related to Hungarian, Finnish, Estonian, and Mongolian. Although dialects exist, the Korean spoken throughout the peninsula is mutually comprehensible. In North Korea, the Korean alphabet (hangul) is used exclusively, unlike in South Korea, where a combination of hangul and Chinese characters is used as the written language.

Korea's traditional religions are Buddhism and Shamanism. Christian missionaries arrived as early as the 16th century, but it was not until the 19th century that they founded schools, hospitals, and other modern institutions throughout Korea. Major centers of 19th-century missionary activity included Seoul and Pyongyang, and there was a relatively large Christian population in the north before 1945. Although religious groups exist in North Korea, most available evidence suggests that the government severely restricts religious activity.

According to legend, the god-king Tangun founded the Korean nation in 2333 BC. By the first century AD, the Korean Peninsula was divided into the kingdoms of Shilla, Koguryo, and Paekche. In 668 AD, the Shilla kingdom unified the peninsula. The Koryo dynasty—from which Portuguese missionaries in the 16th century derived the Western name "Korea"—succeeded the Shilla kingdom in 935. The Choson dynasty, ruled by members of the Yi clan, supplanted Koryo in 1392 and lasted until the Japanese annexed Korea in 1910.

Throughout most of its history, Korea has been invaded, influenced, and fought over by its larger neighbors. Korea was under Mongolian occupation from 1231 until the early 14th century and was plundered by Japanese pirates in 1359 and 1361. The unifier of Japan, Hideyoshi, launched major invasions of Korea in 1592 and 1597. When Western powers focused "gunboat" diplomacy on Korea in the mid-19th century, Korea's rulers adopted a closed-door policy, earning Korea the title of "Hermit Kingdom."

Though the Choson dynasty paid tribute to the Chinese court and recognized China's hegemony in East Asia, Korea was independent until the late 19th century. At that time, China sought to block growing Japanese influence on the Korean Peninsula and Russian pressure for commercial gains there. This competition produced the Sino-Japanese War of 1894-95 and the Russo-Japanese War of 1904-05. Japan emerged victorious from both wars and in 1910 annexed Korea as part of the growing Japanese empire.

Japanese colonial administration was characterized by tight control from Tokyo and ruthless efforts to supplant Korean language and culture. Organized Korean resistance during the colonial era—such as the March 1, 1919, Independence Movement—was unsuccessful, and Japan remained firmly in control until the end of World War II in 1945.

Japan surrendered in August 1945, and Korea was liberated. However, the unexpectedly early surrender of Japan led to the immediate division of Korea into two occupation zones, with the U.S. administering the southern half of the peninsula and the U.S.S.R taking over the area to the north of the 38th parallel. This division was meant to be temporary and to facilitate the Japanese surrender until the U.S., U.K., Soviet Union, and China could arrange a trusteeship administration.

At a meeting in Cairo, it was agreed that Korea would be free "in due course;" at a later meeting in Yalta, it was agreed to establish a four-power trusteeship over Korea. In December 1945, a conference convened in Moscow to discuss the future of Korea. A 5-year trusteeship was discussed, and a joint Soviet-American commission was established. The commission met intermittently in Seoul but deadlocked over the issue of establishing a national government. In September 1947, with no solution in sight, the United States submitted the Korean question to the UN General Assembly.

Initial hopes for a unified, independent Korea quickly evaporated as the politics of the Cold War and domestic opposition to the trusteeship plan resulted in the 1948 establishment of two separate nations with diametrically opposed political, economic, and social systems and the outbreak of war in 1950 (see, under Foreign Relations, Korean war of 1950-53).

# ECONOMY

North Korea's faltering economy and the breakdown of trade relations with the countries of the former socialist bloc—especially following the fall of communism in eastern Europe and the disintegration of the Soviet Union—have confronted Pyongyang with difficult policy choices. Other centrally planned economies in similar straits have opted for domestic economic reform and liberalization of trade and investment. Despite its recent moves toward limited economic opening, North Korea has thus far avoided making any fundamental changes. Its leadership seems determined to maintain tight political and ideological control.

About 80% of North Korea's terrain consists of moderately high mountain ranges and partially forested mountains and hills separated by deep, narrow valleys and small, cultivated plains. The most rugged areas are the north and east coasts. Good harbors are found on the eastern coast. Pyongyang, the capital, near the country's west coast, is located on the Taedong River.

Although most North Korean citizens live in cities and work in factories, agriculture remains a rather high 25% of total GNP, although output has not recovered to early 1990 levels. While trade with the South has expanded since 1988, no physical links between the two remain, and the infrastructure of the North is generally poor and outdated.

North Korea suffers from chronic food shortages, which were exacerbated by record floods in the summer of 1995 and continued shortages of fertilizer and parts. In response to international appeals, the U.S. provided 500,000 tons of humanitarian food aid in the period July 1999-June 2000 through the UN World Food Program and through U.S. private voluntary organizations.

## Colonial Rule and Postwar Division

Beginning in the mid-1920s, the Japanese colonial administration concentrated its industrial development efforts in the comparatively underpopulated and resource-rich northern portion of Korea, resulting in a considerable movement of people northward from the agrarian southern provinces of the Korean Peninsula.

This trend was reversed after the end of World War II, when more than 2 million Koreans moved from North to South following the division of the peninsula into Soviet and American military zones of administration. This southward exodus continued after the establishment of the D.P.R.K. in 1948 and during the 1950-53 Korean war. The North Korean population is now 21.2 million, compared with 46.4 million in South Korea.

The post-World War II division of the Korean Peninsula resulted in imbalances of natural and human resources, with disadvantages for both the North and the South. By most economic measures, after partition the North was better off in terms of industry and natural resources. The South, however, had two-thirds of the work force. In 1945, about 65% of Korean heavy industry was in the North but only 31% of light industry, 37% of agriculture, and 18% of the peninsula's total commerce.

North and South both suffered from the massive destruction caused during the Korean war. In the years immediately after the war, North Korea mobilized its labor force and natural resources in an effort to achieve rapid economic development. Large amounts of aid from other communist countries, notably the Soviet Union and China, helped the regime achieve a high growth rate in the immediate postwar period.

## Efforts at Modernization

During the early 1970s, North Korea attempted a largescale modernization program through the importation of Western technology, principally in the heavy industrial sectors of the economy. Unable to finance its debt through exports that shrank steadily after the worldwide recession stemming from the oil crisis of the 1970s, the D.P.R.K. became the first communist country to default on its loans from free market countries.

In 1979, North Korea was able to renegotiate much of its international debt, but in 1980 it defaulted on all of its loans except those from Japan. By the end of 1986, hard-currency debt had reached more than $4 billion. It also owed nearly $2 billion to communist creditors, principally Russia. The Japanese also declared the D.P.R.K. in default. By 2000, taking into account penalties and accrued inter-

## Travel Notes

**Travel Advice:** For up-to-date information from the U.S. State Department on possible inconvenient or hazardous situations, see the **Travel Warnings and Consular Information Sheets from the U.S. Government** section starting on page 1723. For the latest information on health requirements and conditions, see the **International Travelers' Health Information** section starting on page 1385. For further information dealing with non-urgent matter, see the **Tips for Travelers to...** section starting on page 1588.

est, North Korea's debt was estimated at $10-$12 billion.

Largely because of these debt problems but also because of a prolonged drought and mismanagement, North Korea's industrial growth slowed, and per capita GNP fell below that of the South. By the end of 1979, per capita GNP in the D.P.R.K. was about one-third of that in the R.O.K. The causes for this relatively poor performance are complex, but a major factor is the disproportionately large percentage of GNP (possibly as much as 25%) that the D.P.R.K. devotes to the military.

In April 1982, Kim Il Sung announced a new economic policy giving priority to increased agricultural production through land reclamation, development of the country's infrastructure—especially power plants and transportation facilities—and reliance on domestically produced equipment. There also was more emphasis on trade.

In September 1984, North Korea promulgated a joint venture law to attract foreign capital and technology. The new emphasis on expanding trade and acquiring technology, however, was not accompanied by a shift in priorities away from support of the military. In 1991, the D.P.R.K. announced the creation of a Special Economic Zone (SEZ) in the northeast regions of Najin, Chongjin, and Sonbong. Investment in this SEZ has been slow in coming. Problems with infrastructure, bureaucracy, and

uncertainties about investment security and viability have hindered growth and development.

The D.P.R.K. announced in December 1993 a 3-year transitional economic policy placing primary emphasis on agriculture, light industry, and foreign trade. However, lack of fertilizer, natural disasters, and poor storage and transportation practices have left the country more than a million tons short of grain self-sufficiency each year. Moreover, lack of foreign exchange to purchase spare parts and oil for electrical generation has left many factories shuttered. Without significant opening to the outside world and substantial outside resources, the D.P.R.K. is unlikely to return to a path of sustainable economic growth.

## North-South Economic Ties

Following a 1988 decision by the South Korean Government to allow trade with the D.P.R.K. (see, under Foreign Relations, Reunification Efforts Since 1971), South Korean firms began to import North Korean goods. Direct trade with the South began in the fall of 1990 after the unprecedented September 1990 meeting of the two Korean Prime Ministers. Trade between the countries increased from $18.8 million in 1989 to $333.4 million in 1999, much of it processing or assembly work undertaken in the North.

During this decade, the chairman of the South Korean company Daewoo visited the D.P.R.K. and reached agreement on building a light industrial complex at Nampo. In other negotiations, Hyundai Asan obtained permission to bring tour groups by sea to Kumgangsan on the southeast coast of the D.P.R.K. and more recently to construct an 800-acre industrial complex at Kaesong, near the DMZ, at a cost of more than $1 billion.

In response to the Kim Jong Il/Kim Dae-jung summit, the D.P.R.K. and the R.O.K. agreed in August 2000 to reconnect the Seoul-Sinuiju railroad where it crosses the DMZ. In addition, the two governments said they would build a four-lane highway bypassing the truce village at Panmunjom. Once these projects are completed, the Kaesong industrial park will have ready access to South Korean markets and ports.

## New Commercial Ties

On June 19, 2000, the United States announced easing of sanctions against North Korea and allowed a wide range of exports and imports of U.S. and D.P.R.K. commercial and consumer goods. Imports from North Korea are permitted, subject to an approval process. Direct personal and commercial financial transactions are allowed between U.S. and D.P.R.K. persons. Restrictions on investment also have been eased. Commercial U.S. ships and aircraft carrying U.S. goods are allowed to call at D.P.R.K. ports.

The Departments of Treasury, Commerce, and Transportation have issued regulations, published in the June 19, 2000 Federal Register, affecting sanctions-easing. Points of Contact: Treasury—Dennis P. Wood, Chief of Compliance Programs, Office of Foreign Assets Control, Tel. (202) 622-2490, http://www.treas.gov/ofac; Commerce—James A. Lewis, Director, Office of Strategic Trade, Bureau of Export Administration, Tel. (202) 482-0092; Transportation—Christopher T. Tourtellot, Office of the Assistant General Counsel for International Law, Tel. (202) 366-9183.

This easing of sanctions does not affect U.S. counterterrorism or nonproliferation controls on North Korea, which prohibit exports of military and sensitive dual-use items and most types of U.S. assistance. Statutory restrictions, such as U.S. missile sanctions, remain in place. Restrictions on North Korea based on multilateral arrangements also remain in place.

# GOVERNMENT AND POLITICAL CONDITIONS

North Korea has a centralized government under the rigid control of the communist Korean Workers' Party (KWP), to which all government officials belong. A few minor political parties are allowed to exist in name only. Kim Il Sung ruled North Korea from 1948 until his death in July 1994. Kim served both as Secretary General of the KWP and as President of North Korea. Little is known about the actual lines of power and authority in the North Korean Government despite the formal structure set forth in the constitution. Following the death of Kim Il Sung, his son—Kim Jong Il—inherited supreme power. Kim Jong Il was named General Secretary of the Korean Workers' Party in October 1997, and in September 1998, the SPA reconfirmed Kim Jong Il as Chairman of the National Defense Commission and declared that position as the "highest office of state." North Korea's 1972 constitution was amended in late 1992. The government is led by the president and, in theory, a super cabinet called the Central People's Committee (CPC).

The constitution designates the CPC as the government's top policymaking body. It is headed by the president, who also nominates the other committee members. The CPC makes policy decisions and supervises the cabinet, or State Administration Council (SAC). The SAC is headed by a premier and is the dominant administrative and executive agency.

Officially, the legislature, the Supreme People's Assembly, is the highest organ of state power. Its members are elected every 4 years. Usually only two meetings are held annually, each lasting a few days. A standing committee elected by the SPA performs legislative functions when the Assembly is not in session. In reality, the Assembly serves only to ratify decisions made by the ruling

KWP. North Korea's judiciary is "accountable" to the SPA and the president. The SPA's standing committee also appoints judges to the highest court for 4-year terms that are concurrent with those of the Assembly.

Administratively, North Korea is divided into nine provinces and four provincial-level municipalities—Pyongyang, Chongjin, Nampo, and Kaesong. It also appears to be divided into nine military districts.

## Principal Party and Government Officials

For up-to-date information on Principal Government Officials, see the Chiefs of State and Cabinet Members of Foreign Governments section starting on page 1.

# FOREIGN RELATIONS

North Korea's relationship with the South has informed much of its post-World War II history and still drives much of its foreign policy. North and South Korea have had a difficult and acrimonious relationship in the five decades since the Korean war.

North Korea occupies the northern portion of a mountainous peninsula projecting southeast from China, between the Sea of Japan and the Yellow Sea. Japan lies east of the peninsula across the Sea of Japan. North Korea shares borders with the People's Republic of China along the Yalu River and with China and Russia along the Tumen River.

The military demarcation line (MDL) of separation between the belligerent sides at the close of the Korean war forms North Korea's boundary with South Korea. A demilitarized zone (DMZ) extends for 2,000 meters (just over 1 mile) on either side of the MDL. Both the North and South Korean Governments hold that the MDL is only a temporary administrative line, not a permanent border.

During the postwar period, both Korean Governments have repeatedly affirmed their desire to reunify the Korean Peninsula, but until 1971, the two governments had no direct, official communications or other contact. During former U.S. President Carter's 1994 visit, Kim Il Sung agreed to a first-ever North-South summit. The two sides went ahead with plans for a meeting in July but had to shelve it because of Kim's death.

## Korean war of 1950-53

As noted, differences developed after World War II over the issue of establishing a Korean national government. The Soviet Union and Korean authorities in the North refused to comply with the UN General Assembly's November 1947 resolution on elections and blocked entry of the United Nations Temporary Commission on Korea into the North. Despite this refusal, elections were held in the South under UN observation, and on August 15, 1948, the Republic of Korea was established in the South. Syngman Rhee, a Korean nationalist leader, became the Republic's first president.

On September 9, 1948, the North established the Democratic People's Republic of Korea headed by then-Premier Kim Il Sung, known for his anti-Japanese guerrilla activities in Manchuria during the 1930s. Both administrations claimed to be the only legitimate government on the peninsula. After the establishment of the two states, South Korea experienced several violent uprisings by indigenous, pro-North Korean leftist guerrillas. As Soviet troops left in late 1948 and U.S. troops in the spring of 1949, border clashes along the 38th parallel intensified.

North Korean forces invaded South Korea on June 25, 1950. The United Nations, in accordance with the terms of its Charter, engaged in its first collective action and established the UN Command (UNC), to which 16 member nations sent troops and assistance. Next to South Korea, the United States contributed the largest contingent of forces to this interna-

## Additional Resources

Available from the Superintendent of Documents, U.S. Government Printing Office, Washington, DC 20402:

Library of Congress. *North Korea: A Country Study.* 1994
Department of State. *The Record on Korean Unification 1943-1960.* 1961.
Department of the Army. *Communist North Korea: A Bibliographic Survey.* 1971.

The following titles are provided as a general indication of the material published on this country. The Department of State does not endorse unofficial publications.

Baldwin, Frank, ed. Without Parallel: *The American-Korean Relationship Since 1945.* New York: Pantheon Books, 1974.
Barnds, William J. *The Two Koreas in East Asian Affairs.* New York: New York University Press, 1976.
Chung, Joseph S. *The North Korean Economy: Structure and Development.* Stanford: Hoover Institution Press, 1974.
Clough, Ralph. *Embattled Korea: The Rivalry for International Support.* Colorado: Westview Press, 1987.
Cumings, Bruce. *The Origins of the Korean War, Vol. 2.* Princeton: Princeton University Press, 1990.
Eckert, Carter, Ki-Baik Lee, Young Ick Lew, Michael Robinson, and Edward W. Wagner. *Korea Old and New: A History.* Seoul: Ilchokak Publishers for Harvard University Press, 1990.
Foot, Rosemary. *The Wrong War: American Policy and the Dimensions of the Korean Conflict, 1950-53.* Ithaca: Cornell University Press, 1985.
Hwang, In K. *The Neutralized Unification of Korea.* Cambridge: Schenkman, 1980.
Kihl, Young Hwan. *Politics and Policies in Divided Korea.* Colorado: Westview Press, 1984.
Kim, Hak-joon. *The Unification Policy of South and North Korea, 1948-1976: A Comparative Study.* Seoul: Seoul National University Press, 1977.
Kim, Ilpyong J. *Communist Politics in North Korea.* New York: Praeger, 1975.
Kim, Joungwon Alexander. *Divided Korea: The Politics of Development 1945-1972.* Cambridge: Harvard University Press, 1976.
Kim, Young C. and Abraham M. Halpern. *The Future of the Korean Peninsula.* New York: Praeger, 1976.
Koh, Byung Chul. *The Foreign Policy Systems of North and South Korea.* Berkeley: University of California, 1984.
Lee, Chong-sik. *Korean Workers' Party: A Short History.* Stanford: Hoover Institution Press, 1978.
_____. *Materials on Korean Communist 1945-1947.* Honolulu: Center for Korean Studies, University of Hawaii, 1977.
Lee, Chong-sik and Se-Hee Yoo, ed. *North Korea in Transition.* Berkeley: Institute of East Asian Studies, 1991.
Lee, Ki-baik. *A New History of Korea.* Cambridge: Harvard University Press, 1984.
MacDonald, Donald S. *The Koreans: Contemporary Politics and Society.* Boulder, CO: Westview Press, 1988.
Merrill, John. Korea: *The Peninsular Origins of the War.* Newark: University of Delaware Press, 1988.
Nahm, Andrew C. *North Korea: Her Past, Reality, and Impression.* Kalamazoo: Center for Korean Studies, Western Michigan University, 1978.
Palais, James B. *Politics and Policy in Traditional Korea.* Cambridge: Harvard University Press, 1976.
Scalapino, Robert A. and Jun-yop Kim, eds. *North Korea Today: Strategic and Domestic Issues.* Berkeley: Institute of East Asian Studies, 1983.
Suh, Dae-sook. Kim Il Sung: *A Biography.* Honolulu: University of Hawaii Press, 1989.

tional effort. The battle line fluctuated north and south, and after large numbers of Chinese "People's Volunteers" intervened to assist the North, the battle line stabilized north of Seoul near the 38th parallel.

Armistice negotiations began in July 1951, but hostilities continued until July 27, 1953. On that date, at Panmunjom, the military commanders of the North Korean People's Army, the Chinese People's Volunteers, and the UNC signed an armistice agreement. Neither the United States nor South Korea is a signatory to the armistice per se, although both adhere to it through the UNC. The armistice called for an international conference to find a political solution to the problem of Korea's division. This conference met at Geneva in April 1954 but, after 7 weeks of futile debate, ended without agreement or progress. No comprehensive peace agreement has replaced the 1953 armistice pact;

thus, a condition of belligerency still exists on the peninsula.

## Reunification Efforts Since 1971

In August 1971, North and South Korea agreed to hold talks through their respective Red Cross societies with the aim of reuniting the many Korean families separated following the division of Korea and the Korean war. After a series of secret meetings, both sides announced on July 4, 1972, an agreement to work toward peaceful reunification and an end to the hostile atmosphere prevailing on the peninsula. Officials exchanged visits, and regular communications were established through a North-South coordinating committee and the Red Cross.

However, these initial contacts broke down and ended in 1973 following South Korean President Park Chung Hee's announcement that the South would seek separate entry into the United Nations and after the kidnapping from Tokyo of South Korean opposition leader Kim Dae-Jung by the South Korean intelligence service. There was no other significant contact between North and South Korea until 1984.

Dialogue was renewed on several fronts in September 1984, when South Korea accepted the North's offer to provide relief goods to victims of severe flooding in South Korea. Red Cross talks to address the plight of separated families resumed, as did talks on economic and trade issues and parliamentary-level discussions. However, the North then unilaterally suspended all talks in January 1986, arguing that the annual U.S.-South Korea "Team Spirit" military exercise was inconsistent with dialogue. There was a brief flurry of negotiations on co-hosting the 1988 Seoul Olympics, which ended in failure and was followed by the 1987 KAL flight 858 bombing.

In a major initiative in July 1988, South Korean President Roh Tae Woo called for new efforts to promote North-South exchanges, family reunification, inter-Korean trade, and contact in international forums. Roh followed up this initiative in a UN General Assembly speech in which South Korea offered for the first time to discuss security matters with the North.

Initial meetings that grew out of Roh's proposals started in September 1989. In September 1990, the first of eight prime minister-level meetings between North Korean and South Korean officials took place in Seoul, beginning an especially fruitful period of dialogue. The prime ministerial talks resulted in two major agreements: the Agreement on Reconciliation, Nonaggression, Exchanges, and Cooperation (the "Basic Agreement") and the Declaration on the Denuclearization of the Korean Peninsula (the "Joint Declaration").

The Basic Agreement, signed on December 13, 1991, and calling for reconciliation and nonaggression established four joint commissions. These commissions—on South-North reconciliation, South-North military affairs, South-North economic exchanges and cooperation, and South-North social and cultural exchange—were to work out the specifics for implementing the general terms of the basic agreement. Subcommittees to examine specific issues were created, and liaison offices were established in Panmunjom, but in the fall of 1992, the process came to a halt because of rising tension over the nuclear issue.

The Joint Declaration on denuclearization was initialed on December 31, 1991. It forbade both sides to test, manufacture, produce, receive, possess, store, deploy, or use nuclear weapons and forbade the possession of nuclear reprocessing and uranium enrichment facilities. A procedure for inter-Korean inspection was to be organized and a North-South Joint Nuclear Control Commission (JNCC) was mandated with verification of the denuclearization of the peninsula.

On January 30, 1992, the D.P.R.K. also signed a nuclear safeguards agreement with the IAEA, as it had pledged to do in 1985 when acceding to the nuclear Non-Proliferation Treaty. This safeguards agreement allowed IAEA inspections to begin in June 1992. In March 1992, the JNCC was established in accordance with the joint declaration, but subsequent meetings failed to reach agreement on the main issue of establishing a bilateral inspection regime.

As the 1990s progressed, concern over the North's nuclear program became a major issue in North-South relations and between North Korea and the U.S. The lack of progress on implementation of the joint nuclear declaration's provision for an inter-Korean nuclear inspection regime led to reinstatement of the U.S.-South Korea Team Spirit military exercise for 1993. The situation worsened rapidly when North Korea, in January 1993, refused IAEA access to two suspected nuclear waste sites and then announced in March 1993 its intent to withdraw from the NPT. During the next 2 years, the U.S. held direct talks with the D.P.R.K. that resulted in a series of agreements on nuclear matters (see, under U.S. Policy Toward North Korea, U.S. Efforts on Denuclearization).

## Defense and Military Issues

North Korea now has the fourth-largest army in the world. The North has an estimated 1.2 million armed personnel, compared to about 650,000 in the South. Military spending equals 20%-25% of GNP, with about 20% of men ages 17-54 in the regular armed forces. North Korean forces have a substantial numerical advantage over the South (approximately 2 or 3 to 1) in several key categories of offensive weapons—tanks, long-range artillery, and armored personnel carriers. The North has perhaps the world's second-largest special operations force (55,000), designed for insertion behind the lines in wartime. While the North has a relatively impressive fleet of submarines, its surface fleet has a very limited capability. Its air force has twice the number of aircraft as the South, but, except for a few advanced fighters, the North's air force is obsolete. The North—like the South—deploys the

*A report on important events that have taken place since the last State Department revision of this* Background Note.

In 1996, the North Korean government made the first update since 1983 of its classification system of citizens' loyalty. Each citizen receives one of three designations: "loyal," "wavering," or "hostile." The system is used to keep people who disagree with the government from getting important jobs.

Three years of flooding and the nation's economic collapse hastened a famine that has worsened. The famine also resulted from the country's political isolation. With the fall of most Communist governments, the North Korean regime has found itself with few allies. Financial support from Russia and China disappeared in the early 1990s. The North Korean government refused to allow foreigners to freely see the extent of the famine.

In December 1997, North Korea participated in an initial round of peace talks with South Korea, China, and the United States held in Geneva. The eventual goal is to draw up a treaty that will replace the armistice agreement that ended the fighting in 1953.

Tensions between North Korea and its neighbors increased during August 1998 when Pyongyang test-fired a ballistic missile over the Sea of Japan and part of the Japanese home islands. As a result, Japan froze all of its humanitarian aid for North Korea.

Both former President Bill Clinton and President George W. Bush stated their desires to explore a deal with North Korea to end the production and export of medium- and long-range missiles. The point upon which the deal has been frustrated is how to verify compliance. In September 1999, President Clinton relaxed sanctions against North Korea following their promise to refrain from further nuclear testing.

The United States also continued to express concern over the possibility of nuclear weapons research activity in Kuchang-ri, in violation of the 1994 agreement whereby North Korea agreed to suspend its nuclear program in return for shipments of fuel oil from the United States. The United States continues to demand full access to all suspected nuclear weapons sites.

On June 15, 2000, President Kim Jong Il and South Korean President Kim Dae Jung met for the first time in the capital, Pyongyang. They reached an agreement that recognized the need for reconciliation and possible reunification of the two countries, including cultural and economic exchanges. The agreement also made arrangements for the exchange of families, some who have not seen each other for over 50 years.

In October 2000, Madeleine Albright became the first US Secretary of State to visit North Korea. Talks regarding arms control and sales were expected, but President Clinton wanted it known that serious differences still separate the two countries. President Kim appears ready to seek some accommodation with the non–communist world, as his country suffers from vast food shortages and economic stagnation.

bulk of its forces well forward, along the DMZ. Several North Korean military tunnels under the DMZ were discovered in the 1970s.

In 1953, the Military Armistice Commission (MAC) was created to oversee and enforce the terms of the armistice. The Neutral Nation Supervisory Committee (NNSC)—originally made up of delegations from Poland and Czechoslovakia on the D.P.R.K.-Chinese People's Volunteers side and Sweden and Switzerland on the UN side—monitors the activities of the MAC. In recent years, North Korea has sought to dismantle the MAC in a push for a new "peace mechanism" on the peninsula. In April 1994, it declared the MAC void and withdrew its representatives. Prior to this, it had effectively ended the functions of the NNSC.

Also over the last several years, North Korea has moved even more of its rear-echelon troops to hardened bunkers closer to the DMZ. Given the proximity of Seoul to the DMZ (some 25 miles), South Korean and U.S. forces are likely to have little warning of any attack. The United States and South Korea continue to believe that the U.S. troop presence remains an effective deterrent.

## Relations Outside the Peninsula

After 1945, the Soviet Union supplied the economic and military aid that enabled North Korea to mount its invasion of the South in 1950. Soviet aid and influence continued at a high level during the Korean war; as mentioned, the Soviet Union was largely responsible for rebuilding North Korea's economy after the cessation of hostilities. In addition, the assistance of Chinese "volunteers" during the war and the presence of these troops until 1958 gave China some

degree of influence in North Korea. In 1961, North Korea concluded formal mutual security treaties with the Soviet Union (inherited by Russia) and China, which have not been formally ended.

In the 1970s and early 1980s, the establishment of diplomatic relations between the United States and China, the Soviet-backed Vietnamese occupation of Cambodia, and the Soviet occupation of Afghanistan created strains between China and the Soviet Union and, in turn, in North Korea's relations with its two major communist allies. North Korea tried to avoid becoming embroiled in the Sino-Soviet split, obtaining aid from both the Soviet Union and China and trying to avoid dependence on either. Following Kim Il Sung's 1984 visit to Moscow, there was a dramatic improvement in Soviet-D.P.R.K. relations, resulting in renewed deliveries of advanced Soviet weaponry to

North Korea and increases in economic aid.

The establishment of diplomatic relations by South Korea with the Soviet Union in 1990 and with the P.R.C. in 1992 put a serious strain on relations between North Korea and its traditional allies. Moreover, the fall of communism in eastern Europe in 1989 and the disintegration of the Soviet Union in 1991 resulted in a significant drop in communist aid to North Korea. Despite these changes and its past reliance on this military and economic assistance, North Korea proclaims a militantly independent stance in its foreign policy in accordance with its official ideology of juche, or self-reliance.

At the same time, North Korea maintains membership in a variety of multilateral organizations. It became a member of the UN in September 1991. North Korea also belongs to the Food and Agriculture Organization; the International Civil Aviation Organization; the International Postal Union; the UN Conference on Trade and Development; the International Telecommunications Union; the UN Development Program; the UN Educational, Scientific, and Cultural Organization; the World Health Organization; the World Intellectual Property Organization; the World Meteorological Organization; the International Maritime Organization; the International Committee of the Red Cross; and the Nonaligned Movement.

In July 2000, North Korea began participating in the ASEAN Regional Forum (ARF), as Foreign Minister Paek Nam Sun attended the ARF ministerial meeting in Bangkok July 26-27. The D.P.R.K. also expanded its bilateral diplomatic ties in that year, establishing diplomatic relations with Italy, Australia, and the Philippines. The U.K. and Germany also have announced their intentions to establish diplomatic relations.

## Terrorism

The D.P.R.K. is not known to have sponsored any terrorist acts since 1987, when KAL 858 was bombed in flight. The D.P.R.K. has made several statements condemning terrorism. Most recently, on October 6, 2000, the U.S. and the D.P.R.K. issued a Joint Statement in which "the two sides agreed that international terrorism poses an unacceptable threat to global security and peace, and that terrorism should be opposed in all its forms." The U.S. and D.P.R.K. agreed to support the international legal regime combating international terrorism and to cooperate with each other to fight terrorism. Pyongyang continues to provide sanctuary to members of the Japanese Communist League-Red Army Faction who participated in the hijacking of a Japan Airlines flight to North Korea in 1970.

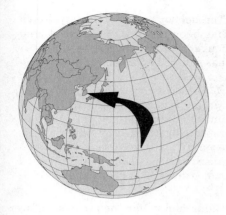

# KOREA (SOUTH)

June 2000

## Official Name:
**Republic of Korea**

# PROFILE

## Geography

**Area:** 98,500 sq. km. (38,000 sq. mi.); about the size of Indiana.

**Cities:** (1998) Capital—Seoul (11 million). Other major cities—Pusan (3.9 million),Taegu (2.5 million), Inchon (2.4 million), Kwangju (1.4 million), Taejon (1.3 million).

**Terrain:** Partially forested mountain ranges separated by deep, narrow valleys; cultivated plains along the coasts, particularly in the west and south.

**Climate:** Temperate.

## People

**Nationality:** Noun and adjective—Korean(s).

**Population:** (1998) 46.9 million.

**Annual growth rate:** (1997) 1.02%.

**Ethnic Groups:** Korean; small Chinese minority.

**Religion:** Christianity, Buddhism, Shamanism, Confucianism, Chondogyo.

**Language:** Korean.

**Education:** Years compulsory—9. Enrollment—11.5 million. Attendance—middle school 99%, high school 95%. Literacy—98%.

**Health:** Infant mortality rate (1997 est.)—8/1,000. Life expectancy (1997 est.)—men 70.1 yrs.; women 77.7 yrs.

**Work force:** (1997 est.) 21.5 million. Services—61%; mining and manufacturing-24%; agriculture—15%.

## Government

**Type:** Republic with powers shared between the president and the legislature.

**Liberation:** August 15, 1945.

**Constitution:** July 17, 1948; last revised 1987.

**Branches:** Executive—president (chief of state). Legislative—unicameral National Assembly. Judicial—Supreme Court and appellate courts; Constitutional Court.

**Subdivisions:** Nine provinces, six administratively separate cities (Seoul, Pusan, Inchon, Taegu, Kwangju, Taejon).

**Political parties:** National Congress for New Politics (NCNP); Grand National Party (GNP); United Liberal Democrats (ULD); Millennium Democratic Party (MDP) vice National Congress for New Politics; Democratic People's Party; North Korea Party of Hope.

**Suffrage:** Universal at 20.

**Central government budget:** (1996) Expenditures—$101 billion (including $20 billion in capital expenditures).

**Defense:** (1996) $17 billion, about 3.3% of nominal GDP and 23.3% of government budget (prior to capital expenditures); about 650,000 troops.

## Economy

**Nominal GDP:** (1999 est.) Approximately $406.7 billion.

**GDP growth rate:** 1999, 10.2%; 2000 est. 7%-8%.

**Per capita GNI:** (1999 est.) $8,581.

**Consumer price index:** 1998 avg. increase, 7.5%; 1999, 1.5%.

**Natural resources:** Limited coal, tungsten, iron ore, limestone, kaolinite, and graphite.

**Agriculture:** (including forestry and fisheries) Products—rice, vegetables, fruit.

**Arable land:** 22% of land area.

**Mining and manufacturing:** Textiles, footwear, electronics and electrical equipment, shipbuilding, motor vehicles, petrochemicals, industrial machinery.

**Trade:** (1999) Exports—$143.7 billion: manufactures, textiles, ships, automobiles, steel, computers, footwear. Major markets—U.S., Japan, ASEAN, European Union. Imports—$119.7 billion: crude oil, food, machinery and transportation equipment, chemicals and chemical products, base metals and articles. Major suppliers—Japan, U.S., European Union, Middle East.

# PEOPLE

The origins of the Korean people are obscure. Korea was first populated by a people or peoples who migrated to the peninsula from the northwestern regions of Asia, some of whom also settled parts of northeast China (Manchuria). Koreans are racially and linguistically homogeneous, with no sizable indigenous minorities, except for some Chinese (about 20,000).

South Korea's major population centers are in the northwest area and in the fertile plain to the south of Seoul-Inchon. The mountainous central and eastern areas are sparsely inhabited. The Japanese colonial administration of 1910-45 concentrated its industrial development efforts in the comparatively underpopulated and resource-rich north, resulting in a considerable migration of people to the north from the southern agrarian provinces. This trend was reversed after World War II as Koreans returned to the south from Japan and Manchuria. In addition, more than 2 million Koreans moved to the south from the north following the division of the peninsula into U.S. and Soviet military zones of administration in 1945. This migration continued after the Republic of Korea was established in 1948 and during the Korean war (1950-53). About 10% of the people now in the Republic of Korea are of northern origin. With 46 million people, South Korea has one of the world's highest population densities—much higher, for example, than India or Japan—while the territorially larger North Korea has only about 22 million people. Ethnic Koreans now residing in other countries live mostly in China (1.9 million), the United States (1.52 million), Japan (681,000), and the countries of the former Soviet Union (450,000).

## Language

The Korean language shares several grammatical features with Japanese, and there are strong similarities with Mongolian, but the exact relationship among these three languages is unclear. Although regional dialects exist, the language spoken throughout the peninsula and in China is comprehensible by all Koreans. Chinese characters were used to write Korean before the Korean Hangul alphabet was invented in the 15th century. Chinese characters are still in limited use in South Korea, but the North uses Hangul exclusively. Many older people retain some knowledge of Japanese from the colonial period, and many educated South Koreans can speak and/or read English, which is taught in all secondary schools.

## Religion

Korea's traditional religions are Buddhism and Shamanism. Buddhism has lost some influence over the years but is still followed by about 27% of the population. Shamanism—traditional spirit worship—is still practiced. Confucianism remains a dominant cultural influence. Since the Japanese occupation, it has existed more as a shared base than as a separate philosophical/religious school. Some sources place the number of adherents of Chondogyo—a native religion founded in the mid-19th century that fuses elements of Confucianism and Christianity—at more than 1 million.

Christian missionaries arrived in Korea as early as the 16th century, but it was not until the 19th century that they founded schools, hospitals, and other modern institutions throughout the country. Christianity is now one of Korea's largest religions. In 1993, nearly 10.5 million Koreans, or 24% of the population, were Christians (about 76% of them Protestant)—the largest figure for any East Asian country, except the Philippines.

# HISTORY

According to Korean legend, the god-king Tangun founded the Korean nation in BC 2333. By the first century AD, the Korean Peninsula was divided into the kingdoms of Silla, Koguryo, and Paekche. The Silla kingdom unified the peninsula in 668 AD. The Koryo dynasty (from which the Western name "Korea" is derived) succeeded the Silla kingdom in 935. The Choson dynasty, ruled by members of the Yi clan, supplanted Koryo in 1392 and lasted until the Japanese annexed Korea in 1910.

Throughout most of its history, Korea has been invaded, influenced, and fought over by its larger neighbors. It has suffered approximately 900 invasions during its 2,000 years of recorded history. Korea was under Mongolian occupation from 1231 until the early 14th century and was repeatedly ravaged by Chinese (government and rebel) armies. The Japanese warlord Hideyoshi launched major invasions in 1592 and 1597.

China had by far the greatest influence of the major powers and was the most acceptable to the Koreans. The Choson Dynasty was part of the Chinese "tribute" system, under which Korea was independent in fact but acknowledged China's theoretical role as "big brother." China was the only exception to Korea's long closed-door policy, adopted to ward off foreign encroachment, which earned it the name of "Hermit Kingdom" in the 19th century.

Korea's isolation finally ended when the major Western powers and Japan sent warships to forcibly open the country. At the same time, Japanese, Chinese, and Russian competition in Northeast Asia led to armed conflict, and foreign intervention established dominance in Korea, formally annexing it in 1910.

The Japanese colonial era was characterized by tight control from Tokyo and ruthless efforts to supplant Korean language and culture. Organized Korean resistance, notably the 1919 Independence Movement, was unsuccessful, and Japan remained firmly in control until the end of World War II.

Near the end of the war, the April 1945 Yalta Conference agreed to establish a four-power trusteeship for Korea. The trusteeship of the U.S., U.K., Soviet Union, and China was intended as a temporary administrative measure pending democratic elections for a Korean Government. With the unexpected early surrender of Japan in September 1945, the United States proposed—and the Soviet Union agreed—that Japanese troops surrender to U.S. forces below the 38th parallel and to Soviet forces above.

At a December 1945 foreign ministers' conference in Moscow, it was proposed that a 5-year trusteeship be established in Korea. The Moscow conference generated a firestorm of protest in the South. Some of its most critical opponents were Korean leaders associated with the provisional government established in Shanghai in 1919 by Korean nationalists living abroad. Most notable among them was nationalist leader Syngman Rhee.

The joint Soviet-American commission provided for by the Moscow Conference met intermittently in Seoul but became deadlocked over the issue of free consultations with representatives of all Korean political groups for establishment of a national government. The U.S. submitted the Korean question to the UN General Assembly for resolution in September 1947. In November, the General Assembly ruled that UN-supervised elections should be held.

The Soviet Union and Korean authorities in the North ignored the UN General Assembly resolution on elections. Nonetheless, elections were carried out under UN observation in the South, and on August 15, 1948, the Republic of Korea (R.O.K.) was established. Syngman Rhee became the Republic of Korea's first president. On September 9, 1948, the Democratic People's Republic of Korea (D.P.R.K.) was established in the North under Kim Il Sung. Both administrations claimed to be the only legitimate government on the peninsula.

Armed uprisings in the South and clashes between southern and northern forces along the 38th parallel began and intensified during 1948-50. Although it continued to provide modest military aid to the South, the U.S. withdrew its occupation forces by June 1949, leaving behind only a military advisory group of 500.

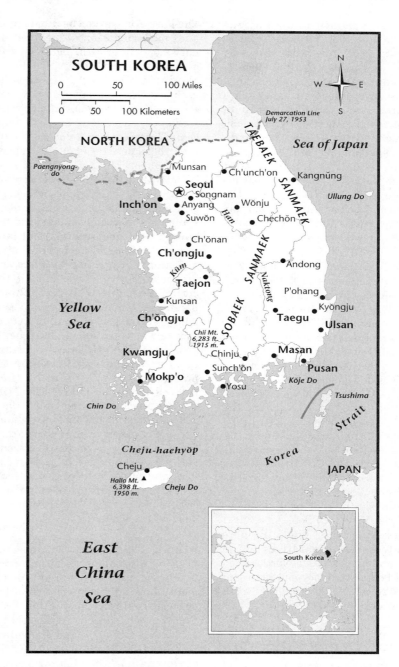

## Korean War of 1950-53

On June 25, 1950, North Korean forces invaded South Korea. The UN, in accord with its Charter, engaged in its first collective action by establishing the UN Command (UNC), under which 16 member nations sent troops and assistance to South Korea. At the request of the UN Security Council, the United States, contributor of the largest contingent, led this international effort.

After initially falling back to the southeastern Pusan perimeter, UN forces conducted a successful surprise landing at Inchon and rapidly advanced up the peninsula. As the main UN force approached the northern Yalu River, however, large numbers of "Chinese People's Volunteers" intervened, forcing UN troops to withdraw south of Seoul. The battle line seesawed back and forth until the late spring of 1951, when a successful offensive by UN forces was halted to enhance cease-fire negotiation prospects. The battle line thereafter stabilized north of Seoul near the 38th parallel.

Although armistice negotiations began in July 1951, hostilities continued until 1953 with heavy losses on both sides. On July 27, 1953 the military commanders of the North Korean Army, the Chinese People's Volunteers, and the UNC signed an armistice agreement at Panmunjom. Neither the United States nor South Korea is a signatory of the armistice per se, though both adhere to it through the UNC. No comprehensive peace agreement has replaced the 1953 armistice pact; thus, a condition of belligerency still technically exists on the divided peninsula.

The Military Armistice Commission (MAC) was created in 1953 to oversee and enforce the terms of the armistice. The Neutral Nation Supervisory Committee (NNSC)—originally made up of delegations from Poland and Czechoslovakia on the D.P.R.K. side and Sweden and Switzerland on the UN side—monitors the activities of the MAC. In recent years, North Korea has sought to undermine the MAC by various means. In April 1994 it declared the MAC void and withdrew its representatives. Prior to this it had forced the Czechs out of the NNSC by refusing to accept the Czech Republic as the successor state of Czechoslovakia, an original member of the NNSC. In September 1994 China recalled the Chinese People's Volunteers representatives to the MAC, and in early 1995 North Korea forced Poland to remove its representatives to the NNSC from the North Korean side of the DMZ.

## Toward Democratization

Syngman Rhee served as president of the Republic of Korea until April 1960, when unrest led by university students forced him to step down. Though the constitution was amended and national elections were held in June, Maj. Gen. Park Chung Hee led an army coup against the successor government and assumed power in May 1961. After 2 years of military government under Park, civilian rule was restored in 1963. Park, who had retired from the army, was elected president and was reelected in 1967, 1971, and 1978 in highly controversial elections.

The Park era, marked by rapid industrial modernization and extraordinary economic growth, ended with his assassination in October 1979. Prime Minister Choi Kyu Ha briefly assumed office, promising a new constitution and presidential elections. However, in December 1979 Maj. Gen. Chun Doo Hwan and close military colleagues staged a coup, removing the army chief of staff and soon effectively controlling the government. University student-led demonstrations against Chun's government spread in the spring of 1980 until the government declared martial law, banning all demonstrations, and arresting many political leaders and dissidents. Special forces units in the city of Kwangju dealt particularly harshly with demonstrators and residents, setting off a chain of events that left at least 200 civilians dead. This became a critically important event in contemporary South Korean political history. Chun, by then retired from the army, officially became president in September 1980. Though martial law ended in January 1981, his government retained broad legal powers to control dissent. Nevertheless, an active and articulate minority of students, intellectuals, clergy, and others remained critical of the Chun government and demonstrated against it.

In April 1986 the President appeared to yield to demands for reform, particularly for a constitutional amendment allowing direct election of his successor. However, in June 1987 Chun suspended all discussion of constitutional revision, and the ruling Democratic Justice Party (DJP) approved Chun's hand-picked successor, Roh Tae Woo. In response, first students and then the general public took to the streets in protest. Then in a surprise move, on June 29, ruling party presidential candidate Roh Tae Woo announced the implementation of democratic reforms. The constitution was revised in October 1987 to include direct presidential elections and a strengthened National Assembly consisting of 299 members.

The main opposition forces soon split into two parties—Kim Dae-jung's Peace and Democracy Party (PPD) and Kim Young Sam's Reunification Democratic Party (RDP). With the opposition vote split, Roh Tae Woo subsequently won the December 1987 presidential election—the first direct one since 1971—with 37% of the vote.

The new constitution entered into force in February 1988 when President Roh assumed office. Elections for the National Assembly were held on April 26. President Roh's ruling Democratic Justice Party was then able to win only 34% of the vote in the April 1988 National Assembly elections—the first time the ruling party had lost control of the Assembly since 1952.

# GOVERNMENT AND POLITICAL CONDITIONS

South Korea is a republic with powers shared between the president and the legislature. The president is chief of state and is elected for a term of 5 years. The 273 members of the unicameral National Assembly are elected to 4-year terms. South Korea's judicial system comprises a Supreme Court, appellate courts, and a Constitutional Court. The country has nine provinces and six administratively separate cities (Seoul, Pusan, Inchon, Taegu, Kwangju, and Taejon). Political parties include the National Congress for New Politics (NCNP); Grand National Party (GNP); United Liberal Democrats (ULD); Millennium Democratic Party (MDP) vice National Congress for New Politics; Democratic People's Party; and the North Korea Party of Hope. Suffrage is universal at age 20.

South Korean politics were changed dramatically by the 1988 legislative elections, the Assembly's greater powers under the 1987 constitution, and the influence of public opinion. After 1987 there was significant political liberalization, including greater freedom of the press, greater freedoms of expression and assembly, and the restoration of the civil rights of former detainees. The new opposition-dominated National Assembly quickly challenged the president's prerogatives.

The trend toward greater democratization continued. In free and fair elections in December 1992, Kim Young Sam, the former opposition leader who joined the ruling party of Roh Tae Woo, received 43% of the vote and became Korea's first civilian president in nearly 30 years. In June 1995, Korea held direct elections for local and provincial executive officials (mayors, governors, county and ward chiefs) for the first time in more than 30 years. In August 1996, ex-Presidents Chun and Roh were convicted on corruption and treason charges but were pardoned by President Kim Young Sam in December 1997.

Kim Dae-jung of the National Congress for New Politics (NCNP) won the December 1997 presidential election, defeating Lee Hoi Chang of the renamed ruling party, the Grand National Party (GNP), and the New Party for the People (NPP) candidate Rhee In Je. Kim's 1997 win was the first true opposition party victory in a Korean presidential election. Kim had previously been a political prisoner who narrowly escaped assassination and execution on several occasions, and who spent time in exile in Japan and the U.S. Kim's political opponents have long charged that he was sympathetic to the D.P.R.K., most recently during the presidential election campaign. Such charges are rooted more firmly in Korea's no-holds-barred political culture than in fact. Kim has articulated an engagement policy toward the North based on the separation of economic and political issues but which takes a firm line on security, with zero tolerance for provocations from the D.P.R.K. Kim has maintained this approach in spite of strong domestic criticism from the opposition GNP and continued provocative behavior by the D.P.R.K., including attempted infiltrations into the South and a clash between D.P.R.K. and R.O.K. naval ships in the Yellow Sea in June 1999, during which several North Korean vessels were damaged or sunk.

One of the most visible fruits of Kim's engagement policy is the Hyundai Corporation's passenger cruise trips to the North's culturally important Mt. Kumgang. In exchange for the right to ferry South Koreans to the mountain, Hyundai will pay the D.P.R.K. nearly $1 billion over 5 years. More than 200,000 people have visited Mt. Kumgang since the program's inception in early 1999. From June 13 to 15, the leaders of the two Koreas held a historic summit meeting in Pyongyang and signed a joint declaration promising a visit to Seoul by Kim Jong-il, continuing government-to-government dialogue, reunion of separated family members, cultural exchanges, and the pursuit of reunification.

President Kim's relations with the opposition have often been contentious, reflecting both substantive disagreements with the opposition and the strongly partisan flavor of R.O.K. domestic politics. Nonetheless, Kim and GNP leader Lee Hoi Chang have attempted to work cooperatively, if not in full agreement, in order to address pressing issues such as the economy.

## Principal Government Officials

For up-to-date information on Principal Government Officials, see the Chiefs of State and Cabinet Members of Foreign Governments section starting on page 1.

Korea maintains an embassy in the United States at 2450 Massachusetts Avenue NW, Washington, DC 20008 (tel. 202-939-5600).

# ECONOMY

South Korea began the postwar period with a per capita gross national product (GNP) far below that of the North. It received large amounts of U.S. foreign assistance for many years, but all direct aid from the United States ended in 1980. The

Republic of Korea's economic growth over the past 30 years has been spectacular. Per capita GNP, only $100 in 1963, exceeded $10,000 in 1997. One of the world's poorest countries only a generation ago, South Korea is now the United States' eighth-largest trading partner and is the 11th-largest economy in the world.

The nation's successful industrial growth program began in the early 1960s, when the Park government instituted sweeping economic reforms emphasizing exports and labor-intensive light industries. The government also carried out a currency reform, strengthened financial institutions, and introduced flexible economic planning. In the 1970s Korea began directing fiscal and financial policies toward promoting heavy and chemical industries, as well as consumer electronics and automobiles. Manufacturing continued to grow rapidly in the 1980s and early 1990s. To meet growing energy demand, Korea has 16 nuclear plants in operation, with two others under construction.

In November 1997, Korea followed Thailand and Indonesia in suffering a loss of international confidence, resulting in a severe foreign exchange liquidity crisis. The Korean won lost over 50% of its value against the dollar by the end of 1997, and foreign currency reserves dropped to dangerously low levels. In December 1997, Korea signed an enhanced $58 billion IMF package, including loans from the IMF, World Bank, and the Asia Development Bank. Under the terms of the IMF program, Korea agreed to accelerate the opening of its financial and equity markets to foreign investment and to reform and restructure its financial and corporate sectors to increase transparency, accountability and efficiency. Since his election in December 1997, President Kim Dae Jung has stressed the need to attract foreign investment and to reduce barriers to both investment and trade.

In the aftermath of the crisis, Korea's GDP shrank 5.8% in real terms in 1998, the worst performance since the Korean war. But the Korean economy bounced back in 1999 with 10.2% GDP growth. Unemployment rose steadily to peak at 8.7% in February 1999, with nearly 1.8 million people unemployed, and another half-million working less than 18 hours per week. Unemployment declined to 4.1% as of April 2000. Wages also showed some recovery in the first 4 months of 1999. Private consumption rose 10.3% in 1999, up 11.2% in 2000. Consumer prices rose less than 1.5% in 1999.

Enormous capital investments made in the 1990s created over-capacity in many industries. Over-capacity and falling demand caused investment to drop sharply, by 21%, in 1998. However, foreign direct investment rose sharply in 1999 to $15.5 billion as a result of recovery from the 1997-98 crisis.

U.S. exports to Korea fell 34.2% in 1998 to $16.5 billion but rose 39.4% in 1999 to $23.0 billion. Korea is the United States' sixth-largest export market. The U.S. is Korea's largest export market (followed by the EU and Japan). Korea's exports to the U.S. were $23.9 billion in 1998 and rose 31% to $31.3 billion in 1999.

Many of Korea's large industrial/commercial conglomerates "chaebol," continue to hold excessive debt and nonmarket-based investments. The high-profile problems of Daewoo in 1999, Korea's second-largest conglomerate, have highlighted these weaknesses. Corporate restructuring, banking reform, and regulatory

transparency will be central to Korea's continued economic recovery.

## North-South Trade

Following the R.O.K.'s 1988 decision to allow trade with the D.P.R.K., South Korean firms began to import North Korean goods, all via third-country contracts. The D.P.R.K. does not acknowledge this trade. Nevertheless, the North publicized a number of visits since 1989 by Hyundai Corporation founder Chung Ju Yong, as well as a private protocol he signed in 1998 to develop tourism and other projects in the North. Since 1998, more than 86,000 South Korean citizens have traveled by Hyundai-operated passenger ships to scenic Mount Kumgang (Diamond Mountain) in the North as part of this tourism initiative.

Trade between the two Koreas increased 16-fold from $18.8 million in 1989 to $310 million in 1995. In 1998 inter-Korean trade measured about $222 million. During this recent period of greater economic cooperation, Daewoo chairman, Kim Woo Choong, visited the North and reached an agreement to build a light industrial complex at Nampo. The establishment of road and rail links has been addressed in other discussions. The first contract directly negotiated by businesspeople of both sides was signed in the spring of 1993. While inter-Korean trade has remained substantial, military tensions and economic problems in North Korea have contributed to a slowdown.

# FOREIGN RELATIONS

In August 1991, South Korea joined the United Nations along with North Korea and since then has been active in most UN specialized agencies and many international fora. The Republic of Korea also has hosted major international events such as the 1988 Summer Olympics and has been chosen to cohost the 2002 World Cup (with Japan). South Korea became a member of the Organization for Economic Cooperation and Development

(OECD) in 1996 and completed a term as a nonpermanent member on the UN Security Council at the end of 1997.

South Korea maintains diplomatic relations with more than 170 countries and a broad network of trading relationships. Former President Roh's policy of Nordpolitik—the pursuit of wideranging relations with socialist nations and contact with North Korea—has been a remarkable success. The R.O.K. now has diplomatic ties with all the countries of eastern and central Europe, as well as the former Soviet republics. The R.O.K. and the People's Republic of China established full diplomatic relations in August 1992.

Since normalizing relations in 1965, Japan and Korea have developed an extensive relationship centering on mutually beneficial economic activity. Although historic antipathies have at times impeded cooperation, relations at the government level have improved steadily and significantly in the past several years. Korea, Japan, and the U.S. consult very closely during periodic U.S.-D.P.R.K. negotiations over the North Korean nuclear issue.

Economic considerations have a high priority in Korean foreign policy. The R.O.K. seeks to build on its economic accomplishments to increase its regional and global role, including playing an increasingly important part in Pacific Rim political and economic activities. It is a founding member of the Asia-Pacific Economic Cooperation (APEC) forum.

## Korean Peninsula: Reunification Efforts Since 1971

Though both Korean governments have repeatedly affirmed their desire for reunification of the Korean Peninsula, the two had no official communication or other contact until 1971. At that time they agreed to hold talks through their respective Red Cross societies with the aim of reuniting the many Korean families separated following the division of Korea and the

Korean war. After a series of secret meetings, both sides announced a 1972 agreement to work toward peaceful reunification and an end to the hostile atmosphere prevailing on the peninsula. These initial contacts ended in August 1973 following President Park's announcement that the South would seek separate entry into the United Nations, and the kidnapping of South Korean opposition leader Kim Dae-jung from Tokyo by the South Korean intelligence service. The breakdown reflected basic differences in approach, with Pyongyang insisting on immediate steps toward reunification before discussing specific issues and Seoul maintaining that, given the long history of mutual distrust, reunification must come through a gradual, step-by-step process.

Tension between North and South Korea increased dramatically in the aftermath of the 1983 North Korean assassination attempt on President Chun in Burma, which killed six members of the R.O.K. cabinet. South Korea's suspicions of the North's motives were not diminished when Pyongyang accepted an earlier U.S.-R.O.K. proposal for tripartite talks on the future of the Korean Peninsula, in which "South Korean authorities" would be permitted to participate. North Korea's provision of relief goods to victims of severe flooding in South Korea in September 1984 led to revived dialogue on several fronts: Red Cross talks to address the plight of separated families, economic and trade talks, and parliamentary talks. However, in January 1986, the North suspended all talks, arguing that annual R.O.K.-U.S. military exercises were inconsistent with dialogue. The North resumed its own large-scale exercises in 1987.

In July 1988, South Korean President Roh Tae Woo called for new efforts to promote exchanges, family reunification, inter-Korean trade, and contact in international fora. President Roh called on Korea's friends and allies to pursue contacts with the North and said that the South intended to seek better relations with the U.S.S.R. and China. The two sides then met several times at Panmunjom in an unsuccessful attempt to arrange a joint meeting of the two Korean Parliaments. Meetings to discuss arrangements for prime ministerial-level talks led to a series of such meetings starting in 1990. In late 1991 the two sides signed the Agreement on Reconciliation, Non-aggression, Exchanges and Cooperation and the Joint Declaration on the Denuclearization of the Korean Peninsula. Nevertheless, there was little progress toward the establishment of a bilateral nuclear inspection regime, and dialogue between the South and North stalled in the fall of 1992.

In 1992 the North agreed to accept International Atomic Energy Agency (IAEA) safeguards as well as a series of IAEA inspections of North Korea's nuclear facilities. In practice though, the North refused to allow special inspections of two areas suspected of holding nuclear waste, and threatened to withdraw from the nuclear Non-Proliferation Treaty (NPT)—bringing North-South progress to an abrupt halt in the process. After a period of high tension brought on by failure to resolve the nuclear issue, as well as UN Security Council discussion of sanctions against the D.P.R.K., former President Carter's visit to Pyongyang in June 1994 helped to defuse tensions and resulted in renewed South-North talks.

The sudden death of North Korean leader Kim Il Sung on July 8, 1994 halted plans for a first-ever South-North presidential summit and led to another period of inter-Korean animosity. U.S.-D.P.R.K. bilateral talks, which began in the spring of 1993, finally resulted in a framework agreement signed by representatives of both nations in Geneva on October 21, 1994. This Agreed Framework committed North Korea to freeze its graphite-moderated reactors and related facilities at Yongbyon and Taechon, which could be used to produce plutonium for nuclear weapons development. In addition, under the Agreed Framework, North Korea agreed to hold expert talks with the U.S. to decide on specific arrangements for the storage of the D.P.R.K.'s spent nuclear fuel rods (which otherwise could be reprocessed into weapons-grade plutonium). In return, the D.P.R.K. was to receive alternative energy, initially in the form of heavy fuel oil (HFO), and eventually two proliferation-resistant light water reactors (LWR).

The 1994 agreement also included gradual improvement of relations between the U.S. and the D.P.R.K., and committed North Korea to engage in South-North dialogue. A few weeks after the signing of the Agreed Framework, President Kim Young Sam loosened restrictions on South Korean firms wanting to pursue business opportunities with the North. Although North Korea continued to refuse official overtures by the South, economic contacts appeared to expand gradually. Shortly after his inauguration, President Kim Dae-jung declared that restraints on investment and communication with North Korea by private entities would be significantly eased. As a result, the Hyundai Corporation has embarked upon an investment plan in North Korea worth approximately $1 billion.

In recent years, several milestones have been reached regarding the implementation of the Agreed Framework. On March 9, 1995, the Governments of the United States, Republic of Korea, and Japan agreed to establish the Korean Peninsula Energy Development Organization, commonly referred to as KEDO. KEDO's task is to implement the LWR and HFO commitments of the Agreed Framework. Since its inception, nine other countries have joined KEDO, making the organization truly international. On December 15, 1995, KEDO concluded a Supply Agreement with the D.P.R.K. concerning the details of implementing the LWR project. Six protocols to the Supply Agreement have already been concluded over the past 2 years. Groundbreaking on the LWR project took place on August 19, 1997. The 15-member European Union joined KEDO and became an executive board member on September 19, 1997. The U.S. Department of Energy at the end of October 1997 essentially completed the safe storage of North

Korea's spent nuclear fuel rods. The freeze on North Korea's graphite-moderated reactors and related facilities has now been in effect since November 1994.

The Agreed Framework prohibits the construction of any new graphite-moderated reactors or related facilities. The Administration became very concerned about reports in mid-1998 of possible surreptitious nuclear-related construction activity at an underground site and engaged the D.P.R.K. intensively on the issue. The Administration made clear to the D.P.R.K. that the future of the Agreed Framework and of our bilateral relationship hinged on the satisfactory resolution of this issue and that a solution would require multiple access by the United States to the suspect site to remove our suspicions. After four difficult rounds of negotiations, on March 16, 1999, the U.S. and D.P.R.K. agreed to an arrangement which provides for multiple access by a team of U.S. experts to the suspect site. The first visit took place in May 1999, a second visit is scheduled to take place in May 2000, and subsequent visits are to be allowed as long as the U.S. concerns about the site remain.

During the May 1999 visit to the suspect underground construction site, the U.S. team was allowed to visit the site "in the manner it deemed necessary." The team found a large, empty underground tunnel complex. Based on the visit, the team determined that the site did not contain a plutonium production reactor or reprocessing plant, either completed or under construction; that it was unsuitable for the installation of a plutonium production reactor, especially a graphite-moderated reactor of the type built previously by the D.P.R.K.; and that it is not well-designed for a reprocessing plant. The U.S. team did not rule out the possibility that the site was intended for other nuclear-related uses, although it did not appear to be configured to support any large industrial nuclear functions. A subsequent technical review by the intelligence community confirmed these findings.

On April 16, 1996, Presidents Clinton and Kim invited the D.P.R.K. and the People's Republic of China to participate in four-party peace talks with the U.S. and R.O.K. on the future of the Korean Peninsula. Following six preparatory meetings, the first four-party plenary session took place in Geneva in December 1997, with subsequent sessions in March 1998, October 1998, January 1999, April 1999, and August 1999. Beginning in January 1999, the four parties have focused their efforts on achieving progress in two subcommittees focusing respectively on tension reduction on the Korean Peninsula and the establishment of a permanent peace regime there that would replace the 1953 military armistice.

# U.S.-KOREAN RELATIONS

The United States believes that the question of peace and security on the Korean Peninsula is, first and foremost, a matter for the Korean people to decide. The U.S. is prepared to assist in this process if the two sides so desire.

In the 1954 U.S.-R.O.K. Mutual Defense Treaty, the United States agreed to help the Republic of Korea defend itself against external aggression. In support of this commitment, the United States currently maintains approximately 37,000 service personnel in Korea, including the Army's Second Infantry Division and several Air Force tactical squadrons. To coordinate operations between these units and the 650,000-strong Korean armed forces, a Combined Forces Command (CFC) was established in 1978. The head of the CFC also serves as Commander in Chief of the United Nations Command (UNC) and the U.S. Forces in Korea (USFK).

Several aspects of the security relationship are changing as the U.S. moves from a leading to a supporting role. South Korea has agreed to pay a larger portion of USFK's stationing costs, and to promote changes in the CFC command structure. On December

ber 1, 1994, peacetime operational control authority over all South Korean military units still under U.S. operational control was transferred to the South Korean Armed Forces.

As Korea's economy has developed, trade has become an increasingly important aspect of the U.S.-Korea relationship. The U.S. seeks to improve access to Korea's expanding market and increase investment opportunities for American business. The implementation of structural reforms contained in the IMF's 1998 program for Korea should improve access to the Korean market. Korean leaders appear determined to successfully manage the complex economic relationship with the United States and to take a more active role in international economic fora as befits Korea's status as a major trading nation.

## Principal U.S. Embassy Officials

**For up-to-date information on Principal U.S. Officials, see the U.S. Embassies, Consulates, and Foreign Service section starting on page 139.**

The U.S. embassy is located at 82 Sejong-Ro, Chongro-Ku, Seoul; Unit 15550, APO AP 96205-0001; tel. 82-2-397-4114; fax 82-2-738-8845.
The U.S. Agricultural Trade Office is located at 146-1, Susong-dong, Chongro-Ku, Leema Bldg., Rm. 303, Seoul 110-140; fax 82-2-720-7921.
The U.S. Export Development Office/U.S. Trade Center is c/o U.S. Embassy; fax 82-2-739-1628. Its director is Camille Sailer.

# ADDITIONAL RESOURCES

The following general country guides are available from the Superintendent of Documents, U.S. Government Printing Office, Washington, DC 20402:

Library of Congress. *North Korea: A Country Study*. 1994. Department of State. *The Record on Korean Unification 1943-1960*. 1961. Department of the Army. *Communist North Korea: A Bibliographic Survey*. 1971.

## Internet Resources on North and South Korea

The following sites are provided to give an indication of Internet sites on Korea. The Department of State does not endorse unofficial publications, including Internet sites.

R.O.K. Embassy page is at http://korea.emb.washington.dc.us. Korea Society page is at http://www.koreasociety.org and links to academic and other sites. Nautilus Institute page is at http://www.nautilus.org; this is produced by the Nautilus Institute in Berkeley, California and includes press round-up Monday through Friday Korea Web Weekly page is at http://www.kimsoft.com/korea.htm and links to North Korean sites. Korea Herald page is at http://www.koreaherald.co.kr; this is a South Korean English-language newspaper. Korea Times page is at http://www.korealink.co.kr/times/times.htm; this is a South Korean English-language newspaper. (North) Korean Central News Agency page is at http://www.kcna.co.jp. Korean Politics page is at http://www.koreanpolitics.com; this provides information on South Korean politics and links to South Korean Government sites.

# KUWAIT

November 1994

## Official Name:
## State of Kuwait

# PROFILE

## Geography

**Area:** 17,820 sq. km. (about 6,880 sq. mi.); slightly smaller than New Jersey.
**Cities:** Capital-Kuwait (pop. about 700,000). Other towns-Ahmadi, Jahra, Fahaheel.
**Terrain:** Flat to slightly undulating desert plain.
**Climate:** Intensely hot and dry in summers; short, cool winters with limited rain.

## People

**Nationality:** Noun and adjective-Kuwaiti(s).
**Population (1993):** 1.8 million, including non-Kuwaiti citizens. Annual growth rate (including immigration): 8.7%.
**Ethnic groups:** Arab 84%, South Asian, Iranian, Southeast Asian.
**Religion:** Islam 85% (Kuwaiti citizens are 100% Muslim).
**Languages:** Arabic (official); English widely spoken.
**Education (free through high school):** Years compulsory—8. Literacy—male 78%, female 69% over age of 15.
**Health:** Infant mortality rate—13 deaths/1,000 births. Life expect-ancy—72 yrs. male, 76 yrs. female.
**Work force (1993):** 731,600.

## Government

**Type:** Constitutional Monarchy.
**Independence:** June 19, 1961.
**Constitution:** 1962.
**Branches:** Executive—Amir (head of state). Legislative—elected National Assembly (Majlis al-'Umma) of 50 members. Judicial—High Court of Appeal.
**Political parties:** None.
**Suffrage:** Adult males who resided in Kuwait before 1920, their male descendants over 21, and Kuwaiti-born sons of naturalized citizens over 21 (eligible voters-over 100,000).
**Subdivisions:** Government is centralized, but for administrative purposes there are five governorates: Kuwait City, Hawalli, Ahmadi, Jahra, and Farwaniya.

## Economy*

**GDP (1993):** $24.7 billion.
**Annual growth rate:** 35%.
**Per capita GDP (1993):** $17,000.
**Natural resources:** Petroleum, fisheries.
**Agriculture:** Most food is imported. Cultivated land—1%.
**Industry:** Types-petroleum extraction and refining, fertilizer, chemicals, some construction materials.
**Water desalinization capacity:** 215 million gallons per day.

**Trade (1993):** Exports and re-exports—$11.4 billion: oil (90%). Major markets—Japan 19%, Netherlands 9%, U.S. 8%, Pakistan 6%. Imports—$6.6 billion: food, construction materials, vehicles and parts, clothing. Suppliers—U.S. 15%, Japan 12%, Germany 8%, U.K. 7%.
**Official exchange rate (Oct. 1994):** 0.30 Kuwaiti dinars=U.S.$1.

# PEOPLE

The people residing in the State of Kuwait are primarily Arab in origin, but less than half of them are from the Arabian Peninsula. Many Arabs from nearby states took up residence in Kuwait because of the prosperity brought by oil production after the 1940s. However, following the liberation of Kuwait from Iraqi occupation in 1991, the Kuwaiti Government undertook a serious effort to reduce the expatriate population. Kuwait still has a sizable Iranian and Indian population. Seventy percent of native Kuwaitis are Sunni Muslims and 30% are Shi'a Muslims. There are very few Kuwaiti Christians. The 74% literacy rate, one of the Arab world's highest, is due to extensive government support for the education

*Note: Some economic data reflect the disruptive 1992 period of the post-invasion reconstruction and recovery.

system. Public school education, including Kuwait University, is free, but access is restricted for foreign residents. The government sends qualified students abroad for degrees not offered at Kuwait University. About 1,000 Kuwaitis are currently studying in U.S. universities.

# HISTORY

Kuwait's modern history began in the 18th century with the founding of the city of Kuwait by the Uteiba section of the Anaiza tribe, who wandered north from Qatar. Its first definite contact with the West was between 1775 and 1779, when the British-operated Persian Gulf-Aleppo Mail Service was diverted through Kuwait from Persian-occupied Basra (in Iraq).

During the 19th century, Kuwait tried to obtain British support to maintain its independence from the Turks and various powerful Arabian Peninsula groups. In 1899, the ruler Sheikh Mubarak Al Sabah—"the Great"—signed an agreement with the United Kingdom pledging himself and his successors neither to cede any territory nor to receive agents or representatives of any foreign power without the British Government's consent. Britain agreed to grant an annual subsidy to support the Sheikh and his heirs and to provide its protection. Kuwait enjoyed special treaty relations with the U.K., which handled Kuwait's foreign affairs and was responsible for its security.

Mubarak was followed as ruler by his son Jabir (1915–17) and another son Salim (1917–21). Subsequent amirs descended from these two brothers. Sheikh Ahmed al-Jabir Al Sabah ruled from 1921 until his death in 1950, and Sheikh Abdullah al-Salim Al Sabah from 1950 to 1965. By early 1961, the British had withdrawn their special court system, which handled the cases of foreigners resident in Kuwait, and the Kuwaiti Government began to exercise legal jurisdiction under new laws drawn up by an Egyptian jurist. On June 19, 1961, Kuwait became fully independent following an exchange of notes with the United Kingdom.

The boundary with Saudi Arabia was set in 1922 with the Treaty of Uqair following the Battle of Jahrah. This treaty also established the Kuwait-Saudi Arabia Neutral Zone, an area of about 5,180 sq. km. (2,000 sq. mi.) adjoining Kuwait's southern border. In December 1969, Kuwait and Saudi Arabia signed an agreement dividing the Neutral Zone (now called the Divided Zone) and demarcating a new international boundary. Both countries share equally the Divided Zone's petroleum, onshore and off-shore.

Kuwait's northern border with Iraq dates from an agreement made with Turkey in 1913. Iraq accepted this claim in 1932 upon its independence from Turkey. However, following Kuwait's independence in 1961, Iraq claimed Kuwait, under the pretense that Kuwait had been part of the Ottoman Empire subject to Iraqi suzerainty. In 1963, Iraq reaffirmed its acceptance of Kuwaiti sovereignty and the boundary it agreed to in 1913 and 1932, in the "Agreed Minutes between the State of Kuwait and the Republic of Iraq Regarding the Restoration of Friendly Relations, Recognition, and Related Matters."

In August 1990, Iraq nevertheless invaded Kuwait, but was forced out seven months later by a UN coalition led by the United States. Following liberation, the UN, under Security Council Resolution 687, demarcated the Iraq-Kuwait boundary on the basis of the 1932 and the 1963 agreements between the two states. Although the demarcation is final and reaffirmed under Chapter VII of the UN Charter by UNSCR 833, Iraq has refused to accept and continues to make claims to Kuwait.

# GOVERNMENT AND POLITICAL CONDITIONS

The State of Kuwait has been ruled by the Sabah family since 1751. The 1962 constitution contains detailed provisions on the powers and rela-

tionships of the branches of government and on the rights of citizens. Upon the death of an amir, the crown prince assumes his position. A new crown prince is then selected by members of the Sabah family from among the direct descendants of Mubarak the Great. Under the constitution, the designation is subject to the approval of the National Assembly. Since independence, successions have been orderly, both in 1965 and 1978.

Kuwait experienced an unprecedented era of prosperity under Amir Sabah al-Salim Al Sabah, who died in 1977 after ruling for 12 years, and under his successor, Amir Jabir Ahmed el-Jaber Al Sabah. The country was transformed into a highly developed welfare state with a free market economy. During the seven-month occupation by Iraq, the Amir, the Government, and many Kuwaitis took refuge in Saudi Arabia or other nations. The Amir and the government successfully managed Kuwaiti affairs from Saudi Arabia, London, and elsewhere during the period, relying on substantial Kuwaiti investments available outside Kuwait for funding and war-related expenses. His return after the liberation in February 1991 was relatively smooth.

Kuwait's first National Assembly was elected in 1963, with follow-on elections held in 1967, 1971, and 1975. From 1976 to 1981, the National Assembly was suspended. Following elections in 1981 and 1985, the National Assembly was again dissolved. Fulfilling a promise made during the period of Iraqi occupation, the Amir held new elections for the National Assembly in 1992. No political parties exist in Kuwait, although there are groupings (such as extended families) that function like parties. The ideological representation in the Kuwaiti National Assembly is broad, with a majority of the 1992 Assembly members being considered as "opposition" in their orientation. Although the Amir maintains the final word on most government policies, the National Assembly plays a real role in decision-making, with powers to initiate legislation, question government ministers, and express lack of confidence in individual ministers. Five of the elected National Assembly members were selected to serve as cabinet ministers.

## Principal Government Officials

For up-to-date information on Principal Government Officials, see the Chiefs of State and Cabinet Members of Foreign Governments section starting on page 1.

Kuwait maintains an embassy in the United States at 2940 Tilden Street NW., Washington, D.C. 20008 (tel. 202-966-0702).

# ECONOMY

Kuwait is a small country with massive oil reserves, whose economy has been traditionally dominated by the state and its oil industry.

During the 1970s, Kuwait benefited from the dramatic rise in oil prices, which Kuwait actively promoted through its membership in the Organization of Petroleum Exporting Countries (OPEC). More recently, the economy has suffered from the triple shock of a 1982 securities market crash, the mid 1980s drop in oil prices, and the 1990 Iraqi invasion and occupation. The Kuwaiti Government-in-exile depended upon its $100 billion in overseas investments during the occupation in order to help pay for the reconstruction. Thus, by 1993, this balance was cut to less than half of its pre-invasion level. The wealth of Kuwait is based primarily on oil and capital reserves, and the Iraqi occupation severely damaged both. In the closing hours of the Gulf war in February 1991, the Iraqi occupation forces set ablaze or damaged 749 of Kuwait's oil wells. All of these fires were extinguished within a year. Production has been restored, and refineries and facilities have been modernized. Oil exports sur-

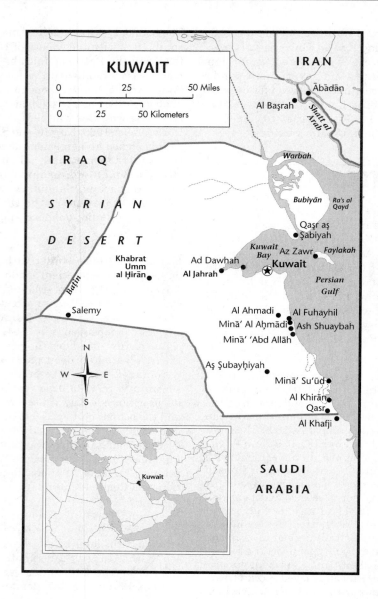

passed their pre-invasion levels in 1993 with production levels only constrained by OPEC quotas.

## Oil

In 1934, the ruler of Kuwait granted an oil concession to the Kuwait Oil Co. (KOC), jointly owned by the British Petroleum Co. and Gulf Oil Corp. In 1976, the Kuwaiti Government nationalized KOC. The following year, Kuwait took over onshore production in the Divided Zone between Kuwait and Saudi Arabia. KOC produces jointly there with Texaco, Inc., which, by its 1984 purchase of Getty Oil Co., acquired the Saudi Arabian

onshore concession in the Divided Zone.

Offshore the Divided Zone, the Arabian Oil Co., 80% owned by Japanese interests and 10% each by the Kuwaiti and Saudi Governments, has produced on behalf of both countries since 1961.

The Kuwait Petroleum Corp. (KPC), an integrated international oil company, is the parent company of the government's operations in the petroleum sector, and includes Kuwait Oil Company, which produced oil and gas; Kuwait National Petroleum Co., refining and domestic sales; Petrochemical Industries Co., producing ammonia and urea; Kuwait Foreign Petroleum Exploration Co., with several concessions in developing countries; Kuwait Oil Tanker Co.; and Santa Fe International Corp. The latter, purchased outright in 1982, gives KPC a worldwide presence in the petroleum industry.

KPC has also purchased from Gulf Oil Co. refineries and associated service stations in the Benelux nations and Scandinavia, as well as storage facilities and a network of service stations in Italy. In 1987, KPC bought a 19% share in British Petroleum, which was later reduced to 10%. KPC markets its products in Europe under the brand Q8 and is interested in the markets of the United States and Japan.

Kuwait has about 77 billion barrels of recoverable oil; Saudi Arabia is the only single country which has larger reserves. Estimated capacity, before the war, was about 2.4 million barrels per day (b/d). During the Iraqi occupation, Kuwait's oil producing capacity was reduced to practically nothing. However, tremendous recovery and improvements have been made. Oil production was 1.5 million b/d by the end of 1992, and pre-war capacity was restored in 1993. Kuwait's OPEC quota in August 1994 is 2 million b/d.

## Social Benefits

The government has sponsored many social welfare, public works, and development plans financed with oil and investment revenues. Among the benefits for Kuwaiti citizens are retirement income, marriage bonuses, housing loans, virtually guaranteed employment, free medical services, and education at all levels. Foreign nationals residing in Kuwait obtain some, but not all, of the welfare services. The right to own stock in publicly traded companies, real estate, and banks or a majority interest in a business is limited to Kuwaiti citizens and citizens of GCC states under limited circumstances.

## Industry and Development

Industry in Kuwait consists of several large export-oriented petrochemical units, oil refineries, and a range of small manufacturers. It also includes large water desalinization, ammonia, desulfurization, fertilizer, brick, block, and cement plants. During the invasion, the Iraqis looted nearly all movable items of worth, especially high technology items and small machinery. Much of this has been replaced with newer equipment.

## Agriculture

Agriculture is limited by the lack of water and arable land. The government has experimented in growing food through hydroponics and carefully managed farms. However, most of the soil which was suitable for farming in south central Kuwait was destroyed when Iraqi troops set fire to oil wells in the area and created vast "oil lakes." Fish and shrimp are plentiful in territorial waters, and large-scale commercial fishing has been undertaken locally and in the Indian Ocean.

## Shipping

The Kuwait Oil Tankers Co. has 35 crude oil and refined product carriers and is the largest tanker company in an OPEC country. Kuwait is also a member of the United Arab Shipping Company.

## Trade, Finance, and Aid

The Kuwaiti dinar is a strong currency pegged to a basket of currencies in which the U.S. dollar has the most weight. Kuwait ordinarily runs a balance-of-payments surplus.

Government revenues are dependent on oil revenues. Revenues for Kuwaiti fiscal year ending in June 1992 were $3 billion, down from a pre-war level of nearly $6 billion. Expenditures, mainly in costs of reconstruction and residual costs of the war, as well as major increases in defense spending, soared to nearly $40 billion, from a pre-war norm of about $10 billion. In

1993, Kuwait resumed pre-war spending levels.

The government's two reserve funds, the Fund for Future Generations and the General Reserve Fund, which totaled nearly $100 billion prior to the invasion in 1990, were the primary source of capital for the Kuwaiti Government during the war. Currently, these funds have been depleted to $40-$50 billion. The bulk of this reserve is invested in the United States, Germany, the United Kingdom, France, Japan, and Southeast Asia. In order of importance, foreign assets are believed to be invested in stocks and bonds, fixed yield instruments (mostly short term), and real estate. Kuwait follows a generally conservative investment policy.

Kuwait has been a major source of foreign economic assistance to other states through the Kuwait Fund for Arab Economic Development, an autonomous state institution created in 1961 on the pattern of Western and international development agencies. In 1974, the fund's lending mandate was expanded to include all-not just Arab-developing countries. Over the years aid was provided to Egypt, Syria, and Jordan, as well as the Palestine Liberation Organization. During the Iran-Iraq war, significant Kuwaiti aid was given to the Iraqis. Due to sizable post-war expenditures, Kuwaiti foreign assistance was limited to $350 million in 1992, but this is expected to rise slowly as budget deficits continue. From 1979–1989, bilateral aid to less developed countries totaled about $18 billion.

# FOREIGN RELATIONS

Following independence in June 1961, Kuwait faced its first major foreign policy problem arising from Iraqi claims to Kuwait's territory. The Iraqis threatened invasion, but were dissuaded by the U.K.'s ready response to the Amir's request for assistance. Kuwait presented its case before the United Nations and preserved its sovereignty. U.K. forces were later withdrawn and replaced by troops from

Arab League nations, which were withdrawn in 1963 at Kuwait's request.

On August 2, 1990, Iraq invaded and occupied Kuwait. Through U.S. efforts, a multinational coalition was assembled, and, under UN auspices, initiated military action against Iraq to liberate Kuwait. Arab states, especially the other five members of the Gulf Cooperation Council (Saudi Arabia, Bahrain, Qatar, Oman, and the United Arab Emirates), Egypt, and Syria, supported Kuwait by sending troops to fight with the coalition. Many European and East Asian states sent either troops, equipment, or financial support.

After liberation, Kuwait concentrated its foreign policy efforts on development of ties to states which had participated in the multinational coalition. Notably, these states were given the lead role in Kuwait's reconstruction. Conversely, Kuwait's relations with those nations that supported Iraq, among them Jordan, Sudan, Yemen, and Cuba, remain strained or non-existent. Palestine Liberation Organization (PLO) Chairman Yasir Arafat's support for Saddam Hussein during the war has also affected Kuwait's attitudes toward the PLO and the peace process.

Since the conclusion of the Gulf war, Kuwait has made efforts to secure allies throughout the world, particularly United Nations Security Council members. In addition to the United States, defense arrangements have been concluded with the United Kingdom, Russia, and France. Close ties to other key Arab members of the Gulf war coalition—Egypt and Syria—have also been sustained.

Kuwait is a member of the UN and some of its specialized and related agencies, including the World Bank (IBRD), International Monetary Fund (IMF), World Trade Organization (WTO), General Agreement on Tariffs and Trade (GATT); African Development Bank (AFDB), Arab Fund for Economic and Social Development (AFESD), Arab League, Arab Monetary Fund (AMF), Council of

## Travel Notes

**Travel Advice:** For up-to-date information from the U.S. State Department on possible inconvenient or hazardous situations, see the **Travel Warnings and Consular Information Sheets from the U.S. Government** section starting on page 1723. For the latest information on health requirements and conditions, see the **International Travelers' Health Information** section starting on page 1385. For further information dealing with non-urgent matter, see the **Tips for Travelers to...** section starting on page 1588.

Arab Economic Unity (CAEU), Economic and Social Commission for Western Asia (ESCWA), Group of 77 (G-77), Gulf Cooperation Council (GCC), INMARSAT, International Development Association (IDA), International Finance Corporation, International Fund for Agricultural Development, International Labor Organization (ILO), International Marine Organization, Interpol, INTELSAT, IOC, Islamic Development Bank (IDB), League of Red Cross and Red Crescent Societies (LORCS), Non-Aligned Movement, Organization of Arab Petroleum Exporting Countries (OAPEC), Organization of the Islamic Conference (OIC), Organization of Petroleum Exporting Countries (OPEC), and the International Atomic Energy Agency (IAEA).

# DEFENSE

Before the Gulf war, Kuwait maintained a small military force consisting of army, navy, and air force units. The majority of equipment for the military was supplied by the United Kingdom. Aside from the few units that were able to escape to Saudi Arabia, including a majority of the air force, all of this equipment was either destroyed or taken by the Iraqis. Much of the property returned by Iraq after the Gulf war was damaged beyond repair. Iraq still retains a substantial amount of captured Kuwaiti military equipment in violation of UN resolutions.

Since the war, Kuwait, with the help of the U.S. and other allies, has made significant efforts to increase the size and modernity of their armed forces. These efforts are succeeding. The government also continues to improve defense arrangements with other Arab states, as well as UN Security Council members.

A separately organized National Guard maintains internal security. Police forces are under the authority of the Ministry of Interior.

# U.S.-KUWAITI RELATIONS

A U.S. consulate was opened at Kuwait in October 1951 and was elevated to embassy status at the time of Kuwait's independence 10 years later. The United States supports Kuwait's sovereignty, security, and independence as well as closer cooperation among the GCC countries.

In 1987, cooperation between the United States and Kuwait increased due to the implementation of the maritime protection regime to ensure freedom of navigation through the Gulf for 11 Kuwaiti tankers that were reflagged with U.S. markings.

The U.S.-Kuwaiti partnership reached dramatic new levels of cooperation after the Iraqi invasion. The United States assumed a leading role in the implementation of Operation Desert Shield. The United States led the UN Security Council to demand Iraqi withdrawal from Kuwait and authorize the use of force, if necessary, to remove Iraqi forces from the occupied country. The United States played a major role in the evolution of Desert Shield into Desert Storm, the multinational military operation to liberate the State of Kuwait.

Eventually, the U.S. provided the bulk of the troops and equipment that were used by the multinational coalition that liberated Kuwait. The U.S.-Kuwaiti relationship has remained strong in the post-war period.

The United States has provided military and defense technical assistance to Kuwait from both foreign military sales (FMS) and commercial sources. All transactions have been made by direct cash sale. The U.S. Office of Military Cooperation in Kuwait is attached to the American Embassy and manages the FMS program. U.S. military sales to Kuwait total $3.1 billion, $1.6 billion of which has been purchased since the close of the Gulf war. Principal U.S. military systems currently purchased by the Kuwait Defense Forces are Patriot missile system, F-18 Hornet fighters, and the M1A2 Main Battle Tank.

## Principal U.S. Officials

**For up-to-date information on Principal U.S. Officials, see the U.S. Embassies, Consulates, and Foreign Service section starting on page 139.**

For up-to-date information on Principal U.S. Officials, see the U.S. Embassies, Consulates, and Foreign Service section starting on page 139.

The United States is currently Kuwait's largest supplier, and Kuwait is the fifth-largest market in the Middle East for U.S. goods and services. U.S. exports to Kuwait totaled $1.2 billion in 1991. Since the Gulf war, Kuwaiti attitudes toward Americans and American products have been excellent. Provided their prices are reasonable, U.S. firms have a competitive advantage in many areas requiring advanced technology, such as oil field equipment and services, electric power generation and distribution equipment, telecommunications gear, consumer goods, and military equipment. In 1993, Kuwait publicly announced abandonment of the secondary and tertiary aspects of the Arab boycott of Israel (those aspects affecting U.S. firms).

The U.S. embassy in Kuwait is located at Bneid al-Gar, Kuwait (opposite the Safir Hotel). The mailing address is P.O. Box 77, SAFAT, 13001 SAFAT, Kuwait; or Unit 69000 APO AE 09880.

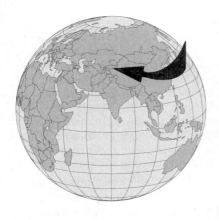

# KYRGYZSTAN

April 1993

## Official Name:
## Republic of Kyrgyzstan

---

**Editor's Note: The U.S. State Department has not yet issued a Background Note on this nation. The information presented here is from the Congressional Research Service of the Library of Congress; it is the latest material available about this nation.**

---

# BACKGROUND

## Area and Population

Land area is 77,415 sq. mi., 0.9 percent of the former U.S.S.R.; about the size of South Dakota. Population is 4.26 million (1989 census); 1.5 percent of the total for the former U.S.S.R. Administrative subdivisions include regions, districts, and cities. In February 1992, Kyrgyz President Askar Akayev proclaimed the establishment of German territorial-cultural enclaves.

# HISTORY

In the tenth century A.D., nomadic Kyrgyz tribes began to migrate south from the region of the Yenisey River in Siberia to present-day Kyrgyzstan. This migration accelerated in the thirteenth century as invading Mongols pushed them south. The Kyrgyz were overrun in the seventeenth century by the Kalmyks, in the mid-eighteenth century by the Manchus, and in the early nineteenth century by the Uzbek Kokand Khanate.

The Russians moved into the area in the mid-nineteenth century, and by 1867, the Kyrgyz were incorporated into the Russian empire as part of

Russian Turkestan, although major uprisings occurred and many Kyrgyz migrated to the Pamirs and Afghanistan. In 1916, a serious revolt against tsarist conscription was forcibly suppressed, resulting in further Kyrgyz migrations to China. After the Bolsheviks defeated determined Kyrgyz opposition forces by 1919, Kyrgyzstan was made part of the new Turkestan Autonomous Republic. In 1924, the Kara-Kyrgyz Autonomous Region was established, renamed the Kyrgyz Autonomous Republic in 1926. In 1936, Stalin upgraded the status of Kyrgyzstan to that of a union republic. While some local self-rule was allowed in the 1920s, by the early 1930s Stalin had begun a process of Russification, including massive purges of local cadres and forced collectivization of the largely nomadic society. Ethnic Russians remained disproportionately represented and influential in the Kyrgyz Communist Party (KCP) for many decades.

The KCP was largely discredited in 1990-1991 for opposing sovereignty, democratization, and market reforms. Akayev resolutely opposed the August 1991 Soviet coup attempt against Gorbachev and moved during the coup to nationalize KCP property. Afterwards, the Kyrgyz Supreme Soviet declared Kyrgyzstan an independent democratic state and scheduled direct presidential elections for October 1991 (the Kyrgyz Supreme

Soviet had approved a declaration on state sovereignty and changed the spelling of the republic's name to Kyrgyzstan in December 1990). Despite the declaration of independence, Akayev and many other Kyrgyz supported maintaining some sort of federal or confederal relationship with the other republics of the Soviet Union. When the Commonwealth of Independent States (CIS) was declared on December 8, Akayev and other Central Asian republic leaders demanded that they be allowed to join as "founding members," and they joined the CIS on December 21, 1991.

## Ethnic Composition and Tensions

2.23 million (52.4%) are Kyrgyz, 917 thousand are Russian (21.5%), 550 thousand are Uzbek (12.9%), 108 thousand Ukrainian (2.5%), 101 thousand German (2.4%), 70 thousand Tatars (1.6%), and others (1989 census). About 420,000 ethnic Kyrgyz reside elsewhere in the former Soviet Union and 170,000 in China. Kyrgyz speak a Turkic language and most are Sunni Moslems. There are major ethnic and clan-based cleavages, including north south clan and regional tensions that threaten fragmentation. According to some reports, one-tenth or more of Russians left Kyrgyzstan during 1991 because of ethnic tensions. Ethnic Germans, deported to Kyrgyzstan by

Stalin during World War II, are also leaving Kyrgyzstan. In June 1990, in the Osh region on the eastern edge of the fertile Fergana Valley, a major ethnic conflict broke out between Kyrgyz and Uzbek inhabitants over land distribution. Approximately 250 people died in what has been termed "the most explosive region of Central Asia," because of its mixed population of Uzbeks and Kyrgyz, poverty, and high unemployment. Periodic clashes also occur between Kyrgyz and Tajiks along the border with Tajikistan over water resources. Beefed-up Kyrgyz security forces were placed in Osh and Alais regions in early 1993 to prevent spillover from fighting going on between Tajik ex-communists and oppositionists in the mountains of northern Tajikistan and to halt the inflow of Tajik refugees.

## Political Leaders

For up-to-date information on Principal Government Officials, see the Chiefs of State and Cabinet Members of Foreign Governments section starting on page 1.

Akayev, an ethnic Kyrgyz, was born in 1944. He received advanced and postdoctoral degrees in optical physics at the Institute of Precision Mechanics and Optics in Leningrad (St. Petersburg). In 1976, Akayev returned to Kyrgyzstan to work as a scientist and teacher. In 1986 he was summoned to Moscow to serve in the Soviet Communist Party (CPSU) Central Committee Department on Science and Education. In 1987, he was elected vice president of the Kyrgyz Academy of Sciences, and in 1989 became its president. In 1989 he was elected to the newly created Soviet Congress of People's Deputies and subsequently selected to serve in the Supreme Soviet. He was elected a full member of the Soviet Communist Party Central Committee in 1990.

In the summer of 1990, ethnic riots in Osh region led to mass demonstrations in Bishkek against KCP rule and demands for the ouster of the hard-line KCP leader Absamat Masaliyev. When the Kyrgyz

## Travel Notes

**Travel Advice:** For up-to-date information from the U.S. State Department on possible inconvenient or hazardous situations, see the **Travel Warnings and Consular Information Sheets from the U.S. Government** section starting on page 1723. For the latest information on health requirements and conditions, see the **International Travelers' Health Information** section starting on page 1385. For further information dealing with non-urgent matter, see the **Tips for Travelers to...** section starting on page 1588.

Supreme Soviet convened in October, 1990, deputies aligned in a democratic bloc narrowly defeated Masaliyev's bid to become president; Akayev's supporters urged him to quickly return to Kyrgyzstan from his legislative duties in Moscow, and after repeated voting elected him to the newly created post. On October 12,1991, Akayev was reaffirmed as president in an uncontested direct popular election, winning 96% of the vote.

## Political Parties and Groups

The Kyrgyzstan Democratic Movement (KDM) is an umbrella group of about 40 parties and organizations, including Erkin (Free) Kyrgyzstan, which calls for elevating the rights of ethnic Kyrgyz, Ashar (Mutual Help), which calls for land for the Kyrgyz and construction of homes for the homeless, and Aqiqat, a student organization calling for democratization. On November 5,1991, a group left the Kyrgyzstan Democratic Movement, declaring itself the Kyrgyz National Revival Party or Asaba (Banner). The Committee for the Defense of Human Rights in Kyrgyzstan also left the Democratic Movement in November 1991. Erkin Kyrgyzstan (also called Erk) split in November 1992, with the liberal wing forming a new party, AltaMekel (Fatherland). The Slavic Fund party upholds the interests of ethnic Russians and other Slavs in Kyrgyzstan. Erkin Kyrgyzstan, Ashar, Asaba, the Committee for the Defense of Human Rights, and the Slavic Fund are legally registered as parties with the Justice Ministry. A

reconstituted KCP, headed by Masaliyev, was registered in January 1993. Islamic fundamentalism has little support among the population. At a congress of democratic parties in late February 1993 consisting of Asaba and several KDM member parties including Erk, they could not agree on uniting to support Akayev's reform program.

## Political Institutions and Policies

A unicameral 350 deputy Supreme Soviet (now called the Supreme Council) was elected in March 1990 in multicandidate elections, although 70 candidates ran unopposed. Ninety-five percent of the deputies elected were KCP members, though many have supported Akayev's reforms. This legislature is ineffective as a deliberative and oversight body since it only meets twice a year for a total of four weeks, though committees may work between sessions. Ten of the deputies work full-time as chairpersons of the 10 standing commissions. Legislative staff number 62. Akayev has resisted opposition calls that he dissolve the ex-communist dominated Supreme Council and move to break the ex-communists' hold on power in the localities, citing the lack of trained personnel to replace them. He has professed his preference for "strong executive power" in Kyrgyzstan. A Presidential Council acts as an advisory body to the President. A Cabinet of Ministers was set up in 1991 directly under the President to carry out administration. It was reorganized in early 1992. Kyrgyzstan is drawing up a new constitution that includes a popularly elected president as head of state, a prime minister as head of government, and a law-making legislature, though not a constitutional court. The president nominates the prime minister and ministers who are approved by the Supreme Council. The prime minister is also confirmed by local government heads. It calls for a mixed private and state-owned economy.

Akayev has assailed widespread crime and corruption in government and society, stating that it has "paralyzed state authority," slowed down reforms, and threatens Kyrgyzstan's

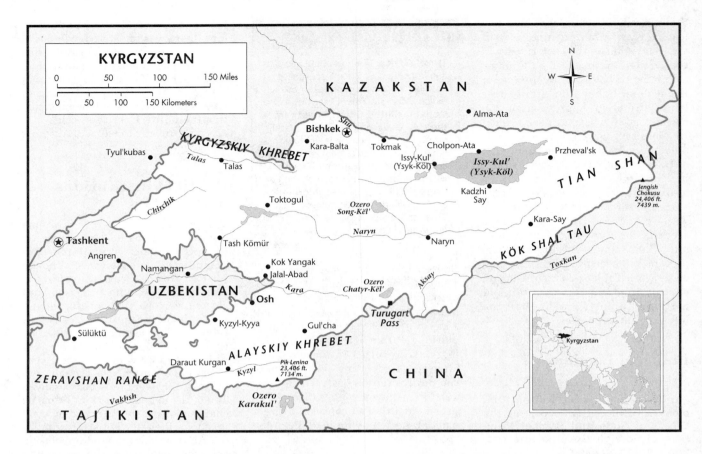

"hard won freedoms." In January 1993, he asserted that corruption was draining Kyrgyzstan of needed revenues, lamenting that his anti-corruption decrees were not being carried out by the police and procuracy. He also condemned the police leadership for approving the arrest of an Uzbek human rights activist in December 1992. To deal with corruption among government officials who are largely holdovers from the communist era, in late January 1993, he appointed ex-KCP head Masaliyev as director of state inspection. This appointment was criticized by Erk chairman Topchubek Turgunaliyev, who accused Akayev of trying to "save the country with the help of people who had earlier brought it to collapse."

## Human Rights and Freedoms

Relative to other Central Asian states, Kyrgyzstan appears more diligent in upholding human rights. Akayev has been cooperative with the Commission on Security and Cooperation in Europe (CSCE), acted to uphold the rights of ethnic minorities

in Kyrgyzstan, refused to suppress opposition party activities, and sponsored an international Human Rights conference in Bishkek in December 1992. A press law passed in July 1992 requires that all media register with the government and eschew "inciting violence or ethnic friction." An opposition party press is allowed to operate, however, and no publications have been banned or censored. A law on religion passed in December 1991 upholds freedom of religion, though its practice must not endanger "public order." Religious parties are banned.

A draft constitution upholds private property rights, freedom of religion, and other rights. The deterioration of the economy has increased public tensions, leading Akayev to contemplate more authoritarian human rights policies against what he termed in January 1993 "political intrigue and the badgering of the president."

## Relations with Commonwealth of Independent States (CIS)

Kyrgyzstan is in favor of establishing beneficial relations with all former Union republics and is the only former Soviet republic to post ambassadors to all CIS capitals. Akayev has particularly stressed close relations with Russia for security, cultural-scientific, and economic assistance reasons, signing a Friendship and Cooperation Treaty with Russia in June 1992. Kyrgyzstan reportedly has sent 500 security personnel to assist Russia in peacekeeping along the Afghan-Tajik border. Kyrgyzstan became a full member of the Commonwealth of Independent States (CIS) on December 21, 1991. Akayev, along with several other Central Asian leaders, has urged that the CIS play a more integrative role. At the Minsk Summit of CIS Heads of State in January 1993, Akayev signed the CIS Charter, supporting its integrative implications. He also supported an agreement on a joint peacekeeping force to the sent to Tajikistan. Before the summit, he argued that while the CIS was useful for "collective security" and consultations on political stability, it had not proved useful in economic cooperation. However, he did sign an agreement on setting up an interstate bank. At the Tashkent meeting of Central Asian states in early January 1993, Kyrgyzstan supported the creation of a regional common market.

## Foreign Policy and Defense

In late December 1991, cooperation agreements with Turkey were concluded. During his visit to Kyrgyzstan in late April 1992, Turkish Prime Minister Suleyman Demirel extended export credits to Kyrgyzstan and the two sides signed investment and other agreements. In October 1992, Akayev attended a Turkic summit in Turkey and visited Saudi Arabia and discussed trade and cooperation issues. He supports businesslike relations with Iran. Akayev has also stressed Kyrgyzstan's relations with the West, visiting Switzerland, Canada, Germany, and Finland during 1992. During his April 1992 visit to Germany, the Germans announced humanitarian and technical aid to encourage Kyrgyz Germans to stay in Kyrgyzstan. Akayev visited Israel in January 1993 to seek agricultural aid and to boost trade relations. In December 1992, the Economic Community (EC) announced about $40 million in credits for food purchases. Kyrgyzstan also seeks to establish strong relations with the Asian countries. Economic contacts with China have steadily grown. Akayev visited India in March 1992, which offered technical aid in banking and business training, and China in May 1992, which offered credits for food and consumer goods purchases. In early May 1992, Japan agreed to train Kyrgyz diplomats and has also extended technical and humanitarian aid to Kyrgyzstan. Kyrgyzstan is a member of the United Nations, the Conference on Security and Cooperation in Europe (CSCE), the International Monetary Fund (IMF), World Bank, International Finance Corporation, and the Economic Cooperation Organization

(ECO), among other international and regional organizations.

In December 1991, the Supreme Soviet declared the creation of a National Guard numbering about 600 troops, and a draft was announced in April 1992. Akayev has called for a unified CIS armed forces, preferring that Kyrgyzstan not be faced with the expense of maintaining its own armed forces. However, with the creation of national armed forces in most of the CIS states, he set up a State Committee for Defense Affairs to manage the possible transition to a Kyrgyz armed forces. Akayev has stated that the Kyrgyz-Russian Friendship Treaty ensures Kyrgyzstan's external security.

## Economy

Estimated GNP in 1991 was 13.8 billion rubles, less than 1.0 percent of the total for the former U.S.S.R. Per capita GNP in 1991 was 3,113 rubles, slightly above that of Uzbekistan and Tajikistan as the third lowest in the former U.S.S.R.; poverty is widespread. Akayev reported that industrial production declined 27 percent in 1992. Because Kyrgyzstan's industries contribute a large share of national income, their decline has sharply affected the overall economy. Kyrgyzstan also must import 95 percent of its oil and gas and 40 percent of its grain. It is a major world extractor and refiner of mercury products. It also produces cotton, wool, and tobacco, ranking third (behind Russia and Kazakhstan) in wool production. It sells some hydroelectric power; it possesses potentially sizable hydroelectric resources. Most uranium mining in the former Soviet Union took place in Kyrgyzstan. Illegal drug production is a growing problem; Kyrgyzstan has appealed to Russia for continued technical aid to combat it.

Akayev has urged Western nations to assist Kyrgyzstan in bolstering its "drastically deteriorating" economy, and has tried to attract foreign investment, by easing tax and custom barriers, as well as export-import regulations. Russia has continued to provide economic subsidies, and in

February 1993, Akayev traveled to Moscow and secured a reported 75 billion rubles in additional credit. In January 1993, Akayev convened an emergency meeting of government ministers to deal with the economic crisis. He noted severe problems in agriculture and growing lawlessness raising the specter of Tajik-style civil conflict. He dismissed the agriculture and economics-finance ministers and the head of the oil production association for ineptitude. The economics-finance minister was accused of proposing emergency economic measures that ran counter to economic reform.

# U.S. POLICY

President George Bush offered to established diplomatic relations with Kyrgyzstan on December 25, 1991, and in February 1992 an American mission was set up in Bishkek. The United States is providing humanitarian and technical assistance to Kyrgyzstan. On May 8, 1992, Kyrgyzstan signed an U.S.-Kyrgyz Trade Agreement providing for most-favored-nation (MFN) status for Kyrgyzstan. This agreement came into force in August 1992 following approval by the Kyrgyz legislature and the exchange of notes. An U.S.-Kyrgyz investment treaty was signed in January 1993. Kyrgyzstan is eligible for Overseas Private Investment Corporation (OPIC) and Commodity Credit Corporation loan guarantees. An agreement on Peace Corps assistance was signed in November 1992, and 25 volunteers are being recruited. In October 1992, Kyrgyzstan signed an agreement with the United States to halt the dumping of uranium on the U.S. market.

## Principal U.S. Officials

**For up-to-date information on Principal U.S. Officials, see the U.S. Embassies, Consulates, and Foreign Service section starting on page 139.**

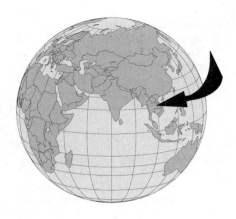

# LAOS
September 2000

## Official Name:
**Lao People's Democratic Republic (LPDR)**

# PROFILE

## Geography
**Area:** 236,800 sq. km. (91,430 sq. mi.); area comparable to Oregon.
**Cities:** Capital—Vientiane (1998 pop. est. 569,000). Other principal towns—Savannakhet, Luang Prabang, Pakse, Thakhek.
**Terrain:** rugged mountains, plateaus, alluvial plains.
**Climate:** tropical monsoon; rainy season (May to November); dry season (November to April).

## People
**Nationality:** Noun and adjective—Lao (sing. and pl.).
**Population:** (1999) 5.4 million.
**Annual growth rate:** (1999) 2.7%.
**Ethnic Groups:** Lao Loum 53%; other lowland Lao 13% (Thai Dam, Phouane); Lao Theung (midslope) 23%; Lao Sung (highland), including Hmong, Akha, and the Yao (Mien) 10%; ethnic Vietnamese/Chinese 1%.
**Religion:** Principally Buddhism, with animism among highland groups.
**Languages:** Lao (official), French, various highland ethnic, English.
**Education:** Literacy—60%.
**Health:** (1999) Infant mortality rate—89.32/1,000. Life expectancy—55.87 years for women, 52.63 years for men.
**Work force:** (2.6 million, 1999) Agriculture—85%; industry and services—15%.

## Government
**Type:** Communist state.
**Branches:** Executive—president (head of state); Chairman, Council of Ministers (prime minister and head of government); nine-member Politburo; 49-member Central Committee. Legislative—99-seat National Assembly. Judicial—district, provincial, and a national Supreme Court.
**Political parties:** Lao People's Revolutionary Party (LPRP)—only legal party.
**Administrative subdivisions:** 16 provinces, one special region, and Vientiane prefecture.
**Flag:** A red band at the top and bottom with a larger blue band between them; a large white circle is centered.

## Economy
**GDP:** (1999) $1.3 billion.
**Per capita income:** (1999) $241.
**GDP growth rate:** (1999) 5.2%.
**Natural resources:** Hydroelectric power, timber, minerals.
**Agriculture:** (51% of GDP) Primary products—glutinous rice, coffee, corn, sugarcane, vegetables, tobacco, ginger, water buffalo, pigs, cattle, and poultry.
**Industry:** (22% of GDP, 1999) Primary types—garment manufacturing, electricity production, gypsum and tin mining, wood and wood processing, cement manufacturing, agricultural processing. Industrial growth rate (1999 est.)—7.5%.
**Services:** (1999)—27% of GDP.
**Trade:** Exports (1999 est.)—$370 million: garments, electricity, wood and wood products, coffee, rattan. Major markets—France, U.K., Germany, Holland, Thailand, Belgium, U.S., Italy, Japan, Vietnam. Imports (1999 est.)—$570 million. Major imports—fuel, food, consumer, goods, machinery and equipment, vehicles and spare parts. Major suppliers—Thailand, Singapore, Japan, Vietnam, China.

# PEOPLE

Laos' population was estimated at about 5.4 million in 1999, dispersed unevenly across the country. Most people live in valleys of the Mekong River and its tributaries. Vientiane prefecture, the capital and largest city, had about 569,000 residents in 1999. The country's population density is 23.4/sq. km. About half the country's people are ethnic Lao, the principal lowland inhabitants and politically and culturally dominant group. The Lao are descended from the Tai people who began migrating southward from China in the first millennium A.D. Mountain tribes of Miao-Yao, Austro-Asiatic, Tibeto-Burman—Hmong, Yao, Akha, and Lahu—and Tai ethnolinguistic heritage are found in northern Laos. Collectively, they are known as Lao Sung or highland Lao. In the central and southern mountains, Mon-Khmer tribes, known as Lao Theung or midslope Lao, predominate. Some Vietnamese and Chinese minorities remain, particularly in the towns, but many left in two waves—after independence in the late 1940s and again after 1975.

The predominant religion is Theravada Buddhism. Animism is common among the mountain tribes. Buddhism and spirit worship coexist easily. There also is a small number of Christians and Muslims.

The official and dominant language is Lao, a tonal language of the Tai linguistic group. Midslope and highland Lao speak an assortment of tribal languages. French, once common in government and commerce, has declined in usage, while knowledge of English—the language of the Association of Southeast Asian Nations (ASEAN)—has increased in recent years.

# HISTORY

Laos traces its first recorded history and its origins as a unified state to the emergence of the Kingdom of Lan Xang (literally, "million elephants") in 1353. Under the rule of King Fa Ngum, the wealthy and mighty kingdom covered much of what today is Thailand and Laos. His successors, especially King Setthathirat in the 16th century, helped establish Buddhism as the predominant religion of the country.

By the 17th century, the kingdom of Lan Xang entered a period of decline marked by dynastic struggle and conflicts with its neighbors. In the late 18th century, the Siamese (Thai) established hegemony over much of what is now Laos. The region was divided into principalities centered on Luang Prabang in the north, Vien-

tiane in the center, and Champassak in the south. Following its colonization of Vietnam, the French supplanted the Siamese and began to integrate all of Laos into the French empire. The Franco-Siamese treaty of 1907 defined the present Lao boundary with Thailand.

During World War II, the Japanese occupied French Indochina, including Laos. King Sisavang Vong of Luang Prabang was induced to declare independence from France in 1945, just prior to Japan's surrender. During this period, nationalist sentiment grew. In September 1945, Vientiane and Champassak united with Luang Prabang to form an independent government under the Free Laos (Lao Issara) banner. The movement, however, was shortlived. By early 1946, French troops reoccupied the country and conferred limited autonomy on Laos following elections for a constituent assembly.

Amidst the first Indochina war between France and the communist movement in Vietnam, Prince Souphanouvong formed the Pathet Lao (Land of Laos) resistance organization committed to the communist struggle against colonialism. Laos was not granted full sovereignty until the French defeat by the Vietnamese and the subsequent Geneva peace conference in 1954. Elections were held in 1955, and the first coalition government, led by Prince Souvanna Phouma, was formed in 1957. The coalition government collapsed in 1958, amidst increased polarization of the political process. Rightist forces took over the government.

In 1960, Kong Le, a paratroop captain, seized Vientiane in a coup and demanded formation of a neutralist government to end the fighting. The neutralist government, once again led by Souvanna Phouma, was not successful in holding power. Rightist forces under Gen. Phoumi Nosavan drove out the neutralist government from power later that same year. Subsequently, the neutralists allied themselves with the communist insurgents and began to receive support from the Soviet Union. Phoumi

Nosavan's rightist regime received support from the U.S.

A second Geneva conference, held in 1961-62, provided for the independence and neutrality of Laos. Soon after accord was reached, the signatories accused each other of violating the terms of the agreement, and with superpower support on both sides, the civil war soon resumed. Although the country was to be neutral, a growing American and North Vietnamese military presence in the country increasingly drew Laos into the second Indochina war (1954-75). For nearly a decade, Laos was subjected to the heaviest bombing in the history of warfare, as the U.S. sought to destroy the Ho Chi Minh Trail that passed through eastern Laos.

In 1972, the communist People's Party renamed itself the Lao People's Revolutionary Party (LPRP). It joined a new coalition government in Laos soon after the Vientiane cease-fire agreement in 1973. Nonetheless, the political struggle between communists, neutralists, and rightists continued. The fall of Saigon and Phnom Penh to communist forces in April 1975 hastened the decline of the coalition in Laos. Months after these communist victories, the Pathet Lao entered Vientiane. On December 2, 1975, the king abdicated his throne in the constitutional monarchy, and the communist Lao People's Democratic Republic (LPDR) was established.

The new communist government imposed centralized economic decisionmaking and broad security measures, including control of the media and the arrest and incarceration of many members of the previous government and military in "re-education camps". These draconian policies and deteriorating economic conditions, along with government efforts to enforce political control, prompted an exodus of lowland Lao and ethnic Hmong from Laos. About 10% of the Lao population sought refugee status after 1975. Many have since been resettled in third countries, including more than 250,000 who have come to the United States. The situation of Lao refugees is nearing its final chapter. Over time, the Lao Government closed the re-education camps and released most political prisoners.

From 1975 to 1996, the U.S. resettled some 250,000 Lao refugees from Thailand, including 130,000 Hmong. By the end of 1999, more than 28,900 Hmong and lowland Lao had repatriated to Laos—3,500 from China, the rest from Thailand. Through the Office of the United Nations High Commissioner for Refugees (UNHCR), the International Organization for Migration (IOM), and nongovernmental organizations, the U.S. has supported a variety of reintegration assistance programs throughout Laos. UNHCR monitors returnees and reports no evidence of systemic persecution or discrimination to date. As of December 1999, about 115 Hmong and lowland Lao remained in Ban Napho camp in Thailand awaiting third-country resettlement by the UNHCR.

# GOVERNMENT

The only legal political party is the Lao People's Revolutionary Party (LPRP). The head of state is President Khamtay Siphandone. The head of government is Prime Minister Sisavath Keobounphanh, who also is Chairman of the LPRP. Government policies are determined by the party through the all-powerful nine-member Politburo and the 49-member Central Committee. Important government decisions are vetted by the Council of Ministers.

Laos adopted a constitution in 1991. The following year, elections were held for a new 85-seat National Assembly with members elected by secret ballot to 5-year terms. This National Assembly, expanded in 1997 elections to 99 members, approves all new laws, although the executive branch retains authority to issue binding decrees. The most recent elections took place in December 1997. The FY 2000 central government budget plan calls for revenue of $180 million and expenditures of $289 million, including capital expenditures of $202 million.

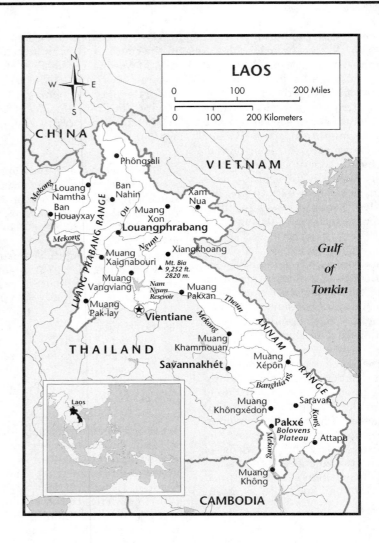

## Principal Government Officials

**For up-to-date information on Principal Government Officials, see the Chiefs of State and Cabinet Members of Foreign Governments section starting on page 1.**

Laos maintains an embassy in the United States at 2222 S Street NW, Washington, D.C. 20009 (tel: 202-332-6416).

# ECONOMY

Laos is a poor, landlocked country with an inadequate infrastructure and a largely unskilled work force.

The country's per capita income in 1999 was estimated to be $241. Agriculture, mostly subsistence rice farming, dominates the economy, employing an estimated 85% of the population and producing 51% of GDP. Domestic savings are low, forcing Laos to rely heavily on foreign assistance and concessional loans as investment sources for economic development. In FY 1999, for example, foreign grants and loans accounted for more than 20% of GDP and more than 75% of public investment. In 1998, the country's foreign debt was estimated at $1.9 billion.

Following its accession to power in 1975, the communist government imposed a harsh, Soviet-style command economy system, replacing the private sector with state enterprises and cooperatives; centralizing investment, production, trade, and pricing;

and creating barriers to internal and foreign trade. Within a few years, the Lao Government realized these types of economic policies were preventing, rather than stimulating, growth and development. No substantive reform was introduced, however, until 1986 when the government announced its "new economic mechanism" (NEM). Initially timid, the NEM was expanded to include a range of reforms designed to create conditions conducive to private sector activity. Prices set by market forces replaced government-determined prices.

Farmers were permitted to own land and sell crops on the open market. State firms were granted increased decisionmaking authority and lost most of their subsidies and pricing advantages. The government set the exchange rate close to real market levels, lifted trade barriers, replaced import barriers with tariffs, and gave private sector firms direct access to imports and credit.

In 1989, the Lao Government reached agreement with the World Bank and the International Monetary Fund on additional reforms. The government agreed to expand fiscal and monetary reform, promote private enterprise and foreign investment, privatize or close state firms, and strengthen banking. In addition, it also agreed to maintain a market exchange rate, reduce tariffs, and eliminate unneeded trade regulations. A liberal foreign investment code was enacted and appears to be slowly making a positive impact in the market. In an attempt to stimulate further international commerce, the Lao Government accepted Australian aid to build a bridge across the Mekong River to Thailand. The "Friendship Bridge," between Vientiane prefecture and Nong Khai, Thailand, was inaugurated in April 1994. Although the bridge has created additional commerce, the Lao Government does not yet permit a completely free flow of traffic across the span.

These reforms led to economic growth and an increased availability of goods. However, the Asian financial crisis, coupled with the Lao Government's own mismanagement of the

## Travel Notes

**Travel Advice:** For up-to-date information from the U.S. State Department on possible inconvenient or hazardous situations, see the **Travel Warnings and Consular Information Sheets from the U.S. Government** section starting on page 1723. For the latest information on health requirements and conditions, see the **International Travelers' Health Information** section starting on page 1385. For further information dealing with non-urgent matter, see the **Tips for Travelers to...** section starting on page 1588.

economy, resulted in spiraling inflation and a steep depreciation of the kip, which lost 87% of its value from June 1997 to June 1999. Tighter monetary policies brought about greater macroeconomic stability in FY 2000, and monthly inflation, which had averaged about 10% during the first half of FY 1999, dropped to an average 1% over the same period in FY 2000. The economy continues to be dominated by an unproductive agricultural sector operating largely outside the money economy and in which the public sector continues to play a dominant role.

# FOREIGN RELATIONS

The new government that assumed power in December 1975 aligned itself with the Soviet bloc and adopted a hostile posture toward the West. In ensuing decades, Laos maintained close ties with the former Soviet Union and its eastern bloc allies and depended heavily on the Soviets for most of its foreign assistance. Laos also maintained a "special relationship" with Vietnam and formalized a 1977 treaty of friendship and cooperation that created tensions with China. With the collapse of the Soviet Union and with Vietnam's decreased ability to provide assistance, Laos has sought to improve relations with its regional neighbors. The Lao Government has focused its efforts on Thailand, Laos' principal means of access to the sea and its primary trading partner. Within a year

of serious border clashes in 1987, Lao and Thai leaders signed a communique, signaling their intention to improve relations. Since then, they have made slow but steady progress, notably the construction and opening of the Friendship Bridge between the two countries.

Relations with China have improved over the years. Although the two were allies during the Vietnam War, the China-Vietnam conflict in 1979 led to a sharp deterioration in Sino-Lao relations. These relations began to improve in the late 1980s. In 1989 Sino-Lao relations were normalized.

Laos' emergence from international isolation has been marked through improved and expanded relations with other nations such as Australia, France, Japan, Sweden, and India. Laos was admitted into the Association of Southeast Asian Nations (ASEAN) in July 1997 and applied to join WTO in 1998.

## Membership in International Organizations

Laos is a member of the following international organizations: Agency for Cultural and Technical Cooperation (ACCT), Association of Southeast Asian Nations (ASEAN), ASEAN Free Trade Area (AFTA), ASEAN Regional Forum, Asian Development Bank, Colombo Plan, Economic and Social Commission for Asia and Pacific (ESCAP), Food and Agriculture Organization (FAO), G-77, International Bank for Reconstruction and Development (World Bank), International Civil Aviation Organization (ICAO), International Development Association (IDA), International Fund for Agricultural Development (IFAD), International Finance Corporation (IFC), International Federation of Red Cross and Red Crescent Societies, International Labor Organization (ILO), International Monetary Fund (IMF), Intelsat (nonsignatory user), Interpol, International Olympic Commission (IOC), International Telecommunications Union (ITU), Mekong Group, Non-Aligned Movement (NAM), Permanent Court of Arbitration (PCA), UN, United Nations Convention on Trade and Development (UNCTAD), United Nations Educational, Social and Cultural Organization (UNESCO), United Nations Industrial Development Organization (UNIDO), Universal Postal Union (UPU), World Federation of Trade Unions, World Health Organization (WHO), World Intellectual Property Organization (WIPO), World Meteorological Organization (WMO), World Tourism Organization, World Trade Organization (observer).

# U.S.-LAO RELATIONS

The United States opened a legation in Laos in 1950. Although diplomatic relations were never severed, U.S.-Lao relations deteriorated badly in the post-Indochina War period. The relationship remained cool until 1982 when efforts at improvement began. For the United States, progress in accounting for Americans missing in Laos from the Vietnam War is a principal measure of improving relations. Counternarcotics activities also have become an important part of the bilateral relationship as the Lao Government has stepped up its efforts to combat cultivation; production; and transshipment of opium, heroin, and marijuana.

Since the late 1980s, progress in these areas has steadily increased. Joint U.S. and Lao teams have conducted a series of joint excavations and investigations of sites related to cases of Americans missing in Laos. In counternarcotics activities, the U.S. and Laos are involved in a multi-million-dollar crop substitution/integrated rural development program. Laos also has formed its own national committee on narcotics, developed a long-range strategy for counternarcotics activities, participated in U.S.-sponsored narcotics training programs, and strengthened law enforcement measures to combat the narcotics problem.

U.S. Government foreign assistance to Laos covers a broad range of efforts. Such aid includes support for Laos' efforts to suppress opium production; training and equipment for a program to clear and dispose of unexploded ordnance; school and hospital construction; public education about the dangers of unexploded ordnance and about HIV/AIDS; support for medical research on hepatitis. Economic relations also are expanding. In August 1997, Laos and the United States initialed a Bilateral Trade Agreement and a Bilateral Investment Treaty.

## Principal U.S. Embassy Officials

**For up-to-date information on Principal U.S. Officials, see the U.S. Embassies, Consulates, and Foreign Service section starting on page 139.**

The American Embassy in Laos is on Rue Bartholonie, B.P. 114, Vientiane, tel: 212-581/582/585; fax: 212-584: country code: (856) city code (21).

Information on the embassy, its work in Laos, and U.S.-Lao relations is available on the Internet at http://www.usembassy.state.gov/laos.

# LATVIA

June 1997

Official Name:
**Republic of Latvia**

# PROFILE

## Geography

**Area:** 64,100 sq. km. (25,640 sq. miles); about the size of West Virginia.

**Cities:** Capital—Riga (1989 pop. 910,455); Daugavpils (124,910); Liepaja (114,486); Jelgava (74,105); Jurmala (60,600); Ventspils (50,646); Rezekne (42,477).

**Terrain:** Fertile low-lying plains predominate in central Latvia, highlands in Vidzeme and Latgale to the east, and hilly moraine in the western Kurzeme region. Forests cover one-third of the country, with over 3,000 small lakes and numerous bogs.

**Land use:** 27% arable land, 13% meadows and pastures, 39% forest and woodland, 21% other.

**Climate:** Temperate, with four seasons of almost equal length. January temperatures average -5°C (23°F); July, 17°C (63°F). Annual precipitation averages 57 centimeters (23 in.).

## People

**Nationality:** Noun and adjective—Latvian(s).

**Population:** 2.5 million.

**Growth rate:** -0.6%.

**Birth rate:** 14/1,000.

**Death rate:** 13/1,000. Divorce Rate: 40%.

**Migration rate:** 4 migrants/1,000.

**Density:** 105/sq. mile. Urban Dwellers: 71%.

**Ethnic groups:** Latvian 51.8%, Russians 33.8%, Belorussians 4.5%, Ukrainians 3.4%, Poles 2.3%.

**Religions:** Lutheran, Orthodox, Roman Catholic.

**State language:** Latvian. Russian also is spoken by most people.

**Education:** Years compulsory—9. By 1989, 60% of the adult populace had finished high school, and 12% had completed college. Attendance—331,100 students at 943 schools, plus 114,200 university students. Literacy—99%.

**Health:** Infant mortality rate—16/1,000. Life expectancy—65 years male, 75 female.

**Work force (1,405,000 people):** Agriculture/Forestry—16%. Industry—30%. Trade/Dining—9%. Transport/Communication—7%. Construction—10%. Financial—1%. Services, other—27%.

## Government

**Type:** Parliamentary democracy.

**Constitution:** The 1922 constitution, the 1990 declaration of renewal of independence, and the 1991 "Basic Law for the Period of Transition" serve until a new constitution is ratified.

**Branches:** Executive—President (Head of State), elected by Parliament every 3 years; Prime Minister (Head of Government). Legislative—Saeima (100-member body). Judicial—Supreme Court.

**Administrative regions:** 26 "rural" districts and 6 districts in Riga.

**Political parties:** Democratic Party "Saimnieks" (Cevers, Kreituss)—18 seats "Fatherland and Freedom" (Maris Grinblats)—14 seats Latvia's Way (Gailis, Birkavs, Pantelejevs)—17 seats Nat'l. Conservatives/Greens (Krastins, Kirsteins)—08 seats Unity Party (Alberts Kauls)—08 seats Farmers Union (Pres. Ulmanis, Rozentals) and Christian Democrats (Predele)—07 seats "For Latvia" (Joachim Siegerist)—16 seats "Harmony" (ex-FM Jurkans, Vulfsons, Kide)—06 seats Socialists (Stroganovs, Rubiks)—06 seats.

**Suffrage:** 18 years, universal

**Government budget:** $939 million (social welfare 41%, education 15%, defense 12%). $73 million deficit.

**National holidays:** November 18—Independence Day.

**Flag:** Two horizontal, maroon bands of equal width divided by a white stripe one-half the width.

## Economy

**GDP:** $3.5 billion.

**Growth rate:** 1%.

**Unemployment:** 6.5%.

**Average annual wages:** $2,230.

**Natural resources:** Peat, limestone, dolomite, gypsum, timber.

**Agriculture/Forestry (10% of GDP):** Products—cattle, dairy foods, cereals, potatoes. Cultivable land—1.36 million ha, of which 60% is arable, 18% meadow, and 13% pasture.

**Manufacturing (14.3% of GDP):** light electrical equipment and fittings, textiles and footwear, technological instruments, construction materials, processed foods. Public Services—11%. Construction—5.3%. Energy/Water—4.5%. Financial Services—3.5%. Rents—2.7%. Other Services—34%. Miscellaneous—14.7%.

**Trade:** Exports—$1.1 billion: transshipment of crude oil; wood/wood products 27%; metals 8%, textiles/apparel 14%, machinery/equipment 9%, food products 11%, chemicals 5%, vehicles 3%. Major markets—Russia 28%, other CIS 15%, Germany 10%, Sweden 7%. Imports—$1.4 billion: energy 52%, minerals 21%, machinery/equipment 17%, chemicals/plastics 11%, food products 8%, textiles/apparel 8%, wood/wood products 4%, metals 3%. Partners—Russia 24%, Germany 13%, Sweden 6.5%, other CIS 6%.

**Official exchange rate:** One lats (Ls) = 100 santimi. 1 USD = .56Ls.

# GEOGRAPHY

Between 55.40 and 58.05 latitude and 20.58 and 28.14 longitude, Latvia lies on the eastern shores of the Baltic Sea on the level northwestern part of the rising East European platform. 98% of the country lies under 200 m elevation (640 ft.). The damp climate resembles New England's. With the exception of the coastal plains, the Ice Age divided Latvia into three main regions: the morainic Western and Eastern uplands and the Middle lowlands. Latvia holds over 12,000 rivers, only 17 of which are longer than 60 miles, and over 3,000 small lakes, most of which are eutrophic. Woodland, more than half of which is pine, covers 41% of the country. Other than peat, dolomite and limestone, natural resources are scarce. Latvia holds 531km (329 mi.) of sandy coastline, and the ports of Liepaja and Ventspils provide important warm-water harbors for the Baltic littoral, although the Bay of Riga itself is rather polluted.

Today, Latvia is slightly larger than Denmark, Estonia, the Netherlands and Switzerland. Its strategic location has instigated many wars between rival powers on its territory. As recently as 1944, the USSR granted Russia the Abrene region on the Livonian frontier, which Latvia still contests.

# PEOPLE

Latvians occasionally refer to themselves by the ancient name of "Latviji," which may have originated from a "Latve" river that presumably flowed through what is now eastern Latvia. A small Finno-Ugric tribe known as the Livs settled among the Latvians and modulated the name to "Latvis," meaning "forest-clearers," which is how medieval German settlers also referred to these peoples. The German colonizers changed this name to "Lette" and called their initially small colony "Livland." The Latin form, "Livonia," gradually referred to the whole of modern-day Latvia as well as southern Estonia, which had fallen under German dominion. Latvians and Lithuanians are the only directly surviving members of the Baltic peoples and languages of the Indo-European family.

Latvians look like, and consider themselves, Nordics, evidenced through the strong cultural and religious influences gained over centuries during Germanic and Scandinavian colonization and settlement. Eastern Latvia (Latgale), however, retains a strong Polish and Russian cultural and linguistic influence. This highly literate society places strong emphasis upon education, which is free and compulsory until age 16. Most Latvians belong to the Evangelical Lutheran Church, a sizable minority are Russian Orthodox, and Eastern Latvia is predominantly Roman Catholic.

Historically, Latvia always has had a fairly large Russian, Jewish, German and Polish minority, but postwar emigration, deportations and Soviet Russification policies from 1939–1989 dropped the percentage of ethnic Latvians in Latvia from 73% to 52%. In an attempt to preserve the Latvian language and avoid ethnic Latvians becoming a minority in their own country, Latvia's strict language law and draft citizenship law have caused many non-citizen resident Russians concern over their ability to assimilate, despite Latvian legal guarantees of universal human and civil rights regardless of citizenship.

Written with the Latin alphabet, Latvian is the language of the Latvian people and the official language of the country. It is an inflective language with several analytical forms, three dialects, and German syntactical influence. The oldest known examples of written Latvian are from a 1585 catechism. The Soviets imposed the official use of Russian, so most Latvians speak Russian as a second or first language while the resident Slavic populace generally speaks Russian as a first language.

# HISTORY

Since 9000 BC ancient peoples of unknown origin had inhabited Latvia, but by 3000 BC the ancestors of the Finns had settled the region. A millennium later, pre-Baltic tribes had arrived and within time evolved into the Baltic Couranian, Latgallian, Selonian and Semigallian groups. These tribes eventually formed local governments independently from the Finno-Ugric Livian tribe until the thirteenth century, when they were conquered by the Germans, who renamed the territory Livonia.

German sailors shipwrecked on the Daugava River in 1054 had inhabited the area, which led to increasing German influence. Founded by the Germanic Bishop Alberth of Livonia in 1201, Riga joined the Hanseatic League in 1285 and shared important cultural and economic ties to the rest of Europe. However, the new German nobility enserfed the peasantry and

accorded non-Germanic peoples only limited trading and property rights.

Subsequent wars and treaties ensured Livonia's partition and colonization for centuries. The Commonwealth's successes during the Livonian Wars (1558–1583) united the Latvian-populated duchies of Pardaugava, Kurzeme and Zemgale, but the Polish-Swedish War (1600–1629) granted Sweden acquisition of Riga and the Duchy of Pardaugava, minus Latgale, leaving Latvia again split ethnically. In turn, victory over Sweden in the Great Northern War (1700–1721) gave Russia control over the Latvian territories. From 1804 onwards, a series of local decrees gradually weakened the grip of German nobility over peasant society, and in 1849 a law granted a legal basis for the creation of peasant-owned farms.

Until the 1860s, there still was little sense of a Latvian national identity, as both serfdom and institutional controls to migration and social mobility limited the boundaries of the peasants' intellectual and social geography. The large baronic estates caused a lack of available farmland for an increasing population, creating a large landless, urban class comprising about 60% of the population. Also in the face of stricter Russification policies, the Baltic German clergy and literati began to take a more benevolent interest in the distinctive language and culture of the Latvian peasantry. These patrons (with such Lettish names as Alunans, Barons, Krastins, Kronvalds, Tomsons and Valdemars) soon formed the Young Latvian Movement, whose aim was to promote the indigenous language and to publicize and counteract the socio-economic oppression of Latvians.

By 1901, "Jauna Strava" had evolved into the Latvian Social Democratic Party. Following the lead of the Austrian Marxists, the LSDP advocated the transformation of the Russian Empire into a federation of democratic states (to include Latvia) and the adoption of cultural autonomy policy for extra-territorial ethnic communities. In 1903, the LSDP split into the more radically internationalist Latvian Social Democratic Worker's Party and the more influential Latvian Social Democratic Union (LSDU), which continued to champion national interests and Latvia's national self-determination, especially during the failed 1905 Revolution in Russia.

The onset of WWI brought German occupation of the western coastal province of Kurzeme, and Latvians heroically countered the invasion with the establishment of several regiments of riflemen commanded by Czarist generals. As a defensive measure, Russia dismantled over 500 local Latvian industries, along with technological equipment, and relocated them to central Russia. The sagging military campaign generally increased Latvian and LSDU support for the Bolsheviks' successful October Revolution in 1917, in the hopes of a "free Latvia within free Russia." These circumstances led to the formation of the soviet "Iskolat Republic" in the unoccupied section of Latvia. In opposition to this government and to the landed barons' German sympathies stood primarily the Latvian Provisional National Council and the Riga Democratic Bloc. These and other political parties formed the Latvian People's Council which on November 18, 1918 declared Latvia's independence and formed an army.

The new Latvian army faced rogue elements of the retreating German army and squared off in civil war against the Soviet Red Army, comprised greatly of the former Latvian Riflemen. Soviet power resumed in Latvia one month later on December 17 by order of the Latvian SSR, which forcefully collectivized all land and nationalized all industries and property. By May 22, 1919 the resurgent German Army occupied and devastated Riga for several days. In response, the Latvian army managed to win a decisive battle over the combined German-Red Army forces and thereafter consolidated its success on the eastern Latgale front. These developments led to the dissolution of the Soviet Latvian government on January 13, 1920 and to a peace treaty between Latvia and Soviet Russia on August 11 later that year. By September 22, 1921, Latvia was admitted to the League of Nations.

Having obtained independent statehood in which Latvians were an absolute majority, the Government headed by Prime Minister Ulmanis declared a democratic, parliamentary republic. It recognized Latvian as the official language, granted cultural autonomy to the country's sizeable minorities, and introduced an electoral system into the Latvian constitution, which was adopted in 1922. The decade witnessed sweeping economic reform, as war had devastated Latvian agriculture, and most Russian factories had been evacuated to Russia. Economic depression heightened political turmoil, and on May 15, 1934, Prime Minister Ulmanis dismissed the parliament, banned outspoken and left-wing political parties and tightened authoritarian state control over Latvian social life and the economy.

The effects of the infamous Molotov-Ribbentrop agreement of 1939 steadily forced Latvia under Soviet influence until August 5, 1940, when the Soviet Union finally annexed Latvia. On June 14 of the following year 15,000 Latvian citizens were forcibly deported and a large number of army officers shot. The subsequent German occupation witnessed the mobilization of many Latvians into Waffen SS legions, while some Latvians joined the Red Army and formed resistance groups; others fled to the West and East. By 1945, Latvia's population dropped by one-third.

After the war, the U.S.S.R. subjected the Latvian republic to a scale of social and economic reorganization which rapidly transformed the rural economy to heavy industry, the strongly ethnically Latvian population into a more multiethnic structure, and the predominantly peasant class into a fully urbanized industrial worker class. As part of the goal to more fully integrate Latvia into the Soviet Union, on March 25, 1949 Stalin again deported another 42,000 Latvians and continued to promote the policy of encouraging Soviet immigration to Latvia. The brief "Krushchev thaw" of the 1950's ended in 1959, when the Soviets dismissed Latvian Communist Party and Government leaders on charges of "bourgeois nationalism" and replaced them with more aggressive hardliners, mostly from Russia.

"Perestroika" enabled Latvians to pursue a bolder nationalistic program, particularly through such general issues as environmental protection. In July 1989, the Latvian Supreme Soviet adopted a "Declaration of Sovereignty" and amended the Constitution to assert the supremacy of its laws over those of the USSR. Pro-independence Latvian Popular Front candidates gained a two-thirds majority in the Supreme Council in the March, 1990 democratic elections. On May 4, the Council declared its intention to restore full Latvian independence after a "transitional" period; three days later, Ivars Godmanis was chosen Council of Ministers Chairman, or Prime Minister.

In January 1991, Soviet political and military forces tried unsuccessfully to overthrow the legitimate Latvian authorities by occupying the central publishing house in Riga and establishing a "Committee of National Salvation" to usurp governmental functions. Seventy-three percent of all Latvian residents confirmed their strong support for independence March 3 in a nonbinding "advisory" referendum. A large number of ethnic Russians also voted for the proposition.

Latvia claimed de facto independence on August 21, 1991 in the aftermath of the failed Soviet coup attempt. International recognition, including the U.S.S.R., followed. The U.S., which had never recognized Latvia's forcible annexation by the U.S.S.R., resumed full diplomatic relations with Latvia on September 2.

# GOVERNMENT AND POLITICAL CONDITIONS

The Saeima, a unicameral legislative body, now is the highest organ of state authority. It initiates and approves legislation sponsored by the Prime Minister. The Prime Minister has full responsibility and control over his cabinet, and the President holds a primarily ceremonial role as Head of State.

In autumn, 1991 Latvia reimplemented significant portions of its 1922 constitution and in spring, 1993 the Government took a census to determine eligibility for citizenship. After almost three years of deliberations, Latvia finalized a citizenship and naturalization law in summer, 1994. By law, those who were Latvian citizens in 1940, and their descendants, could claim citizenship. Forty-six percent of Latvia's population is ethnically non-Latvian, yet about 85% of its ethnic Slavs can pass the residency requirement. Naturalization criteria include a conversational knowledge of Latvian, a loyalty oath, renunciation of former citizenship, a ten-year residency requirement and a knowledge of the Latvian constitution. Dual citizenship is allowed for those who were forced to leave Latvia during the Soviet occupation and adopted another citizenship. Convicted criminals, drug addicts, agents of Soviet intelligence services, and certain other groups also are excluded from becoming citizens.

On March 19, 1991 the Supreme Council passed a law explicitly guaranteeing "equal rights to all nationalities and ethnic groups" and "guarantees to all permanent residents in the Republic regardless of their nationality, equal rights to work and wages." The law also prohibits "any activity directed toward nationality discrimination or the promotion of national superiority or hatred."

In the June 5–6, 1993 elections wherein over 90% of the electorate participated, eight of Latvia's twenty-three registered political parties passed the four percent threshold to enter parliament. The Popular Front, which spearheaded the drive for independence two years ago with a 75% majority in the last parliamentary elections in 1990, did not qualify for representation. The centrist "Latvia's Way" party received a 33% plurality of votes and joined with the Farmer's Union to head a center-right wing coalition government.

Led by the opposition National Conservative Party, right-wing nationalists won a majority of the seats nationwide and also captured the Riga mayoralty in the May 29, 1994 municipal elections. OSCE and COE observers pronounced the elections free and fair, and turnout averaged

about 60%. In February 1995, the Council of Europe granted Latvia membership.

Through President Clinton's initiative, on April 30, 1994 Latvian and Russia signed a troop withdrawal agreement. Russia withdrew its troops by August 31, 1994, and will maintain several hundred technical specialists to man an OSCE-monitored phased-array ABM radar station at Skrunda until the facility is dismantled no later than 1999.

The September 30–October 1, 1995 elections brought forth a deeply fragmented parliament with nine parties represented and the largest party commanding only 18 of 100 seats. Attempts to form right-of-center and leftist governments failed; seven weeks after the election, a broad coalition government of six of the nine parties was voted into office under prime minister Andris Skele, a businessman not in parliament. The publicly popular president, Guntis Ulmanis, has limited constitutional powers but played a key role in leading the various political forces to agree finally to this broad coalition. In June, the saeima re-elected Ulmanis to another three-year term.

## Principal Government Officials

**For up-to-date information on Principal Government Officials, see the Chiefs of State and Cabinet Members of Foreign Governments section starting on page 1.**

Latvia maintains an Embassy in the United States at 4325 17th Street, Washington DC 20011 [tel: (202)726-8213].

# ECONOMY

For centuries under Hanseatic and German influence and then during its inter-war independence, Latvia used its geographic location as an impor-

tant East-West commercial and trading center.

Industry served local markets, while timber, paper and agricultural products supplied Latvia's main exports. Conversely, the years of Russian and Soviet occupation tended to integrate Latvia's economy to serve those empires' large internal industrial needs. Comprising 46% of the populace, ethnic Slavs control about 80% of the economy.

Since reestablishing its independence, Latvia has proceeded with market-oriented reforms, albeit at a measured pace. Its freely-traded currency, the lat, was introduced in 1993 and has held steady, or appreciated, against major world currencies. For the past two years, inflation has been held under a monthly rate of 2–3%. Latvia's economy had contracted substantially since 1991: economic output shrank 34% in 1992 and 20% in 1993. Led by recovery in light industry and a boom in the commerce and finance, the economy appeared to have steadied by late 1994. Modest growth was forecast for 1995. However, a prolonged banking crisis involving what had been Latvia's largest commercial bank, set the economy back in the second half of 1995. The crisis caused the budget deficit for 1995—and projected deficit for 1996—to grow well beyond the 2% target recommended by the IMF.

Replacement of the centrally-planned system imposed during the Soviet period with a structure based on free-market principles has been occurring spontaneously from below much more than through consistently-applied structural adjustment. Official statistics tend to understate the booming private sector, suggesting that the Latvian people and their economy are doing much better than is reflected statistically. A booming private sector, especially in trade and services, accounted for about half of economic activity. Privatization initially proceeded at a good pace in the rural sector; by mid-1994, more than 50% of Latvia's farmland was in private hands, the rest in stock or government-owned companies. In the industrial sector, especially medium and

## Travel Notes

**Customs:** Latvia does not require visas for citizens of the U.S. and most Western countries for visits of less than 90 days. Visitors are encouraged to register at the U.S. Embassy.

Unlimited hard currency, 1 liter of alcohol, 200 cigarettes, and foodstuffs valued at less than one month's minimum wage (3,000 rubles) may be imported. $125 worth of goods not regulated by Latvian or international law requiring special permission may be imported. Export regulations cover hard currency (in unrestricted amounts) and foodstuffs worth less than ten monthly minimum wages). Articles purchased in Latvia for hard currency must be accompanied by a receipt.

**Climate and clothing:** Latvia's climate enjoys seasons of almost equal length. Riga and the coast are temperate, with pleasant, cool summers and damp winters; eastern Latvia is continental, with warmer summers and harsher winters.

**Health:** Medical care does not meet Western standards and faces severe shortages of basic medical supplies, including disposable needles, anesthetics and antibiotics. Recent disruption of energy supplies has decreased the availability of heat and hot water. Raw fruits and vegetables are safe to eat, but avoid drinking unpasteurized milk and tapwater.

**Transportation:** Several international airlines, including SAS and Lufthansa, provide service between European cities and Riga Airport. Train service is available via Moscow, St. Petersburg and Warsaw/Frankfurt, and a bus line connects the Baltic capitals with Warsaw. Bus and taxi services within the capital and its environs are good. Taxis are inexpensive and available at stands or may be ordered by phone. Rental cars are available. Gasoline prices are reaching market rates.

**Telecommunications:** Improved telephone and telegraph services are readily available at standard international rates. Riga is 7 hours ahead of eastern standard time.

**Work week:** 40 hours. Most stores and shops are closed on Sunday, open Monday-Friday from 10:00am–6:00pm and on Saturday from 9:00am–1:00pm.

**National holidays:** Businesses and the U.S. Embassy may be closed on the following Latvian holidays: January 1—New Year's Day; Good Friday; Easter Sunday; May 1—Labor Day; June 24—Midsummer; November 18—Independence Day; December 24–26 (Christmas). The U.S. Embassy also will be closed on U.S. federal holidays.

**Tourist attractions:** Latvia offers a variety of interesting historical and architectural monuments, museums, picturesque scenery and places of interest. Riga features all the appeal of an Old World European capital, with cathedrals, castles and town walls from the Middle Ages and tree-lined boulevards. Also of note are Riga's Freedom Monument and its Outdoor Museum of Ethnography portraying Latvian life through the centuries. Jurmala's seaside resorts are popular for sandy beaches and mudbaths. Numerous castle and church ruins as well as lovely national parks, such as the wildlife refuge in Ligatne, dot the countryside.

**Currency, Weights and Measures:** The transitional national currency is convertible with major Western monies, but some vendors still accept Western cash for purchases. Traveler's checks and some major credit cards can be used primarily at large banks and Western hotels. Latvia uses the metric system.

**Crime:** By U.S. standards, Latvia has a low rate of violent crime. However, the introduction of a market-oriented economy has resulted in an increase in street crime, especially at night near major hotels and restaurants frequented by foreigners. Penalties for possession, use and dealing in illegal drugs are strict, and convicted offenders can expect jail sentences and fines.

**Travel Advice:** For up-to-date information from the U.S. State Department on possible inconvenient or hazardous situations, see the **Travel Warnings and Consular Information Sheets from the U.S. Government** section starting on page 1723. For the latest information on health requirements and conditions, see the **International Travelers' Health Information** section starting on page 1385. For further information dealing with nonurgent matter, see the **Tips for Travelers to...** section starting on page 1588.

large enterprises, progress has been slow. The official unemployment figure has held steady in the 8% range.

Latvia reported a trade surplus of 36.4 million lats in 1993, with exports of 675.6 million lats and imports of 639.2 million lats. Given the persistently strong lat, Latvia is expected to record a larger balance of trade deficit in 1995. Russia remains Latvia's largest trade partner, accounting for 29% of exports and 28% of imports, mostly transit trade. Latvia remains heavily dependent upon Russia and the NIS for about 90 percent of its energy needs. Invisibles flow and net official transfers were positive in 1994, but outflows of mainly Russian portfolio investment in 1995 are likely to hurt the final 1995 balance of payments figure. Direct foreign investment appears to have grown only modestly since January 1994, when the total figure stood at an estimated $140 million. The United States remains at or close to the top in direct foreign investment. Latvia signed a Europe Agreement with the EU in June 1995, with a four-year transition period. In 1995, Latvia signed a bilateral investment treaty with the United States and is currently negotiating a double-taxation treaty.

Structural reform has proceeded most rapidly in agriculture and in the privatization of small enterprises. More than 58,000 private farms have been established and most remaining collective farms transformed into private joint stock companies. However, many of Latvia's new farmers are operating at subsistence levels stemming from a lack of financial resources and credit. Urban and rural property is being returned to former owners, but the legal mechanisms for title registration, sale and mortgaging of real property are not yet fully developed. Other than privatization of the food processing and dairy industries, the pace of privatization of large industrial enterprises has been slow. Only about a dozen of Latvia's largest industrial enterprises have been privatized.

Recovery in light industry and Riga's emergence as a regional financial and commercial center are offsetting shrinkage of the state-owned industrial sector and agriculture. Foreign investment in Latvia is still modest compared with levels in North-Central Europe.

# DEFENSE

Latvia's defense concept is based upon the Swedish-Finnish model of a rapid response force composed of a mobilization base and a small group of career professionals. The armed forces consist of border guards, mobile riflemen, special units, and an air force and navy whose status has not fully been determined financially or administratively. The "zemessardze," or home guard, is an autonomous volunteer paramilitary organization which also performs traditional national guard duties and assists the border guards. Special independent Interior Ministry, intelligence, and civil defense units also exist. Active-duty defense forces stand at 9,000 men. There is a mandatory one-year draft period of active duty, and alternative conscription for conscientious objectors is available.

# FOREIGN RELATIONS

Latvia became a member of the United Nations on September 18, 1991 and is a signatory to a number of UN organizations and other international agreements. It also is a member of the Conference on Security and Cooperation in Europe and of the North Atlantic Coordinating Council. Latvia is unaffiliated directly with any political alliance but welcomes further cooperation and integration with NATO, European Community and other Western organizations. It also seeks more active participation in United Nations peacekeeping efforts worldwide.

Latvia maintains embassies in the United States, Belarus, Belgium, Denmark, Estonia, Finland, France, Germany, Lithuania, Sweden, the United Kingdom, and Russia. It also operates missions to the United Nations in New York City and a Consulate General in Australia. Honorary consuls are located in Australia, Austria, Belgium, Canada, Greece, India, Israel, Italy, Korea, Moldova, Norway, Switzerland, Taiwan, and Venezuela.

Relations with Russia are improving, primarily because Russia withdrew its troops from Latvia by August 31, 1994, according to a bilateral agreement signed on April 30 that year.

Latvia has agreed that Russia may continue to operate the Skrunda radar facility under OSCE supervision strictly for a four-year period. Russia expresses concern for how Latvia's laws on language and naturalization may affect Latvia's ethnic Slavs, who comprise 46% of the population. In turn, Latvia is interested in the welfare of over 210,000 ethnic Latvians still resident in Russia. Neither country allows for dual citizenship.

The United States established diplomatic relations with Latvia on July 28, 1922. The U.S. Legation in Riga officially was established November 13, 1922 and served as the headquarters for U.S. representation in the Baltics during the inter-war era.

The Soviet invasion forced the closure of the legation on September 5, 1940, but Latvian representation in the United States has continued uninterrupted for over seventy years. The U.S. never recognized the forcible incorporation of Latvia into the USSR, and views the present Government of Latvia as a legal continuation of the inter-war republic. Latvia has enjoyed Most-Favored-Nation (MFN) treatment with the U.S. since December, 1991. It annually receives approximately $6 million in humanitarian and medical aid, technical assistance and professional training, along with about $38 million in feed grain credit from the U.S. since 1991.

## Principal U.S. Officials

**For up-to-date information on Principal U.S. Officials, see the U.S. Embassies, Consulates, and Foreign Service section starting on page 139.**

The U.S. Embassy in Latvia is located at Raina Boulevard 7, Riga [tel. (371)782-0046].

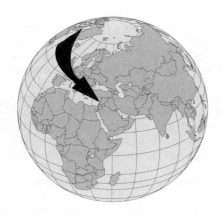

# LEBANON

January 1994

Official Name:
## Republic of Lebanon

# PROFILE

## Geography

**Area:** 10,452 sq. km. (4,015 sq. mi.); about half the size of New Jersey.
**Cities:** Capital—Beirut (pop. 1 million). Other cities—Tripoli (240,000), Sidon (110,000), Tyre (60,000), Zahleh (55,000).
**Terrain:** Narrow coastal plain backed by the Lebanon Mountains, the fertile Biqa' Valley, and the Anti-Lebanon Mountains, which extend to the Syrian border. Land—61% urban, desert, or waste; 21% agricultural; 8% forested.
**Climate:** Typically Mediterranean, resembling that of southern California.

## People

**Nationality:** Noun and adjective—Lebanese (sing. and pl.).
**Population (est.):** 3 million.
**Annual growth rate (est):** 1%.
**Ethnic groups:** Arab 93%, Armenian 6%.
**Religions:** Christian (Maronite, Greek Orthodox, Greek Catholic, Roman Catholic, Protestant, Armenian Apostolic, other), Muslim (Sunni, Shi'a, other), and Druze.
**Languages:** Arabic (official), French, English, Armenian.
**Education:** Years compulsory—5.

Attendance— 93%. Literacy—75%.
**Health:** Infant mortality rate—50/1,000 (1989). Life expectancy—male, 65 years; female, 70 years.
**Work force (750,000 in 1989):** Industry, commerce, services—79%. Agriculture—11%. Government—10%.

## Government

**Type:** Parliamentary republic.
**Independence:** 1943.
**Constitution:** May 26, 1926 (amended).
**Branches:** Executive—president (chief of state, elected by simple majority of parliament for 6-year term), council of ministers (appointed). Legislative—unicameral parliament (128-member National Assembly elected for 4-year renewable terms; last parliamentary elections in 1992). Judicial— secular and religious courts; combination of Ottoman, civil, and canon law; no judicial review of legislative acts.
**Administrative subdivisions:** 5 provinces, each headed by a governor: Beirut, North Lebanon, South Lebanon, Mount Lebanon, and Biqa'.
**Political parties:** Organized along sectarian lines around individuals whose followers are motivated by religious, clan, and ethnic considerations.
**Suffrage:** Males at 21; females with elementary education, at 21.
**Flag:** Two horizontal red bands with

white center band, on which a green and brown cedar tree is centered.

## Economy*

**GDP (1992):** $4 billion.
**Annual growth rate:** (1992) 10%.
**GDP per capita:** $1,500.
**Natural resources:** Limestone.
**Agriculture (7.2% of GDP):** Products—citrus fruit, vegetables, olives, sugar beets, tobacco.
**Industry (21% of GDP):** Types—cement production, ready-made clothing, electrical equipment, light industry, refining.
**Trade (23% of GDP):** Exports—$500 million [f.o.b.—1992]. Major markets—Saudi Arabia, Switzerland, U.A.E., France, Jordan. Imports—$4.8 billion [c.i.f.—1992]. Major suppliers—Italy, Syria, France, Germany, U.S.
**Official exchange rate:** [1992 average] 1,683 Lebanese pounds=US$1; [Dec. 1993] 1,711 Lebanese pounds=US$1.

*Note: Due to drastic fluctuation in exchange rates over 1992, and flaws in the central government's economic database, figures throughout this report are not authoritative, but are estimates based on recent economic performance.

# PEOPLE

The population of Lebanon comprises Christians and Muslims. No official census has been taken since 1932, reflecting the political sensitivity in Lebanon over confessional (religious) balance. The U.S. Government estimate is that more than half of the resident population is Muslim (Shi'a, Sunni and Druze), and the rest is Christian (predominantly Maronite, Greek Orthodox, Greek Catholic, and Armenian). Shi'a Muslims make up the single largest sect. Claims since the early 1970s by Muslims that they are in the majority contributed to tensions preceding the 1975-76 civil strife and have been the basis of demands for a more powerful Muslim voice in the government.

There are over 300,000 Palestinian refugees in Lebanon registered with the United Nations Relief and Works Agency (UNRWA), and about 180,000 stateless undocumented persons resident in the country (mostly Kurds and Syrians). Palestinians and stateless persons are not accorded the legal rights enjoyed by the rest of the population.

With no official figures available, it is estimated that 600,000-900,000 persons fled the country during the initial years of civil strife (1975-76). Although some returned, continuing instability until 1990 sparked further waves of emigration, casting even more doubt on population figures.

Many Lebanese still derive their living from agriculture. The urban population, concentrated mainly in Beirut and Tripoli, is noted for its commercial enterprise, but chronic instability until 1990 in much of the country has had a strong negative impact on both agriculture and commerce. Lebanon has a higher proportion of skilled labor than any other Arab country.

# HISTORY

Lebanon is the historical home of the Phoenicians, Semitic traders whose maritime culture flourished there for more than 2,000 years (c. 2700-450 B.C.). In later centuries, Lebanon's mountains were a refuge for Christians, and Crusaders established several strongholds there. Following the collapse of the Ottoman Empire after World War I, the five Ottoman provinces that had comprised present-day Lebanon were mandated to France by the League of Nations. The country gained independence in 1943, and French troops were withdrawn in 1946.

Lebanon's history from independence can be defined largely in terms of its presidents, each of whom shaped Lebanon by a personal brand of politics: Sheikh Bishara al-Khoury (1943- 52), Camille Chamoun (1952-58), Fuad Shihab (1958-64), Charles Helou (1964-70), Suleiman Franjiyah (1970-76), Elias Sarkis (1976-1982), and Amine Gemayel (1982-88). From the end of the term of Amine Gemayel in September 1988 until the election of Rene Moawad in November 1989, Lebanon had no president.

The terms of the first two presidents ended in political turmoil. In 1958, during the last months of President Chamoun's term, an insurrection broke out, aggravated by external factors. In July 1958, in response to an appeal by the Lebanese Government, U.S. forces were sent to Lebanon. They were withdrawn in October 1958, after the inauguration of President Shihab and a general improvement in the internal and international aspects of the situation.

President Franjiyah's term saw the outbreak of full-scale civil conflict in 1975. Prior to 1975, difficulties had arisen over the large number of Palestinian refugees in Lebanon and the presence of Palestinian fedayeen (commandos). Frequent clashes involving Israeli forces and the fedayeen endangered civilians in south Lebanon and unsettled the country. Following minor skirmishes in the late 1960s and early 1970s, serious clashes erupted between the fedayeen and Lebanese Government forces in May 1973.

Coupled with the Palestinian problem, Muslim and Christian differences grew more intense, with occasional clashes between private sectarian militias. The Muslims were dissatisfied with what they considered an inequitable distribution of political power and social benefits. In April 1975, after shots were fired at a church, a busload of Palestinians was ambushed by gunmen in the Christian sector of Beirut, an incident widely regarded as the spark that touched off the civil war. Palestinian fedayeen forces joined the predominantly leftist-Muslim side as the fighting persisted, eventually spreading to most parts of the country.

Elias Sarkis was elected president in 1976. In October, Arab summits in Riyadh and Cairo set forth a plan to end the war. The resulting Arab Deterrent Force (ADF), composed largely of Syrian troops, moved in at the Lebanese Government's invitation to separate the combatants, and most fighting ended soon thereafter. As an uneasy quiet settled on Beirut and parts of Lebanon, security conditions in southern Lebanon began to deteriorate. A series of clashes occurred in the south in late 1977 and early 1978 between the Palestine Liberation Organization (PLO) and Lebanese leftists on the one hand, and the pro-Israeli, southern Lebanese militia (eventually known as the "Army of South Lebanon," or SLA) on the other.

After a raid on a bus in Northern Israel left large numbers of Israeli and Palestinian guerrilla casualties, Israel invaded Lebanon in March 1978, occupying most of the area south of the Litani river. The UN Security Council passed Resolution 425 calling for withdrawal of Israeli forces from Lebanon and creating a UN Interim Force in Lebanon (UNIFIL), charged with maintaining peace. When the Israelis withdrew, they turned over positions inside Lebanon along the border to their Lebanese ally, the SLA, and formed a "security zone" which exists to this day under the effective control of Israel and the SLA.

In mid-1978, clashes between the ADF and the Christian militias erupted. Arab foreign ministers created the Arab Follow-Up Committee, composed of Lebanon, Syria, Saudi Arabia, and Kuwait, to end fighting between the Syrians and Christians. After the Saudi ambassador was wounded in December 1978, the committee did not meet again formally until June 1981, when it was convened to address security and national reconciliation. The committee was unsuccessful in making progress toward a political settlement and has been inactive since November 1981.

Israeli-Palestinian fighting in July 1981 was ended by a cease-fire arranged by U.S. President Ronald Reagan's special envoy, Philip C. Habib, and announced on July 24, 1981. The cease-fire was respected during the next 10 months, but a string of incidents, including PLO rocket attacks on northern Israel, led to the June 6, 1982, Israeli ground attack into Lebanon to remove PLO forces. Israeli forces moved quickly through south Lebanon, encircling west Beirut by mid-June and beginning a three-month siege of Palestinian and Syrian forces in the city.

Throughout this period, which saw heavy Israeli air, naval, and artillery bombardments of west Beirut, Ambassador Habib worked to arrange a settlement. In August, he was successful in bringing about an agreement for the evacuation of Syrian troops and PLO fighters from Beirut. The agreement also provided for the deployment of a three-nation Multinational Force (MNF) during the period of the evacuation, and by late August, U.S. Marines, as well as French and Italian units, had arrived in Beirut. When the evacuation ended, these units departed. The U.S. Marines left on September 10.

In spite of the invasion, the Lebanese political process continued to function, and Bashir Gemayel was elected President in August, succeeding Elias Sarkis. On September 14, however, Bashir Gemayel was assassinated. On September 15, Israeli troops entered west Beirut. During

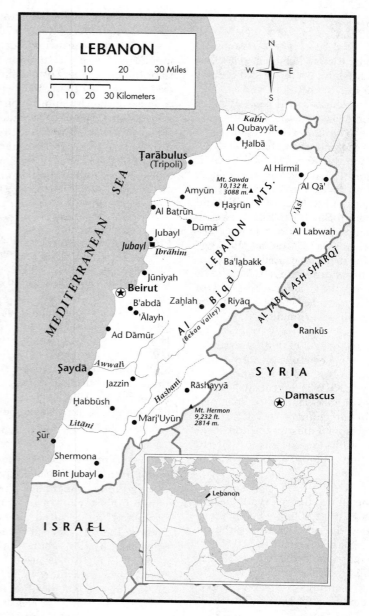

the next three days, Lebanese militiamen massacred hundreds of Palestinian civilians in the Sabra and Shatila refugee camps in west Beirut.

Bashir Gemayel's brother, Amine, was elected President by a unanimous vote of the parliament. He took office September 23, 1982. MNF forces returned to Beirut at the end of September as a symbol of support for the government.

In February 1983, a small British contingent joined the U.S., French, and Italian MNF troops in Beirut. President Gemayel and his government placed primary emphasis on the

withdrawal of Israeli, Syrian, and Palestinian forces from Lebanon, and in late 1982, Lebanese-Israeli negotiations commenced with U.S. participation.

On May 17, 1983, an agreement was signed by the representatives of Lebanon, Israel, and the United States that provided for Israeli withdrawal. Syria declined to discuss the withdrawal of its troops, effectively stalemating further progress. Opposition to the negotiations and to U.S. support for the Gemayel regime led to a series of terrorist attacks in 1983 and 1984 on U.S. interests, including the bombing on April 18, 1983 of the U.S.

embassy in west Beirut (63 dead), of the U.S. and French MNF headquarters in Beirut on October 23, 1983 (298 dead), and of the U.S. embassy annex in east Beirut on September 20, 1984 (8 killed).

Although the general security situation in Beirut remained calm through late 1982 and the first half of 1983, a move by Christian militiamen into the Druze-controlled Shuf area southeast of Beirut following the Israeli invasion led to a series of Druze-Christian clashes of escalating intensity beginning in October 1982. When Israeli forces unilaterally withdrew from the Shuf at the beginning of September 1983, a full-scale battle erupted with the Druze, backed by Syria, pitted against the Christian Lebanese Forces (LF) militia as well as the Lebanese army. U.S. and Saudi efforts led to a cease-fire on September 26. This left the Druze in control of most of the Shuf. Casualties were estimated to be in the thousands.

The virtual collapse of the Lebanese army in February 1984, following the defection of many of its Muslim and Druze units to opposition militias, was a major blow to the government. As it became clear that the departure of the U.S. Marines was imminent, the Gemayel Government came under increasing pressure from Syria and its Muslim Lebanese allies to abandon the May 17 accord. The Lebanese Government announced on March 5, 1984, that it was canceling its unimplemented agreement with Israel. The U.S. Marines left the same month.

Further national reconciliation talks at Lausanne under Syrian auspices failed. A new "government of national unity" under Prime Minister Rashid Karami was declared in April 1984 but made no significant progress toward solving Lebanon's internal political crises or its growing economic difficulties.

The situation was exacerbated by the deterioration of internal security. The opening rounds of the savage "camps war" in May 1985—a war that flared up twice in 1986— pitted the Palestinians living in refugee camps in

Beirut, Tyre, and Sidon against the Shi'ite Amal militia, which was concerned with resurgent Palestinian military strength in Lebanon. Eager for a solution in late 1985, Syria began to negotiate a "tripartite accord" on political reform among the leaders of various Lebanese factions, including the LF.

However, when the accord was opposed by Gemayel and the leader of the LF was overthrown by his hardline anti-Syrian rival, Samir Jaja, in January 1986, Syria responded by inducing the Muslim government ministers to cease dealing with Gemayel in any capacity, effectively paralyzing the government. In 1987, the Lebanese economy worsened, and the pound began a precipitous slide. On June 1, Prime Minister Karami was assassinated, further compounding the political paralysis. Salim al-Huss was appointed acting prime minister.

As the end of President Gemayel's term of office neared, the different Lebanese factions could not agree on a successor. Consequently, when his term expired on September 23, 1988, he appointed Army Commander General Michel Aoun as interim Prime Minister. Gemayel's acting Prime Minister, Salim al-Huss, also continued to act as de facto Prime Minister. Lebanon was thus divided between an essentially Muslim government in west Beirut and an essentially Christian government in east Beirut. The working levels of many ministries, however, remained intact and were not immediately affected by the split at the ministerial level.

In February 1989, General Aoun attempted to close illegal ports run by the LF. This led to several days of intense fighting in east Beirut and an uneasy truce between Aoun's army units and the LF. In March, an attempt by Aoun to close illegal militia ports in predominantly Muslim parts of the country led to a 6-month period of shelling of east Beirut by Muslim and Syrian forces and shelling of west Beirut and the Shuf by the Christian units of the army and the LF. This shelling caused nearly 1,000 deaths, several thousand injuries,

and further destruction to Lebanon's economic infrastructure.

In January 1989, the Arab League appointed a six-member committee on Lebanon, led by the Kuwaiti foreign minister. At the Casablanca Arab summit in May, the Arab League empowered a higher committee on Lebanon—composed of Saudi King Fahd, Algerian President Bendjedid, and Moroccan King Hassan—to work toward a solution in Lebanon. The committee issued a report in July 1989, stating that its efforts had reached a "dead end" and blamed Syrian intransigence for the blockage. After further discussions, the committee arranged for a seven-point cease- fire in September, followed by a meeting of Lebanese parliamentarians in Taif, Saudi Arabia.

After a month of intense discussions, the deputies informally agreed on a charter of national reconciliation, also known as the Taif agreement. The deputies returned to Lebanon in November, where they approved the Taif agreement on November 4, and elected Rene Moawad, a Maronite Christian deputy from Zghorta in north Lebanon, President on November 5. General Aoun, claiming powers as interim Prime Minister, issued a decree in early November dissolving the parliament and did not accept the ratification of the Taif agreement or the election of President Moawad.

President Moawad was assassinated on November 22, 1989, by a bomb that exploded as his motorcade was returning from Lebanese independence day ceremonies. The parliament met on November 24 in the Biqa' Valley and elected Elias Hraoui, a Maronite Christian deputy from Zahleh in the Biqa' Valley, to replace him. President Hraoui named a Prime Minister, Salim al-Huss, and a cabinet on November 25. Despite widespread international recognition of Hraoui and his government, General Aoun refused to recognize Hraoui's legitimacy, and Hraoui officially replaced Aoun as army commander in early December.

In late January 1990, General Aoun's forces attacked positions of the LF in east Beirut in an apparent attempt to remove the LF as a political force in the Christian enclave. In the heavy fighting that ensued in east Beirut and its environs, over 900 people died and over 3,000 were wounded.

In August 1990, the National Assembly approved, and President Hraoui signed into law, constitutional amendments embodying the political reform aspects of the Taif agreement. These amendments gave some presidential powers to the council of ministers, expanded the National Assembly from 99 to 108 seats, and divided those seats equally between Christians and Muslims.

In October 1990, a joint Lebanese-Syrian military operation against General Aoun forced him to capitulate and take refuge in the French embassy. On December 24, 1990, Omar Karami was appointed Lebanon's Prime Minister. General Aoun remained in the French embassy until August 27, 1991 when a "special pardon" was issued, allowing him to leave Lebanon safely and take up residence in exile in France. 1991 and 1992 saw considerable advancement in efforts to reassert state control over Lebanese territory. Militias—with the important exception of Hizballah—were dissolved in May 1991, and the armed forces moved against armed Palestinian elements in Sidon in July 1991. In May 1992 the last of the western hostages taken during the mid-1980s by Islamic extremists was released.

In October 1991, under the sponsorship of the United States and the then-Soviet Union, the Middle East peace talks were convened in Madrid, Spain. This was the first time that Israel and its Arab neighbors had direct bilateral negotiations to seek a just, lasting, and comprehensive peace in the Middle East. Lebanon, Jordan, Syria, and representatives of the Palestinians concluded round 11 of the negotiations in September 1993.

A social and political crisis, fueled by economic instability and the collapse of the Lebanese pound, led to Prime Minister Omar Karami's resignation

May 6, 1992. He was replaced by former Prime Minister Rashid al Sulh, who was widely viewed as a caretaker to oversee Lebanon's first parliamentary elections in 20 years. The elections were not prepared and carried out in a manner to ensure the broadest national consensus.

The turnout of eligible voters in some Christian locales was extremely low, with many voters not participating in the elections because they objected to voting in the presence of non-Lebanese forces. There also were widespread reports of irregularities. The electoral rolls were themselves in many instances unreliable because of the destruction of records and the use of forged identification papers. As a consequence, the results do not reflect the full spectrum of Lebanese politics.

Elements of the 1992 electoral law, which paved the way for elections, represented a departure from stipulations of the Taif agreement, expanding the number of parliamentary seats from 108 to 128 and employing a temporary districting arrangement designed to favor certain sects and political interests. According to the Taif agreement, the Syrian and Lebanese Governments were to agree in September 1992 to the redeployment of Syrian troops from greater Beirut. That date passed without an agreement. In early November 1992, Prime Minister Rafiq al-Hariri formed a new cabinet, retaining for himself the finance portfolio. The formation of the Hariri

Government was widely seen as a sign that the Government of Lebanon would seriously grapple with reconstructing the Lebanese state and reviving the economy.

# GOVERNMENT

Lebanon is a parliamentary democracy in which the people constitutionally have the right to change their government. However, until the parliamentary elections in 1992, the people had not been able to exercise this right during 16 years of civil war. According to the constitution, direct elections must be held for the parliament every 4 years. Parliament, in turn, elects a president every 6 years. The last presidential election was in 1989. The president and parliament choose the cabinet. Political parties may be formed and some in fact flourish.

Since the emergence of the post-1943 state, national policy has been determined largely by a relatively restricted group of traditional regional and sectarian leaders. The 1943 national pact allocated political power on an essentially confessional system, based on the 1932 census. Until 1990, seats in parliament were divided on a 6-to-5 ratio of Christians to Muslims. Positions in the government bureaucracy were allocated on a similar basis.

Efforts to alter or abolish the confessional system of allocating power have been at the center of Lebanese politics for more than 30 years. A series of amendments has substantially altered the constitution of 1926. Among the more significant is Article 95, which provides that the confessional communities of Lebanon shall be equitably represented in public employment and in the composition of the cabinet but that such a measure is not to impair the general welfare of the state. This article supplements the National Covenant of 1943, an unwritten agreement that established the political foundations of modern Lebanon. The covenant provides that public offices shall be distributed among the recognized religious groups and that the three top positions in the governmental systems shall be distributed as follows:

- The president is to be a Maronite Christian;

- The prime minister, a Sunni Muslim, and

- The president of the National Assembly, a Shi'a Muslim.

Those religious groups most favored by the 1943 formula sought to preserve it, while those who perceived themselves to be disadvantaged sought to revise it on the basis of updated demographic data or to abolish it entirely. The struggle gave a strongly sectarian coloration to Lebanese politics and to the continuing civil strife in the country.

Under the national reconciliation agreement reached in Taif, Saudi Arabia, in October 1989, members of parliament agreed to alter the national pact to create a 50-50 Christian-Muslim balance in the parliament and reorder the powers of the different branches of government. The Taif agreement, the political reform aspects of which were signed into law in September 1990, further modified the constitution to permit greater power-sharing and put in writing many of the provisions of the national pact.

Constitutional amendments embodying the political reforms stipulated in the Taif agreement became law in 1990. They included an expansion of the number of seats in parliament and the division of seats equally between Muslims and Christians and the transfer of some powers from the president to the prime minister and council of ministers.

Constitutionally, the president has a strong and influential position. The president appoints the council of ministers and designates one of them to be prime minister. The president also has the authority to promulgate laws passed by the National Assembly, to issue supplementary regulations to ensure the execution of laws and to negotiate and ratify treaties.

The National Assembly, only sporadically active since 1975, is elected by adult suffrage based on a system of proportional representation for the confessional groups of the country. Most deputies do not represent political parties as they are known in the West, nor do they form Western-style groups in the assembly. Political blocs are usually based on confessional and local interests or on personal allegiance rather than on political affinities.

The assembly traditionally has played a significant role in financial affairs, since it has the responsibility for levying taxes and passing the budget. It also exercises political control over the cabinet through formal questioning of ministers on policy issues and by requesting a confidence debate.

Lebanon's judicial system is based on the Napoleonic Code. Juries are not used in trials. The Lebanese court system has three levels—courts of first instance, courts of appeal, and the court of cassation. There also is a system of religious courts having jurisdiction on personal status matters within their own communities, i.e., rules on such matters as marriage, divorce and inheritance.

## Principal Government Officials

**For up-to-date information on Principal Government Officials, see the Chiefs of State and Cabinet Members of Foreign Governments section starting on page 1.**

Lebanon maintains an embassy in the United States at 2560 28th Street, NW, Washington, D.C. 20008, tel. (202) 939-6300. There also are three consulates general in the United States: 1959 East Jefferson, Suite 4A, Detroit, MI 48207, tel. (313) 567-0233/0234; 7060 Hollywood Blvd., Suite 510, Los Angeles, CA 90028, tel. (213) 467-1253/1254; and 9 East 76th Street, New York, N.Y. 10021, tel. (212) 744-7905/7906 and 744-7985.

# POLITICAL CONDITIONS

In addition to its indigenous political groupings, Lebanon contains branches of many other political parties of the Arab world. These cover the political spectrum from far left to far right, from totally secular to wholly religious and often are associated with a particular religion or geographic region. Palestinian refugees, numbering about 400,000 and predominantly Muslim, constitute an important and sensitive minority.

Lebanese political parties are generally vehicles for powerful leaders whose followers are often of the same religious sect. The interplay for position and power among these leaders and groups produces a political tapestry of extraordinary complexity.

In the past, this system worked to produce a viable democracy. Recent events, however, have upset the delicate Muslim-Christian balance and resulted in a tendency for Christians and Muslims to group themselves for safety into distinct zones. All factions have called for a reform of the political system.

Some Christians favor political and administrative decentralization of the government, with separate Muslim and Christian sectors operating within the framework of a confederation. Muslims, for the most part, prefer a unified, central government with an enhanced share of power for themselves commensurate with their percentage of the population. The reforms of the Taif agreement moved in this latter direction.

# ECONOMY

Lebanon's economy is liberal and open, and traditionally heavily oriented toward services. Lebanon served historically as a haven for Arab capital and as a Middle East transit point and enjoyed a vibrant and largely unregulated private sector. Lebanon's banking and tourism sectors flourished between the Gulf oil boom of 1973 and the beginning of Lebanon's civil war in 1975 by serving regional needs. Real GDP growth was 6% per year from 1965 to 1975.

Despite the civil war and mounting government budget deficits resulting from an inability to collect taxes, Lebanon kept its currency stable and inflation rate manageable until the early 1980s. Expatriate workers' remittances, the flow of capital from abroad to support various militias, the PLO's economic activities, and the narcotics trade all contributed to a positive balance of payments.

Events in the early 1980s, including the Israeli invasion of 1982, conspired against the Lebanese economy, resulting in accumulated infrastructure damage, massive dislocations of the population, growing migration of people and capital, and the uprooting of the PLO bureaucracy.

Recession in the Gulf led to a sharp reduction in remittances. Beirut's prominence as a center for finance, commerce, and tourism faded away. A calmer security environment in 1986-87, combined with a sharp depreciation of the Lebanese pound and a decline in labor costs resulting from inflation of 600%, produced a modest economic rebound. Growth was cut short by the general chaos of 1988-90.

Hostilities in 1989-90 in industrial and prosperous areas of Lebanon had a dramatic and negative impact on production and exports, triggered massive outflows of capital and people, and created circumstances resulting in the "dollarization" of the economy.

The end of hostilities in 1990, the beginning of the process of national reconciliation, and the removal of internal barriers to the movements of goods and people produced a short-term economic boom in 1991. This high level of activity proved unsustainable, largely because of enormous state deficits, poor economic management by the government, public sector corruption, the unavailability of commercial credit, and the collapse of public confidence in the nation's leadership.

A large, retroactive public sector salary increase in late 1991, financed through the sale of Treasury bills, precipitated a crisis: From January 1, 1992, to early October, inflation galloped to about 130%, and currency lost 180% of its value. The high cost of living became, and has remained, an issue of acute concern to the Lebanese public.

A surge of optimism swept across Lebanon with the advent of the Hariri Government in October 1992, amidst expectations that the billionaire businessman and his team of advisors would reform state finances and administration, embark on needed emergency infrastructure reconstruction, and attract foreign aid. Demand for Lebanese pounds jumped immediately, despite substantial intervention by the central bank to stabilize the exchange market (the pound was valued at the end of May 1993 at 1,740 to a dollar, after an early October 1992 low of 2,400 to a dollar). There was also evidence of deflation.

The Ministry of Finance has achieved remarkable advances toward closing the budget deficit, despite rigidities in debt servicing, the public sector payroll, and large subsidies to the electricity and telephone companies. The deficit in the first quarter of 1993 amounted to $104 million, compared to $550 million in the first quarter of 1992.

The absence of functioning services is a serious obstacle to growth. The Hariri Government has made infrastructure rehabilitation a centerpiece of its efforts, using the December 1991 emergency rehabilitation plan (ERP) as a blueprint. It calls for spending $2.3 billion in the next 2.5 years, primarily on rejuvenating the electricity, telecommunications, water supply, waste water, and solid waste management sectors.

The government has already begun pre-qualifying international firms for projects in those fields. The government has in hand commitments for over $900 million in allocated and non-allocated foreign assistance, almost entirely in the form of loans.

In February 1993, the World Bank signed an agreement to loan $175 million in support of ERP. Future aid, necessary for partial financing of an ambitious $13-billion, 10-year development plan revealed by the government in March 1993, will depend largely on the Hariri team's ability to point to a record of economic stabilization and well-managed use of current assistance flows for reconstruction.

Hariri's economic policy is firmly rooted in the principle that infrastructure spending and budget austerity will stimulate private-sector growth. The prime minister's advisers hope to develop more sophisticated capital markets to attract a portion of Lebanese capital held abroad, which amounts to tens of billions of dollars, institutionalize exchange rate stability, and help manage a debt burden which is bound to grow as ambitious rehabilitation plans proceed.

The formation of a private real estate company to rebuild the downtown commercial center of Beirut is a centerpiece of the Hariri team's strategy for hooking economic recovery to the engine of private sector investment. The company will expropriate property in the area and compensate owners with shares in the company. The company is to obtain capitalization equal to half of the estimated property value in the development zone, estimated at $4 billion. Gulf Arab businessmen have already committed about $500 million to the controversial project.

Lebanon may have experienced a modest balance of trade deficit in the first quarter of 1993, estimated by a private bank at $1.8 million. A large trade deficit was virtually eliminated by capital inflows. Gold reserves amounted to $3 billion, and foreign exchange reserves at $1.2 billion. Foreign debt may approach $700 million today, and domestic public debt exceeds $2.5 billion.

Another issue bringing increasing attention to Lebanon is its role as a major drug producing and trafficking country. In addition to traditional hashish production, opium is cultivated and processed into heroin in Lebanon, and Lebanese traffickers have become increasingly involved in the cocaine trade.

The dramatic expansion of drug activities in Lebanon can be traced primarily to the breakdown of central government authority. Because of the potential for huge profits from the drug trade, many militias in Lebanon, including known terrorist elements, are thought to be engaged in one or more aspects of the drug trade to finance their operations.

Since 1976, Syrian troops have occupied Lebanon's prime drug-producing area, the Biqa' Valley. They constitute the only formal security authority in this area.

# FOREIGN RELATIONS

Lebanon's foreign policy reflects its geographic location, the composition of its population, and its reliance on commerce and trade. Lebanon hopes to reestablish good ties with Western countries and in the Middle East. Lebanon remains friendly with Western countries and follows a generally cautious course in its relations with countries of the former Soviet bloc.

Lebanon's foreign policy is also heavily influenced by Syria, which maintains forces throughout parts of Lebanon. Lebanon did not participate in the 1967 or 1973 Arab-Israeli war or in the 1991 Gulf War. Lebanon and Israel are now conducting bilateral negotiations in the Arab-Israeli peace process.

# U.S.-LEBANESE RELATIONS

The United States seeks to maintain its traditionally close ties with Lebanon, to help preserve its independence, sovereignty, national unity, and territorial integrity. The United States also supports the withdrawal of all non-Lebanese forces from Lebanon and the disarming and disbanding of all armed militias. The United States believes that a peaceful, prosperous, and stable Lebanon can make an important contribution to stability and peace in the Middle East.

The United States supports the programs of the central government to restore security and unity to Lebanon and to rebuild that country's national institutions. One measure of U.S. concern and involvement has been a program of relief and rehabilitation assistance which, since 1975, has totaled more than $250 million.

This support reflects not only humanitarian concerns and historical ties but the importance the United States attaches to the restoration of a sovereign, independent, unified Lebanon. Current funding is used to support the activities of U.S. and Lebanese private voluntary organizations engaged in humanitarian relief programs.

Over the years, the United States also has helped finance construction of the American University Hospital in Beirut and has assisted the American University of Beirut (AUB) by financing part of its operating budget and by providing scholarships to many of its students. When the AUB administration building was bombed in November 1991, the U.S. allocated an additional $3 million to help defray the costs of rebuilding this symbolic center of the university.

In September 1989, all American officials at the U.S. embassy in Beirut were withdrawn, when safety and operation of the mission could not be guaranteed. A new U.S. ambassador returned to Beirut in November 1990, and the embassy has been continuously open since March 1991. However, due to the size of the staff and security concerns, normal consular and commercial services and other embassy functions are not available in Beirut.

## Principal U.S. Officials

**For up-to-date information on Principal U.S. Officials, see the U.S. Embassies, Consulates, and Foreign Service section starting on page 139.**

For up-to-date information on Principal U.S. Officials, see the U.S. Embassies, Consulates, and Foreign Service section starting on page 139.

The U.S. embassy operates in Awkar, Lebanon (tel. 402-200, 403-300).

# LESOTHO

August 1999

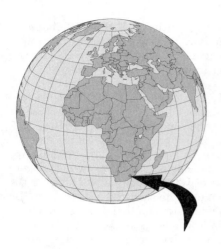

Official Name:
**Kingdom of Lesotho**

# PROFILE

## Geography

**Area:** 30,355 sq. km. (11,718 sq. mi.), about the size of Maryland.
**Cities:** Capital—Maseru (1997 pop. est. 386,000). Other cities—Teyateyaneng (240,754), Leribe (300,160), Mafeteng (211,970), Mohale's Hoek (184,034).
**Terrain:** High veld, plateau and mountains.
**Climate:** Temperate; summers hot, winters cool to cold; humidity generally low and evenings cool year round. Rainy season in summer, winters dry. Southern hemisphere seasons are reversed.

## People

**Nationality:** Noun—Mosotho (sing.); Basotho (pl.) Adjective—Basotho.
**Population (1998 est.):** 2,089,829.
**Annual growth rate (1998 est.):** 1.9%.
**Ethnic groups:** Basotho 99.7%; Europeans 1,600; Asians 800.
**Religions:** 80% Christian, including Roman Catholic (majority), Lesotho Evangelical, Anglican, other denominations.
**Languages:** Official—Sesotho and English; others—Zulu, Xhosa.

**Education:** Years compulsory—None. Literacy (1998)—71.3%.
**Health:** Infant mortality rate (1997 est.)—80.3/1,000. Life expectancy (1997 est.)—51.66 years.
**Work force (1997 est.):** 689,000. 86% subsistence agriculture.

## Government

**Type:** Modified constitutional monarchy.
**Constitution:** April 2, 1993.
**Independence:** October 4, 1966.
**Branches:** Executive—monarch is chief of state; prime minister is head of government and cabinet. Legislative—Bicameral parliament consists of nonelected senate and elected assembly. Judicial—High Court, Court of Appeals, Magistrate's Court, traditional and customary courts.
**Administrative subdivisions:** 10 districts.
**Political parties:** Lesotho Congress for Democracy (LCD), Basotho National Party (BNP), Basotholand Congress Party (BCP), Marematlou Freedom Party (MFP), United Democratic Party (UDP), Popular Front for Democracy (PFD), Sefate Democratic Union (SDU).
**Suffrage:** 18 years of age.
Central government budget (FY 96–97 est.): Revenues—$507 million; Expenditures—$487 million.
**Flag:** Diagonal fields of green and blue with a traditional Basotho shield in brown on a diagonal field of white occupying remaining half of flag.

## Economy

**GDP (1997 est.):** Purchasing power parity—$5.1 billion.
**Annual growth rate (1997 est.):** 9% (although this decreased significantly in 1998 because of political unrest).
**Per capita GDP (1997 est.):** Purchasing power parity—$2,500.
**Average inflation rate (1998 est.):** 8.7%.
**Natural resources:** Water, agricultural and grazing land, some diamonds and other minerals. Lesotho is an exporter of excess labor.
**Agriculture (1997 est.: 14% of GDP):** Products—corn, wheat, sorghum, barley, peas, beans, asparagus, wool, mohair, livestock. Arable land—11%.
**Industry (1997 est.: 46% of GDP):** Products—food, beverages, textiles, handicrafts, construction, tourism.
**Trade (1996 est.):** Exports—$218 million; clothing, furniture, footwear and wool. Partners—South Africa, Botswana, Swaziland, Namibia, North America, EU. Imports—$1.1 billion; corn, clothing, building materials, vehicles, machinery, medicines, petroleum products. Partners—South Africa, Asia, EU.
**Fiscal year:** 1 April – 31 March.
**Economic aid received (1998):** Primary donors—World Bank, IMF,

EU, UN, UK, other bilateral donors. U.S. assistance—$400,000.

# HISTORY

Basutoland (now Lesotho—pronounced le–SOO–too) was sparsely populated by San bushmen (Qhuaique) until the end of the 16th century. Between the 16th and 19th centuries, refugees from surrounding areas gradually formed the Basotho ethnic group.

In 1818, Moshoeshoe I (pronounced mo–SHWAY–shway) consolidated various Basotho groupings and became their King. During Moshoeshoe's reign (1823–1870), a series of wars with South Africa (1856–68) resulted in the loss of extensive Basotho land, now known as the "Lost Territory." In order to protect his people, Moshoeshoe appealed to Queen Victoria for assistance, and in 1868 the land that is present–day Lesotho was placed under British protection. After a 1955 request by the Basutoland Council to legislate its internal affairs, in 1959, a new constitution gave Basutoland its first elected legislature. This was followed in April 1965 with general legislative elections with universal adult suffrage in which the Basutoland National Party (BNP) won 31 and the Basutoland Congress Party (BCP) won 25 of the 65 seats contested.

On October 4, 1966, the Kingdom of Lesotho attained full independence, governed by a constitutional monarchy with a bicameral parliament consisting of a Senate and an elected National Assembly. Early results of the first post–independence elections in January 1970 indicated that the BNP might lose control. Under the leadership of Prime Minister Chief Leabua Jonathan, the ruling Basotho National Party (BNP) refused to cede power to the rival Basotholand Congress Party (BCP), although the BCP was widely believed to have won the elections. Citing election irregularities, Prime Minister Leabua Jonathan nullified the elections, declared a national state of emergency, suspended the constitution,

and dissolved the Parliament. In 1973, an appointed Interim National Assembly was established. With an overwhelming progovernment majority, it was largely the instrument of the BNP, led by Prime Minister Jonathan. In addition to the Jonathan regime's alienation of Basotho powerbrokers and the local population, South Africa had virtually closed the country's land borders because of Lesotho support of cross–border operations of the African National Congress (ANC). Moreover, South Africa publicly threatened to pursue more direct action against Lesotho if the Jonathan government did not root out the ANC presence in the country. This internal and external opposition to the government combined to produce violence and internal disorder in Lesotho that eventually led to a military takeover in 1986.

Under a January 1986 Military Council decree, state executive and legislative powers were transferred to the King who was to act on the advice of the Military Council, a self–appointed group of leaders of the Royal Lesotho Defense Force (RLDF). A military government chaired by Justin Lekhanya ruled Lesotho in coordination with King Moshoeshoe II and a civilian cabinet appointed by the King.

In February 1990, King Moshoeshoe II was stripped of his executive and legislative powers and exiled by Lekhanya, and the Council of Ministers was purged. Lekhanya accused those involved of undermining discipline within the armed forces, subverting existing authority, and causing an impasse on foreign policy that had been damaging to Lesotho's image abroad. Lekhanya announced the establishment of the National Constituent Assembly to formulate a new constitution for Lesotho with the aim of returning the country to democratic, civilian rule by June 1992. Before this transition, however, Lekhanya was ousted in 1991 by a mutiny of junior army officers that left Phisoane Ramaema as Chairman of the Military Council.

Because Moshoeshoe II refused to return to Lesotho under the new rules of the government in which the King was endowed only with ceremonial powers, Moshoeshoe's son was installed as King Letsie III. In 1995, Moshoeshoe II returned to Lesotho as a regular citizen until 1995 when King Letsie abdicated the throne in favor of his father. King Letsie III did ascend to the throne again and was crowned at a coronation in October 1997 following the death of his father the previous year.

In 1993, a new constitution was implemented leaving the King without any executive authority and proscribing him from engaging in political affairs. Multiparty elections were then held in which the BCP ascended to power with a landslide victory. Prime Minister Ntsu Mokhehle headed the new BCP government that had gained every seat in the 65–member National Assembly. In early 1994, political instability increased as first the army, followed by the police and prisons services, engaged in mutinies. In August 1994, King Letsie III, in collaboration with some members of the military, staged a coup, suspended Parliament, and appointed a ruling council. As a result of domestic and international pressures, however, the constitutionally elected government was restored within a month.

In 1995, there were isolated incidents of unrest, including a police strike in May to demand higher wages. For the most part, however, during 1995 and 1996, there were no serious challenges to Lesotho's constitutional order with the exception of a violent police mutiny in January 1997 that was put down by armed soldiers. The mutineers were arrested.

In 1997, tension within the BCP leadership caused a split in which Dr. Mokhehle abandoned the BCP and established the Lesotho Congress for Democracy (LCD) followed by two–thirds of the parliament. This move allowed Mokhehle to remain as Prime Minister and leader of a new ruling party, while relegating the BCP to opposition status. The remaining members of the BCP

## Travel Notes

**Travel Advice:** For up-to-date information from the U.S. State Department on possible inconvenient or hazardous situations, see the **Travel Warnings and Consular Information Sheets from the U.S. Government** section starting on page 1723. For the latest information on health requirements and conditions, see the **International Travelers' Health Information** section starting on page 1385. For further information dealing with non-urgent matter, see the **Tips for Travelers to...** section starting on page 1588.

refused to accept their new status as the opposition party and ceased attending sessions. Multiparty elections were again held in May 1998.

Although Mokhehle completed his term as Prime Minister, due to his failing health, he did not vie for a second term in office. The elections saw a landslide victory for the LCD, gaining 79 of the 80 seats contested in the newly expanded Parliament. As a result of the elections, Mokhehle's Deputy Prime Minister, Pakalitha Mosisili, became the new Prime Minister. The landslide electoral victory caused opposition parties to claim that there were substantial irregularities in the handling of the ballots and that the results were fraudulent. The conclusion of the Langa Commission, a commission appointed by SADC to investigate the electoral process, however, was consistent with the view of international observers and local courts that the outcome of the elections was not affected by these incidents. Despite the fact that the election results were found to reflect the will of the people, opposition protests in the country intensified. On September 11, 1998, protests culminated in a violent demonstration occurring outside the royal palace in early August 1998 and an army mutiny by a number of junior members of the armed service, who were aligned with the opposition. These protests led to an unprecedented level of politically motivated violence, looting, casualties, and destruction of property in the country. They also compromised the neutrality of the

King in political affairs. Consequently, the Government of Lesotho requested that a SADC task force intervene to prevent a military coup and restore stability to the country. To this end, Operation Boleas, consisting of South African and Botswanan troops, entered Lesotho on September 22, 1998 to put down the mutiny and restore the democratically elected government.

After stability returned to Lesotho, the SADC task force withdrew from the country in May 1999, leaving only a small task force (joined by Zimbabwean troops) to provide training to the LDF. In the meantime, an Interim Political Authority (IPA), charged with reviewing the electoral

structure in the country, was created in December 1998. The army mutineers were brought before a court martial. In general, Lesotho's political situation has stabilized substantially, and the next elections are expected to take place in 2000.

# GOVERNMENT AND POLITICAL CONDITIONS

The Lesotho Government is a modified form of constitutional monarchy. The Prime Minister, Pakalitha Mosisili, is head of government and has executive authority. The King serves a largely ceremonial function; he no longer possesses any executive authority and is proscribed from actively participating in political initiatives.

The Lesotho Congress for Democracy (LCD) won the majority in parliament in the May 1998 elections, leaving the once–dominant Basotho National Party (BNP) and Basotholand Congress Party (BCP) far behind in total votes. Although international observers as well as a regional commission declared the elections to have reflected the will of the people, many members of the opposition have accused the LCD of electoral fraud. The 1998 elections were the third multiparty elections in Lesotho's history. The LCD, BNP, and BCP remain the principal rival political organizations in Lesotho. Distinctions and differences in political orientation between the major parties have blurred in recent years.

The constitution provides for an independent judicial system. The judiciary is made up of the High Court, the Court of Appeal, magistrate's courts, and traditional courts that exist predominately in rural areas. There is no trial by jury; rather, judges make rulings alone, or, in the case of criminal trials, with two other judges as observers. The constitution also protects basic civil liberties, including freedom of speech, association, and the press; freedom of peaceful assembly; and freedom of religion.

## Principal Government Officials

For up-to-date information on Principal Government Officials, see the Chiefs of State and Cabinet Members of Foreign Governments section starting on page 1.

For administrative purposes, Lesotho is divided into 10 districts, each headed by a district secretary and a district military officer appointed by

the central government and the RLDF, respectively.

Lesotho maintains an embassy in the United States at 2511 Massachusetts Avenue NW, Washington, DC 20008 (tel: 202–797–5533). Lesotho's mission to the United Nations is located at 204 East 39th Street, New York, NY 10016 (tel: 212–661–1690).

# DEFENSE

The security forces are composed of the Lesotho Defense Force (LDF) and the Lesotho Mounted Police. The LDF consists of an army, an air wing, and a newly formed paramilitary wing. The LDF is answerable to the Prime Minister through the Ministry of Defense, while the Lesotho Mounted Police report to the Minister of Home Affairs. There also is a National Security Service, Intelligence, which is directly accountable to the Prime Minister. Relations between the police and the army have been tense, and in 1997 the army was called upon to put down a serious police mutiny.

# ECONOMY

Lesotho's economy is based on agriculture, livestock, manufacturing, and the earnings of laborers employed in South Africa. Lesotho is geographically surrounded by South Africa and economically integrated with it as well. The majority of households subsist on farming or migrant labor, primarily miners in South Africa for 3 to 9 months. The western lowlands form the main agricultural zone. Almost 50% of the population earn some income through crop cultivation or animal husbandry with nearly two–thirds of the country's income coming from the agricultural sector.

Water is Lesotho's only significant natural resource. This is being exploited through the 30–year, multi–billion dollar Lesotho Highlands Water Project (LHWP). The LHWP, initiated in 1986, has provided approximately 75% of Lesotho's

private investment the following year. It is designed to capture, store, and transfer water from the Orange River system and send it to South Africa's Free State and greater Johannesburg area, which features a large concentration of South African industry, population and agriculture. At the completion of the project, Lesotho should be almost completely self–sufficient in the production of electricity and also gain income from the sale of electricity to South Africa. The World Bank, African Development Bank, European Investment Bank, and many other bilateral donors are financing the project.

Until the political insecurity in September 1998, Lesotho's economy had grown steadily since 1992. The riots, however, destroyed nearly 80% of commercial infrastructure in Maseru and two other major towns in the country, having a disastrous effect on the country's economy. Nonetheless, the country has completed several IMF Structural Adjustment Programs, and inflation declined substantially over the course of the 1990s. Lesotho's trade deficit, however, is quite large, with exports representing only a small fraction of imports.

Lesotho has received economic aid from a variety of sources, including the United States, the World Bank, the United Kingdom, the European Union, and Germany.

Lesotho has nearly 6,000 kilometers of unpaved and modern all–weather roads. There is a short rail line (freight) linking Lesotho with South Africa that is totally owned and operated by South Africa. Lesotho, is a member of the Southern African Customs Union (SACU) in which tariffs have been eliminated on the trade of goods between other member countries, which also include Botswana, Namibia, South Africa, and Swaziland. Lesotho, Swaziland, Namibia, and South Africa also form a common currency and exchange control area known as the Rand Monetary Area that uses the South African Rand as the common currency. In 1980, Lesotho introduced its own currency, the loti (plural: maloti). One hundred lisente equal one loti. The Loti is at par with the Rand.

# FOREIGN RELATIONS

Lesotho's geographic location makes it extremely vulnerable to political and economic developments in South Africa. It is a member of many regional economic organizations including the Southern African Development Community (SADC) and the Southern African Customs Union (SACU). Lesotho also is active in the United Nations, the Organization of African Unity, the Nonaligned Movement, and many other international organizations. In addition to the United States, South Africa, China, the United Kingdom, and the European Union all currently retain resident diplomatic missions in Lesotho.

Lesotho has historically maintained generally close ties with the United States, the United Kingdom, Germany, and other Western states. Although Lesotho decided in 1990 to break relations with the People's Republic of China (P.R.C.) and reestablish relations with Taiwan, it has since restored ties with the P.R.C. Lesotho also recognized Palestine as a state, established relations with Namibia, and was a strong public supporter of the end of apartheid in South Africa.

# U.S.-LESOTHO RELATIONS

The United States was one of the first four countries to establish an embassy in Maseru after Lesotho gained its independence from Great Britain in 1966. Since this time, Lesotho and the United States have consistently maintained warm bilateral relations. In 1996, the United States closed its bilateral aid program in Lesotho. The Southern African regional office of USAID now administers most of the U.S. assistance to Lesotho through SADC regional programs, although estimated U.S. assistance to Lesotho in 1998 was $400,000. The Peace Corps has operated in Lesotho since 1966 and should reach its target of 90 volunteers in country by December 1999, particularly in the sectors of agriculture, education, rural development, and the environment. The Government of Lesotho encourages greater American participation in commercial life and welcomes interest from potential U.S. investors and suppliers.

## Principal U.S. Officials

For up-to-date information on Principal U.S. Officials, see the U.S. Embassies, Consulates, and Foreign Service section starting on page 139.

The mailing address of the U.S. Embassy is P.O. Box 333, Maseru 100, Lesotho. Telephone: (266) 312-666, Fax: (266) 310-116. E-mail: amles@lesoff.co.za.

# LIBERIA

June 1987

## Official Name:
## Republic of Liberia

# PROFILE

## Geography

**Area:** 111,370 sq. km. (43,000 sq. mi.).

**Cities:** Capital—Monrovia (pop. 400,000). Other cities—Harbel (60,000), Buchanan (25,000), Yekepa (16,000).

**Terrain:** Coastal plain rising to rolling plateau, and low mountains near inland borders.

**Climate:** Warm and humid all year.

## People

**Nationality:** Noun and adjective—Liberian(s).

**Population (1986 est.):** 2 million.

**Annual growth rate:** 3%.

**Ethnic groups:** 5% descendants of freed American slaves, 95% indigenous tribes, the largest of which are Kpelle, Bassa, Gio, Kru, Grebo, Mano, Krahn, Gola, Gbandi, Loma, Kissi, Vai, Mandingo, and Belle.

**Religions:** Traditional 65%, Muslim 20%, Christian 15% (est.).

**Languages:** English (official); more than 20 local languages of the Niger-Congo language group.

**Education:** Years compulsory—6. Attendance—primary 35%, secondary 15%. Literacy—25%.

**Health:** Infant mortality rate—132/1,000. Life expectancy—49 yrs.

**Work force:** Agriculture—82%. Industry and commerce—5%. Services—6%. Public sector—7%.

## Government

**Type:** Civilian republic.

**Constitution:** January 6, 1986.

**Branches:** Executive—president, vice president, Cabinet. Legislative—Senate, 26 seats (two from each county). House of Representatives, 62 seats. Judicial—Supreme Court heads civilian appellate court system.

**Administrative subdivisions:** 13 counties.

**Political parties:** National Democratic Party of Liberia (NDPL), Liberia Action Party (LAP)., Liberian Unification Party (LUP), Unity Party (UP).

**Central government budget:** $380 million.

**Defense:** Unknown.

**Flag:** Eleven horizontal red and white stripes, with one white star in a blue field in upper left corner.

## Economy

**GDP:** $320 million at constant factor cost in 1971 dollars (1984 monetary sector est.).

**Annual growth rate (1984):** 0%.

**Per capita income:** $325.

**Inflation rate (1984):** 1%.

**Natural resources:** Iron ore, rubber, timber, diamonds, gold.

**Agriculture (20% of GDP):** Products—rubber, rice, oil palm, cassava, coffee, cocoa, timber.

**Industry (60% of GDP):** Types—iron, gold and diamond mining, food processing, consumer gold production.

**Trade (1984):** Exports—$450 million: iron ore, rubber, timber, diamonds, gold. Major markets—FRG, US, Italy, Belgium. Imports (1984)—$360 million: machinery, petroleum products, transportation equipment, foodstuffs. Major suppliers—US, Western Europe.

**Official exchange rate:** L$1=US$1

**US economic aid received (FY 1985):** $63 million.

**US military aid received (FY 1985):** $13.2 million.

## Membership in International Organizations

UN and most of its specialized agencies, Organization of African Unity (OAU), Economic Community of West African States (ECOWAS), Mano River Union, West African Rice Development Association (WARDA).

# GEOGRAPHY

Liberia lies at the southwestern extremity of the western bulge of

Africa and is bordered by Sierra Leone, Guinea, and the Ivory Coast. It has a 595-kilometer (370-mi.) long coastline on the Atlantic Ocean.

From a narrow, level coastal strip dotted with lagoons, tidal creeks, and marshes, the rolling country rises in a series of plateaus. Low mountains are found intermittently throughout the country but rarely are higher than 914 meters (3,000 ft.) except for the Nimba and Wologisi Mountains, which lie along the country's eastern border and which exceed 1,370 meters (4,500 ft.). Six principal rivers—the Mano, Lofa, St. Paul, Farmington, St. John, and Cestos—flow into the Atlantic Ocean.

Liberia lies within the tropical rain forest belt and has distinct wet and dry seasons. Rainfall, which occurs largely between April and November, averages 380-430 centimeters (150-170 in.). Annually the average daily temperature is about 27°C (80°F).

# PEOPLE

The population of Liberia includes at least 16 distinct ethnic groups and descendants of emancipated slaves from the United States. Some 15,000 foreigners reside in Liberia, most of whom are members of the Lebanese and Indian trading communities. About 3,000 U.S. citizens live there; most are U.S. Government employees and dependents, missionaries, or business representatives.

About 70% of the population are subsistence farmers, who retain traditional cultural values. Of the Liberians who practice Christianity, most are Protestant. In recent years, Islam has gained adherents in some areas, particularly in the northeast counties bordering Guinea.

Education is mandatory between ages 6 and 16, although the percentage of students completing their education is low because of the country's limited resources. Efforts are being made to overcome these obstacles. Liberia has two major 4-year schools: the public University of Liberia,

which has a limited master's degree program, and Cuttington College near Suakoko, linked to the Episcopal Church. There is also a large 4-year Baptist Theological Seminary near Monrovia. Many students study abroad, particularly in the United States.

# HISTORY

It is believed that the forebears of many present-day Liberians migrated into the area from the north and east between the 12th and 17th centuries. None of the sub-Saharan empires of that period encompassed Liberia. Portuguese explorers visited Liberia's coast in 1461, and during the next 300 years, European merchants and coastal Africans engaged in trade.

The history of modern Liberia dates from 1816, when the American Colonization Society, a private U.S. organization, was given a charter by the U.S. Congress to send freed slaves to the west coast of Africa. The U.S. Government, under President James Monroe, provided funds and assisted in negotiations with native chiefs for the ceding of land for this purpose. The first settlers landed at the site of Monrovia in 1822. In 1838, the settlers united to form the Commonwealth of Liberia, under a governor appointed by the American Colonization Society.

In 1847, Liberia became Africa's first independent republic, with a constitution modeled after that of the United States. The United Kingdom officially recognized the Republic of Liberia in 1848, as did France in 1852. The United States granted recognition in 1862. The republic's first 100 years have been described as a "century of survival" because of attempts by neighboring colonial powers (France and Britain) to encroach on Liberia.

William R. Tolbert, Jr., 19th president of Liberia, acceded to office in July 1971, upon the death of his predecessor, William V.S. Tubman, who had served as president since 1944.

Tolbert was overthrown in a coup led by Master Sergeant Samuel K. Doe on April 12, 1980, when the constitution was suspended and martial law imposed. The military government pledged to restore civilian rule in 1985. A new constitution was drafted and reviewed by an elected assembly; the ban on political activity was lifted and an Interim National Assembly appointed in July 1984; and four political parties were able to register and compete in presidential and legislative elections held on October 15, 1985. The new government and the new constitution were inaugurated on January 6, 1986, with Samuel K. Doe as president.

# GOVERNMENT

Administration of the Liberian Government has traditionally been highly centralized. The new national legislature has been working to establish its leadership in the country's affairs under the new constitution. The government's policies are administered with the assistance of a 20-member cabinet, whose ministers are appointed by the president.

The Supreme Court, with a chief justice and four associate justices, hears appeals from the circuit courts and has original jurisdiction over all judicial matters affecting the state. All judges are appointed by the president. The judiciary faces the task of reconciling contradictions in the various sets of laws created and enforced in Liberia's recent past: those in force before the 1980 coup; those imposed by the former ruling People's Redemption Council during the period of martial law; and those subsumed under the new constitution. The judiciary also is being called upon to establish its independence from the other branches of government with the ending of military government.

Each county is administered by a superintendent appointed by the president. Public schools, hospitals, roads, utilities, and police are operated by the central government. Under the constitution, only "persons of Negro descent" can become citizens, and only citizens may own land. However, there is some effort being made to change this provision.

## Principal Government Officials

For up-to-date information on Principal Government Officials, see the Chiefs of State and Cabinet Members of Foreign Governments section starting on page 1.

Liberia maintains an embassy in the United States at 5201—16th Street NW., Washington, D.C. 20011 (tel. 202-723-9437).

# POLITICAL CONDITIONS

Samuel K. Doe is president and commander in chief of the Liberian Armed Forces. He is also the standard bearer of the National Democratic Party of Liberia (NDPL), which holds an overwhelming majority of the country's legislative seats.

The October 15, 1985 elections—the first in Liberia's history based on universal suffrage—were extremely controversial. The government used its authority *inter alia,* to curtail political debate, to limit the number of political parties, and to detain opposition leaders and independent journalists and hold them incommunicado. Although voting on election, day appeared generally free and open, with very high popular interest and participation, there were immediate and widespread allegations of illegal procedures in regard to counting the votes, which was not performed in accordance with the election laws. It was announced that Samuel Doe had won the presidency with 50.9% of the vote and that his party had won 80% of the legislative seats. Opposition parties denounced the results as fraudulent and refused to permit their successful legislative candidates to take their seats under party

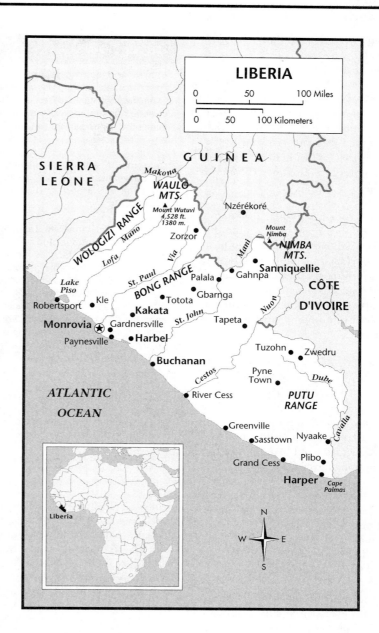

affiliation. There was a bloody, unsuccessful coup attempt on November 12, 1985, which left many dead and most major opposition politicians in prison without charges or trial.

Since the inauguration of the Second Republic on January 6, 1986, efforts at national political reconciliation have continued.

# ECONOMY

Liberia's economy is based primarily on iron ore, rubber, and timber. The iron and rubber industries are well developed. Rubber production was introduced to Liberia in 1926 by Firestone, which manages the world's largest contiguous plantations at Harbel. After World War II, it was joined in Liberia by B. F. Goodrich and Uniroyal. Goodrich sold its investment to Guthrie, a Malaysian company. These large concessions, along with many private Liberian growers, make the labor-intensive rubber industry the largest employer in the country.

A more important source of foreign exchange is iron ore, which constituted 62% of Liberia's total exports in 1984. Iron ore was first mined in Liberia in 1951.

Exploitation of Liberia's extensive timber resources has only recently begun. Until recently, rapid growth in this sector was interrupted by the world recession and the fall in currency values in Europe, the major market.

Other products that may prove increasingly important include diamonds, gold, coffee, cocoa, and palm oil. Liberia is not self-sufficient in food and imports large quantities of rice, its staple. Other major imports are petroleum products, machinery, transport equipment, and manufactured goods.

The worldwide recession in the iron ore industry and historic low prices for rubber have slowed Liberia's economic growth in recent years. However, recovery of the iron ore market and continued expansion in other export sectors would contribute to a resumption of growth.

The United States, for many years Liberia's preeminent trading partner, is expected to remain a leading source of capital and technical assistance. Liberia's currency remains at official par with the U.S. dollar.

In recent years, Liberia's infrastructure has developed, partly as a result of U.S. assistance. Projects completed with the help of U.S. grants or loans include the Freeport of Monrovia, Roberts International Airport, major segments of the interior road system, Monrovia's water supply and sewerage systems, a hydroelectric dam at Mt. Coffee near Monrovia, elementary and secondary schools, and the National Medical Center in Monrovia, which includes the 271-bed John F. Kennedy hospital and training center.

The U.S. Ambassador's Self-Help Fund—a small, U.S. Government fund administered by the U.S. Embassy in Monrovia—has supplied grants to assist small-scale local

## Travel Notes

**Climate and clothing:** Lightweight, loose-fitting, washable clothing is recommended. In the low mountains of the northeast area sweaters or light jackets may be needed during the evenings. Dry cleaning is available in Monrovia.

**Customs:** All Americans entering Liberia must have visas, which are not generally issued at the airport, and international health cards.

**Health:** Medical facilities are chronically short of medications and supplies. By Western standards, facilities are marginal. Some drugs are available in Monrovia but under different names and manufacturers. Many common items used by Americans are not available. Cholera and yellow fever immunizations are required. Drink only boiled water; take malaria suppressants; do not swim in fresh water up-country; and avoid swimming in the ocean.

**Telecommunications:** Long distance telephone service and cable service are available. Monrovia is five standard time zones ahead of the eastern standard time. There is no daylight saving time.

**Transportation:** International flights are available to and from Roberts International Airport, about 57 kilometers (36 miles) from Monrovia. Taxi service is available at the airport. Limited airline service is available to a few points within the country from Spriggs-Payne Airport in Monrovia.

Taxi service is available and reasonably priced in Monrovia. Tipping is not customary. Travelers should agree on a price in advance when traveling outside the metropolitan area. Unpaved interior roads are difficult for travel during the rainy season (May-October). Tourist facilities are available in Monrovia and environs but limited outside the capital.

**Travel Advice:** For up-to-date information from the U.S. State Department on possible inconvenient or hazardous situations, see the **Travel Warnings and Consular Information Sheets from the U.S. Government** section starting on page 1723. For the latest information on health requirements and conditions, see the **International Travelers' Health Information** section starting on page 1385. For further information dealing with non-urgent matter, see the **Tips for Travelers to...** section starting on page 1588.

projects. Through this program, villages have installed water systems and built schools, clinics, public toilets, and fish ponds that otherwise would have been prohibitively expensive. The Agency for International Development (AID) directs its resources toward agriculture, health, human resources, and private-sector development projects. In addition, about 140 Peace Corps volunteers assist Liberia's efforts in education, public health, agriculture, and rural development.

The national economic policy remains largely consistent with that of former governments. The "open-door" policy established in the past officially encourages private foreign investment to stimulate development. This policy and the acceptance of the free market system attracted substantial private investment through the mid-1970s. U.S. investors include Citibank, Chase Manhattan Bank, the International Bank of Washington,

and Firestone Tire and Rubber Company.

# FOREIGN RELATIONS

One of the basic tenets of Liberia's policy is the belief that the future of small nations can best be served by international cooperation. For this reason, Liberia was a charter member of both the League of Nations and the United Nations and remains a staunch supporter of the latter's specialized agencies.

Liberia has been a leader in Pan-African affairs and played an important role in the founding of the Organization of African Unity. The government is represented at most major conferences of African leaders and frequently has taken the initiative in encouraging such gatherings. Liberia's interest in the development of regional economic organizations

## Editor's Update — Dec. 1995–June 2001

*A report on important events that have taken place since the last State Department revision of this Background Note.*

Liberia's four principal militias approved a peace plan on May 8, 1996. The plan requires an immediate halt to fighting, the removal of weapons and ammunition from the capital of Monrovia, and the return of about $20 million worth of vehicles and equipment stolen from international relief organizations in the capital in a month of fighting.

Toward this end, the committee of the Economic Community of West African States (ECOWAS) urged the reinstatement of Roosevelt Johnson, a militia leader and former Minister of Rural Development, to his Cabinet position. Johnson's principal opposition, Charles Taylor, a deputy chairman of the governing council and initiator of the civil war in 1989, said his group would not oppose Johnson's reinstatement.

Additionally, the plan seeks stronger international support for the inadequately equipped 8,500-member West African peacekeeping force in Algeria.

At the end of April 1996, the Clinton Administration expressed willingness to provide $30 million to the West African peacekeepers to increase troop levels, provide more equipment and assist in training. It was still uncertain, however, where these new forces would come from or indeed whether the promised aid would be enough to make a difference.

In an unprecedented move, the regional organization ECOWAS acted with the official sanction of the United Nations to bring about a cease fire in a civil conflict.

Nigeria has been at the forefront of this effort from the beginning, spending about $4 billion. But with major domestic political and economic crises, diplomats say Nigeria is currently unable to carry out Liberia's peace accord without significantly more outside assistance.

After two months of peace, West African leaders in August 1996 brokered a new cease-fire agreement between the warring factions, and selected former Liberian senator Ruth Perry to head an interim government. The leaders were also planning elections for Spring 1997. The peace accord was threatened in October 1996 by a failed assassination attempt against Mr. Taylor. However, there were no reports of fighting in the aftermath. In mid-1997, Mr. Taylor was elected president and he took office in August.

The civil war in Liberia killed as many as 200,000 people and displaced another 700,000. In December 2000, the UN reported that Liberia was providing Sierra Leone's RUF with arms in exchange for looted diamonds. The estimated value of these smuggled gems was $125 million per year. In March 2001, the UN banned the sale of weapons to Liberia, and in May they banned Liberian diamond exports. These sanctions are meant to punish the guns-for-gems trade and are scheduled to remain in effect until May 2002.

was a driving force behind the creation of the Economic Community of West African States. It also cooperates in economic development and customs matters with Sierra Leone and Guinea in the Mano River Union. Liberian leadership supports peaceful settlement of disputes and frequently has used its good offices to encourage moderation.

## U.S.-LIBERIAN RELATIONS

Relations between the United States and Liberia have been friendly since the Republic of Liberia became independent in 1847. Official U.S. policy toward Liberia is based on the desire to maintain and strengthen those close ties.

The United States assists and supports Liberia's efforts to improve the welfare of its people and strengthen its representative institutions. The United States has provided substantial and long-standing AID, Peace Corps, and military assistance programs in Liberia. Additional U.S. support has come from private business, missionary, and educational organizations.

Liberia is the site of important U.S. telecommunications facilities. Located near Monrovia are Voice of America transmitters, which transmit to the entire African Continent, and an Omega navigational station, one of seven such installations in the world. The 427-meter Omega transmission tower is the tallest structure in Africa.

## Principal U.S. Officials

**For up-to-date information on Principal U.S. Officials, see the U.S. Embassies, Consulates, and Foreign Service section starting on page 139.**

The U.S. Embassy in Liberia is located on United Nations Drive, Monrovia (tel. 222991-4).

# LIBYA

July 1994

## Official Name:
## Socialist People's Libyan Arab Jamahiriya

# PROFILE

## Geography

**Area:** 1.8 million sq. km. (700,000 sq. mi.).
**Cities:** Capital—Tripoli (pop. 1.5 million). Other—Benghazi (800,000).
**Terrain:** Desert and semidesert; hills south of Tripoli and east of Benghazi.
**Climate:** Mediterranean on coast; arid.

## People

**Nationality:** Noun and adjective—Libyan(s).
**Population (est.):** 4.9 million.
**Annual growth rate (est.):** 3%.
**Ethnic groups:** Berber and Arab 97%; some Greeks, Maltese, Italians, Egyptians, Pakistanis, Turks, Indians, and Tunisians.
**Religion:** 97% Sunni Muslim.
**Language:** Arabic.
**Education:** Years compulsory—7. Attendance—90%. Literacy—64%.
**Health:** Infant mortality rate—60/1,000. Life expectancy—male, 66 yrs.; female, 71 yrs.

## Government

**Type:** Islamic Arabic Socialist "Jamahiriya" or "state of masses."
**Independence:** December 24, 1951.

**Revolution:** September 1, 1969.
**Constitution:** December 11, 1969 (amended March 2, 1977)—established popular congresses and peoples committees.
**Administrative divisions:** 10 regions controlled by the central government; 25 municipalities (baladiya).
**Political system (political parties are banned):** Based on theory of Maj. Gen. Mu'ammar al-Qadhafi, multilayered popular assemblies (people's congresses) with executive institutions (people's committees) are guided by political cadres (revolutionary committees).
**Suffrage:** Mandatory universal adult.

## Economy

**GDP (1992 est.):** $27.7 billion.
**Per capita GDP:** $5,700.
**Natural resources:** Crude oil, natural gas, gypsum.
**Agriculture:** Products—wheat, barley, olives, citrus fruits, vegetables, dates, peanuts; 75% of Libya's food is imported.
**Industry:** Types—petroleum, food processing, textiles, cement, handicrafts.
**Trade:** Exports (1992)—$10 billion: petroleum, peanuts, hides. Major markets—Italy, countries of the former Soviet Union, Germany, Spain, France, Belgium, Luxembourg, Turkey. Imports—$7.6 billion:

machinery, transport equipment, food, manufactured goods. Major suppliers—Italy, countries of the former Soviet Union, Germany, U.K., Japan.

**Exchange rate (October 1993):** 1 Libyan dinar=U.S. $3.15.

# PEOPLE

Libya has a small population in a large land area. Population density is about 50 persons per sq. km. (80/sq. mi.) in the two northern regions of Tripolitania and Cyrenaica, but falls to less than one person per sq. km. (1.6/sq. mi.) elsewhere. Ninety percent of the people live in less than 10% of the area, primarily along the coast. More than half the population is urban, mostly concentrated in the two largest cities, Tripoli and Benghazi. Fifty percent of the population is under age 15.

Libyans are primarily a mixture of Arabs and Berbers. Small Tebou and Touareg tribal groups in southern Libya are nomadic or semi-nomadic. Among foreign residents, the largest groups are Egyptians (estimates range from 400,000 to 1 million), Tunisians (40,000), Turks, Pakistanis, Indians, Sudanese, Moroccans, Jordanians, South Koreans, and Thais. Other foreign residents include 70,000 from Eastern Europe and 40,000 from Western Europe.

# HISTORY

For most of their history, the peoples of Libya have been subjected to varying degrees of foreign control. The Phoenicians, Carthaginians, Greeks, Romans, Vandals, and Byzantines ruled all or parts of Libya. Although the Greeks and Romans left impressive ruins at Cyrene, Leptis Magna, and Sabratha, little else remains today to testify to the presence of these ancient cultures.

The Arabs conquered Libya in the seventh century A.D. In the following centuries, most of the indigenous peoples adopted Islam and the Arabic language and culture. The Ottoman Turks conquered the country in the 16th century. Libya remained part of their empire—although at times virtually autonomous—until Italy invaded in 1911 and, after years of resistance, made Libya a colony.

In 1934, Italy adopted the name "Libya" (used by the Greeks for all of North Africa, except Egypt) as the official name of the colony, which consisted of the Provinces of Cyrenaica, Tripolitania, and Fezzan. King Idris I, Emir of Cyrenaica, led Libyan resistance to Italian occupation between the two World Wars. From 1943 to 1951, Tripolitania and Cyrenaica were under British administration; the French controlled Fezzan. In 1944, Idris returned from exile in Cairo but declined to resume permanent residence in Cyrenaica until the removal in 1947 of some aspects of foreign control. Under the terms of the 1947 peace treaty with the Allies, Italy relinquished all claims to Libya.

On November 21, 1949, the UN General Assembly passed a resolution stating that Libya should become independent before January 1, 1952. King Idris I represented Libya in the subsequent UN negotiations. When Libya declared its independence on December 24, 1951, it was the first country to achieve independence through the United Nations. Libya was proclaimed a constitutional and a hereditary monarchy under King Idris.

The discovery of significant oil reserves in 1959 and the subsequent income from petroleum sales enabled what had been one of the world's poorest countries to become extremely wealthy, as measured by per capita GDP.

King Idris ruled the Kingdom of Libya until he was overthrown in a military-led coup on September 1, 1969. The new regime, headed by the Revolutionary Command Council (RCC), abolished the monarchy and proclaimed the new Libyan Arab Republic. Col. Mu'ammar al-Qadhafi emerged as leader of the RCC and eventually as de facto chief of state, a position he currently holds. He has no official position.

Seeking new directions, the RCC's motto became "freedom, socialism, and unity." It pledged itself to remove backwardness, take an active role in the Palestinian Arab cause, promote Arab unity, and encourage domestic policies based on social justice, non-exploitation, and an equitable distribution of wealth.

An early objective of the new government was withdrawal of all foreign military installations from Libya. Following negotiations, British military installations at Tobruk and nearby El Adem were closed in March 1970, and U.S. facilities at Wheelus Air Force Base near Tripoli were closed in June 1970. That July, the Libyan Government ordered the expulsion of several thousand Italian residents. By 1971, libraries and cultural centers operated by foreign governments were ordered closed.

During the years since the revolution, Libya claimed leadership of Arab and African revolutionary forces and sought active roles in various international organizations. Late in the 1970s, Libyan embassies were redesignated as "people's bureaus," as Qadhafi sought to portray Libyan foreign policy as an expression of the popular will. The people's bureaus, aided by Libyan religious, political, educational, and business institutions overseas, exported Qadhafi's revolutionary philosophy abroad.

# GOVERNMENT

For seven years, the Government of Libya consisted of Colonel Qadhafi and the Revolutionary Command Council. On March 3, 1977, Qadhafi convened a General People's Congress (GPC) to proclaim the establishment of "people's power," change the country's name to the Socialist People's Libyan Arab Jamahiriya, and to vest, theoretically, primary authority in the GPC.

Qadhafi remained the de facto chief of state and secretary general of the GPC until 1980, when he gave up his office. He continues to control the Libyan Government through direct appeals to the masses, a pervasive security apparatus, and powerful revolutionary committees.

Although he holds no formal office, Qadhafi exercises absolute power with the assistance of a small group of trusted advisers, who include relatives from his home base in the Sirte region, which lies between the rival provinces of Tripolitania and Cyrenaica.

Before the 1969 constitution, Libya had a dual system of civil and religious courts. The new constitution established the primacy of Shari'a, or Islamic law, unifying the two systems. Civil laws now must conform to Shari'a.

The Libyan court system consists of four ascending levels. The GPC appoints justices to the Supreme Court. Military courts and special "revolutionary courts" operate outside the judicial system.

# POLITICAL CONDITIONS

After the revolution, Qadhafi took increasing control of the government,

but he also attempted to achieve greater popular participation in local government. In 1973, he announced the start of a "cultural revolution" in schools, businesses, industries, and public institutions to oversee administration of those organizations in the public interest. The March 1977 establishment of "people's power"—

with mandatory popular participation in the selection of representatives to the GPC—was the culmination of this process.

The GPC is the legislative forum that interacts with the General People's Committee, whose members are secretaries of Libyan ministries. It

serves as the intermediary between the masses and the leadership and is composed of the secretariats of some 600 local "basic popular congresses."

The GPC secretariat and the cabinet secretaries are appointed by the GPC secretary general and confirmed by the annual GPC congress. These cabinet secretaries are responsible for the routine operation of their ministries, but real authority is exercised by Qadhafi directly or through manipulation of the peoples and revolutionary committees.

In the 1980s, competition between the official Libyan Government and military hierarchies and the revolutionary committees was growing. An abortive coup attempt in May 1984, apparently mounted by Libyan exiles with internal support, led to a short-lived reign of terror in which thousands were imprisoned and interrogated. An unknown number were executed. Qadhafi used the revolutionary committees to search out alleged internal opponents following the coup attempt, thereby accelerating the rise of more radical elements inside the Libyan power hierarchy.

In 1988, faced with rising public dissatisfaction with shortages in consumer goods and setbacks in Libya's war with Chad, Qadhafi began to curb the power of the revolutionary committees and to institute some domestic reforms. The regime released many political prisoners and eased restrictions on foreign travel by Libyans. Private businesses were again permitted to operate.

Since the late 1980s, Qadhafi has pursued a harsh anti-Islamic fundamentalist policy domestically, presumably viewing fundamentalism as a potential rallying point for opponents of the regime. Ministerial positions and military commanders are also frequently shuffled to diffuse potential threats to Qadhafi's authority. More recently, the government has sought to counter popular discontent over deteriorating economic conditions with appeals to nationalism in the face of international sanctions.

Despite these measures, internal dissent continues. Qadhafi's security forces launched a pre-emptive strike at alleged coup plotters in the military and among the Warfallah tribe in October 1993. Widespread arrests and government reshufflings followed, accompanied by public "confessions" from regime opponents and allegations of torture and executions.

## Principal Government Officials

For up-to-date information on Principal Government Officials, see the Chiefs of State and Cabinet Members of Foreign Governments section starting on page 1.

# ECONOMY

The General People's Congress continued to pursue the goals of the ruling Revolutionary Command Council soon after the 1984 coup attempt. These goals included a more equitable distribution of income and services, greater government control of the economy, and independence from foreign influence. Libya also dedicated increasing resources to showcase items such as major irrigation projects, overseas interventions, and a military buildup.

In 1992–93, the Libyan Government embarked on a gradual economic liberalization program. Recent developments include the issuance of regulations governing the privatization of selected public enterprises and the lifting of restrictions on private wholesale trade. Its economy remains dependent upon revenues from exported crude oil. Currently, oil production is 1.5 million barrels per day.

During the 1970s, Libyan Government expenditures did not keep pace with the rapid rise in oil revenues. The resulting surplus led to the growth of large central bank foreign exchange reserves. At their peak, these reached $14 billion in 1981, but OPEC's production restraints and softening oil prices led to revenue shortfalls, which have resulted recently in an annual drawdown of foreign exchange reserves by about $2 billion per year. Reserves dropped to $3.5 billion in 1993.

Since 1981, fiscal difficulties associated with declining oil revenues combined with the effects of various socialist schemes have hurt merchants and other business professionals. Although Libyans have experienced a dramatic rise in the standard of living during the past 20 years, more recent economic austerity measures as well as tighter internal security controls have caused a general deterioration in the quality of life for many Libyans. Nonetheless, distribution of national wealth remains more equitable in Libya than in many other developing countries.

Libya's major trading partners are Italy, Germany, Spain, France, and countries of the former Soviet Union. In response to Libyan support of terrorism, the U.S. Government prohibited the importation of Libyan crude oil into the United States in March 1982 and imposed strict controls on U.S.-origin goods intended for export to Libya. A total ban on trade with Libya went into effect in January 1986.

Although agriculture is the second-largest sector in the economy, Libya is self-sufficient in few foods. Higher incomes and a growing population have caused food consumption to rise. Domestic food production meets only about 25% of demand. A long-term objective is to become self-sufficient in agriculture, although the scarcity of water is a serious obstacle. Libya is undertaking a multi-billion-dollar project to tap water resources deep under the Sahara to meet coastal population water needs in the 1990s. However, technical and administrative problems are hindering progress.

# FOREIGN RELATIONS

Since 1969, Qadhafi has determined Libya's foreign policy. His principal foreign policy goals have been Arab unity, elimination of Israel, advancement of Islam, support for Palestinians, elimination of outside—particularly Western—influence in the Middle East and Africa, and support for a range of "revolutionary" causes.

After the 1969 coup, Qadhafi closed American and British bases on Libyan territory and partially nationalized all foreign oil and commercial interests in Libya. He played a key role in introducing oil as a political weapon for challenging the West. He hoped that an oil price rise and embargo in 1973 would persuade the West—especially the United States—to end support for Israel. Qadhafi rejected both Soviet communism and Western capitalism, seeking an allegedly middle course.

Libya's relationship with the former Soviet Union involved massive Libyan arms purchases from the Soviet bloc and the presence of thousands of its advisers. Libya's use—and heavy loss—of Soviet-supplied weaponry in its war with Chad was a notable breach of an apparent Soviet-Libyan understanding not to use the weapons for activities inconsistent with Soviet objectives. As a result, Soviet-Libyan relations reached a nadir in mid-1987.

Since the fall of the Warsaw Pact and the Soviet Union, Libya has concentrated upon expanding diplomatic ties with Third World countries and increasing its commercial links with Europe and East Asia. Libya recently has made substantial investments in international financial institutions and petroleum refining and marketing operations. These foreign investments, however, have been the target of varying enforcement actions under UN Security Council Resolution 883, which imposed a limited freeze on Libyan assets abroad.

## Merger Attempts with Neighbors

In pursuit of his goal of Arab unity, Qadhafi has tried unsuccessfully at various times to merge with Egypt, Sudan, Tunisia, Algeria, and Syria. In August 1981, he signed a treaty with Ethiopia and the then-People's Democratic Republic of Yemen (South Yemen) that attempted to provide a framework for coordinating the foreign policies of the three countries. In 1984, Libya concluded a treaty of union with Morocco. Morocco abrogated this treaty in August 1986. In 1987, Libya once again proposed a bilateral union, with Algeria. Algeria then called on Libya to join a 1983 tripartite pact linking Algeria, Tunisia,

and Mauritania. Qadhafi rejected this offer. Libya and Tunisia subsequently restored diplomatic relations in December 1987, as did Egypt and Libya in 1989. Libya also joined in the 1988 establishment of the Arab Maghreb Union that linked Mauritania, Morocco, Algeria, and Tunisia, in addition to Libya, in a grouping modeled on the European Union.

## Terrorism

In addition to using oil as leverage in his foreign policy, Qadhafi's principal tactics have been destabilization of weaker governments and terrorism. Libya continues to harbor and finance groups all over the world that share Qadhafi's revolutionary and anti-Western views, including the Japanese Red Army and such radical Muslim groups as the Popular Front for the Liberation of Palestine-General Command and Abu Nidal's Fatah Revolutionary Council. Its support for terrorist activity against U.S. citizens and interests resulted in U.S. air strikes against Libya in April 1986; the precipitating event for this U.S. action was the bombing of a Berlin discotheque which killed an American serviceman and for which evidence of Libyan complicity had been discovered.

In October 1987, a Libyan arms shipment was intercepted on its way to the Irish Republican Army. In 1988, operatives of the Abu Nidal Organization, which is headquartered in Libya, launched a grenade attack on a Khartoum hotel and sprayed a Greek passenger ferry with machine-gun fire. Later that year, two Libyan intelligence agents planted an explosive device in Malta on the flight connecting with Pan Am flight 103 in Germany which later exploded over Lockerbie, Scotland, killing 259 passengers and crew and 11 people on the ground. In September 1989, Libya masterminded the bombing of UTA flight 772 over Niger, killing all 171 persons aboard.

Libyan terrorism also has targeted anti-Qadhafi dissidents overseas. Qadhafi's public calls for the deaths of Libyan opponents abroad during the latter half of 1993 raised strong

suspicions of his regime's involvement in the disappearance of prominent Libyan dissident Mansour Kikhya from Cairo in December 1993.

## Subversion

While supporting terrorist groups, Qadhafi also has attempted to undermine other Arab and African states by supporting coups, funding and training opposition political parties and guerrilla groups, and plotting assassinations of rival leaders. He also has sought involvement in Asia and Latin America through support for various subversive groups. Use of such methods has strained Libyan relations with many nations.

Qadhafi's foreign interventions included a bid to prop up former Ugandan dictator Idi Amin in 1979; incursions and intermittent war with Chad throughout the 1980s; continued claims on territory in Chad, Niger, and Algeria; and alleged support of Islamic fundamentalist groups in Sudan, Algeria, and Egypt. Libya withdrew its forces from the disputed Aouzou Strip in mid-1994, after the International Court of Justice ruled Libya's presence an illegal occupation of Chadian territory.

# U.S.-LIBYAN RELATIONS

The United States supported the UN resolution providing for Libyan independence in 1951 and raised the status of its office at Tripoli from a consulate general to a legation. Libya opened a legation in Washington, DC, in 1954. Both countries subsequently raised their missions to embassy level.

After Qadhafi's 1969 coup, U.S.-Libyan relations became increasingly strained because of Libya's foreign policies supporting international terrorism and subversion against moderate Arab and African governments. In 1972, the United States withdrew its ambassador. Export controls on military equipment and civil aircraft were imposed during the 1970s, and

## TRAVEL ADVISORY

Since December 1981, U.S. passports have been declared invalid for travel to, in, or through Libya, unless specifically validated for such travel by the Department of State. Unauthorized use of a U.S. passport for travel to Libya is subject to criminal prosecution under Section 1544 of Title 18, United States Code.

Persons seeking passport validations or further information should contact the Deputy Assistant Secretary of State for Passport Services, Room 300, 1425 K Street, NW, Washington, DC 20522-1705; or, if abroad, the nearest U.S. embassy or consulate. The U.S. Government maintains no diplomatic or consular representation in Libya, and, therefore, cannot provide protective services to American citizens. Very limited services are available through the embassy of Belgium in Tripoli, which acts as the U.S. protecting power in Libya. Further information is available from the Bureau of Consular Affairs, U.S. Department of State.

**Travel Advice:** For up-to-date information from the U.S. State Department on possible inconvenient or hazardous situations, see the **Travel Warnings and Consular Information Sheets from the U.S. Government** section starting on page 1723. For the latest information on health requirements and conditions, see the **International Travelers' Health Information** section starting on page 1385. For further information dealing with non-urgent matter, see the **Tips for Travelers to...** section starting on page 1588.

U.S. embassy staff members were withdrawn from Tripoli after a mob attacked and set fire to the embassy in December 1979. The U.S. Government declared Libya a "state sponsor of terrorism" on December 29, 1979.

In May 1981, the U.S. Government closed the Libyan "people's bureau" (embassy) in Washington, DC, and expelled the Libyan staff in response to a general pattern of conduct by the people's bureau contrary to internationally accepted standards of diplomatic behavior.

In August 1981, two Libyan jets fired on U.S. aircraft participating in a routine naval exercise over international waters of the Mediterranean claimed by Libya. The U.S. planes returned fire and shot down the attacking Libyan aircraft. In December 1981, the State Department invalidated U.S. passports for travel to Libya and, for purposes of safety, advised all U.S. citizens in Libya to leave. In March 1982, the U.S. Government prohibited imports of Libyan crude oil into the United States and expanded the controls on U.S.-origin goods intended for export to Libya. Licenses were required for all transactions, except food and medicine. In March 1984, U.S. export controls were expanded to prohibit future exports to the Ras al-Enf petrochemical complex. In April 1985, all Export-Import Bank financing was prohibited.

Due to Libya's continuing support for terrorism, the United States adopted additional economic sanctions against Libya in January 1986, including a total ban on direct import and export trade, commercial contracts, and travel-related activities. In addition, Libyan Government assets in the United States were frozen. When evidence of Libyan complicity was discovered in the Berlin discotheque terrorist bombing that killed an American serviceman, the United States responded by launching an aerial bombing attack against targets near Tripoli and Benghazi in April 1986. Since then, the United States has maintained its trade and travel embargoes and has sought to bring diplomatic and economic pressure to bear against Libya.

In 1988, Libya was found to be in the process of constructing a chemical weapons plant at Rabta, a plant which is now the largest such facility in the Third World. Libya is currently constructing another chemical weapons production facility at Tarhunah. Libya's support for terrorism and its past regional aggressions made this development a matter of major concern to the United States. In cooperation with like-minded countries, the United States has since sought to bring a halt to the foreign technical assistance deemed essential to the completion of this facility.

In 1991, two Libyan intelligence agents were indicted by federal prosecutors in the U.S. and Scotland for their involvement in the December 1988 bombing of Pan Am flight 103. In January 1992, the UN Security Council approved Resolution 731 demanding that Libya surrender the suspects, cooperate with the Pan Am 103 and UTA 772 investigations, pay compensation to the victims' families, and cease all support for terrorism. Libya's refusal to comply led to the approval of UNSC Resolution 748 on March 31, 1992, imposing sanctions designed to bring about Libyan compliance. Continued Libyan defiance led to passage of UNSC Resolution 883—a limited assets freeze and an embargo on selected oil equipment—in November 1993.

# LIECHTENSTEIN
January 1989

Official Name:
**Principality of Liechtenstein**

# PROFILE

## Geography
**Area:** 160 sq. km. (62 sq. mi.); about the size of Washington, DC.
**Cities:** Capital—Vaduz (pop. 4,920, 1986). Other cities—Schaan, Triesenberg, Triesen, Balzers.
**Terrain:** The Rhine Valley plain 40%; the rest of the country is mountainous.
**Climate:** Mild; winter, rarely below -15°C (5°F); summer, the average high temperature varies between 20°C and 28°C (68°F-82°F).

## People
**Nationality:** Noun—Liechtensteiner(s). Adjective—Liechtenstein.
**Population (1988):** 27,825.
**Annual growth rate:** 0.89%.
**Ethnic groups:** Alemannic 95%, Italian 5%, others.
**Religions:** Roman Catholic 87.1%, Protestant 8.6%.
**Languages:** German (official), Alemannic dialect.
**Education:** Years compulsory—9. Attendance—100%. Literacy—100%.
**Health:** Infant mortality rate—6.3/1,000. Life expectancy—71 yrs. (men), 76 yrs. (women).
**Work force (1985):** 17,121—7,490 domestic; 9,631 foreign. Agriculture, fishing, forestry, horticulture—2.1%. Industry, crafts, and building—52.6%. Services—5.3%.

## Government
**Type:** Hereditary constitutional monarchy.
**Constitution:** October 5, 1921.
**Branches:** Executive—prince (chief of state), Collegial Board (cabinet). Legislative—unicameral Diet. Judicial—three levels of regular courts, administrative court, constitutional court.
**Administrative subdivisions:** 2 districts, 11 communities.
**Political parties:** Patriotic Union *(Vaterlaendische Unzon—VU),* Progressive Citizens' Party *(Fortschrittliche Burgerpartei—FBP).*
**Suffrage:** Universal adult.
**Flag:** Two horizontal bands, blue over red, with a gold crown in the blue field (the colors of the House of Liechtenstein are gold and red).

## Economy
**Per capita income (1980 est.):** $23,200.
**Natural resources:** Hydroelectricity
**Agriculture:** Products—livestock, vegetables, corn, wheat, potatoes, grapes.
**Industry:** Types—electronics, metal manufacturing, textiles, ceramics, pharmaceuticals, food products.
**Trade (1986):** Because Liechtenstein is closely connected with Switzerland by a customs union, Switzerland is its largest single trading partner. Exports—$826 million: metal manufactures, machines and instruments, artificial teeth, chemical products, textiles, ceramics. Major markets—Switzerland (19.2% of exports), other EFTA (European Free Trade Association) countries—primarily Austria (6.6%), European Community (40%), US, and Canada. Imports—$318 million. Major suppliers—Switzerland, EC countries, Austria.

**Official exchange rate (June 1988):** 1.45 Swiss francs US$1 (as part of its customs union, Liechtenstein uses the Swiss franc as its national currency).

## Membership in International Organizations

Although not a member of the UN, Liechtenstein belongs to some of its specialized agencies and programs, including the Universal Postal Union (UPU), International Telecommunication Union (ITU), International Atomic Energy Agency (IAEA), Industrial Development Organization (UNIDO), Children's Fund (UNICEF), Conference on Trade and Development (UNCTAD), consultative status Economic Commission for Europe (ECE), and the International Court of Justice (ICJ); also, the World

Intellectual Property Organization (WIPO); INTELSAT; the European Free Trade Association (EFTA); and the Council of Europe. Liechtenstein's government is currently considering applying for full membership in the UN.

# GEOGRAPHY

The Principality of Liechtenstein is located in central Europe between Switzerland and Austria, in the Alps mountain range that runs east and west through southern Switzerland. One-third of the country lies in the upper Rhine Valley; the rest is mountainous.

# PEOPLE

In 1988, Liechtenstein had a population of 27,825 with an annual growth rate of about 0.89%. The population density for the country as a whole is more than 166 persons per square kilometer (416/sq. mi.). About 18% of the people live in Vaduz, the capital; most of the remainder live in 10 other communities in the Rhine Valley. The social structure of the principality is similar to that of other modern industrialized Western communities, except for the survival of the aristocratic ruling family, the House of Liechtenstein.

The population is homogeneous, stemming almost entirely from a Germanic tribe, the Alemanni. The official language is German, but most Liechtensteiners speak Alemannic, a German dialect similar to that used in eastern Switzerland.

# HISTORY

Because of its strategic location on a north-south and east-west crossroads in central Europe, Liechtenstein has been permanently inhabited since the Neolithic Age. Recorded inhabitants include the Celts, the Romans, and later the Alemanni. The area became

## Travel Notes

**Telecommunications:** Direct-dialing is used throughout the country and includes international service. Telegraph service also is excellent. Vaduz is 6 hours ahead of eastern standard time.

**Transportation:** Modern, comfortable buses have regular service throughout the country and into Austria and Switzerland. A modern, north-south road follows the same route as an ancient Roman one. Five modern bridges and one covered wooden bridge span the Rhine. The country has no airport, and railway facilities are limited.

**Tourist attractions:** Tourist facilities are good. In the Alps, the ski resort of Malbun has 10 hotels and 6 ski lifts.

**Travel Advice:** For up-to-date information from the U.S. State Department on possible inconvenient or hazardous situations, see the **Travel Warnings and Consular Information Sheets from the U.S. Government** section starting on page 1723. For the latest information on health requirements and conditions, see the **International Travelers' Health Information** section starting on page 1385. For further information dealing with non-urgent matter, see the **Tips for Travelers to...** section starting on page 1588.

a direct fief of the Holy Roman Empire in 1396.

The Imperial Principality of Liechtenstein was established in 1719, when the princely House of Liechtenstein, in order to maintain a seat in the Imperial Diet of the Holy Roman Empire, purchased the territory and gave its name to the principality. Liechtenstein was a member of the Confederation of the Rhine during the Napoleonic period and later became a member of the German confederation until its dissolution in 1866. The Austro-Prussian War of 1866 was the last time Liechtenstein fielded an army of 40 men.

Although it has been politically independent since 1815, Liechtenstein joined a customs union with the Austro-Hungarian Empire in 1852. It abrogated this treaty with Austria in

1919. The principality remained neutral in both World Wars. The most important date in recent Liechtenstein history is 1923, when the Swiss-Liechtenstein Customs Treaty was signed, establishing a relationship that has been updated and improved by subsequent agreements.

# GOVERNMENT AND POLITICAL CONDITIONS

Based on the constitution of October 1921, the PrincipalityofLiechtenstein is a hereditary constitutional monarchy. The prince is head of the House of Liechtenstein and thereby chief of state; all legislation must have his concurrence. He also is empowered to dissolve the Diet (parliament). Traditional popular loyalty to the monarchy has assured the stability of the constitutional system.

The highest executive authority of the principality is a five-member Collegial Board (cabinet). Its chairman is the head of government (prime minister), appointed to this position by the prince after being proposed by the Diet from among the members of the majority party. The deputy head of government, traditionally a member of the minority political party, also is appointed by the prince after being proposed by the Diet.

The three other members of the Collegial Board, called government councilors, are proposed by the Diet and appointed by the prince.

The Diet is a unicameral body composed of 15 members, elected by direct suffrage for 4-year terms. Voters in 1987 approved a referendum to raise the size of the Diet to 25 members, effective in 1990. Women are allowed to vote on national questions and, in some areas, on local candidates and issues.

Liechtenstein has an independent judiciary, with three levels of regular courts, an administrative court, and the State Court of Justice. For administrative purposes, the principality is divided into 2 districts and 11 communities.

Liechtenstein has two principal political parties, the Patriotic Union *(Vaterlaend isehe Union—VlJ)* and the Progressive Citizens' Party *(Fortschrittl iche Burgerpartei— FBP)*. Philosophically, they are much alike, and both favor maintenance of the monarchical state.

From 1928 until 1970, the Citizens' Party formed the parliamentary majority; in the 1970 general election, it was superseded as the majority party by the Patriotic Union, but it regained the majority of votes in the 1974 election to the Diet. As a result of the 1978 election, the Patriotic Union resumed power gaining 8 of 15 seats in parliament. Since 1938, both parties have formed a coalition government.

## Principal Government Officials

**For up-to-date information on Principal Government Officials, see the Chiefs of State and Cabinet Members of Foreign Governments section starting on page 1.**

In routine diplomatic matters, Liechtenstein is represented in the United States by the Swiss Embassy, at 2900 Cathedral Avenue NW., Washington, D.C.20008 (tel.202-745-7900).

# ECONOMY

Despite its small size and limited natural resources, Liechtenstein has developed, during the last three decades, from a mainly agricultural to a highly industrialized principality. It now has more than 50 factories, producing a wide range of highly specialized articles, especially in small machinery. Industrial goods are produced almost exclusively for export. In addition to membership in the European Free Trade Association,

the principality has a special trading agreement with the European Community.

Although the domestic labor force of 7,490 is highly skilled, its size has proven inadequate for an industrial economy; therefore, about 9,631 foreign workers (1985 figures) are employed in Liechtenstein, mostly from Switzerland, Austria, Germany, and Italy. Of the total labor force, about 52.6% are employed in industry, crafts, and building; 45.3% in the professions, services, and other occu-

pations; and 2.1% in agriculture and forestry.

The principality was economically integrated with Switzerland by the 1923 Swiss-Liechtenstein Customs Treaty, which provided for a customs union, the use of Swiss currency, and other types of economic cooperation. As a result, Liechtenstein has shared in the prosperity of the Swiss economy. Nominal GNP in 1980 was estimated at 876 million Swiss francs (about $584 million at 1988 exchange rates). Real GNP in 1970 prices was

527.7 million Swiss francs ($352 million). Per capita GNP is difficult to determine because about 25% of the labor force commutes from other countries; however in 1980 it was estimated at $23,200.

Liechtenstein has a market economy. Because of the principality's liberal tax policies, strict bank secrecy, and political stability, several thousand foreign businesses have their nominal headquarters in Liechtenstein. Revenue from the many tourists who visit the principality annually and the sale of postage stamps to collectors also are important sources of revenue.

Liechtenstein's banks form an increasingly important part of its economy. Three banks are domiciled in Liechtenstein with total combined assets of $7.4 billion. (Such combined assets would rank as the seventh largest bank in Switzerland.) Liechtenstein's banks have grown rapidly in recent years. Banking also is becoming an important employed at present accounting for 4.5% of the labor force.

Austrian Federal Railways owns and operates the rail system in Liechtenstein, but few international trains make stops. A major highway runs through the principality, linking Austria and Switzerland. Postal buses are the chief means of public transportation. Liechtenstein has no airport. Two newspapers are published, but there currently are no radio or television broadcasting facilities.

# FOREIGN RELATIONS

Liechtenstein is a member of the Council of Europe at Strasbourg and participates, by virtue of a separate protocol, in the European Free Trade Association. The principality has become an active participant in the Conference on Security and Cooperation in Europe.

In a series of treaties concluded after World War I, Switzerland assumed responsibility for the principality's customs controls, consular matters, and routine diplomatic relations. Liechtenstein deals directly with other states when major treaties or international conferences are involved.

The only diplomatic mission Liechtenstein maintains is its Embassy at Bern, Switzerland, through which the Swiss Foreign Ministry conducts most of the principality's routine foreign affairs. Liechtenstein also has a nonresident ambassador in Vienna and a permanent representative to the Council of Europe in Strasbourg.

# U.S.-LIECHTENSTEIN RELATIONS

The United States has no diplomatic or consular mission in Liechtenstein. The U.S. Consul General at Zurich, Switzerland, has consular accreditation at Vaduz.

## Principal U.S. Officials

**For up-to-date information on Principal U.S. Officials, see the U.S. Embassies, Consulates, and Foreign Service section starting on page 139.**

The Consulate General at Zurich is located at Zollikerstrasse 141 (tel.5525-66).

Background Notes

833

# LITHUANIA

January 1998

Official Name:
**Republic of Lithuania**

# PROFILE

## Geography

**Area:** 65,200 sq. km. (26,080 sq. miles); about the size of West Virginia.
**Cities:** Capital—Vilnius (pop. 592,500); Kaunas (430,000); Klaipeda (206,000); Siauliai (148,000); Panevezys (129,000).
**Terrain:** Lithuania's fertile, central lowland plains are separated by hilly uplands created by glacial drift. 758 rivers (many are navigable) and 2,833 lakes cover the landscape. The coastline is 99 km (62 miles) long. Land use—49.1% arable land, 22.2% meadows and pastures, 16.3% forest and woodland, 12.4% other.
**Climate:** With four distinct seasons, the climate is humid continental, with a moderating maritime influence from the Baltic Sea. January temperatures average -5°C (23°F); July, 17°C (63°F). Annual precipitation averages 54–93 centimeters (21–37 in.).

## People

**Nationality:** Noun and adjective—Lithuanian(s).
**Population:** 3.75 million, 146 people/sq. mile.
**Growth rate:** -0.4%. Birth rate—13/1,000. Death rate—11/1,000. Migra-

tion rate—4 migrants/1,000. Urban dwellers—68%. Density—56 people/sq km (1989). Divorce rate—33% (1989).
**Ethnic groups:** Lithuanian 80.6%, Russians 8.7%, Poles 7%, Belarusians 1.6%, Ukrainians 1.1%.
**Religions:** Catholic (80%), Lutheran/Calvinist (10%), Jewish (7%), Orthodox (3%).
**State language:** Lithuanian. A minority speak Russian and Polish.
**Education:** Years compulsory—9. 60% of the adult population has completed secondary education, and 11% have completed higher education. Attendance—640,000 students at 2,326 schools, plus 55,300 university students at 15 universities and institutes of higher education. Literacy—99%.
**Health:** Infant mortality rate—18/1,000. Life expectancy—66 years male, 76 female.
**Work force:** 1.6 million: Industry—33%, Science, education, culture—14%. Construction—13%. Agriculture, forestry—8%. Health care—7%. Transportation/communications—7%. Trade and government—10%. Other—8%.

## Government

**Type:** Parliamentary democracy.
**Constitution:** On October 25, 1992 Lithuanians ratified a new constitution, which officially was signed on November 6 that year.

**Branches:** Executive—popularly elected President (Chief of State); Prime Minister (Head of Government). Legislative—seimas (Parliament—141 members, 4-year term). Judicial—Supreme Court.

**Administrative regions:** 11 cities, 44 rural districts.

**Principal political parties/coalitions:** Homeland Union/Conservatives (70 seats); Christian Democrats (16 seats); Center Union (13 seats); Democratic Labor Party (12 seats); Social Democrats (12 seats); Democratic Party (2 seats); Independent candidates (12 seats); (4 seats are vacant).

**Suffrage:** 18 years, universal.

**Central government budget:** $1.1 billion (education 20%, public order/safety 9%, social services 8%, defense 3%).

**Public holidays:** Lithuanian businesses and institutions, as well as the U.S. Embassy, will be closed on the following holidays: January 1, January 6 (Epiphany), January 13 (Defenders of Freedom Day), February 16 (Lithuanian Statehood Day), Good Friday, Easter Monday, first Sunday in May (Mother's Day), July 6 (Mindaugas Coronation Day), August 15 (Assumption Day), November 1 (All Saints Day), December 25–26 (Christmas).

**Flag:** horizontal tricolor: yellow, green, red.

## Economy

**GDP:** $5.6 billion. 1996 GDP growth: 3.6%.

**Average annual wages:** $2,322.

**1996 Inflation:** 13.1%.

**Unemployment:** 6.2%

**Natural resources:** Peat, potential for exploiting moderate oil and gas deposits offshore and on the coast.

**Manufacturing:** 25% of GNP (technological instruments, energy, textiles, and footwear, machinery and spare parts, chemicals, food processing, wood/paper/pulp products), trade 17%, transportation 12%, construction 9%, energy 6% (nuclear-powered RBMK electrical plant).

**Agriculture/forestry:** 9% cattle, dairy products, cereals, potatoes), Other 22%. Cultivable land—1.36 million ha, of which 60% arable, 18% meadow, 13% pasture.

**Trade:** Exports—$3 billion: minerals/energy 12%, machinery/electronics 11%, chemicals 12%, textiles 15%. Major partners—Russia 23.8%, Germany 15.7%, Belarus 10.1%, Latvia 9.3%, Ukraine 7.7%, United Kingdom 3.4%, Poland 3.2%. Imports—$3.9 billion: minerals/energy 25%, machinery/electronics 17%, chemicals 9%, textiles 10%. Major partners—Russia 29%, Germany 16%, Poland 4%, United Kingdom 3%, Ukraine 3%, Belarus 2%, Latvia 2%.

**Official exchange rate:** 4 litai (Lt) = $1.00.

# GEOGRAPHY

The largest and most populous of the Baltic states, Lithuania is a generally maritime country with 60 miles of sandy coastline, of which only 24 miles face the open Baltic Sea. Lithuania's major warm-water port of Klaipeda lies at the narrow mouth of Kursiu Gulf, a shallow lagoon extending south to Kaliningrad. The Nemunas River and its dense network of tributaries connect the major inland cities and serve as a great asset to internal shipping. Between 56.27 and 53.54 latitude and 20.56 and 26.51 longitude, Lithuania is glacially flat, except for morainic hills in the western uplands and eastern highlands no higher than 300 meters. The terrain is marked by numerous small lakes and swamps, and a mixed forest zone covers 28% of the country. The growing season lasts 169 days in the east and 202 days in the west, with most farmland consisting of sandy- or clay-loam soils. Limestone, clay, sand and gravel are Lithuania's primary natural resources, but the coastal shelf offers perhaps 10 million barrels' worth of oil deposits, and the southeast could provide high yields of iron ore and granite. Lithuania's capital, Vilnius, lies at the geographical center of Europe.

Border changes initiated by the U.S.S.R. from 1939–1945 have delayed a formal border agreement between Lithuania and Belarus, although a functional border exists based upon Soviet demarcations. The borders with Latvia, Poland and the Kaliningrad district are mutually recognized.

# PEOPLE

The name "Lietuva," or Lithuania, might be derived from the word "lietava," for a small river, or "lietus," meaning rain (or land of rain). Lithuanian still retains the original sound system and morphological peculiarities of the prototypal Indo-European tongue and therefore is fascinating for linguistical study. Between 400–600 AD, the Lithuanian and Latvian languages split from the Eastern Baltic (Prussian) language group, which subsequently became extinct. The first known written Lithuanian text dates from a hymnal translation in 1545. Written with the Latin alphabet, Lithuanian has been the official language of Lithuania again since 1989. The Soviet era had imposed the official use of Russian, so most Lithuanians speak Russian as a second language while the resident Slavic populace generally speaks Russian as a first language.

Lithuanians are neither Slavic nor Germanic, although the union with Poland and Germanic colonization and settlement left cultural and religious influences. This highly literate society places strong emphasis upon education, which is free and compulsory until age 16. Most Lithuanians and ethnic Poles belong to the Roman Catholic Church, but a sizable minority are Russian Orthodox.

Enduring several border changes, Soviet deportations, a massacre of its Jewish population, and postwar German and Polish repatriations, Lithuania has maintained a fairly stable percentage of ethnic Lithuanians (from 84% in 1923 to 80% in 1993). Lithuania's citizenship law and constitution meet international and OSCE standards, guaranteeing universal human and civil rights.

# HISTORY

The earliest evidence of inhabitants in present-day Lithuania dates back to 10,000 BC. Between 3,000–2,000 BC, the cord-ware culture people spread over a vast region of Eastern Europe, between the Baltic Sea and the Vistula River in the west and the Moscow-Kursk line in the east. Merging with the indigenous population, they gave rise to the Balts, a distinct Indo-European ethnic group whose descendants are the present-day Lithuanian and Latvian nations and the now extinct Prussians.

The first written mention of Lithuania occurs in A.D. 1009, although many centuries earlier the Roman historian Tacitus referred to the Lithuanians as excellent farmers. Spurred by the expansion into the Baltic lands of the Germanic monastic military orders (the Order of the Knights of the Sword and the Teutonic Order) Duke Mindaugas united the lands inhabited by the Lithuanians, the Samogitians, Yotvingians and Couranians into the Grand Duchy of Lithuania (GDL) in the 1230s and 40s. In 1251 Mindaugas adopted Catholicism and was crowned King of Lithuania on July 6, 1253; a decade later, civil war erupted upon his assassination until a ruler named Vitenis defeated the Teutonic Knights and restored order.

From 1316–41 Vitenis' brother and successor, Grand Duke Gediminas, expanded the empire as far as Kiev against the Tartars and Russians. He twice attempted to adopt Christianity in order to end the GDL's political and cultural isolation from Western Europe. To that purpose, he invited knights, merchants and artisans to settle in Lithuania and wrote letters to Pope John XXII and European cities maintaining that the Teutonic Order's purpose was to conquer lands rather than spread Christianity. Gediminas' dynasty ruled the GDL until 1572. In the 1300s through the early 1400s, the Lithuanian state expanded eastward. During the rule of Grand Duke Algirdas (1345–77), Lithuania almost doubled in size and achieved major victories over the Teutonic and Livonian Orders at the Battles of Saule (1236) and Durbe (1260). However, backed by the Pope and the Catholic West European countries, the Orders continued their aggression which greatly intensified in the second half of the 14th century. During the period Algirdas' brother, Kestutis (Grand Duke in 1381–82) distinguished himself as the leader of the struggle against the Teutonic Order. The ongoing struggle precipitated the 1385 Kreva Union signed by the Grand Duke of Lithuania Jogaila (ruled in 1377–81 and 1382–92) and the Queen of Poland Jadwyga. Jogaila (Jagiello) married Jadwyga in 1386 and became the King of Poland. One of the conditions of the union was Lithuania's conversion to Christianity (1387) which intensified Lithuania's economic and cultural development, orienting it towards the West. The conversion invalidated the claims by the Teutonic Order and temporarily halted its wars against Lithuania.

Lithuania's independence under the union with Poland was restored by

Grand Duke Vytautas. During his rule (1392–1430) the GDL turned into one of the largest states in Europe, encompassing present-day Belarus, most of Ukraine and the Smolensk region of western Russia. Led by Jogaila and Vytautas, the united Polish-Lithuanian army defeated the Teutonic Order in the Battle of Tannenberg (Gruenwald or Zalgiras) in 1410, terminating the medieval Germanic drive eastward.

The 16th century witnessed a number of wars against the growing Russian state over the Slavic lands ruled by the GDL. Coupled with the need for an ally in those wars, the wish of the middle and petty gentry to obtain more rights already granted to the Polish feudal lords drew Lithuania closer to Poland. The Union of Lublin in 1569 united Poland and Lithuania into a commonwealth in which the highest power belonged to the Sejm of the nobility and its elected King who was also the Grand Duke of Lithuania. Mid-16th century land reform strengthened serfdom and yet promoted the development of agriculture owing to the introduction of a regular three-field rotation system.

The 16th century saw a more rapid development of agriculture, growth of towns, spread of ideas of humanism and the Reformation, book printing, the emergence of Vilnius University in 1579 and the Lithuanian Codes of Law (the Statutes of Lithuania) which stimulated the development of culture both in Lithuania and in neighboring countries.

The rising domination of the big magnates, the 16–18th century wars against Russia and Sweden over Livonia, Ukraine and Byelorussia weakened the Polish-Lithuanian Republic. The end of the 18th century witnessed three divisions of the Commonwealth by Russia, Prussia and Austria; in 1795 most of Lithuania became part of the Russian Empire. Attempts to restore independence in the uprisings of 1794, 1830–31 and 1863 were suppressed and followed by a tightened police regime, increasing Russification, the closure of Vilnius University in 1832 and the 1864 ban on the printing of Lithua-

nian books in traditional Roman characters.

Because of his proclamation of liberation and self-rule, many Lithuanians gratefully volunteered for the French Army when Napoleon occupied Kaunas in 1812 during the fateful invasion of Russia. After the war, Russia imposed extra taxes on Catholic landowners and enserfed an increasing number of peasants. A market economy slowly developed with the abolition of serfdom in 1861. Lithuanian farmers grew stronger, contributing to an increase in the number of intellectuals of peasant origin which led to the growth of a Lithuanian national movement. In German-ruled Lithuania Minor (Konigsberg or Kaliningrad), Lithuanian publications were printed in large numbers and then smuggled into Russian-ruled Lithuania. The most outstanding leaders of the national liberation movement were J. Basanavicius and V. Kudirka. The ban on the Lithuanian press finally was lifted in 1904.

During WW I, the German army occupied Lithuania in 1915, and the occupation administration allowed a Lithuanian Conference to convene in Vilnius in September 1917. The Conference adopted a resolution demanding the restoration of an independent Lithuanian state and elected the Lithuanian Council, a standing body chaired by Antanas Smetona. On February 16, 1918, the Council declared Lithuania's independence. 1919–20 witnessed Lithuania's War for Independence against three factions: the Red Army, which in 1919 controlled territory ruled by a Bolshevist government headed by V. Kapsukas; the Polish army; and the Bermondt army, composed of Russian and German troops under the command of the Germans. Lithuania failed to regain the Polish-occupied Vilnius region.

In the Moscow Treaty of July 12, 1920, Russia recognized Lithuanian independence and renounced all previous claims to it. The Seimas (parliament) of Lithuania adopted a constitution on August 1, 1922, declaring Lithuania a parliamentary republic, and in 1923 Lithuania

annexed the Klaipeda region, the northern part of Lithuania Minor. By then, most countries had recognized Lithuanian independence. After a military coup on December 17, 1926, Nationalist party leader Antanas Smetona became President and gradually introduced an authoritarian regime.

Lithuania's borders posed its major foreign policy problem. Poland's occupation (1920) and annexation (1922) of the Vilnius region strained bilateral relations, and in March 1939 Germany forced Lithuania to surrender the Klaipeda region (the Nurnberg trials declared the treaty null and void). Radical land reform in 1922 considerably reduced the number of estates, promoted the growth of small and middle farms and boosted agricultural production and exports, especially livestock. In particular, light industry and agriculture successfully adjusted to the new market situation and developed new structures.

The inter-war period gave birth to a comprehensive system of education with Lithuanian as the language of instruction and the development of the press, literature, music, arts and theater. On August 23, 1939, the Molotov-Ribbentrop Pact pulled Lithuania first into German influence until the Soviet-German agreement of September 28, 1939 brought Lithuania under Soviet domination. Soviet pressure and a complicated international situation forced Lithuania to sign an agreement with the U.S.S.R. on October 10, 1939, by which Lithuania was given back the city of Vilnius and the part of Vilnius region seized by the Red Army during the Soviet-Polish war; in return, some 20,000 Soviet soldiers were deployed in Lithuania.

On June 14, 1940 the Soviet Government issued an ultimatum to Lithuania, demanding the formation of a new Lithuanian government and permission to station additional Red Army troops. Lithuania succumbed to the Soviet demand, and 100,000 Soviet troops moved into the country the next day. Arriving in Kaunas, the Soviet government's special envoy began implementing the plan for Lithuania's incorporation into the U.S.S.R. On June 17 the alleged People's Government, headed by J. Paleckis, was formed; rump parliamentary elections one month later were held, whereupon Lithuania was proclaimed a Soviet Socialist Republic on August 3.

Totalitarian rule was established, Sovietization of the economy and culture began, and Lithuanian state employees and public figures were arrested and exiled to Russia. During the mass deportation campaign of June 14–18, 1941 about 7,439 families (12,600 people) were deported to Siberia without investigation or trial; 3,600 people were imprisoned and over 1,000 massacred.

Lithuanian revolt against the U.S.S.R. soon followed the outbreak of the war against Germany in 1941. Via Radio Kaunas on June 23, the rebels declared the restoration of Lithuania's independence and actively operated a Provisional Government, without German recognition, from June 24 to August 5. Lithuania became part of the German occupational administrative unit of Ostland. People were repressed and taken to forced labor camps in Germany. The Nazis and local collaborators deprived Lithuanian Jews of their civil rights and massacred about 200,000 of them. Together with Soviet partisans, supporters of independence put up a resistance movement to deflect Nazi recruitment of Lithuanians to the German army.

Forcing the Germans out of Lithuania by 1944, the Red Army reestablished control, and Sovietization continued with the arrival of Communist party leaders to create a local party administration. The mass deportation campaigns of 1941–52 exiled 29,923 families to Siberia and other remote parts of the Soviet Union. Official statistics state that over 120,000 people were deported from Lithuania during this period, while Lithuanian sources estimate the number of political prisoners and deportees at 300,000. In response to these events, an estimated several

ten thousand resistance fighters participated in unsuccessful guerrilla warfare against the Soviet regime from 1944–53. As a measure for integration and industrial development, Soviet authorities encouraged immigration of other Soviet workers, especially Russians.

Until mid-1988, all political, economical and cultural life was controlled by the Lithuanian Communist Party (LCP). First Secretary Antanas Snieckus ruled the LCP from 1940–74. The LCP, in turn, was responsible to the Communist party of the U.S.S.R. In 1947 Lithuanians comprised only 18% of total party membership in 1947 and continued to represent a minority until 1958; by 1986, they made up 70% of the party's 197,000-strong body. During the Khrushchev thaw in the 1950s, the leadership of the LCP acquired limited independence in decision-making.

The political and economic crisis that began in the U.S.S.R. in the mid-1980s also affected Lithuania, and Lithuanians as well as other Balts offered active support to Gorbachev's program of social and political reforms. Under the leadership of intellectuals, the Lithuanian reform movement Sajudis was formed in mid-1988 and declared a program of democratic and national rights, winning nation-wide popularity. On Sajudis' demand, the Lithuanian Supreme Soviet passed constitutional amendments on the supremacy of Lithuanian laws over Soviet legislation, annulled the 1940 decisions on proclaiming Lithuania a part of the U.S.S.R., legalized a multi-party system and adopted a number of other important decisions. A large number of LCP members also supported the ideas of Sajudis, and with Sajudis support, Algirdas Brazauskas was elected First Secretary of the Central Committee of the LCP in 1988. In December 1989, the Brazauskas-led LCP split from the CPSU and became an independent party, renaming itself in 1990 the Lithuanian Democratic Labor Party.

In 1990, Sajudis-backed candidates won the elections to the Lithuanian

Supreme Soviet. On March 11, 1990, its chairman Vytautas Landsbergis proclaimed the restoration of Lithuanian independence, formed a new Cabinet of Ministers headed by Kazimiera Prunskiene, and adopted the Provisional Fundamental Law of the state and a number of by-laws. The U.S.S.R. demanded to revoke the act and began employing political and economic sanctions against Lithuania as well as demonstrating military force. On January 10, 1991, U.S.S.R. authorities seized the central publishing house and other premises in Vilnius and unsuccessfully attempted to overthrow the elected government by sponsoring a local "National Salvation Committee." Three days later the Soviets forcibly took over the TV tower, killing 14 civilians and injuring 700. During the national plebiscite on February 9, 91% of those who took part in the voting (76% of all eligible voters) voted in favor of an independent, democratic Lithuania. Led by the tenacious Landsbergis, Lithuania's leadership continued to seek Western diplomatic recognition of its independence. Soviet military-security forces continued forced conscription, occasional seizure of buildings, attacking customs posts, and sometimes killing customs and police officials.

During the August 19 coup against Gorbachev, Soviet military troops took over several communications and other government facilities in Vilnius and other cities, but returned to their barracks when the coup failed. The Lithuanian government banned the Communist Party and ordered confiscation of its property.

Despite Lithuania's achievement of complete independence, sizable numbers of Russian forces remained on its territory. Withdrawal of those forces was one of Lithuania's top foreign policy priorities. Lithuania and Russia signed an agreement on September 8, 1992 calling for Russian troop withdrawals by August 31, 1993, which now have been completed in full, despite unresolved issues such as Lithuania's compensation claims.

# GOVERNMENT AND POLITICAL CONDITIONS

For over a year after independence, political life was fettered by an unclear delineation of powers between parliament and government. Political polarization increased, and name recognition played a much more significant role in politics than party affiliation. Sajudis remained part of an unofficial ruling coalition with two other politically right-wing parties, but rivalries were heightened by personally divisive political attacks and bureaucratic gridlock.

In an effort to reduce the size and recalcitrance of a government bureaucracy allegedly impeding reform, in April 1992 then-Prime Minister Vagnorius unsuccessfully attempted to enact a measure permitting the dismissal of former Communist party members and of those unwilling to enforce government decrees.

Two deputies and a minister unsuccessfully tendered resignations in support of Vagnorius, but the rest of the cabinet wrote a letter to Chairman Landsbergis complaining of Vagnorius' confrontational governing style. Vagnorius unsuccessfully submitted his resignation in May. When a referendum in May to establish a permanent French-style office of president failed, Landsbergis also threatened to resign. Right-wing members of parliament boycotted legislative sessions to stall attempts to form a quorum and successfully forestalled Vagnorius' resignation until June, when a quorum passed a no-confidence motion. Landsbergis then chose Aleksandras Abisala as Prime Minister.

A constitution was approved by 53% of eligible voters (85% of those who actually voted) in an October 1992 referendum. The results of the October 25 and November 15 runoff elections handed the Democratic Labor Party (LDDP) headed by former Communist Party boss Algirdas Brazauskas a plurality of votes and a clear majority of parliamentary seats. February, 1993 presidential elections gave Brazauskas victory over a non-LDDP coalition led by independent candidate Stasys Lozoraitis, Lithuania's former ambassador to the U.S. Economic mismanagement and collapse, fueled by chronic energy shortages and political factionalism, played a decisive role in the election results.

Since then, the Lithuanian Government has worked steadily to improve relations with its neighbors and to implement necessary Western reforms. In August 1994, the Government, backed by the IMF, lobbied the public successfully to defeat a populist referendum backed by its own far left-wing as well as the opposition which called for the indexation of peoples' savings. However, LDDP candidates took a beating at the hands of the opposition in nationwide municipal elections held in March, 1995. Public perception that the government was not doing enough to promote prosperity and to combat corruption and organized crime again were significant issues.

Caused primarily by a lack of supervision and regulation over the banking sector, a long-simmering financial crisis boiled over in December 1995, leading to the resignation in February of Adolfas Slezevicius as Prime Minister and LDDP Chairman. The new LDDP Prime Minister, Mindaugas Stankevicius, instigated an IMF-backed, comprehensive banking sector bailout plan.

These measures were not enough to persuade voters in the October 25 and November 10, 1996 rounds of parliamentary elections. The Landsbergis-led Conservative Party, gained 70 out of 141 seats, and another 16 seats went to its coalition partner, the Christian Democrats. The new coalition established a new government in early December and won a significant majority in nationwide municipal elections held in March 1997. Valdas Adamkus was elected president in December 1997 and will be sworn in on February 25, 1998.

The seimas (parliament), a unicameral legislative body, is the highest organ of state authority. It initiates and approves legislation sponsored by the Prime Minister. The Prime Minister has full responsibility and control over his cabinet.

## Key Government Officials

**For up-to-date information on Principal Government Officials, see the Chiefs of State and Cabinet Members of Foreign Governments section starting on page 1.**

Lithuania maintains an embassy in the United States at 2622 16th Street, Washington DC 20009 [tel: (202)234-5860].

# ECONOMY

The Soviet era brought Lithuania intensive industrialization and economic integration into the U.S.S.R., although the level of technology and State concern for environmental, health and labor issues sagged far behind Western standards. Urbanization increased from 39% in 1959 to 68% in 1989. From 1949–52 the Soviets abolished private ownership in agriculture, establishing collective and state farms. Production declined and did not reach pre-war levels until the early 1960s. The intensification of agricultural production through intense chemical use and mechanization eventually doubled production but created additional ecological problems.

Industry is Lithuania's largest economic sector. It is being privatized and most small firms are now under private ownership. Large industries, accounting for the bulk of Lithuania's capital investment, are still mainly under state control. Food-processing and light industries dominate but furniture, footwear, and textile manufacturing are important. Machine industries (tools, motors, computers, consumer durables) account for over one-third of the industrial work force but generally suffers from outdated plant and equipment. In agriculture, Lithuania produces for export cattle, hogs and poultry. The principal crops are wheat, feedgrains and rye. Farm production has dropped as a result of difficulties with agricultural privatization and poor weather.

The transportation infrastructure is adequate. Lithuania has one ice-free seaport with ferry services to German ports. There are operating commercial airports with scheduled international services at Vilnius and Kaunas. The road system is good but border crossings may be difficult due to inadequate border facilities at checkpoints with Poland. Telecommunications have improved greatly since independence as a result of heavy investment. The banking/financial sector is weak but improving.

Lithuania recorded a $369 million trade deficit in 1994. Its main trading partners are countries of the former Soviet Union (FSU) and Central Europe, and the main categories of imported products are energy, vehicles for transport and machinery. Exports consist mainly of machinery and food products.

Trade with Western countries increased from 8% of the total in 1992 to over 24% in 1994. In 1996, exports to European countries accounted for 94.3%, and exports to countries of the EU stood at 33.4% of Lithuania's export total.

Although gross national product (GNP) accounts comparable to Western figures are not yet fully available, real GDP has been declining since 1990 and finally broke even in 1994. Inflation is also high due to price deregulation and higher costs of imported energy and other inputs from the traditional suppliers in the FSU. The spread of private sector activity, not always reflected in national accounts statistics, is creating productive jobs and boosting consumer spending. Approximately 50% of Lithuanian workers are in the private sector, which accounts for half of Lithuania's GNP. The introduction in summer 1993 of a stable national currency backed by a currency board and pegged to the U.S. dollar has stimulated investment.

## Travel Notes

**Customs:** Lithuania does not require visas for American, Canadian or British citizens. Visitors are encouraged to register at the U.S. Embassy. Polish border crossings have expanded and improved, but one can expect major delays.

Duty-exempt items include humanitarian aid, foreign currency and securities, goods and valuables unsuitable for consumption, and items temporarily imported and re-exported without "reworking or processing." Besides internationally banned or regulated items requiring special permission, import duties and restrictions are imposed on alcohol (40–100%), tobacco and sugar (30%), foodstuffs and metals (5%). Exports subject to duties are lumber, leather hides (10–15%) and metals (5%).

**Climate and clothing:** Vilnius's climate is temperately continental, with seasons of almost equal length. Summers are pleasant, but winters inland are very cold and snowy.

**Health:** Medical care does not meet Western standards, facing a shortage of basic medical supplies, including disposable needles, anesthetics and antibiotics. Take along your own personal medication. Sometimes heat and hot water are unavailable because of the occasional disruption of energy supplies. Raw fruits and vegetables are safe to eat, but avoid drinking unpasteurized milk and tapwater.

**Transportation:** SAS, LOT, Malev, Swissair, Austrian Air, Lithuanian Airlines and Lufthansa provide service between Vilnius Airport and European cities. Two trains depart daily for Warsaw without crossing into Belarus, but take 12 hours. A bus line connects Warsaw, Vilnius, Riga and Tallinn. Bus and taxi services within the capital and its environs are good. Taxis are inexpensive and available at stands or may be ordered by phone. Rental cars are available. Gasoline prices are at market rates.

**Telecommunications:** Improved telephone and telegraph services are readily available at standard international rates. Vilnius is 7 hours ahead of Eastern Standard Time.

**Work week:** 40 hours. Offices are open 9am–6pm on weekdays, and factories open/close two hours earlier. Food shops are open Monday–Saturday from 8am–8pm, while other shops open two hours later. Stores and shops are closed on Sunday.

**Tourist attractions:** Over 550,000 tourists visited Lithuania in 1989. As Europe's geographic epicenter, Vilnius is the leading attraction, featuring beautiful baroque churches and estates, 16 museums, fortress towers, and historic medieval castles nearby in Trakai and Medininkai. The seaside resorts of Palanga and Kursiu Nerija are famous for clean beaches and natural sand dunes. Ethnographic parks and museums depicting Lithuanian life through the centuries abound, as do scenic national preserves. Historic churches and castles dating to Lithuania's Great Power era are also readily accessible.

**Currency, Weights and Measures:** The national currency, the litas, is convertible with major Western monies. Major credit cards can be used primarily at large banks and Western hotels in Vilnius, but traveler's checks are not accepted everywhere. Lithuania uses the metric system.

**Crime:** By U.S. standards, Lithuania has a low rate of violent crime. However, the introduction of a market-oriented economy has resulted in an increase in street crime, especially at night near major hotels and restaurants frequented by foreigners. Take the same precautions as in any major American city. Penalties for possession, use and dealing in illegal drugs are strict, and convicted offenders can expect jail sentences and fines.

**Travel Advice:** For up-to-date information from the U.S. State Department on possible inconvenient or hazardous situations, see the **Travel Warnings and Consular Information Sheets from the U.S. Government** section starting on page 1723. For the latest information on health requirements and conditions, see the **International Travelers' Health Information** section starting on page 1385. For further information dealing with non-urgent matter, see the **Tips for Travelers to...** section starting on page 1588.

The government focuses its efforts on stabilizing the economy, taking measures to secure supplies of energy and other vital inputs, providing a social safety net to alleviate the worst consequences of the economic depression and combating economic crime. It has enacted legislation providing a reasonably transparent and favorable regulatory regime for private investment.

In 1996, Lithuania exported $34 million in goods to the U.S. and imported $63 million. In 1994, the Government privatized 70% of its state property, and to date has registered 5,300 foreign/joint ventures, whose authorized capital exceeds $400 million. Philip Morris is a major investor. As of January 1997, American companies have invested over $166 million (over 24% of total foreign direct investment) in Lithuania.

Over 139,000 enterprises now exist in Lithuania. State companies are now authorized to sell up to 50% of their shares for hard currency without cabinet approval, and many of over twenty commercial banks offer a full range of international banking services. Monthly inflation in 1996 was about 1%. In acceding to its European Union Association Agreement, the Government removed some restrictions on foreign ownership of land.

# DEFENSE

Lithuania's defense system is based upon the Swedish-Finnish concept of a "total," rapid response force composed of a mobilization base and a small group of career professionals. The defense ministry is responsible for combat forces, border control, customs, civil defense, search/rescue and intelligence operations. The "Iron Wolf" Brigade consists of eight battalions of about 200 men each. The "SKAT," or home guard, consists of over 50–60 units varying in size from company to platoon strength. Perhaps the most prestigious arm of the military, SKAT was born during Lithuania's struggle to regain independence in the early 1990's and consists entirely of volunteers. The 500-

man navy and coast guard use patrol boats and former Russian corvettes and frigates for coastal surveillance; the 800-man air force operates 20–30 helicopters and 35–45 planes used mostly for reconnaissance and border patrol. There is a mandatory one-year active-duty draft period, and alternative service for conscientious objectors is available.

The 5,400 border guards fall under the Interior Ministry's supervision and are responsible for border protection, passport and customs duties, and share responsibility with the navy for smuggling/drug trafficking interdiction. A special security department handles VIP protection and communications security.

# FOREIGN RELATIONS

Lithuania became a member of the United Nations on September 18, 1991 and is a signatory to a number of its organizations and other international agreements. It also is a member of the Organization on Security and Cooperation in Europe, the North Atlantic Coordinating Council and the Council of Europe. Lithuania is unaffiliated directly with any political alliance but welcomes membership in NATO, EU, WTO, OECD, and other Western organizations.

Lithuania maintains Embassies in the United States, Sweden, Finland, the Vatican, Belgium, Denmark, the EC, France, Germany, Poland, the United Kingdom, and Venezuela. It also operates missions in Estonia, Latvia, Russia, the Czech Republic, Italy, Ukraine, and in New York City, to the United Nations and a Consulate. Honorary consuls are located in Argentina, Australia, Canada, Iceland, Korea, Greece, Norway, the Philippines, and in the cities of Los Angeles and Chicago.

Lithuania's liberal "zero-option" citizenship law has substantially erased tensions with its neighbors. Lithua-

nia's suspension of two strongly ethnic Polish district councils on charges of blocking reform or disloyalty during the August 1991 coup had cooled relations with Poland, but bilateral cooperation has markedly increased with the holding of elections in those districts and the signing of a bilateral Friendship Treaty in 1994. A similar agreement has been signed with Belarus in 1995.

The United States established diplomatic relations with Lithuania on July 28, 1922. U.S. representation accredited to Lithuania served from the legation in Riga, Latvia until May 31, 1930, when a legation in Kaunas was established. The Soviet invasion forced the closure of Legation Kaunas on September 5, 1940, but Lithuanian representation in the United States has continued uninterrupted for over 70 years. The U.S. never recognized the forcible incorporation of Lithuania into the U.S.S.R., and views the present Government of Lithuania as a legal continuation of the interwar republic. Lithuania has enjoyed Most-Favored-Nation (MFN) treatment with the U.S. since December, 1991. Through 1996, the U.S. has committed over $100 million to Lithuania's economic and political transformation and to address humanitarian needs. In 1994, the U.S. and Lithuania signed an agreement of bilateral trade and intellectual property protection, and in 1997 a bilateral investment treaty.

## Principal U.S. Officials

**For up-to-date information on Principal U.S. Officials, see the U.S. Embassies, Consulates, and Foreign Service section starting on page 139.**

The U.S. Embassy in Lithuania is located at Akmenu 6, 2600 Vilnius [tel/fax: (370) 670-6083/4].

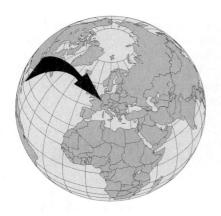

# LUXEMBOURG

July 2000

Official Name:
**Grand Duchy of Luxembourg**

# PROFILE

## Geography

**Area:** 2,586 sq. km. (1,034 sq. mi.; about the size of Rhode Island).
**Cities:** Capital—Luxembourg (pop. 75,800). Other cities—Esch/Alzette, Dudelange, Differdange.
**Terrain:** Continuation of Belgian Ardennes in the north, heavily forested and slightly mountainous; extension of French Lorraine plateau in the south, with open, rolling countryside.
**Climate:** Cool, temperate, rainy; like the U.S. Pacific Northwest.

## People

**Nationality:** Noun—Luxembourger(s). Adjective—Luxembourg.
**Population:** (2000) 452,450.
**Annual growth rate:** Less than 1%.
**Ethnic Groups:** Celtic base with French and German blend; also guest workers from Portugal, Italy, Spain, and other European countries.
**Religion:** Historically Roman Catholic. Luxembourg law forbids the collection of data on religious practices.
**Languages:** Luxembourgish, French, and German (official); English is widely spoken.
**Education:** Years compulsory—9. Attendance—100%. Literacy—100%.
**Health:** Life expectancy—avg. 78 years; males 75 years, females 82 years. Infant mortality rate—5.5/1,000.
**Work force:** (1999, 236,000) Services—62%; agriculture—1%; industry—28%; government—9%.
**Unemployment:** (1999 est.) 2.8%.

## Government

**Type:** Constitutional monarchy.
**Independence:** 1839.
**Constitution:** 1868.
**Branches:** Executive—Grand Duke (chief of state). Legislative—bicameral parliament (Chamber of Deputies and Council of State). Judicial—superior court.
**Political parties:** Christian Socialist Party (CSV), Socialist Party (LSAP), Democratic (liberal) Party (DP), Green Alternative Party (GAP), Party for Pension Rights (ADR).
**Suffrage:** Universal over age of 18.
**Government budget:** (**2000**) $4.73 billion.
**Flag:** Three horizontal stripes—red, white, and sky blue.

## Economy

**GDP:** (2000 est.) $16 .7 billion.
**Annual growth rate:** (2000 est.) 4.5%.
**Per capita income:** (2000 est.) $37,100.
**Inflation rate:** (1999) 1.6%.
**Natural resources:** Iron ore.
**Agriculture:** (1% of GNP) Products—dairy products, corn, wine. Arable land—42%.
**Services:** (1999 est.) 76.7%.
**Industry:** (23% of GDP) Types —chemicals, steel.
**Trade:** (1999) Exports—luf 292,714 million (US$7 billion) steel, plastics, rubber and processed wood products. Major markets—Germany, Belgium, France, and Asia. Imports—luf 409,923 million (US$9.8 billion); minerals, including iron ore, coal, and petroleum products), mechanical and electrical equipment, transportation equipment, scrap metal. Major suppliers—other EU countries (esp. Belgium, the Netherlands, France, and Germany).

# PEOPLE AND HISTORY

The language of Luxembourg is Luxembourgish, a blend of old German and Frankish elements. The official language of the civil service, law, and parliament is French, although criminal and legal debates are conducted partly in Luxembourgish and police case files are recorded in German. German is the primary language of the press. French and German are taught in the schools, with German spoken mainly at the primary level and French at the secondary level.

June 9, 1815, after 400 years of domination by various European nations, Luxembourg was made a grand duchy by the Congress of Vienna. It was granted political autonomy in 1838 under King William I of the Netherlands, who also was the Grand Duke of Luxembourg. The country considers 1835 to be its year of independence. In 1867, Luxembourg was recognized as independent and guaranteed perpetual neutrality. After being occupied by Germany in both World Wars, however, Luxembourg abandoned neutrality and became a charter member of the North Atlantic Treaty Organization (NATO) in 1949.

The present sovereign, Grand Duke Jean, succeeded his mother, Grand Duchess Charlotte, on November 12, 1964. Grand Duke Jean's eldest son, Prince Henri, was appointed "Lieutenant Representative" (Hereditary Grand Duke) on March 4, 1998. On December 24, 1999, Prime Minister Juncker announced Grand Duke Jean's decision to abdicate the throne in September 2000, in favor of Prince Henri who assumed the title and constitutional duties of Grand Duke.

# GOVERNMENT

Luxembourg has a parliamentary form of government with a constitutional monarchy by inheritance. Under the constitution of 1868, as amended, executive power is exercised by the Grand Duke and the Council of Government (cabinet), which consists of a prime minister and several other ministers. The prime minister is the leader of the political party or coalition of parties having the most seats in parliament.

Legislative power is vested in the Chamber of Deputies, elected directly to 5-year terms. A second body, the "Conseil d'Etat" (Council of State), composed of 21 ordinary citizens appointed by the Grand Duke, advises the Chamber of Deputies in the drafting of legislation. The responsibilities of the members of the Conseil d'Etat are extracurricular to their normal professional duties. Luxembourg law is a composite of

local practice, legal tradition, and French, Belgian, and German systems. The apex of the judicial system is the superior court, whose judges are appointed by the Grand Duke.

## Principal Government Officials

**For up-to-date information on Principal Government Officials, see the Chiefs of State and Cabinet Members of Foreign Governments section starting on page 1.**

Luxembourg maintains an embassy in the United States at 2200 Massachusetts Avenue, NW, Washington, DC 20006 (tel. 202-265-4171). Consulates or honorary consulates are located in many U.S. cities.

# POLITICAL CONDITIONS

Since the end of World War II, the Christian Social Party (CSV) has usually been the dominant partner in governing coalitions. The Roman Catholic-oriented CSV resembles Christian Democratic parties in other west European countries and enjoys broad popular support. However, in June 1999, national elections ushered in a new government. For the first time since 1974, the Socialist Party (LSAP) ceded its junior coalition position with the long-reigning CSV majority to the Liberal Democrat Party (DP).

The DP is a center party, drawing support from the professions, merchants, and urban middle class. Like other west European liberal parties, it advocates both social legislation and minimum government involvement in the economy. It also is strongly pro-NATO. In the opposition since 1984, the DP had been a partner in the three previous consecutive coalition governments.

The Communist Party (PCL), which received 10%-18% of the vote in national elections from World War II to the 1960s, won only two seats in the 1984 elections, one in 1989, and none in 1994. Its small remaining support lies in the "steel belt" of the industrialized south.

The Green Party has received growing support since it was officially formed in 1983. It opposes both nuclear weapons and nuclear power and supports environmental and ecological preservation measures. This party generally opposes Luxembourg's military policies, including its membership in NATO.

National elections are held at least every 5 years and municipal elections every 6 years. In the June 1999 parliamentary elections, the CSV won 19, the DP 15, the LSAP 13, the ADR (a single-issue party that emerged from the LSAP focused on pension rights) 6, the "Greens" 5, and the PCL 1. Hence, for the first time since 1974, the Socialists (LSAP) ceded their junior coalition position with the long-reigning Christian Socialist (CSV) majority to the Liberal Democrats. Jean-Claude Juncker (CSV) remained for a second 5-year term as Prime Minister, and Lydie Polfer (DP), the former Luxembourg City mayor, was named Vice Prime Minister and Foreign Minister.

Somewhat unexpectedly, the Socialists gained ground in the October 10, 1999 municipal elections, with candidates taking 34% of municipal seats nationwide, including seven town mayorships. In Luxembourg City, the Grand Duchy's largest municipality, the electorate followed its postwar voting pattern and chose Liberal Democrat Paul Helminger, who had been named to finish Lydie Polfer's term when she became Foreign Minister.

# ECONOMY

Although Luxembourg in tourist literature is aptly called the "Green Heart of Europe," its pastoral land coexists with a highly industrialized and export-intensive economy. Luxembourg enjoys a degree of economic prosperity almost unique among industrialized democracies.

In 1876, English metallurgist Sidney Thomas invented a refining process that led to the development of the steel industry in Luxembourg and the founding of the Arbed company in 1911—now the second-largest steel producer in Europe. The iron and steel industry, located along the French border, is the most important single sector of the economy. Steel accounts for 29% of all exports (excluding services), 1.8% of GDP, 22% of industrial employment, and 3.9% of the work force.

The restructuring of the industry and increasing government ownership in Arbed (31%) began as early as 1974. As a result of timely modernization of facilities, cutbacks in production and employment, government assumption of portions of Arbed's debt, and recent cyclical recovery of the international demand for steel, the company is again profitable. Its productivity is among the highest in the world. U.S. markets account for about 6% of Arbed's output. The company specializes in production of large architectural steel beams and specialized value-added products.

There has been, however, a relative decline in the steel sector, offset by Luxembourg's emergence as a financial center. Banking is especially important. In 1997, there were 215 banks in Luxembourg, with 21,000 employees. Political stability, good communications, easy access to other European centers, skilled multilingual staff, and a tradition of banking secrecy have all contributed to the growth of the financial sector. Germany accounts for the largest-single grouping of banks, with Scandinavian, Japanese, and major U.S. banks also heavily represented. Total assets exceeded $200 billion at the end of 1996, of which some 81% was denominated in foreign currencies, primarily U.S. dollars and German marks. More than 9,000 holding companies are established in Luxembourg. The European Investment Bank—the

financial institution of the European Union—also is located there.

Government policies promote the development of Luxembourg as an audiovisual and communications center. Radio-Television-Luxembourg is Europe's premier private radio and television broadcaster. The govern-

ment-backed Luxembourg satellite company "Societe Europeenne des Satellites" (SES) was created in 1986 to install and operate a satellite telecommunications system for transmission of television programs throughout Europe. The first SES "ASTRA" satellite, a 16-channel RCA 4000, was launched by Ariane Rocket in December 1988. SES presently operates five satellites with two more to be launched before the year 2000.

Luxembourg offers a favorable climate to foreign investment. Successive governments have effectively attracted new investment in medium, light, and high-tech industry. Incentives cover taxes, construction, and plant equipment. U.S. firms are among the most prominent foreign investors, producing tires (Goodyear), chemicals (Dupont), glass (Guardian Industries), and a wide range of industrial equipment. The current value of U.S. direct investment is almost $1.4 billion, on a per capita basis—the highest level of U.S. direct investment outside of North America.

Labor relations have been peaceful since the 1930s. Most industrial workers are organized by unions linked to one of the major political parties. Representatives of business, unions, and government participate in the conduct of major labor negotiations.

Foreign investors often cite Luxembourg's labor relations as a primary reason for locating in the Grand Duchy. Unemployment in 1999 averaged less than 2.8% of the work force.

Luxembourg's small but productive agricultural sector provides employment for about 1%-3% of the work force. Most farmers are engaged in dairy and meat production. Vineyards in the Moselle Valley annually produce about 15 million liters of dry white wine, most of which is consumed locally. Luxembourg's trade account has run a persistent deficit over the last decade, but the country enjoys an overall balance-of-payment surplus, due to revenues from financial services. Government finances are strong, and budgets are normally in surplus.

# FOREIGN RELATIONS

Luxembourg has long been a prominent supporter of European political and economic integration. In efforts foreshadowing European integration, Luxembourg and Belgium in 1921 formed the Belgium-Luxembourg Economic Union (BLEU) to create an inter-exchangeable currency and a common customs regime. Luxembourg is a member of the Benelux Economic Union and was one of the founding members of the European Economic Community (now the European Union). It also participates in the Schengen Group, whose goal is the free movement of citizens among member states. At the same time, Luxembourgers have consistently recognized that European unity makes sense only in the context of a dynamic, transatlantic relationship and have traditionally pursued a pro-NATO, pro-U.S. foreign policy.

Luxembourg is the site of the European Court of Justice, the European Court of Auditors, and other vital EU organs. The Secretariat of the European Parliament is located in Luxembourg, but the Parliament usually meets in nearby Strasbourg.

# DEFENSE

The Luxembourg army is under civilian control. Responsibility for defense matters is vested in the Minister of Cooperation, Humanitarian Action and Defense, Charles Goerens, under the Ministry of Foreign Affairs, Trade, Cooperation and Defense.

Luxembourg has no navy or air force. A 1967 law made the army an all-volunteer force with current strength of approximately 450 professional soldiers, about 340 enlisted recruits and 100 civilians, and a total budget of $120 million. Luxembourg has participated in the European Corps (EUROCORPS) since 1994, has contributed troops to the UNPROFOR and IFOR missions in former Yugoslavia, and participates with a small contingent in the current NATO SFOR mission in Bosnia. The Luxembourg army is integrated into the Multinational Beluga Force under Belgian command. Luxembourg has

## Travel Notes

**Travel Advice:** For up-to-date information from the U.S. State Department on possible inconvenient or hazardous situations, see the **Travel Warnings and Consular Information Sheets from the U.S. Government** section starting on page 1723. For the latest information on health requirements and conditions, see the **International Travelers' Health Information** section starting on page 1385. For further information dealing with non-urgent matter, see the **Tips for Travelers to...** section starting on page 1588.

financially supported international peacekeeping missions during the 1991 Gulf war, in Rwanda and, more recently, Albania. The army also has participated in humanitarian relief missions such as setting up refugee camps for Kurds and providing emergency supplies to Albania.

# U.S.- LUXEMBOURG RELATIONS

Bilateral relations between the United States and Luxembourg are excellent, both historically and through common membership in the Organization for Cooperation and Economic Development (OECD), OSCE, and NATO. More than 5,000 American soldiers, including Gen. George S. Patton, are buried at the American Military Cemetery near the capital.

## Principal U.S. Officials

For up-to-date information on Principal U.S. Officials, see the U.S. Embassies, Consulates, and Foreign Service section starting on page 139.

# MACAU

August 1994

Official Name:
**Macau**

# PROFILE

## Geography

**Area:** 16 sq. km. (6 sq. mi.) on a peninsula connected to China and the southern islands of Taipa (3.4 sq. km.) and Coloane (7.2 sq. km.) linked by bridge and causeway.
**Terrain:** Coastline is flat, inland is hilly and rocky.
**Climate:** Tropical monsoon; cool and humid in winter, hot and rainy from spring through summer.

## People

**Nationality:** Noun—Macanese (sing. and pl.).
**Population:** 400,000.
**Ethnic groups:** Chinese 95%, Portuguese 3%.
**Religions:** Buddhist 45%, Roman Catholic 9%.
**Languages:** In 1992, the government gave the Chinese (Cantonese) language official status and the same legal force as Portuguese, the official language.
**Education:** Literacy—90%.
**Work Force:** Industry and commerce—68%. Services—12%. Agriculture and fishing—9%.

## Government

**Type:** Chinese territory under Portu-guese administration; China regains sovereignty on December 20, 1999.
**Branches:** Executive—governor (head of government), president of Portugal (chief of state), Consultative Council (cabinet). Legislative—Legislative Assembly. Judicial—special courts (administrative), ordinary courts (civil and criminal), Supreme Court.
**Administrative subdivisions:** Two districts—Macau and the islands (Taipa and Coloane).

## Economy

**GDP (1992):** $5 billion.
**Annual growth rate:** 6%.
**Per capita GDP (est.):** $12,500.
**Natural resources:** None.
**Agriculture:** Products—rice and vegetables; most foodstuffs and water are imported.
**Industry:** Tourism and gambling; textiles, construction, and real estate development.
**Trade (1991):** Exports—$2.9 billion: textiles and clothing, manufactured goods (especially toys). Major markets—U.S. 36%, Hong Kong 13%, China 10%. Imports—$1.6 billion: consumer goods, foodstuffs. Major suppliers—Hong Kong 33%, China 21%, Japan 18%, U.S. 5%.
**Exchange rate:** 8 patacas=U.S.$1; officially tied to U.S.-Hong Kong exchange rate, since 1977.

# PEOPLE

Macau's population is 95% Chinese, primarily Cantonese and some Hakka, both from nearby Guangdong Province. The remainder are of Portuguese or mixed Chinese-Portuguese ancestry.

The official languages are Portuguese, and Chinese (Cantonese). English is spoken in tourist areas.

Macau has only one university (University of Macau); most of its 7,700 students are from Hong Kong.

# HISTORY

Chinese records of Macau date back to the establishment in 1152 of Xiangshan County under which Macau was administered, though it remained unpopulated through most of the next century. Members of the South Sung (Song) Dynasty and some 50,000 followers were the first recorded inhabitants of the area, seeking refuge in Macau from invading Mongols in 1277. They were able to defend their settlements and establish themselves there.

The Hoklo Boat people were the first to show commercial interest in Macau as a trading center for the southern provinces. Macau did not develop as a major settlement until the Portuguese arrived in the 16th century. Portuguese traders used Macau as a staging port as early as 1516, making it the oldest European settlement in the Far East. In 1557, the Chinese agreed to a Portuguese settlement in Macau but did not recognize Portuguese sovereignty. Although a Portuguese municipal government was established, the sovereignty question remained unresolved.

Initially, the Portuguese developed Macau's port as a trading post for China-Japan trade and as a staging port on the long voyage from Lisbon to Nagasaki. When Chinese officials banned direct trade with Japan in 1547, Macau's Portuguese traders carried goods between the two countries.

The first Portuguese governor was appointed to Macau in 1680, but the Chinese continued to assert their authority, collecting land and customs taxes. Portugal continued to pay rent to China until 1849, when the Portuguese abolished the Chinese customs house and declared Macau's "independence," a year which also saw Chinese retaliation and finally the assassination of Governor Ferreira do Amaral.

On March 26, 1887, the Manchu Government acknowledged the Portuguese right of "perpetual occupation." The Manchu-Portuguese agreement, known as the Protocol of Lisbon, was signed with the condition that Portugal would never surrender Macau to a third party without China's permission.

Macau enjoyed a brief period of economic prosperity during World War II as the only neutral port in South China, after the Japanese occupied Guangzhou (Canton) and Hong Kong. In 1943, Japan created a virtual protectorate over Macau. Japanese domination ended in August 1945.

When the Chinese communists came to power in 1949, they declared the Protocol of Lisbon to be invalid as an "unequal treaty" imposed by foreigners on China. However, Beijing was

not ready to settle the treaty question, requesting a maintenance of "the status quo" until a more appropriate time. Beijing took a similar position on treaties relating to the Hong Kong territories.

Riots broke out in 1966 when the procommunist Chinese elements and the Macau police clashed. The Portuguese Government reached an agreement with China to end the flow of refugees from China, and to prohibit all communist demonstrations. This move ended the conflict, and relations between the government and the leftist organizations have remained peaceful.

The Portuguese tried once in 1966 after the riots in Macau, and again in 1974, the year of a military revolution in Portugal, to return Macau to Chinese sovereignty. China refused to reclaim Macau however, hoping to settle the question of Hong Kong first.

Portugal and China established diplo-matic relations in 1979. A year later, Gen. Melo Egidio became the first Governor of Macau to visit China. The visit underscored both parties' interest in finding a mutually agreeable solution to Macau's status; negotiations began in 1985, a year after the signing of the Sino-U.K. agreement returning Hong Kong to China in 1997. The result was a 1987 agreement returning Macau to Chinese sovereignty as a Special Administrative Region (SAR) of China on December 20, 1999.

# GOVERNMENT

The governor general of Macau is the ranking civil and military official. Nominated by the president of Portugal, the governor is assisted by five deputy secretaries responsible for the administration of key government sectors. The Legislative Assembly was established in 1974. The assembly consists of 23 members: 8 are elected in universal, direct elections, 8 are indirectly elected by representatives of cultural, economic, and religious groups, and 7 are appointed by the governor. The assembly's powers are limited.

The Consultative Council, an elected and appointed advisory group, advises the governor and provides some measure of popular representation.

Macau's courts are independent of the executive. They are integrated into the Portuguese judicial system, and appeals are directed to the superior Portuguese courts in Lisbon. However, Macau established a High Court of Justice in 1992 which started service in 1993. This will give the enclave nearly complete judicial autonomy, although in cases involving "basic rights of the citizen," defendants may appeal to Portugal's Constitutional Court, where all lower court rulings can be overturned.

In early 1993, the Sino-Portuguese Joint Liaison Group completed work on Macau's mini-constitution that will govern the territory when it reverts to Chinese rule; it was ratified by the Chinese National People's Congress in the spring of 1993.

## Principal Government Officials

**For up-to-date information on Principal Government Officials, see the Chiefs of State and Cabinet Members of Foreign Governments section starting on page 1.**

The embassy of Portugal is located at: 2125 Kalorama Road NW, Washington, DC 20008 (tel. 202-328-8610).

# ECONOMY

Gambling and tourism, textiles, manufacturing, and construction and real estate development sparked the rapid growth of Macau's economy in the late 1980s and early 1990s. Total 1991 export earnings were $1.7 billion. The United States is Macau's leading export market. Portugal receives about 3% of Macau's exports.

Tourism and gambling account for 46% of GDP, manufacturing 35%, construction 9%, government and public authorities 5%, and agriculture and fishing 5%. Macau has many deluxe and first-class hotels. Although small quantities of rice and vegetables are grown locally, Macau imports most of its foodstuffs and all of its water from China. In 1991, imports amounted to about $1.6 billion, one third of which came from Hong Kong.

An international airport is under construction and is projected to open in 1995. There are no rail connections with China, which can be reached by road and ferry. Connections to Hong

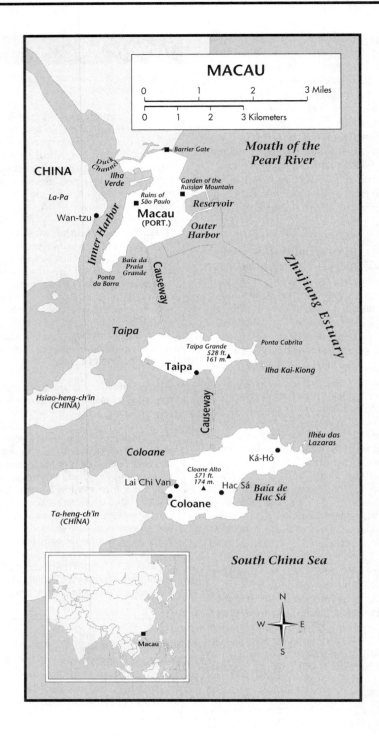

Kong are made by ferry, hydrofoil, or jetfoil. The new bridge between Macau and Taipa, "Bridge of Friendship," was opened officially in April 1994 by the prime minister of Portugal.

Silt from the Pearl River traditionally has clogged Macau's port. However, construction of a deep water port and storage facility are underway and due

to be completed in the mid-1990s. Most of Macau's trade, except with the interior of China, passes through Hong Kong. Several million tourists and business travelers visit Macau each year. Among Macau's tourist attractions are its Mediterranean atmosphere in an oriental setting, resort hotels and gambling casinos, dog and horse racing, and the annual Macau Grand Prix. In addition, one

## Editor's Update                                              June 2001

*A report on important events that have taken place since the last State Department revision of this* Background Note.

On December 20, 1999, Macau's 427,000 inhabitants became Chinese citizens. Macau, a tiny peninsular territory at the mouth of the Zhu River, had been under Portuguese control for 442 years. Most of Macau's residents are ethnic Chinese, and like Hong Kong before them (in July 1997), Macau is reintegrating into China, becoming a Special Administrative Region. Unlike neighboring Hong Kong, though, Macau's transition to Chinese rule was welcomed by most citizens and seemed to go smoothly.

Shortly after the transfer, a new government is to be formed. In its relations with China, the new government will operate under the one-country, two-systems policy, and the new government will follow Macau's Basic Law, which guarantees a high level of autonomy for fifty years after reverting to Chinese rule. However, the power of the Macau Basic Law remains to be seen. Hong Kong had similar protections in place that China did not honor.

Edmund Ho, a banker, was elected chief executive for the post-handover government. Ho was chosen by a Beijing-approved committee. Ho will head an inexperienced and untested government. Most of Macau's top officials and civil servants were Portuguese, and with the turnover, they were replaced by Macanese of Chinese ethnicity. Under post-handover law, in fact, all of Macau's top government positions must be filled by ethnic Chinese.

Competition for the billion-dollar revenue streams that flow from the Asia-Pacific region's big-spending gamblers is increasing as the prospect of the Chinese government granting three additional casino licenses for Macau in 2002 undermines Taiwan's interest in garnering a larger percentage of the money available. There is considerable competition already for the rights to purchase these gambling licenses, with both Australia and the US positioning themselves to acquire at least one of the three being offered in Macau.

can easily cross the border at the historic Barrier Gate to enter China.

Macau's unit of currency is the pataca. Pegged to the value of the U.S. and Hong Kong dollars, a pataca is worth slightly less than one Hong Kong dollar and is valued at 8 patacas to U.S. $1. The state-owned Instituto Emissor de Macau issues currency and controls the money, finance, and foreign exchange markets. There are numerous commercial banks in Macau, many of which are foreign-owned (principally European and Chinese).

# FOREIGN RELATIONS

Recent changes in the relations between the U.K. and China have not affected relations between Portugal and China.

## U.S. Representation

The U.S. Government has no offices in Macau. U.S. interests are represented by the U.S. consulate general in Hong Kong.

## Principal U.S. Officials

**For up-to-date information on Principal U.S. Officials, see the U.S. Embassies, Consulates, and Foreign Service section starting on page 139.**

The American consulate general is located at: 26 Garden Road, Hong Kong (tel. 011-852-523-9011) (FAX 011-852-845-4845 (consular); 001-852-845-1598 (general)).

# MACEDONIA

October 1994

---

**Editor's Note: The U.S. State Department has not yet issued a Background Note on this nation. The information presented here is from the Congressional Research Service of the Library of Congress and the Central Intelligence Agency; it is the latest material available about this nation.**

---

## Geography

**Area:** 24,856 sq km (9,597 sq mi.), slightly larger than Vermont.
**Cities:** Capital—Skopje.
**Climate:** Hot, dry summers and autumns and relatively cold winters with heavy snowfall.
**Terrain:** Mountainous territory covered with deep basins and valleys; there are three large lakes, each divided by a frontier line.
**Environment:** Current issues—air pollution from metallurgical plants.

## People

**Nationality:** Noun and adjective—Macedonian(s).
**Population:** 2,213,785 (July 1994 est.).
**Annual growth rate:** 0.89% (1994 est.).
**Ethnic groups:** Macedonian 65%, Albanian 22%, Turkish 4%, Serb 2%, Gypsies 3%, other 4%.
**Religions:** Eastern Orthodox 67%, Muslim 30%, other 3%.
**Languages:** Macedonian 70%, Albanian 21%, Turkish 3%, Serbo-Croatian 3%, other 3%.
**Health:** Infant mortality rate—27.8 deaths/1,000 live births (1994 est.). Life expectancy at birth—total population, 73.59 years; male, 71.51 years; female 75.85 years (1994 est.).
**Education:** Literacy—NA.
**Work force:** 507,324; by occupation: agriculture 8%, manufacturing and mining 40% (1990).

## Government

**Type:** Emerging democracy.
**Independence:** September 17, 1991 (from Yugoslavia).
**Constitution:** Adopted 17 November 1991, effective 20 November 1991.
**Branches:** Executive—President (chief of state), Prime Minister (head of government), cabinet. Legislative—unicameral, Assembly (Sobranje). Judicial—Constitutional Court, Judicial Court of the Republic.
**Administrative divisions:** 34 counties (opstinas, singular—opstina).
**Political parties:** Social-Democratic Alliance of Macedonia (SDSM; former Communist Party), Party for Democratic Prosperity (PDPM); National Democratic Party (PDP), Alliance of Reform Forces of Macedonia–Liberal Party (SRSM-LP), Socialist Party of Macedonia (SPM), Internal Macedonian Revolutionary Organization– Democratic Party for Macedonian National Unity (VMRO-DPMNE), Party of Yugoslavs in Macedonia (SJM), Democratic Party (DP).
**Suffrage:** 18 years of age; universal.
**Flag:** 16-point gold sun (Vergina, Sun) centered on a red field.

## Economy

**GDP:** $2.2 billion (1993 est.).
**Annual real growth rate:** -14.7% (1992 est.).
**Per capita GDP:** $1,000 (1993 est.).

**Natural resources:** chromium, lead, zinc, manganese, tungsten, nickel, low-grade iron ore, asbestos, sulphur, timber.
**Industry:** Low levels of technology predominate, such as, oil refining by distillation only; produces basic liquid fuels, coal, metallic chromium, lead, zinc, and ferronickel; light industry produces basic textiles, wood products, and tobacco.
**Agriculture:** Provides 12% of GDP and meets the basic needs for food; principal crops are rice, tobacco, wheat, corn, and millet; also grown are cotton, sesame, mulberry leaves, citrus fruit, and vegetables; The Former Yugoslav Republic of Macedonia is one of the seven legal cultivators of the opium poppy for the world pharmaceutical industry, including some exports to the US; agricultural production is highly labor intensive.
**Trade:** Exports—$889 million (1993): manufactured goods 40%, machinery and transport equipment 14%, miscellaneous manufactured articles 23%, raw materials 7.6%, food (rice) and live animals 5.7%, beverages and tobacco 4.5%, chemicals 4.7% (1990). Major markets: principally Serbia and Montenegro and the other former Yugoslav republics, Germany, Greece, Albania. Imports—$963 million (1993): fuels and lubricants 19%, manufactured goods 18%, machinery and transport equipment 15%, food and live ani-

## Editor's Update
## May 2000–June 2001

The conflict in Kosovo and the massive outpouring of refugees—many of them to Macedonia—thrust this small Balkan state into the spotlight in early 1999, with hundreds of thousands of Kosovar Albanian poured over the Macedonian border. Observers believe that the Macedonian government fears that the Kosovar Albanian refugees together with Macedonia's ethnic Albanian population (estimated at over 20 percent of Macedonia's population) may launch a separatist movement. In early 2001, Macedonian security forces skirmished with ethnic Albanian fighters who called themselves a liberation army.

An attempt in May 2001 by the rebels and two Albanians parties from Macedonia to reach a peace accord was denounced by the West. As of Jun3 2001, civilians are suffering as this conflict drags on.

mals 14%, chemicals 11.4%, raw materials 10%, miscellaneous manufactured articles 8.0%, beverages and tobacco 3.5% (1990). Major suppliers: other former Yugoslav republics, Greece, Albania, Germany, Bulgaria. **Exchange rates:** denar per US$1– 865 (October 1992).

## Economic Overview

The Former Yugoslav Republic of Macedonia, although the poorest republic in the former Yugoslav federation, can meet basic food and energy needs through its own agricultural and coal resources. Its economic decline will continue unless ties are reforged or enlarged with its neighbors Serbia and Montenegro, Albania, Greece, and Bulgaria. The economy depends on outside sources for all of its oil and gas and its modern machinery and parts. Continued political turmoil, both internally and in the region as a whole, prevents any swift readjustments of trade patterns and economic programs. The country's industrial output and GDP are expected to decline further in 1994. The Former Yugoslav Republic of Macedonia's geographical isolation, technological backwardness, and potential political instability place it far down the list of countries of interest to Western investors. Resolution of the dispute with Greece and an internal commitment to economic reform would help to encourage foreign investment over the long run. In the immediate future, the worst scenario for the economy would be the spread of fighting across its borders.

## International Status

Due to Greece's objections to the use of the name "Macedonia" by the ex-Yugoslav republic, which Greece believes implies a territorial claim on its own Greek Macedonia, Macedonia has not been recognized by the United States or the European Community. However, the new state has been recognized by several countries, including Bulgaria, Turkey and Russia.

On January 25, 1992, Greek Foreign Minister Michael Papaconstantinou said that his government was prepared in principle to accept the admission of Macedonia to the United Nations under the name of "the Former Yugoslav Republic of Macedonia." The IMF and the World Bank have already admitted Macedonia under this name.

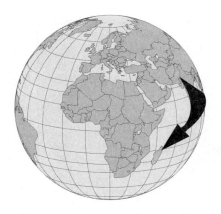

# MADAGASCAR

April 1994

Official Name:
**Republic of Madagascar**

# PROFILE

## Geography

**Area:** 592,800 sq. km. (228,880 sq. mi.).
**Cities:** Capital—Antananarivo (pop. about 850,000). Other cities—Antsirabe (about 120,000), Mahajanga (about 150,000), Toamasina (about 130,000).
**Terrain:** Mountainous central plateau, coastal plain.
**Climate:** Moderate interior, tropical coasts.

## People

**Nationality:** Noun and adjective—Malagasy.
**Population (1993 est.):** 12 million.
**Annual growth rate (1993 est.):** 3.2%.
**Ethnic groups:** 18 Malagasy tribes; small groups of Comorians, French, Indians, and Chinese.
**Religions:** Traditional beliefs 55%, Christian 40%, Muslim 5%.
**Languages:** Malagasy (official), French.
**Education:** Years compulsory—5. Attendance—83%. Literacy—53%.
**Health:** Infant mortality rate—120/1,000. Life expectancy—51 yrs.
**Work force (1992):** 5.8 million. Agriculture—88%. Industry—7%.

## Government

**Type:** Republic.
**Independence:** June 26, 1960.
**Constitution:** Entered into force on September 21, 1992.
**Branches:** Executive—president, prime minister, cabinet. Legislative—National Assembly and Senate. Judicial—Supreme Court, High Court of Justice, Constitutional High Court.
**Subdivisions:** Six provinces (faritany).
**Political parties:** Several dozen, including Active Forces Cartel, Militants for the Development of Madagascar, People United Party, National Union for Development and Democracy, Social Democrat Party, Study and Action Group for Development in Madagascar, Rally for Social Democracy, Liberal Economic and Democratic Action Party, Independence and Renewal Party of Madagascar, The Equal Regional Development Party.
**Suffrage:** Universal at 18.
**National holiday:** June 26.
**Flag:** Vertical white band on staff side; horizontal red and green bands.

## Economy

**GDP (1993 est.):** $1 billion at current prices; $2 billion at constant prices.
**Per capita GDP (1993 est.):** $135.
**Natural resources:** Graphite, chrome, coal, bauxite, ilmenite, tar sands, semiprecious stones, hard wood.
**Agriculture (29% of GDP):** Products—rice, livestock, seafood, coffee, vanilla, sugar, cloves, cotton, sisal, peanuts, tobacco.
**Industry (14% of GDP):** Types—processed food, clothing, textiles, mining, paper, refined petroleum products, glassware, construction, soap, cement, tanning.
**Trade:** Exports (1992)—$328 million: vanilla, sugar, cloves, shrimp, chromite, graphite. Major export markets—France, U.S., Germany, Japan, Singapore, Italy. Imports (1992)—$547 million: consumer goods, foodstuffs, crude oil, machinery and vehicles, iron and steel. Major suppliers—France, Iran, Japan, Germany, Saudi Arabia, Hong Kong.
**Exchange rate (April 1994):** 1,900 FMG=US$1.

# PEOPLE AND HISTORY

Madagascar's population is predominantly of mixed Asian and African origin. Recent research suggests that the island was uninhabited until Indonesian seafarers arrived in roughly the first century A.D., probably by way of southern India and East Africa, where they acquired African wives and slaves. Subsequent migrations from both the Pacific and Africa further consolidated this original mixture, and 18 separate tribal groups emerged. Asian features are most predominant in the central highlands people, the Merina (2 million) and the Betsileo (1 million); the coastal people are of African origin. The largest coastal groups are the Betsimisaraka (1 million) and the Tsimihety and Sakalava (500,000 each).

The Malagasy language is of Malayo-Polynesian origin and is generally spoken throughout the island. French also is spoken among the educated of this former French colony.

Most people practice traditional religions, which tend to emphasize links between the living and the dead. They believe that the dead join their ancestors in the ranks of divinity and that ancestors are intensely concerned with the fate of their living descendants. This spiritual communion is celebrated by the Merina and Betsileo reburial practice of famadihana, or "turning over the dead." In this ritual, relatives' remains are exhumed, rewrapped in new silk shrouds, and reburied following festive ceremonies in their honor.

About 40% of the Malagasy are Christian, divided almost evenly between Roman Catholic and Protestant. Many incorporate the cult of the dead with their religious beliefs and bless their dead at church before proceeding with the traditional burial rites. They also may invite a pastor to attend a famadihana.

An historical rivalry exists between the predominantly Catholic coastal people (cotiers), considered to be underprivileged, and the predominantly Protestant Merina, who tend to prevail in the civil service, business, and professions. A new policy of decentralizing resources and authority is intended to enhance the development potential of all Madagascar's provinces.

The written history of Madagascar began in the seventh century A.D., when Arabs established trading posts along the northwest coast. European contact began in the 1500s, when Portuguese sea captain Diego Dias sighted the island after his ship became separated from a fleet bound for India. In the late 17th century, the French established trading posts along the east coast. From about 1774 to 1824, it was a favorite haunt for pirates, including Americans, one of whom brought Malagasy rice to South Carolina.

Beginning in the 1790s, Merina rulers succeeded in establishing hegemony over the major part of the island, including the coast. In 1817, the Merina ruler and the British governor of Mauritius concluded a treaty abolishing the slave trade, which had been important in Madagascar's economy. In return, the island received British military and financial assistance. British influence remained strong for several decades, during which the Merina court was converted to Presbyterianism, Congregationalism, and Anglicanism.

The British accepted the imposition of a French protectorate over Madagascar in 1885 in return for eventual control over Zanzibar (now part of Tanzania) and as part of an overall definition of spheres of influence in the area. Absolute French control over Madagascar was established by military force in 1895-96, and the Merina monarchy was abolished.

Malagasy troops fought in France, Morocco, and Syria during World War I. After France fell to the Germans in 1942, Madagascar was administered first by the Vichy Government and then by the British, whose troops occupied the strategic island to preclude its seizure by the Japanese. The Free French received the island from the United Kingdom in 1943.

In 1947, with French prestige at low ebb, a nationalist uprising was suppressed only after several months of bitter fighting. The French subsequently established reformed institutions in 1956 under the Loi Cadre (Overseas Reform Act), and Madagascar moved peacefully toward independence.

The Malagasy Republic was proclaimed on October 14, 1958, as an autonomous state within the French Community. A period of provisional government ended with the adoption of a constitution in 1959 and full independence on June 26, 1960.

# GOVERNMENT

In August 1992, Malagasy voters overwhelmingly approved a new, democratic constitution to replace the socialist-oriented 1975 charter. According to the new constitution, the principal institutions of the Republic of Madagascar are a presidency, a parliament (National Assembly and Senate), a prime ministry and government, and an independent judiciary. The president is elected by direct universal suffrage for a five-year term, renewable only once, and is primarily responsible for Madagascar's defense and foreign policy.

The National Assembly consists of 138 representatives elected by direct vote every four years. The selection of the Senate must await the formation of local governments, since two-thirds of the Senate will be elected by local legislatures and one-third appointed by the president, all for four-year terms. Day-to-day management of government is carried out by a prime minister and a council of ministers. A prime minister is elected every four years by a new National Assembly.

In reaction to the concentration of power in the hands of the president during the previous regime, the new constitution contains a number of checks and balances. The prime minister, not the president, initiates and executes legislation. The government and the president, provided they act in concert, can dissolve the National Assembly. For its part, the National Assembly can pass a motion of censure and require the prime minister and council of ministers to step down. The Constitutional Court approves the constitutionality of new laws.

Territorial administration is to be determined by legislation. In an effort to decentralize administration, the current structure of six regions (faritany) are likely to be broken up into more numerous districts, each with increased autonomy. The constitution only provides for the perpetuation of rural village and clan-level entities known as fokonolona, which are accorded the right to protect their traditional fields, pasture lands, and sacred sites.

## Principal Government Officials

**For up-to-date information on Principal Government Officials, see the Chiefs of State and Cabinet Members of Foreign Governments section starting on page 1.**

Madagascar maintains an embassy in the United States at 2374 Massachusetts Avenue NW., Washington, DC 20008 (tel. 202-265-5525).

# POLITICAL CONDITIONS

Madagascar's first President, Philibert Tsiranana, was elected when his Social Democratic Party gained power at independence in 1960 and was reelected without opposition in March 1972. However, he resigned only two months later in response to massive anti-government demonstrations. The unrest continued, and Tsiranana's successor, General Gabriel Ramanantsoa, resigned on February 5, 1975, handing over executive power to Lt. Col. Richard Ratsimandrava, who was assassinated six days later. A provisional military directorate then ruled until a new government was formed in June 1975, under Admiral Didier Ratsiraka.

During the 16 subsequent years of President Ratsiraka's rule, Madagascar continued under a government committed to revolutionary socialism based on the 1975 constitution establishing a highly centralized state. National elections in 1982 and 1989 returned Ratsiraka for a second and

third seven-year presidential term. For much of this period, only limited and restrained political opposition was tolerated, with no direct criticism of the president permitted in the press.

With an easing of restrictions on political expression, beginning in the late 1980s, the Ratsiraka regime came under increasing pressure for fundamental change. In response to a deteriorating economy, Ratsiraka had

MADAGASCAR

0   100   200 Miles

0   100   200 Kilometers

COMOROS

Île de Mayotte (FR.)

Îles Glorieuses (FR.)

Cap d'Ambre

**Antsiranana**

Ambilobe

Nosy Be

Mt. Maromokotro 9,436 ft. 2876 m

MASSIF DU TSARATANANA

Baie de Narinda

Antalaha

Sofia

Maroantsetra

Cap Saint André

Baie de Baly

**Mahajanga**

Rantabe

Cap Masoala

Marovoay

Baie d'Antongila

Île Juan de Nova (FR.)

Lac Kinkony

Antanambe

Mozambique Channel

Besalampy

Lac Alaotra

Nosy Sainte Marie

Betsiboka

Maevatanana

Ambatondrazaka

Mahajamba

Foolpointe

Fenoarivo Be

**Toamasina**

Bemaraha Plateau

**Antananarivo**

Moramanga

Vatomandry

Belo-Tsiribihina

Mania

Ambatolampy

**Antsirabe**

Morondava

Ambositra

Canal des Pangalanes

Manja

INDIAN OCEAN

Mangoky

MASSIF DE L'ISALO

**Fianarantsoa**

Cap Saint Vincent

Atsimo

Manakara

Farafangana

Onilahy

Vangaindrano

**Toliara**

Menarandra

Ranomena

Manantenina

Tolañaro (Fort Dauphin)

Androka

Amboasary

Cap Saint Marie

Bassas da India (FR.)

Mozambique Channel

MADAGASCAR

INDIAN OCEAN

Îles Europa (FR.)

Madagascar

begun relaxing socialist dogma to institute some liberal, private-sector reforms. But these and other political reforms—like the elimination of press censorship in 1989 and the formation of more political parties in 1990—were insufficient to placate a growing opposition force known as Hery Velona or "active forces," centered in the capital city and the surrounding high plateau.

In response to largely peaceful mass demonstrations and crippling general strikes, Ratsiraka replaced his prime minister in August 1991 but suffered an irreparable setback soon thereafter when his troops fired on peaceful demonstrators marching on his suburban palace, killing more than 30.

In an increasingly weakened position, Ratsiraka acceded to negotiations on the formation of a transitional government. The resulting "Panorama Convention" of October 31, 1991, stripped Ratsiraka of nearly all of his powers, created interim institutions, and set an 18-month timetable for completing a transition to a new form of constitutional government. The High Constitutional Court was retained as the ultimate judicial arbiter of the process.

In March 1992, a new constitution was drafted by a widely representative National Forum organized by the Malagasy Christian Council of Churches. Troops guarding the proceedings killed several pro-Ratsiraka "federalists" who tried to disrupt the forum in protest of draft constitutional provisions preventing the incumbent president from running again. The text of the new constitution was put to a nationwide referendum in August 1992 and approved by a wide margin, despite efforts by federalists to disrupt balloting in several coastal areas.

Presidential elections were held on November 25, 1992, after the High Constitutional Court had ruled, over active forces objections, that Ratsiraka could become a candidate. A runoff election was held in February 1993, and active forces leader Albert Zafy defeated Ratsiraka. He was

sworn in as President on March 27, 1993.

A nationwide legislative election was held in June 1993 to elect a new National Assembly, which, under the new constitution, exercises legislative initiative along with the prime minister, whom it elects. On the legislative agenda of the new National Assembly is the redefinition of Madagascar's territorial divisions and the increased devolution of administrative decision making to them.

The proportional representation system for the election of legislators contributed to a significant increase in the number of political parties and special-interest groups. These and a free press promote open and lively discussion of political issues in Madagascar.

# ECONOMY

Agriculture dominates the Malagasy economy, accounting for about 43% of GDP and 80% of exports. Recent estimates are that 88% of the work force is engaged in the agricultural sector. An estimated 65% of the population lives at subsistence level.

Historically, Madagascar's principal export crops have been coffee, vanilla, and cloves. Coffee, which as recently as 1989, was Madagascar's largest earner of foreign exchange, is now a distant second, as both prices and exports have dropped sharply.

Total coffee production has not increased appreciably since the late 1980s. Vanilla exports are the largest source of export earnings, but in recent years this industry has come under intense pressure from foreign competition as well as by increasing use of artificial flavorings.

Clove exports have been highly cyclical in the past; however, prices have changed little in the last six years. Despite price stability, in 1992, exports fell nearly 35% in volume from the previous year.

Price stabilization funds for coffee and cloves were abolished in the late

1980s, but the export price of vanilla remains subject to government control. The recent sharp decline in export receipts from these three cash crops has contributed to a severe shortage of foreign exchange in Madagascar, limiting the import of industrial inputs, capital equipment, and spare parts essential to national economic recovery plans.

The principal food crop in Madagascar is rice. In recent years, one of the main policy objectives in the agriculture sector has been to expand rice production to meet food self-sufficiency targets. During the 1980s, controls on the transport, production, and sale of rice were removed. Although rice imports have not been eliminated, they have declined appreciably from levels reached during the early 1980s.

Other industries showing promise for foreign exchange and employment are tourism, clothing manufacture, fishing, commercial agriculture, and mining. Because of its unique and diverse flora and fauna, Madagascar has the potential of becoming a center of world eco-tourism. The future development of this activity will depend, however, on extensive improvements in the transportation and communication infrastructure in Madagascar. It will also depend on efforts to control deforestation by the population of as much as 80% of existing forests.

Manufacturing accounts for about 14% of the nation's gross domestic product. Low labor costs have encouraged clothing manufacturers to move some operations from Mauritius to Madagascar. A program of duty-free-zones has also attracted some clothing manufacturers. The clothing sector promises to become increasingly important relative to the previous industrial sectors—food processing (currently 50% of industrial activity) and textiles (about 25%). The duty-free program provides for tax benefits and duty-free import of manufacturing inputs for export-oriented industries. By early 1993, about 70 companies established under the provisions of this law were employing more than 17,000 workers.

855

Madagascar's coastal waters, rich in fish and shrimp, have also become an important source of foreign exchange. In 1991, shrimp export receipts overtook those from export of both coffee and cloves for the first time. In the mineral sector, Madagascar has substantial deposits of mica, graphite, and chromite, but exports of these minerals remain comparatively small (less than 10%). It is also a leading producer of semiprecious stones. Large ilmenite deposits in the south may become important sources of titanium dioxide, used for paint pigment. Petroleum exploration continues in Madagascar, but commercially significant quantities of oil have not yet been found.

In the foreign trade sector, Madagascar consistently has run a large trade deficit since the mid-1980s. Severely depressed coffee export receipts and the failure to diversify into new export products have exacerbated the trade imbalance. Energy imports (one-sixth of total imports) are a major drain on foreign exchange resources. Until 1988, the former Soviet Union was Madagascar's principal supplier of crude oil. Supplies are now obtained from Middle Eastern sources and Iran. France remains Madagascar's principal trading partner. The U.S. is an important vanilla market, and Indonesia has been the largest customer for cloves, although its imports recently have decreased as Indonesia's domestic production has increased.

# FOREIGN RELATIONS

Madagascar historically has remained outside the mainstream of African affairs, although it is an active member of the Organization of African Unity and the Non-Aligned Movement.

In contrast to former President Ratsiraka's "all points" policy stressing ties with socialist and radical regimes, including North Korea, Cuba, Libya, and Iran, President Albert Zafy has expressed his desire for diplomatic relations with all countries. Early in his tenure, he established formal ties with South Korea and sent emissaries to Morocco.

## Travel Notes

**Customs:** A valid passport and entry visa are required. Tourists and official travelers should obtain visas before arrival; airport visas can be obtained for official travelers, but problems have been encountered. Travelers should be scrupulous in reporting currency; undeclared currency may be confiscated. Also required is a certificate of immunization against cholera and, if coming from an infected area, yellow fever.

Health requirements change; check latest information. Unauthorized export of protected plant and animal species is severely sanctioned.

**Health:** Avoid raw fruits and vegetables; eat only thoroughly cooked meats. Dairy products generally are not pasteurized and should be avoided. Tapwater is not potable—drink bottled beverages without ice. Do not swim in fresh or salt waters without competent local advice; fresh water is at risk for bilharzia, and coastal waters have sharks. Antimalaria medication is advisable in the capital and indispensable in the coastal areas. The climate in the highland interior tends to provoke colds and bronchitis.

**Telecommunications:** Long-distance telephone and telegraph service is available but expensive and frequently unreliable. Antananarivo is eight time zones ahead of eastern standard time.

**Transportation:** International flights are often fully booked; travel arrangements should be confirmed well in advance.

Domestic air connections are good. Some parts of the country can be covered by train, bus, rural taxi, or hired car, but the road network has deteriorated considerably, and many areas are inaccessible except by four-wheel-drive vehicles.

**Travel Advice:** For up-to-date information from the U.S. State Department on possible inconvenient or hazardous situations, see the **Travel Warnings and Consular Information Sheets from the U.S. Government** section starting on page 1723. For the latest information on health requirements and conditions, see the **International Travelers' Health Information** section starting on page 1385. For further information dealing with non-urgent matter, see the **Tips for Travelers to...** section starting on page 1588.

Active relationships have been maintained with Europe, especially France, Germany, and Switzerland, as well as with Russia, Japan, India, and China.

# U.S.-MALAGASY RELATIONS

Relations with the United States date to the early 1800s. The two countries concluded a commercial convention in 1867 and a treaty of peace, friendship, and commerce in 1881.

These traditionally warm relations suffered considerably during the 1970s, when Madagascar expelled the U.S. ambassador, closed a NASA tracking station, and nationalized two U.S. oil companies. In 1980, relations at the ambassadorial level were restored. Throughout the troubled period, commercial and cultural relations remained active.

In 1990, Madagascar was designated as a priority aid recipient, and assistance increased from $15 million in 1989 to $40 million in 1993. Recent U.S. assistance has contributed to a population census and family planning programs, conservation of Madagascar's remarkable biodiversity, private sector development, agriculture, democracy and governance initiatives, and media training.

## Principal U.S. Officials

For up-to-date information on Principal U.S. Officials, see the U.S. Embassies, Consulates, and Foreign Service section starting on page 139.

The U.S. embassy in Madagascar is at 14 Rue Rainitovo, Antsahavola, Antananarivo (tel. 212-57, 209-56; telex 222-02). The postal address is Ambassade Americaine, B.P. 620, Antananarivo, Madagascar.

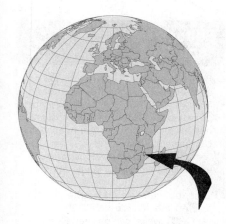

# MALAWI

February 1989

## Official Name:
## Republic of Malawi

# PROFILE

## Geography

**Area:** 118,484 sq. km. (45,747 sq. mi.); about the size of Pennsylvania.

**Cities:** Capital—Lilongwe (pop. 234,000). Other cities—Blantyre (332,000), Zomba (43,000), Mzuzu (44,000).

**Terrain:** Plateaus, high-lands, valleys. Lake Malawi is about 20% total area.

**Climate:** Predominantly subtropical.

## People

**Nationality:** Noun and adjective—Malawian(s).

**Population (1988 est.):** 8.2 million.

**Annual growth rate:** 3.1%.

**Ethnic groups:** Chewa, Nyanja, Tumbuka, Yao, Lomwe, Sena, Tonga, Ngoni, Asians, Europeans.

**Religions:** Protestant 55%, Roman Catholic 20%, Muslim 20%; African traditional religions.

**Languages:** Chichewa (national), English (official); Chitumbuka, Chiyao, Chilomwe.

**Education:** Years compulsory—none. Attendance—42% primary; 3% secondary. Literacy—25% (age 15 and older).

**Health:** Infant mortality rate—151/1,000. Life expectancy—47 yrs.

## Government

**Type:** Republic.

**Independence:** July 6, 1964.

**Constitution:** July 6, 1964.

**Branches:** Executive—president (head of government, chief of state). Legislative—unicameral National Assembly. Judicial—magisterial and traditional courts.

**Administrative subdivisions:** 24 administrative districts.

**Political party:** Malawi Congress Party.

**Suffrage:** Adult over 18.

**Central government budget (1987 est.):** $360 million.

**Defense:** 7% of budget or 2% of GDP (recurrent revenues).

**Flag:** Horizontal tricolor of black, red, and green with a red rising sun in center of black stripe.

## Economy

**GDP (1987 est.):** $1.2 billion.

**Annual growth rate (1987):** -.2%.

**Per capita GDP (1987 est.):** $158.

**Avg. inflation rate (1987 est.):** 26%.

**Natural resources:** Limestone, strontianite, monazite, uranium and coal potential.

**Agriculture (37% of GDP):** Products—tobacco, tea, sugar, corn, coffee, groundnuts, rice, cotton, beans. Arable land—34%, of which 86% is cultivated.

**Industry (manufacturing, 12% of GDP):** Types—food processing, tobacco and tea processing, textiles, footwear, consumer products.

**Trade (1986):** Exports—$245 million: tobacco, tea, sugar, cotton, groundnuts. Major Markets—Western Europe, US, South Africa. Imports—$258 million: fuel, fertilizer, agricultural inputs, machinery, spare parts. Major suppliers—South Africa, UK, Japan, Zimbabwe.

**Official exchange rate (March 1988):** 2.52 Malawi Kwacha=US$1.

**Fiscal year:** April 1-March 31.

## Membership in International Organizations

UN and some of its specialized and related agencies, including the World Bank and the International Monetary Fund (IMF); Organization of African Unity (OAU); Commonwealth; Lome Convention; African Development Bank (AFDB); Southern Africa Development Coordination Conference (SADCC); Nonaligned Movement; Preferential Trade Agreement for East and Southern Africa (PTA).

# GEOGRAPHY

Located in southeastern Africa, Malawi is traversed by part of the Great Rift Valley from north to south. In this deep trough lies Lake Malawi, the third largest lake in Africa, comprising about 20% of Malawi's area. The Shire River flows from the south end of the lake anti joins the Zambezi River 400 kilometers (250 mi.) farther south in Mozambique. East and west of the Rift Valley, the land forms high plateaus, generally between 900 and 1,200 meters (3,000-4,000 ft.) above sea level. In the north, the Nyika Uplands rise as high as 2,600 meters (8,500 ft.); south of the lake lie the Shire Highlands, with an elevation of 600-1,600 meters (2,000-5,000 ft.), rising to Mts. Zomba and Mulanje, 2,130 and 3,048 meters (7,000 and 10,000 ft.). In the extreme south, the elevation is only 60-90 meters (200-300 ft.) above sea level.

Although the new capital, Lilongwe, has expanded rapidly, Blantyre remains Malawi's major commercial center and largest city, having grown from 109,000 inhabitants in 1966 to an estimated 332,000 in 1988. Lilongwe's population has grown from 19,000 in 1966 to 234,000 in 1988 and has attracted increasing commercial activity as well as the government ministries, all of which were relocated in Lilongwe by 1979. The parliament still meets in Zomba.

Malawi's climate is generally subtropical; it is hot and humid only along the lake, in the Shire Valley, and in the far south from October to April. The rest of the country, especially the higher elevations, is warm during those months. From June through August, the lake areas and the far south are comfortably warm, but the rest of Malawi can be quite chilly at night—5°C-14°C (41°F-57°F)

# PEOPLE

Malawi derives its name from the Maravi, a Bantu people who came from the southern Congo about 600 years ago. On reaching the area north of Lake Malawi, the Maravi divided. One branch, the ancestors of the present-day Chewas, moved south to the west bank of the lake, and the other, the ancestors of the Nyanjas, moved down the east bank to the southern part of the country.

By A.D. 1500, the two divisions of the tribe had established a kingdom stretching from north of today's Nkhotakota to the Zambezi River in the south anti from Lake Malawi in the east to the Luangwa River in Zambia in the west.

In recent years, ethnic and tribal distinctions have diminished. Despite some clear differences, no significant friction currently exists between tribal groups, and the concept of a Malawian nationality has begun to take hold.

The Chewas constitute 90% of the population of the central region; the Nyanja tribe predominates in the south anti the Tumbuka in the north. In addition, significant numbers of the Tongas live in the north; Ngonis—an offshoot of the Zulus who came from South Africa in the early 1800s—live in the lower northern and lower central regions; and the Yao, who are mostly Muslim, live along the southeastern border with Mozambique.

Migrations and tribal conflicts precluded the formation of a cohesive Malawian society until the turn of the 20th century. A characteristically Malawian culture is still in the formative stages. Predominantly a rural people, Malawians have begun receiving primary school education in sizable numbers only since independence.

# HISTORY

Hominid remains and stone implements have been identified in Malawi dating back more than 1 million years, and early humans inhabited the vicinity of Lake Malawi 50,000-60,000 years ago. Human remains at a site dated about 8000 B.C. show physical characteristics similar to peoples living today in the Horn of Africa. At another site, dated 1500 B.C., the remains possess features resembling Negro and Bushman people.

Although the Portuguese reached the area in the 16th century, the first sig-

nificant Western contact was the arrival of David Livingston along the shore of Lake Malawi in 1859. Subsequently, Scottish churches established missions in Malawi. One of their objectives was to end the slave trade that continued there as late as the end of the 19th century. In 1878, a number of traders, mostly from Glasgow, formed the African Lakes Company to supply goods and services to the missionaries. Other missionaries, traders, hunters, anti planters soon followed.

In 1883, a consul of the British Government was accredited to the "Kings and Chiefs of Central Africa," and in 1891, the British established the Nyasaland Protectorate (Nyasa is the Chichewa word for "lake"). The British remained in control during the first half of the 1900s; however this period was marked by a number of unsuccessful Malawian attempts to obtain independence. With a growing number of educated African elite voicing its opinions and demands-first through associations, and after 1944, through the Nyasaland African Congress (NAC)—the surge toward nationalism was begun.

During the 1950's, pressure for independence increased when Nyasaland joined with Northern and Southern Rhodesia in 1953 to form the Federation of Rhodesia and Nyasaland. In July 1958, Dr. H. Kamuzu Banda returned to the country after a long absence in the United States (where he had obtained his medical degree at Meharry Medical College in 1937), the United Kingdom, and Ghana. He assumed leadership of the NAC, which later became the Malawi Congress Party (MCP). In 1959, Banda was sent to Gwelo Prison for his political activities but was released in 1960 to join in the constitutional conference in London.

On April 15, 1961, the MCP won an overwhelming victory in elections for a new Legislative Council. It also gained an important role in the new Executive Council and ruled Nyasaland in all but name a year later. In a second constitutional conference in London in November 1962, the British Government agreed to give Nyasaland self-governing status the following year.

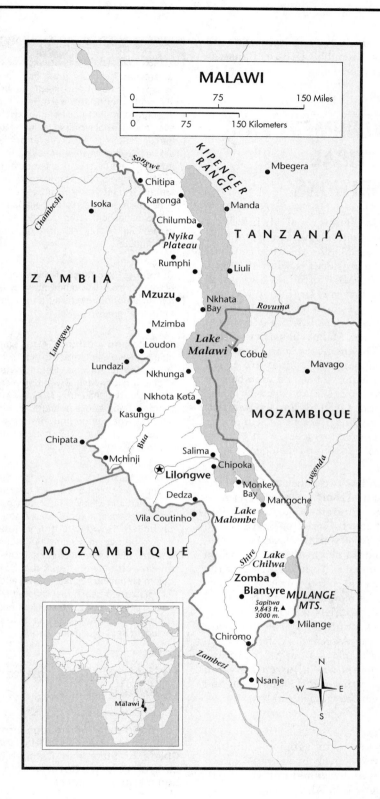

Dr. Banda became prime minister on February 1, 1963, although the British still controlled Malawi's financial, security, and judicial systems. A new constitution took effect in May 1963, providing for virtually complete internal self-government. The Feder-

ation of Rhodesia and Nyasaland was dissolved on December 31, 1963, and Malawi became fully independent under its new name as a member of the Commonwealth (formerly the British Commonwealth) on July 6, 1964. Two years later, Malawi adopted a new constitution and became a republic with Dr. Banda as its first president.

# GOVERNMENT AND POLITICAL CONDITIONS

The Government of Malawi is a greatly modified version of the British system. Under the 1966 constitution, the president is selected every 5 years by MCP officials and tribal chiefs. However, Dr. Banda was proclaimed president for life in 1970 by a unanimous resolution of the MCP convention. Malawi has no vice president. The members of the presidentially appointed Cabinet are either drawn from or become members of parliament. Malawi's unicameral National Assembly (or parliament) currently has 118 seats, the majority being elected members, with 11 presidentially appointed members.

Malawi has two judicial systems: the magisterial courts, headed by a three-member Supreme Court, anti traditional courts," created in 1964 and based largely on the local court system maintained by the British before independence. Unlike officials of the earlier local courts, however a majority of the members of the traditional courts are chiefs who have jurisdiction to hear any type of criminal case involving Africans. Although each system employs an appeals process, no appeals are allowed between courts in the traditional system and courts in the magisterial line.

Local government is carried out in 24 districts within 3 regions administered respectively by district commissioners and regional ministers with Cabinet rank. All are appointed by the central government.

Malawi has only one authorized political party, the MCP. The National Assembly elections were last held in May 1987 on the basis of universal suffrage by secret ballot.

## Travel Notes

**Customs:** Travelers must have a valid passport or travel document, as well as visas for any countries they will pass through en route to or from Malawi; however, a visa is not required to enter Malawi. Immunizations for yellow fever or cholera are required of travelers passing through infected areas. Health requirements change; check latest information. The Malawian Government practices strict censorship, and travelers' luggage is subject to inspection. Journalists are admitted to the country only with prior government clearance.

**Currency:** Exportation of Malawi currency is limited; exporting other currency is limited to amounts declared on a customs form upon arrival.

**Climate and clothing:** Wear summer clothing from September to April, woolen from May to August. Female visitors should arrive in Malawi wearing a skirt or dress covering the knee. The Malawi Government bans slacks or shorts for women (except when engaging in sports or at game parks). Men's hair may not extend below the nape of the neck.

**Health:** Medical facilities are few. Malaria is endemic. Chloroquine resistant malaria is prevalent in Malawi. Tap water in major cities is potable; in rural areas, water must be boiled. Raw fruits and vegetables should be peeled. Freshwater lakes and streams may contain bilharzia (schistosomiasis) organisms. Seek local advice before swimming in Lake Malawi, although its established beach resorts are believed safe. Tsetse flies (and the risk of encephalitis) are present in areas of Malawi, including Kasungu Game Park.

**Telecommunications:** Good long-distance radio/telephone service is available. Telegraph services connect Malawi with the United States. Malawi is seven time zones ahead of eastern standard time.

**Transportation:** Lilongwe's Kamuzu International Airport has regular service from the US via London, Paris, Amsterdam, or Nairobi. Within Malawi, major internal arteries between cities and the road between Lilongwe and Lusaka, Zambia are paved. Traffic moves on the left. Rental cars are usually available in the major urban centers, as are taxis.

**Tourist attractions:** Three major game parks: Lengwe (for antelope), in southern Malawi, 11/2 hrs. from Blantyre by road; Kasungu, in central Malawi, 2 hrs. north of Lilongwe (for elephant, hippopotamus, buck, zebra, and occasional lion and leopard); and Nyika, in the north, one of the world's highest game areas. Lake Malawi offers lovely beaches, a few lodges, and many varieties of tropical fish. Snorkeling is popular. The Dedza, Mulanje, and Zomba Mountains are popular for climbing and hiking.

**Travel Advice:** For up-to-date information from the U.S. State Department on possible inconvenient or hazardous situations, see the **Travel Warnings and Consular Information Sheets from the U.S. Government** section starting on page 1723. For the latest information on health requirements and conditions, see the **International Travelers' Health Information** section starting on page 1385. For further information dealing with non-urgent matter, see the **Tips for Travelers to...** section starting on page 1588.

## Principal Government Officials

**For up-to-date information on Principal Government Officials, see the Chiefs of State and Cabinet Members of Foreign Governments section starting on page 1.**

# ECONOMY

Malawi is a predominantly agricultural economy, operating under a relatively free enterprise environment. Nearly 90% of the population engages in subsistence farming. Smallholder farmers produce a variety of crops, including maize (corn), beans, rice, cassava, tobacco, and groundnuts (peanuts). The main cash crops, grown mostly on estates, are tobacco, tea, coffee, and sugar.

Traditionally, Malawi has relied on an expanding agricultural export sector as its primary vehicle for economic growth. A landlocked country endowed with few exploitable mineral resources, Malawi has developed

**A Malawian fisherman repairs his net.**

Photo credit: Corel Corporation.

since independence into a major exporter of tobacco, tea, sugar groundnuts, coffee, cotton, and most recently, maize (corn). Malawi typically has been self-sufficient in its staple food, maize, and during the mid-1980s exported substantial quantities to its drought-stricken neighbors.

During the 1980s, the Malawian economy was severely affected by the slump in world commodity prices and balance-of-payments problems. Drought, insect infestation, transportation problems, and a massive influx of refugees from Mozambique created further complications.

Real GDP growth declined sharply to minus 0.2% in 1987. In addition to exogenous factors, major structural weaknesses contributed to this economic decline, including:

• Heavy dependency on exports of agricultural products;

• Low producer prices;

• Deteriorating financial situation of parastatal bodies;

• Increasing deficits;

• Formal and informal price controls; and

• Weaknesses in public administration anti management.

Since 1982, the government has implemented a strict program of structural reform with assistance from the International Monetary Find, the World Bank, and bilateral donors, including the United States. During much of this time, Malawi achieved modest rates of economic growth and self-sufficiency in production of its stable food crops. As a result of the progress in economic reform, Malawi has gained broad support and respect among the international donor community.

As a landlocked country, Malawi depends on foreign ports for its imports and exports and is particularly vulnerable to political and economic events within the southern Africa region. The insurgency in Mozambique has blocked direct rail access to Malawi's closest outlets to the sea—the Mozambican Ports of Beira and Nacala. Consequently, Malawi has been forced to rely, for the most part, on the distant Port of Durban in South Africa, which has resulted in substantial increases in transportation costs and has undermined the competitiveness of Malawian exports.

In an agreement with the Mozambican Government, Malawi has contributed to efforts to rehabilitate and secure the Nacala Railroad Line inside Mozambique. The small Malawian Army, providing military protection to part of the line, suffered some casualties from rebel activities aimed at keeping the rail line closed.

Malawi currently hosts one of the largest refugee populations in Africa (about 500,000 in late 1988). Since mid- 1986, when it had almost no refugees, Malawi has experienced a massive influx of Mozambicans fleeing anarchic conditions, famine, and fighting between Mozambican Government forces and insurgents. By late 1987, some 400,000 refugees were in Malawi, and more were arriving at an alarming rate. The refugees, located in heavily populated areas with little available land, have placed a great strain on the economy and on the transportation and social services networks. In some areas, the number of refugees is equal to or slightly greater than the Malawian population. The Government has accepted these refugees and, with the help of international humanitarian organizations, works to provide adequate relief assistance. The government also has devoted many of its own scarce resources to assisting the refugees and permits international and private voluntary organizations to operate relief efforts.

# FOREIGN RELATIONS

Under President Banda, Malawi's foreign policy orientation has been proWestern. It maintains diplomatic relations with principal Western countries but has little contact with communist nations. It is a member of the United Nations and several of its specialized and related agencies, the Organization of African Unity, and the Commonwealth. It also is a signatory to the Lome Convention, which deals with tariff preferences in the European Community.

Malawi has retained diplomatic relations with South Africa since the late 1960s and views itself as a bridge between that government and the rest of Africa. Although Malawi's political ideology is different from that of its three contiguous neighbors, it has pursued normal relations with them and all other states of the region. In recent years, Malawi has exchanged diplomatic representatives with Mozambique and Zimbabwe and established diplomatic representation in Tanzania. Relations with Mozambique have improved markedly, as evidenced by the December 1986 joint security agreement. Malawi has established joint commissions with Zambia, Mozambique, and Zimbabwe to resolve mutual problems.

## Principal U.S. Officials

**For up-to-date information on Principal U.S. Officials, see the U.S. Embassies, Consulates, and For-****eign Service section starting on page 139.**

The U.S. Embassy in Malawi is located in the new capital city development area in Lilongwe. The address is American Embassy, P.O. Box 30016, Capital City, Lilongwe 3, Malawi (tel. 730166).

# U.S.-MALAWIAN RELATIONS

The United States enjoys cordial relations with Malawi, and significant numbers of Malawians study in the United States. An American cultural center in Lilongwe is frequented by many Malawians seeking to expand their knowledge of the United States by using the lending library, attending lectures by visiting American speakers, or viewing films or videotapes. The United States has an active Peace Corps program and an Agency for International Development Mission in Malawi.

U.S. and Malawian views on the necessity of economic and political stability in southern Africa generally coincide. Through a pragmatic assessment of its own national interests and foreign policy objectives, Malawi advocates peaceful solution of the region's problems through negotiation and works with the United States to achieve these objectives in such important arenas as the United Nations.

The two countries maintain a continuing dialogue through diplomatic representatives and in periodic visits by senior officials. President Banda was educated in and has visited the United States several times, most recently in April 1978.

# MALAYSIA
October 2000

Official Name:
**Malaysia**

# PROFILE

## Geography
**Area:** 329,749 sq. km. (127,316 sq. mi.); slightly larger than New Mexico.
**Cities:** Capital—Kuala Lumpur. Other cities—Penang, Ipoh, Malacca, Johor Baru, Kuching, Kota Kinabalu.
**Terrain:** Coastal plains and interior, jungle-covered mountains. The South China Sea separates peninsular Malaysia from East Malaysia on Borneo (400 miles).
**Climate:** Tropical.

## People
**Nationality:** Noun and adjective—Malaysian(s).
**Population:** (1999) 22.7 million.
**Annual growth rate:** 2.4%.
**Ethnic Groups:** Malay 47%, Chinese 24%, Indigenous 11%, Indian 7%, non-Malaysian citizens 7%, others 4%.
**Religion:** Islam, Buddhism, Confucianism, Taoism, Christianity, Hinduism, Sikhism, Baha'i faith.
**Languages:** Malay, Cantonese, Hokkien, Mandarin Chinese, English, Tamil, indigenous.
**Education:** Years compulsory—9. Attendance—99% (primary), 82% (secondary). Literacy (1999)—94%.

**Health:** Infant mortality rate (1999)—7.9/1,000. Life expectancy (2000)—female 75 yrs., male 70.2 yrs
**Work force:** (9.6 million, 2000) Manufacturing—23.2%; services (includes government)—20.8%; trade and tourism—19.2%; agriculture—18.3%; construction—8.9%; finance—4.9%; transportation and communications—4.6%; utilities—0.5%; mining and petroleum—0.3%.

## Government
**Type:** Federal parliamentary democracy with a constitutional monarch.
**Independence:** August 31, 1957. (Malaya, what is now peninsular Malaysia, became independent in 1957. In 1963 Malaya, Sabah, Sarawak, and Singapore formed Malaysia. Singapore became an independent country in 1965.)
**Constitution:** 1957.
**Subdivisions:** 13 states and two federal territories (capital and Labuan). Each state has an assembly and government headed by a chief minister. Nine of these states have hereditary rulers, generally titled "sultans," while the remaining four have appointed governors in counterpart positions.
**Branches:** Executive—Yang di-Pertuan Agong ("paramount ruler," who is head of state and customarily referred to as the king and has ceremonial duties), prime minister (head of government), cabinet. Legisla-

tive—bicameral parliament, comprising 69-member Senate (26 elected by the 13 state assemblies, 43 appointed by the king on the prime minister's recommendation) and 193-member House of Representatives (elected from single-member districts). Judicial—Federal Court, Court of Appeals, high courts, magistrate's courts, session's courts, and juvenile courts. Syariah courts hear cases on certain matters involving Muslims only.
**Political parties:** Barisan Nasional (National Front)—a coalition comprising the United Malays National Organization (UMNO) and 13 other parties, most of which are ethnically based; Democratic Action Party (DAP); Parti Se-Islam Malaysia (PAS); Parti Bersatu Sabah (PBS); Parti KeADILan. There are more than 30 registered political parties, including the foregoing, not all of which are represented in the federal parliament.
**Suffrage:** Universal adult.

## Economy
**Year:** (1999).
**GNP:** $74 billion.
**Annual real GDP growth rate:** 5.8%.
**Per capita income:** $3,238.
**Natural resources:** Petroleum, liquefied natural gas (LNG), tin, minerals.
**Agriculture:** Products—palm oil,

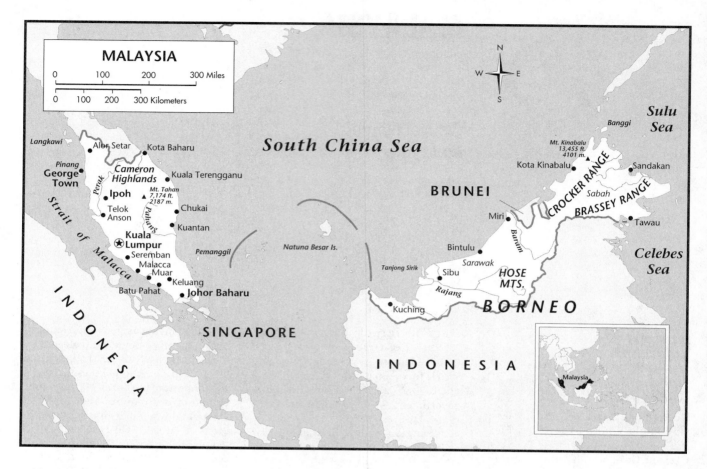

### MALAYSIA

rubber, timber, cocoa, rice, tropical fruit, fish, coconut.

**Industry:** Types—electronics, electrical products, chemicals, food and beverages, metal and machine products, apparel.

**Trade:** Exports—$84.5 billion: electronics, electrical products, palm oil, petroleum, liquid natural gas, apparel, timber and logs, plywood and veneer, natural rubber. Major markets—U.S. 21.9%, Singapore 16.5%, Japan 11.6%. Imports—$65.5 billion: machinery, chemicals, manufactured goods, fuels and lubricants. Major suppliers—U.S. 17.4%, Japan 20.8%, Singapore 14.0%.

# PEOPLE

Malaysia's population of 22.7 million (1999) continues to grow at a rate of 2.4% per annum; about 34% of the population is under the age of 15. Malaysia's population comprises many ethnic groups, with the politically dominant Malays comprising a

plurality. By constitutional definition, all Malays are Muslim. About a quarter of the population is Chinese who have historically played an important role in trade and business.

Malaysians of Indian descent comprise about 7% of the population and include Hindus, Muslims, Buddhists, and Christians. About 85% of the Indian community is Tamil.

Non-Malay indigenous groups make up more than half of Sarawak's population and about 66% of Sabah's. They are divided into dozens of ethnic groups, but they share some general patterns of living and culture. Until the 20th century, most practiced traditional beliefs, but many have become Christian or Muslim. The "other" category includes Malaysians of, inter alia, European and Middle Eastern descent. Population distribution is uneven, with some 15 million residents concentrated in the lowlands of Peninsular Malaysia, an area slightly smaller than the State of Michigan.

# HISTORY

In the first century AD, two far-flung but related events helped stimulate Malaysia's emergence in international trade in the ancient world. At that time, India had two principal sources of gold and other metals: the Roman Empire and China. The overland route from China was cut by marauding Huns, and at about the same time, the Roman Emperor Vespasian cut off shipments of gold to India. As a result, India sent large and seaworthy ships, with crews reported to have numbered in the hundreds, to Southeast Asia, including the Malayan Peninsula, to seek alternative sources. In the centuries that followed, rich Malaysian tin deposits assumed great significance in Indian Ocean trade, and the region prospered. As maritime trade among Middle Eastern, Indian, and Chinese ports flourished, the peninsula benefited from its location as well as from development of its diverse resources, including tropical woods and spices.

Malay ships became prominent in that trade, and Malay ports served as transshipment centers. Indian trade brought Indian culture, economy, religion, and politics, with historic results for what is now Malaysia.

The early Buddhist Malay kingdom of Srivijaya, based at what is now Palembang, Sumatra, dominated much of the Malay Peninsula from the 9th to the 13th centuries AD. The powerful Hindu kingdom of Majapahit, based on Java, gained control of the Malay Peninsula in the 14th century. Conversion of the Malays to Islam, beginning in the early 14th century, accelerated with the rise of the state of Malacca under the rule of a Muslim prince in the 15th century.

Malacca was a major regional entrepot, where Chinese, Arab, Malay, and Indian merchants traded precious goods. Drawn by this rich trade, a Portuguese fleet conquered Malacca in 1511, marking the beginning of European expansion in Southeast Asia. The Dutch ousted the Portuguese from Malacca in 1641 and, in 1795, were themselves replaced by the British, who had occupied Penang in 1786.

In 1826, the British settlements of Malacca, Penang, and Singapore were combined to form the Colony of the Straits Settlements. From these strong points, in the 19th and early 20th centuries, the British established protectorates over the Malay sultanates on the peninsula. Four of these states were consolidated in 1895 as the Federated Malay States.

During British control, a well-ordered system of public administration was established, public services were extended, and largescale rubber and tin production was developed. This control was interrupted by the Japanese invasion and occupation from 1942 to 1945 during World War II.

Popular sentiment for independence swelled during and after the war and, in 1957, the Federation of Malaysia, established from the British-ruled territories of Peninsula Malaysia in 1948, negotiated independence from

the United Kingdom under the leadership of Tunku Abdul Rahman, who became the first prime minister. The British colonies of Singapore, Sarawak, and Sabah (called North Borneo) joined the Federation to form Malaysia on September 16, 1963. Singapore withdrew from the Federation on August 9, 1965, and became an independent republic. Neighboring Indonesia objected to the formation of Malaysia and pursued a program of economic, political, diplomatic, and military "confrontation" against the new country, which ended only after the fall of Indonesia's President Sukarno in 1966.

Following World War II, local communists, nearly all Chinese, launched a long, bitter insurgency, prompting the imposition of a state of emergency in 1948 (later lifted in 1960). Small bands of guerrillas remained in bases along the rugged border with southern Thailand, occasionally entering northern Malaysia. These guerrillas finally signed a peace accord with the Malaysian Government in December 1989. A separate smallscale communist insurgency that began in the mid-1960s in Sarawak also ended with the signing of a peace accord in October 1990.

# GOVERNMENT

Malaysia is a constitutional monarchy, nominally headed by the Yang di-Pertuan Agong ("paramount ruler"), customarily referred to as the king. Kings are elected for 5-year terms from among the nine sultans of the peninsular Malaysian states. The king also is the leader of the Islamic faith in Malaysia.

Executive power is vested in the cabinet led by the prime minister; the Malaysian constitution stipulates that the prime minister must be a member of the lower house of parliament who, in the opinion of the Yang di-Pertuan Agong, commands a majority in parliament. The cabinet is chosen from among members of both houses of parliament and is responsible to that body.

The bicameral parliament consists of the Senate (Dewan Negara) and the House of Representatives (Dewan Rakyat). All 69 Senate members sit for 6-year terms; 26 are elected by the 13 state assemblies, and 43 are appointed by the king. Representatives of the House are elected from single-member districts by universal adult suffrage. The 193 members of the House of Representatives are elected to maximum terms of 5 years. Legislative power is divided between federal and state legislatures.

The Malaysian legal system is based on English common law. The Federal Court reviews decisions referred from the Court of Appeals; it has original jurisdiction in constitutional matters and in disputes between states or between the federal government and a state. Peninsular Malaysia and the East Malaysian states of Sabah and Sarawak each have a high court.

The federal government has authority over external affairs, defense, internal security, justice (except civil law cases among Malays or other Muslims and other indigenous peoples, adjudicated under Islamic and traditional law), federal citizenship, finance, commerce, industry, communications, transportation, and other matters.

## Principal Government Officials

**For up-to-date information on Principal Government Officials, see the Chiefs of State and Cabinet Members of Foreign Governments section starting on page 1.**

Malaysia maintains an embassy in the U.S. at 2401 Massachusetts Ave. NW, Washington, DC 20008, tel. (202) 328-2700; a Consulate General in the World Trade Center, 350 South Figueroa Street, Los Angeles, CA, tel. (213) 621-2991; and a Consulate General at 140 E. 45th Street, New York, NY 10017, tel. (212) 490-2722.

# POLITICAL CONDITIONS

Malaysia's predominant political party, the United Malays National Organization (UMNO), has held power in coalition with other parties since Malaya's independence in 1957. In 1973, an alliance of communally based parties was replaced with a broader coalition—the Barisan Nasional—composed of 14 parties. In early September 1998, Prime Minister Mahathir dismissed Deputy Prime Minister Anwar Ibraham and accused Anwar of immoral and corrupt conduct.

Anwar said his ouster actually owed to political differences and led a series of demonstrations advocating political reforms. Later in September, Anwar was arrested, beaten while in prison, and charged with corrupt practices, i.e., obstruction of justice and sodomy. In April 1999, he was convicted of four counts of corruption and sentenced to 6 years in prison. In August 2000, Anwar was convicted of one count of sodomy and sentenced to 9 years to run consecutively after his earlier 6-year sentence. Both trials were viewed by domestic and international observers as unfair. In the November 1999 general election, the Barisan Nasional was returned to power with three-fourths of the parliamentary seats, but UMNO's seats dropped from 94 to 72. The opposition Barisan Alternatif coalition, led by the Islamic Party of Malaysia (PAS), increased its seats to 42. PAS retained control of the state of Kelantan and won the additional state of Terengganu.

# ECONOMY

After nearly a decade of strong economic growth averaging 8.7% annually, Malaysia was hard hit by the regional financial crisis of 1997-99. The economy suffered a sharp 7.5% contraction in 1998 but rebounded in 1999 to grow by 5.6% for the year. The Government of Malaysia predicts 5.8% real GDP growth in the year

2000, but most analysts predict growth will exceed eight percent for the year. The economic recovery has been led by strong growth in exports, particularly of electronics and electrical products, to the United States, Malaysia's principal trade and investment partner. Inflationary pressures remain benign, and, as a result, Bank Negara, the central bank, has been able to follow a low interest rate policy. Since September 1998, the Malaysian ringgit has been pegged at an exchange rate of RM3.8/U.S.$1.0. Most analysts believe that, with consumer demand and investment finally recovering from the crisis, Malaysia should broaden its economic growth this year.

Malaysia remains an important trading partner for the United States. In 1999, two-way bilateral trade between the U.S. and Malaysia totaled U.S.$30.5 billion, with U.S. exports to Malaysia totaling U.S.$9.1 billion and U.S. imports from Malaysia increasing to U.S.$21.4 billion. Malaysia was the United States' 12th-largest trading partner and its 17th-largest export market. During the first half of 2000, U.S. exports totaled U.S.$5 billion, while U.S. imports from Malaysia reached U.S.$11.6 billion.

At independence, Malaysia inherited an economy dominated by two commodities—rubber and tin. In the 40 years thereafter, Malaysia's economic record had been one of Asia's best. From the early 1980s through the mid-1990s, the economy experienced a period of broad diversification and sustained rapid growth averaging almost 8% annually. By 1999, nominal per capita GDP had reached $3,238. New foreign and domestic investment played a significant role in the transformation of Malaysia's economy. Manufacturing grew from 13.9% of GDP in 1970 to 30% in 1999, while agriculture and mining, which together had accounted for 42.7% of GDP in 1970, dropped to 9.3% and 7.3%, respectively, in 1999. Manufacturing accounted for 30% of GDP (1999). Major products include electronic components—Malaysia is one of the world's largest exporters of

semiconductor devices—electrical goods, and appliances.

The Malaysian Government encourages Foreign Direct Investment (FDI). According to Malaysian statistics, in 1999, the U.S. ranked first among all countries in approved FDI in Malaysia's manufacturing sector with approved new manufacturing investments totaling RM5.2 billion (US$1.37 billion). Principal U.S. investment approved by the Malaysian Investment Development Authority (MIDA) was concentrated in the chemicals, electronics, and electrical sectors. The cumulative value of U.S. private investment in Malaysia exceeds $10 billion, 60% of which is in the oil and gas and petrochemical sectors with the rest in manufacturing, especially semiconductors and other electronic products.

Malaysia's New Economic Policy (NEP), first established in 1971, seeks to eradicate poverty and end the identification of economic function with ethnicity. In particular, it was designed to enhance the economic standing of ethnic Malays and other indigenous peoples (collectively known as "bumiputeras" in Bahasa Malaysia). Rapid growth through the mid-1990s made it possible to expand the share of the economy for bumiputeras without reducing the economic attainment of other groups. One controversial NEP goal was to alter the pattern of ownership of corporate equity in Malaysia, with the government providing funds to purchase foreign-owned shareholdings on behalf of the bumiputera population. In June 1991, after the NEP expired, the government unveiled its National Development Policy, which contained many of the NEP's goals, although without specific equity targets and timetables.

# DEFENSE

In the early 1990s, Malaysia undertook a major program to expand and modernize its armed forces. This included procurement of F/A-18 and C-130 aircraft from the U.S. However, budgetary constraints imposed by the 1997 financial crisis slowed military procurement. The recent economic recovery may lead to relaxation of budgetary constraints on the resumption of major weapons purchases. In October 2000 the Defense Minister announced a review of national defense and security policy to bring it up to date. This review will address new security threats that have emerged in the form of low intensity conflicts, such as the kidnapping of Malaysians and foreigners from resort islands located off the East Malaysian state of Sabah.

# FOREIGN RELATIONS

As a founding member of the Association of Southeast Asian Nations (ASEAN—established 1967), Malaysia views regional cooperation as the cornerstone of its foreign policy. Malaysia was a leading advocate of expanding ASEAN's membership to include Laos, Vietnam, and Burma, arguing that "constructive engagement" with these countries, especially Burma, will help bring political and economic changes. In world affairs, Malaysia maintains cooperative relations with the United States,

the European Union, and Japan. Malaysia is an active member of the Commonwealth, the UN, the Organization of Islamic Conference, and the Non-Aligned Movement. Malaysia also is a member of APEC and hosted the 1998 Leaders' Meeting. Malaysia maintains diplomatic relations with North Korea. In January 1999 Malaysia began a 2-year stint as a non-permanent member of the UN Security Council.

**International affiliations:** UN and many of its specialized agencies, including UNESCO; World Bank, International Monetary Fund, International Atomic Energy Agency; General Agreement on Tariffs and Trade; Association of Southeast Asian Nations; Asian Development Bank; Five-Power Defense Arrangement; South-South Commission (G-15); Asia-Pacific Economic Cooperation (APEC); Commonwealth; Non-Aligned Movement; Organization of Islamic Conference; and INTELSAT.

# U.S.-MALAYSIAN RELATIONS

The United States has maintained friendly relations with Malaysia since its independence in 1957. Despite sometimes strident rhetoric, the U.S. and Malaysia have a solid record of cooperation in many areas, including trade and investment, defense, counter-terrorism, and counter-narcotics.

Cultural and educational exchanges have been another fruitful area of cooperation. Malaysians studying in the U.S., now numbering about 14,000, represent one of the largest foreign student groups enrolled in American colleges and universities. The United States took steps to assist

Malaysian students in the U.S. through the uncertainties of the recent economic downturn.

## Trade and Investment

Malaysia's economic recovery, which began in 1999, appears likely to continue apace into 2001. The U.S. is currently Malaysia's largest trading partner and largest investor. Malaysia possesses abundant resources and land, a well-educated work force, adequate infrastructure, and a relatively stable political environment. The return of economic growth should boost U.S. exports, particularly in priority areas of development, including high-technology fields, industrial automation, medical products and services, education/distance learning, and the environment. Of particular interest to the Malaysian Government is the development of the Multimedia Super Corridor (MSC), Malaysia's effort to create a Silicon Valley in Asia. Malaysia, a member of the World Trade Organization (WTO), has few restraints on trade goods. Its service sector, however, remains protected, particularly in financial services.

## Principal U.S. Embassy Officials

**For up-to-date information on Principal U.S. Officials, see the U.S. Embassies, Consulates, and Foreign Service section starting on page 139.**

The U.S. Embassy in Malaysia is located at 376 Jalan Tun Razak, 50400 Kuala Lumpur (tel. 60-3-2168-5000, fax 60-3-242-2207).

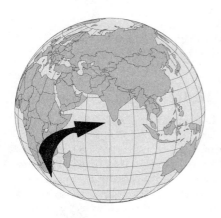

# MALDIVES

June 1996

Official Name:
**Republic of Maldives**

# PROFILE

## Geography

**Area:** 298 sq. km. (115 sq. mi.), over 1,200 islands; twice the size of Washington, DC.
**Cities:** Capital—Male (pop. 62,000).
**Terrain:** Flat islands.
**Climate:** Hot and humid.

## People

**Nationality:** Noun and adjective—Maldivian(s).
**Population:** 245,000.
**Population growth rate:** 3.3%.
**Ethnic groups:** South Indians, Sinhalese, Arabs.
**Religion:** Sunni Islam.
**Languages:** Dhivehi (official); many government officials speak English.
**Education:** Years compulsory—none. Attendance—primary 90%; secondary 35%. Literacy—93%.
**Health:** Infant mortality rate—55/1,000. Life expectancy—62 yrs.
**Work force:** Fishing—20%. Manufacturing—15%. Tourism—11%. Agriculture—5%. Other—49%.

## Government

**Type:** Republic.
**Independence:** July 26, 1965 (formerly a British protectorate).
**Constitution:** November 11, 1968.

**Branches:** Executive—president, cabinet. Legislative—unicameral Majlis (parliament). Judicial—High Court, eight lower courts, 19 atoll courts.
**Administrative subdivisions:** 19 atolls and capital city.
**Political parties:** None.
**Suffrage:** Universal at age 21.

## Economy

**GDP (1995):** $238 million.
**GDP growth rate:** 6.5%.
**Per capita GDP:** $940.
**Inflation:** 16%.
**Percentages of GDP (1994):** Distribution—19%. Tourism—18%. Fishing—12%. Construction—9%. Government—9%. Agriculture—8%. Manufacturing—6%. Other—19%.
**Trade (1994):** Exports—$55 million: fish products, garments. Major markets—Sri Lanka, U.K., U.S. Imports—$257 million: mineral products, machinery, food including vegetables, textiles. Major suppliers—Singapore, Sri Lanka, India, Hong Kong.
**Official exchange rate:** 11.67 rufiyaas=U.S.$1.

# U.S.-MALDIVIAN RELATIONS

The United States has friendly relations with the Republic of Maldives.

The U.S. ambassador and some embassy staff in Sri Lanka are accredited to Maldives and make periodic visits. The United States supports Maldivian independence and territorial integrity and publicly endorsed India's timely intervention on behalf of the Maldivian Government during the November 1988 coup attempt. U.S. Naval vessels have regularly called at Male in recent years.

U.S. contributions to economic development in Maldives have been made principally though international organization programs. Although no bilateral aid agreement exists between the two countries, the United States has directly funded training in airport management and narcotics interdiction and provided desktop computers for Maldivian customs, immigration, and drug-control efforts in recent years. The United States also trains a small number of Maldivian military personnel annually.

Some 25 U.S. citizens are resident in Maldives; about 2,000 Americans visit Maldives annually. Maldives welcomes foreign investment, although the general lack of codified law acts as somewhat of a damper to it. Areas of opportunity for U.S. businesses include tourism, construction, and simple export-oriented manufacturing, such as garments and electrical appliance assembly. There is a shortage of local skilled labor, and most industrial labor has to be imported from Sri Lanka or elsewhere.

## Principal U.S. Embassy Officials

For up-to-date information on Principal U.S. Officials, see the U.S. Embassies, Consulates, and Foreign Service section starting on page 139.

The U.S. embassy in Sri Lanka is at 210 Galle Road, Colombo 3; tel: 94-1-448007; fax: 94-1-437345 or 94-1-446013.

# HISTORICAL AND CULTURAL HIGHLIGHTS

Maldives comprises some 1,200 islands in the Indian Ocean. The earliest settlers were probably from southern India, and they were followed by Indo-European speakers from Sri Lanka in the fourth and fifth centuries BC. In the 12th century AD, sailors from East Africa and Arab countries came to the islands. Today, the Maldivian ethnic identity is a blend of these cultures, reinforced by religion and language.

Originally Buddhists, Maldivians were converted to Sunni Islam in the mid-12th century. Islam is the official religion of nearly the entire population. Strict adherence to Islamic precepts and close community relationships have helped keep crime under control.

The official and common language is Dhivehi, an Indo-European language related to Sinhala, the language of Sri Lanka. The writing system, like Arabic, is from right to left, although alphabets are different. English is used widely in commerce and increasingly as the medium of instruction in government schools.

## Travel Notes

**Travel Advice:** For up-to-date information from the U.S. State Department on possible inconvenient or hazardous situations, see the **Travel Warnings and Consular Information Sheets from the U.S. Government** section starting on page 1723. For the latest information on health requirements and conditions, see the **International Travelers' Health Information** section starting on page 1385. For further information dealing with non-urgent matter, see the **Tips for Travelers to...** section starting on page 1588.

Some social stratification exits on the islands. It is not rigid, since rank is based on varied factors, including occupation, wealth, Islamic virtue, and family ties. Members of the social elite are concentrated in Male.

The early history of the Maldives is obscure. According to Maldivian legend, a Sinhalese prince named Koimale was stranded with his bride—daughter of the king of Sri Lanka—in a Maldivian lagoon and stayed on to rule as the first sultan.

Over the centuries, the islands have been visited and their development influenced by sailors from countries on the Arabian Sea and the Indian Ocean littorals. Mopla pirates from the Malabar Coast—present-day Kerala state in India—harassed the islands. In the 16th century, the Portuguese subjugated and ruled the islands for 15 years (1558-73) before being driven away by the warrior-patriot Muhammad Thakurufar Al-Azam.

Although governed as an independent Islamic sultanate for most of its history from 1153 to 1968, Maldives was a British protectorate from 1887 until July 25, 1965. In 1953, there was a brief, abortive attempt at a republican form of government, after which the sultanate was reimposed.

Following independence from Britain in 1965, the sultanate continued to operate for another three years. On November 11, 1968, it was abolished

and replaced by a republic, and the country assumed its present name.

# ECONOMY

The Maldivian economy is predominantly based on tourism and fishing. Of Maldives' 1,200 islands, only 198 are inhabited. The population is scattered throughout the country, and the greatest concentration is on the capital island, Male. Limitations on potable water and arable land constrain expansion.

Development has been centered upon the tourism industry and its complementary service sectors, transport, distribution, real estate, construction, and government. Taxes on the tourist industry have been plowed into infrastructure and also used to improve technology in the agricultural sector.

GDP in 1995 totaled some $238 million, or about $940 per capita. Inflation accelerated to 20% in 1993, but is now declining toward 10%. Real GDP growth averaged about 10% in the 1980s. It expanded by an exceptional 16.2% in 1990, declined to 4% in 1993, and has since bounced back to the 6% to 7% range.

The merchandise trade deficit widened in 1994 to $202 million as imports increased by 45% to $257 million and exports increased 4.3% to $55 million.

International shipping to and from the Maldives is mainly operated by the private sector with only a small fraction of the tonnage carried on vessels operated by the national carrier, Maldives Shipping Management Ltd.

Over the years, Maldives has received economic assistance from multinational development organizations, including the UN Development Program and the World Bank. Individual donors—including Japan, India, Australia, and European and Arab countries—also have contributed.

A 1956 bilateral agreement gave the United Kingdom the use of Gan—in Addu Atoll in the far south—for 20 years as an air facility in return for British aid. The agreement ended in 1976, shortly after the British closed the Gan air station.

## Economic Sectors

**Tourism.** In recent years, Maldives has successfully marketed its natural assets for tourism—beautiful, unpolluted beaches on small coral islands, diving in blue waters abundant with tropical fish, and glorious sunsets. Tourism now brings in about $180 million a year and contributed 18% of GDP in 1994.

Since the first resort was established in 1972, more than 70 islands have been developed, with a total capacity of some 10,000 beds. The number of tourists (mainly from Europe) visiting the Maldives increased from 1,100 in 1972 to 280,000 in 1994. The hotel occupancy rate is 68%, with the average tourist staying eight or nine days and spending about $650.

**Fishing.** This sector employs about 20% of the labor force and contributes 12% of GDP. The use of nets is illegal, so all fishing is done by line. Production was about 104,000 metric tons in 1994, most of which was skipjack tuna. About 80% is exported, largely to Thailand, Sri Lanka, and Singapore. About 28% of the catch is dried or canned, and another 5% is frozen; 54% of fresh fish is exported. Total export proceeds from fish were about $40 million in 1994. The fishing fleet consists of some 1,550 small, flat-bottomed boats (dhonis). Since the dhonis have shifted from sails to outboard motors, the annual tuna catch per fisherman has risen from 1.4 metric tons in 1983 to 4.5 in 1993.

**Agriculture.** Poor soil and scarce arable land have historically limited agriculture to a few subsistence crops, such as coconut, banana, breadfruit, papayas, mangoes, taro, betel, chilies, sweet potatoes, and onions. Agriculture provides about 8% of GDP.

**Industry.** The industrial sector provides only about 6% of GDP. Tradi-

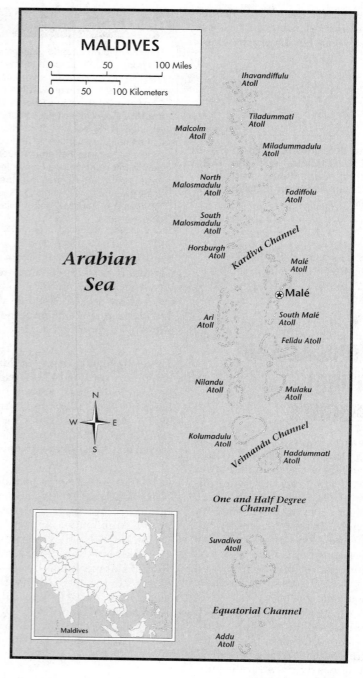

tional industry consists of boat building and handicrafts, while modern industry is limited to a few tuna canneries, five garment factories, a bottling plant, and a few enterprises in the capital producing PVC pipe, soap, furniture, and food products.

## Environmental Concerns

There is growing concern about coral reef and marine life damage because

of coral mining (used for building and jewelry making), sand dredging, and solid waste pollution. Mining of sand and coral have removed the natural coral reef that protected several important islands, making them highly susceptible to the erosive effects of the sea.

In April 1987, high tides swept over the Maldives, inundating much of Male and nearby islands. That event prompted high-level Maldivian interest in global climatic changes, including the "greenhouse effect."

## Investment in Education

The government expenditure for education was 18% of the budget in 1993, with 2,598 employees—1,900 of them teachers, and 450 expatriates. In 1993, there were 78,639 students in 265 institutions, mainly primary schools.

Both formal and non-formal education have made remarkable strides in the last decade. Unique to Maldives, modern and traditional schools exist side by side. The traditional schools are staffed by community-paid teachers without formal training and provide basic numeracy and literacy skills in addition to religious instruction.

The modern schools, run by both the government and private sector, provide primary and secondary education. As the modern English-medium school system expands, the traditional system is gradually being upgraded. There are only two public high schools in the archipelago, one in Male and the other on the southernmost island of Gan.

# GOVERNMENT

A 1968 referendum approved the constitution making Maldives a republic with executive, legislative, and judicial branches of government. The constitution was amended in 1970, 1972, and 1975 and is again under revision.

Ibrahim Nastier, Prime Minister under the pre-1968 sultanate, became President and held office from 1968 to 1978. He was succeeded by Mumoon Abdul Gayoom, who was elected President in 1978 and reelected in 1983, 1988, and 1993.

The president heads the executive branch and appoints the cabinet. Nominated to a five-year term by a secret ballot of the Majlis (parliament), the president must be confirmed by a national referendum.

The unicameral Majlis is composed of 48 members serving five-year terms. Two members from each atoll and Male are elected directly by universal suffrage. Eight are appointed by the president.

The Maldivian legal system—derived mainly from traditional Islamic law—is administered by secular officials, a chief justice, and lesser judges on each of the 19 atolls, who are appointed by the president and function under the Ministry of Justice. There also is an attorney general.

Each inhabited island within an atoll has a chief who is responsible for law and order. Every atoll chief, appointed by the president, functions as a district officer in the British South Asian tradition.

Maldives has no organized political parties. Candidates for elective office run as independents on the basis of personal qualifications.

On November 8, 1988, Sri Lankan Tamil mercenaries tried to overthrow the Maldivian Government. At President Gayoom's request, the Indian military suppressed the coup attempt within 24 hours.

# FOREIGN RELATIONS

Maldives follows a nonaligned policy and is committed to maintaining friendly relations with all countries. The country has a UN Mission in New York and an embassy in Sri Lanka and trade representatives in London and Singapore. India, Pakistan, and Sri Lanka maintain resident embassies in Male. Denmark, Norway, the U.K., Germany, Turkey, and Sweden have consular agencies in Male under the supervision of their embassies in Sri Lanka and India. The UNDP has a representative resident in Male, as do UNICEF and WHO. Like the U.S., many countries have nonresident ambassadors accredited to the Maldives, most of them based in Sri Lanka or India.

Background Notes

871

# MALI

June 2000

Official Name:
**Republic of Mali**

# PROFILE

## Geography

**Area:** 1,240,278 sq. km. (474,764 sq. mi.); about the size of Texas and California combined.
**Cities:** Capital—Bamako (pop. 1,000,000). Other cities—Segou (200,000), Sikasso (120,000), Mopti (90,000), Gao (65,000), Kayes (65,000), Timbuktu (38,000).
**Terrain:** Savannah and desert.
**Climate:** Semitropical in the south; arid in the north.

## People

**Nationality:** Noun and adjective—Malian(s).
**Population:** (1998 est.) 10.1 million.
**Annual growth rate:** 3.1%.
**Ethnic Groups:** Manding (Bambara or Bamana, Malinke, Sarakole) 50%, Fulani 17%, Senoufos/Mianka 12%, Songhai 6%, Tuareg and Maur 5%, other 10%.
**Religion:** Islam 90%, indigenous 6%, Christian 4%.
**Languages:** French (official) and Bambara (spoken by about 80% of the population).
**Education:** Attendance—31% (primary); 9% (secondary). Literacy—31%.
**Health:** Infant mortality rate—106/1,000. Life expectancy—46 yrs.

**Work force:** (4 million) Agriculture—70%; services—15%; industry and commerce—15%.

## Government

**Type:** Republic.
**Independence:** Sept. 22, 1960.
**Constitution:** Approved by referendum January 12, 1991.
**Branches:** Executive—president (chief of state and commander in chief of the armed forces), prime minister (head of government). Legislative—unicameral National Assembly. Judicial—Supreme Court with both judicial and administrative powers.
**Political parties:** Mali is a multiparty democracy. Eight political parties are represented in the National Assembly; others are active in local government.
**Suffrage:** Universal at 18.
**Administrative subdivisions:** Eight regions and capital district.
**Central government budget:** (1998) Revenues—$690 million; expenditures—$724 million; $34 million deficit.
**Flag:** Three vertical bands—green, yellow, and red.

## Economy

**GDP:** (1998) $2.7 billion.
**Avg. annual growth rate:** (1995-98) 5.4%.
**Per capita income:** (1998) $270.
**Annual skilled worker's salary:** $1,200.
**Avg. inflation rate:** (1998) 4.2%.
**Natural resources:** Gold, phosphate, kaolin, salt, and limestone currently mined; deposits of bauxite, iron ore, manganese, lithium, and uranium are known or suspected.
**Agriculture:** (42% of GDP) Products—millet, sorghum, corn, rice, livestock, sugar, cotton, groundnuts (peanuts), and tobacco.
**Industry:** (24% of GDP) Types—food processing, textiles, cigarettes, fish processing, metalworking, light manufacturing, plastics, and beverage bottling.
**Trade:** (1997) Exports—$546 million: cotton and cotton products, animals, fish, tannery products, groundnuts, diamonds, and gold. Major markets—France, Switzerland, Italy, Thailand, Cote d'Ivoire, and Algeria. Imports—$740 million: food, machinery and spare parts, vehicles, petroleum products, chemicals and pharmaceuticals, textiles. Major suppliers—France, Cote d'Ivoire, Belgium, Luxembourg, the U.S. ($26 million), Germany, and Japan.
**Official exchange rate (1999):** CFA franc 600=US$1.

# PEOPLE

Mali's population consists of diverse Sub-Saharan ethnic groups, sharing similar historic, cultural, and religious traditions. Exceptions are the Tuaregs and Maurs, desert nomads, related to the North African Berbers. The Tuaregs traditionally have opposed the central government. Starting in June 1990, armed attacks in the North by Tuaregs seeking greater autonomy led to clashes with the military. In April 1992, the government and most opposing factions signed a pact to end the fighting and restore stability in the north. Its major aims are to allow greater autonomy to the north and increase government resource allocation to what has been a traditionally impoverished region. The peace agreement was celebrated in 1996 in Timbuktu during an official and highly publicized ceremony called "Flamme de la Paix"—(peace flame).

Historically, good interethnic relations throughout the rest of the country were facilitated by easy mobility on the Niger River and across the country's vast savannahs. Each ethnic group was traditionally tied to a specific occupation, all working within close proximity. The Bambara, Malinke, Sarakole, and Dogon are farmers; the Fulani, Maur, and Tuareg are herders; while the Bozo are fishers. In recent years, this linkage has shifted as ethnic groups seek diverse, nontraditional sources of income.

Although each ethnic group speaks a separate language, nearly 80% of Malians communicate in Bambara, the common language of the marketplace. Malians enjoy a relative harmony rare in African states.

# HISTORY

Malians express great pride in their ancestry. Mali is the cultural heir to the succession of ancient African empires—Ghana, Malinke, and Songhai—that occupied the West African savannah. These empires controlled Saharan trade and were in touch with Mediterranean and Middle Eastern centers of civilization.

The Ghana Empire, dominated by the Soninke people and centered in the

---

## Travel Notes

**Customs:** A visa is required for entry and may be obtained at any Malian embassy abroad. Yellow fever inoculations are required prior to arrival.

**Health:** Suppressants for chloroquine-resistant malaria are strongly recommended. Emergency medical care is available in Bamako, but medical facilities are limited. Bring an adequate supply of personal prescription medicines and health-care products, including insect repellent and sun screen. Tap water must be boiled and filtered. Bottled water is available. Meats should be thoroughly cooked. Inquire at the US Public Health Service prior to departure from the United States for latest health information and requirements.

**Climate and clothing:** Summer clothing is suitable for Bamako. Wash-and-wear clothing and sturdy shoes are recommended. Hats and sunglasses should be worn outdoors to protect against overexposure to the sun.

**Telecommunications:** Long-distance telephone and telegraphic service is limited. Public-use telephone, telex, and FAX facilities are available. Mali is on Greenwich Mean Time, 5 hours ahead of Eastern Standard Time.

**Money and Banking:** Banks are open from 7:30-11:30 A.M. and from 1:15-3:30 P.M. Monday through Thursday and from 7:30-12:00 noon on Fridays. Personal checks and credit cards cannot be used for banking transactions, though the major hotels in Bamako do accept credit cards for payment of hotel bills.

**Transportation:** Privately owned automobiles are the principal means of transportation in Bamako for Americans. Bus service within Bamako and to the suburbs was started in 1992. Taxis are also readily available, and vehicles (with drivers) may be chartered for long trips. Roads between major cities in Mali are paved. Bamako is serviced by international flights from Paris, Brussels, and from New York via Dakar. One private airline (Malitas) offers regularly-scheduled internal flights, and two charter airline companies operate in Mali.

**Travel Advice:** For up-to-date information from the U.S. State Department on possible inconvenient or hazardous situations, see the **Travel Warnings and Consular Information Sheets from the U.S. Government** section starting on page 1723. For the latest information on health requirements and conditions, see the **International Travelers' Health Information** section starting on page 1385. For further information dealing with non-urgent matter, see the **Tips for Travelers to...** section starting on page 1588.

---

area along the Malian-Mauritanian frontier, was a powerful trading state from about A.D. 700 to 1075. The Malinke Kingdom of Mali had its origins on the upper Niger River in the 11th century. Expanding rapidly in the 13th century under the leadership of Soundiata Keita, it reached its height about 1325, when it conquered Timbuktu and Gao. Thereafter, the kingdom began to decline, and by the 15th century, it controlled only a small fraction of its former domain.

The Songhai Empire expanded its power from its center in Gao during the period 1465-1530. At its peak under Askia Mohammad I, it encompassed the Hausa states as far as Kano (in present-day Nigeria) and much of the territory that had belonged to the Mali Empire in the west. It was destroyed by a Moroccan invasion in 1591.

French military penetration of the Soudan (the French name for the area) began around 1880. Ten years later, the French made a concerted effort to occupy the interior. The timing and method of their advances were determined by resident military governors. A French civilian governor of Soudan was appointed in 1893, but resistance to French control did not end until 1898, when the Malinke warrior Samory Toure was defeated after 7 years of war. The French attempted to rule indirectly, but in many areas they disregarded traditional authorities and governed through appointed chiefs. As the colony of French Soudan, Mali was administered with other French colonial territories as the Federation of French West Africa.

In 1956, with the passing of France's Fundamental Law (Loi Cadre), the

Background Notes

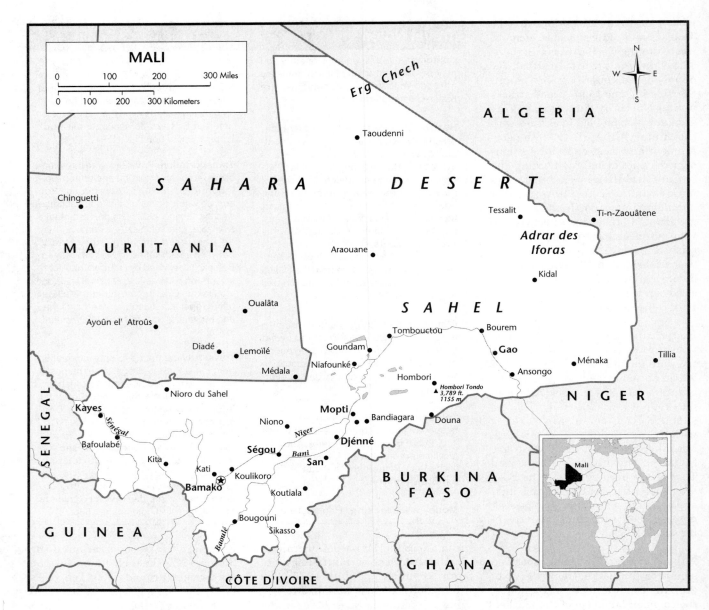

Territorial Assembly obtained extensive powers over internal affairs and was permitted to form a cabinet with executive authority over matters within the Assembly's competence. After the 1958 French constitutional referendum, the "Republique Soudanaise" became a member of the French Community and enjoyed complete internal autonomy.

In January 1959, Soudan joined Senegal to form the Mali Federation, which became fully independent within the French Community on June 20, 1960. The federation collapsed on August 20, 1960, when Senegal seceded. On September 22, Soudan proclaimed itself the Repub-

lic of Mali and withdrew from the French Community.

President Modibo Keita, whose party (Union Soudanaise du Rassemblement Democratique Africain—US/RDA) had dominated preindependence politics, moved quickly to declare a single-party state and to pursue a socialist policy based on extensive nationalization. A continuously deteriorating economy led to a decision to rejoin the Franc Zone in 1967 and modify some of the economic excesses.

On November 19, 1968, a group of young officers staged a bloodless coup and set up a 14-member Military

Committee for National Liberation (CMLN), with Lt. Moussa Traore as president. The military leaders attempted to pursue economic reforms, but for several years faced debilitating internal political struggles and the disastrous Sahelian drought.

A new constitution, approved in 1974, created a one-party state and was designed to move Mali toward civilian rule. However, the military leaders remained in power. In September 1976, a new political party was established, the Democratic Union of the Malian People (UDPM), based on the concept of democratic centralism. Single-party presidential and legislative elections were held in June 1979, and Gen. Moussa Traore received 99% of the votes. His efforts at consolidating the single-party government were challenged in 1980 by student-led anti-government demonstrations, which were brutally put down, and by three coup attempts.

The political situation stabilized during 1981 and 1982, and remained generally calm throughout the 1980s. The UDPM spread its structure to Cercles and Arrondissements across the land. Shifting its attention to Mali's economic difficulties, the government approved plans for cereal marketing liberalization, reform in the state enterprise system, new incentives to private enterprise, and worked out a new structural adjustment agreement with the International Monetary Fund (IMF).

However, by 1990, there was growing dissatisfaction with the demands for austerity imposed by the IMF's economic reform programs and the perception that the president and his close associates were not themselves adhering to those demands.

As in other African countries, demands for multi-party democracy increased. The Traore government allowed some opening of the system, including the establishment of an independent press and independent political associations, but insisted that Mali was not ready for democracy. In early 1991, student-led anti-government rioting broke out again, but this time it was supported also by government workers and others. On March 26, 1991, after 4 days of intense anti-government rioting, a group of 17 military officers arrested President Traore and suspended the constitution. Within days, these officers joined with the Coordinating Committee of Democratic Associations to form a predominantly civilian, 25-member ruling body, the Transitional Committee for the Salvation of the People (CTSP). The CTSP then appointed a civilian-led government. A national conference held in August 1991 produced a draft constitution (approved in a referendum January 12, 1992), a charter for political parties, and an electoral code. Political parties were allowed to form freely. Between January and April 1992, a president, National Assembly, and municipal councils were elected. On June 8, 1992, Alpha Oumar Konare, the candidate of the Association for Democracy in Mali (ADEMA), was inaugurated as the president of Mali's Third Republic.

In 1997, attempts to renew national institutions through democratic elections ran into administrative difficulties, resulting in a court-ordered annulment of the legislative elections held in April 1997. The exercise, nonetheless, demonstrated the overwhelming strength of President Konare's ADEMA party, causing some other historic parties to boycott subsequent elections. President Konare won the presidential election against scant opposition on May 11. In the two-round legislative elections conducted on July 21 and August 3, ADEMA secured over 80% of the National Assembly seats.

# GOVERNMENT AND POLITICAL CONDITIONS

Under Mali's 1992 constitution, the president is chief of state and commander in chief of the armed forces. The president is elected to 5-year terms, with a limit of two terms. The president appoints the prime minister as head of government. The president chairs the Council of Ministers (the prime minister and currently 22 other ministers, including 6 women), which adopts proposals for laws submitted to the National Assembly for approval.

The National Assembly is the sole legislative arm of the government. It currently consists of 147 members. Representation is apportioned according to the population of administrative districts. Election is direct and by party list. The term of office is 5 years. The Assembly meets for two regular sessions each year. It debates and votes on legislation proposed either by one of its members or by the government and has the right to question government ministers about government actions and policies. Eight political parties, aggregated into four parliamentary groups, are represented in the Assembly. ADEMA currently holds the majority; minority parties are represented in all committees and in the Assembly directorate.

Mali's constitution provides for a multi-party democracy, with the only restriction being a prohibition against parties based on ethnic, religious, regional, or gender lines. In addition to those political parties represented in the National Assembly, others are active in municipal councils.

Administratively, Mali is divided into eight regions and the capital district of Bamako, each under the authority of an appointed governor. Each region consists of five to nine districts (or Cercles), administered by commandants. Cercles are divided into communes, which, in turn, are divided into villages or quarters. Plans for decentralization have begun with the establishment of 702 elected municipal councils, headed by elected mayors. Further plans envision election of local officials, greater local control over finances, and the reduction of administrative control by the central government.

Mali's legal system is based on codes inherited at independence from France. New laws have been enacted to make the system conform to Malian life, but French colonial laws not abrogated still have the force of law. The constitution provides for the independence of the judiciary. However, the Ministry of Justice appoints judges and supervises both law enforcement and judicial functions. The Supreme Court has both judicial and administrative powers. Under the constitution, there is a separate constitutional court and a high court of justice with the power to try senior government officials in cases of treason.

Ancient style mosque, Djénné.

Photo credit: Corel Corporation.

## Principal Government Officials

**For up-to-date information on Principal Government Officials, see the Chiefs of State and Cabinet Members of Foreign Governments section starting on page 1.**

Mali maintains an embassy in the United States at 2130 R Street NW, Washington, DC 20008 (tel. 202-332-2249), and a permanent mission to the United Nations at 111 E. 69th Street, New York, NY 10020 (212-734-4150). The Malian Embassy website is http://www.maliembassy-usa.org

# ECONOMY

Mali's per capita gross domestic product (GDP) of $270 (1998) places it among the world's 10 poorest nations. Its potential wealth lies in mining and the production of agricultural commodities, livestock, and fish.

Agricultural activities occupy 70% of Mali's labor force and provide 42% of the GDP. Cotton and livestock make up 75%-80% of Mali's annual exports. Smallscale traditional farming dominates the agricultural sector, with subsistence farming (of cereals, primarily sorghum, millet, and maize) on about 90% of the 1.4 million hectares (3.4 million acres) under cultivation.

The most productive agricultural area lies along the banks of the Niger River between Bamako and Mopti and extends south to the borders of Guinea, Cote d'Ivoire, and Burkina Faso. Average rainfall varies in this region from 50 centimeters per year (20 in.) around Mopti to 140 centimeters (55 in.) in the south near Sikasso. This area is most important for the production of cotton, rice, millet, corn, vegetables, tobacco, and tree crops.

Rice is grown extensively along the banks of the Niger between Segou and Mopti, with the most important rice-producing area at the Office du Niger, located north of Segou toward the Mauritanian border. Using water

diverted from the Niger, the Office du Niger irrigates about 60,000 hectares of land for rice and sugarcane production. About one-third of Mali's paddy rice is produced at the Office du Niger.

The Niger River also is an important source of fish, providing food for riverside communities; the surplus—smoked, salted, and dried—is exported. Due to drought and diversion of river water for agriculture, fish production has steadily declined since the early 1980s.

Sorghum is planted extensively in the drier parts of the country and along the banks of the Niger in eastern Mali, as well as in the lake beds in the Niger delta region. During the dry season, farmers near the town of Dire have cultivated wheat on irrigated fields for hundreds of years. Peanuts are grown throughout the country but are concentrated in the area around Kita, west of Bamako.

Mali's resource in livestock consists of millions of cattle, sheep, and goats. Approximately 40% of Mali's herds were lost during the great drought in 1972-74. The level was gradually restored, but the herds were again decimated in the 1983-85 drought. The overall size of Mali's herds is not expected to reach predrought levels in the north of the country, where encroachment of the desert has forced many nomadic herders to abandon pastoral activities and turn instead to farming. The largest concentrations of cattle are in the areas north of Bamako and Segou extending into the Niger delta, but herding activity is gradually shifting southward, due to the effects of previous droughts. Sheep, goats, and camels are raised to the exclusion of cattle in the dry areas north and east of Timbuktu.

Until the mid-1960s, Mali was self-sufficient in grains—millet, sorghum, rice, and corn. Diminished harvests during bad years, a growing population, changing dietary habits, and, most importantly, policy constraints on agricultural production resulted in grain deficits almost every year from 1965 to 1986. Production has rebounded since 1987, however, thanks to agricultural policy reforms undertaken by the government and supported by the Western donor nations. Liberalization of producer prices and an open cereals market have created incentives to production. These reforms, combined with adequate rainfall, successful integrated rural agriculture programs in the south, and improved management of the Office du Niger, have led to surplus cereal production over the past 5 years.

Annual rainfall, critical for Mali's agriculture, has been at or above average since 1993. Cereal production, including rice, has grown annually, and the 1997-98 cotton harvest reached a record 500,000 tons.

Mining is a rapidly growing industry in Mali, with gold accounting for some 80% of mining activity. There are considerable proven reserves of other minerals not currently exploited. Gold has become Mali's third-largest export, after cotton and livestock. There are two large private investments in gold mining: Anglo-American ($250 million) and Randgold ($140 million), both multinational South African companies located respectively in the western and southern part of the country.

During the colonial period, private capital investment was virtually nonexistent, and public investment was devoted largely to the Office du Niger irrigation scheme and to administrative expenses. Following independence, Mali built some light industries with the help of various donors. Manufacturing, consisting principally of processed agricultural products, accounted for about 8% of the GDP in 1990.

## Economic Reform

With the encouragement of the major donors and international financial institutions, the Government of Mali initiated a series of adjustment and stabilization programs beginning in 1982. Measures were introduced to reduce budgetary deficits, public enterprise operating losses, and public sector arrears. Substantial progress was made in the first few

years of the adjustment program, but the pace of reform slowed considerably in 1987 and required the intervention of donors to avert a financial crisis.

Under the economic reform program signed with the World Bank and the IMF in 1988, the government has taken a number of steps to liberalize the regulatory environment and thereby attract private investment. For example, applications for the establishment of business enterprises now enjoy "one window" (guichet unique) processing through a single ministry, allowing a business to be established in a matter of days. In addition, price controls on consumer goods have been progressively eliminated; the last price control, on petroleum products, was removed on July 1, 1992. Import quotas were eliminated in 1988, and export taxes were dropped in 1991. The Commerce Code was revised in 1991 to remove impediments to commercial activity. The investment and the mining codes also were revised in the early 1990s in order to present a good investment climate. Also in 1991, a system of commercial and administrative courts was established to handle private trade complaints and claims against the government.

During the period 1988-96, the government implemented a large reform program of the public enterprise sector, including the privatization of 16 enterprises, the partial privatization of 12, and the liquidation of 20; others were restructured. Among the 20 enterprises left, five recently were proposed for privatization, and two large companies—Energie du Mali, electricity and water and Societe de Telecommunications du Mali, telecommunications—plan partial privatization.

## Foreign Aid

Mali is a major recipient of foreign aid from many sources, including multilateral organizations (most significantly the World Bank, African Development Bank, and Arab Funds), and bilateral programs funded by the European Union, France, United States, Canada,

Netherlands, and Germany. Before 1991, the former Soviet Union had been a major source of economic and military aid, including construction of a cement plant and the Kalana gold mine. Currently, aid from Russia is restricted mainly to training and provision of spare parts. Chinese aid remains high, and Chinese-Malian joint venture companies have become more numerous in the last 3 years, leading to the opening of a Chinese investment center. The Chinese are major participants in the textile industry and in largescale construction projects, including a bridge across the Niger, a conference center, an expressway in Bamako, and a new national stadium scheduled to be completed for the Africa Cup competition in 2002.

In 1998, U.S. assistance reached over $40 million. This included $39 million in sector support through United States Agency for International Development (USAID) programs, largely channeled to local communities through private voluntary agencies; Peace Corps program budget of $2.2 million for more than 160 Volunteers serving in Mali; Self Help and the Democracy Funds of $170,500; and $650,000 designated for electoral support. Military assistance includes $275,000 for the International Military Education Training (IMET) program, $1.6 million for the African Crisis response Initiative (ACRI), $60,000 for Joint Combined Exercise Training (JCET), and $100,000 for Humanitarian Assistance.

# FOREIGN RELATIONS

Since independence in 1960, Malian governments have shifted from an ideological commitment to socialism and a policy alignment with communist states to a pragmatism that judges issues and their merits, welcomes assistance from all sources, and encourages private investment. The present government, which assumed office in September 1997, is committed to democracy, economic reform, free market policies, and regional integration.

Mali is a member of the UN and many of its specialized agencies, including the International Monetary Fund (IMF) and the World Bank; International Labor Organization (ILO); International Telecommunications Union (ITU); Universal Postal Union (UPU). It also belongs to the Organization of African Unity (OAU); Organization of Islamic Countries (OIC); Non-Aligned Movement (NAM); an associate member of the European Community (EC); African Development Bank (ADB); and INTELSAT.

Mali is active in regional organizations. It participates in the Economic Community of West African States (ECOWAS) and the West African Economic Monetary Union (UEMOA) for regional economic integration; Liptako-Gourma Authority, which seeks to develop the contiguous areas of Mali, Niger, and Burkina Faso; the Niger River Commission; the Permanent Interstate Committee for Drought Control in the Sahel (CILSS); and the Senegal River Valley Development Organization (OMVS).

# DEFENSE

Mali's armed forces number some 7,000 and are under the control of the Minister of Armed Forces and Veter-

ans. The Gendarmerie and local police forces (under the Ministry of Territorial Administration and Security) maintain internal security. In the sixties and seventies, Mali's army and air force relied primarily on the Soviet Union for materiel and training. A few Malians receive military training in the United States, France, and Germany. Military expenditures total about 13% of the national budget.

# U.S.-MALIAN RELATIONS

U.S.-Malian relations are excellent and expanding. They are based on shared goals of averting suffering and strengthening democracy. The bilateral agenda is dominated by efforts to increase broad-based growth, improve health and educational facilities, promote the sustainable use of natural resources, reduce the population growth rate, counter the spread of highly infectious diseases, encourage regional stability, build peacekeeping capabilities, institutionalize respect for human rights, and strengthen democratic institutions in offering good governance. Mali currently is a small market for U.S. trade and investment, but there is potential for considerable growth as its economy expands.

Mali also serves as an important laboratory for testing new anti-malaria medicines for use by American citizen travelers and for research which will have an Africa-wide impact. USAID, Peace Corps, and other U.S. Government programs play a significant role in fostering sustainable economic and social development. USAID programs also strengthen efforts to consolidate the peace process in North Mali and the region's socioeconomic and political integration. Defense Department security assistance programs and training support help permit Mali to achieve its potential in international peacekeeping efforts.

## Principal U.S. Officials

**For up-to-date information on Principal U.S. Officials, see the U.S. Embassies, Consulates, and Foreign Service section starting on page 139.**

The U.S. Embassy is located at Rue Mohamed V and Rue Rochester NY, Bamako, tel.: (223) 22-54-70 or 22-38-33 (after hours), fax: (223) 22-37-12. The mailing address is BP 34, Bamako, Mali. The Embassy website is www.usa.org.ml. Embassy hours are 7:30 a.m - 4:00 p.m., Monday through Friday.

# MALTA

April 1995

## Official Name:
## Malta

## PROFILE

### Geography

**Area:** 316 sq. km. (122 sq. mi.); about one-tenth the size of Rhode Island.
**Major cities:** Valletta (capital), Sliema.
**Terrain:** Low hills.
**Climate:** Subtropical summer; other seasons temperate.

### People

**Nationality:** Noun and adjective—Maltese.
**Population (1994 est.):** 368,000.
**Annual growth rate:** 0.7%.
**Ethnic divisions:** Mixture of Arab, Sicilian, Norman, Spanish, Italian, English.
**Religion:** Roman Catholic, 98%.
**Languages:** Maltese, English.
**Education:** Years compulsory—until age 16. Attendance—96%. Literacy—90%.
**Health:** Infant mortality rate—9.6/1,000. Life expectancy—76 yrs.
**Work force (136,500):** Public sector—37% Services—28%. Manufacturing—21%. Construction—4%. Agriculture and fisheries—2%.

### Government

**Type:** Republic.
**Independence:** September 1964.

**Constitution:** 1964; revised 1974.
**Branches:** Executive—president (chief of state), prime minister (head of government), cabinet. Legislative—unicameral House of Representatives. Judicial—Constitutional Court.
**Administrative subdivisions:** 13 electoral districts.
**Political parties:** Nationalist Party, Malta Labor Party.
**Suffrage:** Universal at 18.

### Economy

**GDP (1994 est.):** $2.9 billion.
**Annual growth rate:** 7%.
**Per capita income:** $7,880.
**Natural resources:** Limestone, salt.
**Agriculture:** Products—fodder crops, potatoes, onions, Mediterranean fruits and vegetables.
**Industry (37% of GDP):** Types—clothing, semiconductors, shipbuilding and repair, furniture, leather, rubber and plastic products, footwear, spectacle frames, toys, jewelry, food, beverages, tobacco products.
**Trade (1993):** Exports—$1.36 billion: clothing, semiconductors, furniture, leather, rubber and plastic products, footwear, bunker fuel. Major markets—Italy, Germany, U.K. Imports—$2.17 billion: finished and semi-finished goods, food and beverages, industrial supplies, petroleum and related products. Major suppliers—Italy, U.K., Germany.
**Official exchange rate:** One Maltese lira=$2.65 (avg. for 1994); rate fluctuates.

## PEOPLE

Malta is one of the most densely populated countries in the world, with about 1,160 inhabitants per square kilometer (3,000 per sq. mi.). This compares with about 21 per square kilometer (55 per sq. mi.) for the United States. Inhabited since prehistoric times, Malta was first colonized by the Phoenicians. Subsequently, Maltese life and culture have been influenced to varying degrees by Arabs, Italians, and the British. Most of the foreign community in Malta, predominantly active or retired British nationals and their dependents, centers around Sliema and surrounding modern suburbs. Roman Catholicism is established by law as the religion of Malta; however, full liberty of conscience and freedom of worship are guaranteed, and a number of faiths have places of worship on the island. Malta has two official languages—Maltese (a Semitic language) and English. The literacy rate has reached 90%, compared to 63% in 1946. Schooling is compulsory until age 16.

# HISTORY

Malta was an important cultic center for earth-mother worship in the 4th millennium B.C. Recent archeological work shows a developed religious center there long before those of Sumer and Egypt. Malta's written history began well before the Christian era. Originally the Phoenicians, and later the Carthaginians, established ports and trading settlements on the island. During the second Punic War (218 B.C.), Malta became part of the Roman Empire. During Roman rule, in A.D. 60, Saint Paul was shipwrecked on Malta at a place now called St. Paul's Bay. In 533 A.D. Malta became part of the Byzantine Empire and in 870 came under Arab control. Arab occupation and rule left a strong imprint on Maltese life, customs, and language. The Arabs were driven out in 1090 by a band of Norman adventurers under Count Roger of Normandy, who had established a kingdom in southern Italy and Sicily. Malta thus became an appendage of Sicily for 440 years. During this period, Malta was sold and resold to various feudal lords and barons and was dominated successively by the rulers of Swabia, Aquitaine, Aragon, Castile, and Spain.

In 1523, a key date in Maltese history, the islands were ceded by Charles V of Spain to the rich and powerful order of the Knights of St. John of Jerusalem. For the next 275 years, these famous "Knights of Malta" made the island their kingdom. They built towns, palaces, churches, gardens, and fortifications and embellished the island with numerous works of art and culture. In 1565, these knights broke the siege of Malta by Suleiman the Magnificent. The power of the knights declined, however, and their rule of Malta was ended by their surrender to Napoleon in 1798.

The people of Malta rose against French rule and, with the help of the British, evicted them in 1800. In 1814, Malta voluntarily became part of the British Empire. Under the United Kingdom, the island became a military and naval fortress, the head-quarters of the British Mediterranean fleet. During World War II, Malta survived a siege at the hands of German and Italian military forces (1940-43). In recognition, King George VI in 1942 awarded the George Cross "to the island fortress of Malta—its people and defenders." President Franklin Roosevelt, describing the wartime period, called Malta "one tiny bright flame in the darkness." Malta obtained independence on September 21, 1964.

# GOVERNMENT

Under its 1964 constitution, Malta became a parliamentary democracy within the Commonwealth. Queen Elizabeth II was sovereign of Malta, and a governor general exercised executive authority on her behalf, while the actual direction and control of the government and the nation's affairs were in the hands of the cabinet under the leadership of a prime minister.

On December 13, 1974, the constitution was revised, and Malta became a republic within the Commonwealth, with executive authority vested in a Maltese president. The president appoints as prime minister the leader of the party with a majority of seats in the House of Representatives. The president also nominally appoints, upon recommendation of the prime minister, the individual ministers to head each of the government departments. The cabinet is selected from among the members of the unicameral House of Representatives. This body consists of between 65 and 69 members elected on the basis of proportional representation. Elections must be held at least every five years. There are no by-elections, and vacancies are filled on the basis of the results of the previous election.

Malta's judiciary is independent. The chief justice and nine judges are appointed by the president on the advice of the prime minister. Their mandatory retirement age is 65. There is a civil court, a commercial court, and a criminal court. In the latter, the presiding judge sits with a jury of nine. The court of appeal hears appeals from decisions of the civil court and of the commercial court. The court of criminal appeal hears appeals from judgments of conviction by the criminal court. The highest court, the Constitutional Court, hears appeals in cases involving violations of human rights, interpretation of the constitution, and invalidity of laws. It also has jurisdiction in cases concerning disputed parliamentary elections and electoral corrupt practices. There also are inferior courts presided over by a magistrate.

Currently, Malta has no local government bodies and few regional branches of the central government, although local advisory councils are being considered. With the exception of the Ministry for Gozo, the police, the post office, and local medical dispensaries, government programs are administered directly from Valletta.

## Principal Government Officials

**For up-to-date information on Principal Government Officials, see the Chiefs of State and Cabinet Members of Foreign Governments section starting on page 1.**

Malta maintains an embassy in the United States at 2017 Connecticut Avenue NW, Washington, DC 20008 (202-462-3611).

# POLITICAL CONDITIONS

Two parties dominate Malta's polarized and evenly divided politics—the Nationalist Party, led by Prime Minister Eddie Fenech Adami, and the Malta Labor Party, led by Alfred Sant. Political views are passionately held, and elections invariably generate a widescale voter turnout exceeding 96%. Political allegiances among the populace are so inflexible and divided that a 52% share of the votes can be considered a "landslide" for the winning party. Prior to the May 1987 election, the Maltese constitution was amended to ensure that the party that obtained more than 50% of the popular vote would have a majority of seats in parliament and would thereby form the government. The then-Labor Party government proposed this constitutional amendment in exchange for Nationalist Party (in opposition at the time) agreement to two other amendments to the constitution: The first stipulates Malta's neutrality status and policy of non-alignment, and the second prohibits foreign interference in Malta's elections.

The February 1992 election resulted in the incumbent Nationalist Party government being re-elected for another five-year term. The Nationalists won 51.8% of the popular vote, with the Labor Party receiving a post-war-low 46.5% share; the remaining 1.7% went to the Labor-breakaway Alternative Movement Party. With its victory, the Nationalist Party established a three-seat majority in the unicameral Maltese parliament.

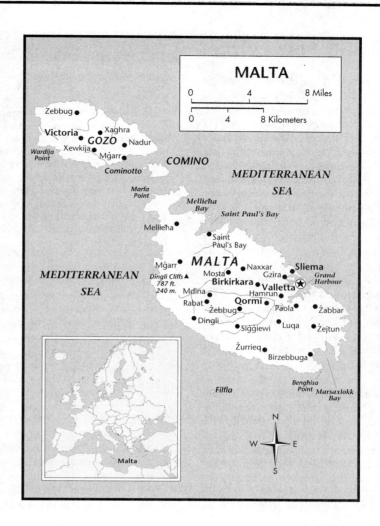

# ECONOMY

Possessing few indigenous raw materials and a very small domestic market, Malta has based its economic development on the promotion of tourism and labor-intensive exports. Since the mid-1980s, expansion in these activities has been the principal engine for strong growth in the Maltese economy. The government's extensive program of infrastructural investment since 1987 has helped alleviate problems that plagued Malta's tourism industry in the early 1980s and has stimulated an impressive upswing in Maltese tourism's economic fortunes.

Tourist arrivals and foreign exchange earnings derived from tourism have steadily increased since the 1987 watershed, in which there was growth from the previous year of, respectively, 30% and 63% (increase in terms of U.S. dollars).

With the help of a favorable international economic climate, the availability of domestic resources, and industrial policies that support foreign export-oriented investment, the economy has been able to sustain a period of rapid growth. During the 1990s, Malta's economic growth has generally continued this brisk pace.

Both domestic demand (mainly consumption), boosted by large increases in government spending, and exports of goods and services contributed to this performance.

Buoyed by continued rapid growth, the economy has maintained a relatively low rate of unemployment. Labor market pressures have increased as skilled labor shortages have become more widespread, despite illegal immigration, and real earnings growth has accelerated.

Growing public and private sector demand for credit has led—in the context of interest rate controls—to credit rationing to the private sector and the introduction of non-interest charges by banks. Despite these pressures, consumer price inflation has remained low, reflecting the impact of a fixed exchange rate policy and lingering price controls.

The Maltese Government has pursued a policy of gradual economic liberalization, taking some steps to shift the emphasis in trade and financial policies from reliance on direct government intervention and control to policy regimes that allow a greater role for market mechanisms. However, by international standards, the economy remains highly regulated and continues to be hampered by some long-standing structural weaknesses.

## FOREIGN RELATIONS

For the first several years of independence, Malta followed a policy of close cooperation with the United Kingdom and other NATO countries. This relationship changed with the election of the Mintoff Labor Party government in June 1971. The NATO sub-headquarters in Malta was closed at the request of the Labor Party government, and the U.S. 6th Fleet discontinued recreational visits to the country. After substantially increased financial contributions from several NATO countries (including the United States), British forces remained in Malta until 1979. Following their departure, the Labor government charted a new course of neutrality and became an active member of the Non-Aligned Movement.

Malta is an active participant in the United Nations, the Commonwealth, the Council of Europe, OSCE, the Non-Aligned Movement, and various other international organizations. In these fora, Malta has frequently expressed its concern for the peace and economic development of the Mediterranean region. The National-ist Party government is continuing a policy of neutrality and nonalignment, but in a Western context. The government desires improved relations with the United States and Western Europe, with an emphasis on increased trade and private investment.

Malta is an associate member of the EU. The government has made clear that its primary foreign policy objective is to seek full membership in the EU, under the right conditions, and it has actively pursued increased political and economic ties to the EU.

### Travel Notes

**Travel Advice:** For up-to-date information from the U.S. State Department on possible inconvenient or hazardous situations, see the **Travel Warnings and Consular Information Sheets from the U.S. Government** section starting on page 1723. For the latest information on health requirements and conditions, see the **International Travelers' Health Information** section starting on page 1385. For further information dealing with non-urgent matter, see the **Tips for Travelers to...** section starting on page 1588.

## U.S.-MALTESE RELATIONS

Malta and the United States established full diplomatic relations upon Malta's independence in 1964; overall relations are currently active and cordial. The United States has been sympathetic to Malta's campaign to attract private investment, and some firms operating in Malta have U.S. ownership or investment. These include two major hotels and four manufacturing and repair facilities, a water desalinization plant, and some offices servicing regional operations.

### Principal U.S. Embassy Officials

For up-to-date information on Principal U.S. Officials, see the U.S. Embassies, Consulates, and Foreign Service section starting on page 139.

The U.S. embassy in Malta is located in Development House, St. Anne Street, Floriana (tel: 620424).

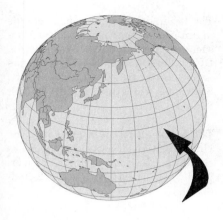

# MARSHALL ISLANDS

July 2000

## Official Name:
## Republic of the Marshall Islands

# PROFILE

## Geography

**Area:** 181 sq. km. (about 70 sq. mi.) of land area scattered over 500,000 sq. mi. of the Western Pacific.
**Cities:** Capital—Majuro (pop. 23,676). Other towns—Ebeye, Jaluit.
**Terrain:** 29 low-lying coral atolls and five islands.
**Climate:** Tropical with a wet season from May to November.

## People

**Nationality:** Noun and adjective—Marshallese.
**Population:** (1999 est.) 50,840. (Figures not adjusted for migration to the U.S., where Marshallese colonies of unknown size exist.)
**Annual growth rate:** 1.5%.
**Ethnic Groups:** 90% Marshallese, 10% estimated U.S., Filipino, Chinese, New Zealander, and Korean.
**Religion:** Christian, mostly Protestant.
**Languages:** Two major Marshallese dialects from Malayo-Polynesian family; English; Japanese.
**Education:** Literacy (1999)—97%.
**Health:** Infant mortality rate—50/1,000. Life expectancy—men 66 yrs.; women 69 yrs.
**Work force:** (about 15,000) Services, including government—58%; con-

struction and services—21%; agriculture and fishing—21%.

## Government

**Type:** Parliamentary democracy in free association with the U.S.; the Compact of Free Association entered into force October 21, 1986.
**Independence:** October 21, 1986 from the U.S.-administered UN trusteeship.
**Constitution:** May 1, 1979.
**Branches:** Executive—president (chief of state), cabinet. Legislative—unicameral parliament (Nitijela) and consultative Council of Iroij (traditional leaders). Judicial—Supreme Court, high court, district and community courts, traditional rights court.
**Political parties:** United Democratic and unnamed opposition.
**Suffrage:** Universal at age 18.
**Administrative subdivisions:** 24 local governments.
**Flag:** Deep blue background with two rays, one orange and one white, and a 24-point star.

## Economy

**GDP:** (current market prices, 1997) $92.1 million est.
**Natural resources:** Marine resources, including mariculture and possible deep seabed minerals.
**Agriculture:** Products—Copra (dried coconut meat); taro and bread-

fruit are subsistence crops.
**Industry:** Types—Copra processing, tuna loining.
**Trade:** Major trading partners—U.S., Japan, Australia, China, Hong Kong, New Zealand, Taiwan.
**Official currency:** U.S. dollar.

# GEOGRAPHY AND PEOPLE

The Marshalls are comprised of 29 atolls and five major islands, which form two parallel groups—the "Ratak" (sunrise) chain and the "Ralik"(sunset) chain. Two-thirds of the nation's population lives in Majuro and Ebeye. The outer islands are sparsely populated due to lack of employment opportunities and economic development.

The Marshallese are of Micronesian origin, which is traced to a combination of peoples who emigrated from Southeast Asia in the remote past. The matrilineal Marshallese culture revolves around a complex system of clans and lineages tied to land ownership.

Virtually all Marshallese are Christian, most of them Protestant. Other Christian denominations include Roman Catholic, Seventh-day Adventist, Mormon, Salvation Army, and

Jehovah's Witness. A small Bahai community also exists. Both Marshallese and English are official languages. English is spoken by most of the urban population. However, both the Nitijela (parliament) and national radio use Marshallese.

The public school system provides education through grade 12, although admission to secondary school is selective. The elementary program employs a bilingual/bicultural curriculum. English is introduced in the fourth grade. There is one post-secondary institution in the Marshall Islands—the College of the Marshall Islands.

# HISTORY

Little is clearly understood about the prehistory of the Marshall Islands. Researchers agree on little more than that successive waves of migratory peoples from Southeast Asia spread across the Western Pacific about 3,000 years ago and that some of them landed on and remained on these islands. The Spanish explorer de Saavedra landed there in 1529. They were named for English explorer John Marshall, who visited them in 1799. The Marshall Islands were claimed by Spain in 1874.

Germany established a protectorate in 1885 and set up trading stations on the islands of Jaluit and Ebon to carry out the flourishing copra (dried coconut meat) trade. Marshallese Iroij (high chiefs) continued to rule under indirect colonial German administration.

At the beginning of World War I, Japan assumed control of the Marshall Islands. Their headquarters remained at the German center of administration, Jaluit. U.S. Marines and Army troops took control from the Japanese in early 1944, following intense fighting on Kwajalein and Enewetak atolls. In 1947, the United States, as the occupying power, entered into an agreement with the UN Security Council to administer Micronesia, including the Marshall Islands, as the Trust Territory of the Pacific Islands.

On May 1, 1979, in recognition of the evolving political status of the Marshall Islands, the United States recognized the constitution of the Marshall Islands and the establishment of the Government of the Republic of the Marshall Islands. The constitution incorporates both American and British constitutional concepts.

# GOVERNMENT

The legislative branch of the government consists of the Nitijela (parliament) with an advisory council of high chiefs. The Nitijela has 33 members from 24 districts elected for concurrent 4-year terms. Members are called senators. The president is elected by the Nitijela from among its members. Presidents pick cabinet members from the Nitijela. Amata Kabua was elected as the first president of the republic in 1979. Subsequently, he was re-elected to 4-year terms in 1983, 1987, 1991, and 1996. After Amata Kabua's death in office, his first cousin, Imata Kabua, won a special election in 1997. The current president was elected in the general elections of November 1999 and took office in January 2000.

The Republic of the Marshall Islands has four court systems: Supreme Court, high court, district and community courts, and the traditional rights court. Trial is by jury or judge. Jurisdiction of the traditional rights court is limited to cases involving titles or land rights or other disputes arising from customary law and traditional practice.

## Principal Government Officials

**For up-to-date information on Principal Government Officials, see the Chiefs of State and Cabinet Members of Foreign Governments section starting on page 1.**

The Republic of the Marshall Islands maintains an embassy at 2433 Massachusetts Avenue NW, Washington, DC 20008 (tel. 202-234-5414). It has a consulate at 1888 Lusitana St., Suite 301, Honolulu, HI 96813 (tel. 808-545-7767).

The Marshall Islands' mission to the United Nations is located at the News Building, 220 E. 42nd St., 31st Floor, New York, NY 10017 (tel. 212-983-3040).

# POLITICAL CONDITIONS

Citizens of the Marshall Islands live with a relatively new democratic political system combined with a hierarchical traditional culture. The first two presidents were chiefs. Kessai Note is a commoner.

There have been a number of local and national elections since the Republic of the Marshall Islands was founded, and in general, democracy has functioned well. There have been some incidents of human rights concern, however, such as undue government pressure on the judiciary and the press. The United Democratic Party, running on a reform platform, won the 1999 parliamentary election, taking control of the presidency and cabinet. The new government has publicly confirmed its commitment to an independent judiciary.

# ECONOMY

The government is the largest employer, employing 30.6% of the work force, down by 3.4% since 1988. GDP is derived mainly from payments made by the United States under the terms of the Compact of Free Association. Direct U.S. aid accounted for 60% of the Marshalls' $90 million budget.

The economy combines a small subsistence sector and a modern urban sector. In short, fishing and breadfruit, banana, taro, and pandanus cultivation constitute the subsistence sector. On the outer islands, production of copra and handicrafts income provide cash income. The modern service-oriented economy is located in Majuro and Ebeye. It is sustained by government expenditures and the U.S. Army installation at Kwajalein Atoll. The airfield there also serves as a second national hub for international flights.

The modern sector consists of wholesale and retail trade; restaurants; banking and insurance; construction, repair, and professional services; and copra processing. Copra cake and oil are by far the nation's largest exports. A tuna loining plant employs 300 workers, mostly women, at $1.50 per hour. Copra production, the most important single commercial activity for the past 100 years, now depends on government subsidies. The subsidies, more a social policy than an economic strategy, help reduce migration from outer atolls to densely populated Majuro and Ebeye.

Marine resources, including fishing, aquaculture, tourism development, and agriculture, are top government development priorities. The Marshall Islands sells fishing rights to other nations as a source of income. In recent years, the Marshall Islands has begun to offer ship registrations under the Marshall Islands flag. As a small nation, the Marshall Islands must import a wide variety of goods, including foodstuffs, consumer goods, machinery, and petroleum products.

# FOREIGN RELATIONS

While the Government of the Marshall Islands is free to conduct its own foreign relations, it does so under the terms of the Compact of Free Association. Since independence, the Republic of the Marshall Islands has established relations with 67 nations, including most other Pacific Island nations. Regional cooperation, through membership in various regional and international organizations, is a key element in its foreign policy.

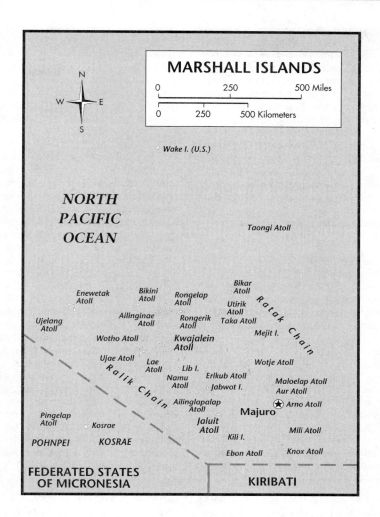

The Marshall Islands became a member of the United Nations in September 1991. The Marshall Islands maintains embassies in the U.S., Fiji, Japan, and Taiwan.

# U.S.-MARSHALLESE RELATIONS

After more than a decade of negotiation, the Marshall Islands and the United States signed the Compact of Free Association on June 25, 1983. The people of the Marshall Islands approved the compact in a UN-observed plebiscite on September 7, 1983. The U.S. Congress subsequently approved the compact, adding several amendments which were accepted by the Government of the Marshall Islands.

The compact was signed into U.S. law on January 14, 1986 (PL 99-239), and entered into force on October 21, 1986. The Republic of the Marshall Islands is a sovereign nation in "free association" with the United States. Under the compact, the United States has full authority and responsibility for security and defense of the Marshall Islands, and the Government of the Marshall Islands is obligated to refrain from taking actions that would be incompatible with these security and defense responsibilities. The duration of the compact's economic provisions is 15 years (ending in 2001); renegotiations regarding these provisions began late in 1999.

A major subsidiary agreement of the compact allows the United States continued use of the U.S. Army Kwajalein Atoll (USAKA) missile test range until 2016. Kwajalein, an atoll consisting of approximately 90 islets

## Travel Notes

**Customs:** Proof of U.S. citizenship, preferably a passport, but not visas, are required of American citizens traveling to the Marshall Islands. Visitors can obtain permits to stay up to three months by presenting an onward or return ticket and evidence of sufficient funds to cover the period of stay.

Immunizations against cholera and yellow fever may be required of travelers coming from infected areas. AIDS testing may be required of visitors staying longer than 3 months.

**Climate and clothing:** Climate is tropical, with high humidity, an average temperature of 84 degrees, and little seasonal change. Rainfall varies from 6-14 inches monthly. Dress is casual. Shorts are not acceptable as street wear for either sex.

**Health:** Typhoid, hepatitis B, and venereal diseases are endemic in the Marshall Islands. Typhoid and polio shots are recommended. Health care is adequate for minor medical problems. Tap water is not potable; bottled water is available. Travelers should consult latest information.

**Telecommunications:** Domestic and international telephone service is available. Telephone service outside Majuro and Kwajalein is unavailable. Outer islands are linked by an HF radio net. Majuro is across the international date line, 16 standard time zones ahead of eastern standard time.

**Transportation:** Flights arrive in Majuro from Honolulu, Guam, and Fiji several times a week. Domestic flights service 25 airstrips on 22 inhabited atolls. Transportation between islands is also available by sea. Taxis are available during normal work hours in Majuro, and public transportation is exceedingly limited. Rental cars are available, but there are only 152 km. (95 mi.) of paved roads in the Marshalls (mostly on Majuro and Ebeye).

**Travel Advice:** For up-to-date information from the U.S. State Department on possible inconvenient or hazardous situations, see the **Travel Warnings and Consular Information Sheets from the U.S. Government** section starting on page 1723. For the latest information on health requirements and conditions, see the **International Travelers' Health Information** section starting on page 1385. For further information dealing with non-urgent matter, see the **Tips for Travelers to...** section starting on page 1588.

around the largest lagoon in the world, is used by the Department of Defense under a government-to-government agreement with the Marshall Islands. The U.S. Department of Defense controls the use of some islands within Kwajalein atoll. Another major subsidiary agreement of the compact provides for settlement of all claims arising from the U.S. nuclear tests conducted at Bikini and Enewetak Atolls from 1946 to 1958. Under the terms of the compact, more than 40 U.S. Government agencies such as the Federal Aviation Administration, U.S. Postal Service, the Small Business Administration, and the Federal Emergency Management Agency operate programs or render assistance to the Marshall Islands.

The United States and the Marshall Islands have full diplomatic relations. The Marshall Islands have expressed an interest in attracting U.S. investment.

## Principal U.S. Embassy Officials

For up-to-date information on Principal U.S. Officials, see the U.S. Embassies, Consulates, and Foreign Service section starting on page 139.

The U.S. Embassy in the Marshall Islands is located on Lagoon Road, Majuro (tel. 692-247-4011). Mailing Address: P.O. Box 1379, Majuro, MH 96960-1379.

# MAURITANIA

July 1995

**Official Name:**
## Islamic Republic of Mauritania

## PROFILE

### Geography

**Area:** 1.1 million sq. km. (419,212 sq. mi.); slightly larger than Texas and New Mexico combined.
**Cities:** Capital—Nouakchott (pop. 600,000). Other cities—Nouadhibou (70,000), Kaedi (74,000), Zouerate (27,000), Kiffa (65,000), Rosso (50,000).
**Terrain:** Northern four-fifths barren desert; southern 20% mainly Sahelian with small scale irrigated and rain-fed agriculture in the Senegal River basin.
**Climate:** Predominantly hot and dry.

### People

**Nationality:** Noun and adjective—Mauritanian(s).
**Population (1995):** 2.3 million.
**Annual growth rate:** 2.9%.
**Ethnic groups:** Arab-Berber, Arab-Berber-Negroid, Pulaar, Soninke, Wolof.
**Religion:** Islam.
**Languages:** Hassaniya Arabic (official), French, Pular, Wolof, and Soninke.
**Education:** Years compulsory—none. Attendance—Student population enrolled in primary school 83%. Adult literacy—33%.
**Health:** Infant mortality rate—125/

1,000. Life expectancy—46 yrs.
**Work force:** Agriculture and fisheries—50%. Services and commerce—20%. Government—20%. Industry and transportation—5%. Other—5%.

### Government

**Type:** Republic.
**Independence:** November 28, 1960.
**Constitution:** Promulgated 1961, abolished by decree July 10, 1978. New constitution approved by referendum July 20, 1991.
**Branches:** Executive—president (chief of state). Legislative—bicameral national assembly, elected lower house (79 members), and upper house (56 members) chosen indirectly by municipal councilors. Judicial—a supreme court and lower courts are subject to control of executive branch; judicial decisions are rendered mainly on the basis of shari'a (Islamic law) for social/family matters and a western style legal code, applied in commercial and some criminal cases.
**Political parties:** Officially 19.
**Suffrage:** Universal at 18.

### Economy

**GDP (1994 est.):** $1.1 billion.
**Annual growth rate:** 5.6%.
**Per capita income:** $480.
**Natural resources:** Fish, iron ore, gypsum.
**Agriculture (24% of GDP):** Prod-

ucts—livestock, millet, maize, wheat, dates, rice.
**Industry (30% of GDP):** Types—iron mining, fishing.
**Trade (1994) (40% of GDP):** Exports—$419 million. Major markets—Japan 29%; Italy 14%; France 14%; Spain 10%, Belgium/Luxembourg 7%; Switzerland 5%. Imports—$384 million: foodstuffs, machinery, tools, cloth, consumer goods. Major suppliers—France 33%; U.S. 10%; Spain 9%; Germany 6%; Algeria 6%; Belgium/Luxembourg 5%; Italy 4%.

## U.S.-MAURITANIAN RELATIONS

Before June 7, 1967, the United States maintained cordial relations with Mauritania and provided a small amount of economic assistance. However, Mauritania broke diplomatic and consular relations with the United States during the June 1967 Middle East war. Relations were restored two years later, and ties were relatively friendly until the late 1980s, despite disagreement over the Arab-Israeli issue..

Between 1983 and 1991, when the USAID (U.S. Agency for International Development) mission in Mauritania ceased operations, the United States provided $67.3 million in development assistance. The U.S. also pro-

# MAURITANIA

| 0 | 75 | 150 | 225 | 300 Miles |

| 0 | 75 | 150 | 225 | 300 Kilometers |

ATLANTIC
OCEAN

ALGERIA

Dayet el
Khadra

Erg Iguidi

Al Bir Lahlou

Agmar

Chegga

WESTERN
SAHARA

Bîr Mogreïn

'Ayoûn 'Abd
el Mâlek

SAHARA DESERT

Fdérik      Zouérat

▲ Kediet ej Jill
3,002 ft.
915 m.

MALI

Awaday

El Moueïla

El Mrâyer

Bir Gandús

Ouadane

El Djouf

Cap
Blanc  Nouadhibou

Atar      Chinguetti

Baie de
Lévrier      Tánoudert

Île Tidra

Akjoujt

Cap
Timiris  Nouamrhar

Tidjikdja      Tîchît

Tijti

Nouakchott

Qualâta

Boutilimit

'Ayoûn
el 'Atroûs

Néma

Lac
Rkiz      Aleg

Kîfa

Diadé      Lemoïlé

Rosso  Senegal  Bogué

Médala

Kaédi

Mbout

Maghama

Nioro du Sahel

Maurítania

Bakel  Sélibaby

Niono

Kayes

SENEGAL

MALI

N
W       E
S

Bafoulabé

vided emergency food assistance through bilateral channels until 1992 and, subsequently, through multilateral channels. Since 1981, the United States has provided about $100 million in economic and food assistance

The 1989 rupture between Mauritania and Senegal that resulted in the deportation of tens of thousands of Mauritanian citizens negatively affected U.S.-Mauritanian relations. Moreover, Mauritania's perceived support of Iraq prior to and during the Gulf war of 1991 further weakened the strained ties.

Relations between the U.S. and Mauritania reached a low in the spring of 1991, as details of the Mauritanian military's role in widespread human rights abuses surfaced. The United States responded by formally halting USAID operations and all military assistance to Mauritania.

Since late 1991, the Government of Mauritania has expressed a desire to restore good relations with the United States. It has implemented democratic reforms such as the legalization of political parties, a free press, and presidential and legislative elections. The government has also improved its overall performance on human rights.

## Trade and Investment

In 1995, an American firm was awarded a $17 million contract for projects in Mauritania in telecommunications and other fields, indicating that bilateral commercial ties are expanding.

Mauritanians would welcome U.S. investment, particularly in fisheries. U.S. exporters have been active in the mining sector, although primarily through European offices or agents. Export opportunities exist in transportation, agriculture, boat repair, and port handling equipment.

## Principal U.S. Officials

For up-to-date information on Principal U.S. Officials, see the U.S. Embassies, Consulates, and Foreign Service section starting on page 139.

The address of the U.S. embassy in Mauritania is BP 222, Nouakchott, Islamic Republic of Mauritania. Tel. (222)(2) 526-60/526-63; Telex AMEMB 5558 MTN; Fax (222)(2) 515-92.

# GOVERNMENT AND POLITICAL CONDITIONS

From July 1978 to April 1992, Mauritania was governed by a military junta. The ruling group was composed of military officers holding ministerial portfolios or important positions in the defense establishment. The chairman of the committee was also chief of state. A new constitution was approved by referendum in July 1991; in early 1992, faced with internal crisis in the form of ethnic strife, as well as a cutoff of military and development assistance from abroad, the government reverted to civilian rule and the military committee was disbanded. Maaouya Ould Sid'Ahmed Taya remained at the head of government. As of June 1995, only one military officer remained in the Council of Ministers.

Politics in Mauritania have always been heavily influenced by personalities, with any leader's ability to exercise political power dependent upon control over resources, perceived ability or integrity, and tribal, ethnic, family, and personal considerations. It is likely that during the civilian transition still underway, the chief of state, though very powerful, will continue to be subject to tribal and ethnic pressures. Conflict between Moor and non-Moor ethnic groups, centering on language, land tenure, and other issues, continues to be the dominant challenge to national unity.

The government bureaucracy is composed of traditional ministries, special agencies, and parastatal companies. The Ministry of Interior

controls a system of regional governors and prefects modeled on the French system of local administration. Under this system, Mauritania is divided into 13 regions (wilayas) and one district (Nouakchott). Control is tightly centralized in Nouakchott. However, partly because of 1992 national elections and 1994 municipal elections, a decentralizing trend in the bureaucracy is underway.

Political parties, illegal during the military period, were legalized again in 1991, as a sign of democratic reform. By April 1992, when the civilian transition occurred, 15 political parties had been recognized. Although most are small, there are two main opposition parties. Most opposition parties boycotted the first legislative election in 1992, and the parliament is dominated by one party, President Taya's PRDS (Parti Republicain et Democratique Social). The opposition participated in municipal elections in January-February 1994 and subsequent Senate elections, gaining representation at the local level as well as one seat in the Senate.

Much social status is determined by descent from either the region's Arab-Berber conquerors or the Caucasoid-Negroid peoples they enslaved. A distinction between aristocracy and servant historically defined Maure (Moor) society as "white" and "black"—traditionally the enslaved indigenous class came to be called black Moors—although such status differences are declining.

The ethnic conflict that troubled Mauritania in the late 1980s and early 1990s has lessened, although political parties still reflect the country's social division. Many of the country's non-Arabic-speaking black citizens support opposition parties, while others are active in the PRDS.

## Principal Government Officials

**For up-to-date information on Principal Government Officials, see the Chiefs of State and Cabinet Members of Foreign Governments section** **starting on page 1.**

Mauritania maintains an embassy in the United States at 2129 Leroy Place NW, Washington, DC 20008 (tel. 202-232-5700).

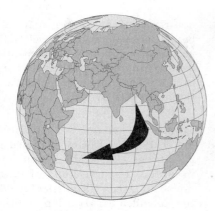

# MAURITIUS

December 1999

Official Name:
**Republic of Mauritius**

# PROFILE

## Geography

**Area:** 1,865 sq. km. (720 sq. mi.), about the size of Rhode Island; 500 miles east of Madagascar in the Indian Ocean.

**Dependencies:** Rodrigues Island, the Agalega Islands and Cargados Carajos Shoals; Mauritius also claims sovereignty over the Chagos Archipelago, part of the British Indian Ocean Territory, where U.S. Naval Base Diego Garcia is located.

**Cities (1996):** Capital—Port Louis (pop.146,000). Other cities—Beau Bassin and Rose Hill (98,000), Vacoas–Phoenix (96,000), Curepipe (78,000), Quatre Bornes (75,000).

**Terrain:** Volcanic island surrounded by coral reefs. A central plateau is rimmed by mountains. Climate: Tropical; cyclone season mid–December–April.

## People

**Nationality:** Noun and adjective—Mauritian(s).

**Population (1997):** 1.1 million.

**Population density:** 1,500/sq. mi.

**Avg. annual population growth (1997):** 1.2%.

**Ethnic groups:** Indo–Mauritians 68%, Creoles 27%, Sino–Mauritians 3%, Franco–Mauritians 2%.

**Religions:** Hindu, Roman Catholic, Muslim.

**Languages:** Creole (common), French, English (official), Hindi, Urdu, Hakka, Bhojpuri.

**Education:** Years compulsory—6 (primary school). Attendance (primary school)—virtually universal. Literacy—adult population 80%; school population 90%.

**Health (1996):** Infant mortality rate—22/1,000. Life expectancy—male 66 yrs., female 74 yrs.

**Work force (1997):** 505,000. Manufacturing—25%. Trade and tourism—18%. Government services—10%. Agriculture and fishing—9%. Other—48%.

## Government

**Type:** Republic.

**Independence:** March 12, 1968 (became a republic in 1992).

**Constitution:** March 12, 1968.

**Branches:** Executive—President (head of state), prime minister (head of government), Council of Ministers. Legislative—Unicameral National Assembly. Judicial—Supreme Court. Administrative subdivisions: 10.

**Major political parties:** Mauritian Labor Party (MLP), Militant Socialist Movement (MSM), Mauritian Militant Movement (MMM), and the Mauritian Social Democratic Party (PMSD).

**Suffrage:** Universal over 18.

**Defense (1997):** 1.7 % of GDP.

**Flag:** Four horizontal stripes—red, blue, yellow, green.

## Economy

**GDP (1997):** $4.1 billion.

**Real growth rate (1997):** 5%.

**Per capita income (1997):** $3,600.

**Avg. inflation rate (1997):** 6.6%.

**Natural resources:** None.

**Manufacturing (including export processing zone):** 25% of GDP. Types—labor–intensive goods for export, including textiles and clothing, pearls, cut and polished diamonds, semiprecious stones, optical goods, cut flowers, leather products, electronic goods, watches, and toys. Tourism sector—12% of GDP. Main countries of origin—France, including nearby French island Reunion, South Africa, and West European countries.

**Agriculture:** 9% of GDP. Products—sugar, sugar derivatives, tea, tobacco, vegetables, fruits, and flowers.

**Trade (1997):** Exports—$1.6 billion: textiles and clothing, sugar, canned tuna, jewelry, leather products, and flowers. Major markets—Europe and the U.S. Imports—$2.2 billion: foodstuffs, petroleum products, machinery and transport equipment, construction materials, manufactured goods, and textile raw materials. Major suppliers—South Africa, Great Britain, France, Australia,

India.

**Fiscal year:** July 1–June 30.

# HISTORY

While Arab and Malay sailors knew of Mauritius as early as the 10th century AD and Portuguese sailors first visited in the 16th century, the island was not colonized until 1638 by the Dutch. Mauritius was populated over the next few centuries by waves of traders, planters and their slaves, indentured laborers, merchants, and artisans. The island was named in honor of Prince Maurice of Nassau by the Dutch, who abandoned the colony in 1710.

The French claimed Mauritius in 1715 and renamed it Ile de France. It became a prosperous colony under the French East India Company. The French Government took control in 1767, and the island served as a naval and privateer base during the Napoleonic wars. In 1810, Mauritius was captured by the British, whose possession of the island was confirmed 4 years later by the Treaty of Paris. French institutions, including the Napoleonic code of law, were maintained. The French language is still used more widely than English.

Mauritian Creoles trace their origins to the plantation owners and slaves who were brought to work the sugar fields. Indo–Mauritians are descended from Indian immigrants who arrived in the 19th century to work as indentured laborers after slavery was abolished in 1835. Included in the Indo–Mauritian community are Muslims (about 15% of the population) from the Indian subcontinent. The Franco–Mauritian elite controls nearly all of the large sugar estates and is active in business and banking. As the Indian population became numerically dominant and the voting franchise was extended, political power shifted from the Franco–Mauritians and their Creole allies to the Hindus.

Elections in 1947 for the newly created Legislative Assembly marked Mauritius' first steps toward self–rule. An independence campaign gained momentum after 1961, when the British agreed to permit additional self–government and eventual independence. A coalition composed of the Mauritian Labor Party (MLP), the Muslim Committee of Action (CAM), and the Independent Forward Bloc (IFB)—a traditionalist Hindu party—won a majority in the 1967 Legislative Assembly election, despite opposition from Franco–Mauritian and Creole supporters of Gaetan Duval's Mauritian Social Democratic Party (PMSD). The contest was interpreted locally as a referendum on independence. Sir Seewoosagur Ramgoolam, MLP leader and chief minister in the colonial government, became the first prime minister at independence, on March 12, 1968. This event was preceded by a period of communal strife, brought under control with assistance from British troops.

# GOVERNMENT AND POLITICAL CONDITIONS

Mauritian politics are vibrant and characterized by coalition and alliance building. All parties are centrist and reflect a national consensus that supports democratic politics and a relatively open economy with a strong private sector.

Alone or in coalition, the Mauritian Labor Party (MLP) ruled from 1947 through 1982 and returned to power in 1995. The Mauritian Militant Movement/Mauritian Socialist Party (MMM/PSM) alliance won the 1982 election. In 1983, defectors from the MMM joined with the PSM to form the Militant Socialist Movement (MSM) and won a working majority. In July 1990, the MSM realigned with the MMM and in September 1991 national elections won 59 of the 62 directly elected seats in parliament. In December 1995, the MLP returned to power, this time in coalition with the MMM. Labor's Navinchandra Ramgoolam, son of the country's first prime minister, became prime minister himself. Ramgoolam dismissed his MMM coalition partners in mid–1997, leaving Labor in power save for several small parties allied with it.

Mauritius became a republic on March 12, 1992. The most immediate result was that a Mauritian–born president became head of state, replacing Queen Elizabeth II. Under the amended constitution, political power remained with parliament. The Council of Ministers (cabinet), responsible for the direction and control of the government, consists of the prime minister (head of government), the leader of the majority party in the legislature, and about 20 ministries.

The unicameral National Assembly has up to 70 deputies. Sixty–two are elected by universal suffrage, and as many as eight "best losers" are chosen from the runners–up by the Electoral Supervisory Commission using a formula designed to give at least minimal representation to all ethnic communities and under–represented parties. Elections are scheduled at least every 5 years.

Mauritian law is an amalgam of French and British legal traditions. The Supreme Court—a chief justice and five other judges—is the highest judicial authority. There is an additional right of appeal to the Queen's Privy Council. Local government has nine administrative divisions, with municipal and town councils in urban areas and district and village councils in rural areas. The island of Rodrigues forms the country's 10th administrative division.

## Principal Government Officials

**For up-to-date information on Principal Government Officials, see the Chiefs of State and Cabinet Members of Foreign Governments section starting on page 1.**

Mauritius maintains an embassy at 4301 Connecticut Avenue NW, Washington, DC 20008 (tel. 202–244–1491).

# ECONOMY

Mauritius has one of the strongest economies in Africa, with a GDP of $4.1 billion in 1997 and per capita income of $3,600. It is heavily reliant on exports of sugar and textiles, but tourism, offshore business, and financial services are growing. Independent surveys typically characterize the Mauritian business environment as among the best in Africa.

Economic performance has been impressive for the past 15 years, with real growth averaging 7% between 1985–90 and 5.4% between 1990–97. GDP grew 5% in 1997, with strong performances in all major sectors. Annual economic growth is likely to hover between 5% and 6% over the medium term; neither a recession nor a boom is forecast. Inflation was 6.6% in 1997 and is likely to remain in single digits over the medium term. Unemployment is growing but manageable. The jobless rate was about 6% in 1997, nearly double previous estimates. The upward trend is causing concern in a society grown accustomed to full employment. Chronic trade deficits are normally offset by surpluses in tourism and other services. The Mauritian rupee is freely convertible.

The economy faces daunting challenges. The country's two principal exports—textiles and sugar—rely on preferential access to markets in Europe and the United States. As World Trade Organization regulations come into force and textile quotas disappear, Mauritius will face increased competition from low–cost producers in Asia and South America. The price it receives for its sugar in Europe and the United States— two or three times the world market price—will almost certainly fall. Both industries are responding by placing more emphasis on productivity. Also, many of the country's most successful companies and banks are expanding

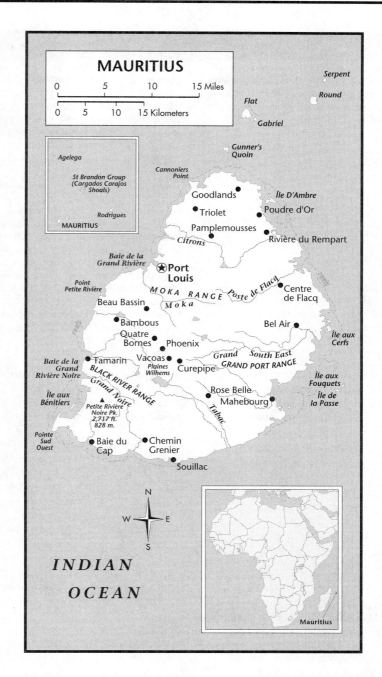

outside the country and establishing operations in India and Africa. For its part, the government is encouraging investment in services with the goal of establishing Mauritius as a regional trade and financial center for commerce between Africa and the Far East.

There are about 275 textile factories in Mauritius exporting to Europe and the United States. Products range from simple garments to fashionable sweaters and other apparel sold in the finest shops. Raw material—yarn and fabric—comes primarily from India and China.

The sugar industry comprises 20 estates, 17 mills, and 35,000 small planters. Production ranges between 600,000 and 650,000 tons per year. More than 90% is sold to Europe, the remainder to the United States. An increasing number of mills are investing in power plants fueled by coal and bagasse, the residue left from crushed sugarcane.

More than 90 hotels serve the tourism industry. They range from mod-

Mauritius

## Travel Notes

**Customs:** Visas are not required for US citizens, but travelers should have onward or return tickets. Immunization certificates are not required unless the traveler arrives in Mauritius from an infected area.

**Currency, exchange, and banking:** Travelers may bring in any amount of foreign notes or travelers checks.

**Health:** Mauritius has no major health hazards. Local clinics and pharmacies are adequate. Precautions should be taken before consuming raw fruits and vegetables or tap water.

**Telecommunications:** Reliable international mail, telephone, FAX, and telegraph services are available. Mauritius is nine time zones ahead of eastern standard time.

**Transportation:** Regular flights serve Europe, East and Southern Africa, India, Singapore, Hong Kong, and Australia. Rental cars and taxis are readily available. Traffic moves on the left. Bus service is regular and inexpensive throughout Mauritius. Most roads, though paved, are narrow, twisting, and poorly lit at night.

**Travel Advice:** For up-to-date information from the U.S. State Department on possible inconvenient or hazardous situations, see the **Travel Warnings and Consular Information Sheets from the U.S. Government** section starting on page 1723. For the latest information on health requirements and conditions, see the **International Travelers' Health Information** section starting on page 1385. For further information dealing with non-urgent matter, see the **Tips for Travelers to...** section starting on page 1588.

est bed–and–breakfasts to five–star resorts. Tourist arrivals exceeded 500,000 in 1997 and are expected to reach 600,000 before the turn of the century.

Banking and other financial services form the most rapidly growing economic sector. Some 6,000 offshore companies were registered as of 1997. Freeport facilities, including warehouses, commercial exhibition space, and modern cargo handling systems, opened in 1997, primarily to serve trade between Asia and Africa.

# FOREIGN RELATIONS

Mauritius has strong and friendly relations with the West, as well as with India and the countries of southern and eastern Africa. It is a member of the World Trade Organization, the Commonwealth, La Francophonie, the Southern Africa Development Community, the Indian Ocean Commission, COMESA, and the recently formed Indian Ocean Rim Association.

Trade, commitment to democracy, and the country's small size are driving forces behind Mauritian foreign policy. The country's political heritage and dependence on Western markets have led to close ties with the European Union and its member states, particularly the United Kingdom and France, which exercises sovereignty over neighboring Reunion.

Considered part of Africa geographically, Mauritius has friendly relations with other African states in the region, particularly South Africa, by far its largest continental trading partner. Mauritian investors are gradually entering African markets, notably Madagascar and Mozambique. Mauritius coordinates much of its foreign policy with the Southern Africa Development Community and the Organization of African Unity.

Relations with India are strong for both historical and commercial reasons. Foreign embassies in Mauritius include Australia, the United Kingdom, China, Egypt, France, India, Madagascar, Pakistan, Russia, and the United States.

# DEFENSE

Mauritius does not have a standing army. All military, police, and security functions are carried out by 10,000 active–duty personnel under the command of the Commissioner of Police. The 8,000–member National Police is responsible for domestic law enforcement. The 1,400–member Special Mobile Force (SMF) and the 500–member National Coast Guard are the only two paramilitary units in Mauritius. Both units are composed of police officers on lengthy rotations to those services.

The SMF is organized as a ground infantry unit and engages extensively in civic works projects. The Coast Guard has four patrol craft for search–and–rescue missions and surveillance of territorial waters. A 100–member police helicopter squadron assists in search–and–rescue operations. There also is a special supporting unit of 270 members trained in riot control.

Military advisers from the United Kingdom and India work with the SMF, the Coast Guard, and the Police Helicopter Unit, and Mauritian police officers are trained in the United Kingdom, India, and France. The United States provides training to Mauritian Coast Guard officers in such fields as seamanship and maritime law enforcement.

## Principal U.S. Officials

**For up-to-date information on Principal U.S. Officials, see the U.S. Embassies, Consulates, and Foreign Service section starting on page 139.**

The U.S. embassy in Mauritius is located in the Rogers House, 4th floor, John Kennedy Street, Port Louis (tel. 230 208–2347; Fax 230–208–9534; E–mail: usembass@bow.intnet.mu.).

# U.S.-MAURITIAN RELATIONS

Official U.S. representation in Mauritius dates from the end of the 18th century. An American consulate was established in 1794 but closed in 1911. It was reopened in 1967 and elevated to embassy status upon the country's independence in 1968.

894

Since 1970, the mission has been directed by a resident U.S. ambassador.

Relations between the United States and Mauritius are cordial and largely revolve around trade. U.S. exports to Mauritius are modest but growing, particularly in telecommunications and other high–technology fields. In 1996, Mauritius imported U.S goods valued at $25 million; the same year, the United States imported $238 million in Mauritian products—mostly knitwear, other textiles, and sugar.

The U.S. funds a small military assistance program focused on Coast Guard training. The embassy also manages special self–help funds for community groups and non–governmental organizations and a democracy and human rights fund.

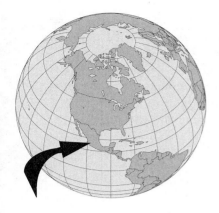

# MEXICO
February 2001

## Official Name:
## United Mexican States

## PROFILE

### Geography
**Area:** 1,972,500 sq. km. (761,600 sq. mi.); about three times the size of Texas.
**Cities:** Capital—Mexico City (13 million, 2000 census metro area). Other cities—Guadalajara, Monterrey, Puebla, Leon.
**Terrain:** Coastal lowlands, central high plateaus, and mountains up to 5,400 m. (18,000 ft.).
**Climate:** Tropical to desert.

### People
**Nationality:** Noun and adjective—Mexican(s).
**Population:** (2000 census) 97.3 million.
**Annual growth rate:** (net 2000) 1.6%.
**Ethnic groups:** Indian-Spanish (mestizo) 60%, Indian 30%, Caucasian 9%, other 1%.
**Religions:** Roman Catholic 89%, Protestant 6%, other 5%.
**Language:** Spanish.
**Education:** Years compulsory—12. Literacy—89.4% Health (1996 est.): Infant mortality rate—31/1,000. Life expectancy—male 73 years; female 77 years.
**Work force:** (1999, 41 million) Agriculture, forestry, hunting, fishing—

21.0%; services—32.2%; commerce—16.9%; manufacturing—18.7%; construction—5.6%; transportation and communication—4.5%; mining and quarrying—1.0%.

### Government
**Type:** Federal republic.
**Independence:** First proclaimed September 16, 1810; republic established 1824.
**Constitution:** February 5, 1917.
**Branches:** Executive—president (chief of state and head of government). Legislative—bicameral. Judicial—Supreme Court, local and federal systems. Administrative subdivisions: 31 states and a federal district.
**Political parties:** Green Ecological Party (PVEM), Institutional Revolutionary Party (PRI), Labor Party (PT), National Action Party (PAN), Party of the Democratic Revolution (PRD), and several small parties.
**Suffrage:** Universal at 18.

### Economy
**Nominal GDP:** (2000 est.) $557 billion.
**Per capita GDP:** (2000 est.) $5,223.
**Annual real GDP growth:** (2000 est.) 7.2%; 1999, 3.7%; 1998, 4.9%; 1997, 6.8%.
**Avg. annual real GDP growth:** (1994-2000) 5%.
**Inflation rate:** (2000 est.) 8.8%;

1999, 12.3%; 1998, 18.6%; 1994-2000, 18.2%.
**Natural resources:** Petroleum, silver, copper, gold, lead, zinc, natural gas, timber.
**Agriculture:** (5% of GDP) Products—corn, beans, oilseeds, feedgrains, fruit, cotton, coffee, sugarcane, winter vegetables.
**Industry:** (21% of GDP) Types—manufacturing (21.1%), petroleum and mining.
**Services:** (66.8% of GDP) Types—commerce and tourism (20.7%), transportation and communications (9.5%).
**Trade:** (2000 est.) Exports—$167.6 billion: manufacturing 89.6%, petroleum and derivatives 7.3%, agriculture 2.9%, other 0.2%. Major Markets—U.S. (82%, $261.7 billion in 2000), Europe (3.5%), South America (2.6%), Canada (1.3%). Imports—$174.9 billion: intermediate goods 77.0%, capital goods 14.5%, consumer goods 8.5%. Major source—U.S. (70%, $123.2 billion in 2000), Europe (9.0%), Asia (8.6%), Canada (1.8%).

## PEOPLE

Mexico is the most populous Spanish-speaking country in the world and the second most-populous country in Latin America after Portuguese-speaking Brazil. About 70% of the people live in urban areas. Many Mexicans emigrate from rural areas that lack job opportunities—such as the underdeveloped southern states and the crowded central plateau—to the industrialized urban centers and the developing areas along the U.S.-Mexico border. According to some estimates, the population of the area around Mexico City is about 18 million, which would make it the largest concentration of population in the world. Cities bordering on the United States—such as Tijuana and Ciudad Juarez—and cities in the interior—such as Guadalajara, Monterrey, and Puebla—have undergone sharp rises in population.

# HISTORY

Highly advanced cultures, including those of the Olmecs, Mayas, Toltecs, and Aztecs existed long before the Spanish conquest. Hernando Cortes conquered Mexico during the period 1519-21 and founded a Spanish colony that lasted nearly 300 years. Independence from Spain was proclaimed by Father Miguel Hidalgo on September 16, 1810; this launched a war for independence. An 1821 treaty recognized Mexican independence from Spain and called for a constitutional monarchy. The planned monarchy failed; a republic was proclaimed in December 1822 and established in 1824.

Prominent figures in Mexico's war for independence were Father Jose Maria Morelos; Gen. Augustin de Iturbide, who defeated the Spaniards and ruled as Mexican emperor from 1822-23; and Gen. Antonio Lopez de Santa Ana, who went on to control Mexican politics from 1833 to 1855. Santa Ana was Mexico's leader during the conflict with Texas, which declared itself independent from Mexico in 1836, and during Mexico's war with the United States (1846-48). The presidential terms of Benito Juarez (1858-71) were interrupted by the Hapsburg monarchy's rule of Mexico (1864-67). Archduke Maximilian of Austria, whom Napoleon III of France established as Emperor of Mexico, was deposed by Juarez and

executed in 1867. Gen. Porfirio Diaz was president during most of the period between 1877 and 1911.

Mexico's severe social and economic problems erupted in a revolution that lasted from 1910-20 and gave rise to the 1917 constitution. Prominent leaders in this period—some of whom were rivals for power—were Francisco I. Madero, Venustiano Carranza, Pancho Villa, Alvaro Obregon, Victoriano Huerta, and Emiliano Zapata. The Institutional Revolutionary Party (PRI), formed in 1929 under a different name, continues to be the most important political force in the nation. It emerged as a coalition of interests after the chaos of the revolution as a vehicle for keeping political competition in peaceful channels. For almost 70 years, Mexico's national government has been controlled by the PRI, which has won every presidential race and most gubernatorial races.

# GOVERNMENT

The 1917 constitution provides for a federal republic with powers separated into independent executive, legislative, and judicial branches. Historically, the executive is the dominant branch, with power vested in the president, who promulgates and executes the laws of the Congress. The Congress has played an increasingly important role since 1997 when opposition parties made major gains. The president also legislates by executive decree in certain economic and financial fields, using powers delegated from the Congress. The president is elected by universal adult suffrage for a 6-year term and may not hold office a second time. There is no vice president; in the event of the removal or death of the president, a provisional president is elected by the Congress.

The Congress is composed of a Senate and a Chamber of Deputies. Consecutive re-election is prohibited. Senators are elected to 6-year terms, and deputies serve 3-year terms. In the lower chamber, 300 deputies are directly elected to represent single-

member districts, and 200 are selected by a modified form of proportional representation from five electoral regions created for this purpose across the country. The 200 proportional representation seats were created to help smaller parties gain access to the Chamber.

The judiciary is divided into federal and state court systems, with federal courts having jurisdiction over most civil cases and those involving major felonies. Under the constitution, trial and sentencing must be completed within 12 months of arrest for crimes that would carry at least a 2-year sentence. In practice, the judicial system often does not meet this requirement. Trial is by judge, not jury, in most criminal cases. Defendants have a right to counsel, and public defenders are available. Other rights include defense against self-incrimination, the right to confront one's accusers, and the right to a public trial. Supreme Court justices are appointed by the president and approved by the Senate.

## National Security

Mexico's armed forces number about 225,000. The army makes up about three-fourths of that total. Principal military roles include national defense, narcotics control, and civic action assignments such as road-building, search and rescue, and disaster relief.

## Principal Government Officials

**For up-to-date information on Principal Government Officials, see the Chiefs of State and Cabinet Members of Foreign Governments section starting on page 1.**

Mexico maintains an embassy in the United States at 1911 Pennsylvania Ave. NW, Washington, DC 20006 (tel. 202-728-1600).
Consular offices are located at 2827 - 16th St. NW, 20009 (tel. 202-736-1012), and the trade office is co-

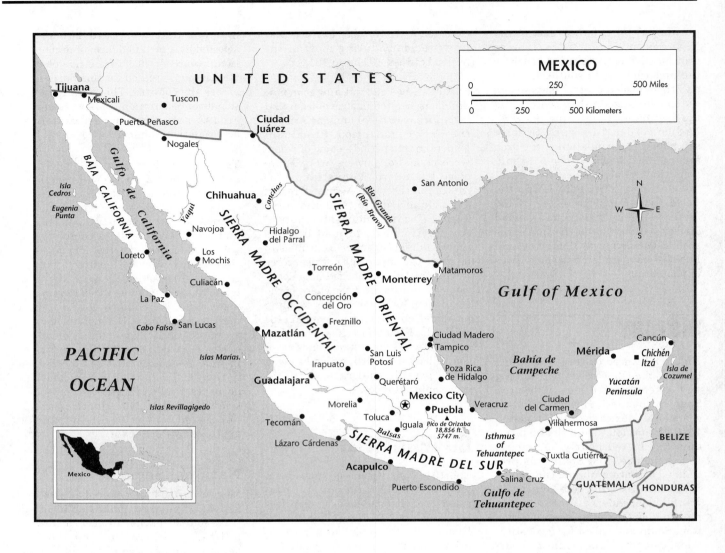

located at the embassy (tel. 202-728-1686).

Consulates general are located in Chicago, Dallas, Denver, El Paso, Houston, Los Angeles, Miami, New Orleans, New York, San Antonio, San Diego, and San Francisco; consulates are (partial listing) in Atlanta, Boston, Detroit, Philadelphia, Seattle, St. Louis, and Tucson.

# POLITICAL CONDITIONS

On July 2, 2000, Vicente Fox Quesada of the opposition Alliance for Change coalition, mainly headed by the National Action Party (PAN), was elected president, in what are consid-ered to have been the freest and fair-est elections in Mexico's history. Fox began his 6-year term on December 1. His victory ended the Institutional Revolutionary Party's (PRI) 71-year hold on the presidency.

Fox has proposed major changes in the relationship between the individ-ual and the state as well as between the individual states and the federal government. The President named a diverse cabinet and vowed to main-tain a prudent fiscal policy, empha-size job creation, promote more legal emigration into the United States, initiate negotiations with the rebels in the southern state of Chiapas, and move ahead with constitutional reforms, such as the reelection of members of Congress.

## Recent Elections

The July 2, 2000 elections marked the first time since the 1910 Mexican Revolution that the opposition defeated the party in government. Election officials declared Fox the winner with 43% of the vote, followed by PRI candidate Francisco Labas-tida with 36%, and Cuauhtemoc Cardenas of the Party of the Demo-cratic Revolution (PRD) with 17%. Despite some isolated incidents of irregularities and problems, there was no evidence of systematic attempts to manipulate the elections or their results, and critics concluded that the irregularities that occurred did not alter the outcome of the pres-idential vote. Civic organizations fielded more than 80,000 trained electoral observers; foreigners—many from the United States—were invited to witness the process, and numerous independent "quick count" operations and exit polls validated the official vote tabulation.

Numerous electoral reforms implemented since 1989 aided in the opening of the Mexican political system, and opposition parties have made historic gains in elections at all levels. Many of the concerns shifted from fraud to campaign fairness issues. During 1995-96 the political parties negotiated constitutional amendments to address these issues. Implementing legislation included major points of consensus that had been worked out with the opposition parties. The thrust of the new laws has public financing predominate over private contributions to political parties, tightens procedures for auditing the political parties, and strengthens the authority and independence of electoral institutions. The court system also was given greatly expanded authority to hear civil rights cases on electoral matters brought by individuals or groups. In short, the extensive reform efforts have "leveled the playing field" for the parties.

Even before the new electoral law was passed, opposition parties had obtained an increasing voice in Mexico's political system. A substantial number of candidates from opposition parties had won election to the Chamber of Deputies and senate. As a result of the 2000 elections, the Congress will be more diverse than ever. In the new Chamber, 211 seats belong to the PRI, 206 to the PAN, 50 to the PRD, 17 for the Green Party, and the remaining 16 are split among four smaller parties. In the 128-seat Senate, the upper house of Congress, the PRI still holds the most seats at 60, but the PAN holds 46, the PRD 15, the Greens 5, and two smaller parties each have one seat. Senators serve 6 years in office and Deputies 3 years; neither can be elected to consecutive terms.

In the aftermath of the July 2, 2000 elections, many political analysts assumed that the PRI, having lost its first presidential election, was a dying party. This rush to judgment has not been borne out by the facts. Certainly, the first state election in Chiapas, after July 2 appeared to confirm that prediction. Chiapas has long been a treasury of reliable votes for the PRI, but the opposition parties there joined in a broadbased coalition, including the PRD and the PAN. On August 20, around 50% of the eligible voters in Chiapas chose the coalition opposition candidate Pablo Salazar over the PRI's Sami David David by a six-point margin.

Yet, on September 3 in the coastal state of Veracruz, the PRI won more than half of the 210 municipal presidencies at stake, highlighting the party's underlying strength. On October 15, the PRI appeared to retain the governorship in the southeastern state of Tabasco, although the race was very tight and the results are still in dispute. On November 12, the PAN maintained the governorship of the western state of Jalisco, but again the race is being contested, this time by the PRI. The bottom line is that reports of the PRI's demise have been greatly exaggerated, and it will continue to be a major force for the foreseeable future.

## Other Reforms

Constitutional and legal changes have been adopted in recent years to improve the performance and accountability of the Supreme Court and the Office of the Attorney General and the administration of federal courts. The Supreme Court, relieved of administrative duties for lower courts, was given responsibilities for judicial review of certain categories of law and legislation. A variety of laws also was passed in 1995-96 to help control organized crime.

Although the constitution provides for three branches of government, the Mexican presidency traditionally occupies a dominant position. In order to overcome this "presidentialism," the administration of President Ernesto Zedillo sought to develop a greater role for the Congress, notably by inviting the participation of a multi-party legislative commission in the Chiapas peace negotiations and seeking congressional approval of the financial assistance package signed by the U.S. and Mexico in February 1995. Congress' role as a coequal balance to the Executive also received a boost after the July 1997 elections, which gave the opposition the strength to command a majority in the Chamber of Deputies. The judicial reforms mentioned above were designed in part to allow the judicial branch of government to become a more effective counterweight to the other two branches. The Zedillo administration also promoted a "new federalism" to devolve more power to state and local governments, starting with pilot programs in education and health.

## Chiapas

A lingering political conflict exists in the southernmost state of Chiapas. In January 1994, insurgents in the state of Chiapas briefly took arms against the government, protesting alleged oppression and governmental indifference to poverty. After 12 days of fighting, a cease-fire was negotiated that remains in effect. The government and the Zapatista Army of National Liberation (EZLN) reached accords in 1996 that are still under consideration in the Congress. Following the massacre of 45 indigenous peasants in the village of Acteal in December 1997, tensions increased; sporadic clashes continued to occur between armed civilian groups, usually over disputed land claims. As a presidential candidate, Fox promised to renew dialogue with the EZLN and address unresolved problems in the state. Following his inauguration, he ordered many troops out of Chiapas, dismantled roadblocks, and submitted the peace accords to Congress.

## Education

Although educational levels in Mexico have improved substantially in recent decades, the country still faces daunting problems. Education is one of the Government of Mexico's highest priorities. The education budget for 2000—$23 billion—represented a 6.8% increase over the previous year's figure and 23% more funding in real terms for education in 2000 than in 1994. Educational funding now represents 27% of the budget. Education in Mexico also is being decentralized from federal to state authority in order to improve accountability.

Education is mandatory from ages 6 through 18. The increase in school enrollments during the past two decades has been dramatic. By 1999, 94% of the population between the ages of 6 and 14 were enrolled in school. Primary, including preschool, enrollment totaled 17.2 million in 2000. Enrollment at the secondary public school level rose from 1.4 million in 1972 to 5.4 million in 2000. A rapid rise also occurred in higher education. Between 1959-2000 college enrollments rose from 62,000 to more than 2.0 million.

# ECONOMY

Sustained economic growth is vital to Mexico's prospects for a successful evolution to a more competitive democracy. Mexico's level of economic prosperity has a direct, though proportionally smaller impact on the U.S. as it affects trade and migration. In recent years, Mexico has sought economic prosperity through liberalization of its trade regime. In January 1994, Mexico joined Canada and the United States in the North American Free Trade Agreement (NAFTA), which will phase out all tariffs over a 15-year period. Four months later, in April 1994, Mexico joined the Organization for Economic Cooperation and Development (OECD). Mexico was the first Latin American member of the Asia-Pacific Economic Cooperation forum (APEC), joining in 1993, and in January 1996, became a founding member of the World Trade Organization (WTO).

Mexico's NAFTA membership helped the Mexican economy grow at an annualized rate of 2.3% in 1994-99. Following the December 1994 devaluation of the peso, Mexico experienced a severe financial crisis that also threatened the stability of other emerging market economies, especially in Latin America. The United States responded by leading a group of international lenders in making

**Travel Notes**

**Travel Advice:** For up-to-date information from the U.S. State Department on possible inconvenient or hazardous situations, see the **Travel Warnings and Consular Information Sheets from the U.S. Government** section starting on page 1723. For the latest information on health requirements and conditions, see the **International Travelers' Health Information** section starting on page 1385. For further information dealing with non-urgent matter, see the **Tips for Travelers to...** section starting on page 1588.

available to Mexico more than $40 billion in international financial assistance, including $20 billion from the United States. This action helped stabilize the Mexican economy, allowing Mexico to repay the loans to the United States more than 3 years ahead of schedule. The oil revenue windfall from Mexico's oil exports in 2000 reduced its recourse to the international capital market and allowed Mexico to pay off its debt to the International Monetary Fund and to liquidate some $7.9 billion in Brady bonds ahead of time.

Other indicators show that Mexico achieved the objectives of the emergency economic program developed to cope with the 1995 peso crisis. Although the 1995 recession was severe-real GDP fell 6.2%—tough stabilization measures averted a more serious collapse and brought about a rapid recovery. Mexican real GDP grew 7.2% in 2000, 3.7% in 1999, and 4.9% in 1998. The outlook is 7.0% for 2000. During these years, inflation and unemployment fell, and the value of the peso stabilized. NAFTA contributed to the process of adjustment by enabling Mexico to reduce its current account deficit through increased exports rather than through slashing imports from the United States, as it had following the 1982 debt crisis.

## Trade

Mexico ranks second as a United States trading partner in 2000, accounting for 10% of U.S. trade. In

2000, $123.2 billion in merchandise exports to Mexico dramatically surpassed U.S. exports to Japan, even though the Mexican economy is just one-tenth the size of Japan's. That year, the United States was Mexico's predominant trading partner, accounting for 82% of Mexican exports and 70% of Mexican imports. The chief U.S. exports to Mexico were motor vehicle parts, electronic equipment, and agricultural products; the top imports from Mexico included petroleum, motor vehicles, and electronic equipment.

U.S.-Mexico trade has increased dramatically since NAFTA. In 1993, the year before NAFTA took effect, U.S. exports to Mexico totaled $41.6 billion and U.S. imports from Mexico $40.7 billion. By the end of 1999, U.S. exports had risen to $87 billion and imports from Mexico to $110 billion. From 1994-2000, according to U.S. data, two-way trade increased from $82.3 billion to $261.7 billion.

Although trade deficits characterize U.S. trade with Mexico, U.S. exports to Mexico have been rising at a much faster rate than U.S. exports with the rest of the world. Between 1993 and 1999, U.S. exports to Mexico grew three times as fast as its exports to the rest of the world. Much of this trade is complementary intra-industry trade, a pattern of trade that shows that specialization in manufactured goods is progressing. As Mexico broadens and deepens its economic base, U.S. exports to Mexico will continue to rise in the interest of both countries.

NAFTA eliminates restrictions on the flow of goods, services, and investments in North America. In addition to phasing out tariffs, NAFTA eliminates, as far as possible, non-tariff barriers and promotes safeguards for intellectual property rights—patents, copyrights, and trademarks. This pact also includes provisions on trade rules and dispute settlements, and its parallel labor agreement seeks to ensure full protection of worker's rights.

Through its supplemental environment cooperation agreement, NAFTA marked the first time in the history of U.S. trade policy that environmental concerns have been addressed in a comprehensive trade agreement. The pact also serves as a basis for enhancing ongoing U.S.-Mexico cooperation on a host of other issues that do not respect national borders.

## Agriculture

Mexico's agrarian reform program began in 1917, when the government began distribution of land to farmers. Extended further in the 1930s, this cooperative agrarian reform, which guaranteed small farmers a means of subsistence livelihood, also caused land fragmentation and lack of capital investment, since commonly held land could not be used as collateral. This, combined with poor soil, several recent years of low rainfall, and rural population growth, has made it difficult to raise the productivity and living standards of Mexico's subsistence farmers.

There have been programs that provide money to pay off loans and help banks with their debt burdens. While high credit costs are still a major problem impeding agricultural development, the burden of debt has been reduced. High interest rates for loans have compounded the difficulty for producers, and the 1994 peso crisis exacerbated the decline in productivity. Agriculture accounted for 5.8% of GDP in 1999.

In an effort to raise rural productivity and living standards, Article 27 of the Mexican Constitution was amended in 1992 to allow for the transfer of communal land to the farmers cultivating it. They then could rent or sell it, opening the way for larger farms and economies of scale. By early 1996, however, only six farmers' cooperatives had voted to dissolve themselves, perhaps because the government provides subsidies for communal land seeded by farmers. (The subsidy was 700 pesos per hectare in 1999.) Since communal land use is formally reviewed only every 2 years, privatization of these communal lands may continue to be very slow.

In the past, the government encouraged production of basic crops such as corn and beans by maintaining support prices. In order to rationalize its agricultural sector, Mexico is phasing out its support price scheme. Corn production dropped in 1995 and 1996 as more was imported. The government in 1996 crafted federal-to-state agreements targeted at each states' most urgent needs, with the goal of increasing the use of modern equipment and technology in order to increase per-acre productivity. In addition to this new initiative, the government is continuing PRO-CAMPO, the rural support program which provides the approximately 3.5 million farmers who produce basic commodities—about 64% of all farmers—with a fixed payment per hectare of cropland.

## Manufacturing and Foreign Investment

Mexico's manufacturing sector accounted for 21% of Mexico's GDP in 1999 and 19% of employment in 1999. Manufacturing output grew at an annual rate of 7.3% in 1998, 4.1% in 1999, and may attain 6.7% in 2000.

The industrial sector as a whole, which along with manufacturing includes construction, electricity, and mining, grew 6.6% rate in 1998, 4.2% in 1999, and may rise by 6.4% in 2000. Construction grew 4.2% rate in 1998, 4.5% in 1999, and may rise by 6.6% in 2000.

In December 1993, Mexico passed a new foreign investment law which promotes competitiveness and established clear rules for the entry of international capital into productive activities. The law permits foreigners to own nonresidential property in the "restricted zones"—within 100 kilometers (62 miles) of the border and 50 kilometers of the coasts. Residential property in these zones still must be acquired via a trust through a Mexican financial institution. Total direct foreign investment in 1999 was $11.6 billion, 60% of which was of U.S. origin. In 2000, direct foreign investment may rise to $14.0 billion.

## Transportation and Communications

The Zedillo administration continued the previous government's modernization of infrastructure and services, deregulation and development of more efficient transport systems, and increased privatization. Mexico's land transportation network is one of the most extensive in Latin America. More than 4,000 kilometers (2,400 miles) of four-lane highway have been built through government concessions to private sector contractors since 1989, of which 3,500 kilometers (2,100 miles) have been constructed since 1994. The 26,622 kilometers (16,268 miles) of government-owned railroads in Mexico have been privatized through the sale of 50-year operating concessions.

Tampico and Veracruz, on the Gulf of Mexico, are Mexico's two primary seaports. Recognizing that the low productivity of Mexico's 108 ports poses a threat to trade development, the government has steadily been privatizing port operations to improve their efficiency. A number of international airlines serve Mexico, with direct or connecting flights from most major cities in the United States, Canada, Europe, Japan, and Latin America. Most Mexican regional capitals and resorts have direct air services to Mexico City or the United States. Airport privatization, based on Mexico's successful experience with seaports, is nearly complete.

Mexico has taken significant steps to modernize its telecommunications system. A key element was the privatization in 1990 of the national telephone company, Telefonos de Mexico (TELMEX), which was sold to a consortium of Mexican investors, Southwestern Bell, and France Telecom. A positive result has been the increase in telephone lines and telephones for the general population. The government has opened the telecommunications sector to greater foreign investment. Competition in long-distance telecommunications service began in 1997, and competitors quickly gained a 30% share of the market. Eleven companies provide cellular telephone service to various parts of Mexico, resulting in a dramatic expansion of cellular telephone services to various parts of Mexico and a dramatic expansion of cellular telephone users. Three communications satellites were in use in Mexico in 1999. One satellite ceased operating in 2000.

# FOREIGN RELATIONS

Traditionally, the Government of Mexico has sought to maintain its interests abroad and project its influence largely through moral persuasion. In particular, Mexico champions the principles of nonintervention and self-determination. In its efforts to revitalize its economy and open up to international competition, Mexico has sought closer relations with the U.S., western Europe, and the Pacific Basin. While the United States and Mexico are often in agreement on foreign policy issues, some differences remain—in particular, relations with Cuba. The U.S. and Mexico agree on the ultimate goal of establishing a democratic, free-market regime in Cuba but disagree on tactics to reach that goal. Fox has promised to more actively promote international human rights and democracy and increase Mexico's participation in international affairs.

Mexico actively participates in several international organizations. It is a supporter of the United Nations and Organization of American States systems and also pursues its interests through a number of ad hoc international bodies. Mexico has been selective in its membership in other international organizations. It declined, for example, to become a member of Organization of Petroleum Exporting Countries (OPEC). Nevertheless, Mexico does seek to diversify its diplomatic and economic relations, as demonstrated by its accession to GATT in 1986; its joining APEC in 1993; becoming, in April 1994, the first Latin American member of the OECD; and a founding member of the World Trade Organization (WTO) in 1996. Mexico attended the 1994 Summit of the Americas, held in Miami,

and managed coordination of the agenda item on education for the 1998 Summit of the Americas in Santiago, Chile.

# U.S.-MEXICAN RELATIONS

U.S. relations with Mexico are as important and complex as with any country in the world. A stable, democratic, and economically prosperous Mexico is fundamental to U.S. interests. U.S. relations with Mexico have a direct impact on the lives and livelihoods of millions of Americans— whether the issue is trade and economic reform, drug control, migration, or the promotion of democracy. The U.S. and Mexico are partners in NAFTA, and enjoy a rapidly developing trade relationship.

The scope of U.S.-Mexican relations goes far beyond diplomatic and official contacts; it entails extensive commercial, cultural, and educational ties, as demonstrated by the annual figure of nearly 340 million legal crossings from Mexico to the United States in the fiscal year 1999. In addition, more than a half-million American citizens live in Mexico. More than 2,600 U.S. companies have operations there, and the U.S. accounts for 60% of all foreign direct investment in Mexico. Along the 2,000-mile shared border, state and local governments interact closely.

Since 1981, the management of the broad array of U.S.-Mexico issues has been formalized in the U.S.-Mexico Binational Commission, composed of numerous U.S. cabinet members and their Mexican counterparts. The commission holds annual plenary meetings, and many subgroups meet during the course of the year to discuss trade and investment opportunities, financial cooperation, consular issues and migration, legal affairs and anti-narcotics cooperation, cultural relations, education, energy, border affairs, environment and natural resources, labor, agriculture, health, housing and urban development, transportation, fisheries, tour-

ism, and science and technology. The commission met most recently on May 2000 in Washington D.C.

A strong partnership with Mexico is critical to controlling the flow of illicit drugs into the United States. The U.S. has certified Mexico as fully cooperating in this effort based on the level of cooperation on counternarcotics and Mexico's own initiatives in fighting drug trafficking. The U.S. will continue working with Mexico to help ensure that Mexico's cooperation and anti-drug efforts grow even stronger.

During 1996, the U.S. and Mexico established a High-Level Contact Group (HLCG) on narcotics control to explore joint solutions to the shared drug threat, to coordinate the full range of narcotics issues, and to promote closer law enforcement coordination. President Zedillo formalized his government's commitment to counternarcotics cooperation with the United States by signing the "Declaration of the Mexican-U.S. Alliance Against Drugs" with President Clinton in May 1997. The U.S. and Mexico continue to cooperate on narcotics interdiction, demand reduction, and eradication. Mexican Government authorities have seized a record number of drugs over the past few years. Marijuana and heroin seizures in 2000 have increased by 50% and 61% respectively, while cocaine seizures are 34% lower than last year.

## Border and Environmental Affairs

The "New Border Vision" report issued at the June 1998 Binational Commission meeting in Washington responded to the call by Presidents Clinton and Zedillo for a comprehensive and long-lasting strategy to transform the border into a model area of bilateral cooperation. It has become the blueprint for enhancing collaboration at all levels of government.

Cooperation between the United States and Mexico along the 2,000-mile common border includes state and local problem-solving mechanisms; transportation planning; and institutions to address resource, environment, and health issues. In 1993, the Border Liaison Mechanism (BLM) was established; now 10 BLMs chaired by U.S. and Mexican consuls operate in "sister city" pairs. BLMs have proven to be effective means of dealing with a variety of local issues ranging from accidental violation of sovereignty by law enforcement officials and charges of mistreatment of foreign nationals to coordination of port security and cooperation in public health matters such as tuberculosis. The BLMs form an integral part of the "New Border Vision."

As the number of people and the volume of cargo crossing the U.S.-Mexico border grow, so, too, does the need for coordinated infrastructure development. The multi-agency U.S.-Mexico Binational Group on Bridges and Border Crossings meets twice yearly to improve the efficiency of existing crossings and coordinate planning for new ones. The 10 U.S. and Mexican Border States have become active participants in these meetings. The U.S. and Mexico also conduct an annual "Border Walk" to gain a first-hand impression of how border crossings are working.

The United States and Mexico have a long history of cooperation on environmental and natural resource issues, particularly in the border area, where there are serious environmental problems caused by rapid population growth, urbanization, and industrialization. Cooperative activities between the U.S. and Mexico take place under a number of agreements such as:

•An 1889 convention establishing the International Boundary Commission, reconstituted by the Water Treaty of 1944 as the International Boundary and Water Commission, United States and Mexico (IBWC). The IBWC has settled many difficult U.S.-Mexico boundary and water problems, including the regularization of the Rio Grande near El Paso through the 1967 Chamizal settlement. The IBWC divides the use of international waters, builds and operates water conservation and flood control projects, and constructs and maintains boundary markers on the land boundary and on international bridges. In recent years, the IBWC has worked to resolve longstanding border sanitation problems, to monitor the quantity and quality of border waters, and to address water delivery and sedimentation problems of the Colorado River. Current issues include Mexico's water debt to the U.S. on the Rio Grande, and the impact on Mexican groundwater sources which may be caused by the lining of the All-American Canal.

•A series of agreements on border health (since 1942), wildlife and migratory birds (since 1936), national parks, forests, marine and atmospheric resources. In July of 2000, the U.S. and Mexico signed an agreement to establish a binational Border Health Commission. The new Border Health Commission is scheduled to hold its inaugural meeting before the end of 2000.

•The 1983 La Paz Agreement to protect and improve the border environment and Border XXI, a binational, interagency planning program, begun in 1996, to address environmental, natural resource, and environmental health concerns in the border area. Border XXI concludes this year; hope is to develop a new border plan early in the new U.S. and Mexican administrations that will build on the progress of Border XXI while enhancing decentralization and stakeholders' involvement.

•The 1993 North American Agreement on Environmental Cooperation (NAAEC), creating the North American Commission on Environmental Cooperation under NAFTA by the U.S., Mexico, and Canada, to improve enforcement of environmental laws and to address common environmental concerns.

•A November 1993 agreement between the U.S. and Mexico, also related to NAFTA, establishing the Border Environment Cooperation Commission (BECC) which works with local communities to develop and certify environmental infrastructure projects such as wastewater treatment plants, drinking water systems, and solid waste disposal facilities. The sister organization, the North American Development Bank (NADBank), uses capital and grant funds contributed by partner governments to help finance border environmental infrastructure projects certified by the BECC. BECC has certified more than 40 environment infrastructure projects, 29 of which are now built or are under construction.

## Principal U.S. Officials

For up-to-date information on Principal U.S. Officials, see the U.S. Embassies, Consulates, and Foreign Service section starting on page 139.

## Other Contact Information

### American Chamber of Commerce of Mexico
A.C. Lucerna 78-4 06600 Mexico D.F. Mexico
Tel: (525) 724-3800
Fax: (525) 703-3908
E-Mail: amchammxamcham.com.mx
(Branch offices also in Guadalajara and Monterrey)

### U.S. Department of Commerce
International Trade Administration Office of Latin America and the Caribbean
14th and Constitution, NW
Washington, DC 20230
Tel: 202-482-0305; 202-USA-TRADE
Fax: 202-482-0464
Internet: http://www.ita.doc.gov

# MICRONESIA

February 2001

Official Name:
**Federated States of Micronesia (FSM)**

# PROFILE

### Geography
**Area:** 702 sq. km (about 270 sq. mi.) in four major island groups (Pohnpei, Chuuk, Yap and Kosrae) totaling 607 islands.
**Cities:** Capital—Palikir. Other cities—Kolonia, Moen, Lelu.
**Terrain:** Varies from mountainous to low coral atolls.
**Climate:** Tropical.

### People
**Nationality:** Noun and adjective—Micronesian.
**Population:** 116,268.
**Growth rate:** 2.0%.
**Ethnic groups:** Nine ethnic Micronesian and Polynesian groups.
**Religion:** Roman Catholic 50%, Protestant 47%.
**Language:** English (official and common), and all four states have their own ethnic language.
**Education:** Literacy—89%.
**Health:** Life expectancy—male—66.7 years; female—70.6 years. Infant mortality rate—33.5/1,000.
**Work force:** More than one-half of workers are government employees.

### Government
**Type:** Constitutional government in free association with the U.S. Independence (from U.S.-administered UN trusteeship): November 3, 1986.
**Constitution:** May 10, 1979.
**Branches:** Executive—president (chief of state and head of government), cabinet. Legislative—unicameral Congress with 14 seats. Judicial—Supreme Court. Major political parties: No formal parties.

### Economy
**GDP:** $224 million.
**GDP per capita:** (nominal) $1,977.
**National income:** (GDP + foreign assistance) $340 million.
**National income per capita:** $2,925.
**GDP composition by sector:** Services 77%, agriculture 19%, industry 4%. Industry: Types—government, fishing.
**Trade:** Exports ($33 million)—fish, garments and buttons, betel nut. Export markets—Japan (80%), U.S. Imports ($85 million)—food, manufactured goods, fuel. Import sources—U.S. (73%), Japan, Australia.
**External debt:** $111 million. Currency: U.S. dollar.

# GEOGRAPHY AND PEOPLE

The Federated States of Micronesia (FSM) consists of 607 islands extending 1,800 miles across the archipelago of the Caroline Islands east of the Philippines. The four constituent island groups are Yap, Chuuk (called Truk until January 1990), Pohnpei (called Ponape until November 1984), and Kosrae. The federal capital is Palikir, on Pohnpei.

The indigenous population, which is predominantly Micronesian, consists of various ethno-linguistic groups. English has become the common language. Population growth remains high at more than 3%, ameliorated somewhat by net emigration.

# HISTORY

The ancestors of the Micronesians settled the Caroline Islands over 4,000 years ago. A decentralized chieftain-based system eventually evolved into a more centralized economic and religious empire centered on Yap. European explorers—first the Portuguese in search of the Spice Islands (Indonesia) and then the Spanish—reached the Carolines in

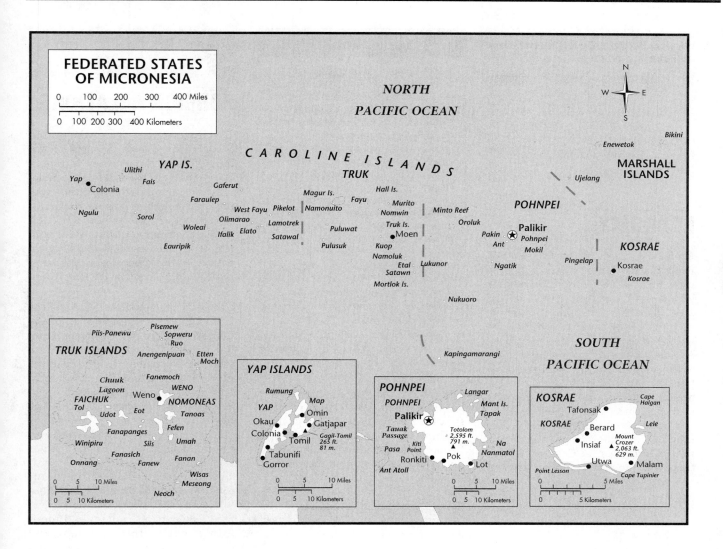

**FEDERATED STATES OF MICRONESIA**

the 16th century, with the Spanish establishing sovereignty. The current FSM passed to German control in 1899, then to the Japanese in 1914, and finally to the U.S. under UN auspices in 1947 as part of the Trust Territory of the Pacific Islands.

On May 10, 1979, four of the Trust Territory districts ratified a new constitution to become the Federated States of Micronesia. The neighboring trust districts of Palau, the Marshall Islands, and the Northern Mariana Islands chose not to participate. The FSM signed a Compact of Free Association with the U.S., which entered into force on November 3, 1986, marking Micronesia's emergence from trusteeship to independence.

# GOVERNMENT

The internal workings of FSM are governed by the 1979 constitution, which guarantees fundamental human rights and establishes a separation of governmental powers. The unicameral Congress has 14 members elected by popular vote. Four senators—one from each state—serve 4-year terms; the remaining 10 senators represent single-member districts based on population, and serve 2-year terms. The President and vice president are elected by Congress from among the four state-based senators to serve 4-year terms in the executive branch. Their congressional seats are then filled by special elections. The president and vice president are supported by an

appointed cabinet. There are no formal political parties.

Each of FSM's four states has its own constitution, elected legislature, and governor. The state governments maintain considerable power, particularly regarding the implementation of budgetary policies.

The judiciary is headed by the Supreme Court, which is divided into trial and appellate divisions. The president appoints judges with the advice and consent of the Congress.

## Principal Government Officials

**For up-to-date information on Principal Government Officials, see the**

Chiefs of State and Cabinet Members of Foreign Governments section starting on page 1.

FSM maintains an embassy at 1725 N Street NW, Washington, DC 20036 (tel: 202–223–4383).
It also maintains consulates in Honolulu and Guam.

# ECONOMY

Under the terms of the Compact of Free Association, the U.S. will provide FSM with over $1 billion in grants and services from 1986 to 2001. The largest single item is an annual block grant, which has declined in three 5-year phases. Annual payments for seven specific categories of programs, including health and education, have been made in fixed amounts since the Compact's inception. The entire package is adjusted each year for inflation. In 1997 the U.S. provided more than $78 million in Compact assistance—an amount equivalent to over one-third of FSM's GDP—plus another $11 million through other federal programs. Total official development assistance from all sources was $101 million in 1997, with nearly 90% of that total coming from the U.S.

The FSM public sector plays a central role in the economy as the administrator of the Compact money. The national and state-level governments employ over one-half of the country's workers and provide services accounting for more than 40%of GDP. Faced with the potential decrease or cessation of some of the assistance programs upon the Compact's expiry in 2001, the Government of the FSM in 1996 began to implement a program of economic reforms designed to reduce the role of the public sector in the economy.

The fishing industry also is highly important. Foreign commercial fishing fleets pay over $20 million annu-

## Travel Notes

**Travel Advice:** For up-to-date information from the U.S. State Department on possible inconvenient or hazardous situations, see the **Travel Warnings and Consular Information Sheets from the U.S. Government** section starting on page 1723. For the latest information on health requirements and conditions, see the **International Travelers' Health Information** section starting on page 1385. For further information dealing with non-urgent matter, see the **Tips for Travelers to...** section starting on page 1588.

ally for the right to operate in FSM territorial waters. These licensing fees account for nearly 30% of domestic budgetary revenue. Additionally, exports of marine products, mainly reexports of fish to Japan, account for nearly 85% of export revenue.

The tourist industry is present but has been hampered by a lack of infrastructure. Visitor attractions include scubadiving (notably in Chuuk Lagoon), World War II battle sites, and the ancient ruined city of Nan Madol on Pohnpei. Some 15,000 tourists visit the islands each year. The Asian Development Bank has identified tourism as one of FSM's highest potential growth industries.

Farming is mainly subsistence, and its importance is declining. The principal crops are coconuts, bananas, betel nuts, cassava, and sweet potatoes. Less than 10% of the formal labor force and less than 7% of export revenue come from the agriculture sector. Manufacturing activity is modest, consisting mainly of a garment factory in Yap and production of buttons from trochus shells.

The large inflow of official assistance to FSM allows it to run a substantial trade deficit and to have a much lighter tax burden than other states in the region (11% of GDP in FSM compared to 18%-25% elsewhere). The government also borrowed against future Compact disbursements in the early 1990s, yielding an

external debt of $111 million in 1997 (over 50% of GDP).

# FOREIGN RELATIONS

The Government of the Federated States of Micronesia conducts its own foreign relations. Since independence, the FSM has established diplomatic relations with a number of nations, including most of its Pacific neighbors. Regional cooperation through various multilateral organizations is a key element in its foreign policy. The FSM became a member of the United Nations in 1991.

The Governments of the FSM and the U.S. signed the final version of the Compact of Free Association on October 1, 1982. The Compact went into effect on November 3, 1986, and the FSM became a sovereign nation in free association with the United States. Under the Compact, the U.S. has full authority and responsibility for the defense of the FSM. This security relationship can be changed or terminated by mutual agreement. The Compact provides U.S. grant funds and federal program assistance to the FSM. The basic relationship of free association continues indefinitely, but certain economic and defense provisions of the Compact expire in 2001, subject to renegotiation. Negotiations on extending the Compact began in November 1999.

## Principal U.S. Officials

For up-to-date information on Principal U.S. Officials, see the U.S. Embassies, Consulates, and Foreign Service section starting on page 139.

The mailing address for the U.S. Embassy is P.O. Box 1286, Kolonia, Pohnpei, Federated States of Micronesia 96941. Telephone: 691–320–2187. Fax: 691–320–2186. Email: USEmbassy@mail.fm.

# MOLDOVA

February 1996

Official Name:
**Republic of Moldova**

# PROFILE

## Geography
**Area:** 33,700 sq km; slightly more than twice the size of Hawaii.
**Cities:** Capital—Chisinau.
**Climate:** moderate winters, warm summers.
**Terrain:** rolling steppe, gradual slope south to Black Sea.

## People
**Nationality:** Noun and adjective—Moldovan(s).
**Population (1995 est.):** 4,489,657.
**Annual growth rate (1995 est.):** 0.36% .
**Languages:** Moldovan (official; virtually the same as the Romanian language), Russian, Gagauz (a Turkish dialect).
**Ethnic groups (1989):** Moldavian/Romanian 64.5%, Ukrainian 13.8%, Russian 13%, Gagauz 3.5%, Jewish 1.5%, Bulgarian 2%, other 1.7%.
**Religions (1991):** Eastern Orthodox 98.5%, Jewish 1.5%, Baptist (only about 1,000 members).
**Education:** Literacy—male, 99%; female, 94%.
**Health:** Infant mortality rate—29.8 deaths/1,000 live births (1995 est.). Life expectancy at birth—68 years.
**Labor force (1994) 2.03 million:** Agriculture 34.4%. Industry 20.1%. Other 45.5%.

## Government
**Type:** Republic.
**Independence:** August 27, 1991 (from Soviet Union).
**Constitution:** New constitution adopted NA July 1994; replaces old Soviet constitution of 1979.
**Branches:** Executive—president (chief of state), Prime Minister, and cabinet (appointed by the president on recommendation of the prime minister). Legislative—unicameral. Judicial branch: Supreme Court.
**Administrative divisions:** previously divided into 40 rayons; new districts possible under new constitution in 1994.
**Political parties:** Christian Democratic Popular Front (formerly Moldovan Popular Front), Yedinstvo Intermovement, Social Democratic Party, Agrarian-Democratic Party, Democratic Party, Democratic Labor Party, Reform Party, Republican Party, Socialist Party, Communist Party, Peasants and Intellectuals Bloc.
**Suffrage:** 18 years of age; universal.
**Flag:** same color scheme as Romania—3 equal vertical bands of blue (hoist side), yellow, and red; emblem in center of flag is of a Roman eagle of gold outlined in black with a red beak and talons carrying a yellow cross in its beak and a green olive branch in its right talons and a yellow scepter in its left talons; on its breast is a shield divided horizontally red over blue with a stylized ox head, star, rose, and crescent all in black-outlined yellow.

## Economy
**GDP:** $11.9 billion (1994 est.).
**Annual growth rate:** -30% (1994 est.).
**Per capita GDP:** $2,670 (1994 est.).
**Natural resources:** lignite, phosphorites, gypsum.
**Agriculture (40% of GDP):** Products—fruits, wine, grain, sugar beets, sunflower seed, meat, milk, tobacco. Arable land—50% of land use.
**Industry:** Types—canned food, agricultural machinery, foundry equipment, refrigerators and freezers, washing machines, hosiery, refined sugar, vegetable oil, shoes, textiles.
**Trade:** Exports—$144 million: foodstuffs, wine, tobacco, textiles and footwear, machinery, chemicals. Major markets: Russia, Kazakhstan, Ukraine, Romania, Germany. Imports—$174 million: oil, gas, coal, steel, machinery, foodstuffs, automobiles, and other consumer durables. Major suppliers: Russia, Ukraine, Uzbekistan, Romania, Germany.
**Currency:** the leu (plural lei) was introduced in late 1993.
**Exchange rates:** lei per US$1— 4.277 (22 December 1994).

# BACKGROUND

Moldova is a landlocked area bounded by Ukraine on the east and Romania to the west. Because of its close ties to Romania, Moldovan culture and language reflect the make-up of its population: Romanian and Russian are spoken, as well as Ukrainian, Bulgarian, and Turkic (Gagauz). With an area of only 34,000 square kilometers (13,000 square miles, roughly equal to Maryland), Moldova is the second smallest of the former Soviet republics and the most densely populated.

A hilly plain, Moldova occupies most of what has been known as Bessarabia. About two-thirds of the republic's 4.3 million people are Moldovans with Ukrainian (14%), Russian (13%), Gagauz (4%), Bulgarian, and Jewish minorities.

Moldova's location has made it a historic passageway between Asia and Southern Europe, as well as the victim of frequent warfare. Greeks, Romans, Huns, and Bulgars invaded the area, which in the 13th century became part of the Mongol empire. An independent Moldovan state emerged briefly in the 14th century but fell under Ottoman Turkish rule in the 16th century.

After the Russo-Turkish War of 1806-12, the eastern half of Moldova (Bessarabia) between the Prut and the Dniester Rivers was ceded to Russia, while Romanian Moldova (west of the Prut) remained with the Turks. Romania, which gained independence in 1878, took control of the Russian half of Moldova in 1918. The Soviet Union never recognized the seizure, creating an autonomous Moldavian republic on the east side of the Dniester River in 1924.

In 1940, Romania was forced to cede eastern Moldova to the U.S.S.R., which established the Moldavian Soviet Socialist Republic. Romania sought to regain it by joining with Germany in the 1941 attack on the U.S.S.R. Moldova was ceded back to Moscow when hostilities between the U.S.S.R and Romania ceased at the end of World War II. The present boundary between Moldova and Romania was established in 1947. Moldova declared independence on August 27, 1991.

## Principal Government Officials

For up-to-date information on Principal Government Officials, see the Chiefs of State and Cabinet Members of Foreign Governments section starting on page 1.

# U.S.-MOLDOVAN RELATIONS

The dissolution of the Soviet Union in December 1991 brought an end to the Cold War and created the opportunity to build bilateral relations with the New Independent States (NIS) as they began a political and economic transformation. The United States recognized the independence of Moldova on December 25, 1991, and opened an embassy in the capital of Chisinau in March 1992. The U.S. Ambassador to Moldova, John Todd Stewart, assumed the post on November 14, 1995.

In January 1992 the U.S. initiated the Coordinating Conference on Assistance to the New Independent States in response to the humanitarian emergencies facing these States. The resulting Operation Provide Hope provided desperately needed food, fuel, medicine and shelter. More recently the focus of U.S. assistance to Moldova has shifted to technical assistance in support of Moldova's transition to a market economy and democratic society. From 1992 through September 1995 total U.S. assistance to Moldova included approximately $61 million in technical assistance, $104 million in U.S. Department of Agriculture food assistance and $59 million in humanitarian shipments to Moldova.

Through January 1, 1996 the U.S. had provided approximately $61 million in humanitarian medical supplies, food and clothing. In November 1995 the U.S. provided equipment that allowed for mass immunization of the Moldovan population against diphtheria. Other initiatives include donation of a warm-based military hospital, worth $13 million, to Moldova in 1994 and an $8.1 million shipment of Department of Defense excess medical supplies in 1993. The U.S. Department of Agriculture provided about 80,000 metric tons of food aid, valued at $20 million, in FY 1994-1995.

The establishment of a Western NIS Enterprise Fund was announced by President Clinton in January 1994, providing investment capital to privatizing firms in Ukraine, Moldova and Belarus. The Fund's Chisinau office opened in October 1995 and as of early 1996 had committed investment capital of over $3 million to companies in Moldova.

The Enterprise Fund is the capstone of an assistance effort that has focused on creating the institutions necessary to support a market economy. In 1995 the U.S. provided assistance and training that played an important role in the Moldovan parliament's passage of the Law on the Circulation of Securities and Stock Exchanges. In July 1995 U.S. advisors were placed at Moldova's Central Bank to help with the bank sector's transition to international accounting standards. The U.S. has also provided training in a variety of related areas including entrepreneurship, agribusiness development, and international trade and investment. In addition, technical assistance has been provided to support implementation of Moldova's privatization programs.

Training and technical assistance programs have been provided in law school curriculum reform, rule of law, law enforcement, assessment of the draft Moldovan constitution, municipal organization and staffing, political parties and elections, independent media, pluralism, protection of minority rights and diplomacy and foreign policy. Educational exchanges play an important role in these areas. Resident advisors have worked with the executive and legislative branches of the Moldovan Government. Peace Corps volunteers are working in Moldova with a focus on teaching English and advising small businesses.

## Bilateral Trade Issues

A trade agreement providing reciprocal most-favored-nation tariff treatment became effective on July 2, 1992. An Overseas Private Investment Corporation agreement, which encourages U.S. private investment by providing direct loans and loan guarantees, was signed in June 1992. A bilateral investment treaty was signed in April 1993. GSP status was granted in August 1995 and some Ex-Im bank coverage became available in November 1995.

# MILITARY ISSUES

Moldova has accepted all relevant arms control obligations of the former Soviet Union. On October 30, 1992, Moldova ratified the Conventional Armed Forces in Europe Treaty, which establishes comprehensive limits on key categories of conventional military equipment and provides for the destruction of weapons in excess of those limits. It acceded to the provisions of the nuclear Non-Proliferation Treaty in October 1994 in Washington. It does not have nuclear, biological, or chemical weapons. Moldova joined the North Atlantic Treaty Organization's Partnership for Peace on March 16, 1994.

# POLITICAL CONDITIONS

Moldova declared its independence from the former Soviet Union on August 27, 1991. Parliament elected Mircea Snegur to be president in October 1990. A former Communist Party official, he endorsed independence and actively sought Western

recognition. However, Snegur's opposition to immediate reunification with Romania led to a split with the Moldovan Popular Front in October 1991 and to his decision to run as an independent candidate in a December 1991 presidential election. Running unopposed, he won after the Popular Front's efforts to organize a voter boycott failed.

Moldova's transition to democracy has been impeded by an ineffective parliament, the lack of a new constitution, a separatist movement led by the Gagauz (Christian Turkic) minority in the south, and continued unrest in the Trans-Dniester region where a separatist movement, assisted by uniformed Russian military forces in the region, and led by supporters of the 1991 attempted coup in Moscow, has declared a "Dniester republic." The population of this ethnic area is 40% Moldovan, 28% Ukrainian, and 23% Russian. Moldova has attempted to meet the Russian minority's demands by offering the region rather broad cultural and political autonomy. Although the dispute strained Moldova's relations with Russia, on July 21, 1992, the government negotiated a cease-fire arrangement with Russian and Trans-Dniestrian officials. The agreement established a tripartite peace-keeping force comprised of Moldovan, Russian, and Trans-Dniestrian units. Negotiations to resolve the conflict continue, and the cease-fire is still in effect. The Organization for Security and Cooperation in Europe (OSCE) also is attempting to facilitate a negotiated settlement and has sent an observer mission. The conflict with the Gagauz was settled peacefully by granting the region local autonomy in 1995.

The ineffective parliament elected in 1990 to a five-year term was replaced after new elections were held on February 27, 1994. The election for the new parliament was conducted peacefully and received good ratings from international observers for its fairness. Authorities in the Trans-Dniester region, however, refused to allow balloting there and tried to discourage inhabitants from participating. Inhabitants of the Gagauz separatist region did participate in the elections. The new parliament is considerably smaller than the previous one, numbering only 104 deputies.

The largest political group in parliament is the Agrarian Party, which currently has a plurality in the legislature of 46 seats, following the departure of 10 deputies in August 1995. The 10 left the ruling Agrarians to join a new party, the Party of Renewal and Conciliation, founded by President Snegur. The Socialist-Edinstvo Bloc has 28 seats, while the pro-Romanian parties—the Peasants and Intellectuals Bloc and the Popular Front—have 11 and 9 seats, respectively. Several other parties did not receive a sufficient percentage of

the popular vote to be represented in the new parliament. Former speaker of parliament, Petru Lucinschi, was re-elected as speaker on March 29, 1994. The previous Prime Minister, Andrei Sangheli, was re-elected to his post on March 31, 1994. The government was restructured somewhat with parliament's approval of a new cabinet on April 5, 1994. The new 1994 Constitution and the law provide for freedom of speech, press, assembly, and religion, though with some restrictions.

Political parties and other groups publish newspapers which often criticize government policies. There are several independent news services, radio stations, and an independent television station. Peaceful assembly is allowed, though permits for demonstrations must be obtained, and private organizations, including political parties, are required to register with the government. Legislation passed in 1992 codified religious freedom but required that religious groups be recognized by the government.

A 1990 Soviet law and a 1991 parliamentary decision authorizing formation of social organizations provide for independent trade unions. However, the Federation of Independent Trade Unions of Moldova, successor to the former organizations of the Soviet trade union system, is the sole structure. It has attempted to influence government policy in labor issues and has been critical of many economic policies. Moldovan labor law, which is based on former Soviet

legislation, provides for collective bargaining rights.

Tensions continue among the ethnic minorities of the region due to the ongoing dispute between the government and Transdniester separatists, but no serious violations of human rights have been reported in the areas controlled by the Moldovan government. Tension over a new language law was defused when parliament in 1994 voted to delay until 1997 implementation of the 1989 language law, which would have made Romanian the official language, replaced the Cyrillic alphabet with the Latin, and would have meant language testing. Although the law protects the use of Russian and other languages, it raised much skepticism, especially among Russian speakers. The independence of the judiciary has increased since the dissolution of the Soviet Union, partly due to provisions for judicial tenure designed to increase judicial independence. A series of reforms approved in 1995 have begun to be implemented, including creation of a constitutional court to deal with constitutional issues and a system of appeals courts.

# FOREIGN RELATIONS

Parliament approved Moldova's membership in the Commonwealth of Independent States (CIS) and a CIS charter on economic union on April 8, 1994. Moldova is a member of the United Nations, the OSCE, the North Atlantic Cooperation Council, and in 1995 became the first NIS admitted to the Council of Europe. President Snegur signed the North Atlantic Treaty Organization's Partnership for Peace agreement on March 16, 1994.

Moldova has worked with Romania, Ukraine, and Russia to seek a peaceful resolution to the conflict in the Trans-Dniester region. It has cooperated with OSCE and UN fact-finding and observer missions and called for international mediation.

25

# ECONOMIC OUTLOOK

Like many other former Soviet republics, Moldova has experienced economic difficulties. Since its economy is highly dependent on the rest of the former Soviet Union for energy and raw materials, the breakdown in trade has had a serious effect, which was exacerbated by drought and civil conflict. Despite its difficult economic situation, Moldova has made substantial progress in economic reform. The government has liberalized most prices and has phased out subsidies on most basic consumer goods. A privatization program begun in March 1993 has privatized 80% of all housing units, and nearly 2,000 small, medium and large enterprises. Inflation has been brought down from over 105% in 1994 to about 24% in 1995. The Moldovan leu, introduced in November 1993, is fully convertible, and its value has remained relatively stable against the dollar since introduction. A stock market opened in June 1995. Moldova has International Monetary Fund standby and systemic transformation programs in effect. Moldova's economy resembles those of the Central Asian republics more than those of the other states on the western edge of the former Soviet Union. Industry accounts for only 20% of its labor force, and agriculture's share is more than one-third.

Moldova's proximity to the Black Sea gives it a mild and sunny climate, making the area ideal for agriculture. Its fertile soil supports wheat, corn, barley, tobacco, sugar beets, and soybeans. Beef and dairy cattle are raised, and beekeeping and silkworm breeding are widespread.

Moldova's best-known product comes from its extensive and well-developed vineyards, which are concentrated in the central and southern regions. In addition to world-class wine, Moldova produces liquors and champagne and is known for its sunflower seeds, prunes, and other fruits.

Moldova is a member of the International Monetary Fund, the World Bank, and the European Bank for Reconstruction and Development.

## U.S. Embassy Officials

**For up-to-date information on Principal U.S. Officials, see the U.S. Embassies, Consulates, and Foreign Service section starting on page 139.**

# MONACO

January 1999

Official Name:
**Principality of Monaco**

## PROFILE

### Geography

**Area:** 1.95 sq. km. (0.8 sq. mi); about the size of New York City's Central Park.
**Cities:** Capital—Monaco-Ville, pop. 1,151 (1990).
**Terrain:** Hilly.
**Climate:** Mediterranean.

### People

**Nationality:** Noun and adjective—Monegasque.
**Population (1995):** 30,744.
**Annual growth rate (1996 est.):** 0.59% .
**Ethnic groups (1995):** Monegasque 22%, French 35%, Italian 18%, other 25%.
**Religion:** Roman Catholic 95%, other 5%.
**Languages:** French (official), English, Italian, and Monegasque (a blend of French and Italian).
**Education:** Years compulsory—10, ages 6-16. Attendance—99%. Literacy—99%.
**Health (1997):** Infant mortality—7/1,000. Life expectancy—74.18 male; 81.8 female.
**Number of births (1997):** 713.
**Number of deaths (1997):** 485.
**Work force (32,691):** Private sector—29,311; public sector—3,380.
Services—46%, banking—7%, tourism and hotel—17%, retail—12%, construction and public works—7%, industry—11%.

### Government

**Type:** Constitutional monarchy.
**Constitution:** December 17, 1962.
**Branches:** Executive—Prince Rainier III (chief of state). Legislative—National Council (18 members). Judicial—Court of First Instance, Court of Appeal, High Court of Appeal, Criminal Court, Supreme Court.
**Subdivisions:** Four quarters (quartiers)—Monaco-Ville, La Condamine, Monte-Carlo, Fontvieille.
**Political parties:** National and Democratic Union (UND), Campora List, Medecin List.
**Suffrage:** Universal adult at age 25.
**Flag:** Top band red; bottom white.

### Economy

**GDP:** Monaco does not publish economic figures such as gross domestic product, though estimates placed GDP at $788 million in 1994.
**Average annual growth rate:** Not available.
**Per capita GDP:** Estimated at $25,000.
**Agriculture:** None.
**Industry:** Types—tourism, construction, chemicals, food products, plastics, precision instruments, cosmetics, ceramics.
**Trade:** Imports—about $415,272; Exports—about $415,272.
**Currency:** Monaco used the French franc as its currency until January 1999, when Monaco switched to the Euro with others of the European Union. As in the past, special Monegasque coins will continue to circulate.

## PEOPLE

In 1995, Monaco's population was estimated at 30,744, with an estimated average growth rate of 0.59%. Monaco-Ville has a population of 1,151.

French is the official language; English, Italian, and Monegasque (a blend of French and Italian) are also spoken. The literacy rate is 99%. Roman Catholicism is the official religion, with freedom of other religions guaranteed by the constitution.

## GEOGRAPHY

The Principality of Monaco is the second-smallest independent state in the world, after Vatican City. It is located on the Mediterranean coast, 18 kilometers (11 mi.) east of Nice, France, and is surrounded on three sides by France. Monaco is divided into four sections: Monaco-Ville, the old city on a rocky promontory extending into the Mediterranean; La Condamine, the section along the port; Monte-Carlo, the principal residential and resort area; and Fontvieille, a newly constructed area reclaimed from the sea.

The principality is noted for its beautiful natural scenery and mild, sunny climate. The average minimum temperature in January and February is 8° C (47° F); in July and August the average maximum temperature is 26° C (78° F).

# HISTORY

Founded in 1215 as a colony of Genoa, Monaco has been ruled by the House of Grimaldi since 1297, except when under French control from 1789 to 1814. Designated as a protectorate of Sardinia from 1815 until 1860 by the Treaty of Vienna, Monaco's sovereignty was recognized by the Franco-Monegasque Treaty of 1861. The Prince of Monaco was an absolute ruler until a constitution was promulgated in 1911.

In July 1918, a treaty was signed providing for limited French protection over Monaco. The treaty, written into the Treaty of Versailles, established that Monegasque policy would be aligned with French political, military, and economic interests.

Prince Rainier III, the current ruler of Monaco, acceded to the throne following the death of his grandfather, Prince Louis II, in 1949. The current heir apparent, Prince Albert, was born in 1958.

A new constitution, proclaimed in 1962, abolished capital punishment, provided for female suffrage, and established a Supreme Court to guarantee fundamental liberties.

In 1993, Monaco became an official member of the United Nations with full voting rights.

# GOVERNMENT

Monaco has been governed as a constitutional monarchy since 1911, with the Prince as chief of state. The executive branch consists of a Minister of State (head of government), who presides over a four-member Council of Government (cabinet). The Minister of State, who is a French citizen appointed by the Prince for a 3-year term from among several senior French civil servants proposed by the French Government, is responsible for foreign relations. As the Prince's representative, the Minister of State also directs the executive services, commands the police, and presides (with voting powers) over the Council of Government. The three other members of the Council are responsible for financial and economic affairs, internal affairs, and public works and social affairs, respectively.

Under the 1962 constitution, the Prince shares his power with the unicameral National Council. The 18 members of this legislative body are elected from lists by universal suffrage for 5-year terms. If the Prince dissolves the National Council, new elections must be held within 3 months. Usually meeting twice annually, the Council votes on the budget and endorses laws proposed by the Prince.

Ordinances passed by the National Council are debated in the Council of Government, as are the ministerial decrees signed by the Minister of State. Once approved, the ordinances must be submitted to the Prince within 80 days for his signature, which makes them legally enforceable. If he does not express opposition within 10 days of submission, they become valid.

Legal power is invested in the Prince, who delegates legal procedures to the various courts, which dispense justice in his name. The independence of the judges is guaranteed by the constitution. The Supreme Court is composed of five chief members and two assistant judges named by the Prince on the basis of nominations by the National Council and other govern-

## Travel Notes

**Travel Advice:** For up-to-date information from the U.S. State Department on possible inconvenient or hazardous situations, see the **Travel Warnings and Consular Information Sheets from the U.S. Government** section starting on page 1723. For the latest information on health requirements and conditions, see the **International Travelers' Health Information** section starting on page 1351. For further information dealing with non-urgent matter, see the **Tips for Travelers to...** section starting on page 1588.

ment bodies. The Supreme Court is the highest court for judicial appeals and also interprets the Constitution when necessary. Monaco's legal system is patterned after the Napoleonic Code.

The principality's local affairs are directed by the Communal Council, which consists of 15 elected members and is presided over by the Mayor.

## Principal Government Officials

**For up-to-date information on Principal Government Officials, see the Chiefs of State and Cabinet Members of Foreign Governments section starting on page 1.**

# ECONOMY

Monaco, located on the Mediterranean coast, has an economy primarily geared toward finance, commerce, and tourism. Low taxes have drawn many foreign companies to Monaco and account for around 50% of the $586 million annual government income (1997). Similarly, tourism accounts for close to 25% of the annual revenue, as the Principality of Monaco also has been a major center for tourism ever since its famed casino was established in 1856.

Customs, postal services, telecommunications, and banking in Monaco are governed by an economic and customs union with France. Although Monegasque coins are minted and circulated, the official currency is the euro (as of January 1999).

Though official economic statistics are not published, 1994 estimates place the national product at $788 million and the per capita income at $25,000.

Monaco is noted for its activity in the field of marine sciences. Its Oceanographic Museum, formerly directed by Jacques Cousteau, is one of the most renowned institutions of its kind in the world. Monaco imports and exports products and services from all over the world. There is no commercial agriculture in Monaco.

# FOREIGN RELATIONS

Monaco actively participates in the United Nations, which it joined in 1993. Monaco is also a member of many international and intergovernmental organizations, including Interpol, UNESCO, and WHO. The International Hydrographic Bureau (IHB) is headquartered in Monaco.

The Principality of Monaco is a sovereign and independent state, linked closely to France by the Treaty of 1918, the text of which has international recognition because it is confirmed by Article 436 of the Treaty of Versailles of 1919, which instituted a contractual, bilateral, and reciprocal regime between the two states. The foreign policy of Monaco is one illustration of this accord: France has agreed to defend the independence and sovereignty of Monaco, while the Monegasque Government has agreed to exercise its sovereign rights in conformity with French interests. Since then, the relations between the sovereign states of France and Monaco have been further defined in the Treaty of 1945 and the Agreement of 1963.

Although not a member of the European Union (EU), Monaco is closely associated with the economic apparatus of the EU through its customs

**MONACO**

union with France and its reliance upon the French franc (euro as of January 1999) as its official currency.

Monaco has 10 diplomatic missions in Western Europe and a permanent representation at the United Nations. It maintains honorary consulates in 106 cities in 45 countries. Sixty-one countries have consulates general, consulates, or honorary consulates in or accredited to Monaco.

# U.S.–MONACO RELATIONS

The United States and Monaco enjoy excellent relations, which both countries seek to maintain and strengthen. From 1956 until her

death in 1982, the American Grace Kelly was married to Prince Rainier III. The United States does not have a diplomatic mission located in Monaco. The U.S. Consul General in Marseille, France, is formally accredited to Monaco.

## Principal U.S. Official

For up-to-date information on Principal U.S. Officials, see the U.S. Embassies, Consulates, and Foreign Service section starting on page 139.

The U.S. Consulate General at Marseille is located at 12 Boulevard Paul Peytral, 13286 Marseille Cedex (tel. [33]-(4)-91-54-92-00).

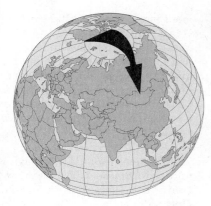

# MONGOLIA
November 2000

## Official Name:
**Mongolia**

# PROFILE

## Geography

**Area:** 1,566,500 sq. km. (604,103 sq. mi.); slightly larger than Alaska (land boundaries 8,114 km.).
**Cities:** Capital—Ulaanbaatar (pop. 680,000). Other cities—Darhan (90,000), Erdenet (65,000).
**Terrain:** Almost 90% of land area is pasture or desert wasteland, of varying usefulness; 1% arable; 9% forested.
**Climate:** Continental, with little precipitation and sharp seasonal fluctuations.

## People

**Nationality:** Noun and adjective—Mongolian(s).
**Population:** (2000) 2.4 million.
**Annual growth rate:** (1996 est.) 1.40%.
**Health:** (1999) Infant mortality rate—37.3/1,000. Life expectancy (1998 est.)—65.1 yrs.
**Ethnic groups:** (1995) 85% Mongol (predominantly Khalkha), 7% Turkic (largest group, Kazakh) 4.6% Tungusic, and 3.4% others, including Chinese and Russian.
**Languages:** Khalkha Mongol, more than 90%; minor languages include Kazakh, Chinese, and Russian.
**Religion:** Tibetan Buddhist Lama-ism 96%, Muslim 4% (primarily in the southwest), and Shamanism.
**Education:** Years compulsory—8 (provided free by the government). Literacy—over 85%.

## Government

**Type:** Parliamentary form of government, president second in authority to the State Great Hural.
**Independence:** 1921; democratic reform and shift from dependence on the former Soviet Union declared 1990.
**Constitutions:** 1960 and February 12, 1992.
**Branches:** Executive—power is divided between a president (elected by a popular election in May 1997) and prime minister (current cabinet nominated by the prime minister was formed in August 2000 by the State Great Hural, which was elected in July 2000). Legislative—State Great Hural (76 deputies). Judicial—Constitutional Court is empowered to supervise the implementation of the constitution, makes judgment on the violation of its provisions, and solves disputes. Legal code based on Continental and Russian law is under revision. No provision for judicial review of legislative acts. Legal education at Mongolian State Univ. and private universities. Mongolia accepts ICJ jurisdiction.
**Political parties:** 24 announced political parties.

**Suffrage:** Universal at 18.
**Administrative subdivisions:** 18 aimags (provinces) and 3 autonomous cities (Ulaanbaatar, Darhan, and Erdenet).
**Flag:** Three vertical bands—red, sky-blue, red; on the left red band the Mongolian national emblem, the Soyombo, in yellow.

## Economy

**GDP:** (1997) $970 million.
**Per capita GDP:** (1998 est.) $430.
**Natural resources:** Coal, copper, molybdenum, iron, phosphates, tin, nickel, zinc, wolfram, fluorspar, gold, uranium, petroleum.
**Agriculture:** (37.3% of 1998 GDP, livelihood for approximately 50% of population) Products—livestock and byproducts, hay fodder, vegetables.
**Industry:** (32% of 1997 GDP) Types—Minerals (primarily copper), animal-derived products, building materials, food/beverage, mining (esp. coal) (can't confirm 1998 data).
**Trade:** (1999) Exports—$462 million: livestock, animal products, wool, hides, fluorspar, nonferrous metals, minerals. Markets—Russia 12.5%, China 58.2%, U.S. 13.8%, Japan 4.5%. Imports—$524 million: machinery and equipment, fuels, food products, industrial consumer goods, tea, chemicals, building equipment, sugar. Suppliers—Russia 45.9%, China 16.9%, Japan 12.5%, U.S. 6.8%.

**Aid received:** Donors promised $291 million in aid, loans, and technical assistance at 1999 Donor's Conference in Ulaanbaatar.

**Fiscal year:** Calendar year.

# PEOPLE

Life in sparsely populated Mongolia has become more urbanized. Nearly half of the people live in the capital, Ulaanbaatar, and in other provincial centers. Seminomadic life still predominates in the countryside, but settled agricultural communities are becoming more common. Mongolia's birth rate is estimated at 1.4% (2000 census). About two-thirds of the total population are under age 30, 36% of whom are under 14.

Ethnic Mongols account for about 85% of the population and consist of Khalkha and other groups, all distinguished primarily by dialects of the Mongol language. Mongol is an Altaic language—from the Altaic Mountains of Central Asia, a language family comprising the Turkic, Tungusic, and Mongolic subfamilies—and is related to Turkic (Uzbek, Turkish, and Kazakh), Korean, and, possibly, Japanese. The Khalkha make up 90% of the ethnic Mongol population. The remaining 10% include Durbet Mongols and others in the north and Dariganga Mongols in the east. Turkic speakers (Kazakhs, Turvins, and Khotans) constitute 7% of Mongolia's population, and the rest are Tungusic-speakers, Chinese, and Russians. Most Russians left the country following the withdrawal of economic aid and collapse of the Soviet Union in 1991.

Traditionally, Tibetan Buddhist Lamaism was the predominant religion. However, it was suppressed under the communist regime until 1990, with only one showcase monastery allowed to remain. Since 1990, as liberalization began, Buddhism has enjoyed a resurgence. About 4 million Mongols live outside Mongolia; about 3.4 million live in China, mainly in the Inner Mongolia Autonomous Region; and some 500,000 live in Russia, primarily in Buryatia and Kalmykia.

# HISTORY

In 1203 AD, a single Mongolian state was formed based on nomadic tribal groupings under the leadership of Genghis Khan. He and his immediate successors conquered nearly all of Asia and European Russia and sent armies as far as central Europe and Southeast Asia. Genghis Khan's grandson Kublai Khan, who conquered China and established the Yuan dynasty (1279-1368 AD), gained fame in Europe through the writings of Marco Polo.

Although Mongol-led confederations sometimes exercised wide political power over their conquered territories, their strength declined rapidly after the Mongol dynasty in China was overthrown in 1368. The Manchus, a tribal group which conquered China in 1644 and formed the Qing dynasty, were able to bring Mongolia under Manchu control in 1691 as Outer Mongolia when the Khalkha Mongol nobles swore an oath of allegiance to the Manchu emperor. The Mongol rulers of Outer Mongolia enjoyed considerable autonomy under the Manchus, and all Chinese claims to Outer Mongolia following the establishment of the republic have rested on this oath. In 1727, Russia and Manchu China concluded the Treaty of Khiakta, delimiting the border between China and Mongolia that exists in large part today.

Outer Mongolia was a Chinese province (1691-1911), an autonomous state under Russian protection (1912-19), and again a Chinese province (1919-21). As Manchu authority in China waned, and as Russia and Japan confronted each other, Russia gave arms and diplomatic support to nationalists among the Mongol religious leaders and nobles. The Mongols accepted Russian aid and proclaimed their independence of Chinese rule in 1911, shortly after a successful Chinese revolt against the Manchus. By agreements signed in 1913 and 1915, the Russian Government forced the new Chinese Republican Government to accept Mongolian autonomy under continued Chinese control, presumably to discourage other foreign powers from approaching a newly independent Mongolian state that might seek support from as many foreign sources as possible.

The Russian revolution and civil war afforded Chinese warlords an opportunity to re-establish their rule in Outer Mongolia, and Chinese troops were dispatched there in 1919. Following Soviet military victories over White Russian forces in the early 1920s and the occupation of the Mongolian capital Urga in July 1921, Moscow again became the major outside influence on Mongolia. The Mongolian People's Republic was proclaimed on November 25, 1924. Between 1925 and 1928, power under the communist regime was consolidated by the Mongolian Peoples Revolutionary Party (MPRP). The MPRP left gradually undermined rightist elements, seizing control of the party and the government. Several factors characterized the country during this period: the society was basically nomadic and illiterate; there was no industrial proletariat; the aristocracy and the religious establishment shared the country's wealth; there was widespread popular obedience to traditional authorities; the party lacked grassroots support; and the government had little organization or experience.

In an effort at swift socioeconomic reform, the leftist government applied extreme measures which attacked the two most dominant institutions in the country—the aristocracy and the religious establishment. Between 1932 and 1945, their excess zeal, intolerance, and inexperience led to anti-communist uprisings. In the late 1930s, purges directed at the religious institution resulted in the desecration of hundreds of Buddhist institutions and imprisonment of more than 10,000 people.

During World War II, because of a growing Japanese threat over the Mongolian-Manchurian border, the Soviet Union reversed the course of

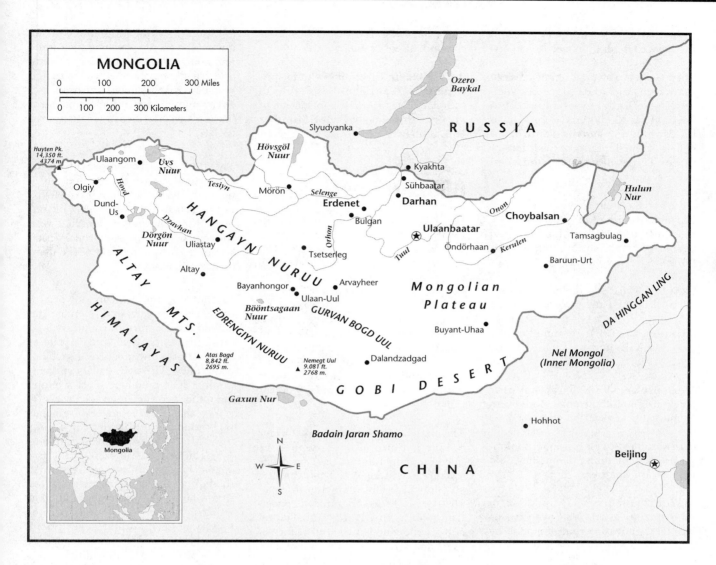

**MONGOLIA**

| 0 | 100 | 200 | 300 Miles |
| 0 | 100 | 200 | 300 Kilometers |

Huyten Pk.
14,350 ft.
4374 m

Ulaangom

Olgiy

Dund-
Us

*Uvs
Nuur*

*Hovd*

*Dzavhan*

*Dörgön
Nuur*

A L T A Y

M T S.

H I M A L A Y A S

Atas Bagd
8,842 ft.
2695 m.

*Hövsgöl
Nuur*

Slyudyanka

*Tesiyn*

Mörön

Uliastay

Altay

Bayanhongor

*Bööntsagaan
Nuur*

Ulaan-Uul

EDRENGIYN NURUU

Nemegt Uul
9,081 ft.
2768 m.

Gaxun Nur

H A N G A Y N     N U R U U

*Selenge*

Erdenet

Bulgan

*Orhon*

Tsetserleg

Arvayheer

GURVAN BOGD UUL

*Ozero
Baykal*

R U S S I A

Kyakhta

Sühbaatar

**Darhan**

☆ **Ulaanbaatar**

*Tuul*

*Onon*

Ondörhaan

*Kerulen*

Dalandzadgad

G O B I     D E S E R T

*Mongolian
Plateau*

Buyant-Uhaa

Badain Jaran Shamo

N
W  E
S

*Choybalsan*

*Hulun
Nur*

Tamsagbulag

Baruun-Urt

D A   H I N G G A N   L I N G

*Nel Mongol
(Inner Mongolia)*

Hohhot

Beijing ☆

C H I N A

Mongolia

Background Notes

Mongolian socialism in favor of a new policy of economic gradualism and buildup of the national defense. The Soviet-Mongolian army defeated Japanese forces that had invaded eastern Mongolia in the summer of 1939, and a truce was signed setting up a commission to define the Mongolian-Manchurian border in the autumn of that year.

Following the war, the Soviet Union reasserted its influence in Mongolia. Secure in its relations with Moscow, the Mongolian Government shifted to postwar development, focusing on civilian enterprise. International ties were expanded, and Mongolia established relations with North Korea and the new communist governments in eastern Europe. It also increased its participation in communist-spon-

sored conferences and international organizations. Mongolia became a member of the United Nations in 1961.

In the early 1960s, Mongolia attempted to maintain a neutral position amidst increasingly contentious Sino-Soviet polemics; this orientation changed in the middle of the decade. Mongolia and the Soviet Union signed an agreement in 1966 that introduced large scale Soviet ground forces as part of Moscow's general buildup along the Sino-Soviet frontier.

During the period of Sino-Soviet tensions, relations between Mongolia and China deteriorated. In 1983, Mongolia systematically began expelling some of the 7,000 ethnic Chinese

in Mongolia to China. Many of them had lived in Mongolia since the 1950s, when they were sent there to assist in construction projects.

# CHRONOLOGY OF MONGOIAN HISTORY 1921-PRESENT

**March 13, 1921:** Provisional People's Government declares independence of Mongolia.

**May 31, 1924:** U.S.S.R. signs agreement with Peking government, referring to Outer Mongolia as an "integral part of the Republic of

917

China," whose "sovereignty" therein the Soviet Union promises to respect.

**May-September 16, 1939:** Large scale fighting takes place between Japanese and Soviet-Mongolian forces along Khalkhyn Gol on Mongolia-Manchuria border, ending in defeat of the Japanese expeditionary force. Truce negotiated between U.S.S.R. and Japan.

**October 6, 1949:** Newly established People's Republic of China accepts recognition accorded Mongolia and agrees to establish diplomatic relations.

**October 1961:** Mongolia becomes a member of the United Nations.

**January 27, 1987:** Diplomatic relations established with the United States.

**December 1989:** First popular reform demonstrations. Mongolian Democratic Association organized.

**January 1990:** Largescale demonstrations demanding democracy held in sub-zero weather.

**March 2, 1990:** Soviets and Mongolians announce that all Soviet troops will be withdrawn from Mongolia by 1992.

**May 1990:** Constitution amended to provide for multi-party system and new elections.

**July 29, 1990:** First democratic elections held.

**September 3, 1990:** First democratically elected People's Great Hural takes office.

**February 12, 1992:** New constitution goes into effect.

**April 8, 1992:** New election law passed.

**June 28, 1992:** Election for the first unicameral legislature (State Great Hural).

**June 6, 1993:** First direct presidential election.

**June 30, 1996:** Election of first non-communist government.

**July 2, 2000:** Election of the former communist Mongolian Peoples Revolutionary Party (MPRP); formation of new government by Prime Minister N. Enkhbayar.

# GOVERNMENT

Until 1990, the Mongolian Government was modeled on the Soviet system; only the communist party—the MPRP—officially was permitted to function. After some instability during the first two decades of communist rule in Mongolia, there was no significant popular unrest until December 1989. Collectivization of animal husbandry, introduction of agriculture, and the extension of fixed abodes were all carried out without perceptible popular opposition.

The birth of perestroika in the former Soviet Union and the democracy movement in Eastern Europe were mirrored in Mongolia. The dramatic shift toward reform started in early 1990 when the first organized opposition group, the Mongolian Democratic Union, appeared. In the face of extended street protests in sub-zero whether and popular demands for faster reform, the politburo of the MPRP resigned in March 1990. In May, the constitution was amended, deleting reference to the MPRP's role as the guiding force in the country, legalizing opposition parties, creating a standing legislative body, and establishing the office of president.

Mongolia's first multi-party elections for a People's Great Hural were held on July 29, 1990. The MPRP won 85% of the seats. The People's Great Hural first met on September 3 and elected a president (MPRP), vice president (SDP—Social Democrats), prime minister (MPRP), and 50 members to the Baga Hural (small Hural). The vice president also was chairman of the Baga Hural. In November 1991, the People's Great Hural began discussion on a new constitution, which entered into force February 12. In

addition to establishing Mongolia as an independent, sovereign republic and guaranteeing a number of rights and freedoms, the new constitution restructured the legislative branch of government, creating a unicameral legislature, the State Great Hural (SGH).

The 1992 constitution provided that the president would be elected by popular vote rather than by the legislature as before. In June 1993, incumbent Punsalmaagiyn Ochirbat won the first popular presidential election running as the candidate of the democratic opposition.

As the supreme government organ, the SGH is empowered to enact and amend laws, determine domestic and foreign policy, ratify international agreements, and declare a state of emergency. The SGH meets semiannually. SGH members elect a chairman and vice chairman who serve 4-year terms. SGH members are popularly elected by district for 4-year terms. In the most recent parliamentary election on June 30, 1996, the opposition, running together under the banner of the Democratic Union, won a landslide victory, taking 50 of 76 seats in the SGH. The first completely noncommunist government was installed in July 1996, headed by Prime Minister M. Enkhsaihan.

The president is the head of state, commander in chief of the armed forces, and head of the national security council. He is popularly elected by a national majority for a 4-year term and limited to two terms. The constitution empowers the president to propose a prime minister, call for the government's dissolution, initiate legislation, veto all or parts of legislation (the SGH can override the veto with a two-thirds majority), and issue decrees, which become effective with the prime minister's signature. In the absence, incapacity, or resignation of the president, the SGH chairman exercises presidential power until inauguration of a newly elected president. In the most recent presidential election on May 18, 1997, the MPRP candidate, N. Bagabandi, was elected with 57% of the vote.

The government, headed by the prime minister, has a 4-year term. The prime minister is nominated by the president and confirmed by the SGH. The prime minister chooses a cabinet, subject to SGH approval. Dissolution of the government occurs upon the prime minister's resignation, simultaneous resignation of half the cabinet, or after an SGH vote for dissolution. Local hurals are elected by the 18 aimags (provinces) plus the capital, Ulaanbaatar, and cities of Darhan and Erdenet. On the next lower administrative level, they are elected by provincial subdivisions and urban subdistricts in Ulaanbaatar and the municipalities, Darhan and Erdenet.

## Political Parties
- Mongolian People's Revolutionary Party
- Mongolian Social Democratic Party
- Mongolian National Democratic Party
- Mongolian People's Party
- Mongolian Green Party
- Mongolian Religious Democratic Party
- Party for Mongolia
- Mongolian Republican Party
- Mongolian Workers' Party
- Mongolian Traditional United Party
- Mongolian Democratic Renaissance Party
- Mongolian Solidarity Party
- Mongolian Party for Tradition and Justice
- Mongolian Democratic Socialist Party
- Mongolian Youth Party
- Mongolian Liberal Democratic Party
- Mongolian Democratic New Socialist Party
- Mongolian Communist Party
- Mongolian Rural Development Party
- Mongolian Local Development Party
- Mongolian Civil Democratic New Liberal Party
- Mongolian Citizens's Will Party
- Mongolian Democratic Party
- Mongolian New Social Democratic Party

## Legal System
The new constitution empowered a General Council of Courts (GCC) to select all judges and protect their rights. The Supreme Court is the highest judicial body. Justices are nominated by the GCC and confirmed by the SGH and president. The court is constitutionally empowered to examine all lower court decisions—excluding specialized court rulings—upon appeal and provide official interpretations on all laws except the constitution.

Specialized civil, criminal, and administrative courts exist at all levels and are not subject to Supreme Court supervision. Local authorities—district and city governors—ensure that these courts abide by presidential decrees and SGH decisions. At the apex of the judicial system is the Constitutional Court, which consists of nine members, including a chairman, appointed for 6-year terms, whose jurisdiction extends solely over the interpretation of the constitution.

## Principal Government Officials

**For up-to-date information on Principal Government Officials, see the Chiefs of State and Cabinet Members of Foreign Governments section starting on page 1.**

Mongolia maintains an embassy in the U.S. at 2833 M Street, NW, Washington, DC, 20007; tel. (202) 333-7117, fax (202) 298-9227.

# ECONOMY

The rapid political changes of 1990-91 marked the beginning of Mongolia's efforts to develop a market economy, but these efforts have been complicated and disrupted by the dissolution and continuing deterioration of the economy of the former Soviet Union. Prior to 1991, 80% of Mongolia's trade was with the former Soviet Union, and 15% was with other Council for Mutual Economic Assistance (CMEA) countries. Mongolia was heavily dependent upon the former Soviet Union for fuel, medicine, and spare parts for its factories and power plants.

The former U.S.S.R. also served as the primary market for Mongolian industry. In the 1980s, Mongolia's industrial sector became increasingly important. By 1989, it accounted for an estimated 34% of material products, compared to 18% from agriculture. However, minerals, animals, and animal-derived products still constitute a large proportion of the country's exports. Principal imports included machinery, petroleum, cloth, and building materials.

In the late 1980s, the government began to improve links with noncommunist Asia and the West, and a tourism sector developed. As of January 1, 1991, Mongolia and the former Soviet Union agreed to conduct bilateral trade in hard currency at world prices.

Despite its external trade difficulties, Mongolia has continued to press ahead with reform. Privatization of small shops and enterprises is largely complete, and most prices have been freed. Privatization of large state enterprises has begun. Tax reforms also have begun, and the barter and official exchange rates were unified in early 1992.

Between 1990 and 1993, Mongolia suffered triple-digit inflation, rising unemployment, shortages of basic goods and food rationing. During that period, economic output contracted by one-third. As market reforms and private enterprise took hold, economic growth began again in 1994-95. Unfortunately, since this growth was fueled in part by over-allocation of bank credit, especially to the remaining state-owned enterprises, economic growth was accompanied by a severe weakening of the banking sector. GDP grew by about 6% in 1995, thanks largely to a boom in copper prices. Average real economic growth leveled off to about 3.5 in 1996-99 due to the Asian financial crisis, the collapse of the Russian ruble in mid-1999, and worsening commodity prices, especially copper and gold.

Prospects for development outside the traditional reliance on nomadic, livestock-based agriculture are constrained by Mongolia's landlocked location and lack of basic infrastructure. Mongolia's best hope for accelerated growth is to attract more foreign investment. New foreign investment in the first half of 1997 totaled $16.7 million, a figure that the Mongolian Government seeks to increase dramatically.

## Environment

As a result of rapid urbanization and industrial growth policies under the communist regime, Mongolia's deteriorating environment has become a major concern. The burning of soft coal coupled with thousands of factories in Ulaanbaatar has resulted in severely polluted air. Deforestation, overgrazed pastures, and efforts to increase grain and hay production by plowing up more virgin land has increased soil erosion from wind and rain. Most recently, with the rapid growth of newly privatized herds, overgrazing in selected areas also is a concern.

# FOREIGN RELATIONS

In the wake of the international socialist economic system's collapse and the disintegration of the former Soviet Union, Mongolians began to pursue an independent and non-aligned foreign policy. The Prime Minister called for coexistence with all nations, and Mongolia follows a general policy of expanding relations with as many countries as possible.

Due to Mongolia's landlocked position between the new independent states (NIS) of the former Soviet Union and China, it was essential to continue and improve relations with these countries. At the same time, Mongolia is reaching out to advance its regional and global relations.

As part of its aim to establish a more balanced nonaligned foreign policy, Mongolia is seeking active supporters and friends beyond its neighbors and looking to take a more active role in the United Nations and other international organizations. While it is downgrading relations with most of its former east European allies, it is pursuing a more active role in Asian and Northeast Asian affairs. Mongolia is seeking to join APEC and became a full participant in the ASEAN Regional Forum (ARF) in July 1998. Mongolia became a full member of the Pacific Economic Cooperation Council in April 2000.

High-level Mongolian officials and/or parliamentarians have made official visits to countries, including the United States, China, Japan, South Korea, Australia, Nepal, the Philippines, Pakistan, and several west European countries, as well as Russian and the former Soviet Union countries. Mongolia also has established diplomatic relations with a number of other nations, among them Oman, Brunei, and Israel, and in early 2000 opened an embassy in Bangkok, Thailand. An embassy is to be opened in Ottawa, Canada, in late 2000.

## Asia

Mongolian relations with China began to improve in the mid-1980s when consular agreements were reached and crossborder trade contacts expanded. In 1989, China and Mongolia exchanged visits of foreign ministers. In May 1990, a Mongolian head of state visited China for the first time in 28 years. The cornerstone of the Mongolian-Chinese relationship is a 1994 Treaty of Friendship and Cooperation, which codifies mutual respect for the independence and territorial integrity of both sides. Today, relations between Mongolia and China are correct. The two foreign ministers exchanged visits in 1997, as did the leaders of the two countries' parliaments. President Jiang Zemin visited Mongolia in July 1999.

Mongolia is expanding relations with Japan and South Korea. Its Prime Minister visited Japan in March 1990 and Prime Minister Obuchi reciprocated with a visit to Mongolia in July 1999. Japan has provided more than $100 million in grants and loans since 1991 and coordinated international assistance to Mongolia.

Diplomatic relations were established with South Korea in 1991, and during the Mongolian President's visit, seven agreements and treaties were signed, providing the legal basis for further expanding bilateral relations. Japan is Mongolia's largest bilateral aid donor.

## Russia

After the disintegration of the former Soviet Union, Mongolia developed relations with the new independent states. Links with Russia and other republics were essential to contribute to stabilization of the Mongolian economy. The primary difficulties in developing fruitful coordination occurred because the NIS were experiencing the same political and economic restructuring as Mongolia.

Despite these difficulties, Mongolia and Russia successfully negotiated both a 1991 Joint Declaration of Cooperation and a bilateral trade agreement. This was followed by a 1993 Treaty of Friendship and Cooperation establishing a new basis of equality in the relationship. President Bagabandi visited Moscow in 1999, and there have been frequent bilateral visits since then.

## Europe

Mongolia seeks closer relations with countries in Europe and hopes to receive most-favored-nation status from the European Union (EU). During 1991, Mongolia signed investment promotion and protection agreements with Germany and France and an economic cooperation agreement with the United Kingdom. Germany continued former East German cooperative programs and also provided loans and aid. The Prime Minister has traveled to Germany, France, Belgium, and EU headquarters in Brussels seeking economic cooperation. President Bagabandi visited several European capitals in 1999-2000.

# U.S.-MONGOLIAN RELATIONS

The U.S. Government recognized Mongolia in January 1987 and established its first embassy in Ulaanbaatar in June 1988. It formally opened in September 1988. The first U.S. ambassador to Mongolia, Richard L. Williams, was not resident there; Joseph E. Lake, the first resident ambassador, arrived in July 1990. Secretary of State James A. Baker, III visited Mongolia in August 1990, and again in July 1991. Mongolia accredited its first ambassador to the United States in March 1989. Most recently, Prime Minister Enkhsaihan visited the United States in October 1996.

The United States has sought to assist Mongolia's movement toward democracy and market-oriented reform and to expand relations with

**Travel Notes**

**Travel Advice:** For up-to-date information from the U.S. State Department on possible inconvenient or hazardous situations, see the **Travel Warnings and Consular Information Sheets from the U.S. Government** section starting on page 1723. For the latest information on health requirements and conditions, see the **International Travelers' Health Information** section starting on page 1385. For further information dealing with non-urgent matter, see the **Tips for Travelers to...** section starting on page 1588.

Mongolia primarily in the cultural and economic fields. The United States granted Mongolia most-favored-nation status and has supported Mongolia's transition to political democracy and a market economy. In 1989 and 1990, a cultural accord, Peace Corps accord, consular convention, and Overseas Private Investment Corporation (OPIC) agreement were signed. A trade agreement was signed in January 1991 and a bilateral investment treaty in 1994. Mongolia was granted permanent NTR status and GSP eligibility in June 1999.

USAID has provided more than $100 million over the past 7 years in technical assistance and training for Mongolia's democratic and economic reform program. Of that total, some $38 million has gone for emergency energy assistance, which has been instrumental in keeping Mongolia's power and heating system operable through the country's harsh winters. By FY 2000, rural development replaced energy as USAID's main program emphasis. Nearly half of USAID's annual program—$10.8 million in FY 1999 and $12 million in FY 2000—is devoted to the Gobi Regional Economic Growth Initiative and the farmer-to-farmer program of ACDI/VOCA.

The U.S. also is directly supporting Mongolia's democratization by working with U.S. non-governmental organizations to provide training for parliamentary committee organization and constituent service and has recently launched a program to establish public affairs organizations and legislative relations offices in every ministry. U.S. assistance also provided technical assistance for the drafting of the 1992 constitution, nonpartisan voter education guides, and an election- observer mission for the July 2000 elections.

The U.S. provides support for the Mongolian Government's economic reforms through its Economic Policy Support Project that includes a full-time American policy adviser in the Prime Minister's office. The adviser has worked closely with the Government of Mongolia to set the policy agenda of the current government and provides policy advice and expert technical assistance for the government's major reform initiatives, including privatization, energy, pension, and banking reforms.

The Peace Corps currently has more than 80 volunteers in Mongolia. They are engaged primarily in English teaching and teacher training activities. At the request of the Government of Mongolia, the Peace Corps has developed programs in the areas of public health and the environment.

## Principal U.S. Embassy Official

For up-to-date information on Principal U.S. Officials, see the U.S. Embassies, Consulates, and Foreign Service section starting on page 139.

The U.S. embassy is located in Micro Region 11, Big Ring Road, Ulaanbaatar; tel. [976] (1) 329-095 or 329-606, fax 320-776.
Consular and commercial information are available at the embassy's web site: www.us-mongolia.com.

# MOROCCO
November 1994

## Official Name:
**Kingdom of Morocco**

# PROFILE

## Geography

**Area:** 446,550 sq. km. (172,413 sq. mi.); slightly larger than California.
**Cities:** Capital—Rabat (pop. 1.2 million in urban prefecture of Rabat-Sale). Other cities—Casablanca (3 million), Marrakech, Fez, Tangier.
**Terrain:** Coastal plain, mountains, desert.
**Climate:** Mediterranean, becoming more extreme in the interior.

## People

**Nationality:** Noun and adjective—Moroccan(s).
**Population (est.):** 28 million.
**Annual growth rate (est.):** 2.2%.
**Ethnic groups:** Arab-Berber 99%.
**Religions:** Muslim, Christian 1%, Jewish 0.2%.
**Languages:** Arabic (official), several Berber dialects; French is often the language of business, government, and diplomacy.
**Education:** Years compulsory—7. Literacy—43%.
**Health:** Infant mortality rate—53/1,000. Life expectancy—66 years male, 69 years female.
**Work force (7.4 million):** Agriculture—50%. Services—26%. Industry—15%. Other—9%.

## Government

**Type:** Constitutional monarchy.
**Constitution:** September 1992.
**Independence:** March 2, 1956.
**Branches:** Executive—king (chief of state), prime minister (head of government). Legislative—unicameral legislature (6-yr. term). Judicial—Supreme Court.
**Political parties:** Socialist Union of Popular Forces (USFP), Istiqlal (independence) Party (PI), Popular Movement (MP), National Popular Movement (MNP), National Rally of Independents (RNI), Constitutional Union Party (UC), National Democratic Party (PND), Party of Progress and Socialism (PPS), Organization for Democratic and Popular Action (OADP).
**Suffrage:** Universal over 20.

## Economy

**GDP (1992):** $27.7 billion.
**Per capita GDP:** $1,030.
**Natural resources:** Phosphates, fish, manganese, lead, silver, copper.
**Agriculture (18% of GDP):** Products—barley, wheat, citrus fruits, wine, vegetables, olives, livestock, fishing.
**Industry (34% of GDP):** Types—phosphate mining, manufacturing and handicrafts, construction and public works, energy.
**Trade (1992):** Exports—$4.7 billion: food and beverages 28%, semiprocessed goods 25%, consumer goods 26%, phosphates 8%. Major markets—EU 62%, India 7%, Japan 5%, U.S. 2%. Imports—$7.6 billion: capital goods 27%, semiprocessed goods 16%, raw materials 12%, fuel and lubricants 15%, food and beverages 13%, consumer goods 9%. Major suppliers—EU 54%, U.S. 6%, Canada 3%, Japan 2%.
**Official exchange rate (October 1994):** 8.6 Dirham (Dh)=U.S.$1.

# PEOPLE

Most Moroccans are Sunni Muslims of Arab, Berber, or mixed Arab-Berber stock. The Arabs invaded Morocco in the 7th and 11th centuries and established their culture there. Morocco's Jewish minority numbers about 7,000. Most of the 100,000 foreign residents are French or Spanish; many are teachers or technicians.

Arabic is the official and principal language, but French is widely used in government and commerce, except in the northern zone, where Spanish is spoken. In rural areas, any of three Berber dialects—which are not mutually intelligible—are spoken.

Most people live west of the Atlas Mountains, a range which insulates the country from the Sahara Desert. Casa-blanca is the center of commerce and industry and the leading port; Rabat is the seat of government; Tangier is the gateway to Morocco from Spain and also a major port; "Arab" Fez is the cultural and religious center; and "Berber" Marrakech is a major tourist center.

Education is free and compulsory through primary school. Education now surpasses national defense as the largest item in the government's budget. Of Morocco's several universities, the most important is Muhammad V University in Rabat. Its students study medicine, law, liberal arts, and the sciences. Most university students benefit from government stipends. In Fez, Morocco's religious capital, students from around the world study Islamic law and theology at Karaouine University, which is more than 1,000 years old.

# HISTORY

Morocco's strategic location has shaped its history. Beginning with the Phoenicians, many foreigners have come to this area, some to trade or settle, others as invaders sweeping the land and dominating it. Romans, Vandals, Visigoths, and Byzantine Greeks successively ruled the area. Arab forces began occupying Morocco in the seventh century A.D., bringing with them Arab civilization and Islam. Other invasions followed. The Alaouite dynasty, which has ruled Morocco since 1649, claims descent from the Prophet Muhammad.

Morocco's location and resources led to early competition among European powers in Africa, beginning with successful Portuguese efforts to control the Atlantic coast in the 15th century. France showed a strong interest in Morocco as early as 1830. Following recognition by the United Kingdom in 1904 of France's "sphere of influence" in Morocco, the Algeciras Conference (1906) formalized France's "special position" and entrusted policing of Morocco to France and Spain jointly. The Treaty of Fez (1912) made Morocco a protectorate of France. By the same treaty, Spain assumed the role of protecting power over the

## Travel Notes

**Climate and clothing:** Morocco has wide daily variations in temperature. The coastal climate, though temperate, is damp. Wear clothing suitable for the eastern U.S.

**Customs and currency:** Passports are required. U.S. tourists do not need visas for visits of 3 months or less. Dirhams may not be imported or exported. All currency or travelers checks must be declared upon entry.

**Health:** Although not meeting U.S. standards, public health is improving steadily. Eat prepared fruits and vegetables and drink bottled water, which is widely available, when traveling outside the main cities.

**Telecommunications:** Local and international telephone and telegraph service is available. A working knowledge of French or Arabic is essential. Morocco is on Greenwich mean time (five standard time zones ahead of eastern standard time); and remains on GMT throughout the year.

**Transportation:** Direct flights are available from New York. Adequate public transportation by air, rail, and bus is available to and from principal cities. The highway system is good, and directions are clearly marked.

**Travel Advice:** For up-to-date information from the U.S. State Department on possible inconvenient or hazardous situations, see the **Travel Warnings and Consular Information Sheets from the U.S. Government** section starting on page 1723. For the latest information on health requirements and conditions, see the **International Travelers' Health Information** section starting on page 1385. For further information dealing with non-urgent matter, see the **Tips for Travelers to...** section starting on page 1588.

northern and southern (Saharan) zones.

The first nationalist political parties based their arguments for Moroccan independence on such World War II declarations as the Atlantic Charter (a joint statement issued by President Franklin D. Roosevelt and Prime Minister Winston Churchill that sets forth, among other things,

the right of all people to choose the form of government under which they will live). A manifesto of the Istiqlal (Independence) Party in 1944 was one of the earliest public demands for independence. That party subsequently provided most of the leadership for the nationalist movement.

France's exile of the highly respected Sultan Muhammad V in 1953 and his replacement by the unpopular Muhammad Ben Aarafa, whose reign was perceived as illegitimate, sparked active opposition to the French protectorate. France allowed Muhammad V to return in 1955; negotiations leading to independence began the following year.

The Kingdom of Morocco recovered its political independence from France on March 2, 1956. By agreements with Spain in 1956 and 1958, Moroccan control over certain Spanish-ruled areas was restored. On October 29, 1956, the signing of the Tangier Protocol politically reintegrated the former international zone. Spain, however, retained control over the small enclaves of Ceuta and Melilla in the north and the enclave of Ifni in the south. Ifni became part of Morocco in 1969.

After the death of his father, Muhammad V, King Hassan II succeeded to the throne on March 3, 1961. He recognized the Royal Charter proclaimed by his father on May 8, 1958, which outlined steps toward establishing a constitutional monarchy.

A constitution providing for representative government under a strong monarchy was approved by referendum on December 7, 1962. Elections were held in 1963. In June 1965, following student riots and civil unrest, the king invoked article 35 of the constitution and declared a "state of exception." He assumed all legislative and executive powers and named a new government not based on political parties. In July 1970, King Hassan submitted to referendum a new constitution providing for an even stronger monarchy. Its approval and the subsequent elections formally ended the 1965 "state of exception."

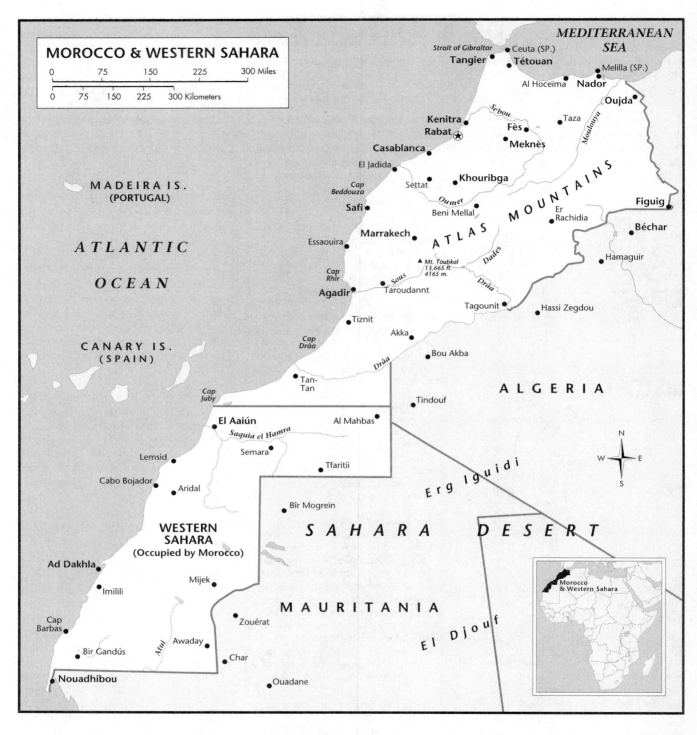

## MOROCCO & WESTERN SAHARA

0   75   150   225   300 Miles

0   75   150   225   300 Kilometers

MEDITERRANEAN SEA

Strait of Gibraltar
Ceuta (SP.)
Tangier
Tétouan
Melilla (SP.)
Al Hoceima
Nador
Oujda

Kenitra
Rabat ★
Fès
Taza
Casablanca
Meknès
El Jadida
Khouribga
Cap Beddouza
Settat
Safi
Beni Mellal
Er Rachidia
Figuig

Marrakech
ATLAS MOUNTAINS
Béchar

Essaouira
Oumer
Dadès
Hamaguir

Cap Rhir
Mt. Toubkal 13,665 ft. 4165 m.
Sous
Dràa

Agadir
Taroudannt
Tagounit
Hassi Zegdou

Tiznit
Akka
MADEIRA IS. (PORTUGAL)

ATLANTIC OCEAN

Cap Dràa
Bou Akba

Dràa
Tan-Tan
Tindouf

CANARY IS. (SPAIN)

Cap Juby
El Aaiún
Al Mahbas

Saquia el Hamra
ALGERIA
Lemsid
Semara
Tfaritii

Cabo Bojador
Aridal

Bîr Mogreïn
Erg Iguidi

WESTERN SAHARA (Occupied by Morocco)

SAHARA DESERT

Ad Dakhla
Mijek

Imilili

Cap Barbas
Zouérat
MAURITANIA

Bir Gandús
Atui
Awaday
El Djouf

Nouadhibou
Char

Ouadane

Morocco & Western Sahara

An unsuccessful coup on July 10, 1971, organized by senior military officers at Skhirat, was followed by Morocco's third constitution, approved by popular referendum in early 1972. The new constitution kept King Hassan's powers intact but enlarged from one-third to two-thirds the number of directly elected parliamentary representatives.

In August 1972, after a second coup attempt by Moroccan Air Force dissidents and the King's powerful Interior Minister General Oufkir, relations between the opposition and the Crown deteriorated, due to disagreement on opposition participation in elections. The king subsequently appointed a series of

nonpolitical cabinets responsible only to him.

Stemming from cooperation on the Sahara issue, rapprochement between the king and the opposition began in mid-1974 and led to elections for local councils, with opposition party participation, in November 1976. Parliamentary elections, deferred because of tensions with Spain and Algeria over the Sahara dispute, were held in 1977, resulting in a two-thirds majority for the government-backed independent candidates and their allies, the Istiqlal and the Popular Movement. The Constitutional Union finished first in local elections in June 1983 and parliamentary elections in 1984.

# GOVERNMENT

The King is head of state, and his son, the Crown Prince, is heir apparent. Under the 1992 constitution, a prime minister appointed by the King is head of government. Of the 333-seat unicameral parliament, two-thirds of the members are chosen directly by universal adult suffrage; the remaining one-third is indirectly elected by community councils and business, labor, artisan, and farmer groups. The parliament's powers, though limited, were expanded by the 1992 constitution and include budgetary matters, approving bills presented by the King and establishing ad hoc commissions of inquiry to investigate actions by the executive branch.

The highest court in the independent judicial structure is the Supreme Court, the judges of which are appointed by the King. Each province is headed by a governor appointed by the King. Morocco has divided the former Spanish Sahara into four provinces.

## Principal Government Officials

**For up-to-date information on Principal Government Officials, see the Chiefs of State and Cabinet Members of Foreign Governments section starting on page 1.**

Morocco maintains an embassy in the United States at 1601 21st Street NW., Washington, D.C. 20009 (tel. 202-462-7979).

# POLITICAL CONDITIONS

The pro-government RNI and UC parties won the largest number of seats in local elections in 1992. In 1993, parliamentary elections gave 50% of the vote to the six parties of the previous governing coalition but the two largest opposition parties, the Istiqlal and USFP, which ran common candidates, received the highest individual party vote totals. Together they took 41% of the seats contested (four smaller parties and independents won the remainder). These elections demonstrated a significant increase in the opposition's representation. The expansion of parliament's authority under the September 1992 constitution was another indicator of Morocco's political liberalization.

The most prominent political parties are:

* The Istiqlal (PI), Morocco's oldest political party, was founded in 1944 and helped lead the fight for independence from French and Spanish colonial domination. The party retains its strongly nationalistic philosophy and also is among the most active on pan-Arab issues.

* The Union of Socialist Popular Forces (USFP), established in 1974, is to the left of the Istiqlal, and its leaders present it as being in the tradition of the social democratic parties in Europe. It is strong in urban centers, among organized labor, and among youth groups.

* The Berber-based Popular Movement (MP) and breakaway National Popular Movement (MNP) have as their main issue the promotion and protection of Berber culture and interests.

* The National Rally of Independents (RNI) was founded in 1977 by then Prime Minister Ahmed Osman, who continues to lead the party.

* The Center Right Constitutional Union Party (UC), was founded in April 1983. Its president is former Prime Minister Maati Bouabid.

* The National Democratic Party (PND) was formed in 1981 when it broke off from the RNI. Led by former cabinet member Arsalane El Jadidi, it is principally rural based.

* The Party of Progress and Socialism (PPS) is the latest label for the small Moroccan communist party. Although tolerated, the party has been officially illegal at various times since its founding in 1943, the latest from 1969 to late 1974. The party bases its main support in urban areas and among younger, disaffected elements of society, and is led by Secretary General Ali Yata.

* The Organization for Democratic and Popular Action (OADP), has traditionally adopted strongly leftist positions on most domestic issues. However, like all the other Moroccan parties, it strongly supports Morocco's claim of sovereignty over the Western Sahara. Party Secretary General Mohammed Ben Said leads the formation.

# ECONOMY

The Moroccan economy is becoming increasingly diversified. Morocco has the largest phosphate reserves in the world. Other mineral resources include copper, fluorine, lead, barite, iron, and anthracite. It has a diverse agricultural (including fishing) sector, a large tourist industry, a growing manufacturing sector (especially clothing), and considerable inflows of funds from Moroccans working abroad.

The export of phosphates and its derivatives account for more than a quarter of Moroccan exports. Morocco is increasing production of phosphoric acid and fertilizers. About one-third of the Moroccan manufacturing sector is related to phosphates and one-third to agriculture with virtually all of the remaining third divided between textiles, clothing, and metal-working. The clothing sector, in particular, has shown consistently strong growth over the last few years as foreign companies established large-scale operations geared toward exporting garments to Europe.

Agriculture plays a leading role in the Moroccan economy, generating between 15 and 20% of GDP (depending on the harvest) and employing about 40% of the work force. Morocco is a net exporter of fruits and vegetables, and a net importer of cereals; over 90% of agriculture is rain-fed. Fishing is also important to Morocco, employing more than 100,000 people, including the canning and packing industries, and accounting for $520 million of exports in 1992.

The Moroccan Government has pursued an economic reform program supported by the International Monetary Fund (IMF) and the World Bank since the early 1980s. It has restrained spending, revised the tax system, reformed the banking system, followed appropriate monetary policies, lifted import restrictions, lowered tariffs, and liberalized the foreign exchange regime. Over the last decade, the reforms have contributed to rising per capita incomes, lower inflation, and narrower fiscal and current account deficits.

Nonetheless, population growth, rural-urban migration, and higher labor force participation rates (particularly among women) are contributing to rising urban unemployment, in spite of generally strong economic growth and job creation. The rapid increase in secondary and university (but not primary) enrollments in the 1980s exceeded the economy's capacity to create jobs, resulting in rising unemployment rates for graduates, which are about 33% for high school graduates and 11% for university graduates.

As part of its IMF program, the Moroccan Government has reduced its budget deficit. The central bank operates as an independent entity, and, following economic reform measures, has been remarkably successful in restoring domestic and

Photo credit: Corel Corporation.
**Fès medina or bazaar. Fès is Morocco's cultural capital and second largest city.**

international confidence in the value of the kingdom's currency. The government has made the dirham convertible for an increasing number of transactions over the last few years. The central bank sets the exchange rate for the dirham against a basket of currencies of its principal trading partners. The rate against the basket has been steady since a 9% devaluation in May 1990, with changes against the dollar being due to movement of the dollar against major European currencies.

The Moroccan Government actively encourages foreign investment. It has opened virtually all sectors (other than those reserved for the state such as air transport and public utilities) to foreign investment. The government also has made a number of regulatory changes designed to improve the investment climate in recent years, including tax breaks, streamlined approval procedures, and access to foreign exchange for the repatriation of dividends and invested capital.

## FOREIGN RELATIONS

Since Morocco attained independence, its foreign policy has been sympathetic to the West. Long-term goals are to strengthen its influence in the Arab world and Africa and to maintain its close relations with Europe and the United States. It is a member of the UN and some of its specialized and related agencies, including the International Monetary Fund (IMF). Morocco served a two-year term as a non-permanent member of the UN Security Council from January 1992 to December 1993. It also belongs to the Arab League; Arab Maghreb Union (UMA); Organization of the Islamic Conference (OIC); INTELSAT; and Non-Aligned Movement.

The major issue in Morocco's foreign relations is its claim to the Western Sahara relinquished by Spain in 1976. This has involved the country in a costly war against the Polisario forces seeking creation of an independent Saharan Republic. Since September 1991, Moroccan and Polisario forces have observed a cease-fire, established under the UN Secretary General's plan to hold a referendum in the Western Sahara in order to resolve the dispute. No date has been set for holding the referendum because of differences between the two parties over voter eligibility, although identification of potential voters by the UN has begun. The U.S. Government fully supports the efforts of the UN Secretary General to work with the parties to overcome these differences.

In 1984, Morocco signed a Treaty of Union with Libya, primarily aimed at ensuring a cessation of Libyan support for the Polisario. This disturbed some of Morocco's traditional friends, including the United States. Morocco described the union as a limited tactical alliance, and the King terminated the agreement in mid-1986.

Morocco adheres to sanctions imposed by the UN Security Council on Libya in April 1992 in the wake of the Pan Am 103 bombing. Relations between Morocco and Algeria have improved in recent years, as reflected in the 1988 resumption of diplomatic relations and in King Hassan's 1992 ratification of the long-pending border agreement with Algeria.

Morocco continues to play a significant role in the search for peace in the Middle East, participating in the multilateral phase of the peace talks and urging Arab moderation in the bilateral phase. King Hassan is Acting Chairman of the Arab League until the next regular Arab League Summit and Chairman of the Organization of the Islamic Conference's (OIC) Jerusalem committee. In 1986, he took the daring step of inviting then-Israeli Prime Minister Peres for talks, becoming the second Arab leader to do so. Following the September 1993 signing of the Israeli-Palestinian Declaration of Principles, Morocco's economic ties and political contacts with Israel accelerated. In September 1994, Morocco and Israel announced the opening of liaison offices in each other's countries.

Morocco has expanded its regional role. In May 1989, the King hosted the Casablanca summit which reintegrated Egypt into the Arab fold and endorsed a moderate Palestinian approach to the peace process. In February 1989, Morocco played a leading role in the formation of the Arab Maghreb Union (UMA) made up of Algeria, Tunisia, Libya, Mauritania, and Morocco. The UMA's formation

owed much to the May 1988 restoration of diplomatic relations between Morocco and Algeria after a 13-year hiatus.

Morocco has close relations with Saudi Arabia and the Persian Gulf states, which have provided Morocco with substantial amounts of financial assistance. Morocco was the first Arab state to condemn Iraq's invasion of Kuwait and sent troops to help defend Saudi Arabia. Morocco follows the UN Security Council-imposed sanctions on Iraq. Morocco remains active in African affairs, contributing troops to the UN peace-keeping force in Somalia in 1992. The Moroccans have worked to promote reconciliation between the Angolan Government and UNITA.

# U.S.-MOROCCAN RELATIONS

Moroccans are proud to have recognized the Government of the United States in 1777. Formal U.S. relations with Morocco date from 1787, when the two nations negotiated a Treaty of Peace and Friendship. Renegotiated in 1836, it is still in force, constituting the longest unbroken treaty relationship in U.S. history.

U.S.-Moroccan relations are characterized by mutual respect and friendship. They were strengthened by King Hassan's visits to the United States in March 1963, February 1967, November 1978, and May and October 1982, and September 1991.

The U.S. and Morocco share key foreign policy objectives, such as promoting regional peace and development. Morocco's strategic location on the Strait of Gibraltar, its moderate and constructive positions on Middle East issues, its religious tolerance, and its past opposition to communist aggression are factors contributing to harmonious bilateral relations.

U.S. objectives include maintaining cordial and cooperative relations; promoting respect for human rights

and continued-democratization; supporting Moroccan efforts to develop an increasingly effective administration; and aiding its domestic, social, and economic progress.

In addition to U.S. Navy port visits, Morocco has granted rights of transit through its airfields for U.S. forces and conducts joint exercises with various U.S. Armed Forces. The recently completed $225-million Voice of America (VOA) transmitter in Morocco will be the world's largest VOA transmitter.

Since independence, more than $1.5 billion in U.S. grants and loans has been provided to Morocco. Total U.S. economic and military assistance (foreign military funds, economic support funds, development assistance, and PL 480 loans) to Morocco has averaged around $100 million annually. The assistance programs are aimed at increasing the food supply, improving food distribution, reducing population growth, improving health care, promoting the private sector, and assisting Morocco in meeting its legitimate defense needs.

The Peace Corps has been active in Morocco for more than 30 years, and its program is among the largest in the world, with 100-140 volunteers in 1994. Peace Corps volunteers are involved in English language instruction, medical and veterinary care, sanitation, and environmental education.

## Principal U.S. Embassy Officials

For up-to-date information on Principal U.S. Officials, see the U.S. Embassies, Consulates, and Foreign Service section starting on page 139.

The U.S. embassy in Morocco is located at 2 Avenue de Marrakech, Rabat (tel. 212 (7) 76-22-65.

## Western Sahara

The Western Sahara, scene of a decade-long conflict between the Polisario and Morocco, comprises 267,028 square kilometers (102,703 sq. mi.)—an area about the size of Colorado—of wasteland and desert, bordered on the north by Morocco, on the west by the Atlantic Ocean, on the east and south by Mauritania, and for a few kilometers on the east by Algeria. From 1904 until 1975, Spain occupied the entire territory, which is divided into a northern portion, the Saguia el Hamra, and the southern two-thirds, known as Rio de Oro. Calls for the decolonization of these territories began in the 1960s, first from the surrounding nations and then from the United Nations.

The discovery of phosphates in Bou Craa in the Saguia el Hamra heightened demands for Spanish withdrawal from the territory. Morocco's occupation after Spain's 1975 withdrawal led to long-term armed conflict between Morocco and the Polisario, an independence movement based in the region of Tindouf, Algeria.

Morocco's claim to sovereignty over the Western Sahara is based largely on the historical argument of traditional loyalty of the Saharan tribal leaders to the Moroccan sultan as spiritual leader and ruler. The International Court of Justice, to which the issue was referred, delivered its opinion in 1975 that while historical ties exist between the inhabitants of the Western Sahara and Morocco, they are insufficient to establish Moroccan sovereignty.

The Polisario claims to represent the aspirations of the Western Saharan inhabitants for independence. Algeria claims none of the territory for itself but maintains that a popular referendum on self-determination should determine the territory's future status. In 1969, the Polisario Front (Popular Front for the Liberation of the Saguia el Hamra and Rio de Oro) was formed to combat Spanish colonization. After the Spanish left and the Moroccans and, initially, the Mauritanians

moved in, the Polisario turned its guerrilla operations against them.

In November 1975, 350,000 unarmed Moroccan citizens staged what came to be called the "Green March" into the Western Sahara. The march was designed to both demonstrate and strengthen Moroccan claims to the territory. On November 9, 1975, King Hassan requested that the marchers withdraw. On November 14, Spain, Morocco, and Mauritania announced a tripartite agreement for an interim administration under which Spain agreed to share administrative authority with Morocco and Mauritania, leaving aside the question of sovereignty. With the establishment of a Moroccan and Mauritanian presence throughout the territory, however, Spain's role in the administration of the Western Sahara ceased altogether. Mauritania withdrew from the territory in 1978 after several defeats by the Polisario.

Mauritania signed a peace treaty with the Polisario in Algiers in 1979 renouncing all claims and vacating the territory. Thereupon, Moroccan troops occupied the vacated region, and tribal leaders pledged allegiance to King Hassan. Later, local elections and the election of representatives to the National Assembly took place and Morocco proclaimed the area reintegrated into Morocco. It has since built fortifications that control about three-fourths of the Western Sahara and protect the economic and population centers, including the phosphate mine at Bou Craa.

At the Organization of African Unity (OAU) summit in June 1981, King Hassan announced his willingness to hold a referendum in the Western Sahara. He took this decision, he explained, in deference to African and other leaders who had urged him to permit a referendum as the accepted way to settle such issues. Subsequent meetings of an OAU Implementation Committee proposed a

cease-fire, a UN peace-keeping force, and an interim administration to assist with an OAU-UN-supervised referendum on the issue of independence or annexation.

Domestically, King Hassan's agreement in 1981 to hold a referendum evoked criticism from Morocco's socialist party (USFP), leading to the arrest and conviction at that time of USFP leaders for actions considered detrimental to national security and public order.

In 1984, the OAU seated a delegation of the Sahara Democratic Arab Republic (SDAR), the shadow government of the Polisario; consequently, Morocco withdrew from the OAU.

In late August 1988, Moroccan and Polisario representatives, meeting separately with UN officials, agreed on a peace plan proposed by UN Secretary General Perez de Cuellar. A UN-brokered cease-fire and project for a referendum went into effect on September 6, 1991, between Morocco and the Polisario. The referendum, which aims at determining whether the region will choose integration with Morocco or independence, was originally scheduled for 1992 but has yet to be held because of differences between the two parties regarding the details of implementation.

The United States has consistently supported efforts to end the war through negotiations between the concerned parties leading to a cease-fire and referendum. While recognizing Morocco's administrative control of the Western Sahara, the United States has not endorsed Morocco's claims of sovereignty there. It is the U.S. position that a political solution to the Western Sahara should take into account the views of its inhabitants. The UN initiative to foster the referendum continued to struggle in early 2000 as diplomats found it difficult to find common ground between the parties.

# MOZAMBIQUE

July 1996

Official Name:
## Republic of Mozambique

## PROFILE

### Geography

**Area:** 789,800 sq. km. (303,769 sq. mi.); about twice the size of California.
**Major cities:** Maputo (Capital, pop. 1,100,000 est.) Beira, Quelimane, Tete, Nampula, Nacala.
**Terrain:** Varies from lowlands to high plateau.
**Climate:** Tropical to subtropical.

### People

**Nationality:** Noun and adjective—Mozambican(s).
**Population (1996 est.):** 17 million.
**Annual growth rates (1995):** Population—2.9%; Economy—3.6%.
**Ethnic groups:** Makua, Tsonga, Makonde, Shangaan, Shona, Sena, and other indigenous tribal groups; about 10,000 Europeans, 35,000 Euro-Africans, 15,000 Indians.
**Religions:** Christian 30%, Muslim 30%, indigenous African and other beliefs 40%.
**Languages:** Portuguese (official), indigenous.
**Education:** Mean years of schooling (adults over 25): men—2.1, women—1.2. Attendance—40%. Literacy—about one-third.
**Health:** Infant mortality rate—140-173/1,000. Life expectancy—44 yrs. male. 48 yrs. female.(1995).

**Work force (8.5 million est. 1995):** Agriculture—85%. Industry and commerce—10%. Services—5%.

### Government

**Type:** Multiparty democracy.
**Independence:** June 25, 1975.
**Constitution:** November 1990.
**Branches:** Executive—President, Council of Ministers. Legislative—National Assembly. Judicial—Supreme Court; provincial, district, and municipal courts.
**Administrative subdivisions:** 10 provinces and the capital, Maputo.
**Political parties:** Front for Liberation of Mozambique (FRELIMO). Mozambican National Resistance (RENAMO).
**Suffrage:** Universal adult-18 years and older.
**Flag:** Horizontal green, black, and yellow bars separated by white stripes. The national emblem—a book covered by a crossed weapon and hoe superimposed on a yellow star—is on a red triangle at left.

### Economy

**GDP (1996):** $1.58 billion.
**Per capita income (1996 est.):** $87.
**Natural resources:** Coal, iron ore, natural gas, titanium sands, semi-precious stones.
**Agriculture (50% of GDP):** Products—cashews, maize, cotton, sugar, copra, tea.

**Industry (35% of GDP):** Types—consumer goods, light machinery.
**Trade (1995):** Exports—$160 million: shrimp (accounting for over one-third of exports), cashews, cotton, sugar, and tea. Major markets—South Africa and Western Europe. Imports (1995)—$960 million: refined petroleum products, machinery, vehicles, spare parts and consumer goods. Major suppliers—South Africa, Zimbabwe, Saudi Arabia, U.K., Portugal, and Japan.
**Official exchange rate (July 1996):** 11,175 meticais=U.S. $1.

## PEOPLE

Mozambique's 10 major ethnic groups encompass numerous subgroups with diverse languages, dialects, cultures, and history; the largest are the Makua and Tsonga.

The north-central provinces of Zambezia and Nampula are the most populous, with about 40% of the population. The estimated 4 million Makua are the dominant group in the northern part of the country—the Sena and Ndau are prominent in the Zambezi valley, and the Tsonga dominate in southern Mozambique.

Despite the influence of Islamic coastal traders and European colonizers, the people of Mozambique have

929

largely retained an indigenous culture based on subsistence agriculture. Mozambique's most highly developed art forms have been wood sculpture, for which the Makonde in northern Mozambique are particularly renowned, and dance. The modern elite continues to be heavily influenced by the Portuguese colonial and linguistic heritage.

During the colonial era, Christian missionaries were active in Mozambique, and many foreign clergy remain in the country. While precise statistics are impossible to obtain, most observers believe that about 20 to 30% of the population is Christian, 20-30% Muslim, with the rest mainly influenced by traditional beliefs.

Under the colonial regime, educational opportunities for black Mozambicans were limited, and 93% of the population was illiterate. After independence, the government placed a high priority on expanding education, reducing the illiteracy rate to about two-thirds as primary school enrollment increased. Unfortunately, in recent years, school enrollments have not kept up with population increases and the quality of education has decreased.

# HISTORY

Mozambique's first inhabitants were Bushmanoid hunters and gatherers, ancestors of the Khoisani peoples. Between the first and fourth centuries AD., waves of Bantu-speaking peoples migrated from the north through the Zambezi River Valley and then gradually into the plateau and coastal areas. The Bantu were farmers and ironworkers.

When Portuguese explorers reached Mozambique in 1498, Arab trading settlements had existed along the coast for several centuries. From about 1500, Portuguese trading posts and forts became regular ports of call on the new route to the east. Later, traders and prospectors penetrated the hinterland seeking gold and slaves. Although Portuguese influence gradually expanded, its power was limited and exercised through

individual settlers who were granted extensive autonomy. As a result, development lagged while Lisbon devoted itself to the more lucrative trade with India and the Far East and to colonization of Brazil.

In the early 20th century, the Portuguese shifted the administration of much of the country to large private companies, controlled and financed mostly by the British, which established railroad lines to neighboring countries and by supplied cheap—often forced—African labor to the mines and plantations of the nearby British colonies. Because policies were designed to benefit white settlers and the Portuguese homeland, little attention was paid until the last years of colonial rule, to the development Mozambique's economic infrastructure or the skills of its population.

After World War II, while many European nations were granting independence to their colonies, Portugal clung to the concept that Mozambique and other Portuguese possessions were overseas provinces of the mother country and immigration to the colonies soared. Mozambique's Portuguese population at the time of independence was over 200,000. The drive for Mozambican independence developed apace, and in 1962 several anti-Portuguese political groups formed the Front for the Liberation of Mozambique (FRELIMO), which initiated an armed campaign against Portuguese colonial rule in September 1964. After 10 years of sporadic warfare and major political changes in Portugal, Mozambique became independent on June 25, 1975. FRELIMO quickly established a one-party Marxist state and outlawed rival political activity.

A civil war between the FRELIMO government and the Mozambican National Resistance (RENAMO) began in 1976. RENAMO originally emerged as a creation of the Ian Smith regime in Southern Rhodesia to destabilize the Mozambican government which supported Zimbabwean and South African liberation movements. After Southern Rhodesia became Zimbabwe in 1980, the South African government took over the external sponsorship of RENAMO

and began providing the insurgents with logistical support and training. Despite its brutal methods and documented human rights abuses, RENAMO was also able to draw upon strong internal dissatisfaction with FRELIMO to garner some support among local populations.

On March 5, 1984, the Government's of Mozambique and South Africa signed the Nkomati accords, which committed both countries to cease hostilities against the other and to search for ways to increase economic cooperation. Thereafter, Mozambique severely restricted African National Congress (ANC) activities within Mozambique, and the volume of official South African support for RENAMO diminished.

Mozambique's first president, Samora Machel, died when his aircraft crashed near Mbunzi on South Africa's border with Mozambique in October 1986. Machel was succeeded by Joaquim Alberto Chissano, who had served as Foreign Minister from 1975 until Machel's death.

Despite a reduction in external support to RENAMO, the government was unable to defeat the insurgents. As early as 1980, the war's stalemate had led the two sides to begin peace talks in Rome under the auspices of Italy and the Catholic Church. Not until December 1990, however, did FRELIMO and RENAMO agree to a partial cease-fire covering two of the country's principal transportation arteries: the Limpopo and Beira corridors. The partial cease-fire continued through mid-1992. Though the negotiations only progressed slowly during 1991 and 1992, the parties were able to agree on three protocols regarding the electoral system, political parties, and the structure of the talks. In June 1992, the United States was invited to become an official observer to the talks, and the General Peace Accord was signed in October 1992. A UN Peacekeeping Force (ONUMOZ) successfully oversaw the cease-fire and the two year transition to multiparty elections. The last ONUMOZ contingents departed Mozambique in early 1995.

By mid-1995, the over 1.7 million refugees who had sought asylum in

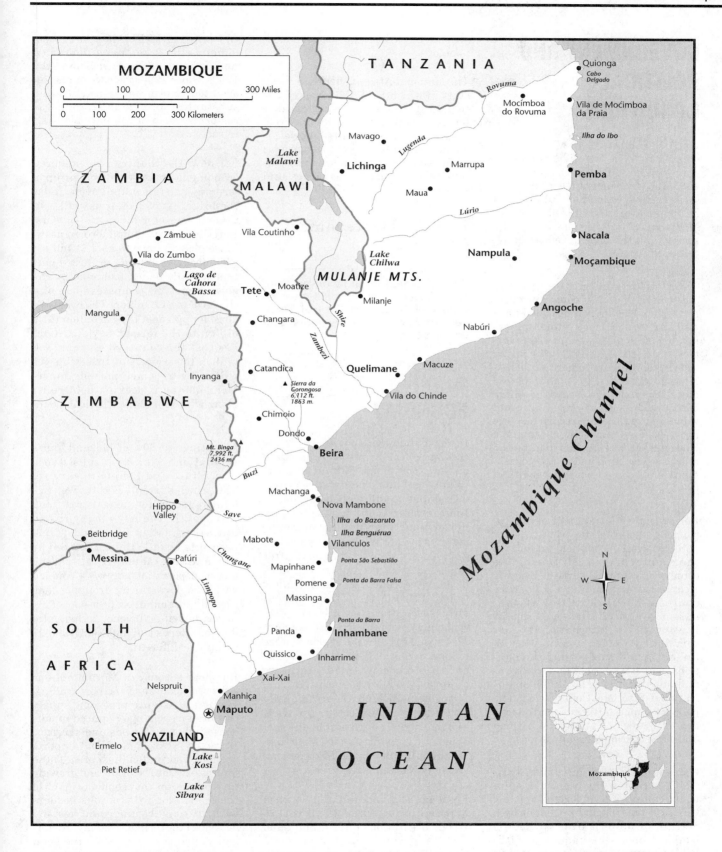

neighboring Malawi, Zimbabwe, Swaziland, Zambia, Tanzania, and South Africa as a result of war and drought had returned to Mozambique, as part of the largest repatriation witnessed in sub-Saharan Africa. Additionally, a further estimated 4 million internally displaced persons had largely returned to their areas of origin.

# GOVERNMENT AND POLITICAL CONDITIONS

Until November 1990, Mozambique was formally a socialist, one-party state ruled by FRELIMO. As early as 1983, the government began to introduce various economic and political reforms aimed at transforming Mozambique into a more pluralistic society and the pace of reform accelerated after 1987.

Those efforts culminated in the enactment of a new constitution in November 1990 which provided for a multiparty political system, a market-based economy, and free elections. In 1991, FRELIMO party activities and government responsibilities were officially separated, and mass organizations created by FRELIMO (such as the worker, youth, and women's groups) declared themselves independent, autonomous entities. However, FRELIMO has maintained a de facto monopoly over the government and many societal organizations.

Following enactment of constitutional guarantees for a multiparty political system, political activity in the country increased. During the country's first multi-party democratic elections in October 1994, 14 parties contested seats in the National Assembly and 12 candidates ran for President. The international donor community played a major role in financing and supervising the elections, which were held under the formal supervision of an independent National Elections Commission. The polls were monitored and pronounced generally free and fair by the UN and other international organizations.

Opposition parties, including RENAMO, accepted the results despite their complains of irregularities. Chissano was elected president by a margin of 53-34% over RENAMO leader Afonso Dhlakama and FRELIMO gained a narrow majority in the National Assembly. RENAMO made a strong showing, outpolling FRELIMO in five central and north-ern provinces, including the two most populous.

The National Assembly, after a rocky start in which RENAMO walked out to protest the election of the Speaker by secret vote, has steadily matured. Its effectiveness is limited, however, as the Assembly has yet to develop as a check on executive power and suffers from a lack of resources and experience.

## Principal Government Officials

For up-to-date information on Principal Government Officials, see the Chiefs of State and Cabinet Members of Foreign Governments section starting on page 1.

# ECONOMY

Prior to independence in 1975, the economy of Mozambique was based on the export of agricultural products to Portugal and associated services, e.g. shipping and transportation. A limited manufacturing sector produced some products for domestic consumption. With the exodus of 250,000 resident Portuguese after independence, the country lost most of its entrepreneurial and technical talent. FRELIMO's political leadership immediately embarked on replacing colonial mercantilism with Marxism. Private enterprises were nationalized, collective farms created, and centralized planning adopted. Armed resistance from opposition RENAMO forces easily succeeded in rapidly choking off trade and industry through systematic sabotage of the country's infrastructure. By the mid-1980s, the Mozambican economy was in disarray.

Economic reform began in 1984 when Mozambique joined the Bretton Woods institutions (World Bank and IMF) and the Lome Convention. Until 1993, progress was painstakingly slow and shrouded by ongoing civil war, seasonal droughts, and a lingering distrust of free market prin-ciples within FRELIMO. Corruption found fertile ground and flourished until it became a real problem in the 1990s. Since 1993, the pace of market oriented reform has quickened and substantial foreign assistance was restoring much of the nation's basic infrastructure.

For now, the country's beleaguered economy is entirely dependent upon foreign assistance and, even under the brightest of scenarios, will continue to be so for the next 3-5 years. In recent years, annual foreign assistance pledges have totaled $1 billion, with about two-thirds to three-quarters actually being disbursed in any given year. This compares to an official GDP of $1.6 billion. The country's large foreign debt of $5.2 billion ($1.6 billion to the former Soviet Union) has cost the country less than $50 million to service, but these charges will grow as grace periods lapse. Mozambique is seeking debt relief along with many other African countries.

An estimated 80% of Mozambique's population relies upon subsistence agriculture and fishing to survive. The principal staple is corn; wet rice is also grown in the natural flood plains of the country's many rivers; but all wheat is imported. Time needed to resettle those displaced by war and reestablish rural trading and transportation networks, coupled with two devastating droughts, has slowed Mozambique's post-war effort to regain self-sufficiency in food production. Hopes run high that 1996-97 will prove different.

Business activity in Mozambique is centered upon import/export trading. Foreign assistance programs supply the foreign exchange required to purchase imports of goods and services. At nearly $1 billion, official imports are five times official exports. These figures exclude a vibrant and growing informal sector that conducts much of the trade along the porous borders with six neighboring countries and outside of the formal economy. Historically, principal exports have been shrimp, cashews, copra, sugar, cotton, tea, and citrus fruits. Private initiatives in each of these areas are currently being undertaken. These initiatives, coupled with the rehabilitation of electricity transmission from the giant Cahora Bassa hydroelectric dam in South Africa and Zimbabwe; proposed construction of a natural gas pipeline to South Africa; and reform of transportation services could make a major impact on foreign exchange earnings in the future. The export of minerals could also be a source of future foreign exchange earnings.

What manufacturing industry there is has either recently been privatized or is currently undergoing privatization. Obsolete and poorly maintained capital equipment coupled with the lack of managerial capacity and an excess of employees has caused a number of privatizations to immediately fail. On the other hand, foreign managed privatizations, most notable Portuguese and South African, have been scoring some successes, particularly in plastic products, tires, cashew processing, milling, beverages, and construction materials. Practically all manufacturing is located in the major urban areas of Maputo, Beira, and Nampula, which are situated along historic transportation corridors to neighboring countries.

All transportation corridors are receiving increased attention from neighboring states and foreign investors, but none more than the Maputo (or Limpopo) corridor, the object of a high level bilateral initiative between the South African and Mozambican governments. A major sticking point, however, has been the desire of the Mozambican government to limit the level of private management in port and rail operations. The port and rail authority continues to be widely criticized for inefficiency, mismanagement, and corruption..

In the past few years, over 500 privatizations have been accomplished, most of which involve small enterprises. More recently, larger enterprises have been subject to privatization. In 1996, the government plans to privatize the country's largest commercial bank, and a number of sizable manufacturing companies. Other reform measures being considered include the privatization of customs operations, customs and

tax reform, and the introduction of competition and/or private participation to the transportation, energy, and telecommunications sectors.

# FOREIGN RELATIONS

While allegiances dating back to the liberation struggle remain relevant, Mozambique's foreign policy has become increasingly pragmatic and less ideological. The twin pillars of Mozambique's foreign policy are its desire for good relations with its neighbors and the need to maintain and expand ties to current and potential donor states.

During its first two decades, Mozambique's foreign policy was inextricably linked to the struggles for majority rule in Rhodesia and South Africa as well as superpower competition and the Cold War. Mozambique's principled decision to enforce UN sanctions against Southern Rhodesia and deny that country access to the sea, led Ian Smith's regime to undertake overt and covert actions to destabilize the country. While majority rule in Zimbabwe in 1980 removed this threat, the apartheid regimes in South Africa continued to keep the pressure on Mozambique. The 1984 Nkomati accord, which provided the beginnings of a political and economic

accommodation with South Africa thus marked a watershed in Mozambique's history. This process gained momentum with South Africa's own implementation of internal political reforms, which culminated in the establishment of full diplomatic relations in October 1993. While relations with neighboring Zimbabwe, Malawi, Zambia and Tanzania show occasional strains, Mozambique's ties to these countries remain strong.

In the years immediately following its independence, Mozambique benefited from considerable assistance from some western countries, notable the Scandinavians, but quickly fell under the Soviet Union's sphere of influence. During these years, Moscow and its allies became Mozambique's primary economic, military, and political supporters. In exchange, Mozambique's foreign policy was closely linked to the goals of its patrons. This began to change in the mid-1980s and notably, in 1984, when Mozambique joined the World Bank and International Monetary Fund. Western aid quickly displaced Soviet largess in supporting the Mozambican state. While the Scandinavians continue to provide significant amounts of aid, the United States, the Netherlands, and the European Union are increasingly important sources of development assistance. Italy also maintains a high profile in Mozambique as a result of its key role during the peace process. Relations with Portugal, the former colonial power, are close and of increasing importance as Portuguese investors play a significant role in Mozambique's economy. Mozambique is a member of the Non-Aligned Movement and ranks among the moderate members of the African Bloc in the United Nations and other international organizations. Mozambique also belongs to the Organization of African Unity and the Southern African Development Community, which is increasingly assuming a political, as well as economic role. In 1994, the government became a full member of the Organization of the Islamic Conference, in part to broaden its base of international support but also to please the country's sizable Muslim population. Similarly, in early-1996 Mozambique joined the Commonwealth, an organization which includes all of its anglophone neighbors. At the same time, Mozambique will be a founding member of the community of Portuguese language countries when that organization is launched in mid-1996.

# U.S.-MOZAMBICAN RELATIONS

Although the United States was quick to recognize Mozambique's independence from Portugal (establishing diplomatic relations with the new country on September 23, 1975), the relationship between he two countries quickly soured. The turnaround began in the mid-1980s with Mozambique's shift out of the Soviet orbit. By the early-1990s, the relationship was markedly improved. The U.S. played a leading role in providing assistance during Mozambique's worst drought this century in the early-1990s and was also a key actor in the peace process that led to elections in October 1994.

## Principal U.S. Officials

**For up-to-date information on Principal U.S. Officials, see the U.S. Embassies, Consulates, and Foreign Service section starting on page 139.**

The U.S. embassy opened in Maputo on November 8, 1975 and the first American Ambassador arrived in March 1976. In that same year, the United States extended a $10 million grant to the government of Mozambique to help compensate for the costs of enforcing Rhodesia sanctions. In 1977, however, largely motivated by a concern with human rights violations, the U.S. Congress prohibited the provision of development aid to Mozambique without a Presidential certification that such aid would be in the foreign policy interests of the United States. Relations hit a nadir in March 1981, when the government of Mozambique expelled four members of the U.S. embassy staff. In response, the U.S. suspended plans to provide development aid and to name a new ambassador to Mozambique.

## Travel Notes

**Customs and currency:** Visas are required and can be obtained for a fee through the Mozambican Embassy in Washington, its Mission in New York, through the government agency or firm in Mozambique that the traveler intends to visit, or by applying directly by cable with prepaid response to the Ministry of Foreign Affairs in Maputo at least six weeks in advance. The government imposes exorbitant fines for overstaying visas. Money can be exchanged at the airport, banks and money-changing firms, and should not be exchanged on the black market. Mozambican currency may not be taken in or out of the country. Travelers may not take out of the country any foreign exchange that they do not declare upon entry.

**Climate and clothing:** Light summer clothing is worn generally from mid-August to mid-May; light woolens are suitable the rest of the year.

**Health:** Standards in Maputo and other urban areas are better than other parts of the country, but exercise caution. In Maputo, boil water before drinking; many find it prudent to drink bottled water. There are a limited number of doctors, and hospitals are overcrowded and poorly equipped. Adequate medical care can only be obtained in Maputo at the private Sommerchield clinic. Malaria suppressants are required, vaccinations for tetanus and typhoid are highly recommended, and a gamma globulin injection should be obtained.

**Telecommunications:** International telephone and telegram services are usually adequate but very costly. Maputo is seven time zones ahead of Eastern Standard Time.

**Transportation:** Most Americans enter Mozambique by air from Johannesburg or Lisbon. Direct connections also are available to Manzini, Harare, Luanda and Paris. The Mozambican airline, LAM, has been the subject of travel advisories due to inadequate maintenance practices. When possible, travelers should avoid using LAM. There are also a number of small charter companies that service domestic routes in addition to LAM.

A passenger railway links Mozambique with South Africa. Paved roads connect major towns south of the Zambezi River and extend to the South African, Swazi, and Zimbabwean frontiers.

The security situation in Mozambique requires caution. Road travel can be hazardous and should not be undertaken after daylight hours. The abundance of weapons remaining from the country's civil war and police who are poorly trained, equipped, and motivated contribute to a serious crime situation. Additionally, up to one million land mines were planted throughout Mozambique during the last three decades of conflict, and mine clearing operations are currently in their initial stages. Before visiting Mozambique, consult the consular information sheet. Visit the consular section of the Embassy after arrival for security updates and to register.

Traffic moves on the left. Rental cars are available in Maputo and there is a growing taxi service. Buses are few, dangerously overcrowded, and follow erratic schedules.

**National holidays.** Businesses and the U.S. Embassy are closed on the following Mozambican holidays.

New Year's Day—January 1
Mozambican Heroes Day—February 3
Mozambican Women's Day—April 7
Workers Day—May 1
Independence Day—June 25
Lusaka Agreement—September 7
Armed Forces Day—September 25
Family/Christmas Day—December 25

**Travel Advice:** For up-to-date information from the U.S. State Department on possible inconvenient or hazardous situations, see the **Travel Warnings and Consular Information Sheets from the U.S. Government** section starting on page 1723. For the latest information on health requirements and conditions, see the **International Travelers' Health Information** section starting on page 1385. For further information dealing with nonurgent matter, see the **Tips for Travelers to...** section starting on page 1588.

Relations between the two countries were then firmly mired in a climate of stagnation and mutual suspicion.

Contacts between the two countries continued in the early 1980s as part of the U.S. Administration's conflict resolution efforts in the region. In late 1983, a new U.S. ambassador arrived in Maputo and the first Mozambican envoy to the United States arrived in Washington, signaling a thaw in the bilateral relationship. The U.S. subsequently responded to Mozambique's economic reform and drift away from Moscow's embrace by initiating an aid program in 1984. President Samora Machel paid a symbolically important official working visit to the United States in 1985. For his part, President Chissano has met with Presidents Reagan (October 1987) and Bush (March 1990), and also with Secretary of State Baker (July 1992) since replacing Machel.

The bilateral relationship has been fostered by the end of the superpower confrontation on the continent, South Africa democratic transition, and most importantly, Mozambique's own internal changes. By 1993, Mozambique had become one of the largest recipients of U.S. aid in sub-Saharan Africa, due in part to significant emergency food assistance in the wake of the 1991-93 southern African drought. During the U.N.-financed peace process leading up to elections in October 1994, the U.S. served as a member of several of the most important commissions established to monitor implementation of the Rome Accords. The United States continues to play a leading role in donor efforts to assist Mozambique's on-going economic and political transitions and is currently the largest bilateral donor to the country. Vocal U.S. support for reform at times is perceived as an irritant in the bilateral relationship, especially by hard-liners within the government who are resisting these changes.

## Offices of the U.S. Mission

**U.S. Embassy**—193 Avenida Kenneth Kaunda, P.O. Box 783; Tel.: (258) (1) 492-797, after hours (258) (1) 490-723; Fax: (258) (1) 490-114; Telex: 6-143 AMEMB MO.

**USAID Mission**—107 Rua Faria de Sousa; Tel.: (258) (1) 490-726, after hours (258) (1) 491-677; Fax: (258) (1) 492-098; Telex: 6-180 USAID/MO.

**USIS Office**—542 Avenida Mao Tse Tung; Tel.: (258) (1) 491-916; Fax: (258) (1) 491-918.

Background Notes

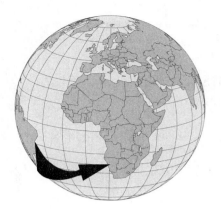

# NAMIBIA
April 1995

Official Name:
**Republic of Namibia**

# PROFILE

## Geography
**Area:** 823,145 sq. km. (320,827 sq. mi.); the size of Texas and Louisiana combined.
**Cities:** Capital—Windhoek (1991) pop. 160,000. Other cities—Keetmanshoop, Luderitz, Oranjemund, Oshakati, Otjivarongo, Swakopmund, Tsumeb, Walvis Bay.
**Terrain:** Varies from coastal desert to semiarid mountains and plateau.
**Climate:** Semi-desert and high plateau.

## People
**Nationality:** Noun and adjective—Namibian(s).
**Population (1995 est.):** 1.6 million.
**Annual growth rate (1995 est.):** 3.4%.
**Ethnic groups:** Black 87%; White 6%; mixed race 7%.
**Religions:** Predominantly Christian; also indigenous beliefs.
**Languages:** English is the official language of Namibia; Afrikaans, German, and various indigenous languages also are spoken.
**Education:** Years compulsory—to age 16. Attendance—whites nearly 100%; others 16%. Literacy—whites nearly 100%; others 30%.
**Work force:** Est. 200,000 in 1992.

## Government
**Type:** Republic as of March 21, 1990. Branches: Executive—President (elected for 5-year term). Legislative—bicameral: National Assembly (78 members) and the National Council (26 members). Judicial—Supreme Court, the High Court, and lower courts.
**Subdivisions:** 13 administrative regions.
**Major political parties:** South West Africa People's Organization (SWAPO), Democratic Turnhalle Alliance (DTA), United Democratic Front of Namibia (UDF), Democratic Coalition of Namibia (DCN), Monitor Action Group (MAG).
**Suffrage:** Universal adult.

## Economy
**GDP (1994):** $5.8 billion.
**Annual growth rate (1994):** 5.8%.
**Per capita GDP (1994):** $3,600.
**Inflation rate (1994):** 11%.
**Natural resources:** diamonds, copper, gold, uranium, lead, tin, zinc, salt, vanadium, fisheries, and wildlife.
**Agriculture (8% of GDP in 1993):** Products—beef , karakul (sheep) pelts, wool, other meat, fish.
**Mining (18% of GDP in 1993):** Gem-quality diamonds, other.
**Trade:** Exports (1993)—$1.3 billion: diamonds, copper, lead, uranium, beef, cattle, fish, karakul pelts. Imports (1993)—$1.1 billion: food stuffs, construction material, manufactured goods. Major partners—South Africa, Angola, Botswana, Germany, UK, US.
**Official exchange rate: (1994):** 3.5 Namibia dollars=U.S. $1.

# PEOPLE

Africans are of diverse ethnic origins. The principal groups are the Ovambo, Kavango, Herero/Himba, Damara, mixed race ("Colored" and Rehoboth Baster), white (Afrikaner, German, and Portuguese), Nama, Caprivian (Lozi), Bushman, and Tswana.

The Ovambo make up about half of Namibia's people. The Ovambo, Kavango, and East Caprivian peoples, who occupy the relatively well-watered and wooded northern part of the country, are settled farmers and herders. Historically, they have shown little interest in the central and southern parts of Namibia, where conditions do not suit their traditional way of life.

Until the early 1900s, these tribes had little contact with the Nama, Damara, and Herero, who roamed the central part of the country vying for control of sparse pastureland. German colonial rule destroyed the war-making ability of the tribes but did not erase their identities or traditional organization. People from the more populous north have settled throughout the country in recent decades as a result of urbanization, industrialization, and the demand for labor.

The modern mining, farming, and industrial sectors of the economy, controlled by the white minority, have affected traditional African society without transforming it. Urban and migratory workers have adopted Western ways, but in rural areas, traditional society remains intact.

Missionary work during the 1800s drew many Namibians to Christianity. While most Namibian Christians are Lutheran, there are also Roman Catholic, Methodist, Anglican, African Methodist Episcopal, and Dutch Reformed Christians represented.

Modern education and medical care have been extended in varying degrees to most rural areas in recent years. The literacy rate of Africans is generally low except in sections where missionary and government education efforts have been concentrated, such as Ovamboland. The Africans speak various indigenous languages.

The minority white population is primarily of South African, British, and German descent. About 60% of the whites speak Afrikaans (a variation of Dutch); 30% speak German; and 10% speak English.

# HISTORY

Bushmen (or San) are generally assumed to have been the earliest inhabitants of the region. Later inhabitants include the Nama and the Damara or Berg Dama. The Bantu-speaking Ovambo and Herero migrated from the north in about the 14th century A.D.

The inhospitable Namib Desert constituted a formidable barrier to European exploration until the late 18th century, when successions of travelers, traders, hunters, and missionaries explored the area. The 1878, the

## Travel Notes

**Travel Advice:** For up-to-date information from the U.S. State Department on possible inconvenient or hazardous situations, see the **Travel Warnings and Consular Information Sheets from the U.S. Government** section starting on page 1723. For the latest information on health requirements and conditions, see the **International Travelers' Health Information** section starting on page 1385. For further information dealing with non-urgent matter, see the **Tips for Travelers to...** section starting on page 1588.

United Kingdom annexed Walvis Bay on behalf of Cape Colony, and the area was incorporated into the Cape of Good Hope in 1884. In 1883, a German trader, Adolf Luderitz, claimed the rest of the coastal region after negotiations with a local chief. Negotiations between the United Kingdom and Germany resulted in Germany's annexation of the coastal region, excluding Walvis Bay. The following year, the United Kingdom recognized the hinterland up to 20o east longitude as a German sphere of influence. A region, Caprivi Strip, became a part of South West Africa after an agreement on July 1, 1890, between the United Kingdom and Germany. The British recognized that the strip would fall under German administration to provide access to the Zambezi River and German colonies in East Africa. In exchange, the British received the islands of Zanzibar and Heligoland.

German colonial power was consolidated, and prime grazing land passed to white control as a result of the Herero and Nama wars of 1904-08. German administration ended during World War I following South African occupation in 1915.

On December 17, 1920, South Africa undertook administration of South West Africa under the terms of Article 22 of the Covenant of the League of Nations and a mandate agreement by the League Council. The mandate agreement gave South Africa full power of administration and legislation over the territory. It required

that South Africa promote the material and moral well being and social progress of the people.

When the League of Nations was dissolved in 1946, the newly formed United Nations inherited its supervisory authority for the territory. South Africa refused UN requests place the territory under a trusteeship agreement. During the 1960s, as the European powers granted independence to their colonies and trust territories in Africa, pressure mounted on South Africa to do so in Namibia, which was then South West Africa. In 1966, the UN General Assembly revoked South Africa's mandate.

Also in 1966, the South West Africa People's Organization (SWAPO) began guerrilla attacks on Namibia, infiltrating the territory from bases in Zambia. After Angola became independent in 1975, SWAPO established bases in the southern part of the country. Hostilities intensified over the years, especially in Ovamboland.

In a 1971 advisory opinion, the International Court of Justice upheld UN authority over Namibia, determining that the South African presence in Namibia was illegal and that South Africa therefore was obligated to withdraw its administration from Namibia immediately. The Court also advised UN member states to refrain from implying legal recognition or assistance to the South African presence.

## International Pressure for Independence

In 1977, Western members of the UN Security Council, including Canada, France, the Federal Republic of Germany, the United Kingdom, and the United States (known as the Western Contact Group), launched a joint diplomatic effort to bring an internationally acceptable transition to independence for Namibia. Their efforts led to the presentation in April 1978 of Security Council Resolution 435 for settling the Namibian problem. The proposal, known as the UN Plan, was worked out after lengthy consultations with South Africa, the front-line states (Angola, Botswana,

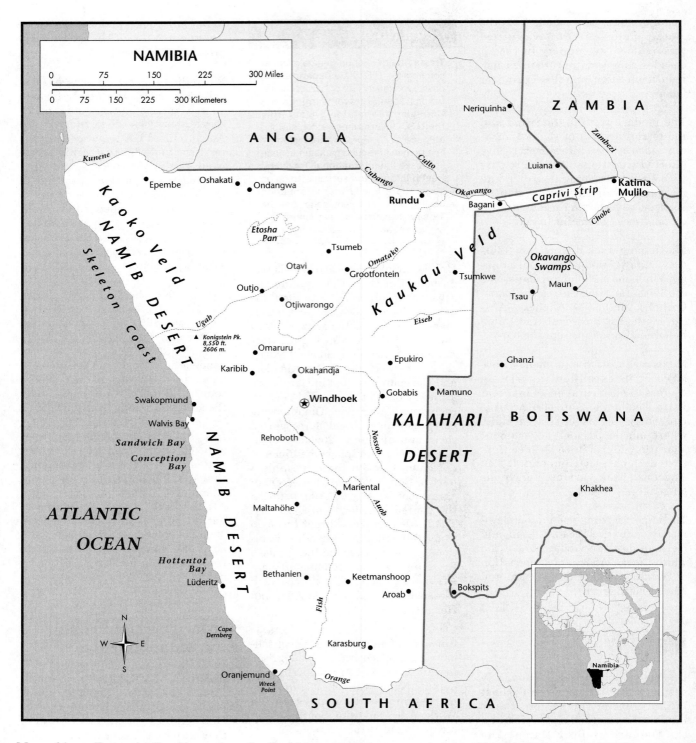

## NAMIBIA

| | | | | | |
|---|---|---|---|---|---|
| 0 | 75 | 150 | 225 | 300 Miles | |
| 0 | 75 | 150 | 225 | 300 Kilometers | |

Mozambique, Tanzania, Zambia, and Zimbabwe), SWAPO, UN officials, and the Western Contact Group. It called for the holding of elections in Namibia under UN supervision and control, the cessation of all hostile acts by all parties, and restrictions on the activities of South African and Namibian military, paramilitary, and police.

South Africa agreed to cooperate in achieving the implementation of Resolution 435. Nonetheless, in December 1978, in defiance of the UN proposal, it unilaterally held elections in Namibia which were boycotted by SWAPO and a few other political parties. South Africa continued to administer Namibia through its installed multi-racial coalitions.

Negotiations after 1978 focused on issues such as supervision of elections connected with the implementation of the UN Plan.

## Negotiations and Transition

Intense discussions between the concerned parties continued during the

1978-88 period, with the UN Secretary General's Special Representative, Martti Ahtisaari, playing a key role. The 1982 Constitutional Principles, agreed upon by the front-line states, SWAPO, and the Western Contact Group created the framework for Namibia's democratic constitution. The U.S. Government's role as mediator was critical throughout the period, one example being the intense efforts in 1984 to obtain withdrawal of South African defense forces from Southern Angola.

In May 1988, a U.S. mediation team, headed by Assistant Secretary of State for African Affairs Chester A. Crocker, brought negotiators from Angola, Cuba, and South Africa, and observers from the Soviet Union together in London. Intense diplomatic maneuvering characterized the next 7 months, as the parties worked out agreements to bring peace to the region and make implementation of UN Security Council Resolution 435 possible. On December 13, Cuba, South Africa, and the People's Republic of Angola agreed to a total Cuban troop withdrawal from Angola. The protocol also established a Joint Commission, consisting of the parties with the United States and the Soviet Union as observers, to oversee implementation of the accords. A bilateral agreement between Cuba and the People's Republic of Angola was signed in New York on December 22, 1988. On the same day a tripartite agreement, in which the parties recommended initiation of the UN Plan on April 1 and the Republic of South Africa agreed to withdraw its troops, was signed. Implementation of Resolution 435 officially began on April 1, 1989, when South African-appointed Administrator General Louis Pienaar officially began administering the territory's transition to independence. Special Representative Martti Ahtisaari arrived in Windhoek to begin performing his duties as head of the UN Transition Assistance Group (UNTAG).

The transition got off to a shaky start on April 1 because, in contravention to SWAPO President Sam Nujoma's written assurances to the UN Secretary General to abide by a cease-fire and repatriate only unarmed insurgents, approximately 2,000 armed members of the People's Liberation Army of Namibia (PLAN), SWAPO's military wing, crossed the border from Angola in an apparent attempt to establish a military presence in northern Namibia. The special representative authorized a limited contingent of South African troops to aid the South West African police in restoring order. A period of intense fighting followed, during which 375 PLAN fighters were killed. At Mt. Etjo, a game park outside Windhoek, in a special meeting of the Joint Commission on April 9, a plan was put in place to confine the South African forces to base and return PLAN elements to Angola. While the problem was solved, minor disturbances in the north continued throughout the transition period. In October, under order of the UN Security Council, Pretoria demobilized members of the disbanded counterinsurgency unit, Koevoet (Afrikaans for crowbar), who had been incorporated into the South West African police.

The 11-month transition period went relatively smoothly. Political prisoners were granted amnesty, discriminatory legislation was repealed, South Africa withdrew all its forces from Namibia, and some 42,000 refugees returned safely and voluntarily under the auspices of the Office of the UN High Commissioner for Refugees (UNHCR). Almost 98% of registered voters turned out to elect members of the constituent assembly. The elections were held in November 1989 and were certified as free and fair by the special representative, with SWAPO taking 57% of the vote, just short of the two-thirds necessary to have a free hand in drafting the constitution. The Democratic Turnhalle Alliance, the opposition party, received 29% of the vote. The Constituent Assembly held its first meeting on November 21 and its first act unanimously resolved to use the 1982 Constitutional Principles as the framework for Namibia's new constitution.

By February 9, 1990, the Constituent Assembly had drafted and adopted a constitution. March 21, independence day, was attended by Secretary of State James A. Baker III to represent President Bush. On that same day, he inaugurated the U.S. Embassy in Windhoek in recognition of the establishment of diplomatic relations.

On March 1, 1994, the coastal enclave of Walvis Bay and 12 offshore islands were transferred to Namibia by South Africa. This followed three years of bilateral negotiations between the two governments and the establishment of a transitional Joint Administrative Authority (JAA) in November 1992 to administer the 300 square mile territory. The peaceful resolution of this territorial dispute, which dated back to 1878, was praised by the U.S. and the international community, as it fulfilled the provisions of U.N. Security Council 432 (1978) which declared Walvis Bay to be an integral part of Namibia.

# GOVERNMENT

After 80 days, the Constituent Assembly produced a constitution which established a multi-party system and a bill of rights. It also limited the executive president to two five-year terms and provided for the private ownership of property. The three branches of government are subject to checks and balances, and a provision is made for judicial review. The constitution also states that Namibia should have a mixed economy, and foreign investment should be encouraged.

While the ethnic-based three-tier South African-imposed governing authorities have been dissolved, the current government pledged for the sake of national reconciliation to retain civil servants employed during the colonial period. The government is still organizing itself both on a national and regional level.

The Constituent Assembly converted itself into the National Assembly on February 16, 1990, retaining all the members elected on a straight party ticket.

The judicial structure in Namibia parallels that of South Africa. In 1919, Roman-Dutch law was declared the common law of the territory and remains so to the present.

Elections were held in 1992, to elect members of 13 newly established Regional Councils, as well as new municipal officials. Two members from each Regional Council serve simultaneously as members of the National Council, the country's second house of Parliament. Nineteen of its members are from the ruling SWAPO party, and seven are from the Democratic Turnhalle Alliance (DTA). In December 1994, elections were held for the President and the National Assembly.

## National Security

The constitution defined the role of the military as "defending the territory and national interests." Namibia formed the National Defense Force (NDF), comprised of former enemies in a 23-year bush war: the PLAN and South West African territorial force. The British formulated the force integration plan and began training the NDF, which consists of five battalions and a small headquarters element. The UNTAG Kenyan infantry battalion remained in Namibia for 3 months after independence to assist in training the NDF and stabilize the north. According to the Namibian Defense Ministry, enlistments of both men and women will number no more than 7,500. Currently, Namibia has no air force or navy. Defense and security account for less than 8% of government spending.

Defense cooperation at various levels has been explored with several governments, including the United States. Areas of cooperation include military education, training, and a fisheries program. A bilateral International Military Education and Training (IMET) program was concluded between the United States and Namibia in January 1991.

On May 21, 1990, Namibia signed a border-control agreement with Angola but to date has not entered into defense agreements with any country.

## Principal Government Officials

**For up-to-date information on Principal Government Officials, see the Chiefs of State and Cabinet Members of Foreign Governments section starting on page 1.**

# POLITICAL CONDITIONS

Namibia has about 40 political groups, ranging from modern political parties to traditional groups based on tribal authority. Some represent single tribes or ethnic groups while others encompass several. Most participate in political alliances, some of which are multi-racial, with frequently shifting membership.

SWAPO is the ruling party, and all but one of the new government's first cabinet posts went to SWAPO members. Two deputy ministers are from other parties. Formerly a Marxist oriented movement, SWAPO now espouses the principles of multiparty democracy and a mixed economy. SWAPO has been a legal political party since its formation and was cautiously active in Namibia, although before implementation of the UN Plan, it was forbidden to hold meetings of more than 20 people, and its leadership was subject to frequent detention. SWAPO draws its strength principally, but not exclusively, from within the Ovambo tribe. In December 1976, the UN General Assembly recognized SWAPO as "the sole and authentic representative of the Namibian people," a characterization other internal parties did not accept.

The principal opposition party is the Democratic Turnhalle Alliance (DTA), a coalition of several ethnically based parties, tribal chiefs, and former SWAPO members. The DTA, which governed Namibia under Pre-

toria's supervision for 10 years, holds 21 seats in the National Assembly. Some of the smaller parties in the National Assembly also are ethnically based. The United Democratic Front (4 seats), led by Justus Garoeb of the Damara group, is comprised of ethnically based parties and former SWAPO members allegedly tortured in SWAPO camps in Angola. The Monitor Action Group (3 seats) is a conservative party with support from the white community; it favors legislation to protect minority rights, which comprises around 50% of Namibia's population.

# ECONOMY

The Namibian economy has a modern market sector, which produces most of the country's wealth, and a traditional subsistence sector. Namibia's average GDP per capita is relatively high among developing countries but obscures one of the most unequal income distributions on the African continent. Although the majority of the population engages in subsistence agriculture and herding, Namibia has more than 200,000 skilled workers, as well as a small, well-trained professional and managerial class.

The country's sophisticated formal economy is based on capital-intensive industry and farming. However, Namibia's economy is heavily dependent on the earnings generated from primary commodity exports in a few vital sectors, including minerals, livestock, and fish. Furthermore, the Namibian economy remains integrated with the economy of South Africa, as the bulk of Namibia's imports originate there.

Since independence, the Namibian government has pursued free market economic principles designed to promote commercial development and job creation to bring disadvantaged Namibians into the economic mainstream. To facilitate this goal, the government has actively courted donor assistance and foreign investment. The liberal Foreign Investment Act of 1990 provides for freedom from nationalization, freedom to remit capital and profits, currency convertibility, and a process for settling disputes equitably. Namibia is also addressing the sensitive issue of agrarian land reform in a pragmatic manner.

In September 1993, Namibia introduced its own currency, the Namibia dollar, which will remain linked to the South African Rand. There has been widespread acceptance of the Namibia dollar throughout the country and, while Namibia remains a part of the Southern African Common Monetary Area, it now enjoys much greater flexibility in monetary policy.

Given its small domestic market but favorable location and a superb transport and communications base, Namibia is a leading advocate of regional economic integration. In addition to its membership in the Southern African Development Community (SADC), Namibia presently belongs to the Southern African Customs Union (SACU) with South Africa, Botswana, Lesotho, and Swaziland. Within SACU, no tariffs exist on goods produced in and moving among the member.

Ninety percent of Namibia's imports originate in South Africa, and many Namibian exports are destined for the South African market or transit that country. Namibia's exports consist mainly of diamonds and other minerals, fish products, beef and meat products, karakul sheep pelts, and light manufactures. In recent years, Namibia has accounted for about 5% of total SACU exports, and a slightly higher percentage of imports.

Namibia is seeking to diversify its trading relationships away from its heavy dependence on South African goods and services. Europe has become a leading market for Namibian fish and meat, while mining concerns in Namibia have purchased heavy equipment and machinery from Germany, the United Kingdom, the United States, and Canada. However, most imports from outside the customs union are subject to tariff rates which are usually quite restric-

tive. Recently, some of the smaller SACU members have called for reform of the customs union, which is viewed by many as a protectionist vestige of South Africa's apartheid past. Also, the General Agreement on Tariffs and Trade (GATT) is putting pressure on SACU to reduce its prohibitive tariffs and other barriers to trade, which have tended to inhibit true competition within the region.

In 1993, Namibia itself became a GATT signatory, and the Minister of Trade and Industry represented Namibia at the Marrakech signing of the Uruguay Round Agreement in April 1994. Namibia is also a member of the International Monetary Fund and the World Bank, and has acceded to the European Community/Union's Lome Convention.

## Mining and Energy

Although beset in recent years by increasing global competition, slack demand, and falling prices, mining remains Namibia's most important economic sector. In 1993, mining contributed about 18% of GDP and 54% of exports.

High value, gem-quality diamonds remain Namibia's leading generator of export earnings. Other important mineral resources are uranium, copper, lead, and zinc. The country is also a source of gold, silver, tin, vanadium, semi-precious gemstones, tantalite, phosphate, sulfur, and salt.

During the pre-independence period, large areas of Namibia (including offshore) were leased for oil prospecting. Some natural gas was discovered in 1974 in the Kudu Field off the mouth of the Orange River, but the extent of this find is not fully known. The Namibian government has invited foreign firms to explore for hydrocarbons in Namibia, with a view to lessening its dependence on South Africa for its energy supply.

Early in 1993, the government awarded the first round of licenses to several foreign consortia (including Chevron) to undertake offshore exploration for oil. One of the concessionaires, Norsk Hydro, sank its first

exploratory well in late 1993, but the company has yet to reveal whether this initial effort was successful. The government is conducting a second petroleum licensing round, from October 1, 1994, to July 31, 1995, during which all available offshore and onshore blocks will be open for international bidding.

In November 1993, the Minister of Mines and Energy announced his government's intention to proceed with the feasibility study of the major Epupa Falls hydropower project on the Kunene River border with Angola.

## Agriculture

Namibian agriculture contributes only 8% of Namibia's GDP, but approximately 70% of the Namibian population depends on agricultural activities for livelihood, mostly in the subsistence sector. In 1993, agriculture products constituted roughly 7% of total Namibian exports.

In the largely white-dominated commercial sector, agriculture consists primarily of livestock ranching. Cattle raising is predominant in the central and northern regions, while karakul sheep, goat, and ostrich farming are concentrated in the more arid southern regions. Subsistence farming is confined to the "communal lands" of the country's populous north, where roaming cattle herds are prevalent and the main crops are mahango (millet), sorghum, corn, and peanuts.

The government introduced its longawaited agricultural land reform legislation in September 1994, and a companion bill dealing with the communal areas will be presented later. As the government addresses the vital land and range management questions, water use issues and availability considered.

## Fishing

The clean, cold South Atlantic waters off the coast of Namibia are home to some of the richest fishing grounds in the world, with the potential for sustainable yields of up to 1.5 million metric tons per year. Commercial fishing and fish processing is becoming the fastest-growing sector of the Namibian economy in terms of employment, export earnings, and contribution to GDP.

The main species found in abundance off Namibia are pilchards (sardines), anchovy, hake, and horse mackerel. There are also smaller but significant quantities of sole, squid, deepsea crab, rock lobster, and tuna. However, due to the lack of protection and conservation of the fisheries and the overexploitation of these resources in the pre-independence era, fish stocks have fallen to dangerously low levels. This trend appears to have been halted and reversed since independence, as the Namibian government is now pursuing a conservative resource management policy along with an aggressive fisheries enforcement campaign.

## Manufacturing and Infrastructure

In 1993, Namibia's manufacturing sector contributed approximately 9% of GDP. Namibian manufacturing is inhibited by a small domestic market, dependence on imported goods, limited supply of local capital, widely dispersed population, small skilled labor force and high relative wage rates, and subsidized competition from South Africa.

Since the March 1994 return of Walvis Bay from South Africa, there has been interest in developing a free trade zone or export processing zone in the harbor town. Walvis Bay is a well-developed, deep-water port, and Namibia's fishing infrastructure is most heavily concentrated there. The Namibian government expects Walvis Bay to become an important commercial gateway to the Southern African region.

Namibia also boasts world-class civil aviation facilities and an extensive, well-maintained land transportation network. Construction is underway on two new arteries—the Trans-Caprivi and Trans-Kalahari Highways—which will open up the region's access to Walvis Bay. Furthermore, Telecom Namibia is in the process of procuring state-of-the-art technology to modernize its already impressive communications infrastructure, including the erection of three new satellite earth stations which will link Namibia with the world.

# FOREIGN RELATIONS

Namibia follows a non-aligned foreign policy. Former SWAPO offices abroad began performing some diplomatic functions after Namibia's independence, and the government established 11 overseas embassies in the first year of independence.

With a small army and a fragile economy, the Namibian government's principal foreign policy concern is getting along with its powerful neighbors. As its economy is closely tied to South Africa, Namibia's relations with its former colonial metropole have been pragmatic. Namibia's warm relations with Zambia and Angola, and other black-ruled neighboring countries, are the result of those countries' support of SWAPO during its 23-year war with South Africa. Relations with Botswana are excellent; Namibia has looked to Botswana's democratic institutions and market-based economy as models.

Namibia became the 160th member of the United Nations on April 23, 1990, and the 50th member of the British Commonwealth upon independence.

# U.S.-NAMIBIAN RELATIONS

U.S.-Namibian relations are characterized by shared democratic values and the active role the United States played in helping Namibia reach independence. Namibian independence had been a major U.S. foreign policy goal for more than 10 years.

In keeping with its support of UN resolutions and International Court of Justice advisory opinions regarding Namibia, the U.S. government believed that the South African government should end its administration of Namibia. The United States advocated a resolution of the Namibian problem by peaceful means and supported practical efforts to enable the people of Namibia to exercise their right to self-determination and independence on the basis of UN Security Council Resolution 435.

In the ensuing years, the United States played the principal role in negotiations to achieve Namibian independence, a process that enjoyed virtually unanimous international support. In 1988, U.S. diplomats mediated a set of interlocking agreements that allowed implementation of Resolution 435. Those agreements constituted a "peace without losers," in which all parties achieved their security objectives in southwestern Africa. The United States contributed over $100 million toward UNTAG.

From May 1970 until Namibia's independence, the U.S. government discouraged American investment in Namibia. It announced that investment rights acquired through the South African government following termination of the mandate of 1966 would not be protected against the claims of a future, lawful government in the territory. In 1986, Comprehensive Anti Apartheid Act sanctions were applied against Namibia because it was a territory administered by South Africa. All sanctions were lifted when Namibia reached independence.

## Principal U.S. Embassy Officials

For up-to-date information on Principal U.S. Officials, see the U.S. Embassies, Consulates, and Foreign Service section starting on page 139.

The U.S. Embassy in Namibia is located at 14 Lossen Street, Windhoek, (tel. 22-1601).

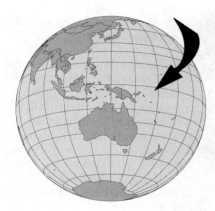

# NAURU
June 1988

Official Name:
**Republic of Nauru**

# PROFILE

## Geography

**Area:** 21 sq. km. (8 sq. mi.).
**Cities:** No capital city; government offices in Yaren District.
**Terrain:** Raised coral reefs, composed largely of phosphate-bearing rock.
**Climate:** Tropical monsoon.

## People

**Nationality:** Noun and adjective—Nauruan(s).
**Population (1987 est.):** 8,748.
**Annual growth rate:** 1.80%.
**Ethnic groups:** Nauruan 58%, other Pacific Island peoples 26%, Chinese 8%, European 8%.
**Religions:** Christian-Nauruan Congregational Church, Nauru Independent Church, Roman Catholic Church.
**Languages:** Nauruan (official), a distinct Pacific language; English widely spoken and is used for most government and commercial purposes.
**Education:** Years compulsory—ages 6-16 for Nauruans, ages 6-15 for others; free. Literacy—99%.

## Government

**Type:** Republic.

**Constitution:** Jan. 29, 1968.
**Independence:** Jan. 31, 1968.
**Branches:** Executive—president (head of state; de facto prime minister) elected by Parliament. Legislative—unicameral Parliament; 18 members elected every 3 yrs. Judicial—Supreme Court, District Court, Family Court.
**Administrative subdivisions:** The Nauru Local Government Council of nine elected councilors governs the 14 administrative districts.
**Political parties:** Democratic Party.
**Suffrage:** Universal and compulsory for all adult citizens.
**National holiday:** In addition to religious holidays, 3 national holidays—Independence Day, Jan. 31; Constitution Day, May 17; and Angam Day, Oct. 26.
**Flag:** Royal blue field with a gold stripe across the center representing the Equator. In the lower left quarter, below the gold stripe, a 12-pointed white star indicates the country's position in relation to the Equator and symbolizes the original 12 tribes of Nauru.

## Economy

Nauru does not publish GNP, export, or import figures; these figures are 1984 estimates.
**GNP:** More than $160 million; varies greatly with world price of phosphate.
**Per capita income:** $20,000.

**Agriculture:** Negligible.
**Industry:** Phosphate mining.
**Trade (1983):** Exports—$120.9 million: phosphate. Imports—$27.9 million: food, water, other necessities. Major trade partners—Australia, New Zealand, Japan.
**Official exchange rate:** Nauru uses Australian currency; 1 Australian=US$.71 (June 1987).
**Fiscal year:** July 1-June 30.

## Membership in International Organizations

Special member of the Commonwealth, South Pacific Forum, South Pacific Commission, International Telecommunication Union (ITU), Universal Postal Union (UPU), International Civil Aviation Organization (ICAO), INTERPOL, Economic and Social Council for Asia and the Pacific (ESCAP).

# GEOGRAPHY

Nauru, an oval island in the west-central Pacific Ocean, lies 53 kilometers (33 mi.) south of the Equator, 3,540 kilometers (2,200 mi.) northeast of Sydney, Australia, and 3,930 kilometers (2,445 mi.) southwest of Honolulu, Hawaii. The island is about 19 kilometers (12 mi.) in circumference and contains 21 square kilometers (8 sq. mi.) of land.

Nauru is one of the three great phosphate-rock islands of the Pacific (the others are Ocean Island, part of Kiribati, and Makatea Island in French Polynesia). The coast has a sandy beach rising gradually to form a fertile section several hundred meters wide encircling the island. A coral reef reaches 60 meters (200ft.) above sea level on the inner side of the fertile area. An extensive plateau bearing high-grade phosphate is above the cliff.

Although phosphate mining has provided Nauru's major source of income in recent years, it has done considerable environmental damage and left large areas of tall coral pinnacles above a coral stratum. In May 1987, a Nauruan commission of inquiry began a series of hearings to explore the possibilities of rehabilitation and revegetation of mined lands on the island.

Nauru, however still boasts considerable rich tropical vegetation that covers much of the coastal belt and the area that has not been mined. Pandanus and coconut palms are found in these areas. There also has been rejuvenation of secondary growth in the older mined out areas.

The climate is hot but not unpleasant. Temperatures range between 24°C and 33°C (76°F-93°F) and the humidity between 70% and 80%. The average annual rainfall is 45 centimeters (18 in.), but it fluctuates greatly. For example, in 1950, only 30 centimeters (12 in.) of rain fell, but in 1930 and 1940, rainfall measured more than 457 centimeters (180 in.). The temperature and humidity vary little during the year except during the wet season (November-February), when storms and winds bring a slight fall in temperature.

Nauru has no capital city; Parliament House and government houses are on the coast and opposite the airport in Yaren District.

# PEOPLE

The population includes more than 4,000 indigenous Nauruans, nearly 2,000 workers from other Pacific islands, and 1,500 Europeans and Chinese. Inhabitants live in small settlements scattered throughout the island. Nauruans are a mixture of the three basic Pacific ethnic groups: Melanesian, Micronesian, and Polynesian; through centuries of intermarriage, a homogenous people evolved. Their language, a fusion of elements from the Gilbert, Caroline, Marshall, and Solomon Islands, is distinct from all other Pacific languages. Most of the people speak English, and all understand it. All Nauruans are professed Christians.

Education is free and compulsory for Nauruan children between ages 6 and 16 and between 6 and 15 for non-Nauruan children. In addition, numerous government scholarships are given for students to attend boarding schools and universities abroad, principally in Australia. Literacy is virtually universal.

In the past 100 years, the existence of the Nauruans as a people has been threatened on several occasions. Tribal disputes in the 1870s reduced the population to fewer than 1,000 after 10 years of strife. An influenza epidemic in 1919 reduced the population by one-third in a few weeks. During World War II, the Nauruan community again lost two-thirds of its population when the Japanese deported many Nauruans to the Caroline Islands to build airstrips. Since the war however the population has increased substantially. Angam Day on October 26 commemorates the various occasions when the Nauruan population has reached 1,500, the minimum the Nauruans consider necessary for their survival.

# HISTORY

Little is known of Nauru's early history. The origin of the inhabitants and the circumstances of their coming are unknown, but they are believed to be castaways who drifted there from some other island.

The island was discovered in 1798 by John Fearn, captain of the British whaling ship "Hunter," on a voyage from New Zealand to the China Seas. He noted that the attractive island was "extremely populous," with many houses, and named it Pleasant Island.

The isolated island remained free of European contact for much longer than other Pacific islands. During the 19th century, however, European traders and beachcombers established themselves there. The Europeans were useful to the Nauruans as intermediaries with visiting ships; however, the Europeans obtained firearms and alcohol for the islanders, exacerbating intertribal warfare.

Pleasant Island came under German control in 1851 under an Anglo-German Convention and reverted to its native name, Nauru. By 1881, when the Germans first sent an administrator to the island, continual warring between the 12 tribes had reduced the population from about 1,400 in 1842 to little more than 900. Alcohol was banned and arms and ammunition confiscated in an effort to restore order. With the arrival in 1899 of the first missionaries, Christianity and Western education were introduced. The translation of the Bible into Nauruan standardized the language.

When World War I broke out in 1914, German authorities surrendered Nauru to an Australian expeditionary force that landed on the island, and in 1919 Germany formally renounced its title to it. A League of Nations mandate was granted to Australia, Britain, and New Zealand, and Nauru was there after administered by Australia on behalf of the three governments.

The island's rich deposits of high-grade phosphates had been discovered during the German administration, and a British company, the Pacific Phosphate Company. mined the deposits under license from Nauruan landowners. After the establishment of the mandate, the three governments purchased the company's interests and appointed a phosphate commissioner for each government to run the industry.

In 1940, during World War II, German raiders sank British phosphate ships waiting off the island and shelled the phosphate installations. Less than a year later the Japanese bombed Nauru and landed there in August 1942. In 1943, the Japanese restored the phosphate works and built an airstrip. Later that year, 1,200 of the 1,800 Nauruans were deported to Truk Island in the Carolines to build an airstrip. Only 737 Nauruans survived the brutal treatment by the Japanese on Truk and returned to Nauru on January 31, 1946—among them Hammer DeRoburt, current president of Nauru. Those who had stayed behind on Nauru also suffered privations, aggravated by food shortages that became even more acute when Japanese supply ships were sunk in 1944.

After the war, Australia restored the Nauruan settlements, and phosphate mining resumed. On November 1, 1947, the United Nations made Nauru a trust territory of Australia, New Zealand, and Great Britain, again under Australian administration.

The political advancement of the Nauruans began in December 1951 when the Council of Chiefs, a largely hereditary body with no powers, was replaced by the Nauru Local Government Council (NLGC). The council's formation and the emergence of strong leaders, particularly Timothy Detudamo and Hammer DeRoburt, accelerated the Nauruans' desire to control their own affairs. They began to press their claim for independence and ownership of the phosphate industry.

Throughout the 1960s, the Nauruans were given an increasing share in the island's administration. In 1966, the Legislative and Executive Councils were established, and a large mea-

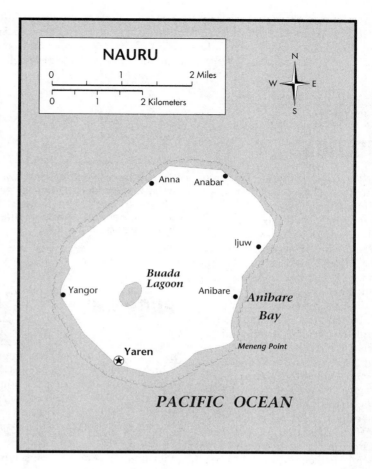

sure of internal self-government was granted. In the following year, agreement was reached that Nauru should become an independent republic, and on January 31, 1968, the trusteeship agreement was terminated and independence was celebrated. The date chosen for the inauguration was the 22d anniversary of the return from Truk of the islanders deported by the Japanese.

Independence negotiations included an agreement for the sale of the assets of the British Phosphate Company at 21 million over 3 years. In July 1970, the Nauru Phosphate Corporation took full control of the phosphate operations.

# GOVERNMENT

Nauru's constitution, adopted by an elected constitutional convention on January 29, 1968, and amended May 17, 1968, established a republic with a parliamentary system of government.

The unicameral Nauruan Parliament has 18 members, elected for 3-year terms. Voting is compulsory for all Nauruans over age 20. The island is divided into eight electoral districts, most electing two members. After each election, Parliament elects the republic's president, who chooses and serves as executive of the five- or six-member cabinet. The president is thus head of state and de facto prime minister.

Nauru is divided into 14 administrative districts, governed by the NLGC. Much overlap has developed between the central and local governments— many members of Parliament also are elected as NLGC councilors, and President DeRoburt has served as head chief of the NLGC since 1956.

The judicial arm of government is composed of the Supreme Court, presided over by a chief justice, the District Court, presided over by a resident magistrate, and the Family Court.

# POLITICAL CONDITIONS

Soon after independence, Hammer DeRoburt was elected the first president. He was reelected in May 1971 and December 1973. In December 1976, Bernard Dowiyogo was chosen president. Eleven months later on October 7, 1977, he dissolved Parliament to seek a mandate for his government because former President DeRoburt had refused to accept the 1976 election as constitutional. Although he received the mandate, his period of control was limited, and in April 1978, he resigned under pressure from DeRoburt's supporters Dowiyogo's successor Lagumot Harris, remained in office only 2 weeks before resigning. In the election following Harris' resignation, DeRoburt again became president and was reelected in December 1980 and December 1983.

In September 1986, DeRoburt was defeated on an important bill in Parliament and resigned the presidency. Prominent opposition parliamentarian Kennan Adeang then became president, but 14 days later was replaced by DeRoburt.

Elections held in December 1986 resulted in government and opposition forces tied nine to nine in Parliament. During several weeks of political maneuvering, Adeang became president for 8 days before an impasse forced another election in January 1987. Although Parliament was again deadlocked, DeRoburt put together a 10-8 majority and was reelected president. All transfers of power have been peaceful and in accordance with the constitution. In February 1987, Adeang announced the formation of the opposition "Democratic Party."

Traditionally, politics in Nauru have not been based on organized political parties, but rather on friendship, family ties, and business interests. Persons with diverse points of view run for and are elected to Parliament and the NLGC.

## Principal Government Officials

**For up-to-date information on Principal Government Officials, see the Chiefs of State and Cabinet Members of Foreign Governments section starting on page 1.**

# ECONOMY

Nauru has based its economy on exploiting its phosphate deposits, which are among the richest in the world. It exports about 1.8 million metric tons a year and its gross national product (GNP) varies with the world market price of phosphate.

Phosphate resources total some $40.5 million. At the present rate of removal, these resources are expected to be exhausted by the early 1990s. A large portion of the revenue from phosphate sales has been invested in long-term trust funds established to support Nauruans when the phosphate is depleted. Some of the better-known investments include Nauru House, a $48 million, 52-story office complex in Melbourne, a 19-floor resort-hotel on Guam, and 17 acres of prime land in Honolulu to be developed into a major office and shopping complex.

Nauru has no taxes, and costs of government and the large statutory trust fund for the future are paid from phosphate revenues. In the government's 1987 budget estimates presented to Parliament, phosphate dividends were projected to be $30.5 million. Out of a total budget of $69.6 million, a "resource gap" or deficit of $29 million, or about 40% of planned expenditures, was forecast. Some $25.3 million, or 36% of the budget was earmarked for debt servicing.

In recent years, the country has undertaken a program of enterprises, as well as investment. Its national airline owns and operates several Boeing 737s, which fly to a number of Pacific destinations and are an important transportation link for otherwise remote island states. In budget estimates for 1986-87, however Air Nauru was projected to lose $16.7 million. The NLGC owns the Nauru Pacific Shipping Line, which owns and charters several vessels providing services to Nauru and to other points in the Pacific.

Nauru has no natural port but has excellent deep-water anchorages served by lighters and a cantilever system to handle phosphate and other cargo.

The government subsidizes all imports so that food and other necessities are available at nominal cost. Virtually everything must be imported, including fresh water brought from Australia as ballast in the vessels that take the phosphate from Nauru.

Of Nauru's limited plateau area undamaged by mining, about 5,000 acres are available for cultivation. Coconuts are the main crop, and small quantities of vegetables are grown, principally by the Chinese population. Pigs and chickens are raised, and fish are caught along the coast from canoes. All other food is imported, largely from Australia and New Zealand.

Electricity is available throughout the island from the Nauru Phosphate Company, and housing is available at nominal rents. A short railroad carries the phosphate from the mines in the interior to the coast, and a paved road circles the island.

# DEFENSE

Nauru does not belong to any defense pact or treaty. Australia assures Nauru's defense, but no formal agreement exists. Nauru has no military forces; it does maintain a police force of about 60 officers, under civilian control.

# FOREIGN RELATIONS

At the Nauru Government's request, the status of "special member" of the

## Further Information

These titles are provided as a general indication of material published on this country. The Department of State does not endorse unofficial publications.

Baker, Mark. "The Dying Island." Melbourne: *The Age Saturday Extra,* February 28, 1987.

Carter, John (ed.). *Pacific Islands Year Book.* (15th ed.) Sydney: Pacific Publications, 1984.

Oliver, Douglas. *The Pacific Islands.* rev. ed. Garden City, N.Y.: Doubleday, 1961.

Osborne, Charles, ed. *Australia, New Zealand and the South Pacific: A Handbook.* New York: Praeger, 1970.

Petit-Skinner, Solange. *The Nauruans.* San Francisco: Macduff, 1981.

Skinner, Cariton. "Nauru, the Remarkable Community." Paris: *Journal de la Societe des Oceanistes,* March 1976.

Data Paper #5. Santa Cruz: University of California, Center for South Pacific Studies, December 1977.

Trumbull, Robert. "Worlds Richest Little Isle." *The New York Times Magazine,* March 7, 1982.

Viviani, Nancy. *Nauru: Phosphate and Political Progress.* Canberra, Australian National University Press, 1970.

Williams, Maslyn. *Three Islands.* Melbourne: British Phosphate Commissioners, 1971.

Williams, Maslyn and Barrie Macdonald. *The Phosphateers.* Melbourne: Melbourne University Press, 1985.

Commonwealth was devised in November 1968 for the Republic of Nauru. As a special member Nauru is not represented at meetings of the Commonwealth heads of government but may participate in all Commonwealth functional meetings and activities and is eligible for Commonwealth technical assistance, usually in the form of advice on phosphate marketing.

Nauru's main regional political interests are expressed in the South Pacific Forum, while its economic and social interests are served by membership in the South Pacific Commission, and specialized agencies such as the UN Economic and Social Commission for Asia and the Pacific. Nauru has not applied for UN membership. Nauru also is a member of the International Criminal Police Organization. In April 1987, President DeRoburt represented the South Pacific island countries at signing ceremonies for the multilateral fisheries treaty with the United States.

Under trusteeship, Nauru's external ties were almost exclusively with Australia. Many Nauruans still travel frequently to Australia, particularly to Melbourne, for vacation and shopping trips, medical care, and university-level education. Since independence, however Nauru has developed relations with a number of other countries. Although Nauru has no embassies abroad, it has honorary consuls or offices in Honolulu, Guam, and Pago Pago, as well as in a number of other Pacific cities. The U.S. Ambassador to Australia, residing in Canbera, is accredited to Nauru. No U.S. or international aid programs are active on the island.

## Principal U.S. Officials

**For up-to-date information on Principal U.S. Officials, see the U.S. Embassies, Consulates, and Foreign Service section starting on page 139.**

The U.S. Embassy in Australia is at Moonah Place, Canberra, ACT 2600 (tel. 062-73-3711).

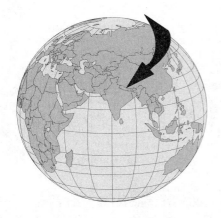

# NEPAL

January 1995

Official Name:
## Kingdom of Nepal

# PROFILE

## Geography

**Area:** 147,181 sq. km. (56,136 sq. mi.); about the size and shape of Tennessee, bordering China and India.

**Cities:** Capital—Kathmandu (pop. 600,000). Other cities—Biratnagar, Patan, Pokhara, Birganj, Dharan, Nepalganj.

**Terrain:** Flat and fertile in the southern Terai region; terraced cultivation and swiftly flowing mountain rivers in the central hills; and the high Himalayas in the north. Eight of the world's ten highest peaks are in Nepal. Kathmandu, the capital, is in a broad valley at 1,310 meters (4,300 ft.) elevation.

**Climate/Time Zone:** Subtropical in the south to cool summers and severe winters in the northern mountains. The monsoon season is from June through September and brings 75 to 150 centimeters (30-60 in.) of rain. Showers occur almost every day. Nepal is 10 hours and 45 minutes ahead of Eastern Standard Time and does not observe daylight saving time.

## People

**Nationality:** Noun—Nepalese (sing. and pl.). Adjective—Nepalese or Nepali.

**Population (1993 est.):** 19 million.
**Annual growth rate:** 2.5%.
**Ethnic groups (caste and ethnicity are often used interchangeably):** Brahman, Chetri, Newar, Gurung, Magar, Tamang, Rai, Limbu, Sherpa, Tharu, and others.
**Religions:** Hinduism (86.2%), Buddhism (7.8%), Islam (3.8%) and others (2.2%). Languages: Nepali and more than 12 others.
**Education:** Years compulsory—0. Attendance—primary 81%, secondary 30%. Literacy—38% (52% male, 18% female).
**Health:** Infant mortality rate—102/1,000. Life expectancy—54 yrs. (male), 52 yrs. (female).
**Work Force:** Agriculture—81%. Industry—3%. Services—11%. Other—5%.

## Government

**Type:** Parliamentary Democracy and Constitutional Monarchy.
**Constitution:** November 9, 1990.
**Branches:** Executive—prime minister (head of government), king (head of state). Legislative—Parliament consisting of House of Representatives (Lower House: 205 members) and National Assembly (Upper House: 60 members). Judicial—Supreme Court, 11 appellate courts, 75 district courts.
**Subdivisions:** 5 development regions, 14 zones and 75 districts.
**Political parties (Lower House representation):** United Marxist-Leninist (Communist Party of Nepal), Nepali Congress Party, National Democratic Party, others.
**Elections:** At least every five years.
**Suffrage:** Universal over 18.
**Defense/Police (1994):** $114 million
**National Day:** Democracy Day, Falgun 7 (mid-February).
**Flag:** Two blue-edged red triangles pointing away from staff, with symbols of the sun and moon in white.

## Economy

**GDP (1994-est.):** $4.1 billion.
**Annual growth rate:** 6%.
**Per capita income:** $200.
**Avg. inflation rate (1993-94):** 9.6%.
**Natural resources:** Water, hydropower, scenic beauty, limited but fertile agricultural land, timber.
**Agriculture (42% of GDP):** Products—rice, wheat, maize, sugarcane, oilseed, jute, millet, potatoes. Land—25% cultivated.
**Industry (20% of GDP):** Types—carpets, garments, cement, cigarettes, bricks, sugar, soap, matches, jute, hydroelectric power.
**Trade (1994-est.):** Exports—$460 million: carpets, garments. Major markets—Germany, U.S. Imports—$1.3 million: manufactured goods. Major supplier—India.
**Official exchange rate (December 1994):** 49 Nepalese rupees=US$1.00.
**Fiscal Year:** July 16-July 15.

# PEOPLE

Perched on the southern slopes of the Himalayan Mountains, the Kingdom of Nepal is as ethnically diverse as its terrain of fertile plains, broad valleys, and the highest mountain peaks in the world. The Nepalese are descendants of three major migrations from India, Tibet, and Central Asia.

Among the earliest inhabitants were the Newars of the Kathmandu Valley and aboriginal Tharus in the southern Terai region. The ancestors of the Brahman and Chetri caste groups came from India, while other ethnic groups trace their origins to central Asia and Tibet, including the Gurungs and Magars in the west, Rais and Limbus in the east, and Sherpas and Bhotias in the north.

In the Terai, a part of the Ganges Basin with 20% of the land, much of the population is physically and culturally similar to the Indo-Aryan people of northern India. People of Indo-Aryan and Mongoloid stock live in the hill region. The mountainous highlands are sparsely populated. Kathmandu Valley, in the middle hill region, constitutes a small fraction of the nation's area but is the most densely populated, with almost 5% of the population.

Religion is important in Nepal—Kathmandu Valley has more than 2,700 religious shrines alone. Nepal is 90% Hindu, the official state religion. Hinduism, however, has synthesized with Buddhism in Nepal. As a result, Buddhist and Hindu shrines and festivals are respected and celebrated by all. Nepal also has small Muslim and Christian minorities. Certain animistic practices of old indigenous religions survive.

Nepali is the official language, although a dozen different languages and about 30 major dialects are spoken throughout the country. Derived from Sanskrit, Nepali is related to the Indian language, Hindi, and is spoken by about 90% of the population. Many Nepalese in government and business also speak English.

# HISTORY

Modern Nepal was created in the latter half of the 18th century when Prithvi Narayan Shah, the ruler of the small principality of Gorkha, formed a unified country from a number of independent hill states. The country was frequently called the Gorkha Kingdom, the source of the term "Gurkha" used for Nepalese soldiers.

After 1800, the heirs of Prithvi Narayan Shah proved unable to maintain firm political control over Nepal. A period of internal turmoil followed, heightened by Nepal's defeat in a war with the British from 1814 to 1816. Stability was restored after 1846 when the Rana family gained power, entrenched itself through hereditary prime ministers, and reduced the monarch to a figurehead. The Rana regime, a tightly centralized autocracy, pursued a policy of isolating Nepal from external influences. This policy helped Nepal maintain its national independence during the colonial era, but it also impeded the country's economic development.

In 1950, King Tribhuvan, a direct descendant of Prithvi Narayan Shah, fled his "palace prison" to newly independent India, touching off an armed revolt against the Rana administration. This allowed the return of the Shah family to power and, eventually, the appointment of a non-Rana as prime minister. A period of quasi-constitutional rule followed, during which the monarch, assisted by the leaders of fledgling political parties, governed the country. During the 1950s, efforts were made to frame a constitution for Nepal that would establish a representative form of government, based on a British model.

## Democracy Develops

In early 1959, King Mahendra issued a new constitution and the first democratic elections for a national assembly were held. The Nepali Congress Party, a moderate socialist group, gained a substantial victory in the election. Its leader, B.P. Koirala,

formed a government and served as prime minister.

Declaring parliamentary democracy a failure 18 months later, King Mahendra dismissed the Koirala government and promulgated a new constitution on December 16, 1962. The new constitution established a "partyless" system of panchayats (councils) which King Mahendra considered to be a democratic form of government closer to Nepalese traditions. As a pyramidal structure progressing from village assemblies to a Rastriya Panchayat (National Parliament), the panchayat system enshrined the absolute power of the monarchy and kept the King as head of state with sole authority over all governmental institutions, including the Cabinet (Council of Ministers) and the parliament.

King Mahendra was succeeded by his 27-year-old son, King Birendra, in 1972. Amid student demonstrations and anti-regime activities in 1979, King Birendra called for a national referendum to decide on the nature of Nepal's government—either the continuation of the panchayat system with democratic reforms or the establishment of a multiparty system. The referendum was held in May 1980, and the panchayat system won a narrow victory. The king carried out the promised reforms, including selection of the prime minister by the Rastriya Panchayat.

## Movement To Restore Democracy

In 1990, the political parties again pressed the king and the government for change. Leftist parties united under a common banner of the United Left Front and joined forces with the Nepali Congress Party to launch strikes and demonstrations in the major cities of Nepal. This "Movement to Restore Democracy" was initially dealt with severely, with more than 50 persons killed by police gunfire and hundreds arrested. In April, the king capitulated. Consequently, he dissolved the panchayat system, lifted the ban on political parties, and released all political prisoners.

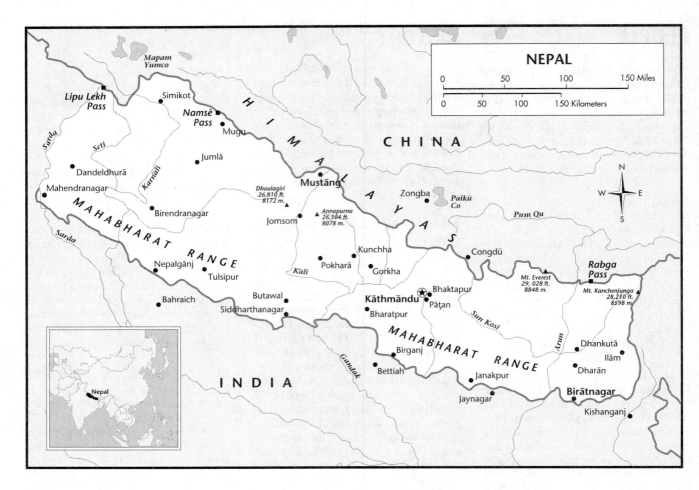

An interim government was sworn in on April 19, 1990, headed by Krishna Prasad Bhattarai as prime minister presiding over a cabinet made up of members of the Nepali Congress Party, the communist parties of Nepal, royal appointees and independents.

The new government drafted and promulgated a new constitution in November 1990, which enshrined fundamental human rights and established Nepal as a parliamentary democracy under a constitutional monarch. International observers characterized the May 1991 elections as free and fair in which the Nepali Congress won 110 seats out of 205 to form the government. The largest opposition, the United Marxist and Leninist Party (UML), won 69 seats. Girija Prasad Koirala became prime minister and formed the government. In May/June of 1992 the structure of Nepal's new democratic government was completed following local elec-

tions in which the Nepali Congress Party scored a convincing victory.

# GOVERNMENT AND POLITICAL CONDITIONS

Nepal is a constitutional monarchy with a democratic, parliamentary form of government that is multiethnic, multilingual, Hindu, and retains the king in the role of head of state. The former "partyless" panchayat system of government was abolished in April 1990.

The 1994 election defeat of the Nepali Congress Party by the UML has made Nepal the world's first Communist monarchy. The politically-moderate UML also was a champion of multiparty democracy during the years of struggle, and has supported

the country's free-market reforms. Man Mohan Adhikary, 72, the president of the Communist Party who spent 17 years in prison for fighting to restore democracy, is the new prime minister.

The Communist Party formed a minority government in December 1994. The new Government's major policy statements call for continued, if somewhat slower, economic liberalization and privatization of state enterprises, land reform, and the establishment of a Human Rights Commission.

Political parties agreed in 1991 that the monarchy would remain to enhance political stability and provide an important symbol of national identity for the culturally diverse Nepali people.

Nepal's judiciary is legally separate from the executive and legislative branches and has increasingly shown the will to be independent of political influence. The judiciary has the right of judicial review under the constitution. The king appoints the chief justice and all other judges to the supreme, appellate, and district courts upon the recommendation of the judicial council. All lower court decisions, including acquittals, are subject to appeal. The Supreme Court is the court of last appeal. The king may grant pardons and may suspend, commute, or remit any sentence by any court.

There are hundreds of small privately-owned newspapers in addition to the two state-owned newspapers. Views expressed since the 1990 move to democracy are extremely varied and vigorous. Radio and television media remain state owned and normally follow the views of the government. The law strictly forbids the media to criticize or satirize the king or any member of the royal family.

## Principal Government Officials

**For up-to-date information on Principal Government Officials, see the Chiefs of State and Cabinet Members of Foreign Governments section starting on page 1.**

Nepal maintains an embassy in the United States at 2131 Leroy Place, NW, Washington, DC 20008 (tel. 202-667-4550; fax: 202-667-5534). The Nepalese Mission to the United Nations is at 300 E. 46th Street, New York, NY 10017.

# ECONOMY

Nepal ranks among the world's poorest countries with a per capita income of under $200. An isolated, agrarian society until the mid-20th century, Nepal entered the modern era in 1951 without schools, hospitals, roads, telecommunications, electric power, industry, or civil service. The country has, however, made progress toward sustainable economic growth since the 1950s and is committed to a program of economic liberalization.

Nepal has completed seven economic development plans and began its eighth in 1991; its currency was recently made convertible, and a number of state enterprises have been earmarked for privatization. Government priorities over the years have been the development of transportation and communication facilities, agriculture, and industry. Since 1975, improved government administration and rural development efforts have been emphasized.

Agriculture remains Nepal's principal economic activity, employing 81% of the population and providing almost half of the country's income. Only about 20% of the total area is cultivable; another 33% is forested; most of the rest is mountainous. Rice and wheat are the main food crops. The lowland Terai region produces an agricultural surplus, part of which supplies the food-deficient hill areas.

Economic development in social services and infrastructure have made progress. A countrywide primary education system is under development and Tribhuvan University has several campuses. Although eradication efforts continue, malaria had been controlled in the fertile but previously uninhabitable Terai region in the south. Kathmandu is linked to India and nearby hill regions by road and an expanding highway network.

Major towns are connected to the capital by telephone and domestic air services. A system of internal finance and public administration has been established. The export-oriented carpet and garment industries have grown rapidly in recent years and together now account for some 80% of merchandise exports.

Nepal's merchandise trade balance has improved somewhat in recent years with the growth of the carpet and garment industries. The trade deficit steadily rose in the early 1990s, fueled by the results of trade disputes with India and erratic monsoons. Despite a rapid increase in manufactured exports during the

**Travel Notes**

**Travel Advice:** For up-to-date information from the U.S. State Department on possible inconvenient or hazardous situations, see the **Travel Warnings and Consular Information Sheets from the U.S. Government** section starting on page 1723. For the latest information on health requirements and conditions, see the **International Travelers' Health Information** section starting on page 1385. For further information dealing with non-urgent matter, see the **Tips for Travelers to...** section starting on page 1588.

past five years, particularly carpets and garments, imports have increased even faster and trade deficit has accordingly climbed from $432 million in 1992 to $687 million in 1993 and may reach $840 million in 1994. The annual monsoon rain or lack of it strongly influences economic growth. Real GDP growth fell from 6% in 1990 to 3% in 1992 and 1993 before recovering to 8% in 1994.

Strong export performance, including earnings from tourism, and external aid have helped improve the overall balance of payments situation and increase international reserves. Nepal receives substantial amounts of external assistance from India, the People's Republic of China, the United Kingdom, the United States, Japan, and Germany. Several multilateral organizations, such as the World Bank, the Asian Development Bank, and the UN Development Program also provide assistance. By 1994, Nepal had foreign exchange reserves equal to eight months of imports.

Progress has been made in exploiting Nepal's major economic resources—tourism and hydroelectricity. With eight of the world's ten highest mountain peaks—including Mt. Everest at 8,800 m (29,000 ft)—hiking, mountain climbing, and other tourism is growing. Swift rivers flowing south through the Himalayas have massive hydroelectricity potential to service domestic needs and the growing demand from India. The two countries have joint irrigation-hydroelectric projects on the Kosi, Trisuli, and

Background Notes

Gandaki rivers. Several other hydro-electric projects, at Kulekhani and Marsyangdi, have been completed; still others are planned.

The environmental impact of Nepal's hydroelectric projects (HEP) has been limited by the fact that most are "run-of-river" with no water storage. The largest under active consideration is the controversial Arun III 201 mega-watt project. A national electricity grid is in place and consumption is increasing at 15% to 20% a year.

Population pressure on natural resources is increasing. At current rates of growth, Nepal's population will reach 20-22 million by the turn of the century. Over-population is already straining the "carrying capacity" of the middle hill areas, particularly the Kathmandu Valley, resulting in the depletion of forest cover for crops, fuel, and fodder and contributing to erosion and flooding. Although steep mountain terrain makes exploitation difficult, mineral surveys have found small deposits of limestone, magnesite, zinc, copper, iron, mica, lead, and cobalt.

# DEFENSE

Nepal's military consists of an army of about 35,000 troops organized into a royal guards brigade, seven infantry brigades, a special forces unit, an air wing, four support brigades (logistics, engineer, signal, and artillery), and 44 independent infantry companies. Training assistance is provided by India, Pakistan, Bangladesh, and the United Kingdom. U.S. training assistance is provided via an annual $100,000 International Military Education and Training Program (IMET) grant.

The Royal Nepalese Army has served with distinction in numerous UN peacekeeping missions and currently has contingents deployed with the UN Interim Force in Lebanon (UNIFIL), the UN Protective Force (UNPROFOR), and in Somalia with UNOSOM II. Nepalese troops have fought in the British army since 1814 and for the Indian army since 1947, which inherited some of the British

army's regiments at independence. Agreements allowing the British and Indians to recruit in Nepal still exist.

# HUMAN RIGHTS

Progress has been achieved in the transition to a more open society and greater respect for human rights since political reform began in 1990; however, substantial problems remain. Poorly trained police forces often use indiscriminate force in quelling leftist-inspired protests. In addition, there have been reports of torture under detention and widespread reports of custodial abuse. The Government's unwillingness to investigate or enforce accountability for recent and past abuses remains a concern.

Some restrictions continue on freedom of expression. Trafficking in women and child labor remain serious problems. Discrimination against women and lower castes is prevalent.

# FOREIGN RELATIONS

As a small, landlocked country wedged between two larger and far stronger powers, Nepal seeks good relations with both India and China. Nepal formally established relations with China in 1956 and since then their bilateral relations have generally been very good. Because of strong cultural, religious, linguistic, and economic ties, Nepal's association with India traditionally has been closer than with China. India and Nepal restored trade relations in 1990, after a break caused by India's security concerns over Nepal's relations with China. The two countries have since undertaken renegotiations regarding trade and transit terms.

Nepal has played an active role in the formation of the economic development-oriented South Asian Association for Regional Cooperation (SAARC) and is the site of its secretariat. On international issues, Nepal follows a non-aligned policy and often votes with the Non-aligned Movement in the United Nations. The country also participates in a number

of UN specialized agencies and is a member of the World Bank, International Monetary Fund, Colombo Plan, and the Asian Development Bank.

# U.S.-NEPALESE RELATIONS

The United States established official relations with Nepal in 1947 and opened its Kathmandu embassy in 1959. Relations between the two countries have always been friendly. U.S. policy objectives toward Nepal include supporting democratic institutions and economic liberalization, promoting peace and stability in South Asia, supporting Nepalese independence and territorial integrity, and the alleviation of poverty.

The United States has provided more than $500 million in bilateral economic assistance to Nepal since 1951. In recent years, annual bilateral U.S. economic assistance through the Agency for International Development (AID) has averaged $15 million. AID supports agriculture, health, family planning, environmental, democratization, and economic liberalization efforts in Nepal. The United States also contributes to international institutions and private voluntary organizations working in Nepal. Multilateral contributions to date approach an additional $500 million, including humanitarian assistance.

## Principal U.S. Officials

**For up-to-date information on Principal U.S. Officials, see the U.S. Embassies, Consulates, and Foreign Service section starting on page 139.**

The U.S. embassy in Nepal is located in Pani Pokhari, Kathmandu (tel: [977] (1) 411179. Fax: [977] (1) 419963). The U.S. Agency for International Development is located at the embassy (tel: [977] (1) 411179. Fax: [977] (1) 272357.

# NETHERLANDS ANTILLES AND ARUBA

January 1989

Official Name:
**Netherlands Antilles and Aruba**

# PROFILE

## Geography

**Area:** Netherlands Antilles—839 sq. km. (324 sq. mi.); Aruba—181 sq. km. (70 sq. mi.).
**Capital cities:** Netherlands Antilles—Willemstad, Curacao; Aruba—Oranjestad.
Other island capitals—Philipsburg, St. Maarten; Kralendijk, Bonaire; Oranjestad, St. Eustatius; The Bottom, Saba.
**Climate:** Mildly tropical with little annual variation; arid in Aruba, Bonaire, and Curacao, which have steady trade winds and lie outside the hurricane belt. Curacao—average temperature 28°C (82°F), rainfall 56 cm. (22 in.), humidity 75.9%. Aruba—temperature 27°C (81°F), rainfall 60 cm. (24 in.), humidity 75.9%. St. Maarten—temperature 27°C (80°F), rainfall 114.3 cm. (45 in.).

## People

**Nationality:** Noun and adjective—Netherlands Antilles, Netherlands Antillean; Aruba, Aruban.
**Population:** Netherlands Antilles—187,500 (Curacao 150,000, St. Maarten 25,000, Bonaire 10,000, St. Eustatius 1,500, Saba 1,000); Aruba—60,000.

**Annual growth rate:** 1%.
**Ethnic groups:** Netherlands Antilles—African 85%, European, Carib Indian; Aruba—mixed European and Carib Indian 85%, African.
**Religions:** Roman Catholic, Protestant, Jewish.
**Languages:** Papiamento, English, Dutch, Spanish.
**Literacy:** 95%.
**Work force:** Netherlands Antilles—70,000: government, tourism, petroleum refining and transshipment, financial services; Aruba—23,000: government, tourism.

## Government

**Type:** Aruba and the Netherlands Antilles are autonomous parts of the Kingdom of the Netherlands. Each has a parliamentary system of government.
**Constitution:** December 29, 1954, Charter of the Kingdom of the Netherlands, as amended; also country constitutions.
**Branches:** Executive—governors, appointed by the sovereign of the Netherlands, serve as de facto chiefs of state in both the Netherlands Antilles and Aruba. Minister presidents, chosen by the parties in the governing coalition, serve as heads of government. In addition, each island in the Netherlands Antilles has a lieutenant governor appointed by the Crown. Legislative—both Aruba and the Netherlands Antilles have

elected unicameral "Statens" (22 members in the Antilles and 21 in Aruba). Judicial—a single Supreme Court of Justice with members appointed by the Crown serves both the Netherlands Antilles and Aruba.
**Subdivisions:** Five island territories in the Netherlands Antilles, each governed by an island council. None in Aruba.
**Political parties:** Each island has parties that compete for seats in the national legislature and, in the Netherlands Antilles, in the island councils.
**Suffrage:** Universal, age 18 and older. National elections must be held at least every 4 years.
**Central government budget (Netherlands Antilles 1987 est.):**
Revenues, $169 million; expenditures, $221 million; deficit, $52 million. Curacao—revenues, $359 million; expenditures, $374 million; deficit, $15 million. Aruba (1986)—revenues, $111 million; expenditures, $125 million; deficit, $14 million.
**Defense:** The responsibility of the Kingdom of the Netherlands. Dutch military bases are in Aruba and Curacao.
**Flag:** Netherlands Antilles—a vertical red stripe crossed by a horizontal blue stripe on a white field, with a circle of five stars at the crossing. Aruba—a four-pointed red star in the upper-left quadrant and two horizontal yellow stripes across the lower half of a blue field.

## Economy

**GDP (est.):** Netherlands Antilles (1985)—$940 million. Aruba (1986)—$377 million.

**Per capital income:** Approximately $5,000 in both Aruba and the Netherlands Antilles.

**Inflation rate:** Netherlands Antilles (1986)—3.5%. Aruba (1986)—1.7%.

**Natural resources:** Limestone (Curaeao), salt (Bonaire).

**Agriculture:** Products—aloe (Aruba).

**Industry:** Types—tourism (all islands), petroleum refining, ship repairing, limestone mining (Curacao), petroleum transshipment (Curacao, Bonaire, St. Eustatius) offshore financial services (Curacao, Aruba, St. Maarten), textiles, salt production (Bonaire).

**Trade:** Netherlands Antilles (1985, data for Curacao and Bonaire only): Exports—$956 million, of which $922 million are petroleum products. Imports—$1.125 billion, of which $758 million are petroleum products. Major markets—US, Latin America. Aruba (1986): Exports—$30 million. Imports—$211 million. Major market—US (57% of exports).

**Fiscal year:** Calendar year.

**Official exchange rates:** 1.78 Netherlands Antilles (florins—or guilders)= US$1. 1.79 Aruban florins= US$1.

**Economic aid received:** From Netherlands annually, about $75 million for the Netherlands Antilles and $25 million for Aruba. Much smaller amounts from the European Economic Communities and the UN Development Program. No US aid, but both jurisdictions are beneficiaries of the Caribbean Basin Initiative.

## Membership in International Organizations

The Kingdom of the Netherlands is responsible for foreign policy and represents Aruba and the Netherlands Antilles in the United Nations and other international bodies. Both Aruba and the Netherlands Antilles are associate members of the European Community.

# GEOGRAPHY

The Netherlands Antilles consist of two groups of islands located about 880 kilometers (550 mi.) apart in the Caribbean Sea. The "Leeward Islands" group, composed of Curacao and Bonaire, is just off the northwestern coast of Venezuela. The "Windward Islands" group St. Maarten, St. Eustatius, and Saba—is about 352 kilometers (220 mi.) east of Puerto Rico and some 96 kilometers (60 mi.) from the US Virgin Islands. Aruba, a separate part of Kingdom of the Netherlands is located 24 kilometers (15 mi.) off the coast of Venezuela, West of Curacao. Aruba, Bonaire, and Curacao are called the "ABC" islands.

Curacao (462 sq. km.—178 sq. mi.) is the largest of the five islands in the Netherlands Antilles. Most of the population of about 150,000 is centered around Willemstad, the capital of the country and of the island. Curacao is a low, hilly island of volcanic origin. The natural vegetation consists primarily of cacti, aloes, and divi-divi trees. Bonaire, 40 kilometers (25 mi.) east of Curacao, has an area of 291 square kilometers (112 sq. mi.) and a population of about 10,000.

St. Maarten is the largest and most populous of the lushly tropical Windward group. Only the southern half of the island (41 sq. km. 16 sq. mi.) is administered by the Dutch. The northern portion (called St. Martin) is part of France, although no border control divides the island. Some 25,000 people now live in Dutch St. Maarten.

Near St. Maarten are the small volcanic islands of St. Eustatius and Saba. St. Eustatius (31 sq. km. 12 sq. mi.) has some 1,500 inhabitants in Oranjestad, the capital. Mountainous Saba (13 sq. km.—5 sq. mi.) has a population of about 1,000.

Aruba (181 sq. km.—70 sq. mi.) is the westernmost of the ABC islands. It lies 67 kilometers (42 mi.) west of Curacao and 24 kilometers (15 mi.) from Venezuela. The population is about 60,000, of which one-third live in Oranjestad. Like the other ABC islands, the climate is arid, and vegetation is sparse.

# PEOPLE

Some 40 nationalities are represented in the Netherlands Antilles and Aruba but the mixture varies from island to island. The people of the Netherlands Antilles primarily are of African or mixed African and European descent. They also include Dutch, Scots, Irish, Indians, Chinese, Lebanese, and other nationalities. Arubans mostly are a mixture of European and Caribbean Indian.

Several languages are widely spoken. Dutch is an official language, as is Papiamento in Bonaire and Curacao and English in the Windward group. Papiamento, closely related to Spanish and Portuguese, is the native language of the ABC islands.

Roman Catholicism dominates in the ABC islands, but the people of the Windward group are largely Protestant. Curacao has a long-established and influential Jewish community.

# HISTORY

Alonzo de Ojeda, a Spanish navigator, landed in Curacao in 1499, and in 1527 the Spanish took possession of Curacao Bonaire, and Aruba. In 1634, the three islands passed to the Netherlands, where they have remained except for two short periods of British rule during the Napoleonic Wars. The Windward Islands changed hands often during the 17th and 18th centuries but have been under Dutch control since the early 19th century. Curacao was the center of the Caribbean slave trade until emancipation in 1863.

In the early 20th century, the establishment of oil refineries brought prosperity to Aruba and Curacao. Venezuelan crude oil was refined and served as a major source of petroleum products used by Allied forces in Europe during the Second World War. American forces helped defend the islands during the war. A large financial services industry was established when Dutch companies relocated from occupied Holland to Curacao.

Before the war, the six Dutch Caribbean islands were administered as Dutch colonies; afterward, negotiations to confer a greater measure of self-government began. With the signing of the Charter of the kingdom on December 15, 1954, the Netherlands Antilles became an autonomous part of the kingdom. In a 1983 agreement, Aruba sought autonomy from the Netherlands Antilles. On January 1, 1986, it achieved separate status equal to that of the Antilles and is slated to become fully independent in 1996.

# GOVERNMENT

Aruba and the Netherlands Antilles have a constitutional and parliamentary form of government. Each has domestic autonomy, while control over foreign policy and defense is vested in the Council of Ministers in The Hague. Each is represented in the Council by a minister plenipotentiary with full voting powers.

The highest power in the Kingdom of the Netherlands is the Sovereign. The Crown is represented in the Netherlands and Aruba by governors, who are appointed for 6-year terms after nomination by the local governments. The governor, chief of state in the Sovereign's absence, plays a key role in forming the new coalition government after an election. Principal executive power, however, lies with the Minister President and the other members of the Council of Ministers, who are chosen by the party or coalition of parties with a majority in the legislature (Staten). The Minister President is typically the leader of the largest party in the ruling coalition.

The Antillean Legislature has 22 members—15 from Curacao, 3 from St. Maarten, 2 from Bonaire, and 1 each from St. Eustatius and Saba. The Aruban Legislature has 21 members. Legislative elections must be held at least every 4 years and may occur any time a government fails to maintain a majority in the legislature.

A single independent court system, serving both Aruba and the Netherlands Antilles, is controlled by a chief justice of the Supreme Court. Judges are appointed by the Dutch Sovereign, and the legal system is based on the Napoleonic Code. In some cases, appeal to the Supreme Court in The Hague is possible. Both Aruba and

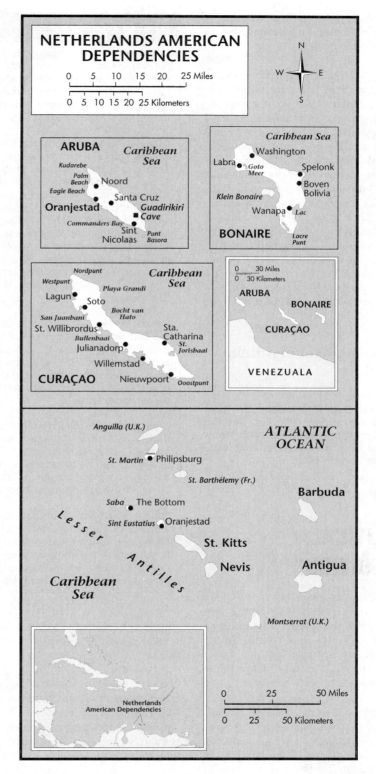

NETHERLANDS AMERICAN DEPENDENCIES

0   5   10   15   20   25 Miles
0   5  10  15 20 25 Kilometers

ARUBA   Caribbean Sea
Kudarebe
Palm Beach
Eagle Beach   Noord
Santa Cruz
Oranjestad   Guadirikiri Cave
Commanders Bay
Sint Nicolaas   Punt Basora

Caribbean Sea
Labra   Washington
Goto Meer   Spelonk
Boven Bolivia
Klein Bonaire
Wanapa   Lac
BONAIRE   Lacre Punt

Nordpunt   Caribbean Sea
Westpunt   Playa Grandi
Lagun   Soto
San Juanbani   Bocht van Hato
St. Willibrordus
Bullenbaai   Sta. Catharina
Julianadorp   St. Jorisbaai
Willemstad
CURAÇAO   Nieuwpoort   Ooostpunt

0   30 Miles
0   30 Kilometers
ARUBA   BONAIRE
CURAÇAO
VENEZUALA

Anguilla (U.K.)   ATLANTIC OCEAN
St. Martin   Philipsburg
St. Barthélemy (Fr.)
Barbuda
Saba   The Bottom
Sint Eustatius   Oranjestad
St. Kitts
Lesser Antilles
Nevis   Antigua
Caribbean Sea
Montserrat (U.K.)

Netherlands American Dependencies

0   25   50 Miles
0   25   50 Kilometers

the Netherlands Antilles have ministers of justice and attorneys general who enforce the laws..

In the Netherlands Antilles, many governmental functions are performed not by the central government, but by individual island governments. Each island territory has its own Island Council, comparable to the national legislature. Members are elected to 4year terms, but island elections rarely coincide with national elections. The party or parties with a majority in the Island Council choose commissioners to head the major departments of government and sit in the island Executive Council. It is headed by the Lieutenant Governor, who is appointed by the Crown for a 6-year term.

## Principal Government Officials

**For up-to-date information on Principal Government Officials, see the Chiefs of State and Cabinet Members of Foreign Governments section starting on page 1.**

# POLITICAL CONDITIONS

Politics centers on personalities rather than platforms. Parties are identified with certain individuals, as well as with individual islands. In the Antilles, no national parties exist; parties peculiar to each island form coalitions at the national level.

The political spectrum is narrow, with no extreme parties of the right or left represented in national or island legislatures. Some parties are affiliated with the international Christian Democrat or socialist movements. The National People's Party (PNP) on Curacao and the Aruba People's Party (AVP) lean toward the Christian Democrats, while the New Antillean Movement (MAN) in Curacao and the People's

---

## Travel Notes

**Customs and immigration:** Visas are not required for the Netherlands Antilles or Aruba. An American entering for a temporary visit must have a valid passport, birth certificate or other proof of citizenship, and a ticket indicating onward passage.

**Climate:** Aruba, Bonaire, and Curacao are arid and lie below the hurricane belt. They resemble the American southwest. August, September, and October are the warmest months, and December, January, and February the coolest. Temperatures seldom rise above 90 F or fall below 80 F, and almost constant northeast trade winds lessen the effect of heat and humidity. St. Maarten, Saba, and St. Eustatius have more rainfall but a similar temperature pattern. Summer clothes are worn year round.

**Health:** Drinking water in Aruba, Bonaire, and Curacao, distilled from the sea, is consequently of high quality. Most food is imported and subject to adequate public health controls. Overexposure to the sun is probably the main health hazard facing the temporary visitor.

**Transportation:** US airlines have daily flights to Aruba, Curacao, and St. Maarten. Major car rental companies are represented on the larger islands. Roads are in generally good condition. Taxis and buses are available on major islands.

**Tourist attractions:** Tourists are basically attracted by the warm weather, but each island has special features, from the beaches of Aruba to the architecture of Curacao; scuba diving in Bonaire; the sophisticated ambiance of St. Maarten;

St. Eustatius' history; and Saba's picturesque setting. Carnival at the start of Lent brings street processions with colorful costumes, floats, and dancing. In October, Bonaire hosts an annual International Sailing Regatta. New Year's Eve is the occasion for spectacular fireworks. Hotel prices are lower in the off-season (May-November). Atlantic standard time is observed year round, 1 hour ahead of eastern standard time and eastern daylight time.

**Holidays:** Netherlands Antilles-Carnival Jan. l; Good Friday; Easter Monday (date varies); Queen's Birthday April 30; Labor Day May l; Ascension Day (date varies); Christmas Dec. 25; Boxing Day Dec. 26. In addition, July 2 is a holiday in Curacao, Sept. 6 in Bonaire, Nov. 11 in St. Maarten, Nov. 16 in St. Eustatius, and Dec. 2 in Saba. Aruba-Carnival Jan. 1; Aruba Day March 18; Good Friday; Easter Monday (date varies); Queen's Birthday April 30; Labor Day May 1; Ascension Day (date varies); Christmas Dec. 25; Boxing Day Dec. 26.

**Travel Advice:** For up-to-date information from the U.S. State Department on possible inconvenient or hazardous situations, see the **Travel Warnings and Consular Information Sheets from the U.S. Government** section starting on page 1723. For the latest information on health requirements and conditions, see the **International Travelers' Health Information** section starting on page 1385. For further information dealing with non-urgent matter, see the **Tips for Travelers to...** section starting on page 1588.

---

Electoral Movement (MEP) in Aruba lean toward the Socialist International.

National elections in both Aruba and the Netherlands Antilles took place in November 1985, on the eve of separate status for Aruba. In each case, the party receiving a plurality of the vote was, nevertheless, excluded from the government in preference for a coalition of smaller parties. In the Antilles the PNP led by Maria Liberia-Peters, was forced into opposition by a coalition anchored by Don Martina's MAN party and Claude Wathey's Democratic Party of St. Maarten. Martina succeeded Liberia-

Peters as Minister President. The Martina government fell in March 1988, when the governing coalition lost its one-vote majority with the withdrawal of the Frente Obrero party over planned civil service cutbacks. On the instructions of the governor, Maria Liberia-Peters formed a new coalition government based on a simple majority in May 1988. In Aruba, the MEP led by the leading advocate of separate status, Betico Croes, won a plurality in 1985, but a coalition led by Eman's AVP formed the first government. (Croes was injured in an automobile accident on the eve of separate status and died 11 months later.)

# ECONOMY

Major sectors are oil refining and transshipment, tourism, and offshore financial services. Agriculture is almost nonexistent because the climate is too arid on the major islands. Manufacturing also is minimal due to lack of natural resources and relatively high wage and utility costs. Most foodstuffs and manufactured goods are imported, often from the United States. The currencies are pegged to the dollar, and inflation rates tend to mirror those in the United States.

The Aruban and Antillean economies are struggling to maintain relatively high standards of living. Both have been hit by the downturn in the market for petroleum products. The devaluation of the Venezuelan bolivar in 1983 led to a severe reduction in the flow of Venezuelan tourists to Aruba and the Antilles. Changes in U.S. tax policy have reduced employment and government tax receipts from the offshore financial sector in Curacao. Unemployment in Curacao and Aruba approaches 30%. Both governments offer tax holidays to attract new investments.

In Aruba, closure of the island's Exxon oil refinery in 1985 increased unemployment and left tourism as almost the only base of the economy. The government passed a law in 1987 to regulate exploration for petroleum in the waters off Aruba. It intends to double hotel capacity (to 4,000 rooms) by 1990 and has succeeded in attracting major new hotel chains.

St. Maarten is experiencing an economic boom based on tourism. The central government is encouraging import substitution in Curacao and Bonaire by offering protection to indigenous manufacturers. Curacao's Free Zone is expanding, and the new International Trade Center opened in 1988. Curacao's repair drydock, the largest in the Western Hemisphere, is again showing profits after a period of cost cutting. The Venezuelan Petroleum Company, which began operating Curacao's oil refinery after Shell closed in 1985, has a lease on the property until 1994. The refinery has a capacity of 300,000 barrels per day.

# FOREIGN RELATIONS

Aruban and the Netherlands Antillean foreign relations are the responsibility of the Government of the Netherlands. Each jurisdiction, however, has a Foreign Relations Office, which coordinates closely with the Dutch Government. In some capitals, including Washington, D.C., representatives of the Netherlands Antilles serve on the Netherlands Embassy's staff.

U.S.–Netherlands Antilles relations date back to 1776, when Fort Orange on St. Eustatius gave the first salute by a foreign nation to an American warship, the brig *Andrea Doria*. In the last century, Leonard B. Smith, an American businessman who served as the American honorary consul in Curacao, built the first floating bridge across the harbor entrance as well as the first electric and water distribution systems on the island. In 1950, in appreciation for the protection by American troops during World War II, the Netherlands Antilles gave the United States property in Curacao that now houses the Consulate General.

## Principal U.S. Officials

For up-to-date information on Principal U.S. Officials, see the U.S. Embassies, Consulates, and Foreign Service section starting on page 139.

The U.S. Consulate General serving Aruba and the Netherlands Antilles is located at Romulo Betancourt Boulevard 19, Willemstad, Curacao (tel. 599-9-613-066, telex 1062 AMCONNA).

# NETHERLANDS

May 1999

Official Name:

## Kingdom of the Netherlands

# PROFILE

## Geography

**Area:** 41,526 sq. km. (16,485 sq. mi.).
**Cities:** Capital—Amsterdam (pop. 1.1 million). Other cities—The Hague, seat of government, (pop. 699,000); Rotterdam, the world's largest port (1.1 million); Utrecht (554,000).
**Terrain:** Coastal lowland.
**Climate:** Northern maritime.

## People

**Population:** 15.7 million.
**Nationality:** Noun—Dutchmen and Dutchwomen. Adjective—Dutch.
**Ethnic groups:** Predominantly Dutch; largest minority communities are Moroccans, Turks, Surinamese.
**Religions:** Roman Catholic, Protestant, Muslim, other.
**Language:** Dutch.
**Education:** Years compulsory—10. Attendance—nearly 100%. Literacy—99%.
**Health:** Infant mortality rate—6.6/1,000. Life expectancy—78 yrs.
**Work force:** 6.7 million. Services—49%. Industry—16%. Government—7%. Agriculture—2%.

## Government

**Type:** Parliamentary democracy under a constitutional monarch. Constitution: 1814 and 1848.
**Branches:** Executive—monarch (chief of state), prime minister (head of government), cabinet. Legislative—bicameral parliament (First and Second Chambers). Judicial—Supreme Court.
**Subdivisions:** 12 provinces.
**Political parties:** Christian Democratic Appeal (CDA), Labor Party (PvdA), Liberal Party (VVD), Democrats '66 (D'66), other minor parties.
**Suffrage:** Universal at 18.

## Economy

**GDP (1998):** $372.1 billion (nominal, market prices).
**GDP real growth rate (1998):** 3.8%.
**GDP per capita (1998):** $23,853.
**Natural resources:** Natural gas, petroleum, fertile soil.
**Agriculture (3% of GDP):** Products—dairy, poultry, meat, flower bulbs, cut flowers, vegetables and fruits, sugar beets, potatoes, wheat, barley.
**Industry (28% of GDP):** Types—agro-industries, steel and aluminum, metal and engineering products, electric machinery and equipment, bulk chemicals, natural gas, petroleum products, transport equipment, microelectronics.

**Trade (1998):** Exports—$170 billion (f.o.b): mineral fuels, chemicals, machinery and transport equipment, processed food and tobacco, agricultural products. Imports—$155.1 billion (c.i.f): mineral fuels and crude petroleum, machinery, transportation equipment, consumer goods, foodstuffs. Major trading partners—EU, Germany, Belgium, Luxembourg, France, U.K., U.S.

# HISTORY

The Dutch are primarily of Germanic stock with some Gallo–Celtic mixture. Their small homeland frequently has been threatened with destruction by the North Sea and has often been invaded by the great European powers.

Julius Caesar found the region which is now the Netherlands inhabited by Germanic tribes in the first century B.C. The western portion was inhabited by the Batavians and became part of a Roman province; the eastern portion was inhabited by the Frisians. Between the fourth and eighth centuries A.D., most of both portions were conquered by the Franks. The area later passed into the hands of the House of Burgundy and the Austrian Hapsburgs. Falling under harsh Spanish rule in the 16th century, the Dutch revolted in 1558 under the leadership of Willem of Orange. By virtue of the Union of Utrecht in 1579, the seven northern Dutch provinces became the Republic of the United Netherlands.

During the 17th century, considered its "golden era," the Netherlands became a great sea and colonial power. Among other achievements, this period saw the emergence of some of painting's "Old Masters," including Rembrandt and Hals, whose works—along with those of later artists such as Mondriaan and Van Gogh—are today on display in museums throughout the Netherlands.

The country's importance declined, however, with the gradual loss of Dutch technological superiority and after wars with Spain, France, and England in the 18th century. The Dutch United Provinces supported the Americans in the Revolutionary War. In 1795, French troops ousted Willem V of Orange, the Stadhouder under the Dutch Republic and head of the House of Orange.

Following Napoleon's defeat in 1813, the Netherlands and Belgium became the "Kingdom of the United Netherlands" under King Willem I, son of Willem V of Orange. The Belgians withdrew from the union in 1830 to form their own kingdom. King Willem II was largely responsible for the liberalizing revision of the constitution in 1848.

The Netherlands prospered during the long reign of Willem III (1849–1890). At the time of his death, his daughter Wilhelmina was 10 years old. Her mother, Queen Emma, reigned as regent until 1898, when Wilhelmina reached the age of 18 and became the monarch.

The Netherlands proclaimed neutrality at the start of both world wars. Although it escaped occupation in World War I, German troops overran the country in May 1940. Queen Wilhelmina fled to London and established a government-in-exile. Shortly after the Netherlands was liberated in May 1945, the Queen returned. Crown Princess Juliana

acceded to the throne in 1948 upon her mother's abdication. In April 1980, Queen Juliana abdicated in favor of her daughter, now Queen Beatrix. Crown Prince Willem Alexander was born in 1967.

Elements of the Netherlands' once far–flung empire were granted either full independence or nearly complete autonomy after World War II. Indonesia formally gained its independence in 1949, and Suriname became independent in 1975. The five islands of the Netherlands Antilles (Curacao, Bonaire, Saba, St. Eustatius, and a part of St. Maarten) are an integral part of the Netherlands realm but enjoy a large degree of autonomy. Aruba, which had been a part of the Netherlands Antilles, was granted in January 1986 a separate status within the kingdom on par with, but apart from, the Netherlands Antilles.

# GOVERNMENT AND POLITICAL CONDITIONS

The present constitution—which dates from 1848 and has been amended several times—protects individual and political freedoms, including freedom of religion. Although church and state are separate, a few historical ties remain; the royal family belongs to the Dutch Reformed Church (Protestant). Freedom of speech also is protected.

## Government Structure

The country's government is based on the principles of ministerial responsibility and parliamentary government. The national government comprises three main institutions: the Monarch, the Council of Ministers, and the States General. There also are local governments.

**The Monarch.** The monarch is the titular head of state. The Queen's function is largely ceremonial, but she does have some influence deriving from the traditional veneration of

the House of Orange—from which Dutch monarchs for more than three centuries have been chosen; the personal qualities of the Queen; and her power to appoint the formateur, who forms the Council of Ministers following elections.

The Council of Ministers plans and implements government policy. The Monarch and the Council of Ministers together are called the Crown. Most ministers also head government ministries, although ministers without portfolio exist. The ministers, collectively and individually, are responsible to the States General (parliament). Unlike the British system, Dutch ministers cannot simultaneously be members of parliament.

The Council of State is a constitutionally established advisory body to the government which consists of members of the royal family and crown–appointed members generally having political, commercial, diplomatic, or military experience. The Council of State must be consulted by the cabinet on proposed legislation before a law is submitted to the parliament. The Council of State also serves as a channel of appeal for citizens against executive branch decisions.

**States General (Parliament).** The Dutch parliament consists of two houses, the First Chamber and the Second Chamber. Historically, Dutch governments have been based on the support of a majority in both houses of parliament. The Second Chamber is by far the more important of the two houses. It alone has the right to initiate legislation and amend bills submitted by the Council of Ministers. It shares with the First Chamber the right to question ministers and state secretaries.

The Second Chamber consists of 150 members, elected directly for a 4–year term—unless the government falls prematurely—on the basis of a nationwide system of proportional representation. This system means that members represent the whole country—rather than individual districts as in the United States—and are normally elected on a party slate, not on a personal basis. There is no

threshold for small–party representation. Campaigns usually last 6 weeks, and the election budgets of each party tend to be less than $500,000. The electoral system makes a coalition government almost inevitable. The last election of the Second Chamber was in May 1998.

The First Chamber is composed of 75 members elected for 4–year terms by the 12 provincial legislatures. It cannot initiate or amend legislation, but its approval of bills passed by the Second Chamber is required before bills become law. The First Chamber generally meets only once a week, and its

members usually have other full–time jobs. The current First Chamber was elected following provincial elections in March 1995.

**Courts.** The judiciary comprises 62 cantonal courts, 19 district courts, five courts of appeal, and a Supreme

Court which has 24 justices. All judicial appointments are made by the crown. Judges nominally are appointed for life but actually are retired at age 70.

**Local Government.** The first–level administrative divisions are the 12 provinces, each governed by a locally elected provincial council and a provincial executive appointed by members of the provincial council. The province is formally headed by a queen's commissioner appointed by the crown.

The current government, formed in August 1998, is a three–way "Purple Coalition" of the Labor (PvdA), Liberal (VVD), and Democrats '66 (D'66) parties headed by Prime Minister Kok of the PvdA. The coalition parties hold 97 of the 150 seats in the Second Chamber of Parliament. The main opposition parties are the Christian Democrats with 29 seats, and the Greens with 13 seats. Given the consensus–based nature of Dutch government, elections do not result in any drastic change in foreign or domestic policy. Descriptions of the four main parties follow.

The Labor Party, a European social democratic party, is left of center. Labor has 45 seats in the current Second Chamber, which makes it the largest party. Labor's program is based on greater social, political, and economic equality for all citizens, although in recent years the party has begun to debate the role of central government in that process. Although called the Labor Party, it has no formal links to the trade unions.

The Christian Democratic Appeal was formed from the merger of the Catholic People's Party and two Protestant parties, the Anti–Revolutionary Party and the Christian–Historical Union. The merger process, begun in the early 1970s to try to stem the tide of losses suffered by religiously based parties, was completed in 1980. The CDA supports free enterprise and holds to the principle that government activity should supplement but not supplant communal action by citizens. On the political

spectrum, the CDA sees its philosophy as standing between the "individualism" of the Liberals and the "statism" of the Labor Party. The CDA won 29 seats in the 1998 parliamentary elections, which was a significant drop from 1994. For the first time in 76 years, the CDA was excluded from government.

The Liberal Party is "liberal" in the European, rather than American, sense of the word. It thus attaches great importance to private enterprise and the freedom of the individual in political, social, and economic affairs. The VVD is generally seen as the most conservative of the major parties. The VVD was the junior partner in two governing coalitions with the CDA from 1982–89, and is now in the three–way coalition with 38 seats in the Second Chamber.

Democrats 66, the largest of the "small" parties in the Dutch parliament, has grown in size and influence. The electoral fortunes of D'66 have fluctuated widely since the party's founding in 1966. The 14 seats it currently holds reflect the party's average showing over the last 20 years. D'66 is a center–left party, generally portrayed as between the CDA and PvdA, with its strongest support among young, urban, professional voters. It professes a pro–European platform of ethnic and religious toleration.

## Domestic Drug Policy

The Dutch Government continues to give priority to fighting narcotics trafficking, including the production and trade in XTC and other designer drugs. The XTC action plan, which reflects the serious concern of Dutch authorities about this growing problem, appears to be increasingly effective. A special synthetic–drug unit, set up to coordinate the fight against designer drugs, became operational in 1997. The Dutch Government has also stepped up border controls and intensified cooperation with neighbouring countries.

All illicit drugs are illegal in the Netherlands. The Dutch Opium Act,

however, distinguishes between "hard" drugs, having "unacceptable" risks (heroin, cocaine etc.), and "soft" drugs (canabis). One of the main aims of this policy is to separate the markets for soft and hard drugs so that soft drugs users are less likely to come into contact with hard drugs. The sale of a small quantity (no more than five grams per person) of soft drugs in "coffeeshops" is tolerated, albeit under strict criteria and increasing government control. Although drug abuse is seen primarily as a public health issue in the Netherlands, responsibility for drug policy is shared by both the Ministries of Health, Welfare, and Sports and Justice.

The Netherlands spend more than $150 million on facilities for addicts, of which about 50% goes to drug addicts. The Netherlands has extensive demand reduction programs, reaching about 75% of the country's 25,000 hard drug users. The number of hard drug addicts has stabilized in the past few years and their average age has risen to 36. The number of drug–related deaths in the country remains the lowest in Europe.

## Principal Government Officials

**For up-to-date information on Principal Government Officials, see the Chiefs of State and Cabinet Members of Foreign Governments section starting on page 1.**

The Netherlands' embassy in the U.S. is at 4200 Wisconsin Ave., NW, Washington, DC 20016; tel: 202–244–5300; fax: 202–362–3430.

# ECONOMY

After growing above the trend rate for several years, the Dutch economy is currently showing sings of weakening activity and growing tension in the labor market. The economy peaked in 1998, with strong 4% consumer–spending led GDP growth, sharply falling unemployment, and modest inflation. Slackening world demand is forecast to dampen business investment while causing export growth to decelerate. This will lead the economy to slow to 2% GDP growth in 1999 and 2000. The economic slowdown is likely to affect the labor market and cause unemployment to edge up to roughly 5% of the labor force in 1999. Decelerating import prices will, on the other hand, soften consumer price inflation from 2% in 1998 to slightly over 1% in 1999 and 2000. A current account surplus of more than 6% of GDP continues as one of the strong features of the Dutch economy. The Netherlands is firmly committed to Economic and Monetary Union (EMU), and public finances are well within the official and EMU targets. Dutch fiscal policy aims at striking a balance between a further reduction of public spending and lowering taxes and social security contributions. The fiscal deficit is expected to stabilize at 1.75% in 1999. The stock of public debt is forecast to fall from a high of 67.3% in 1998 to 67.1% in 1999 and 2000.

## Government Role

Although the private sector is the cornerstone of the economy, the Netherlands has an important and vibrant public sector. The Government plays a significant role through the many permit requirements and regulations pertaining to almost every aspect of economic activity. Public spending, including social security transfer payments and subsidy programs, still accounts for more than 50% of GDP. The Government has gradually reduced its role in the economy since the 1980s, and privatization and deregulation continue with little debate or opposition.

## Trade and Investment

The Netherlands, which derives more than two–thirds of its GDP from merchandise trade, continues to have a strongly positive balance of payments for 1999 estimated at $30 billion – 4% of GDP, the main contributor to a current account surplus of close to 6% of GDP. Since there are no significant trade or investment barriers, the Netherlands remains a receptive market for U.S. exports and an important investment partner. The Netherlands is the eighth–largest U.S. export market, as well as the third–largest direct investor in the United States, behind the United Kingdom and Japan. Dutch accumulated direct investment in the United States in 1997 was $85 billion. The United States is the largest investor in the Netherlands with direct investment of $65 billion. There are more than 1,600 U.S. companies with subsidiaries or offices in the Netherlands. The Dutch are strong proponents of free trade and the staunchest allies of the U.S. in international fora such as the World Trade Organization (WTO) and the OECD.

## Sectors of the Economy

Services account for more than half of the national income and are primarily in transportation, distribution, and logistics, and in financial areas, such as banking and insurance. Industrial activity (including mining) generates about 20% of the national product and is dominated by the metalworking, oil refining, chemical, and food–processing industries. Construction amounts to about 6% of GDP. Agriculture and fishing, although visible and traditional Dutch activities, account for just 4%.

Although Dutch crude oil production is insignificant, the Netherlands ranks among the largest producers and distributors of natural gas. The Slochteren gasfields in Groningen Province are among the world's largest producing natural gasfields. At present, total proven natural gas reserves—on the mainland and on the North Sea continental shelf—amount to close to 2 trillion cubic meters, of which about 80% is accounted for by reserves on the mainland. Current gas production is running at an annual average of about 80 billion cubic meters, roughly half of which is exported to EU member countries. General government revenues from natural gas totaled about $2 billion in 1997.

## Environmental Policy

The Netherlands is a small and densely populated country. Its economy depends on industry, particularly chemicals and metal processing, intensive agriculture and horticulture, and on its infrastructure which takes advantage of the country's geographical position at the heart of Europe's transportation network. These factors have led to major pressure on the environment.

The National Environmental Policy Plan (NMP) sets out Dutch environmental policy. The first version was published in 1989, followed by second and third versions in 1993 and 1998, respectively. Under the NMP, the government seeks to cut back on all forms of pollution by 80–90% within one generation, meaning that by 2010 the present generation should be able to pass on a clean enviroment to the next one.

Although the environmental quality in the Netherland has improved significantly, some important targets, particularly with respect to NOX and ammonia emissions, climate change, and noise reduction, will not be realized within the timeframe set in the NMPs. The main reason for this is the close relation between economic growth and its negative effects on the environment. The NMP–3, therefore, proposes drastic measures in order to be able to meet the targets.

The Dutch government works closely with industry and NGOs on implementation of environmental policy. To be able to reach environmental targets, the government has signed agreements with the private sector and other relevant organizations.

# FOREIGN RELATIONS

The Netherlands abandoned its traditional policy of neutrality after World War II. The Dutch have since become engaged participants in international affairs. Dutch foreign policy is geared to promoting a variety of goals: transatlanticism; European integration; Third World development; and respect for international law, human rights, and democracy. The Dutch Government conducted a review of foreign policy main themes, organization, and funding in 1995. The document "The Foreign Policy of the Netherlands: A Review" outlined the new direction of Dutch foreign policy. The Netherlands prioritizes enhancing European integration, maintaining relations with neighboring states, ensuring European security and stability (mainly through the mechanism of NATO and emphasizing the important role the United States plays in the security of Europe), and participating in conflict management, and peacekeeping missions. The foreign policy review also resulted in the reorganization of the Ministry of Foreign Affairs. Through the creation of Regional Departments, the Ministry coordinates tasks previously divided among the International Cooperation, Foreign Affairs, and Economic Affairs sections.

As a relatively small country, the Netherlands generally pursues its foreign policy interests within the framework of multilateral organizations. The Netherlands is an active and responsible participant in the United Nations system as well as other multilateral organizations such as the Organization for Security and Cooperation in Europe (OSCE), Organization for Economic Cooperation and Development (OECD), World Trade Organization (WTO), and International Monetary Fund. A centuries–old tradition of legal scholarship has made the Netherlands the home of the International Court of Justice; the Iran Claims Tribunal; the Yugoslavia and Rwanda War Crime Tribunals; and the European police organization, Europol.

Dutch security policy is based primarily on membership in NATO, which the Netherlands joined in 1949. The Dutch also pursue defense cooperation within Europe, both multilaterally—in the context of the Western European Union—and bilaterally—as in the German–Netherlands Corps. In recent years, the Dutch have become significant contributors to United Nations peacekeeping efforts around the world.

The Dutch have been strong advocates of European integration, and most aspects of their foreign, economic, and trade policies are coordinated through the EU. The Netherlands' postwar customs union with Belgium and Luxembourg (the Benelux group) paved the way for the formation of the European Community (precursor to the EU), of which the Netherlands was a founding member. Likewise, the Benelux abolition of internal border controls was a model for the wider Schengen Accord, which today has 10 European signatories—including the Netherlands—pledged to common visa policies and free movement of people across common borders.

The Dutch stood at the cradle of the 1992 Maastricht Treaty and have been the architects of the Treaty of Amsterdam concluded in 1998. The Dutch thus have been playing an important role in European political and monetary integration. A Dutchman currently heads the European Central Bank (ECB) and the Dutch will continue to play an important role in further economic and monetary intergration in the EU.

## Foreign Aid

The Netherlands is among the world's leading aid donors, giving about 1% of its gross national product in development assistance. The country consistently contributes large amounts of aid through multilateral channels, especially the UN Development Program, the international financial institutions, and EU programs. A large portion of Dutch aid funds also are channeled through private ("co–financing") organizations that have almost total autonomy in choice of projects.

In 1998, Dutch development assistance—as defined by the OECD—was about $3 billion. The policy priorities of Dutch aid for 1998 are basic social facilities, reproductive health care, the environment, and aid to least developed countries. Dutch aid is also

targeted on emergency aid, programs for the private sector, and international education.

The Netherlands is a member of the European Bank for Reconstruction and Development, which recently initiated economic reforms in Central Europe. The Dutch strongly support the Middle East Peace Process and in 1998 earmarked $29 million in contributions to international donor–coordinated activities for the occupied territories and also for projects in which they worked directly with Palestinian authorities. These projects included improving environmental conditions and support for multilateral programs in cooperation with local non–governmental organizations. In 1998, the Dutch provided significant amounts of aid to former Yugoslavia and Africa. The Dutch also provided significant amounts of relief aid to victims of hurricane Mitch in Central America.

## International Drug–Trafficking Control

Narcotics trafficking is a global issue that the Netherlands has deemed a priority. The Netherlands is considered a major transit point for narcotics; it has a large international airport hub, and Rotterdam is the world's largest container port. The Dutch Government has been working to tighten controls on its airports and harbors.

The Dutch also work closely with the U.S. and other countries on international programs against drug trafficking and organized crime. The Netherlands is a signatory to international counter–narcotics agreements, a member of the UN International Drug Control Program, the UN Commission on Narcotic Drugs, and is a leading contributor to international counter–narcotics projects.

# U.S.-NETHERLANDS RELATIONS

The United States' partnership with the Netherlands is its oldest continuous relationship and dates back to the American revolution. The excellent bilateral relations are based on close historical and cultural ties and a common dedication to individual freedom and human rights. An outward–looking nation, the Netherlands shares with the U.S. a commitment to an open market and free trade. The U.S. attaches great value to its strong economic and commercial ties with the Dutch. The Netherlands is the United States' eighth–largest export market. The

U.S. currently runs an annual trade surplus with the Netherlands of more than $11 billion. The Netherlands is the third–largest direct investor in the U.S. ($85 billion in 1997). The U.S. is the largest direct foreign investor in the Netherlands ($65 billion in 1997).

The United States and the Netherlands often have similar positions on issues and work together bilaterally and through the UN and other multilateral organizations on matters concerning NATO. The Dutch have worked with the U.S. in the Uruguay round, at the WTO, in the OECD, and within the EU to advance the main U.S. goal of a more open, honest, and market–led global economy. The Dutch play a decisive role in European political and monetary integration. The Dutch also strongly support keeping EU markets open to CEE and expanding the EU eastward, both of which are major U.S. goals.

The Dutch were among the first to join the GLOBE Project, initiated by Vice President Gore, under which schools around the world cooperate in collecting environmental data and

entering it into a computer network for use by scientists and other researchers. The Clinton Administration works closely with the Dutch on climate change, biodiversity issues, global deforestation, the sustainable development of rainforests, ozone layer depletion, and trade and environment issues.

## Principal U.S. Embassy Officials

**For up-to-date information on Principal U.S. Officials, see the U.S. Embassies, Consulates, and Foreign Service section starting on page 139.**

For up-to-date information on Principal U.S. Officials, see the U.S. Embassies, Consulates, and Foreign Service section starting on page 139.

The U.S. Embassy is located at Lange Voorhout 102, 2514 EJ The Hague; tel: 31–70–310–9209; fax: 31–70–361–4688. The Consulate General is at Museumplein 13, 1071 DJ Amsterdam; tel: 31–20–5755– 309; fax: 31–20–5755–310.

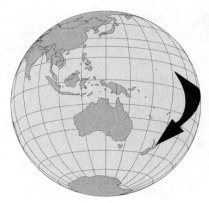

# NEW ZEALAND

October 2000

Official Name:
**New Zealand**

# PROFILE

## Geography

**Area:** 270,534 sq. km. (104,440 sq. mi.); about the size of Colorado.
**Cities:** (2000) Capital—Wellington (346,000). Other cities—Auckland (1,090,000), Christchurch (341,000), Hamilton (169,000).
**Terrain:** Highly varied, from snow-capped mountains to lowland plains.
**Climate:** Temperate to subtropical.

## People

**Nationality:** Noun—New Zealander(s). Adjective—New Zealand.
**Population:** (2000) 3,829,600.
**Annual growth rate:** (2000) 0.5%.
**Ethnic Groups:** European 75%, Maori 14.5%, other Polynesian 5.6%.
**Religion:** Anglican 18%, Presbyterian 13%, Roman Catholic 14%.
**Languages:** English, Maori.
**Education:** Years compulsory—ages 6-16. Attendance—100%. Literacy—99%.
**Health:** (1996) Infant mortality rate—7.3/1,000. Life expectancy—males 73 yrs., females 79 yrs.
**Work force:** (2000, 1.8 million) Services and government—68%; manufacturing and construction—23%; agriculture, forestry and mining—8%.

## Government

**Type:** Parliamentary.
**Constitution:** No formal, written constitution.
**Independence:** Declared a dominion in 1907.
**Branches:** Executive—Queen Elizabeth II (chief of state, represented by a governor general), prime minister (head of government), cabinet. Legislative—unicameral House of Representatives, commonly called parliament. Judicial—three-level system: District Courts, the High Court, and the Court of Appeals, with further appeal possible to the Judicial Committee of the Privy Council. There also are specialized courts, such as employment court, family courts, youth courts, and the Maori Land Court.
**Administrative subdivisions:** 12 regions with directly elected councils and 74 districts (15 of which are designated as cities) with elected councils. There are also a number of community boards and special-purpose bodies with partially elected, partially appointed memberships.
**Political parties:** Labour, National, the Alliance, New Zealand Green Party, New Zealand First, ACT, United New Zealand, and several smaller parties not represented in Parliament.
**Suffrage:** Universal at 18.

## Economy

**GDP:** (1999) $53.4 billion.
**Real annual GDP growth rate:** (1999) 3.4%.
**Per capita income:** (1999) $14,008.
**Natural resources:** Natural gas, iron sand, coal, timber.
**Agriculture:** (9.7% of GDP) Products—meat, dairy products, forestry products, wool.
**Industry:** (46.1% of GDP) Types—food processing, textiles, machinery, transport equipment, fish, forestry products.
**Trade:** (1999) Exports—$12 billion: meat, dairy products, manufactured products, forest products, fish, fruit and vegetables, wool. Major markets—Australia, U.S., Japan, U.K. Imports—$12 billion: machinery, manufactured goods, transportation equipment, chemicals, mineral fuels. Major suppliers—Australia, U.S., Japan, U.K.

# PEOPLE

Most of the 3.8 million New Zealanders are of British origin. About 15% claim descent from the indigenous Maori population, which is of Polynesian origin. Nearly 75% of the people, including a large majority of Maori, live on the North Island. In addition, 167,000 Pacific Islanders also live in New Zealand. During the late 1870s, natural increase permanently replaced immigration as the chief contributor to population growth and has accounted for more than 75% of population growth in the 20th century. Nearly 85% of New Zealand's population lives in urban areas (with almost one-third in Auckland alone), where the service and manufacturing industries are growing rapidly. New Zealanders colloquially refer to themselves as "Kiwis," after the country' native bird.

# HISTORY

Archaeological evidence indicates that New Zealand was populated by fishing and hunting people of East Polynesian ancestry perhaps 1,000 years before Europeans arrived. Known to some scholars as the Moahunters, they may have merged with later waves of Polynesians who, according to Maori tradition, arrived between 952 and 1150. Some of the Maoris called their new homeland "Aotearoa," usually translated as "land of the long white cloud."

In 1642, Abel Tasman, a Dutch navigator, made the first recorded European sighting of New Zealand and sketched sections of the two main islands' west coasts. English Captain James Cook thoroughly explored the coastline during three South Pacific voyages beginning in 1769. In the late 18th and early 19th centuries, lumbering, seal hunting, and whaling attracted a few European settlers to New Zealand. In 1840, the United Kingdom established British sovereignty through the Treaty of Waitangi signed that year with Maori chiefs.

In the same year, selected groups from the United Kingdom began the colonization process. Expanding European settlement led to conflict with Maori, most notably in the Maori land wars of the 1860s. British and colonial forces eventually overcame determined Maori resistance. During this period, many Maori died from disease and warfare, much of it intertribal.

Constitutional government began to develop in the 1850s. In 1867, Maori won the right to a certain number of reserved seats in parliament. During this period, the livestock industry began to expand, and the foundations of New Zealand's modern economy took shape. By the end of the 19th century, improved transportation facilities made possible a great overseas trade in wool, meat, and dairy products.

By the 1890s, parliamentary government along democratic lines was well- established, and New Zealand's social institutions assumed their present form. Women received the right to vote in national elections in 1893. The turn of the century brought sweeping social reforms that built the foundation for New Zealand's version of the welfare state.

Maori gradually recovered from population decline and, through interaction and intermarriage with settlers and missionaries, adopted much of European culture. In recent decades, Maori have become increasingly urbanized and have become more politically active and culturally assertive.

New Zealand was declared a dominion by a royal proclamation in 1907. It achieved full internal and external autonomy by the Statute of Westminster Adoption Act in 1947, although this merely formalized a situation that had existed for many years.

# GOVERNMENT

New Zealand has a parliamentary system of government closely patterned on that of the United Kingdom and is a fully independent member of the Commonwealth. It has no written constitution.

Executive authority is vested in a cabinet led by the prime minister, who is the leader of the political party or coalition of parties holding the majority of seats in parliament. All cabinet ministers must be members of parliament and are collectively responsible to it.

The unicameral parliament (House of Representatives) has 120 seats, six of which currently are reserved for Maori elected on a separate Maori roll. However, Maori also may run for, and have been elected to, nonreserved seats. Parliaments are elected for a maximum term of 3 years, although elections can be called sooner.

The judiciary consists of the Court of Appeals, the High Court, and the District Courts. New Zealand law has three principal sources—English common law, certain statutes of the UK Parliament enacted before 1947, and statutes of the New Zealand Parliament. In interpreting common law, the courts have been concerned with preserving uniformity with common law as interpreted in the United Kingdom.

This uniformity is ensured by the maintenance of the Privy Council in London as the final court of appeal and by judges' practice of following British decisions, even though, technically, they are not bound by them.

Local government in New Zealand has only the powers conferred upon it by parliament. The country's 12 regional councils are directly elected, set their own tax rates, and have a chairman elected by their members. Regional council responsibilities include environmental management, regional aspects of civil defense, and transportation planning. The 74 "territorial authorities"—15 city councils, 58 district councils in rural areas, and one county council for the Chatham Islands—are directly elected, raise local taxes at rates they themselves set, and are headed by popularly elected mayors. The territorial authorities may delegate powers to local community boards. These boards, instituted at the behest either local citizens or territorial authorities, advocate community views but cannot levy taxes, appoint staff, or own property.

## Principal Government Officials

For up-to-date information on Principal Government Officials, see the Chiefs of State and Cabinet Members of Foreign Governments section starting on page 1.

New Zealand maintains an embassy in the United States at 37 Observatory Circle NW, Washington, DC 20008 (tel. 202-328-4800, fax 202-667-5227).

A consulate general is located in Los Angeles (tel. 310-207-1605, fax 310-207-3605).

Tourism information is available through the New Zealand Tourism Board office in Santa Monica, California (toll-free tel. 800-388-5494) or through the following website: http://www.tourisminfo.govt.nz.

# POLITICAL CONDITIONS

The conservative National Party and left-leaning Labour Party have dominated New Zealand political life since a Labour government came to power in 1935. During 14 years in office, the Labour Party implemented a broad array of social and economic legislation, including comprehensive social security, a largescale public works program, a 40-hour work week, a minimum basic wage, and compulsory unionism. The National Party won control of the government in 1949 and adopted many welfare measures instituted by the Labour Party. Except for two brief periods of Labour governments in 1957-60 and 1972-75, National held power until 1984. After regaining control in 1984, the Labour government instituted a series of radical market-oriented reforms in response to New Zealand's mounting external debt. It also enacted anti-nuclear legislation that effectively brought about New Zealand's suspension from the ANZUS security alliance with the United States and Australia.

In October 1990, the National Party again formed the government, for the first of three, 3-year terms. In 1996, New Zealand inaugurated a mixed-member proportional (MMP) system to elect its Parliament. The system was designed to increase representation of smaller parties in Parliament and appears to have done so in the MMP elections to date. Since 1996, neither the National nor the Labour Party has had an absolute majority in Parliament, and for all but one of those years, the government has been a minority one. After 9 years in office, the National Party lost the November 1999 election. Labour outpolled National by 39% to 30% and formed a coalition, minority government with the left-wing Alliance Party. The government relies on support from minor parties (typically the New Zealand Green Party or New Zealand First) to pass legislation.

# ECONOMY

New Zealand's economy has traditionally been based on a foundation of exports from its very efficient agricultural system. Leading agricultural exports include meat, dairy products, forest products, fruit and vegetables, fish, and wool. New Zealand was a direct beneficiary of many of the reforms achieved under the Uruguay Round of trade negotiations, with agriculture in general and the dairy sector in particular enjoying many new trade opportunities. The country has substantial hydroelectric power and sizable reserves of natural gas. Leading manufacturing sectors are food processing, metal fabrication, and wood and paper products.

Since 1984, government subsidies have been eliminated; import regulations have been liberalized; exchange rates have been freely floated; controls on interest rates, wages, and prices have been removed; and marginal rates of taxation reduced. Tight monetary policy and major efforts to reduce the government budget deficit cut inflation from an annual rate of more than 18% in 1987 to about 1.1% in early 2000. The restructuring and sale of government-owned enterprises in the 1990s reduced government's role in the economy and permitted the retirement of some public debt.

Economic growth slowed in 1997 and 1998, due in large part to the negative effects of the Asian financial crisis and two successive years of drought. Real gross domestic product (GDP) growth picked up in 1999, with the economy growing by 4.4% in the year ending March 2000. This compared to flat growth in the preceding 12-month period. The return of substantial economic growth led the unemployment rate to drop from 7.8% in 1999 to 6.6% in early 2000.

Analysts expect growth to slow somewhat in the second half of 2000 and early 2001 in response to low business confidence and the effects of rising oil and import prices. Some of the uncertainty in the economy has been linked to new economic policies of the Labour-Alliance coalition government elected in November 1999. Several of these policies, such as raising the top income tax rate, renationalizing the accident compensation scheme and overhauling labor relations laws, were strongly opposed by the business sector. The substantial depreciation of the NZ dollar, which fell over 20% in value against the U.S. dollar in the first 9 months of 2000, should boost export growth in 2001 and compensate for the weak domestic sector. The large current account deficit, which stood at over eight percent of GDP in 2000, has been a constant source of concern for NZ policy makers. The rebound in the export sector is expected to help narrow the deficit to lower levels.

New Zealand's economy has been helped by strong economic relations with Australia. Australia and New Zealand are partners in "Closer Economic Relations" (CER), which allows for free trade in goods and most services. Since 1990, CER has created a single market of more than 22 million people, and this has provided new opportunities for New Zealand exporters. Australia is now the destination of 21% of New Zealand's exports, compared to 14% in 1983. Both sides also have agreed to con-

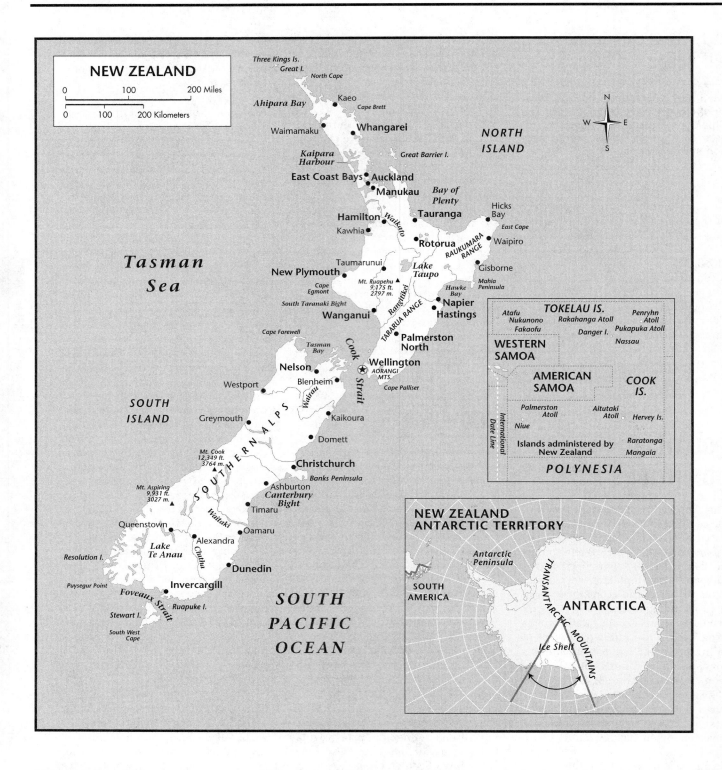

**NEW ZEALAND**

sider extending CER to product standardization and taxation policy. New Zealand initialed a free trade agreement with Singapore in September 2000 and is seeking other bilateral/regional trade agreements in the Pacific area.

U.S. goods and services have been competitive in New Zealand, though the strong U.S. dollar has created challenges for U.S. exporters in 2000. The market-led economy offers many opportunities for U.S. exporters and investors. Investment opportunities exist in chemicals, food preparation, finance, tourism, and forest products, as well as in franchising. The best sales prospects are for medical equipment, information technology, and general consumer goods. On the agricultural side, the best prospects are for fresh fruit, snack foods, and soy-bean meal.

New Zealand welcomes and encourages foreign investment without discrimination. The Overseas Investment Commission (OIC) must give consent to foreign investments that would control 25% of more of businesses or property worth more than NZ$ 50 million. Restrictions and approval requirements also apply to certain investments in land and in the commercial fishing industry. In practice, OIC approval requirements have not been an obstacle for U.S. investors. OIC consent is based on a national interest determination, but no performance requirements are attached to foreign direct investment after consent is given. Full remittance of profits and capital is permitted through normal banking channels.

A number of U.S. companies have subsidiary branches in New Zealand. Many operate through local agents, and some are in association in joint ventures. The American Chamber of Commerce is active in New Zealand, with its main office in Auckland and a branch committee in Wellington.

# NATIONAL SECURITY

New Zealand has three defense policy objectives: defend New Zealand against low-level threats; contribute to regional security; and play a part in global security efforts. New Zealand considers its own national defense needs to be modest. Its defense budget provides for selected upgrades in equipment, most of which is devoted to the army. Shortly after winning the 1999 election, the Labour government cancelled a lease-to-buy agreement with the U.S. for 28 F-16 aircraft, and in September 2000 scrubbed a planned upgrade of its P3-C aircraft. New Zealand states it maintains a "credible minimum force," although critics maintain that the country's defense forces have fallen below this standard. With a claimed area of direct strategic concern that extends from Australia to Southeast Asia to the South Pacific,

and with defense expenditures that total around 1% of GDP, New Zealand necessarily places substantial reliance on its defense relationship with other countries, in particular Australia.

New Zealand is an active participant in multilateral peacekeeping. It has taken a leading role in trying to bring peace, reconciliation, and reconstruction to the Solomon Islands and the neighboring island of Bougainville. New Zealand maintains a contingent in the Sinai Multinational Force and Observers and has contributed to UN peacekeeping operations in Angola, Cambodia, Somalia, and the former Yugoslavia. It also participated in the Multilateral Interception Force in the Persian Gulf. New Zealand's most recent PKO experience has been in East Timor, where it initially dispatched almost 10% of its entire defense force and continues to be the second largest force contributor.

New Zealand participates in Mutual Assistance Programs (MAP), sharing training facilities, personnel exchanges, and joint exercises with the Philippines, Thailand, Indonesia, Papua New Guinea, Malaysia, Singapore, Brunei, Tonga, and other South Pacific states. It also exercises with its Five-Power Defense Arrangement partners (Australia, the United Kingdom, Malaysia, and Singapore), as well as with Korea. Due to New Zealand's anti-nuclear policy, defense cooperation with the U.S., including training exercises has been significantly restricted since 1986.

# FOREIGN RELATIONS

New Zealand's foreign policy is oriented chiefly toward developed democratic nations and emerging Pacific economies. The country's major political parties have generally agreed on the broad outlines of foreign policy, and the current coalition government has been active in multilateral fora on issues of recurring interest to New Zealand: trade liberalization, disarmament, and arms control. New Zealand values the United Nations

and its participation in that organization.

It also values its participation in the World Trade Organization (WTO); World Bank; International Monetary Fund (IMF); Organization for Economic Cooperation and Development (OECD); International Energy Agency; Asian Development Bank; South Pacific Forum; The Pacific Community; Colombo Plan; Asia Pacific Economic Cooperation (APEC); INTELSAT; and the International Whaling Commission. New Zealand also is an active member of the Commonwealth. Despite the 1985 rupture in the ANZUS alliance, New Zealand has maintained good working relations with the United States and Australia on a broad array of international issues. In the past, New Zealand's geographic isolation and its agricultural economy's general prosperity tended to minimize public interest in world affairs. However, growing global trade and other international economic events have made New Zealanders increasingly aware of their country's dependence on stable overseas markets.

New Zealand's economic involvement with Asia has been increasingly important, first through aid, mainly to Southeast Asia, and through expanding trade with the growing economies of Asia. New Zealand is a "dialogue partner" with the Association of South East Asian Nations (ASEAN) and an active participant in APEC.

As a charter member of the Colombo Plan, New Zealand has provided Asian countries with technical assistance and capital. It also contributes through the Asian Development Bank and through UN programs and is a member of the UN Economic and Social Council for Asia and the Pacific.

New Zealand has focused its bilateral economic assistance resources on projects in the South Pacific island states, especially on Bougainville. The country's long association with Samoa (formerly known as Western Samoa), reflected in a treaty of friendship signed in 1962, and its close association with Tonga have resulted in a flow of immigrants and visitors under work permit schemes from both countries. New Zealand administers the Tokelau Islands and provides foreign policy and economic support when requested for the freely associated self-governing states of the Cook Islands and Niue. Inhabitants of these areas hold New Zealand citizenship.

In 1947, New Zealand joined Australia, France, the United Kingdom, and the United States to form the South Pacific Commission, a regional body to promote the welfare of the Pacific region. New Zealand has been a leader in the organization. In 1971, New Zealand joined the other independent and self-governing states of the South Pacific to establish the South Pacific Forum (now known as the Pacific Islands Forum), which meets annually at the "heads of government" level.

# U.S.-NEW ZEALAND RELATIONS

Bilateral relations are excellent. The United States and New Zealand share common elements of history and culture and a commitment to democratic principles. Senior-level officials regularly consult with each on issues of mutual importance.

The United States established consular representation in New Zealand in 1839 to represent and protect American shipping and whaling interests. Since the U.K. was responsible for New Zealand's foreign affairs, direct U.S.-New Zealand diplomatic ties were not established until 1942, when the Japanese threat encouraged close U.S.-New Zealand cooperation in the Pacific campaign. During the war, more than 400,000 American military personnel were stationed in New Zealand to help bolster its defenses and to prepare for crucial battles such as Tarawa and Guadalcanal.

## Travel Notes

**Travel Advice:** For up-to-date information from the U.S. State Department on possible inconvenient or hazardous situations, see the **Travel Warnings and Consular Information Sheets from the U.S. Government** section starting on page 1723. For the latest information on health requirements and conditions, see the **International Travelers' Health Information** section starting on page 1385. For further information dealing with non-urgent matter, see the **Tips for Travelers to...** section starting on page 1588.

New Zealand's relationship with the United States in the post-World War II period was closely associated with the Australian, New Zealand, United States (ANZUS) security treaty of 1951, under which signatories agreed to consult in case of an attack in the Pacific and to "act to meet the common danger." During the postwar period, access to New Zealand ports by U.S. vessels contributed significantly to the flexibility and effectiveness of U.S. naval forces in the Pacific.

Growing concern about nuclear testing in the South Pacific and arms control issues contributed to the 1984 election of a Labour government committed to barring nuclear-armed and nuclear-powered warships from New Zealand ports. The government's anti-nuclear policy proved incompatible with longstanding, worldwide U.S. policy of neither confirming nor denying the presence or absence of nuclear weapons onboard U.S. vessels.

Implementation of New Zealand's policy effectively prevented practical alliance cooperation under ANZUS, and after extensive efforts to resolve the issue proved unsuccessful, in August 1986 the United States suspended its ANZUS security obligations to New Zealand. Even after President Bush's 1991 announcement that U.S. surface ships do not normally carry nuclear weapons, New Zealand's legislation prohibiting

visits of nuclear-powered ships continues to preclude a bilateral security alliance with the U.S. The United States would welcome New Zealand's reassessment of its legislation to permit that country's return to full ANZUS cooperation.

Despite suspension of U.S. security obligations, the New Zealand Government has reaffirmed the importance it attaches to continued close political, economic, and social ties with the United States and Australia. The United States is New Zealand's second-largest trading partner after Australia. Total bilateral trade for 1999 was $4.1 billion (with a $545 million surplus in favor of the U.S.) and U.S. merchandise exports to New Zealand were $2.3 billion. U.S. direct foreign investment in New Zealand (as of March 2000) totaled $6.2 billion, largely concentrated in manufacturing, forestry, telecommunications services, transportation, and finance.

New Zealand has worked closely with the U.S. to promote free trade in the GATT/WTO, the Asia-Pacific Economic Cooperation (APEC) forum, and other multilateral fora.

The U.S. and New Zealand work together closely on scientific research in the Antarctic. Christchurch is the staging area for joint logistical support operations serving U.S. permanent bases at McMurdo Station and South Pole, and New Zealand's one base, (located just three kilometers from McMurdo Station in the Ross Sea region).

## Principal U.S. Embassy Officials

For up-to-date information on Principal U.S. Officials, see the U.S. Embassies, Consulates, and Foreign Service section starting on page 139.

The U.S. Embassy in New Zealand is located at 29 Fitzherbert Terrace, Thorndon, Wellington (tel. 64-4-472-2068, fax 64-4-471-2380).
The Embassy website is http://usembassy.state.gov/wellington.
The U.S. Consulate General is located on the 3rd Floor, Citibank Building, 23 Customs Street East, Auckland (tel. 64-9-303-2724, fax 64-9-366-0870).

For information on foreign economic trends, commercial development, production, trade regulations, and tariff rates, contact the Bureau of Export Development, International Trade Administration, U.S. Department of Commerce, Washington, DC 20230. This information also is available from any Commerce Department district office.

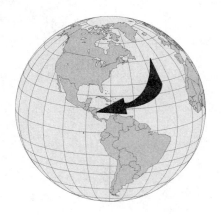

# NICARAGUA

September 2000

## Official Name:
## Republic of Nicaragua

# PROFILE

## Geography

**Area:** 130,688 sq. km. (50,446 sq. mi.); slightly larger than New York State.
**Cities:** Capital—Managua (pop. 1 million). Other cities—Leon, Granada, Jinotega, Matagalpa, Chinandega, Masaya.
**Terrain:** Extensive Atlantic coastal plains rising to central interior mountains; narrow Pacific coastal plain interrupted by volcanoes.
**Climate:** Tropical in lowlands; cooler in highlands.

## People

**Nationality:** Noun and adjective—Nicaraguan(s).
**Population:** (1999 est.) 4.7 million.
**Annual growth rate:** (1999 est.) 2.84%. Density—33 per sq. km.
**Ethnic Groups:** Mestizo (mixed European and indigenous) 69%, white 17%, black (Jamaican origin) 9%, indigenous 5%.
**Religion:** Roman Catholic 95%.
**Languages:** Spanish (official), English and indigenous languages on Caribbean coast.
**Education:** Years compulsory—none enforced (28% first graders eventually finish sixth grade). Literacy—75%.

**Health:** Life expectancy—62 yrs. Infant mortality rate—50/1,000.
**Work force:** (1996) 1.7 million. Unemployed—14%. Underemployed—36%.

## Government

**Type:** Republic.
**Independence:** 1821.
**Constitution:** The 1995 reforms to the 1987 Sandinista-era Constitution provide for a more even distribution of power among the four branches of government.
**Branches:** Executive—president and vice president. Legislative—National Assembly (unicameral). Judicial—Supreme Court; subordinate appeals, district and local courts; separate labor and administrative tribunals. Electoral—Supreme Electoral Council, responsible for organizing and holding elections.
**Administrative subdivisions:** 15 departments and two autonomous regions on the Atlantic coast; 145 municipalities.
**Major political parties:** Liberal Alliance (AL), Sandinista National Liberation Front (FSLN).
**Suffrage:** Universal at 16.

## Economy

**GDP:** (1996) $2.3 billion.
**Annual growth rate:** (1998 est.) 4.0%.

**Per capita GDP:** (1998 est.) $438.
**Inflation rate:** (1998 est.) 16%.
**Natural resources:** Arable land, livestock, fisheries, gold, timber.
**Agriculture:** (32% of GDP) Products—corn, coffee, sugar, meat, rice, beans, bananas.
**Industry:** (24% of GDP) Types—processed food, beverages, textiles, petroleum, and metal products.
**Services:** (44% of GDP) Types—commerce, construction, government, banking, transportation, and energy.
**Trade:** (1997) Exports—$704 million (FOB) coffee, seafood, beef, sugar, industrial goods, gold, bananas, sesame. Markets—U.S. 43%, European Union 33%, Central American Common Market (CACM) 17%, Mexico 2%. Imports—$1.45 billion (FOB 1997) petroleum, agricultural supplies, manufactured goods. Suppliers—U.S. 32%, CACM 21%, Venezuela 11%, European Union 9%.

# PEOPLE

Most Nicaraguans have both European and Indian ancestry, and the culture of the country reflects the Ibero-European and Indian heritage of its people. Only the Indians of the eastern half of the country remain ethnically distinct and retain tribal customs and languages. A large black minority (of Jamaican origin) is concentrated on the Caribbean coast. In the mid-1980s, the central government divided the eastern half of the country—the former department of Zelaya—into two autonomous regions and granted the people of the region limited self-rule. The 1995 constitutional reform guaranteed the integrity of the regions' several unique cultures and gave the inhabitants a say in the use of the area's natural resources. Roman Catholicism is the major religion, but Evangelical Protestant groups have grown recently, and there are strong Anglican and Moravian communities on the Caribbean coast. Most Nicaraguans live in the Pacific lowlands and the adjacent interior highlands. The population is 54% urban.

# HISTORY

Nicaragua takes its name from Nicarao, chief of the indigenous tribe then living around present-day Lake Nicaragua. In 1524, Hernandez de Cordoba founded the first Spanish permanent settlements in the region, including two of Nicaragua's two principal towns: Granada on Lake Nicaragua and Leon east of Lake Managua. Nicaragua gained independence from Spain in 1821, briefly becoming a part of the Mexican Empire and then a member of a federation of independent Central American provinces. In 1838, Nicaragua became an independent republic.

Much of Nicaragua's politics since independence has been characterized by the rivalry between the Liberal elite of Leon and the Conservative elite of Granada, which often spilled into civil war. Initially invited by the Liberals in 1855 to join their struggle against the Conservatives, an American named William Walker and his "filibusters" seized the presidency in 1856. The Liberals and Conservatives united to drive him out of office in 1857, after which a period of three decades of Conservative rule ensued.

Taking advantage of divisions within the Conservative ranks, Jose Santos Zelaya led a Liberal revolt that brought him to power in 1893. Zelaya ended the longstanding dispute with Britain over the Atlantic Coast in 1894, and reincorporated that region into Nicaragua. However, due to differences over an isthmian canal and concessions to Americans in Nicaragua as well as a concern for what was perceived as Nicaragua's destabilizing influence in the region, in 1909 the United States provided political support to Conservative-led forces rebelling against President Zelaya and intervened militarily to protect American lives and property. Zelaya resigned later that year. With the exception of a 9-month period in 1925-26, the United States maintained troops in Nicaragua from 1912 until 1933. From 1927 until 1933, U.S. marines stationed in Nicaragua engaged in a running battle with rebel forces led by renegade Liberal General Augusto Sandino, who rejected a 1927 negotiated agreement brokered by the United States to end the latest round of fighting between Liberals and Conservatives.

After the departure of U.S. troops, National Guard Cmdr. Anastasio Somoza Garcia out maneuvered his political opponents, including Sandino, who was assassinated by National Guard officers, and took over the presidency in 1936. Somoza, and two sons who succeeded him, maintained close ties with the U.S. The Somoza dynasty ended in 1979 with a massive uprising led by the Sandinista National Liberation Front (FSLN), which, since the early 1960s, had conducted a lowscale guerrilla war against the Somoza regime.

The FSLN established an authoritarian dictatorship soon after taking power. U.S.-Nicaraguan relations deteriorated rapidly as the regime nationalized many private industries, confiscated private property, supported Central American guerrilla movements, and maintained links to international terrorists. The United States suspended aid to Nicaragua in 1981. The Reagan Administration provided assistance to the Nicaraguan Resistance and in 1985 imposed an embargo on U.S.-Nicaraguan trade.

In response to both domestic and international pressure, the Sandinista regime entered into negotiations with the Nicaraguan Resistance and agreed to nationwide elections in February 1990. In these elections, which were proclaimed free and fair by international observers, Nicaraguan voters elected as their president the candidate of the National Opposition Union, Violeta Barrios de Chamorro.

During President Chamorro's nearly 7 years in office, her government achieved major progress toward consolidating democratic institutions, advancing national reconciliation, stabilizing the economy, privatizing state-owned enterprises, and reducing human rights violations. In February 1995, Sandinista Popular Army Cmdr. Gen. Humberto Ortega was replaced, in accordance with a new military code enacted in 1994 by Gen. Joaquin Cuadra, who has espoused a policy of greater professionalism in the renamed Army of Nicaragua. A new police organization law, passed by the National Assembly and signed into law in August 1996, further codified both civilian control of the police and the professionalization of that law enforcement agency.

The October 20, 1996 presidential, legislative, and mayoral elections also were judged free and fair by international observers and by the ground-breaking national electoral observer group Eticay Transparencia—Ethics and Transparency—despite a number of irregularities, due largely to logistical difficulties and a baroquely complicated electoral law. This time Nicaraguans elected former-Managua Mayor Arnoldo Aleman, leader of the center-right Liberal Alliance. More than 76% of Nicaragua's 2.4 million eligible voters participated in the elections. The first transfer of power in recent Nicaraguan history from one democratically elected president to another took place on January 10, 1997, when the Aleman government was inaugurated.

# GOVERNMENT AND POLITICAL CONDITIONS

Nicaragua is a constitutional democracy with executive, legislative, judicial, and electoral branches of government. In 1995, the executive and legislative branches negotiated a reform of the 1987 Sandinista constitution which gave impressive new powers and independence to the legislature—the National Assembly—including permitting the Assembly to override a presidential veto with a simple majority vote and eliminating the president's ability to pocket veto a bill. Both the president and the members of the unicameral National Assembly are elected to concurrent 5-year terms. The National Assembly consists of 90 deputies elected from party lists drawn at the department and national level, plus the defeated presidential candidates who obtained a minimal quotient of votes. In the 1996 elections, the Liberal Alliance won a plurality of 42 seats, the FSLN won 36 seats, and nine other political parties and alliances won the remaining 15 seats.

The Supreme Court supervises the functioning of the still largely ineffective and overburdened judicial system. As part of the 1995 constitutional reforms, the independence of the Supreme Court was strengthened by increasing the number of magistrates from 9 to 12. Supreme Court justices are elected to 7-year terms by the National Assembly.

Led by a council of five magistrates, the Supreme Electoral Council is the coequal branch of government responsible for organizing and conducting elections, plebiscites, and referendums. The magistrates and their alternates are elected to 5-year terms by the National Assembly.

Freedom of speech is a right guaranteed by the Nicaraguan constitution and vigorously exercised by its people. Diverse viewpoints are freely and openly discussed in the media and in academia. There is no state censorship in Nicaragua. Other constitutional freedoms include peaceful assembly and association, freedom of religion, and freedom of movement within the country, as well as foreign travel, emigration, and repatriation. The government also permits domestic and international human rights monitors to operate freely in Nicaragua. The constitution prohibits discrimination based on birth, nationality, political belief, race, gender, language, religion, opinion, national origin, economic condition, or social condition. All public and private sector workers, except the military and the police, are entitled to form and join unions of their own choosing, and they exercise this right extensively. Nearly half of Nicaragua's work force, including agricultural workers, is unionized. Workers have the right to strike. Collective bargaining is becoming more common in the private sector.

## Political Parties

In all, Nicaragua's 35 political parties participated in the 1996 elections, independently or as part of one of five electoral coalitions. With nearly 52% of the vote, the Liberal Alliance, a coalition of five political parties and sectors of another two, won the presidency, a plurality in the national legislature, and a large majority of the mayoral races. The FSLN ended in second place with 38%. Most other parties fared poorly. A new political party, the Nicaraguan Christian Path, ended a distant third with 4% of the vote and four seats in the 93-member National Assembly. The traditional alternative to the Liberals, the National Conservative Party, ended in fourth place with slightly over 2% of the vote and three seats in the National Assembly. The remaining 24 parties and alliances together obtained less than 5% of the vote. Seven of these smaller parties control eight seats in the National Assembly. Only two of 145 mayors belong to third parties.

According to Nicaraguan law, those political parties that did not win at least one seat in the National Legislature automatically lose their legal status and must repay government campaign financing. There are 19 parties represented in the National Assembly independently or as part of an alliance.

## Principal Government Officials

For up-to-date information on Principal Government Officials, see the Chiefs of State and Cabinet Members of Foreign Governments section starting on page 1.

Nicaragua maintains an embassy in the United States at 1627 New Hampshire Avenue, NW, Washington, DC 20009 (tel. 202-387-4371).

# ECONOMY

Nicaragua began free market reforms in 1991 after 12 years of economic free-fall under the Sandinista regime. Despite some setbacks, it has made dramatic progress: privatizing 351 state enterprises, reducing inflation from 13,500% to 12%, and cutting the foreign debt in half. The economy began expanding in 1994 and grew a strong 4.5% in 1996 (its best performance since 1977). As a result, GDP reached $1.969 billion.

Despite this growing economy, Nicaragua remains the second-poorest nation in the hemisphere with a per capita GDP of $438 (below where it stood before the Sandinista take-over in 1979). Unemployment, while falling, is 16%, and another 36% are underemployed. Nicaragua suffers from persistent trade and budget deficits and a high debt-service burden, leaving it highly dependent on foreign assistance (22% of GDP in 1996).

One of the key engines of economic growth has been production for export. Exports rose to $671 million in 1996, up 27% from 1995. Although traditional products such as coffee, meat, and sugar continued to lead the list of Nicaraguan exports, during

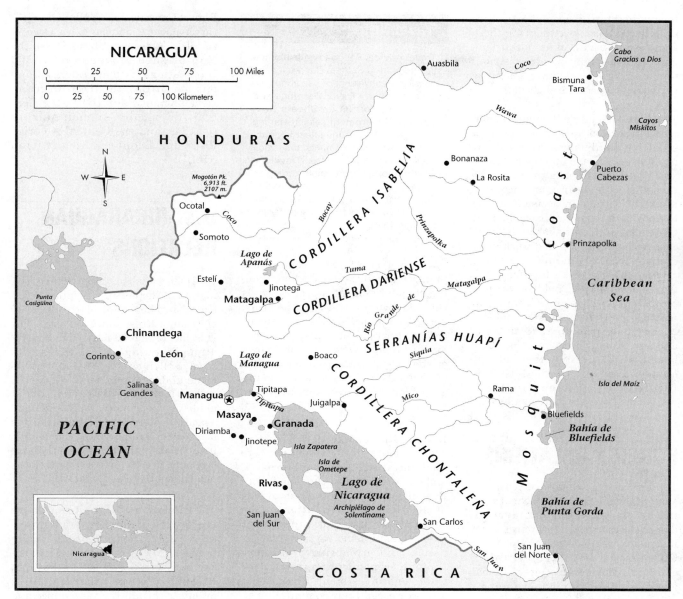

## NICARAGUA

0   25   50   75   100 Miles
0   25   50   75   100 Kilometers

HONDURAS

Mogotón Pk.
6,913 ft.
2107 m.

Ocotal

Somoto

Coco

Lago de
Apanás

Estelí

Jinotega

Matagalpa

CORDILLERA ISABELIA

Bocay

Tuma

CORDILLERA DARIENSE

Matagalpa

Río Grande de

Auasbila

Coco

Cabo
Gracias a Dios

Bismuna
Tara

Wawa

Cayos
Miskitos

Prinzapolka

Bonananza

La Rosita

Puerto
Cabezas

Prinzapolka

Caribbean
Sea

SERRANÍAS HUAPÍ

Punta
Cosigüina

Chinandega

Corinto

León

Salinas
Geandes

Managua

Masaya

Diriamba

Jinotepe

PACIFIC
OCEAN

Tipitapa

Tipitapa

Lago de
Managua

Boaco

Siquia

CORDILLERA CHONTALEÑA

Mico

Juigalpa

Granada

Isla Zapatera

Isla de
Ometepe

Rivas

San Juan
del Sur

Lago de
Nicaragua

Archipiélago de
Solentiname

San Carlos

San Juan

COSTA RICA

Rama

Isla del Maíz

Bluefields

Bahía de
Bluefields

Bahía de
Punta Gorda

San Juan
del Norte

Mosquito Coast

Nicaragua

1996 the fastest growth came in non-traditional exports: maquila goods (apparel); bananas; gold; seafood; and new agricultural products such as sesame, melons, and onions.

Nicaragua is primarily an agricultural country, but construction, mining, fisheries, and general commerce also have been expanding strongly during the last few years. Foreign private capital inflows saw a net increase in 1996, totaling an estimated $215 million. The private banking sector continues to expand and now holds 70% of the nation's deposit base.

Rapid expansion of the tourist industry has made it the nation's third-largest source of foreign exchange. Some 51,000 Americans visited Nicaragua in 1996 (primarily business people, tourists, and those visiting relatives). An estimated 5,300 U.S. citizens reside in the country. The U.S. Embassy's consular section provides a full range of consular services, from passport replacement and veteran's assistance to prison visitation and repatriation assistance.

Nicaragua now appears poised for rapid economic growth. However, long-term success at attracting

investment, creating jobs, and reducing poverty depend on its ability to comply with an International Monetary Fund (IMF) program, resolve the thousands of Sandinista-era property confiscation cases, and open its economy to foreign trade.

The U.S. is the country's largest trading partner by far—the source of 32% of Nicaragua's imports and the destination of 42% of its exports. About 25 wholly or partly owned subsidiaries of U.S. companies operate in Nicaragua. The largest of those investments are in the energy, communications, manufacturing, fisheries, and shrimp farming sectors. Good opportunities exist for further investments in those same sectors, as well as in tourism, mining, franchising, and the distribution of imported consumer, manufacturing, and agricultural goods.

The U.S. embassy's Economic/Commercial Section advances American economic and business interests by briefing U.S. firms on opportunities and stumbling blocks to trade and investment in Nicaragua; encouraging key Nicaraguan decisionmakers to work with American firms; helping to resolve problems that affect U.S. commercial interests; and working to change local economic and trade ground rules in order to afford U.S. firms a level playing field on which to compete. The Economic/Commercial Section counseled 112 U.S. and 148 Nicaraguan firms in 1996 on trade and investment opportunities. U.S. businesses may access key Embassy economic reports via the Mission's Internet home page at http://www.usia.gov/posts/managua.html.

## FOREIGN RELATIONS

The 1990 election victory of President Violeta Chamorro placed Nicaragua in the ranks of Latin American democracies. Nicaragua pursues an independent foreign policy. President Chamorro was instrumental in obtaining considerable international assistance for her government's efforts to improve living conditions for Nicaraguans (the country is the second-poorest in the Western Hemisphere after Haiti). Her administration also negotiated substantial reductions in the country's foreign debt burden. A participant of the Central American Security Commission (CASC), Nicaragua also has taken a leading role in pressing for regional demilitarization and peaceful settlement of disputes within states in the region.

The Aleman administration has expressed a commitment to follow the major tenets of its predecessor's foreign policy, to promote Central Amer-

---

### Travel Notes

**Travel Advice:** For up-to-date information from the U.S. State Department on possible inconvenient or hazardous situations, see the **Travel Warnings and Consular Information Sheets from the U.S. Government** section starting on page 1723. For the latest information on health requirements and conditions, see the **International Travelers' Health Information** section starting on page 1385. For further information dealing with non-urgent matter, see the **Tips for Travelers to...** section starting on page 1588.

---

ican political and economic integration, and to resolve outstanding boundary disputes peacefully. At the 1994 Summit of the Americas, Nicaragua joined six Central American neighbors in signing the Alliance for Sustainable Development, known as the Conjunta Centroamerica-USA or CONCAUSA, to promote sustainable economic development in the region.

In Costa Rica in May 1997, President Aleman met with President Clinton, his Central American counterparts, and the president of the Dominican Republic to celebrate the remarkable democratic transformation in the region and reaffirm support for strengthening democracy, good governance, and promoting prosperity through economic integration, free trade, and investment. The leaders also expressed their commitment to the continued development of just and equitable societies and responsible environmental policies as an integral element of sustainable development.

Nicaragua belongs to the UN and several specialized and related agencies, including the World Bank, the International Monetary Fund (IMF), World Trade Organization (WTO), UN Educational, Scientific, and Cultural Organization (UNESCO), World Health Organization (WHO), Food and Agriculture Organization (FAO), International Labor Organization (ILO), and the UN Human

---

Rights Commission (UNHRC). Nicaragua also is a member of the Organization of American States (OAS), the Non-aligned Movement (NAM), International Atomic Energy Commission (IAEA), the Inter-American Development Bank (IDB), the Central American Common Market (CACM), and the Central America Bank for Economic Integration (CABEI).

## U.S.-NICARAGUAN RELATIONS

U.S. policy aims to support the consolidation of the democratic process initiated in Nicaragua with the 1990 election of President Chamorro. The U.S. has promoted national reconciliation, encouraging Nicaraguans to resolve their problems through dialogue and compromise. It recognizes as legitimate all political forces that abide by the democratic process and eschew violence. U.S. assistance is focused on strengthening democratic institutions, stimulating sustainable economic growth, and supporting the health and basic education sectors.

The resolution of U.S. citizen claims arising from Sandinista-era confiscations and expropriations still figure prominently in bilateral policy concerns. Section 527 of the Foreign Relations Authorization Act (1994) prohibits certain U.S. assistance and support for a government of a country that has confiscated U.S. citizen property, unless the government has taken certain remedial steps. In July 1997, the Secretary of State issued a fourth annual national interest waiver of the Section 527 prohibition because of Nicaragua's record in resolving U.S. citizen claims as well as its overall progress in implementing political and economic reforms.

Other key U.S. policy goals for Nicaragua are:

Improving respect for human rights and resolving outstanding high-profile human rights cases; Development of a free market economy with respect for property and intellectual property rights; Ensuring effective civilian control over defense and security policy; Increased effectiveness of Nicaragua's efforts to combat narcotics trafficking, illegal alien smuggling, international terrorist and criminal organizations; and Reforming the judicial system. Since 1990, the U.S. has provided $1.2 billion in assistance to Nicaragua. Approximately $260 million of that was for debt relief and another $450 million was for balance-of-payments support. The levels of assistance have fallen incrementally to reflect the improvements in Nicaragua, and FY 1997 assistance was about $25 million. This assistance was focused on promoting more citizen political participation, compromise, and government transparency; stimulating

sustainable growth and income; and fostering better educated, healthier, and smaller families.

## Principal U.S. Officials

**For up-to-date information on Principal U.S. Officials, see the U.S. Embassies, Consulates, and Foreign Service section starting on page 139.**

The U.S. Embassy in Nicaragua is located at Kilometer 4.5, Carretera Sur, Managua (tel. country code 505, phone 266-6010).
Letters mailed in the U.S. should be addressed to American Embassy Managua, APO AA 34021. Internet: http://www.usia.gov/posts/managua.html.

## Other Contact Information

**U.S. Department of Commerce**
International Trade Administration
Trade Information Center
14th and Constitution, NW
Washington, DC 20230
Tel: 1-800-USA-TRADE

**American Chamber of Commerce in Nicaragua**
Apartado Postal 202
Managua, Nicaragua
Tel: (5052) 67-30-99
Fax: (5052) 67-30-98

**Caribbean/Latin American Action**
1818 N Street, NW, Suite 310
Washington, D.C. 20036
Tel: 202-466-7464
Fax: 202-822-0075

Background Notes

# NIGER

July 1994

Official Name:
**Republic of Niger**

# PROFILE

## Geography

**Area:** 1,267,000 sq. km. (490,000 sq. mi.); about three times the size of California.
**Cities:** Capital—Niamey (pop. approx. 500,000). Other cities—Tahoua, Maradi, Zinder, Arlit, and Agadez.
**Terrain:** About two-thirds desert and mountains, one-third savanna.
**Climate:** Hot, dry, and dusty. Rainy season June-September.

## People

**Nationality:** Noun and adjective—Nigerien(s).
**Population (1993 est.):** 8.6 million.
**Annual growth rate (1992):** 3.5%.
**Ethnic groups:** Hausa 53%, Djerma-Songhai 21%, Fulani 10%, Tuareg 10%, Beri Beri (Kanouri) 4.4%; Arab, Toubou, and Gourmantche 1.6%.
**Religions:** Islam (98%); remainder traditional and Christian.
**Languages:** French (official), Hausa, Djerma.
**Education:** Years compulsory—6, attendance—19%, literacy—12.5%.
**Health:** Infant mortality rate (1992)—123/1,000. Life expectancy—44 yrs.
**Work force (3.5 million):** Self-employed/work for family (primarily agriculture and herding)—90%; employed by private sector—8%; government—2%.

## Government

**Type:** Republic.
**Independence:** August 3, 1960.
**Constitution:** Approved by referendum December 26, 1992.
**Branches:** Executive—president and prime minister. Legislative—unicameral national assembly (83 MP's). Judicial—Court of Appeals, Supreme Court, High Court of Justice, and Court of State Security.
**Political parties:** 18; 9 are represented in the National Assembly.
**Suffrage:** The 1992 constitution provides for universal suffrage for Nigeriens age 18 or older.
**Administrative subdivisions:** Eight departments subdivided into 36 districts (arrondissements).
**Central government budget (Post devaluation adjustment of FY 1993):** $291.4 million (167.6 billion CFA (Communaute Financiere Africaine) francs at 575 CFA=US$1). Investment budget (capital and development expenditures)—$190 million. Current Operations (personnel wages plus material and transport)—$141 million.
**Flag:** Three horizontal bands—orange, white, and green from top to bottom—with orange orb representing the sun centered on white band.

## Economy

*All figures pre-devaluation.*
**GDP (1993):** $2.3 billion.
**Annual growth rate (1990-91):** 1.9%.
**Per capita GDP (1993):** $285.
**Avg. inflation rate (1993):** less than 0.4%. (Figure for the first 2 months after devaluation is 6-8% per month).
**Natural resources:** Uranium, gold, oil, coal, iron, tin, phosphates.
**Agriculture (20% of GDP):** Products—millet, sorghum, cowpeas, peanuts, cotton, rice.
**Industry (1% of GDP):** Types—textiles, cement, soap, beverages.
**Trade (1993 est.):** Exports (Freight on Board (FOB))—$235.5 million: uranium, livestock, cowpeas, onions. Major markets—France, other EC countries, Nigeria. Imports (FOB)—$241.4 million: petroleum, foodstuffs, industrial products. Major suppliers—France, other EC countries, Nigeria.
**Official exchange rate (April 1994):** 575 CFA francs=US$1.

## Membership in International Organizations

UN and some of its specialized and related agencies, Council of the Entente, West African Economic Community (CEAO), West African Monetary Union (UMOA), Liptako-

Gourma Authority, Niger River Basin Commission, Lake Chad Basin Commission, Organization of African Unity (OAU), Economic Organization of West African States (ECOWAS), Organization of the Islamic Conference, Nonaligned Movement.

# PEOPLE

The largest ethnic groups in Niger are the Hausa, who also constitute the major ethnic group in northern Nigeria, and the Djerma-Songhai, who are also found in parts of Mali. Both groups are sedentary farmers who live in the arable, southern tier. The remainder of the Nigerien people are nomadic or seminomadic livestock-raising peoples—Fulani, Tuareg, Kanouri, and Toubou. With rapidly growing populations and the consequent competition for meager natural resources, lifestyles of these two types of peoples have come increasingly into conflict in Niger in recent years.

Niger's high infant mortality rate is comparable to levels recorded in neighboring countries. However, the child mortality rate (deaths among children between the ages of 1 and 4) is exceptionally high (222 per 1,000) due to generally poor health conditions and inadequate nutrition for most of the country's children. Niger's very high fertility rate (7.4%) nonetheless means that nearly half (49%) of the Nigerien population is under age 15. School attendance is very low (19%), including 23% of males and only 15% of females. Additional education occurs through Koranic schools.

# HISTORY

Considerable evidence indicates that about 600,000 years ago, humans inhabited what has since become the desolate Sahara of northern Niger. Long before the arrival of French influence and control in the area, Niger was an important economic crossroads, and the empires of Songhai, Mali, Gao, Kanem, and Bornu, as well as a number of Hausa states, claimed control over portions of the area.

During recent centuries, the nomadic Tuareg formed large confederations, pushed southward, and, siding with various Hausa states, clashed with the Fulani Empire of Sokoto, which had gained control of much of the Hausa territory in the late 18th century.

In the 19th century, contact with the West began when the first European explorers—notably Mungo Park (British) and Heinrich Barth (German)—explored the area searching for the mouth of the Niger River. Although French efforts at pacification began before 1900, dissident ethnic groups, especially the desert Tuareg, were not subdued until 1922, when Niger became a French colony.

Niger's colonial history and development parallel that of other French West African territories. France administered her West African colonies through a governor general at Dakar, Senegal, and governors in the individual territories, including Niger. In addition to conferring French citizenship on the inhabitants of the territories, the 1946 French constitution provided for decentralization of power and limited participation in political life for local advisory assemblies.

A further revision in the organization of overseas territories occurred with the passage of the Overseas Reform Act (Loi Cadre) of July 23, 1956, followed by reorganizational measures enacted by the French Parliament early in 1957. In addition to removing voting inequalities, these laws provided for creation of governmental organs, assuring individual territories a large measure of self-government. After the establishment of the Fifth French Republic on December 4, 1958, Niger became an autonomous state within the French Community. Following full independence on August 3, 1960, however, membership was allowed to lapse.

For its first 14 years as an independent state, Niger was run by a single-party civilian regime under the presidency of Hamani Diori. In 1974, a combination of devastating drought and accusations of rampant corruption resulted in a military coup which overthrew the Diori regime. Col. Seyni Kountche and a small group of military ruled the country until Kountche's death in 1987. He was succeeded by his Chief of Staff, Col. Ali Saibou, who released political prisoners, liberalized some of Niger's laws and policies, and promulgated a new constitution. However, President Saibou's efforts to control political reforms failed in the face of union and student demands to institute a multiparty democratic system. The Saibou regime acquiesced to these demands by the end of 1990. New political parties and civic associations sprang up and a National Conference was convened in July 1991 to prepare the way for the adoption of a new constitution and the holding of free and fair elections. A transition government was installed in November 1991 to manage the affairs of state until the institutions of the Third Republic were put in place in April 1993.

# GOVERNMENT AND POLITICAL CONDITIONS

Niger's new constitution was approved in December 1992. It provides for a semi-presidential system of government in which executive power is shared by the president of the republic, elected by universal suffrage for a five-year term, and a prime minister named by the president. The unicameral legislature is comprised of 83 deputies elected for a five-year term under a proportional system of representation.

Niger's independent judicial system is composed of four higher courts—the court of appeals, the supreme court, the high court of justice and the court of state security.

The country is divided into 8 departments, which are subdivided into 36 districts (arrondissements). The chief

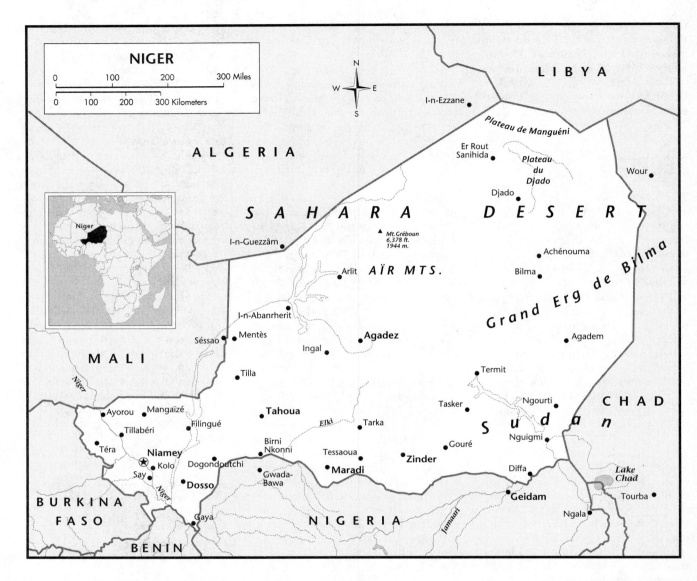

NIGER

0   100   200   300 Miles

0   100   200   300 Kilometers

administrator (prefet) in each territorial unit is appointed by the government and functions primarily as the local agent of the central authorities. The 1992 constitution provides for the popular election of municipal and local officials.

## Principal Government Officials

For up-to-date information on **Principal Government Officials,** see the **Chiefs of State and Cabinet Members of Foreign Governments** section starting on page 1.

Niger's 1991 National Conference allowed political voices that had been silenced for years to express themselves freely and publicly. The debate was often contentious and accusatory, but under the leadership of Professor Andre Salifou, the conference developed consensus on the modalities of a transition government. It established three governmental organs to run the country during a 15-month period. The government's primary tasks were to stabilize the economy, deal with a growing rebellion by Tuareg rebels, and pave the way for multi-party elections. While the economy deteriorated over the course of the transition, certain accomplishments stand out, including the successful conduct of a constitutional referendum, the adoption of key legislation

such as the electoral and rural codes, and the holding of three nationwide elections, all of which were free, fair and non-violent. Freedom of the press flourished with the appearance of several new independent newspapers.

The first multi-party legislature since independence, containing nine political parties, was elected on February 14, and installed on April 9. Mahamane Ousmane was elected President of the Republic on March 27, 1993, and took the oath of office on April 16.

On the eve of the establishment of the Third Republic, Northern-based rebels of the FLAA (Front for the Liberation of Air and Azawak) released their hostages and gave renewed hope that a peaceful settlement could be reached with the new authorities. Since then, rebel factions have agreed to a number of cease-fires, but talks between the Government and various rebel factions have stalled.

Niger maintains an embassy in the United States at 2204 R Street, NW, Washington, D.C. 20008 (tel. 202-483-4224/25/26/27) and a permanent mission to the United Nations at 417 East 50th Street, New York, NY 10022 (tel. (212-421-3260).

# ECONOMY

One of the poorest countries in the world, Niger's economy is based largely on subsistence crops, livestock, and some of the world's largest uranium deposits. Drought cycles, desertification, a 3.3 percent population growth rate and the declining world demand for uranium have undercut an already marginal economy. Deteriorating terms of trade due to persistently high domestic wage levels and currency devaluations in Nigeria have also contributed to economic decline. Many of the modern sector's private and parastatal industries have shut down, leaving only a handful of companies engaged in light industry that mostly transform imported inputs (textile manufacturing, corrugating steel sheets, drink bottling, soap production). The northern-based Tuareg rebellion has impacted negatively on tourism since early 1992.

Niger's agricultural and livestock sectors are the mainstay of all but 10-15 percent of the population. 12-13 percent of Niger's GDP is generated by livestock production (camels, goats, sheep and cattle), said to support 29 percent of the population. Only about 12 percent of land is arable. Rainfall varies, though Niger has seen relatively good rains in recent years. When there is not sufficient rainfall, Niger has difficulty feeding its population and must rely on grain purchases and food aid to meet food requirements. Rains, which were good in 1990 and 1991, were less

Photo credit: Corel Corporation.

**A street merchant from Niger.**

well-distributed in 1992 and 1993, creating food deficits in certain regions. Millet, sorghum and cassava are Niger's principal rain-fed subsistence crops. Irrigated rice for internal consumption, while expensive, has, since the devaluation of the CFA franc, sold for below the price of imported rice, encouraging additional production. Cowpeas and onions are grown for commercial export, as are small quantities of garlic, peppers, potatoes and wheat.

Of Niger's exports, foreign exchange earnings from livestock, although impossible to quantify, are second only to those from uranium; actual exports far exceed official statistics, which often fail to detect large herds of animals informally crossing into Nigeria. Some hides and skins are exported and some are transformed into handicrafts.

The persistent uranium price slump has brought lower revenues for Niger's uranium sector, although uranium still provides 68 percent of national export proceeds. Industry officials have been working to reduce excessive costs of production, including personnel, electricity, transportation, hospital administration, mining town management fees and debt. Niger's two uranium mines (SOMAIR's open pit mine and COMI-

NAK's underground mine) are primarily owned and operated by French interests. COMINAK is partially by other shareholders including Japan, Germany, Spain and Niger, all of which negotiate to purchase and sell certain quantities of uranium. In recent years, only France and Germany have contracted to sell uranium. American participation in Niger's uranium industry ended in 1983, when CONOCO gave its shares in the Imouraren concession back to Niger. Large reserves of low-grade uranium at Imouraren remain untapped due to the depressed state of the global uranium market.

Hunt Oil of Texas began exploring for petroleum in 1992 in the Djado plateau in northeastern Niger. The French company Elf Aquitaine (62.5 percent) and Exxon (37.5 percent) have a joint exploration permit for the Agadem basin, north of Lake Chad. Elf conducts the actual exploration and has found significant quantities of petroleum to justify further exploration and development.

Exploitable deposits of gold are known to exist in Niger in the region between the Niger River and the border with Burkina Faso. The government of Niger recently adopted a new Mining Code and hopes to obtain commitments soon

Niger

from interested foreign investors. Niger's known coal reserves, with low energy and high ash content, cannot compete against higher quality coal on the world market. However, the parastatal SONICHAR (Societe Nigerienne de Charbon) in Tchirozerine (north of Agadez) extracts coal from an open pit and fuels an electricity generating plant that supplies energy to the uranium mines. Parastatal tin production stopped in 1991 and tin is currently produced at artisanal levels.

While France and Taiwan provided significant budgetary assistance in 1992, Niger accrued lower total assistance in 1991-1992 from its other major donors, which include the United States, Germany, Canada, Saudi Arabia, the European Community and the UN Development Program (UNDP). In early 1994, the IMF and Niger agreed to a stand-by agreement which ended Niger's isolation from the international financial community.

Niger shares a common currency, the CFA Franc, and a common central bank, the Central Bank of West African States (BCEAO), with six other members of the West African Monetary Union. The Treasury of the Government of France supplements the BCEAO's international reserves in order to maintain a fixed rate of 100 CFA (Communaute Financiere Africaine) to the French franc.

## Economic Reform

In 1993, Niger's newly elected government inherited a tangle of financial and economic problems including: past-due salary and scholarship payments (5 months of arrears), increased debt, reduced revenue performance, and lower public investment. The CFA franc was devalued in January 1994, doubling Niger's external debt (quantified in dollars) overnight. The rectification of exchange rates should increase demand for Nigerien exports and create a larger domestic market.

The government of Niger is also currently taking actions to streamline civil services, reduce corruption,

reorient expenditures in the education sector, and enhance revenues. In February 1994, Niger signed a stand by agreement with the IMF. They are currently negotiating for an Enhanced Structural Adjustment Facility.

## Foreign Aid

The United States was the third largest bilateral donor to Niger and the fourth largest donor overall. Total U.S. aid in averages around $15 million per year though this figure is expected to increase. Other major donors include: France, Germany, The World Bank, The European Economic Community, and The United Nations. The importance of donor

activity in Niger's development plans is best demonstrated by the fact that about 97 percent of the GON's investment budget derives from donor resources.

Niger's 1993 elections were smooth and successful, in part due to the donors' 56 percent contribution (25 percent of the total from the French) to the election budget.

# FOREIGN RELATIONS

Niger pursues a moderate foreign policy and maintains friendly relations with both East and West. It belongs to the United Nations and its main specialized agencies and in 1980-81 served on the UN Security Council. Niger maintains a special relationship with France and enjoys close relations with its West African neighbors. It is a charter member of the Organization of African Unity and the West African Monetary Union and also belongs to the Niger River and Lake Chad Basin Commissions, the Economic Community of West African States, the Nonaligned Movement, and the Organization of the Islamic Conference.

# DEFENSE

The Niger Armed Forces total 3,500 personnel, in addition to 1,500 national gendarmes and 1,500 members of the Garde Republicaine. The air force has four operational transport aircraft, including two C-130s. The armed forces include a general staff, two paratroop companies, two light armored squadrons, and six motorized infantry companies located in Tahoua, Agadez, Dirkou, Zinder, N'Guigmi, and N'Gourti.

Niger's defense budget is modest, accounting for less than 3% of government expenditures. France provides the largest share of military assistance to Niger: approximately 55 French military advisers are in Niger, many Nigerien military personnel receive training in France, and the Nigerien Armed Forces are equipped mainly with materiel either given by or purchased in France. Germany provides general engineering assistance. U.S. assistance has focused on training pilots and aviation support personnel, professional military education for staff officers, and initial specialty training for junior officers. A small foreign military assistance program was initiated in 1983 and a U.S. Defense Attache office opened in June 1985. In 1987 the attache office was converted to a Security Assistance Office.

## Principal U.S. Officials

**For up-to-date information on Principal U.S. Officials, see the U.S. Embassies, Consulates, and For-eign Service section starting on page 139.**

The U.S. Embassy in Niger is located on the Avenue des Ambassadeurs. The telephone numbers for the Embassy are (227) 72-26-61 through 65 and the fax number is (227) 73-31-67. The mailing address is B.P. 11201, Niamey.

# U.S.-NIGERIEN RELATIONS

U.S. relations with Niger have been close and friendly since Niger attained independence. A substantial U.S. Agency for International Development (AID) program focuses on agriculture and natural resource management as well as demography and family health. The U.S. Peace Corps program, started in Niger in 1962, has about 106 volunteers.

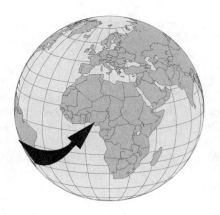

# NIGERIA

August 2000

Official Name:
**Federal Republic of Nigeria**

# PROFILE

## Geography

**Area:** 923,768 sq. km. (356,700 sq. mi.) about the size of California, Nevada, and Arizona.
**Cities:** Capital—Abuja (pop. est. 100,000). Other cities—Lagos (12 million), Ibadan (5 million), Kano (1 million), Enugu (500,000).
**Terrain:** Ranges from southern coastal swamps to tropical forests, open woodlands, grasslands, and semidesert in the far north. The highest regions are the Jos Plateau 1,200-2,000 meters above sea level and the mountains along the border with Cameroon.
**Climate:** Annual rainfall ranges from 381 cm. along the coast to 64 cm. or less in the far north.

## People

**Nationality:** Noun and adjective—Nigerian(s).
**Population:** (est. 1999) 100 million.
**Total fertility rate:** (avg. number of children per woman) 6.0.
**Ethnic groups:** (250) Hausa-Fulani, Igbo, and Yoruba are the largest.
**Religion:** Muslim, Christian, indigenous African.
**Languages:** English (official), Hausa, Igbo, Yoruba, others.
**Education:** Attendance (second-ary)—male 32%, female 27%.
**Literacy:** 39%-51 %.
**Health:** Life expectancy—56 years.

## Government

**Type:** An elected civilian government took office on May 29, 1999, following 15 years of military rule.
**Independence:** October 1, 1960.
**Constitution:** The 1979 constitution was suspended after 1983, the May 3, 1989 constitution never implemented, and the 1999 constitution (based largely on the 1979 constitution) was promulgated by decree on May 5, 1999. The 1999 constitution came into force on May 29, 1999.
**Subdivisions:** 36 states plus Federal Capital Territory (Abuja); states divided into a total of 774 local government areas.
**Total government expenditure:** $9.47 billion.
**Defense:** 10% of 1996 budget.
**Flag:** Green, white, green, three vertical bands.

## Economy

**GDP:** (1998 est.) $36 billion.
**Estimated real growth rate:** (2000) 2.7%.
**Per capita GDP:** (1999 est.) $300.
**Inflation:** (2000 est.) 6.6 %.
**Natural resources:** Petroleum, natural gas, tin, columbite, iron ore, coal, limestone, lead, zinc.
**Agriculture:** Products—cocoa, palm oil, yams, cassava, sorghum, millet, corn, rice, livestock, groundnuts, cotton.
**Industry:** Types—textiles, cement, food products, footwear, metal products, lumber, beer, detergents, car assembly.
**Trade:** (1997) Exports—$15.2 billion: petroleum (98.4%), cocoa, rubber.

# PEOPLE

The most populous country in Africa, Nigeria accounts for one-quarter of West Africa's people. Although less than 25% of Nigerians are urban dwellers, at least 24 cities have populations of more than 100,000. The variety of customs, languages, and traditions among Nigeria's 250 ethnic groups gives the country a rich diversity. The dominant ethnic group in the northern two-thirds of the country is the Hausa-Fulani, most of whom are Muslim. Other major ethnic groups of the north are the Nupe, Tiv, and Kanuri. The Yoruba people are predominant in the southwest. About half of the Yorubas are Christian and half Muslim. The predominantly Catholic Igbo are the largest ethnic group in the southeast, with the Efik, Ibibio, and Ijaw (the country's fourth-largest ethnic group) comprising a substantial segment of the population in that area as well.

Persons of different language backgrounds most commonly communicate in English, although knowledge of two or more Nigerian languages is widespread. Hausa, Yoruba, and Igbo are the most widely used.

# HISTORY

Before the colonial period, the area which comprises modern Nigeria had an eventful history. More than 2,000 years ago, the Nok culture in the present Plateau state worked iron and produced sophisticated terra cotta sculpture. In the northern cities of Kano and Katsina, recorded history dates back to approximately 1000 AD. In the centuries that followed, these Hausa kingdoms and the Bomu empire near Lake Chad prospered as important terminals of north-south trade between North African Berbers and forest people who exchanged slaves, ivory, and kola nuts for salt, glass beads, coral, cloth, weapons, brass rods, and cowrie shells used as currency.

In the southwest, the Yoruba kingdom of Oyo was founded about 1400, and at its height from the 17th to 19th centuries attained a high level of political organization and extended as far as modern Togo. In the south central part of present-day Nigeria, as early as the 15th and 16th centuries, the kingdom of Benin had developed an efficient army; an elaborate ceremonial court; and artisans whose works in ivory, wood, bronze, and brass are prized throughout the world today. In the 17th through 19th centuries, European traders established coastal ports for the increasing traffic in slaves destined for the Americas. Commodity trade, especially in palm oil and timber, replaced slave trade in the 19th century, particularly under anti-slavery actions by the British navy. In the early 19th century the Fulani leader, Usman dan Fodio, launched an Islamic crusade that brought most of the Hausa states and other areas in the north under the loose control of an empire centered in Sokoto.

## A British Sphere of Influence

Following the Napoleonic wars, the British expanded their trade with the Nigerian interior. In 1885, British claims to a sphere of influence in that area received international recognition and, in the following year, the Royal Niger Company was chartered. In 1900, the company's territory came under the control of the British Government, which moved to consolidate its hold over the area of modern Nigeria. In 1914, the area was formally united as the "Colony and Protectorate of Nigeria."

Administratively, Nigeria remained divided into the northern and southern provinces and Lagos colony. Western education and the development of a modern economy proceeded more rapidly in the south than in the north, with consequences felt in Nigeria's political life ever since. Following World War II, in response to the growth of Nigerian nationalism and demands for independence, successive constitutions legislated by the British Government moved Nigeria toward self-government on a representative, increasingly federal, basis.

Nigeria was granted full independence in October 1960, as a federation of three regions (northern, western and eastern) under a constitution that provided for a parliamentary form of government. Under the constitution, each of the three regions retained a substantial measure of self-government. The federal government was given exclusive powers in defense and security, foreign relations, and commercial and fiscal policies. In October 1963, Nigeria altered its relationship with the United Kingdom by proclaiming itself a federal republic and promulgating a new constitution. A fourth region (the Midwest) was established that year. From the outset, Nigeria's ethnic, regional, and religious tensions were magnified by the significant disparities in economic and educational development between the south and the north. On January 15, 1966, a small group of army officers, mostly southeastern Ibos, overthrew the government and assassinated the federal

prime minister and the premiers of the northern and western regions. A federal military government assumed power, but it was unable to quiet ethnic tensions or produce a new constitution acceptable to all sections of the country. In fact, its efforts to abolish the federal structure greatly raised tensions and led to another coup in July. The massacre of thousands of Igbo in the north prompted hundreds of thousands of them to return to their homeland in the southeast, where increasingly strong Igbo secessionist sentiment emerged.

In a move that gave greater autonomy to minority ethnic groups, the military replaced the four regions with 12 states. The Igbo rejected attempts at constitutional revisions and insisted on full autonomy for the east. Finally, in May 1967, Lt. Col. Emeka Ojukwu, the military governor of the eastern region, who emerged as the leader of increasing Igbo secessionist sentiment, declared the independence of the eastern region as the "Republic of Biafra." The civil war, which ensued, was bitter and bloody, ending in the defeat of Biafra in 1970. Following the civil war, reconciliation was rapid and effective, and the country turned to the task of economic development. Foreign exchange earnings and government revenues increased spectacularly with the oil price rises of 1973-74.

On July 29, 1975, Gen. Murtala Muhammed and a group of fellow officers staged a bloodless coup, accusing the military government of delaying the promised return to civilian rule and becoming corrupt and ineffective. General Muhammed replaced thousands of civil servants and announced a timetable for the resumption of civilian rule by October 1, 1979. Muhammed also announced the government's intention to create new states and to construct a new federal capital in the center of the country.

General Muhammed was assassinated on February 13, 1976, in an abortive coup, and his chief of staff, Lt. Gen. Olusegun Obasanjo, became head of state. Obasanjo adhered

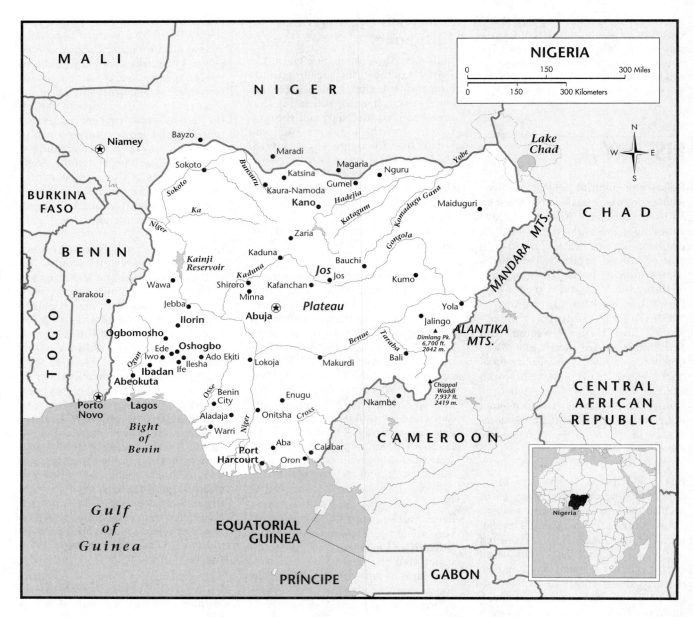

meticulously to the schedule for return to civilian rule, moving to modernize and streamline the armed forces and seeking to use oil revenues to diversify and develop the country's economy. Seven new states were created in 1976, bringing the total to 19. The process of carving out additional states continued until, in 1996, there were 36.

## The Second Republic

A constituent assembly was elected in 1977 to draft a new constitution, which was published on September 21, 1978, when the ban on political activity, in effect since the advent of military rule, was lifted. Political parties were formed, and candidates were nominated for president and vice president, the two houses of the National Assembly, governorships, and state houses of assembly. In 1979, five political parties competed in a series of elections in which a northerner, Alhaji Shehu Shagari of the National Party of Nigeria (NPN), was elected president. All five parties won representation in the National Assembly.

In August 1983, Shagari and the NPN were returned to power in a landslide victory, with a majority of seats in the National Assembly and control of 12 state governments. But the elections were marred by violence and allegations of widespread vote rigging and electoral malfeasance led to legal battles over the results.

On December 31, 1983, the military overthrew the Second Republic. Maj. Gen. Muhammadu Buhari emerged as the leader of the Supreme Military Council (SMC), the country's new ruling body. He charged the civilian government with economic mismanagement, widespread corruption, election fraud, and a general lack of concern for the problems of Nigerians. He also pledged to restore prosperity to Nigeria and to return the government to civilian rule but proved unable to deal with Nigeria's severe economic problems. The Buhari government was peacefully overthrown by the SMC's third-ranking member, Army Chief of Staff Maj. Gen. Ibrahim Babangida, in August 1985.

Babangida cited the misuse of power, violations of human rights by key officers of the SMC, and the government's failure to deal with the country's deepening economic crisis as justifications for the takeover. During his first few days in office, President Babangida moved swiftly to restore freedom of the press and to release political detainees being held without charge. As part of a 15-month economic emergency, he announced stringent paycuts for the military, police, and civil servants and proceeded to enact similar cuts for the private sector.

Imports of rice, maize, and later wheat were banned. President Babangida demonstrated his intent to encourage public participation in government decisionmaking by opening a national debate on proposed economic reform and recovery measures. The public response convinced Babangida of intense opposition to an economic recovery package dependent on an International Monetary Fund (IMP) loan and an apparent preference for self-imposed austerity.

## Third Republic

President Babangida promised to return the country to civilian rule by 1990; this date was later extended until January 1993. In early 1989, a constituent assembly completed work on a constitution for the Third Republic. In the spring of 1989, political activity was again permitted. In October 1989 the government decreed the establishment of two "grassroots" parties: the National Republican Convention (NRC), which was to be "a little to the right," and the Social Democratic (SDP), "a little to the left." Babangida rejected other parties, and they were not allowed to register.

In April 1990, mid-level officers attempted to overthrow the Babangida government. The coup failed, and 69 accused coup plotters were later executed after secret trials before military tribunals. The transition resumed after the failed coup. In December 1990 the first stage of partisan elections was held at the local government level. While turnout was low, there was no violence, and both parties demonstrated strength in all regions of the country, with the SDP winning control of a majority of local government councils.

In December 1991, gubernatorial and state legislative elections were held throughout the country. Babangida decreed in December 1991 that previously banned politicians would be allowed to contest in primaries scheduled for August 1992. These were canceled due to fraud and subsequent primaries scheduled for September also were canceled. All announced candidates were disqualified from again standing for president once a new election format was selected. The presidential election was finally held on June 12, 1993, with the inauguration of the new president scheduled to take place August 27, 1993, the eighth anniversary of President Babangida's coming to power.

In the historic June 12, 1993 presidential elections, which most observers deemed to be Nigeria's fairest, early returns indicated that wealthy Yoruba businessman M.K.O. Abiola would win a decisive victory. However, on June 23, Babangida, using several pending lawsuits as a pretense, annulled the election and threw Nigeria into turmoil. Over 100 persons were killed in riots before Babangida agreed to hand over power to an "interim government" on August 27, 1993. Babangida then had second thoughts and attempted to renege on his decision, but without popular and military support he was forced to hand over to Ernest Shonekan, a nonpartisan businessman. Shonekan was to rule until new elections, scheduled for February 1994. Although he had led Babangida's Transitional Council since early 1993, Shonekan was unable to tackle

Nigeria's ever-growing economic problems.

With the country sliding into chaos, Defense Minister Sani Abacha quickly assumed power and engineered Shonekan's "resignation" on November 17, 1993. He dissolved all democratic political institutions and replaced elected governors with military officers. Abacha promised to return the government to civilian rule but refused to announce a timetable until his October 1, 1995 Independence Day address.

Following the annulment of the June 12 election, the United States and other nations imposed various sanctions on Nigeria, including restrictions on travel by government officials and their families and suspension of arms sales and military assistance. Additional sanctions were imposed as a result of Nigeria's failure to gain full certification for its counter-narcotics efforts. In addition, direct flights between Nigeria and the United States were suspended on August 11, 1993, when the Secretary of Transportation determined that Lagos' Murtala Muhammed International Airport did not meet the security standards established by the FAA. The FAA in December 1999 certified security at MMIA, opening the way for operation of direct flights between Lagos and U.S. airports.

Although Abacha's takeover was initially welcomed by many Nigerians who thought he could lead the country out of its morass, disenchantment grew rapidly. A number of opposition figures united to form a new organization, the National Democratic Coalition (NADECO), which campaigned for an immediate return to civilian rule. The government arrested NADECO members who attempted to reconvene the Senate and other disbanded democratic institutions. Most Nigerians boycotted the elections for delegates to the Constitutional Conference, which were held from May 23-28, 1994.

On June 11, 1994, using the groundwork laid by NADECO, Abiola declared himself president and went into hiding. He reemerged and was promptly arrested on June 23. With Abiola in prison and tempers rising, Abacha convened the Constitutional Conference June 27, but it almost immediately went into recess and did not reconvene until July 11, 1994.

On July 4, a petroleum workers union called a strike demanding that Abacha release Abiola and hand over power to him. Other unions then joined the strike, which brought economic life in the Lagos area and much of the southwest to a standstill. After calling off a threatened general strike in July, the Nigeria Labor Congress (NLC) began to consider a general strike in August, after the government imposed "conditions" on Abiola's release. On August 17, 1994, the government dismissed the leadership of the NLC and the petroleum unions, placed the unions under appointed administrators, and arrested Frank Kokori and a number of other labor leaders. Although striking unions returned to work, the government arrested opponents, closed media houses, and moved strongly to curb dissent.

The government alleged in early 1995 that some 40 military officers and civilians were engaged in a coup plot. Security officers quickly rounded up the accused, including former head of state Obasanjo and his erstwhile deputy, retired General Shehu Musa Yar'Adua. After a secret tribunal, most of the accused were convicted, and several death sentences were handed down. The tribunal also charged, convicted, and sentenced prominent human rights activists, journalists, and others, including relatives of the coup suspects, for their alleged "antiregime" activities. In October, the government announced that the Provisional Ruling Concil (PRC—see below: Abubakar's Transition to Civilian Rule) and Abacha had approved final sentences for those convicted of participation in the coup plot.

In late 1994 the government set up the Ogoni Civil Disturbances Special Tribunal to try prominent author and Ogoni activist Ken Saro-lh'iwa and others for their alleged roles in the killings of four prominent Ogoni politicians in May 1994. Saro-lh'iwa and 14 others pleaded not guilty to charges that they procured and counseled others to murder the politicians. On October 31, 1995, the tribunal sentenced Saro-Wiwa and eight others to death by hanging. In November Abacha and the PRC confirmed the death sentence. Saro-Wiwa and his eight co-defendants were executed on November 10.

In an October 1, 1995 address to the nation, Gen. Sani Abacha announced the timetable for a 3-year transition to civilian rule. Only five of the political parties which applied for registration were approved by the regime. In local elections held in December 1997, turnout was under 10%. By the April 1998 state assembly and gubernatorial elections, all five of the approved parties had nominated Abacha as their presidential candidate in controversial party conventions. Public reaction to this development in the transition program was apathy and a near-complete boycott of the elections.

On December 21, 1997, the government announced the arrest of the country's second highest-ranking military officer, Chief of General Staff Lt. Gen. Oladipo Diya, 10 other officers, and eight civilians on charges of coup plotting. Subsequently, the government arrested a number of additional persons for roles in the purported coup plot and tried the accused before a closed-door military tribunal in April in which Diya and eight others were sentenced to death. Abacha, widely expected to succeed himself as a civilian president on October 1, 1998, remained head of state until his death on June 8 of that year. He was replaced by General Abdulsalami Abubakar, who had been third in command until the arrest of Diya. The PRC, under new head of state Abubakar, commuted the sentences of those accused in the alleged 1997 coup in July 1998. In March 1999, Diya and 54 others accused or convicted of participation in coups in 1990, 1995, and 1997 were released.

Following the death of former head of state Abacha in June, Nigeria has released almost all known civilian political detainees, including the Ogoni 19.

During the last months of the Abacha regime, the government continued to enforce its arbitrary authority through the federal security system (the military, the state security service, and the courts). Under Abacha, all branches of the security forces committed serious human rights abuses. After Abubakar's assumption of power and consolidation of support within the PRC, human rights abuses decreased.

Other human rights problems included infringements on freedom of speech, press, assembly, association, and travel; violence and discrimination against women; and female genital mutilation. Worker rights suffered as the government continued to interfere with organized labor by restricting the fundamental rights of association and the independence of the labor movement. After it came to power in June 1998, the Abubakar government took several important steps toward restoring worker rights and freedom of association for trade unions, which had deteriorated seriously between 1993 and June 1998 under the Abacha regime. The Abubakar government released two imprisoned leaders of the petroleum sector unions, Frank Kokori and Milton Dabibi; abolished two decrees that had removed elected leadership from the Nigeria Labour Congress and the oil workers unions; and allowed leadership elections in these bodies.

## Abubakar's Transition to Civilian Rule

During both the Abacha and Abubakar eras, Nigeria's main decisionmaking organ was the exclusively military Provisional Ruling Council (PRC) which governs by decree. The PRC oversaw the 32-member federal executive council composed of civilians and military officers. Pending the promulgation of the constitution written by the constitutional conference in 1995, the government observed some provisions of the 1979 and 1989 constitutions. Neither Abacha nor Abubakar lifted the decree suspending the 1979 constitution, and the 1989 constitution was not implemented. The judiciary's authority and independence was significantly impaired during the Abacha era by the military regime's arrogation of judicial power and prohibition of court review of its action. The court system continued to be hampered by corruption and lack of resources after Abacha's death. In an attempt to alleviate such problems, Abubakar's government implemented a civil service pay raise and other reforms.

In August 1998, the Abubakar government appointed the independent National Electoral Commission (NEC) to conduct elections for local government councils, state legislatures and governors, the national assembly, and president. NEC successfully held these elections on December 5, 1998, January 9, 1999, February 20, and February 27, 1999, respectively. For the local elections, a total of nine parties were granted provisional registration, with three fulfilling the requirements to contest the following elections. These parties were the People's Democratic Party (PDP), the All Peoples Party (APP), and the predominantly Yoruba Alliance for Democracy (AD). Former military head of state Olusegun Obasanjo, freed from prison by Abubakar, ran as a civilian candidate and won the presidential election. Irregularities marred the vote, and the defeated candidate, Chief Olu Falae, challenged the electoral results in court.

The PRC planned to promulgate a new constitution based largely on the suspended 1979 constitution, before the May 29, 1999 inauguration of the new civilian president. The draft constitution includes provisions for a bicameral legislature, the National Assembly, consisting of a 360-member House of Representatives and a 109-member Senate. The executive branch and the office of president will

## Travel Notes

**Clothing:** Tropical wash-and-wear clothing and rainwear are recommended.

**Customs:** Persons arriving in Nigeria must have valid passports and visas obtained from the Nigerian embassy or consulates.

**Health:** Public health facilities, private clinics, dental care, and optical services are available in major cities, but most fall short of American standards. Malaria is endemic and suppressants are recommended. Tapwater is not potable. Fruits and vegetables should be carefully prepared and meats cooked until well done.

**Telecommunications:** Telephone calls to the US and Europe are via satellite. Facilities exist for overseas cables, telexes, and radiotelephone messages to ships at sea. Lagos is 6 hours ahead of Eastern Standard Time.

**Transportation:** Several international airlines provide regular service to Nigeria. Nigeria Airways and private carriers provide domestic air service. The country has about 16,000 kilometers of paved roads, including some fourlane highways. Railways are used primarily to transport agricultural and commercial goods. Passenger service is available but very slow. Within cities and towns, taxis and buses are commonly used.

**National holidays:** The US embassy and consulate general observe the following American holidays-New Year's Day, Martin Luther King's Birthday, Presidents' Day, Memorial Day, Independence Day, Labor Day. Columbus Day, Veteran's Day, Thanksgiving, and Christmas.

The embassy and consulate general also observe the following Nigerian holidays—Good Friday, Easter Monday, Worker's Day (May 1), National Day (October and boxing Day (December 26). The embassy and consulate general offices are also closed for 2 days each during the Muslim feasts of Id-el-Fitr and Id-el-Kabir, and on the Prophet's birthday. (Exact dates of the Muslim feasts vary.)

**Travel Advice:** For up-to-date information from the U.S. State Department on possible inconvenient or hazardous situations, see the **Travel Warnings and Consular Information Sheets from the U.S. Government** section starting on page 1723. For the latest information on health requirements and conditions, see the **International Travelers' Health Information** section starting on page 1385. For further information dealing with non-urgent matter, see the **Tips for Travelers to...** section starting on page 1588.

retain strong federal powers. The legislature and judiciary, having suffered years of neglect, must be rebuilt as institutions.

## Principal Government Officials

**For up-to-date information on Principal Government Officials, see the Chiefs of State and Cabinet Members of Foreign Governments section starting on page 1.**

Nigeria maintains an embassy in the United States at 1333 - 16th Street, NW, Washington, DC 20036, (tel. 202-986-8400, fax-202-775-1385) and a consulate general in New York at 575 Lexington Ave., New York, NY 10022, (tel. 212-715-7200).

# ECONOMY

## Dominated by Oil

The oil boom of the 1970s led Nigeria to neglect its strong agricultural and light manufacturing bases in favor of an unhealthy dependence on oil for more than 97% of export earnings and 80% of federal revenue. New oil wealth and general economic decline fueled massive migration to the cities and did little to reverse widespread poverty, especially in rural areas, and the collapse of even basic infrastructure and social services. Nigerian oil reserves are 25 billion barrels, and gas reserves are over 100 trillion cubic feet. Due to OPEC quota cutbacks and mounting community problems in oil producing areas, daily

*A report on important events that have taken place since the last State Department revision of this* Background Note.

Democratic rule is returning gradually to Nigeria after years of corrupt military rule, most recently under the control of General Sani Abacha, who died on June 8, 1998. Abacha systematically halted Nigeria's movement toward democracy, arresting in late June 1994 Moshood Abiola, the top vote-getter in the 1993 president election. After Abacha annulled the results of the contest in December 1993, Abiola declared himself president of Nigeria and began forming a government. Hundreds took to the streets demanding Abiola's release, but Abacha responded by cracking down on opposition and suspending a conference on Nigeria's transition to democracy. On July 6 Abiola pleaded not guilty to three counts of treason; the following day oil laborers went on strike to protest the Abacha regime. In the following months millions of Nigerian workers reportedly walked out in support of Abiola and refused to attend scheduled government talks. Abiola remained in prison through June 1996, when his outspoken wife Kudirat Abiola was assassinated. Strikes and protests continued on Abiola's behalf. Independent journalists have been arrested, physically abused, sent into exile, and even killed.

Abacha announced efforts in November 1996 to spur economic change and raise living standards in the country, a pronouncement met with skepticism by an increasingly angry opposition. By December, opponents of the government stepped up their campaign against the Abacha with two bomb attacks in a one-week span. Both attacks were aimed at Col. Mohammed Marwa, head of the Nigerian military. Col. Marwa escaped both attacks.

Abacha, however, maintained a tight grip on power. Quick to punish opposition, the General fired in August 1994 his army and navy commanders. Two weeks later he banned several newspapers, declaring that his government had absolute power and would not give in to pro-democracy demonstrators. Late in September 1994,

claiming that it was part of his plan to "rejuvenate the machinery of government," Abacha removed all civilians from his ruling council. Three months later he suspended habeas corpus and continued to round up and jail opponents. At the same time he rejected a court order demanding the release of Abiola from prison for medical treatment. In March 1995 Abacha ordered the arrest of former Nigerian leader Olusegun Obasanjo on suspicion of treason. Later in the month he dissolved labor unions and jailed their leaders. On April 25 Abacha canceled a January 1, 1996 deadline for the return of civilian rule and refused to discuss the matter. Though he lifted a ban on political parties in June 1995, Abacha placed tight restrictions on their operations. The July convictions in secret trials of forty suspected traitors brought international condemnation and demands of leniency from critics of the Nigerian government. Ultimately Abacha relented on October 1, commuting the death sentences of his convicted opponents and declaring that he would relinquish power to an elected government in 1998.

Despite these promises, many outside observers remained skeptical, largely due to fallout from the case of Ken Saro-Wiwa, leader of the Movement for the Survival of Ogoni People. Sentenced to death in October 1995 for a quadruple murder, many believed Saro-Wiwa had been convicted on trumped-up charges simply because he led opposition to a proposed drilling agreement in Nigeria's main oil-producing region. The executions in early November of Saro-Wiwa and eight others brought a torrent of criticism from the international community and resulted in Nigeria's suspension from the British Commonwealth and an embargo from the European Union on arms and aid to Nigeria. Bowing to this pressure, the Abacha government amended in May 1996 the law under which Saro-Wiwa and the others had been convicted and offered to hold talks on the matter with the UK.

In February 1998, Nigeria led an intervention force of several West African nations that marched on Freetown, Sierra Leone. A military junta in Sierra Leone had seized power from the elected government in May 1997.

In March 1998, Pope John Paul II visited Nigeria for the beatification of a Nigerian priest who had died in 1964. Hundreds of thousands of Nigerians came out to greet the Pope, and about one million attended the beatification ceremony. The Pope appealed for an improvement in the country's human rights situation and a return to democracy. The visit temporarily upstaged General Abacha and the authoritarian military government.

Abacha died suddenly on June 8, 1998 and was succeeded by General Abdulsalam Abubakar, an officer with no interest in governing longer than it took to restore civilian rule. General Abubakar began his rule by releasing many political prisoners and vowing to restore democracy to his corrupt, impoverished country. One prisoner not released was Moshood Abiola, winner of the aborted 1993 elections. Mr. Abiola, died in prison reportedly of natural causes shortly after General Abacha's death.

In early December 1998, Nigerians went to the polls in local elections. On February 27, 1999, Olusegun Obasanjo won the presidential elections over Olu Falae. Mr. Obasanjo is a former general who ruled the country from 1976 to 1979 when he became the first Nigerian military ruler to return power freely to an elected civilian government. Since then, however, Nigeria has been plagued by ethnic and religious violence. Unfortunately, Nigeria's understaffed, underpaid, and undertrained police force is more of a problem than a solution. The forces are corrupt and brutal, prone to extortion and bribes, and contribute to the general lawlessness in the country.

production has fallen to about two million barrels, of which 40% is exported to the United States.

The United States is Nigeria's main trading partner and foreign investor (nearly $7 billion), mostly in the energy sector. Exxon-Mobil, Chevron,

and Texaco are prominent producers. Exxon-Mobil also is a major player in offshore exploration. Significant exports of liquefied natural gas are started in late 1999.

Agriculture has suffered from years of poor management, inconsistent

and poorly implemented government policy, and lack of basic infrastructure, but it still accounts for 40.6% of GDP and 65% of employment. Nigeria is no longer a major exporter of cocoa, peanuts, rubber, and palm products. Cocoa production, mostly from obsolete varieties and overaged trees, is stagnant at around 150,000 tons annually; 25 years ago it was 300,000 tons. There has been a similar decline in peanuts and palm oil. Once the biggest poultry producer in Africa, inefficient corn production, coupled with a corn import ban, slashed output from 40 million birds on feed annually to about six million today. Import constraints limit the availability of many agricultural and food processing inputs. Land tenure in general does not favor long-term investment in technology or modern production methods.

Oil dependency, and the allure it generated of great wealth through government contracts, spawned other distortions. A greatly overvalued naira, fall in domestic purchasing power, the rising costs of imported inputs, and the expense of duplicating infrastructure like power generation fueled consumer imports and has pushed local industry to less than 30% capacity utilization. Many more Nigerian factories would have closed except for low labor costs (10%-15 %), and most—especially pharmaceuticals and textiles—have lost their ability to compete in traditional regional markets. Nigeria's foreign debt is about $30 billion and rising because of new arrears (the precise figure is disputed); about 75% is owed to Paris Club institutions, and much of it went to abandoned or nonperforming public sector projects.

Constraints after years of decline and policy inconsistency, the Nigerian Government's return to reformist policies in 1994 led to some macroeconomic stability but at the cost of new recession due to public sector budget cuts (the formal economy hinges on government spending) and new arrears on domestic and foreign debt. In part because of slumping oil revenue stemming from falling world prices, the government failed to fund its full share of oil joint venture operations, thereby compromising future production, or repair basic infrastructure like oil refineries and power generation. From its peak in 1980 of $25 billion, oil revenue dropped to less than $10 billion in 1998. Faced with falling revenues, falling foreign reserves (from nearly $8 billion in

1998 to $5 billion in March 1999), heavy pressure on the naira, new inflationary pressures, and the prospect of negative GDP growth in 1999, the government in January 1999 agreed to an IMF Staff Monitored Program as an essential first step toward its desire for significant debt relief. Increased oil prices in 2000 have raised government revenues. The IMF is considering a Standby Arrangement with Nigeria this year.

In addition to weak consumer spending, major development and investment constraints include the high cost of doing business in Nigeria, in large part because of the need to duplicate infrastructure, crime, lack of effective due process, and lack of transparency in economic decision-making, especially in contracting. Corruption is endemic and has resulted in projects that are either abandoned or completed at exorbitant costs; contract commissions of more than 100% are reportedly common. There has been notable progress in stabilizing the troubled banking sector, though it remains plagued by poor transparency and an unwillingness to acknowledge its many nonperforming loans.

Nigeria's overwhelmed transportation infrastructure is a major constraint to development. Principal ports are at Lagos (Apapa and Tin Can Island), Port Harcourt, and Calabar. The 8,577 kilometers (5,331-mi.) of navigable inland waterways, utilizing principally the Niger and Benue Rivers and their tributaries, are an important waterway system, though long-delayed dredging in several key areas limits their utility. Of the 80,500 kilometers (50,000 mi.) of roads, more than 15,000 kilometers (10,000 mi.) are officially paved, but many are in poor shape.

However, extensive road repairs and construction by the parastatal Petroleum Trust Fund have greatly improved many major interurban routes. There are 3,500 kilometers (2,180 mi.) of railroad track, which fell into near total disuse but are now slowly coming back into service after extensive renovation by a Chinese company. Three of Nigeria's airports

(Lagos, Kano, and Port Harcourt) receive international flights. The government-owned Nigeria Airways is virtually moribund due to high debt and a vastly shrunken fleet and is now primarily a domestic carrier. There are several private Nigerian carriers, including one with international routes, but all reportedly are losing money due to high costs and weak demand.

## Gradual Reform

Nigerian Government undertakings to privatize large parastatals have yet to be implemented or even detailed, despite many missed target dates. However, there has been slow but important progress on reform, including abolition of most foreign exchange and import controls in favor of a more open market; abolition of most price controls; privatization of some state-owned enterprises; abolition of the dual exchange rate system, which distorted budgets and spawned corruption; and liberalized rules for foreign investment. In late 1998, the government effectively ended indirect fuel subsidies by allowing domestic fuel prices to double to the equivalent of $1 per gallon (the government cut its tax take to give more to hard-pressed down-stream operators). For 3 years, Nigerians and their economy have endured painful and costly fuel shortages caused by the inability of Nigeria's dilapidated refineries to produce anywhere near capacity. Available fuel is often diverted to the domestic and regional black markets. Long-deferred maintenance of Nigeria's four refineries, resulting from the desire of Abacha regime insiders to boost their commissions from fuel imports, began in 1998 and will likely continue well into 1999.

## Investment

Although grappling with the sobering reality of falling oil revenue, Nigeria continues to represent an important market. It is Africa's most populous nation, and it is extremely well endowed with human and mineral resources (especially hydrocarbon). Profitable niche markets outside the energy sector, like specialized tele-communication providers, have developed under the government's reform program, and there is a Nigerian consensus that foreign investment is essential to realizing Nigeria's vast but squandered potential. Companies interested in long-term investment and joint ventures, especially those that use locally available raw materials, will find potential opportunities in the large national market. Sustaining political reforms and its transition to democratic, civilian rule is essential to enhancing Nigeria's investment climate.

## Economic Assistance

The United States assisted with Nigeria's economic development from 1954 through June 1974, when concessional assistance was phased out because of a substantial increase in Nigeria's per capita income resulting from rising oil revenue. By 1974, the United States had provided Nigeria with approximately $360 million in assistance, which included grants for technical assistance, development assistance, relief and rehabilitation, and food aid. Disbursements continued into the late 1970s, bringing total bilateral economic assistance to roughly $445 million.

The sharp decline in oil prices, the deterioration of the economy, and continued military rule characterized Nigeria in the 1980s. In 1983, USAID began providing assistance to the Nigerian Federal and State Ministries of Health to develop and implement programs in family planning and child survival. In 1992, an HIV/AIDS prevention and control program was added to existing health activities. USAID committed $135 million to bilateral assistance programs for the period of 1986 to 1996. Plans to commit $150 million in assistance from 1993 to 2000 were interrupted by strains in U.S.-Nigerian relations over human rights abuses, the failed transition to democracy, and a lack of cooperation from the Nigerian Government on anti-narcotics trafficking issues. By the mid-1990s, these problems resulted in the curtailment of USAID activities which might benefit the Nigerian Government. Existing health programs were re-designed to focus on working through grassroots Nigerian non-governmental organizations and community groups. As a response to the Nigerian military government's plans for delayed transition to civilian rule, the Peace Corps closed its program in Nigeria in 1994.

In response to the increasingly repressive political situation, USAID established a Democracy and Governance (DG) program in 1996. This program integrates themes focusing on basic participatory democracy, human and civil rights, women's empowerment, accountability, and transparency with other health activities to reach Nigerians at the grassroots level in 14 of Nigeria's 36 states.

The sudden death of Gen. Sani Abacha and the assumption of power by Gen. Abdulsalami Abubakar in June 1998, marked a turning point in U.S.-Nigerian relations. USAID provided significant support to the electoral process by providing some $4 million in funding for international election observation, the training of Nigerian election observers and political party polling agents, as well as voter education activities. A Vital National Interest Certification was submitted to Congress in February 1999 by President Clinton to lift restrictions on U.S. Government interaction with and support to the Government of Nigeria. During a transitional period of 18 to 24 months, USAID planned to continue its active support to Nigeria by providing training on the roles and responsibilities of elected officials in a representative democracy for newly elected officials at the federal, state, and local levels prior to their installation in May 1999. Plans also call for assisting in the areas of conflict prevention and resolution in the Niger Delta, civil military relations, civil society, political party development, and encouraging private sector development and economic reform. In addition, health, HIV/AIDS, education, transportation infrastructure, and improving civil-military relations are priorities for bilateral assistance. Overall assistance for FY 2000 should total about $108 million.

# DEFENSE

Active duty personnel in the three Nigerian armed services total approximately 76,000. The Nigerian army, the largest of the services, has about 60,000 personnel deployed in two mechanized infantry divisions, one composite division (airborne and amphibious), the Lagos Garrison Command (a division size unit), and the Abuja-based Brigade of Guards. It has demonstrated its capability to mobilize, deploy, and sustain battalions in support of peacekeeping operations in Liberia, Yugoslavia, Angola, Rwanda, Somalia, and Sierra Leone. The Nigerian navy (7,000) is equipped with frigates, fast attack Pratt, convenes, and coastal patrol boats. The Nigerian air force (9,000) flies transport, trainer, helicopter, and fighter aircraft, but most are currently not operational. Nigeria also has pursued a policy of developing domestic training and military production capabilities. After the imposition of sanctions by many Western nations, Nigeria turned to China, Russia, North Korea, and India for the purchase of military equipment and training.

# FOREIGN RELATIONS

Since independence, Nigerian foreign policy has been characterized by a focus on Africa and by attachment to several fundamental principles: African unity and independence; peaceful settlement of disputes; nonalignment and nonintentional interference in the internal affairs of other nations; and regional economic cooperation and development. In carrying out these principles, Nigeria participates in the Organization of African Unity (OAU), the Economic Community of West African States (ECOWAS), the Nonaligned Movement, and the United Nations.

In pursuing the goal of regional economic cooperation and development, Nigeria helped create ECOWAS, which seeks to harmonize trade and investment practices for its 16 West African member countries and ultimately to achieve a full customs union. Nigeria also has taken the lead in articulating the views of developing nations on the need for modification of the existing international economic order.

Nigeria has played a central role in the ECOWAS efforts to end the civil war in Liberia and contributed the bulk of the ECOWAS peacekeeping forces sent there in 1990. Nigeria also has provided the bulk of troops for ECOMOG forces in Sierra Leone.

Nigeria has enjoyed generally good relations with its immediate neighbors. A longstanding border dispute with Cameroon over the potentially oil-rich Bakassi Peninsula is to be resolved by the International Court of Justice in The Hague. Nigeria released about 150 Cameroonian prisoners of war in late 1998.

Nigeria is a member of the following international organizations: UN and several of its special and related agencies, Organization of Petroleum Exporting Countries (OPEC), Economic Community of West African States (ECOWAS), Organization of African Unity (OAU), Organization of African Trade Union Unity (OATUU), Commonwealth, INTEL-SAT, Nonaligned Movement, several other West African bodies. The Babangida regime joined the Organization of the Islamic Conference (OIC), though President-elect Obasanjo has indicated he might reconsider Nigeria's membership.

# U.S.-NIGERIAN RELATIONS

After the June 12, 1993 presidential election was annulled, and in light of human rights abuses and the failure to embark on a meaningful democratic transition, the U.S. imposed numerous sanctions on Nigeria. These sanctions included the imposition of Section 212(f) of the Immigration and Nationality Act to refuse entry into the U.S. of senior government officials and others who formulated, implemented, or benefited from policies impeding Nigeria's transition to democracy; suspension of all military assistance; and a ban on the sale and repair of military goods and refinery services to Nigeria. The U.S.

Ambassador was recalled for consultations for four months after the execution of the Ogoni Nine on November 10, 1995.

After a period of increasingly strained relations, the death of General Abacha in June 1998 and his replacement by General Abubakar opened a new phase of improved bilateral relations. As the transition to democracy progressed, the removal of visa restrictions, increased high-level visits of U.S. officials, discussions of future assistance, and the granting of a Vital National Interest Certification on counter-narcotics, effective in March, 1999, paved the way for re—establishment of closer ties between the U.S. and Nigeria, as a key partner in the region and the continent.

## Principal U.S. Officials

For up-to-date information on Principal U.S. Officials, see the U.S. Embassies, Consulates, and Foreign Service section starting on page 139.

# NORWAY

May 1999

Official Name:
**Kingdom of Norway**

# PROFILE

## Geography

**Area (including the island territories of Svalbard and Jan Mayen):** 385,364 sq. km. (150,000 sq. mi.); slightly larger than New Mexico.
**Cities:** Capital—Oslo (pop. 499,000). Other cities—Bergen (200,000), Trondheim (136,000), Stavanger (107,000).
**Terrain:** Rugged with high plateaus, steep fjords, mountains, and fertile valleys.
**Climate:** Temperate along the coast, colder inland.

## People

**Nationality:** Noun and adjective—Norwegian(s).
**Population (1997 est.):** 4.4 million.
**Annual growth rate (1997):** 0.5%.
**Density:** 13 per sq. km.
**Ethnic groups:** Norwegian (Nordic, Alpine, Baltic), Lapp (or Sami), a racial–cultural minority of 20,000; foreign nationals (225,000) from Nordic and other countries.
**Religion:** Evangelical Lutheran 94%.
**Languages:** Norwegian (official), Lapp.
**Education:** Years compulsory—9.

Literacy—100%.
**Health:** Infant mortality rate—4/1,000. Life expectancy—men 75 yrs; women 81 yrs.
**Work force (1997, 2.3 million):** Government, social, personal services—39%. Wholesale and retail trade, hotels, restaurants—17%. Manufacturing—15%. Transport and communications—8%. Financing, insurance, real estate, business services—8%. Agriculture, forestry, fishing—5%. Construction—6%. Oil extraction—1%.

## Government

**Type:** Hereditary constitutional monarchy.
**Independence:** 1905.
**Constitution:** May 17, 1814.
**Branches:** Executive—king (chief of state), prime minister (head of government), Council of Ministers (cabinet). Legislative—modified unicameral parliament (Storting). Judicial—Supreme Court, appellate courts, city and county courts.
**Political parties:** Labor, Conservative, Center, Christian Democratic, Liberal, Socialist Left, Progress.
**Suffrage:** Universal over 18.
**Administrative subdivisions:** 18 fylker (counties), the city of Oslo, and Svalbard.
**National holiday:** May 17.
**Flag:** White cross with blue inner cross on red field. The white cross and red field are derived from the Danish flag; the blue cross was added to symbolize Norway's independence.

## Economy

**GDP (1997):** $151 billion.
**Annual growth rate (1997):** 1.9%.
Per capita GDP (1997): $33,300.
**Natural resources:** Oil, gas, fish, timber, hydroelectric power, mineral ores.
**Agriculture and fishing (2% of GDP):** Arable land—3%. Products—dairy, livestock, grain (barley, oats, wheat), potatoes and other vegetables, fruits and berries, furs, wool.
**Industry (manufacturing, 12% of GNP:** oil, gas, shipping 16%; construction 4%) Types—food processing, pulp and paper, ships, aluminum, ferroalloys, iron and steel, nickel, zinc, nitrogen, fertilizers, transport equipment, hydroelectric power, refinery products, petrochemicals, electronics.
**Trade (1997):** Exports (f.o.b.)—$47 billion: crude oil, natural gas, pulp and paper, metals, chemicals, fish and fish products. Major markets—U.K., Germany, Sweden, U.S. (6%). Imports (c.i.f.)—$35 billion: machinery and transport equipment, foodstuffs, iron and steel, textiles and clothing. Major suppliers—Sweden, Germany, U.K., U.S.(8%).

# PEOPLE

Ethnically, Norwegians are predominantly Germanic, although in the far north there are communities of Sami (Lapps) who came to the area more than 10,000 years ago, probably from central Asia. In recent years, Norway has become home to increasing numbers of immigrants, foreign workers, and asylum–seekers from various parts of the world. Immigrants now total nearly 150,000; some have obtained Norwegian citizenship.

Although the Evangelical Lutheran Church is the state church, Norway has complete religious freedom. Education is free through the university level and is compulsory from ages 7 to 16. At least 12 months of military service and training are required of every eligible male. Norway's health system includes free hospital care, physician's compensation, cash benefits during illness and pregnancy, and other medical and dental plans. There is a public pension system.

Norway is in the top rank of nations in the number of books printed per capita, even though Norwegian is one of the world's smallest language groups. Norway's most famous writer is the dramatist Henrik Ibsen. Artists Edvard Munch and Christian Krogh were Ibsen's contemporaries. Munch drew part of his inspiration from Europe and in turn exercised a strong influence on later European expressionists. Sculptor Gustav Vigeland has a permanent exhibition in the Vigeland Sculpture Park in Oslo. Musical development in Norway since Edvard Grieg has followed either native folk themes or, more recently, international trends.

# HISTORY

The Viking period (9th to 11th centuries) was one of national unification and expansion. The Norwegian royal line died out in 1387, and the country entered a period of union with Denmark. By 1586, Norway had become part of the Danish Kingdom. In 1814, as a result of the Napoleonic wars, Norway was separated from Denmark and combined with Sweden. The union persisted until 1905, when Sweden recognized Norwegian independence.

The Norwegian Government offered the throne of Norway to Danish Prince Carl in 1905. After a plebiscite approving the establishment of a monarchy, the parliament unanimously elected him king. He took the name of Haakon VII, after the kings of independent Norway. Haakon died in 1957 and was succeeded by his son, Olav V, who died in January 1991. Upon Olav's death, his son Harald was crowned as King Harald V. Norway was a nonbelligerent during World War I, but as a result of the German invasion and occupation during World War II, Norwegians generally became skeptical of the concept of neutrality and turned instead to collective security. Norway was one of the signers of the North Atlantic Treaty in 1949 and was a founding member of the United Nations. The first UN General Secretary, Trygve Lie, was a Norwegian. Under the terms of the will of Alfred Nobel, the *Storting* (Parliament) elects the five members of the Norwegian Nobel Committee who award the Nobel Peace Prize to champions of peace.

# GOVERNMENT

The functions of the King are mainly ceremonial, but he has influence as the symbol of national unity. Although the 1814 constitution grants important executive powers to the king, these are almost always exercised by the Council of Ministers in the name of the King (King's Council). The Council of Ministers consists of a prime minister—chosen by the political parties represented in the *Storting*—and other ministers.

The 165 members of the *Storting* are elected from 18 *fylker* (counties) for 4–year terms according to a complicated system of proportional representation. After elections, the *Storting* divides into two chambers, the *Odelsting* and the *Lagting*, which meet separately or jointly depending on the legislative issue under consideration.

The special High Court of the Realm hears impeachment cases; the regular courts include the Supreme Court (17 permanent judges and a president), courts of appeal, city and county courts, the labor court, and conciliation councils. Judges attached to regular courts are appointed by the King in council after nomination by the Ministry of Justice.

Each *fylke* is headed by a governor appointed by the King in council, with one governor exercising authority in both Oslo and the adjacent county of Akershus.

# POLITICAL CONDITIONS

## Principal Government Officials

For up-to-date information on Principal Government Officials, see the Chiefs of State and Cabinet Members of Foreign Governments section starting on page 1.

Norway maintains an embassy in the United States at 2720 – 34th Street NW, Washington, DC 20008, tel .202–333–6000 and consulates in Houston, Los Angeles, Minneapolis, New York, and San Francisco.

Until the 1981 election, Norway had been governed by Labor Party governments since 1935, except for three periods (1963, 1965–71, and 1972–73). The Labor Party lost its majority in the *Storting* in the 1981 elections. Since that time, minority and coalition governments have been the rule.

From 1981 to 1997, governments alternated between Labor minority governments and Conservative–led governments. Labor leader Gro Harlem Brundtland served as Prime Minister from 1990 until October 1996 when she decided to step out of politics. Labor Party leader Thorbjorn Jagland formed a new Labor government that stayed in office until October 1997. A three–party minority coalition government headed by Christian Democrat Prime Minister Kjell Magne Bondevik moved into

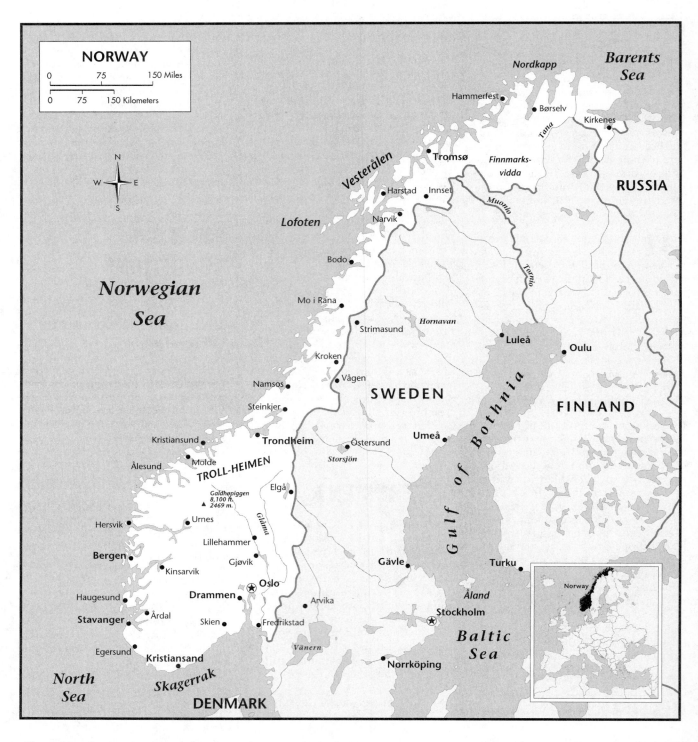

## NORWAY

0    75    150 Miles

0    75    150 Kilometers

Barents Sea

Nordkapp

Hammerfest

Børselv

Kirkenes

Tromsø

Finnmarks-vidda

RUSSIA

Vesterålen

Harstad    Innset

Lofoten

Narvik

Tana

Muonio

Bodo

Mo i Rana

Torne

Norwegian Sea

Strimasund

Hornavan

Luleå

Oulu

Kroken

Vågen

SWEDEN

Namsos

FINLAND

Steinkjer

Kristiansund

Trondheim

Östersund

Umeå

Ålesund    Molde

Storsjön

TROLL-HEIMEN

Gulf of Bothnia

Galdhøpiggen
8,100 ft.
2469 m.

Elgå

Hersvik    Urnes

Gløma

Lillehammer

Bergen

Gjøvik

Gävle

Turku

Kinsarvik

Åland

Oslo

Haugesund

Drammen

Arvika

Stavanger    Årdal

Stockholm

Skien

Fredrikstad

Baltic Sea

Egersund

Kristiansand

Vänern

North Sea

Skagerrak

Norrköping

DENMARK

Norway

office when Jagland, after the September 1997 election, declared that his government would step down because the Labor Party failed to win at least 36.9% of the national vote, the percentage Labor had won in the 1993 election. Bondevik's nonsocialist coalition is composed of the Center Party, the Christian Democratic Party, and the Liberal Party. The coa-

lition parties control only 42 seats in the 165–member National Assembly, and the coalition governs on the basis of shifting alliances in Parliament.

## ECONOMY

Norway is one of the world's richest countries. It has an important stake

in promoting a liberal environment for foreign trade. Its large shipping fleet is one of the most modern among maritime nations. Metals, pulp and paper products, chemicals, shipbuilding, and fishing are the most significant traditional industries.

Norway's emergence as a major oil and gas producer in the mid–1970s transformed the economy. Large sums of investment capital poured into the offshore oil sector, leading to greater increases in Norwegian production costs and wages than in the rest of Western Europe up to the time of the global recovery of the mid–1980s. The influx of oil revenue also permitted Norway to expand an already extensive social welfare system.

High oil prices from 1983 to 1985 led to significant increases in consumer spending, wages, and inflation. The subsequent decline in oil prices since 1985 sharply reduced tax revenues and required a tightening of both the government budget and private sector demand. As a result, the nonoil economy showed almost no growth during 1986–88, and the current account went into deficit. As oil prices recovered sharply in 1990 following the Persian Gulf crisis, the 1990 current account posted a large surplus which continued through 1997. Unemployment fell gradually to 4.1%. Given the volatility of the oil and gas market, Norway is seeking to restructure its nonoil economy to reduce subsidies and stimulate efficient, nontraditional industry.

Norway's exports have continued to grow, largely because of favorable world demand for oil and gas. Moreover, the flight of Norwegian–owned ships from the country's traditional register ended in 1987, as the government established an international register, replete with tax breaks and relief from national crewmember requirements.

Norway voted against joining the European Union (EU) in a 1994 referendum. With the exception of the agricultural and fisheries sectors, however, Norway enjoys free trade with the EU under the framework of the European Economic Area. This agreement aims to apply the four freedoms of the EU's internal market (goods, persons, services, and capital) to Norway. As a result, Norway normally adopts and implements most EU directives. Norwegian monetary policy is aimed at maintaining a stable exchange rate for the krone against European currencies, of which the "euro" is a key operating parameter. Norway is not a member of the EU's Economic and Monetary Union and does not have a fixed exchange rate. Its principle trading partners are in the EU; the United States ranks sixth.

## Energy Resources

Offshore hydrocarbon deposits were discovered in the 1960s, and development began in the 1970s. The growth of the petroleum sector has contributed significantly to Norwegian economic vitality. Current petroleum production capacity is more than 3 million barrels per day. Production has increased rapidly during the past several years as new fields are opened. Total production in 1997 was about 237 million cubic meters of oil equivalents, nearly 81% of which was crude oil. Hydropower provides nearly all of Norway's electricity, and all of the gas and most of the oil produced were exported. Production is expected to increase significantly in the 1990s as new fields come onstream.

Norway is the world's second–largest oil exporter and provides about 40% of Western Europe's crude oil requirements and 20% of its gas requirements. In 1997, Norwegian oil and gas exports accounted for 48% of total merchandise exports. In addition, offshore exploration and production have stimulated onshore economic activities. Foreign companies, including many American ones, participate actively in the petroleum sector.

# FOREIGN RELATIONS

Norway supports international cooperation and the peaceful settlement of disputes, recognizing the need for maintaining a strong national defense through collective security. Accordingly, the cornerstones of Norwegian policy are active membership in NATO and support for the United Nations and its specialized agencies. Norway also pursues a policy of economic, social, and cultural cooperation with other Nordic countries—Denmark, Sweden, Finland, and Iceland—through the Nordic Council. On January 1, 1999, Foreign Minister Knut Vollebaek became Chairman In Office of the Organization for Security and Cooperation in Europe.

**Travel Notes**

**Travel Advice:** For up-to-date information from the U.S. State Department on possible inconvenient or hazardous situations, see the **Travel Warnings and Consular Information Sheets from the U.S. Government** section starting on page 1723. For the latest information on health requirements and conditions, see the **International Travelers' Health Information** section starting on page 1385. For further information dealing with non-urgent matter, see the **Tips for Travelers to...** section starting on page 1588.

In addition to strengthening traditional ties with developed countries, Norway seeks to build friendly relations with developing countries and has undertaken humanitarian and development aid efforts with selected African and Asian nations. Norway also is dedicated to encouraging democracy, assisting refugees, and protecting human rights throughout the world.

# U.S.-NORWAY RELATIONS

The United States and Norway enjoy a long tradition of friendly association. The relationship is strengthened by the millions of Norwegian–Americans in the United States and by about 10,000 U.S. citizens who reside in Norway. The two countries enjoy an active cultural exchange, both officially and privately.

## Principal U.S. Officials

**For up-to-date information on Principal U.S. Officials, see the U.S. Embassies, Consulates, and Foreign Service section starting on page 139.**

The U.S. Embassy is located at Drammensveien 18, 0244 Oslo (tel. 47–22–44– 85–50; FAX: 47–22–43–07–77).

# OMAN

December 1994

## Official Name:
## Sultanate of Oman

# PROFILE

## Geography
**Area:** 212,457 sq. km. (82,030 sq. mi.); about the size of Colorado. It is bordered on the north by the United Arab Emirates (U.A.E.), on the northwest by Saudi Arabia, and on the southwest by the Republic of Yemen. The Omani coastline stretches 2,092 km.
**Cities:** Capital—Muscat. Other cities—Matrah, Ruwi, Nizwa, Salalah, Sohar.
**Terrain:** Mountains, plains, and arid plateau.
**Climate:** Hot, humid along the coast; hot, dry in the interior; summer monsoon in far south.

## People
**Nationality:** Noun—Oman. Adjective—Omani.
**Population:** 1.6 million (1993).
**Annual growth rate:** 3.6% (est.).
**Ethnic groups:** Arab, Baluchi, East African (Zanzabari), South Asian (Indian, Pakistani, Bangladeshi). Religions: Ibadhi and Sunni Muslim: 95%, Shia Muslim, Hindu.
**Languages:** Arabic (official), English, Baluchi, Urdu, Hindi and Indian dialects.
**Education:** Literacy—41% ( est.).
**Health:** Infant mortality rate (est.)—33/1,000. Life expectancy—66 years.
**Work force:** 750,000. Agriculture and fishing—50%.

## Government
**Type:** Monarchy.
**Constitution:** none.
**Branches:** Executive—sultan. Legislative—Majlis Ash-Shura (Consultative Council). Judicial—civil courts handle criminal cases; Shari'a (Islamic law) courts oversee family law.
**Political parties:** None.
**Suffrage:** None.
**Administrative subdivisions:** eight administrative regions: Muscat, Al-Batinah, Musandam, A'Dhahirah, A'Dakhliya, A'Shariqiya, Al Wusta, Dhofar Governorate. There are 59 districts (wilayats).

## Economy
**GDP (1992):** $11.6 billion.
**Per capita GDP:** $5,800.
**Natural resources:** Oil, natural gas, copper, marble, limestone, gypsum, chromium.
**Agriculture and fisheries:** (3.66% of GDP).
**Agriculture:** Products—dates, limes, bananas, mangoes, alfalfa, other fruits and vegetables. Fisheries—Kingfish, tuna, other fish, shrimp, lobster, abalone.
**Industry:** Types—crude petroleum over 750,000 b/d; construction, petroleum refinery, copper mines and smelter, cement and various light industries.
**Trade (1992):** Exports—$5.5 billion; Oil—83%. Major markets—Japan (35%), South Korea (21%), Singapore (7%), U.S. (6%), Taiwan (4%). Imports—$3.6 billion: machinery, transportation equipment, manufactured goods, food, livestock, lubricants. Major suppliers—Japan 21%, U.A.E. 20%, U.K. 10%, U.S. 7%.
**Exchange rate (1994):** 38 Rials= U.S.$1.

# PEOPLE

About 50% of the population lives in Muscat and the Batinah coastal plain northwest of the capital; about 200,000 live in the Dhofar (southern) region, and about 30,000 live in the remote Musandam peninsula on the Strait of Hormuz. At least 550,000 expatriates live in Oman, of whom about 455,000 are guest workers from South Asia, Egypt, Jordan, and the Philippines.

Since 1970, the government has given especially high priority to education to develop a domestic work force, which the government considers a vital factor in the country's economic and social progress. In 1986, Oman's first university, Sultan Qaboos University, opened. Other post-secondary institutions include a technical college, banking institute, teachers training college, and health sciences institute. As many as 200 scholarships are awarded each year for study abroad.

# HISTORY

Muscat and Oman (as the country was called before 1970) was converted to Islam in the seventh century A.D., during the lifetime of Muhammad. Ibadhism, a form of Islam tracing its roots to the Kharijite movement, became the dominant religious sect in Oman by the eighth century. Contact with Europe was established in 1508, when the Portuguese conquered parts of the coastal region. Portugal's influence predominated for more than a century, with only a short interruption by the Turks. Fortifications built during the Portuguese occupation can still be seen at Muscat.

After the Portuguese were expelled in 1650 and while resisting Persian attempts to establish hegemony, Muscat and Oman extended its conquests to Zanzibar (now part of Tanzania), other parts of the eastern coast of Africa, and portions of the southern Arabian peninsula. During this period, political leadership shifted from the Ibadhi imams, who were elected religious leaders, to hereditary sultans who established their capital in Muscat. The Muscat rulers established trading posts on the Persian coast (now Iran) and also exercised a measure of control over the Makran coast (now Pakistan) of mainland Asia. By the early 19th century, Muscat and Oman was the most powerful state in Arabia and on the East African coast.

Muscat and Oman was the object of Franco-British rivalry throughout the 18th century. The British developed the stronger position in 1908 through an agreement of friendship. During the 19th century, Muscat and Oman and the United Kingdom concluded several treaties of friendship and commerce. Their traditional association was confirmed in 1951

through a new treaty of friendship, commerce, and navigation by which the United Kingdom recognized the sultanate as a fully independent state.

When Sultan Sa'id Sayyid died in 1856, his sons quarreled over his succession. As a result of this struggle, the empire—through the mediation of the British Government under the "Canning Award"—was divided in 1861 into two separate principalities—Zanzibar, with its East African dependencies, and Muscat and Oman. Zanzibar paid an annual subsidy to Muscat and Oman until its independence in early 1964.

During the late 19th and early 20th centuries, the sultan in Muscat faced rebellion by members of the Ibadhi sect residing in the interior who wanted to be ruled exclusively by their religious leader, the Imam of Oman. This conflict was resolved temporarily by the Treaty of Seeb, which granted the imam autonomous rule in the interior, while recognizing the nominal sovereignty of the sultan.

The conflict flared up again in 1954, when the new imam led a sporadic five-year rebellion against the sultan's efforts to extend government control into the interior. The insurgents were defeated in 1959 with British help. The sultan then terminated the Treaty of Seeb and voided the office of the imam. In the early-1960s, the exiled imam obtained support from Saudi Arabia and other Arab governments, but this support ended in the 1980s.

In 1964, a separatist revolt began in Dhofar Province. Aided by communist and leftist governments such as the former South Yemen (People's Democratic Republic of Yemen), the rebels formed the Dhofar Liberation Front, which later merged with the Marxist-dominated Popular Front for the Liberation of Oman and the Arab Gulf (PFLOAG). The PFLOAG's declared intention was to overthrow all traditional Arab Gulf regimes in the Persian Gulf.

In mid-1974, PFLOAG shortened its name to the Popular Front for the Liberation of Oman (PFLO) and embarked on a political rather than a military approach to gain power in the other Persian Gulf states, while continuing the guerrilla war in Dhofar.

Sultan Qaboos bin Sa'id assumed power on July 24, 1970, in a palace coup directed against his father, Sa'id bin Taymur, who later died in exile in London. The new sultan was confronted with insurgency in a country plagued by endemic disease, illiteracy, and poverty.

One of the new sultan's first measures was to abolish many of his father's harsh restrictions, which had caused thousands of Omanis to leave the country, and offer amnesty to opponents of the previous regime, many of whom returned to Oman. He also established a modern government structure; and launched a major development program to upgrade educational and health facilities, build a modern infrastructure, and develop the country's resources.

In an effort to curb the Dhofar insurgency, Sultan Qaboos expanded and re-equipped the armed forces and granted amnesty to all surrendered rebels while vigorously prosecuting the war in Dhofar. He obtained direct military support from Iran and Jordan. By early-1975, the guerrillas were confined to a 50-square-kilometer (20-sq.-mi.) area and shortly thereafter were defeated. As the war drew to a close, civil action programs were given increasing priority throughout the province and since then have become major elements in winning the allegiance of the people. The PFLO threat appeared to diminish further with the establishment of diplomatic relations in October 1983 between South Yemen and Oman, and South Yemen's subsequent diminution of propaganda and subversive activities against Oman. In late-1987, Oman opened an embassy in Aden, South Yemen, and appointed its first resident ambassador to the country.

# GOVERNMENT AND POLITICAL CONDITIONS

Sultan Qaboos bin Sa'id, the monarch, rules with the aid of his ministers. His dynasty, the Al Sa'id, was founded about 250 years ago by Imam Ahmed bin Sa'id. The sultan is a direct descendant of the 19th-century ruler, Sa'id bin Sultan. The sultanate has no constitution, Western-style legislature, or legal political parties.

Oman's judicial system traditionally has been based on the Shari'a—the Koranic laws and the oral teachings of the Islamic Prophet Muhammad. The Shari'a courts fall under the jurisdiction of the Ministry of Justice, Awqaf, and Islamic Affairs. Oman's first criminal code was not enacted until 1974. The current structure of the criminal court system was established in 1984 and consists of a magistrate court in the capital and four additional magistrate courts in Sohar, Sur, Salalah, and Nizwa. In the less-populated areas and among the nomadic bedouin, tribal custom often is the law.

Administratively, the populated regions are divided into numerous districts (wilayats) presided over by governors (walis) responsible for settling local disputes, collecting taxes, and maintaining peace. Most wilayats are small; an exception is the wilayat of Dhofar, which comprises the whole province. The wali of Dhofar is an important government figure, holding cabinet rank, while other walis operate under the guidance of the ministry of interior.

In November 1991, Sultan Qaboos established the Majlis ash-Shura (Council of Deliberation/Consultation), which replaced the 10-year-old State Consultative Council, in an effort to systematize and broaden public participation in government. Representatives were chosen in the following manner: Local caucuses in each of the 59 districts sent forward the names of three nominees, whose credentials were reviewed by a cabi-

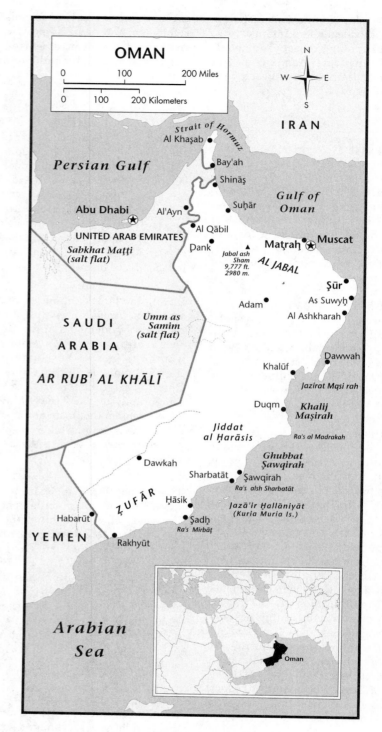

net committee. These names were then forwarded to the sultan, who made the final selection. The Council serves as a conduit of information between the people and the government ministries. It is empowered to review drafts of economic and social legislation prepared by service ministries, such as communications and housing, and to provide recommenda-

tions. Service ministers may also be summoned before the Majlis to respond to representatives' questions. It has no authority in the areas of foreign affairs, defense, security, and finances.

After North and South Yemen merged in May 1990, Oman settled its border disputes with the new

Republic of Yemen on October 1, 1992. The two neighbors have cooperative bilateral relations.

Although Oman enjoys a high degree of internal stability, regional tensions in the aftermath of the Persian Gulf war and the Iran-Iraq war continue to necessitate large defense expenditures. In 1992, Oman budgeted $1.73 billion for defense—about 15% of its GDP. Oman maintains a small but effective military, supplied mainly with British equipment in addition to items from the United States, France, and other countries. British officers, on loan or on contract to the sultanate, help staff the armed forces, although a program of "Omanization" has steadily increased the proportion of Omani officers over the past several years.

## Principal Government Officials

For up-to-date information on Principal Government Officials, see the Chiefs of State and Cabinet Members of Foreign Governments section starting on page 1.

Oman maintains an embassy in the United States at 2535 Belmont Rd. NW, Washington, DC 20008 (tel. 202-387-1980).

# ECONOMY

When Oman declined as an entrepot for arms and slaves in the mid-19th century, much of its former prosperity was lost, and the economy relied almost exclusively on agriculture, camel and goat herding, fishing, and traditional handicrafts. Today, oil fuels the economy and revenues from petroleum products have enabled Oman's dramatic development over the past 20 years.

Oil was first discovered in the interior near Fahud in the western desert in 1964. Petroleum Development (Oman) Ltd. (PDO) began production in August 1967. The Omani Govern-

## Travel Notes

**Visas and Customs:** A visa or a "No Objection Certificate" is required of U.S. citizens for entry, and sponsorship by a resident of Oman is normally necessary. Visa application may be made at the Omani Embassy in Washington, D.C. Application for a No Objection Certificate can be made only by the traveler's sponsor in Oman. Customs regulations prohibit importation of liquor, firearms, or pornographic material. Incoming baggage may be inspected, including carry-ons.

**Climate and Clothing:** Wear summer clothing almost year round, but bring a sweater for the cool winter evenings. Because of cultural sensitivities, conservative dress is advised—no sleeveless tops, short skirts, shorts, or tight-fitting clothing for women. Men should only wear tank tops or shorts when engaged in athletic activity.

**Health:** Basic, modern care and most medicines are available. Typhoid and gamma globulin shots are recommended, as well as up-to-date tetanus and polio. Take malaria suppressants. Tapwater, including ice, is not reliable.

**Telecommunications:** Telephone service is available in the capital area, in Salalah, and several other towns. Telegraphic and telex service is available; telefax and mobile telephones are also available. Oman is nine hours ahead of eastern standard time.

**Transportation:** Flights are available from several regional and European cities to the international airport at Seeb, about 42 km. (26 mi.) west of Muscat. Taxis can be rented for the ride or by the day. Rental cars also are readily available. Driving is on the right.

**Hotel Accommodations:** There are several international-class hotels in the Muscat area, but they often are heavily booked during the cooler months (October-March), and reservations should be made well ahead of travel. The Omani Government promotes limited tourism. Tourists who wish to visit Oman must be sponsored; hotels may arrange visas and sponsorship. Contact your hotel for further information. Business people are welcome under proper sponsorship.

**Travel Advice:** For up-to-date information from the U.S. State Department on possible inconvenient or hazardous situations, see the **Travel Warnings and Consular Information Sheets from the U.S. Government** section starting on page 1723. For the latest information on health requirements and conditions, see the **International Travelers' Health Information** section starting on page 1385. For further information dealing with non-urgent matter, see the **Tips for Travelers to...** section starting on page 1588.

ment owns 60% of PDO production, and foreign interests own 40% (Royal Dutch Shell owns 34%; the remaining 6% is owned by Compagnie Francaise des Petroles [Total] and Partex). In 1976, Oman's oil production rose to 366,000 barrels per day (b/d) but declined gradually to about 285,000 b/d in late 1980 due to the slow depletion of recoverable reserves. From 1981 to 1986, Oman was able to compensate for declining oil prices by increasing its production levels, which reached 600,000 b/d. With the collapse of oil prices in 1986, however, revenues dropped dramatically. Production was cut back temporarily in coordination with the Organization of Petroleum Exporting Countries (OPEC), and production levels again reached 600,000 b/d by mid-1987, which helped increase revenues. By

mid-1993, production had climbed to more than 750,000 b/d but falling oil prices may necessitate further adjustment. Oman is not a member of OPEC but is a leader of Independent Petroleum Exporting Countries.

Oman does not have the immense oil resources of some of its neighbors. Nevertheless, recently, it has found more oil than it has produced, and total proven reserves rose from 2.9 billion barrels in January 1982 to 4.6 billion barrels by the end of 1992. The outlook for additions to reserves is promising, although Oman's complex geology makes exploration and production a challenge. Recent improvements in technology, however, have enhanced recovery. Natural gas reserves, which will increasingly provide the fuel for power generation and desalination, stand at 17 trillion cubic feet. Studies are currently underway to supply export of gas for liquefied natural gas after processing in Oman.

Agriculture and fishing are the traditional way of life in Oman. Dates and limes, grown extensively in the Batinah coastal plain and the highlands, make up most of the country's agricultural exports. Coconut palms, wheat, and bananas also are grown, and cattle are raised in Dhofar. Other areas grow cereals and forage crops. Poultry production is steadily rising. Fish and shellfish exports reached $35 million in 1991.

The government is undertaking many development projects to modernize the economy and improve the standard of living. Increases in agriculture and especially fish production are believed possible with the application of modern technology. The Muscat capital area has both an international airport at Seeb and a deepwater port at Mina Qaboos. An airport in Salalah, capital of the Dhofar Governate, and a seaport at nearby Raysut were recently completed. A national road network includes a $400-million highway linking the northern and southern regions. In an effort to diversify, the government built a $200-million copper mining and refining plant at Sohar. Other large industrial projects include an 80,000 b/d oil refinery and two cement factories. An industrial zone at Rusayl is the showcase of the country's modest light industries. Marble, lime-stone, and gypsum may prove commercially valuable in the future.

Some of the largest budgetary outlays are in the areas of health services and basic education. The number of schools rose from three in 1970 to more than 840 by 1993, while hospital and clinic beds increased during this period from 12 to 4,355.

The subsequent drop in oil prices over the 1980s, combined with rapidly growing recurrent outlays and ambitious spending programs for development and defense usually have

created budget deficits every year (except 1990) since 1982.

Economic growth surged in Oman in 1992. This was the direct result of the improvement in Oman's oil sector, which experienced higher prices and an increased production level. The other key sector of the economy, government spending, is directly driven by the amount of oil revenues the government receives.

The economic outlook for the remainder of the 1990s is good, although falling oil prices once again will require budget cutbacks. The Omani Government is continuing to pursue its fourth five-year plan, launched in 1991, to reduce its dependence on oil and expatriate labor. The plan focuses on income diversification, job creation for Omanis in the private sector, and development of Oman's interior. Government programs offer soft loans and propose the building of new industrial estates in population centers outside the capital area. The government is giving greater emphasis to the "Omanization" of the labor force, particularly in sectors such as banking, hotels, and municipally-sponsored shops benefiting from government subsidies. Currently, efforts are underway to liberalize investment opportunities in order to attract foreign capital.

U.S. firms face a small and highly competitive market dominated by trade with Japan and Britain and re-exports from the United Arab Emirates. The sale of U.S. products also is hampered by higher transportation costs and the lack of familiarity with Oman on the part of U.S. exporters. However, the traditional U.S. market in Oman, oil field supplies and services, should grow as the country's major oil producer continues a major expansion of fields and wells.

# FOREIGN RELATIONS

Except for a brief period of Persian rule, the Omanis have remained independent since 1650. Under its previous ruler, Oman had limited contacts with the outside world,

including neighboring Arab states. When Sultan Qaboos assumed power in 1970, only two countries, the United Kingdom and India, maintained a diplomatic presence in the country. A special treaty relationship permitted the United Kingdom close involvement in Oman's civil and military affairs. Ties with the United Kingdom have remained friendly under Sultan Qaboos.

Oman pursues a moderate foreign policy. It supported the Camp David accords and was one of three Arab League states, along with Somalia and Sudan, that did not break relations with Egypt after the signing of the Egyptian-Israeli Peace Treaty in 1979. Oman supports the current Middle East peace initiatives, as it did those in 1983. In April 1994, Oman hosted the plenary meeting of the water working group of the peace process, the first Gulf state to do so During the Persian Gulf crisis, Oman assisted the UN coalition effort. Oman has developed close ties to its neighbors; it joined the six-member Gulf Cooperation Council when it was established in 1980.

For many years, Oman avoided relations with communist countries because of the communist support connection to the insurgency in Dhofar. Recently, however, Oman has undertaken diplomatic initiatives in the Central Asian republics, particularly in Kazakhstan, where it is involved in a joint oil pipeline project. In addition, Oman maintains a low-key relationship with Iran, its northern neighbor, and the two countries regularly exchange delegations. Oman is an active member in international and regional organizations, notably the Arab League. Oman is a temporary member of the UN Security Council for 1994–95.

# U.S.-OMANI RELATIONS

The United States has maintained relations with the sultanate since the early years of American independence. A treaty of friendship and navigation, one of the first agreements of its kind with an Arab state, was concluded between the United States and Muscat in 1833. This treaty was replaced by the treaty of amity, economic relations, and Consular Rights signed at Salalah on December 20, 1958.

A U.S. Consulate was maintained in Muscat from 1880 until 1915. Thereafter, U.S. interests in Oman were handled by U.S. diplomats resident in other countries. In 1972, the U.S. ambassador in Kuwait was accredited also as the first U.S. ambassador to Oman, and the U.S. embassy, headed by a resident charge d'affaires, was opened. The first resident U.S. ambassador took up his post in July 1974. The Oman embassy was opened in Washington, DC, in 1973.

U.S.-Omani relations were strengthened in 1980 by the conclusion of two important agreements. One provided access to Omani military facilities by U.S. forces under agreed upon conditions. The other agreement established a Joint Commission for Economic and Technical Cooperation, located in Muscat, to provide U.S. economic assistance to Oman. A Peace Corps program, which assisted Oman mainly in the fields of health and education, was initiated in 1973 and phased out in 1983. A team from the Federal Aviation Administration worked with Oman's Civil Aviation Department on a reimbursable basis but was phased out in 1992.

In April 1983, Sultan Qaboos made a state visit to the United States. Vice President Bush visited Oman in 1984 and 1986.

## Principal U.S. Officials

For up-to-date information on Principal U.S. Officials, see the U.S. Embassies, Consulates, and Foreign Service section starting on page 139.

The address of the U.S. embassy in Oman is P.O. Box 202, Postal Code No. 115, Muscat, Sultanate of Oman. Telephone: (011) (968) 698-989, 699-094. FAX: (011)(968) 604-316.

# PAKISTAN

March 2000

## Official Name:
## Islamic Republic of Pakistan

# PROFILE

## Geography

**Area:** 803,943 sq. km. (310,527 sq. mi.); about twice the size of California.
**Cities:** Capital—Islamabad and adjacent Rawalpindi comprise a national capital area with a combined population of 3.7 million. Other cities—Karachi (10 million), Lahore (5.7 million), Faisalabad (6.5 million).

## People

**Nationality:** Noun and adjective—Pakistan(i).
**Population (1998 estimate):** 135 million.
**Annual growth rate (1998):** 2.6%.
**Ethnic groups:** Punjabi, Sindhi, Pathan (Pushtun), Baloch, Muhajir (i.e., Urdu-speaking immigrants from India and their descendants), Saraiki, Hazara.
**Religions:** Muslim 97%; small minorities of Christians, Hindus, and others.
**Languages:** Urdu (national and official), English, Punjabi, Sindhi, Pushtu, Baloch.
**Education:** Literacy (1999) 45%. Unofficial estimates are as low as 35%.
**Health:** Infant mortality rate (1997)—85/1,000. Life expectancy (1999)—men 63 yrs., women 63 yrs.
**Work force (1999):** Agriculture—44%. Services—30%. Industry—26%.

## Government

**Type:** Military. Parliamentary democracy suspended on October 12, 1999.
**Independence:** August 14, 1947.
**Branches:** Executive—The Chief of Army Staff serves as Chief Executive and is advised by a mixed civilian/military National Security Council and civilian Cabinet. Provinces are headed by a Governor and provincial cabinet, who are civilians appointed by the Chief Executive. Judicial—Supreme Court, provincial high courts, and Federal Islamic Court. On January 26, 2000, justices were required to take an oath of loyalty to the Chief Executive and the Provisional Constitutional Order that placed the constitution in abeyance.
Political parties: the Pakistan Muslim League (PML) and the Pakistan People's Party (PPP) are national political parties. Other parties with a strong regional, ethnic or religious base include the Awami National Party (ANP), the Muttahida Qaumi Movement (MQM), and the Jamaat-i-Islami (JI).
**Suffrage:** Universal at 21. Following the October 12, 1999, ouster of the government of Prime Minister Nawaz Sharif, the military-led government stated its intention to restructure the political and electoral systems. Elections for local government are anticipated in late 2000. No time frame has yet been provided for provincial and national elections.
**Political subdivisions:** Each of the four provinces—Punjab, Sindh, Northwest Frontier, and Balochistan—comes under the authority of the Governor and provincial cabinet, appointed by the Chief Executive. The Northern Areas and Federally Administered Tribal Areas (FATA) are administered by the federal government, but enjoy considerable autonomy.

## Economy

**GDP (1998-99):** $59 billion.
**Real annual growth rate 1998-99:** 3.1%.
**Per capita GDP (1998-99):** $441.
**Natural resources:** Arable land, natural gas, limited petroleum, substantial hydropower potential, coal, iron ore.
**Agriculture:** Products—wheat, cotton, rice, sugarcane, tobacco.
**Industry:** Types—textiles, fertilizer, steel products, chemicals, food processing, oil and gas products, cement.
**Trade (FY 1998-99):** Exports—$7.8 billion: raw cotton, rice, cotton yarn, textiles, fruits, vegetables. Major partners—U.S., Japan, U.K., Saudi Arabia, Germany. Imports—$9.4 billion: wheat, crude oil, cooking oil, fertilizers, machinery. Major partners—

U.S., Japan, Saudi Arabia, Malaysia, U.K., Sri Lanka.

# PEOPLE

The majority of Pakistan's population lives along the Indus River valley and along an arc formed by the cities of Faisalabad, Lahore, Rawalpindi/ Islamabad, and Peshawar.

Although the official language of Pakistan is Urdu, it is spoken as a first language by only 9% of the population; 65% speak Punjabi, 11% Sindhi, and 24% speak other languages (Pushtu, Saraiki, Baloch, Brahui). Urdu, Punjabi, Pushtu, and Baloch are Indo-European languages; Brahui is believed to have Dravidian (pre-Indo-European) origins. English is widely used within the government, the officer ranks of the military, and in many institutions of higher learning.

# HISTORY

Archeological explorations have revealed impressive ruins of a 4,500-year old urban civilization in Pakistan's Indus River valley. The reason for the collapse of this highly developed culture is unknown. A major theory is that it was crushed by successive invasions (circa 2000 B.C. and 1400 B.C.) of Aryans, Indo-European warrior tribes from the Caucasus region in what is now Russia. The Aryans were followed in 500 B.C. by Persians and, in 326 B.C., by Alexander the Great. The "Gandhara culture" flourished in much of present-day Pakistan.

The Indo-Greek descendants of Alexander the Great saw the most creative period of the Gandhara (Buddhist) culture. For 200 years after the Kushan Dynasty was established in A.D. 50, Taxila (near Islamabad) became a renowned center of learning, philosophy, and art.

Pakistan's Islamic history began with the arrival of Muslim traders in the 8th century. During the 16th and 17th centuries, the Mogul Empire dominated most of South Asia, including much of present-day Pakistan.

British traders arrived in South Asia in 1601, but the British Empire did not consolidate control of the region until the latter half of the 18th century. After 1850, the British or those influenced by them governed virtually the entire subcontinent.

In the early 20th century, South Asian leaders began to agitate for a greater degree of autonomy. Growing concern about Hindu domination of the Indian National Congress Party, the movement's foremost organization, led Muslim leaders to form the all-India Muslim League in 1906. In 1913, the League formally adopted the same objective as the Congress—self-government for India within the British Empire—but Congress and the League were unable to agree on a formula that would ensure the protection of Muslim religious, economic, and political rights.

## Pakistan and Partition

The idea of a separate Muslim state emerged in the 1930s. On March 23, 1940, Muhammad Ali Jinnah, leader of the Muslim League, formally endorsed the "Lahore Resolution," calling for the creation of an independent state in regions where Muslims constituted a majority. At the end of World War II, the United Kingdom moved with increasing urgency to grant India independence. However, the Congress Party and the Muslim League could not agree on the terms for a constitution or establishing an interim government. In June 1947, the British Government declared that it would bestow full dominion status upon two successor states—India and Pakistan. Under this arrangement, the various princely states could freely join either India or Pakistan. Consequently, a bifurcated Muslim nation separated by more than 1,600 kilometers (1,000 mi.) of Indian territory emerged when Pakistan became a self-governing dominion within the Commonwealth on August 14, 1947. West Pakistan comprised the contiguous Muslim-major-

ity districts of present-day Pakistan; East Pakistan consisted of a single province, which is now Bangladesh.

The Maharaja of Kashmir was reluctant to make a decision on accession to either Pakistan or India. However, armed incursions into the state by tribesman from the NWFP led him to seek military assistance from India. The Maharaja signed accession papers in October 1947 and allowed Indian troops into much of the state. The Government of Pakistan, however, refused to recognize the accession and campaigned to reverse the decision. The status of Kashmir has remained in dispute.

## After Independence

With the death in 1948 of its first head of state, Muhammad Ali Jinnah, and the assassination in 1951 of its first Prime Minister, Liaqat Ali Khan, political instability and economic difficulty became prominent features of post-independence Pakistan. On October 7, 1958, President Iskander Mirza, with the support of the army, suspended the 1956 constitution, imposed martial law, and canceled the elections scheduled for January 1959. Twenty days later the military sent Mirza into exile in Britain and Gen. Mohammad Ayub Khan assumed control of a military dictatorship. After Pakistan's loss in the 1965 war against India, Ayub Khan's power declined. Subsequent political and economic grievances inspired agitation movements that compelled his resignation in March 1969. He handed over responsibility for governing to the Commander-in-Chief of the Army, General Agha Mohammed Yahya Khan, who became President and Chief Martial Law Administrator.

General elections held in December 1970 polarized relations between the eastern and western sections of Pakistan. The Awami League, which advocated autonomy for the more populous East Pakistan, swept the East Pakistan seats to gain a majority in Pakistan as a whole. The Pakistan Peoples Party (PPP), founded and led by Ayub Khan's former Foreign Minister, Zulfikar Ali Bhutto,

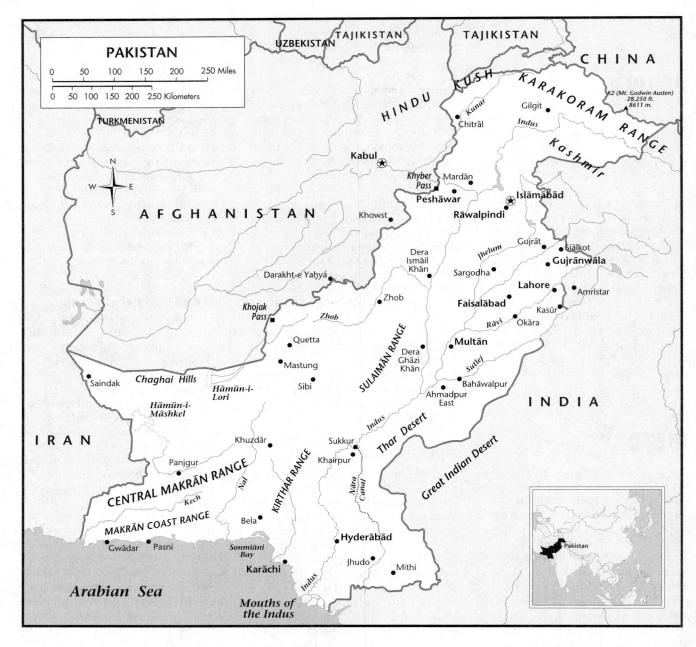

**PAKISTAN**

0 50 100 150 200 250 Miles

0 50 100 150 200 250 Kilometers

UZBEKISTAN
TAJIKISTAN
TAJIKISTAN
CHINA

TURKMENISTAN

HINDU KUSH
KARAKORAM RANGE
K2 (Mt. Godwin Austen)
28,250 ft.
8611 m.

Kunar
Gilgit
Chitrāl
Indus

Kashmir

Kabul
Khyber Pass
Mardān
Peshāwar
Islāmābād
Rāwalpindi

AFGHANISTAN

Khowst

Dera Ismāil Khān
Jhelum
Gujrāt
Siālkot
Gujrānwāla

Darakht-e Yaḥyá
Sargodha
Lahore
Amristar

Zhob
Faisalābād
Kasūr

Khojak Pass
Zhob
Rāvi
Okāra

Quetta
Dera Ghāzi Khān
Multān
Sutlej

Mastung
Sibi
Bahāwalpur
Ahmadpur East

Saindak
Chaghai Hills
Hāmūn-i-Lori

SULAIMĀN RANGE

INDIA

Hāmūn-i-Māshkel

IRAN

Khuzdār
Indus
Sukkur
Khairpur
Thar Desert

Panjgur

Great Indian Desert

Nal
KIRTHĀR RANGE
Nāra Canal

CENTRAL MAKRĀN RANGE
Kech

MAKRĀN COAST RANGE
Bela

Gwādar
Pasni
Sonmiāni Bay
Hyderābād

Karāchi
Jhudo
Mithi

Indus

Arabian Sea

Mouths of the Indus

Pakistan

won a majority of the seats in West Pakistan, but the country was completely split with neither major party having any support in the other area. Negotiations to form a coalition government broke down and a civil war ensued. India attacked East Pakistan and captured Dhaka in December 1971, when the eastern section declared itself the independent nation of Bangladesh. Yahya Khan then resigned the presidency and handed over leadership of the western part of Pakistan to Bhutto, who became President and the first civilian Chief Martial Law Administrator.

Bhutto moved decisively to restore national confidence and pursued an active foreign policy, taking a leading role in Islamic and Third World forums. Although Pakistan did not formally join the non-aligned movement until 1979, the position of the Bhutto government coincided largely with that of the non-aligned nations. Domestically, Bhutto pursued a populist agenda and nationalized major industries and the banking system. In 1973, he promulgated a new constitution accepted by most political elements and relinquished the presidency to become Prime Minister.

Although Bhutto continued his populist and socialist rhetoric, he increasingly relied on Pakistan's urban industrialists and rural landlords. Over time the economy stagnated, largely as a result of the dislocation and uncertainty produced by Bhutto's frequently changing economic policies. When Bhutto proclaimed his own victory in the March 1977 national elections, the opposition Pakistan National Alliance (PNA) denounced the results as fraudulent and demanded new elections. Bhutto resisted and later arrested the PNA leadership.

## 1977-1985 Martial Law

With increasing anti-government unrest, the army grew restive. On July 5, 1977, the military removed Bhutto from power and arrested him, declared martial law, and suspended portions of the 1973 constitution. Chief of Army Staff Gen. Muhammad Zia ul-Haq became Chief Martial Law Administrator and promised to hold new elections within three months.

Zia released Bhutto and asserted that he could contest new elections scheduled for October 1977. However, after it became clear that Bhutto's popularity had survived his government, Zia postponed the elections and began criminal investigations of the senior PPP leadership. Subsequently, Bhutto was convicted and sentenced to death for alleged conspiracy to murder a political opponent. Despite international appeals on his behalf, Bhutto was hanged on April 6, 1979.

Zia assumed the Presidency and called for elections in November. However, fearful of a PPP victory, Zia banned political activity in October 1979 and postponed national elections.

In 1980, most center and left parties, led by the PPP, formed the Movement for the Restoration of Democracy (MRD). The MRD demanded Zia's resignation, an end to martial law, new elections, and restoration of the constitution as it existed before Zia's takeover. In early December 1984, President Zia proclaimed a national referendum for December 19 on his "Islamization" program. He implicitly linked approval of "Islamization" with a mandate for his continued presidency. Zia's opponents, led by the MRD, boycotted the elections. When the government claimed a 63% turnout, with more than 90% approving the referendum, many observers questioned these figures.

On March 3, 1985, President Zia proclaimed constitutional changes designed to increase the power of the President vis-a-vis the Prime Minister (under the 1973 constitution the President had been mainly a figurehead). Subsequently, Zia nominated Muhammad Khan Junejo, a Muslim League member, as Prime Minister. The new National Assembly unanimously endorsed Junejo as Prime Minister and, in October 1985, passed Zia's proposed eighth amendment to the constitution, legitimizing the actions of the martial law government, exempting them from judicial review (including decisions of the military courts), and enhancing the powers of the President.

## The Democratic Interregnum

On December 30, 1985, President Zia removed martial law and restored the fundamental rights safeguarded under the constitution. He also lifted the Bhutto government's declaration of emergency powers. The first months of 1986 witnessed a rebirth of political activity throughout Pakistan. All parties—including those continuing to deny the legitimacy of the Zia/Junejo government—were permitted to organize and hold rallies. In April 1986, PPP leader Benazir Bhutto, daughter of Zulfiqar Ali Bhutto, returned to Pakistan from exile in Europe.

Following the lifting of martial law, the increasing political independence of Prime Minister Junejo and his differences with Zia over Afghan policy resulted in tensions between them. On May 29, 1988, President Zia dismissed the Junejo government and called for November elections. In June, Zia proclaimed the supremacy in Pakistan of Shari'a (Islamic law), by which all civil law had to conform to traditional Muslim edicts.

On August 17, a plane carrying President Zia, American Ambassador Arnold Raphel, U.S. Brig. General Herbert Wassom, and 28 Pakistani military officers crashed on a return flight from a military equipment trial near Bahawalpur, killing all of its occupants. In accordance with the constitution, Chairman of the Senate Ghulam Ishaq Khan became Acting President and announced that elections scheduled for November 1988 would take place.

After winning 93 of the 205 National Assembly seats contested, the PPP, under the leadership of Benazir Bhutto, formed a coalition government with several smaller parties, including the Muhajir Qaumi Movement (MQM). The Islamic Democratic Alliance (IJI), a multi-party coalition led by the PML and including religious right parties such as the Jamaat-i-Islami (JI), won 55 National Assembly seats.

Differing interpretations of constitutional authority, debates over the powers of the central government relative to those of the provinces, and the antagonistic relationship between the Bhutto Administration and opposition governments in Punjab and Balochistan seriously impeded social and economic reform programs. Ethnic conflict, primarily in Sindh province, exacerbated these problems. A fragmentation in the governing coalition and the military's reluctance to support an apparently ineffectual and corrupt government were accompanied by a significant deterioration in law and order.

In August 1990, President Khan, citing his powers under the eighth amendment to the constitution, dismissed the Bhutto government and dissolved the national and provincial assemblies. New elections, held in October of 1990, confirmed the political ascendancy of the IJI. In addition to a two-thirds majority in the National Assembly, the alliance acquired control of all four provincial parliaments and enjoyed the support of the military and of President Khan. Muhammad Nawaz Sharif, as leader of the PML, the most prominent Party in the IJI, was elected Prime Minister by the National Assembly.

Sharif emerged as the most secure and powerful Pakistani Prime Minister since the mid-1970s. Under his rule, the IJI achieved several important political victories. The implementation of Sharif's economic reform program, involving privatization, deregulation, and encouragement of private sector economic growth, greatly improved Pakistan's economic performance and business climate. The passage into law in May 1991 of a Shari'a bill, providing for widespread Islamization, legitimized the IJI government among much of Pakistani society.

After PML President Junejo's death in March 1993, Sharif loyalists unilaterally nominated him as the next party leader. Consequently, the PML divided into the PML Nawaz (PML/N) group, loyal to the Prime Minister, and the PML Junejo group (PML/J), supportive of Hamid Nasir Chatta, the President of the PML/J group.

However, Nawaz Sharif was not able to reconcile the different objectives of the IJI's constituent parties. The largest religious party, Jamaat-i-Islami (JI), abandoned the alliance because of its perception of PML hegemony. The regime was weakened further by the military's suppression of the MQM, which had entered into a coalition with the IJI to contain PPP influence, and allegations of corruption directed at Nawaz Sharif. In April 1993, President Khan, citing "maladministration, corruption, and nepotism" and espousal of political violence, dismissed the Sharif government, but the following month the Pakistan Supreme Court reinstated the National Assembly and the Nawaz Sharif government. Continued tensions between Sharif and Khan resulted in governmental gridlock and the Chief of Army Staff brokered an arrangement under which both the President and the Prime Minister resigned their offices in July 1993.

An interim government, headed by Moeen Qureshi, a former World Bank Vice President, took office with a mandate to hold national and provincial parliamentary elections in October. Despite its brief term, the Qureshi government adopted political, economic, and social reforms that generated considerable domestic support and foreign admiration.

In the October 1993 elections, the PPP won a plurality of seats in the National Assembly and Benazir Bhutto was asked to form a government. However, because it did not acquire a majority in the National

Assembly, the PPP's control of the government depended upon the continued support of numerous independent parties, particularly the PML/J. The unfavorable circumstances surrounding PPP rule—the imperative of preserving a coalition government, the formidable opposition of Nawaz Sharif's PML/N movement, and the insecure provincial administrations—presented significant difficulties for the government of Prime Minister Bhutto. However, the election of Prime Minister Bhutto's close associate, Farooq Leghari, as President in November 1993 gave her a stronger power base.

In November 1996, President Leghari dismissed the Bhutto government, charging it with corruption, mismanagement of the economy, and implication in extra-judicial killings in Karachi. Elections in February 1997 resulted in an overwhelming victory for the PML/Nawaz, and President Leghari called upon Nawaz Sharif to form a government. In March 1997, with the unanimous support of the National Assembly, Sharif amended the constitution, stripping the President of the power to dismiss the government and making his power to appoint military service chiefs and provincial governors contingent on the "advice" of the Prime Minister. Another amendment prohibited elected members from "floor crossing" or voting against party lines. The Sharif government engaged in a protracted dispute with the judiciary, culminating in the storming of the Supreme Court by ruling party loyalists and the engineered dismissal of the Chief Justice and the resignation of President Leghari in December 1997. The new President elected by Parliament, Rafiq Tarar, was a close associate of the Prime Minister. A one-sided accountability campaign was used to target opposition politicians and critics of the regime. Similarly, the government moved to restrict press criticism and ordered the arrest and beating of prominent journalists. As domestic criticism of Sharif's administration intensified, Sharif attempted to replace Chief of Army Staff General Pervez Musharraf on October 12, 1999, with a family loyalist, Director General ISI Lt. Gen.

Ziauddin. Although General Musharraf was out of the country at the time, the Army moved quickly to depose Sharif.

On October 14, 1999, General Musharraf declared a state of emergency and issued the Provisional Constitutional Order (PCO), which suspended the federal and provincial parliaments, held the constitution in abeyance, and designated Musharraf as Chief Executive. While delivering an ambitious seven-point reform agenda, Musharraf has not yet provided a timeline for a return to civilian, democratic rule, although local elections are anticipated at the end of calendar year 2000. Musharraf has appointed a National Security Council, with mixed military/civilian appointees, a civilian Cabinet, and a National Reconstruction Bureau (think tank) to formulate structural reforms. A National Accountability Bureau (NAB), headed by an active duty military officer, is prosecuting those accused of willful default on bank loans and corrupt practices, whose conviction can result in disqualification from political office for twenty-one years. The NAB Ordinance has attracted criticism for holding the accused without charge and, in some instances, access to legal counsel. While military trial courts were not established, on January 26, 2000, the government stipulated that Supreme, High, and Shari'a Court justices should swear allegiance to the Provisional Constitutional Order and the Chief Executive. Approximately 85 percent of justices acquiesced, but a handful of justices were not invited to take the oath and were forcibly retired. Political parties have not been banned, but a couple of dozen ruling party members remain detained, with Sharif and five colleagues facing charges of attempted hijacking.

# GOVERNMENT

The Pakistan Constitution of 1973, amended substantially in 1985 under Zia, was suspended by the military government on October 12, 1999. Musharraf has committed to return

Pakistan to democratic, civilian rule but the implications of his promised structural reforms on the country's previous parliamentary system are unknown.

Under the Provisional Constitutional Order and its amendments, all power flows from and to the Chief Executive, who also holds the posts of Chief of Army Staff and Chairman, Joint Chiefs of Staff. The Judiciary is proscribed from issuing any order contrary to the decisions of the Chief Executive, and the President, Cabinet, National Security Council, and Governors serve at his discretion. In practice, Musharraf consults extensively with his civilian appointees and Corps Commanders and in certain policy areas (e.g., economic reform) civilian appointees have exhibited wide policy latitude.

Although the Judiciary was compelled to take an oath to the PCO and the Chief Executive, courts continue to function and exercise that authority which does not conflict with the PCO. The Supreme Court is Pakistan's highest court. The President, in consultation with the Chief Executive, appoints the Chief Justice and they together determine the other judicial appointments. Each province has a high court, the justices of which are appointed by the President after conferring with the Chief Justice of the Supreme Court and the provincial chief justice.

## National Security

Pakistan's 610,000-member armed forces, the world's eighth largest, are well trained and disciplined. However, budget constraints and nation-building duties have reduced Pakistan's normal robust training tempo, which if not reversed, will eventually impact on the operational readiness of the Armed Forces. Likewise, Pakistan has had an increasingly difficult time maintaining their aging fleet of United States, Chinese, United Kingdom and French equipment. While the industrial base capabilities have expanded significantly, limited fiscal resources and various sanctions have significantly constrained the govern-

ment's efforts to modernize the armed forces.

Until 1990, the United States provided military aid to Pakistan to modernize its conventional defensive capability. The United States allocated about 40% of its assistance package to non-reimbursable credits for military purchases, the third largest program behind Israel and Egypt. The remainder of the aid program was devoted to economic assistance. While sanctions have been in effect since 1990, various amendments have authorized return of spare parts and end items already paid for by Pakistan. In addition, the U.S. and Pakistan have come to a financial agreement on the non-delivery of F-16s. However, Pakistan's nuclear tests in response to India's May 1998 tests and the recent military coup have placed additional sanctions on Pakistan.

## Principal Government Officials

**For up-to-date information on Principal Government Officials, see the Chiefs of State and Cabinet Members of Foreign Governments section starting on page 1.**

Pakistan maintains an embassy in the United States at 2315 Massachusetts Avenue, N.W., Washington, DC 20008 (Tel. 202-939-6200).

# ECONOMY

Extreme poverty and underdevelopment in Pakistan, as well as fiscal mismanagement that has produced a large foreign debt, obscure the potential of a country which has the resources and entrepreneurial skill to support rapid economic growth. In fact, the economy averaged an impressive growth rate of 6 percent per year during the 1980s and early 1990s. However, the economy is extremely vulnerable to Pakistan's external and internal shocks, such as in 1992-93, when devastating floods

and political uncertainty combined to depress economic growth sharply and the financial crisis in Asia which hit major markets for Pakistani textile exports. Average real GDP growth from 1992 to 1998 dipped to 4.1 percent annually.

Since the early 1980s, the government has pursued market-based economic reform policies. Market-based reforms began to take hold in 1988, when the government launched an ambitious IMF-assisted structural adjustment program in response to chronic and unsustainable fiscal and external account deficits. Since that time the government has removed barriers to foreign trade and investment, begun to reform the financial system, eased foreign exchange controls, and privatized dozens of state-owned enterprises. Pakistan continues to struggle with these reforms, having mixed success, especially in reducing its budget and current account deficits. The budget deficit in FY 1996-97 was 6.4% of GDP. Initial data implied a reduction in 1997-98 to 5.4% and in 1998-99 to 4.3%, but revised data indicates that the deficit is probably still over 5.0%. In that same 2-year period, the rupee was devalued against the dollar 12% and 10.5% respectively.

Economic reform was further set back by Pakistan's nuclear tests in May 1998 and the subsequent economic sanctions imposed by the G-7. International default was narrowly averted by the partial waiver of sanctions and the subsequent reinstatement of Pakistan's IMF ESAF/EFF in early 1999, followed by Paris Club and London Club reschedulings. The Sharif government had difficulty meeting the conditionality of the IMF program, which was suspended in July 1999. The current government has announced a program of reforms and is in discussion with the IMF regarding a Poverty Reduction and Growth Facility to begin in July 2000.

With a per capita GDP of about USD 441, the World Bank considers Pakistan a low-income country. No more than 39 percent of adults are literate, and life expectancy is about 62 years or less. The population, currently about 130 million, is growing at about 2.6%, very close to the GDP growth rate. Relatively few resources have been devoted to socio-economic development on infrastructure projects. Inadequate provision of social services and high population growth have contributed to a persistence of poverty and unequal income distribution.

## Agriculture and Natural Resources

Pakistan's principal natural resources are arable land and water. About 25% of Pakistan's total land area is under cultivation and is watered by one of the largest irrigation systems in the world. Agriculture accounts for about 24% of GDP and employs about 50% of the labor force. The most important crops are wheat, sugarcane, cotton, and rice, which together account for more than 75% of the value of total crop output. Despite intensive farming practices, Pakistan remains a net food importer. Pakistan exports rice, cotton, fish, fruits, and vegetables and imports vegetable oil, wheat, cotton, pulses and consumer foods.

The economic importance of agriculture has declined since independence, when its share of GDP was around 53%. Following the poor harvest of 1993, the government introduced agriculture assistance policies, including increased support prices for many agricultural commodities and expanded availability of agricultural credit. From 1993 to 1997, real growth in the agricultural sector averaged 5.7% but has since declined to less than 4%. Agricultural reforms, including increased wheat and oilseed production, play a central role in the new government's economic reform package.

Pakistan has extensive energy resources, including fairly sizable natural gas reserves, some proven oil reserves, coal, and large hydropower potential. However, the exploitation of energy resources has been slow due to a shortage of capital and domestic political constraints. For instance, domestic petroleum production totals only about half the country's oil

needs. The need to import oil also contributes to Pakistan's persistent trade deficits and the shortage of foreign exchange. The current government has announced that privatization in the oil and gas sector is a priority, as is the substitution of indigenous gas for imported oil, especially in the production of power.

## Industry

Pakistan's manufacturing sector accounts for about 26% of GDP. Cotton textile production and apparel manufacturing are Pakistan's largest industries, accounting for about 64% of total exports. Other major industries include cement, fertilizer, edible oil, sugar, steel, tobacco, chemicals, machinery, and food processing. Despite ongoing government efforts to privatize large-scale parastatal units, the public sector continues to account for a significant proportion of industry. In FY 1998-99, gross fixed capital formation in the public sector accounted for about 38% of the total. In the face of an increasing trade deficit, the government hopes to diversify the country's industrial base and bolster export industries.

## Foreign Trade and Aid

Weak world demand for its exports and domestic political uncertainty have contributed to Pakistan's high trade deficit. In FY 1998-99, Pakistan recorded a current account deficit of $1.7 billion, only a slight improvement over the FY 1997-98 current account deficit of $1.9 billion. Pakistan's exports continue to be dominated by cotton textiles and apparel, despite government diversification efforts. Major imports include petroleum and petroleum products, edible oil, wheat, chemicals, fertilizer, capital goods, industrial raw materials, and consumer products. External imbalance has left Pakistan with a growing foreign debt burden. Principal and interest payments in FY 1998-99 totaled $2.6 billion, more than double the amount paid in FY 1989-90. Annual debt service now exceeds 34% of export earnings.

Pakistan receives about $2.5 billion per year in loan/grant assistance

from international financial institutions (e.g., the IMF, the World Bank, and the Asian Development Bank) and bilateral donors. Increasingly, the composition of assistance to Pakistan has shifted away from grants toward loans repayable in foreign exchange. All new U.S. economic assistance to Pakistan was suspended after October 1990, when then-President Bush could no longer certify under the Pressler Amendment to the Foreign Assistance Act (Section 620e[e]) "that Pakistan does not possess a nuclear explosive device and that the proposed assistance package reduces significantly the risk that Pakistan will acquire a nuclear explosive device."

# FOREIGN RELATIONS

Pakistan is a prominent member of the Organization of the Islamic Conference (OIC) and an active member of the United Nations. Its foreign policy encompasses historically difficult relations with India, a desire for a stable Afghanistan, long-standing close relations with China, extensive security and economic interests in the Persian Gulf, and wide-ranging bilateral relations with the United States and other Western countries.

## India

Since partition, relations between Pakistan and India have been characterized by rivalry and suspicion. Although many issues divide the two countries, the most sensitive one since independence has been the status of Kashmir.

At the time of partition, the princely state of Kashmir, though ruled by a Hindu Maharajah, had an overwhelmingly Muslim population. When the Maharajah hesitated in acceding to either Pakistan or India in 1947, some of his Muslim subjects, aided by tribesmen from Pakistan, revolted in favor of joining Pakistan. In exchange for military assistance in containing the revolt, the Kashmiri ruler offered his allegiance to India. Indian troops occupied the eastern portion of Kashmir, including its capital, Srinagar, while the western part came under Pakistani control.

India addressed this dispute in the United Nations on January 1, 1948. One year later, the UN arranged a cease-fire along a line dividing Kashmir, but leaving the northern end of the line undemarcated and the vale of Kashmir (with the majority of the population) under Indian control. India and Pakistan agreed with Indian resolutions which called for a UN-supervised plebiscite to determine the state's future.

Full-scale hostilities erupted in September 1965, when India alleged that insurgents trained and supplied by Pakistan were operating in India-controlled Kashmir. Hostilities ceased three weeks later, following mediation efforts by the UN and interested countries. In January 1966, Indian and Pakistani representatives met in Tashkent, U.S.S.R., and agreed to attempt a peaceful settlement of Kashmir and their other differences.

Following the 1971 Indo-Pakistan conflict, President Zulfiqar Ali Bhutto and Indian Prime Minister Indira Gandhi met in the mountain town of Shimla, India, in July 1972. They agreed to a line of control in Kashmir resulting from the December 17, 1971 cease-fire, and endorsed the principle of settlement of bilateral disputes through peaceful means. In 1974, Pakistan and India agreed to resume postal and telecommunications linkages, and to enact measures to facilitate travel. Trade and diplomatic relations were restored in 1976 after a hiatus of five years.

India's nuclear test in 1974 generated great uncertainty in Pakistan and is generally acknowledged to have been the impetus for Pakistan's nuclear weapons development program. In 1983, the Pakistani and Indian governments accused each other of aiding separatists in their respective countries, i.e., Sikhs in India's Punjab state and Sindhis in Pakistan's Sindh province. In April 1984, tensions erupted after troops were deployed to the Siachen Glacier, a high-altitude

desolate area close to the China border left undemarcated by the cease-fire agreement (Karachi Agreement) signed by Pakistan and India in 1949.

Tensions diminished after Rajiv Gandhi became Prime Minister in November 1984 and after a group of Sikh hijackers was brought to trial by Pakistan in March 1985. In December 1985, President Zia and Prime Minister Gandhi pledged not to attack each other's nuclear facilities. (A formal "no attack" agreement was signed in January 1991.) In early 1986, the Indian and Pakistani governments began high-level talks to resolve the Siachen Glacier border dispute and to improve trade.

Bilateral tensions increased in early 1990, when Kashmiri militants began a campaign of violence against Indian Government authority in Jammu and Kashmir. Subsequent high-level bilateral meetings relieved the tensions between India and Pakistan, but relations worsened again after the destruction of the Ayodhya Mosque by Hindu extremists in December 1992 and terrorist bombings in Bombay in March 1993. Talks between the Foreign Secretaries of both countries in January 1994 resulted in deadlock.

In the last several years, the Indo-Pakistani relationship has veered sharply between rapprochement and conflict. After taking office in February 1997, Prime Minister Nawaz Sharif moved to resume official dialog with India. A number of meetings at the foreign secretary and prime ministerial level took place, with positive atmospherics but little concrete progress. The relationship improved markedly when Indian Prime Minister Vajpayee traveled to Lahore for a summit with Sharif in February 1999. There was considerable hope that the meeting could lead to a breakthrough. Unfortunately, in spring 1999 infiltrators from Pakistan occupied positions on the Indian side of the Line of Control in the remote, mountainous area of Kashmir near Kargil, threatening the ability of India to supply its forces on Siachen Glacier. By early summer, serious fighting flared in the Kargil

## Travel Notes

**Travel Advice:** For up-to-date information from the U.S. State Department on possible inconvenient or hazardous situations, see the **Travel Warnings and Consular Information Sheets from the U.S. Government** section starting on page 1723. For the latest information on health requirements and conditions, see the **International Travelers' Health Information** section starting on page 1385. For further information dealing with non-urgent matter, see the **Tips for Travelers to...** section starting on page 1588.

sector. The infiltrators withdrew following a meeting between Prime Minister Sharif and President Clinton in July. Relations between India and Pakistan have since been particularly strained, especially since the October 12, 1999 coup in Islamabad.

## Afghanistan

Following the 1979 Soviet invasion of Afghanistan, the Pakistani Government played a vital role in supporting the Afghan resistance movement and assisting Afghan refugees. After the Soviet withdrawal in February 1989, Pakistan, with cooperation from the world community, continued to provide extensive support for displaced Afghans. In 1999, the United States provided approximately $70 million in humanitarian assistance to Afghanistan and Afghan refugees in Pakistan, mainly through multilateral organizations and NGOs. As such, the United States in 1999 was the largest single donor. In 1999, more than 1.2 million registered Afghan refugees remained in Pakistan, as fighting between rival factions continued. Pakistan has recognized the Taliban as the government in Afghanistan and provides the Taliban assistance. Pakistan has periodically offered to try to help bring Afghanistan's warring factions to the negotiating table, thus far with negligible results.

## Russian Federation

Under military leader Ayub Khan, Pakistan sought to improve relations with the Soviet Union; trade and cultural exchanges between the two countries increased between 1966 and 1971. However, Soviet criticism of Pakistan's position in the 1971 war with India weakened bilateral relations, and many Pakistanis believed that the August 1971 Indo-Soviet Treaty of Friendship, Peace and Cooperation encouraged Indian belligerency. Subsequent Soviet arms sales to India, amounting to billions of dollars on concessional terms, reinforced this argument.

During the 1980s, tensions increased between the Soviet Union and Pakistan because of the latter's key role in helping to organize political and material support for the Afghan rebel forces. The withdrawal of Soviet forces from Afghanistan and the collapse of the former Soviet Union resulted in significantly improved bilateral relations, but Pakistan's support for and recognition of the Taliban regime in neighboring Afghanistan is an ongoing source of tension.

## People's Republic of China

In 1950, Pakistan was among the first countries to recognize the People's Republic of China (P.R.C.). Following the Sino-Indian hostilities of 1962, Pakistan's relations with China became stronger; since then, the two countries have regularly exchanged high-level visits resulting in a variety of agreements. China has provided economic, military, and technical assistance to Pakistan.

Favorable relations with China have been a pillar of Pakistan's foreign policy. The P.R.C. strongly supported Pakistan's opposition to Soviet involvement in Afghanistan and is perceived by Pakistan as a regional counterweight to India and Russia.

## Iran and the Persian Gulf

Historically, Pakistan has had close geopolitical and cultural-religious linkages with Iran. However, strains in the relationship appeared in the last decade. Pakistan and Iran sup-

port opposing factions in the Afghan conflict. Also, some Pakistanis suspect Iranian support for the sectarian violence which has plagued Pakistan. Nevertheless, Pakistan pursues an active diplomatic relationship with Iran, including recent overtures to seek a negotiated settlement between Afghanistan's warring factions.

Despite popular support for Iraq in 1991, the Pakistani government supported the coalition against Iraq's invasion of Kuwait and sent 11,600 troops to defend Saudi Arabia. Pakistan provides military personnel to strengthen Gulf-state defenses and to reinforce its own security interests in the area.

# U.S.-PAKISTAN RELATIONS

## Principal U.S. Embassy Officials

**For up-to-date information on Principal U.S. Officials, see the U.S. Embassies, Consulates, and Foreign Service section starting on page 139.**

For up-to-date information on Principal U.S. Officials, see the U.S. Embassies, Consulates, and Foreign Service section starting on page 139.

The U.S. Embassy is located at the Diplomatic Enclave, Ramna 5, Islamabad [Tel. (92)-(51)-2080-2000; telex 82-5-864].

The United States and Pakistan established diplomatic relations in 1947. The U.S. agreement to provide economic and military assistance to Pakistan and the latter's partnership in the Baghdad Pact/CENTO and SEATO strengthened relations between the two nations. However, the U.S. suspension of military assistance during the 1965 Indo-Pakistan war generated a widespread feeling in Pakistan that the United States was not a reliable ally. Even though the United States suspended military assistance to both countries involved in the conflict, the suspension of aid affected Pakistan much more

severely. Gradually, relations improved and arms sales were renewed in 1975. Then, in April 1979, the United States cut off economic assistance to Pakistan, except food assistance, as required under the Symington Amendment to the Foreign Assistance Act of 1961, due to concerns about Pakistan's nuclear program.

The Soviet invasion of Afghanistan in December 1979 highlighted the common interest of Pakistan and the United States in peace and stability in South Asia. In 1981, the United States and Pakistan agreed on a $3.2-billion military and economic assistance program aimed at helping Pakistan deal with the heightened threat to security in the region and its economic development needs.

Recognizing national security concerns and accepting Pakistan's assurances that it did not intend to construct a nuclear weapon, Congress waived restrictions (Symington Amendment) on military assistance to Pakistan. In March 1986, the two countries agreed on a second multi-year (FY 1988-93) $4-billion economic development and security assistance program. On October 1, 1990, however, the United States suspended all military assistance and new economic aid to Pakistan under the Pressler Amendment, which required that the President certify annually that Pakistan "does not possess a nuclear explosive device."

There have been several incidents of violence against American officials and U.S. mission employees in Pakistan. In November 1979, false rumors that the United States had participated in the seizure of the Grand Mosque in Mecca provoked a mob attack on the U.S. embassy in Islamabad. The government's delayed response enabled the mob to burn the embassy. Four people died, two of them U.S. nationals. The American Cultural Center in Lahore also was destroyed by fire. In 1989, there was an attack on the American Center in Islamabad, where six Pakistanis were killed in the crossfire with the police. In March of 1995, two American employees of the consulate in

Karachi were killed and one wounded in an attack on the home-to-office shuttle. In November of 1997, four U.S. businessmen were brutally murdered while being driven to work in Karachi. In November 1999, the Embassy and the American Center were the targets of rocket attacks that wounded one local national security guard.

The decision by India to conduct nuclear tests in May 1998 and Pakistan's matching response set back U.S. relations in the region, which had seen renewed U.S. Government interest during the second Clinton Administration. A presidential visit scheduled for the first quarter of 1998 was postponed and, under the Glenn Amendment, sanctions restricted the provision of credits, military sales, economic assistance, and loans to the government. An intensive dialogue on nuclear nonproliferation and security issues between Deputy Secretary Talbott and Foreign Secretary Shamshad Ahmad was initiated, with discussions focusing on CTBT signature and ratification, FMCT negotiations, export controls, and a nuclear restraint regime. The October 1999 overthrow of the democratically elected Sharif government triggered an additional layer of sanctions under Section 508 of the Foreign Appropriations Act which include restrictions on foreign military financing and economic assistance. Presently, U.S. Government assistance to Pakistan is limited mainly to refugee and counter-narcotics assistance.

# PALAU

February 2001

Official Name:
**Republic of Palau**

# PROFILE

## Geography

**Area:** 458 sq. km (about 190 sq. mi.) in eight main islands plus more than 250 islets.
**Cities:** Capital—Koror (pop. 13,303).
**Terrain:** varies from mountainous main island to smaller, reef-rimmed coral islands.
**Climate:** tropical.

## People

**Nationality:** Noun and adjective—Palauan.
**Population:** 19,129. Age structure—35.4% under 18, 6.6% over 65.
**Growth rate:** 2.3%.
**Ethnic groups:** Palauans are Micronesian with Malayan and Melanesian elements.
**Religion:** Roman Catholic, Protestant, Modekngei (an indigenous Palauan religion)
**Languages:** English (official in all 16 states), Palauan.
**Education:** Literacy—92%.
**Health:** Life expectancy—male 64.5 yrs.; female 70.8 yrs. Infant mortality rate—20/1,000.
**Work force:** Government—30%, tourism—10%; other services—35%; industry—15%, agriculture—10%.

## Government

**Type:** Constitutional republic in free association with United States.
**Independence** (from U.S.-administered UN trusteeship): October 1, 1994
**Constitution:** January 1, 1981.
**Branches:** Executive—president (head of state and government), vice president, cabinet. Legislative—bicameral parliament elected by popular vote. Judicial—Supreme Court, National Court, Court of Common Pleas, and the Land Court.
**Political parties:** Palau Nationalist Party, Ta Belau Party.

## Economy

**GDP:** $125.3 million. GDP per capita: $6,550.
**National income:** (GDP + foreign assistance) $150.3 million.
**National income per capita:** $7,850.
**GDP composition by sector:** Services 80%, industry 12%, agriculture 8%.
**Industry:** Types—Government, tourism.
**Trade:** Exports ($5.5 million)—fish, garments, handicraft. Export markets—U.S., Japan, Taiwan. Imports ($126 million)—fuel, food and beverages, manufactured goods. Import sources—U.S. + Guam (48%), Japan, Singapore, Taiwan, Korea.
**External debt:** $20 million.
**Currency:** U.S. dollar.

# GEOGRAPHY AND PEOPLE

The Republic of Palau consists of eight principal islands and more than 250 smaller ones lying roughly 500 miles southeast of the Philippines. The islands of Palau constitute part of the Caroline Islands chain. About 70% of the Palauan population lives in the capital city of Koror on Koror Island. The constitution calls for a new capital to be established on the bigger but less developed island of Babeldaob—the second-largest island in Micronesia after Guam.

# HISTORY

Palau was initially settled over 4,000 years ago, probably by migrants from what today is Indonesia. British traders became prominent visitors in the 18th century, followed by expanding Spanish influence in the 19th century. Following its defeat in the Spanish-American War, Spain sold Palau and most of the rest of the Caroline Islands to Germany in 1899. Control passed to Japan in 1914 and then to the United States under UN auspices in 1947 as part of the Trust Territory of the Pacific Islands.

Four of the Trust Territory districts formed a single federated Micronesian state in 1979, but the districts of Palau and the Marshall Islands declined to participate. Palau instead approved a new constitution and became the Republic of Palau in 1981, signing a Compact of Free Association with the United States in 1982. After eight referenda and an amendment to the Palauan constitution, the Compact went into effect on October 1, 1994, marking Palau's emergence from trusteeship to independence.

# GOVERNMENT

Palau is a democratic republic with directly elected executive and legislative branches. Presidential elections take place every 4 years to select the president and the vice president, who run on separate tickets. The Palau National Congress (Olbiil era Kelulau) has two houses. The Senate has nine members elected nationwide. The House of Delegates has 16 members, one each from Palau's 16 states. All of the legislators serve 4-year terms. Each state also elects its own governor and legislature.

The Council of Chiefs is an advisory body to the president containing the highest traditional chiefs from each of the 16 states. The Council is consulted on matters concerning traditional laws and customs.

The judicial system consists of the Supreme Court, National Court, the Court of Common Pleas, and the Land Court. The Supreme Court has trial and appellate divisions and is presided over by the Chief Justice.

## Principal Government Officials

**For up-to-date information on Principal Government Officials, see the Chiefs of State and Cabinet Members of Foreign Governments section starting on page 1.**

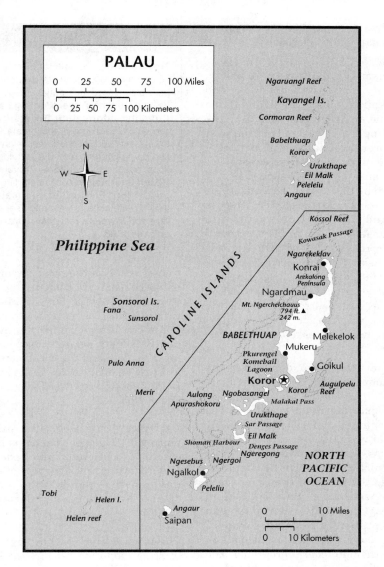

Palau maintains an embassy at 1150 18th Street NW, Suite 750, Washington, DC 20036. Tel: 202–452–6814.

# POLITICAL CONDITIONS

While calm in recent years, Palau witnessed several instances of political violence in the 1980s. The republic's first president, Haruo I. Remeliik, was assassinated in 1985, with the Minister of State eventually found to be complicit in the crime. Palau's third president, Lazurus Salii, committed suicide in September 1988 amidst bribery allegations. Salii's personal assistant had been imprisoned several months earlier after being convicted of firing shots into the home of the Speaker of the House of Delegates.

Legislation making Palau an "offshore" financial center was passed by the Senate in 1998. Opponents fear that the country will become a haven for money launderers and other sorts of criminal activity.

# ECONOMY

Palau's per capita GDP of $6,550 makes it one of the wealthier Pacific Island states. Nominal GDP increased by an annual average of nearly 14% from 1983 to 1990, and by an annual rate of over 10% from 1991 to 1997. Growth turned sharply negative in 1998 and 1999 as a result of the Asian financial crisis.

Tourism is Palau's main industry. Activity focuses on scubadiving and snorkeling among the islands' rich marine environment, including the Floating Garden Islands to the west of Koror. The number of visitors—85% of whom come from Japan, Taiwan, and the U.S.—reached nearly 67,000 in 1997, more than quadruple the level of a decade earlier. Tourism earned $67 million in foreign exchange for Palau in 1996, accounting for roughly half of GDP. Arrivals from Asian countries dropped in 1998 and 1999 due to the regional economic downturn and the depreciation of many Asian currencies against the dollar, which made Palau's dollar-denominated prices more expensive.

The service sector dominates the Palauan economy, contributing more than 80% of GDP and employing three-quarters of the work force. The government alone employs nearly 30% of workers. One of the government's main responsibilities is administering external assistance. Under the terms of the Compact of Free Association with the United States, Palau will receive more than $450 million in assistance over 15 years and is eligible to participate in more than 40 federal programs. The first grant of $142 million was made in 1994. Further annual payments in lesser amounts will be made through 2009. U.S. grants in 1999 totaled $24 million.

**Travel Notes**

**Travel Advice:** For up-to-date information from the U.S. State Department on possible inconvenient or hazardous situations, see the **Travel Warnings and Consular Information Sheets from the U.S. Government** section starting on page 1723. For the latest information on health requirements and conditions, see the **International Travelers' Health Information** section starting on page 1385. For further information dealing with non-urgent matter, see the **Tips for Travelers to...** section starting on page 1588.

Construction is the most important industrial activity, contributing over 9% of GDP. Several large infrastructure projects, including the rebuilding of the bridge connecting Koror and Babeldaob Islands after its collapse in 1996 and the construction of a highway around the rim of Babeldaob, boosted activity at the end of 1990s.

Agriculture is mainly on a subsistence level, the principal crops being coconuts, root crops, and bananas. Fishing is a potential source of revenue, but the islands' tuna output dropped by over one-third during the 1990s.

The main economic challenge confronting Palau is to ensure the long-term viability of its economy by reducing its reliance on foreign assistance. Palau has created a trust fund to be drawn upon after the cessation of Compact grants, the value of which

had grown to $140 million by the beginning of 2000.

# FOREIGN RELATIONS

Palau gained its independence October 1, 1994 with the entry into force of the Compact of Free Association with the United States. Palau was the last Trust Territory of the Pacific Islands territories to gain its independence. Under the Compact, the U.S. remains responsible for Palau's defense for 50 years.

Palau is a sovereign nation and conducts its own foreign relations. Since independence, Palau has established diplomatic relations with a number of nations, including many of its Pacific neighbors. Palau was admitted to the United Nations on December 15, 1994, and has since joined several other international organizations.

## Principal U.S. Officials

**For up-to-date information on Principal U.S. Officials, see the U.S. Embassies, Consulates, and Foreign Service section starting on page 139.**

The mailing address for the U.S. Embassy is P.O. Box 6028, Republic of Palau 96940. Telephone: 680–488–2920. Fax: 680–488–2911. Email: usembassy@palaunet.com.

# PANAMA

April 2001

## Official Name:
## Republic of Panama

# PROFILE

## People

**Nationality:** Noun and adjective—Panamanian(s).

**Population:** (July 2000 est.) 2.808 million.

**Annual growth rate:** 1.34%.

**Ethnic groups:** Mestizo (mixed Indian and European ancestry) 70%, West Indian 14%, Caucasian 10%, Indian 6%.

**Religions:** Roman Catholic 85%, Protestant (Evangelical) 15%.

**Languages:** Spanish (official); 14% speak English as their native tongue; various Indian languages.

**Education:** Years compulsory—6. Attendance—95% for primary school-age children, 96% for secondary. Literacy—about 90% overall: urban 94%, rural 62%.

**Health:** Infant mortality rate—17/1,000. Life expectancy—75 yrs.

**Work force:** (1,086,598) Commerce (wholesale and retail)—19.1%; agriculture, cattle, hunting, silviculture—14%; industries (manufactures)—8.8%; construction—7.7%; transportation, storage, communications—7.2%; public and defense administration—6.9%; other community and social activities—5.8%; hotels and restaurants—3.7%; financial intermediation—2.6%.

## Geography

**Area:** 77,381 sq. km. (29,762 sq. mi.); slightly smaller than South Carolina. Panama occupies the southeastern end of the isthmus forming the land bridge between North and South America.

**Cities:** Capital—Panama City (827,828). Other cities—Colon (140,908), David (102,678).

**Terrain:** Mountainous (highest elevation Cerro Volcan, 3,475 m.—11,468 ft.); coastline 2,857 km. (1,786 mi.).

**Climate:** Tropical, with average daily rainfall 28 mm. (1 in.) in winter.

## Government

**Type:** Constitutional democracy.

**Independence:** November 3, 1903.

**Constitution:** October 11, 1972; amended 1983 and 1994.

**Branches**: Executive—president (chief of state), two vice presidents. Legislative—Legislative Assembly (unicameral, 72 members). Judicial—Supreme Court.

**Subdivisions:** Nine provinces and two (Indian) territories.

**Political parties:** President Mireya Moscoso belongs to the Arnulfista Party (PA). Principal opposition parties include the Democratic Revolutionary Party (PRD) of the former president, Ernesto Perez Balladares. The PRD, in coalition with smaller parties, holds a slim majority in the Legislative Assembly.

**Suffrage:** Universal and compulsory at 18.

## Economy

**GDP:** (1998) (PPP) $8.96 billion.

**Annual growth rate:** (2000 est.) 2.3%; 3.0% (1999).

**Per capita GDP:** (1998) (PPP) $3,199.

**Natural resources:** Timber, seafood, copper. Services (76.5% of GDP): Finance, insurance, canal-related services, Colon Free Zone.

**Agriculture (7% of GDP):** Products—bananas and other fruit, corn, sugar, rice, coffee, shrimp, timber, vegetables, livestock.

**Industry:** (16.5% of GDP) Types—food and drink processing, metalworking, petroleum refining and products, chemicals, paper and paper products, printing, mining, refined sugar, clothing, furniture, construction.

**Trade:** Exports (1999)—$707 million: bananas, shrimp, sugar, coffee, clothing. Major markets—U.S. 42%. Imports (1999)—$3.5 billion: capital goods, crude oil, foodstuffs, chemicals, other consumer and intermediate goods. Major suppliers—U.S. 35.3%.

# PEOPLE

The culture, customs, and language of the Panamanians are predominantly Caribbean Spanish. Ethnically, the majority of the population is mestizo (mixed Spanish and Indian) or mixed Spanish, Indian, Chinese, and West Indian. Spanish is the official and dominant language; English is a common second language spoken by the West Indians and by many in business and the professions. More than half the population lives in the Panama City-Colon metropolitan corridor.

Panama is rich in folklore and popular traditions. Brightly colored national dress is worn during local festivals and the pre-Lenten carnival season, especially for traditional folk dances like the tanborito. Lively salsa—a mixture of Latin American popular music, rhythm and blues, jazz, and rock—is a Panamanian specialty. Indian influences dominate handicrafts such as the famous Kuna textile molas. Artist Roberto Lewis' Presidential Palace murals and his restoration work and ceiling in the National Theater are well known and admired.

More than 65,000 Panamanian students attend the University of Panama, the Technological University, and the University of Santa Maria La Antigua, a private Catholic institution. Including smaller colleges, there are 14 institutions of higher education in Panama.

The first 6 years of primary education are compulsory, and there are about 357,000 students currently enrolled in grades one through six. The total enrollment in the six secondary grades is about 207,000. Nearly 90% of Panamanians are literate.

# HISTORY

Panama's history has been shaped by the evolution of the world economy and the ambitions of great powers. Rodrigo de Bastidas, sailing westward from Venezuela in 1501 in search of gold, was the first European to explore the isthmus of Panama. A year later, Christopher Columbus visited the isthmus and established a short-lived settlement in the Darien. Vasco Nunez de Balboa's tortuous trek from the Atlantic to the Pacific in 1513 demonstrated that the isthmus was, indeed, the path between the seas, and Panama quickly became the crossroads and marketplace of Spain's empire in the New World. Gold and silver were brought by ship from South America, hauled across the isthmus, and loaded aboard ships for Spain. The route became known as the Camino Real, or Royal Road.

Panama was part of the Spanish empire for 300 years (1538–1821). From the outset, Panamanian identity was based on a sense of "geographic destiny," and Panamanian fortunes fluctuated with the geopolitical importance of the isthmus. The colonial experience also spawned Panamanian nationalism as well as a racially complex and highly stratified society, the source of internal conflicts that ran counter to the unifying force of nationalism.

## Building the Canal

Modern Panamanian history has been shaped by its transisthmian canal, which had been a dream since the beginning of Spanish colonization. From 1880 to 1900, a French company under Ferdinand de Lesseps attempted unsuccessfully to construct a sea-level canal on the site of the present Panama Canal. In November 1903, with U.S. encouragement and French financial support, Panama proclaimed its independence and concluded the Hay/Bunau-Varilla Treaty with the United States.

The treaty granted rights to the United States "as if it were sovereign" in a zone roughly 10 miles wide and 50 miles long. In that zone, the U.S. would build a canal, then administer, fortify, and defend it "in perpetuity." In 1914, the United States completed the existing 83-kilometer (50-mi.) lock canal, which today is one of the world's greatest engineering triumphs. The early 1960s saw the beginning of sustained pressure in Panama for the renegotiation of this treaty. (See discussion of United States-Panama relations and the 1977 Panama Canal Treaties below.)

## Military Coups and Coalitions

From 1903 until 1968, Panama was a constitutional democracy dominated by a commercially oriented oligarchy. During the 1950s, the Panamanian military began to challenge the oligarchy's political hegemony. In October 1968, Dr. Arnulfo Arias Madrid, twice elected president and twice ousted by the Panamanian military, was again ousted as president by the National Guard after only 10 days in office. A military junta government was established, and the commander of the National Guard, Brig. Gen. Omar Torrijos, emerged as the principal power in Panamanian political life. Torrijos' regime was harsh and corrupt, but he was a charismatic leader whose populist domestic programs and nationalist foreign policy appealed to the rural and urban constituencies largely ignored by the oligarchy.

Torrijos' death in 1981 altered the tone but not the direction of Panama's political evolution. Despite 1983 constitutional amendments which appeared to proscribe a political role for the military, the Panama Defense Force (PDF), as they were then known, continued to dominate Panamanian political life behind a facade of civilian government. The PDF's hand-picked candidate won the presidential election in 1984. Progovernment parties also won a majority of Legislative Assembly seats, in races tainted by charges of corruption. By this time, Gen. Manuel Noriega was firmly in control of both the PDF and the civilian government.

The rivalry between civilian elites and the Panamanian military, a recurring theme in Panamanian political life since the 1950s, developed into a grave crisis in the 1980s. Prompted by government restrictions on media and civil liberties, in the summer of 1987 more than 100 busi-

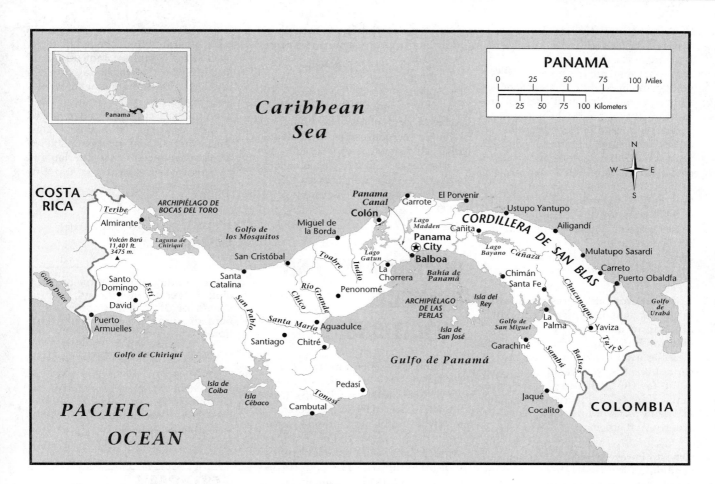

ness, civic, and religious groups formed a loose coalition that organized widespread anti-government demonstrations.

Panama's developing domestic crisis was paralleled by rising tensions between the Panamanian Government and the United States. The United States froze economic and military assistance to Panama in the summer of 1987 in response to the political crisis and an attack on the U.S. embassy. The Government of Panama countered by ousting the U.S. Agency for International Development in December 1987; before the end of the year, the U.S. Congress cut off all assistance to Panama. General Noriega's February 1988 indictment in U.S. courts on drug-trafficking charges sharpened tensions. In April 1988, President Reagan invoked the International Emergency Economic Powers Act, freezing Panamanian Government assets in U.S. banks and prohibiting payments by American

agencies, firms, and individuals to the Noriega regime.

When national elections were held in May 1989, Panamanians voted for the anti-Noriega candidates by a margin of over three-to-one. Although the size of the opposition victory and the presence of international observers thwarted regime efforts to control the outcome of the vote, the Norieiga regime promptly annulled the election and embarked on a new round of repression.

By the fall of 1989, the regime was barely clinging to power. An unsuccessful PDF coup attempt in October produced bloody reprisals. Deserted by all but a small number of cronies, and distrustful of a shaken and demoralized PDF, Noriega began increasingly to rely on irregular paramilitary units called Dignity Battalions. In December 1989, the regime's paranoia made daily existence unsafe for U.S. forces and other U.S. citizens.

On December 20, President Bush ordered the U.S. military into Panama to protect U.S. lives and property, to fulfill U.S. treaty responsibilities to operate and defend the Canal, to assist the Panamanian people in restoring democracy, and to bring Noriega to justice. The U.S. troops involved in Operation Just Cause achieved their primary objectives quickly, and troop withdrawal began on December 27. Norieiga eventually surrendered to U.S. authorities voluntarily. He is now serving a 40-year sentence for drug trafficking.

## Rebuilding Democracy

Panamanians moved quickly to rebuild their civilian constitutional government. On December 27, 1989, Panama's Electoral Tribunal invalidated the Norieiga regime's annulment of the May 1989 election and confirmed the victory of opposition candidates under the leadership of President Guillermo Endara and Vice

Presidents Guillermo Ford and Ricardo Arias Calderon. President Endara took office as the head of a four-party minority government, pledging to foster Panama's economic recovery, transform the Panamanian military into a political force under civilian control, and strengthen democratic institutions. During its 5-year term, the Endara government struggled to meet the public's high expectations. Its new police force proved to be a major improvement in outlook and behavior over its thuggish predecessor but was not fully able to deter crime. Its overall record was not enough to convince a skeptical public that it deserved re-election in 1994.

Ernesto Perez Balladares was sworn in as President on September 1, 1994, after an internationally monitored election campaign. The campaign was Panama's largest, with seven candidates for the presidency; over 2,500 for the legislature; 2,000 for mayoral posts; and more than 10,000 at the local level and was peaceful, orderly, and efficient.

Ernesto Perez Balladares ran as the candidate for a three-party coalition dominated by the Democratic Revolutionary Party (PRD), the erstwhile political arm of the military dictatorship during the Torrijos and Norieiga years. A long-time member of the PRD, Perez Balladares worked skillfully during the campaign to rehabilitate the PRD's image, emphasizing the party's populist Torrijos roots rather than its association with Noriega. He won the election with only 33% of the vote when the major non-PRD forces, unable to agree on a joint candidate, splintered into competing factions.

Perez Balladares governed with a multiparty cabinet that included prominent experts in their fields as well as several members who publicly opposed Noriega. His administration carried out economic reforms and often worked closely with the U.S. on implementation on the Canal treaties. In August 1998, a Perez Balladares-blocked referendum to allow presidential reelection failed by a large margin. Soon after, the Government of Panama asked that the 2-

year-long negotiations to establish a multilateral counter-narcotics center be ended.

On May 2, 1999, Mireya Moscoso, the widow of former President Arnulfo Arias Madrid who had lost narrowly to Perez Balladares in 1994, defeated PRD candidate Martin Torrijos, son of the late dictator. The elections were considered free and fair. Moscoso took office on September 1, 1999.

# GOVERNMENT AND POLITICAL CONDITIONS

Panama is a representative democracy with three branches of government: executive and legislative branches elected by direct, secret vote for 5-year terms, and an independent appointed judiciary. The executive branch includes a president and two vice presidents. The legislative branch consists of a 72-member unicameral Legislative Assembly. The judicial branch is organized under a nine-member Supreme Court and includes all tribunals and municipal courts. An autonomous Electoral Tribunal supervises voter registration, the election process, and the activities of political parties. Everyone over the age of 18 is required to vote, although those who fail to do so are not penalized.

## National Security

The Panamanian Government has converted the former Panama Defense Forces (PDF) into a civilian "public force," subordinate to civilian officials and composed of four independent units: the Panamanian National Police, the National Maritime Service (Coast Guard), the National Air Service, and the Institutional Protective Service (VIP Security). A constitutional amendment, passed in 1994, abolished the military permanently.

Law enforcement units that have been separated from the public force, such as the Technical Judicial Police, also are directly subordinate to civilian authorities. The public force budget—in contrast to the former PDF—is on public record and under control of the executive. The United States, with congressional approval, is delivering assistance to help develop and maintain truly professional law enforcement agencies.

## Principal Government Officials

For up-to-date information on Principal Government Officials, see the Chiefs of State and Cabinet Members of Foreign Governments section starting on page 1.

Panama maintains an embassy in the United States at 2862 McGill Terrace, N.W., Washington, D.C. 20008 (tel: 202–483–1407).

# ECONOMY

Panama's economy is based primarily on a well-developed services sector that accounts for nearly 80% of GDP. Services include the Panama Canal, banking, the Colon Free Zone, insurance, container ports, and flagship registry. Tourism is becoming increasingly important.

Panama's previous government under Ernesto Perez Balladares made important advances toward opening its economy to trade and free competition, in part by embarking on a major privatization program that attracted over $1 billion worth of U.S. investment. Though this privatization mostly has been concluded, more U.S. investment is anticipated with the signing of the OPIC Agreement and the amendment to the Bilateral Investment Treaty in 2000.

However, a slump in Colon Free Zone and agricultural exports, high oil prices, and the withdrawal of U.S. military forces precipitated an economic slowdown in 2000. A major challenge facing the current government under President Mireya Moscoso is turning to productive use the 70,000 acres of former U.S. military land and the more than 5,000 buildings that reverted to Panama at the end of 1999. Administratively, this job falls to the Panamanian Inter-Oceanic Regional Authority (ARI). Estimates of U.S. Department of Defense contribution to the Panamanian economy through employing Panamanians, local procurement, and expenditures by personnel range from $170 to $350 million.

GDP growth for 2000 was about 2.3%, compared to 3.0% in 1999. Though Panama has the highest GDP per capita in Central America, approximately 37% of its population lives in poverty. The unemployment rate in 2000 was 13.3%.

Beginning March 1, 2001, Panama will serve as host for the 2001–03 Free Trade Area of the Americas negotiations. Additionally, Panama is negotiating free trade areas with Costa Rica and Mexico, among others.

# FOREIGN RELATIONS

Panama is a member of the UN General Assembly, most major UN agencies, and has served three terms as a member of the UN Security Council. It maintains membership in several international financial institutions, including the World Bank, the Inter-American Development Bank, and the International Monetary Fund.

Panama is a member of the Organization of American States and was a founding member of the Rio Group. Although it was suspended from the Latin American Economic System—known informally both as the Group of Eight and the Rio Group—in 1988 due to its internal political system under Noriega, Panama was readmitted in September 1994 as an acknowledgment of its present democratic credentials.

Panama also is one of the founding members of the Union of Banana Exporting Countries and belongs to the Inter-American Tropical Tuna Commission. Panama is an active participant in Central American regional meetings, although it is not a formal participant in integration activities. Panama is a member of the Central American Parliament (PARLACEN) as well as the Central American Integration System (SICA). Panama joined its six Central American neighbors at the 1994 Summit of the Americas in signing the Alliance for Sustainable Development known as the Conjunta Centroamerica-USA or CONCAUSA to promote sustainable economic development in the region and participates in some Miami summit follow-on meetings.

Panama strongly backed efforts by the United States to implement UN Security Council Resolution 940, which was designed to facilitate the departure of Haiti's de facto authorities from power. Panama offered to contribute personnel to the Multinational Force, which restored the democratically elected government to Haiti in October 1994, and granted asylum to some former Haitian military leaders. Also in 1994, Panama agreed to accept 9,000 Cuban "rafters," who were housed temporarily on U.S. military range areas until 1995.

# U.S.-PANAMANIAN RELATIONS

The Panama Canal Treaties provided the foundation for an enduring partnership. The U.S. and Panama implemented the treaties by preparing for the transfer to Panama of the Canal and the U.S. base properties. Headquarters of the U.S. Southern Command transferred to Miami in 1997 and the withdrawal of all U.S. military forces from Panama was completed in 1999.

The United States cooperates with the Panamanian Government in promoting economic, political, and social development through U.S. and international agencies. Cultural ties between the two countries are strong, and many Panamanians come to the United States for higher education and advanced training. About 6,000 Americans reside in Panama, most of whom are retirees from the Panama Canal Commission and individuals who hold dual nationality.

Panama continues to fight against illegal narcotics. The country's proximity to major cocaine-producing nations and its role as a commercial and financial crossroads make it a country of special importance in this regard. Although money laundering remains a problem, Panama passed significant reforms in 2000 intended to strengthen its cooperation against international financial crimes. Panama has worked closely with the U.S. Treasury Department's Financial Crimes Enforcement Network and is a member of the Egmont Group.

## The Panama Canal Treaties

The 1977 Panama Canal Treaties entered into force on October 1, 1979. They replaced the 1903 Hay/Bunau-Varilla Treaty between the United States and Panama, and all other U.S.-Panama agreements concerning the Panama Canal which were in force on that date. The treaties comprise:

* A basic treaty governing the operation and defense of the Canal from October 1, 1979, to December 31, 1999 (Panama Canal Treaty); and * A treaty guaranteeing the permanent neutrality of the Canal (Neutrality Treaty). The details of the arrangements for U.S. operation and defense of the Canal under the Panama Canal Treaty are spelled out in separate implementing agreements.

## Purpose of the Treaties

In negotiating the Panama Canal Treaties, four successive U.S. administrations acted to protect a fundamental national interest in long-term access to a secure and efficient Canal. Panama's cooperation is fundamental to this objective. By meeting Panamanian aspirations for eventual control of the Canal, the United States sought a new relationship with Panama based on friendship and mutual respect. The treaties make Panama a partner in the continued safe and efficient operation of the Canal. In serving the best interests of both nations, the treaties serve the interests of all users of the Canal.

## History of the Negotiations

Our bilateral relationship with Panama has centered on the Panama Canal since the beginning of the century. Under the 1903 treaty, the United States acquired unilateral rights to build and operate a canal in perpetuity. It also acquired the Canal Zone—a 553-square mile area in which the United States exercised the rights, power, and authority of a sovereign state. In January 1964, Panamanian dissatisfaction with this relationship boiled over into riots that resulted in the deaths of four U.S. Marines and more than 20 Panamanians. A 3-month suspension of diplomatic relations followed.

The growing bilateral tension in the 1960s gave weight to the views of those who believed that a new Canal Treaty was needed to replace the 1903 treaty and to establish a new relationship with Panama. In June 1967, United States and Panamanian negotiators completed draft treaties dealing with the existing Canal, a possible sea-level Canal through Panama, and defense matters. Neither country ratified the treaties, however, and they were publicly rejected by the new Torrijos government in 1970.

A resumption of treaty negotiations led to a declaration of principles signed in 1973 by Secretary of State Henry Kissinger and his Panamanian counterpart, Juan Antonio Tack. On September 7, 1977, President Carter and General Torrijos signed the Panama Canal Treaties at the headquarters of the Organization of American States in Washington, DC. The Panamanian people approved the new treaties in a plebiscite held on October 23, 1977. The U.S. Senate ratified the Neutrality Treaty on March 16, 1978, and the Panama Canal Treaty on April 18, 1978. The treaties entered into force on October 1, 1979. The protocol to the Neutrality Treaty is open to accession by all nations, and more than 35 have subscribed.

## Basic Provisions of the Treaties

The United States had primary responsibility for the operation and defense of the Canal until December 31, 1999. At noon on that date, Panama assumed sole responsibility for operating the waterway. The United States and Panama continue to maintain a regime of neutrality for the Canal, including nondiscriminatory access and tolls for merchant and naval vessels of all nations. A U.S. Senate condition attached to the instruments of ratification allows the U.S. and Panama to negotiate a post-1999 defense-sites treaty, if both countries find such a treaty in their mutual interest. Negotiations for a possible post-1999 U.S. presence in Panama in a proposed multinational counter-narcotics center (MCC) ended in September 1998, and no further negotiations are planned.

Under the terms of the Neutrality Treaty, U.S. warships are entitled to expeditious passage through the Canal at all times, and the United States continues to have the obligation to ensure that the Canal remains open and secure.

The United States operated the Canal through the Panama Canal Commission (PCC), which was a U.S. Government agency supervised by a Board of Directors consisting of five American and four Panamanian members, appointed by the President (the Panamanian members are initially nominated by their government). Until 1990, the Canal Administrator was an American, and the Deputy Administrator was Panamanian; these nationalities reversed for the final decade of the treaty on September 20, 1990, when Gilberto Guardia was installed as the first Panamanian Administrator. He was succeeded in 1996 by another Panamanian, Alberto Aleman Zubieta. Pursuant to treaty obligations, the PCC trained Panamanians in all areas of Canal operations prior to the transfer of the Canal in 1999. In 1997 President Perez Balladares named the members of the Panama Canal Authority (PCA), which became the successor agency to the PCC. During the life of the treaty, Panama received the following payments from Canal revenues:

A fixed annual payment of $10 million; An annual payment of $10 million, adjustable for inflation, for public services provided to Canal operating areas by the Government of Panama (the Canal Zone and its government ceased to exist when the treaties entered into force, and Panama assumed jurisdiction over Canal Zone territories and functions); An annual percentage of toll revenues assessed at $0.39 (since October 1, 1996) per Panama Canal net ton transiting the Canal, worth $84.6 million in 1996; and A payment of up to $10 million in the event that revenues exceeded PCC expenditures in a given year.

Under U.S. implementing legislation (the Panama Canal Act), the PCC was required to be self-sustaining; its costs could not exceed its revenues, nor could U.S. taxpayer funds be used for Canal operations or payments to Panama.

## Principal U.S. Officials

**For up-to-date information on Principal U.S. Officials, see the U.S. Embassies, Consulates, and Foreign Service section starting on page 139.**

The U.S. Embassy in Panama is located at Avenida Balboa y Calle 38, Panama City (tel: 507–207–7000). Personal and official mail for the Embassy and members of the mission may be sent to: U.S. Embassy Panama, Unit 0945, APO AA 34002. E-mail: U.S. Information Service (USIS): usispan@pty.com Political/Economic Section—embpol@sinfo.net

## Other Contact Information

**American Chamber of Commerce & Industry in Panama**
Estafeta Balboa Apartado 168 Panama, Republica de Panama Tel: (507) 269–3881
Fax: (507) 223–3508
E-mail: amcham@pan.gbm.net

**U.S. Department of Commerce**
International Trade Administration
Office of Latin American and the Caribbean
14th and Constitution, NW
Washington, D.C. 20230
Tel: (202) 482–0057 800-USA-TRADE
Fax: (202) 482–0464
Home Page: http://www.ita.doc.gov

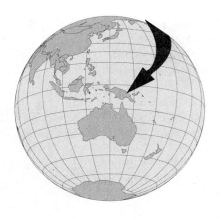

# PAPUA NEW GUINEA

August 1999

## Official Name:
## Independent State of Papua New Guinea

# PROFILE

## Geography

**Land area:** 452,860 sq. km.; about the size of California.
**Cities:** Capital—Port Moresby (pop. 300,000). Other cities—Lae (88,172), Mt. Hagen (70,850).
**Terrain:** Mostly mountains with coastal lowlands and rolling foothills.
**Climate:** Tropical. NW Monsoon, Dec–Mar. SE Monsoon, May–Oct.

## People

**Population:** 4.5 million.
**Annual growth rate:** 2.3%.
**Languages:** English, Tok Pisin, Motu (official), and about 715 other languages.
**Education:** Years compulsory—0. Literacy—72.2%.
**Health:** Infant mortality rate—59/1,000. Life expectancy—men 57 yrs.; women 58 yrs.

## Government

**Type:** Constitutional monarchy with parliamentary democracy.
**Constitution:** September 16, 1975.
**Branches:** Executive—British monarch (chief of state), represented by governor general; prime minister (head of government). Legislative—unicameral parliament. Judicial—independent; highest is Supreme Court.
**Administrative subdivisions:** 19 provinces and the national capital district (Port Moresby).
**Major political parties:** People's Progress Party (PPP); Pangu Parti; People's Democratic Movement (PDM); Advance Papua New Guinea; and Melanesian Alliance (MA).
**Suffrage:** Universal over 18 years of age.

## Economy (1998 est.)

**GDP:** $3.872 billion.
**Growth rate:** 1.9%.
**Per capita GDP:** $860.
**Natural resources:** Gold, copper ore, oil, natural gas, timber, fish.
**Agriculture (28% of GDP):** Major products—coffee, cocoa, coconuts, palm oil, timber, tea.
**Industry (32% of GDP):** Major sectors—copra crushing, palm oil processing, plywood production, wood chip production, mining of gold, silver and copper, construction, tourism, crude oil production.
**Trade (1998):** Exports—$1.7 billion: gold, copper ore, oil, timber, palm oil, coffee. Major markets—Australia, Japan, Germany, U.K., South Korea, China. Imports—$1.2 billion: machinery and transport equipment, manufactured goods, food, fuels, chemicals. Major suppliers—Australia, Singapore, Japan, U.S., New Zealand, Malaysia.

# PEOPLE

The indigenous population of Papua New Guinea is one of the most heterogeneous in the world. Papua New Guinea has several thousand separate communities, most with only a few hundred people. Divided by language, customs, and tradition, some of these communities have engaged in tribal warfare with their neighbors for centuries.

The isolation created by the mountainous terrain is so great that some groups, until recently, were unaware of the existence of neighboring groups only a few kilometers away. The diversity, reflected in a folk saying, "For each village, a different culture," is perhaps best shown in the local languages. Spoken mainly on the island of New Guinea—composed of Papua New Guinea and Irian Jaya, Indonesia (the term "New Guinea" is applied both to the northern two-thirds of the main island of Papua New Guinea and to the entire island)—about 650 of these languages have been identified; of these, only 350–450 are related. The remainder seem to be totally unrelated either to each other or to the other major groupings. Native languages are spoken by a few hundred to a few thousand, although Enga, used in Enga Province, is spoken by some 130,000 people. Most native languages are extremely complex grammatically.

Melanesian Pidgin serves as lingua francas. English is spoken by educated people and in Milne Bay Province.

The overall population density is low, although pockets of overpopulation exist. Papua, with almost half the area of Papua New Guinea, has only 20% of the population. The Western Province of Papua averages one person per square kilometer (3 per sq. mi.). The Chimbu Province in the New Guinea highlands averages 20 persons per square kilometer (60 per sq. mi.) and has areas containing up to 200 people farming a square kilometer of land. The highlands have 40% of the population.

A considerable urban drift toward Port Moresby and other major centers has occurred in recent years. Between 1978 and 1988, Port Moresby grew nearly 8% per year, Lae 6%, Mount Haven 6.5%, Goroka 4%, and Madang 3%. The trend towards urbanization has accelerated in the 90s, bringing in its wake squatter settlements, unemployment and attendant social problems.

Almost two–thirds of the population is nominally Christian. Of these, more than 700,000 are Catholic, more than 500,000 Lutheran, and the balance are members of other Protestant sects. Although the major churches are under indigenous leadership, a large number of missionaries remain in the country. The bulk of the estimated 2,500 Americans resident in Papua New Guinea are missionaries and their families. The non–Christian portion of the indigenous population practices a wide variety of religions, which are an integral part of traditional culture and consist mainly of animism (spirit worship) and ancestor cults.

Foreign residents are just over 1% of the population. More than half are Australian; others are from the United Kingdom, New Zealand, the Philippines, and the United States. Since independence, about 900 foreigners have become naturalized citizens.

The traditional Papua New Guinea social structure includes the following characteristics:

- The practice of subsistence economy;

- Recognition of bonds of kinship with obligations extending beyond the immediate family group;

- Generally egalitarian relationships with an emphasis on acquired, rather than inherited, status; and

- A strong attachment of the people to land.

Most Papua New Guineans still adhere strongly to this traditional social structure, which has its roots in village life.

# HISTORY

Archeological evidence indicates that humans arrived on New Guinea at least 60,000 years ago, probably by sea from Southeast Asia during an ice age period when the sea was lower and distances between islands shorter. Although the first arrivals were hunters and gatherers, early evidence shows that people managed the forest environment to provide food. There also are indications of gardening having been practiced at the same time that agriculture was developing in Mesopotamia and Egypt. Early garden crops—many of which are indigenous—included sugarcane, Pacific bananas, yams, and taros, while sago and pandanus were two commonly exploited native forest crops. Today's staples—sweet potatoes and pigs—are later arrivals, but shellfish and fish have long been mainstays of coastal dwellers' diets.

When Europeans first arrived, inhabitants of New Guinea and nearby islands—while still relying on bone, wood, and stone tools—had a productive agricultural system. They traded along the coast, where products mainly were pottery, shell ornaments, and foodstuffs, and in the interior, where forest products were exchanged for shells and other sea products.

The first Europeans to sight New Guinea were probably the Portuguese and Spanish navigators sailing in the South Pacific in the early part of the 16th century. In 1526–27, Don Jorge de Meneses accidentally came upon the principal island and is credited with naming it "Papua," a Malay word for the frizzled quality of Melanesian hair. The term "New Guinea" was applied to the island in 1545 by a Spaniard, Ynigo Ortis de Retez, because of a fancied resemblance between the islands' inhabitants and those found on the African Guinea coast. Although European navigators visited the islands and explored their coastlines for the next 170 years, little was known of the inhabitants until the late 19th century.

## New Guinea

With Europe's growing need for coconut oil, Godeffroy's of Hamburg, the largest trading firm in the Pacific, began trading for copra in the New Guinea Islands. In 1884, Germany formally took possession of the northeast quarter of the island and put its administration in the hands of a chartered company. In 1899, the German imperial Government assumed direct control of the territory, thereafter known as German New Guinea. In 1914, Australian troops occupied German New Guinea, and it remained under Australian military control until 1921. The British Government, on behalf of the Commonwealth of Australia, assumed a mandate from the League of Nations for governing the Territory of New Guinea in 1920. It was administered under this mandate until the Japanese invasion in December 1941 brought about the suspension of Australian civil administration. Following the surrender of the Japanese in

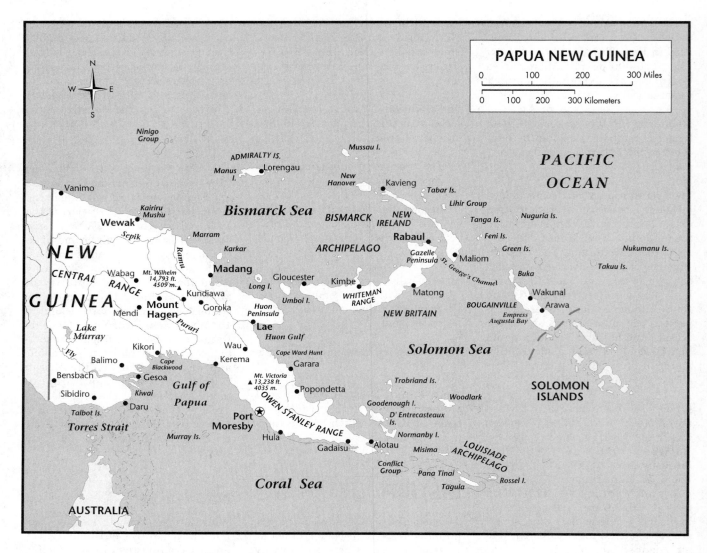

1945, civil administration of Papua as well as New Guinea was restored, and under the Papua New Guinea Provisional Administration Act, 1945–46, Papua and New Guinea were combined in an administrative union.

## Papua

On November 6, 1884, a British protectorate was proclaimed over the southern coast of New Guinea (the area called Papua) and its adjacent islands. The protectorate, called British New Guinea, was annexed outright on September 4, 1888. The possession was placed under the authority of the Commonwealth of Australia in 1902. Following the passage of the Papua Act of 1905, British New Guinea became the Territory of

Papua and formal Australian administration began in 1906. Papua was administered under the Papua Act until it was invaded by the Japanese in 1942 and civil administration suspended. During the war, Papua was governed by a military administration from Port Moresby, where Gen. Douglas MacArthur occasionally made his headquarters. As noted, it was later joined in an administrative union with New Guinea during 1945–46 following the surrender of Japan.

## Postwar Developments

The Papua and New Guinea Act of 1949 formally approved the placing of New Guinea under the international trusteeship system and confirmed the administrative union of New Guinea and Papua under the title of "The

Territory of Papua and New Guinea." The act provided for a Legislative Council (established in 1951), a judicial organization, a public service, and a system of local government. A House of Assembly replaced the Legislative Council in 1963, and the first House of Assembly opened on June 8, 1964. In 1972, the name of the territory was changed to Papua New Guinea.

Elections in 1972 resulted in the formation of a ministry headed by Chief Minister Michael Somare, who pledged to lead the country to self–government and then to independence. Papua New Guinea became self–governing in December 1973 and achieved independence on September 16, 1975. The 1977 national elections confirmed Michael Somare as Prime Minister at the head of a coalition led by the Pangu Party. However, his government lost a vote of confidence in 1980 and was replaced by a new cabinet headed by Sir Julius Chan as Prime Minister. The 1982 elections increased Pangu's plurality, and parliament again chose Somare as Prime Minister. In November 1985, the Somare government lost a vote of no confidence, and the parliamentary majority elected Paias Wingti, at the head of a five–party coalition, as Prime Minister. A coalition, headed by Wingti, was victorious in very close elections in July 1987. In July 1988, a no confidence vote toppled Wingti and brought to power Rabbie Namaliu, who a few weeks earlier had replaced Somare as leader of the Pangu Party.

Such reversals of fortune and a revolving–door succession of Prime Ministers continue to characterize Papua New Guinea's national politics. A plethora of political parties, coalition governments, shifting party loyalties and motions of no–confidence in the leadership all lend an air of instability to political proceedings. Under legislation intended to enhance stability, new governments remain immune from no–confidence votes for the first 18 months of their incumbency.

# GOVERNMENT AND POLITICAL CONDITIONS

Papua New Guinea, a constitutional monarchy, recognizes the Queen of England as head of state. She is represented by a governor–general who is elected by parliament and who performs mainly ceremonial functions. Papua New Guinea has three levels of government—national, provincial, and local. There is a 109–member unicameral parliament, whose members are elected every 5 years. The parliament in turn elects the prime minister, who appoints his cabinet from members of his party or coalition.

Members of parliament (MP's) are elected from 19 provinces and the national capital district of Port Moresby. Parliament introduced reforms in June 1995 to change the provincial government system, with regional (at–large) MP's becoming provincial governors, while retaining their national seats in parliament.

Papua New Guinea's judiciary is independent of the government. It protects constitutional rights and interprets the laws. There are several levels, culminating in the Supreme Court.

Papua New Guinea's politics are highly competitive. MP's are elected on a "first past the post" system, with winners frequently gaining less than 15% of the vote. There are several parties, but party allegiances are not strong. Winning candidates are usually courted in efforts to forge the majority needed to form a government, and allegiances are fluid. No single party has yet won enough seats to form a government in its own right.

Papua New Guinea has a history of changes in government coalitions and leadership from within Parliament during the 5–year intervals between national elections. New governments are protected by law from votes of no confidence for the first 18 months of their incumbency, and no votes of no confidence may be moved in the 12 months preceding a national election.

The last national election was held in June, 1997. The election was characterized by a large turnover in sitting members of Parliament and a number of veteran politicians, including former Prime Ministers Sir Julius Chan and Pias Wingti, lost their seats. A large number of independents were elected. Eighty–eight of the 109 election victories have been challenged by losing candidates in the courts and some elections have been annulled. The government was formed by a coalition of several parties. Bill Skate, the leader of the People's Congress Party, was elected Prime Minister. In July, 1999, Skate resigned under threat of a motion of no confidence and the Parliament

elected Sir Mekere Morauta Prime Minister, leaving Skate leader of the Opposition. Many members of the Morauta cabinet served Skate as ministers.

On Bougainville Island, a rebellion had been under way from early 1989 until a truce came into effect in October 1997 and a permanent cease fire was signed in April 1998. Under the eyes of a regional peace monitoring force and a UN observer mission, the government and provincial leaders have established an interim government and are working toward election of a provincial government.

## Principal Government Officials

**For up-to-date information on Principal Government Officials, see the Chiefs of State and Cabinet Members of Foreign Governments section starting on page 1.**

Papua New Guinea maintains an Embassy at 1779 Massachusetts Ave. NW, Washington, DC 20036 (tel. 202–745–3680; fax 202–745–3679). The Papua New Guinea mission to the United Nations is at 801 Second Avenue, New York, NY 10017 (tel. 212–682–6447).

# ECONOMY

Papau New Guinea is rich in natural resources, including minerals, timber and fish, and produces a variety of commercial agricultural products. The economy generally can be separated into subsistence and market sectors, although the distinction is blurred by small–holder cash cropping of coffee, cocoa, and copra. About 75% of the country's population relies primarily on the subsistence economy. The minerals, timber and fish sectors are dominated by foreign investors. Manufacturing is limited, and the formal labor sector is consequently also limited.

## Mineral Resources

In 1998 mineral production accounted for 23% of GDP. Government revenues and foreign exchange earning depend heavily on mineral exports. Indigenous land owners in areas affected by minerals projects also receive royalties from those operations. Papua New Guinea is richly endowed with gold, copper, oil, natural gas, and other minerals. Although Bougainville copper and gold mines are currently in production at Progera, Ok Tedi, Misima and Lihir. New nickel, copper and gold projects have been identified and are awaiting a rise in commodity prices to begin development. A consortium led by Chevron is producing and exporting oil from south–western Papua New Guinea. In 2000, it expects to begin the commercialization of the country's estimated 22.5 trillion cubic feet of natural gas reserves through the construction of a gas pipeline from Papua New Guinea to Queensland, Australia.

## Agriculture, Timber and Fish

Papua New Guinea also produces and exports valuable agricultural, timber and fish products. Agriculture currently accounts for 28% of GDP and supports over 80% of the population. Cash crops ranked by value are coffee, oil, cocoa, copra, tca, rubber and sugar. The timber industry was not active in 1998, due to low world prices, but is rebounding in 1999. About 40% of the country is covered with exploitable trees and a domestic wood working industry has been slow to develop and fish exports are confined primarily to shrimp. Fishing boats of other nations catch tuna in PNG waters under license.

## Industry

In general, the Papua New Guinea economy is highly dependent on imports for manufacturing goods. Its industrial sector (exclusive of mining) accounts for only 9% of GDP, and contributes little to exports. Small–scale industries produce beer, soap, concrete products, clothing, paper prod-

ucts, matches, ice cream, canned meat, fruit juices, furniture, plywood and pain. The small domestic market, relatively high wages, and high transport costs are constraints to industrial development.

## Trade and Investment

Australia, Singapore, and Japan are the principal exporters to Papua New Guinea. Petroleum and mining machinery and aircraft are perennially the strongest U.S. exports to Papua New Guinea. In 1998, as mineral exploration and new minerals investments declined, so did U.S. exports.

Australia is Papua New Guinea's most important export market followed by Japan and European Union. Crude oil is the largest U.S. import from Papua New Guinea, followed by gold, cocoa, coffee and copper ore.

U.S. companies are active in developing Papua New Guinea's mining and petroleum sectors. Chevron operates the Kutubu and Gobe oil projects and is developing its natural gas reserves. Battle Mountain Gold is a principal owner of Papua New Guinea Gold, which operates the Lihir gold mine, and Cyprus–Amex is the developer of a gold and copper project in the Sepik region. A 30,000–40,000 barrel–per–day oil refinery project in which there is an American interest is also under development in Port Moresby.

Papua New Guinea became a participating economy in the Asia–Pacific Economic Cooperation (APEC) Forum in 1993. It joined the World Trade Organization (WTO) in 1996.

## Development Programs and Aid

Australia is the largest bilateral aid donor to Papua New Guinea, offering about $200 million a year in assistance. Budgetary support, which has been provided in decreasing amounts since independence, will stop altogether in 2000, with aid concentrated on project development.

**Travel Notes**

**Travel Advice:** For up-to-date information from the U.S. State Department on possible inconvenient or hazardous situations, see the **Travel Warnings and Consular Information Sheets from the U.S. Government** section starting on page 1723. For the latest information on health requirements and conditions, see the **International Travelers' Health Information** section starting on page 1385. For further information dealing with non-urgent matter, see the **Tips for Travelers to...** section starting on page 1588.

Other major sources of aid to PNG are Japan, the European Union, the People's Republic of China, the Republic of China, the United Nations, the Asian Development Bank, and the World Bank. At mid–1999, the GPNG is negotiating an economic support loan from the International Monetary Fund.

Volunteers from a number of countries, including the United States, and mission church workers also provide education, health and development assistance throughout the country.

## Current Economic Conditions

By mid–1999, Papua New Guinea's economy was in crisis. Although its agricultural sector had recovered from the 1997 drought and timber prices were rising as most Asian economies were recovered from their 1998 slump, Papua New Guinea's foreign currency earnings suffered from low world mineral and petroleum prices. Estimates of minerals in exploration expenditure in 1999 were one third of what was spent in 1997. The resulting lower foreign exchange earnings, capital flight and general government mismanagement resulted in a precipitous drop in the value of Papua New Guinea's currency, the kina, leading to a dangerous decrease in foreign currency reserves. The kina has been floated since 1994. Economic activity decreased in most sectors, imports of all kinds shrunk, and inflation, which had been over 21% in 1998, slowed to an estimated annual rate of 8% in 1999. Citing the previous government's failure to successfully negotiate acceptable commercial loans or bond sales to cover its budget deficit, the government formed in July, 1999, announced its intention to request emergency assistance from the International Monetary Fund and the World Bank. Such assistance had been denied to the previous government largely because of habitual unbudgeted spending and question over spending priorities.

# FOREIGN RELATIONS

Papua New Guinea's foreign policy reflects close ties with Australia and other traditional allies and cooperative relations with neighboring countries. Its views on international political and economic issues are generally moderate. Papua New Guinea has diplomatic relations with 56 countries.

# U.S.-PAPUA NEW GUINEA RELATIONS

The United States and Papua New Guinea established diplomatic relations upon the latter's independence on September 16, 1975. The two nations belong to a variety of regional organizations, including the Asia–Pacific Economic Cooperation (APEC) forum; the ASEAN Regional Forum (ARF); the South Pacific Commission; and the South Pacific Regional Environmental Program (SPREP).

One of the most successful cooperative multilateral efforts linking the U.S. and Papua New Guinea is the U.S.-Pacific Islands Multilateral Tuna Fisheries Treaty, under which the U.S. grants $18 million per year to Pacific Island parties and the latter provide access for U.S. fishing vessels.

The United States has provided significant humanitarian assistance to Papua New Guinea during the past five years, and has contributed to the rehabilitation of Bougainville.

The U.S. also supports Papua New Guinea's efforts to protect bio–diversity. The U.S. Government supports the International Coral Reef Initiative aimed at protecting reefs in tropical nations such as Papua New Guinea.

U.S. military forces, through the Pacific Theater Command in Honolulu, Hawaii, carry out annual bilateral meeting with the Papua New Guinea Defense Force (PNGDF). The U.S. also provides police and other education and training courses to national security officials.

The U.S. Peace Corps sent its first group of volunteers to Papua New Guinea in September 1981. Currently over 80 volunteers serve throughout the country. Volunteer work is concentrated in rural community development and education.

About 2,500 U.S. citizens live in Papua New Guinea, with major concentrations at two missionary headquarters in Eastern Highlands Province.

## Principal U.S. Embassy Officials

**For up-to-date information on Principal U.S. Officials, see the U.S. Embassies, Consulates, and Foreign Service section starting on page 139.**

The U.S. embassy in Papua New Guinea is located on Douglas Street, Port Moresby (tel. 675–321–1455; fax 675–321–3423). The mailing address is P.O. Box 1492, Port Moresby, U.S. Department of State, Washington, DC 20521–4240.

# PARAGUAY

March 2001

Official Name:
**Republic of Paraguay**

## PROFILE

### Geography

**Area:** 406,752 sq. km. (157,047 sq. mi.); about the size of California.
**Cities:** Capital—Asuncion (pop. 502,000). Other cities—Caaguazu, Coronel Oviedo, Pedro Juan Caballero, Encarnacion, and Ciudad del Este.
**Terrain:** East of the Paraguay River—grassy plains, wooded hills, tropical forests; west of the Paraguay River (Chaco region)—low, flat, marshy plain.
**Climate:** Temperate east of the Paraguay River, semiarid to the west.

### People

**Nationality:** Noun and adjective—Paraguayan(s).
**Population:** 4.8 million. Annual population growth rate: 2.7%.
**Ethnic groups:** Mixed Spanish and Indian descent (mestizo) 95%.
**Religions:** Roman Catholic 90%; Mennonite and other Protestant denominations.
**Languages:** Spanish, Guarani.
**Education:** Years compulsory—6. Attendance—86.6%. Literacy—90.7%.
**Health:** Infant mortality rate—38/1,000. Life expectancy—68 years male; 75 years female.

**Work force:** (1995, 1.7 million) Agriculture—45%; industry and commerce—31%; services—19%; government—4%.

### Government

**Type:** Constitutional Republic. Independence: May 1811.
**Constitution:** June 1992.
**Branches:** Executive—President. Legislative—Senate and Chamber of Deputies. Judicial—Supreme Court of Justice. Administrative subdivisions: 17 departments.
**Political parties:** Colorado (National Republican Association), Authentic Radical Liberal, National Encounter, Christian Democratic, and numerous smaller parties not represented in Congress.
**Suffrage:** 18 years of age; universal and compulsory up to age 75.

### Economy (2000 Central Bank Preliminary.)

**GDP:** $7.8 billion.
**Annual growth rate:** 1.5%.
**Per capita GDP:** $1,500.
**Natural resources:** Hydroelectric sites, forests. Agriculture (28% of GDP): Products—soybeans, cotton, beef, cereals, sugarcane. Arable land—9 million hectares, of which 30% is in production.
**Manufacturing:** (14% of GDP) Types—sugar, cement, textiles, beverage, wood products.

**Trade:** (1998) Exports—$852 million*: soybeans, cotton, grains, meat and meat products, lumber, vegetable oil, and yerba mate. Major markets—Brazil, Argentina, EU. Imports—$2 billion*: machinery, fuels and lubricants, electronics, consumer goods. Major suppliers—Brazil (25%), Argentina (24 %), U.S. (14%).

**Market exchange rate:** (February 20, 2001) 3,750 guaranies=U.S.$1. (*Source: Government of Paraguay)

## PEOPLE

Paraguay's population is distributed unevenly throughout the country. The vast majority of the people live in the eastern region, most within 160 kilometers (100 miles) of Asuncion, the capital and largest city. The Chaco, which accounts for about 60% of the territory, is home to less than 2% of the population. Ethnically, culturally, and socially, Paraguay has one of the most homogeneous populations in South America. About 95% of the people are of mixed Spanish and Guarani Indian descent. Little trace is left of the original Guarani culture except the language, which is understood by 90% of the population. About 75% of all Paraguayans speak Spanish. Guarani and Spanish are official languages. Germans, Japanese, Koreans, ethnic Chinese, Arabs, Brazil-

## HISTORY

Pre-Columbian civilization in the fertile, wooded region that is now Paraguay consisted of numerous seminomadic, Guarani-speaking tribes of Indians, who were recognized for their fierce warrior traditions. They practiced a mythical polytheistic religion, which later blended with Christianity. Spanish explorer Juan de Salazar founded Asuncion on the Feast Day of the Assumption, August 15, 1537. The city eventually became the center of a Spanish colonial province. Paraguay declared its independence by overthrowing the local Spanish authorities in May 1811.

The country's formative years saw three strong leaders who established the tradition of personal rule that lasted until 1989: Jose Gaspar Rodriguez de Francia, Carlos Antonio Lopez, and his son, Francisco Solano Lopez. The younger Lopez waged a war against Argentina, Uruguay, and Brazil (War of the Triple Alliance, 1864–70) in which Paraguay lost half its population; afterwards, Brazilian troops occupied the country until 1874. A succession of presidents governed Paraguay under the banner of the Colorado Party from 1880 until 1904, when the Liberal party seized control, ruling with only a brief interruption until 1940.

In the 1930s and 1940s, Paraguayan politics were defined by the Chaco War against Bolivia, a civil war, dictatorships, and periods of extreme political instability. Gen. Alfredo Stroessner took power in May 1954. Elected to complete the unexpired term of his predecessor, he was re-elected president seven times, ruling almost continuously under the state-of-siege provision of the constitution with support from the military and the Colorado Party. During Stroessner's 34-year reign, political freedoms were severely limited, and opponents of the regime were systematically harassed and persecuted in the name of national security and anticommunism. Though a 1967 constitution gave dubious legitimacy to Stroessner's control, Paraguay became progressively isolated from the world community.

On February 3, 1989, Stroessner was overthrown in a military coup headed by Gen. Andres Rodriguez. Rodriguez, as the Colorado Party candidate, easily won the presidency in elections held that May and the Colorado Party dominated the Congress. In 1991 municipal elections, however, opposition candidates won several major urban centers, including Asuncion. As president, Rodriguez instituted political, legal, and economic reforms and initiated a rapprochement with the international community.

The June 1992 constitution established a democratic system of government and dramatically improved protection of fundamental rights. In May 1993, Colorado Party candidate Juan Carlos Wasmosy was elected as Paraguay's first civilian president in almost 40 years in what international observers deemed fair and free elections. The newly elected majority-opposition Congress quickly demonstrated its independence from the executive by rescinding legislation passed by the previous Colorado-dominated Congress. Wasmosy worked to consolidate Paraguay's democratic transition, reform the economy and the state, and improve respect for human rights. His major accomplishments were exerting civilian control over the armed forces and undertaking fundamental reform of the judicial and electoral systems. With support from the United States, the Organization of American States, and other countries in the region, the Paraguayan people rejected an April 1996 attempt by then-Army Chief Gen. Lino Oviedo to oust President Wasmosy, taking an important step to strengthen democracy.

Oviedo became the Colorado candidate for president in the 1998 election, but when the Supreme Court upheld in April his conviction on charges related to the 1996 coup attempt, he was not allowed to run and remained in confinement. His former running mate, Raul Cubas Grau, became the Colorado Party's candidate and was elected in May in elections deemed by international observers to be free and fair. Cubas included among his priorities reducing the growing budget deficit and fighting corruption and narcotics trafficking. However, his brief presidency was dominated by conflict over the status of Oviedo, who had significant influence over the Cubas government. One of Cubas' first acts after taking office in August was to commute Oviedo's sentence and release him from confinement. In December 1998, Paraguay's Supreme Court declared these actions unconstitutional. After delaying for 2 months, Cubas openly defied the Supreme Court in February 1999, refusing to return Oviedo to jail. In this tense atmosphere, the murder of Vice President and long-time Oviedo rival Luis Maria Argana on March 23, 1999, led the Chamber of Deputies to impeach Cubas the next day. The March 26 murder of eight student antigovernment demonstrators, widely believed to have been carried out by Oviedo supporters, made it clear that the Senate would vote to remove Cubas on March 29, and Cubas resigned on March 28. Despite fears that the military would not allow the change of government, Senate President Luis Gonzalez Macchi, a Cubas opponent, was peacefully sworn in as president the same day. Oviedo fled the same day to Argentina, where he was granted political asylum. Cubas left for Brazil the next day and has since received asylum.

Gonzalez Macchi offered cabinet positions in his government to senior representatives of all three political parties in an attempt to create a coalition government. While the Liberal Party pulled out of the government in February 2000, the Gonzalez Macchi government has achieved a consensus among the parties on many controversial issues, including economic reform.

# GOVERNMENT AND POLITICAL CONDITIONS

Paraguay's highly centralized government was fundamentally changed by the 1992 constitution, which provides for a division of powers. The president, popularly elected for a 5-year term, appoints a cabinet. The next presidential elections are scheduled for 2003. The bicameral Congress consists of an 80-member Chamber of Deputies and a 45-member Senate, elected concurrently with the president through a proportional representation system. Deputies are elected by department and senators nationwide. Paraguay's highest court is the Supreme Court. The Senate and the president select its nine members on the basis of recommendations from a constitutionally created Magistrates Council. Each of Paraguay's 17 departments is headed by a popularly elected governor.

## Principal Government Officials

For up-to-date information on Principal Government Officials, see the Chiefs of State and Cabinet Members of Foreign Governments section starting on page 1.

Paraguay maintains an embassy in the United States at 2400 Massachusetts Avenue, NW, Washington, DC 20008 (tel. 202–483–6960).
Consulates are in Miami, New York, and Kansas City, Kansas.

# ECONOMY

Paraguay has a predominantly agricultural economy, with an important commercial sector. There is a large subsistence sector, including sizable urban underemployment, and a large underground re-export sector. The country has vast hydroelectric resources, including the world's largest hydroelectric generation facility built and operated jointly with Brazil (Itaipú Dam), but it lacks significant mineral or petroleum resources. The government welcomes foreign investment and provides national treatment to foreign investors. The economy is dependent on exports of soybeans, cotton, grains, cattle, timber, and sugar; electricity generation; and to a decreasing degree on re-exporting to Brazil and Argentina products made elsewhere. It is therefore vulnerable to the vagaries of weather and to the fortunes of the Argentine and Brazilian economies.

According to Paraguayan Government statistics, Paraguay's GDP of $7.8 billion in 2000 represented a real increase of 1.5% from 1999. However, given the importance of the informal sector, accurate economic measures are difficult to obtain. Paraguay generally maintains a small balance-of-payments surplus. In early 2000, official foreign exchange reserves were below $775 million, and foreign official debt remained about $2.2 billion. On a per capita basis, GDP declined by about 1% during 2000, and inflation rose to 9.6%.

## Agriculture and Commerce

Agricultural activities, most of which are for export, represent about 27% of GDP. More than 200,000 families depend on subsistence farming activities and maintain marginal ties to the larger productive sector of the economy. The commercial sector is primarily engaged in the import of goods from Asia and the United States for re-export to neighboring countries. The recorded activities of this sector have declined significantly in recent years, placing a strain on government finances, which depend heavily on taxes on this trade. In general, Paraguayans prefer imported goods, and local industry relies on imported capital goods. The underground economy, which is not included in the national accounts, may equal the formal economy in size. The bulk of underground activ-ity centers on the unregistered sale of imported goods—including computers, sound equipment, cameras, liquor, and cigarettes—to Argentina and Brazil.

## Post-Stroessner Reforms

Since 1989, the government has deregulated the economy, which had been tightly controlled by President Stroessner's authoritarian regime. The Rodriguez and Wasmosy administrations eliminated foreign exchange controls and implemented a dirty floating exchange rate system, reformed the tax structure and established tax incentives to attract investment, reduced tariff levels, launched a stock market, and began a process of financial reform.

Though the short-lived Cubas administration was hampered by political conflicts, it attempted to reduce the rising government deficit by cutting spending, to fight intellectual property piracy in order to attract foreign investment, and to address a financial sector crisis that had simmered since 1995. The Gonzalez Macchi government has made some progress on state reform and privatization, but the fiscal deficit has grown as has Paraguay's external debt. The central government budget in 2000, excluding decentralized agencies and store-owned enterprises represented 20% of GDP.

# DEFENSE

The constitution designates the president as commander-in-chief of the armed forces. Military service is compulsory, and all 18-year-old males—and 17 year olds in the year of their 18th birthday—are liable for one year of active duty. Although the 1992 constitution allows for conscientious objection, no enabling legislation has yet been approved. Of the three services, the army has the majority of personnel, resources, and influence. With about 9,000 personnel, it is organized into three corps, with six infantry divisions and three cavalry divisions. The army has two primary

functions: to maintain the national defense, including internal order, and to manage some civic action projects in the countryside. The navy consists of about 2,000 personnel divided into three service branches. The air force, the newest and smallest of the services, has about 1,500 personnel.

# FOREIGN RELATIONS

Paraguay is a member of the United Nations and several of its specialized agencies. It also belongs to the Organization of American States, the Latin American Integration Association (ALADI), the Rio Group, INTEL-SAT, INTERPOL, and MERCOSUR (the Southern Cone Common Market). Its foreign policy has followed closely the Rio Group's lead on many issues of wideranging political importance.

# U.S.-PARAGUAY RELATIONS

The United States and Paraguay have an extensive relationship at the government, business, and personal level. Paraguay is a partner in hemispheric initiatives to improve counternarcotics cooperation, combat money laundering and other illicit cross-border activities, and adequately protect intellectual property rights. The U.S. looks to Paraguay, which has substantial rainforest and riverine resources, to engage in hemispheric efforts to ensure sustainable development. As a member of MERCOSUR, Paraguay supports the move toward a Free Trade Area of the Americas early in the next century. The U.S. and Paraguay also cooperate in a variety of international organizations.

The U.S. strongly supports consolidation of Paraguay's democracy and continued economic reform, the cornerstones of cooperation among countries in the hemisphere. The U.S. has played important roles in defending Paraguay's democratic institutions, in helping resolve the April 1996 crisis, and in ensuring that the March 1999 change of government took place without further bloodshed.

Although U.S. imports from Paraguay are only about $40 million per year, U.S. exports to Paraguay approached $450 billion in 2000, according to U.S. Customs data. (Not all of the U.S. exports are reflected in Paraguayan government data.) More than a dozen U.S. multinational firms have subsidiaries in Paraguay. These include firms in the computer, agroindustrial, telecom, and banking and other service industries. Some 75 U.S. businesses have agents or representatives in Paraguay, and more than 3,000 U.S. citizens reside

## Travel Notes

**Travel Advice:** For up-to-date information from the U.S. State Department on possible inconvenient or hazardous situations, see the **Travel Warnings and Consular Information Sheets from the U.S. Government** section starting on page 1723. For the latest information on health requirements and conditions, see the **International Travelers' Health Information** section starting on page 1385. For further information dealing with non-urgent matter, see the **Tips for Travelers to...** section starting on page 1588.

there. In November 1998, U.S. and Paraguayan officials signed a memorandum of understanding on steps to improve protection of intellectual property rights in Paraguay.

## U.S. Assistance

The U.S. Government has assisted Paraguayan development since 1942. The U.S. Agency for International Development (USAID) currently supports a variety of programs to strengthen Paraguay's democratic institutions in the areas of civil society, local government and decentralization, and national reform of the state. Other important areas of intervention are the environment and reproductive health. Current plans call for the development of new activities supporting economic growth. The total amount of the program is $12 million in fiscal year 2001.

The U.S. Department of State and the Drug Enforcement Administration provide technical assistance, equipment, and training to strengthen counternarcotics enforcement and to assist in the development and implementation of money laundering legislation. The U.S. Department of Defense provides technical assistance and training to help modernize, professionalize, and democratize the military. The Peace Corps has about 180 volunteers working throughout Paraguay on projects ranging from agriculture and natural resources to education, rural health, and urban youth development. The Office of Public Diplomacy also is active in Paraguay, providing information on the United States to the press and public, as well as helping to arrange educational and citizen exchanges to promote democracy.

## Principal U.S. Officials

**For up-to-date information on Principal U.S. Officials, see the U.S. Embassies, Consulates, and Foreign Service section starting on page 139.**

The U.S. embassy in Paraguay is located at 1776 Avenida Mariscal Lopez, Asuncion (tel. (595) (21) 213–715, Fax (595) (21) 213–728). The embassy's home page address on the World Wide Web is: http://www.usembparaguay.gov.py/

## Other Contact Information

**U.S. Department of Commerce**
International Trade Administration Office of Latin America and the Caribbean
14th & Constitution Ave., NW
Washington, DC 20230
Tel: (202) 482–0477, 800-USA-TRADE
Fax: (202) 482–0464

**Paraguayan-American Chamber of Commerce**
Edif. El Faro Internacional, Piso 4
Asuncion, Paraguay
Tel: (595) 21–442–136
Fax: (595) 21–442–135
E-mail: pamcham@infonet.com.py
(Branch office in Ciudad del Este)

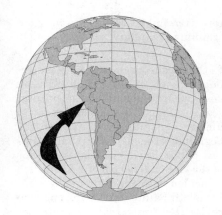

# PERU
April 2001

Official Name:
**Republic of Peru**

# PROFILE

## Geography

**Area:** 1.28 million sq. km. (496,225 sq. mi.); three times larger than California.

**Cities:** Capital—Lima/Callao metropolitan area (pop. 8.27 million, 2000). Other cities—Arequipa, Chiclayo, Cuzco, Huancayo, Truujillo, Ayacucho, Piura, Iquitos, Chimbote.

**Terrain:** Western coastal plains, central rugged mountains (Andes), eastern lowlands with tropical forests.

**Climate:** Coastal area, arid and mild; Andes, temperate to frigid; eastern lowlands, tropically warm and humid.

## People

**Nationality:** Noun and adjective—Peruvian(s).

**Population:** (2000 est.) 25.7 million (72.3 % urban).

**Annual growth rate:** (2000 est.) 1.7%.

**Ethnic groups:** (1961) Indian 45%. Mestizo 37%. White 15%. Black, Japanese, Chinese, and other 3%.

**Religion:** (1993) Roman Catholic (89%).

**Languages:** Spanish (official), Quechua (official), Aymara and a large number of minor Amazonian languages.

**Education:** Years compulsory—11.

Literacy—about 87.5% (1999).

**Health (2000):** Infant mortality rate—37/1,000. Life expectancy—67 male; 72 female.

**Employed work force:** (1999, 7.2 million) Manufacturing—12.7%; commerce—26.4%; agriculture—5.8%; mining—0.4%; construction—5.2%; government—9.1% (est.); other services—40.4%.

## Government

**Type:** Constitutional republic.

**Independence:** 1821.

**Constitution:** December 1993.

**Branches**: Executive—president, two vice presidents, Council of Ministers. Legislative—unicameral Congress. Judicial—Supreme Court and lower courts, Tribunal of Constitutional Guarantees.

**Administrative subdivisions:** 12 regions, 24 departments, 1 constitutional province.

**Political parties and movements:** Peru Possible, National Unity, We Are Peru, Change 90/New Majority/ Let's Go Neighbor/People's Solution, Union For Peru (UPF), American Popular Revolutionary Alliance (APRA), Independent Moralizing Front (FIM), Popular Christian Party (PPC), Popular Action (AP).

**Suffrage:** Universal over 18; compulsory until age 70 (members of the military may not vote).

## Economy (2000)

**GDP:** (est.) $53.9 billion.

**Annual growth rate:** 3.6%. Per capita GDP: $2,101.

Inflation rate: 3.8%.

**Natural resources:** Minerals, metals, fish, petroleum, natural gas, and forests.

**Agriculture (7% of GDP):** Products—sugar, potatoes, rice, yellow corn, cotton, coffee, poultry, beef, milk.

**Manufacturing:** (15% of GDP) Types—fish meal, nonferrous metals, steel, textiles, chemicals, wood, nonmetallic minerals, cement, paper.

Trade: Exports—$7.0 billion: gold, copper, fishmeal, textiles, zinc, lead, coffee, petroleum products. Major markets—U.S. (29%), U.K. (9%), Switzerland (9%), Japan (4%) Germany (4%). Imports—$7.3 billion: machinery and parts, cereals, chemicals, pharmaceuticals, crude oil and petroleum products, mining equipment, household appliances and automobiles. Major suppliers—U.S. (27%), Andean Pact countries (16%), Argentina (3%), EU (16%), and Japan (7%).

# PEOPLE

Most Peruvians are "mestizo," a term that usually refers to a mixture of Amerindians and Peruvians of European descent. Peruvians of European descent make up about 15% of the population; there also are smaller numbers of persons of African, Japanese, and Chinese descent. In the past decade, Peruvians of Asian heritage have made significant advancements in business and political fields; a past president, several past cabinet members, and several members of the Peruvian congress are of Japanese or Chinese descent. Socioeconomic and cultural indicators are increasingly important as identifiers. For example, Peruvians of Amerindian descent who have adopted aspects of Hispanic culture also are considered "mestizo." With economic development, access to education, intermarriage, and largescale migration from rural to urban areas, a more homogeneous national culture is developing, mainly along the relatively more prosperous coast.

Peru has two official languages— Spanish and the foremost indigenous language, Quechua. Spanish is used by the government and the media and in education and commerce. Amerindians who live in the Andean highlands speak Quechua and Aymara and are ethnically distinct from the diverse indigenous groups who live on the eastern side of the Andes and in the tropical lowlands adjacent to the Amazon basin.

Peru's distinct geographical regions are mirrored in a socioeconomic divide between the coast's mestizo-Hispanic culture and the more diverse, traditional Andean cultures of the mountains and highlands. The indigenous populations east of the Andes speak various languages and dialects. Some of these groups still adhere to traditional customs, while others have been almost completely assimilated into the mestizo-Hispanic culture.

## Education

Under the 1993 constitution, primary education is free and compulsory. The system is highly centralized, with the Ministry of Education appointing all public school teachers. Eighty-three percent of Peru's students attend public schools at all levels. School enrollment has been rising sharply for years, due to a widening educational effort by the government and a growing school-age population. The illiteracy rate is estimated at 12.5% (17.4% for women), 28.0% in rural areas and 5.6% in urban areas. Elementary and secondary school enrollment is approximately 7.7 million. Peru's 74 universities (1999), 39% public and 61% private institutions, enrolled about 322,000 students in 1999.

## Culture

The relationship between Hispanic and Indian cultures has shaped the face of Peru. During pre-Columbian times, Peru was one of the major centers of artistic expression in America, where pre-Inca cultures, such as Chavin, Paracas, Wari, Nazca, Chimu, and Tiahuanaco developed high-quality pottery, textiles, jewelry, and sculpture. Drawing upon earlier cultures, the Incas continued to maintain these crafts but made even more impressive achievements in architecture. The mountain town of Machu Picchu and the buildings at Cuzco are excellent examples of Inca architectural design.

Peru has passed through various intellectual stages—from colonial Hispanic culture to European Romanticism after independence. The early 20th century brought "indigenismo," expressed in a new awareness of Indian culture. Since World War II, Peruvian writers, artists, and intellectuals have participated in worldwide intellectual and artistic movements, drawing especially on U.S. and European trends.

During the colonial period, Spanish baroque fused with the rich Inca tradition to produce mestizo or creole art. The Cusco school of largely anonymous Indian artists followed the Spanish baroque tradition with influence from the Italian, Flemish, and French schools. Painter Francisco Fierro made a distinctive contribution to this school with his portrayals of typical events, manners, and customs of mid-19th-century Peru. Francisco Lazo, forerunner of the indigenous school of painters, also achieved fame for his portraits. Peru's 20th-century art is known for its extraordinary variety of styles and stunning originality.

In the decade after 1932, the "indigenous school" of painting headed by Jose Sabogal dominated the cultural scene in Peru. A subsequent reaction among Peruvian artists led to the beginning of modern Peruvian painting. Sabogal's resignation as director of the National School of Arts in 1943 coincided with the return of several Peruvian painters from Europe who revitalized "universal" and international styles of painting in Peru. During the 1960s, Fernando de Szyszlo, an internationally recognized Peruvian artist, became the main advocate for abstract painting and pushed Peruvian art toward modernism. Peru remains an art-producing center with painters such as Gerardo Chavez, Alberto Quintanilla, and Jose Carlos Ramos, along with sculptor Victor Delfin, gaining international stature. Promising young artists continue to develop now that Peru's economy allows more promotion of the arts.

# HISTORY

When the Spanish landed in 1531, Peru's territory was the nucleus of the highly developed Inca civilization. Centered at Cuzco, the Inca Empire extended over a vast region from northern Ecuador to central Chile. In search of Inca wealth, the Spanish explorer Francisco Pizarro, who arrived in the territory after the Incas had fought a debilitating civil war, conquered the weakened people. The Spanish had captured the Incan capital at Cuzco by 1533 and consolidated their control by 1542. Gold and silver from the Andes enriched the conquerors, and Peru became the principal source of Spanish wealth and power in South America.

Pizarro founded Lima in 1535. The viceroyalty established at Lima in 1542 initially had jurisdiction over all of South America except Portuguese Brazil. By the time of the wars of independence (1820–24), Lima had become the most distinguished and

aristocratic colonial capital and the chief Spanish stronghold in America.

Peru's independence movement was led by Jose de San Martin of Argentina and Simon Bolivar of Venezuela. San Martin proclaimed Peruvian independence from Spain on July 28, 1821. Emancipation was completed in December 1824, when Gen. Antonio Jose de Sucre defeated the Span-ish troops at Ayacucho, ending Spanish rule in South America. Spain made futile attempts to regain its former colonies, but in 1879 it finally recognized Peru's independence.

After independence, Peru and its neighbors engaged in intermittent territorial disputes. Chile's victory over Peru and Bolivia in the War of the Pacific (1879–83) resulted in a territorial settlement. Following a clash between Peru and Ecuador in 1941, the Rio Protocol—of which the United States is one of four guarantors—sought to establish the boundary between the two countries. Continuing boundary disagreement led to brief armed conflicts in early 1981 and early 1995, but in 1998 the governments of Peru and Ecuador signed a historic peace treaty and demarcated the border. In late 1999, the governments of Peru and Chile likewise finally implemented the last outstanding article of their 1929 border agreement.

The military has been prominent in Peruvian history. Coups have repeatedly interrupted civilian constitutional government. The most recent period of military rule (1968–80) began when Gen. Juan Velasco Alvarado overthrew elected President Fernando Belaunde Terry of the Popular Action Party (AP). As part of what has been called the "first phase" of the military government's nationalist program, Velasco undertook an extensive agrarian reform program and nationalized the fish meal industry, some petroleum companies, and several banks and mining firms.

Because of Velasco's economic mismanagement and deteriorating health, he was replaced by Gen. Francisco Morales Bermudez Cerruti in 1975. Morales Bermudez moved the revolution into a more pragmatic "second phase," tempering the authoritarian abuses of the first phase and beginning the task of restoring the country's economy. Morales Bermudez presided over the return to civilian government in accordance with a new constitution drawn up in 1979. In the May 1980 elections, President Belaunde Terry was returned to office by an impressive plurality.

Nagging economic problems left over from the military government persisted, worsened by an occurrence of the "El Niño" weather phenomenon in 1982–83, which caused widespread flooding in some parts of the country, severe droughts in others, and decimated the schools of ocean fish that are one of the country's major resources. After a promising beginning, Belaunde's popularity eroded under the stress of inflation, economic hardship, and terrorism.

During the 1980s, cultivation of illicit coca was established in large areas on the eastern Andean slope. Rural terrorism by Sendero Luminoso (SL) and the Tupac Amaru Revolutionary Movement (MRTA) increased during this time and derived significant financial support from alliances with the narcotraffickers. In 1985, the American Popular Revolutionary Alliance (APRA) won the presidential election, bringing Alan Garcia Perez to office. The transfer of the presidency from Belaunde to Garcia on July 28, 1985, was Peru's first exchange of power from one democratically elected leader to another in 40 years. Economic mismanagement by the Garcia administration led to hyperinflation from 1988 to 1990. Concerned about the economy, the increasing terrorist threat from Sendero Luminoso, and allegations of official corruption, voters chose a relatively unknown mathematician-turned-politician, Alberto Fujimori, as president in 1990. Fujimori implemented drastic orthodox measures that caused inflation to drop from 7,650% in 1990 to 139% in 1991. Faced with opposition to his reform efforts, Fujimori dissolved Congress in the "auto-coup" of April 4, 1992. He then revised the constitution; called new congressional elections; and implemented substantial economic reform, including privatization of numerous state-owned companies, creation of an investment-friendly climate, and sound management of the economy. Fujimori's constitutionally questionable decision to seek a third term and subsequent tainted victory in June 2000 brought political and economic turmoil. A bribery scandal that broke just weeks after he took office in July forced Fujimori to call new elections in which he would not run. Fujimori fled the country and resigned from office in November 2000. A caretaker government presided over by Valentin Paniagua Corazao took on the responsibility of conducting new presidential and congressional elections, scheduled for April 2001. The new elected government will take office July 28, 2001.

# GOVERNMENT

The president is popularly elected for a 5-year term, and the 1993 constitution permits one consecutive re-election. The first and second vice presidents also are popularly elected but have no constitutional functions unless the president is unable to discharge his duties. The principal executive body is the Council of Ministers, headed by a prime minister, all appointed by the president. All presidential decree laws or draft bills sent to Congress must be approved by the Council of Ministers.

The legislative branch consists of a unicameral Congress of 120 members. In addition to passing laws, Congress ratifies treaties, authorizes government loans, and approves the government budget. The president has the power to block legislation with which the executive branch does not agree.

The judicial branch of government is headed by a 16-member Supreme Court seated in Lima. The Constitutional Tribunal interprets the constitution on matters of individual rights. Superior courts in departmental capitals review appeals from decisions by lower courts. Courts of first instance are located in provincial capitals and are divided into civil, penal, and special chambers. The judiciary has created several temporary specialized courts, in an attempt to reduce the large backlog of cases pending final court action. In 1996 a Human Rights Ombudsman's office was created to address human rights issues.

Peru is divided into 24 departments and the constitutional province of Callao, the country's chief port, adjacent to Lima. The departments are subdivided into provinces, which are composed of districts. Authorities below the departmental level are elected.

## Principal Government Officials

**For up-to-date information on Principal Government Officials, see the Chiefs of State and Cabinet Members of Foreign Governments section starting on page 1.**

Peru maintains an embassy in the United States at 1700 Massachusetts Avenue, NW, Washington, DC 20036 (tel. 202–833–9860/67, consular section: 202–462–1084).

Peru has consulates in New York; Paterson, NJ; Miami; Chicago; Houston; Los Angeles; San Francisco; and San Juan, Puerto Rico.

# POLITICAL CONDITIONS

Peru is a republic with a dominant executive branch. Congress President Valentin Paniagua was selected according to Peru's constitution to head an interim government after President Alberto Fujimori fled the country and resigned in November 2000 in the wake of a bribery scandal and political turmoil resulting from his tainted re-election to a third term in June 2000.

The Paniagua government's principal objective is to conduct free and fair presidential and congressional elections in April 2001. A new 5-year government will take office in July 2001. The interim government is also investigating a web of corruption under the Fujimori administration run by Fujimori's closest adviser, Vladimiro Montesinos, and involving a wide range of government, political and business leaders.

Human rights violations by the security forces dropped considerably over the last several years, although there have been numerous accusations of human rights infractions. Reports of torture, and the lack of accountability and due process remain areas of concern. In 1995, the Peruvian congress passed a law that granted amnesty from prosecution to those who committed human rights abuses during the war on terrorism from May 1980 to June 1995. The Peruvian Government established in 1996 the Human Rights Ombudsman's office to address human rights issues and an ad hoc commission to review and recommend for presidential pardon those unjustly detained for terrorism or treason.

# ECONOMY

From 1994 through 1997, the economy recorded robust growth driven by foreign direct investment, almost 40% of which was related to the privatization program. In 1998, real GDP fell 0.4%, largely as a result of the "El Niño" weather phenomenon, which led to sharp declines in fishmeal exports, disrupted agriculture, and damaged infrastructure. A stalled privatization program, increased government intervention in markets, and worsening terms of trade also contributed to the poor economic performance. Financial turmoil in Asia, Russia, and Brazil added to the problem, leading to a sharp decline in privatization-related foreign direct investment and dramatic outflows of short-term capital. The economy recovered somewhat in 1999 and 2000, registering growth rates of 1.4% and 3.5%, respectively. But political turmoil dampened growth and investment, and the economy is expected to grow less than 2% in 2001. The Lima Stock Exchange general index fell 34.5% in 2000, but had recovered somewhat by the end of the first quarter of 2001. Inflation remained at record lows, registering about 3.7% in 1999 and 2000. The government's overall budget deficit rose sharply in 1999 and 2000 to about 3.0% of GDP, the result of hikes in government salaries, expenditures related to the 2000 election campaign, higher foreign debt service payments, and lower tax revenues. Peru's macroeconomic stability brought about a substantial reduction in underemployment, from and average of 74% from the late 1980s through 1994 to 43% in the 1995–2000 period. The poverty rate has fallen slightly over the years but remained at 54% in 2000. Foreign Trade and Balance of Payments.

The current account deficit dropped in 2000 to about 2.3% of GDP ($1.3 billion)—from 3.0% in 2000—while merchandise trade registered a small surplus of $100 million compared to a $2.5 billion deficit (4.3% of GDP) in 1998. Exports grew by 7.6% to $7.54 billion, while imports grew 1.7% to $7.46 billion. After being hit hard by El Niño in 1998, fisheries exports have recovered, and minerals and metals exports should record an increase of about 10% in 2001. Imports may register a small increase in all categories in 2001. After several years of substantial growth, foreign direct investment not related to privatization has fallen dramatically to levels not seen in a decade. Short-term capital and portfolio investment are expected to register a combined outflow of $600 million, continuing a trend that began in 1998 with the Russian financial crisis. Net international reserves at the end of March 2001 stood at $8.0 billion, down from $8.2 billion at the end of 2000.

## Foreign Investment

The Peruvian Government actively seeks to attract both foreign and domestic investment in all sectors of the economy. International investment was spurred by the significant progress Peru made during the 1990s toward economic, social, and political stability, but it slowed again after the government delayed privatizations and as political uncertainty increased in 2000. While Peru was previously marked by terrorism, hyperinflation, and government intervention in the economy, the Government of Peru under former President Alberto Fujimori took the steps necessary to bring those problems under control. Democratic institutions, especially the judiciary, remain weak. The Government of Peru's economic stabilization and liberalization program lowered trade barriers, eliminated restrictions on capital flows, and opened the economy to foreign investment, with the result that Peru now has one of the most open investment regimes in the world. Between 1990 and 2000, Peru attracted more than $15 billion in foreign direct investment in Peru, after negligible investment during the 1980s, mainly from Spain, the United States, the United Kingdom, Panama, and Netherlands. The basic legal structure for foreign investment in Peru is formed by the 1993 constitution, the Private Investment Growth Law, and the November 1996 Investment Promotion Law. Although Peru does not have a bilateral investment treaty with the United States, it has signed an agreement (1993) with the Overseas Private Investment Corporation concerning OPIC-financed loans, guarantees, and investments. Peru also has committed itself to arbitration of government-to-government investment disputes under the auspices of ICSID—the World Bank's International Center for the Settlement of Investment Disputes.

## Economic Outlook

Forecasts for the medium- and long-term remain bright, as political uncertainty diminishes with the inauguration of a new government. In the near term, real GDP is expected to grow 1.5% in 2001. Inflation is likely to fall again slightly, to about 3.6%, while the budget deficit is expected to fall to about 1.9% of GDP as the result of a reduced government spending. Private investment is estimated to drop further, by some 1.5% in 2001, also as a result of near-term political uncertainty, but is likely to increase after the new government takes office in July 2001. Exports are expected to rise by 4.6%. The unemployment and underemployment indexes (7.4 % and 42.9%, respectively, in the third quarter of 2000) are expected to rise in 2001. However, the country is likely to attract both domestic and foreign investment in the tourism, mining, petroleum and natural gas, and electric power industries once the new government takes office.

## Narcotics

The fight against narcotics trafficking in Peru has resulted in an unprecedented 70% reduction since 1995 in the number of acres of illegal coca leaf under cultivation. The impact of this illicit industry to the national economy is difficult to measure, but estimates range from $300-$600 million. An estimated 200,000 Peruvians are engaged in the production, refining, or distribution of the narcotic. Many economists believe that large flows of dollars into the banking system contribute to the traditional depression in the dollar exchange rate vis-a-vis the sol, and create a climate in which

money-laundering can flourish. The Central Bank engages in open market activities to prevent the price of the sol from rising to levels that would otherwise hurt Peruvian exports.

Hurt economically by successful Peruvian Air Force interdiction efforts in the mid-1990s, drug traffickers are now using land and river routes as well as aircraft to transport cocaine paste and, increasingly, cocaine hydrochloride (HCL) around and out of the country. Peru continues to arrest drug traffickers and seize drugs and precursor chemicals, destroy coca labs, disable clandestine airstrips, and prosecute officials involved in narcotics corruption.

Working with the U.S. Agency for International Development (USAID), the Peruvian Government carries out alternative development programs in the leading coca-growing areas in an effort to convince coca farmers not to grow that crop. Although the government previously eradicated only coca seed beds, in 1998 and 1999 it began to eradicate mature coca being grown in national parks and elsewhere in the main coca growing valleys. In 1999 the government eradicated over 15,000 hectares of coca; this figure declined to 6,500 hectares in 2000, due largely to political instability. The government agency "Contradrogas," founded in 1996, facilitates coordination among Peruvian Government agencies working on counternarcotics issues.

# FOREIGN RELATIONS

In October 1998, Peru and Ecuador signed a peace accord which definitively resolved border differences which had, over the years, resulted in armed conflict. Peru and Ecuador are now jointly coordinating an internationally sponsored border integration project. The United States Government, as one of four guarantor states, was actively involved in facilitating the 1998 peace accord between Peru and Ecuador and remains committed to its implementation. The United States has pledged $40 million to the Peru-Ecuador border integration project and another $4 million to support Peruvian and Ecuadorian demining efforts along their common border.

In November 1999, Peru and Chile signed three agreements which put to rest the remaining obstacles holding up implementation of the 1929 Border Treaty. (The 1929 Border Treaty officially ended the 1879 War of the Pacific.) In December 1999, President Fujimori made the first visit ever to Chile by a Peruvian head of state.

Peru has been a member of the United Nations since 1949, and Peruvian Javier Perez de Cuellar served as UN Secretary General from 1981 to 1991. Former President Fujimori's tainted re-election to a third term in June 2000 strained Peru's relations with the United States and with many Latin American and European countries, but relations improved with the installation of an interim government determined to ensure free and fair elections in 2001. Peru is planning full integration into the Andean Free Trade Area. In addition, Peru is a standing member of APEC and the WTO, and is an active participant in negotiations toward a Free Trade Area of the Americas (FTAA).

# U.S.-PERUVIAN RELATIONS

The United States enjoys strong and cooperative relations with Peru. Relations were strained following the tainted re-election of former President Fujimori in June 2000, but improved with the installation of an interim government committed to holding free and fair presidential and congressional elections in April 2001. The United States continues to promote the strengthening of democratic institutions and human rights safeguards in Peru.

The United States and Peru cooperate on efforts to interdict the flow of narcotics, particularly cocaine, to the United States. The Peruvian Air Force has successfully interdicted narcotics trafficking via air to surrounding countries. Bilateral programs are now in effect to reduce the flow of drugs on Peru's extensive river system and to perform ground interdiction in tandem with successful law enforcement operations. The United States and Peru cooperate on promoting programs of alternative development in coca-growing regions.

U.S. investment and tourism in Peru have grown substantially in recent years. U.S. exports to Peru were valued at $2.4 billion in 2000, accounting for about 30% of Peru's imports. In the same year, Peru exported $2 billion in goods to the United States, accounting for about 30% of Peru's exports to the world.

About 200,000 U.S. citizens visit Peru annually for business, tourism , and study. About 10,000 Americans reside in Peru, and more than 400 U.S. companies are represented in the country.

## U.S. Economic Assistance

U.S. bilateral assistance to Peru, including food aid and disaster relief and rehabilitation, totaled more than $1.3 billion during the 1990–2000 period. The USAID program in Peru is its second-largest in Latin America.

U.S. assistance to Peru is focused on six strategic objectives: broader citizen participation in democratic processes; increased incomes of the poor; improved health of high-risk populations, including family planning;

improved environmental management; reduced illicit coca production in target areas of Peru; and expanded educational opportunities for women. Additionally, a new initiative is being developed to support the consolidation of the peace agreement signed between Peru and Ecuador. The initiative would contribute to improved living conditions of the population in the border region and thus show tangible benefits of the peace accords.

Democracy. U.S. assistance seeks to strengthen democratic institutions; promote more effective local governments; promote and protect human rights; foster citizen participation; and strengthen women's participation in decisionmaking processes. Through USAID, the United States is providing more than $7 million to support the 2001 election process.

Reducing poverty. USAID aims to improve the policy environment for private sector-led growth; expand access to markets; improve production; improve access to and distribution of food resources; and improve access to public utilities in poverty areas. U.S. food assistance programs reach about 1.7 million poor Peruvians annually in rural highlands and jungle areas, where the majority of the extreme poverty is found.

Health. U.S. assistance is improving child survival and maternal health services—such as immunization, diarrheal control, and prenatal care—and strengthening and expanding the participation of public and private sector entities in HIV/AIDS prevention. In family planning, activities with the NGO sector include efforts to strengthen the capacity of NGOs to supply family planning methods in urban and rural areas; increase the sustainability of the supply of contraceptives; and disseminate information on family planning methods and services. USAID's support to the Ministry of Health has made substantial improvements in this area. Infant mortality rate fell from 57 per 1,000 births in 1991 to 42 in 1997 while immunization campaigns for children younger than 1 reached 97.5% coverage.

Environment. USAID's strategy focuses on improving the legal, policy, regulatory, and normative environment and natural resource framework; promoting pollution prevention in selected peri-urban and industrial settings; and protecting natural resources, including biological diversity and fragile ecosystems. USAID has provided important assistance to the Peruvian Government to improve the legal, regulatory, and policy framework that established clearer rules on environmentally sustainable natural resource use. Among these were the National Environmental Council's Structural Framework for Environmental Management, the Ministry of Industry's Environmental Regulation, the Framework Law for Sustainable Use of Natural Resources, and the Pollution Prevention Oriented Environmental Framework Legislation for the Fisheries and related industries.

Alternative development. USAID seeks to reduce coca leaf cultivation through alternative development and environmental protection programs, as well as to reduce drug use and addition through prevention, awareness and rehabilitation programs. It also seeks to increase the commitment of farmers and communities to reduce illicit coca production voluntarily. USAID, together with Peruvian and U.S. law enforcement actions, has contributed to a 70% reduction of hectares devoted to coca cultivation (from 115,300 Ha in 1995 to 34,000 Ha in 2000). As a result, over the same period the capacity of Peru to produce cocaine hydrochloride, or HCl, declined from 525 tons to 145 tons. As of 1998, the total gross agricultural production value of the alternative crops in targeted areas outweighed the total gross production value of coca leaf by 39%. As a result, over 2,600 new jobs were created and more than 20,000 farmers were assisted in production, quality improvement, processing and marketing for licit crops such as coffee, cacao, livestock, and agroforestry, on nearly 25,000 hectares.

## Education

This strategic objective is aimed at assisting the Government of Peru and civil society organizations to develop initiatives that address critical constraints to basic education of girls in rural areas in Peru. As a result, USAID has contributed to the establishment of a National Network for Girls' Education in Peru, with the participation of GOP sectoral ministries, NGOs, universities, the business community, and donors. This national network has been very active in increasing consciousness about the importance of girls' education in Peru.

## Principal U.S. Embassy Officials

**For up-to-date information on Principal U.S. Officials, see the U.S. Embassies, Consulates, and Foreign Service section starting on page 139.**

The U.S. embassy in Peru is located at Avendia la Encalada, Cuadra 17 s/n, Monterrico (Surco), Lima 33 (tel. (511) 434–3000; fax. (511) 434–3037). Home page: http://usembassy.state.gov/lima

The embassy is open from 8:00 a.m. to 5:00 p.m., Monday-Friday, except U.S. and some Peruvian holidays.
The mailing address from the United States is American Embassy Lima, APO AA 34031 (use U.S. domestic postage rates).
The American Citizen Services section is open to the public from 8:00 a.m. to 12:00 p.m.
The Consular Agency in Cuzco is located at Anda Tullamayu 125 (tel. (51) (84) 224112 or (51) (84) 239451; fax. (51) (84) 233541).

## Other Contact Information

### U.S. Department of State
Bureau of Western Hemisphere Affairs
Office of Andean Affairs (Room 5906)
2201 C Street N.W.
Washington, D.C. 20520–6263
Tel: 202–647–3360
Fax: 202–647–2628
Home Page: http://www.state.gov

### U.S. Department of Commerce
International Trade Administration
Office of Latin America and the Caribbean
14th and Constitution, NW
Washington, DC 20230
Tel: (202) 482–0475
(800) USA-TRADE
Fax: (202) 482–0464
Home Page: http://www.ita.doc.gov

### American Chamber of Commerce of Peru
Avenida Ricardo Palma 836, Miraflores
Lima 18, Peru
Tel: (511) 241–0708
Fax: (511) 241–0709
E-Mail: amcham@amcham.tci.net.pe
Home Page: http://www.amcham.org.pe

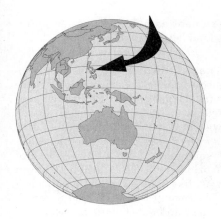

# PHILIPPINES

October 2000

Official Name:
**Republic of the Philippines**

## PROFILE

### Geography

**Area:** 300,000 sq. km. (117,187 sq. mi.).
**Cities:** (1997) Capital—Manila (pop. 10.4 million in metropolitan area); Davao (1.3 million), Cebu (3.1 million).
**Terrain:** Islands, 65% mountainous, with narrow coastal lowlands.
**Climate:** Tropical, astride typhoon belt.

### People

**Nationality:** Noun—Filipino(s). Adjective—Philippine.
**Population:** (1999) 75 million.
**Annual growth rate:** 2.3%.
**Ethnic Groups:** Malay, Chinese.
**Religion:** Catholic 83%, Protestant 9%, Muslim 5%, Buddhist and other 3%.
**Languages:** Pilipino (based on Tagalog), national language; English, language of government and instruction in higher education.
**Education:** Years compulsory—6. Attendance—above 97% in elementary grades, 55% in secondary grades. Literacy—94.6%.
**Health:** Infant mortality rate (1997)—35.2/1,000. Life expectancy (1997)—66.5 yrs.
**Work force:** (1997) 30 million. Agri-

culture—38%; government and services—37%; industry and commerce—16%.

### Government

**Type:** Republic.
**Independence:** 1946.
**Constitution:** February 11, 1987.
**Branches:** Executive—president and vice president. Legislative—bicameral legislature. Judicial—independent.
**Administrative subdivisions:** 13 regions and Manila, 78 provinces, 61 chartered cities.
**Political parties:** Laban Ng Masang Pilipino (LAMP), Lakas Ng Bayan (Lakas/NUCD), and other small parties.
**Suffrage:** Universal, but not compulsory, at age 18.

### Economy

**GDP:** (1999) $76.5 billion.
**Annual growth rate:** (1999) 3.2%.
**GDP per capita:** (1999) $1,017.
**Natural resources:** Timber, copper, nickel, iron, cobalt, silver, gold.
**Agriculture:** Products—sugar, coconut products, rice, corn, pineapples, bananas, aquaculture, mangoes, pork, eggs.
**Industry:** Types—textiles and garments, pharmaceuticals, chemicals, wood products, food processing, electronics assembly, petroleum refining, fishing.

**Trade:** (1999) Exports—$35.0 billion. Imports—$30.7 billion.

## PEOPLE

The majority of Philippine people are of Malay stock, descendants of Indonesians and Malays who migrated to the islands long before the Christian era. The most significant ethnic minority group is the Chinese, who have played an important role in commerce since the ninth century, when they first came to the islands to trade. As a result of intermarriage, many Filipinos have some Chinese and Spanish ancestry. Americans and Spaniards constitute the next largest alien minorities in the country.

About 90% of the people are Christian; most were converted and Westernized to varying degrees during nearly 400 years of Spanish and American rule. The major non-Hispanicized groups are the Muslim population, concentrated in the Sulu Archipelago and in central and western Mindanao, and the mountain groups of northern Luzon. Small forest tribes live in the more remote areas of Mindanao.

About 87 native languages and dialects are spoken, all belonging to the Malay-Polynesian linguistic family. Of these, eight are the first languages of more than 85% of the population. The three principal indigenous languages are Cebuano, spoken in the Visayas; Tagalog, predominant in the area around Manila; and Ilocano, spoken in northern Luzon. Since 1939, in an effort to develop national unity, the government has promoted the use of the national language, Pilipino, which is based on Tagalog. Pilipino is taught in all schools and is gaining acceptance, particularly as a second language.

English, the most important nonnative language, is used as a second language by many, including nearly all professionals, academics, and government workers. Only a few Filipino families retain Spanish usage.

Despite this multiplicity of languages, the Philippines has one of the highest literacy rates in the East Asian and Pacific area. About 90% of the population 10 years of age and older are literate.

# HISTORY

The history of the Philippines may be divided into four distinct phases: the pre-Spanish period (before 1521); the Spanish period (1521-1898); the American period (1898-1946); and the years since independence (1946-present).

## Pre-Spanish Period

The first people in the Philippines, the Negritos, are believed to have come to the islands 30,000 years ago from Borneo and Sumatra, making their way across then-existing land bridges. Subsequently, people of Malay stock came from the south in successive waves, the earliest by land bridges and later in boats called barangays. The Malays settled in scattered communities, also called barangays, which were ruled by chieftains known as datus. Chinese merchants and traders arrived and settled in the ninth century A.D. In the 14th century, Arabs arrived, introducing Islam in the south and extending some influence even into Luzon. The Malays, however,

remained the dominant group until the Spanish arrived in the 16th century.

## Spanish Period

Ferdinand Magellan claimed the Philippines for Spain in 1521, and for the next 377 years, the islands were under Spanish rule. This period was the era of conversion to Roman Catholicism. A Spanish colonial social system was developed, complete with a strong centralized government and considerable clerical influence. The Filipinos were restive under the Spanish, and this long period was marked by numerous uprisings. The most important of these began in 1896 under the leadership of Emilio Aguinaldo and continued until the Americans defeated the Spanish fleet in Manila Bay on May 1, 1898, during the Spanish-American War. Aguinaldo declared independence from Spain on June 12, 1898.

## American Period

Following Admiral Dewey's defeat of the Spanish fleet in Manila Bay, the United States occupied the Philippines. Spain ceded the islands to the United States under the terms of the Treaty of Paris (December 10, 1898) that ended the war.

A war of resistance against U.S. rule, led by Revolutionary President Aguinaldo, broke out in 1899. Although Americans have historically used the term "the Philippine Insurrection" Filipinos and an increasing number of American historians refer to these hostilities as the Philippine-American War (1899-1902), and in 1999 the U.S. Library of Congress reclassified its references to use this term. In 1901, Aguinaldo was captured and swore allegiance to the United States, and resistance gradually died out.

U.S. administration of the Philippines was always declared to be temporary and aimed to develop institutions that would permit and encourage the eventual establishment of a free and democratic government. Therefore, U.S. officials concentrated on the creation of such practical supports for democratic gov-

ernment as public education and a sound legal system.

The first legislative assembly was elected in 1907. A bicameral legislature, largely under Philippine control, was established. A civil service was formed and was gradually taken over by the Filipinos, who had effectively gained control by the end of World War I. The Catholic Church was disestablished, and a considerable amount of church land was purchased and redistributed.

In 1935, under the terms of the Tydings-McDuffie Act, the Philippines became a self-governing commonwealth. Manuel Quezon was elected president of the new government, which was designed to prepare the country for independence after a 10-year transition period. World War II intervened, however, and in May 1942, Corregidor, the last American/Filipino stronghold, fell. U.S. forces in the Philippines surrendered to the Japanese, placing the islands under Japanese control.

The war to regain the Philippines began when Gen. Douglas MacArthur landed on Leyte on October 20, 1944. Filipinos and Americans fought together until the Japanese surrender in September 1945. Much of Manila was destroyed during the final months of the fighting, and an estimated 1 million Filipinos lost their lives in the war.

As a result of the Japanese occupation, the guerrilla warfare that followed, and the battles leading to liberation, the country suffered great damage and a complete organizational breakdown. Despite the shaken state of the country, the United States and the Philippines decided to move forward with plans for independence. On July 4, 1946, the Philippine Islands became the independent Republic of the Philippines, in accordance with the terms of the Tydings-McDuffie Act. In 1962, the official Independence Day was changed from July 4 to June 12, commemorating the date independence from Spain was declared by General Aguinaldo in 1898.

## Post-Independence Period

The early years of independence were dominated by U.S.-assisted postwar reconstruction. A communist-inspired Huk Rebellion (1945-53) complicated recovery efforts before its successful suppression under the leadership of President Ramon Magsaysay. The succeeding administrations of Presidents Carlos P. Garcia (1957-61) and Diosdado Macapagal (1961-65) sought to expand Philippine ties to its Asian neighbors, implement domestic reform programs, and develop and diversify the economy.

In 1972, President Ferdinand E. Marcos (1965-86) declared martial law, citing growing lawlessness and open rebellion by the communist rebels as his justification. Marcos governed from 1973 until mid-1981 in accordance with the transitory provisions of a new constitution that replaced the commonwealth constitution of 1935. He suppressed democratic institutions and restricted civil liberties during the martial law period, ruling largely by decree and popular referenda. The government began a process of political normalization during 1978-81, culminating in the reelection of President Marcos to a 6-year term that would have ended in 1987. The Marcos government's respect for human rights remained low despite the end of martial law on January 17, 1981. His government retained its wide arrest and detention powers. Corruption and favoritism contributed to a serious decline in economic growth and development under Marcos.

The assassination of opposition leader Benigno (Ninoy) Aquino upon his return to the Philippines in 1983, after a long period of exile, coalesced popular dissatisfaction with Marcos and set in motion a succession of events that culminated in a snap presidential election in February 1986. The opposition united under Aquino's widow, Corazon Aquino, and Salvador Laurel, head of the United Nationalist Democratic Organization (UNIDO). The election was marred by widespread electoral fraud on the part of Marcos and his supporters. International observers, including a U.S. delegation led by Sen. Richard Lugar (R-Indiana), denounced the official results. Marcos was forced to flee the Philippines in the face of a peaceful civilian-military uprising that ousted him and installed Corazon Aquino as president on February 25, 1986.

Under Aquino's presidency progress was made in revitalizing democratic institutions and respect for civil liberties. However, the administration was also viewed by many as weak

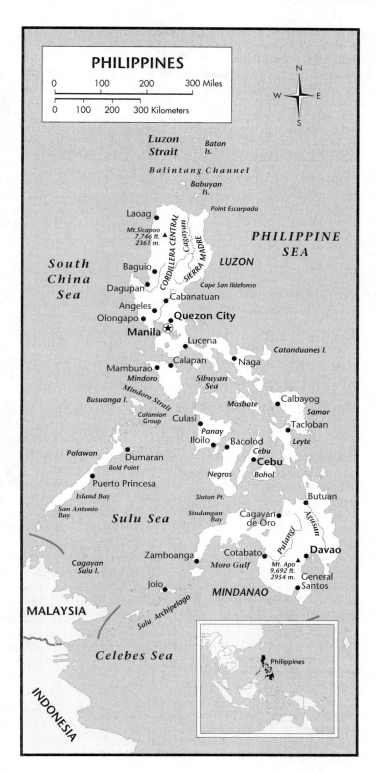

and fractious, and a return to full political stability and economic development was hampered by several attempted coups staged by disaffected members of the Philippine military.

Fidel Ramos was elected president in 1992. Early in his administration, Ramos declared "national reconciliation" his highest priority. He legalized the communist party and created the National Unification Commission (NUC) to lay the groundwork for talks with communist insurgents, Muslim separatists, and military rebels. In June 1994, President Ramos signed into law a general conditional amnesty covering all rebel groups, as well as Philippine military and police personnel accused of crimes committed while fighting the insurgents. In October 1995, the government signed an agreement bringing the military insurgency to an end. A peace agreement with one major Muslim insurgent group was signed in 1996.

Joseph Ejercito Estrada's election as President in May 1998, marked the Philippines' third democratic succession since the ouster of Marcos. Estrada was elected with overwhelming mass support on a platform promising poverty alleviation and an anti-crime crackdown.

# GOVERNMENT AND POLITICAL CONDITIONS

The Philippines has a representative democracy modeled on the U.S. system. The 1987 constitution, adopted during the Aquino administration, re-established a presidential system of government with a bicameral legislature and an independent judiciary. The president is limited to one 6-year term. Provision also was made in the constitution for autonomous regions in Muslim areas of Mindanao and in the Cordillera region of northern Luzon.

The Philippine Senate is elected at large. There are currently 22 senators rather than the usual 24, since Senator Gloria Macapagal-Arroyo became Vice President in the May 1998 elections and another died—replacements cannot be chosen without a national election. The next election is scheduled for May 2001. Two hundred six of a possible 250 members of the House of Representatives are elected from the single-member districts. The remainder of the House seats are designated for sectoral representatives elected at large through a complex "party list" system.

Joseph Estrada took office June 30, 1998, succeeding Fidel Ramos, under whom he had served as Vice President. Despite coalitions and party identification, members of the Philippine congress tend to be independent, changing party affiliation with ease.

Following his election, President Estrada formed the LAMP party out of a tri-partite alliance that had helped him get elected. Some members of former President Ramos's Lakas Party defected to LAMP. President Estrada's priorities include battling poverty, crime, and corruption. The government remains confronted with both Muslim and communist insurgencies, and in May-June 2000 stepped up its military campaign against the Muslim-separatist Moro Islamic Liberation Front (MNLF). In late April 2000, the Philippines also became embroiled in an international hostage crisis, after the extremist Filipino Muslim rebel group, Abu Sayaaf, snatched a group of mostly foreign hostages from a resort in Malaysian waters and transported them to the southern Philippine Island of Jolo. The Communist New Peoples Army continues to operate in remote areas throughout the country but is badly splintered and therefore less effective than it was formerly. The anti-insurgency campaign is a drain on Philippine Government resources and hampers development efforts. However, these rebel groups do not fundamentally threaten government stability.

## Principal Government Officials

**For up-to-date information on Principal Government Officials, see the Chiefs of State and Cabinet Members of Foreign Governments section starting on page 1.**

The Republic of the Philippines maintains an embassy in the United States at 1600 Massachusetts Avenue NW, Washington, DC 20036 (tel. 202-467-9300).
Consulates general are in New York, Chicago, San Francisco, Los Angeles, Honolulu, and Agana (Guam).

# ECONOMY

Since the end of the Second World War, the Philippine economy has had a mixed history of growth and development. Over the years, the Philippines has gone from being one of the richest countries in Asia (following Japan) to being one of the poorest. Growth immediately after the war was rapid, but slowed over time. A severe recession in 1984-85 saw the economy shrink by more than 10%, and perceptions of political instability during the Aquino administration further dampened economic activity. During his administration, President Ramos introduced a broad range of economic reforms and initiatives designed to spur business growth and foreign investment. As a result, the Philippines saw a period of rapid sustained growth, but the spreading Asian financial crisis has slowed economic development in the Philippines once again. President Estrada has tried to resist protectionist measures; efforts to continue the reforms begun by the Ramos administration have made significant progress.

Important sectors of the Philippine economy include agriculture and industry (particularly food processing, textiles and garments, and electronics and automobile parts). Most industries are concentrated in the urban areas around metropolitan

Manila. Mining also is important in the Philippines, which possesses significant reserves of chromite, nickel, and copper. Recent natural gas finds off the islands of Palawan add to the country's substantial geothermal, hydro, and coal energy reserves.

## Today's Economy

The Philippines was less severely affected by the Asian financial crisis than its neighbors, due in considerable part to remittances of approximately $5 billion annually from overseas workers. Nonetheless, the country continues to be a weak economic performer. The government has recently reiterated its target of 4.5%-5.5% real GNP growth (4%-5% for GDP), but private forecasts are somewhat lower. In 1999, the Philippines GDP increased by 3.2%.

Agriculture accounts for one-fifth of the Philippine economy. Output fell in 1997 and early 1998 due to an El-Nino-related drought but increased by 6.6% in 1999 (over 1998s low base).

The Philippines continues to record monthly export figures up significantly on year-earlier levels, but examination of the month-by-month export figures had suggested that the export boom is running out of steam. Monthly exports continue to grow but at increasingly slower rates. Electronic and auto parts exports account for most of this growth. The Philippines' traditional exports are stagnant or declining.

The commercial banking sector suffered from high interest rates and higher nonperforming loan levels during the Asian financial crisis, but the banking system remains sound. Interest rates have been brought under control, but loan growth remains slow as banks continue to exercise caution and clean up their balance sheets.

The Philippine peso has lost more than 40% of its value vis-a-vis the U.S. dollar since mid-1997 and currently trades at about 44/$. Inflation, perennially a problem in the Philip-

pines, is under control and will likely average 6%-7% in 2000.

Despite slower than hoped for growth, the Philippines' longer term prospects remain bright. The Aquino and Ramos administrations opened up the relatively closed Philippine economy and provided a firmer base for sustainable economic growth. After a slow start, President Estrada and his cabinet have continued with, and expanded, liberalization and market-based policies and reforms. Efforts to reform the constitution to encourage foreign investment, particularly foreign ownership of land, were abandoned amidst nationalist opposition. Initial optimism about prospects for economic reform also had dimmed amid concerns of governmental corruption. Recent scandals involving the Philippine Stock Exchange, and the President's close ties to certain businessmen, have shaken confidence of investors and other members of the business community. However, the pace of economic reform, particularly the passage of key legislation in areas such as retail trade, electronic commerce, banking reform, and securities regulation, suggests that the investment and business climate can be expected to continue to improve.

## Agriculture and Forestry

Arable farmland comprises an estimated 26% of the total land area. Although the Philippines is rich in agricultural potential, inadequate infrastructure, lack of financing, and past government policies have limited productivity gains. Philippine farms produce food crops for domestic consumption and cash crops for export. The agricultural sector employs about 38% of the work force but only provides about one-fifth of GDP.

Decades of uncontrolled logging and slash-and-burn agriculture in marginal upland areas have stripped forests, with critical implications for the ecological balance. The government has instituted conservation programs, but deforestation remains a severe problem.

With its 7,107 islands, the Philippines has a very diverse range of fishing areas. Notwithstanding good prospects for the aquaculture subsector, the fishing industry continues to face a bleak future due to destructive fishing methods, a lack of funds, and an absence of government support.

## Industry

Industrial production is centered on processing and assembly operations of the following: food, beverages, tobacco, rubber products, textiles, clothing and footwear, pharmaceuticals, paints, plywood and veneer, paper and paper products, small appliances, and electronics. Heavier industries are dominated by the production of cement, glass, industrial chemicals, fertilizers, iron and steel, and refined petroleum products.

The industrial sector is concentrated in the urban areas, especially in the metropolitan Manila region and has only weak linkages to the rural economy. Inadequate infrastructure, transportation, communication, and electrical power shortages have so far inhibited faster industrial growth.

## Mining

The country is well-endowed with mineral and thermal energy resources. A recent discovery of natural gas reserves off Palawan Island will soon be brought on-line to generate electricity. Philippine copper and chromite deposits are among the largest in the world. Other important minerals include gold, nickel, silver, coal, gypsum, and sulfur. Significant deposits of clay, limestone, marble, silica, and phosphate exist. About 60% of total mining production is accounted for by nonmetallic minerals, which contributed substantially to the industry's steady output growth between 1993 and 1998, with the value of production growing 58%. In 1999, however, mineral production declines 16% to $793 million. Mineral exports have slowed steadily since 1996. Led by copper cathodes, Philippine mineral exports amounted to $645 million in 1999, down 16% from 1998 levels. Low metal prices, high production costs, and lack of investment in infrastructure have contributed to the mining industry's overall decline.

# FOREIGN RELATIONS

In its foreign policy, the Philippines cultivates constructive relations with its Asian neighbors, with whom it is linked through membership in ASEAN, the ASEAN Regional Forum (ARF), and the Asia-Pacific Economic Cooperation (APEC) forum. The Philippines is a member of the UN and some of its specialized agencies, the Non-Aligned Movement (NAM, since 1992), and has close links with the Organization of Islamic Conference (OIC). The Philippines has played a key role in ASEAN in recent years and also values its relations with the countries of the Middle East, in no small part because hundreds of thousands of Filipinos are employed in that region. The fundamental Philippine attachment to democracy and human rights is reflected in its foreign policy. Philippine soldiers and police have participated in a number of multilateral civilian police and peacekeeping operations, and a Philippine Army general served as the first commander of the UN Peacekeeping Operation in East Timor. The Philippine Government also has been active in efforts to reduce tensions among rival claimants to the territories and waters of the resource-rich South China Sea.

# U.S.-PHILIPPINE RELATIONS

U.S.-Philippine relations are based on shared history and commitment to democratic principles, as well as on economic ties. The historical and cultural links between the Philippines and the U.S. remain strong. The Philippines modeled its governmental institutions on those of the U.S., and continues to share a commitment to democracy and human rights. At the most fundamental level of bilateral relations, human links continue to

## Travel Notes

**Travel Advice:** For up-to-date information from the U.S. State Department on possible inconvenient or hazardous situations, see the **Travel Warnings and Consular Information Sheets from the U.S. Government** section starting on page 1723. For the latest information on health requirements and conditions, see the **International Travelers' Health Information** section starting on page 1385. For further information dealing with non-urgent matter, see the **Tips for Travelers to...** section starting on page 1588.

form a strong bridge between the two countries. There are an estimated 2 million Americans of Philippine ancestry in the United States and more than 100,000 American citizens in the Philippines.

Until November 1992, pursuant to the 1947 Military Bases Agreement, the United States maintained and operated major facilities at Clark Air Base, Subic Bay Naval Complex, and several small subsidiary installations in the Philippines. In 1983 and 1988, the United States and the Philippines completed successful reviews and extensions of the Military Bases Agreement, as amended. In August 1991, negotiators from the two countries reached agreement on a draft treaty providing for use of Subic Bay Naval Base by U.S. forces for 10 years. The draft treaty did not include use of Clark Air Base, which had been so heavily damaged by the 1991 eruption of Mt. Pinatubo that the U.S. decided to abandon it.

On September 16, 1991, the Philippine Senate rejected the bases treaty, and despite further efforts to salvage the situation, the two sides could not reach agreement. As a result, the Philippine Government informed the U.S. on December 6, 1991, that it would have 1 year to complete withdrawal. That withdrawal went smoothly and was completed ahead of schedule, with the last U.S. forces departing on November 24, 1992. On departure, the U.S. Government turned over assets worth more than

$1.3 billion to the Philippines, including an airport and ship-repair facility. Agencies formed by the Philippine Government have converted the former military bases for civilian commercial use, with Subic Bay serving as a flagship for that effort.

The post-U.S. bases era has seen U.S.-Philippine relations improved and broadened, focusing more prominently on economic and commercial ties while maintaining the importance of the security dimension. Philippine domestic political stability has resulted in increased U.S. investment in the country, while a strong security relationship rests on the U.S.-Philippines Mutual Defense Treaty (MDT). In February 1998, U.S. and Philippine negotiators concluded the Visiting Forces Agreement (VFA), paving the way for increased military cooperation under the MDT. The agreement was approved by the Philippine Senate in May 1999 and entered into force on June 1, 1999. Under the VFA, the U.S. is conducting an active program of ship visits to Philippine ports and has resumed large combined military exercises with Philippine forces. Although U.S. aid to the Philippines has taken on a far less prominent role than in the past, assistance programs continue, highlighted by the July 1996 opening of a major airport and harbor project in General Santos City with U.S. Agency for International Development funding. Then-President Ramos underscored the strength of the bilateral relationship by declaring July 4, 1996 to be Philippine-American Friendship Day in commemoration of the 50th anniversary of Philippine independence. Ramos visited the United States in April 1998.

## Trade and Investment

Two-way U.S. trade with the Philippines amounted to nearly $17 billion in 1999. The strong trade ties between the U.S. and the Philippines is reflected in the fact that some 20% of the Philippines' imports in 1999 came from the U.S., and about one-third of its exports were bound for America. Key exports to the U.S. are semiconductor devices and computer peripherals, automobile parts, electric machinery, textiles and garments, and coconut oil. In addition to other goods, the Philippines imports raw and semiprocessed materials for the manufacture of semiconductors, electronics and electrical machinery, transport equipment, and cereals and cereal preparations.

U.S. investment in the Philippines is estimated at some $2.8 billion, slightly more than 25% of all foreign investment in the Philippines. Since the late 1980s, the Philippines has committed itself to reforms that encourage foreign investment as a basis for economic development, subject to certain guidelines and restrictions in specified areas. Under President Ramos, the Philippines expanded reforms, opening the power

generation and telecommunications sectors to foreign investment, as well as securing ratification of the Uruguay Round agreement and membership in the World Trade Organization. As noted earlier, President Estrada's administration is continuing such reforms, a position which generally enjoys domestic political support.

During the last few years, the relatively closed Philippine economy has been opened significantly by foreign exchange deregulation, foreign investment and banking liberalization, and tariff and market barrier reduction. President Estrada continues to support further economic reform, and congressional action is now furthering these efforts. Trade

opportunities for exporters exist in a broad range of industries.

## Principal U.S. Embassy Officials

**For up-to-date information on Principal U.S. Officials, see the U.S. Embassies, Consulates, and Foreign Service section starting on page 139.**

The U.S. embassy is located at 1201 Roxas Boulevard, Manila; tel. (63)(2)521-7116; fax 522-4361; telex 722-27366 AME PH. Website: http://www.usembassy.state.gov/manila

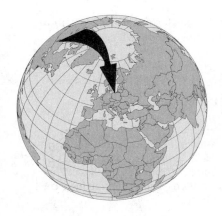

# POLAND

June 2000

Official Name:
**Republic of Poland**

# PROFILE

## Geography

**Area:** 312,683 sq. km. (120,725 sq. mi.); about the size of New Mexico.
**Cities:** (2000) Capital—Warsaw (pop. 1,626,100). Other cities—Lodz (825,600), Krakow (746,000), Wroclaw (641,000), Poznan (582,800), Gdansk (463,000).
**Terrain:** Flat plain, except mountains along southern border.
**Climate:** Temperate continental.

## People

**Nationality:** Noun—Pole(s). Adjective—Polish.
**Population:** 39 million.
**Annual growth rate:** Negligible.
**Ethnic Groups:** Polish 98%, German, Ukrainian, Belorussian, Lithuanian.
**Religion:** Roman Catholic 90%, Eastern Orthodox, Uniate, Protestant, Judaism.
**Language:** Polish.
**Literacy:** 98%.
**Health:** (2000) Infant mortality rate—15/1,000. Life expectancy—males 66 yrs., females 75 yrs.
**Work force:** 18.0 million. Industry and construction—30.4%; agriculture—27%; trade and business—25.1%; government and other—17.6%.

## Government

**Type:** Republic.
**Constitution:** The constitution now in effect was approved by the national referendum on May 25, 1997. The constitution codifies Poland's democratic norms and establishes checks and balances among the president, prime minister, and parliament. It also enhances several key elements of democracy including judicial review and the legislative process, while continuing to guarantee the wide range of civil rights, such as the right to free speech, press, and assembly, which Poles have enjoyed since 1989.
**Branches:** Executive—head of state (president), head of government (prime minister). Legislative—bicameral National Assembly (lower house—Sejm, upper house—Senate). Judicial—Supreme Court, provincial and local courts, constitutional tribunal.
**Administrative subdivisions:** 16 provinces (voivodships).
**Political parties:** (in Parliament) Solidarity Electoral Action, Democratic Left Alliance, Freedom Union, Polish Peasant Party, Polish Alliance, Confederation for an Independent Poland, Movement for Reconstruction of Poland, Polish Socialist Party, and Polish Raison d'Etats.
**Suffrage:** Universal at 18.
**Flag:** Upper half white; lower red.

## Economy

**GDP:** (1999) $154.2 billion.
**Per capita GDP:** (1999) $4,000.
**Growth rate:** (1999) 4.1%.
**Rate of Inflation:** (1999) 7.3%.
**Natural resources:** Coal, copper, sulfur, natural gas, silver, lead, salt.
**Agriculture:** Products—grains, hogs, dairy, potatoes, horticulture, sugarbeets, oilseed.
**Industry:** Types—machine building, iron and steel, mining, shipbuilding, automobiles, textiles and apparel, chemicals, food processing, glass, beverages.
**Trade:** (1999) Exports—$27.4 billion: furniture, cars, ships, coal, apparel. Imports—$45.9 billion: crude oil, passenger cars, pharmaceuticals, car parts, computers.

# PEOPLE

Poland today is ethnically almost homogeneous (98% Polish), in contrast with the pre-World War II period, when there were significant ethnic minorities—4.5 million Ukrainians, 3 million Jews, 1 million Belorussians, and 800,000 Germans. The majority of the Jews were murdered during the German occupation in World War II, and many others emigrated in the succeeding years.

Most Germans left Poland at the end of the war, while many Ukrainians and Belorussians lived in territories incorporated into the then-U.S.S.R. Small Ukrainian, Belorussian, Slovakian, and Lithuanian minorities reside along the borders, and a German minority is concentrated near the southwest city of Opole.

# HISTORY

Poland's written history begins with the reign of Mieszko I, who accepted Christianity for himself and his kingdom in AD 966. The Polish state reached its zenith under the Jagiellonian dynasty in the years following the union with Lithuania in 1386 and the subsequent defeat of the Teutonic Knights at Grunwald in 1410. The monarchy survived many upheavals but eventually went into a decline, which ended with the final partition of Poland by Prussia, Russia, and Austria in 1795.

Independence for Poland was one of the 14 points enunciated by President Woodrow Wilson during World War I. Many Polish-Americans enlisted in the military services to further this aim, and the United States worked at the postwar conference to ensure its implementation.

However, the Poles were largely responsible for achieving their own independence in 1918. Authoritarian rule predominated for most of the period before World War II.

On August 23, 1939, Germany and the Soviet Union signed the Ribbentrop-Molotov nonaggression pact, which secretly provided for the dismemberment of Poland into Nazi and Soviet-controlled zones. On September 1, 1939, Hitler ordered his troops into Poland. On September 17, Soviet troops invaded and then occupied eastern Poland under the terms of this agreement. After Germany invaded the Soviet Union in June 1941, Poland was completely occupied by German troops.

The Poles formed an underground resistance movement and a government-in-exile, first in Paris and later in London, which was recognized by the Soviet Union. During World War II, 400,000 Poles fought under Soviet command, and 200,000 went into combat on Western fronts in units loyal to the Polish government-in-exile.

In April 1943, the Soviet Union broke relations with the Polish government-in-exile after the German military announced that they had discovered mass graves of murdered Polish army officers at Katyn, in the U.S.S.R. (The Soviets claimed that the Poles had insulted them by requesting that the Red Cross investigate these reports.) In July 1944, the Soviet Red Army entered Poland and established a communist-controlled "Polish Committee of National Liberation" at Lublin.

Resistance against the Nazis in Warsaw, including uprisings by Jews in the Warsaw ghetto and by the Polish underground, was brutally suppressed. As the Germans retreated in January 1945, they leveled the city.

During the war, about 6 million Poles were killed, and 2.5 million were deported to Germany for forced labor. More than 3 million Jews (all but about 100,000 of the Jewish population) were killed in death camps like those at Oswiecim (Auschwitz), Treblinka, and Majdanek.

Following the Yalta Conference in February 1945, a Polish Provisional Government of National Unity was formed in June 1945; the U.S. recognized it the next month. Although the Yalta agreement called for free elections, those held in January 1947 were controlled by the Communist Party. The communists then established a regime entirely under their domination.

## Communist Party Domination

In October 1956, after the 20th ("de-Stalinization") Soviet Party Congress at Moscow and riots by workers in Poznan, there was a shakeup in the communist regime. While retaining most traditional communist economic and social aims, the regime of First Secretary Wladyslaw Gomulka liberalized Polish internal life.

In 1968, the trend reversed when student demonstrations were suppressed and an "anti-Zionist" campaign initially directed against Gomulka supporters within the party eventually led to the emigration of much of Poland's remaining Jewish population. In December 1970, disturbances and strikes in the port cities of Gdansk, Gdynia, and Szczecin, triggered by a price increase for essential consumer goods, reflected deep dissatisfaction with living and working conditions in the country. Edward Gierek replaced Gomulka as First Secretary.

Fueled by large infusions of Western credit, Poland's economic growth rate was one of the worlds highest during the first half of the 1970s. But much of the borrowed capital was misspent, and the centrally planned economy was unable to use the new resources effectively. The growing debt burden became insupportable in the late 1970s, and economic growth had become negative by 1979.

In October 1978, the Bishop of Krakow, Cardinal Karol Wojtyla, became Pope John Paul II, head of the Roman Catholic Church. Polish Catholics rejoiced at the elevation of a Pole to the papacy and greeted his June 1979 visit to Poland with an outpouring of emotion.

In July 1980, with the Polish foreign debt at more than $20 billion, the government made another attempt to increase meat prices. A chain reaction of strikes virtually paralyzed the Baltic coast by the end of August and, for the first time, closed most coal mines in Silesia. Poland was entering into an extended crisis that would change the course of its future development.

## The Solidarity Movement

On August 31, 1980, workers at the Lenin Shipyard in Gdansk, led by an electrician named Lech Walesa, signed a 21-point agreement with the government that ended their strike.

Background Notes

imilar agreements were signed at Szczecin and in Silesia. The key provision of these agreements was the guarantee of the workers' right to form independent trade unions and the right to strike. After the Gdansk agreement was signed, a new national union movement—"Solidarity"—swept Poland.

The discontent underlying the strikes was intensified by revelations of widespread corruption and mismanagement within the Polish state and party leadership. In September 1980, Gierek was replaced by Stanislaw Kania as First Secretary.

Alarmed by the rapid deterioration of the PZPR's authority following the Gdansk agreement, the Soviet Union proceeded with a massive military buildup along Poland's border in December 1980. In February 1981, Defense Minister Gen. Wojciech Jaruzelski assumed the position of Prime Minister as well, and in October 1981, he also was named party First Secretary. At the first Solidarity national congress in September-October 1981, Lech Walesa was elected national chairman of the union.

On December 12-13, the regime declared martial law, under which the army and special riot police were used to crush the union. Virtually all Solidarity leaders and many affiliated intellectuals were arrested or detained. The United States and other Western countries responded to martial law by imposing economic sanctions against the Polish regime and against the Soviet Union. Unrest in Poland continued for several years thereafter.

In a series of slow, uneven steps, the Polish regime rescinded martial law. In December 1982, martial law was suspended, and a small number of political prisoners were released. Although martial law formally ended in July 1983 and a general amnesty was enacted, several hundred political prisoners remained in jail.

In July 1984, another general amnesty was declared, and 2 years later, the government had released nearly all political prisoners. The authorities continued, however, to harass dissidents and Solidarity activists. Solidarity remained proscribed and its publications banned. Independent publications were censored.

## Roundtable Talks and Elections

The government's inability to forestall Poland's economic decline led to waves of strikes across the country in April, May, and August 1988. In an attempt to take control of the situation, the government gave de facto recognition to Solidarity, and Interior Minister Kiszczak began talks with Lech Walesa on August 31. These talks broke off in October, but a new series—the "roundtable" talks—began in February 1989.

These talks produced an agreement in April for partly open National Assembly elections. The June election produced a Sejm (lower house), in which one-third of the seats went to communists and one-third went to the two parties which had hitherto been their coalition partners. The remaining one-third of the seats in the Sejm and all those in the Senate were freely contested; virtually all of these were won by candidates supported by Solidarity.

The failure of the communists at the polls produced a political crisis. The roundtable agreement called for a communist president, and on July 19, the National Assembly, with the support of some Solidarity deputies, elected General Jaruzelski to that office. Two attempts by the communists to form governments failed, however.

On August 19, President Jaruzelski asked journalist/Solidarity activist Tadeusz Mazowiecki to form a government; on September 12, the Sejm voted approval of Prime Minister Mazowiecki and his cabinet. For the first time in more than 40 years, Poland had a government led by non-communists.

In December 1989, the Sejm approved the government's reform program to transform the Polish economy rapidly from centrally planned to free-market, amended the constitution to eliminate references to the "leading role" of the Communist Party, and renamed the country the "Republic of Poland." The Polish United Workers' (Communist) Party dissolved itself in January 1990, creating in its place a new party, Social Democracy of the Republic of Poland. Most of the property of the former Communist Party was turned over to the state.

The May 1990 local elections were entirely free. Candidates supported by Solidarity's Citizens' Committees won most of the races they contested, although voter turnout was only a little over 40%. The cabinet was reshuffled in July 1990; the national defense and interior affairs ministers—hold-overs from the previous communist government—were among those replaced.

In October 1990, the constitution was amended to curtail the term of President Jaruzelski. In December, Lech Walesa became the first popularly elected President of Poland.

## Poland in the 1990s

Poland in the early 1990s made great progress toward achieving a fully democratic government and a market economy. In November 1990, Lech Walesa was elected President for a 5-year term. Jan Krzysztof Bielecki, at Walesa's request, formed a government and served as its Prime Minister until October 1991, introducing world prices and greatly expanding the scope of private enterprise.

Poland's first free parliamentary elections were held in 1991. More than 100 parties participated, representing a full spectrum of political views. No single party received more than 13% of the total vote. After a rough start, 1993 saw the second group of elections, and the first parliament to actually serve a full term. The Democratic Left Alliance (SLD) received the largest percentage of votes.

After the election, the SLD and PSL formed a governing coalition. Waldemar Pawlak, leader of the junior partner PSL, became Prime Minister. Relations between President Walesa and the Prime Minister remained poor throughout the Pawlak government, with President Walesa charging Pawlak with furthering personal and party interests while neglecting matters of state importance. Following a number of scandals implicating Pawlak and increasing political tension over control of the armed forces, President Walesa demanded Pawlak's resignation in January 1995. In the ensuing political crisis, the coalition removed Pawlak from office and replaced him with the SLD's Jozef Oleksy as the new Prime Minister.

In November 1995, Poland held its second post-war free presidential elections. SLD leader Aleksander Kwasniewski defeated Walesa by a narrow margin—51.7% to 48.3%. Soon after Walesa's defeat, Interior Minister Andrzej Milczanowski accused then-Prime Minister Oleksy of longtime collaboration with Soviet and later Russian intelligence. In the ensuing political crisis, Oleksy resigned. For his successor, The SLD-PSL coalition turned to deputy Sejm speaker Wlodzimierz Cimoszewicz—who was linked to, but not a member of, the SLD. Polish prosecutors subsequently decided that there was insufficient evidence to charge Oleksy, and a parliamentary commission decided in November 1996 that the Polish intelligence services may have violated rules of procedure in gathering evidence in the Oleksy case.

Poland's most recent parliamentary elections were in September 1997 when two parties with roots in the Solidarity movement—Solidarity Electoral Action (AWS) and the Freedom Union (UW)—won 261 of the 460 seats in the Sejm and formed a coalition government. Jerzy Buzek of the AWS has been Prime Minister since these elections in 1997. Today the AWS and the Democratic Left Alliance (SLD) hold the majority of the seats in the Sejm. Marian Krzaklewski is the leader of the AWS, and Leszek Miller leads the SLD. In June 2000, UW withdrew from the governing collation, leaving AWS at the helm of a minority government.

# GOVERNMENT AND POLITICAL CONDITIONS

The current government structure consists of a council of ministers led by a Prime Minister, typically chosen from a majority coalition in the bicameral legislature's lower house. The president elected every 5 years is head of state. The judicial branch plays a minor role in decisionmaking.

Former SLD leader Aleksander Kwasniewski was elected President in November 1995. President Kwasniewski has supported Polish membership in NATO and the EU and backed the SLD's legislative agenda on issues such as redrafting of the constitution and abortion liberalization.

The parliament, consisting of 460 members of the Sejm and 100 members of the Senate, was elected in September 1997 in free and fair elections in which 16 political parties participated. A 1993 electoral law stipulated that with the exception of guaranteed seats for small German and Ukrainian ethnic parties, only parties receiving at least 5% of the total vote could enter parliament. As of June 2000, nine parties are represented in the Sejm.

Currently, Poland is lead by a minority government, comprised of the AWS party, under the leadership of Prime Minister Jerzy Buzek. The coalition has maintained generally pro-market economic policies and made clear its commitment to a democratic political system. The Democratic Left Alliance (SLD) is the opposition to the ruling coalition and holds 161 seats in the Sejm and 26 seats in the Senate. The UW and SLD currently dominate the Warsaw municipal council, which has lead to some clashes recently between the three dominant political parties.

Along with AWS, other parties represented in parliament are the Polish Peasant Party (PSL), the Polish Alliance (PP), the Independent Party, the Confederation for an Independent Poland (KPNO), the Movement for the Reconstruction of Poland (ROP), the Polish Socialist Party-Movement of Labor People (PPS-RLP), and the Polish Raison d'Etat (PRS).

General parliamentary elections are scheduled for September of 2001. Poland's next presidential election is scheduled for October 8, 2000.

## National Security

Poland's top national security goal is to further integrate with NATO and other west European defense, economic, and political institutions via a modernization and reorganization of its military. Polish military doctrine reflects the same defense nature as its NATO partners.

Poland maintains a sizable armed force currently numbering about 198,000 troops divided among an army of 138,500, an air and defense force of 43,000, and a navy of 16,500. The Ministry of Defense has announced that the armed forces of Poland will number 150,000 by 2006. Poland relies on military conscription for the majority of its personal strength. All males (with some exceptions) are subject to a 12-month term of military service.

The Polish military continues to restructure and to modernize its equipment. The Polish Defense Ministry General Staff and the Land Forces staff have recently reorganized the latter into a NATO-compatible J/G-1 through J/G-6 structure. Budget constraints hamper such priority defense acquisitions as a multi-role fighter, improved communications systems, and an attack helicopter.

Poland continues to be a regional leader in support and participation in the NATO Partnership for Peace Program and has actively engaged most of its neighbors and other regional actors to build stable foundations for future European security arrangements. Poland continues its long record of strong support for UN Peacekeeping Operations by maintaining a unit in Southern Lebanon, a battalion in NATO's Kosovo Force (KFOR), and by providing and actually deploying the KFOR strategic reserve to Kosovo.

## Principal Government Officials

**For up-to-date information on Principal Government Officials, see the Chiefs of State and Cabinet Members of Foreign Governments section starting on page 1.**

Poland maintains an embassy in the United States at 2640 16th St. NW, Washington, DC 20009 (tel. 202-234-3800/3801/3802); the consular annex is at 2224 Wyoming Ave. NW, Washington, DC 20008 (tel. 202-234-3800). Poland has consulates in Chicago, New York City, and Los Angeles.

# ECONOMY

The Polish economy recorded growth of 4.1% in gross domestic product (GDP) in 1999, and an estimated 5.1% growth is expected for 2000. Other economic indicators continue to improve; however, the unemployment rate at the end of 1999 was 13%. This is up considerably since 1998's 10.4%. This can be attributed to mass layoffs due to enterprise restructuring, and the rate of inflation in 1999 declined to 7.3% from the 1998 figure of 8.6%. However, some budgetary concerns remain. The Finance Ministry has set a goal of balancing the budget, excluding privatization revenues, by the year 2003. The budget deficit was 2.0% of GDP in 1999 and is expected to be at 2.3% in 2000. Since 1995, Poland has run a steadily rising current account deficit—4.3% of GDP in 1998, 6.8% in 1999, and an estimated 8% in 2000. Although the government had expected this deficit to decline beginning 2000 to about 6.1%, it is not a source of concern at this time because of substantial official reserves and coverage by capital inflows.

The United States and other Western countries have supported the growth of a free enterprise economy by reducing Poland's enormous foreign debt burden, providing economic aid, and lowering trade barriers. Poland will graduate from USAID assistance in 2000.

## Agriculture

Agriculture employs 27% of the work force but contributes only 5% to the gross domestic product (GDP), reflecting a relatively low level of productivity compared to other sectors of the economy. Unlike the industrial sector, Poland's agricultural sector remained largely in private hands during the decades of communist rule. Most of the former state farms are now being leased to farmer tenants. Lack of credit is hampering efforts to sell former state farmland. Currently, Poland's 2 million private farms occupy 90% of all farmland and account for roughly the same percentage of total agricultural production. These farms are small—8 hectares (ha) on average—and often fragmented. Farms with an area exceeding 15 ha accounted only for 9% of the total number of farms but cover 45% of total agricultural area. Over half of all farming households in Poland produce only for their own needs with little, if any, commercial marketing's.

Privatization within the food processing sector is the most advanced in the food concentrate, brewery, and confectionery industries and the weakest in the grain milling, sugar refining, and potato processing industries. Poland net exports confectionery, processed fruit and vegetables, meat, and dairy products. Processors often rely on imports to supplement domestic supplies of wheat, feed grains, vegetable oil, and protein meals, which are generally insufficient to meet domestic demand. However, Poland is the leading producer in Europe of potatoes and rye and is one of the ten-largest producers of sugarbeets. Poland also is a significant producer of rapeseed, grains, hogs, and cattle. Attempts to increase domestic feed grain production are hampered by the short growing season, poor soil, and the small size of farms.

## Travel Notes

**Travel Advice:** For up-to-date information from the U.S. State Department on possible inconvenient or hazardous situations, see the **Travel Warnings and Consular Information Sheets from the U.S. Government** section starting on page 1723. For the latest information on health requirements and conditions, see the **International Travelers' Health Information** section starting on page 1385. For further information dealing with non-urgent matter, see the **Tips for Travelers to...** section starting on page 1588.

Pressure to restructure the agriculture sector is intensifying as Poland prepares to accede to the European Union, which is unwilling to subsidize the vast number of subsistence farms that do not produce for the market. The changes in agriculture are likely to strain Poland's social fabric, tearing at the heart of the traditional, family-based small farm as the younger generation drifts toward the cities.

## Industry

Before World War II, Poland's industrial base was concentrated in the coal, textile, chemical, machinery, iron, and steel sectors. Today it extends to fertilizers, petrochemicals, machine tools, electrical machinery, electronics, and shipbuilding.

Poland's industrial base suffered greatly during World War II, and many resources were directed toward reconstruction. The communist economic system imposed in the late 1940s created large and unwieldy economic structures operated under a tight central command. In part, because of this systemic rigidity, the economy performed poorly even in comparison with other economies in central Europe.

In 1989, the Mazowiecki government began a comprehensive reform program to replace the centralized command economy with a market-oriented system. Many largescale state-owned industrial enterprises, particularly in the mining and steel

sectors, have remained resistant to the change and downsizing required to survive in an open market economy.

In the past years, the percentage of those employed in Polish industry has declined. Some possible reasons for this are that the mining industry has been experiencing internal conflicts. There also has been somewhat of an attempt to restructure agriculture.

## Economic Reform Program

Poland was the first former centrally planned economy in central Europe to end its recession and return to growth after a deep recession in the late 1980s and early 1990s. Since 1992, the Polish economy has enjoyed an accelerated recovery. The private sector now accounts for nearly two-thirds of GDP and employs some 60% of the work force. However, unemployment remains relatively high (13.7% as of April 2000), especially in rural areas.

The sweeping economic reforms introduced in 1989 removed price controls, eliminated most subsidies to industry, opened markets to international competition, and imposed strict budgetary and monetary discipline. These reforms have achieved positive results in reducing inflation—from almost 600% in 1990 to an estimated 7.3% in 1999—and in bringing budget deficits under control. Poland's GDP grew by 4.1% in 1999 and is estimated to grow by over 5.1% in 2000.

As a result of Poland's growth and investment-friendly climate, foreign investment flows are now increasing at record levels. However, the restructuring of industry to adapt to the new conditions of a market economy, a necessary accompaniment to macroeconomic stabilization, has often proceeded more slowly than expected. In certain sectors, such as coal and steel, state-owned enterprises continue to operate at a loss. Efforts to privatize them have encountered many snags, including worker apprehensions about large job losses and management fears of bankruptcy. Government budget deficits have been brought under control, but spending cuts in areas such as education, health care, infrastructure, and public safety were necessary to reduce the deficit. Meanwhile, the burden on the budget for subsidies to the Social Insurance Fund has mushroomed, especially due to the massive number of workers retiring early since 1989.

Poland became a full member of NATO in March 1999 and has set an objective of joining the European Union in 2003. The Polish economy continues to grow, and new investment continues to be strong. Government reforms are making progress in many areas. A growing middle class and rapidly developing distribution networks are turning Poland into a more attractive market for small and medium exporters. With a population of 39 million, Poland's market potential is huge. Many European firms have recognized this potential and are beginning to expand operations and sales in Poland, and there is a high level of direct American investment.

### Foreign Trade

With the collapse of the ruble-based COMECON trading bloc in 1990, Poland scrambled to reorient its trade. By 1996, 70% of its trade was with European Union (EU) members, with Germany alone accounting for more than 30%. While membership in the EU is Poland's primary goal, it has fostered regional integration and trade through the Central European Free Trade Agreement (CEFTA), which includes Hungary, the Czech and Slovak Republics, and Slovenia.

Poland faced a growing trade and current account deficit in 1996, despite nearly $7 billion in unrecorded cross-border exports (mostly to Germany but also to the Ukraine, Belarus, and the Czech Republic). Much of this trade consists of imports of capital goods needed for industrial retooling and for manufacturing inputs, rather than imports for consumption. Therefore, a deficit is expected, and even

positive at this point. Poland, a member of the World Trade Organization (WTO), has been steadily lowering tariffs in line with its WTO and EU commitments.

Opportunities for trade and investment continue to exist across virtually all sectors of Poland. The American Chamber of Commerce in Poland, founded in 1991 with seven members, now has more than 300 members. Constant economic growth, the size of the Polish market, and a high level of political stability are the top reasons the U.S. and other foreign companies do business in Poland. Most believe that Poland is the best market in central and eastern Europe for their products and investments.

# FOREIGN RELATIONS

Poland became a full member of NATO in March 1999 and has set an objective of joining the European Union in 2003. Poland promoted its NATO candidacy through energetic participation in the Partnership for Peace (PfP) program and through intensified individual dialogue between Poland and NATO. Poland was invited in the first wave of NATO enlargement at the July 1997 NATO Summit in Madrid.

Poland also has forged ahead on its economic integration with the West. Poland became an associate member of the European Union (EU) and its defensive arm, the Western European Union (WEU) in 1994. In 1996 Poland achieved full OECD membership and submitted preliminary documentation for full EU membership. Poland is negotiating for early entry into join the European Union.

Changes since 1989 have redrawn the map of central Europe, and Poland has had to forge relationships with seven new neighbors. Poland has actively pursued good relations with all its neighbors, signing friendship treaties replacing links severed by the collapse of the Warsaw Pact. The Poles have forged special rela-

tionships with Lithuania and particularly Ukraine in an effort to firmly anchor these states to the West.

# U.S.-POLISH RELATIONS

The United States established diplomatic relations with the newly formed Polish Republic in April 1919. After Gomulka came to power in 1956, relations with the United States began to improve. However, during the 1960s, reversion to a policy of full and unquestioning support for Soviet foreign policy objectives and anti-Semitic feelings in Poland caused those relations to stagnate.

U.S.-Polish relations improved significantly after Gierek succeeded Gomulka and expressed his interest in improving relations with the United States. A consular agreement was signed in 1972.

In 1974 Gierek was the first Polish leader to visit the United States. This action, among others, demonstrated both sides wish to facilitate better relations.

The birth of Solidarity in 1980 raised the hope that progress would be made in Poland's external relations as well as in its domestic development. During this time, the U.S. provided $765 million in agricultural assistance. Human rights and individual freedom issues, however, were not improved upon, and the U.S. revoked Poland's most-favored-nation (MFN) status in response to the Polish Government's decision to ban solidarity. MFN status was reinstated in 1987, and diplomatic relations were upgraded.

The United States and Poland have enjoyed warm bilateral relations since 1989. Every post-1989 Polish government has been a strong supporter of continued American military and economic presence in Europe and has identified membership in NATO, the European Union and other Western security and economic structures as Poland's principal foreign policy priority. Poland became a member of the OECD in November 1996 and served successfully as the Chairman in Office of the Organization for Security and Cooperation in Europe (OSCE) in 1998. It has done a superb job as the formal protector of American interests in Iraq since the Gulf War and cooperates closely with American diplomacy on such issues as nuclear proliferation, human rights, regional cooperation in central and eastern Europe, and United Nations reform.

## Principal U.S. Embassy Officials

**For up-to-date information on Principal U.S. Officials, see the U.S. Embassies, Consulates, and Foreign Service section starting on page 139.**

The street address and international mailing address of the U.S. embassy in Poland is Aleje Ujazdowskie 29/31, 00540 Warsaw, Poland; tel: 48-22-628-3041; fax 48-22-628-8298.

The Consulate General in Krakow is at Ulica Stolarska 9, 31043 Krakow, Poland; tel: 48-12-211-400, 216-767, 226-040 or 229-764; fax: 48-12-218-292; and a Consular Agency in Poznan is at Ulica Paderewskiego 8, 61708 Poznan, Poland; tel: 48-61-518-516; fax: 48-61-518-966.

# PORTUGAL

May 2000

Official Name:
**Portuguese Republic**

# PROFILE

## Geography

**Area:** 92,391 sq. km., including the Azores and Madeira Islands; slightly smaller than the State of Indiana.
**Cities:** Lisbon (capital, pop. 1.9 million), Oporto (1.7 million), Faro.
**Terrain:** Mountainous in the north; rolling plains in the central south.
**Climate:** Maritime temperate, average annual temperature is 16°C (61°F).

## People

**Nationality:** Noun and adjective—Portuguese (singular and plural).
**Population:** (1999) 9.9 million.
**Population density:** 105 per sq. km. (272 per sq. mi.).
**Annual growth rate:** 0.0%.
**Ethnic Groups:** Homogeneous Mediterranean stock with a small black African minority.
**Religion:** Roman Catholic, 97%.
**Language:** Portuguese.
**Education:** Years compulsory—9.
**Literacy:** 90%.
**Health:** Infant mortality rate—6.73/1, 000. Life expectancy—76 years.
**Work force:** (4.7 million) Government and services—56%; industry—32%; agriculture—12%.

## Government

**Type:** Republic.
**Constitution:** Effective April 25, 1976; revised October 30, 1982, June 1, 1989, November 25, 1992, and September 3, 1997.
**Branches:** Executive—president (head of state), Council of State (presidential advisory body), prime minister (head of government), Council of Ministers. Legislative—unicameral Assembly of the Republic (230 deputies). Judicial—Supreme Court, district courts, appeals courts, Constitutional Tribunal.
**Administrative subdivisions:** 18 districts, 2 autonomous regions.
**Major political parties:** Socialist Party (PS), Social Democratic Party (PSD), Popular Party (CDS/PP), Portuguese Communist Party (PCP).
**Suffrage:** Universal at age 18.

## Economy

**GDP:** (1999) $108.9 billion.
**Annual growth rate:** 3.1%.
**Per capita GDP:** (1999) $10,901.
**Avg. inflation rate:** (1999) 2.2%.
**Natural resources:** Fish, tungsten, iron, copper, tin, and uranium ores.
**Agriculture:** Forestry, fisheries, cork, wine.
**Industry:** Textiles, clothing, footwear, wood and cork, paper, chemicals, manufacturing, food and beverages.
**Services:** Commerce, government, housing, banking and finance.

**Trade:** Exports—$25 billion; clothing, footwear, machinery, vehicles, cork and paper products, food products. Imports—$34.9 billion; machinery, vehicles, agricultural products, chemicals. Partners—European Union (81%), United States, Portuguese-speaking African countries, European Free Trade Area (EFTA), Middle East.

# GOVERNMENT

Portugal's April 25, 1976 constitution reflected the country's 1974-76 move from authoritarian rule to provisional military government to a parliamentary democracy with some initial communist and left-wing influence. The military coup in 1974 was a result of the colonial wars and removed the authoritarian dictator, Marcello Caetano, from power. The threat of a communist takeover in Portugal generated considerable concern among the country's NATO allies. The revolution also led to the country abruptly abandoning its colonies overseas and to the return of an estimated 600,000 Portuguese citizens from abroad. The 1976 constitution, which defined Portugal as a "Republic...engaged in the formation of a classless society," was revised in 1982, 1989, 1992, and 1997.

The 1982 revision of the constitution placed the military under strict civilian control, trimmed the powers of the president, and abolished the Revolutionary Council (a non-elected committee with legislative veto powers). The country joined the European Union in 1986, beginning a path toward greater economic and political integration with its richer neighbors in Europe. The 1989 revision of the constitution eliminated much of the remaining Marxist rhetoric of the original document, abolished the communist-inspired "agrarian reform," and laid the groundwork for further privatization of nationalized firms and the government-owned communications media.

The current Portuguese constitution provides for progressive administrative decentralization and calls for future reorganization on a regional

Background Notes

basis. The Azores and Madeira Islands have constitutionally mandated autonomous status. A regional autonomy statute promulgated in 1980 established the Government of the Autonomous Region of the Azores; the Government of the Autonomous Region of Madeira operates under a provisional autonomy statute in effect since 1976. Apart from the Azores and Madeira, the country is divided into 18 districts, each headed by a governor appointed by the Minister of Internal Administration. Macau, a former dependency, reverted to Chinese sovereignty in December 1999.

The four main organs of the national government are the presidency, the prime minister and Council of Ministers (the government), the Assembly of the Republic (the parliament), and the judiciary. The president, elected to a 5-year term by direct, universal suffrage, also is commander in chief of the armed forces. Presidential powers include appointing the prime minister and Council of Ministers, in which the president must be guided by the assembly election results; dismissing the prime minister; dissolving the assembly to call early elections; vetoing legislation, which may be overridden by the assembly; and declaring a state of war or siege.

The Council of State, a presidential advisory body, is composed of six senior civilian officers, any former presidents elected under the 1976 constitution, five members chosen by the assembly, and five selected by the president.

The government is headed by the presidentially appointed prime minister, who names the Council of Ministers. A new government is required to define the broad outline of its policy in a program and present it to the assembly for a mandatory period of debate. Failure of the assembly to reject the program by a majority of deputies confirms the government in office.

The Assembly of the Republic is a unicameral body composed of up to 235 deputies. Elected by universal suffrage according to a system of proportional representation, deputies serve terms of office of 4 years, unless the president dissolves the assembly and calls for new elections.

The national Supreme Court is the court of last appeal. Military, administrative, and fiscal courts are designated as separate court categories. A nine-member Constitutional Tribunal reviews the constitutionality of legislation.

# CURRENT ADMINISTRATION

The Socialist Party, under the leadership of Antonio Guterres, came to power with a coalition government following the October 1995 parliamentary elections. The Socialists won a new mandate by winning exactly half the parliamentary seats in the latest election in October 1999. Socialist Jorge Sampaio won the February 1996 presidential elections with nearly 54% of the vote. Sampaio's election marked the first time since the 1974 revolution that a single party held the prime ministership, the presidency, and a plurality of the municipalities. Local elections were held in December 1997.

Prime Minister Guterres has continued the privatization and modernization policies begun by his predecessor. Guterres has been a vigorous proponent of the effort to include Portugal in the first round of countries to collaborate and put into effect the "euro" in 1999. In international relations, Guterres has pursued strong ties with the United States and greater Portuguese integration with the European Union while continuing to raise Portugal's profile through an activist foreign policy. One of his first decisions as Prime Minister was to send 900 troops to participate in the IFOR peacekeeping mission in Bosnia. Portugal later contributed 320 troops to SFOR, the follow-up Bosnia operation. Portugal also contributed aircraft and personnel to NATO's Operation Allied Force in Kosovo.

## Principal Government Officials

For up-to-date information on Principal Government Officials, see the Chiefs of State and Cabinet Members of Foreign Governments section starting on page 1.

Portugal maintains an embassy in the United States at 2125 Kalorama Road, NW, Washington, DC 20008 (tel. 202-328-8610); consulates general in New York City, Boston, San Francisco, and Newark, NJ; consulates in Providence, RI and New Bedford, MA; and honorary consulates in Honolulu, Los Angeles, Houston, New Orleans, Chicago, Philadelphia, Miami, San Juan, and Waterbury. The Portuguese National Tourist Office in the United States is located at 590 Fifth Avenue, New York, NY 10036 (tel: 212-354-4403).

# ECONOMY

Membership in the European Union (EU) has brought robust economic growth, largely through increased trade ties and an inflow of structural adjustment funds to improve the country's infrastructure. Since the last recession in 1993, the economy has grown at an average annual rate of 3.3%, well above EU averages. Much of the recent growth has occurred as a result of the European Monetary Union (EMU). In order to qualify, Portugal agreed to cut its fiscal deficit and undertake structural reforms. As a result of EMU, however, the country witnessed exchange rate stability, falling inflation, and falling interest rates. Falling interest rates, in turn, lowered the cost of public debt and made it relatively easy for the country to achieve its fiscal targets. Another result of falling interest rates has been the rapid expansion of household debt and the overheating economy. The European Commission, OECD, and others have advised the Portuguese Government to exercise more fiscal restraint to bring the situation under control.

Portugal's economy is based on traditional industries such as textiles, clothing, footwear, cork and wood products, beverages (wine), porcelain and earthenware, and glass and glassware. In addition, the country has increased its role in Europe's automotive sector. Services, particularly tourism, are playing an increasingly important role in the economy.

Portugal's privatization program has reduced the weight of the state-owned sector in the economy from 20% in 1989 to 10% in 1998 and yielded $21.5 billion in total proceeds to the government.

Portugal has made significant progress in raising its standard of living closer to that of its EU partners. GDP per capita on a purchasing power parity basis rose from 53% of the EC average in 1985 to 70% of the EU average in 1998.

Unemployment stood at 4.1% at the end of 1999, which is low compared to the EU average. Real wages are flexible, but high social costs and severance packages raise fixed labor costs and make new job creation difficult.

# U.S.-PORTUGUESE RELATIONS

The United States encourages a stable and democratic Portugal that is closely associated with the industrial democracies of western Europe and NATO; it has supported Portugal's successful entry into the West European economic and defense mainstream. Although it was a neutral country during World War II, Portugal was a founding member of NATO and has been a strong supporter of transatlantic ties. Portugal's commitment to democratic values is demonstrated by the country's successful transition from authoritarian rule to

## Travel Notes

**Travel Advice:** For up-to-date information from the U.S. State Department on possible inconvenient or hazardous situations, see the **Travel Warnings and Consular Information Sheets from the U.S. Government** section starting on page 1723. For the latest information on health requirements and conditions, see the **International Travelers' Health Information** section starting on page 1385. For further information dealing with non-urgent matter, see the **Tips for Travelers to...** section starting on page 1588.

constitutional democracy and its excellent human rights record.

Bilateral ties date from the earliest years of the United States. Following the Revolutionary War, Portugal was the first neutral country to recognize the United States. On February 21, 1791, President George Washington opened formal diplomatic relations, naming Col. David Humphreys as U.S. minister. A shared perspective promotes close contact between the two nations. Emigration and sizable Portuguese communities in Massachusetts, Rhode Island, New Jersey, and California has contributed to strong cultural ties. There also are about 16,000 Americans living in Portugal. This exchange was promoted in 1999 when Portugal entered the U.S. Visa Waiver Pilot Program.

U.S.-Portuguese trade is relatively small, with the U.S. exporting $1.05 billion worth of goods in 1999 and importing $1.2 billion. While total Portuguese trade has increased dramatically over the last 10 years, the U.S. percentage of it—both exports and imports—has declined. The Portuguese Government is seeking to increase exports of textiles and footwear to the United States and is encouraging greater bilateral investment.

## Principal U.S. Officials

**For up-to-date information on Prin-** cipal U.S. Officials, see the U.S. Embassies, Consulates, and Foreign Service section starting on page 139.

---

The U.S. embassy is located at Avenida das Forcas Armadas, 1600 Lisbon, Portugal (tel.: 351-21-727-3300). The embassy homepage is located at www.usia.gov/posts/lisbon.html.
The Ponta Delgada consulate is located at Avenida Infante D. Henrique, Ponta Delgada, Sao Miguel, Azores 9502 (tel.: 296-282216).
The consular agent in Funchal, Madeira is Antonio Drummond Borges (tel.: 291-741088).

# FOREIGN RELATIONS

As Portuguese democracy has matured, the country has taken a more active role in international issues. Portugal has proportionally large contingents in both SFOR and KFOR, and the government backed the NATO operations in Kosovo although 60% of the population opposed the campaign. Portugal has created an organization, the CPLP, to improve its ties with other Portuguese-speaking countries, and has participated, along with Spain, in a series of Ibero-American summits. Most importantly, Portugal lobbied long and hard for independence for East Timor, a former Portuguese colony. The violence that followed East Timor's vote for independence triggered the largest demonstrations seen since the revolution. Following the restoration of peace to the territory, Portugal has committed troops and money to help bring stability and economic development to East Timor in close cooperation with the United States.

Although Portugal has long seen itself as an Atlantic, rather than European state, that focus is clearly shifting as Portugal moves toward greater integration with Europe. The saying goes that Europe was the last continent discovered by the Portuguese. Portugal has been one of the greatest beneficiaries of the European Union and is now one of its strongest proponents. In 1998, Portugal met the financial criteria for joining the European Monetary Union and the country's exchange rates, along with those of 10 other EU countries have been tied to the "euro" since January 1, 1999.

Portugal held the presidency of the European Union for the second time during the first half of 2000. Portugal has used its term to launch a dialogue between the EU and Africa and to begin to take steps to make the European economy dynamic and competitive. Portugal's tenure also has been important in making progress on a number of internal EU issues, such as institutional reforms and beginning negotiations with new candidate countries.

# QATAR

November 1997

## Official Name:
## State of Qatar

# PROFILE

## Geography

**Area:** 11,437 sq. km. (4,427 sq. mi.); about the size of Connecticut and Rhode Island combined.
**Cities:** Capital—Doha 313,600 (1992). Other Cities—Umm Said, Al-Khor, Dukhan, Ruwais.
**Terrain:** Mostly desert, flat, barren.
**Climate:** Hot and dry, sultry in summer.

## People

**Nationality:** Noun and adjective—Qatari(s).
**Population:** 550,000 (est.) 80% foreign workers.
**Population growth rate (1996 est):** 2.39%.
**Ethnic groups:** Arab 40%, Pakistani 18%, Indian 18%, Iranian 10%, other 14%.
**Religion:** Islam (state religion, claimed by virtually all of the indigenous population).
**Languages:** Arabic (official); English (widely spoken).
**Literacy:** 79.4%—total population, 79.2%—male, 79.9%—female.
**Education:** Compulsory—ages 6-16. Attendance—98%.
**Health:** Infant Mortality Rate—20.4 deaths/1,000 live births. Life expectancy at birth—73.03 years.

**Work force (primarily foreign):** 290,000. Industry, services and commerce—70%, Government—20%, Agriculture—10%.

## Government

**Type:** Traditional emirate.
**Independence:** September 3, 1971.
**Constitution:** 1970 Basic Law, revised 1972.
**Branches:** Executive—Council of Ministers. Legislative—Advisory Council (appointed; has assumed only limited responsibility to date). Judicial—independent.
**Subdivisions:** Fully centralized government; nine municipalities.
**Political parties:** None.
**Suffrage:** None.
**Flag:** Maroon with white serrated band (nine white points) on the hoist side.

## Economy

**GDP:** $10.7 billion
**Real growth rate:** -1%
**Per capita income:** $20,820
**Natural resources:** Petroleum, natural gas, fish.
**Agriculture:** Accounts for less than 2% of GDP. Products—fruits and vegetables (most food is imported).
**Industry:** Oil production and refining (31% of GDP), natural gas development, mining, manufacturing, construction, and power.
**Trade:** Exports—$3.26 billion (1996 est.), principally oil (75-80%). Partners—Japan 61%, Australia 5%, UAE 4%, Singapore 4% (1994). Imports—$4.9 billion (1996 est.), principally consumer goods, machinery, food. Partners—Germany 14%, Japan 12%, UK 11%, U.S. 9%, Italy 5% (1994).

# PEOPLE

Natives of the Arabian Peninsula, most Qataris are descended from a number of migratory tribes that came to Qatar in the 18th century to escape the harsh conditions of the neighboring areas of Nejd and Al-Hasa. Some are descended from Omani tribes. Qatar has over 0.5 million people, the majority of whom live in Doha, the capital. Foreign workers with temporary residence status make up about four-fifths of the population. Most of them are South Asians, Egyptians, Palestinians, Jordanians, and Iranians. About 3,000 U.S. citizens resided there as of 1996.

For centuries, the main sources of wealth were pearling, fishing, and trade. At one time, Qataris owned nearly one-third of the Persian Gulf fishing fleet. With the Great Depression and the introduction of Japan's cultured-pearl industry, pearling in Qatar declined drastically.

The Qataris are mainly Sunni "Wahhabi" Muslims. Islam is the official religion, and Islamic jurisprudence is the basis of Qatar's legal system. Arabic is the official language and English is the lingua franca. Education is compulsory and free for all Arab residents 6-16 years old. Qatar has an increasingly high literacy rate.

# HISTORY

Qatar has been inhabited for millennia. In the 19th century, the Bahraini Al Khalifa family dominated until 1868 when, at the request of Qatari nobles, the British negotiated the termination of the Bahraini claim, except for the payment of tribute. The tribute ended with the occupation of Qatar by the Ottoman Turks in 1872.

When the Turks left, at the beginning of World War I, the British recognized Sheikh Abdullah bin Jassim Al Thani as Ruler. The Al Thani family had lived in Qatar for 200 years. The 1916 treaty between the United Kingdom and Sheikh Abdullah was similar to those entered into by the British with other Gulf principalities. Under it, the Ruler agreed not to dispose of any of his territory except to the U.K. and not to enter into relationships with any other foreign government without British consent. In return, the British promised to protect Qatar from all aggression by sea and to lend their good offices in case of a land attack. A 1934 treaty granted more extensive British protection.

In 1935, a 75-year oil concession was granted to Qatar Petroleum Company, a subsidiary of the Iraq Petroleum Company, which was owned by Anglo-Dutch, French, and U.S. interests. High-quality oil was discovered in 1940 at Dukhan, on the western side of the Qatari peninsula. Exploitation was delayed by World War II, and oil exports did not begin until 1949.

During the 1950s and 1960s gradually increasing oil reserves brought prosperity, rapid immigration, substantial social progress, and the beginnings of Qatar's modern history.

When the U.K. announced a policy in 1968 (reaffirmed in March 1971) of ending the treaty relationships with the Gulf sheikdoms, Qatar joined the other eight states then under British protection (the seven trucial sheikdoms—the present United Arab Emirates—and Bahrain) in a plan to form a union of Arab emirates. By mid-1971, however, the nine still had not agreed on terms of union, and the termination date (end of 1971) of the British treaty relationship was approaching. Accordingly, Qatar sought independence as a separate entity and became the fully independent State of Qatar on September 3, 1971.

# GOVERNMENT AND POLITICAL CONDITIONS

The ruling Al Thani family continued to hold power following the declaration of independence in 1971. The head of state is the Emir, and the right to rule Qatar is passed on within the Al Thani family. Politically, Qatar is evolving from a traditional society into a modern welfare state. Government departments have been established to meet the requirements of social and economic progress. The Basic Law of 1970 institutionalized local customs rooted in Qatar's conservative Wahhabi heritage, granting the Emir preeminent power. The Emir's role is influenced by continuing traditions of consultation, rule by consensus, and the citizen's right to appeal personally to the Emir. The Emir, while directly accountable to no one, cannot violate the *Shari'a* (Islamic law) and, in practice, must consider the opinions of leading notables and the religious establishment. Their position was institutionalized in the Advisory Council, an appointed body that assists the Emir in formulating policy. There is no electoral system. Political parties are banned.

The influx of expatriate Arabs has introduced ideas that call into question the tenets of Qatar's traditional society, but there has been no serious challenge to Al Thani rule.

In February 1972, the Deputy Ruler and Prime Minister, Sheikh Khalifa bin Hamad, deposed his cousin, Emir Ahmad, and assumed power. This move was supported by the key members of Al Thani and took place without violence or signs of political unrest.

On June 27, 1995, the Deputy Ruler, Sheikh Hamad bin Khalifa, deposed his father Emir Khalifa in a bloodless coup. Emir Hamad and his father reconciled in 1996.

## Principal Government Officials

**For up-to-date information on Principal Government Officials, see the Chiefs of State and Cabinet Members of Foreign Governments section starting on page 1.**

Qatar maintains an embassy in the United States at 4200 Wisconsin Ave. NW, Suite 200, Washington, DC 20016 (tel. 202-274-1600) and expects to open a consulate in Houston in November 1997. Qatar's Permanent Mission to the United Nations is at 747 Third Ave., 22nd floor, New York, NY 10017 (tel. 212-486-9335).

# DEFENSE

Qatar's defense expenditures accounted for approximately 4.2% of GNP in 1993. Qatar maintains a modest military force of approximately 11,800 men, including an army (8,500), navy (1,800) and air force (1,500). In August 1994, Qatar signed a defense agreement with France in which it agreed to purchase several Mirage 2000-5 aircraft. Qatar has also recently signed defense pacts with the U.S. and U.K. Qatar plays an active role in the collective defense efforts of the Gulf Cooperation Coun-

## Travel Notes

**Travel Advice:** For up-to-date information from the U.S. State Department on possible inconvenient or hazardous situations, see the **Travel Warnings and Consular Information Sheets from the U.S. Government** section starting on page 1723. For the latest information on health requirements and conditions, see the **International Travelers' Health Information** section starting on page 1385. For further information dealing with non-urgent matter, see the **Tips for Travelers to...** section starting on page 1588.

cil (the regional organization of the Arab states in the Gulf; the other five members are Saudi Arabia, Kuwait, Bahrain, the UAE, and Oman). Qatari forces played a disproportionately important role in the Gulf War.

# ECONOMY

Oil is the cornerstone of Qatar's economy and accounts for more than 70% of total government revenue. In 1973, oil production and revenues increased sizeably, moving Qatar out of the ranks of the world's poorest countries and providing it with one of the highest per capita incomes. Despite a marked decline in levels of oil production and prices since 1982, Qatar remains a wealthy country.

Qatar's economy was in a downturn from 1982 to 1989. OPEC (Organization of Petroleum Exporting Countries) quotas on crude oil production, the lower price for oil, and the generally unpromising outlook on international markets reduced oil earnings. In turn, the Qatari Government's spending plans had to be cut to match lower income. The resulting recessionary local business climate caused many firms to lay off expatriate staff. With the economy recovering in the 1990s, expatriate populations, particularly from Egypt and South Asia, have grown again.

Oil production will not long return to peak levels of 500,000 barrels per day (b/d), as oil fields are projected to be

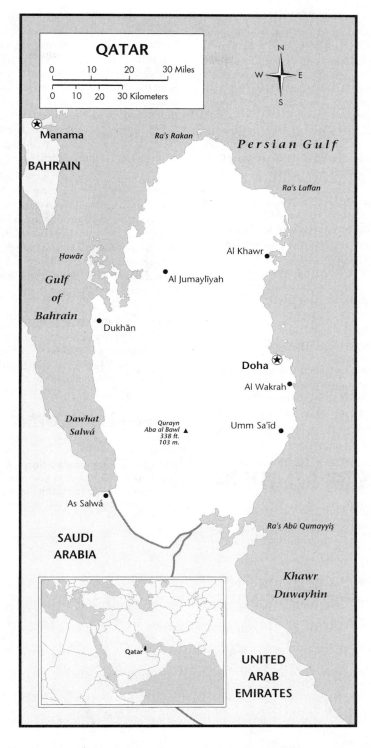

mostly depleted by 2023. Fortunately, large natural gas reserves have been located off Qatar's northeast coast. Qatar's proved reserves of gas are the third-largest in the world, exceeding 7 trillion cubic meters. The economy was boosted in 1991 by completion of the $1.5-billion Phase I of North Field gas development. In 1996, the Qatar-

gas project began exporting liquefied natural gas (LNG) to Japan. Further phases of North Field gas development costing billions of dollars are in various stages of planning and development.

Qatar's heavy industrial projects, all based in Umm Said, include a refinery with a 50,000 b/d capacity, a fertilizer plant for urea and ammonia, a steel plant, and a petrochemical plant. All these industries use gas for fuel. Most are joint ventures between European and Japanese firms and the state-owned Qatar General Petroleum Corporation (QGPC). The U.S. is the major equipment supplier for Qatar's oil and gas industry, and U.S. companies are playing a major role in North Field gas development.

Qatar pursues a vigorous program of "Qatarization," under which all joint venture industries and government departments strive to move Qatari nationals into positions of greater authority. Growing numbers of foreign-educated Qataris, including many educated in the U.S., are returning home to assume key positions formerly occupied by expatriates. In order to control the influx of expatriate workers, Qatar has tightened the administration of its foreign manpower programs over the past several years. Security is the principal basis for Qatar's strict entry and immigration rules and regulations.

# FOREIGN RELATIONS

Qatar achieved full independence in an atmosphere of cooperation with the U.K. and friendship with neighboring states. Most Arab states, the U.K., and the U.S. were among the first countries to recognize Qatar, and the state promptly gained admittance to the United Nations and the Arab League. Qatar established diplomatic relations with the U.S.S.R. and China in 1988. It was an early member of OPEC and a founding member of the GCC, whose rotating presidency it holds until December 1997.

In September 1992 tensions arose with Saudi Arabia when a Qatari border post was allegedly attacked by Saudi forces resulting in two deaths. Relations have since improved and a joint commission has been set up to demarcate the border as agreed between the two governments.

Qatar and Bahrain dispute ownership of the Hawar islands. The case is before the International Court of Justice in The Hague, while Saudi-led mediation efforts continue.

## Principal U.S. Officials

For up-to-date information on Principal U.S. Officials, see the U.S. Embassies, Consulates, and Foreign Service section starting on page 139.

The U.S. Embassy in Qatar is located in Doha at 149 Ahmed bin Ali Street, Fariq bin Omran. Mailing address: P.O. Box 2399, Doha. Telephone: 974-864701/2/3; fax 861669. The embassy is open Saturday through Wednesday (Qatar's workweek), closed for U.S. and Qatari holidays.

# U.S.-QATARI RELATIONS

Bilateral relations are cordial. The U.S. Embassy was opened in March 1973. The first resident U.S. ambassador arrived in July 1974. In the summer of 1986, the then-Minister of Education, Sheikh Mohammed bin Hamad Al Thani, third-ranking official in the government, visited the U.S. as a guest of U.S. Secretary of Education William J. Bennett. In October 1987, Energy Secretary John S. Herrington led a delegation on a visit to Qatar that included calls on the Emir and the Heir Apparent and meetings at the Ministry of Finance and Petroleum. Secretary of Energy Henson Moore led a delegation to Doha in October 1991. The late Secretary of Commerce Ron Brown visited Doha in February 1995, and Secretary of Defense Perry visited in November 1996. More than 400 Qataris study at U.S. universities.

# ROMANIA

July 2000

Official Name:
**Romania**

## PROFILE

### Geography

**Area:** 237,499 sq. km. (91,699 sq. mi.); somewhat smaller than New York and Pennsylvania combined.
**Cities:** Capital—Bucharest (pop. 2.02 million). Other cities—Constanta (344,000), Iasi (350,000), Timisoara (327,000), Cluj-Napoca (334,000), Galati (331,000), Brasov (316,000).
**Terrain:** Consists mainly of rolling, fertile plains; hilly in the eastern regions of the middle Danube basin; and major mountain ranges running north and west in the center of the country, which collectively are known as the Carpathians.
**Climate:** Moderate.

### People

**Nationality:** Noun and adjective—Romanian(s).
**Population:** 22.5 million (est.).
**Annual population growth rate:** -2.7%
**Ethnic Groups:** Romanians 89%, Hungarians 7.1%, Germans 0.5%, Ukrainians, Serbs, Croats, Russians, Turks, and Gypsies 2.5%.
**Religion:** Orthodox 86.8%, Roman Catholic 5%, Reformed Protestant, Baptist, and Pentecostal 5%, Greek Catholic (Uniate) 1%, Jewish less

than 0.1%.
**Languages:** Romanian (official). Other languages—Hungarian, German.
**Education:** Years compulsory—10. Attendance—98%. Literacy—98%.
**Health:** Infant mortality rate (1998 est.)—22/1,000. Life expectancy—men 69.5 yrs., women 73.9 yrs.
**Work force:** (9 million) Agriculture—42.3%. Industry and commerce—38%. Other—34%.

### Government

**Type:** Republic.
**Constitution:** November 21, 1991.
**Branches:** Executive—president (head of state), prime minister (head of government), Council of Ministers. Legislative—bicameral Parliament. Judicial—Constitutional Court, Supreme Court, and lower courts.
**Subdivisions:** 40 counties plus the city of Bucharest.
**Political parties:** Political parties recognized as such with members in Parliament include the Party of Social Democracy of Romania (PDSR); Democratic Convention of Romania (CDR), a coalition of the National Peasant-Christian Democrat Party (PNTCD); the National Liberal Party (PNL); the Democratic Party (PD); the Hungarian Democratic Union of Romania (UDMR); Social Democrat Party (PSDR); Social Democratic Party (PSDR); the

Party of Romanian National Unity (PUNR); and the Greater Romania Party (PRM). There are a number of other political parties, some with members in Parliament, which are officially designated as Independents in Parliament. These smaller political parties include the Alternative Party (APR), the Union of Right Wing Forces (UFD), and the National Party of Romania (PNR).
**Suffrage:** Universal from age 18.
**Defense:** 1.8% of GDP.

### Economy

**GDP:** 1997, $32.1 billion; 1998, $38.2 billion.
**Annual GDP growth rate:** 1997, 6.6%; 1998; 7.3%, 1999 est., 4.5%.
**Per Capita GDP:** 1998, $1,695.6; 1999 est., $1,328.8.
**Natural resources:** Oil, timber, natural gas, coal, salt, iron ore.
**Agriculture:** (1998) 16.4% of GDP. Products—corn, wheat, potatoes, oilseeds, vegetables, livestock.
**Industry:** (1998) 40.1%: Types—machine building, mining, construction materials, metal production and processing, chemicals, food processing, textiles, clothing.
**Services:** (1998) 43.4%.
**Trade:** (1998) Exports—$8.3 billion: textiles, chemicals, light manufactures, wood products, fuels, processed metals. Major markets—Germany, Italy, France, and Turkey. Imports—$11.8 billion: Imports—fuel, cooking

coal, iron ore, machinery, wheat, cotton, and potatoes. Major suppliers—Italy, Germany, Russia, France, and U.K.

**Exchange rate:** (January 2000) 18,288 lei=US$1.

# GEOGRAPHY

Extending inland halfway across the Balkan Peninsula and covering a large elliptical area of 237,499 square kilometers (91,699 sq. mi.), Romania occupies the greater part of the lower basin of the Danube River system and the hilly eastern regions of the middle Danube basin. It lies on either side of the mountain systems collectively known as the Carpathians, which form the natural barrier between the two Danube basins.

Romania's location gives it a continental climate, particularly in the Old Kingdom (east of the Carpathians and south of the Transylvanian Alps) and to a lesser extent in Transylvania, where the climate is more moderate. A long and at times severe winter (December-March), a hot summer (April-July), and a prolonged autumn (August-November) are the principal seasons, with a rapid transition from spring to summer. In Bucharest, the daily minimum temperature in January averages -7°C (20°F), and the daily maximum temperature in July averages 29°C (85°F).

# PEOPLE

About 89% of the people are ethnic Romanians, a group that—in contrast to its Slav or Hungarian neighbors—traces itself to Latin-speaking Romans, who in the second and third centuries A.D. conquered and settled among the ancient Dacians, a Thracian people. As a result, the Romanian language, although containing elements of Slavic, Turkish, and other languages, is a romance language related to French and Italian.

Primarily a rural, agricultural population, the medieval Wallachians and Moldavians maintained their language and culture despite centuries of rule by foreign princes. Once independent, the population of the unified Romanian state took their modern name to emphasize their connection with the ancient Romans.

Hungarians and Gypsies are the principal minorities, with a declining German population and smaller numbers of Serbs, Croats, Ukrainians, Greeks, Turks, Armenians, Great Russians, and others. Minority populations are greatest in Transylvania and the Banat, areas in the north and west, which belonged to the Austro-Hungarian Empire until World War I. Even before union with Romania, ethnic Romanians comprised the overall majority in Transylvania. However, ethnic Hungarians and Germans were the dominant urban population until relatively recently, and still are the majority in a few districts.

Before World War II, minorities represented more than 28% of the total population. During the war that percentage was halved, largely by the loss of the border areas of Bessarabia and northern Bukovina (to the former Soviet Union—now Moldova and Ukraine) and southern Dobrudja (to Bulgaria), as well as by the postwar flight or deportation of ethnic Germans.

Though Romanian troops participated in the destruction of the Jewish communities of Bessarabia and Bukovina, most Jews from Romania properly survived the Holocaust. Mass emigration, mostly to Israel, has reduced the surviving Jewish community from over 300,000 to less than 15,000. In recent years, more than two-thirds of the ethnic Germans in Romania have emigrated to Germany.

Religious affiliation tends to follow ethnic lines, with most ethnic Romanians identifying with the Romanian Orthodox Church. The Greek Catholic or Uniate church, reunified with the Orthodox Church by fiat in 1948, was restored after the 1989 revolution. The 1992 census indicates that 1% of the population is Greek Catholic, as opposed to about 10% prior to 1948. Roman Catholics, largely ethnic Hungarians and Germans, constitute about 5% of the population; Calvinists, Baptists, Pentecostals, and Lutherans make up another 5%. There are smaller numbers of Unitarians, Muslims, and other religions.

Romania's rich cultural traditions have been nourished by many sources, some of which predate the Roman occupation. The traditional folk arts, including dance, wood carving, ceramics, weaving and embroidery of costumes and household decorations, and fascinating folk music, still flourish in many parts of the country. Despite strong Austrian, German, and especially French influence, many of Romania's great artists, such as the painter Nicolae Grigorescu, the poet Mihai Eminescu, the composer George Enescu, and the sculptor Constantin Brancusi, drew their inspiration from Romanian folk traditions.

The country's many Orthodox monasteries, as well as the Transylvanian Catholic and Evangelical Churches, some of which date back to the 13th century, are repositories of artistic treasures. The famous painted monasteries of Bukovina make an important contribution to European architecture.

Poetry and the theater play an important role in contemporary Romanian life. Classic Romanian plays, such as those of Ion Luca Caragiale, as well as works by modern or avant-garde Romanian and international playwrights, find sophisticated and enthusiastic audiences in the many theaters of the capital and of the smaller cities.

# HISTORY

From about 200 B.C., when it was settled by the Dacians, a Thracian tribe, Romania has been on the path of a series of migrations and conquests. Under the emperor Trajan early in the second century A.D., Dacia was incorporated into the Roman Empire, but was abandoned by a declining

ROMANIA

| | | |
|---|---|---|
| 0 | 50 | 100 Miles |
| 0 | 50 | 100 Kilometers |

Rome less than two centuries later. Romania disappeared from recorded history for hundreds of years, to reemerge in the medieval period as the Principalities of Moldavia and Wallachia. Heavily taxed and badly administered under the Ottoman Empire, the two Principalities were unified under a single native prince in 1859, and had their full independence ratified in the 1878 Treaty of Berlin. A German prince, Carol of Hohenzollern, was crowned first King of Romania in 1881.

The new state, squeezed between the Ottoman, Austro-Hungarian, and Russian empires, with Slav neighbors on three sides, looked to the West,

particularly France, for its cultural, educational, and administrative models. Romania was an ally of the Entente and the U.S. in World War I, and was granted substantial territories with Romanian populations, notably Transylvania, Bessarabia, and Bukovina, after the war.

Most of Romania's pre-World War II governments maintained the forms, but not the substance, of a liberal constitutional monarchy. The quasi-mystical fascist Iron Guard movement, exploiting nationalism, fear of communism, and resentment of alleged foreign and Jewish domination of the economy, was a key factor in the creation of a dictatorship in 1938. In

1940-41, the authoritarian General Antonescu took control. Romania entered World War II on the side of the Axis Powers in June 1941, invading the Soviet Union to recover Bessarabia and Bukovina, which had been annexed in 1940.

In August 1944, a coup led by King Michael, with support from opposition politicians and the army, deposed the Antonescu dictatorship and put Romania's battered armies on the side of the Allies. Romania incurred additional heavy casualties fighting the Germans in Transylvania, Hungary, and Czechoslovakia.

The peace treaty, signed at Paris on February 10, 1947, confirmed the Soviet annexation of Bessarabia and northern Bukovina, but restored the part of northern Transylvania granted to Hungary in 1940 by Hitler. The treaty required massive war reparations by Romania to the Soviet Union, whose occupying forces left in 1958.

The Soviets pressed for inclusion of Romania's heretofore negligible Communist Party in the post-war government, while non-communist political leaders were steadily eliminated from political life. King Michael abdicated under pressure in December 1947, when the Romanian People's Republic was declared, and went into exile.

In the early 1960s, Romania's communist government began to assert some independence from the Soviet Union. Nicolae Ceausescu became head of the Communist Party in 1965 and head of state in 1967. Ceausescu's denunciation of the 1968 Soviet invasion of Czechoslovakia and a brief relaxation in internal repression helped give him a positive image both at home and in the West. Seduced by Ceausescu's "independent" foreign policy, Western leaders were slow to turn against a regime that, by the late 1970s, had become increasingly harsh, arbitrary, and capricious. Rapid economic growth fueled by foreign credits gradually gave way to wrenching austerity and severe political repression.

After the collapse of communism in the rest of Eastern Europe in the late summer and fall of 1989, a mid-December protest in Timisoara against the forced relocation of a Hungarian minister grew into a country-wide protest against the Ceausescu regime, sweeping the dictator from power. Ceausescu and his wife were executed on December 25, 1989, after a cursory military trial. About 1,500 people were killed in confused street fighting. An impromptu governing coalition, the National Salvation Front (FSN), installed itself and proclaimed the restoration of democracy and freedom. The Communist Party was outlawed, and Ceausescu's most unpopular measures, such as

bans on abortion and contraception, were repealed.

Ion Iliescu, a former Communist Party official demoted by Ceausescu in the 1970s, emerged as the leader of the NSF. Presidential and parliamentary elections were held on May 20, 1990. Running against representatives of the pre-war National Peasants' Party and National Liberal Party, Iliescu won 85% of the vote. The NSF captured two-thirds of the seats in Parliament, named a university professor, Petre Roman, as Prime Minister, and began cautious free market reforms.

The new government made a crucial early misstep. Unhappy at the continued political and economic influence of members of the Ceausescu-era elite, anti-Communist protesters camped in University Square in April 1990. When miners from the Jiu Valley descended on Bucharest two months later and brutally dispersed the remaining "hooligans," President Iliescu expressed public thanks, thus convincing many that the government had sponsored the miners' actions. The miners also attacked the headquarters and houses of opposition leaders. The Roman Government fell in late September 1991, when the miners returned to Bucharest to demand higher salaries and better living conditions. A technocrat, Theodor Stolojan, was appointed to head an interim government until new elections could be held.

Parliament drafted a new democratic constitution, approved by popular referendum in December 1991. The FSN split into two groups, led by Ion Iliescu (FDSN) and Petre Roman (FSN) in March 1992; Roman's party subsequently adopted the name Democratic Party (PD). National elections in September 1992 returned President Iliescu by a clear majority, and gave his party, the FDSN, a plurality. With parliamentary support from the nationalist PUNR and PRM parties, and the ex-communist PSM party, a technocratic government was formed in November 1992 under Prime Minister Nicolae Vacaroiu, an economist. The FDSN became the Party of Social Democracy of Romania (PDSR) in

July 1993. The Vacaroiu government ruled in coalition with three smaller parties, all of which abandoned the coalition by the time of the November 1996 elections. Emil Constantinescu of the Democratic Convention (CDR) electoral coalition defeated President Iliescu in the second round of voting by 9% and replaced him as chief of state. The PDSR won the largest number of seats in Parliament, but the constituent parties of the CDR joined the Democratic Party, the National Liberal Party, and the Hungarian Democratic Union of Romania (UDMR) to form a centrist coalition government, holding 60% of the seats in Parliament. Victor Ciorbea was named Prime Minister. Ciorba remained in office until March 1998, when he was replaced by Radu Vasile (PNTCD).

# GOVERNMENT

Romania's 1991 constitution proclaims Romania a democracy and market economy, in which human dignity, civic rights and freedoms, the unhindered development of human personality, justice, and political pluralism are supreme and guaranteed values. The constitution directs the state to implement free trade, protect the principle of competition, and provide a favorable framework for production. The constitution provides for a President, a Parliament, a Constitutional Court and a separate system of lower courts that includes a Supreme Court.

The two-chamber Parliament, consisting of the Chamber of Deputies and the Senate, is the law-making authority. Deputies and senators are elected for 4-year terms by universal suffrage.

The president is elected by popular vote for a maximum of two 4-year terms. He is the Chief of State, charged with safeguarding the constitution, foreign affairs, and the proper functioning of public authorities. He is supreme commander of the armed forces and chairman of the Supreme Defense Council. According to the constitution, he acts as mediator among the power centers within the state, as well as between the state and society. The president nominates the prime minister, who in turn appoints the government, which must be confirmed by a vote of confidence from Parliament.

The Constitutional Court adjudicates the constitutionality of challenged laws, and decides on appeals from the regular court system concerning the unconstitutionality of laws and decrees. The court consists of nine judges, appointed for a term of 9 years. Three judges are appointed by the Chamber of Deputies, three by the Senate, and three by the president of Romania.

The Romanian legal system is based on the Napoleonic Code. The judiciary is to be independent, and judges appointed by the president are not removable. The president and other judges of the Supreme Court are appointed for a term of 6 years and may serve consecutive terms. Proceedings are public, except in special circumstances provided for by law.

The Ministry of Justice represents "the general interests of society" and defends the legal order as well as citizens' rights and freedoms. The ministry is to discharge its powers through independent, impartial public prosecutors.

For territorial and administrative purposes, Romania is divided into 40 counties and the city of Bucharest. Each county is governed by an elected county council. Local councils and elected mayors are the public administration authorities in villages and towns. The county council is the public administration authority that coordinates the activities of all village and town councils in a county.

The central government appoints a prefect for each county and Bucharest municipality. The prefect is the representative of the government at the local level and directs any public services of the ministries and other central agencies at the county level. A prefect may block the action of a local authority if he deems it unlawful or

unconstitutional. The matter is then decided by an administrative court.

Under new legislation in force since January 1999, local councils have control over spending of their allocations from the central government budget as well as authority to raise additional revenue locally. Central government-appointed prefects formerly significant authority over the budget is limited to a review of expenditures to ascertain their constitutionality.

## Principal Government Officials

For up-to-date information on Principal Government Officials, see the Chiefs of State and Cabinet Members of Foreign Governments section starting on page 1.

Romania maintains an embassy in the United States at 1607 23rd St., NW, Washington, DC 20008 (tel. 202-332-4846).

# POLITICAL CONDITIONS

Romania has made great progress in institutionalizing democratic principles, civil liberties, and respect for human rights since the revolution. Nevertheless, the legacy of 44 years of communist rule cannot quickly be eliminated. Membership in the Romanian Communist Party was usually the prerequisite for higher education, foreign travel, or a good job, while the extensive internal security apparatus subverted normal social and political relations. To the few active dissidents, who suffered gravely under Ceausescu, most of those who came forward as politicians after the revolution seemed tainted by cooperation with the previous regime.

Over 200 new political parties sprang up after 1989, gravitating around

personalities rather than programs. All major parties espoused democracy and market reforms, but the governing National Salvation Front proposed slower, more cautious economic reforms and a social safety net. In contrast, the opposition's main parties, the National Liberal Party (PNL), and the National Peasant-Christian Democrat Party (PNTCD) favored quick, sweeping reforms, immediate privatization, and reducing the role of the ex-communist elite. There is no law banning communist parties (the Communist Party ceased to exist).

In the 1990 general elections, the FSN and its candidate for presidency, Ion Iliescu, have won with a large majority of the votes (66.31% and, respectively 85.07%). The strongest parties in opposition were the Democratic Alliance of Hungarians in Romania (UDMR), with 7.23%, and the PNL, with 6.41%.

Following the FSN Prime Minister Petre Roman's brutal sacking (due to the miners' descent on Bucharest late 1991), few months before the 1992 general elections, the FSN broke in two. President Iliescu's followers have formed a new party called the Democratic Front of National Salvation (FDSN), while Roman's supporters have kept the party's original title, FSN.

The 1992 local and national elections revealed a political cleavage between major urban centers and the countryside. Rural voters, who were grateful for the restoration of most agricultural land to farmers but fearful of change, strongly favored President Ion Iliescu and the FDSN, while the urban electorate favored the CDR (a coalition made up by several parties—among which the PNTCD and the PNL were the strongest—and civic organizations) and quicker reform. Iliescu easily won reelection over a field of five other candidates. The FDSN won a plurality in both chambers of Parliament. With the CDR, the second-largest parliamentary group, reluctant to take part in a national unity coalition, the FDSN (now PDSR) formed a government under Prime Minister Nicolae Vacaroiu, an economist, with parliamentary support from the PUNR, PRM, and PSM. In January 1994, the stability of the governing coalition became problematic when the PUNR threatened to withdraw its support unless given cabinet portfolios. In August 1994, two members of the nationalist PUNR received cabinet portfolios in the Vacaroiu government. In September, the incumbent justice minister announced that he had become a PUNR member. PRM and PSM left the government in October and December 1995, respectively.

The 1996 local elections realized a major shift in the political orientation of the Romanian electorate. Opposition parties swept Bucharest and most of the larger cities in Transylvania and Dobrogea. This trend continued in the national elections, where the opposition dominated the cities and made steep inroads into rural areas theretofore dominated by President Iliescu and the PDSR, which have lost many voters in their traditional stronghold constituency outside Transylvania. The campaign of the opposition hammered away on the twin themes of the need to squelch corruption and to launch economic reform. The message resonated with the electorate, which swept Constantinescu and parties allied to him to power in free and fair elections. The coalition government formed in December 1996 took the historic step of inviting the UDMR and its Hungarian ethnic backers into government. Since its victory, the coalition has had three prime ministers. Despite these leadership changes, and constant internal frictions, the governing parties have managed to preserve their coalition.

Romania has made great progress in consolidating democratic institutions. The press is free and outspoken. Independent radio networks have proliferated, and a private television network now operates nationwide. The reorganized and security services have a much reduced role in civil society, but still maintain sole control over the secret police files of the former Communist regime.

# ECONOMY

Romania is a country of considerable potential: rich agricultural lands; diverse energy sources (coal, oil, natural gas, hydro, and nuclear); a substantial, if aging, industrial base encompassing almost the full range of manufacturing activities; an intelligent, well-trained work force; and opportunities for expanded development in tourism on the Black Sea and in the mountains.

In 1993, the economy reached the end of a decline in output that had begun well before the 1989 revolution. The Romanian Government had borrowed heavily from the West in the 1970s to build a massive state-owned industrial base. Following the 1979 oil price shock and a debt rescheduling in 1981, Ceausescu decreed that Romania would no longer be subject to foreign creditors. By the end of 1989, Romania had paid off a foreign debt of about $10.5 billion through an unprecedented effort that wreaked havoc on the economy. Vital imports were slashed, and food and fuel strictly rationed, while the government exported everything it could to earn hard currency. With investment slashed, Romania's technological infrastructure rapidly fell behind that of even its Balkan neighbors.

Since the fall of the Ceausescu regime in 1989, successive governments have sought to build a Western-style market economy. The pace of restructuring has been slow, but by 1994 the legal basis for a market economy was largely in place. After the 1996 elections, the coalition government attempted to move rapidly and eliminate consumer subsidies, float prices, liberalize exchange rates, and put in place a tight monetary policy. The Parliament has enacted laws permitting foreign entities incorporated in Romania to purchase land and has identified a large number of government enterprises for rapid privatization or restructuring. Foreign capital investment in Romania has been decreasing and is significantly less than in some other Central European countries.

Privatization of industry was pursued with the transfer in 1992 of 30% of the shares of some 6,000 state-owned enterprises to five private ownership funds, in which each adult citizen received certificates of ownership. The remaining 70% ownership of the enterprises was transferred to a state ownership fund, with a mandate to sell off its shares at the rate of at least 10% per year. The privatization law also called for direct sale of some 30 specially selected enterprises and the sale of "assets" (i.e., commercially viable component units) of larger enterprises.

Subsidies to loss-making state-owned enterprises continue to be a serious drain on the state budget. Despite delays in privatizing certain large companies, the State Ownership Fund has made progress. Altogether, the private sector now accounts for an estimated 55% of GDP and employs approximately 52% of the work force.

The return of collectivized farmland to its cultivators, one of the first initiatives of the post-December 1989 revolution government, resulted in a short-term decrease in agricultural production. Some four million small parcels representing 80% of the arable surface were returned to original owners or their heirs. Many of the recipients were elderly or city dwellers, and the slow progress of granting formal land titles was an obstacle to leasing or selling land to active farmers.

An acute shortage of foreign exchange and a poorly developed financial sector have also been obstacles to rapid economic transition. Outside factors such as the collapse of trade with Soviet bloc trading partners, economic slowdown in the industrialized West, increases in imported energy costs, and large losses from UN sanctions against Iraq and the Former Republic of Yugoslavia, contributed to a precipitous drop in industrial output after 1989. The fact that the Danube River remains blocked from the Kosovo conflict denies Romania an important transportation route for its goods and has further hampered economic recovery.

In 1993, Romania embarked upon an adjustment program that showed some results. GDP, which had fallen for three consecutive years, stabilized in 1993 and registered 3.4% growth in 1994, 6.9% in 1995, and 4% in 1996. Since 1997, there has again been a decline in GDP of -6.6% in 1997, -7.3% in 1998, and (est.) -4.5% in 1999. Monthly retail price inflation, which averaged 12.1% in 1993 (the equivalent of 256% annually), declined to 28% in 1995. However, inflation picked up again in 1996 and 1997 due to excessive government spending in late 1996, and price and exchange rate liberalization in early 1997. Inflation in 1999 hovered around 50%. The government has committed itself to reduce the inflation rate by half in 2000.

Subsidies on most basic consumer goods were lifted in May 1993, but support for underproductive and loss-making state-owned industries continues to be a serious drain on the budget. The government nonetheless managed to cut the deficit, which totaled almost 4% of GDP in 1992, to only 1.7% in 1993. By 1995, however, the budget deficit had again risen to about 4% of GDP. The consolidated deficit, including internal arrearages, climbed to more than 10% of GDP in 1996.

Financial and technical assistance continue to flow in from the U.S., European Union, other industrial nations, and international financial institutions facilitating Romania's reintegration into the world economy. The International Monetary Fund (IMF), World Bank (IBRD), the European Bank for Reconstruction and Development (EBRD), and the U.S. Agency for International Development (USAID) all have programs and resident representatives in Romania. Romania has also attracted foreign direct investment, which in 1997 rose to $2.5 billion.

Romania was the largest U.S. trading partner in Eastern Europe until Ceausescu's 1988 renunciation of Most Favored Nation (non-discriminatory) trading status resulted in high U.S. tariffs on Romanian products. Congress approved restoration of MFN status effective November 8, 1993, as part of a new bilateral trade agreement. Tariffs on most Romanian products dropped to zero in February 1994 with the inclusion of Romania in the Generalized System of Preferences (GSP). Major Romanian exports to the U.S. include shoes and clothing, steel, and chemicals. Romania signed an Association Agreement with the EU in 1992 and a free trade agreement with the European Free Trade Association (EFTA) in 1993, codifying Romania's access to European markets and creating the basic framework for further economic integration. At its Helsinki Summit in December 1999, the European Union invited Romania to formally begin accession negotiations.

# FOREIGN RELATIONS

Since December 1989, Romania has actively pursued a policy of strengthening relations with the West in general, more specifically with the U.S. and the European Union. Romania was a helpful partner to the allied forces during the Gulf war, particularly during its service as president of the UN Security Council. Romania has been active in peacekeeping operations in UNAVEM in Angola, IFOR/SFOR in Bosnia, and in Albania.

Romania diligently enforces United Nations' sanctions against the Former Republic of Yugoslavia (FRY). Despite divisions within the Parliament and among the people, Romania supported NATO in the Kosovo campaign and granted approval for NATO to overfly Romanian airspace. While Romania does not belong to any military alliance, it is a member of the Organization for Security and Cooperation in Europe (OSCE) and the North Atlantic Cooperation Council (NACC), and was the first country to enroll in the NATO Partnership for Peace program.

In 1996, Romania signed and ratified a basic bilateral treaty with Hungary that settled outstanding contentions and laid the foundation for closer, more cooperative relations. In June 1997, Romania signed a bilateral treaty with Ukraine that resolved territorial and minority issues, among others.

Romania has been actively involved in regional organizations, such as the Southeast Europe Cooperation Initiative (SECI) and the Stability Pact for Southeast Europe, and has been a positive force in supporting stability and cooperation in the area.

Romania maintains good diplomatic relations with Israel and was supportive of the Middle East peace negotiations initiated after the Gulf conflict in 1991. Romania also is a founding member of the Black Sea Consortium for Economic Development. It joined the International Monetary Fund and the World Bank in 1972, and is a member of the World Trade Organization.

Romanian Missions in the United States:

Embassy of Romania
1607 23rd Street NW
Washington, DC 20008
Tel. 202-332-4846

Romanian Mission to the UN
573 Third Avenue

New York, NY 10016
Tel. 212-682-3273

Romanian National Tourist Office
573 Third Avenue
New York, NW 10016
Tel. 212-697-6971

Romanian Cultural Center
200 E. 38th Street
New York, NY 10016
Tel. 212-687-0180

# DEFENSE

In accordance with the December 1991 Romanian constitution, the Romanian armed forces have the defensive mission of ensuring the territorial integrity of the country. The military enjoys popular support, largely because of its role in supporting the December 1989 revolution. The army is the largest service. Total armed forces strength is currently at 180,000, and is maintained through conscription. The Romanian Parliament has approved a plan to decrease the size of the armed forces from the current 180,000 to 112,000 by 2004. In 1993, the U.S. military began limited training of Romanian military and civilian officials through IMET and other exchange programs, emphasizing civilian democratic control over the military. The Romanian Government has expressed a strong desire to join NATO and has seriously focused on the NATO Membership Action Plan (MAP) to prepare itself for membership.

# U.S.-ROMANIAN RELATIONS

Cold during the early post-war period, U.S. bilateral relations with Romania began to improve in the early 1960s with the signing of an agreement providing for partial settlement of American property claims. Cultural, scientific, and educational exchanges were initiated, and in 1964 the legations of both nations were promoted to full embassies.

Responding to Ceausescu's cautious distancing of Romania from Soviet foreign policy, particularly continued diplomatic relations with Israel and denunciation of the 1968 Soviet intervention in Czechoslovakia, President Nixon paid an official visit to Romania in August 1969. Despite political differences, high-level contacts continued between U.S. and Romanian leaders throughout the decade of the 1970s, culminating in the 1978 state visit to Washington by President and Mrs. Ceausescu.

In 1972, a consular convention to facilitate protection of citizens and their property in both countries was signed. Overseas Private Investment Corporation (OPIC) facilities were granted, and Romania became eligible for U.S. Export-Import Bank credits.

A trade agreement signed in April 1975 accorded Most Favored Nation (MFN) status to Romania under section 402 of the Trade Reform Act of 1974 (the Jackson-Vanik amendment that links MFN to a country's performance on emigration.) This status was renewed yearly after Congressional review of a presidential determination that Romania was making progress toward freedom of emigration. Subsequently, the two countries signed a long-term agreement on economic, industrial, and technical cooperation.

In the mid-1980s, criticism of Romania's deteriorating human rights record, particularly allegations of mistreatment of religious and ethnic minorities, spurred attempts by Congress to withdraw MFN status. In 1988, to preempt Congressional action, Ceausescu renounced MFN treatment, calling Jackson-Vanik and other human rights requirements unacceptable interference in Romanian sovereignty.

After welcoming the revolution of December 1989 with a brief visit by Secretary of State Baker in February 1990, the U.S. Government expressed concern that opposition parties had faced discriminatory treatment in the May 1990 elections, when the National Salvation Front won a sweeping victory. The slow progress of subsequent political and economic reform increased that concern, and relations with Romania cooled sharply after the June 1990 intervention of the miners in University Square.

Anxious to cultivate better relations with the U.S. and Europe, and disappointed at the poor results from its gradualist economic reform strategy, the Stolojan government undertook some economic reforms and conducted free and fair parliamentary and presidential elections in September 1992. Encouraged by the conduct of local elections in February 1992, Deputy Secretary of State Lawrence Eagleburger paid a visit in May 1992. Congress voted down a 1992 attempt to restore MFN status, but restored MFN in November 1993 in recognition of Romania's progress in institut-

ing political and economic reform. In 1996, the U.S. Congress voted to extend permanent MFN graduation to Romania.

As Romania's policies have become unequivocally pro-Western, the United States has moved to deepen relations. President Clinton visited Bucharest in 1997 and announced a strategic partnership between the U.S. and Romania, through which the two countries could strengthen bilateral relations and deepen cooperation on shared goals in economic and political development, regional security, defense reform, and non-traditional threats (such as trans-border crime and non-proliferation).

The United States maintains Agency for International Development (USAID) and Peace Corps missions in Bucharest, and provides humanitar-

ian, economic, and technical assistance to help Romania in its transition to democracy and a market economy.

## Principal U.S. Officials

**For up-to-date information on Principal U.S. Officials, see the U.S. Embassies, Consulates, and Foreign Service section starting on page 139.**

The U.S. embassy in Romania is located at Strada Tudor Arghezi 7-9, Bucharest (tel. 40-1 210-4042, fax 40-1 210-0395, consular fax 211-3360). A U.S. embassy Branch Office was opened in Cluj-Napoca in January 1994 (tel. 40-64 19-38-15, fax 40-64-19-38-68).

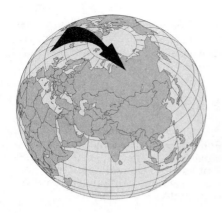

# RUSSIA

May 2000

Official Name:
**Russian Federation**

## PROFILE

### Geography

**Area:** 17 million sq. km. (6.5 million sq. mi.); about 1.8 times the size of the U.S.
**Cities:** Capital—Moscow (pop. 9 million). Other cities—St. Petersburg (5 million), Novosibirsk (1.4 million), Nizhniy Novgorod (1.3 million).
**Terrain:** Broad plain with low hills west of Urals; vast coniferous forest and tundra in Siberia; uplands and mountains (Caucasus range) along southern borders.
**Climate:** Northern continental, from subarctic to subtropical.

### People

**Nationality:** Noun and adjective—Russian(s).
**Population:** (1997 est.) 147.5 million.
**Annual growth rate:** Negative.
**Ethnic Groups:** Russian 81%, Tatar 4%, Ukrainian 3%, other 12%.
**Religion:** Russian Orthodox, Islam, Judaism, Roman Catholicism, Protestant, Buddhist, other.
**Language:** Russian (official); more than 140 other languages and dialects.
**Education:** (total pop.) Literacy—98%.
**Health:** Life expectancy—(1996) 58 yrs. men, 72 yrs. women.
**Work force:** (85 million) Production and economic services—84%. Government—16%.

### Government

**Type:** Federation.
**Independence:** August 24, 1991.
**Constitution:** December 12, 1993.
**Branches:** Executive—president, prime minister (chairman of the government). Legislative—Federal Assembly (Federation Council, State Duma). Judicial—Constitutional Court, Supreme Court, Supreme Court of Arbitration, Office of Procurator General.
**Political parties:** Shifting. The 1999 elections were contested by Conservative Movement of Russia, Russian All-Peoples Union, Women of Russia, Stalin Bloc-For the USSR, Yabloko, Working Russia, Peace-Labor-May, Bloc of Nikolayev and Federov, Spiritual Heritage, Congress of Russian Communities, Peace and Unity Party, Party for the Protection of Women, Unity Interregional Movement, Social Democrats, Movement in Support of the Army, Zhirinovskiy's Bloc, For Civic Dignity, Fatherland-All Russia, Communist Party, Russian Cause, All-Russian Political Party of the People, Union of Right Forces, Our Home is Russia, Socialist Party of Russia, Party of Pensioners and the Russian Socialist Party.
**Subdivisions:** 21 autonomous republics and 68 autonomous territories and regions.
**Suffrage:** Universal at 18 years.

### Economy

**Year:** 1999.
**GDP:** $183 billion.
**Growth rate:** 3.2%.
**Per capita GDP:** (exchange rate method) $1,241.
**Natural resources:** Petroleum, natural gas, timber, furs, precious and nonferrous metals.
**Agriculture:** Grain, sugarbeets, sunflower seeds, meat, dairy products.
**Industry:** Complete range of manufactures: automobiles, trucks, trains, agricultural equipment, advanced aircraft, aerospace, machine and equipment products; mining and extractive industry; medical and scientific instruments; construction equipment.
**Trade:** Exports (f.o.b.), $74 billion: petroleum and petroleum products, natural gas, woods and wood products, metals, chemicals. Major markets—EU, NIS, China, Japan. Imports (c.i.f.), $41 billion: machinery and equipment, chemicals, consumer goods, medicines, meat, sugar, semi-finished metal products. Major partners—EU, U.S., NIS, Japan, China. Principal U.S. exports ($1.85 billion)—meat, machinery, tobacco. Principal U.S. imports ($5.81 bil-

Background Notes

lion)—aluminum, precious stones and metals, iron, and steel.

# PEOPLE

Russia's area is about 17 million sq. km. (6.5 million sq. mi.). It remains the largest country in the world by more than 2.5 million sq. mi. Its population density is about 23 persons per square mile (9 per sq. km.), making it one of the most sparsely populated countries in the world. Its population is predominantly urban.

Most of the roughly 150 million Russians derive from the Eastern Slavic family of peoples, whose original homeland was probably present-day Poland. Russian is the official language of Russia, and an official language in the United Nations. As the language of writers such as Tolstoy, Dostoevsky, Chekov, Pushkin, and Solzhenitsyn, it has great importance in world literature.

Russia's educational system has produced nearly 100% literacy. About 3 million students attend Russia's 519 institutions of higher education and 48 universities. As a result of great emphasis on science and technology in education, Russian medical, mathematical, scientific, and space and aviation research is generally of a high order. The number of doctors in relation to the population is high by American standards, although medical care in Russia, even in major cities, is far below Western standards.

The Russian labor force is undergoing tremendous changes. Although well-educated and skilled, it is largely mismatched to the rapidly changing needs of the Russian economy. Millions of Russian workers are under-employed. Unemployment is highest among women and young people. Many Russian workers compensate by working other part-time jobs. Following the collapse of the Soviet Union and the economic dislocation it engendered, the standard of living fell dramatically, and one third of the population lives on just over $1 a day.

Moscow is the largest city (population 9 million) and is the capital of the Federation. Moscow continues to be the center of Russian Government and is increasingly important as an economic and business center. Its cultural tradition is rich, and there are many museums devoted to art, literature, music, dance, history, and science. It has hundreds of churches and dozens of notable cathedrals; it has become Russia's principal magnet for foreign investment and business presence.

St. Petersburg, established in 1703 by Peter the Great as the capital of the Russian Empire, was called Petrograd during World War I, and Leningrad after 1924. In 1991, as the result of a city referendum, it was renamed St. Petersburg. Under the Tsars, the city was Russia's cultural, intellectual, commercial, financial and industrial center. After the capital was moved back to Moscow in 1918, the city's political significance declined, but it remained a cultural, scientific and military-industrial center. The Hermitage is one of the world's great fine arts museums. Finally, Vladivostok, located in the Russian Far East, is becoming an important center for trade with the Pacific Rim countries.

# HISTORY

Human experience on the territory of present-day Russia dates back to Paleolithic times. Greek traders conducted extensive commerce with Scythian tribes around the shores of the Black Sea and the Crimean region. In the third century B.C., Scythians were displaced by Sarmatians, who in turn were overrun by waves of Germanic Goths. In the third century A.D., Asiatic Huns replaced the Goths and were in turn conquered by Turkic Avars in the sixth century. By the ninth century, Eastern Slavs began to settle in what is now Ukraine, Belarus and the Novgorod and Smolensk regions.

In 862, the political entity known as Kievan Rus was established in what is now Ukraine and lasted until the 12th century. In the 10th century, Christianity became the state religion under Vladimir, who adopted Greek Orthodox rites. Consequently, Byzantine culture predominated, as is evident in much of Russia's architectural, musical, and artistic heritage. Over the next centuries, various invaders assaulted the Kievan state and, finally, Mongols under Batu Khan destroyed the main population centers except for Novgorod and Pskov and prevailed over the region until 1480.

In the post-Mongol period, Muscovy gradually became the dominant principality and was able, through diplomacy and conquest, to establish suzerainty over European Russia. Ivan III (1462-1505) was able to refer to his empire as the "Third Rome" and heir to the Byzantine tradition, and a century later the Romanov dynasty was established under Tsar Mikhail in 1613.

During Peter the Great's reign (1689-1725), Russia began modernizing, and European influences spread in Russia. Peter created Western-style military forces, subordinated the Russian Orthodox Church hierarchy to the Tsar, reformed the entire governmental structure, and established the beginnings of a Western-style education system. His introduction of European customs generated nationalistic resentments in society and spawned the philosophical rivalry between "Westernizers" and nationalistic "Slavophiles" that remains a key dynamic of current Russian social and political thought.

Peter's expansionist policies were continued by Catherine the Great, who established Russia as a continental power. During her reign (1762-96), power was centralized in the monarchy and administrative reforms concentrated great wealth and privilege in the hands of the Russian nobility.

Napoleon failed in his attempt in 1812 to conquer Russia after occupying Moscow; his defeat and the continental order that emerged following the Congress of Vienna (1814-15) set the stage for Russia and Austria-

Hungary to dominate the affairs of eastern Europe for the next century.

During the 19th century, the Russian Government sought to suppress repeated attempts at reform from within. Its economy failed to compete with those of Western countries. Russian cities were growing without an industrial base to generate employment, although emancipation of the serfs in 1861 foreshadowed urbanization and rapid industrialization late in the century. At the same time, Russia expanded across Siberia until the port of Vladivostok was opened on the Pacific coast in 1860. The Trans-Siberian Railroad opened vast frontiers to development late in the century. In the 19th century, Russian culture flourished as Russian artists made significant contributions to world literature, visual arts, dance, and music.

Imperial decline was evident in Russia's defeat in the unpopular Russo-Japanese war in 1905. Subsequent civic disturbances forced Tsar Nicholas II to grant a constitution and introduce limited democratic reforms. The government suppressed opposition and manipulated popular anger into anti-Semitic pogroms. Attempts at economic reform, such as land reform, were incomplete.

## 1917 Revolution and the U.S.S.R.

The ruinous effects of World War I, combined with internal pressures, sparked the March 1917 uprising, which led Tsar Nicholas II to abdicate the throne. A provisional government came to power, headed by Aleksandr Kerenskiy. On November 7, 1917, the Bolshevik Party, led by Vladimir Lenin, seized control and established the Russian Soviet Federated Social-

ist Republic. Civil war broke out in 1918 between Lenin's "Red" army and various "White" forces and lasted until 1920, when, despite foreign interventions, the Bolsheviks triumphed. After the Red army conquered Ukraine, Belorussia, Azerbaijan, Georgia, and Armenia, a new nation was formed in 1922, the Union of Soviet Socialist Republics.

The U.S.S.R. lasted 69 years. In the 1930s, tens of millions of its citizens were collectivized under state agricultural and industrial enterprises. Millions died in political purges, the vast penal and labor system, or in state-created famines. During World War II, as many as 20 million Soviet citizens died. In 1949, the U.S.S.R. developed its own nuclear arsenal.

First among its political figures was Lenin, leader of the Bolshevik Party and head of the first Soviet Government, who died in 1924. In the late 1920s, Josif Stalin emerged as General Secretary of the Communist Party of the Soviet Union (CPSU) amidst intraparty rivalries; he maintained complete control over Soviet domestic and international policy until his death in 1953. His successor, Nikita Khrushchev, served as Communist Party leader until he was ousted in 1964. Aleksey Kosygin became Chairman of the Council of Ministers, and Leonid Brezhnev was made First Secretary of the CPSU Central Committee in 1964, but in 1971, Brezhnev rose to become "first among equals" in a collective leadership. Brezhnev died in 1982 and was succeeded by Yuriy Andropov (1982-84), Konstantin Chernenko (1984-85), and Mikhail Gorbachev, who resigned as Soviet President on December 25, 1991. On December 26, 1991, the U.S.S.R. was formally dissolved.

## The Russian Federation

After the December 1991 dissolution of the Soviet Union, the Russian Federation became its largest successor state, inheriting its permanent seat on the United Nations Security Council, as well as the bulk of its foreign assets and debt.

Boris Yeltsin was elected President of Russia by popular vote in June 1991. By the fall of 1993, politics in Russia reached a stalemate between President Yeltsin and the parliament. The parliament had succeeded in blocking, overturning, or ignoring the President's initiatives on drafting a new constitution, conducting new elections, and making further progress on democratic and economic reforms.

In a dramatic speech in September 1993, President Yeltsin dissolved the Russian parliament and called for new national elections and a new constitution. The standoff between the executive branch and opponents in the legislature turned violent in October after supporters of the parliament tried to instigate an armed insurrection. Yeltsin ordered the army to respond with force to capture the parliament building (known as the White House).

In December 1993, voters elected a new parliament and approved a new constitution that had been drafted by the Yeltsin government. Yeltsin has remained the dominant political figure, although a broad array of parties, including ultra-nationalists, liberals, agrarians, and communists, have substantial representation in the parliament and compete actively in elections at all levels of government.

In late 1994, the Russian security forces launched a brutal operation in the Republic of Chechnya against rebels who were intent on separation from Russia. Along with their opponents, Russian forces committed numerous violations of human rights. The Russian Army used heavy weapons against civilians. Tens of thousands of them were killed and more than 500,000 displaced during the course of the war. The protracted conflict, which received close scrutiny in the Russian media, raised serious human rights and humanitarian concerns abroad as well as within Russia.

After numerous unsuccessful attempts to institute a cease-fire, in August 1996 the Russian and Chechen authorities negotiated a settlement that resulted in a complete withdrawal of Russian troops and the holding of elections in January 1997. The Organization for Security and Cooperation in Europe (OSCE) played a major role in facilitating the negotiation. A peace treaty was concluded in May 1997. Following an August 1999 attack into Dagestan by Chechan separatists and the September 1999 bombings of two apartment buildings in Moscow, the federal government launched a military campaign into Chechnya. Russian authorities accused the Chechan government of failing to stop the growth of the rebels activities and failure to curb widespread banditry and hostage taking in the republic. By spring 2000, federal forces claimed control over Chechan territory, but fighting continues as rebel fighters regularly ambush Russian forces in the region.

# GOVERNMENT AND POLITICAL CONDITIONS

In the political system established by the 1993 constitution, the president wields considerable executive power. There is no vice president, and the legislative is far weaker than the executive. The president nominates the highest state officials, including the prime minister, who must be approved by the Duma. The president can pass decrees without consent from the Duma. He also is head of the armed forces and of the national security council.

Duma elections were on December 19, 1999 and presidential elections March 26, 2000. While the Communist Party won a narrow plurality of seats in the Duma, the pro-government party Unity and the centrist Fatherland-All Russia also won substantial numbers of seats in the legislature. In the presidential election, Vladimir Putin, named Acting President following the December 31 resignation of Boris Yeltsin, was elected in the first round with 53% of the vote. Both the presidential and parliamentary elections were judged generally free and fair by international observers.

Russia is a federation, but the precise distribution of powers between the central government and the regional and local authorities is still evolving. The Russian Federation consists of 89 components, including two federal cities, Moscow and St. Petersburg. The constitution explicitly defines the federal government's exclusive powers, but it also describes most key regional issues as the joint responsibility of the federal government and the Federation components.

## Judicial System

Russia's judiciary and justice system are weak. Numerous matters which are dealt with by administrative authority in European countries remain subject to political influence in Russia. The Constitutional Court was reconvened in March 1995 following its suspension by President Yeltsin in October 1993. The 1993 constitution empowers the court to arbitrate disputes between the executive and legislative branches and between Moscow and the regional and local governments. The court is also authorized to rule on violations of constitutional rights, to examine appeals from various bodies, and to participate in impeachment proceedings against the president. The July 1994 Law on the Constitutional Court prohibits the court from examining cases on its own initiative and limits the scope of issues the court can hear.

In the past 3 years, the Russian Government has begun to reform the criminal justice system and judicial institutions, including the reintroduction of jury trials in certain criminal cases. Despite these efforts, judges are only beginning to assert their constitutionally mandated independence from other branches of government.

## Human Rights

Russia's human rights record remains uneven and worsened in some areas. Despite significant improvements in conditions following the end of the Soviet Union, problem areas remain. In particular, the Russian government's military policy in Chechnya is a cause for international concern. Government forces have killed numerous civilians through the use of indiscriminate force in Chechnya. There have been credible allegations of violations of international human rights and humanitarian law by Russian forces. Chechen groups also have committed abuses.

Although the government has made progress in recognizing the legitimacy of international human rights standards, the institutionalization of procedures to safeguard these rights has lagged. Implementation of the constitutional provisions for due process and timely trials, for example, has made little progress. There are indications that the law is becoming an increasingly important tool for those seeking to protect human rights; after a lengthy trial and eight separate indictments, environmental whistleblower Alexander Nikitin was acquitted of espionage charges relating to publication of material exposing hazards posed by the Russian Navy's aging nuclear fleet earlier this year. Nonetheless, serious problems remain. The judiciary is often subject to manipulation by political authorities and is plagued by large case backlogs and trial delays. Lengthy pretrial detention remains a serious problem. There are credible reports of beating and torturing of inmates and detainees by law enforcement and correctional officials. Prison conditions fall well below international standards and, according to human rights groups, in 1996 between 10,000 and 20,000 prisoners and detainees died, most because of overcrowding, disease, and lack of medical care.

Efforts to institutionalize official human rights bodies have been mixed. In 1996, human rights activist Sergey Kovalev resigned as chairman of the Presidential Human Rights Commission to protest the government's record, particularly the war in Chechnya. Parliament in 1997 passed a law establishing a "human rights ombudsman," a position that is provided for in Russia's constitution and is required of members of the Council of Europe, to which Russia was admitted in February 1996. The Duma finally selected Duma deputy Oleg Mironov in May 1998. A member of the Communist Party, Mironov resigned from both the Party and the Duma after the vote, citing the law's stipulation that the Ombudsman be nonpartisan. Because of his party affiliation, and because Mironov had no evident expertise in the field of human rights, his appointment was widely criticized at the time by human rights activists. International human rights groups operate freely in Russia, although the government has hindered the movements and access to information of some individuals investigating the war in Chechnya.

The Russian Constitution provides for freedom of religion and the equality of all religions before the law as well as the separation of church and state. Although Jews and Muslims continue to encounter prejudice and societal discrimination, they have not been inhibited by the government in the free practice of their religion. High-ranking federal officials have condemned anti-Semitic hate crimes, but law enforcement bodies have not effectively prosecuted those responsible. The influx of missionaries over the past several years has led to pressure by groups in Russia, specifically nationalists and the Russian Orthodox Church, to limit the activities of these "nontraditional" religious groups. In response, the Duma passed a new, restrictive, and potentially discriminatory law in October 1997. The law is very complex, with many ambiguous and contradictory provisions. The law's most controversial provisions separates religious "groups" and "organizations" and introduce a 15-year rule, which allows groups that have been in existence for 15 years or longer to obtain accredited status. Senior Russian officials have pledged to implement the 1997 law on religion in a manner that is not in conflict with Russia's international human rights obligations. Some local officials, however, have used the law as a pretext to restrict religious liberty.

The constitution guarantees citizens the right to choose their place of residence and to travel abroad. Some big-city governments, however, have restricted this right through residential registration rules that closely resemble the Soviet-era "propiska" regulations. Although the rules were touted as a notification device rather than a control system, their implementation has produced many of the same results as the propiska system. The freedom to travel abroad and emigrate is respected although restrictions may apply to those who have had access to state secrets. Recognizing this progress, since 1994, President Clinton has found Russia to be in full compliance with the provisions of the Jackson-Vanik amendment.

## Principal Government Officials

For up-to-date information on Principal Government Officials, see the Chiefs of State and Cabinet Members of Foreign Governments section starting on page 1.

The Russian Federation maintains an embassy at 2650 Wisconsin Ave. NW, Washington, DC 20007 (tel. 202-298-5700) and a consular section at 2641 Tunlaw Road, Washington DC (tel. 202-939-8907/8913/8918). Russian consulates also are located in New York, San Francisco, and Seattle.

# ECONOMY

The Russian economy has undergone tremendous stress as it has moved from a centrally planned economy toward a free market system. Difficulties in implementing fiscal reforms aimed at raising government revenues and a dependence on short term borrowing to finance budget deficits led to a serious financial crisis in 1998. Lower prices for Russia's major export earners (oil and minerals) and a loss of investor confidence due to the Asian financial crisis exacerbated financial problems. The result was a rapid decline in the value of the ruble, flight of foreign investment, delayed payments on sovereign and private debts, a breakdown of commercial transactions through the banking system and the threat of runaway inflation. However, Russia appears to have weathered the crisis relatively well. Real GDP increased by the highest percentage since the fall of the Soviet Union, the ruble stabilized, inflation was moderate, and investment began to increase again. Russia is making progress in meeting its foreign debts obligations. In 1999, with limited access to financing from international financial institutions or bilateral sources, the GOR serviced around half its external debt payments due, and sought delays in servicing Soviet-era debt pending negotiations in the Paris and London Clubs. In early 2000 Russia negotiated a 35% write off of its commercial debt with the London Club. Russia's current Paris Club agreement expires at the end of 2000.

## Gross Domestic Product

Russia's GDP, estimated at $183 billion at exchange rates current in 1999, increased by 3.2% in 1999 compared to 1998. The major factors behind this strong growth were the earlier devaluation of the ruble (spurring production of Russian products as substitutes for more expensive imports); record high commodity prices on international markets, particularly oil (Russia's principal export); low inflation; and strict government budget discipline. For 1999 the unemployment rate was 12.6% (using International Labor Organization methodology). Combined unemployment and underemployment may exceed that figure. Industrial output in 1999 was up sharply (to 8.1%) compared to 1998, aided by the devalued ruble.

## Monetary Policy

The exchange rate stabilized in 1999—after falling from 6.5 rubles/dollar in August 1998 to approximately 25 rubles/dollar by April 1999, one year later it had further depreciated only to approximately 28.5 rubles/dollar. After some large spikes in inflation following the August 1998 economic crisis, inflation declined steadily throughout 1999, with an overall figure of 36.5 percent; inflation for the first quarter of 2000 was an estimated 4.1 percent. Factors dampening price increases include weak domestic demand, a relatively stable ruble, and the absence to date of a federal budget deficit for the Central Bank of Russia to monetize.

## Government Spending/ Taxation

Fiscal policy has been very disciplined in 1999 and early 2000. The overall budget deficit for 1999 was 1.7 percent of GDP, with a primary surplus of 2 percent; 1999 was the first year the federal budget was fully implemented. The primary surplus during the first quarter of 2000 was 3.5 percent of GDP. The GOR estimates that it will exceed budgeted revenue forecasts for 2000 by about 100 billion rubles, collecting 897.2 billion rubles. In part, the increase in cash revenues reflects increased receipts from large taxpayers, e.g. oil companies and natural monopolies, as well as growing economic activity.

## Law

Lack of legislation in many areas of economic activity is a pressing issue. Taxation and business regulations are unpredictable, and legal enforcement of private business agreements is weak. Government decisions affecting business have often been arbitrary and inconsistent. Crime has increased costs for both local and foreign businesses. On the positive side, Russian businesses are increasingly turning to the courts to resolve disputes. The passage of an improved bankruptcy code in January 1998 was a positive step; the government is advocating further improvements to this legislation.

## Natural Resources

The mineral-packed Ural mountains and the vast oil, gas, coal and timber reserves of Siberia and the Russian Far East make Russia rich in natural resources. However, most such resources are located in remote and climactically unfavorable areas that are difficult to develop and far from Russian ports. Oil and gas exports continue to be the main source of hard currency, but declining energy prices have hit Russia hard. Russia is a leading producer and exporter of minerals, gold and all major fuels. The Russian fishing industry is the world's fourth-largest, behind Japan, the U.S. and China. Russia accounts for one-quarter of the world's production of fresh and frozen fish and about one-third of world output of canned fish.

## Industry

Russia is one of the most industrialized of the former Soviet republics. However, much of its industry is antiquated and highly inefficient. Besides its resource-based industries, it has developed large manufacturing capacities, notably in machinery. Russia inherited most of the defense industrial base of the Soviet Union. Efforts have been made with varying success over the past few years to convert defense industries to civilian use.

## Agriculture

Russia comprises roughly three-quarters of the territory of the former Soviet Union, but has relatively little area suited for agriculture because of its arid climate and inconsistent rainfall. Northern areas concentrate mainly on livestock, and the southern parts and western Siberia produce grain. Restructuring of former state farms has been an extremely slow process, partially due to the lack of a land code allowing for the free sale, purchase and mortgage of agricultural land. Private farms and garden plots of individuals account for over one-half of all agricultural production.

## Investment

In 1999, investment increased by 4.5 percent, the first such growth since 1990. The increase came in the last half of 1999, and has continued in the opening months of 2000, up 5.9 percent year-on-year in the first quarter. Higher retained earnings, increased cash transactions, the positive outlook for sales and political stability have contributed to these favorable trends. Over the medium-to-long term, Russian companies that do not invest to increase their competitiveness will find it harder either to expand exports or protect their recent domestic market gains from higher quality imports.

Foreign direct investment rose slightly in 1999, but remains small. Foreign direct investment in Russia in 1999 was USD 2.9 billion, up from USD 2.8 billion in 1998, but still well below the USD 6.6 billion of FDI received in 1997.

A significant drawback for investment is the banking sector, which has

**Travel Notes**

**Travel Advice:** For up-to-date information from the U.S. State Department on possible inconvenient or hazardous situations, see the **Travel Warnings and Consular Information Sheets from the U.S. Government** section starting on page 1723. For the latest information on health requirements and conditions, see the **International Travelers' Health Information** section starting on page 1385. For further information dealing with non-urgent matter, see the **Tips for Travelers to...** section starting on page 1588.

neither the resources, capability, nor the trust of the population to attract substantial savings and intermediate them to productive investments. While ruble lending has doubled since the October 1998 financial crisis, loans are still only 28 percent of total bank assets, the same percentage as before the crisis. The CBR has reduced its refinancing rate three times in 2000, to 33 percent, signaling its interest in lower lending rates. Banks still perceive commercial lending as risky, and some banks are inexperienced with assessing credit risk.

## Trade

The major factor contributing to Russia's significant economic growth in 1999 was trade performance. Exports were up slightly to USD74.3 billion, while imports slumped by 30.5 percent to USD 41.1 billion. As a consequence, the trade surplus ballooned to USD 33.2 billion, more than double the previous year's level. After a weak start, both imports and exports recovered somewhat in the second half of the year, as the economy began to stabilize. The effect of higher oil prices had a major effect on export performance, particularly in the latter half of the year. Even though volumes of crude oil exports (to non-CIS countries) were down by 2.9 percent, prices jumped up 45.9 percent. Fuels and energy comprise 42 percent of Russian exports. Other exports performed better in 1999: fertilizer exports were up 16.7 percent, forestry products up 38 percent, copper up 17.6 percent, and aluminum up 10.5

percent. On the import side, food and consumer goods suffered especially, with food imports dropping by 28 percent.

Most analysts predict these trade trends will continue to some extent in 2000. The GOR forecasts export increases of about 4 percent and, as the ruble strengthens in real terms and purchasing power slowly recovers, a slightly larger recovery in imports of about 8 percent. However, imports in the first quarter remained flat at USD 9.4 billion, compared to USD 9.5 billion in the same period in 1999. The devaluation of the ruble and difficulties in completing transactions through the Russian banking system continue to depress imports. The combination of import duties, a 20% value-added tax and excise taxes on imported goods (especially automobiles, alcoholic beverages, and aircraft) and an import licensing regime for alcohol further restrain demand for imports. Frequent changes in customs regulations also have created problems for foreign and domestic traders and investors. Exports have continued to benefit from higher oil prices, bolstered by higher natural gas prices. In the first quarter of 2000, exports were up USD 6 billion, driving the trade surplus to USD 12.1 billion from USD 6.1 billion higher than the same period last year.

# FOREIGN RELATIONS

Russia has taken important steps to become a full partner in the world's principal political groupings. On December 27, 1991, Russia assumed the seat formerly held by the Soviet Union in the UN Security Council. Russia also is a member of the Organization for Security and Cooperation in Europe (OSCE) and the North Atlantic Cooperation Council (NACC). It signed the NATO Partnership for Peace initiative on June 22, 1994. On May 27, 1997, NATO and Russia signed the NATO-Russia Founding Act, which provides the basis for an enduring and robust partnership between the Alliance and Russia—one that can make an important contribution to European security architecture in the 21st century. On June 24, 1994, Russia and the European Union (EU) signed a partnership and cooperation agreement.

Russia has played an important role in helping mediate international conflicts and has been particularly actively engaged in trying to promote a peace following the conflict in Kosovo. Russia is a co-sponsor of the Middle East peace process and supports UN and multilateral initiatives in the Persian Gulf, Cambodia, Angola, the former Yugoslavia, and Haiti. Russia is a founding member of the Contact Group and (since the Denver Summit in June 1997) a member of the G-8. In November 1998, Russia joined APEC. Russia has contributed troops to the NATO-led stabilization force in Bosnia and has affirmed its respect for international law and OSCE principles. It has accepted UN and/or OSCE involvement in instances of regional conflict in neighboring countries, including the dispatch of observers to Georgia, Moldova, Tajikistan, and Nagorno-Karabakh.

# DEFENSE

Since the breakup of the U.S.S.R., the Russians have discussed rebuilding a viable, cohesive fighting force out of the remaining parts of the former Soviet armed forces. A new Russian military doctrine, promulgated in November 1993, implicitly acknowledges the contraction of the old Soviet military into a regional military power without global imperial ambitions. In keeping with its emphasis on the threat of regional conflicts, the doctrine calls for a Russian military that is smaller, lighter, and more mobile, with a higher degree of professionalism and with greater rapid deployment capability. Such a transformation has proven difficult.

The challenge of this task has been magnified by difficult economic conditions in Russia, which have resulted in reduced defense spending. This has led to training cutbacks, wage arrears, and severe shortages of housing and other social amenities for military personnel, with a conse-

quent lowering of morale, cohesion, and fighting effectiveness. The poor combat performance of the Russian armed forces in the Chechen conflict in part reflects these breakdowns.

The actual strength of the Russian armed forces probably falls between 1.4 and 1.6 million and is scheduled to fall to 1.2 million by the end of 1999. Weapons production in Russia has fallen dramatically over the past few years; between 1988 and 1993, it fell by at least 50% for virtually every major weapons system. Weapons spending in 1992 was approximately 75% less than in 1988. Almost all of Russia's arms production is for sales to foreign governments, and procurement of major end items by the Russian military has all but stopped.

About 70% of the former Soviet Union's defense industries are located in the Russian Federation. A large number of state-owned defense enterprises are on the brink of collapse as a result of cuts in weapons orders and insufficient funding to shift to production of civilian goods, while at the same time trying to meet payrolls. Many defense firms have been privatized; some have developed significant partnerships with U.S. firms.

# U.S.- RUSSIA RELATIONS

The United States remains committed to maintaining a constructive relationship with Russia in which we seek to expand areas of cooperation and effectively work through differences. The United States continues to support Russia's political and economic transformation and its integration into major international organizations. These steps, in conjunction with achievements in considerably reducing nuclear weapons, have greatly enhanced the security of the United States.

The intensity and frequency of contacts between President Yeltsin and President Clinton, most recently the Moscow Summit in August 1998, are

indicative of the strong commitment to working together on a broad range of issues. These include European security, reducing the threat to our countries posed by weapons of mass destruction, and economic cooperation, especially American investment in Russia.

## Economic Relations

*U.S.- Russia Joint Commission on Economic and Technological Cooperation.* Under the leadership of Vice President Gore and the Russian Prime Minister, the U.S. and Russia are working to advance bilateral cooperation through nine working committees and several working groups known collectively as the U.S.-Russian Joint Commission on Economic and Technological Cooperation. Committees address issues in the fields of science and technology, business development, space, energy policy, environmental protection, health, defense conversion, capital markets, and agriculture. In addition, the commission provides a forum for high-level discussions of priority security and economic issues. The commission held its 10th session in Washington in March 1998 and an executive session in Washington in July 1999.

*Trade and Investment.* In 1999, the U.S. trade deficit with Russia was $3.96 billion, up $1.76 billion over 1998. U.S. merchandise exports to Russia were nearly $1.85 billion in 1999. Russia was the United States' 41st largest export market in 1999. U.S. imports from Russia were $5.81 billion in 1999, making Russia the 28th largest supplier of U.S. imports. The 1992 U.S.-Russia trade agreement provides mutual most-favored-nation status and includes commitments on intellectual property rights protection. In 1992, the two countries also signed treaties on the avoidance of double taxation and on bilateral investment. In 1992, the two countries also signed treaties on the avoidance of double taxation and on bilateral investment. As of spring 2000, however, the Russian parliament has not ratified the bilateral investment treaty. It has been ratified by the U.S. Senate.

The U.S. actively supports Russia's efforts to join the World Trade Organization on commercially viable terms. Russia is currently in the process of negotiating terms of accession to the WTO. By the end of 1999 it had completed ten working party meetings. It tables its initial services market access offer in October 1999 and has conducted negotiations on its goods market access offer. These offers contain Russia's proposed commitments to maximum tariff rates and opening of its markets to foreign providers of services. The U.S. actively supported Russian membership in the Asia-Pacific Economic Cooperation (APEC) forum. Russia became a member of APEC in November 1998.

## Security Cooperation

*NATO/Russia Founding Act.* Russia signed the NATO Partnership for Peace initiative in June 1994. U.S. and Russian troops are serving together in the Implementation Force in Bosnia and its successor, the Stabilization Force. Building on these steps, NATO and Russia signed the NATO-Russia Founding Act on May 27, 1997, in Paris. The act defines the terms of a fundamentally new and sustained relationship in which NATO and Russia will consult and coordinate regularly, and where appropriate, act jointly. Cooperation between NATO and Russia exists in scientific and technical fields.

*Agreements/Cooperation/Nuclear Arms.* The U.S. and Russia signed a memorandum of understanding on defense cooperation in September 1993 that institutionalized and expanded relations between defense ministries, including establishing a broad range of military-to-military and scientist to scientist contacts. The U.S. and Russia carried out a joint peacekeeping training exercise in Totskoye, Russia, in September 1994. Based on the January 14, 1994, agreement between Presidents Clinton and Yeltsin, the two nations stopped targeting their strategic nuclear missiles at each other as of May 30, 1994. U.S. and Russian security cooperation emphasizes strategic stability, nuclear safety, dismantling

nuclear weapons, preventing proliferation of weapons of mass destruction and their delivery systems, and enhancing military-to-military contacts. The START I Treaty was signed by the United States and the Soviet Union on July 31, 1991. Five months later, the Soviet Union dissolved, and in May 1992, Belarus, Kazakhstan, Russia and Ukraine signed the Lisbon Protocol to the START I Treaty, making them Parties to the START I Treaty. Belarus, Kazakhstan and Ukraine have also fulfilled their commitment to accede to the Nuclear Non-Proliferation Treaty (NPT) as non-nuclear weapon states in the shortest possible time, and to return all nuclear weapons on their territory to Russia for dismantlement. The START I Treaty entered into force on December 5, 1994. START I requires reductions in strategic offensive arms to 6,000 accountable warheads on each side as of December 4, 2001. All Parties to the Treaty have been successful in meeting the Treaty's reduction requirements.

*START II.* The START II Treaty was signed by the United States and Russia on January 3, 1993. START II builds on the START I Treaty, requiring reductions in two phases to 3,000-3,500 deployed strategic nuclear warheads on each side, a two-thirds reduction from Cold War levels. At the September 1994 summit, the two nations agreed to begin removing nuclear warheads due to be scrapped under START II immediately, once START I takes effect and the START II Treaty is ratified by both countries, instead of taking the 9 years allowed. At their May 1995 summit, Presidents Clinton and Yeltsin agreed on a set of principles that would guide further discussion in the field of demarcation between anti-ballistic missile systems and theater missile defenses. They also agreed on steps to increase the transparency and irreversibility of nuclear arms reduction and committed not to use newly produced fissile materials or to reuse the fissile materials removed from nuclear weapons being eliminated and excess to national security requirements in nuclear weapons. Since that time, all strategic nuclear weapons have been

removed from Ukraine, Belarus, and Kazakhstan to Russia. Under START II, all heavy ICBMs and MIRVed ICBMs must be eliminated from each side's deployed forces. In January 1996, the U.S. Senate provided its advice and consent to ratification of the START II Treaty.

The deadline for START II reductions was extended to December 2007 by the START II Protocol signed by the United States and Russia on September 26, 1997. The Protocol has not been submitted to the U.S. Senate for ratification. On April 14, 2000, the Russian Duma approved the START II Treaty and the START II Protocol, and on May 5, President Putin signed the ratification document. In ratifying the START II Treaty, the Russian Duma passed a federal law containing a number of conditions. Among them is a requirement that the United States ratify the START II Protocol before the START II Treaty can enter into force. The Duma's ratification law and the relationship between the 1997 agreements, including those related to the ABM Treaty, and START III and changes to the ABM Treaty, will be considered before the START II Protocol is submitted to the Senate for approval.

In March 1997, in Helsinki, Finland, Presidents Clinton and Yeltsin agreed that a START III agreement would include the following basic elements, among others:

lower aggregate levels of 2,000-2,500 strategic nuclear warheads— 80 percent below the Cold War peak—for each of the parties transparency measures related to strategic nuclear warheads inventories and the destruction of strategic nuclear warheads resolving issues related to the goal of making the current START treaties of unlimited duration exploration of possible measures relating to nuclear long-range sea-launched cruise missiles and tactical nuclear systems, including confidence-building and transparency measures. early deactivation of all strategic nuclear delivery vehicles to be eliminated under START II by December 31, 2003, by removing their nuclear warheads or taking other jointly agreed steps; In June 1999, in Cologne, Germany, Presidents Clinton and Yeltsin reaffirmed their readiness to conduct new negotiations on strategic offensive arms aimed at further reducing the level of strategic nuclear warheads on each side, elaborating measures of transparency concerning existing strategic nuclear warheads and their elimination, as well as other agreed technical and organizational measures. Presidents Clinton and Yeltsin also agreed at this Summit to begin discussions on START III and the ABM Treaty.

*START III.* As agreed at Cologne, the United States and Russia began discussions on both START III and ABM issues during the summer of 1999. Since then extensive discussions have been held on these matters at senior levels of both governments. On July 23, 1999, the President signed into law H.R. 4, the National Missile Defense (NMD) Act of 1999. We are continuing substantive discussions with Russia on START III, in parallel with discussions on changes to the ABM Treaty. These discussions are continuing and, with Russia's ratification of START II, are expected to intensify.

*CFE.* Following ratification by Russia and the other NIS, the Conventional Armed Forces in Europe Treaty entered into force on November 9, 1992. This treaty establishes comprehensive limits on key categories of military equipment—tanks, artillery, armored combat vehicles, combat aircraft, and combat helicopters—and provides for the destruction of weaponry in excess of these limits. An adapted CFE Treaty was adopted at the November 1999 Istanbul Summit. The adapted Treaty takes account of the changes in Europe since CFE was signed. Politically, the process of adaptation has played a pivotal role in managing Russian concerns and expectations regarding NATO enlargement, through both the Madrid and Washington NATO Summits. NATO Allies addressed deeply-held Russian concerns by accepting provisions in CFE which demonstrated that NATO did not contemplate a massive eastward shift in peacetime military potential as a

result of enlargement. But this remains a very NATO-friendly Treaty.

*Cooperative Threat Reduction (CTR).* Often called Nunn-Lugar assistance, this type of assistance is provided to Russia (as well as Belarus, Kazakhstan and Ukraine) to aid in the dismantling of weapons of mass destruction and to prevent the proliferation of such weapons. More than $730 million has been allocated for assistance to Russia during fiscal years 1997 and 1998 under this program, and 13 implementing agreements have been signed. Key projects have included assistance in the elimination of strategic offensive arms ($184 million), design and construction of a fissile material storage facility ($127 million), provision of fissile material containers ($45 million), material control and accounting and physical protection of nuclear materials ($51 million), and development of a chemical weapons destruction facility and provision of equipment for a pilot laboratory for the safe and secure destruction of chemical weapons ($106 million).

Under the highly enriched uranium agreement, the U.S. is purchasing uranium from Russian weapons for use in power reactors. Also, both the U.S. and Russia will cooperate to dispose of excess military plutonium. The U.S. also is assisting Russia in the development of export controls, providing emergency response equipment and training to enhance Russia's ability to respond to accidents involving nuclear weapons, providing increased military-to-military contacts.

In a multilateral effort (the European Union, Japan, and Canada also are involved), the U.S. also has provided over $60 million to establish and support the International Science and Technology Center (ISTC), which provides alternative peaceful civilian employment opportunities to scientists and engineers of the former Soviet Union involved with weapons of mass destruction and their delivery systems.

## U.S. Assistance to Russia

*Cumulative U.S. Assistance Figures.* Since 1992, the U.S. Government has allocated more than $8.2 billion in grant assistance to Russia, funding a variety of programs in four key areas: security programs, humanitarian assistance, economic reform and democratic reform. The U.S. Government is also providing assistance in such areas as nuclear reactor safety and the environment. The grant assistance provided by the U.S. Government to date can be broken down as follows: almost $3.3 billion in security assistance (weapons dismantlement and nonproliferation), over $2.2 billion in humanitarian assistance, over $1.4 billion in economic reform programs, almost $650 million in democratic reform programs, and $615 million in cross-sectoral and other programs. The U.S. Government has also supported approximately $8.9 billion in commercial financing and insurance for Russia. Nearly 40,000 Russians have traveled to the United States under U.S. Government-funded training and exchange programs. The annual level of FREEDOM Support Act-funded assistance for Russia, which declined from a peak of $1.6 billion in FY 1994 to $95 million in FY 1997, is about $178 million in FY 2000. For more detailed information on these programs, please see the FY 1999 Annual Report to Congress on U.S. Government Assistance to and Cooperative Activities with the New Independent States of the Former Soviet Union, which is available on the State Department's website at the following address: http://www.state.gov/www/regions/nis/nis_assist_index.html

*How U.S. Assistance Has Evolved.* The U.S. Government's strategy for assistance to Russia is based on the premise that Russia's transition to democracy and free markets will be a long-term process. The U.S. will need to remain engaged throughout this process, and therefore U.S. assistance emphasizes activities that promote the establishment of lasting ties between Russians and Americans at all levels of society. Over the past three years, the U.S. assistance program has moved away from technical assistance to the central government, although such assistance is still provided when it is appropriate and will help to advance reform. An increasing proportion of U.S. assistance is focused at the regional and municipal level, where programs are helping to build the infrastructure of a market economy, remove impediments to trade and investment, and strengthen civil society. In general, U.S. assistance programs in Russia are working at the grassroots level by bolstering small business through training and enhanced availability of credit; expanding exchanges so that more Russian citizens can learn about America's market democracy on a first-hand basis; and increasing the number of partnerships between Russian and U.S. cities, universities, hospitals, business associations, charities, and other civic groups. In FY 1999, humanitarian assistance accounted for approximately 60% of U.S. assistance to Russia, in response to the increased need for such assistance in the aftermath of Russia's August 1998 financial crisis. However, in FY 2000, security and nonproliferation programs represent over two-thirds of U.S assistance to Russia.

Security programs help demilitarize facilities; eliminate weapons of mass destruction and prevent their proliferation, as well as the proliferation of weapons materials, delivery systems, technology and weapons expertise; and enable compliance with arms accords.

U.S. Government-funded humanitarian assistance consists mainly of food assistance provided by the U.S. Department of Agriculture (see below). The U.S. Government also transports food, medical equipment and other humanitarian assistance donated by U.S. private voluntary organizations (PVOs), as well as Defense Department excess commodities.

Increasingly, U.S. Government-funded economic reform programs are focused in Russia's regions. A limited amount of assistance is targeted at promoting reforms at the national level, particularly with regard to tax administration and Russia's efforts to accede to the World Trade Organization (WTO).

Democratic reform programs are helping Russians develop the building blocks of a democratic society based on the rule of law by providing support to non-governmental organizations (NGOs), independent media the judiciary and other key institutions. To support this long-term generational transition, the U.S. Government is increasingly promoting links between U.S. and Russian communities and institutions, including universities, hospitals and professional associations, and is establishing public-access Internet sites throughout Russia. The U.S. Government will also be awarding a grant to support a curriculum development program for the Institute of Public Administration and Social Studies at Moscow State University. In addition, the U.S. Government is helping Russia combat crime and corruption through cooperation with U.S. law enforcement agencies and community-based groups.

*Regional Initiative (RI).* The RI concentrates an array of U.S. government technical assistance, business development, and exchange programs in a small group of progressive Russian regions, with the goal of helping to create successful models of economic and political development at the regional level. Over time, it is hoped that these regions will achieve broad-based economic growth, attract outside investment, and build a strong civil society, and that they will participate in efforts to disseminate their experience to other regions of Russia. Three RI sites are up and running, in Novgorod, Samara, and Khabarovsk/Sakhalin in the Russian Far East, and a new site is currently being established in Tomsk.

## Cooperative Threat Reduction (CTR) Program

The Defense Department's (DoD) CTR or "Nunn-Lugar" Program was initiated in FY 1992 to reduce the threat posed to the United States by the weapons of mass destruction (WMD) remaining on the territory of the former Soviet Union. CTR promotes denuclearization and demilitarization, and seeks to prevent WMD proliferation.

Through FY 1999, DoD has notified the U.S. Congress of over $1.6 billion in CTR assistance to Russia, of which over $1.2 billion has been obligated through FY 1999 and over $790 million disbursed. Cooperation has evolved and strengthened over the years in DoD's interaction with the Russian ministries administering the CTR program, including the Ministry of Defense (MoD), the Ministry of Atomic Energy (MinAtom), the now-disbanded Ministry for Defense Industry (MDI), and the Ministry of Economy (MinEcon). In June 1999, the U.S. and Russian Governments extended the CTR Umbrella Agreement through 2006.

Since FY 1997, the CTR Program has focused increasingly on Russia. About $383 million of the $440.4 million appropriated for CTR in FY 1999 was earmarked for Russia. To position Russia to reduce its force structure to START II or potential START III levels, DoD, MoD and MinEcon agreed in December 1997 on new CTR projects to support the required missile systems dismantlement, strategic submarine elimination, and enhance nuclear weapons and fissile material security. Several of these projects are underway. In 1999, projects were being developed to help the Russians process and package fissile material in the post-dismantlement stage and to prevent the proliferation of biological weapons (BW) expertise and technology.

The CTR Program is providing Russia equipment, training, services and logistical support to expedite the elimination of strategic offensive arms pursuant to the START Treaties. This includes assistance with liquid rocket-fuel disposition, SLBM launcher and associated submarine elimination, solid rocket-motor elimination, SS-18 and heavy-bomber dismantlement, and other projects. This also includes provision of equipment for emergency support in case of an accident involving the transport or elimination of missiles. Under the CTR Program, the U.S. is helping Russia destroy its CW stockpile and associated infrastructure. Efforts have focused on designing a CW destruction facility at Shchuchye that the U.S. Government plans to help construct. Construction is under way on a Central Analytical Laboratory (CAL) that will enhance Russia's ability to conduct chemical-agent monitoring at CW storage and destruction sites. The U.S. Government procured and delivered three mobile analytical laboratories to support Russian CW destruction projects. U.S. Government-funded efforts also continued to eliminate CW infrastructure at the KhimProm Volgograd and Novocheboksarsk chemical complexes.

Construction continues on a facility for the storage of fissile material derived from dismantled Russian weapons at Mayak in the Southern Urals. DoD is providing design assistance, construction support and equipment, and facility equipment. The U.S. Government is also providing Russia's Ministry of Atomic Energy (MinAtom) with containers for the transport and storage of fissile materials from dismantled weapons. Production of the containers began in October 1995, and initial shipments to Russia began in December 1995. Through FY 1999, more than 32,000 fissile material containers have been produced and delivered.

*CTR Weapons Protection Control and Accounting (WPC&A) Program.* This program is improving security of nuclear weapons during transportation and interim storage. The project was started in April 1995 under two CTR implementing agreements with Russia. Assistance provided includes supercontainers, railcar upgrades, emergency support equipment, automated inventory control and management systems, computer modeling, a personnel reliability program, 50 sets of "quick-fix" fencing and sensors for storage sites, and the development of a Security Assessment and Training Center to test and evaluate new security systems for storage sites. This

project is planned to expand to protect over 70 additional storage sites.

*CTR Materials Protection, Control and Accounting Program.* Since 1993, the United States and Russia have worked together to prevent the theft or loss of nuclear material by improving nuclear materials protection, control, and accounting (MPC&A). MPC&A improvements are designed to keep nuclear materials secured in the facilities that are authorized to contain them, and are the first line of defense against nuclear smuggling that could lead to nuclear proliferation and/or nuclear terrorism. DOE took over the program from DOD and is seeking to enhance the security of weapons-grade fissile materials at more than 40 sites in Russia.

In addition, under the highly enriched uranium agreement, the U.S. is purchasing uranium from Russian weapons for use in power reactors. Also, both the U.S. and Russia will cooperate to dispose of excess military plutonium.

*Export Control Assistance.* Since the early 1990s, the U.S. has provided assistance to Russia to help it develop more effective export control systems and capabilities in order to prevent, deter and detect the potential proliferation of weapons of mass destruction (WMD) and associated materials. The objective is to help Russia build export control institutions, infrastructure and legislation to help prevent weapons proliferation. Initial funding from the CTR program has been augmented by funds from the Departments of Commerce, Energy, State and Treasury (Customs Service). In FY 1996, overall responsibility for export control assistance shifted to the Department of State, which provides policy direction and coordinates all agencies providing export control and border security assistance, capitalizing in particular on the unique capabilities of the U.S. Coast Guard to support export control and border security assistance programs. Recent State Department funded programs with Russia include supporting the Russian Center for Export Controls (CEC) work with the Department of

Commerce to install internal compliance programs (ICPs) in key Russian defense and high-technology enterprises and facilitating the adoption of a new, comprehensive export control law and other legal/regulatory changes in Russia. DOE export control efforts in Russia include traditional activities such as workshops, studies and regulatory development. DOE also initiated the Second Line of Defense program for Russia to combat the trafficking of illicit nuclear materials across border and control points to strengthen its overall capability to prevent nuclear materials, equipment and technology from getting into the hands of would-be proliferators. This program entails procuring Russian-manufactured detection equipment for key border crossings and training programs for Russian Customs officials.

*International Science and Technology Center (ISTC).* In a multilateral effort involving the European Union, Japan, and Canada, the U.S. has provided over $100 million to the Moscow-based ISTC for redirection activities in Russia in addition to millions of dollars in contributions from the EU, Canada, Norway, Japan and South Korea. The ISTC provides alternative peaceful civilian employment opportunities to scientists and engineers of the former Soviet Union involved with weapons of mass destruction and their delivery systems. To date, the ISTC has funded more than 500 projects involving more than 20,000 Russian scientists.

*Biotechnical Redirection Program.* In FY 1999, the U.S. Government implemented a State Department-led pilot project aimed at increasing transparency in former Soviet biological weapons (BW) facilities and redirecting their scientists to civilian commercial, agricultural and public health activities. All activity under this project is subject to strict oversight by an interagency working group. Facilities and government officials in countries where the U.S. Government is pursuing redirection activities are explicitly informed that any cooperation with countries of proliferation concern or terrorist entities, or any behavior inconsistent with the Biological and Toxin Weapons Convention (BWC), would have an immediate and negative impact on U.S. Government assistance. The majority of U.S. Government-funded redirection activities are taking place under the auspices of the International Science and Technology Center (ISTC), which has access to facilities, provides tax-exempt assistance directly to scientists, and can engage multilateral funding. Agencies involved in these efforts include the U.S. Departments of State, Energy (DOE), Defense (DoD), Agriculture (USDA) and Health and Human Services (HHS). Most of these activities are oriented toward Russian institutes and scientists. The State Department has allocated over $22 million since FY 1998 for these activities. DoD also has initiated a CTR program to fund collaborative biotechnical research with former biological weapons scientists to prevent the proliferation of biological weapons expertise and technology, increase access to Russian scientists, and to enhance the transparency of their work. CTR also is enhancing the security of Russian biotechnical facilities through initiation in FY 1999 of a Biological Material Protection, Control and Accountability Program.

## Implementing Agencies

*U.S. Agency for International Development (USAID).* USAID has implemented the lion's share of U.S. Government-funded technical assistance to Russia—over $1.8 billion since 1992. USAID has devoted its assistance efforts to helping Russia develop democratic institutions and transform its state-controlled economy to one based on market principles. USAID has been active in the areas of privatization and private-sector development, agriculture, energy, housing reform, health, environmental protection, economic restructuring, independent media, and the rule of law.

*U.S. Department of State - Public Diplomacy Exchanges (formerly the U.S. Information Agency).* Approximately 27,000 Russians have traveled to the United States on USIA-

funded exchanges since 1992. Public diplomacy exchanges promote the growth of democracy and civil society, encourage economic reform and growth of a market economy in Russia. USIA's professional and academic exchanges cover such diverse fields as journalism, public administration, local government, business management, education, political science, and civic education.

*Library of Congress.* In FY 2000, the Russian Leadership Program will bring 1,800 Russians from throughout Russia to the United States for short-term study tours, including up to 150 members of the Russian Parliament for meetings with their counterparts in the U.S. Congress.

*U.S. Department of Commerce.* The Special American Business Internship Training (SABIT) Program places Russian managers for short-term internships with U.S. companies. To date, over 1,000 Russians have participated in the SABIT Program. The Commerce Department also operates the Business Information Service for the New Independent States (BISNIS), which provides market information, trade leads, and partnering services to U.S. companies interested in the Russian market.

*U.S. Export-Import Bank (Eximbank).* Eximbank has approved more than $3.6 billion in loans, loan guarantees, and insurance for transactions in Russia since 1991. Of this total, more than $1 billion was approved under its Oil and Gas Framework Agreement.

*U.S. Overseas Private Investment Corporation (OPIC).* OPIC has provided more than $4.0 billion in loans, loan guarantees, and political investment insurance to American companies investing in Russia.

*Trade and Development Agency (TDA).* TDA has approved approximately $55 million in funding for feasibility studies on more than 135 investment projects.

*U.S. Department of Agriculture (USDA).* In FY 1999, in response to a

request by the Russian Government, USDA provided more than 3.7 million metric tons of food valued at more than $1 billion, including 100,000 metric tons of nonperishable food donated through U.S. private voluntary organizations (PVOs), 1.7 million tons of wheat on a grant basis, and 1.55 million tons of commodities (including beef, pork, poultry, corn, rice, wheat and soybeans) on a concessional basis under USDA's P.L. 480, Title I Program. USDA also donated 15,000 tons of corn and vegetable seeds to the Russian Government for the 1999 planting season. In FY 2000, USDA will be providing approximately $225 million in food assistance to Russia, which will consist of approximately 300,000 metric tons of government-to-government commodities targeted at institutions such as orphanages and hospitals, and approximately 200,000 metric tons of commodities provided by U.S. PVOs. In addition, USDA provides training to Russian agriculturists and agricultural faculty through its Cochran Fellowship and Faculty Exchange Programs, with the goal of helping to familiarize the Russian agricultural sector with Western-style agribusiness management, marketing, and other issues, while at the same time increasing U.S. agricultural exports to Russia. Since 1992, over 500 Russians have traveled to the U.S. under these two programs.

*U.S. Department of Defense (DoD).* DoD implements the majority of the U.S. Government's security-related assistance programs through its Cooperative Threat Reduction (CTR) Program (see above). DoD also implements the Foreign Military Financing (FMF) and International Military Education and Training (IMET) programs in support of the Partnership for Peace.

*U.S. Department of Energy (DOE).* DOE funds and implements a wide range of programs in the security area, including the provision of Material Protection Control and Accounting (MPC& A) assistance to secure and prevent proliferation of nuclear materials and plutonium disposition assistance. DOE is also focusing on preventing proliferation of weapons expertise, facilitating the downsizing of Russia's nuclear cities, and improving the safety of Russia's nuclear reactors.

*Initiatives for Proliferation Prevention (IPP).* DOE's IPP Program provides meaningful, sustainable, non-weapons-related work for former Soviet weapons-of-mass-destruction (WMD) scientists, engineers and technicians in the NIS through commercially viable market opportunities. IPP provides seed funds for the identification and maturation of technology and facilitates interactions between U.S. industry and NIS institutes for developing industrial partnerships, joint ventures and other mutually beneficial arrangements. Since 1994, IPP has funded over 440 projects involving more than 7,000 former Soviet weapons scientists at over 170 NIS institutes. Since establishing the IPP program, DOE has allocated over $100 million to support IPP projects in Russia.

*Nuclear Cities Initiative (NCI).* NCI was established by DOE in late FY 1998 to help Russia provide new employment opportunities to the workers who are displaced through downsizing of the Russian nuclear weapons complex. DOE has initially concentrated its efforts on three focus cities of Sarov, Snezhinsk and Zheleznogorsk, which house the two Russian weapons-design laboratories and a plutonium production enterprise. NCI is helping create the conditions under which new jobs can be created through economic diversification in these closed cities. DOE has allocated $20 million through FY 2000 for this program.

*Eurasia Foundation.* The Eurasia Foundation, a private, non-profit, grant-making organization supported by the U.S. Government and private foundations, has awarded more than 1,600 grants totaling more than $40 million to Russian non-governmental organizations (NGOs) and U.S.-Russian NGO partnerships since 1993. The Foundation's grants have been targeted in three main programmatic areas: economic reform, governmental reform and the non-profit sector, and media and communications. The Foundation has also implemented targeted grant initiatives to address specific issues, such as the rule of law and alternative dispute resolution.

## Principal U.S. Embassy Officials

**For up-to-date information on Principal U.S. Officials, see the U.S. Embassies, Consulates, and Foreign Service section starting on page 139.**

The U.S. embassy in Russia is located at Bolshoy Devyatinskiy Perenlok, Number 8, 121099 Moscow (tel. [7](095) 728-5000; fax: [7] (095) 728-5090).

## Consulates General

Consulate General, St. Petersburg (Furshtatskaya Ulitsa 15), tel. [7] (812) 275-1701—Paul Smith, Consul General.

Consulate General, Vladivostok (Mordovtseva Ulitsa 12), tel. [7] (4232) 268-458/554—Lysbeth Rickerman, Consul General.

Consulate General, Yekaterinburg (Ulitsa Gogolya 15A), tel. [7] (3432) 60-11-43—James Bigus, Consul General.

In Moscow, the U.S. Commercial Office is located at Novinskiy Bulvar 15 (tel. [7] (095) 255-4848/4660 or 9564255, fax: [7] (095) 230-2101). In St. Petersburg, the U.S. Commercial Office is located at Bolshaya Morskaya Ulitsa 57 (tel. [7] (812) 110-6042, fax: [7] (812) 1106479).

# RWANDA

March 1998

## Official Name:
## Republic of Rwanda

---

# PROFILE

## Geography

**Area:** 26,338 sq. km. (10,169 sq. km.); about the size of Maryland.
**Cities:** Capital—Kigali (est. pop. 236,000). Other cities—Gitarama, Butare, Ruhengeri, Gisenyi.
**Terrain:** Uplands and hills.
**Climate:** Mild and temperate, with two rainy seasons.

## People

**Nationality:** Noun and adjective—Rwandan(s).
**Population (1997 est.):** 7.6 million.
**Annual growth rate:** Over 3%.
**Ethnic groups:** Hutu 85%, Tutsi 14%, Twa 1%.
**Religions:** Christian 80%, traditional African 10%, Muslim 10%.
**Languages:** French, English, Kinyarwanda.
**Education:** Years compulsory—6. Attendance—70% (prewar). Literacy—50%.
**Health:** Infant mortality rate—123/1,000. Life expectancy—49 yrs.
**Work force:** Agriculture—92%. Industry and commerce, services and government—8%.

## Government

**Type:** Republic.

**Independence:** July 1, 1962.
**Constitution:** June 10, 1991.
**Branches:** Executive—president (chief of state), prime minister (head of government). Broad-based government of national unity formed after the 1994 civil war for transition to multi-party parliamentary democracy. Legislative—National Assembly. Judicial—Supreme Court, Constitutional Court, Council of State, Court of Appeals.
**Administrative subdivisions:** 12 prefectures, 154 communes.
**Political parties:** Five parties comprise the government: the Rwandan Popular Front (RPF), the Democratic Republican Movement (MDR), the Social Democratic Party (PSD), the Liberal Party (PL), and the Christian Democratic Party (PDC).
**Suffrage:** Suspended.
**Central government budget (1997 est.—billions of Rwandan francs):** Revenues—50 billion. Expenditures—62 billion, excluding an estimated 80 billion in capital expenditures financed by donors.

## Economy

**GDP (1996 est.):** 425 billion Rwandan francs.
**Real GDP growth rate (1996 est.):** 13%.
**Per capita income (1997 est.):** $234.
**Average inflation rate (1996 est.):** 9%.

**Natural resources:** Cassiterite, wolfram, methane.
**Agriculture (1996 est.):** 35% of GDP. Products—coffee, tea, cattle, hides and skin, pyrethrum. Arable land—48%, 90% of which is cultivated.
**Industry (1996 est.):** 17% of GDP. Type—beer production, soft drink, soap, furniture, shoes, plastic goods, textiles, cigarettes, pharmaceuticals.
**Trade (1996 est.):** Exports—$68 million: coffee, tea, hides and skins, cassiterite, pyrethrum. Major markets—Germany, Belgium, Netherlands, Pakistan. Imports—$275 million: food, consumer goods, capital equipment, petroleum products. Major suppliers—Belgium, U.S., Tanzania, Kenya, France.
**Official exchange rate:** Approx. 300 Rwandan francs=U.S.$1 (fluctuates daily).

# GEOGRAPHY

Rwanda's countryside is covered by grasslands and small farms extending over rolling hills, with areas of rugged mountains that extend southeast from a chain of volcanoes in the northwest. The divide between the Congo and Nile drainage systems extends from north to south through western Rwanda at an average elevation of almost 9,000 feet. On the western slopes of this ridgeline, the land slopes abruptly toward Lake Kivu and the Ruzizi River valley, which form the western boundary with the People's Democratic Republic of Congo (formerly Zaire) and constitute part of the Great Rift valley. The eastern slopes are more moderate, with rolling hills extending across central uplands at gradually reducing altitudes, to the plains, swamps, and lakes of the eastern border region.

Although located only two degrees south of the Equator, Rwanda's high elevation makes the climate temperate. The average daily temperature near Lake Kivu, at an altitude of 4,800 feet (1,463 meters) is 73° F (23° C). During the two rainy seasons (February-May and September-December), heavy downpours occur almost daily, alternating with sunny weather. Annual rainfall averages 80 centimeters (31 in.) but is generally heavier in the western and north western mountains than in the eastern savannas.

# PEOPLE

Rwanda's population density, even after the 1994 genocide, is among the highest in Sub-Saharan Africa (230 per sq. km.—590 per sq. mi.). Nearly every family in this country with few villages lives in a self-contained compound on a hillside. The urban concentrations are grouped around administrative centers. The indigenous population consists of three ethnic groups. The Hutus, who comprise the majority of the population (85%), are farmers of Bantu origin. The Tutsis (14%) are a pastoral people who arrived in the area in the 15th century. Until 1959, they formed the dominant caste under a feudal system based on cattleholding. The Twa (1%) are thought to be the remnants of the earliest settlers of the region. About half of the adult population is literate, but not more than 5% have received secondary education. During 1994-95, most primary schools and more than half of prewar secondary schools reopened. The national university in Butare reopened in April 1995; enrollment is over 4,000. Rebuilding the educational system

continues to be a high priority of the Rwandan Government.

# HISTORY

According to folklore, Tutsi cattle breeders began arriving in the area from the Horn of Africa in the 15th century and gradually subjugated the Hutu inhabitants. The Tutsis established a monarchy headed by a mwami (king) and a feudal hierarchy of Tutsi nobles and gentry. Through a contract known as ubuhake, the Hutu farmers pledged their services and those of their descendants to a Tutsi lord in return for the loan of cattle and use of pastures and arable land. Thus, the Tutsi reduced the Hutu to virtual serfdom. However, boundaries of race and class became less distinct over the years as some Tutsi declined until they enjoyed few advantages over the Hutu. The first European known to have visited Rwanda was German Count Von Goetzen in 1894. He was followed by missionaries, notably the "White Fathers." In 1899, the mwami submitted to a German protectorate without resistance. Belgian troops from Zaire chased the small number of Germans out of Rwanda in 1915 and took control of the country.

After World War I, the League of Nations mandated Rwanda and its southern neighbor, Burundi, to Belgium as the territory of Ruanda-Urundi. Following World War II, Ruanda-Urundi became a UN trust territory with Belgium as the administrative authority. Reforms instituted by the Belgians in the 1950s encouraged the growth of democratic political institutions but were resisted by the Tutsi traditionalists who saw in them a threat to Tutsi rule. An increasingly restive Hutu population, encouraged by the Belgian military, sparked a revolt in November 1959, resulting in the overthrow of the Tutsi monarchy. Two years later, the Party of the Hutu Emancipation Movement (PARMEHUTU) won an overwhelming victory in a UN-supervised referendum.

## Travel Notes

**Travel Advice:** For up-to-date information from the U.S. State Department on possible inconvenient or hazardous situations, see the **Travel Warnings and Consular Information Sheets from the U.S. Government** section starting on page 1723. For the latest information on health requirements and conditions, see the **International Travelers' Health Information** section starting on page 1385. For further information dealing with non-urgent matter, see the **Tips for Travelers to...** section starting on page 1588.

During the 1959 revolt and its aftermath, more than 160,000 Tutsis fled to neighboring countries. The PARMEHUTU government, formed as a result of the September 1961 election, was granted internal autonomy by Belgium on January 1, 1962. A June 1962 UN General Assembly resolution terminated the Belgian trusteeship and granted full independence to Rwanda (and Burundi) effective July 1, 1962.

Gregoire Kayibanda, leader of the PARMEHUTU Party, became Rwanda's first elected president, leading a government chosen from the membership of the directly elected unicameral National Assembly. Peaceful negotiation of international problems, social and economic elevation of the masses, and integrated development of Rwanda were the ideals of the Kayibanda regime. Relations with 43 countries, including the United States, were established in the first 10 years. Despite the progress made, inefficiency and corruption began festering in government ministries in the mid-1960s. On July 5, 1973, the military took power under the leadership of Maj. Gen. Juvenal Habyarimana, who dissolved the National Assembly and the PARMEHUTU Party and abolished all political activity.

In 1975, President Habyarimana formed the National Revolutionary Movement for Development (MRND) whose goals were to promote peace, unity, and national development. The movement was organized from the "hillside" to the national level and included elected and appointed officials.

Under MRND aegis, Rwandans went to the polls in December 1978, overwhelmingly endorsed a new constitution, and confirmed President Habyarimana as president. President Habyarimana was re-elected in 1983 and again in 1988, when he was the sole candidate. Responding to public pressure for political reform, President Habyarimana announced in July 1990 his intention to transform Rwanda's one-party state into a multi-party democracy.

On October 1, 1990, Rwandan exiles banded together as the Rwandan Patriotic Front (RPF) and invaded Rwanda from their base in Uganda. The rebel force, composed primarily of ethnic Tutsis, blamed the government for failing to democratize and resolve the problems of some 500,000 Tutsi refugees living in diaspora around the world. The war dragged on for almost two years until a ceasefire accord was signed July 12, 1992, in Arusha, Tanzania, fixing a timetable for an end to the fighting and political talks, leading to a peace accord and power-sharing, and authorizing a neutral military observer group under the auspices of the Organization for African Unity. A ceasefire took effect July 31, 1992, and political talks began August 10, 1992.

On April 6, 1994, the airplane carrying President Habyarimana and the President of Burundi was shot down as it prepared to land at Kigali. Both presidents were killed. As though the shooting down was a signal, military and militia groups began rounding up and killing all Tutsis and political moderates, regardless of their ethnic background.

The prime minister and her 10 Belgian bodyguards were among the first victims. The killing swiftly spread from Kigali to all corners of the country; between April 6 and the beginning of July, a genocide of unprecedented swiftness left up to 1 million Tutsis and moderate Hutus dead at the hands of organized bands of militia—Interahamwe. Even ordi-

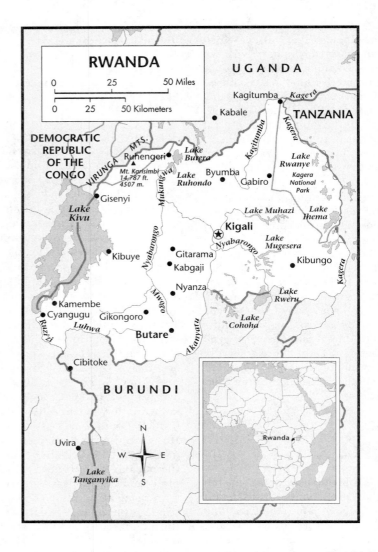

nary citizens were called on to kill their neighbors by local officials and government-sponsored radio. The president's MRND Party was implicated in organizing many aspects of the genocide.

The RPF battalion stationed in Kigali under the Arusha accords came under attack immediately after the shooting down of the president's plane. The battalion fought its way out of Kigali and joined up with RPF units in the north. The RPF then resumed its invasion, and civil war raged concurrently with the genocide for two months. French forces landed in Goma, Zaire, in June 1994 on a humanitarian mission. They deployed throughout southwest Rwanda in an area they called "Zone Turquoise," quelling the genocide and stopping the fighting there. The

Rwandan army was quickly defeated by the RPF and fled across the border to Zaire followed by some 2 million refugees who fled to Zaire, Tanzania, and Burundi. The RPF took Kigali on July 4, 1994, and the war ended on July 16, 1994. The RPF took control of a country ravaged by war and genocide. Up to 800,000 had been murdered, another 2 million or so had fled, and another million or so were displaced internally.

The international community responded with one of the largest humanitarian relief efforts ever mounted. The U.S. was one of the largest contributors. The UN peacekeeping operation, UNAMIR, was drawn down during the fighting but brought back up to strength after the RPF victory. UNAMIR remained in Rwanda until March 8, 1996.

Following an uprising by the ethnic Tutsi Banyamulenge people in Eastern Zaire in October 1996, a huge movement of refugees began which brought over 600,000 back to Rwanda in the last two weeks of November. This massive repatriation was followed at the end of December 1996 by the return of another 500,000 from Tanzania, again in a huge, spontaneous wave. Less than 100,000 Rwandans are estimated to remain outside of Rwanda in late 1997, and they are thought to be the remnants of the defeated army of the the former genocidal government and its allies in the civilian militias known as Interahamwe.

With the return of the refugees, a new chapter in Rwandan history began. The government began the long-awaited genocide trials, which got off to an uncertain start in the closing days of 1996 and inched forward in 1997. The success or failure of the Rwandan social compact will be decided over the next few years, as Hutu and Tutsi try to find ways to live together again.

# GOVERNMENT AND POLITICAL CONDITIONS

After its military victory in July 1994, the RPF organized a coalition government similar to that established by President Habyarimana in 1992. Called The Broad Based Government of National Unity, its fundamental law is based on a combination of the constitution, the Arusha accords, and political declarations by the parties. The MRND Party was outlawed. Political organizing is banned until 1999.

The biggest problems facing the government are reintegration of more than 2 million refugees returning from as long ago as 1959; the end of the insurgency and counter-insurgency among ex-military and Interahamwe militia and the Rwandan Patriotic Army, which is concentrated in the northwest; and the shift away

from crisis to medium- and long-term development planning. The prison population will continue to be an urgent problem for the foreseeable future, having swelled to over 100,000 in the three years after the war. Trying this many suspects of genocide will tax Rwanda's resources sorely.

## Principal Government Officials

**For up-to-date information on Principal Government Officials, see the Chiefs of State and Cabinet Members of Foreign Governments section starting on page 1.**

Rwanda maintains an embassy in the United States at 1714 New Hampshire Avenue NW., Washington, DC 20009 (tel. 202-232-2882).

# ECONOMY

The Rwandan economy is based on the largely rain-fed agricultural production of small, semi-subsistence, and increasingly fragmented farms. It has few natural resources to exploit and a small, uncompetitive industrial sector. While the production of coffee and tea is well-suited to the small farms, steep slopes, and cool climates of Rwanda and has ensured access to foreign exchange over the years, farm size continues to decrease.

Prewar population was growing at the high rate of 3% a year. By 1994, farm size, on average, was smaller than one hectare, while population density was more than 450 persons per square kilometer of arable land.

In the 1960s and 1970s, Rwanda's prudent financial policies, coupled with generous external aid and relatively favorable terms of trade, resulted in sustained growth in per capita income and low inflation rates. However, when world coffee prices fell sharply in the 1980s, growth became erratic.

Compared to an annual GDP growth rate of 6.5% from 1973 to 1980, growth slowed to an average of 2.9% a year from 1980 through 1985 and was stagnant from 1986 to 1990. The crisis peaked in 1990 when the first measures of an IMF structural adjustment program were carried out. While the program was not fully implemented before the war, key measures such as two large devaluations and the removal of official prices were enacted. The consequences on salaries and purchasing power were rapid and dramatic. This crisis particularly affected the educated elite, most of whom were employed in civil service or state-owned enterprises.

During the five years of civil war that culminated in the 1994 genocide, GDP declined in three out of five years, posting a dramatic decline at more than 40% in 1994, the year of the genocide. The 9% increase in real GDP for 1995, the first post-war year, signaled the resurgence of economic activity.

The Government of Rwanda posted a 13% GDP growth rate in 1996 through improved collection of tax revenues, accelerated privatization of state enterprises to stop their drain on government resources, and continued improvement in export crop and food production. It is estimated that in 1997 that food production levels will reach 81% of prewar levels, and should continue to improve as more returned refugees continue to put land back into cultivation.

Tea plantations and factories continue to be rehabilitated, and coffee, always a smallholder's crop, is being more seriously rehabilitated and tended as the farmers' sense of security returns. However, the road to recovery will be slow. Coffee production of about 15,000 tons in 1996 compares to a pre-civil war variation between 35,000 and 40,000 tons, while 1996 tea production reached 11,000 tons, compared to prewar production of about 13,000 tons. Rwanda's natural resources are limited. A small mineral industry provides about 5% of foreign exchange earnings. Concentrates of the heavy minerals cassiterite, columbite-tantalite, and wolframite are most important, followed by small amounts of gold and sapphires. Production of methane from Lake Kivu began in 1983, but to date has been used only by a brewery. Depletion of the forests will eventually pressure Rwandans to turn to fuel sources other than charcoal for cooking and heating, given the abundance of mountain streams and lakes, the potential for hydroelectric power is substantial. Rwanda is exploiting these natural resources through joint hydroelectric projects with Burundi and the People's Democratic Republic of the Congo.

Rwanda's manufacturing sector contributes about 15%-18% of GDP and is dominated by the production of import substitutes for internal consumption. The larger enterprises produce beer, soft drinks, cigarettes, hoes, wheelbarrows, soap, cement, mattresses, plastic pipe, roofing materials and textiles. By mid-1997, up to 70% of the factories functioning before the war had returned to production, at an average of 75% of their capacity. Investments in the industrial sector continue to mostly be limited to the repair of existing industrial plants. Retail trade, devastated by the war, has revived quickly, with many new small businesses established by Rwandan returnees from Uganda, Burundi, and the People's Democratic Republic of the Congo.

Industry received little external assistance from the end of the war through 1995. In 1996-97, the government has become increasingly active in helping the industrial sector to restore production through technical and financial assistance, including loan guarantees, economic liberalization, and the privatization of state-owned enterprises. In early 1998, the government will set up a one-stop investment promotion center and implement a new investment code that should create an enabling environment for foreign and local investors. An autonomous revenue authority should also begin operation, improving collections and accountability.

Possibilities for economic expansion, however, are limited by inadequate infrastructure and transport and the small available market in this predominantly subsistence economy. Existing foreign investment is concentrated in commercial establishments, mining, tea, coffee, and tourism. Minimum wage and social security regulations are in force, and the four prewar independent trade unions are back in operation. The largest union, CESTRAR, was created as an organ of the government but became fully independent with the political reforms introduced by the 1991 constitution. As security in Rwanda improves, the country's nascent tourism sector may expand. Centered around the attractions of a population of mountain gorillas and a game park, tourism has potential as a source of foreign exchange if the country's tourism infrastructure is improved.

In the immediate postwar period—mid-1994 through 1995—emergency humanitarian assistance of over U.S. $307.4 million was largely directed to relief efforts in Rwanda and in the refugee camps in neighboring countries where Rwandans fled during the war. In 1996, humanitarian relief aid began to shift to reconstruction and development assistance. The United States, Belgium, the Federal Republic of Germany, Holland, France, China, the World Bank, the UN Development Program and the European Development Fund will continue to account for the substantial aid. Rehabilitation of government infrastructure, in particular the justice system, is an international priority, as is the continued repair and expansion of infrastructure, health facilities, and schools.

## MEDIA

Rwanda's government-run radio broadcasts 15 hours a day in English, French and Kinyarwanda, the national languages. News programs include regular re-broadcasts from international radio such as Voice of America and Radio France International. There is a fledgling television station. There are several independent newspapers, mostly in Kinyarwanda, that publish on a weekly, biweekly, or monthly basis. Several Western nations, including the U.S., are working to encourage freedom of the press, the free exchange of ideas, and responsible journalism.

## DEFENSE

The military establishment is comprised of an army and a paramilitary gendarmerie. Defense spending continues to represent a disproportionate share of the national budget, largely due to continuing security problems along the frontiers with the People's Democratic Republic of the Congo and Burundi in the aftermath of the war. The government has launched an ambitious plan to demobilize thousands of soldiers. Under the International Military and Training program, the U.S. has provided professional training for Rwandan military officers, especially in civil-military relations and respect for human rights.

## FOREIGN RELATIONS

Rwanda has been the center of much international attention since the war and genocide of 1994. Rwanda is an active member of the UN, having presided over the Security Council during part of 1995. The UN assistance mission in Rwanda, a UN chapter 6 peace-keeping operation, involved personnel from over a dozen countries. Most of the UN development and humanitarian agencies have had a large presence here.

At the height of the emergency, more than 200 non-governmental organizations were carrying out humanitarian operations. Several Western European and African nations, Canada, China, Egypt, Libya, Russia, The Vatican, and the European Union maintain diplomatic missions in Kigali.

# U.S.-RWANDAN RELATIONS

In the post-crisis period, U.S. Government interests have shifted from strictly humanitarian to include the prevention of renewed regional conflict, the promotion of internal stability, and renewed economic development. A major focus of bilateral relations is the Agency for International Development's (USAID) "transition" program, which aims to promote internal stability and to increase confidence in the society.

To achieve this, USAID is trying to achieve three strategic objectives under an integrated strategic plan:

- Increased rule of law and transparency in governance;

- Increased use of health and social services and changed behavior related to sexually transmitted infections and human immunodeficiency virus and maternal and child health by building service capacity in target regions; and

- Increased ability of rural families in targeted communities to improve household food security.

The mission currently is implementing activities in humanitarian assistance and rehabilitation—women's income-generating initiatives, shelter, family relocation for children—administration of justice, increased local government capacity, improved health service delivery, AIDS and STI prevention, and enhanced food security.

The U.S. Information Service maintains a cultural center in Kigali, which offers public access to English-language publications and information on the United States. American business interests have been small; currently, private U.S. investment is limited to the tea industry. Annual U.S. exports to Rwanda, under $10 million annually from 1990-93, have exceeded $40 million in 1994 and 1995.

## Principal U.S. Officials

**For up-to-date information on Principal U.S. Officials, see the U.S. Embassies, Consulates, and Foreign Service section starting on page 139.**

The U.S. embassy is located on Boulevard de la Revolution, P.O. Box 28, Kigali (tel. 250-75601/02; fax 250-72128).

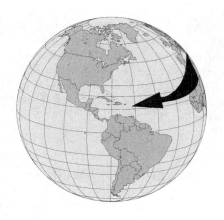

# ST. KITTS AND NEVIS

May 2001

Official Name:
**Federation of St. Kitts and Nevis**

# PROFILE

## Geography

**Area:** St. Kitts 168 sq. km. (65 sq. mi.); Nevis 93 sq. km. (36 sq. mi.).

**Cities:** Capital—Basseterre (pop. about 15,000).

**Terrain:** Generally mountainous; highest elevations are 1,156 m. (3,792 ft.) at Mt. Liamuiga on St. Kitts and 985 m. (3,232 ft.) at Nevis peak on Nevis.

**Climate:** Tropical.

## People

**Nationality:** Noun and adjective—Kittitian(s), Nevisian(s).

**Population (1999 est.):** 42,500.

**Annual growth rate (1999 est.):** 2.8%.

**Ethnic groups:** Predominantly of African origin; some of British, Portuguese, and Lebanese descent.

**Religions:** Principally Anglican, with Evangelical Protestant and Roman Catholic minorities.

**Languages:** English (official).

**Education (1999):** Years compulsory—9. Literacy—98%.

**Health (1999 est.):** Infant mortality rate—12.7/1,000. Life expectancy—70 yrs.

## Government

**Type:** Constitutional monarchy with Westminster-style Parliament.

**Constitution:** 1983.

**Independence:** September 19, 1983.

**Branches:** Executive—governor general (representing Queen Elizabeth II, head of state), prime minister (head of government), cabinet. Legislative—an 11-member senate appointed by the governor general (mainly on the advice of the prime minister and the leader of the opposition) and an 11-member popularly elected house of representatives. Judicial—magistrate's courts, Eastern Caribbean supreme court (high court and court of appeals), final appeal to privy council in London.

**Administrative subdivisions:** 14 parishes.

**Political parties:** St. Kitts and Nevis Labor Party (ruling), People's Action Movement (PAM), Concerned Citizens Movement (a Nevis-based party), and Nevis Reformation Party.

**Suffrage:** Universal at 18.

## Economy

**GDP (1999):** $300.7 million.

**GDP growth rate (1999):** 2.8%.

**Per capita GDP (1999):** US$7,075.

**Natural resources:** Negligible.

**Agriculture:** Products—sugarcane, cotton, peanuts, vegetables.

**Industry (1999):** Types—Financial and business services, tourism, construction, sugar processing, cotton, salt, copra, clothing, beverages, and tobacco. Unemployment—12%.

**Trade (1999):** Exports—US$47.9 million. Major markets—U.K., U.S. and CARICOM. Imports—US$144.3 million.

**Exchange rate:** Eastern Caribbean $2.70=U.S.$1.

# HISTORY

At the time of European discovery, the islands of St. Kitts and Nevis were inhabited by Carib Indians. Christopher Columbus landed on the larger island in 1493 on his second voyage and named it after St. Christopher, his patron saint. Columbus also discovered Nevis on his second voyage, reportedly calling it Nevis because of its resemblance to a snow-capped mountain (in Spanish, nuestra senora de las nieves or our lady of the snows). European colonization did not begin until 1623-24, when first English, then French colonists arrived on St. Christopher's island, whose name the English shortened to St. Kitt's island. As the first English colony in the Caribbean, St. Kitts served as a base for further colonization in the region.

St. Kitts was held jointly by the English and French from 1628-1713.

During the 17th century, intermittent warfare between French and English settlers ravaged its economy. Meanwhile Nevis, settled by English settlers in 1628, grew prosperous under English rule. St. Kitts was ceded to Great Britain by the treaty of Utrecht in 1713. Both St. Kitts and Nevis were seized by the French in 1782.

The Treaty of Paris in 1783 definitively awarded both islands to Britain. They were part of the colony of the Leeward Islands from 1871-1956, and of the West Indies Federation from 1958-62. In 1967, together with Anguilla, they became a self-governing state in association with Great Britain; Anguilla seceded late that year and remains a British dependency. The federation of St. Kitts and Nevis attained full independence on September 19, 1983.

# GOVERNMENT AND POLITICAL CONDITIONS

As head of state, Queen Elizabeth II is represented in St. Kitts and Nevis by a governor general, who acts on the advice of the prime minister and the cabinet. The prime minister is the leader of the majority party of the house, and the cabinet conducts affairs of state. St. Kitts and Nevis has a bicameral legislature: An 11-member senate appointed by the governor general (mainly on the advice of the prime minister and the leader of the opposition) and an 11-member popularly elected house of representatives which has eight St. Kitts seats and three Nevis seats. The prime minister and the cabinet are responsible to the Parliament.

St. Kitts and Nevis, like most of the region, faces a threat from narco-traffickers who see the country as a potential drug transshipment point. In 1994, a controversy related to drug trafficking by two sons of the then-deputy prime minister was partially responsible for a prison riot which extensively damaged the prison. With the assistance of the Regional

## Travel Notes

**Travel Advice:** For up-to-date information from the U.S. State Department on possible inconvenient or hazardous situations, see the **Travel Warnings and Consular Information Sheets from the U.S. Government** section starting on page 1723. For the latest information on health requirements and conditions, see the **International Travelers' Health Information** section starting on page 1385. For further information dealing with non-urgent matter, see the **Tips for Travelers to...** section starting on page 1588.

Security System (RSS), a cooperative defense organization of seven small eastern Caribbean island nations (including St. Kitts and Nevis), the riot ended soon after it began. Also in 1994, the chief of the special branch and criminal investigation division was killed while investigating a politically sensitive murder. In 2000, crime figure Charles "Little Nut" Miller was successfully brought to the United States by U.S. law enforcement authorities and convicted of criminal charges involving narcotics trafficking and murder.

St. Kitts and Nevis has enjoyed a long history of free and fair elections, although the outcome of elections in 1993 was strongly protested by the opposition, and the RSS was briefly deployed to restore order. The elections in 1995 were contested by the two major parties, the ruling People's Action Movement (PAM) and the St. Kitts and Nevis Labor Party. Labor won seven of the 11 seats, with Dr. Denzil Douglas becoming prime minister. In March 2000 elections, Denzil Douglas and the Labour Party were returned to power, winning eight of the 11 seats in Parliament. The Nevis-based Concerned Citizens Movement (CCM) won two seats and the Nevis Reformation Party (NRP) won one seat. The PAM party was unable to obtain a seat.

Under the constitution, Nevis has considerable autonomy and has an island assembly, a premier, and a deputy governor general. Under certain specified conditions, it may

secede from the federation. In June 1996, the Nevis Island Administration under the concerned citizens movement of Premier Vance Amory announced its intention to do so. Secession requires approval by two-thirds of the assembly's five elected members and also by two-thirds of voters in a referendum. After the Nevis Reformation Party blocked the bill of secession, the premier called for elections for February 24, 1997. Although the elections produced no change in the composition of the assembly, Premier Amory pledged to continue his efforts toward Nevis' independence. In August 1998, a referendum on the question of independence for Nevis failed and Nevis presently remains in the Federation. The March 2000 election results placed Vance Armory, as head of the CCM, the leader of the country's opposition party.

Constitutional safeguards include freedom of speech, press, worship, movement, and association. Like its neighbors in the English-speaking Caribbean, St. Kitts and Nevis has an excellent human rights record. Its judicial system is modeled on British practice and procedure and its jurisprudence on English common law. The Royal St. Kitts and Nevis police force has about 340 members.

## Principal Government Officials

**For up-to-date information on Principal Government Officials, see the Chiefs of State and Cabinet Members of Foreign Governments section starting on page 1.**

The embassy of St. Kitts and Nevis is located at 3216 New Mexico Ave., NW, Washington, DC 20016 (tel. 202-686-2636).

# ECONOMY

St. Kitts and Nevis was the last sugar monoculture in the Eastern Caribbean. Faced with a sugar industry, which was finding it increasingly difficult to earn a profit, the Government of St. Kitts and Nevis embarked on a program to diversify the agricultural sector and stimulate the development of other sectors of the economy.

The government instituted a program of investment incentives for businesses considering locating in St. Kitts or Nevis, encouraging both domestic and foreign private investment. Government policies provide liberal tax holidays, duty-free import of equipment and materials, and subsidies for training provided to local personnel. Tourism has shown the greatest growth. By 1987, tourism had surpassed sugar as the major foreign exchange earner for St. Kitts and Nevis.

The economy of St. Kitts and Nevis experienced strong growth for most of the 1990s, but hurricanes in 1998 and 1999 contributed to a sharp slowdown in growth. Growth was only 1% in 1998 and 2.8% in 1999, compared to 7.3% in 1997. Tourism in particular suffered in 1998 and 1999 as a result of the hurricanes which forced the closure of one of the major hotels and heavily damaged the cruiseship pier. Significant new investment in tourism as well as continued government efforts to diversify the economy are expected to improve economic performance.. Consumer prices have risen marginally over the past few years. The inflation rate was 3%-4% for most of the 1990s. St. Kitts and Nevis is a member of the Eastern Caribbean Currency Union (ECCU). All members of the ECCU, The Eastern Caribbean Central Bank (ECCB) issues a common currency for all members of the ECCU. The ECCB also manages monetary policy, and regulates and supervises commercial banking activities in its member countries.

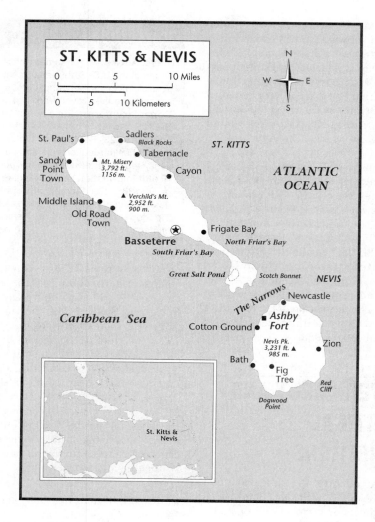

# FOREIGN RELATIONS

St. Kitts and Nevis maintains diplomatic relations with the United States, Canada, the United Kingdom, Taiwan, and South Korea, as well as with many Latin American countries and neighboring Eastern Caribbean states. It is a member of the Commonwealth, the United Nations and several of its specialized and related agencies, the World Bank and the International Monetary Fund, the Organization of American States, the Organization of Eastern Caribbean States, the Eastern Caribbean Regional Security System (RSS), and the Caribbean Community and Common Market (CARICOM). The Eastern Caribbean Central Bank is headquartered in St. Kitts.

As a member of CARICOM, St. Kitts and Nevis strongly backed efforts by the United States to implement UN Security Council Resolution 940, designed to facilitate the departure of Haiti's de facto authorities from power. The country agreed to contribute personnel to the multinational force, which restored the democratically elected Government of Haiti in October 1994. In May 1997, President Clinton met with Prime Minister Douglas and 14 other Caribbean leaders during the first-ever U.S.-regional summit in Bridgetown, Barbados. The summit strengthened the basis for regional cooperation on justice and counternarcotics issues, finance and development, and trade.

# U.S.-ST. KITTS AND NEVIS RELATIONS

Since St. Kitts and Nevis attained full independence in 1983, relations with the U.S. have been friendly. The U.S. embassy in Bridgetown, Barbados, conducts bilateral relations with St. Kitts and Nevis. The United States seeks to help St. Kitts and Nevis develop economically and to help strengthen its moderate, democratic, parliamentary form of government. St. Kitts and Nevis is a beneficiary of the U.S. Caribbean Basin Initiative. U.S. assistance is primarily channeled through multilateral agencies such as the World Bank, and the Caribbean Development Bank (CDB), and the newly opened USAID satellite office in Bridgetown, Barbados. In addition, St. Kitts and Nevis receives counternarcotics assistance and benefits from U.S. military exercise-related and humanitarian civic action construction projects.

St. Kitts and Nevis are strategically placed in the Leeward Islands, near maritime transport lanes of major importance to the United States. St. Kitts and Nevis' location close to Puerto Rico and the U.S. Virgin Islands makes the two-island federation attractive to narcotics traffickers. To counter this threat, the Government of St. Kitts and Nevis cooperates with the U.S. in the fight against illegal narcotics. In 1995, the government signed a maritime law enforcement treaty with the United States, later amended with an over-flight/order-to-land amendment in 1996. St. Kitts and Nevis also signed an updated extradition treaty with the U.S. in 1996, and a mutual legal assistance treaty in 1997.

St. Kitts and Nevis are popular American tourist destinations. In 1999, more than 40% of the 84,000 stayover visitors were from the U.S. The majority of the 143,800 yacht and cruiseship passengers also were from the U.S. Fewer than 1,000 U.S. citizens reside on the island, and students and staff of Ross University Veterinary School constitute a significant population of U.S. citizens.

## Principal U.S. Embassy Officials

**For up-to-date information on Principal U.S. Officials, see the U.S. Embassies, Consulates, and Foreign Service section starting on page 139.**

The United States maintains no official presence in St. Kitts and Nevis.

The ambassador and embassy officers are resident in Barbados and frequently travel to St. Kitts and Nevis. However, a U.S. consular agent residing in nearby Antigua assists U.S. citizens in St. Kitts and Nevis.

The U.S. embassy in Barbados is located in the Canadian Imperial Bank of Commerce Building, Broad Street, Bridgetown (tel: 246-436-4950; fax: 246-429-5246). Consular Agent: Juliet Ryder Hospital Hill, English Harbor, Antigua Tel: (268) 463-6531.

## Other Contact Information

**U.S. Department of Commerce**
International Trade Administration
Trade Information Center
14th and Constitution, NW
Washington, DC 20230
Tel: 1-800-USA-TRADE

**Caribbean/Latin American Action**
1818 N Street, NW, Suite 310
Washington, DC 20036
Tel: (202) 466-7464
Fax: (202) 822-0075

# ST. LUCIA

April 2001

## Official Name:
## Saint Lucia

## PROFILE

### Geography

**Area:** 619 sq. km. (238 sq. mi.).
**Cities:** Capital—Castries (pop. est. 67,000); Micoud, Gros-Islet; Vieux Fort; Soufriere.
**Terrain:** Mountainous.
**Climate:** Tropical.

### People

**Nationality:** Noun and adjective—St. Lucian(s).
**Population (1999):** 155,000.
**Annual growth rate (est. 2000):** 2.0%.
**Ethnic groups:** African descent 90%, mixed 6%, East Indian 3%, European 0.8%.
**Religions:** Roman Catholic 90%, Church of England 3%, various Protestant denominations.
**Languages:** English (official); a French patois is common throughout the country.
**Education:** Literacy—85%. Years compulsory—ages 5-15. Attendance—more than 80% urban, 75% rural.
**Health (1999):** Life expectancy—74 years female; 68 years male. Infant mortality rate—16/1,000.
**Work force (1998):** Agriculture—62%; industry and commerce—20%; services—18%. Unemployment (2000) 15%.

### Government

**Type:** Westminster-style parliamentary democracy.
**Independence:** February 22, 1979.
**Constitution:** 1979.
**Branches:** Executive—governor general (representing Queen Elizabeth II, head of state), prime minister (head of government), cabinet. Legislative—bicameral parliament. Judicial—district courts, Eastern Caribbean Supreme Court (High Court and Court of Appeals), final appeal to privy council in London.
**Administrative subdivisions:** 11 parishes.
**Political parties:** St. Lucia Labor Party (SLP, ruling); in power since 1997, United Workers' Party (UWP, official opposition).
**Suffrage:** Universal at 18.

### Economy (2000)

**GDP:** U.S. $707 million.
Annual growth rate: 2.0%.
**Per capita GDP:** US $4,560.
**Natural resources:** Forests, beaches, minerals (pumice), mineral springs. Agriculture (7.9% of GDP): Products—bananas, cocoa, coconut, citrus fruits, livestock.
**Industry:** Manufacturing 5.5% of GDP. Types—garments, electronic components, beverages, corrugated boxes. Tourism—13% of GDP.

**Trade:** Exports US $63.3 million—bananas, cocoa, vegetables, fruits, other agricultural products, oils and fats, manufactured goods. Major markets—U.K., U.S., CARICOM countries. Imports US $327.6 million—food, fuel, manufactured goods, machinery and transport equipment. Major suppliers—U.S., CARICOM countries, U.K., Japan.

## PEOPLE

St. Lucia's population is predominantly of African and mixed African-European descent, with small East Indian and European minorities. English is the official language, although many St. Lucians speak a French patois. Ninety percent of the population is Roman Catholic, a further reflection of early French influence on the island. The population of just over 147,000 is evenly divided between urban and rural areas, although the capital, Castries, contains more than one-third of the population. Despite a high emigration rate, the population is growing rapidly, about 1.6% per year.

## HISTORY

St. Lucia's first known inhabitants were Arawaks, believed to have come from northern South America 200-400 A.D. Numerous archaeological sites on the island have produced specimens of the Arawaks' well-developed pottery. Caribs gradually replaced Arawaks during the period 800-1000 A.D. Europeans first landed on the island in either 1492 or 1502 during Spain's early exploration of the Caribbean. The Dutch, English, and French all tried to establish trading outposts on St. Lucia in the 17th century but faced opposition from hostile Caribs.

The English, with their headquarters in Barbados, and the French, centered on Martinique, found St. Lucia attractive after the sugar industry developed in 1765. Britain eventually triumphed, with France permanently ceding St. Lucia in 1815. In 1838, St. Lucia was incorporated into the British windward islands administration, headquartered in Barbados. This lasted until 1885, when the capital was moved to Grenada.

St. Lucia's 20th-century history has been marked by increasing self-government. A 1924 constitution gave the island its first form of representative government, with a minority of elected members in the previously all-nominated legislative council. Universal adult suffrage was introduced in 1951, and elected members became a majority of the council. Ministerial government was introduced in 1956, and in 1958 St. Lucia joined the short-lived West Indies Federation, a semi-autonomous dependency of the United Kingdom. When the federation collapsed in 1962, following Jamaica's withdrawal, a smaller federation was briefly attempted. After the second failure, the United Kingdom and the six windward and leeward islands—Grenada, St. Vincent, Dominica, Antigua, St. Kitts-Nevis-Anguilla, and St. Lucia—developed a novel form of cooperation called associated statehood.

As an associated state of the United Kingdom from 1967 to 1979, St. Lucia had full responsibility for internal self-government but left its external affairs and defense responsibilities to the United Kingdom. This interim arrangement ended on February 22, 1979, when St. Lucia achieved full independence. St. Lucia continues to recognize Queen Elizabeth II as titular head of state and is an active member of the Commonwealth. The island continues to cooperate with its neighbors through the Caribbean community and common market (CARICOM), the East Caribbean Common Market (ECCM), and the Organization of Eastern Caribbean States (OECS).

# GOVERNMENT AND POLITICAL CONDITIONS

St. Lucia is a parliamentary democracy modeled on the Westminster system. The head of state is Queen Elizabeth II, represented by a Governor General, appointed by the Queen as her representative. The Governor General exercises basically ceremonial functions, but residual powers, under the constitution, can be used at the governor general's discretion. The actual power in St. Lucia lies with the prime minister and the cabinet, usually representing the majority party in parliament.

The bicameral parliament consists of a 17-member House of Assembly whose members are elected by universal adult suffrage for 5-year terms and an 11-member senate appointed by the governor general. The parliament may be dissolved by the governor general at any point during its 5-year term, either at the request of the prime minister—in order to take the nation into early elections—or at the governor general's own discretion, if the house passes a vote of no confidence in the government.

St. Lucia has an independent judiciary composed of district courts and a high court. Cases may be appealed to the Eastern Caribbean Court of Appeals and, ultimately, to the Judicial Committee of the Privy Council in London. The island is divided into 10 administrative divisions, includ-

ing the capital, Castries. Popularly elected local governments in most towns and villages perform such tasks as regulation of sanitation and markets and maintenance of cemeteries and secondary roads. St. Lucia has no army but maintains a paramilitary Special Service Unit within its police force and a coast guard.

Politics in St. Lucia has been dominated by the United Workers Party (UWP), which has governed the country for all but 3 years since independence. John Compton was premier of St. Lucia from 1964 until independence in February 1979 and remained prime minister until elections later that year. The St. Lucia Labor Party (SLP) won the first post-independence elections in July 1979, taking 12 of 17 seats in parliament. A period of turbulence ensued, in which squabbling within the party led to several changes of prime minister. Pressure from the private sector and the unions forced the government to resign in 1982. New elections were then called and were won resoundingly by Compton's UWP, which took 14 of 17 seats. The UWP was elected for a second time in April 16, 1987, but with only nine of 17 seats. Seeking to increase his slim margin, Prime Minister Compton suspended parliament and called new elections on April 30. This unprecedented snap election, however, gave Compton the same results as before—the UWP retained nine seats and the SLP eight. In April 1992, Prime Minister Compton's government again defeated the SLP. In this election, the government increased its majority in parliament to 11 seats.

In 1996, Compton announced his resignation as prime minister in favor of his chosen successor Dr. Vaughan Lewis, former director general of the Organization of Eastern Caribbean States (OECS). Dr. Lewis became prime minister and minister of finance, planning and development on April 2, 1996. The SLP also had a change of leadership with former CARICOM official Dr. Kenny Anthony succeeding businessman Julian Hunte. In elections held May 23, 1997, the St. Lucia Labor Party won all but one of the 17 seats in Parliament, and Dr. Kenny Anthony became Prime Minister and Minister of Finance, Planning and Development on May 24, 1997.

## Principal Government Officials

**For up-to-date information on Principal Government Officials, see the Chiefs of State and Cabinet Members of Foreign Governments section starting on page 1.**

St. Lucia maintains an embassy at 3216 New Mexico Ave., NW, Washington, DC 20016 (tel. 202-364-6792).

# ECONOMY

St. Lucia's economy depends primarily on revenue from banana production and tourism with some input from smallscale manufacturing. There are numerous small and medium-sized agricultural enterprises. Revenue from agriculture has supported the noticeable socioeconomic changes that have taken place in St. Lucia since the 1960s. Eighty percent of merchandise trade earnings came from banana exports to the United Kingdom in the 1960s. In view of the European Union's announced phase-out of preferred access to its markets by Windward

Island bananas by 2006, agricultural diversification is a priority. An attempt is being made to diversify production by encouraging the establishment of tree crops such as mangos and avocados. A variety of vegetables are produced for local consumption. Recently, St. Lucia added small computer-driven information technology

and financial services as development objectives.

St. Lucia's leading revenue producers—agriculture, tourism and small-scale manufacturing—benefited from a focus on infrastructure improvements in roads, communications, water supply, sewerage, and port facilities. Foreign investors also have been attracted by the infrastructure improvements as well as by the educated and skilled work force and relatively stable political conditions. The largest investment is in a petroleum storage and transshipment terminal built by Hess Oil. The Caribbean Development Bank (CDB) funded and airport expansion project.

The tourism sector has made significant gains, experiencing a boom during the last few years despite some untimely and destructive hurricanes.. In 1999, 50% more tourists visited the island than in 1996, including 261,000 stayover tourists and 423,000 cruise- ship visitors. The development of the tourism sector has been helped by the government's commitment to providing a favorable investment environment. Incentives are available for building and upgrading tourism facilities. There has been liberal use of public funds to improve the physical infrastructure of the island, and the government has made efforts to attract cultural and sporting events and develop historical sites.

St. Lucia is a member of the Eastern Caribbean Currency Union (ECCU). The Eastern Caribbean Central Bank (ECCB) issues a common currency for all members of the ECCU. The ECCB also manages monetary policy, and regulates and supervises commercial banking activities in its member countries. St. Lucia is a beneficiary of the U.S. Caribbean Basin Initiative and is a member of the Caribbean Community and Common Market (CARICOM) and the Organization of Eastern Caribbean States (OECS)

# FOREIGN RELATIONS

The major thrust of foreign affairs for St. Lucia is economic development. The government is seeking balanced international relations with emphasis on mutual economic cooperation and trade and investment. It seeks to conduct its foreign policy chiefly

through its membership in the OECS. St. Lucia participated in the 1983 Grenada mission, sending members of its Special Services Unit into active duty. St. Lucia is a member of the Commonwealth, the Organization of American States, and the United Nations. It seeks pragmatic solutions to major international issues and maintains friendly relations with the major powers active in the Caribbean, including the United States, the United Kingdom, Canada, and France. St. Lucia has been active in eastern Caribbean regional affairs through the OECS and CARICOM. As a member of CARICOM, St. Lucia strongly backed efforts by the United States to implement UN Security Council Resolution 940, designed to restore democracy to Haiti. The country agreed to contribute personnel to the multinational force, which restored the democratically elected government of Haiti in October 1994.

St. Lucia participated, along with 14 other Caribbean nations, in a summit with President Clinton in Bridgetown, Barbados in May 1997. The summit, which was the first-ever meeting in the region between the U.S. and Caribbean heads of government, strengthened the basis for regional cooperation on justice and counternarcotics, finance and development, and trade issues.

There are currently four diplomatic missions in St. Lucia—People's Republic of China, France, Venezuela, and an office of the Barbados-based British High Commission. Some countries with which St. Lucia has diplomatic relations have representatives resident in Barbados, Jamaica, Trinidad, and Guyana.

# U.S.-ST. LUCIAN RELATIONS

The United States and St. Lucia have a cooperative relationship. The United States supports the St. Lucian Government's efforts to

expand its economic base and improve the lives of its citizens.

U.S. assistance is primarily channeled through multilateral agencies such as the the World Bank, the Caribbean Development Bank (CDB), and the newly opened USAID satellite office in Bridgetown, Barbados. The Peace Corps, whose Eastern Caribbean regional headquarters is in Castries, has 25-30 volunteers in St. Lucia, working primarily in education, agriculture, and health. U.S. security assistance programs provide limited training to the paramilitary Special Services Unit and the coast guard. In addition, St. Lucia receives U.S. counternarcotics assistance and benefits from U.S. military exercise-related and humanitarian civic action construction projects.

St. Lucia and the United States share interest in combating international crime, the flow of illegal drugs, and narcotics trafficking. Because of St. Lucia's geographical location, it is an appealing transit point for traffickers. In response to this threat, the Government of St. Lucia has concluded various bilateral treaties with the United States, including a Maritime Law Enforcement Agreement (subsequently amended to include overflight and order-to-land provisions), a Mutual Legal Assistance Treaty, and an Extradition Treaty.

In 1999, more than 30% of the stayover tourists and a majority of the cruiseship passengers were from the U.S. A relatively small number of American citizens—fewer than 1,000— reside in St. Lucia.

## Principal U.S. Embassy Officials

For up-to-date information on Principal U.S. Officials, see the U.S. Embassies, Consulates, and Foreign Service section starting on page 139.

The United States maintains no diplomatic presence in St. Lucia. The ambassador and embassy officers are resident in Barbados and frequently travel to St. Lucia.

The U.S. embassy in Barbados is located in the Canadian Imperial Bank of Commerce Building, Broad Street, Bridgetown (tel: 246-436-4950; fax: 246-429-5246).

## Other Contact Information

### U.S. Department of Commerce
International Trade Administration
Trade Information Center
14th and Constitution, NW
Washington, DC 2230
Tel: 1-800-USA-TRADE

### Caribbean/Latin American Action
1818 N Street, NW, Suite 310
Washington, DC 20036
Tel: (202) 466-7464
Fax: (202) 822-0075